# SCHOLARSHIPS,
## FELLOWSHIPS
## AND LOANS

ISSN 1058-5699

# SCHOLARSHIPS, FELLOWSHIPS AND LOANS

## A GUIDE TO EDUCATION-RELATED FINANCIAL AID PROGRAMS FOR STUDENTS AND PROFESSIONALS

**Valerie J. Webster**
**Editor**

**Fifteenth Edition**

GALE GROUP

Detroit
San Francisco
London
Boston
Woodbridge, CT

Valerie J. Webster, *Editor*
Katy Balcer, *Associate Editor*

Evi Seoud, *Assistant Production Manager*
Nekita McKee, *Buyer*

Mary Claire Krzewinski, *Cover Designer*
Christine O'Bryan, *Desktop Publisher*
Cover Photo: David G. Toerge/Black Star

Theresa A. Rocklin, *Technical Support Services Manager*
Venus Little, *Programmer/Analyst*

Ronald D. Montgomery, *Manager, Data Entry Services*
Constance J. Wells, *Data Entry Associate*

ISBN 0-7876-2648-1
ISSN 1058-5699

Published in the United States by Gale Group, Inc.

# Contents

# *Highlights*

With the addition of over 250 new awards, this edition of *Scholarships, Fellowships, and Loans (SFL)* provides access to over 6,000 sources of education-related financial aid for students and professionals at all levels of study from undergraduate and vocational/technical to post doctorate and professional study. Students, their parents and counselors, and others interested in education funding will find comprehensive information on a variety of programs in all areas of study, including:

| | | |
|---|---|---|
| Agriculture | Health Science | Life science |
| Architecture | Humanities | Medicine |
| Area and ethnic studies | Industrial arts | Mathematics |
| Art | Language | Performing arts |
| Business | Law | Philosophy |
| Communications | Literature | Physical sciences |
| Computer Science | Liberal Arts | Social sciences |
| Education | Library science | Theology and religion |
| Engineering | | |

*SFL* provides detailed information on awards, including:

    administering organization name and address
    purpose of the award
    qualifications and restrictions
    selection criteria
    award amount and number of awards granted
    application details and deadlines
    contact information

Look for the section on federal financial aid following the User's Guide for a quick summary of programs sponsored by the U.S. government, and also the information on the AmeriCorps program. We have also added a state-by-state listing of agencies that you can contact in your home state.

## *Six Indexes Allow Fast Access to Awards*

Whether you are a high school student looking for basic undergraduate financial aid, a scientist investigating research grants, or a professional attempting to finance additional career training, *SFL* facilitates your search by providing access to awards through the following indexes:

*Vocational Goals Index* -- offers a quick reference to all listed awards and their eligibility requirements in a convenient topical arrangement

*Field of Study Index* -- categorizes awards by very specific subject fields

*Legal Resident Index* -- targets awards restricted to applicants from specific geographic locations

*Place of Study Index* -- provides a handy guide to awards granted for study within specific states, provinces, or countries

*Special Recipient Index* -- lists awards that are reserved for candidates who qualify by virtue of their gender, organizational affiliation, or minority or ethnic background.

*Sponsor and Scholarship Index* -- provides a complete alphabetical listing of all awards and their administering organizations

# Preface

## *Practical Tips on How to Find Financial Aid*

There are many education-related financial aid programs for students of all types, but the competition for available funds keeps increasing along with the rising cost of education. You will increase the likelihood of meeting your aid-related financial goals if you plan ahead and:
carefully assess your particular needs and preferences;
consider any special circumstances or conditions that might qualify you for aid targeted for special audiences; and
carefully research available aid programs.

What follows are some guidelines for making your way through the search and application process.

### 1. Start Your Search Early

Any search for financial aid is likely to be more successful if it is started early. If you allow enough time to complete all of the necessary steps, you will be more likely to identify, and be able to meet application deadlines for, a wide variety of awards for which you may qualify. This in turn will increase your chances of obtaining aid.

Some experts recommend that you start this process as early as two years before you think you will need financial assistance. While you will probably be able to obtain some support if you allow less time, you might overlook or run out of time for some important opportunities.

Some awards are given on a first-come, first-served basis, and if you do not file your application early enough, the aid will already be distributed. In many cases, if your application is late you will not be considered, even if you meet all of the other criteria.

An early start may also allow you to identify organizations that offer scholarships to members or participants, such as student or professional associations, in time to establish membership or otherwise meet their qualifying criteria.

### 2. Assess Your Needs and Goals

The intended recipients for financial aid programs, and the purposes for which these awards were established, can vary greatly. Some programs are open to almost anyone; others are restricted to very specific categories of recipients. The majority of awards fall somewhere in between.

Your first step in seeking financial aid should be to establish your basic qualifications as a potential recipient. To help you do this, here are some general questions that you should ask yourself in order to define your educational and financial needs and goals:

• What kinds of colleges or universities interest me?
• What careers or fields of study interest me?
• Do I plan to earn a degree?
• Am I only interested in financial aid that is a gift, or am I willing to consider a loan or exchanging work for assistance?
• In what parts of the country am I willing to live and study?

### 3. Leave No Stone Unturned

Once you have defined your goals, the next step is to identify any special factors that might make you eligible for aid programs that are offered only to a restricted group. Examine this area carefully, and remember that even slight or unlikely connections may be worth checking out.

The most common qualifications and restrictions involve:

gender
race or ethnic group
place of residence
citizenship
employer
membership in an organization
   (such as a union, association,
      or fraternal group)

religious affiliation
military or veteran status
financial need
merit or academic achievement
creative or professional
   accomplishment
community involvement or
   volunteer work

Some of these qualifiers may apply to the applicant as well as his/her parents, step-parents, guardians, and/or spouse. If your parents are divorced, you should be aware of both parents' affiliations--even if you don't live with one (or both) of them. If your parents are deceased, you may be eligible for some awards based on their status or affiliations. And given enough lead time, it may be possible for you (or your parents) to join a particular organization, or establish residence, in time for you to be eligible for certain funds.

4. **Contact the Financial Aid Office of the Schools and Other Educational Institutions That You Are Considering**

Most colleges, universities, and other educational institutions offer their own, institution-specific financial aid programs. Their financial aid offices may also have information on privately sponsored awards that are specifically designated for students at those institutions. Contact the financial aid offices of all institutions in which you have an interest and request applications and detailed information on all of the aid programs that they sponsor or administer.

5. **Use *Scholarships, Fellowships and Loans* to Identify Awards Sponsored by Private Organizations and Corporations**

*Scholarships, Fellowships and Loans* (SFL) is the most comprehensive single source of information on major education-related financial aid programs sponsored and administered by private organizations and companies for use by students and professionals. Using *SFL* as a starting point, you can quickly compile a substantial list of financial aid programs for which you may qualify by following these simple steps:

Start by reading the **Introduction** and the **"User's Guide"** to learn about the kinds of information that is provided.

Compile an initial list of awards offered in your field of study.

If you have not yet chosen a specific area of study, look in the **"Guide to Subjects Used in the Vocational Goals Index"** to find the general topic--such as *Business and Management*, or *Communications*--that most closely matches your area of interest. Then, look under that subject in the **"Vocational Goals Index"** to find a list of awards that may be of interest. Be sure to also look under the subject *Liberal/General Studies*, since awards that are offered without restrictions on study area are listed here.

If you have already specifically defined your field, look in the **"Field of Study Index"** to find listings of awards grouped by more precise disciplines--such as *Accounting* or *Journalism*. If you choose this approach, your initial list is likely to be shorter, but more focused.

Eliminate awards that can't be used at your chosen level of study, and awards of a type that don't meet your financial needs. Are you an undergraduate only interested in a scholarship? Are you a graduate student willing to participate in an internship or take out a loan? Consult the **"User's Guide"** to determine which of the study level categories and award types apply to your particular situation. Both indexes clearly note the study levels for which awards can be used; the **"Field of Study Index"** also lists the type of financial aid provided.

Eliminate awards with citizenship, residence and other restrictions (such as minority status or ethnic background, gender, and organizational affiliation) that make you ineligible.

This information is also clearly stated in the **"Vocational Goals Index."** If your list is based on the **"Field of Study Index,"** you will need to look under *"Qualifications"* in each descriptive listing to see what requirements may apply.

Read the descriptive listings for each of the award programs left on your list. The descriptive listings should contain all the information you need to decide if you may qualify, and apply for, each of the awards on your list.

## 6. Expand Your List of Possibilities

If you are willing to take the initiative and do a little extra digging, you should be able to add to your list of institution-related and privately sponsored programs. In most cases, the best possibilities fall into these two areas:

**Government Agencies and Programs**. *Scholarships, Fellowships and Loans* includes a broad representation of award programs sponsored by federal and state governments. Since these listings are not meant to be exhaustive, you should be able to identify additional programs by contacting the government agencies responsible for the education-related financial aid programs listed here. On the federal level, contact the **U.S. Department of Education** at **600 Maryland Ave., S.W., Washington, DC 20202**, for up-to-date information on U.S. Government award programs. Similarly, you should contact your state department of education for details on what is offered in your particular state.

**Local Sources of Awards.** A surprisingly large number of financial aid programs are sponsored by small or local organizations. *SFL* contains a representative sampling of such programs, in the hopes that this information will encourage you to seek similar programs in your own geographic area. High school guidance counselors are often aware of local programs, and they can usually tell you how to get in touch with the sponsoring or administering organizations. Local newspapers are also rich sources of information on financial aid programs.

## 7. Allow Enough Time for the Application Process

The amount of time needed to complete the application process for individual awards will vary, so you should pay close attention to application details and deadlines. Some awards carry application deadlines that require you to apply more than a year before study will actually begin. In general, it is wise to allow plenty of time to:

- Write for official applications. You won't be considered for some awards unless you apply using the correct forms.
- Read all instructions carefully.
- Take note of application deadlines.
- Accurately and completely file all required supporting material, such as essays and resumes. If you fail to answer certain questions, you may be disqualified even though you are a worthy candidate.
- Give references enough time to submit their recommendations. Teachers, in particular, get many requests for letters of recommendation and should be given as much advance notice as possible.

### 8. Don't Apply Unless You Are Sure You Qualify

Finally, don't submerge yourself under needless paperwork. If you find you don't qualify for a particular award, don't apply for it. Instead, use your time and energy to unearth and apply for more likely sources of aid.

### A Word of Encouragement

By doing your homework, you'll greatly increase your chances of finding the necessary funding. The personal labor involved in securing financial support for school is much like the resume shuffling and door knocking that occurs during a job hunt. Success is likely to come to those who make themselves aware of the opportunities available, and who pursue those opportunities in a dedicated, continuous, and systematic manner. Frustration, of course, is part of the game and should not bring your search to a halt. In the quest for funding, as in most of life's endeavors, your most valuable resource is you.

# *Introduction*

As we enter the twenty-first century, there is an increasing focus on the need for a more highly-trained and educated work force. From political discussions and debates to reports from future-oriented think tanks and other groups, there is agreement that postsecondary education of some type is the key to the future, both for individual and national success. Yet how are students and their families to afford the already high and ever-growing cost of higher education? Searching for financial aid can be very time-consuming and difficult, though hundreds of millions of dollars in aid reportedly go unclaimed every year.

### Scholarships, Fellowships and Loans Identifies Sources of Aid

*Scholarships, Fellowships and Loans (SFL)*, the most comprehensive single directory of education-related financial aid available, can save you time, effort, and money by helping you to focus your search within the largest pool of awards and avoid pursuing aid for which you do not qualify. In most cases, *SFL*'s detailed descriptions contain enough information to allow you to decide if a particular scholarship is right for you and begin the application process. *SFL* lists almost 3,900 major awards available to U.S. and Canadian students for study throughout the world. Included are:

- *scholarships, fellowships,* and *grants*, which do not require repayment;
- *loans*, which require repayment either monetarily or through service;
- *scholarship loans*, which are scholarships that become loans if the recipient does not comply with the award's terms;
- *internships* and *work study programs*, which provide training, work experience, and (for awards listed in this directory) monetary compensation;
- *awards* and *prizes* that recognize excellence in a particular field;

and other forms of assistance offered by associations, corporations, religious groups, fraternal organizations, foundations, and other private organizations and companies. *SFL* also includes a broad representation of government-backed awards at the national and state levels, as well as a representative sampling of lesser-known and more narrowly focused awards, such as those of a strictly local nature or programs sponsored by small organizations. Financial aid programs administered and funded by individual colleges or universities are not included in *SFL*. Both need- and merit-based awards are included. Competition-based awards and prizes are included when they offer funds that support study or research and are intended to encourage further educational or professional growth.

### Students of All Types Can Benefit

Traditional students as well as those returning to school, non-degree learners, those in need of retraining, and established professionals can use the funding sources listed in *SFL* for formal and non-formal programs of study at all levels:

high school
undergraduate
graduate
postgraduate
doctorate
postdoctorate
professional development

### New Edition Is Improved and Expanded

Major features of the fourteenth edition of *Scholarships, Fellowships and Loans* include:

> *Expanded coverage. SFL* includes over 4,100 awards, 250 of which are new to this edition.

> *More Information.* Many of the sponsoring organization entries now feature email and web page addresses which make contacting these groups even easier.

### Content and Arrangement

*Scholarships, Fellowships and Loans* is organized into a main section containing descriptive listings on award programs and their administering organizations, and six indexes.

The main section, Sponsors and Their Scholarships, is arranged alphabetically by name of administering organization. Entries for its awards appear immediately following the entry on the organization. Each entry contains detailed contact and descriptive information, often providing users with all the information they need to make a decision about applying.

The indexes provide a variety of specific access points to the information contained in the organization and award listings, allowing users to easily identify awards of interest.

Consult the "User's Guide" following this introduction for details on the content, arrangement, and indexing of entries.

### Compilation Methods

Information for all listings in this edition of *Scholarships, Fellowships and Loans* was obtained from the administering organizations through mail, telephone, web page, and email contact. Questionnaires completed by organization officials were augmented by brochures, information sheets, and other printed materials supplied by the organizations.

### Suggestions Welcome

We welcome reader suggestions regarding new and previously unlisted organizations and awards.

# User's Guide

**Scholarships, Fellowships and Loans** is comprised of a main section containing descriptive listings on award programs and their administering organizations, and six indexes. Each of these sections is described in detail below.

## Sponsors and Their Scholarships

**Scholarships, Fellowships and Loans** contains two types of descriptive listings:
- brief entries on the organizations that sponsor or administer specific award programs
- descriptive entries on the award programs themselves

Entries are arranged alphabetically by administering organization; awards administered by each organization follow that organization's listings.

Entries contain detailed contact and descriptive information. *Users are strongly encouraged to read the descriptions carefully and pay particular attention to the various eligibility requirements before applying for awards.*

The organization and award entries shown below illustrate the kind of information that is or might be included in these entries. Each item of information is preceded by a number, and is explained in the paragraph of the same number following the sample entries.

*Sample Entries*

---

[1] • **3445** •

[2] *Microscopy Spcoety of America*

[3] 4 Barlows Landing Rd., Ste. 8          [4] Ph: (508)563-1155
Woods Hole, MA  02543                    [5] Fax: (508)563-1211
                                         [6] Free: 800-538-3672

[7] E-mail: businessoffice@msa.microscopy.com
[8] URL: http://www.msa.microscopy.com

[9] **The Microscopy Society of America was formerly known as the Electron Microscopy Society of America**

[10] • 3446 •   [11] MSA Presidential Student Awards
[12] (Graduate, [13] Undergraduate/Award)

[14] *Purpose:* To recognize outstanding original research by students. [15] *Focus:* Biological Clinical Sciences—Microscopy, Physical Sciences—Microscopy. [16] *Qualif.:* Candidate may be of any nationality, but must be enrolled at a recognized college or university in the United States at the time of the MSA annual meeting. [17] *Criteria:* Award winners will be selected on the basis of the completed application.

[18] *Funds Avail.:* Registration and round-trip travel to the MSA annual meeting, plus a stipend to defray lodging and other expenses. [19] *Duration:* 1 year. [20] *No. of Awards:* Up to 20. [21] *To Apply:* Write to MSA for application form and guidelines. [22] *Deadline:* March 15.

[23] *Remarks:* Research programs for which funds are awarded must be carried out in the U.S. [24] *Contact:* Alternate phone number: 800-538-EMSA.

---

**[1]** *Organization Entry Number:* Entries on administering organizations are listed alphabetically. Each is followed by an alphabetical listing of its awards. All entries—organization and award—are numbered in a single sequence. These numbers are used as references in the indexes.

**[2]** *Organization Name:* The name of the organization administering the awards that follow.

**[3]** *Mailing Address:* The organization's permanent mailing address is listed when known; in some cases an award address is given.

**[4]** *Telephone Number:* The general telephone number for the administering organization. Phone numbers pertaining to specific awards are listed under "Contact" in the award description.

**[5]** *Fax Number:* The facsimile number for the administering organization. Fax numbers pertaining to specific awards are included under "Contact" in the award description

**[6]** *Toll-free Number:* The toll-free number for the administering organization. Toll-free numbers pertaining to specific awards are included under "Contact" in the award description.

**[7]** *E-mail Address:* The electronic mail address for the administering organization. Electronic mail addresses pertaining to specific awards are included under "Contact" in the award description.

**[8]** *URL:* The website address for the administering organization.

**[9]** *Former Name:* Indicates any previous names used by the administering organization.

**[10]** *Award Entry Number:* Entries on awards are listed alphabetically following the entry for their administering organizations. All entries—organization and award—are numbered in a single sequence. These numbers are used as references in the indexes.

**[11]** *Award Name:* Names of awards are listed as given whenever possible. Organization titles or acronyms have been added to generic award names (for example, MSA Undergraduate Scholarships, Canadian Council Fiction Writing Grant, etc.) to avoid confusion.

**[12]** *StudyLevel:* Indicates the level of study for which the award may be used. One or more of the following terms will be listed:

*All*—not restricted to a particular level.

*Doctorate*—study leading to a Ph.D., Ed.D., Sc.D., M.D., D.D.S., D.O., J.D., and other terminal degrees.

*Graduate*—study leading to a M.A., M.S., LL.B., LL.M., and other intermediate degrees.

*High School*—study at the secondary level.

*Other*—study outside the other levels listed.

*Postdoctorate*—study beyond the doctorate level; includes awards intended for professional development when candidates must hold a doctoral degree to qualify.

*Postgraduate*—study beyond the graduate level not specifically leading to a degree.

*Professional Development*—career development not necessarily restricted by study.

*Undergraduate*—study immediately beyond the secondary level, including study at:
- the associate level
- colleges or universities
- junior colleges
- technical institutes leading to a bachelor's degree

• vocational technical schools

[13] **Award Type:** Indicates the type or category of award. One or more of the following terms will be listed:

**Award**—generally includes aid given in recognition and support of excellence, including awards given through music and arts competitions. Non-monetary awards and awards given strictly for recognition are not included.

**Fellowship**—awards granted for graduate- or postgraduate-level research and/or education that does not require repayment.

**Grant**—includes support for research, travel, and creative, experimental, or innovative projects.

**Internship**—training and work experience programs. Internships that do not include compensation of some type are not included.

**Loan**—aid that must be repaid either monetarily or through service. Some loans are interest-free, others are not.

**Other**—anything that does not fit the other categories, such as travel awards.

**Prize**—funds awarded as the result of a competition or contest. Prizes that are not intended to be used for study or to support professional development are not included.

**Scholarships**—support for formal educational programs that does not require repayment.

**Scholarship Loan**—a scholarship that becomes a loan if the recipient does not comply with the terms.

**Work Study**—combined study and work program for which payment is received.

[14] **Purpose:** The purpose for which the award is granted is listed here when known.

[15] **Focus:** Lists the field(s) of study award winners must be pursuing

[16] **Qualif.:** Information regarding applicant eligibility, including the following:

- academic record
- citizenship
- financial need
- organizational affiliation
- minority or ethnic background
- residency
- gender

[17] **Criteria:** When available, an explanation of how award winners are selected.

[18] **Funds Avail.:** The number of awards granted and their dollar amounts are included here along with other relevant funding information, such as: the time period covered by the award; a breakdown of expenses covered (e.g., stipends, tuition and fees, travel and living allowances, equipment funds, etc.); amount awarded to the institution; loan repayment schedules; and service-in-return-for-funding agreements and other obligations.

[19] **Duration:** Indicates the length of time an award is active.

[20] **No. of Awards**: Lists the number of awards given at each presentation.

[21] **To Apply:** Information concerning how to apply for the award.

**[22] Deadline:** Includes specific application due dates, notification dates (date when applicant will be notified of receipt or denial of award), disbursement dates, and other relevant dates.

**[23] Remarks:** Additional information of interest, such as award history, co-sponsors, average number of applicants, and any obligations that must be met by award winners.

**[24] Contact:** When contact information differs from that given for the administering organization, relevant addresses, telephone and fax numbers, and names of specific contact persons are listed here. When the address is that of the administering organization, the entry number for the organization is provided.

# Indexes

*Scholarships, Fellowships and Loans* contains six indexes that make it easy to narrow the search for appropriate awards. The numbers used to refer to the descriptive listings in all of the indexes refer to entry numbers, not page numbers.

### Vocational Goals Index

The Vocational Goals Index preceding the main Sponsors and Their Scholarships section is arranged by level of study and broad subject category to help students quickly focus on the most pertinent awards. It provides a quick overview of each award's purpose and specific eligibility requirements to further fine-tune a search strategy.

The following sample from this index shows the categories of information provided. The items of information preceded by numbers are explained in the paragraph of the same number following the sample:

| [1]<br>Vocational Goal and Award | [2]<br>Geographic Restrictions<br>(Citizenship, Legal Residence, Place of Study) | [3]<br>Affiliation/Special Recipient Requirements |
|---|---|---|
| *Liberal/General Studies* | | |
| Military Order of the Purple Heart Scholarships (2750) | Citizenship: US | Other |
| Mortar Board Foundation Fellowships (2822) | | Association |
| Barbara S. Mosbacher Fellowship (1121) | Study: RI | Association |
| National Consortium for Educational Access Fellowship (2971) | | African American |
| National Fraternal Society of the Deaf Awards (3182) | | Association, Handicapped |
| Nevada Women's Fund Scholarships (3427) | Legal: NV | |
| Opportunities for the Blind Grants (3647) | Citienship: US | Handicapped |
| Oregon Educational Aid for Veterans (3656) | Citizenship: US; Legal: OR | Veteran |
| ORS Awards (3681) | Study: England | |
| Henry J. Reilly Memorial Scholarship (3894) | | Military |
| Western Interstate Commission Graduate Awards (92) | Legal: AK; Study: AK, AZ, CO, HI, ID, MT, ND, NM, NV, OR, UT, WA, WY | |
| Nancy B. Woolridge Graduate Fellowship (4788) | | Fraternal |
| Zuni Higher Education Scholarships (4794) | | Native American |

**[1] VocatioinalGoal, Award Name, and Entry Number.** Citations in this index are classified by one or more of 28 broad vocational goals or categories, which are used as subject headings. These categories are based on the U.S. Department of Education's Office of Educational Research and Improvement's Classification of Instructional Programs (CIP). Categories appear in boldface and are listed alphabetically; citations to relevant awards follow, along with the award's entry number in the main section.

It is important to note that many awards are offered without any restrictions on the field of study. These are listed under the category "Liberal/General Studies" along with awards that are specifically granted for liberal arts studies. Additionally, awards that cover a wide range of study fields are listed under this category. All users should look under "Liberal/General Studies" as well as other relevant categories.

For a complete list of the categories used and the specific subjects covered by each category, consult the "Guide to Subjects Used in the Vocational Goals Index" immediately preceding the index. The Field of Study Index, which is described below, classifies the award listings by some 330 subject terms and should be used for more direct access to awards pertaining to specific fields of study.

[2] **Geographic Restrictions.** This column provides information on citizenship and residency requirements as explained below.

> **Citizenship.** Some awards have citizenship requirements as a qualification for aid When citizenship requirements exist, they are indicated by the following codes:
>
> - US—United States citizenship is required
> - Canada—Canadian citizenship is required
> - US/CA—Either United States or Canadian citizenship is required
> - PermRes—must be a permanent resident; if U.S., must have an I-151, I-551, or I-551C Alien Registration Receipt Card (or "green card")
> - Other—includes citizens of countries other than the U.S. or Canada
>
> **Residence.** Some awards have residence requirements as a condition for aid. These requirements fall into two categories:
>
> - Legal Residence—noted after the word "Legal," the geographic location(s) in which a recipient must maintain residence of legal record.
> - Residence During Study—noted after the word "Study," the geographic location(s) in which the award may be used. The specific requirements noted may include states in the U.S. (U.S. Postal Service abbreviations are used to designate states) specific countries (including the U.S.; permanent residence may also be required), or geographic areas (such as North America, Eastern Europe, abroad, etc.).

Some awards require residence for a particular length of time; consult the award entries in the main section for detailed information on residence requirements. If no requirements are listed following a particular award, there are no clearly stated limitations on eligibility due to residence.

[3] **Affiliation/Special Recipient Requirements.** Provides information on restrictions or requirements that limit eligibility to applicants and their parents, guardians, or spouses who are participants, members, or those affiliated with the following twelve specific groups or categories:

- Association membership
- Employer affiliation
- Ethnic group membership or heritage
- Female
- Fraternal organization membership
- Male
- Military service or status
- Minority status (includes African American, Asian American, Hispanic, Native American, and Handicapped)

- Other (includes required affiliations not covered by the other categories)
- Religious affiliation
- Union membership
- Veteran status or affiliation

In some cases these requirements will apply to the applicant; in others, the requirements apply to parents (may include divorced and deceased parents), step-parents, guardians, or spouses. Generally, there are specific lengths of time that parents or students must be members of an organization or work for a company before they or their families are eligible to apply for aid. Consult the award entries in the Sponsors and Their Scholarships section for detailed information on these special requirements or restrictions.

## Field of Study Index

The Field of Study Index classifies awards by one or more of some 330 specific subject categories, allowing users to easily target their search by specific areas of study. Citations are arranged alphabetically under all appropriate subject terms. Each citation is followed by the study level and award type, which appear in parentheses and can be used to narrow the search even further.

## Legal Residence Index

The Legal Residence Index lists awards that are restricted by the applicant's residence of legal record. Award citations are arranged alphabetically by country and subarranged by state or province (for U.S. and Canada). Each citation is followed by the study level and award type, which appear in parentheses and can be used to eliminate inappropriate awards.

## Place of Study Index

The Place of Study Index lists awards that carry restrictions on where study can take place. Award citations are arranged alphabetically under the following geographic headings.

- United States
- United States—by State
- Canada
- Canada—by Province
- International
- International—by Region
- International—by Country

Each citation is followed by the study level and award type, which appear in parentheses.

## Special Recipient Index

The Special Recipient Index lists awards that carry restrictions or special qualifying factors relating to applicant affiliation. Awards of particular interest to users in the following categories can be quickly identified by this index:

| | |
|---|---|
| African American | Male |
| Asian American | Military |
| Association | Minority |
| Employer | Native American |
| Ethnic | Religion |
| Female | Union |
| Fraternal | Veteran |
| Handicapped | Other |
| Hispanic | |

Awards are listed under all appropriate headings. Each citation includes information on study level and award type, which appear in parentheses and can be used to further narrow the search. Users interested in awards restricted to particular minorities should also look under the general "Minorities" heading, which lists awards targeted for minorities but not restricted to any particular minority group.

**Sponsor and Scholarship Index**

The Sponsor and Scholarship Index lists, in a single alphabetic sequence, all of the administering organizations, awards, and acronyms included in *SFL*.

# Federal Programs

Federal aid for college students is available through a variety of programs administered by the U.S. Department of Education. Most colleges and universities participate with federal programs, but there are exceptions. Contact the school's financial aid office to find out if it is a participating institution. If it participates, the student works with financial aid counselors to determine how much aid can be obtained.

Aid for students comes in three forms, grants (gifts to the student), loans (funds which must be repaid), and work-study jobs (a job for the student while enrolled in which his/her pay is applied to his school account). These types of aid are further explained below.

### Grants

•*Pell Grants:* These grants are intended to provide funds for any undergraduate student (who does not already have a degree) who wishes to attend college regardless of family financial background. It is available through the financial aid office at the college

•*Federal Supplemental Educational Opportunity Grants (FSEOG)*: Intended for students with exceptional financial need, these grants are typically for smaller amounts (between $100 and $4,000) than Pell Grants. They are available on a limited basis.

### Loans

Student loans are available in a variety of ways. Loans may not be taken out for any more than the cost of attendance at the school, which is determined by the financial aid administrator. Grants and other forms of aid are considered when the amount to be borrowed is determined. If other forms of aid are sufficient, then the amount that can be borrowed will be reduced.

These loans are divided into two types: subsidized and unsubsidized loans. If the loan is subsidized, then the federal government pays the interest on the loan until after the schooling is completed. If it is unsubsidized, then the student incurs the interest charges while in school, but payment of the charges may be deferred until school is completed. The advantage of unsubsidized loans is that there are usually fewer restrictions against obtaining them. Amounts available through these programs vary depending on academic level.

The total debt a student or a student's parents may accumulate for that student is $23,000 for a dependent undergraduate student, $46,000 for an independent undergraduate student (with a limit of $23,000 in subsidized loans), and $138,500 for a graduate or professional student (with a limit of $65,500 in subsidized loans).

•*Direct Loan Program*: These low-interest loans bypass lending institutions such as banks. They are a direct arrangement between the government and the student (through the school). Direct subsidized loans may be taken out for a maximum of $2,625 by incoming freshmen while juniors and seniors may borrow through this program up to a maximum of $5,500. The amounts for independent undergraduate students range from $6,625 minimum to $10,500 maximum per year. Independent students face some restrictions on the amounts of subsidized funds they can receive from the program. At least half of the funds borrowed through the Direct Loan program by independent students must come from unsubsidized loans. Graduate students may borrow up to $18,500 directly of which $10,000 must be in unsubsidized loans.

There are four repayment options for the Direct Loan Program: the Income Contingent Repayment Plan, the Extended Repayment Plan, the Graduated Repayment Plan, and the Standard Repayment Plan.

•**Federal Family Education Loans (FFEL)/Stafford Loans**: This program provides funds to the students' lending institutions of their choice. Before borrowing the funds, the student must obtain an application for federal student aid and a Federal Stafford Loan Application and Promissory Note from the school's financial aid office.

This program is also divided into subsidized and unsubsidized loans. However, students may not borrow simultaneously from this program and the Direct Loan program. Students may borrow separately subsidized and unsubsidized funds from either program. The maximum amounts that can be borrowed through this program are the same as through the Direct Loan program.

There are three repayment options for FFEL/Stafford Loans: Fixed, Graduated, and Income-Sensitive. Any FFEL/Stafford loan must be paid back within ten years.

•**Direct and FFEL/Stafford Program Loans for Parents (PLUS)**: Parents may borrow for their children's education through the aforementioned Federal Loan programs. They are responsible for the repayment of the loans. The maximum amount to be borrowed is the cost of attending the school minus other forms of aid already obtained. The interest rate on the loans is variable and has a slightly higher ceiling (9%) than when students themselves bear the responsibility of repayment (8.25%).

With the Direct PLUS loan, parents fill out a Direct PLUS Loan Application and Promissory Note available at the school's financial aid office. The funds are disbursed to the school. Parents may choose from three repayment plans: Standard, Extended, or Graduated. To obtain funds for their children through the FFEL/Stafford Program, parents make the arrangements with the lending institution. The school is not involved in the application process. Parents who borrow through the FFEL/Stafford program make arrangements with the lender for repayment.

•**Perkins Loan Program**: The Perkins Loan allows students who have unusual financial need to borrow funds not otherwise available from other loan or grant programs. Up to $3,000 is available to undergraduates each year (up to $5,000 for graduate students). It has a fixed interest rate of 5%. Perkins Loans must be repaid within ten years.


### Other Types of Funding

**Federal Work-Study Program**: Work-study is an arrangement that allows students to work on (and off) campus while they are enrolled to help pay their expenses. The federal government pays for the majority of the student's wages although the department where the student works also contributes. The employment must be relevant to the student's field of study and only so much time per semester may be devoted to the job. If the student earns the amount of aid prior to the end of the semester, then work is terminated for the duration of the award period.


### Other Considerations

**Application**: Applying for federal student aid is free. All federal aid is obtained by first completing a Free Application for Federal Student Aid (FAFSA). After the application is submitted, it will be processed by the Department of Education. The student then receives a Student Aid Report, which contains a figure for Expected Family Contribution. This is the amount that the student should plan on providing from non-federal sources in order to attend school.

**Dependency**: If a student is eligible for independent status, more money may be available to attend school in the form of loans. The interest rates and the programs for repayment, however, are the same. The purpose of distinguishing between the status of dependent or independent is to allow students who do not have the benefit of parental financial contributions more leeway in obtaining federal funds for education.

***Deadline***: The FAFSA must be received by May 1 for the following school year. Applicants are encouraged to apply as soon as possible after January 1 of the year they plan to enroll, but no earlier.

***Special Circumstances***: The financial aid counselor at the school will often listen to extenuating circumstances such as unexpected medical expenses, private education expenses for other family members, or recent unemployment when evaluating requests for assistance.

***Telephone Numbers***:

- 1-800-433-3243 to have questions answered about how to apply;
- 1-319-337-5665 to find out if your application has been processed;
- 1-800-730-8913 (TDD) if you are hearing impaired; and
- 1-800-647-8733 to report fraud, waste, or abuse of federal student aid funds.

***Additional Information:*** For more information about Federal student financial aid, write to:

Federal Student Aid Information Center
PO Box 84
Washington, DC 20044

and ask for ***The Student Guide to Financial Aid from the U.S. Department of Education.***

# AmeriCorps

President Clinton launched this volunteer community service program in
through the National and Community Service Trust Act, aimed at helping co...
people pay for their education and get a sense of community service. Volu...
minimum wage, health benefits, and a grant toward college (for up to two years).

Funds for the program are distributed by the Federal government to qualifying organization...
community groups with the goal of achieving direct results in addressing the nation's criti...
education, human services, public safety, and environmental needs at the community level. The
program provides meaningful opportunities for Americans of all ages and backgrounds to serve
their country in organized efforts, fostering citizen responsibility, building community, and
providing educational opportunity for those who make a substantial commitment to service.

The AmeriCorps programs are run by not-for-profit organizations or partnerships, institutions of
higher learning, local governments, school or police districts, states, Native American tribes, or
federal agencies. State commissions assist programs in recruiting participants, disseminate
information about service opportunities, and provide technical assistance to communities
organizing service programs.

### Am I eligible to serve in AmeriCorps?

Probably. Citizens and legal resident aliens who are 17 years of age or older are eligible to serve
in AmeriCorps before, during, or after post-secondary education. In general, participants must be
high school graduates or agree to achieve their GED prior to receiving education awards.

### How will participants be selected?

Individual programs select service participants on a non-discriminatory and non-political basis.
There are national and state-wide recruiting information systems and a national pool of potential
service volunteers.

### How will I be compensated?

Full-time participants not otherwise covered receive
basic health insurance and may receive a child
care allowance if they need it to be able to participate.
For one year of full-time or two years of part-time service
in a designated national service program, participants
will also receive $4,725 as an education award
and repayment of any interest on student loans during
their service. These awards may be used to pay for
higher education or for vocational training. Awards must
be used within seven years of completion of service.
For those participants who have outstanding loan
obligations for qualified educational activities, the
post-service educational awards may be paid directly to
the lender.

> **The AmeriCorps Pledge**
>
> I will get things done for America to make our people safer, smarter, and healthier.
>
> I will bring Americans together to strengthen our     communities.
>
> Faced with apathy, I will take action.
>
> Faced with conflict, I will seek a common ground.
>
> Faced with adversity, I will persevere.
>
> I will carry this commitment with me this year and beyond.
>
> I am an AmeriCorps Member and I am going to get things done.

### How long is a term of service?

The program requires a commitment intensive in hours but limited in years. Participants can
perform a 1,700 hour full-time term over nine months to a year, or a part-time term of 900 hours
over one to two years (or one to three years in the case of full-time college students).

*Individuals interested in participating in AmeriCorps national service programs should apply directly to grant recipients.*
*For basic program information, individuals can call the AmeriCorps Information Hotline at 1-800-942-2677.*

# State Agencies

The following is an alphabetic state-by-state listing of agencies located in the United States. Many of these agencies administer special federal award programs, such as the Robert C. Byrd Honors Scholarship Program offered by about 20 states, as well as state-specific awards, such as the Tuition Incentive Program (TIP) offered by the state of Michigan for low-income students to receive free tuition at community colleges. Financial aid seekers should contact the agency in their home state for more information.

## Alabama
Commission on Higher Education
100 N. Main St.
One Court Sq., Ste. 221
Montgomery, AL 36130
(334)242-1998
Fax: (334)242-0268
http://www.ache.state.al.us/index.htm

## Alaska
ACPE
Student Loan Program
3030 Vintage Blvd.
907465-2962
http://www.state.ak.us/acpe

## Arizona
Arizona Dept. of Education
1535 W. Jefferson
Phoenix, AZ 85007
(602)542-5393

## Arkansas
Student Loan Authority
101 E. Capitol Ave., Ste. 401
Little Rock, AR 72201
(501)682-2952
Toll-Free: (800)443-6030
httpP//www.asla.state.ar.us/student/other.htm

## California
Student Aid Commission
PO Box 419026
Rancho Cordova, CA 95741-9026
(916)526-7200
http://www.csac.ca.gov

## Colorado
Colorado Student Loan Program
One Denver Pl., S. Ter.
999 18th St., No. 425
Denver, CO 80202
(303)294-5050
http://www.cslp.org

## Connecticut
Connecticut Student Loan Foundation
525 Brook St.
PO Box 1009
Rocky Hill, CT 06067
(860)257-4001
Fax: (860)563-3247

Toll-Free: (800)237-9721
http://cslf.com

## Delaware
Higher Education Commission
Carvel State Office Bldg.
820 N. French St.
Wilmington, DE 19801
(302)577-3240
Fax: (302)577-6765
Toll-Free: (800)292-7935
http://www.doc.state.dc.us/high-ed/

## District of Columbia
Higher Education Loan Program
1850 K St., NW, Ste. 215
Washington, DC 20006
(202)289-4500

## Florida
Office of Student Financial Assist.
Department of Education
325 W. Gaines St.
Collins Bldg., Rm. 255
Tallahassee, FL 32399-0400
(904)487-0049

## Georgia
Student Finance Commission
2082 E. Exchange Pl., No. 200
Tucker, GA 30084
(770)414-3000
Fax: (770)414-3133
Toll-Free: (800)776-6878
http://www.gsfc.org

## Hawaii
Hawaii Education Loan Program
1314 S. King St., Ste. 861
Honolulu, HI 96814
(808)593-2262

## Idaho
Idaho Student Loan Fund
PO Box 730
Fruitland, ID 83619
(208)452-4058

## Illinois
Student Assistance Commission
1755 Lake Cook Rd.
Deerfield, IL 60015-5209
(847)948-8500

Toll –Free: (800)899-ISAC
http://www.isac1.org/

## Indiana
State Student Assist. Comm.
150 W. Market St., Ste. 500
Indianapolis, IN 46204
(317)232-2350

## Iowa
Iowa College Student Aid Comm.
200 10th St., 4th Fl.
Des Moines, IA 50309
(515)281-3501
http://www.sos.state.ia.us/register/r4/r4studya.htm

## Kentucky
Higher Education Assist. Authority
1050 US 127 South
Frankfort, KY 40601-4323
(502)564-7990
Fax: (502)696-7345
http://www.kheaa.state.ky.us/

## Louisiana
Student Financial Assistance Comm.
PO Box 91202
Baton Rouge, LA 70821-9202
(225)922-1011
Fax: (225)922-0790
http://www.gov.state.la.us/depts.osfa

## Maine
Finance Authority of Maine
Educational Assistance Div.
State House, Sta. 119
One Weston Ct.
Augusta, ME 04333
(207)287-2183

## Massachusetts
Office of Student Financial Assist.
330 Stuart St., Ste. 304
Boston,MA 02116
(617)727-9420
http://www.osfa.mass.edu

## Michigan
Great Lakes Higher Education Corp.
4700 S. Hagadon Rd., Ste. 190
East Lansing, MI 48823

**Minnesota**
Dept of Children, Families & Learning
1500 Hwy. 36 W.
Roseville, MN 55113-4266
(651)582-8200

**Missouri**
Dept of Higher Education
3515 Amazona Dr.
Jefferson City. MO 65109-5717
(573)751-2361
Fax: (573)751-6635

**Montana**
Guaranteed Student Loan Program
2500 Broadway
PO Box 203101
Helena, MT 59620-3101
(406)444-6594
http://www.mgslp.state.mt.us/

**Nebraska**
Nebraska Student Loan Program
PO Box 82507
Lincoln, NE 68501-2507
(402)475-8686
http://www.nslp.org

**New Hampshire**
Higher Educatioin Assistance
Foundation
44 Warren St.
PO Box 877
Concord, NH 03302
(603)225-6612

**New Jersey**
New Jersey Office of Student
Assistance
4 Quakerbridge Plz.
Trenton, NJ 08625
(609)588-3200

**New Mexico**
Student Loan Guarantee Corp.
PO Box 92230
Albuquerque, NM 87199-2230
(505)345-3371
Toll-Free: (800)279-5083

**New York**
New York State Higher Education
Services Commission
99 Wasington Ave.
Albany, NY 12255
(518)473-7087

**North Carolina**
Education Assistance Authority

PO Box 2688
Chapel Hill, NC 27515-2688
(919)549-8614

**North Dakota**
Dept. of Public Instruction
North Dakota Capitol Bldg.
600 E. Boulevard Ave., Dept. 201
Bismarck, ND 58505-0440
(701)328-2260
Fax: (701)328-2461

**Ohio**
Ohio Board of Regents
30 E. Broad St., 36th Fl.
Columbus, OH 43266-0417
(614)466-6000
Fax: (614)466-5866
http://www.bor.ohio.gov/

**Oklahoma**
State Regents for Higher Education
500 Education Bldg.
State Capital Complex
Oklahoma City, OK 73105
(405)524-9100
Fax: (405)524-9234
http://www.okhighered.org/

**Oregon**
State Scholarship Commission
1500 Valley River Dr., Ste. 100
Eugene, OR 97401
(541)687-7400

**Pennsylvania**
Higher Education Assistance Agency
1200 N 7th St.
Harrisburgh, PA 17102
(717)720-2860
http://www.pheaa.org/index.htm

**Rhode Island**
Higher Education Assistance
Authority
560 Jefferson Blvd.
Warwick, RI 02886
(401)736-1100

**South Carolina**
SEAA
PO Box 210219
Columbia, SC 29221
(803)798-7960

**South Dakota**
Education Assistance Corp.
115 1st Ave., SW
Aberdeen, SD 57401

(605)225-6423

**Tennessee**
Student Assistance Corp.
Parkway Towers
404 James Robertson Pkwy., Ste.
1950
Nashville, TN 37243-0820
(615)741-1346

**Texas**
Texas Guaranteed Student Loan
Corp.
Box 201725
Austin, TX 78720-1725
(512)219-5700

**Utah**
Student Loan Programs
PO Box 45202
Salt Lake City, UT 84145
(801)321-7200

**Vermont**
Student Assistance Corp.
Champlain Mill
Box 2000
Winooski, VT 05404
(802)655-9602

**Virginia**
Student Assistance Authorities
411 E. Franklin St., Ste. 300
Richmond, VA 23218
(804)775-4000

**Washington**
NW Education Loan Guarantee
Association
500 Colman Bldg.
811 First Ave.
Seattle, WA 98104
(206)461-5300

**West Virginia**
West Virginia Education Loan
Services
PO Box 591
Charleston, WV 25322
(304)345-7211

**Wisconsin**
Great Lakes Higher Education Corp.
2401 International LN.
Madison, WI 53704-3192
(608)246-1800
http://www.glhec.org/

# Abbreviations

### Geographic Abbreviations— United States

| | | | |
|---|---|---|---|
| AK | Alaska | MT | Montana |
| AL | Alabama | NC | North Carolina |
| AR | Arkansas | ND | North Dakota |
| AZ | Arizona | NE | Nebraska |
| CA | California | NH | New Hampshire |
| CO | Colorado | NJ | New Jersey |
| CT | Connecticut | NM | New Mexico |
| DC | District of Columbia | NV | Nevada |
| DE | Delaware | NY | New York |
| FL | Florida | OH | Ohio |
| GA | Georgia | OK | Oklahoma |
| GU | Guam | OR | Oregon |
| HI | Hawaii | PA | Pennsylvania |
| IA | Iowa | PR | Puerto Rico |
| ID | Idaho | RI | Rhode Island |
| IL | Illinois | SC | South Carolina |
| IN | Indiana | SD | South Dakota |
| KS | Kansas | TN | Tennessee |
| KY | Kentucky | TX | Texas |
| LA | Louisiana | UT | Utah |
| MA | Massachusetts | VA | Virginia |
| MD | Maryland | VI | Virgin Islands |
| ME | Maine | VT | Vermont |
| MI | Michigan | WA | Washington |
| MN | Minnesota | WI | Wisconsin |
| MO | Missouri | WV | West Virginia |
| MS | Mississippi | WY | Wyoming |

### Geographic Abbreviations—Canadian Provinces

| | | | |
|---|---|---|---|
| AB | Alberta | NT | Northwest Territories |
| BC | British Columbia | ON | Ontario |
| MB | Manitoba | PE | Prince Edward Island |
| NM | New Brunswick | PQ | Quebec |
| NF | Newfoundland | SK | Saskatchewan |
| NS | Nova Scotia | YT | Yukon Territory |

### Other Abbreviations

| | | | |
|---|---|---|---|
| ACT | American College Testing Program | | Science/Surgery |
| | | D.O. | Doctor of Osteopathy |
| B.A. | Bachelor of Arts | D.Sc. | Doctor of Science |
| B.Arch. | Bachelor of Architecture | D.S.W. | Doctor of Social Work |
| B.F.A. | Bachelor of Fine Arts | D.V.M. | Doctor of Veterinary Medicine |
| B.S. | Bachelor of Science | D.V.M.S. | Doctor of Veterinary Medicine and Surgery |
| B.Sc. | Bachelor of Science | | |
| CSS | College Scholarship Service | D.V.S. | Doctor of Veterinary Science |
| D.D.S. | Doctor of Dental | FAFSA | Free Application for Federal |

| | | | |
|---|---|---|---|
| | Student Aid | M.S. | Master of Science |
| FSEOG | Federal Supplemental Educational Opportunity Grants | M.Sc. | Master of Science |
| | | M.S.W. | Master of Social Work |
| | | O.D. | Doctor of Optometry |
| FWS | Federal Work Study | Pharm.D. | Doctor of Pharmacy |
| GED | General Education Development Certificate | Ph.D. | Doctor of Philosophy |
| | | POW | Prisoner of War |
| GPA | Grade Point Average | PSAT | Preliminary Scholastic Aptitude Test |
| GRE | Graduate Record Examination | | |
| J.D. | Doctor of Jurisprudence | ROTC | Reserve Officers Training Corps |
| LL.B. | Bachelor of Law | | |
| LL.M. | Master of Law | SAR | Student Aid Report |
| LSAT | Law School Admission Test | SAT | Scholastic Aptitude Test |
| M.A. | Master of Arts | Sc.D. | Doctor of Science |
| M.Arch. | Master of Architecture | TDD | Telephone Device for the Deaf |
| M.B.A. | Master of Business Administration | Th.d. | Doctor of Theology |
| | | U.N. | United Nations |
| M.D. | Doctor of Medicine | U.S. | United States |
| M.Div. | Master of Divinity | | |
| M.F.A. | Master of Fine Arts | | |
| MIA | Missing in Action | | |
| M.L.S. | Master of Library Science | | |
| M.N. | Master of Nursing | | |

## Currency Abbreviations

| | | | |
|---|---|---|---|
| A$ | Australian dollar | IR | Irish Pound |
| BDS$ | Barbados dollar | ¥ | Japanese Yen |
| C$ | Canadian dollar | S$ | Singapore dollar |
| DM | German mark | £ | United Kingdom pound |
| Fr | French franc | | |

# Guide to Subjects Used in the Vocational Goals Index

The following is an alphabetical listing of the 28 broad subject fields used in the Vocational Goals Index. Specific subjects covered by each broad subject term are listed alphabetically beneath them. All of the terms listed below are also used to classify awards in the Field of Study Index.

## Agriculture

Agribusiness
Agricultural sciences
Animal science and
  behavior
Dairy science
Fisheries
  sciences/management
Food science and
  technology
Forestry
Horticulture
Poultry science
Wildlife conservation,
  management, and science

## Architecture and Environmental Design

Architecture
Architecture, naval
Environmental design
Historic preservation
Interior design
Land management
Landscape architecture
  and design
Urban design/planning

## Area and Ethnic Studies

African American studies
African studies
Armenian studies
Asian studies
British studies
Byzantine studies
Canadian studies
Central Eurpoean studies
Chinese studies
Classical studies
Cross-cultural studies
Demography
East European studies
Ethnology
European studies
Finnish studies
French studies

German studies
Greek studies
Italian studies
Japanese studies
Jewish studies
Latin American studies
Native American studies
Near Eastern studies
Portuguese studies
Romanian studies
Soviet studies
Spanish studies
Swedish studies
Welsh studies

## Business and Management

Accounting
Advertising
Banking
Business
Business administration
Economics
Finance
Food service careers
Funeral services
Hotel, institutional, and
  restaurant management
Industrial and labor
  relations
Insurance and insurance
  related fields
Management
Marketing and
  related fields
Personnel administration
Public relations
Publishing
Real estate
Travel and tourism

## Communications

Advertising
Broadcasting
Communications
  technologies

Graphic art and design
Journalism
Media arts
Public relations
Publishing
Radio and television
Telecommunications
  systems

## Computer and Information Sciences

Data processing
Information science
  and technology
Operations research

## Education

Early childhood education
Education, bilingual
  and cross-cultural
Education, elementary
Education, English as a
  second language
Education, industrial
Education, physical
Education, Rrligious
Education, secondary
Education, special
Education, vocational
  technical
Educational administration

## Engineering

Aviation
Electronics
Engineering, aerospace/
  aeronautical/astronautical
Engineering, biomedical
Engineering, chemical
Engineering, civil
Engineering, electrical
Engineering, geological
Engineering, industrial
Engineering, marine
Engineering, mechanical

### Engineering (cont.)

Engineering,
  metallurgical
Engineering, mineral
  and mining
Engineering, naval
Engineering, nuclear
Engineering, ocean
Technology

### Foreign Languages

### Health Care Services

Art therapy
Dental hygiene
Health services
  administration
Medical assisting
Medical laboratory
  technology
Medical record
  administration/
  technology
Nutrition
Occupational therapy
Physical therapy
Rehabilitation
Respiratory therapy
Substance abuse

### Health Sciences

Dental hygiene
Gerontology
Immunology
Immunopharmacology
Medical technology
Medicine, chiropractic
Mental health
Nursing administration
Nursing, cardiovascular
  and cerebrovascular
Nursing, psychiatric
Nursing, pulmonary
Pharmaceutical
  sciences
Pharmacology
Pharmacy
Public health
Speech and language
  pathology/Audiology

### Home Economics

Culinary arts
Fashion design
Food science and
  technology
Food service careers
Interior design
Nutrition
Textile science

### Humanities

### Industry and Trade

Aviation
Construction
Education, vocational-
  technical
Electronics
Energy-related areas
Industrial and labor
  relations
Industrial design
International trade
Manufacturing
Marketing and
  distribution
Materials
  research/science
Mechanics and repairs
Transportation

### Language and Literature

English language and
  literature
Linguistics
Literature
Literature, children's
Playwriting
Poetry
Publishing
Screenwriting
Sports writing
Translating
Writing

### Law

Criminal justice
Law enforcement

### Liberal/General Studies

General Studies
Interdisciplinary studies
Liberal arts

### Library and Archival Sciences

Archival science
Library science
Museum science

### Life Sciences

Behavioral sciences
Biochemistry
Biological and clinical
  sciences
Biology
Biology, marine
Biology, molecular
Biomedical research
Biomedical sciences

Biophysics
Botany
Chemistry
Clinical laboratory sciences
Ecology
Entomology
Environmental conservation
Environmental science
Equine studies
Genetics
Microbiology
Mortuary science
Natural history
Ocean management
Oceanography
Ornithology
Paleontology
Pathology
Primatology
Toxicology
Wildlife conservation,
  management, and
  science
Zoology

### Mathematics

Actuarial sciences
Statistics

### Medicine

Acquired Immune
  Deficiency Syndrome
Allergies
Alzheimer's disease
Amyotrophic lateral
  disease
Anesthesiology
Arthritis
Asthma
Biological and clinical
  sciences
Biomedical research
Biomedical sciences
Cooley's anemia
Cystic fibrosis
Dentistry
Dermatology
Diabetes
Endocrinology
Engineering
  biomedical
Epidemiology
Epilepsy
Ethics and bioethics
Gastroenterology
Genetics
Gerontology

### Medicine (cont.)
- Hemophilia
- Hepatology
- Herpatology
- History, medical
- Hodgkin's disease
- Huntington's disease
- Ileitis and Colitis
- Immunology
- Immunopharmacology
- Infectious disease
- Internal cystitis
- Leprosy
- Leukemia
- Medical research
- Medicine cerebrovascular
- Medicine, geriatric
- Medicine gynocological and obstetrical
- Medicine, internal
- Medicine, orthopedic
- Medicine, osteopathic
- Medicine, pediatric
- Medicine, pulmonary
- Medicine, sports
- Mental health
- Multiple sclerosis
- Muscular dystrophy
- Myasthenia Gravis
- Nephrology
- Neuroscience
- Oncology
- Ophthalmology
- Optometry
- Otolarynclogy
- Otology
- Parkinson's disease
- Plastic surgery
- Podiatry
- Psychiatry
- Rheumatology
- Spinal cord injuries and research
- Sudden infant death syndrome
- Surgery
- Tourette syndrome
- Tuberculosis
- Urology
- Veterinary science and medicine
- Visual impairment

### Military Sciences
- History, military
- Military science and education
- National security

### Parks and Recreation
- Crafts
- Numismatics

### Philosophy, Theology and Religion
- Bible studies
- Education, religious
- Philosophy
- Religion
- Theology

### Physical Sciences
- Aeronautics
- Aerospace sciences
- Astronautics
- Astronomy and astronomical sciences
- Atmospheric science
- Cartography/surveying
- Chemistry
- Earth sciences
- Electrochemistry
- Energy-related areas
- Environmental science
- Geology
- Geophysics
- Geosciences
- Hydrology
- Metallurgy
- Meteorology
- Mineralogy
- Mining
- Natural history
- Natural resources
- Natural sciences
- Nuclear science
- Oceanography
- Optics
- Paleontology
- Photogrammetry
- Physics
- Science technologies
- Space and planetary sciences
- Vacuum science and technology

### Protective Services and Public Affairs
- Consumer affairs
- Criminal justice
- Law enforcement
- Leadership, institutional and community
- Protective services
- Public administration
- Public affairs
- Public health
- Public service
- Social work

### Social Sciences
- Aggression and violence
- Anthropology
- Archeology
- Byzantine studies
- Counseling/guidance
- Criminology
- Cross-cultural studies
- Economics
- Ethnology
- Geography
- Government
- History
- History, American
- History, Economic
- History, Medical
- History, Military
- Human relations
- International affairs and relations
- International development
- Maritime studies
- Medieval studies
- Parapsychology
- Peace studies
- Political science
- Pre-Columbian studies
- Psychology
- Renaissance studies
- Sociology
- Soviet studies
- Women's studies

### Visual and Performing Arts
- Art
- Art, caricatures, and cartoons
- Art conservation
- Art history
- Choreography
- Crafts
- Criticism (art, drama, literary)
- Dance
- Drawing
- Filmmaking
- Graphic art and design
- Media arts
- Music
- Music, bass
- Music, cello
- Music, chamber
- Music, classical
- Music composition
- Music, jazz

## *Visual and Performing Arts (cont.)*

Musicology
Music, orchestral
Music, piano
Music therapy
Music, viola
Music, violin
Music, vocal
Opera
Painting
Photography
Playwriting
Poetry
Printmaking
Puppetry
Radio and television
Screenwriting
Sculpture
Theater arts
Video
Visual arts
Writing

# Vocational Goals Index

This index classifies awards first by level of study, and then by one or more of 28 broad vocational goals or subject fields (see the "Guide to Subjects Used in the Vocational Goals Index" immediately preceding this index for a complete list of terms used). Awards not restricted by vocational goal are listed in the *Liberal/General Studies* category. Vocational goals, relevant awards, and award entry numbers are listed in the first column of the index. Subsequent columns indicate specific restrictions or requirements as indicated by the column headings. See the "Users Guide" for additional information on how to use this index.

## All

| Vocational Goal, Award, and Entry Number | Geographic Restrictions (Citizenship, Legal Residence, Place of Study) | Affiliation/Special Recipients Requirements |
|---|---|---|
| **Business and Management** | | |
| Chartered Institute of Management Accountants Research Foundation Grants (1834) | | |
| **Education** | | |
| American Council of the Blind Scholarship Program (399) | Citizenship: US, PermRes | Handicapped |
| Phyllis P. Harris Scholarships (4956) | Legal: Canada; Study: Canada | |
| NSCA Challenge Scholarships (4415) | | Association |
| **Engineering** | | |
| Doris Mullen Memorial Scholarships (3203) | | |
| The Payzer Scholarship (2423) | | |
| **Health Care Services** | | |
| NSCA Challenge Scholarships (4415) | | Association |
| **Health Sciences** | | |
| Health Sciences Student Fellowships (2401) | | |
| **Industry and Trade** | | |
| Herbert L. Cox Memorial Scholarship (5692) | | |
| EAA Aviation Achievement Scholarship (2422) | | |
| Teledyne Continental Aviation Excellence Scholarship (5693) | | |
| Richard Lee Vernon Aviation Scholarship (5694) | | |
| **Language and Literature** | | |
| Bibliographical Society of America Fellowships (1430) | | |
| IREX Bulgarian Studies Seminar (3184) | Citizenship: US, PermRes; Study: Bulgaria | |
| **Liberal/General Studies** | | |
| 102nd Infantry Division Scholarship (6) | | Veteran |
| American Council of the Blind Scholarship Program (399) | Citizenship: US, PermRes | Handicapped |
| AMF/Signet Bank Educational Loans (99) | Citizenship: US, PermRes | Military, Veteran |
| Baldridge Scholarship (5942) | | Association |
| Citizens' Scholarship Foundation of Wakefield Scholarships (1960) | Legal: MA | |
| Marion Wright Edelman Scholarship (3490) | | Minority |
| Educational Enrichment Grant (2893) | | Native American |
| FEAT Loans (2607) | | Other |

| Vocational Goal, Award, and Entry Number | Geographic Restrictions (Citizenship, Legal Residence, Place of Study) | Affiliation/Special Recipients Requirements |
|---|---|---|
| *Liberal/General Studies (continued)* | | |
| Federal Consolidation Loan Program (3688) | Legal: MI | |
| George Grotefend Scholarships (2754) | Study: CA | Other |
| Halton Foundation Scholarships (2784) | | Employer |
| The Hauss-Helms Foundation Scholarships (2817) | Legal: OH | |
| Jaycee War Memorial Fund Scholarship (5943) | Citizenship: US | |
| Jaycee War Memorial Scholarships (3257) | Citizenship: US | |
| Maine Veterans Dependents Educational Benefits (3538) | Legal: ME | Veteran |
| New Hampshire Alternative Loans for Parents and Students (2736) | | |
| Leo S. Rowe Pan American Fund (4810) | Legal: United States | |
| San Mateo County Farm Bureau Scholarships (5243) | | Association |
| SRI Multi-Cultural Scholarship (5264) | | |
| Lloyd D. Sweet Education Scholarships (5658) | | |
| Carol Thomson Memorial Fund Scholarship (3447) | Study: Canada | Handicapped |
| Nicholas C. Vrataric Scholarships (5810) | | Union |
| Washington State Student Financial Aid Programs State Need Grant (6103) | Legal: WA; Study: WA | |

**Library and Archival Sciences**

| Bibliographical Society of America Fellowships (1430) | | |
|---|---|---|

**Life Sciences**

| Phyllis P. Harris Scholarships (4956) | Legal: Canada; Study: Canada | |
|---|---|---|
| The Payzer Scholarship (2423) | | |

**Mathematics**

| The Payzer Scholarship (2423) | | |
|---|---|---|

**Medicine**

| Mary Rowena Cooper Scholarship Fund (6195) | | Veteran |
|---|---|---|
| Phyllis P. Harris Scholarships (4956) | Legal: Canada; Study: Canada | |
| NSCA Challenge Scholarships (4415) | | Association |

**Physical Sciences**

| The Payzer Scholarship (2423) | | |
|---|---|---|

**Social Sciences**

| Phyllis P. Harris Scholarships (4956) | Legal: Canada; Study: Canada | |
|---|---|---|

**Visual and Performing Arts**

| Errol Garner Memorial Foundation Scholarship Awards (2626) | | |
|---|---|---|
| Japanese American Citizens League Performing Arts Award (3247) | | Ethnic |
| Stefan and Wanda Wilk Prizes for Research in Polish Music (4973) | | |
| Young American Creative Patriot Art Award (6038) | | Association |

# Doctorate

**Agriculture**

| John G. Bene Fellowship in Social Forestry (3150) | Citizenship: Canada; Legal: Canada | |
|---|---|---|
| Andrew J. Boehm Fellowships (466) | | |
| A & E Capelle LN Herfords Scholarship (150) | Legal: Canada | |
| Dr. Allan P. Chan Scholarship (2225) | Citizenship: Canada | |
| Herb Society Research Grants (2862) | | |

| Vocational Goal, Award, and Entry Number | Geographic Restrictions (Citizenship, Legal Residence, Place of Study) | Affiliation/Special Recipients Requirements |
|---|---|---|
| *Agriculture (continued)* | | |
| New York State Professional Opportunity Scholarships (4592) | Citizenship: US, PermRes; Legal: NY; Study: NY | |
| Edwin G. Nourse Award (3952) | | |
| Outstanding Doctoral and Master's Thesis Awards (248) | | |
| Young Canadian Researchers Awards (3151) | Citizenship: Canada, PermRes | Other |

### Architecture and Environmental Design

| Vocational Goal, Award, and Entry Number | Geographic Restrictions | Affiliation/Special Recipients Requirements |
|---|---|---|
| John G. Bene Fellowship in Social Forestry (3150) | Citizenship: Canada; Legal: Canada | |
| Fellowships in Byzantine Studies, Pre-Columbian Studies and Landscape Architecture (2288) | Study: DC | |
| Paul Mellon Centre Fellowship (6276) | Study: England | |
| New York State Professional Opportunity Scholarships (4592) | Citizenship: US, PermRes; Legal: NY; Study: NY | |
| New York State Regents Professional Opportunity Scholarships (4577) | Legal: NY; Study: NY | |

### Area and Ethnic Studies

| Vocational Goal, Award, and Entry Number | Geographic Restrictions | Affiliation/Special Recipients Requirements |
|---|---|---|
| ACLS Grants for East European Studies - Dissertation Fellowships (407) | Citizenship: US, PermRes | |
| AIIS Junior Fellowships (586) | Study: India | |
| AIMS Small Grants (590) | Citizenship: US/CA, Mexico | Association |
| Alexander von Humboldt Research Fellowships (2679) | Study: Germany | |
| American Institute of Pakistan Studies Predoctoral and Postdoctoral Fellowships (596) | Citizenship: US; Study: Pakistan | |
| American Jewish Studies Fellowships (598) | Study: United States | |
| American Research Center in Egypt Research Fellowships for Study in Egypt (843) | Citizenship: US, PermRes; Legal: United States; Study: Egypt | |
| American Research Center in Egypt Research Fellowships for Study in the U.S. or Canada (844) | Citizenship: Egypt; Study: Canada, United States | |
| Ancient India and Iran Trust Travel and Research Grants (1035) | | |
| ARIT Fellowships (846) | Study: Canada, Turkey, United States | |
| Leo Baeck Institute-DAAD Grants (2680) | Study: Germany | |
| BAEF Predoctoral Fellowships (1397) | Citizenship: US; Study: Belgium | |
| George A. Barton Fellowship (865) | | |
| Bulgarian Studies Seminar (3183) | Citizenship: US, PermRes | |
| Canadian Studies Graduate Student Fellowships (1626) | Citizenship: US, PermRes; Legal: Canada, United States; Study: Canada | |
| Canadian Studies for Indian Scholars (5315) | | |
| Gilbert Chinard Scholarships (3041) | Study: France | |
| Cultural Cooperation Grants (6004) | | |
| Czech Education Scholarships (3708) | Study: Slovakia | |
| Helen Darcovich Memorial Doctoral Fellowship (1657) | Study: Canada | |
| Minda de Gunzburg Center for European Studies Program for the Study of Germany and Europe Dissertation Research Fellowships (2769) | | Other |
| Doctoral Thesis Fellowship in Ukrainian History (1658) | | |
| Endowment for Biblical Research, Summer Research and Travel Grants (868) | | |
| Ford Foundation Fellowships (1178) | Citizenship: Other; Study: United States | |
| German Studies Research Grant (2687) | Study: Germany | |
| Fritz Halbers Fellowships (1356) | | |
| Humanities Fellowships (1179) | Citizenship: US | |

| Vocational Goal, Award, and Entry Number | Geographic Restrictions (Citizenship, Legal Residence, Place of Study) | Affiliation/Special Recipients Requirements |
| --- | --- | --- |
| *Area and Ethnic Studies (continued)* | | |
| IAF Field Research Fellowships Program at the Doctoral Level (3090) | | |
| Institute of American Cultures Graduate and Predoctoral Fellowships (3012) | Study: CA | |
| International Doctoral Scholarships for Studies Specializing in Jewish Fields (3644) | | |
| Islamic Studies Fellowship (872) | | |
| Kress Fellowship in the Art and Archaeology of Jordan (873) | Citizenship: US | |
| LBI/DAAD Fellowships (1357) | Citizenship: US; Study: United States | |
| LBI/DAAD Fellowships for Research in Germany (1358) | Citizenship: US; Study: Germany | |
| National Foundation for Jewish Culture Doctoral Dissertation Grants (4167) | Citizenship: US, PermRes | |
| National Program for Advanced Study and Research in China - Senior Advanced Studies (2017) | Citizenship: US, PermRes; Study: People's Republic of China | |
| National Welsh-American Foundation Exchange Scholarships (4450) | Citizenship: US; Study: Wales | Ethnic |
| Near and Middle East Research and Training Program Pre-Doctoral Fellowships (880) | Citizenship: US | |
| Phillips Grants for North American Indian Research (769) | | |
| Pre- and Postdoctoral Fellowships in International and Area Studies (2804) | Study: United States | |
| Queen's Fellowship (5424) | Citizenship: Canada, PermRes | |
| Research Support Opportunities in Arctic Environmental Studies (1682) | Citizenship: Canada, PermRes; Legal: Canada; Study: Canada | |
| Mary Isabel Sibley Fellowships (4894) | | |
| SSRC Africa Predissertation Fellowships (5394) | Citizenship: US, PermRes | |
| SSRC African Humanities Fellowships (5396) | Study: IL | |
| SSRC Bangladesh Studies Fellowships (5397) | Study: Bangladesh | |
| SSRC Berlin Program for Advanced German and European Studies Fellowships (5398) | Citizenship: US, PermRes; Study: Germany | |
| SSRC Grants for Advanced Area Research (5399) | | |
| SSRC International Predissertation Fellowships (5402) | | |
| SSRC Japan Fellowships for Dissertation Write-Up (5404) | Study: United States | |
| SSRC-MacArthur Foundation Dissertation Fellowships on Peace and Security in a Changing World (5409) | | |
| SSRC Near and Middle East Dissertation Research Fellowships (5412) | | |
| SSRC South Asia Dissertation Fellowships for Bangladesh (5415) | | |
| SSRC Southeast Asia Predissertation Fellowships (5417) | Citizenship: US, PermRes | |
| SSRC Soviet Union and Its Successor States Dissertation Fellowships (5418) | Citizenship: US | |
| SSRC Soviet Union and Its Successor States Workshop Grants (5422) | | |
| Sub-Saharan African Dissertation Internship Award (5154) | Legal: Canada, United States | |
| Touro National Heritage Trust Fellowship (1517) | Study: RI | |
| United States Information Agency (USIA) Fellowships (884) | Citizenship: US | |
| USIA Fellowships, AIAR, Jerusalem (885) | Citizenship: US | |
| Vincent and Anna Visceglia Fellowship (4268) | | |

| Vocational Goal, Award, and Entry Number | Geographic Restrictions (Citizenship, Legal Residence, Place of Study) | Affiliation/Special Recipients Requirements |
|---|---|---|
| **Business and Management** | | |
| American Accounting Association Fellowship Program in Accounting (246) | Legal: Canada, United States; Study: Canada, United States | |
| Andersen Fellowships for Doctoral Candidates at the Dissertation Stage (1039) | | |
| Applebaum Master's and Ph.D. Programs Awards (2549) | | |
| Avis Rent a Car Scholarship (972) | Citizenship: US/CA; Study: Canada, United States | |
| Michael J. Barrett Doctoral Dissertation Grant (3065) | | |
| Luray Caverns Research Grant (4430) | | |
| Joseph L. Fisher Dissertation Awards (5111) | | |
| FORE Graduate Scholarships (517) | Citizenship: US, PermRes | |
| Albert Gallatin Fellowships in International Affairs (2613) | Citizenship: US; Study: Switzerland | |
| John Grenzebach Awards for Outstanding Research in Philanthropy for Education (12) | | |
| Huebner Foundation Doctoral Fellowships (2918) | Citizenship: US/CA; Study: PA, United States | |
| Institute for the Study of World Politics Fellowships (3079) | Study: United States | |
| Richard D. Irwin Fellowship Awards (3230) | Study: Canada, United States | |
| Herman Kahn Fellowships (2910) | Study: United States | |
| Laurels Fund Scholarships (2350) | | |
| NAPM Doctoral Grants (3895) | Citizenship: US, PermRes; Study: United States | |
| NAPM Senior Research Fellowship Grants (3896) | Citizenship: US, PermRes; Study: United States | |
| New York State Regents Professional Opportunity Scholarships (4577) | Legal: NY; Study: NY | |
| Outstanding Doctoral and Master's Thesis Awards (248) | | |
| Petro-Canada Inc. Graduate Research Awards (1284) | Citizenship: Canada, PermRes; Study: Canada | |
| Quebec Scholarship (4438) | Citizenship: Canada; Legal: Canada; Study: Canada | |
| Simmons Scholarship (981) | Citizenship: US/CA, PermRes | |
| Society of Actuaries Ph.D. Grants (5431) | | |
| U.S. Department of Energy Integrated Manufacturing & Processing Predoctoral Fellowships (4361) | | |
| Wharton Doctoral and Postdoctoral Fellowships In Risk & Insurance (2920) | Citizenship: US/CA; Study: PA | |
| Young Canadian Researchers Awards (3151) | Citizenship: Canada, PermRes | Other |
| **Communications** | | |
| AEJMC Communication Theory and Methodology Division Minority Doctoral Scholarships (1232) | | Association |
| Public Interest Internships (1803) | Study: United States | |
| The Slack Award for Medical Journalism (4307) | Study: United States | African American |
| Della A. Whittaker Scholarships (5504) | | |
| **Computer and Information Sciences** | | |
| The AFCEA Educational Foundation Fellowship (1099) | Citizenship: US | |
| Andersen Fellowships for Doctoral Candidates at the Dissertation Stage (1039) | | |
| ASIS Doctoral Dissertation Scholarships (933) | | |
| ASIS Student Paper Award (935) | | |
| AT & T Bell Laboratories Graduate Research Fellowships for Women (1303) | Citizenship: US, PermRes; Study: NJ | |

| Vocational Goal, Award, and Entry Number | Geographic Restrictions (Citizenship, Legal Residence, Place of Study) | Affiliation/Special Recipients Requirements |
|---|---|---|
| *Computer and Information Sciences (continued)* | | |
| AT & T Bell Laboratories Graduate Research Grants for Women (1304) | Citizenship: US, PermRes; Study: NJ | |
| AT & T Bell Laboratories University Relations Summer Program (1306) | | |
| Doctoral Dissertation Scholarship (1422) | | |
| Engineer Degree Fellowships; Howard Hughes Doctoral Fellowships (2922) | Citizenship: US; Study: United States | |
| FORE Graduate Scholarships (517) | Citizenship: US, PermRes | |
| Laboratory-Graduate Participantships; Thesis Parts Appointment (1084) | Legal: United States; Study: United States | |
| National Physical Science Consortium Graduate Fellowships for Minorities and Women (4338) | Citizenship: US | Native American, Hispanic American, African American |
| Adelle and Erwin Tomash Fellowship in the History of Information Processing (1353) | | |
| **Education** | | |
| Animal Health Trust of Canada Research Grants (1046) | Study: Canada | |
| ASME Graduate Teaching Fellowships (943) | Citizenship: US, PermRes | Association |
| Bossing-Edwards Research Scholarships (3871) | | |
| Jeanne S. Chall Research Fellowship (3176) | | Association |
| Civil Air Patrol Graduate Scholarship (3915) | | |
| ETS Summer Program in Research for Graduate Students (2354) | Study: NJ, United States | |
| Excellence in Arc Welding Awards; Graduate and Professional Awards for Achievement in Arc-Welded Design, Engineering and Fabrication (3482) | Legal: United States | |
| FORE Graduate Scholarships (517) | Citizenship: US, PermRes | |
| Hollingworth Award Competition (3877) | | |
| Iota Lambda Sigma Grand Chapter Scholarship (3213) | | Fraternal |
| Donald L. McCullough Memorial Scholarships (3866) | | |
| Mississippi African-American Doctoral Teacher Loan/Scholarship Program (3730) | Legal: MS; Study: MS | African American |
| NACADA Scholarship (3825) | | Association |
| Oklahoma State Regents for Higher Education Doctoral Study Grants (4739) | Study: OK | Minority |
| Spencer Foundation Dissertation Fellowships for Research Related to Education (5586) | Study: United States | |
| United Commercial Travelers Retarded Citizens Teacher Scholarship (5787) | | |
| Constance Dorothea Weinman Scholarship Trust for Graduate Study in Instructional Technology (5839) | | |
| **Engineering** | | |
| The AFCEA Educational Foundation Fellowship (1099) | Citizenship: US | |
| AIAA/Gordon C. Oates Air Breathing Propulsion Award (566) | Citizenship: US | |
| American Water Works Association Academic Achievement Awards (1015) | | |
| American Water Works Association Scholarship Program (1017) | Legal: Canada, Guam, Mexico, Puerto Rico, United States | |
| ASME Graduate Teaching Fellowships (943) | Citizenship: US, PermRes | Association |
| AT & T Bell Laboratories Graduate Research Fellowships for Women (1303) | Citizenship: US, PermRes; Study: NJ | |
| AT & T Bell Laboratories Graduate Research Grants for Women (1304) | Citizenship: US, PermRes; Study: NJ | |

| Vocational Goal, Award, and Entry Number | Geographic Restrictions (Citizenship, Legal Residence, Place of Study) | Affiliation/Special Recipients Requirements |
|---|---|---|
| *Engineering (continued)* | | |
| AT & T Bell Laboratories University Relations Summer Program (1306) | | |
| AWU Graduate Research Fellowships (1201) | Citizenship: US, PermRes; Study: CA, CO, ID, MT, ND, NM, NV, OK, UT, WA, WY | |
| AWU Post-Graduate Fellowship (1202) | Citizenship: US, PermRes; Study: CA, CO, ID, ND, NM, OK | |
| F.M. Becket Memorial Award (2366) | Study: Canada, United States | |
| H. Fletcher Brown Scholarship (4967) | Legal: DE | |
| Chateaubriand Scholarship (Scientifique) (2372) | Citizenship: US; Study: France | |
| CIC Predoctoral Fellowships (2013) | Citizenship: US; Study: United States | African American, Hispanic American, Native American |
| Civil Air Patrol Graduate Scholarship (3915) | | |
| Electrochemical Society Energy Research Fellowships (2367) | Study: Canada, United States | |
| Electrochemical Society Summer Fellowships (2368) | Study: Canada, United States | |
| Engineer Degree Fellowships; Howard Hughes Doctoral Fellowships (2922) | Citizenship: US; Study: United States | |
| Ford Foundation Predoctoral and Dissertation Fellowships for Minorities (4357) | Citizenship: US; Study: United States | Native American, Asian American, Hispanic American, African American |
| GEM Ph.D. Engineering Fellowships for Minorities (3942) | Citizenship: US | Native American, African American, Hispanic American |
| Government of Canada Awards (3145) | Citizenship: France, Germany, Japan, Mexico; Study: Canada | |
| Hertz Foundation Graduate Fellowships (2866) | Citizenship: US, PermRes; Study: United States | |
| IEEE Fellowship in Electrical History (3033) | | |
| Iota Lambda Sigma Grand Chapter Scholarship (3213) | | Fraternal |
| Laboratory-Graduate Participantships; Thesis Parts Appointment (1084) | Legal: United States; Study: United States | |
| LARS Scholarships (1020) | Study: Canada, Guam, Mexico, Puerto Rico, United States | |
| Magnetic Fusion Energy Technology Fellowship Program (5901) | | |
| Magnetic Fusion Science Fellowship Program (5902) | | |
| New York State Professional Opportunity Scholarships (4592) | Citizenship: US, PermRes; Legal: NY; Study: NY | |
| New York State Regents Professional Opportunity Scholarships (4577) | Legal: NY; Study: NY | |
| Nuclear Engineering/Health Physics Fellowship Program (5915) | | |
| Oak Ridge National Laboratory Professional Internship Program (5918) | | |
| Elisabeth M. and Winchell M. Parsons Scholarships (950) | Citizenship: US; Legal: United States | Association |
| Petro-Canada Inc. Graduate Research Awards (1284) | Citizenship: Canada, PermRes; Study: Canada | |
| Eleanor Roosevelt Teacher Fellowships (338) | Citizenship: US, PermRes | |
| Savannah River Technology Center Professional Internship Program (5924) | | |
| Von Karman Institute Doctoral Fellowship (6073) | | |
| Young Canadian Researchers Awards (3151) | Citizenship: Canada, PermRes | Other |

**Health Care Services**

| | | |
|---|---|---|
| AOTF Dissertation Research Award for Occupational Therapists (743) | Citizenship: US | Association |
| Richard P. Covert Scholarships (2833) | | Association |
| ESRI Doctoral Training Grants; ESRI Postdoctoral Fellowships (2316) | Citizenship: Canada; Legal: Canada; Study: Canada | |

| Vocational Goal, Award, and Entry Number | Geographic Restrictions (Citizenship, Legal Residence, Place of Study) | Affiliation/Special Recipients Requirements |
|---|---|---|
| *Health Care Services (continued)* | | |
| Florida Dental Health Foundation Student Loans (2492) | Study: FL | |
| FORE Graduate Scholarships (517) | Citizenship: US, PermRes | |
| William F. Grupe Foundation Scholarships (2756) | | |
| Indian Health Career Awards (4935) | | Ethnic |
| W. K. Kellogg Community Medicine Training Fellowship Program for Minority Medical Students (4297) | | African American, Hispanic American, Native American |
| Grace Whiting Myers/Malcolm T. MacEachern Student Loans (520) | Citizenship: US | |
| New York State Professional Opportunity Scholarships (4592) | Citizenship: US, PermRes; Legal: NY; Study: NY | |
| New York State Regents Professional Opportunity Scholarships (4577) | Legal: NY; Study: NY | |
| Public Interest Internships (1803) | Study: United States | |

## Health Sciences

| Vocational Goal, Award, and Entry Number | Geographic Restrictions (Citizenship, Legal Residence, Place of Study) | Affiliation/Special Recipients Requirements |
|---|---|---|
| AACN Educational Advancement Scholarships for Graduates (278) | | |
| Academia-Oriented "Springboard to Teaching" Fellowship (487) | Citizenship: US, PermRes; Study: United States | |
| AFPE Graduate Fellowships (488) | Citizenship: US | |
| AIHP Grant-in-Aid Toward Thesis Expenses Related to the History of Pharmacy (583) | Study: United States | |
| American Heart Association, California Affiliate - Predoctoral Fellowship (532) | Citizenship: US | |
| American Speech-Language-Hearing Foundation Graduate Student Scholarships (989) | Study: United States | |
| American Speech-Language-Hearing Foundation Research Grants for New Investigators (990) | Study: United States | |
| AORN Scholarships (1252) | | Association |
| Arthritis Society Clinical Fellowships (1154) | Citizenship: Canada; Study: Canada | |
| Canadian Nurses Foundation Study Awards (1687) | Citizenship: Canada, PermRes; Study: Canada | Association |
| Cancer Prevention and Control Research Small Grant Program (3922) | | |
| Dr. Alfred C. Fones Scholarships (425) | | Association |
| Foundation for Physical Therapy Doctoral Award (2575) | | |
| William F. Grupe Foundation Scholarships (2756) | | |
| Health Canada Research Personnel Training Awards (Regular Program) (2829) | Citizenship: Canada, PermRes; Legal: Canada | |
| Dr. Harold Hillenbrand Scholarships (426) | | Association |
| HP/AACN Critical-Care Nursing Research Grants (2868) | | |
| HRSA-BHP Professional Nurse Traineeship (5971) | | |
| HRSA-BHP Scholarships for Disadvantaged Students (5972) | Citizenship: US, PermRes, Other | |
| HSFC Nursing Research Fellowships (2842) | | |
| Indian Health Career Awards (4935) | | Ethnic |
| Leslie Isenberg Graduate Scholarship (992) | | Handicapped |
| Mary Connolly Livingston Grant (3415) | | Fraternal |
| Mead Johnson Nutritional Perinatal Research Grants Program (5337) | Citizenship: US | |
| Mississippi Nursing Education DSN Program (3735) | Legal: MS | |
| MLA Doctoral Fellowship (3633) | Citizenship: US/CA, PermRes | |

| Vocational Goal, Award, and Entry Number | Geographic Restrictions (Citizenship, Legal Residence, Place of Study) | Affiliation/Special Recipients Requirements |
|---|---|---|
| *Health Sciences (continued)* | | |
| NEF Scholarships (4703) | Citizenship: US, PermRes | Association |
| New York State Professional Opportunity Scholarships (4592) | Citizenship: US, PermRes; Legal: NY; Study: NY | |
| New York State Regents Professional Opportunity Scholarships (4577) | Legal: NY; Study: NY | |
| Irene E. Newman Scholarships (428) | | Association |
| NINR Individual National Research Service Awards Predoctoral Fellowship (4202) | | |
| Nursing Research Training Award (Cancelled) (681) | Citizenship: US/CA, PermRes; Study: United States | |
| Oncology Nursing Foundation Doctoral Scholarship (4764) | | |
| Oncology Nursing Foundation/Rhone Poulenc Rorer New Investigator Research Grants (4771) | | |
| Public Interest Internships (1803) | Study: United States | |
| Regular AFPE Fellowships and Scholarships in the Pharmaceutical Sciences (492) | Citizenship: US, PermRes; Study: United States | |
| Sandoz-AFPE First Year Graduate Scholarships (493) | | |
| Kala Singh Graduate Scholarship (994) | | |
| Summer Fellowship Grants (215) | Legal: Canada, United States | |
| Margaret E. Swanson Scholarships (432) | | Association |
| UpJohn-AFPE First Year Graduate Scholarships (496) | Citizenship: US, PermRes | |
| Washington Health Professional Loan Repayment and Scholarship Program (6099) | | |
| Western Interstate Commission for Higher Education Student Exchanges (135) | Legal: AK | |

## Home Economics

| | | |
|---|---|---|
| AVA Home Economics Education Graduate Fellowships (1013) | | Association |
| A & E Capelle LN Herfords Scholarship (150) | Legal: Canada | |
| CHEA Fiftieth Anniversary Scholarship (1645) | Citizenship: Canada, Other | Association |
| Kappa Omicron Nu Doctoral Fellowships (3335) | | Fraternal |

## Humanities

| | | |
|---|---|---|
| ACLS Grants for East European Studies - Dissertation Fellowships (407) | Citizenship: US, PermRes | |
| Frances C. Allen Fellowships (4615) | Study: United States | Native American |
| ARIT Fellowships (846) | Study: Canada, Turkey, United States | |
| Artists Fellowship; Japan Foundation Cultural Properties Specialists Fellowship; Japan Foundation Doctoral Fellowship; Japan Foundation Research Fellowship (3240) | Study: Japan | |
| Oscar Broneer Fellowship (856) | Study: Greece | Other |
| Chateaubriand Fellowships (Humanities) (2375) | Citizenship: US; Study: France | |
| CIC Predoctoral Fellowships (2013) | Citizenship: US; Study: United States | African American, Hispanic American, Native American |
| Anna C. and Oliver C. Colburn Fellowship (857) | Study: Greece | Other |
| Helen Darcovich Memorial Doctoral Fellowship (1657) | Study: Canada | |
| Ecole des Chartes Exchange Fellowship (4604) | | |
| The Eta Sigma Phi Summer Scholarships (2414) | Study: Greece, Italy | |
| Faculty Graduate Study Fellowships for Historically Black Colleges and Universities (3984) | Citizenship: US, PermRes | |

| Vocational Goal, Award, and Entry Number | Geographic Restrictions (Citizenship, Legal Residence, Place of Study) | Affiliation/Special Recipients Requirements |
|---|---|---|
| *Humanities (continued)* | | |
| Fellowships in Byzantine Studies, Pre-Columbian Studies and Landscape Architecture (2288) | Study: DC | |
| Alison M. Frantz Fellowship (858) | | |
| Getty Center Predoctoral Fellowships (2700) | Study: United States | |
| Government of Canada Awards (3145) | Citizenship: France, Germany, Japan, Mexico; Study: Canada | |
| Jacob Hirsch Fellowship (859) | Legal: Israel, United States; Study: Greece | Other |
| Institute for European History Fellowships (3035) | Study: Germany | |
| Jacob K. Javits Fellowship (3255) | | |
| Kress Research Fellowship in Art History (3404) | Study: United States | |
| Kress Research Fellowships at Foreign Institutions (3405) | Study: Cyprus, France, Germany, Israel, Italy, Netherlands, Switzerland, United Kingdom | |
| NEH Interpretive Research Grants (3987) | Citizenship: US, PermRes | |
| NEH Reference Materials Grants (3988) | Citizenship: US, PermRes | |
| Professional Development Fellowship Program for Artists and Art Historians (1982) | Citizenship: US, PermRes | |
| Social Sciences and Humanities Research Council Doctoral Fellowships (5425) | Citizenship: Canada, PermRes | |
| SSRC Africa Predissertation Fellowships (5394) | Citizenship: US, PermRes | |
| SSRC African Humanities Fellowships (5396) | Study: IL | |
| SSRC Bangladesh Studies Fellowships (5397) | Study: Bangladesh | |
| SSRC Berlin Program for Advanced German and European Studies Fellowships (5398) | Citizenship: US, PermRes; Study: Germany | |
| SSRC Grants for Advanced Area Research (5399) | | |
| SSRC-MacArthur Foundation Dissertation Fellowships on Peace and Security in a Changing World (5409) | | |
| SSRC Near and Middle East Dissertation Research Fellowships (5412) | | |
| SSRC South Asia Dissertation Fellowships for Bangladesh (5415) | | |
| SSRC Southeast Asia Predissertation Fellowships (5417) | Citizenship: US, PermRes | |
| SSRC Soviet Union and Its Successor States Dissertation Fellowships (5418) | Citizenship: US | |
| Whiting Fellowships in the Humanities (6171) | Study: CA, CT, IL, MA, NJ, NY, PA | |

### Industry and Trade

| Vocational Goal, Award, and Entry Number | Geographic Restrictions | Affiliation/Special Recipients Requirements |
|---|---|---|
| Dwight David Eisenhower Transportation Fellowship (6052) | Citizenship: US; Study: United States | |
| Joseph L. Fisher Dissertation Awards (5111) | | |
| Hudson River Fellowships (2912) | | |
| LARS Scholarships (1020) | Study: Canada, Guam, Mexico, Puerto Rico, United States | |
| Young Canadian Researchers Awards (3151) | Citizenship: Canada, PermRes | Other |

### Language and Literature

| Vocational Goal, Award, and Entry Number | Geographic Restrictions | Affiliation/Special Recipients Requirements |
|---|---|---|
| Blakemore Foundation Asian Language Fellowship Grants (1440) | Citizenship: US, PermRes | |
| Stephen Botein Fellowships (254) | Study: United States | |
| Chateaubriand Fellowships (Humanities) (2375) | Citizenship: US; Study: France | |
| The Eta Sigma Phi Summer Scholarships (2414) | Study: Greece, Italy | |
| General Semantics Foundation Project Grants (2645) | | |

| Vocational Goal, Award, and Entry Number | Geographic Restrictions (Citizenship, Legal Residence, Place of Study) | Affiliation/Special Recipients Requirements |
|---|---|---|
| *Language and Literature (continued)* | | |
| Phillips Grants for North American Indian Research (769) | | |
| Helen M. Robinson Award (3179) | | Association |
| Thesaurus Linguae Latinae Fellowship (764) | Legal: United States | |
| **Law** | | |
| Maxwell Boulton Junior Fellowship (3626) | Study: Canada | |
| H. Fletcher Brown Scholarship (4967) | Legal: DE | |
| Chateaubriand Fellowships (Humanities) (2375) | Citizenship: US; Study: France | |
| Family Court Services Dissertation Grant Competition (3304) | Study: CA | |
| FORE Graduate Scholarships (517) | Citizenship: US, PermRes | |
| Albert Gallatin Fellowships in International Affairs (2613) | Citizenship: US; Study: Switzerland | |
| Celia M. Howard Fellowships (2964) | Legal: IL | |
| Elaine Osborne Jacobson Award for Women in Health Care (5163) | | |
| National Association of Black Women Attorneys Scholarships (3862) | Citizenship: US | |
| Public Interest Internships (1803) | Study: United States | |
| **Liberal/General Studies** | | |
| American Sociological Association Minority Fellowships (986) | Citizenship: US, PermRes; Legal: United States | Minority |
| Armenian Professional Society Scholarship (1114) | Citizenship: US; Legal: CA | Ethnic |
| Armenian Students' Association of America Reading Scholarships (1138) | Study: United States | Ethnic |
| BIA Higher Education/Hopi Supplemental Grants (2892) | | Native American |
| Boyle Research Scholarships (1468) | | |
| John Carter Brown Library Associates Fellowship (1512) | Study: RI | |
| Sally Butler Memorial Fund for Latina Research (1549) | | Association, Hispanic American |
| CCSFC India Scholarships (3141) | Citizenship: Canada, PermRes; Study: India | |
| CCSFC New Zealand Scholarships (3142) | Citizenship: Canada, PermRes; Study: New Zealand | |
| CCSFC Sri Lanka Scholarships (3143) | Citizenship: Canada, PermRes; Study: Sri Lanka | |
| CCSFC United Kingdom Scholarships (3144) | Citizenship: Canada, PermRes; Study: United Kingdom | |
| Lady Davis Graduate and Postdoctoral Fellowships (2193) | Study: Israel | |
| Evrytanian Association Scholarship (2418) | | Ethnic |
| Five Colleges Fellowship Program (2470) | Study: United States | Minority |
| Gallaudet University Alumni Association Graduate Fellowship Funds (2615) | | Handicapped |
| Grants for Canadians (1640) | Citizenship: Canada, PermRes; Study: Israel | |
| Kathern F. Gruber Scholarships (1444) | | Veteran |
| Patricia Roberts Harris Fellowships (2796) | | |
| Harvard Travellers Club Grants (2802) | | |
| ICCS Foreign Government Awards (3146) | Citizenship: Canada; Legal: Canada | |
| IGCC Dissertation Fellowships (3043) | Study: United States | |
| Japanese American Citizens League Graduate Scholarships (3246) | | Association |
| Jewish Federation of Metropolitan Chicago Academic Scholarships (3265) | Legal: IL, IN | Religion |
| Steven Knezevich Trust Grants (3381) | | Ethnic |
| Minnie L. Maffett Scholarship (4466) | Legal: TX; Study: TX | |
| McKnight Doctoral Fellowships (2519) | Citizenship: US; Study: FL | African American |

| Vocational Goal, Award, and Entry Number | Geographic Restrictions (Citizenship, Legal Residence, Place of Study) | Affiliation/Special Recipients Requirements |
|---|---|---|
| *Liberal/General Studies (continued)* | | |
| Paul W. McQuillen Memorial Fellowship (1515) | Study: RI | |
| Margaret McWilliams Predoctoral Fellowship (1635) | Citizenship: Canada; Legal: Canada; Study: Canada | |
| Ministry of the Flemish Community in Belgium Fellowships (2483) | Citizenship: US | |
| Montana Indian Student Fee Waiver (557) | Study: MT | Native American |
| Mortar Board Foundation Fellowships (3782) | | Association |
| Barbara S. Mosbacher Fellowship (1516) | Study: RI | |
| National Art Materials Trade Association Scholarships (3848) | | Employer |
| National Consortium for Educational Access Fellowship (3939) | | African American |
| National Fourth Infantry Division Association Scholarship (4171) | | Veteran |
| National Fraternal Society of the Deaf Scholarships (4173) | | Association, Handicapped |
| Nevada Women's Fund Scholarships (4521) | Legal: NV | |
| New Jersey State Federation of Women's Clubs Margaret Yardley Fellowship (4543) | Legal: NJ | |
| OAS-PRA Fellowships (4809) | | |
| Opportunities for the Blind, Inc. Grants (4785) | Citizenship: US | Handicapped |
| Oregon Educational Aid for Veterans (4799) | Citizenship: US; Legal: OR | Veteran |
| ORS Awards (4824) | Study: England | |
| J. H. Stewart Reid Memorial Fellowship (1605) | Citizenship: Canada, PermRes; Study: Canada | |
| Henry J. Reilly Memorial Graduate Scholarships (5105) | Study: United States | Military |
| Research Grants for Recent PhDs and PhD Candidates (2690) | Legal: Germany | |
| Schlesinger Library, Radcliffe College Honorary Visiting Scholar Appointments (5257) | | |
| Scholarships for Study in Israel (2851) | Citizenship: US; Study: Israel | |
| Sikh Education Aid Fund Scholarship (5349) | | |
| Study Visit Research Grants for Faculty (2691) | Study: Germany | |
| Sub-Saharan African Dissertation Internship Award (5154) | Legal: Canada, United States | |
| War Memorial Scholarships (3935) | Citizenship: Canada; Study: Canada | |
| Warner Trust Loan Program (6079) | Legal: CA; Study: CA | |
| Charles H. Watts Memorial Fellowship (1519) | Study: RI | |
| Western Interstate Commission for Higher Education Western Regional Graduate Program (136) | Legal: AK; Study: AK, AZ, CO, HI, ID, MT, ND, NM, NV, OR, UT, WA, WY | |
| Nancy B. Woolridge Graduate Fellowship (6308) | | Fraternal |
| Young Canadian Researchers Awards (3151) | Citizenship: Canada, PermRes | Other |
| Zeta Phi Beta General Graduate Fellowship (6309) | | |
| Zuni Higher Education Scholarships (6314) | | Native American |

## Library and Archival Sciences

| | | |
|---|---|---|
| ALA Doctoral Dissertation Fellowship (1225) | | |
| ALISE Doctoral Forum (1244) | | |
| ALISE Doctoral Students' Dissertation Competition Prizes; ALISE Research Paper Competition Prizes (1245) | | Association |
| Doctoral Dissertation Scholarship (1422) | | |
| Hagley-Winterthur Fellowship (2780) | | |
| ISI Scholarship (5577) | Study: Canada, United States | Association |
| Law Degree Scholarships for Library School Graduates (312) | Citizenship: US/CA; Study: Canada, United States | |
| MLA Doctoral Fellowship (3633) | Citizenship: US/CA, PermRes | |

| Vocational Goal, Award, and Entry Number | Geographic Restrictions (Citizenship, Legal Residence, Place of Study) | Affiliation/Special Recipients Requirements |
|---|---|---|
| *Library and Archival Sciences (continued)* | | |
| Smithsonian Institution Predoctoral Fellowships (5378) | | |
| World Book Graduate Scholarships in Library Science (1668) | Citizenship: Canada; Study: Canada, United States | |
| **Life Sciences** | | |
| Agency for Toxic Substances and Disease Registry Student Internship Program (5860) | | |
| American Foundation for Aging Research Predoctoral Awards (469) | Study: United States | |
| ASM Predoctoral Minority Fellowships (954) | Citizenship: US, PermRes; Study: United States | Minority |
| Alfred D. Bell, Jr. Visiting Scholars Program (2553) | | |
| Capranica Foundation Award in Neuroethology (1723) | Citizenship: US | |
| Carnegie Institution of Washington Postdoctoral and Predoctoral Fellowships (1737) | Study: United States | |
| Chateaubriand Scholarship (Scientifique) (2372) | Citizenship: US; Study: France | |
| John K. Cooper Ornithology Research Grants (2079) | Citizenship: Canada; Study: Canada | |
| Environmental Protection Agency Tribal Lands Science Scholarship (560) | | Native American |
| Fellowships in Cereal Chemistry (275) | | |
| Joseph L. Fisher Dissertation Awards (5111) | | |
| GCA Awards in Tropical Botany (2621) | | |
| Grass Fellowships in Neurophysiology (2742) | Study: MA | |
| Hudson River Fellowships (2912) | | |
| JOI/USSAC Ocean Drilling Fellowships (3291) | Study: United States | |
| Laboratory-Graduate Participantships; Thesis Parts Appointment (1084) | Legal: United States; Study: United States | |
| LARS Scholarships (1020) | Study: Canada, Guam, Mexico, Puerto Rico, United States | |
| Mycological Society of America Graduate Fellowships (3815) | Study: Canada, United States | Association |
| Mycological Society of America Graduate Research Prizes (3816) | | Association |
| New York Botanical Garden Fellowships for Graduate Study in Systemic and Economic Botany (4560) | Study: NY | |
| NIDA Individual National Research Service Awards (4192) | Citizenship: US, PermRes | |
| NIMH Individual Predoctoral National Research Service Awards (4199) | Citizenship: US, PermRes | |
| Nuclear Engineering/Health Physics Fellowship Program (5915) | | |
| NYZS/Wildlife Conservation Society Research Fellowship Program (RFP) (6177) | Study: Belize, Costa Rica, El Salvador, Guatemala, Honduras, Nicaragua, Panama | |
| Ortho/McNeil Predoctoral Minority Fellowship in Antimicrobial Chemotherapy (955) | Citizenship: US, PermRes | Minority |
| Research Support Opportunities in Arctic Environmental Studies (1682) | Citizenship: Canada, PermRes; Legal: Canada; Study: Canada | |
| SSRC-MacArthur Foundation Dissertation Fellowships on Peace and Security in a Changing World (5409) | | |
| Welder Wildlife Fellowships (6127) | Study: Canada, United States | |
| Young Canadian Researchers Awards (3151) | Citizenship: Canada, PermRes | Other |
| **Mathematics** | | |
| The AFCEA Educational Foundation Fellowship (1099) | Citizenship: US | |
| ASA/USDA/NASS Research Fellowships and Associateships (1001) | Study: United States | |

| Vocational Goal, Award, and Entry Number | Geographic Restrictions (Citizenship, Legal Residence, Place of Study) | Affiliation/Special Recipients Requirements |
|---|---|---|
| *Mathematics (continued)* | | |
| CIC Predoctoral Fellowships (2013) | Citizenship: US; Study: United States | African American, Hispanic American, Native American |
| Engineer Degree Fellowships; Howard Hughes Doctoral Fellowships (2922) | Citizenship: US; Study: United States | |
| ETS Summer Program in Research for Graduate Students (2354) | Study: NJ, United States | |
| Ford Foundation Predoctoral and Dissertation Fellowships for Minorities (4357) | Citizenship: US; Study: United States | Native American, Asian American, Hispanic American, African American |
| Hertz Foundation Graduate Fellowships (2866) | Citizenship: US, PermRes; Study: United States | |
| Laboratory-Graduate Participantships; Thesis Parts Appointment (1084) | Legal: United States; Study: United States | |
| Magnetic Fusion Energy Technology Fellowship Program (5901) | | |
| Magnetic Fusion Science Fellowship Program (5902) | | |
| National Physical Science Consortium Graduate Fellowships for Minorities and Women (4338) | Citizenship: US | Native American, Hispanic American, African American |
| Society of Actuaries Ph.D. Grants (5431) | | |
| **Medicine** | | |
| ABMAC/Clerkship in Taiwan Award (358) | Study: People's Republic of China | |
| ACOG/Ortho-McNeil Academic Training Fellowships in Obstetrics and Gynecology (382) | Citizenship: US; Study: United States | Association |
| ADA Medical Student Diabetes Research Fellowship Program (437) | | |
| AFUD Summer Student Fellowships (501) | Study: Canada, United States | |
| Agency for Toxic Substances and Disease Registry Student Internship Program (5860) | | |
| Allied Health Doctoral Fellowships (3368) | Citizenship: Canada | |
| Alzheimer's Association Pioneer Award for Alzheimer's Disease Research (207) | | |
| American Association for Dental Research-Student Research Fellowships (285) | Study: United States | |
| American Foundation for Aging Research Predoctoral Awards (469) | Study: United States | |
| American Heart Association, California Affiliate - Predoctoral Fellowship (532) | Citizenship: US | |
| American Liver Foundation Student Research Fellowships (674) | | |
| AMWA Medical Education Loans (699) | Citizenship: US, PermRes | |
| Arthritis Foundation Doctoral Dissertation Award for Arthritis Health Professionals (1148) | | |
| Arthritis Society Clinical Fellowships (1154) | Citizenship: Canada; Study: Canada | |
| Beale Family Memorial Scholarship (3533) | Legal: ME | |
| Behavioral Science Dissertation Grants (Cancelled) (679) | Citizenship: US/CA, PermRes; Study: United States | |
| Biomedical Scholarship (3373) | Citizenship: Canada; Study: Canada | |
| William Blair-Bell Memorial Lectureships in Obstetrics and Gynecology (5179) | | Association |
| M.D.K. Bremner Student Award for Dental History Essay (231) | | |
| H. Fletcher Brown Scholarship (4967) | Legal: DE | |
| William and Charlotte Cadbury Award (4288) | Citizenship: US; Study: United States | African American, Hispanic American, Native American |
| Canadian Liver Foundation Graduate Studentships (1672) | Study: Canada | |
| Cancer Prevention and Control Research Small Grant Program (3922) | | |
| Cancer Research Society Fellowships (1718) | Study: Canada | |
| A & E Capelle LN Herfords Scholarship (150) | Legal: Canada | |

| Vocational Goal, Award, and Entry Number | Geographic Restrictions (Citizenship, Legal Residence, Place of Study) | Affiliation/Special Recipients Requirements |
|---|---|---|
| *Medicine (continued)* | | |
| Center for Mental Health Services Minority Fellowship Program (803) | Citizenship: US, PermRes; Study: United States | |
| Chateaubriand Scholarship (Scientifique) (2372) | Citizenship: US; Study: France | |
| Children's Medical Research Institute Ph.D. Scholarships; Children's Medical Research Institute Postdoctoral Research Fellowships (1941) | | |
| Paul C. Cole Scholarships (5475) | Study: United States | |
| Colgate-Palmolive Research Award (340) | | |
| Cystic Fibrosis Foundation Student Traineeships (2159) | Citizenship: US, PermRes | |
| Delaware Academy of Medicine Student Financial Aid Program (2207) | Legal: DE | |
| Lord Dowding Grant (2278) | | |
| Eden Traveling Fellowship in Obstetrics and Gynecology (5180) | | |
| Endodontic Graduate Student Grants (288) | Legal: Canada, United States | Association |
| Epilepsy Foundation of America Research Training Fellowships (2400) | | |
| ESRI Doctoral Training Grants; ESRI Postdoctoral Fellowships (2316) | Citizenship: Canada; Legal: Canada; Study: Canada | |
| Established Investigator Grant (527) | Citizenship: US | |
| William C. Ezell Fellowship (746) | | |
| Fellowship Program in Academic Medicine (4289) | Citizenship: US; Study: United States | African American, Hispanic American, Native American |
| FFS-NSPB Student Fellowships (2451) | | |
| Gina Finzi Memorial Student Summer Fellowships for Research (3519) | | |
| Fresno-Madera Medical Society Scholarships (2597) | Legal: CA | |
| Fyssen Foundation Research Grants (2610) | | |
| Edgar Gentilli Prize (5181) | | |
| Gerber Prize for Excellence in Pediatrics (4291) | Study: MI | African American, Hispanic American, Native American |
| Benn and Kathleen Gilmore Scholarship (4292) | Legal: DC, IL, IN, MI, OH; Study: MI | African American |
| Glenn Foundation/AFAR Scholarships for Research in the Biology of Aging (459) | | |
| Irving Graef Memorial Scholarship (4293) | Citizenship: US | |
| William F. Grupe Foundation Scholarships (2756) | | |
| Henry G. Halladay Awards (4294) | Citizenship: US; Study: United States | African American |
| Senator Mark Hatfield Award for Clinical Research in Alzheimer's Disease (208) | | |
| Health Care Policy Clinical Career Development Award (2240) | | |
| Health Education Loan Program (5709) | | |
| George Hill Memorial Scholarship (4295) | Legal: NY; Study: United States | African American |
| HRSA-BHP Exceptional Financial Need Scholarship (5966) | Citizenship: US, PermRes | |
| HRSA-BHP Health Professions Student Loans (5967) | | |
| HRSA-BHP National Health Service Corps Scholarships (5969) | Citizenship: US | |
| HRSA-BHP Scholarships for Disadvantaged Students (5972) | Citizenship: US, PermRes, Other | |
| HSFC Career Investigator Awards (2839) | Study: ON | |
| HSFC Junior Personnel Medical Scientist Traineeships (2841) | | |
| HSFC PhD Research Traineeships (2843) | | |

| Vocational Goal, Award, and Entry Number | Geographic Restrictions (Citizenship, Legal Residence, Place of Study) | Affiliation/Special Recipients Requirements |
|---|---|---|
| *Medicine (continued)* | | |
| Hugh J. Andersen Memorial Scholarship (4296) | Legal: MN; Study: MN | |
| Indian Health Career Awards (4935) | | Ethnic |
| W. K. Kellogg Community Medicine Training Fellowship Program for Minority Medical Students (4297) | | African American, Hispanic American, Native American |
| Kent Medical Foundation Student Loans Program (3354) | Legal: MI | |
| Krebs Memorial Scholarships (1434) | | |
| Ralph Lombardi Memorial Scholarship (4236) | Legal: DC | |
| Andrew M. Longley, Jr., D.O. Scholarship (3534) | Legal: ME | |
| Lupus Foundation of America Research Grants (3520) | Study: United States | |
| Irene and Daisy MacGregor Memorial Scholarship (4401) | Citizenship: US; Study: United States | |
| The MacKenzie Foundation (3526) | Study: CA | |
| Minnie L. Maffett Scholarship (4466) | Legal: TX; Study: TX | |
| Maine Osteopathic Association Memorial Scholarship (3535) | Legal: ME | |
| Maine Osteopathic Association Scholarship (3536) | Legal: ME | |
| Russell C. McCaughan Education Fund Scholarship (4335) | Legal: United States | |
| Franklin C. McLean Award (4298) | | |
| The Mead Johnson/NMA Scholarship (4299) | Study: United States | African American |
| Medical Student Diabetes Research Fellowships (443) | | |
| Metropolitan Life Foundation Awards for Academic Excellence in Medicine (4300) | | African American, Hispanic American, Native American |
| Arthur Minden Predoctoral Fellowship (3804) | Study: Canada | |
| Minority Dental Student Scholarship Program (43) | Citizenship: US; Study: United States | African American, Hispanic American, Native American, Minority |
| Minority Fellowships in Neuroscience (806) | Citizenship: US, PermRes | Minority |
| Mississippi Graduate and Professional Degree Loan/Scholarship Program (3731) | Legal: MS | |
| Mississippi Southern Regional Education Board Loan/Scholarship Program (3741) | Legal: MS | |
| Mississippi Special Medical Education Loan/Scholarship Program (3742) | Legal: MS; Study: MS | Other |
| Mississippi State Dental Education Loan/Scholarship Program (3743) | Legal: MS; Study: MS | Other |
| Mississippi State Medical Education Loan/Scholarship Program (3744) | Legal: MS; Study: MS | Other |
| MMA Medical Student Loans (3712) | Study: United States | Association |
| MSNJ Medical Student Loan Fund (3641) | Citizenship: US; Legal: NJ; Study: Canada, United States | Association |
| Multiple Sclerosis Society Research Studentships (3792) | | |
| New York State Professional Opportunity Scholarships (4592) | Citizenship: US, PermRes; Legal: NY; Study: NY | |
| New York State Regents Professional Opportunity Scholarships (4577) | Legal: NY; Study: NY | |
| NIH Predoctoral Fellowship Awards for Minority Students (3722) | | Minority |
| NMA Merit Scholarships (4301) | | African American |
| The NMA Special Awards Program (4303) | Study: United States | African American |
| NMF Scholarships for Minority Students (4304) | Citizenship: US; Study: United States | African American, Hispanic American, Native American |
| Oklahoma Resident Rural Scholarship Loans (4939) | Legal: OK; Study: OK | |

| Vocational Goal, Award, and Entry Number | Geographic Restrictions (Citizenship, Legal Residence, Place of Study) | Affiliation/Special Recipients Requirements |
|---|---|---|
| *Medicine (continued)* | | |
| Oklahoma Rural Medical Education Scholarship Loans (4940) | Legal: OK | |
| Oncology Nursing Foundation/Rhone Poulenc Rorer New Investigator Research Grants (4771) | | |
| Otological Research Fellowships (2199) | Study: Canada, United States | |
| Jerry L. Pettis Memorial Scholarship (689) | | |
| Presidential Scholar Awards (218) | | |
| The Primary Care Resource Initiative for Missouri (PRIMO) (3755) | Legal: MO | |
| Program for Minority Research Training in Psychiatry (804) | | Minority |
| RCPSC International Travelling Fellowship (5187) | Citizenship: Canada | Association |
| RCPSC-MRC/PMAC-Novartis Clinical Research Fellowship (5188) | Citizenship: Canada | Association |
| James H. Robinson Memorial Prize (4305) | Citizenship: US; Study: United States | African American, Hispanic American, Native American |
| Royal College Fellowship for Studies in Medical Education (5189) | Citizenship: Canada | Association |
| Rural Kentucky Medical Scholarship Fund (RKMSF) (3364) | Legal: KY; Study: KY | |
| Vincent Salierno Scholarship (747) | | |
| Samsun Medical Research Institute Student Internships (5224) | | |
| Savoy Foundation Postdoctoral and Clinical Research Fellowships; Savoy Foundation Research Grants; Savoy Foundation Studentships (5252) | Study: Canada | |
| George Scanlon Medical Student Loans (2987) | Legal: IA | |
| Scientist Development Grant (528) | Citizenship: US | |
| Dr. Sydney Segal Research Grants (1638) | Study: Canada | |
| Aura E. Severinghaus Award (4306) | Citizenship: US | African American, Hispanic American, Native American |
| The Slack Award for Medical Journalism (4307) | Study: United States | African American |
| Society of Nuclear Medicine Student Fellowship Awards (5477) | | |
| Student Travel Fellowships (748) | | |
| Summer Fellowship Grants (215) | Legal: Canada, United States | |
| Dr. Max Thorek Student Loans (3138) | | |
| Tylman Research Grant (222) | Citizenship: US/CA | |
| USA British Isles Traveling Fellowship (5182) | Study: United States | |
| Lee C. Van Wagner Scholarship (1909) | Legal: NY | |
| Dr. Henry R. Viets Medical Student Research Fellowships (3812) | Legal: United States; Study: United States | |
| Virginia Dental Scholarships (6065) | Study: VA | |
| WAMI Medical Education Program (134) | Legal: AK; Study: AK, WA | |
| Washington Osteopathic Foundation Student Loans (6087) | Legal: WA | |
| Western Interstate Commission for Higher Education Student Exchanges (135) | Legal: AK | |
| Arthur N. Wilson, M.D. Scholarship (691) | Study: AK | |
| Women's Medical Association of New York Financial Assistance Fund Loans (6232) | Study: NY | |
| Wyeth-Ayerst Prize in Women's Health (4308) | | Minority |
| Zeneca Pharmaceuticals Underserved Healthcare Grant (4336) | | |
| Zenith Fellows Award Program (209) | | |

| Vocational Goal, Award, and Entry Number | Geographic Restrictions (Citizenship, Legal Residence, Place of Study) | Affiliation/Special Recipients Requirements |
|---|---|---|
| **Military Sciences** | | |
| U.S. Army Center of Military History Dissertation Year Fellowships (5821) | Citizenship: US | |
| **Parks and Recreation** | | |
| American Numismatic Society Graduate Fellowships (736) | Study: NY | |
| **Philosophy, Theology, and Religion** | | |
| Animal Health Trust of Canada Research Grants (1046) | Study: Canada | |
| Sidney E. Mead Prize (899) | | |
| **Physical Sciences** | | |
| Agency for Toxic Substances and Disease Registry Student Internship Program (5860) | | |
| AIAA/Gordon C. Oates Air Breathing Propulsion Award (566) | Citizenship: US | |
| American Association of Petroleum Geologists Foundation Grants-in-Aid (319) | | |
| American Museum of Natural History Collection Study Grants (712) | Study: United States | |
| Association for Women Geoscientists Thesis Support Scholarships (Chrysalis) (1296) | | |
| AT & T Bell Laboratories Graduate Research Fellowships for Women (1303) | Citizenship: US, PermRes; Study: NJ | |
| AT & T Bell Laboratories Graduate Research Grants for Women (1304) | Citizenship: US, PermRes; Study: NJ | |
| AT & T Bell Laboratories University Relations Summer Program (1306) | | |
| AWU Graduate Research Fellowships (1201) | Citizenship: US, PermRes; Study: CA, CO, ID, MT, ND, NM, NV, OK, UT, WA, WY | |
| AWU Post-Graduate Fellowship (1202) | Citizenship: US, PermRes; Study: CA, CO, ID, ND, NM, OK | |
| F.M. Becket Memorial Award (2366) | Study: Canada, United States | |
| H. Fletcher Brown Scholarship (4967) | Legal: DE | |
| Carnegie Institution of Washington Postdoctoral and Predoctoral Fellowships (1737) | Study: United States | |
| Frank M. Chapman Memorial Fellowships and Grants (714) | | |
| Chateaubriand Scholarship (Scientifique) (2372) | Citizenship: US; Study: France | |
| CIC Predoctoral Fellowships (2013) | Citizenship: US; Study: United States | African American, Hispanic American, Native American |
| Energy Fellowships (3488) | | |
| Engineer Degree Fellowships; Howard Hughes Doctoral Fellowships (2922) | Citizenship: US; Study: United States | |
| Environmental Protection Agency Tribal Lands Science Scholarship (560) | | Native American |
| Joseph L. Fisher Dissertation Awards (5111) | | |
| Ford Foundation Predoctoral and Dissertation Fellowships for Minorities (4357) | Citizenship: US; Study: United States | Native American, Asian American, Hispanic American, African American |
| GEM Ph.D. Science Fellowship Program (3943) | Citizenship: US; Study: United States | Native American, African American, Hispanic American |
| Government of Canada Awards (3145) | Citizenship: France, Germany, Japan, Mexico; Study: Canada | |
| Guggenheim Fellowships (5380) | Study: United States | |
| Hertz Foundation Graduate Fellowships (2866) | Citizenship: US, PermRes; Study: United States | |
| Hydrology (Horton) Research Grant (511) | | Association |
| International Astronomical Union Travel Grants (3121) | | |
| International Travel Grants (344) | Legal: United States | |
| Jessup and McHenry Awards (26) | Study: United States | |

| Vocational Goal, Award, and Entry Number | Geographic Restrictions (Citizenship, Legal Residence, Place of Study) | Affiliation/Special Recipients Requirements |
|---|---|---|
| *Physical Sciences (continued)* | | |
| JOI/USSAC Ocean Drilling Fellowships (3291) | Study: United States | |
| Dean John A. Knauss Marine Policy Fellowships (4328) | Study: United States | |
| Laboratory-Graduate Participantships; Thesis Parts Appointment (1084) | Legal: United States; Study: United States | |
| Leakey Foundation Fellowships for Great Ape Research and Conservation (3442) | | |
| Leakey Foundation General Grants (3443) | | |
| Magnetic Fusion Energy Technology Fellowship Program (5901) | | |
| Magnetic Fusion Science Fellowship Program (5902) | | |
| National Physical Science Consortium Graduate Fellowships for Minorities and Women (4338) | Citizenship: US | Native American, Hispanic American, African American |
| New Focus Research Awards (4787) | Study: United States | |
| Nuclear Engineering/Health Physics Fellowship Program (5915) | | |
| Oak Ridge National Laboratory Professional Internship Program (5918) | | |
| Petro-Canada Inc. Graduate Research Awards (1284) | Citizenship: Canada, PermRes; Study: Canada | |
| Predoctoral Fellowships in Biological Sciences (2927) | | |
| Research Support Opportunities in Arctic Environmental Studies (1682) | Citizenship: Canada, PermRes; Legal: Canada; Study: Canada | |
| Theodore Roosevelt Memorial Grants (716) | | |
| SAO Predoctoral Fellowships (5371) | Study: United States | |
| Savannah River Technology Center Professional Internship Program (5924) | | |
| John Clarke Slater Fellowship (770) | | |
| SSRC-MacArthur Foundation Dissertation Fellowships on Peace and Security in a Changing World (5409) | | |
| Tesla Award (5702) | | |
| Young Canadian Researchers Awards (3151) | Citizenship: Canada, PermRes | Other |

## Protective Services and Public Affairs

| | | |
|---|---|---|
| Dwight David Eisenhower Transportation Fellowship (6052) | Citizenship: US; Study: United States | |
| International Foundation of Employee Benefit Plans Grants for Research (3155) | Citizenship: Canada | |
| Dean John A. Knauss Marine Policy Fellowships (4328) | Study: United States | |
| National Institute of Justice Graduate Research Fellowships (4194) | | |
| New York State Professional Opportunity Scholarships (4592) | Citizenship: US, PermRes; Legal: NY; Study: NY | |
| Presidential Scholar Awards (218) | | |
| Public Interest Internships (1803) | Study: United States | |

## Social Sciences

| | | |
|---|---|---|
| AAS Joint Fellowships with the Newberry Library (253) | Study: MA | |
| ACLS Grants for East European Studies - Dissertation Fellowships (407) | Citizenship: US, PermRes | |
| Afro-American and African Studies Fellowships (6251) | Study: United States | |
| American Jewish Studies Fellowships (598) | Study: United States | |
| American Museum of Natural History Collection Study Grants (712) | Study: United States | |

| Vocational Goal, Award, and Entry Number | Geographic Restrictions (Citizenship, Legal Residence, Place of Study) | Affiliation/Special Recipients Requirements |
|---|---|---|
| *Social Sciences (continued)* | | |
| American Research Center in Egypt Research Fellowships for Study in the U.S. or Canada (844) | Citizenship: Egypt; Study: Canada, United States | |
| American Sociological Association Research Doctoral Fellowships in Sociology (987) | Citizenship: US, PermRes | Minority |
| Ancient India and Iran Trust Travel and Research Grants (1035) | | |
| Annual Grants; Dr. John Pine Memorial Award; Dr. A. F. Zimmerman Award (4890) | | Fraternal |
| APSA Graduate Fellowships for African-American Students (781) | | African American |
| APSA Graduate Fellowships for Latino Students (782) | | Hispanic American |
| ARIT Fellowships (846) | Study: Canada, Turkey, United States | |
| Artists Fellowship; Japan Foundation Cultural Properties Specialists Fellowship; Japan Foundation Doctoral Fellowship; Japan Foundation Research Fellowship (3240) | Study: Japan | |
| Jeannette D. Black Memorial Fellowship (1511) | Study: RI | |
| The Jeanne Humphrey Block Dissertation Award (3796) | | |
| Stephen Botein Fellowships (254) | Study: United States | |
| Mildred Cater Bradham Social Work Fellowship (6303) | | Fraternal |
| John Carter Brown Library Travel Grants (1514) | Study: RI | |
| National Council on Family Relations Ernest W. Burgess Award (3947) | | |
| California Psychological Association Foundation Minority Scholarships (1572) | Study: CA | Minority |
| Chateaubriand Fellowships (Humanities) (2375) | Citizenship: US; Study: France | |
| Chateaubriand Scholarship (Scientifique) (2372) | Citizenship: US; Study: France | |
| CIC Predoctoral Fellowships (2013) | Citizenship: US; Study: United States | African American, Hispanic American, Native American |
| Clark Library Predoctoral Fellowship (1762) | Study: CA | |
| Anna C. and Oliver C. Colburn Fellowship (1064) | Legal: Canada, United States; Study: Greece | Association |
| Congressional Fellowships on Women and Public Policy (6236) | Legal: United States; Study: United States | |
| Council for European Studies Pre-Dissertation Fellowships in the Social Sciences (2102) | Citizenship: US/CA, PermRes | |
| Council for European Studies Pre-Dissertation Fellowships for Topics Related to the European Community (2103) | Citizenship: US; Study: United States | |
| Council on Social Work Education Minority Fellowships (3724) | Citizenship: US, PermRes | Native American, African American, Hispanic American, Asian American |
| Minda de Gunzburg Center for European Studies Program for the Study of Germany and Europe Dissertation Research Fellowships (2769) | | Other |
| Christopher DeCormier Scholarship (3075) | Study: NY | Other |
| Friedreich Ebert Stiftung Pre Dissertation/Advanced Graduate Fellowshps (2332) | Citizenship: US; Study: Germany | |
| Albert Einstein Institution Fellowships (2361) | | |
| Kenan T. Erim Award (1065) | | |
| ETS Summer Program in Research for Graduate Students (2354) | Study: NJ, United States | |
| Fellowship in Aerospace History (537) | Citizenship: US; Study: United States | |
| Fellowship for the Study of Foraging Peoples (3441) | | |

| Vocational Goal, Award, and Entry Number | Geographic Restrictions (Citizenship, Legal Residence, Place of Study) | Affiliation/Special Recipients Requirements |
|---|---|---|
| *Social Sciences (continued)* | | |
| Fellowships in Byzantine Studies, Pre-Columbian Studies and Landscape Architecture (2288) | Study: DC | |
| Ford Foundation Predoctoral and Dissertation Fellowships for Minorities (4357) | Citizenship: US; Study: United States | Native American, Asian American, Hispanic American, African American |
| Foreign Policy Research Fellowships (1509) | Study: United States | |
| Fyssen Foundation Research Grants (2610) | | |
| Albert Gallatin Fellowships in International Affairs (2613) | Citizenship: US; Study: Switzerland | |
| Getty Center Predoctoral Fellowships (2700) | Study: United States | |
| Government of Canada Awards (3145) | Citizenship: France, Germany, Japan, Mexico; Study: Canada | |
| H. F. Guggenheim Foundation Dissertation Fellowships (2758) | | |
| Louise Wallace Hackney Fellowship for the Study of Chinese Art (757) | Citizenship: US | |
| Charles U. and Janet C. Harris Fellowship (871) | | |
| Robert D. Hodgson Memorial Ph.D. Dissertation Grant (1208) | | Association |
| Hollingworth Award Competition (3877) | | |
| Celia M. Howard Fellowships (2964) | Legal: IL | |
| Humanities Fellowships (1179) | Citizenship: US | |
| Hubert H. Humphrey Doctoral Fellowships in Arms Control and Disarmament (5819) | Citizenship: US | |
| Institute Postdoctoral NEH Fellowship (4751) | | |
| Institute for the Study of World Politics Fellowships (3079) | Study: United States | |
| Institute of Turkish Studies Dissertation Writing Grants (3081) | | |
| IREX Individual Advanced Research Opportunities (3185) | Citizenship: US, PermRes | |
| Olivia James Traveling Fellowship (1066) | Citizenship: US, PermRes; Study: Greece, Italy | |
| Jacob K. Javits Fellowship (3255) | | |
| Samuel H. Kress Foundation Fellowship (874) | Citizenship: US | |
| Katrin H. Lamon Resident Scholarship for Native Americans (5274) | Study: United States | Native American |
| Leakey Foundation General Grants (3443) | | |
| Henry Luce Foundation/ACLS Dissertation Fellowship in American Art (412) | Citizenship: US | |
| Marine Corps Historical Center Doctoral Dissertation Fellowship (3557) | | |
| Paul Mellon Centre Fellowship (6276) | Study: England | |
| Andrew W. Mellon Foundation Fellowships (877) | Legal: Czech Republic, Hungary, Poland | |
| Institute Andrew W. Mellon Postdoctoral Research Fellowship (4752) | | |
| Mesopotamian Fellowship (878) | | Association |
| Minority Fellowships in Psychology (807) | Citizenship: US, PermRes | Minority |
| The Henry A. Murray Dissertation Award (3797) | | |
| National Tax Association Doctoral Dissertation Awards (4422) | Study: Canada, United States | |
| NEH Fellowships (6200) | Citizenship: US, PermRes; Legal: United States; Study: United States | |
| New York State Professional Opportunity Scholarships (4592) | Citizenship: US, PermRes; Legal: NY; Study: NY | |
| New York State Regents Professional Opportunity Scholarships (4577) | Legal: NY; Study: NY | |
| NWSA Graduate Scholarships in Lesbian Studies (4452) | | |

| Vocational Goal, Award, and Entry Number | Geographic Restrictions (Citizenship, Legal Residence, Place of Study) | Affiliation/Special Recipients Requirements |
|---|---|---|
| *Social Sciences (continued)* | | |
| OTA Congressional Fellowship (2040) | | |
| Paleoanthropology Award (3444) | | |
| Peace Scholars Award (5077) | | |
| Pergamon-NWSA Graduate Scholarships in Women's Studies (4453) | | |
| Kate B. and Hall J. Peterson Fellowships (256) | Study: United States | |
| Petro-Canada Inc. Graduate Research Awards (1284) | Citizenship: Canada, PermRes; Study: Canada | |
| Phi Alpha Theta Graduate Scholarship (4892) | | Fraternal |
| Pre- and Postdoctoral Fellowships in International and Area Studies (2804) | Study: United States | |
| Pre- and Postdoctoral Fellowships on Nonviolent Sanctions; Visiting Scholar Affiliations (2806) | Study: United States | |
| Psychology Internships (5228) | Study: United States | |
| Research Fellowships in American History and Culture (3460) | Study: United States | |
| Barbara Rosenblum Cancer Dissertation Award (5525) | | Association |
| Rundell Graduate Student Award (6155) | | |
| William B. Schallek Memorial Graduate Study Fellowships (5132) | Citizenship: US | |
| Schlesinger Library, Radcliffe College Dissertation Grants (5256) | | |
| Schlesinger Library, Radcliffe College Honorary Visiting Scholar Appointments (5257) | | |
| James R. Scobie Memorial Awards (3071) | | |
| Social Sciences and Humanities Research Council Doctoral Fellowships (5425) | Citizenship: Canada, PermRes | |
| SPSSI Social Issues Dissertation Award (5498) | | |
| SSRC Advanced Postdoctoral Training and Research Awards (5393) | Citizenship: US, PermRes | |
| SSRC Africa Predissertation Fellowships (5394) | Citizenship: US, PermRes | |
| SSRC African Humanities Fellowships (5396) | Study: IL | |
| SSRC Bangladesh Studies Fellowships (5397) | Study: Bangladesh | |
| SSRC Berlin Program for Advanced German and European Studies Fellowships (5398) | Citizenship: US, PermRes; Study: Germany | |
| SSRC Grants for Advanced Area Research (5399) | | |
| SSRC International Predissertation Fellowships (5402) | | |
| SSRC Japan Fellowships for Dissertation Write-Up (5404) | Study: United States | |
| SSRC-MacArthur Foundation Dissertation Fellowships on Peace and Security in a Changing World (5409) | | |
| SSRC Near and Middle East Dissertation Research Fellowships (5412) | | |
| SSRC Predoctoral and Dissertation Training and Research Awards (5413) | Citizenship: US, PermRes | |
| SSRC South Asia Dissertation Fellowships for Bangladesh (5415) | | |
| SSRC Southeast Asia Predissertation Fellowships (5417) | Citizenship: US, PermRes | |
| SSRC Soviet Union and Its Successor States Dissertation Fellowships (5418) | Citizenship: US | |
| SSRC Soviet Union and Its Successor States Workshop Grants (5422) | | |
| Otis Paul Starkey Grant (1209) | | Association |

| Vocational Goal, Award, and Entry Number | Geographic Restrictions (Citizenship, Legal Residence, Place of Study) | Affiliation/Special Recipients Requirements |
|---|---|---|
| **Social Sciences (continued)** | | |
| Robert G. Stone Fellowships in American Maritime History (6182) | Study: CT | |
| Student Research Grants for the Scientific Study of Sex (5502) | | |
| U.S. Air Force Dissertation Year Fellowship in U.S. Military Aerospace History (5814) | Citizenship: US; Study: DC | |
| U.S. Army Center of Military History Dissertation Year Fellowships (5821) | Citizenship: US | |
| Alexander O. Vietor Memorial Fellowship (1518) | Study: RI | |
| Paul Vouras Grant (1210) | | Association |
| WAWH Graduate Student Fellowship (6147) | | Association |
| Weatherhead Fellowships (5276) | | |
| Wenner-Gren Foundation Predoctoral Grants (6136) | | |
| Winterthur Research Fellowships (6201) | Study: United States | |
| Helen M. Woodruff Fellowship of the Archaeological Institute of America (1068) | Citizenship: US, PermRes | |
| Woodruff Traveling Fellowship (1069) | | |
| Manfred Worner Fellowship (4657) | | |
| Young Canadian Researchers Awards (3151) | Citizenship: Canada, PermRes | Other |
| **Visual and Performing Arts** | | |
| Animal Health Trust of Canada Research Grants (1046) | Study: Canada | |
| Artists Fellowship; Japan Foundation Cultural Properties Specialists Fellowship; Japan Foundation Doctoral Fellowship; Japan Foundation Research Fellowship (3240) | Study: Japan | |
| The Classical Fellowship; The Norbert Schimmel Fellowship for Mediterranean Art and Archaeology (3652) | Legal: United States; Study: United States | |
| Consortium College University Media Centers Annual Research Grants (2065) | Legal: United States | |
| Mary Davis Fellowship (1770) | | |
| David E. Finley Fellowship (1771) | | |
| Ford Foundation Fellowships (1178) | Citizenship: Other; Study: United States | |
| Getty Museum Graduate Internships (2702) | Study: United States | |
| Louise Wallace Hackney Fellowship for the Study of Chinese Art (757) | Citizenship: US | |
| Humanities Fellowships (1179) | Citizenship: US | |
| The Ittleson Fellowship (1774) | Study: United States | |
| Olivia James Traveling Fellowship (1066) | Citizenship: US, PermRes; Study: Greece, Italy | |
| Jacob K. Javits Fellowship (3255) | | |
| Kress Research Fellowship in Art History (3404) | Study: United States | |
| Kress Research Fellowships at Foreign Institutions (3405) | Study: Cyprus, France, Germany, Israel, Italy, Netherlands, Switzerland, United Kingdom | |
| Henry Luce Foundation/ACLS Dissertation Fellowship in American Art (412) | Citizenship: US | |
| Paul Mellon Centre Fellowship (6276) | Study: England | |
| Andrew W. Mellon Fellowship (1775) | Study: United States | |
| Paul Mellon Fellowship (1776) | Study: United States | |
| Andrew W. Mellon Fellowships in Art History (3658) | Study: United States | |
| Metropolitan Museum of Art Classical Fellowship (3660) | Study: NY | |
| Professional Development Fellowship Program for Artists and Art Historians (1982) | Citizenship: US, PermRes | |
| Theodore Rousseau Fellowships (3667) | | |
| Robert H. and Clarice Smith Fellowship (1779) | Study: United States | |

| Vocational Goal, Award, and Entry Number | Geographic Restrictions (Citizenship, Legal Residence, Place of Study) | Affiliation/Special Recipients Requirements |
|---|---|---|
| *Visual and Performing Arts (continued)* | | |
| Polaire Weissman Fund Fellowship (3669) | Study: United States | |
| Wyeth Fellowship (1782) | Study: United States | |

# Graduate

**Agriculture**

| | | |
|---|---|---|
| American Horticultural Society Horticultural Career Internship (545) | | |
| American Society for Enology and Viticulture Scholarships (928) | | |
| John G. Bene Fellowship in Social Forestry (3150) | Citizenship: Canada; Legal: Canada | |
| Harold Bettinger Memorial Scholarship (1382) | Study: Canada, United States | |
| Biggs and Gilmore Communications Scholarships (4030) | Study: IA, IL, MI, OH, WI | Association |
| Andrew J. Boehm Fellowships (466) | | |
| Howard S. Brembeck Scholarship in Agricultural Engineering (892) | | |
| A.W. "Winn" Brindle Memorial Scholarship Loans (131) | | |
| A & E Capelle LN Herfords Scholarship (150) | Legal: Canada | |
| John Carew Memorial Scholarship (1383) | Study: Canada, United States | |
| Certified Angus Beef Scholarship (4274) | | Association |
| Dr. Allan P. Chan Scholarship (2225) | Citizenship: Canada | |
| Dog Writers' Educational Trust Scholarships (2264) | | Other |
| Grace and Robert Fraser Landscape Heritage Award (3423) | | |
| Herb Society Research Grants (2862) | | |
| Institute of Food Technologists Graduate Fellowships (3038) | | |
| Interchange Fellowship in Horticulture and Landscape Design (2622) | Citizenship: United Kingdom, US, PermRes; Study: United States | |
| Fran Johnson Scholarships (1385) | Citizenship: US, Canada; Study: Canada, United States | |
| LAF Student Research Grant (3429) | | |
| LANDCADD, Inc. Scholarship (3430) | | |
| William J. Locklin Scholarship (3431) | | |
| Kenneth D. Naden Award (3950) | | |
| National Wool Growers Memorial Fellowships (887) | | |
| National Zoological Park Minority Traineeships (4456) | | |
| National Zoological Park Traineeship in BioPark Horticulture (4458) | | |
| NCSGC National Scholarships (3959) | | |
| New York State Professional Opportunity Scholarships (4592) | Citizenship: US, PermRes; Legal: NY; Study: NY | |
| Ohio State University Extension Internship (4733) | | |
| Raymond E. Page Scholarship (3432) | | |
| Piancone Family Agriculture Scholarship (4254) | Legal: DC, DE, MA, MD, NJ, NY, PA, VA | Ethnic |
| Purina Research Fellowships (5033) | | |
| James K. Rathmell, Jr., Memorial Scholarship to Work/Study Abroad (1387) | Legal: United States | |
| Abbie Sargent Memorial Scholarships (5250) | Legal: NH | |
| Statler Foundation Scholarship (5622) | Study: NY, United States | |
| E.A. Stokdyk Award (3953) | | |

| Vocational Goal, Award, and Entry Number | Geographic Restrictions (Citizenship, Legal Residence, Place of Study) | Affiliation/Special Recipients Requirements |
|---|---|---|
| *Agriculture (continued)* | | |
| Ed Taylor Memorial Scholarship (6153) | Study: CA | |
| United Nations Educational Training Scholarships for Southern Africans (5798) | Legal: Namibia, Republic of South Africa | |
| Lester Walls III Scholarship (3435) | | Handicapped |
| Wood Awards (2555) | | |
| Worcester County Horticultural Society Scholarship (6257) | | |
| Young Canadian Researchers Awards (3151) | Citizenship: Canada, PermRes | Other |
| **Architecture and Environmental Design** | | |
| AAUW Educational Foundation Selected Professions Fellowship (336) | Citizenship: US, PermRes | |
| AHA/American Institute of Architects Fellowships in Health Facilities Design (547) | Citizenship: US | |
| AIA/AAF Scholarship for Advanced Study and Research (571) | | |
| AIA/AAF Scholarship for Professional Degree Candidates (572) | | |
| AIA/AHA Fellowship in Health Facilities Design (573) | Citizenship: US/CA | |
| The American Architectural Foundation Minority/Disadvantaged Scholarship (574) | Legal: United States | Minority |
| Association for Women in Architecture Scholarship (1292) | Legal: CA; Study: CA | |
| John G. Bene Fellowship in Social Forestry (3150) | Citizenship: Canada; Legal: Canada | |
| Mabelle Wilhelmina Boldt Memorial Scholarship (938) | | |
| John Dinkeloo Bequests/American Academy in Rome Traveling Fellowship in Architectural Technology (6023) | Study: Italy | |
| Fellowships in Byzantine Studies, Pre-Columbian Studies and Landscape Architecture (2288) | Study: DC | |
| Edith H. Henderson Scholarship (3424) | Study: GA | |
| Historically Black Colleges and Universities Building Technology Summer Research Participation Program (5889) | | |
| Interchange Fellowship in Horticulture and Landscape Design (2622) | Citizenship: United Kingdom, US, PermRes; Study: United States | |
| Kate Neal Kinley Memorial Fellowshsip (5998) | | |
| The Lippincott and Margulies Summer Internship (5385) | | |
| Paul Mellon Centre Fellowship (6276) | Study: England | |
| National Zoological Park Minority Traineeships (4456) | | |
| National Zoological Park Traineeship in Exhibit Interpretation (4460) | | |
| National Zoological Park Traineeship in Facilities Design (4461) | | |
| National Zoological Park Traineeship in Landscaping (4462) | | |
| NCSGC National Scholarships (3959) | | |
| New York State Professional Opportunity Scholarships (4592) | Citizenship: US, PermRes; Legal: NY; Study: NY | |
| New York State Regents Professional Opportunity Scholarships (4577) | Legal: NY; Study: NY | |
| NIAE/ATBCB Student Design Competition Prizes (6024) | Study: United States | |
| RTKL Traveling Fellowship (576) | | |
| Robert Schreck Memorial Fund Scholarship (5280) | Legal: TX | |

| Vocational Goal, Award, and Entry Number | Geographic Restrictions (Citizenship, Legal Residence, Place of Study) | Affiliation/Special Recipients Requirements |
|---|---|---|
| **Architecture and Environmental Design (continued)** | | |
| Society of American Registered Architects Student Design Competition/Emily Munson Memorial Student Award (5433) | | |
| Robert Thunen Memorial Educational Scholarships (2983) | Study: CA, NV, OR, WA | |
| Van Alen Institute Fellowship in Public Architecture (Loyd Warren Fellowships/Paris Prize) (6026) | Citizenship: US, PermRes | |
| David T. Woolsey Scholarship (3437) | Legal: HI | |
| **Area and Ethnic Studies** | | |
| AGBU Education Loan Program in the U.S. (1133) | | Ethnic |
| AGBU Graduate Loan Program (1134) | | |
| Lorraine Allison Scholarships; Jennifer Robinson Scholarships (1081) | Citizenship: Canada; Study: Canada | |
| American Jewish League for Israel University Scholarship Fund (600) | | |
| American School of Classical Studies Summer Sessions Scholarships (855) | Legal: Canada, United States; Study: Greece | Association |
| Ancient India and Iran Trust Travel and Research Grants (1035) | | |
| Stella Blum Research Grant (2089) | | Association |
| Bulgarian Studies Seminar (3183) | Citizenship: US, PermRes | |
| Camargo Foundation Residential Fellowships (1588) | Study: France | |
| CFUW Awards (1631) | Citizenship: Canada; Legal: Canada | |
| CIBC Youthvision Graduate Research Award Program (1270) | Citizenship: Canada, PermRes; Study: Canada | |
| Community Service Scholarships (3643) | | |
| Cultural Cooperation Grants (6004) | | |
| Czech Education Scholarships (3708) | Study: Slovakia | |
| Helen Darcovich Memorial Doctoral Fellowship (1657) | Study: Canada | |
| Minda de Gunzburg Center for European Studies Dissertation Exploration Grants (2766) | | Other |
| Minda de Gunzburg Center for European Studies Graduate Summer Research Travel Grants (2768) | | Other |
| Minda de Gunzburg Center for European Studies Short-Term Opportunity Grants (2770) | | Other |
| Marusia and Michael Dorosh Masters Fellowship (1659) | Study: Canada | |
| EMGIP Internships (2380) | Study: Germany | |
| Endowment for Biblical Research, Summer Research and Travel Grants (868) | | |
| Ford Foundation Fellowships (1178) | Citizenship: Other; Study: United States | |
| German Studies Research Grant (2687) | Study: Germany | |
| IAF Field Research Fellowships Program at the Master's Level (3091) | | |
| Institute of Holy Land Studies Scholarships (3047) | Study: Israel | |
| Inter-University Center Fellowships (3095) | Study: Japan | Association |
| Inter-University Program Fellowships (3097) | Study: People's Republic of China | |
| U. Alexis Johnson Scholarship (3238) | Study: DC, MD, VA, WV, Japan | |
| Krupp Foundation Fellowship (2773) | | Other |
| National Program for Advanced Study and Research in China - Senior Advanced Studies (2017) | Citizenship: US, PermRes; Study: People's Republic of China | |
| National Welsh-American Foundation Exchange Scholarships (4450) | Citizenship: US; Study: Wales | Ethnic |

| Vocational Goal, Award, and Entry Number | Geographic Restrictions (Citizenship, Legal Residence, Place of Study) | Affiliation/Special Recipients Requirements |
|---|---|---|
| **Area and Ethnic Studies (continued)** | | |
| King Olav Norwegian-American Heritage Fund (5535) | | |
| Post-Rabbinic Scholarships (3646) | | |
| Research Support Opportunities in Arctic Environmental Studies (1682) | Citizenship: Canada, PermRes; Legal: Canada; Study: Canada | |
| Scholarship in Jewish Women's Studies (4454) | | |
| Society Farsarotul Grants (5449) | | |
| SSRC Bangladesh Studies Fellowships (5397) | Study: Bangladesh | |
| SSRC Soviet Union and Its Successor States Graduate Training Fellowships (5419) | Citizenship: US, PermRes | |
| SSRC Soviet Union and Its Successor States Institutional Awards for First-Year Fellowships (5420) | | |
| Studentships in Northern Studies (1684) | Citizenship: Canada, PermRes; Study: Canada | |
| Study Abroad Scholarships (4263) | Study: Italy | |
| James A. Swan Fund Grants (5652) | | |
| Vincent and Anna Visceglia Fellowship (4268) | | |
| **Business and Management** | | |
| AAUW Educational Foundation Selected Professions Engineering Dissertation Fellowship (335) | Citizenship: US, PermRes | Minority |
| AFL-CIO Research Internship (464) | Citizenship: US, PermRes; Study: United States | |
| AFLSE Scholarships (506) | Citizenship: US, PermRes; Study: England | |
| African Graduate Fellowships (47) | Study: United States | |
| AIER Summer Fellowships (580) | Study: United States | |
| AISES A.T. Anderson Memorial Scholarship (559) | | Native American, Association |
| American Economic Association/Federal Reserve System Minority Graduate Fellowships in Economics (453) | Citizenship: US | African American, Hispanic American, Native American |
| Applebaum Master's and Ph.D. Programs Awards (2549) | | |
| Appraisal Institute Education Trust Scholarships (1060) | Citizenship: US | |
| Aspen Systems Graduate Scholarship (515) | | |
| Avis Rent a Car Scholarship (972) | Citizenship: US/CA; Study: Canada, United States | |
| Avon Products Foundation Scholarship Program for Women in Business Studies (1545) | Citizenship: US | |
| Batten Fellowships (6013) | Citizenship: US | |
| Harold Bettinger Memorial Scholarship (1382) | Study: Canada, United States | |
| BPW/Sears Roebuck Loans for Women in Graduate Business Studies (1548) | Citizenship: US; Study: United States | |
| Business Press Educational Foundation Student Intern Program (1543) | | |
| Luray Caverns Research Grant (4430) | | |
| Central Intelligence Agency Graduate Studies Internships (1811) | Citizenship: US | |
| CERT Scholarship (2100) | Study: United States | Native American |
| Consortium Graduate Study Management Fellowships for Minorities (2067) | Citizenship: US; Study: United States | African American, Hispanic American, Native American |
| Council of Logistics Management Graduate Scholarships (2123) | | |
| Keith Davis Graduate Scholarship Awards (5334) | | Fraternal |
| Fellowships in National Security (2812) | Study: United States | |
| FORE Graduate Scholarships (517) | Citizenship: US, PermRes | |
| A.P. Giannini Scholarship (4228) | | Ethnic |

| Vocational Goal, Award, and Entry Number | Geographic Restrictions (Citizenship, Legal Residence, Place of Study) | Affiliation/Special Recipients Requirements |
|---|---|---|
| **Business and Management (continued)** | | |
| GOALS Fellowships (3001) | Citizenship: US; Study: IA, IL, MA, MI, MN, NJ, NY, OH, OR, SC, WI, WV | African American, Hispanic American, Native American |
| David Hallissey Memorial Scholarships (973) | Citizenship: US/CA, PermRes | |
| Harwood Memorial Real Estate Scholarship (5083) | | |
| India Studies Student Fellowships (5319) | Citizenship: Canada; Study: India | |
| Jacob's Pillow Dance Festival Internships (3234) | Study: United States | |
| Robert Kaufman Memorial Scholarships (2989) | | |
| Laurels Fund Scholarships (2350) | | |
| Mackenzie King Travelling Scholarships (3529) | Legal: Canada; Study: United States | |
| The Frederick T. Metcalf Award Program (1283) | Citizenship: Canada; Study: Canada | |
| Minority Student Administrative Summer Internship Program (5903) | | Minority |
| National Association of Black Accountants National Scholarship (3857) | | Minority |
| National Zoological Park Traineeship in Public Affairs (4463) | | |
| NBMBAA National MBA Scholarship/PhD Fellowship (3910) | | Minority |
| New York State Regents Professional Opportunity Scholarships (4577) | Legal: NY; Study: NY | |
| Petro-Canada Inc. Graduate Research Awards (1284) | Citizenship: Canada, PermRes; Study: Canada | |
| Phi Chi Theta Scholarships (4896) | | Association |
| Quebec Scholarship (4438) | Citizenship: Canada; Legal: Canada; Study: Canada | |
| Rockefeller Archive Center Research Grants (5142) | Study: United States | |
| William B. Ruggles Journalism Scholarship (4196) | Study: United States | |
| Karla Scherer Foundation Scholarships (5254) | | |
| Edwin P. Shaunessy Memorial Scholarships (4989) | | Employer |
| Simmons Scholarship (981) | Citizenship: US/CA, PermRes | |
| Statler Foundation Scholarship (5622) | Study: NY, United States | |
| Stanley H. Stearman Scholarships (4406) | | Association |
| Wolcott Foundation Fellowships (2870) | Study: DC | |
| Young Canadian Researchers Awards (3151) | Citizenship: Canada, PermRes | Other |

## Communications

| Vocational Goal, Award, and Entry Number | Geographic Restrictions (Citizenship, Legal Residence, Place of Study) | Affiliation/Special Recipients Requirements |
|---|---|---|
| AGBU Education Loan (1136) | | Ethnic |
| AGBU Education Loan Program in the U.S. (1133) | | Ethnic |
| AIAA/Command, Control, Communications and Intelligence Graduate Scholarship Award (565) | | |
| Len Allen Award of Merit for Radio News (5051) | | |
| Alpha Epsilon Rho Scholarships (196) | | Fraternal |
| Asian American Journalists Association Scholarship (1172) | | Ethnic |
| Atlanta Press Club Journalism Scholarship (1310) | Study: GA | |
| Batten Fellowships (6013) | Citizenship: US | |
| The BBM Scholarship (1601) | Study: Canada | |
| WCVB TV Leo L. Beranek Fellowship for Newsreporting (6123) | | |
| Blethen Family Newspaper Internship Program for Minorities (5295) | Study: WA | Minority |
| Broadcast Pioneers Scholarships (1495) | | |

| Vocational Goal, Award, and Entry Number | Geographic Restrictions (Citizenship, Legal Residence, Place of Study) | Affiliation/Special Recipients Requirements |
|---|---|---|
| *Communications (continued)* | | |
| Mary Butler Scholarship (6221) | Legal: MI; Study: MI | |
| Cable Telecommunications Research Fellowship Program (1267) | Citizenship: Canada; Study: Canada | |
| College Conference and Summer Fellowship Program (3174) | | |
| Lucy Corbett Scholarship (6222) | Legal: MI; Study: MI | |
| Raymond Crepault Scholarship (1602) | Citizenship: Canada; Study: Canada | |
| Dirksen Congressional Research Grants (2253) | | |
| Dog Writers' Educational Trust Scholarships (2264) | | Other |
| Bob East Scholarship (4343) | | |
| Editing Internships (2275) | Citizenship: US; Study: United States | |
| Harold E. Fellows Scholarships (1496) | | Employer |
| Florida Chapter of the Association of Women in Communications Christina Saralegui Scholarship (1294) | Legal: FL | Hispanic American |
| James Lawrence Fly Scholarships (1497) | | |
| Grants for Research in Broadcasting (3864) | | |
| Hoover Library Fellowships and Grants (2890) | Study: United States | |
| Ken Inouye Scholarship (5488) | | Minority |
| Inter-American Press Association Scholarships (3093) | Citizenship: US, Canada, PermRes; Study: Canada, United States | |
| William E. Jackson Award (5198) | | |
| Journalists in Europe Study Program (3302) | | |
| Julia Kiene Fellowship (2363) | | |
| Kit C. King Graduate Scholarship (4345) | | |
| Claude R. Lambe Fellowships (3058) | | |
| Lyle Mamer Fellowship (2364) | | |
| Anne O'Hare McCormick Scholarship (3618) | Citizenship: US; Study: NY | |
| The Frederick T. Metcalf Award Program (1283) | Citizenship: Canada; Study: Canada | |
| NAHJ Scholarships (2879) | | |
| National Association of Black Journalists Scholarship (3859) | | Minority |
| National Scholarship Trust Fund of the Graphic Arts Fellowships (4373) | | |
| Northwestern University Journalism Minority Scholarships (4698) | | Minority |
| Online Newspaper Intern Program (2276) | | |
| Walter Patterson Scholarships (1498) | | |
| Politics and Journalism Internship (6083) | | |
| Public Interest Internships (1803) | Study: United States | |
| Pulliam Journalism Fellowships (1814) | Citizenship: US, PermRes; Study: United States | |
| Garth Reeves Jr. Memorial Scholarships (5490) | Legal: FL | Minority |
| Reporters Committee for Freedom of the Press Clinical Internship Program (5094) | | |
| Richard J. Roth Journalism Fellowship (4600) | Citizenship: US; Legal: NY; Study: NY | |
| RTNDF Presidential Memorial Scholarship (5066) | | |
| RTNDF Six-Month Entry Level Internships for Minority Students (5067) | | Minority |
| RTNDF Undergraduate Scholarships (5069) | | |
| William B. Ruggles Journalism Scholarship (4196) | Study: United States | |
| San Francisco Chronicle Summer Newsroom Internships (5230) | | |

| Vocational Goal, Award, and Entry Number | Geographic Restrictions (Citizenship, Legal Residence, Place of Study) | Affiliation/Special Recipients Requirements |
|---|---|---|
| *Communications (continued)* | | |
| San Francisco Chronicle Two-Year Editing Internships (5231) | | |
| San Francisco Chronicle Two-Year Newsroom Internships (5232) | | |
| Abe Schechter Graduate Scholarship (5070) | | |
| Seattle Professional Chapter of Women in Communications Annual Communications Scholarship (6224) | | |
| The *Seattle Times* Summer Newsroom Internships (5296) | | |
| Shane Media Scholarships (1499) | | |
| Carole Simpson Scholarship (5071) | | Minority |
| Stoody-West Fellowship in Journalism (5795) | Study: United States | Religion |
| Sun Chemical Corporation Flexographic Research Scholarship (2569) | | |
| Thomson Fellowship (5727) | | Minority |
| *U* The National College Magazine Internships/Fellowships (5763) | | |
| Virginia Press Association Minority Internship (6063) | Legal: VA; Study: VA | Minority |
| *The Washington Post* Summer Journalism Internships (6090) | | |
| Vincent T. Wasilewski Scholarships (1500) | | Association |
| WCVB TV Hearst Broadcast News Fellowship (6125) | | Minority |
| Della A. Whittaker Scholarships (5504) | | |
| Mark Zambrano Scholarship (2880) | | Minority |
| **Computer and Information Sciences** | | |
| AAUW Educational Foundation Selected Professions Fellowship (336) | Citizenship: US, PermRes | |
| The AFCEA Educational Foundation Fellowship (1099) | Citizenship: US | |
| ASIS Student Paper Award (935) | | |
| Aspen Systems Graduate Scholarship (515) | | |
| AT & T Bell Laboratories Cooperative Research Fellowships for Minorities (1302) | Citizenship: US, PermRes; Study: NJ | African American, Native American, Hispanic American |
| AT & T Bell Laboratories Graduate Research Grants for Women (1304) | Citizenship: US, PermRes; Study: NJ | |
| AT & T Bell Laboratories University Relations Summer Program (1306) | | |
| BPW Career Advancement Scholarships (1546) | Citizenship: US; Study: United States | |
| Bureau of Engraving and Printing Graduate Student Research Participation Program (5862) | | |
| Central Intelligence Agency Graduate Studies Internships (1811) | Citizenship: US | |
| Electronic Industries Foundation Scholarships (2370) | Citizenship: US | Handicapped |
| FORE Graduate Scholarships (517) | Citizenship: US, PermRes | |
| Fossil Energy Professional Internship Program (5878) | | |
| FSD Student Grant (2578) | | Handicapped |
| Graduate U.S. Army Environmental Hygiene Internship Program (5885) | | |
| Grants for Physically Disabled Students in the Sciences (2579) | | Handicapped |
| Dr. Theodore von Karman Graduate Scholarship (45) | Study: United States | Military |
| Laboratory-Graduate Participantships; Thesis Parts Appointment (1084) | Legal: United States; Study: United States | |

| Vocational Goal, Award, and Entry Number | Geographic Restrictions (Citizenship, Legal Residence, Place of Study) | Affiliation/Special Recipients Requirements |
|---|---|---|
| **Computer and Information Sciences (continued)** | | |
| Richard E. Merwin Scholarships (2950) | | Association |
| Microsoft Corporation Scholarships (5516) | | |
| Minority Student Administrative Summer Internship Program (5903) | | Minority |
| NAACP Willems Scholarship (3851) | | Minority, Association |
| National Center for Toxicological Research Graduate Student Research Participation (5906) | | |
| National Physical Science Consortium Graduate Fellowships for Minorities and Women (4338) | Citizenship: US | Native American, Hispanic American, African American |
| Naval Air Warfare Center Training Systems Division Graduate Research Participation Program (5912) | | |
| NRAO Summer Student Research Assistantships (4352) | Citizenship: US; Study: United States | |
| Adelle and Erwin Tomash Fellowship in the History of Information Processing (1353) | | |
| U.S. Nuclear Regulatory Commission Historically Black Colleges and Universities Graduate Student Research Participation (5935) | | |
| Upsilon Pi Epsilon/Computer Society Award for Academic Excellence (2952) | | Association |

## Education

| Vocational Goal, Award, and Entry Number | Geographic Restrictions | Affiliation/Special Recipients Requirements |
|---|---|---|
| AASA and Convention Exhibitors Scholarships (321) | Legal: Canada, United States | |
| AGBU Education Loan (1136) | | Ethnic |
| AGBU Education Loan Program in the U.S. (1133) | | Ethnic |
| AGBU Graduate Loan Program (1134) | | |
| AISES A.T. Anderson Memorial Scholarship (559) | | Native American, Association |
| American Montessori Society Scholarship Fund (710) | | |
| Assistantships in France (2374) | Citizenship: US | |
| Ruth Binnie Scholarships (1644) | Citizenship: Canada, Other | Association |
| Blaine House Scholars Loans (2455) | Legal: ME | |
| Bossing-Edwards Research Scholarships (3871) | | |
| BPW Career Advancement Scholarships (1546) | Citizenship: US; Study: United States | |
| The British Universities Summer Schools Scholarships (2384) | Study: United Kingdom | |
| CEASD Ethic Student Scholarship (2038) | | |
| Cherokee Nation Graduate Scholarship (1911) | | Native American |
| Civil Air Patrol Graduate Scholarship (3915) | | |
| CSAC Assumption Program of Loans for Education (1580) | Legal: CA | |
| Arthur Davis Fellowship; Charles E. Merrill Trust Fellowship (3806) | Study: United States | |
| Delta Gamma Foundation - Florence Margaret Harvey Memorial Scholarship (480) | Citizenship: US | Handicapped |
| Delta Psi Kappa Research Awards (2223) | | Fraternal |
| Rudolph Dillman Scholarship (481) | Citizenship: US | Handicapped |
| Paul Douglas Teacher Scholarship (1583) | Legal: CA; Study: CA | |
| Excellence in Arc Welding Awards; Graduate and Professional Awards for Achievement in Arc-Welded Design, Engineering and Fabrication (3482) | Legal: United States | |

| Vocational Goal, Award, and Entry Number | Geographic Restrictions (Citizenship, Legal Residence, Place of Study) | Affiliation/Special Recipients Requirements |
|---|---|---|
| *Education (continued)* | | |
| Florida Critical Teacher Shortage Scholarship Loans (2501) | Study: FL | |
| Florida Critical Teacher Shortage Tuition Reimbursement Program (2502) | Study: FL | |
| Florida Teacher Scholarship and Forgivable Loan Program (2506) | Study: FL | |
| FORE Graduate Scholarships (517) | Citizenship: US, PermRes | |
| French Government Teaching Awards (2376) | Study: France | |
| Georgia Student Finance Commission Service-Cancellable Stafford Loan (2666) | Legal: GA; Study: GA | |
| Georgia Student Finance Commission State-Sponsored Loan (2669) | Legal: GA; Study: GA | |
| Bishop Charles P. Greco Graduate Fellowships (3385) | | Religion, Association |
| Isabel M. Herson Scholarship in Education (6305) | | |
| Hollingworth Award Competition (3877) | | |
| Iota Lambda Sigma Grand Chapter Scholarship (3213) | | Fraternal |
| Doreen Kronick Scholarship (3446) | | |
| Albert H. Marckwardt Travel Grants (5680) | | Association |
| Sharon Christa McAuliffe Education Scholarship (3583) | Legal: MD; Study: MD | |
| Donald L. McCullough Memorial Scholarships (3866) | | |
| McKnight Junior Faculty Developmment Fellowships (2520) | Citizenship: US; Study: FL | |
| NACA Prize Papers Competition (3868) | | |
| NACADA Research Award (3824) | | |
| NACADA Scholarship (3825) | | Association |
| NAJA Graduate Scholarships (3881) | Citizenship: US; Legal: AL, AR, LA, MO, MS, TN, TX; Study: United States | |
| National Restaurant Association Graduate Degree Scholarship (4365) | | |
| National Scholarship Trust Fund of the Graphic Arts Fellowships (4373) | | |
| National Zoological Park Traineeship in Education (4459) | | |
| NCTE Research Foundation Research Grant-in-Aid (3961) | | |
| NDCS Scholarship Grant (3970) | Legal: England | Handicapped |
| Order of Alhambra Scholarships (4789) | Legal: CA; Study: United States | Religion |
| Pi Lambda Theta Graduate Student Scholar Award (4943) | | |
| Billy D. Pounds Scholarships and Bobby Jones Scholarships (3322) | | Fraternal |
| Power Systems Inc./NSCA Strength and Conditioning Professional Scholarship (4417) | | Association |
| Polingaysi Qoyawayma Scholarship (562) | | Native American |
| Retarded Citizens Teachers Scholarships (4793) | Citizenship: US, Canada | |
| Rockefeller Archive Center Research Grants (5142) | Study: United States | |
| SAE Doctoral Scholars Program (5435) | | |
| Scholarships for Blind and Visually Impaired Postsecondary Students (483) | Citizenship: US | Handicapped |
| Service Cancelable Student Loan (2660) | | |
| South Carolina Teachers Loan Program (5547) | | |
| Robert C. Thomas Memorial Scholarship (133) | | |
| United Commercial Travelers Retarded Citizens Teacher Scholarship (5787) | | |

| Vocational Goal, Award, and Entry Number | Geographic Restrictions (Citizenship, Legal Residence, Place of Study) | Affiliation/Special Recipients Requirements |
|---|---|---|
| **_Education (continued)_** | | |
| United Nations Educational Training Scholarships for Southern Africans (5798) | Legal: Namibia, Republic of South Africa | |
| Constance Dorothea Weinman Scholarship Trust for Graduate Study in Instructional Technology (5839) | | |
| Margaret Wight Scholarships (3324) | | Fraternal |
| **Engineering** | | |
| AAAS Directorate for Science & Policy Administrative Internship (264) | | |
| AAUW Educational Foundation Selected Professions Fellowship (336) | Citizenship: US, PermRes | |
| ACI Fellowships: ACI/W.R. Grace Fellowship; V. Mohan Malhotra Fellowship; Katherine Bryant Mather Fellowship; Stewart C. Watson Fellowship (388) | Study: Canada, United States | |
| Advanced Industrial Concepts (AIC) Materials Science Program (5857) | | African American, Native American |
| The AFCEA Educational Foundation Fellowship (1099) | Citizenship: US | |
| AIAA/Command, Control, Communications and Intelligence Graduate Scholarship Award (565) | | |
| AIAA/Gordon C. Oates Air Breathing Propulsion Award (566) | Citizenship: US | |
| AIAA Liquid Propulsion Award (567) | Citizenship: US | |
| Air Force Civilian Cooperative Work-Study Program (66) | | |
| Air Traffic Control Association Scholarships (72) | Citizenship: US | |
| AISES A.T. Anderson Memorial Scholarship (559) | | Native American, Association |
| The American Society of Mechanical Engineers Auxiliary Student Loans (948) | | |
| American Society of Naval Engineers Scholarships (959) | Citizenship: US, PermRes | |
| American Water Works Association Academic Achievement Awards (1015) | | |
| American Water Works Association Holy A. Cornell Grant (1016) | | Minority |
| American Water Works Association Scholarship Program (1017) | Legal: Canada, Guam, Mexico, Puerto Rico, United States | |
| ANS Graduate Scholarships (722) | Citizenship: US, PermRes | |
| Applied Health Physics Fellowship Program (5861) | | |
| ASHRAE Grants-in-Aid for Graduate Students (930) | | |
| Associated General Contractors Education Research Foundation Graduate Scholarship (401) | | |
| AT & T Bell Laboratories Cooperative Research Fellowships for Minorities (1302) | Citizenship: US, PermRes; Study: NJ | African American, Native American, Hispanic American |
| AT & T Bell Laboratories Graduate Research Grants for Women (1304) | Citizenship: US, PermRes; Study: NJ | |
| AT & T Bell Laboratories University Relations Summer Program (1306) | | |
| AWU Graduate Research Fellowships (1201) | Citizenship: US, PermRes; Study: CA, CO, ID, MT, ND, NM, NV, OK, UT, WA, WY | |
| AWU Student Research Fellowships (1203) | Citizenship: US, PermRes; Study: CA, CO, ID, MT, ND, NM, NV, OK, UT, WA, WY | |
| F.M. Becket Memorial Award (2366) | Study: Canada, United States | |
| BPW Career Advancement Scholarships (1546) | Citizenship: US; Study: United States | |

| Vocational Goal, Award, and Entry Number | Geographic Restrictions (Citizenship, Legal Residence, Place of Study) | Affiliation/Special Recipients Requirements |
|---|---|---|
| *Engineering (continued)* | | |
| BPW Loans for Women in Engineering Studies (1547) | Citizenship: US | |
| Joseph Bramah Scholarship; Raymond Coleman Prescott Scholarship (3086) | | Association |
| H. Fletcher Brown Scholarship (4967) | Legal: DE | |
| Bureau of Engraving and Printing Graduate Student Research Participation Program (5862) | | |
| Cable Telecommunications Research Fellowship Program (1267) | Citizenship: Canada; Study: Canada | |
| Cape Canaveral Chapter Scholarships (5114) | Legal: FL | Minority |
| Central Intelligence Agency Graduate Studies Internships (1811) | Citizenship: US | |
| CERT Scholarship (2100) | Study: United States | Native American |
| Renate W. Chasman Scholarship (1507) | Citizenship: US, PermRes; Legal: NY | |
| Cherokee Nation Graduate Scholarship (1911) | | Native American |
| CIC Predoctoral Fellowships (2013) | Citizenship: US; Study: United States | African American, Hispanic American, Native American |
| Civil Air Patrol Graduate Scholarship (3915) | | |
| Civilian Radioactive Waste Management Fellowship Program (5866) | | |
| Robert A. Dannels Scholarships (726) | Citizenship: US, PermRes | |
| Verne R. Dapp Scholarship (727) | Citizenship: US, PermRes | |
| Raymond Davis Scholarship (5461) | | |
| DOE Student Research Participation (4705) | Citizenship: US, PermRes | |
| Amelia Earhart Fellowship Awards (6312) | | |
| Electrochemical Society Energy Research Fellowships (2367) | Study: Canada, United States | |
| Environmental Restoration/Waste Management Fellowship Program (5870) | | |
| Charles LeGeyt Fortescue Fellowship (3031) | Study: Canada, United States | |
| Fossil Energy Professional Internship Program (5878) | | |
| FSD Student Grant (2578) | | Handicapped |
| GEM Master's Engineering Fellowships for Minorities (3941) | Citizenship: US; Study: United States | Native American, African American, Hispanic American |
| Frank and Lillian Gilbreth Memorial Fellowships (3061) | Study: Canada, Mexico, United States | Association |
| Dr. Robert H. Goddard Scholarships (4408) | Citizenship: US; Study: United States | |
| Louis Goldberg Scholarship (2069) | Citizenship: US | |
| Government of Canada Awards (3145) | Citizenship: France, Germany, Japan, Mexico; Study: Canada | |
| Graduate Student Research Participation Program (5884) | | |
| Graduate U.S. Army Environmental Hygiene Internship Program (5885) | | |
| Grants for Physically Disabled Students in the Sciences (2579) | | Handicapped |
| Paul A. Greebler Scholarship (730) | Citizenship: US, PermRes; Study: United States | |
| Mark O. Hatfield Scholarship (5138) | Study: United States | |
| Hertz Foundation Graduate Fellowships (2866) | Citizenship: US, PermRes; Study: United States | |
| Historically Black Colleges and Universities Building Technology Summer Research Participation Program (5889) | | |
| Historically Black Colleges and Universities Faculty and Student Research Participation Program in Fusion. (5890) | | |
| Historically Black Colleges and Universities Fossil Energy Faculty and Student Research Training (5891) | | |

| Vocational Goal, Award, and Entry Number | Geographic Restrictions (Citizenship, Legal Residence, Place of Study) | Affiliation/Special Recipients Requirements |
|---|---|---|
| *Engineering (continued)* | | |
| Historically Black Colleges and Universities Nuclear Energy Training Program (5894) | | |
| IEEE Fellowship in Electrical History (3033) | | |
| Iota Lambda Sigma Grand Chapter Scholarship (3213) | | Fraternal |
| William E. Jackson Award (5198) | | |
| Dr. Theodore von Karman Graduate Scholarship (45) | Study: United States | Military |
| Wayne Kay Graduate Fellowships (5466) | | |
| Julia Kiene Fellowship (2363) | | |
| Laboratory-Graduate Participantships; Thesis Parts Appointment (1084) | Legal: United States; Study: United States | |
| Laboratory Graduate Participation Program (5899) | | |
| John and Muriel Landis Scholarships (732) | Study: United States | |
| LARS Scholarships (1020) | Study: Canada, Guam, Mexico, Puerto Rico, United States | |
| Lyle Mamer Fellowship (2364) | | |
| Marliave Scholarships (2382) | | Association |
| Mass Media Science and Engineering Fellowships (268) | Study: United States | |
| The Frederick T. Metcalf Award Program (1283) | Citizenship: Canada; Study: Canada | |
| MHEF Scholarship (3607) | Citizenship: US | |
| Microsoft Corporation Scholarships (5516) | | |
| NAACP Willems Scholarship (3851) | | Minority, Association |
| NASA Graduate Student Research Fellowships (3839) | Citizenship: US; Study: United States | |
| National Defense Science and Engineering Graduate Fellowship Program (5855) | Citizenship: US; Study: United States | |
| National Oceanic and Atmospheric Administration/Historically Black Colleges and Universities Faculty/Student Research Participation Program (5910) | | |
| National Scholarship Trust Fund of the Graphic Arts Fellowships (4373) | | |
| Naval Air Warfare Center Training Systems Division Graduate Research Participation Program (5912) | | |
| New York State Professional Opportunity Scholarships (4592) | Citizenship: US, PermRes; Legal: NY; Study: NY | |
| New York State Regents Professional Opportunity Scholarships (4577) | Legal: NY; Study: NY | |
| NRAO Summer Student Research Assistantships (4352) | Citizenship: US; Study: United States | |
| NSERC Research Scholarships, Fellowships, and Grants (4474) | Citizenship: Canada, PermRes; Study: Canada | |
| Nuclear Engineering/Health Physics Fellowship Program (5915) | | |
| Nuclear Regulatory Commission Graduate Fellowship Program (5916) | | |
| Oak Ridge National Laboratory Professional Internship Program (5918) | | |
| Parenteral Drug Association Foundation Research Grants (4835) | Citizenship: US, PermRes; Study: United States | |
| Arthur & Doreen Parrett Scholarship Fund (4848) | Legal: WA | |
| Petro-Canada Inc. Graduate Research Awards (1284) | Citizenship: Canada, PermRes; Study: Canada | |
| Petroleum Research Fund Grants (369) | Legal: United States; Study: United States | |
| Al Qoyawayma Award (561) | | Native American |

| Vocational Goal, Award, and Entry Number | Geographic Restrictions (Citizenship, Legal Residence, Place of Study) | Affiliation/Special Recipients Requirements |
|---|---|---|
| *Engineering (continued)* | | |
| Rice-Cullimore Scholarships (951) | Study: United States | |
| Marjorie Roy Rothermel Scholarships (952) | Citizenship: US; Study: United States | Association |
| SAE Doctoral Scholars Program (5435) | | |
| Olive Lynn Salembier Scholarship (5520) | | |
| Savannah River Technology Center Professional Internship Program (5924) | | |
| Robert Schreck Memorial Fund Scholarship (5280) | Legal: TX | |
| SHPE Foundation Education Grant (5454) | | |
| E.J. Sierleja Memorial Fellowship (3063) | | Association |
| Sigma Xi Grants-in-Aid of Research (5347) | | |
| SPIE Educational Scholarships and Grants in Optical Engineering (5589) | | |
| Sumner Memorial Fellowships (5646) | Citizenship: Canada; Legal: Canada; Study: Canada | |
| Tau Beta Pi Fellowships for Graduate Study in Engineering (5677) | | Fraternal |
| Arthur S. Tuttle Memorial National Scholarship (906) | | Association |
| U.S. Nuclear Regulatory Commission Historically Black Colleges and Universities Graduate Student Research Participation (5935) | | |
| Upsilon Pi Epsilon/Computer Society Award for Academic Excellence (2952) | | Association |
| Vertical Flight Foundation Engineering Scholarships (534) | | |
| Vertical Flight Foundation Scholarships (6036) | | |
| James R. Vogt Scholarship (734) | Citizenship: US, PermRes | |
| WAAIME Scholarship Loans (592) | Study: United States | |
| Western Dredging Association Scholarships (6149) | Study: TX | |
| Young Canadian Researchers Awards (3151) | Citizenship: Canada, PermRes | Other |
| **Foreign Languages** | | |
| Alpha Mu Gamma Scholarships (200) | | Fraternal |
| Assistantships in France (2374) | Citizenship: US | |
| Central Intelligence Agency Graduate Studies Internships (1811) | Citizenship: US | |
| Cultural Ambassadorial Scholarship (5168) | | |
| Minda de Gunzburg Center for European Studies German Language Training Grants (2767) | | Other |
| French Government Teaching Awards (2376) | Study: France | |
| Germanistic Society of America Quadrille Grants (2697) | | |
| Hochschulsommerkurse at German Universities (2688) | Citizenship: US, Canada; Study: Germany | |
| Institute of Holy Land Studies Scholarships (3047) | Study: Israel | |
| Linguistic Employment Scholarship Program (1281) | Citizenship: Canada; Study: Canada | |
| Norwich Jubilee Esperanto Foundation Travel Grants (4701) | | |
| Phi Sigma Iota Scholarships (4904) | | Fraternal |
| Root Foreign Language Scholarship (3333) | Citizenship: US/CA | Fraternal |
| St. David's Scholarship (5220) | | Ethnic |
| Service Cancelable Student Loan (2660) | | |
| Summer Language Course at the University of Leipzig (2692) | Study: Germany | |

| Vocational Goal, Award, and Entry Number | Geographic Restrictions (Citizenship, Legal Residence, Place of Study) | Affiliation/Special Recipients Requirements |
|---|---|---|
| *Foreign Languages (continued)* | | |
| Summer Language Courses at Goethe Institutes (2693) | Study: Germany | |
| **Health Care Services** | | |
| ADHA Certificate/Associate Degree, Baccalaureate and Graduate Scholarships (418) | | |
| ADHA Part-Time Scholarship (420) | | |
| AISES A.T. Anderson Memorial Scholarship (559) | | Native American, Association |
| John D. Archbold Scholarship (1073) | | |
| Aspen Systems Graduate Scholarship (515) | | |
| John O. Butler Scholarships (422) | | |
| Cancer Research Institute Science Writing Internship (1716) | | |
| Richard P. Covert Scholarships (2833) | | Association |
| F. Stanton Deland Fellowships in Health Care and Society (1478) | Study: United States | |
| Delta Gamma Foundation - Florence Margaret Harvey Memorial Scholarship (480) | Citizenship: US | Handicapped |
| Albert W. Dent Scholarship (373) | Citizenship: US/CA | Other |
| Albert W. Dent Scholarship (2561) | Citizenship: US/CA | Association, Minority |
| William and Dorothy Ferrell Scholarship (1235) | | |
| Florida Dental Association Student Loan Program (2488) | Legal: FL | |
| FORE Graduate Loan (516) | | |
| FORE Graduate Scholarships (517) | Citizenship: US, PermRes | |
| Georgia Student Finance Commission Service-Cancellable Stafford Loan (2666) | Legal: GA; Study: GA | |
| Georgia Student Finance Commission State-Sponsored Loan (2669) | Legal: GA; Study: GA | |
| Graduate Awards in Dietetics (2249) | | Association |
| William F. Grupe Foundation Scholarships (2756) | | |
| Indian Health Career Awards (4935) | | Ethnic |
| Rolfe B. Karlsson Scholarships (2321) | Legal: IA | |
| Foster G. McGaw Student Scholarship (374) | Citizenship: US/CA | |
| Foster G. McGaw Student Scholarship (2562) | Citizenship: US/CA | Association |
| Mississippi Psychology Apprenticeship Program (3738) | Legal: MS; Study: MS | |
| Grace Whiting Myers/Malcolm T. MacEachern Student Loans (520) | Citizenship: US | |
| New York State Health Service Corps Scholarships (4589) | Citizenship: US; Legal: NY; Study: NY | |
| New York State Professional Opportunity Scholarships (4592) | Citizenship: US, PermRes; Legal: NY; Study: NY | |
| New York State Regents Professional Opportunity Scholarships (4577) | Legal: NY; Study: NY | |
| Occupational Therapist and Physical Therapist Scholarship Loan Program (2513) | | |
| E.L. Peterson Scholarships (2323) | Legal: IA | |
| Power Systems Inc./NSCA Strength and Conditioning Professional Scholarship (4417) | | Association |
| Public Interest Internships (1803) | Study: United States | |
| Scholarships for Blind and Visually Impaired Postsecondary Students (483) | Citizenship: US | Handicapped |
| Sigma Phi Alpha Graduate Scholarship (430) | | |
| Rawley Silver Scholarship (261) | | |
| Telesensory Scholarship (1236) | | Association |

| Vocational Goal, Award, and Entry Number | Geographic Restrictions (Citizenship, Legal Residence, Place of Study) | Affiliation/Special Recipients Requirements |
|---|---|---|
| *Health Care Services (continued)* | | |
| Transcriptions, Ltd. Scholarship for Health Information Management and Graduate Students (524) | | |
| Lynn Marie Vogel Scholarships (2324) | Legal: IA | |
| WHO Fellowships and Research Training Grants (6261) | | |
| David A. Winston Fellowship (1290) | Study: DC | |
| Wisconsin Dental Foundation Achievement Scholarship (6205) | Citizenship: US; Legal: WI | |
| Wisconsin Dental Foundation/Marquette University Dental Scholarships (6206) | Legal: WI; Study: WI | |
| **Health Sciences** | | |
| AACN Educational Advancement Scholarships for Graduates (278) | | |
| AACP-AFPE Gateway Scholarships (485) | Citizenship: US, PermRes | Minority |
| AAPS-AFPE Gateway Scholarships (486) | | |
| AIHP Grant-in-Aid Toward Thesis Expenses Related to the History of Pharmacy (583) | Study: United States | |
| AMBUCS Scholars (3854) | Citizenship: US | |
| American Speech-Language-Hearing Foundation Graduate Student Scholarships (989) | Study: United States | |
| American Speech-Language-Hearing Foundation Research Grants for New Investigators (990) | Study: United States | |
| American Speech-Language-Hearing Foundation Student Research Grant in Audiology (991) | | |
| AORN Scholarships (1252) | | Association |
| John D. Archbold Scholarship (1073) | | |
| Armenian American Pharmacists' Association Scholarship (1108) | Study: MA | Ethnic |
| The Albert Baker Fund (1362) | | Religion |
| Fay L. Bower Nursing Student Scholarship (1563) | | |
| Canadian Nurses Foundation Small Research Grants (1686) | Citizenship: Canada, PermRes | Association |
| Canadian Nurses Foundation Study Awards (1687) | Citizenship: Canada, PermRes; Study: Canada | Association |
| Centennial Scholars Awards (1690) | Legal: Canada; Study: Canada | |
| Dr. B. Olive Cole Graduate Educational Grant (3413) | | Fraternal |
| Connecticut League for Nursing Scholarships (2052) | Legal: CT; Study: CT | |
| Cora E. Craven Educational Grants (3414) | | Fraternal |
| Cuyahoga County Medical Foundation Scholarship (2146) | Legal: OH | |
| Rudolph Dillman Scholarship (481) | Citizenship: US | Handicapped |
| Eight and Forty Nurses Scholarships (630) | Citizenship: US; Study: United States | |
| Endowment Fund Dental Hygiene Scholarship Program (42) | Citizenship: US | |
| Dr. Alfred C. Fones Scholarships (425) | | Association |
| Foundation for Chiropractic Education and Research Fellowships, Scholarships, and Residency Stipends (2564) | | |
| Foundation of Research and Education (FORE) of AHIMA Graduate Scholarship (693) | | Association |
| Foundation of Research and Education Loan (695) | Citizenship: US | Association |
| Franks Foundation Loan (5832) | Legal: OR | |

| Vocational Goal, Award, and Entry Number | Geographic Restrictions (Citizenship, Legal Residence, Place of Study) | Affiliation/Special Recipients Requirements |
|---|---|---|
| *Health Sciences (continued)* | | |
| Georgia Student Finance Commission Service-Cancellable Stafford Loan (2666) | Legal: GA; Study: GA | |
| Georgia Student Finance Commission State-Sponsored Loan (2669) | Legal: GA; Study: GA | |
| GFWC of MA Communication Disorder Scholarships (2637) | Legal: MA | |
| GLAXO AACP-AFPE Graduate Studies Scholarships (489) | | |
| Grants for Physically Disabled Students in the Sciences (2579) | | Handicapped |
| William F. Grupe Foundation Scholarships (2756) | | |
| Health Canada Research Personnel Training Awards (Regular Program) (2829) | Citizenship: Canada, PermRes; Legal: Canada | |
| Dr. Harold Hillenbrand Scholarships (426) | | Association |
| HP/AACN Critical-Care Nursing Research Grants (2868) | | |
| HRSA-BHP Professional Nurse Traineeship (5971) | | |
| HRSA-BHP Scholarships for Disadvantaged Students (5972) | Citizenship: US, PermRes, Other | |
| HSFC Nursing Research Fellowships (2842) | | |
| Indian Health Career Awards (4935) | | Ethnic |
| International Order of the King's Daughters and Sons Health Careers Scholarships (3169) | Citizenship: US/CA; Legal: Canada, United States; Study: Canada, United States | |
| Leslie Isenberg Graduate Scholarship (992) | | Handicapped |
| Kansas City Speech Pathology Award (3327) | Citizenship: US/CA; Study: NY | |
| Dr. Dorothy J. Kergin Research Grant in Primary Health Care (1688) | Citizenship: Canada, PermRes | Association |
| S. Evelyn Lewis Memorial Scholarship in Medical Health Sciences (6306) | | |
| Maryland House of Delegates Scholarship (3575) | Legal: MD | |
| Maryland Professional Scholarship (3578) | Legal: MD; Study: MD | |
| Maryland Senatorial Scholarship (3580) | Legal: MD | |
| Maryland State Nursing Scholarships (3581) | Legal: MD; Study: MD | |
| Marguerite Mc Alpin Memorial Scholarships (640) | Legal: WA | Veteran |
| Charlotte McGuire Scholarships (543) | | Association |
| MERCK-AFPE Gateway Scholarships (490) | Citizenship: US, PermRes | |
| Mississippi Nursing Education MSN Program (3736) | Legal: MS | |
| NAJA Graduate Scholarships (3881) | Citizenship: US; Legal: AL, AR, LA, MO, MS, TN, TX; Study: United States | |
| National Association of Hispanic Nurses National Scholarship Award (3879) | | Hispanic American, Association |
| NEF Scholarships (4703) | Citizenship: US, PermRes | Association |
| New York State Health Service Corps Scholarships (4589) | Citizenship: US; Legal: NY; Study: NY | |
| New York State Professional Opportunity Scholarships (4592) | Citizenship: US, PermRes; Legal: NY; Study: NY | |
| New York State Regents Professional Opportunity Scholarships (4577) | Legal: NY; Study: NY | |
| Irene E. Newman Scholarships (428) | | Association |
| NSDAR Occupational Therapy Scholarship (4403) | Citizenship: US; Study: United States | |
| Nursing Education Loan Repayment (5938) | | |
| Oncology Nursing Foundation Masters Scholarship (4766) | | |

| Vocational Goal, Award, and Entry Number | Geographic Restrictions (Citizenship, Legal Residence, Place of Study) | Affiliation/Special Recipients Requirements |
|---|---|---|
| *Health Sciences (continued)* | | |
| Oncology Nursing Foundation/Rhone Poulenc Rorer New Investigator Research Grants (4771) | | |
| Arthur & Doreen Parrett Scholarship Fund (4848) | Legal: WA | |
| PRN Grants (202) | | Fraternal |
| Public Interest Internships (1803) | Study: United States | |
| San Joaquin County Medical Society Scholarship Loans (5241) | Legal: CA | |
| Service Cancelable Student Loan (2660) | | |
| Bertha B. Singer Nurses Scholarship (5835) | Legal: OR; Study: OR | |
| Kala Singh Graduate Scholarship (994) | | |
| Stokoe Scholarships (3873) | | Handicapped |
| Student Research Grant in Early Childhood Language Development (995) | | |
| Margaret E. Swanson Scholarships (432) | | Association |
| SYNTEX-AFPE Gateway Scholarships (495) | Citizenship: US, PermRes | |
| Texas Health Education Loan (5714) | Study: TX | |
| The Tova Fellowship (4745) | | |
| U.S. Nuclear Regulatory Commission Historically Black Colleges and Universities Graduate Student Research Participation (5935) | | |
| Zelda Walling Vicha Memorial Scholarship (967) | | |
| Western Interstate Commission for Higher Education Student Exchanges (135) | Legal: AK | |
| WHO Fellowships and Research Training Grants (6261) | | |
| Wisconsin Dental Foundation Achievement Scholarship (6205) | Citizenship: US; Legal: WI | |
| Wisconsin Dental Foundation/Marquette University Dental Scholarships (6206) | Legal: WI; Study: WI | |
| **Home Economics** | | |
| AIN Predoctoral Fellowships (594) | | |
| AVA Home Economics Education Graduate Fellowships (1013) | | Association |
| Ruth Binnie Scholarships (1644) | Citizenship: Canada, Other | Association |
| Stella Blum Research Grant (2089) | | Association |
| A & E Capelle LN Herfords Scholarship (150) | Legal: Canada | |
| CHEA Silver Jubilee Scholarship (1646) | Citizenship: Canada, Other | Association |
| Mary A. Clarke Memorial Scholarship (1647) | Citizenship: Canada, PermRes | Association |
| Mary Josephine Cochran Fellowship (291) | Citizenship: US, PermRes | |
| Jeannette H. Crum Fellowship; Jewell L. Taylor Fellowships (293) | Citizenship: US, PermRes | |
| Mildred B. Davis Memorial Fellowship (294) | Citizenship: US, PermRes | Association |
| Freda A. DeKnight Memorial Fellowship (295) | Citizenship: US | African American |
| Margaret Drew Alpha Fellowship (4917) | | Fraternal |
| General Fellowship (296) | Citizenship: US; Study: United States | |
| Kappa Omicron Nu Masters Fellowships (3336) | | Fraternal |
| Flemmie P. Kittrell Memorial Fellowship for Minorities (297) | Citizenship: US | Minority |
| Ella H. McNaughton Memorial Fellowship (298) | Citizenship: US | |
| National Restaurant Association Graduate Degree Scholarship (4365) | | |
| Nestle Canada Scholarship (1650) | Citizenship: Canada, PermRes | Association |
| Ohio State University Extension Internship (4733) | | |

| Vocational Goal, Award, and Entry Number | Geographic Restrictions (Citizenship, Legal Residence, Place of Study) | Affiliation/Special Recipients Requirements |
|---|---|---|
| **Home Economics (continued)** | | |
| Ethel L. Parker International Memorial Fellowship; Marion K. Piper Fellowship (301) | Study: United States | |
| Inez Eleanor Radell Sole Donor Memorial Fellowship (302) | Citizenship: US, PermRes | |
| Effie I. Raitt Memorial Fellowship (303) | Citizenship: US | |
| Ellen H. Richards Fellowship (304) | Citizenship: US | Association |
| Hazel Putnam Roach Memorial Fellowships (305) | Citizenship: US | |
| Robin Hood Multifoods Scholarship (1651) | Citizenship: Canada, PermRes | Association |
| Abbie Sargent Memorial Scholarships (5250) | Legal: NH | |
| Tony's Foodservice Scholarships (5278) | | Association |
| YMA Scholarships (6295) | Study: NC, NY, PA | |
| **Humanities** | | |
| Frances C. Allen Fellowships (4615) | Study: United States | Native American |
| Oscar Broneer Fellowship (856) | Study: Greece | Other |
| CIC Predoctoral Fellowships (2013) | Citizenship: US; Study: United States | African American, Hispanic American, Native American |
| Helen Darcovich Memorial Doctoral Fellowship (1657) | Study: Canada | |
| Marusia and Michael Dorosh Masters Fellowship (1659) | Study: Canada | |
| H.B. Earhart Fellowships (2301) | | |
| The Eta Sigma Phi Summer Scholarships (2414) | Study: Greece, Italy | |
| Fellowships in Byzantine Studies, Pre-Columbian Studies and Landscape Architecture (2288) | Study: DC | |
| Government of Canada Awards (3145) | Citizenship: France, Germany, Japan, Mexico; Study: Canada | |
| Jacob Hirsch Fellowship (859) | Legal: Israel, United States; Study: Greece | Other |
| Humane Studies Foundation Summer Residential Program Fellowships (3053) | Study: VA | |
| Claude R. Lambe Fellowships (3058) | | |
| Andrew W. Melon Fellowships in Humanistic Studies (6187) | Citizenship: US, PermRes | |
| National Program for Advanced Study and Research in China - General Advanced Studies (2015) | Citizenship: US, PermRes; Study: People's Republic of China | |
| Professional Development Fellowship Program for Artists and Art Historians (1982) | Citizenship: US, PermRes | |
| Thomas Day Seymour Fellowship (860) | Legal: Canada, United States; Study: Greece | Other |
| SSRC Bangladesh Studies Fellowships (5397) | Study: Bangladesh | |
| Summer Session Awards (861) | | |
| Lewis Walpole Library Fellowship (6277) | Study: CT | |
| Richard M. Weaver Fellowship (3099) | Citizenship: US | |
| **Industry and Trade** | | |
| ACI Fellowships: ACI/W.R. Grace Fellowship; V. Mohan Malhotra Fellowship; Katherine Bryant Mather Fellowship; Stewart C. Watson Fellowship (388) | Study: Canada, United States | |
| Associated General Contractors Education Research Foundation Graduate Scholarship (401) | | |
| DEED Scholarships (811) | Study: United States | Association |
| Ginger & Fred Deines Canada Scholarships (5741) | Citizenship: Canada; Study: Canada | |
| Ginger and Fred Deines Mexico Scholarships (5742) | Study: Mexico, United States | Hispanic American |
| Dwight David Eisenhower Transportation Fellowship (6052) | Citizenship: US; Study: United States | |

| Vocational Goal, Award, and Entry Number | Geographic Restrictions (Citizenship, Legal Residence, Place of Study) | Affiliation/Special Recipients Requirements |
|---|---|---|
| *Industry and Trade (continued)* | | |
| Hooper Memorial Scholarship(s) (5743) | | |
| Hudson River Fellowships (2912) | | |
| Industrial Hygiene Graduate Fellowship Program (5897) | | |
| Julia Kiene Fellowship (2363) | | |
| LARS Scholarships (1020) | Study: Canada, Guam, Mexico, Puerto Rico, United States | |
| Denny Lydic Scholarship (5744) | | |
| Lyle Mamer Fellowship (2364) | | |
| National Association of Water Companies - New Jersey Chapter Scholarship (3904) | Citizenship: US; Legal: NJ; Study: NJ | |
| Nebraska Space Grant Scholarships and Fellowships (4505) | Citizenship: US | |
| Helene Overly Scholarship (6243) | Legal: United States | |
| James F. Schumar Scholarship (733) | Citizenship: US | |
| SEMA Scholarship (5581) | | |
| Shared Research Equipment Program (5926) | | |
| TAC Scholarships (5739) | Citizenship: Canada, PermRes; Study: Canada, United States | |
| Texas Transportation Scholarship (5745) | | |
| University of Delaware-Hagley Program Fellowship (2777) | | |
| Wood Awards (2555) | | |
| Charlotte Woods Memorial Scholarship (5746) | | Association |
| Young Canadian Researchers Awards (3151) | Citizenship: Canada, PermRes | Other |
| **Language and Literature** | | |
| AGBU Graduate Loan Program (1134) | | |
| American Numismatic Society Graduate Seminar (737) | Study: Canada, United States | |
| Blakemore Foundation Asian Language Fellowship Grants (1440) | Citizenship: US, PermRes | |
| Business Press Educational Foundation Student Intern Program (1543) | | |
| Cancer Research Institute Science Writing Internship (1716) | | |
| Center for Arabic Study Abroad Fellowship (1787) | | |
| CFUW Awards (1631) | Citizenship: Canada; Legal: Canada | |
| Chicago Association of Black Journalists Scholarships (1916) | | Minority |
| Columbia Journalism Review Internship Program (2009) | | |
| The Eta Sigma Phi Summer Scholarships (2414) | Study: Greece, Italy | |
| Huntington Library Research Awards (2939) | Study: United States | |
| Inter-University Program Fellowships (3097) | Study: People's Republic of China | |
| John M. Will Memorial Journalism Scholarships (6180) | Legal: AL, FL, MS | |
| Claude R. Lambe Fellowships (3058) | | |
| Online Newspaper Intern Program (2276) | | |
| Service Cancelable Student Loan (2660) | | |
| Student Research Grant in Early Childhood Language Development (995) | | |
| **Law** | | |
| AAUW Educational Foundation Selected Professions Engineering Dissertation Fellowship (335) | Citizenship: US, PermRes | Minority |
| AGBU Education Loan Program in the U.S. (1133) | | Ethnic |

| Vocational Goal, Award, and Entry Number | Geographic Restrictions (Citizenship, Legal Residence, Place of Study) | Affiliation/Special Recipients Requirements |
|---|---|---|

*Law (continued)*

| Vocational Goal, Award, and Entry Number | Geographic Restrictions | Affiliation/Special Recipients Requirements |
|---|---|---|
| AGBU Graduate Loan Program (1134) | | |
| TELACU/Richard Alatorre Fellowship (5686) | Legal: CA; Study: United States | Minority |
| Ida and Benjamin Alpert Scholarships (192) | Legal: MI | |
| Viscount Bennett Fellowship (1609) | Citizenship: Canada | |
| Donald Bogie Prize (3051) | | |
| BPW Career Advancement Scholarships (1546) | Citizenship: US; Study: United States | |
| H. Fletcher Brown Scholarship (4967) | Legal: DE | |
| Cherokee Nation Graduate Scholarship (1911) | | Native American |
| James F. Connolly Congressional Informaton Service Scholarship (311) | | |
| Council On Legal Education Opportunities (2119) | Citizenship: US | Minority |
| James Lawrence Fly Scholarships (1497) | | |
| FORE Graduate Scholarships (517) | Citizenship: US, PermRes | |
| Fredrikson & Byron Minority Scholarships (2589) | | Minority |
| Graduate Scholarships at University of Cambridge (1655) | Legal: Canada; Study: England | |
| Justice Pauline Davis Hanson Memorial Scholarship (2595) | | |
| Mark O. Hatfield Scholarship (5138) | Study: United States | |
| Celia M. Howard Fellowships (2964) | Legal: IL | |
| Humane Studies Foundation Summer Residential Program Fellowships (3053) | Study: VA | |
| IHS-Eberhard Student-Writing Competition (3054) | | |
| IHS John M. Olin Fellowships (3056) | Citizenship: US; Study: England | |
| Elaine Osborne Jacobson Award for Women in Health Care (5163) | | |
| Claude R. Lambe Fellowships (3058) | | |
| Law Fellowship (4235) | | Ethnic |
| Law Internship Program (5900) | | |
| Library Degree Scholarships for Law School Graduates (313) | Citizenship: US/CA | |
| Hatton Lovejoy Graduate Studies Fund (1585) | | |
| Mackenzie King Travelling Scholarships (3529) | Legal: Canada; Study: United States | |
| MALDEF Scholarships (3675) | Citizenship: US, PermRes | |
| Maryland Professional Scholarship (3578) | Legal: MD; Study: MD | |
| Michael Murphy Memorial Scholarship Loans (132) | Legal: AK | |
| NIAF/FIERI D.C. Matching Scholarship (4245) | | |
| Oklahoma State Regents for Higher Education Professional Study Grants (4740) | Study: OK | Minority |
| Oregon State Bar Scholarships (4803) | Study: OR | Minority |
| Post-Rabbinic Scholarships (3646) | | |
| Preventive Law Prizes (Discontinued) (3933) | | |
| PRLDEF Scholarship (5023) | | Hispanic American |
| Public Interest Internships (1803) | Study: United States | |
| The Puerto Rican Bar Association Scholarship Fund, Inc. (5021) | | |
| Rocky Mountain Mineral Law Foundation Scholarship Program Including the Joe Rudd Scholarship (5159) | | |
| Scalia Scholarship (4260) | Legal: NY | |
| Otto M. Stanfield Legal Scholarship (5785) | | Religion |
| Earl Warren Legal Training Scholarships (6081) | Citizenship: US | African American |

| Vocational Goal, Award, and Entry Number | Geographic Restrictions (Citizenship, Legal Residence, Place of Study) | Affiliation/Special Recipients Requirements |
|---|---|---|

**Liberal/General Studies**

| Vocational Goal, Award, and Entry Number | Geographic Restrictions | Affiliation/Special Recipients Requirements |
|---|---|---|
| 1989 Polytechnique Commemorative Award (1630) | Citizenship: Canada; Legal: Canada | |
| AAUW Educational Foundation International Fellowships (334) | | Association |
| Academic-Year Ambassadorial Scholarship (5167) | | |
| ACB Scholarships (398) | Citizenship: US | Handicapped |
| AIGC Fellowships (553) | Citizenship: US, PermRes; Legal: United States | Native American |
| Alabama G.I. Dependents' Scholarships (119) | Study: AL | Veteran |
| Alabama Stafford Loans (109) | Citizenship: US, PermRes | |
| Alaska Family Education Loans (127) | Legal: AK | |
| Alaska Student Loans (129) | Legal: AK | |
| American Baptist Financial Aid Program (348) | | Religion |
| American Indian Endowed Scholarships (551) | Legal: WA; Study: WA | |
| AMVETS National Scholarship for Graduate Students (1030) | Citizenship: US | Veteran |
| AOSC Scholarships (1250) | | Employer |
| AOUW Student Loan (1037) | | Fraternal |
| Arkansas Department of Higher Education Scholarship (1091) | Study: AR | |
| Armenian American Middle East Club Scholarship (1107) | Study: CA | Ethnic |
| Armenian General Benevolent Union (AGBU) Loans and Grants (1112) | | Ethnic |
| Armenian Professional Society Scholarship (1114) | Citizenship: US; Legal: CA | Ethnic |
| Armenian Students Association of America, Inc. Grant (1116) | Study: United States | Ethnic |
| Armenian Students' Association of America Reading Scholarships (1138) | Study: United States | Ethnic |
| ASA Stafford Loan (1003) | | |
| Awards for Advanced Study and Research in Scandinavia (852) | Citizenship: US, PermRes | |
| Awards for Advanced Study or Research in the U.S.A. (853) | Study: United States | |
| The Albert Baker Fund (1362) | | Religion |
| Walter S. Barr Fellowships (5363) | Legal: MA | |
| Alexander G. Bell Scholarship Awards (1399) | | Handicapped |
| Beta Theta Pi Founders Fund Scholarship-Leadership Awards (1428) | | Fraternal |
| Mary McLeod Bethune Scholarship (2494) | Citizenship: US; Legal: FL; Study: FL | |
| BIA Higher Education/Hopi Supplemental Grants (2892) | | Native American |
| David Birenbaum Scholarship Fund of the AAB Associate Member Section (10) | | Association |
| Blind Service Association Scholarship Awards (1442) | Legal: IL | Handicapped |
| British Marshall Scholarships (1230) | Citizenship: US; Study: United Kingdom | |
| British Marshall Scholarships (1483) | Citizenship: US | |
| British Marshall Scholarships (1487) | Citizenship: US; Study: England | |
| George M. Brooker Collegiate Scholarship for Minorities (1502) | Citizenship: US, Canada | |
| Gabriel J. Brown Trust Fund Loans (1521) | Legal: ND | |
| General Buxton/St. Michael's Scholarships (6032) | | Military |
| Campbell-Non-Linfield Scholarship Fund (5830) | Legal: OR; Study: OR | |
| Canadian Soroptimist Grants for Women (5539) | Citizenship: Canada, PermRes; Study: Canada | |
| Cape Canaveral Chapter Scholarships (5114) | Legal: FL | Minority |

| Vocational Goal, Award, and Entry Number | Geographic Restrictions (Citizenship, Legal Residence, Place of Study) | Affiliation/Special Recipients Requirements |
|---|---|---|
| *Liberal/General Studies (continued)* | | |
| Vikki Carr Scholarship (1741) | Legal: CA, United States | Hispanic American |
| Karen D. Carsel Memorial Scholarship (479) | Citizenship: US | Handicapped |
| CCSFC Australian Scholarships (3140) | Citizenship: Canada; Legal: Canada; Study: Australia | |
| CCSFC India Scholarships (3141) | Citizenship: Canada, PermRes; Study: India | |
| CCSFC New Zealand Scholarships (3142) | Citizenship: Canada, PermRes; Study: New Zealand | |
| CCSFC Sri Lanka Scholarships (3143) | Citizenship: Canada, PermRes; Study: Sri Lanka | |
| CCSFC United Kingdom Scholarships (3144) | Citizenship: Canada, PermRes; Study: United Kingdom | |
| Anthony J. Celebrezze Scholarship (4213) | Legal: OH | Ethnic |
| Central Scholarship Bureau Interest-Free Loans (1816) | Legal: MD | |
| CEW Scholarships for Returning Women (6002) | Study: MI | |
| CFUW Professional Fellowship (1632) | Citizenship: Canada; Legal: Canada; Study: Canada | |
| Chicana Dissertation Fellowship (2233) | | Hispanic American |
| Chicana Latina Foundation Scholarships (1931) | Legal: CA | Hispanic American |
| Child of Disabled Veteran Grant or Purple Heart Recipient, Grant (2996) | Legal: IN; Study: IN | Veteran |
| Ferdinand Cinelli Etruscan Scholarship (4214) | | Ethnic |
| Civitan Scholarships (1964) | | Association |
| CMT Scholarships (1830) | | Other |
| College Access Loan (5708) | Study: TX | |
| Commonwealth Scholarship Plan (2021) | Citizenship: Commonwealth | |
| Connecticut Family Education Loan Program (CT FELP) (2044) | Legal: CT; Study: CT | |
| (Connecticut) Federal Subsidized Stafford Loans (2056) | | |
| Edward T. Conroy Memorial Scholarship (3568) | Study: MD | Military, Veteran |
| NIAF/NOIAW Cornaro Scholarship (4218) | | |
| John Cornelius and Max English Memorial Scholarship (3564) | | Military |
| Crawford Scholarship Fund (5831) | Legal: OR | |
| CSAC Graduate Fellowships (1581) | Legal: CA; Study: CA | |
| CSAC Law Enforcement Personnel Dependents Scholarships (1582) | | Employer |
| DAAD-Canadian Government Grants and Grants of Quebec (2684) | Citizenship: Canada; Study: Germany | |
| DAAD and DAAD-Fulbright Grants (2685) | Citizenship: US; Legal: Germany | |
| Daughters of Penelope Graduate Student Award (2182) | | Ethnic, Association |
| Henry N. and Sydney T. Davenport Loan Fund (1822) | Citizenship: US; Legal: NC | |
| Lady Davis Graduate and Postdoctoral Fellowships (2193) | Study: Israel | |
| Minda de Gunzburg Center for European Studies Graduate Summer Research Travel Grants (2768) | | Other |
| Delta Gamma Foundation Fellowships (2218) | | Fraternal |
| Descendants of the Signers of the Declaration of Independence Scholarship (2243) | Study: United States | Association |
| Dog Writers' Educational Trust Scholarships (2264) | | Other |
| East-West Center Graduate Degree Fellowships (2308) | Study: HI | |
| Educational Communications Scholarship Foundation (2348) | | |

| Vocational Goal, Award, and Entry Number | Geographic Restrictions (Citizenship, Legal Residence, Place of Study) | Affiliation/Special Recipients Requirements |
|---|---|---|
| *Liberal/General Studies (continued)* | | |
| Edwards Scholarship (2357) | Legal: MA | |
| Emergency Aid and Health Professions Scholarships (1214) | | Native American |
| Epsilon Sigma Phi Mini-Grants (2406) | | Fraternal |
| Epsilon Sigma Phi Scholarship Loans (2408) | | Fraternal |
| Esperanza Scholarships (2412) | Legal: OH | Hispanic American |
| Evrytanian Association Scholarship (2418) | | Ethnic |
| FAR Scholarships (2559) | | |
| Federal Stafford Loan under the North Carolina Insured Student Loan Program (1992) | | |
| Federal Stafford Loan (Subsidized and Unsubsidized) (2341) | | |
| Federal Unsubsidized Stafford Loan (2057) | | |
| FEEA Federal Plus Loan (2431) | | Employer |
| FEEA Federal SLS Loan (2432) | | Employer |
| FEEA Federal Stafford Loan (2433) | | Employer |
| FEEA Federal Unsubsidized Stafford Loan (2434) | | Employer |
| FEEA Scholarship Award (2435) | | Employer |
| Virginia Student Financial Assistance Award (5606) | Legal: VA; Study: VA | |
| First Catholic Slovak Ladies Association Fraternal Scholarship Awards (2461) | Study: Canada, United States | Association |
| Raquel Marquez Frankel Scholarship Fund (3542) | | Hispanic American |
| Gerard S. Fudge Scholarship (2946) | | |
| Carmela Gagliardi Fellowship (4226) | | Ethnic |
| Gallaudet University Alumni Association Graduate Fellowship Funds (2615) | | Handicapped |
| Georgia State Regents Scholarship (2657) | Legal: GA; Study: GA | |
| Georgia Student Finance Commission Perkins Loan (2664) | Legal: GA | |
| Georgia Student Finance Commission SLS Loan (2667) | Legal: GA | |
| Georgia Student Finance Commission Stafford Loan (2668) | Legal: GA | |
| Germanistic Society of America Quadrille Grants (2697) | | |
| GFWC of MA International Affairs Scholarships (2638) | Legal: MA | |
| GFWC of MA Memorial Education Fellowships (2639) | Legal: MA | |
| Giargiari Fellowship (4229) | | Ethnic |
| Dr. Marion Elder Grant Fellowship (1633) | Citizenship: Canada; Legal: Canada | |
| Grants for Canadians (1640) | Citizenship: Canada, PermRes; Study: Israel | |
| Kathern F. Gruber Scholarships (1444) | | Veteran |
| Guido-Zerilli-Marimo Scholarships (4233) | Study: NY | |
| John T. Hall Student Loan Fund (2782) | Legal: GA; Study: GA | |
| Harness Tracks of America Scholarship (2794) | | Other |
| Patricia Roberts Harris Fellowships (2796) | | |
| Harvard Travellers Club Grants (2802) | | |
| Hawaii's Federal Stafford Loans (2822) | | |
| A. A. Heaps Scholarships (1663) | Citizenship: Canada; Study: Canada | |
| Hinson-Hazlewood College Student Loan Program/Federal Stafford Student Loan Program (5710) | Study: TX | |
| Hopi Scholarship (2894) | | Native American |
| ICCS Foreign Government Awards (3146) | Citizenship: Canada; Legal: Canada | |
| IGCC Dissertation Fellowships (3043) | Study: United States | |

| Vocational Goal, Award, and Entry Number | Geographic Restrictions (Citizenship, Legal Residence, Place of Study) | Affiliation/Special Recipients Requirements |
|---|---|---|
| *Liberal/General Studies (continued)* | | |
| Illinois Federal PLUS Loan (2970) | Legal: IL; Study: IL | |
| Illinois Federal Subsidized Stafford Loan (2971) | Study: IL | |
| Illinois Federal Supplemental Loans for Students (2972) | Legal: IL; Study: IL | |
| Illinois Federal Unsubsidized Stafford Loan (2973) | Study: IL | |
| Illinois National Guard Grant (2976) | Study: IL | Military |
| Illinois unILoan (2979) | Legal: IL; Study: IL | |
| International Peace Scholarships (4877) | Study: Canada, United States | |
| Beverley Jackson Fellowship (1634) | Citizenship: Canada; Legal: Canada | |
| Agnes Jones Jackson Scholarship (3850) | | Minority, Association |
| Japanese American Citizens League Graduate Scholarships (3246) | | Association |
| Japanese American Citizens League Student Aid Award (3248) | | Ethnic |
| Jenkins Loan (5834) | Legal: ID, OR, WA | |
| Jewish Educational Loans Fund (3269) | Citizenship: US, PermRes; Legal: DC, MD, VA; Study: United States | Ethnic |
| Jewish Federation of Metropolitan Chicago Academic Scholarships (3265) | Legal: IL, IN | Religion |
| Roy Johnson Trust Graduate School Grants (3681) | Study: United States | Handicapped |
| Kansas State Program of Benefits for Dependents of POWs and MIAs (3315) | | Veteran |
| Kappa Kappa Gamma Chapter Consultant Scholarships (3328) | Citizenship: US/CA | Fraternal |
| Kappa Kappa Gamma Graduate Fellowships (3330) | Citizenship: US/CA | Fraternal |
| Lucille R. Keller Foundation Loans (3343) | Legal: IN | |
| Keystone Stafford and Keystone Direct Student Loans (4863) | Citizenship: US | |
| Steven Knezevich Trust Grants (3381) | | Ethnic |
| Knights of Columbus Student Loan Program (3388) | Citizenship: US, PermRes | Religion |
| Knights of Lithuania Scholarships (3392) | | Association, Ethnic |
| Frank Knox Memorial Fellowships (1280) | Citizenship: Canada, PermRes; Study: United States | |
| Peter and Alice Koomruian Armenian Education Fund (1125) | Study: United States | Ethnic |
| Kosciuszko Foundation Graduate/Postgraduate Study and Research in Poland Scholarships (3400) | Study: Poland | |
| Kottis Family Scholarships (2184) | | Association |
| Latin American Educational Foundation Scholarships (3439) | Legal: CO | Hispanic American |
| Samuel Lemberg Scholarship Loan Fund, Inc. (3451) | | Ethnic |
| The Lighthouse Career Incentive Award for Graduate Students (3476) | Citizenship: US; Legal: CT, MA, ME, NH, NJ, NY, PA, RI, VT; Study: CT, MA, ME, NH, NJ, NY, PA, RI, VT | Handicapped |
| Franklin Lindsay Student Loans (3486) | Citizenship: US; Study: TX | |
| Lindstrom Foundation Student Service Scholarships (876) | | |
| Louisiana State Aid Dependents Educational Assistance (3500) | Legal: LA; Study: LA | Veteran |
| Luce Scholars Program (3512) | Citizenship: US | |
| Lynden Memorial Scholarship (3522) | | Employer |
| Minnie L. Maffett Scholarship (4466) | Legal: TX; Study: TX | |
| Maltese-American Benevolent Society Scholarship (3540) | Legal: MI | Association |

| Vocational Goal, Award, and Entry Number | Geographic Restrictions (Citizenship, Legal Residence, Place of Study) | Affiliation/Special Recipients Requirements |
|---|---|---|
| *Liberal/General Studies (continued)* | | |
| Marin County American Revolution Bicentennial Scholarship (3551) | Legal: CA | |
| Jose Marti Scholarship Challenge Grants (2511) | Citizenship: US; Legal: FL; Study: FL | Other |
| Maryland House of Delegates Scholarship (3575) | Legal: MD | |
| Maryland Senatorial Scholarship (3580) | Legal: MD | |
| Massachusetts Family Education Loan (3598) | Legal: MA; Study: MA | |
| Massachusetts Indian Association Scholarships (3595) | | Native American |
| John T. McCraw Scholarship (3996) | | Handicapped |
| Louise McKinney Post-Secondary Scholarships (177) | Legal: AB, Canada | |
| Michigan Indian Tuition Waiver (3683) | Legal: MI; Study: MI | Native American |
| Michigan Tuition Grants (3686) | Citizenship: US, PermRes; Legal: MI; Study: MI | |
| Ministry of the Flemish Community in Belgium Fellowships (2483) | Citizenship: US | |
| Miss America Pageant Scholarships (3726) | Citizenship: US | |
| Mississippi Law Enforcement Officers and Firemen Scholarship Program (3733) | Legal: MS; Study: MS | |
| Mississippi Southeast Asia POW/MIA Scholarship Program (3740) | Legal: MS; Study: MS | Military |
| Montana Indian Student Fee Waiver (557) | Study: MT | Native American |
| Mortar Board Foundation Fellowships (3782) | | Association |
| Multi-Year Ambassadorial Scholarship (5170) | | |
| NAPWPT Scholarships (3891) | | |
| National Alliance for Excellence Honored Scholars Awards (3841) | Citizenship: US; Study: United States | |
| National Art Materials Trade Association Scholarships (3848) | | Employer |
| National Association for Armenian Studies and Research, Inc. Fund (1126) | Citizenship: US | Ethnic |
| National Association of Executive Secretaries Scholarships (3875) | | Association |
| National Association for Women in Education Women's Research Awards (3908) | | |
| National Fourth Infantry Division Association Scholarship (4171) | | Veteran |
| National Fraternal Society of the Deaf Scholarships (4173) | | Association, Handicapped |
| National Miss Indian U.S.A. Scholarship (555) | | Native American |
| Native American Education Grants (4992) | Citizenship: US | Native American |
| James Z. Naurison Scholarship Fund (2472) | Legal: CT, MA | |
| Navajo Code Talkers Scholarship (4479) | | Native American |
| Naval Officers' Spouses' Association of Mayport Scholarships (4487) | Legal: FL | Military |
| Nevada Women's Fund Scholarships (4521) | Legal: NV | |
| New England Regional Student Program (4525) | Legal: CT, MA, ME, NH, RI, VT; Study: CT, MA, ME, NH, RI, VT | |
| New Hampshire Charitable Foundation Statewide Student Aid Program (4533) | Legal: NH | |
| New Jersey State Federation of Women's Clubs Margaret Yardley Fellowship (4543) | Legal: NJ | |
| New Mexico Federal Stafford Loans (4551) | Legal: NM; Study: NM | |
| New Mexico Unsubsidized Loan for Students (4552) | Citizenship: US, PermRes | |
| New York State Parent Loans for Students (4591) | Citizenship: US, PermRes | |
| New York State Senate Legislative Fellows Program (4598) | Citizenship: US | |

| Vocational Goal, Award, and Entry Number | Geographic Restrictions (Citizenship, Legal Residence, Place of Study) | Affiliation/Special Recipients Requirements |
|---|---|---|
| *Liberal/General Studies (continued)* | | |
| New York State Stafford Loan (4594) | Citizenship: US, PermRes | |
| New York State Supplemental Loans for Students (4595) | Citizenship: US, PermRes | |
| New York State Tuition Assistance Program (4596) | Citizenship: US, PermRes; Legal: NY; Study: NY | |
| Newberry Library Joint Fellowships with the American Antiquarian Society (4621) | | |
| NHSF Scholarships (4179) | Citizenship: US, PermRes; Study: United States | Hispanic American |
| Northern Alberta Development Council Bursaries (182) | Legal: AB, Canada | |
| NSCA Student Research Grant (4416) | | |
| OAS-PRA Fellowships (4809) | | |
| Ohio Regents Graduate/Professional Fellowships (4725) | Study: OH | |
| Oklahoma State Regents Academic Scholars Scholarships (4736) | Legal: OK; Study: OK | |
| Ontario Graduate Scholarships (4781) | Citizenship: Canada, PermRes; Study: Canada | |
| Opportunities for the Blind, Inc. Grants (4785) | Citizenship: US | Handicapped |
| Oregon Educational Aid for Veterans (4799) | Citizenship: US; Legal: OR | Veteran |
| ORS Awards (4824) | Study: England | |
| Overseas Postgraduate Research Scholarships for Study in Australia (1339) | Study: Australia | |
| Pellegrini Scholarship Grants (5662) | Legal: CT, DE, NJ, NY, PA | Ethnic |
| Phi Kappa Phi Graduate Fellowships (4900) | | Fraternal |
| Minnie Stevens Piper Foundation Student Loan (4951) | Citizenship: US; Legal: TX; Study: TX | |
| PPGA Family Member Scholarship (1386) | | Association |
| PVR Scholarship Award (4388) | | Association |
| QuikTrip Scholarships (5046) | | Employer |
| Realty Foundation of New York Scholarships (5085) | Citizenship: US; Study: NY | Employer |
| Red River Valley Fighter Pilot Association Scholarships (5087) | | Veteran |
| Regents' Opportunity Scholarship (2659) | | |
| Henry J. Reilly Memorial Graduate Scholarships (5105) | Study: United States | Military |
| Rhodes Scholarships (5129) | Citizenship: US/CA; Study: England | |
| Sid Richardson Memorial Fund Scholarship (5134) | | |
| David Rogers Bursary (3971) | Legal: England | Handicapped |
| Admiral Roland Student Loan (5849) | Citizenship: US | Other |
| The Leo S. Rowe Pan American Fund Loan (5174) | Legal: United States | |
| St. Andrews Society of the State of New York Scholarships (5218) | Citizenship: US; Legal: NY | Ethnic |
| St. David's Scholarship (5220) | | Ethnic |
| Peter Sammartino Scholarship (4258) | | |
| SCAMP Grants & Scholarships (5266) | | Veteran |
| Scholarship for Children of Disabled, Deceased and POW/MIA Veterans (4676) | Legal: NC | Veteran |
| Scholarship Foundation of St. Louis Loan (5262) | Legal: MO | |
| Scholarships for Study in Israel (2851) | Citizenship: US; Study: Israel | |
| Seminole-Miccosukee Indian Scholarships (2515) | Legal: FL; Study: FL | Native American |
| Sequoyah Graduate Fellowships (1215) | | Native American |
| Sikh Education Aid Fund Scholarship (5349) | | |
| Smithsonian Institution Minority Internship (5386) | | Minority |

| Vocational Goal, Award, and Entry Number | Geographic Restrictions (Citizenship, Legal Residence, Place of Study) | Affiliation/Special Recipients Requirements |
|---|---|---|
| *Liberal/General Studies (continued)* | | |
| Sons of Italy Foundation National Leadership Grants (5533) | | Ethnic |
| State Student Incentive Grant For Students at Private Non-Profit Institutions (5712) | Study: TX | |
| State Student Incentive Grant For Students at Public Institutions (5713) | Study: TX | |
| Sonja Stefanadis Graduate Student Award (2187) | | Association |
| Emanuel Sternberger Educational Loan (5628) | Legal: NC | |
| Hattie M. Strong College Loan Program (5638) | Citizenship: US | |
| Texas Tuition Equalization Grant (5717) | Study: TX | |
| Virginia Tuition Assistance Grant (5609) | Legal: VA; Study: VA | |
| United Daughters of the Confederacy Scholarships (5790) | | Veteran |
| U.S. Air Force Academy Graduate Dependent Scholarship (1240) | | Military |
| United States Naval Academy Class of 1963 Foundation Scholarship (5947) | | Association |
| University of Delaware-Hagley Program Fellowship (2777) | | |
| Utah State Student Incentive Grant (6019) | Study: UT | |
| Adolph Van Pelt Special Fund for Indian Scholarships (1216) | | Native American |
| Virgin Islands Territorial Loan/Grant Program and Special Legislative Grants (6046) | Legal: VI | |
| Virginia War Orphans Education Program (6054) | Legal: VA; Study: VA | Veteran |
| Flora M. Von Der Ahe Scholarship (5838) | Legal: OR; Study: OR | |
| Warner Trust Loan Program (6079) | Legal: CA; Study: CA | |
| Washington State Work Study (6105) | Legal: WA; Study: WA | |
| Wasie Foundation Scholarships (6109) | | Ethnic |
| Westchester Community Scholarship (4271) | Legal: NY | |
| Western Interstate Commission for Higher Education Western Regional Graduate Program (136) | Legal: AK; Study: AK, AZ, CO, HI, ID, MT, ND, NM, NV, OR, UT, WA, WY | |
| Western Regional Graduate Program (6159) | Legal: AK, AZ, CO, HI, ID, MT, ND, NM, NV, OR, SD, UT, WA, WY | |
| Alice E. Wilson Award (1636) | Citizenship: Canada | |
| Maude Winkler Scholarship Awards (1407) | | Handicapped |
| Wisconsin Department of Veterans Affairs Part-Time Study Grants (6209) | Legal: WI; Study: WI | Veteran |
| Deborah Partridge Wolfe International Fellowship (6307) | | |
| Women of the ELCA Scholarship (6226) | | Religion |
| The Women's Sports Foundation Minority Internship Program (6241) | | Other, Minority |
| Harold S. Wood Award for Excellence (4205) | | |
| Nancy B. Woolridge Graduate Fellowship (6308) | | Fraternal |
| Xerox Technical Minority Scholarship (5682) | | Minority |
| YLD Scholarships (6287) | Citizenship: US; Study: NC | Employer |
| Young Canadian Researchers Awards (3151) | Citizenship: Canada, PermRes | Other |
| Zeta Phi Beta General Graduate Fellowship (6309) | | |
| Zuni Higher Education Scholarships (6314) | | Native American |

## Library and Archival Sciences

| Vocational Goal, Award, and Entry Number | Geographic Restrictions | Affiliation/Special Recipients Requirements |
|---|---|---|
| AALL Law Librarians in Continuing Education Courses Scholarship (310) | | Association |
| Affirmative Action Scholarship Program (5575) | Study: Canada, United States | Asian American, African American, Hispanic American, Native American |

| Vocational Goal, Award, and Entry Number | Geographic Restrictions (Citizenship, Legal Residence, Place of Study) | Affiliation/Special Recipients Requirements |
|---|---|---|
| **Library and Archival Sciences (continued)** | | |
| Alabama Library Association Scholarships and Loans (121) | Legal: AL | |
| ALISE Research Grant Awards (1246) | | Association |
| Arkansas Library Association Scholarship for Graduate Study in Library Science (1095) | Legal: AR | |
| Carroll Preston Baber Research Grants (659) | | Association |
| Bound to Stay Bound Books Scholarships (648) | Citizenship: US | |
| Bound-to-Stay-Bound Books Scholarship (661) | Citizenship: US/CA | |
| Reverend Andrew L. Bouwhuis Memorial Scholarship (1751) | | |
| CLA Scholarship for Minority Students in Memory of Edna Yelland (1565) | Citizenship: US, PermRes; Legal: CA | Asian American, African American, Hispanic American, Native American, Other |
| David H. Clift Scholarship (662) | Citizenship: US/CA, Canada, PermRes | |
| James F. Connolly Congressional Informaton Service Scholarship (311) | | |
| CLA DaFoe Scholarships (1665) | Study: Canada | |
| EBSCO/NMRT Scholarship (663) | Citizenship: US/CA | |
| Friends of the Library of Hawaii Memorial Scholarship (2599) | Legal: HI; Study: HI | |
| Louise Giles Minority Scholarship (664) | Citizenship: US, Canada | Minority |
| Hagley Fellowships/Grants-in-Aid (2779) | | |
| Hagley-Winterthur Fellowship (2780) | | |
| Caroline M. Hewins Scholarship (2800) | | |
| Hubbards Scholarships (2651) | Citizenship: US; Study: United States | |
| Peter Krueger Summer Internships (5384) | Study: NY | |
| Sheila Suen Lai Scholarships (1945) | | Asian American |
| Harold Lancour Scholarship for Foreign Study (1423) | | |
| Christian Larew Memorial Scholarship in Library Information Technology (3464) | | |
| Library of Congress Junior Fellowship (3462) | Citizenship: US | |
| Library Degree Scholarships for Law School Graduates (313) | Citizenship: US/CA | |
| Library Degree Scholarships for Non-Law School Graduates (314) | Citizenship: US/CA | |
| LITA/GEAC-CLSI Scholarship (665) | | |
| LITA/GEAC Scholarships in Library and Information Technology (3465) | | |
| LITA/LSSI Minority Scholarship; LITA/OCLC Minority Scholarship (666) | Citizenship: US, Canada | Other |
| LITA/OCLC and LITA/LSSI Minority Scholarships in Library and Information Technology (3466) | Citizenship: US/CA | Minority |
| Louisiana Library Association Scholarship in Librarianship (3502) | Legal: LA; Study: LA | |
| Master of Library Science Degree Training Grants (2966) | Citizenship: US, Other; Legal: IL; Study: IL | |
| Frederic G. Melcher Scholarship (667) | Citizenship: US/CA | |
| Frederic G. Melcher Scholarships (649) | Legal: Canada, United States | |
| MLA Scholarship (3635) | Citizenship: US/CA, PermRes | |
| MLA Scholarship for Minority Students (3636) | Citizenship: US/CA, PermRes | Asian American, African American, Hispanic American, Native American |
| Gerd Muehsam Memorial Award (1145) | | |
| National Museum of American Art Summer Internships (5388) | Study: NY | |
| NMRT EBSCO Scholarship (656) | Citizenship: US/CA | Association |
| Pennsylvania Library Association Library Science Scholarships (4868) | Legal: PA | |
| Sarah Rebecca Reed Scholarships (1424) | | |

| Vocational Goal, Award, and Entry Number | Geographic Restrictions (Citizenship, Legal Residence, Place of Study) | Affiliation/Special Recipients Requirements |
|---|---|---|
| *Library and Archival Sciences (continued)* | | |
| Reference Service Press Fellowships (1566) | | |
| REFORMA Scholarships (5091) | Legal: United States | |
| David Rozkuszka Scholarship (Godort) (668) | | |
| School Librarian's Workshop Scholarship (646) | | |
| School Librarian's Workshop Scholarship (669) | | |
| Frances M. Schwartz Fellowships (741) | Study: United States | |
| SLA Scholarships (5579) | Study: Canada, United States | |
| Smithsonian Institution Graduate Fellowships (5376) | | |
| George A. Strait Minority Stipend (315) | Citizenship: US/CA | Minority |
| U.S. Marine Corps Historical Center College Internships (5945) | | |
| Virginia Library Association Scholarships (6059) | | |
| The H.W. Wilson Scholarships (1667) | Citizenship: Canada, PermRes | |
| **Life Sciences** | | |
| AFAR Fellowships (468) | Study: United States | |
| Agency for Toxic Substances and Disease Registry Student Internship Program (5860) | | |
| Air Force Civilian Cooperative Work-Study Program (66) | | |
| AISES A.T. Anderson Memorial Scholarship (559) | | Native American, Association |
| American Foundation for Aging Research Predoctoral Awards (469) | Study: United States | |
| American Society for Clinical Laboratory Science Scholarships (908) | Citizenship: US, PermRes | |
| Applied Health Physics Fellowship Program (5861) | | |
| Archbold Biological Station Undergraduate and Graduate Internships (1071) | | |
| Lester Armour Graduate Fellowships (2443) | | |
| Alfred Bader Scholarship (1905) | Study: Canada | |
| Alfred D. Bell, Jr. Visiting Scholars Program (2553) | | |
| Bermuda Biological Station Summer Course Scholarships (1417) | Study: Bermuda | |
| Bermuda Biological Station Visiting Graduate Internships (1418) | Study: Bermuda | |
| Beverly and Qamanirjaq Caribou Management Scholarship (1678) | Citizenship: Canada, PermRes; Study: Canada | |
| Canadian Water Resources Association Scholarships (1708) | Citizenship: Canada; Study: Canada | |
| CIIT Summer Internships (1903) | Study: NC | |
| John Henry Comstock Graduate Student Awards (2388) | | Association |
| Conchologists of America Grants (25) | | |
| John K. Cooper Ornithology Research Grants (2079) | Citizenship: Canada; Study: Canada | |
| Entomological Society Postgraduate Awards (2394) | Citizenship: Canada; Study: Canada | |
| Environmental Protection Agency Tribal Lands Science Scholarship (560) | | Native American |
| Explorers Club Exploration Fund Grants (2425) | | |
| Fellowships in Cereal Chemistry (275) | | |
| Field Museum Graduate Fellowships (2444) | | |
| FSD Student Grant (2578) | | Handicapped |
| Graduate Fellowships for Global Change (5883) | | |

| Vocational Goal, Award, and Entry Number | Geographic Restrictions (Citizenship, Legal Residence, Place of Study) | Affiliation/Special Recipients Requirements |
|---|---|---|
| *Life Sciences (continued)* | | |
| Graduate Student Research Participation Program (5884) | | |
| Graduate U.S. Army Environmental Hygiene Internship Program (5885) | | |
| Grants for Physically Disabled Students in the Sciences (2579) | | Handicapped |
| U.P. Hedrick Award (786) | | |
| Herpetologists' League Best Student Paper (2864) | | Association |
| Hudson River Fellowships (2912) | | |
| Huyck Station Research Grants (2944) | Study: United States | |
| Dean John Knauss Marine Policy Fellowship (4386) | | |
| Laboratory-Graduate Participantships; Thesis Parts Appointment (1084) | Legal: United States; Study: United States | |
| Laboratory Graduate Participation Program (5899) | | |
| Jeffrey P. LaFage Graduate Student Research Award (2390) | | |
| LARS Scholarships (1020) | Study: Canada, Guam, Mexico, Puerto Rico, United States | |
| McKinley Research Fund Scholarships (5035) | Study: United States | |
| MSA Presidential Student Awards (3696) | Legal: United States | |
| Mycological Society of America Graduate Research Prizes (3816) | | Association |
| National Center for Toxicological Research Graduate Student Research Participation (5906) | | |
| National Defense Science and Engineering Graduate Fellowship Program (5855) | Citizenship: US; Study: United States | |
| National Oceanic and Atmospheric Administration/Historically Black Colleges and Universities Faculty/Student Research Participation Program (5910) | | |
| National Zoological Park Minority Traineeships (4456) | | |
| National Zoological Park Research Traineeships (4457) | | |
| National Zoological Park Traineeship in Education (4459) | | |
| National Zoological Park Traineeship in Exhibit Interpretation (4460) | | |
| Naval Air Warfare Center Training Systems Division Graduate Research Participation Program (5912) | | |
| North American Bluebird Society Research Grants (4642) | | |
| Nuclear Engineering/Health Physics Fellowship Program (5915) | | |
| NYZS/Wildlife Conservation Society Research Fellowship Program (RFP) (6177) | Study: Belize, Costa Rica, El Salvador, Guatemala, Honduras, Nicaragua, Panama | |
| Sigurd T. Olson Common Loon Research Awards (4747) | | |
| Parenteral Drug Association Foundation Research Grants (4835) | Citizenship: US, PermRes; Study: United States | |
| Arthur & Doreen Parrett Scholarship Fund (4848) | Legal: WA | |
| Pestcon Graduate Scholarship (1906) | Citizenship: Canada; Study: Canada | |
| Tibor T. Polgar Fellowship (2916) | | |
| Research Support Opportunities in Arctic Environmental Studies (1682) | Citizenship: Canada, PermRes; Legal: Canada; Study: Canada | |

| Vocational Goal, Award, and Entry Number | Geographic Restrictions (Citizenship, Legal Residence, Place of Study) | Affiliation/Special Recipients Requirements |
|---|---|---|
| *Life Sciences (continued)* | | |
| William A. and Stella M. Rowley Graduate Fellowship (2447) | | |
| Scholarships for Marine Sciences (3206) | | |
| Seaspace Scholarship (5293) | Study: United States | |
| Marie Selby Internships (5304) | Study: FL | |
| Service Cancelable Student Loan (2660) | | |
| Sigma Xi Grants-in-Aid of Research (5347) | | |
| Slocum-Lunz Foundation Scholarships and Grants (5359) | Legal: United States; Study: SC, United States | |
| Smithsonian Environmental Research Center Work-Learn Opportunities in Environmental Studies (5374) | Legal: United States; Study: MD | |
| Snodgrass Memorial Research Grant (2392) | | Association |
| James A. Swan Fund Grants (5652) | | |
| Walton Scholarships (3787) | Study: United States | |
| Welder Wildlife Fellowships (6127) | Study: Canada, United States | |
| Young Canadian Researchers Awards (3151) | Citizenship: Canada, PermRes | Other |
| **Mathematics** | | |
| AAUW Educational Foundation Selected Professions Fellowship (336) | Citizenship: US, PermRes | |
| The AFCEA Educational Foundation Fellowship (1099) | Citizenship: US | |
| Applied Health Physics Fellowship Program (5861) | | |
| The BBM Scholarship (1601) | Study: Canada | |
| Cape Canaveral Chapter Scholarships (5114) | Legal: FL | Minority |
| Central Intelligence Agency Graduate Studies Internships (1811) | Citizenship: US | |
| Renate W. Chasman Scholarship (1507) | Citizenship: US, PermRes; Legal: NY | |
| CIC Predoctoral Fellowships (2013) | Citizenship: US; Study: United States | African American, Hispanic American, Native American |
| Fossil Energy Professional Internship Program (5878) | | |
| FSD Student Grant (2578) | | Handicapped |
| Graduate Student Research Participation Program (5884) | | |
| Grants for Physically Disabled Students in the Sciences (2579) | | Handicapped |
| Hertz Foundation Graduate Fellowships (2866) | Citizenship: US, PermRes; Study: United States | |
| Dr. Theodore von Karman Graduate Scholarship (45) | Study: United States | Military |
| Laboratory-Graduate Participantships; Thesis Parts Appointment (1084) | Legal: United States; Study: United States | |
| Laboratory Graduate Participation Program (5899) | | |
| Logistics Education Foundation Scholarship (5463) | | |
| Martino Scholars Program (4239) | | Ethnic |
| NAACP Willems Scholarship (3851) | | Minority, Association |
| National Center for Toxicological Research Graduate Student Research Participation (5906) | | |
| National Defense Science and Engineering Graduate Fellowship Program (5855) | Citizenship: US; Study: United States | |
| National Physical Science Consortium Graduate Fellowships for Minorities and Women (4338) | Citizenship: US | Native American, Hispanic American, African American |
| National Scholarship Trust Fund of the Graphic Arts Fellowships (4373) | | |

| Vocational Goal, Award, and Entry Number | Geographic Restrictions (Citizenship, Legal Residence, Place of Study) | Affiliation/Special Recipients Requirements |
|---|---|---|
| *Mathematics (continued)* | | |
| Smithsonian Environmental Research Center Work-Learn Opportunities in Environmental Studies (5374) | Legal: United States; Study: MD | |
| **Medicine** | | |
| AAUW Educational Foundation Selected Professions Engineering Dissertation Fellowship (335) | Citizenship: US, PermRes | Minority |
| ACNM Scholarships (3267) | Legal: United States; Study: United States | Association |
| ADHF Student Research Fellowship Awards (447) | | |
| AFAR Fellowships (468) | Study: United States | |
| AFVA(MOA) Scholarships (504) | Legal: MI | |
| AGBU Education Loan Program in the U.S. (1133) | | Ethnic |
| AGBU Graduate Loan Program (1134) | | |
| Agency for Toxic Substances and Disease Registry Student Internship Program (5860) | | |
| Albert Ellis Institute Clinical Fellowships, Internships (143) | Citizenship: US, PermRes; Study: United States | |
| Allied Health Scholarships (3370) | Citizenship: Canada; Legal: Canada; Study: Canada | |
| American Foundation for Aging Research Predoctoral Awards (469) | Study: United States | |
| American Liver Foundation Student Research Fellowships (674) | | |
| American Osteopathic Association/National Osteopathic Foundation Student Loans (4333) | | Association |
| APA/Lilly Psychiatric Research Fellowship (800) | | |
| The Applied Social Issues Internship Program (5493) | | |
| John D. Archbold Scholarship (1073) | | |
| Armed Forces Health Professions Scholarship (4483) | | Military |
| Association for Women Veterinarians Student Scholarships (1298) | Study: Canada, United States | |
| AVMF Auxiliary Student Loan (1011) | | |
| Norman Barwin Scholarships (4955) | Citizenship: Canada, PermRes; Study: Canada | |
| Berkshire District Medical Society Medical School Scholarship Loan (1414) | Legal: MA | |
| H. Fletcher Brown Scholarship (4967) | Legal: DE | |
| California Pharmacists Association Educational Foundation Trust Fund (1570) | Citizenship: US; Study: CA | Association |
| Canadian Liver Foundation Graduate Studentships (1672) | Study: Canada | |
| Canadian Liver Foundation Summer Studentship Award (1674) | Study: Canada | |
| A & E Capelle LN Herfords Scholarship (150) | Legal: Canada | |
| Charles River District Medical Society Scholarship (1832) | Legal: MA; Study: United States | |
| Cherokee Nation Graduate Scholarship (1911) | | Native American |
| Ty Cobb Scholarships (1976) | Legal: GA | |
| Joseph Collins Foundation Scholarships (1994) | | |
| "Country Doctor" Scholarship Program (5619) | Legal: GA; Study: GA | |
| Cuyahoga County Medical Foundation Scholarship (2146) | Legal: OH | |
| Cystic Fibrosis Foundation Student Traineeships (2159) | Citizenship: US, PermRes | |
| Dental Student Scholarship Program (41) | Citizenship: US | |

| Vocational Goal, Award, and Entry Number | Geographic Restrictions (Citizenship, Legal Residence, Place of Study) | Affiliation/Special Recipients Requirements |
|---|---|---|
| *Medicine (continued)* | | |
| Dental Teaching and Research Fellowships (2229) | Citizenship: Canada, PermRes; Study: Canada | |
| William E. Dochterman Medical Student Scholarship (5213) | | |
| Dog Writers' Educational Trust Scholarships (2264) | | Other |
| Lord Dowding Grant (2278) | | |
| Endowment Fund Dental Hygiene Scholarship Program (42) | Citizenship: US | |
| William C. Ezell Fellowship (746) | | |
| FFS-NSPB Student Fellowships (2451) | | |
| Gina Finzi Memorial Student Summer Fellowships for Research (3519) | | |
| Morris Fishbein Fellowship in Medical Journalism (688) | | |
| FSD Student Grant (2578) | | Handicapped |
| Georgia Student Finance Commission Service-Cancellable Stafford Loan (2666) | Legal: GA; Study: GA | |
| Georgia Student Finance Commission State-Sponsored Loan (2669) | Legal: GA; Study: GA | |
| Grants for Physically Disabled Students in the Sciences (2579) | | Handicapped |
| G. Layton Grier Scholarship (2211) | Legal: DE | |
| William F. Grupe Foundation Scholarships (2756) | | |
| John A. Hartford Afar Medical Student Geriatric Scholarship Program (460) | | |
| Health Education Loan Program (5709) | | |
| HRSA-BHP Health Professions Student Loans (5967) | | |
| HRSA-BHP Scholarships for Disadvantaged Students (5972) | Citizenship: US, PermRes, Other | |
| HSFC Graduate Research Traineeships (2840) | Citizenship: Canada, PermRes; Study: Canada | |
| Howard Hughes Medical Institute Research Training Fellowships for Medical Students (2925) | | |
| Indian Health Career Awards (4935) | | Ethnic |
| International Order of the King's Daughters and Sons Health Careers Scholarships (3169) | Citizenship: US/CA; Legal: Canada, United States; Study: Canada, United States | |
| Clem Jaunich Education Trust Scholarships (3253) | Legal: MN | |
| S. Evelyn Lewis Memorial Scholarship in Medical Health Sciences (6306) | | |
| Lilly International Fellowships (3479) | Citizenship: United Kingdom, Japan, France; Study: Canada, United States | |
| Lupus Foundation of America Research Grants (3520) | Study: United States | |
| Minnie L. Maffett Scholarship (4466) | Legal: TX; Study: TX | |
| Maine Osteopathic Association Memorial Scholarship (3535) | Legal: ME | |
| Maine Osteopathic Association Scholarship (3536) | Legal: ME | |
| Maryland Professional Scholarship (3578) | Legal: MD; Study: MD | |
| Russell C. McCaughan Education Fund Scholarship (4335) | Legal: United States | |
| Minority Dental Student Scholarship Program (43) | Citizenship: US; Study: United States | African American, Hispanic American, Native American, Minority |
| National Center for Toxicological Research Graduate Student Research Participation (5906) | | |
| National Zoological Park Minority Traineeships (4456) | | |

| Vocational Goal, Award, and Entry Number | Geographic Restrictions (Citizenship, Legal Residence, Place of Study) | Affiliation/Special Recipients Requirements |
|---|---|---|
| *Medicine (continued)* | | |
| New York State Health Service Corps Scholarships (4589) | Citizenship: US; Legal: NY; Study: NY | |
| New York State Professional Opportunity Scholarships (4592) | Citizenship: US, PermRes; Legal: NY; Study: NY | |
| New York State Regents Health Care Opportunity Scholarships (4593) | Citizenship: US, PermRes; Legal: NY | |
| New York State Regents Professional Opportunity Scholarships (4577) | Legal: NY; Study: NY | |
| NMA Scholarships (4302) | Citizenship: US | Minority, African American, Hispanic American, Native American |
| Nursing Scholarship Program (2512) | | Minority |
| Occupational Therapist and Physical Therapist Scholarship Loan Program (2513) | | |
| Oklahoma State Regents for Higher Education Professional Study Grants (4740) | Study: OK | Minority |
| Oncology Nursing Foundation/Rhone Poulenc Rorer New Investigator Research Grants (4771) | | |
| Maurice J. Oringer Awards (224) | | |
| Osteopathic Medical Students Loans (2003) | Legal: CO | |
| Parkinson's Disease Foundation Summer Fellowship (4845) | | |
| Arthur & Doreen Parrett Scholarship Fund (4848) | Legal: WA | |
| Poncin Scholarship Fund (4977) | Study: WA | |
| Colin L. Powell Minority Postdoctoral Fellowship in Tropical Disease Research (4164) | Citizenship: US | African American, Hispanic American, Asian American, Native American |
| Power Systems Inc./NSCA Strength and Conditioning Professional Scholarship (4417) | | Association |
| The Primary Care Resource Initiative for Missouri (PRIMO) (3755) | Legal: MO | |
| The Professional and Practical Nursing Student Loan Program (3756) | Legal: MO | |
| Program for Minority Research Training in Psychiatry (804) | | Minority |
| Royal College Fellowship for Studies in Medical Education (5189) | Citizenship: Canada | Association |
| Vincent Salierno Scholarship (747) | | |
| Samsun Medical Research Institute Student Internships (5224) | | |
| San Joaquin County Medical Society Scholarship Loans (5241) | Legal: CA | |
| Abbie Sargent Memorial Scholarships (5250) | Legal: NH | |
| Savoy Foundation Postdoctoral and Clinical Research Fellowships; Savoy Foundation Research Grants; Savoy Foundation Studentships (5252) | Study: Canada | |
| Robert Schreck Memorial Fund Scholarship (5280) | Legal: TX | |
| Dr. Sydney Segal Research Grants (1638) | Study: Canada | |
| Service Cancelable Student Loan (2660) | | |
| Society of Nuclear Medicine Student Fellowship Awards (5477) | | |
| Stokoe Scholarships (3873) | | Handicapped |
| STTI Scholarships (5345) | | |
| Student Travel Fellowships (748) | | |
| Texas Health Education Loan (5714) | Study: TX | |
| William W. Tucker Medical Student Scholarship (5214) | | |
| Tylman Research Grant (229) | | |

| Vocational Goal, Award, and Entry Number | Geographic Restrictions (Citizenship, Legal Residence, Place of Study) | Affiliation/Special Recipients Requirements |
|---|---|---|
| *Medicine (continued)* | | |
| United Nations Educational Training Scholarships for Southern Africans (5798) | Legal: Namibia, Republic of South Africa | |
| Lee C. Van Wagner Scholarship (1909) | Legal: NY | |
| Dr. Henry R. Viets Medical Student Research Fellowships (3812) | Legal: United States; Study: United States | |
| Western Interstate Commission for Higher Education Student Exchanges (135) | Legal: AK | |
| WHO Fellowships and Research Training Grants (6261) | | |
| Arthur N. Wilson, M.D. Scholarship (691) | Study: AK | |
| Wisconsin Dental Foundation Achievement Scholarship (6205) | Citizenship: US; Legal: WI | |
| Wisconsin Dental Foundation/Marquette University Dental Scholarships (6206) | Legal: WI; Study: WI | |

### Military Sciences

| | | |
|---|---|---|
| Fellowships in National Security (2812) | Study: United States | |

### Parks and Recreation

| | | |
|---|---|---|
| American Numismatic Society Graduate Seminar (737) | Study: Canada, United States | |
| American Numismatic Society Grants-in-Aid (738) | Legal: Canada, United States; Study: United States | |
| Delta Psi Kappa Research Awards (2223) | | Fraternal |
| Tom and Ruth Rivers International Scholarships (6264) | | |

### Philosophy, Theology, and Religion

| | | |
|---|---|---|
| The Albert Baker Fund (1362) | | Religion |
| Donald Bogie Prize (3051) | | |
| Christian Church Hispanic Scholarship (1947) | | Hispanic American, Religion |
| Disciple Chaplain's Scholarship Grant (1948) | | Religion |
| Fellowship of United Methodists in Worship, Music and Other Arts Scholarship (2439) | | Religion |
| Franks Foundation Loan (5832) | Legal: OR | |
| Greek Orthodox Ladies Philoptochos Society Scholarships for Hellenic College and Holy Cross Greek Orthodox School of Theology (2749) | | Religion |
| Humane Studies Foundation Summer Residential Program Fellowships (3053) | Study: VA | |
| IHS John M. Olin Fellowships (3056) | Citizenship: US; Study: England | |
| Institute of Holy Land Studies Scholarships (3047) | Study: Israel | |
| Clem Jaunich Education Trust Scholarships (3253) | Legal: MN | |
| David Tamotsu Kagiwada Memorial Fund Award (1949) | | Asian American, Religion |
| Jesse Lee Prizes (2630) | | |
| Lett Scholarships (4720) | | Religion, African American |
| Verne Catt McDowell Corporation Scholarships (3622) | | Religion |
| Ministerial Education Scholarship (5782) | | Religion |
| Native American Seminary Scholarships (4993) | Citizenship: US, PermRes; Study: United States | Native American, Religion |
| John Harrison Ness Memorial Awards (2631) | | Religion |
| New England Education Society Loan (4527) | Study: CT, MA, ME, NH, RI, VT | |
| Ohio Baptist Education Society Scholarships (4721) | | Religion |
| Presbyterian Church Native American Seminary Scholarships (4994) | Citizenship: US | Native American, Religion |
| Presbyterian Church Student Loans (4995) | Citizenship: US | Religion |

| Vocational Goal, Award, and Entry Number | Geographic Restrictions (Citizenship, Legal Residence, Place of Study) | Affiliation/Special Recipients Requirements |
|---|---|---|
| *Philosophy, Theology, and Religion (continued)* | | |
| Presbyterian Study Grants (4997) | Citizenship: US, PermRes; Study: Canada, United States | Religion |
| Racial/Ethnic Leadership Supplemental Grants (4998) | Citizenship: US, PermRes; Study: Canada, United States | Asian American, African American, Hispanic American, Native American, Religion |
| Rockefeller Archive Center Research Grants (5142) | Study: United States | |
| Charles M. Ross Trust (5165) | Study: IL, KY, LA, TN, TX, WI | |
| Rowley Ministerial Education Scholarship (1951) | | Religion |
| Robert Schreck Memorial Fund Scholarship (5280) | Legal: TX | |
| Katherine J. Schutze Memorial Scholarship (1952) | | Religion |
| Stoody-West Fellowship in Journalism (5795) | Study: United States | Religion |
| Lillian E. Whitmore Scholarship (6173) | | |

## Physical Sciences

| | | |
|---|---|---|
| AAAS Directorate for Science & Policy Administrative Internship (264) | | |
| Advanced Industrial Concepts (AIC) Materials Science Program (5857) | | African American, Native American |
| Agency for Toxic Substances and Disease Registry Student Internship Program (5860) | | |
| AIAA/Gordon C. Oates Air Breathing Propulsion Award (566) | Citizenship: US | |
| AIAA Liquid Propulsion Award (567) | Citizenship: US | |
| AIAA/William T. Piper, Sr. General Aviation Systems Award (569) | Citizenship: US | |
| Air Force Civilian Cooperative Work-Study Program (66) | | |
| Air & Waste Management Scholarship Endowment Trust Fund (75) | | |
| AISES A.T. Anderson Memorial Scholarship (559) | | Native American, Association |
| Alabama Space Grant Consortium Graduate Student Fellowship Program (123) | Citizenship: US | Asian American, African American, Hispanic American, Minority, Native American |
| Alaska Space Grant Program Graduate Research Assistantships (138) | | |
| Alaska Space Grant Program Internships (139) | | |
| Robert E. Altenhofen Memorial Scholarship (963) | | Association |
| American Association for Geodetic Surveying Graduate Fellowship (391) | | Association |
| American Association of Petroleum Geologists Foundation Grants-in-Aid (319) | | |
| AMS/Industry Government Graduate Fellowships (701) | | |
| ANS Graduate Scholarships (722) | Citizenship: US, PermRes | |
| Applied Health Physics Fellowship Program (5861) | | |
| Lester Armour Graduate Fellowships (2443) | | |
| Association for Women Geoscientists Thesis Support Scholarships (Chrysalis) (1296) | | |
| AT & T Bell Laboratories Cooperative Research Fellowships for Minorities (1302) | Citizenship: US, PermRes; Study: NJ | African American, Native American, Hispanic American |
| AT & T Bell Laboratories Graduate Research Grants for Women (1304) | Citizenship: US, PermRes; Study: NJ | |
| AT & T Bell Laboratories University Relations Summer Program (1306) | | |
| AVS Student Prize; Russel and Sigurd Varian Fellowship (1008) | | |

| Vocational Goal, Award, and Entry Number | Geographic Restrictions (Citizenship, Legal Residence, Place of Study) | Affiliation/Special Recipients Requirements |
|---|---|---|
| *Physical Sciences (continued)* | | |
| AWU Graduate Research Fellowships (1201) | Citizenship: US, PermRes; Study: CA, CO, ID, MT, ND, NM, NV, OK, UT, WA, WY | |
| AWU Student Research Fellowships (1203) | Citizenship: US, PermRes; Study: CA, CO, ID, MT, ND, NM, NV, OK, UT, WA, WY | |
| Alfred Bader Scholarship (1905) | Study: Canada | |
| F.M. Becket Memorial Award (2366) | Study: Canada, United States | |
| J. Bolton Scholarships (5527) | Legal: Canada; Study: Canada | |
| BPW Career Advancement Scholarships (1546) | Citizenship: US; Study: United States | |
| H. Fletcher Brown Scholarship (4967) | Legal: DE | |
| Bureau of Engraving and Printing Graduate Student Research Participation Program (5862) | | |
| Canadian Society of Petroleum Geologists Graduate Scholarships (1704) | Legal: Canada; Study: Canada | |
| Canadian Water Resources Association Scholarships (1708) | Citizenship: Canada; Study: Canada | |
| Robert A. Canham Award (6117) | | |
| Cape Canaveral Chapter Scholarships (5114) | Legal: FL | Minority |
| Central Intelligence Agency Graduate Studies Internships (1811) | Citizenship: US | |
| CERT Scholarship (2100) | Study: United States | Native American |
| Renate W. Chasman Scholarship (1507) | Citizenship: US, PermRes; Legal: NY | |
| CIC Predoctoral Fellowships (2013) | Citizenship: US; Study: United States | African American, Hispanic American, Native American |
| Civilian Radioactive Waste Management Fellowship Program (5866) | | |
| Violet Cressey-Marcks Fisher Travel Fellowship (5192) | Legal: England | |
| Robert A. Dannels Scholarships (726) | Citizenship: US, PermRes | |
| Verne R. Dapp Scholarship (727) | Citizenship: US, PermRes | |
| Arthur Davis Fellowship; Charles E. Merrill Trust Fellowship (3806) | Study: United States | |
| Raymond Davis Scholarship (5461) | | |
| DOE Student Research Participation (4705) | Citizenship: US, PermRes | |
| Amelia Earhart Fellowship Awards (6312) | | |
| Electronic Industries Foundation Scholarships (2370) | Citizenship: US | Handicapped |
| Environmental Protection Agency Tribal Lands Science Scholarship (560) | | Native American |
| Explorers Club Exploration Fund Grants (2425) | | |
| Field Museum Graduate Fellowships (2444) | | |
| William A. Fischer Memorial Scholarship (964) | | Association |
| Donald W. Fogarty International Student Paper Competition (1052) | | |
| Donald W. Fogarty International Student Paper Competition (2539) | | |
| Fossil Energy Professional Internship Program (5878) | | |
| FSD Student Grant (2578) | | Handicapped |
| Geological Society of America Research Grants (2649) | Study: Canada, Mexico, United States | |
| Georgia Space Grant Consortium Fellowships (2655) | | |
| GITA (2705) | | |
| Government of Canada Awards (3145) | Citizenship: France, Germany, Japan, Mexico; Study: Canada | |
| Graduate Student Fellowships (5560) | | |
| Graduate Student Research Participation Program (5884) | | |

| Vocational Goal, Award, and Entry Number | Geographic Restrictions (Citizenship, Legal Residence, Place of Study) | Affiliation/Special Recipients Requirements |
|---|---|---|
| *Physical Sciences (continued)* | | |
| Graduate U.S. Army Environmental Hygiene Internship Program (5885) | | |
| Grants for Physically Disabled Students in the Sciences (2579) | | Handicapped |
| Paul A. Greebler Scholarship (730) | Citizenship: US, PermRes; Study: United States | |
| Hertz Foundation Graduate Fellowships (2866) | Citizenship: US, PermRes; Study: United States | |
| High Temperatures Materials Laboratory (HTML) Graduate Student Fellowships (5888) | | |
| Historically Black Colleges and Universities Building Technology Summer Research Participation Program (5889) | | |
| Historically Black Colleges and Universities Faculty and Student Research Participation Program in Fusion. (5890) | | |
| Historically Black Colleges and Universities Fossil Energy Faculty and Student Research Training (5891) | | |
| Historically Black Colleges and Universities Nuclear Energy Training Program (5894) | | |
| Anna Louise Hoffman Awards for Outstanding Achievement in Graduate Research (3216) | | |
| International Astronomical Union Travel Grants (3121) | | |
| Dr. Theodore von Karman Graduate Scholarship (45) | Study: United States | Military |
| Dean John A. Knauss Marine Policy Fellowships (4328) | Study: United States | |
| Laboratory-Graduate Participantships; Thesis Parts Appointment (1084) | Legal: United States; Study: United States | |
| Laboratory Graduate Participation Program (5899) | | |
| John and Muriel Landis Scholarships (732) | Study: United States | |
| Leakey Foundation Fellowships for Great Ape Research and Conservation (3442) | | |
| Leakey Foundation General Grants (3443) | | |
| LH Systems Internship (965) | | Association |
| Lunar and Planetary Institute Visiting Graduate Fellows (3515) | Study: United States | |
| Maryland Space Grant Consortium Graduate Level Fellowship (3588) | | |
| Mass Media Science and Engineering Fellowships (268) | Study: United States | |
| Minority Geoscience Scholarships (508) | Citizenship: US; Study: United States | African American, Hispanic American, Native American |
| Montana Space Grant Consortium Scholarship-Fellowship Program (3771) | | |
| MSA Presidential Student Awards (3696) | Legal: United States | |
| NASA/DESGC Graduate Student Fellowships (2204) | Citizenship: US | |
| NASA Graduate Student Research Fellowships (3839) | Citizenship: US; Study: United States | |
| National Defense Science and Engineering Graduate Fellowship Program (5855) | Citizenship: US; Study: United States | |
| National Oceanic and Atmospheric Administration/Historically Black Colleges and Universities Faculty/Student Research Participation Program (5910) | | |
| National Physical Science Consortium Graduate Fellowships for Minorities and Women (4338) | Citizenship: US | Native American, Hispanic American, African American |
| National Scholarship Trust Fund of the Graphic Arts Fellowships (4373) | | |

| Vocational Goal, Award, and Entry Number | Geographic Restrictions (Citizenship, Legal Residence, Place of Study) | Affiliation/Special Recipients Requirements |
|---|---|---|
| *Physical Sciences (continued)* | | |
| NRAO Summer Student Research Assistantships (4352) | Citizenship: US; Study: United States | |
| NSERC Research Scholarships, Fellowships, and Grants (4474) | Citizenship: Canada, PermRes; Study: Canada | |
| Nuclear Engineering/Health Physics Fellowship Program (5915) | | |
| Nuclear Regulatory Commission Graduate Fellowship Program (5916) | | |
| Oak Ridge National Laboratory Professional Internship Program (5918) | | |
| Parenteral Drug Association Foundation Research Grants (4835) | Citizenship: US, PermRes; Study: United States | |
| Petro-Canada Inc. Graduate Research Awards (1284) | Citizenship: Canada, PermRes; Study: Canada | |
| Tibor T. Polgar Fellowships (2914) | Study: NY | |
| Al Qoyawayma Award (561) | | Native American |
| Research Support Opportunities in Arctic Environmental Studies (1682) | Citizenship: Canada, PermRes; Legal: Canada; Study: Canada | |
| Rocky Mountain Mineral Law Foundation Scholarship Program Including the Joe Rudd Scholarship (5159) | | |
| Theodore Roosevelt Memorial Grants (716) | | |
| William A. and Stella M. Rowley Graduate Fellowship (2447) | | |
| Savannah River Technology Center Professional Internship Program (5924) | | |
| Robert Schreck Memorial Fund Scholarship (5280) | Legal: TX | |
| Seaspace Scholarship (5293) | Study: United States | |
| SEG Scholarships (5300) | Study: United States | |
| Marie Selby Internships (5304) | Study: FL | |
| SHPE Foundation Education Grant (5454) | | |
| Sigma Xi Grants-in-Aid of Research (5347) | | |
| Smithsonian Environmental Research Center Work-Learn Opportunities in Environmental Studies (5374) | Legal: United States; Study: MD | |
| Space and Aerospace Graduate Fellowships (3508) | Citizenship: US | |
| Space Grant Graduate Fellowship Program (5125) | | |
| SPIE Educational Scholarships and Grants in Optical Engineering (5589) | | |
| Ralph W. Stone Research Award (4410) | | Association |
| Sumner Memorial Fellowships (5646) | Citizenship: Canada; Legal: Canada; Study: Canada | |
| Tennessee Space Grant Consortium Fellowships and Scholarships (5698) | Citizenship: US; Study: TN | |
| UA/NASA Space Grant Graduate Fellowship Program (1086) | | |
| James R. Vogt Scholarship (734) | Citizenship: US, PermRes | |
| West Virginia Space Consortium Graduate Fellowship Program (6144) | Citizenship: US | |
| Nellie Yeoh Whetten Award (1009) | | |
| Wisconsin Space Grant Consortium Graduate Fellowships (6214) | Citizenship: US | |
| Young Canadian Researchers Awards (3151) | Citizenship: Canada, PermRes | Other |

### Protective Services and Public Affairs

| | | |
|---|---|---|
| Charles Abrams Scholarships (774) | Citizenship: US; Study: United States | |
| AGBU Education Loan (1136) | | Ethnic |
| TELACU/Richard Alatorre Fellowship (5686) | Legal: CA; Study: United States | Minority |

| Vocational Goal, Award, and Entry Number | Geographic Restrictions (Citizenship, Legal Residence, Place of Study) | Affiliation/Special Recipients Requirements |
|---|---|---|

### Protective Services and Public Affairs (continued)

| Vocational Goal, Award, and Entry Number | Geographic Restrictions | Affiliation/Special Recipients Requirements |
|---|---|---|
| APA Planning Fellowships (776) | Citizenship: US/CA; Study: United States | African American, Hispanic American, Native American |
| Dwight David Eisenhower Transportation Fellowship (6052) | Citizenship: US; Study: United States | |
| Emergency Preparedness Canada Research Fellowship Program (1274) | Citizenship: Canada, PermRes | |
| Federation Executive Recruitment and Education Program (FEREP) Scholarships (2117) | | |
| Government Scholars Summer Program (4562) | Study: NY, United States | |
| International Foundation of Employee Benefit Plans Grants for Research (3155) | Citizenship: Canada | |
| Dean John A. Knauss Marine Policy Fellowships (4328) | Study: United States | |
| Law Enforcement Career Scholarships (1238) | | |
| LES Fellowships (3468) | Study: Canada, United States | |
| Maryland Reimbursement of Firefighters and Rescue Squad Members (3579) | Legal: MD; Study: MD | Employer, Other |
| Mississippi Public Management Graduate Internship Program (3739) | Citizenship: US; Legal: MS; Study: MS | |
| Michael Murphy Memorial Scholarship Loans (132) | Legal: AK | |
| National Urban/Rural Fellows (4446) | Citizenship: US | |
| New York City Urban Fellowships (4563) | Study: NY, United States | |
| New York State Professional Opportunity Scholarships (4592) | Citizenship: US, PermRes; Legal: NY; Study: NY | |
| Population Sciences Fellowships (5149) | | |
| Public Interest Internships (1803) | Study: United States | |
| Summer Graduate Internships (4564) | Study: NY, United States | |
| Robert C. Thomas Memorial Scholarship (133) | | |
| Lent D. Upson-Loren B. Miller Fellowships (1958) | Study: MI | |
| John Charles Wilson Scholarship (3107) | | Association |
| David A. Winston Fellowship (1290) | Study: DC | |
| Wolcott Foundation Fellowships (2870) | Study: DC | |
| Women and Public Policy Fellowship (1809) | Study: NY | |

### Social Sciences

| Vocational Goal, Award, and Entry Number | Geographic Restrictions | Affiliation/Special Recipients Requirements |
|---|---|---|
| Advanced Research Grants in Military History (5823) | Study: PA, United States | |
| AGBU Graduate Loan Program (1134) | | |
| Gordon Allport Intergroup Relations Prize (5492) | | |
| American Numismatic Society Graduate Seminar (737) | Study: Canada, United States | |
| American Society of Crime Laboratory Scholarship Award (916) | | |
| Ancient India and Iran Trust Travel and Research Grants (1035) | | |
| Annual Grants; Dr. John Pine Memorial Award; Dr. A. F. Zimmerman Award (4890) | | Fraternal |
| ANS Fellowship in Roman Studies (739) | | |
| ASC Gene Carte Student Paper Competition (918) | | |
| Bliss Prize Fellowship in Byzantine Studies (2286) | Study: Canada, United States | |
| Donald Bogie Prize (3051) | | |
| Mildred Cater Bradham Social Work Fellowship (6303) | | Fraternal |
| Robert G. Buzzard Scholarships (2617) | | Fraternal |
| J.E. Caldwell Centennial Scholarships (4394) | Citizenship: US; Study: United States | |

| Vocational Goal, Award, and Entry Number | Geographic Restrictions (Citizenship, Legal Residence, Place of Study) | Affiliation/Special Recipients Requirements |
|---|---|---|
| *Social Sciences (continued)* | | |
| Canadian Soroptimist Grants for Women (5539) | Citizenship: Canada, PermRes; Study: Canada | |
| Candle Fellowships (4911) | | Fraternal |
| Central Intelligence Agency Graduate Studies Internships (1811) | Citizenship: US | |
| CIBC Youthvision Graduate Research Award Program (1270) | Citizenship: Canada, PermRes; Study: Canada | |
| CIC Predoctoral Fellowships (2013) | Citizenship: US; Study: United States | African American, Hispanic American, Native American |
| The Clara Mayo Grant (5494) | | |
| Geraldine Clewell Fellowship I (4912) | | Fraternal |
| Monica Cole Research Grant (5191) | Legal: England | |
| Congressional Fellowships on Women and Public Policy (6236) | Legal: United States; Study: United States | |
| Minda de Gunzburg Center for European Studies Dissertation Exploration Grants (2766) | | Other |
| Minda de Gunzburg Center for European Studies German Language Training Grants (2767) | | Other |
| Minda de Gunzburg Center for European Studies Graduate Summer Research Travel Grants (2768) | | Other |
| Minda de Gunzburg Center for European Studies Short-Term Opportunity Grants (2770) | | Other |
| Diamond Anniversary Fellowships (4915) | | Fraternal |
| Jean Dearth Dickerscheid Fellowship (4916) | | Fraternal |
| Dirksen Congressional Research Grants (2253) | | |
| H.B. Earhart Fellowships (2301) | | |
| Friedreich Ebert Stiftung Pre Dissertation/Advanced Graduate Fellowshps (2332) | Citizenship: US; Study: Germany | |
| Federated Women's Institutes of Ontario International Scholarship (1648) | Study: ON, Canada | |
| Federation Executive Recruitment and Education Program (FEREP) Scholarships (2117) | | |
| Rabbi Robert Feinberg Scholarship (4223) | | |
| Fellowship for the Study of Foraging Peoples (3441) | | |
| Fellowships in Byzantine Studies, Pre-Columbian Studies and Landscape Architecture (2288) | Study: DC | |
| The Feminist Majority Internships (2441) | | |
| Florida House of Representatives Intern Program (2522) | Legal: FL; Study: FL | |
| Founders Fellowship (4918) | | Fraternal |
| Eileen J. Garrett Scholarship (4832) | | |
| John C. Geilfuss Fellowship (5615) | | |
| Geraldine Clewell Fellowship II (4919) | | Fraternal |
| Germanistic Society of America Quadrille Grants (2697) | | |
| Government of Canada Awards (3145) | Citizenship: France, Germany, Japan, Mexico; Study: Canada | |
| Graduate Student Research Participation Program (5884) | | |
| Jennifer C. Groot Fellowship (869) | Citizenship: US, Canada | |
| Harrell Family Fellowship (870) | | |
| Lullelia W. Harrison Scholarship in Counseling (6304) | | |

| Vocational Goal, Award, and Entry Number | Geographic Restrictions (Citizenship, Legal Residence, Place of Study) | Affiliation/Special Recipients Requirements |
| --- | --- | --- |
| *Social Sciences (continued)* | | |
| Harvard University Pre-Doctoral Fellowships in European Studies (2772) | | |
| Hollingworth Award Competition (3877) | | |
| Hoover Library Fellowships and Grants (2890) | Study: United States | |
| AGBU Hirair and Anna Hovnanian Fellowship (1123) | | Ethnic |
| Celia M. Howard Fellowships (2964) | Legal: IL | |
| Humane Studies Foundation Summer Residential Program Fellowships (3053) | Study: VA | |
| Amy Louise Hunter Fellowship (5616) | | |
| Huntington Library Research Awards (2939) | Study: United States | |
| IHS Excellence in Liberty Prizes (3055) | | |
| IHS John M. Olin Fellowships (3056) | Citizenship: US; Study: England | |
| India Studies Student Fellowships (5319) | Citizenship: Canada; Study: India | |
| Institute Postdoctoral NEH Fellowship (4751) | | |
| Internships (5805) | Study: United States | |
| Johnson Foundation Photocopying Grants (3283) | Legal: United States; Study: United States | |
| Otto Klineberg Intercultural and International Relations Award (5496) | | |
| Kosciuszko Foundation Domestic Scholarships (3399) | Citizenship: US, PermRes; Study: United States | |
| Krupp Foundation Fellowship (2773) | | Other |
| Laboratory Graduate Participation Program (5899) | | |
| Claude R. Lambe Fellowships (3058) | | |
| Leakey Foundation General Grants (3443) | | |
| Ottis Lock Endowment Scholarships (2306) | Study: TX | |
| Mackenzie King Travelling Scholarships (3529) | Legal: Canada; Study: United States | |
| James Madison Fellowships (3531) | Citizenship: US | |
| Marine Corps Historical Center Master's Thesis Fellowship (3558) | | |
| Marine Corps Historical Center Research Grants (3559) | | |
| Mass Media Science and Engineering Fellowships (268) | Study: United States | |
| Paul Mellon Centre Fellowship (6276) | Study: England | |
| National Council on Family Relations Student Award (3948) | | Association |
| National Council for Geographic Education Committee for Women in Geographic Education Scholarship (3955) | | |
| National Program for Advanced Study and Research in China - General Advanced Studies (2015) | Citizenship: US, PermRes; Study: People's Republic of China | |
| New York State Professional Opportunity Scholarships (4592) | Citizenship: US, PermRes; Legal: NY; Study: NY | |
| New York State Regents Professional Opportunity Scholarships (4577) | Legal: NY; Study: NY | |
| NWSA Graduate Scholarships in Lesbian Studies (4452) | | |
| Pergamon-NWSA Graduate Scholarships in Women's Studies (4453) | | |
| Petro-Canada Inc. Graduate Research Awards (1284) | Citizenship: Canada, PermRes; Study: Canada | |
| Phi Alpha Theta Graduate Scholarship (4892) | | Fraternal |
| Presidents Research Fellowship (4923) | | Fraternal |
| Public Employees Roundtable Public Service Scholarships (5017) | | |

| Vocational Goal, Award, and Entry Number | Geographic Restrictions (Citizenship, Legal Residence, Place of Study) | Affiliation/Special Recipients Requirements |
|---|---|---|
| *Social Sciences (continued)* | | |
| Rhode Island Commission on State Government Summer Internships (5122) | Legal: RI | |
| Benjamin F. Richason III Scholarship (2618) | | Fraternal |
| Rockefeller Archive Center Research Grants (5142) | Study: United States | |
| Roosevelt Institute Grants-in-Aid (5161) | Study: United States | |
| Kenneth W. Russell Fellowship (883) | | |
| William B. Schallek Memorial Graduate Study Fellowships (5132) | Citizenship: US | |
| Scholarship in Jewish Women's Studies (4454) | | |
| Ellen Setterfield Memorial Scholarship (4008) | | Handicapped |
| Alice E. Smith Fellowship (5617) | | |
| Society for the Psychological Study of Social Issues Grants-In-Aid Program (5497) | | |
| SSRC Bangladesh Studies Fellowships (5397) | Study: Bangladesh | |
| SSRC Soviet Union and Its Successor States Graduate Training Fellowships (5419) | Citizenship: US, PermRes | |
| SSRC Soviet Union and Its Successor States Institutional Awards for First-Year Fellowships (5420) | | |
| Statten Fellowship (5624) | Study: Canada | |
| Student Research Grants for the Scientific Study of Sex (5502) | | |
| Truman Scholarships (5752) | Citizenship: US | |
| United Nations Educational Training Scholarships for Southern Africans (5798) | Legal: Namibia, Republic of South Africa | |
| U.S. Marine Corps Historical Center College Internships (5945) | | |
| Jesse Marvin Unruh Assembly Fellowships (1574) | Study: United States | |
| Richard M. Weaver Fellowship (3099) | Citizenship: US | |
| Wolcott Foundation Fellowships (2870) | Study: DC | |
| Jesse Wrench Scholarship (3748) | Study: MO | |
| Young Canadian Researchers Awards (3151) | Citizenship: Canada, PermRes | Other |

## Visual and Performing Arts

| Vocational Goal, Award, and Entry Number | Geographic Restrictions | Affiliation/Special Recipients Requirements |
|---|---|---|
| Academy of Motion Picture Arts and Sciences Student Academy Awards (22) | | |
| Gladys Agell Award for Excellence in Research (258) | | |
| American Watercolor Society Scholarship Award (1022) | | |
| Central Intelligence Agency Graduate Studies Internships (1811) | Citizenship: US | |
| Chautauqua Institution Scholarship (1842) | | |
| Chigiana Summer Course Scholarships (1935) | Study: Italy | |
| Community Arts Administration Internships (4662) | Legal: NC | |
| Consortium College University Media Centers Annual Research Grants (2065) | Legal: United States | |
| Delta Psi Kappa Research Awards (2223) | | Fraternal |
| Pauly D'Orlando Memorial Art Scholarship (5781) | | Religion |
| Cay Drachnik Minorities Fund (259) | | Minority |
| Fellowship of United Methodists in Worship, Music and Other Arts Scholarship (2439) | | Religion |
| Morris Fishbein Fellowship in Medical Journalism (688) | | |
| Folklife Internships (4665) | Legal: NC | |
| Ford Foundation Fellowships (1178) | Citizenship: Other; Study: United States | |

| Vocational Goal, Award, and Entry Number | Geographic Restrictions (Citizenship, Legal Residence, Place of Study) | Affiliation/Special Recipients Requirements |
|---|---|---|
| **Visual and Performing Arts (continued)** | | |
| Sergio Franchi Music Scholarship in Voice Performance (4225) | | Ethnic |
| Getty Museum Graduate Internships (2702) | Study: United States | |
| Roswell L. Gilpatric Internship (3655) | | |
| The Elizabeth Greenshields Grant (2751) | | |
| Henry Luce Foundation/ACLS Dissertation Fellowship Program in American Art (411) | Citizenship: US | |
| Huntington Library Research Awards (2939) | Study: United States | |
| Independent and Student Filmmakers Competition (1436) | | African American |
| India Studies Student Fellowships (5319) | Citizenship: Canada; Study: India | |
| Jacob's Pillow Dance Festival Internships (3234) | Study: United States | |
| Kate Neal Kinley Memorial Fellowshsip (5998) | | |
| Peter Krueger Summer Internships (5384) | Study: NY | |
| Myra Levick Scholarship (260) | | |
| Lifchez/Stronach Curatorial Internship (3656) | | |
| Paul Mellon Centre Fellowship (6276) | Study: England | |
| Metropolitan Museum of Art Nine-Month Internship (3661) | Citizenship: US; Study: NY | Minority |
| Metropolitan Museum of Art Six Month Internship (3662) | | |
| Metropolitan Museum of Art Summer Internship for Graduate Students (3664) | | |
| Metropolitan Museum of Art Volunteer Internships (3665) | | |
| Monitor/Technical Assistant Scholarships (2826) | Study: United States | |
| Gerd Muehsam Memorial Award (1145) | | |
| National Alliance for Excellence Honored Scholars Awards (3841) | Citizenship: US; Study: United States | |
| National Museum of American Art Summer Internships (5388) | Study: NY | |
| National Orchestral Institute Scholarships (4330) | Study: United States | |
| National Zoological Park Traineeship in Zoo Photography (4464) | | |
| Pavarotti Scholarship (4252) | | Ethnic |
| Posey Foundation Graduate Art Scholarships (4985) | | |
| Professional Development Fellowship Program for Artists and Art Historians (1982) | Citizenship: US, PermRes | |
| Al Qoyawayma Award (561) | | Native American |
| Theodore Rousseau Fellowships (3667) | | |
| Louis J. Salerno, M.D. Memorial Scholarship (4257) | | |
| Swann Foundation Fellowship (5654) | | |
| Robert Thunen Memorial Educational Scholarships (2983) | Study: CA, NV, OR, WA | |
| Tuition Grants for Apprenticeships (3280) | Study: United States | |
| University Film and Video Association Student Grants (5992) | | |
| Polaire Weissman Fund Fellowship (3669) | Study: United States | |
| Polaire Weissman Fund (3670) | | |
| Jane and Morgan Whitney Fellowships (3671) | | |
| Harriet Hale Woolley Scholarships (2545) | Citizenship: US; Study: France | |

| Vocational Goal, Award, and Entry Number | Geographic Restrictions (Citizenship, Legal Residence, Place of Study) | Affiliation/Special Recipients Requirements |
|---|---|---|
| *Area and Ethnic Studies (continued)* | | |

# High School

**Area and Ethnic Studies**

| | | |
|---|---|---|
| AATG/PAD Travel/Study Awards (327) | Citizenship: US; Study: Germany | |
| AFS Intercultural Global Teenager Program Scholarships (49) | Citizenship: US, PermRes | |
| International Student Identity Card Travel Grants for Educational Programs in Developing Countries (2113) | Citizenship: US, PermRes | |

**Business and Management**

| | | |
|---|---|---|
| Academy of Travel and Tourism Award (4426) | | |
| Service Merchandise Scholarship Program (5310) | | |

**Communications**

| | | |
|---|---|---|
| Lisa Bjork Memorial Scholarship (2028) | Legal: FL | |
| Dallas-Fort Worth Association of Black Communicators Scholarships (2170) | | Minority |
| FFTA Scholarship Competition (2568) | | |
| Stephen H. Gayle Memorial Scholarship (4558) | Legal: NY | Minority |
| The National Scholarship Trust Fund Scholarships for High School Students (4374) | | |
| Quill and Scroll National Writing/Photo Contest (5049) | | |
| Sacramento Bee Journalism Scholarships for Community College Students (5206) | Study: CA | |
| Specs Howard High School Scholarships (5583) | Study: MI | |
| Young Feminist Scholarship Program (5591) | | |

**Education**

| | | |
|---|---|---|
| Newtonville Woman's Club Scholarships (2641) | Legal: MA | |

**Engineering**

| | | |
|---|---|---|
| The DuPont Challenge: Science Essay Awards Program (2643) | | |
| Thomas Edison/Max McGraw Scholarship (4379) | | |
| Maryland MESA Scholarships (3586) | Legal: MD | |
| Spence Reese Scholarship (5089) | | |

**Foreign Languages**

| | | |
|---|---|---|
| AATG/PAD Travel/Study Awards (327) | Citizenship: US; Study: Germany | |

**Health Sciences**

| | | |
|---|---|---|
| Median School Scholarship (3629) | | |

**Home Economics**

| | | |
|---|---|---|
| ProStart Scholarships (4369) | | |

**Industry and Trade**

| | | |
|---|---|---|
| NAPHCC Educational Foundation Scholarships (3887) | Study: United States | |
| The National Scholarship Trust Fund Scholarships for High School Students (4374) | | |
| New England Graphic Arts Scholarships (4531) | Legal: CT, MA, ME, NH, RI, VT | |

**Language and Literature**

| | | |
|---|---|---|
| Lisa Bjork Memorial Scholarship (2028) | Legal: FL | |
| John M. Will Memorial Journalism Scholarships (6180) | Legal: AL, FL, MS | |
| Scholastic Art and Writing Awards (5268) | | |

| Vocational Goal, Award, and Entry Number | Geographic Restrictions (Citizenship, Legal Residence, Place of Study) | Affiliation/Special Recipients Requirements |
|---|---|---|
| *Language and Literature (continued)* | | |
| World of Expression Scholarship Program (1420) | Legal: NY | |
| **Law** | | |
| Spence Reese Scholarship (5089) | | |
| **Liberal/General Studies** | | |
| Adult High School Equivalency Scholarships (171) | Legal: AB | |
| AFS Intercultural Global Teenager Program Scholarships (49) | Citizenship: US, PermRes | |
| Americanism Essay Contest Scholarships (610) | Legal: IL | |
| Association of the Sons of Poland Scholarships (1260) | | Association |
| Burlington Northern Santa Fe Scholarships (1531) | | Employer |
| Allen C. Clark Memorial Scholarship (2030) | Legal: FL | |
| Congress Bundestag Youth Exchange Program Scholarships (6297) | Citizenship: US; Study: Germany | |
| Terry Darby Memorial Scholarship (2032) | Legal: FL | |
| Daughters of Penelope Past Grand President's Award (2183) | | Association |
| James H. Davis Memorial Scholarship (2033) | Legal: FL; Study: FL | |
| Voice of Democracy Scholarship Contest (6040) | | |
| William C. Doherty Scholarships (3883) | | Employer |
| Duracell/NSTA Scholarship Competition (4381) | Legal: United States | |
| Ellen Beth Eddleman Memorial Scholarship (2034) | Legal: FL | |
| Finland U.S. Senate Youth Exchange Scholarships (6298) | Citizenship: US; Legal: CA, FL, MA, MI, MN, OR, WA; Study: Finland | |
| First Catholic Slovak Ladies Association High School Fraternal Scholarship Awards (2462) | Study: Canada, United States | Association |
| Gardner Foundation Scholarship Grants (2624) | Legal: OH | |
| The Jerome L. Hauck Scholarship (2792) | | |
| ILGWU National College Award Program (3161) | | Union |
| International Student Identity Card Travel Grants for Educational Programs in Developing Countries (2113) | Citizenship: US, PermRes | |
| Japanese American Citizens League Freshman Awards (3245) | | Ethnic |
| Japanese American Citizens League Student Aid Award (3248) | | Ethnic |
| Lehigh Valley Workers Memorial Scholarship Fund (3449) | | Other |
| James L. and Lavon Madden Mallory Disability Scholarship (2322) | Legal: IA | Handicapped |
| Mazda National Scholarship (6299) | Legal: United States; Study: Japan | |
| Multi-Cultural Scholarship (5270) | | |
| National High School Oratorical Contest (619) | | |
| National High School Oratorical Contest (623) | | |
| National High School Oratorical Contest (631) | Citizenship: US; Study: United States | |
| National Society of the Sons of the American Revolution George S. and Stella M. Knight Essay Contest (5531) | | |
| Native Sons of the Golden West High School Public Speaking Scholarships (4472) | Legal: CA | |
| NCOA Scholarships (4639) | | Military, Association |
| Northeastern Loggers' Association Annual Scholarships (4688) | | Association |

| Vocational Goal, Award, and Entry Number | Geographic Restrictions (Citizenship, Legal Residence, Place of Study) | Affiliation/Special Recipients Requirements |
|---|---|---|
| *Liberal/General Studies (continued)* | | |
| Past Grand Presidents Award (2185) | | Association |
| Private High School Scholarship (2895) | | Native American |
| Rutherford Scholars (184) | Legal: Canada | |
| Secondary School Exchange (2386) | Study: United Kingdom, United States | |
| Service Merchandise Scholarship Program (5310) | | |
| Alexandra Apostolides Sonenfeld Award (2186) | | Association |
| Telluride Association Summer Program Scholarships (5696) | Study: MA, NY | |
| Texas History Essay Contest (5537) | | |
| United World College Scholarships (186) | Legal: Canada | |
| USCG Chief Petty Officers Association Captain Caliendo College Assistance Fund Scholarship Program (5847) | | Handicapped, Association |
| Voice of Democracy Scholarships (6069) | | |
| Washington State Student Financial Aid Programs Washington Scholars (6104) | Study: WA | |
| West Virginia War Orphans Education Benefits (6141) | Legal: WV; Study: WV | Veteran |
| David & Dovetta Wilson Scholarship Fund (6191) | Legal: United States | Religion |
| World of Expression Scholarship Program (1420) | Legal: NY | |
| XX Olympiad Memorial Award (3275) | | |
| Mary & Harry Zimmerman Scholarship Program (5311) | | Employer |

**Life Sciences**

| | | |
|---|---|---|
| The DuPont Challenge: Science Essay Awards Program (2643) | | |
| Hancock County Scholars Program (3784) | Legal: ME; Study: ME | |
| Maryland MESA Scholarships (3586) | Legal: MD | |

**Mathematics**

| | | |
|---|---|---|
| The DuPont Challenge: Science Essay Awards Program (2643) | | |
| Maryland MESA Scholarships (3586) | Legal: MD | |

**Medicine**

| | | |
|---|---|---|
| ADHF Student Research Fellowship Awards (447) | | |
| The DuPont Challenge: Science Essay Awards Program (2643) | | |
| Spence Reese Scholarship (5089) | | |

**Physical Sciences**

| | | |
|---|---|---|
| The DuPont Challenge: Science Essay Awards Program (2643) | | |
| Thomas Edison/Max McGraw Scholarship (4379) | | |
| Maryland MESA Scholarships (3586) | Legal: MD | |
| New Jersey Academy of Science Research Grants-in-Aid to High School Students (4537) | Legal: NJ; Study: NJ | |

**Social Sciences**

| | | |
|---|---|---|
| The DuPont Challenge: Science Essay Awards Program (2643) | | |
| National High School Oratorical Contest (631) | Citizenship: US; Study: United States | |
| National Peace Essay Contest (5075) | | |
| Native Sons of the Golden West High School Public Speaking Scholarships (4472) | Legal: CA | |
| Spence Reese Scholarship (5089) | | |
| United States Senate Youth Program (2835) | Citizenship: US, PermRes; Study: DC | |

| Vocational Goal, Award, and Entry Number | Geographic Restrictions (Citizenship, Legal Residence, Place of Study) | Affiliation/Special Recipients Requirements |
|---|---|---|
| **Visual and Performing Arts** | | |
| Ralph Brewster Vocal Scholarship/Jack Pullen Memorial Scholarship (3705) | | |
| Chautauqua Institution Scholarship (1842) | | |
| Delius Composition Contest for High School Composers (2214) | | |
| Dorchester Woman's Club Scholarships (2635) | Legal: MA | |
| GFWC of MA Art Scholarships (2636) | Legal: MA | |
| GFWC of MA Music Scholarships (2640) | Legal: MA | |
| The Elizabeth Greenshields Grant (2751) | | |
| Frances Hook Scholarship (2886) | | |
| Interlochen Arts Academy and Arts Camp Scholarships (3101) | Study: MI | |
| Glenn Miller Birthplace Society Instrumental Scholarships (3706) | | |
| National Symphony Young Soloists' Competition, High School Division (4420) | | |
| Jean Pratt Scholarship (1453) | Study: KS | |
| Scholastic Art and Writing Awards (5268) | | |
| World of Expression Scholarship Program (1420) | Legal: NY | |
| Young American Creative Patriotic Art Awards (3409) | Citizenship: US | |
| Young Feminist Scholarship Program (5591) | | |

# Other

| Vocational Goal, Award, and Entry Number | Geographic Restrictions | Affiliation/Special Recipients Requirements |
|---|---|---|
| **Agriculture** | | |
| Bedding Plants Foundation Vocational Scholarships (1381) | Citizenship: US, Canada | |
| Caribou Research Bursary (1680) | Citizenship: Canada | |
| Dairy Management Inc. Nutrition Research Projects (2168) | | |
| Lindbergh Grants (3484) | | |
| Scottish Gardening Scholarship (4277) | Study: Scotland | |
| Summer Internship Program (2551) | | |
| **Architecture and Environmental Design** | | |
| MacDowell Colony Residencies (3524) | Study: United States | |
| New York Foundation for the Arts Artists' Fellowships (4570) | Legal: NY | |
| **Area and Ethnic Studies** | | |
| James W. Bourque Studentship in Northern Geography (1679) | | |
| Bundeskanzler Scholarships (2681) | Study: Germany | |
| Dante B. Fascell Inter-American Fellowships (3089) | | |
| Pew Fellowships in International Journalism (4854) | Study: United States | |
| The Spalding Trust (5570) | | |
| SSRC Grants for Advanced Area Research (5399) | | |
| **Aviation** | | |
| Bell Helicopter Scholarship (3201) | | Association |
| Flight Safety International Instrument Refresher Course Scholarship (3202) | | Association |
| Lowell Gaylor Memorial Scholarship (85) | | |

| Vocational Goal, Award, and Entry Number | Geographic Restrictions (Citizenship, Legal Residence, Place of Study) | Affiliation/Special Recipients Requirements |
|---|---|---|
| **Business and Management** | | |
| American Institute for Economic Research Visiting Research Fellowship (581) | | |
| Harwood Memorial Real Estate Scholarship (5083) | | |
| **Communications** | | |
| American Bankers Association Fellowships (346) | Citizenship: US | |
| American Political Science Association-MCI Communications Fellowships for Scholars and Journalists (778) | | |
| American Press Institute Minority Journalism Educators Fellowship (791) | | Minority |
| American Society of Newspaper Editors Institute for Journalism Excellence (961) | | |
| Asian American Journalists Association National Internship Grant (1171) | | Association, Asian American |
| Barach Teaching Fellowships in Non-Fiction (6139) | | |
| Cissy Patterson Fellowship (792) | | |
| Donrey Media Group Internships (2270) | | |
| Walter Everett Fellowship (793) | | |
| Gannett Center Fellowships (2593) | Study: NY | |
| Hawaii Society of Professional Journalists Internships (2824) | Legal: HI | |
| John E. Heselden Fellowship (794) | | |
| Investigative Reporters and Editors Minority Conference Fellowships (6006) | | Minority |
| *Arizona Daily Star* Frank E. Johnson Scholarship (795) | | Minority |
| Kaiser Media Internships in Urban Health Reporting (3313) | | Minority |
| Lindbergh Grants (3484) | | |
| *The Nation* Internships Program (3822) | | |
| The National Scholarship Trust Fund Scholarships for Undergraduates (4375) | | |
| *Omaha World-Herald* Intern Scholarships (4749) | | |
| The Oregonian Minority Internship Program (4805) | | Minority |
| James H. Ottaway Sr. Fellowships (797) | | |
| Philip S. Weld Sr. Fellowship (798) | | |
| **Education** | | |
| Civil Air Patrol Technical/Vocational Scholarships (3916) | | Association |
| Contemplative Practice Fellowship (410) | | |
| John Haynes Holmes Memorial Fund (2023) | | Religion |
| Lindbergh Grants (3484) | | |
| Robert H. Michel Civic Education Grants (2254) | | |
| Margaret & Charles E. Stewart Grant (5630) | | |
| Teacher as Researcher Grant (3181) | | Association |
| U.S. Department of Education OERI Visiting Scholars Fellowship (4360) | | |
| William Winter Teacher Scholar Loan Program (3746) | Legal: MS; Study: MS | |
| **Engineering** | | |
| Major General Lucas Beau Flight Scholarship (3914) | | Military |

| Vocational Goal, Award, and Entry Number | Geographic Restrictions (Citizenship, Legal Residence, Place of Study) | Affiliation/Special Recipients Requirements |
|---|---|---|
| *Engineering (continued)* | | |
| Civil Air Patrol Technical/Vocational Scholarships (3916) | | Association |
| Lindbergh Grants (3484) | | |
| NASA Administrator's Fellowship Program (4359) | | |
| NSF-DAAD Grants for the Natural, Engineering and Social Sciences (2689) | Study: Germany | |
| Eleanor Roosevelt Teacher Fellowships (338) | Citizenship: US, PermRes | |

**Foreign Languages**

| | | |
|---|---|---|
| Arabic Translation Contest (323) | | |
| Contemporary Literature Grant (2682) | Study: Germany | |

**Health Care Services**

| | | |
|---|---|---|
| Dairy Management Inc. Nutrition Research Projects (2168) | | |
| Florida Dental Association Dental Hygiene Scholarship Program (2487) | Legal: FL | |
| WHO Fellowships and Research Training Grants (6261) | | |
| Maxine Williams Scholarships (317) | | |

**Health Sciences**

| | | |
|---|---|---|
| Foundation for Physical Therapy Research Grant (2576) | | |
| HRSA-BHP Nursing Student Loan (5970) | Citizenship: US | |
| International Founders' Fund Awards (1702) | | Association |
| Lindbergh Grants (3484) | | |
| Nursing Research Fellowship (3811) | | |
| Oklahoma State Regents Chiropractic Education Assistance (4737) | Legal: OK; Study: OK | |
| M. K. Wang Visiting Professorships (360) | Study: Taiwan | |
| WHO Fellowships and Research Training Grants (6261) | | |

**Home Economics**

| | | |
|---|---|---|
| Industry Assistance Grants (4363) | | |
| Kappa Omicron Nu Research/Project Grant (3337) | | Fraternal |
| ProMgmt. Scholarship (4368) | | |

**Humanities**

| | | |
|---|---|---|
| Konrad Adenauer Research Award (6071) | Legal: Canada; Study: Germany | |
| Chinese Fellowships for Scholarly Development (409) | Legal: People's Republic of China | |
| Lindbergh Grants (3484) | | |
| SSRC Grants for Advanced Area Research (5399) | | |

**Industry and Trade**

| | | |
|---|---|---|
| Marin Education Grant for Short-Term and Long-Term Occupational Study (3553) | Citizenship: US, PermRes; Legal: CA | |
| The National Scholarship Trust Fund Scholarships for Undergraduates (4375) | | |

**Language and Literature**

| | | |
|---|---|---|
| Coast Guard Essay Contest (5950) | | |
| Dobie-Paisano Fellowships (2262) | Study: TX | |
| Iowa School of Letters Award for Short Fiction (3225) | | |
| Lindbergh Grants (3484) | | |
| MacDowell Colony Residencies (3524) | Study: United States | |

| Vocational Goal, Award, and Entry Number | Geographic Restrictions (Citizenship, Legal Residence, Place of Study) | Affiliation/Special Recipients Requirements |
|---|---|---|
| *Language and Literature (continued)* | | |
| New York Foundation for the Arts Artists' Fellowships (4570) | Legal: NY | |
| W.D. Weatherford Award (1054) | | |

## Liberal/General Studies

| | | |
|---|---|---|
| Academic-Year Ambassadorial Scholarship (5167) | | |
| Association on American Indian Affairs Displaced Homemaker Scholarships (1212) | | Native American |
| Blind Service Association Scholarship Awards (1442) | Legal: IL | Handicapped |
| Child of Disabled Veteran Grant or Purple Heart Recipient, Grant (2996) | Legal: IN; Study: IN | Veteran |
| Cooperatives Bursary (1681) | Citizenship: Canada | |
| CSF Special Purpose Grants (1697) | Citizenship: Canada | |
| Voice of Democracy Scholarship Contest (6040) | | |
| Displaced Homemaker Scholarships (1213) | | |
| Duracell/NSTA Scholarship Competition (4381) | Legal: United States | |
| Florida Division of Blind Services Vocational Rehabilitation Program (2517) | Legal: FL | Handicapped |
| Gerber Companies Foundation Scholarships (2677) | | Employer |
| Loan Assistant Repayment Program (3571) | Legal: MD | |
| Louisiana Rehabilitation Services Award (3506) | Legal: LA | Handicapped |
| Louisiana State Aid Dependents Educational Assistance (3500) | Legal: LA; Study: LA | Veteran |
| Marine Corps Essay Contest (5954) | | |
| Mellon Resident Research Fellowships (767) | | |
| Multi-Year Ambassadorial Scholarship (5170) | | |
| National Fourth Infantry Division Association Scholarship (4171) | | Veteran |
| Nevada Women's Fund Scholarships (4521) | Legal: NV | |
| N. Neal Pike Prize for Service to People with Disabilities (4947) | | Handicapped |
| Colin L. Powell Joint Warfighting Essay Contest (5956) | | |
| Quaker Chemical Foundation Scholarships (5037) | | Employer |
| The Spalding Trust (5570) | | |
| Special Bursary For Northern Residents (1683) | Citizenship: Canada | |
| Irene Stambler Vocational Opportunities Grants (3271) | Legal: DC, MD, VA | Ethnic |
| Tuition/Book Scholarship (2896) | | |
| Venture Student Aid Award for Physically Disabled Students (6028) | | Handicapped |
| Warner Trust Loan Program (6079) | Legal: CA; Study: CA | |
| Watson Fellowships (6119) | | |
| Wisconsin Department of Veterans Affairs Retraining Grant (6210) | Legal: WI; Study: WI | Veteran |
| YLD Scholarships (6287) | Citizenship: US; Study: NC | Employer |

## Library and Archival Sciences

| | | |
|---|---|---|
| AASL/Highsmith Research Grant (642) | | Association |
| ABC-CLIO Leadership Grant (643) | | Association |
| Blance E. Woolls Scholarship for School Library Media Service (1426) | | |

## Life Sciences

| | | |
|---|---|---|
| Cancer Research Institute Clinical Investigator Award (1714) | | |

| Vocational Goal, Award, and Entry Number | Geographic Restrictions (Citizenship, Legal Residence, Place of Study) | Affiliation/Special Recipients Requirements |
|---|---|---|
| *Life Sciences (continued)* | | |
| Lindbergh Grants (3484) | | |
| North American Loon Fund Grants (4644) | | |
| **Medicine** | | |
| American Liver Foundation Student Research Fellowships (674) | | |
| Cancer Research Fellowship Program (3407) | | |
| CFF/NIH Funding Award (2150) | | |
| Cystic Fibrosis Foundation Research Grants (2156) | | |
| Grant Foundation Faculty Scholars Program (2739) | | |
| H. William Harris Visiting Professorship (359) | Study: Taiwan | |
| JDFI Innovative Grants (3309) | | |
| Loan Assistant Repayment Program for Medical Residents in Primary Care (3572) | Legal: MD | |
| Pilot and Feasibility Awards (2163) | | |
| Research Fellowships (3196) | | |
| Therapuetics Development Grants (2166) | | |
| WHO Fellowships and Research Training Grants (6261) | | |
| **Military Sciences** | | |
| Vincent Astor Memorial Leadership Essay Contest (5949) | | Military |
| Coast Guard Essay Contest (5950) | | |
| Enlisted Essay Contest (5951) | | Military |
| International Navies Essay Contest (5952) | | |
| International Navies Photo Contest (5953) | | |
| **Philosophy, Theology, and Religion** | | |
| American Academy of Religion Research Assistance and Collaborative Research Grants (242) | | Association |
| John Haynes Holmes Memorial Fund (2023) | | Religion |
| The Spalding Trust (5570) | | |
| Women in United Methodist History Research Grants (2632) | | |
| Women in United Methodist History Writing Awards (2633) | | |
| **Physical Sciences** | | |
| American Alpine Club Grants (250) | | |
| Chemical Heritage Foundation Travel Grants (1899) | Study: PA | |
| Lindbergh Grants (3484) | | |
| Summer Faculty Fellowships (5561) | | |
| A. Verville Fellowship (5381) | Study: United States | |
| **Social Sciences** | | |
| AAUW Educational Foundation Community Action Grants (333) | Citizenship: US, PermRes | |
| Konrad Adenauer Research Award (6071) | Legal: Canada; Study: Germany | |
| Weston A. Cate, Jr. Annual Research Fellowship (6030) | | |
| Center for Strategic and Budgetary Assessments Internship (1805) | Study: DC | |
| Chemical Heritage Foundation Travel Grants (1899) | Study: PA | |
| Chinese Fellowships for Scholarly Development (409) | Legal: People's Republic of China | |

| Vocational Goal, Award, and Entry Number | Geographic Restrictions (Citizenship, Legal Residence, Place of Study) | Affiliation/Special Recipients Requirements |
|---|---|---|
| *Social Sciences (continued)* | | |
| Paul Cuffe Memorial Fellowship for the Study of Minorities in American Maritime History (3794) | Study: MA | |
| Dante B. Fascell Inter-American Fellowships (3089) | | |
| NSF-DAAD Grants for the Natural, Engineering and Social Sciences (2689) | Study: Germany | |
| Pew Fellowships in International Journalism (4854) | Study: United States | |
| SSRC Grants for Advanced Area Research (5399) | | |
| A. Verville Fellowship (5381) | Study: United States | |
| Women in United Methodist History Research Grants (2632) | | |
| Women in United Methodist History Writing Awards (2633) | | |
| Woodswomen Scholarship Fund (6255) | | Association |

## Visual and Performing Arts

| | | |
|---|---|---|
| Curtis Institute of Music Scholarships (2144) | Study: PA | |
| Chester Dale Fellowship (1769) | Study: United States | |
| Delius Composition Contest (2213) | | |
| Delta Omicron International Triennial Composition Competition (2221) | | |
| Emergency Assistance Grants (2719) | | |
| The Fund for U.S. Artists at International Festivals and Exhibitions (1164) | | |
| The Elizabeth Greenshields Grant (2751) | | |
| Greenshields Grants (2752) | | |
| Japanese American Citizens League Creative Arts Award (3244) | | Ethnic |
| Lindbergh Grants (3484) | | |
| MacDowell Colony Residencies (3524) | Study: United States | |
| National Sculpture Society Scholarships (4384) | | |
| Walter W. Naumburg Awards (4477) | | |
| Naval and Maritime Photo Contest (5955) | | |
| NEA/TCG Career Development Program for Designers (5724) | Citizenship: US, PermRes | |
| NEA/TCG Career Development Program for Directors (5725) | Citizenship: US | |
| New Hampshire Individual Artist Fellowships (4535) | Legal: NH; Study: NH | |
| New York Foundation for the Arts Artists' Fellowships (4570) | Legal: NY | |
| Travel Grants for Independent Short-Term Research (3190) | Study: Union of Soviet Socialist Republics | |
| Visiting Senior Research Fellowship Program for Scholars from East and South Asia (1781) | Citizenship: Other | |
| World Model Awards (6266) | | |

# Postdoctorate

## Agriculture

| | | |
|---|---|---|
| AIBS Congressional Science Fellowship (476) | Citizenship: US, PermRes; Study: United States | Association |
| Biotechnology Career Fellowships (5147) | | |
| Competitive Grants-in-Aid for Original Research (4286) | Study: United States | |
| Corn Refiners Association Research Funds (2087) | | |
| Horticultural Research Institute Grants (2898) | | |

| Vocational Goal, Award, and Entry Number | Geographic Restrictions (Citizenship, Legal Residence, Place of Study) | Affiliation/Special Recipients Requirements |
|---|---|---|
| *Agriculture (continued)* | | |
| NAS/NRC Collaboration in Basic Science and Engineering Long-Term Grants (3831) | Citizenship: US | |
| NAS/NRC Collaboration in Basic Science and Engineering Short-Term Project Development Grants (3832) | Citizenship: US | |
| Research Grants in Wildlife Conservation (6178) | | |
| Shade Tree Research Grants (3192) | | |
| Social Science Research Fellowships in Agriculture (5152) | | |

## Architecture and Environmental Design

| | | |
|---|---|---|
| Center for Advanced Study in the Visual Arts Senior Fellowships and Senior Visiting Fellowships (1767) | Study: United States | |
| Fellowships in Byzantine Studies, Pre-Columbian Studies and Landscape Architecture (2288) | Study: DC | |
| Frese Senior Research Fellowship Program (1773) | Citizenship: Germany; Study: DC | |
| Andrew W. Mellon Fellowships in Conservation (3659) | Study: United States | |
| Michael Ventris Memorial Award (3017) | | |

## Area and Ethnic Studies

| | | |
|---|---|---|
| AAS-NEAC U.S. Research Travel Grants (1220) | Citizenship: US, PermRes; Study: United States | |
| ACLS Grants for East European Studies - Fellowships for Postdoctoral Research (408) | Citizenship: US, PermRes | |
| AIATSIS Research Grants (1327) | Study: Australia | |
| AIIS Fellowship for Senior Scholarly Development (585) | Study: India | |
| AIIS Senior Research Fellowships (587) | Study: India | |
| AIMS Small Grants (590) | Citizenship: US/CA, Mexico | Association |
| American Institute of Pakistan Studies Predoctoral and Postdoctoral Fellowships (596) | Citizenship: US; Study: Pakistan | |
| American Jewish Studies Fellowships (598) | Study: United States | |
| American Research Center in Egypt Research Fellowships for Study in Egypt (843) | Citizenship: US, PermRes; Legal: United States; Study: Egypt | |
| Ancient India and Iran Trust Travel and Research Grants (1035) | | |
| Annual Professorship in Jerusalem (864) | | |
| APDC Visiting Fellowships (1182) | Study: Malaysia | |
| ARIT Fellowships (846) | Study: Canada, Turkey, United States | |
| Asian American Studies Center Postdoctoral Fellowship/Visiting Scholars Awards (1174) | Study: United States | |
| Asian Art and Religion Fellowships (1176) | Citizenship: US | |
| George A. Barton Fellowship (865) | | |
| David Baumgardt Memorial Fellowships (1355) | | |
| Harry J. Benda Prize (1223) | | |
| Bulgarian Studies Seminar (3183) | Citizenship: US, PermRes | |
| Canadian Studies Faculty Research Grants (1625) | Legal: United States | |
| Gilbert Chinard Scholarships (3041) | Study: France | |
| The James Bryant Conant Fellowships for Postdoctoral Research (2765) | Citizenship: US/CA; Study: MA | |
| Czech Education Scholarships (3708) | Study: Slovakia | |
| Davis Center for Russian Studies Postdoctoral Fellowships (2191) | Study: MA | |
| Dorot Research Fellowship (867) | | |
| Rose and Isidore Drench Fellowships (6284) | Study: United States | |

| Vocational Goal, Award, and Entry Number | Geographic Restrictions (Citizenship, Legal Residence, Place of Study) | Affiliation/Special Recipients Requirements |
|---|---|---|
| *Area and Ethnic Studies (continued)* | | |
| Du Bois Mandela Rodney Postdoctoral Fellowships (1784) | Study: United States | |
| Dublin Institute for Advanced Studies Research Scholarships (2282) | Study: Ireland | |
| East-West Center Visiting Fellowships (2311) | Study: United States | |
| Endowment for Biblical Research, Summer Research and Travel Grants (868) | | |
| Ford Foundation Fellowships (1178) | Citizenship: Other; Study: United States | |
| Grants-in-Aid of Publication (4879) | | |
| Humanities Fellowships (1179) | Citizenship: US | |
| Institute of American Cultures Postdoctoral and Visiting Scholars Fellowships (3013) | Study: CA | |
| IREX Research Residencies (3186) | Citizenship: US, PermRes | |
| IREX Short-Term Travel Grants for Independent Short-Term Research (3187) | Citizenship: US, PermRes; Study: Union of Soviet Socialist Republics | |
| H. Kellogg Institute Residential Fellowships (3347) | Study: United States | |
| Joseph Levenson Prizes (1218) | | |
| The National Council Research Contracts (3945) | Citizenship: US, PermRes; Legal: United States | |
| National Program for Advanced Study and Research in China - Research Program (2016) | Study: People's Republic of China | |
| Near and Middle East Research and Training Program Senior Research Grants (881) | Citizenship: US | |
| NEH Fellowships for Research in Turkey (847) | Study: Canada, Turkey, United States | |
| Neporany Research and Teaching Fellowship (1661) | | |
| Phillips Grants for North American Indian Research (769) | | |
| Pre- and Postdoctoral Fellowships in International and Area Studies (2804) | Study: United States | |
| Rockefeller Fellows Programs (1785) | | |
| Short-term Travel Grants to Japan (1221) | Citizenship: US; Study: Japan | |
| Mary Isabel Sibley Fellowships (4894) | | |
| SSRC African Advanced Research Grants (5395) | Citizenship: US, PermRes | |
| SSRC African Humanities Fellowships (5396) | Study: IL | |
| SSRC Berlin Program for Advanced German and European Studies Fellowships (5398) | Citizenship: US, PermRes; Study: Germany | |
| SSRC Japan Advanced Research Grants (5403) | Citizenship: US, PermRes | |
| SSRC Japan Grants for Research Planning Activities (5405) | | |
| SSRC Korea Advanced Research Grants (5406) | Citizenship: US, PermRes | |
| SSRC Korea Grants for Research Planning Activities (5407) | | |
| SSRC Latin America and the Caribbean Advanced Research Grants (5408) | Citizenship: US, PermRes | |
| SSRC Near and Middle East Advanced Research Fellowships (5411) | Citizenship: US, PermRes | |
| SSRC South Asia Advanced Research Grants (5414) | Citizenship: US, PermRes | |
| SSRC Southeast Asia Advanced Research Grants (5416) | Citizenship: US, PermRes | |
| SSRC Soviet Union and Its Successor States Postdoctoral Fellowships (5421) | Citizenship: US | |
| SSRC Soviet Union and Its Successor States Workshop Grants (5422) | | |
| Touro National Heritage Trust Fellowship (1517) | Study: RI | |

| Vocational Goal, Award, and Entry Number | Geographic Restrictions (Citizenship, Legal Residence, Place of Study) | Affiliation/Special Recipients Requirements |
|---|---|---|
| ***Area and Ethnic Studies (continued)*** | | |
| United States Information Agency (USIA) Fellowships (884) | Citizenship: US | |
| USIA Fellowships, AIAR, Jerusalem (885) | Citizenship: US | |
| Moritz and Charlotte Warbourg Research Fellowships (2849) | Study: Israel | |
| **Business and Management** | | |
| APDC Visiting Fellowships (1182) | Study: Malaysia | |
| CIR Postdoctoral Fellowship (5986) | Study: United States | |
| Fellowships in Ethics (5015) | Study: United States | |
| Fellowships in National Security (2812) | Study: United States | |
| William C. Foster Fellows Visiting Scholars Competition (5818) | Citizenship: US | |
| John Grenzebach Awards for Outstanding Research in Philanthropy for Education (12) | | |
| Harvard-Newcomen Postdoctoral Fellowship (4627) | Study: MA | |
| Huebner Foundation Postdoctoral Fellowships (2919) | Citizenship: US/CA; Study: PA, United States | |
| Institute of Developing Economies Visiting Research Fellowships (3027) | Study: Japan | |
| Ministry of the Flemish Community Fellowships (3710) | Citizenship: US, PermRes | |
| Population Council Fellowships in the Social Sciences (4981) | | |
| Reflections on Development Fellowships (5150) | | |
| Rockefeller Archive Center Research Grants (5142) | Study: United States | |
| Social Science Research Fellowships in Population (5153) | Citizenship: US/CA | |
| UNITAR Internships (5803) | Study: United States | |
| Upjohn Institute Grants (6015) | | |
| Wharton Doctoral and Postdoctoral Fellowships In Risk & Insurance (2920) | Citizenship: US/CA; Study: PA | |
| **Communications** | | |
| R.C. Hoiles and IHS Postdoctoral Fellowships (3052) | | |
| Hoover Library Fellowships and Grants (2890) | Study: United States | |
| Rennie Taylor/Alton Blakeslee Memorial Fellowship in Science Writing (2091) | Citizenship: US | |
| **Computer and Information Sciences** | | |
| Argonne National Laboratory Faculty Research Leave; Faculty Research Participation Awards (1083) | Citizenship: US, PermRes; Legal: United States; Study: United States | |
| ASIS Doctoral Forum Awards (934) | | |
| Bunting Institute Science Scholars Fellowships and Biomedical Research Fellowships (1529) | Citizenship: US, PermRes; Study: MA | |
| Center for Judaic Studies Postdoctoral Fellowships (1799) | | |
| Department of Energy Distinguished Postdoctoral Research Program (5868) | | |
| William C. Foster Fellows Visiting Scholars Competition (5818) | Citizenship: US | |
| Global Change Distinguished Postdoctoral Fellowships (5882) | | |
| Human Genome Distinguished Postdoctoral Fellowships (5896) | | |
| IBM Postdoctoral Research Fellowships in Mathematical Sciences (2948) | Study: NY | |
| Jansky Fellowships (4351) | Study: United States | |

| Vocational Goal, Award, and Entry Number | Geographic Restrictions (Citizenship, Legal Residence, Place of Study) | Affiliation/Special Recipients Requirements |
|---|---|---|
| *Computer and Information Sciences (continued)* | | |
| NAS/NRC Collaboration in Basic Science and Engineering Long-Term Grants (3831) | Citizenship: US | |
| NAS/NRC Collaboration in Basic Science and Engineering Short-Term Project Development Grants (3832) | Citizenship: US | |
| Oak Ridge National Laboratory Postdoctoral Research Associates Program (5917) | | |
| U.S. Air Force Phillips Laboratory Scholar Program (4686) | Citizenship: US; Study: MA | |
| U.S. Department of Energy Distinguished Postdoctoral Research Fellowship (4708) | Citizenship: US, PermRes | |
| U.S. Department of Energy Global Change Distinguished Postdoctoral Fellowships (4709) | Citizenship: US, PermRes | |
| **Education** | | |
| ETS Center for Performance Assessment Postdoctoral Fellowships (2352) | Study: NJ, United States | |
| ETS Postdoctoral Fellowships (2353) | Study: NJ, United States | |
| Hollingworth Award Competition (3877) | | |
| Hoover Institution National Fellowships (2888) | Study: United States | |
| Juniper Gardens Post-Doctoral Fellowship in Research with Minority Handicapped Children (3306) | | |
| National Assessment of Educational Progress Visiting Scholar Program (2355) | Study: NJ, United States | |
| NCTE Teacher-Researcher Grants (3962) | | Association |
| Rockefeller Archive Center Research Grants (5142) | Study: United States | |
| Spencer Foundation Small Grants (5587) | Study: United States | |
| Spencer Postdoctoral Fellowships (3829) | | |
| **Engineering** | | |
| AAAS Congressional Science and Engineering Fellowships (263) | Study: United States | |
| AAAS-EPA Environmental Science and Engineering Fellowships (265) | Legal: United States | |
| AAAS Science, Engineering, and Diplomacy Fellows Program (266) | Citizenship: US | |
| AAAS Technology Policy Science and Engineering Fellowships (267) | Citizenship: US; Study: United States | |
| Annual Travel Fellowship (6116) | Study: England | |
| Argonne National Laboratory Faculty Research Leave; Faculty Research Participation Awards (1083) | Citizenship: US, PermRes; Legal: United States; Study: United States | |
| Army Research Laboratory Postdoctoral Fellowship Program (922) | | |
| AWU Post-Graduate Fellowship (1202) | Citizenship: US, PermRes; Study: CA, CO, ID, ND, NM, OK | |
| Bunting Institute Science Scholars Fellowships and Biomedical Research Fellowships (1529) | Citizenship: US, PermRes; Study: MA | |
| Center for Judaic Studies Postdoctoral Fellowships (1799) | | |
| Chateaubriand Scholarship (Scientifique) (2372) | Citizenship: US; Study: France | |
| Trent R. Dames and William W. Moore Fellowship (903) | | |
| Department of Energy Distinguished Postdoctoral Research Program (5868) | | |
| DOE Student Research Participation (4705) | Citizenship: US, PermRes | |
| Environmental Monitoring Systems Laboratory Research Participation Program (5869) | | |
| Ford Foundation Postdoctoral Fellowships for Minorities (4356) | Citizenship: US | Minority |

| Vocational Goal, Award, and Entry Number | Geographic Restrictions (Citizenship, Legal Residence, Place of Study) | Affiliation/Special Recipients Requirements |
|---|---|---|
| **Engineering (continued)** | | |
| William C. Foster Fellows Visiting Scholars Competition (5818) | Citizenship: US | |
| Fusion Energy Postdoctoral Research Program (5881) | | |
| Global Change Distinguished Postdoctoral Fellowships (5882) | | |
| Government of Canada Awards (3145) | Citizenship: France, Germany, Japan, Mexico; Study: Canada | |
| IEEE Fellowship in Electrical History (3033) | | |
| Jansky Fellowships (4351) | Study: United States | |
| Killam Research Fellowships (3375) | Legal: Canada | |
| Manulife Financial Scholarships (1617) | Study: Canada | Association |
| Meloche-Monnex Scholarship (1618) | Study: Canada | Association |
| NAS/NRC Collaboration in Basic Science and Engineering Long-Term Grants (3831) | Citizenship: US | |
| NAS/NRC Collaboration in Basic Science and Engineering Short-Term Project Development Grants (3832) | Citizenship: US | |
| NASA Field Center Resident Research Associateships (3838) | Citizenship: US; Study: United States | |
| National Research Council of Canada Research Associateships (4354) | | |
| Naval Research Laboratory Postdoctoral Fellowship Program (924) | Citizenship: US | |
| NSERC Research Scholarships, Fellowships, and Grants (4474) | Citizenship: Canada, PermRes; Study: Canada | |
| Oak Ridge National Laboratory Postdoctoral Research Associates Program (5917) | | |
| Petroleum Research Fund Grants (369) | Legal: United States; Study: United States | |
| Postdoctoral Fellowships in the Atmospheric Sciences (3931) | Study: United States | |
| Risk Reduction Engineering Research Laboratory Research Participation Program (5923) | | |
| J. Waldo Smith Hydraulic Fellowship (905) | | Association |
| Tennessee Valley Authority Research Participation Program (5927) | | |
| Tyndall Air Force Base Research Participation Program (5928) | | |
| Morris K. Udall OTA Congressional Fellowship (5851) | | |
| U.S. Air Force Phillips Laboratory Scholar Program (4686) | Citizenship: US; Study: MA | |
| U.S. Army Construction Engineering Research Laboratory Research Participation Program (5930) | | |
| U.S. Army Environmental Hygiene Agency Internship Program (5931) | | |
| U.S. Department of Energy Distinguished Postdoctoral Research Fellowship (4708) | Citizenship: US, PermRes | |
| U.S. Navy ONR-ASEE Postdoctoral Fellowship (926) | Citizenship: US; Study: CA, CT, DC, FL, MD, MS, PA, RI, VA | |

### Foreign Languages

| Vocational Goal, Award, and Entry Number | Geographic Restrictions | Affiliation/Special Recipients Requirements |
|---|---|---|
| South Central Modern Languages Association Fellowship (4624) | Study: IL | Association |

### Health Care Services

| Vocational Goal, Award, and Entry Number | Geographic Restrictions | Affiliation/Special Recipients Requirements |
|---|---|---|
| AHCPR Individual National Research Service Awards (62) | Citizenship: US, PermRes | |
| ESRI Doctoral Training Grants; ESRI Postdoctoral Fellowships (2316) | Citizenship: Canada; Legal: Canada; Study: Canada | |

| Vocational Goal, Award, and Entry Number | Geographic Restrictions (Citizenship, Legal Residence, Place of Study) | Affiliation/Special Recipients Requirements |
|---|---|---|
| **Health Care Services (continued)** | | |
| Florida Dental Health Foundation Student Loans (2492) | Study: FL | |
| Postdoctoral Fellowships in Health Policy and Health Services Research (3045) | Citizenship: US, PermRes; Study: United States | |
| WHO Fellowships and Research Training Grants (6261) | | |
| **Health Sciences** | | |
| American Speech-Language-Hearing Foundation Research Grants for New Investigators (990) | Study: United States | |
| Arthritis Society Research Fellowships (1155) | Study: Canada | |
| Arthritis Society Research Grants (1156) | Citizenship: Canada, PermRes; Legal: Canada; Study: Canada | |
| Arthritis Society Research Scientist Award (1158) | Study: Canada | |
| Behavioral Sciences Research Training Fellowship (2396) | | |
| Biotechnology Career Fellowships (5147) | | |
| Cancer Prevention and Control Research Small Grant Program (3922) | | |
| Career Development Fellowships (1611) | Citizenship: Canada, PermRes; Study: Canada | |
| Clinical Research Fellowship (2398) | Study: United States | |
| EORTC/NCI Exchange Program (3923) | | |
| Epilepsy Foundation of America Research Grants (2399) | | |
| FIC Bilateral Exchanges (2525) | | |
| FIC International Research Fellowships (2528) | Study: United States | |
| FIC Senior International Fellowships (2529) | Citizenship: US, PermRes | |
| FIC Visiting Fellowships (2531) | Study: United States | |
| Fogarty International Research Collaboration Award (2532) | | |
| Health Canada Research Personnel Career Awards (2828) | Citizenship: Canada, PermRes; Legal: Canada | |
| HRC Postdoctoral Fellowship (2831) | Study: New Zealand | |
| Killam Research Fellowships (3375) | Legal: Canada | |
| William G. Lennox International Clinical Research Fellowship; Fritz E. Dreifuss International Visiting Professorships (2402) | | |
| Mead Johnson Nutritional Perinatal Research Grants Program (5337) | Citizenship: US | |
| NCI International Bilateral Program (3924) | | |
| NINR Individual National Research Service Awards Postdoctoral Fellowship (4201) | | |
| NINR Individual National Research Service Awards Senior Fellowship (4203) | | |
| Metro A. Ogryzlo International Fellowship (1159) | Study: Canada | |
| Oncology Research Faculty Development Program (3925) | | |
| Gustavus A. Pfeiffer Faculty Development Postdoctoral Research Fellowship (491) | | |
| Population Council Fellowships in the Social Sciences (4981) | | |
| Research Grant in Speech Science (993) | | |
| G. D. Searle & Co. Faculty Development Research Fellowship in Pharmacoeconomics (494) | | |
| Washington Health Professional Loan Repayment and Scholarship Program (6099) | | |
| WHO Fellowships (6259) | | |

| Vocational Goal, Award, and Entry Number | Geographic Restrictions (Citizenship, Legal Residence, Place of Study) | Affiliation/Special Recipients Requirements |
|---|---|---|
| *Health Sciences (continued)* | | |
| WHO Fellowships for Canadian Citizens (6260) | Citizenship: Canada | |
| WHO Fellowships and Research Training Grants (6261) | | |
| WHO Fellowships for U.S. Citizens (6262) | Citizenship: US | |
| **Humanities** | | |
| ACLS Fellowships (406) | Citizenship: US, PermRes | |
| ACLS Grants for East European Studies - Fellowships for Postdoctoral Research (408) | Citizenship: US, PermRes | |
| ARIT Fellowships (846) | Study: Canada, Turkey, United States | |
| Artists Fellowship; Japan Foundation Cultural Properties Specialists Fellowship; Japan Foundation Doctoral Fellowship; Japan Foundation Research Fellowship (3240) | Study: Japan | |
| Australian National University Visiting Fellowships (1333) | Study: Australia | |
| Beinecke Library Visiting Fellowships (1393) | Study: United States | |
| British Academy Visiting Professorships for Overseas Scholars (1480) | | |
| Oscar Broneer Fellowship (856) | Study: Greece | Other |
| Lester J. Cappon Fellowship in Documentary Editing (4602) | | |
| Anna C. and Oliver C. Colburn Fellowship (857) | Study: Greece | Other |
| President Francisco Cossiga Fellowship (4603) | Legal: Italy | |
| Du Bois Mandela Rodney Postdoctoral Fellowships (1784) | Study: United States | |
| Earhart Foundation Fellowship Research Grants (2302) | | |
| Fellowships in Byzantine Studies, Pre-Columbian Studies and Landscape Architecture (2288) | Study: DC | |
| Getty Center Postdoctoral Fellowships (2699) | | |
| Government of Canada Awards (3145) | Citizenship: France, Germany, Japan, Mexico; Study: Canada | |
| R.C. Hoiles and IHS Postdoctoral Fellowships (3052) | | |
| Hoover Institution National Fellowships (2888) | Study: United States | |
| Humanities Research Centre Visiting Fellowships (2933) | Study: Australia | |
| Institute for Advanced Studies Visiting Research Fellowships (3007) | Study: Scotland | |
| Institute for European History Fellowships (3035) | Study: Germany | |
| IREX Short-Term Travel Grants for Independent Short-Term Research (3187) | Citizenship: US, PermRes; Study: Union of Soviet Socialist Republics | |
| Neil Ker Memorial Fund Grants (1481) | | |
| Audrey Lumsden-Kouvel Fellowship (4605) | | |
| Andrew W. Mellon Postdoctoral Fellowships in the Humanities (5597) | Study: United States | |
| Mellon Postdoctoral Research Fellowships (4607) | | |
| National Endowment for the Humanities Post-Doctoral Fellowships, Nicosia (879) | Citizenship: US | |
| National Humanities Center Residential, Advanced Postdoctoral Fellowships (4184) | Study: United States | |
| National Program for Advanced Study and Research in China - Research Program (2016) | Study: People's Republic of China | |
| NEH Fellowship for University Teachers (3985) | | |
| NEH Fellowships for College Teachers and Independent Scholars (3986) | | |
| NEH Fellowships for Research in Turkey (847) | Study: Canada, Turkey, United States | |

| Vocational Goal, Award, and Entry Number | Geographic Restrictions (Citizenship, Legal Residence, Place of Study) | Affiliation/Special Recipients Requirements |
|---|---|---|
| *Humanities (continued)* | | |
| NEH Interpretive Research Grants (3987) | Citizenship: US, PermRes | |
| NEH Post-Doctoral Research (882) | Citizenship: US | |
| NEH Reference Materials Grants (3988) | Citizenship: US, PermRes | |
| NEH Summer Stipend (3990) | | |
| Newberry-British Academy Fellowship (4620) | | |
| Rockefeller Fellows Programs (1785) | | |
| Rockefeller Foundation Residential Fellowships in Gender Studies in Early Modern Europe (4608) | | |
| Rockefeller Humanities Fellowship (5151) | Study: United States | |
| Social Sciences and Humanities Research Council Postdoctoral Fellowships (5426) | Citizenship: Canada, PermRes | |
| Society for the Humanities Fellowships (5459) | | |
| Society for the Humanities Postdoctoral Fellowships (5456) | Study: United States | |
| South Central Language Association Fellowship (4610) | | Association |
| Spencer Foundation Fellowships in the History of Education (4611) | | |
| SSRC Abe Fellowship Program (5392) | Study: Japan, United States | |
| SSRC African Advanced Research Grants (5395) | Citizenship: US, PermRes | |
| SSRC African Humanities Fellowships (5396) | Study: IL | |
| SSRC Berlin Program for Advanced German and European Studies Fellowships (5398) | Citizenship: US, PermRes; Study: Germany | |
| SSRC Japan Advanced Research Grants (5403) | Citizenship: US, PermRes | |
| SSRC Korea Advanced Research Grants (5406) | Citizenship: US, PermRes | |
| SSRC Korea Grants for Research Planning Activities (5407) | | |
| SSRC Latin America and the Caribbean Advanced Research Grants (5408) | Citizenship: US, PermRes | |
| SSRC Near and Middle East Advanced Research Fellowships (5411) | Citizenship: US, PermRes | |
| SSRC Southeast Asia Advanced Research Grants (5416) | Citizenship: US, PermRes | |
| SSRC Soviet Union and Its Successor States Postdoctoral Fellowships (5421) | Citizenship: US | |
| Villa I Tatti Fellowships (6044) | | |
| Lewis Walpole Library Fellowship (6277) | Study: CT | |
| Woodrow Wilson Center Residential Fellowship (6184) | | |

### Industry and Trade

| Vocational Goal, Award, and Entry Number | Geographic Restrictions | Affiliation/Special Recipients Requirements |
|---|---|---|
| Canadian Transportation Education Foundation Scholarships and Research Grants (1706) | Citizenship: Canada | |
| Hudson River Research Grants (2913) | | |
| Shared Research Equipment Program (5926) | | |
| Upjohn Institute Grants (6015) | | |
| Gilbert F. White Postdoctoral Fellowships (5112) | Study: DC | |

### Language and Literature

| Vocational Goal, Award, and Entry Number | Geographic Restrictions | Affiliation/Special Recipients Requirements |
|---|---|---|
| Beinecke Library Visiting Fellowships (1393) | Study: United States | |
| Bunting Fellowship (1526) | Study: MA | |
| Bunting Institute Affiliation Program (1527) | Study: MA | |
| Center for Hellenic Studies Fellowships (1793) | Study: DC | |
| ChLA Research Fellowships (1939) | | Association |
| Fellowship in Latin Lexicography (762) | Citizenship: US, PermRes; Study: Germany | |

| Vocational Goal, Award, and Entry Number | Geographic Restrictions (Citizenship, Legal Residence, Place of Study) | Affiliation/Special Recipients Requirements |
|---|---|---|
| **Language and Literature (continued)** | | |
| General Semantics Foundation Project Grants (2645) | | |
| Huntington Library Research Awards (2939) | Study: United States | |
| Neil Ker Memorial Fund Grants (1481) | | |
| NCTE Teacher-Researcher Grants (3962) | | Association |
| NEH Fellowships for Research in Turkey (847) | Study: Canada, Turkey, United States | |
| NHPRC/Fellowships in Historical Editing (4182) | | |
| Phillips Grants for North American Indian Research (769) | | |
| Reading/Literacy Research Fellowship (3178) | | Association |
| Yale Center for British Art Fellowships (6278) | Study: United States | |
| **Law** | | |
| ABA Mini-Grants (350) | | |
| Maxwell Boulton Junior Fellowship (3626) | Study: Canada | |
| DAAD Young Lawyers Program (2686) | Citizenship: US/CA; Study: Germany | |
| Fellowships in Ethics (5015) | Study: United States | |
| R.C. Hoiles and IHS Postdoctoral Fellowships (3052) | | |
| Hoover Institution National Fellowships (2888) | Study: United States | |
| Junior Research Program Grants Exchange with China (5980) | Citizenship: US; Study: People's Republic of China | |
| Ministry of the Flemish Community Fellowships (3710) | Citizenship: US, PermRes | |
| NAPIL Fellowships for Equal Justice (3893) | | |
| Henry M. Phillips Grants in Jurisprudence (768) | | |
| Specialist Program Grants Exchange with China (5981) | Citizenship: US; Study: People's Republic of China | |
| Teaching/Research Program Grants Exchange with China (5982) | Citizenship: US; Study: People's Republic of China | |
| Morris K. Udall OTA Congressional Fellowship (5851) | | |
| **Liberal/General Studies** | | |
| AAUW Educational Foundation American Fellowships (331) | Citizenship: US, PermRes | |
| AAUW Educational Foundation Career Development Grants (332) | Citizenship: US; Legal: United States | |
| AAUW Postdoctoral Fellowships (337) | Citizenship: US; Legal: United States | |
| Association of Commonwealth Universities Fellowships (1229) | Citizenship: Commonwealth | |
| Australian Postdoctoral Research Fellowships (1335) | Study: Australia | |
| Australian Research Fellowship (1336) | Study: Australia | |
| Australian Senior Research Fellowships (1337) | Study: Australia | |
| John Carter Brown Library Associates Fellowship (1512) | Study: RI | |
| Brown Library Long-Term Research Fellowships (1513) | Citizenship: US; Legal: United States; Study: United States | |
| Bunting Fellowship (1526) | Study: MA | |
| Bunting Institute Affiliation Program (1527) | Study: MA | |
| Sally Butler Memorial Fund for Latina Research (1549) | | Association, Hispanic American |
| Carnegie Grants (1739) | Study: Scotland | |
| Center for Advanced Study in the Behavioral Sciences Fellowship (1765) | Study: CA | |
| Lady Davis Graduate and Postdoctoral Fellowships (2193) | Study: Israel | |
| Lady Davis Visiting Professorships (2194) | Study: Israel | |

| Vocational Goal, Award, and Entry Number | Geographic Restrictions (Citizenship, Legal Residence, Place of Study) | Affiliation/Special Recipients Requirements |
|---|---|---|
| *Liberal/General Studies (continued)* | | |
| Friedreich Ebert Foundation, Post-Doctoral/Young Scholar Fellowships (2331) | Citizenship: US | |
| Queen Elizabeth II Fellowships (1338) | Study: Australia | |
| Fulbright Senior Scholar Program (2115) | Citizenship: US | |
| General Research Grant Program (766) | Study: United States | |
| Hebrew University Postdoctoral Fellowships (2853) | Study: Israel | |
| The Audrey Lumsden-Kouvel Fellowship (4618) | Study: IL | |
| Paul W. McQuillen Memorial Fellowship (1515) | Study: RI | |
| Mellon Postdoctoral Fellowships (5458) | Citizenship: US/CA, PermRes | |
| Michigan Society Postdoctoral Fellowships (3692) | Study: United States | |
| Monticello College Foundation Fellowship for Women (4619) | Citizenship: US, PermRes; Study: IL | |
| Barbara S. Mosbacher Fellowship (1516) | Study: RI | |
| Newberry-British Academy Fellowship (4620) | | |
| Newberry Library National Endowment for the Humanities Fellowships (4622) | Citizenship: US, Other; Study: IL | |
| Newberry Library Short-Term Resident Fellowships (4623) | Study: IL | |
| OAS-PRA Fellowships (4809) | | |
| Radcliffe Research Support Program (3798) | | |
| Research Fellowships in Marine Policy (6248) | | |
| Research Grants for Recent PhDs and PhD Candidates (2690) | Legal: Germany | |
| Schlesinger Library, Radcliffe College Honorary Visiting Scholar Appointments (5257) | | |
| Schlesinger Library, Radcliffe College Research Support Grants (5258) | | |
| University of California President's Postdoctoral Fellowship (5978) | Citizenship: US, PermRes | |
| Charles H. Watts Memorial Fellowship (1519) | Study: RI | |
| Zeta Phi Beta General Graduate Fellowship (6309) | | |

### Library and Archival Sciences

| | | |
|---|---|---|
| Hagley Fellowships/Grants-in-Aid (2779) | | |
| Hagley-Winterthur Fellowship (2780) | | |
| IREX Short-Term Travel Grants for Independent Short-Term Research (3187) | Citizenship: US, PermRes; Study: Union of Soviet Socialist Republics | |
| Munby Fellowship in Bibliography (1592) | Study: England | |
| Plenum Scholarship (5578) | Study: Canada, United States | Association |
| Short-Term Fellowships in the History of Cartography (4609) | | |
| Smithsonian Institution Postdoctoral Fellowships (5377) | | |

### Life Sciences

| | | |
|---|---|---|
| AAAS-EPA Environmental Science and Engineering Fellowships (265) | Legal: United States | |
| AIBS Congressional Science Fellowship (476) | Citizenship: US, PermRes; Study: United States | Association |
| AIDS Fellowships (2524) | | |
| Alexopoulos Prize (3814) | | Association |
| Argonne National Laboratory Faculty Research Leave; Faculty Research Participation Awards (1083) | Citizenship: US, PermRes; Legal: United States; Study: United States | |
| Army Research Laboratory Postdoctoral Fellowship Program (922) | | |
| Behavioral Sciences Research Training Fellowship (2396) | | |

| Vocational Goal, Award, and Entry Number | Geographic Restrictions (Citizenship, Legal Residence, Place of Study) | Affiliation/Special Recipients Requirements |
|---|---|---|

*Life Sciences (continued)*

| Vocational Goal, Award, and Entry Number | Geographic Restrictions (Citizenship, Legal Residence, Place of Study) | Affiliation/Special Recipients Requirements |
|---|---|---|
| Alfred D. Bell, Jr. Visiting Scholars Program (2553) | | |
| Biotechnology Career Fellowships (5147) | | |
| BNL Postdoctoral Research Associateships (1504) | Study: NY | |
| Bunting Institute Science Scholars Fellowships and Biomedical Research Fellowships (1529) | Citizenship: US, PermRes; Study: MA | |
| Cancer Research Institute Postdoctoral Fellowship (1715) | | |
| Capranica Foundation Award in Neuroethology (1723) | Citizenship: US | |
| Carnegie Institution of Washington Postdoctoral and Predoctoral Fellowships (1737) | Study: United States | |
| CCMS Fellowships (4653) | Citizenship: Other | |
| Centre for Interdisciplinary Studies in Chemical Physics Senior Visiting Fellowships (1795) | Study: Canada | |
| Chateaubriand Scholarship (Scientifique) (2372) | Citizenship: US; Study: France | |
| CIIT Postdoctoral Trainee Fellowships (1902) | Study: United States | |
| W. Storrs Cole Memorial Research Awards (2648) | | Association |
| Conservation Science Fellowship (2060) | Study: United States | |
| Eastburn Fellowships (2314) | Citizenship: Canada, PermRes; Study: Canada | |
| E. B. Eastburn Fellowships (2788) | Citizenship: Canada; Study: Canada | |
| Edelstein International Fellowship in the History of Chemical Sciences and Technology (1900) | Study: PA, Israel | |
| Eppley Foundation Support for Advanced Scientific Research (2404) | | |
| FIC International Research Fellowships (2528) | Study: United States | |
| FIC Senior International Fellowships (2529) | Citizenship: US, PermRes | |
| FIC Senior International Fellowships in Biomedical Sciences (2530) | Citizenship: US, PermRes | |
| Field Museum Visiting Scholar Funds (2446) | | |
| Fondation Fyssen Post-Doctoral Study Grants (2609) | | |
| Grant in Biotechnology (4834) | Citizenship: US, PermRes; Study: United States | |
| Grass Fellowships in Neurophysiology (2742) | Study: MA | |
| Alexander Hollaender Distinguished Postdoctoral Fellowships (4706) | Citizenship: US, PermRes | |
| Hudson River Research Grants (2913) | | |
| Human Genome Distinguished Postdoctoral Fellowships (5896) | | |
| Israeli Ministry of Health Fellowships (2533) | Study: Israel | |
| Japan Society for the Promotion of Science Fellowships (2534) | Study: Japan | |
| Miller Institute Research Fellowships (5984) | Study: CA | |
| NAS/NRC Collaboration in Basic Science and Engineering Long-Term Grants (3831) | Citizenship: US | |
| NAS/NRC Collaboration in Basic Science and Engineering Short-Term Project Development Grants (3832) | Citizenship: US | |
| NASPE Full-Year Fellowships (4649) | | |
| NASPE Traveling Fellowships (4650) | | |
| NIDA Individual National Research Service Awards (4192) | Citizenship: US, PermRes | |
| NIDAY Fellowships (3786) | Study: United States | |
| NIMH Individual Postdoctoral National Research Service Awards (4198) | Citizenship: US, PermRes | |
| NYZS/Wildlife Conservation Society Research Fellowship Program (RFP) (6177) | Study: Belize, Costa Rica, El Salvador, Guatemala, Honduras, Nicaragua, Panama | |

| Vocational Goal, Award, and Entry Number | Geographic Restrictions (Citizenship, Legal Residence, Place of Study) | Affiliation/Special Recipients Requirements |
|---|---|---|
| *Life Sciences (continued)* | | |
| Olfactory Research Fund Grants (4744) | | |
| Postdoctoral Fellowships in the Atmospheric Sciences (3931) | Study: United States | |
| Postdoctoral Fellowships in the History and Philosophy of Science (4699) | Study: United States | |
| Postdoctoral Fellowships in Ocean Science and Engineering (6247) | Study: United States | |
| Postdoctoral Research Fellowships for Physicians (2926) | | |
| Henry and Sylvia Richardson Research Grant (2391) | | Association |
| Swedish Medical Research Council Fellowships (2535) | Study: Sweden | |
| Taiwan National Science Council Fellowships (2536) | Study: Taiwan | |
| Taste & Clinic Fellowship (1801) | | |
| Tyndall Air Force Base Research Participation Program (5928) | | |
| Morris K. Udall OTA Congressional Fellowship (5851) | | |
| U.S. Department of Energy Global Change Distinguished Postdoctoral Fellowships (4709) | Citizenship: US, PermRes | |
| U.S. Department of Energy Human Genome Distinguished Postdoctoral Fellowships (4710) | | |
| Alexander von Humboldt Foundation Fellowship (2537) | Study: Germany | |
| Whitehall Foundation Grants-in-Aid (6168) | | |
| Whitehall Foundation Research Grants (6169) | | |
| Ziskind-Sommerfeld Research Award (5440) | | Association |
| **Mathematics** | | |
| Argonne National Laboratory Faculty Research Leave; Faculty Research Participation Awards (1083) | Citizenship: US, PermRes; Legal: United States; Study: United States | |
| ASA/NCES/NSF Research Fellowships (997) | Study: United States | |
| ASA/NSF/BLS Senior Research Fellowship (998) | Study: United States | |
| ASA/NSF/Census Research Fellowship (999) | Study: United States | |
| ASA/NSF/NIST Senior Research Fellowships and Associateships (1000) | Study: United States | |
| ASA/USDA/NASS Research Fellowships and Associateships (1001) | Study: United States | |
| Centennial Research Fellowships (686) | Citizenship: PermRes, US/CA, Mexico | |
| ETS Center for Performance Assessment Postdoctoral Fellowships (2352) | Study: NJ, United States | |
| ETS Postdoctoral Fellowships (2353) | Study: NJ, United States | |
| Ford Foundation Postdoctoral Fellowships for Minorities (4356) | Citizenship: US | Minority |
| William C. Foster Fellows Visiting Scholars Competition (5818) | Citizenship: US | |
| IBM Postdoctoral Research Fellowships in Mathematical Sciences (2948) | Study: NY | |
| ICTP Research Grants for Postdoctoral Students (3135) | Study: Italy | |
| Institute for Advanced Study Postdoctoral Research Fellowships (3009) | Study: United States | |
| Institute for Advanced Study Postdoctoral Study Awards (3010) | | |
| Solomon Lefschetz Instructorships in Mathematics (1818) | Study: Mexico | |

| Vocational Goal, Award, and Entry Number | Geographic Restrictions (Citizenship, Legal Residence, Place of Study) | Affiliation/Special Recipients Requirements |
|---|---|---|
| *Mathematics (continued)* | | |
| Mathematical Sciences Research Institute Postdoctoral Fellowships in Mathematics (3611) | Legal: United States; Study: United States | |
| Mathematical Sciences Research Institute Research Professorships in Mathematics (3612) | Legal: United States; Study: United States | |
| NAS/NRC Collaboration in Basic Science and Engineering Long-Term Grants (3831) | Citizenship: US | |
| NAS/NRC Collaboration in Basic Science and Engineering Short-Term Project Development Grants (3832) | Citizenship: US | |
| National Assessment of Educational Progress Visiting Scholar Program (2355) | Study: NJ, United States | |
| Oak Ridge National Laboratory Postdoctoral Research Associates Program (5917) | | |
| Postdoctoral Fellowships in the Atmospheric Sciences (3931) | Study: United States | |
| Research Associateships and Fellowships in Statistics (1321) | Study: Australia | |
| U.S. Air Force Phillips Laboratory Scholar Program (4686) | Citizenship: US; Study: MA | |
| **Medicine** | | |
| AAO-HNSF Academy Resident Research Grant (233) | | |
| AAP Residency Scholarships (238) | Legal: Canada, United States | |
| ACOG/3M Pharmaceuticals Research Awards in Lower Genital Infections (376) | | Association |
| ACOG/Cytyc Corporation Research Award for the Prevention of Cervical Cancer (377) | | Association |
| ACOG/Ethicon Research Award for Innovations in Gynecologic Surgery (378) | | Association |
| ACOG/Merck Award for Research in Migraine Management in Women's Health Care (379) | | Association |
| ACOG/Novartis Pharmaceuticals Fellowship for Research in Endocrinology of the Postreproductive Woman (380) | Citizenship: US | Association |
| ACOG/Organon Inc. Research Award in Contraception (381) | | Association |
| ACOG/Pharmacia & Upjohn Research Award in Urognecology of the Postreproductive Woman (383) | | Association |
| ACOG/Solvay Pharmaceuticals Research Award in Menopause (384) | | Association |
| ACOG/Zeneca Pharmaceuticals Research Award in Breast Cancer (385) | | Association |
| Action Research Program and Project Grants (30) | | |
| ADA Career Development Awards (435) | Citizenship: US, PermRes | |
| ADA Clinical Research Grant Program (436) | Citizenship: US, PermRes | |
| ADA Mentor-Based Postdoctoral Fellowship Program (438) | Citizenship: US | |
| ADA Research Awards (439) | Citizenship: US, PermRes | |
| ADHF/Elsevier Research Initiative Awards (445) | | |
| ADHF/Industry Research Scholar Awards (446) | | |
| AES/EFA Research Grants (455) | Study: Canada, United States | |
| AES Research Fellowships (456) | Study: Canada, United States | |
| AFUD/NKF Resident Fellowship (498) | Study: Canada, United States | |
| AFUD/Ph.D. Research Scholar Program (499) | | |
| AFUD Research Scholars Program (500) | Study: Canada, United States | |

| Vocational Goal, Award, and Entry Number | Geographic Restrictions (Citizenship, Legal Residence, Place of Study) | Affiliation/Special Recipients Requirements |
|---|---|---|
| *Medicine (continued)* | | |
| AGA Foundation/SmithKline Beecham Clinical Research Awards (Discontinued) (449) | Study: United States | |
| Agency for Toxic Substances and Disease Registry Clinical Fellowships in Environmental Medicine (5858) | | |
| AHA Grant-in-Aid (526) | | |
| AIBS Congressional Science Fellowship (476) | Citizenship: US, PermRes; Study: United States | Association |
| ALA Career Investigator Awards (677) | Citizenship: US/CA, PermRes; Study: United States | |
| ALA Research Grants (678) | Citizenship: US/CA, PermRes; Study: United States | |
| Albert Ellis Institute Clinical Fellowships, Internships (143) | Citizenship: US, PermRes; Study: United States | |
| Allergy and Clinical Immunology Fellowship Program (1300) | | |
| ALSA Research Grants (1033) | | |
| Alzheimer's Association Faculty Scholar Awards (204) | | |
| Alzheimer's Association Investigator Initiated Research Grants (205) | | |
| Alzheimer's Association Pilot Research Grants for New Investigators (206) | | |
| Alzheimer's Association Pioneer Award for Alzheimer's Disease Research (207) | | |
| Ambulatory Pediatric Association Special Projects Program (213) | | Association |
| The American Academy of Periodontology Student Loan Program (240) | Citizenship: US/CA | Association |
| American Brain Tumor Association Fellowships (356) | Citizenship: US, PermRes | |
| American Cancer Society Clinical Research Professorships (363) | Citizenship: US, PermRes | |
| American Cancer Society Postdoctoral Fellowships (364) | Citizenship: US, PermRes | |
| American Fund for Dental Health Dental Faculty Development Fellowships (35) | Citizenship: US | |
| American Fund for Dental Health Dental Teacher Training Fellowships (36) | Citizenship: US; Study: United States | |
| American Fund for Dental Health Grants for Research and Special Projects in Dentistry (37) | | |
| American Fund for Dental Health/Hillenbrand Fellowship in Dental Administration (38) | Citizenship: US; Study: United States | |
| American Heart Association, California Affiliate - Grants-in-Aid (530) | | |
| American Heart Association, California Affiliate - Postdoctoral Research Fellowships (531) | | |
| American Kidney Fund Clinical Scientist in Nephrology (606) | Citizenship: US | |
| American Liver Foundation Postdoctoral Supplementary Fellowships (673) | | |
| American Otological Society Research Fellowship and Medical Student Training Grants (759) | Study: Canada, United States | |
| American Otological Society Research Grants (760) | Legal: Canada, United States | |
| American Society for Dermatologic Surgery Grants (2235) | Study: Canada, United States | |
| AmFAR Pediatric AIDS Foundation Grants (471) | | |
| AmFAR Research Grants (472) | | |
| AmFAR Scholar Awards (473) | | |

| Vocational Goal, Award, and Entry Number | Geographic Restrictions (Citizenship, Legal Residence, Place of Study) | Affiliation/Special Recipients Requirements |
| --- | --- | --- |
| *Medicine (continued)* | | |
| AmFAR Small Grants (474) | | |
| APA/SmithKline Beecham Junior Faculty Fellowship for Research Development in Biological Psychiatry (801) | | |
| APA/Wyeth-Ayerst M.D. Ph.D. Psychiatric Research Fellowship (802) | | |
| The Applied Social Issues Internship Program (5493) | | |
| Arthritis Biomedical Science Grants (1147) | Citizenship: US, PermRes | |
| Arthritis Foundation New Investigator Grant for Arthritis Health Professionals (1149) | | |
| Arthritis Foundation Physician Scientist Development Award (1150) | Study: United States | |
| Arthritis Foundation Postdoctoral Fellowships (1151) | | |
| Arthritis Investigator Awards (1152) | Citizenship: US, PermRes | |
| Arthritis Society Research Fellowships (1155) | Study: Canada | |
| Arthritis Society Research Grants (1156) | Citizenship: Canada, PermRes; Legal: Canada; Study: Canada | |
| Arthritis Society Research Scientist Award (1158) | Study: Canada | |
| ASHA Postdoctoral Fellowships (889) | Legal: United States; Study: United States | |
| Astra/Merck Fellowship/Faculty Transition Award (450) | Study: United States | |
| BARD Postdoctoral Fellowships; BARD Research Fellows Program (1432) | Citizenship: US, Israel; Study: Israel, United States | |
| Benevolent Foundation Dissertation Research Fellowships (1411) | | |
| Benevolent Foundation Research Grants (1412) | | |
| A. E. Bennett Research Awards (5438) | | |
| Wilfred G. Bigelow Traveling Fellowship (4646) | Legal: Canada; Study: Canada | |
| Michael Bilitch Fellowship in Cardiac Pacing and Electrophysiology (4647) | Citizenship: US/CA, Mexico, PermRes | |
| Biomedical Fellowships (3371) | Citizenship: Canada; Legal: Canada; Study: Canada | |
| Biomedical Research Grant (3372) | Citizenship: Canada; Study: Canada | |
| Biomedical Scholarship (3373) | Citizenship: Canada; Study: Canada | |
| William Blair-Bell Memorial Lectureships in Obstetrics and Gynecology (5179) | | Association |
| British Leprosy Relief Association Research Grants (1491) | | |
| Burroughs Wellcome Young Investigator Award in Virology (3003) | Citizenship: US, PermRes | |
| Canadian Liver Foundation Establishment Grants (1670) | Citizenship: Canada; Study: Canada | |
| Canadian Liver Foundation Fellowships (1671) | Citizenship: Canada, PermRes; Study: Canada | |
| Canadian Liver Foundation Operating Grant Program (1673) | Legal: Canada | |
| Cancer Prevention and Control Research Small Grant Program (3922) | | |
| Cancer Research Society Fellowships (1718) | Study: Canada | |
| Career Development Fellowships (1611) | Citizenship: Canada, PermRes; Study: Canada | |
| Cassen Postdoctoral Fellowship (5474) | Study: United States | |
| CDA Fellowships (1621) | Citizenship: Canada, PermRes; Study: Canada | |
| CDA Scholarships (1622) | Citizenship: Canada, PermRes; Study: Canada | |
| Chateaubriand Scholarship (Scientifique) (2372) | Citizenship: US; Study: France | |

| Vocational Goal, Award, and Entry Number | Geographic Restrictions (Citizenship, Legal Residence, Place of Study) | Affiliation/Special Recipients Requirements |
|---|---|---|
| *Medicine (continued)* | | |
| Children's Medical Research Institute Ph.D. Scholarships; Children's Medical Research Institute Postdoctoral Research Fellowships (1941) | | |
| Childs Postdoctoral Fellowships (1943) | Study: United States | |
| CLA/MRC Scholarships (3638) | Citizenship: Canada, PermRes | |
| Clinical Career Development Award (2236) | Study: Canada, United States | |
| Clinical Dental Fellowships (2328) | Study: United States | |
| Combined AAOA/AAO-HNSF Research Grant (234) | | Association |
| Combined PSEF/AAO-HNSF Research Grant (235) | | |
| Cooley's Anemia Foundation Research Fellowship (2077) | | |
| Jeanne Timmins Costello Fellowship (3775) | | |
| Crohn's & Colitis Foundation Career Development Awards (2138) | Study: United States | |
| Crohn's & Colitis Foundation Research Fellowships (2139) | Study: United States | |
| Crohn's & Colitis Foundation Research Grants (2140) | | |
| Cystic Fibrosis Foundation Clinical Fellowships (2151) | Citizenship: US, PermRes; Study: United States | |
| Cystic Fibrosis Foundation/National Institute of Diabetes and Digestive and Kidney Diseases Funding Award (2153) | | |
| Cystic Fibrosis Foundation New Investigator Grants (2154) | | |
| Cystic Fibrosis Foundation Research Fellowships (2155) | | |
| Cystic Fibrosis Foundation Research Scholar Awards (2157) | Citizenship: US, PermRes | |
| Cystic Fibrosis Foundation Third Year Clinical Fellowship Awards for Research Training (2160) | | |
| Dalsemer Research Scholar Award (680) | Citizenship: US, PermRes | |
| Deafness Research Foundation Grants (2198) | | |
| Dermatologist Investigator Research Fellowship Award (2237) | Study: Canada, United States | |
| Dermatology Foundation Research Fellowships (2238) | Study: Canada, United States | |
| Dermatology Foundation Research Grants (2239) | Study: Canada, United States | |
| Detweiler Travelling Fellowships (5184) | Legal: Canada | Association |
| Dysautonomia Research Grants (2292) | | |
| Eastburn Fellowships (2314) | Citizenship: Canada, PermRes; Study: Canada | |
| E. B. Eastburn Fellowships (2788) | Citizenship: Canada; Study: Canada | |
| Eastern European Visiting Scholarships (2814) | Study: United States, Wales | |
| Eden Traveling Fellowship in Obstetrics and Gynecology (5180) | | |
| Endodontic Faculty Grants (287) | Legal: Canada, United States | |
| EORTC/NCI Exchange Program (3923) | | |
| Eppley Foundation Support for Advanced Scientific Research (2404) | | |
| ESRI Doctoral Training Grants; ESRI Postdoctoral Fellowships (2316) | Citizenship: Canada; Legal: Canada; Study: Canada | |
| Faculty Research Award in Oncology (365) | Citizenship: US, PermRes | |
| Fellowship in Infectious Diseases (4160) | Citizenship: US | |
| Fellowships for Careers in Clinical Pharmacology (4888) | Citizenship: US; Study: United States | |
| Fellowships in Ethics (5015) | Study: United States | |

| Vocational Goal, Award, and Entry Number | Geographic Restrictions (Citizenship, Legal Residence, Place of Study) | Affiliation/Special Recipients Requirements |
|---|---|---|
| *Medicine (continued)* | | |
| Fellowships in Spinal Cord Injury Research (4830) | Legal: Canada, United States | |
| FFS-NSPB Grants-In-Aid (2449) | | |
| FFS-NSPB Postdoctoral Research Fellowships (2450) | | |
| FIC Foreign-Funded Fellowships (2526) | Citizenship: US, PermRes; Study: Finland, France, Germany, Ireland, Israel, Japan, Norway, Sweden, Switzerland, Taiwan | |
| FIC International Neuroscience Fellowships (2527) | Study: United States | |
| Parker B. Francis Fellowships (2587) | Citizenship: US/CA | |
| R. Robert and Sally Funderburg Research Scholar Award in Gastric Biology Related to Cancer (451) | | |
| Edgar Gentilli Prize (5181) | | |
| Georgia State Loan Repayment Program (5620) | | |
| Duncan L. Gordon Fellowships (2900) | Citizenship: Canada; Legal: Canada | |
| Grant Foundation Research Grants (2740) | | |
| Hastings Center International Fellowships (2815) | Study: United States | |
| Senator Mark Hatfield Award for Clinical Research in Alzheimer's Disease (208) | | |
| Heiser Postdoctoral Research Fellowships (2857) | | |
| Heiser Research Grants (2858) | | |
| Leonard W. Horowitz Fellowship in Cardiac Pacing and Electrophysiology (4648) | Citizenship: US/CA, Mexico, PermRes | |
| Howard Hughes Medical Institute Predoctoral Fellowships in Biological Sciences (4358) | | |
| HSFC PhD Research Traineeships (2843) | | |
| HSFC Research Fellowships (2844) | | |
| HSFC Research Scholarships (2845) | Citizenship: Canada, PermRes; Study: Canada | |
| HSFC Senior Personnel Research Scholarship/McDonald Scholarship (2846) | | |
| Human Growth Foundation Small Grants (2929) | | |
| Huntington's Disease Society Research Fellowships (2941) | | |
| IBRO/Unesco Research Fellowships (3125) | | |
| ICA Pilot Research Project Grants (3208) | | |
| ICRF Postdoctoral Fellowships (2985) | Study: England | |
| ICS Research Scholarships (3137) | | |
| J. Franklin Jameson Fellowship in American History (538) | Study: United States | |
| JDFI Career Development Awards (3308) | | |
| JDFI Postdoctoral Fellowships (3310) | | |
| JDFI Research Grants (3311) | | |
| Viola Kerr Fellowship (4841) | | |
| Lalor Foundation Postdoctoral Research Grants (3411) | | |
| Leukemia Society Fellow Awards (3456) | | |
| Leukemia Society Scholar Awards (3457) | | |
| Leukemia Society Special Fellow Awards (3458) | | |
| Life Sciences Research Foundation Fellowships (3470) | | |
| Lions SightFirst Diabetic Retinopathy Research Program - LCIF Clinical Research Grant Program (440) | | |

| Vocational Goal, Award, and Entry Number | Geographic Restrictions (Citizenship, Legal Residence, Place of Study) | Affiliation/Special Recipients Requirements |
|---|---|---|
| *Medicine (continued)* | | |
| Lions SightFirst Diabetic Retinopathy Research Program - LCIF Equipment Grant Program (441) | | |
| Lions SightFirst Diabetic Retinopathy Research Program - LCIF Training Grant Program (442) | Citizenship: US | |
| Liver Scholar Awards (675) | | |
| Walter C. MacKenzie, Johnson and Johnson Fellowship (5185) | Legal: Canada | Association |
| March of Dimes Research Grants (3548) | | |
| Leroy Matthews Physician/Scientist Awards (2161) | Citizenship: US, PermRes | |
| Mayo Foundation Postdoctoral Training Fellowships (3616) | Study: United States | |
| McEachern Awards (1614) | Citizenship: Canada | |
| Mead Johnson Awards for Graduate Education in Family Practice (226) | | |
| Medical Education Travelling Fellowship (5186) | Legal: Canada | Association |
| H. Houston Merritt Fellowship (4842) | Study: NY | |
| Milheim Foundation for Cancer Research Project Grants in Oncology (3701) | Study: United States | |
| Ministry of the Flemish Community Fellowships (3710) | Citizenship: US, PermRes | |
| Multiple Sclerosis Society Career Development Awards (3789) | Study: Canada | |
| Multiple Sclerosis Society Postdoctoral Fellowships (3790) | | |
| Multiple Sclerosis Society Research Grants (3791) | | |
| Myasthenia Gravis Osserman Fellowship Grants (3810) | Citizenship: US, PermRes | |
| NARSAD Established Investigator Award (3843) | | |
| NARSAD Young Investigator Award (3844) | | |
| National Cancer Institute of Canada Research Fellowships (3927) | Citizenship: Canada, PermRes; Study: Canada | |
| National Cancer Institute of Canada Research Grants (3928) | Citizenship: Canada, PermRes; Legal: Canada; Study: Canada | |
| National Cancer Institute of Canada Research Scientist Career Appointments (3929) | Legal: Canada; Study: Canada | |
| National Heart, Lung, and Blood Institute's Minority School Faculty Development Award (4175) | | |
| National Institute of Diabetes and Digestive and Kidney Diseases Fellowship Program-Sabbatical (2162) | | |
| National Kidney Foundation Research Fellowships (4279) | | |
| National Kidney Foundation Young Investigator Grant (4280) | | |
| National Leukemia Research Association Research Awards (4284) | Legal: United States | |
| National Multiple Sclerosis Society Advanced Postdoctoral Fellowships (4313) | | |
| National Multiple Sclerosis Society Postdoctoral Fellowships (4318) | Study: United States | |
| NCI International Bilateral Program (3924) | | |
| New Investigator Matching Grants (4161) | | |
| NIAMS Academic Research Enhancement Awards (4186) | | |
| NIAMS National Research Service Award (NRSA) Fellowships (4187) | | |

| Vocational Goal, Award, and Entry Number | Geographic Restrictions (Citizenship, Legal Residence, Place of Study) | Affiliation/Special Recipients Requirements |
|---|---|---|
| *Medicine (continued)* | | |
| NIAMS National Research Service Award (NRSA) Senior Fellowships (4188) | | |
| NIAMS Regular Research Grants (4189) | | |
| NIAMS Research Career Development Awards (4190) | | |
| Basil O'Connor Starter Scholar Awards (3549) | | |
| OFAS Research Grants (4807) | Study: United States | |
| Metro A. Ogryzlo International Fellowship (1159) | Study: Canada | |
| Olfactory Research Fund Grants (4744) | | |
| Oncology Research Faculty Development Program (3925) | | |
| Parke-Davis Teacher Development Awards (227) | | Association |
| Parkinson's Disease Foundation Postdoctoral Fellowship (4843) | | |
| Parkinson's Disease Foundation Research Grants (4844) | | |
| Pediatric Pulmonary Research Training Fellowships (Cancelled) (682) | Citizenship: US/CA, PermRes; Study: United States | |
| Percy Memorial Research Award (236) | | Association |
| Jerry L. Pettis Memorial Scholarship (689) | | |
| The Pfizer American Geriatrics Society Postdoctoral Outcomes Research Fellowships (4883) | Citizenship: US, PermRes | |
| The Pfizer Postdoctoral Fellowships (4884) | | |
| The Pfizer Scholars Program for New Faculty (4885) | Citizenship: US, PermRes | |
| Physician Student Loan Repayment Program (5711) | | |
| Poncin Scholarship Fund (4977) | Study: WA | |
| Judith Graham Pool Postdoctoral Research Fellowships (4177) | Citizenship: US, PermRes; Legal: United States | |
| Postdoctoral Fellowship in Emerging Infectious Diseases (4162) | Citizenship: US | |
| Postdoctoral Fellowship in Nosocomial Infection Research and Training (4163) | Citizenship: US | |
| Postdoctoral Research Fellowships for Basic and Physician Scientists (5200) | | |
| Practicing Urologist's Research Award (502) | Study: Canada, United States | |
| Psychologists Supplemental Sabbatical Awards (1756) | Study: Canada, United States | |
| Public Policy Fellowships in Mental Retardation (3352) | Study: United States | |
| Research Career Development Award (2241) | Study: Canada, United States | |
| Research Grants in Orthopaedic Surgery (4815) | Legal: Canada, United States; Study: United States | |
| Research Training Fellowships (683) | Citizenship: US/CA, PermRes; Study: United States | |
| Resident Research Fellowships in Orthopaedic Surgery (4816) | Study: Canada, United States | |
| Preston Robb Fellowship (3776) | | |
| Robinson/Cunningham Awards (219) | | |
| Kenneth M. Rosen Fellowship in Cardiac Pacing and Electrophysiology (4651) | Citizenship: US/CA, Mexico, PermRes | |
| Royal College Fellowship for Studies in Medical Education (5189) | Citizenship: Canada | Association |
| Lillian Shorr Fellowship (4846) | | |
| Harry Shwachman Clinical Investigator Award (2164) | Citizenship: US, PermRes | |
| Rock Sleyster Memorial Scholarship (690) | Citizenship: US; Study: Canada, United States | |

| Vocational Goal, Award, and Entry Number | Geographic Restrictions (Citizenship, Legal Residence, Place of Study) | Affiliation/Special Recipients Requirements |
|---|---|---|
| *Medicine (continued)* | | |
| Society of Nuclear Medicine Pilot Research Grants (5476) | | |
| Summer Scholarships in Epidemiology (2165) | Citizenship: US, PermRes | |
| Tetalman Award (5478) | | |
| Edward Livingston Trudeau Scholar Awards (Cancelled) (684) | Citizenship: US/CA; Study: Canada, United States | |
| TSA Clinical Studies Grants; TSA Postdoctoral Training Fellowships; TSA Research Grants (5735) | | |
| Underrepresented Minority Investigators Award in Asthma and Allergy (216) | Citizenship: US, PermRes | African American, Hispanic American, Native American |
| USA British Isles Traveling Fellowship (5182) | Study: United States | |
| John P. Utz Postdoctoral Fellowship in Medical Mycology (4165) | Citizenship: US | |
| Warren H Pearse/Wyeth-Ayerst Women's Health Policy Research Award (386) | | Association |
| Harry Weaver Neuroscience Scholarships (4322) | Study: United States | |
| Whitney Postdoctoral Research Fellowships (6175) | | |
| WHO Fellowships (6259) | | |
| WHO Fellowships for Canadian Citizens (6260) | Citizenship: Canada | |
| WHO Fellowships and Research Training Grants (6261) | | |
| WHO Fellowships for U.S. Citizens (6262) | Citizenship: US | |
| Simon Wile Awards (220) | | |
| Zecchino Post-Graduate Orthopaedic Fellowship (4272) | Study: Italy | |
| Zenith Fellows Award Program (209) | | |

### Military Sciences

| | | |
|---|---|---|
| Army Research Laboratory Postdoctoral Fellowship Program (922) | | |
| Fellowships in National Security (2812) | Study: United States | |
| William C. Foster Fellows Visiting Scholars Competition (5818) | Citizenship: US | |
| Naval Research Laboratory Postdoctoral Fellowship Program (924) | Citizenship: US | |
| U.S. Army Construction Engineering Research Laboratory Research Participation Program (5930) | | |

### Philosophy, Theology, and Religion

| | | |
|---|---|---|
| Asian Art and Religion Fellowships (1176) | Citizenship: US | |
| Beinecke Library Visiting Fellowships (1393) | Study: United States | |
| Cushwa Center Research Travel Grants (6008) | Study: United States | |
| Fellowships in Ethics (5015) | Study: United States | |
| Sidney E. Mead Prize (899) | | |
| Rockefeller Archive Center Research Grants (5142) | Study: United States | |

### Physical Sciences

| | | |
|---|---|---|
| AAAS Congressional Science and Engineering Fellowships (263) | Study: United States | |
| AAAS-EPA Environmental Science and Engineering Fellowships (265) | Legal: United States | |
| AAAS Science, Engineering, and Diplomacy Fellows Program (266) | Citizenship: US | |
| AAAS Technology Policy Science and Engineering Fellowships (267) | Citizenship: US; Study: United States | |
| AIBS Congressional Science Fellowship (476) | Citizenship: US, PermRes; Study: United States | Association |

| Vocational Goal, Award, and Entry Number | Geographic Restrictions (Citizenship, Legal Residence, Place of Study) | Affiliation/Special Recipients Requirements |
|---|---|---|
| *Physical Sciences (continued)* | | |
| American Astronomical Society Small Research Grants (342) | Citizenship: US | |
| American Museum of Natural History Collection Study Grants (712) | Study: United States | |
| American Museum of Natural History Research and Museum Fellowships (713) | Study: United States | |
| Argonne National Laboratory Faculty Research Leave; Faculty Research Participation Awards (1083) | Citizenship: US, PermRes; Legal: United States; Study: United States | |
| Army Research Laboratory Postdoctoral Fellowship Program (922) | | |
| AWU Faculty Fellowships (1199) | Citizenship: US, PermRes; Study: CA, CO, ID, MT, ND, NM, NV, OK, UT, WA, WY | |
| AWU Faculty Sabbatical Fellowships (1200) | Citizenship: US, PermRes; Study: CA, CO, ID, MT, ND, NM, NV, OK, WA, WY | |
| AWU Post-Graduate Fellowship (1202) | Citizenship: US, PermRes; Study: CA, CO, ID, ND, NM, OK | |
| BARD Postdoctoral Fellowships; BARD Research Fellows Program (1432) | Citizenship: US, Israel; Study: Israel, United States | |
| BNL Postdoctoral Research Associateships (1504) | Study: NY | |
| BNL Research Fellowship in Physics (1505) | Citizenship: US, PermRes; Study: United States | Minority |
| Bunting Institute Science Scholars Fellowships and Biomedical Research Fellowships (1529) | Citizenship: US, PermRes; Study: MA | |
| Carnegie Institution of Washington Postdoctoral and Predoctoral Fellowships (1737) | Study: United States | |
| The Center for Field Research Grants (1791) | | |
| Centre for Interdisciplinary Studies in Chemical Physics Senior Visiting Fellowships (1795) | Study: Canada | |
| Frank M. Chapman Memorial Fellowships and Grants (714) | | |
| Chateaubriand Scholarship (Scientifique) (2372) | Citizenship: US; Study: France | |
| Chretien International Research Grants (343) | | |
| CIR Postdoctoral Fellowship (5986) | Study: United States | |
| CIRES Visiting Fellowships (2085) | Study: United States | |
| Gladys W. Cole Memorial Research Awards (2647) | | |
| Trent R. Dames and William W. Moore Fellowship (903) | | |
| Department of Energy Distinguished Postdoctoral Research Program (5868) | | |
| DOE Student Research Participation (4705) | Citizenship: US, PermRes | |
| Dublin Institute for Advanced Studies Research Scholarships (2282) | Study: Ireland | |
| Eastburn Fellowships (2314) | Citizenship: Canada, PermRes; Study: Canada | |
| E. B. Eastburn Fellowships (2788) | Citizenship: Canada; Study: Canada | |
| Edelstein International Fellowship in the History of Chemical Sciences and Technology (1900) | Study: PA, Israel | |
| Environmental Monitoring Systems Laboratory Research Participation Program (5869) | | |
| Eppley Foundation Support for Advanced Scientific Research (2404) | | |
| Fellowships in Theoretical Neurobiology (4517) | Study: United States | |
| Field Museum Visiting Scholar Funds (2446) | | |
| Ford Foundation Postdoctoral Fellowships for Minorities (4356) | Citizenship: US | Minority |
| William C. Foster Fellows Visiting Scholars Competition (5818) | Citizenship: US | |
| Government of Canada Awards (3145) | Citizenship: France, Germany, Japan, Mexico; Study: Canada | |

| Vocational Goal, Award, and Entry Number | Geographic Restrictions (Citizenship, Legal Residence, Place of Study) | Affiliation/Special Recipients Requirements |
|---|---|---|
| *Physical Sciences (continued)* | | |
| ICA Pilot Research Project Grants (3208) | | |
| ICTP Research Grants for Postdoctoral Students (3135) | Study: Italy | |
| ILZRO Postdoctoral Fellowships (3164) | | |
| Institute for Advanced Study Postdoctoral Research Fellowships (3009) | Study: United States | |
| Institute for Advanced Study Postdoctoral Study Awards (3010) | | |
| International Astronomical Union Travel Grants (3121) | | |
| International Travel Grants (344) | Legal: United States | |
| Jackson Laboratory Postdoctoral Traineeships (3232) | Study: United States | |
| Jansky Fellowships (4351) | Study: United States | |
| Jessup and McHenry Awards (26) | Study: United States | |
| JILA Postdoctoral Research Associateships for Laboratory Astrophysics (3277) | | |
| JILA Visiting Fellowships for Laboratory Astrophysics (3278) | | |
| Killam Research Fellowships (3375) | Legal: Canada | |
| Leakey Foundation Fellowships for Great Ape Research and Conservation (3442) | | |
| Leakey Foundation General Grants (3443) | | |
| Lerner-Gray Grants (715) | | |
| Lunar and Planetary Institute Visiting Postdoctoral Fellowships (3516) | Study: United States | |
| Lunar and Planetary Institute Visiting Scientist Program (3517) | Study: United States | |
| Miller Institute Research Fellowships (5984) | Study: CA | |
| NAS/NRC Collaboration in Basic Science and Engineering Long-Term Grants (3831) | Citizenship: US | |
| NAS/NRC Collaboration in Basic Science and Engineering Short-Term Project Development Grants (3832) | Citizenship: US | |
| NAS/NRC Radioactive Waste Management Program Grants (3833) | Citizenship: US | |
| NASA Field Center Resident Research Associateships (3838) | Citizenship: US; Study: United States | |
| NASPE Full-Year Fellowships (4649) | | |
| NASPE Traveling Fellowships (4650) | | |
| National Humanities Center Residential, Advanced Postdoctoral Fellowships (4184) | Study: United States | |
| National Research Council of Canada Research Associateships (4354) | | |
| NSERC Research Scholarships, Fellowships, and Grants (4474) | Citizenship: Canada, PermRes; Study: Canada | |
| Oak Ridge National Laboratory Postdoctoral Research Associates Program (5917) | | |
| Postdoctoral Fellowships in the Atmospheric Sciences (3931) | Study: United States | |
| Postdoctoral Fellowships in the History and Philosophy of Science (4699) | Study: United States | |
| Postdoctoral Fellowships in Ocean Science and Engineering (6247) | Study: United States | |
| Risk Reduction Engineering Research Laboratory Research Participation Program (5923) | | |
| Theodore Roosevelt Memorial Grants (716) | | |
| SAO Postdoctoral Fellowships (5370) | Study: United States | |
| SAO Visiting Scientist Awards (5372) | Study: United States | |

| Vocational Goal, Award, and Entry Number | Geographic Restrictions (Citizenship, Legal Residence, Place of Study) | Affiliation/Special Recipients Requirements |
|---|---|---|
| *Physical Sciences (continued)* | | |
| Tennessee Valley Authority Research Participation Program (5927) | | |
| Tyndall Air Force Base Research Participation Program (5928) | | |
| Morris K. Udall OTA Congressional Fellowship (5851) | | |
| U.S. Air Force Phillips Laboratory Scholar Program (4686) | Citizenship: US; Study: MA | |
| U.S. Department of Energy Distinguished Postdoctoral Research Fellowship (4708) | Citizenship: US, PermRes | |
| U.S. Department of Energy Global Change Distinguished Postdoctoral Fellowships (4709) | Citizenship: US, PermRes | |
| U.S. Navy ONR-ASEE Postdoctoral Fellowship (926) | Citizenship: US; Study: CA, CT, DC, FL, MD, MS, PA, RI, VA | |
| Gilbert F. White Postdoctoral Fellowships (5112) | Study: DC | |
| Whitney Postdoctoral Research Fellowships (6175) | | |
| **Protective Services and Public Affairs** | | |
| AAAS Science, Engineering, and Diplomacy Fellows Program (266) | Citizenship: US | |
| ACS Congressional Fellowship Program (367) | Study: United States | Association |
| International Foundation of Employee Benefit Plans Grants for Research (3155) | Citizenship: Canada | |
| Population Sciences Fellowships (5149) | | |
| Morris K. Udall OTA Congressional Fellowship (5851) | | |
| **Social Sciences** | | |
| AAAS Technology Policy Science and Engineering Fellowships (267) | Citizenship: US; Study: United States | |
| AAS Joint Fellowships with the Newberry Library (253) | Study: MA | |
| ACLS Fellowships (406) | Citizenship: US, PermRes | |
| ACLS Grants for East European Studies - Fellowships for Postdoctoral Research (408) | Citizenship: US, PermRes | |
| Advanced Research Fellowships in U.S.-Japan Relations (2808) | Study: United States | |
| Afro-American and African Studies Fellowships (6251) | Study: United States | |
| AIBS Congressional Science Fellowship (476) | Citizenship: US, PermRes; Study: United States | Association |
| American Jewish Studies Fellowships (598) | Study: United States | |
| American Museum of Natural History Collection Study Grants (712) | Study: United States | |
| American Museum of Natural History Research and Museum Fellowships (713) | Study: United States | |
| American Society for 18th-Century Studies Fellowships (4616) | Study: IL | Association |
| Ancient India and Iran Trust Travel and Research Grants (1035) | | |
| APA Congressional Fellowships (809) | Study: United States | Association |
| APDC Visiting Fellowships (1182) | Study: Malaysia | |
| ARIT Fellowships (846) | Study: Canada, Turkey, United States | |
| Artists Fellowship; Japan Foundation Cultural Properties Specialists Fellowship; Japan Foundation Doctoral Fellowship; Japan Foundation Research Fellowship (3240) | Study: Japan | |
| ASA/NSF/BLS Senior Research Fellowship (998) | Study: United States | |
| ASECS/Clark Fellowship (1761) | Study: CA | Association |
| Australian Institute of Archaeology Grants (1329) | | |

| Vocational Goal, Award, and Entry Number | Geographic Restrictions (Citizenship, Legal Residence, Place of Study) | Affiliation/Special Recipients Requirements |
|---|---|---|
| *Social Sciences (continued)* | | |
| Behavioral Sciences Research Training Fellowship (2396) | | |
| Beinecke Library Visiting Fellowships (1393) | Study: United States | |
| Berkshire Summer Fellowships (1525) | Study: MA | |
| The Albert J. Beveridge Grant (536) | | Association |
| Jeannette D. Black Memorial Fellowship (1511) | Study: RI | |
| British Academy Visiting Professorships for Overseas Scholars (1480) | | |
| John Carter Brown Library Travel Grants (1514) | Study: RI | |
| Brown University, The Future of Gender (5990) | | |
| R. B. Byers Postdoctoral Fellowship Program (1266) | Citizenship: Canada; Study: Canada | |
| Center for Advanced Study in the Visual Arts Senior Fellowships and Senior Visiting Fellowships (1767) | Study: United States | |
| Center for Hellenic Studies Fellowships (1793) | Study: DC | |
| Chateaubriand Scholarship (Scientifique) (2372) | Citizenship: US; Study: France | |
| CIR Postdoctoral Fellowship (5986) | Study: United States | |
| Clark Library Short-Term Fellowship (1763) | Study: CA | |
| CMRS Summer Fellowships (5988) | Study: United States | |
| Anna C. and Oliver C. Colburn Fellowship (1064) | Legal: Canada, United States; Study: Greece | Association |
| Arthur H. Cole Grants-in-Aid (2334) | | |
| Arthur H. Cole Grants-In-Aid for Research in Economic History (2359) | | |
| Council of American Overseas Research Centers Fellowships (866) | Citizenship: US | |
| Shelby Cullom Davis Center Research Fellowships (2189) | Study: NJ | |
| Du Bois Mandela Rodney Postdoctoral Fellowships (1784) | Study: United States | |
| Earhart Foundation Fellowship Research Grants (2302) | | |
| Edelstein International Fellowship in the History of Chemical Sciences and Technology (1900) | Study: PA, Israel | |
| Albert Einstein Institution Fellowships (2361) | | |
| Kenan T. Erim Award (1065) | | |
| ETS Center for Performance Assessment Postdoctoral Fellowships (2352) | Study: NJ, United States | |
| ETS Postdoctoral Fellowships (2353) | Study: NJ, United States | |
| Faculty Development Awards in Clinical Pharmacology and Toxicology (4887) | Citizenship: US; Study: United States | |
| Fellowship in Aerospace History (537) | Citizenship: US; Study: United States | |
| Fellowship for the Study of Foraging Peoples (3441) | | |
| Fellowships in Byzantine Studies, Pre-Columbian Studies and Landscape Architecture (2288) | Study: DC | |
| Fellowships in Ethics (5015) | Study: United States | |
| Folger Library Long-Term Fellowships (2541) | Study: United States | |
| Folger Library Short-Term Fellowships (2542) | Study: United States | |
| Ford Foundation Postdoctoral Fellowships for Minorities (4356) | Citizenship: US | Minority |
| Lena Lake Forrest Fellowships/BPW Research Grants (1550) | Citizenship: US | Association |
| William C. Foster Fellows Visiting Scholars Competition (5818) | Citizenship: US | |
| Frese Senior Research Fellowship (1772) | Citizenship: Germany, PermRes; Study: United States | |

| Vocational Goal, Award, and Entry Number | Geographic Restrictions (Citizenship, Legal Residence, Place of Study) | Affiliation/Special Recipients Requirements |
|---|---|---|
| *Social Sciences (continued)* | | |
| Getty Center Postdoctoral Fellowships (2699) | | |
| Government of Canada Awards (3145) | Citizenship: France, Germany, Japan, Mexico; Study: Canada | |
| H. F. Guggenheim Foundation Research Grants (2759) | | |
| Louise Wallace Hackney Fellowship for the Study of Chinese Art (757) | Citizenship: US | |
| Charles U. and Janet C. Harris Fellowship (871) | | |
| Harvard-Newcomen Postdoctoral Fellowship (4627) | Study: MA | |
| R.C. Hoiles and IHS Postdoctoral Fellowships (3052) | | |
| Hollingworth Award Competition (3877) | | |
| Hoover Library Fellowships and Grants (2890) | Study: United States | |
| Humanities Fellowships (1179) | Citizenship: US | |
| Richard Carley Hunt Memorial Postdoctoral Fellowships (6134) | | |
| Huntington Library Research Awards (2939) | Study: United States | |
| Institute for Advanced Study Postdoctoral Research Fellowships (3009) | Study: United States | |
| Institute for Advanced Study Postdoctoral Study Awards (3010) | | |
| Institute of Developing Economies Visiting Research Fellowships (3027) | Study: Japan | |
| Institute of Irish Studies Junior Fellowships (3069) | | |
| Institute Postdoctoral Fellowship (4754) | Citizenship: US, PermRes; Study: United States | |
| International Collaborative Research Grants (6135) | | |
| IREX Research Residencies (3186) | Citizenship: US, PermRes | |
| IREX Short-Term Travel Grants for Independent Short-Term Research (3187) | Citizenship: US, PermRes; Study: Union of Soviet Socialist Republics | |
| Olivia James Traveling Fellowship (1066) | Citizenship: US, PermRes; Study: Greece, Italy | |
| Jamestown Prize (4755) | | |
| H. Kellogg Institute Residential Fellowships (3347) | Study: United States | |
| The Louise Kidder Early Career Award (5495) | | |
| Killam Research Fellowships (3375) | Legal: Canada | |
| Samuel H. Kress Joint Athens-Jerusalem Fellowship (875) | Citizenship: US | |
| Katrin H. Lamon Resident Scholarship for Native Americans (5274) | Study: United States | Native American |
| Leakey Foundation General Grants (3443) | | |
| Lloyd Lewis Fellowships in American History (4617) | Study: IL | |
| Materials Analysis Fellowships (2061) | Study: United States | |
| Andrew W. Mellon Foundation Fellowships (877) | Legal: Czech Republic, Hungary, Poland | |
| Institute Andrew W. Mellon Postdoctoral Research Fellowship (4752) | | |
| Institute Andrew W. Mellon Postdoctoral Research Fellowship (4756) | | |
| Mesopotamian Fellowship (878) | | Association |
| Ministry of the Flemish Community Fellowships (3710) | Citizenship: US, PermRes | |
| NAS/NRC Collaboration in Basic Science and Engineering Long-Term Grants (3831) | Citizenship: US | |
| NAS/NRC Collaboration in Basic Science and Engineering Short-Term Project Development Grants (3832) | Citizenship: US | |

| Vocational Goal, Award, and Entry Number | Geographic Restrictions (Citizenship, Legal Residence, Place of Study) | Affiliation/Special Recipients Requirements |
|---|---|---|
| *Social Sciences (continued)* | | |
| National Assessment of Educational Progress Visiting Scholar Program (2355) | Study: NJ, United States | |
| National Endowment for the Humanities Fellowships (2543) | Citizenship: US; Study: United States | |
| National Endowment for the Humanities Fellowships (5275) | | |
| National Humanities Center Residential, Advanced Postdoctoral Fellowships (4184) | Study: United States | |
| National Program for Advanced Study and Research in China - Research Program (2016) | Study: People's Republic of China | |
| NATO Euro-Atlantic Partnership Council Fellowships Programme (4655) | Citizenship: US | |
| NEH Fellowships for Research in Turkey (847) | Study: Canada, Turkey, United States | |
| Neporany Research and Teaching Fellowship (1661) | | |
| Olfactory Research Fund Grants (4744) | | |
| Phi Alpha Theta Faculty Advisor Research Grant (4891) | | Fraternal |
| Pontifical Institute of Mediaeval Studies Research Associateships (4979) | Study: Canada | |
| Population Council Fellowships in the Social Sciences (4981) | | |
| Postdoctoral Fellowships in the Atmospheric Sciences (3931) | Study: United States | |
| Postdoctoral Fellowships in the History and Philosophy of Science (4699) | Study: United States | |
| Postgraduate Study Visits Scheme (1493) | Citizenship: United Kingdom | |
| Pre- and Postdoctoral Fellowships in International and Area Studies (2804) | Study: United States | |
| Pre- and Postdoctoral Fellowships on Nonviolent Sanctions; Visiting Scholar Affiliations (2806) | Study: United States | |
| Radcliffe Research Support Program (3798) | | |
| Reflections on Development Fellowships (5150) | | |
| Research Fellowships in American History and Culture (3460) | Study: United States | |
| Rockefeller Archive Center Research Grants (5142) | Study: United States | |
| Roosevelt Institute Grants-in-Aid (5161) | Study: United States | |
| Schlesinger Library, Radcliffe College Honorary Visiting Scholar Appointments (5257) | | |
| Schlesinger Library, Radcliffe College Research Support Grants (5258) | | |
| Social Science Research Fellowships in Population (5153) | Citizenship: US/CA | |
| Social Sciences and Humanities Research Council Postdoctoral Fellowships (5426) | Citizenship: Canada, PermRes | |
| SSRC Abe Fellowship Program (5392) | Study: Japan, United States | |
| SSRC Advanced Postdoctoral Training and Research Awards (5393) | Citizenship: US, PermRes | |
| SSRC African Advanced Research Grants (5395) | Citizenship: US, PermRes | |
| SSRC African Humanities Fellowships (5396) | Study: IL | |
| SSRC Berlin Program for Advanced German and European Studies Fellowships (5398) | Citizenship: US, PermRes; Study: Germany | |
| SSRC Japan Advanced Research Grants (5403) | Citizenship: US, PermRes | |
| SSRC Japan Grants for Research Planning Activities (5405) | | |
| SSRC Korea Advanced Research Grants (5406) | Citizenship: US, PermRes | |

| Vocational Goal, Award, and Entry Number | Geographic Restrictions (Citizenship, Legal Residence, Place of Study) | Affiliation/Special Recipients Requirements |
|---|---|---|
| *Social Sciences (continued)* | | |
| SSRC Korea Grants for Research Planning Activities (5407) | | |
| SSRC Latin America and the Caribbean Advanced Research Grants (5408) | Citizenship: US, PermRes | |
| SSRC-MacArthur Foundation Postdoctoral Fellowships on Peace and Security in a Changing World (5410) | | |
| SSRC Near and Middle East Advanced Research Fellowships (5411) | Citizenship: US, PermRes | |
| SSRC South Asia Advanced Research Grants (5414) | Citizenship: US, PermRes | |
| SSRC Southeast Asia Advanced Research Grants (5416) | Citizenship: US, PermRes | |
| SSRC Soviet Union and Its Successor States Postdoctoral Fellowships (5421) | Citizenship: US | |
| SSRC Soviet Union and Its Successor States Workshop Grants (5422) | | |
| Robert G. Stone Fellowships in American Maritime History (6182) | Study: CT | |
| Summer Travel/Research in Turkey Grants (3082) | Legal: United States; Study: Turkey | |
| Morris K. Udall OTA Congressional Fellowship (5851) | | |
| UNITAR Internships (5803) | Study: United States | |
| Venetian Research Program (2216) | Citizenship: US, PermRes; Study: Italy | |
| Alexander O. Vietor Memorial Fellowship (1518) | Study: RI | |
| Visiting Scholar Postdoctoral Stipend (1789) | | |
| Weatherhead Fellowships (5276) | | |
| Woodrow Wilson Center Residential Fellowship (6184) | | |
| Helen M. Woodruff Fellowship of the Archaeological Institute of America (1068) | Citizenship: US, PermRes | |
| Manfred Worner Fellowship (4657) | | |
| Yale Center for British Art Fellowships (6278) | Study: United States | |
| Ziskind-Sommerfeld Research Award (5440) | | Association |

## Visual and Performing Arts

| Vocational Goal, Award, and Entry Number | Geographic Restrictions | Affiliation/Special Recipients Requirements |
|---|---|---|
| Artists Fellowship; Japan Foundation Cultural Properties Specialists Fellowship; Japan Foundation Doctoral Fellowship; Japan Foundation Research Fellowship (3240) | Study: Japan | |
| Asian Art and Religion Fellowships (1176) | Citizenship: US | |
| Asian Cultural Council Fellowship Grants (1177) | Citizenship: US, Other; Study: United States | |
| Bunting Fellowship (1526) | Study: MA | |
| Bunting Institute Affiliation Program (1527) | Study: MA | |
| Center For Advanced Study in the Visual Arts Associate Appointments (1768) | Study: DC | |
| Ford Foundation Fellowships (1178) | Citizenship: Other; Study: United States | |
| Frese Senior Research Fellowship (1772) | Citizenship: Germany, PermRes; Study: United States | |
| Frese Senior Research Fellowship Program (1773) | Citizenship: Germany; Study: DC | |
| Getty Museum Guest Scholar Grants (2703) | Study: United States | |
| Louise Wallace Hackney Fellowship for the Study of Chinese Art (757) | Citizenship: US | |
| Humanities Fellowships (1179) | Citizenship: US | |
| Huntington Library Research Awards (2939) | Study: United States | |
| Olivia James Traveling Fellowship (1066) | Citizenship: US, PermRes; Study: Greece, Italy | |
| Andrew W. Mellon Fellowships (3657) | | |

| Vocational Goal, Award, and Entry Number | Geographic Restrictions (Citizenship, Legal Residence, Place of Study) | Affiliation/Special Recipients Requirements |
|---|---|---|
| *Visual and Performing Arts (continued)* | | |
| Andrew W. Mellon Fellowships in Art History (3658) | Study: United States | |
| Andrew W. Mellon Fellowships in Conservation (3659) | Study: United States | |
| J. Clawson Mills Scholarships (3666) | | |
| Ministry of the Flemish Community Fellowships (3710) | Citizenship: US, PermRes | |
| NEH Fellowships for Research in Turkey (847) | Study: Canada, Turkey, United States | |
| Samuel H. Kress/Ailsa Mellon Bruce Paired Fellowship for Research in Conservation and Art History/Archaeology (1777) | | |
| Scholarships for Young Researchers and University Teaching Staff (1797) | Study: Finland | |
| Senior Fellowships (1778) | Study: DC | |
| Visiting Senior Fellowships (1780) | Study: DC | |
| Jane and Morgan Whitney Fellowships (3671) | | |
| Yale Center for British Art Fellowships (6278) | Study: United States | |

# Postgraduate

### Agriculture

| | | |
|---|---|---|
| Fellowship Progamme of the Netherlands Ministry of Agriculture, Nature Management and Fisheries (3103) | Study: Netherlands | |
| Interchange Fellowship in Horticulture and Landscape Design (2622) | Citizenship: United Kingdom, US, PermRes; Study: United States | |
| International Arabian Horse Foundation Scholarship Application (3105) | | |
| Outstanding Doctoral and Master's Thesis Awards (248) | | |
| Wood Awards (2555) | | |

### Architecture and Environmental Design

| | | |
|---|---|---|
| AIA/AAF Scholarship for Advanced Study and Research (571) | | |
| John Dinkeloo Bequests/American Academy in Rome Traveling Fellowship in Architectural Technology (6023) | Study: Italy | |
| Interchange Fellowship in Horticulture and Landscape Design (2622) | Citizenship: United Kingdom, US, PermRes; Study: United States | |
| Van Alen Institute Fellowship in Public Architecture (Loyd Warren Fellowships/Paris Prize) (6026) | Citizenship: US, PermRes | |
| Michael Ventris Memorial Award (3017) | | |

### Area and Ethnic Studies

| | | |
|---|---|---|
| Bilateral Scholarships (2110) | Study: Finland | |
| Cultural Cooperation Grants (6004) | | |
| Germanistic Society of America Fellowships (3067) | Citizenship: US; Study: Germany | |
| Irish American Cultural Institute Visiting Fellowship in Irish Studies (3227) | Legal: United States; Study: Ireland | |
| James A. Swan Fund Grants (5652) | | |
| U.S. Japan Media Fellowship (3242) | Citizenship: US | |

### Business and Management

| | | |
|---|---|---|
| African Graduate Fellowships (47) | Study: United States | |
| American Economic Association/Federal Reserve System Minority Graduate Fellowships in Economics (453) | Citizenship: US | African American, Hispanic American, Native American |
| Bosch Foundation Fellowships (1459) | Citizenship: US; Study: Germany | |
| Fellowships in Ethics (5015) | Study: United States | |

| Vocational Goal, Award, and Entry Number | Geographic Restrictions (Citizenship, Legal Residence, Place of Study) | Affiliation/Special Recipients Requirements |
|---|---|---|
| *Business and Management (continued)* | | |
| David Hallissey Memorial Scholarships (973) | Citizenship: US/CA, PermRes | |
| Mackenzie King Travelling Scholarships (3529) | Legal: Canada; Study: United States | |
| Robert S. McNamara Fellowships (5140) | | |
| Outstanding Doctoral and Master's Thesis Awards (248) | | |
| Phi Chi Theta Scholarships (4896) | | Association |
| UNDP Summer Internships (5801) | Study: United States | |

## Communications

| | | |
|---|---|---|
| Bosch Foundation Fellowships (1459) | Citizenship: US; Study: Germany | |
| The Chicago Reporter Minority Fellowship in Urban Journalism (1920) | | Minority |
| Dirksen Congressional Research Grants (2253) | | |

## Computer and Information Sciences

| | | |
|---|---|---|
| Bureau of Engraving and Printing Graduate Student Research Participation Program (5862) | | |
| Bureau of Engraving and Printing Postgraduate Research Program (5863) | | |
| Center for Devices and Radiological Health Postgraduate Research Program (5864) | | |
| Fossil Energy Professional Internship Program (5878) | | |
| Laboratory Cooperative Postgraduate Research Training Program (5898) | | |
| National Center for Toxicological Research Graduate Student Research Participation (5906) | | |
| Naval Air Warfare Center Training Systems Division Graduate Research Participation Program (5912) | | |
| Naval Air Warfare Center Training Systems Division Postgraduate Research Participation Program (5913) | | |
| SDE Fellowships (5330) | | |

## Education

| | | |
|---|---|---|
| American Montessori Society Scholarship Fund (710) | | |
| AOSA Tap Fund (753) | | Association |
| Bilateral Scholarships (2110) | Study: Finland | |
| Emblem Club Scholarship Grants (2378) | | |
| Gunild Keetman Assistance Grants (754) | | Association |
| NCTE Research Foundation Research Grant-in-Aid (3961) | | |
| Retarded Citizens Teachers Scholarships (4793) | Citizenship: US, Canada | |
| Scholarships for Advanced Finnish Studies and Research (2111) | Study: Finland | |
| Shields-Gillespie Scholarships (755) | Legal: United States | Association |
| United Commercial Travelers Retarded Citizens Teacher Scholarship (5787) | | |

## Engineering

| | | |
|---|---|---|
| Bureau of Engraving and Printing Graduate Student Research Participation Program (5862) | | |
| Bureau of Engraving and Printing Postgraduate Research Program (5863) | | |
| Center for Devices and Radiological Health Postgraduate Research Program (5864) | | |

| Vocational Goal, Award, and Entry Number | Geographic Restrictions (Citizenship, Legal Residence, Place of Study) | Affiliation/Special Recipients Requirements |
|---|---|---|
| *Engineering (continued)* | | |
| Churchill Scholarships (1954) | Citizenship: US, PermRes; Legal: United States; Study: England | |
| ENCON Endowment (1616) | Study: Canada | Association |
| Environmental Monitoring Systems Laboratory Research Participation Program (5869) | | |
| Environmental Restoration/Waste Management Fellowship Program (5870) | | |
| Fossil Energy Professional Internship Program (5878) | | |
| Graduate Student Research Participation Program (5884) | | |
| Laboratory Cooperative Postgraduate Research Training Program (5898) | | |
| Manulife Financial Scholarships (1617) | Study: Canada | Association |
| Meloche-Monnex Scholarship (1618) | Study: Canada | Association |
| Naval Air Warfare Center Training Systems Division Graduate Research Participation Program (5912) | | |
| Naval Air Warfare Center Training Systems Division Postgraduate Research Participation Program (5913) | | |
| NSERC Research Scholarships, Fellowships, and Grants (4474) | Citizenship: Canada, PermRes; Study: Canada | |
| Office of Ground Water and Drinking Water Postgraduate Internship Program (5921) | | |
| Arthur & Doreen Parrett Scholarship Fund (4848) | Legal: WA | |
| Risk Reduction Engineering Research Laboratory Research Participation Program (5923) | | |
| Sumner Memorial Fellowships (5646) | Citizenship: Canada; Legal: Canada; Study: Canada | |
| Tennessee Valley Authority Research Participation Program (5927) | | |
| Tyndall Air Force Base Research Participation Program (5928) | | |
| U.S. Army Construction Engineering Research Laboratory Research Participation Program (5930) | | |
| U.S. Army Environmental Hygiene Agency Internship Program (5931) | | |
| J.E. Zajic Postgraduate Scholarship in Biochemical Engineering (1907) | Citizenship: Canada; Study: Canada | |

### Foreign Languages

| | | |
|---|---|---|
| Germanistic Society of America Quadrille Grants (2697) | | |

### Health Care Services

| | | |
|---|---|---|
| F. Stanton Deland Fellowships in Health Care and Society (1478) | Study: United States | |
| USP Fellowship Award (5964) | | |

### Health Sciences

| | | |
|---|---|---|
| American Speech-Language-Hearing Foundation Research Grants for New Investigators (990) | Study: United States | |
| American Speech-Language-Hearing Foundation Student Research Grant in Audiology (991) | | |
| Cancer Prevention and Control Research Small Grant Program (3922) | | |
| Career Development Fellowships (1611) | Citizenship: Canada, PermRes; Study: Canada | |

| Vocational Goal, Award, and Entry Number | Geographic Restrictions (Citizenship, Legal Residence, Place of Study) | Affiliation/Special Recipients Requirements |
|---|---|---|
| *Health Sciences (continued)* | | |
| Hazel Corbin Assistance Fund Scholarships (3609) | Study: United States | |
| International Order of the King's Daughters and Sons Health Careers Scholarships (3169) | Citizenship: US/CA; Legal: Canada, United States; Study: Canada, United States | |
| Maurice Legault Awards (1613) | Citizenship: Canada, PermRes | |
| Mead Johnson Nutritional Perinatal Research Grants Program (5337) | Citizenship: US | |
| Arthur & Doreen Parrett Scholarship Fund (4848) | Legal: WA | |
| Sigma Theta Tau International Small Research Grant (5344) | | |
| Student Research Grant in Early Childhood Language Development (995) | | |
| **Humanities** | | |
| Frances C. Allen Fellowships (4615) | Study: United States | Native American |
| D'Arcy McNickle Center for the History of the American Indian Fellowships (4606) | | |
| National Endowment for the Humanities Fellowships (255) | Study: MA | |
| Sir Arthur Sims Scholarships (5196) | Citizenship: Canada | |
| **Industry and Trade** | | |
| EAIA Research Grants Program (2304) | Citizenship: US | |
| SEMA Scholarship (5581) | | |
| USAIG PDP Scholarships (6017) | Citizenship: US | |
| Wood Awards (2555) | | |
| **Language and Literature** | | |
| Elva Knight Research Grants (3177) | | Association |
| The Harper-Wood Studentship for English Poetry and Literature (5222) | | |
| Student Research Grant in Early Childhood Language Development (995) | | |
| **Law** | | |
| Viscount Bennett Fellowship (1609) | Citizenship: Canada | |
| Fellowships in Ethics (5015) | Study: United States | |
| Law Fellowship (4235) | | Ethnic |
| Mackenzie King Travelling Scholarships (3529) | Legal: Canada; Study: United States | |
| **Liberal/General Studies** | | |
| Anglo-Jewish Association Grants (1044) | | Religion |
| John Dana Archbold Fellowship (3820) | Citizenship: US, PermRes; Study: Norway | |
| Awards for Advanced Study and Research in Scandinavia (852) | Citizenship: US, PermRes | |
| Freda Bage Fellowships; Commemorative Fellowships (1323) | Study: Australia | |
| Beit Trust Postgraduate Fellowships (1395) | Citizenship: Zimbabwe, PermRes; Study: England, Ireland, Republic of South Africa | |
| BIA Higher Education/Hopi Supplemental Grants (2892) | | Native American |
| British Marshall Scholarships (1230) | Citizenship: US; Study: United Kingdom | |
| Carnegie Grants (1739) | Study: Scotland | |
| Beatrice Fincher Scholarship; Lady Leitch Scholarship (1325) | | Association |
| Germanistic Society of America Quadrille Grants (2697) | | |
| Hopi Scholarship (2894) | | Native American |
| Steven Knezevich Trust Grants (3381) | | Ethnic |
| Kosciuszko Foundation Graduate/Postgraduate Study and Research in Poland Scholarships (3400) | Study: Poland | |

| Vocational Goal, Award, and Entry Number | Geographic Restrictions (Citizenship, Legal Residence, Place of Study) | Affiliation/Special Recipients Requirements |
|---|---|---|
| *Liberal/General Studies (continued)* | | |
| Latin American Educational Foundation Scholarships (3439) | Legal: CO | Hispanic American |
| Lynden Memorial Scholarship (3522) | | Employer |
| MacKenzie King Open Scholarship (3528) | Legal: Canada | |
| Ministry of the Flemish Community in Belgium Fellowships (2483) | Citizenship: US | |
| National Association for Armenian Studies and Research, Inc. Fund (1126) | Citizenship: US | Ethnic |
| National Fraternal Society of the Deaf Scholarships (4173) | | Association, Handicapped |
| Navajo Code Talkers Scholarship (4479) | | Native American |
| NCAA Postgraduate Scholarships (3937) | Legal: United States | |
| New York State Senate Legislative Fellows Program (4598) | Citizenship: US | |
| James R. Nicholl Memorial Grant (4635) | Legal: OH | |
| Opportunities for the Blind, Inc. Grants (4785) | Citizenship: US | Handicapped |
| ORS Awards (4824) | Study: England | |
| Admiral Roland Student Loan (5849) | Citizenship: US | Other |
| Scholarships and Awards for Overseas Students (1590) | Study: England | |
| Women of the ELCA Scholarship (6226) | | Religion |
| The Women's Sports Foundation Minority Internship Program (6241) | | Other, Minority |

### Library and Archival Sciences

| | | |
|---|---|---|
| Mary Adeline Connor Professional Development Scholarship Program (5576) | | Association |
| Hagley Fellowships/Grants-in-Aid (2779) | | |
| Gerd Muehsam Memorial Award (1145) | | |
| World Book Graduate Scholarships in Library Science (1668) | Citizenship: Canada; Study: Canada, United States | |

### Life Sciences

| | | |
|---|---|---|
| Agency for Toxic Substances and Disease Registry Postgraduate Research Program (5859) | | |
| Bermuda Biological Station Visiting Graduate Internships (1418) | Study: Bermuda | |
| Center for Devices and Radiological Health Postgraduate Research Program (5864) | | |
| Center for Drug Evaluation and Research Postgraduate Research (5865) | | |
| CIIT Summer Internships (1903) | Study: NC | |
| Conservation Science Fellowship (2060) | Study: United States | |
| Continental European Fellowships (1956) | Citizenship: United Kingdom, Ireland, PermRes | |
| Environmental Protection Agency Tribal Lands Science Scholarship (560) | | Native American |
| Explorers Club Exploration Fund Grants (2425) | | |
| Eloise Gerry Fellowships (5329) | | |
| Graduate Fellowships for Global Change (5883) | | |
| Graduate Student Research Participation Program (5884) | | |
| Historically Black Colleges and Universities Health and Environmental Research Opportunities for Faculty and Students (5892) | | |
| National Center for Toxicological Research Graduate Student Research Participation (5906) | | |
| National Center for Toxicological Research Postgraduate Research Program (5907) | | |

| Vocational Goal, Award, and Entry Number | Geographic Restrictions (Citizenship, Legal Residence, Place of Study) | Affiliation/Special Recipients Requirements |
|---|---|---|
| *Life Sciences (continued)* | | |
| Naval Air Warfare Center Training Systems Division Graduate Research Participation Program (5912) | | |
| Naval Air Warfare Center Training Systems Division Postgraduate Research Participation Program (5913) | | |
| NIDAY Fellowships (3786) | Study: United States | |
| Sigurd T. Olson Common Loon Research Awards (4747) | | |
| Arthur & Doreen Parrett Scholarship Fund (4848) | Legal: WA | |
| SDE Fellowships (5330) | | |
| Sport Fishery Research Grants and Fellowships (5593) | Citizenship: US; Study: United States | |
| James A. Swan Fund Grants (5652) | | |
| Tyndall Air Force Base Research Participation Program (5928) | | |

## Mathematics

| | | |
|---|---|---|
| Churchill Scholarships (1954) | Citizenship: US, PermRes; Legal: United States; Study: England | |
| Fossil Energy Professional Internship Program (5878) | | |
| Graduate Student Research Participation Program (5884) | | |
| Laboratory Cooperative Postgraduate Research Training Program (5898) | | |
| National Center for Toxicological Research Graduate Student Research Participation (5906) | | |
| National Center for Toxicological Research Postgraduate Research Program (5907) | | |
| SDE Fellowships (5330) | | |

## Medicine

| | | |
|---|---|---|
| Action Research Training Fellowships (31) | | |
| Agency for Toxic Substances and Disease Registry Postgraduate Research Program (5859) | | |
| Albert Ellis Institute Clinical Fellowships, Internships (143) | Citizenship: US, PermRes; Study: United States | |
| Allied Health Scholarships (3370) | Citizenship: Canada; Legal: Canada; Study: Canada | |
| AVMF Auxiliary Student Loan (1011) | | |
| E. A. Baker Foundation Fellowships and Research Grants (1676) | Citizenship: Canada | |
| Cancer Prevention and Control Research Small Grant Program (3922) | | |
| Career Development Fellowships (1611) | Citizenship: Canada, PermRes; Study: Canada | |
| Cystic Fibrosis Foundation Clinical Research Grants (2152) | | |
| Cystic Fibrosis Foundation Special Research Awards (2158) | | |
| Dermatologist Investigator Research Fellowship Award (2237) | Study: Canada, United States | |
| Fellowships in Ethics (5015) | Study: United States | |
| Morris Fishbein Fellowship in Medical Journalism (688) | | |
| Fyssen Foundation Research Grants (2610) | | |
| Heed Ophthalmic Foundation Fellowships (2855) | Citizenship: US; Study: United States | |
| HSFC Graduate Research Traineeships (2840) | Citizenship: Canada, PermRes; Study: Canada | |

| Vocational Goal, Award, and Entry Number | Geographic Restrictions (Citizenship, Legal Residence, Place of Study) | Affiliation/Special Recipients Requirements |
|---|---|---|
| *Medicine (continued)* | | |
| International Order of the King's Daughters and Sons Health Careers Scholarships (3169) | Citizenship: US/CA; Legal: Canada, United States; Study: Canada, United States | |
| Life Sciences Research Foundation Fellowships (3470) | | |
| Medical Student Loan Repayment Program (3753) | | |
| National Center for Toxicological Research Graduate Student Research Participation (5906) | | |
| NCAFP Foundation Medical Student Loan (4659) | Study: NC | |
| James R. Nicholl Memorial Grant (4635) | Legal: OH | |
| Nurse Loan Repayment Program (3754) | Legal: MO | |
| Arthur & Doreen Parrett Scholarship Fund (4848) | Legal: WA | |
| Scleroderma Research Grants (5284) | | |
| Society of Nuclear Medicine Pilot Research Grants (5476) | | |
| Society for Pediatric Dermatology Grant (5480) | | |
| Tylman Research Grant (229) | | |

**Military Sciences**

| | | |
|---|---|---|
| Department of National Defense Security and Defense Forum Internships (1272) | Citizenship: Canada | |
| U.S. Army Construction Engineering Research Laboratory Research Participation Program (5930) | | |

**Parks and Recreation**

| | | |
|---|---|---|
| American Numismatic Society Grants-in-Aid (738) | Legal: Canada, United States; Study: United States | |

**Philosophy, Theology, and Religion**

| | | |
|---|---|---|
| Fellowships in Ethics (5015) | Study: United States | |
| Greek Orthodox Ladies Philoptochos Society Scholarships for Hellenic College and Holy Cross Greek Orthodox School of Theology (2749) | | Religion |
| Spalding Trust Postgraduate Scholarship/Grant (5571) | | |

**Physical Sciences**

| | | |
|---|---|---|
| Annual Student Paper Competition (6115) | | |
| Bureau of Engraving and Printing Graduate Student Research Participation Program (5862) | | |
| Bureau of Engraving and Printing Postgraduate Research Program (5863) | | |
| Carnegie Postdoctoral Research Fellowship in Astronomy (4713) | | |
| Center for Drug Evaluation and Research Postgraduate Research (5865) | | |
| The Center for Field Research Grants (1791) | | |
| Churchill Scholarships (1954) | Citizenship: US, PermRes; Legal: United States; Study: England | |
| Environmental Monitoring Systems Laboratory Research Participation Program (5869) | | |
| Environmental Protection Agency Tribal Lands Science Scholarship (560) | | Native American |
| Explorers Club Exploration Fund Grants (2425) | | |
| Fossil Energy Postgraduate Research Training Program (5877) | | |
| Fossil Energy Professional Internship Program (5878) | | |

| Vocational Goal, Award, and Entry Number | Geographic Restrictions (Citizenship, Legal Residence, Place of Study) | Affiliation/Special Recipients Requirements |
| --- | --- | --- |
| *Physical Sciences (continued)* | | |
| Geological Society of America Research Grants (2649) | Study: Canada, Mexico, United States | |
| Graduate Student Research Participation Program (5884) | | |
| ILZRO Lead-Acid Battery Fellowship (3163) | | |
| Laboratory Cooperative Postgraduate Research Training Program (5898) | | |
| NSERC Research Scholarships, Fellowships, and Grants (4474) | Citizenship: Canada, PermRes; Study: Canada | |
| Office of Ground Water and Drinking Water Postgraduate Internship Program (5921) | | |
| Risk Reduction Engineering Research Laboratory Research Participation Program (5923) | | |
| SDE Fellowships (5330) | | |
| Sumner Memorial Fellowships (5646) | Citizenship: Canada; Legal: Canada; Study: Canada | |
| Tennessee Valley Authority Research Participation Program (5927) | | |
| Tyndall Air Force Base Research Participation Program (5928) | | |

**Protective Services and Public Affairs**

| | | |
| --- | --- | --- |
| American Cancer Society Clinical Oncology Social Work Training Grants (362) | Citizenship: US, PermRes | |
| Phoenix Management Internships (4933) | | |

**Social Sciences**

| | | |
| --- | --- | --- |
| Advanced Research Grants in Military History (5823) | Study: PA, United States | |
| Gordon Allport Intergroup Relations Prize (5492) | | |
| Richard Barnett Memorial Travel Awards (1042) | Study: Israel | |
| Bosch Foundation Fellowships (1459) | Citizenship: US; Study: Germany | |
| Bunting Institute Peace Fellowships (1528) | Study: MA | |
| Dirksen Congressional Research Grants (2253) | | |
| EAIA Research Grants Program (2304) | Citizenship: US | |
| Friedreich Ebert Foundation Doctoral Research Fellowships (2330) | Citizenship: US | |
| Fellowships in Ethics (5015) | Study: United States | |
| Fyssen Foundation Research Grants (2610) | | |
| John C. Geilfuss Fellowship (5615) | | |
| Germanistic Society of America Quadrille Grants (2697) | | |
| Graduate Student Research Participation Program (5884) | | |
| Amy Louise Hunter Fellowship (5616) | | |
| Otto Klineberg Intercultural and International Relations Award (5496) | | |
| Mackenzie King Travelling Scholarships (3529) | Legal: Canada; Study: United States | |
| Marine Corps Historical Center Research Grants (3559) | | |
| Materials Analysis Fellowships (2061) | Study: United States | |
| National Endowment for the Humanities Fellowships (255) | Study: MA | |
| New York State Assembly Graduate Scholarships (4574) | Legal: NY; Study: NY | |
| Peace Fellowships (5076) | Study: United States | |
| Sir Arthur Sims Scholarships (5196) | Citizenship: Canada | |

| Vocational Goal, Award, and Entry Number | Geographic Restrictions (Citizenship, Legal Residence, Place of Study) | Affiliation/Special Recipients Requirements |
|---|---|---|
| *Social Sciences (continued)* | | |
| Society for the Psychological Study of Social Issues Grants-In-Aid Program (5497) | | |
| UNDP Summer Internships (5801) | Study: United States | |
| Jesse Marvin Unruh Assembly Fellowships (1574) | Study: United States | |
| Venetian Research Program (2216) | Citizenship: US, PermRes; Study: Italy | |

**Visual and Performing Arts**

| | | |
|---|---|---|
| Associated Board of the Royal Schools of Music International Scholarships (1191) | | |
| Banff Centre for the Arts Scholarships (1370) | Study: Canada | |
| Chester Dale Fellowships (3654) | | |
| Morris Fishbein Fellowship in Medical Journalism (688) | | |
| Interlochen Arts Academy and Arts Camp Scholarships (3101) | Study: MI | |
| Gerd Muehsam Memorial Award (1145) | | |
| National Orchestral Institute Scholarships (4330) | Study: United States | |
| NATS Artist Awards (3902) | | Association |
| Don and Gee Nicholl Fellowships in Screenwriting (23) | | |
| OPERA America Fellowship Program (4783) | Citizenship: US/CA | |
| Oregon College of Art & Craft Artists-in-Residence Program (4797) | Citizenship: US, PermRes; Study: OR, United States | |
| Scholarships for Young Researchers and University Teaching Staff (1797) | Study: Finland | |
| Swann Foundation Fellowship (5654) | | |
| Jane and Morgan Whitney Fellowships (3671) | | |

# Professional Development

**Agriculture**

| | | |
|---|---|---|
| American Horticultural Society Horticultural Career Internship (545) | | |
| CIEA Grants-in-Aid (3133) | Study: Switzerland | |
| Grants for Orchid Research (750) | | |
| International Affairs Fellowships (2105) | Citizenship: US, PermRes | |
| Sarah B. Tyson Fellowship (6234) | Study: United States | |

**Architecture and Environmental Design**

| | | |
|---|---|---|
| AIA/AAF Scholarship for Advanced Study and Research (571) | | |
| AILA Yamagami Hope Fellowship (3421) | | |
| Cintas Fellowships (1163) | | Ethnic |
| Dumbarton Oaks Project Grants (2287) | | |
| Graham Foundation Grants (2726) | | |
| Ralph Hudson Environmental Fellowship (3425) | Legal: Canada, Mexico, United States | |
| The Richard Morris Hunt Fellowship (575) | | |
| MacDowell Colony Residencies (3524) | Study: United States | |
| Andrew W. Mellon Fellowships in Conservation (3659) | Study: United States | |
| Netz Hilai Visiting Artists Fellowships (4515) | Study: Israel | |
| Revson Fellowships (5118) | Citizenship: US, PermRes; Study: United States | |
| Society of Naval Architects and Marine Engineers Scholarships (5472) | Citizenship: US/CA | |
| Starr Fellowships in Asian Paintings Conservation (3668) | Study: United States | |

| Vocational Goal, Award, and Entry Number | Geographic Restrictions (Citizenship, Legal Residence, Place of Study) | Affiliation/Special Recipients Requirements |
|---|---|---|
| *Architecture and Environmental Design (continued)* | | |
| Steedman Traveling Fellowship in Architecture (5626) | | |

**Area and Ethnic Studies**

| | | |
|---|---|---|
| AATF Summer Institute in France (325) | Citizenship: US, PermRes; Study: France, United States | Association |
| AIATSIS Research Grants (1327) | Study: Australia | |
| American School of Classical Studies Summer Sessions Scholarships (855) | Legal: Canada, United States; Study: Greece | Association |
| Amity Institute Internships (1026) | Study: United States | |
| Canadian Studies Faculty Enrichment Awards (1624) | Legal: United States; Study: Canada, United States | |
| Canadian Studies for Indian Scholars (5315) | | |
| Canadian Studies Sabbatical Fellowship Program (1627) | Legal: United States; Study: Canada | |
| Cultural Cooperation Grants (6004) | | |
| Cultural Grants (1596) | Citizenship: Canada | Native American |
| Dumbarton Oaks Project Grants (2287) | | |
| East-West Center Professional Associateships (2310) | Study: United States | |
| EMGIP Internships (2380) | Study: Germany | |
| The Freedom Forum Asia Studies Fellowships (5996) | Citizenship: US, PermRes, Other | |
| Friendship Commission Prize for the Translation of Japanese Literature (3341) | Citizenship: US, PermRes | |
| International Fellowships in Jewish Studies (3645) | | |
| Irish in America Publication Award; Notre Dame Studies in Catholicism Publication Award (6009) | | |
| Irish Research Funds (3228) | | |
| Jacobs Research Fund Grants (3236) | | |
| Neporany Research and Teaching Fellowship (1661) | | |
| NNAC Gifted/Talented Artist Sponsorships (4324) | | Native American |
| Post-Rabbinic Scholarships (3646) | | |
| Bernadette Schmitt Grants (541) | | Association |
| Schomburg Center Scholars-in-Residence (5272) | Citizenship: US; Study: United States | |
| Senior Performing Arts Fellowships (588) | Legal: United States; Study: India | |
| Dorothy Silver Playwriting Competition Prize (3261) | Study: United States | |
| Elizabeth A. Whitehead Visiting Professorships (862) | Legal: Canada, United States; Study: Greece | |

**Business and Management**

| | | |
|---|---|---|
| AERF Individual Grants (33) | | Association |
| Andersen Foundation Faculty Residencies (1040) | | |
| Henry A. Applegate Scholarships (2201) | | Association |
| Avis Rent a Car Scholarship (972) | Citizenship: US/CA; Study: Canada, United States | |
| Avon Products Foundation Scholarship Program for Women in Business Studies (1545) | Citizenship: US | |
| Boleslaw Monic Fund Prizes (1457) | | |
| Robert Bosch Foundation Fellowships (1758) | | |
| Direct Marketing Institute for Professors Scholarships (2251) | Study: United States | |
| Charles Fitzsimmons Award; IAHA General Scholarships; Frances Tally Award (3115) | | |

| Vocational Goal, Award, and Entry Number | Geographic Restrictions (Citizenship, Legal Residence, Place of Study) | Affiliation/Special Recipients Requirements |
|---|---|---|
| *Business and Management (continued)* | | |
| William C. Foster Fellows Visiting Scholars Competition (5818) | Citizenship: US | |
| India Studies Faculty Fellowships (5316) | Citizenship: Canada; Study: India | |
| India Studies Postdoctoral Research Fellowships (5318) | Citizenship: Canada; Study: India | |
| Institute of Chartered Accountants Research Grants (3015) | | |
| IPMA Graduate Study Fellowships (3172) | | Association |
| NAA Foundation Minority Fellowships (4631) | | Minority |
| National Awards for the Teaching of Economics (2336) | Study: United States | |
| Aviation Management Wilfred M. "Wiley" Post Scholarship (1351) | Legal: PA | |
| Rockefeller Archive Center Research Grants (5142) | Study: United States | |
| United Nations Fellowships (5799) | | |
| Visiting Scholar Awards (4441) | | |
| **Communications** | | |
| APSA Congressional Fellowships for Journalists (780) | Study: DC | |
| Asian American Journalists Association Fellowships (1170) | | Association, Asian American |
| Sherlee Barish Fellowship (5052) | | |
| The Joan Shorenstein Barone Congressional Fellowship (783) | Citizenship: US | |
| Blethen Family Newspaper Internship Program for Minorities (5295) | Study: WA | Minority |
| Robert Bosch Foundation Fellowships (1758) | | |
| Boston Globe One-Year Minority Development Program (1461) | | Minority |
| Arthur F. Burns Fellowships (3131) | Citizenship: US, Germany, PermRes; Study: Germany, United States | |
| Capital Cities/ABC Inc. Newspaper Internship (1721) | | Minority |
| Howard Chapnick Grant (5367) | | |
| The Chicago Reporter Minority Fellowship in Urban Journalism (1920) | | Minority |
| Michele Clark Fellowship (5057) | | |
| Dance Screen Competition Awards (3166) | Study: France | |
| The Walt Disney Studios Fellowship Program (2258) | Study: United States | |
| Editing Program for Minority Journalists (2338) | | Minority |
| The Freedom Forum Media Studies Center Residential Fellowships (2592) | Study: United States | |
| Gannett Center Fellowships (2593) | Study: NY | |
| Sandra Freeman Geller and Alfred Geller Fellowship (5059) | | |
| Hartford Courant Minority Internship (2798) | | Minority |
| Inter-American Press Association Scholarships (3093) | Citizenship: US, Canada, PermRes; Study: Canada, United States | |
| International Affairs Fellowships (2105) | Citizenship: US, PermRes | |
| Jefferson Fellowships (2312) | Legal: United States; Study: United States | |
| Knight-Bagehot Fellowships in Economics and Business Journalism (2011) | Study: United States | |
| Knight-Ridder Minority Specialty Development Program (4928) | | Minority |
| Knight Science Journalism Fellowships (3383) | Study: MA | |
| Landmark Communications Minority Internships (3419) | | Minority |
| Rollan D. Melton Fellowship (796) | | Minority |

| Vocational Goal, Award, and Entry Number | Geographic Restrictions (Citizenship, Legal Residence, Place of Study) | Affiliation/Special Recipients Requirements |
|---|---|---|
| **Communications (continued)** | | |
| Edward R. Murrow Fellowship for American Foreign Correspondents (2106) | Citizenship: US; Study: NY, United States | |
| NAA Foundation Minority Fellowships (4631) | | Minority |
| National Court Reporters Association Scholarships (3964) | | |
| Vada and Barney Oldfield Fellowship for National Security Reporting (5063) | | |
| Patterson Fellowships (4852) | Citizenship: US | |
| The Poynter Fellowship (784) | Citizenship: US | |
| Rennie Taylor/Alton Blakeslee Memorial Fellowship in Science Writing (2091) | Citizenship: US | |
| Reporters Committee Fellowship (5093) | Study: DC | |
| RTNDF Environmental and Science Reporting Fellowship (5065) | | |
| Times Mirror Minority Editorial Training Program (3496) | | Minority |
| Washington Press Association Annual Scholarships (6093) | Study: WA | |
| World Press Institute Fellowships (6268) | | |

## Computer and Information Sciences

| | | |
|---|---|---|
| Andersen Foundation Faculty Residencies (1040) | | |
| Engineering Rotation Program (2923) | Citizenship: US; Study: United States | |
| Faculty Research Participation Program at the National Center for Toxicological Research (5874) | | |
| Faculty Research Participation Program at the Naval Air Warfare Center Training Systems Division. (5875) | | |
| Fossil Energy Faculty Research Participation (5876) | | |
| William C. Foster Fellows Visiting Scholars Competition (5818) | Citizenship: US | |
| U.S. Department of Energy Faculty Research Participation Fellowship (5932) | | |

## Education

| | | |
|---|---|---|
| ACE Fellows Program (404) | | |
| ACRSE Scholarships (414) | | |
| All Saints Educational Trust Grants (190) | | |
| American Orff Schulwerk Association Research Grants (752) | | Association |
| Arts Education Fellowships (2093) | Citizenship: US | |
| The British Universities Summer Schools Scholarships (2384) | Study: United Kingdom | |
| Ruth Crymes Fellowship (5679) | | Association |
| Division II Arc Welding Awards (3481) | Legal: United States | |
| Excellence in Arc Welding Awards; Graduate and Professional Awards for Achievement in Arc-Welded Design, Engineering and Fabrication (3482) | Legal: United States | |
| Exhibitor Scholarships (1258) | | Association |
| Faculty Research Participation Program at the Agency for Toxic Substances and Disease Registry (5872) | | |
| Fellowships for Basic Study in the Humanities/Fellowships for Principals (2094) | | Other |
| Florida Critical Teacher Shortage Tuition Reimbursement Program (2502) | Study: FL | |
| Fulbright Teacher Exchange Program (2605) | Citizenship: US | |

| Vocational Goal, Award, and Entry Number | Geographic Restrictions (Citizenship, Legal Residence, Place of Study) | Affiliation/Special Recipients Requirements |
|---|---|---|
| *Education (continued)* | | |
| Grants for University Teachers to Serve in Developing Countries (5169) | | Association |
| Hollingworth Award Competition (3877) | | |
| IBE Scholars-in-Residence Awards (3129) | Study: Switzerland | |
| International Fellowships in Medical Education (2345) | Study: United States | |
| Joseph Klingenstein Fellowships (3379) | Study: United States | |
| McKnight Junior Faculty Developmment Fellowships (2520) | Citizenship: US; Study: FL | |
| NACA Multi-Cultural Scholarship (3867) | | Minority |
| NACA Prize Papers Competition (3868) | | |
| NACADA Research Award (3824) | | |
| National Fellowships in Education Reporting (2343) | | |
| National Restaurant Association Teacher Work/Study Grant (4366) | | |
| Piano Teaching Fellowship (4556) | Study: United States | |
| Retarded Citizens Teachers Scholarships (4793) | Citizenship: US, Canada | |
| Rockefeller Archive Center Research Grants (5142) | Study: United States | |
| Shields-Gillespie Scholarships (755) | Legal: United States | Association |
| United States Space Foundation Teacher Course Fellowship (5974) | Study: CO | |

**Engineering**

| | | |
|---|---|---|
| AAAS Congressional Science and Engineering Fellowships (263) | Study: United States | |
| AAAS Technology Policy Science and Engineering Fellowships (267) | Citizenship: US; Study: United States | |
| O.H. Ammann Research Fellowship in Structural Engineering (902) | | Association |
| ASME Federal Government Fellowships (942) | Citizenship: US | Association |
| Aviation Technology Scholarship (1349) | Legal: PA; Study: PA | |
| BPW Loans for Women in Engineering Studies (1547) | Citizenship: US | |
| Joseph Bramah Scholarship; Raymond Coleman Prescott Scholarship (3086) | | Association |
| Civilian Radioactive Waste Management/Historically Black Colleges and Universities Faculty Fellowship Program (5867) | | |
| Clayton Grants (3087) | | Association |
| Engineering Rotation Program (2923) | Citizenship: US; Study: United States | |
| Faculty Research Participation Program at the Naval Air Warfare Center Training Systems Division. (5875) | | |
| Fossil Energy Faculty Research Participation (5876) | | |
| William C. Foster Fellows Visiting Scholars Competition (5818) | Citizenship: US | |
| Freeman Fellowship (904) | | Association |
| Historically Black Colleges and Universities Faculty and Student Research Participation Program in Fusion. (5890) | | |
| Historically Black Colleges and Universities Fossil Energy Faculty and Student Research Training (5891) | | |
| Historically Black Colleges and Universities Nuclear Energy Faculty Research Participation Program (5893) | Citizenship: US | |
| ICE Overseas Travel Awards (3084) | | Association |

| Vocational Goal, Award, and Entry Number | Geographic Restrictions (Citizenship, Legal Residence, Place of Study) | Affiliation/Special Recipients Requirements |
|---|---|---|
| *Engineering (continued)* | | |
| International Association of Fire Chiefs Foundation Scholarships (3113) | | Employer |
| Professional Pilot John W. "Reds" Macfarlane Scholarship (1350) | Legal: PA; Study: PA | |
| NASA-ASEE Summer Faculty Fellowship (923) | Citizenship: US; Study: United States | |
| National Oceanic and Atmospheric Administration/Historically Black Colleges and Universities Faculty/Student Research Participation Program (5910) | | |
| National Oceanic and Atmospheric Administration Scholar in Residence Program (5911) | | |
| NATO Senior Guest Fellowships (4656) | Study: France, Italy, Luxembourg, Spain, Turkey | |
| NSERC Research Scholarships, Fellowships, and Grants (4474) | Citizenship: Canada, PermRes; Study: Canada | |
| Part-time Fossil Energy Faculty Research Participation Program (5922) | | |
| Petroleum Research Fund Grants (369) | Legal: United States; Study: United States | |
| Society of Naval Architects and Marine Engineers Scholarships (5472) | Citizenship: US/CA | |
| U.S. Department of Energy Faculty Research Participation Fellowship (5932) | | |
| U.S. Navy-ASEE Summer Faculty Research Program (925) | Citizenship: US; Study: CA, CT, DC, FL, LA, MS, PA, RI | |
| U.S. Nuclear Regulatory Commission Historically Black Colleges and Universities Faculty Research Participation (5934) | | |

## Foreign Languages

| | | |
|---|---|---|
| AATF Summer Institute in France (325) | Citizenship: US, PermRes; Study: France, United States | Association |
| NEH Summer Fellowships for Foreign Language Teachers K-12 (3989) | | |
| St. David's Scholarship (5220) | | Ethnic |

## Health Care Services

| | | |
|---|---|---|
| ADHA Institute Research Grants (419) | | |
| AOTF Research Grants (744) | | Association |
| Florida Dental Association Dental Hygiene Scholarship Program (2487) | Legal: FL | |
| Robert Wood Johnson Health Policy Fellowships (3073) | | Employer |
| Elizabeth St. Louis Award (2317) | Citizenship: Canada | |
| Miriam Neveren Summer Studentship (2318) | Citizenship: Canada | |
| Ray Woodham Visiting Fellowship Program (549) | | |

## Health Sciences

| | | |
|---|---|---|
| AACN Clinical Practice Grant (277) | | Association |
| AACN-Sigma Theta Tau Critical Care Grant (280) | | Association |
| Behavioral Sciences Student Fellowship (2397) | Study: United States | |
| CSLT Founders Fund Awards (1701) | | Association |
| Data-Driven Clinical Practice Grant (281) | | Association |
| Faculty Research Participation Program at the Agency for Toxic Substances and Disease Registry (5872) | | |
| Carl Foley Scholarships (2097) | | |
| Foundation for Chiropractic Education and Research Fellowships, Scholarships, and Residency Stipends (2564) | | |
| Health Canada Research Personnel Career Awards (2828) | Citizenship: Canada, PermRes; Legal: Canada | |

| Vocational Goal, Award, and Entry Number | Geographic Restrictions (Citizenship, Legal Residence, Place of Study) | Affiliation/Special Recipients Requirements |
|---|---|---|
| *Health Sciences (continued)* | | |
| Health Physics Faculty Research Award Program (5886) | | |
| KCI-AACN Critical Care Research Grant (282) | | Association |
| Maryland House of Delegates Scholarship (3575) | Legal: MD | |
| Nellcor Puritan Bennett Inc. AACN Mentorship Grant (283) | | Association |
| Oncology Nursing Foundation/Amgen, Inc. Research Grant (4758) | | |
| Oncology Nursing Foundation/Bristol- Myers Oncology Chapter Research Grant (4760) | | |
| Oncology Nursing Foundation/Bristol- Myers Oncology Division Community Health Research Grant (4761) | | |
| Oncology Nursing Foundation/Bristol- Myers Oncology Division Research Grant (4762) | | |
| Oncology Nursing Foundation/Cetus Oncology Grants for Research Involving Biotherapy or Immunotherapy (4763) | | |
| Oncology Nursing Foundation/Glaxo Research Grants (4765) | | |
| Oncology Nursing Foundation/Oncology Nursing Certification Corporation Nursing Education Research Grants (4767) | | |
| Oncology Nursing Foundation/Oncology Nursing Society Research Grant (4768) | | |
| Oncology Nursing Foundation/Ortho Biotech Research Grant (4769) | | |
| Oncology Nursing Foundation/Purdue Frederick Research Grant (4770) | | |
| Oncology Nursing Foundation/Sigma Theta Tau International and Oncology Nursing Society Research Grant (4772) | | |
| Oncology Nursing Society/SmithKline Beecham Research Grant (4773) | | Association |
| Scholarships for Therapists (3855) | Citizenship: US | |
| Sigma Theta Tau International/American Association of Diabetes Educators Grant (5338) | | |
| Sigma Theta Tau International/American Nephrology Nurses' Association Grant (5339) | | |
| Sigma Theta Tau International/American Nurses' Foundation Grant (5340) | | |
| Sigma Theta Tau International/Emergency Nursing Foundation Grant (5341) | | |
| Sigma Theta Tau International/Glaxo Wellcome New Investigator/Mentor Grant (5342) | | |
| Sigma Theta Tau International/Glaxo Wellcome Prescriptive Practice Grant (5343) | | |
| Archie Vinitsky ET Scholarship (5807) | | |
| WHO Fellowships (6259) | | |
| **Home Economics** | | |
| All Saints Educational Trust Grants (190) | | |
| American Institute of Baking and Maintenance Engineering Scholarships (578) | | |
| Malcolm Bird Commemorative Award (1331) | | Association |
| Borden Award (290) | Citizenship: US, Canada | |
| Commemorative Lecture Award (292) | | Association |
| GRI/ICIF Culinary Scholarships (4232) | | |
| Edward T. Hanley Scholarships (2903) | Study: United States | |
| IACP Foundation Scholarships (3111) | | |

| Vocational Goal, Award, and Entry Number | Geographic Restrictions (Citizenship, Legal Residence, Place of Study) | Affiliation/Special Recipients Requirements |
|---|---|---|
| **Home Economics (continued)** | | |
| James D. Moran Memorial Research Award (299) | Legal: United States | |
| National Restaurant Association Teacher Work/Study Grant (4366) | | |
| Ruth O'Brien Project Grants (300) | | Association |
| Joel Polsky/Fixtures Furniture/FIDER Endowment Research Award (2571) | | |
| Tony's Foodservice Scholarships (5278) | | Association |
| Wiley-Berger Memorial Award for Volunteer Service (306) | | |

## Humanities

| | | |
|---|---|---|
| Artists Fellowship; Japan Foundation Cultural Properties Specialists Fellowship; Japan Foundation Doctoral Fellowship; Japan Foundation Research Fellowship (3240) | Study: Japan | |
| Fellowships for Basic Study in the Humanities/Fellowships for Principals (2094) | | Other |
| Fellowships for Independent Study in the Humanities (2095) | | |
| Fraenkel Prizes in Contemporary History (3023) | | |
| Society for the Humanities Postdoctoral Fellowships (5456) | Study: United States | |
| Summer Session Awards (861) | | |

## Industry and Trade

| | | |
|---|---|---|
| Canadian Transportation Education Foundation Scholarships and Research Grants (1706) | Citizenship: Canada | |
| Chartered Institute of Transport to New Zealand Scholarships (1838) | Study: New Zealand | |
| Ginger and Fred Deines Mexico Scholarships (5742) | Study: Mexico, United States | Hispanic American |
| R & E Council Graphic Arts Educators' Programs (5101) | | |
| Shared Research Equipment Program (5926) | | |
| Henry Spurrier Scholarship (1836) | | |
| U.S. Nuclear Regulatory Commission Historically Black Colleges and Universities Faculty Research Participation (5934) | | |
| Whirly-Girls Memorial Flight Scholarships (3204) | | |

## Language and Literature

| | | |
|---|---|---|
| Albee Foundation Residencies (141) | Study: United States | |
| Nelson Algren Awards (1924) | Citizenship: US | |
| Amity Institute Internships (1026) | Study: United States | |
| Artists Fellowships and Residencies (3766) | Study: United States | |
| AWP Award in Poetry, Short Fiction, Novel, and Creative Nonfiction (1205) | | |
| George Bennett Fellowships (4931) | Study: United States | |
| Stephen Botein Fellowships (254) | Study: United States | |
| Bread Loaf Writers' Conference Fellowships; Bread Loaf Writers' Conference Scholarships (1476) | Study: United States | |
| Bunting Fellowship (1526) | Study: MA | |
| Bunting Institute Affiliation Program (1527) | Study: MA | |
| Bush Artist Fellowships (1539) | Legal: MN, ND, SD, WI | |
| Cintas Fellowships (1163) | | Ethnic |
| Bernard F. Conners Poetry Prize (4839) | | |
| Cummington Community of the Arts Residencies (2142) | Study: United States | |

119

| Vocational Goal, Award, and Entry Number | Geographic Restrictions (Citizenship, Legal Residence, Place of Study) | Affiliation/Special Recipients Requirements |
|---|---|---|
| *Language and Literature (continued)* | | |
| Discovery/*The Nation* Contest; The Joan Leiman Jacobson Poetry Prizes (4969) | Study: United States | |
| Don Freeman Memorial Grant-in-Aid (5444) | | Association |
| Friendship Commission Prize for the Translation of Japanese Literature (3341) | Citizenship: US, PermRes | |
| Tony Godwin Award (2711) | | |
| Joseph Henry Jackson Award (5234) | Legal: CA, NV | |
| Ezra Jack Keats/Kerlan Collection Memorial Fellowship (3339) | Study: United States | |
| Letras de Oro Spanish Speaking Literary Prizes (3453) | Legal: United States | |
| Amy Lowell Poetry Travelling Scholarship (3510) | Legal: United States | |
| MacDowell Colony Residencies (3524) | Study: United States | |
| National Endowment for the Arts - Fellowships for Playwrights (3976) | Citizenship: US, PermRes | |
| National Endowment for the Arts - Literature Program Creative Writing Fellowships (3977) | Citizenship: US, PermRes | |
| National Endowment for the Arts - Literature Program Translators' Fellowships (3978) | Citizenship: US, PermRes | |
| National Poetry Competition Prizes (3293) | Citizenship: US/CA; Legal: United States | |
| North Carolina Arts Council Artist Fellowships (4668) | Legal: NC | |
| Flannery O'Connor Awards for Short Fiction (5994) | | |
| Oregon Humanities Center Summer Visiting Research Fellowships (6011) | Study: United States | |
| PEN Fund for Writers and Editors with AIDS Grants and Loans (4858) | | Other |
| PEN Writers Fund (4856) | Legal: United States | |
| James D. Phelan Award in Literature (5235) | | |
| Resident Fellowships (2786) | Study: United States | |
| SCBWI Work-in-Progress Grants (5445) | | Association |
| Frances Shaw Fellowship (5073) | | |
| Dorothy Silver Playwriting Competition Prize (3261) | Study: United States | |
| Nila Banton Smith Research Dissemination Support Grant (3180) | | Association |
| John Ben Snow Prize (5668) | | |
| Thurber House Residencies (5731) | Study: United States | |
| Vermont Studio Center Residency Fellowships (6034) | Study: United States | |
| Elizabeth A. Whitehead Visiting Professorships (862) | Legal: Canada, United States; Study: Greece | |
| Yale Center for British Art Fellowships (6278) | Study: United States | |
| Yale Series of Younger Poets Prizes (6280) | Citizenship: US | |

**Law**

| | | |
|---|---|---|
| Robert Bosch Foundation Fellowships (1758) | | |
| Maxwell Boulton Senior Fellowship (3627) | Study: Canada | |
| James F. Connolly Congressional Informaton Service Scholarship (311) | | |
| Gordon F. Henderson/SOCAN Copyright Competition Award (5390) | Citizenship: Canada; Legal: Canada | |
| International Affairs Fellowships (2105) | Citizenship: US, PermRes | |
| Judicial Fellowships (5650) | Study: United States | |
| Liberal Arts Fellowships in Law (2810) | | |
| The Littleton-Griswold Research Grant (540) | | Association |
| Oregon Humanities Center Summer Visiting Research Fellowships (6011) | Study: United States | |

| Vocational Goal, Award, and Entry Number | Geographic Restrictions (Citizenship, Legal Residence, Place of Study) | Affiliation/Special Recipients Requirements |
|---|---|---|
| *Law (continued)* | | |
| Post-Rabbinic Scholarships (3646) | | |
| Preventive Law Prizes (Discontinued) (3933) | | |
| Reporters Committee Fellowship (5093) | Study: DC | |

## Liberal/General Studies

| Vocational Goal, Award, and Entry Number | Geographic Restrictions | Affiliation/Special Recipients Requirements |
|---|---|---|
| AAUW Educational Foundation Career Development Grants (332) | Citizenship: US; Legal: United States | |
| John Dana Archbold Fellowship (3820) | Citizenship: US, PermRes; Study: Norway | |
| Asahi Fellowships (1166) | | |
| Bicentennial Swedish-American Exchange Fund Travel Grants (5656) | Citizenship: US, PermRes; Legal: Sweden | |
| Bunting Fellowship (1526) | Study: MA | |
| Bunting Institute Affiliation Program (1527) | Study: MA | |
| CEW Scholarships for Returning Women (6002) | Study: MI | |
| Chase Manhattan Scholarship (2457) | | Association |
| Circle Key Grants of Rose McGill (3326) | Citizenship: US/CA | Fraternal |
| Connecticut Family Education Loan Program (CT FELP) (2044) | Legal: CT; Study: CT | |
| Epsilon Sigma Phi Mini-Grants (2406) | | Fraternal |
| Epsilon Sigma Phi Professionalism Scholarship (2407) | | Fraternal |
| Epsilon Sigma Phi Scholarship Loans (2408) | | Fraternal |
| Fulbright Teacher Exchange Program (2605) | Citizenship: US | |
| John Simon Guggenheim Fellowships (2761) | Legal: Canada, United States | |
| Humanitarian Trust Research Awards (2931) | | |
| Lester Educational Trust Loans (2133) | Legal: VA | |
| Maryland House of Delegates Scholarship (3575) | Legal: MD | |
| Montana Indian Student Fee Waiver (557) | Study: MT | Native American |
| Mosal Scholar Program (4907) | | Fraternal |
| National Fraternal Society of the Deaf Scholarships (4173) | | Association, Handicapped |
| Navajo Code Talkers Scholarship (4479) | | Native American |
| Nevada Women's Fund Scholarships (4521) | Legal: NV | |
| Nieman Fellowships for Journalists (4637) | Study: United States | |
| Opportunities for the Blind, Inc. Grants (4785) | Citizenship: US | Handicapped |
| Parnell Scholar Programs (4909) | | Fraternal |
| Rangeley Educational Trust Loans (2134) | Legal: VA | |
| Z. Smith Reynolds Fellowship (5120) | Legal: NC; Study: NC | |
| Rockefeller Fellowships in Violence, Culture and Survival (6056) | | |
| St. David's Scholarship (5220) | | Ethnic |
| Soroptimist Women's Opportunity Award (5541) | | |
| John N. Stern Fellowships for Oberlin College Faculty (4625) | Legal: OH; Study: IL | Employer |
| Tolbert Grant (3584) | Legal: MD | |
| VFH Center for the Humanities Affiliate Fellowships (6057) | | |
| Women in Scholarly Publishing Career Development Fund (6228) | | Association |
| Xerox Technical Minority Scholarship (5682) | | Minority |

## Library and Archival Sciences

| Vocational Goal, Award, and Entry Number | Geographic Restrictions | Affiliation/Special Recipients Requirements |
|---|---|---|
| 3M/NMRT Professional Development Grant (655) | | Association |
| AIMHS Scholarship (1242) | | Association |
| ALA/USIA Library Fellows (652) | Citizenship: US | Association |

| Vocational Goal, Award, and Entry Number | Geographic Restrictions (Citizenship, Legal Residence, Place of Study) | Affiliation/Special Recipients Requirements |
|---|---|---|
| *Library and Archival Sciences (continued)* | | |
| ALISE Doctoral Students' Dissertation Competition Prizes; ALISE Research Paper Competition Prizes (1245) | | Association |
| ALTA/Gale Outstanding Trustee Conference Grant (671) | | Association |
| Baker & Taylor Conference Grants (6291) | | Association |
| Bogle International Library Travel Fund (653) | | Association |
| CLR Fellows Program (2121) | Citizenship: US/CA, PermRes | |
| Connecticut Library Association Education Grants (2054) | Legal: CT | Association |
| James F. Connolly Congressional Informaton Service Scholarship (311) | | |
| Cunningham Memorial International Fellowship (3631) | Study: Canada, United States | |
| Hagley-Winterthur Fellowship (2780) | | |
| Frances Henne Award (644) | | Association |
| Information Plus Continuing Education Scholarship (645) | | Association |
| Samuel Lazerow Fellowship for Research in Acquisitions or Technical Services (1226) | | |
| Library Research and Development Grants (1666) | | Association |
| MLA Continuing Education Grant (3632) | Citizenship: US/CA, PermRes | Association |
| MLA Research, Development, and Demonstration Project Grant (3634) | Citizenship: US/CA, PermRes | Association |
| NHPRC/Fellowships in Archival Administration (4181) | | |
| Martinus Nijhoff International West European Specialist Study Grant (1227) | | Association |
| Shirley Olofson Memorial Award (657) | | Association |
| Pennsylvania Library Association Library Science Continuing Education Grants (4867) | | Association |
| Putnam & Grosset Group Award (650) | | Association |
| Readex/GODORT/ALA Catherine J. Reynolds Grant (2722) | | |
| Frank B. Sessa Scholarship for Continuing Education (1425) | | Fraternal |
| Support for Special Projects in the Study of Library and Information Science (3189) | | |
| World Book, Inc., Grants (1752) | | Association |
| **Life Sciences** | | |
| Kathleen S. Anderson Award (3546) | | |
| ASET Scholarships (920) | | |
| ASN Young Investigator's Award (957) | | |
| Alfred D. Bell, Jr. Visiting Scholars Program (2553) | | |
| Bermuda Biological Station Grants-in-Aid (1416) | Study: Bermuda | |
| Civilian Radioactive Waste Management/Historically Black Colleges and Universities Faculty Fellowship Program (5867) | | |
| Conservation and Research Foundation Research Grants (2063) | | |
| del Duca Foundation Maintenance and Travel Grants (2284) | | |
| Faculty Research Participation Program at the National Center for Toxicological Research (5874) | | |
| Faculty Research Participation Program at the Naval Air Warfare Center Training Systems Division. (5875) | | |

| Vocational Goal, Award, and Entry Number | Geographic Restrictions (Citizenship, Legal Residence, Place of Study) | Affiliation/Special Recipients Requirements |
|---|---|---|
| *Life Sciences (continued)* | | |
| Hilgenfeld Research and Publications Grants; Hilgenfeld Scholarship Grants (2874) | | |
| Historically Black Colleges and Universities Health and Environmental Research Opportunities for Faculty and Students (5892) | | |
| Historically Black Colleges and Universities Nuclear Energy Faculty Research Participation Program (5893) | Citizenship: US | |
| International Scientific Prize (2611) | | |
| National Oceanic and Atmospheric Administration/Historically Black Colleges and Universities Faculty/Student Research Participation Program (5910) | | |
| National Oceanic and Atmospheric Administration Scholar in Residence Program (5911) | | |
| North American Bluebird Society Research Grants (4642) | | |
| Olin Fellowships (1312) | Citizenship: US/CA; Legal: Canada, United States | |
| Sigurd T. Olson Common Loon Research Awards (4747) | | |
| Sport Fishery Research Grants and Fellowships (5593) | Citizenship: US; Study: United States | |
| SSRC Grants for Collaborative Activities between American and Japanese Scholars (5400) | Citizenship: US, PermRes, Japan | |

**Mathematics**

| Vocational Goal, Award, and Entry Number | Geographic Restrictions | Affiliation/Special Recipients Requirements |
|---|---|---|
| AERF Individual Grants (33) | | Association |
| Engineering Rotation Program (2923) | Citizenship: US; Study: United States | |
| Fossil Energy Faculty Research Participation (5876) | | |
| William C. Foster Fellows Visiting Scholars Competition (5818) | Citizenship: US | |
| NATO Senior Guest Fellowships (4656) | Study: France, Italy, Luxembourg, Spain, Turkey | |
| U.S. Department of Energy Faculty Research Participation Fellowship (5932) | | |

**Medicine**

| Vocational Goal, Award, and Entry Number | Geographic Restrictions | Affiliation/Special Recipients Requirements |
|---|---|---|
| Allied Health Doctoral Fellowships (3368) | Citizenship: Canada | |
| Allied Health Research Grants (3369) | Citizenship: Canada; Legal: Canada; Study: Canada | |
| Apex Foundation Research Grants (1050) | Study: Australia | |
| Ruth Aziz Clinical Fellowship (3802) | Study: Canada | |
| Bernhard Baron Traveling Scholarship (5178) | | |
| Bristol-Myers Squibb Outstanding Resident Awards (4334) | | |
| British Digestive Foundation Project Grants (1485) | | |
| Cancer Research Campaign Research Grants (1712) | | |
| Cancer Research Society Grants (1719) | Study: Canada | |
| Career Development Awards in Orthopaedic Surgery (4814) | Legal: Canada, United States | |
| The College of Family Physicians of Canada Awards/DM Robb Research and Family Physician Research Grants (1986) | | Association |
| The College of Family Physicians of Canada/Family Physician Study Grants (1987) | Study: Canada | Association |
| The College of Family Physicians of Canada Practice Enrichment Awards (1988) | Study: Canada | Association |

| Vocational Goal, Award, and Entry Number | Geographic Restrictions (Citizenship, Legal Residence, Place of Study) | Affiliation/Special Recipients Requirements |
|---|---|---|
| *Medicine (continued)* | | |
| Council for Tobacco Research Grants-in-Aid (2125) | | |
| Creative Investigator Grants (458) | Study: United States | |
| del Duca Foundation Maintenance and Travel Grants (2284) | | |
| Eastern European Visiting Scholarships (2814) | Study: United States, Wales | |
| Endodontic Faculty Grants (287) | Legal: Canada, United States | |
| Faculty Research Participation Program at the Agency for Toxic Substances and Disease Registry (5872) | | |
| Faculty Research Participation Program at the National Center for Toxicological Research (5874) | | |
| Generalist Physician Faculty Grants (3285) | Citizenship: US; Study: United States | |
| Dr. David Green Postdoctoral Fellowship (3803) | Study: Canada | |
| The Hospital for Sick Children Foundation External Grants Program (2901) | Citizenship: Canada | |
| HSFC Visiting Scientist Program (2847) | | |
| Huntington's Disease Society Research Grants (2942) | | |
| International Cancer Technology Transfer Fellowships (3194) | | |
| International Oncology Nursing Fellowships (3195) | | |
| JDFI Career Development Awards (3308) | | |
| JDFI Research Grants (3311) | | |
| Leukemia Society of America Short-term Scientific Awards (3455) | | |
| March of Dimes Research Grants (3548) | | |
| MDA Research Grants; MDA Research Development Grants; MDA Genetics Research Grants (3800) | Study: United States | |
| Medical Research Council Travel Grants (3639) | Legal: Canada | |
| Medical Student Loans (4871) | Legal: PA | |
| Robert S. Morison Fellowships (2743) | | |
| National Multiple Sclerosis Society Biomedical Research Grants (4314) | | |
| National Multiple Sclerosis Society Health Services Research Grants (4315) | | |
| National Multiple Sclerosis Society Patient Management Care and Rehabilitation Grants (4316) | | |
| National Multiple Sclerosis Society Pilot Research Grants (4317) | | |
| National Multiple Sclerosis Society Research Grants (4319) | | |
| National Multiple Sclerosis Society Senior Faculty Awards (4320) | | |
| Oncology Nursing Foundation/Amgen, Inc. Research Grant (4758) | | |
| Oncology Nursing Foundation/Bristol-Myers Oncology Chapter Research Grant (4760) | | |
| Oncology Nursing Foundation/Bristol-Myers Oncology Division Community Health Research Grant (4761) | | |
| Oncology Nursing Foundation/Bristol-Myers Oncology Division Research Grant (4762) | | |
| Oncology Nursing Foundation/Cetus Oncology Grants for Research Involving Biotherapy or Immunotherapy (4763) | | |

| Vocational Goal, Award, and Entry Number | Geographic Restrictions (Citizenship, Legal Residence, Place of Study) | Affiliation/Special Recipients Requirements |
|---|---|---|
| *Medicine (continued)* | | |
| Oncology Nursing Foundation/Glaxo Research Grants (4765) | | |
| Oncology Nursing Foundation/Oncology Nursing Certification Corporation Nursing Education Research Grants (4767) | | |
| Oncology Nursing Foundation/Oncology Nursing Society Research Grant (4768) | | |
| Oncology Nursing Foundation/Ortho Biotech Research Grant (4769) | | |
| Oncology Nursing Foundation/Purdue Frederick Research Grant (4770) | | |
| Oncology Nursing Foundation/Sigma Theta Tau International and Oncology Nursing Society Research Grant (4772) | | |
| Oncology Nursing Society/SmithKline Beecham Research Grant (4773) | | Association |
| Patient Management, Care and Rehabilitation Grants (4321) | | |
| Plastic Surgery Educational Foundation Scholarships (4958) | | |
| Donald I. Rice Merit Award (1989) | Study: Canada | |
| Elizabeth St. Louis Award (2317) | Citizenship: Canada | |
| Miriam Neveren Summer Studentship (2318) | Citizenship: Canada | |
| Well Being (6129) | | |
| WHO Fellowships (6259) | | |
| Arizona WICHE Professional Student Exchange Program (1089) | Citizenship: US; Legal: AZ | |
| Yamagiwa-Yoshida Memorial International Cancer Study Grants (3197) | | |

## Military Sciences

| | | |
|---|---|---|
| William C. Foster Fellows Visiting Scholars Competition (5818) | Citizenship: US | |

## Philosophy, Theology, and Religion

| | | |
|---|---|---|
| ARIL Research Colloquium Fellowships (1256) | Study: United States | Religion |
| Frank S. and Elizabeth D. Brewer Prize (897) | | |
| Jane Dempsey Douglass Prize (898) | | |
| International Affairs Fellowships (2105) | Citizenship: US, PermRes | |
| Irish in America Publication Award; Notre Dame Studies in Catholicism Publication Award (6009) | | |
| Oregon Humanities Center Summer Visiting Research Fellowships (6011) | Study: United States | |
| Albert C. Outler Prize in Ecumenical Church History (900) | | |
| Rockefeller Archive Center Research Grants (5142) | Study: United States | |

## Physical Sciences

| | | |
|---|---|---|
| AAAS Congressional Science and Engineering Fellowships (263) | Study: United States | |
| AAAS Technology Policy Science and Engineering Fellowships (267) | Citizenship: US; Study: United States | |
| ACPSEM Scholarship (1316) | | Association |
| ASN Young Investigator's Award (957) | | |
| Bank of Sweden Tercentenary Foundation Project Grants (1372) | Study: Sweden | |
| Chretien International Research Grants (343) | | |
| CIRA Fellowships in Atmospheric Science and Related Research (2083) | | |
| CIRES Visiting Fellowships (2085) | Study: United States | |

| Vocational Goal, Award, and Entry Number | Geographic Restrictions (Citizenship, Legal Residence, Place of Study) | Affiliation/Special Recipients Requirements |
|---|---|---|
| *Physical Sciences (continued)* | | |
| Civilian Radioactive Waste Management/Historically Black Colleges and Universities Faculty Fellowship Program (5867) | | |
| Conservation and Research Foundation Research Grants (2063) | | |
| Cottrell Scholars Science Awards (5096) | Legal: United States | |
| Engineering Rotation Program (2923) | Citizenship: US; Study: United States | |
| Environmental Protection Agency Fellowships (5940) | | Employer |
| Faculty Research Participation Program at the Bureau of Engraving and Printing (5873) | | |
| Fossil Energy Faculty Research Participation (5876) | | |
| William C. Foster Fellows Visiting Scholars Competition (5818) | Citizenship: US | |
| Grants for Overseas Scientific Expeditions (5194) | Legal: England | |
| Health Physics Faculty Research Award Program (5886) | | |
| Historically Black Colleges and Universities Faculty and Student Research Participation Program in Fusion. (5890) | | |
| Historically Black Colleges and Universities Fossil Energy Faculty and Student Research Training (5891) | | |
| Historically Black Colleges and Universities Nuclear Energy Faculty Research Participation Program (5893) | Citizenship: US | |
| Leakey Foundation General Grants (3443) | | |
| NASA-ASEE Summer Faculty Fellowship (923) | Citizenship: US; Study: United States | |
| National Oceanic and Atmospheric Administration/Historically Black Colleges and Universities Faculty/Student Research Participation Program (5910) | | |
| National Oceanic and Atmospheric Administration Scholar in Residence Program (5911) | | |
| NATO Senior Guest Fellowships (4656) | Study: France, Italy, Luxembourg, Spain, Turkey | |
| NSERC Research Scholarships, Fellowships, and Grants (4474) | Citizenship: Canada, PermRes; Study: Canada | |
| Part-time Fossil Energy Faculty Research Participation Program (5922) | | |
| Prince Rainier III de Monaco Bursary (3049) | | |
| Research Opportunity Awards (5097) | Legal: United States | |
| SSRC Grants for Collaborative Activities between American and Japanese Scholars (5400) | Citizenship: US, PermRes, Japan | |
| U.S. Department of Energy Faculty Research Participation Fellowship (5932) | | |
| U.S. Nuclear Regulatory Commission Historically Black Colleges and Universities Faculty Research Participation (5934) | | |

## Protective Services and Public Affairs

| | | |
|---|---|---|
| ACS Congressional Fellowship Program (367) | Study: United States | Association |
| ACS Science Policy Fellowship (368) | | Association |
| International Association of Fire Chiefs Foundation Scholarships (3113) | | Employer |
| New York City Urban Fellowships (4563) | Study: NY, United States | |
| The Lois and Samuel Silberman Awards (5351) | | |
| Summer Graduate Internships (4564) | Study: NY, United States | |

| Vocational Goal, Award, and Entry Number | Geographic Restrictions (Citizenship, Legal Residence, Place of Study) | Affiliation/Special Recipients Requirements |
|---|---|---|
| **Social Sciences** | | |
| AAAS Technology Policy Science and Engineering Fellowships (267) | Citizenship: US; Study: United States | |
| AAG General Fund Research Grants (1207) | | Association |
| AAS/American Society for Eighteenth Century Studies Fellowships (252) | Study: United States | Association |
| APSA Congressional Fellowships for Federal Executives (779) | Study: DC | Employer |
| Artists Fellowship; Japan Foundation Cultural Properties Specialists Fellowship; Japan Foundation Doctoral Fellowship; Japan Foundation Research Fellowship (3240) | Study: Japan | |
| The Joan Shorenstein Barone Congressional Fellowship (783) | Citizenship: US | |
| Behavioral Sciences Student Fellowship (2397) | Study: United States | |
| The Albert J. Beveridge Grant (536) | | Association |
| Robert Bosch Foundation Fellowships (1758) | | |
| Stephen Botein Fellowships (254) | Study: United States | |
| National Council on Family Relations Ernest W. Burgess Award (3947) | | |
| Canadian Studies Sabbatical Fellowship Program (1627) | Legal: United States; Study: Canada | |
| Crane-Rogers Fellowships (3025) | | |
| Eben Demarest Fund (2227) | | |
| Dudley Stamp Memorial Trust (5193) | Legal: England | |
| East-West Center Internships (2309) | Study: HI | |
| Albert Einstein Institution Fellowships (2361) | | |
| Fellowships for Taft Seminar for Teachers (5670) | Study: United States | |
| The Feminist Majority Internships (2441) | | |
| William C. Foster Fellows Visiting Scholars Competition (5818) | Citizenship: US | |
| Donald Groves Fellowship (740) | | |
| Hollingworth Award Competition (3877) | | |
| Howard Foundation Fellowships (2908) | Legal: United States | |
| IHS Summer Faculty Fellowships (3057) | | |
| India Studies Faculty Fellowships (5316) | Citizenship: Canada; Study: India | |
| India Studies Postdoctoral Research Fellowships (5318) | Citizenship: Canada; Study: India | |
| International Affairs Fellowships (2105) | Citizenship: US, PermRes | |
| Irish in America Publication Award; Notre Dame Studies in Catholicism Publication Award (6009) | | |
| Johnson Foundation Grants-in-Aid of Research (3282) | Study: United States | |
| Michael Kraus Research Grant in History (539) | | Association |
| Leakey Foundation General Grants (3443) | | |
| Materials Analysis Fellowships (2061) | Study: United States | |
| Phillip Morris Public Policy Fellowship (4349) | | |
| NATO Senior Guest Fellowships (4656) | Study: France, Italy, Luxembourg, Spain, Turkey | |
| Neporany Research and Teaching Fellowship (1661) | | |
| Oregon Humanities Center Summer Visiting Research Fellowships (6011) | Study: United States | |
| Paleoanthropology Award (3444) | | |
| Parliamentary Internships (1692) | Citizenship: Canada; Study: Canada | |
| Peace Fellowships (5076) | Study: United States | |
| Kate B. and Hall J. Peterson Fellowships (256) | Study: United States | |
| Harriet and Leon Pomerance Fellowship (1067) | Legal: Canada, United States | |

| Vocational Goal, Award, and Entry Number | Geographic Restrictions (Citizenship, Legal Residence, Place of Study) | Affiliation/Special Recipients Requirements |
|---|---|---|
| *Social Sciences (continued)* | | |
| The Poynter Fellowship (784) | Citizenship: US | |
| Jennings Randolph Senior Fellow Award (5078) | | |
| Benjamin F. Richason III Scholarship (2618) | | Fraternal |
| Rockefeller Archive Center Research Grants (5142) | Study: United States | |
| Bernadette Schmitt Grants (541) | | Association |
| Herbert Scoville Jr. Peace Fellowship (5288) | Citizenship: US; Study: United States | |
| SSRC Grants for Collaborative Activities between American and Japanese Scholars (5400) | Citizenship: US, PermRes, Japan | |
| SSRC International Peace and Security Research Workshop Competition (5401) | | |
| United Nations Fellowships (5799) | | |
| United States Institute of Peace Distinguished Fellows (5079) | Study: United States | |
| Arthur Weinberg Fellowship for Independent Scholars (4612) | | |
| Elizabeth A. Whitehead Visiting Professorships (862) | Legal: Canada, United States; Study: Greece | |
| World Press Institute Fellowships (6268) | | |
| Manfred Worner Fellowship (4657) | | |
| Yale Center for British Art Fellowships (6278) | Study: United States | |

**Visual and Performing Arts**

| Vocational Goal, Award, and Entry Number | Geographic Restrictions (Citizenship, Legal Residence, Place of Study) | Affiliation/Special Recipients Requirements |
|---|---|---|
| Academy of Vocal Arts Scholarships (28) | Study: United States | |
| Adler Fellowships (5237) | | |
| Albee Foundation Residencies (141) | Study: United States | |
| American Orff Schulwerk Association Research Grants (752) | | Association |
| Artists Fellowship; Japan Foundation Cultural Properties Specialists Fellowship; Japan Foundation Doctoral Fellowship; Japan Foundation Research Fellowship (3240) | Study: Japan | |
| Artists Fellowships and Residencies (3766) | Study: United States | |
| Artists Workplace Fellowships (6253) | | |
| Artpark Residencies (1161) | | |
| Arts Education Fellowships (2093) | Citizenship: US | |
| ASCAP Foundation Grants to Young Composers (912) | Citizenship: US, PermRes | Other |
| ASCAP Foundation Morton Gould Awards to Young Composers (913) | | |
| Assistant Directors Training Program Apprenticeships (1189) | | |
| Austrian Federal Ministry for Science and Research Grants (1341) | Study: Austria | |
| Ballet Prizes (3123) | | |
| Baltimore Opera Studio & Residency Program (1368) | Citizenship: US/CA, Mexico; Study: MD | |
| Banff Centre for the Arts Scholarships (1370) | Study: Canada | |
| Frank Huntington Beebe Awards (1391) | | |
| Leslie Bell Scholarship for Choral Conducting (4777) | Citizenship: Canada; Legal: ON | |
| Black American Cinema Society Award (6163) | | Minority |
| Blue Mountain Center Residencies (1446) | | |
| BMI Student Composer Awards (1450) | | |
| Nadia and Lili Boulanger Scholarship (2547) | | |
| Herbert and Patricia Brodkin Scholarship (4775) | Citizenship: US; Study: NY, United States | |
| Brucebo Fine Arts Summer Scholarship (1696) | Citizenship: Canada; Study: Sweden | |

| Vocational Goal, Award, and Entry Number | Geographic Restrictions (Citizenship, Legal Residence, Place of Study) | Affiliation/Special Recipients Requirements |
|---|---|---|
| *Visual and Performing Arts (continued)* | | |
| Bunting Fellowship (1526) | Study: MA | |
| Bunting Institute Affiliation Program (1527) | Study: MA | |
| Bush Artist Fellowships (1539) | Legal: MN, ND, SD, WI | |
| Canadian Council for the Arts Grants Program (1594) | Citizenship: Canada, PermRes | |
| Carmel Music Society Competition (1733) | Legal: CA; Study: CA | |
| Pete Carpenter Film Composing Internship (1451) | Study: CA | |
| Centrum Residencies (1820) | Study: United States | |
| Chalmers Performing Arts Training Grants (4778) | Legal: ON | |
| Howard Chapnick Grant (5367) | | |
| Chigiana Summer Course Scholarships (1935) | Study: Italy | |
| Choreographers Fellowship (4661) | Legal: NC | |
| Cintas Fellowships (1163) | | Ethnic |
| Cleveland International Piano Competition (1968) | | |
| Van Cliburn International Piano Competition (1972) | | |
| Composer's Composition Prizes (244) | | |
| Consortium College University Media Centers Annual Research Grants (2065) | Legal: United States | |
| Contemporary Record Society National Festival for the Performing Arts (2071) | | |
| Cummington Community of the Arts Residencies (2142) | Study: United States | |
| Dance Screen Competition Awards (3166) | Study: France | |
| Eben Demarest Fund (2227) | | |
| Dramatists Guild Fund Scholarships (2280) | | |
| Emergency Assistance Grants (2719) | | |
| Alex J. Ettl Grant (4383) | Citizenship: US, PermRes | |
| Faculty Research Participation Program at the Bureau of Engraving and Printing (5873) | | |
| Fellowships in Art Conservation (3403) | | |
| Film/Video Artists Fellowship (4663) | Legal: NC | |
| Fine Arts Grants (194) | | |
| Fine Arts Work Center Fellowships (2459) | Study: United States | |
| Folklife Documentary Program (4664) | Legal: NC | |
| Harvey Gaul Composition Contest (4953) | Citizenship: US | |
| Martha Graham Dance Scholarships (2728) | Study: United States | |
| Grant in Humanistic Photography (5368) | | |
| Grants to Individual Artists (3762) | Citizenship: US/CA | |
| Headlands Center for the Arts Residency (4666) | Legal: NC | |
| High Temperature Materials Laboratory Faculty Fellowship (5887) | | |
| Howard Foundation Fellowships (2908) | Legal: United States | |
| Vaclav Huml International Violin Competition Prizes (2136) | Study: Croatia | |
| Independent and Student Filmmakers Competition (1436) | | African American |
| India Studies Faculty Fellowships (5316) | Citizenship: Canada; Study: India | |
| India Studies Performing Arts Fellowships (5317) | Citizenship: Canada; Study: India | |
| India Studies Postdoctoral Research Fellowships (5318) | Citizenship: Canada; Study: India | |
| Individual Support Grants (2720) | | |
| Inter-American Music Awards (5327) | | |

| Vocational Goal, Award, and Entry Number | Geographic Restrictions (Citizenship, Legal Residence, Place of Study) | Affiliation/Special Recipients Requirements |
|---|---|---|
| *Visual and Performing Arts (continued)* | | |
| International Biennial Competition of Humour and Satire in the Arts (2906) | | |
| International Book Translation and Publishing Program (1318) | | |
| International Competition Prizes (4476) | | |
| International Magazine Publishing Program (1319) | | |
| International Music Contest of Rio de Janeiro Prizes (1474) | Study: Brazil | |
| International Playwrights' Competition (5325) | Study: United States | |
| JCC of Metropolitan New Jersey Patrons Award and Florence Ben-Asher Memorial Award (3259) | Legal: NJ | |
| Jerome Playwright-in-Residence Fellowships (4962) | Citizenship: US, PermRes; Study: United States | |
| Edward Johnson Music Competition (3287) | Citizenship: Canada, PermRes | |
| Margaret Fairbank Jory Copying Assistance Program (718) | Citizenship: US, PermRes | |
| Kosciuszko Foundation Chopin Piano Competition/Scholarships (3398) | Citizenship: US, PermRes | |
| La Napoule Residency for Visual Artists and Writers (4667) | Legal: NC | |
| Lotte Lehmann Fellowship in Voice/Vocal Accompanying; Gabor Rejto Fellowship in Cello (3808) | Study: United States | |
| Light Work Artist-in-Residence Program (3472) | Study: United States | |
| The Little Emo Awards (3492) | | |
| Amy Lowell Poetry Travelling Scholarship (3510) | Legal: United States | |
| MacDowell Colony Residencies (3524) | Study: United States | |
| McKnight Advancement Grants (4963) | Citizenship: US, PermRes; Legal: MN | |
| McKnight Fellowships (4964) | Citizenship: US; Study: United States | |
| Andrew W. Mellon Fellowships in Conservation (3659) | Study: United States | |
| Merola Opera Program (5238) | | |
| Minnesota Artist Assistance Fellowships (3714) | Legal: MN | |
| Minnesota Career Opportunity Grants (3715) | Legal: MN | |
| Minnesota Folk Arts Apprenticeship (3716) | Legal: MN | |
| MISSIM/ASCAP Composers Competition (914) | | |
| Thelonious Monk International Jazz Instrumental Competition (3764) | | |
| Multi-Arts Production Fund Grants (5148) | | |
| Music Assistance Fund Orchestral Fellowships (1005) | Citizenship: US | African American |
| National Endowment for Arts - Choreographers' Fellowships (3973) | Citizenship: US, PermRes | |
| National Endowment for the Arts - Design Arts Program USA Fellowships (3974) | Citizenship: US, PermRes; Study: United States | |
| National Endowment for the Arts - Director Fellows (3975) | Citizenship: US, PermRes | |
| National Endowment for the Arts - National Heritage Fellowships (3979) | Citizenship: US, PermRes | |
| National Endowment for the Arts - U.S./France Exchange Fellowship (3980) | Citizenship: US, PermRes; Study: France | |
| National Endowment for the Arts - U.S./Japan Exchange Fellowships (3981) | Citizenship: US, PermRes; Study: Japan | |
| National Endowment for the Arts - Visual Artists Fellowships (3982) | Citizenship: US, PermRes | |
| National Playwrights' Award (5772) | | |
| National Poetry Competition Prizes (3293) | Citizenship: US/CA; Legal: United States | |
| National Sculpture Society Scholarships (4384) | | |

| Vocational Goal, Award, and Entry Number | Geographic Restrictions (Citizenship, Legal Residence, Place of Study) | Affiliation/Special Recipients Requirements |
|---|---|---|
| *Visual and Performing Arts (continued)* | | |
| National Stage Combat Workshop Fellowship (3349) | | |
| National Symphony Young Soloists' Competition, College Division (4419) | Legal: DC; Study: DC | |
| National Theatre Artist Residency Grants (5723) | | |
| National Vocal Competition for Young Opera Singers (6301) | | |
| NATS Artist Awards (3902) | | Association |
| Netz Hilai Visiting Artists Fellowships (4515) | Study: Israel | |
| New Jersey State Opera Annual Vocal Competition (4547) | | |
| New Letters Literary Awards (4549) | | |
| New Play Competition Prizes (3703) | Study: United States | |
| New York International Ballet Competition (4572) | | |
| Lionel Newman Conducting Fellowship (1452) | Study: CA | |
| NNAC Gifted/Talented Artist Sponsorships (4324) | | Native American |
| North Carolina Arts Council Artist Fellowships (4668) | Legal: NC | |
| Opera Screen Competition Awards (3167) | | |
| Orchestra Management Fellowships (1006) | Legal: United States; Study: United States | |
| Oregon Humanities Center Summer Visiting Research Fellowships (6011) | Study: United States | |
| OSM Competition (3778) | Citizenship: Canada; Legal: Canada; Study: Canada | |
| Pastel Society of America Scholarships (4850) | | |
| Piano Teaching Fellowship (4556) | Study: United States | |
| Playwrights' Center PlayLabs (4965) | Citizenship: US, PermRes | |
| Pollock-Krasner Grants (4975) | | |
| Promising Playwright Award (1996) | Legal: United States; Study: United States | |
| Regional Artist Project Grants Program (4669) | | |
| Resident Fellowships (2786) | Study: United States | |
| RTMF Career Grants/Sara Tucker Study Grant (5754) | | |
| Scholarships for Mature Women (4282) | | |
| Senior Performing Arts Fellowships (588) | Legal: United States; Study: India | |
| ShenanArts Fellowships (5323) | Study: United States | |
| Sinfonia Foundation Research Assistance Grant (5353) | | |
| Skowhegan School Fellowships (5355) | Study: United States | |
| Sorantin Young Artist Award (5226) | | |
| John F. and Anna Lee Stacey Scholarships (3966) | Citizenship: US; Study: United States | |
| Stanley Drama Award (6075) | | |
| Starr Fellowships in Asian Paintings Conservation (3668) | Study: United States | |
| Sundance Theater Laboratory Fellowship (3350) | | |
| Thurber House Residencies (5731) | Study: United States | |
| Richard Tucker Award (5755) | Citizenship: US | |
| Tuition Grants for Apprenticeships (3280) | Study: United States | |
| Heinz Unger Award for Conducting (4779) | Citizenship: Canada | |
| UNIMA-USA Scholarship (5774) | Study: France | Association |
| The University of Maryland International Music Competitions (4331) | | |
| Elizabeth Harper Vaughn Concerto Competition Prizes (3377) | Citizenship: US; Study: United States | |

| Vocational Goal, Award, and Entry Number | Geographic Restrictions (Citizenship, Legal Residence, Place of Study) | Affiliation/Special Recipients Requirements |
|---|---|---|
| *Visual and Performing Arts (continued)* | | |
| V.C.C. Fuchs Scholarship Award (6042) | Legal: CA | |
| Vermont Studio Center Residency Fellowships (6034) | Study: United States | |
| Virginia Museum of Fine Arts Fellowship (6061) | | |
| Visual Artists Fellowship (4670) | Legal: NC | |
| We Don't Need No Stinkin' Dramas (3758) | | |
| Arnold Weissberger Playwrighting Competition (4523) | | |
| WESTAF/NEA Regional Fellowships for Visual Artists (6161) | Citizenship: US, PermRes; Legal: AK, AZ, CA, CO, HI, ID, MT, NM, NV, OR, UT, WA, WY | |
| Western Opera Theater Program (5239) | | |
| World Model Awards (6266) | | |
| Wayne Wylie Scholarship (5172) | | Association |
| Yale Center for British Art Fellowships (6278) | Study: United States | |
| The Yard Residencies for Choreographers (6282) | Study: United States | |
| Harry and Sarah Zelzer Fellowship and Prize (4613) | | |

# Undergraduate

**Agriculture**

| | | |
|---|---|---|
| 21st Century Genetics Cooperative Scholarships (4012) | Legal: IA, MN, ND, NE, SD, WI | Association |
| AgRadio Network Scholarships (4013) | Legal: CT, MA, ME, NH, NY, RI, VT | Association |
| Airline Pilots Association Scholarship (96) | | Association |
| Alberta Salers Association Scholarship (146) | Legal: Canada | Association |
| Alberta Wheat Pool Scholarships (148) | Study: AB, Canada | |
| Alfa-Laval Agri Scholarships (4014) | | Association |
| Allflex USA Scholarship (4015) | | Association |
| Alpha Gamma Rho Education Foundation Scholarship (4016) | | Association |
| American Association of Cereal Chemists Scholarships (274) | | |
| American Farm Bureau Federation Scholarship (4019) | | Association |
| American Floral Endowment Scholarship (4020) | | Association |
| American Grain and Related Industries Scholarship (4021) | Legal: IA | Association |
| American Horticultural Society Horticultural Career Internship (545) | | |
| American Morgan Horse Institute Scholarships (4022) | | Association |
| American Seed Trade Association Scholarship (4023) | | Association |
| American Society for Enology and Viticulture Scholarships (928) | | |
| Anchor Division Boehringer Ingelheim Animal Health Scholarship (4024) | | Association |
| Associated Milk Producers and Babson Bros. Co./SURGE Scholarships (4026) | | Association |
| Award Design Medals Scholarship (4027) | | Association |
| Jerry Baker College Freshman Scholarships (1380) | | |
| Bedding Plants Foundation Scholarship (4028) | | Association |
| Harold Bettinger Memorial Scholarship (1382) | Study: Canada, United States | |
| Big R. Stores and Fleet Supply Company Scholarship (4029) | Legal: IN; Study: IN | Association |

| Vocational Goal, Award, and Entry Number | Geographic Restrictions (Citizenship, Legal Residence, Place of Study) | Affiliation/Special Recipients Requirements |
|---|---|---|
| *Agriculture (continued)* | | |
| Biggs and Gilmore Communications Scholarships (4030) | Study: IA, IL, MI, OH, WI | Association |
| Ardell Bjugstad Memorial Scholarships (5551) | Legal: ND, SD | Native American |
| Blue Seal Feeds Scholarship (4031) | Legal: CT, MA, MD, ME, NH, NJ, NY, OH, PA, RI, VT | Association |
| Borden Foundation Scholarships (4032) | Study: MS, TX | Association |
| B.R.I.D.G.E. Endowment Fund Scholarships (4033) | | Association, Handicapped |
| A.W. "Winn" Brindle Memorial Scholarship Loans (131) | | |
| Bunge Corporation Scholarship (4037) | | |
| Business Men's Assurance Company of America Scholarships (4038) | | Association |
| CAL Stores Companies Scholarships (4039) | Legal: ID | Association |
| California Farm Bureau Scholarships (1557) | Study: CA | |
| A & E Capelle LN Herfords Scholarship (150) | Legal: Canada | |
| Capital Agricultural Property Services, Inc. Scholarship (4040) | | Association |
| Capitol American Scholarships (4041) | Legal: AK, CO, IA, IL, IN, KS, MO, MT, ND, NE, OK, SD, WY | Association |
| Wilson W. Carnes Scholarships (4043) | | Association |
| Casey's General Stores, Inc. Scholarships (4045) | Legal: IA, IL, MO | Association |
| Celanese Canada Inc. Scholarships (1269) | Citizenship: Canada, PermRes; Study: Canada | |
| Certified Angus Beef Scholarship (4274) | | Association |
| Champions Choice/AKZO Salt Scholarships (4046) | | Association |
| Chevron USA, Inc. Scholarship (4047) | Legal: FL, GA | Association |
| Chicago and North Western Transportation Company Scholarship (4049) | Legal: IA | Association |
| Chief Industries Inc. Scholarships (4050) | Legal: NE | Association |
| Chilean Nitrate Corporation Scholarship (4051) | Legal: NC, VA | Association |
| ConAgra Scholarships (4052) | Legal: United States; Study: NE | Association |
| Countrymark Cooperative, Inc. Scholarships (4053) | Legal: IN, MI, OH | Association |
| County of Forty Mile Agricultural Committee Bursaries (2127) | Legal: AB | Other |
| Creswell, Munsell, Fultz & Zirbel Scholarships (4054) | Study: IA, IL, IN, KS, MN, MO, NC, NE, OH, SC, WI | Association |
| Curtice Burns and Pro-Fac Scholarships (4055) | | Association |
| D & B Supply Company, Inc. Scholarships (4056) | Legal: ID, OR, WA | Association |
| Darigold Scholarships (4057) | Legal: CA, ID, OR, WA | Association |
| Data Transmission Network Corporation Scholarship (4058) | | Association |
| Harold Davis Memorial Endowment Scholarship (4059) | | Association |
| DEKALB Genetic Corporation Scholarships (4060) | | Association |
| Delmar Publishers Scholarship (4061) | | Association |
| Delta and Pine Land Company Scholarship (4062) | Legal: AL, AR, AZ, CA, FL, GA, KS, LA, MO, MS, NC, NM, OK, SC, TN, TX, VA | Association |
| Howard and Marjorie DeNise Memorial Scholarships (4580) | Legal: NY | |
| Carl F. Dietz Memorial Scholarship (1384) | Study: Canada, United States | |
| Dodge Trucks Scholarships (4063) | | Association |
| Dog Writers' Educational Trust Scholarships (2264) | | Other |

| Vocational Goal, Award, and Entry Number | Geographic Restrictions (Citizenship, Legal Residence, Place of Study) | Affiliation/Special Recipients Requirements |
|---|---|---|
| *Agriculture (continued)* | | |
| Douglas Products and Packaging Scholarships (4064) | Legal: MO | Association |
| Drysdales Scholarships (4065) | | Association |
| Dueutz-Allis Corporation, Hesston Corporation, and White Tractor Scholarships (4066) | | |
| Eastern Apiculture Society of North America Scholarship (4067) | Study: CT, DE, MA, MD, ME, NC, NH, NJ, NY, OH, PA, RI, TN, VA, VT, WV | Association |
| The Ertl Company Scholarship (4069) | Legal: IA, IL, IN, KS, KY, MI, MN, MO, ND, NE, OH, SD, WI | Association |
| Excel Corporation, Geo. A. Hormel & Company, and Oscar Mayer Food Corporation Scholarship (4070) | | Association |
| FARM AID Scholarships (4071) | | Association |
| Farm King Supply Scholarship (4072) | Legal: IA, IL | Association |
| Farmers Mutual Hail Insurance Company of Iowa Scholarships (4073) | Legal: IA, IL, IN, MI, MN, MO, ND, NE, OH, WI | Association |
| Federated Genetics Scholarship (4075) | | Association |
| Fermenta Animal Health Company Scholarships (4076) | | Association |
| First Mississippi Corporation Scholarships (4077) | Legal: LA, MS | Association |
| FISCO Farm and Home Stores Scholarships (4078) | Legal: CA; Study: CA | Association |
| Fleishman-Hillard, Inc. Scholarship (4079) | | Association |
| Grace and Robert Fraser Landscape Heritage Award (3423) | | |
| Future Farmers of America Scholarships (1532) | Legal: AZ, CA, CO, IA, IL, KS, MN, MO, MT, ND, NE, NM, OK, OR, SD, TX, WA | Association |
| Golden Harvest Seeds, Inc. Scholarships (4082) | Citizenship: US; Legal: CO, IA, IL, IN, KS, MI, MN, MO, NE, OH, SD, WI; Study: CO, IA, IL, IN, KS, MI, MN, MO, NE, OH, SD, WI | Association |
| Growmark, Inc. Scholarships (4083) | Legal: IA, IL, WI; Study: IA, IL, WI | Association |
| Gustafson, Inc. Scholarship (4084) | Study: CO, IA, MS | Association |
| Hardie Irrigation Scholarships (4085) | | Association |
| Hawkeye Steel Products, Inc. Scholarship (4086) | Legal: IA; Study: IA | Association |
| Helena Chemical Company Scholarships (4087) | | Association |
| Georgia M. Hellberg Memorial Scholarships (4088) | | Association |
| Hillshire Farm & Kahn's Scholarship (4090) | Legal: WI; Study: WI | Association |
| Hoard's Dairyman Scholarship (4091) | | Association |
| Hoechst Canada Bursary (155) | Study: AB | Association |
| Hydro Agri North America, Inc. Scholarships (4092) | | Association |
| Institute of Food Technologists Freshman/Sophomore Scholarships (3037) | | |
| Institute of Food Technologists Junior/Senior Scholarships (3039) | | |
| International Arabian Horse Foundation Scholarship Application (3105) | | |
| Fran Johnson Scholarships (1385) | Citizenship: US, Canada; Study: Canada, United States | |
| Ladies of the ABBA American Junior Brahman Association Scholarships (602) | | Association |
| LAF Student Research Grant (3429) | | |
| LANDCADD, Inc. Scholarship (3430) | | |
| Lextron, Inc. Scholarships (4094) | Legal: AL, AR, AZ, CA, CO, FL, GA, IA, ID, KS, LA, MI, MN, MO, MT, ND, NE, NM, NV, OK, OR, SD, TX, UT, WA, WY | Association |
| Lilydale Co-operative Scholarship (157) | Legal: AB | Association |

| Vocational Goal, Award, and Entry Number | Geographic Restrictions (Citizenship, Legal Residence, Place of Study) | Affiliation/Special Recipients Requirements |
|---|---|---|
| *Agriculture (continued)* | | |
| Livestock Marketing Association and Local LMA Member Market Scholarship (4095) | | Association |
| Marilyn Sue Lloyd Memorial Scholarship (158) | Legal: AB | Association |
| William J. Locklin Scholarship (3431) | | |
| Earl May Seed & Nursery L.P. Scholarship (4096) | Study: IA, KS, MO, NE, SD | Association |
| Metropolitan Life Foundation Scholarships (4097) | Study: IA, IN, KS, MO, NE | Association |
| Mid-America Dairymen, Inc., National Dairy Promotion and Research Board and Patz Sales, Inc. Scholarships (4098) | | Association |
| Mid-State Wool Growers Cooperative Scholarship (4099) | Legal: IA, IL, IN, KS, KY, MI, MN, MO, NE, OH, OK, SD | Association |
| Miller Meester Advertising Scholarship (4100) | | Association |
| Mississippi Farm Bureau Foundation Scholarship (4101) | Legal: MS | Association |
| Monrovia Nursery Co. Scholarship (4102) | | Association |
| Moorman Scholarship in Agriculture (3780) | | |
| National Dairy Shrine/Dairy Management Scholarships, Inc. (3968) | | |
| National FFA Alumni Scholarships (4103) | | Association |
| National FFA Foundation Minority Scholarships (4104) | | Association, Minority, Native American, Asian American, African American, Hispanic American, Ethnic |
| National Junior Angus Scholarships (4275) | | Association |
| National Mastitis Council Scholarship (4105) | | Association |
| National Pork Producers Council Scholarships (4106) | | Association |
| National Suffolk Sheep Association Scholarship (4107) | | Association |
| National Zoological Park Minority Traineeships (4456) | | |
| National Zoological Park Traineeship in BioPark Horticulture (4458) | | |
| Nationwide Foundation Scholarships (4108) | | Association |
| NC+ Hybrids Scholarship (4109) | | Association |
| NCFC Undergraduate Term Paper Awards (3951) | | |
| NCSGC National Scholarships (3959) | | |
| NCSU - Pulp & Paper Merit Scholarships (5031) | | |
| New York State Professional Opportunity Scholarships (4592) | Citizenship: US, PermRes; Legal: NY; Study: NY | |
| Kenneth and Ellen Nielsen Cooperative Scholarships (4110) | Legal: CO, IA, IL, KS, MN, MO, ND, NE, OK, SD, TX, WI, WY; Study: CO, IA, IL, KS, MN, MO, ND, NE, OK, SD, TX, WI, WY | |
| Norfolk Southern Foundation Scholarships (4111) | | |
| North American Limousin Foundation Scholarship (4112) | | Association |
| Northrup King Company Scholarships (4113) | Legal: IA, IL, MN, NE, WI | Association |
| Ohio State University Extension Internship (4733) | | |
| Oklahoma Natural Gas Company Scholarship (4114) | Legal: OK; Study: OK | Association |
| Raymond E. Page Scholarship (3432) | | |
| Pennington Memorial Scholarships (162) | Legal: Canada | Association |
| Piancone Family Agriculture Scholarship (4254) | Legal: DC, DE, MA, MD, NJ, NY, PA, VA | Ethnic |
| Prairie Farms Dairy, Inc. Scholarship (4115) | Legal: IA, IL, IN, MO | Association |
| Precision Laboratories, Inc. Scholarship (4116) | Legal: IL; Study: IL | Association |

| Vocational Goal, Award, and Entry Number | Geographic Restrictions (Citizenship, Legal Residence, Place of Study) | Affiliation/Special Recipients Requirements |
|---|---|---|
| *Agriculture (continued)* | | |
| Professional Products & Services, Inc. Scholarship (4117) | Legal: WI | Association |
| Purina Mills Scholarships (4118) | | Association |
| Quality Stores, Inc. Scholarships (4119) | Legal: IN, MI, OH | Association |
| Rain Bird Sprinkler Manufacturing Corp. Scholarships (4120) | | Association |
| James K. Rathmell, Jr., Memorial Scholarship to Work/Study Abroad (1387) | Legal: United States | |
| Rhone-Poulenc Animal Nutrition Scholarships (4121) | | Association |
| Ritchie Industries, Inc. Scholarship (4122) | Legal: IA | Association |
| Royal Bath & West of England Society Scholarships (5176) | | |
| Ruetgers-Nease Chemical Company, Inc. Scholarship (4123) | Study: PA | Association |
| Sandoz Agro, Inc. Scholarships (4124) | Study: CA, FL, IA, IL, IN, MI, MN, NY, TX, VI, WI | Association |
| Santa Fe Pacific Foundation Scholarships (4125) | Legal: AZ, CA, CO, IL, KS, MO, NM, OK, TX | |
| Abbie Sargent Memorial Scholarships (5250) | Legal: NH | |
| SIGCO Research Scholarships (4126) | Legal: MN, ND, SD | Association |
| Silgan Containers Corporation Scholarships (4127) | Legal: CA, IA, IL, KY, MO, OR, PA, WI | Association |
| Earl J. Small Growers, Inc. Scholarships (1388) | Citizenship: US/CA; Study: Canada, United States | |
| Souvenir Shirts, Etc. Scholarships (4128) | | Association |
| Spraying Systems Company Scholarships (4129) | | Association |
| State Farm Companies Foundation Scholarships (4130) | Legal: IL | Association |
| Statler Foundation Scholarship (5622) | Study: NY, United States | |
| Sun Company Scholarships (4131) | | Association |
| Syracuse Pulp and Paper Foundation Scholarship (5666) | Citizenship: US, PermRes; Study: NY | |
| George Tanaka Memorial Scholarship Program (1288) | Citizenship: Canada, PermRes; Study: Canada | |
| Ed Taylor Memorial Scholarship (6153) | Study: CA | |
| TCS, Farm, Home and Auto Stores Scholarship (4132) | | |
| Tetra Park Scholarship (4133) | | |
| Theisen Supply, Inc. Scholarships (4134) | Legal: IA | Association |
| Tri-State Breeders Scholarships (4135) | | Association |
| Tyson Foods, Sanofi Animal Health and American Proteins Scholarships (4136) | | Association |
| Union Pacific Foundation Scholarship (4137) | Legal: AR, CA, CO, IA, ID, IL, KS, LA, MO, NE, NV, OK, OR, TX, UT, WA, WY | Association |
| United Dairymen of Idaho Scholarship (4138) | Legal: ID | Association |
| United Farmers of Alberta Scholarship (165) | Legal: AB; Study: Canada | Association |
| United Feeds Scholarships (4139) | Legal: IL, IN, MI, OH; Study: IL, IN, MI, OH | Association |
| United Nations Educational Training Scholarships for Southern Africans (5798) | Legal: Namibia, Republic of South Africa | |
| Universal Dairy Equipment, Inc. Scholarships (4140) | Legal: KS | |
| Universal Leaf Tobacco Company Scholarship (4141) | Legal: NC | Association |
| University of Maine Pulp and Paper Foundation Scholarships (6000) | Study: ME | |
| Valmont Irrigation Scholarships (4142) | | Association |
| Wal-Mart Scholarship (4144) | | |
| Walco International, Inc. Scholarship (4145) | | Association |
| Lester Walls III Scholarship (3435) | | Handicapped |

| Vocational Goal, Award, and Entry Number | Geographic Restrictions (Citizenship, Legal Residence, Place of Study) | Affiliation/Special Recipients Requirements |
|---|---|---|
| *Agriculture (continued)* | | |
| Wells Fargo Bank Scholarship (4146) | Legal: CA | Association |
| Western Dairymen - John Elway - Melba FFA Scholarship Fund (4147) | Legal: ID | Association |
| Western Seedmen's Association Scholarships (4148) | Legal: AZ, CA, CO, IA, ID, KS, MN, MO, MT, ND, NE, NM, NV, OK, OR, SD, TX, UT, WA, WY | Association |
| Williams Pipe Line Company Scholarship (4150) | Legal: IA, IL, KS, MN, MO, ND, NE, OK, SD, WI | Association |
| Jerry Wilmot Scholarship (1389) | Study: Canada, United States | |
| WIX Corporation Scholarships (4151) | | Association |
| Wolf's Head Oil Company Scholarships (4152) | Legal: CT, DE, GA, IL, IN, KY, MA, MD, ME, MI, MN, MO, NC, NH, NJ, NY, OH, PA, RI, SC, TN, VA, VT, WI, WV | Association |
| Worcester County Horticultural Society Scholarship (6257) | | |
| Wyandott, Inc. Snacks and Popcorn Scholarship (4153) | Legal: OH | Association |
| Yetter Manufacturing Co. Scholarship (4154) | | Association |

## Architecture and Environmental Design

| Vocational Goal, Award, and Entry Number | Geographic Restrictions | Affiliation/Special Recipients Requirements |
|---|---|---|
| AIA/AAF Scholarship for Professional Degree Candidates (572) | | |
| AIA/AHA Fellowship in Health Facilities Design (573) | Citizenship: US/CA | |
| The American Architectural Foundation Minority/Disadvantaged Scholarship (574) | Legal: United States | Minority |
| APA Planning & the Black Community Division Scholarship (775) | | African American, Native American, Hispanic American |
| Architects League Scholastic Award (1075) | Legal: NJ | |
| Architects Registration Council Student Maintenance Grants (1079) | | |
| Associated Landscape Contractors of America Scholarsip (4025) | | Association |
| Association for Women in Architecture Scholarship (1292) | Legal: CA; Study: CA | |
| California Landscape Architectural Student Scholarships (3422) | Study: CA | |
| Fellowships in Byzantine Studies, Pre-Columbian Studies and Landscape Architecture (2288) | Study: DC | |
| Albert Halse Memorial Scholarship (1076) | Legal: NJ | |
| Edith H. Henderson Scholarship (3424) | Study: GA | |
| Frank Walton Horn Memorial Scholarships (4000) | | Handicapped |
| LAF/CLASS Cal Poly Scholarships (3426) | Study: CA | |
| LAF/CLASS Fund Scholarships and Internships (3427) | Study: CA | |
| LAF/CLASS University Program (3428) | Study: CA | |
| LIFE Scholarship Award (3417) | | |
| The Lippincott and Margulies Summer Internship (5385) | | |
| Theodore Mazza Scholarship (5769) | | |
| National Roofing Foundation Scholarship Award (4371) | Citizenship: US | |
| National Zoological Park Minority Traineeships (4456) | | |
| National Zoological Park Traineeship in Exhibit Interpretation (4460) | | |
| National Zoological Park Traineeship in Facilities Design (4461) | | |
| National Zoological Park Traineeship in Landscaping (4462) | | |
| NCSGC National Scholarships (3959) | | |

| Vocational Goal, Award, and Entry Number | Geographic Restrictions (Citizenship, Legal Residence, Place of Study) | Affiliation/Special Recipients Requirements |
|---|---|---|
| *Architecture and Environmental Design (continued)* | | |
| New York State Professional Opportunity Scholarships (4592) | Citizenship: US, PermRes; Legal: NY; Study: NY | |
| New York State Regents Professional Opportunity Scholarships (4577) | Legal: NY; Study: NY | |
| NIAE/ATBCB Student Design Competition Prizes (6024) | Study: United States | |
| Rain Bird Company Scholarship (3433) | | |
| Howard Brown Rickard Scholarship (4007) | | Handicapped |
| RTKL Traveling Fellowship (576) | | |
| Robert Schreck Memorial Fund Scholarship (5280) | Legal: TX | |
| Society of American Registered Architects Student Design Competition/Emily Munson Memorial Student Award (5433) | | |
| Edward D. Stone Jr. and Associates Minority Scholarship (3434) | | Minority |
| Student Store Interior Design Competition Prizes (3077) | | |
| Clarence Tabor Memorial Scholarship (1077) | Legal: NJ | |
| Robert Thunen Memorial Educational Scholarships (2983) | Study: CA, NV, OR, WA | |
| Harriett Barnhardt Wimmer Scholarship (3436) | | |
| David T. Woolsey Scholarship (3437) | Legal: HI | |
| **Area and Ethnic Studies** | | |
| Joseph Adams Scholarships (5428) | | Association |
| American Jewish League for Israel University Scholarship Fund (600) | | |
| Stella Blum Research Grant (2089) | | Association |
| Community Service Scholarships (3643) | | |
| Minda de Gunzburg Center for European Studies Undergraduate Summer Travel Grants (2771) | | Other |
| EMGIP Internships (2380) | Study: Germany | |
| Garikian University Scholarship Fund (1119) | | Ethnic |
| German Studies Research Grant (2687) | Study: Germany | |
| Inter-University Center Fellowships (3095) | Study: Japan | Association |
| Inter-University Program Fellowships (3097) | Study: People's Republic of China | |
| International Student Identity Card Travel Grants for Educational Programs in Developing Countries (2113) | Citizenship: US, PermRes | |
| U. Alexis Johnson Scholarship (3238) | Study: DC, MD, VA, WV, Japan | |
| Leo J. Krysa Family Foundation Undergraduate Scholarship (1660) | Citizenship: Canada; Study: Canada | |
| National Welsh-American Foundation Exchange Scholarships (4450) | Citizenship: US; Study: Wales | Ethnic |
| King Olav Norwegian-American Heritage Fund (5535) | | |
| Society Farsarotul Grants (5449) | | |
| Studentships in Northern Studies (1684) | Citizenship: Canada, PermRes; Study: Canada | |
| Study Abroad Scholarships (4263) | Study: Italy | |
| George Tanaka Memorial Scholarship Program (1288) | Citizenship: Canada, PermRes; Study: Canada | |
| **Aviation** | | |
| David Arver Memorial Scholarship (77) | Study: IA, IL, IN, KS, MI, MN, MO, NB, ND, SD, WI | |
| BFGoodrich Component Services Scholarship (78) | | |
| Bose Corporation Avionics Scholarship (79) | | |
| Bud Glover Memorial Scholarship (80) | | |

| Vocational Goal, Award, and Entry Number | Geographic Restrictions (Citizenship, Legal Residence, Place of Study) | Affiliation/Special Recipients Requirements |
|---|---|---|
| *Aviation (continued)* | | |
| College of Aeronautics Scholarship (81) | Study: NY | |
| Dutch and Ginger Arver Scholarship (82) | | |
| Field Aviation Co., Inc. Scholarship (83) | Study: Canada | |
| GARMIN Scholarship (84) | | |
| Gulf Coast Avionics Scholarships to Fox Valley Technical College (86) | Study: WI | |
| Russell Leroy Jones Memorial Scholarship to Colorado Aero Tech (87) | | |
| Leon Harris/Les Nichols Memorial Scholarship to Spartain School of Aeronautics (88) | Study: OK | |
| Mid-Continent Instrument Scholarship (89) | | |
| Monte Mitchell Global Scholarship (90) | | |
| Northern Airborne Technology Scholarship (91) | Study: Canada | |
| Plane & Pilot Magazine Germin Scholarship (92) | | |
| Lee Tarbox Memorial Scholarship (93) | | |
| Paul and Blanche Wulfsberg Scholarship (94) | | |

### Business and Management

| | | |
|---|---|---|
| AAAA Minority Advertising Internships (270) | Citizenship: US; Study: CA, IL, MI, NY | Minority |
| AAHCPA Scholarship (308) | | Hispanic American |
| AIER Summer Fellowships (580) | Study: United States | |
| Air Force ROTC Scholarships (5816) | Citizenship: US | Military |
| Air Travel Card Grant (969) | Citizenship: US/CA | |
| Airline Pilots Association Scholarship (96) | | Association |
| AISES A.T. Anderson Memorial Scholarship (559) | | Native American, Association |
| Alabama/Birmingham Legacy Scholarship (4427) | | |
| American Express Travel Scholarship (970) | Citizenship: US/CA; Legal: United States | |
| A.A. Amidon Scholarship (1848) | Legal: NY | |
| Dr. Tom Anderson Memorial Scholarship (4428) | | |
| Applebaum Master's and Ph.D. Programs Awards (2549) | | |
| Appraisal Institute Education Trust Scholarships (1060) | Citizenship: US | |
| Arizona Chapter Dependent Employee Membership Scholarship (971) | Citizenship: US/CA; Study: United States | Association |
| Avis Rent a Car Scholarship (972) | Citizenship: US/CA; Study: Canada, United States | |
| Avon Products Foundation Scholarship Program for Women in Business Studies (1545) | Citizenship: US | |
| Harold Bettinger Memorial Scholarship (1382) | Study: Canada, United States | |
| Business Press Educational Foundation Student Intern Program (1543) | | |
| Call to Action Opportunity Scholarship (1568) | Citizenship: US; Legal: CA; Study: CA | |
| Canadian Hospitality Foundation Scholarships (1653) | Study: NS, ON | |
| Bill Carpenter Memorial Certificate School Scholarship (4429) | | |
| Central Intelligence Agency Undergraduate Scholars Program (1812) | Study: DC | Minority, Handicapped |
| CERT Scholarship (2100) | Study: United States | Native American |
| Cleveland Legacy Scholarship (4431) | Legal: OH | |
| Weeta F. Colebank Scholarship (4432) | Legal: MS; Study: MS | |
| Colorado Society of CPAs Educational Foundation High School Scholarship (2000) | Study: CO | |

| Vocational Goal, Award, and Entry Number | Geographic Restrictions (Citizenship, Legal Residence, Place of Study) | Affiliation/Special Recipients Requirements |
|---|---|---|
| *Business and Management (continued)* | | |
| Colorado Society of CPAs Educational Foundation Scholarships (2001) | Study: CO | |
| Cox Minority Journalism Scholarship (2131) | Legal: GA; Study: GA | Minority |
| Louise Dessureault Memorial Scholarship (4433) | Citizenship: Canada | |
| Duracell/National Urban League Scholarship and Intern Program for Minority Students (4448) | | Minority |
| Engalitcheff Institute on Comparative Political and Economic Systems Internship (3019) | | |
| Exceptional Student Fellowship Award (5613) | Citizenship: US | |
| First Interstate Bank Scholarship (2468) | Legal: WA; Study: WA | |
| FORE Undergraduate Scholarships (519) | Citizenship: US | |
| Four-Shra-Nish Foundation Loan (2583) | Legal: OH | |
| Eric and Bette Friedheim Scholarship (4434) | | |
| Fukunaga Scholarship Foundation Annual Four-Year Scholarships in Business Administration (2603) | Legal: HI | |
| A.P. Giannini Scholarship (4228) | | Ethnic |
| Golden State Minority Foundation Scholarships (2713) | Citizenship: US, PermRes; Legal: CA | Minority |
| George L. Graziadio Fellowship for Business (4230) | | |
| Bryce Harlow Institute on Business and Government Affairs Internship (3020) | | |
| Harwood Memorial Real Estate Scholarship (5083) | | |
| Healy Scholarship (974) | Citizenship: US/CA | |
| Holland-America Line Westours Scholarships (975) | Citizenship: US/CA | |
| Institute on Political Journalism Summer Program (3021) | | |
| Jacob's Pillow Dance Festival Internships (3234) | Study: United States | |
| Jewel/Taylor C. Cotton Scholarship (1927) | Legal: IL | Minority |
| Robert Kaufman Memorial Scholarships (2989) | | |
| H. Neil Mecaskey Scholarship (4435) | | |
| Mercedes-Benz of North America Scholarship Program (1928) | Legal: IL | Minority |
| Merrill Lynch Scholarship (4241) | Legal: NY | |
| Mexican American Grocers Association Foundation Scholarships (3673) | | Hispanic American |
| Ed S. Miller Scholarship in Industrial and Labor Relations (2904) | Study: CA, NY | Union |
| Ministry of the Flemish Community Fellowships (3710) | Citizenship: US, PermRes | |
| Minority Student Administrative Summer Internship Program (5903) | | Minority |
| Patrick Murphy Internship (4436) | | |
| National Association of Black Accountants National Scholarship (3857) | | Minority |
| National Dairy Shrine/Dairy Management Scholarships, Inc. (3968) | | |
| National Restaurant Association Undergraduate Scholarships (4367) | | |
| National Scholarships for Funeral Service (354) | Citizenship: US | |
| National Zoological Park Traineeship in Public Affairs (4463) | | |
| New York State Regents Professional Opportunity Scholarships (4577) | Legal: NY; Study: NY | |

| Vocational Goal, Award, and Entry Number | Geographic Restrictions (Citizenship, Legal Residence, Place of Study) | Affiliation/Special Recipients Requirements |
|---|---|---|
| **Business and Management (continued)** | | |
| Northern California/Richard Epping Scholarships (976) | Citizenship: US/CA; Legal: CA; Study: CA | |
| Vennera Noto Scholarship (4249) | | |
| NSPA Scholarship Awards (4405) | Citizenship: US/CA | |
| NTF Internship (4437) | | |
| Orange County Chapter/Harry Jackson Scholarship (977) | Citizenship: US/CA; Study: CA | Association |
| Phi Chi Theta Scholarships (4896) | | Association |
| Pollard Scholarships (978) | Citizenship: US/CA | |
| Aviation Management Wilfred M. "Wiley" Post Scholarship (1351) | Legal: PA | |
| President's Committee on Employment of People with Disabilities Scholarships for Students with Disabilities (5001) | | Handicapped |
| Princess Cruises and Princess Tours Scholarship (979) | Citizenship: US/CA | |
| Professional Secretaries International Scholarships (5011) | | Association |
| George Reinke Scholarships (980) | Citizenship: US/CA | |
| William B. Ruggles Journalism Scholarship (4196) | Study: United States | |
| Sacramento Hispanic Chamber of Commerce Scholarships (5216) | Citizenship: US | Hispanic American |
| Santa Fe Pacific Foundation Scholarships (563) | Legal: AZ, CA, CO, KS, NM, OK | Association, Native American |
| Karla Scherer Foundation Scholarships (5254) | | |
| Harold W. Schloss Memorial Scholarship (1745) | Study: IA | |
| Service Merchandise Scholarship Program (5310) | | |
| Sigma Iota Epsilon Undergraduate Scholarship Awards (5335) | | Fraternal |
| Southern California Chapter/Pleasant Hawaiian Holidays Scholarship (982) | Citizenship: US | Employer |
| A.J. (Andy) Spielman Scholarships (983) | Citizenship: US/CA | |
| Statler Foundation Scholarship (5622) | Study: NY, United States | |
| Stanley H. Stearman Scholarships (4406) | | Association |
| E.D. Stella Scholarship (4262) | | Ethnic |
| Joseph R. Stone Scholarships (984) | Citizenship: US/CA | Employer |
| Sutherland/Purdy Scholarship (4925) | | Fraternal |
| William Toto Scholarship (4265) | | Ethnic |
| Treadway Inns, Hotels, and Resorts Scholarship (4439) | | |
| Tulsa Legacy Scholarship (4440) | Legal: OK; Study: OK | |
| Jerry Wilmot Scholarship (1389) | Study: Canada, United States | |
| Yellow Ribbon Scholarship (4442) | | |
| Harry and Angel Zerigian Scholarship (1130) | | Ethnic |
| **Communications** | | |
| AEJ Summer Internships for Minorities (3029) | Study: NJ, NY | African American, Hispanic American, Asian American, Minority |
| Albuquerque Amateur Radio Club Scholarship (815) | Legal: NM | |
| Jim Allard Broadcast Journalism Scholarship (1600) | Citizenship: Canada; Study: Canada | |
| Len Allen Award of Merit for Radio News (5051) | | |
| Alpha Epsilon Rho Scholarships (196) | | Fraternal |
| American Society of Magazine Editors Magazine Internship Program (940) | | |

| Vocational Goal, Award, and Entry Number | Geographic Restrictions (Citizenship, Legal Residence, Place of Study) | Affiliation/Special Recipients Requirements |
|---|---|---|
| *Communications (continued)* | | |
| Earl I. Anderson Scholarship (816) | Study: FL, IL, IN, MI | |
| Asbury Park Press Scholarships for Minority Students (1168) | Legal: NJ | Minority |
| Asian American Journalists Association National Internship Grant (1171) | | Association, Asian American |
| Asian American Journalists Association Scholarship (1172) | | Ethnic |
| Associated Press Summer Minority Internships (1197) | | Minority |
| Atlanta Association of Media Women Scholarship (1308) | Study: GA | Minority |
| Atlanta Press Club Journalism Scholarship (1310) | Study: GA | |
| WCVB TV Leo L. Beranek Fellowship for Newsreporting (6123) | | |
| Lisa Bjork Memorial Scholarship (2028) | Legal: FL | |
| Reid Blackburn Scholarship (4342) | | |
| Bookbuilders West Annual Scholarship (2581) | | |
| Ed Bradley Scholarships (5053) | | Minority |
| Broadcast Pioneers Scholarships (1495) | | |
| William A. Brower Scholarship (4694) | Legal: OH; Study: OH | Minority |
| Mary Lou Brown Scholarship (817) | Legal: AK, ID, MT, OR, WA | |
| Business Reporting Intern Program for College Sophomores and Juniors (2274) | | Minority |
| Mary Butler Scholarship (6221) | Legal: MI; Study: MI | |
| Jim Byron Scholarship (5054) | | |
| Wilson W. Carnes Scholarships (4043) | | Association |
| Ben Chatfield Scholarship (5055) | | |
| Richard Cheverton Scholarship (5056) | | |
| Chicago FM Club Scholarship (818) | Citizenship: US; Legal: IL, IN, WI | |
| Chicago Heights Star Publications Minority Internship (5603) | | Minority |
| Chicago Sun-Times Minority Scholarships and Internships (1922) | Legal: IL | Minority |
| Chips Quinn Scholars Program (2591) | | |
| College Conference and Summer Fellowship Program (3174) | | |
| Concerned Media Professionals Scholarships (5976) | | Hispanic American |
| Irving W. Cook, WA0CGS Scholarship (820) | Legal: KS | |
| Lucy Corbett Scholarship (6222) | Legal: MI; Study: MI | |
| Cox Minority Journalism Scholarship (2131) | Legal: GA; Study: GA | Minority |
| Creswell, Munsell, Fultz & Zirbel Scholarships (4054) | Study: IA, IL, IN, KS, MN, MO, NC, NE, OH, SC, WI | Association |
| Dallas-Fort Worth Association of Black Communicators Scholarships (2170) | | Minority |
| *Detroit Free Press* Minority Journalism Scholarships (2247) | | Minority, African American, Asian American, Hispanic American, Native American |
| Dog Writers' Educational Trust Scholarships (2264) | | Other |
| Maurice and Robert Early Scholarship (2999) | Study: IN | |
| Bob East Scholarship (4343) | | |
| Editing Internships (2275) | Citizenship: US; Study: United States | |
| Joseph Ehrenreich Scholarships (4344) | | |
| Engalitcheff Institute on Comparative Political and Economic Systems Internship (3019) | | |
| Harold E. Ennes Scholarship (5442) | | |
| Harold E. Fellows Scholarships (1496) | | Employer |
| FFTA Scholarship Competition (2568) | | |

| Vocational Goal, Award, and Entry Number | Geographic Restrictions (Citizenship, Legal Residence, Place of Study) | Affiliation/Special Recipients Requirements |
|---|---|---|
| *Communications (continued)* | | |
| Martin Fischbein Fellowship (2601) | | |
| Charles N. Fisher Memorial Scholarship (822) | Legal: AZ, CA | |
| Fleishman-Hillard, Inc. Scholarship (4079) | | Association |
| Florida Chapter of the Association of Women in Communications Christina Saralegui Scholarship (1294) | Legal: FL | Hispanic American |
| Michael J. Flosi Memorial Scholarship (823) | Citizenship: US; Legal: IL, IN, WI | |
| James Lawrence Fly Scholarships (1497) | | |
| Fort Wayne News-Sentinel Minority Journalism Scholarship (2557) | | |
| Joel Garcia Memorial Scholarship (1555) | Legal: CA; Study: CA | Hispanic American |
| Garikian University Scholarship Fund (1119) | | Ethnic |
| Stephen H. Gayle Memorial Scholarship (4558) | Legal: NY | Minority |
| Georgia Press Education Foundation Scholarships (2653) | Study: GA | |
| ARRL Scholarship Honoring Senator Barry Goldwater (825) | | |
| Grants for Research in Broadcasting (3864) | | |
| Paul and Helen L. Grauer Scholarship (826) | Legal: IA, KS, MO, NE; Study: IA, KS, MO, NE | |
| K2TEO Martin J. Green Sr. Memorial Scholarship (827) | | |
| Perry F. Hadlock Memorial Scholarship (828) | Study: NY | |
| Ruth Hancock Scholarships (1603) | Citizenship: Canada; Study: Canada | |
| Bryce Harlow Institute on Business and Government Affairs Internship (3020) | | |
| Hawaii Society of Professional Journalists Internships (2824) | Legal: HI | |
| Hearst Foundation Journalism Writing Competition (2837) | | |
| Hispanic Link News Service Internships (2878) | | Hispanic American |
| John Hogan Scholarship (5060) | | |
| Indiana Professional Chapter of SPJ Minority Scholarship (5486) | Legal: IN; Study: IN | Minority |
| Ken Inouye Scholarship (5488) | | Minority |
| Institute on Political Journalism Summer Program (3021) | | |
| Iowa Broadcasters Association Scholarship (3219) | Legal: IA; Study: IA | |
| Journalism Institute for Minorities Scholarships (3300) | | Minority |
| Kentucky School of Journalism Foundation Internships (3362) | Legal: KY | |
| KNTV Minority Scholarships (3394) | Legal: CA; Study: CA | Minority |
| Theodore Koop Scholarship (5061) | | |
| James McCulla Scholarship (5062) | | |
| Mercedes-Benz of North America Scholarship Program (1928) | Legal: IL | Minority |
| Miller Meester Advertising Scholarship (4100) | | Association |
| Mississippi Scholarship (832) | Legal: MS; Study: MS | |
| Modesto Bee Summer Internships (3760) | | |
| NAHJ Scholarships (2879) | | |
| *The Nation* Internships Program (3822) | | |
| National Association of Black Journalists Scholarship (3859) | | Minority |
| National Association of Black Journalists Summer Internships (3860) | | African American |
| National Association of Media Women Scholarship (3885) | | Minority |
| National Newspaper Publishers Association Grants (4326) | | Minority |

| Vocational Goal, Award, and Entry Number | Geographic Restrictions (Citizenship, Legal Residence, Place of Study) | Affiliation/Special Recipients Requirements |
|---|---|---|
| *Communications (continued)* | | |
| National Press Club Ellen Masin Persina Scholarship (4340) | | Minority |
| The National Scholarship Trust Fund Scholarships for High School Students (4374) | | |
| The National Scholarship Trust Fund Scholarships for Undergraduates (4375) | | |
| Native American Journalists Association Scholarships (4470) | | Native American |
| Edward J. Nell Memorial Scholarships in Journalism (5048) | | |
| North Texas - Bob Nelson KB5BNU Memorial Scholarship (833) | Legal: OK, TX | |
| New England Press Association Internships (4529) | Study: CT, MA, ME, NH, RI, VT | |
| New York Financial Writers' Association (4568) | Study: NY | |
| News-Sentinel Minority Scholarship (4629) | | Minority |
| NPPF Still Scholarship (4346) | | |
| NPPF Television News Scholarship (4347) | | |
| Oak Ridge National Laboratory Professional Internship Program (Undergrad) (5919) | | |
| Father Anthony J. O'Driscoll Memorial Scholarship Award (633) | Legal: NJ | |
| Ohio Newspaper Women's Association Scholarship (4731) | Legal: OH; Study: OH | |
| Online Newspaper Intern Program (2276) | | |
| Bruce Palmer Scholarship (5064) | | |
| Walter Patterson Scholarships (1498) | | |
| Leonard M. Perryman Communications Scholarship for Ethnic Minority Students (5794) | Citizenship: US | Minority, Religion |
| Art Peters Minority Internships (4929) | Study: PA | Minority |
| Politics and Journalism Internship (6083) | | |
| Press Club of Dallas Foundation Scholarship (5003) | Study: TX | |
| Public Interest Internships (1803) | Study: United States | |
| Chips Quinn Scholars Program Internship (1438) | | Minority |
| Garth Reeves Jr. Memorial Scholarships (5490) | Legal: FL | Minority |
| Reporters Committee for Freedom of the Press Clinical Internship Program (5094) | | |
| Nelson A. Rockefeller Minority Internships (6270) | Legal: NY | Asian American, African American, Hispanic American, Native American |
| Richard J. Roth Journalism Fellowship (4600) | Citizenship: US; Legal: NY; Study: NY | |
| RTNDF Presidential Memorial Scholarship (5066) | | |
| RTNDF Summer Internships for Minority Students (5068) | | Minority |
| RTNDF Undergraduate Scholarships (5069) | | |
| William B. Ruggles Journalism Scholarship (4196) | Study: United States | |
| Fred Russell-Grantland RICE TRA Sports Writing (5729) | Study: TN | |
| Sacramento Bee Journalism Scholarships for Community College Students (5206) | Study: CA | |
| Sacramento Bee Minority Media Scholarships (5207) | Legal: CA | Minority |
| Eugene "Gene" Sallee, W4YFR Memorial Scholarship (839) | Legal: GA | |
| San Francisco Chronicle Summer Newsroom Internships (5230) | | |

| Vocational Goal, Award, and Entry Number | Geographic Restrictions (Citizenship, Legal Residence, Place of Study) | Affiliation/Special Recipients Requirements |
|---|---|---|
| *Communications (continued)* | | |
| Seattle Professional Chapter of Women in Communications Annual Communications Scholarship (6224) | | |
| The *Seattle Times* Summer Newsroom Internships (5296) | | |
| Shane Media Scholarships (1499) | | |
| Dennis and Elizabeth Shattuck Internships (2429) | | |
| Carole Simpson Scholarship (5071) | | Minority |
| Six Meter Club of Chicago Scholarship (840) | Legal: IL; Study: IL | |
| South Carolina Press Association Foundation Scholarships (5545) | Study: SC | |
| Specs Howard High School Scholarships (5583) | Study: MI | |
| Specs Howard School of Broadcast Arts Industry Scholarships (5584) | Study: MI | Other |
| *Sports Illustrated* for Kids Internships (5595) | | |
| Syracuse Newspapers Journalism Scholarship (5664) | Legal: NY; Study: NY | Minority |
| Virginia Press Association Minority Internship (6063) | Legal: VA; Study: VA | Minority |
| The *Washington Post* Summer Journalism Internships (6090) | | |
| Washington Press Association Annual Scholarships (6093) | Study: WA | |
| Vincent T. Wasilewski Scholarships (1500) | | Association |
| Muddy Waters Scholarship (1448) | Study: IL | |
| WCVB TV 5 Broadcasting Internships (6124) | Citizenship: US | |
| WCVB TV Hearst Broadcast News Fellowship (6125) | | Minority |
| Della A. Whittaker Scholarships (5504) | | |
| L. Phil Wicker Scholarship (841) | Legal: NC, SC, VA, WV; Study: NC, SC, VA, WV | |
| Young Feminist Scholarship Program (5591) | | |
| Mark Zambrano Scholarship (2880) | | Minority |

## Computer and Information Sciences

| Vocational Goal, Award, and Entry Number | Geographic Restrictions (Citizenship, Legal Residence, Place of Study) | Affiliation/Special Recipients Requirements |
|---|---|---|
| AFCEA ROTC Scholarship Program (1100) | | Military |
| Airline Pilots Association Scholarship (96) | | Association |
| ASIS Student Paper Award (935) | | |
| AT & T Bell Laboratories Summer Research Program for Minorities & Women (1305) | Citizenship: US, PermRes; Study: NJ | African American, Hispanic American, Native American |
| AT & T Bell Laboratories University Relations Summer Program (1306) | | |
| BPW Career Advancement Scholarships (1546) | Citizenship: US; Study: United States | |
| Central Intelligence Agency Undergraduate Scholars Program (1812) | Study: DC | Minority, Handicapped |
| Electronic Industries Foundation Scholarships (2370) | Citizenship: US | Handicapped |
| Hewlett-Packard Scholarships (5512) | Citizenship: US | |
| Admiral Grace Murray Hopper Scholarship (5513) | Citizenship: US | |
| LPI Summer Intern Program in Planetary Science (3514) | | |
| Ruth A. & G. Elving Lundine Scholarship (1879) | | Employer |
| Richard E. Merwin Scholarships (2950) | | Association |
| Microsoft Corporation Scholarships (5516) | | |
| Minority Student Administrative Summer Internship Program (5903) | | Minority |
| NAACP Willems Scholarship (3851) | | Minority, Association |

| Vocational Goal, Award, and Entry Number | Geographic Restrictions (Citizenship, Legal Residence, Place of Study) | Affiliation/Special Recipients Requirements |
|---|---|---|
| *Computer and Information Sciences (continued)* | | |
| National Association for the Advancement of Colored People Scholarship Program (5905) | | |
| Naval Air Warfare Center Training Systems Division Undergraduate Research Participation Program (5914) | | |
| NRAO Summer Student Research Assistantships (4352) | Citizenship: US; Study: United States | |
| General Emmett Paige Scholarship (1101) | Citizenship: US | |
| Sacramento Hispanic Chamber of Commerce Scholarships (5216) | Citizenship: US | Hispanic American |
| The SHL Systemhouse President's Award for Education Technology Program (1286) | | |
| Lance Stafferd Larson Student Scholarship (2951) | | Association |
| Tandy Technology Scholars (5672) | | |
| Undergraduate U.S. Army Environmental Hygiene Internship Program (5929) | | |
| U.S. Department of Energy Internship (4711) | Citizenship: US, PermRes; Study: CA, IL, NM, NY, TN, WA | |
| U.S. Nuclear Regulatory Commission Historically Black Colleges and Universities Student Research Participation (5936) | | |
| Upsilon Pi Epsilon/Computer Society Award for Academic Excellence (2952) | | Association |
| **Education** | | |
| AISES A.T. Anderson Memorial Scholarship (559) | | Native American, Association |
| Alaska Teacher Loans (130) | Legal: AK | |
| Assistantships in France (2374) | Citizenship: US | |
| ATA Undergraduate Scholarships (1093) | Study: AR | African American |
| Thomas William Bennett Memorial Scholarship (2027) | Citizenship: US; Legal: FL | |
| Eva Betschart Scholarships (3319) | | Fraternal |
| Blaine House Scholars Loans (2455) | Legal: ME | |
| BPW Career Advancement Scholarships (1546) | Citizenship: US; Study: United States | |
| Brookmire-Hastings Scholarship (6203) | Legal: WI | |
| Call to Action Opportunity Scholarship (1568) | Citizenship: US; Legal: CA; Study: CA | |
| Patricia Chesebro Scholarships (3320) | | Fraternal |
| CSAC Assumption Program of Loans for Education (1580) | Legal: CA | |
| Delta Gamma Foundation - Florence Margaret Harvey Memorial Scholarship (480) | Citizenship: US | Handicapped |
| Rudolph Dillman Scholarship (481) | Citizenship: US | Handicapped |
| Paul Douglas Teacher Scholarship (Illinois) (2968) | Legal: IL | |
| Paul Douglas Teacher Scholarship (1583) | Legal: CA; Study: CA | |
| Paul Douglas Teacher Scholarship (2498) | Citizenship: US; Legal: FL; Study: FL | |
| Paul Douglas Teacher Scholarship (4585) | Citizenship: US, PermRes; Legal: NY; Study: NY | |
| Paul Douglas Teacher Scholarships (4735) | Study: OK | |
| Dusendon Scholarship Grants (3494) | Legal: OH | |
| Florida Critical Teacher Shortage Scholarship Loans (2501) | Study: FL | |
| Florida Teacher Scholarship and Forgivable Loan Program (2506) | Study: FL | |
| Four-Shra-Nish Foundation Loan (2583) | Legal: OH | |
| French Government Teaching Awards (2376) | Study: France | |
| Garikian University Scholarship Fund (1119) | | Ethnic |
| Georgia Student Finance Commission Service-Cancellable Stafford Loan (2666) | Legal: GA; Study: GA | |

| Vocational Goal, Award, and Entry Number | Geographic Restrictions (Citizenship, Legal Residence, Place of Study) | Affiliation/Special Recipients Requirements |
|---|---|---|
| *Education (continued)* | | |
| Georgia Student Finance Commission State-Sponsored Loan (2669) | Legal: GA; Study: GA | |
| Greater Peace Alberta Teachers' Associatioin No. 13 Scholarship (188) | Legal: AB, Canada; Study: AB | |
| Haines Memorial Scholarships (5552) | Study: SD | |
| Isabel M. Herson Scholarship in Education (6305) | | |
| Margaret Holland Scholarships (3321) | | Fraternal |
| Wilma Hoyal/Maxine Chilton Scholarships (614) | Citizenship: US; Legal: AZ; Study: AZ | |
| Anna & John Kolesar Memorial Scholarships (176) | Legal: Canada; Study: AB, Canada | |
| Leo J. Krysa Family Foundation Undergraduate Scholarship (1660) | Citizenship: Canada; Study: Canada | |
| Lois T. Larson Scholarship (1877) | | |
| Marin Education Grants (3554) | Citizenship: US, PermRes; Legal: CA | |
| Maryland Teacher Education Distinguished Scholar Scholarship (3582) | Legal: MD; Study: MD | |
| Sharon Christa McAuliffe Education Scholarship (3583) | Legal: MD; Study: MD | |
| Minority Educator Scholarship (1886) | Study: NY | |
| Minority Teachers of Illinois Scholarship (2981) | Study: IL | Minority |
| Missouri Minority Teacher Education Scholarship (3750) | Legal: MO | Minority |
| Missouri Teacher Education Scholarship (3751) | Legal: MO | |
| Mary Morrow-Edna Richards Scholarships (4672) | Legal: NC; Study: NC | |
| Ruth E. Munson Music Scholarship (1891) | | |
| NACA Prize Papers Competition (3868) | | |
| National Board Civil Air Patrol Undergraduate/Advanced Undergraduate College Scholarship (3918) | | Association |
| National Federation of the Blind Educator of Tomorrow Award (4002) | | Handicapped |
| National Zoological Park Traineeship in Education (4459) | | |
| Newtonville Woman's Club Scholarships (2641) | Legal: MA | |
| Oklahoma State Regents Future Teacher Scholarships (4738) | Legal: OK | |
| Order of Alhambra Scholarships (4789) | Legal: CA; Study: United States | Religion |
| Oregon PTA Teacher Education Scholarships (4801) | Legal: OR; Study: OR | |
| Phi Delta Kappa Scholarship Grant for Prospective Educators (4898) | | Fraternal |
| Pi Lambda Theta Distinguished Student Scholar Award (4942) | | |
| Billy D. Pounds Scholarships and Bobby Jones Scholarships (3322) | | Fraternal |
| Power Systems Inc./NSCA Strength and Conditioning Professional Scholarship (4417) | | Association |
| Retarded Citizens Teachers Scholarships (4793) | Citizenship: US, Canada | |
| Rockefeller Brothers Fund Fellowships for Minority Students (5144) | | Minority |
| Santa Fe Pacific Foundation Scholarships (563) | Legal: AZ, CA, CO, KS, NM, OK | Association, Native American |
| Scholarships for Blind and Visually Impaired Postsecondary Students (483) | Citizenship: US | Handicapped |
| Second Marine Division Memorial Scholarships (5298) | | Veteran |

| Vocational Goal, Award, and Entry Number | Geographic Restrictions (Citizenship, Legal Residence, Place of Study) | Affiliation/Special Recipients Requirements |
|---|---|---|
| *Education (continued)* | | |
| Service Cancelable Student Loan (2660) | | |
| Kathryn G. Siphers Scholarships (6218) | | |
| South Carolina Teachers Loan Program (5547) | | |
| Elizabeth Stadtlander Scholarships (3323) | | Fraternal |
| Lord Strathcona Trust Fund Scholarship Alberta (5634) | Study: Canada | |
| Teacher Education Scholarship Program (125) | Citizenship: US | Minority, Handicapped |
| Robert C. Thomas Memorial Scholarship (133) | | |
| Marguerite Tremblay Cote Scholarships (1726) | Legal: ME; Study: ME | Ethnic |
| United Commercial Travelers Retarded Citizens Teacher Scholarship (5787) | | |
| United Nations Educational Training Scholarships for Southern Africans (5798) | Legal: Namibia, Republic of South Africa | |
| Virginia Volkwein Memorial Scholarships (6219) | | |
| William Winter Teacher Scholar Loan Program (3746) | Legal: MS; Study: MS | |

## Engineering

| Vocational Goal, Award, and Entry Number | Geographic Restrictions (Citizenship, Legal Residence, Place of Study) | Affiliation/Special Recipients Requirements |
|---|---|---|
| AAAS Directorate for Science & Policy Administrative Internship (264) | | |
| ACEC Cotton Scholarships (396) | Citizenship: US | |
| Marijane E. and William J. Adams, Jr. Scholarship (891) | | |
| AFSA Scholarship Awards (68) | | Military |
| AIAA Scholarship Program (568) | Citizenship: US, PermRes | Association |
| Air Force Civilian Cooperative Work-Study Program (66) | | |
| Air Force ROTC Scholarships (5816) | Citizenship: US | Military |
| Air Traffic Control Association Scholarships (72) | Citizenship: US | |
| Airline Pilots Association Scholarship (96) | | Association |
| AISES A.T. Anderson Memorial Scholarship (559) | | Native American, Association |
| The American Society of Mechanical Engineers Auxiliary Student Loans (948) | | |
| American Society of Naval Engineers Scholarships (959) | Citizenship: US, PermRes | |
| ANS Environmental Sciences Division Scholarship (720) | Citizenship: US, PermRes | |
| ANS Fuel Cycle and Waste Management Scholarship (721) | Citizenship: US, PermRes | |
| ANS Nuclear Operations Division Scholarship (723) | Citizenship: US, PermRes | |
| ANS Power Division Scholarship (724) | Citizenship: US, PermRes | |
| ANS Undergraduate Scholarships (725) | Citizenship: US, PermRes | |
| APEGGA Entrance Scholarships (1254) | Study: AB | |
| ASCET Small Cash Grant (895) | | |
| ASDSO Scholarship (1262) | | |
| ASHRAE Scholarships (931) | | |
| ASM Foundation Scholarship (1184) | Citizenship: US/CA | |
| ASME Student Assistance Loans (944) | Citizenship: US | Association |
| Associated General Contractors Education and Research Foundation Undergraduate Scholarship (402) | | |
| AT & T Bell Laboratories Summer Research Program for Minorities & Women (1305) | Citizenship: US, PermRes; Study: NJ | African American, Hispanic American, Native American |
| AT & T Bell Laboratories University Relations Summer Program (1306) | | |
| Aviation Technology Scholarship (1349) | Legal: PA; Study: PA | |

| Vocational Goal, Award, and Entry Number | Geographic Restrictions (Citizenship, Legal Residence, Place of Study) | Affiliation/Special Recipients Requirements |
|---|---|---|
| *Engineering (continued)* | | |
| AWU Student Research Fellowships (1203) | Citizenship: US, PermRes; Study: CA, CO, ID, MT, ND, NM, NV, OK, UT, WA, WY | |
| Anne Maureen Whitney Barrow Memorial Scholarship (5506) | Citizenship: US | |
| Henry Boh Memorial Scholarships (51) | | |
| BPW Career Advancement Scholarships (1546) | Citizenship: US; Study: United States | |
| BPW Loans for Women in Engineering Studies (1547) | Citizenship: US | |
| H. Fletcher Brown Scholarship (4967) | Legal: DE | |
| The Build America Scholarships (52) | | |
| G.E. Byrne Memorial Scholarships (53) | | |
| Cape Canaveral Chapter Scholarships (5114) | Legal: FL | Minority |
| Billy R. Carter Memorial Scholarships (54) | | |
| Caterpillar Scholars Award (5465) | | |
| CCC Scholarships (55) | | |
| Celanese Canada Inc. Scholarships (1269) | Citizenship: Canada, PermRes; Study: Canada | |
| Central Intelligence Agency Undergraduate Scholars Program (1812) | Study: DC | Minority, Handicapped |
| CERT Scholarship (2100) | Study: United States | Native American |
| Renate W. Chasman Scholarship (1507) | Citizenship: US, PermRes; Legal: NY | |
| CHROME Scholarship (2081) | | Association |
| Herbert L. Cox Memorial Scholarship (2294) | | |
| Raymond Davis Scholarship (5461) | | |
| Alexander Defilippis Scholarship (4219) | | |
| Delayed Education for Women Scholarship (728) | Citizenship: US; Study: United States | |
| Joseph R. Dietrich Scholarships (729) | Citizenship: US, PermRes | |
| Digital Equipment Corporation Scholarship (5507) | Citizenship: US, PermRes; Study: CT, MA, ME, NH, NY, RI, VT | Association |
| DOE Student Research Participation (4705) | Citizenship: US, PermRes | |
| Dueutz-Allis Corporation, Hesston Corporation, and White Tractor Scholarships (4066) | | |
| Duracell/National Urban League Scholarship and Intern Program for Minority Students (4448) | | Minority |
| EAA Aviation Achievement Scholarship (2295) | | |
| Thomas Edison/Max McGraw Scholarship (4379) | | |
| Sylvia W. Farny Scholarships (949) | Citizenship: US; Study: United States | |
| Florida National Science Scholars Program (2503) | Citizenship: US; Legal: FL; Study: FL | |
| Fossil Energy Professional Internship Program (Undergrad) (5879) | | |
| Fossil Energy Technology Internship Program (5880) | | |
| Dwight D. Gardner Memorial Scholarship (3060) | Study: Canada, Mexico, United States | Association |
| General Electric Foundation Scholarships (5508) | Citizenship: US | |
| General Motors Foundation Scholarships for Graduates (5509) | Citizenship: US | |
| General Motors Foundation Scholarships for Undergraduates (5510) | Citizenship: US | |
| Lillian Moller Gilbreth Scholarship (5511) | | |
| Dr. Robert H. Goddard Scholarships (4408) | Citizenship: US; Study: United States | |
| Barry M. Goldwater Scholarship (2715) | Citizenship: US | |
| John and Elsa Gracik Scholarships (945) | Citizenship: US | |
| Hewlett-Packard Scholarships (5512) | Citizenship: US | |

| Vocational Goal, Award, and Entry Number | Geographic Restrictions (Citizenship, Legal Residence, Place of Study) | Affiliation/Special Recipients Requirements |
|---|---|---|
| *Engineering (continued)* | | |
| Historically Black Colleges and Universities Faculty and Student Research Participation Program in Fusion. (5890) | | |
| Historically Black Colleges and Universities Fossil Energy Faculty and Student Research Training (5891) | | |
| Historically Black Colleges and Universities Nuclear Energy Training Program (Undergrad) (5895) | | |
| Admiral Grace Murray Hopper Scholarship (5513) | Citizenship: US | |
| Frank Walton Horn Memorial Scholarships (4000) | | Handicapped |
| Dorothy Lemke Howarth Scholarship (5514) | Citizenship: US | |
| C.D. Howe Memorial Foundation Engineering Awards Program (1276) | Citizenship: Canada, PermRes; Study: Canada | |
| JDS FITEL Scholarship Program (1279) | Citizenship: Canada; Study: Canada | |
| Jewel/Taylor C. Cotton Scholarship (1927) | Legal: IL | Minority |
| Wayne Kay Scholarship (5467) | | |
| Samuel C. Kraus, Jr. Memorial Scholarship (4412) | | Other |
| Herbert Frank and Bertha Maude Laird Memorial Foundation Scholarships (4690) | Legal: CA | |
| John R. Lamarsh Scholarship (731) | Citizenship: US, PermRes; Study: United States | |
| John and Muriel Landis Scholarships (732) | Study: United States | |
| Vernie G. Lindstron, Jr. Memorial Scholarships (56) | | |
| LPI Summer Intern Program in Planetary Science (3514) | | |
| Ruth A. & G. Elving Lundine Scholarship (1879) | | Employer |
| Professional Pilot John W. "Reds" Macfarlane Scholarship (1350) | Legal: PA; Study: PA | |
| Maryland MESA Scholarships (3586) | Legal: MD | |
| MASWE Memorial Scholarships (5515) | | |
| Fred R. McDaniel Memorial Scholarship (830) | | |
| Robert B. McEachem Memorial Scholarships (57) | | |
| Mercedes-Benz of North America Scholarship Program (1928) | Legal: IL | Minority |
| Edmond A. Metzger Scholarship (831) | | Association |
| Allen H. Meyers Scholarship (3677) | Legal: MI | |
| MHEF Scholarship (3607) | Citizenship: US | |
| Microsoft Corporation Scholarships (5516) | | |
| Minority Students Hazardous Materials Management Training Program (5904) | | Minority |
| Ted Moll Flight Scholarship (1887) | | |
| MTM Fellowships (3062) | | Association |
| NAACP Willems Scholarship (3851) | | Minority, Association |
| NACME Corporate Scholars Program (3835) | | African American, Hispanic American, Native American |
| NACME TechForce Scholarships (3836) | | African American, Hispanic American, Native American |
| Robert H. Nagel Scholarships (5676) | | Association |
| National Association for the Advancement of Colored People Scholarship Program (5905) | | |
| National Board Civil Air Patrol Undergraduate/Advanced Undergraduate College Scholarship (3918) | | Association |
| National Library of Medicine Undergraduate Research Study Program (5909) | | |

| Vocational Goal, Award, and Entry Number | Geographic Restrictions (Citizenship, Legal Residence, Place of Study) | Affiliation/Special Recipients Requirements |
|---|---|---|
| *Engineering (continued)* | | |
| National Oceanic and Atmospheric Administration/Historically Black Colleges and Universities Faculty/Student Research Participation Program (5910) | | |
| Naval Air Warfare Center Training Systems Division Undergraduate Research Participation Program (5914) | | |
| NDDOT Educational Grants (4682) | Study: ND | |
| Nemal Electronics Scholarship (834) | | |
| New York State Professional Opportunity Scholarships (4592) | Citizenship: US, PermRes; Legal: NY; Study: NY | |
| New York State Regents Professional Opportunity Scholarships (4577) | Legal: NY; Study: NY | |
| Northeast Chapter of the American Association of Airport Executives (AAAE) Post Scholarship (272) | | |
| Northrop Corporation Founders Scholarship (5517) | | Association |
| NRAO Summer Student Research Assistantships (4352) | Citizenship: US; Study: United States | |
| Oak Ridge National Laboratory Professional Internship Program (Undergrad) (5919) | | |
| Oak Ridge National Laboratory Technology Internship Program (5920) | | Association |
| General Emmett Paige Scholarship (1101) | Citizenship: US | |
| Ivy Parker Memorial Scholarship (5518) | | |
| Arthur & Doreen Parrett Scholarship Fund (4848) | Legal: WA | |
| The Payzer Scholarship (2296) | | |
| Stanley F. Pepper Memorial Scholarships (58) | | |
| Petroleum Research Fund Grants (369) | Legal: United States; Study: United States | |
| Pitcock Scholarships (59) | | |
| Al Qoyawayma Award (561) | | Native American |
| Quarry Engineering Scholarship Program (4413) | | |
| Spence Reese Scholarship (5089) | | |
| Judith Resnik Memorial Scholarship (5519) | | Association |
| Paul B. Richards Memorial Scholarship (60) | | |
| Howard Brown Rickard Scholarship (4007) | | Handicapped |
| Rocky Mountain Coal Mining Institute Scholarships (5157) | Citizenship: US; Legal: AZ, CO, MT, ND, NM, TX, UT, WY | |
| Kenneth Andrew Roe Scholarships (946) | Citizenship: US; Study: Canada, Mexico, United States | Association |
| Sacramento Hispanic Chamber of Commerce Scholarships (5216) | Citizenship: US | Hispanic American |
| SAE Engineering Scholarships (5436) | | |
| St. Louis SME Chapter No. 17 Scholarships (5468) | Study: MO | |
| Olive Lynn Salembier Scholarship (5520) | | |
| Savannah River Technology Center Professional Internship Program (Undergrad) (5925) | | |
| Robert Schreck Memorial Fund Scholarship (5280) | Legal: TX | |
| The SHL Systemhouse President's Award for Education Technology Program (1286) | | |
| SHPE Foundation Education Grant (5454) | | |
| Sigma Xi Grants-in-Aid of Research (5347) | | |
| Society of Plastics Engineers Foundation Scholarships (5484) | | |

Vocational Goals Index - Undergraduate

| Vocational Goal, Award, and Entry Number | Geographic Restrictions (Citizenship, Legal Residence, Place of Study) | Affiliation/Special Recipients Requirements |
|---|---|---|
| *Engineering (continued)* | | |
| Spartan School of Aeronautics Scholarship (2297) | | |
| SPIE Educational Scholarships and Grants in Optical Engineering (5589) | | |
| Student Engineer of the Year Scholarship (893) | Citizenship: US, Canada | |
| Syracuse Pulp and Paper Foundation Scholarship (5666) | Citizenship: US, PermRes; Study: NY | |
| Teledyne Continental Aviation Excellence Scholarship (2298) | | |
| Texaco Scholarships (5521) | | Association |
| William Toto Scholarship (4265) | | Ethnic |
| TRW Scholarships (5522) | | |
| Undergraduate U.S. Army Environmental Hygiene Internship Program (5929) | | |
| U.S. Coast Guard Academy Appointment (5845) | | |
| U.S. Department of Energy Internship (4711) | Citizenship: US, PermRes; Study: CA, IL, NM, NY, TN, WA | |
| U.S. Department of Energy Student Research Participation Program (5933) | | |
| U.S. Nuclear Regulatory Commission Historically Black Colleges and Universities Student Research Participation (5936) | | |
| University of Maine Pulp and Paper Foundation Scholarships (6000) | Study: ME | |
| Upsilon Pi Epsilon/Computer Society Award for Academic Excellence (2952) | | Association |
| Richard Lee Vernon Aviation Scholarship (2299) | | |
| Vertical Flight Foundation Engineering Scholarships (534) | | |
| Vertical Flight Foundation Scholarships (6036) | | |
| James R. Vogt Scholarship (734) | Citizenship: US, PermRes | |
| WAAIME Scholarship Loans (592) | Study: United States | |
| Myrtle and Earl Walker Scholarships (5469) | | |
| William E. Weisel Scholarship (5470) | Citizenship: US/CA | |
| Westinghouse Bertha Lamme Scholarships (5523) | Citizenship: US | |
| Westinghouse Science Talent Search (5282) | | |
| **Foreign Languages** | | |
| Joseph Adams Scholarships (5428) | | Association |
| Alpha Mu Gamma Scholarships (200) | | Fraternal |
| Assistantships in France (2374) | Citizenship: US | |
| Central Intelligence Agency Undergraduate Scholars Program (1812) | Study: DC | Minority, Handicapped |
| Cultural Ambassadorial Scholarship (5168) | | |
| French Government Teaching Awards (2376) | Study: France | |
| Hochschulsommerkurse at German Universities (2688) | Citizenship: US, Canada; Study: Germany | |
| Official Languages Part-Time Monitor Program (4716) | Legal: Canada | |
| Phi Sigma Iota Scholarships (4904) | | Fraternal |
| Queen Elizabeth Silver Jubilee Endowment Fund for Study in a Second Official Language Awards (1285) | Citizenship: Canada, PermRes | |
| Root Foreign Language Scholarship (3333) | Citizenship: US/CA | Fraternal |
| St. David's Scholarship (5220) | | Ethnic |
| Service Cancelable Student Loan (2660) | | |
| Summer Language Bursary Program (4717) | Legal: Canada; Study: Canada | |

| Vocational Goal, Award, and Entry Number | Geographic Restrictions (Citizenship, Legal Residence, Place of Study) | Affiliation/Special Recipients Requirements |
|---|---|---|
| *Foreign Languages (continued)* | | |
| Summer Language Bursary Program for Francophones (4718) | Legal: Canada; Study: Canada | |
| Summer Language Course at the University of Leipzig (2692) | Study: Germany | |
| **Health Care Services** | | |
| ADHA Certificate/Associate Degree, Baccalaureate and Graduate Scholarships (418) | | |
| ADHA Part-Time Scholarship (420) | | |
| Airline Pilots Association Scholarship (96) | | Association |
| AISES A.T. Anderson Memorial Scholarship (559) | | Native American, Association |
| Allied Health Student Loans (4870) | Legal: PA; Study: PA | |
| American Medical Technologists Scholarships (697) | | |
| American Society of Clinical Pathologists Scholarships (910) | Citizenship: US, PermRes | |
| John D. Archbold Scholarship (1073) | | |
| Carol Bauhs Benson Memorial Scholarship (421) | Legal: MN, ND, SD, WI | |
| Celanese Canada Inc. Scholarships (1269) | Citizenship: Canada, PermRes; Study: Canada | |
| Richard P. Covert Scholarships (2833) | | Association |
| Delta Gamma Foundation - Florence Margaret Harvey Memorial Scholarship (480) | Citizenship: US | Handicapped |
| Morton B. Duggan Jr. Memorial Education Recognition Award (849) | Citizenship: US, PermRes | |
| William and Dorothy Ferrell Scholarship (1235) | | |
| Rebecca Fisk Scholarship (424) | | |
| Florida Dental Health Foundation Dental Assisting Scholarship (2490) | Legal: FL | |
| Florida Dental Health Foundation Dental Hygiene Scholarship (2491) | Legal: FL | |
| FORE Undergraduate Loan (518) | | |
| Georgia Student Finance Commission Service-Cancellable Stafford Loan (2666) | Legal: GA; Study: GA | |
| Georgia Student Finance Commission State-Sponsored Loan (2669) | Legal: GA; Study: GA | |
| Indian Health Career Awards (4935) | | Ethnic |
| Oliver Joel and Ellen Pell Denny Student Loan Fund (6196) | Legal: NC; Study: NC | |
| Rolfe B. Karlsson Scholarships (2321) | Legal: IA | |
| Louie LeFlore/Grant Foreman Scholarship (5306) | Legal: OK | Native American |
| Maryland Physical and Occupational Therapists and Assistants Scholarships (3577) | Legal: MD | |
| Mississippi Psychology Apprenticeship Program (3738) | Legal: MS; Study: MS | |
| Birdell Chew Moore Scholarships (6121) | Legal: CA | |
| Wilma E. Motley Scholarship (427) | | |
| Grace Whiting Myers/Malcolm T. MacEachern Student Loans (520) | Citizenship: US | |
| Ida L., Mary L., and Ervin R. NePage Foundation (4513) | Legal: WA; Study: WA | |
| New York Life Foundation Scholarships for Women in the Health Professions (1551) | Citizenship: US; Study: United States | |
| New York State Professional Opportunity Scholarships (4592) | Citizenship: US, PermRes; Legal: NY; Study: NY | |
| New York State Regents Professional Opportunity Scholarships (4577) | Legal: NY; Study: NY | |

| Vocational Goal, Award, and Entry Number | Geographic Restrictions (Citizenship, Legal Residence, Place of Study) | Affiliation/Special Recipients Requirements |
|---|---|---|
| **Health Care Services** *(continued)* | | |
| Oral-B Laboratories Dental Hygiene Scholarships (429) | | |
| E.L. Peterson Scholarships (2323) | Legal: IA | |
| Power Systems Inc./NSCA Strength and Conditioning Professional Scholarship (4417) | | Association |
| Public Interest Internships (1803) | Study: United States | |
| Scholarships for Blind and Visually Impaired Postsecondary Students (483) | Citizenship: US | Handicapped |
| Sigma Phi Alpha Undergraduate Scholarship (431) | | |
| SMART Corporation Scholarship (521) | | |
| Juliette A. Southard Scholarship (416) | Citizenship: US | |
| Telesensory Scholarship (1236) | | Association |
| Barbara Thomas Enterprises, Inc. Scholarship (522) | | Other |
| Transcriptions, Ltd. Scholarship (523) | | |
| Transcriptions, Ltd. Scholarship for Health Information Management and Graduate Students (524) | | |
| Lynn Marie Vogel Scholarships (2324) | Legal: IA | |
| Warner Lambert Joint Oral Hygiene Group Scholarships (433) | | |
| David A. Winston Fellowship (1290) | Study: DC | |
| Wisconsin Dental Foundation Two-Year Scholarships (6207) | Legal: WI; Study: WI | |
| Jimmy A. Young Memorial Education Recognition Award (850) | Citizenship: US, Other | Minority, Native American, Asian American, African American, Hispanic American |
| **Health Sciences** | | |
| AACN Educational Advancement Scholarships for Undergraduates (279) | | Association |
| AAPS-AFPE Gateway Scholarships (486) | | |
| Air Force ROTC Scholarships (5816) | Citizenship: US | Military |
| Alabama Nursing Scholarship (105) | Legal: AL; Study: AL | |
| Allied Health Student Loans (4870) | Legal: PA; Study: PA | |
| AMBUCS Scholars (3854) | Citizenship: US | |
| American Legion Auxiliary Nurses, Physical Therapists and Respiratory Therapists Scholarship (626) | Legal: MI | Military |
| American Legion Auxiliary Past Presidents' Parley Nurses Scholarships (613) | Citizenship: US; Legal: AZ; Study: AZ | |
| John D. Archbold Scholarship (1073) | | |
| Armenian American Pharmacists' Association Scholarship (1108) | Study: MA | Ethnic |
| The Albert Baker Fund (1362) | | Religion |
| Fay L. Bower Nursing Student Scholarship (1563) | | |
| Call to Action Opportunity Scholarship (1568) | Citizenship: US; Legal: CA; Study: CA | |
| Madeline Pickett Halbert Cogswell Nursing Scholarships (4395) | Citizenship: US | Association |
| Colgate "Bright Smile, Bright Futures" Minority Scholarship/ADHA Institute Minority Scholarship (423) | | |
| Connecticut League for Nursing Scholarships (2052) | Legal: CT; Study: CT | |
| Rudolph Dillman Scholarship (481) | Citizenship: US | Handicapped |
| James D. Durante Nurse Scholarship Program (4169) | | Association |
| Environmental Restoration/Waste Management Technical Degree Scholarship Program (5871) | | |

| Vocational Goal, Award, and Entry Number | Geographic Restrictions (Citizenship, Legal Residence, Place of Study) | Affiliation/Special Recipients Requirements |
|---|---|---|
| *Health Sciences (continued)* | | |
| J. Hugh & Earle W. Fellows Memorial Fund Loans (2437) | Legal: FL | |
| Dr. Alfred C. Fones Scholarships (425) | | Association |
| Foundation of Research and Education (FORE) of AHIMA Undergraduate Scholarship (694) | | Association |
| Foundation of Research and Education Loan (695) | Citizenship: US | Association |
| Franks Foundation Loan (5832) | Legal: OR | |
| Georgia Student Finance Commission Service-Cancellable Stafford Loan (2666) | Legal: GA; Study: GA | |
| Georgia Student Finance Commission State-Sponsored Loan (2669) | Legal: GA; Study: GA | |
| Dr. Harold Hillenbrand Scholarships (426) | | Association |
| Caroline Holt Nursing Scholarships (4399) | Citizenship: US | |
| HRSA-BHP Nursing Student Loan (5970) | Citizenship: US | |
| HRSA-BHP Scholarships for Disadvantaged Students (5972) | Citizenship: US, PermRes, Other | |
| IHS Health Professions Compensatory Preprofessional Scholarship (2993) | | Native American |
| Illinois AMVETS Sad Sacks Nursing Scholarships (2956) | Study: IL | Veteran |
| Independent Order of Odd Fellows Nurses Training Scholarships (2991) | Study: ME | |
| Indian Health Career Awards (4935) | | Ethnic |
| International Order of the King's Daughters and Sons Health Careers Scholarships (3169) | Citizenship: US/CA; Legal: Canada, United States; Study: Canada, United States | |
| Oliver Joel and Ellen Pell Denny Student Loan Fund (6196) | Legal: NC; Study: NC | |
| Harvey and Bernice Jones Scholarships (3295) | Legal: AR | |
| Kelley Foundation Scholarships (3345) | Study: MA | |
| Louie LeFlore/Grant Foreman Scholarship (5306) | Legal: OK | Native American |
| S. Evelyn Lewis Memorial Scholarship in Medical Health Sciences (6306) | | |
| MARILN Scholarship (3603) | Legal: MA, RI | |
| Mary Marshall Nurse Practitioner/Nurse Midwife Scholarship Program (6048) | Legal: VA; Study: VA | |
| Mary Marshall Nursing Scholarship for Student Nurses Practical Nursing Program (6049) | Legal: VA; Study: VA | |
| Mary Marshall Nursing Scholarship for Student Nurses Registered Nurse Program (6050) | Legal: VA; Study: VA | |
| Maryland House of Delegates Scholarship (3575) | Legal: MD | |
| Maryland Professional Scholarship (3578) | Legal: MD; Study: MD | |
| Maryland Senatorial Scholarship (3580) | Legal: MD | |
| Maryland State Nursing Scholarships (3581) | Legal: MD; Study: MD | |
| Marguerite Mc Alpin Memorial Scholarships (640) | Legal: WA | Veteran |
| McFarland Charitable Foundation Registered Nursing Scholarship (3624) | | |
| McFarland Charitable Foundation Scholarship (2819) | | |
| Charlotte McGuire Scholarships (543) | | Association |
| MERCK-AFPE Gateway Scholarships (490) | Citizenship: US, PermRes | |
| Michigan League for Nursing Student Achievement Scholarship Awards (3690) | | Association |
| Mississippi Health Care Professions Loan/Scholarship Program (3732) | Legal: MS; Study: MS | |
| Mississippi Nursing Education BSN Program (3734) | Legal: MS | |

| Vocational Goal, Award, and Entry Number | Geographic Restrictions (Citizenship, Legal Residence, Place of Study) | Affiliation/Special Recipients Requirements |
| --- | --- | --- |
| *Health Sciences (continued)* | | |
| Mississippi Nursing Education RN to BSN Program (3737) | Legal: MS | |
| National Association of Hispanic Nurses National Scholarship Award (3879) | | Hispanic American, Association |
| The National Society of the Colonial Dames of America American Indian Nurse Scholarship Awards (4390) | | Native American |
| New York Life Foundation Scholarships for Women in the Health Professions (1551) | Citizenship: US; Study: United States | |
| New York State Professional Opportunity Scholarships (4592) | Citizenship: US, PermRes; Legal: NY; Study: NY | |
| New York State Regents Professional Opportunity Scholarships (4577) | Legal: NY; Study: NY | |
| Irene E. Newman Scholarships (428) | | Association |
| NJSCLS Scholarships (4541) | Study: NJ | |
| Northwest Pharmacist Coalition Pre-Pharmacy Scholarship (4696) | | Minority |
| NSDAR Occupational Therapy Scholarship (4403) | Citizenship: US; Study: United States | |
| Nursing Education Loan Repayment (5938) | | |
| Oklahoma State Regents Chiropractic Education Assistance (4737) | Legal: OK; Study: OK | |
| Oncology Nursing Foundation Bachelors Scholarship (4759) | | |
| Arthur & Doreen Parrett Scholarship Fund (4848) | Legal: WA | |
| Past Presidents Parley Nursing Scholarship (635) | Legal: VT | |
| Physician Assistant Foundation Annual Scholarship Program (4937) | | Association |
| Iris Pollock Memorial Scholarship (2734) | Legal: AB | |
| PRN Grants (202) | | Fraternal |
| Public Interest Internships (1803) | Study: United States | |
| Lucretia H. Richter Nursing Scholarship (6157) | Study: NY | |
| SBNA Scholarship (5209) | | African American |
| Service Cancelable Student Loan (2660) | | |
| Bertha B. Singer Nurses Scholarship (5835) | Legal: OR; Study: OR | |
| Margaret E. Swanson Scholarships (432) | | Association |
| SYNTEX-AFPE Gateway Scholarships (495) | Citizenship: US, PermRes | |
| Virginia Elizabeth and Alma Vane Taylor Fund (6197) | Legal: NC; Study: NC | |
| U.S. Nuclear Regulatory Commission Historically Black Colleges and Universities Student Research Participation (5936) | | |
| USA National Educational Grants (3273) | | Veteran |
| Wisconsin Dental Foundation Two-Year Scholarships (6207) | Legal: WI; Study: WI | |
| Wisconsin League for Nursing Scholarships (6212) | Legal: WI; Study: WI | |

## Home Economics

| | | |
| --- | --- | --- |
| Alberta Wheat Pool Scholarships (148) | Study: AB, Canada | |
| ASID Educational Foundation/S Harris Memorial Scholarship (937) | | |
| Stella Blum Research Grant (2089) | | Association |
| A & E Capelle LN Herfords Scholarship (150) | Legal: Canada | |
| County of Forty Mile Agricultural Committee Bursaries (2127) | Legal: AB | Other |
| IACP Foundation Scholarships (3111) | | |
| Kraft Canada Inc. Undergraduate Scholarship (1649) | Citizenship: Canada | |

| Vocational Goal, Award, and Entry Number | Geographic Restrictions (Citizenship, Legal Residence, Place of Study) | Affiliation/Special Recipients Requirements |
|---|---|---|
| *Home Economics (continued)* | | |
| Maryland Child Care Provider Scholarship (3573) | Legal: MD; Study: MD | |
| National Restaurant Association Educational Foundation Undergraduate Scholarship for High School Seniors (4364) | | |
| National Restaurant Association Undergraduate Scholarships (4367) | | |
| Ohio State University Extension Internship (4733) | | |
| Abbie Sargent Memorial Scholarships (5250) | Legal: NH | |
| Sutherland/Purdy Scholarship (4925) | | Fraternal |
| Tony's Foodservice Scholarships (5278) | | Association |
| Gianni Versace Scholarship in Fashion Design (4267) | | |

## Humanities

| | | |
|---|---|---|
| Thomas Joseph "Willie" Ambrosole Scholarship (4207) | Legal: NJ, NY | |
| Engalitcheff Institute on Comparative Political and Economic Systems Internship (3019) | | |
| Fellowships in Byzantine Studies, Pre-Columbian Studies and Landscape Architecture (2288) | Study: DC | |
| Italian Cultural Society and NIAF Matching Scholarship (4234) | Study: DC, MD, VA | |
| Leo J. Krysa Family Foundation Undergraduate Scholarship (1660) | Citizenship: Canada; Study: Canada | |
| National Board Civil Air Patrol Undergraduate/Advanced Undergraduate College Scholarship (3918) | | Association |
| National Federation of the Blind Humanities Scholarship (4003) | | Handicapped |
| Research Science Institute Internship (5103) | | |
| Summer Session Awards (861) | | |
| Xerox Scholarships (6272) | | |

## Industry and Trade

| | | |
|---|---|---|
| ABCI Scholarships (1343) | Study: CO, MI | |
| American Postal Workers Union Vocational Scholarship (788) | | Union |
| AMT's Two-Year Scholarships (1248) | | |
| Associated General Contractors Education and Research Foundation Undergraduate Scholarship (402) | | |
| Children of Air Traffic Control Specialists (73) | Citizenship: US | Military, Employer |
| CN Native Education Awards (1974) | Legal: Canada | |
| Construction Education Foundation Scholarship Awards (16) | | |
| DEED Scholarships (811) | Study: United States | Association |
| Ginger & Fred Deines Canada Scholarships (5741) | Citizenship: Canada; Study: Canada | |
| Ginger and Fred Deines Mexico Scholarships (5742) | Study: Mexico, United States | Hispanic American |
| Desk and Derrick Educational Trust Scholarship (2245) | | |
| El Camino Real No. 158 NAWIC Scholarship (3906) | Citizenship: US; Study: CA | |
| Gravure Education Foundation Cooperative Education Grant (2745) | | Other |
| Hooper Memorial Scholarship(s) (5743) | | |
| Jewel/Taylor C. Cotton Scholarship (1927) | Legal: IL | Minority |

| Vocational Goal, Award, and Entry Number | Geographic Restrictions (Citizenship, Legal Residence, Place of Study) | Affiliation/Special Recipients Requirements |
|---|---|---|
| *Industry and Trade (continued)* | | |
| William D. Krenkler Working Scholar Program (5099) | | |
| Denny Lydic Scholarship (5744) | | |
| Marin Education Grant for Short-Term and Long-Term Occupational Study (3553) | Citizenship: US, PermRes; Legal: CA | |
| McAllister Memorial Scholarship (1048) | Citizenship: US | |
| McFadden Family Automotive Scholarship (1882) | Study: MI | |
| Mercedes-Benz of North America Scholarship Program (1928) | Legal: IL | Minority |
| Col. Louisa Spruance Morse CAP Scholarship (3917) | | Military |
| NAPHCC Educational Foundation Scholarships (3887) | Study: United States | |
| National Association of Water Companies - New Jersey Chapter Scholarship (3904) | Citizenship: US; Legal: NJ; Study: NJ | |
| National Roofing Foundation Scholarship Award (4371) | Citizenship: US | |
| The National Scholarship Trust Fund Scholarships for High School Students (4374) | | |
| The National Scholarship Trust Fund Scholarships for Undergraduates (4375) | | |
| NDDOT Educational Grants (4682) | Study: ND | |
| Nebraska Space Grant Scholarships and Fellowships (4505) | Citizenship: US | |
| New England Graphic Arts Scholarships (4531) | Legal: CT, MA, ME, NH, RI, VT | |
| Pacific Printing and Imaging Association Scholarship (4826) | | |
| Packaging Education Forum (PEF) Packaging Scholarships (4828) | | |
| Plastic Pioneers Association Scholarships (4960) | Citizenship: US | |
| SEMA Scholarship (5581) | | |
| Texas Graphic Arts Education Foundation Scholarships (5706) | Study: TX | |
| Texas Transportation Scholarship (5745) | | |
| USAIG PDP Scholarships (6017) | Citizenship: US | |
| Washington Printing Guild Scholarships (6095) | Citizenship: US; Legal: DC | |
| Charlie Wells Memorial Aviation Scholarship (6131) | | |
| Charlotte Woods Memorial Scholarship (5746) | | Association |

## Language and Literature

| Vocational Goal, Award, and Entry Number | Geographic Restrictions | Affiliation/Special Recipients Requirements |
|---|---|---|
| AATI National College Essay Contest (329) | | |
| Lisa Bjork Memorial Scholarship (2028) | Legal: FL | |
| Business Press Educational Foundation Student Intern Program (1543) | | |
| Center for Arabic Study Abroad Fellowship (1787) | | |
| Chicago Association of Black Journalists Scholarships (1916) | | Minority |
| Columbia Journalism Review Internship Program (2009) | | |
| Cox Minority Journalism Scholarship (2131) | Legal: GA; Study: GA | Minority |
| Bruce Dennis Scholarship (5058) | | |
| Garikian University Scholarship Fund (1119) | | Ethnic |
| R.L. Gillette Scholarship (482) | Citizenship: US | Handicapped |
| Hispanic Link News Service Internships (2878) | | Hispanic American |
| Inter-University Program Fellowships (3097) | Study: People's Republic of China | |
| John M. Will Memorial Journalism Scholarships (6180) | Legal: AL, FL, MS | |

| Vocational Goal, Award, and Entry Number | Geographic Restrictions (Citizenship, Legal Residence, Place of Study) | Affiliation/Special Recipients Requirements |
|---|---|---|
| *Language and Literature (continued)* | | |
| Edna Meudt Memorial Scholarship (4010) | Study: United States | |
| Mola Foundation of Chicago Scholarships (4243) | Legal: IA, IL, IN, KY, MI, MN, ND, OH, SD, WI | |
| Online Newspaper Intern Program (2276) | | |
| Paragano Scholarship (4250) | Legal: NJ | |
| The Lionel Pearson Fellowship (763) | | |
| Service Cancelable Student Loan (2660) | | |
| Theodore Ward Prize (2007) | | African American |
| World of Expression Scholarship Program (1420) | Legal: NY | |

## Law

| | | |
|---|---|---|
| ABA Mini-Grants (350) | | |
| ABF Summer Research Fellowships in Law and Social Science for Minority Undergraduate Students (352) | Citizenship: US, PermRes; Study: IL | African American, Native American, Hispanic American |
| Air Force ROTC Scholarships (5816) | Citizenship: US | Military |
| BPW Career Advancement Scholarships (1546) | Citizenship: US; Study: United States | |
| H. Fletcher Brown Scholarship (4967) | Legal: DE | |
| James Lawrence Fly Scholarships (1497) | | |
| Garikian University Scholarship Fund (1119) | | Ethnic |
| Law Scholarships (3250) | | Ethnic |
| Maryland Professional Scholarship (3578) | Legal: MD; Study: MD | |
| Ministry of the Flemish Community Fellowships (3710) | Citizenship: US, PermRes | |
| Michael Murphy Memorial Scholarship Loans (132) | Legal: AK | |
| Public Interest Internships (1803) | Study: United States | |
| Spence Reese Scholarship (5089) | | |
| Howard Brown Rickard Scholarship (4007) | | Handicapped |
| Sho Sato Memorial Law Scholarship (3251) | | Ethnic |

## Liberal/General Studies

| | | |
|---|---|---|
| 4-H Foundation of Alberta Scholarship (145) | Legal: Canada | |
| 37th Infantry Division Award (2) | | Veteran |
| AAAA Minority Advertising Internships (270) | Citizenship: US; Study: CA, IL, MI, NY | Minority |
| A.A.R.P. Jamestown Chapter 334 Scholarship (1844) | Legal: NY | |
| Clara Abbott Foundation Scholarships (14) | | Employer |
| Academic-Year Ambassadorial Scholarship (5167) | | |
| ACB Scholarships (398) | Citizenship: US | Handicapped |
| AEJMC Correspondence Fund Scholarships (1233) | | Employer |
| AFSA Scholarship Awards (68) | | Military |
| AGF Financial Life Skills Scholarship Program (1264) | Citizenship: Canada, PermRes | |
| Agnes Home Scholarship (1845) | Legal: NY | |
| Air Force Aid Society Education Grants (64) | | Military |
| Airmen Memorial Scholarships (98) | | Military, Veteran |
| Glenn Lee Akam, Jr. Memorial Scholarship (1846) | | |
| Alabama G.I. Dependents' Scholarships (119) | Study: AL | Veteran |
| Alabama Junior and Community College Athletic Scholarships (102) | Study: AL | |
| Alabama Junior and Community College Performing Arts Scholarships (103) | Study: AL | |
| Alabama National Guard Educational Assistance Program (104) | Study: AL | Military |

| Vocational Goal, Award, and Entry Number | Geographic Restrictions (Citizenship, Legal Residence, Place of Study) | Affiliation/Special Recipients Requirements |
|---|---|---|
| *Liberal/General Studies (continued)* | | |
| Alabama Police Officer's and Firefighter's Survivor's Educational Assistance (106) | Study: AL | |
| Alabama Scholarships for Dependents of Blind Parents (107) | Legal: AL; Study: AL | Other |
| Alabama Senior Adult Scholarships (108) | Citizenship: Other; Legal: AL; Study: AL | |
| Alabama Stafford Loans (109) | Citizenship: US, PermRes | |
| Alabama Student Assistance Program (110) | Legal: AL; Study: AL | |
| Alabama Student Grant Program (111) | Legal: AL; Study: AL | |
| Alabama Two-Year College Academic Scholarships (112) | Study: AL | |
| Alaska Family Education Loans (127) | Legal: AK | |
| Alaska State Educational Incentive Grants (128) | Legal: AK | |
| Alaska Student Loans (129) | Legal: AK | |
| Alberta Educational Grants for Disabled Persons (172) | Legal: Canada | Handicapped |
| Alberta Educational Maintenance Grants (173) | Legal: Canada | Handicapped |
| Alberta Educational Opportunity Equalization Grants (174) | Legal: Canada | |
| Alberta Salers Association Scholarship (146) | Legal: Canada | Association |
| Alberta Treasury Branches Scholarship (147) | Study: AB, Canada | Association |
| Alberta Wheat Pool Scholarships (148) | Study: AB, Canada | |
| Alexander Scholarship Loans (3119) | Study: United States | |
| All-Inland Scholarship (3005) | | Employer |
| Allied Fire Protection System, Inc. Scholarship (1847) | Legal: NY | |
| Alpha Kappa Alpha Educational Advancement Foundation Scholarships (198) | Study: United States | African American, Asian American, Hispanic American, Native American |
| Amarillo Area Foundation Scholarship (211) | | |
| American Baptist Financial Aid Program (348) | | Religion |
| American Family Insurance Company Scholarships (4018) | Legal: MN, MO, WI | Association |
| American Federation of Grain Millers International Union Scholarship (462) | | Association |
| American Indian Endowed Scholarships (551) | Legal: WA; Study: WA | |
| American Indian Scholarship (4392) | Citizenship: US | Native American |
| American Legion Auxiliary Department Gift Scholarships (637) | Legal: WA | Veteran |
| American Legion Auxiliary Department of Minnesota Scholarships (628) | Legal: MN | Veteran |
| American Legion Auxiliary Department Scholarship (616) | | Association |
| American Legion Auxiliary Memorial Scholarship (617) | Legal: FL; Study: FL | Veteran |
| American Legion Auxiliary Memorial Scholarship (625) | Legal: MI; Study: MI | |
| American Legion Auxiliary Scholarships (113) | Legal: AL; Study: AL | Veteran |
| American Legion Boy Scout Scholarships (608) | Legal: IL | Association |
| American Legion Oratorical Contest (609) | Legal: IL | |
| American Legion Scholarships (114) | Legal: AL; Study: AL | Veteran |
| America's National Teenager Scholarship (4424) | | |
| America's Young Woman of the Year Scholarships (1024) | Citizenship: US | |
| Amoco Canada Petroleum Company Scholarships (1028) | Study: Canada, United States | Employer |
| Dr. William L. Amoroso, Jr. Scholarship (4208) | Legal: United States | |
| AMVETS Auxiliary Department of Illinois Memorial Scholarship (2954) | Legal: IL | |

| Vocational Goal, Award, and Entry Number | Geographic Restrictions (Citizenship, Legal Residence, Place of Study) | Affiliation/Special Recipients Requirements |
|---|---|---|
| *Liberal/General Studies (continued)* | | |
| AMVETS National Scholarships for Undergraduate Students (1031) | Citizenship: US | Veteran |
| Angela Scholarship (4209) | | |
| Anheuser-Busch Scholarship Fund (1926) | Legal: IL; Study: IL | Minority |
| AOSC Scholarships (1250) | | Employer |
| AOUW Student Loan (1037) | | Fraternal |
| Appaloosa Youth Educational Scholarships (1056) | | Association |
| AQHYA Scholarships (813) | | Association |
| K. Arakelian Foundation Scholarship (1103) | | Ethnic |
| Arby's Scholarships (1062) | Legal: Canada, United States | Other |
| Arkansas Department of Higher Education Scholarship (1091) | Study: AR | |
| Arkansas Student Assistance Grants (1097) | Legal: AR | |
| Armenian-American Citizens' League Scholarship (1105) | Citizenship: US | Ethnic |
| Armenian American Middle East Club Scholarship (1107) | Study: CA | Ethnic |
| Armenian Bible College Scholarship (1109) | Study: CA | Ethnic |
| Armenian Cultural Society of Akron/Canton Scholarship (1110) | Legal: OH | Ethnic |
| Armenian General Athletic Union Scholarship (1111) | Legal: NY | Ethnic |
| Armenian General Benevolent Union (AGBU) Loans and Grants (1112) | | Ethnic |
| Armenian Professional Society of the Bay Area Scholarship (1113) | | Ethnic |
| Armenian Relief Society of North America Scholarship (1115) | | Ethnic |
| Armenian Students Association of America, Inc. Grant (1116) | Study: United States | Ethnic |
| Armenian Students' Association of America Reading Scholarships (1138) | Study: United States | Ethnic |
| Army Emergency Relief Scholarships (1140) | Citizenship: US, PermRes; Legal: United States | Military, Veteran |
| Army Engineer Memorial Awards (1143) | | Military |
| William C. Arrison Memorial Scholarship (1849) | | |
| ASA Stafford Loan (1003) | | |
| Association on American Indian Affairs Displaced Homemaker Scholarships (1212) | | Native American |
| Association of the Sons of Poland Scholarships (1260) | | Association |
| Athletes of the Year (5684) | | |
| Automotive Hall of Fame Educational Fund Scholarships (1345) | | |
| Avenor Maritimes Scholarship Program (1265) | Citizenship: Canada | |
| Wendy Sue Axelson & Theodore Moll II Frewsburg School Scholarship (1850) | Legal: NY | |
| Aztec Scholarship (5573) | Legal: CA | |
| Mercer Silas Bailey Memorial Scholarships (1360) | Study: United States | Other |
| The Albert Baker Fund (1362) | | Religion |
| J.H. Baker Trust Student Loan Program (1364) | Legal: KS | |
| Balso Foundation Scholarships (1366) | Legal: CT | |
| Barnett Bank of Palm Beach County Minority Student Scholarship Fund (2025) | Legal: FL | |
| Walter S. Barr Scholarships (5364) | Legal: MA | |
| Bausch & Lomb Science Awards (1378) | | |
| Alexander G. Bell Scholarship Awards (1399) | | Handicapped |
| Bement Educational Grants (1409) | | Religion |

| Vocational Goal, Award, and Entry Number | Geographic Restrictions (Citizenship, Legal Residence, Place of Study) | Affiliation/Special Recipients Requirements |
|---|---|---|
| *Liberal/General Studies (continued)* | | |
| Maura and William Benjamin Scholarship (2026) | Legal: FL | |
| Frank F. Bentley Scholarship (5757) | Legal: OH | |
| Beta Theta Pi Founders Fund Scholarship-Leadership Awards (1428) | | Fraternal |
| Mary McLeod Bethune Scholarship (2494) | Citizenship: US; Legal: FL; Study: FL | |
| BIA Higher Education/Hopi Supplemental Grants (2892) | | Native American |
| Marija Bileta Scholarship (4210) | | |
| David Birenbaum Scholarship Fund of the AAB Associate Member Section (10) | | Association |
| Kathleen A. Black Memorial Scholarship (1851) | Legal: NY | |
| Blind Service Association Scholarship Awards (1442) | Legal: IL | Handicapped |
| Walter and Adi Blum Scholarship (2029) | Legal: FL; Study: United States | |
| Glen Bodell Memorial Scholarship (149) | Legal: AB | Association |
| Boettcher Foundation Scholarship (1455) | Study: CO | |
| Hagop Bogigian Scholarship Fund (1117) | | Ethnic |
| Bolla Wines Scholarship (4211) | | Ethnic |
| William L. Boyd IV, Florida Resident Access Grant (2495) | Legal: FL; Study: FL | |
| BP America Scholarship (1472) | Citizenship: US, PermRes; Study: United States | Employer |
| Mildred Louise Brackney Scholarships (4393) | Citizenship: US | |
| Claude & Ina Brey Scholarships (3648) | | Association |
| B.R.I.D.G.E. Kraft General Foods Scholarship (4034) | | Association, Handicapped |
| B.R.I.D.G.E. Quaker Oats Foundation Scholarship (4035) | | Association, Handicapped |
| Bridgestone/Firestone Agricultural Mechanics Scholarships (4036) | | Association |
| British Marshall Scholarships (1483) | Citizenship: US | |
| Gabriel J. Brown Trust Fund Loans (1521) | Legal: ND | |
| Dodd and Dorothy L. Bryan Loan (1523) | Legal: MT, WY | |
| Susan Burdett Scholarhips (638) | Legal: WA | Other |
| Burlington Northern Santa Fe Scholarships (1531) | | Employer |
| Burns Scholarships (1537) | Legal: AB | Employer |
| Florence Evans Bushee Foundation Scholarship Grants (1541) | Legal: MA | |
| Butler Manufacturing Company Foundation Scholarship (1553) | | Employer |
| General Buxton/St. Michael's Scholarships (6032) | | Military |
| Robert C. Byrd Honors Scholarship (115) | | |
| Robert C. Byrd Honors Scholarship (1576) | Legal: CA; Study: United States | |
| Robert C. Byrd Honors Scholarship (2496) | Citizenship: US; Legal: FL; Study: FL | |
| Robert C. Byrd Honors Scholarship (3498) | Citizenship: US; Legal: LA | |
| Robert C. Byrd Honors Scholarship (4584) | Citizenship: US, PermRes; Legal: NY | |
| Robert C. Byrd Honors Scholarships (2042) | Legal: CT | |
| Robert C. Byrd Honors Scholarships (4862) | Citizenship: US; Legal: PA | |
| Alyce M. Cafaro Scholarship (4212) | Legal: OH | |
| Cal Grant A (1577) | Legal: CA; Study: CA | |
| Cal Grant B (1578) | Citizenship: US, PermRes; Legal: CA; Study: CA | |
| Cal Grant C (1579) | Legal: CA; Study: CA | |
| Hermione Grant Calhoun Scholarship (3998) | | Handicapped |
| California-Hawaii Elks Disabled Student Scholarships (1559) | Citizenship: US; Legal: CA, HI | Handicapped |
| California Junior Miss Scholarship Program (1561) | Citizenship: US; Legal: CA | Other |

| Vocational Goal, Award, and Entry Number | Geographic Restrictions (Citizenship, Legal Residence, Place of Study) | Affiliation/Special Recipients Requirements |
|---|---|---|
| *Liberal/General Studies (continued)* | | |
| Cal Callahan Memorial Bursary (4949) | Legal: Canada | Association, Employer |
| Vivienne Camp College Scholarship Fund (3263) | Legal: CA; Study: CA | Ethnic, Religion |
| Campbell-Non-Linfield Scholarship Fund (5830) | Legal: OR; Study: OR | |
| Canada Trust Scholarship Program for Outstanding Community Leadership (1268) | Citizenship: Canada, PermRes; Study: Canada | |
| Canadian Golf Foundation Scholarships (1642) | Study: Canada | Other |
| Canadian Soroptimist Grants for Women (5539) | Citizenship: Canada, PermRes; Study: Canada | |
| Cape Canaveral Chapter Scholarships (5114) | Legal: FL | Minority |
| Cargill National Merit Scholarships (1728) | Citizenship: US | Employer |
| Cargill Scholars Program Scholarships (1729) | Citizenship: US | Employer |
| Cargill Scholarships for Rural America (4042) | | |
| Charles Reed Carlson Business Education Fund (1852) | Legal: NY | |
| Nellie Martin Carman Scholarships (1731) | Citizenship: US; Legal: WA; Study: WA | |
| CARQUEST Corporation Scholarships (4044) | | Association |
| Vikki Carr Scholarship (1741) | Legal: CA, United States | Hispanic American |
| Marjorie S. Carter Boy Scout Scholarship (1743) | Legal: CT, MA, ME, NH, RI, VT | Association |
| Thomas Caryk Memorial Scholarship (151) | Legal: AB | Association |
| Catholic Aid Association Tuition Scholarships (1747) | | Association, Religion |
| Catholic Workman College Scholarships (1754) | | Association, Religion |
| Anthony J. Celebrezze Scholarship (4213) | Legal: OH | Ethnic |
| Central Scholarship Bureau Interest-Free Loans (1816) | Legal: MD | |
| Century Three Leaders Scholarships (3898) | Legal: United States | |
| CEW Scholarships for Returning Women (6002) | Study: MI | |
| Chairscholars Foundation Scholarship (1826) | | Handicapped |
| Chautauqua County Basketball Officials Scholarship (1855) | Legal: NY; Study: NY | |
| Cesar Chavez Memorial Leadership Award (5687) | Legal: CA; Study: CA | Minority |
| Cherokee National Higher Education Undergraduate Grant Program (1912) | | |
| Chevy Trucks Scholarships (4048) | | Association |
| Cheyenne-Arapaho Higher Education Assistance Program Grant (1914) | Legal: OK | Native American |
| Chicago FM Club Scholarship (818) | Citizenship: US; Legal: IL, IN, WI | |
| Chicana Latina Foundation Scholarships (1931) | Legal: CA | Hispanic American |
| Child of Disabled Veteran Grant or Purple Heart Recipient, Grant (2996) | Legal: IN; Study: IN | Veteran |
| Children of Deaf Adults Scholarship (1937) | | |
| Children of Deceased Active Duty Servicemembers Grants (4495) | | Veteran |
| Children of Deceased or Disabled Veterans or Children of Servicemen Classified as Prisoners of War or Missing in Action Scholarship (2497) | Legal: FL; Study: FL | Veteran |
| Children of Deceased, Retired Servicemembers Grants (4496) | | Veteran |
| Children of Unitarian Universalist Ministers Scholarship (5780) | | Religion |
| CIBC Youthvision Scholarship Program (1271) | Citizenship: Canada, PermRes; Study: Canada | Other |
| Ferdinand Cinelli Etruscan Scholarship (4214) | | Ethnic |
| Circle Key Grants of Rose McGill (3326) | Citizenship: US/CA | Fraternal |

| Vocational Goal, Award, and Entry Number | Geographic Restrictions (Citizenship, Legal Residence, Place of Study) | Affiliation/Special Recipients Requirements |
|---|---|---|
| *Liberal/General Studies (continued)* | | |
| Civic Service Union No. 52 Charitable Assistance Fund (1962) | | Union |
| Civitan Scholarships (1964) | | Association |
| Cleveland Scholarship Programs (1970) | | Other |
| CMSAF Richard D. Kisling Scholarships (100) | | Military |
| Coca-Cola Scholars (1978) | | |
| Coca-Cola Youth Bowling Championships Scholarships (5005) | | |
| Julian and Eunice Cohen Scholarship (2031) | Legal: FL | |
| James W. Colgan Educational Loan (1980) | Legal: MA | |
| College Access Loan (5708) | Study: TX | |
| Lance G. Colvin Memorial Scholarship (1857) | Legal: NY | |
| Commonwealth of Pennsylvania Educational Gratuity Program Grants (2019) | Citizenship: US; Legal: PA; Study: PA | Veteran |
| Communications Scholarship (4215) | Legal: United States | |
| Tom and Judith Comstock Scholarship (819) | | Association |
| Jimmie Condon Athletic Scholarships (175) | Legal: Canada | Other |
| Confederate Memorial Scholarships (5789) | Study: FL | Veteran |
| Congress-Bundestag Youth Exchange for Young Professionals (1759) | Citizenship: US | |
| Connecticut Aid for Public College Students (2043) | Legal: CT; Study: CT | |
| Connecticut Family Education Loan Program (CT FELP) (2044) | Legal: CT; Study: CT | |
| (Connecticut) Federal Subsidized Stafford Loans (2056) | | |
| Connecticut Independent College Student Grants (2045) | Legal: CT; Study: CT | |
| Connecticut Scholastic Achievement Grants (2046) | Citizenship: US, PermRes; Legal: CT | |
| Connecticut Tuition Aid for Needy Students (2047) | Study: CT | |
| Connecticut Tuition Waiver for Senior Citizens (2048) | Legal: CT; Study: CT | Other |
| Connecticut Tuition Waiver for Veterans (2049) | Legal: CT; Study: CT | Veteran |
| James Conover Neighbors of Woodcraft Scholarship (4509) | | Association |
| Edward T. Conroy Memorial Scholarship (3568) | Study: MD | Military, Veteran |
| Constantinople Armenian Relief Society (CARS) Scholarship (1118) | | Ethnic |
| Silvio Conte Internship (4216) | | Ethnic |
| Continental Society Daughters of Indian Wars Scholarship (2180) | | Native American |
| Continental Society Daughters of Indian Wars Scholarships (2073) | | Native American |
| Carle C. Conway Scholarships (2075) | | Employer |
| Terry Gane Coon Scholarship (1858) | Legal: NY | |
| Arthur E. and Helen Copeland Scholarships (5828) | | Handicapped, Association |
| Charles Clarke Cordle Memorial Scholarship (821) | | |
| Cornaro Scholarship (4217) | | Ethnic |
| NIAF/NOIAW Cornaro Scholarship (4218) | | |
| John Cornelius and Max English Memorial Scholarship (3564) | | Military |
| Council of Europe Scholarships (2683) | Study: Germany | |
| Henry Cozen Scholarship (3889) | | Association |
| Crawford Scholarship Fund (5831) | Legal: OR | |
| P.V. Croken Matriculation Scholarships (2732) | Legal: AB | Other |

| Vocational Goal, Award, and Entry Number | Geographic Restrictions (Citizenship, Legal Residence, Place of Study) | Affiliation/Special Recipients Requirements |
|---|---|---|
| *Liberal/General Studies (continued)* | | |
| Grover T. Cronin Memorial Scholarship (3210) | Legal: MA | |
| Alberta E. Crowe Star of Tomorrow Scholarship (5006) | | |
| CSAC Law Enforcement Personnel Dependents Scholarships (1582) | | Employer |
| Nathan Cummings Scholarships (Canada) (5245) | Citizenship: Canada | Employer |
| Nathan Cummings Scholarships (United States) (5246) | Study: United States | Employer |
| Cymdeithas Gymreig/Philadelphia Scholarships (2148) | | Ethnic |
| Nathan and Harry Daly Scholarship (2172) | | |
| Barbara D'Angelo Memorial Teaching Scholarship (1860) | Legal: NY | |
| Gordon & Mabel Morse Danielson Memorial Scholarship (1861) | | |
| Verland & Doris Danielson Scholarship (1862) | Legal: NY | |
| Danish Sisterhood in America National Scholarships (2174) | | Association |
| May Darling Scholarship/Asa T. Williams/N.W. Labor Press Scholarship (4795) | Legal: OR | |
| Daughters of the Cincinnati Scholarships (2178) | | Military |
| Daughters of Penelope Past Grand President's Award (2183) | | Association |
| Henry N. and Sydney T. Davenport Loan Fund (1822) | Citizenship: US; Legal: NC | |
| William C. Davini Scholarship (5767) | | |
| Ezra Davis Memorial Scholarship (3999) | | Handicapped |
| Davis-Roberts Scholarships (2196) | | Association |
| Bert Day/Acu-Rite Memorial Scholarship (1863) | | |
| Johnson & Wales Governor Christopher Del Sesto/NIAF Scholarship (4220) | | |
| Delaware Higher Education Benefits for Children of Veterans and Others (2209) | Legal: DE | Veteran, Employer |
| Delta Gamma Foundation Scholarships (2219) | | Fraternal |
| Department of New York Scholarship (2256) | | Military |
| Department of Veterans Affairs Free Tuition for Children of POW/MIA's in Vietnam (2997) | Legal: IN; Study: IN | Military |
| Dependent Children of Soldiers Scholarship Program (1141) | | Veteran |
| Frank DePietro Memorial Scholarship (4221) | Study: CA | |
| Betty Derby Memorial Scholarship (1864) | | Religion |
| Descendants of the Signers of the Declaration of Independence Scholarship (2243) | Study: United States | Association |
| Robert J. Di Pietro Scholarship (4222) | | Ethnic |
| Dog Writers' Educational Trust Scholarships (2264) | | Other |
| William C. Doherty Scholarships (3883) | | Employer |
| Dolphin Scholarship (2266) | | Military |
| Stanley A. Doran Memorial Scholarship (2474) | | Association |
| Dow Chemical Canada Higher Education Awards (2272) | Study: Canada | Employer |
| Dunkin' Donuts Charitable Trust Scholarships (2290) | Citizenship: US | Employer |
| Rita A. Dunn & Mollie Dunn McKee Scholarship (1865) | | |
| Lillian and Arthur Dunn Scholarships (4396) | Citizenship: US; Study: United States | Association |
| Maurice and Robert Early Scholarship (2999) | Study: IN | |

| Vocational Goal, Award, and Entry Number | Geographic Restrictions (Citizenship, Legal Residence, Place of Study) | Affiliation/Special Recipients Requirements |
|---|---|---|
| *Liberal/General Studies (continued)* | | |
| Easley National Scholarship Awards (3827) | Citizenship: US, PermRes | |
| Easter Seal Society of Iowa Disability Scholarship (2320) | Legal: IA | Handicapped |
| Benjamin Eaton Scholarships (4156) | | Other |
| Ellen Beth Eddleman Memorial Scholarship (2034) | Legal: FL | |
| Ken Edgerton Memorial Scholarship (152) | Legal: AB | Association |
| Acoma Higher Education Grants (5019) | | Ethnic |
| Educational Assistance Grant (3569) | Legal: MD | |
| Educational Communications Scholarship (2347) | Citizenship: US | |
| Educational Communications Scholarship Foundation (2348) | | |
| Edwards Scholarship (2357) | Legal: MA | |
| Elks National Foundation Eagle Scout Scholarship (1463) | | Association |
| Emergency Aid and Health Professions Scholarships (1214) | | Native American |
| Esperanza Scholarships (2412) | Legal: OH | Hispanic American |
| Evans Caddie Scholarships (6151) | Legal: AZ, CO, IL, IN, KY, MI, MN, MO, OH, WI; Study: AZ, CO, IL, IN, KY, MI, MN, MO, OH, WI | Other |
| Evrytanian Association Scholarship (2418) | | Ethnic |
| H.T. Ewald Scholarships (2420) | Legal: MI | |
| Thomas Ewing Memorial Educational Grants for Newspaper Carriers (6089) | | Employer |
| FAR Scholarships (2559) | | |
| Farm Credit Corporation Scholarships (153) | Legal: AB | Association |
| Gloria Fecht Memorial Scholarship (6238) | Legal: CA | |
| Federal Plus Loans (2340) | | |
| Federal PLUS Loans to Parents under the North Carolina Insured Student Loan Program (1991) | | |
| Federal PLUS (Parent Loans for Undergraduate Students) (116) | Citizenship: US, PermRes, Other | |
| Federal Stafford Loan under the North Carolina Insured Student Loan Program (1992) | | |
| Federal Stafford Loan (Subsidized and Unsubsidized) (2341) | | |
| Federal Unsubsidized Stafford Loan (2057) | | |
| FEEA Federal Plus Loan (2431) | | Employer |
| FEEA Federal SLS Loan (2432) | | Employer |
| FEEA Federal Stafford Loan (2433) | | Employer |
| FEEA Federal Unsubsidized Stafford Loan (2434) | | Employer |
| FEEA Scholarship Award (2435) | | Employer |
| Herbert P. Feibelman Jr. (IPO) Award (1400) | | Handicapped |
| Fessenden-Trott Scholarships (1275) | Citizenship: Canada | |
| Fifth Marine Division Association Scholarships (3561) | | Association, Veteran |
| Fifty Men and Women of Toledo Scholarships (4) | Legal: OH | |
| FINA/Dallas Morning News All-Texas Scholar-Athlete Team Scholarships (2453) | Legal: TX | |
| Undergraduate Student Financial Aid Program Grant (5605) | Study: VA | Minority |
| Virginia Student Financial Assistance Award (5606) | Legal: VA; Study: VA | |
| First Catholic Slovak Ladies Association Fraternal Scholarship Awards (2461) | Study: Canada, United States | Association |

| Vocational Goal, Award, and Entry Number | Geographic Restrictions (Citizenship, Legal Residence, Place of Study) | Affiliation/Special Recipients Requirements |
|---|---|---|
| *Liberal/General Studies (continued)* | | |
| First Cavalry Division Association Scholarship (2464) | | Veteran |
| First Commercial Bank National Advisory Board Scholarship (2466) | Legal: AR; Study: AR | |
| Fleet Reserve Association Scholarship (2475) | | Association |
| Peter G. Flinn Scholarships (2485) | Legal: IN | |
| Florida Bright Futures Scholarship Program (2500) | Legal: FL; Study: FL | |
| Florida Resident Access Grant (2504) | Legal: FL; Study: FL | |
| Florida Student Assistance Grants (2505) | Citizenship: US; Study: FL | |
| Florida Undergraduate Scholars' Fund (2507) | Legal: FL; Study: FL | |
| Florida Vocational Gold Seal Endorsement Scholarship Program (2508) | Legal: FL; Study: FL | |
| Florida Work Experience Program (2509) | Study: FL | |
| Michael J. Flosi Memorial Scholarship (823) | Citizenship: US; Legal: IL, IN, WI | |
| Charlie Floyd Memorial Scholarship (2129) | | Association |
| Ford Motor Company Fund Scholarship (4080) | | Association |
| Ford New Holland Scholarship (4081) | | Association |
| Terry Fox Humanitarian Award (2585) | Citizenship: Canada; Study: Canada | |
| Raquel Marquez Frankel Scholarship Fund (3542) | | Hispanic American |
| Susan W. Freestone Vocational Education Award (4581) | Legal: NY; Study: NY | Association |
| French Fellowships (4715) | Legal: Canada | |
| Gerard S. Fudge Scholarship (2946) | | |
| Future Farmers of America Scholarships (1532) | Legal: AZ, CA, CO, IA, IL, KS, MN, MO, MT, ND, NE, NM, OK, OR, SD, TX, WA | Association |
| Gamewardens of Vietnam Association Scholarships (5958) | | Military, Veteran |
| GAR Living Memorial Scholarship (2176) | | Veteran |
| Gardner Foundation Scholarship Grants (2624) | Legal: OH | |
| Frank W. Garner Scholarship (69) | | Veteran |
| General Fund Scholarship (824) | | |
| General Undergraduate Scholarships (4227) | Legal: United States | |
| Major Don S. Gentile Scholarship (5768) | | |
| Georgia State Regents Scholarship (2657) | Legal: GA; Study: GA | |
| Georgia Student Finance Commission Governor's Scholarship (2662) | Legal: GA; Study: GA | |
| Georgia Student Finance Commission Pell Grant (2663) | Legal: GA | |
| Georgia Student Finance Commission Perkins Loan (2664) | Legal: GA | |
| Georgia Student Finance Commission PLUS Loan (2665) | Legal: GA | |
| Georgia Student Finance Commission SLS Loan (2667) | Legal: GA | |
| Georgia Student Finance Commission Stafford Loan (2668) | Legal: GA | |
| Georgia Student Finance Commission Student Incentive Grant (2670) | Legal: GA; Study: GA | |
| Georgia Student Finance Commission Supplemental Educational Opportunity Grant (2671) | Legal: GA | |
| Georgia Tuition Equalization Grant (2672) | Legal: GA; Study: GA | |
| GFWC of MA International Affairs Scholarships (2638) | Legal: MA | |
| Morton A. Gibson Memorial Scholarships (3268) | Study: United States | Ethnic |
| Gilbert Matching Scholarship (3597) | Legal: MA; Study: MA | |

| Vocational Goal, Award, and Entry Number | Geographic Restrictions (Citizenship, Legal Residence, Place of Study) | Affiliation/Special Recipients Requirements |
|---|---|---|
| *Liberal/General Studies (continued)* | | |
| Gleaner Life Insurance Society Scholarship Award (2709) | | Employer |
| GMP Memorial Scholarships (2707) | Study: Canada, United States | Union |
| Charles M. Goethe Memorial Scholarships (5211) | | Association |
| Thomas Googooian Memorial Scholarship (1120) | | Ethnic |
| Graco Scholarship Program (2724) | | Employer |
| AMA/Charles H. Grant Scholarship (18) | | Association |
| Grants for Canadians (1640) | Citizenship: Canada, PermRes; Study: Israel | |
| Robert Hampton Gray Memorial Bursary (4485) | Legal: AB | Military |
| M. Geneva Gray Scholarship (2747) | | |
| Norma Jean Gray Scholarships (154) | Legal: Canada | Association |
| Rose Basile Green Scholarship (4231) | | Ethnic |
| Amelia Greenbaum Scholarships (3957) | Legal: MA; Study: MA | Religion |
| Elsie Bell Grosvenor Scholarship Awards (1401) | Study: DC, MD, VA | Handicapped |
| Kathern F. Gruber Scholarships (1444) | | Veteran |
| Guaranteed Access Grant (3570) | Legal: MD | |
| Guideposts Magazine's Youth Writing Contest (2763) | | |
| Guido-Zerilli-Marimo Scholarships (4233) | Study: NY | |
| Guistwhite Scholar Program (4906) | | Fraternal |
| Calouste Gulbenkian Foundation (1121) | | Ethnic |
| Barbara Mae Gustafson & Bridget Mary Drew (B&B) Scholarship (1866) | Legal: NY; Study: NY | |
| Paul and Mary Haas Foundation Student Scholarship Grants (2775) | Legal: TX | |
| Hai Guin Scholarship Association (1122) | Legal: MA; Study: MA | Ethnic |
| Chuck Hall Star of Tomorrow Scholarship (5007) | | |
| John T. Hall Student Loan Fund (2782) | Legal: GA; Study: GA | |
| E.C. Hallbeck Memorial Scholarship (789) | | Union |
| John D. Hamilton Scholarship (1867) | Legal: NY | |
| Margaret Howard Hamilton Scholarships (4398) | Citizenship: US; Study: AR | Handicapped |
| Charles Hardy Memorial Scholarship Awards (5308) | | Union |
| Harness Tracks of America Scholarship (2794) | | Other |
| Harvard Travellers Club Grants (2802) | | |
| The Jerome L. Hauck Scholarship (2792) | | |
| Hawaii's Federal PLUS Loans (2821) | Legal: HI | |
| Hawaii's Federal Stafford Loans (2822) | | |
| Walter & Grace Hazzard Scholarship (1868) | | |
| A. A. Heaps Scholarships (1663) | Citizenship: Canada; Study: Canada | |
| Charles R. Hemenway Scholarship (2860) | Study: HI | |
| Cheryl Dant Hennesy Scholarship (4089) | Legal: GA, KY, TN | Association |
| Robert A. Hine Memorial Scholarship (5564) | Citizenship: US, PermRes; Legal: CA | Minority |
| Hinson-Hazlewood College Student Loan Program/Federal Stafford Student Loan Program (5710) | Study: TX | |
| Orris C. and Beatrice Dewey Hirtzel Memorial Foundation Scholarship (2876) | Legal: NY, PA | |
| Hispanic American Scholarship Program (1533) | | Hispanic American |
| Hispanic Education Foundation Matching Funds Award (513) | | |

| Vocational Goal, Award, and Entry Number | Geographic Restrictions (Citizenship, Legal Residence, Place of Study) | Affiliation/Special Recipients Requirements |
|---|---|---|
| *Liberal/General Studies (continued)* | | |
| Jostens Our Town Jack M. Holt Memorial Scholarship (3297) | | Employer |
| Charles H. Hood Fund Scholarships (2884) | | Employer |
| Hope Scholarship (2658) | Legal: GA | |
| HOPE Scholarships (2882) | Legal: MA | Hispanic American |
| Hopi Scholarship (2894) | | Native American |
| Frank Walton Horn Memorial Scholarships (4000) | | Handicapped |
| Randy Hough Scholarship (1869) | | |
| House of Commons Page Programme (1598) | Citizenship: Canada; Study: Canada | |
| Oliver and Esther R. Howard Scholarship (2476) | | Association |
| C.D. Howe Scholarship Program (1277) | Citizenship: Canada, PermRes | |
| Carrie and Luther Huffines Loan Fund (1823) | Citizenship: US; Legal: NC | |
| Hunt Manufacturing Company Foundation Scholarships (2937) | | Employer |
| The Allie Raney Hunt Memorial Scholarship (1402) | | Handicapped |
| Tom Hutchinson Memorial Scholarship (19) | | Association |
| IAM Scholarships (3117) | Legal: Canada, United States | Union |
| Idaho Guaranteed Student Loans (5640) | | |
| IFDA Educational Foundation Scholarship (3157) | | Association |
| ILGWU Local 23-25 College Textbook Scholarship (3159) | | Union |
| ILGWU National College Award Program (3161) | | Union |
| Illinois American Legion Scholarships (611) | Legal: IL | Association |
| Illinois AMVETS Auxiliary WORCHID Scholarships (2955) | Legal: IL | Veteran |
| Illinois AMVETS Service Foundation Scholarship Award (2957) | Legal: IL | Veteran |
| Illinois Correctional Officer's Grant (2969) | Study: IL | Other |
| Illinois Federal PLUS Loan (2970) | Legal: IL; Study: IL | |
| Illinois Federal Subsidized Stafford Loan (2971) | Study: IL | |
| Illinois Federal Supplemental Loans for Students (2972) | Legal: IL; Study: IL | |
| Illinois Federal Unsubsidized Stafford Loan (2973) | Study: IL | |
| Illinois Merit Recognition Scholarship (2974) | Legal: IL; Study: IL | |
| Illinois MIA/POW Scholarship (2961) | Study: IL | Veteran |
| Illinois Monetary Award Program (2975) | Study: IL | |
| Illinois National Guard Grant (2976) | Study: IL | Military |
| Illinois Police Officer/Fire Officer Grant (2977) | Legal: IL; Study: IL | Other |
| Illinois Student-to-Student Grant (2978) | Study: IL | |
| Illinois unILoan (2979) | Legal: IL; Study: IL | |
| Illinois Veteran Grant (2980) | Legal: IL; Study: IL | Veteran |
| Illinois Veterans' Children Educational Opportunities (2962) | Legal: IL | Veteran |
| Imasco Scholarships for Disabled Students (1278) | Citizenship: Canada, PermRes; Legal: Canada; Study: Canada | Handicapped |
| International Brotherhood of Teamsters Scholarships (3127) | | Union |
| International Student Identity Card Travel Grants for Educational Programs in Developing Countries (2113) | Citizenship: US, PermRes | |
| Iowa Federation of Labor, AFL-CIO High School Scholarships (3223) | Legal: IA | |
| Lee-Jackson Foundation Award (5607) | Study: VA | |

| Vocational Goal, Award, and Entry Number | Geographic Restrictions (Citizenship, Legal Residence, Place of Study) | Affiliation/Special Recipients Requirements |
|---|---|---|
| *Liberal/General Studies (continued)* | | |
| Maria C. Jackson & General George A. White Scholarships (5833) | Citizenship: US; Legal: OR; Study: OR | Military |
| Agnes Jones Jackson Scholarship (3850) | | Minority, Association |
| Stanley E. Jackson Scholarship Awards (2566) | | Handicapped |
| JACS Annual Scholarship (3289) | | Other |
| Jamestown School of Practical Nursing Scholarship (1871) | | |
| Japanese American Citizens League Student Aid Award (3248) | | Ethnic |
| Japanese American Citizens League Undergraduate Awards (3249) | | Ethnic |
| Jaycee War Memorial Scholarships (3257) | Citizenship: US | |
| Jenkins Loan (5834) | Legal: ID, OR, WA | |
| Jewish Educational Loans Fund (3269) | Citizenship: US, PermRes; Legal: DC, MD, VA; Study: United States | Ethnic |
| Jewish Federation of Metropolitan Chicago Academic Scholarships (3265) | Legal: IL, IN | Religion |
| Jewish Undergraduate Scholarships (3270) | Legal: DC, MD, VA | Religion |
| John A. Johnson Memorial Scholarship (1872) | Legal: NY | |
| Martha V. Johnson Memorial Scholarship (2260) | | |
| Hazel A. and H. Margaret Johnson Scholarship (1873) | Legal: NY | |
| Percy J. Johnson Scholarships (3386) | | Religion, Association |
| Jostens Our Town Scholarship (3298) | | Employer |
| Kansas State Program of Benefits for Dependents of POWs and MIAs (3315) | | Veteran |
| Charlotte and Lazare Kaplan Foundation Scholarship (3317) | Legal: NY | |
| Kappa Kappa Gamma Emergency Assistance Grants (3329) | Citizenship: US/CA | Fraternal |
| Kappa Kappa Gamma Undergraduate Scholarships (3332) | Citizenship: US/CA | Fraternal |
| Lucille R. Keller Foundation Loans (3343) | Legal: IN | |
| Ted Kenney Memorial Scholarships (1918) | Legal: IL; Study: United States | Union |
| Maude Grant Kent Scholarship (1874) | | |
| Kentucky Center for Veterans Affairs State Tuition Waivers (3358) | Study: KY | Veteran, Handicapped |
| Kentucky Department of Veterans Affairs Tuition Waivers (3356) | Citizenship: US; Study: KY | Veteran |
| James J. Kerrigan Memorial Scholarships (3366) | | Employer |
| Keystone Stafford and Keystone Direct Student Loans (4863) | Citizenship: US | |
| Blue Klein Memorial Scholarship (156) | Legal: AB | Association |
| Steven Knezevich Trust Grants (3381) | | Ethnic |
| Knights of Columbus Educational Trust Program Scholarships (3387) | | Religion, Association |
| Knights of Columbus Student Loan Program (3388) | Citizenship: US, PermRes | Religion |
| Knights of Lithuania Scholarships (3392) | | Association, Ethnic |
| Knights of Varton, Fresno Lodge 9 Scholarship (1124) | | Ethnic |
| Kodak Scholarship Award (5688) | Citizenship: US, PermRes; Legal: CA; Study: CA | Minority |
| Kohler Co. College Scholarship (3396) | | Employer |
| Peter and Alice Koomruian Armenian Education Fund (1125) | Study: United States | Ethnic |
| Kova Fertilizer, Inc. Scholarships (4093) | Legal: IN; Study: IN | Association |
| Father Krewitt Scholarship Awards (1749) | | Association |

| Vocational Goal, Award, and Entry Number | Geographic Restrictions (Citizenship, Legal Residence, Place of Study) | Affiliation/Special Recipients Requirements |
|---|---|---|
| *Liberal/General Studies (continued)* | | |
| William R. & Catherine Joann Krishock Scholarship (1875) | | |
| Kuchler-Killian Memorial Scholarship (4001) | | Handicapped |
| LA FRA National President's Scholarship (2477) | | Association |
| Ladies Auxiliary of Fleet Reserve Association Scholarship (2478) | | Association |
| Ladies Auxiliary to the VFW Junior Girls Scholarships (3408) | | Association |
| Herbert Frank and Bertha Maude Laird Memorial Foundation Scholarships (4690) | Legal: CA | |
| Ann Lane Home Economics Scholarships (5704) | Legal: TX; Study: TX | Association |
| Samuel J. Lasser Scholarship (1878) | | |
| Latin American Educational Foundation Scholarships (3439) | Legal: CO | Hispanic American |
| Law Enforcement Personnel Dependents Grant (2673) | Legal: GA; Study: GA | Employer |
| Dr. James L. Lawson Memorial Scholarship (829) | | |
| Herbert Lehman Education Fund Scholarships (3818) | Citizenship: US | African American |
| Samuel Lemberg Scholarship Loan Fund, Inc. (3451) | | Ethnic |
| Lester Educational Trust Loans (2133) | Legal: VA | |
| The Lighthouse Career Incentive Award for Adult Undergraduates (3474) | Citizenship: US; Legal: CT, MA, ME, NH, NJ, NY, PA, RI, VT; Study: CT, MA, ME, NH, NJ, NY, PA, RI, VT | Handicapped, Other |
| The Lighthouse Career Incentive Award for College-Bound Students (3475) | Citizenship: US; Legal: CT, MA, ME, NH, NJ, NY, PA, RI, VT; Study: CT, MA, ME, NH, NJ, NY, PA, RI, VT | Handicapped |
| The Lighthouse Career Incentive Award for Undergraduates (3477) | Citizenship: US; Legal: CT, MA, ME, NH, NJ, NY, PA, RI, VT; Study: CT, MA, ME, NH, NJ, NY, PA, RI, VT | Handicapped |
| Limited Access Competitive Grant (2510) | Legal: FL; Study: FL | |
| Franklin Lindsay Student Loans (3486) | Citizenship: US; Study: TX | |
| Lindstrom Foundation Student Service Scholarships (876) | | |
| Charlie Logan Scholarship for Dependents (5290) | | Union |
| Charlie Logan Scholarship for Seafarers (5291) | | Union |
| Longman-Harris Scholarship (4400) | Citizenship: US; Legal: AL | |
| Louisiana National Guard Tuition Exemption Program (3504) | Legal: LA; Study: LA | Military |
| Louisiana State Aid Dependents Educational Assistance (3500) | Legal: LA; Study: LA | Veteran |
| Inez Peppers Lovett Scholarship (2035) | Legal: FL | |
| Lucy Dalbiac Luard Scholarship (2385) | Study: United Kingdom | |
| Luce Scholars Program (3512) | Citizenship: US | |
| Cletus E. Ludden Memorial Scholarships (2231) | Legal: CO | Union |
| Lutheran Life University Scholarships (1314) | Study: Canada | Association |
| Lynden Memorial Scholarship (3522) | | Employer |
| John H. Lyons, Sr. Scholarship Program (3109) | Study: Canada, United States | Union, Association |
| M.A. Hanna Company Scholarship (3170) | | Employer |
| MACESA Awards (3699) | | Association, African American, Hispanic American, Native American |
| Minnie L. Maffett Scholarship (4466) | Legal: TX; Study: TX | |
| James L. and Lavon Madden Mallory Disability Scholarship (2322) | Legal: IA | Handicapped |

| Vocational Goal, Award, and Entry Number | Geographic Restrictions (Citizenship, Legal Residence, Place of Study) | Affiliation/Special Recipients Requirements |
|---|---|---|
| *Liberal/General Studies (continued)* | | |
| Maltese-American Benevolent Society Scholarship (3540) | Legal: MI | Association |
| Horace Mann Scholarship (3544) | | Employer |
| Marianas Naval Officers' Wives' Club Scholarships (5959) | Legal: GU | Military, Veteran |
| Marin County American Revolution Bicentennial Scholarship (3551) | Legal: CA | |
| Marine Corps Foundation Scholarships (3562) | | Military, Veteran |
| Antonio M. Marinelli Founders' Scholarship (4237) | Study: DC | |
| Marinelli Scholarships (4238) | | Ethnic |
| Inga Marr Memorial Scholarship (159) | Legal: AB | Other |
| Marsh Scholarship (2326) | | Association |
| Thurgood Marshall Scholarship (3566) | Citizenship: US; Study: United States | African American |
| Jose Marti Scholarship Challenge Grants (2511) | Citizenship: US; Legal: FL; Study: FL | Other |
| Maryland Distinguished Scholar Scholarship (3574) | Legal: MD; Study: MD | |
| Maryland Higher Education Commission Distinguished Scholar Program (3591) | Legal: MD; Study: MD | |
| Maryland House of Delegates Scholarship (3575) | Legal: MD | |
| Maryland Part-Time Grant Program (3576) | Legal: MD; Study: MD | |
| Maryland Senatorial Scholarship (3580) | Legal: MD | |
| Joseph Mason Memorial Scholarship (1881) | Study: NY | |
| Masonic Bursaries (2730) | Study: AB | |
| Massachusetts Family Education Loan (3598) | Legal: MA; Study: MA | |
| Massachusetts Indian Association Scholarships (3595) | | Native American |
| Massachusetts Public Service Scholarship (3599) | Legal: MA | Employer, Veteran |
| Massachusetts Tuition Waiver (3600) | Legal: MA; Study: MA | |
| MassGrant Program (3601) | Legal: MA; Study: CT, DC, MA, MD, ME, NH, PA, RI, VT | |
| Masters, Mates & Pilots Health & Benefit Plan Scholarship Program (3605) | | Employer |
| Don Matthews Scholarship (160) | Legal: AB | Association |
| Mattinson Endowment Fund Scholarship for Disabled Students (1282) | Citizenship: Canada, PermRes; Legal: Canada | Handicapped |
| Edmund F. Maxwell Foundation Scholarship (3614) | Legal: WA | |
| Howard E. May Memorial Scholarships (3992) | | Handicapped |
| Jonathan May Memorial Scholarships (3993) | Study: CT | Handicapped |
| McCabe Awards (5286) | | Employer |
| John T. McCraw Scholarship (3996) | | Handicapped |
| McDonnell Douglas Scholarships (3620) | | Employer |
| Louise McKinney Post-Secondary Scholarships (177) | Legal: AB, Canada | |
| Charles D. Melhuish Scholarship (1883) | | |
| Memmott-Langhans Scholarship (1884) | | |
| Memorial Scholarships for Children of Deceased Police Officers and Firefighters (4586) | Citizenship: US; Legal: NY; Study: NY | |
| Merit Gasoline Foundation College Scholarships (3650) | Study: United States | Employer |
| Mexican American Grocers Association Foundation Scholarships (3673) | | Hispanic American |
| Edwin G. and Lauretta M. Michael Scholarship (1950) | | Religion |

| Vocational Goal, Award, and Entry Number | Geographic Restrictions (Citizenship, Legal Residence, Place of Study) | Affiliation/Special Recipients Requirements |
|---|---|---|

### Liberal/General Studies (continued)

| Vocational Goal, Award, and Entry Number | Geographic Restrictions | Affiliation/Special Recipients Requirements |
|---|---|---|
| Michigan Association for Deaf, Hearing, and Speech Services Scholarships (3679) | Citizenship: US; Legal: MI | Handicapped |
| Michigan Competitive Scholarships (3685) | Citizenship: US; Legal: MI; Study: MI | |
| Michigan Indian Tuition Waiver (3683) | Legal: MI; Study: MI | Native American |
| Michigan Tuition Grants (3686) | Citizenship: US, PermRes; Legal: MI; Study: MI | |
| Michigan Veterans Trust Educational Tuition Grants (3694) | Legal: MI | Veteran |
| Alphonse A. Miele Scholarship (5770) | | |
| Leon S. Miller Memorial Scholarship (1885) | Legal: NY | |
| Larry Miller Transportation Scholarship Program (5750) | | Employer |
| Roger Milliken Scholarships (5642) | | Association |
| Milo High School Alumni Scholarships (4875) | Legal: ME | |
| Minburn Wild Rose Scholarship (161) | | Association |
| Minnesota State Department of Veterans Affairs Educational Assistance Grants (3718) | Study: MN | Veteran |
| Minnesota Teamsters Joint Council No. 32 Scholarship Awards (3720) | Study: MN | Union |
| Helen Lancaster Minton Educational Fund (1824) | Citizenship: US; Legal: NC; Study: NC | |
| Miss America Pageant Scholarships (3726) | Citizenship: US | |
| Mississippi Law Enforcement Officers and Firemen Scholarship Program (3733) | Legal: MS; Study: MS | |
| Mississippi Southeast Asia POW/MIA Scholarship Program (3740) | Legal: MS; Study: MS | Military |
| Mississippi State Student Incentive Grant Program (3745) | Legal: MS; Study: MS | |
| Montana Indian Student Fee Waiver (557) | Study: MT | Native American |
| Montana State Student Incentive Grants (3768) | Legal: MT | |
| Montana University System Fee Waivers (3769) | Study: MT | Native American, Other, Association, Veteran |
| Montgomery GI Bill (5825) | | Veteran |
| Montgomery G.I. Bill and U.S. Army College Fund (5826) | Citizenship: US | Military |
| Brenda L. Morrow Memorial Scholarship (1888) | Legal: NY | |
| Alberta M. Morse Memorial Scholarship (1889) | Legal: NY | |
| Multi-Cultural Scholarship (5270) | | |
| Multi-Year Ambassadorial Scholarship (5170) | | |
| NACA Scholarships for Student Leaders (3869) | | |
| NAPWPT Scholarships (3891) | | |
| National Achievement Scholarship Program for Outstanding Negro Students (4310) | Citizenship: US, PermRes | African American |
| National Alliance for Excellence Honored Scholars Awards (3841) | Citizenship: US; Study: United States | |
| National Amputation Foundation Scholarship (3846) | | Handicapped |
| National Art Materials Trade Association Scholarships (3848) | | Employer |
| National Association of Executive Secretaries Scholarships (3875) | | Association |
| National Broadcasting Society Member Scholarship (3920) | | Association |
| The National Bursaries (5039) | Citizenship: Canada; Legal: Canada; Study: ON | |
| National Eagle Scout Scholarships (1464) | | Association |
| National Federation of the Blind Scholarships (4004) | | Handicapped |
| National Fourth Infantry Division Association Scholarship (4171) | | Veteran |

| Vocational Goal, Award, and Entry Number | Geographic Restrictions (Citizenship, Legal Residence, Place of Study) | Affiliation/Special Recipients Requirements |
|---|---|---|
| *Liberal/General Studies (continued)* | | |
| National Fraternal Society of the Deaf Scholarships (4173) | | Association, Handicapped |
| National Guard Association of New Jersey Scholarship (4539) | | Military |
| National Hispanic Scholar Recognition Program (1984) | | Hispanic American |
| National Honor Society Scholarships (3899) | | Other |
| National Latin Exam Scholarship (371) | | |
| National Merit Scholarship Program (4311) | Citizenship: US, PermRes | |
| National Miss Indian U.S.A. Scholarship (555) | | Native American |
| National Presbyterian College Scholarships (4991) | Citizenship: US, PermRes | Religion |
| Native American Education Grants (4992) | Citizenship: US | Native American |
| James Z. Naurison Scholarship Fund (2472) | Legal: CT, MA | |
| Navajo Code Talkers Scholarship (4479) | | Native American |
| Naval Academy Women's Club Scholarship (4481) | | Military |
| Naval Officers' Spouses' Association of Mayport Scholarships (4487) | Legal: FL | Military |
| Navy League Scholarship Program (4491) | Citizenship: US | |
| Navy-Marine Corps ROTC College Scholarships (4489) | Citizenship: US | |
| Navy Supply Corps Foundation Scholarships (4501) | | Military, Veteran |
| Navy Wives Club of America Scholarships (5960) | | Military, Veteran |
| NCAA Postgraduate Scholarships (3937) | Legal: United States | |
| NCOA Scholarships (4639) | | Military, Association |
| Nebraska Department of Veterans' Affairs Waiver of Tuition (4503) | Legal: NE; Study: NE | Veteran |
| NEED Scholarships (4507) | Legal: PA | |
| Nevada Hispanic Services Scholarships (4519) | Legal: NV | Hispanic American |
| Nevada Women's Fund Scholarships (4521) | Legal: NV | |
| New England FEMARA Scholarship (835) | | |
| New England Regional Student Program (4525) | Legal: CT, MA, ME, NH, RI, VT; Study: CT, MA, ME, NH, RI, VT | |
| New Hampshire Charitable Foundation Statewide Student Aid Program (4533) | Legal: NH | |
| New Hampshire Federal PLUS Loans (2737) | Legal: NH; Study: NH | |
| New Jersey State Golf Association Caddie Scholarships (4545) | Legal: NJ | |
| New Mexico Federal Stafford Loans (4551) | Legal: NM; Study: NM | |
| New Mexico Unsubsidized Loan for Students (4552) | Citizenship: US, PermRes | |
| New Mexico Veterans' Service Commission Scholarships (4554) | | Veteran |
| New York Council Navy League Scholarships (4566) | Legal: CT, NJ, NY | Military |
| New York State Child of Deceased Police Officer-Firefighter-Correction Officer Awards (4587) | Citizenship: US; Legal: NY; Study: NY | Employer |
| New York State Child of Veteran Awards (4588) | Citizenship: US; Legal: NY; Study: NY | Veteran |
| New York State Grange Student Loans (4582) | Legal: NY | Association |
| New York State Higher Education Opportunity Program (4590) | Study: NY | |
| New York State Indian Aid (4468) | Legal: NY; Study: NY | Native American |
| New York State Parent Loans for Students (4591) | Citizenship: US, PermRes | |

| Vocational Goal, Award, and Entry Number | Geographic Restrictions (Citizenship, Legal Residence, Place of Study) | Affiliation/Special Recipients Requirements |
|---|---|---|
| *Liberal/General Studies (continued)* | | |
| New York State Regents Scholarship at Cornell University (4578) | Citizenship: US, PermRes; Legal: NY; Study: NY | |
| New York State Senate Sessions Assistance Program (4599) | Citizenship: US; Legal: NY; Study: NY | |
| New York State Stafford Loan (4594) | Citizenship: US, PermRes | |
| New York State Supplemental Loans for Students (4595) | Citizenship: US, PermRes | |
| New York State Tuition Assistance Program (4596) | Citizenship: US, PermRes; Legal: NY; Study: NY | |
| Clarence Newlun Memorial Scholarship Award (2958) | Legal: IL | Veteran |
| NFB of CT Academic Sholarship (3994) | Study: CT | Handicapped |
| NHSF Scholarships (4179) | Citizenship: US, PermRes; Study: United States | Hispanic American |
| NIAF/FIERI National Matching Scholarship (4246) | | Ethnic |
| NIAF/Pepperdine University Scholarship (4247) | | |
| NIAF/Sacred Heart University Matching Scholarship (4248) | | Ethnic |
| Niccum Educational Trust Foundation Scholarship (4633) | Legal: IN | |
| Charles S. Noble Awards for Student Leadership (178) | Legal: AB | |
| Charles S. Noble Junior A Hockey Scholarships (179) | Legal: Canada; Study: AB, Canada | Other |
| Charles S. Noble Junior Football Scholarships (180) | Legal: Canada; Study: AB, Canada | |
| Charles S. Noble Scholarships for Study at Harvard (181) | Legal: AB, Canada; Study: MA, United States | |
| North Carolina Scholarships for Children of War Veterans (4674) | | Veteran |
| North Carolina State Legislative Tuition Grants (4680) | Legal: NC; Study: NC | |
| North Dakota Indian Scholarships (4684) | Study: ND | Native American |
| North Georgia College ROTC Grant (2675) | Legal: GA; Study: GA | Military |
| Northeastern Loggers' Association Annual Scholarships (4688) | | Association |
| Northern Alberta Development Council Bursaries (182) | Legal: AB, Canada | |
| NSCA Student Research Grant (4416) | | |
| NSSA Scholarship (4377) | | Association |
| Allie Mae Oden Memorial Scholarship (2479) | | Association |
| Ohio Academic Scholarships (4723) | Legal: OH; Study: OH | |
| Ohio American Legion Scholarship (621) | | Military |
| Ohio Instructional Grants (4724) | Legal: OH; Study: OH, PA | |
| Ohio National Guard Tuition Grant (4729) | Legal: OH; Study: OH | Military |
| Ohio Student Choice Grants (4726) | Legal: OH; Study: OH | |
| Ohio War Orphans Scholarships (4727) | Legal: OH; Study: OH | Veteran |
| Oklahoma State Regents Academic Scholars Scholarships (4736) | Legal: OK; Study: OK | |
| Oklahoma State Regents Tuition Aid Grants (4741) | Legal: OK; Study: OK | |
| OMC Foundation Scholarship (2416) | | Employer |
| Opportunities for the Blind, Inc. Grants (4785) | Citizenship: US | Handicapped |
| Oral Hearing Impaired Section Scholarship Award (1403) | | Handicapped |
| Oregon Educational Aid for Veterans (4799) | Citizenship: US; Legal: OR | Veteran |
| Steve Orlowski Memorial Scholarships (4908) | | Fraternal |
| Orphan Foundation of America Scholarship (4812) | | Other |
| Oshkosh Foundation Scholarships (4818) | Legal: WI | |

| Vocational Goal, Award, and Entry Number | Geographic Restrictions (Citizenship, Legal Residence, Place of Study) | Affiliation/Special Recipients Requirements |
|---|---|---|
| *Liberal/General Studies (continued)* | | |
| The Francis Ouimet Scholarships (4820) | Legal: MA | Other |
| Melva T. Owen Memorial Scholarship (4005) | | Handicapped |
| Palm Beach Kennel Club Scholarship (2036) | Legal: FL | |
| Parent Loan for Undergraduate Students (PLUS) (2058) | | |
| John and Anne Parente Matching Scholarship (4251) | | Ethnic |
| Parents Without Partners International Scholarship (4837) | | Association |
| Parke-Davis Epilepsy Scholarship (3211) | | |
| Helen Wegman Parmalee Educational Foundation Scholarships (4691) | Legal: CA | |
| Past Grand Presidents Award (2185) | | Association |
| Anne Pekar Memorial Scholarship (4006) | | Handicapped |
| Pellegrini Scholarship Grants (5662) | Legal: CT, DE, NJ, NY, PA | Ethnic |
| Pennsylvania Bureau for Veteran's Affairs Educational Gratuity (4860) | Legal: PA; Study: PA | Veteran |
| (Pennsylvania) Federal PLUS Loans (4864) | | |
| (Pennsylvania) Federal Stafford Loans (4865) | Citizenship: US | |
| Pennsylvania Steel Foundry Foundation Awards (4873) | | Employer |
| "Persons Case" Scholarships (183) | Legal: AB; Study: Canada | |
| Norman R. Peterson Scholarship (John Cabot University) (4253) | Legal: United States | |
| Petro-Canada Education Awards for Native Students (4881) | Citizenship: Canada | Native American |
| PHD Scholarship (836) | | |
| Phi Kappa Theta National Foundation Scholarships (4902) | | Fraternal |
| Philippines Subic Bay-Cubi Point Scholarship (4492) | Citizenship: US | Military |
| Pickett & Hatcher Educational Loans (4945) | Citizenship: US; Legal: AL, FL, GA, KY, MS, NC, SC, TN, VA; Study: AL, FL, GA, KY, MS, NC, SC, TN, VA | |
| George Pimm Memorial Scholarship (163) | Legal: AB | Association |
| Minnie Stevens Piper Foundation Student Loan (4951) | Citizenship: US; Legal: TX; Study: TX | |
| Polaroid Foundation National Merit Scholarship (4971) | | Employer |
| Robert "Bobby" Guy Pollino II Memorial Scholarship (1895) | Legal: NY | |
| Portuguese Continental Union Scholarships (4983) | | Association |
| Potlatch Foundation for Higher Education Scholarships (4987) | Legal: AR, ID, MN; Study: United States | |
| Paul Powell Memorial AMVETS Scholarships (2959) | Legal: IL | |
| PPGA Family Member Scholarship (1386) | | Association |
| Presbyterian Church Student Opportunity Scholarships (4996) | Citizenship: US, PermRes | African American, Asian American, Hispanic American, Native American, Religion |
| Herschel C. Price Scholarship (2872) | | |
| Principal's Leadership Award (3900) | Citizenship: US | |
| Private Colleges & Universities Community Service Scholarship (1735) | | Minority |
| Pro Deo and Pro Patria (Canada) Scholarships (3389) | Study: Canada | Religion, Association |
| Pro Deo and Pro Patria Scholarships (3390) | | Religion, Association |
| Puerto Rico Council on Higher Education Educational Funds (5025) | Legal: PR | |
| Puerto Rico Council on Legislative Funds (5026) | Citizenship: US; Legal: PR | |

| Vocational Goal, Award, and Entry Number | Geographic Restrictions (Citizenship, Legal Residence, Place of Study) | Affiliation/Special Recipients Requirements |
|---|---|---|
| *Liberal/General Studies (continued)* | | |
| Puerto Rico Council State Student Incentive Grant (5027) | Citizenship: US | |
| Schuler S. Pyle Scholarship (2480) | | Association |
| Quaker Chemical Foundation Scholarships (5037) | | Employer |
| Queen Elizabeth Silver Jubilee Endowment Fund for Study in a Second Official Language Awards (1285) | Citizenship: Canada, PermRes | |
| QuikTrip Scholarships (5046) | | Employer |
| Michael J. Quill Scholarship (5737) | | Union |
| Rangeley Educational Trust Loans (2134) | Legal: VA | |
| Jeannette Rankin Award (5081) | Citizenship: US | |
| Realty Foundation of New York Scholarships (5085) | Citizenship: US; Study: NY | Employer |
| Alex and Henry Recine Scholarships (4255) | Legal: NY | |
| Red River Valley Fighter Pilot Association Scholarships (5087) | | Veteran |
| Henry J. Reilly Memorial Undergraduate Scholarship for College Attendees (5106) | Study: United States | Military |
| Henry J. Reilly Memorial Undergraduate Scholarship for Graduating High School Students (5107) | Study: United States | Military |
| The Retired Officers Association Educational Assistance Program (5116) | | Military |
| Dr. Syngman Rhee Scholarship (2268) | Legal: HI | Ethnic |
| Rhodes Scholarships (5129) | Citizenship: US/CA; Study: England | |
| David Carlyle Richards III Scholarships (5131) | | |
| Sid Richardson Memorial Fund Scholarship (5134) | | |
| Richland County Foundation Scholarships (5136) | Study: OH | |
| Donald R. Riebhoff Memorial Scholarship (837) | | |
| Samuel Robinson Scholarships (4999) | | Religion |
| David Rogers Bursary (3971) | Legal: England | Handicapped |
| Admiral Roland Student Loan (5849) | Citizenship: US | Other |
| Sam Rose Memorial Scholarship (2481) | | Association |
| Rosewood Family Scholarship Fund (2514) | | Minority |
| Bettsy Ross Educational Grants (4640) | | Military, Association |
| Richard D. Rousher Scholarship (70) | | Veteran |
| The Leo S. Rowe Pan American Fund Loan (5174) | Legal: United States | |
| Royal Canadian Legion Camrose Branch No. 57 Bursaries (5040) | Legal: Canada | Association |
| Royal Canadian Legion Ladies Auxiliary Alberta-N.W.T. Command Awards (5041) | Legal: Canada | Military |
| Royal Canadian Legion Ladies Auxiliary Camrose Branch No. 57 Bursaries (5042) | Legal: Canada | Military, Veteran |
| F. Charles Ruling/N6FR Memorial Scholarship (838) | | |
| Alexander Rutherford Scholarships for High School Achievement (185) | Citizenship: Canada; Legal: AB, Canada | |
| Edward Rutledge Charity Scholarships (5202) | Legal: WI | |
| Sachs Foundation Grants (5204) | Citizenship: US; Legal: CO | African American |
| St. Anslem's College Scholarship (4256) | | |
| St. David's Scholarship (5220) | | Ethnic |
| St. James Armenian Church Memorial Scholarship (1127) | | Ethnic, Religion |
| Santa Fe Pacific Foundation Scholarships (563) | Legal: AZ, CA, CO, KS, NM, OK | Association, Native American |

| Vocational Goal, Award, and Entry Number | Geographic Restrictions (Citizenship, Legal Residence, Place of Study) | Affiliation/Special Recipients Requirements |
|---|---|---|
| *Liberal/General Studies (continued)* | | |
| Santa Fe Pacific Native American Scholarships (1534) | Legal: AZ, CA, CO, KS, NM, OK | Native American |
| Santa Fe Pacific Special Scholarships (1535) | | Employer |
| Sara Lee Corporation Student Loan Program (5247) | Citizenship: US, PermRes | Employer |
| Sara Lee National Achievement Scholarships (5248) | | African American, Employer |
| SBS Scholarships (5660) | Legal: IL, WI | Ethnic |
| Scaife Foundation Scholarships (4692) | Citizenship: US; Legal: CA | |
| SCAMP Grants & Scholarships (5266) | | Veteran |
| Marlin Scarborough Memorial Scholarship (5554) | Legal: SD; Study: SD | |
| Conrad & Marcel Schlumberger Scholarships (5260) | | Employer |
| Scholarship for Children of Disabled, Deceased and POW/MIA Veterans (4676) | Legal: NC | Veteran |
| Scholarship Foundation of St. Louis Loan (5262) | Legal: MO | |
| Scholarships for Study in Israel (2851) | Citizenship: US; Study: Israel | |
| Seabee Memorial Association Scholarships (5961) | | Association, Veteran |
| Second Marine Division Memorial Scholarships (5298) | | Veteran |
| Secondary School Exchange (2386) | Study: United Kingdom, United States | |
| Seibel Foundation Interest Free Educational Loan (5302) | Legal: TX; Study: TX | |
| Seminole-Miccosukee Indian Scholarships (2515) | Legal: FL; Study: FL | Native American |
| Service Merchandise Scholarship Program (5310) | | |
| Dr. Forrest Shaklee Memorial Scholarship (5313) | | Employer |
| Sheet Metal Workers' International Scholarship (5321) | | Association |
| Sig Memorial Scholarship (20) | | Association |
| Sigma Gamma Rho National Education Fund Scholarship (5332) | | |
| Sikh Education Aid Fund Scholarship (5349) | | |
| Six Meter Club of Chicago Scholarship (840) | Legal: IL; Study: IL | |
| C. Bascom Slemp Scholarship (5357) | | Other |
| Slovenian Women's Union Scholarships (5361) | | Association |
| Horace Smith Fund Loans (5365) | Legal: MA | |
| Joseph Sumner Smith Scholarship (5783) | | Religion |
| Smithsonian Institution Minority Internship (5386) | | Minority |
| Society of Daughters of the United States Army Scholarship Program (5447) | | Military, Veteran |
| Society of the First Division Foundation Scholarships (5451) | | Veteran |
| Alexandra Apostolides Sonenfeld Award (2186) | | Association |
| Annie Sonnenblick Scholarship (5529) | | Employer |
| Sons of the First Division Scholarship Fund (5452) | | Veteran |
| Sons of Italy Foundation National Leadership Grants (5533) | | Ethnic |
| South Carolina Press Association Foundation Scholarships (5545) | Study: SC | |
| South Carolina Tuition Grant Awards (5549) | Legal: SC; Study: SC | |
| South Carolina Tuition Program (5543) | Legal: SC; Study: SC | Veteran |

| Vocational Goal, Award, and Entry Number | Geographic Restrictions (Citizenship, Legal Residence, Place of Study) | Affiliation/Special Recipients Requirements |
|---|---|---|
| *Liberal/General Studies (continued)* | | |
| South Dakota Board of Regents National Guard Tuition Assistance (5555) | Legal: SD; Study: SD | Military |
| South Dakota Board of Regents Senior Citizens Tuition Assistance (5556) | Legal: SD; Study: SD | Other |
| South Dakota Board of Regents State Employee Tuition Assistance (5557) | Legal: SD; Study: SD | Employer |
| South Dakota Board of Regents Veterans Tuition Exemption (5558) | Legal: SD; Study: SD | Veteran |
| Southeast Asia POW/MIA Scholarship (3728) | | Veteran |
| Southern California Edison Company College Scholarships (5565) | Citizenship: US, PermRes; Legal: CA | |
| Southern California Edison Company Community College Achievement Awards (5566) | Citizenship: US, PermRes; Legal: CA | |
| Southern California Edison Company Educational Grants (5567) | Citizenship: US, PermRes; Legal: CA | |
| Southern California Edison Company Independent Colleges of Southern California Scholarships (5568) | Citizenship: US, PermRes; Legal: CA; Study: CA | Minority |
| The Spina Bifida Association of Northern Alberta Scholarship (5043) | Citizenship: Canada; Legal: AB | |
| Stanhome Scholarship (5599) | | Employer |
| Star Bank, N.A. Scholarship (5601) | Legal: OH | |
| State Student Incentive Grant For Students at Private Non-Profit Institutions (5712) | Study: TX | |
| State Student Incentive Grant For Students at Public Institutions (5713) | Study: TX | |
| Jerome B. Steinbach Scholarship (5836) | Citizenship: US; Legal: OR | |
| Daniel Stella Scholarship (4261) | | Ethnic |
| Emanuel Sternberger Educational Loan (5628) | Legal: NC | |
| Harley & Mertie Stevens Memorial Fund (5837) | Legal: OR; Study: OR | |
| Ney Stineman Memorial Scholarship (1896) | | |
| Levi Strauss Foundation Scholarship Program (5636) | | Employer |
| Hattie M. Strong College Loan Program (5638) | Citizenship: US | |
| Student Access Awards Program (1287) | Citizenship: Canada, PermRes; Study: Canada | Handicapped |
| CDR William S. Stuhr Scholarship (5644) | Legal: NY | Military |
| Supplemental Education Loans for Families (4511) | | |
| Supplemental Educational Opportunity Grant (2050) | | |
| Joe Tangaro Memorial Athletic Scholarship (4264) | Legal: MO | |
| Hope Pierce Tartt Scholarship (5674) | | |
| Edith Taylor Memorial Scholarship (164) | Legal: AB | Association |
| TELACU Scholarships (5690) | Legal: CA; Study: CA | Minority |
| Telesensory Scholarship (2098) | | Handicapped |
| Tennessee Federal Parent Loan for Undergraduate Students (5700) | Citizenship: US; Legal: TN | |
| Texas Black Scholarships (1374) | Legal: TX; Study: TX | African American, Religion |
| Texas Public Educational Grant Program (5715) | Study: TX | |
| Texas State Scholarship Program for Ethnic Recruitment (5716) | Legal: TX | Minority |
| Texas Tuition Equalization Grant (5717) | Study: TX | |
| Texas Veterans Educational Benefits (5721) | | Military |
| Al Thompson Junior Bowler Scholarships (5008) | | |
| Rosalie Tiles Scholarship (5733) | Legal: MO | |
| Americo Toffoli Scholarships (1998) | Legal: CO | Union |

| Vocational Goal, Award, and Entry Number | Geographic Restrictions (Citizenship, Legal Residence, Place of Study) | Affiliation/Special Recipients Requirements |
|---|---|---|
| *Liberal/General Studies (continued)* | | |
| Tolbert Grant (3584) | Legal: MD | |
| Virginia Transfer Grant (5608) | Study: VA | Minority |
| Travel and Training Grant (6240) | | Other |
| Vice Admiral E.P. Travers Scholarships and Loan Program (4497) | | Military |
| Virginia Tuition Assistance Grant (5609) | Legal: VA; Study: VA | |
| Tuition/Book Scholarship (2896) | | |
| Twenty and Four Memorial Scholarships (4444) | | Veteran |
| Two/Ten International Footwear Foundation Scholarships (5759) | | Employer |
| Tyson Scholarship (5761) | Legal: AK, AL, AR, FL, GA, IA, IL, IN, MI, MN, MO, MS, NC, OK, OR, PA, TN, TX, VA, WA | |
| UFCW Scholarships (5792) | Citizenship: US/CA | Union |
| Mark Ulmer Native American Scholarships (5748) | Legal: NC; Study: NC | Native American |
| Union of Hadjin Fund (1128) | Study: CA | Ethnic |
| Union of Marash Fund (1129) | | Ethnic |
| Union Pacific Railroad Employee Dependent Scholarships (5778) | | Employer |
| UNITE Scholarships (5776) | | Association, Union |
| United Daughters of the Confederacy Scholarships (5790) | | Veteran |
| United Paperworkers International Union Scholarships (5809) | | Union |
| U.S. Air Force Academy Graduate Dependent Scholarship (1240) | | Military |
| U.S. Bureau of Indian Affairs Scholarship Grant (5843) | | Native American |
| U.S. Coast Guard Academy Appointment (5845) | | |
| United States Naval Academy Class of 1963 Foundation Scholarship (5947) | | Association |
| U.S. Submarine Veterans of World War II Scholarships (5962) | | Association, Veteran |
| USCG Chief Petty Officers Association Captain Caliendo College Assistance Fund Scholarship Program (5847) | | Handicapped, Association |
| USET Scholarships (5812) | | Native American |
| USS Lake Champlain Foundation Scholarships (5648) | Citizenship: US | Military |
| USS Stark Memorial Scholarships (4498) | | Veteran |
| USS Tennessee Scholarships (4499) | Study: TN | Veteran |
| Utah State Student Incentive Grant (6019) | Study: UT | |
| UWUA Scholarships (6021) | | Employer |
| Agnes E. Vaghi-Cornaro Scholarship (4266) | | Ethnic |
| Adolph Van Pelt Special Fund for Indian Scholarships (1216) | | Native American |
| Vermilion River 4-H District Scholarship (166) | Legal: AB | Association |
| Virgin Islands Territorial Loan/Grant Program and Special Legislative Grants (6046) | Legal: VI | |
| Virginia College Scholarship (5610) | Legal: VA; Study: VA | |
| Virginia Graduate and Undergraduate Assistance Award (5611) | Study: VA | |
| Virginia War Orphans Education Program (6054) | Legal: VA; Study: VA | Veteran |
| Viscosity Oil Company Scholarships (4143) | | |
| Visionaries Achievement Award (6067) | Legal: FL | |
| Vocational Rehabilitation Assistance for Postsecondary Training (4678) | Legal: NC | Handicapped |

| Vocational Goal, Award, and Entry Number | Geographic Restrictions (Citizenship, Legal Residence, Place of Study) | Affiliation/Special Recipients Requirements |
|---|---|---|
| *Liberal/General Studies (continued)* | | |
| Vocational Rehabilitation Grants (3360) | Legal: KY | Handicapped |
| Voice of Democracy Scholarships (6069) | | |
| John A. Volpe Scholarship (4269) | | |
| Volta Scholarship Award (1404) | | Handicapped |
| Flora M. Von Der Ahe Scholarship (5838) | Legal: OR; Study: OR | |
| David J. Von Hagen Scholarship Award (1405) | | Handicapped |
| Wallace-Folsom Prepaid College Tuition Program (117) | | |
| Raoul Wallenberg Scholarships (3274) | | Veteran, Religion |
| War Orphans Educational Fund (3221) | Legal: IA; Study: IA | Veteran |
| Wilbur H.H. Ward Educational Trust Scholarship (6077) | Legal: MA; Study: MA | |
| Washington Crossing Foundation Scholarships (6085) | Citizenship: US | |
| Washington Scholars Grants (6100) | Legal: WA; Study: WA | |
| Washington State Educational Opportunity Grant (6101) | Legal: WA | |
| Washington State Need Grant (6102) | Legal: WA; Study: WA | |
| Washington State PTA Scholarships (6107) | Legal: WA | |
| Washington State Student Financial Aid Programs Washington Scholars (6104) | Study: WA | |
| Washington State Work Study (6105) | Legal: WA; Study: WA | |
| Wasie Foundation Scholarships (6109) | | Ethnic |
| David Wasserman Scholarships (6111) | Legal: NY | |
| W.C.A. Care and Share Scholarship (1897) | Legal: NY, PA | Employer |
| Robert H. Weitbrecht Scholarship Award (1406) | | Handicapped |
| Billy Welu Scholarship (5009) | | |
| West Virginia Italian Heritage Festival Scholarships (4270) | Legal: WV | |
| West Virginia War Orphans Education Benefits (6141) | Legal: WV; Study: WV | Veteran |
| Westchester Community Scholarship (4271) | Legal: NY | |
| Wetaskiwin District 4-H Scholarships (167) | Legal: AB | Association |
| Weyerhaeuser Company Foundation College Scholarship (6165) | | Employer |
| Weyerhaeuser Company Foundation Community Education Scholarship (6166) | | Employer |
| Wheat Board Surplus Monies Trust Scholarships (168) | Legal: AB | Association |
| Who's Who Among American High School Students Scholarships (4149) | | Association |
| Roy Wilkins Scholarships (3852) | | Association, Minority |
| William P. Willis Scholars Scholarships (4742) | Study: OK | |
| David and Dovetta Wilson Scholarship (6190) | | |
| Windham Foundation Scholarship (6193) | Legal: VT | |
| Maude Winkler Scholarship Awards (1407) | | Handicapped |
| The Winston-Salem Foundation Loans (6198) | Legal: NC | |
| Wisconsin Department of Veterans Affairs Part-Time Study Grants (6209) | Legal: WI; Study: WI | Veteran |
| Deborah Partridge Wolfe International Fellowship (6307) | | |
| Woman's Board Scholarship (1470) | Legal: IL | Association |
| Women of the ELCA Scholarship (6226) | | Religion |
| The Women's Sports Foundation Minority Internship Program (6241) | | Other, Minority |
| Women's Western Golf Foundation Scholarship (6245) | | Other |
| Harold S. Wood Award for Excellence (4205) | | |

| Vocational Goal, Award, and Entry Number | Geographic Restrictions (Citizenship, Legal Residence, Place of Study) | Affiliation/Special Recipients Requirements |
|---|---|---|
| *Liberal/General Studies (continued)* | | |
| Woodgrove Unifarm Local Scholarship (169) | Study: AB | Association, Other |
| Honourable W.C. Woodward Scholarships (5044) | Citizenship: Canada; Study: AB, BC | Employer |
| World of Expression Scholarship Program (1420) | Legal: NY | |
| Xerox Technical Minority Scholarship (5682) | | Minority |
| YLD Scholarships (6287) | Citizenship: US; Study: NC | Employer |
| Yoshiyama Award for Exemplary Service to the Community (6289) | | |
| Whitney M. Young Memorial Scholarship (1929) | Legal: IL | Minority |
| Coleman A. Young Scholarship (6293) | Legal: MI | |
| Zeta Phi Beta General Undergraduate Scholarship (6310) | | |
| Mary & Harry Zimmerman Scholarship Program (5311) | | Employer |
| Charles K. and Pansy Pategian Zlokovich Scholarship (1131) | | Ethnic |
| Zuni Higher Education Scholarships (6314) | | Native American |
| **Library and Archival Sciences** | | |
| Cooper-Hewitt Museum Internships (5383) | Study: NY | |
| Ethics in Business Scholarship Program (2499) | Study: FL | |
| Peter Krueger Summer Internships (5384) | Study: NY | |
| Library of Congress Junior Fellowship (3462) | Citizenship: US | |
| Marine Corps Historical Center College Internships (3556) | Study: DC, VA | |
| Massachusetts Black Librarians Network Scholarship. (3593) | Citizenship: US | Minority |
| National Museum of American Art Summer Internships (5388) | Study: NY | |
| Ida L., Mary L., and Ervin R. NePage Foundation (4513) | Legal: WA; Study: WA | |
| Pennsylvania Library Association Library Science Continuing Education Grants (4867) | | Association |
| U.S. Marine Corps Historical Center College Internships (5945) | | |
| **Life Sciences** | | |
| AFAR Fellowships (468) | Study: United States | |
| Air Force Civilian Cooperative Work-Study Program (66) | | |
| AISES A.T. Anderson Memorial Scholarship (559) | | Native American, Association |
| American Cyanamid Scholarship (4017) | | Association |
| American Foundation for Aging Research Predoctoral Awards (469) | Study: United States | |
| Archbold Biological Station Undergraduate and Graduate Internships (1071) | | |
| Bermuda Biological Station Summer Course Scholarships (1417) | Study: Bermuda | |
| Beverly and Qamanirjaq Caribou Management Scholarship (1678) | Citizenship: Canada, PermRes; Study: Canada | |
| Call to Action Opportunity Scholarship (1568) | Citizenship: US; Legal: CA; Study: CA | |
| Cancer Federation Scholarships (1710) | | |
| CIIT Summer Internships (1903) | Study: NC | |
| Delmar Publishers Scholarship (4061) | | Association |
| Environmental Science Amoco Foundation Scholarships (4068) | | Association |
| ESA Undergraduate Scholarships (2389) | Study: Canada, Mexico, United States | |

| Vocational Goal, Award, and Entry Number | Geographic Restrictions (Citizenship, Legal Residence, Place of Study) | Affiliation/Special Recipients Requirements |
|---|---|---|
| *Life Sciences (continued)* | | |
| GCA Awards For Summer Environmental Studies; Clara Carter Higgins Scholarship (2620) | Legal: United States | |
| Harness Horse Youth Foundation Scholarships (2790) | | |
| U.P. Hedrick Award (786) | | |
| Italian Cultural Society and NIAF Matching Scholarship (4234) | Study: DC, MD, VA | |
| Maryland MESA Scholarships (3586) | Legal: MD | |
| Allen H. Meyers Scholarship (3677) | Legal: MI | |
| MSA Presidential Student Awards (3696) | Legal: United States | |
| MSA Undergraduate Research Scholarships (3697) | | |
| National Center for Toxicological Research Undergraduate Program (5908) | | |
| National Oceanic and Atmospheric Administration/Historically Black Colleges and Universities Faculty/Student Research Participation Program (5910) | | |
| National Zoological Park Minority Traineeships (4456) | | |
| National Zoological Park Research Traineeships (4457) | | |
| National Zoological Park Traineeship in Education (4459) | | |
| National Zoological Park Traineeship in Exhibit Interpretation (4460) | | |
| Naval Air Warfare Center Training Systems Division Undergraduate Research Participation Program (5914) | | |
| Our World - Underwater Scholarships (4822) | | Association |
| Arthur & Doreen Parrett Scholarship Fund (4848) | Legal: WA | |
| Tibor T. Polgar Fellowship (2916) | | |
| Research Science Institute Internship (5103) | | |
| Howard Brown Rickard Scholarship (4007) | | Handicapped |
| Santa Fe Pacific Foundation Scholarships (563) | Legal: AZ, CA, CO, KS, NM, OK | Association, Native American |
| Seaspace Scholarship (5293) | Study: United States | |
| Marie Selby Internships (5304) | Study: FL | |
| Service Cancelable Student Loan (2660) | | |
| Sigma Xi Grants-in-Aid of Research (5347) | | |
| Smithsonian Environmental Research Center Work-Learn Opportunities in Environmental Studies (5374) | Legal: United States; Study: MD | |
| U.S. Department of Energy Internship (4711) | Citizenship: US, PermRes; Study: CA, IL, NM, NY, TN, WA | |
| U.S. Department of Energy Student Research Participation Program (5933) | | |
| Walton Scholarships (3787) | Study: United States | |
| WERC Undergraduate Scholarships (6113) | Study: NM | |
| Westinghouse Science Talent Search (5282) | | |
| Woods Hole Oceanographic Institution Summer Student Fellowships (6249) | Study: United States | |
| **Mathematics** | | |
| AFCEA ROTC Scholarship Program (1100) | | Military |
| Air Force ROTC Scholarships (5816) | Citizenship: US | Military |
| Call to Action Opportunity Scholarship (1568) | Citizenship: US; Legal: CA; Study: CA | |
| Cape Canaveral Chapter Scholarships (5114) | Legal: FL | Minority |

| Vocational Goal, Award, and Entry Number | Geographic Restrictions (Citizenship, Legal Residence, Place of Study) | Affiliation/Special Recipients Requirements |
|---|---|---|
| *Mathematics (continued)* | | |
| Casualty Actuarial Scholarships for Minority Students (5430) | Citizenship: US, PermRes | Minority |
| Central Intelligence Agency Undergraduate Scholars Program (1812) | Study: DC | Minority, Handicapped |
| Renate W. Chasman Scholarship (1507) | Citizenship: US, PermRes; Legal: NY | |
| CHROME Scholarship (2081) | | Association |
| Florida National Science Scholars Program (2503) | Citizenship: US; Legal: FL; Study: FL | |
| Fossil Energy Professional Internship Program (Undergrad) (5879) | | |
| Fossil Energy Technology Internship Program (5880) | | |
| Barry M. Goldwater Scholarship (2715) | Citizenship: US | |
| Logistics Education Foundation Scholarship (5463) | | |
| LPI Summer Intern Program in Planetary Science (3514) | | |
| Maryland MESA Scholarships (3586) | Legal: MD | |
| NAACP Willems Scholarship (3851) | | Minority, Association |
| National Association for the Advancement of Colored People Scholarship Program (5905) | | |
| National Center for Toxicological Research Undergraduate Program (5908) | | |
| General Emmett Paige Scholarship (1101) | Citizenship: US | |
| The Payzer Scholarship (2296) | | |
| Smithsonian Environmental Research Center Work-Learn Opportunities in Environmental Studies (5374) | Legal: United States; Study: MD | |
| Tandy Technology Scholars (5672) | | |
| U.S. Department of Energy Student Research Participation Program (5933) | | |
| U.S. Nuclear Regulatory Commission Historically Black Colleges and Universities Student Research Participation (5936) | | |
| Westinghouse Science Talent Search (5282) | | |

## Medicine

| Vocational Goal, Award, and Entry Number | Geographic Restrictions (Citizenship, Legal Residence, Place of Study) | Affiliation/Special Recipients Requirements |
|---|---|---|
| ADHF Student Research Fellowship Awards (447) | | |
| AFAR Fellowships (468) | Study: United States | |
| Allied Health Student Loans (4870) | Legal: PA; Study: PA | |
| American Foundation for Aging Research Predoctoral Awards (469) | Study: United States | |
| American Kennel Clubs Veterinary Scholarship (604) | Study: United States | |
| The Applied Social Issues Internship Program (5493) | | |
| John D. Archbold Scholarship (1073) | | |
| Armenian American Medical Association Scholarship (1106) | Citizenship: US; Study: United States | Ethnic |
| H. Fletcher Brown Scholarship (4967) | Legal: DE | |
| A & E Capelle LN Herfords Scholarship (150) | Legal: Canada | |
| Celanese Canada Inc. Scholarships (1269) | Citizenship: Canada, PermRes; Study: Canada | |
| Joan C. Chiappetta Scholarship for a Career In Practical Nursing (1856) | Legal: NY | |
| Ty Cobb Scholarships (1976) | Legal: GA | |
| Dental Assisting Scholarship Program (39) | Citizenship: US | |
| Dental Lab Tech Scholarship Program (40) | Citizenship: US | |
| Dog Writers' Educational Trust Scholarships (2264) | | Other |

| Vocational Goal, Award, and Entry Number | Geographic Restrictions (Citizenship, Legal Residence, Place of Study) | Affiliation/Special Recipients Requirements |
|---|---|---|
| *Medicine (continued)* | | |
| J. Hugh & Earle W. Fellows Memorial Fund Loans (2437) | Legal: FL | |
| Fellowship Program in Academic Medicine for Minority Students (4290) | | Minority |
| FFS-NSPB Student Fellowships (2451) | | |
| Gina Finzi Memorial Student Summer Fellowships for Research (3519) | | |
| Four-Shra-Nish Foundation Loan (2583) | Legal: OH | |
| Georgia Student Finance Commission Service-Cancellable Stafford Loan (2666) | Legal: GA; Study: GA | |
| Georgia Student Finance Commission State-Sponsored Loan (2669) | Legal: GA; Study: GA | |
| Good Samaritan Foundation Scholarship for Nursing (2717) | Study: TX | |
| HRSA-BHP Loans for Disadvantaged Students (5968) | Citizenship: US, PermRes, Other | |
| HRSA-BHP Scholarships for Disadvantaged Students (5972) | Citizenship: US, PermRes, Other | |
| IHS Health Professions Pre-Graduate Scholarships (2994) | | Native American |
| Indian Health Career Awards (4935) | | Ethnic |
| International Order of the King's Daughters and Sons Health Careers Scholarships (3169) | Citizenship: US/CA; Legal: Canada, United States; Study: Canada, United States | |
| Jamestown General Hospital Auxiliary Scholarship (1870) | Legal: NY | |
| Clem Jaunich Education Trust Scholarships (3253) | Legal: MN | |
| Sharon Kunkel Nursing Scholarship (1876) | Legal: NY | |
| S. Evelyn Lewis Memorial Scholarship in Medical Health Sciences (6306) | | |
| Minnie L. Maffett Scholarship (4466) | Legal: TX; Study: TX | |
| Maine Osteopathic Association Memorial Scholarship (3535) | Legal: ME | |
| Maine Osteopathic Association Scholarship (3536) | Legal: ME | |
| Maryland Professional Scholarship (3578) | Legal: MD; Study: MD | |
| Allen H. Meyers Scholarship (3677) | Legal: MI | |
| Ministry of the Flemish Community Fellowships (3710) | Citizenship: US, PermRes | |
| National Zoological Park Minority Traineeships (4456) | | |
| Margarete E. Nelson Scholarship (1892) | | |
| New York State Professional Opportunity Scholarships (4592) | Citizenship: US, PermRes; Legal: NY; Study: NY | |
| New York State Regents Professional Opportunity Scholarships (4577) | Legal: NY; Study: NY | |
| Nursing Scholarship Program (2512) | | Minority |
| Maurice J. Oringer Awards (224) | | |
| Parkinson's Disease Foundation Summer Fellowship (4845) | | |
| Arthur & Doreen Parrett Scholarship Fund (4848) | Legal: WA | |
| Jane Hultquist Pearson Medical Scholarship (1894) | Legal: NY | |
| Power Systems Inc./NSCA Strength and Conditioning Professional Scholarship (4417) | | Association |
| The Primary Care Resource Initiative for Missouri (PRIMO) (3755) | Legal: MO | |
| The Professional and Practical Nursing Student Loan Program (3756) | Legal: MO | |
| Spence Reese Scholarship (5089) | | |

| Vocational Goal, Award, and Entry Number | Geographic Restrictions (Citizenship, Legal Residence, Place of Study) | Affiliation/Special Recipients Requirements |
|---|---|---|
| **Medicine (continued)** | | |
| Howard Brown Rickard Scholarship (4007) | | Handicapped |
| Samsun Medical Research Institute Student Internships (5224) | | |
| Abbie Sargent Memorial Scholarships (5250) | Legal: NH | |
| Robert Schreck Memorial Fund Scholarship (5280) | Legal: TX | |
| Service Cancelable Student Loan (2660) | | |
| Society of Nuclear Medicine Student Fellowship Awards (5477) | | |
| Frances Tompkins Scholarships (2573) | | |
| Undergraduate U.S. Army Environmental Hygiene Internship Program (5929) | | |
| United Nations Educational Training Scholarships for Southern Africans (5798) | Legal: Namibia, Republic of South Africa | |
| **Military Sciences** | | |
| ADM Mike Boorda Seaman-to-Admiral Educational Assistance Program (4494) | | Military |
| Air Force ROTC Scholarships (5816) | Citizenship: US | Military |
| Falcon Foundation Scholarship (2427) | Citizenship: US | |
| North Georgia College Military Scholarship (2674) | Legal: GA; Study: GA | Military |
| Washington Crossing Foundation Scholarships (6085) | Citizenship: US | |
| **Parks and Recreation** | | |
| RCRA Internship Program (5109) | | |
| Tom and Ruth Rivers International Scholarships (6264) | | |
| **Philosophy, Theology, and Religion** | | |
| The Albert Baker Fund (1362) | | Religion |
| Eastern Star Educational and Religious Scholarship (4791) | Citizenship: US; Legal: CA; Study: CA | |
| J. Hugh & Earle W. Fellows Memorial Fund Loans (2437) | Legal: FL | |
| Fellowship of United Methodists in Worship, Music and Other Arts Scholarship (2439) | | Religion |
| Four-Shra-Nish Foundation Loan (2583) | Legal: OH | |
| Franks Foundation Loan (5832) | Legal: OR | |
| Clem Jaunich Education Trust Scholarships (3253) | Legal: MN | |
| Lois T. Larson Scholarship (1877) | | |
| Lett Scholarships (4720) | | Religion, African American |
| Ohio Baptist Education Society Scholarships (4721) | | Religion |
| Leonard M. Perryman Communications Scholarship for Ethnic Minority Students (5794) | Citizenship: US | Minority, Religion |
| Presbyterian Church Student Loans (4995) | Citizenship: US | Religion |
| Robert Schreck Memorial Fund Scholarship (5280) | Legal: TX | |
| Ullery Charitable Trust Scholarship (5765) | | |
| UMF Annual Conference Scholars Program (5796) | | Religion |
| Lillian E. Whitmore Scholarship (6173) | | |
| **Physical Sciences** | | |
| AAAS Directorate for Science & Policy Administrative Internship (264) | | |
| ACA Scholarship Award (390) | | |
| AFCEA ROTC Scholarship Program (1100) | | Military |
| AIAA Scholarship Program (568) | Citizenship: US, PermRes | Association |

| Vocational Goal, Award, and Entry Number | Geographic Restrictions (Citizenship, Legal Residence, Place of Study) | Affiliation/Special Recipients Requirements |
|---|---|---|
| *Physical Sciences (continued)* | | |
| Air Force Civilian Cooperative Work-Study Program (66) | | |
| AISES A.T. Anderson Memorial Scholarship (559) | | Native American, Association |
| Alabama Space Grant Consortium Undergraduate Fellowship Program (124) | Citizenship: US | Asian American, African American, Handicapped, Minority, Hispanic American, Native American |
| Alaska Space Grant Program Internships (139) | | |
| Robert E. Altenhofen Memorial Scholarship (963) | | Association |
| AMS/Industry Minority Scholarships (702) | | Minority, Hispanic American, Native American, African American |
| AMS/Industry Undergraduate Scholarship (703) | Citizenship: US, PermRes | |
| AMS Undergraduate Scholarship (704) | | |
| ANS Environmental Sciences Division Scholarship (720) | Citizenship: US, PermRes | |
| ANS Fuel Cycle and Waste Management Scholarship (721) | Citizenship: US, PermRes | |
| ANS Nuclear Operations Division Scholarship (723) | Citizenship: US, PermRes | |
| ANS Power Division Scholarship (724) | Citizenship: US, PermRes | |
| ANS Undergraduate Scholarships (725) | Citizenship: US, PermRes | |
| APEGGA Entrance Scholarships (1254) | Study: AB | |
| ASM Foundation Scholarship (1184) | Citizenship: US/CA | |
| ASM Outstanding Scholars (1185) | Citizenship: US/CA | |
| AT & T Bell Laboratories Summer Research Program for Minorities & Women (1305) | Citizenship: US, PermRes; Study: NJ | African American, Hispanic American, Native American |
| AT & T Bell Laboratories University Relations Summer Program (1306) | | |
| AWU Student Research Fellowships (1203) | Citizenship: US, PermRes; Study: CA, CO, ID, MT, ND, NM, NV, OK, UT, WA, WY | |
| BPW Career Advancement Scholarships (1546) | Citizenship: US; Study: United States | |
| Brown-NASA Space Grant Scholars Program (5124) | | |
| H. Fletcher Brown Scholarship (4967) | Legal: DE | |
| Call to Action Opportunity Scholarship (1568) | Citizenship: US; Legal: CA; Study: CA | |
| Canadian Society of Exploration Geophysicists Scholarships (1699) | Study: Canada | |
| Cape Canaveral Chapter Scholarships (5114) | Legal: FL | Minority |
| Celanese Canada Inc. Scholarships (1269) | Citizenship: Canada, PermRes; Study: Canada | |
| Central Intelligence Agency Undergraduate Scholars Program (1812) | Study: DC | Minority, Handicapped |
| CERT Scholarship (2100) | Study: United States | Native American |
| Renate W. Chasman Scholarship (1507) | Citizenship: US, PermRes; Legal: NY | |
| CHROME Scholarship (2081) | | Association |
| Corporate Sponsored Scholarships for Minority Undergraduate Physics Majors (772) | Citizenship: US | African American, Hispanic American, Native American |
| Violet Cressey-Marcks Fisher Travel Fellowship (5192) | Legal: England | |
| Raymond Davis Scholarship (5461) | | |
| Delaware NASA Space Grant Undergraduate Tuition Scholarships (2203) | Citizenship: US | |
| Delayed Education for Women Scholarship (728) | Citizenship: US; Study: United States | |
| Joseph R. Dietrich Scholarships (729) | Citizenship: US, PermRes | |
| DOE Student Research Participation (4705) | Citizenship: US, PermRes | |
| Joseph F. Dracup Scholarship Award (392) | | |
| Thomas Edison/Max McGraw Scholarship (4379) | | |

| Vocational Goal, Award, and Entry Number | Geographic Restrictions (Citizenship, Legal Residence, Place of Study) | Affiliation/Special Recipients Requirements |
|---|---|---|
| *Physical Sciences (continued)* | | |
| Electronic Industries Foundation Scholarships (2370) | Citizenship: US | Handicapped |
| Gladys Anderson Emerson Scholarships (3215) | | Fraternal |
| Environmental Restoration/Waste Management Technical Degree Scholarship Program (5871) | | |
| Federal Cartridge Company Scholarship (4074) | | Association |
| Field Museum of Natural History Undergraduate Internships (2445) | Study: IL | |
| Florida National Science Scholars Program (2503) | Citizenship: US; Legal: FL; Study: FL | |
| Donald W. Fogarty International Student Paper Competition (1052) | | |
| Donald W. Fogarty International Student Paper Competition (2539) | | |
| Fossil Energy Professional Internship Program (Undergrad) (5879) | | |
| Fossil Energy Technology Internship Program (5880) | | |
| Georgia Space Grant Consortium Fellowships (2655) | | |
| GITA (2705) | | |
| Barry M. Goldwater Scholarship (2715) | Citizenship: US | |
| N.J. Grant Scholarship (1186) | Citizenship: US/CA | |
| Howard H. Hanks, Jr. Scholarship in Meteorology (705) | | |
| Historically Black Colleges and Universities Faculty and Student Research Participation Program in Fusion. (5890) | | |
| Historically Black Colleges and Universities Fossil Energy Faculty and Student Research Training (5891) | | |
| Historically Black Colleges and Universities Nuclear Energy Training Program (Undergrad) (5895) | | |
| International Desalination Association Scholarship (3148) | | |
| Iota Sigma Pi Undergraduate Awards for Excellence in Chemistry (3217) | | |
| Samuel C. Kraus, Jr. Memorial Scholarship (4412) | | Other |
| Paul H. Kutschenreuter Scholarship (706) | Citizenship: US, PermRes | |
| John R. Lamarsh Scholarship (731) | Citizenship: US, PermRes; Study: United States | |
| John and Muriel Landis Scholarships (732) | Study: United States | |
| LPI Summer Intern Program in Planetary Science (3514) | | |
| Father James B. Macelwane Annual Awards (707) | Citizenship: US, PermRes | |
| Maryland MESA Scholarships (3586) | Legal: MD | |
| Masonic-Range Science Scholarship (5500) | | |
| Allen H. Meyers Scholarship (3677) | Legal: MI | |
| Miami University Pulp and Paper Foundation Scholarships (5029) | Study: OH | |
| Minority Geoscience Scholarships (508) | Citizenship: US; Study: United States | African American, Hispanic American, Native American |
| Minority Students Hazardous Materials Management Training Program (5904) | | Minority |
| Montana Space Grant Consortium Scholarship-Fellowship Program (3771) | | |
| MSA Presidential Student Awards (3696) | Legal: United States | |
| MSA Undergraduate Research Scholarships (3697) | | |

| Vocational Goal, Award, and Entry Number | Geographic Restrictions (Citizenship, Legal Residence, Place of Study) | Affiliation/Special Recipients Requirements |
|---|---|---|
| *Physical Sciences (continued)* | | |
| NASA/DESGC Undergraduate Summer Scholarships (2205) | Citizenship: US | |
| National Oceanic and Atmospheric Administration/Historically Black Colleges and Universities Faculty/Student Research Participation Program (5910) | | |
| NRAO Summer Student Research Assistantships (4352) | Citizenship: US; Study: United States | |
| Oak Ridge National Laboratory Professional Internship Program (Undergrad) (5919) | | |
| Howard T. Orville Scholarship in Meteorology (708) | | |
| General Emmett Paige Scholarship (1101) | Citizenship: US | |
| The Payzer Scholarship (2296) | | |
| Tibor T. Polgar Fellowships (2914) | Study: NY | |
| Al Qoyawayma Award (561) | | Native American |
| Research Science Institute Internship (5103) | | |
| Howard Brown Rickard Scholarship (4007) | | Handicapped |
| G.A. Roberts Scholarship (1187) | Citizenship: US/CA | |
| Rocky Mountain Coal Mining Institute Scholarships (5157) | Citizenship: US; Legal: AZ, CO, MT, ND, NM, TX, UT, WY | |
| Santa Fe Pacific Foundation Scholarships (563) | Legal: AZ, CA, CO, KS, NM, OK | Association, Native American |
| Savannah River Technology Center Professional Internship Program (Undergrad) (5925) | | |
| The Schonstedt Scholarship in Surveying (393) | | |
| Robert Schreck Memorial Fund Scholarship (5280) | Legal: TX | |
| Seaspace Scholarship (5293) | Study: United States | |
| SEG Scholarships (5300) | Study: United States | |
| Marie Selby Internships (5304) | Study: FL | |
| SHPE Foundation Education Grant (5454) | | |
| Sigma Xi Grants-in-Aid of Research (5347) | | |
| Smithsonian Environmental Research Center Work-Learn Opportunities in Environmental Studies (5374) | Legal: United States; Study: MD | |
| Society of Physics Students Scholarships (5482) | | Association |
| Space Grant Undergraduate Scholar Program (5126) | | |
| Space Grant Undergraduate Summer Scholar Program (5127) | | |
| Space Scholars Program (3589) | | |
| SPIE Educational Scholarships and Grants in Optical Engineering (5589) | | |
| Tandy Technology Scholars (5672) | | |
| Tennessee Space Grant Consortium Fellowships and Scholarships (5698) | Citizenship: US; Study: TN | |
| TSGC Fellowship and Scholarship (5719) | | |
| Undergraduate NASA Space Grant Fellowship (6143) | Citizenship: US; Legal: WV | |
| Undergraduate Student Assistantships and Scholarships (5562) | | |
| Undergraduate U.S. Army Environmental Hygiene Internship Program (5929) | | |
| U.S. Department of Energy Internship (4711) | Citizenship: US, PermRes; Study: CA, IL, NM, NY, TN, WA | |
| U.S. Department of Energy Student Research Participation Program (5933) | | |

| Vocational Goal, Award, and Entry Number | Geographic Restrictions (Citizenship, Legal Residence, Place of Study) | Affiliation/Special Recipients Requirements |
|---|---|---|
| *Physical Sciences (continued)* | | |
| U.S. Nuclear Regulatory Commission Historically Black Colleges and Universities Student Research Participation (5936) | | |
| The University of Arizona/NASA Space Grant Undergraduate Research Internship Program (1087) | Citizenship: US | |
| James R. Vogt Scholarship (734) | Citizenship: US, PermRes | |
| Washington Pulp & Paper Foundation Scholarships (6097) | Study: WA | |
| West Virginia Space Grant Consortium Undergraduate Scholarship Program (6145) | Citizenship: US; Legal: WV | |
| Westinghouse Science Talent Search (5282) | | |
| The Wild Leitz Surveying Scholarship (394) | Citizenship: US | |
| Wisconsin Space Grant Consortium Undergraduate Research Awards (6215) | Citizenship: US | |
| Wisconsin Space Grant Consortium Undergraduate Scholarships (6216) | Citizenship: US | |
| Woods Hole Oceanographic Institution Summer Student Fellowships (6249) | Study: United States | |

## Protective Services and Public Affairs

| | | |
|---|---|---|
| ATF Special Agents' Scholarships (5841) | | |
| Call to Action Opportunity Scholarship (1568) | Citizenship: US; Legal: CA; Study: CA | |
| Alphonso Deal Scholarship Award (3912) | Citizenship: US | African American |
| Government Scholars Summer Program (4562) | Study: NY, United States | |
| Law Enforcement Career Scholarships (1238) | | |
| Law Enforcement Explorer Scholarships (5853) | | Other |
| Hatton Lovejoy Scholarship Plan (1586) | Legal: GA | |
| Maryland Reimbursement of Firefighters and Rescue Squad Members (3579) | Legal: MD; Study: MD | Employer, Other |
| Michael Murphy Memorial Scholarship Loans (132) | Legal: AK | |
| New York State Professional Opportunity Scholarships (4592) | Citizenship: US, PermRes; Legal: NY; Study: NY | |
| Public Interest Internships (1803) | Study: United States | |
| Robert C. Thomas Memorial Scholarship (133) | | |
| David A. Winston Fellowship (1290) | Study: DC | |

## Social Sciences

| | | |
|---|---|---|
| ABF Summer Research Fellowships in Law and Social Science for Minority Undergraduate Students (352) | Citizenship: US, PermRes; Study: IL | African American, Native American, Hispanic American |
| American Society of Crime Laboratory Scholarship Award (916) | | |
| APA Planning & the Black Community Division Scholarship (775) | | African American, Native American, Hispanic American |
| ASC Gene Carte Student Paper Competition (918) | | |
| Canadian Soroptimist Grants for Women (5539) | Citizenship: Canada, PermRes; Study: Canada | |
| Central Intelligence Agency Undergraduate Scholars Program (1812) | Study: DC | Minority, Handicapped |
| Geraldine Clewell Scholarship (4913) | | Fraternal |
| Closs/Parnitzke/Clarke Scholarship (4914) | | Fraternal |
| Monica Cole Research Grant (5191) | Legal: England | |
| Cox Minority Journalism Scholarship (2131) | Legal: GA; Study: GA | Minority |
| Minda de Gunzburg Center for European Studies Undergraduate Summer Travel Grants (2771) | | Other |
| Federated Women's Institutes of Ontario International Scholarship (1648) | Study: ON, Canada | |
| Rabbi Robert Feinberg Scholarship (4223) | | |

| Vocational Goal, Award, and Entry Number | Geographic Restrictions (Citizenship, Legal Residence, Place of Study) | Affiliation/Special Recipients Requirements |
|---|---|---|
| *Social Sciences (continued)* | | |
| Fellowships in Byzantine Studies, Pre-Columbian Studies and Landscape Architecture (2288) | Study: DC | |
| The Feminist Majority Internships (2441) | | |
| Garikian University Scholarship Fund (1119) | | Ethnic |
| Eileen J. Garrett Scholarship (4832) | | |
| E. Urner Goodman Professional Scouter Scholarship (1466) | | Association |
| Grand Army of the Republic Memorial Scholarship (1347) | | Veteran |
| Enid Hall Griswold Memorial Scholarship (4397) | Citizenship: US; Study: United States | |
| Jennifer C. Groot Fellowship (869) | Citizenship: US, Canada | |
| Tommie J. Hamner Scholarship (4920) | | Fraternal |
| Bryce Harlow Institute on Business and Government Affairs Internship (3020) | | |
| Lullelia W. Harrison Scholarship in Counseling (6304) | | |
| Wilma Hoyal/Maxine Chilton Scholarships (614) | Citizenship: US; Legal: AZ; Study: AZ | |
| IHS Excellence in Liberty Prizes (3055) | | |
| Institute on Political Journalism Summer Program (3021) | | |
| Treva C. Kintner Scholarships (4921) | | Fraternal |
| Leo J. Krysa Family Foundation Undergraduate Scholarship (1660) | Citizenship: Canada; Study: Canada | |
| Ottis Lock Endowment Scholarships (2306) | Study: TX | |
| Margaret Jerome Sampson Scholarships (4922) | | Fraternal |
| Marine Corps Historical Center College Internships (3556) | Study: DC, VA | |
| Assunta Lucchetti Martino Scholarship for International Studies (4240) | | |
| Ministry of the Flemish Community Fellowships (3710) | Citizenship: US, PermRes | |
| National Council for Geographic Education Committee for Women in Geographic Education Scholarship (3955) | | |
| Ida L., Mary L., and Ervin R. NePage Foundation (4513) | Legal: WA; Study: WA | |
| New York State Assembly Session Internships (4575) | Legal: NY; Study: NY | |
| New York State Professional Opportunity Scholarships (4592) | Citizenship: US, PermRes; Legal: NY; Study: NY | |
| New York State Regents Professional Opportunity Scholarships (4577) | Legal: NY; Study: NY | |
| NSDAR American History Scholarship (4402) | Citizenship: US | |
| Margaret E. Olson Memorial Scholarship (1893) | Legal: NY | |
| Public Employees Roundtable Public Service Scholarships (5017) | | |
| Spence Reese Scholarship (5089) | | |
| Rhode Island Commission on State Government Summer Internships (5122) | Legal: RI | |
| Edith Nourse Rogers Scholarship Fund (6230) | Study: MA | Veteran |
| Lillian P. Schoephoerster Scholarship (4924) | | Fraternal |
| Silver Dart Aviation History Award (1607) | Legal: Canada | |
| George Tanaka Memorial Scholarship Program (1288) | Citizenship: Canada, PermRes; Study: Canada | |
| Truman Scholarships (5752) | Citizenship: US | |

| Vocational Goal, Award, and Entry Number | Geographic Restrictions (Citizenship, Legal Residence, Place of Study) | Affiliation/Special Recipients Requirements |
|---|---|---|
| **Social Sciences (continued)** | | |
| United Nations Educational Training Scholarships for Southern Africans (5798) | Legal: Namibia, Republic of South Africa | |
| U.S. Department of Energy Student Research Participation Program (5933) | | |
| U.S. Marine Corps Historical Center College Internships (5945) | | |
| Washington Crossing Foundation Scholarships (6085) | Citizenship: US | |
| Muddy Waters Scholarship (1448) | Study: IL | |
| Mary Welking Franken Scholarship (4926) | | Fraternal |
| Jesse Wrench Scholarship (3748) | Study: MO | |
| Xerox Scholarships (6272) | | |
| **Visual and Performing Arts** | | |
| Academy of Motion Picture Arts and Sciences Student Academy Awards (22) | | |
| Thomas Joseph "Willie" Ambrosole Scholarship (4207) | Legal: NJ, NY | |
| American Watercolor Society Scholarship Award (1022) | | |
| Gladys C. Anderson Scholarship (478) | Citizenship: US | Handicapped |
| Armenian Allied Arts Association Scholarship (1104) | | Ethnic |
| Arts Recognition and Talent Search (ARTS) (4158) | Citizenship: US, PermRes | |
| Associated Board of the Royal Schools of Music International Scholarships (1191) | | |
| Associated Male Choruses of America Scholarship (1195) | | |
| Ralph Brewster Vocal Scholarship/Jack Pullen Memorial Scholarship (3705) | | |
| Canadian Printing Industries Scholarships (1694) | Study: Canada | |
| Hanna Carola Art Scholarship (1853) | | |
| Constance E. Casey Scholarship (1854) | Study: NY | |
| Central Intelligence Agency Undergraduate Scholars Program (1812) | Study: DC | Minority, Handicapped |
| CFGP Radio Station Scholarships (8) | Legal: AB | |
| Chancellor's Talent Award Program (1828) | Legal: MA | |
| Chautauqua Institution Scholarship (1842) | | |
| The Cleveland Institute of Art Portfolio Scholarships (1966) | Study: OH | |
| The Cloisters Summer Internship Program for College Students (3653) | | |
| Consortium College University Media Centers Annual Research Grants (2065) | Legal: United States | |
| Emily Harrington Crane Scholarship (1859) | Legal: NY | |
| Dorchester Woman's Club Scholarships (2635) | Legal: MA | |
| Pauly D'Orlando Memorial Art Scholarship (5781) | | Religion |
| Fellowship of United Methodists in Worship, Music and Other Arts Scholarship (2439) | | Religion |
| Cesare Fera Memorial Scholarship (4224) | | |
| Sergio Franchi Music Scholarship in Voice Performance (4225) | | Ethnic |
| Garikian University Scholarship Fund (1119) | | Ethnic |
| GFWC of MA Art Scholarships (2636) | Legal: MA | |
| GFWC of MA Music Scholarships (2640) | Legal: MA | |
| R.L. Gillette Scholarship (482) | Citizenship: US | Handicapped |
| Roswell L. Gilpatric Internship (3655) | | |

| Vocational Goal, Award, and Entry Number | Geographic Restrictions (Citizenship, Legal Residence, Place of Study) | Affiliation/Special Recipients Requirements |
|---|---|---|
| **Visual and Performing Arts (continued)** | | |
| Gravure Education Foundation Cooperative Education Grant (2745) | | Other |
| The Elizabeth Greenshields Grant (2751) | | |
| Frances Hook Scholarship (2886) | | |
| Hungarian Arts Club Scholarships (2935) | | Ethnic |
| Independent and Student Filmmakers Competition (1436) | | African American |
| Interlochen Arts Academy and Arts Camp Scholarships (3101) | Study: MI | |
| Jacob's Pillow Dance Festival Internships (3234) | Study: United States | |
| Peter Krueger Summer Internships (5384) | Study: NY | |
| Lois T. Larson Scholarship (1877) | | |
| Florence Lemke Memorial Scholarships in Fine Arts (639) | Legal: WA | Veteran |
| William J. Mariner Working Scholar Program (5100) | Study: NY | |
| Elizabeth Warner Marvin Music Scholarship (1880) | | |
| Theodore Mazza Scholarship (5769) | | |
| Metropolitan Museum of Art Nine-Month Internship (3661) | Citizenship: US; Study: NY | Minority |
| Metropolitan Museum of Art Six Month Internship (3662) | | |
| Metropolitan Museum of Art Summer Internship for College Students (3663) | | |
| Metropolitan Museum of Art Volunteer Internships (3665) | | |
| Glenn Miller Birthplace Society Instrumental Scholarships (3706) | | |
| Ministry of the Flemish Community Fellowships (3710) | Citizenship: US, PermRes | |
| Vincent Minnelli Scholarship (4242) | Legal: CA | |
| Rae Mitsuoka Photography Scholarships (6092) | | |
| Montreal International Music Prizes (3773) | | |
| Mozart Club Music Scholarship (1890) | Legal: NY | |
| Pillsbury Music Scholarship (2410) | Legal: CA | |
| National Alliance for Excellence Honored Scholars Awards (3841) | Citizenship: US; Study: United States | |
| National Museum of American Art Summer Internships (5388) | Study: NY | |
| National Orchestral Institute Scholarships (4330) | Study: United States | |
| National Zoological Park Traineeship in Zoo Photography (4464) | | |
| Nerone/NIAF Matching Art Scholarship (4244) | | |
| Stanley Paul/Raelene Mittelman Fashion Design Scholarship Fund (1058) | | |
| Pavarotti Scholarship (4252) | | Ethnic |
| Al Qoyawayma Award (561) | | Native American |
| Minna Kaufmann Ruud Scholarship (1840) | | |
| Louis J. Salerno, M.D. Memorial Scholarship (4257) | | |
| Nina Santavicca Scholarship (4259) | | |
| Kathryn G. Siphers Scholarships (6218) | | |
| Ida Speyrer Stahl Scholarships (1725) | Legal: NY; Study: NY | Ethnic |
| Marion Barr Stanfield Art Scholarship (5784) | | Religion |
| Anne Bradshaw Stokes Foundation Scholarships (5632) | Citizenship: US; Study: TX | |

| Vocational Goal, Award, and Entry Number | Geographic Restrictions (Citizenship, Legal Residence, Place of Study) | Affiliation/Special Recipients Requirements |
|---|---|---|
| *Visual and Performing Arts (continued)* | | |
| George Tanaka Memorial Scholarship Program (1288) | Citizenship: Canada, PermRes; Study: Canada | |
| TELACU Arts Award (5689) | Legal: CA; Study: CA | Minority |
| Robert Thunen Memorial Educational Scholarships (2983) | Study: CA, NV, OR, WA | |
| University Film and Video Association Student Grants (5992) | | |
| Virginia Volkwein Memorial Scholarships (6219) | | |
| Muddy Waters Scholarship (1448) | Study: IL | |
| World of Expression Scholarship Program (1420) | Legal: NY | |
| Young Feminist Scholarship Program (5591) | | |

# Sponsors and Their Scholarships

## • 1 •

**37th Division Veterans Association**
83 E. Mound St., Ste. 103
Columbus, OH 43215-5420          *Ph:* (614)228-3788

### • 2 • 37th Infantry Division Award *(Undergraduate/ Award)*

**Qualif.:** Applicants must be a son or daughter of a 37th Infantry Division veteran who served in World War I, World War II, or the Korean Conflict. Applicants may be seniors in high school, enrolled in a college program or enrolled in a fully accredited, state-approved trade school.

**Funds Avail.:** Two awards of not less than $500 are given annually. **To Apply:** Candidates must complete and return application form and supply a transcript of the senior year of high school. ACT, SAT, or comparable test score is required. The company or regiment of the father must be furnished when requesting an application. **Deadline:** April 1. **Contact:** The 37th Division Veterans Association at the above address (see entry 1).

## • 3 •

**50 Men and Women of Toledo, Inc.**
4201 Stickney Ave.
PO Box 3357          *Ph:* (419)729-4654
Toledo, OH 43608-2016          *Fax:* (419)729-4004

### • 4 • Fifty Men and Women of Toledo Scholarships *(Undergraduate/Scholarship)*

**Focus:** General studies. **Qualif.:** Applicants must be minority students attending school in the Toledo, Ohio area. **No. of Awards:** 6. **To Apply:** Write or call for further details. **Deadline:** March 1. **Contact:** Fifty Men and Women of Toledo at the above address (see entry 3).

## • 5 •

**102nd Infantry Division Association**
821 Shackleford Rd.
Nashville, TN 37215          *Ph:* (615)292-2469

### • 6 • 102nd Infantry Division Scholarship *(All/ Scholarship)*

**Qualif.:** Applicant must be a child or grandchild of a member of the 102nd Infantry Div. who is an active member of the association (or active at time of death). **No. of Awards:** 14. **Deadline:** May 15. **Contact:** Scholarship department.

## • 7 •

**97.7 Sun FM**
Scholarship Awards
200 Windsor Ct.
9835-101 Ave.          *Ph:* (780)539-9700
Grande Prairie, AB, Canada T8V 5V4          *Fax:* (780)532-1600
*E-mail:* sunfm@ccinet.ab.ca
*URL:* http://www.97.7sufm.com

### • 8 • CFGP Radio Station Scholarships *(Undergraduate/Scholarship)*

**Purpose:** To help students further their skills and expertise in music or performing arts through full-time or short course study at an institution of their choice. **Qualif.:** Applicants must be students attending school in the city or county of Grande Prairie who have demonstrated outstanding talent in the areas of music or drama.

**Funds Avail.:** Varies. **To Apply:** All applications should be marked confidential upon submission. **Deadline:** April 28. **Contact:** Scholarship Awards, CFGP Radio, at the above address (see entry 7).

## • 9 •

**AAB Associate Member Section**
917 Locust St., Ste. 1100          *Ph:* (314)241-1445
St. Louis, MO 63101-1413          *Fax:* (314)241-1449
*E-mail:* aab1445@primary.net
*URL:* http://www.aab.org

### • 10 • David Birenbaum Scholarship Fund of the AAB Associate Member Section *(Graduate, Undergraduate/Scholarship)*

**Purpose:** To help members and their children further their education. **Focus:** General Studies. **Qualif.:** Applicants must be AAB Associate members in good standing, their spouse or their children. They must also be graduates of an accredited high school or its equivalent. **Criteria:** Applications are reviewed by an Honorary Awards and Scholarship Committee. Candidates are evaluated on scholastic ability, financial need, and community involvement.

**Funds Avail.:** Award amounts vary. **No. of Awards:** 2-3. **To Apply:** A completed application and a black and white photo must be submitted. Students who are currently enrolled in high school may apply and submit a partial transcript of their high school credits. All other applicants must submit a complete transcript of credits from high school, college or other school attended, as well as two character references. **Deadline:** April 1. **Contact:** LeAnn M. Hampton at the above address (see entry 9).

## AAFRC Trust for Philanthropy
23 W. 43rd St.                          *Ph:* (212)354-5799
New York, NY 10036-7406                 *Fax:* (212)768-1795

#### • 12 •  John Grenzebach Awards for Outstanding Research in Philanthropy for Education *(Doctorate, Postdoctorate/Award)*

**Purpose:** To broaden the dissemination of outstanding works in the scholarly analysis of fund raising, and to encourage even more improvement in the quality of educational philanthropic scholarly exploration.

**Funds Avail.:** Awards of $2,000 each are given to an author of an outstanding dissertation and an author of an outstanding published scholarly work. In addition, recipients will receive funds for travel and lodging for the CASE Annual Assembly in Washington, D.C. for award presentation. Selections from the works of winning authors are printed in Trust and Council for Advancement and Support of Education (CASE) publications. **No. of Awards:** 2 awards are available. **To Apply:** For the Outstanding Doctoral Dissertation Award, applicants must submit a letter from a faculty member outlining the applicant's contribution to the field; a curriculum vitae; five copies of an abstract; and one full copy of the dissertation. For the Outstanding Published Scholarship Award, applicants must submit five copies of the published work and their curriculum vitae. **Deadline:** February 28.

**Remarks:** The program is cosponsored by Council for Advancement and Support of Education (CASE) and is named in honor of the late John Grenzebach, founding chairman of Grenzebach and Associates, Inc., development consultants to educational institutions. **Contact:** Paul Chewning, CASE, Ste. 400, 11 Dupont Circle, Washington, D.C., 20036-1261. Telephone: (202)328-5985.

## Clara Abbott Foundation
c/o Executive Dir.
200 Abbott Park Rd.                     *Ph:* (847)937-1090
D579, Bldg. AMJ37                       *Fax:* (847)938-6511
Abbott Park, IL 60064                   *Free:* 800-972-3859
*E-mail:* barry.wojtak@ln.ssw.abbott.com

#### • 14 •  Clara Abbott Foundation Scholarships *(Undergraduate/Scholarship)*

**Purpose:** To help students fund a college education. **Focus:** General Studies. **Qualif.:** Applicants must be sons, daughters, or dependents of current or retired employees of Abbott Laboratories. They must also be full-time students between the ages of 17 and 29. **Criteria:** Selection is based on financial need and academic record.

**Funds Avail.:** Awards may total a maximum of $13,000 each. **No. of Awards:** A maximum of 5. **To Apply:** A completed application must be submitted. **Deadline:** March 15. **Contact:** Barry Wojtak at the above address (see entry 13).

## ABC/CEF
Atten: College Relations Mgr.
1300 N. 17th St., No. 800               *Ph:* (703)812-2010
Rosslyn, VA 22209                       *Fax:* (703)812-8235
*E-mail:* deanna@abc.org
*URL:* http://www.abc.org/student

*The Construction Education Foundation is the education arm of the Associated Builders and Contractors. It promotes the merit shop philosophy through education, research, and training. It was formerly known as the Merit Shop Foundation.*

#### • 16 •  Construction Education Foundation Scholarship Awards *(Undergraduate/Scholarship)*

**Purpose:** To ensure that this generation and future generations of construction managers and craftsmen can tackle even the largest technical or manpower problem. **Focus:** Construction Management. **Qualif.:** Candidates must be currently enrolled students who have successfully completed at least one year in a baccalaureate degree program in construction (other than a design discipline). Students enrolled in a two-year college construction degree program may be eligible in the event that an award has been designated for that specific school. If the college or university has an ABC Student Chapter, the student must be an active member of that chapter. **Criteria:** Scholarships are awarded on the basis of academic performance, extracurricular activities, employment experience, and financial need.

**Funds Avail.:** Varies. **To Apply:** Applications for the scholarship competition are available on January 1 of each year. **Deadline:** June 1. **Contact:** DeAnna McCray, College Relations, at the above address (see entry 15).

## Academy of Model Aeronautics
Education Coordinator
5151 E. Memorial Dr.                    *Ph:* (765)287-1256
Muncie, IN 47302                        *Fax:* (765)289-4248
*E-mail:* mvojslav@modelaircraft.org
*URL:* http://www.modelaircraft.org

#### • 18 •  AMA/Charles H. Grant Scholarship *(Undergraduate/Scholarship)*

**Qualif.:** Any current AMA member is eligible, providing they have been a member for at least three years, they are to graduate from high school in the year the award will be granted, and they are enrolled in a college or university certificate or degree program. **Criteria:** Based upon AMA modeling activities, scholastic achievement (class rank, grades, test scores), and citizenship achievement. An exceptionally high rating in all categories may result in the maximum amount of the scholarship.

**Funds Avail.:** A total of $20,000 is available. **To Apply:** Available from the Academy.

#### • 19 •  Tom Hutchinson Memorial Scholarship *(Undergraduate/Scholarship)*

**Qualif.:** Any current AMA member is eligible, providing they have been a member for three years, are to graduate in the same year the award will be given, and are enrolled in a college or university certificate or degree program. **Criteria:** The scholarship is based entirely on Free Flight modeling activity.

**Funds Avail.:** A total of $20,000 is given by the academy to various recipients. **Deadline:** April 30.

## • 20 • Sig Memorial Scholarship (Undergraduate/ Scholarship)

**Qualif.:** Any current AMA member is eligible, providing they have been a member for three years, they are to graduate from high school in the same year the award is to be given, and are enrolled in a college or university certificate or degree program. **Criteria:** Based upon modeling performance and financial need. Grades are not a determining factor.

**Funds Avail.:** A total of $20,000 is given by the academy yearly. **To Apply:** Applicants must submit a one page statement concerning personal need for financial assistance. **Deadline:** April 30.

## 21 •

## :ademy of Motion Picture Arts and Sciences - :ademy Foundation

49 Wilshire Blvd.      *Ph:* (310)247-3000
verly Hills, CA 90211-1972      *Fax:* (310)859-9619
*mail:* ampas@oscars.org
RL: http://ampas.org/academy/nichollindex.html

## • 22 • Academy of Motion Picture Arts and Sciences Student Academy Awards (Graduate, Undergraduate/Award, Internship)

**Purpose:** To support and encourage film makers with no previous professional experience who are enrolled in accredited colleges and universities. **Focus:** Film **Qualif.:** Films must have been made in a student-teacher relationship within the curricular structure of an accredited U.S. college, university, film school, or art school. Prizes are awarded in the animation, documentary, narrative, and alternative disciplines. Advertising films, promotional films, and films previously submitted for Academy Award consideration are not eligible. All regional finalist films in the narrative category automatically become eligible for the Directors Guild of America Student Film Award. The American Society of Cinematography Award gives an award to a cinematographer chosen from the finalist films (animated film excerpts). **Criteria:** Selection is made on the basis of resourcefulness, originality, entertainment, and production quality, with regard to cost of production or subject matter.

**Funds Avail.:** Gold ($2,000), Silver ($1,500), and Bronze ($1,000) awards are given in each of four categories. The winner of the Directors Guild of America Student Film Award receives $1,000 cash, a directing internship of up to 13 weeks on a feature motion picture, a stipend for living expenses, and a travel allowance. American Society of Cinematographers awardee receives $1,000 cash and paid trip to Los Angeles for awards week. **To Apply:** Films and entry forms must be submitted to the region where the educational institution at which the film was made is located. No entry may be longer than 60 minutes and must be composite in 16mm gauge or larger, with optical or magnetic sound. Entry forms must list the person or persons (no more than two) responsible for the creative production of the picture. Rules and entries can be accessed at: www.oscars.org/saa. In the event of two winners, cash awards will be divided. **Deadline:** All entries must be received, not postmarked, on or before midnight, April 3.

**Remarks:** This is not a fellowship or loan or scholarship. Please send stamped self-addressed business-sized envelope to Student Academy Awards to receive entry form. **Contact:** Richard Miller, Awards Administrator, at the above address;(see entry 21) or rmiller@oscars.org.

## • 23 • Don and Gee Nicholl Fellowships in Screenwriting (Postgraduate/Fellowship)

**Purpose:** To support the development of the art of screen writing. **Focus:** screen writing. **Qualif.:** Candidate may be of any nationality. Applicant must not have earned money as a screenwriter for theatrical films or television, or sold or optioned screen or television rights to any original story, treatment, screenplay, or teleplay. The fellowship is tenable anywhere, and supports screen writing only. Funds are not available for scholarships or the completion of degree requirements. **Criteria:** Screen writing talent as judged by entrant's feature script submission.

**Funds Avail.:** $25,000. **No. of Awards:** Up to 5. **To Apply:** Send stamped, self-addressed, business-sized envelope to Nicholl Fellowships to receive application form. Submit form with a copy of a feature screenplay (100-130 pages), and entry fee ($30). A downloadable application is available on the society's web page. **Deadline:** May 1. Recipients are notified in mid-October. **Contact:** The organization at the above address (see entry 21).

## • 24 •

## Academy of Natural Sciences of Philadelphia

1900 Benjamin Franklin Pkwy.      *Ph:* (215)299-1000
Philadelphia, PA 19103-1195      *Fax:* (215)299-1028
*E-mail:* Schuyler@say.acnatsci.org

## • 25 • Conchologists of America Grants (Graduate/ Grant)

**Purpose:** To assist qualified students with research projects dealing with mollusks. **Focus:** Biology, Geology. **Qualif.:** Applicants must be in good standing and undertaking research under the supervision of a professor of biology or geology. **Criteria:** Selection is based upon the worthiness of the research project.

**Funds Avail.:** Approximately $9,000. Awards rarely exceed $10,000. **No. of Awards:** 15-20. **To Apply:** Student should outline project, project expenses, and submit a letter of recommendation. **Deadline:** May 1.

**Remarks:** There are usually 40-60 applicants each year. **Contact:** Dr. Rosenberg, Chairman of Grants, at the above address (see entry 24).

## • 26 • Jessup and McHenry Awards (Doctorate, Postdoctorate/Award)

**Purpose:** To assist graduate students and recent recipients of the Ph.D. to conduct research at the Academy. **Focus:** Botany. **Qualif.:** Applicant may be of any nationality. Candidate must be either a predoctoral student or a postdoctoral scholar who received his/her degree within the past several years. Individuals already living within the Philadelphia area are ineligible. Awards are tenable at the Academy. Awardees work under the supervision or sponsorship of a member of the curatorial staff; therefore, proposed research must be in a specialty in which the curators have expertise. Research should also result in a publishable report. Award recipients must give a seminar at the Academy. **Criteria:** Applicants are judged on quality of proposal and academic credentials.

**Funds Avail.:** $250/week, plus $500 travel allowance. $500 for North American, Mexican, and Caribbean applicants. $1,000 for applicants from elsewhere. **To Apply:** Write to the Academy for a listing of curators and their specialties. After arranging for a curator to sponsor the proposed project, write to the chair of the Awards Committee for application form and guidelines. Submit form with three letters of recommendation, including one from the Academy sponsor. **Deadline:** March 1, October 1. Notification by April 1, November 1. **Contact:** Dr. A. E. Schuyler, Jessup-McHenry Fund Committee Chair, at the above address (see entry 24).

---

**• 27 •**

## Academy of Vocal Arts
1920 Spruce St.                             *Ph:* (215)735-1685
Philadelphia, PA 19103-6685          *Fax:* (215)732-2189
*URL:* http://sevenarts.voicenet.com/bef_vocal.html

**• 28 •   Academy of Vocal Arts Scholarships**
*(Professional Development/Scholarship)*

**Purpose:** To enable young people to undertake vocal training at the Academy. **Focus:** Voice. **Qualif.:** Candidate may be of any nationality. Applicant must be a vocalist with operatic career potential who has a bachelor's degree in any discipline. Preference is given to candidates with master's degrees. Female applicants must be under the age of 28 years; male applicants must be 30 years or younger. Previous operatic experience is required. Scholarships are tenable at the Academy. Scholars are selected on the basis of competitive auditions, which are held as part of the admissions process.

**Funds Avail.:** Full tuition (valued at $25,000). **To Apply:** Write to the Director for Academy catalogue and application guidelines. **Deadline:** Mid-March, mid-May. Notification by June 1. **Contact:** K. James McDowell, Director, at the above address (see entry 27).

---

**• 29 •**

## Action Research
Vincent House, North Parade
Horsham, W. Sussex RH12 2DP,          *Ph:* 1403 210406
England                                        *Fax:* 1403 210541

**• 30 •   Action Research Program and Project Grants**
*(Postdoctorate/Grant)*

**Purpose:** To support research into the prevention of disability and alleviation of physical handicaps. **Focus:** Basic and clinical research including medical engineering. **Qualif.:** Grants are tenable at universities and teaching hospitals in the United Kingdom. Awards are not offered to support higher education conferences, or publications.

**Funds Avail.:** £52,904 average. **To Apply:** Write a brief outline to the Research Grants Officer for application form and guidelines. **Deadline:** March 15, July 20, and November 15. Assessment of program grants usually takes one year.

**Remarks:** Applications for research into cancer, cardiovascular diseases, AIDS and HIV are not accepted. **Contact:** Research Grants Officer at the above address (see entry 29).

**• 31 •   Action Research Training Fellowships**
*(Postgraduate/Fellowship)*

**Purpose:** To support training for research into the prevention of disability and alleviation of physical handicaps. **Focus:** Basic and clinical research including medical engineering. **Qualif.:** Candidate must be a graduate or have equivalent experience. Fellowships are tenable at universities and teaching hospitals in the United Kingdom. Awards are not offered to support higher education, conferences, or publications.

**Funds Avail.:** £66,745 average. **To Apply:** Write to the Research Grants Officer for application form and guidelines. **Deadline:** January 31.

**Remarks:** Applications from those working in the fields of cancer, cardiovascular diseases, AIDS and HIV research are not accepted. **Contact:** Dr. K. Walsh, Research Grants Officer, at the above address (see entry 29).

---

**• 32 •**

## Actuarial Education and Research Fund
475 N. Martingale, Ste. 800            *Ph:* (847)706-3584
Schaumburg, IL 60173-2226           *Fax:* (847)706-3599
*E-mail:* phaberstroh@soa.org
*URL:* http://www.aerf.org

**• 33 •   AERF Individual Grants** *(Professional Development/Grant)*

**Purpose:** To encourage research in actuarial science and education. **Focus:** Actuarial Sciences **Qualif.:** Candidate may be of any nationality. Applicant must be a member of a sponsoring AERF organization, a faculty member in actuarial or related fields, or have otherwise qualified to conduct research appropriate to the AERF's interests. **Criteria:** Based on the applicant's project's potential to contribute significantly to the advancement of knowledge in actuarial science.

**Funds Avail.:** $4,000-10,000. **No. of Awards:** 1 to 5 per year. **To Apply:** Contact AERF for application form and guidelines. **Deadline:** December 30. Grants awarded by April 5. **Contact:** Paulette Haberstroh (847)706-3584. Send Proposals to Curtis Huntington, AERF Executive Director, U of M, Dept. of Mathematics, 2864 East Hall, 525 E. University Ave., Ann Arbor, MI, 48109-1109.

---

**• 34 •**

## ADA Endowment Fund and Assistance Fund Inc.
211 E. Chicago Ave., 17th Fl.           *Ph:* (312)440-2567
Chicago, IL 60611                          *Fax:* (312)440-2822
                                                 *Free:* 800-621-8099
*URL:* http://ada.org/dnewdig/newsprev/960923/np-16.html

**• 35 •   American Fund for Dental Health Dental Faculty Development Fellowships** *(Postdoctorate/Fellowship)*

**Purpose:** To help dental faculty to improve their research and teaching skills. **Focus:** Dentistry **Qualif.:** Applicants must be U.S. citizens with a D.D.S. or D.M.D. degree. They must also be full-time instructors, associates or assistant professors, at an accredited dental school in the United States.

**Funds Avail.:** $20,000. **To Apply:** Write for application form. Submit completed application with curriculum vitae; a detailed outline of proposed course study; a research proposal, including methodology and a supporting statement from a qualified mentor; an outline of personal goals and objectives for the fellowship year; three letters of recommendation; and a letter of acceptance from a postdoctoral program, if applicable. **Deadline:** September 1. Notification in mid-December. **Contact:** Program Coordinator, at the above address (see entry 34).

**• 36 •   American Fund for Dental Health Dental Teacher Training Fellowships** *(Postdoctorate/Fellowship)*

**Purpose:** To support postdoctoral research and teacher training. **Focus:** Dentistry. **Qualif.:** Applicants must be U.S. citizens with a D.D.S. or D.M.D. degree. They must also be in the final year of a postdoctoral research or teacher training program. Fellowships are tenable in the United States.

**Funds Avail.:** $20,000. **To Apply:** Write for application forms. Submit completed application with curriculum vitae; dental school transcripts, including verification of class standing; verification of enrollment in the final year of a postdoctoral program; and three letters of recommendation, including one from the program director. **Deadline:** September 1. Notification in mid-December.

Contact: Program Coordinator, at the above address (see entry 34).

## • 37 • American Fund for Dental Health Grants for Research and Special Projects in Dentistry (Postdoctorate/Grant)

**Purpose:** To support research linking dentistry and medicine with community interests. **Focus:** Dentistry. **Qualif.:** Applicants must be qualified researchers who are affiliated with a nonprofit organization in the United States or its protectorates. The organization must agree to assume fiscal responsibility for the proposed research. Proposed project should be national in scope and show promise of impacting one or more of the established goals of the Fund.

**Funds Avail.:** $35,000 maximum. **To Apply:** Write for application guidelines. Submit a grant proposal, including a project summary and an annual budget. **Deadline:** July 15. Notification in mid-March. **Contact:** Program Coordinator, at the above address (see entry 34).

## • 38 • American Fund for Dental Health/Hillenbrand Fellowship in Dental Administration (Postdoctorate/Fellowship)

**Purpose:** To provide an individual with a year of study and practical experience in the field of dental administration. **Focus:** Dental Administration (specific topic varies). **Qualif.:** Applicants must be U.S. citizens with a graduate degree from an accredited dental school. Fellowship is tenable in Chicago.

**Funds Avail.:** $40,000. **No. of Awards:** One biennially. **To Apply:** Write for application form. Submit completed application with dental school transcripts, three letters of recommendation, and a one-page statement describing area of interest and goals and objectives for career development. Applicants may be interviewed. **Deadline:** Varies; December 1 in odd years. **Contact:** Program Coordinator

## • 39 • Dental Assisting Scholarship Program (Undergraduate/Scholarship)

**Purpose:** To assist students entering dental assisting that need financial assistance. **Focus:** Dental Assisting. **Qualif.:** Applicants must be U.S. citizens entering an accredited dental assisting program. **Criteria:** 2.8 GPA, 2 letters of reference, financial need, and a typed summary of personal/professional goals.

**Funds Avail.:** $1,000. **No. of Awards:** 25. **To Apply:** Contact the Fund for guidelines. Applications are sent to schools. **Deadline:** September 15. **Contact:** Marsha Mountz, at the above address (see entry 34).

## • 40 • Dental Lab Tech Scholarship Program (Undergraduate/Scholarship)

**Purpose:** To assist students who are in need of financial assistance. **Focus:** Dental Lab technology. **Qualif.:** Applicants must be U.S. citizens enrolled as entering or first year students at an accredited laboratory technology school. **Criteria:** 2.8 GPA; demonstrate financial need; 21 letters of reference; and a typed summary of personal/professional goals.

**Funds Avail.:** $1,000. **No. of Awards:** 25. **To Apply:** Contact the Fund for guidelines. Applications are sent to schools. **Deadline:** August 15. **Contact:** Marsha Mountz, at the above address (see entry 34).

## • 41 • Dental Student Scholarship Program (Graduate/Scholarship)

**Purpose:** To assist students in need of financial assistance in the field of dentistry. **Focus:** Dentistry. **Qualif.:** Applicants must be U.S. citizens in their second year of dental school. **Criteria:** Applicants must have a 3.0 GPA, demonstrate financial need, and submit 2 letters of reference, and typed summary of personal/professional goals.

**Funds Avail.:** $2,500. **No. of Awards:** 25. **To Apply:** Contact the Fund for guidelines. Applications are sent to schools. **Deadline:** June 15. **Contact:** Marsha Mountz, at the above address (see entry 34).

## • 42 • Endowment Fund Dental Hygiene Scholarship Program (Graduate/Scholarship)

**Purpose:** To assist students in need of financial assistance in the field of dental hygiene. **Focus:** Dental Hygiene. **Qualif.:** Applicants must be U.S. citizens entering or in the first year of an accredited dental hygiene program. **Criteria:** 2.8 GPA; demonstrate financial need; 21 letters of reference; and a typed summary of personal/professional goals.

**Funds Avail.:** $1,000. **No. of Awards:** 25. **To Apply:** Contact the Fund for guidelines. Applications are sent to schools. **Deadline:** August 15. **Contact:** Marsha Mountz, at the above address (see entry 34).

## • 43 • Minority Dental Student Scholarship Program (Doctorate, Graduate/Scholarship)

**Purpose:** To assist students from minority groups that are traditionally under-represented in the fields of medicine and dentistry. **Focus:** Dentistry. **Qualif.:** Applicants must be U.S. citizens entering the second year of a U.S. dental school. They must also be African-Americans, Native Americans, or Hispanics. **Criteria:** 2.5 GPA; demonstrate financial need; 2 letters of reference; and a typed summary of personal/professional goals.

**Funds Avail.:** $2,000. **No. of Awards:** 15-20. **To Apply:** Write to the Fund for guidelines. Applications are sent to schools. **Deadline:** July 1. Notification in mid-August. **Contact:** Marsha Mountz, at the above address (see entry 34).

## • 44 •
## Aerospace Education Foundation

1501 Lee Hwy.                    Ph: (703)247-5839
Arlington, VA 22209-1109         Fax: (703)247-5853
E-mail: AEFstaff@aef.org
URL: http://www.aef.org

## • 45 • Dr. Theodore von Karman Graduate Scholarship (Graduate/Scholarship)

**Purpose:** To assist Air Force Reserve Officer Training Corps (ROTC) cadets who are pursuing advanced degrees in the fields of science, math and engineering. **Qualif.:** Candidates must be Air Force ROTC (4th year) cadets who have already been accepted into graduate, fully-accredited academic/administrative programs at United States colleges or technical institutions and have been granted delay from the USAF. **Criteria:** Based on scholastic ability or potential, leadership abilities, and apparent personal qualities of excellence.

**Funds Avail.:** $5,000 is available. **No. of Awards:** 10 awards are available. **To Apply:** Applicants must submit complete grade transcript, three letters of reference, autobiography, application for delayed entry, birth certificate, letter from PAS, and a resume. **Deadline:** Applications are due by February 10. **Contact:** Arthur C. Hyland, Contributions and Public Affairs Associate, at the above address (see entry 44).

• 46 •

## African-American Institute

833 United Nations Plz.  
New York, NY 10017-3518

*Ph:* (212)949-5666  
*Fax:* (212)682-6174  
*Free:* 800-745-3899

*URL:* http://charity.org/aai.html

### • 47 • African Graduate Fellowships *(Graduate, Postgraduate/Fellowship)*

**Purpose:** To support African nationals who wish to pursue graduate and postgraduate degrees in the United States. **Focus:** Development. **Qualif.:** Applicant must be a national of a sub-Saharan African country and have an undergraduate degree. Candidate's proposed course of study must be relevant to the economic and social development of his/her home country. Fellowships are tenable in graduate degree programs at U.S. universities. The African-American Institute arranges placement for the student. Candidate should not apply directly to the university for admission. The host institution provides free tuition; other basic expenses are covered by the Institute. Fellows who do not already know English will be provided with language training. Fellows are expected to return to their home countries on completion of the degree.

**Funds Avail.:** Tuition, plus living, travel and book allowances. **To Apply:** The Institute does not accept applications directly from students; candidates must be nominated by an African government or employer. Contact local United States Agency for International Development office for AF-GRAD application guidelines. **Deadline:** January. Awards are made in September.

**Remarks:** The Institute also offers POST-AF support to Africans who have completed a master's or doctoral degree and who would like to conduct a short-term (less than six-month) advanced research project in the United States. Awards include living, travel, and book allowances. Contact a university placement office in home country for further information. **Contact:** Yolanda Zahler, Director of Placement and Programming, at the above address (see entry 46).

• 48 •

## AFS Intercultural Programs

71 W. 23rd St., 17th Fl.  
New York, NY 10010-4102  
*URL:* http://afs.org

*Free:* 800-AFS-INFO

### • 49 • AFS Intercultural Global Teenager Program Scholarships *(High School/Other)*

**Purpose:** To help students finance their AFS experience in a foreign country. **Focus:** Area and Ethnic Studies. **Qualif.:** Candidates must be high school students ages 15 to 18 who are United States citizens or legal residents. Program lengths are 4 weeks, 6-10 weeks, 4-6 months (semester) and 10-12 months (year). The short-term programs (3-10 weeks) may include specialized topics of learning such as Language Study, Outdoor Education and Environmental Studies. **Criteria:** Awards are offered only for AFS participants. AFS does not award scholarships for students attending undergraduate or graduate study programs.

**Funds Avail.:** AFS offers financial aid and scholarship assistance with AFS participation fees which vary depending upon the length and type of program. Fees range from $2,395 to $5,895. There is a non-refundable registration fee of $75 for all applications. All participation fees include round trip international travel, medical insurance, orientation and counseling serves. Additional costs include domestic travel to and from point of departure or arrival in the U.S., personal allowance while abroad, and visa fees. **Contact:** AFS Intercultural Program, Inc. at the above address:(see entry 48) Toll-free telephone: (800)AFS-INFO.

• 50 •

## AGC Education & Research Foundation

Director of Programs  
1957 E St., NW  
Washington, DC 20006

*Ph:* (202)393-2040  
*Fax:* (202)347-4004

*URL:* http://2.cac.washington.edu/home/uwin/services/  
scholar/arch/AGC

### • 51 • Henry Boh Memorial Scholarships *(Undergraduate/Scholarship)*

**Qualif.:** Applicants must be college freshmen, sophomores, or juniors enrolled, or planning to enroll, in a four- or five-year degree program in construction and/or civil engineering. High school seniors are no longer eligible. **Criteria:** Selection is based on academic performance, extracurricular activities, employment experience, financial need, and a demonstrated interest in a construction industry career.

**Funds Avail.:** $1,500 per year for each year of undergraduate education, for a maximum of $6,000. **To Apply:** Applications are available after September 1. One completed application allows applicants to compete for all undergraduate scholarship awards sponsored by the AGC Education and Research Foundation (see separate entries). Applications may be obtained by writing or faxing the Foundation office at the above address. **Deadline:** November 15. Finalists are selected in January and are subject to a personal interview with an AGC contractor member. **Contact:** Director of Programs, AGC Education and Research Foundation, at the above address (see entry 50).

### • 52 • The Build America Scholarships *(Undergraduate/Scholarship)*

**Qualif.:** Applicants must be college freshmen, sophomores, or juniors enrolled, or planning to enroll, in a four- or five-year degree program in construction and/or civil engineering. High school seniors are no longer eligible. **Criteria:** Selection is based on academic performance, extracurricular activities, employment experience, financial need, and a demonstrated interest in a construction industry career.

**Funds Avail.:** $1,500 per year for each year of undergraduate education, for a maximum of $6,000. **To Apply:** Applications are available after September 1. One completed application allows applicants to compete for all undergraduate scholarship awards sponsored by the AGC Education and Research Foundation (see separate entries). Applications may be obtained by writing or faxing the Foundation office at the above address. **Deadline:** November 15. Finalists are selected in January and are subject to a personal interview with an AGC contractor member. **Contact:** Director of Programs, AGC Education and Research Foundation, at the above address (see entry 50).

### • 53 • G.E. Byrne Memorial Scholarships *(Undergraduate/Scholarship)*

**Qualif.:** Applicants must be college freshman, sophomores, or juniors enrolled, or planning to enroll, in a four- or five-year degree program in construction and/or civil engineering. High school seniors are no longer eligible. **Criteria:** Selections are based on academic performance, extracurricular activities, employment experience, financial need, and a demonstrated interest in a construction industry career.

**Funds Avail.:** $1,500 per year for each year of undergraduate education, up to a maximum of $6,000. **To Apply:** Applications are available on September 1. One application completed and submitted before the deadline will allow the applicant to compete for all undergraduate scholarship awards sponsored by the AGC Education and Research Foundation (see separate entries). Applications may be obtained by writing or faxing the Foundation office at the above address. **Deadline:** November 15. Finalists are selected in January. **Contact:** For applications and additional information contact the Director of Programs, AGC Education and Research Foundation, at the above address (see entry 50).

### • 54 • Billy R. Carter Memorial Scholarships
*(Undergraduate/Scholarship)*

**Focus:** Civil engineering or construction related studies. **Qualif.:** Applicants must be college freshmen, sophomores, or juniors enrolled, or planning to enroll, in a four- or five-year degree program in construction and/or civil engineering. High school seniors are no longer eligible. **Criteria:** Selection is based on academic performance, extracurricular activities, employment experience, financial need, and a demonstrated interest in a construction industry career.

**Funds Avail.:** $1,500 per year for each year of undergraduate education, for a maximum of $6,000. **To Apply:** Applications are available after September 1. One completed application allows applicants to compete for all undergraduate scholarship awards sponsored by the AGC Education and Research Foundation (see separate entries). Applications may be obtained by writing or faxing the Foundation office at the above address. **Deadline:** November 15. Finalists are selected in January and are subject to a personal interview with an AGC contractor member. **Contact:** Director of Programs, AGC Education and Research Foundation, at the above address (see entry 50).

### • 55 • CCC Scholarships *(Undergraduate/Scholarship)*

**Focus:** Civil engineering or construction related studies. **Qualif.:** Applicants must be college freshman, sophomores, or juniors enrolled, or planning to enroll, in a four- or five-year degree program in construction and/or civil engineering. High school seniors are no longer eligible. **Criteria:** Selections are based on academic performance, extracurricular activities, employment experience, financial need, and a demonstrated interest in a construction industry career.

**Funds Avail.:** $1,500 per year for each year of undergraduate education, up to a maximum of $6,000. **To Apply:** Applications are available on September 1. One application completed and submitted before the deadline will allow the applicant to compete for all undergraduate scholarship awards sponsored by the AGC Education and Research Foundation (see separate entries). Applications may be obtained by writing or faxing the Foundation office at the above address. **Deadline:** November 15. Finalists are selected in January. **Contact:** For applications and additional information contact the Director of Programs, AGC Education and Research Foundation, at the above address (see entry 50).

### • 56 • Vernie G. Lindstron, Jr. Memorial Scholarships *(Undergraduate/Scholarship)*

**Focus:** Civil engineering or construction related studies. **Qualif.:** Applicants must be college freshmen, sophomores, or juniors enrolled, or planning to enroll, in a four- or five-year degree program in construction and/or civil engineering. High school seniors are no longer eligible. **Criteria:** Selection is based on academic performance, extracurricular activities, employment experience, financial need, and a demonstrated interest in a construction industry career.

**Funds Avail.:** $1,500 per year for each year of undergraduate education, for a maximum of $6,000. **To Apply:** Applications are available after September 1. One completed application allows applicants to compete for all undergraduate scholarship awards sponsored by the AGC Education and Research Foundation (see separate entries). Applications may be obtained by writing or faxing the Foundation office at the above address. **Deadline:** November 15. Finalists are selected in January and are subject to a personal interview with an AGC contractor member. **Contact:** Director of Programs, AGC Education and Research Foundation, at the above address (see entry 50).

### • 57 • Robert B. McEachem Memorial Scholarships
*(Undergraduate/Scholarship)*

**Focus:** Civil engineering or construction related studies. **Qualif.:** Applicants must be college freshman, sophomores, or juniors enrolled, or planning to enroll, in a four- or five-year degree program in construction and/or civil engineering. High school seniors are no longer eligible. **Criteria:** Selections are based on academic performance, extracurricular activities, employment experience, financial need, and a demonstrated interest in a construction industry career.

**Funds Avail.:** $1,500 per year for each year of undergraduate education, up to a maximum of $6,000. **To Apply:** Applications are available on September 1. One application completed and submitted before the deadline will allow the applicant to compete for all undergraduate scholarship awards sponsored by the AGC Education and Research Foundation (see separate entries). Applications may be obtained by writing or faxing the Foundation office at the above address. **Deadline:** November 15. Finalists are selected in January. **Contact:** For applications and additional information contact the Director of Programs, AGC Education and Research Foundation, at the above address (see entry 50).

### • 58 • Stanley F. Pepper Memorial Scholarships
*(Undergraduate/Scholarship)*

**Focus:** Civil engineering or construction-related studies. **Qualif.:** Applicants must be college freshmen, sophomores, or juniors enrolled, or planning to enroll, in a four- or five-year degree program in construction and/or civil engineering. High school seniors are no longer eligible. **Criteria:** Selection is based on academic performance, extracurricular activities, employment experience, financial need, and a demonstrated interest in a construction industry career.

**Funds Avail.:** $1,500 per year for each year of undergraduate education, for a maximum of $6,000. **To Apply:** Applications are available after September 1. One application allows applicants to compete for all undergraduate scholarship awards sponsored by the AGC Education and Research Foundation (see separate entries). Applications may be obtained by writing or faxing the Foundation office at the above address. **Deadline:** November 15. Finalists are selected in January and are subject to a personal interview with an AGC contractor member. **Contact:** Director of Programs, AGC Education and Research Foundation, at the above address (see entry 50).

### • 59 • Pitcock Scholarships *(Undergraduate/Scholarship)*

**Focus:** Civil engineering or construction related studies. **Qualif.:** Applicants must be college freshmen, sophomores, or juniors enrolled, or planning to enroll, in a four- or five-year degree program in construction and/or civil engineering. High school seniors are no longer eligible. **Criteria:** Selection is based on academic performance, extracurricular activities, employment experience, financial need, and a demonstrated interest in a construction industry career.

**Funds Avail.:** $1,500 per year for each year of undergraduate education, for a maximum of $6,000. **To Apply:** Applications are available after September 1. One application allows applicants to compete for all undergraduate scholarship awards sponsored by the AGC Education and Research Foundation (see separate entries). Applications may be obtained by writing or faxing the Foundation office at the above address. **Deadline:** November 15. Finalists are selected in January and are subject to a personal interview with an AGC contractor member. **Contact:** Director of Programs, AGC Education and Research Foundation, at the above address (see entry 50).

## AGC Education & Research Foundation (continued)

### • 60 • Paul B. Richards Memorial Scholarship
*(Undergraduate/Scholarship)*

**Focus:** Civil engineering or construction related studies. **Qualif.:** Applicants must be college freshmen, sophomores, or juniors enrolled, or planning to enroll, in a four- or five-year degree program in construction and/or civil engineering. High school seniors are no longer eligible. **Criteria:** Selection is based on academic performance, extracurricular activities, employment experience, financial need, and a demonstrated interest in a construction industry career.

**Funds Avail.:** $1,500 per year for each year of undergraduate education, for a maximum of $6,000. **To Apply:** Applications are available after September 1. One application allows applicants to compete for all undergraduate scholarship awards sponsored by the AGC Education and Research Foundation (see separate entries). Applications may be obtained by writing or faxing the Foundation office at the above address. **Deadline:** November 15. Finalists are selected in January and are subject to a personal interview with an AGC contractor member. **Contact:** Director of Programs, AGC Education and Research Foundation, at the above address (see entry 50).

### • 61 •
## Agency for Health Care Policy and Research
2101 E. Jefferson St., Ste. 602     *Ph:* (301)594-1449
Rockville, MD 20852     *Fax:* (301)594-0154

### • 62 • AHCPR Individual National Research Service Awards *(Postdoctorate/Grant)*

**Purpose:** To provide opportunities for academic training and experience in applying research methods to the systematic analysis of the delivery of health care services. **Focus:** Health Care Delivery. **Qualif.:** Applicants must be U.S. citizens or permanent residents who have received the M.D., D.D.S., Ph.D., or equivalent doctoral degree. They must also have been accepted by an appropriate institution and sponsor.

**Funds Avail.:** $18,600-32,300. **To Apply:** Write to the Division of Research Grants for application form and guidelines. **Deadline:** December 5, April 5, August 5.

**Remarks:** We announce all research grant programs in the NIH Guide to Contracts and Grants. **Contact:** William Maas, D.D.S., NRSA Project Officer, (301)594-1449, at the above address (see entry 61).

### • 63 •
## Air Force Aid Society
National Headquarters
1745 Jefferson Davis Hwy., No. 202     *Ph:* (703)607-3072
Arlington, VA 22202-3402     *Free:* 800-429-9475
*URL:* http://www.afas.org

### • 64 • Air Force Aid Society Education Grants
*(Undergraduate/Grant)*

**Focus:** General Studies. **Qualif.:** Applicants must be dependent sons and daughters of Air Force members in one of the following categories: active duty and Title 10 Reservists on extended active duty (all other Guard and Reserve are not eligible); retired due to length of active duty service or disability, or retired Guard/Reserve age 60 and receiving retirement pay; and deceased while on active duty or in retired status. Spouses of active duty members and Title

10 Reservists on extended active duty, residing in Continental U.S., and surviving spouses of deceased members are also eligible. Applicants must be enrolled or accepted for the coming school year as a full-time undergraduate student in a college, university, or a vocational/trade school whose accreditation is accepted by the Department of Education. They must also maintain a minimum grade point average of 2.0 on a 4.0 scale. Applicants who are recipients of previous grants must demonstrate satisfactory progress by promotion in school grade level. **Criteria:** Selection is based on need, tailored to recognize the proper weighting of family income and education cost factors.

**Funds Avail.:** $1,500 grants. **No. of Awards:** 5,000. **To Apply:** Applicants and the Air Force member, or parent or guardian, will complete a preliminary application form. Attached to the application form, applicants will include a copy of assignment orders to present duty station. Title 10 Reserve attach extended active duty order showing active duty status. If member is retired, they will attach a copy of military retirement orders. Retired Guard/Reserve attach retirement orders showing attainment of age 60 and receiving retirement pay. If member is deceased, applicant will attach copy of DD13 Statement of Service form; or death certificate with copy of most current military orders. After the preliminary application has been sent in and processed, ACT, Inc. will mail to the student an application packet consisting of two forms: a Family Financial Data Form (FFDF) and a Grade Point Average Verification form which must be completed and mailed to ACT Recognition Program Services. All grant awards will be made co-payable to both the applicant and the school, and will be sent directly to the schools financial aid office by September, of the award year. **Deadline:** Late March for the preliminary application form, and by April 15 for the FFDF data and GPA forms. **Contact:** Applications are sent to Air Force Aid Society's Education Assistance Department at the above address (see entry 63). For questions regarding the preliminary application or processing procedures, call AFAS at (800)429-9475 or DSN at (703)327-3072. Questions regarding the status of FFDF and GPA forms should be directed to ACT Recognition Program Services at (800)205-6372. Overseas applicants should call (319)337-1204.

### • 65 •
## Air Force Civilian Cooperative Work-Study Programs - Air Force Material Command (DPCF)
Wright-Patterson Air Force Base
Dayton, OH 45433-5000     *Ph:* (513)257-4136

### • 66 • Air Force Civilian Cooperative Work-Study Program *(Graduate, Undergraduate/Work Study)*

**Qualif.:** Applicants must be pursuing a career in a technical field, including engineering and physical/life sciences.

### • 67 •
## Air Force Sergeants Association
PO Box 50     *Ph:* (301)899-3500
Temple Hills, MD 20757-0050     *Fax:* (301)899-8136
    *Free:* 800-638-0594
*URL:* http://phobos.kiss.de:81/~afsa/

### • 68 • AFSA Scholarship Awards *(Undergraduate/Scholarship)*

**Purpose:** To foster academic or technical excellence. **Focus:** General Studies. **Qualif.:** Applicants must be single, dependent children, including stepchildren and legally adopted children, of Air Force Sergeants Association members or members of the

Association's Auxiliary. Applicants must be high school graduates or in-college students. Pre-freshmen who have not previously attended college and in-college freshmen who will not have completed one full-year of college work by the end of the next spring semester or quarter, must submit the Scholastic Aptitude Test (SAT) Results Report. **Criteria:** Criteria for selection are academic ability, character, leadership, writing ability, and potential for success. Financial need is not a consideration. Faculty members from George Washington University and from the Capitol Institute of Technology review applications from college students and from technical or trade school students, respectively. Final selection is made by the Air Force Sergeants Association Scholarship Fund trustees.

**Funds Avail.:** Scholarships are available for assistance to attain college education or training and for study at accredited trade and technical schools. Scholarship amounts range from $1,500-2,500. A technology scholarship, sponsored by the Capitol Institute of Technology at its Laurel, Maryland, campus for study in the field of electronic engineering is valued at $600. Unless otherwise approved by the trustees, the total amount of the award is sent to the student's college with instructions that the money is to be used for any of the following expenses: tuition, fees, room and board (which may be on or off campus), books, supplies, lunches, and student transportation costs commuting from home. The scholarships are not transferable from one school to another at any time during a semester or term. **To Apply:** Application forms must be requested by sending a self-addressed, postage paid ($1.21), 9 by 12 inch, envelope after November 1. Candidates must submit the formal application along with their Scholastic Aptitude Test scores (ACT not accepted); a recommendation from their high school principal if they are freshmen candidates; a recommendation from a teacher for high school students or a professor for in-college applicants; a certificate of admission from the school to be attended; a complete, official transcript of all grades of those who are currently freshmen, sophomores, or juniors in undergraduate or technical school; and a brief handwritten statement of educational objectives. Candidates are required to include a two-page handwritten reply to any one of the following questions: What do you expect to gain by attending college? Do you think a college education is as important to women as it is to men? What did you like and dislike most in high school? Are you proud of your parents and why? Since you have spent most of your life as a dependent of an enlisted man, what do you think of the Air Force in general? Would you choose the Air Force as a career? What do you think of your fellow man? or a two-page handwritten comment on any issue of a controversial nature. All information requested in the application, as well as other material required, must be furnished. If it is not, the application is considered incomplete and the applicant is ineligible for consideration. Applications are not accepted without the applicant's signature. **Deadline:** Completed applications, with all supporting documents, must be filed between January 1 and April 15.

**Remarks:** Students who qualify for an AFSA Scholarship are also eligible for consideration in the Airmen Memorial Foundation (AMF) Scholarship Program (see separate entry). AMF Scholarship application materials are automatically sent with all AFSA Scholarship packages. Median SAT scores for recipients in the past has been 1150 and above; median high school and college GPA has been 3.65 and above. **Contact:** Scholarship Administrator at the above address (see entry 67).

## • 69 • Frank W. Garner Scholarship (Undergraduate/ Scholarship)

**Qualif.:** Candidates must be a single dependent, less than 23 years of age, of an association member or auxiliary member. **Criteria:** Selection is based on academic ability, character, leadership, writing ability, and potential success factors.

**Funds Avail.:** $2000 awarded annually. **To Apply:** April 15. **Contact:** Scholarship Administrator.

## • 70 • Richard D. Rousher Scholarship (Undergraduate/Scholarship)

**Qualif.:** Candidates must be single dependents of an Air Force Sergeant Association member or Auxiliary member under the age of 23. **Criteria:** Selection is based on academic ability, character, leadership, writing ability, and success potential.

**Funds Avail.:** Awarded annually. **Deadline:** April 15. **Contact:** Scholarship Administrator.

## • 71 •
## Air Traffic Control Association
Arlington Courthouse Plz. II
2300 Clarendon Blvd., Ste. 711
Arlington, VA 22201-3367

*Ph:* (703)522-5717
*Fax:* (703)527-7251

## • 72 • Air Traffic Control Association Scholarships (Graduate, Undergraduate/Scholarship)

**Purpose:** The scholarship is awarded to promising men and women who are enrolled in programs leading to a bachelor's degree or higher in aviation-related courses of study and to full-time employees engaged in advanced study to improve their skills in an air traffic control or aviation discipline. **Focus:** Aviation. **Qualif.:** Student applicants must be U.S. citizens, be enrolled or accepted in an accredited college or university pursuing a bachelor's degree, or higher plan to continue the following year, have course work related to a planned aviation-related career leading to a degree, have attendance equal to at least half time (6 hours), and have a minimum of 30 semester or 45 quarter hours still to be completed before graduation. Full-time employee candidates must engage in full-time employment in an aviation-related field and their course work must be designed to enhance their skills in an ATC or aviation discipline. **Criteria:** The Scholarship Awards Committee shall in all cases take the applicant's need for financial aid into consideration and in cases where qualifications of candidates are reasonably equivalent, make a selection in favor of the candidate with the greatest need.

**Funds Avail.:** Scholarships range from $1,500 to $2,500 for half- to full-time students. Full-time employee scholarships are up to $600. The number and amount of scholarship awards will vary depending upon the qualifications, financial need, and number of outstanding candidates. They must be used within four years of the date awarded. If the recipient should change academic major, resubmission of intended program of study to the ATCA scholarship committee is required for continued reimbursement. **To Apply:** Applicants must submit a completed application form, a recommendation, and a certified transcript of all college course work. If less than 30 semester or 45 quarter hours of college course work have been completed, all high school transcripts are also required. Half- to full-time students must also submit a paper on a designated topic. **Deadline:** Applications must be received by May 1. **Contact:** The Air Traffic Control Association at the above address (see entry 71).

## • 73 • Children of Air Traffic Control Specialists (Undergraduate/Scholarship)

**Qualif.:** Must be a U.S. Citizen, the child, natural or by adoption, of a person serving or having served as an air traffic control specialist, be it with the U.S. Government, U.S. Military, or in a private facility in the United States. Must also be enrolled (or accepted) in an accredited college or univeristy and planning to continue the following year. Attendance must be at least half-time (6 hours). Must have a minimum of 30 semester or 45 quarter hours till to be completed before graduation. Course of study leads to a bachelors degree or higher. **Deadline:** May 1.

**Air and Waste Management Association**
1 Gateway Ctr., 3rd Fl.                    *Ph:* (412)232-3444
Pittsburgh, PA 15222                       *Fax:* (412)232-3450
*E-mail:* info@awma.org
*URL:* http://www.awma.org

**• 75 •   Air & Waste Management Scholarship
Endowment Trust Fund** *(Graduate/Scholarship)*

**Qualif.:** Applicants must be full-time graduate students pursuing courses of study and research leading to careers in air pollution control and/or waste management.

**Funds Avail.:** Varies (averages $2,000-$5,000). **No. of Awards:** Varies (previously 56). **To Apply:** Mailed in September **Deadline:** First week in December. **Contact:** Nancy Eiben.

**• 76 •**
**Aircraft Electronics Association**
4217 S. Hocker
PO Box 1963
Independence, MO 64055-0963               *Ph:* (816)373-6565
                                          *Fax:* (816)478-3100
*E-mail:* tracyw@aea.net
*URL:* http://www.AEAavnews.org

**• 77 •   David Arver Memorial Scholarship**
*(Undergraduate/Scholarship)*

**Purpose:** To provide youth with the opportunity to seek avionics as a career. **Focus:** Avionics. **Qualif.:** Applicants must be students planning to attend an accredited vocational/technical school located in AEA Region 3 (Illinois, Indiana, Iowa, Kansas, Michigan, Minnesota, Missouri, Nebraska, North Dakota, South Dakota, or Wisconsin) and are enrolled in an avionics or aircraft repair program. **Criteria:** Based on mechanical ability, aviation interests, class attendance, technical aptitude, scholastic record, responsibility, and commitment to the aviation industry.

**Funds Avail.:** $1000. **To Apply:** A completed application form, 3 letters of recommendation, grade transcripts, and a 300 word essay must be submitted. **Deadline:** February 15.

**Remarks:** Given by Dutch and Ginger Arver in memory of their son, David.

**• 78 •   BFGoodrich Component Services Scholarship**
*(Undergraduate/Scholarship)*

**Purpose:** To provide youth with the opportunity to seek avionics as a career. **Focus:** Avionics. **Qualif.:** Applicants must be attending or planning to attend an accredited school in an avionics or aircraft repair program. **Criteria:** Based on mechanical ability, aviation interests, class attendance, technical aptitude, scholastic record, responsibility, and commitment to the aviation industry.

**Funds Avail.:** $2500. **To Apply:** A completed application form, 3 letters of recommendation, grade transcripts, and a 300 word essay must be submitted. **Deadline:** February 15.

**• 79 •   Bose Corporation Avionics Scholarship**
*(Undergraduate/Scholarship)*

**Purpose:** To provide youth with the opportunity to seek avionics as a career. **Focus:** Avionics. **Qualif.:** Applicants must be attending or planning to attend Embry-Riddle Aeronautical University in an avionics program. **Criteria:** Based on mechanical ability, aviation interests, class attendance, technical aptitude, scholastic record, responsibility, and commitment to the aviation industry.

**Funds Avail.:** $1500. **To Apply:** A completed application form, 3 letters of recommendation, grade transcripts, and a 300 word essay must be submitted. **Deadline:** February 15.

**• 80 •   Bud Glover Memorial Scholarship**
*(Undergraduate/Scholarship)*

**Purpose:** To provide youth with the opportunity to seek avionics as a career. **Focus:** Avionics. **Qualif.:** Applicants must plan to attend or already be attending an accredited school in avionics or aircraft repair. **Criteria:** Based on mechanical ability, aviation interests, class attendance, technical aptitude, scholastic record, responsibility, and commitment to the aviation industry.

**Funds Avail.:** $1000. **To Apply:** A completed application form, 3 letters of recommendation, grade transcripts, and a 300 word essay must be submitted. **Deadline:** February 15.

**• 81 •   College of Aeronautics Scholarship**
*(Undergraduate/Scholarship)*

**Purpose:** To provide youth with the opportunity to seek avionics as a career. **Focus:** Avionics. **Qualif.:** Applicants must be in the two-year avionics program at the College of Aeronautics in Flushing, NY. **Criteria:** Based on mechanical ability, aviation interests, class attendance, technical aptitude, scholastic record, responsibility, and commitment to the aviation industry.

**Funds Avail.:** $3000. Students receive $750 per semester. **To Apply:** A completed application form, 3 letters of recommendation, grade transcripts, and a 300 word essay must be submitted. **Deadline:** February 15.

**• 82 •   Dutch and Ginger Arver Scholarship**
*(Undergraduate/Scholarship)*

**Purpose:** To provide youth with the opportunity to seek avionics as a career. **Focus:** Avionics. **Qualif.:** Applicants must be attending or planning to attend an accredited school in avionics. **Criteria:** Based on mechanical ability, aviation interests, class attendance, technical aptitude, scholastic record, responsibility, and commitment to the aviation industry.

**Funds Avail.:** $1000. **To Apply:** A completed application form, 3 letters of recommendation, grade transcripts, and a 300 word essay must be submitted. **Deadline:** February 15.

**• 83 •   Field Aviation Co., Inc. Scholarship**
*(Undergraduate/Scholarship)*

**Purpose:** To provide youth with the opportunity to seek avionics as a career. **Focus:** Avionics. **Qualif.:** Applicants must be high school seniors and/or college students who plan to or are attending an accredited college/university in an avionics or aircraft repair program in Canada. **Criteria:** Based on mechanical ability, aviation interests, class attendance, technical aptitude, scholastic record, responsibility, and commitment to the aviation industry.

**Funds Avail.:** $1000. **To Apply:** A completed application form, 3 letters of recommendation, grade transcripts, and a 300 word essay must be submitted. **Deadline:** February 15.

**• 84 •   GARMIN Scholarship** *(Undergraduate/Scholarship)*

**Purpose:** To provide youth with the opportunity to seek avionics as a career. **Focus:** Avionics. **Qualif.:** Applicants must be attending or planning to attend an accredited school in avionics or aircraft repair. **Criteria:** Based on mechanical ability, aviation interests, class attendance, technical aptitude, scholastic record, responsibility, and commitment to the aviation industry.

**Funds Avail.:** $2000. **To Apply:** A completed application form, 3 letters of recommendation, grade transcripts, and a 300 word essay must be submitted. **Deadline:** February 15.

**• 85 • Lowell Gaylor Memorial Scholarship** *(Other/Scholarship)*

**Purpose:** To provide youth with the opportunity to seek avionics as a career. **Focus:** Avionics or aircraft repair. **Qualif.:** Applicants must be attending or planning to attend an accredited school in a related area of study. **Criteria:** Based on mechanical ability, aviation interests, class attendance, technical aptitude, scholastic record, responsibility, and commitment to the aviation industry. **Funds Avail.:** $1000. **To Apply:** Completed application form, 3 letters of recommendation, grade transcripts, and a 300 word essay must be submitted. **Deadline:** February 15.

**• 86 • Gulf Coast Avionics Scholarships to Fox Valley Technical College** *(Undergraduate/Scholarship)*

**Purpose:** To provide youth with the opportunity to seek avionics as a career. **Focus:** Avionics. **Qualif.:** Applicants must be planning to attend Fox Valley Technical College in Oshkosh, WI, in the avionics program. **Criteria:** Based on mechanical ability, aviation interests, class attendance, technical aptitude, scholastic record, responsibility, and commitment to the aviation industry. **Funds Avail.:** $1000. **To Apply:** A completed application form, 3 letters of recommendation, grade transcripts, and a 300 word essay must be submitted. **Deadline:** February 15. **Remarks:** Applicants may not currently be enrolled in Fox Valley.

**• 87 • Russell Leroy Jones Memorial Scholarship to Colorado Aero Tech** *(Undergraduate/Scholarship)*

**Purpose:** For attendance at Colorado Aero Tech in Broomfield, CO. **Focus:** Avionics. **Criteria:** Based on mechanical ability, aviation interests, class attendance, technical aptitude, scholastic record, responsibility, and commitment to the aviation industry. **Funds Avail.:** $6000 for tuition only. All other costs (tools, fees, room and board) will be the responsibility of the student. **No. of Awards:** 3. **To Apply:** A completed application form, 3 letters of recommendation, grade transcripts, and a 300 word essay must be submitted. **Deadline:** February 15. **Remarks:** The applicant may not currently be enrolled in the avionics program at Colorado Aero Tech.

**• 88 • Leon Harris/Les Nichols Memorial Scholarship to Spartain School of Aeronautics** *(Undergraduate/Scholarship)*

**Purpose:** To provide youth with the opportunity to seek avionics as a career. **Focus:** Avionics. **Qualif.:** Applicants must be planning to pursue an associates degree at NEEC Spartan School of Aeronautics. **Criteria:** Based on mechanical ability, aviation interests, class attendance, technical aptitude, scholastic record, responsibility, and commitment to the aviation industry. **Funds Avail.:** Students receive $750 per semester for full tuition. Possibly over $16,000. All other costs (tools, living expenses, and student fees) will be the responsibility of the student. **To Apply:** A completed application form, 3 letters of recommendation, grade transcripts, and a 300 word essay must be submitted. **Deadline:** February 15. **Remarks:** Applicants may not be currently enrolled in the avionics program at Spartan's School of Aeronautics.

**• 89 • Mid-Continent Instrument Scholarship** *(Undergraduate/Scholarship)*

**Purpose:** To provide youth with the opportunity to seek avionics as a career. **Focus:** Avionics. **Qualif.:** Applicants must be attending or planning to attend an accredited school in avionics. **Criteria:** Based on mechanical ability, aviation interests, class attendance, technical aptitude, scholastic record, responsibility, and commitment to the aviation industry.

**Funds Avail.:** $1000. **To Apply:** A completed application form, 3 letters of recommendation, grade transcripts, and a 300 word essay must be submitted. **Deadline:** February 15.

**• 90 • Monte Mitchell Global Scholarship** *(Undergraduate/Scholarship)*

**Purpose:** To provide youth with the opportunity to seek avionics as a career. **Focus:** Avionics. **Qualif.:** Applicants must be European students pursuing a degree in aviation maintenance, technology, avionics, or aircraft repair at an accredited school located in Europe or the United States. **Criteria:** Based on mechanical ability, aviation interests, class attendance, technical aptitude, scholastic record, responsibility, and commitment to the aviation industry. **To Apply:** A completed application form, 3 letters of recommendation, grade transcripts, and a 300 word essay must be submitted. **Deadline:** February 15. **Remarks:** Sponsored by Mid-Continent Instrument Co.

**• 91 • Northern Airborne Technology Scholarship** *(Undergraduate/Scholarship)*

**Purpose:** To provide youth with the opportunity to seek avionics as a career. **Focus:** Avionics. **Qualif.:** Applicants must be high school seniors and/or college students planning to or attending an accredited college/university in avionics or aircraft repair program in Canada. **Criteria:** Based on mechanical ability, aviation interests, class attendance, technical aptitude, scholastic record, responsibility, and commitment to the aviation industry. **Funds Avail.:** $1000. **To Apply:** A completed application form, 3 letters of recommendation, grade transcripts, and a 300 word essay must be submitted. **Deadline:** February 15.

**• 92 • Plane & Pilot Magazine Germin Scholarship** *(Undergraduate/Scholarship)*

**Purpose:** To provide youth with the opportunity to seek avionics as a career. **Focus:** Avionics. **Qualif.:** Applicants must be high school, college or vocational/technical school students who plan to attend or are already attending an accredited vocational/technical school in avionics or aircraft repair. **Criteria:** Based on mechanical ability, aviation interests, class attendance, technical aptitude, scholastic record, responsibility, and commitment to the aviation industry. **Funds Avail.:** $2000. **To Apply:** A completed application form, 3 letters of recommendation, grade transcripts, and a 300 word essay must be submitted. **Deadline:** February 15.

**• 93 • Lee Tarbox Memorial Scholarship** *(Undergraduate/Scholarship)*

**Purpose:** To provide youth with the opportunity to seek avionics as a career. **Focus:** Avionics. **Qualif.:** Applicants must be attending or planning to attend an accredited school in avionics or aircraft repair. **Criteria:** Based on mechanical ability, aviation interests, class attendance, technical aptitude, scholastic record, responsibility, and commitment to the aviation industry. **Funds Avail.:** $2500. **To Apply:** A completed application form, 3 letters of recommendation, grade transcripts, and a 300 word essay must be submitted. **Deadline:** February 15. **Remarks:** Given by Pacific Southwest Instruments.

**• 94 • Paul and Blanche Wulfsberg Scholarship** *(Undergraduate/Scholarship)*

**Purpose:** To provide youth with the opportunity to seek avionics as a career. **Focus:** Avionics. **Qualif.:** Applicants must be attending or planning to attend an accredited school in avionics or aircraft repair. **Criteria:** Based on mechanical ability, aviation interests, class attendance, technical aptitude, scholastic record, responsibility, and commitment to the aviation industry.

## *Aircraft Electronics Association (continued)*

**Funds Avail.:** $1000. **To Apply:** A completed application form, 3 letters of recommendation, grade transcripts, and a 300 word essay must be submitted. **Deadline:** February 15.

**Remarks:** Sponsored by the Paul & Blanche Wulfsberg Foundation.

---

### • 95 •
**Airline Pilots Association**
1625 Massachusetts Ave. NW, 8th Fl.
Washington, DC 20036                    **Ph:** (202)797-4050

#### • 96 • Airline Pilots Association Scholarship
*(Undergraduate/Scholarship)*

**Focus:** General studies. **Qualif.:** Applicants must be sons or daughters of medically retired, long-term disabled, or deceased pilot members of the Air Line Pilots Association. Although the program envisions selection of a student enrolling as a college freshman, eligible individuals who are already enrolled in college may also apply. **Criteria:** Awards are made based on academic capability and financial need.

**Funds Avail.:** $12,000 with $3000 disbursed annually. **No. of Awards:** 1. **To Apply:** Applications should be submitted prior to applicant's senior year in high school and preferably after the first semester of that senior year. Applicants already enrolled in college must submit a copy of all college courses and course grades received to date in addition to the application and required high school performance data. **Deadline:** April 1. **Contact:** Jan Redden at the above address (see entry 95)for applications.

---

### • 97 •
**Airmen Memorial Foundation**
5211 Auth Rd.                          **Ph:** (301)899-8386
Suitland, MD 20746-4339               **Fax:** (301)899-8136
                                       **Free:** 800-638-0594
*URL:* http:////association.com/afsa/amf/amfc$he.htm

#### • 98 • Airmen Memorial Scholarships
*(Undergraduate/Scholarship)*

**Qualif.:** Applicant must be an unmarried dependent child of an enlisted member, current or retired status, of the Air Force, Air National Guard, or Air Force Reserve. Dependent child is defined as a natural, step, or legally adopted youth under the age of 25. Recipients must attend an accredited academic or trade/technical institution at the undergraduate level. **Criteria:** Recipients are selected on the basis of academic ability, character, leadership, writing ability, and potential for success. Financial need is not a consideration. Faculty members from the University of Maryland and from the Capitol Institute of Technology review applications from college students and from technical or trade school students, respectively.

**Funds Avail.:** The number of scholarships depends upon the amount of money collected annually for scholarships. Normally, the grant $1,000. Unless otherwise approved by the board of directors, the total amount of the award is sent to the student's college with instructions that the money is to be used for any of the following expenses: tuition, fees, room and board (which may be on or off campus), books, supplies, lunches, and student transportation costs commuting from home. The scholarships are not transferable from one school to another at any time during a semester or term. **To Apply:** Application forms must be requested by sending a self-addressed postage paid ($1.21) 9x12 envelope after November 1. Candidates must submit the formal application along with their Scholastic Aptitude Test (SAT) scores; a recommendation from their high school principal if they are freshmen candidates or from a teacher or professor for in-college applicants; a certificate of admission from the school to be attended; a complete, official transcript of all grades of those who are currently freshmen, sophomores, or juniors in undergraduate or technical school; and a brief handwritten statement of educational objectives. Candidates are required to include a two-page handwritten reply to any one of the following questions: What do you expect to gain by attending college? Do you think a college education is as important to women as it is to men? What did you like and dislike most in high school? Are you proud of your parents? If you have spent most of your life as a dependent of an enlisted man, what do you think of the Air Force in general? Would you choose the Air Force as a career? What do you think of your fellow man? Or commentary on any issue of a controversial nature. All information requested in the application, as well as other material required, must be furnished. If it is not, the application is considered incomplete and the applicant is ineligible for consideration. Applications are not accepted without the applicant's signature. **Deadline:** Completed applications, with all supporting documents, must be postmarked no later than April 15.

**Remarks:** Median SAT score for selectives in past has been 1200 and above; median high school GPA, 3.65 and above; and Median College GPA 3.65 and above. **Contact:** Scholarship Administrator at the above address (see entry 97). The Foundation's toll-free number is: (800)638-0594.

#### • 99 • AMF/Signet Bank Educational Loans *(All/Loan)*

**Purpose:** This Student Loan Program is designed to permit maximum flexibility when the student or family members are ineligible for other types of loans or more is needed to borrow than is allowed under existing programs. **Focus:** All areas of study are eligible. **Qualif.:** Applicants must be enlisted members of the Air Force, Air National Guard, Air Force Reserves on active duty, retired, or veteran status, or their spouses or dependents. There is no family income test. The borrower and/or co-signer must be United States citizens or permanent residents of the United States. **Criteria:** Any student enrolled at least half-time is eligible for the Federal Subsidized Stafford and/or the Federal Unsubsidized Stafford Loans. The parent or legal guardian of a dependent half-time student is eligible for a Federal PLUS loan.

**Funds Avail.:** Funds vary depending on specific educational situation. **To Apply:** Processing time varies, although applications may be filed at any time. Checks are made co-payable to both borrower(s) and the institution and must be endorsed by all parties. Completed application with all required documentation is sent to the student's school for the required school certification. **Deadline:** None.

**Remarks:** Using the Federally Subsidized, Unsubsidized Stafford loans together with the Federal PLUS loan program provides for the total cost of education minus scholarships and school-based financial aid. **Contact:** AMF Scholarship Administration at the above address (see entry 97).

#### • 100 • CMSAF Richard D. Kisling Scholarships
*(Undergraduate/Scholarship)*

**Purpose:** To recognize academic and technical excellence among Air Force enlisted dependents. **Qualif.:** Applicants must be unmarried dependent children of an enlisted member, current or retired status, of the Air Force, Air National Guard, or Air Force Reserve. Dependent child is defined as a natural, step, or legally adopted youth under the age of 25. Recipients must attend accredited academic or trade/technical institutions at the undergraduate level. **Criteria:** Recipients are selected on the basis of academic ability, character, leadership, writing ability, and potential for success. Financial need is not a consideration. Kisling Scholarship recipients are selected from the participants in the

Airmen Memorial Scholarship Program. Faculty members from the University of Maryland and from the Capitol Institute of Technology review applications from college students and from technical or trade school students, respectively. Final selection is made by the Kisling Scholarship Committee chaired by the Chief Master Sergeant of the Air Force.

**Funds Avail.:** The number of scholarships depends upon the amount of money collected annually for scholarships. Amounts vary from $1,000 to $3,000, with a total of $11,00 available. **No. of Awards:** Normally there are seven grants. Unless otherwise approved by the board of directors, the total amount of the award is sent to the student's college with instructions that the money is to be used for any of the following expenses: tuition, fees, room and board (which may be on or off campus), books, supplies, lunches, and student transportation costs commuting from home. The scholarships are not transferable from one school to another at any time during a semester or term. **To Apply:** Application forms must be requested by sending a self-addressed postage paid ($1.21) 9x12 envelope after November 1. No separate application is required for the AFSA or AMF Scholarship program. Candidates must submit the formal application along with their Scholastic Aptitude Test scores; and a recommendation from a high school principal for freshmen candidates or a recommendation from a teacher or a professor for in-college applicants; a certificate of admission from the school to be attended; a complete, official transcript of all grades of those who are currently freshmen, sophomores, or juniors in undergraduate or technical school; and a brief handwritten statement of educational objectives. Candidates are required to include a two-page handwritten reply to any one of the following questions: What do you expect to gain by attending college? Do you think a college education is as important to women as it is to men? What did you like and dislike most in high school? Are you proud of your parents? If you have spent most of your life as a dependent of an enlisted man, what do you think of the Air Force in general? Would you choose the Air Force as a career? What do you think of your fellow man? or commentary on any issue of a controversial nature. All information requested in the application, as well as other material required, must be furnished. If it is not, the application is considered incomplete and the applicant is ineligible for consideration. Applications are not accepted without the applicant's signature. **Deadline:** Completed applications, with all supporting documents, must be postmarked no later than April 15.

**Remarks:** Median SAT score for selectees in the past has been 1200, median high school GPA, 3.65 or above; and median college GPA, 3.65 or above. Approximately 600 applications are received annually. **Contact:** Scholarship Administrator at the above address (see entry 97).

---

**• 101 •**

**Alabama Commission on Higher Education**

PO Box 302000
00 N. Union St., 7th Fl.          *Ph:* (334)242-2274
Montgomery, AL 36130-2000        *Fax:* (334)242-0270

**• 102 •   Alabama Junior and Community College Athletic Scholarships** *(Undergraduate/Award)*

**Focus:** General Studies. **Qualif.:** Applicants must be full-time students enrolled in public junior and community colleges in Alabama. **Criteria:** Selection based on demonstrated athletic ability determined through try-outs. Awards are not based on financial aid.

**Funds Avail.:** Awards do not exceed total tuition and the cost of books.

**Remarks:** Awards may be renewed on the basis of continued participation in the designated sport or activity. **Contact:** Applicants must contact a coach, athletic director, or financial aid officer, at appropriate institutions.

**• 103 •   Alabama Junior and Community College Performing Arts Scholarships** *(Undergraduate/Award)*

**Focus:** General Studies. **Qualif.:** Full-time students attending public junior and community colleges in Alabama are eligible. **Criteria:** Selection is based on demonstrated talent determined through competitive auditions.

**Funds Avail.:** Awards do not exceed in-state tuition for attendance at public junior or community colleges in Alabama. **To Apply:** Applicants must contact the financial aid office at appropriate institutions. Competitive auditions will be scheduled as part of the application process.

**• 104 •   Alabama National Guard Educational Assistance Program** *(Undergraduate/Award)*

**Focus:** General Studies. **Qualif.:** Applicants must be students who are active members in good standing with a federally-recognized unit of the Alabama National Guard. They must attend a postsecondary educational institution in Alabama. Participants may receive federal veterans benefits, but must show a cost less aid amount of at least $25. **Criteria:** Selection is not based on need.

**Funds Avail.:** Awards are limited to $500 a term, and no more than $1,000 a year, to be used for tuition, educational fees, and books and supplies. **To Apply:** A formal application, signed by a representative of the Alabama Military Department and the financial aid officer at the college or university the student plans to attend, must be submitted. **Deadline:** Funds are limited, so students who are Guard members are encouraged to apply early. **Contact:** Applications are available from Alabama National Guard Units.

**• 105 •   Alabama Nursing Scholarship** *(Undergraduate/Loan, Scholarship)*

**Focus:** Nursing. **Qualif.:** Applicants must be Alabama residents admitted to a nursing program at an Alabama institution participating in this program.

**Funds Avail.:** Scholarship/loan amounts vary. Students must agree to practice nursing for at least one year in Alabama following completion of the nursing program. **To Apply:** Formal application required. **Deadline:** Application deadline dates vary from institution to institution. Applicants are encouraged to apply early. **Contact:** The financial aid offices at the institutions offering this award.

**• 106 •   Alabama Police Officer's and Firefighter's Survivor's Educational Assistance** *(Undergraduate/Grant)*

**Focus:** General Studies. **Qualif.:** Applicants must be dependents or spouses of police officers or firefighters killed in the line of duty in Alabama and enrolled in an undergraduate program at a public postsecondary educational institution in Alabama.

**Funds Avail.:** No limit on the grant to cover tuition, fees, books, and supplies. **To Apply:** Formal application required. **Contact:** The Alabama Commission on Higher Education at the above address (see entry 101).

**• 107 •   Alabama Scholarships for Dependents of Blind Parents** *(Undergraduate/Award)*

**Focus:** General Studies. **Qualif.:** Applicants must be Alabama residents from families in which the head of the family is blind and whose family income is insufficient to provide educational benefits. Students must attend a state institution of higher learning.

**Funds Avail.:** Awards cover instructional fees and tuition. **To Apply:** Formal applications must be filed within two years of high school graduation. **Contact:** State of Alabama Department of Education, Administrative and Financial Services Division, Gordon Persons Bldg., 50 N Ripley, Montgomery, AL 36130.

*Alabama Commission on Higher
Education (continued)*

### • 108 • Alabama Senior Adult Scholarships
*(Undergraduate/Scholarship)*

**Focus:** General Studies. **Qualif.:** Applicants must be Alabama residents who are 60 years of age or older and must attend public two-year postsecondary educational institutions in Alabama.

**Funds Avail.:** Free tuition. **Contact:** The financial aid office at any public two-year postsecondary educational institution in Alabama.

### • 109 • Alabama Stafford Loans *(Graduate, Undergraduate/Loan)*

**Focus:** General Studies. **Qualif.:** Applicants must be United States citizens or permanent residents enrolled or accepted in a participating school at least half-time. They cannot be in default on any student loan or owe a refund on a grant or scholarship. **Criteria:** Selection based on financial need.

**Funds Avail.:** Up to $2,625 per academic year for the first and second years of undergraduate study, up to $4,000 per academic year for students who have completed the first two years of undergraduate study, and up to $7,500 per academic year for graduate or professional students. Maximum of $17,250 for undergraduate study; $54,750 for graduate and undergraduate combined. **To Apply:** Formal applications must be filed. **Contact:** Applications are available from lending institutions (banks, savings and loan companies, credit unions) or from the financial aid office at educational institutions.

### • 110 • Alabama Student Assistance Program
*(Undergraduate/Grant)*

**Focus:** General Studies. **Qualif.:** Applicants must be Alabama residents attending eligible Alabama institutions. Awards are limited to undergraduate study. **Criteria:** Selection based on financial need.

**Funds Avail.:** Grants range from $300 to $2,500 per academic year. **To Apply:** Applicants must submit the Free Application for Federal Student Aid (FAFSA) to the processing center. **Deadline:** These forms should be filed early. **Contact:** FAFSA forms are available from high school guidance offices or the financial aid offices at Alabama institutions.

### • 111 • Alabama Student Grant Program
*(Undergraduate/Grant)*

**Focus:** General Studies. **Qualif.:** Alabama residents attending Birmingham-Southern College, Concordia College, Faulkner University, Huntingdon College, Judson College, Miles College, Mobile College, Oakwood College, Samford University, Southeastern Bible College, Southern Vocational College, Spring Hill College, or Stillman College at the undergraduate level at least half-time are eligible. **Criteria:** Selection is not based on need.

**Funds Avail.:** Grants of up to $1,200 per academic year may be awarded when sufficient funds are available. **To Apply:** Formal applications must be submitted. **Contact:** Applications are available from the financial aid office at the above mentioned institutions.

### • 112 • Alabama Two-Year College Academic
Scholarships *(Undergraduate/Award)*

**Focus:** General Studies. **Qualif.:** Applicants must be accepted for enrollment at public two-year postsecondary educational institutions in Alabama. **Criteria:** Selection based on demonstrated academic merit as determined by the institutional scholarship committee. Priority is given to in-state residents.

**Funds Avail.:** Awards do not exceed in-state tuition and books. Awards may be renewed if students demonstrate academic excellence. **Contact:** Financial aid office at any public two-year

postsecondary educational institution in Alabama for application details.

### • 113 • American Legion Auxiliary Scholarships
*(Undergraduate/Grant)*

**Focus:** General Studies. **Qualif.:** Applicants must be sons, daughters, grandsons, or granddaughters of veterans of World War I, World War II, Korea, Vietnam, Beirut Granada Emergency, or Panama Emergency. They must also be residents of Alabama and must attend a public postsecondary educational institution in Alabama that has on-campus housing.

**Funds Avail.:** Grant awards must be used for tuition, fees, and board. Scholarship amounts vary. Renewable annually. **To Apply:** Formal application required. **Deadline:** April 1. **Contact:** The American Legion Department Headquarters, American Legion Auxiliary, 120 N Jackson St., PO Box 1069 , Montgomery, AL, 36104 for applications.

### • 114 • American Legion Scholarships
*(Undergraduate/Scholarship)*

**Focus:** General Studies. **Qualif.:** Applicants must be sons, daughters, grandsons, or granddaughters of veterans of World War I, World War II, Korea, Vietnam, Beirut Granada Emergency, or Panama Emergency. They must be residents of Alabama and must attend a public postsecondary educational institution in Alabama that has on-campus housing.

**Funds Avail.:** Grants for tuition, fees, and board expenses vary. Renewable annually. **No. of Awards:** 37. **To Apply:** Applicants must file a formal application. Send SASE for application. **Deadline:** April 1. **Contact:** The Department Adjutant, The American Legion, PO Box 1069, Montgomery, AL, 36192 for applications.

### • 115 • Robert C. Byrd Honors Scholarship
*(Undergraduate/Scholarship)*

**Focus:** General Studies. **Qualif.:** Applicants must be high school seniors who have been admitted for enrollment at an institution of higher education. **Criteria:** Selection based on academic achievement and show of promise of continued academic achievement.

**Funds Avail.:** $1,500 one-time scholarships for the first year of study. **Contact:** Alabama high school guidance counselors for applications.

### • 116 • Federal PLUS (Parent Loans for
Undergraduate Students) *(Undergraduate/Loan)*

**Focus:** General Studies. **Qualif.:** Applicants must be natural or adoptive parents, or legal guardians of an eligible student. They must also be U.S. citizens, U.S. nationals, or eligible non-citizens, and cannot be in default on another student loan or owe a refund to an education grant program. Loans are primarily for students whose financial circumstances disqualify them for federally subsidized loans or who still need some financial assistance. Students cannot be in default on another student loan or owe a refund to an education grant program.

**Funds Avail.:** Up to $4,000 per year. Aggregate maximum is $20,000. Interest rate is adjusted annually, not to exceed 12 percent. Repayment begins 60 days after the funds are disbursed. **To Apply:** Contact financial aid offices or lenders for applications.

### • 117 • Wallace-Folsom Prepaid College Tuition
Program *(Undergraduate/Other)*

**Purpose:** To guarantee four years of fully-paid undergraduate tuition at any public junior college, college, or university in Alabama. **Focus:** General Studies. **Qualif.:** Age limits apply to students enrolled in the program.

**Funds Avail.:** Any sponsor may purchase a contract to guarantee tuition payment for a determined number of credit hours for a baccalaureate degree. Lump-sum or periodic payment plans may be selected. **Contact:** State Treasurer's Office, 204 Alabama State House, Montgomery, AL, 36130. Telephone: (205)242-7514 or (800)ALA-PACT.

• 118 •

## Alabama Department of Veterans Affairs
PO Box 1509        *Ph:* (334)242-5077
Montgomery, AL 36102-1509      *Fax:* (334)242-5102
*E-mail:* Ed.Minter@vaonline.va.gov
*URL:* http://www.agencies.state.al.US/VA

• 119 •    **Alabama G.I. Dependents' Scholarships**
*(Graduate, Undergraduate/Scholarship)*

**Focus:** General Studies. **Qualif.:** Applicants must be dependents of disabled veterans who were permanent civilian residents of the State of Alabama for at least one year immediately prior to their initial entry into active military service or for at least one year prior to any subsequent period of military service in which a break in service occurred and the civilian residency was established. Permanently service-connected veterans rated at 100 percent may qualify after establishing at least five years of permanent residency in Alabama prior to filing of an application or immediately prior to death, if deceased. Veteran must have honorably served at least 90 or more days of continuous active federal military service and must be rated 20 percent or more due to service-connected disabilities or have held the qualifying rating at the time of death or be a former POW, or declared missing in action, or died as the result of a service-connected disability, or died while on active military duty in the line of duty. Children or stepchildren must initiate training under the program prior to their 26th birthday. There is no deadline for spouses or unremarried widows or widowers.

**Funds Avail.:** Children or stepchildren are entitled to four standard academic years or part-time equivalents at any Alabama state-supported institution of higher learning or a prescribed course of study at any Alabama state-supported trade/technical school without payment of any tuition or required books. Spouses or unremarried widow or widowers of a veterans rated 20-90 percent or 100 percent temporary rated are entitled to two standard academic years or a prescribed technical course that does not exceed 18 months in duration. Scholarships do not pay for noncredit courses, placement testing, GED preparation, continuing educational courses, pre-technical courses, or state board examinations. **To Apply:** Formal application is required. **Contact:** Veteran Service Officers of the Alabama Department of Veterans Affairs located in each county, courthouse, or nearby vicinity.

• 120 •

## Alabama Library Association - Scholarship and Loan Fund, Inc.
400 S. Union St., Ste. 255
Montgomery, AL 36104-4316      *Ph:* (334)262-5210

• 121 •    **Alabama Library Association Scholarships and Loans** *(Graduate/Loan, Scholarship)*

**Purpose:** To have aid available to those pursuing a career in librarianship. **Focus:** Library and Archival Sciences. **Qualif.:** Applicants must demonstrate academic achievement and financial need. They must be residents of Alabama or be attending the University of Alabama.

**Funds Avail.:** Two awards of $1,000 each and one for $2,000. Loans are for up to $2,000. **No. of Awards:** 3. **Contact:** President, Scholarship and Loan Board, at the above address (see entry 120).

• 122 •

## Alabama Space Grant Cosortium
University of Alabama in Huntsville    *Ph:* (205)895-6800
Huntsville, AL 35899      *Fax:* (205)895-6061

• 123 •    **Alabama Space Grant Consortium Graduate Student Fellowship Program** *(Graduate/Fellowship)*

**Purpose:** To encourage interdisciplinary training and research; to train professionals for careers in related areas of study; and to encourage individuals from underrepresented groups to consider careers in related fields. **Focus:** Space related fields, including physical, natural, and biological sciences; engineering; education; economics; business; sociology; behavioral sciences; computer science; communications; law; international affairs; and public administration. **Qualif.:** Applicants must be US citizens sponsored by a consortium member institution. Individuals from underrepresented groups, specifically African Americans, Hispanics, American Indians, Pacific Islanders, Asian Americans, and women of all races are encouraged to apply. **Criteria:** Based on academic excellence.

**Funds Avail.:** Up to $20,000. **To Apply:** 7 copies of all materials must be submitted. Online applications is available from the Consortium's web site. **Deadline:** March 2.

• 124 •    **Alabama Space Grant Consortium Undergraduate Fellowship Program** *(Undergraduate/Fellowship)*

**Purpose:** To improve the understanding, assessment, development, and utilization of space. **Focus:** Space related fields. **Qualif.:** Applicants must be US citizens, attending a Consortium institution, full time undergraduate. Blacks, Hispanics, American Indians, Pacific Islanders Asian Americans, and women of all races are encourage to apply. **Criteria:** Based on academic records. **To Apply:** 7 copies of the application form, cover sheet with appropriate signatures, career goal statement, personal references, brief resume and transcripts must be submitted. **Deadline:** March 2.

• 125 •    **Teacher Education Scholarship Program** *(Undergraduate/Scholarship)*

**Purpose:** To encourage individuals to pursue careers in teaching. To reward educational excellence. To increase minority, female, and disabled participation in selected areas of study. **Focus:** Science and mathematics, including earth, space, and environmental science. **Qualif.:** Applicants must be full time undergraduate students at one of six Consortium institutions and US citizens. High school seniors planning to attend one of the six Consortium institutions and meeting other criteria may apply.

**Funds Avail.:** Up to $1000. **To Apply:** 7 copies of the application; statement of academic goals and course of study; two letters of recommendation; and a resume of education, significant accomplishments and other relevant information must be submitted. One copy of a certified transcript plus six copies must also be submitted. **Deadline:** March 2.

• 126 •
## Alaska Commission on Post-Secondary Education

3030 Vintage Blvd.                           *Ph:* (907)465-2854
Juneau, AK 99801-7109                        *Fax:* (907)586-4002
                                             *Free:* 800-441-2962

### • 127 • Alaska Family Education Loans *(Graduate, Undergraduate/Loan)*

**Purpose:** Established as an alternative to the Alaska Student Loan Program, this program provides low interest loans to students with repayment guaranteed by the student's parent, guardian, or spouse to enable a student's family to share the cost of education and reduce indebtedness faced by the student upon completion of schooling or training. **Focus:** General Studies. **Qualif.:** The family member guaranteeing the loan must meet residency requirements (one year of physical presence) at the time of application and be able to claim the student as a dependent for tax purposes for the year immediately preceding application. Continuing eligibility for loans requires continued residency by the family member guaranteeing the loan and maintenance of full-time study in good academic standing by the student. Loans may not be received under this program and the Alaska Student Loan Program for the same student for the same academic year.

**Funds Avail.:** The annual maximum award for undergraduates and graduates is $8,500 and $9,500 respectively. Loans may be awarded for up to five years of undergraduate study, or up to five years of graduate study, but not more than eight years combined, inclusive of any Alaska Student or Teacher Loans. Funds may only be used for the cost of tuition and fees, books and supplies, and room and board. Loan repayment begins the first of the month immediately following loan disbursement. Repayment is over a ten-year period with a provision for extending to 15 years if necessary. Interest rate is five percent per annum. **To Apply:** Formal application required.

### • 128 • Alaska State Educational Incentive Grants *(Undergraduate/Grant)*

**Focus:** General Studies. **Qualif.:** Applicants must be residents of Alaska for at least one year prior to SEIG application, and must be enrolled, or eligible for admission, as full-time students in a first undergraduate degree or comparable certificate program at an accredited postsecondary educational institution. If enrolled, they must be maintaining satisfactory academic progress. Students who owe a refund on a grant previously received under the Pell Grant, Supplemental Educational Opportunity Grant, or the State Educational Incentive Grant Program or who are in default on loans made, insured, or guaranteed under the Perkins Loan Act or Guaranteed Student Loan Program at the institution to be attended are not eligible. Applicants must be able to establish financial need.

**Funds Avail.:** Grant awards range from $100-1,500 depending upon financial need. Between 300 and 320 grants are awarded each year. **To Apply:** Free Application for Federal Student Aid (FAFSA) and SEIG application must be filed. Free Application for Federal Student Aid (FAFSA) must be sent to Federal Student Aid Programs, PO Box 60006, East St. Louis, IL 62206-6006. **Deadline:** Application and supporting materials must be postmarked by May 31. Students should note that the processing time for FAFSA is four to six weeks, so early applications are advisable.

### • 129 • Alaska Student Loans *(Graduate, Undergraduate/Loan)*

**Purpose:** To provide low-cost educational loans to students who have established financial need. **Focus:** General Studies. **Qualif.:** Applicants must be enrolled full-time in an undergraduate, graduate, or career degree program which is accredited by a regional or national accrediting association or approved by the Alaska Commission on Postsecondary Education. They must have physically resided in Alaska for a period of one year, or be a

dependent of a resident who has been physically present for one year (the dependent student in this case must have been present for one year out of the last five). Students with previous loans under this program, or in combination with the Family Education Loan and Teacher Scholarship Loan programs, for more than eight full school years (not more than five years of undergraduate study or five years of graduate study) are not eligible. **Criteria:** Selection is based on financial need.

**Funds Avail.:** Maximum award for each year is $8,500 for undergraduate and $9,500 for graduate students. Interest will vary each year based upon the unpaid balance of the loan. **To Apply:** Formal application is required.

### • 130 • Alaska Teacher Loans *(Undergraduate/Loan)*

**Purpose:** To encourage rural Alaska high school graduates to pursue teaching careers in rural elementary and secondary schools in the state. **Focus:** General Studies. **Qualif.:** Alaska high school graduates who are enrolled or plan to enroll full-time in a Bachelor's degree program in elementary or secondary teacher education or in a teacher certification program offered by a school accredited by a regional or national accrediting association or approved by the Alaska Commission on Postsecondary Education are eligible. Applicants must have physically resided in the State of Alaska for a continuous period of one year, or be dependents of residents who have been physically present for one year (the dependent student in this case must have been present for one out of the last five years). Students cannot receive a Teacher Loan and an Alaska Student Loan simultaneously. Full-time status and satisfactory academic progress must be maintained for eligibility. **Criteria:** Selection is based on financial need. The Alaska Commission on Postsecondary education will allocate new loan awards giving preference to rural districts. The local school districts will select loan recipients based on high school academic performance and the student's intent to enter a teaching career in a rural area of the state.

**Funds Avail.:** The maximum award is $7,500 per year. Loans may be awarded for a maximum of five years of undergraduate study and may be used for tuition, room and board, books and supplies, and transportation costs. The borrower may be eligible for forgiveness benefits of up to 100 percent of the total loan, if after graduation they are employed as teachers in a rural elementary or secondary school and meet Alaska Student Loan conditions. **To Apply:** Application forms will be sent by the Commission only to nominated recipients for completion and submission. Applications are not available for general distribution.

### • 131 • A.W. "Winn" Brindle Memorial Scholarship Loans *(Graduate, Undergraduate/Loan)*

**Focus:** Fishery Science and related disciplines. **Qualif.:** Applicants must be enrolled for full-time undergraduate or graduate study at accredited schools in fisheries, fishery science, fishery management, seafood processing, food technology, or other related fields. **Criteria:** Selection is made by the Student Financial Aid Committee of the Alaska Commission on Postsecondary Education. Applicants nominated by donors will be given preference.

**Funds Avail.:** The number of awards each year is based upon contributions. Loans may be made for up to five years of undergraduate study, five years of graduate study, or a combined maximum of eight years of study. Interest rate is eight percent and borrowers have up to ten years to repay. Scholarship loans are awarded to cover the costs of tuition and fees, books and supplies, room and board, and transportation costs for up to two round trips between the recipient's home and school each year.

**Remarks:** This program is in memory of A.W. "Winn" Brindle who was president of the Wards Cove Packing Company and Columbia Wards Fisheries. It is funded by private donations and contributions from fisheries businesses in exchange for tax credits.

## • 132 • Michael Murphy Memorial Scholarship Loans *(Graduate, Undergraduate/Loan)*

**Focus:** Law and related disciplines. **Qualif.:** Alaska residents who are undergraduate or graduate full-time students in a degree program at an accredited college or university in law enforcement, law, probation and parole, penology, or closely related fields are eligible.

**Funds Avail.:** Loans of up to $1,000 per year are non-interest-bearing. Upon degree completion, scholarship loan recipients shall receive forgiveness of 20 percent of total loan indebtedness for each one- year period they are employed full-time in Alaska law enforcement or related fields. **To Apply:** Formal application is required. **Deadline:** Application deadline is April 1.

**Remarks:** The Alaska State Legislature has established the Michael Murphy Scholarship Loan Fund for eligible Alaska residents. This scholarship loan is funded by private donations and by voluntary contributions from state employees who may contribute one or more days of annual leave to the fund. The Department of Administration credits the memorial with funds equal to the value of the donated leave and furnishes the employee with a statement reflecting the value of the donation. The statement may be used for income tax purposes. **Contact:** Lieutenant Robin Lown, Alaska State Troopers, ATTN: Michael Murphy Scholarship Fund, 2760 Sherwood Lane, Juneau, AK, 99801; (907)789-2161.

## • 133 • Robert C. Thomas Memorial Scholarship *(Graduate, Undergraduate/Loan)*

**Focus:** Education, Public Administration and related disciplines. **Qualif.:** Alaska residents who are full-time undergraduate or graduate students at an accredited college or university pursuing a career in education, public administration, or other closely related fields are eligible.

**Funds Avail.:** Scholarship loans up to $1,000 per year. The loans are non-interest-bearing and, upon degree completion, recipients shall receive forgiveness of 20 percent of total loan indebtedness for each one- year period they are employed full-time in Alaska in an education or public administration field. **To Apply:** Application required. **Deadline:** Applications are due each spring for fall enrollment. **Contact:** Rosemary Hagevig, Department of Education, 801 W. 10th St., Juneau, AK, 99801-1894.

## • 134 • WAMI Medical Education Program *(Doctorate/Other)*

**Purpose:** The WAMI Program, named for the participant states of Washington, Alaska, Montana, and Idaho, provides access to medical school for residents of these states. **Focus:** Medicine. **Qualif.:** Admission as a freshman medical student at the University of Washington School of Medicine (UWSM) is a prerequisite. Ten places in each entering class are reserved for Alaskan residents. **Criteria:** An admissions committee that includes representatives nominated by the University of Alaska reviews all applications.

**Funds Avail.:** Students pay resident tuition for the state in which they are studying. **To Apply:** Applicants must take the Medical College Admission Test (MCAT) and complete the American Medical College Application Service (AMCAS) medical school application form. AMCAS will send a copy of the application to UWSM who will request an autobiographical statement, three letters of recommendation from instructors or one from a premedical committee, a $35 fee, and a supplemental application form from the student. Applicants must also provide certification of Alaskan residency. **Deadline:** Deadline for submission of AMCAS medical school application changes from year to year; approximately November 1. Students are notified if and when they should come in for an interview. Notification of final action normally occurs no later than May 15.

**Remarks:** After admission, Alaskan students attend the University of Alaska Anchorage for the first year of medical school. Students attend the second through fourth year of medical school in Seattle, with the option of clinical clerkship during this time at clinics in towns in the WAMI states. **Contact:** Director, WAMI Program, University of Alaska Anchorage, 3211 Providence Dr., Anchorage, AK, 99508.

## • 135 • Western Interstate Commission for Higher Education Student Exchanges *(Doctorate, Graduate/Other)*

**Purpose:** Helps Alaska residents obtain access to eight fields of professional education not available in Alaska, but made available at participating institutions in other western states at a reduced tuition rate. **Focus:** Dentistry, Medicine, Osteopathic Medicine, Occupational Therapy, Optometry, Podiatry, Veterinary Science and Medicine. **Qualif.:** Applicants must have at least one continuous year of Alaska residency. Fields of study include dentistry, medicine, occupational therapy, optometry, osteopathy, physical therapy, podiatry, and veterinary medicine.

**Funds Avail.:** Reduced tuition usually amounts to the in-state rate at public schools and one-third the tuition rate at private schools. Alaska reimburses the institution where a WICHE student enrolls with a set support fee that covers the non-resident portion of the tuition and a portion of the institution's operating costs. The student does not receive any direct payment. Eligible students will receive final certification pending sufficient funding from the State Legislature. Support will continue throughout the student's program of professional or graduate study as long as he or she remains in good academic standing, maintains Alaska residency, and providing that sufficient funds are available. **Deadline:** Interested students should apply for certification to participate in the program by October 15. **Contact:** WICHE Certifying Office, Alaska Commission on Postsecondary Education, at the above address (see entry 126).

## • 136 • Western Interstate Commission for Higher Education Western Regional Graduate Program *(Doctorate, Graduate/Other)*

**Purpose:** Enables Alaska residents to enroll at reduced tuition rates in certain masters and doctoral programs selected by participating institutions in 14 western states. Residents from the western states, in turn, may enroll at the University of Alaska Fairbanks in selected degree programs at in-state tuition rates. **Focus:** General Studies. **Qualif.:** Students must meet all departmental requirements and deadlines.

**Remarks:** Eligible programs have been selected by a review committee because they serve the western region in a distinctive way.

## • 137 •
### Alaska Space Grant Progam
University of Alaska, Fairbanks
Duckering Bldg., Rm. 225
PO Box 755919                                    *Ph:* (907)474-6833
Fairbanks, AK 99775-5919                          *Fax:* (907)474-5135
*URL:* http://asgp.uafsoe.alaska.edu/index2.html

## • 138 • Alaska Space Grant Program Graduate Research Assistantships *(Graduate/Grant)*

**Purpose:** To encourage students to work closely with faculty members to propose new research initiatives for new research programs at UAF. **Focus:** Aerospace related fields. **Qualif.:** Applicants must be graduate students.

**Funds Avail.:** Stipend and tuition waiver. **Deadline:** January.

*Alaska Space Grant Progam (continued)*

### • 139 • Alaska Space Grant Program Internships *(Graduate, Undergraduate/Internship)*

**Focus:** Aerospace related fields not directly related to the applicants degree. **Qualif.:** Applicants must be graduate or undergraduate students with the UAF working on related projects. **Criteria:** Internships are generally granted to students who have already put in several months of volunteer hours on the project and have shown an active leadership role.

**Remarks:** Internships consist of 50 hours per week during the academic year and 200 hours per week during the summer.

### • 140 •
## Edward F. Albee Foundation, Inc.
William Flanagan Memorial Creative
  Persons Center
14 Harrison St.
New York, NY 10013                    *Ph:* (212)226-2020
*URL:* http://under.org/cpcc/0120.htm

### • 141 • Albee Foundation Residencies *(Professional Development/Other)*

**Purpose:** To offer writers and visual artists a private and peaceful atmosphere in which to work. **Focus:** Drama, Fiction, Music Composition, Nonfiction, Painting, Poetry, Sculpture. **Qualif.:** Qualified artists of any nationality and from all backgrounds are eligible. Awards are tenable at the Flanagan Center in New York. **Criteria:** Standards for admission are talent and need.

**Funds Avail.:** Residency. **No. of Awards:** 8 in the visual arts; 12 in writing. **To Apply:** Write to the Foundation for application forms. Submit completed forms with work samples, resume, letter of intent, and two letters of recommendation. Include a self-addressed, stamped envelope. **Deadline:** Applications accepted from January 1 to April 1. Notification by May 1. **Contact:** David Briggs, Foundation Secretary, at the above address (see entry 140).

### • 142 •
## Albert Ellis Institute
45 E. 65th St.                        *Ph:* (212)535-0822
New York, NY 10021                    *Fax:* (212)249-3582
                                      *Free:* 800-323-4738

*E-mail:* info@rebt.org
*URL:* http://www.rebt.org

### • 143 • Albert Ellis Institute Clinical Fellowships, Internships *(Graduate, Postdoctorate, Postgraduate/Fellowship)*

**Purpose:** To assist therapists to develop clinical proficiency in an active psychotherapy approach emphasizing rational-emotive behavior psychotherapy and allied cognitive-behavioral techniques. **Focus:** Psychotherapy. **Qualif.:** Applicants must be U.S. citizens or permanent residents, or have U.S. visas. They must either have an M.S.W. degree; hold a Ph.D. in psychology or counseling; or be registered nurses or medical doctors with at least one year of training in psychiatric or family practice. Candidates must be license-eligible in their respective states/countries. Selected predoctoral students with only the dissertation requirement remaining to complete their degrees may also be eligible. Fellowships are tenable at the Institute, where award recipients participate in clinical practice; study individual

psychotherapy cases; assist with public education workshops; and conduct research projects. Fellows ordinarily take two years to complete the fellowship program, but individuals from outside of the New York City area, as well as those on sabbatical leaves, may choose to double their weekly clinical workload in order to finish in one year.

**Funds Avail.:** One-year full fellowship: $1,000/month; two-year part-time fellowship: $500/month; One-year part-time internship: $500. **No. of Awards:** 6 a year. **To Apply:** Write to the training coordinator for application form and guidelines. **Deadline:** April 1.

### • 144 •
## Alberta Agriculture - 4-H Branch
Rm. 200, J.G. O'Donoghue Building
7000-113 St.                          *Ph:* (403)427-4444
Edmonton, AB, Canada T6H 5T6          *Fax:* (403)422-7755
*URL:* http://www.agric.gov.ab.ca/4h

### • 145 • 4-H Foundation of Alberta Scholarship *(Undergraduate/Scholarship)*

**Qualif.:** Applicants must be pursuing officially recognized post-secondary education, must be a resident of Alberta, Canada and must be a past 4-H member in Alberta. **Criteria:** Selection is based on 4-H achievement and academic excellence.

**Funds Avail.:** One $325 scholarship. **Deadline:** May 15.

**Remarks:** Available for Canadian residents only. **Contact:** Alberta Agriculture, 4-H Branch, at the above address (see entry 144).

### • 146 • Alberta Salers Association Scholarship *(Undergraduate/Scholarship)*

**Qualif.:** Candidates must be present or past 4-H members. Must be residents of Alberta, Canada. **Criteria:** Preference is given to applicants who have used Saler cattle and are pursuing a career in agriculture. Consideration is given to past 4-H achievements. Must have been in Alberta 4-H for 3 years.

**Funds Avail.:** One $500 scholarship. **To Apply:** Applicants must submit a 200-word essay describing their future plans and how they relate to agriculture. **Deadline:** May 15.

**Remarks:** Available for Canadian residents only. **Contact:** Alberta Agriculture, 4-H Branch, at the above address (see entry 144).

### • 147 • Alberta Treasury Branches Scholarship *(Undergraduate/Scholarship)*

**Qualif.:** Applicants must have been a 4-H member in Alberta for at least two years immediately preceding application and be enrolled in a first year degree program at an Alberta university or college offering degree credits. **Criteria:** Selection is based on 4-H achievement, community involvement and contributions, and academic standing. Must be a resident of Alberta for 5 years and a canadian citizen.

**Funds Avail.:** Seven (one per region) $1,000 scholarships. **Deadline:** May 15. **Contact:** Alberta Agriculture, 4-H Branch, at the above address (see entry 144).

### • 148 • Alberta Wheat Pool Scholarships *(Undergraduate/Scholarship)*

**Qualif.:** Applicants must be first or second year students attending an Alberta university or affiliated college offering transfer credits. Candidates' parents must derive a major portion of their income from farming. **Criteria:** Preference is given to students enrolled in a human ecology or agricultural, forestry program.

Funds Avail.: Four $500 scholarships. **No. of Awards: 4 Deadline:** May 15. **Contact:** Alberta Agriculture, 4-H Club, at the above address (see entry 144).

• **149** • **Glen Bodell Memorial Scholarship** (Undergraduate/Scholarship)

**Qualif.:** Must be a resident from Alberta (Northwest region). **Criteria:** Preference is given to a suitable 4-H candidate from Strathcona County. Otherwise, to an applicant from the Northwest 4-H Region of Alberta. Equal consideration will be given to 4-H achievement and academic excellence.

**Funds Avail.:** One award of $300. **Deadline:** May 15. **Contact:** Alberta Agriculture, 4-H Branch, at the above address (see entry 144).

• **150** • **A & E Capelle LN Herfords Scholarship** (Doctorate, Graduate, Undergraduate/Scholarship)

**Focus:** Agriculture, Veterinary Science or Human Ecology. **Qualif.:** Applicants must be pursuing a degree in agriculture, veterinary science, or home economics. **Criteria:** Preference is given to students from the counties of Lac St. Anne and Barrhead. If suitable candidate is not found, $175 award will be given to an applicant from the Northwest region.

**Funds Avail.:** One $175 scholarship. **Deadline:** May 15. **Contact:** Alberta Agriculture, 4-H Branch, at the above address (see entry 144).

• **151** • **Thomas Caryk Memorial Scholarship** (Undergraduate/Scholarship)

**Qualif.:** Candidates must have a minimum of three years 4-H experience in the Peace Region. **Criteria:** Selection is based on 4-H achievement, academic performance, and financial need. Pursuit of a diploma or degree in agriculture is preferred.

**Funds Avail.:** One $500 scholarship. **Deadline:** July 15. **Contact:** Alberta Agriculture, 4-H Branch, at the above address (see entry 144).

• **152** • **Ken Edgerton Memorial Scholarship** (Undergraduate/Scholarship)

**Qualif.:** Candidates must be past or present members of 4-H clubs in the Peace Region of Alberta with at least three years of 4-H membership. **Criteria:** Award based upon 4-H involvement, community involvement, leadership skills, and financial need.

**Funds Avail.:** One scholarship of approximately $350. **Deadline:** May 15. **Contact:** Alberta Agriculture, 4-H Branch, at the above address (see entry 144).

• **153** • **Farm Credit Corporation Scholarships** (Undergraduate/Scholarship)

**Focus:** Diploma or degree program. **Qualif.:** Applicants must be students entering the first year of a post-secondary program. Candidates must have a minimum two-year involvement in 4-H. Must be a resident of Alberta. **Criteria:** Awarded on the basis of community involvement and outstanding 4-H achievements.

**Funds Avail.:** Seven scholarships of $300 are awarded to one person from each region. **Deadline:** May 15. **Contact:** Alberta Agriculture, 4-H Branch, at the above address (see entry 144).

• **154** • **Norma Jean Gray Scholarships** (Undergraduate/Scholarship)

**Qualif.:** Candidates must be enrolled in the first year of a post-secondary program. Must be a resident of Alberta. **Criteria:** Selection is based on 4-H club leadership, community responsibility, and communication skills, particularly in the area of public speaking. Candidates must notify the 4-H office within 30 days of using the scholarship or the scholarship will be awarded to another applicant.

**Funds Avail.:** Seven awards of $1,500 each. **Deadline:** May 15. **Contact:** Alberta Agriculture, 4-H Branch, at the above address (see entry 144).

• **155** • **Hoechst Canada Bursary** (Undergraduate/Scholarship)

**Qualif.:** Candidates must be current 4-H members undertaking a degree or diploma program in agriculture at an Alberta college or university. **Criteria:** Recipients are selected on the basis of 4-H achievement, academic standing, and leadership abilities.

**Funds Avail.:** One award of $500. **Deadline:** July 15. **Contact:** Alberta Agriculture, 4-H Branch, at the above address (see entry 144).

• **156** • **Blue Klein Memorial Scholarship** (Undergraduate/Scholarship)

**Focus:** Diploma or certificate. **Qualif.:** Candidates must be past or present 4-H members, in good standing for a minimum of four years, live in the West Central Region of Alberta, and have been residents of Alberta for at least five years, and must have experience in farming.

**Funds Avail.:** One scholarship of $100. **Deadline:** May 15. **Contact:** Alberta Agriculture, 4-H Branch, at the above address (see entry 144).

• **157** • **Lilydale Co-operative Scholarship** (Undergraduate/Scholarship)

**Qualif.:** Candidates must be second year students pursuing a degree program, preferably in agriculture. They must demonstrate good leadership skills, an interest in community activities, and be from a family that derives the major portion of its income from farming. They must also have a minimum of three years of 4-H involvement.

**Funds Avail.:** One scholarship of $800. **Deadline:** July 15. **Contact:** Alberta Agriculture, 4-H Branch, at the above address (see entry 144).

• **158** • **Marilyn Sue Lloyd Memorial Scholarship** (Undergraduate/Scholarship)

**Focus:** Post-secondary institution. **Qualif.:** Candidates must be past or present 4-H members in Alberta. Preference is given to students taking equine studies. **Criteria:** Consideration given to students with 4-H achievement and high academic marks.

**Funds Avail.:** One award of $400. **Deadline:** May 15. **Contact:** Alberta Agriculture, 4-H Branch, at the above address (see entry 144).

• **159** • **Inga Marr Memorial Scholarship** (Undergraduate/Scholarship)

**Qualif.:** Candidates must be first year post-secondary students with a background in farming.

**Funds Avail.:** One award of $300. **Deadline:** May 15. **Contact:** Alberta Agriculture, 4-H Branch, at the above address (see entry 144).

• **160** • **Don Matthews Scholarship** (Undergraduate/Scholarship)

**Qualif.:** Applicants must be past or present 4-H members in Alberta displaying leadership abilities, community responsibility, and communication skills and must be a resident of Alberta.

*Alberta Agriculture - 4-H Branch (continued)*

**Funds Avail.:** One scholarship at $300. **Deadline:** May 15. **Contact:** Alberta Agriculture, 4-H Branch, at the above address (see entry 144).

### • 161 • Minburn Wild Rose Scholarship
*(Undergraduate/Scholarship)*

**Qualif.:** Candidates must have been a member of the Minburn 4-H District for a minimum of five years in Alberta. **Criteria:** Awarded based on leadership skills and 4-H and community involvement. Preference is given to students in the first year of a post-secondary program. Award wil only be given to candidate from Minburn district.

**Funds Avail.:** One award of $500. **Deadline:** May 15. **Contact:** Alberta Agriculture, 4-H Branch, at the above address (see entry 144).

### • 162 • Pennington Memorial Scholarships
*(Undergraduate/Scholarship)*

**Qualif.:** Applicants must be pursuing post-secondary study in agriculture or a related field. **Criteria:** Preference is given to applicants from Barrhead and Mayerthorpe (counties of Lac St. Anne and Improvement district) agricultural areas. Selection is based on 4-H achievement, academic standing, moral character, and financial need and must be used in year received along with notification to trustee within 30 days of use.

**Funds Avail.:** Two awards of $500 each. **Deadline:** May 15. **Contact:** Alberta Agriculture, 4-H Branch, at the above address (see entry 144).

### • 163 • George Pimm Memorial Scholarship
*(Undergraduate/Scholarship)*

**Qualif.:** Candidates must have at least three years of 4-H membership in Alberta Preference is given to candidates from the Peace Region Mackenzie 4-H district and must be a resident of Alberta. **Criteria:** Awarded on the basis of 4-H achievements and leadership skills.

**Funds Avail.:** One award of approximately $300 is offered. **Deadline:** May 15. **Contact:** Alberta Agriculture, 4-H Branch, at the above address (see entry 144).

### • 164 • Edith Taylor Memorial Scholarship
*(Undergraduate/Scholarship)*

**Qualif.:** Candidates must be from the Peace River region and have a minimum two-year involvement with the 4-H program in Alberta. **Criteria:** Selection is based on 4-H achievements, community involvement and financial need and must be a resident of Alberta.

**Funds Avail.:** One award of approximately $375. **Deadline:** May 15. **Contact:** Alberta Agriculture, 4-H Branch, at the above address (see entry 144).

### • 165 • United Farmers of Alberta Scholarship
*(Undergraduate/Scholarship)*

**Qualif.:** Candidates must be second year students pursuing a degree in agriculture or a related field at any recognized university or college in Canada. Candidates are chosen from different areas of the province each year. Parents must be actively farming. Applicant must be either a past or present 4-H member in Alberta and have a UFA membership. Applicant should have lived in Alberta for the past 5 years.

**Funds Avail.:** Two awards of $1,000 each. **Deadline:** May 15. **Contact:** Alberta Agriculture, 4-H Branch, at the above address (see entry 144).

### • 166 • Vermilion River 4-H District Scholarship
*(Undergraduate/Scholarship)*

**Qualif.:** Candidates must have been a 4-H member in Alberta for three years. They must have been active beyond club level and must have been a member of the Vermilion River 4-H District. Mature students are eligible.

**Funds Avail.:** One award of $200 ($100 per semester). **Deadline:** May 15. **Contact:** Alberta Agriculture, 4-H Branch, at the above address (see entry 144).

### • 167 • Wetaskiwin District 4-H Scholarships
*(Undergraduate/Scholarship)*

**Criteria:** Preference is given to first year students entering a post-secondary institution and who were active 4-H members who are residents of Alberta and living a minimum of three years in the Wetaskiwin 4-H District. Subject to review by the Wetaskiwin county.

**Funds Avail.:** Three awards of approximately $500 each. **Deadline:** May 15. **Contact:** Alberta Agriculture, 4-H Branch, at the above address (see entry 144).

### • 168 • Wheat Board Surplus Monies Trust Scholarships *(Undergraduate/Scholarship)*

**Criteria:** Selection is based on community involvement and outstanding achievement in 4-H who resides in Alberta.

**Funds Avail.:** Seven awards of $250 each are presented to recipients from each region and must be used in the year awarded. **Deadline:** July 15. **Contact:** Alberta Agriculture, 4-H Branch, at the above address (see entry 144).

### • 169 • Woodgrove Unifarm Local Scholarship
*(Undergraduate/Scholarship)*

**Qualif.:** Candidates must be second year post-secondary students pursuing degrees at an Alberta university or through a college transfer program. They must have a farming background and have a minimum of two years of 4-H membership. **Criteria:** Preference is given to residents of Sturgeon or Thorhild Counties.

**Funds Avail.:** One award of approximately $400. **Deadline:** July 15. **Contact:** Alberta Agriculture, 4-H Branch, at the above address (see entry 144).

---

## • 170 •
### Alberta Heritage Scholarship Fund
9th Fl, 9940 106 St.
Box 28000 Station Main                  *Ph:* (403)427-8640
Edmonton, AB, Canada T5J 4R4            *Fax:* (403)422-4516

### • 171 • Adult High School Equivalency Scholarships
*(High School/Scholarship)*

**Purpose:** To recognize outstanding achievement in the attainment of high school equivalency. **Focus:** General Studies. **Qualif.:** Applicants must have been out of school for three years, have achieved a minimum GPA of 80 percent as full-time students in courses required for entry into a post-secondary program, and be nominated by their Alberta institution.

**Funds Avail.:** $500. **No. of Awards:** 200. **To Apply:** The applicant must be nominated by the school. **Deadline:** September 1. **Contact:** The Alberta Heritage Scholarship Fund at the above address (see entry 170).

## • 172 • Alberta Educational Grants for Disabled Persons (Undergraduate/Grant)

**Focus:** General Studies. **Qualif.:** Applicants must be students who require special assistance due to physical or mental disabilities.

**Funds Avail.:** $1,000. **Contact:** Student Finance Board at the above address (see entry 170).

## • 173 • Alberta Educational Maintenance Grants (Undergraduate/Grant)

**Focus:** General Studies. **Qualif.:** Applicants must have physical, mental, or social handicaps and, in the opinion of the Students Finance Board, require special assistance. They must additionally be in special needs groups, such as single parents, disabled persons, and individuals of Native ancestry.

**Funds Avail.:** Up to $6,000 for an 8-month academic year and up to $9,000 for a 12-month academic year. Support is normally limited to a maximum of four years of undergraduate study. During the first three years of study, students are normally expected to take full advantage of student loan programs before accessing the grant. During subsequent years of study, students may not be required to take the maximum loan before receiving the Maintenance Grant. Throughout the program, students are eligible for remission benefits. **Contact:** Director, Client Services, at the above address (see entry 170).

## • 174 • Alberta Educational Opportunity Equalization Grants (Undergraduate/Grant)

**Focus:** General Studies. **Qualif.:** Applicants must be dependent students whose program of study is not available within normal commuting distance of their parent's home and demonstrate financial need.

**Funds Avail.:** $2,000 per 8-month academic year. **Contact:** Director, Client Services, at the above address (see entry 170).

## • 175 • Jimmie Condon Athletic Scholarships (Undergraduate/Scholarship)

**Focus:** General Studies. **Qualif.:** Applicants must be members of designated teams, or be recognized under the Alberta Athlete Development Program as members of a provincial disabled athlete team. **Criteria:** Student are nominated by their coach.

**Funds Avail.:** $1,000. **No. of Awards:** Approximately 1,400. **To Apply:** Alberta residents at designated Alberta schools. **Deadline:** October 15. **Contact:** The Alberta Heritage Scholarship Fund at the above address (see entry 170).

## • 176 • Anna & John Kolesar Memorial Scholarships (Undergraduate/Scholarship)

**Focus:** Education. **Qualif.:** Applicants must be Alberta residents in a family where neither parent has received a university degree and who are studying in a Faculty of Education in Alberta full-time. **Criteria:** Selection is based on academic standing in three Grade 12 matriculation subjects, one of which must be English 30.

**Funds Avail.:** $1,200. **No. of Awards:** 1. **Deadline:** July 1. **Contact:** The Alberta Heritage Scholarship Fund at the above address (see entry 170).

## • 177 • Louise McKinney Post-Secondary Scholarships (Graduate, Undergraduate/Scholarship)

**Focus:** General Studies. **Qualif.:** Applicants must be Alberta residents enrolled in undergraduate programs. **Criteria:** Applicant must be nominated by their institution.

**Funds Avail.:** $1,500 at the undergraduate level and $3,500 at the professional level. **No. of Awards:** 930. **To Apply:** Students enrolled within the province may apply directly to the awards office of their institution. Those Alberta students enrolled in programs outside the province because their program of study is not offered in Alberta should apply directly to the Alberta Heritage Scholarship Fund office. **Deadline:** June 1. **Contact:** Financial aid offices or Alberta Heritage Scholarship Fund at the above address (see entry 170).

## • 178 • Charles S. Noble Awards for Student Leadership (Undergraduate/Award)

**Focus:** General Studies. **Qualif.:** Students must exhibit outstanding leadership in the areas of student government, student societies, clubs, or organizations at the post-secondary level in Alberta. **Criteria:** Applicant must be nominated by their school.

**Funds Avail.:** $300 awards. **No. of Awards:** 80. **Deadline:** March 1. **Contact:** The Alberta Heritage Scholarship Fund at the above address (see entry 170).

## • 179 • Charles S. Noble Junior A Hockey Scholarships (Undergraduate/Scholarship)

**Focus:** General Studies. **Qualif.:** Applicants must have participated in Junior A Hockey, be currently enrolled in full-time post-secondary study in Alberta, and be nominated by their team.

**Funds Avail.:** $650. **No. of Awards:** 5. **Deadline:** December 1.

**Remarks:** The awards are co-sponsored by the Junior A Hockey League. **Contact:** The Alberta Heritage Scholarship Fund at the above address (see entry 170).

## • 180 • Charles S. Noble Junior Football Scholarships (Undergraduate/Scholarship)

**Focus:** General Studies. **Qualif.:** Applicants must be junior football players who are currently enrolled full-time in a post-secondary institution in Alberta and are nominated by their team.

**Funds Avail.:** $1,000 each. **No. of Awards:** 30. **Deadline:** October 1. **Contact:** The Alberta Heritage Scholarship Fund at the above address (see entry 170).

## • 181 • Charles S. Noble Scholarships for Study at Harvard (Undergraduate/Scholarship)

**Focus:** General Studies. **Qualif.:** Applicants must be Alberta residents who are studying at Harvard University.

**Funds Avail.:** $10,000. **No. of Awards:** 3. **Deadline:** May 15.

**Remarks:** The awards are co-sponsored from an endowment established by Edmonton businessman Sandy Mactaggart. **Contact:** The Alberta Heritage Scholarship Fund at the above address (see entry 170).

## • 182 • Northern Alberta Development Council Bursaries (Graduate, Undergraduate/Scholarship)

**Focus:** General Studies. **Qualif.:** Applicants must be long-term residents of Alberta (3 year minimum), enrolled full-time in post-secondary pursuits which will prepare them for an occupation that has high employment potential in northern Alberta, and enrolled in the latter stage of their education. They must sign an agreement to live and work one year in northern Alberta for each year of bursary support.

**Funds Avail.:** $3,000 ($1,500 if study period is less than an academic year). **No. of Awards:** Varies. **Deadline:** May 31. **Contact:** The Alberta Heritage Scholarship Fund, at the above address (see entry 170).

## • 183 • "Persons Case" Scholarships (Undergraduate/Scholarship)

**Purpose:** To promote studies that will contribute to the advancement of women. **Focus:** General Studies. **Qualif.:** Applicants must be Albertans whose studies will contribute to the

## Alberta Heritage Scholarship Fund (continued)

advancement of women, or who are studying in fields where members of their sex are traditionally few in number. **Criteria:** Awards are given based on program of study, academic achievement, and financial need.

**Funds Avail.:** $1,000 to $5,000. Yearly budget is $20,000. **To Apply:** Applicant must be a resident of Alberta and studying in Alberta. **Deadline:** September 30. **Contact:** The Alberta Heritage Scholarship Fund at the above address (see entry 170).

### • 184 • Rutherford Scholars (High School/ Scholarship)

**Focus:** General Studies. **Qualif.:** Applicants must be the top ten Alberta students graduating from grade 12, as determined solely on the basis of Diploma Examination results in English 30 or Francais 30, Social Studies 30, and 3 other subjects. **Criteria:** Applicant must apply for an Alexander Rutherford Scholarship.

**Funds Avail.:** $1,500. **No. of Awards:** 10. **Contact:** The Alberta Heritage Scholarship Fund at the above address (see entry 170).

### • 185 • Alexander Rutherford Scholarships for High School Achievement (Undergraduate/Scholarship)

**Purpose:** To recognize and reward exceptional achievement at the senior high school level and to encourage students to continue their studies. **Focus:** General Studies. **Qualif.:** Applicants must be Alberta residents who plan to enroll or are enrolled full-time in a post-secondary program of at least one semester in length. **Criteria:** Scholarships are awarded to students who have achieved a minimum average of 80 percent in five designated subjects in grades 10, 11, and 12.

**Funds Avail.:** $300 for grade 10, $500 for grade 11, and $700 for grade 12, with a total value of up to $1,500. **No. of Awards:** Over 6,000. **Deadline:** May 1 for September entry; December 1 for January entry. **Contact:** The Alberta Heritage Scholarship Fund at the above address (see entry 170).

### • 186 • United World College Scholarships (High School/Scholarship)

**Focus:** General Studies. **Qualif.:** Applicants must be Alberta residents in the process of completing Grade 11. **Criteria:** Awards are given based on academic ability, leadership capability, references, and an interview.

**Funds Avail.:** Two years of study at United World Colleges. **No. of Awards:** 6 new awards available each year. **Deadline:** March 1. **Contact:** The Alberta Heritage Scholarship Fund at the above address (see entry 170).

## • 187 •
## Alberta Teacher's Association Local No. 13
c/o Peace River School Division No.
 10
PO Box 6960                          *Ph:* (403)624-3601
Peace River, AB, Canada T8S 1S7      *Fax:* (403)624-5941

### • 188 • Greater Peace Alberta Teachers' Associatioin No. 13 Scholarship (Undergraduate/Scholarship)

**Focus:** Education. **Qualif.:** Applicants must be students entering the third year of a bachelor of education program or the first year of an after-degree program in education and who are attending school in Alberta. Applicants must have graduated from a high school in the Greater Peace Teachers' Alberta Peace Teachers' Association Local No. 13 Area.

**Funds Avail.:** $500. **No. of Awards:** 2. **To Apply:** Applicants must provide proof of official acceptance and official transcript from the appropriate post-secondary institution, three letters of reference, and a letter of application stating why they are applying for the scholarship and why they have selected teaching as a career. **Deadline:** May 31. **Contact:** President, Local No. 13, at the above address (see entry 187).

## • 189 •
## All Saints Educational Trust
St. Katharine Cree Church
86 Leadenhall Street
London EC3A 3DH, England        *Ph:* 171 283 4485

### • 190 • All Saints Educational Trust Grants (Professional Development/Grant)

**Purpose:** To further the education of persons who are, or who intend to become, teachers. **Focus:** Education, Home Economics, Religious Education. **Qualif.:** Candidate may be of any nationality. Applicant must be a teacher who wishes to take courses held in the United Kingdom. Priority is given to applicants who wish to become qualified, or better qualified, to teach religious education or home economics, especially those who wish to change their specialty to these subjects. Teachers of other subjects may apply, but must show in what way their courses or projects benefit the Church of England, or enhance the Church's contribution to education.

**Funds Avail.:** Usually £500-1,500, including allowances for fees, books, and maintenance. Awards are usually paid in installments from 1 September. **No. of Awards:** 84. **To Apply:** Write to the secretary of the Trust for application form and guidelines. **Deadline:** December for following academic year. **Contact:** Secretary at the above address (see entry 189).

## • 191 •
## Ida and Benjamin Alpert Foundation
c/o David Caplan
27600 NW Hwy., Ste. 214
Southfield, MI 48034-2184        *Ph:* (248)350-8330

### • 192 • Ida and Benjamin Alpert Scholarships (Graduate/Scholarship)

**Purpose:** To assist legal education. **Qualif.:** Applicants must be Michigan residents attending or accepted to law school. Law school need not be in Michigan. **Criteria:** Selection based on quality of required essay.

**Funds Avail.:** Scholarship amount varies. Eight scholarships of between $500 and $3,500 are awarded. **To Apply:** Application form and written essay required. **Deadline:** May 15. **Contact:** David Caplan, at the above address (see entry 191).

## • 193 •
**Alpha Delta Kappa Foundation**
International Headquarters
1615 W. 92nd St.
Kansas City, MO 64114-3210
*Ph:* (816)363-5525
*Fax:* (816)363-4010

### • 194 • Fine Arts Grants *(Professional Development/ Grant)*

**Purpose:** To recognize outstanding talent in the performing and visual arts. **Focus:** Performing Arts, Visual Arts (exact categories vary). **Qualif.:** Every two years, grants are awarded in both the performing and visual arts categories. Grants are targeted to graduate level and mid-career artists. Membership in Alpha Delta Kappa is not a prerequisite for application. Artists who have received grants from the Foundation during the last five years are not eligible to apply. Preference is given to individuals committed to teaching the arts. Other requirements may apply to specific categories of competition. **Criteria:** Selection based on submitted works (visual arts) and competition held in Kansas, MO (performing arts).

**Funds Avail.:** First place: $5,000; second place: $3,000; third place: $1,000. **No. of Awards:** Three in performing arts and three in visual arts. **To Apply:** Write the coordinator for application guidelines. Specify art category. **Deadline:** April 1 of even-numbered years. **Contact:** Dee Frost, Scholarships and Grants Coordinator, at the above address (see entry 193).

## • 195 •
**Alpha Epsilon Rho - The National Broadcasting Society**
c/o Paula C. Briggs
NBS National Office
PO Box 1058
St. Charles, MO 63302-1058
*Free:* 888-627-1266
*URL:* http://www.onu.edu/org/nbs

### • 196 • Alpha Epsilon Rho Scholarships *(Graduate, Undergraduate/Scholarship)*

**Focus:** Broadcasting. **Qualif.:** Applicants must be undergraduate or graduate members of the National Broadcasting Society - Alpha Epsilon Rho. **Criteria:** Selection is based on scholarship and service to the Society.

**Funds Avail.:** Scholarships are in the amount of $1,500. **To Apply:** Candidates should apply through local chapters. **Contact:** Local chapters of Alpha Epsilon Rho or the above address.

## • 197 •
**Alpha Kappa Alpha Educational Advancement Foundation**
5656 S. Stony Island Ave.
Chicago, IL 60637
*Ph:* (312)947-0026
*Fax:* (312)947-0277
*Free:* 800-653-6528

### • 198 • Alpha Kappa Alpha Educational Advancement Foundation Scholarships *(Undergraduate/Scholarship)*

**Purpose:** To pay for tuition, books, and education related materials. **Focus:** General Studies. **Qualif.:** To qualify for the Merit Scholarship, Applicants must have completed at least one full year of undergraduate studies and demonstrated academic excellence.

The Financial Assistance Scholarship is available to individuals currently enrolled in a course of study beyond the first year, or engaged in a program which may or may not be in a degree granting institution. Applicants need not be a member of Alpha Kappa Alpha. **Criteria:** Financial need and merit.

**Funds Avail.:** $1,500. **No. of Awards:** Approximately 40. **To Apply:** Three letters of recommendation and official transcript(s) from all colleges attended are required for application. **Deadline:** February 15. **Contact:** Doris S. Parker at the above address (see entry 197).

## • 199 •
**Alpha Mu Gamma National**
855 N. Vermont Ave.
Los Angeles, CA 90029
*Ph:* (323)644-9752
*Fax:* (323)644-9752
*E-mail:* amgnat@citymail.lacc.ce.ca.us
*URL:* http://citywww.lacc.ce.ca.us/amg/homepage.htm

### • 200 • Alpha Mu Gamma Scholarships *(Graduate, Undergraduate/Scholarship)*

**Purpose:** To further the studies of Alpha Mu Gamma members who are students of foreign languages. **Focus:** Foreign Languages. **Qualif.:** Applicants must be members of Alpha Mu Gamma.

**Funds Avail.:** Three $500 scholarships are awarded. One student of French is also nominated to receive tuition for a summer session at Laval University in Quebec along with a $400 scholarship. One $200 scholarship to study Esperants or Spanish. **No. of Awards:** 4. **To Apply:** Applicants must request scholarship information from their chapter sponsors. Official transcripts and three recommendations must be submitted with a completed application. **Deadline:** First week of January.

**Remarks:** Will reply to enquirers concerning the organization only and not concerning the scholarship. **Contact:** Hisham Malek, Administrative Assistant, at the above address (see entry 199).

## • 201 •
**Alpha Tau Delta - National Fraternity for Professional Nurses**
150 Cruickshank Dr.
Folsom, CA 95630
*Ph:* (916)984-9150
*URL:* http://www.ATDnursing.org

### • 202 • PRN Grants *(Graduate, Undergraduate/Scholarship)*

**Focus:** Nursing **Qualif.:** Applicants must be members of Alpha Tau Delta in good standing. **Criteria:** Applicants will be judged on their participation in the fraternity, level of financial need, and academic standing.

**Funds Avail.:** $1,000. **No. of Awards:** Varies. **Deadline:** April 15.

• 203 •
## Alzheimer's Association
Medical and Scientific Affairs
919 N. Michigan Ave., Ste. 1000          *Ph:* (312)335-5747
Chicago, IL 60611-1676                   *Fax:* (312)335-1110
*URL:* http://www.alz.org/

### • 204 • Alzheimer's Association Faculty Scholar Awards *(Postdoctorate/Award)*

**Purpose:** To support research relevant to degenerative brain diseases such as Alzheimer's. **Focus:** Alzheimer's Disease. **Qualif.:** Candidate may be of any nationality. Applicant must be an investigator at the junior academic level or its equivalent. Candidate should have completed at least two years of postdoctoral research and be committed to a career in basic, clinical, or social research. Proposed research need not involve direct studies of Alzheimer's disease, but it must be relevant to research being conducted in the field. Research may be in the biological, behavioral, or social sciences. Awards are tenable at any nonprofit institution worldwide.

**Funds Avail.:** Up to $50,000/year maximum is available. **To Apply:** Write to the grants coordinator for application form and guidelines. **Deadline:** Materials must be in by January 13, with Notification in June.

### • 205 • Alzheimer's Association Investigator Initiated Research Grants *(Postdoctorate/Grant)*

**Purpose:** To support research projects related to Alzheimer's disease. All applications must focus on questions around the early detection of the disease. **Focus:** Alzheimer's Disease. **Qualif.:** Applicant must be a qualified investigator, working on an ongoing, independent research project in pursuit of leads garnered from previous studies. Grants are intended to support biological, clinical, or social/behavioral research relevant to degenerative brain diseases such as Alzheimer's disease. Grants are tenable at any nonprofit institution worldwide.

**Funds Avail.:** Up to $60,000/year maximum is available. **To Apply:** Write to the grants coordinator for application form and guidelines. **Deadline:** February 13.

### • 206 • Alzheimer's Association Pilot Research Grants for New Investigators *(Postdoctorate/Grant)*

**Purpose:** To provide new investigators with funding which will allow them to develop preliminary or pilot data, to test procedures and develop hypotheses which will then underpin the preparation of research grant applications to the National Institutes of Health and other funding agencies and groups, including future proposals to the Alzheimer's Association. **Focus:** Alzheimer's Disease. **Qualif.:** Eligibility is restricted to investigators who have less than 10 years of research experience, including postdoctoral fellowships or residencies, after receipt of the doctoral degree. Proposals are accepted for biological, clinical, or social/behavioral research relevant to degenerative brain diseases such as Alzheimer's disease.

**Funds Avail.:** Grants of $40,000 are available. **To Apply:** Write to the grants coordinator for application form and guidelines. **Deadline:** January 30.

### • 207 • Alzheimer's Association Pioneer Award for Alzheimer's Disease Research *(Doctorate, Postdoctorate/Grant)*

**Purpose:** Offers investigators the opportunity of obtaining substantial research and research support funding. **Qualif.:** Investigators who have made important, ground-breaking contributions to Alzheimer's disease are encouraged to apply. It is anticipated that the successful applicants will hold senior academic rank, have international recognition of their research contributions, have lengthy peer reviewed publications in major scientific journals, and have long track records of substantial funding from the National Institutes of Health or other national funding agencies. All applications submitted to the Pioneer Award program must focus on a question or questions in the early detection of Alzheimer's disease to be considered responsive to the program announcement.

**Funds Avail.:** Award is limited to $1,000,000. Requests in any year may not exceed $300,000. **Deadline:** March 6.

### • 208 • Senator Mark Hatfield Award for Clinical Research in Alzheimer's Disease *(Doctorate, Postdoctorate/Grant)*

**Purpose:** To support clinical research by new investigators in Alzheimer's disease. **Qualif.:** Applicants for the Hatfield Award are limited to those investigators who have fewer than 10 years research experience since the receipt of the doctoral degree. The award is aimed at investigators whose goal is to establish careers focused on clinical issues in Alzheimer's disease.

**Funds Avail.:** $75,000 per year. **Deadline:** January 9.

### • 209 • Zenith Fellows Award Program *(Doctorate, Postdoctorate/Grant)*

**Purpose:** To provide a vehicle for research support for donors with a substantial personal commitment to the advancement of Alzheimer's disease. **Qualif.:** Only established independent investigators are eligible. The proposed research must be on the cutting edge of basic biomedical research and therefore may not fit current conventional scientific wisdom or may challenge the prevailing orthodoxy. The proposed research should address fundamental problems related to early detection, etiology, pathogenesis, treatment and prevention of Alzheimer's disease.

**Funds Avail.:** $200,000. **Deadline:** February 6.

• 210 •
## Amarillo Area Foundation
801 S. Fillmore St., No. 700             *Ph:* (806)376-4521
Amarillo, TX 79101-3545                  *Fax:* (806)373-3656

### • 211 • Amarillo Area Foundation Scholarship *(Undergraduate/Scholarship)*

**Focus:** General studies. **Qualif.:** Applicants must be graduating high school seniors of the 26 northernmost counties of the Texas Panhandle. **Criteria:** Awards are made based on financial need.

**Funds Avail.:** Varies. **No. of Awards:** Varies. **To Apply:** Write for further details. **Deadline:** April 1. **Contact:** Sylvia Artho, Scholarship Coordinator, at the above address (see entry 210).

• 212 •
## Ambulatory Pediatric Association
6728 Old McLean Village Dr.             *Ph:* (703)556-9222
Mc Lean, VA 22101-3906                  *Fax:* (703)556-8729

### • 213 • Ambulatory Pediatric Association Special Projects Program *(Postdoctorate/Grant)*

**Purpose:** To encourage, promote, and facilitate improved patient care, teaching, and research in General Pediatrics. **Focus:** General Pediatrics. **Qualif.:** The principle investigator must be a member of the Ambulatory Pediatric Association (APA), including in-training members. **Criteria:** Preference is given to those proposals that have the potential of leading to projects of a larger or longer-term nature. The review panel, comprised of the Chairperson of the Special Projects Program, the past APA president, and the Chairs of the four standing committees (education, research, public policy, and health care delivery) review the submitted proposals and identify those that warrant further elaboration. All applicants receive feedback from the review panel.

**Funds Avail.:** Maximum one-time grants of $10,000 per project are awarded, multiple-year funding requests are not considered. The number of awards is dependent upon the funds available from Association and the Special Projects Program and the size of the grant requests. Awardees are required to submit to the APA Board a progress report of the funded project at the end of one year and upon completion of the project. **No. of Awards:** 3-4. **To Apply:** Initial proposals of no more than two pages must include a brief overview of the project describing purpose, methods, evaluation, and estimated budget. Second proposals must be no more than ten pages in length including tables and appendices and should describe background, purpose, hypothesis methods including evaluation in educational and health care proposals, descriptions of key personnel, and a detailed budget with justification. **Deadline:** Initial proposals must be received by January 15. Applicants with proposals selected for elaboration are notified by February 15. The postmark deadline for re-submission is March 15. **Contact:** Marge Degnon at the above address (see entry 212).

---

• 214 •

## American Academy of Allergy, Asthma & Immunology

611 E. Wells St., 4th Fl.　　　　　　*Ph:* (414)272-6071
Milwaukee, WI 53202-3889　　　　　*Fax:* (414)272-6070
*E-mail:* info@aaaai.org
*URL:* http://www.aaaai.org

### • 215 • Summer Fellowship Grants *(Doctorate/Fellowship)*

**Purpose:** To fund medical students interested in pursuing research in allergy and immunology during their summer recess. **Focus:** Physiology of Allergic Diseases, Pharmacology of Allergy and Inflammation, Immunology, AIDS. **Qualif.:** Applicants must have successfully completed at least eight months of medical school by deadline and be AAAAI residents of the U.S. or Canada.

**Funds Avail.:** $2,000. **To Apply:** Write to the AAAAI for application form and information. Application must include a biographical sketch and curriculum vitae and description of research. Original and eight copies of application should be sent to the Undergraduate and Graduate Medical Education Committee Summer Fellowship Grant. **Deadline:** March 15.

**Remarks:** The AAAAI offers a variety of AAAAI Educational Grants and Awards for AAAAI members. Write for further information.

### • 216 • Underrepresented Minority Investigators Award in Asthma and Allergy *(Postdoctorate/Award)*

**Purpose:** To assist underrepresented minority postdoctoral scientists to concentrate research efforts in the fields of asthma and allergy. **Focus:** Asthma, Allergy. **Qualif.:** Applicants must be U.S. citizens or permanent residents and members of a minority group traditionally underrepresented in biomedical or behavioral research such as African Americans, Hispanics, Native Americans or Pacific Islanders. Applicants should also be postdoctoral scientists in NIH and non-NIH funded programs with an M.D.

**Funds Avail.:** $30,000/year. **No. of Awards:** 2. **To Apply:** Write for further information and application form. Original application plus five copies should be submitted to: Sri Ram, Ph.D., Director of Lung Diseases, NHLBI, 5333 W. Bard Ave., Rm. 6A09, Bethesda, MD 20892 U.S.A. **Deadline:** March 31.

**Remarks:** This award is cosponsored with the National Institute of Allergy and Infectious Diseases and the National Heart, Lung, and Blood Institute. The NIAID and NHLBI component of the award is open to Ph.D.s also and provides up to $50,000 per year. **Contact:** Jerome Schultz at the above address (see entry 214).

---

• 217 •

## American Academy of Child and Adolescent Psychiatry

c/o Office of Research　　　　　　　　*Ph:* (202)966-7300
3615 Wisconsin Ave. NW　　　　　　*Fax:* (202)966-2891
Washington, DC 20016　　　　　　　*Free:* 800-333-7636
*URL:* http://www.cuit.cpmc.columbia.edu/dept/ps/memos/
　　awards/awrd0011.html

### • 218 • Presidential Scholar Awards *(Doctorate/Award)*

**Purpose:** To recognize specialized competence among child and adolescent psychiatry residents in research, public policy, and innovative service systems. **Focus:** Psychiatry Child and Adolescent, Public Affairs.

**Funds Avail.:** Up to $2,500 for travel and lodging for one week's tutorial/exchange with a senior Academy leader in the specified area of interest, as well as participation in the Academy's Annual Meeting. **No. of Awards:** 3. **To Apply:** Nominations are made by the Program or Training Director and must include a statement in support of the nomination, the curriculum vitae of the nominee, and a statement by the nominee about a specific area of interest, plans for the tutorial/exchange, and plans for the presentation to the home program. Letters should not exceed two pages; four copies must be submitted. **Deadline:** All materials must be received by March 15, selections and announcements are made in July. **Contact:** Deputy Director of Research Development, at the above address (see entry 217).

### • 219 • Robinson/Cunningham Awards *(Postdoctorate/Award)*

**Purpose:** To recognize a paper on some aspect of child and adolescent psychiatry. **Focus:** Psychiatry—Child and Adolescent. **Qualif.:** Paper must have been started during child and adolescent psychiatry residency and completed within three years of graduation. If research is done as part of a collaborative team, the resident or recently trained resident should be the first author/principal investigator. **Criteria:** Preference is given to independent work.

**Funds Avail.:** Winner will be invited to attend the Annual Meeting of the Academy. Expenses to this meeting will be paid and the winner will be awarded a $100 honorarium. **To Apply:** Applicants must submit four copies of their manuscript. **Deadline:** June 1. **Contact:** Deputy Director of Research Development, at the above address (see entry 217).

### • 220 • Simon Wile Awards *(Postdoctorate/Award)*

**Purpose:** To acknowledge outstanding leadership and continuous contributions in the field of liaison child and adolescent psychiatry. **Focus:** Psychiatry—Child and Adolescent.

**Funds Avail.:** An $1,000 honorarium requires the recipient to make a scholarly presentation at the Annual Meeting of the Academy. **No. of Awards:** One. **To Apply:** Nominations should include a description of the nominee's work and reasons for the nomination. **Deadline:** June 1. **Contact:** Deputy Director of Research Development, at the above address (see entry 217).

---

## • 221 •
### American Academy of Crown and Bridge Prosthodontics

c/o Dr. Robert S. Staffanou     *Ph:* (707)875-3040
PO Box 1409     *Fax:* (707)875-2927
Bodega Bay, CA 94923-1409     *Free:* 800-785-9188
*E-mail:* secaafp@worldnet.att.net

#### • 222 • Tylman Research Grant *(Doctorate/Grant)*

**Purpose:** To encourage postgraduate study in crown and bridge prosthodontics. **Focus:** Prosthetic Dentistry. **Qualif.:** Applicants may be citizens of the U.S. or Canada, but must be enrolled in an accredited program. They must also receive the permission of the program director to undertake the grant. Upon completion of the grant, the student must submit a manuscript which is appropriate for publication in the *Journal of Prosthetic Dentistry*. **Criteria:** Competitive - judged by committee of 6.

**Funds Avail.:** $2,000. **No. of Awards:** 6. **To Apply:** Write to: Dr. Peter S. Lund, Chairman, 333 S. 7th St., Ste. 110, Minneapolis, MN 55402. Prosthodontic Program Directors, Tylman Graduate Student Research Support Award Committee. **Deadline:** April 1.

## • 223 •
### American Academy of Dental Electro Surgery

PO Box 374
Planetarium Station
New York, NY 10024     *Ph:* (212)595-1925

#### • 224 • Maurice J. Oringer Awards *(Graduate, Undergraduate/Award)*

**Purpose:** To motivate and reward excellence in clinical and/or research that contributes to the improvement of clinical techniques and circuitry to enhance the safety, effectiveness, and use of electrosurgery for dental therapy. **Focus:** Dentistry. **Qualif.:** Candidates must be dental school undergraduate or graduate American or Canadian students at grade A. **Criteria:** Undergraduate students must be nominated by the deans of their schools. Graduate students must be nominated by the chairpersons of their departments.

**Funds Avail.:** $1,000 per year for each award (one graduate and one undergraduate award). **No. of Awards:** 2 awards are available annually. **To Apply:** Applicants should provide detailed information about the nature, objective, and results of their efforts supported by photographic roentgenologic, and/or histologic or other pertinent laboratory confirmation in a 500-1,000 word thesis suitable for publication. **Deadline:** Candidate nominations are due by March 15; candidate thesis is due by June 15. **Contact:** M.J. Oringer, Executive Secretary, or J.D. Harrison, Chairman, Awards Committee, at the above address (see entry 223).

## • 225 •
### American Academy of Family Physicians

8880 Ward Pkwy.     *Ph:* (816)333-9700
Kansas City, MO 64114-2797     *Free:* 800-274-2237
*E-mail:* pfletche@aafp.org
*URL:* http://www.aafp.org

#### • 226 • Mead Johnson Awards for Graduate Education in Family Practice *(Postdoctorate/Award)*

**Purpose:** To assist residents entering the family practice of medicine. **Focus:** Medicine. **Qualif.:** Awards are given only for the third year of training. Applicant must currently be a second-year resident in an accredited family practice residency, with intentions to enter family practice in the United States.

**Funds Avail.:** $2,000. **No. of Awards:** 20 **To Apply:** Write to the Academy for application form. Submit completed form with a curriculum vitae, a statement of reason for study and for choice of family practice. Letters of recommendation are also required. **Deadline:** March 2. Notification in July. **Contact:** Penny Fletcher at the above address (see entry 225).

#### • 227 • Parke-Davis Teacher Development Awards *(Postdoctorate/Award)*

**Purpose:** To assist physicians beginning part-time teaching of family practice after completion of a family practice residency. **Focus:** Medicine. **Qualif.:** Applicant must be a graduate of an approved family practice residency and have been out of residency no more than three years. Candidate must plan to begin teaching of family practice part-time in a medical school and/or family practice residency. Full-time faculty, defined as teaching more than 500 hours per year, and past winners are not eligible to apply. Candidate must be a member of the American Academy of Family Physicians.

**Funds Avail.:** $1,500, plus funding to attend AAFP's Annual Scientific Assembly. **To Apply:** Write to the Academy for application form. Submit form with resume, statement of purpose, and references. **Deadline:** January 17. Awards are announced in May. **Contact:** Susie Monrante at the above address (see entry 225).

## • 228 •
### American Academy of Fixed Prosthodontics - Tylman Research Committee

c/o Kent L. Knoernschild, DMD, MS, Chm.
Dept. of Restorative Dentistry (M/C555)
Univ. of Illinois at Chicago
801 S. Paulina St.     *Ph:* (312)413-1181
Chicago, IL 60612-7212     *Fax:* (312)996-3535
*E-mail:* kentk@uic.edu
*URL:* http://www.prosthodontics.org

*Formerly known as the American Academy of Crown and Bridge Prosthodontics.*

#### • 229 • Tylman Research Grant *(Graduate, Postgraduate/Grant)*

**Purpose:** To support student research in the field of fixed prosthodontics. **Qualif.:** Full-time students in any graduate or post-graduate programs conducting research that pertains to fixed prosthodontics are eligible. Pre-doctoral dental students are not eligible. **Criteria:** Significance to the clinical practice of fixed prosthatentics (40%); scientific merit (60%). Priority will be given to students in prothodontic programs.

**Funds Avail.:** Up to six grants of $2,000. **To Apply:** Proposals from both prosthodontic and non-prosthodontic students must be endorsed by the program dir. of an accredited prosthodontic program, who will assume responsibility for ensuring timely completion of the research and compliance with all grant guidelines and obligations. **Deadline:** March 1; funded May 1. **Contact:** Prosthodontic Program Directors or Dr. Kent L. Knoernschild, Chairman, at the above address (see entry 228).

• 230 •

## American Academy of the History of Dentistry
100 S. Vail Ave.
Arlington Heights, IL 60005-1866          *Ph:* (847)670-7561

• 231 • **M.D.K. Bremner Student Award for Dental History Essay** *(Doctorate/Prize)*

**Purpose:** To encourage the study of the sciences and the art of dentistry. **Focus:** Dentistry. **Qualif.:** Open to all pre-doctoral students of dentistry from the United States and Canada.

**Funds Avail.:** The annual award is a cash prize of $500 plus one year's membership dues in the Academy. **No. of Awards:** 1. **To Apply:** Entries must be original essays certified by the dean or a responsible faculty member of the dental school in which the student is enrolled. While there is no limitation on the length of the essay, 15 double-spaced pages are recommended. **Deadline:** June 1. **Contact:** Dr. Arden Christen, 7112 Sylvan Ridge Rd. Indianapolis, IN 46240.

• 232 •

## American Academy of Otolaryngology - Head & Neck Surgery Foundation
Dept. of Research Development
1 Prince St.                           *Ph:* (703)836-4444
Alexandria, VA 22314-3357              *Fax:* (703)683-5100
*URL:* http://www.netdoor.com/entinfo/AAOHNS.htm

• 233 • **AAO-HNSF Academy Resident Research Grant** *(Postdoctorate/Grant)*

**Purpose:** To encourage research by otolaryngology residents. **Focus:** Otolaryngology. **Qualif.:** Applicant must be a resident, preferably third- or fourth-year, enrolled in an accredited otolaryngology training program. All applicants must be members in good standing of AAO-HNSF.

**Funds Avail.:** $10,000. **No. of Awards:** 5. **To Apply:** Write or call the Foundation's Department of Research Development for application, available September through January. **Deadline:** Letter of Intent January 15. Application deadline February 1.

**Remarks:** Number of grants awarded varies, depending on available funding. **Contact:** Sharon Hooper, Research Resource Coordinator, (703)519-1541, at the above address (see entry 232).

• 234 • **Combined AAOA/AAO-HNSF Research Grant** *(Postdoctorate/Grant)*

**Purpose:** To encourage research by otolaryngology residents. **Focus:** Otolaryngic Allergy. **Qualif.:** All applicants must be members in good standing of AAO-HNSF. Applicant must be a senior resident, fellow, or junior faculty member. Research must be specifically directed toward studies in otolaryngic allergy.

**Funds Avail.:** $10,000. **No. of Awards:** 1. **To Apply:** Write or call the Foundation's Department of Research Development for application, available September through January. **Deadline:** Letter of Intent January 15. Application deadline February 1.

**Remarks:** This award is cosponsored by the American Academy of Otolaryngic Allergy (AAOA) and the American Academy of Otolaryngology - Head & Neck Surgery Foundation. **Contact:** Sharon Hooper, Research Resource Coordinator, (703)519-1541, at the above address (see entry 232).

• 235 • **Combined PSEF/AAO-HNSF Research Grant** *(Postdoctorate/Grant)*

**Purpose:** To encourage collaborative research between otolaryngology and plastic surgery. **Focus:** Otolaryngology and Plastic Surgery. **Qualif.:** Applicant must be a senior resident, fellow, or junior faculty member. Research must be to demonstrate a collaborative effort between specialties.

**Funds Avail.:** $10,000. **No. of Awards:** 1. **To Apply:** Write or call the Foundation's Department of Research Development for application, available September through January. **Deadline:** Letter of Intent January 15. Application deadline February 1.

**Remarks:** This award cosponsored by the American Academy of Otolaryngology - Head and Neck Surgery Foundation and the Plastic Surgery Educational Foundation. **Contact:** Sharon Hooper, Research Resource Coordinator, (703)519-1541, at the above address (see entry 232).

• 236 • **Percy Memorial Research Award** *(Postdoctorate/Award)*

**Purpose:** To support advanced research. **Focus:** Otolaryngology. **Qualif.:** Applicant must be an experienced investigator in otolaryngology. All applicants must be members in good standing of AAO-HNSF.

**Funds Avail.:** $30,000. **No. of Awards:** 1. **To Apply:** Write or call the Foundation's Department of Research Development for application, available September through January. **Deadline:** Letter of Intent January 15. Application deadline February 1. **Contact:** Sharon Hooper, Research Resource Coordinator, (703)519-1541, at the above address (see entry 232).

• 237 •

## American Academy of Pediatrics - Resident Scholarship Program
141 NW Point Blvd.
PO Box 927                             *Ph:* (847)228-5005
Elk Grove Village, IL 60007-1019       *Fax:* (847)228-7035
*URL:* http://www.aap.org

• 238 • **AAP Residency Scholarships** *(Postdoctorate/Scholarship)*

**Purpose:** To enable young physicians to complete their pediatric training. **Focus:** Pediatrics. **Qualif.:** Applicants must be legal residents of the United States, Canada, or Puerto Rico and in pediatric residency. They must also have completed, by July 1, an approved qualifying internship, or one year of internship with a definite commitment for a first-year pediatric residency accredited by the Residency Review Committee for Pediatrics. Candidate must demonstrate financial need. Awards are tenable at institutions offering pediatric residency programs.

**Funds Avail.:** Scholars may receive $1,000, $3,000 or $5,000. **To Apply:** Write to the Academy for application form. **Deadline:** All materials must be received by the first Friday of February each year. **Contact:** Jackie Burke, at the above address (see entry 237).

• 239 •
## American Academy of Peridontology
737 N. Michigan Ave., Ste. 800
Chicago, IL 60611
*URL:* http://www.perio.org

### • 240 • The American Academy of Periodontology Student Loan Program *(Postdoctorate/Loan)*

**Purpose:** To assist in any expense required to continue or complete the student's education. **Qualif.:** Applicants must be student members of the academy; dentists and citizens of the U.S. or Canada; and be enrolled in a program approved by the Council on Dental Education of the American Dental Association in postdoctoral training for the specialty of Periodontics. **Criteria:** Selection is made by the Membership Committee and is based on financial need; and assessment of assets/liabilities, program director and applicant's comments.

**Funds Avail.:** $5,000. **To Apply:** Applications must be typed and complete. A copy of the applicants most current IRS Form 1040 (and spouses) must be included. If none were filed, please include a statement that none were filed.

### • 241 •
## American Academy of Religion
1703 Clifton Rd., NE, Ste. G5          *Ph:* (404)727-7920
Atlanta, GA 30329-4037                  *Fax:* (404)727-7959
*E-mail:* aar@emory.edu
*URL:* http://www.aar-site.org

### • 242 • American Academy of Religion Research Assistance and Collaborative Research Grants *(Other/Grant)*

**Purpose:** To stimulate research in the academic field of religion by members of the AAR or joint members of the AAR/SBL (Society of Biblical Literature). **Focus:** Religious Studies. **Qualif.:** Members of AAR or joint AAR/SBL members are eligible for funds to support individual or collaborative group research within the field of religion. No awards will be given for dissertations or scholarship support. **Criteria:** Selection based on coherence of the project, feasibility within the budget and time frame, impact of project on the field of religion, and competence of the applicant(s).

**Funds Avail.:** Individual and collaborative grants are between $500-$5,000. **No. of Awards:** 16. **To Apply:** See Religious Studies News for guidelines or contact the executive office to request brochure. **Deadline:** August 15. **Contact:** Associate Executive Director at the above address (see entry 241).

### • 243 •
## American Accordion Musicological Society
334 South Broadway
Pitman, NJ 08071                        *Ph:* (609)854-6628

### • 244 • Composer's Composition Prizes
*(Professional Development/Prize)*

**Purpose:** To encourage the composition of music for the classical accordion. **Focus:** Music Composition. **Qualif.:** Candidates may be of any nationality and must be composers who wish to create classical works for the accordion. New and young composers compete separately from those who are older and more experienced. **Criteria:** Applicants are chosen based on composition.

**Funds Avail.:** New and young composers: $250; older and experienced composers: $500. **No. of Awards:** 4. **To Apply:** Write for application form and guidelines. Submit application with $10 entry fee. **Deadline:** August.

**Remarks:** Winning composition will be published. **Contact:** Stanley Darrow at the above address (see entry 243).

### • 245 •
## American Accounting Association
5717 Bessie Dr.                         *Ph:* (941)921-7747
Sarasota, FL 34233-2399                 *Fax:* (941)923-4093
*E-mail:* aaahqpolitical actionket.net
*URL:* http://www.aaa-edu.org

### • 246 • American Accounting Association Fellowship Program in Accounting *(Doctorate/Fellowship)*

**Purpose:** To encourage and increase the supply of qualified teachers of accounting at the University level in the United States and Canada. **Focus:** Accounting. **Qualif.:** Candidate must have been accepted into a doctoral program. Awards will only go to those students in their first year. Foreign students are eligible if a resident of the U.S. or Canada at the time of application and are enrolled in or have a degree from a U.S. or Canadian accredited graduate program and plan to teach in the U.S. or Canada.

**Funds Avail.:** $2,500. **To Apply:** Contact the office manager for application guidelines, available in September. **Deadline:** February 1. Notification by March 31. **Contact:** Mary Cole, Office Manager, at the above address (see entry 245).

### • 247 •
## American Agricultural Economics Association
1110 Buckeye Ave.                       *Ph:* (515)233-3202
Ames, IA 50010-8063                     *Fax:* (515)233-3101
*E-mail:* lchristo@iastate.edu

### • 248 • Outstanding Doctoral and Master's Thesis Awards *(Doctorate, Postgraduate/Award)*

**Purpose:** To recognize superior papers written by graduate students. **Focus:** Agricultural Economics, Rural Economics. **Qualif.:** Candidate may be of any nationality. Applicant must have written a master's or doctoral thesis, or a comparable paper, in one of the areas of study listed above. The paper must have partially fulfilled the graduate degree requirements of a U.S. institution.

**Funds Avail.:** $250. **No. of Awards:** Six **To Apply:** Write for application guidelines. Three copies of the thesis must be submitted by the chair or head of the department at the home institution. **Deadline:** February 1.

### • 249 •
## American Alpine Club
710 10th St., Ste. 100                  *Ph:* (303)384-0110
Golden, CO 80401-1022                   *Fax:* (303)384-0111
*E-mail:* amalpine@ix.netcom.com

### • 250 • American Alpine Club Grants *(Other/Grant)*

**Purpose:** To support advanced scientific research in mountain and polar environments. **Focus:** Arctic and Alpine Environments.

**Qualif.:** Applicants must be currently engaged in arctic or alpine environmental research.

**Funds Avail.:** $250-600. **To Apply:** Write to the above address for application form. **Deadline:** March 1.

---

• **251** •

**American Antiquarian Society**
185 Salisbury St.                                        *Ph:* (508)755-5221
Worcester, MA 01609-1634                    *Fax:* (508)754-9069
*E-mail:* cfs@mwa.org
*URL:* http://www.acls.org/aantiqs.htm

• **252** • **AAS/American Society for Eighteenth Century Studies Fellowships** *(Professional Development/Fellowship)*

**Purpose:** To support and encourage research at the Antiquarian Society's library. **Focus:** American Eighteenth Century Studies. **Qualif.:** Applicants may be of any nationality, and need not be degree candidates. Topic of study must be appropriate to the Society's library collection. Membership in the American Society for Eighteenth Century Studies is not required for application, but successful candidates are expected to become members. **Criteria:** The fellowship awards will be made on the basis of the applicant's scholarly qualifications, the general interest of the project, and the appropriateness of the inquiry to the Society's holdings.

**Funds Avail.:** $950 per month. **No. of Awards:** One or two. **To Apply:** Write for application form and guidelines. Submit completed form with two letters of reference. **Deadline:** January 15. Notification by March 30. **Contact:** John B. Hench, Vice President for Academic and Public Programs, at the above address (see entry 251).

• **253** • **AAS Joint Fellowships with the Newberry Library** *(Doctorate, Postdoctorate/Fellowship)*

**Purpose:** To use the resources of the American Antiquarian Society library and the Newberry Library. **Focus:** American History. **Qualif.:** Candidates must be scholars who seek short-term fellowships at the American Antiquarian Society and at the Newberry Library. Recipients are expected to be in regular and continuous residence at the Society's library during the period of the grant. **Criteria:** Selection is based on the applicant's qualifications and the appropriateness of inquiry to the Society's holdings.

**Funds Avail.:** $950 a month. **To Apply:** Candidates may apply for a joint short-term fellowship at either the American Antiquarian Society or at Newberry Library with which the Society has a joint fellowship. Applications must be requested. **Deadline:** Applicants must meet each institution's deadline in order to be considered for awards by both libraries. The Newberry Library closing date is January 31. The AAS deadline is January 15. **Contact:** John B. Hench, Vice President for Academic and Public Programs, at the above address (see entry 251). Questions about The Newberry's collections and fellowship program should be directed to The Committee on Awards, The Newberry Library, 60 W. Walton St., Chicago, Illinois 60610. Telephone: (312)943-9090.

• **254** • **Stephen Botein Fellowships** *(Doctorate, Professional Development/Fellowship)*

**Purpose:** To support and encourage research on the history of the book in American culture at the Society's library. **Focus:** History of the Book in American Culture. **Qualif.:** Applicants may be of any nationality and must be scholars engaged in research and writing in any field of American history and culture through 1876. Applicants who are working on a doctoral dissertation are also

eligible to apply. Candidates' research topics must be the history of the book.

**Funds Avail.:** $950 per month. **No. of Awards:** 1-2. **To Apply:** Write for application forms and guidelines. Submit completed form with two letters of reference. **Deadline:** January 15.

**Remarks:** Notification by March 30. **Contact:** John B. Hench, Vice President for Academic and Public Programs, at the above address (see entry 251).

• **255** • **National Endowment for the Humanities Fellowships** *(Postgraduate/Fellowship)*

**Purpose:** To provide funds for long-term fellowships from four to twelve months. The fellowships are designed for both senior scholars working on broad subject areas and younger scholars at work on more narrowly focused monographs. Fellowships are not awarded to degree candidates, for study leading to an advanced degree. AAS-NEH Fellows must devote full time to their study and may not accept teaching assignments or undertake any other major activities during the tenure of the award. Fellows are expected to be in regular and continuous residence at the Society's library during the period of the grant. They may not hold any other major fellowships, except sabbaticals or other grants from their own institutions. **Focus:** American History up to 1876. **Qualif.:** Applicants must be U.S. citizens or three year residents of the U.S. Ph.D. required. **Criteria:** The fellowship awards will be made on the basis of the applicant's scholarly qualifications, the general interest of the project, and the appropriateness of the inquiry to the Society's holdings.

**Funds Avail.:** $30,000. **No. of Awards:** 2 to 3. **To Apply:** Candidates must request the AAS/NEH application form. Two letters of reference are required. **Deadline:** January 15. Notification by March 15. **Contact:** John B. Hench, Vice President for Academic and Public Programs, at the above address (see entry 251).

• **256** • **Kate B. and Hall J. Peterson Fellowships** *(Doctorate, Professional Development/Fellowship)*

**Purpose:** To support scholarly research in the Society's collections. **Focus:** American History, American Studies. **Qualif.:** Applicants may be of any nationality and must be scholars engaged in research and writing in any field of American history and culture through 1876. Applicants who are working on a doctoral dissertation are also eligible to apply. **Criteria:** The fellowship awards will be made on the bases of the applicant's scholarly qualications, the general interest of the project, and the appropriateness of the inquiry to the Society's holdings.

**Funds Avail.:** $950 per month. **No. of Awards:** 6-10. **To Apply:** Write for application forms and guidelines. Submit completed form with two letters of reference. **Deadline:** January 15. Notification by March 30. **Contact:** John B. Hench, Vice President for Academic and Public Programs, at the above address (see entry 251).

---

• **257** •

**American Art Therapy Association, Inc.**
1202 Allanson Rd.                                       *Ph:* (847)949-6064
Mundelein, IL 60060-3808                      *Fax:* (847)566-4580

• **258** • **Gladys Agell Award for Excellence in Research** *(Graduate/Award)*

**Purpose:** To encourage student research. **Qualif.:** The award goes to the most outstanding project, completed within the past year, by an art therapist using a statistical measure in the area of applied art therapy. They must be enrolled in an AATA-approved program and be a member of the AATA. **To Apply:** Applicants must submit a publishable description of the research project, proof of student status in an AATA-approved program, and proof of student

## *American Art Therapy Association, Inc. (continued)*

membership in AATA. They must submit the original and one copy of all application forms. **Deadline:** July 1. **Contact:** American Art Therapy Association at the above address (see entry 257).

### • 259 • Cay Drachnik Minorities Fund *(Graduate/Award)*

**Purpose:** To encourage professionalism in the field of art therapy. **Qualif.:** Applicants must demonstrate financial need and be accepted into an AATA-approved graduate program.

**Funds Avail.:** $200 for books. **To Apply:** Applicants must submit demonstration of financial need through letters of reference, copies of financial aid forms, etc., proof of acceptance into an approved program, and a one- or two-page essay that includes a brief biography and career goals. **Deadline:** July 1. **Contact:** American Art Therapy Association at the above address (see entry 257).

### • 260 • Myra Levick Scholarship *(Graduate/Scholarship)*

**Purpose:** To encourage professionalism and scholarship in the field of art therapy. **Qualif.:** Applicants must demonstrate financial need and be accepted into an AATA-approved graduate art therapy program and must have an undergraduate grade point average of at least 3.0.

**Funds Avail.:** $500 award and $200 for books. **To Apply:** Applicants must submit academic records, two letters of reference, proof of acceptance into an approved program, a Student Financial Information form, and a one- or two-page essay that includes a brief biography and career goals. **Deadline:** July 1. **Contact:** American Art Therapy Association at the above address (see entry 257).

### • 261 • Rawley Silver Scholarship *(Graduate/Award)*

**Purpose:** To encourage professionalism and scholarship in the field of art therapy. **Qualif.:** Applicants must be enrolled in, or accepted by, a graduate level, AATA approved art therapy program with an excellent academic record and prior experience. Applicants must also demonstrate financial need.

**Funds Avail.:** $500 award and $200 for books. **To Apply:** Applicants must submit academic records, two letters of reference, proof of acceptance into an approved program, student financial information form, and a one to two page essay which includes a brief biography and career goals. **Deadline:** July 1. **Contact:** Mr. William More, Chair, Scholarship and Grants, at the above address (see entry 257).

### • 262 •
## American Association for the Advancement of Science

1333 H St., NW                          Ph: (202)326-6600
Washington, DC 20005                     Fax: (202)289-4950
*E-mail:* science-policy@aaas.org
*URL:* http://www.aaas.org/spp/dspp/stg/fellow.htm

### • 263 • AAAS Congressional Science and Engineering Fellowships *(Postdoctorate, Professional Development/Fellowship)*

**Purpose:** To enable scientists and engineers to make practical contributions to the more effective use of scientific and technical knowledge in the government. **Focus:** Engineering, Science, U.S. Congress. **Qualif.:** Candidate must have a Ph.D. in science or engineering and demonstrate sensitivity toward political and social

issues. Scholars from the postdoctoral to mid-career levels are eligible. Awards are tenable in Washington, D.C. Fellows spend the term working as special legislative assistants on the staffs of members of Congress or congressional committees. Participation in seminars is also required.

**Funds Avail.:** $40,000 plus relocation and travel allowance. **No. of Awards:** 2. **To Apply:** Write to the AAAS Congressional Science and Engineering Fellows Program for application guidelines. **Deadline:** January 15. Notification in early April.

**Remarks:** AAAS also offers a number of awards in recognition of outstanding achievements and careers in the sciences and engineering. Write for further information. **Contact:** Project Director at the above address (see entry 262).

### • 264 • AAAS Directorate for Science & Policy Administrative Internship *(Graduate, Undergraduate/Internship)*

**Focus:** Science and Public Policy. **Qualif.:** Applicants should have a serious interest in science and public policy, and in promoting the goals of this professional society. They should have completed at least two years of college, including some course work in the areas of science, technology, public policy, and public understanding of science. **Criteria:** Priority will be given to seniors and graduate students in the natural and social sciences and engineering. Word-processing skills and telephone etiquette are appreciated.

**Funds Avail.:** $7 per hour (full- or part-time). During the academic year, starting dates are flexible and can be arranged on an individual basis. **To Apply:** Candidates must submit a resume, names and addresses of two references, and a detailed letter stating why they are interested in working for AAAS and how this opportunity might meet their overall career objective. They should also include approximate time period in which they are interested. **Deadline:** The Directorate hires interns throughout the year.

**Remarks:** The intern will assist staff in the Directorate on a wide range of projects including a R&D budget and policy project, science and technology planning, congressional information seminars, and the science and engineering fellows program. Conference and seminar organization, questionnaire survey analysis, computer data entry (training provided), and helping administer the fellows program will absorb most of the intern's time, although there may be an opportunity to conduct research and write reports. **Contact:** La Verne Evans-MacDonald, Administrative Associate, Science and Policy Programs, at the above address (see entry 262).

### • 265 • AAAS-EPA Environmental Science and Engineering Fellowships *(Postdoctorate/Fellowship)*

**Purpose:** To provide an opportunity to learn firsthand how scientific and technological information is used in environmental policy-making. Broad areas of research interest within EPA include human and environmental risk assessment; environmental socioeconomic concerns; hazardous air pollutants; global environmental hazards; pesticides, including biologicals; municipal waste water; drinking water; management and control of hazardous substances; chemical testing and assessment; radiation; and innovative technologies such as green technologies. **Focus:** Environmental Science, Engineering. **Qualif.:** Applicants must be residents of the United States and show exceptional competence in a relevant professional area, usually at the doctoral level, have a broad professional background, and have a strong interest and some experience in applying scientific or other professional knowledge toward the identification and assessment of future environmental problems. Fellows are expected to be critical thinkers, articulate, adaptable, and able to work with a variety of people from different professional backgrounds. Applicants may have any physical, biological, or behavioral science, engineering background as well as other relevant professional fields. Minorities and persons with disabilities are especially encouraged to apply.

**Funds Avail.:** Ten summer fellowships with a stipend of $950 per week each for ten weeks, plus nominal relocation and travel expenses, and up to five Environmental Science and Engineering Fellows for the year long program with a stipend of $40,000, plus allowances for moving, health and professional travel. **To Apply:** Completed applications must include a letter from the candidate indicating desire to apply; addresses and telephone numbers of two references as well as two letters of reference; a statement describing candidate's qualifications for the fellowship and career goals; a full curriculum vitae. **Deadline:** January 15. **Contact:** Environmental Science and Engineering Fellows Program at the above address (see entry 262).

• 266 • **AAAS Science, Engineering, and Diplomacy Fellows Program** (Postdoctorate/Fellowship)

**Purpose:** To provide a unique public policy learning experience in order to demonstrate the value of the interface of government, policy, and science, and to make practical contributions to the more effective use of scientific and technical knowledge in government. Fellows are either assigned to work in the U.S. State Department, working on international affairs on scientific and technical subjects, or to the U.S. Agency for International Development working on science and technology issues relevant to developing countries. **Focus:** Science. **Qualif.:** Applicants must be United States citizens and obtain security clearance. They must also be postdoctoral to mid-career scientists or engineers. They must demonstrate exceptional competence in some area of science or engineering; be cognizant of many matters in nonscientific areas; demonstrate sensitivity toward political and social issues; and have a strong interest and some experience in applying knowledge toward the solution of societal problems.

**Funds Avail.:** One year appointment with a stipend consistent with education and experience, typically starting at approximately $45,000. The fellowships are potentially renewable for a second year and may provide international travel opportunities. **Deadline:** January 15. **Contact:** American Association for the Advancement of Science, Fellowship Programs, at the above address (see entry 262).

• 267 • **AAAS Technology Policy Science and Engineering Fellowships** (Postdoctorate, Professional Development/Fellowship)

**Purpose:** To encourage collaboration between industrial scientists and engineers and the U.S. Government on issues involving scientific and technical policy. **Focus:** Science Policy. **Qualif.:** Candidate must be an industrial scientist or engineer with a graduate or professional degree and a minimum of five years professional experience. Applicant should have a strong interest and some experience in applying technical knowledge to public policies involving U.S. technology and industry. Applications are invited from candidates with a minimum of five years industrial experience, through mid-level and senior executives. Applicants must be U.S. citizens. The fellowships are tenable at the RAND Critical Technologies Institute or possibly in the White House Office of Science and Technology Policy. Fellowships include an orientation on executive branch and congressional operations and foreign affairs. Participation in seminars is also required. The program operates in parallel with the AAAS Congressional Science and Engineering Fellowships.

**Funds Avail.:** Stipends are negotiable, depending on qualifications and experience. **To Apply:** Write for application guidelines. **Deadline:** January 15. **Contact:** Project Director at the above address (see entry 262).

• 268 • **Mass Media Science and Engineering Fellowships** (Graduate/Fellowship)

**Purpose:** To enable students in the natural and social sciences and engineering to cover science and technology issues for print and broadcast media organizations. **Focus:** Engineering, Natural Sciences, Social Sciences. **Qualif.:** Applicant may be of any nationality. Candidate must ordinarily be a graduate student in the natural or social sciences or engineering, although qualified undergraduates and postdoctoral scholars are also considered. Candidate must be enrolled in a university or college at the time of application, and have a demonstrated talent for communicating technical ideas to a general audience. Students majoring in English, journalism or other nontechnical fields are not eligible to apply. During the fellowship term, each award recipient is assigned to a radio or television station, a newspaper, or a magazine in the United States, where he/she works as a reporter, researcher, and/or production assistant covering science and technology issues.

**Funds Avail.:** Weekly stipend, plus travel allowances. **No. of Awards:** 20. **To Apply:** Write to the AAAS Mass Media Science and Engineering Fellows Program for application form and guidelines. Submit form with resume, brief writing samples, transcripts, and three letters of recommendation. **Deadline:** January 15. Notification by March 15.

**Remarks:** AAAS also offers a number of awards in recognition of outstanding achievements and careers in the sciences and engineering. Write for further information. **Contact:** Amie E. King, Program Coordinator, at the above address (see entry 262).

• 269 •
**American Association of Advertising Agencies**
*Fax:* (212)573-8968
The Chrysler Bldg.
405 Lexington Ave.
New York, NY 10174-1801          *Free:* 800-676-9333
*URL:* http://www.commercepark.com/AAAA/maip/student/manager_letter.html

• 270 • **AAAA Minority Advertising Internships** (Undergraduate/Internship)

**Purpose:** The Program, a ten week (June-August) summer experience in Chicago, Detroit, Los Angeles, San Francisco, and New York, is designed to provide student interns with a realistic job experience in an advertising agency and to help prepare them for an entry-level professional position in advertising. Advertising agencies also gain an opportunity to identify talented minority students with an interest in advertising. **Focus:** Advertising, marketing, communications, general studies. **Qualif.:** Applicants must be African-American, Asian-American, Hispanic-American, or Native-American students in an undergraduate or graduate program who will have completed at least their junior year by the summer for which they are applying. They must be citizens of the United States, have a minimum GPA of 3.0 on a 4.0 scale, and plan to return to school in the fall to complete their studies. Applicants must show a commitment to a career in advertising.

**Funds Avail.:** Undergraduates receive a salary of $300 per week for a ten week internship. A higher salary is set for graduate students. Sixty percent of dormitory housing and transportation expenses are paid for students who do not live in the cities where they are placed. Between 40 and 50 internships are available. **To Apply:** Candidates must submit an application form, undergraduate school transcript, letters of recommendation from a professor and a previous employer, and two essays supporting material, e.g., sample art work. Initial screening is conducted by the AAAA Equal Employment Opportunities Committee. Semi-finalists are interviewed by the participating agencies. **Deadline:** January 3.

**Remarks:** The Minority Advertising Intern Program is administered by the American Association of Advertising Agencies. Individual agencies select interns who may be assigned to any geographical area. The student's summer position is determined by the needs of the participating agencies, and in the past have included assignments in account management, art direction, copywriting, research and media. In addition to working full-time, interns participate in seminars held at various participating agencies.

*American Association of Advertising Agencies (continued)*

Contact: Rhonda Jackman, Manager, Minority Advertising Intern Program, at the above address (see entry 269).

## • 271 •

## American Association of Airport Executives-Northeast Chapter

PO Box 1253
Rockville, MD 20849

### • 272 • Northeast Chapter of the American Association of Airport Executives (AAAE) Post Scholarship *(Undergraduate/Scholarship)*

Focus: Aviation management. Qualif.: Applicants must be juniors and seniors enrolled in colleges and universities offering an aviation management program. Criteria: Preference given to residence in the Northeast Region of the AAAE. To Apply: Write for further details. Deadline: December 31. Contact: AAAE-Northeast Chapter at the above address (see entry 271).

## • 273 •

## American Association of Cereal Chemists

3340 Pilot Knob Rd.          *Ph:* (612)454-7250
St. Paul, MN 55121-2097      *Fax:* (612)454-0766
*E-mail:* acc@scisoc.org

### • 274 • American Association of Cereal Chemists Scholarships *(Undergraduate/Scholarship)*

Purpose: To encourage scholastically outstanding undergraduate students in academic preparation for a career in cereal chemistry and technology including oilseeds, to attract and encourage outstanding students to enter the field of cereal and oilseed science and technology, and to serve as a recruitment tool for colleges and universities. Focus: Science and Technology. Qualif.: Applicants must have completed at least one term of college or university enrollment at the time of application, and hold a grade point average of at least 3.0 (4.0 scale), both cumulatively in all courses and in all science and mathematics courses. They must have at least one term remaining at the time the scholarship is awarded and have a demonstrated interest in and intent to pursue a career in cereal chemistry and technology, or in a related area, including oilseeds in industry, academia, or government. Applicants must have completed or projected a plan of work that would support their intentions to pursue such a career, and must include how the course work would do this. Students' academic schedule must meet the minimum requirements of the college or university being attended and reflect an approved course of study leading to a degree from that institution. The educational institution must be conducting fundamental investigations for the advancement of cereal science and technology or related areas, including oilseeds. Scholarships are not available to recent high school graduates nor for culinary arts majors. Criteria: GPA, relevance of course work (completed or planned) to cereal science and technology, career plans, referee appraisal of scholarship, extracurricular activities, and abilities.

Funds Avail.: $1,000-$2,000. Scholarships are awarded directly to the winners in two installments after AACC receives verification of recipients registration from appropriate department head. An AACC scholarship and the attending cash award is tenable with any other award or scholarship aid that the individual may receive. No. of Awards: 15. To Apply: Formal application and additional supporting materials required. Deadline: Application and supporting materials, including department head endorsement, are due on or before March 15. Contact: Scholarship Department at the above address (see entry 273).

### • 275 • Fellowships in Cereal Chemistry *(Doctorate, Graduate/Fellowship)*

Purpose: To encourage graduate research in cereal- and oilseed related areas. Focus: Chemistry—Cereal. Qualif.: Applicant must be enrolled in a graduate study program where fundamental research is underway. Program must lead to the M.S. or Ph.D.

Funds Avail.: $2,000-3,000. No. of Awards: 15. To Apply: Write to the Scholarship Department for formal application form. Deadline: March 15 to academic department head; April 1 to AACC. Contact: Award Jury Chair at the above address (see entry 273).

## • 276 •

## American Association of Critical Care Nurses

101 Columbia          *Ph:* (714)362-2000
Aliso Viejo, CA 92656-1491   *Fax:* (714)362-2020
                             *Free:* 800-899-2226
*URL:* http://brooklyn.cuny.edu/bc/grant/v1n5/aaccn/21994.html

### • 277 • AACN Clinical Practice Grant *(Professional Development/Grant)*

Focus: Nursing. Qualif.: Applicants must be nurses with current AACN membership. Members of the AACN Board of Directors, the AACN Research Committee, and employees of AACN are not eligible.

Funds Avail.: Up to $6,000 is available. To Apply: Grant proposals must be relevant to critical care nursing practice. Research conducted in fulfillment of an academic degree is acceptable. Applications and copies of the research priorities are available upon request. Specific proposal descriptions are outlined in the application package. Deadline: Application materials must be received by October 1. Contact: Department of Research at the above address (see entry 276).

### • 278 • AACN Educational Advancement Scholarships for Graduates *(Doctorate, Graduate/Scholarship)*

Focus: Nursing. Qualif.: Candidates must be current AACN members, licensed as registered nurses, enrolled in a masters or doctorate level program, have a cumulative GPA of at least 3.0 on a 4.0 scale, and currently work in a critical unit or have worked in a critical care unit for at least one year in the last three years. Previous recipients are eligible to reapply, but may receive no more than a total of $3,000. Members of the Board of Directors, Education Committee, and ACCN staff are not eligible.

Funds Avail.: 18 $1,500 scholarships are available. A minimum of 20 percent will be allocated to ethnic minorities. Recipients must also agree to participate in a follow-up study to discuss the impact of their degree on care of patients/families in critical care unit. No. of Awards: 18. To Apply: Completed application forms (typed only) should include official transcripts of all coursework, verification of enrollment in a planned course of graduate study, verification of employment in a critical care unit for at least one year in the last three years, a curriculum vitae, a statement regarding how applicants see their nursing practice changing as a result of their graduate degree, and an exemplar (a situation where applicant's intervention made a difference in a patient's outcome). Deadline: The deadline is May 15. Contact: AACN at the above address (see entry 276).

**• 279 •   AACN Educational Advancement Scholarships for Undergraduates** *(Undergraduate/ Scholarship)*

**Focus:** Nursing. **Qualif.:** Candidates must be current AACN members, licensed as registered nurses, enrolled in an NLN-accredited baccalaureate degree program in nursing with at least junior status, have a cumulative GPA of at least 3.0 on a 4.0 scale, and currently work in a critical unit or have worked in a critical care unit for at least one year in the last three years. Previous recipients are eligible to reapply, but may receive no more than a total of $3,000. Members of the Board of Directors, Education Committee, and AACN staff are not eligible.

**Funds Avail.:** $1,500 scholarships are available. A minimum of 20 percent will be allocated to ethnic minorities. Recipients must also agree to participate in a follow-up study to discuss impact of degree on care of patients/families in critical care units. **No. of Awards:** 37. **To Apply:** Completed application forms (typed only) should include official transcripts of all coursework; verification of employment in a critical care unit for at least one year in the last three years; letter of enrollment from school of nursing director, faculty, or advisor that verifies junior or senior status; verification from Nursing Director of NLN accreditation status; and a statement regarding goals in returning to school and past and projected contributions to critical care nursing. **Deadline:** The deadline is May 15. **Contact:** AACN at the above address (see entry 276).

**• 280 •   AACN-Sigma Theta Tau Critical Care Grant** *(Professional Development/Grant)*

**Focus:** Nursing. **Qualif.:** Applicants must be nurses with current AACN membership. Members of the AACN Board of Directors, the AACN Research Committee, and employees of AACN are not eligible.

**Funds Avail.:** $10,000 is available to qualified applicants. **No. of Awards:** One. **To Apply:** Applications outlining specific proposal descriptions are available upon request. Grant proposals must be relevant to critical care nursing practice and may be used to fund research for an academic degree. **Deadline:** Application materials must be received by October 1.

**Remarks:** This $10,000 grant is co-sponsored by AACN and Sigma Theta Tau, International. **Contact:** Department of Research at the above address (see entry 276).

**• 281 •   Data-Driven Clinical Practice Grant** *(Professional Development/Grant)*

**Purpose:** To stimulate the use of patient-focused data and/or previously generated research findings to develop, implement, and evaluate changes in acute and critical care nursing practice. **Qualif.:** Applicants must be nurses with current AACN membership. Members of the AACN Board of Directors, the AACN Research Committee, and employees of AACN are not eligible.

**Funds Avail.:** $1,000. **To Apply:** Applications outlining specific proposal descriptions and procedures are available upon request. Grant proposals must be relevant to critical care nursing practice. **Deadline:** Application materials must be received by February 1. **Contact:** Department of Research at the above address (see entry 276).

**• 282 •   KCI-AACN Critical Care Research Grant** *(Professional Development/Grant)*

**Focus:** Nursing. **Qualif.:** Applicants must be nurses with current AACN membership. Members of the AACN Board of Directors, the AACN Research Committee, and employees of AACN are not eligible.

**Funds Avail.:** Up to $15,000. **To Apply:** Applications outlining specific proposal descriptions and procedures are available upon request. Grant proposals must be relevant to critical care nursing practice and may not be used to fund research for an academic

degree. **Deadline:** February 1. **Contact:** Department of Research at the above address (see entry 276).

**• 283 •   Nellcor Puritan Bennett Inc. AACN Mentorship Grant** *(Professional Development/Grant)*

**Purpose:** To provide research support for a novice researcher with limited or no research experience working under the direction of a mentor with expertise in the area of proposed investigation. **Qualif.:** Applicants must be nurses with current AACN membership. Novice researchers may be conducting the research as part of academic requirements for a degree while mentors may not. Mentors must show strong evidence of research in the proposed area and cannot be designated on an AACN Mentorship Grant in two consecutive years. Members of the AACN Board of Directors, the AACN Research Committee, and employees of AACN are not eligible.

**Funds Avail.:** Up to $10,000 will be given to the principal investigator. **To Apply:** Applications outlining specific proposal descriptions and procedures are available upon request. Grant proposals must be relevant to critical care nursing practice. **Deadline:** Application materials must be received by February 1.

**Remarks:** This grant is sponsored by Nellcor, Inc. **Contact:** Department of Research at the above address (see entry 276).

**• 284 •**
**American Association for Dental Research**
1619 Duke St.                                  Ph: (703)548-0066
Alexandria, VA 22314-3406                Fax: (703)548-1883
*E-mail:* pat@iadr.com
*URL:* http://www.idar.com

**• 285 •   American Association for Dental Research-Student Research Fellowships** *(Doctorate/Fellowship)*

**Purpose:** To encourage dental students living in the United States to consider careers in oral health research. **Focus:** Dentistry. **Qualif.:** Students must be enrolled in an accredited DDS/DMD or hygiene program in a dental (health associated) institution within the United States and must be sponsored by a faculty member at that institution. Students should not have received their degree, nor should they be due to receive their degree in the year of the award. Applicants may have an advanced degree in a basic science subject. **Criteria:** Selection is based on scientific merit, creativity, feasibility, and potential significance to oral health research.

**Funds Avail.:** Each fellowship includes a stipend of $2,100. In addition, each preceptor receives $300 for supplies and funds for travel when research is presented. **No. of Awards:** Approximately 25. **To Apply:** Five sets of the following material must be submitted: a proposal no longer than eight pages, cover letter from the applicant's sponsor, curriculum vitae no longer than two pages, and a copy of the sponsor's biographical sketch. **Deadline:** All materials must be received by January 15. **Contact:** Ms. Patricia J. Reynolds, AADR Central Office, at the above address (see entry 284).

---

**• 286 •**

## American Association of Endodontists Foundation

211 E. Chicago Ave., Ste. 1100     *Ph:* (312)266-7255
Chicago, IL 60611-2691     *Fax:* (312)266-9867
*E-mail:* webmaster@aae.org

**• 287 • Endodontic Faculty Grants** *(Postdoctorate, Professional Development/Grant)*

**Purpose:** To strengthen the endodontic research environment for endodontic faculties and their institutions. **Focus:** Endodontics, Pulp Biology. **Qualif.:** Applicants must be full-time members of the endodontic faculty at an American Dental Association-accredited institution in the United States or Canada.

**Funds Avail.:** $6,000, maximum. **To Apply:** Write for application form and guidelines to preparing research proposal. **Deadline:** March 10. Notification by June 1.

**Remarks:** Number of awards granted varies, depending on available funding. **Contact:** Mary Bernhardt, Administrative Secretary, at the above address (see entry 286).

**• 288 • Endodontic Graduate Student Grants** *(Doctorate/Grant)*

**Purpose:** To encourage graduate dental students in endodontic programs to conduct meaningful research in endodontics/pulp biology during their specialty education. **Focus:** Endodontics, Pulp Biology. **Qualif.:** Applicants must be in the first or second year of an American Dental Association-accredited endodontic graduate program in the United States or Canada. They must also be student members of the American Association of Endodontics. Priority is given to students in the first year of training.

**Funds Avail.:** $2,000, maximum. **No. of Awards:** Depends on funds available. **To Apply:** Write for application form and guidelines to preparing research proposal. **Deadline:** March 20. Notification by June 1.

**Remarks:** Number of awards granted varies, depending on available funding. **Contact:** Mary Bernhardt, Administrative Secretary, at the above address (see entry 286).

**• 289 •**

## American Association of Family and Consumer Sciences

1555 King St.     *Ph:* (703)706-4600
Alexandria, VA 22314     *Fax:* (703)706-4663
*E-mail:* staff@aafcs.org

*Formerly known as American Home Economics Association Foundation.*

**• 290 • Borden Award** *(Professional Development/ Award)*

**Purpose:** This award, offered by Borden, Inc. through the American Home Economics Association Foundation, is presented in recognition of significant research in nutrition and/or experimental foods. This award honors an outstanding home economist for the impact the recipient's work has had on the quality of life for others. **Qualif.:** Home economists in the United States or Canada who have published research are nominated for this award. Preference is given to members of the American Home Economics Association. **Criteria:** Nominations are reviewed by a jury composed of researchers who have recognized competence in food science or nutrition. The quality of research and its fundamental contribution to knowledge is the most important consideration in the jury making its decision.

**Funds Avail.:** A $2,000 award, a gold medal, and his or her name engraved on a plaque at the Association's headquarters. **Deadline:** Nominations must be postmarked by February 1st. **Contact:** Awards Committee Chairman at the above address (see entry 289).

**• 291 • Mary Josephine Cochran Fellowship** *(Graduate/Fellowship)*

**Purpose:** To support students studying textiles and clothing. **Focus:** Textiles, Clothing. **Qualif.:** Applicant must be a U.S. citizen or permanent resident pursuing a graduate degree in textiles and clothing.

**Funds Avail.:** $3,000. **No. of Awards:** One. **To Apply:** Write to the AHEAF for application forms. A non-refundable application fee ($15 for AHEAF members, $30 for non-members) must accompany each request for forms. Eight copies of the completed application form must be submitted. **Deadline:** December 30. Awards announced in May. **Contact:** Foundation Administrator at the above address (see entry 289).

**• 292 • Commemorative Lecture Award** *(Professional Development/Award)*

**Purpose:** Recognizes and honors the professional and intellectual achievements of AHEA members and is designed to stimulate critical thinking and articulation of home economics subject matter and its relationship to society. **Qualif.:** To be eligible for the award, applicants must have made formal, scholarly presentations before large professional societies or public meetings, published in the scholarly or popular print media or have given scholarly presentations in the broadcast media, participated in programs/ activities of the Association at the national and state levels, and made significant contributions to the field of home economics through professional endeavors. Applicants must be able to attend the AHEA Annual Meeting, which is held in June. **Criteria:** The applicant's knowledge of the subject of the lecture and the quality of the prospectus of the lecture.

**Funds Avail.:** The recipient receives $2,000, financial support of up to $600 to attend the AHEA Annual Meeting, and a plaque which will be presented at the Annual Meeting, where the recipient will deliver the Commemorative Lecture. **To Apply:** Application criteria and forms are available from AHEA Headquarters. **Deadline:** Applications must be submitted to the Awards Committee Chairman by December 10. **Contact:** American Home Economics Association Foundation at the above address (see entry 289).

**• 293 • Jeannette H. Crum Fellowship; Jewell L. Taylor Fellowships** *(Graduate/Fellowship)*

**Purpose:** To promote home economics education and research **Focus:** Home Economics. **Qualif.:** Applicants must be U.S. citizens or permanent residents pursuing a graduate degree in home economics.

**Funds Avail.:** Crum: $3,000; Richards: $3,000; Taylor: $5,000. **No. of Awards:** Crum and Richards: One; Taylor: Two. **To Apply:** Write to the AHEAF for application forms. A non-refundable application fee ($15 for AHEAF members, $30 for non-members in 1994) must accompany each request for forms. **Deadline:** January 15. Awards announced in April. **Contact:** Foundation Administrator at the above address (see entry 289).

**• 294 • Mildred B. Davis Memorial Fellowship** *(Graduate/Fellowship)*

**Purpose:** To support a student majoring in nutrition **Focus:** Nutrition. **Qualif.:** Applicant must be a U.S. citizen or permanent resident who is an active student member of AHEA. Candidate must have clearly defined plans to major in nutrition at the graduate level.

**Funds Avail.:** $3,000. **No. of Awards:** One. **To Apply:** Write to the AHEAF for application forms. A non-refundable application fee ($15 for AHEAF members, $30 for non-members in 1994) must accompany each request for forms. **Deadline:** January 15. Awards announced in April. **Contact:** Foundation Administrator at the above address (see entry 289).

• **295** • **Freda A. DeKnight Memorial Fellowship** *(Graduate/Fellowship)*

**Purpose:** To promote home economics education and research by Black Americans. **Focus:** Home Economics. **Qualif.:** Applicant must be a U.S. citizen or a permanent resident. Applicant must be an African-American, and a full-time graduate student. Preference is given to applicants who plan careers in home economic communications or cooperative extension, and to candidates with professional home economics experience.

**Funds Avail.:** $3,000. **To Apply:** Write to the AHEAF for application forms. A non-refundable application fee ($15) must accompany each request for forms. Eight copies of the application must be submitted. **Deadline:** January 15. Awards will be announced in April.

**Remarks:** The names of the AHEAF programs and the value of the awards may vary from year to year. Write to the AHEAF for further information. **Contact:** Foundation Administrator at the above address (see entry 289).

• **296** • **General Fellowship** *(Graduate/Fellowship)*

**Purpose:** To promote home economics education and research. **Focus:** Home Economics. **Qualif.:** Applicant must be a U.S. citizen or permanent resident. Applicant must be a full-time graduate student in the area of home economics. Applicants with professional home economics experience are preferred. Fellowship is tenable in the United States.

**Funds Avail.:** $3,000. **To Apply:** Write to the AHEAF for application forms. A non-refundable application fee ($15 for AHEA members, $30 for non-members) must accompany each request for forms. Nine copies of the application must be submitted. **Deadline:** January 15. Awards will be announced in April.

**Remarks:** The names of the AHEAF programs, the number and value of the awards may vary from year to year. Write to the AHEAF for further information. **Contact:** Foundation Administrator at the above address (see entry 289).

• **297** • **Flemmie P. Kittrell Memorial Fellowship for Minorities** *(Graduate/Fellowship)*

**Purpose:** To promote home economics education and research by minority students. **Focus:** Home Economics. **Qualif.:** Applicant must be a U.S. citizen or permanent resident. Applicant must be a minority and a full-time graduate student in home economics. Preference is given to candidates with professional home economics experience.

**Funds Avail.:** $3,000. **To Apply:** Write to the AHEAF for application forms. A non-refundable application fee ($15 for AHEA members; $30 for non-members) must accompany each request for forms. Eight copies of the application must be submitted. **Deadline:** January 15. Awards will be announced in April.

**Remarks:** The names of the AHEAF programs and the value of the awards may vary from year to year. Write to the AHEAF for further information. **Contact:** Foundation Administrator at the above address (see entry 289).

• **298** • **Ella H. McNaughton Memorial Fellowship** *(Graduate/Fellowship)*

**Purpose:** Provides a fellowship for study in the area of aging. **Qualif.:** Applicants must be citizens or permanent residents of the United States, and must show clearly defined plans for graduate study (as defined by the applicant's university) during the time for which the fellowship is awarded. It is suggested, but not required, that applicants have completed at least one year of professional home economics experience (including a graduate assistantship, traineeship, or internship) by the time of application. The fellowship recipient will be asked to submit an annual progress report to the Foundation, and upon completing the required investigation or study, submit its title, date of completion, and the location where a written report is available. Should the study or its results be published, the name of the fellowship and the AHEA Foundation must be acknowledged. **Criteria:** Criteria used to select fellowship recipients includes scholarship and special aptitudes for advanced study and research, educational and/or professional experiences, professional and personal characteristics, professional contributions to home economics, and significance of the proposed research problem or area to the public well-being and the advancement of home economics.

**Funds Avail.:** One award of $3,000 is granted as funds allow. **To Apply:** Candidate's request for application materials must include an application fee ($15 for AHEA members, $30 for nonmembers). Nine copies of the completed application must be submitted. **Deadline:** Applications must be postmarked by January 15; awards are announced in April.

**Remarks:** In recognition of Ella McNaughton's dedicated service to the home economics profession in general, and in appreciation for her widespread support of individual members of the AHEA, this fund was established by her friends and family. **Contact:** American Home Economics Association Foundation at the above address (see entry 289).

• **299** • **James D. Moran Memorial Research Award** *(Professional Development/Award)*

**Purpose:** To recognize significant research in the area of family relations and/or child development. **Qualif.:** Applicants may be any home economist in the United States who has published research. Any AHEA member may nominate a candidate for this award. An individual may receive this award a second time only for research on a different subject. **Criteria:** The award is based on research available in published form. Nominations are reviewed by a jury composed of researchers who have recognized competence in family relations/child development. The most important consideration of the jury in making its selection is the quality of research and its fundamental contribution to knowledge.

**Funds Avail.:** The award of $1,000 and a plaque are presented at the AHEA's Annual Meeting. **To Apply:** Nomination criteria and forms are available from AHEA Headquarters. **Deadline:** Nominations must be submitted to the Awards Committee Chairman by February 1.

**Remarks:** The award recipient will be invited to submit a report of her or his research, which may be published in an issue of the *Home Economics Research Journal*. **Contact:** American Home Economics Association Foundation at the above address (see entry 289).

• **300** • **Ruth O'Brien Project Grants** *(Professional Development/Grant)*

**Purpose:** To assist home economists in developing and using their own potential to serve all members of society, and to support education, study, and scientific research relating to home economics, and improve the usefulness and effectiveness of home economics in all its aspects. **Qualif.:** Applicants must be AHEA members. Beginning researchers are encouraged to apply.

**Funds Avail.:** Up to $3,000 per grant. Funding amount changes each year. **Deadline:** Applications and all supporting materials must be filed by the second week of December.

**Remarks:** Upon completion of the project, a final report must be submitted to the Foundation. **Contact:** American Home Economics Association Foundation at the above address (see entry 289).

## American Association of Family and Consumer Sciences (continued)

### • 301 • Ethel L. Parker International Memorial Fellowship; Marion K. Piper Fellowship (Graduate/Fellowship)

**Purpose:** To promote home economics education and research. **Focus:** Home Economics. **Qualif.:** Applicant must be a citizen of a country outside of the United States who wishes to study home economics in the United States. Fellowships are generally intended for study at the graduate level, but exceptions may be made for an applicant from a country that offers little or no college training in home economics.

**Funds Avail.:** $3,000 each. **No. of Awards:** One Piper Fellowship; two Parker Fellowships. **To Apply:** Write to the AHEAF for the application. An international student residing in the United States must submit an application fee ($15) with each request for application materials, and must submit eight copies of the application. An international student living outside of the United States will not be charged a fee, and need only submit one copy of the application. **Deadline:** January 15. Awards will be announced in April.

**Remarks:** The names of the AHEAF programs and the value of the awards may vary from year to year. Write to the AHEAF for further information. **Contact:** Foundation Administrator at the above address (see entry 289).

### • 302 • Inez Eleanor Radell Sole Donor Memorial Fellowship (Graduate/Fellowship)

**Purpose:** To promote the design, construction, and marketing of clothing for handicapped and/or aging adults. **Focus:** Clothing (Construction, Design, and Marketing), Home Economics. **Qualif.:** Applicant must be a U.S. citizen or permanent resident. Applicant must have an undergraduate degree in home economics with a major in clothing, art, merchandising, business, or a related field, and must be enrolled full-time in a graduate school. Graduate study must be in the area of design, construction, and/or marketing of clothing for the aging and/or handicapped adult. Preference is given to candidates with professional home economics experience.

**Funds Avail.:** $3,000. **To Apply:** Write to the AHEAF for application forms. A non-refundable application fee ($15 in) must accompany each request for forms. Eight copies of the application must be submitted. **Deadline:** January 15. Awards will be announced in April.

**Remarks:** The names of the AHEAF programs and the value of the awards may vary from year to year. Write to the AHEAF for further information. **Contact:** Foundation Administrator at the above address (see entry 289).

### • 303 • Effie I. Raitt Memorial Fellowship (Graduate/Fellowship)

**Focus:** Home Economics. **Qualif.:** Applicants must be graduate students majoring in any area of home economics. They must also be U.S. citizens or permanent residents, and must show clearly defined plans for study (as defined by the applicant's university) for the time during which the fellowship is awarded. It is suggested, but not required, that applicants have at least one year of professional home economics experience (including a graduate assistantship, traineeship, or internship) by the time of application. The fellowship recipient will be asked to submit an annual progress report to the Foundation, and upon completing the required investigation or study, submit its title, date of completion, and the location where a written report is available. Should the study or its results be published, the name of the fellowship and the AHEA Foundation must be acknowledged. **Criteria:** Criteria used to select fellowship recipients include: scholarship and special aptitudes for advanced study and research; educational and/or professional experiences; professional and personal characteristics; professional contributions to home economics;

and significance of the proposed research problem or area to the public well-being and the advancement of home economics.

**Funds Avail.:** One $3,000 fellowship is awarded. **To Apply:** Requests for application materials must include an application fee ($15 for AHEA members, $30 for nonmembers). Eight copies of the completed application must be submitted. **Deadline:** Applications must be postmarked by January 15; awards are announced in April.

**Remarks:** This fellowship was established in memory of Effie I. Raitt, a 33-year faculty member and Dean of the School of Home Economics at the University of Washington and Past President of AHEA. **Contact:** Foundation Administrator at the above address (see entry 289).

### • 304 • Ellen H. Richards Fellowship (Graduate/Fellowship)

**Purpose:** This fellowship honors the founder of the American Home Economics Association. **Focus:** Home Economics. **Qualif.:** The award is granted to home economics graduates who plan to pursue advanced study with emphasis on administration. Applicants must be members of the American Home Economics Association and citizens or permanent residents of the United States. In addition, candidates must have at least one year of professional home economics experience (which may include a graduate assistantship, traineeship, or internship) by the beginning of the year for which the award is granted. For this fellowship, candidates must also have had work experience in an administrative area such as supervision, college or university administration, cooperative extension, or business. Candidates must show clearly defined plans for full-time graduate study during the award period. The recipient of this fellowship must submit an annual progress report to the Foundation, and upon completing the required investigation or study, must submit its title, date of completion, and the location where a written report is available. **Criteria:** Applicants are selected on the basis of scholarship and special aptitudes for advanced study and research, educational and/or professional experiences, professional and personal characteristics, professional contributions to home economics, and significance of the proposed research problems or areas to the public well-being and the advancement of home economics.

**Funds Avail.:** One fellowship of $3,000 is granted annually. **To Apply:** An application fee ($15 for AHEA members, $30 for nonmembers) must accompany each request for fellowship materials. **Deadline:** Six copies of the application must be filed by January 15. Recipient is notified in April. **Contact:** The American Home Economics Association Foundation at the above address (see entry 289).

### • 305 • Hazel Putnam Roach Memorial Fellowships (Graduate/Fellowship)

**Purpose:** To promote home economics education and research. **Focus:** Home Economics. **Qualif.:** Applicant must be a U.S. citizen or permanent resident. Applicant must be a full-time graduate student pursuing a master's degree in any area of home economics. Preference is given to candidates with professional home economics experience.

**Funds Avail.:** $3,000. **To Apply:** Write to the AHEAF for application forms. An application fee ($15) must accompany each request for forms. Eight copies of the application must be submitted. **Deadline:** January 15. Awards will be announced in April.

**Remarks:** The names of the AHEAF programs and the value of the awards may vary from year to year. Write to the AHEAF for further information. **Contact:** Foundation Administrator at the above address (see entry 289).

### • 306 • Wiley-Berger Memorial Award for Volunteer Service (Professional Development/Award)

**Purpose:** Given in recognition of outstanding effort in a volunteer capacity to improve the public well-being. **Criteria:** The most important consideration of the jury is evidence that the nominee has demonstrated how home economics can contribute to the community through either consistent volunteer service over a period of years, or through the implementation of an exemplary volunteer service project.

**Funds Avail.:** The recipient receives a cash award of $1,000 and a commemorative certificate. Both are presented at the AHEA Annual Meeting. **To Apply:** Nominations may be submitted by any individual or organization using the nomination procedures and forms. Self-nominations, nominations by AHEA state affiliates, and nominations by local, state, national, and community service organizations are especially encouraged. Nomination criteria and forms are available from AHEA headquarters. **Deadline:** Nominations must be submitted to the Awards Committee Chairman by February 1. **Contact:** American Home Economics Association Foundation at the above address (see entry 289).

---

**• 307 •**

## American Association of Hispanic CPA'S
19726 E. Columa Rd., Ste. 270
Rowland Heights, CA 20037          *Ph:* (202)337-4069
*E-mail:* 104124,553@compupserve.com

**• 308 •   AAHCPA Scholarship** (*Undergraduate/Scholarship*)

**Purpose:** To promote the advancement of Hispanics in the accounting profession. **Focus:** Accounting. **Qualif.:** Candidates must be Hispanic students majoring in accounting. **Criteria:** Academic achievement, financial need and community involvement.

**Funds Avail.:** Varies (approximately $5,000 per year). **No. of Awards:** Varies. **To Apply:** Applicants must send a completed scholarship application with essay; an official transcript; one letter of recommendation; a copy of financial aid offer letter; and a copy of a current class schedule. **Deadline:** September 30. **Contact:** John R. Hernandez, Executive Director at the above address (see entry 307).

---

**• 309 •**

## American Association of Law Libraries
53 W. Jackson Blvd., Ste. 940       *Ph:* (312)939-4764
Chicago, IL 60604                   *Fax:* (312)431-1097
*E-mail:* aallhq@aall.org
*URL:* http://aallnet.org

**• 310 •   AALL Law Librarians in Continuing Education Courses Scholarship** (*Graduate/Scholarship*)

**Qualif.:** Candidates must be members of AALL and registrants of a course in law librarianship taken for credit at an accredited library school. **Criteria:** Scholarships are awarded on the basis of proven ability, promise of future usefulness, permanence in the law library profession, and financial need. Preference is given to permanent residents of the United States and Canada.

**Funds Avail.:** One or more scholarships of up to $500 for tuition, plus $25 for incidentals are awarded annually. **To Apply:** Applicants should submit a completed application with a statement (typed on 8 x 11 paper) discussing interest in law librarianship, reasons for this interest, reason applying for the scholarship, and career goals; three letters of recommendation; a self-addressed, stamped envelope and a postcard for receipt of application and committee's decision; and eight collated and stapled copies of the entire application package. **Deadline:** April 1.

**Contact:** Scholarships Committee at the above address (see entry 309).

**• 311 •   James F. Connolly Congressional Informaton Service Scholarship** (*Graduate, Professional Development/Scholarship*)

**Focus:** Law. **Qualif.:** Applicants must be law librarians interested in pursuing a law degree. **Criteria:** Preference will be given to a librarian who had demonstrated an interest in government publications.

**Funds Avail.:** $3,000.

**• 312 •   Law Degree Scholarships for Library School Graduates** (*Doctorate/Scholarship*)

**Purpose:** To support students who plan to pursue careers in law librarianship. **Focus:** Law Librarianship. **Qualif.:** Candidate should preferably be a U.S. or Canadian citizen. Applicant must be a graduate of an accredited library school who is working toward a law degree in an accredited law school, with no more than 36 semester (or 54 quarter) credit hours of study remaining before qualifying for the degree. Candidate must have meaningful law library experience. Scholarships are tenable at a law school accredited by the American Bar Association.

**Funds Avail.:** $1,500-$3,500. **To Apply:** Write for application form and guidelines. **Deadline:** April 1.

**Remarks:** Funds are also available to law librarians for a course related to law librarianship. Write the Association for further details. **Contact:** Scholarship Committee at the above address (see entry 309).

**• 313 •   Library Degree Scholarships for Law School Graduates** (*Graduate/Scholarship*)

**Purpose:** To support students who plan to pursue careers in law librarianship. **Focus:** Law Librarianship. **Qualif.:** Candidate should preferably be a U.S. or Canadian citizen. Applicant must be a graduate of an accredited law school who is a degree candidate in an accredited library school.

**Funds Avail.:** $1,500-$3,500. **To Apply:** Write for application form and guidelines. **Deadline:** April 1. Notification by May 31.

**Remarks:** Funds are also available to law librarians for a course related to law librarianship. Write the Association for further details. **Contact:** Scholarship Committee at the above address (see entry 309).

**• 314 •   Library Degree Scholarships for Non-Law School Graduates** (*Graduate/Scholarship*)

**Purpose:** To support students who plan to pursue careers in law librarianship. **Focus:** Law Librarianship. **Qualif.:** Candidate should preferably be a U.S. or Canadian citizen. Applicant must be a graduate of an accredited college; a degree candidate in an accredited library school; and have some law library experience.

**Funds Avail.:** $2,500 maximum. **To Apply:** Write for application form and guidelines. **Deadline:** April 1. Notification by May 31.

**Remarks:** Funds are also available to law librarians for a course related to law librarianship. Write the Association for further details. **Contact:** Scholarship Committee at the above address (see entry 309).

**• 315 •   George A. Strait Minority Stipend** (*Graduate/Award*)

**Purpose:** To support minority students who plan to pursue careers in law librarianship. **Focus:** Law Librarianship. **Qualif.:** Applicant must be a U.S. or Canadian citizen, or submit evidence that naturalization proceedings have begun by the beginning of the year of application. Applicant must be a member of a minority

---

Awards are arranged alphabetically below their administering organizations

*American Association of Law Libraries (continued)*

group, and a college graduate with library experience. Applicant must be working toward an advanced degree to further a library career. Preference will be given to candidates with previous service to, or interest in, law librarianship.

**Funds Avail.:** $1,500-$3,500. **To Apply:** Write for application form and guidelines. **Deadline:** April 1. Notification by May 31.

**Remarks:** Funds are also available to law librarians for a course related to law librarianship. Write the Association for further details. **Contact:** Scholarship Committee at the above address (see entry 309).

---

**• 316 •**
**American Association of Medical Assistants'**
**Endowment**
20 N. Wacker Dr., Ste. 1575          *Ph:* (312)899-1500
Chicago, IL 60606          *Free:* 800-228-2262

**• 317 •   Maxine Williams Scholarships** *(Other/Scholarship)*

**Purpose:** To support students pursuing careers as medical assistants. **Focus:** Medical Assisting. **Qualif.:** Candidate may be of any nationality. Applicant must hold a high school diploma or the equivalent and must be committed to a career as a medical assistant. Candidate must demonstrate financial need. Scholarships are tenable at postsecondary medical assistant training programs accredited by the Commission on Accreditation of Allied Health Education Programs (CAAHEP).

**Funds Avail.:** $500. **No. of Awards:** 4-6. **To Apply:** Write to the assistant executive director for application form and guidelines. Submit form with letter of recommendation from the medical assisting program director with most recent transcripts, reasons for wanting to become a medical assistant, and a statement of financial need. **Deadline:** February 1 and June 1. Candidates will be notified six weeks after the deadline. **Contact:** Anna L. Johnson, Assistant Executive Director, at the above address (see entry 316).

---

**• 318 •**
**American Association of Petroleum Geologists**
**Foundation - Grants-in-Aid Committee**
PO Box 979          *Ph:* (918)584-2555
Tulsa, OK 74101-0979          *Fax:* (918)560-2642
*E-mail:* rgriffin@aapg.org
*URL:* http://www.aapg.org/fdn.html

**• 319 •   American Association of Petroleum**
**Geologists Foundation Grants-in-Aid** *(Doctorate, Graduate/Grant)*

**Purpose:** To support research projects in the geosciences leading to M.S. degrees (or in some cases Ph.D.s) that are related to the search and development of petroleum and energy minerals resources, and to related environmental geology issues. **Focus:** Petroleum Sciences. **Qualif.:** Candidate may be of any nationality. Applicant must be a qualified graduate student whose project is endorsed by his/her faculty supervisor and department chairperson or graduate advisor. Grants are tenable worldwide. Funds cannot be used to purchase capital equipment or as salary.

**Funds Avail.:** Up to $2,000. **No. of Awards:** 50. **To Apply:** Write for application forms. Submit forms with a summary of the proposed project and how funds would be used, and faculty endorsements. **Deadline:** Mid-January. Awards will be announced by April 30.

**Remarks:** The Grants-in-Aid Program includes named grants with specific restrictions. The Gustavus E. Archie Grant supports studies related to petrophysics and development geology. The Thomas A. Hendricks Grant supports studies of the Ouachitas, the Arkoma Basin, and/or the Marathon/Solitario areas. The Hugh D. Miser Grant is limited to the studies of the geology of Arkansas and Oklahoma. The Raymond C. Moore Grant is awarded for significant involvement with paleontology. **Contact:** Rebecca Griffin at the above address (see entry 318).

---

**• 320 •**
**American Association of School Administrators**
1801 N. Moore St.          *Ph:* (703)875-0714
Arlington, VA 22209          *Fax:* (703)528-2146
*E-mail:* dpierce@aasa.org

**• 321 •   AASA and Convention Exhibitors**
**Scholarships** *(Graduate/Scholarship)*

**Purpose:** To encourage and support outstanding graduate students who intend to pursue careers in public school administration. **Focus:** Education **Qualif.:** Applicant must be a graduate student in the field of school administration enrolled at a U.S. or Canadian institution. Candidate must intend to pursue the public school superintendency as a career. Candidate must be nominated by the dean of the department.

**Funds Avail.:** $2,000. **No. of Awards:** Six. **To Apply:** Write for nomination guidelines. Contact the Dept. of Education at local university. **Deadline:** September 15.

**Remarks:** AASA gives numerous awards in recognition of outstanding contributions by educators, and to honor positive role models from all fields. Candidates for most awards must be nominated. Write to AASA for further information. **Contact:** Darlene Pierce, at the above address (see entry 320).

---

**• 322 •**
**American Association of Teachers of Arabic**
c/o R. Kirk Belhap, Executive
     Director
280 HRCB - Brigham Young
     University          *Ph:* (801)378-3723
Provo, UT 84602          *Fax:* (801)378-5866
*E-mail:* aata@byu.edu
*URL:* http://humanities.byu.edu/aata/aata_homepage.html

**• 323 •   Arabic Translation Contest** *(Other/Prize)*

**Purpose:** To address the need for capable translators who can produce accurate, fluent, and when appropriate, artistic English renditions of Arabic literary and nonliterary texts. **Qualif.:** Current students in a program of Arabic instruction at any level or individuals who have been participating in such a program within the last two years are eligible. **Criteria:** A committee of judges will be appointed from among the active membership of AATA. This committee, in particular cases, will solicit additional evaluations of translations from individuals specially qualified in the areas in question, and these evaluations will be given full consideration by the committee in its final decision.

**Funds Avail.:** First place prize of $600 and one second place prize of $400 will be given. **To Apply:** Applicants must submit a translation of approximately 15 to 20 pages. Length is only a suggestion, individuals are free to submit longer or shorter translations as the difficulty, complexity, continuity, or other circumstances might dictate. Translation must be accompanied by a simple note attesting to the student's participation signed by their instructor or another responsible person within the program, short resume, a copy of the translated text, and a short prefatory essay. Applicants are discouraged from submitting translations of texts that have already been translated into English or any other major European language, they must explain convincingly the need for a new translation and provide a copy of the appropriate portion of the earlier translation. Six copies of the entire application must be submitted. **Deadline:** September 1. **Contact:** Professor Mona Mikhail, Kevorkian Center for Near East Studies, New York University, 50 Washington Square South, New York, NY, 10012.

## • 324 •
## American Association of Teachers of French
57 E. Armory Ave.           *Ph:* (217)333-2842
Champaign, IL 61820          *Fax:* (217)333-2842

### • 325 •   AATF Summer Institute in France
*(Professional Development/Fellowship)*

**Purpose:** To enable American teachers of French to improve their communicative skills and to learn about the history, literature, and culture of France. **Focus:** French Language. **Qualif.:** Candidate must be a U.S. citizen, a member of AATF, and a teacher of French at the elementary, secondary, or university level. Applicants must plan to continue teaching French for five years after the program. The program begins at Indiana University and is completed in France.

**Funds Avail.:** Room and board and $300 toward airfare. **No. of Awards:** 22. **To Apply:** Write for current application forms and instructions. **Deadline:** December 1; recipients will be notified by April 1. **Contact:** Margot Steinhart, Vice President for Scholarships, at the above address (see entry 324).

## • 326 •
## American Association of Teachers of German
112 Haddontowne Ct., No. 104     *Ph:* (609)795-5553
Cherry Hill, NJ 08034        *Fax:* (609)795-9398
*E-mail:* 73740,3231@compuserve.com
*URL:* http://www.stolaf.edu/stolaf/depts/german/aatg

### • 327 •   AATG/PAD Travel/Study Awards *(High School/Award)*

**Purpose:** To stimulate interest in German Studies. **Focus:** German Studies, Foreign Languages. **Qualif.:** Students must score in the 90 percentile on the National German test to qualify. They must be at least 16 years old as of December 31 of the year in which they compete, and must not live in a household where regular conversation is in German, nor have lived or traveled for more than a total of eight weeks in German-speaking countries since the age of six. Eligible candidates must be in their second, third, or fourth year or level of German language study. **Criteria:** Local interviews are conducted.

**Funds Avail.:** In the past, Germany, through its Pedagogical Exchange Service, has made travel-study awards available to students selected by the Association. Students will live with German families and receive formal instruction in the German language and culture, in addition to excursions to places of historic and cultural interest. No cash awards are available, nor is financial aid available for post-secondary education. **No. of Awards:** 54. **To Apply:** Contestants take tests designed for their level of German study. **Deadline:** High school German teachers must submit an order registration with a $4 registration fee for each test to the AATG by December 2. The test is administered in December/January. Those students who score in the 90th

percentile or above and who wish to apply for the AATG/PAD awards must return their application forms the beginning of March. Recipients are notified in mid-March.

**Remarks:** Please add: no cash awards are available, nor is financial aid available for post-secondary education. **Contact:** AATG Test Director at the above address (see entry 326).

## • 328 •
## American Association of Teachers of Italian
c/o Prof. Anthony S. Mollica
Faculty of Education
Brock University           *Ph:* (905)688-3345
St. Catharines, ON, Canada L2S 3A1    *Fax:* (905)788-2674

### • 329 •   AATI National College Essay Contest
*(Undergraduate/Prize)*

**Qualif.:** Contestants must be enrolled in a junior, community, or four-year college or university in the United States, Canada, or Mexico. Applicants must have completed one year of Italian in college or its equivalent by June 30th of the test year.

**Funds Avail.:** Prizes are awarded by the national association for top essays with $250 for first place. Some local chapters also award prizes. **To Apply:** A ten- to twelve-page typed essay must be submitted on one of the following topics: a critical appreciation of an Italian author; a study on the post World War II Italian cinema; a study on contemporary Italian theatre, music or art; the industrialization of modern Italy, history, and effects; modern Italian politics; of the Italian in North America today. The essay must include a bibliography and research. It may be written in Italian or English and the rules of the MLA Handbook must be followed. In addition to the essay, contestants must submit a signed statement by a permanent member of the Italian department or section of their college that verifies one year of college or its equivalent will have been completed by June 30th. Contestants must also sign a personal pledge stating that the essay is their own. A home address must also be given for the mailing of test results. **Deadline:** Essays and accompanying materials must be submitted by June 30th. **Contact:** The American Association of Teachers of Italian at the above address (see entry 328).

## • 330 •
## American Association of University Women Educational Foundation
2201 N. Dodge St.           *Ph:* (319)337-1716
Iowa City, IA 52243-4030       *Fax:* (319)463-1204
*E-mail:* foundation@mail.aauw.org; info@mail.aauw.org
*URL:* http://www.aauw.org

### • 331 •   AAUW Educational Foundation American Fellowships *(Postdoctorate/Fellowship)*

**Purpose:** To assist in the research or final year of dissertation. **Focus:** All s/fields except engineering. **Qualif.:** Applicants must be women who are citizens or permanent residents of the United States. A postdoctoral fellowship candidate must hold a doctoral degree at the time of application. Scholars in any field of study may apply. One fellowship is designated for a woman from an under represented minority group. Dissertation fellowships are for women who are in the final year of writing their dissertation. Applicants must have successfully completed all required course work, passed all preliminary examinations, and have their dissertation research proposal (or plan) approved by November 15 of the year of application. Applicants are expected to receive a

## American Association of University Women Educational Foundation (continued)

doctoral degree at the end of the fellowship year. The fellowship is not intended to fund extended field research. Students holding a fellowship for the purpose of writing a dissertation the year before the AAUW fellowship year are ineligible. There are no restrictions as to place of study. **Criteria:** Selection is based primarily on scholarly excellence, quality of applicants' proposals, and their commitment to helping women through service in their community, profession, and/or field of research.

**Funds Avail.:** Postdoctoral fellowships are $27,000 each. Dissertation fellowships are $15,000 each. **No. of Awards:** 16 postdoctoral fellowships and 51 dissertation fellowships. **To Apply:** American Fellowships (postdoctoral and dissertation) applications are available from August 1 through November 1. Applicants may apply up to 2 times for a dissertation fellowship on the same topic. **Deadline:** Materials must be postmarked by November 15. Fellowship year starts July 1. **Contact:** AAUW Educational Foundation at the above address (see entry 330).

## • 332 • AAUW Educational Foundation Career Development Grants (Masters, Professional Development/Grant)

**Purpose:** To assist women in preparing for reentry into the workforce, or for career change or career advancement. **Focus:** General Studies. **Qualif.:** Applicant must be a woman scholar who is a U.S. citizen or permanent resident; have a bachelor's degree; and have completed her most recent degree at least five years before the start of the award. Coursework must be undertaken at an accredited institution and be a prerequisite for professional employment plans. Preference is given to applicants seeking to enter nontraditional career fields and to women of color. **Criteria:** Based on academic excellence and quality of proposal.

**Funds Avail.:** $2,000-8,000. **No. of Awards:** Approximately 60. **To Apply:** Write to AAUW for application form and guidelines, available from August 1 to December 1. **Deadline:** Materials must be in by December 15. **Contact:** AAUW Educational Foundation at the above address (see entry 330).

## • 333 • AAUW Educational Foundation Community Action Grants (Other/Grant)

**Purpose:** To provide seed money to AAUW branches, states, or individual women for community based projects or non-degree research that addresses the contemporary needs of women and girls or provides information to educate and benefit the public on those issues. **Qualif.:** Applicants must be U.S. citizens or permanent residents. Proposed activity must have direct community or public impact and support the advancement of education and equity for women and girls. AAUW branch and AAWU state projects must be approved and signed by the AAUW branch or state president. Applicants are encouraged to collaborate with local schools, businesses, and community groups. **Criteria:** Criteria is detailed in the application packet.

**Funds Avail.:** One year grants between $2,000 to $7,000 are awarded for project related expenses. Applicants may apply up to two times for the same proposed grant project. Funds cannot cover salaries for project directors. Two year grants between $5,000 and $10,000 are awarded for coalition-based projects that involve planning and implementation activities and are designed to improve K-12 girls' achievement in math/science/technology. **No. of Awards:** 30-40 one-year grants; up to 5 two-year grants. **To Apply:** Write or call for application packet from August 1 to January 31. **Deadline:** Applications must be postmarked by February 1. Notifications ae made by April 30.

**Remarks:** Community Action Grant projects may not seek to influence new or pending legislation or favor a particular political candidate or party. **Contact:** AAUW Educational Foundation at the above address (see entry 330).

## • 334 • AAUW Educational Foundation International Fellowships (Graduate/Fellowship, Grant)

**Purpose:** To provide assistance for advanced study and research to women of outstanding ability who are citizens of countries other than the United States. **Focus:** General Studies. **Qualif.:** Applicant must be a woman scholar who is not a U.S. citizen or permanent resident. Candidate must have completed an academic degree equivalent to a U.S. bachelor's degree by time of application. Study or research may take place at any approved institution in the United States. Six fellowships are available to members of the International Federation of University Women National affiliates for study in any country other than the applicant's own. **Criteria:** Based on academic excellence and quality of proposal.

**Funds Avail.:** $16,500 is available for fellowships and $5,000-$7,000 for project grants. **No. of Awards:** 46 fellowships; 5 grants. **To Apply:** Write or call for application form and guidelines, August 1 through November 15. **Deadline:** Materials must be postmarked by December 15.

**Remarks:** Applicants who will be in their final year of study during the fellowship year may also apply for a grant to support the implementation of a project to benefit women/girls in their home country the year immediately following the fellowship year. **Contact:** AAUW Educational Foundation at the above address (see entry 330).

## • 335 • AAUW Educational Foundation Selected Professions Engineering Dissertation Fellowship (Graduate/Fellowship)

**Purpose:** To assist women with the completion of their research and the writing of their dissertation. **Focus:** Engineering. **Qualif.:** Awarded to women who are citizens or permanent residents of the United States pursuing a doctoral degree in engineering and who will complete all required course work and have pass all preliminary exams by the application postmark deadline. Doctoral degree is expected at the end of the fellowship year. Students holding any fellowship for the purpose of writing a dissertation in the year prior to the AAUW fellowship year are not eligible. Tuition for additional course work is not available through the fellowship. No restrictions on the age of the applicant or place of study (among accredited U.S. institutions). **Criteria:** Based on scholarly excellence, scope/complexity/innovation of the research or project, feasibility of research plan, and potential of applicant to make a significant contribution to the field.

**Funds Avail.:** Fellowships stipends are $15,000 each for full-time work on the dissertation. **No. of Awards:** 8-9. **To Apply:** Call or write, at least two weeks before the deadline, for application packets. **Deadline:** Completed application material must be postmarked by Nov. 15. **Contact:** AAUW Educational Foundation at the above address (see entry 330).

## • 336 • AAUW Educational Foundation Selected Professions Fellowship (Graduate/Fellowship)

**Purpose:** To assist women with the completion of graduate degrees in science and technology disciplines. **Focus:** Architecture, business administration, computer/information science, engineering, mathematics/statistics, general medicine, or osteopathic medicine. **Qualif.:** The fellowship is awarded to women who are citizens or permanent residents of the United States for the final year of a masters degree program, including one-year programs. Fellowships are also available for the first year of a master's in engineering. There are no restrictions on the age of the applicant or place of study (among accredited U.S. institutions). Fellowships in law, medicine, and business administration are restricted to women of color who have historically been under represented in these fields. Eligible minority candidates are African American, Mexican American, Puerto Rican and other Latino, Native American, Alaskan Natives, Asian American, and Pacific Islanders. **Criteria:** Based on academic excellence, professional promise, and financial need. Special consideration is given to applicants who demonstrate professional promise in innovative or neglected areas of research and/or practice, public interest concerns, or those specialties in which women are under represented.

**Funds Avail.:** Fellowships stipends range from $5,000-12,000 for full-time study. **No. of Awards:** 38-42. **To Apply:** Write or call for details from August 1 to December 20. **Deadline:** Completed application materials must be postmarked by January 10. **Contact:** AAUW Educational Foundation at the above address (see entry 330).

### • 337 • AAUW Postdoctoral Fellowships
*(Postdoctorate/Fellowship)*

**Purpose:** To provide research funds to women who have achieved distinction or the promise of distinction in their fields. **Focus:** General Studies. **Qualif.:** Applicant must be a woman scholar who has successfully completed a doctorate. Applicant must be a U.S. citizen or permanent resident.

**Funds Avail.:** $20,000-$25,000. **No. of Awards:** Nine. **To Apply:** Write to AAUW for application form and guidelines, available from August 1 to November 1. **Deadline:** November 15. **Contact:** AAUW at the above address (see entry 330).

### • 338 • Eleanor Roosevelt Teacher Fellowships
*(Doctorate, Other/Fellowship)*

4

**Purpose:** Designed for K-12 public school teachers who are seeking to advance gender equity in the classroom, increase their effectiveness at teaching math, science, and technology to girls and/or tailor their teaching to the needs of minority students and girls at risk of dropping out. **Qualif.:** Women teachers who are U.S. citizens or permanent residents, teach full time at U.S. public schools in grades K through 12, have at least three consecutive years fill time teaching experience, plan to continue teaching for the next three years, and are able to demonstrate commitment to educational opportunities for women and girls through work are eligible. **Criteria:** Quality of the proposal.

**Funds Avail.:** $1,000-9,000. **No. of Awards:** Approximately 25. **Deadline:** Applications must be in by January 10. **Contact:** AAUW Educational Foundation at the above address (see entry 330).

---

### • 339 •
## American Association of Women Dentists
645 N. Michigan Ave., No. 800　　*Ph:* (312)280-9296
Chicago, IL 60611　　　　　　　*Fax:* (312)280-9893
　　　　　　　　　　　　　　　*Free:* 800-920-2293

*E-mail:* info@womendentists
*URL:* http://www.womendentists.org

### • 340 • Colgate-Palmolive Research Award
*(Doctorate/Scholarship)*

**Purpose:** To recognize excellence in the field of dentistry and research. **Focus:** Dentistry. **Qualif.:** Must be a junior or a senior student in good standing at dental school. **Criteria:** Ten dental students are selected annually be AAWD Awards Committee and are notified of their selection.

**Funds Avail.:** Ten $500 scholarships annually. **No. of Awards:** 10. **To Apply:** Students cannot apply directly, but must be nominated through the dental college. **Deadline:** February 1. **Contact:** The American Association of Women Dentists at the above address (see entry 339)for additional information.

---

### • 341 •
## American Astronomical Society
2000 Florida Ave., NW, Ste. 400　　*Ph:* (202)328-2010
Washington, DC 20009-1231　　　　*Fax:* (202)234-2560
*E-mail:* aas@aas.org

### • 342 • American Astronomical Society Small Research Grants *(Postdoctorate/Grant)*

**Purpose:** To support astronomical research. **Focus:** Astronomy. **Qualif.:** Candidate must be a U.S. citizen. Applicant must be an astronomer with a Ph.D. or its equivalent. Institutional affiliation is not a prerequisite for applying, but preference is given to applicants from smaller, less endowed institutions. Graduate students are not eligible. Funds must be used to cover research expenses; grants are not offered for salaries or overhead. Normally, investigator may not hold federal research grants concurrently with a Society award.

**Funds Avail.:** $300-4,000. **No. of Awards:** Varies, according to funds available. **To Apply:** Write to the Small Research Grant Committee for application guidelines. Submit a two-page proposal, budget, and curriculum vitae. **Deadline:** May 12 and December 1. Awards are announced 8 to 12 weeks after deadlines. **Contact:** Small Research Grant Committee at the above address (see entry 341).

### • 343 • Chretien International Research Grants
*(Postdoctorate, Professional Development/Grant)*

**Purpose:** To encourage and support international collaboration in observational astronomy. **Focus:** Observational Astronomy. **Qualif.:** Applicant may be of any nationality. Candidate must be an astronomer qualified to conduct research on a long-term, international basis. Grants may be used to cover travel costs, salary, publication costs, small pieces of research equipment, and other reasonable expenses. Awardees are expected to collaborate with astronomers in the host country.

**Funds Avail.:** $20,000 maximum. **No. of Awards:** Varies, according to funds available. **To Apply:** Write to the Chretien International Research Grant Committee for guidelines. Submit proposal with description of research project, statement of ability to conduct proposed research, budget, curriculum vitae, list of publications, two letters of reference, and other relevant information. **Deadline:** April 1. Awards will be announced in September. **Contact:** Chretien International Research Grant Committee at the above address (see entry 341).

### • 344 • International Travel Grants *(Doctorate, Postdoctorate/Grant)*

**Purpose:** To enable astronomers from the United States to present papers at astronomical meetings abroad. **Focus:** Astronomy. **Qualif.:** Applicant must be an astronomer working in the United States. Applicant must have a Ph.D. or its equivalent; or be an especially meritorious graduate student. Graduate students must attend a meeting related to thesis topic. Preference is given to applicants requesting partial support. Grants are intended to cover travel expenses only; funds may not be used for per diem or registration costs.

**Funds Avail.:** Varies, according to cost of travel; $200-1,200. **No. of Awards:** Varies, according to funds available. **To Apply:** Write to the Travel Grant Selection Committee for application form and guidelines. Graduate students must submit a letter of recommendation from their thesis advisor attesting to the meeting's relevance. **Deadline:** To be announced on Web site. **Contact:** Travel Grant Selection Committee at the above address (see entry 341).

---

• 345 •
## American Bankers Association
1120 Connecticut Ave. NW
8th Fl.
Washington, DC 20036      *Ph:* (202)663-5311

### • 346 • American Bankers Association Fellowships
*(Other/Fellowship)*

**Purpose:** To provide an industry professional with the opportunity to attend the Stonier Graduate School of Banking at the University of Delaware, Newark. **Focus:** Journalism. **Qualif.:** Applicants must be active members of the financial press with at least three years writing experience and U.S. citizens.

**Funds Avail.:** Approximately $4000 covering tuition, travel and living expenses, and a $300 stipend. **No. of Awards:** 2.

### • 347 •
## American Baptist Financial Aid Program - Educational Ministries
PO Box 851      *Ph:* (610)768-2067
Valley Forge, PA 19482-0851      *Fax:* (610)768-2056
     *Free:* 800-334-1427

*E-mail:* lynne.eckman@abc-usa.org

### • 348 • American Baptist Financial Aid Program
*(Graduate, Undergraduate/Loan)*

**Focus:** General studies. **Qualif.:** Applicants must be members of American Baptists churches.

**Funds Avail.:** $500 - $1,000 per award. **To Apply:** Applicants must submit a completed application form. Write for further details. **Deadline:** May 31. **Contact:** Lynne Eckman, Director of Financial Aid.

### • 349 •
## American Bar Association - Commission on College and University Legal Studies
Public Education Division
541 North Fairbanks Court      *Ph:* (312)988-5734
Chicago, IL 60611-3314      *Fax:* (312)988-5032
*URL:* http://abanet.org/barserv/barawards.html

### • 350 • ABA Mini-Grants *(Postdoctorate, Undergraduate/Grant)*

**Purpose:** To stimulate projects designed to enhance undergraduate liberal arts education about the legal process and its role in society. **Focus:** Law. **Qualif.:** Candidates may be of any nationality but must be full- or part-time faculty members at an accredited 2 year or 4 year college. Proposed projects must use a liberal art approach; projects using a pre-law, pre-professional, or para-legal approach will not be funded. Grants are not offered for indirect costs. **Criteria:** All proposals will be judged on: enhancement of student understanding of law, the legal system, and the role of law in society; the improved quality or innovativeness of approaches; and generalizability and utility to other campuses, departments, or teaching settings.

**Funds Avail.:** $1,500 maximum. **No. of Awards:** 7-8. **To Apply:** Write to the staff director for application guidelines. Submit four copies of the following: a curriculum vitae, a one-page budget, and a three-page project proposal. **Deadline:** March 29. Grants are

announced June 15. **Contact:** ABA at the above address (see entry 349).

### • 351 •
## American Bar Foundation
750 N. Lake Shore Dr.      *Ph:* (312)988-6500
Chicago, IL 60611-4403      *Fax:* (312)988-6579
*URL:* http://www.abf-sociolegal.org

### • 352 • ABF Summer Research Fellowships in Law and Social Science for Minority Undergraduate Students *(Undergraduate/Fellowship)*

**Purpose:** To acquaint undergraduate minority students with research in the field of law and social science. **Focus:** Law, Social Sciences. **Qualif.:** Applicants must be citizens or permanent residents of the United States. They must be of American Indian, African, Mexican, or Puerto Rican descent. Candidates should have completed at least the sophomore year of college and must not have received a bachelor's degree by the time the fellowship begins. Applicants must have a grade point average of at least 3.0 on a 4.0 scale and be moving toward an academic major in one of the social science disciplines. They must be able to work at the American Bar Foundation's offices in Chicago for 35 hours per week during the period of the fellowship.

**Funds Avail.:** $3,500. **To Apply:** A formal application must be submitted, along with a personal statement, official transcripts, and one letter of reference from a faculty member familiar with the student's work. **Deadline:** March 1. Recipients are announced by April 15.

**Remarks:** Students work at the offices of the American Bar Foundation in Chicago, Illinois. Each recipient is assigned to a Foundation Research Fellow who acts as a mentor. **Contact:** Summer Research Fellowships for Minority Undergraduates at the above address (see entry 351).

### • 353 •
## American Board of Funeral Service Education
PO Box 1305
Brunswick, ME 04011-1305      *Ph:* (207)798-5801

### • 354 • National Scholarships for Funeral Service
*(Undergraduate/Scholarship)*

**Focus:** Mortuary Science. **Qualif.:** Applicants must be citizens of the United States and have completed at least one term of study in a program in Funeral Service or Mortuary Science Education that is accredited by the American Board of Funeral Service Education. **Criteria:** Recipients are chosen on the basis of financial need, academic performance, extracurricular and/or community activities, recommendations, and the articulateness of the scholarship application.

**Funds Avail.:** Either $250 or $500 and is remitted directly to the college upon satisfactory proof of enrollment. **No. of Awards:** 25-50. **To Apply:** Applicants are required to file an application (including one essay), one letter of recommendation, transcripts of all previous college work attempted, and their federal 1040 tax form. **Deadline:** March 15 and September 15. **Contact:** Committee on Scholarships at the above address (see entry 353).

**• 355 •**

**American Brain Tumor Association**

2720 River Rd., Ste. 146      *Ph:* (847)827-9910
Des Plaines, IL 60018      *Fax:* (847)827-9918
               *Free:* 800-886-2282

*E-mail:* info@abta.org
*URL:* http://www.abta.org

**• 356 •**   **American Brain Tumor Association**
**Fellowships** *(Postdoctorate/Fellowship)*

**Purpose:** To encourage talented junior investigators to enter, or remain in, the field of brain tumor research. **Focus:** Neuro-oncology, brain tumor research. **Qualif.:** Applicants must be postdoctoral candidates who intend to pursue careers in brain tumor research. They must also be U.S. citizens or permanent residents. Clinical training applications will not be considered. Qualified applications will be reviewed by the Association's Scientific Advisory Council. Awards will be determined by ABTA's Board of Directors based upon the Advisor's recommendations.

**Funds Avail.:** $60,000. **No. of Awards:** Varies each year. **To Apply:** Applications are available in August. **Deadline:** January 6. **Contact:** Naomi Berkowitz, Executive Director, at the above address (see entry 355).

**• 357 •**

**American Bureau for Medical Advancement in China**

New York Academy of Medicine
  Bldg.
2 E. 103rd St.      *Ph:* (212)860-1990
New York, NY 10029      *Fax:* (212)860-1994
*URL:* http://www.cait.columbia.edu/dept/ps/memos/awards/
  awrd0013.html

*The American Bureau for Medical Advancement in China, Inc. (ABMAC) is a non-political, medical and scientific service organization that facilitates the exchange of medical and scientific knowledge and fosters cooperation between the Republic of China and the United States in biomedical teaching, research, and health care.*

**• 358 •**   **ABMAC/Clerkship in Taiwan Award**
*(Doctorate/Other)*

**Purpose:** To provide exposure for fourth-year medical school students to do research-oriented work, observe in clinical situations, participate in rounds, and in some cases encounter disease entities seen much less commonly in Western medical practices. **Focus:** Medicine. **Qualif.:** Applicants must be fourth-year medical students. Opportunities exist particularly in departments of family practice, infectious diseases, pediatrics, internal medicine, and psychiatry.

**Funds Avail.:** $1,250 to be used toward round-trip air fare to and from the Republic of China (Taiwan). **To Apply:** Application includes essay, curriculum vitae, two letters of recommendation, a letter of good standing from the dean, and interview (optional). Contact ABMAC for specifications regarding the application. **Deadline:** May 15. **Contact:** Julia C. Grammar, Associate Director, at the above address (see entry 357).

**• 359 •**   **H. William Harris Visiting Professorship**
*(Other/Other)*

**Purpose:** To assist in the advancement of clinical teaching of internal medicine in the Republic of China (Taiwan). **Focus:** Medicine. **Qualif.:** Applicants must be United States senior medical professionals with experience in bedside medical teaching.

**Funds Avail.:** Travel expenses, housing, and a stipend of $1,200 per month for six visiting teachers and their spouses.

**Remarks:** ABMAC in conjunction with faculty members of Taiwan teaching hospitals and medical schools, has developed a special program permitting American clinical teachers to teach in Taiwan hospitals. The program was named for Dr. H. William Harris to acknowledge his clinical teaching in Taiwan during the past 14 years. **Contact:** Julia C. Grammar, Associate Director, at the above address (see entry 357).

**• 360 •**   **M. K. Wang Visiting Professorships** *(Other/ Other)*

**Purpose:** To assist in supplying expert nurses to serve as visiting professors and consultants to institutions in the Republic of China (Taiwan). **Focus:** Nursing. **Qualif.:** Applicants must be very senior, expert nurses.

**Funds Avail.:** Professorship will provide for at least one nurse to spend three months in hospitals and schools of nursing. The Fund will provide travel expenses and a stipend. Host institutions will contribute lodging.

**Remarks:** Mamie Kwoh Wang, R.N., M.S., has been a long time advocate of advances in nursing education and practice in Taiwan. She has taken the initiative to supply American expert nurse consultants to their counterparts in Taiwan and to raise funds to support educational opportunities for the nursing community. The clinical practice of the visiting professor will focus on areas of need identified by the Science and Technology Advisory Group (STAG), the Department of Health of the Republic of China, and by a comprehensive 1985 ABMAC study. These areas currently include occupational health nursing, critical care, care of the chronically/terminally ill (hospice), and pain management. **Contact:** Julia C. Grammar at the above address (see entry 357).

**• 361 •**

**American Cancer Society**

Extramural Grants and Awards      *Ph:* (404)329-7558
1599 Clifton Rd., NE      *Fax:* (404)321-4669
Atlanta, GA 30329      *Free:* 800-ACS-2345
*E-mail:* grants@cancer.org
*URL:* http://www.cancer.org

**• 362 •**   **American Cancer Society Clinical Oncology Social Work Training Grants** *(Postgraduate/Grant)*

**Purpose:** To support hospital-based training in either a master's or post-master's program. **Qualif.:** Master's trainees must be second-year students in a social work master's program with demonstrated interest in needs of oncology patients and their families. Prior social work experience in health or mental health care is desirable. Post-master's trainees must have master's degree from a program that provided clinical oncology social work experience and have demonstrated interest in psychosocial needs of cancer patients and their families. The proposed program for the trainee must include an opportunity to concentrate in oncology and a multidisciplinary hospital cancer program. It must name, as preceptor to the trainee, a social worker with a degree from an accredited school of social work, with ACSW or documentation of equivalent credentials and two years of supervisory and/or field instructor experience as well as a minimum of two years oncology practice experience. For master's trainees, the program must indicate that the trainee will experience and develop clinical skills in the management of the cancer patient and family. For post-master's trainees, the program must provide concrete examples of advanced clinical practice and research experience. A doctoral-prepared preceptor is required. Applicants must be citizens or permanent residents of the United States. Permanent residents must request form G-639 from the U.S. Department of Immigration and Naturalization. Only one traineeship per institution will be

*American Cancer Society (continued)*

awarded. The sponsoring institutions must be hospitals or medical centers with close ties to accredited schools of social work. Institutions should have organized oncology sections; a functioning multidisciplinary hospital cancer program; active social work services that are well-integrated in the institution's health care delivery programs; approval from the Commission on Cancer for hospital cancer programs; for master's training, affiliations as a training site with accredited schools of social work having a health care or mental health concentration; for post-master's training a demonstrated commitment to research in clinical oncology social work. **Criteria:** The Medical Affairs Advisory Group on Clinical Oncology Social Work Training reviews applications and submits recommendations to the Medical Affairs Committee and the Society Executive Committee for the winter meeting. Institutions awarded training grants are then asked to nominate candidates.

**Funds Avail.:** Twenty grants of $8,000 each for the master's level social work traineeship and four grants of $12,000 for the post-master's traineeship paid in monthly installments. At the end of the calendar year, the Society will send a tax statement indicating the amount paid. **To Apply:** Institutions, not prospective trainees, must submit an original typewritten application and three copies, a letter of support from the local Division of the American Cancer Society, condensed resume of the preceptor (must not exceed two pages), and if applicable, required reports from the previous year trainees. **Deadline:** October 1. Awardees are notified by March or April. Awards begin September 1 of the following year. **Contact:** Virginia Krawiec, M.P.A., Professional Education Department, at the above address (see entry 361).

**• 363 •   American Cancer Society Clinical Research Professorships** *(Postdoctorate/Grant)*

**Purpose:** To provide salaries for cancer research scientists working in academic institutions. **Focus:** Oncology. **Qualif.:** Grants are awarded to academic institutions to support individual faculty members; application must originate jointly from the institution and the nominee. Applicant must be a U.S. citizen or permanent resident. Candidate for a Research Professorship must have at least ten years of experience beyond the doctoral level. In general, candidate should have the rank of full professor or equivalent. Applicant for a Clinical Research Professorship must be a clinical scientist involved in patient care, usually in a teaching capacity, and have at least ten years of experience beyond the medical degree. Candidate should have the rank of associate or full professor. Professorships are intended to encourage research activities; recipients cannot have significant administrative or service responsibilities.

**Funds Avail.:** $50,000/year maximum. **To Apply:** Write for application form and guidelines. The instruction booklet should be followed closely when preparing forms. Application must describe fully all proposed research and teaching activities. Consultation between the Dean or official of the Institution is required. Submit five copies of application with the following: official transcripts; research proposal with budget, including a proposed annual salary; curriculum vitae; the names of three references; and supplemental materials. **Deadline:** March 1 and October 1.

**Remarks:** The Society also offers Research and Clinical Investigation Grants for research projects. Write for further details. **Contact:** Peter Ove, Ph.D.; Donella Wilson, Ph.D.; T.J. Koerner, Ph.D.; Scientific Program Directors, at the above address (see entry 361).

**• 364 •   American Cancer Society Postdoctoral Fellowships** *(Postdoctorate/Award, Fellowship)*

**Purpose:** To provide cancer-research training opportunities for new investigators and physicians with limited experience. **Focus:** Oncology. **Qualif.:** Applicant must be a U.S. citizen or permanent resident, and have a doctoral degree. Applicant should be a beginning investigator with limited research experience. A fellow's training can be in either basic or clinical research and must be full-

time. A plan of training, formulated and agreed upon by applicant and mentor, must be described in detail in the application. Awards may be used in other countries when suitable for training objectives.

**Funds Avail.:** PRTA $40,000 first year, $42,000 second year, $44,000 third year; PF $22,000, $24,000, $26,000. **To Apply:** Write for application form and guidelines. The instruction booklet should be followed closely when preparing forms. Application must be signed by the proposed mentor and the head of the department in which the training will be received. Submit four copies of application with the following: official transcripts, research proposal with budget and requested travel funds, curriculum vitae, the names of three references, and supplemental materials. **Deadline:** March 1 and October 1.

**Remarks:** The Society also offers Research and Clinical Investigation Grants for research projects. Write for further details. **Contact:** Peter Ove, Ph.D.; Donella Wilson, Ph.D.; T.J. Koerner; Scientific Program Directors, at the above address (see entry 361).

**• 365 •   Faculty Research Award in Oncology** *(Postdoctorate/Award)*

**Purpose:** To provide salaries for cancer research scientists working in academic institutions. **Focus:** Oncology. **Qualif.:** Grants are awarded to academic institutions to support individual faculty members; application must originate jointly from the institution and the nominee. Applicant must be a U.S. citizen or permanent resident, and have a doctoral degree. A junior faculty applicant should have recently completed his/her postdoctoral training, and have a faculty appointment at the nominating institution. Applicant for the Faculty Research Award must be a qualified scientist with demonstrated research experience, and have a continuing faculty appointment at the host institution. However, the awards are not intended for scientists who are substantially advanced in their careers, such as senior associate professors or full professors. Individuals who have held an equivalent award from another agency for a substantial period of time are not eligible.

**Funds Avail.:** Faculty Research Award: $205,000 maximum; Junior Faculty Research Award: $90,500 maximum. **To Apply:** Write for application form and guidelines. The instruction booklet should be followed closely when preparing forms. Application must describe fully all proposed research and teaching activities. The endorsement of the department head and the dean is required. Submit five copies of application with the following: official transcripts, research proposal with budget and requested travel funds, curriculum vitae, the names of three references, and supplemental materials. **Deadline:** March 1 and October 1.

**Remarks:** The Society also offers Research and Clinical Investigation Grants for research projects. Write for further details. **Contact:** Peter Ove, Ph.D.; Donella Wilson, Ph.D.; T.J. Koerner, Ph.D.; Scientific Program Directors, at the above address (see entry 361).

**• 366 •**
**American Chemical Society**
1155 16th St., NW
Washington, DC 20036

*Ph:* (202)452-8917
*Fax:* (202)872-6206
*Free:* 800-227-5558

*E-mail:* mcarey@acs.org;  longfellow@acs.org
*URL:* http://www.acs.org/govt

**• 367 •   ACS Congressional Fellowship Program** *(Postdoctorate, Professional Development/Fellowship)*

**Purpose:** To place a person with an interest in science and public policy in the office of a U.S. senator, representative, congressional committee or subcommittee. **Focus:** Government/Public Policy. **Qualif.:** Applicants are selected on a competitive basis from among members of the ACS who have significant familiarity with one of the chemical sciences or engineering (e.g., a doctorate or equivalent work experience); a working understanding of the chemical community; and experience in civic activities or public affairs. Past involvement in ACS activities also is taken into account.

**Funds Avail.:** Stipend depends on work experience. **No. of Awards:** 2. **To Apply:** A candidate for the Fellowship must submit a letter of intent and a resume directly to the ACS. In addition, two letters of recommendation are to be sent to the ACS by their authors. **Deadline:** January 1, for term beginning the following September. **Contact:** Deitra Jackson, at the above address (see entry 366).

### • 368 • ACS Science Policy Fellowship (Professional Development/Fellowship)

**Purpose:** To provide an opportunity for ACS members to work with the Government Affairs and Policy Staff. **Focus:** Public Policy. **Qualif.:** Applicant may be of any nationality, but must be a member of ACS with a demonstrated interest in science and public policy. Applicants must have some scientific knowledge as well as being well versed in nonscientific areas. A Ph.D. is not required.

**Funds Avail.:** Salary in the mid $40,000 range, plus benefits. **No. of Awards:** 1. **To Apply:** Write to the manager for application form and guidelines. **Deadline:** January 8. **Contact:** Deitra Jackson.

### • 369 • Petroleum Research Fund Grants (Graduate, Postdoctorate, Professional Development, Undergraduate/Grant)

**Purpose:** To encourage advanced scientific research relevant to the petroleum field. **Focus:** Engineering/Sciences. **Qualif.:** Applicant must be a regularly appointed member of the science faculty at a college or university. Candidate's research proposal must be in a field of pure science which may afford a basis for subsequent research directly connected with the petroleum field. There are three kinds of Petroleum Research Fund Grants. Type AC Grants support faculty research that is assisted by undergraduate, graduate and postdoctoral students. Type B Grants are only given to faculty in departments that do not offer doctoral-level degrees. Proposed research must include opportunities for meaningful participation by undergraduate students. Type G Grants are intended for new faculty at U.S. institution within the first three years of teaching who do not have extensive postdoctoral research experience. All grants are tenable at the award recipient's home institution.

**Funds Avail.:** Type AC Grants: $30,000/year; Type B Grants: $15,000/year; Type G Grants: $12,500/year. **No. of Awards:** Varies. **To Apply:** Write to the program manager for application form and guidelines. **Deadline:** None. Grant proposals are considered in February, May, and November.

---

## • 370 •
## American Classical League/NJCL National Latin Exam
PO Box 95        *Ph:* (703)360-4354
Mount Vernon, VA 22121     *Free:* 888-378-7721
*URL:* http://acs.rhodes.edu/~nle

### • 371 • National Latin Exam Scholarship (Undergraduate/Scholarship)

**Purpose:** To promote the study of Latin. **Focus:** General studies. **Qualif.:** Applicants must be high school seniors who are gold medal winners in Latin III-IV Prose, III-IV Poetry, Latin V, or Latin VI.

**Funds Avail.:** $20,000. $1,000 per scholarship. Recipients must agree to take at least one year of Latin or classical Greek in college

(a classics in translation course does not fulfill this requirement). Scholarships are renewable. **No. of Awards:** 20. **To Apply:** Write for further details. **Deadline:** January 10. **Contact:** Jane J. Hall.

---

## • 372 •
## American College of Healthcare Executives Foundation
1 N. Franklin St., Ste. 1700     *Ph:* (312)943-0544
Chicago, IL 60606-3491      *Fax:* (312)943-3791
*URL:* http://www.health.swt.edu/ACHE/1995.html

### • 373 • Albert W. Dent Scholarship (Graduate/Scholarship)

**Purpose:** To provide financial aid and increase the enrollment of minority and physically disabled students in healthcare management graduate programs and to encourage them to obtain middle- and upper-level positions in health care management. **Qualif.:** Applicants must be United States or Canadian citizens who are either Student Associates in good standing in the American College of Healthcare Executives, minority or physically disabled undergraduate students who either have been accepted for full-time study for the fall term in a health care management graduate program accredited by the Accrediting Commission on Education for Health Services Administration, or students enrolled full-time and in good academic standing in an accredited graduate program in health care management. Previous recipients are not eligible. Financial need must be demonstrated.

**Funds Avail.:** Each scholarship is $3,000. The number of awards varies from year to year. **Deadline:** Completed applications must be filed between January 1 and March 31.

**Remarks:** This scholarship was established and named in honor of Dr. Albert W. Dent, the foundation's first Black Fellow, and President Emeritus of Dillard University, New Orleans. **Contact:** Albert W. Dent Scholarship, Foundation of the American College of Healthcare Executives, at the above address (see entry 372).

### • 374 • Foster G. McGaw Student Scholarship (Graduate/Scholarship)

**Purpose:** To assist financially needy persons to better prepare for health care management careers, thereby contributing to improvements in the field. **Qualif.:** Applicants must be enrolled full-time and in good academic standing in graduate programs in healthcare management that are accredited by the Accrediting Commission on Education for Health Services Administration; student associates in good standing in the ACHE may also apply. Candidates must also be United States or Canadian citizens. Previous recipients are not eligible. Applicants must provide evidence of financial need. **Criteria:** The Director of each graduate program must recommend students with the greatest financial need. **To Apply:** Applications may be obtained from the Program Director. **Deadline:** Applications are accepted each year between January 1 and March 31.

**Remarks:** Foster G. McGraw was the founder of the American Hospital Supply Corporation. **Contact:** Director of program in which candidate is enrolled.

---

Awards are arranged alphabetically below their administering organizations

## • 375 •
## American College of Obstetricians and Gynecologists

Lee Cassidy, Dir. of Development
Dept. of Development and Industry
  Relations
409 12th St., SW                    Ph: (202)863-2577
Washington, DC 20024-2188           Fax: (202)554-3490
*E-mail:* lcassidy@acog.org
*URL:* http://www.acog.org

### • 376 • ACOG/3M Pharmaceuticals Research Awards in Lower Genital Infections *(Postdoctorate/ Award)*

**Purpose:** To provide grant funds to junior investigators with the opportunity to improve the understanding of genital health through clinical research in the area of lower genital infections (examples include bacterial vaginosis, trichomoniasis, candidal infections, and post-surgical infections). **Focus:** Medical Research — Lower Genital Infections. **Qualif.:** Applicants who are Junior Fellows or Fellows of ACOG and enrolled in an approved obstetrics/ gynecology residency program or within three years postresidency will qualify. Grant award is for research costs and not intended to supplement physician stipends.

**Funds Avail.:** $15,000 award plus travel expenses for round-trip coach airfare to attend the ACOG Annual Clinical Meeting. **No. of Awards:** 2. **To Apply:** Applications must include a one-page budget sheet, curriculum vitae, letter of support from program director, departmental chair, or laboratory director, and a six page research proposal including: hypothesis, objective, scientific aim, background and significance, experimental design, and references. Six copies of the application must be submitted. **Deadline:** October 1.

**Remarks:** A final written report is required and due by September 1 after the grant concludes. This report is to include a brief account of final expenditures.

### • 377 • ACOG/Cytyc Corporation Research Award for the Prevention of Cervical Cancer *(Postdoctorate/ Grant)*

**Purpose:** To provide seed grant funds to junior investigators for clinical research. **Focus:** Cervical cancer prevention. **Qualif.:** Applicants must be Fellows or Junior Fellows of ACOG and in an approved obstetrics/gynecology residency program or within three years postresidency. **Criteria:** All applicants are reviewed by a committee of ACOG members.

**Funds Avail.:** $15,000 plus travel expenses to attend the ACOF Annual Clinical Meeting. Grant award is for research costs and not intended to supplement physician stipends. **No. of Awards:** 1. **To Apply:** Six copies of a one-page budget sheet; curriculum vitae; letter of support from a program director, departmental chair or laboratory director; and a six typewritten pages scientific research proposal which should include the following: hypotheses; objective; specific aims; background and significance; experimental design; and references must be submitted. **Deadline:** October 1.

**Remarks:** A final written report is required and due by September 1 after the grant concludes. This report is to include a brief account of final expenditures.

### • 378 • ACOG/Ethicon Research Award for Innovations in Gynecologic Surgery *(Postdoctorate/ Award)*

**Purpose:** To encourage Junior Fellows or Fellows of ACOG to perform research which will advance the knowledge of gynecologic surgery. Proposals may include investigation of, but are not limited to, disorders of endocrinology, fertility/infertility, neoplastic and inflammatory disease, and diseases of aging. **Focus:** Medical Research — Gynecologic Surgery. **Qualif.:** Applicants must be Junior Fellows or Fellows of ACOG at the time of application. Candidate must have completed at least one year of training and be considered by his/her residency program director to be fit for a career in academic ob/gyn. Award is intended for direct research costs; grants are not offered to supplement physician stipends or to cover overhead expenses.

**Funds Avail.:** $20,000 plus travel expenses to attend the ACOG Annual Clinical Meeting. **No. of Awards:** 1. **To Apply:** Applications should include six copies of a one-page budget, curriculum vitae, IRB approvals, a letter of support from mentor, a copy of mentor's curriculum vitae, and a research proposal including hypothesis, objective, scientific aims, background and significance, experimental design, and references. **Deadline:** October 1.

### • 379 • ACOG/Merck Award for Research in Migraine Management in Women's Health Care *(Postdoctorate/Grant)*

**Purpose:** To provide an opportunity for a junior investigator to perform clinical research related to the area of migraine management. **Focus:** Pathophysiology, pharmacologic and nonpharmacologic treatment, and epidemiology. **Qualif.:** Applicants must be Fellows or Junior Fellows of ACOG who are in an approved obstetrics/gynecology residency program or within three years of postresidency. **Criteria:** All applications are reviewed by a committee of ACOG members.

**Funds Avail.:** $15,000 plus a $1000 travel stipend to attend the ACOG Annual Clinical Meeting. **No. of Awards:** 1. **To Apply:** Six copies of a curriculum vitae; supervisor's curriculum vitae; letter of support from the program director, department chair, or laboratory director; a one-page budget; and a 6-8 typewritten pages scientific research proposal which should include the following: hypothesis, objectives, specific aims, background and significance, experimental design, and references must be submitted. **Deadline:** October 1.

**Remarks:** Research must be conducted under the sponsorship of a recognized specialist in headache or pain. A progress report on work completed is required at the end of six months. A final written report, including financial expenditures, must be submitted by September 1 following completion of the award year.

### • 380 • ACOG/Novartis Pharmaceuticals Fellowship for Research in Endocrinology of the Postreproductive Woman *(Postdoctorate/Fellowship)*

**Purpose:** To provide opportunities for reseach studies relating to some aspect of the endocrinology of the aging woman. **Focus:** Endocrinology, Medicine—Gynecological and Obstetrical. **Qualif.:** Residents who are Fellows or Junior Fellows of ACOG who have completed at least one year of graduate medical education but are not more than two years past completion of residency or fellowship are eligible. Applicants must be considered by the director of the residency program to be especially fitted for a career in ob/gyn.

**Funds Avail.:** $25,000 plus a $750 travel stipend to attend the ACOG Annual Clinical Meeting. **No. of Awards:** 1. **To Apply:** Applications should be in the form of a detailed letter that includes basic personal data, educational background, present position, institution in which the fellowship is to be held and the name of the director of the program, description of long-range career goals and a statement of how the fellowship will enhance these goals. The research proposal should include: hypothesis, objective, scientific aims, background and significance, experimental design, and references. A separate letter of support from the program director, department chair, or laboratory director is required. Five copies of the complete application must be submitted. **Deadline:** October 1.

### • 381 • ACOG/Organon Inc. Research Award in Contraception *(Postdoctorate/Grant)*

**Purpose:** To provide seed grant funds to junior investigators for clinical research. **Focus:** Obstetrics and gynecology. **Qualif.:** Applicants must be Fellows or Junior Fellows of ACOG who are in an approved obstetrics/gynecology residency program or within three years postresidency. **Criteria:** Applications are reviewed by a committee of ACOG members.

**Funds Avail.:** $25,000 plus travel expenses to attend the ACOF Annual Clinical Meeting. **No. of Awards:** 1. **To Apply:** Six copies of the completed application; a one-page budget sheet, curriculum vitae; letter of support from program director, department chair, or laboratory director; and a sixty page typewritten scientific research proposal which should include the following: hypotheses, objective, specific aims, background and significance, experimental design, and references must be submitted. **Deadline:** October 1.

**Remarks:** A final written report is required and due by September 1 after the grant concludes. This report is to include a brief account of final expenditures.

### • 382 • ACOG/Ortho-McNeil Academic Training Fellowships in Obstetrics and Gynecology *(Doctorate/Fellowship)*

**Purpose:** To enable qualified obstetric/gynecologic residents or fellows to spend an extra year involved in responsibilities that will prepare them for academic positions in their specialty. **Focus:** Medicine, Gynecological and Obstetrical. **Qualif.:** Applicants who are Fellows or Junior Fellows of ACOG at the time of application are eligible. Candidate must have completed at least one year of training and be fit for a career in medical education or academic obstetrics and gynecology. Investigative projects are not restricted to the area of basic research; they may include studies in the broader aspects of the discipline, such as teaching and the delivery of health care. Findings of the investigation must be published. Fellow may engage in limited teaching and patient care, consistent with the objectives of the award.

**Funds Avail.:** $30,000 plus award travel expenses to attend the ACOG Annual Clinical Meeting. **No. of Awards:** 2. **To Apply:** Applications should be in the form of a detailed letter that includes basic personal data, present position, educational background, institution at which the fellowship is to be held and the name of the director of the program, description of long-range career goals and a statement of how the fellowship will enhance these goals. The research proposal should include: hypothesis, objective, scientific aims, background and significance, experimental design, and references. A letter of recommendation from the program director, department chair, or laboratory director is also required. **Deadline:** October 1.

### • 383 • ACOG/Pharmacie & Upjohn Research Award in Urognecology of the Postreproductive Woman *(Postdoctorate/Grant)*

**Purpose:** To provide seed grant funds to junior investigators for clinical research in the area of urognecology of the postreproductive woman. **Focus:** Urogynecology. **Qualif.:** Applicants must be Fellows or Junior Fellows of ACOG who are in an approved obstetrics/gynecology residency program or within three years postresidency. **Criteria:** All applicantions are reviewed by a committee of ACOG members.

**Funds Avail.:** $15,000 plus travel and $1000 stipend to attend the ACOG Annual Clinical Meeting. **No. of Awards:** 1. **To Apply:** Six copies of the completed application; a one-page budget sheet; curriculum vitae, letter of support from program director, departmental chair, or laboratory director; and a six typewritten pages scientific research proposal which should includ the following: hypotheses, objective, specific aims, background and significance, experimental design, and references must be submitted. **Deadline:** October 1.

**Remarks:** A final written report is required and due by September 1 after the grant concludes. This report is to include a brief account of final expenditures.

### • 384 • ACOG/Solvay Pharmaceuticals Research Award in Menopause *(Postdoctorate/Fellowship)*

**Purpose:** To advance knowledge in the field of ob/gyn through encouraging basic research on issues related to menopause. Relevant subject include physiological changes of the postreproductive woman, hormonal receptor site distribution, or other investigation deemed appropriate to furthering the basic understanding of menopause. **Focus:** Gynecological and obstetrical medicine. **Qualif.:** Applicants must be Fellows or Junior Fellows of ACOG who are in an approved obstetrics/gynecology residency program or within three years of postresidency. **Criteria:** All applications are reviewed by a committee of ACOG members.

**Funds Avail.:** $20,000 plus travel and a $1000 travel stipend to attend the ACOG Annual Clinical Meeting. **No. of Awards:** 1. **To Apply:** Applications should be in the form of a detailed letter that includes basic personal data, educational background, present position, institution in which the Fellowship is to be held and the name of the director of the program, description of long-range career goals and a statement of how this Fellowship will enhance these goals. The scientific research proposal should include the following: hypotheses, objective, specific aims, background and significance, experimental design, and references. A separate letter of support fromt he program director, department chair, or laboratory director and a one-page budget are required. Five copies must be submitted. **Deadline:** October 1.

**Remarks:** A progress report on work done during the Fellowship will be required at the end of six months. A final written report is required and due by September 1 after the grant concludes.

### • 385 • ACOG/Zeneca Pharmaceuticals Research Award in Breast Cancer *(Postdoctorate/Grant)*

**Purpose:** To provide seed grant funds to junior investigators for research in the area of breast cancer. **Focus:** Oncology, specifically breast cancer. **Qualif.:** Applicants must be Fellows or Junior Fellows of ACOG who are in an approved obstetrics/gynecology residency program or within three years postresidency. **Criteria:** All applications are reviewed by a committee of ACOG members.

**Funds Avail.:** $15,000 plus travel expenses and travel expenses to attend the ACOG Annual Clinical Meeting of up to $2000. **No. of Awards:** 1. **To Apply:** Six copies of a one-page budget sheet; curriculum vitae; letter of support from program director, departmental chair, or laboratory director; and a six typewritten pages scientific research proposal which should include the following: hypotheses, objective, specific aims, background and significance, experimental design, and references must be submitted. **Deadline:** October 1.

**Remarks:** A final written report is required and due by September 1 after the grant concludes. This report is to include a brief account of final expenditures.

### • 386 • Warren H Pearse/Wyeth-Ayerst Women's Health Policy Research Award *(Postdoctorate/Grant)*

**Purpose:** To provide seed grant funds to junior investigators for research in the area of health care policy. The research should be about an aspect of policy that either defines, assists or restricts the ability of the physician to deliver health care to women in general or in a specific area. **Focus:** Health care policy. **Qualif.:** The principal or co-principal investigator must be a Fellow or Junior Fellow of the ACOG. **Criteria:** Applications are reviewd by a committee of ACOG members looking at innovation, potential utility of the research, ability to generalize results, and demonstrated capability of investigator.

**Funds Avail.:** $15,000 plus travel expenses and travel expenses to attend the ACOG Annual Clinical Meeting. **No. of Awards:** 1. **To**

## American College of Obstetricians and Gynecologists (continued)

**Apply:** Six copies of a one-page budget sheet, curriculum vitae, letter of support from program director, departmental chair, or laboratory director; and a six typewritten pages scientific research proposal which should include the following: hypotheses, objective, specific aims, background and significance, experimental design, and references must be submitted. **Deadline:** October 1.

**Remarks:** A final written report is required and due by September 1 after the grant concludes. This report is to include a brief account of final expenditures.

## • 387 •

## American Concrete Institute - Concrete Research and Education Foundation

PO Box 9094     *Ph:* (248)848-3700
Farmington Hills, MI 48333     *Fax:* (248)848-3701
*URL:* http://www.ce.ecn.purdue.edu/~aci/text/
committee.html

**• 388 • ACI Fellowships: ACI/W.R. Grace Fellowship; V. Mohan Malhotra Fellowship; Katherine Bryant Mather Fellowship; Stewart C. Watson Fellowship** *(Graduate/Fellowship)*

**Purpose:** To support graduate study in the field of concrete. **Focus:** Engineering, Architectural or Materials Science, Concrete Materials Research, Research and Grad study of joints and bearings for concrete structures. **Qualif.:** Applicant may be of any nationality, but must be proficient in the English language (or French as required in the Canadian Province of Quebec or Spanish in Puerto Rico). Applicant must have completed a bachelor's degree in a field of engineering related to concrete construction, such as design or materials and be in the first or second year of graduate study during the entire scholarship in an accredited engineering, architectural, or material science program at an accredited college or university in the U.S. or Canada which offers a graduate program in concrete design, materials, or construction, with the exception of the V. Mohan Malhorta Fellowship which is available only to an applicant majoring in concrete materials science research and the Stewart C. Watson Fellowship which is available only for research and graduate study of joints and bearings for concrete structures.

**Funds Avail.:** $3,000. **No. of Awards:** Six. **To Apply:** Write for application form and guidelines. **Deadline:** January 15. Notification by March 1.

**Remarks:** It is necessary to submit only one application to be considered for all of these awards. **Contact:** Concrete Research and Education Foundation (ConREF) at the above address (see entry 387).

## • 389 •

## American Congress on Surveying and Mapping

5410 Grosvenor Ln., Ste. 100     *Ph:* (301)493-0200
Bethesda, MD 20814-2160     *Fax:* (301)493-8245
*URL:* http://www.sgi.ursus.maine.edu/gisweb/acsm/
asprsyears.html

**• 390 • ACA Scholarship Award** *(Undergraduate/ Scholarship)*

**Purpose:** The objective of the American Cartographic Association (ACA) Scholarship Award is to recognize outstanding cartography and mapping science students and to encourage the completion of an undergraduate program and/or pursuit of graduate education in cartography or other mapping sciences. **Qualif.:** Applicants must be full-time students of junior or senior standing enrolled in a cartography or other mapping sciences curriculum in a 4-year degree granting institution. Nominees should have had a minimum of three courses in cartography or other mapping sciences participated in professional societies. **Criteria:** Any ACSM member may nominate a qualified student with appropriate documentation. Students may nominate themselves by completing the ACSM Fellowship or Scholarship Awards Application and by providing all other necessary documentation.

**Funds Avail.:** $1,000. **To Apply:** Applicants must submit application form, academic transcripts, three letters of recommendation, two of which should be from the faculty members familiar with the nominee's academic performance, and a personal statement of course of study and its relationship to career goals prepared by the nominee. **Deadline:** January 1. **Contact:** ACSM Award Director at the above address (see entry 389).

**• 391 • American Association for Geodetic Surveying Graduate Fellowship** *(Graduate/Fellowship)*

**Purpose:** To promote geodetic surveying. **Focus:** Surveying, Mapping. **Qualif.:** Candidates may be of any nationality, but must be a graduate student and a member of the ACSM or the American Society for Photogrammetry and Remote Sensing. Applicants should be accepted by a graduate program with significant focus on geodetic surveying or geodesy.

**Funds Avail.:** $2,000. **To Apply:** Candidates must be nominated by members of ACSM or ASPRS. Write to the Awards director for application form and guidelines. **Deadline:** December 1. **Contact:** Awards Director at the above address (see entry 389).

**• 392 • Joseph F. Dracup Scholarship Award** *(Undergraduate/Scholarship)*

**Purpose:** To encourage and recognize outstanding students committed to a career in geodetic surveying. **Qualif.:** Applicants must be enrolled in or accepted by a undergraduate program with a significant focus upon geodetic surveying. **Criteria:** Nominations will be received from any member of ACSM or ASPRS. Nominations of previous recipients are eligible. The recipient will be selected annually by the American Association for Geodetic Surveying Awards Committee.

**Funds Avail.:** $2,000. **To Apply:** Applicants must submit application form, academic transcripts, letters of recommendation from the faculty member familiar with the nominee's academic performance, letter of recommendation form the nominee's previous or current employer in the surveying profession, a personal statement of course of study and its relationship to career goals prepared by the nominee. **Deadline:** January 1. **Contact:** ACSM Awards Director.

**• 393 • The Schonstedt Scholarship in Surveying** *(Undergraduate/Scholarship)*

**Qualif.:** Applicants must have completed at least 2 years of 4-year undergraduate curriculum leading to a degree in surveying. **Criteria:** Selection will be based on the applicant's statement of merit, educational and career plans, prior academic record, and recommendation of faculty member.

**Funds Avail.:** $1,500. **Deadline:** January 1.

**Remarks:** Scholarship is funded by the Schonstedt Instrument Company of Reston, Virginia. **Contact:** ACSM Awards Director at the above address (see entry 389).

**• 394 • The Wild Leitz Surveying Scholarship** *(Undergraduate/Scholarship)*

**Purpose:** To encourage qualified candidates to pursue undergraduate education in surveying and to promote the development of the field of surveying and mapping science. **Qualif.:** Applicants must be enrolled as undergraduates in a program at an institution with a two- or four-year degree program in surveying or related fields. Students enrolled in foreign training programs are eligible. Applicants must be U.S. citizens who have completed at least one undergraduate course in surveying prior to the receipt of the scholarship. Applicants must be members of the American Congress on Surveying and Mapping, or the American Society for Photogrammetry and Remote Sensing, or regular students of an accredited school who are sponsored by a member of ACSM or ASPRS. **Criteria:** Selection will be made by the ACSM Scholarship Awards Committee and will be based on the following criteria: 30 percent previous academic record; 30 percent applicant's statement of study objectives; 15 percent applicability of previous courses to a degree in surveying; 20 percent recommendation of faculty member; and 5 percent financial need.

**Funds Avail.:** Two awards of $1,000 each. Recipients may reapply for an extension in the succeeding years. **Deadline:** January 1. Recipients will be announced by March 31.

**Remarks:** The award will be presented at the Annual Convention of the ACSM-ASPRS. In June following the award, the recipient is expected to submit to ACSM a brief summary of academic accomplishments during the year.

**• 395 •**
**American Consulting Engineers Council of Metropolitan Washington, D.C.**
8811 Colesville Rd., Ste. G106         *Ph:* (301)588-6616
Silver Spring, MD 20910                 *Fax:* (301)589-2017

**• 396 • ACEC Cotton Scholarships** *(Undergraduate/Scholarship)*

**Focus:** Engineering. **Qualif.:** Applicants must be United States citizens pursuing a Bachelor's degree in an ABET-approved engineering program or in an accredited land surveying program. Students must be entering their junior, senior, or fifth year to qualify. **Criteria:** Selection is based on GPA, written essay, work experience, recommendations, and college activities.

**Funds Avail.:** $1,000 each. **No. of Awards:** 1. **To Apply:** Applicants must submit a certified grade transcript identifying cumulative grade point average based on a 4.0 grading scale; a typed or neatly printed essay of approximately 500 words; a list of recent work experiences, including the year in high school during which an applicant held a position and indicating if the work was in the form of work study, co-op, or practicum, and the nature of the business of the listed employers; a list of college activities, including offices held in any organizations; and a recommendation form completed by an engineering professor, consulting engineer, or land surveyor. The evaluator must send the recommendation directly to the Washington, D.C., office. Incomplete applications will not be considered. **Deadline:** February 17. **Contact:** Marcia L. Bachner, Executive Director, at the above address (see entry 395).

**• 397 •**
**American Council of the Blind**
1155 15th St., NW, Ste. 720         *Ph:* (202)467-5081
Washington, DC 20005                *Free:* 800-424-8666
*E-mail:* jbeach@access.digex.net
*URL:* http://acb.org

**• 398 • ACB Scholarships** *(Graduate, Undergraduate/Scholarship)*

**Purpose:** To provide financial assistance to blind or visually impaired students. **Focus:** General Studies. **Qualif.:** Applicant must be a legally blind U.S. citizen or resident alien. Applicant may be an undergraduate or graduate student; or a vocational/technical student at the postsecondary level.

**Funds Avail.:** $500-4,000. **No. of Awards:** 21. **To Apply:** Contact the coordinator for application form and guidelines. Submit form with a two-page autobiographical statement, transcripts, certificate of legal blindness, and a letter of recommendation. Selected candidates will be interviewed by telephone. **Deadline:** March 1.

**Remarks:** Six ACB Scholarships are named awards: the Anne Pekar Scholarship, the Grant M. Mack Memorial Schools, the Melva T. Owen Memorial Scholarship, the Floyd Qualls Memorial Scholarship, and Arnold Oswald Memorial Science Scholarship, Xerox Imaging Systems Scholarship, John Hebner Memorial Scholarship. All eligibility and application information is the same as that listed above. **Contact:** Scholarship Coordinator at the above address (see entry 397).

**• 399 • American Council of the Blind Scholarship Program** *(All/Scholarship)*

**Focus:** General Studies. **Qualif.:** The awards are given to outstanding legally-blind students enrolled in academic, vocational, technical, or professional training programs beyond the high school level. The students must be United States citizens or resident aliens. **Criteria:** Applicants must be legally blind in both eyes.

**Funds Avail.:** 25 awards ranging from $500 to $4,000 are presented to Scholars in each of four categories; entering freshmen in academic programs, sophomores, juniors and seniors in academic programs, graduate students in academic or professional programs, and vocational and technical school students. **No. of Awards:** 25. **To Apply:** Students must submit a completed application, an autobiographical sketch, a certified school transcript, and a letter of recommendation from a current or recent instructor. An entering or transferred student must show proof of acceptance in a post-secondary school. **Deadline:** All required documents must be postmarked by March 1. Recipients are announced in July at the national convention of the ACB. **Contact:** American Council of the Blind at the above address (see entry 397).

**• 400 •**
**American Council for Construction Education**
1957 E St. NW
Washington, DC 20006                 *Ph:* (202)393-2040

**• 401 • Associated General Contractors Education Research Foundation Graduate Scholarship** *(Graduate/Scholarship)*

**Focus:** Construction, civil engineering. **Qualif.:** Applicants must be college seniors enrolled in an undergraduate or civil engineering degree program, or graduates possessing degrees in civil engineering or construction. Applicants must be enrolled or planning to enroll in a graduate level construction or civil

## American Council for Construction Education (continued)

engineering degree program as full-time students. **Criteria:** Awards are made based on personal interview.

**Funds Avail.:** $7,500. Paid in two installments of $3,750. **To Apply:** Applicants must submit an application form, transcripts, three adult evaluations, and a completed and stamped "Notification of Receipt" card. Incomplete packages will not be considered; no exceptions. **Deadline:** November 1. Finalists selected in January and are subject to personal interview with an AGC contractor member representing the AGC Foundation.

**Remarks:** Scholarships include the Saul Horowitz, Jr. Memorial Graduate Award and the Heffner Scholarships for Graduate Students. **Contact:** Director of Programs at the above address (see entry 400).

## • 402 • Associated General Contractors Education and Research Foundation Undergraduate Scholarship (Undergraduate/Scholarship)

**Focus:** Construction, civil engineering. **Qualif.:** Applicants must be college freshman, sophomores, and juniors enroled or planning to enroll in a four or five-year degree program in construction or civil engineering.

**Funds Avail.:** $1,500. Renewable up to a maximum of $6,000. **To Apply:** Applicants must submit application, transcript, three adult evaluations, and a completed and stamped "Notification of Receipt" card. Incomplete packages will not be considered; no exceptions. Write or fax for further information. **Deadline:** November 1.

**Remarks:** Special awards offered in the Undergraduate Scholarship Program are the B.B. & Betty Ellen Armstrong Scholarships; Henry M. Boh Memorial Scholarships; Bowen Engineering Minority Scholarships; Build America Scholarships; G.E. Burne Memorial Scholarships; Billy R. Carter Memorial Scholarships; CCC Undergraduate Scholarships; Ival R. Cianchette Scholarships; Ralph E. Daily Scholarships; Owen H. Emme Scholarships; Carl W. Erickson Scholarships; General Fund Scholarships; Robert B. & Celine Fay Scholarships; Humphrey Folk Scholarships; J.T. Folk Scholarships; Richard and Elizabeth Hall Scholarships; Harry R. Halloran/The Conduit & Foundation Corporation Scholarships; Vernie & Flora Lindstrom Scholarships; Vernie G. Lindstrom, Jr. Scholarships; Robert B. McEachern Memorial Scholarships; William S. & Shirley C. McIntyre Scholarships; Stanley F. Pepper Memorial Scholarships; Pfaffmann Family Scholarships; James D. Pitcock, Jr. Scholarships; Pizzagalli Construction Company Scholarships; Paul B. Richards Memorial Scholarships; Tom & Mary Steele Scholarships; and U.S. F&G Foundation Scholarships; Willis Corroon Scholarship. Only one application is needed to compete for all of the above scholarships. **Contact:** Director of Programs at the above address (see entry 400).

## • 403 •
## American Council on Education

1 Dupont Circle                    Ph: (202)939-9420
Washington, DC 20036-1193          Fax: (202)785-8056
E-mail: fellows@ace.nche.edu
URL: http://www.ACENET.edu

## • 404 • ACE Fellows Program (Professional Development/Fellowship)

**Purpose:** To identify and prepare senior faculty and mid-level administrators at colleges and universities for more senior administrative positions through an internship; seminars focusing on financial planning, budgeting, personnel management, and legal issues; campus visits and development of an extensive

national and international network. **Focus:** Higher Education. **Qualif.:** Nominees must have a minimum of five years of college-level experience as faculty members or as administrators and must have a record of leadership accomplishments. **Criteria:** Candidates are nominated by their institution's chief executive or chief academic officer. After an initial screening of candidates' credentials by a committee of higher education leaders, finalists are interviewed and approximately 30 fellows are selected by a panel of presidents and senior officers in higher education.

**Funds Avail.:** The nominating institution continues to pay the fellow's salary and benefits during the fellowship year. The institution hosting a fellow is responsible for providing funds to cover the fellow's professional development expenses, which amount to approximately $10,000. The institution providing the internship experience is also responsible for a $3,000 program fee payable to ACE. Several grants are available on a competitive basis to nominating institutions that are ACE members and release their fellows for an off-campus fellowship. The grants range between $7,000 and $12,000 and are intended to help offset the institution's expense in replacing the fellow. Institutions that are not ACE members may nominate a candidate, but must pay an additional fee if the candidate is selected as a fellow. **No. of Awards:** Approximately 30 each academic year. **To Apply:** Nominations and candidates' application materials are sent to presidents and chief academic officers of all regionally accredited institutions during the summer. **Deadline:** November 1. Finalists are selected and notified by January 15. Finalists are interviewed in Washington, DC, in late January and early February. Approximately 30 ACE Fellows are selected and notified of their appointment by March 1.

**Remarks:** Fellows serve their internship with the president and other senior administrators at either the host institution or home campus where they have access to the highest level of decision making on campus and involvement in a wide variety of administrative activities. They also participate in three week-long seminars sponsored by ACE, where they meet with national leaders and learn the latest theories and practice in higher education administration. They also attend regional seminars in which higher education leaders help fellows understand specific problems or topic areas selected by the fellows themselves. **Contact:** The American Council on Education at the above address (see entry 403).

## • 405 •
## American Council of Learned Societies

228 E. 45th St.                    Ph: (212)697-1505
New York, NY 10017-3398            Fax: (212)949-8058
E-mail: grants@acls.org
URL: http://www.acls.org

*The General Programs of the American Council of Learned Society support postdoctoral research in the humanities. The following fields of specialization are included: philosophy (including the philosophy of law and science), aesthetics, philology, languages, literature, and linguistics, archaelogy, art history, musicology, history (including the history of science, law, and religions) cultural anthropology, and folklore. Proposals with a predominantly humanistic emphasis in economics, geography, political science, psychology, sociology, and the natural sciences will also be considered.*

## • 406 • ACLS Fellowships (Postdoctorate/Fellowship)

**Purpose:** To support postdoctoral research in the humanities. **Focus:** Humanities and humanities-related social sciences. **Qualif.:** Applicants must be U.S. citizens or permanent residents who have not undertaken supported research leave within the five years prior to application. Applicants for a General Fellowship must have held the Ph.D. for at least two years. Fellowships are intended as salary replacement for the provision of free time for research. Awardees may hold ACLS fellowships concurrently with other fellowships or grants but the total support may not exceed the fellow's normal academic year salary.

**Funds Avail.:** $25,000 for junior scholars, and up to $35,000 for senior scholars. **To Apply:** Write for application form and guidelines. **Deadline:** October 2. Notification in late March. **Contact:** Office of Fellowships and Grants at the above address (see entry 405).

### • 407 • ACLS Grants for East European Studies - Dissertation Fellowships *(Doctorate/Fellowship)*

**Qualif.:** Applicants must be doctoral candidates working on Ph.D. dissertations focusing on Eastern Europe in the social sciences and humanities. Applicants must be United States citizens or permanent legal residents of the United States.

**Funds Avail.:** Stipends will be up to $15,000 plus expenses per year. Candidates may apply initially for support for one year, with reapplication for a second year possible. **No. of Awards:** Approximately 10. **To Apply:** Individuals must request application forms in writing and provide the following information: highest academic degree held and date received; country of citizenship or permanent legal residence; academic or other position; field of specialization; proposed subject of research or study; proposed date for beginning tenure of the award and duration requested; specific award program for which application is requested. **Deadline:** Completed application forms must be postmarked no later than November 2. Decisions are announced in April. Fellowships are tenable beginning June.

**Remarks:** This program is subject to funding. **Contact:** Office of Fellowships and Grants at the above address (see entry 405).

### • 408 • ACLS Grants for East European Studies - Fellowships for Postdoctoral Research *(Postdoctorate/ Fellowship)*

**Purpose:** To enable scholars in the humanities and social sciences to undertake a period of at least six consecutive months of full-time research focusing on Eastern Europe. **Qualif.:** Candidates must hold a Ph.D. or its equivalent as of the application deadline date. They must be United States citizens or permanent legal residents of the United States. All proposals should be for scholarly work, the product of which is to be disseminated in English. These programs are not intended to support research within East Europe. In special circumstances untenured scholars or younger independent scholars without an academic appointment may apply for support to be used over any period of one to three years. **Criteria:** Fellows will be selected on the basis of the scholarly merit of the proposal, its importance to the development of East European studies, and the scholarly potential, accomplishments, and financial need of the applicants.

**Funds Avail.:** Stipends of up to $25,000 are intended primarily as salary replacement to provide free time for research; the funds may be used to supplement sabbatical salaries or awards from other sources, provided they would intensify or extend the contemplated research. **No. of Awards:** Five to seven. **To Apply:** Individuals must request application forms in writing and provide the following information: highest academic degree held and date received; country of citizenship or permanent legal residence; academic or other position; field of specialization; proposed subject of research or study; proposed date for beginning tenure of the award and duration requested; specific award program for which application is requested. **Deadline:** Completed application forms must be postmarked no later than November 2. Decisions are announced in April. Fellowships are tenable during six to twelve months between July 1 and September 1.

**Remarks:** This program is subject to funding. **Contact:** Office of Fellowships and Grants at the above address (see entry 405).

### • 409 • Chinese Fellowships for Scholarly Development *(Other/Fellowship)*

**Focus:** Social sciences and humanities. **Qualif.:** Applicants must be Chinese scholars in a related area of study with a MA or PhD or equivalent.

**Funds Avail.:** Living allowance, health insurance , and international airfare. **No. of Awards:** 8. **Deadline:** October 31.

**Remarks:** Directed at younger scholars for whom a period of research in the US at this time in their careers would enhance their scholarly potential after returning to China and is offered only if funding is available.

### • 410 • Contemplative Practice Fellowship *(Other/ Fellowship)*

**Purpose:** To develop courses and teaching materials that explore contemplative practice from a variety of disciplinary and interdisciplinary perspectives. **Focus:** Education. **Qualif.:** Applicants must be regular full-time faculty members at academic institutions in the United States.

**Funds Avail.:** Up to 10,000. **No. of Awards:** 10 to 15. **Deadline:** October 30.

**Remarks:** Made possible by the Nathan Cummings Foundation and the Fetzer Institute.

### • 411 • Henry Luce Foundation/ACLS Dissertation Fellowship Program in American Art *(Graduate/ Fellowship)*

**Purpose:** To assist in dissertation research or writing. **Focus:** American art history. **Qualif.:** Applicants must have completed all requirements for the PhD except the dissertation and be U.S. citizens or permanent residents.

**Funds Avail.:** $18,500. **Deadline:** November 16.

**Remarks:** Funds can not be used for tuition costs.

### • 412 • Henry Luce Foundation/ACLS Dissertation Fellowship in American Art *(Doctorate/Fellowship)*

**Purpose:** To assist graduate students in any stage of Ph.D. dissertation research or writing. **Focus:** History of the visual arts in the United States. **Qualif.:** Applicants must be a Ph.D. candidate in a department of Art History, a U.S. citizen and have completed all requirements for the Ph.D. except the dissertation before beginning tenure.

**Funds Avail.:** $15,000. **To Apply:** Write for application form and guidelines. **Deadline:** November 15. Notification in April. **Contact:** Office of Fellowships and Grants at the above address (see entry 405).

### • 413 •
## American Council on Rural Special Education
Gonzaga University
Department of Teacher Education     *Ph:* (509)328-4220
Spokane, WA 99258-0001     *Fax:* (509)324-5812
*E-mail:* jlemke@soe.gonzaga.edu

### • 414 • ACRSE Scholarships *(Professional Development/Scholarship)*

**Purpose:** To offer practicing rural teachers an opportunity to pursue education and training that would not otherwise be available. **Qualif.:** Applicants must be currently employed by a rural school district as certified teachers. They must be teachers who work with students with disabilities, or regular education teachers

## American Council on Rural Special Education (continued)

who are "retooling" for work in a special education setting. **Criteria:** A selection committee made up of ACRES members evaluates academic and leadership potential. **No. of Awards:** 1. **To Apply:** A completed application and two letters of reference must be submitted in addition to an essay describing the advantages and disadvantages of rural special education and the proposed use of the scholarship funds. **Deadline:** February 1. **Contact:** Dr. June Canty Lemke, ACRES Scholarship Program, at the above address (see entry 413).

## • 415 •
### American Dental Assistants Association

203 N. La Salle St., No. 1320  
Chicago, IL 60601-1210  

*Ph:* (312)541-1550  
*Fax:* (312)541-1496  
*Free:* 800-733-2322  

*E-mail:* adaa1@aol.com

#### • 416 • Juliette A. Southard Scholarship
*(Undergraduate/Scholarship)*

**Purpose:** To further education in the field of dental assisting. **Focus:** Dental Assisting. **Qualif.:** Applicants must be U.S. citizens, high school graduates or equivalent, and enrolled in an accredited dental assisting program. **Criteria:** Candidates are considered on the basis of academic achievement, ability, interest in dentistry, and personal attributes.

**Funds Avail.:** $100-$500. Candidates who receive funds must complete their dental assisting education. In the event that they do not, the scholarship becomes a non-interest bearing loan that must be repaid within 12 months from the date the funds were granted. **No. of Awards:** 10. **To Apply:** Attached to the application form, candidates must submit official transcripts of high school and any other previous academic work, and proof of graduation. They must also send or have the school send proof of acceptance to the dental assisting program, a statement of intent indicating their goals to pursue a long-range career in dental assisting, and a current passport-size photograph of themselves. Also required are two letters of reference: one from a dental professional who is a member of the ADAA or ADA endorsing the applicant's qualities as they relate to being an effective dental assistant; the other from a person of the applicant's choice endorsing integrity and conscientiousness with a brief summary of the applicant's cooperation, leadership, good sportsmanship, and application of efforts. **Deadline:** September 1. **Contact:** Tina Grikmanis at the above address (see entry 415).

## • 417 •
### American Dental Hygienists' Association - Institute for Oral Health

444 N. Michigan Ave., Ste. 3400  
Chicago, IL 60611  

*Ph:* (312)440-8944  
*Fax:* (312)440-8929  
*Free:* 800-735-4916  

*URL:* http://www.adha.org/

#### • 418 • ADHA Certificate/Associate Degree, Baccalaureate and Graduate Scholarships *(Graduate, Undergraduate/Scholarship)*

**Purpose:** To assist students pursuing education related to careers in dental hygiene. **Focus:** Dental Hygiene. **Qualif.:** Applicant must be enrolled full-time in a dental hygiene program in the United States; and have completed a minimum of one year in a dental

hygiene curriculum with a grade point average of 3.0 (on a 4.0 scale) prior to receiving an award. Candidate must also document financial need. Applicant for the graduate scholarships must be a licensed dental hygienist with a bachelor's degree.

**Funds Avail.:** $1,500 maximum. **No. of Awards:** Varies. **To Apply:** Write or call the ADHA Institute for an application packet. **Deadline:** June 1. Recipients will be notified in early fall.

**Remarks:** In addition to the general scholarships, the ADHA Institute offers several designated scholarships, including one for minorities. Write to the ADHA Institute for details. About 400 apply each year. **Contact:** Beatrice Pedersen, Associate Administrator, at the above address (see entry 417).

#### • 419 • ADHA Institute Research Grants
*(Professional Development/Grant)*

**Purpose:** To offer research opportunities to dental hygienists. **Focus:** Dental Hygiene. **Qualif.:** Applicant must be a licensed dental hygienist or dental hygiene student. Grants are tenable at any research site.

**Funds Avail.:** $1,000-5,000. **No. of Awards:** Varies. **To Apply:** Write or call the ADHA Institute to request proposal guidelines. **Deadline:** January 15. Notification after June 30. **Contact:** Beatrice Pederson, at the above address (see entry 417).

#### • 420 • ADHA Part-Time Scholarship *(Graduate, Undergraduate/Scholarship)*

ARS Dental hygiene. **Qualif.:** Applicants must be part-time students enrolled in a Certificate/Associate, Baccalaureate, or Graduate Degree in the United States; have completed a minimum of one year in the curriculum; **Criteria:** Based on financial need.

**Funds Avail.:** $1000. **No. of Awards:** 1. **To Apply:** A document of financial need a career goals statement must be submitted. **Deadline:** June 1.

#### • 421 • Carol Bauhs Benson Memorial Scholarship
*(Undergraduate/Scholarship)*

**Focus:** Dental hygiene. **Qualif.:** Applicants must be from Minnesota, North Dakota, South Dakota, or Wisconsin; be enrolled in an accredited program in the United States; have completed a minimum of one year in the curriculum; **Criteria:** Based on financial need.

**Funds Avail.:** $1000. **No. of Awards:** 1. **To Apply:** A document of financial need a career goals statement must be submitted. **Deadline:** June 1.

#### • 422 • John O. Butler Scholarships *(Graduate/Scholarship)*

**Focus:** Dental hygiene or dental hygiene education. **Qualif.:** Applicants must currently be enrolled full-time in a master's degree program in the United States; have a minimum GPA of 3.0; and must demonstrate financial need.

**Funds Avail.:** $2000. **No. of Awards:** 7. **To Apply:** Documentation of financial need; a completed career goals statement; evidence of dental hygiene licensure; evidence of acceptance as a full-time Master's or Doctoral Degree application in a university graduate program ; and statement of research interests must be submitted. **Deadline:** June 1.

**Remarks:** Graduate Scholarship recipients are encouraged to submit a final thesis or dissertation manuscript format to be considered for publication in the *Journal of Dental Hygiene*. Sponsored by the John O Butler Co.

## • 423 • Colgate "Bright Smile, Bright Futures" Minority Scholarship/ADHA Institute Minority Scholarship *(Undergraduate/Scholarship)*

**Purpose:** To provide financial assistance for minority groups currently underrepresented in the dental hygiene program. **Focus:** Dental Hygiene. **Qualif.:** Applicants must be members of minority groups, including Native Americans, African-Americans, Hispanics, Asians, and males. Male applicants are not required to be members of minority groups. Applicants must have completed a minimum of one year in a dental hygiene curriculum. They must have a minimum grade point average of 3.0 on a 4.0 scale for the time they have been enrolled in a dental hygiene curriculum. Applicants must be full-time students during the academic year for which they are applying. Candidates must be able to document financial need of at least $1,500.

**Funds Avail.:** Funds for financial assistance are limited because they consist of donations and grants from various sources. Average scholarship will be $1,250. **To Apply:** A formal application must be filed. Upon request, a scholarship application packet is sent to interested candidates. **Deadline:** Completed packets and all other application materials must be filed by June 1. All applicants are notified in September whether or not they have been selected as recipients.

## • 424 • Rebecca Fisk Scholarship *(Undergraduate/Scholarship)*

ARS Dental hygiene. **Qualif.:** Applicants must be enrolled in an accredited program in the United States; have completed a minimum of one year in the curriculum. **Criteria:** Based on financial need.

**Funds Avail.:** $1000. **No. of Awards:** 1. **To Apply:** A document of financial need a career goals statement must be submitted. **Deadline:** June 1.

## • 425 • Dr. Alfred C. Fones Scholarships *(Doctorate, Graduate, Undergraduate/Scholarship)*

**Focus:** Dental Hygiene. **Qualif.:** Applicants must be members of ADHA and either have evidence of a dental hygiene certificate, be entering their senior year of a dental hygiene bachelor's program, or be a licensed dental hygienist with a bachelor's degree. Those who will qualify for a certificate in the current year are also eligible. Applicants who can provide evidence of acceptance as full-time bachelor's, master's, or doctoral degree candidates in accredited four-year colleges or universities are also eligible. Applicants must have a minimum grade point average of 3.0 on a 4.0 scale for the time they have been enrolled in a dental hygiene curriculum, and be full-time students during the academic year for which they are applying, and able to document financial need of at least $1,500.

**Funds Avail.:** $1,500 maximum. **No. of Awards:** 1. **To Apply:** Formal application from an ADHA Institute and a FAFSA Aid form must be filed. Upon request, a scholarship application packet is sent to interested candidates. **Deadline:** Completed scholarship application packets must be mailed and postmarked no later than June 1. Completed financial aid forms must reach College Scholarship Service by March 1. All applicants are notified in September whether or not they have been selected as recipients. **Contact:** Linda Caradine.

## • 426 • Dr. Harold Hillenbrand Scholarships *(Doctorate, Graduate, Undergraduate/Scholarship)*

**Purpose:** Awarded to a candidate who demonstrates specific academic excellence and outstanding clinical performance. **Focus:** Dental Hygiene. **Qualif.:** Applicants must have completed a minimum of one year's study in a dental hygiene curriculum prior to receiving an award and have maintained at least a 3.0 (on a 4.0 scale) grade point average while enrolled. Candidates must be full-time students during the academic year for which they are applying and be able to document financial need of at least $1,500.

They must be enrolled in a dental hygiene program in the United States. **Criteria:** Based on assessed need as determined by the Financial Aid Office and on how well the candidate demonstrates academic excellence.

**Funds Avail.:** The maximum for any scholarship is $1,500. **To Apply:** Formal application must be filed. Applicants must also file a FAFSA form. **Deadline:** Applicants must file the Financial Aid Form of FAFSA by March 1. Completed applications and supporting materials must be postmarked by June 1. Applicants are notified in early fall. **Contact:** Linda Caradine at the above address (see entry 417).

## • 427 • Wilma E. Motley Scholarship *(Undergraduate/Scholarship)*

**Focus:** Dental hygiene. **Qualif.:** Applicants must be pursuing a baccalaureate degree in dental hygiene at a four-year institution with an accredited dental hygiene program in the United States. Must be full-time and have a 4.0 GPA.

**Funds Avail.:** $1000. **No. of Awards:** 1. **To Apply:** Documentation of financial need; and career goals statement must be submitted. **Deadline:** June 1.

## • 428 • Irene E. Newman Scholarships *(Doctorate, Graduate, Undergraduate/Scholarship)*

**Purpose:** Awarded to a candidate who demonstrates strong potential in public health or community dental health. **Focus:** Dental Hygiene. **Qualif.:** Applicants must either have evidence of a dental hygiene certificate, be entering their senior year of a dental hygiene bachelor's program, or be a licensed dental hygienists with a bachelor's degree. Those who will qualify for a certificate in the current year are also eligible. Students who can provide evidence of acceptance as full-time bachelor's, master's, or doctoral degree candidates in accredited four-year colleges or universities are also eligible. Applicants must have a minimum grade point average of 3.0 on a 4.0 scale for the time they have been enrolled in a dental hygiene curriculum, be full-time students during the academic year for which they are applying, able to document financial need of at least $1,500, and be members of ADHA.

**Funds Avail.:** $1,500 maximum. **No. of Awards:** 1. **To Apply:** Formal application from ADHA and a FAFSA Aid form must be filed. Upon request, a scholarship application packet is sent to interested candidates. **Deadline:** Completed scholarship application packets must be mailed and postmarked no later than June 1. Completed financial aid forms must reach FAFSA by March 1. All applicants are notified in September whether or not they have been selected as recipients. **Contact:** Linda Caradine.

## • 429 • Oral-B Laboratories Dental Hygiene Scholarships *(Undergraduate/Scholarship)*

**Purpose:** To encourage professional, excellence, and scholarship; promote quality research; and support dental hygiene through public and private education. **Focus:** Dental hygiene and related fields. **Qualif.:** Applicants must have a 3.5 GPA. Be enrolled in an accredited program in the United States; be a full-time student. **Criteria:** Based on financial need.

**Funds Avail.:** $1000 and $1500. **No. of Awards:** 2. **To Apply:** Documentation of financial need and a career goals statement must be submitted. **Deadline:** June 1.

## • 430 • Sigma Phi Alpha Graduate Scholarship *(Graduate/Scholarship)*

**Focus:** Dental hygiene or dental hygiene education. **Qualif.:** Applicants must currently be enrolled full-time in a master's degree program in the United States; have a minimum GPA of 3.0; and must demonstrate financial need.

## American Dental Hygienists' Association - Institute for Oral Health (continued)

**Funds Avail.:** $1000. **No. of Awards:** 1. **To Apply:** Documentation of financial need; a completed career goals statement; evidence of dental hygiene licensure; evidence of acceptance as a full-time Master's or Doctoral Degree application in a university graduate program ; and statement of research interests must be submitted. **Deadline:** June 1.

**Remarks:** Graduate Scholarship recipients are encouraged to submit a final thesis or dissertation manuscript format to be considered for publication in the *Journal of Dental Hygiene*.

### • 431 •  Sigma Phi Alpha Undergraduate Scholarship
*(Undergraduate/Scholarship)*

**Focus:** Dental hygiene or related fields. **Qualif.:** Applicants must be full-time students attending an accredited school with an active chapter of the Sigma Phi Alpha Dental Hygiene Honor Society; pursuing a baccalaureate degree in the United States; be eligible for licensure in the academic year the award is being made; entered in a Degree Completion Program; or currently licensed or will be eligible for licensure in the current year.

**Funds Avail.:** $1000. **No. of Awards:** 1. **To Apply:** Documentation of financial need and complete career goals statement must be submitted. **Deadline:** June 1.

### • 432 •  Margaret E. Swanson Scholarships
*(Doctorate, Graduate, Undergraduate/Scholarship)*

**Purpose:** Awarded to a candidate who demonstrates exceptional organizational leadership potential. **Focus:** Dental Hygiene. **Qualif.:** Applicants must have completed a minimum of one year's study in a dental hygiene curriculum prior to receiving an award and have maintained at least a 3.0 on a 4.0 scale grade point average while enrolled. Candidates must be full-time students during the academic year for which they are applying and be able to document financial need of at least $1,500. Applicants must be enrolled in a dental hygiene program in the United States. **Criteria:** Based on assessed need as determined by the Financial Aid Office and on how well the candidate demonstrates leadership potential.

**Funds Avail.:** The maximum for any scholarship is $1,500. **No. of Awards:** 1. **To Apply:** Formal application must be filed. Applicants must also file a FAFSA form. **Deadline:** Applicants must file the Financial Aid Form of the FAFSA by March 1. Completed applications and supporting materials must be postmarked by June 1. Applicants are notified in early fall. **Contact:** Linda Caradine at the above address (see entry 417).

### • 433 •  Warner Lambert Joint Oral Hygiene Group Scholarships *(Undergraduate/Scholarship)*

**Focus:** Dental hygiene. **Qualif.:** Applicants must be pursuing a baccalaureate degree in dental hygiene at a four-year institution with an accredited dental hygiene program in the United States. Must be full-time and have a 4.0 GPA.

**Funds Avail.:** $1000. **No. of Awards:** 1. **To Apply:** Documentation of financial need; and career goals statement must be submitted. **Deadline:** June 1.

**Remarks:** Sponsored by Warner Lambert Co.

## • 434 •
## American Diabetes Association - Research Program

National Service Center
1660 Duke St.                              Ph: (703)549-1500
PO Box 25757                              Fax: (703)549-1715
Alexandria, VA 22314-3427               Free: 800-676-4065
E-mail: research@diabetes.org
URL: http://www.diabetes.org/default.htm

### • 435 •  ADA Career Development Awards
*(Postdoctorate/Grant)*

**Purpose:** These awards are designed to assist exceptionally-promising new investigators to conduct diabetes-related research. The award supports such individual's salary for up to four years to enable the investigator to initiate an independent research effort that would yield accomplishments sufficient to qualify for long-term research funding. **Focus:** Medical Research, Diabetes. **Qualif.:** Applicants must have only 2 to 5 years of postdoctoral/postfellowship research experience, must be U.S. citizens or have (or have applied for) permanent resident status, and hold full-time or clinical faculty positions at U.S. university-related institutions. At the time of the award, applicants must hold an assistant professor or justified equivalent academic position within their institution. Investigators holding awards with similar intent from NIH or other agencies are not eligible for this award. **Criteria:** Special emphasis in the evaluation of the application will be given to the following: intent of the applicant to pursue a career in diabetes-related research; evidence of commitment of the institution toward this purpose; tangible evidence of the applicant's independent performance in diabetes-related research in the form of peer-reviewed scientific publications or equivalent; quality of the research proposal, its relevance to diabetes, novelty of the idea, and experimental approach.

**Funds Avail.:** Applications for four years of support up to $100,000 (including 15% for indirect costs) will be considered. The funds are to be divided by the recipient between the salary of the principal investigator (maximum of $50,000 per year) and other grant support. Grant support may be used to defray the cost of technicians and/or for supplies. Travel support is restricted to a maximum of $1,000 per year and equipment to a maximum of $5,000 per year. **To Apply:** Applicants must agree to devote at least 70 percent of their time and effort to their research projects during the period of the award, and inform the ADA of professional status, research support, and publications for five years following completion of the award. The applicants' institutions must, through the chairperson of the sponsoring department, provide assurance of an academic commitment to the applicants and their research proposal, outline a plan for allocating the applicants' responsibilities so that at least 70 percent of their time and effort is allocated to the research project for the term of the award, and confirm the commitment of both adequate space and other facilities for the conduct of the research proposal. The institution must also provide accurate and complete information regarding all other sources of research grant support (current or pending, federal and non-federal) for the applicants. In addition, it must outline the institution's plans for the longer-term development of the applicants and specific expectations of their near-term career course. **Deadline:** August 1 (for January funding); February 1 (for July funding).

### • 436 •  ADA Clinical Research Grant Program
*(Postdoctorate/Grant)*

**Purpose:** Provides funding for studies that directly involve humans. **Focus:** Medical Research. **Qualif.:** Studies must focus on intact human subjects in which the effect of a change in the individual's external or internal environment is evaluated. In-vitro research on human blood or tissue samples does not qualify unless there has been a major in vivo intervention (e.g. diet, drugs, exercise, etc.) and the protocol is designed specifically to quantitate the effect of this manipulation on the tissue being examined in-vitro. The program is intended for any investigator with or without NIH or other significant support. Applicants must be U.S. citizens or have (or have applied for) permanent resident status and hold full-time faculty positions at U.S. university-related institutions. **Criteria:** All other factors being equal, preference will be given to newly-independent investigators (i.e. those with five years or less post fellowship training). Applications submitted for the Clinical Research Grant program will be considered for funding under the Research Award program, if not awarded under the Clinical Research Grant program. In such a case the Research Award program criteria for support levels and duration of the award will apply.

**Funds Avail.:** $20,000-$100,000 (including 15% for indirect costs) per year. Funds may be used for equipment, supplies or technician salary support. Up to $20,000 may be used for the investigator's salary. **To Apply:** Applications from investigators with fewer than five years post fellowship research experience must include three letters of reference assessing the scientific abilities and potential of the applicant and a letter from the chairman of the applicant's department that outlines the institution's commitment to the applicant's career development and provides assurances of adequate research space and other facilities for the conduct of this research proposal. Applications must include accurate and complete information regarding all other sources of research grant support (current or pending) including titles of grants, annual and total amounts of support and inclusive funding periods, and the role of the investigator in each grant. **Deadline:** February 1 (July funding) or August 1 (January funding).

### • 437 • ADA Medical Student Diabetes Research Fellowship Program *(Doctorate/Fellowship)*

**Purpose:** To promote medical student interest in careers of diabetes-related clinical investigation or basic research. **Focus:** Medical Research, Diabetes. **Qualif.:** The student must have completed at least one year of medical school.

**Funds Avail.:** Stipend is $30,000 to cover the 1 year period of research experience. **To Apply:** Application must be made by the student, who must have a qualified sponsor. **Deadline:** February 1 (July funding). **Contact:** The American Diabetes Association at the above address,(see entry 434) or telephone the above number, extension 376 or 362.

### • 438 • ADA Mentor-Based Postdoctoral Fellowship Program *(Postdoctorate/Fellowship)*

**Purpose:** To support the training of scientists in an environment most conductive to beginning a career in diabetes research. An award will be given to an established and active investigator in diabetes research for the annual stipend support of a postdoctoral fellow to work closely with the mentor. The applicant investigator will be responsible for the selection of the qualified fellow. The term of the award is three years. **Focus:** Medical Research, Diabetes. **Qualif.:** The investigator must be a U.S. citizen or permanent resident and hold an appointment at a U.S. research institution and have sufficient research support to provide an appropriate training environment for the fellow. This must be documented by the head of the investigator's administrative unit at the institution. The applicant investigator must be a member of the Professional Section of the American Diabetes Association; the fellow must be, or agree to become, a member. There are no citizenship requirements for the fellow. The fellow must have a M.D. or Ph.D. degree, no more than three years of postdoctoral research experience in the field of diabetes/endocrinology at the commencement of this fellowship, and cannot serve an internship or residency during the award period. The fellow cannot receive support from this program for more than four years. Although clinical training to meet the requirements for certification in endocrinology is acceptable, the fellow must devote at least 80 percent of time and effort to his or her diabetes research under this fellowship. **Criteria:** Particular attention will be paid to the quality and activity of the applicant investigator's diabetes research

program, and evidence of sufficient research support and adequate facilities to provide an appropriate training environment for a postdoctoral fellow.

**Funds Avail.:** The award will be made for the stipend support of a single postdoctoral fellow in a given year, as well as laboratory supplies and travel costs. The salary of the fellow is to be determined by the applicant investigator, but the total amount of the award cannot exceed $30,000 per year. Laboratory supply costs are restricted to a maximum of $3,000 per year and travel for the fellow to attend diabetes-related scientific meetings is restricted to a maximum of $1,000. The salary portion of the award may include health insurance and social security benefits, if applicable. The American Diabetes Association does not pay indirect costs. An award year commences on July 1 and ends on June 30. Funds will be paid to the institution in quarterly payments beginning July 1 for up to four years, dependent upon identification of the postdoctoral fellow(s). A progress report is required by August 30 following the four-year award period. These awards are renewable. **To Apply:** Applications must be made on proper application form. Eight copies of the application form and supporting documents must be submitted. The applicant may submit a self-addressed, stamped postal card for confirmation of the application's receipt. **Deadline:** October 1 (July funding). Successful applicants will be notified of the award by January 6.

**Remarks:** Acknowledgment of support from the American Diabetes Association must be made in all research publications arising, in whole or in part, from funds provided by this award or in publicity given to the research. The fellow must agree to inform the American Diabetes Association of his or her professional status, research support and all publications for a period of five years following completion of the fellowship. **Contact:** Director, Research Programs, at the above address,(see entry 434) or telephone the above number, extension 2376 or 2362.

### • 439 • ADA Research Awards *(Postdoctorate/Grant)*

**Purpose:** To provide assistance for three years to investigators, new or established, who have a particularly novel and exciting idea for which they need support. The proposal may be related to a current area of investigation, as long as it represents a novel idea. Feasibility studies will be considered under this category. **Focus:** Medical Research, Diabetes. **Qualif.:** Applicants must be U.S. citizens or have (or have applied for) permanent resident status, and hold full-time faculty positions at U.S. university-related institutions. Investigators who have not previously worked in the field of diabetes and have an imaginative proposal related to any aspect of diabetes research are eligible to apply for this award. Investigators who previously received ADA Research Awards (previously called Feasibility Grant) may not reapply for Research Award support for work in the same area. A recipient will not be eligible to receive an ADA Career Development Award or Clinical Research Grant during the term of the ADA Research Award. Preference will be given to funding new investigators.

**Funds Avail.:** Between $20,000-$100,000 (including 15% for indirect costs) per year for two years. Funds may be used for equipment, supplies, and salary for technical assistance. **To Apply:** Applications from investigators with less than five years of postdoctoral research experience must include three letters of reference assessing the scientific abilities and potential of the applicant and a letter from the chairman of the applicant's department outlining the institution's commitment to the applicant's career development and providing assurance of adequate space and other facilities for conduct of the research proposal. Applicants from institutions with a Diabetes Endocrinology Research Center (DERC) or a Diabetes Research and Training Center (DRTC) must provide a letter from the Program Director indicating the extent of available support to the applicant, and specifying whether or not the applicant has access to pilot and feasibility study funds from the institution's diabetes center. If funds are available, the applicant must give information delineating whether an application of such funds is pending, including a statement which indicates a willingness to return to the ADA any overlapping funds. Ambiguity in the matter of other funding will result in administrative disapproval of the application. Applications

*American Diabetes Association - Research Program (continued)*

must include accurate and complete information regarding all other sources of research grant support (current or pending) including titles of grants, annual and total amounts of support and inclusive funding periods, and the role of the investigator in each grant. **Deadline:** August 1 (for January funding); February 1 (for July funding).

## • 440 • Lions SightFirst Diabetic Retinopathy Research Program - LCIF Clinical Research Grant Program *(Postdoctorate/Grant)*

**Purpose:** To support clinical or applied research in diabetic retinopathy in the Unites States and abroad, including new treatment regimens, epidemiology, and translation research. **Focus:** Diabetic Retinopathy. **Qualif.:** Applicants may be any investigator with or without NIH or other significant support. They must have M.D.s or a Ph.D.s, or, in the case of other health professions, appropriate health or science related degrees. Applicants must hold faculty level appointments or its equivalent at a research institution. A new investigator (i.e. one having five years or less postdoctoral research experience) at the time of the award should have an independent faculty position or equivalent, but should not have held such a position for more than four years.

**Funds Avail.:** Up to $60,000 per year for two years. The funds may be used for equipment and/or supplies and/or salary support. The funds may not be used for the principal investigator's salary. Travel, to diabetic retinopathy-related scientific meetings, is restricted to a maximum of $1,000 per year. **To Apply:** Applications from new investigators (i.e. those with 5 years or less of postdoctoral research experience) must include: three letters from persons assessing the scientific abilities and potential of the applicant, a letter from the Chairman of the applicant's department outlining the institution's commitment to the applicant's career development and providing assurance of adequate research space and other facilities for conduct of the research proposal, and a clear statement regarding all research support in terms of dollar (U.S.) amounts and the role of the applicant in each project. Applications from established investigators must include accurate and complete information regarding all other sources of research grant support (current or pending) including titles of grants, annual and total amounts of support and inclusive funding periods, the role of the investigator and the percentage of the investigator's time devoted to each grant. The recommended way to provide this information is to attach the summary paragraph from other grants on which the applicant is a principal investigator to each copy of the application. Ambiguity in the matter of other funding will result in administrative disapproval of the application. Applicants from U.S. institutions with a DERC or DRTC must provide a letter from the Program Director that indicates the extent of support available to the applicant and specifies whether or not the applicant had access to pilot and feasibility study funds from their institution's diabetes center. If funds were available, the applicant must state whether an application for such funds is pending. All overlapping funds must be returned to the Lions SightFirst Diabetic Retinopathy Research Program. **Deadline:** February 1 (July funding).

**Remarks:** The program is funded through a research grant from the Lions Clubs International Foundation. **Contact:** Director, Research Programs, at the above address,(see entry 434) or telephone the above number, extension 362 or 376.

## • 441 • Lions SightFirst Diabetic Retinopathy Research Program - LCIF Equipment Grant Program *(Postdoctorate/Grant)*

**Purpose:** To provide funds to be used for the purchase of equipment necessary for the conduct of clinical research in diabetic retinopathy. **Focus:** Diabetic Retinopathy. **Qualif.:** Applicants must hold M.D.s or Ph.D.s or, in the case of other health

professions, appropriate health or science degrees. Applicants must hold faculty level appointments at research institutions.

**Funds Avail.:** Up to $15,000. The funds will be paid to the institution in one payment in July. A report from the investigator's fiscal office, showing the final disposition of funds, should be filed within six months of receipt of the funds. Recipients may not transfer grants, in whole or in part, between institutions without prior written approval of the American Diabetes Association. The equipment purchased shall remain the property of the investigator and can be transferred to another institution upon written notification to the American Diabetes Association. **To Apply:** A detailed justification for the need to purchase the equipment and its intended use must be submitted. **Deadline:** February 1 (July funding).

**Remarks:** The program is funded through a research grant from the Lions Clubs International Foundation. Acknowledgment of support from the Lions SightFirst Diabetic Retinopathy Research Program of the American Diabetes Association must be made when findings are reported or publicly given to the work in which the equipment is used. **Contact:** Director, Research Programs, at the above address,(see entry 434) or telephone the above number, extension 2376 or 2362.

## • 442 • Lions SightFirst Diabetic Retinopathy Research Program - LCIF Training Grant Program *(Postdoctorate/Grant)*

**Purpose:** To enable U.S. investigators to visit foreign research institutions (particularly in underdeveloped countries) and conduct training in clinical research in diabetic retinopathy and implement public health programs (e.g. screening). **Focus:** Diabetic Retinopathy. **Qualif.:** Applicants must be U.S. citizens and hold M.D.s or Ph.D.s or, in the case of other health professions, appropriate health or science related degrees. Applicants must hold faculty level appointments at U.S. research institutions.

**Funds Avail.:** Up to $60,000 per year for two years. The funds are to be used for salary support as well as supplies and travel. Laboratory supply costs are restricted to a maximum of $1,000 per year. Travel, to include one round-trip coach airfare to the designated country, is restricted to a maximum of $3,000 the first year and $1,000 the second year. The American Diabetes Association does not pay indirect costs. Funding for the second year is contingent upon approval by the American Diabetes Association of the recipient's research progress report and budget, and the availability of funds. Funds will be paid to the U.S. institution in quarterly payments starting July 1 and ending June 30. The applicants' institutions will be responsible for issuing payments to the foreign institutions. At the end of the two year funding period, the recipient must file a report indicating the benefit of this training opportunity and his/her future career plans. This should be received no later than 60 days following the end of the grant period. A brief report from the investigator's fiscal office, showing the financial disposition of funds, should be filed at the same time. Recipients may not transfer grants, in whole or in part, between institutions without prior written approval. **Deadline:** February 1 (July funding).

**Remarks:** The program is funded through a research grant from the Lions Clubs International Foundation. Acknowledgment of support from the Lions SightFirst Diabetic Retinopathy Research Program must be made when findings are reported or publicity given to the work. **Contact:** Director, Research Programs, at the above address,(see entry 434) or telephone the above number, extension 2362 or 2376.

## • 443 • Medical Student Diabetes Research Fellowships *(Doctorate/Fellowship)*

**Purpose:** To promote medical student interest in careers of diabetes-related clinical investigation or basic research. **Focus:** Diabetes. **Qualif.:** Applicant must have completed at least one year of medical school, and have a qualified sponsor. Candidate's sponsor must be a U.S. citizen or permanent resident, and must hold a faculty position within an accredited medical school in the United States.

**Funds Avail.:** $3,000 stipend, plus $1,000 for supplies. **To Apply:** Write to the director for application materials. Application must be initiated by the student. **Deadline:** March 1. **Contact:** Director, Research Program, at the above address,(see entry 434) or telephone the above number, extension 362 or 376.

---

• **444** •
## American Digestive Health Foundation
7910 Woodmont Ave., Ste. 700    *Ph:* (301)654-2635
Bethesda, MD 20814    *Fax:* (301)654-1140
*URL:* http://www.adhf.org

### • 445 • ADHF/Elsevier Research Initiative Awards
*(Postdoctorate/Award)*

**Purpose:** To provide funds for new investigators to help them establish their research careers, and to support pilot projects that represent new research directions for established investigators, which will permit investigators to obtain new data which can ultimately provide the basis for subsequent grant applications of more substantial funding and duration. **Focus:** Gastroenterology. **Qualif.:** Investigators who hold an M.D. or Ph.D. degree and hold faculty positions at an accredited North American institution are eligible to apply. Investigators may not hold awards on a similar topic from other agencies. Applications from women and minority students are encouraged.

**Funds Avail.:** $25,000/year. **No. of Awards:** 1 **To Apply:** Write to the contact for application form and guidelines. **Deadline:** September 1. **Contact:** Candace Blank at the above address (see entry 444).

### • 446 • ADHF/Industry Research Scholar Awards
*(Postdoctorate/Award)*

**Purpose:** To ensure that a major portion of young investigators' time is protected for research, thus enabling him/her to develop independent and productive research careers in gastroenterology-related fields. **Focus:** Gastroenterology, Hepatology. **Qualif.:** Applicants must hold full-time faculty positions at North American universities or professional institutions. Candidates must devote at least 70 percent of their effort to research related to the gastrointestinal tract or liver. They should be early in their careers and, commonly, will have recently completed their fellowship training. Applications from women and minority students are encouraged.

**Funds Avail.:** $50,000/year. **To Apply:** Write to the contact for application form and guidelines. **Deadline:** September 10.

### • 447 • ADHF Student Research Fellowship Awards
*(Graduate, High School, Undergraduate/Fellowship)*

**Purpose:** To stimulate interest in research careers in digestive diseases by providing salary support for summer research projects. **Focus:** Gastroenterology. **Qualif.:** Candidates may be high school, undergraduate, medical, or graduate students (not yet engaged in thesis research) in accredited North American institutions. Candidates holding advanced degrees must be enrolled as undergraduates, medical, or graduate students, and may not hold similar salary support awards from other agencies. Applications from women and minority students are encouraged.

**Funds Avail.:** $2,500. **To Apply:** Write to the contact for application form and guidelines. **Deadline:** March 3. **Contact:** Candace Blank at the above address (see entry 444).

### • 448 • AGA Foundation Advanced Research Training Awards (Discontinued) *(Postdoctorate/Award)*

**Purpose:** To allow physicians to undertake full-time research training in preparation for individual research. **Focus:** Gastroenterology, Hepatology. **Qualif.:** Candidates may be of any nationality, but must be M.D.s currently in a Fellowship who have completed at least two years of research. Candidates must be sponsored by an AGA member who directs a gastroenterology-related unit at an American medical school, teaching hospital, or research institute. Applications from women and minorities are encouraged.

**Funds Avail.:** $36,000/year. **No. of Awards:** 3. **To Apply:** Write to the contact for application form and guidelines. **Deadline:** September 1.

**Remarks:** Award has been discontinued, 1999.

### • 449 • AGA Foundation/SmithKline Beecham Clinical Research Awards (Discontinued) *(Postdoctorate/Award)*

**Purpose:** To attract investigators to study fundamental problems in clinical gastroenterology. The intent is to provide funds to initiate clinical research pilot projects, the data from which can ultimately provide the basis for subsequent grant applications of more substantial funding and duration. **Focus:** Gastroenterology. **Qualif.:** Investigators interested in clinical research who do not hold awards on a similar topic from other agencies are eligible. For this program, clinical research is defined as direct interaction between an investigator and a patient or human subject. The research project must be performed at a U.S. institution. Applications from women and minority students are encouraged.

**Funds Avail.:** $25,000/year. **To Apply:** Write to the contact for application form and guidelines.

**Remarks:** Discontinued in 1999.

### • 450 • Astra/Merck Fellowship/Faculty Transition Award *(Postdoctorate/Award)*

**Purpose:** To encourage the career development of young investigators in the field of digestive diseases. **Focus:** Gastroenterology, Hepatology, Nutrition. **Qualif.:** Candidates may be of any nationality, but must be M.D. currently in Fellowships who have completed at least one but less than two years of research. Candidates must be sponsored by an AGA member who directs a gastroenterology-related unit at an American medical school, teaching hospital, or research institute. Applications from women and minorities are encouraged.

**Funds Avail.:** $36,000/year. **To Apply:** Write to the contact for application form and guidelines. **Deadline:** September 10. **Contact:** Candace Blank at the above address (see entry 444).

### • 451 • R. Robert and Sally Funderburg Research Scholar Award in Gastric Biology Related to Cancer *(Postdoctorate/Award)*

**Purpose:** To attract young investigators into careers in gastric cancer biology, to protect the investigator's research time, and to attract established investigators from various disciplines into careers in the study of gastric cancer. **Focus:** Gastric Cancer Biology. **Qualif.:** Candidates must hold faculty positions at accredited institutions, and may not hold other exclusively salary support awards on a similar topic from other agencies. Applications from women and minority students are encouraged.

**Funds Avail.:** $25,000/year. **No. of Awards:** 1. **To Apply:** Write to the contact for application form and guidelines. **Deadline:** September 1 **Contact:** Candace Blank, at the above address (see entry 444).

---

*Awards are arranged alphabetically below their administering organizations*

• 452 •
## American Economic Association
c/o Joint Center for Political and
   Economic Studies
1090 Vermont Ave., Ste. 1100
Washington, DC 20005

### • 453 • American Economic Association/Federal Reserve System Minority Graduate Fellowships in Economics (Graduate, Postgraduate/Fellowship)

**Qualif.:** Applicants must be U.S. citizens who are African American, Hispanic or Native American and are enrolled in an accredited graduate program in economics in the United States. Preference will be given to applicants whose areas of concentration are of special interest to the Federal Reserve System. The applicant must also be in residence at the institution and cannot be employed without prior permission from the fellowship committee. **Criteria:** Based on academic performance.

**Funds Avail.:** The fellowships provide a monthly stipend of $900. **To Apply:** Applicants must send the following information: a completed application form; GRE scores; copies of undergraduate and graduate transcripts; current resume, which should include a complete employment history; a detailed description of the proposed dissertation (3-5 pages); a personal statement from the nominee which discusses the nominee's career plans or aspirations; copies of letters of recommendation for graduate school; a letter of recommendation from the nominee's primary dissertation advisor; a statement from the director of graduate studies or chairman of the Economics Department listing the requirements for the PhD in Economics and specifying the candidate's progress toward fulfilling each of those requirements. The application must be signed by the director of graduate studies or the chairman of the Department of Economics. Either signature indicates compliance with the following three conditions: the nominee is enrolled in full-time study toward a PhD in Economics in an accredited U.S. institution; the nominee is a U.S. citizen and; the nominating institution agrees to provide a tuition waiver without requiring research or teaching assistantship. **Deadline:** March 1. **Contact:** Dr. Susan M. Collins, AEA Committee on the Status of Minority Groups in the Economics Profession, c/o The Brookings Institution.

• 454 •
## American Epilepsy Society
Research Grants and Fellowship
   Program
638 Prospect Ave.
638 Prospect Ave.
Hartford, CT 06105-4250     Ph: (860)232-4825
   Fax: (860)586-7550

### • 455 • AES/EFA Research Grants (Postdoctorate/ Grant)

**Purpose:** To support basic or clinical research which will advance understanding, treatment, or prevention of epilepsy. **Focus:** Epilepsy. **Qualif.:** Applicants must be investigators in the early stages of a career, or be involved in a new, innovative project concerning epilepsy. They must be either a clinical investigator or basic scientist conducting biological or behavioral research. Research grants are not intended as support for postdoctoral fellows, nor are established investigators ordinarily funded. The proposed research must take place at a facility with an epilepsy research program within the United States, its territories or Canada, and must be approved by the sponsoring institution.

**Funds Avail.:** $30,000. **No. of Awards:** Six. **To Apply:** Write or call the Research Administration, Epilepsy Foundation of America, 4351 Garden City Dr., Landover, MD 20785 USA (301)459-3700 for

application form and guidelines, available after 1 December. **Deadline:** September 1. Notification in December.

**Remarks:** AES also sponsors an Awards Program to recognize outstanding researchers in the field of pediatric epilepsy. Recipients must be nominated by their peers. Write for further details. **Contact:** Joe Giffels, at the above address (see entry 454).

### • 456 • AES Research Fellowships (Postdoctorate/ Fellowship)

**Purpose:** To support research in epilepsy by investigators in the early stages of their careers. **Focus:** Epilepsy. **Qualif.:** Applicants must be physicians or neuroscientists with a Ph.D. degree. Research fellowships are designed as training opportunities; individuals holding faculty appointments at the level of assistant professor or higher are ineligible. Preference is given to research proposals that focus on developmental or pediatric aspects of epilepsy. Research must take place at a facility with an epilepsy research program within the United States, its territories, or Canada, and must be approved by the sponsoring institution.

**Funds Avail.:** $30,000. **No. of Awards:** Eight. **To Apply:** Write to the Research Administration, Epilepsy Foundation of America, 4351 Garden City Dr., Landover, MD 20785 USA (301)459-3700 for application form and guidelines. Submit 20 copies of the following: form, curriculum vitae, a statement of intent, a detailed description of the proposed first-year research and training experience, preceptor's curriculum vitae and letter of support, and the AES Protection of Animals Subjects Assurance Form. **Deadline:** September 1. Notification in December.

**Remarks:** AES also sponsors an AES Awards Program to recognize outstanding researchers in the field of pediatric epilepsy. Recipients must nominated by their peers. Write for further details. **Contact:** Joe Giffles, at the above address (see entry 454).

• 457 •
## American Federation for Aging Research
1414 Avenue of the Americas, 18th
   Fl.     Ph: (212)752-2327
New York, NY 10019     Fax: (212)832-2298
*E-mail:* amfedaging@aol.com
*URL:* http://www.afar.org/

### • 458 • Creative Investigator Grants (Professional Development/Grant)

**Purpose:** To assist research in the field of aging. **Focus:** Medicine—Geriatric, Gerontology. **Qualif.:** Applicant must be a qualified investigator employed by a U.S. university or research institution. Grants will be made both to initiate and continue research related to the bio-medical aspects of aging. Awards are tenable at the investigator's home institution.

**Funds Avail.:** $40,000. **No. of Awards:** 25. **To Apply:** Write to AFAR for application guidelines, available in July. **Deadline:** December 15. **Contact:** Odette Van Der Willik at the above address (see entry 457).

### • 459 • Glenn Foundation/AFAR Scholarships for Research in the Biology of Aging (Doctorate/ Scholarship)

**Focus:** Geriatric medicine. **Qualif.:** Applicants must be MD's or PhD's.

**Funds Avail.:** $5,500. **No. of Awards:** 25. **Deadline:** February. **Contact:** American Federation for Aging Research at the above address (see entry 457).

**• 460 • John A. Hartford Afar Medical Student Geriatric Scholarship Program** *(Graduate/Scholarship)*

**Focus:** Geriatric medicine **Qualif.:** Applicants must be medical students. **Deadline:** February 5. **Contact:** American Federation for Aging Research at the above address (see entry 457).

**• 461 •**
**American Federation of Grain Millers**
4949 Olson Memorial Hwy.          *Ph:* (612)545-0211
Minneapolis, MN 55422-5199          *Fax:* (612)545-5489

**• 462 • American Federation of Grain Millers International Union Scholarship** *(Undergraduate/ Scholarship)*

**Qualif.:** Applicants must be members of AFGM in good standing; or the dependent son, daughter, stepchild or legally adopted child of an AFGM member in good standing. All applicants must be in the last year of high school planning to attend college or vocational school in the fall, or must already have a high school diploma (or equivalent) and are planning to enter college or vocational school for the first time. **Criteria:** Awards will be made based on scholastic achievement, character, and academic or vocational potential.

**Funds Avail.:** $1,000 per award. Non-renewable. **To Apply:** Applicants must submit an official AFGM Scholarship Program Preliminary Application Form (which needs to carry the endorsement of the Local Union indicating the applicant or parent of an applicant is a member of the Local Union in good standing). Upon receipt of the preliminary application, properly endorsed, the International Union Scholarship Program will send the applicant a final application package. The final application package will include a final form, including essay; character reference form ; and an official transcript, including SAT or ACT scores. **Deadline:** December 31. **Contact:** AGFM International Union Scholarship Program at the above address (see entry 461).

**• 463 •**
**American Federation of Labor Congress of Industrial Organization**
Research Department
815 16th St., NW          *Ph:* (202)637-5315
Washington, DC 20006          *Fax:* (202)637-5263
*E-mail:* 7112.2112@compuserve.com; feedback@afkio.org
*URL:* http://solar.rtd.utk.edu/~ccsi/csusa/proassoc/afl-cio.html

**• 464 • AFL-CIO Research Internship** *(Graduate/ Internship)*

**Purpose:** To enable U.S. graduate students to participate in the economic research activities of the AFL-CIO. **Focus:** Economics, Labor. **Qualif.:** Applicant must be a U.S. citizen or permanent resident who has completed one year of graduate studies, and who has a strong background in labor relations and economics. The internship is tenable at the AFL-CIO Research Department.

**Funds Avail.:** $525/week, plus limited health insurance. **No. of Awards:** One. **To Apply:** Write to the Research Department for application form and guidelines. Submit form, transcripts, resume, and a 500-word statement of interests in organized labor. **Deadline:** January 1 to March 1. Interns are selected by the end of April. **Contact:** Ruby Oswald at the above address (see entry 463).

**• 465 •**
**American Fishing Tackle Manufacturers Association**
1033 N. Fairfax St., Ste. 200          *Ph:* (703)519-9691
Alexandria, VA 22314          *Fax:* (703)519-1872

**• 466 • Andrew J. Boehm Fellowships** *(Doctorate, Graduate/Fellowship)*

**Purpose:** To encourage graduate students who have made a commitment to a professional career in fisheries management or research. **Focus:** Fisheries Sciences. **Qualif.:** Candidate may be of any nationality. Applicant must be a graduate student with a grade point average of 3.0/4.0 or higher. Candidate must be preparing to conduct research for an M.S. or Ph.D. thesis on some aspect of the life history, ecology, population dynamics, or behavior of some species of fish or fish-food organisms or their environmental requirements. Proposals for research that has the potential of improving understanding or management of recreational fisheries will receive special consideration. Preference is also given to research projects that may be completed during the fellowship year.

**Funds Avail.:** $1,000-10,000. **To Apply:** Write to the Association for application guidelines. Application must be submitted by the responsible supervising professor with an informative synopsis of the research project. **Deadline:** March 15. Fellows are selected by June 1. **Contact:** Robert G. Kavanaugh at the above address (see entry 465).

**• 467 •**
**American Foundation for Aging Research**
PO Box 7622
North Carolina State University          *Ph:* (919)515-5679
Raleigh, NC 27695          *Fax:* (919)515-2047
*E-mail:* afar@bchserver.bch.ncsu.edu
*URL:* http://www4.ncsu.edu/unity/users/a/agris/afar/afar.htm

**• 468 • AFAR Fellowships** *(Graduate, Undergraduate/ Fellowship)*

**Purpose:** To motivate young researchers in the field of the biology of aging. **Focus:** Neurobiology, Cancer, Autoimmunity, Biochemistry, Cell and Molecular Biology. **Qualif.:** Candidates must be undergraduate, graduate, or pre-doctoral students at a college or university in the United States. No awards are given to those already having an M.D. or Ph.D. Applicants must be actively involved or planning active involvement in a specific biomedical research project in the field of aging. No sociological or psychological research is funded through the Foundation. **Criteria:** Selection is based on application, transcript, test scores, references, and research proposal.

**Funds Avail.:** The number of fellowships and size of awards vary on the basis of the number of qualified applicants and the money available from private and corporate donations. $500 to $1,000 are available per semester. **No. of Awards:** Varies. **To Apply:** Applicants must request application forms in writing and should include $3 for processing and handling. There are no other application fees. They should specify their year in school and the type of research project they propose. **Deadline:** There is no deadline for applications. **Contact:** The American Foundation for Aging Research at the above address (see entry 467).

**• 469 • American Foundation for Aging Research Predoctoral Awards** *(Doctorate, Graduate, Undergraduate/Award)*

**Purpose:** To support and encourage study of the field of the biology of aging and age-related diseases. **Focus:** Biomedicine, Biochemistry, Biophysics, Molecular and Cell Biology. **Qualif.:**

## American Foundation for Aging Research (continued)

Students must be undergraduates, graduates, or predoctoral students conducting research at U.S. institutions. Students must be actively involved in a research project in the listed areas using modern innovative approaches.

**Funds Avail.:** $1,000 per semester. **No. of Awards:** Varies. **To Apply:** Write for preliminary screening application form. **Deadline:** None.

**Remarks:** Special awards are available to students conducting cancer research.

## • 470 •
## American Foundation for AIDS Research
5900 Wilshire Blvd., 23rd Fl.          *Ph:* (213)857-5900
Los Angeles, CA 90036-5013          *Fax:* (213)857-5920
*URL:* http://www.amfar.org/

### • 471 • AmFAR Pediatric AIDS Foundation Grants
*(Postdoctorate/Grant)*

**Purpose:** To provide funds for research programs not funded by the federal government. **Focus:** AIDS. **Qualif.:** Varies.

**Funds Avail.:** Varies. **To Apply:** Write to the Grants Officer for application form and guidelines. **Deadline:** Varies. **Contact:** Grants Officer at the above address (see entry 470).

### • 472 • AmFAR Research Grants *(Postdoctorate/Grant)*

**Purpose:** To provide funds the direct costs of AIDS research. **Focus:** AIDS. **Qualif.:** Applicant must be an M.D. or Ph.D. affiliated with an institution. The Grant is highly competitive. Only 100 letters of intent will be selected for actual application.

**Funds Avail.:** $50,000 for direct costs (equipment, supplies, salaries, etc). **To Apply:** Applicants must submit a letter of intent (original plus eight copies) containing: cover sheet available from above address; 200 word, one page abstract of the proposed project; research plan of not more than three pages which must contain background and rational of project, preliminary studies, specific aims and experimental designs, procedures and data analysis, and biographical data containing not more than 15 publications. Write or call for further information. **Deadline:** Varies. **Contact:** Grants Officer at the above address (see entry 470).

### • 473 • AmFAR Scholar Awards *(Postdoctorate/Award)*

**Purpose:** To encourage new investigators within the field by providing 3 years of postdoctoral salary support. **Focus:** AIDS. **Qualif.:** Applicant must be an M.D. or Ph.D. with two to three years postdoctoral experience. Applicant does not have to be tenured. The Award is highly competitive.

**Funds Avail.:** $32,000 first year; $34,000 second year; $36,000 third year. **To Apply:** Applicants are solicited twice annually during the months and November. Write for more information. **Deadline:** Varies. **Contact:** Grants Officer at the above address (see entry 470).

### • 474 • AmFAR Small Grants *(Postdoctorate/Grant)*

**Purpose:** To facilitate short-term periods of study or specialized training. **Qualif.:** Grants are intended for established investigators qualified in the sciences, medicine, or the humanities.

**Funds Avail.:** The maximum award is $5,000. **To Apply:** A letter of intent must be submitted for a pre-application review process. This process is highly competitive. Only 100 or fewer letters of intent will be selected for solicitation of a full application. A letter of intent

consists of collated sets of the original and eight copies of the following: cover sheet (available from AmFAR); a 200-word one-page abstract of the proposed project; research plan of not more than three pages, which must include background and rationale, preliminary studies, specific aims, and experimental design, procedures, and date analysis to be used; biographical sketch of the principal investigator, including not more than 15 relevant and/or recent publications. **Deadline:** Letters of intent must be received by August 3. **Contact:** AmFAR at the above address (see entry 470).

## • 475 •
## American Foundation for Biological Sciences
730 11th St., NW                    *Ph:* (202)628-1500
Washington, DC 20001-4521          *Fax:* (202)628-1509
*E-mail:* aibs@aibs.org

### • 476 • AIBS Congressional Science Fellowship
*(Postdoctorate/Fellowship)*

**Purpose:** To enable U.S. scientists interested in biology to participate in policy-making at the Congressional level. **Focus:** Agriculture, Biology, Environmental Policy, Medicine, U.S. Congress. **Qualif.:** Applicant must be a U.S. citizen or permanent resident, and be a member of the American Institute for Biological Sciences (AIBS). Candidate must have a doctoral degree in one of the life sciences, public policy experience, and a background in a relevant biological discipline. The fellowship is tenable in Washington, D.C., where award recipient works as a scientific adviser to a Congressional committee or office.

**Funds Avail.:** $40,000 maximum. **To Apply:** Write to the Foundation for application guidelines. Submit application materials with letters of reference. **Deadline:** February 15. **Contact:** Jennie Moehlmann, Coordinator, at the above address (see entry 475).

## • 477 •
## American Foundation for the Blind, Inc.
11 Penn Plz., Ste. 300              *Ph:* (212)232-5463
New York, NY 10001-2018            *Fax:* (212)502-7777
*E-mail:* afbinfo@afb.org
*URL:* http://dots.physics.orst.edu/tactile/nodel8.html

### • 478 • Gladys C. Anderson Scholarship
*(Undergraduate/Scholarship)*

**Qualif.:** Candidates must be women who are United States citizens, legally blind, and studying religious or classical music at the college level.

**Funds Avail.:** Two $1,000 scholarships are awarded annually. **To Apply:** Applicants must submit evidence of legal blindness; official transcripts of grades; proof of acceptance at a college or university; three letters of recommendation; a sample performance tape of voice or instrumental selection (not to exceed 30 minutes); and a typewritten statement of no more than two double-spaced pages describing educational and personal goals, work experience, extra-curricular activities, and how scholarship monies will be used. **Contact:** Elga Joffee, Director, Information Center/Scholarships, at the above address (see entry 477). Telephone: (212)502-7661.

**• 479 • Karen D. Carsel Memorial Scholarship**
*(Graduate/Scholarship)*

**Qualif.:** The scholarship is awarded to a full-time graduate student who presents evidence of economic need. Applicants must be legally blind United States citizens. **Criteria:** Economic need.

**Funds Avail.:** $1,000. **To Apply:** Applicants must submit evidence of legal blindness; official transcripts of grades; evidence of acceptance into a full-time graduate program; three letters of recommendation; and a typewritten statement of not more than two double-spaced pages describing personal and educational goals, work experience, extracurricular activities, and how scholarship monies will be utilized. **Contact:** Elga Joffee, Director, Information Center/Scholarships, at the above address (see entry 477). Telephone: (212)502-7661.

**• 480 • Delta Gamma Foundation - Florence Margaret Harvey Memorial Scholarship** *(Graduate, Undergraduate/Scholarship)*

**Qualif.:** The Delta Gamma Foundation Florence Margaret Harvey Memorial Scholarship is awarded to undergraduate or graduate students who are legally blind, of good character, have exhibited academic excellence, and are studying in the field of rehabilitation and/or education of persons who are visually impaired and blind. Applicants must be United States citizens, and legally blind.

**Funds Avail.:** $1,000. **To Apply:** Applicants must submit evidence of legal blindness; official transcripts of grades; proof of acceptance at a college or university; three letters of recommendation; and a typewritten statement of not more than two double-spaced pages describing personal and educational goals, work experience, extracurricular activities, and how scholarship monies will be utilized. **Contact:** Elga Joffee, Director, Information Center/Scholarships, at the above address (see entry 477). Telephone: (212)502-7661.

**• 481 • Rudolph Dillman Scholarship** *(Graduate, Undergraduate/Scholarship)*

**Qualif.:** Scholarships are awarded to undergraduate or graduate students who are legally blind and studying in the field of rehabilitation and/or education of persons who are visually impaired and blind. Applicants must be United States citizens.

**Funds Avail.:** Three grants of $2,500 are awarded annually. **To Apply:** The applicant must submit evidence of legal blindness; official transcripts of grades; proof of acceptance in an accredited undergraduate or graduate training program within the broad field of rehabilitation and/or education of persons who are blind and visually impaired; three letters of recommendation; and a typewritten statement of no more than two double-spaced pages describing educational and personal goals, work experience, extra-curricular activities, and how scholarship monies will be used. **Contact:** Elga Joffee, Director, Information Center/Scholarships, at the above address (see entry 477). Telephone: (212)502-7661.

**• 482 • R.L. Gillette Scholarship** *(Undergraduate/Scholarship)*

**Qualif.:** Candidates must be women who are legally blind and enrolled in a four-year undergraduate degree program in literature or music. Applicants must also be United States citizens.

**Funds Avail.:** Two $500 scholarships are awarded annually. **To Apply:** Applicants must also submit evidence of legal blindness; official transcripts of grades; proof of acceptance at a college or university; three letters of recommendation; a sample performance tape not over 30 minutes, or a creative writing sample; and a typewritten statement of no more than two double-spaced pages describing educational and personal goals, work experience, extra-curricular activities, and how scholarship monies will be used. **Contact:** Elga Joffee, Director, Information Center/Scholarships, at the above address (see entry 477). Telephone: (212)502-7661.

**• 483 • Scholarships for Blind and Visually Impaired Postsecondary Students** *(Graduate, Undergraduate/Scholarship)*

**Purpose:** To support blind students studying. **Focus:** Blindness, Education, Impaired Vision, Music, Rehabilitation. **Qualif.:** Applicant must be a U.S. citizen, and be legally blind. Candidate must be an undergraduate or graduate student of high standing, studying in the field of rehabilitation and/or education of visually impaired and blind persons.

**Funds Avail.:** Varies, according to merit and needs; $500-3,000. **To Apply:** Write for the application form and guidelines. Submit form with evidence of legal blindness, certified transcripts, proof of acceptance at a college or university, three letters of recommendation, and a statement of goals. **Deadline:** April 1. Awards are announced by August 1.

**Remarks:** Applicant may apply for more than one award, but will not receive more than one. Individual awards are named, and requirements may differ slightly: one Karen D. Carsel Memorial Scholarship ($500); one Delta Gamma Foundation Florence Margaret Harvey Memorial Scholarship ($1,000); three Rudolph Dillman Memorial Scholarships ($2,500); and one Telesensory Scholarship ($1,000). Please identify the AFB scholarship for which you are applying. The Foundation also offers several Louis H. Rives, Jr., Memorial Scholarships (valued up to $2,500) to legally blind U.S. citizens interested in attending law school. Application procedures and deadlines are the same as those listed above. **Contact:** Leslie Rosen, Director, Information Center/Scholarships, at the above address (see entry 477). Telephone: (212)502-7661.

**• 484 •**

**American Foundation for Pharmaceutical Education**
1 Church St., Ste. 202
Rockville, MD 20850-4158

**• 485 • AACP-AFPE Gateway Scholarships**
*(Graduate/Scholarship)*

**Purpose:** To encourage minority undergraduates in pharmacy colleges to continue their education and pursue a Ph.D. in one of the pharmaceutical sciences. **Focus:** Pharmacy. **Qualif.:** Applicants must have participated in the American Association of Colleges of Pharmacy (AACP) Undergraduate Research Participation Program for Minorities and Merek Undergraduate Scholar Programs. Candidates must be U.S. citizens or permanent residents and demonstrate proof of acceptance into a graduate program leading to a Ph.D. degree in any pharmaceutical discipline. **Criteria:** Selection is made by the AFPE Boards of Grants.

**Funds Avail.:** $5,000, funded through a grant from GLAXO, Inc. is available. **No. of Awards:** 4. **To Apply:** Applicants must send the following information: letter providing a summary of research conducted as a recipient of the Research Participation Program award, additional research experience gained while a pharmacy undergraduate, and reasons for wishing to earn a Ph.D. degree; letter of recommendation from the pharmacy college/school dean; name of the graduate school applicant has been accepted into and the major area of study to be undertaken, (pharmaceutics, pharmacy administration, pharmaceutical chemistry, etc.); transcript of all completed pharmacy course work; list of special honors, awards, accomplishments in high school and pharmacy college reflecting achievement and an ability to succeed in graduate school. **Deadline:** All information must be received by AFPE by July 1. Recipients will be notified by August 1. Award will be provided anytime after September 1 and after confirmation that the student is enrolled in a graduate program for the Ph.D.

## American Foundation for Pharmaceutical Education *(continued)*

**Contact:** The American Foundation for Pharmaceutical Education at the above address (see entry 484).

### • 486 • AAPS-AFPE Gateway Scholarships *(Graduate, Undergraduate/Scholarship)*

**Purpose:** To encourage undergraduates from any discipline to pursue the Ph.D. in a pharmacy graduate program. **Focus:** Pharmacy. **Qualif.:** Candidates must be undergraduate students enrolled in the last three years of a baccalaureate or doctor of pharmacy degree program in an accredited school of pharmacy or a baccalaureate degree program in a related field of scientific study. Applicants must have demonstrated interest in and potential for a career in any of the pharmaceutical sciences. U.S. citizenship or permanent residency is not required. **Criteria:** Finalists are selected by the AAPS Awards Committee from which recipients are chosen by the AFPE Board of Grants.

**Funds Avail.:** $3,750 is provided for an undergraduate research project, $500 to attend an AAPS Annual Meeting, and $5,000 when the student enrolls in graduate school to help cover first year expenses. The $3,750 may be used for any purpose decided by the awardee and faculty sponsor that will enable the student to have a successful program, including student stipend, laboratory supplies or materials related to the project, and travel. None of the funds may be used for indirect costs by the institution. **No. of Awards:** 9. **To Apply:** Applicants must send the following information to AAPS: a letter from a faculty sponsor who will supervise the research experience; brief description of the research to be carried out and the time period involved; a letter from the dean of the college or one other faculty member supporting the application; a letter from the applicant outlining career goals and reasons for applying for the scholarship; a list of special honors, awards, accomplishments in high school and college reflecting achievement and an ability to carry out the research project and succeed in graduate school; an official transcript of all collegiate grades and, if available, copies of GPA and SAT and/or other national achievement test scores. **Deadline:** All information must be received by AAPS by December 1. Recipients are notified by January 15 for scholarships beginning after February 1.

**Remarks:** The AAPS-AFPE Gateway Scholarship program is a collaborative program between the Foundation and the American Association of Pharmaceutical Scientists. **Contact:** Application material must be sent to American Association of Pharmaceutical Scientists, 1650 King St., Alexandria, VA 22314-2747.

### • 487 • Academia-Oriented "Springboard to Teaching" Fellowship *(Doctorate/Fellowship)*

**Purpose:** To support Ph.D. candidates interested in pursuing a career in teaching. **Focus:** Pharmacy, Pharmacology. **Qualif.:** Applicant must be a U.S. citizen or permanent resident currently enrolled in a doctoral program administered by or affiliated with a U.S. college of pharmacy. Applicant must intent on pursuing a career in teaching.

**Funds Avail.:** Fellowships: $22,500 maximum. **To Apply:** Write to AFPE for application forms and guidelines. **Deadline:** March 1. Notification by April 15. **Contact:** Dr. Richard E. Faust, President, at the above address (see entry 484).

### • 488 • AFPE Graduate Fellowships *(Doctorate/Fellowship)*

**Focus:** Pharmacy. **Qualif.:** The candidate must be a citizen of the United States who holds a B.S. or Pharm.D., is pursuing a Ph.D. Degree in one of the fields of pharmacy, and has completed one term of graduate study.

**Funds Avail.:** Approximately 50 fellowships of $6,000 each, 50 of $7,500 each and 20 at $10,000 each are awarded annually. While fellowships are renewable twice, recipients must request renewal.

It is hoped that the recipients of Fellowships will wish to repay the amount provided, if and when possible, so that other worthy students may be similarly helped. There is no legal or other obligation to do so, however. **No. of Awards:** 50 new, 50 renewals, 20 extensions. **To Apply:** Along with the completed application, the candidate must supply three references, statement of plans, certificate of graduate school registration, and transcripts. **Deadline:** Applications must be filed by March 1. Awards are made the end of March and begin the following September 1. Fellows wishing to renew their Fellowships must reapply before March 1. **Contact:** The American Foundation for Pharmaceutical Education at the above address (see entry 484).

### • 489 • GLAXO AACP-AFPE Graduate Studies Scholarships *(Graduate/Scholarship)*

**Purpose:** To encourage undergraduate students in pharmacy colleges to continue their education in a graduate or professional program leading to an advanced degree that will provide a valuable background for careers in the pharmaceutical industry. **Focus:** Pharmacy. **Qualif.:** Applicants must be in the final year of a B.S. or Pharm.D. program in a pharmacy college and planning to continue their education in pursuit of any graduate or professional degree (not a Pharm.D.) in the pharmaceutical sciences, or in business administration, law, public health, or engineering. **Criteria:** Recipients will be selected by the Foundation's Board of Grants.

**Funds Avail.:** $5,000 each. **No. of Awards:** 1 to 8. **To Apply:** Application deadline is May 1. Awardees will be notified by June 15 and funds provided on September 1. **Contact:** The American Foundation for Pharmaceutical Education at the above address (see entry 484).

### • 490 • MERCK-AFPE Gateway Scholarships *(Graduate, Undergraduate/Scholarship)*

**Purpose:** To encourage undergraduates in a pharmacy college to pursue the Ph.D. in a graduate program within a pharmacy college. **Focus:** Pharmacy. **Qualif.:** Applicants must be undergraduate students enrolled in the last three years of a B.S. or Pharm.D. program in a college of pharmacy. U.S. citizenship or permanent resident status is required.

**Funds Avail.:** Scholarship of $9,250; $4,250 is provided for an undergraduate research project and $5,000 when the student enrolls in a graduate program in a pharmacy college. The $5,000 can be received anytime within two years after completion of the undergraduate program. The $4,250 may be used for any purpose decided by the awardee and faculty sponsor that will enable the student to have a successful program, including student stipend, laboratory supplies or materials related to the project, or travel. None of the funds may be used for indirect costs by the institution. **To Apply:** Applicants must send the following information to AFPE: letter from faculty sponsor who will supervise research; description of the research and the time period involved; letter from the dean or one other faculty member supporting the application; letter from the student outlining career goals and reasons for applying for the scholarship; list of special honors, awards, accomplishments in high school and college; official transcript of all collegiate grades; and, if available, copies of GPA and SAT and/or other national achievement test scores. **Deadline:** Applications must be received by December 1. The awardee will be notified by January 15 for the scholarship beginning after February 1. Recipient must submit a brief final report of the accomplishments at the conclusion of the undergraduate research experience. **Contact:** The American Foundation for Pharmaceutical Education at the above address (see entry 484).

### • 491 • Gustavus A. Pfeiffer Faculty Development Postdoctoral Research Fellowship *(Postdoctorate/Fellowship)*

**Qualif.:** Applicants must be faculty members in a college of pharmacy holding the Ph.D. or Pharm.D. Applicants should have extensive record of research achievements and a well-defined research proposal in any of the pharmaceutical disciplines.

**Funds Avail.:** Stipend of up to $22,500. **Deadline:** A recipient is announced March 1. The Fellowship starts the following September. **Contact:** Richard E. Faust, Ph.D., President, American Foundation for Pharmaceutical Education, at the above address (see entry 484).

**• 492 • Regular AFPE Fellowships and Scholarships in the Pharmaceutical Sciences** *(Doctorate/Fellowship, Scholarship)*

**Purpose:** To support graduate study in the Pharmaceutical Sciences. **Focus:** Pharmacy. **Qualif.:** Applicant must be a U.S. citizen or permanent resident currently enrolled in a doctoral program administered by or affiliated with a U.S. college of pharmacy. Applicant must usually have completed at least one term in the program before applying; however, some first-year scholarships are available.

**Funds Avail.:** Fellowships: $6,000-10,000; scholarships: $1,000-7,500. **To Apply:** Write to AFPE for application forms and guidelines. **Deadline:** March 1. Notification by April 15. **Remarks:** The AFPE awards a total of about 90 fellowships each year, including renewals. These include collaborative fellowships with sponsoring organizations, industry-oriented fellowships, and Association Fellowships. **Contact:** Dr. Richard E. Faust, President, at the above address (see entry 484).

**• 493 • Sandoz-AFPE First Year Graduate Scholarships** *(Doctorate/Scholarship)*

**Purpose:** To encourage undergraduate students to continue their education in a graduate program for the Ph.D. in a pharmacy college. **Focus:** Pharmacy. **Qualif.:** Applicants must be in the final year of an undergraduate program and planning to pursue the Ph.D. in any pharmaceutical discipline in a pharmacy college. **Criteria:** Dean may select a senior student who intends to study in a pharmacy college graduate program. Selection should be based on academic excellence and financial need. The student may be one from the institution's graduating senior class and/or one who will be enrolled in an institution's pharmacy graduate program. The awardees will be selected by the AFPE Board of Grants.

**Funds Avail.:** $5,000 each. **No. of Awards:** 2. **To Apply:** Nominated students should send the following information: letter of recommendation from the dean (either the dean where the student is graduating or the dean where the student is enrolling); name of the graduate school student plans to attend and the major areas of study to be undertaken (if known); transcript of all grades for undergraduate work; special honors, awards, accomplishments in high school and pharmacy college that reflect the excellence of the candidate and ability to succeed in graduate school; Graduate Record Examination (GRE) and SAT scores, if known, and other national achievement tests; one- or two-page statement elaborating reasons for wishing to attend graduate school. **Deadline:** Documentation and application should be sent to the Foundation by May 1. Recipients will be notified by June 15. Funds will be provided on September 1. **Contact:** The American Foundation for Pharmaceutical Education at the above address (see entry 484).

**• 494 • G. D. Searle & Co. Faculty Development Research Fellowship in Pharmacoeconomics** *(Postdoctorate/Fellowship)*

**Focus:** Pharmacy. **Qualif.:** Applicants must be pharmacy faculty members holding the Ph.D. or Pharm.D. Candidates must have a strong record of research in an area encompassing such topics as cost-benefit and cost-effectiveness of pharmaceuticals, the impact of current or future legislation on drug innovation and/or healthcare in the nation, the economics of healthcare and the quality of life in changing patterns of healthcare delivery systems, the contribution of the pharmaceutical industry and the economic

impact of research and new drugs, and healthcare cost-containment issues.

**Funds Avail.:** Stipend of up to $22,500. **Deadline:** March 1. **Contact:** Richard E. Faust, Ph.D., President, American Foundation for Pharmaceutical Education, at the above address (see entry 484).

**• 495 • SYNTEX-AFPE Gateway Scholarships** *(Graduate, Undergraduate/Scholarship)*

**Purpose:** To encourage undergraduates in a pharmacy college to pursue the Ph.D. in a graduate program within a pharmacy college. **Focus:** Pharmacy. **Qualif.:** Applicants must be undergraduate students enrolled in the last 3 years of a B.S. or Pharm.D. program in a college of pharmacy. U.S. citizenship or permanent resident status is required.

**Funds Avail.:** Scholarship of $9,250; $4,250 is provided for an undergraduate research project and $5,000 is provided anytime within two years after completion of undergraduate program when the student enrolls in a graduate program in a pharmacy college. The $4,250 may be used for any purpose decided by the awardee and faculty sponsor that will enable the student to have a successful program. None of the funds may be used for indirect costs by the institution. **To Apply:** Applicants must send the following information: letter from a faculty sponsor who will supervise research including a description of the research and the time period involved; letter from the dean or one other faculty member supporting the application; letter from the applicant outlining career goals and reasons for applying for the scholarship; list of special honors, awards, accomplishments in high school and college; official transcript of all collegiate grades; and if available, copies of GPA and SAT and/or other national achievement test scores. **Deadline:** Applications must be received by AFPE by December 1. The awardee is be notified by January 1 for the scholarship beginning after February 1. Recipient must submit a final report of the accomplishments at the conclusion of the undergraduate research. **Contact:** The American Foundation for Pharmaceutical Education at the above address (see entry 484).

**• 496 • UpJohn-AFPE First Year Graduate Scholarships** *(Doctorate/Scholarship)*

**Purpose:** To encourage undergraduate students to continue their education in a graduate program for the Ph.D. in one of the nation's pharmacy colleges. **Focus:** Pharmacy. **Qualif.:** Applicants must be United States citizens or permanent residents in their final year of an undergraduate degree program and planning to pursue a Ph.D. in pharmaceutics or pharmacy administration in a pharmacy college. **Criteria:** A dean may select, based on academic excellence and financial need, a senior student from the institution's graduating senior class and/or one who will be enrolled in an institution's pharmacy graduate program who intends to study in a pharmacy college graduate program. Awardees will be selected by the AFPE Board of Grants. **To Apply:** Applicants should submit a letter of recommendation from the dean (either the dean where the student is graduating or the dean where the student is enrolling), name of the graduate school applicant plans to attend and the major areas of study to be undertaken (if known), transcript of all grades for undergraduate work, special honors, awards, accomplishments in high school and pharmacy college that reflect the excellence of the candidates and their ability to succeed in graduate school, Graduate Record Examination (GRE) and SAT scores, if available, and any other national achievement tests, and a one- or two-page statement elaborating reasons for wishing to attend graduate school. **Deadline:** May 1. Recipients will be notified by June 15. Funds will be provided on September 1. **Contact:** AFPE at the above address (see entry 484).

## American Foundation for Urologic Disease, Inc.
1128 N. Charles St.                    *Ph:* (410)727-2908
Baltimore, MD 21201-5506               *Fax:* (410)528-0550
*URL:* http://www.orge.ufl.edu/fyi/v23n03/fyi036.html

### • 498 •  AFUD/NKF Resident Fellowship
*(Postdoctorate/Fellowship)*

**Purpose:** To enable urological residents in training to undertake full-time research. **Focus:** Urology. **Qualif.:** Applicant may be of any nationality. Applicant must be a urological resident in training at a Canadian or U.S. institution.

**Funds Avail.:** $25,000. **No. of Awards:** 4. **To Apply:** Write: A.F.U.D. Fellowship Committee, National Kidney Foundation, Two Park Avenue, New York, NY, 10016, USA, 800-622-9010 for application form and guidelines. **Deadline:** September 15. Notification in January. **Contact:** Meg Habenicht, Program Coordinator Fellowship Committee, at the above address (see entry 497).

### • 499 •  AFUD/Ph.D. Research Scholar Program
*(Postdoctorate/Award)*

**Purpose:** To support postdoctoral scientists engaged in basic research related to the prevention and cure of urologic diseases. **Focus:** Urology. **Qualif.:** Candidate must be a postdoctoral scientist with a research interest in urologic or related diseases and dysfunctions. Applicant must be sponsored by a urology department that provides space, laboratory equipment, and supplies for the proposed research. Applicant's preceptor should be a senior Ph.D. or M.D. engaged in urological research at an established laboratory, and must agree to accept direct responsibility for the candidate. Continued support is subject to yearly review and evaluation by the Scientific and Education Committee. Recipient must undertake full-time research during the award term. Funds are not intended for junior faculty member support.

**Funds Avail.:** $23,000/year matched by institution. **No. of Awards:** 5. **To Apply:** Write to AFUD for application form and guidelines. Submit original and four copies. **Deadline:** September 1. Awards are announced in February. **Contact:** Meg Habenicht, Program Coordinator, at the above address (see entry 497).

### • 500 •  AFUD Research Scholars Program
*(Postdoctorate/Award)*

**Purpose:** To support post-residency in scientific techniques, preferably in a basic research laboratory. **Focus:** Urology. **Qualif.:** Candidate may be of any nationality. Applicant must be a urologist who has completed his/her residency. The proposed research project must be approved by AFUD, and awards must be matched by the scholar's sponsoring institution. Awards are tenable at U.S. and Canadian academic research institutions. The program is not intended as a source of funding for junior clinical faculty.

**Funds Avail.:** $22,000, matched by institution. **No. of Awards:** 7. **To Apply:** Write the AFUD for application forms and guidelines. **Deadline:** September 1. Notification by February 15. **Contact:** Meg Habenicht, Program Coordinator, at the above address (see entry 497).

### • 501 •  AFUD Summer Student Fellowships
*(Doctorate/Fellowship)*

**Purpose:** To encourage medical students to work in an urological research laboratory for the summer. **Focus:** Urology. **Qualif.:** Applicant may be of any nationality. Applicant must be a medical student who plans to work in a Canadian or U.S. urological research laboratory during the summer.

**Funds Avail.:** $2,000. **No. of Awards:** 20. **To Apply:** Write or call AFUD for application form and guidelines. Submit form with a letter of recommendation from the sponsoring institution. **Deadline:** April 15. Notification by May 31.

### • 502 •  Practicing Urologist's Research Award
*(Postdoctorate/Award)*

**Purpose:** To encourage urologists to undertake collaborative investigations at a urological research laboratory. **Focus:** Urology. **Qualif.:** Applicant may be of any nationality. Applicant must be a practicing urologist who wishes to conduct research at a U.S. or Canadian urological research laboratory. Awards must be matched by the sponsoring institution.

**Funds Avail.:** $5,000 matched by institution. **No. of Awards:** 1. **To Apply:** Write AFUD for application forms and guidelines. **Deadline:** September 1. Notification by February 15. **Contact:** Meg Habenicht, Program Coordinator, at the above address (see entry 497).

## American Foundation for Vision Awareness (MOA)
530 W. Ionia St., No. A                *Ph:* (517)482-0616
Lansing, MI 48933                      *Fax:* (517)482-1611

### • 504 •  AFVA(MOA) Scholarships *(Graduate/Scholarship)*

**Purpose:** To supplement fourth-year internship tuition for optometry students. **Focus:** Optometry. **Qualif.:** Applicants must be third-year optometry students and Michigan residents carrying a "B" average or better. **Criteria:** Selection is based upon grade point average and need.

**Funds Avail.:** The amount of the scholarship varies; it is usually $500 or more. **To Apply:** Applicants must submit college transcripts and a letter of recommendation from a professor. **Deadline:** March 1. **Contact:** Linda M. Moleski, Scholarship Chair, at the above address (see entry 503).

## American Friends of the London School of Economics
Scholarship Office
733 15th St., NW, Ste. 700
Washington, DC 20005                   *Ph:* (202)347-3232
*E-mail:* plakias@aol.com

### • 506 •  AFLSE Scholarships *(Graduate/Scholarship)*

**Purpose:** To enable graduate students from the United States to study at the London School of Economics and Political Science. **Focus:** Social Sciences. **Qualif.:** Applicant must be a U.S. citizen or permanent resident who is qualified to undertake graduate studies in a discipline offered by the London School of Economics. An applicant must not wait for acceptance to the School before applying to AFLSE for scholarship support. Awards and admission are decided independently. Scholarships are not finalized until admission to the School is confirmed. Current or former students of the School are not eligible, except those who attended only summer school. Funds are only available for tuition support. **Criteria:** Applicant must have financial need and meet academic requirements.

**Funds Avail.:** Full-tuition. **No. of Awards:** 2-4. **To Apply:** Write to AFLSE for scholarship application form and guidelines, available in early October. Applications for admission to the School are not available from AFLSE. The scholarship office has no information on other sources of funds for study at the London School of Economics or elsewhere. **Deadline:** Mid-February. Scholars are selected in mid-April.

**Remarks:** For London School of Economics admission forms and catalogues, write the Graduate Admissions Office, London School of Economics, Houghton St., London WC2A 2A, England. **Contact:** Jane P. Plakias at the above address (see entry 505).

---

• 507 •
**American Geological Institute**
4220 King St.
Alexandria, VA 22302-1502
*Ph:* (703)379-2480
*Fax:* (703)379-7563
*URL:* http://www.agiweb.org/ehr/mgsftp.html

• 508 • **Minority Geoscience Scholarships** *(Graduate, Undergraduate/Scholarship)*

**Purpose:** To aid outstanding minority students in the geosciences. **Focus:** Geosciences, including Geochemistry, Geology, Geophysics, Geoscience Education, Hydrology, Meteorology, Physical Oceanography, Planetary Geology. **Qualif.:** Applicant must be a U.S. citizen, and be a geoscience or geoscience-education major. Candidate must be a member of one of the following groups in the geosciences: Black, Hispanic, Native American (American Indian, Eskimo, Hawaiian, and Samoan). Applicant must have a good academic record, meet financial need criteria, and be currently enrolled in an accredited institution in the United States.

**Funds Avail.:** $10,000 maximum. **To Apply:** Write for application form. Submit form with official transcripts from all colleges attended (SAT, ACT, and/or GRE scores are requested), and three letters of recommendation from persons qualified to judge applicant's academic performance and character. **Deadline:** February 1.

**Remarks:** Applications may be obtained from the website. **Contact:** Mike Smith at the above address (see entry 507).

---

• 509 •
**American Geophysical Union**
2000 Florida Ave., NW
Washington, DC 20009
*Ph:* (202)462-6900
*Fax:* (202)328-0566
*Free:* 800-966-2481

*E-mail:* dtate@agu.org; wsinghatch@agu.org
*URL:* http://www.agu.org

• 510 • **AGU Congressional Science Fellowship Program** *(Postdoctorate/Fellowship)*

**Purpose:** To provide an opportunity for early to mid-career scientists to work as regular staff members in Congress. **Focus:** Science and Public Policy. **Qualif.:** Candidates must be members of the AGU and American citizens or permanent residents of the U.S. Candidates should hold a Ph.D. and have a strong background in science with some knowledge of public policy. **Criteria:** The top five candidates will be called for an interview at AGU Headquarters. The interview will be conducted by the Committee on Public Affairs.

**Funds Avail.:** $42,000, plus $2,000 for vouchered travel and moving expenses incurred during relocation, and $2,000 for vouchered travel during year, plus $1,000 for travel to AGU meetings. **No. of Awards:** One. **To Apply:** Submit a letter of intent, curriculum vitae, and three letters of recommendation from individuals who are in a position to evaluate the candidate's

professional competence. **Deadline:** February 20. **Contact:** Daryl Tate at the above address (see entry 509).

• 511 • **Hydrology (Horton) Research Grant** *(Doctorate/Grant)*

**Purpose:** To support the reasearch in hydrology and or water resources. **Focus:** Hydrology. **Qualif.:** Applicants must be Ph.D. candidates who are members or student members of the American Geophysical Union pursuing research in hydrology and water resources leading to the completion of a doctoral dissertation. Appropriate topics may be hydrology, including its physical, chemical, or biological aspects or water resources policy sciences, including economics, systems analysis, sociology, and law. **Criteria:** The selection committee will consider the technical merits of the project, the clarity of presentation, and the feasibility of meeting objectives during the period of the award.

**Funds Avail.:** The number and amount of awards varies depending on available income from the Horton Fund. Payment is in two installments, the first at or before the spring meeting in May and the second in December upon receipt of a brief progress report. **No. of Awards:** Two. **To Apply:** Applications should be accompanied by an executive summary of the project no more than two pages in length, two letters of recommendation from the main faculty research supervisor and one from another member of the thesis committee, a one-page statement of purpose, and a detailed budget. **Deadline:** Proposals signed by the candidate and by the faculty supervisor must be filed by March 1. **Contact:** Wynetta Singhateh at the above address (see entry 509).

---

• 512 •
**American GI Forum Hispanic Education Fund**
3301 Mountain Rd. NW
Albuquerque, NM 87104
*Ph:* (505)243-7551
*Fax:* (505)247-4910
*E-mail:* agiforum@aol.com
*URL:* http://www.nmt.edu/~larranag/hef/hef.html

• 513 • **Hispanic Education Foundation Matching Funds Award** *(Undergraduate/Scholarship)*

**Focus:** General studies. **No. of Awards:** Varies. **To Apply:** Applicants must seek scholarship through a local chapter in Arizona, California, Colorado, Kansas, Michigan, Nebraska, New Mexico, Oklahoma, Texas, Utah and Washington. Applicants must submit school transcripts and proof of enrollment. Write for further details. **Contact:** Isabelle Ogaz Tellez.

---

• 514 •
**American Health Information Management Association - Foundation of Research and Education**
919 N. Michigan Ave., Ste. 1400
Chicago, IL 60611-1683
*Ph:* (312)787-2672
*Fax:* (312)787-9793
*URL:* http://www.va.gov/publ/standard/health/ahima.htm

• 515 • **Aspen Systems Graduate Scholarship** *(Graduate/Scholarship)*

**Purpose:** To assist credentialed HIM professionals to obtain advanced degrees. **Focus:** Computer sciences, medical record administration, and business administration. **Qualif.:** Applicants must be graduate students whose course of study is directly related to health information management, medical informatics, computer science, or business management. **Criteria:** Selection is

## American Health Information Management Association - Foundation of Research and Education (continued)

based on financial need, ability to write, professionalism and activities.

**Funds Avail.:** $1,000 scholarship. **Deadline:** August 1. Scholarships are awarded in September. **Contact:** American Health Information Management Association at the above address (see entry 514). Toll-free telephone: 800-621-6828.

### • 516 • FORE Graduate Loan (Graduate/Loan)

**Purpose:** To assist credentialed HIM professionals to obtain advanced degrees. **Focus:** Computer Sciences, Medical Record Administration, and Business Administration. **Qualif.:** Applicants must be graduate students whose course of study is directly related to health information management, medical informatics, computer science, or business management. **Criteria:** Selection is based on financial need, ability to write, professionalism and activities.

**Funds Avail.:** Up to $5,000. **Deadline:** June 15 and October 15. Loans are awarded in August and December, respectively. **Contact:** American Health Information Management Association at the above address (see entry 514).

### • 517 • FORE Graduate Scholarships (Doctorate, Graduate/Scholarship)

**Focus:** Health Services Administration. **Qualif.:** Applicants must be credentialed medical record professionals (RRA or CCS), be active members of AHIMA, hold a bachelor's degree, be citizens or permanent residents of the United States, and be enrolled full-time or part-time in an accredited college or university in a program leading to a master's, law, or doctoral degree. The area of study should be relevant to health information management. Eligible areas include business, or health care, finance, information science, education, law, public health, or other related disciplines. **Criteria:** Selection is based on financial need, ability to write, professionalism and activities.

**Funds Avail.:** $3,000 scholarship. **To Apply:** Applicants must submit a formal application accompanied by an official transcript of each college attended and three letters of reference from persons not related to the applicant who are knowledgeable of the applicant's character, education, and abilities. **Deadline:** August 1. **Contact:** AHIMA, Foundation of Record Education, Graduate Scholarship Committee, at the above address (see entry 514). Toll-free telephone: (800)621-6828.

### • 518 • FORE Undergraduate Loan (Undergraduate/Loan)

**Focus:** Medical Record Administration. **Qualif.:** Applicants must be enrolled in health information management, technology, or coding specialist programs. Independent study program students are not eligible.

**Funds Avail.:** Up to $1,000 for coding; up to $2,000 for technology; up to $5,000 for management. **Deadline:** June 15 and October 15. Loans will be awarded in August and December. **Contact:** American Health Information Management Association at the above address (see entry 514).

### • 519 • FORE Undergraduate Scholarships (Undergraduate/Scholarship)

**Focus:** Medical Records Administration. **Qualif.:** Applicants must have been accepted for enrollment in a program for health information management or health information technology approved by the Committee on Allied Health and Accreditation and must be beginning their final year of undergraduate study or they must have been accepted for admission to the Independent Study Program of the American Health Information Management

Association and have successfully completed the third module. Applicants must be citizens of the United States or its territories. **Criteria:** Based on educational achievement, financial need, assessment of applicant's statement of objectives, and references.

**Funds Avail.:** $1,500 scholarships. **To Apply:** Application forms must be accompanied by three letters of reference, a letter of acceptance from the school program director, transcripts from all college work completed, and evidence of acceptance from the program or completion of the enclosed form by the program director. **Deadline:** July 1. Applicants are notified of decision on August 15. **Contact:** Barbara Manny, RRA, Professional Practice Division, at the above address (see entry 514). Toll-free telephone: (800)621-6828.

### • 520 • Grace Whiting Myers/Malcolm T. MacEachern Student Loans (Doctorate, Graduate, Undergraduate/Loan)

**Qualif.:** Applicants must either have been accepted for full-time enrollment in a program of health information management or technology approved by the Committee on Allied Health and Accreditation; be registered record administrators or accredited record technicians who are active members of AHIMA and enrolled in a baccalaureate degree program related to the health information field; be working towards a master's or doctoral degree related to the health information field; or must be enrolled in a coding specialist program affiliated with a regionally-accredited college or university. Applicants must be citizens of the United States or its territories. Independent Study Program students are not eligible.

**Funds Avail.:** Loans for students in a health information management program, baccalaureate, master's, or doctoral degree program will not exceed $5,000. Loans for students in a health information technology program will not exceed $2,000. Loans for students in a coding specialist program will not exceed $1,000. The interest rate on the unpaid balance of the loan will be eight percent per year. **To Apply:** Applicants should submit an application form, three letters of reference, a letter of acceptance from the school program director, and transcripts for all college work completed. **Deadline:** Students should submit all application materials no later than June 15 to be eligible for loans awarded in September, and no later than October 15 for loans awarded in December. **Contact:** Foundation of Record Education of AHIMA at the above address (see entry 514).

### • 521 • SMART Corporation Scholarship (Undergraduate/Scholarship)

**Focus:** Medical Record Administration. **Qualif.:** Applicants must be undergraduates studying health information technology or management.

**Funds Avail.:** $1,100 scholarship. **Deadline:** July 1. Scholarships are awarded in August. **Contact:** American Health Information Management Association at the above address (see entry 514).

### • 522 • Barbara Thomas Enterprises, Inc. Scholarship (Undergraduate/Scholarship)

**Purpose:** To assist a single parent to return to school. **Focus:** Medical record administration. **Qualif.:** Applicants must be single parents enrolled in a health information technology or management program.

**Funds Avail.:** $5,000 scholarship. **Deadline:** July 1. The scholarship is awarded in August. **Contact:** American Health Information Management Association at the above address (see entry 514).

### • 523 • Transcriptions, Ltd. Scholarship (Undergraduate/Scholarship)

**Focus:** Medical Record Administration. **Qualif.:** Applicants must be students enrolled in a health information technology program.

**Funds Avail.:** One $1,000 scholarship. **Contact:** American Health Information Management Association at the above address (see entry 514).

• 524 • **Transcriptions, Ltd. Scholarship for Health Information Management and Graduate Students** *(Graduate, Undergraduate/Scholarship)*

**Focus:** Medical Record Administration. **Qualif.:** Applicants must be enrolled in a health information management or graduate program.

**Funds Avail.:** One $3,000 scholarship. **Deadline:** July 1. The scholarship is awarded in August. **Contact:** American Health Information Management Association at the above address (see entry 514).

• 525 •

**American Heart Association, Inc.**
7272 Greenville Ave.          *Ph:* (214)706-1453
Dallas, TX 75231-4596         *Fax:* (214)706-1341
*E-mail:* ncrp@heart.org
*URL:* http://www.americanheart.org

• 526 • **AHA Grant-in-Aid** *(Postdoctorate/Grant)*

**Purpose:** To support well-defined research projects broadly related to cardiovascular function and diseases, stroke or related basic science, clinical, and public health problems and to encourage development of research projects by junior investigators and new areas of research by established investigators. **Focus:** Cardiology and related disciplines **Qualif.:** Applicant must be a U.S. citizen, exchange visitor, or permanent resident, with a doctorate. Grants-in-aid are available to investigators in all basic disciplines related to cardiology, including biochemistry, epidemiology, pathology, and physiology. Grants-in-aid are tenable at academic and nonprofit research institutions. Only U.S. citizens may use the award to conduct research outside of the United States. An individual may hold only one grant-in-aid from the AHA at any given time. Not restricted by seniority or academic rank.

**Funds Avail.:** $71,500 annually including 10% indirect costs; up to $15,000 per year for principal investigator salary and fringe benefits. **To Apply:** Write or call for application disk information. The AHA revises applications each year and only the latest form is acceptable. Pick up disk at Institution's grants offices or go to the internet site at www.americanheart.org. **Deadline:** June 15. Notification by December 1.

**Remarks:** There are 15 AHA affiliates in the United States that also support research. Write the AHA for a listing, or go to website: www.americanheart.org. **Contact:** Division of Research Administration at the above address (see entry 525).

• 527 • **Established Investigator Grant** *(Doctorate/Grant)*

**Purpose:** To support the career development of clinician-scientists and PhD's who have recently acquired independent status by funding high quality innovative research projects for which no previous financial support has been obtained from other granting agencies. **Qualif.:** Applicants must be MD's, PhD's, DO's or persons with equivalent doctoral degrees, U.S. citizens or permanent residents, and can not have completed or currently hold an equivalent award. It also must be 4 to 9 years since applicant's first full-time faculty/staff appointment at the Assistant Professor level or equivalent (at the time of award activation).

**Funds Avail.:** $75,000 annual salary, fringe benefits, indirect costs, and project costs (at least $40,000 for project support). R 4 years.

• 528 • **Scientist Development Grant** *(Doctorate/Grant)*

**Purpose:** To support beginning scientists in their progress toward independence; to bridge the gap between completion of research training and readiness for competition as an independent investigator. **Qualif.:** Applicants must be MD's, PhD's, DO's or have equivalent doctoral degrees; be U.S. citizens or permanent residents, and can not hold or ever have held any other national award. It must be no more than 4 years since the first full-time faculty/staff appointment at the Assistant Professor level or its equivalent (at time of award activation).

**Funds Avail.:** $65,000 annual salary, fringe benefits, indirect costs, and project costs (at least $35,00 for project support). **To Apply:** Applications may be submitted for review in the final year of postdoctoral research fellowship or in initial years of first full-time faculty/staff appointment.

• 529 •

**American Heart Association Inc., California Affiliate**
1710 Gilbreth Rd.          *Ph:* (415)259-6700
Burlingame, CA 94010-1317  *Fax:* (415)259-6891

• 530 • **American Heart Association, California Affiliate - Grants-in-Aid** *(Postdoctorate/Grant)*

**Purpose:** To support research projects related to cardiovascular function and disease, including basic cardiovascular mechanisms, stroke or the causes, diagnosis, treatment or prevention of cardiovascular disease. Research may involve basic and clinical biomedical sciences, epidemiology, or public health. **Qualif.:** Applicants must hold a doctoral degree and be faculty or staff of nonprofit institutions within the geographic area served by the California Affiliate. Individuals may hold only one Grant-in-Aid at a time. **Criteria:** Priority is given to beginning investigators.

**Funds Avail.:** $50,000, including 10% overhead, is available yearly. **Deadline:** Application materials must be in by November 1. Funding activation is on July 1.

**Remarks:** Approximately 110 applications are received per year. **Contact:** Research Department at the above address (see entry 529).

• 531 • **American Heart Association, California Affiliate - Postdoctoral Research Fellowships** *(Postdoctorate/Fellowship)*

**Purpose:** To further research training and experience in the field of cardiovascular research. The proposed research may be in clinical biomedical sciences, social and behavioral sciences, epidemiology, or public health. **Qualif.:** A doctoral degree is required. Fellows must work in a nonprofit institution within the geographic area served by the California Affiliate. **Criteria:** Selection is based on the qualifications of the applicant, the quality of the training program and environment, and the scientific merit of the proposed project.

**Funds Avail.:** Awards range from an $19,600 to $33,000 stipend (depending on years of relevant postdoctoral training), plus a $3,000 annual departmental grant for medical insurance and other project support. Fellow must spend at least 80 percent of time in research. **Deadline:** Materials must be received by October 1. Funding activation is on July 1.

**Remarks:** Approximately 150 applications are received per year. **Contact:** Research Department at the above address (see entry 529).

*American Heart Association Inc., California Affiliate (continued)*

**• 532 •　American Heart Association, California Affiliate - Predoctoral Fellowship** *(Doctorate/Fellowship)*

**Purpose:** To inspire individuals to initiate careers in cardiovascular research and support students conducting doctoral dissertation projects which broadly relate to the cardiovascular area. **Qualif.:** Applicants must be doctoral candidates enrolled in an accredited, nonprofit institution within the geographic area served by the California Affiliate and pursuing cardiovascular research in basic or clinical biomedical sciences, social or behavioral sciences, epidemiology, or public health. United States citizenship or a visa is required. Applicants must be supported by a dissertation sponsor who is a faculty member at the institution where the research is to be conducted. **Criteria:** Women and minorities are encouraged to apply.

**Funds Avail.:** Fellows receive a $16,500 stipend. **Deadline:** Application materials must be in by October 1. Funding activation is July 1. **Contact:** Research Department at the above address (see entry 529).

**• 533 •**
**American Helicopter Society**
217 N. Washington St.
Alexandria, VA 22314

**• 534 •　Vertical Flight Foundation Engineering Scholarships** *(Graduate, Undergraduate/Scholarship)*

**Focus:** Engineering. **Criteria:** Based on merit.

**Funds Avail.:** $2000-4000. **No. of Awards:** 2; 1 graduate and 1 undergraduate. **To Apply:** Application, transcripts, and references from a professor or dean must be submitted. **Deadline:** February 1.

**• 535 •**
**American Historical Association**
400 A St., SE　　　　　　　Ph: (202)544-2422
Washington, DC 20003　　　Fax: (202)544-8307
*E-mail:* aha@aha.msu.edu
*URL:* http://www.aols.org/ahista.htm

**• 536 •　The Albert J. Beveridge Grant** *(Postdoctorate, Professional Development/Grant)*

**Purpose:** To support research in progress of the history of the Western Hemisphere. **Focus:** The history of the U.S., Canada and Latin America. **Qualif.:** Only members of the association are eligible. Grants may be used for travel to a library or archive. Preference will be given to Ph.D. candidates and senior scholars.

**Funds Avail.:** $1,000 maximum. **To Apply:** Write for application form. **Deadline:** February 1. **Contact:** Administrative Assistant.

**• 537 •　Fellowship in Aerospace History** *(Doctorate, Postdoctorate/Fellowship)*

**Purpose:** To provide research opportunities using the documentary resources of the National Aeronautics and Space Administration (NASA). **Focus:** Aerospace History. **Qualif.:** Applicant must be a U.S. citizen. Candidate must have a Ph.D. in history or a related field, or be a doctoral student who has completed all course work. Research may cover any aspect of aerospace history from earliest times to present, including cultural and intellectual history, economic history, history of law and public policy, or history of science, engineering, and management. Fellowship is tenable at NASA headquarters, or a NASA center.

**Funds Avail.:** $25,000 maximum, postdoctoral recipients; $16,000 maximum, graduate students. **To Apply:** Write for application form and guidelines. Submit form with detailed research proposal. **Deadline:** Please contact the AHA at the above address.

**Remarks:** The fellowship is cosponsored by NASA. **Contact:** Administrative Assistant.

**• 538 •　J. Franklin Jameson Fellowship in American History** *(Postdoctorate/Fellowship)*

**Purpose:** To support scholarly research in the Library of Congress collections. **Focus:** American History. **Qualif.:** Applicant must have received a doctoral degree or its equivalent within the last five years. Candidate may not have published a book-length historical work. Fellowship is tenable at the Library of Congress.

**Funds Avail.:** $10,000. **To Apply:** Write for application form and guidelines. Submit form with curriculum vitae, description of research and its relevance to the Library of Congress collections, project schedule, and names of three references. **Deadline:** Please contact the AHA, at the above address.

**Remarks:** Fellowship is cosponsored by the Library of Congress. **Contact:** Administrative Assistant.

**• 539 •　Michael Kraus Research Grant in History** *(Professional Development/Grant)*

**Purpose:** To support research in progress on American colonial history. **Focus:** American Colonial History. **Qualif.:** Applicant must be a member of the Society who is conducting research in American colonial history with reference to the intercultural aspects of American and European relations. Grants may be used for travel, clerical assistance, or material reproduction.

**Funds Avail.:** $1,000 maximum. **To Apply:** Write for application form and guidelines. Submit form with a curriculum vitae, a description of proposed project, and a list of other supporting funds. **Deadline:** February 1. **Contact:** Administrative Assistant.

**• 540 •　The Littleton-Griswold Research Grant** *(Professional Development/Grant)*

**Purpose:** To further research in progress. **Focus:** American legal history and the field of law and society. **Qualif.:** Only numbers of the association are eligible. Grants may be used for travel to a library or archive for research.

**Funds Avail.:** $1,000. **To Apply:** American legal history and the field of law and society. **Deadline:** February 1. **Contact:** Administrative Assistant.

**• 541 •　Bernadette Schmitt Grants** *(Professional Development/Grant)*

**Purpose:** To support research in progress on the history of Europe, Africa, and Asia. **Focus:** African History, Asian History, European History. **Qualif.:** Applicant must be a member of the Society who is conducting research in the history of Europe, Africa, and/or Asia. Grants may be used for travel, clerical assistance, or material reproduction.

**Funds Avail.:** $1,000 maximum. **To Apply:** Write for application form and guidelines. Submit form with a curriculum vitae, a description of proposed project, and a list of other supporting funds. **Deadline:** September 15.

## • 542 •

### American Holistic Nurses Association

PO Box 2130
Flagstaff, AZ 86003-2130      *Free:* 800-278-AHNA
*URL:* http://ahna.org

#### • 543 • Charlotte McGuire Scholarships *(Graduate, Undergraduate/Scholarship)*

**Purpose:** This award celebrates the commitment of nurses to a holistic path. Scholarships may be used for: college tuition and expenses for an accredited nursing program (AND, BSN, MSN, or PhD); tuition and expenses for accredited programs in holistic health or alternative modalities (these programs must be approved by the AHNA Education Committee); AHNA Certificate Programs; and research related to holistic health. **Focus:** Holistic Nursing. **Qualif.:** Scholarships are available to any licensed nurse or nursing student who is pursuing holistic education for personal and professional growth. Experience in holistic health care or alternative health practices is preferred. Membership (minimum six months) in the American Holistic Nurses' Association is required. If applying for a school scholarship, nursing prerequisites should be completed, with a minimum grade point average of 3.0 on a 4.0 scale.

**Funds Avail.:** $500 awards are made each year (one for AND or BSN programs, and one for graduate study); amounts may vary due to available funds. **No. of Awards:** 2. **To Apply:** Applicants must request an application form from AHNA Headquarters. Completed application will contain: personal data; list of educational institutions attended and degrees received; employment history; description of personal interests, including community, political, professional or spiritual activities; explanation of purpose for requesting financial assistance (projected/estimated income and expenses for school term; other scholarships/financial aid applied for and/or received); copy of catalog description or program bulletin with explanation of program for which funds will be used; official copy of transcript (sent directly to AHNA Headquarters); an application essay describing the applicant's plans for integration of the AHNA Standards of Holistic Nursing Practice into educational, professional, and personal life; and two letters of reference. **Deadline:** Completed applications are accepted only between January 1 and March 15 of the year in which the scholarship is to be awarded. Scholarships are presented to recipients and the membership at the annual AHNA Conference. These conferences are held in late May or early June at sites rotates among the AHNA regions. **Contact:** Charlotte McGuire Scholarship Program at the above address (see entry 542).

## • 544 •

### American Horticultural Society

7931 East Boulevard Dr.      *Ph:* (703)768-5700
Alexandria, VA 22308      *Fax:* (703)768-8700
     *Free:* 800-777-7931

*E-mail:* mpatterson@ahs.org
*URL:* http://www.ahs.org

#### • 545 • American Horticultural Society Horticultural Career Internship *(Graduate, Professional Development, Undergraduate/Internship)*

**Purpose:** To provide hands-on experience in horticulture at a 25-acre garden estate and education institution. **Focus:** Horticulture. **Qualif.:** Applicants must desire a career in horticulture, preferably studying or graduating from a horticultural program at a university. **Criteria:** Selection is based on application and phone interview.

**Funds Avail.:** A stipend of $7.00 per hour for a 37.5-hour work week is provided. **No. of Awards:** 6-7 annually. **To Apply:** Write to

AHS for application materials and directions, or visit the website. **Deadline:** Three months before desired start date of internship. **Contact:** Patrick Larkin, Director of Horticulture & River Farm Operations at the above address (see entry 544).

## • 546 •

### American Hospital Association

1 N. Franklin      *Ph:* (312)422-3807
Chicago, IL 60606      *Fax:* (312)422-4571

#### • 547 • AHA/American Institute of Architects Fellowships in Health Facilities Design *(Graduate/Fellowship)*

**Purpose:** To encourage research and study related to the architectural design of health care facilities. **Focus:** Health Care Architecture. **Qualif.:** Candidate must be a U.S. citizen. Applicant must be a graduate-level student in architecture with an interest in the design of health care facilities. Fellowships, which are co-sponsored by the American Institute of Architecture, may be used for graduate study at an accredited school of architecture associated with a school of hospital administration or near hospital resources adequate to supplement prescribed graduate architecture courses in health facilities design. Awards may also be used for independent graduate-level study, research, or design in the health facilities field; or for travel with in-residence research at selected hospitals in a predetermined area.

**Funds Avail.:** $20,000. **To Apply:** Write to AHA for application materials. **Deadline:** January 15. Awards are announced in March.

**Remarks:** The American Institute of Architects also administers several scholarships for graduate and postgraduate students of architecture. **Contact:** Fellowship Coordinator at the above address (see entry 546).

## • 548 •

### American Hospital Association - Section for Health Care Systems

1 N. Franklin      *Ph:* (312)422-3317
Chicago, IL 60606      *Fax:* (312)422-4583

#### • 549 • Ray Woodham Visiting Fellowship Program *(Professional Development/Fellowship)*

**Purpose:** To encourage interest in research of multi-institutional activities and to provide practicing multi-institutional executives with an opportunity to pursue a specific interest related to the financing, organization, or delivery of health care services. **Focus:** Health Care Systems. **Qualif.:** Applicants must be practicing executives within a multi-institutional organization and have an interest, knowledge, and background in research. They must also arrange with their employer sufficient time for research and completion of project. The research project should result in a product suitable for publication in a scholarly management or research journal.

**Funds Avail.:** $3,000; awardee's salary would continue to be paid by his/her organization. **No. of Awards:** One. **To Apply:** Write for application materials. **Deadline:** February 1. Awards are announced in March. **Contact:** Coordinator at the above address (see entry 548).

# • 550 •
## American Indian Endowed Scholarship Program
c/o Washington State Higher
Education Coordinating Board
PO Box 43430
Olympia, WA 98504-3430

*Ph:* (360)753-7800
*Fax:* (360)753-7808

### • 551 • American Indian Endowed Scholarships
*(Graduate, Undergraduate/Scholarship)*

**Qualif.:** Applicants must have close social and cultural ties to an American Indian tribe or community within Washington state, be Washington residents in need of financial assistance, and promise to use their education to benefit other American Indians. Candidates must also be enrolled as full-time students in Washington at the time of scholarship, but cannot be enrolled in a program that includes religious worship, exercise, or instruction, or be working towards a degree in religious, seminarian, or theological studies. **Criteria:** Selection is based on ties to an American Indian community, academic achievement, and commitment to return service to the American Indian community within Washington state. Priority is given to upper-level undergraduates or graduate students.

**Funds Avail.:** Amount varies. **No. of Awards:** Varies. **To Apply:** Applicants should submit a completed application with high school and college grade transcripts, a statement of close social and cultural ties, a statement of commitment to return service, three letters of recommendation, and release of information form. **Deadline:** May 15. **Contact:** John Klacik, Associate Director of Student Financial Aid; Rick Page, Associate Director of Minority Affairs; or Ann McLendon, Program Manager of Student Financial Aid, at the above address (see entry 550).

# • 552 •
## American Indian Graduate Center
4520 Montgomery Blvd. NE, Ste. 1-
B
Albuquerque, NM 87109-1291
*URL:* http://www.ucla.edu/student/grapes/doc.00266.html

*Ph:* (505)881-4584

### • 553 • AIGC Fellowships *(Graduate/Fellowship)*

**Purpose:** To provide supplemental financial aid to Native American and Alaska Native graduate students pursuing master's and doctoral degrees. **Focus:** All graduate-level degree fields **Qualif.:** Applicant must be a member of a federally-recognized Native American or Alaska Native group, and enrolled full-time at an accredited graduate program in the United States. Fellowship's value is determined by applicant's level of unmet financial need. Applicants must apply for campus-based aid, including loans.

**Funds Avail.:** Amounts ranged from $250 to $3,000. **To Apply:** Write or phone AIGC for application packet, available from January through May. **Deadline:** June 1. **Contact:** American Indian Graduate Center at the above address (see entry 552).

# • 554 •
## American Indian Heritage Foundation
6051 Arlington Blvd.
Falls Church, VA 22044

*Ph:* (703)237-7500
*Fax:* (703)532-1921

### • 555 • National Miss Indian U.S.A. Scholarship
*(Graduate, Undergraduate/Scholarship)*

**Purpose:** To promote young Indian women who continue with their Indian culture and heritage along with making a place for

themselves in the white man's world. **Qualif.:** Women must be 18-26 years old, never married, pregnant, or cohabitated, and must be high school graduates. Applicant must have an Indian sponsor such as: tribe, business, or organization with a valid governing board. The women must also have a belief of and practice tribal culture and heritage. They must exhibit such positive characteristics as: listening to their elders, joining in pow-wows, and promoting Indian language if possible.

**Funds Avail.:** First place winner receives a $12,000 cash award, $7,000 to the school of choice, and $5,000 for wardrobe. **To Apply:** Applications must be requested. There is a $500 application fee. **Deadline:** September 15. **Contact:** Barbara Butler, Pageant Director, at the above address (see entry 554)for applications and further information.

# • 556 •
## American Indian Minority Achievement
Office of the Commissioner of
Higher Education
2500 Broadway
Helena, MT 59620-3101
*E-mail:* eswaney@oche.montana.edu
*URL:* http://www.montana.edu/~wwwoche/

*Ph:* (406)444-6570
*Fax:* (406)444-1469

### • 557 • Montana Indian Student Fee Waiver
*(Doctorate, Graduate, Professional Development, Undergraduate/Scholarship)*

**Purpose:** To increase accessibility to public higher education for citizens who would not be able to matriculate or to continue an educational program without financial assistance. Also to recognize meritorious achievement or service, whether academic or through exceptional accomplishment, and to assure uniform and equitable administration of fee waiver policies of students in the Montana University System. **Qualif.:** Applicants must be one-fourth or more Indian blood who are bona fide residents of the state of Montana for at least one year prior to enrollment in the Montana University System. They must also demonstrate financial need.

**Funds Avail.:** Approximately $1,759.60 - $2,565. **No. of Awards:** 591.4 FTE. **To Apply:** Students should request an Indian Student Fee Waiver application form when applying to any Montana System campus. **Deadline:** Requests should be coordinated with Federal financial aid deadlines. **Contact:** Melina Hawkins, Financial Aid Director, Montana State University-Billings. Telephone: (406)657-2188; Mike Richardson, Montana Tech. Telephone: (406)496-4213; James Craig, Montana State University. Telephone: (406)994-2845; Steve Jamruska, Montana State University-Northern. Telephone (406)265-4190; Mick Hanson, University of Montana. Telephone: (406)243-5373; Arlene Williams, Western Montana College of the University of Montana. Telephone: (406)683-7511; Brenda Sebastian, MSuCotGF. Telephone: (406)771-4304; Victoria Glass, Helena CoT. Telephone: (406)444-6800.

## • 558 •
## American Indian Science and Engineering Society

5661 Airport Blvd.                          *Ph:* (303)939-0023
Boulder, CO 80301-2339                      *Fax:* (303)939-8150
*E-mail:* aiseshq@spot.colorado.edu
*URL:* http://www.colorado.edu/AISES

### • 559 •  AISES A.T. Anderson Memorial Scholarship
*(Graduate, Undergraduate/Scholarship)*

**Qualif.:** Applicants must be American Indian or Alaskan native college students pursuing academic programs in the sciences, engineering, health related fields, business, natural resources, and math and science secondary education. Applicants must be members of AISES recognized as a member of a tribe and full-time students maintaining a GPA of 2.0 or higher.

**Funds Avail.:** $1,000 award for undergraduate study; $2,000 award for graduate study. **To Apply:** Candidates must provide proof of tribal enrollment. **Deadline:** June 15. **Contact:** Scholarship Coordinator, American Indian Science & Engineering Society, at the above address (see entry 558).

### • 560 •  Environmental Protection Agency Tribal Lands Science Scholarship *(Doctorate, Graduate, Postgraduate/Scholarship)*

**Purpose:** To increase the number of degreed American Indians in the biological and environmental sciences. **Qualif.:** Applicants must be Native Americans.

**Funds Avail.:** $4,000 per semester. **Deadline:** June 15. **Contact:** The American Indian Science and Engineering Society at the above address (see entry 558).

### • 561 •  Al Qoyawayma Award *(Graduate, Undergraduate/Award)*

**Qualif.:** Applicants must be undergraduate or graduate students who are members of the AISES. They must be double majors in science or engineering and be pursuing a degree in the arts. **Criteria:** Awards are based on leadership and academic achievement. **To Apply:** Applications must include the applicants official academic transcript, a typed personal essay, two letters of recommendation, and a Certificate of Indian Blood (CIB)/Tribal Enrollment. Prior scholarship recipients are not required to submit their CIB and are not given special consideration during the application evaluation. **Deadline:** June 15.

**Remarks:** The award is sponsored by the George Bird Grinnell American Indian Children's Education Foundation, and honors AL Qoyawayma, a distinguished engineer, Hopi artist, and one of six founders of AISES. **Contact:** Scholarship Coordinator, American Indian Science and Engineering Society, at the above address (see entry 558).

### • 562 •  Polingaysi Qoyawayma Scholarship
*(Graduate/Scholarship)*

**Purpose:** To promote excellence in teaching, in memory of Polingaysi Qoyawayma (Elizabeth White), who taught for 30 years on the Hopi and Navajo reservations, and who in 1954 was awarded the U.S. Department of the Interior Distinguished Service Award for teaching excellence. **Qualif.:** Applicants must be American Indian students or teachers pursuing continued teacher education in science or math. **To Apply:** Information is available by writing to the AISES. **Deadline:** June 15. **Contact:** AISES at the above address (see entry 558).

### • 563 •  Santa Fe Pacific Foundation Scholarships
*(Undergraduate/Scholarship)*

**Qualif.:** Applicants must be American Indians and recent high school graduates with a GPA of 2.0 or higher. They must plan to be full-time undergraduate students at a college or university majoring in the sciences, business, education, or health administration. They must also reside in states serviced by the Santa Fe Pacific Corporation and its affiliated companies, including Arizona, Colorado, Kansas, New Mexico, Oklahoma, and California. **Criteria:** Selection is based on leadership and academic achievement.

**Funds Avail.:** $2,500 for four years (8 semesters) or until baccalaureate degree is obtained, whichever occurs first. **To Apply:** Applicants must be recognized as a member of a tribe. **Deadline:** March 31. **Contact:** American Indian Science and Engineering Society at the above address (see entry 558).

## • 564 •
## American Institute of Aeronautics and Astronautics

Suite 500                                   *Ph:* (703)264-7500
1801 Alexander Bell Dr.                      *Fax:* (703)264-7551
Reston, VA 20191-4344                        *Free:* 800-NEW-AIAA
*URL:* http://www.aiaa.org/

### • 565 •  AIAA/Command, Control, Communications and Intelligence Graduate Scholarship Award
*(Graduate/Scholarship)*

**Focus:** Astronautics, Engineering, Communications, Information Science and Technology. **Qualif.:** Applicants must have completed at least one academic year of full-time graduate college work and have in place or under way a university-approved research or thesis project in the field of command, control, communications, and intelligence or related disciplines. Candidates for the award must have a graduate grade point average of not less than the equivalent of a 3.0 on a 4.0 scale. Applicants must be enrolled in a university graduate program having command, control, communications, and intelligence and/or its associated disciplines or courses of study.

**Funds Avail.:** One or more Graduate Master of Science and/or Doctor of Philosophy Fellowship of $1,000 is awarded. **To Apply:** Application includes a 250-500 word essay, which serves to provide evidence of the candidate's C3I related technical work in support of his/her research or best project. Advisor approval of the project is required. The student's academic record will be examined along with a 100-200 word essay on career objectives, which must be submitted with the application and three letters of recommendation. **Deadline:** Application and accompanying papers must be submitted by January 31. **Contact:** Student Programs Department at the above address (see entry 564).

### • 566 •  AIAA/Gordon C. Oates Air Breathing Propulsion Award *(Doctorate, Graduate/Award)*

**Focus:** Astronautics, Aeronautics. **Qualif.:** Applicants must be U.S. citizens, have completed at least one academic year of full-time graduate college work, and have in place or under way a university-approved research or thesis project in the field of air-breathing propulsion or related disciplines. Candidates for the Award must have a graduate grade point average of not less than the equivalent of a 3.0 on a 4.0 scale. They must be enrolled in an accredited college or university graduate program having air breathing propulsion and/or related courses of study in air breathing propulsion. Applicants do not have to be AIAA student members in good standing to apply, but must become so before receiving an award.

**Funds Avail.:** One or more Graduate Master of Science and/or Doctor of Philosophy Fellowships of $1,000 are awarded. These are non-renewable awards. **To Apply:** Application includes a 500-1000 word essay, which will serve to provide evidence of the candidate's technical work in support of his/her research or best project. Advisor approval of the project is required. An official college transcript, 100-150 word essay on career objectives, and

## American Institute of Aeronautics and Astronautics (continued)

three letters of recommendation must be submitted. **Deadline:** Application and accompanying papers must be submitted by February 1. **Contact:** Student Programs Department at the above address (see entry 564).

### • 567 • AIAA Liquid Propulsion Award (Graduate/Scholarship)

**Purpose:** To provide one or more yearly scholarship awards to qualified students actively participating in liquid rocket propulsion research endeavors as part of their graduate studies. **Focus:** Astronautics, Aeronautics. **Qualif.:** Applicants must be citizens of the United States who have completed at least one academic year of full-time graduate work. In addition, they must have a university approved thesis or research project specializing in the field of liquid propulsion, or its related disciplines, in progress. Applicants cannot be previous winners of this award. If they applied and were not selected, then they may reapply. Postdoctoral candidates are not eligible. Applicants must have a GPA of not less than the equivalent of a 3.0 on a 4.0 scale, and be enrolled in an accredited college or university graduate program having liquid propulsion and/or related technical courses of study. Applicants do not have to be AIAA student members to apply, but they must become members before receiving a scholarship award. Application packages must be endorsed and/or cosigned by the applicant's graduate advisor and the appropriate university department head. **Criteria:** The recipients are selected on the basis of the following criteria, listed in order of importance: essay describing the research program, graduate program being pursued by the candidate, and letters of recommendation.

**Funds Avail.:** One or more Graduate Master of Science and/or Doctor of Philosophy fellowships of $1,000 are awarded. **To Apply:** Applications must include a 500 to 1000 word essay which will serve to provide evidence of liquid propulsion technical work in support of candidate's research. Advisor approval of project is required. Candidates must also submit an official college transcript, a 100 to 500 word essay on career objectives, and three letters of recommendation. Advisor endorsement/approval of the research as required above may serve as one of the letters of recommendation. One letter of recommendation may come from the sponsoring head of the candidate's department. Since a key requirement of this award is the conduct of research in the field of liquid propulsion, letters of recommendation from persons knowledgeable in the area and familiar with the candidate's research activity are encouraged. All letters of recommendation may be attached to the application or sent directly to the Director of Student Programs at AIAA. **Deadline:** Application and accompanying papers must be postmarked by February 1 to be considered.

**Remarks:** The LPTC will request and strongly encourage recipients to present and publish their research work as a technical paper at a subsequent AIAA conference. Acceptance of this request is not essential for candidate eligibility. Arrangements for such a presentation will be discussed with recipients following their selection. **Contact:** Student Programs Department at the above address (see entry 564).

### • 568 • AIAA Scholarship Program (Undergraduate/Scholarship)

**Purpose:** To further the objective of the American Institute of Aeronautics and Astronautics to advance the arts, sciences, and technology of aeronautics. **Focus:** Astronautics, Aeronautics. **Qualif.:** Applicants must be either citizens or permanent residents of the United States. They do not have to be student members to apply, but must become members before receiving a scholarship. The scholastic plan shall be such as to provide entry into some field of science or engineering related to the technical activities of the AIAA. Candidates must be enrolled in, or eligible for entry into, an accredited college or university and have completed at least one academic quarter or semester of full-time college. **Criteria:**

Selection of recipients is based on the following criteria: a grade point average of not less than 3.0, a 500 to 1000 word essay on applicant's career objectives and an outline of the academic program necessary to meet the objectives, and three recommendations. High school, college, and community activities, offices, awards, and work experience are also considered.

**Funds Avail.:** Each scholarship is worth $1,000. Applicants must not have or subsequently receive another award which, combined with the AIAA scholarship, would provide a stipend greater than tuition plus direct educational expenses such as books and lab fees. Sophomore and junior students who receive one of these awards are eligible for yearly continuation until completion of their senior year provided they maintain at least a 3.0 average on a 4.0 scale. Continuation is not automatic; students must reapply each year. **To Apply:** Application form, essay, and three recommendations must be submitted. College transcripts must be sent directly. **Deadline:** Applications and related materials must be postmarked by January 31. Candidates will be notified of the results by July 15. **Contact:** Mr. Wil Vargas, Student Programs Department, at the above address (see entry 564).

### • 569 • AIAA/William T. Piper, Sr. General Aviation Systems Award (Graduate/Scholarship)

**Purpose:** To provide one or more yearly scholarship awards to worthy graduate students actively participating in research endeavors in general aviation as part of their graduate studies. **Focus:** Astronautics, Aeronautics, Aerospace Science. **Qualif.:** Applicants must be citizens of the United States who have completed at least one academic year of full-time graduate work. In addition, they must have a university approved thesis or research project specializing in the technical field of general aviation, or its related disciplines, in progress. Applicants cannot be previous winners of this award. If they applied and were not selected, then they may reapply. Postdoctoral candidates are not eligible. Applicants must have a GPA of not less than the equivalent of a 3.0 on a 4.0 scale. Applicants do not have to be AIAA student members in good standing to apply, but they must become members before receiving a scholarship award. Application packages must be endorsed and/or cosigned by the applicant's graduate advisor and the appropriate university department head. **Criteria:** Recipients are selected on the basis of the following criteria listed in order of importance: essay describing the research program, graduate program being pursued by the candidate, career goals essay, and the letters of recommendation.

**Funds Avail.:** $1,000 scholarship plus travel expenses to attend a national AIAA meeting. The award is nonrenewable. **To Apply:** Applications must include an official college transcript, and a 100 to 500 word essay on career objectives, and three letters of recommendation. Advisor endorsement/approval of research as required above may serve as one of the letters of recommendation. One letter of recommendation may come from the sponsoring head of the candidate's department. Since a key requirement of this award is the conduct of research in the field of general aviation, letters of recommendation from persons knowledgeable in the area and familiar with the candidate's research activity are encouraged. All letters of recommendation may be attached to the application or sent directly to the Director of Student Programs at AIAA. **Deadline:** Application and accompanying papers must be postmarked by January 31 to be considered.

**Remarks:** The General Aviation Systems Technical Committee (GASTC) will request and strongly encourage recipients to present and publish their research work as a technical paper at a subsequent AIAA conference. Acceptance of this request is not essential for candidate eligibility. Arrangements for such a presentation will be discussed with recipients following their selection. **Contact:** Student Programs Department at the above address (see entry 564).

**• 570 •**

## The American Institute of Architects

1735 New York Ave., NW
Washington, DC 20006-5292

*Ph:* (202)626-7511
*Fax:* (202)626-7420

### • 571 • AIA/AAF Scholarship for Advanced Study and Research *(Graduate, Postgraduate, Professional Development/Scholarship)*

**Purpose:** To support advanced study and research by those who have already earned a professional degree. **Focus:** Architecture **Qualif.:** Applicants must be either in the final year of a degree program resulting in a bachelor or master of architecture, or practitioners, interns, or educators who wish to pursue an advanced degree or conduct research under the auspices of a United States university. **Criteria:** Selections are based on the merits of a project proposal.

**Funds Avail.:** Awards generally range from $1,000 to $2,500. Scholarships are awarded to the individual and the school under whose sponsorship the research or advanced study will be done. The award is to be used for the full academic year and may not be used retroactively or deferred for later use. **No. of Awards:** Varies. **Deadline:** February 15. Winners are announced in April. **Contact:** AIA/AAF Scholarship Program Director, The American Architectural Foundation, at the above address (see entry 570).

### • 572 • AIA/AAF Scholarship for Professional Degree Candidates *(Graduate, Undergraduate/ Scholarship)*

**Purpose:** To assist students in one of the two final years of a professional degree in architecture. **Focus:** Architecture **Qualif.:** Candidates must be in the third or fourth year of a five year program resulting in a bachelor of architecture degree, or in the fourth or fifth year of a six year program resulting in a master of architecture degree, or in the second or third year of a three-to-four year program resulting in a master of architecture degree and whose undergraduate degree is in a discipline other than architecture. **Criteria:** Selection is based on a personal statement, recommendations, academic performance, and financial need.

**Funds Avail.:** Varies from year to year. Awards are generally between $500 to $2,500. **To Apply:** Applications are only available from the architecture departments at schools accredited by the National Architectural Accrediting Board (NAAB), or the Royal Architectural Institute of Canada (RAIC). **Deadline:** February 3. **Contact:** The dean or department head at an NAAB- or RAIC-accredited school of architecture.

### • 573 • AIA/AHA Fellowship in Health Facilities Design *(Graduate, Undergraduate/Fellowship)*

**Purpose:** To support study in the field of health facilities design in one of the following settings: Option A - graduate study for one academic year in any accredited school of architecture associated with a school of hospital administration or near hospital resources adequate to supplement prescribed graduate architecture courses in health facilities design; Option B - Independent graduate-level study, research, or design in the health facilities field, to be completed within one calendar year; or Option C - travel with in-residence research at selected hospitals in a predetermined area, to be completed within one calendar year. **Qualif.:** Applicants must be US or Canadian citizens and have either received a professional degree from an accredited school of architecture or be in the final year of undergraduate work leading to a professional degree. **Criteria:** Fellowship recipients are selected on the basis of the proposed study program and the applicant's potential ability to make future contributions in the field of health-care architecture.

**Funds Avail.:** Two or more fellowships are awarded for a total of $17,000. **Deadline:** January 15; awards are announced March 1. **Contact:** Director of Architecture for Health, The American Institute of Architects, 1735 New York Ave. N.W., Washington D.C. 20006.

### • 574 • The American Architectural Foundation Minority/Disadvantaged Scholarship *(Graduate, Undergraduate/Scholarship)*

**Purpose:** To financially assist minority and/or disadvantaged students in their pursuit of a professional degree in architecture at schools of architecture accredited by The National Architectural Accrediting Board (NAAB). **Focus:** Architecture **Qualif.:** Qualified applicants are high school seniors, technical school/junior college students transferring to an NAAB school, or college freshmen beginning a program that will lead to either a bachelor's or master's degree. Applicants must be residents of the United States. Students who have completed heir first year of a standard four-year curriculum are not eligible. **Criteria:** Financial need, GPA, drawing, essays.

**Funds Avail.:** The award amount is determined by the financial need of the student and in cooperation with the scholarship program director and the directors of financial aid at the school. The scholarship is not intended to cover the full cost of education. Twenty scholarships are awarded each year and may be renewed for an additional two years, provided the student remains in good standing at an accredited school of architecture, has continued financial need, and adheres to all program requirements. **To Apply:** Candidates must first be nominated and submit a nomination form in order to receive an application. Nominations may be made by an architect or architectural firm, a local chapter of The American Institute of Architects, a community design center, a guidance counselor or teacher, a dean, department head, or professor from an accredited school of architecture, or a director of a community, civic, or religious organization. **Deadline:** Nominations must be postmarked no later than December 4, and completed applications postmarked by January 15. Finalists are announced in April. **Contact:** For nomination forms, write to The Minority/Disadvantaged Scholarship, AIA/AAF Scholarship Program Director, at the above address,(see entry 570) or contact Mary Felber, Program Director. Telephone: (202)626-7511.

### • 575 • The Richard Morris Hunt Fellowship *(Professional Development/Fellowship)*

**Purpose:** To financially support an architect and encourage the stewardship of American and French heritage. **Focus:** Historic preservation **Qualif.:** Applicants must be pursuing a career in historic preservation. **No. of Awards:** 1.

**Remarks:** The fellowship is alternately awarded to French and American scholars and consists of a six-month work/study program in the United States or France. **Contact:** AAF at the above address (see entry 570).

### • 576 • RTKL Traveling Fellowship *(Graduate, Undergraduate/Fellowship)*

**Purpose:** To encourage and support foreign travel undertaken to further education toward a professional degree in architecture. **Focus:** Architecture **Qualif.:** Applicants should be in the second-to-last year of a bachelor or master of architecture program and plan to travel outside the United States in an established school program, or be accepted in a professional degree program and plan foreign travel that will have a beneficial and direct relationship to educational goals. **Criteria:** Applicants are evaluated on a statement of purpose, relevance of travel plans to educational goals, strong academic performance, and letters of recommendation.

**Funds Avail.:** $1,500. **No. of Awards:** One. **To Apply:** Applications are available through any NAAB-accredited architecture school or The American Architectural Foundation. **Deadline:** February 15. The winner is announced in April.

**Remarks:** The fellowship was established with funds contributed by the architecture firm RTKL in honor of one of its founders, Francis T. Taliaferro. **Contact:** Refer to appropriate school or AAF at the above address (see entry 570).

## American Institute of Baking
1213 Bakers Way                                    *Ph:* (913)537-4750
Manhattan, KS 66502                                *Fax:* (913)537-1493
                                                   *Free:* 800-633-5137
*E-mail:* webmaster@aibonline.org; kembers@aibonline.org
*URL:* http://www.bakery_net.com/rdocs/aib.html

### • 578 • American Institute of Baking and Maintenance Engineering Scholarships *(Professional Development/Scholarship)*

**Purpose:** To provide scholarships for students who want to study at AIB. **Focus:** Baking Science, Maintenance Engineering. **Qualif.:** Applicants must be high school graduates or hold a G.E.D. and have two years experience in baking or a mechanical background. **Criteria:** Scholarships are based on merit (formal education, baking/maintenance experience, and letters of recommendation).

**Funds Avail.:** $500-$2,500. Scholarships are applied to tuition at the American Institute of Baking Resident Courses. Courses are 16 or 10 weeks in duration. **No. of Awards:** 20 per class. **Deadline:** May 1 and November 1. Applications are accepted on a first come first serve basis after each deadline. **Contact:** Ken Embers at the above address (see entry 577).

## American Institute for Economic Research
Division St.
PO Box 1000                                        *Ph:* (413)528-1216
Great Barrington, MA 01230                          *Fax:* (413)528-0103
*E-mail:* info@aier.org
*URL:* http://www.aier.org

### • 580 • AIER Summer Fellowships *(Graduate, Undergraduate/Fellowship)*

**Purpose:** To foster the training of economic scientists. **Focus:** Economics. **Qualif.:** Applicants must be college seniors applying to graduate programs in economics or students already enrolled in such programs. Awards are tenable at AIER; fellows live, work, and study in residence. The course of study focuses on monetary economics and on scientific procedures of inquiry. Business-cycle analysis and forecasting also receive attention. **Criteria:** First priority for summer fellowships will be given to U.S. citizens, but awards are often granted to foreign nationals. Foreign applicants must be able to speak and write English with native fluency.

**Funds Avail.:** $1000 stipend, plus room and board. **No. of Awards:** 10-15. **To Apply:** Applicants must write to the assistant to the director for application form and guidelines. Submit form with information about professional and educational background, transcripts, and an academic writing sample. Two letters of recommendation are also required. **Deadline:** March 31. Notification in early April.

**Remarks:** Participants in the Summer Fellowship Program may be eligible to apply to AIER for In-Abstentia Awards, which help cover the costs of tuition and living expenses during the school year. **Contact:** Susan Gillette, Assistant to the Director, at the above address (see entry 579).

### • 581 • American Institute for Economic Research Visiting Research Fellowship *(Other/Fellowship)*

**Focus:** Open, but especially welcomes applicants in the areas of banking and credit; public and personal finance; economic and monetary history; the role of government in society; the methodology of economics; and the role of individual freedom, private property, and free enterprise in economic progress. **Qualif.:**

Candidates must have strong writing skills, and the ideal candidate will be able to communicate their research findings to a general audience. Applicants who have a PhD or have completed all but their dissertation are preferred, but those with demonstrably strong writing skills will be considered.

**Funds Avail.:** Full room and board and a cash stipend. **To Apply:** Applicants should send a cover letter, a 500-word outline of their proposed course of research, a resume, and a copy of a recent publication or unpublished manuscript. Candidates must also arrange to have two confidential letters of reference sent directly to AIER by the referees. **Deadline:** March 31.

## American Institute of the History of Pharmacy
University of Wisconsin School of
  Pharmacy
Pharmacy Bldg.
425 N. Charter St.
Madison, WI 53706-1508                             *Ph:* (608)262-5378
*E-mail:* aihp@macc.wisc.edu
*URL:* http://www.wiscinfo.wisc.edu/pharmacy/aihp/
  welcome.html

### • 583 • AIHP Grant-in-Aid Toward Thesis Expenses Related to the History of Pharmacy *(Doctorate, Graduate/Grant)*

**Purpose:** To encourage academic research within the Institute's scope. **Focus:** History of Pharmacy, History of Medicine, History of Technology. **Qualif.:** Any graduate student in good standing at an institution of the United States may apply, regardless of the department through which the Master's degree or Doctor of Philosophy degree will be granted. However, for many projects some scientific or pharmaceutical background is advantageous. Therefore an application is strengthened by indicating clearly the applicant's qualifications to undertake the particular research proposed. American citizenship is not required and the research topic does not need to be in the field of American history. The thesis research must be clearly and significantly related to some aspect of pharmaceutical history (including the history of medicaments and dosage forms, from ancient to modern times) or some other branch of humanistic investigation that significantly utilizes a pharmo-historical approach. For the present purpose, the history of pharmacy includes at least five main categories of historical study: the profession of pharmacist (e.g., professional structuring, professional policy, legal aspects, organizations, education, literature, industry, economics, military and other public service); pharmaceutical disciplines basic to the profession (e.g., pharmaceutical botany, pharmacology, pharmaceutical chemistry, pharmaceutics, clinical pharmacy); pharmaceutical technology and processes; pharmacy's interaction with the arts (architecture and interior decor, painting and sculpture, literature and music); and pharmacists and pharmaceutical work (e.g., biography, and pharmaceutical establishments and institutions). **Criteria:** Applications are referred to an evaluating committee of the AIHP. The ratings of the panel guide the Director in the award of funds available in this program at a particular time. Principal criteria used in evaluating an application are: originality and significance of the proposed master's or doctoral thesis, relevance to the history of pharmacy, and demonstrated need for outside funds to enhance or complete the research project.

**Funds Avail.:** Grants total $5,000 annually. Funds are intended solely to help eligible graduate students defray the direct costs of thesis research attributable to supplies and other expenses that cannot normally be reimbursed by the degree-granting institution. Examples of eligible expenses are: computer time and assistance in programming; travel and maintenance at site removed from home university for research in sources necessary to the project; obtaining a photocopy or microform of essential sources; and application of investigative methods unusual in the history of pharmacy. Ineligible expenses include: living expenses of the applicant at the home university; routine typing to produce research notes or the thesis manuscript; routine illustrations for the manuscript; publication of research results; and indirect expenses such as overhead and other institution-related costs. **To Apply:** The following categories of information must be included in a typed application of not more than four single-spaced pages: applicant's name, address, telephone number, social security number, date of birth, nationality, education since high school, including the expected graduate degree, and the major area of specialization; name, address and telephone number of the graduate faculty member responsible for supervising the applicant's thesis research; tentative title and short prospectus of the thesis (designation of the degree and the major for which the thesis is a requirement must be included); concrete explanation of the significance of the research for the history of pharmacy (including the history of drugs) or for other humanistic study that relies upon pharmaco-historical approach; itemized annotated estimate of expenses for which a grant is being sought; other information the applicant considers important to proper consideration of the application; signature of the graduate student and date of application; and co-signature of faculty supervisor of thesis research. Four copies of the application must be sent by first-class mail to the AIHP. **Deadline:** February 1. Applications postmarked after that date are evaluated individually if any funds remain unawarded. If funds are unavailable, late applications are considered in the following year's program. Awards are announced by May 1, with funds available after July 1. If all funds for the current year are not awarded at that time, later applicants are ordinarily notified within three months of application.

**Remarks:** Most of our recipients are enrolled in History or History Of Science programs, Not Pharmacy or Pharmaceutical Sciences. **Contact:** Greg Higby at the above address (see entry 582).

---

• 584 •

## American Institute of Indian Studies

1130 E. 59th St.  
Chicago, IL 60637  
*E-mail:* aiis@uchicago.edu  
*Ph:* (773)702-8638  
*Fax:* (773)702-6636

### • 585 • AIIS Fellowship for Senior Scholarly Development *(Postdoctorate/Fellowship)*

**Purpose:** To support established scholars to conduct independent research in India. **Focus:** Indian Studies. **Qualif.:** Applicant must be a U.S. citizen or foreign national teaching full time at a U.S. college or university. Research proposals should have a substantial research or project component with clearly defined anticipated results. While in India, each Fellow will be formally affiliated with an Indian University.

**Funds Avail.:** Funds are made available in Indian currency only. **No. of Awards:** Varies. **To Apply:** Write AIIS for application form and guidelines. **Deadline:** July 1. Awards announced the following summer.

**Remarks:** AIIS is a cooperative nonprofit organization of 49 American colleges and universities with a special interest in Indian Studies. Write AIIS for a listing of the cooperating universities. **Contact:** Fellowship Coordinator at the above address (see entry 584).

### • 586 • AIIS Junior Fellowships *(Doctorate/ Fellowship)*

**Purpose:** To support Ph.D. Candidates who wish to conduct dissertation research in India. **Focus:** Indian Studies. **Qualif.:** Applicant must be a U.S. citizen or foreign national enrolled full-time at a U.S. college or university. Applicant must be researching Indian aspects of an academic discipline for a dissertation.

Applicant must have completed all requirements toward the Ph.D. except dissertation. Junior fellows will have formal affiliation with Indian universities and Indian research supervisors. All research projects and programs must be approved by the government of India.

**Funds Avail.:** Award funds are made available in Indian currency only. **No. of Awards:** Varies. **To Apply:** Write to AIIS for application form and guidelines. **Deadline:** July 1. Awards are announced the following summer.

**Remarks:** AIIS is a cooperative nonprofit organization of 49 American colleges and universities with a special interest in Indian Studies. Write AIIS for a listing of the cooperating universities. **Contact:** Fellowship Coordinator at the above address (see entry 584).

### • 587 • AIIS Senior Research Fellowships *(Postdoctorate/Fellowship)*

**Purpose:** To support scholars specializing in Indian studies to conduct research in India. **Focus:** Indian Studies. **Qualif.:** Applicant may be a scholar of any nationality at a U.S. university or a U.S. citizen. Applicant must be a specialist in Indian studies with a doctorate or its equivalent. While in India, each fellow will be formally affiliated with an Indian university. All research projects and programs must be approved by the government of India.

**Funds Avail.:** Award funds are made available in Indian currency only. **No. of Awards:** Varies depending on the amount of support received by AIIS. **To Apply:** Write AIIS for application form and guidelines. **Deadline:** July 1. Awards are announced the following summer.

**Remarks:** AIIS is a cooperative nonprofit organization of 49 American colleges and universities with a special interest in Indian studies. Write AIIS for a listing of the cooperating universities. **Contact:** Fellowship Coordinator at the above address (see entry 584).

### • 588 • Senior Performing Arts Fellowships *(Professional Development/Fellowship)*

**Purpose:** To support American artists to study the performing arts of India. **Focus:** Indian Performing Arts. **Qualif.:** Applicant may be of any nationality but must normally be resident in the United States. Applicant must be an accomplished practitioner of the performing arts of India who can demonstrate that studying in India will enhance these skills and develop capabilities to teach or perform in the United States. All programs must be approved by the government of India. Graduate students are not eligible.

**Funds Avail.:** Award funds are made available in Indian currency only. **No. of Awards:** Varies depending on the amount of support received by AIIS. **To Apply:** Write AIIS for application form and guidelines. **Deadline:** July 1. Awards are announced the following summer.

**Remarks:** AIIS is a cooperative nonprofit organization of 49 American colleges and universities with a special interest in Indian Studies. Write AIIS for a listing of the cooperating universities. **Contact:** Fellowship Coordinator at the above address (see entry 584).

---

• 589 •

**American Institute for Maghrib Studies**
c/o School of Advanced
   International Studies
Johns Hopkins University
1740 Massachusetts Ave., NW          *Ph:* (202)663-5676
Washington, DC 20036                  *Fax:* (202)663-5683

**• 590 •  AIMS Small Grants** *(Doctorate, Postdoctorate/Grant)*

**Purpose:** To enable North American scholars and students to conduct research in North Africa. **Focus:** African Studies, Islamic Studies, Middle Eastern Studies. **Qualif.:** Candidate must be an AIMS member and a citizen of the United States, Canada, or Mexico. Applicant must be a predoctoral student or a scholar with a Ph.D. affiliated with a North American university or college. Candidates from all disciplines with an interest in topics relevant to North Africa's past, present, or future are welcome. Applicant should be able to read and write in a language of the countries to be studied. Awards are tenable in North Africa: AIMS administers the Center for Maghrib Studies in Tunis and is associated with the Tangier American Legation Museum in Morocco; scholars may also conduct research in other North African countries through individual arrangements. **Criteria:** Candidate judged on quality of proposal.

**Funds Avail.:** $60,000. **No. of Awards:** 15. **To Apply:** Submit to the above address three copies of the following: a curriculum vitae, including language abilities and institutional affiliation; names of two referees; a 1,500-word research proposal; proposed itinerary with dates; proposed budget from all income sources; and a one-page summary written in French or Arabic. **Deadline:** March 1. Notification by April 1.

• 591 •

**American Institute of Mining, Metallurgical and Petroleum Engineers, Inc. - Woman's Auxiliary**
345 E. 47th St., 14th Fl.              *Ph:* (212)705-7695
New York, NY 10017-2396               *Fax:* (212)371-9622
*E-mail:* aime.ny@aol.com
*URL:* http://206.168.59.66/aime

**• 592 •  WAAIME Scholarship Loans** *(Graduate, Undergraduate/Scholarship loan)*

**Qualif.:** Applicants must be undergraduate students studying for a degree at an accredited United States engineering school in engineering science as applied to industries within the mineral field. These include mining, geology, metallurgy, petroleum, mineral science, materials science, mining economics and other related fields that further the interests of the mineral industry. Scholarship loans also are available for graduate students on the same terms as for undergraduates. These cannot be given to students who have also had an undergraduate grant from WAAIME unless that loan has been repaid. Graduate scholarship loans are limited to two years. **Criteria:** Each applicant is considered on an individual basis by a local Section Scholarship Loan Fund Chairman through personal interviews and research of academic standing, character, need, and personality, and then by the National Scholarship Loan Fund Committee. Preference is given to college juniors and seniors.

**Funds Avail.:** The amount of the scholarship loans is individually determined. Each recipient is expected to repay 50 percent of the monies loaned without interest. Repayment starts after graduation and is to be completed within six years. **To Apply:** Applications should not be sent before the interview. Applications must be accompanied by recent grade transcripts, supporting letters including the personal evaluation by the Section Scholarship Loan

Fund Chairman. **Deadline:** All application material must be in the hands of the Chairman of the National Scholarship Loan Fund Committee by March 15.

---

• 593 •

**American Institute of Nutrition**
9650 Rockville Pke.                    *Ph:* (301)530-7050
Bethesda, MD 20814                    *Fax:* (301)571-1892
*URL:* http://www.orge.ufl.edu/fyi/v23n02/fyi018.html

**• 594 •  AIN Predoctoral Fellowships** *(Graduate/Fellowship)*

**Focus:** Nutrition. **Qualif.:** Applicants must be enrolled in a graduate program of nutrition that is listed in the AIN Directory of Graduate Programs in Nutritional Sciences. **Criteria:** Selection is made by the AIN Graduate Nutrition Education Committee. The Committee will evaluate significance, feasibility, communication and clarity, as well as the overall scientific technical quality of the proposal.

**Funds Avail.:** $5,000. Fellowships are non-renewable. **No. of Awards:** 4. **To Apply:** Application forms are available from the AIN office. Forms must be accompanied by a summary of the research proposal not to exceed four single-spaced typewritten pages including objective, experimental approach, and selected references. **Deadline:** December 1. **Contact:** Dr. Richard G. Allison at the above address (see entry 593).

---

• 595 •

**American Institute of Pakistan Studies**
PO Box 7568
Wake Forest University               *Ph:* (336)758-5453
Winston-Salem, NC 27109              *Fax:* (336)758-6104
*E-mail:* ckennedy@wfu.edu
*URL:* http://www.vill.edu/academic/artsci/arts/pak/pak.htm

**• 596 •  American Institute of Pakistan Studies Predoctoral and Postdoctoral Fellowships** *(Doctorate, Postdoctorate/Fellowship)*

**Purpose:** To enhance scholarship on Pakistan by supporting research in that country. **Focus:** Pakistan, Asian Studies, Humanities, Social Sciences. **Qualif.:** Applicant must be a U.S. citizen who is either a predoctoral or postdoctoral scholar whose research would benefit from a trip to Pakistan. Fellowships are usually tenable at an institution in Pakistan. **Criteria:** Award based on the validity and strength of applicant's proposal.

**Funds Avail.:** Varies. **No. of Awards:** Approximately per year. **To Apply:** Write to the director for application form and guidelines. Submit form with a curriculum vitae, a research proposal, and names of three references. Predoctoral candidates also should supply graduate transcripts. **Deadline:** All materials should be in by February 1. Notification by April 30.

**Remarks:** An alternate phone number is (910)758-5449. **Contact:** Director, American Institute of Pakistan Studies, at the above address (see entry 595).

---

• 597 •
**American Jewish Archives**
3101 Clifton Ave.                    *Ph:* (513)221-7444
Cincinnati, OH 45220-2488           *Fax:* (513)221-7812
*E-mail:* AJA@fuse.net
*URL:* http://home.fuse.net/aja/

• 598 • **American Jewish Studies Fellowships**
*(Doctorate, Postdoctorate/Award, Fellowship)*

**Purpose:** To support doctoral and postdoctoral research or writing at the American Jewish Archives. **Focus:** Jewish Studies—Western Culture. **Qualif.:** Candidate may be of any nationality. Applicant must be a doctoral or postdoctoral scholar, and be conducting research that would benefit from the use of the Archives' collection.

**Funds Avail.:** Doctoral: $1,000; postdoctoral: $2,000. **To Apply:** Write for application guidelines; there is no official application form. Submit curriculum vitae, research proposal, and evidence of published research, where possible. Doctoral students must provide three faculty recommendations (including that of dissertation supervisor). Postdoctoral candidates must provide two recommendations from academic colleagues. **Deadline:** April 1. Notification by May 15.

**Remarks:** The Archives offer fellowship programs: the Marguerite R. Jacobs Memorial Fellow in American Jewish Studies; The Loewenstein-Weiner Fellowship Awards in American Jewish Studies; The Bernard and Audre Rapoport Fellowships in American Jewish Studies; The Rabbi Theodore S. Levy Tribute Fellowship in American Jewish Studies; The Rabbi Frederic A. Doppelt Memorial Fellowship in American Jewish Studies; and The Ethel Marcus Memorial Fellowship in American Jewish Studies. The information listed above is the same for each award. **Contact:** Administrative Director at the above address (see entry 597).

• 599 •
**American Jewish League for Israel**
130 E 59th St.                       *Ph:* (212)371-1583
New York, NY 10022-1301              *Fax:* (212)371-3265

• 600 • **American Jewish League for Israel University Scholarship Fund** *(Graduate, Undergraduate/ Scholarship)*

**Purpose:** To foster Jewish spiritual and cultural values. **Focus:** Jewish studies, Law, Medicine, and all Liberal Arts. **Qualif.:** Applicants must be high school graduates who have been accepted or are enrolled in an American college and all graduate and undergraduate students planning to spend one year of academic study, one year program in Israel. The scholarship is limited to students accepted for study in the following institutions in Israel: Bar Ilan University, Ben Gurion University of Negev, Haifa University, the Hebrew University of Jerusalem, Technion, Tel Aviv University, and the Weizmann Institute of Science. **Criteria:** Awards are granted based on merit and financial need.

**Funds Avail.:** Varies. **No. of Awards:** 5-6. **To Apply:** Write for further details. **Deadline:** May 1. **Contact:** Mrs. Judith Struhl, Executive Director.

• 601 •
**American Junior Brahman Association**
1313 La Concha Ln.                   *Ph:* (713)795-4444
Houston, TX 77054-1809               *Fax:* (713)795-4450
*E-mail:* tsmith@brahman.org
*URL:* http://www.abba.wt.net

• 602 • **Ladies of the ABBA American Junior Brahman Association Scholarships** *(Undergraduate/ Scholarship)*

**Purpose:** To further the careers of American Junior Brahman Association members in the field of agriculture. **Focus:** Agricultural Sciences. **Qualif.:** Candidates must be graduating high school seniors with at least a 2.0 grade point average who are active members of the American Junior Brahman Association. They must also be studying a field related to the agriculture/cattle industry.

**Funds Avail.:** One to four scholarships equaling up to $1,000. **To Apply:** Students must submit a scholarship questionnaire, which includes a brief essay section and questions concerning involvement in clubs and other organizations. Recommendations are also helpful. Applications must be requested in writing by the applicant. **Deadline:** April 30 of the year scholarship is awarded. **Contact:** Todd Smith, AJBA Youth Activities Department, at the above address (see entry 601).

• 603 •
**American Kennel Clubs**
260 Madison Ave.                     *Ph:* (212)696-8234
New York, NY 10016                   *Fax:* (212)696-8299
*E-mail:* jxc@akc.com
*URL:* http://www.dkis.dk/dogworld/akc.htm

• 604 • **American Kennel Clubs Veterinary Scholarship** *(Undergraduate/Scholarship)*

**Focus:** Veterinary medicine. **Qualif.:** Applicants must be students of accredited veterinary schools in the United States. **Criteria:** Awards are made based on academic achievement, financial need and involvement with purebred dogs.

**Funds Avail.:** $60,000 per year. **No. of Awards:** 20-30. **To Apply:** Write for further details. **Deadline:** May 1. **Contact:** James Crowley, secretary, at the above address (see entry 603).

• 605 •
**American Kidney Fund**
6110 Executive Blvd., Ste. 1010      *Ph:* (301)881-3052
Rockville, MD 20852-3915             *Fax:* (301)881-0898
                                     *Free:* 800-638-8299

• 606 • **American Kidney Fund Clinical Scientist in Nephrology** *(Postdoctorate/Fellowship)*

**Purpose:** To foster the development of a cadre of nephrology professionals whose expertise will lend understanding to the entire spectrum of concerns that surround patients with kidney disease. The goal of this program is to enhance the training of nephrologists who desire to pursue an academic career and whose primary professional commitments to scholarship in the provision of clinical care. It is the Fund's intent that this program ultimately will contribute to the overall improvement in the quality of care provided to patients with kidney disease, in the amount and quality of clinical research in Nephrology and all related fields, and in the academic recognition and professional standing of clinical

## American Kidney Fund (continued)

nephrologists among their peers. **Focus:** Clinical Nephrology. **Qualif.:** The program is open to anyone who is a citizen of the United States or who is a resident alien in the United States. Applicants must have completed a residency in internal medicine or pediatric medicine, and must be in the process of completing or have completed at least one year of training in clinical nephrology in an accredited program. Candidates should demonstrate aptitude for and a commitment to developing special expertise in an area of knowledge applicable to clinical nephrology, and intend to pursue a professional career with emphasis on the provision of care to patients with kidney disease, possibly within the confines of an academic medical center where they will be exposed to continued learning and teaching. Successful candidates will identify an area of knowledge broadly applicable to clinical nephrology, in which they will develop expertise and conduct research resulting in publication in a peer-reviewed journal. Such areas of study will be primarily in the non-biological sciences and will include disciplines in public health and preventive medicine, in the humanities, and in the social and behavioral sciences. It is expected that all recipients of the Fellowship will participate in a yearly meeting of the members of the AKF Board of Trustees during their one or two years of training as AKF Clinical Scientists, and that they will commit themselves to remain available to act as a resource of information in their own field of expertise for the AKF or other organizations dedicated to the improvement of care of patients with kidney disease. The training institution must operate an accredited training program in Nephrology. Successful sponsoring institutions will be those that have direct access to comprehensive clinical facilities, and where a well-developed scholarly environment exists. The Director of the Program must certify the candidate's credentials and capabilities and develop a program of studies. The clinical scientist must have continued exposure to the clinical practice of nephrology in a scholarly environment. This ongoing clinical exposure should take up at least half a day but not more than one day per week for the duration of the fellowship. A collaborative effort must be present with faculty members at the same or other institutions who can offer reasonable guarantees of availability and dedication to the training of the clinical scientists in their specific area of study. Assurance must be given that the appropriate supervision will be provided to maintain the quality of training, and that yearly progress reports detailing the Clinical Scientist's performance in the clinical and research areas will be submitted to the Quality Control Committee of the American Kidney Fund.

**Funds Avail.:** A fellowship may be granted yearly. The maximum duration of each fellowship is two years. The level of funding is a maximum of $50,000 per year. The sum will be expected to cover the individual Fellow's salary (which will be set to equal that of a fifth year postgraduate trainee at the same institution, but not to exceed $36,000 including benefits) and training-related expenses. These may include expenditures for enrollment in academic courses, computer hardware and software, and support for research, clerical, supplies, and travel expenses as required by the plan of studies and justified in the budget outlined in the application. The American Kidney Fund will not provide support for institutional overhead expenses and will not fund expenditures for technical or clerical personnel. **No. of Awards:** 1 per year. **To Apply:** Candidates must submit a completed application form and a statement of intent detailing the plan of studies, the area of research, and an overall career plan and expectations, a statement of support from the director of the division of nephrology, a statement from the preceptor that will supervise the training of the candidate in the chosen (non-nephrological) area of study, and the curricula vitae of all main parties involved in the plan of studies. Three additional letters of support are required, including one from the chairman of medicine or the program director of the residency program in internal medicine or pediatric medicine where the candidate trained. **Deadline:** Documents must reach the American Kidney Fund by December 1. The AKF Selection Committee reviews the applications and proceeds to a preliminary ranking in December. Finalists are interviewed in January and up to three successful candidates are notified by February 15. For those recipients who apply for a two-year fellowship, granting of a continuation fellowship for a second year of training, beginning on July 1, will depend on submission of evidence by April 30 that the plan of study is proceeding according to the goals outlined in the application and is consistent with the overall intent of the American Kidney Fund. **Contact:** Carol Lynn Halal, Director of Programs, at the above address (see entry 605).

---

• 607 •

## The American Legion
PO Box 2910
Bloomington, IL 61702
*E-mail:* webmasterillinoisegion.org
*URL:* http://www.illegion.org

• **608** • **American Legion Boy Scout Scholarships**
*(Undergraduate/Scholarship)*

**Focus:** General Studies. **Qualif.:** Candidates must be Illinois residents, graduating high school seniors, and qualified senior Boy Scouts or Explorers. **Criteria:** Applicants are judged on a 500-word essay on Legion's Americanism and Boy Scout programs.

**Funds Avail.:** One $1,000 award and four $200 awards are given. **No. of Awards:** 5. **Deadline:** April 30. **Contact:** Local Boy Scout office or Legion Boy Scout Chairman, Department Headquarters, at the above address (see entry 607).

• **609** • **American Legion Oratorical Contest**
*(Undergraduate/Award)*

**Focus:** General Studies. **Qualif.:** Applicants must be in the 9th, 10th, 11th, or 12th grade at an accredited high school in Illinois. **Criteria:** Applicants are judged on speeches.

**Funds Avail.:** First place: $1,600. Second place: $1,300. Third place: $1,200. Fourth place: $1,000. Fifth place: $1,000. For each division: Five $150 awards are given for second place. $100 for third place. $75 for fourth place. For each district: $125 for first palce. $100 for second place. $75 for third place. **To Apply:** Speech contests begin in January. Oratorical contest starts at the Post level and goes on to District, then to Division, Department, and National. **Contact:** Local American Legion post or department headquarters at the above address (see entry 607).

• **610** • **Americanism Essay Contest Scholarships**
*(High School/Award)*

**Focus:** General Studies. **Qualif.:** Candidates must be in 8th, 9th, 10th, 11th, or 12th grade at an accredited high school in Illinois. **Criteria:** Applicants are judged on a 500-word essay on a selected topic.

**Funds Avail.:** $50 to $75 depending on grade level. **To Apply:** Applicants must submit a 500-word essay on a selected topic. **Deadline:** February 12. **Contact:** Local American Legion unit, or American Legion Auxiliary at PO Box 1426, Bloomington, IL 61702.

• **611** • **Illinois American Legion Scholarships**
*(Undergraduate/Scholarship)*

**Focus:** General Studies. **Qualif.:** Applicants must be graduating high school seniors who are sons or daughters of an American Legion member in Illinois. **Criteria:** Awards are based on merit and financial need.

**Funds Avail.:** $1,000 each. **No. of Awards:** 20. **To Apply:** Applications are available September 15. **Deadline:** March 15. **Contact:** The American Legion Scholarship Program at the above address (see entry 607).

• 612 •

## American Legion - Arizona Auxiliary

4701 N. 19th Ave., Ste. 100     *Ph:* (602)241-1080
Phoenix, AZ 85015-3727     *Fax:* (602)264-0029

• 613 • **American Legion Auxiliary Past Presidents' Parley Nurses Scholarships** *(Undergraduate/ Scholarship)*

**Focus:** Nursing. **Qualif.:** Applicants must be in at least their second year as nursing students, have at least a C grade point average, be enrolled in accredited institutions in Arizona which award Registered Nursing degrees, be residents of Arizona for at least one year and citizens of the United States. **Criteria:** Awards are made based on character, financial need, scholarship and initiative. First consideration is given to former recipients continuing a degree program in nursing (R.N., B.A., M.A.).

**Funds Avail.:** $400 per award. **No. of Awards:** Varies. **To Apply:** Applicants must submit a photograph of self; transcripts of previous year's nursing grades; three letters of reference from persons who can testify to character, study and work habits; and a statement, in narrative form, not to exceed 500 words, giving family background, civic, social, school, and church activities, including reasons applicant feels qualified for the scholarship and why a nursing career is pursued. **Deadline:** May 15. **Contact:** Past Presidents' Parley Chairman.

• 614 • **Wilma Hoyal/Maxine Chilton Scholarships** *(Undergraduate/Scholarship)*

**Focus:** Political science, public programs, special education. **Qualif.:** Applicants must be residents of Arizona for at least one year who are enrolled as second year or upper division students at Arizona State University or Northern Arizona University, studying political science, public programs or special education, and carrying at least twelve hours with a grade average of B or better. Applicants must also be U.S. citizens. **Criteria:** Awards are granted based on scholarship, financial need, character, and leadership.

**Funds Avail.:** $400 per award. **No. of Awards:** Varies. **To Apply:** Applicants must submit three letters of reference from persons who can testify to character, aptitude, initiative, and need; transcripts of previous year's grades; resume of not more than 300 words giving family background, civic, social, school, and church activities, including statement of applicant's career goals. Preference given to honorably discharged veterans or immediate family members of veterans. **Deadline:** May 15. **Contact:** American Legion Auxiliary Department of Arizona at the above address (see entry 612).

• 615 •

## American Legion Auxiliary - Dept. of Florida

c/o Department Sec.
PO Box 547917
Orlando, FL 32854-7917     *Ph:* (407)293-7411
    *Fax:* (407)299-6522

• 616 • **American Legion Auxiliary Department Scholarship** *(Undergraduate/Scholarship)*

**Focus:** General studies. **Qualif.:** Applicants must be children of honorably discharged Veterans.

**Funds Avail.:** $1,000 maximum for four-year university grants; $500 maximum for technical-vocational school grants. **No. of Awards:** 15/-8. **To Apply:** Please write for further details. **Deadline:** January 1. **Contact:** American Legion Auxiliary at the above address (see entry 615).

• 617 • **American Legion Auxiliary Memorial Scholarship** *(Undergraduate/Scholarship)*

**Focus:** General studies. **Qualif.:** Applicants must be daughters and granddaughters of American Legion Auxiliary members in good standing for three years, who are Florida residents planning to attend a Florida university, college or technical school. Applicants must be sponsored by official action of a local American Legion Auxiliary unit in the state of Florida.

**Funds Avail.:** $1,000 maximum for four-year university grants; $500 maximum for technical-vocational school grants. **To Apply:** Write for further details. **Contact:** American Legion Auxiliary at the above address (see entry 615).

• 618 •

## American Legion, Department of Hawaii

c/o Department Headquarters
612 McCully St.     *Ph:* (808)946-6383
Honolulu, HI 96826-3935     *Fax:* (808)947-3957
*E-mail:* aldepthi@gte.net

• 619 • **National High School Oratorical Contest** *(High School/Prize)*

**Focus:** General studies. **Criteria:** Awards are based on merit of an oratorical presentation. **To Apply:** Write for further details. **Contact:** American Legion, Department of Hawaii at the above address (see entry 618).

• 620 •

## American Legion, Department of Ohio

c/o Department Scholarship
  Committee
4060 Indiaola Ave.
PO Box 14348     *Ph:* (614)268-7072
Columbus, OH 43214-3160     *Fax:* (614)268-3048

• 621 • **Ohio American Legion Scholarship** *(Undergraduate/Scholarship)*

**Focus:** General studies. **Qualif.:** Applicants must Legionnaires, direct descendants of Legionnaires, direct descendants of decease Legionnaires, and/or surviving spouses or children of deceased U.S. military persons who died on active duty or of injuries received on active duty.

**Funds Avail.:** Varies. **No. of Awards:** Varies. **To Apply:** Write for further details. **Deadline:** April 15. **Contact:** Donald R. Lanthorn.

• 622 •

## American Legion, Department of Texas

PO Box 789
Austin, TX 78767     *Ph:* (512)472-4138

• 623 • **National High School Oratorical Contest** *(High School/Scholarship)*

**Focus:** General studies. **Qualif.:** Applicants must be high school students who are residents of Texas. **Criteria:** Awards granted based on merit of presentation.

*American Legion, Department of Texas (continued)*

Funds Avail.: $250 to $1,000. Non-renewable. **No. of Awards:** 4. **To Apply:** Write for further details. **Deadline:** November 1. **Contact:** Department Oratorical Chairman.

---

**• 624 •**

## American Legion - Michigan Auxiliary
212 N. Verlinden St.
Lansing, MI 48915

### • 625 • American Legion Auxiliary Memorial Scholarship *(Undergraduate/Scholarship)*

**Focus:** General studies. **Qualif.:** Applicants must be daughters, granddaughters, and great-granddaughters of any honorably discharged or deceased men/women veterans of World War I, World War II, Korean Conflict, Vietnam Hostilities, Grenada and Lebanon Hostilities, Panama Hostilities, and Persian Gulf Conflict. Applicants must also be Michigan residents at the time of application and for one year preceding the date of the award, be enrolled in a university in the state of Michigan, and at least 16 years of age but not over 21. **Criteria:** Awards are granted based on scholastic standing.

**Funds Avail.:** $500 to be used for tuition and fees, room and board, books and supplies. **To Apply:** Applicants must submit a completed application and a copy of parent or guardian's income tax form (1040). **Deadline:** November 15. **Contact:** American Legion Auxiliary at the above address (see entry 624).

### • 626 • American Legion Auxiliary Nurses, Physical Therapists and Respiratory Therapists Scholarship *(Undergraduate/Scholarship)*

**Focus:** Nursing, physical therapy, respiratory therapy. **Qualif.:** Applicants must be daughters, granddaughters, great-granddaughters, sons, grandsons, great-grandsons, wives or widows of honorably discharged or deceased men or women veterans of World War I, World War II, Korean Conflict, Vietnam Hostilities, Grenada and Lebanon Hostilities, Panama Hostilities, and Persian Gulf. Applicants must also be in the top quarter of their class and residents of the State of Michigan. **Criteria:** Awards are granted based on financial need and academic achievement.

**Funds Avail.:** $500 to be used toward tuition, books and supplies, and room and board fees. Recipients who drop out during the year must repay the American Legion Auxiliary the unused portion of the scholarship. **To Apply:** Applicants must submit a completed application with grade transcript and a copy of veteran's discharge papers. **Deadline:** May 15. **Contact:** Chairman.

---

**• 627 •**

## American Legion - Minnesota Auxiliary
State Veterans Service Bldg.
St. Paul, MN 55155-4013                    *Ph:* (651)224-7634

### • 628 • American Legion Auxiliary Department of Minnesota Scholarships *(Undergraduate/Scholarship)*

**Focus:** General Studies. **Qualif.:** Candidates must have a parent or grandparent who served in the Armed Forces during one of the following time periods: April 6, 1917 to November 11, 1918; December 7, 1941 to December 31, 1946; June 25, 1950 to January 31, 1955; December 22, 1961 to May 7, 1975; August 24, 1982 to July 31, 1984; December 20, 1989 to January 31, 1990; August 2, 1990 to present. Candidates must also be Minnesota residents

who are high school seniors or graduates with at least a C average. Must attend institution of higher learning in Minnesota. **Criteria:** Selection is based on character, academic ambition, and financial need.

**Funds Avail.:** Scholarships of $750 are given each year. **No. of Awards:** 7. **To Apply:** Candidates must submit a completed application, letter from a school superintendent, principal or counselor regarding scholastic record, letter from a professional person, brief essay outlining educational and career goals, and a copy of high school grade transcripts. Applications must be submitted to the Unit President and forwarded to Department Headquarters. **Deadline:** March 5. **Contact:** American Legion Auxiliary at the above address (see entry 627).

---

**• 629 •**

## American Legion - National Headquarters
PO Box 7197                            *Ph:* (317)630-1323
Indianapolis, IN 46207-7197            *Fax:* (317)630-1369
                                       *Free:* 800-424-FLAG

*URL:* http://www.legion.org/

### • 630 • Eight and Forty Nurses Scholarships *(Graduate/Scholarship)*

**Purpose:** To support nurses seeking graduate training in lung and respiratory diseases. **Focus:** Pulmonary Nursing. **Qualif.:** Applicant must be a U.S. citizen and a registered nurse. Scholarships are tenable at accredited schools of nursing in the United States.

**Funds Avail.:** $2,500. **No. of Awards:** 20-22. **To Apply:** Write to the director for application guidelines, available after September 1. **Deadline:** May 15. **Contact:** Lee A. Hardy, Assistant Director, at the above address (see entry 629).

### • 631 • National High School Oratorical Contest *(High School/Award, Scholarship)*

**Purpose:** To develop a deeper knowledge and appreciation of the Constitution of the United States on the part of high school students. To promote the development of leadership qualities, the ability to think and speak clearly and intelligently, and the preparation for acceptance of the duties and responsibilities, and the rights and privileges of American citizenship. **Focus:** Government. **Qualif.:** Applicants must be citizens of the United States who are under the age of 20, and are bona fide students in a high school or junior high school that has a high-school level curriculum from grade nine through grade 12. The four finalists of the National Contest are ineligible to enter again. **Criteria:** Applicants are judged on: originality; freshness and directness of approach; application of knowledge on topic; skill in selecting examples; use of description, analogies, specific data, and logic; comprehensiveness of knowledge; voice and diction; style (language use, word arrangement transition, word selection); and body action (poise, eye contact, posture, gestures).

**Funds Avail.:** National Final scholarship awards are presented as follows: first place $18,000; 2nd place, $16,000; third place, $14,000; and fourth place, $12,000. Each Department (State) winner who is certified into the next (Regional) level of the national contest will receive a $1,500 scholarship. Each Regional winner who advances to the Sectional level but not to the National Finals will receive an additional $1,500 scholarship to pursue education beyond high school. The scholarships awarded by the National Organization of The American Legion to four finalists, to the Department winners, and to the Regional winners who are eliminated at the Sectional level of the competition may be used to attend any college or university in the United States. Funds for the scholarships awarded by the National Organization are provided by the American Legion Life Insurance Trust Fund. In addition, several hundred scholarships of varying amounts are also available through local organizations. **No. of Awards:** 54. **To Apply:** The contest starts early in the school year through local posts. Each contestant gives a prepared oration of between 8 and 10 minutes on a topic relating to the United States Constitution and an extemporaneous discourse of 3 to 5 minutes on an assigned topic. **Contact:** State Headquarters in the states of residence.

---

## • 632 •
### American Legion Press Club of New Jersey
68 Merrill Rd.
Clifton, NJ 07012          *Ph:* (201)473-5176

#### • 633 • Father Anthony J. O'Driscoll Memorial Scholarship Award *(Undergraduate/Scholarship)*

**Purpose:** To further studies in communication. **Focus:** Communications. **Qualif.:** Applicants must be New Jersey residents who are members of The Sons of The American Legion or graduates of American Legion Jersey boys state or auxiliary girls state, or Auxiliary Juniors, or children or grandchildren of members of The American Legion or the Auxiliary, or of deceased members of either group. Each candidate must be entering an accredited four-year college as a freshman and working toward a degree in communications.

**Funds Avail.:** $500 award. **No. of Awards:** 1. **To Apply:** An essay of not less than 500 words as to why candidate chose a communications major as well as proof of required qualifications must be submitted along with a completed application. Financial need and class standing information is not required. Send SASE with request for application. **Deadline:** July 15 of the year of graduation from high school. **Contact:** Jack W. Kuepfer, Scholarship Chairman, at the above address (see entry 632).

---

## • 634 •
### American Legion - Vermont Auxiliary
c/o Department Headquarters
PO Box 396
Montpelier, VT 05601-0396

#### • 635 • Past Presidents Parley Nursing Scholarship *(Undergraduate/Scholarship)*

**Focus:** Nursing. **Qualif.:** Applicants must be Vermont residents who are children, grandchildren or great-grandchildren of veterans and who are high school seniors planning to pursue study within the field of nursing.

**Funds Avail.:** $500. **To Apply:** Applicants must submit a completed application form. **Deadline:** April 10. **Contact:** American Legion at the above address (see entry 634).

---

## • 636 •
### American Legion - Washington Auxiliary
3600 Ruddell Rd., SE
PO Box 5867        *Ph:* (360)456-5995
Lacey, WA 98503-3801      *Fax:* (360)491-7442

#### • 637 • American Legion Auxiliary Department Gift Scholarships *(Undergraduate/Scholarship)*

**Focus:** General Studies. **Qualif.:** Candidates must be seniors or graduates of an accredited high school in the state of Washington, but they cannot have attended an institution of higher learning.

Applicants must also be the children of a deceased or incapacitated veteran. **Criteria:** Judging is based on character, leadership, scholastic achievement, financial need, and desire for education.

**Funds Avail.:** $300 scholarships are awarded annually. **No. of Awards:** 3. **To Apply:** Applications may be requested from your local American Legion Auxiliary. Each American Legion Auxiliary Unit may submit only one candidate. Candidates must complete the application form and provide a list of organizations to which the applicant belongs, three letters of recommendation, a 300-word essay on "My Desire to Further My Education," a certified transcript of grades, and a brief statement of the military service of the veteran parent through whom the applicant is eligible. All materials must be typed. **Deadline:** Application packets are due to the local American Legion Auxiliary Unit Education Chairman by March 15. **Contact:** The American Legion Auxiliary, Department of Washington, at the above address (see entry 636).

#### • 638 • Susan Burdett Scholarhips *(Undergraduate/Scholarship)*

**Focus:** General Studies. **Qualif.:** Candidates must be former citizens of Evergreen Girls State and residents of the state of Washington. **Criteria:** Selection is based on character, leadership, scholastic achievement, financial need, and an essay.

**Funds Avail.:** $500 is awarded annually and is renewable for another year upon reapplication. **No. of Awards:** 1. **To Apply:** Applications may be obtained from your local American Legion Auxiliary. Each American Legion Auxiliary Unit may submit only one candidate. Candidates must complete the application form and provide a list of organizations to which the applicant belongs, three letters of recommendation, a 500-word essay on "How I Benefited from Attending Evergreen Girls State," and a certified transcript of grades. All materials must be typed. **Deadline:** Application packets are due to the Unit Education Chairman by March 15. **Contact:** The American Legion Auxiliary, Department of Washington, at the above address (see entry 636).

#### • 639 • Florence Lemke Memorial Scholarships in Fine Arts *(Undergraduate/Scholarship)*

**Focus:** Art. **Qualif.:** Applicants must be from the state of Washington and be seniors or graduates of an accredited high school. They must also be children or grandchildren of a veteran. **Criteria:** Winners are selected based on character, leadership, scholastic achievement, financial need, and desire for education.

**Funds Avail.:** $600 scholarship is awarded annually. **No. of Awards:** 1. **To Apply:** Applications may be obtained from your local American Legion Auxiliary Unit. Each American Legion Auxiliary Unit may submit only one candidate. Candidates must complete the application form and provide a list of organizations to which the applicant belongs, three letters of recommendation, a 300-word essay detailing applicant's proposed course of study and educational goals in the field of Fine Arts, a certified transcript of grades, and a brief statement of the military service of the veteran parent through whom the applicant is eligible. All materials must be typed. **Deadline:** Application packets are due to the Unit Education Chairman by March 15. Unit winners must submit applications to the Department Chairman by April 1. **Contact:** The American Legion Auxiliary, Department of Washington, at the above address (see entry 636).

#### • 640 • Marguerite Mc Alpin Memorial Scholarships *(Graduate, Undergraduate/Scholarship)*

**Focus:** Nursing. **Qualif.:** Applicants must be residents of the state of Washington and must be graduate or undergraduate students who are studying and/or training in the field of nursing. They must also children or grandchildren of a veteran or have served in the armed forces. **Criteria:** Selection is based on character (as determined by letters of reference), statement expressing desire for education, scholastic history, resume, and financial need.

---

## American Legion - Washington Auxiliary (continued)

**Funds Avail.:** $800 is given annually. **No. of Awards:** 1. **To Apply:** Applications may be obtained from your local American Legion Auxiliary Unit. Each American Legion Auxiliary Unit may submit only one candidate. Candidates must complete the application form and provide a list of organizations to which the applicant belongs, three letters of recommendation, a 300-word essay on their desire to study nursing, a certified transcript of grades, and a brief statement of the military service of the veteran parent through whom the applicant is eligible. All materials must be typed. **Deadline:** Application packets are due to the Unit Education Chairman by March 15. **Contact:** The American Legion Auxiliary, Department of Washington, at the above address (see entry 636).

## • 641 •
## American Library Association - American Association of School Libraries

| | |
|---|---|
| 50 E. Huron St. | *Ph:* (312)280-4383 |
| Chicago, IL 60611-2795 | *Fax:* (312)664-7459 |
| | *Free:* 800-545-2433 |

*E-mail:* dcatten@ala.org
*URL:* http://www.ala.org/aasl/

### • 642 • AASL/Highsmith Research Grant (Other/Grant)

**Purpose:** To conduct innovative research aimed at measuring and evaluating the impact of school library media programs on learning and education. **Focus:** Library media. **Qualif.:** Applicants must be library media specialists, library educators, or library information science or education professors who are also AASL personal members. **Criteria:** Based on the projects potential to measure and/or evaluate the impact of school library media programs on learning and education; originality; potential for replication; ability of applicant(s) to undertake and successfully complete the project; evidence that sufficient time and resources have been allocated; support and commitment by institutions and organizations; clarity and completeness of the proposal; and applicants personal resume. Special attention is given to pilot research studies that employ experimental methodologies.

**Funds Avail.:** Up to $2500 for individuals. Up to $5000 for a joint or group project. **No. of Awards:** Varies, at least one is awarded each year. **To Apply:** 10 copies of the application and all attachments must be submitted. Attachments consist of a application narrative of no more than 2 typewritten pages including the statement of the problem goals and objectives of the project, planned activities, and possibilities for dissemination and a budget of no more than 1 typewritten page including salaries and wages, consultant services, travel for work on the project, supplies and materials, space and equipment rental, computer services, and dissemination costs. **Deadline:** February 1.

**Remarks:** Awardees are expected to present the project results at the ALA Annual Conference the year following the year of the grant. They also are expected to publish a summary in the *School Library Media Research* and/or *Knowledge Quest*.

### • 643 • ABC-CLIO Leadership Grant (Other/Grant)

**Purpose:** For planning and implementing leadership programs at the state, regional, or local levels. **Focus:** Library media. **Qualif.:** Applicants must be school library media associations that are AASL affiliates. **Criteria:** Based on clarity of program objectives; nature and importance of desired leadership qualities; intended group participation; plan of action (including a calendar); budget; validity of evaluation plan and appropriate follow-up activities; program merit for replication by other affiliates.

**Funds Avail.:** Up to $1750 of each grant. **To Apply:** 10 copies of the application must be submitted. **Deadline:** February 1.

**Remarks:** Donated by ABC-CLIO.

### • 644 • Frances Henne Award (Professional Development/Award)

**Purpose:** To enable one school library media specialist to attend the ALA Annual Conference. **Focus:** Library and Information Science. **Qualif.:** Applicants must be current members in good standing of the ALA and the AASL Division and be employed as school library media specialists at the building level with one to five years experience as school library media specialists. Applicants should not have attended a previous ALA Conference nor a national AASL Conference. They must have demonstrated leadership qualities in working with students, teachers, and administrators.

**Funds Avail.:** A grant of $1,250 will be given to the recipient. **No. of Awards:** 1. **To Apply:** Seven copies of the completed application and supporting statement must be submitted to the AASL Office. **Deadline:** Applications and all support data must be received by February 1; the winner is notified by April 15.

**Remarks:** The award is made possible by an annual gift from the R.R. Bowker Company. **Contact:** Darlene Cattenhead at the above address (see entry 641).

### • 645 • Information Plus Continuing Education Scholarship (Professional Development/Scholarship)

**Purpose:** To provide financial assistance for the continuing education and professional development of a school library media specialist, supervisor, or educator. **Focus:** Library and Information Science. **Qualif.:** Applicants must have current personal memberships in the ALA and the AASL Division, and must hold positions as full-time school library media specialists at the building or district level, or as full-time faculty members in a program for educating school library media specialists.

**Funds Avail.:** A $500 grant to enable an AASL member to attend an ALA or AASL pre/post conference or an ALA- or AASL-sponsored regional workshop. **No. of Awards:** 1. **To Apply:** Seven copies of the completed application as well as certification that the applicant is receiving no other financial support for the pre/post conference workshop attendance must be submitted. **Deadline:** Applications must be received by February 1; the winner is notified by April 15.

**Remarks:** The scholarship is made possible through a donation from Information Plus. **Contact:** Darlene Cattenhead at the above address (see entry 641).

### • 646 • School Librarian's Workshop Scholarship (Graduate/Scholarship)

**Purpose:** To encourage students who have demonstrated an interest in working with children or young adults in a school library media program. **Focus:** Librarianship, Information Science, School Library Media. **Qualif.:** Applicant must be a student entering a ALA-accredited master's program of library education.

**Funds Avail.:** $2,500. **No. of Awards:** 1. **To Apply:** Write to the AASL at the above address for application form and guidelines. **Deadline:** February 1.

**Remarks:** The Scholarship is co-sponsored by the Library Learning Resources Company. **Contact:** Darlene Cattenhead at the above address (see entry 641).

**• 647 •**
## American Library Association - Association for Library Service to Children
50 E. Huron St.
Chicago, IL 60611-2729

*Ph:* (312)280-2163
*Fax:* (312)280-3257
*Free:* 800-545-2433

*URL:* http://www.ala.org/alsc

### • 648 • Bound to Stay Bound Books Scholarships *(Graduate/Scholarship)*

**Purpose:** To encourage advanced degree study in the field of library service to children. **Focus:** Library and Archival Sciences. **Qualif.:** Applicant must be a U.S. citizen. Applicant must be planning to work in the field of library service to children. The scholarships may be used for study toward the M.L.S. degree or other graduate work at an ALA-accredited library school.

**Funds Avail.:** $5,000 is available. **To Apply:** Write for the ALA handbook, which lists all awards available, application form and guidelines. For application form, send postcard to: ALSC Bound to Stay Bound, 50 E. Huron, Chicago, IL 60611. **Deadline:** Application must be received by March 1.

**Remarks:** More than 100 awards-many in the form of cash, scholarships, and research grants—are sponsored by the ALA and its units to honor distinguished service and foster professional growth. The deadline for most awards is December 1. Write the ALA for further details and application guidelines. **Contact:** Susan Roman, Staff Liaison, at the above address (see entry 647).

### • 649 • Frederic G. Melcher Scholarships *(Graduate/Scholarship)*

**Purpose:** To encourage advanced degree study in the field of library service to children. **Focus:** Library and Archival Sciences. **Qualif.:** Applicant must reside in the U.S. or Canada. Applicant must be planning to work in the field of library service to children for at least two years upon graduation. The scholarships may be used for study toward the M.L.S. degree or other graduate work at an ALA-accredited library school.

**Funds Avail.:** $5,000; Melcher: $5,000 is available. **To Apply:** Write for the ALA handbook, which lists all awards available, application form and guidelines. For application form, send a postcard to ALSC Melcher Scholarship, 50 E. Huron, Chicago, IL 60611. **Deadline:** Application must be received by March 1.

**Remarks:** More than 100 awards-many in the form of cash, scholarships, and research grants—are sponsored by the ALA and its units to honor distinguished service and foster professional growth. The deadline for most awards is December 1. Write the ALA for further details and application guidelines. **Contact:** Susan Roman, Staff Liaison, at the above address (see entry 647).

### • 650 • Putnam & Grosset Group Award *(Professional Development/Award)*

**Purpose:** To enable recipients to attend the ALA Annual Conference for the first time. **Qualif.:** Applicants must be children's librarians in schools or public libraries with ten or fewer years of experience. They must also be members of the ALSC.

**Funds Avail.:** $600 is available. **No. of Awards:** 4 awards are available. **To Apply:** For application, send a postcard to Putnam and Grosset Award - ALSC, 50 E. Huron St., Chicago, IL 60611. **Deadline:** Applications must be in by December 1.

**Remarks:** Funding provided by Putnam & Grosset Group. **Contact:** ALA at the above address (see entry 647).

**• 651 •**
## American Library Association - International Relations Committee
50 E. Huron St.
Chicago, IL 60611-2729

*Ph:* (312)280-3200
*Fax:* (312)944-3897
*Free:* 800-545-2433

*E-mail:* U58539@UICVM.EDU
*URL:* http://www.ala.org

*The American Library Association is a private, nongovernmental, educational organization. Founded in 1876, it is the oldest and largest library association in the world with more than 55,000 members representing all types of libraries.*

### • 652 • ALA/USIA Library Fellows *(Professional Development/Fellowship)*

**Purpose:** To place library professionals in institutions overseas. The program's purposes are to increase international understanding through the establishment of professional and personal relationships and the accomplishment of mutual goals, to promote the sharing of resources and to increase access to U.S. materials, and to enable librarians to enrich and broaden their career experiences through a short period of overseas service. **Focus:** Library and Archival Sciences. **Qualif.:** Fellows must be U.S. citizens for positions outside the United States at the time of application (status as a permanent resident is not sufficient). Applicants must have education and experience in library or information science or in other fields directly related to the interests and needs of specific projects, with demonstrated competency as required. A command of the language of the host country is desired for all applicants and may be required for some specific assignments. Persons who have lived abroad for a ten-year continuous period immediately preceding application are not eligible. Good physical and mental health, the ability to adapt to new situations, and a breadth of interests are needed. Certification of good health may be required. A previous Library Fellow may apply for a second time if three years have elapsed between projects. **Criteria:** Applications undergo a three-stage review process. Initially, the applications are sorted and reviewed to eliminate those who do not meet minimum qualifications. A screening committee representing a cross-section of librarians then determines the candidates to be interviewed. An interview committee conducts in-depth interviews. Final selection is made by the ALA. Needs of the host institutions abroad and other factors, such as a candidate's health or the extent and recency of previous experience abroad, are considered in all stages of the selection process. Selection is made without regard to age, gender, race, ethnic origin, or religion. To the extent program requirements and selection standards permit, fellows are chosen to represent a broad geographic distribution by home state and institution. Other factors equal, preference is given to veterans. In some cases, in-country residence at the time of application may reduce the chances for selection for a project in that country. Preference will be given to persons who have not already been Library Fellows.

**Funds Avail.:** Stipends are $34,000 per year. The grant provides for international and in-country travel as required, and medical insurance. The grant also provides for one dependent's round-trip transport to the assigned country. **No. of Awards:** 8 to 10 U.S. fellows are sent abroad each year. **To Apply:** After host institutions' proposals are reviewed and ranked, the ALA announces the positions available to U.S. librarians in late December or early January. References and endorsements from the applicant's current and previous employers and schools will be required and considered. **Deadline:** For U.S. librarians, applications must be submitted by March 15. The screening committee determines candidates to be interviewed by April 1; interviews take place in late April. In most cases, fellows begin overseas assignments by September. For non-U.S. librarians, applications are due to the U.S. embassy by October 1.

**Remarks:** The program is funded by the U.S. Information Agency and is administered by the American Library Association. The

*American Library Association - International Relations Committee (continued)*

United States Information Agency, an independent agency within the executive branch, is responsible for the U.S. government's overseas cultural and information programs, including the Voice of America and the Fulbright scholarship program. **Contact:** Robert P. Doyle, Director, Library Fellows Program, American Library Association, (800)545-2433.

## • 653 • Bogle International Library Travel Fund
*(Professional Development/Grant)*

**Purpose:** To encourage librarians to attend their first international library conferences. **Focus:** Library and Archival Sciences. **Qualif.:** Applicants must be members of the ALA who plan to attend an international library conference for the first time.

**Funds Avail.:** $500. **No. of Awards:** 2. **To Apply:** Write to the ALA at the above address for application form and guidelines. **Deadline:** December 1.

**Remarks:** More than 100 awards, many in the forms of cash prizes, scholarships, and research grants, are sponsored by the ALA and its units to honor distinguished service and foster professional growth. The deadline for most awards is December 1. Write the ALA for further details and application guidelines. **Contact:** Can also be reached at 800-545-2433 (inside the U.S.) Robert P. Doyle, Director, at the above address (see entry 651).

## • 654 •
## American Library Association New Members Round Table
50 E. Huron St.                          *Ph:* (312)944-6780
Chicago, IL 60611-2729                   *Fax:* (312)280-3257
                                          *Free:* 800-545-2433

*URL:* http://www.ala.org

## • 655 • 3M/NMRT Professional Development Grant
*(Professional Development/Grant)*

**Purpose:** To encourage professional development and participation by new librarians in national ALA and NMRT activities. **Qualif.:** Recipients must be current members of the ALA and the New Members Round Table. Eligible applicants may apply more than once and may have attended previous ALA conferences.

**Funds Avail.:** Cash awards are presented to librarians to attend an annual conference of the ALA. **Deadline:** November 15. **Contact:** Heleni Marques Pedersoli, 3259 McKeldin Library, Univ. of Maryland, College Park, MD 20742, or Peggy Barber, ALA Liaison, American Library Association, at the above address (see entry 654).

## • 656 • NMRT EBSCO Scholarship *(Graduate/Scholarship)*

**Qualif.:** Applicants must enroll at a library school accredited by the ALA in a formal program of library education leading to a master's degree. Candidates must be U.S. or Canadian citizens and members of the ALA and NMRT or must join prior to acceptance of the award.

**Funds Avail.:** $1,000. **Deadline:** December 15.

**Remarks:** The scholarship is made possible through the support of EBSCO Subscription Services. **Contact:** Angela Jones, Univ. of South Mississippi, McCain Library and Archives, S. Sta. Box 5148, Hattiesburg, MS 39406-5148, or Peggy Barber, ALA Liaison, American Library Association, at the above address (see entry 654).

## • 657 • Shirley Olofson Memorial Award
*(Professional Development/Grant)*

**Purpose:** To allow individuals to attend their second annual conference of the ALA. **Qualif.:** Recipients must be members of the ALA and be potential or current members of the New Members Round Table.

**Funds Avail.:** Up to $500. **Deadline:** November 15. **Contact:** Richard C. Dickey, Ref. Dept., Willis Library, Univ. of North Texas, PO Box 5188, Denton, TX 76203-5188, or Peggy Barber, ALA Liaison, American Library Association, at the above address (see entry 654).

## • 658 •
## American Library Association - Office for Research
50 E. Huron St.                          *Ph:* (312)280-4273
Chicago, IL 60611                        *Fax:* (312)280-3256
                                          *Free:* 800-545-2433

*E-mail:* mary.j.lynch@ala.org
*URL:* http://www.ala.org

## • 659 • Carroll Preston Baber Research Grants
*(Graduate/Grant)*

**Purpose:** For innovative research that could lead to an improvement in library services to any specified group(s) of people. **Focus:** Library and Archival Sciences. **Qualif.:** Applicants must be ALA members. The project should have the potential to serve as a model for the library community and the researchers should provide documentation of the results of their work. **Criteria:** Projects that involve a practicing librarian are given special consideration. Preference is also given to those proposals that pay special attention to the uses of technology and efforts involving cooperation between libraries and other agencies, or librarians and persons in other disciplines. Selection is based on potential to improve library services to specific groups of users; innovative quality and/or use of technology in a new way; originality of research question and strategy; potential to address pressing library service needs which are national in scope; cooperative nature of project; potential for replication; demonstrated ability of applicants to undertake and successfully complete the project; evidence that sufficient time and resources have been allocated to the effort; institutional commitment to the project; and clarity and completeness of the proposal.

**Funds Avail.:** $7,500 and a citation. **No. of Awards:** 1. **To Apply:** Applicants must send six copies of their proposals, complete cover sheets, and updated resumes. **Deadline:** December.

**Remarks:** Funding provided by Eric R. Baber. **Contact:** American Library Association, Office for Research, at the above address (see entry 658).

## • 660 •
## American Library Association - Scholarship Juries
50 E. Huron St.                          *Ph:* (312)440-0901
Chicago, IL 60611                        *Fax:* (312)280-3256
                                          *Free:* 800-545-2433

*URL:* http://www.ala.org

## • 661 • Bound-to-Stay-Bound Books Scholarship
*(Graduate/Scholarship)*

**Focus:** Librarianship. **Qualif.:** Recipients are expected to work directly with children in any type of library for at least one year following completion of education program. U.S. or Canadian citizens pursuing a master's or advanced degree in a school offering an ALA-accredited program are eligible. **Criteria:** Based on academic excellence and leadership qualities.

**Funds Avail.:** $5,000. **To Apply:** Applications are available from the Association for Library Service to Children, ALA, at the above address or telephone (312)280-2165. **Deadline:** March 1. **Contact:** Association for Library Service to Children, ALA at the above address (see entry 660).

• 662 • David H. Clift Scholarship *(Graduate/Scholarship)*

**Purpose:** To permit worthy students to begin an MLS degree at an ALA-accredited program. **Focus:** Librarianship. **Qualif.:** Applicants must be United States or Canadian citizens or permanent residents who have not completed more than twelve semester hours toward a master's degree in library science the June prior to the award year. **Criteria:** Academic excellence, leadership qualities, and evidence of a commitment to a career in librarianship.

**Funds Avail.:** $3,000. **Deadline:** January. **Contact:** Staff Liaison, ALA Scholarship Juries, at the above address (see entry 660).

• 663 • EBSCO/NMRT Scholarship *(Graduate/Scholarship)*

**Focus:** Librarianship. **Qualif.:** Applicants must be ALA/New Members Round Table members at the time of receiving the award. They must also be U.S. or Canadian citizens entering an ALA-accredited program leading to a master's degree. **Criteria:** Based on academic credentials, financial need, and professional goals.

**Funds Avail.:** $1,000. **To Apply:** Applications are available by calling NMRT staff liaison at 1-800545-2433. **Deadline:** December 1. **Contact:** Write to the address above or call 1-800-545-2433.

• 664 • Louise Giles Minority Scholarship *(Graduate/Scholarship)*

**Purpose:** To permit a worthy minority student to begin an MLS degree at an ALA-accredited program. **Focus:** Librarianship. **Qualif.:** Applicants must be members of a minority group, and must be United States or Canadian citizens who have not completed more than twelve semester hours toward a masters degree in library science prior to June of the award year. **Criteria:** Academic excellence, leadership qualities, and commitment to a career in librarianship.

**Funds Avail.:** $3,000. **Deadline:** January. **Contact:** Staff Liaison, ALA Scholarship Juries, at the above address (see entry 660).

• 665 • LITA/GEAC-CLSI Scholarship *(Graduate/Scholarship)*

**Focus:** Librarianship. **Qualif.:** Applicants must be entering an ALA-accredited master's degree program with an emphasis on library automation. **Criteria:** Based on academic excellence, leadership, evidence of a commitment to a career in library automation and information technology, and prior activity and experience in those fields.

**Funds Avail.:** $2,500. **To Apply:** Applications are available from the Library and Information Technology Association of the ALA at the above address. **Deadline:** April 1. **Contact:** ALA at the above address (see entry 660)or telephone (312)280-4270.

• 666 • LITA/LSSI Minority Scholarship; LITA/OCLC Minority Scholarship *(Graduate/Scholarship)*

**Focus:** Librarianship. **Qualif.:** Applicants must be U.S. or Canadian citizens who are members of any principal minority group (African American, American Indian, Alaskan Native, Asian or Pacific Islander, or Hispanic). Recipients must enter an ALA-accredited master's degree program, with an emphasis on library automation. **Criteria:** Based on academic excellence, leadership, evidence of a

commitment to a career in library automation and information technology, and prior activity and experience in those fields.

**Funds Avail.:** $2,500 each. **To Apply:** Applications are available from the Library and Information Technology Association of the ALA at the above address. **Deadline:** April 1. **Contact:** ALA at the above address (see entry 660)or telephone (312)280-4270.

• 667 • Frederic G. Melcher Scholarship *(Graduate/Scholarship)*

**Focus:** Librarianship. **Qualif.:** U.S. and Canadian citizens entering ALA-accredited master's degree programs are eligible. **Criteria:** Based on academic excellence, leadership qualities, and desire to work with children in any type of library. Upon graduation, recipients are expected to work in library service to children for at least one year.

**Funds Avail.:** $5,000. **To Apply:** Applications are available from the Association for Library Services to Children, ALA, at the above address. **Deadline:** March 1. **Contact:** ALA at the above address (see entry 660)or telephone (312)280-2165.

• 668 • David Rozkuszka Scholarship (Godort) *(Graduate/Scholarship)*

**Focus:** Librarianship. **Qualif.:** Applicants must currently work in a library specifically with government documents. They must be accepted into an ALA-accredited master's degree program, display evidence of commitment to government documents librarianship.

**Funds Avail.:** $3,000. **To Apply:** Applications are available from Jan Swanbeck, George A. Smathers Libraries, University of Florida, Gainesville, FL 326-2048; telephone (904)392-0366. **Deadline:** December 1. **Contact:** The address listed above.

• 669 • School Librarian's Workshop Scholarship *(Graduate/Scholarship)*

**Focus:** Librarianship. **Qualif.:** Applicants must plan to enter full-time in an ALA-accredited master's degree program or a school library media program that meets the ALA curriculum guidelines for an NCATE-accredited unit. **Criteria:** Based on demonstrated interest in working with children or young adults in a school library media program in either a public or private educational setting; academic excellence; and leadership potential.

**Funds Avail.:** $2,500. **To Apply:** Applications are available from the American Association of School Librarians at ALA at the above address. **Deadline:** February 1. **Contact:** ALA at the above address (see entry 660)or telephone (312)280-4381.

---

• 670 •
**American Library Trustee Association**
50 E. Huron St.                          Ph: (312)280-2161
Chicago, IL 60611-2729                   Fax: (312)280-3257
                                         Free: 800-545-2433

*E-mail:* alta@ala.org
*URL:* http://www.ala.org/alta

• 671 • ALTA/Gale Outstanding Trustee Conference Grant *(Professional Development/Grant)*

**Purpose:** To enable recipients to attend the ALA Annual Conference for the first time. **Focus:** Library and Archival Sciences. **Qualif.:** Applicants must be ALTA members who are also members of a public library board.

**Funds Avail.:** $750. **No. of Awards:** 2. **Deadline:** December 1.

**Remarks:** Funding provided by The Gale Group. **Contact:** Kerry Ward, Deputy Director, at the above address (see entry 670).

## • 672 •
**American Liver Foundation**
1425 Pompton Ave.  Ph: (201)256-2550
Cedar Grove, NJ 07009-1000  Fax: (201)256-3214
 Free: 800-223-0179
*URL:* http://cait.cpmc.columbia.edu/dept/ps/memos/awards/
awrd0025/html

### • 673 • American Liver Foundation Postdoctoral Supplementary Fellowships *(Postdoctorate/Fellowship)*

**Focus:** Medical Research, Hepatology. **Qualif.:** Candidates must be M.D.s or Ph.D.s pursuing research related to problems in liver physiology or disease.

**Funds Avail.:** A supplementary award of $7,500. **To Apply:** Applicants must submit ten copies of all application requirements and indicate the name and address of their sponsors, the medical school or hospital of the sponsor, their previous education and research experience, and the length of time that will be spent on the research project. Candidates must also submit a protocol of no more than two typewritten pages. It should include the aims of the research, the methods of procedure, the rationale of investigation, the importance of the study, an estimate provided by the sponsor as to what portion of the study the candidate will be able to accomplish during the period of the fellowship, the facilities and equipment available for the study, and the role of the candidate in the study. All publications resulting from research performed during the Fellowship must acknowledge Foundation support. **Deadline:** December 15. **Contact:** Alan P. Brownstein, CEO, at the above address (see entry 672).

### • 674 • American Liver Foundation Student Research Fellowships *(Doctorate, Graduate, Other/Fellowship)*

**Focus:** Medical Research, Hepatology, Veterinary Science, Medicine. **Qualif.:** Candidates may be medical, premedical, non-terminal Ph.D. or veterinary students who are in full-time research for a period of 10 to 12 weeks under the supervision of a preceptor in hepatic physiology or disease. Candidates must pursue research related to a problem in liver physiology or disease.

**Funds Avail.:** Fellowships of $2,500. **To Apply:** Applicants must submit ten copies of all application requirements and indicate the name and address of their sponsors and the medical school or hospital of the sponsor, their previous education and research experience, and the length of time that will be spent on the research project. Candidates must also submit a protocol that is no more than two typewritten pages. It should include the aims of the research, the methods of procedure, the rationale of investigation, the importance of the study, an estimate provided by the sponsor as to what portion of the study the candidate will be able to accomplish during the period of the fellowship, the facilities and equipment available for the study, and the role of the candidate in the study. All publications resulting from research performed during the Fellowship must acknowledge Foundation support. **Deadline:** The deadline for receipt of all requirements is December 15. **Contact:** Alan P. Brownstein, CEO, at the above address (see entry 672).

### • 675 • Liver Scholar Awards *(Postdoctorate/Grant)*

**Focus:** Medical Research, Hepatology. **Qualif.:** Candidates must be at the junior faculty level and pursuing research related to a problem in liver physiology or disease.

**Funds Avail.:** $30,000 per year. **To Apply:** Applicants must submit ten copies of all required materials and indicate the name and address and the medical school or hospital of their sponsors, their previous education and research experience, and the length of time that will be spent on the research project. Candidates must also submit a protocol of no more than two typewritten pages. It should include the aims of the research, the methods of procedure,

the rationale of investigation, the importance of the study, an estimate provided by the sponsor as to what portion of the study the candidate will be able to accomplish during the period of the award, the facilities and equipment available for the study, and the role of the candidate in the study. All publications resulting from research performed during the period of the award must acknowledge Foundation support. **Deadline:** February 1. **Contact:** Alan P. Brownstein, CEO, at the above address (see entry 672).

## • 676 •
**American Lung Association - Medical Affairs Div.**
1740 Broadway  Ph: (212)315-8793
New York, NY 10019-4374  Fax: (212)315-6498
*URL:* http://www.lungusa.org/homepage.html

### • 677 • ALA Career Investigator Awards *(Postdoctorate/Award)*

**Purpose:** Provides salary and/or project suport for investigators making the transition from junior to mid-level faculty. Designed to support physician investigators, but applications will be accepted from other scientists. **Focus:** Pulmonary Medicine.

**Funds Avail.:** $35,000 for the first year and may be renewed for an additional two years, depending on the availability of funds. **Deadline:** October 1.

### • 678 • ALA Research Grants *(Postdoctorate/Grant)*

**Purpose:** Provides starter or seed money to new investigators working on problems relevant to lung disease. **Focus:** Physiological, epidemiological or other types of studies directly related to patient care, health services, research or bioethics. **Qualif.:** Applicants must be individuals who have completed at least two years of research training and are at the instructor or assistant professor level.

**Funds Avail.:** $25,000 maximum the first year and may be renewed for an additional year, depending on availability of funds. **Deadline:** November 1.

### • 679 • Behavioral Science Dissertation Grants (Cancelled) *(Doctorate/Grant)*

**Purpose:** To support training in a field of behavioral science related to lung health. **Focus:** Pulmonary Medicine. **Qualif.:** Candidate must be a U.S. or Canadian citizen or a U.S. permanent resident enrolled in a doctoral program at a U.S. institution. Noncitizens must have a permit to stay or work in the United States. Candidate's dissertation must be in a field related to the social, behavioral, epidemiologic or educational aspects of lung health. Grantee may not simultaneously hold another national ALA award. Award funds may not be used for institution overhead or equipment, payment of dues, purchase of textbooks or periodicals, or payment for secretarial support. There are also restrictions on the amount of funds expendable for travel and publication costs.

**Funds Avail.:** $21,000/year ($16,000 stipend and $5,000 for research project). Award payments are issued semiannually. **To Apply:** Write for application form and guidelines, available in July. **Deadline:** October 1. **Contact:** Director of Medical Affairs at the above address (see entry 676).

### • 680 • Dalsemer Research Scholar Award *(Postdoctorate/Award)*

**Purpose:** To support research in interstitial lung disease. **Focus:** Interstitial Lung Disease. **Qualif.:** Applicants must be physicians who have completed graduate training in pulmonary disease and are beginning a faculty track at a school of medicine.

**Funds Avail.:** $25,000 maximum for the first year, for research and salary support and may be renewed for an additional year, depending on the availability of funds. **Deadline:** November 1. Notification in March.

### • 681 • Nursing Research Training Award (Cancelled) *(Doctorate/Award)*

**Purpose:** To encourage professional nurses to undertake doctoral studies in fields of scientific investigation in order to promote greater clinical research in respiratory care by nurses. **Focus:** Pulmonary Nursing. **Qualif.:** Applicant must be a U.S. or Canadian citizen, or hold a U.S. permanent visa. Applicant must be a licensed professional nurse holding a master's degree who is matriculated in a full-time doctoral program leading to a Ph.D, D.N.Sc., or Sc.D. degree with a focus on respiratory physiology, epidemiological or behavioral science physiology, epidemiology or behavioral science. Sponsorship is required from a recognized authority in the applicant's field of study and possess the necessary laboratory and training resources. Candidate must be accepted for full-time study in a doctoral program at a U.S. institution at the time of application. Applicant must have a program sponsor and a dissertation topic directly applicable to the conquest of lung disease and/or the promotion of lung health. Preference is given to applicants who plan to pursue academic careers. No other fellowship may be held concurrently with the award.

**Funds Avail.:** $11,000 maximum. **To Apply:** Write to the Medical Affairs Division for application form and guidelines. Specify the type of application and quantity needed; state whether national or local support is sought. National applications should be submitted directly to the national office, local applications to the local associations. **Deadline:** October 1. Notification in March. **Contact:** Director of Medical Affairs at the above address (see entry 676).

### • 682 • Pediatric Pulmonary Research Training Fellowships (Cancelled) *(Postdoctorate/Fellowship)*

**Purpose:** To stimulate the training of academic pulmonary physicians in the field of pediatrics. **Focus:** Pulmonary Medicine. **Qualif.:** Applicant must be a U.S. or Canadian citizen, or hold a U.S. permanent visa. Applicant should be a doctor of medicine or osteopathy who has completed a residency in pediatrics. Preference is given to applicants who plan to pursue academic careers. Sponsorship is required from an established investigator within the applicant's field of research and possess the necessary laboratory and training resources. Awards are normally limited to training in U.S. institutions. Under unusual circumstances, an award for study abroad may be granted if the appointment will provide a unique experience not available in the United States or Canada. Although one-third of the fellowship training time may be devoted to clinical activities, the major emphasis should be on research training. No other award may be held concurrently, nor may the fellow engage in private practice of medicine during the award.

**Funds Avail.:** $32,500 for each of two years. **To Apply:** Write to the Medical Affairs Division for application form and guidelines. Specify the type of application and quantity needed; state whether national or local support is sought. National applications should be submitted directly to the national office, local applications to the local associations. **Deadline:** October 1. Notification in March. **Contact:** Director of Medical Affairs at the above address (see entry 676).

### • 683 • Research Training Fellowships *(Postdoctorate/Fellowship)*

**Purpose:** To stimulate the training of teachers and scientific investigators in the field of lung biology. **Focus:** Pulmonary Medicine. **Qualif.:** Applicant must be a U.S. or Canadian citizen, or hold a U.S. permanent visa. Applicant must be a doctor of medicine or osteopathy who has completed residency in Internal Medicine, Pediatrics, Thoracic Surgery or other specialties relevant to lung disease. Candidates with other doctoral degrees must be interested in further training as a scientific investigator in fields relevant to the prevention and control of lung disease. Preference is given to applicants who plan to pursue academic careers. Sponsorship is required from a recognized authority in applicant's field of research and possess the necessary laboratory and training resources. Applicant is expected to have obtained an appointment, effective at the starting time of the award, at a U.S. university, medical center, or hospital for training under a qualified teacher or investigator. Under unusual circumstances, an award for study abroad may be granted if the appointment will provide a unique experience not available in the United States or Canada. No other award may be held concurrently, nor may the fellow engage in private practice of medicine during the award.

**Funds Avail.:** $32,500 a year for two years. Award payments are issued semiannually. **To Apply:** Write to the Medical Affairs Division for application form and guidelines. Specify the type of application and quantity needed; state whether national or local support is sought. National applications should be submitted directly to the national office, local applications to the local associations. **Deadline:** October 1. Notification in March. **Contact:** Director of Medical Affairs at the above address (see entry 676).

### • 684 • Edward Livingston Trudeau Scholar Awards (Cancelled) *(Postdoctorate/Award)*

**Purpose:** To give promising young physicians in schools of medicine or osteopathy an opportunity to stay in academic medicine and to prove themselves as teachers and investigators in fields relevant to the conquest of lung disease and promotion of lung health. **Focus:** Pulmonary Medicine. **Qualif.:** Applicant must be a U.S. or Canadian citizen. Applicant must have an M.D. or D.O. degree and should have completed formal training in the study of lung disease. Applicant must be assured of a faculty appointment in a U.S. or Canadian school of medicine or osteopathy during the award year, and the home institution must agree to supplement the award in order to demonstrate its continued interest in the candidate's academic career. Scholars are expected to be devoted full-time to teaching and research. Scholars should have some responsibility for organizing and correlating the instruction in lung disease in their department. No other award may be held concurrently, nor may the scholar engage in private practice of medicine during the award.

**Funds Avail.:** $25,000. **To Apply:** Write to the Medical Affairs Division for the current application forms and guidelines. Specify the type of application and quantity needed; applications must clearly state whether national or local support is sought. National applications should be submitted directly to the national office, local applications to the local associations. **Deadline:** October 1. Notification in March. **Contact:** Director of Medical Affairs at the above address (see entry 676).

### • 685 •
### American Mathematical Society
PO Box 6248
Providence, RI 02940-6248

Ph: (401)455-4000
Fax: (401)331-3842
Free: 800-321-4267

E-mail: ams@ams.org
URL: http://www.ams.org

### • 686 • Centennial Research Fellowships *(Postdoctorate/Fellowship)*

**Purpose:** To provide enhanced opportunities for research to outstanding mathematicians to help further their careers in research. **Focus:** Mathematics. **Qualif.:** Applicants must be citizens or permanent residents of a North American nation who have held their doctoral degree for at least two years at the time of the

## American Mathematical Society (continued)

award, have not had permanent tenure, and have held less than two years of research support at the time of the award.

**Funds Avail.:** $37,000 stipend, plus $1,500 expense allowance. **To Apply:** Available upon request from AMS. Must be submitted to the chair of the Fellowship Committee at the address listed on the application form. **Deadline:** December 1. Fellowships are announced in February.

---

## • 687 •
## American Medical Association - Education and Research Foundation

515 N. State St.        *Ph:* (312)464-4470
Chicago, IL 60610-4325      *Fax:* (312)464-5839

### • 688 • Morris Fishbein Fellowship in Medical Journalism *(Graduate, Postgraduate/Fellowship)*

**Purpose:** To provide physicians with training in medical editing. **Focus:** Medical Editing. **Qualif.:** Applicants must hold a medical degree and have proven their writing ability prior to the beginning of the Fellowship. Fellows will be required to learn and put into practice all the skills necessary in publishing The Journal of the American Medical Association, including copy editing, page layout, manuscript selection, research, etc.

**Funds Avail.:** $40,000. **To Apply:** Write to the Deputy Editor, for application form and guidelines, or see the announcement in the fall issues of AMA. **Deadline:** January 15. Announcement in March. **Contact:** Richard M. Glass M.D. Deputy Editor, JAMA, at the above address (see entry 687).

### • 689 • Jerry L. Pettis Memorial Scholarship *(Doctorate, Postdoctorate/Scholarship)*

**Focus:** Medical Communication. **Qualif.:** The award is for a junior or senior medical student with a demonstrated interest in the communication of science. Financial need is not a consideration. **Criteria:** Candidates are selected from nominees proposed by the deans of AMA-approved medical schools. Each school may propose one student.

**Funds Avail.:** $2,500. **No. of Awards:** One. **To Apply:** The following materials should be submitted: letter of nomination from the office of the dean; letter and curriculum vitae from the student; letter from the director of the library, Audio-Visual unit, or other appropriate person professional interested in communications; and reprints or other materials prepared by the student to support the nomination. **Deadline:** All documentation should be submitted by January 28.

**Remarks:** The scholarship is in honor of Jerry L. Pettis, a deceased Congressman from California, and a founder of the Audio-Digest Foundation. **Contact:** Rita M. Palulonis at the above address (see entry 687).

### • 690 • Rock Sleyster Memorial Scholarship *(Postdoctorate/Scholarship)*

**Focus:** Psychiatry Medicine. **Qualif.:** Applicants must be United States citizens who are third-year medical students enrolled in accredited American or Canadian medical schools planning to specialize in psychiatry.

**Funds Avail.:** $2,500. **To Apply:** Each medical school in the United States or Canada is invited to submit one to three nominations in accordance with the size of the third year class. Application papers should include: application form, letter from the medical school dean outlining the basis of the nomination, letter from the student outlining career goals in the field of psychiatry, letter from a member of the psychiatry department of the medical school

supporting the nomination, AMA-ERF Student's Financial Statement to be completed by the medical school's financial aid office, and medical school transcript. **Deadline:** Nominations must be submitted by May 1; recipients are announced by September 1.

**Remarks:** This memorial scholarship is from a bequest in honor of Rock Sleyster, former president of the AMA. **Contact:** Harry S. Jonas, M.D., Director, Division of Undergraduate Medical Education, (312)464-4657, at the above address (see entry 687).

### • 691 • Arthur N. Wilson, M.D. Scholarship *(Doctorate, Graduate/Scholarship)*

**Focus:** Medicine. **Qualif.:** Applicants must be qualified medical students who are graduates of a high school in southeast Alaska.

**Funds Avail.:** The scholarship is for $3,000 for one year. Recipients may apply in subsequent years of their medical education. **To Apply:** The following materials should be submitted to AMA-ERF: application and CV from the student; school transcript from the high school in southeast Alaska; and three letters of recommendation from the president of one of the local societies in Ketchikan, Juneau, or Sitka, Alaska. **Deadline:** Materials should be forwarded to the Foundation by January 28.

**Remarks:** The grant is funded by a bequest from the late Arthur N. Wilson, M.D., who practiced in Southeast Alaska, and gifts from his wife. **Contact:** Rita M. Paululonis at the above address (see entry 687).

---

## • 692 •
## American Medical Record Association

919 N Michigan Ave., Ste. 1400
Chicago, IL 60611       *Ph:* (312)787-2672

### • 693 • Foundation of Research and Education (FORE) of AHIMA Graduate Scholarship *(Graduate/Scholarship)*

**Focus:** Health information management, health information technology. **Qualif.:** Applicants must be members of AHIMA with minimum cumulative grade point averages of 2.5 on a 4.0 scale who are credentialed HIM professionals (RRA, ART, or CCS) and hold bachelor's degree. Applicants must be enrolled in a college or university accredited by a nationally recognized accrediting agency, and be pursuing, at a minimum, a master's degree in a program related to HIM.

**Funds Avail.:** $1,000 - $5,000. **To Apply:** Write for further details. **Deadline:** May 31, June 30. **Contact:** Foundation of Research and Education at the above address (see entry 692).

### • 694 • Foundation of Research and Education (FORE) of AHIMA Undergraduate Scholarship *(Undergraduate/Scholarship)*

**Focus:** Health information management, health information technology. **Qualif.:** Applicants must be AHIMA members with cumulative grade point averages of 2.5 or higher on a 4.0 scale, and be accepted for admission to a health information management (HIM) or technology (HIT) program accredited by the Commission on Accreditation of Allied Health Education Programs, or applicants must be accepted for admission to AHIMA's Independent Study Program and have successfully completed three individual models.

**Funds Avail.:** $1,000-$5,000 per award. **To Apply:** Write for further details. **Deadline:** May 31. **Contact:** Foundation of Research and Education at the above address (see entry 692).

## • 695 • Foundation of Research and Education
**Loan** *(Graduate, Undergraduate/Loan)*

**Focus:** Health information management, health information technology. **Qualif.:** Applicants must be AHIMA members with minimum cumulative grade point averages of 2.5 on a 4.0 scale, be accepted or enrolled in a program for HIM or HIT approved by the Commission on Accreditation of Allied Health Education Programs. Graduate applicants must be enrolled in a credentialed HIM professional (RRA, ART, or CCS), hold a bachelor's degree and be pursuing a master's degree in an HIM-related field, or be enrolled in a coding specialist program affiliated with a regionally accredited college or university. All applicants must be U.S. citizens.

**Funds Avail.:** $1,000 $5,000. **To Apply:** Write for further details. **Deadline:** June 30. **Contact:** Foundation of Research and Education at the above address (see entry 692).

## • 696 •
## American Medical Technologists
710 Higgins Rd.
Park Ridge, IL 60068-5765        *Ph:* (708)823-5169
*URL:* http://www.careers.com/A/0069.html

### • 697 • American Medical Technologists
**Scholarships** *(Undergraduate/Scholarship)*

**Focus:** Medical Technology, Medical Assisting, Dental Assisting. **Qualif.:** Applicants must be high schools seniors or graduates in good standing who are planning to attend a college, university, or school accredited by the Accrediting Bureau of Health Education Schools or a regionally accredited university or college in the United States. They must be enrolled in a medical technology, medical assisting, or dental assisting program.

**Funds Avail.:** $250. Winners must furnish proof of enrollment and good standing. **To Apply:** Applicants must submit completed application with transcript of grades an essay on their career choice, and two letters of personal reference. Applications are available by writing to the above address. Requests should be accompanied by a legal-size, self-addressed, stamped envelope. **Deadline:** April 1. Winners are determined at the Annual Convention of the American Medical Technologists each summer and notified thereafter. **Contact:** Linda Kujbida, American Medical Technologists, at the above address (see entry 696).

## • 698 •
## American Medical Women's Association, Inc. - National Office
801 N. Fairfax, Ste. 400        *Ph:* (703)838-0500
Alexandria, VA 22314        *Fax:* (703)549-3864
*E-mail:* mglanz@amwa-doc.org
*URL:* http://www.amwa-doc.org

### • 699 • AMWA Medical Education Loans *(Doctorate/ Loan)*

**Purpose:** To provide financial assistance to women attending medical school. **Focus:** Medicine. **Qualif.:** Applicants must be women who are enrolled in accredited U.S. medical or osteopathic medicine schools, U.S. citizens or permanent residents, and Student Life members of national AMWA. **Criteria:** Based on financial need.

**Funds Avail.:** Loans of $2,000 or $2,500 per student per year. Student can receive a maximum of $5,000 during medical school. Payment on the principal commences the January 15 after graduation. Interest at 10 percent begins December 15 after graduation. Payment is to be completed within a three-year period. **No. of Awards:** 50 to 60. **To Apply:** Formal application must be filed. **Deadline:** April 30. **Contact:** Marie Glanz, Special Programs Director, at the above address (see entry 698).

## • 700 •
## American Meteorological Society
45 Beacon St.        *Ph:* (617)227-2425
Boston, MA 02108-3693        *Fax:* (617)642-8718
*E-mail:* armstrong@ametsoc.org
*URL:* http://www.ametsoc.org/AMS

### • 701 • AMS/Industry Government Graduate
**Fellowships** *(Graduate/Fellowship)*

**Purpose:** To encourage first year graduate students to pursue advanced degrees in the meteorological, oceanic, and hydrologic fields. **Qualif.:** Applicants must be entering their first year of graduate study by the time the Fellowship is awarded and be pursuing advanced degrees in the atmospheric and related oceanic and hydrologic sciences. Candidates currently studying chemistry, computer sciences, engineering, environmental sciences, mathematics, and physics who intend to pursue careers in the atmospheric or related oceanic or hydrologic sciences are also encouraged to apply.

**Funds Avail.:** Eleven non-renewable Fellowships of $15,000 each. **To Apply:** Applicants must submit an official application, an official transcript, GRE scores, and three written references from faculty or others familiar with the applicant's academic work. **Deadline:** The application request deadline is January 15; the application due deadline is January 30. The winner is notified April 30.

### • 702 • AMS/Industry Minority Scholarships
*(Undergraduate/Scholarship)*

**Purpose:** To provide funding for minority students who have been traditionally underrepresented in the sciences especially Hispanic, Native American, and Black students. **Focus:** Atmospheric or related oceanic and hydrologic sciences. **Qualif.:** Applicants must be minority, high school students planning to pursue a career in one of the required areas of study.

**Funds Avail.:** $3000 per year. R 2 years.

### • 703 • AMS/Industry Undergraduate Scholarship
*(Undergraduate/Scholarship)*

**Purpose:** To encourage outstanding undergraduate students to pursue careers in the atmospheric and related oceanic and hydrologic sciences. **Qualif.:** Applicants must be in sophomore standing at the time of the application and must be either enrolled or planning to enroll in a course of study leading to a bachelor's degree in the atmospheric or related oceanic and hydrologic sciences, or enrolled in a program leading to a bachelor's degree in science or engineering and have demonstrated a clear intent to pursue a career in the atmospheric or related oceanic and hydrologic sciences following completion of appropriate specialized education at the graduate level. Clear intent must be demonstrated by a presentation of a proposed program of study for the junior and senior years designed to prepare the student's plans by one or more faculty members familiar with the student's objectives. Applicants must also be citizens or permanent residents of the United States who have successfully completed two years of study at an accredited institution with a grade point average of at least 3.0 on a scale of 4.0. There is no age limit.

**Funds Avail.:** The awards are $2,000 non-renewable scholarships. **No. of Awards:** 13 awards are available. **To Apply:** Applicants must submit an official application form, an official transcript, and three

## American Meteorological Society (continued)

references from faculty or others that are familiar with the candidates studies. **Deadline:** The application request deadline is February 3; the application due deadline is February 17. The winner is notified May 5.

### • 704 • AMS Undergraduate Scholarship
*(Undergraduate/Scholarship)*

**Focus:** Atmospheric or related oceanic or hydrologic sciences. **Qualif.:** Applicants must be entering their final year of undergraduate study in one of the required areas of study, have a cumulative GPA of 3.0 on a 4.0 scale, and plan to pursue a career in atmospheric or related science.

**Funds Avail.:** Varies. **No. of Awards:** Varies.

### • 705 • Howard H. Hanks, Jr. Scholarship in Meteorology *(Undergraduate/Scholarship)*

**Purpose:** To encourage outstanding undergraduate students to pursue careers in the atmospheric and related oceanic and hydrologic sciences. **Qualif.:** Applicants must be in junior standing at the time of the application must be enrolled full time in an accredited United States institution, and must have a cumulative grade point average of at least 3.0 on a scale of 4.0. **Criteria:** Scholarship selection is based on financial need.

**Funds Avail.:** One $700 non-renewable scholarship. **To Apply:** Applicants must submit an official application form that includes a statement, in fewer than 500 words, of the candidate's future goals and aspirations; a letter of recommendation from the chairman or another designated faculty member of the major department, reflecting the department faculty's overall view; and an official transcript showing all coursework completed through June 1. **Deadline:** The application request deadline is June 1; the application due deadline is June 15. The winner is notified in October. **Contact:** Stephanie Kehoe, Fellowship/Scholarship Coordinator, at the above address (see entry 700).

### • 706 • Paul H. Kutschenreuter Scholarship
*(Undergraduate/Scholarship)*

**Purpose:** To encourage outstanding undergraduate students to pursue careers in the atmospheric and related oceanic and hydrologic sciences. **Qualif.:** Applicants must be in junior standing at the time of the application. They must be citizens or permanent residents of the United States. There are no age limits. **Criteria:** Scholarship selection is based on financial need.

**Funds Avail.:** One $5,000 non-renewable scholarship. **To Apply:** Applicants must submit an official application form that includes a statement, in fewer than 500 words, of the candidate's future goals and aspirations; a letter of recommendation from the chairman or another designated faculty member of the major department, reflecting the department faculty's overall view; and an official transcript showing all course work completed through June 1. **Deadline:** The application request deadline is June 1; the application due deadline is June 15. The winner is notified in October. **Contact:** Stephanie Kehoe, Fellowship/Scholarship Coordinator, at the above address (see entry 700).

### • 707 • Father James B. Macelwane Annual Awards
*(Undergraduate/Award)*

**Purpose:** To stimulate interest in meteorology among college students through the encouragement of original student papers concerned with some phase of the atmospheric sciences. **Qualif.:** Applicants must be undergraduates at the time the paper is written, and no more than two students from any one institution may enter papers in any one contest. Candidates must be citizens or permanent residents of the United States. There is no age restriction.

**Funds Avail.:** Three non-renewable awards: first place is $300; second place is $200; and third place is $100. **To Apply:** The paper with a letter of application from the author, and a letter from the department head or other faculty member of the major department, confirming that the author was an undergraduate student at the time the paper was written and indicating the elements of the paper that represent the original contributions by the student. **Deadline:** The application request deadline is June 1; the application due deadline is June 15. The winner is notified in October.

### • 708 • Howard T. Orville Scholarship in Meteorology *(Undergraduate/Scholarship)*

**Purpose:** To encourage outstanding undergraduate students to pursue careers in the atmospheric and related oceanic and hydrologic sciences. **Qualif.:** Applicants must be in junior standing at the time of the application enrolled full time in an accredited United States institution, and have a cumulative grade point average of at least 3.0 on a scale of 4.0. **Criteria:** Scholarship selection is based on academic excellence.

**Funds Avail.:** Award is a $2,000 non-renewable scholarship. **No. of Awards:** 1 award is offered. **To Apply:** Applicants must submit an official application form that includes a statement, in fewer than 500 words, of the candidate's future goals and aspirations; a letter of recommendation from the chairman or another designated faculty member of the major department, reflecting the department faculty's overall view; and an official transcript showing all coursework completed through June 1. **Deadline:** The application request deadline is June 1; the application due deadline is June 15. The winner is notified in October. **Contact:** Stephanie Kehoe, Fellowship/Scholarship Coordinator, at the above address (see entry 700).

### • 709 •
## American Montessori Society
281 Park Ave. S, 6th Fl.      *Ph:* (212)358-1250
New York, NY 10011      *Fax:* (212)358-1256
*E-mail:* montessori@internetsite.com
*URL:* http://www.seattleu.edu/~jcm/montessori/arms_ helping.html

### • 710 • American Montessori Society Scholarship Fund *(Graduate, Postgraduate/Scholarship)*

**Purpose:** To financially support aspiring Montessori teachers accepted into American Montessori Society (AMS) teacher education programs. **Focus:** Early Childhood Education. **Qualif.:** Applicants must have been accepted into an AMS-affiliated program, but not yet enrolled. Teacher education opportunities include programs for children from birth to three, three to six, six to nine, or six to 12, and 12 to 15 years of age. **Criteria:** Financial need and ability to express oneself in writing.

**Funds Avail.:** Varies. **No. of Awards:** Varies. **To Apply:** Applications are available from course directors, AMS office, or fund administrator. The following are required: a financial statement, three general recommendations and one from the course director, and a personal statement. **Deadline:** May 1. **Contact:** AMS at the above address (see entry 709).

• **711** •

## American Museum of Natural History
Office of Grants and Fellowships
Central Park West at 79th St.
New York, NY 10024-5192          *Ph:* (212)769-5467
*E-mail:* grants.and.fellowship@amnh.org
*URL:* http://www.research.amhn.org/grants/index.html

• **712** • **American Museum of Natural History Collection Study Grants** *(Doctorate, Postdoctorate/ Grant)*

**Purpose:** To enable investigators to study any of the scientific collections at the Museum. **Focus:** Anthropology, Invertebrate Zoology, Mineral Sciences, Paleozoology, Vertebrate Zoology. **Qualif.:** Candidates may be of any nationality but must be predoctoral or recent postdoctoral investigators who wish to use the Museum collections. The visit must be arranged through and approved by the appropriate scientific department of the Museum. Only one Collection Study Grant will be awarded to an individual. They are not available to investigators residing within daily commuting distance of the Museum.

**Funds Avail.:** $1000 maximum, including partial travel and subsistence support. **No. of Awards:** 50. **To Apply:** First, contact the appropriate scientific department of the Museum to discuss the feasibility of the proposed visit. Approval by the department chairman is required. Request the special Collection Study Grants application form from the Office of Grants and Fellowships. Submit form with a project description including a brief statement of the purpose and scope of research, its significance, collections to be studied, facilities needed, and the names of Museum staff members who have been consulted. Submit application at least two months prior to the intended date of the visit. **Deadline:** None. Decisions will be made within two months of submission. **Contact:** Diane Bynum, Administrator, at the above address.

• **713** • **American Museum of Natural History Research and Museum Fellowships** *(Postdoctorate/ Fellowship)*

**Purpose:** To provide support to investigators, scientists, and other scholars whose research would benefit from use of the Museum's resources. **Focus:** Anthropology, Astronomy, Invertebrate Zoology, Mineral Sciences, Museum Studies, Paleontology, Paleozoology, Vertebrate Zoology. **Qualif.:** Candidates may be of any nationality but must be postdoctoral researchers or established scholars with the equivalent of a doctorate in experience, training, and accomplishment. Project must fit into the above areas of study. Fellows are expected to be in residence at the Museum or one of its field stations.

**Funds Avail.:** $28,000, including limited relocation, research, and publication support. **To Apply:** Write for a special Research-Museum Fellowship application form. Submit with a project description, budget, curriculum vitae, bibliography, and letters of recommendation. **Deadline:** January 15. Notification by April 1. **Contact:** Diane Bynum, Administrator, at the above address (see entry 711).

• **714** • **Frank M. Chapman Memorial Fellowships and Grants** *(Doctorate, Postdoctorate/Fellowship, Grant)*

**Purpose:** To support and foster research in neontological and paleontological ornithology. **Focus:** Neontological and Paleontological Ornithology. **Qualif.:** Candidate may be of any nationality but usually should be advanced predoctoral or postdoctoral researchers, but there are no formal educational requirements. Museum awards are mutually exclusive. Candidates will not receive support from more than one fund for the same project during the same grant year.

**Funds Avail.:** Write for an application form and guidelines. Submit form with proposal description, budget, and two letters of recommendation. $200-2,000; $700 average. **Deadline:** January 15. Awards are announced in early April. **Contact:** Administrator at the above address (see entry 711).

• **715** • **Lerner-Gray Grants** *(Postdoctorate/Grant)*

**Purpose:** To assist individuals beginning a marine zoology career. **Focus:** Marine Zoology. **Qualif.:** Candidates may be of any nationality but must be highly qualified researchers starting a career in marine zoology. Support is limited to projects dealing with systematics, evolution, ecology, and field-oriented behavioral studies of marine animals. Awards are not made to support research in botany and biochemistry. Museum grants are mutually exclusive. Candidates will not receive support from more than one fund for the same project during the same grant year.

**Funds Avail.:** $200-2,000; $700 average. **To Apply:** Write for application form and guidelines. Submit form with proposal description, budget, and two letters of recommendation. **Deadline:** March 15. Awards are announced in mid-May. **Contact:** Diane Bynum, Administrator, at the above address (see entry 711).

• **716** • **Theodore Roosevelt Memorial Grants** *(Doctorate, Graduate, Postdoctorate/Grant)*

**Purpose:** To provide financial assistance to individuals for research on North American fauna. **Focus:** North American Fauna and related disciplines. **Qualif.:** Candidates may be of any nationality but must be qualified students or scientists whose research on North American fauna relates to the wildlife conservation or natural history activities of the Museum. Museum grants are mutually exclusive; candidates will not receive support from more than one fund for the same project during the same grant year.

**Funds Avail.:** $200-2,000; $700 average. **To Apply:** Write for application form and guidelines. Submit form with two letters of recommendation, a budget, and a description of the proposed investigation. **Deadline:** February 15. Notification by April 15. **Contact:** Diane Bynum, Administrator, at the above address (see entry 711).

• **717** •

## American Music Center
30 W. 26th St., Ste. 1001          *Ph:* (212)366-5260
New York, NY 10010-2011          *Fax:* (212)366-5265
*E-mail:* center@amc.net
*URL:* http://www.amc.net

• **718** • **Margaret Fairbank Jory Copying Assistance Program** *(Professional Development/Award)*

**Purpose:** To assist composers with the costs of copying parts for the premiere performance of one of their works. **Focus:** Music Composition. **Qualif.:** Applicant must be a U.S. citizen or permanent resident. There are no stylistic restrictions on the nature of the composition, except that work must be for four or more players. Candidate must have a written commitment for at least one public performance of the submitted composition by a professional ensemble in the United States or abroad. Funds are available for copying fees and/or the purchase of music notation computer software/hardware.

**Funds Avail.:** $750 average. **To Apply:** Contact the Center for application form and guidelines. Submit application form with professional resume, the complete score for which support is requested, a written estimate from the copyist of the cost of extracting and reproducing parts, and a letter of commitment from the performing ensemble. **Deadline:** February 1, May 1, October 1. Notification around April 1, July 1, or December 1. **Contact:** Grants Manager at the above address (see entry 717).

• 719 •
**American Nuclear Society**
555 N. Kensington Ave.                    *Ph:* (708)352-6611
La Grange, IL 60526                       *Fax:* (708)352-0499
*URL:* http://neutrino.nuc.berkeley.edu/ans/old.ANS.html

### • 720 • ANS Environmental Sciences Division Scholarship *(Undergraduate/Scholarship)*

**Focus:** Nuclear Science, Nuclear Engineering. **Qualif.:** Applicants must be undergraduate students at an accredited institution in the United States who have completed two or more years in a course of study leading to a degree in nuclear science or nuclear engineering. They must be U.S. citizens or possess permanent resident visas.

**Funds Avail.:** Varies. **To Apply:** Transcript, application form and 3 reference letters must be submitted. **Deadline:** March 1. **Contact:** Scholarship Program, American Nuclear Society, at the above address (see entry 719). Send a self-addressed, stamped envelope.

### • 721 • ANS Fuel Cycle and Waste Management Scholarship *(Undergraduate/Scholarship)*

**Focus:** Nuclear Science, Nuclear Engineering. **Qualif.:** Applicants must be undergraduate students at an accredited institution in the United States who have completed two or more years in a course of study leading to a degree in nuclear science or nuclear engineering. They must be U.S. citizens or possess permanent resident visas.

**Funds Avail.:** Varies. **To Apply:** Transcript, application form and three reference letters must be submitted. **Deadline:** March 1. **Contact:** Scholarship Program, American Nuclear Society, at the above address (see entry 719). Send a self-addressed, stamped envelope.

### • 722 • ANS Graduate Scholarships *(Graduate/Scholarship)*

**Focus:** Nuclear Science, Nuclear Engineering. **Qualif.:** Candidates must be graduate students at an accredited institution in the United States who are enrolled full-time in a program leading to an advanced degree in nuclear science or nuclear engineering, and must be sponsored by an ANS Local Section, Division, Student Branch, Committee, Member, or Organization Member. They must be U.S. citizens or possess permanent resident visas.

**Funds Avail.:** Varies. **No. of Awards:** 7. **To Apply:** Transcript, application form and three reference letters must be submitted. **Deadline:** March 1. **Contact:** Scholarship Program, American Nuclear Society, at the above address (see entry 719). Send a self-addressed, stamped envelope.

### • 723 • ANS Nuclear Operations Division Scholarship *(Undergraduate/Scholarship)*

**Focus:** Nuclear Science, Nuclear Engineering. **Qualif.:** Applicants must be undergraduate students at an accredited institution in the United States who have completed two or more years in a course of study leading to a degree in nuclear science or nuclear engineering. They must be U.S. citizens or possess permanent resident visas.

**Funds Avail.:** Varies. **To Apply:** Transcript, application form and three reference letters must be submitted. **Deadline:** March 1. **Contact:** Scholarship Program, American Nuclear Society, at the above address (see entry 719). Send a self-addressed, stamped envelope.

### • 724 • ANS Power Division Scholarship *(Undergraduate/Scholarship)*

**Focus:** Nuclear Science, Nuclear Engineering. **Qualif.:** Applicants must be undergraduate students at an accredited institution in the United States who have completed two or more years in a course of study leading to a degree in nuclear science or nuclear engineering. They must be a U.S. citizens or possess permanent resident visas.

**Funds Avail.:** Varies. **To Apply:** Transcript and application form must be submitted. **Deadline:** March 1. **Contact:** Scholarship Program, American Nuclear Society, at the above address (see entry 719). Send a self-addressed, stamped envelope.

### • 725 • ANS Undergraduate Scholarships *(Undergraduate/Scholarship)*

**Focus:** Nuclear Science, Nuclear Engineering. **Qualif.:** Candidates must be undergraduate students at an accredited institution in the United States who have completed one year in a course of study leading to a degree in nuclear science, or nuclear engineering. They must be U.S. citizens or possess permanent resident visas.

**Funds Avail.:** Varies. **No. of Awards:** 4 for sophomores and 11 for students who will be entering as juniors or seniors. **To Apply:** Transcript, application form and three reference letters must be submitted. **Deadline:** March 1. **Contact:** Scholarship Program, American Nuclear Society, at the above address (see entry 719). Send a self-addressed, stamped envelope.

### • 726 • Robert A. Dannels Scholarships *(Graduate/Scholarship)*

**Focus:** Nuclear Science, Nuclear Engineering. **Qualif.:** Applicants must be a graduate students in an accredited institution in the United States who are enrolled full-time in a program leading to an advanced degree in nuclear science or nuclear engineering. They must be U.S. citizens or possess permanent resident visas. **Criteria:** Nominations of handicapped persons is encouraged.

**Funds Avail.:** Varies. **No. of Awards:** 1. **To Apply:** Transcript, application form and three reference letters must be submitted. **Deadline:** March 1. **Contact:** Scholarship Program, American Nuclear Society, at the above address (see entry 719). Send a self-addressed, stamped envelope.

### • 727 • Verne R. Dapp Scholarship *(Graduate/Scholarship)*

**Qualif.:** Applicants must be graduate students in an accredited institution in the United States who are enrolled full-time in a program leading to an advanced degree in nuclear science or nuclear engineering. They must be U.S. citizens or possess permanent resident visas.

**Funds Avail.:** Varies. **To Apply:** Transcript, application form and three reference letters must be submitted. **Deadline:** March 1.

**Remarks:** The American Nuclear Society also offers the Walter Meyer scholarship for students who are enrolled in or have been accepted to a graduate program in nuclear science, nuclear engineering, or a nuclear-related field **Contact:** Scholarship Program, American Nuclear Society, at the above address (see entry 719).

### • 728 • Delayed Education for Women Scholarship *(Undergraduate/Scholarship)*

**Qualif.:** Applicants must be mature women whose formal studies in the field of nuclear science, nuclear engineering, or a nuclear-related field have been delayed or interrupted at least one-year. They must also be United States citizens or permanent residents, enrolled in a U.S. college or university, and sponsored by an ANS local section, division, student branch, committee, or organization member. **Criteria:** Based on academic ability and financial need.

**Funds Avail.:** Award amount varies. Awards may be used for any bona fide education costs including tuition, books, and room and board. **To Apply:** Application requests should include name of univeristy that will be attended, letter of commitment from that school, student's status (sophomore, junior) for the next fall semester, and major course of study. Completed applications should be returned with a grade transcript and sponsoring organization form. **Deadline:** March 1. **Contact:** H&A Scholarship Program at the above address (see entry 719).

### • 729 • Joseph R. Dietrich Scholarships
*(Undergraduate/Scholarship)*

**Focus:** Nuclear Science, Nuclear Engineering. **Qualif.:** Applicants must be undergraduate students in an accredited institution in the United States who have completed two or more years in a course of study leading to a degree in nuclear science or nuclear engineering. They must be U.S. citizens or possess permanent resident visas.

**Funds Avail.:** Varies. **To Apply:** Transcript, application form and three reference letters must be submitted. **Deadline:** March 1.

**Remarks:** The American Nuclear Society also offers the following undergraduate scholarships for students who have completed two or more years in a course of study leading to a degree in nuclear science, nuclear engineering, or a nuclear-related field: Robert T. Liner Scholarship; Raymond DiSalvo Scholarship. **Contact:** Scholarship Program, American Nuclear Society, at the above address (see entry 719). Send a self-addressed, stamped envelope.

### • 730 • Paul A. Greebler Scholarship *(Graduate/Scholarship)*

**Focus:** Nuclear Science, Nuclear Engineering. **Qualif.:** Applicants must be graduate students at an accredited institution in the United States who are enrolled in a full-time program in nuclear engineering. They must be U.S. citizens or possess permanent resident visas.

**Funds Avail.:** Varies. **To Apply:** Transcript, application form and three reference letters must be submitted. **Deadline:** March 1. **Contact:** Scholarship Program, American Nuclear Society, at the above address (see entry 719). Send a self-addressed, stamped envelope.

### • 731 • John R. Lamarsh Scholarship
*(Undergraduate/Scholarship)*

**Focus:** Nuclear Science, Nuclear Engineering. **Qualif.:** Applicants must be undergraduate students at an accredited institution in the United States who have completed two or more years in a course of study leading to a degree in nuclear science or nuclear engineering. They must be U.S. citizens or possess permanent resident visas.

**Funds Avail.:** Varies. **To Apply:** Transcript, application form and three reference letters must be submitted. **Deadline:** March 1. **Contact:** Scholarship Program, American Nuclear Society, at the above address (see entry 719). Send a self-addressed, stamped envelope.

### • 732 • John and Muriel Landis Scholarships
*(Graduate, Undergraduate/Scholarship)*

**Qualif.:** Applicants must be United States citizens or permanent residents and undergraduate or graduate students in any U.S. college or university who are planning to pursue a career in nuclear engineering, nuclear science, or a nuclear-related field. They must be sponsored by an ANS local section, division, student branch, committee, member, or organization member. Applicants must have a greater than average financial need or exhibit conditions or experiences that render them disadvantaged, such as poor high school or undergraduate preparation due to family poverty. Qualified high school seniors are also eligible to apply. **Criteria:**

Based on financial need. Minorities and women are especially encouraged to apply, although selections are made without regard to race, creed, or gender.

**Funds Avail.:** Varies. **No. of Awards:** A maximum of eight. **To Apply:** Application requests should include name of university that will be attended, letter of commitment from that school, status (sophomore, junior) for the next fall semester, and major course of study. Completed applications should include a transcript of grades and a sponsoring organization form. **Deadline:** March 1. **Contact:** Scholarship Program at the above address (see entry 719). Send a self-addressed, stamped envelope.

### • 733 • James F. Schumar Scholarship *(Graduate/Scholarship)*

**Purpose:** To encourage graduate study in materials science and technology. **Focus:** Materials Science, Nuclear Science, Nuclear Engineering. **Qualif.:** Applicant must be a U.S. citizen enrolled in a materials science graduate program.

**Funds Avail.:** Varies. **To Apply:** Transcript, application form and three letters of reference must be submitted. **Deadline:** March 1. **Contact:** Scholarships Program, at the above address (see entry 719). Send a self-addressed, stamped envelope.

### • 734 • James R. Vogt Scholarship *(Graduate, Undergraduate/Scholarship)*

**Focus:** Nuclear Science, Nuclear Engineering. **Qualif.:** Applicants must be undergraduate students at an accredited institution in the United States who are enrolled in or proposing to undertake research in radio-analytical chemistry or analytical applications of nuclear science. They must be U.S. citizens or possess permanent resident visas.

**Funds Avail.:** Varies. **To Apply:** Transcript, application form and three reference letters must be submitted. **Deadline:** March 1. **Contact:** Scholarship Program, American Nuclear Society, at the above address (see entry 719). Send a self-addressed, stamped envelope.

---

### • 735 •
## The American Numismatic Society
Broadway at 155th St.          Ph: (212)234-3130
New York, NY 10032          Fax: (212)234-3381
*E-mail:* nyc@mediabridge.com
*URL:* http://www.mediabridge.com/nyc/museums/
    american.numismatic. society.html

### • 736 • American Numismatic Society Graduate Fellowships *(Doctorate/Fellowship)*

**Purpose:** To support doctoral dissertation work employing numismatic evidence. **Focus:** Numismatics. **Qualif.:** Candidates must have completed the general examinations (or the equivalent) for the doctorate and must be writing a dissertation during the academic year on a topic in which the use of numismatics evidence plays a significant part. Candidates should have attended one of the American Numismatic Society's Graduate Seminars. The Council of the American Numismatic Society may waive the Seminar requirement.

**Funds Avail.:** $3,500 is awarded. The fellowship may be held in addition to any other support the applicant may receive. **No. of Awards:** 1. **To Apply:** Further information and application form may be obtained from the society. **Deadline:** Application must be completed by March 1 and announcement of the award is made prior to April 1. **Contact:** The American Numismatic Society at the above address (see entry 735).

## The American Numismatic Society (continued)

### • 737 • American Numismatic Society Graduate Seminar (Graduate/Other)

**Purpose:** To familiarize students with numismatic methodology and scholarship and to provide them with a deeper understanding of the contributions made by numismatics to other fields of study. **Focus:** Numismatics, Archeology, Art History, Classical Studies, History, History-Economic. **Qualif.:** Students must be of demonstrated competence and must have completed at least one year of graduate work in classical studies, history, archaeology, art history, economic history, or related disciplines. Applications will also be accepted from junior faculty members with an advanced degree in one of these fields. This offer is restricted to individuals affiliated with colleges and universities in the United States and Canada.

**Funds Avail.:** Stipends of $2,000 will be available to the recipients. The Society will also endeavor to provide round-trip travel fare from each student's home institution. **To Apply:** Information and application forms may be obtained from the Society. **Deadline:** Applications must be completed by March 1 and announcement of the awards will be made by April 1.

**Remarks:** The seminar, held at the museum of the American Numismatic Society, is an intensive program of study including lectures and conferences conducted by specialists in various fields, preparation and oral delivery of a paper on a topic of the student's choice, and actual contact with the coinages related to that topic. Curators of the American Numismatic Society and experts from this country and abroad will participate in the seminar. Grants in support of attendance at the Seminar are made possible by a generous donation from Mr. and Mrs. Eric P. Newman.

### • 738 • American Numismatic Society Grants-in-Aid (Graduate, Postgraduate/Grant)

**Purpose:** To provide graduate students with the opportunity to attend the Society's annual Graduate Seminar in Numismatics. **Focus:** Numismatics. **Qualif.:** Applicant must have completed at least one year of graduate study. Junior faculty members with an advanced degree may also apply. Grants are restricted to individuals affiliated with universities in the United States and Canada. The Seminar involves an intensive program of study which includes lectures and conferences conducted by specialists in various fields, preparation and oral delivery of a paper on a topic of the student's choice, and actual contact with the coinages related to that topic.

**Funds Avail.:** $2,000. **To Apply:** Write the Society for application guidelines and form. Submit form with three letters of recommendation. **Deadline:** March 1. Notification by April 1.

**Remarks:** Graduate students who successfully complete the seminar may seek a $3,500 fellowship from the Society for dissertation work in which the use of numismatic evidence plays a significant part. Donald Groves Fund Grants are also offered to promote publication in the field of Early American numismatics involving material dating no later than 1800. Funding is available for travel and other research-related expenses, as well as for publication costs. Write to the secretary of the Society for further details. **Contact:** William E. Metcalf, Chief Curator, at the above address (see entry 735).

### • 739 • ANS Fellowship in Roman Studies (Graduate/Fellowship)

**Purpose:** To promote use of the Society's library and collections on the Roman world. **Focus:** Numismatics. **Qualif.:** Applicants must be U.S. citizens affiliated with a North American institution of higher learning and must demonstrate academic competency. There is no minimum age or degree requirement, but preference will be given to those seeking advanced degrees.

**Funds Avail.:** $5,000 maximum. **To Apply:** Applicants must submit a detailed proposal of their work. **Deadline:** March 1. Winners will

be announced by April 1. **Contact:** American Numismatic Society at the above address (see entry 735).

### • 740 • Donald Groves Fellowship (Professional Development/Fellowship)

**Purpose:** To promote publication in the field of early American numismatics involving material dating no later than 1800. **Focus:** Numismatics.

**Funds Avail.:** Travel expenses, publication and research costs. **To Apply:** Applications must be addressed to the secretary of the society and should include an outline of the proposed research, methods involved, funding requested, and the specific use of funds. **Deadline:** March 1. **Contact:** American Numismatic Society at the above address (see entry 735).

### • 741 • Frances M. Schwartz Fellowships (Graduate/ Fellowship)

**Purpose:** To educate qualified students in museum practice and to train them in numismatics. **Focus:** Museum Science, Numismatics. **Qualif.:** Applicant must have completed a bachelor's degree or its equivalent. Fellowships are tenable in the Greek, Roman, and Byzantine departments of the Society.

**Funds Avail.:** Up to $2,000. **No. of Awards:** One. **To Apply:** Write the Society for application materials. **Deadline:** March 1. Notification by April 1.

**Remarks:** Donald Groves Fund Grants are also offered to promote publication in the field of Early American numismatics involving material dating no later than 1800. Funding is available for travel and other research-related expenses, as well as for publication costs. Write to the secretary of the Society for further details. **Contact:** William E. Metcalf, Chief Curator, at the above address (see entry 735).

### • 742 •

## American Occupational Therapy Foundation, Inc.
4720 Montgomery Ln.
PO Box 31220
Bethesda, MD 20824-1220
*E-mail:* ngillette@aotf.org
*URL:* http://www.aotf.org

*Ph:* (301)652-6611
*Fax:* (301)656-3620

### • 743 • AOTF Dissertation Research Award for Occupational Therapists (Doctorate/Grant)

**Purpose:** To encourage research in occupational therapy. **Focus:** Occupational Therapy. **Qualif.:** Candidates must be registered therapists, members of the AOTA, minimum five years experience in occupational therapy practice and education, minimum GPA of 3.5 in doctoral studies, presentation of an approved dissertation proposal, and the dissertation shall contribute clearly to the knowledge base in occupation science and therapy.

**Funds Avail.:** From $5,000-20,000. **No. of Awards:** 1-3. **To Apply:** Available in September. Check homepage for more information. **Deadline:** December 1. Contact the AOTF office for further information. **Contact:** Research Resources at the above address (see entry 742).

### • 744 • AOTF Research Grants (Professional Development/Grant)

**Purpose:** To support research and other clinical investigations. **Focus:** Occupational Therapy. **Qualif.:** Applicant must be an occupational therapist who is a member of the American Occupational Therapy Association. Grant proposals may be submitted in three categories: Impact Studies, Innovation Grants, and Student Research.

**Funds Avail.:** Impact Studies: $15,000-30,000; Innovation Grants: up to $8,000; Student Research Grants: up to $1,000. **To Apply:** Visit homepage to download applications. **Deadline:** Impact Studies, Innovation Grants: February 1, June 1, October 1. Student Research Grants: February 10, April 10, June 10, August 10, October 10, December 10.

**Remarks:** Consult website for current submission deadlines. **Contact:** Research Resources at the above address (see entry 742).

• 745 •
**American Optometric Foundation**
6110 Executive Blvd., Ste. 506          *Ph:* (301)984-4734
Rockville, MD 20852                      *Fax:* (301)984-4737
*E-mail:* aaoptom@aol.com
*URL:* http://www.aaopt.org

• 746 •  **William C. Ezell Fellowship** *(Doctorate, Graduate/Fellowship)*

**Purpose:** To encourage talented persons to pursue full-time careers in optometric research and education at schools and colleges of optometry. **Qualif.:** Post-graduate students entering or continuing a full-time program of study and training in research that leads to the masters of Ph.D are eligible.

**Funds Avail.:** Up to $6,000. R One year.

• 747 •  **Vincent Salierno Scholarship** *(Doctorate, Graduate/Scholarship)*

**Qualif.:** Any first year student pursuing a Doctorate of Optometry through full-time study is eligible. Scholarship is automatically renewed for four years as long as the continuing eligibility requirements are met.

**Funds Avail.:** $1,500 per year. **Deadline:** March 1.

• 748 •  **Student Travel Fellowships** *(Doctorate, Graduate/Fellowship)*

**Purpose:** To promote research aims, infuse an appropriate mix of young members into the Academy, and encourage optometry students. **Qualif.:** Eligible students are those who are currently enrolled full-time or have graduated within a year of the award.

**Funds Avail.:** A number of $500 fellowships are awarded for students to attend the annual meeting of the American Academy of Optometry.

**Remarks:** Students need not apply for a specific fellowship among the following: the Frank W. Weymouth Student Travel Fellowship, the Academy Program Committee Student Travel Fellowship, the Academy Student Travel Fellowship, the Irvin M. and Beatrice Borish Student Travel Fellowship, the Vistakon Student Travel Fellowship, the Wesley-Jessen Student Travel Fellowship, the Cornea and Contact Lens Student Fellowship, and the Bausch & Lomb Student Travel Fellowship.

• 749 •
**American Orchid Society**
6000 S. Olive Ave.                       *Ph:* (561)585-8666
West Palm Beach, FL 33405-4159           *Fax:* (561)585-0654
*E-mail:* theaos@compuserve.com
*URL:* http://www.orchidweb.org

• 750 •  **Grants for Orchid Research** *(Professional Development/Grant)*

**Purpose:** To advance the study of orchids in every aspect, including classification, taxomomy, genetics, anatomy, physiology, development, pathology, and tissue culture, and to assist in the publication of scholarly and popular scientific literature on orchids. **Focus:** Orchids. **Qualif.:** Applicant may be of any nationality. Candidate must be a qualified researcher sponsored by an accredited institution of higher learning or by an appropriate research institute. Candidate may be a graduate student, if his/her research is appropriate to the interests of the Society. Grants are tenable worldwide.

**Funds Avail.:** $500-12,000. **To Apply:** Write to the executive director for application instructions; there is no application form. Submit 25 copies of the following: a cover page on institutional letterhead, an abstract of the research proposal, an expanded research plan, a description of research facilities, a budget, a curriculum vitae, and information about other research support. **Deadline:** January 1, August 1. Results of grant evaluations are available at the end of March and October, respectively. **Contact:** Lee S. Cooke, Executive Director, at the above address (see entry 749).

• 751 •
**American Orff Schulwerk Association**
PO Box 391089                            *Ph:* (440)543-5366
Cleveland, OH 44139-8089                 *Fax:* (440)543-4057
*E-mail:* hdqtrsaosa@aol.com
*URL:* http://www.aosa.com

• 752 •  **American Orff Schulwerk Association Research Grants** *(Professional Development/Grant)*

**Purpose:** To encourage music teachers trained in Orff Schulwerk to promote the philosophy and practices of Carl Orff and Gunild Keetman, and to make available, through the Isabel McNeill Carley Library, the findings, evidence, and documentation of the sponsored research projects. **Focus:** Music, Education. **Qualif.:** Candidates must be members of the American Orff Schulwerk Association who show documented evidence of expertise in Orff Schulwerk (children's music education method) through training and experience. **Criteria:** Awards are given based on the validity of the project and importance to AOSA members.

**Funds Avail.:** Grant amounts are individually determined. Full funding may be available for qualifying low-budget projects. Limited funding may be available for some other qualifying projects. The pledged financial assistance is available to the applicant for up to 12 months from notification, pending the acquisition of the remaining budget requirements from other sources. **No. of Awards:** 1-2. **To Apply:** A formal application must be submitted detailing work experience and proposed research project. **Deadline:** Applications must be received by January 1. Winners are notified in late March. **Contact:** The American Orff Schulwerk Association Executive Headquarters at the above address (see entry 751).

• 753 •  **AOSA Tap Fund** *(Postgraduate/Scholarship)*

**Purpose:** To promote elementary or junior high school level music programs serving low income populations. **Focus:** Orff-Schulwerk.

## American Orff Schulwerk Association (continued)

**Qualif.:** Applicants must be current members of the American Orff-Schoolwerk Association and must have been an AOSA member in good standing for one year prior to application. Applicants must also be United States or have resided in the United States of America for the past five years; and must have a personal financial need or must present evidence that the proposed project will benefit the low-income population they teach.

**Funds Avail.:** $200-$600. **No. of Awards:** 1-2. **To Apply:** Necessary forms include, application, financial report (if relevant) and three character references. Forms must be typed, completed and returned by the deadline date. **Deadline:** January 1. **Contact:** Office of the Executive Director.

### • 754 • Gunild Keetman Assistance Grants
*(Postgraduate/Scholarship)*

**Purpose:** To further the growth of Orff Schulwerk. **Focus:** Orff-Schulwerk. **Qualif.:** Applicants must be current members of the American Orff-Schulwerk Association and must have been an AOSA member in good standing for the one year prior to the application. Applicants also must be citizens of the United States of America or have resided in the United States of America for the past five years; and must need financial aid to further their education in Orff Schulwerk, or financial aid to develop a valid, creative project.

**Funds Avail.:** Varies. **No. of Awards:** 6-10. **To Apply:** Necessary forms include, application, financial report and three character references. All forms must be typed, completed and returned by the deadline date. **Deadline:** January 1. Notification by April 1. **Contact:** Office of the Executive Director.

### • 755 • Shields-Gillespie Scholarships *(Postgraduate, Professional Development/Scholarship)*

**Purpose:** To provide financial aid to teachers of preschool and kindergarten children from minority/low-income populations. **Focus:** Music, Education, Orff-Schulwerk teacher training. **Qualif.:** Applicants must have been active members of the American Orff Schulwerk Association for the previous two years and involved in preschool or kindergarten education programs of minority and low-income populations. They must demonstrate strong motivation to advance the study and use of music, particularly the Orff Schulwerk process in early childhood education. They must also have financial need and must have resided in the United States for the past five years. **Criteria:** Priority will be given to applicants demonstrating financial need.

**Funds Avail.:** The amount of the award is individually determined. **No. of Awards:** 3-4. **To Apply:** A formal application must be completed. **Deadline:** January 1. **Contact:** The American Orff-Schulwerk Association at the above address (see entry 751).

### • 756 •
## American Oriental Society
Harlan Hatcher Graduate Library
University of Michigan                    *Ph:* (734)747-4760
Ann Arbor, MI 48109-1205                  *Fax:* (734)763-6743
*URL:* http://www.acls.org/aorients.htm

### • 757 • Louise Wallace Hackney Fellowship for the Study of Chinese Art *(Doctorate, Postdoctorate/Fellowship)*

**Purpose:** To support the study of Chinese art, with special relation to painting and its reflection of Chinese culture; and to support the translation into English of works on this subject. **Focus:** Chinese Art, Painting, and Culture. **Qualif.:** Applicant must be a doctoral or postdoctoral scholar and a U.S. citizen. Applicant must have

completed three years of Chinese language study or its equivalent, and demonstrate a commitment to this area. The fellowship is not intended for well-established scholars.

**Funds Avail.:** $8,000. **To Apply:** Write for application guidelines; there is no application form. The following must be submitted in duplicate: Submit the following in duplicate: transcripts of coursework; statement of personal finances; summary of the proposed project, appended with a budget proposal; and a minimum of three letters of recommendation. **Deadline:** February 1. Fellowship is announced at the end of April. **Contact:** Secretary-Treasurer at the above address (see entry 756).

### • 758 •
## American Otological Society - Research Fund
Dept. of Otolaryngology - Head and
  Neck Surgery
The Emory Clinic, A2325
1365 Clifton Rd.                          *Ph:* (404)778-5724
Atlanta, GA 80322                         *Fax:* (404)778-4295
*URL:* http://www.ortge.ufl.edu/fyi/v23n09/fyi.018.html

### • 759 • American Otological Society Research Fellowship and Medical Student Training Grants
*(Postdoctorate/Grant)*

**Purpose:** To foster academic training in sciences related to research on Otosclerosis and Meniere's disease. **Focus:** Medical Research. **Qualif.:** Applicants must be medical students or resident physicians who are planning to conduct full-time research involving Otosclerosis or Meniere's disease at United States or Canadian institutions.

**Funds Avail.:** Awards are made to institutions on behalf of the grantees. A maximum award request is a $40,000 for one year. The amount requested for the stipend is based on the applicant's position and on institutional norms. **No. of Awards:** Varies. **To Apply:** The applicant should describe correlations between proposed research and the clinical pathological entity of Otosclerosis or Meniere's disease. A formal, detailed application must be filed, along with a specific research proposal explaining how the research may lead to the amelioration of the consequences of Otosclerosis or Meniere's disease. Applicants must provide documentation that appropriate facilities and faculties are available. **Deadline:** Applications must be received by January 31. **Contact:** Douglas E. Mattox, M.D., Secretary-Treasurer, at the above address (see entry 758).

### • 760 • American Otological Society Research Grants *(Postdoctorate/Grant)*

**Purpose:** To encourage academic research in sciences related to the investigation of the diagnosis, management, and pathogenesis of Otosclerosis or Meniere's disease, as well as underlying processes. **Focus:** Medical Research. **Qualif.:** Candidates must be physicians or doctoral-level investigators in the United States or Canada.

**Funds Avail.:** Awards are made to an institution on behalf of the grantee. The maximum Research Grant is $40,000 per year, including indirect costs, and is annually and competitively renewable. No funds may be requested or used for investigators' travel or salary, except under very unusual circumstances. **No. of Awards:** Varies. **To Apply:** Applicants should describe correlations between proposed research and the clinical pathological entity of Otosclerosis or Meniere's disease. A formal, detailed application must be filed, along with a specific research proposal explaining how the research may lead to the amelioration of the consequences of Otosclerosis or Meniere's disease. **Deadline:** Applications must be received by January 31. The project period is for one year, beginning July 1. **Contact:** Douglas E. Mattox, M.D., Secretary-Treasurer, at the above address (see entry 758).

---

• **761** •

## American Philological Association
Department of Classics
Holy Cross College                    *Ph:* (508)793-2203
Worcester, MA 01610-2395              *Fax:* (508)793-3428
*E-mail:* ziobro@holycross.edu

### • 762 •  Fellowship in Latin Lexicography
*(Postdoctorate/Fellowship)*

**Purpose:** To enable an American scholar to conduct research at the Thesaurus Linguae Latinae in Munich. **Focus:** Latin Lexicography. **Qualif.:** Applicant must be a U.S. citizen or permanent resident who possesses a familiarity with and a special interest in the Latin language. Candidate must have a Ph.D., or anticipate earning one before the starting date of the fellowship. Generally, the fellowship is intended for someone newly graduated or still at the assistant professor level. Applicant should be able to read and speak German. Fellowship is tenable at the Thesaurus Linguae Latinae in Munich.

**Funds Avail.:** $31,500. **No. of Awards:** 1. **To Apply:** There is no application form. Submit a letter of application to the APA secretary with a curriculum vitae and a statement of interest in Latin lexicography. Indicate on the envelope that an application is enclosed. Two letters of recommendation should be sent directly from the referees to the secretary. Short-listed candidates will be interviewed. **Deadline:** Varies. Fellowship will be announced in January. **Contact:** William J. Ziobro, APA Secretary-Treasurer, at the above address (see entry 761).

### • 763 •  The Lionel Pearson Fellowship
*(Undergraduate/Fellowship)*

**Qualif.:** Applicants must be in the final year of undergraduate study.

**Funds Avail.:** The total reimbursement for all expenses will not exceed $25,000. **Deadline:** November 11. **Contact:** American Philological Association at the above address (see entry 761).

### • 764 •  Thesaurus Linguae Latinae Fellowship
*(Doctorate/Fellowship)*

**Focus:** Latin language and literature, Roman law, Roman history, and the literature of early Christianity. **Qualif.:** Applicants must be PhDs.

**Funds Avail.:** Stipend of $31,500. **Contact:** American Philological Association at the above address (see entry 761).

---

• **765** •

## American Philosophical Society
104 S. 5th St.
Philadelphia, PA 19106-3387
*URL:* http://www.amphilsoc.org

### • 766 •  General Research Grant Program
*(Postdoctorate/Grant)*

**Purpose:** To support scholarly research. **Focus:** Research all fields, except those where funding by government or corporate enterprise is more appropriate. **Qualif.:** Applicant must be a U.S. citizen, or a national of another country whose research can only be carried out in the United States. Applicant must have a doctorate for at least one year. Grants are rarely made to persons who have had the doctorate less than a year; and never for predoctoral study or research. Funds are only intended for travel and supplies necessary for scholarly research. Awards are not available for journalistic work, creative or performing arts projects, the preparation of materials for classroom use by students, attendance at conferences, fellowships or scholarships, or costs of publication. Nor may grants be applied to institutional costs, salaries, permanent equipment, clerical support, or living expenses while working at home. The Committee will seldom approve more than two grants to an individual within any five-year period.

**Funds Avail.:** $6,000 maximum. **To Apply:** Interested candidates should write to the Society for forms, stating area of research and proposed use of grant funds in an itemized budget. Telephone requests for forms cannot be honored. **Deadline:** December 1, March 1, and October 1. Candidates are notified four months after deadline.

**Remarks:** Additional information and forms may also be downloaded from www.amphilsoc.org. **Contact:** Committee on Research at the above address (see entry 765).

### • 767 •  Mellon Resident Research Fellowships
*(Other/Fellowship)*

**Purpose:** To provide a research opportunity in the Library's collections lasting one to three months. **Focus:** General Studies.

**Funds Avail.:** $1,900 per month stipend. **To Apply:** Requests concerning this fellowship must be addressed directly to the library. When placing telephone requests, candidates must ask the receptionist for a connection to the person responsible for handling Mellon questions, not to the grants office. **Deadline:** March 1. **Contact:** For application information write A.P.S. Library, 105 S. 5th St., Philadelphia, PA 19106-3387.

### • 768 •  Henry M. Phillips Grants in Jurisprudence
*(Postdoctorate/Grant)*

**Purpose:** To support research in jurisprudence. **Focus:** Jurisprudence. **Qualif.:** Applicant must be a U.S. citizen, or a national of another country whose research can only be carried on in the United States. Applicant must have a Ph.D. or J.D. Grants are never for predoctoral study or research. The Committee will seldom approve more than two grants to a researcher within any five-year period. Eligible expenses are generally limited to necessary travel, room and board, and photocopying.

**Funds Avail.:** $6,000 maximum. **To Apply:** Applicants should write the Society for an application form and guidelines, specifying interest in the Phillips Grant in Jurisprudence and including a proposed budget. No telephone requests for forms can be honored. **Deadline:** December 1. Notification by March.

**Remarks:** Information and forms may be downloaded from www.amphilsoc.org. **Contact:** Phillips-Jurisprudence Committee at the above address (see entry 765).

### • 769 •  Phillips Grants for North American Indian Research *(Doctorate, Postdoctorate/Grant)*

**Focus:** Native American Ethnohistory, Linguistics. **Qualif.:** Candidates should be graduate students or postdoctoral candidates conducting research on North American Indian linguistics and ethnohistory. Because funds are limited, grants are not made for projects in archaeology, ethnography, psycho linguistics, or for the preparation of pedagogical materials.

**Funds Avail.:** Awards average $1,300, and are ordinarily given for only one year (the 12 months following the date of the award). Grants support extra costs such as travel, tapes, and films, but are not for general maintenance or purchase of equipment. **To Apply:** Applicants must submit four copies of a formal application, and three letters of support. Applications must be requested in writing, specifying linguistics or ethnohistory. **Deadline:** Application and

---

## American Philosophical Society (continued)

letters of support must be filed by March 1. Decisions are announced in mid-May.

**Remarks:** Information and forms are available from www.amphilsoc.org. **Contact:** Phillips Fund for Native American Research at the above address (see entry 765).

### • 770 • John Clarke Slater Fellowship (Doctorate/Fellowship)

**Focus:** History, Physical Sciences. **Qualif.:** Applicants must be doctoral candidates conducting research in the history of modern physical sciences who have passed their preliminary exams by the time of application and are writing their dissertations on a topic in the history of the physical sciences in the 20th century. It is open to candidates for the doctorate at an American institution or to those in universities abroad who propose to spend the fellowship year in association with an American university or research institution. Recipients must agree to submit a completed copy of their dissertation for the Society's Library.

**Funds Avail.:** Stipends are $12,000. Awards are for one year and coincide with the academic school year. **To Apply:** Applicants must submit a formal application, a five-page summary of the project, a copy or outline of the dissertation proposal, two references, and official graduate and undergraduate transcripts. **Deadline:** The application deadline is December 1. Notification is mailed by early March.

**Remarks:** The John Clark Slater Fellowship is named for John Clark Slater, a member of the Society and a leader in the development of quantum mechanics and solid state physics. Information and forms are downloadable from www.amphilsoc.org. **Contact:** The American Philosophical Society at the above address (see entry 765).

## • 771 •
## American Physical Society
Minority Scholarship Program
1 Physics Ellipse                         Ph: (301)209-3232
College Park, MD 20740-3232        Fax: (301)209-0865
E-mail: modeste@aps.org
URL: http://www.aps.org/educ/index.html

### • 772 • Corporate Sponsored Scholarships for Minority Undergraduate Physics Majors (Undergraduate/Scholarship)

**Purpose:** To significantly increase the level of under represented minority participation in physics in this country. **Focus:** Physics. **Qualif.:** Any black, Hispanic, or American Indian U.S. citizen who is majoring or plans to major in physics and who is a high school senior or college freshman or sophomore is eligible. **Criteria:** A selection committee of the APS Committee on Minorities in Physics appointed by the APS president will choose the scholarship recipients. The selection committee will assign an accomplished physicist as a mentor to each scholarship recipient, and encourages applications from students attending historically or predominantly black, Hispanic, or American Indian institutions.

**Funds Avail.:** $2,000 for tuition, room, or board, and $500 awarded to each college or university physics department that hosts one or more APS minority undergraduate scholars. The scholarship may be renewed one time. **No. of Awards:** 10-15. **To Apply:** Applicants must submit a completed application form with a personal statement. Two completed reference forms, one must be from a science or math professor/teacher, and a copy of applicant's high school and/or college transcripts should be mailed directly to the APS office. ACT, SAT, and any other scholastic aptitude test scores must be sent directly to the APS office by the testing

service. **Deadline:** First Friday in February. **Contact:** APS Minorities Scholarship Program at the above address (see entry 771).

## • 773 •
## American Planning Association
122 South Michigan Ave., Ste. 1600        Ph: (312)431-9100
Chicago, IL 60603-6107                    Fax: (312)431-9985
URL: http://www.planning.org/html/welcome.html

### • 774 • Charles Abrams Scholarships (Graduate/Scholarship)

**Purpose:** To support study toward a master's degree in planning at one of the five schools at which Charles Abrams taught. **Focus:** Transportation or Urban Planning. **Qualif.:** The scholar is selected from among nominees of the following five institutions: Columbia University, Harvard University, Massachusetts Institute of Technology, New School for Social Research, and University of Pennsylvania. Applicants must be U.S. citizens and be accepted to or enrolled in the urban planning department or school of one of the eligible institutions. They must also demonstrate financial need. The scholarship may only be used to defray tuition costs. **Criteria:** Applicants are chosen based on merit, financial need and recommendation by department chairperson.

**Funds Avail.:** $2,000 **To Apply:** Write to APA for a financial aid application. Submit form through the urban and regional planning department or school at one of the designated universities. The institution will forward nomination for approval by APA. **Deadline:** April 30 for receipt of nomination by APA.

### • 775 • APA Planning & the Black Community Division Scholarship (Undergraduate/Scholarship)

**Purpose:** To recognize outstanding minority students in undergraduate planning programs in the United States. **Focus:** Urban Planning. **Qualif.:** Applicants must be African American, Hispanic American, or Native American students with a demonstrated interest in working in the planning profession or as an advocate for improving, enhancing, or maintaining the quality of life in black communities. He or she must apply in the second or third year of undergraduate study, be working towards a baccalaureate degree in planning or related field (architecture, community development, environmental science, public administration, or urban studies), have a minimum of 30 semester hours or 45 quarter hours at the time of application, have demonstrated financial need, and have a minimum GPA of 2.85 on a 4.0 scale. **Criteria:** Preference is given to applicants who demonstrate a record of service to the black community, are enrolled in planning programs and those recognized by the Planning Accreditation Board, and are members of the American Planning Association and/or the Planning and the Black Community Division.

**Funds Avail.:** $2,500. **To Apply:** Applicants must send a completed application accompanied by a two to five-page, double-spaced essay that identifies critical problems facing minority communities in the 21st century and indicates alternative planning strategies to resolve these problems; at least two letters of recommendation (for nominated candidates, one of the two letters must be from a professor or school official); and an official copy of college or university transcripts. **Deadline:** May 15. Award decisions are made in July.

**Remarks:** Planning Accreditation Board approved schools only.

### • 776 • APA Planning Fellowships (Graduate/Fellowship)

**Purpose:** To encourage minority students to enter the planning profession and to support graduate studies in planning. **Focus:**

Regional and Urban Planning. **Qualif.:** Applicants must be Hispanic, African American, or Native American citizens of the United States or Canada. They must be enrolled or accepted for enrollment in a graduate planning program accredited by the Planning Accreditation Board. They must also document the need for financial assistance. Preference will be given to full-time students. Candidates must be nominated, but self-nominations are accepted. Fellowships are tenable for the first or second year of a graduate planning program. **Criteria:** Applicants are chosen based on financial need, merit, and essay.

**Funds Avail.:** $2,000-5,000. **No. of Awards:** Varies. **To Apply:** Write for application form and guidelines. Submit form with a letter of nomination from a professor or school official (unless self-nominated); resume; personal statement describing academic and career goals; transcripts; statement of financial independence; letter of acceptance into a graduate planning program; and verification of expenses for one academic year of graduate study. **Deadline:** May 15. Award decisions are made in mid-June.

---

• 777 •

## American Political Science Association

1527 New Hampshire Ave., NW            *Ph:* (202)483-2512
Washington, DC 20036                   *Fax:* (202)483-2657
*E-mail:* cfp@apsanet.org
*URL:* http://www.apsanet.org

### • 778 • American Political Science Association-MCI Communications Fellowships for Scholars and Journalists *(Other/Fellowship)*

**Purpose:** To provide qualified journalists and scholars the opportunity to work as a full-time aide to members of the House and/or Senate. **Focus:** Journalism. **Qualif.:** Scholar applicants must have completed a PhD in the last 15 years or be near completion of the dissertation. Journalist applicants must have a bachelors degree, minimum of 2 years experience in any media form, and show interest in communications and public policy. **Criteria:** Preference is given to applicants without much Washington experience.

**Funds Avail.:** $30,000 stipend plus a small travel allowance. **Deadline:** December 1.

### • 779 • APSA Congressional Fellowships for Federal Executives *(Professional Development/Fellowship)*

**Purpose:** To provide opportunities for mid to upper-level Federal executives to learn more about the legislative process by working as Congressional aides for nine months. **Focus:** Political Science, Government, Public Administration. **Qualif.:** Applicants must have a minimum grade of GS-13 or equivalent; at least two years of Federal service in the executive branch; ability to work in an unstructured environment; and an interest in the legislative process and public affairs. Candidates must be nominated by the agency in which they work. Agencies with substantial activity with foreign governments may nominate employees for the Foreign Affairs Fellows section of the Congressional Fellowship Program, which adds eight weeks to the regular Congressional Fellows Programs prior to its start. Fellowships are available, also for those with the above qualifications and a demonstrated, professional interest in telecommunications.

**Funds Avail.:** During the Fellowship year, Fellows receive their regular salaries from the agency for which they work. The cost to the nominating agency is $4,000 per participant plus an additional $2,250 per recipient for Foreign Affairs Fellows. Other costs such as travel funds for assignments in the district of the Member of Congress to which they are assigned may be negotiated between the Fellow and his/her agency. **To Apply:** Each agency submits, for each nominated candidate, an Optional Training Form 37 or 170 or other approved agency training form and five copies of each of the

following: a detailed resume or current SF-171; an assessment by supervisors of the nominee's executive potential and need for training; a statement by the nominee of the need for the training, its relevance to career goals; and how the training will be utilized in the agency. An additional Optional Training Form 37 or 170 must be submitted for Foreign Affairs Fellows. **Deadline:** Nominations must be submitted by March 1; nominees are interviewed; and recipients are selected by June 1. Except for Foreign Affairs Fellows, whose program starts in September, the Program commences in early November with an orientation period.

**Remarks:** Program includes seminars with numerous legislators, administrators, lobbyists, reporters, and scholars covering a wide range of topics relating to Congress and public policy making. During this time, Fellows also begin work in their House or Senate offices in December. They serve in each house of Congress for approximately four and a half months. A continuing series of seminars are scheduled during the entire year to supplement the intern experience. Fellows also travel with their Representative and Senator to the Congressional district or state during the course of the year. **Contact:** Headquarters-level training officer or coordinator for executive development of the Federal agency, or the Director at the above address (see entry 777).

### • 780 • APSA Congressional Fellowships for Journalists *(Professional Development/Fellowship)*

**Purpose:** To provide journalists with an opportunity to learn about the legislative process by working as Congressional aides for nine months. **Focus:** Political Science, Government, Journalism. **Qualif.:** Applicants must have a bachelor's degree and two to ten years full-time professional experience in newspaper, magazine, radio, or television reporting. College part-time work is not considered professional experience. Fellowships are also available for those with the above qualifications and have a demonstrated, professional interest in telecommunications. **Criteria:** Preference is given to those without extensive Washington experience.

**Funds Avail.:** The stipend is $30,000 plus travel allowance. **To Apply:** Applicants must submit eight copies each of a detailed resume; a personal statement of about 500 words explaining how the program relates to professional career goals; names of three professional references who will send their letter of recommendation to APSA; a sample of their best professional writing (six copies of one clip or radio/TV script or a single copy of a VHS tape). **Deadline:** Applications and all supporting materials must be submitted between October and December 1 of the year prior to the beginning of the Fellowship. Awards are announced by March 15.

**Remarks:** The program commences in early November with an orientation period. Program includes seminars with numerous legislators, administrators, lobbyists, reporters, and scholars covering a wide range of topics relating to Congress and public policymaking. During this time, Fellows also begin exploring individual office assignments. Negotiations are conducted by the individual participants with Congressional offices of their choice. Fellows begin work in their House or Senate offices in December. They serve in each house of Congress for approximately four and a half months. A continuing series of seminars are scheduled during the entire year to supplement the intern experience. Fellows also travel with their Representative and Senator to the Congressional district or state during the course of the year. **Contact:** Director, Congressional Fellowship Program, at the above address (see entry 777).

### • 781 • APSA Graduate Fellowships for African-American Students *(Doctorate/Fellowship)*

**Purpose:** To identify and to aid prospective African-American political science graduate students, encourage other institutions to provide financial assistance to these students, and to increase the number of African-American Ph.D.'s in political science. **Qualif.:** Applicants must be African-American students who qualify for acceptance at accredited institutions of higher learning and who have a potential for graduate work in political science. Students

## American Political Science Association (continued)

are free to attend the university of their choice. **Criteria:** Priority is given to persons about to enter graduate school. Applicants with the greatest financial need are given preference.

**Funds Avail.:** APSA Fellows are chosen and ranked. The first three are offered stipends of approximately $6,000 each for one year of study. These Fellows usually receive a waiver of tuition and fees. The graduate school attended by the recipient is encouraged to support the future years of study. The remaining Fellows are designated as Fellows without stipend and are recommended to graduate departments of political science for fellowships at the department level. **No. of Awards:** 3. **Deadline:** Applications must be received prior to November 1.

**Remarks:** The American Political Science Association authorized the establishment of the African-American Graduate Fellowship Program in 1969. The Program originated out of the recognition for the need to make a special effort to overcome some of the obstacles that have hampered recruitment of African-Americans to higher education. **Contact:** The American Political Science Association at the above address (see entry 777).

### • 782 • APSA Graduate Fellowships for Latino Students (Doctorate/Fellowship)

**Purpose:** To identify and aid prospective Latino political science graduate students, encourage other institutions to provide financial assistance for these students, and increase the number of Latino Ph.D's in political science. **Qualif.:** Applicants must be Latino students who qualify for acceptance at accredited institutions of higher learning and who will enroll in doctoral programs in political science. Priority is given to those about to enter graduate school. Major consideration is given to candidates with potential for academic success and with financial need.

**Funds Avail.:** Fellowships of approximately $6,000 are awarded annually. One APSA Fellow is given a stipend to attend the university of his or her choice. Requests are made of graduate departments to provide assistance for the remaining Fellows. **No. of Awards:** 1. **To Apply:** The formal application requests information about candidates' income and resources, last three jobs including summer and/or part-time, teaching experience (if any), skills in foreign languages, and computer or statistical tools. References from three persons, two of whom have taught the candidate, and school transcripts must be sent directly to APSA. The Graduate Record Examination should be taken. Listing of five Ph.D. degree granting departments to which the application folder should be sent and a biographical essay of 400 words or less that summarizes past experience, current interests, and career goals are also required. **Deadline:** Applications and all supporting materials including references must be filed before December 1. **Contact:** APSA Graduate Fellowships for Latino Students at the above address (see entry 777).

### • 783 • The Joan Shorenstein Barone Congressional Fellowship (Professional Development/Fellowship)

**Purpose:** To provide support to a broadcast journalist of special merit. **Focus:** Broadcast Journalism, Political Science. **Qualif.:** Candidate must be a U.S. citizen and a broadcast journalist. **No. of Awards:** One. **To Apply:** Write to the APSA, specifying interest in the Fellowship, for application form and guidelines. **Deadline:** December 1. **Contact:** Dr. Maurice Woodard, Staff Associate, at the above address (see entry 777).

### • 784 • The Poynter Fellowship (Professional Development/Fellowship)

**Purpose:** To provide support to a print journalist who shows the most promise of making a significant contribution to the public's understanding of the political process. **Focus:** Political Science, Print Journalism. **Qualif.:** Candidate must be a U.S. citizen and a print journalist. **No. of Awards:** One. **To Apply:** Write to the APSA, specifying interest in the Fellowship, for application form and

guidelines. **Deadline:** December 1. **Contact:** Dr. Maurice Woodard, Staff Associate, at the above address (see entry 777).

### • 785 •
## American Pomological Society

| | |
|---|---|
| 102 Tyson Bldg. | **Ph:** (814)863-6163 |
| University Park, PA 16802-4200 | **Fax:** (814)863-6139 |

**E-mail:** aps@agcs.cas.psu.edu; dottie@ihl.state.ms.us

### • 786 • U.P. Hedrick Award (Graduate, Undergraduate/Award)

**Purpose:** To encourage promising and gifted students to specialize in the field of pomology. **Focus:** Botany, Horticulture. **Qualif.:** Applicants must be graduate or undergraduate students writing alone or co-authoring with an advisor a paper related to cultivators of deciduous, tropical or subtropical fruits as related to climate, soil, rootstocks, or a specific experiment. Maximum length should be 1,000 words. Winning papers will be published in *Fruit Vanities Journal*. **Criteria:** Papers submitted are judged by a three-member panel.

**Funds Avail.:** $300 for first place; $50 for second place. **To Apply:** Papers should be sent to: Dr. Robert M. Crassweller no later than 60 days before the annual APS meeting. **Contact:** Dr. Robert M. Crassweller, at the above address (see entry 785).

### • 787 •
## American Postal Workers Union, AFL-CIO

| | |
|---|---|
| 1300 L St., NW | **Ph:** (202)842-4200 |
| Washington, DC 20005-4107 | **Fax:** (202)842-4297 |

### • 788 • American Postal Workers Union Vocational Scholarship (Undergraduate/Scholarship)

**Purpose:** To help students interested in programs of study leading to definite trade, technical, industrial, or vocational occupations. **Focus:** Vocation-Technical Education. **Qualif.:** Applicants must be children, stepchildren or legally adopted children of active or deceased members of the American Postal Workers Union. Parents must be members in good standing for at least one year immediately preceding application deadline or must have been members for one year immediately preceding death. Applicants must also be seniors attending high school or other corresponding secondary school and must plan to attend an accredited vocational school on a full-time basis. **Criteria:** Winners are judged on the basis of school records, personal qualifications, evidence of a commitment to an occupation, response to contemporary questions, and an essay. The Scholarship Selection Committee selects the top five candidates. A drawing is held to determine the winner from the top five.

**Funds Avail.:** One scholarship of up to $1,000 is awarded for three consecutive years or until completion of courses. Winners may not accept more than $5,000 annually from other scholarships. **To Apply:** Applicants must submit completed application forms, answer sheets, essays, official transcripts, SAT or ACT scores, and school's report on the student. **Deadline:** Applications should be postmarked no later than March 1 and received no later than March 15 prior to the applicant's high school graduation. **Contact:** The Union at the above address.

### • 789 • E.C. Hallbeck Memorial Scholarship (Undergraduate/Scholarship)

**Focus:** General Studies. **Qualif.:** Applicants must be children, stepchildren, or legally adopted children of active or deceased members of the American Postal Workers Union. Parents must be members in good standing for at least one year immediately preceding the application deadline or must have been members for one year immediately preceding death. Applicants must also be seniors attending high school or other corresponding secondary school and be accepted at an accredited college on a full-time basis. **Criteria:** Winners are judged on the basis of school records, personal qualifications, SAT/ACT scores, and total family income.

**Funds Avail.:** Five geographic area winners will be selected and awarded $1,000 for each of four consecutive years of college providing that a satisfactory academic record is maintained. An award winner may not accept more than $5,000 annually from other scholarships. **No. of Awards:** 5 required by rules; 10 awarded last year. **To Apply:** Applicants must submit a completed application form, biographical questionnaire, secondary school report, official transcript, and SAT or ACT scores. **Deadline:** Applications should be postmarked no later than March 1 and received no later than March 15 prior to high school graduation.

**Remarks:** The scholarship was established in January 1969 and first awarded in 1970 as a living memorial and permanent tribute to E.C. "Roy" Hallbeck, President of the former United Federation of Postal Clerks. **Contact:** The Union at the above address.

---

**• 790 •**

**American Press Institute Fellowships**
Fellowships
11690 Sunrise Valley Dr.     *Ph:* (703)620-3611
Reston, VA 22191-1498     *Fax:* (703)620-5814

**• 791 • American Press Institute Minority Journalism Educators Fellowship** *(Other/Fellowship)*

**Purpose:** To allow a college-level journalism educator who is a member of a recognized minority group, to attend an API seminar.

**Funds Avail.:** Covers tuition, room, and meals.

**• 792 • Cissy Patterson Fellowship** *(Other/Fellowship)*

**Purpose:** Given as part of the American Press Institute Seminar Fellowships program. **Focus:** Journalism. **Qualif.:** Applicants must be female reporters/editors from a newspaper with a circulation of under 25,000.

**Funds Avail.:** May cover tuition, room, meals, and possibly travel. **To Apply:** Write for details.

**• 793 • Walter Everett Fellowship** *(Other/Fellowship)*

**Purpose:** Given as part of the American Press Institute Seminar Fellowships program. **Focus:** Journalism. **Qualif.:** Applicants must be city editors.

**Funds Avail.:** Tuition, room, meals, and travel may be covered. **To Apply:** Write for details.

**• 794 • John E. Heselden Fellowship** *(Other/Fellowship)*

**Purpose:** Given as part of the American Press Institute Seminar Fellowships program. **Focus:** Journalism. **Qualif.:** Applicants must be newspaper executives interested in marketing or general management. **To Apply:** Write for details.

**• 795 •** *Arizona Daily Star* Frank E. Johnson Scholarship *(Other/Scholarship)*

**Focus:** Journalism. **Qualif.:** Applicants must be minority students at Pima Community College. **Criteria:** Based on scholarship, need, and interest in journalism.

**Funds Avail.:** Up to $500.

**• 796 • Rollan D. Melton Fellowship** *(Professional Development/Fellowship)*

**Purpose:** To enable college-level journalism educators who are members of a minority race to attend an American Press Institute seminar of their choice. To help develop a closer association between journalism faculty and working newspaper men and women. To provide faculty members an opportunity to update knowledge on current newspaper practices. **Focus:** Journalism. **Qualif.:** Nominations are invited from all schools and departments of journalism and mass communication. Nominations must be approved by the head of the school or department. Selections will be made by API. Two of the three fellowships are for minority applicants only.

**Funds Avail.:** The fellowship covers tuition, room, and meals. **No. of Awards:** 1 award is offered each year. **Deadline:** Application materials must be in by November 15. **Contact:** The address above.

**• 797 • James H. Ottaway Sr. Fellowships** *(Other/Fellowship)*

**Purpose:** Given as part of the American Press Institute Seminar Fellowships. **Focus:** Journalism. **Qualif.:** Applicants must be college-level journalism educators.

**Funds Avail.:** Tuition, room, meals, and travel may be covered. **No. of Awards:** 2. **To Apply:** Write for details.

**• 798 • Philip S. Weld Sr. Fellowship** *(Other/Fellowship)*

**Purpose:** Given as part of the American Press Institute Seminar Fellowships program. **Focus:** Journalism. **Qualif.:** Applicants must be college-level educators.

**Funds Avail.:** Tuition, room, meals, and travel may be covered. **To Apply:** Write for details.

---

**• 799 •**

**American Psychiatric Association**
1400 K St. NW     *Ph:* (202)682-6316
Washington, DC 20005     *Fax:* (202)789-1874
*URL:* http://www.psych.org

**• 800 • APA/Lilly Psychiatric Research Fellowship** *(Graduate/Fellowship)*

**Purpose:** To allow a post-graduate medical trainee to focus on research and personal scholarship. **Qualif.:** Applicants must be APA members who have earned either an M.D. or D.O. degree and have completed residency training in general psychiatry or child psychiatry. **Criteria:** Applications are evaluated on the basis of the applicant's qualifications, preceptor's qualifications, quality of research training plan, and adequacy of institutional resources and facilities.

**Funds Avail.:** $35,000 stipend. **Deadline:** October 14. **Contact:** American Psychiatric Association at the above address (see entry 799).

## American Psychiatric Association (continued)

### • 801 • APA/SmithKline Beecham Junior Faculty Fellowship for Research Development in Biological Psychiatry (Postdoctorate/Fellowship)

**Purpose:** To support the research of a junior faculty member in biology and psychopharmacology of mood disorders and/or anxiety disorders.

**Funds Avail.:** $35,000 is paid to the institution for the disbursement to the fellow.

**Remarks:** The institution must agree not to deduct indirect costs from this award, but may augment this award for further salary support for the faculty member. Established in 1995.

### • 802 • APA/Wyeth-Ayerst M.D. Ph.D. Psychiatric Research Fellowship (Postdoctorate/Fellowship)

**Purpose:** To focus on research and personal scholarship on a post-graduate level. **Focus:** Psychiatry. **Qualif.:** Applicants must be members of the APA; have received a M.D. or D.O. and a PhD degree; and have completed residency training in general psychiatry or child psychiatry immediately prior to the time the fellowship starts. Fellowship is designed for a resident who has demonstrated significant research potential; had research training; and is not already an established investigator. **Criteria:** Based on applicant's qualifications, preceptor's qualification; quality of research training plan; and adequacy of institutional resources and facilities. **No. of Awards:** 1. **To Apply:** Each chairman of a Department of Psychiatry can nominate one resident. The chairman should send a letter of recommendation providing details about the candidate's accomplishments and activities that justify the nomination and the institutional resources available to support the application in his/her research training endeavors. Accompanying this should be a copy of the nominee's specific objectives for his/her research training fellowship and the specific plans for meeting those objectives. A statement by the candidate's preceptor is also required which describes the preceptor's accomplishments as both a researcher and mentor as well as a description of the specific responsibilities that preceptor would have with regard to the applicant's research training program. Five copies of all of the above material should be sent. **Deadline:** October 14.

### • 803 • Center for Mental Health Services Minority Fellowship Program (Doctorate/Fellowship)

**Purpose:** To provide enriching training experience for psychiatric residents and stimulate interest in pursuing training areas of psychiatry where minority groups are under represented such as research, child psychiatry, and addiction psychiatry. **Focus:** Psychiatry. **Qualif.:** Applicants must be U.S. citizens or permanent residents and psychiatric residents who will be at least a PGY 2 at the start of the fellowship term in July. Fellows join in deliberations of selected APA committees and attend the APA annual meeting.

**Funds Avail.:** Dependent upon years of relevant experience. **No. of Awards:** Varies. **To Apply:** Write to the APA for application form and guidelines. Submit form with three letters of reference, medical school transcripts, curriculum vitae, and an essay outlining career goals. An interview with a practicing psychiatrist will be arranged by APA staff. **Deadline:** January 31. **Contact:** Marilyn King, at the above address (see entry 799).

### • 804 • Program for Minority Research Training in Psychiatry (Doctorate, Graduate/Fellowship)

**Purpose:** To increase the number of men and women in the field of psychiatric research. **Focus:** Psychiatry **Qualif.:** Applicant must be a medical student, resident, or post-residency fellow interested in psychiatric research. Preference is given to underrepresented minorities, American Indians, African-Americans, Hispanics or Pacific Islanders. **Criteria:** Based on scholarship and promise as a researcher, class ranking, research and/or publication experience, honors and awards, personal essay, minority status.

**Funds Avail.:** $14,685 for medical students, $26,250 - $36,030 for residents, up to $41,265 for post-residents. **No. of Awards:** Up to 12 full-time. **To Apply:** Applicants for full-year fellowships will be interviewed by Advisory Committee members. **Deadline:** December 1 for full-time fellowships; all others, 3 months prior to start of training. **Contact:** Ernesto Guerra.

---

### • 805 •
## American Psychological Association - Minority Fellowship Program
750 1st St., NE
Washington, DC 20002-4242
*E-mail:* webmaster@apa.org
*URL:* http://www.apa.org

*Ph:* (202)336-5500
*Fax:* (202)336-6012

### • 806 • Minority Fellowships in Neuroscience (Doctorate/Fellowship)

**Purpose:** To support doctoral study in neuroscience by minority students. **Focus:** Neuroscience. **Qualif.:** Applicant must be a U.S. citizen or permanent resident and a member of a minority group. Applicant must be accepted and enrolled in a doctoral program in a field of neuroscience. Fellowships may include a full tuition scholarship.

**Funds Avail.:** $10,000/year. **To Apply:** Write to APA for application form and guidelines, available in August. **Deadline:** January 15. Notification in March. **Contact:** Joe L. Martinez Jr., PhD, Director, at the above address (see entry 805).

### • 807 • Minority Fellowships in Psychology (Doctorate/Fellowship)

**Purpose:** To support doctoral study in psychology by minority students. **Focus:** Psychology. **Qualif.:** Applicant must be a U.S. citizen or permanent resident and a member of a minority group. Applicant must be enrolled in a full-time APA-approved academic program leading to a doctoral degree in a field of psychology. Candidate may apply for support in either research or clinical training. Candidate should have an interest in a career in mental health research, and/or services relevant to ethnic and racial minority groups. Fellowships may include a full tuition scholarship.

**Funds Avail.:** $8,340/year. **To Apply:** Write to APA for application form and guidelines. **Deadline:** January 15. Notification in April. **Contact:** Dr. James M. Jones, Director, at the above address (see entry 805).

---

### • 808 •
## American Psychological Association - Public Policy Office
750 1st St., NE
Washington, DC 20002
*E-mail:* AZS.APA@EMAIL.APA.ORG
*URL:* http://www.apa.org/

*Ph:* (202)336-5500
*Fax:* (202)336-6063

### • 809 • APA Congressional Fellowships (Postdoctorate/Fellowship)

**Purpose:** To provide psychologists with the opportunity to participate in Congressional policy making in psychology-related areas. **Focus:** Psychology, Government, U.S. Congress. **Qualif.:** Applicant may be of any nationality, but must be a member of APA who has a Ph.D. degree in psychology and a minimum of two years postdoctoral experience. Fellowships are tenable in Washington, D.C., where fellows work as legislative assistants on the staff of a member of Congress or on a Congressional committee, and attend a seminar series on issues involving science and public policy. **Criteria:** Selection is based on demonstrated competence in scientific and/or professional psychology; sensitivity toward policy issues and a strong interest in applying psychological knowledge to the solution of societal problems.

**Funds Avail.:** $37,000 - $47,000, plus $2,500 for moving and travel expenses is available, depending on postdoctoral experience. **No. of Awards:** 5. **To Apply:** Write for application guidelines. Submit the following: a detailed curriculum vitae listing educational background, professional employment, and publications; a statement of interest and career goals; and three letters of reference. **Deadline:** Materials must be submitted by mid-January. **Contact:** Brian Wilcox, Coordinator, at the above address (see entry 808).

**• 810 •**
**American Public Power Association -**
**Demonstration of Energy-Efficient Developments**
2301 M St., NW                    *Ph:* (202)467-2960
Washington, DC 20037              *Fax:* (202)467-2910
*URL:* http://www.appanet.org

**• 811 • DEED Scholarships** *(Graduate, Undergraduate/Scholarship)*

**Purpose:** To encourage student research and study related to the interests of electric power or energy services industries. **Focus:** Energy Sciences, Electrical Engineering. **Qualif.:** Applicants may be of any nationality, but must be undergraduate or graduate students who are sponsored by a municipally owned electric utility that is a member of DEED. Write for a list of participating utilities. Awards are tenable at accredited U.S. institutions, and may be applied to tuition or research costs. Successful applicants are expected to conduct research on a project approved by the sponsoring utility and submit a final report. **Criteria:** Awards are given based on broad applicability of benefits to public power systems, close involvement of host utility in project management, superior academic performance, generalizable methodologies, and promotion of energy-efficiency.

**Funds Avail.:** $3,000. **No. of Awards:** 10. **To Apply:** Contact administrator for application form. Application must be signed and returned by the sponsoring utility. Student transcript must be mailed to the administrator directly from the school. **Deadline:** December, July.

**Remarks:** At least one-third of the award is withheld until completion of the project. **Contact:** Holly Riester, DEED Administrator, at the above address (see entry 810).

**• 812 •**
**American Quarter Horse Youth Association**
PO Box 3211
Amarillo, TX 79120-2111          *Ph:* (806)376-5181
*URL:* http://www.aqha.com

**• 813 • AQHYA Scholarships** *(Undergraduate/Scholarship)*

**Purpose:** To reward outstanding members of the AQHYA. **Focus:** General Studies. **Qualif.:** Applicants must have been members of the American Quarter Horse Youth Association for the past three years, not older than 21 or have completed more than one year of college, and have at least a 2.5 GPA or be in the upper 20th percentile of their graduating class. **Criteria:** High school grades, involvement in AQHYA, and financial need.

**Funds Avail.:** $1,000 per year through four years of college. **No. of Awards:** 13. **To Apply:** Applicant must supply letters of recommendation from school and horse interests, extracurricular information, and standard information about home and school. In addition, parents' total net worth income tax form must accompany application. **Deadline:** May 15. **Contact:** Heath Miller, Director of Youth Activities and AQHYA, at the above address (see entry 812).

**• 814 •**
**American Radio Relay League**
225 Main St.                      *Ph:* (860)594-0230
Newington, CT 06111               *Fax:* (860)594-0259
*E-mail:* foundation@arrl.org
*URL:* http://www.arrl.org

**• 815 • Albuquerque Amateur Radio Club Scholarship** *(Undergraduate/Scholarship)*

**Qualif.:** For a resident of New Mexico working on an undergraduate degree.

**Funds Avail.:** $500. **To Apply:** Applicants must supply a one page essay on the role amateur radio has played in their lives. **Deadline:** February 1.

**• 816 • Earl I. Anderson Scholarship** *(Undergraduate/Scholarship)*

**Qualif.:** To an ARRL radio operator with any class license attending electronic engineering or related classes in IL, IN, MI, or FL.

**Funds Avail.:** $1,250. **Deadline:** February 1.

**• 817 • Mary Lou Brown Scholarship** *(Undergraduate/Scholarship)*

**Qualif.:** A minimum of a general radio operator's license is required. Must be a resident of ARRL Northwest Division and have a grade point average of 3.0 or higher. Must also have demonstrated interest in promoting the Amateur Radio Service.

**Funds Avail.:** $2,500. **Deadline:** February 1.

**• 818 • Chicago FM Club Scholarship** *(Undergraduate/Scholarship)*

**Qualif.:** For an applicants holding a technician's radio license and residing in the FCC Ninth Call District. Student must be enrolled in a two or four year college or trade school.

**Funds Avail.:** $500. **Deadline:** February 1.

**• 819 • Tom and Judith Comstock Scholarship** *(Undergraduate/Scholarship)*

**Focus:** General studies. **Qualif.:** Applicants must be members of the American Radio Relay League, and high school seniors accepted at or students attending two- or four-year colleges and universities. **Criteria:** Preference given to residents of Texas and Oklahoma.

**Funds Avail.:** $500 **No. of Awards:** Varies. **To Apply:** Write for further details. **Deadline:** February. **Contact:** AARL Foundation Scholarship Program at the above address (see entry 814).

*American Radio Relay League (continued)*

• 820 • **Irving W. Cook, WA0CGS Scholarship**
*(Undergraduate/Scholarship)*

**Qualif.:** To a resident of Kansas who holds a radio operator's license of any class and is studying electronics or communications.

**Funds Avail.:** $1,000. **Deadline:** February 1.

• 821 • **Charles Clarke Cordle Memorial Scholarship**
*(Undergraduate/Scholarship)*

**Focus:** General studies. **Qualif.:** Applicants must be licensed amateur radio operators. **Criteria:** Preference given to residents of Georgia and Alabama, and attending school in that region who have grade point averages of 2.5 and higher.

**Funds Avail.:** $1000. **No. of Awards:** Varies. **To Apply:** Write for further details. **Deadline:** February. **Contact:** AARL Foundation Scholarship Program at the above address (see entry 814).

• 822 • **Charles N. Fisher Memorial Scholarship**
*(Undergraduate/Scholarship)*

**Qualif.:** Must be a radio operator with any class license and a resident of ARRL Southwestern Division enrolled in a regionally accredited electronics or communication study program.

**Funds Avail.:** $1,000. **Deadline:** February 1.

• 823 • **Michael J. Flosi Memorial Scholarship**
*(Undergraduate/Scholarship)*

**Qualif.:** To a resident of the FCC Ninth Call District who is a high school senior or graduate holding a technician's license.

**Funds Avail.:** $500. **Deadline:** February 1.

• 824 • **General Fund Scholarship** *(Undergraduate/ Scholarship)*

**Focus:** General studies. **Qualif.:** Applicants must be licensed amateur radio operators.

**Funds Avail.:** $1000. **No. of Awards:** 2. **To Apply:** Write for further details. **Deadline:** February. **Contact:** AARL Foundation Scholarship Program at the above address (see entry 814).

• 825 • **ARRL Scholarship Honoring Senator Barry Goldwater** *(Undergraduate/Scholarship)*

**Qualif.:** Minimum of a novice radio license is required.

**Funds Avail.:** $5,000 per year for study at a regionally accredited institution. **Deadline:** February 1.

• 826 • **Paul and Helen L. Grauer Scholarship**
*(Undergraduate/Scholarship)*

**Qualif.:** Must have at least a novice radio operator's license and be a resident of ARRL Midwest Division attending classes in electronics or communications.

**Funds Avail.:** $1,000. **Deadline:** February 1.

• 827 • **K2TEO Martin J. Green Sr. Memorial Scholarship** *(Undergraduate/Scholarship)*

**Qualif.:** Must have at least a general radio operator's license. **Criteria:** Preference is given to a student ham from a ham family.

**Funds Avail.:** $1,000. **Deadline:** February 1.

• 828 • **Perry F. Hadlock Memorial Scholarship**
*(Undergraduate/Scholarship)*

**Qualif.:** Must have a general radio operator's license and be following a course of study in electronic engineering at Clarkson University in Potsdam, NY.

**Funds Avail.:** $1,000. **Deadline:** February 1.

• 829 • **Dr. James L. Lawson Memorial Scholarship**
*(Undergraduate/Scholarship)*

**Focus:** General studies. **Qualif.:** Applicants must be amateur radio operators holding general licenses. **Criteria:** Preference given to residents of ARRL Midwest Division (Iowa, Kansas, Missouri, Nebraska) attending schools in that Division, and studying electronics, communications or related fields. Preference also given to residents of New England Division (Connecticut, Massachusetts, Maine, New Hampshire, Rhode Island, and Vermont) and also entire New York State, and attending school within that Division and/or state.

**Funds Avail.:** $500 **No. of Awards:** Varies. **To Apply:** Write for further details. **Deadline:** February. **Contact:** AARL Foundation Scholarship Program at the above address (see entry 814).

• 830 • **Fred R. McDaniel Memorial Scholarship**
*(Undergraduate/Scholarship)*

**Focus:** General studies. **Qualif.:** Applicants must be amateur radio operators holding general licenses. **Criteria:** Preference given to applicants residing in the FCC Fifth Call District (Texas, Oklahoma, Arkansas, Louisiana, Mississippi, and New Mexico) and attending schools within that Call district, studying electronics, communications or related fields who have grade point averages of 3.0 and higher and hold baccalaureate or higher degrees.

**Funds Avail.:** $500. **No. of Awards:** Varies. **To Apply:** Write for further details. **Deadline:** February. **Contact:** AARL Foundation Scholarship Program at the above address (see entry 814).

• 831 • **Edmond A. Metzger Scholarship**
*(Undergraduate/Scholarship)*

**Focus:** Electrical engineering. **Qualif.:** Applicants must be amateur radio operators with general licenses who are current members of the American Radio Relay League, current residents of and attend school within the ARRL Central Division (Illinois, Indiana, Wisconsin), studying electrical engineering. **Criteria:** Preference given to applicants with baccalaureate or higher degrees.

**Funds Avail.:** $500. **No. of Awards:** Varies. **To Apply:** Write for further details. **Deadline:** February. **Contact:** AARL Foundation Scholarship Program at the above address (see entry 814).

• 832 • **Mississippi Scholarship** *(Undergraduate/ Scholarship)*

**Qualif.:** For a resident of Mississippi studying electronics or communication who holds a radio operator's license of any class. Student must be under 30 years of age.

**Funds Avail.:** $500. **Deadline:** February 1.

• 833 • **North Texas - Bob Nelson KB5BNU Memorial Scholarship** *(Undergraduate/Scholarship)*

**Qualif.:** To a radio operator of any class in Texas or Oklahoma. Decision is based on character, humanitarianism, and active amateur radio participation. Nominee must also be enrolled in a full time degree program.

**Funds Avail.:** $750. **Deadline:** February 1.

• 834 • **Nemal Electronics Scholarship**
*(Undergraduate/Scholarship)*

**Focus:** General studies. **Qualif.:** Applicants must be amateur radio operators holding general licenses. **Criteria:** Preference given to applicants studying electronics, communications or related fields who hold baccalaureate or higher degrees and who have grade point averages of 3.0 and higher.

**Funds Avail.:** $500. **No. of Awards:** Varies. **To Apply:** Applicants must submit a brief letter explaining background and educational plans. Write for further details. **Deadline:** February. **Contact:** AARL Foundation Scholarship Program at the above address (see entry 814).

• 835 • **New England FEMARA Scholarship**
*(Undergraduate/Scholarship)*

**Focus:** General studies. **Qualif.:** Applicants must be amateur radio operators holding technician licenses. **Criteria:** Preference given to residents of the six New England states.

**Funds Avail.:** $600. **No. of Awards:** Varies. **To Apply:** Write for further details. **Deadline:** February. **Contact:** AARL Foundation Scholarship Program at the above address (see entry 814).

• 836 • **PHD Scholarship** *(Undergraduate/Scholarship)*

**Focus:** General studies. **Qualif.:** Applicants must be licensed amateur radio operators. **Criteria:** Preference given to residents of ARRL Midwest Division (Iowa, Kansas, Missouri, Nebraska) attending schools in that Division, studying journalism, computer science or electronic engineering, and children of deceased Radio Amateurs.

**Funds Avail.:** $1000. **No. of Awards:** Varies. **To Apply:** Write for further details. **Deadline:** February. **Contact:** AARL Foundation Scholarship Program at the above address (see entry 814).

• 837 • **Donald R. Riebhoff Memorial Scholarship**
*(Undergraduate/Scholarship)*

**Focus:** General studies. **Qualif.:** Applicants must be licensed amateur radio operators. **Criteria:**

**Funds Avail.:** Pending. **No. of Awards:** Varies. **To Apply:** Write for further details. **Deadline:** February. **Contact:** AARL Foundation Scholarship Program at the above address (see entry 814).

• 838 • **F. Charles Ruling/N6FR Memorial Scholarship** *(Undergraduate/Scholarship)*

**Focus:** General studies. **Qualif.:** Applicants must be amateur radio operators holding general licenses. **Criteria:** Preference given to students in electronics, communications and related fields.

**Funds Avail.:** $1000. **No. of Awards:** Varies. **To Apply:** Write for further details. **Deadline:** February. **Contact:** AARL Foundation Scholarship Program at the above address (see entry 814).

• 839 • **Eugene "Gene" Sallee, W4YFR Memorial Scholarship** *(Undergraduate/Scholarship)*

**Qualif.:** To a Georgia resident who holds a technician plus radio operator's license and a minimum 3.0 grade point average.

**Funds Avail.:** $500. **Deadline:** February 1.

• 840 • **Six Meter Club of Chicago Scholarship**
*(Undergraduate/Scholarship)*

**Qualif.:** For a resident of Illinois who holds a radio license of any class and who is enrolled in a post-secondary education program in Illinois.

**Funds Avail.:** $500. **Deadline:** February 1.

• 841 • **L. Phil Wicker Scholarship** *(Undergraduate/Scholarship)*

**Qualif.:** Must hold a general radio operator's license and be attending school in ARRL Roanoke Division. Must also be following a course of study in electronics or communications.

**Funds Avail.:** $1,000. **Deadline:** February 1.

---

• 842 •
**American Research Center in Egypt**
30 E. 20th St., Ste. 401          *Ph:* (212)529-6661
New York, NY 10003-1310          *Fax:* (212)529-6856
*E-mail:* walz@acfcluster.nyu.edu
*URL:* http://www.arce.org/home.html

• 843 • **American Research Center in Egypt Research Fellowships for Study in Egypt** *(Doctorate, Postdoctorate/Fellowship)*

**Purpose:** To support U.S. students and scholars who wish to study in Egypt. **Focus:** Egyptian Studies, Near Eastern Studies, Middle Eastern Studies, African Studies. **Qualif.:** Applicants must be U.S. citizens or permanent residents and Ph.D. students or more advanced scholars affiliated with a U.S. academic institution. Fellowships are tenable in Egypt. A fellow's research may be in any relevant humanities social science or fine arts discipline and may focus on any period of history.

**Funds Avail.:** $1,150-3,325/month stipend and round-trip travel allowance **No. of Awards:** 10. **To Apply:** Write to the Executive Director for application guidelines. **Deadline:** November 1. **Contact:** The American Research Center in Egypt at the above address (see entry 842).

• 844 • **American Research Center in Egypt Research Fellowships for Study in the U.S. or Canada** *(Doctorate/Fellowship)*

**Purpose:** To assist and support Egyptian doctoral students in U.S. institutions research topics relating to development issues in Egypt. **Focus:** Developmental Studies **Qualif.:** Candidates must be Egyptians with student visas who are enrolled at U.S. or Canadian universities. Applicants must have completed all requirements for a doctorate except the dissertation. Dissertation proposals must have direct relevance to the economic and social development of Egypt or current policy issues related to development. Specific topics vary. Proposals were accepted in the fields of economics, developmental studies, health, education, and women's studies. Fellowships are tenable only in Egypt.

**Funds Avail.:** International airfare, living stipend, and some research expenses. **No. of Awards:** 4. **To Apply:** Write to the Executive Director for application guidelines. Submit application with letters of recommendation. **Deadline:** November 1. **Contact:** The American Research Center in Egypt at the above address (see entry 842).

---

## • 845 •
### American Research Institute in Turkey
c/o University of Pennsylvania
  Museum
33rd and Spruce St.                    *Ph:* (215)898-3474
Philadelphia, PA 19104-6324            *Fax:* (215)898-0657
*E-mail:* leinwand@sas.upenn.edu
*URL:* http://mec.sas.upenn.edu

### • 846 • ARIT Fellowships *(Doctorate, Postdoctorate/ Fellowship)*

**Purpose:** To encourage scholars conducting research projects in Turkey. **Focus:** Near Eastern Studies, Humanities—Turkish Studies, Social Sciences—Turkish Studies. **Qualif.:** Applicants may be of any nationality, but must be scholars or advanced graduate students at an educational institution in the United States or Canada. Graduate student applicants must have completed all preliminary Ph.D. degree requirements. Candidate's research on Turkey may concentrate on ancient, medieval, or modern times in any field of the humanities or social sciences. Awards are tenable for travel and maintenance in Turkey. Fellowship applicants are personally responsible for obtaining permission from the Turkish government (through the Cultural Office at the Turkish Embassy, 1714 Massachusetts Avenue, N.W., Washington, D.C. 20036) to conduct research in Turkey. Candidates should contact the Embassy at least six months prior to the proposed start of research. **Criteria:** Applications are judged on excellence of their proposal and preparation of the researcher.

**Funds Avail.:** Varies. **No. of Awards:** Between 8 and 12. **To Apply:** Write to the Institute for application instructions. **Deadline:** November 15. Notification by January. **Contact:** Administrator at the above address (see entry 845).

### • 847 • NEH Fellowships for Research in Turkey *(Postdoctorate/Fellowship)*

**Purpose:** To encourage scholars conducting research projects in Turkey. **Focus:** Archaeology, Art, History, Linguistics, Literature, Humanities, Near Eastern Studies. **Qualif.:** Applicants may be of any nationality, but must be scholars or advanced graduate students at an educational institution in the United States or Canada. Graduate student applicants must have completed all preliminary Ph.D. degree requirements. Candidate's research on Turkey may concentrate on ancient, medieval, or modern times in any field of the humanities or social sciences. Awards are tenable at ARIT-Istanbul or ARIT-Ankara, depending on field of study. Fellowship applicants are personally responsible for obtaining permission from the Turkish government (through the Cultural Office at the Turkish Embassy, 1714 Massachusetts Avenue, N.W., Washington, D.C. 20036) to conduct research in Turkey. Candidates should contact the Embassy at least six months prior to the proposed start of research. **Criteria:** Based on excellence of proposed research and preparation of the scholar.

**Funds Avail.:** $10,000-30,000. **No. of Awards:** 2-3. **To Apply:** Write to the Institute for application instructions. **Deadline:** November 15. Notification by January 25. **Contact:** Administrator at the above address (see entry 845).

## • 848 •
### American Respiratory Care Foundation
11030 Ables Ln.                        *Ph:* (972)243-2272
Dallas, TX 75229-4593                  *Fax:* (972)484-2720
*E-mail:* info@aarc.org
*URL:* http://www.aarc.org/awards

### • 849 • Morton B. Duggan Jr. Memorial Education Recognition Award *(Undergraduate/Scholarship)*

**Purpose:** To assist students enrolled in respiratory therapy training programs. **Focus:** Respiratory Therapy. **Qualif.:** Candidates must be United States citizens or submit a copy of an immigration visa and be enrolled in an AMA-approved respiratory care training program. **Criteria:** Applications are accepted from all states with preference to Georgia and South Carolina candidates.

**Funds Avail.:** The scholarship award is $1,000. **No. of Awards:** 1. **To Apply:** The application must be accompanied by an official grade transcript showing a 3.0 average at the minimum, on a 4.0 scale or the equivalent, and at least two letters of recommendation, one attesting to the candidate's worthiness and potential in the field of respiratory care. One letter must be from the program director or a senior faculty member and the other from the medical director or other physician instructor. Submission of six copies of an original referenced paper on some facet of respiratory care accompanied by letters of approval by knowledgeable persons is also required. **Deadline:** Deadline for receipt of application is June 30; the scholarship is awarded September 1.

**Remarks:** The award is given in memory of Morton B. Duggan. **Contact:** Norma Hernandez, Administrative Coordinator, American Respiratory Care Foundation, at the above address (see entry 848).

### • 850 • Jimmy A. Young Memorial Education Recognition Award *(Undergraduate/Scholarship)*

**Purpose:** To assist minority students in respiratory therapy programs based on academic achievement. **Focus:** Respiratory Therapy. **Qualif.:** Applicants must be United States citizens or submit a copy of their immigrant visa. They must be members of minority groups, which include American Indians, Asian or Pacific Islanders, Black-Americans, Spanish-Americans, and Mexican-Americans. They must provide evidence of enrollment in an AMA-approved respiratory care program and have a minimum grade point average of 3.0 on a 4.0 scale. **Criteria:** Applicant must be of minority origin.

**Funds Avail.:** $1,000. **No. of Awards:** 1 each year. **To Apply:** Candidates must submit official transcripts of grades, and two letters of recommendation from the program director and medical director that verifies the applicant is deserving and a member of a designated minority group. An original essay on some facet of respiratory care is also required. **Deadline:** Applications are accepted between April 1 and June 30. Scholarships are awarded by September 1.

**Remarks:** These scholarships are given in memory of Jimmy A. Young who contributed greatly to respiratory therapy education. **Contact:** Norma Hernandez, Administrative Coordinator, at the above address (see entry 848).

---

• 851 •

## American-Scandinavian Foundation
725 Park Ave.    *Ph:* (212)879-9779
New York, NY 10021   *Fax:* (212)249-3444
*E-mail:* grants@amscan.org
*URL:* http://www.amscan.org

### • 852 • Awards for Advanced Study and Research in Scandinavia *(Graduate, Postgraduate/Fellowship, Grant)*

**Purpose:** To encourage advanced study and research and increase understanding between the United States and Scandinavia. **Focus:** General Studies. **Qualif.:** Applicant must be a U.S. citizen or permanent resident who holds a bachelor's degree. Applicant must be planning a project or study course that would be best pursued in one of the Scandinavian countries (Denmark, Finland, Iceland, Norway, Sweden). Competence in the language of the country is expected. Preference is given to candidates working on dissertations. The number and value of the awards vary annually. Other factors being equal, priority (for fellowships) will be given candidates at the dissertation level.

**Funds Avail.:** $3,000 for grants, $15,000 for fellowships. **To Apply:** Write for application form and guidelines. **Deadline:** November 1.

**Remarks:** Awards are also available to citizens of the Scandinavian countries who wish to undertake programs of study or research in the United States. Candidates are recommended by agencies cooperating with the ASF. **Contact:** Exchange Division at the above address (see entry 851).

### • 853 • Awards for Advanced Study or Research in the U.S.A. *(Graduate/Award)*

**Purpose:** To enable Scandinavians to undertake study or research in the U.S. **Focus:** General Studies. **Qualif.:** Applicants must be citizens of Denmark, Finland, Iceland, Norway or Sweden. Applicants must be at the graduate level. Awards are tenable in the U.S.

**Funds Avail.:** Varies depending on total funds available by country. **To Apply:** Danish applicants should contact The Denmark-America Foundation, Dronningens Fiolstraede 24, 1171 3.Sal, Copenhagen K, Denmark. Finnish applicants should contact The League of Finnish-American Societies, Mechelininkatu 10, SF 00100 Helsinki, Finland. Icelandic applicants should contact The Icelandic-American Society, c/o The U.S.-Icelandic Educational Commission, Laugavegi 26, 101 Reykjavik, Iceland. Norwegian applicants should contact The Norway-America Association, Drammensveien 20 C, 0255 Oslo 2, Norway. Swedish applicants should contact The Sweden-American Foundation, Box 5280, S-102 46 Stockholm, Sweden.

---

• 854 •

## American School of Classical Studies at Athens
6-8 Charlton St.    *Ph:* (609)683-0800
Princeton, NJ 08540-5232  *Fax:* (609)924-0574
*E-mail:* ascsa@ascsa.org
*URL:* http://www.ascsa.org

### • 855 • American School of Classical Studies Summer Sessions Scholarships *(Graduate, Professional Development/Scholarship)*

**Purpose:** To support study in Greece. **Focus:** Antiquities and Topography of Greece. **Qualif.:** Candidate must reside in the United States or Canada. Applicant must qualify for and obtain summer session membership in the School. Scholarships are tenable at the summer course run by the School in Greece.

**Funds Avail.:** All fees, room, and partial board. **To Apply:** Write to the Committee for application forms and guidelines. **Deadline:** February 15. **Contact:** Committee on the Summer Sessions, at the above address (see entry 854).

### • 856 • Oscar Broneer Fellowship *(Doctorate, Graduate, Postdoctorate/Fellowship)*

**Purpose:** For study at the American School of Classical Studies at Athens or the American Academy at Rome. **Focus:** Classical Studies. **Qualif.:** Applicants must be recent alumni of the American Academy in Rome or the American School of Classical Studies at Athens, and will study at the opposite institution.

**Funds Avail.:** Stipend of $8,840, plus fees, room and partial board. **No. of Awards:** 1. **To Apply:** Updated curriculum vitae, either a project statement or a statement of why the candidate wishes to attend the other institution and two letters of reference must be sent in duplicate to each of the following. **Deadline:** March 1. **Contact:** Dr. James D. Muhly, Director, American School of Classical Studies, 54 Souidias St., GR-106 76 Athens, Greece, or Dr. Lester K. Little, Director, American Academy in Rome, via Angelo Masina 5, Rome, Italy 00153.

### • 857 • Anna C. and Oliver C. Colburn Fellowship *(Doctorate, Postdoctorate/Fellowship)*

**Focus:** Classical Studies. **Qualif.:** Applicants must be accepted as Student Associate Members or as Senior Associate Members of the American School of Classical Studies at Athens (ASCSA). They may not be members of ASCSA during year of application. Student membership is open to graduate students who have passed their qualifying examinations for a Ph.D. degree. **No. of Awards:** 1. **To Apply:** Applicants must submit formal application, transcripts and letters of recommendation. Candidates must apply to both ASCSA and the Archeological Institute of America (AIA). **Deadline:** February 1. **Contact:** Archeological Institute of America, 656 Beacon St., Boston, MA, 02215 and ASCSA at the above address (see entry 854).

### • 858 • Alison M. Frantz Fellowship *(Doctorate/Fellowship)*

**Purpose:** To support doctorate or post-doctorate work in one of the fields represented by the Gennadius Library in Athens. **Focus:** Late Antiquity, Byzantine Studies, post-Byzantine, and Modern Greek. **Qualif.:** Applicants must be PhD candidates or recent PhDs from the United States or Canada.

**Funds Avail.:** Room, board, waiver of school fees, and a stipend of $8,840. **Contact:** American School of Classical Studies at Athens at the above address (see entry 854). ATTEN: Prof. James R. McCredie, Chm., Committee on the Gennaduis Library.

### • 859 • Jacob Hirsch Fellowship *(Doctorate, Graduate/Fellowship)*

**Purpose:** To allow students to study at the American School of Classical Studies at Athens. **Focus:** Archeology. **Qualif.:** Candidates must be Student Associate Members who are graduate students writing a dissertation in archeology or a recent Ph.D. completing a project, such as a dissertation, for publication. Students in the United States or Israel are eligible. The project requires substantial residence in Greece.

**Funds Avail.:** Stipend of $8,840, plus fees, room and partial board. **No. of Awards:** 1. **To Apply:** Applicant must submit transcripts, three letters of recommendation and a detailed description of the project to be pursued. Application must be made for membership in the School at the same time. **Deadline:** January 31. **Contact:** American School of Classical Studies, Committee on Admissions and Fellowships, at the above address (see entry 854).

---

*American School of Classical Studies at Athens (continued)*

### • 860 • Thomas Day Seymour Fellowship *(Graduate/Fellowship)*

**Purpose:** To allow students to study at the American School of Classical Studies in Athens in Greece. **Focus:** Greek Literature, Greek History. **Qualif.:** Candidates must be regular members of the school, that is, graduate students in classical studies (literature, archeology, history) in the United States or Canada. They preferably will have finished at least one year of graduate work but will have not completed their Ph.D. The Seymour Fellowship is specifically for the study of Greek literature and history. **Criteria:** Selection is based upon transcripts, recommendations and examinations in Greek language, history and archeology or literature.

**Funds Avail.:** A stipend of $8,840, plus fees, room, and partial board. **No. of Awards:** 1. **Deadline:** January 15. **Contact:** Admissions Coordinator, American School of Classical Studies at Athens, at the above address (see entry 854).

### • 861 • Summer Session Awards *(Graduate, Professional Development, Undergraduate/Scholarship)*

**Purpose:** American School of Classical Studies at Athens offers two six-week sessions emphasizing the topography and antiquities of Greece. **Qualif.:** Applicants may be graduate or undergraduate students or high school and college teachers.

**Funds Avail.:** Five scholarships to cover cost of program plus room and partial board. **Deadline:** February 1. **Contact:** Committee on the Summer Session, American School of Classical Studies at Athens, at the above address (see entry 854).

### • 862 • Elizabeth A. Whitehead Visiting Professorships *(Professional Development/Award)*

**Purpose:** To provide research opportunities at the School. **Focus:** Greek Archaeology, Greek History, Greek Literature. **Qualif.:** Applicant may be of any nationality. Applicant must normally be a member of the School's Managing Committee, but applications are also accepted from faculty members at institutions that cooperate with the School. There are 148 cooperating institutions in the United States and Canada. Professorships are honorary in nature and are intended to allow scholars to engage in their own research. Awardees are expected to offer a seminar during the winter term and to participate in some of the School trips in the fall.

**Funds Avail.:** $6,000, housing and fees. **To Apply:** Write for guidelines and application form two years before the appointment is to take place. **Deadline:** February 15. **Contact:** Chairperson of the Committee on Personnel, at the above address (see entry 854).

---

### • 863 •

## American Schools of Oriental Research
656 Beacon Street, 5th Fl.            *Ph:* (617)353-6570
Boston, MA 02215-2010                *Fax:* (617)353-6575
*E-mail:* asor@bu.edu

### • 864 • Annual Professorship in Jerusalem *(Postdoctorate/Fellowship)*

**Purpose:** To provide for professorship for a post-doctoral scholar at the W.F. Albright Institute of Archaeological Research. **Qualif.:** Open to scholars in Near-Eastern archaeology, geography, history, and Biblical studies.

**Funds Avail.:** $23,000 maximum. **Deadline:** October 13.

### • 865 • George A. Barton Fellowship *(Doctorate, Postdoctorate/Fellowship)*

**Purpose:** To provide one research fellowship for seminarians, predoctoral, or recent post-doctoral students. **Funds Avail.:** $2,000 stipend plus free room and half board for the fellow. **Deadline:** October 13.

**Remarks:** Residence at the Albright Institute is required. The award may not be used in the summer.

### • 866 • Council of American Overseas Research Centers Fellowships *(Postdoctorate/Fellowship)*

**Purpose:** To support advanced multi-country research. **Qualif.:** Open to scholars pursuing research in broad questions of multi-country significance in the fields of humanities, social sciences, and related natural sciences in countries in the Near and Middle East and South Asia. Doctoral candidates and established scholars with U.S. citizenship are eligible to apply as individuals or in teams. **Criteria:** Preference is given to candidates examing comparative and/or cross-regional questions requiring research in two or more countries.

**Funds Avail.:** $6,000 plus $3,000 for travel. **Deadline:** January 1.

### • 867 • Dorot Research Fellowship *(Postdoctorate/Fellowship)*

**Purpose:** To encourage the development of a major research project by senior scholars in the field of ancient Near Eastern studies.

**Funds Avail.:** Stipend is $22,000, plus room and half board. R Ten months to a year.

### • 868 • Endowment for Biblical Research, Summer Research and Travel Grants *(Doctorate, Graduate, Postdoctorate/Grant)*

**Purpose:** To provide for summer research. **Qualif.:** Must be seminarians, graduate students, or recent post-doctoral scholars from any country outside the Middle East and the Eastern Mediterranean.

**Funds Avail.:** Each grant is $1,000.

### • 869 • Jennifer C. Groot Fellowship *(Graduate, Undergraduate/Fellowship)*

**Purpose:** To assist an undergraduate or graduate student of archaeology to participate in an archaeological excavation in Jordan. **Qualif.:** Open to U.S. or Canadian students with little or no prior archaeological field experience.

**Funds Avail.:** $1,500. **Deadline:** February 1.

### • 870 • Harrell Family Fellowship *(Graduate/Fellowship)*

**Purpose:** To support a graduate student in an ACOR-supported archaeological project which has passed an academic review process, or an ACOR-funded archaeological research project. **Qualif.:** Open to enrolled graduate students of any nationality.

**Funds Avail.:** $1,500. **Deadline:** Februray 1.

### • 871 • Charles U. and Janet C. Harris Fellowship *(Doctorate, Postdoctorate/Fellowship)*

**Purpose:** To support participation in any phase or aspect of a project in Cyprus which has been approved by ASOR's Committee on Archaeological Policy.

**Funds Avail.:** $1,500. **Deadline:** February 1.

• 872 • **Islamic Studies Fellowship** *(Doctorate/ Fellowship)*

**Qualif.:** Candidates must have expertise in research and teaching in Islamic archaeology, art, and architecture.

**Funds Avail.:** $12,200 stipend plus room and half board. **Deadline:** October 13.

• 873 • **Kress Fellowship in the Art and Archaeology of Jordan** *(Doctorate/Fellowship)*

**Qualif.:** For pre-doctoral students (American Ph.D. candidates) completing dissertation research in an art historical topic. A topic should be focused on some aspect of the artistic legacy of a specific culture, site, or period. The candidate should make a strong case for residency at the American Center or Oriental Research in Amman, Jordan to do one's research.

**Funds Avail.:** $14,000. **Deadline:** February 1.

• 874 • **Samuel H. Kress Foundation Fellowship** *(Doctorate/Fellowship)*

**Purpose:** To provide for one ten-month dissertation research fellowship of art history, architecture, or archaeology. **Qualif.:** Applicants must be U.S. citizens well advanced in their dissertation research and be able to demonstrate the need of benefit of continuing research in Jerusalem.

**Funds Avail.:** A stipend of $6,000 plus room and half board for the fellow is provided. R Ten months.

• 875 • **Samuel H. Kress Joint Athens-Jerusalem Fellowship** *(Postdoctorate/Fellowship)*

**Purpose:** For research at the American School of Classical Studies, Athens, and the W.F. Albright Institute of Archaeological research, Jerusalem. **Qualif.:** Applicants may be pre-doctoral students researching art history, architecture, archaeology, or classical studies.

**Funds Avail.:** $5,500 stipend plus room and board. **Deadline:** November 1.

• 876 • **Lindstrom Foundation Student Service Scholarships** *(Graduate, Undergraduate/Scholarship)*

**Purpose:** To award up to 20 hours of service. **Qualif.:** For ASOR student members.

**Funds Avail.:** Maximum award is $500. **Deadline:** September 15.

• 877 • **Andrew W. Mellon Foundation Fellowships** *(Doctorate, Postdoctorate/Fellowship)*

**Qualif.:** Open to Czech, Hungarian, Polish, and Slovak scholars. Candidates should not be permanently resident outside the four countries concerned, and should have obtained a doctorate by the time the fellowship is awarded. **Deadline:** October 13.

• 878 • **Mesopotamian Fellowship** *(Doctorate, Postdoctorate/Fellowship)*

**Purpose:** To provide scholars with the opportunity to do independent research on Mesopotamian civilization. **Focus:** Anthropology, Archaeology, Architecture, Biblical Studies, Epigraphy, History, History of Art, Literature, Philology. **Qualif.:** Candidate may be of any nationality, but must be a member of ASOR or one of its affiliated institutions and be a seminarian, or be a pre- or postdoctoral scholar. Special consideration is given to those scholars whose research is affiliated with a ASOR institution.

**Funds Avail.:** $5,000. **To Apply:** Write to the Coordinator of Academic Programs for application form and guidelines. **Deadline:**

February 1. Notification in April. **Contact:** Coordinator of Academic Programs at the above address (see entry 863).

• 879 • **National Endowment for the Humanities Post-Doctoral Fellowships, Nicosia** *(Postdoctorate/ Fellowship)*

**Purpose:** To support any field of humanistic research requiring residence in Cyprus. **Qualif.:** U.S. citizens who are humanities scholars holding a Ph.D. as of January 1 of the year of the award are eligible.

**Funds Avail.:** Up to $30,000. **Deadline:** January 15.

• 880 • **Near and Middle East Research and Training Program Pre-Doctoral Fellowships** *(Doctorate/ Fellowship)*

**Purpose:** To support graduate students of political science, economics, international relations, history, or journalism to conduct research in Jordan. **Qualif.:** For students who are U.S. citizens and who have not yet chosen a dissertation topic and who have had little or no prior experience in the Middle East.

**Funds Avail.:** Maximum award is $10,100. **Deadline:** February 1.

• 881 • **Near and Middle East Research and Training Program Senior Research Grants** *(Postdoctorate/Grant)*

**Qualif.:** For senior post-doctoral scholars who are U.S. citizens pursuing research or publication projects in the social sciences, humanities, and associated disciplines relating to the Middle East. **Criteria:** Preference is given to scholars with limited prior experience in the Middle East.

**Funds Avail.:** $34,700 maximum grant. **Deadline:** February 1.

• 882 • **NEH Post-Doctoral Research** *(Postdoctorate/ Fellowship)*

**Purpose:** To support humanities research in Jordan. **Qualif.:** For post-doctoral scholars in modern and classical languages, linguistics, literature, history, jurisprudence, philosophy, archaeology, comparative religion, ethics, and the history, criticism, and theory of the arts. **Deadline:** February 1.

• 883 • **Kenneth W. Russell Fellowship** *(Graduate/ Fellowship)*

**Purpose:** To assist a student in Jordan with graduate studies.

**Funds Avail.:** $1,500. **Deadline:** February 1.

• 884 • **United States Information Agency (USIA) Fellowships** *(Doctorate, Postdoctorate/Fellowship)*

**Purpose:** To provide for research in the social sciences and humanities in Near Eastern studies. **Qualif.:** For pre-doctoral and recent post-doctoral scholars.

**Funds Avail.:** Maximum award is $14,000. **Deadline:** February 1.

• 885 • **USIA Fellowships, AIAR, Jerusalem** *(Doctorate, Postdoctorate/Fellowship)*

**Purpose:** To provide for research in Jerusalem in any Near Eastern studies field from pre-history to modern. **Qualif.:** Available to U.S. citizens who are pre-doctoral students or recent Ph.D. recipients.

**Funds Avail.:** $6,800 plus room and half board. **Deadline:** October 13.

## • 886 •
## American Sheep Industry Association

6911 S. Yosemite St., Ste. 200          *Ph:* (303)771-3500
Englewood, CO 80112-2142                *Fax:* (303)771-8200
*E-mail:* mjensen@sheepusa.org
*URL:* http://www.sheepusa.org

### • 887 • National Wool Growers Memorial Fellowships *(Graduate/Fellowship)*

**Purpose:** To advance the sheep, lamb, and wool industry. **Focus:** Agricultural Sciences, Textile Science. **Qualif.:** Applicants must be graduate students involved in lamb or wool research.

**Funds Avail.:** There is a $2,500 stipend. **No. of Awards:** One annually. **To Apply:** Applications are available from the American Sheep Industry Association. **Deadline:** June 1. **Contact:** Mary Jensen, at the above address (see entry 886).

## • 888 •
## American Social Health Association

PO Box 13827                            *Ph:* (919)361-8418
Durham, NC 27709-3827                   *Fax:* (919)361-8425

### • 889 • ASHA Postdoctoral Fellowships *(Postdoctorate/Fellowship)*

**Purpose:** To encourage research training in the field of sexually transmitted diseases. **Focus:** Sexually Transmitted Diseases. **Qualif.:** Applicants must be residents in the United States, and be recent recipients of a Ph.D., M.D., or D.Sc. degree in a relevant field. Fellowships are tenable at U.S. research institutions. Candidates must seek the sponsorship of an established investigator at the host institution, who is willing to supervise research training during the award term.

**Funds Avail.:** $27,500-$28,750. **To Apply:** Write to ASHA for application materials. **Deadline:** Spring or summer. **Contact:** Kay Flaminio at the above address (see entry 888).

## • 890 •
## American Society of Agricultural Engineers

2950 Niles Rd.                          *Ph:* (616)429-0300
St. Joseph, MI 49085-8607               *Fax:* (616)429-3852
*E-mail:* asae@asae.org

### • 891 • Marijane E. and William J. Adams, Jr. Scholarship *(Undergraduate/Scholarship)*

**Purpose:** To assist a student of biological or agricultural engineering. **Qualif.:** Applicant must be a declared major in biological or agricultural engineering at a school accredited by ABET or CEAB. They must be student members of ASAE, in at least the second year of study toward a degree, have a GPA of at least 2.5 out of 4.0, be able to show need for financial aid, and have a special interest in agricultural machinery product design and development.

**Funds Avail.:** $1,000. **No. of Awards:** 1. **To Apply:** In a letter, applicants should formally request the scholarship, state how the money will be used, outline the extent of financial need, and tell of their interest in the design and development of new agricultural machinery products. The letter should be no more than two pages long. Applicants should also have their college dean or department chair send a statement on official college stationary to the ASAE Foundation corroborating that applicant is a biological or agricultural engineering major, a student member of ASAE, that the

curriculum is accredited by ABET or CEAB, that applicant's GPA is at least 2.5, and that financial need can be demonstrated. **Deadline:** April 15. **Contact:** Carol Flautt, Administrator, The Adams Scholarship Fund, ASAE Foundation, at the above address (see entry 890).

### • 892 • Howard S. Brembeck Scholarship in Agricultural Engineering *(Graduate/Scholarship)*

**Purpose:** To promote interest in the development of poultry related equipment. **Focus:** Agricultural engineering. **Qualif.:** Applicants must be graduates of an accredited college or university with a degree in agricultural engineering. They must also have a desire to pursue a graduate degree in a field that is related to the development of poultry equipment. Poultry equipment would include specializing in any and all equipment that would be considered necessary to sustain the life of the animal during the production process. Scholarship is open to applicants of any nationality but they must attend graduate school in the United States. **Criteria:** Recipients are chosen by a scholarship committee convened by the Midwest Poultry Consortium.

**Funds Avail.:** $5,000. **To Apply:** Applicants must provide proof of acceptance into a graduate program and a resume to CTB, Inc., PO Box 2000, Milford, IN 46526 or Midwest Poultry Consortium, Box 191, 13033 Ridgedale Dr., Minneapolis, MN 55343. **Contact:** Richard Gentry, Director of Corporate Relations, CTB, Inc., (219) 658-9323 for further information.

### • 893 • Student Engineer of the Year Scholarship *(Undergraduate/Scholarship)*

**Purpose:** To recognize an outstanding engineering undergraduate student in one of the engineering departments in the United States or Canada. **Qualif.:** Applicants must be engineering students who will have enrolled in school as an undergraduate at least an academic year prior to the award date. **Criteria:** The winner will be judged on scholarship, character, student membership in the ASAE, other activities, and level of financial self-support.

**Funds Avail.:** $1,000. **Deadline:** January 30.

## • 894 •
## American Society of Certified Engineering Technicians

Small Cash Grant Program
PO Box 1348                             *Ph:* (770)967-9173
Flowery Branch, GA 30542-1348           *Fax:* (770)967-8049

### • 895 • ASCET Small Cash Grant *(Undergraduate/Grant)*

**Focus:** Engineering technology. **Qualif.:** Applicants must be high school seniors entering an engineering technology post high school program.

**Funds Avail.:** $100 per award. **No. of Awards:** 4 maximum per year. **To Apply:** Applicants must submit a completed application from and letter(s) of recommendation. **Deadline:** April 1. **Contact:** American Society of Certified Engineering Technicians.

**• 896 •**
**American Society of Church History**
PO Box 8517
Red Bank, NJ 07701-8517

*Ph:* (908)932-9638
*Fax:* (908)932-1271

**• 897 • Frank S. and Elizabeth D. Brewer Prize**
*(Professional Development/Prize)*

**Purpose:** To assist an author publishing a work in church history. **Focus:** Congregationalism, History of Christianity. **Qualif.:** Candidates may be of any nationality but must have written an unpublished book-length manuscript on church history. Preference may be given to submissions relating to the history of Congregationalism. Award must be used to subsidize the cost of publishing manuscript.

**Funds Avail.:** $1,000. **To Apply:** Write to the secretary for application guidelines. Submit complete manuscript in final form. **Deadline:** November 1. The prize is announced in the spring. **Contact:** Henry W. Bowden, Secretary, at the above address (see entry 896).

**• 898 • Jane Dempsey Douglass Prize** *(Professional Development/Prize)*

**Purpose:** To recognize the best unpublished essay about the role of women in the history of Christianity. **Focus:** Women in Christianity. **To Apply:** Write to the secretary for application guidelines.

**Remarks:** This prize is undergoing redefinition. Please write for details. **Contact:** Henry W. Bowden, Secretary, at the above address (see entry 896).

**• 899 • Sidney E. Mead Prize** *(Doctorate, Postdoctorate/Prize)*

**Purpose:** To recognize the best essay in church history written by a doctoral candidate or recent degree recipient. **Focus:** History of Christianity. **Qualif.:** Candidates may be of any nationality but must be doctoral candidates or recent recipients of the Ph.D. Submissions must include an unpublished essay, under 25 pages in length, based directly on doctoral research in church history. Winning manuscript will be published in *Church History*.

**Funds Avail.:** $250. **No. of Awards:** One. **To Apply:** Write to the secretary for application guidelines. Submit manuscript to Secretary. **Deadline:** July 1. The prize will be announced in January. **Contact:** Henry W. Bowden, Secretary, at the above address (see entry 896).

**• 900 • Albert C. Outler Prize in Ecumenical Church History** *(Professional Development/Prize)*

**Purpose:** To assist with publication expenses. **Focus:** Ecumenicism, History of Christianity. **To Apply:** Write to the secretary for application guidelines.

**Remarks:** This prize is undergoing severe changes. Please write for complete details. **Contact:** Henry W. Bowden, Secretary, at the above address (see entry 896).

**• 901 •**
**American Society of Civil Engineers**
1801 Alexander Bell Dr.
Reston, VA 20191-4400

*Ph:* (703)295-6300
*Fax:* (703)295-6222
*Free:* 800-548-2723

*URL:* http://www.asce.org

**• 902 • O.H. Ammann Research Fellowship in Structural Engineering** *(Professional Development/Fellowship)*

**Purpose:** To support research on structural design and construction. **Focus:** Civil Engineering. **Qualif.:** Applicant for must be a national member of ASCE; applications for membership may be submitted with scholarship applications. Applicant may be of any nationality. Candidate's research must be in the field of structural design and construction. Fellowships are tenable at institutions with appropriate research facilities. Candidate must seek institutional approval for research prior to submitting application to ASCE.

**Funds Avail.:** $5,000-$7,000. **To Apply:** Write to Student Services for application form and guidelines. Submit form with transcripts, evidence of ability in relevant field of civil engineering, a description of proposed research with proof of institutional support, and a budget. **Deadline:** March 1. Notification in June. **Contact:** Student Services Department at the above address (see entry 901).

**• 903 • Trent R. Dames and William W. Moore Fellowship** *(Postdoctorate/Fellowship)*

**Purpose:** To provide research funds for qualified researchers. **Focus:** Engineering, Earth Science. **Qualif.:** Applicants must be practicing engineers or earth scientists, professors or graduate students. Membership in ASCE is not a requirement for this award. Previous awardees are eligible to reapply.

**Funds Avail.:** Varies based on funds available; $10,000. **To Apply:** Write to the Student Services Department for application form and guidelines. Application must include application form, description of proposed research and its objectives, budget. **Deadline:** February 15.

**Remarks:** Fellowship is awarded biennially. **Contact:** Student Services Dept. at the above address (see entry 901).

**• 904 • Freeman Fellowship** *(Professional Development/Fellowship)*

**Purpose:** To aid and encourage young engineers. **Focus:** Engineering. **Qualif.:** Applicant may be of any nationality. Candidate must be a national member of ASCE; applications for membership may be submitted with scholarship applications. The fellowship supports a variety of activities related to engineering: Grants may be made toward experiments, observations and compilations to discover new and accurate data that will be useful in engineering, or to recognize a useful paper relating to the art or science of hydraulic construction. The fellowship may also be used to underwrite the cost of publishing works pertaining to hydraulics which might not be published otherwise, or for the translation and publication in English of works on hydraulics written in other languages. Finally, the fellowship may be used by engineers younger than 45 years as a traveling scholarship for study visits to engineering works worldwide. Preference is given to research-related proposals.

**Funds Avail.:** $3,000-$5,000. **To Apply:** Write to Student Services Department for application form and guidelines. Submit form with a statement of purpose for which funds are expected to be used and a budget. **Deadline:** March 1. Notification in June. **Contact:** Student Services Department at the above address (see entry 901).

## American Society of Civil Engineers (continued)

### • 905 • J. Waldo Smith Hydraulic Fellowship (Postdoctorate/Fellowship) ·

**Purpose:** To encourage research in the field of experimental hydraulics. **Focus:** Hydraulic Engineering. **Qualif.:** Applicant may be of any nationality. Candidate must be a graduate student and an associate member of ASCE. The fellowship is tenable at the student's home institution. Research must be in the field of experimental hydraulics, as distinguished from that of purely theoretical hydraulics. Special consideration is given to experiments designed and executed for the purpose of advancing knowledge with respect to the laws of hydraulic flow.

**Funds Avail.:** $4,000 stipend, plus up to $1,000 equipment grant. **No. of Awards:** One. **To Apply:** Write to Student Services Department for application form and guidelines. Submit form with a statement of purpose for which funds are expected to be used and a budget. **Deadline:** February 1; Notification in June. The fellowship is offered triennially. **Contact:** Student Services Department at the above address (see entry 901).

### • 906 • Arthur S. Tuttle Memorial National Scholarship (Graduate/Scholarship)

**Purpose:** To support civil engineering students during the first year of graduate study. **Focus:** Civil Engineering. **Qualif.:** Applicant may be of any nationality. Candidate must be a national member of ASCE; applications for membership may be submitted with scholarship applications. Scholarships are tenable during the first year of graduate study in civil engineering at accredited educational institutions.

**Funds Avail.:** $3,000-$5,000. **To Apply:** Write to Student Services Department for application materials. Submit application form with statement of financial need and interest in the scholarship, a detailed financial plan for funding education, transcripts, and three recommendations, including one from an ASCE student chapter faculty advisor. **Deadline:** March 1. Notification in June. **Contact:** Student Services Department at the above address (see entry 901).

### • 907 •

## American Society for Clinical Laboratory Science

7910 Woodmont Ave., No. 530  
Bethesda, MD 20814  
*E-mail:* ascls@ascls.org  
*URL:* http://www.ascls.org  

*Ph:* (301)657-2768  
*Fax:* (301)657-2909

### • 908 • American Society for Clinical Laboratory Science Scholarships (Graduate/Scholarship)

**Purpose:** To assist experienced professionals who wish to pursue graduate, continuing, or advanced studies relevant to the interests of the Society. **Focus:** Biomedical Science, Hematology, Medical Technology. **Qualif.:** Applicant for most ASCLS scholarships must be a U.S. citizen or permanent resident, and be a clinical laboratory practitioner or educator, who has performed clinical laboratory functions for at least one year. For the Baxter Healthcare Scientific Products Division Graduate Scholarship candidate must be pursuing master's or doctoral study in the clinical laboratory or related sciences.

**Funds Avail.:** $250-$1,000. **To Apply:** Write to the executive secretary for application form and guidelines. **Deadline:** March.

**Remarks:** ASCLS also offers a number of awards recognizing outstanding on-going and completed projects in fields related to clinical laboratory science and medical technology, including health care administration and clinical science education. Write to the executive secretary for further information and application guidelines. **Contact:** The Education Department at the above address (see entry 907).

### • 909 •

## American Society of Clinical Pathologists

2100 W. Harrison St.  
Chicago, IL 60612-3798  
*E-mail:* info@ascp.org  
*URL:* http://www.ascp.org  

*Fax:* (312)738-0102  

*Free:* 800-621-4142

### • 910 • American Society of Clinical Pathologists Scholarships (Undergraduate/Scholarship)

**Purpose:** To financially assist students entering their final year of clinical education. **Focus:** Medical Technology, Medical Laboratory Technician, Cytotechnology, Histotechnology, Histologic Technician. **Qualif.:** Applicants must be enrolled in an accredited program in one of the following areas: Medical Technologist, Medical Laboratory Technician, Cytotechnologist, Histologic Technician, and Histotechnologist. They must also be U.S. citizens or permanent U.S. residents in their final year of education. **Criteria:** Scholarships awarded based on GPA, financial need, and recommendations.

**Funds Avail.:** $1,000. **No. of Awards:** 50. **To Apply:** A completed application, official school transcripts, three letters of recommendation, and two self-addressed, stamped envelopes must be submitted in one packet. **Deadline:** October 31. **Contact:** Program Registration and Member Services, at the above address (see entry 909).

### • 911 •

## American Society of Composers, Authors, and Publishers

C/O Frances Richard,  
VP President of Concert Music  
ASCAP Bldg, 1 Lincoln Plaza  
New York, NY 10023  
*E-mail:* frichard@ascap.com  
*URL:* http://www.ascap.com  

*Ph:* (212)621-6327  
*Fax:* (212)621-6504

### • 912 • ASCAP Foundation Grants to Young Composers (Professional Development/Grant)

**Purpose:** To recognize and encourage young music creators of any style or category. **Focus:** Composition. **Qualif.:** Grants are offered to young composers who are under 30 years old by March 15 of the year of application. Candidates must be United States citizens or permanent residents.

**Funds Avail.:** Grant amounts are individually determined. A year after receipt of the grant, recipients must report to the Foundation on how the grant was used, progress toward improved skills, and accomplishments. **No. of Awards:** Varies. **To Apply:** Candidates must submit a formal application with education, experience, and background in the field of music, and the score of one composition. In the case of electronic or graphic works, tapes must be accompanied by written description of source material and electronic equipment used. **Deadline:** Materials must be received by March 15; winners are announced by April 30.

**Remarks:** The program is funded by the Jack and Amy Norworth Memorial Fund. Jack Norworth is best remembered for his contributions of such standards as "Shine on Harvest Moon" and "Take Me Out to the Ball Game." Royalties from his compositions were left to the Foundation. **Contact:** Frances Richard, Director, at the above address (see entry 911).

### • 913 • ASCAP Foundation Morton Gould Awards to Young Composers *(Professional Development/Grant)*

**Purpose:** To encourage the development of talented young American composers. **Focus:** Music composition. **Qualif.:** Applicants must be younger than thirty years of age and be US citizens or permanent residents. **Criteria:** Awards are granted based on merit of work.

**Funds Avail.:** $20,000. **No. of Awards:** Varies. **To Apply:** Applicants must submit a completed application form; one reproduction of a manuscript or score; biographical information listing prior music studies, background and experience; and a list of compositions to date. Only one composition per composer may be submitted. The score reproduction submitted must be legible, must bear the applicant's name and may be submitted either on regular music paper or reproduced by an accepted reproduction process. Only copies or reproductions should be submitted and the original of the composition should be held by the applicant. A cassette tape of the composition submitted for the competition may be included if it is marked with the composer's name and the title of the work. Tapes of electronic music must also be accompanied by written information concerning source material and electronic equipment used. A score containing a tape part should be accompanied, insofar as it is possible, by a cassette tape of the complete work. A composition that involves a text must be accompanied by information about the source of the text with evidence that is in the public domain or by written permission from the copyright proprietor. All scores and tapes shall remain the property of the composers. So that musical materials may be returned, each entry must be accompanied by self-addressed envelope with sufficient postage. Proper care will be taken to protect all musical materials submitted, but each applicant releases all persons connected with the ASCAP Foundation Grants to Young Composer from any claims resulting from possible loss and/or destruction of works/tapes/materials submitted. **Deadline:** March 15. **Contact:** Frances Richard.

### • 914 • MISSIM/ASCAP Composers Competition *(Professional Development/Award)*

**Purpose:** To recognize excellent compositions. **Focus:** Music composition. **Qualif.:** Applicants must be living concert composer members of ASCAP. **Criteria:** Award is based on merit of work as judged by three conductors.

**Funds Avail.:** $5000. **No. of Awards:** 1. **To Apply:** Applicants must submit the score of one published or unpublished concert work requiring a conductor scored for full orchestra, chamber orchestra, or large wind/brass ensemble (with or without soloists and/or chorus) not previously performed professionally. A work with a performance history will be eligible only if earlier performances were, in the judgment of the Committee, clearly non-professional. For this exception to be granted, information regarding previous performances must be submitted with the score, in a separate envelope. Where protected text is used, formal permission from copyright proprietors must be included. **Deadline:** November 15. **Contact:** Frances Richard, Vice President, Concert Music.

---

### • 915 •
## American Society of Crime Laboratory Directors - Education & Training Committee
c/o Chief Kenneth Jonmaire
PO Box 496
Lockport, NY 14094

*Ph:* (716)438-3360
*Fax:* (716)229-3948

### • 916 • American Society of Crime Laboratory Scholarship Award *(Graduate, Undergraduate/Scholarship)*

**Purpose:** For the recognition of outstanding graduate and undergraduate forensic science students. **Focus:** Forensic Science. **Qualif.:** Applicants must be enrolled in a forensic science program in an accredited university, at either graduate or undergraduate level of study, and must maintain a B average. **Criteria:** The Education Committee reviews coursework, grades, internships, and goals, and makes recommendations to the Board of Directors, who make the final decision.

**Funds Avail.:** $2,000. **No. of Awards:** 2. **To Apply:** Students must provide documentation of coursework, internships, grades, and must give a narrative concerning themselves, their goals, and their future plans in forensic science. **Deadline:** April 1. **Contact:** The American Society of Crime Laboratory Directors at the above address (see entry 915).

---

### • 917 •
## The American Society of Criminology
1314 Kinnear Rd., Ste. 212
Columbus, OH 43212
*E-mail:* cwellford@bss2.umd.edu
*URL:* http://www.bsos.umd.edu/asc/

*Ph:* (614)292-9207
*Fax:* (614)292-6767

### • 918 • ASC Gene Carte Student Paper Competition *(Graduate, Undergraduate/Other)*

**Qualif.:** Any student currently enrolled on a full-time basis in an academic program at either the undergraduate or graduate level may enter the competition. All entries must be empirical and/or theoretical papers related to criminology.

**Funds Avail.:** Awards of $300, $150, and $100 are made to the first, second, and third place papers, which are eligible for presentation at the annual meeting of the American Society of Criminology. **To Apply:** Ten copies of the paper, which must not be more than 7,500 words in length, typewritten, double spaced on 8.5x11 paper, and with standard format for organization of text, citations, and references, must be submitted. Author(s) name(s), department(s), and (optional) advisor(s) must appear only on the title page as papers will be evaluated anonymously. Paper must be accompanied by a letter that indicates the student's status and is cosigned by the dean, department chair, or program chair. **Deadline:** Applications and supporting materials must be filed by April 15. Recipients are notified by August 1. **Contact:** The American Society of Criminology at the above address (see entry 917).

---

### • 919 •
## American Society of Electroneurodiagnostic Technologists, Inc.
204 West 7th St.
Carroll, IA 51401
*E-mail:* aset@netins.net
*URL:* http://www.aset.org

*Ph:* (712)792-2978
*Fax:* (712)792-6962

### • 920 • ASET Scholarships *(Professional Development/Scholarship)*

**Purpose:** To defray the cost of attending ASET courses. **Focus:** Life Sciences. **Qualif.:** Applicants must be members of ASET for one year prior to applying for scholarships. **Criteria:** Based on financial need.

**Funds Avail.:** $300 or $500. **No. of Awards:** 7. **To Apply:** Applications form may be obtained from the ASET Executive office. **Deadline:** February 1 for spring; June 1 for annual; October 1 for fall focus. **Contact:** M. Fran Pedelty at the above address (see entry 919).

---

# American Society for Engineering Education
1818 N St., NW, Ste. 600      Ph: (202)331-3525
Washington, DC 20036      Fax: (202)265-8504
E-mail: projects@asee.org

## • 922 • Army Research Laboratory Postdoctoral Fellowship Program (Postdoctorate/Fellowship)

**Purpose:** To significantly increase the involvement of creative and highly trained scientists and engineers from academia and industry in scientific and technical areas of interest and relevance to the Army. **Qualif.:** Each participant must present evidence of having received a Ph.D., Sc.D., or other earned research doctoral degree recognized in U.S. academic circles as equivalent to a Ph.D. Applicants must submit a proposal that relates to a specific research opportunity at ARL. **Criteria:** Fellows are selected based on their overall qualifications and technical proposal addressing specific needs defined by ARL.

## • 923 • NASA-ASEE Summer Faculty Fellowship (Professional Development/Fellowship)

**Purpose:** To further the professional knowledge of scientists and engineers who are members of university faculties. **Focus:** Engineering, Science. **Qualif.:** Applicant must be a U.S. citizen holding a research or teaching assignment at a U.S. university or college with at least two years of experience. The Fellowship is design in order that the National Aeronautic and Space Administration (NASA) may exchange ideas with faculty members.

**Funds Avail.:** $900, plus travel allowance. **To Apply:** Write the Contact for application form and guidelines. Application must be accompanied by a curriculum vitae, a letter of recommendation from the applicant's dean, and the names and addresses of two professional references. **Deadline:** February 15.

## • 924 • Naval Research Laboratory Postdoctoral Fellowship Program (Postdoctorate/Fellowship)

**Purpose:** To significantly increase the involvement of creative and highly trained scientists and engineers from academia and industry in scientific and technical areas of interest and relevance to the Navy. **Qualif.:** Applicants must be U.S. citizens and must present evidence of having received the Ph.D., Sc.D., or other earned research doctoral degree. **Criteria:** Fellowship awards will be based upon the technical quality and relevance of the proposed research, recommendations by the Navy laboratories or centers, academic qualifications, reference reports, and availability of funds. **Deadline:** January 1, April 1, July 1, and October 1.

## • 925 • U.S. Navy-ASEE Summer Faculty Research Program (Professional Development/Fellowship)

**Purpose:** To engage university faculty members in research programs of naval laboratories; to develop the basis for continuing research of interest to the Navy at the recipients' institutions; to establish continuing relations between faculty members and their professional peers in the Navy; and to enhance the research interests and capabilities of science and engineering faculty members. **Qualif.:** Applicants must be United States citizens who either have or are eligible for a Department of Defense Security Clearance of SECRET. Two years of experience in teaching or research at the college or university level is preferred.

**Funds Avail.:** Stipends vary between $1,230 and $1,730 per week, depending upon the level of appointment, for ten weeks during the summer. A travel allowance is paid for a pre-program visit to the research site and for the summer program. Recipients have access to laboratory, computational, and specialized library facilities at 17 Navy Research and Development Centers in the Washington, D.C. metropolitan area, California, Connecticut, Florida, Louisiana, Mississippi, Pennsylvania, and Rhode Island. **To Apply:** An application must be filed and accompanied by a separate sheet that contains a list of the colleges attended with dates of attendance, degrees received, area and titles of theses and dissertations, and chronology of professional employment and significant academic and professional activities; list of publications; research experience, courses taught, and any other information the candidate feels may be helpful. Applicants must supply the names and addresses of three professional references, the first being their current department head or dean. Each of the 17 centers has areas of special interest; details are included with information sent to applicants. Candidates must indicate in order of preference and/or qualifications the organization and field of work in which they would like to be placed. **Deadline:** Applications must be filed by January 15; recipients are notified around March 1.

**Remarks:** The U.S. Navy-ASEE Summer Faculty Research Program was established in 1979 at four Navy Research and Development Centers in the Washington, D.C. area.

## • 926 • U.S. Navy ONR-ASEE Postdoctoral Fellowship (Postdoctorate/Fellowship)

**Purpose:** To increase the involvement of highly-trained scientists and engineers to meet the increased needs of naval technology. **Qualif.:** Applicants must be United States citizens who either have or are eligible for a Department of Defense Security Clearance of SECRET. Candidates must have received a Ph.D. or other earned research doctoral degree within seven years of the date of application.

**Funds Avail.:** Annual stipends vary between $36,000 to $42,000 depending on experience and are paid in 13 installments. Subsequent year stipends will be paid in 12 monthly installments. Awards are for one year and renewable for a second. At the discretion of the laboratory, third-year appointments may be arranged. A negotiable relocation allowance is paid depending upon participant's personal situation, and a travel allowance is available for limited professional travel. Forty postdoctoral appointments are made each year. **To Apply:** Applicants are encouraged to work with a Navy laboratory to develop a suitable research proposal. The proposal should be prepared on a problem of mutual interest to the applicant and the Navy research facility. Awards are based upon the technical quality of the proposal, recommendations by the Navy laboratories or centers, academic qualifications and reference reports. Three reference reports must be submitted, the first from the applicant's doctoral thesis advisor, and the others from those who are familiar with the applicant's academic and professional background. They may not be from persons employed by the naval facility where the Fellowship is pursued. Applicants should order undergraduate and graduate transcripts that bear the original seal and signature of the university as early as possible. Applicants are encouraged to correspond with the staff at the various laboratories, which will help develop a suitable research project. **Deadline:** An application must be filed and must be accompanied by the research proposal by January 1, April 1, July 1, or October 1. Applicants are notified of awards by February 20, May 20, August 20, or November 20, respectively.

**Remarks:** There are presently 17 Navy host facilities located in California, Connecticut, Florida, Maryland, Mississippi, Pennsylvania, Rhode Island, Virginia, and Washington, D.C.

## • 927 •

## American Society for Enology and Viticulture

PO Box 1855                          Ph: (916)753-3142
Davis, CA 95617-1855                 Fax: (916)753-3318
E-mail: asevdavis@aol.com
URL: http://wineserver.ucdavis.edu/asev1.html

### • 928 • American Society for Enology and Viticulture Scholarships (Graduate, Undergraduate/Scholarship)

**Purpose:** To encourage and support scientific research directly applicable to the wine and grape industry. **Focus:** Enology, Viticulture. **Qualif.:** Candidates may be of any nationality but must be full-time undergraduates of junior status or higher with an overall GPA of 3.0 or higher, or graduate students at an accredited North American university with an overall GPA of 3.2 or higher. They must also be enrolled in a field of study emphasizing enology, viticulture, or another science basic to the wine and grape industry. **To Apply:** Write to the chair for application form and guidelines. Submit form with transcripts, a schedule of classes, a statement describing career goals, and two letters of recommendation. An interview may be required. **Deadline:** March 1. **Contact:** Scholarship Committee Chair at the above address (see entry 927).

## • 929 •

## American Society of Heating, Refrigerating and Air-Conditioning Engineers, Inc.

1791 Tullie Circle, NE               Ph: (404)636-8400
Atlanta, GA 30329                    Fax: (404)321-5478
E-mail: bseaton@ashrae.org
URL: http://ashrae.org

### • 930 • ASHRAE Grants-in-Aid for Graduate Students (Graduate/Grant)

**Purpose:** To encourage heating, refrigeration, and air-conditioning students to continue preparation for service in the industry. **Focus:** Heating, Refrigeration, Air Conditioning, Energy Conservation, Air Quality. **Qualif.:** Applicants must be full-time students of ASHRAE-related technologies. **Criteria:** The grant-in-aid is not intended as an award for excellence or for support of a particular research project, although the relevance of the candidate's research will be taken into consideration.

**Funds Avail.:** $7,500. Grants-in-aid are made to universities solely for the support of students. **No. of Awards:** 24. **To Apply:** Applications are available from the Manager of Research at ASHRAE. The application is submitted by the student's faculty advisor and should include the student history (name, address, scholastic achievement, rank in class, membership in professional societies, and transcripts) as well as an assessment of the student's personal and professional qualifications. It should also describe the research project, including the significance of research, plan of procedure, approximate budget, institution's contribution, and plan for publication of research results. Finally, it should state the amount of grant needed; this should include only the student's stipend and not fringe benefits or project costs. Qualifications of the institution and faculty advisor will be taken into account in relation to whether the institution has or has had ASHRAE funded research and whether the advisor is an ASHRAE member. **Deadline:** December 15. Recipients are notified by April 1. Funds are available after July 1.

### • 931 • ASHRAE Scholarships (Undergraduate/Scholarship)

**Purpose:** To encourage and assist heating, ventilating, air-conditioning, and refrigeration education at the undergraduate level and to serve the public interest in aiding in the education of men and women to become qualified to practice as engineers in HVAC and/or the refrigeration field. **Focus:** Engineering. **Qualif.:** Applicants must be undergraduate students enrolled in any school provided the curriculum in which the student is enrolled is accredited by ABET (Accreditation Board for Engineering and Technology) or another accrediting agency recognized by ASHRAE. Students must be pursuing a course of study that has traditionally been a preparatory curriculum for the profession of HVAC and/or refrigeration. **Criteria:** Basic criteria on which all scholarships are granted are as follows: need for financial assistance; prior academic performance (candidates must have a grade point average of at least 3.0 or Dean's List, whichever is higher, where 4.0 is the highest); performance on tests designed to measure ability and aptitude for college work; recommendations from instructors; character; leadership ability; potential service to the HVAC and/or refrigeration profession; and at least one full year of undergraduate study remaining.

**Funds Avail.:** $3,000 to $5,000 for each of three scholarships currently awarded. **To Apply:** Applications must be made to the Scholarship Fund Trustees at the ASHRAE address. The following data must be submitted: completed and signed application form; official transcript of grades; letter of recommendation from Professor or Faculty Advisor; and two additional letters of recommendation from individuals familiar with applicant's character, accomplishments, and likelihood of success in the HVAC and/or refrigeration industry. **Deadline:** December 1. Funds are available to scholarship recipients in the spring.

## • 932 •

## American Society for Information Science

8720 Georgia Ave., Ste. 501         Ph: (301)495-0900
Silver Spring, MD 20910-3610        Fax: (301)495-0810
E-mail: Mdevine!@cni.org

### • 933 • ASIS Doctoral Dissertation Scholarships (Doctorate/Scholarship)

**Purpose:** To foster information science research by encouraging and supporting doctoral students with their dissertation research. **Focus:** Computer and Information Sciences. **Qualif.:** All active information science doctoral students enrolled in institutions granting doctoral degrees are eligible. Students must have completed all coursework and have received acceptance of their dissertation proposals. **Criteria:** Potential significance, validity of methodology, originality, clarity, presentation of a convincing plan of completion. **To Apply:** Nomination packages should, in ten pages or less, include a description of the research, schedule for completion, budget and budget justification, names of dissertation advisor and committee members, a letter of endorsement from the student's advisor, and a curriculum vitae. **Deadline:** July 1. **Contact:** Michele Devine at the above address (see entry 932).

### • 934 • ASIS Doctoral Forum Awards (Postdoctorate/Award)

**Purpose:** To honor outstanding achievements by information scientists in the completion of dissertation projects. **Focus:** Computer and Information Sciences. **Qualif.:** All information scientists who have completed their dissertation within the past year are eligible.

**Funds Avail.:** Cash reimbursement. **To Apply:** Nomination packages must include a manuscript providing a comprehensive account of the dissertation or a full dissertation in a loose-leaf,

*American Society for Information Science (continued)*

reproducible format. **Deadline:** June 1. **Contact:** Michele Devine at the above address (see entry 932).

### • 935 • ASIS Student Paper Award *(Doctorate, Graduate, Undergraduate/Award)*

**Purpose:** To recognize substantial work performed by students in the field of information science. **Qualif.:** Any student in a degree-granting program may submit a paper that falls within the scope of the *Journal of the American Society for Information Science* (doctoral dissertations are not eligible).

**Funds Avail.:** Round trip expenses and conference registration at ASIS Annual Meeting not to exceed $500. **To Apply:** The author's name should not appear on the paper itself. The author should be identified only in the accompanying cover letter. The package should include endorsement of the paper by a faculty member. **Deadline:** June 15. **Contact:** Michele Devine at the above address (see entry 932).

## • 936 •
### American Society of Interior Designers - Educational Foundation, Inc.

608 Massachusetts Ave., NE    *Ph:* (202)546-3480
Washington, DC 20002-6006    *Fax:* (202)546-3240
    *Free:* 800-775-2743
*URL:* http://www.interiors.org/four.html

### • 937 • ASID Educational Foundation/S Harris Memorial Scholarship *(Undergraduate/Scholarship)*

**Purpose:** To assist students in meeting their educational costs. To encourage and support professional development. **Focus:** Interior design. **Qualif.:** Applicants must be undergraduate students at a degree-granting institution in at least the second term of studies. **Criteria:** Based on financial need and academic accomplishment.

**Funds Avail.:** $1500. **No. of Awards:** 1. **To Apply:** Academic transcripts and letters of recommendation from faculty must be submitted. **Deadline:** March 10.

### • 938 • Mabelle Wilhelmina Boldt Memorial Scholarship *(Graduate/Scholarship)*

**Purpose:** To assist practicing designers in returning to graduate school. **Focus:** Interior Design. **Qualif.:** Applicant must be a practicing residential or commercial interior designer with at least five years of experience prior to returning to the graduate level. Applicant must be enrolled in or applied to a graduate level interior design program at a degree-granting institution. The scholarship will be awarded on the basis of academic/creative accomplishment, as demonstrated by school transcripts and a letter of recommendation. Preference will be given to students with a focus on design research.

**Funds Avail.:** $2,000. **No. of Awards:** 1. **To Apply:** Write the Educational Foundation for application form and guidelines. **Deadline:** March 10.

**Remarks:** Send legal sized SASE with all inquiries. **Contact:** Educational Foundation, at the above address (see entry 936).

## • 939 •
### American Society of Magazine Editors

919 3rd Ave.    *Ph:* (212)872-3700
New York, NY 10022-3902    *Fax:* (212)906-0128

### • 940 • American Society of Magazine Editors Magazine Internship Program *(Undergraduate/ Internship)*

**Purpose:** To integrate the interests of magazine editors and their staffs, college students working toward careers in magazine journalism and schools of journalism. **Qualif.:** Applicants must have completed their junior year of college by June and be entering a full senior year in the fall after the internship program. Their interest in journalism must be evident from such activities as: academic courses in journalism, especially reporting, writing and editing; participation in campus journalism, especially as editor or senior staff member; previous summer internships or jobs at magazines or newspapers; and published articles in magazines or newspapers. **Criteria:** Strong consideration is given to heavy involvement in journalism and interest in magazine work.

**Funds Avail.:** Interns become employees of the magazines to which they are assigned at a minimum weekly stipend of $300 before deductions. The program runs ten weeks from June to August. Interns are responsible for their own travel expenses between assignment and home or school. They are also responsible for their own housing and maintenance. Arrangements are made with New York University or elsewhere for dormitory accommodations. Students who live in the area may live at home. **To Apply:** Invitations to participate are sent to deans of journalism schools and heads of journalism departments; deans or department heads of liberal arts universities and colleges which have previously participated; university and college offices handling summer internships for students that have requested information; and individual students who have requested information. Each dean or department head may nominate one candidate, except those having a magazine sequence accredited by the American Council on Education for Journalism, which may submit two nominations. Submission of a formal application is required. Each application must include an application form signed by the nominee and by a dean or department head; a letter from the nominee expanding on the application, such as relevant experience, why the nominee wants to be an intern, what is expected from the experience and what the nominee hopes to contribute to the assigned magazine, the attitude of candidates towards magazines, and their willingness to dig-in as full-time employees; a supporting letter from a dean, department head, or professor who personally knows the nominees journalistic excellence; writing samples; a letter from a former intern (if possible); a recent black and white photograph (passport photo size); and a self-addressed stamped postcard for notification of receipt of application material. **Deadline:** December 15. Recipients will be notified no later than March 1.

## • 941 •
### American Society of Mechanical Engineers

c/o Allian Pratt
Public Affairs Dept.
1828 L St., NW, Ste. 906    *Ph:* (202)785-3756
Washington, DC 20036-5104    *Fax:* (202)429-9417
*E-mail:* pratta@asme.org
*URL:* http://www.asme.org

### • 942 • ASME Federal Government Fellowships *(Professional Development/Fellowship)*

**Purpose:** To provide opportunity for Society members to work with the U.S. Congress; to support the state-federal technology partnership activities aimed at enhancing state-federal cooperation and technology-based economic growth. **Focus:** Technology, environment, energy policy. **Qualif.:** Candidates are ASME members who are United States citizens. **Criteria:** Mid-career engineers are preferred.

**Funds Avail.:** The Fellowship is a stipend of $40,000 plus some relocation expenses. The remaining salary and relocation expenses plus fringe benefits are provided by the Fellow's employer. **No. of Awards:** 3. **To Apply:** A formal application and a statement of 500 to 1,000 words describing why the candidate is applying, what experience and ability qualifies the candidate, applicant's expectation of the program, and any other pertinent thoughts are required. The employer must submit a statement approving a one-year leave of absence. Also required are three completed reference forms from people who know the candidate's technical and professional abilities. **Deadline:** April 1. **Contact:** Allian Pratt, Public Affairs Department

### • 943 • ASME Graduate Teaching Fellowships
*(Doctorate/Fellowship)*

**Purpose:** To encourage outstanding graduate students, especially women and minorities, to pursue a doctorate in mechanical engineering and to select engineering education as a profession. **Focus:** Mechanical Engineering, Education. **Qualif.:** Applicants must be United States citizens or permanent residents pursuing a Ph.D in mechanical engineering with a demonstrated interest in a teaching career. They must also have an undergraduate degree from an ABET accredited program, be a student member of ASME, and have a teaching assistantship from their department.

**Funds Avail.:** Stipends are $5,000 initially for a maximum of three years. **No. of Awards:** Maximum of 2 per year. **To Apply:** Applicants must submit an undergraduate GPA, GRE scores, two letters of recommendation, a graduate transcript, and a written statement. **Deadline:** October 15. **Contact:** Thomas J. Perry, Director, (212)705-8234.

### • 944 • ASME Student Assistance Loans
*(Undergraduate/Loan)*

**Purpose:** To provide timely financial assistance to ASME Student Members experiencing difficulty. **Focus:** Mechanical Engineering. **Qualif.:** Eligible students are ASME student members who are attending school full time as candidates for an undergraduate degree in Mechanical Engineering or Mechanical Technology and are in good academic standing. Loans are made for educational purposes in cases where normal student financial aids are unavailable or insufficient.

**Funds Avail.:** The maximum amount borrowed by an individual must not exceed $2,500 per semester to a maximum of $5,000 overall. The loan does not bear interest until six months after completion of full-time study or termination of full-time student status. Repayment is made monthly beginning six months after graduation or stop of schooling. The Board approves a promissory note which is signed by the borrower and an endorser, who assumes an obligation for repayment of the loan. **To Apply:** The loan application must include a recommendation by the applicant's Department Head. **Deadline:** April 15 and October 15.

**Remarks:** There are approximately 87-90 applicants. **Contact:** Thomas J. Perry, Director, Engineering Education, (212)705-7234.

### • 945 • John and Elsa Gracik Scholarships
*(Undergraduate/Scholarship)*

**Focus:** Mechanical Engineering. **Qualif.:** Applicants must be United States citizens enrolled in an ABET accredited Mechanical Engineering or related program. **Criteria:** Recipients will be selected on the basis of scholastic ability, financial need, character, leadership, and potential contribution to the mechanical engineering profession.

**Funds Avail.:** $1,500. **No. of Awards:** Up to 4. **To Apply:** Applicants must submit an application from a nomination by Department-

Head and a letter of recommendation by their faculty advisor, official academic record transcript. **Deadline:** April 15. **Contact:** Thomas J. Perry, Director of Engineering Education, (212)705-7234.

### • 946 • Kenneth Andrew Roe Scholarships
*(Undergraduate/Scholarship)*

**Focus:** Mechanical Engineering. **Qualif.:** Applicants must be ASME student members studying in the junior or senior year for a Baccalaureate in Mechanical Engineering in an ABET accredited or substantially equivalent program. They must also be North American residents and United States citizens. **Criteria:** Selection is based on scholastic ability, character, integrity, leadership potential contribution to the mechanical engineering profession and financial need.

**Funds Avail.:** $5,000 annually. **No. of Awards:** One. **To Apply:** Applicants must submit an application from a nomination by Department-Head. **Deadline:** April 15. **Contact:** Thomas J. Perry, Director of Engineering Education, (212)705-7234. (212)705-7234.

---

### • 947 •
## The American Society of Mechanical Engineers Auxiliary, Inc.
United Engineering Center
345 E. 47th St.
New York, NY 10017-2330
*URL:* http://www.asme.org

Ph: (212)705-7733
Fax: (212)705-7739

### • 948 • The American Society of Mechanical Engineers Auxiliary Student Loans *(Graduate, Undergraduate/Loan)*

**Purpose:** To provide mechanical engineering loans. **Focus:** Mechanical Engineering. **Qualif.:** Candidates must be college juniors, seniors, or graduate students in good standing. Applicants must be enrolled as candidates for degrees at schools with accredited mechanical engineering curricula and with student sections of The American Society of Mechanical Engineers. Candidates must also be endorsed by their respective Deans of Engineering and three other responsible persons. **Criteria:** Based on grades and extra curricular activities.

**Funds Avail.:** The maximum loan is $2,500. The loans are interest free while the recipients are in college. After graduation, recipients are charged low interest rates until the loans are repaid in full. **No. of Awards:** 1. **To Apply:** Write for application and further details. **Deadline:** None. **Contact:** The American Society of Mechanical Engineers Auxiliary, Inc. at the above address (see entry 947).

### • 949 • Sylvia W. Farny Scholarships
*(Undergraduate/Scholarship)*

**Purpose:** Helps with maintenance. **Focus:** Mechanical Engineering. **Qualif.:** Candidates must be U.S. citizens and undergraduates in mechanical engineering in accredited United States colleges or universities that have student sections of the American Society of Mechanical Engineers. **Criteria:** Selection is based on character, scholastic achievement, and financial need.

**Funds Avail.:** At least one scholarship of $1,500 is awarded annually. The number of awards depends upon the funds available. The award is for use in the recipient's final (fourth or fifth) year of study. **No. of Awards:** 10. **To Apply:** Each fall the colleges are notified that application forms are available. **Deadline:** Applications must be received on or before February 15 of the student's junior year. **Contact:** The American Society of Mechanical Engineers Auxiliary, Inc. at the above address (see entry 947).

## The American Society of Mechanical Engineers Auxiliary, Inc. (continued)

### • 950 • Elisabeth M. and Winchell M. Parsons Scholarships (Doctorate/Scholarship)

**Purpose:** To enable graduate students to pursue the Ph.D. in mechanical engineering. **Focus:** Mechanical Engineering **Qualif.:** Applicants must be U.S. citizens enrolled at a school with an accredited mechanical engineering program. They must also be members of The American Society of Mechanical Engineers at the time of application. **Criteria:** Based on grades.

**Funds Avail.:** $1,500. **No. of Awards:** 10. **To Apply:** Write to Mrs. Walter Leroy, 802 Academy Ave., Waynesboro, GA 30830 U.S.A. for application form and guidelines. **Deadline:** 15 February. Notification 15 April. **Contact:** Parsons chairperson at the above address (see entry 947).

### • 951 • Rice-Cullimore Scholarships (Graduate/Scholarship)

**Purpose:** To enable foreign graduate students to pursue a master's degree in mechanical engineering in the United States. **Focus:** Mechanical Engineering. **Qualif.:** Applicant may be of any nationality except the United States, but must hold a degree in mechanical engineering and have been selected by their school for the Scholarship. The sponsor must have a contract with the International Institute of Education.

**Funds Avail.:** $2,000. **To Apply:** Applications are obtained from sponsors who have contracts with the International Institute of Education. **Deadline:** February 15. Notification is made by April 15. **Contact:** Committee chairperson at the above address (see entry 947).

### • 952 • Marjorie Roy Rothermel Scholarships (Graduate/Scholarship)

**Purpose:** To enable graduate students to pursue a master's degree in mechanical engineering. **Focus:** Mechanical Engineering **Qualif.:** Applicants must be U.S. citizens enrolled at a school with an accredited mechanical engineering program. They must also be members of The American Society of Mechanical Engineering at the time of application.

**Funds Avail.:** $1,500 **To Apply:** Write to Mrs. Otto Prochaska, 332 Valencia St., Gulf Breeze, FL 32561 USA, for application form and guidelines. **Deadline:** February 15. Notification is made by April 15. **Contact:** Rothermel chairperson at the above address (see entry 947).

### • 953 •
## American Society for Microbiology
1325 Massachusetts Ave., NW      *Ph:* (202)942-9295
Washington, DC 20005-4171      *Fax:* (202)942-9329
*E-mail:* Fellowships-CareerInformation@asmusa.org
*URL:* http://www.asmusa.org/asm.htm

### • 954 • ASM Predoctoral Minority Fellowships (Doctorate/Fellowship)

**Purpose:** To support doctoral studies by minorities. **Focus:** Microbiology and related fields, including Bacteriology, Biochemistry, Biotechnology, Immunology, Microbial Genetics, Microbial Physiology, Molecular Biology, Virology. **Qualif.:** Applicant must be a U.S. citizen or permanent resident and a member of an ethnic minority, including: Blacks, Hispanics, Native American Indians, Alaskan Natives, and Pacific Islanders. Candidate must be enrolled full-time in a doctoral program at a U.S. institution. Studies must be related to the clinical, medical, veterinary, or industrial aspects of microbiology. **Criteria:** Selection

is based on academic achievement, evidence of a successful research plan, and relevant career goals in the microbiological sciences.

**Funds Avail.:** $12,000. **No. of Awards:** 3. **To Apply:** Write or call the assistant for application form and guidelines. **Deadline:** May 1.

**Remarks:** The fellowship is sponsored by the American Society for Microbiology and the American Cyanamid Company. **Contact:** Coordinator , Minority Program - Graduate Fellowships, at the above address (see entry 953).

### • 955 • Ortho/McNeil Predoctoral Minority Fellowship in Antimicrobial Chemotherapy (Doctorate/Fellowship)

**Purpose:** To support a graduate student conducting research in antimicrobial chemotherapy who is a member of a recognized racial or ethnic minority group in the United States. **Focus:** Microbiology. **Qualif.:** To be eligible, applicants must be U.S. citizens or permanent residents, members of the African American, Hispanic, Native Alaskan, Native American, or Native Pacific Islander group, and formally admitted as candidates for a doctoral degree in microbiology at an accredited U.S. institution at the time of application.

**Funds Avail.:** A two-year fellowship of $10,000 per year is awarded. A portion of the fellowship must be used for tuition and fees. Leaving the approved program during an award year forfeits that portion of the stipend, tuition, and fees remaining to be disbursed. Awardees will be required to provide an accounting of pre-doctoral progress at the end of each semester for which they receive the fellowship support. The fellowship is offered every other year. **No. of Awards:** 1. **To Apply:** Applications must consist of a nomination cover page, a nominating letter, proof of admission to a doctoral program in microbiology at an accredited U.S. institution, a one- to two-page description of the research project, copies of the nominee's undergraduate and graduate transcripts and GRE scores supplied by the university, and three letters of recommendation, one of which should be from the nominee's research advisor. **Deadline:** May 1.

**Remarks:** The fellowship is sponsored by the Ortho Pharmaceutical Corporation. **Contact:** Coordinator, Minority Programs, at the above address (see entry 953).

### • 956 •
## American Society of Naturalists
c/o Dr. Nancy T. Burley
Ecology and Evolutionary Biology
University of California, Irvine      *Ph:* (714)856-8130
Irvine, CA 92717-2557      *Fax:* (714)725-2181
*E-mail:* ntburley@gandalf.bio.uci.edu

### • 957 • ASN Young Investigator's Award (Professional Development/Award)

**Purpose:** To recognize outstanding research by a young Ph.D. in ecological or evolutionary studies. **Focus:** Ecology. **Qualif.:** Applicants must be either one year from completion of their Ph.D. or up to three years postdoctoral. **Criteria:** Selection is based upon the originality and high quality of research.

**Funds Avail.:** An honorarium is awarded to cover expenses in order to present a paper at the annual meeting. **Deadline:** May. **Contact:** Peter C. Chabora at the above address (see entry 956).

## • 958 •
### American Society of Naval Engineers
1452 Duke St.  *Ph:* (703)836-6727
Alexandria, VA 22314-3458  *Fax:* (703)836-7491
*E-mail:* scholarships@navalengineers.org
*URL:* http://www.navalengineers.org

### • 959 • American Society of Naval Engineers Scholarships *(Graduate, Undergraduate/Scholarship)*

**Purpose:** To support students and naval engineers pursuing studies directed toward a naval engineering career. **Focus:** Aeronautical Engineering, Civil Engineering, Electrical/Electronic Engineering, Marine Engineering, Mechanical Engineering, Naval Architecture, Ocean Engineering, Physical Sciences. **Qualif.:** Applicant must be a U.S. citizen pursuing graduate or advanced undergraduate study leading to a designated engineering or physical science degree in an accredited college or university. Candidate must have demonstrated interest in a naval engineering career, or be a practicing naval engineer seeking to further his/her career. Award is for the last year of an undergraduate program or for one year of graduate study leading to a master's degree. **Criteria:** Selection is based on the candidate's academic record, work history, professional promise, and interest in naval engineering, extracurricular activities, and recommendations of college faculty, employers, and other character references. Financial need may also be considered.

**Funds Avail.:** $2,500-$3,500. **No. of Awards:** 20-22. **To Apply:** Write for application form. Submit completed form with three references and official transcripts. **Deadline:** February 15. Awards are announced in early May. **Contact:** Capt. Dennis A. Pignotti, USN (Ret.), at the above address (see entry 958).

## • 960 •
### American Society of Newspaper Editors
PO Box 17004
Washington, DC 20041

### • 961 • American Society of Newspaper Editors Institute for Journalism Excellence *(Other/Fellowship)*

**Focus:** Journalism. **Qualif.:** Applicants must be senior and junior full-time faculty or administrators whose newspaper experience was before 1993.

**Funds Avail.:** Certificate program with $5500 stipend plus travel and housing expenses. **No. of Awards:** 20.

## • 962 •
### American Society for Photogrammetry and Remote Sensing - The Imaging and Geospatial Information Society
5410 Grosvenor Ln., Ste. 210  *Ph:* (301)493-0290
Bethesda, MD 20814-2160  *Fax:* (301)493-0208
*E-mail:* asprs@asprs.org
*URL:* http://www.asprs.org

### • 963 • Robert E. Altenhofen Memorial Scholarship *(Graduate, Undergraduate/Scholarship)*

**Purpose:** To encourage and commend college students who display exceptional ability in the theoretical aspects of photogrammetry and/or remote sensing. **Focus:** Photogrammetry, Remote Sensing. **Qualif.:** Applicant must be an undergraduate or graduate student in an accredited college or university in the U.S. or elsewhere who is either a Student Member or Active Member of ASPRS.

**Funds Avail.:** $1,000. **No. of Awards:** 1. **To Apply:** Write to ASPRS for application form and guidelines. Additional application items will be required. Information is available of the ASPRS website. **Deadline:** December 1.

### • 964 • William A. Fischer Memorial Scholarship *(Graduate/Scholarship)*

**Purpose:** To facilitate graduate-level studies and career goals adjudged to address new and innovative uses of remote sensing data/techniques that relate to the natural, cultural, or agricultural resources of the Earth. **Focus:** Photogrammetry. **Qualif.:** Applicant must be a member of ASPRS and currently pursuing graduate-level studies or who plans to enroll for graduate studies in an accredited college or university. Awards are tenable at school of recipient's choice.

**Funds Avail.:** $2,000 **No. of Awards:** 1. **To Apply:** Write the awards director for application form. Submit completed form with transcripts, letters of recommendation, and statement of goals. Application information is available on the ASPRS website. **Deadline:** December 1.

### • 965 • LH Systems Internship *(Graduate/Internship)*

**Purpose:** To provide an opportunity for a graduate student to carry out a small research project of his or her choice, or to work on an existing LH Systems project as part of a team. **Focus:** Photogrammetry, Surveying. **Qualif.:** Applicant must be a graduate student and a member of ASPRS.

**Funds Avail.:** $2,500 plus an allowance for travel and living expenses for the period of the internship. **No. of Awards:** One. **To Apply:** Write the program manager for application form and guidelines. Submit completed form with transcripts, letters of recommendation, and statement of goals. **Deadline:** December 1.

**Remarks:** Candidate may apply for more than one ASPRS award. Submit a separate application for each.

## • 966 •
### American Society of Podiatric Medical Assistants
c/o Linda L. Smith, PMAC
235 Brisbane Ave.
Westerville, OH 43081-3474  *Fax:* (614)291-7720
*E-mail:* lsmithPMAC@aol.com

### • 967 • Zelda Walling Vicha Memorial Scholarship *(Graduate/Scholarship)*

**Purpose:** To give financial assistance in Podiatric Education. **Focus:** Podiatric Medicine. **Qualif.:** Applicants must be fourth year podiatry students. **Criteria:** Outstanding scholastic achievement and financial need.

**Funds Avail.:** $1000. **No. of Awards:** 1. **To Apply:** Applications are sent to each of the seven podiatry colleges in December of each year. They may be obtained at the financial aid offices of those colleges or by contacting the chairman of the scholarship fund. **Deadline:** February 15.

**Remarks:** The awards, formerly reserved for female students, are now available to both male and female fourth year students. **Contact:** Linda Smith, PMAC, Chairman, at the above address (see entry 966).

## • 968 •
## American Society of Travel Agents

1101 King St.
Alexandria, VA 22314
*Ph:* (703)739-2782
*Fax:* (703)684-8319
*E-mail:* astasysop@astanet.com
*URL:* http://www.astanet.com

### • 969 • Air Travel Card Grant *(Undergraduate/Grant)*

**Purpose:** Encourage education in travel and tourism, with emphasis in the area of business travel engagement. **Focus:** Travel and Tourism. **Qualif.:** Applicants must be United States or Canadian citizens who are undergraduates enrolled in an accredited two- or four-year college (not a proprietary school). A 2.5 grade point average on a 4.0 scale is required. **Criteria:** Essay/GPA/Transcripts.

**Funds Avail.:** One annual award of $3,000. **No. of Awards: 1. To Apply:** Students must submit an essay (minimum of 500 words) on the challenges of managing business travel in the 1990's which should contain a brief description of career goals and proof of enrollment in a qualified college. Applicants must also submit transcripts from the last academic year. Students must send brochures describing the travel curriculum, tuition, and length of their programs. Statements from at least one professor and/or employer in the travel and tourism field attesting to the applicant's dedication and interest in the travel industry are required. **Deadline:** June or July. **Contact:** American Society of Travel Agents at the above address (see entry 968).

### • 970 • American Express Travel Scholarship *(Undergraduate/Scholarship)*

**Purpose:** To encourage the pursuit of education in the field of travel and tourism, and to support the growth and quality development of tomorrow's travel and tourism workforce. **Focus:** Travel and Tourism. **Qualif.:** Applicants must be citizens of the United States or Canada enrolled in a two- or four-year college or proprietary travel school in the United States that offers a travel and tourism program. A 2.5 grade point average on a 4.0 scale is required. **Criteria:** Essay, GPA, and Transcripts.

**Funds Avail.:** The fund will offer one scholarship of $2,500. **No. of Awards: 1. To Apply:** Students must provide a 500-word essay detailing their plans in travel and tourism, as well as their views of the travel industry's future. Proof of enrollment in a qualified school or program must be submitted. Transcripts from the last academic year must be attached. Students must send official school printed description of travel curriculum, tuition, and length of their programs. Statements from at least one professor and/or employer in the travel and tourism field attesting to the applicant's dedication and interest in the travel industry are required. **Deadline:** June/July. **Contact:** The American Society of Travel Agents at the above address (see entry 968).

### • 971 • Arizona Chapter Dependent Employee Membership Scholarship *(Undergraduate/Scholarship)*

**Purpose:** To promote professionalism in the travel industry by providing scholarships for continued education in the field of travel and tourism. **Focus:** Travel and Tourism. **Qualif.:** Applicants must be enrolled either in their final year in a two-year college or as juniors or seniors in a four-year university in the United States. An educational major in travel and tourism is not required; however, the student must be a dependent of an ASTA Arizona Chapter agency member whose ASTA dues are current. Proof of parent's involvement with ASTA is required. Students must also have a 2.5 grade point average (4.0 scale), and be residents, citizens, or legal aliens of the United States or Canada. **Criteria:** Essay, GPA, and transcripts.

**Funds Avail.:** $1,000. **No. of Awards: 1. To Apply:** A 500-word essay entitled "My Career Goals" is required. Students must also submit proof of enrollment or acceptance to a school, an official school-printed description or listing of the travel curriculum, an official statement of the tuition amount, and a letter of recommendation. Application materials must be mailed in triplicate; faxed entries are not accepted. **Deadline:** July 15. Winners are notified by August 31. **Contact:** Myriam Lechuga, Coordinator, ASTA Scholarship Foundation, at the above address (see entry 968).

### • 972 • Avis Rent a Car Scholarship *(Doctorate, Graduate, Professional Development, Undergraduate/Scholarship)*

**Purpose:** To support further studies related to the travel industry. **Focus:** Tourism, Travel. **Qualif.:** Candidates must be a citizen, resident, or legal alien of the United States or Canada pursuing further studies in the field of travel and tourism at a U.S. or Canadian institution. Applicants for the Avis Scholarship must be an upper-class undergraduate or graduate student who has worked part time in the travel industry. Candidate must submit a 500-word essay on the benefits of automation for travel agents and industry suppliers. **Criteria:** Essay, transcripts.

**Funds Avail.:** $2,000. **No. of Awards:** One. **To Apply:** Write to the Foundation for application form and guidelines. **Deadline:** June 14.

**Remarks:** Write ASTA Scholarship Foundation for further information. **Contact:** Myriam Lechuga, Coordinator: (703)739-2782, Ext. 392.

### • 973 • David Hallissey Memorial Scholarships *(Graduate, Postgraduate/Scholarship)*

**Purpose:** To encourage serious academic research in the tourism field. **Focus:** Travel and Tourism. **Qualif.:** Candidates must be either graduate students or a professors of tourism at a recognized college, university, or proprietary travel school and submit proof of such. They must also be residents, citizens, or legal aliens of the United States or Canada.

**Funds Avail.:** $1,500 ($750 will be awarded in September and the second installment of $750 will be awarded upon completion of the report no later than June of the next year). **To Apply:** A 500-word essay on an intended topic of research incorporating methodology and objectives is required. Graduate students must submit proof of enrollment, an official school-printed description or listing of the travel curriculum, an official statement of the tuition amount, and a letter of recommendation. Application materials must be mailed in triplicate; faxed entries are not accepted. **Deadline:** June or July. Winner are notified in September. **Contact:** ASTA Scholarship Foundation at the above address (see entry 968).

### • 974 • Healy Scholarship *(Undergraduate/Scholarship)*

**Purpose:** To promote professionalism in the travel industry. **Focus:** Travel and Tourism. **Qualif.:** Applicants must be citizens of the United States or Canada. They must be enrolled in a recognized college, and be a sophomore, junior, or senior. Applicants must be enrolled in travel and tourism courses. A 2.5 grade point average on a 4.0 scale is required. **Criteria:** Essay, GPA, transcripts.

**Funds Avail.:** The fund offers one award of $2,000 to dedicated undergraduate students. **No. of Awards: 1. To Apply:** Students must provide a 500-word essay suggesting improvements for the travel industry. Proof of enrollment in a qualified school or program must be submitted. Transcripts from the last academic year must be attached. Students must send brochures describing the travel curriculum, tuition, and length of their programs. Statements from at least one professor and/or employer in the travel and tourism field attesting to the applicant's dedication and interest in the travel industry are also required. **Deadline:** June/July. **Contact:** American Society of Travel Agents at the above address (see entry 968).

**• 975 • Holland-America Line Westours Scholarships** (Undergraduate/Scholarship)

**Purpose:** To promote professionalism in the travel industry. **Focus:** Travel and Tourism. **Qualif.:** Applicants must be citizens or legal aliens of the United States or Canada enrolled in a travel and tourism program in either a two-or four-year college or university or proprietary travel school. A 2.5 grade point average on a 4.0 scale is required. **Criteria:** Essay, GPA, transcripts.

**Funds Avail.:** This fund offers two awards of $2,000. **No. of Awards:** 2. **To Apply:** Students must provide a 500-word essay on the future of the cruise industry, proof of enrollment in a qualified school or program, recommendations from at least one professor and/or employer in the travel and tourism field that can attest to the applicants' dedication and interest in the travel industry, and brochures describing the travel curriculum, tuition, and length of their programs. Transcripts from the last academic year must also be submitted. **Deadline:** June or July. **Contact:** American Society of Travel Agents at the above address (see entry 968).

**• 976 • Northern California/Richard Epping Scholarships** (Undergraduate/Scholarship)

**Purpose:** To promote professionalism in the travel industry. **Focus:** Travel and Tourism. **Qualif.:** Applicants must be currently enrolled in a travel or tourism curriculum at a college, university, or proprietary travel and tourism school. The establishment must be located within the geographic boundaries of California. In addition, applicants must have a 2.5 grade point average (4.0 scale) and be residents, citizens, or legal aliens of the United States or Canada. **Criteria:** Essay, GPA, transcripts.

**Funds Avail.:** One $2000 award is given annually. **No. of Awards:** 1. **To Apply:** A 500-word essay entitled, "Why I Desire a Profession in the Travel and Tourism Industry," is required. Students must also submit proof of enrollment or acceptance to a school, an official school-printed description or listing of the travel curriculum, an official statement of the tuition amount, and a letter of recommendation. Application materials must be mailed in triplicate; faxed entries are not accepted. **Deadline:** July. Winners are notified by August 31. **Contact:** Myriam Lechuga, Coordinator, ASTA Scholarship Foundation at the above address (see entry 968).

**• 977 • Orange County Chapter/Harry Jackson Scholarship** (Undergraduate/Scholarship)

**Purpose:** To help educate tomorrow's travel industry leaders. **Focus:** Travel and Tourism. **Qualif.:** Students must be citizens of the United States or Canada and be enrolled as sophomores, juniors, or seniors in an accredited two-year college or four-year university in Orange County, California. Students must also be enrolled in a minimum of one travel vocational/industry class per semester and have a 2.5 grade point average on a 4.0 scale. They must also become involved in the Orange County ASTA and make a presentation to the Chapter in the fall.

**Funds Avail.:** Scholarships will be available for amounts up to $250 each with maximum of $2,000 being awarded per year. **To Apply:** Applicants must submit a letter of interest and/or need, letter of recommendation and employee status confirmation from their official ASTA employer and application. **Deadline:** June/July.

**Remarks:** Scholarship qualifications and requirements may change substantially. **Contact:** The ASTA Scholarship Foundation for current information at the above address (see entry 968).

**• 978 • Pollard Scholarships** (Undergraduate/Scholarship)

**Purpose:** To promote professionalism in travel by supporting persons reentering the job market via attendance in recognized proprietary travel schools or two-year junior colleges that specialize in travel or tourism studies. **Focus:** Travel and Tourism. **Qualif.:** Students must be citizens of the United States or Canada who have been out of high school for at least five years. **Criteria:** Essay, GPA, transcripts.

**Funds Avail.:** The fund currently awards two $2,000 scholarships. **No. of Awards:** 2. **To Apply:** Students must provide proof of registration in a recognized travel school or two-year college, a 500-word essay on objectives in the travel and tourism industry, and proof that they have been out of high school for at least 5 years. **Deadline:** June/July. **Contact:** The American Society of Travel Agents at the above address (see entry 968).

**• 979 • Princess Cruises and Princess Tours Scholarship** (Undergraduate/Scholarship)

**Purpose:** To promote professionalism in the travel industry. **Focus:** Travel and Tourism. **Qualif.:** Candidates must be sophomores, juniors, or seniors studying travel and tourism in a four-year college or university, and they must be a resident, citizen, or legal alien of the United States or Canada. **Criteria:** Essay, GPA, transcripts.

**Funds Avail.:** Two awards of $2000. **No. of Awards:** 2. **To Apply:** Submit a 500-word essay on the two features that cruise ships will need to offer passengers in the next ten years. Applicants should also submit proof of enrollment; provide and official statement of their tuition; provide an official school-printed description of their travel curriculum; possess at least a 2.5 grade point average on a 4.0 scale. Provide a letter of recommendation from a professor, employer, or business colleague that attests to the student's desire to pursue a profession in the travel and tourism industry. **Deadline:** July. **Contact:** ASTA Scholarship Foundation at the above address (see entry 968).

**• 980 • George Reinke Scholarships** (Undergraduate/Scholarship)

**Purpose:** To promote professionalism in the travel industry. **Focus:** Travel and Tourism. **Qualif.:** Students must be citizens of the United States or Canada. **Criteria:** Essay, GPA, transcripts.

**Funds Avail.:** The fund currently awards three $1,000 scholarships. The award may not exceed 50 percent of the annual tuition. **No. of Awards:** 3. **To Apply:** Students must provide proof of registration in a recognized proprietary travel school or junior college. A copy of the tuition fee is required. A 500-word essay must also be submitted. **Deadline:** July. **Contact:** The American Society of Travel Agents, Scholarship Foundation, at the above address (see entry 968).

**• 981 • Simmons Scholarship** (Doctorate, Graduate/Scholarship)

**Purpose:** To promote professionalism in the travel industry by providing scholarships for continued education in the field of travel and tourism. **Focus:** Travel and Tourism. **Qualif.:** Applicants must be graduate students who are pursuing a Master's or Doctorate degree with an emphasis in travel and tourism. They must have a minimum 2.5 grade point average (4.0 scale) and be residents, citizens, or legal aliens of the United States or Canada.

**Funds Avail.:** Two awards of $1,500 each are given. **To Apply:** An upper-level paper or thesis (15 to 20 pages) written on some travel and tourism topic that has been or will be submitted to a professor must be provided. Candidates must also submit proof of enrollment, an official school-printed description or listing of the travel curriculum, an official statement of the tuition amount, and a letter of recommendation. Application materials must be mailed in triplicate; faxed entries are not accepted. **Deadline:** June or July. Winners are notified in September. **Contact:** ASTA Scholarship Foundation at the above address (see entry 968).

## American Society of Travel Agents (continued)

### • 982 • Southern California Chapter/Pleasant Hawaiian Holidays Scholarship (Undergraduate/Scholarship)

**Purpose:** To promote professionalism in the travel industry by providing scholarships for continued education in the field of travel and tourism. **Focus:** Travel and Tourism. **Qualif.:** Applicants must be undergraduate students enrolled or accepted to an accredited college, junior college, university, or proprietary travel school in preparation for a profession in the travel and tourism industry. They must also have a 3.0 grade point average (4.0 scale), and submit proof of U.S. citizenship. **Criteria:** Essay, GPA, transcripts.

**Funds Avail.:** $2,000. **No. of Awards:** 1. **To Apply:** A 500-word essay entitled, "My Goals in the Travel Industry," is required, as well as a statement as to why applicant should be chosen to receive the award. Students must submit proof of enrollment, an official school-printed description or listing of the travel curriculum, an official statement of the tuition amount, and a letter of recommendation. Application materials must be mailed in triplicate; faxed entries are not accepted. **Deadline:** July. Winners are notified by August 31. **Contact:** Myriam Lechuga, Coordinator, ASTA Scholarship Foundation at the above address (see entry 968).

### • 983 • A.J. (Andy) Spielman Scholarships (Undergraduate/Scholarship)

**Purpose:** To promote professionalism in the travel industry. **Focus:** Travel and tourism. **Qualif.:** Applicants must be citizens of the United States or Canada who are currently enrolled in or scheduled to attend a recognized proprietary travel school for the purpose of re-entering the work force in the field of travel. **Criteria:** Essay, GPA, transcripts.

**Funds Avail.:** The fund currently awards two $3,000 scholarships. **No. of Awards:** 2. **To Apply:** Applicants must submit a 500-word essay entitled, "Why I have chosen the Travel Profession for my Re-entry into the Work Force," and provide proof of registration at a recognized proprietary travel school. **Deadline:** June/July. **Contact:** ASTA at the above address (see entry 968).

### • 984 • Joseph R. Stone Scholarships (Undergraduate/Scholarship)

**Purpose:** To promote professionalism in the travel industry by providing scholarships for continued education in the field of travel and tourism. **Focus:** Travel and tourism. **Qualif.:** Applicants must be citizens of the United States or Canada. They must be undergraduates in a college or university and pursuing a travel/tourism degree. A 2.5 grade point average on a 4.0 scale is required. One parent must be employed in the travel industry (i.e. hotel, car rental, airlines, travel agency, etc.). **Criteria:** Essay, GPA, transcripts.

**Funds Avail.:** Three $2,400 scholarships. **No. of Awards:** 3. **To Apply:** Students must provide a 500-word essay on their goals in the travel industry. Proof of enrollment in a qualified school or program must be submitted. Transcripts from the last academic year must be attached. Students must send brochures describing the travel curriculum, tuition, and length of their programs. A statement from the parent's employer must also accompany the application. **Deadline:** June/July. **Contact:** The American Society of Travel Agents at the above address (see entry 968).

## American Sociological Association - Minority Fellowship Program

1307 New York Ave., Ste. 700      *Ph:* (202)383-9005
Washington, DC 20005      *Fax:* (202)638-0882
*E-mail:* minorityaffairs@asanet.org
*URL:* http://www.asanet.org

### • 986 • American Sociological Association Minority Fellowships (Doctorate/Fellowship)

**Purpose:** To encourage research in the areas of Sociology of Mental Health. **Qualif.:** Applicant must be a U.S. citizen or permanent resident, and a member of a minority group. Applicant must be a Ph.D. student whose research interests and training are in the field of Sociology of Mental Health. If the fellowship is extended beyond one year, fellow must agree to engage in postdoctoral behavior research and/or training for a period equal to the extension.

**Funds Avail.:** $14,688. **To Apply:** Candidates should write to the Association for application form and guidelines. **Deadline:** December 31. **Contact:** Edward Murgvia, Director.

### • 987 • American Sociological Association Research Doctoral Fellowships in Sociology (Doctorate/Fellowship)

**Purpose:** To encourage research in the area of Sociology. **Qualif.:** Candidates must be American citizens, permanent visa residents, or alien card holders and minorities, including, but not limited to, persons who are African Americans, Latino-Hispanic, American Indian, Asian American, and Pacific Islanders (e.g., Filipino, Samoan, Hawaiian, Guamanian). They must also be beginning or continuing doctoral study in sociology departments. There are two competitions: one is for students interested in the sociology of mental health illness; the other is for applicants whose research interests and training are outside the sociology of mental health. These fellowships do not stipulate a special area or focus. **Criteria:** Selection is based on financial need and potential for success in graduate studies.

**Funds Avail.:** Depending upon the availability of funds, fellowships of $11,496 are awarded. Upon completion of their Ph.D., ASA Fellows are required to engage in behavioral research and/or training for a period equal to the length of support beyond 12 months. **To Apply:** Required documentation includes official transcripts for each college and university attended, three references (at least two from persons whom have taught the applicant), an essay of not more than three double-spaced pages that includes a statement of career goals and aspirations, anticipated date of receipt of doctorate, and how the candidate thinks the attainment of the Ph.D. relates to goals. Individuals applying for the fellowship in the sociology of mental health should document their commitment to teaching, research, and service careers on the sociological aspects of mental health. **Deadline:** Materials must be in by December 31; recipients are notified by April 15.

**Remarks:** Funding for the mental health/illness awards is provided by the National Institute of Mental Health. Funding for the general sociological awards is provided by ASA member's contributions.

• 988 •
## American Speech-Language-Hearing Foundation
10801 Rockville Pike                    *Ph:* (301)897-5700
Rockville, MD 20852                     *Fax:* (301)571-0457
*E-mail:* foundation@asha.org
*URL:* http://www.asha.org

• 989 • **American Speech-Language-Hearing Foundation Graduate Student Scholarships** *(Doctorate, Graduate/Scholarship)*

**Purpose:** To support graduate studies in communication sciences and disorders. **Focus:** Audiology, Communication Sciences and Disorders, Speech-Language Pathology. **Qualif.:** Candidate may be of any nationality. Applicant must be accepted for full-time graduate study in an ASHA Educational Standards Board accredited communication sciences and disorders program at a U.S. institution; this requirement is not mandatory for doctoral degree candidates. The student must be enrolled full-time. Applicants must submit an official application packet and forms. This includes: University transcripts of course work, credits, and grades, plus recommendations of a committee of two or more persons who are: faculty at the student's current college or university program; or faculty at the student's past college or university program if the student is a recent undergraduate; and colleagues at the student's current place of employment. Candidate may not have previously received a scholarship from the Foundation. In addition to general graduate scholarships, the Foundation administers two scholarships with additional stipulations. The Kala Singh Memorial Scholarship gives priority to a non-U.S. citizen or a U.S. minority student applicant must be studying in the continental United States. The Leslie Isenberg Fund Scholarship gives priority to a disabled student. Separate applications are not necessary for these awards; students will be automatically considered for all awards for which they are eligible.

**Funds Avail.:** General scholarships award $4,000; Isenberg scholarships award $2,000, Singh Scholarships award $2,000 and the Young Scholars Award for Minority Students awards $2,000. **No. of Awards:** Usually up to 7. **To Apply:** Write to the Foundation for application materials and guidelines. **Deadline:** Application materials must be received by June 11. Scholarship recipients will be announced in November. **Contact:** Gina Smolka, Administrative Assistant, at the above address (see entry 988).

• 990 • **American Speech-Language-Hearing Foundation Research Grants for New Investigators** *(Doctorate, Graduate, Postdoctorate, Postgraduate/Grant)*

**Purpose:** To encourage research in audiology or speech pathology areas. **Focus:** Audiology, Communication Sciences and Disorders, Speech Pathology. **Qualif.:** Applicant for a new investigator grant must have received his/her master's or doctoral level degree within the past five years, and may not have received prior funding for research, with the exception of internal university funding. Candidate's research should have particular clinical relevance to speech-language and pathology. Grants are tenable in the continental United States.

**Funds Avail.:** $4,000 is available. **No. of Awards:** Up to 4 grants are available. **To Apply:** Write for application form and guidelines for preparation of proposal. **Deadline:** Materials must be submitted by July 14. Grant recipients are announced in November. **Contact:** Nancy J. Minghetti, Director of Programs and Corporate Development, at the above address (see entry 988).

• 991 • **American Speech-Language-Hearing Foundation Student Research Grant in Audiology** *(Graduate, Postgraduate/Grant)*

**Purpose:** To support research in the areas of clinical and/or rehabilitative audiology. **Focus:** Audiology. **Qualif.:** Applicants

must be graduate or postgraduate students working in the area of clinical and/or rehabilitative audiology.

**Funds Avail.:** $2,000 are available. **No. of Awards:** 1 award is offered. **To Apply:** Applicants should write to the Foundation for application materials which contain specific guidelines to be followed by all applicants. **Deadline:** Application materials must be received by July 3. Grant recipients will be announced in November. **Contact:** Nancy J. Minghetti, Director of Programs and Corporate Development, at the above address (see entry 988).

• 992 • **Leslie Isenberg Graduate Scholarship** *(Doctorate, Graduate/Scholarship)*

**Purpose:** To support graduate studies in comm sciences disorders. **Qualif.:** Applicants must be accepted or enrolled full-time in a graduate study in a communication sciences and disorders program. Master's degree candidates must be in an ASHA Educational Standards Board (ESB) accredited program; this is not mandatory for doctoral degree candidates. If the full-time standard is less than twelve credit hours, the student must provide documentation from the college or university stating its standard. Students who have received a prior scholarship from the Foundation are not eligible. Priority is given to disabled students.

**Funds Avail.:** One $2,000 scholarship is awarded each year. **No. of Awards:** 1. **To Apply:** Applicants must submit a cover letter; student information form which should include a statement of good standing, transcripts, and GPA; recommendations; and an essay. **Deadline:** June 11. Recipients are announced in November at the ASHA Convention.

**Remarks:** This scholarship is underwritten by the Leslie Isenberg Fund. **Contact:** Graduate Student Scholarship Competition at the above address (see entry 988).

• 993 • **Research Grant in Speech Science** *(Postdoctorate/Grant)*

**Purpose:** To encourage research by new investigators into the acoustic properties of speech production and perception. **Focus:** Speech Science. **Qualif.:** Applicant must have received a doctoral degree within the past five years. The research proposal must be in the area of speech science, such as speech perception, synthesis, and acoustics, with an emphasis on an interdisciplinary research approach.

**Funds Avail.:** The award is $2,000. **No. of Awards:** 1. **To Apply:** Write to the Foundation for application materials and guidelines. This is a biannual award. **Deadline:** Application materials must be received by July 7. Grant recipients will be announced in November. **Contact:** Nancy J. Minghetti, Director of Programs and Corporate Development, at the above address (see entry 988).

• 994 • **Kala Singh Graduate Scholarship** *(Doctorate, Graduate/Scholarship)*

**Purpose:** To support graduate studies in comm sciences and disorders. **Qualif.:** Applicants must be students who are accepted or enrolled full-time in a graduate study in a communication sciences and disorders program. Master's degree candidates must be in an ASHA Educational Standards Board (ESB) accredited program; this is not mandatory for doctoral degree candidates. If the full-time standard is less than twelve credit hours, the student must provide documentation from the college or university stating its standard. Students who have received a prior scholarship from the Foundation are not eligible. **Criteria:** Priority is given to minority or foreign students.

**Funds Avail.:** One $2,000 scholarship is awarded annually. **No. of Awards:** 1. **To Apply:** Applicants must submit a cover letter; student information form which should include a statement of good standing, transcripts, and GPA; recommendations; and an essay. **Deadline:** June 11. Recipients are announced in November at the ASHA Convention.

## American Speech-Language-Hearing Foundation (continued)

**Remarks:** This scholarship is underwritten by the Kala Singh Memorial Scholarship Fund. **Contact:** Graduate Student Scholarship Competition at the above address (see entry 988).

### • 995 • Student Research Grant in Early Childhood Language Development *(Graduate, Postgraduate/Grant)*

**Purpose:** To encourage research in early childhood language development. **Focus:** Language Development. **Qualif.:** Applicant must be a graduate or postgraduate student doing research in the area of early childhood language development.

**Funds Avail.:** The award is $2,000. **To Apply:** Write for application form and guidelines for preparation of proposal. **Deadline:** Application materials must be received by July 3. Grant recipients are announced in November. **Contact:** Nancy J. Minghetti, Director of Programs and Corporate Development, at the above address (see entry 988).

---

## • 996 •
## American Statistical Association

1429 Duke St.
Alexandria, VA 22314-3402
*E-mail:* asainfo@amstat.org
*URL:* http://www.amstat.org/

*Ph:* (703)684-1221
*Fax:* (703)684-2036

### • 997 • ASA/NCES/NSF Research Fellowships *(Postdoctorate/Fellowship)*

**Purpose:** To help bridge the gap between academic scholars and government social scientists by exposing the research fellow to methodological problems and policy issues faced by a federal statistical agency. **Focus:** Statistics. **Qualif.:** Applicants should have a recognized research record and expertise in their proposed area of research. Fellowship is tenable in Washington, D.C.

**Funds Avail.:** Stipend commensurate with salary plus appropriate moving and travel allowances **To Apply:** Write to the ASA for guidelines. All applicants will have to provide a curriculum vitae and a statement identifying and discussing areas of research interest. **Deadline:** March 1 for program beginning in September; July 1 for program beginning in January.

**Remarks:** This award is offered by the ASA and the National Center for Education Statistics, Office of Education Research and Improvement under a grant from the National Science Foundation.

### • 998 • ASA/NSF/BLS Senior Research Fellowship *(Postdoctorate/Fellowship)*

**Purpose:** To bridge the gap between academic scholars and government social science research. **Focus:** Statistics, Social Sciences. **Qualif.:** Applicants should have a recognized research record and considerable expertise in their area of proposed research. Applicants must submit a detailed research proposal for review. Qualified women and members of minority groups are encouraged to apply. Fellowship is tenable at the Bureau of Labor Statistics in Washington, D.C.

**Funds Avail.:** Salaries are commensurate with qualifications and experience; fringe benefits and travel allowances are provided. **To Apply:** Write to the Program Director for guidelines. In addition, applicants must provide a detailed research proposal, a curriculum vitae, and names and addresses of three referees. **Deadline:** January 14. Notification by March 14.

**Remarks:** This award is offered by the ASA under a grant from the National Science Foundation in cooperation with the Bureau of Labor Statistics.

### • 999 • ASA/NSF/Census Research Fellowship *(Postdoctorate/Fellowship)*

**Purpose:** To help bridge the gap between government and academic social science. **Focus:** Statistics. **Qualif.:** Applicants should be senior statisticians or social scientists who have recognized research records and considerable expertise in their areas of proposed research. They must submit a detailed research proposal as part of the application. Awards are tenable at the Bureau of the Census in Suitland, Maryland.

**Funds Avail.:** Salary is commensurate with qualifications and experience, fringe benefits and travel allowances are negotiable. **No. of Awards:** Three to five per year. **To Apply:** Write to ASA for guidelines. Applications should include a curriculum vitae, names and addresses of three referees, and a detailed research proposal. **Deadline:** January 4. Final decisions by March 4.

**Remarks:** Fellowships are offered by the ASA under a grant from the National Science Foundation in cooperation with the Bureau of the Census.

### • 1000 • ASA/NSF/NIST Senior Research Fellowships and Associateships *(Postdoctorate/Fellowship)*

**Purpose:** To encourage research projects by academics that use the statistical resources of the U.S. government and address federal issues and problems. **Focus:** Statistics. **Qualif.:** Candidate for a fellowship must be a senior academic statistician or social scientist. Associateship candidate should have completed at least two years of graduate study; recent recipients of the Ph.D. may also apply. Awards are tenable at the facilities of one of six U.S. government departments: the Bureau of Labor Statistics, the Census Bureau, the National Agricultural Statistics Service, the National Institute of Standards and Technology, or the National Center for Educational Statistics. During the award term, fellows lead independent research projects using the data collection and analysis resources of the chosen facility. Associates participate in a fellow's project and acquire research training. The Census Bureau, National Center for Educational Statistics, do not have Associates.

**Funds Avail.:** Stipend, plus fringe benefits and travel allowances. **To Apply:** Write to the ASA for overviews of the five fellowship/associateship programs and their research priorities. Applicants for associateships must submit an application form (which is also available from ASA) with transcripts, two letters of recommendation and a statement of interest. There is no application form for fellowship candidates. They must submit a curriculum vitae, names of three references, and a detailed research proposal. **Deadline:** Fellowships: January 14; associateships: February 15. Notification by March 30.

**Remarks:** These awards are cosponsored by the American Statistical Association and the National Institute of Standards and Technology under a grant from the National Science Foundation. **Contact:** Carolee Bush, ASA/NSF/NIST Research Program, at the above address (see entry 996).

### • 1001 • ASA/USDA/NASS Research Fellowships and Associateships *(Doctorate, Postdoctorate/Fellowship)*

**Purpose:** To supplement graduate education and research in statistics with experience at the National Agricultural Statistics Service. **Focus:** Statistics. **Qualif.:** Applicants for fellowships should have a Ph.D. and an established, recognized research record and considerable expertise in their area of proposed research. Applicants for associateships should have completed a Ph.D. or have at least two years of graduate study toward the Ph.D. Awards are tenable at NASS in Washington, D.C.

**Funds Avail.:** Stipend for Fellow will be commensurate with current salary plus moving and travel allowance; stipend for Associates will be set at the equivalent G.S. rate and include moving and travel allowance. **To Apply:** Write to the ASA for guidelines. Fellows must include a curriculum vitae and letter stating area of proposed research or interests. Associates must include both, plus a university transcript and two letters of recommendation. **Deadline:** March 1 for program beginning in September; June 1 for program beginning in January.

**Remarks:** These awards are offered by the ASA in cooperation with the National Agricultural Statistics Service of the U.S. Department of Agriculture.

## • 1002 •
## American Student Assistance
330 Stuart St.
Boston, MA 02116

Ph: (617)426-9434
Fax: (617)728-4265
Free: 800-999-9080

E-mail: webmaster@amsa.com
URL: http://www.amsa.com/

### • 1003 • ASA Stafford Loan (Graduate, Undergraduate/Loan)

**Qualif.:** Massachusetts residency is not required if the student attends a Massachusetts school or borrows from an ASA lender. Student must attend an eligible school at least half-time.

**Funds Avail.:** Award amounts vary as follows: up to $2,635 per year for freshman; up to $3,500 per year to sophomores; up to $5,500 per year for juniors and seniors; and up to $8,500 per year for graduate students at a variable interest rate. **To Apply:** Students may apply through local lenders. Applications must be filed several weeks before the funds are needed. Applicants must file a FAFSA. **Contact:** Local lenders or American Student Assistance at the above address (see entry 1002).

## • 1004 •
## American Symphony Orchestra League
1156 15th St., NW, Ste. 800
Washington, DC 20005-1704
E-mail: league@symphony.org

Ph: (202)628-0099
Fax: (202)873-7228

### • 1005 • Music Assistance Fund Orchestral Fellowships (Professional Development/Fellowship)

**Purpose:** To encourage and support gifted student musicians and young professionals of African-American descent who wish to pursue careers in U.S. symphony orchestras. **Focus:** Instrumental Music. **Qualif.:** Applicant must be of African descent and a U.S. citizen. Candidate must be a student musician. Students must be enrolled at accredited conservatories and university schools of music. Support is for players of orchestral instruments only. Pianists are not eligible to apply. Awards may be used for tuition, additional instruction, and other expenses used to advance the fellow's musical career. Funds can be applied to academic-year or summer study. **Criteria:** Scholarship awards are based on audition, financial need, and written recommendations.

**Funds Avail.:** $2,500 maximum. **No. of Awards:** Varies. **To Apply:** Write or phone for application form and guidelines. Financial aid forms, a teacher recommendation, and an audition are required. **Deadline:** December 15. **Contact:** Alberto Gutierrez, Coordinator, at the above address (see entry 1004).

### • 1006 • Orchestra Management Fellowships (Professional Development/Fellowship)

**Purpose:** To provide on-the-job practical training to individuals interested in pursuing a career in orchestra management. **Focus:**

Orchestra Management. **Qualif.:** Candidates must be U.S. citizens, residents or authorized by INS to be employed in the U.S. They must also have an undergraduate degree or equivalent experience. Candidates should have knowledge in the areas of business procedures and music as related to the orchestral repertoire. Fellowship programs are tailored to provide the best training for individual recipients. Fellowship term may include 15-week assignments at three different professional orchestras, a management seminar, or a one-week assignment with a small-budget orchestra. Fellows should expect to be employed by a U.S. orchestra upon completion of the program.

**Funds Avail.:** $15,000 stipend, plus travel, and some relocation costs. **To Apply:** Write or phone the fellowship program coordinator for application package. Submit form, university transcripts, three references, application fee ($45), and two essays. Finalists are interviewed in Washington, DC in March. **Deadline:** November 1. **Contact:** Anita H. Weisburger, Fellowship Program Coordinator, at the above address (see entry 1004).

## • 1007 •
## American Vacuum Society
120 Wall St., 32nd Fl.
New York, NY 10005
E-mail: angela@vacuum.org
URL: http://www.vaccum.org/

Ph: (212)248-0200
Fax: (212)248-0245

### • 1008 • AVS Student Prize; Russel and Sigurd Varian Fellowship (Graduate/Fellowship, Prize)

**Purpose:** To recognize and encourage excellence in graduate studies in vacuum science and technology. **Focus:** Vacuum Science and Technology. **Qualif.:** For each of these awards, candidate may be of any nationality but must be a registered graduate student in an accredited academic institution in North America. Applicants are normally not expected to graduate before the award selection. Candidates working directly with a member of the Scholarship and Awards Trustees are not eligible. The Whetten Award is reserved for women.

**Funds Avail.:** AVS Awards: $1,000; Varian Fellowship: $1,500. Award recipients also receive up to $750 for travel to the Society's National Symposium. **No. of Awards:** Nine. **To Apply:** Write to the scholarship secretary for application form and guidelines. Submit form with two letters of reference. **Deadline:** March.

**Remarks:** The American Vacuum Society also offers five awards to recognize outstanding contributors to the fields of vacuum science and technology: the Medard W. Welch Award, the Albert Nerken Award, the John A. Thornton Memorial Award and Lecture, the Peter Mark Award, and the Gaede-Langmuir Award. Candidates may be of any nationality but must be nominated by a qualified colleague. Other requirements and prize values vary. Write to the Society for further information. **Contact:** Angela Mulligan, Scholarship Secretary, at the above address (see entry 1007).

### • 1009 • Nellie Yeoh Whetten Award (Graduate/Award)

**Purpose:** To recognize and encourage excellence in graduate studies in vacuum science and technology. **Focus:** Vacuum Science and Technology. **Qualif.:** For each of these awards, candidate may be of any nationality but must be a registered graduate student in an accredited academic institution in North America. Applicants are normally not expected to graduate before the award selection. Candidates working directly with a member of the Scholarship and Awards Trustees are not eligible. The Whetten Award is reserved for women.

**Funds Avail.:** $1,000. Award recipients also receive up to $750 for travel to the Society's National Symposium. **No. of Awards:** Nine. **To Apply:** Write to the scholarship secretary for application form

## American Vacuum Society (continued)

and guidelines. Submit form with two letters of reference. **Deadline:** March 1.

**Remarks:** The American Vacuum Society also offers five awards to recognize outstanding contributors to the fields of vacuum science and technology: the Medard W. Welch Award, the Albert Nerken Award, the John A. Thornton Memorial Award and Lecture, the Peter Mark Award, and the Gaede-Langmuir Award. Candidates may be of any nationality but must be nominated by a qualified colleague. Other requirements and prize values vary. Write to the Society for further information. **Contact:** Angela Mulligan, Scholarship Secretary, at the above address (see entry 1007).

## • 1010 •
## American Veterinary Medical Foundation

1931 N. Meacham Rd., Ste. 100     *Ph:* (847)925-8070
Schaumburg, IL 60173              *Fax:* (847)925-1329
                                  *Free:* 800-248-2862

*E-mail:* avmfmail@aol.com
*URL:* http://www.avma.org/avmf

### • 1011 • AVMF Auxiliary Student Loan *(Graduate, Postgraduate/Loan)*

**Purpose:** To assist students of veterinary medicine pay for books and tuition. **Focus:** Veterinary Science, Veterinary Medicine. **Qualif.:** Candidates must be sophomore, junior, or senior veterinary students. **Criteria:** First priority is given to senior veterinary students, although sophomore and junior students are encouraged to apply.

**Funds Avail.:** Up to $4,000 per student. The loan carries an 8 percent interest rate. **To Apply:** Interested students may request an application packet. Along with the application, a personal statement, two faculty recommendations, and the signature of a co-signer must be submitted. **Deadline:** None. **Contact:** Program Manager at the above address (see entry 1010).

## • 1012 •
## American Vocational Association - Home Economics Education Division

1410 King St.           *Ph:* (703)683-3111
Alexandria, VA 22314    *Fax:* (703)683-7424
*URL:* http://www.ngi-net.com/mgilists/ava.htm

### • 1013 • AVA Home Economics Education Graduate Fellowships *(Doctorate, Graduate/Fellowship)*

**Focus:** Home Economics. **Qualif.:** Students must be members of the AVA Home Economics Education Division and have the qualifications for admission to a graduate master's or doctoral program in an accredited institution. **Criteria:** Preference is given to doctoral candidates.

**Funds Avail.:** The number and value of Fellowships are determined by the Home Economics Education Division Policy and Planning Board upon recommendation of the Fellowship Fund Committee. In recent years an average of three fellowships of $3000 each have been awarded. **To Apply:** A formal application, letter of recommendation from three persons knowledgeable as to the candidate's professional and academic qualifications for graduate study, a transcript, a brief autobiographical sketch, and, if possible, the likely research topic must be filed by November 1. **Contact:** The American Vocational Association, Home Economics Education Division, at the above address (see entry 1012).

## American Water Works Association

Attn: Scholarship Coordinator
6666 W Quincy Ave.        *Ph:* (303)794-7711
Denver, CO 80235-3098     *Fax:* (303)794-6303
*E-mail:* vbaca@awwa.org
*URL:* http://www.awwa.org

### • 1015 • American Water Works Association Academic Achievement Awards *(Doctorate, Graduate/Award)*

**Purpose:** To encourage academic excellence by recognizing contributions to the field of public water supply. **Focus:** Water supply-related fields. **Qualif.:** All master's theses and doctoral dissertations that are relevant to the water supply industry are eligible. The manuscript must reflect the work of a single author and be submitted during the competition year in which it was submitted for the degree. The competition is open to students majoring in any subject provided the work is directly related to the drinking water supply industry. **Criteria:** Entries are read by a panel of judges appointed by the American Water Works Association, and are evaluated on the basis of originality, practical application, value to the water supply field, potential value as a reference, and overall clarity of the presentation.

**Funds Avail.:** For the Doctoral Dissertation First Place is $1,000 and Second Place is $500. For the Master's Thesis, First Place is $1,000 and Second Place is $500. **No. of Awards:** 4 **To Apply:** Applicants must submit an unbound manuscript. An entry form with the name of the author, name of the school and department, name of the major professor, the degree sought, a one-page abstract of the manuscript plus a letter of endorsement from the major professor or department chair must be included. **Deadline:** January 15. **Contact:** American Water Works Association Scholarship Coordinator.

### • 1016 • American Water Works Association Holy A. Cornell Grant *(Graduate/Scholarship)*

**Purpose:** To encourage and support outstanding female and/or minority students to pursue advanced training in the field of water supply and treatment. **Qualif.:** Applicants must be female and/or minority students who are currently Master's degree students and anticipate completion of the requirements for a Master's degree in engineering no sooner than January 15 are eligible. Students who have been accepted into graduate school but have not yet begun graduate school but have not yet begun graduate school but have not yet begun graduate study are encouraged to apply. **Criteria:** Members of the University Student Activities Subcommittee of the American Water Works Association will evaluate the applicants and select the scholarship recipient based on: the quality of the applicant's academic record; and potential to provide leadership in the field of water supply and treatment.

**Funds Avail.:** A one time grant of $5,000. **No. of Awards:** 1. **To Apply:** Applicants must submit the following: official application form; official transcripts of all university education; official copies of GRE scores; three letters of recommendation (one of which must be from the advisor); proposed curriculum of study and; a brief(1-2 page) statement describing the student's career objectives. **Deadline:** January 15. **Contact:** Scholarship Coordinator American Water Works Association at the above address (see entry 1014).

### • 1017 • American Water Works Association Scholarship Program *(Doctorate, Graduate/Scholarship)*

**Purpose:** To honor the memory of Dr. Larson by providing support and encouragement to outstanding graduate students preparing for careers in the fields of science or engineering. **Qualif.:** Applicants must be pursuing an advanced degree at an institution of higher education located in Canada, Guam, Puerto Rico, Mexico or the United States. In addition, applicants must complete the requirements for your Master's degree sometime after August 1. Doctoral students should complete their requirements after December 1. **Criteria:** A selection committee with representation from the American Water Works Association, the American Chemical Society, and Aquatic Chemistry Section of the Illinois State Water Survey will evaluate the applicants and select the scholarship recipients based on excellence of their academic record and their potential to provide leadership in one of the fields served by Dr. Larson.

**Funds Avail.:** $5,000 scholarship for an MS student and $7,000 scholarship for PhD student. **No. of Awards:** 2. **To Apply:** Applicants must submit the following: an official application form; a resume (including educational history); official transcripts of all post-secondary education; official copies of GRE Scores(quantitative, verbal, and analytical); three letters of recommendation; a proposed plan of study and; a statement of educational plans and career objectives demonstrating or declaring an interest in an appropriate field of endeavor or, if applicable, a research plan. **Deadline:** January 15. **Contact:** Scholarship Coordinator American Water Works Association.

### • 1018 • American Water Works Association Scholarship Program Abel Wolman Fellowship Award *(Doctorate/Fellowship)*

**Purpose:** To support promising students in the U.S., Canada and Mexico pursuing advanced training and research in the field of water supply and treatment. **Qualif.:** You are eligible to apply if you are anticipating completing the requirements for a PhD., within two years of the award, and have citizenship or permanent residence in Canada, Mexico or the United States. Applicants will be considered without regard to color, gender, race, creed or country of origin. **Criteria:** A selection committee from the American Water Works Association's University Student Activities Subcommittee will evaluate the applicants and select the fellowship recipient based on the quality of the applicant's academic record, the significance of the proposed research to water supply and treatment, and the applicant's potential to do high quality research.

**Funds Avail.:** A $15,000 stipend, plus $1,000 for research supplies and equipment, and an education allowance of up to $4,000 to cover the cost of tuition and other fees. **No. of Awards:** 1. **To Apply:** Applicants must submit the following: Official application form; official transcripts of all university education; official copies of GRE scores; three letters of recommendation, one of which must be from the dissertation advisor; proposed curriculum of study; brief plans of dissertation research study, including statement describing how research will relate specifically to water supply and treatment. **Deadline:** January 15. **Contact:** Scholarship Coordinator at the above address (see entry 1014)or check the Events & Chalndars Scholarship section of the association's home page.

### • 1019 • American Water Works Association Thomas R. Camp Scholarship *(Graduate/Scholarship)*

**Purpose:** To honor the memory of Dr. Camp by supporting and encouraging outstanding graduate students doing applied research in the drinking water field. **Focus:** Water-related areas. **Qualif.:** You are eligible if you are pursuing a Master's degree at an institution of higher education located in Canada, Guam, Puerto Rico, Mexico or the United States. **Criteria:** A selection committee from the American Water Works Association, Student/University Affairs Subcommittee and Camp Dresser and McKee Inc, will evaluate the applicants and select the scholarship recipient based on the excellence of his or her academic record and potential to provide leadership in applied research in drinking water field.

**Funds Avail.:** $5,000 **To Apply:** Applicants must submit the following: Official application form; a resume (including educational history); official transcripts of all post-secondary education; official copies of GRE scores; Three letters of recommendation; a one-page statement of educational plans and career objectives demonstrating or declaring an interest in the

drinking water field and; a two-page proposed plan of research. **Deadline:** January 15 **Contact:** Scholarship Coordinator at the above address (see entry 1014)or download information from the association's webs site.

### • 1020 • LARS Scholarships *(Doctorate, Graduate/ Scholarship)*

**Purpose:** To provide encouragement and support to graduate students in water chemistry and related fields. **Focus:** Water Supply Industry—Resource Management, Chemistry—Analytical and Aquatic, Engineering, Chemistry—Environmental. **Qualif.:** Applicant may be of any nationality, but must be an M.S. or Ph.D. student at an institution in the United States, Canada, Mexico, Guam, or Puerto Rico. Master's candidates must have at least one semester of degree work left at the time of application. Doctoral candidates must have at least one more year of schooling to complete. **Criteria:** Selection is based on academic excellence and leadership potential.

**Funds Avail.:** M.S. scholarship: $5,000; Ph.D. scholarship: $7,000 **To Apply:** Write to the scholarships coordinator for application form and guidelines. Submit form with a resume, including educational history; transcripts; three letters of recommendation; a proposed plan of study and/or research; and a statement of educational plans and career objectives. **Deadline:** January 15. Recipients are announced by May. **Contact:** Scholarship Coordinator at the above address (see entry 1014)or download information from the association's web site.

### • 1021 • American Watercolor Society
47 5th Ave.
New York, NY 10003-4303     *Ph:* (212)206-8986

### • 1022 • American Watercolor Society Scholarship Award *(Graduate, Undergraduate/Scholarship)*

**Purpose:** To advance the art of watercolor painting. **Focus:** Painting. **Qualif.:** Applicants must be pursuing studies in watercolor.

**Funds Avail.:** $1,000 to $1,500 per award. **To Apply:** Schools may apply on behalf of student and supervise student's progress in watercolor painting. Included with each application should be a small portfolio of 4-6 slides of recent watercolors. Individuals may not apply. **Contact:** Ilda De Sanblas at the above address (see entry 1021).

### • 1023 • America's Junior Miss
PO Box 2786     *Ph:* (334)438-3621
Mobile, AL 36652-2786     *Fax:* (334)431-0063
*E-mail:* dave@circa3k.com
*URL:* http://www.circa3k.com/ajm/default.htm

### • 1024 • America's Young Woman of the Year Scholarships *(Undergraduate/Scholarship)*

**Purpose:** To honor the nation's outstanding high school senior girls while promoting self-esteem among young women. **Qualif.:** Candidates must be high school juniors or seniors in the United States. **Criteria:** Selection is based on panel evaluation, scholastic achievement, talent in creative and performing arts, fitness, and poise.

**America's Junior Miss (continued)**

**Funds Avail.:** Each year more than $3.5 million is presented at the local, state and national levels. **To Apply:** Students should consult with their high school guidance counselors early in their junior years or write for information. **Deadline:** Dates vary by state. **Contact:** Write to Contestant Inquiry at the above address (see entry 1023).

---

• 1025 •

**Amity Institute**
10671 Roselle St., Ste. 101      *Ph:* (619)455-6364
San Diego, CA 92121      *Fax:* (619)455-6597
*E-mail:* amity@cris.com
*URL:* http://www.amity.org/contact.html

• 1026 • **Amity Institute Internships** *(Professional Development/Internship)*

**Purpose:** Internships are awarded during the school year to exceptional candidates for the opportunity to teach their native language and culture in American elementary and secondary schools, colleges and universities. Interns gain teaching experience, immerse themselves in American culture and improve their English skills while they volunteer approximately 15 hours per week as teaching assistants. **Focus:** Spanish, French, German, Japanese, Chinese, Russian, and other languages. **Qualif.:** Applicant's must be single, between the ages of 20 to 30, students or graduates of a university, professional or technical institution, have the ability to communicate effectively in English, interested in working with children or young people, and possess the desire to encourage international understanding and friendship.

**Funds Avail.:** Free room and board with a host family or on campus as well as the opportunity to attend American Studies and English classes are provided by the host school. School also pays small spending allowance, arranges free lunches and local transportation, and overseas teaching activities. **To Apply:** Prospective applicants must obtain and carefully read the Amity Bulletin and Applicant Brochure from the above address before applying. Applications are accepted year-round. **Contact:** Debra C. Hinman, Executive Director, at the above address (see entry 1025).

---

• 1027 •

**Amoco Canada Petroleum Company**
Benefits Coordinator, Human
  Resources
PO Box 200, Sta. M
Calgary, AB, Canada T2P 2H8

• 1028 • **Amoco Canada Petroleum Company Scholarships** *(Undergraduate/Scholarship)*

**Focus:** General Studies. **Qualif.:** Candidates must be children of current or retired employees or employees on long-term disability leave from the Amoco Canada Petroleum Company. They should be enrolled at a Canadian or American university, college, or technical institute.

**Funds Avail.:** Thirty-five scholarships of $1,000 each are awarded annually. **Deadline:** June 1. **Contact:** Benefits Coordinator, Human Resources, Amoco Canada Petroleum Company Ltd., at the above address (see entry 1027).

---

• 1029 •

**AMVETS - National Headquarters**
Attn: Scholarships
4647 Forbes Blvd.      *Ph:* (301)459-9600
Lanham, MD 20706-4380      *Fax:* (301)459-7924

• 1030 • **AMVETS National Scholarship for Graduate Students** *(Graduate/Scholarship)*

**Focus:** General **Qualif.:** Candidates must be children of American veterans who have exhausted all government financial aid. They must also be United States citizens, accepted or currently enrolled in an accredited graduate program, and able to demonstrate academic achievement and financial need. **Criteria:** Awards are based on scholastic aptitude and financial need.

**Funds Avail.:** $1,000 scholarship. **To Apply:** Scholarship application requests must be accompanied by a stamped, self-addressed envelope. **Deadline:** April 15. **Contact:** AMVETS National Scholarship Program at the above address (see entry 1029).

• 1031 • **AMVETS National Scholarships for Undergraduate Students** *(Undergraduate/Scholarship)*

**Qualif.:** Candidates must be children of American veterans who have exhausted all government financial aid. They must also be United States citizens, high school seniors (current year) entering a four-year course of study at an accredited college or university, and able to demonstrate academic achievement and financial need. **Criteria:** Awards are based on scholastic aptitude and financial need.

**Funds Avail.:** Fifteen $4,000 scholarships payable in grants of $1,000 per year for four years. **To Apply:** Scholarship application requests must be accompanied by a stamped, self-addressed envelope. **Deadline:** April 15. **Contact:** AMVETS National Scholarship Program at the above address (see entry 1029).

---

• 1032 •

**Amyotrophic Lateral Sclerosis Association**
27001 Agoura Rd., Ste. 150
Calabasas Hills, CA 91301-5104
*E-mail:* bro@huey.met.fsu.edu
*URL:* http://www.familyvillage.wisc.edu/lib_als.htm

• 1033 • **ALSA Research Grants** *(Postdoctorate/ Grant)*

**Purpose:** To support research into the cause and cure of amyotrophic lateral sclerosis. **Focus:** Amyotrophic Lateral Sclerosis. **Qualif.:** Candidate may be of any nationality. Applicant must be a qualified principal investigator associated with a medical institution or university. Awards are tenable worldwide but must be used at the investigator's home institution.

**Funds Avail.:** Varies; $25,000-35,000 for short-term (12-18 month) projects. **To Apply:** Submit three copies of a brief abstract of proposed project to the chair of the ALSA Research Committee. If the Committee is interested, further application instructions will be forwarded. **Deadline:** Abstract: September 15; application: December 31. Grant recipients are selected in May. **Contact:** Robert V. Abendroth, ALSA Research Committee Chairperson, at the above address (see entry 1032).

## • 1034 •
## The Ancient India and Iran Trust
Brooklands House
23 Brooklands Avenue       *Ph:* 1223 356841
Cambridge CB2 2BG, England      *Fax:* 1223 61125

### • 1035 • Ancient India and Iran Trust Travel and Research Grants *(Doctorate, Graduate, Postdoctorate/ Grant)*

**Purpose:** To support research on Ancient India and Iran. **Focus:** India and Iranian Art History, Indo-Iranian Languages, and Pre-History Archaeology of India and Iran. **Qualif.:** Applicant's field(s) of research must fall within the scope of subjects and areas covered by the trust. Applicant's should normally be established scholars or graduate students registered for a higher degree, although undergraduate students attending relevant conferences, or taking part in excavations or field work will be considered.

**Funds Avail.:** Varies. **To Apply:** Applications must be made to the Secretary and include a short statement of applicant's research project, the purpose for which the grant is required, a budget, and in the case of students a supporting letter from his/her supervisor. **Deadline:** Michaelmas, Lent, Easter Terms. **Contact:** Secretary at the above address (see entry 1034).

## • 1036 •
## Ancient Order United Workmen
12819 SE 38th St., Ste. 136
Bellevue, WA 98006       *Ph:* (206)277-1603

### • 1037 • AOUW Student Loan *(Graduate, Undergraduate/Loan)*

**Focus:** General Studies. **Qualif.:** Candidates must be active members of AOUW and have held membership for at least one year.

**Funds Avail.:** $2,000. **Contact:** Carol Benton at the above address (see entry 1036).

## • 1038 •
## Andersen Foundation
Recruiting and College and
  University Relations
69 West Washington St., 26th Floor    *Ph:* (312)507-3402
Chicago, IL 60602       *Fax:* (312)507-2548
*URL:* http://www.brooklyn.cuny.edu/bc/grant/vln5/aac/aacf.html

### • 1039 • Andersen Fellowships for Doctoral Candidates at the Dissertation Stage *(Doctorate/ Fellowship)*

**Purpose:** To enable prospective faculty who are outstanding candidates for the Ph.D. or an equivalent degree, to complete their dissertations. To support predoctoral students interested in careers as professors in fields related to accounting, tax or information sciences. **Focus:** Accounting, Business Administration, Computer Sciences, Information Sciences, Taxation. **Qualif.:** Applicants may be of any nationality but must be doctoral candidates at an accredited institution (usually a business school) who have completed all degree requirements except the writing of the dissertation. Candidates must intend to pursue a university career immediately after completion of their Ph.D. Fellows may not simultaneously accept other forms of financial assistance, engage in teaching or other employment, or enroll in university courses. Fellows who are not engaged in academic careers for at least five years after completing the award term are obligated to repay all or part of the fellowship.

**Funds Avail.:** $1,500/month, plus an in-state tuition grant. **To Apply:** Write to the Foundation for application form and guidelines. Applications should include (but are not limited to): a description of previous business, professional, and teaching experience; transcripts, graduate-level test scores and honors; a dissertation proposal (not to exceed 2,500 words); and five personal references, including one from the chair of the dissertation committee. **Deadline:** March 1, October 1. Fellows are announced within five weeks of deadline. **Contact:** Managing Director at the above address (see entry 1038).

### • 1040 • Andersen Foundation Faculty Residencies *(Professional Development/Award)*

**Purpose:** To enable full-time university faculty members to obtain diversified field experience working as members of the Arthur Andersen or Andersen Consulting organization while on sabbatical or on leave from a university position. **Focus:** Accounting, Business Administration, Computer Sciences, Information Sciences, Taxation. **Qualif.:** Applicant must be from a country where Arthur Andersen & Co. operates. Candidate must be a university faculty member. Individuals working on doctoral degrees are not eligible to apply. There are two types of residencies available: regular and short-term. Regular residencies are available in accounting, auditing, taxation, management information consulting, and professional education (involving course development). Regular residencies are usually undertaken during sabbaticals. Short-term residencies are primarily offered in auditing, and are available during sabbaticals or university vacations. We will arrange, whenever possible, for the faculty resident to attend one of our mainline staff training schools. Upon completion of the training course, residents gain field experience as Arthur Andersen or Andersen Consulting staff members. Individuals in the regular residency program may also undertake research projects, either independently or as a joint effort with a professional at the firm, during the last two or three months of their residency. Residents' salaries will not exceed their regular base salary at their home institution.

**Funds Avail.:** Varies. **To Apply:** Write to the managing director for application form and guidelines. **Deadline:** January 15. Notification by February 1. **Contact:** Managing Director at the above address (see entry 1038).

## • 1041 •
## Anglo-Israel Archaeological Society
3 St. John's Wood Rd.
London NW8 8RB, England      *Ph:* 171 286 1176

### • 1042 • Richard Barnett Memorial Travel Awards *(Postgraduate/Award)*

**Purpose:** To enable a postgraduate student of archaeology to travel to the country of his/her studies in order to carry out research. **Focus:** Archaeology. **Qualif.:** Applicant must be a postgraduate candidate studying archaeology of the Middle East, Anatolia, or Cyprus. Preference will normally be given to candidates who plan to conduct research in Israel.

**Funds Avail.:** £800. **No. of Awards:** Varies, not more than one per year. **To Apply:** Write to the secretary for application form and guidelines. Submit form with two academic references and a detailed description of the project. **Deadline:** April 30; Notification in July.

**Remarks:** The Society also offers several travel awards each year to both graduate and undergraduate students. The awards cover

*Anglo-Israel Archaeological Society (continued)*
the cost of travel to and from the country of study (normally Israel). **Contact:** Secretary at the above address (see entry 1041).

---

## • 1043 •
### Anglo-Jewish Association
Woburn House, 5th Floor
Upper Woburn Place
London WC1H OEP, England          *Ph:* 171 387 5937

#### • 1044 • Anglo-Jewish Association Grants
*(Postgraduate/Grant)*

**Purpose:** To support non-British Jewish students who wish to study in the United Kingdom. **Focus:** General Studies. **Qualif.:** Applicant must be Jewish and from a country other than the United Kingdom. Grants are tenable for postgraduate study in the United Kingdom.

**Funds Avail.:** £250-500. **To Apply:** Write the AJA general secretary for application form and guidelines. **Deadline:** May 1. **Contact:** Mrs. Salasnik, General Secretary, at the above address (see entry 1043).

---

## • 1045 •
### Animal Health Trust of Canada
1 Yonge Street, Suite 1801          *Ph:* (416)368-7914
Toronto, ON, Canada M5E 1W7          *Fax:* (416)369-0515

#### • 1046 • Animal Health Trust of Canada Research Grants *(Doctorate/Award)*

**Purpose:** To support research in animal health in Canada. **Focus:** Animal Husbandry, Veterinary Medicine. **Qualif.:** Applicant may be of any nationality, but must be qualified researcher in Canada, but not necessarily a veterinarian. Current priorities are (1) companion animals, (2) wildlife, and (3) animals in industry and agriculture. Preference will be given to those areas of clinical research that are not receiving adequate support from other sources.

**Funds Avail.:** Varies. **To Apply:** Write for application form and guidelines. **Deadline:** April 1. **Contact:** Laurie Lloyd, Executive Director, at the above address (see entry 1045).

---

## • 1047 •
### AOPA Air Safety Foundation
421 Aviation Way          *Ph:* (301)695-2170
Frederick, MD 21701-4798          *Fax:* (301)695-2375
*URL:* http://www.aopq.org/asf/

#### • 1048 • McAllister Memorial Scholarship
*(Undergraduate/Scholarship)*

**Purpose:** To provide promising young men and women interested in aviation with financial assistance for college. **Qualif.:** Candidates must be of college junior or senior standing at the time of application, have a 3.25 GPA, and be enrolled in a college aviation (non-engineering) baccalaureate degree program at an organization described in section 170 of the Internal Revenue Code of 1954. They must be pursuing a curriculum designed for a career in aviation. Previous recipients are not eligible.

**Funds Avail.:** $1,000. **No. of Awards:** 1. **To Apply:** Applicants must submit a 250-word essay on topic that is chosen on an annual basis, and applicant is interested in pursuing a career in aviation along with an official transcript from the applicant's college or university. A self-addressed stamped envelope should accompany applications. **Deadline:** March 31.

**Remarks:** The McAllister Memorial Scholarship is awarded annually and administered jointly by the AOPA Air Safety Foundation and the University Aviation Association. **Contact:** An original and five copies of the application packet should be sent to Ms. Mary Ann Eiff, 314 Wildwood Lane, Lafayette, Indiana 47905.

---

## • 1049 •
### Apex Foundation for Research into Intellectual Disability
PO Box 311
Mt. Evelyn, VIC 3796, Australia          *Ph:* 3 736 1261

#### • 1050 • Apex Foundation Research Grants
*(Professional Development/Grant)*

**Purpose:** To assist research related to intellectual disability. **Focus:** Intellectual Disability. **Qualif.:** Applicant may be of any nationality, but research must be conducted in Australia. Candidate must wish to conduct research into the causes, diagnosis, treatment or prevention of intellectual disability.

**Funds Avail.:** A$30,000-A$35,000. **To Apply:** Write to the honorary secretary for application form and guidelines. **Deadline:** July 31. **Contact:** K. Morrish, Honorary Secretary, at the above address (see entry 1049).

---

## • 1051 •
### APICS - Educational & Research Foundation
500 W. Annandale Rd.          *Ph:* (703)354-8851
Falls Church, VA 22046-4274          *Fax:* (703)354-8794
          *Free:* 800-444-2742
*E-mail:* foundation@apics-hq.org
*URL:* http://www.apics.org

#### • 1052 • Donald W. Fogarty International Student Paper Competition *(Graduate, Undergraduate/Award)*

**Purpose:** To encourage students to become more knowledgeable in the principles and techniques that can be applied to the field of resource management. **Focus:** Production and Operations Management. **Qualif.:** All full-time and part-time undergraduate and graduate students are eligible. **Criteria:** Papers are judged on relevance of the topic to resource management, timeliness of material presented, apparent understanding of topic and depth of coverage, accuracy of material, organization and clarity of the presentation, and originality of treatment.

**Funds Avail.:** $100-$1700. **No. of Awards:** Varies, up to 672. **To Apply:** Papers must conform to all contest rules and must be submitted to a local APICS chapter. **Deadline:** May 15.

**Remarks:** High school students are not eligible; prefer calls for info (800); return envelopes will not be used.

## • 1053 •
## Appalachian Center
Berea College
College Box 2336
Berea, KY 40404

*Ph:* (606)986-9341
*Fax:* (606)986-4506

*URL:* http://www.cn.edu/cncweb/appcenter.html

### • 1054 • W.D. Weatherford Award *(Other/Award)*

**Focus:** Writing. **Qualif.:** The work submitted as a candidate for the Weatherford Award must have been first published during the year for which the award is made. The work may have been published anywhere in the United States. In the opinion of the judges, it must best illustrate the problems, personalities, and unique qualities of the Appalachian South. In recognition of the diversity of works published each year, the judges if they see fit, may present a second award to a deserving work or to ongoing works that make special contributions to the region but might not be eligible for the regular award. Unpublished or reprinted works are not eligible. Works submitted may be fact, fiction, or poetry of any length, from magazine articles or story-length to book-length. They may consist of one individual piece or series of pieces. They may be published in newspapers, magazines, or anthologies, or they may in themselves be complete books. **Criteria:** Best work of the year.

**Funds Avail.:** The Weatherford Award is in the amount of $500. A special award of $200 to honor other outstanding work may be made. The awards are made to the authors. **No. of Awards:** 1 annually. **To Apply:** A work may be nominated by its publisher, by a member of the Award Committee or by any reader. Persons making award nominations send at least one and preferably seven copies of the nominated work. If this cannot be done, complete and full information about the work is necessary. **Deadline:** Nominations must be received by December 31. **Contact:** Chairman, Weatherford Award Committee, at the above address (see entry 1053).

## • 1055 •
## Appaloosa Horse Club, Inc. - Appaloosa Youth Program
PO Box 8403
5070 Hwy. 8 W.
Moscow, ID 83843

*Ph:* (208)882-5578
*Fax:* (208)882-8150

*URL:* http://www.maroon.com/horses/appalossa/

### • 1056 • Appaloosa Youth Educational Scholarships *(Undergraduate/Scholarship)*

**Focus:** General Studies. **Qualif.:** Applicants must be members of the Appaloosa Youth Association or the Appaloosa Horse Club, sons or daughters of a member of the Appaloosa Horse Club, or they must be sponsored by a regional club or a racing association. Every regional club and racing association should make it known to all their members that these scholarships are available so interested youth can submit their applications for consideration. The procedure for determining its two applicants shall be at the discretion of the regional club or racing association. **Criteria:** Based on scholastic aptitude, leadership potential, sportsmanship, community and civic responsibility, plus general knowledge and accomplishments in horsemanship.

**Funds Avail.:** $1,000 scholarships. One will be awarded in each of the five territories of the Appaloosa Horse Club, Inc., two will be awarded at large, and one will be awarded to a past-year winner in the form of a continuing scholarship. The check from the Scholarship Fund will be payable only to the educational institution the recipient wishes to attend. **No. of Awards:** 8. **To Apply:** Two applications will be provided to each regional club and racing association. An official grade transcript from the applicant's last high school or college and a picture of the nominee must

accompany the application. **Deadline:** June 10. **Contact:** Appaloosa Youth Foundation Scholarship Committee at the above address (see entry 1055).

## • 1057 •
## Apparel Industry Foundation
350 N Orleans St., Ste. 1047
Chicago, IL 60654-1501

*Ph:* (312)836-1041

### • 1058 • Stanley Paul/Raelene Mittelman Fashion Design Scholarship Fund *(Undergraduate/Award)*

**Purpose:** To further charitable and educational programs related to the fashion design industry. **Focus:** Fashion design. **Qualif.:** Applicants must be graduating public or private high school seniors attending school in the state of Illinois with overall grade point averages of 2.0. **Criteria:** Finalists must submit a finished garment of one of the previously submitted original sketches by May 10. Write for further details.

**Funds Avail.:** $10,000. **No. of Awards:** 1-4. **To Apply:** Applicants must submit a brief biographical description written relating to the reasons the applicant plans to enter the field of fashion design and listing fashion activities both in and outside of school; one letter of recommendation; and 2-5 original design sketches (11"x14" sketch-size matted; fabric swatches; and colors, name school, teacher contact) **Deadline:** March 15. **Contact:** Nancy Berman, executive director.

## • 1059 •
## Appraisal Institute Education Trust
875 N. Michigan Ave., Ste. 2400
Chicago, IL 60611-1980

*Ph:* (312)335-4100
*Fax:* (312)335-4400

*URL:* http://www.appraisalinstitute.org

### • 1060 • Appraisal Institute Education Trust Scholarships *(Graduate, Undergraduate/Scholarship)*

**Focus:** Land Economics, Real Estate, or allied fields. **Qualif.:** Applicants must be U.S. citizens, graduate or undergraduate students majoring in real estate appraisal, land economics, real estate, or an allied fields. **Criteria:** The scholarships are awarded on the basis of academic excellence.

**Funds Avail.:** $3,000 graduate and $2,000 undergraduate. **To Apply:** Write to the Institute for application form and guidelines. Applications are available in beginning September for the following year's deadline. The following documents are required at the time of application: a written statement from the Dean of the college; a signed statement regarding applicant's general activities and intellectual interests, college training, activities and employment, a future plans; official copies of transcripts; proposed program of study; and two letters of recommendation. **Deadline:** March 15. **Contact:** Charlotte Timms, Project Coordinator, at the above address,(see entry 1059) Telephone: (312)335-4136.

# • 1061 •
## Arby's Foundation - Big Brothers Big Sisters of America

230 North 13th St.
Philadelphia, PA 19107

*Ph:* (215)567-7000
*Fax:* (215)567-0394

### • 1062 • Arby's Scholarships *(Undergraduate/ Scholarship)*

**Purpose:** Arby's Scholarships are part of Big Brother Big Sisters of America's continuing corporate partnership with Arby's. Scholarships are awarded to people who have benefited from being a Little Brother/Little Sister, and in turn have volunteered their time. Although not restricted to low and middle income families headed by one parent, scholarships are designed to help those who might not have the financial means to otherwise attend college. **Focus:** General Studies. **Qualif.:** Each applicant must have been a matched Little Brother or Little Sister in an affiliated Big Brother/Big Sister program for at least one year. The match does not have to be current. **Criteria:** Application forms must be submitted by an affiliated Big Brothers Big Sisters agency. Applicants are selected based on academic achievement, volunteer and community involvement, and financial need.

**Funds Avail.:** $5,000. **No. of Awards:** 2. **To Apply:** Candidates must submit transcripts from their last two years of school, a parental agreement form, letter(s) of recommendation, student application form, agency application form and a picture of the applicant. **Deadline:** April 30 for the following school year. **Contact:** Local Big Brothers Big Sisters agencies.

# • 1063 •
## Archaeological Institute of America

656 Beacon St.
Boston, MA 02215-2010
*E-mail:* aia@bu.edu
*URL:* http://www.archaeology.org

*Ph:* (617)353-9361
*Fax:* (617)353-6550

### • 1064 • Anna C. and Oliver C. Colburn Fellowship *(Doctorate, Postdoctorate/Fellowship)*

**Purpose:** To support attendance at the American School of Classical Studies in Athens, Greece. **Focus:** Archaeology. **Qualif.:** Applicant must be a citizen or permanent resident of the United States or Canada who is at the pre-doctoral stage or who has received the Ph.D. degree within the last five years. Award is contingent upon acceptance as an incoming Associate Member of the American School of Classical Studies in Athens. Candidate's must apply concurrently to the American School for Associate Membership. Applicants may not be members of the American School during the year of application. The recipient is required to submit a report on the use of the stipend both to the president of the Archaeological Institute of American and to the Director of the American School. Other major fellowships may not be held during the requested tenure of the award.

**Funds Avail.:** $13,000. **No. of Awards:** One. **To Apply:** Write for application form and guidelines. **Deadline:** February 1. Fellowship is announced April 15.

### • 1065 • Kenan T. Erim Award *(Doctorate, Postdoctorate/Fellowship)*

**Qualif.:** Applicants must be American or international research and/or excavating scholars in a doctoral program or with a recent Ph.D. who are currently working on material from the American Friends of Aphrodisias. Current officers and members of the Governing Board of the Institute are not eligible.

**Funds Avail.:** $4,000 for one year of research. **No. of Awards:** 1. **To Apply:** Candidates must submit written approval from the field director if the project involves work at Aphrodisias along with three letters of reference from persons familiar with the candidate's work. Recipients must submit a final report to the president of the Archaeological Institute of America and to the President of the American Friends of Aphrodisias. **Deadline:** November 1. **Contact:** Archaeological Institute at the above address (see entry 1063)or the American Friends of Aphrodisias, Box 989, Lenox Hill Station, New York, NY 10021.

### • 1066 • Olivia James Traveling Fellowship *(Doctorate, Postdoctorate/Fellowship)*

**Purpose:** To support research and travel in the Mediterranean. **Focus:** Archaeology, Architecture, Classics, History, Sculpture. **Qualif.:** Applicant must be a U.S. citizen or permanent resident. Candidate does not have to be registered in an academic institution, but preference will be given to applicants engaged in dissertation research and to recent recipients of the Ph.D. Fellowship is intended for travel and study in Greece, the Aegean Islands, Sicily, southern Italy, Asia Minor, or Mesopotamia. The fellowship may not be used for field excavation projects. Fellow may not hold other major awards during the requested tenure of the fellowship. **Criteria:** Preference will be given to projects of at least a half year's duration.

**Funds Avail.:** $20,000. **No. of Awards:** 1. **To Apply:** Write for application form and guidelines. Submit ten copies of the form with three letters of reference. **Deadline:** November 1. Fellowship is announced February 1.

### • 1067 • Harriet and Leon Pomerance Fellowship *(Professional Development/Fellowship)*

**Purpose:** To support a project of a scholarly nature relating to Aegean Bronze Age archaeology. **Focus:** Archaeology of the Aegean Bronze Age. **Qualif.:** Applicant must be a resident of the United States or Canada. **Criteria:** Preference will be given to applicants whose projects require travel to the Mediterranean.

**Funds Avail.:** $4,000. **No. of Awards:** One. **To Apply:** Write for application form and guidelines. Submit ten copies of the form with three letters of reference. **Deadline:** November 1. Fellowship is announced February 1.

### • 1068 • Helen M. Woodruff Fellowship of the Archaeological Institute of America *(Doctorate, Postdoctorate/Fellowship)*

**Qualif.:** Applicants must be United States citizens or permanent residents pursuing, or who have recently obtained a doctoral degree in archaeology or classical studies. Current officers and members of the Governing Board of the Institute are not eligible.

**Funds Avail.:** This Fellowship, along with other funds from the Institute from the American Academy in Rome, supports a Rome Prize Fellowship. Recipients must submit a report to the President of the Institute and the President of the American Academy in Rome at the conclusion of the Fellowship tenure. **No. of Awards:** 1. **To Apply:** Applications are available from the American Academy in Rome. Candidates must submit three letters of reference from persons familiar with their work. **Deadline:** February 1. **Contact:** American Academy in Rome, 7 E. 60th St., New York, NY 10022, (212)751-7200.

### • 1069 • Woodruff Traveling Fellowship *(Doctorate/ Fellowship)*

**Purpose:** To support archaeological dissertation research in Italy (outside of Sicily and Magna Graecia) and the western Mediterranean. **Focus:** Archeology. **Qualif.:** Applicants must have completed all requirements for the PhD except the dissertation at the time of application. Preference will be given to field oriented projects.

**Funds Avail.:** $6000 usable for travel, room and board, and other legitimate research expenses. **Deadline:** November 1.

---

### • 1070 •
**Archbold Biological Station - Internship Committee**
PO Box 2057      *Ph:* (941)465-2571
Lake Placid, FL 33852-2057      *Fax:* (941)699-1927
*E-mail:* hswain@ct.net
*URL:* http://acc.imok.ufl.edu/bock/c-5270.html

**• 1071 •** **Archbold Biological Station Undergraduate and Graduate Internships** *(Graduate, Undergraduate/Internship)*

**Purpose:** To help students develop their research skills. The program involves assisting half-time in assigned duties and half-time conducting an independent research project under the guidance of a staff member. **Focus:** Ecology—Plant, Arthropod, Fire, and Agriculture, Biological, and Clinical Sciences, Environmental Science—Population Biology, Demography, Conservation, and Endangered Species. **Qualif.:** Applicants must be undergraduates at any level or students who have recently obtained their bachelor's degree and are planning to go into graduate school or a career in biology.

**Funds Avail.:** Students receive free room and board and a stipend of $50 to $100 per week for expenses. The Station does not qualify for J-1 Visas, therefore, foreign students do not receive a stipend. Research equipment and supplies are also provided. Students must arrange their own travel to and from the Station. **To Apply:** Applicants should indicate a first and second choice of fields in which they would like to work. They should also include a letter giving a summary of general biological background, interests, and the type of research project in which they would be interested; a resume; and two letters of recommendation. **Deadline:** Applications for the summer period are due April 1.

**Remarks:** Students are encouraged to make arrangements with their home institutions for academic credit. **Contact:** Internship Committee at the above address (see entry 1070).

---

### • 1072 •
**John D. Archbold Memorial Hospital**
PO Box 1018
116 Mimosu Dr.      *Ph:* (912)228-2970
Thomasville, GA 31792      *Fax:* (912)228-8584
*URL:* http://www.assoc-cancer-ctrs.org/members/116.html

**• 1073 •** **John D. Archbold Scholarship** *(Graduate, Undergraduate/Scholarship)*

**Qualif.:** Applicant must be within two years of completion of a college degree that can be utilized by the hospital and must agree to work full-time for the hospital for three years following the completion of education. Applicant must reside in southwest Georgia or north Florida.

**Funds Avail.:** $6,000. **No. of Awards:** 50. **To Apply:** Applicants should submit an application to the Department of Education along with a degree program acceptance letter and a copy of their transcript. **Contact:** Donna McMillan at the above address (see entry 1072).

---

### • 1074 •
**Architects League of Northern New Jersey**
c/o Albert Zaconne, AIA
24 Webster St.      *Ph:* (201)440-0058
Ridgefield Park, NJ 07660      *Fax:* (201)440-5230

**• 1075 •** **Architects League Scholastic Award** *(Undergraduate/Scholarship)*

**Focus:** Architecture. **Qualif.:** Applicants must be permanent residents of Bergen, Hudson, Passaic, Sussex, and certain areas of Essex and the northern part of Morris counties of New Jersey (Architects League's territory) who are fourth and fifth year architectural majors. **Criteria:** Awards are made based on scholastic excellence in architectural design.

**Funds Avail.:** $1,000. Non-renewable. **No. of Awards:** 2. **To Apply:** Applicants must submit a completed application, college transcript, two letters of reference, financial statement and examples of work. **Deadline:** June 1. **Contact:** Albert Zaccone.

**• 1076 •** **Albert Halse Memorial Scholarship** *(Undergraduate/Scholarship)*

**Focus:** Architecture. **Qualif.:** Applicants must be permanent residents of Bergen, Hudson, Passaic, Sussex, and certain areas of Essex and the northern part of Morris counties of New Jersey (Architects League's territory) who are fourth and fifth year architectural majors. **Criteria:** Awards are made based on excellence in architectural delineation and/or architectural models.

**Funds Avail.:** $1,500. Non-renewable. **No. of Awards:** 1. **To Apply:** Applicants must submit a completed application, college transcript, two letters of reference, financial statement and examples of work. **Deadline:** June 1. **Contact:** Albert Zaccone.

**• 1077 •** **Clarence Tabor Memorial Scholarship** *(Undergraduate/Scholarship)*

**Focus:** Architecture. **Qualif.:** Applicants must be permanent residents of Bergen, Hudson, Passaic, Sussex or certain areas of Essex and the northern part of Morris Counties in New Jersey (Northern New Jersey Architects League's territory) who are in their last year of undergraduate study in architecture. **Criteria:** Awards are made based on scholastic excellence, attitude toward profession, probable success as an architect and financial need.

**Funds Avail.:** $1,500. Non-renewable. **No. of Awards:** 1. **To Apply:** Applicants must submit a completed application form, college transcript, two letters of reference, financial statement and examples of work. **Deadline:** June 1. **Contact:** Albert Zaccone.

---

### • 1078 •
**Architects Registration Council of the United Kingdom**
73 Hallam Street      *Ph:* 171 580 5861
London W1N 6EE, England      *Fax:* 171 436 5269

**• 1079 •** **Architects Registration Council Student Maintenance Grants** *(Undergraduate/Grant)*

**Purpose:** To provide assistance to students of architecture. **Focus:** Architecture. **Qualif.:** Applicant may be of any nationality, but must be pursuing a degree in architecture at a recognized U.K. institution. Applicants who have been accepted to a school of architecture but have not yet started studies are eligible to apply. Candidate must demonstrate financial need which cannot be met through other sources, and must intend to practice architecture in the United Kingdom after completing studies.

---

### Architects Registration Council of the United Kingdom (continued)

**Funds Avail.:** Varies, according to financial need. **To Apply:** Write to the education secretary for application form and guidelines. Submit form with a letter concerning financial hardship and reason for studying architecture; a letter from the local authority indicating ineligibility for a local authority grant; and a letter confirming acceptance to a school of architecture, if applicable. **Deadline:** None. **Contact:** Education Secretary at the above address (see entry 1078).

---

### • 1080 •
### Arctic Institute of North America

2500 University Drive, NW
University of Calgary     *Ph:* (403)220-7515
Calgary, AB, Canada T2N 1N4     *Fax:* (403)282-4609

#### • 1081 • Lorraine Allison Scholarships; Jennifer Robinson Scholarships *(Graduate/Scholarship)*

**Purpose:** To support graduate studies in Northern issues. **Focus:** Arctic Studies. **Qualif.:** Applicants must be Canadian citizens and graduate students enrolled in a Canadian university who are studying a field related to Northern issues.

**Funds Avail.:** Allison Scholarship: $2,000; Robinson Scholarship: $5,000. **To Apply:** Write for application guidelines. **Deadline:** May 1. **Contact:** Executive Director at the above address (see entry 1080).

---

### • 1082 •
### Argonne National Laboratory - Division of Educational Programs

9700 S. Cass Ave.     *Ph:* (708)252-4579
Argonne, IL 60439-4803     *Fax:* (708)252-3193
*URL:* http://www.anl.gov/

#### • 1083 • Argonne National Laboratory Faculty Research Leave; Faculty Research Participation Awards *(Postdoctorate/Award)*

**Purpose:** To provide academic scientists with the opportunity to conduct collaborative projects with the researchers at the Laboratory. **Focus:** Engineering, Physical Science, Life Sciences, Mathematics, Computer Science, Conservation, Ecology. **Qualif.:** Candidate must be a U.S. citizen or permanent resident. Applicant must be a full-time faculty member at an accredited U.S. college or university. Research Participation Awards are intended to support summer projects at Argonne; Research Leave Awards are given to faculty members who wish to spend their sabbatical leave at the Laboratory.

**Funds Avail.:** Participation Awards: varies, according to academic salary. Leave Awards: up to one-half of usual academic salary; some reimbursement. **To Apply:** Write to Faculty Programs for application guidelines and forms. **Deadline:** Participation Awards: January 10; Leave Awards: six to nine months before anticipated visit. **Contact:** Faculty Programs at the above address (see entry 1082).

#### • 1084 • Laboratory-Graduate Participantships Thesis Parts Appointment *(Doctorate, Graduate/Grant)*

**Purpose:** To support master's or doctoral thesis research at the Laboratory. **Focus:** Engineering, Science. **Qualif.:** Applicant must be a graduate student enrolled in a U.S. college or university.

Candidate must wish to conduct thesis/dissertation research that would benefit from the Laboratory's facilities and scientists. Participantships are intended for students who wish to undertake all of their research at Argonne. Appointments are for short-term research visits.

**Funds Avail.:** Stipend varies; recipients of participantships are also granted $4,000/year tuition scholarship. **To Apply:** Write to Graduate Student Programs for application guidelines. **Deadline:** Completed application due two months prior to proposed starting date. **Contact:** Graduate Student Programs at the above address (see entry 1082).

---

### • 1085 •
### Arizona Space Grant Consortium

The University of Arizona
Lunar and Planetary Laboratory, Rm. 345
PO Box 210092
Tucson, AZ 85721     *Ph:* (520)621-8556
*E-mail:* sbrew@seds.org
*URL:* http://www.seds.org/spacegrant/azoffice.htm

#### • 1086 • UA/NASA Space Grant Graduate Fellowship Program *(Graduate/Fellowship)*

**Focus:** Space engineering and global change-related fields. **Qualif.:** Applicants must be graduate students.

**Funds Avail.:** $16,000 stipend, in- and out-of-state tuition waivers; and $1500 for travel to scientific meetings. **No. of Awards:** 6.

#### • 1087 • The University of Arizona/NASA Space Grant Undergraduate Research Internship Program *(Undergraduate/Grant, Internship)*

**Purpose:** To provide paid research experience, develop professional interests, and develop understanding of scientific work. **Focus:** Aerospace fields. **Qualif.:** Applicants must be U.S. citizens and at least sophomore undergraduate students. Applications are encouraged from under-represented minority groups and women. **To Apply:** An application is available on the Consortium's website. **Deadline:** July 5.

---

### • 1088 •
### Arizona State Board of Regents

2020 N. Central, Rm. 1400
Phoenix, AZ 85012

#### • 1089 • Arizona WICHE Professional Student Exchange Program *(Professional Development/Work Study)*

**Purpose:** To provide funding in six medical fields for students to go out of state for training which is not available in Arizona. **Focus:** Medicine. **Qualif.:** Applicants must be a five year resident of the State of Arizona; US citizen; average grades. **Criteria:** Admission to a WICHE participating school and program, and Arizona certification.

**Funds Avail.:** Varies by field. **No. of Awards:** 50 new per year. **To Apply:** The 6 fields currently supported are: Dentistry, Occupational Therapy, Optometry, Osteopathy, Physician Assistant, and Veterinary Medicine. **Deadline:** October 15 of the year prior to commencement of training.

**Remarks:** The student is required to practice in Arizona one year for each year of support or repay Arizona one-half of all funds expended on his/her behalf plus interest. **Contact:** Louise Lynch, Certifying Officer.

## • 1090 •
### Arkansas Department of Higher Education

| | |
|---|---|
| 114 E. Capitol | *Ph:* (501)371-2050 |
| Little Rock, AR 72201 | *Fax:* (501)371-2001 |
| | *Free:* 800-547-8839 |

*E-mail:* finaid@adhe.arknet.edu
*URL:* http://www.arscholarships.com

#### • 1091 • Arkansas Department of Higher Education Scholarship *(Graduate, Undergraduate/Scholarship)*

**Purpose:** To aid with educational costs for students working toward degrees within the state of Arkansas. **Focus:** General studies. **Qualif.:** Applicants must be high school seniors planning to attend or undergraduate or graduate students attending Arkansas colleges and universities.

**Funds Avail.:** Up to $7,500. **No. of Awards:** Varies. **To Apply:** Write for further details. **Deadline:** March 1 through October 1. **Contact:** Melissa Goff, Coordinator, Financial Aid.

## • 1092 •
### Arkansas Education Association

| | |
|---|---|
| 1500 W. 4th St. | *Ph:* (501)375-4611 |
| Little Rock, AR 72201-1034 | *Fax:* (501)375-4620 |

#### • 1093 • ATA Undergraduate Scholarships *(Undergraduate/Scholarship)*

**Purpose:** To provide a living memorial to the Arkansas Teachers Association which was organized to secure equality of educational opportunities for every child, equality of professional status for every teacher in Arkansas, and to aid in providing motivation and developing opportunities for young people of African-American descent to enter the teaching profession. **Focus:** Education. **Qualif.:** Applicants must be African-American juniors or seniors enrolled in an accredited teacher education program at an Arkansas college or university.

**Funds Avail.:** $500. **No. of Awards:** 5. **To Apply:** Applications are available in the winter each year from the Student AEA Advisors, College of Education Department Heads, or the AEA. **Contact:** Annette Thomas-Jones at the above address (see entry 1092).

## • 1094 •
### Arkansas Library Association

| | |
|---|---|
| 9 Shackleford Plz., Ste. 1 | *Ph:* (501)228-0775 |
| Little Rock, AR 72211-1855 | *Fax:* (501)228-5535 |

*E-mail:* jcole10145@aol.com
*URL:* http://pw2.netcom.com/~runruss/arias.html

#### • 1095 • Arkansas Library Association Scholarship for Graduate Study in Library Science *(Graduate/Scholarship)*

**Focus:** Library and Archival Studies. **Qualif.:** Applicants must be legal residents of the state of Arkansas; accept professional employment in an Arkansas library within one year after completing the graduate program; continue to work in an Arkansas

library for at least one year, in a capacity related to their training and education, after accepting such employment; hold or be completing work toward a bachelor's degree from an accredited college or university; and have been accepted at an American Library Association accredited program leading to a master's degree in library science, with the course of study to be completed within three academic years after the receipt of the award. Applications will also be considered from persons already in service as librarians as well as from other college graduates. **Criteria:** Selection of recipients is based on the applicant's interest in librarianship as a profession. It is also based on personality, character, academic record, references, and personal interviews. Awards are made without regard to race, sex, age, religion, or ethnic background.

**Funds Avail.:** $1,500. **To Apply:** Applicants must submit a program of study to the Scholarship Committee, and must supply Arkansas Library Association with written proof that all of the above requirements have been met. Scholarship recipients will be required to sign a promissory note agreeing to repay the Association the amount of the scholarship unless the conditions set out herein are met. **Deadline:** April 15. **Contact:** Application forms may be obtained from the Arkansas Library Association at the above address (see entry 1094).

## • 1096 •
### Arkansas Student Assistance Grant Program

| | |
|---|---|
| Department of Higher Education | *Ph:* (501)371-2050 |
| 114 E. Capitol | *Fax:* (501)371-2001 |
| Little Rock, AR 72201-3818 | *Free:* 800-547-8839 |

*E-mail:* finaid@adhe.arknet.edu
*URL:* http://www.adhe.arknet.edu

#### • 1097 • Arkansas Student Assistance Grants *(Undergraduate/Grant)*

**Focus:** General Studies. **Qualif.:** Applicants must be Arkansas undergraduate residents with financial need who are full-time in accredited institutions. **Criteria:** Selection is based on financial need and cost of attendance.

**Funds Avail.:** Approximately $3.9 million in grants are available. **No. of Awards:** Varies. **To Apply:** Applicants must submit an FAFSA. **Contact:** Philip Axelroth, Assistant Coordinator of Financial Aid, at the above address (see entry 1096).

## • 1098 •
### The Armed Forces Communications & Electronics Association - Educational Foundation

| | |
|---|---|
| 766 Shresbury Ave. | *Ph:* (908)758-9009 |
| Tinton Falls, NJ 07724 | *Fax:* (908)747-6474 |
| | *Free:* 800-336-4583 |

*E-mail:* jedelman@neo.sytexinc.com
*URL:* http://www.afeea-ftmonmouth.org/

#### • 1099 • The AFCEA Educational Foundation Fellowship *(Doctorate, Graduate/Fellowship)*

**Purpose:** To support the development of students pursuing an advanced degree in Electrical, Electronic or Communications Engineering, Physics, Mathematics or Computer Science. **Qualif.:** Applicants must be United States citizens pursuing masters or doctorate degrees in the areas of electronics, electrical or communications engineering, mathematics, physics or computer science. **Criteria:** Awards are based foremost on academic excellence, thesis subject, potential for service to the United States, leadership abilities, and financial need.

---

*The Armed Forces Communications & Electronics Association - Educational Foundation (continued)*

**Funds Avail.:** $25,000. **To Apply:** Applications are available through the AFCEA Education Foundation at 800-336-4583, ext. 6149. Applicants must be nominated by the Dean of the College of Engineering of their university. Only one candidate per university is permitted. **Deadline:** April 1.

**Remarks:** The fellowship will be provided directly to the recipient and is in addition to any other funds which the student may receive. **Contact:** Phyllis R. Lau at the above address (see entry 1098).

• 1100 • **AFCEA ROTC Scholarship Program**
*(Undergraduate/Scholarship)*

**Purpose:** To encourage and reward outstanding and deserving students in the ROTC program. **Focus:** Candidates must be engaged in the study of electronics, electrical or communications engineering, mathematics, physics, computer science or technology, information management, or in the intelligence field. **Qualif.:** Applicants must be United States citizens enrolled in an ROTC program. Candidates must also be of good moral character, have proven academic excellence, and demonstrate motivation and potential for completing a college education and serving as an officer of the Armed Forces of the United States. The student's need for financial assistance is also considered. **Criteria:** Selection is made by a board of active duty officers representing the four services. Scholarship recipients are chosen based on merit and financial need and distributed equally among the Army, Navy/Marine Corps, and Air Force ROTC programs.

**Funds Avail.:** Sixty awards are given annually. Thirty scholarships of $1,000 each are presented to ten Army, ten Navy/Marine Corps, and ten Air Force ROTC students from the junior class for the year they matriculate as seniors. Thirty $1,000 scholarships are given to ten Army, ten Navy/Marine Corps, and ten Air Force ROTC students from the sophomore class for the year they matriculate as juniors. Each scholarship is paid in full to the recipients in August. **To Apply:** Application forms are available from school ROTC units. Professors of Military Science, Naval Science, and Aerospace studies review applications and submit nominations to the AFCEA. **Deadline:** May 1 for nominations. All individuals nominated are notified. Scholarship recipients are notified in June. **Contact:** Phyllis R. Lau at the above address (see entry 1098).

• 1101 • **General Emmett Paige Scholarship**
*(Undergraduate/Scholarship)*

**Purpose:** To promote excellence in scientific and engineering education. **Focus:** Recipients must be working toward a degree in electrical engineering, electronics, mathematics, physics, photometries, communications engineering or technology, computer science or technology, or information management systems. **Qualif.:** Applicants must be United States citizens enrolled in an accredited four-year college or university and working toward a bachelor degree. **Criteria:** The scholarship is awarded on the basis of demonstrated academic achievement, high moral character, leadership ability, and potential to contribute to the defense of the United States. Financial need is also a consideration.

**Funds Avail.:** $1,500. Except under unusual circumstances, students may receive only one award from AFCEA per year. **To Apply:** Application forms are available from school ROTC units or by contacting Mrs. Phyllis R. Lau, Administrator of Scholarships and Awards, Toll-free telephone: 800-336-4583, ext. 6149. Students competing for other AFCEA scholarships are automatically considered for the General Emmett Paige Scholarship. **Deadline:** Applications must be received by May 1.

**Remarks:** This scholarship was founded by the personnel of the U.S. Army Information Systems Command (USAISC) to honor Lieutenant General Emmett Paige, Jr., USA (Ret.), who served for more than 40 years in the Army. **Contact:** Phyllis R. Law,

Administrator of Scholarships and Awards, at the above address (see entry 1098).

• 1102 •
**Armenian Assembly of America**
122 C St., Ste. 350                         Ph: (202)393-3434
Washington, DC 20001-2109                    Fax: (202)638-4904
*URL:* http://www.interaction.org/mb/aaa.html

• 1103 • **K. Arakelian Foundation Scholarship**
*(Undergraduate/Scholarship)*

**Focus:** General studies. **Qualif.:** Applicants must be San Joaquin Valley high school graduates who are of Armenian descent.

**Funds Avail.:** $250 per award. **No. of Awards:** 8. **To Apply:** Write for further details. **Deadline:** February 1. **Contact:** Director of Academic Affairs, Armenian Assembly at the above address (see entry 1102).

• 1104 • **Armenian Allied Arts Association Scholarship** *(Undergraduate/Award)*

**Focus:** Art, literature, dance, music, voice, composition. **Qualif.:** Applicants must have at least one parent of Armenian descent and must not yet have had a professional debut or exhibit. **Criteria:** Awards are made based on merit of work.

**Funds Avail.:** $50 - $1,000. Fund are to bet used to further study at an accredited school or with a recognized private instructor of the winner's choice. **To Apply:** Write for further details. **Deadline:** April. **Contact:** Director of Academic Affairs, Armenian Assembly at the above address (see entry 1102).

• 1105 • **Armenian-American Citizens' League Scholarship** *(Undergraduate/Scholarship)*

**Focus:** General studies. **Qualif.:** Applicants must be Armenian residents of California for at least two years who are enrolled full-time in accredited colleges and universities, and have minimum grade point averages of 3.0. Applicants must be U.S. citizens. **Criteria:** Awards are made based on academic achievement, financial need and involvement in school and community activities.

**Funds Avail.:** $500 - $1,500. Renewable. **To Apply:** Write for further details. **Deadline:** May 1. **Contact:** Director of Academic Affairs, Armenian Assembly at the above address (see entry 1102).

• 1106 • **Armenian American Medical Association Scholarship** *(Undergraduate/Scholarship)*

**Focus:** Medicine. **Qualif.:** Applicants must be Armenian students enrolled in U.S. medical schools who are U.S. citizens. **Criteria:** Awards are granted on the basis of financial need, merit and involvement in Armenian cultural affairs. Preference given to students residing and studying a private New England medical schools.

**Funds Avail.:** $750 - $1,000. **To Apply:** Write for further details. **Deadline:** October 15. **Contact:** Director of Academic Affairs, Armenian Assembly at the above address (see entry 1102).

• 1107 • **Armenian American Middle East Club Scholarship** *(Graduate, Undergraduate/Scholarship)*

**Focus:** General studies. **Qualif.:** Applicants must be of Armenian descent and be full-time juniors, seniors or graduate students in accredited colleges and universities in California who carry 12 or more semester credits. **Criteria:** Awards are granted on the basis of academic excellence, extracurricular activities with an emphasis on the Armenian community.

Funds Avail.: $500 $750. **To Apply:** Write for further details. **Deadline:** February 28. **Contact:** Director of Academic Affairs, Armenian Assembly at the above address (see entry 1102).

• **1108** • **Armenian American Pharmacists' Association Scholarship** *(Graduate, Undergraduate/ Scholarship)*

**Focus:** Pharmacology. **Qualif.:** Applicants must be of Armenian parentage and residents in the New England area who are enrolled at the undergraduate and graduate level at colleges of pharmacy in the Commonwealth of Massachusetts. **Criteria:** Awards are made on the basis of academic excellence and financial need.

**Funds Avail.:** $500. Non-renewable. **To Apply:** Write for further details. **Deadline:** Ongoing. **Contact:** Director of Academic Affairs, Armenian Assembly at the above address (see entry 1102).

• **1109** • **Armenian Bible College Scholarship** *(Undergraduate/Scholarship)*

**Focus:** General studies. **Qualif.:** Applicants must be of Armenian descent and students of the Armenian Bible College who pledge to work as ministers, evangelists, missionaries or youth directors after graduation. **To Apply:** Write for further details. **Deadline:** June 30. **Contact:** Director of Academic Affairs, Armenian Assembly at the above address (see entry 1102).

• **1110** • **Armenian Cultural Society of Akron/Canton Scholarship** *(Undergraduate/Scholarship)*

**Focus:** General studies. **Qualif.:** Applicants must be of students of Armenian descent who live in Northeast Ohio and are enrolled in colleges and universities. **Funds Avail.:** $250 - $500. Renewable **To Apply:** Write for further details. **Deadline:** June 1. **Contact:** Director of Academic Affairs, Armenian Assembly at the above address (see entry 1102).

• **1111** • **Armenian General Athletic Union Scholarship** *(Undergraduate/Scholarship)*

**Focus:** General studies. **Qualif.:** Applicants must be high school students within a 300-mile radius of New York City who are entering college. **Criteria:** Awards are granted on the basis of merit and financial need. **Funds Avail.:** $1,200. Non-renewable. **To Apply:** Write for further details. **Deadline:** April 30. **Contact:** Director of Academic Affairs, Armenian Assembly at the above address (see entry 1102).

• **1112** • **Armenian General Benevolent Union (AGBU) Loans and Grants** *(Graduate, Undergraduate/ Loan)*

**Focus:** General studies. **Qualif.:** Applicants must be full matriculated students of Armenian descent enrolled in accredited American colleges or universities. **Funds Avail.:** $1,000. Payable in one installment, at the beginning of the fall semester. Repayment of loans, without interest, is to begin one year after leaving school and must be completed within three years. Limited funds exist for graduate studies in law, medicine, pharmacy, international relations and Armenian studies. **To Apply:** Write for further details. **Deadline:** April 30. **Contact:** Director of Academic Affairs, Armenian Assembly at the above address (see entry 1102).

• **1113** • **Armenian Professional Society of the Bay Area Scholarship** *(Undergraduate/Scholarship)*

**Focus:** General studies. **Qualif.:** Applicants must be of Armenian descent of full-time status at accredited universities or four-year colleges at sophomore or higher level, with minimum grade point averages of 3.2. This requirement is waived for teachers of

Armenian subjects who are studying on a part-time basis to obtain a teaching credential or toward a degree in education or other related fields. **Criteria:** Preference given to students interested in Armenian studies programs, elementary and secondary level teaching careers in Armenian schools and the arts.

**Funds Avail.:** $1,000. Non-renewable. **To Apply:** Write for further details. **Deadline:** November 15. **Contact:** Director of Academic Affairs, Armenian Assembly at the above address (see entry 1102).

• **1114** • **Armenian Professional Society Scholarship** *(Doctorate, Graduate/Scholarship)*

**Focus:** General studies. **Qualif.:** Applicants must be California residents who are full-time students of Armenian descent and who are enrolled at accredited colleges and universities. Applicants must maintain a minimum grade point average of 3.2. **Criteria:** Awards are granted on the basis of financial need and academic record.

**Funds Avail.:** $1,000. Renewable. **To Apply:** Applicants must interview. Write for further details. **Deadline:** March. **Contact:** Director of Academic Affairs, Armenian Assembly at the above address (see entry 1102).

• **1115** • **Armenian Relief Society of North America Scholarship** *(Undergraduate/Scholarship)*

**Focus:** General studies. **Qualif.:** Applicants must be of Armenian descent who are undergraduate and graduate students enrolled at accredited colleges and universities. **Criteria:** Awards are granted on the basis of financial need, academic merit, and involvement in the Armenian community. **To Apply:** Applicants must submit three letters of recommendation, transcript and tax returns. Write for further details. **Deadline:** April 1. **Contact:** Director of Academic Affairs, Armenian Assembly at the above address (see entry 1102).

• **1116** • **Armenian Students Association of America, Inc. Grant** *(Graduate, Undergraduate/Grant)*

**Focus:** General studies. **Qualif.:** Applicants must be of Armenian descent and be full-time students who have completed at least one year at accredited fouryear colleges and universities in the U.S. **Criteria:** Awards are granted on the basis of financial need, academic achievement, character, self-assurance, and extracurricular activities.

**Funds Avail.:** $500 - $1,500. Renewable. **To Apply:** Write for further details. **Deadline:** April 1. **Contact:** Director of Academic Affairs, Armenian Assembly at the above address (see entry 1102).

• **1117** • **Hagop Bogigian Scholarship Fund** *(Undergraduate/Scholarship)*

**Focus:** General studies. **Qualif.:** Applicants must be students of Armenian descent who are enrolled in four-year Bachelor of Arts degree programs, and maintain a 3.0 grade point average or high. **Criteria:** Awards are granted on the basis of academic achievement and financial need.

**Funds Avail.:** Renewable. **To Apply:** Write for further details. **Deadline:** March 1. **Contact:** Director of Academic Affairs, Armenian Assembly at the above address (see entry 1102).

• **1118** • **Constantinople Armenian Relief Society (CARS) Scholarship** *(Undergraduate/Scholarship)*

**Focus:** General studies. **Qualif.:** Applicants must be Armenian students enrolled in accredited colleges or universities, and at least the sophomore level. **Criteria:** Awards are made on the basis of financial need and academic merit.

**Funds Avail.:** $400 - $600 per award. **No. of Awards:** 10 approximately. **To Apply:** Write for further details. **Deadline:** August 30. **Contact:** Director of Academic Affairs, Armenian Assembly at the above address (see entry 1102).

*Armenian Assembly of America (continued)*

**• 1119 • Garikian University Scholarship Fund**
*(Undergraduate/Scholarship)*

**Focus:** Armenian studies, law, sociology, psychology, political science, history, literature, journalism, education, music. **Qualif.:** Applicants must be Armenian students who have completed their first academic year at colleges or universities in California and are pursuing degrees in the following areas: Armenian studies, law, sociology, psychology, political science, history, literature, journalism, education or music. **Criteria:** Awards are granted on the basis of academic merit, financial need and community involvement.

**Funds Avail.:** $750 - $1,000. **To Apply:** Write for further details. **Deadline:** July 31. **Contact:** Director of Academic Affairs, Armenian Assembly at the above address (see entry 1102).

**• 1120 • Thomas Googooian Memorial Scholarship**
*(Undergraduate/Scholarship)*

**Focus:** General studies. **Qualif.:** Applicants must be Armenian studies who are enrolled in programs leading to bachelor's degrees.

**Funds Avail.:** $500. **To Apply:** Write for further details. **Deadline:** February 1. **Contact:** Director of Academic Affairs, Armenian Assembly at the above address (see entry 1102).

**• 1121 • Calouste Gulbenkian Foundation**
*(Undergraduate/Grant)*

**Focus:** General studies. **Qualif.:** Applicants must be Armenian students who are sophomore or above and enrolled full-time in accredited colleges or universities. **Criteria:** Awards are granted on the basis of academic merit and financial need. Preference given to those candidates who immediate family has not previously received a scholarship.

**Funds Avail.:** Renewable up to five years. **To Apply:** Write for further details. **Deadline:** April 30. **Contact:** Director of Academic Affairs, Armenian Assembly at the above address (see entry 1102).

**• 1122 • Hai Guin Scholarship Association**
*(Undergraduate/Scholarship)*

**Focus:** General studies. **Qualif.:** Applicants must be Armenians residing and attending college in Massachusetts. **Criteria:** Awards are made on the basis of scholastic and financial need.

**Funds Avail.:** $500. **To Apply:** Write for further details. **Deadline:** December 15. **Contact:** Director of Academic Affairs, Armenian Assembly at the above address (see entry 1102).

**• 1123 • AGBU Hirair and Anna Hovnanian Fellowship** *(Graduate/Fellowship)*

**Focus:** Politics, government, international affairs. **Qualif.:** Applicants must be students of Armenian descent pursuing graduate studies leading to a career in politics, government or international affairs.

**Funds Avail.:** $3,000. **To Apply:** Write for further details. **Deadline:** April 30. **Contact:** Director of Academic Affairs, Armenian Assembly at the above address (see entry 1102).

**• 1124 • Knights of Varton, Fresno Lodge 9 Scholarship** *(Undergraduate/Scholarship)*

**Focus:** General studies. **Qualif.:** Applicants must be of full-time students of Armenian descent who have grade point averages of at least 3.0.

**Funds Avail.:** $500 per award. Recipients must enroll in at least one class in Armenian studies, Armenian language or Armenian history. **To Apply:** Write for further details. **Deadline:** February 1.

**Contact:** Director of Academic Affairs, Armenian Assembly at the above address (see entry 1102).

**• 1125 • Peter and Alice Koomruian Armenian Education Fund** *(Graduate, Undergraduate/Scholarship)*

**Focus:** General studies. **Qualif.:** Applicants must be of Armenian descent who are enrolled in accredited U.S. colleges and universities at the undergraduate or graduate level. **Criteria:** Funds are awarded on the basis of financial need and academic achievement. **To Apply:** Write for further details. **Contact:** Director of Academic Affairs, Armenian Assembly at the above address (see entry 1102).

**• 1126 • National Association for Armenian Studies and Research, Inc. Fund** *(Graduate, Postgraduate/ Fellowship, Grant)*

**Focus:** General studies. **Qualif.:** Applicants must be of Armenian descent and pursuing graduate or post-graduate studies as residents of the United States.

**Funds Avail.:** Grants for travel, cost of microfilms or other research materials, and for similar expenses. **To Apply:** Applicants must state in full details the purpose and scope of their research. Applicants must provide a detailed proposal including a budget, details of any travel required, and whether other sources have been approached for funds. In addition, a curriculum vitae and recommendations from at least two persons of academic standing familiar with the applicant's previous work and proposed research. Write for further details. **Deadline:** Early spring for fall grants, early fall for spring grants; early winter for summer grants. **Contact:** Director of Academic Affairs, Armenian Assembly at the above address (see entry 1102).

**• 1127 • St. James Armenian Church Memorial Scholarship** *(Undergraduate/Scholarship)*

**Focus:** General studies. **Qualif.:** Applicants must be Armenians affiliated with St. James Armenian Church by being graduates of the Sunday School, a Sunday School teacher, a church choir member for at least one year, or in some way acceptable to the Scholarship Committee. **Criteria:** Scholarships are awarded on the basis of academic achievement, financial need, service to school, community and church, and seriousness of purpose.

**Funds Avail.:** $300 $500. **No. of Awards:** 4. **To Apply:** Write for further details. **Deadline:** May 1. **Contact:** Director of Academic Affairs, Armenian Assembly at the above address (see entry 1102).

**• 1128 • Union of Hadjin Fund** *(Undergraduate/ Scholarship)*

**Focus:** General studies. **Qualif.:** Applicants must be Armenian full-time students who have at least one parent who is Hadjintsi, and who are matriculated in accredited California colleges or universities, carrying 12 or more semester quarter units and engaged in courses of study with the objective of obtaining degrees.

**Funds Avail.:** $500. **To Apply:** Write for further details. **Deadline:** June 30. **Contact:** Director of Academic Affairs, Armenian Assembly at the above address (see entry 1102).

**• 1129 • Union of Marash Fund** *(Undergraduate/ Scholarship)*

**Focus:** General studies. **Qualif.:** Applicants must be of Marashtzi background and descent, and be enrolled full-time in accredited institutions of higher learning. **Criteria:** Awards are granted on the basis of moral character, financial need, and high school achievement.

**Funds Avail.:** Varies. Renewable up to three times. **To Apply:** Write for further details. **Deadline:** July 31. **Contact:** Director of

Academic Affairs, Armenian Assembly at the above address (see entry 1102).

**• 1130 •  Harry and Angel Zerigian Scholarship**
*(Undergraduate/Scholarship)*

**Focus:** Accounting. **Qualif.:** Applicants must be of Armenian descent who are full-time students and have satisfactorily completed their sophomore year and majoring in accounting. **Criteria:** Awards are granted on the basis of financial need and academic achievement. Preference given to students from Haverhill, Lawrence, Waltham or Watertown, Massachusetts. **To Apply:** Write for further details. **Contact:** Director of Academic Affairs, Armenian Assembly at the above address (see entry 1102).

**• 1131 •  Charles K. and Pansy Pategian Zlokovich Scholarship** *(Undergraduate/Scholarship)*

**Focus:** General studies. **Qualif.:** Applicants must be of Armenian descent and interested in Armenian culture.

**Funds Avail.:** Varies. **To Apply:** Write for further details. **Deadline:** February 1. **Contact:** Director of Academic Affairs, Armenian Assembly at the above address (see entry 1102).

**• 1132 •**
**Armenian General Benevolent Union**
Education Dept.
55 E. 59th St.                              *Ph:* (212)319-6383
New York, NY 10022-1112            *Fax:* (212)319-6507
*E-mail:* agbuny@aol.com
*URL:* http://www.armino.com/Armenia/HDR/abrev.htm

**• 1133 •  AGBU Education Loan Program in the U.S.**
*(Graduate/Loan)*

**Qualif.:** Candidates must be of Armenian descent and enrolled in highly competitive colleges and universities. They must have a GPA of at least 3.5 during undergraduate study. Loans will be considered for those pursuing masters degrees in communication, education administration, public administration, international relations, or Armenian studies. A limited number of loans for study in law and medicine could be dispensed by the most selective institutions.

**Funds Avail.:** $5,000-$7,000. **To Apply:** Request forms from the AGBU. **Deadline:** April 1.

**• 1134 •  AGBU Graduate Loan Program** *(Graduate/Loan)*

**Purpose:** To support American students of Armenian descent. **Focus:** Armenian Studies, International Relations, Educational Administration, Journalism, Public Administration, Communication, Law, Medicine. **Qualif.:** Applicants must be of Armenian descent and enrolled full-time at a highly competitive and accredited U.S. college or university. Candidates may be graduate students in any of the areas of study listed above. They must also have a GPA of 3.5 or better during their undergraduate study.

**Funds Avail.:** $5,000-7,500. **To Apply:** Write to AGBU for application form and guidelines. **Deadline:** May 15. **Contact:** Maral Achian, Administrator, Scholarship Program, at the above address (see entry 1132).

**• 1135 •**
**Armenian General Benevolent Union**
c/o Maral Achian, Adm. of
Scholarship Program
55 E. 59th St.                              *Ph:* (212)319-6383
New York, NY 10022-1112            *Fax:* (212)319-6507

**• 1136 •  AGBU Education Loan** *(Graduate/Loan)*

**Focus:** Communication, education administration, public administration, international relations. **Qualif.:** Full time students of Armenian heritage enrolled at competitive universities and pursuing their master's degree are eligible. This is a merit-based award. **Criteria:** Applicants must have a GPA of 3.5 or better in their undergraduate years. **No. of Awards:** 10. **To Apply:** Students must request applications in writing. **Deadline:** April 1. **Contact:** Mrs. Maral Achian.

**• 1137 •**
**Armenian Students' Association of America, Inc.**
395 Concord Ave.
Belmont, MA 02178                      *Ph:* (617)484-9548
*URL:* http://www.asainc.org/

**• 1138 •  Armenian Students' Association of America Reading Scholarships** *(Doctorate, Graduate, Undergraduate/Scholarship)*

**Focus:** General Studies. **Qualif.:** Applicants must be of Armenian ancestry, be full-time students (at least a sophomore), plan to attend a four-year accredited college or university in the United States during the next academic year, demonstrate financial need, have good academic performance, show self sufficiency, and participate in extracurricular activities.

**Funds Avail.:** Scholarships range from $500-$2,500. **No. of Awards:** Approximately 30. **To Apply:** Applicants must submit a $15 application fee with their completed C.S.S. Profile form. **Deadline:** January 15 for application requests and March 15 for completed application packages.

**• 1139 •**
**Army Emergency Relief**
National Headquarters
Attn: MG James Ursanos
Scholarship Fund
200 Stovall St.
Alexandria, VA 22332-0600          *Ph:* (703)428-0035
*URL:* http://144.246.28.35/aer/aer.html

**• 1140 •  Army Emergency Relief Scholarships**
*(Undergraduate/Scholarship)*

**Focus:** General Studies. **Qualif.:** Applicants must be unmarried dependent children, including step-children, or legally adopted children of soldiers who are on extended active duty, or in the U.S. Army Reserve or Army National Guard and who will be on continuous active duty during the school year for which assistance is requested; who is on the retired list because of length of service on active duty, physical disability, or having attained age 60 (Reserve Components); or who died on active duty or in retired status. Applicants must not have reached their 22rd birthday before June 1st of the school year that begins following September. **Criteria:** Financial need is the primary criteria;

## Army Emergency Relief *(continued)*

academic achievement and individual accomplishments are also considered.

**Funds Avail.:** The amount of the scholarship may be up to $1,500 per academic year, but is individually determined. Re-application is required for renewal. **To Apply:** Applicants must send in a completed SAR, College Scholarship Service Financial Aid Form which requires data on parental assets, size of family, educational costs incurred by siblings, financial obligations or circumstances, the applicant's assets, including projected summer earnings, and total costs of the year's college education. Accompanying this information a 500 word essay outlining personal ambitions and goals (optional), extracurricular activities, and offices and leadership positions held. In addition, the applicant must submit official high school or college grade transcripts. Complete scholarship applications must be postmarked by March 1. **Deadline:** Application with supporting documentation should be submitted by March 1 and SAR by April 15. **Contact:** AER National Headquarters at the above address (see entry 1139).

### • 1141 • Dependent Children of Soldiers Scholarship Program *(Undergraduate/Scholarship)*

**Qualif.:** Candidates must be single, under the age of 22, and a dependent of a soldier on active duty, retired, or deceased while on active duty or retired. **Criteria:** A GPA of 2.0 and financial need are required to retain the scholarship.

**Funds Avail.:** $500-1,500 awarded annually. **Deadline:** March 1. **Contact:** Army Emergency Relief at the above address (see entry 1139).

### • 1142 •
## Army Engineer Officers Wives Club

Asst. Treas., AEOWC
PO Box 313
Fort Belvoir, VA 22060

### • 1143 • Army Engineer Memorial Awards *(Undergraduate/Scholarship)*

**Purpose:** To serve as a living memorial to Engineer officers who die in the line of duty. **Focus:** General Studies. **Qualif.:** Applicants must be sons or daughters of an officer on active duty with the U.S. Army Corps of Engineers, a retired officer, or an officer who died while on active duty. They must also be high school seniors. **Criteria:** Selection is based on academic achievement and extracurricular activities.

**Funds Avail.:** Several $1,000 awards are given annually to be used for tuition or scholastic expenses at a college, university, technical or vocational school. **No. of Awards:** 2-3. **To Apply:** A completed application, academic transcript, SAT/ACT scores, and documentation of academic or extracurricular recognition must be submitted. **Deadline:** March 1. **Contact:** AEMA Treasurer, at the above address (see entry 1142).

### • 1144 •
## Art Libraries Society of North America

4101 Lake Boone Trail, Ste. 201      *Ph:* (919)787-5181
Raleigh, NC 27607-7506      *Fax:* (919)787-4916
*URL:* http://caroline.eastlib.ufl.edu/arlis/04m.much.html

### • 1145 • Gerd Muehsam Memorial Award *(Graduate, Postgraduate/Award)*

**Purpose:** To recognize excellence in a graduate paper on a topic relevant to art or visual resources librarianship. **Focus:** Art Librarianship. **Qualif.:** Applicant may be of any nationality, but must have written his/her paper while enrolled in either a graduate program of library science accredited by the American Library Association, or in a post-M.L.S. graduate program in art history or a related discipline. The submitted paper must be 2,000 to 2,500 words in length, and have been written during the 18 months prior to the deadline. Papers written in conjunction with a course assignment are eligible for submission. An abstract of the winning paper will be published in ARLIS/NA's quarterly journal.

**Funds Avail.:** $500. **To Apply:** Submit a copy of the paper with an abstract of 250 words. Title page should include the name of entrant, date submitted, institution attended, and if applicable, the name of the faculty member and course title for which the paper was written. **Deadline:** December 1. **Contact:** Penney DePas, CAE, Executive Director, at the above address (see entry 1144).

### • 1146 •
## Arthritis Foundation

1330 W. Peachtree St.      *Ph:* (404)965-7637
Atlanta, GA 30309      *Fax:* (404)872-9559
*E-mail:* adeleon@arthritis.org
*URL:* http://www.arthritis.org/

### • 1147 • Arthritis Biomedical Science Grants *(Postdoctorate/Grant)*

**Purpose:** To encourage and support original biomedical research on arthritis. **Focus:** Rheumatology. **Qualif.:** Applicant must be U.S. citizen or permanent resident and must have a Ph.D., M.D., D.O., or equivalent, and be at least at the assistant professor level at a nonprofit U.S. institution. Research must be related to the etiology, pathogenic mechanisms and control of arthritis and related rheumatic diseases.

**Funds Avail.:** $75,000/year maximum. **To Apply:** Write for application form and guidelines. **Deadline:** September 1. Notification by mid-February. **Contact:** Research Department at the above address (see entry 1146).

### • 1148 • Arthritis Foundation Doctoral Dissertation Award for Arthritis Health Professionals *(Doctorate/Award)*

**Purpose:** To advance the research training of arthritis health professionals in investigative or clinical teaching careers as they relate to the rheumatic diseases. **Focus:** Arthritis. **Qualif.:** The Doctoral Dissertation Awards are designed for doctoral candidates entering the research phase of their programs. The doctoral chairman must approve the project. A dissertation project is preferred. The research project must be related to arthritis management and/or comprehensive patient care in rheumatology practice, research, or education. Suitable studies include, but are not limited to, functional, behavioral, nutritional, occupational, or epidemiological aspects of patient care and management. Drug studies and laboratory in vitro studies are not appropriate. Candidates must have membership or eligibility for membership in their professional organization. **Criteria:** Projects are rated on the basis of proposed research environment, background and potential of the researcher, and significance and relevance of the project to the rheumatic diseases.

**Funds Avail.:** Awards may be made for up to $10,000 per year depending on the amount of time committed to research. Stipends are paid in monthly installments by the Arthritis Foundation. Checks, earmarked for the awardee, are sent directly to the sponsoring institution. **No. of Awards:** 1-4. **To Apply:** A formal application must be filed. Applications are available on the website after May 1. **Deadline:** September 1. Applicants will be notified by mid-February of any action taken on their application. **Contact:** Research Department at the above address (see entry 1146).

• **1149** • **Arthritis Foundation New Investigator Grant for Arthritis Health Professionals** *(Postdoctorate/Grant)*

**Purpose:** To encourage Ph.D. level health professionals who have research expertise to design and carry out innovative research projects related to the rheumatic diseases. The grant is intended to provide support for the period between completion of doctorate work and establishment as an independent investigator. **Focus:** Arthritis. **Qualif.:** Applicants should have Ph.D. or equivalent doctoral degree and demonstrated research experience. These awards are meant to encourage investigators who have received a doctoral degree within the last five years. M.D.s are not eligible. The research project must be related to arthritis management and/or comprehensive patient care in rheumatology practice, research or education. Applicants must have membership or eligibility for membership in his/her professional organization. Approval of each application and research project is required from an academic institution. Endorsement of an application by the institution constitutes agreement to allow the necessary time for completion of the project within the alloted term. **Criteria:** Projects are rated on the basis of design, originality, potential significance and relevance to the rheumatic diseases and the principal investigator's background and experience as an investigator. Applications are reviewed by the National Peer Review System of the Arthritis Foundation, which is made up of six study sections with experts from relevant research disciplines.

**Funds Avail.:** Grants are in the amount of $25,000 annually. Payments are made quarterly to the investigator's institution. Awards are for a term of one or two years and may be renewed for a third year on a competitive basis. Renewal support is based on demonstration of substantial accomplishment during the first years of the grant. **To Apply:** A formal application must be submitted. **Deadline:** September 1. Applicants will be notified by mid-February of any action taken on their application. **Contact:** Arthritis Foundation at the above address (see entry 1146).

• **1150** • **Arthritis Foundation Physician Scientist Development Award** *(Postdoctorate/Award)*

**Purpose:** To encourage qualified physicians without significant prior research experience to embark on careers in biomedical and/or clinical research related to the understanding of arthritis and the rheumatic diseases. **Focus:** Rheumatology **Qualif.:** Applicant must be a U.S. citizen or permanent resident and must have an M.D., D.O., or equivalent from an accredited institution within the past seven years. They must also have completed training in internal medicine or pediatrics and have completed one year of specialty training in rheumatology. Before submitting an application, the candidate must arrange for an appointment to an appropriate institution and acceptance by a supervisor who will oversee the training and research experience. Only physicians with not more than one year of research training at the time of the award are eligible. Award is tenable only at U.S. institutions.

**Funds Avail.:** $27,000-32,000, plus $500 institutional grant. **To Apply:** Write for application form and guidelines. **Deadline:** September 1. Notification by mid-February.

**Remarks:** Award is co-sponsored by American College of Rheumatology. **Contact:** Research Department at the above address (see entry 1146).

• **1151** • **Arthritis Foundation Postdoctoral Fellowships** *(Postdoctorate/Fellowship)*

**Purpose:** To encourage physicians and scientists to embark on careers in research broadly relating to arthritis and the rheumatic diseases. **Focus:** Rheumatology **Qualif.:** Applicant may be of any nationality, but must have an M.D., Ph.D., or equivalent doctoral degree. Individuals with an M.D. who have more than six years of laboratory training or a Ph.D. with more than four years of post-degree laboratory experience are not eligible. Individuals at or above the assistant professor level, or those who have tenured positions are also ineligible. Candidate must plan to pursue a program in a research field broadly related to the rheumatic diseases under the supervision of a qualified supervisor. Fellowships may sometimes be awarded to U.S. citizens for study abroad. Citizens of other countries are occasionally funded, but only when their training is conducted at a U.S. institution. Fellows are expected to devote 90% of their professional time to activities related to the fellowship.

**Funds Avail.:** $35,000/year plus $500 grant. **No. of Awards:** 32. **To Apply:** Write for application form and guidelines. **Deadline:** September 1. Notification by mid-February. **Contact:** Research Department at the above address (see entry 1146).

• **1152** • **Arthritis Investigator Awards** *(Postdoctorate/Award)*

**Purpose:** To support physicians and scientists in research fields related to arthritis during the early stages of their careers. **Focus:** Rheumatology. **Qualif.:** Applicants must be U.S. citizens or permanent residents. U.S. citizens may use the award in other countries, if appropriate training is unavailable in the United States. Applicant must have a Ph.D., M.D., D.O., or the equivalent, and have between three years and seven years of postdoctoral research experience. Applicant may not hold other major awards at the time of application. Individuals with tenured positions are ineligible. Candidate must be sponsored by a senior scientist at the host institution familiar with the proposed area of research. The investigator is expected to devote 80% time to activities related to research.

**Funds Avail.:** $74,000/year, plus an institutional grant of $1,000/year. **No. of Awards:** 20. **To Apply:** Write for application form and guidelines. **Deadline:** September 1. Notification by mid-February. **Contact:** Research Department at the above address (see entry 1146).

• **1153** •
**Arthritis Society**
393 University Ave., Ste. 1700     Ph: (416)979-7228
Toronto, ON, Canada M5G 1E6      Fax: (416)979-1149
*E-mail:* bthorn@arthritis.ca
*URL:* http://www.arthritis.ca

• **1154** • **Arthritis Society Clinical Fellowships** *(Doctorate/Fellowship)*

**Purpose:** To support medical residents who wish to undertake sub-specialty training in rheumatology. **Focus:** Rheumatology, Arthritis. **Qualif.:** Applicant for a clinical fellowship must be a Canadian citizen or a permanent resident who has completed three years of graduate training in internal medicine or pediatrics in an approved program. Candidate must be qualified for residency training in rheumatology. Awards are tenable at Canadian medical schools that have Rheumatic Disease Units. Clinical fellows may apply to use the award outside of Canada if he/she has completed at least one year of training in rheumatology in Canada.

**Funds Avail.:** $45,000-60,000 **No. of Awards:** 6. **To Apply:** Write to the Society for application form and guidelines. Submit form with transcripts; a letter of acceptance from proposed supervisor at

## Arthritis Society *(continued)*

host institution, including an outline of the proposed training program; letters of recommendation from current or most recent supervisor and two other sponsors; and a statement from the Royal College of Physicians and Surgeons or the Corporation of Physicians and Surgeons of Quebec providing an assessment of training. **Deadline:** September 15. **Contact:** Bonnie D. Thorn, Medical and Scientific Programs, at the above address (see entry 1153).

### • 1155 • Arthritis Society Research Fellowships *(Postdoctorate/Fellowship)*

**Purpose:** To support training in research related to arthritis, and to enhance the research training of rheumatologists likely to embark on careers in academic medicine. **Focus:** Arthritis. **Qualif.:** Applicant may be of any nationality, although preference is given to candidates who are planning to embark on a research career in Canada. Candidate must have a doctoral degree, or the equivalent. Fellowships are normally tenable at Canadian medical schools, unless the candidate can demonstrate that suitable training is not available in Canada. Fellows are expected to dedicate at least 90% of their time to research related to arthritis.

**Funds Avail.:** Ph.D. fellows: $27,300-31,100; M.D. fellows: $27,600-43,400. **To Apply:** Write to the Society for application form and guidelines. Submit form with a letter of acceptance from proposed supervisor, including an outline of training program; applicant and supervisor's curriculum vitae and letters from three sponsors. **Deadline:** November 1.

**Remarks:** Society has extended program to include joint funding with arthritis and MRC. Applicants applying to joint program should submit applications directly to MRC. **Contact:** Bonnie D. Thorn, Vice President, Medical and Scientific Programs, at the above address (see entry 1153).

### • 1156 • Arthritis Society Research Grants *(Postdoctorate/Grant)*

**Purpose:** To promote and support research relevant to arthritis. **Focus:** Rheumatology/Arthritis. **Qualif.:** Applicant must be a Canadian citizen or permanent resident and must hold a staff appointment at a Canadian university or other recognized Canadian institution. Appropriate space and basic facilities at the host institution are a prerequisite to an application. Grants may be used for supplies; service and maintenance contracts; research-related travel expenses; salaries of summer students, technical, non-professional, and specialized professional assistants; and other necessary costs. Funds are not available for investigator's salary or fellowships.

**Funds Avail.:** $25,000-65,000. **To Apply:** Write to the Society for application forms and guidelines. **Deadline:** December 15.

**Remarks:** The Society also offers grants for collaborative research projects, both between scientists in a single institution, and between scientists at two or more sites. Write for further information. **Contact:** Bonnie D. Thorn, Vice President, Medical and Scientific Programs, at the above address (see entry 1153).

### • 1157 • Arthritis Society Research Scholarships *(Postdoctorate/Scholarship)*

**Purpose:** To support newly appointed junior faculty members who are planning careers in research related to arthritis. **Focus:** Arthritis. **Qualif.:** Candidate may be of any nationality, but must have either a Ph.D. with several years of postdoctoral training, or an M.D. with extensive post-doctoral training in their chosen field. Candidates should have a major interest in research and a full-time academic career in medical science. Awards are tenable at Canadian medical schools. Recipients must devote at least 75% of their time to research. Application must be made on behalf of the candidate by the department chair or director of the host institution.

**Funds Avail.:** Varies **To Apply:** Write for application form and guidelines. Application should include the following: form; curriculum vitae; a statement of interests; a detailed research proposal; and letters of recommendation from department head, Rheumatic Disease Unit director, and three other sponsors. **Deadline:** December 15. **Contact:** Bonnie D. Thorn, Vice President, Medical and Scientific Programs, at the above address (see entry 1153).

### • 1158 • Arthritis Society Research Scientist Award *(Postdoctorate/Award)*

**Purpose:** To support independent research scientists. **Focus:** Arthritis. **Qualif.:** Candidate may be of any nationality, but must be an independent research scientist who is pursuing a full-time academic career in medical science. Awards are not intended to replace the current salary support for investigators who have held a faculty appointment for longer than five years. Awards are tenable at Canadian medical schools. Recipients must devote at least 75% of their time to research. Application must be made on behalf of the candidate by the department chair or director of the host institution.

**Funds Avail.:** Varies. **To Apply:** Write for application form and guidelines. Application should include the following: form; curriculum vitae; a statement of interests; a detailed research proposal; and letters of recommendation from department head, Rheumatic Disease Unit director, and three other sponsors. **Deadline:** December 15 **Contact:** Bonnie D. Thorn Vice President, Medical and Scientific Programs, at the above address (see entry 1153).

### • 1159 • Metro A. Ogryzlo International Fellowship *(Postdoctorate/Fellowship)*

**Purpose:** To provide advanced training in clinical rheumatology at a Canadian Rheumatic Disease Unit. **Focus:** Rheumatology/Arthritis. **Qualif.:** Applicants for an Ogryzlo Fellowship may be a citizen or permanent resident of any country except Canada. Applicants must anticipate graduation from medical school before receipt of the Fellowship. Preference is given to applicants who have a substantial prospect of returning to an academic position in his/her own country.

**Funds Avail.:** $31,000 maximum. **No. of Awards:** 1. **To Apply:** Write to the Society for application form and guidelines. Submit form with a transcripts, if available; a letter of acceptance from proposed supervisor at host institution; and letters of recommendation from three sponsors, one of whom should be current or most recent supervisor. **Deadline:** November 1. **Contact:** Bonnie D. Thorn, Vice President, Medical and Scientific Programs, at the above address (see entry 1153).

---

### • 1160 •
## Artpark

PO Box 28      *Ph:* (716)754-9000
Lewiston, NY 14092      *Fax:* (716)754-2741
*URL:* http://www.artpark-ny.org/index.html

### • 1161 • Artpark Residencies *(Professional Development/Award)*

**Purpose:** To provide visual and performing artists with opportunities to work and display their work at Artpark. **Focus:** Performing Arts, Visual Arts. **Qualif.:** Applicants must be U.S. citizens or have a visa to work in the United States. They must also be professional artists; students and individuals who pursue art as a hobby are not eligible to apply. There are three types of awards available. Visual Artists work in semi-enclosed studios at Artpark. Artists retain the work produced. Workshop Artists conduct public participatory workshops for visitors to Artpark. Artists in both the visual and performance media may apply. Performing Artists are employed to work outdoors at Artpark. Proposed projects should have potential for generating interaction with the public.

**Funds Avail.:** $450/week, plus living, material and travel allowances. **No. of Awards:** Varies, approximately 36-100. **To Apply:** Write to the Park Program Department for application form and guidelines, indicating which program of interest. Submit form with resume, a project proposal, and slides or taped evidence of artistic work. **Deadline:** Performing Arts: December 31; Visual Arts: October 31, December 31.

**Remarks:** The Pollock-Krasner Foundation considers applications from visual artists who, in order to accept and fully utilize a colony residency, will need financial help beyond that which a colony can offer. **Contact:** Joan McDonough, Supervisor, at the above address (see entry 1160).

## • 1162 •
## Arts International - Institute of International Education

809 United Nations Plaza  
New York, NY 10017-3580  
*E-mail:* ainternational@iie.org  
*URL:* http://www.iie.org/ai  

*Ph:* (212)984-5370  
*Fax:* (212)984-5574

*Arts International is a division of the Institute of International Education (IIE), the largest and most active international, educational, and cultural exchange organization in the United States. IIE has administered the Fulbright Student Exchange on behalf of the federal government (USIA) for over half of its 70-year history. The Institute's resources include offices throughout the U.S. and overseas in Hong Kong, Mexico City, Bangkok, Jakarta, and Sri Lanka.*

### • 1163 • Cintas Fellowships *(Professional Development/Fellowship)*

**Purpose:** To acknowledge demonstrated creative accomplishments and to encourage the professional development of talented creative artists in the fields of architecture, literature, music composition, and the visual arts. **Focus:** Creative Arts. **Qualif.:** Applicants must be professionals in the above-mentioned arts, who are of Cuban citizenship or direct lineage (having a Cuban parent or grandparent), and are living outside Cuba. The fellowships are not awarded toward the furtherance of academic study, research, or writing, nor to performing artists. Fellowships are not awarded more than twice to the same person. **Criteria:** Artists are selected by panels of qualified members of each artistic discipline. The final decision is made by the board of the Cintas Foundation.

**Funds Avail.:** $10,000 fellowships are awarded. **No. of Awards:** 3-5 **To Apply:** A formal application and two letters of recommendation must be submitted. Visual art professionals must submit a maximum of 10 slides, in standard 2x2 mountings. Architecture professionals must submit no more than one portfolio 15x20x4 containing architectural renderings and project descriptions. Music composition professionals must submit a score accompanied by a new audio cassette (1 7/8 inches per second) containing 15-20 minutes of music. Literature professionals must submit no more than one original manuscript, twenty-five pages in length and clearly reproduced on white 8 1/2x11 paper. One sample publication may also accompany the manuscript. **Deadline:** Materials for application must be postmarked by March 1, with notification by August 1.

**Remarks:** Cintas Fellows are free to pursue their arts activities as they wish, either in the United States or in other countries approved by the Cintas Foundation, Inc. Fellows will be asked to submit interim and final reports to the Arts International division of the Institute of International Education and to contribute or dedicate one work completed during the fellowship year to the Cintas Foundation, Inc. The Cintas Foundation, Inc. supports this fellowship program in memory of Oscar B. Cintas (1887-1957), a prominent Cuban industrialist and patron of the arts. **Contact:** Program Officer at the above address (see entry 1162).

### • 1164 • The Fund for U.S. Artists at International Festivals and Exhibitions *(Other/Other)*

**Purpose:** To help ensure that the excellence, diversity, and vitality of the arts in the United States is represented at major international events. **Focus:** Music Theatre and Dance **Qualif.:** Applicants must be individual performing artists or organizations that have been invited to participate in international festivals around the world.

**Funds Avail.:** Support for travel expenses. **No. of Awards:** varies **To Apply:** Guidelines and application form are available in November from Arts International. **Deadline:** Deadlines for the performing arts portion of The Fund are January 15, May 3, and September 1.

**Remarks:** The Fund is supported by The U.S. Information Agency, The National Endowment for the Arts, The Pew Charitable Trusts, and The Rockefeller Foundation. **Contact:** Applicants who wish to receive requests for exhibition proposals should contact the International Program of the National Endowment for the Arts, 1100 Pennsylvania Ave., NW, Washington, D.C. 20506.

## • 1165 •
## Asahi Shimbun Foundation

Attn: Cultural Projects Division  
(Kikaku Dani-bu)  
5-3-2, Tsukiji  
Chuo-ku  
Tokyo 104-11, Japan  

*Ph:* 33 5450131  
*Fax:* 33 5461894

### • 1166 • Asahi Fellowships *(Professional Development/Fellowship)*

**Purpose:** To provide promising scholars, journalists, artists, and others with the opportunity of a year's stay in Japan in order to develop their academic or professional expertise, as well as their personal knowledge of Japan. **Focus:** General, as related to Japan. **Qualif.:** Candidates must not be Japanese citizens or permanent residents. Candidates must hold a bachelor's degree or its equivalent. Applicants must desire to enrich their expertise through a stay in Japan for research and study which cannot be taken elsewhere. Candidates must not have lived in Japan for an extended period of time, nor intend to do so. No age or citizenship restrictions apply. Fellowship is tenable in Japan. Fellows may not hold any other scholarship or have received any other research grant concurrently with the Asahi Fellowship.

**Funds Avail.:** *yn15 million, plus round-trip airfare to Japan, and traveler's insurance. **No. of Awards:** 2-4 per year. **To Apply:** Write to the fellowship office for application form and guidelines, available from December through February. Submit application with designated reference form. **Deadline:** February 28. Notification by end of June. **Contact:** Asahi Fellowship Office, Kikaku Daini-bu (Department II, Cultural Projects Division).

---

**Asbury Park Press**
Editorial Dept.
3601 Hwy. 66
PO Box 1550
Neptune, NJ 07754
*Ph:* (908)922-6000
*Fax:* (908)922-4818
*URL:* http://www.nj.com/forms/get/groups/ted2421.html

**• 1168 • Asbury Park Press Scholarships for Minority Students** *(Undergraduate/Scholarship)*

**Purpose:** To encourage college study by minority students. **Focus:** Newspaper Reporting, Editing. **Qualif.:** Candidates must be graduating high school minority students from Monmouth County and Ocean County, New Jersey, who will enter college seeking a career in the field of newspaper reporting and/or editing.

**Funds Avail.:** Two $2,000 scholarships are awarded annually and are renewable for one year dependent upon continued satisfactory work. **No. of Awards:** 2. **Deadline:** Last Friday of April. **Contact:** Asbury Park Press, Editorial Department at the above address (see entry 1167).

**• 1169 •**
**Asian American Journalists Association**
c/o Hein Nguyen
1765 Sutter St., Rm. 1000
San Francisco, CA 94115
*E-mail:* aaja1@aol.com
*URL:* http://www.aaja.org
*Ph:* (415)346-2051
*Fax:* (415)931-4671

**• 1170 • Asian American Journalists Association Fellowships** *(Professional Development/Fellowship)*

**Purpose:** To enable AAJA members to attend short-term journalism training and skills development programs by providing funds to defray tuition, travel, food, lodging, and other related program costs. **Qualif.:** Applicants must be members of AAJA and able to provide proof of registration at, or acceptance to, the training program. **Deadline:** Applications are reviewed quarterly (January, April, July, and October).

**Remarks:** Fellowships must be used within 12 months of the award date. Recipients must have been granted a leave of absence to attend the program. **Contact:** AAJA at the above address (see entry 1169).

**• 1171 • Asian American Journalists Association National Internship Grant** *(Other, Undergraduate/Grant)*

**Qualif.:** Applicants must be students who are working as an intern for a newspaper, magazine, television station, radio station, or other news organization.

**Funds Avail.:** $1,000 stipend. **Deadline:** Mid-April.

**Remarks:** The intent is to supplement the intern's moving and living expenses during the internship period. **Contact:** AAJA, at the above address (see entry 1169).

**• 1172 • Asian American Journalists Association Scholarship** *(Graduate, Undergraduate/Scholarship)*

**Purpose:** To assist high school seniors, college students, and graduate students pursuing journalism careers; to increase the number of Asian Pacific American students pursuing journalism; and to improve coverage of the Asian Pacific American community. **Qualif.:** Applicants must be attending an accredited college or university full-time during the upcoming academic year and must be pursuing a journalism career. **Criteria:** Based on

commitment to journalism, commitment to and understanding of Asian Pacific American community, scholastic achievement, letters of recommendation, and financial need.

**Funds Avail.:** Ranges from $250 to $2,000. **To Apply:** Applications include two essay questions and a work exercise. **Deadline:** Around mid-April. **Contact:** The Asian American Journalists Association at the above address (see entry 1169).

**• 1173 •**
**Asian American Studies Center**
University of California, Los Angeles
Institute of American Cultures
3230 Campbell Hall
Los Angeles, CA 90024
*E-mail:* dtn@ucla.edu
*URL:* http://www.sscnet.ucla.edu/aasc/
*Ph:* (310)825-2974
*Fax:* (310)206-9844

**• 1174 • Asian American Studies Center Postdoctoral Fellowship/Visiting Scholars Awards** *(Postdoctorate/Award, Fellowship)*

**Purpose:** To support research on Asian American experience and culture. **Focus:** Asian American Studies. **Qualif.:** Candidate may be of any nationality. Applicant must have a Ph.D.; both recent recipients of the degree and senior scholars on sabbatical leave are eligible to apply. UCLA faculty are ineligible for support. Awards are tenable at UCLA. In addition to conducting an original research project, award recipients must participate in the activities of the Center.

**Funds Avail.:** $24,000-28,000. **No. of Awards:** One. **To Apply:** Write to the assistant director for application materials. **Deadline:** December 31. **Contact:** Enrique De La Cruz, Assistant Director, at the above address (see entry 1173).

**• 1175 •**
**Asian Cultural Council**
437 Madison Ave.
New York, NY 10022-7001
*E-mail:* acc@accny.org
*URL:* http://www.asianculturalcouncil.org
*Ph:* (212)812-4300
*Fax:* (212)312-4299

**• 1176 • Asian Art and Religion Fellowships** *(Postdoctorate/Fellowship)*

**Purpose:** To support Americans undertaking interdisciplinary analyses of Asian arts and religious systems. **Focus:** Asian Art, Asian Religions. **Qualif.:** Applicant must be a U.S. citizen. Candidate must be an established scholar, art specialist, or artist with at least five years of professional experience who is interested in studying the connections between art and religion in Asia. Awards are tenable in Asia.

**Funds Avail.:** $2,500-20,000. **No. of Awards:** 3-5. **To Apply:** Submit a brief description of the activity for which assistance is being sought. If the proposed activity falls within the Council's guidelines, application materials will be forwarded. **Deadline:** February 1 and August 1. **Contact:** Director at the above address (see entry 1175).

**• 1177 • Asian Cultural Council Fellowship Grants** *(Postdoctorate/Fellowship)*

**Purpose:** To promote cultural exchange between the United States and Asia in the performing and visual arts. **Focus:** Architecture, Art Criticism, Art History, Museum Studies, Performing Arts, Visual

Arts. **Qualif.:** Applicant must be a U.S. citizen or a citizen of an Asian country. Candidate must be a scholar, arts specialist, creative artist, or graduate student in one of the areas of study listed above. Individuals seeking funds for lecture programs, personal exhibitions, or individual performance tours are not eligible. Awards to U.S. citizens are tenable in Asia. Citizens of Asian countries must use the grants in the United States. Awards support research, study, specialized training, observation tours, or creative activities.

**Funds Avail.:** Round-trip international airfare, domestic travel, maintenance, and medical insurance allowances, plus an allocation for miscellaneous expenses. **To Apply:** Submit a brief description of the activity for which assistance is being sought. If the proposed activity falls within the Council's guidelines, application materials will be forwarded. **Deadline:** February 1 and August 1.

**Remarks:** The Council offers Starr Foundation Fellowships to contemporary visual artists and arts specialists in Asia who wish to conduct research or participate in creative activities in the United States. Application procedures are the same as those listed above. Fellowships are also available through the Council's Hong Kong Arts Program to especially promising artists, students, and scholars from Hong Kong for research, study and creative work in the United States. For application guidelines, write to the Hong Kong office of the Council at the following address: Asian Arts Council, One Hysan Avenue, 22nd Floor; Hong Kong (phone: 5-895-0407). The Council also grants the John D. Rockefeller 3rd Award annually to an individual from Asia or the United States who has made an especially significant contribution to the understanding, practice, or study of the visual or performing arts of Asia. This international research and travel grant is not open to direct application. For information about the nomination process, write the Council. **Contact:** Ralph Samuelson, Director, at the above address (see entry 1175).

• **1178** • **Ford Foundation Fellowships** *(Doctorate, Graduate, Postdoctorate/Fellowship)*

**Purpose:** To support training, travel and research by individuals from Asia engaged in the documentation and preservation of traditional Asian arts. **Focus:** Traditional Asian Performing and Visual Arts. **Qualif.:** Applicant must be a citizen of an Asian nation. Candidate must be a graduate student, visual or performing artist, art historian, archaeologist, art conservator, museum professional, or other specialist involved in the preservation of traditional Asian arts. Awards are tenable in the United States. Fellowships support independent projects, research training, relevant travel, and/or graduate studies.

**Funds Avail.:** Research, travel, and living allowances. **No. of Awards:** Seven. **To Apply:** Submit a brief description of the activity for which assistance is being sought. If the proposed activity falls within the Council's guidelines, application materials will be forwarded. **Deadline:** February 1, August 1. **Contact:** Ralph Samuelson, Director, at the above address (see entry 1175).

• **1179** • **Humanities Fellowships** *(Doctorate, Postdoctorate/Fellowship)*

**Purpose:** To assist American scholars, doctoral students, and specialists in the humanities to undertake research, training, and study relevant to performing and visual arts in Asia. **Focus:** Archaeology, Art Conservation, Art Criticism, Art History, History of Architecture, History of Performing Arts, Museum Studies. **Qualif.:** Applicant must be a U.S. citizen. Candidate must be a scholar, Ph.D. student, or specialist in a humanistic discipline who wishes to conduct research or pursue training in one of the areas of study listed above. Fellowships are tenable in Asia.

**Funds Avail.:** Research, travel and living allowances. **No. of Awards:** 12. **To Apply:** Submit a brief description of the activity for which assistance is being sought. If the proposed activity falls within the Council's guidelines, application materials will be forwarded. **Deadline:** February 1, August 1.

**Remarks:** Asian scholars and doctoral students who wish to participate in conferences, exhibitions, visiting professorships, or similar projects may also qualify for support through the Humanities Fellowship Program. Write to the Council for further information. **Contact:** Ralph Samuelson, Director, at the above address (see entry 1175).

• **1180** • **Japan-United States Art Fellowships** *(Postdoctorate, Professional Development/Fellowship)*

**Purpose:** To promote cultural exchange between the United States and Japan in the visual and performing arts. **Focus:** Architecture, Art Criticism, Art History, Literature, Museum Studies, Performing Arts, Visual Arts. **Qualif.:** Applicant must be a U.S. or Japanese citizen. Candidate must be an artist, arts specialist, or scholar in one of the areas of study listed above. Students are not eligible to apply. Awards to U.S. citizens are tenable in Japan. Japanese fellows must use their awards in the United States.

**Funds Avail.:** Round-trip international airfare, domestic travel, maintenance, and medical insurance allowances, plus an allocation for miscellaneous expenses. **No. of Awards:** 17. **To Apply:** Submit a brief description of the activity for which assistance is being sought. If the proposed activity falls within the Council's guidelines, application materials will be forwarded. **Deadline:** February 1, August 1.

**Remarks:** The Council offers Starr Foundation Fellowships to contemporary visual artists and arts specialists in Asia who wish to conduct research or participate in creative activities in the United States. Application procedures are the same as those listed above. **Contact:** Japan-United States Arts Program at the above address (see entry 1175).

• **1181** •
**Asian and Pacific Development Centre**
Pesiaran Duta
PO Box 12224
50770 Kuala Lumpur, Malaysia          *Ph:* 3 254 8088

• **1182** • **APDC Visiting Fellowships** *(Postdoctorate/ Fellowship)*

**Purpose:** To provide opportunities for senior and middle level researchers and policy makers to obtain a regional perspective of development issues and problems through research at the Centre. **Focus:** Economic and Social Development. **Qualif.:** Candidate may be of any nationality. Applicant must be at least 30 years old and must have a Ph.D. degree. Candidate should have substantial experience as a researcher or policy-maker. Awards are tenable at the Centre. While in residence, fellows cooperate with the Centre's staff on policy research projects on topics relevant to development in the Asian and Pacific region. Preference is given to projects that focus on economic management/information technology, employment/poverty alleviation, energy/environment, gender/ human development, public management/human resource development and regional cooperation/trade.

**Funds Avail.:** Varies. **No. of Awards:** Two. **To Apply:** Write to the director for application guidelines. **Deadline:** Varies. **Contact:** Dr. Harka Gurung, Director, at the above address (see entry 1181).

## • 1183 •
## ASM International Foundation for Education and Research

9639 Kinsman Rd.
Materials Park, OH 44073-0002
E-mail: asmif@poasm-intl.org
URL: http://www.asm-intl.org

Fax: (440)338-5151

Free: 800-336-5152

### • 1184 • ASM Foundation Scholarship (Undergraduate/Scholarship)

Focus: Metallurgy, materials engineering. Qualif.: Applicants must be enrolled at colleges and universities in the U.S., Canada, and Mexico; intended or declared majors in metallurgy/materials; must complete at least one year of college by June 15; be undergraduate sophomores, juniors and seniors or final year community college students; and be citizens of the U.S., Canada, and Mexico. Criteria: Awards are made based on interest in metallurgy/materials engineering, motivation, scholarship, citizenship, achievement, and potential.

Funds Avail.: $17,000. One-time renewal. No. of Awards: 34. To Apply: Applicants must submit an official application form completed and signed; personal essay (maximum of two pages); up-to-date transcripts or facsimile of college academic records; and three letters of recommendation from teachers and/or employers. Contact: ASM Foundation at the above address (see entry 1183).

### • 1185 • ASM Outstanding Scholars (Undergraduate/Scholarship)

Focus: Metallurgy, materials engineering. Qualif.: Applicants must be enrolled at colleges and universities in the U.S., Canada, and Mexico; intended or declared majors in metallurgy/materials; must complete at least one year of college by June 15; be undergraduate sophomores, juniors or seniors or in final year at community college; and be citizens of the U.S., Canada, and Mexico. Criteria: Awards are made based on interest in metallurgy/materials engineering, motivation, scholarship, citizenship, achievement, and potential.

Funds Avail.: $6,000. One-time renewal. No. of Awards: 3. To Apply: Applicants must submit an official application form completed and signed; personal essay (maximum of two pages); up-to-date transcripts or facsimile of college academic records; and no more than two letters of recommendation from teachers and/or employers. Contact: ASM Foundation at the above address (see entry 1183).

### • 1186 • N.J. Grant Scholarship (Undergraduate/Scholarship)

Focus: Metallurgy, materials engineering. Qualif.: Applicants must be enrolled at colleges and universities in the U.S., Canada, and Mexico; intended or declared majors in metallurgy/materials; must complete at least one year of college by June 15; be undergraduate juniors and seniors; and be citizens of the U.S., Canada, and Mexico. Criteria: Awards are made based on interest in metallurgy/materials engineering, motivation, scholarship, citizenship, achievement, and potential.

Funds Avail.: Full tuition. One-time renewal. No. of Awards: 1. To Apply: Applicants must submit an official application form completed and signed; personal essay (maximum of two pages); up-to-date transcripts or facsimile of college academic records; no more than two letters of recommendation from teachers and/or employers; and name fax and phone number of Financial Aid Officer. Contact: ASM Foundation at the above address (see entry 1183).

### • 1187 • G.A. Roberts Scholarship (Undergraduate/Scholarship)

Focus: Metallurgy, materials engineering. Qualif.: Applicants must be enrolled at colleges and universities in the U.S., Canada, and Mexico; intended or declared majors in metallurgy/materials; must complete at least one year of college by June 15; and be citizens of the U.S., Canada, and Mexico. Criteria: Awards are made based on interest in metallurgy/materials engineering, motivation, scholarship, citizenship, achievement, and potential.

Funds Avail.: $5,000; travel and housing allowances up tp $300 for attendance at the award ceremony during Materials Week. One-time renewal. No. of Awards: 7. To Apply: Applicants must submit an official application form completed and signed; personal essay (maximum of two pages); up-to-date transcripts or facsimile of college academic records; and no more than two letters of recommendation from teachers and/or employers.

Remarks: Funded by Teledyne, Inc. Retired Chairman & ASM Past President Dr. George A. Roberts. Awards include a framed certificate of recognition. Contact: ASM Foundation at the above address (see entry 1183).

## • 1188 •
## Assistant Directors Training Program

15260 Ventura Blvd., Ste. 1200-A
Sherman Oaks, CA 91403
E-mail: trainingprogram@dgpt.org
URL: http://www.dgpt.org

Ph: (818)386-2545

### • 1189 • Assistant Directors Training Program Apprenticeships (Professional Development/Internship)

Purpose: To train second assistant directors for the motion picture and television industry. The program is designed to give trainees a basic knowledge of the organization and logistics of motion picture and television production, including set operations, paperwork, and the working conditions and collective bargaining agreements of more than 20 guilds and unions. Trainees learn to deal with cast and crew members and to solve problems in a day-to-day working environment. Trainees learn on the job in highly varied and sometimes difficult situations. Applicants should be aware that trainee work, in general, is physically demanding and is characterized by long hours. Focus: Television, Filmmaking. Qualif.: All program applicants must have the legal right to work in the United States and be a minimum of 21 years of age. In addition, a baccalaureate degree from an accredited four-year college or university, or an associate of arts or sciences degree from an accredited two-year college is required. In lieu of a degree, two years (520 days) of paid work in film or television production may be treated as equivalent to a baccalaureate degree. College credits and work experience may be combined to meet the program's eligibility requirements. An applicant who has been discharged from a branch of the U.S. military at a level of E-5 or higher is also eligible. Criteria: The final selection of trainees is based on test scores and group and individual interviews.

Funds Avail.: Trainees are paid by the production companies and studios for which they work. Upon satisfactory completion of the program, trainees' names are placed on the Southern California Area Qualification List, making them eligible to join the Directors Guild of America as Second Assistant Directors. No. of Awards: 10 to 20. To Apply: Program applicants who meet the basic eligibility requirements must first take a written test administered by a neutral testing agency. Approximately 1,000 people are accepted for testing each year. The examination does not test knowledge of the motion picture industry. It consists of a battery of tests that assess job-related skills, including, but not limited to verbal, reasoning, and mathematical abilities. The test is given once per year, usually in January. It is administered in Los Angeles, California, and Chicago, Illinois. Eligible applicants must pay a $50 non-refundable testing fee. The applicants who achieve the highest test scores are invited for group and individual interviews with the Screening and Admissions Committee. Trainees are accepted into the program once a year, usually in mid-summer. **Deadline:** November.

**Remarks:** The Program was established in 1965 and is currently sponsored by the Directors Guild of America and the Alliance of Motion Picture and Television Producers in Los Angeles. During training, trainees are assigned to work on episodic television, television movies, pilots, mini-series, and features with various studios and production companies. All such employment is subject to collective bargaining agreements, training plan rules, and studio/producer regulations. Assistant Director trainees are not junior directors or directors-in-training. The career ladder most frequently followed by Second Assistant Directors is Second Assistant Director, First Assistant Director, Unit Production Manager. Therefore, this program emphasizes administrative, managerial, and interpersonal skills. **Contact:** Kate Carroll, Administrator, Assistant Directors Training Program, at the above address (see entry 1188).

**• 1190 •**
**Associated Board of the Royal Schools of Music**
14 Bedford Sq.    *Ph:* 171 636 5400
London WC1B 3JG, England    *Fax:* 171 436 4520
*URL:* http://www.dmd.co.nz/rsm/

**• 1191 •  Associated Board of the Royal Schools of Music International Scholarships** *(Postgraduate, Undergraduate/Scholarship)*

**Focus:** Music. **Qualif.:** Applicants must be undergraduate or postgraduate students studying music performance at any of the Royal Schools of Music. **Criteria:** Awards are made based on musical promise in graded examinations of the Associated Board of the Royal Schools of Music.

**Funds Avail.:** $1,000 per award, per term, plus return air travel at end of course. **No. of Awards:** 8 per year. **To Apply:** Write the Associated Board's London office for further details and an application form. **Deadline:** December 31. **Contact:**

**• 1192 •**
**The Associated General Contractors of America - Education and Research Foundation**
c/o Floretta D. Slade, Program
  Coord.
1957 E St., NW    *Ph:* (202)393-2040
Washington, DC 20006    *Fax:* (202)347-4004
*E-mail:* sladef@agc.org
*URL:* http://www.agcfoundation.org

**• 1193 •  AGC Foundation Graduate Awards** *(Graduate, Undergraduate/Award)*

**Purpose:** To support work toward a graduate degree in construction or civil engineering. **Focus:** Civil Engineering, Construction. **Qualif.:** Applicant must be enrolled or planning to enroll in a graduate level construction or civil engineering degree program as a full-time student.

**Funds Avail.:** $7,500. **No. of Awards:** 2-5. **To Apply:** Write or fax the Program Coordinator for application form and guidelines, available September 1. Submit application with three references, transcripts, and supporting essays. **Deadline:** November 1.

**Remarks:** Undergraduate awards are also available. **Contact:** Program Coordinator at the above address (see entry 1192).

**• 1194 •**
**Associated Male Choruses of America - Scholarship Fund**
43 Freemont Ave.
Etobicoke, ON, Canada M9P 2W4
*E-mail:* dthomas@pclink.com
*URL:* http://members.aol.com/AMCAschol

**• 1195 •  Associated Male Choruses of America Scholarship** *(Undergraduate/Scholarship)*

**Purpose:** To assist promising students of music at the college level. **Focus:** Music. **Qualif.:** Applicants must be full-time college students enrolled in a Bachelor's degree program as a voice or instrumental music major. The applicants must be sponsored by a chorus of the Associated Male Choruses of America.

**Funds Avail.:** A scholarship of $500 is awarded for use towards tuition, books, music, texts, or private lessons. Any unused amount of the scholarship award is returned to the AMCA Scholarship Fund for future use. Scholarships may be renewed, but are not automatic and must be reapplied for each year. **No. of Awards:** 6. **Deadline:** March 1. **Contact:** Chairman, at the above address (see entry 1194).

**• 1196 •**
**Associated Press**
50 Rockefeller Plaza    *Ph:* (212)621-1500
New York, NY 10020    *Fax:* (212)621-5447
*URL:* http://www.ldc.upenn.edu/ldc/about/text/appress.html

**• 1197 •  Associated Press Summer Minority Internships** *(Undergraduate/Internship)*

**Qualif.:** Black, Asian American, Native American, and Hispanic college juniors, seniors, and graduate students who are in school full time at the time of application.

**Funds Avail.:** Interns attend a 13-week work program at one of AP's domestic bureaus. Upon successful completion of the program, students are offered full-time employment with AP after graduation. **Contact:** Jack Stokes, Director of Recruiting at the above address (see entry 1196).

**• 1198 •**
**Associated Western Universities, Inc.**
4190 S. Highland Dr., Ste. 211    *Ph:* (801)273-8900
Salt Lake City, UT 84124    *Fax:* (801)277-5632
*E-mail:* info@awu.sl.org
*URL:* http://www.awu.org

**• 1199 •  AWU Faculty Fellowships** *(Postdoctorate/ Fellowship)*

**Purpose:** To provide opportunities for college and university science and engineering faculty to participate in research and develop collaborative proposals with scientists at government and industrial facilities. **Qualif.:** Applicants must be faculty members with instructional and research responsibilities at an accredited

## Associated Western Universities, Inc. (continued)

college or university in the U.S. and a continuing career commitment to teaching and research. U.S. citizenship may be required at some facilities.

**Funds Avail.:** Stipend up to the faculty member's certified college/university salary, travel expenses, and modest relocation allowance. Award funding may be allocated for research participation by undergrad and grad students. A stipend may be provided only when the award recipient is not otherwise supported, usually during summer or authorized sabbatical or other leaves. **To Apply:** Contact AWU for application and info on participating facilities. Info is also available via the AWU home page. **Deadline:** February 15 postmark. **Contact:** AWU Faculty Program at the above address (see entry 1198).

## • 1200 • AWU Faculty Sabbatical Fellowships
*(Postdoctorate/Fellowship)*

**Purpose:** To provide opportunities for college and university science and engineering faculty to participate in research and develop collaborative proposals with scientists at government and industrial facilities. Opportunities are available at over fifty government and industrial facilities. **Qualif.:** Applicants must be faculty members with instructional and research responsibilities at an accredited college or university in the U.S. and a continuing career commitment to teaching and research. U.S. citizenship may be required by some facilities. Evidence of sabbatical leave authorization is essential before an award can be granted.

**Funds Avail.:** Fellowship stipends and travel and relocation allowances are provided. The home institution must contribute at least 50 percent of the stipend, with AWU and the facility each contributing one-half of the balance. The maximum term of a fellowship sponsored in part by AWU is nine months. However, up to six additional months may be available under laboratory sponsorship. **To Apply:** Contact AWU for application and information on participating facilities. Info is also available via the AWU Home Page. **Deadline:** February 15 postmark. **Contact:** AWU Faculty Program at the above address (see entry 1198).

## • 1201 • AWU Graduate Research Fellowships
*(Doctorate, Graduate/Fellowship)*

**Purpose:** To provide education and training in the fields of science and engineering, and to facilitate the exchange of technical expertise and scientific information between facility scientists and the nation's educational institutions. Qualified graduate students are offered access to the unique resources for the completion of their thesis research and to share the expertise of facility scientists and engineers. **Qualif.:** Candidates must be enrolled in a master's or doctoral degree program in science or engineering and have completed all advanced-degree requirements except those directly related to the thesis. U.S. citizenship is required at some facilities.

**Funds Avail.:** Awards may include stipends ($1,300 per month and up) tuition assistance, and allowance for travel. The fellowship term ranges from one to twelve months. Renewals are competitive and require reapplication annually. **To Apply:** Contact AWU for application and information about participating facilities. Info is also available at the AWU home page. **Deadline:** February 15. **Contact:** AWU at the above address (see entry 1198).

## • 1202 • AWU Post-Graduate Fellowship *(Doctorate, Postdoctorate/Fellowship)*

**Purpose:** To encourage recent advanced-degree graduates to select a professional career in a science or engineering field. It offers such individuals the opportunity to conduct research at one of the participating facilities, often as a continuation of work done for the thesis or dissertation. **Qualif.:** Candidates must be graduates who have been awarded the master's or doctoral degree within 4 years of applying. U.S. citizenship is required at some facilities.

**Funds Avail.:** The stipend level is determined by the host facility and may include travel and relocation allowances. **To Apply:** The western U.S. currently participate in this program. Applicants or their thesis advisor are required to contact the facility their choice before submitting an application to AWU. Cooperating facilities are: Idaho National Engineering Laboratory (Idaho Falls, ID), Inhalation Toxicology Research Institute (Albuquerque, NM), Lawrence Livermore National Laboratory (Livermore, CA), National Institute for Petroleum & Energy Research (Bartlesville, OK), National Renewable Energy Laboratory (Golden, CO), Sandia National Laboratories (Albuquerque, NM and Livermore, CA), and UND Energy & Environmental Research Center (Grand Forks, ND). The application requires the identification of the prospective facility and host scientist, and a description of the research project and how it will contribute to the candidate's professional development and fulfillment of career goals. The application must be supported by graduate transcripts and recommendations from the prospective host scientist, Department Chair, thesis advisor, and one other person acquainted with the candidate's academic achievements and research potential. **Deadline:** Application may be made at any time; however, AWU recommends filing at least four months prior to the requested starting date. **Contact:** Dr. R. Norman Orava at the above address (see entry 1198).

## • 1203 • AWU Student Research Fellowships
*(Graduate, Undergraduate/Fellowship)*

**Purpose:** To give qualified undergraduate students the opportunity to take part, normally during the summer, in energy-related science or engineering research at a U.S. Department of Energy facility in the western United States, and to encourage students to go on to graduate school and a career as a scientist or engineer. **Qualif.:** At least two years of college is preferred. U.S. citizenship is normally required; some facilities may accept participants with permanent resident status. A cumulative GPA of 3.0/4.0 and a commitment to completion of degree requirements are expected. This program is open also to graduate students who wish to participate in non-thesis research.

**Funds Avail.:** Funds are provided for fellowship stipends and limited, qualifying, travel costs. This AWU program is sponsored by DOE and several of its facilities. **To Apply:** More than 20 facilities participate in this program. Applicants are encouraged to contact the facility of their choice before submitting an application to AWU. Cooperating facilities and centers are: Bartlesville Project Office (Bartlesville, OK), Chem-Nuclear Geotech (Grand Junction, CO), Crocker Nuclear Laboratory (Davis, CA), Denver Support Office, Idaho National Engineering Laboratory (Idaho Falls, ID)— EG&G-Idaho Inc., Radiological & Environmental Sciences Laboratory, and Westinghouse Idaho Nuclear Company — Inhalation Toxicology Research Institute (Albuquerque, NM), Jet Propulsion Laboratory (Pasedena, CA), Laboratory for Energy-Related Health Research (Davis, CA), Laboratory of Biomedical & Environmental Sciences (Los Angeles, CA), Lawrence Berkeley Laboratory (Berkeley, CA), Lawrence Livermore National Laboratory (Livermore, CA), Los Alamos National Laboratory (Los Alamos, NM), MSE Inc. (Butte, MT), National Institute for Petroleum & Energy Research (Bartlesville, OK), Pacific Northwest Laboratory (Richland, WA), National Renewable Energy Laboratory (Golden, CO), Sandia National Laboratories (Albuquerque, NM and Livermore, CA), Stanford Linear Accelerator Center (Stanford, CA), UND Energy & Environmental Research Center (Grand Forks, ND), U.S. Army White Sands Missile Range (White Sands, NM), Waste Isolation Pilot Plant (Carlsbad, NM), and Western Research Institute (Laramie, WY). The application requires the identification of the prospective host facility and research topic and a description of relevant background and experience; a proposed plan of study; career goals; anticipated benefits of the research experience; and how the results of the research will be publicized. The application must be supported by college/university transcripts and letters or standard forms of recommendation from three persons acquainted with the candidate's professional and academic achievements. **Deadline:** March 1. For Lawrence Livermore National Laboratory, preliminary applications are due by November 1. **Contact:** Dr. Varien R. Tilton at the above address (see entry 1198).

## • 1204 •

### Associated Writing Programs - A Series in Poetry, Short Fiction, Novel and Creative Nonfiction

TallwoodHouse
Mail Stop 1E3
George Mason University
Fairfax, VA 22030                    *Ph:* (703)993-4301
*E-mail:* awp@gmu.edu
*URL:* http://www.awpwriter.org

#### • 1205 • AWP Award in Poetry, Short Fiction, Novel, and Creative Nonfiction *(Professional Development/ Award)*

**Purpose:** Annual competition to recognize outstanding book-length manuscripts. **Focus:** Writing-Fiction, Nonfiction, Poetry. **Qualif.:** Applicant may be of any nationality or residence, but must write in English. Candidate must enter a novel or a book-length work of poetry, short stories, or creative nonfiction. Each of the four genres is judged separately. Criticism, scholarly monographs, works of mixed genre, and manuscripts previously published in book form are not eligible for submission. Applicant may submit manuscript to other publishers while competing for the awards, but must notify AWP if work is accepted elsewhere. Entries will be subject to blind review. Winning manuscripts will be placed by AWP with participating university presses for publication.

**Funds Avail.:** $2,000. **No. of Awards:** 4. **To Apply:** Write to the publications assistant for entry requirements and manuscript format guidelines. Submit manuscript with processing fee (AWP member, $10, nonmember, $15) and self-addressed, stamped envelope and postcard for notification of receipt and results. Manuscript will not be returned. **Deadline:** Submissions are accepted with postmark dates of January and February only. Winners of the awards will be notified in September.

**Remarks:** AWP will also act as a literary agent for those manuscripts that are selected as finalists. **Contact:** Beth Jarock, Assistant Editor, at the above address (see entry 1204).

## • 1206 •

### The Association of American Geographers

1710 16th St. NW                    *Ph:* (202)234-1450
Washington, DC 20009-3198          *Fax:* (202)234-2744
*E-mail:* gaia@aag.org; ebeetsch@aag.org
*URL:* http://www.aag.org; http://www.ads.org/

#### • 1207 • AAG General Fund Research Grants *(Professional Development/Grant)*

**Purpose:** To support research and field work. **Focus:** Geography. **Qualif.:** Applicant may be of any nationality, but must have been a member of AAG for at least two years at the time of application. Preference is given to research projects that deal with important gaps in geography. Grants are tenable worldwide. Grants may not be used to support doctoral dissertation work. Funds must be used for direct research expenses, and are not available for overhead costs.

**Funds Avail.:** $1,000 maximum. **No. of Awards:** 6. **To Apply:** Write for application form and guidelines. **Deadline:** December 31 with notification by March 1. **Contact:** Ehsan M. Khater, at the above address (see entry 1206).

#### • 1208 • Robert D. Hodgson Memorial Ph.D. Dissertation Grant *(Doctorate/Grant)*

**Purpose:** This fund was established by AAG in memory of Dr. Hodgson to support dissertation research in Geography. **Focus:** Geography. **Qualif.:** Candidates must be members of the

Association of American Geographers for at least one year at the time of grant application. At the time the grant is awarded, applicants must not have a Ph.D. degree. All the requirements of a Ph.D., except for the dissertation research, must be completed no later than the term or semester following the date the grant is awarded. **Criteria:** The Hodgson Fund gives preference to topics that best reflect Hodgson's belief that the understanding of geographical knowledge may lead to international cooperation.

**Funds Avail.:** Each grant awarded is not likely to exceed $500. If funds are insufficient or if no application of merit is received, a grant will not be awarded for that year. **No. of Awards:** 2. **To Apply:** Applicants must submit a formal application, a statement of eligibility from the Ph.D. advisor, a background form, and a dissertation proposal of not more than three typed double-spaced pages that includes a statement of the problem, a synthesis of methodology to be used, and expected results. **Deadline:** Application materials must be filed by December 31. Recipients are notified around March 1.

**Remarks:** A written progress report to the Executive Director of the AAG must be submitted within 12 months of receiving the award. **Contact:** Ph.D. Dissertation Grant Program at the above address (see entry 1206).

#### • 1209 • Otis Paul Starkey Grant *(Doctorate/Grant)*

**Purpose:** To support doctoral dissertations or research papers devoted to regional study or significant problem areas in the United States or its possessions. **Focus:** Geography. **Qualif.:** Candidates must be members of the Association of American Geographers for at least one year at the time of grant application. At the time the grant is awarded, applicants must not have a Ph.D. All the requirements of a Ph.D., except for the dissertation research, must be completed no later than the term or semester following the date the grant is awarded.

**Funds Avail.:** Each grant awarded is not likely to exceed $500. If funds are insufficient or if no application of merit is received, a grant will not be awarded for that year. **No. of Awards:** 4. **To Apply:** Applicants must submit a formal application, a statement of eligibility form from the Ph.D. advisor, a background form, and a dissertation proposal of not more than three typed double-spaced pages that includes a statement of the problem, and a synthesis of methodology to be used, and expected results. **Deadline:** Application materials must be filed by December 31. Recipients are notified around March 1.

**Remarks:** A written progress report to the Executive Director of the AAG must be submitted within 12 months of receiving the award. **Contact:** Elizabeth Beetschen, Ph.D. Dissertation Grant Program at the above address (see entry 1206).

#### • 1210 • Paul Vouras Grant *(Doctorate/Grant)*

**Purpose:** To support dissertation research in Geography. **Focus:** Geography. **Qualif.:** Candidate must be a member of the Association of American Geographers for at least one year at the time of application. At the time the grant is awarded, applicant must not have a Ph.D. All the requirements of a Ph.D., except for the dissertation research, must be completed no later than the term or semester following the date the grant is awarded. The Fund gives preference to minority student applications.

**Funds Avail.:** Each grant awarded is not likely to exceed $500. In any year if funds are insufficient or if no application of merit is received, a grant will not be awarded. **No. of Awards:** 1. **To Apply:** Applicants must submit a formal application, a statement of eligibility from the Ph.D. advisor, a background form, and a dissertation proposal of not more than three typed double-spaced pages that includes a statement of the problem, a synthesis of methodology to be used, and expected results. **Deadline:** Application materials must be filed by December 31. Recipients are notified around March 1.

**Remarks:** A written progress report must be submitted to the Executive Director of the AAG within 12 months of receiving the

**The Association of American Geographers** *(continued)*

award. **Contact:** Ph.D. Dissertation Grant Program at the above address (see entry 1206).

---

### • 1211 •
## Association on American Indian Affairs, Inc.
PO Box 268                              *Ph:* (605)698-3998
Sisseton, SD 57262-0268                 *Fax:* (605)698-3316
*E-mail:* mrc@radcliffe.edu
*URL:* http://www.radcliffe.edu/murray; http://www.doi.gov/bia/aioday/aitoday.html

**• 1212 • Association on American Indian Affairs Displaced Homemaker Scholarships** *(Other, Undergraduate/Scholarship)*

**Purpose:** To help mid-life homemakers, both men and women, who are otherwise unable to fulfill their educational goals by providing support for up to three years with scholarships that financially account for their special needs as heads of households, as single parents, or as displaced homemakers. **Focus:** General Studies. **Qualif.:** Applicants must be mid-life Native Americans who would not otherwise be able to finish their education. They must also provide evidence of at least 25 percent American Indian heritage. **Criteria:** Applicants are selected based on their special needs as head of households, as single parents, or as displaced home makers.

**Funds Avail.:** The program augments the usual and expected financial sources of educational money. It provides funds for child care, transportation, and some basic living expenses. **No. of Awards:** 10. **To Apply:** Application forms must be submitted with two letters of recommendation, a one- to two-page essay outlining applicant's life experience, personal monthly budget, copy of transcripts, most recent Financial Aid letter, and copy of either a Certificate of degree of Indian blood or Tribal enrollment card. **Deadline:** September 10 of each academic year. **Contact:** Elena Stops, Scholarship Coordinator, at the above address.

**• 1213 • Displaced Homemaker Scholarships** *(Other/Scholarship)*

**Purpose:** Assist both men and women who are unable to fill their educational goals. The program will augment the usual and expected financial sources of educational money to assist those students with child care, transportation, and some basic living expenses. **Deadline:** September 10.

**• 1214 • Emergency Aid and Health Professions Scholarships** *(Graduate, Undergraduate/Scholarship)*

**Qualif.:** Applicants must be full-time undergraduate American Indian or Alaskan Native students in need of emergency aid. **Criteria:** Candidates are selected based on financial need and limited by the availability of funds.

**Funds Avail.:** When funds are available, individual grants average between $50 and $300. **No. of Awards:** Varies. **To Apply:** Applicants must submit a completed application, certificate of degree of Indian blood, a one- to two-page essay describing the specific nature of the emergency need, a budget of educational costs and resources, and a most recent copy of transcripts. **Deadline:** May 1. **Contact:** Association of American Indian Affairs at the above address.

**• 1215 • Sequoyah Graduate Fellowships** *(Graduate/Fellowship)*

**Purpose:** To support graduate study by Native Americans. **Focus:** General Studies. **Qualif.:** Applicant must be an American Indian or Alaska Native pursuing a graduate degree in one of many diverse fields. Candidate must be enrolled full time and provide a class schedule. Must be minimally 1/4 degree Indian blood from a federally recognized tribe. **Criteria:** Applicants are selected based on scholastic achievement.

**Funds Avail.:** $1,500. Scholarship is paid in two installments. **No. of Awards:** 10. **To Apply:** Students must submit completed application, certificate of degree of Indian blood, two letters of recommendation, a one- to two-page essay describing educational goals, most recent copy of transcripts, and a budget of educational costs and resources. **Deadline:** October 1.

**Remarks:** The Association also offers small emergency grants. Write for further details. Fellows will be announced in October.

**• 1216 • Adolph Van Pelt Special Fund for Indian Scholarships** *(Graduate, Undergraduate/Scholarship)*

**Purpose:** To support study by Native Americans. **Focus:** General Studies. **Qualif.:** Applicant must be an American Indian or Alaska Native Indian affiliated with a tribe. Candidate must be enrolled in an accredited U.S. university or college, as either a graduate or undergraduate student. **Criteria:** Candidates are selected based on financial aid need and merit.

**Funds Avail.:** $500-800 **No. of Awards:** 14. **To Apply:** Write for application form and guidelines. Submit form with personal essay, proof of tribal affiliation and enrollment, two letters of recommendation, budget of educational costs and resources, and most recent copy of transcripts. **Deadline:** August 15. **Contact:** Olivia Tiger, Scholarship Coordinator, at the above address (see entry 1211).

---

### • 1217 •
## Association for Asian Studies, Inc. - China and Inner Asia Council
1 Lane Hall
University of Michigan
Ann Arbor, MI 48109                     *Ph:* (734)665-3801
*E-mail:* postmaster@aasianst.org
*URL:* http://www.acls.org/aasianst.htm

**• 1218 • Joseph Levenson Prizes** *(Postdoctorate/Prize)*

**Purpose:** To support scholarly works that broaden understanding of China. **Focus:** China. **Qualif.:** Applicant must be a U.S. citizen or permanent resident. Applicant must have recently published a scholarly work on China. **No. of Awards:** Two. **To Apply:** Write to the above address for application information. **Contact:** Carol Hansen at the above address (see entry 1217).

• 1219 •

## Association for Asian Studies, Inc. - Northeast Asia Council

1 Lane Hall
University of Michigan     *Ph:* (734)665-2490
Ann Arbor, MI 48109     *Fax:* (734)665-3801
*E-mail:* postmaster@aasianst.org
*URL:* http://www.acls.org/aasianst.htm

### • 1220 • AAS-NEAC U.S. Research Travel Grants (Postdoctorate/Grant)

**Purpose:** To support postdoctoral and dissertation research on Japan. **Focus:** Japanese Studies. **Qualif.:** Applicant must be a U.S. citizen or permanent resident. Applicant must be a postdoctoral scholar or Ph.D. candidate engaged in research on Japan. Grants are tenable at museums, libraries, and archives in the United States. Funds may be used for research materials, assistance, and reasonable subsistence costs.

**Funds Avail.:** $1,500 maximum. **To Apply:** Write to NEAC for application form and guidelines. Submit form with curriculum vitae. **Deadline:** March 1 and November 1.

**Remarks:** Small grants of up to $500 are also available to Japanese studies scholars for small-scale research needs that are not covered by smaller academic institutions and outside funding agencies. Write to NEAC for further information. **Contact:** Karen Fricke at the above address (see entry 1219).

### • 1221 • Short-term Travel Grants to Japan (Postdoctorate/Grant)

**Purpose:** To support travel to Japan for specific research projects. **Focus:** Japanese Studies. **Qualif.:** Applicant must be a U.S. citizen or permanent resident and a scholar who is already familiar with Japan and his/her proposed area of research. The grantee must undertake a research project that specifically requires study in Japan and that can be completed during the tenure of the award. Grants may be used to cover basic transportation costs or per diem costs for travel in Japan. Awards may not be used for international transportation.

**Funds Avail.:** Up to *yn200,000. **To Apply:** Write to NEAC for application form and guidelines. Submit form with curriculum vitae. **Deadline:** March 1 and 1 November.

**Remarks:** Small grants of up to $500 are also available to Japanese studies scholars for small-scale research needs that are not covered by smaller academic institutions and outside funding agencies. Write to NEAC for further information. **Contact:** Karen Fricke at the above address (see entry 1219).

• 1222 •

## Association for Asian Studies, Inc. - Southeast Asia Council

1021 E. Huron St.     *Ph:* (734)665-2490
Ann Arbor, MI 48104     *Fax:* (734)665-3801
*E-mail:* postmaster@aasianst.org
*URL:* http://www.aasianst.org

### • 1223 • Harry J. Benda Prize (Postdoctorate/Prize)

**Purpose:** To recognize an outstanding young scholar in Southeast Asian studies. **Focus:** Southeast Asian Studies. **Qualif.:** Candidate may be of any nationality or residence. Candidate must be an outstanding new scholar in any field specializing in Southeast Asian studies. Candidate must be nominated. Self-nominations are not accepted.

**Funds Avail.:** $1,000. **No. of Awards:** 1. **To Apply:** Write to the chair of the Benda Prize Committee for nomination guidelines. General information about AAS may be obtained from the address above. **Deadline:** August.

• 1224 •

## Association of College and Research Libraries

50 E. Huron St.     *Ph:* (312)280-2516
Chicago, IL 60611-2729     *Fax:* (312)280-2520
    *Free:* 800-545-7433
*E-mail:* jbriody@ala.org
*URL:* http://www.ala.org/acrl.html

### • 1225 • ALA Doctoral Dissertation Fellowship (Doctorate/Fellowship)

**Purpose:** To provide doctoral students with assistance in completion of doctoral dissertation. **Focus:** Academic Librarianship **Qualif.:** Applicants must be doctoral students in the field of academic librarianship whose research indicates originality, creativity, and interest in scholarship. **Criteria:** Applicants will be judged on their potential significance to the academic librarianship field, validity of the methodology and proposed methods of analysis, originality and creativity, presentation of a convincing plan for completion in a reasonable amount of time, and evidence of continuing interest in scholarship.

**Funds Avail.:** $1,500. **To Apply:** Applicants brief proposals shall be less than five page and should include description of research, travel or writing project, schedule of project, estimate of expenses, and an up-to-date curriculum vitae should accompany proposal. **Deadline:** 01 December.

**Remarks:** Funding provided by the Institute for Scientific Information **Contact:** The American Library Association, Association of College and Research Libraries

### • 1226 • Samuel Lazerow Fellowship for Research in Acquisitions or Technical Services (Professional Development/Fellowship)

**Purpose:** To foster advances in acquisitions or technical services by providing librarians a fellowship for travel or writing within those fields. **Qualif.:** Evidence of an interest through past publication.

**Funds Avail.:** $1,000. **No. of Awards:** 1 annually. **To Apply:** Candidates must submit a description of project, schedule, expense estimate and an up-to-date curriculum vitae. **Deadline:** 01 December.

**Remarks:** Funding provided by the Institute for Scientific Information **Contact:** The American Library Association, Association of College and Research Libraries, at the above address (see entry 1224).

### • 1227 • Martinus Nijhoff International West European Specialist Study Grant (Professional Development/Grant)

**Purpose:** To enable recipients to visit the Netherlands and two other West European countries to study West European librarianship or bibliography. **Focus:** Library and Archival Sciences. **Qualif.:** Applicants must be ALA members. **Criteria:** Candidates are selected based on the clarity of their proposals and qualifications.

**Funds Avail.:** Grant covers travel expenses, room, and board. **No. of Awards:** One annually. **To Apply:** Candidates must submit a proposal, budget and curriculum vitae. **Deadline:** December 1.

**Remarks:** Funding provided by Martinus Nijhoff International. **Contact:** The American Library Association, Association of College and Research Libraries.

• 1228 •
## Association of Commonwealth Universities - Marshall Aid Commemoration Commission

John Foster House, 36 Gordon Sq.    *Ph:* 44 171 3878572
London WC1H 0PF, England    *Fax:* 44 171 3872655

*URL:* http://www.acu.ac.uk/marshall

### • 1229 • Association of Commonwealth Universities Fellowships *(Postdoctorate/Fellowship)*

**Purpose:** To support advanced study and research at Commonwealth universities; and exchange of expertise between, and assistance in the optimal development of their human resources. **Focus:** General Studies. **Qualif.:** Applicant must be a citizen of a Commonwealth country and a staff member at a Commonwealth university. Fellowships are available for travel, research, and academic exchange at Commonwealth universities outside of the fellow's home country. Some fellowships are reserved for candidates from developing countries in the Commonwealth. Write to the Association for a complete list of opportunities.

**Funds Avail.:** £2,500-5,000. **To Apply:** Application procedures vary, depending on the type of fellowship. Contact the executive head of home institution for application materials, or write the Association for further information and addresses of regional partners. **Deadline:** Varies. **Contact:** Deputy Secretary-General (CAA/TA) at the above address (see entry 1228).

### • 1230 • British Marshall Scholarships *(Graduate, Postgraduate/Scholarship)*

**Purpose:** To enable young Americans of high ability to study at a British university for a period of two years (in certain circumstances renewable to three) to read for a degree at either the undergraduate or postgraduate level. The scholarships were founded by an Act of Parliament in 1953 and commemorate the humane ideals of the European Recovery Program (Marshall Plan). The objectives of the program are as follows: to express the gratitude of the British people to the American people for the Marshall Plan; to bring for study in the United Kingdom intellectually distinguished young Americans who will one day become leaders, opinion formers, and decision makers in their own country; to expose them to British social and academic values so as to enable them to gain an understanding and appreciation of the British way of life; to encourage them to be ambassadors to the United Kingdom for their own way of life; and to establish long-lasting bridges and ties between the peoples of the United States and the United Kingdom, at a personal level; and to raise the profile of the United Kingdom in the United States, particularly among its young people. **Focus:** General Studies. **Qualif.:** Applicants must have graduated from a four-year American university/college with a grade point average of 3.7 or above. Candidates must be U.S. citizens and normally be below the age of 26 on activation of award. **Criteria:** In addition to intellectual distinction and strong motivation of purpose, candidates should display an ability to make their mark in their chosen career and the potential to make a continuing contribution to British-American understanding.

**Funds Avail.:** The total value of a scholarship varies according to the circumstances (place of residence, selected university, etc.) of each scholar, but the average figure tends to be approximately L16,500 a year. This comprises: a personal allowance to cover residence and cost of living expenses at the rate of L533 per month (L636 for Scholars at Central London institutions); payment of tuition fees; a grant for books of L357 in the first year and L214 in subsequent years; an annual grant of up to L175 for approved travel in connection with studies; payment of necessary daily expenses in excess of L7.20 a month for travel between place of residence and place of study, provided the distance between the two is reasonable; L235 towards the cost of preparation of any thesis submitted for examination, if required; and fares to and from the United States. An amount not exceeding L3,192 a year may be added in certain circumstances as a contribution to the support of a dependent spouse. British Marshall Scholarships are not subject to U.K. income tax but may be considered taxable income by the Internal Revenue Service. **No. of Awards:** Up to 40 per year. **To Apply:** Candidates may apply in one region only: either that in which they have their permanent home address or ordinary place of residence/employment, or that in which they are studying. Any candidate applying in more than one region will automatically be disqualified. Each candidate must submit his/her application on the forms prescribed. Application materials, if not available from the applicant's college or university, may be obtained from the British Council at the British Embassy in Washington, DC, or British Consulates-General in Atlanta, Boston, Chicago, or San Francisco. Electronic application forms and other documentation also available at: http://www.acu.ac.uk/marshall. The competition is conducted entirely in the United States. Applications must be endorsed by the President or Dean of the applicant's educational institution or employer, accompanied by academic references, and submitted in complete form. Candidates invited for interview must bring with them evidence of date of birth and citizenship (e.g. passport) and (in the case of married candidates) of marriage. **Deadline:** October of preceding year. **Contact:** British Embassy in Washington DC or British Consulates General in Atlanta, Boston, Chicago or San Francisco for applications, guidelines, deadlines, and additional information. Details also available at: http://www.acu.ac.uk/marshall

## • 1231 •
## Association for Education in Journalism and Mass Communication

University of South Carolina
1621 College St.    *Ph:* (803)777-2005
Columbia, SC 29208-0251    *Fax:* (803)777-4728

### • 1232 • AEJMC Communication Theory and Methodology Division Minority Doctoral Scholarships *(Doctorate/Scholarship)*

**Focus:** Communications, Journalism. **Qualif.:** Applicants must be members of AEJMC or the Communication Theory and Methodology Division and enrolled in a Ph.D. program in mass communication that reflects the interest of the division. **No. of Awards:** 1. **To Apply:** Applicants must submit two letters of recommendation, a resume, and a brief letter outlining research interests and career plans. **Contact:** AEJMC at the above address (see entry 1231).

### • 1233 • AEJMC Correspondence Fund Scholarships *(Undergraduate/Scholarship)*

**Purpose:** To assist children of present and former foreign correspondents who wish to study in institutions of higher learning in the United States. **Focus:** General Studies. **Qualif.:** Applicants must be children of U.S. citizens who work or have worked for an American or foreign bona fide news organization in print or broadcast media as a foreign correspondent. Children of foreign nationals who work as correspondents for American news organizations are eligible, but with secondary consideration.

**Funds Avail.:** Up to $2,000. **Deadline:** April 30. **Contact:** Jennifer McGill, AEJMC Executive Director, at the above address (see entry 1231).

## • 1234 •

### Association for Education and Rehabilitation of the Blind and Visually Impaired

206 N. Washington St., Ste. 320     *Ph:* (703)548-1884
Alexandria, VA 22314     *Fax:* (703)683-2926

#### • 1235 • William and Dorothy Ferrell Scholarship *(Graduate, Undergraduate/Scholarship)*

**Qualif.:** Applicants must be legally blind and studying at a post-secondary level for a career in the field of services to blind and visually impaired people. **Criteria:** Varies.

**Funds Avail.:** Two scholarships are offered in even-numbered years. The amounts of scholarship awards are individually determined. **To Apply:** A formal application, a certificate of visual status, and an autobiography not exceeding three double-spaced typewritten pages must be submitted. The autobiography should include a statement about the candidate's vocational goals, the kinds of blind persons with whom the applicant would like to work, and any other important details about the student's goals that they feel are important. **Deadline:** Applications must be filed by April 15 of even numbered years.

**Remarks:** The association typically receives approximately 40 applications. **Contact:** The Association for Education and Rehabilitation of the Blind and Visually Impaired at the above address (see entry 1234).

#### • 1236 • Telesensory Scholarship *(Graduate, Undergraduate/Scholarship)*

**Qualif.:** Applicants must be studying at a post-secondary level for a career in the field of services to blind and visually impaired people. Candidates must be current members of the Association at the time of filing the application. **Criteria:** Varies.

**Funds Avail.:** $1,000. **To Apply:** A formal application and an autobiography not exceeding three double-spaced typewritten pages must be submitted. The autobiography should include a statement about candidate's vocational goals, the kinds of blind persons with whom the applicant would like to work, and any other details about goals that they feel are important. **Deadline:** Application must be filed by April 15th of even numbered years. **Contact:** The Association for Education and Rehabilitation of the Blind and Visually Impaired at the above address (see entry 1234).

## • 1237 •

### Association of Former Agents of the U.S. Secret Service, Inc.

PO Box 848
Annandale, VA 22003-0848     *Ph:* (703)256-0188

#### • 1238 • Law Enforcement Career Scholarships *(Graduate, Undergraduate/Scholarship)*

**Purpose:** To assist and encourage higher education. **Focus:** Police Administration, Law Enforcement. **Qualif.:** Candidates must be students who are enrolled in a Law Enforcement or Police Administration course at an accredited college or university that offers a degree in these studies. Applicants must have completed one year of study at that school. Students working toward an advanced degree are eligible if their graduate study is in Law Enforcement or Police Administration. Applications are accepted from more than one member of the same family, but only one scholarship is awarded to any one family. Past recipients of a scholarship are ineligible for an award. High school students and college freshmen are not eligible. **Criteria:** Selection is based on scholastic standing.

**Funds Avail.:** From one to three awards of $750 to $1,500. The amount of the scholarship is individually determined. **No. of Awards:** 2-5. **To Apply:** Candidates must explain why they chose the law enforcement field, how they would use the grant, their previous work experience, and their post-graduation career goals. They must also submit a current academic transcript. Two letters of recommendation from instructors or professors and two letters of personal reference (not from teachers) must be sent directly to the Association. Incomplete applications, with attachments, letters, etc., are not considered. **Deadline:** Applications must be filed by May 1. Recipients are notified after August 1.

**Remarks:** Formerly known as the Dietrich/Cross/Hanly Scholarships. **Contact:** AFAUSSS, at the above address (see entry 1237).

## • 1239 •

### Association of Graduates of the United States Air Force Academy

3116 Academy Dr., Ste. 100     *Ph:* (719)472-0300
USAF Academy, CO 80840-4475     *Fax:* (719)472-4194

#### • 1240 • U.S. Air Force Academy Graduate Dependent Scholarship *(Graduate, Undergraduate/Scholarship)*

**Purpose:** To directly support postsecondary education for the children of Air Force Academy graduates. **Focus:** General Studies. **Qualif.:** Parent of applicant must be a graduate of the United States Air Force Academy. Applicant must be enrolled full-time at a college or university accredited by an appropriate regional or national accrediting body. **Criteria:** A minimum cumulative GPA between 3.0 and 4.0 for the six most recent semesters of full-time academic work, SAT/ACT scores, extracurricular activities, employment history, and educational goals.

**Funds Avail.:** Ranging from $500 to $1,500. The number and size of awards will grow annually. **To Apply:** Application forms must be requested. **Deadline:** March 1.

**Remarks:** Approximately 75 fully-qualified candidates apply. **Contact:** Vice President, Services, at the above address (see entry 1239).

## • 1241 •

### Association of Illinois Museums and Historical Societies

1 Old State Capitol Plaza     *Ph:* (217)782-2635
Springfield, IL 62701-1507     *Fax:* (217)524-8042
*E-mail:* ishs@eosinc.com
*URL:* http://www.prairienet.org/ishs

#### • 1242 • AIMHS Scholarship *(Professional Development/Scholarship)*

**Purpose:** To provide a AIMHS member the opportunity to attend the American Law Institute-American Bar Association/American Association of Museums seminar. **Focus:** Museum Law. **Qualif.:** Recipient must be a member of AIMHS and MMC. If not a member of both at the time of application, the recipient may pay dues at the time of the award. The recipient must sign a contract agreeing to disseminate information gained from the seminar with AIMHS organizations. Failure to do so will require the recipient to reimburse AIMHS for the scholarship. The scholarship is intended to go to an individual or institution that may not have the resources to attend otherwise. **Criteria:** Recipients are selected based on need.

## Association of Illinois Museums and Historical Societies (continued)

**Funds Avail.:** A $420 scholarship is available. The recipient is responsible for local arrangements and travel. **No. of Awards:** One per year. **To Apply:** Applications should include a resume with description of current responsibilities with museum/organization, a statement concerning the need for the scholarship, a letter of support from a member of a board of trustees or a top administrator in the applicant's organization. **Deadline:** December 1 prior to seminar. **Contact:** John Austin at the above address (see entry 1241).

---

## • 1243 •
## Association for Library and Information Science Education

PO Box 7640  
Arlington, VA 22207  
*URL:* http://www.alise.org

*Ph:* (703)243-8040  
*Fax:* (703)243-4551

### • 1244 • ALISE Doctoral Forum *(Doctorate/Award)*

**Purpose:** To provide an opportunity for the exchange of research ideas between doctoral students who have recently graduated and established researchers in the field of education for library and information science. Up to two outstanding dissertations completed during the previous year are selected by members of the ALISE Research Committee for summary presentation at the Doctoral Forum held during the ALISE annual conference. **Qualif.:** Eligible students who have recently graduated in any field of study or are about to finish their dissertations are invited to submit papers summarizing their dissertation research in areas dealing with substantive issues in library and information science. **Criteria:** Significance of the research problem, application of the appropriate research methods, and clarity and organization of the presentation.

**Funds Avail.:** As an honorarium, winners receive $400 to defray travel expenses, plus personal membership in ALISE and conference registration for the following year. **To Apply:** The dissertation should be summarized in a paper of no more than 20 double-spaced pages. The paper should include a title page with author's name followed by a title page without author's name so that the first page can be removed for the purpose of committee review. The summary must be accompanied by a letter from the author's dissertation chairperson stating that the dissertation is completed or is expected to be completed by December 31 of the year preceding the award. A copy of the signed title page can be used as evidence that the dissertation has been completed. Seven copies of the summary, plus an abstract of no more than 200 words, must be submitted. **Deadline:** Submissions must be postmarked no later than October 1. **Contact:** Dr. Debra Wilcox Johnson, School of Library and Information Studies, University of Wisconsin, Madison, H.C. White Hall, 600 N. Park St., Madison, WI 53706.

### • 1245 • ALISE Doctoral Students' Dissertation Competition Prizes; ALISE Res earch Paper Competition Prizes *(Doctorate, Professional Development/Prize)*

**Purpose:** To encourage the presentation of research at ALISE meetings. **Focus:** Information Science, Librarianship. **Qualif.:** Applicant for the Research Paper Competition may be of any nationality, but must be a member of ALISE. Research paper must represent completed research not previously published; a research paper completed in the pursuit of master's or doctoral studies is not eligible for submissions. For the Doctoral Students' Dissertation Competition, applicant may be of any nationality, but must be a doctoral student who has recently graduated or is about

to finish dissertation. Award is intended to defray travel expenses to the ALISE Conference and pay for membership.

**Funds Avail.:** Research Paper: $500 honorarium; Doctoral Students' Dissertation: $400 honorarium. **No. of Awards:** Two for each award. **To Apply:** Write to ALISE for application guidelines, available in February. **Deadline:** October 1. **Contact:** Executive Director at the above address (see entry 1243).

### • 1246 • ALISE Research Grant Awards *(Graduate/Grant)*

**Qualif.:** Applicants must be personal members of ALISE as of the deadline date. The award cannot be used to support a doctoral dissertation. **Criteria:** Proposals are evaluated by the ALISE Research Committee and other appropriate and knowledgeable ALISE members as needed. Proposals will be judged on: appropriateness of the proposed project to issues in library/information science education in its broadest context; significance of the problem; appropriateness of the proposed method to the problem; the investigator's qualifications (how likely he/she is to be successful, based on previous work and/or possession of the requisite skills); and the reasonableness of the schedule (the likelihood that the work will be accomplished on time).

**Funds Avail.:** An award of one or more grants totaling $2,500 can be made. Recipients will normally receive the grant in periodic payments as the research progresses. Recipients of the award must present a progress report at the ALISE Annual Conference, and will submit written quarterly progress reports to the Executive Secretary of ALISE. The results of the funded study must be submitted to the Association's Journal for possible publication prior to submission to other publications; that is, the Journal will have first option on publication. Any publicity or presentation based on the funded study must acknowledge the support of ALISE. If recipients of the award receive funding in addition to that provided by ALISE they should so inform the Executive Secretary. **To Apply:** Proposals must include the following information to be considered in the competition: an abstract of the project no greater than 200 words; a Problem Statement and Literature Review (including justification and need for the research); project objectives; project description; research design, methodology, and analysis techniques; detailed budget (including institutional or departmental contributions if any); expected benefits and impact from the research; and vita of project investigators. Proposals should be succinct and precise (no more than 20 double-spaced, typed pages). If necessary, supporting information may be included in an appendix. Seven copies of the proposal must be submitted. **Deadline:** Proposals must be postmarked no later than October 1. **Contact:** Dr. Debra Wilcox Johnson, School of Library and Information Studies, University of Wisconsin, Madison, H.C. White Hall, 600 N. Park St., Madison, WI 53706.

---

## • 1247 •
## The Association for Manufacturing Technology

7901 Westpark Dr.  
Mc Lean, VA 22102-4206  
*E-mail:* amt@capcon.net  
*URL:* http://members.Nems.org/AMT.html

*Ph:* (703)827-2900  
*Fax:* (703)893-1151

### • 1248 • AMT's Two-Year Scholarships *(Undergraduate/Scholarship)*

**Purpose:** To encourage students to pursue careers in the machine tool industry and to foster a closer working relationship between AMT member companies and the educational institutions in their communities. **Focus:** Industry and Trade. **Qualif.:** Applicants must be recent or upcoming high school graduates who are planning to enroll full-time in a two-year public community, junior, or technical college and are interested in seeking a career in a manufacturing technology related discipline. They must also be employable in the machine tool industry. **Criteria:** The AMT member companies that wish to participate will work with a regionally accredited colleges or high schools in its geographic area to select a deserving student and will act as the student's sponsor by providing work-training employment during the two summers of the scholarship, working with the school and student to assure appropriateness of the student's course of study, maintaining contact with the school in monitoring student's academic progress, and to monitor student's work-training performance to assure that work assignments contribute to the student's educational development. Selection is based on academic performance, demonstrated interest in a manufacturing technology related discipline, and ability to meet entrance requirements of the participating college and employment standards of the participating member company. Each participating member company can only select one recipient.

**Funds Avail.:** Up to $2,000 per year for two years for tuition, academic fees, and books. **To Apply:** Students should apply through the participating colleges. Each candidate should have an endorsement and recommendation from the secondary school. **Deadline:** None. **Contact:** David E. Horn, Continuous Improvement Director, at the above address (see entry 1247).

---

### • 1249 •
### Association of Oilwell Servicing Contractors

6060 N. Central Expy., Ste. 428  
Dallas, TX 75206

*Ph:* (214)692-0771  
*Fax:* (214)692-0162  
*Free:* 800-692-0771

#### • 1250 • AOSC Scholarships (Graduate, Undergraduate/Scholarship)

**Purpose:** To provide financial assistance to employees and their dependents so that they may further their education beyond secondary school. **Focus:** General Studies. **Qualif.:** Applicants must be employees or legal dependents of an employee of a member company. **Criteria:** Selection is based on grades, test scores, an essay, and financial need.

**Funds Avail.:** $1,000 each. **To Apply:** Applications must be obtained from a member company and submitted to the local AOSC chapter for preliminary screening, it is then sent to the national office for final selection. **Deadline:** April 15. **Contact:** Local AOSC chapters or the National Headquarters at the above address (see entry 1249).

---

### • 1251 •
### Association of Operation Room Nurses, Inc. - AORN Scholarship Board

2170 S. Parker Rd., Ste. 300  
Denver, CO 80231-5711

*Ph:* (303)755-6300  
*Fax:* (303)368-4460  
*Free:* 800-755-2676

*URL:* http://stti-web.iupui.edu/stti/aorn.html

#### • 1252 • AORN Scholarships (Doctorate, Graduate/Scholarship)

**Purpose:** To assist registered nurse members of AORN to further their educational goals, further the practice of perioperative nursing, and expand the activities of the association. **Focus:** Nursing. **Qualif.:** Applicants must be registered nurses who are current members of AORN and have been a member for 12 consecutive months prior to the application deadline. **Criteria:** When awarding scholarships, selection is based on personal goals, references, financial need, contributions to AORN, perspective nursing practice, research and education.

**Funds Avail.:** Varies. **No. of Awards:** Varies. **To Apply:** Applications and instructions may be obtained from AORN. **Deadline:** April 1 and October 1. **Contact:** AORN Scholarship Board Staff Consultant at the above address (see entry 1251).

---

### • 1253 •
### Association of Professional Engineers, Geologists and Geophysicists of Alberta

Honours and Awards Committee  
15th Fl., Scotia Pl., Tower One  
10060 Jasper Ave.  
Edmonton, AB, Canada T5J 4A2  
*E-mail:* bjensen@apegga.com  
*URL:* http://www.apegga.com

*Ph:* (403)426-3990  
*Fax:* (403)426-1877  
*Free:* 800-661-7020

#### • 1254 • APEGGA Entrance Scholarships (Undergraduate/Award)

**Focus:** Engineering, Geology, Geophysics. **Qualif.:** Candidates must be students undertaking post-secondary studies in engineering, geology, or geophysics at the University of Calgary, the University of Alberta, or an institution in the province offering a university-transfer program, who have achieved a high academic standing in grade 12 mathematics, science and engineering.

**Funds Avail.:** Twelve awards that cover tuition costs are presented annually. **No. of Awards:** 12. **To Apply:** Applications for this award must be accompanied by a letter of recommendation from the student's high school principal. **Deadline:** July 15. **Contact:** Honours and Awards Committee, Association of Professional Engineers, Geologists and Geophysicists of Alberta, at the above address (see entry 1253).

---

### • 1255 •
### Association for Religion and Intellectual Life

c/o Charles P. Henderson, Exec.Dir.  
College of New Rochelle  
New Rochelle, NY 10805-2339  
*E-mail:* aril@ecunet.org  
*URL:* http://www.aril.org

*Ph:* (914)235-1439  
*Fax:* (914)235-1584

#### • 1256 • ARIL Research Colloquium Fellowships (Professional Development/Fellowship)

**Purpose:** To give Scholars the opportunity to share in critical dialogue, worship, and study while pursuing individual projects related to religion and intellectual life. The Colloquium seeks to create a gender-balanced group, with diversity in age, race, ethnic background, denominational affiliation, and areas of intellectual endeavor. **Focus:** Religion and Intellectual Life. **Qualif.:** Candidates may be of any nationality, academic discipline or religious tradition. At the Colloquium, Fellows share a common life of religious reflection and worship while they pursue individual projects related to religion and intellectual life. Recipients are responsible for all travel expenses to and from the Colloquium and for a $125 registration fee.

**Funds Avail.:** Room and board, plus access to facilities and resources at Columbia University. **No. of Awards:** 25. **To Apply:** Write to the director for brochure; there is no application form. Submit a letter of application, including educational and employment background, relevant accomplishments, a project proposal, and names of two references. **Deadline:** March 1. Notification by April 1.

**Remarks:** General information about ARIL's activities and mission may be obtained from the above address. **Contact:** Charles P.

---

*Association for Religion and Intellectual Life (continued)*

Henderson, Executive Director, at the above address (see entry 1255).

## • 1257 •
## Association of School Business Officials International

| | |
|---|---|
| 11401 North Shore Dr. | *Ph:* (703)478-0405 |
| Reston, VA 22090-4232 | *Fax:* (703)478-0205 |

### • 1258 • Exhibitor Scholarships *(Professional Development/Scholarship loan)*

**Purpose:** To recognize and encourage individuals employed in school business management. **Focus:** Educational Administration. **Qualif.:** Applicant may be of any nationality. For at least 36 consecutive months prior to the year of application, applicant must have been both a member of ASBO and a full-time employee in a school business management position. Scholarships may be used at accredited colleges and universities for academic courses that improve technical skills and competence. Scholars are required to repay the funds awarded if they do not complete a minimum of six semesters of academic credit within three years of the date of receipt of the scholarship.

**Funds Avail.:** $1,200. **To Apply:** Write to the scholarship coordinator for application form and guidelines. Transcripts and a letter of recommendation from the chief school administrator at the employing institution are required. **Deadline:** August 1.

**Remarks:** The Exhibitors' Scholarships are also known as the Charles W. Foster Scholarship, the Frederick W. Hill Scholarship, and the Schuyler C. Joyner Scholarship. **Contact:** Executive Director at the above address (see entry 1257).

## • 1259 •
## Association of the Sons of Poland, Inc.

| | |
|---|---|
| 333 Hackensack St. | *Ph:* (201)935-2807 |
| Carlstadt, NJ 07072-1043 | *Fax:* (201)935-2752 |

### • 1260 • Association of the Sons of Poland Scholarships *(High School, Undergraduate/Award, Scholarship)*

**Focus:** General Studies. **Qualif.:** Applicants must have been insured members of the Association for two years. They must be entering an accredited college in September of the year of graduation from high school. **Criteria:** Selection is based upon the high school transcript, letter of application, character, and leadership.

**Funds Avail.:** $500 and an Achievement Award of $50 are presented. **No. of Awards:** 2. **To Apply:** The applicants should submit a letter to the Association, outlining their activities while in high school and specifying the college that they plan to enter in the fall. In addition, applicants should ask their high school principal or student advisor to send a transcript of their high school record directly to the Association no later than early May. **Deadline:** The entire file must be complete by May 14. **Contact:** Scholarship Committee, Association of the Sons of Poland, at the above address (see entry 1259).

## • 1261 •
## Association of State Dam Safety Officials

| | |
|---|---|
| 450 Old East Vine St., 2nd Floor | *Ph:* (606)257-5140 |
| Lexington, KY 40507-1544 | *Fax:* (606)323-1958 |

*E-mail:* 72130,2130@compuserve.com; damsafety@aol.com
*URL:* http://www.members.aol.com/damsafety/
homepage.htm

### • 1262 • ASDSO Scholarship *(Undergraduate/Scholarship)*

**Purpose:** To make students more aware of careers in dam safety engineering, and to award those who have excelled in engineering and who plan to go into dam safety engineering. **Focus:** Civil engineering, hydrology, geology, and environmental engineering. **Qualif.:** Applicants must be juniors or seniors majoring in civil or agricultural engineering, or related fields such as geology. **Criteria:** Financial need, extracurricular activities, and GPA.

**Funds Avail.:** Two scholarships of $2,500 per year are awarded annually; one to a junior, and the other to a senior. **No. of Awards:** Two. **Deadline:** February 13 for Fall/Spring of following school year. **Contact:** Sarah Mayfield at the above address (see entry 1261).

## • 1263 •
## Association of Universities and Colleges of Canada - Canadian Awards Programs - International and Canadian Programs Division

| | |
|---|---|
| 350 Albert St., Ste. 600 | *Ph:* (613)563-1236 |
| Ottawa, ON, Canada K1R 1B1 | *Fax:* (613)563-9745 |

*E-mail:* taskforce@aucc.ca
*URL:* http://www.aucc.ca

### • 1264 • AGF Financial Life Skills Scholarship Program *(Undergraduate/Scholarship)*

**Purpose:** To provide a two part scholarship for persons' seeking post-secondary education in Canada. **Focus:** All disciplines. **Qualif.:** Applicants must be Canadian citizens or permanent residents graduating from high school with a 75% average in their final and next-to-final year courses. They also must show involvement in the areas of community leadership; extra-curricular activities; special projects; volunteer service; outside interests or hobbies; and career and education objectives.

**Funds Avail.:** $1000 for the first year of a post-secondary education program and $1080 investment for a period of three years. **No. of Awards:** 40. **Deadline:** May 28.

**Remarks:** The award will be invested in the AGF fund(s) of the winner's choice - $30 a month over three years. There are no acquisition or redemption fees applied to the award, but the winner must remain in a university or college program to receive the total amount.

### • 1265 • Avenor Maritimes Scholarship Program *(Undergraduate/Scholarship)*

**Purpose:** To provide post-secondary educational opportunities for Canadian high school graduates. **Focus:** General studies. **Qualif.:** Applicants must be high school graduates from New Brunswick's School Districts Numbers 5 and 14 bordered by the towns of Jacquet River in the east and Tide Head in the west. They also must be entering the first year of a full-time degree/diploma program of at least one year duration. Applicants must have completed the course work of the final two years of schooling required for admission to the qualifying education institution in not more than two years and must have obtained a minimum academic standing of 60% in their final and next to final year courses and be planning to start post-secondary education within the year they graduate from high school.

**Funds Avail.:** $1500. **No. of Awards:** 2, one to a froncophone student from School District Number 5 and one to a Anglophone student from School District Number 14. **Deadline:** June 1.

**Remarks:** Scholarships are tenable at Canadian degree-granting institutions, Canadian community colleges, vocational, and trade schools.

## • 1266 • R. B. Byers Postdoctoral Fellowship Program *(Postdoctorate/Fellowship)*

**Purpose:** To support Canadians conducting research in national security strategic studies. **Focus:** National Security. **Qualif.:** Candidate must be a Canadian citizen and hold a Ph.D. or its equivalent. Individuals holding tenured or tenure-track appointments are not eligible to apply. Fellows must be affiliated with educational institutions in Canada. On completion of the research, a written report must be submitted.

**Funds Avail.:** $27,000. **No. of Awards:** One. **To Apply:** Write to the AUCC Awards Division, Canadian Awards Programs for application form and guidelines. **Deadline:** February 1. **Contact:** Alison Craig, Program Officer, Canadian Awards Programs, at the above address (see entry 1263).

## • 1267 • Cable Telecommunications Research Fellowship Program *(Graduate/Fellowship)*

**Focus:** Electrical engineering communications systems for video, voice and data signals, or for computer applications to Cable TV requirements. **Qualif.:** Applicants must be Canadian citizens or permanent residents, enrolled in or planning to enroll in a Canadian university and intend to use the fellowship to assist in completing a graduate degree in an applicable area of study.

**Funds Avail.:** $5000. **No. of Awards:** 2. **Deadline:** February 1.

**Remarks:** Fellowships are tenable at any university which is a member, or affiliated with a member, of AUCC.

## • 1268 • Canada Trust Scholarship Program for Outstanding Community Leadership *(Undergraduate/Scholarship)*

**Purpose:** To provide post-secondary educational opportunities for Canadian high school graduates. **Focus:** General studies. **Qualif.:** Applicants must be Canadian citizens or permanent residents who are graduating from high school (and/or cegep in Quebec) and have demonstrated involvement in community leadership.

**Funds Avail.:** $3500 living stipend plus full tuition and compulsory fees; summer employment and a $500 Award of Merit. **No. of Awards:** 20 renewable scholarships and 60 one time Certificate of Merit awards. **Deadline:** November 6.

**Remarks:** Scholarships are tenable at any Canadian educational institution.

## • 1269 • Celanese Canada Inc. Scholarships *(Undergraduate/Scholarship)*

**Focus:** Administration/commerce, Chemical Engineering, Chemistry, Mechanical Engineering. **Qualif.:** Applicants must be students entering the final year of an undergraduate program or a professional program. Eligible undergraduate fields of study are: Administration/commerce, tenable at any university that is a member or affiliated member of the AUCC with faculties of Administration; Chemical Engineering and Chemistry, tenable at the University of Alberta and the University of Calgary; Mechanical Engineering, tenable in the province of Quebec at any university that is a member or affiliated with a member of AUCC. Candidates must also be Canadian citizens or have held permanent resident status for one year prior to application, have achieved a high level of academic excellence, and have superior intellectual ability and judgement. **Criteria:** Academic excellence and superior intellectual

ability and judgement. Applications are by nomination only (three per institution). Selection is made by a committee of university representatives chosen by the AUCC with appropriate regard to geographical distribution.

**Funds Avail.:** $1,500, nonrenewable. **No. of Awards:** Six. **Deadline:** July 2. **Contact:** Alison Craig, Program Officer, Awards Division, at the above address (see entry 1263).

## • 1270 • CIBC Youthvision Graduate Research Award Program *(Graduate/Award)*

**Focus:** Business administration, economics, geography, political studies, psychology, sociology, and anthropology. **Qualif.:** Applicants must be Canadian citizens or permanent residents at the time of application, hold a Bachelors degree in a related field, have record high academic achievement, and be working full-time on a master's or doctoral degree in an area related to youth employment.

**Funds Avail.:** $15,000. **No. of Awards:** 6. **Deadline:** February 1.

**Remarks:** Awards are tenable at any member university or any university affiliated with a member of the AUCC. In some circumstances, permission may be granted to study abroad.

## • 1271 • CIBC Youthvision Scholarship Program *(Undergraduate/Scholarship)*

**Purpose:** To provide post-secondary educational opportunities for Canadian high school graduates. **Focus:** General studies. **Qualif.:** Applicants must be Canadian citizens or permanent residents graduating or have graduated with a minimum average of 60 % who are also enrolled in a Big Brothers and Sisters of Canada agency program.

**Funds Avail.:** $4000 or actual tuition fees, plus summer employment. **No. of Awards:** 30. **To Apply:** Application information and forms are available from the BBSC at 1-800-263-9133 or visit the CIBC's web site at www.cibc.com.

**Remarks:** Scholarships are tenable at any Canadian education institution.

## • 1272 • Department of National Defense Security and Defense Forum Internships *(Postgraduate/Internship)*

**Purpose:** To help recent graduates with a background in the strategic studies to obtain work experience in that field by working for a year in a research or similarly valuable position in the private sector or in a non-governmental organization. **Focus:** National Security. **Qualif.:** Applicants must be Canadian citizens and hold a master's degree. They must be entering fields of Strategic and Military (MSS) studies of relevance to current and future Canadian national security problems, including their political, international, historical, social, military, industrial, and economic dimensions in a wide range of disciplines.

**Funds Avail.:** Internships are valued at up to $16,000 for 12 months (prorated for shorter periods of time). Recipients may concurrently hold other awards or receive a salary, as long as the cumulative value does not exceed two-thirds of the value of this scholarship. The award is not renewable. Upon completion of the award, recipients must submit a reasonably detailed account of the year's experience and of any research undertaken. This report is forwarded to the Department of National Defense. **To Apply:** Applicants must clearly explain the relationship of their plans to the field of Canadian national security problems. **Deadline:** February 1. **Contact:** Alison Craig, Program Officer, Awards Division, at the above address (see entry 1263).

**Association of Universities and Colleges of Canada - Canadian Awards Programs - International and Canadian Programs Division (continued)**

### • 1273 • Department of National Defense Security and Defense Forum MA and Ph.D Scholarships *(Doctorate, Graduate/Scholarship)*

**Purpose:** To encourage postgraduate research relevant to national security in Canada. **Focus:** Canadian Politics, Military Studies, National Security. **Qualif.:** Applicant must be a Canadian citizen who holds a minimum of an Honors Bachelor's degree or its equivalent and has a knowledge of both official languages. Candidate must be undertaking research for a master's or Ph.D. degree on a topic of relevance to Canada's national security. Research may be on the political, international, historical, social, military, industrial, or economic dimensions of security policies and problems. MA scholarships are tenable only in Canada. On completion of the scholarship, one copy of a thesis or a detailed account of the research must be submitted to the AUCC.

**Funds Avail.:** Ph.D. scholarships: $16,000 maximum; M.A. scholarships: $12,000 maximum, renewable. **To Apply:** Write to the AUCC Awards Division, Canadian Awards Programs for application form and guidelines. **Deadline:** February 1. **Contact:** Alison Craig, Program Officer, Canadian Awards Programs, at the above address (see entry 1263).

### • 1274 • Emergency Preparedness Canada Research Fellowship Program *(Graduate/Fellowship)*

**Focus:** Disaster and Emergency studies, preferably in urban and regional planning, economics, earth sciences, risk analysis and management, systems science, social science, business administration and health administration. Multidisciplines are encouraged. **Qualif.:** Applicants must be Canadian citizens or permanent residents. Preference is given to those holding a master's degree and are pursuing doctoral studies.

**Funds Avail.:** $10,000. **No. of Awards:** 1. **Deadline:** February 1.

**Remarks:** Applicants in Business administration or health administration must have already completed their master's degree. Fellowship is tenable at any university in Canada or abroad.

### • 1275 • Fessenden-Trott Scholarships *(Undergraduate/Scholarship)*

**Focus:** General Studies. **Qualif.:** Applicants must be undergraduate students who are completing their first year of a university program, have obtained high academic standing, and are Canadian citizens or permanent residents. The awards are restricted to certain regions each year. **Criteria:** Applicants are chosen based on academic excellence, extracurricular activities, letters of reference, and leadership qualities. Selection of award recipients is made by a committee of university representatives chosen by the AUCC with appropriate regard to geographical distribution.

**Funds Avail.:** $9,000 to four recipients. The scholarships are valid for three years or until the recipients obtain their first degree, whichever comes first. Recipients must pass all courses in order to be considered for renewal. **To Apply:** Applications are by nomination and each eligible university may nominate only one candidate. **Deadline:** July 2. **Contact:** Alison Craig, Program Officer, Awards Division, at the above address (see entry 1263).

### • 1276 • C.D. Howe Memorial Foundation Engineering Awards Program *(Undergraduate/Scholarship)*

**Focus:** Engineering. **Qualif.:** Applicants must be Canadian citizens or permanent residents who have completed the first year of an engineering program.

**Funds Avail.:** $6000. **No. of Awards:** 2 (one for a male student and one for a female student). **To Apply:** Applications are by nomination by deans of engineering only. **Deadline:** July 2.

**Remarks:** Scholarships are tenable at any university that is a member, or affiliated with a member, of AUCC. Each university may nominate two candidates (one male and one female).

### • 1277 • C.D. Howe Scholarship Program *(Undergraduate/Scholarship)*

**Purpose:** To provide post-secondary educational opportunities for Canadian high school graduates. **Focus:** General studies. **Qualif.:** Applicants must be Canadian citizens or permanent residents who are graduating or have graduated within the last year, with a minimum average of A minus in their top OAC. They also must be residents of Thunder Bay or one of the following school boards: Lakehead, Lakehead District Roman Catholic, Lake Superior, North of Superior District Roman Catholic Separate School, Geraldton, Geraldton District Roman Catholic Separate School, Nipigon-Red Rock, or Hornepayne.

**Funds Avail.:** $5000. **No. of Awards:** 2. **Deadline:** June 1.

### • 1278 • Imasco Scholarships for Disabled Students *(Undergraduate/Scholarship)*

**Purpose:** To assist young disabled Canadian students to pursue university degrees. **Focus:** General Studies. **Qualif.:** Applicants must be disabled, Canadian citizens or permanent residents who have lived in Canada for at least two years, and enrolled in an undergraduate degree program at a Canadian post-secondary institution. Candidates who already have an undergraduate degree or are employees, franchisees, or dependents of employees or franchisees of Imasco or any of its subsidiaries are not eligible. **Criteria:** Candidates are judged on academic excellence and their level of motivation and maturity.

**Funds Avail.:** Each renewable scholarship is worth $5,000 annually. **To Apply:** Applicants must send four copies of their application form accompanied by a letter from a medical doctor describing the type and extent of their disability, two letters or reference (one from a past teacher and one from a person other than a relative who has known the applicant for more than one year), and official transcripts covering the last two years of study. **Deadline:** June 1. Winners are notified in September.

**Remarks:** The recipients must attend school in the year of application and complete each academic term. Requests for deferments will be considered only in unusual circumstances. **Contact:** Alison Craig, Program Officer, Awards Division, at the above address (see entry 1263).

### • 1279 • JDS FITEL Scholarship Program *(Undergraduate/Scholarship)*

**Focus:** Physics or engineering physics. **Qualif.:** Applicants must be currently enrolled in a qualifying program; be entering the second, third, or fourth year of study; and be a Canadian citizen.

**Funds Avail.:** $3000. **No. of Awards:** 18. **To Apply:** Applications are nominated by Deans of eligible faculties or Department Heads from each eligible educational institution. Each institution may nominate up to two candidates. **Deadline:** July 2.

**Remarks:** Scholarships are tenable at any Canadian degree-granting educational institution offering programs in the required fields of study.

### • 1280 • Frank Knox Memorial Fellowships *(Graduate/Fellowship)*

**Purpose:** To enable Canadians to study at Harvard University. **Focus:** General Studies. **Qualif.:** Applicant must be a Canadian citizen or permanent resident who has graduated, or is about to graduate, from a university or college in Canada. Individuals already studying in the United States are not eligible. Fellowships are tenable in any of the faculties of Harvard University: Arts and Sciences (including Engineering), Business Administration, Design, Divinity, Education, Law, Public Administration (John F. Kennedy School of Government), Medicine, Dental Medicine, and Public Health. Candidate is responsible for gaining admission to Harvard.

**Funds Avail.:** $15,500 stipend plus tuition fees and health insurance. **No. of Awards:** One or two. **To Apply:** Write to the AUCC, Awards Division, Canadian Awards Programs for application form and guidelines. Submit application materials with endorsement of department head. **Deadline:** February 1. Fellowships are announced in May.

## • 1281 • Linguistic Employment Scholarship Program *(Graduate/Scholarship)*

**Focus:** Translation of an oriental language at the master's level. **Qualif.:** At the time of application, candidates must be Canadian citizens holding a bachelor's degree in a related field with a record of high academic achievement. **Criteria:** Based on applicants advanced ability in an Oriental language or basic knowledge of an Oriental language and proven talent for acquiring languages as demonstrated by the Modern Language Aptitude Test.

**Funds Avail.:** $12,000. **No. of Awards:** 2.

**Remarks:** Scholarship is tenable at any Canadian university that is a member of the AUCC or is affiliated with a member.

## • 1282 • Mattinson Endowment Fund Scholarship for Disabled Students *(Undergraduate/Scholarship)*

**Purpose:** To assist young disabled Canadian students to pursue university degrees. **Focus:** General Studies. **Qualif.:** Applicants must be disabled, Canadian citizens or permanent residents who have lived in Canada for at least two years, and enrolled in an undergraduate degree program at a Canadian post-secondary institution. Candidates who already have an undergraduate degree or are employees, franchisees, or dependents of employees or franchisees of Imasco or any of its subsidiaries are not eligible. **Criteria:** Candidates are judged on academic excellence and their level of motivation and maturity.

**Funds Avail.:** Each renewable scholarship is worth $2,500 annually. **To Apply:** Applicants must send four copies of their application form accompanied by a letter from a medical doctor describing the type and extent of their disability, two letters of reference (one from a past teacher and one from a person other than a relative, who has known the applicant for more than one year), and official transcripts covering the last two years of study. **Deadline:** June 1. Winners are notified in September.

**Remarks:** The recipients must attend school in the year of application and complete each academic term. Requests for deferments will be considered only in unusual circumstances.

## • 1283 • The Frederick T. Metcalf Award Program *(Graduate/Award)*

**Focus:** Any field of study directly related to the development and delivery of cable television in Canada, including engineering, economics, and finance. **Qualif.:** Applicants must be Canadian citizens or permanent residents who are full-time students pursuing a master's degree in a qualifying field.

**Funds Avail.:** $5000. **No. of Awards:** 1. **Deadline:** February 1.

**Remarks:** The award is tenable at any Canadian university which is a member of the AUCC or affiliated to a member.

## • 1284 • Petro-Canada Inc. Graduate Research Awards *(Doctorate, Graduate/Award)*

**Purpose:** To support Canadians conducting graduate research in fields relating to the petroleum industry. **Focus:** Sciences, Engineering, Social Sciences, Business Administration. **Qualif.:** Applicant must be a Canadian citizen or permanent resident who is working toward a master's or doctoral degree on a subject related

to the oil and gas industry. Awards are tenable at Canadian universities and colleges which are members of AUCC.

**Funds Avail.:** $10,000. **No. of Awards:** Up to four. **To Apply:** Write to the AUCC Awards Division, Canadian Awards Programs for application form and guidelines. **Deadline:** February 1. **Contact:** Alison Craig, Program Officer, Awards Division, Canadian Awards Programs, at the above address (see entry 1263).

## • 1285 • Queen Elizabeth Silver Jubilee Endowment Fund for Study in a Second Official Language Awards *(Undergraduate/Scholarship)*

**Purpose:** To encourage young Canadians who wish to improve their proficiency in their second official language to pursue full-time studies at another university that functions in the other official language and in a milieu in which that language predominates. **Focus:** Language. **Qualif.:** Applicants must be Canadian citizens or permanent residents enrolled in their second or third year of an undergraduate program during the year of application, and have abilities in their second language sufficient for pursuit of studies in that language. (Candidates attending a Quebec institution may be in their first year of a first undergraduate program.) Permanent residents are required to submit proof of status with their applications. Recipients may not concurrently hold any other major awards. **Criteria:** Preference is given to candidates who wish to study at another educational institution where their second language is predominant.

**Funds Avail.:** $5,000 each and transportation expenses for one return trip (economy) between place of residence and the university to be attended. **No. of Awards:** A maximum of six non-renewable awards are made annually. **To Apply:** Applications are by nomination only. **Deadline:** The deadline for nomination is February 15.

## • 1286 • The SHL Systemhouse President's Award for Education Technology Program *(Undergraduate/Scholarship)*

**Focus:** Computer science and engineering. **Qualif.:** Applicants must have maintained a honors level (70% for colleges) average on a full academic workload in their previous year of study and must also be entering the final year of a honors degree or college diploma program.

**Funds Avail.:** $5000 for university studies and $2500 for college studies. **No. of Awards:** 28 (20 for university and 8 for college). **To Apply:** Applications are by nomination from an eligible institution only. Each institution may nominate 3 candidates. **Deadline:** July 2.

**Remarks:** Scholarships are tenable at SHL Systemhouse selected institutions which offer programs in the required fields of study.

## • 1287 • Student Access Awards Program *(Undergraduate/Scholarship)*

**Focus:** General studies. **Qualif.:** Applicants must be disabled persons who are Canadian citizens or permanent residents for at least two years.

**Funds Avail.:** $2500. **No. of Awards:** Determined annually. **Deadline:** June 1.

**Remarks:** Scholarships are tenable at any Canadian university or college.

## • 1288 • George Tanaka Memorial Scholarship Program *(Undergraduate/Scholarship)*

**Focus:** Architecture, landscape architecture, art and culture. **Qualif.:** Applicants must be full-time students enrolled in an undergraduate program of an accepted discipline, entering their second, third, or fourth year of study. Applicants also must be Canadian citizens or permanent residents for one year prior to submitting an application.

---

*Association of Universities and Colleges of Canada - Canadian Awards Programs - International and Canadian Programs Division (continued)*

**Funds Avail.:** $2000. **No. of Awards:** 1. **To Apply:** Applications are by nomination only. Deans of eligible faculties or Departments Heads from each eligible educational institution may nominate up to two candidates. **Deadline:** July 2.

**Remarks:** Scholarships are tenable at The University of Columbia, University of Guelph, McGill University, and The University of Toronto.

## • 1289 •
**Association of University Programs in Health Administration**
430 11th St. NW, 4th Fl.     *Ph:* (202)638-1448
Washington, DC 20005-3500     *Fax:* (202)638-3429
*E-mail:* aaupha.aupha.org
*URL:* http://www.aupha.org

### • 1290 • David A. Winston Fellowship *(Graduate, Undergraduate/Fellowship)*

**Purpose:** To provide an opportunity to promising young people to learn about the political system through direct exposure to public and private sector roles in health policy developments. **Focus:** Health services administration and health policy. **Qualif.:** The Fellowship is open to any student in a college or university that has a program of health services administration and policy and is a full or associate member of the Association of University Programs in Health Administration. Candidates must graduate in the year the application is made. The degree may be in any discipline, field, or profession. The applicant must not have had any previous public policy experience in Washington, DC. Each university may nominate one candidate.

**Funds Avail.:** The stipend is $2,700 monthly. The Fellowship also provides $2,000 for relocation expenses. The Fellowship offers a nine month postgraduate experience in Washington, D.C. and starts between May 15 and July 1. The first portion of the Fellowship is a planned rotation of at least three months through various centers of government health policy development at the national level. It may include activities at nearby state capitals. During the final months the Fellow will pursue a personal interest project under the guidance of an advisory committee of key policy makers from the private and public sectors. **No. of Awards:** 1 per year. **To Apply:** Applicants should submit a short summary of personal experience, educational and work background; a letter to the Campus Selection Committee about how the Fellowship can assist their career; and a letter of recommendation from the dean, director or chairman of the department of the school involved. They must also submit transcripts of grades, a summary of community activities, and a resume. **Deadline:** The chairman of the health administration program on each campus, who is the nominating committee contact person, must receive the candidate's application materials early in October. Three nominees are invited to Washington, DC during the first half of January. The recipient is announced in late January.

**Remarks:** The David A. Winston Fellowship Board of Directors sponsors the Fellowship and the Association of University Programs in Health Administration administers the Fellowship. The Fellowship expresses Mr. Winston's commitment to the public/private partnership required for a high quality, market oriented health care system. **Contact:** Director or Chairman of the Health Administration Program on campus at the above address.

## • 1291 •
**Association for Women in Architecture**
2550 Beverly Blvd.
Los Angeles, CA 90057     *Ph:* (213)389-6490
*URL:* http://www.awa-la.org

### • 1292 • Association for Women in Architecture Scholarship *(Graduate, Undergraduate/Scholarship)*

**Purpose:** To promote the education of women. **Focus:** Architecture and related fields. **Qualif.:** California residents or those attending school in California must have completed at least their first year in architectural or related studies such as civil, structural, mechanical, or electrical engineering as related to architecture; landscape architecture; urban and land planning; interior design; or architectural rendering and illustration. A maximum of ten finalists are chosen, and they must appear, at their own expense, in Los Angeles for a mandatory interview. **Criteria:** Selection is based on financial need, scholarship, personal statement, and letters of recommendation from professors.

**Funds Avail.:** Scholarships amounts vary from $200 to $2,500 are awarded based on available funds. **No. of Awards:** 3. **To Apply:** Applications are usually available in February. Write or phone for an application. **Deadline:** April 29.

## • 1293 •
**Association of Women in Communications - Florida Chapter**
FIU, International II
Room 323 School of Journalism and
   Mass Comm.
3000 NE 151st St.
North Miami, FL 33181-3000

### • 1294 • Florida Chapter of the Association of Women in Communications Christina Saralegui Scholarship *(Graduate, Undergraduate/Scholarship)*

**Focus:** Communications. **Qualif.:** Applicants must be female, bilingual, Hispanic residents of Dade County who are also a junior, senior, or graduate student with a minimum 3.2 GPA. Preference will be given to students attending a Florida institution. **To Apply:** Write for application details. **Deadline:** April 1.

## • 1295 •
**Association for Women Geoscientists**
4779 126th St. N     *Ph:* (651)426-3316
White Bear Lake, MN 55110-5910     *Fax:* (651)426-5449
*E-mail:* scholarships@awg.org; leete@macalstr.edu
*URL:* http://www.awg.org; http://flint.mines.edu:4502/

### • 1296 • Association for Women Geoscientists Thesis Support Scholarships (Chrysalis) *(Doctorate, Graduate/Scholarship)*

**Purpose:** To assist female geoscientists with the completion of their theses. **Focus:** Geoscience. **Qualif.:** Applicants must be women who have completed the academic requirements for the degree and who plan to complete their theses within the academic year. **Criteria:** Based on service to community and promise as a geoscientist, as shown in letters of recommendation.

**Funds Avail.:** At least three scholarships of $750 each. **No. of Awards:** At least 3 per year. **To Apply:** A letter of application and letters of recommendation (one from thesis advisor, the others may be persons of applicant's choice). There is no application form. **Deadline:** February 28. **Contact:** Jeanne Harris, (303)534-0708, at the above address (see entry 1295).

---

• **1297** •

## Association for Women Veterinarians
32205 Allison Dr.
Union City, CA 94587                    *Ph:* (510)797-2323

• **1298** • **Association for Women Veterinarians Student Scholarships** *(Graduate/Scholarship)*

**Purpose:** To provide financial assistance to students of veterinary medicine currently enrolled in a veterinary program. **Focus:** Veterinary Studies. **Qualif.:** Candidates must be second- or third-year students currently attending veterinary schools in the United States or Canada. **Criteria:** Selection is based on an essay, grades, need, leadership, and letters of recommendation.

**Funds Avail.:** $1,500. **No. of Awards:** Four. **To Apply:** Applications are available from the Deans of Veterinary Schools after January 1. **Deadline:** February 21. **Contact:** Dr. Chris Stone Payne at the above address (see entry 1297).

---

• **1299** •

## Asthma and Allergy Foundation of America
242 Merrick Rd., Ste. 401              *Ph:* (516)536-8032
Rockville Center, NY 11570             *Fax:* (516)536-7650
*URL:* http://www.li.net/~respcare/aafa.htm

• **1300** • **Allergy and Clinical Immunology Fellowship Program** *(Postdoctorate/Fellowship)*

**Purpose:** To encouraged young physicians to study the causes and treatment of asthma and allergies. **Focus:** Asthma, Allergies. **Qualif.:** Candidate may be of any nationality, but must be a postgraduate and nominated by the dean of their medical school and by the preceptor in charge of research.

**Funds Avail.:** $5,000-20,000. **To Apply:** Write the Executive Director for application form. **Deadline:** November 1. **Contact:** Mary Worstell, Executive Director, at the above address (see entry 1299).

---

• **1301** •

## AT & T Bell Laboratories - Special Programs
600 Mountain Ave., Rm. 3D316          *Ph:* (908)582-4822
Murray Hill, NJ 07974                 *Fax:* (908)582-7383
*URL:* http://www.research.att.com/lateinfo/research/
  summer/

*AT&T Bell Laboratories is the research and development unit of AT&T. Its mission is to provide basic and applied research, development and design, systems engineering, and information and operations systems for AT&T.*

• **1302** • **AT & T Bell Laboratories Cooperative Research Fellowships for Minorities** *(Graduate/Fellowship)*

**Purpose:** To identify and develop scientific and engineering research ability among members of underrepresented minority groups, and to increase their representation in the sciences and engineering. **Qualif.:** Applicants must be members of underrepresented minority groups (Blacks, Native American Indians, and Hispanics) who are graduate students in programs leading to doctoral degrees in the following disciplines: chemistry, chemical engineering, communications science, computer science and engineering, electrical engineering, information science, materials science, mathematics, mechanical engineering, operations research, physics, and statistics. Awards are made only to U.S. citizens or permanent residents, and who are admitted to full-time study in a graduate program approved by AT&T Bell Laboratories. **Criteria:** Candidates are selected on the basis of scholastic attainment in their field of specialization, and other evidence of their ability and potential as research scientists. A personal interview with AT&T Bell Laboratories scientists and engineers is arranged to select an appropriate summer mentor.

**Funds Avail.:** Nine to 12 fellowships are awarded annually. The fellowship provides full tuition, an annual stipend of $13,200 (paid bi-monthly September through May), books, fees, and related travel expenses. Fellowship recipients may not accept any other fellowship support. Fellowships may be renewed on a yearly basis for four years, contingent upon satisfactory progress toward the doctoral degree. If needed, the fellowship will be renewed after four years subject to an annual review by the CRFP committee. Fellowship holders are invited to resume employment at AT&T Bell Laboratories during subsequent summers, but may elect to continue supervised university study or research; fellowship support would be continued (with the exception of the living stipend). During periods of summer employment, fellowship holders receive salaries commensurate with those earned by employees at approximately the same level of training. **To Apply:** Applications should include: a completed application form; official transcripts of grades from all undergraduate schools attended; a statement of interest; letters of recommendation from college professors who can evaluate the applicant's scientific aptitude and potential for research (additional letters of recommendation are also invited); Graduate Record Examination scores on the Aptitude Test and the appropriate Advanced Test (scores are required and should be submitted by listing on the GRE registration form Institution Code R2041, AT&T Bell Laboratories). **Deadline:** Applications and all supporting documentation, preferably in one package, must be received by January 15. **Contact:** AT&T Bell Laboratories, Special Programs, at the above address (see entry 1301).

• **1303** • **AT & T Bell Laboratories Graduate Research Fellowships for Women** *(Doctorate/Fellowship)*

**Qualif.:** Applicants must be women who are United States citizens or permanent residents pursuing full-time doctoral studies in chemistry, chemical engineering, communications science, computer science/engineering, electrical engineering, information science, materials science, mathematics, mechanical engineering, operations research, physics, and statistics. **Criteria:** First consideration is given to seniors. Participants are selected on the basis of scholastic attainment in their field of specialization, and other evidence of their ability and potential as research scientists. Finalists are invited to visit AT&T Bell Laboratories for personal interviews. At that time they speak with members of the technical staff in their field of interest to aid in the selection of award winners and in the choice of a mentor.

**Funds Avail.:** Four fellowships are awarded annually, providing a stipend of $13,200 plus tuition, books, fees, and related travel and housing expenses. Summer employment is provided. An AT&T scientist serves as a mentor during the Fellowship period. **To Apply:** Applications should include a statement of interest, information on scholastic background, academic standing, and

---

## AT & T Bell Laboratories - Special Programs (continued)

related job experience. Candidates should arrange for official transcripts of grades to be sent from their institutions, and three letters of recommendation from college professors who can evaluate the applicant's scientific aptitude and potential for research. Letters of recommendation from others familiar with the candidate's qualifications are also encouraged (forms are included with the application). In addition, Graduate Record Examination scores on the Aptitude Test and the appropriate Advanced Test are required and should be submitted by listing on the GRE registration form Institution Code R2041. **Deadline:** January 15. **Contact:** AT&T Bell Laboratories at the above address (see entry 1301).

### • 1304 • AT & T Bell Laboratories Graduate Research Grants for Women (Doctorate, Graduate/ Grant)

**Purpose:** To identify and develop research ability in women and to increase their representation in science and engineering. **Qualif.:** Applicants must be women students who are pursuing full-time doctoral studies in the following disciplines: chemistry, chemical engineering, communications science, computer science and engineering, electrical engineering, information science, materials science, mathematics, mechanical engineering, operations research, physics, and statistics. Awards are made only to women who are U.S. citizens or permanent residents, and who are admitted to full-time study in a doctoral program agreed to by AT&T Bell Laboratories. The program is primarily directed to graduating seniors, but applications from first-year graduate students will be considered. **Criteria:** Participants are selected on the basis of scholastic attainment in their field of specialization, and other evidence of their ability and potential as research scientists. Finalists are invited to visit AT&T Bell Laboratories for personal interviews. At that time, they speak with members of the technical staff in their field of interest to aid in the selection of award winners and in the choice of a mentor.

**Funds Avail.:** Six grants are awarded annually. Each grant provides an annual award of $1,500, which is used to support aspects of the recipients' professional development that would not normally be covered by other awards, i.e. expenses for childcare, personal computing equipment, and software, or to visit other university research laboratories. The grant is intended to be in addition to any other financial support. Grants are renewed on a yearly basis for the normal duration of the graduate program, subject to the participant's satisfactory progress toward the doctoral degree. **To Apply:** Applications should include a statement of interest, information on scholastic background, academic standing, and related job experience, and arrange for official transcripts of grades to be sent from their institutions, and three letters of recommendation from college professors who can evaluate the applicant's scientific aptitude and potential for research. Letters of recommendation from others familiar with the candidate's qualifications are also encouraged (forms are included with the application). In addition, Graduate Record Examination scores on the Aptitude Test and the appropriate Advanced Test are required and should be submitted by listing on the GRE registration form Institution Code R2041-2-00, AT&T Bell Laboratories. **Deadline:** Applications and all supporting documentation, preferably in one package, must be received by January 15. **Contact:** AT&T Bell Laboratories, Special Programs, at the above address (see entry 1301).

### • 1305 • AT & T Bell Laboratories Summer Research Program for Minorities & Women (Undergraduate/Fellowship)

**Purpose:** To attract students into scientific careers, including patent law, by placing participants in working contact with experienced research scientists, engineers, and patent lawyers. **Qualif.:** Applicants must be women and/or members of under represented minority groups (Blacks, Native American Indians, and Hispanics). The program is primarily directed toward undergraduate students who have completed their third year of college. Emphasis is placed on the following disciplines: ceramic engineering, chemistry, chemical engineering, communications science, computer science and engineering, electrical engineering, information science, materials science, mathematics, mechanical engineering, operations research, physics, and statistics. Applicants should be U.S. citizens or permanent residents of the United States. **Criteria:** Candidates are selected based on academic achievement, personal motivation, and compatibility of student interests with current AT&T Bell Laboratories activities.

**Funds Avail.:** Salaries are commensurate with those of regular AT&T Bell Laboratories employees of comparable education. During the summer, living accommodations at a nearby college are arranged for students who desire them. Bus transportation between campus housing facilities and AT&T Bell Laboratories is provided. Participants are free to make their own arrangements for board and transportation. Upon reporting to work, each summer employee will be reimbursed for air or surface travel expenses to New Jersey, in an amount not to exceed the cost of round trip economy class airfare. **No. of Awards:** 60-100 annually. **Deadline:** Applications and all supporting documentation, preferably in one package, must be received by December 1. **Contact:** AT &T Bell Laboratories, Special Programs, at the above address (see entry 1301).

### • 1306 • AT & T Bell Laboratories University Relations Summer Program (Doctorate, Graduate, Undergraduate/Work Study)

**Purpose:** To provide work experience for talented students on a well-defined project in an R&D environment. **Qualif.:** Candidates should be outstanding B.S., M.S., and Ph.D. candidates who are within two years of graduation and are pursuing studies in the fields of ceramic engineering, chemistry, computer science, electrical engineering, mechanical engineering, operations research, chemical engineering, physics, mathematics, information science, communications science, statistics, or materials science.

**Funds Avail.:** Funding covers summer housing arrangements and transportation. **No. of Awards:** 200-300. **Deadline:** Applications and all supporting documentation, preferably in one package, must be received by February 15. **Contact:** AT&T UR Summer Programs, 101 Crawford Corner Rd., Rm. 1B222, Holmdel, NJ, 07733.

### • 1307 •
## Atlanta Association of Media Women

A.S. Reeves, Journal/Constitution
PO Box 4689
Atlanta, GA 30302                     *Ph:* (404)526-5091

### • 1308 • Atlanta Association of Media Women Scholarship (Undergraduate/Scholarship)

**Focus:** Mass communications. **Qualif.:** Applicants must be a minority female undergraduate student attending a college or university in Georgia.

**Funds Avail.:** Minimum of $1000. **Deadline:** March 15.

## • 1309 •

**Atlanta Press Club**
260 14th St. NW, Ste. 300
Atlanta, GA 30318
*URL:* http://www.atlpressclub.org

Ph: (404)577-7377
Fax: (404)892-2637

**• 1310 • Atlanta Press Club Journalism Scholarship**
*(Graduate, Undergraduate/Scholarship)*

**Focus:** Journalism. **Qualif.:** Applicants must be graduate or undergraduate students attending or planning to attend a Georgia institution of higher learning, majoring in journalism.

**Funds Avail.:** $1,000 per award. **No. of Awards:** 4. **To Apply:** Applicants must submit a essay, official transcript, and completed application form. **Deadline:** February 16. **Contact:** Lisa Johnson or Ann Wright.

## • 1311 •

**Atlantic Salmon Federation**
Headquarters
12 Evergreen Ct.
Truro, NS, Canada B2N 5H9
*URL:* http://is.dal.ca/~stanet/database/salmon.html

Ph: (902)897-9390
Fax: (902)897-9390

**• 1312 • Olin Fellowships** *(Professional Development/ Fellowship)*

**Focus:** Biology—Marine. **Qualif.:** Applicants must be legal residents of the United States or Canada who are seeking to improve their knowledge or skills in Atlantic salmon biology, management, and conservation. Candidates need not be in a degree program.

**Funds Avail.:** Fellowships of $1,000 to $3,000 each are awarded and may be applied toward a wide range of endeavors including salmon management, graduate studies, and research. Fellowships are tenable at any accredited university or research laboratory or in an active management program. **To Apply:** A formal application must be submitted. If an applicant has graduated from an academic or technical course in the past three years, or is currently a student, a copy of the most recent transcript of grades must either be attached to the application or forwarded. Candidates must attach a concise statement of their qualifications for the program for which they are seeking a fellowship. They must include information regarding their present employment or course of study and a brief biographical sketch of their educational and professional achievements, including degrees or certificates received, awards for achievements or service, and recent grants or scholarships. Information on their previous or present work/study projects that have particular relevance to their proposed program must be included. Candidates must provide a description of their proposed program. This should include the title of the program; the title of the specific study/research project, if different; site of the program including the institution and mailing address; the dates of the program; and a proposal describing the program. The proposal must include precise information on all of the following: program/ project content, specific objectives and timetable; justification including background and/or future implications; proposed budget; cooperating organizations, if any, and the extent of funding from these sources including a list of grants received or sought; and the amount and specific use of the grant sought from the International Atlantic Salmon Foundation. A letter of acceptance or other documentation indicating approval of the program from the institution where the fellowship is to be held must be attached to the proposal, if such approval is a prerequisite of the program. Recommendations are required from two persons not related to the candidate. One person should be an individual under whom the applicant has studied or worked and the other should be from the organization with which the applicant is

currently associated. Applications must be received at the St. Andrews office (see below) by March 15. Applicants are advised of fellowship awards by May 15. **Contact:** Dr. John M. Anderson, Vice-President, Operations, Atlantic Salmon Federation, PO Box 429, St. Andrews, N.B., E09 2X0, Canada, or above address.

## • 1313 •

**Augustana University College**
Financial Aid Office
4901-46 Ave.
Camrose, AB, Canada T4V 2R3
*URL:* http://marcello.auguatana.ab.ca/

Ph: (403)679-1117
Fax: (403)679-1129

**• 1314 • Lutheran Life University Scholarships**
*(Undergraduate/Scholarship)*

**Focus:** General Studies. **Qualif.:** Applicants must be members of the Lutheran Life Insurance Society of Canada undertaking degree programs at a university or affiliated college. **Criteria:** Selection is based on academic standing, community involvement, and citizenship qualities.

**Funds Avail.:** $1,200. **No. of Awards:** Varies. **Deadline:** December 31. **Contact:** Financial Aid Office, Augustana University College, at the above address (see entry 1313).

## • 1315 •

**Australasian College of Physical Scientists and Engineers in Medicine**
c/o Department of Physical Sciences
Peter MacCallum Cancer Institute
Locked Bag 1, A'Beckett St.
Melbourne, VIC 3000, Australia

Ph: 3 656 1253
Fax: 3 656 1444

**• 1316 • ACPSEM Scholarship** *(Professional Development/Scholarship)*

**Purpose:** To support research and study by medical engineers and scientists. **Focus:** Physical Sciences. **Qualif.:** Candidate may be of any nationality. Applicant must be a member of ACPSEM who wishes to undertake a specific course of study or investigation.

**Funds Avail.:** A$2,000 maximum. **To Apply:** Write to the secretary for application guidelines. **Deadline:** March 31. **Contact:** Secretary at the above address (see entry 1315).

## • 1317 •

**Australia Council - Literature Board**
PO Box 788
Strawberry Hills, NSW 2012,
Australia

Ph: 2 950 9000
Fax: 2 950 9111

**• 1318 • International Book Translation and Publishing Program** *(Professional Development/Award)*

**Purpose:** To extend the overseas market for Australian literature and to ensure royalty payments are made to Australian writers. **Focus:** Publishing, Translation, Writing. **Qualif.:** Applicant may be of any nationality who plans to translate and publish works by living Australian writers of poetry, fiction, drama, and books for children and young people. Applications for assistance with books of literature criticism, essays, autobiography, biography, and

## Australia Council - Literature Board (continued)

general cultural significance that are substantially by or about living Australian writers will also be considered. Candidate can apply for assistance with translation costs, permission fees and/or publication costs. **Criteria:** The literary quality of writer, ability of translator, details of print run and distribution, standard of production.

**Funds Avail.:** A$1,000 minimum. **No. of Awards:** Varies. **To Apply:** Write to the administrator for application form and guidelines. **Deadline:** March 1 and September 15. **Contact:** Administrator, Literature, at the above address (see entry 1317).

### • 1319 • International Magazine Publishing Program (Professional Development/Award)

**Purpose:** To extend the overseas market for Australian literature and to ensure royalty payments are made to Australian writers. **Focus:** Publishing, Translation, Magazines, Writing. **Qualif.:** Applicant may be of any nationality who plans to translate and publish works by living Australian writers. International literary magazines which feature Australian writing on a regular basis can also apply for assistance with the publication of the Australian writing section. **Criteria:** Factors considered when assessing applications are: literary and editorial quality: proportion of Australian creative writing in the magaine; payments to Australian writers; print run and circulation; distribution and production standards.

**Funds Avail.:** Minimum of A$1,000. **No. of Awards:** Varies. **To Apply:** Write to the administrator for application form and guidelines. **Deadline:** August 2. **Contact:** Administrator, Literature, at the above address (see entry 1317).

## • 1320 •
## Australian Bureau of Statistics
PO Box 10
Belconnen, ACT 2616, Australia            *Ph:* 6 252 7020

### • 1321 • Research Associateships and Fellowships in Statistics (Postdoctorate/Fellowship)

**Purpose:** To encourage statisticians to investigate problems of interest to the Bureau. **Focus:** Statistics. **Qualif.:** Applicant may be of any nationality, although preference is given to Australian citizens and residents. Candidate must be a statistician qualified to conduct research in statistical methodology, social and demographic studies, economic studies, or applications of technology. Fellowships are usually tenable at the Canberra office of the Bureau; proposals for research at other sites may occasionally be approved.

**Funds Avail.:** A$27,800-63,700/year. **To Apply:** Write to the director for application form and guidelines. Submit form with a description of proposed research and details of professional and personal background. **Deadline:** July. Notification by October. **Contact:** Administrative Support Unit, Statistical and Information Support Unit, at the above address (see entry 1320).

## • 1322 •
## Australian Federation of University Women - Queensland
Fellowship Committee
Box 8/217 Hawken Drive
St. Lucia, QLD 4067, Australia            *Ph:* 74 494 1021

### • 1323 • Freda Bage Fellowships Commemorative Fellowships (Postgraduate/Fellowship)

**Purpose:** To support postgraduate research and study by women. **Focus:** General Studies. **Qualif.:** Candidate may be of any nationality. Applicant for either fellowship must be a female graduate and must not be fully employed or entitled to be paid study or long-service leave during tenure of the fellowship. Both awards are tenable at any university or approved institute in Australia with one exception; the Bage Fellowship may not be used at the applicant's alma mater. If an award is made to an Australian citizen, it is also tenable overseas.

**Funds Avail.:** A$15,000/year (Bage) $13,000/year (Commemorative). **To Apply:** Write to the administrator for application form and guidelines. **Deadline:** September 30. **Contact:** Administrator at the above address (see entry 1322).

## • 1324 •
## Australian Federation of University Women - Victoria
PO Box 816
Mount Eliza, VIC 3199, Australia
*URL:* http://www.ecom.unimelb.edu.au/ecowww/scholar/

### • 1325 • Beatrice Fincher Scholarship Lady Leitch Scholarship (Postgraduate/Scholarship)

**Purpose:** To support study and research by Australian women. **Focus:** General Studies. **Qualif.:** Applicant must be an AFUW member who wishes to conduct research or study at the postgraduate level. Scholarships are not usually awarded to individuals on paid study or related programs from academic institutions. Awards are tenable in any country. Candidate for the Fincher Scholarship must be a member of AFUW or of the International Federation of University Women. The Fincher Scholarship is tenable at a recognized Victorian tertiary institution. Victorian recipients may use the scholarship for interstate or overseas studies and research.

**Funds Avail.:** A$5,000. **To Apply:** Write to the scholarship secretary for application materials. Submit application form with a detailed report of academic record; names of three academic references; research or study proposal; values of other awards sought or granted; a self-addressed stamped envelope; and evidence of membership in AFUW. An interview may be requested. **Deadline:** March 1. Recipient will be notified by June 30. **Contact:** Mrs. M.R. Endersbee at the above address (see entry 1324).

## • 1326 •
## Australian Institute of Aboriginal and Torres Strait Islander Studies
GPO Box 553
Canberra, ACT 2601, Australia          Ph: 6 246 1111

### • 1327 • AIATSIS Research Grants (Postdoctorate, Professional Development/Grant)

**Purpose:** To support research into Aboriginal and Torres Strait Islander Studies. **Focus:** Aboriginal and Torres Strait Island Studies. **Qualif.:** Applicant may be of any nationality. Proposed research project must endeavor to secure short-term and long-term benefits to Aboriginal and Torres Strait Islands Peoples, and must have the support of relevant community organizations. Funds are available for investigator's cost of living expenses, local travel, and field expenses. Both limited (short-term) and full grants are available.

**Funds Avail.:** Full grants, no limit; limited grants: A$5,000. **No. of Awards:** No limit. **To Apply:** Write to the Principal for application materials. The Director of Research should be contacted if there are specific questions about topics and procedures for research. **Deadline:** Limited grants: February 14, full grants: June 30. Awardees are selected in April and November, respectively. **Contact:** Dr. Mary Edmunds at the above address (see entry 1326).

## • 1328 •
## Australian Institute of Archaeology
174 Collins Street          Ph: 3 650 3477
Melbourne, VIC 3000, Australia     Fax: 3 654 2774

### • 1329 • Australian Institute of Archaeology Grants (Postdoctorate/Grant)

**Purpose:** To assist with excavations or travel grants to present papers at conferences relating to Biblical archaeology. **Focus:** Biblical Archaeology. **Qualif.:** Applicants may be of any nationality. Grants are made to fund archaeological excavations or conference travel, not individual research. Applicant must have a Ph.D. degree and at least five years of experience in directing excavations. Conference papers must be submitted to the director upon return. **Criteria:** Conference paper on excavations with particular relevance to biblical background will be considered more favorably.

**Funds Avail.:** A$1,000 maximum. **To Apply:** Write to the director for application guidelines. Submit a description of qualifications for leading an excavation, purpose of proposed project, and a budget. **Deadline:** Six months before the commencement of excavation. **Contact:** P. T. Crocker, Director, at the above address (see entry 1328).

## • 1330 •
## Australian Institute of Food Science and Technology Ltd.
PO Box 319
Noble Park, VIC 3174, Australia          Ph: 3 706 3337

### • 1331 • Malcolm Bird Commemorative Award (Professional Development/Award)

**Purpose:** To recognize outstanding papers by young food scientists and technologists. **Focus:** Food Science/Technology, Nutrition. **Qualif.:** Candidate may be of any nationality. Applicant

must be a member of the Institute under 30 years of age on 30 June of the year of the award.

**Funds Avail.:** A$350; plus all costs of attending the convention. **To Apply:** Write to the executive secretary for application guidelines. Submit paper. The top candidates present their papers at the Institute's annual convention. **Deadline:** December 31. The award winner is selected at the annual convention in May or June. **Contact:** Christian Harfield, Executive Secretary, at the above address (see entry 1330).

## • 1332 •
## The Australian National University
Humanities Research Centre          Ph: 6 249 2700
Canberra, ACT 0200, Australia      Fax: 6 248 0054
E-mail: administrator.hrc@anv.edu.an

### • 1333 • Australian National University Visiting Fellowships (Postdoctorate/Fellowship)

**Purpose:** To promote research into the humanities in Australia. **Focus:** Humanities. **Qualif.:** Applicant may be of any nationality but must have earned the Ph.D. and be an established scholar. The University establishes a new theme annually.

**Funds Avail.:** A$420/week and a travel allowance up to A$2,000. **No. of Awards:** 20. **To Apply:** Write the Director for application form and guidelines. A proposal is required upon filing of the application. **Deadline:** October 31. **Contact:** Professor Graeme Clarke, Director, at the above address (see entry 1332).

## • 1334 •
## Australian Research Council - Institutional Grants Section - Research Branch
Department of Employment,
  Education and Training
GPO Box 9880
Canberra, ACT 2601, Australia          Ph: 6 276 7182

### • 1335 • Australian Postdoctoral Research Fellowships (Postdoctorate/Fellowship)

**Purpose:** To provide opportunities for scholars to undertake research of national and international significance. **Focus:** General Studies. **Qualif.:** Applicant may be of any nationality, but preference will be given to Australian residents. Applicant must hold a Ph.D. or equivalent. Fellowships are tenable at any Australian institution, including government and industrial research organizations, that has the facilities to support the research. Fellows work with or manage a research team at the host facility.

**Funds Avail.:** Postdoctoral fellowships: A$36,285-38,950, plus A$3,500/year research support grant. **To Apply:** Write for application form and guidelines. **Deadline:** March 1. **Contact:** Institutional Grants Section Director at the above address (see entry 1334).

### • 1336 • Australian Research Fellowship (Postdoctorate/Fellowship)

**Purpose:** To provide opportunities for scholars of national significance. **Focus:** General Studies. **Qualif.:** Applicant may be of any nationality, but preference will be given to Australian residents. Applicant must hold a Ph.D. or equivalent with at least three years of postdoctoral experience. Fellowships are tenable at only at Unified National System approved higher education institutions. Fellows work with or manage a research team at the institution.

## Australian Research Council - Institutional Grants Section - Research Branch *(continued)*

**Funds Avail.:** A$41,000-48,688, plus A$5,500 research support grant. **To Apply:** Write for application form and guidelines. **Deadline:** March 1. **Contact:** Institutional Grants Section Director at the above address (see entry 1334).

### • 1337 • Australian Senior Research Fellowships *(Postdoctorate/Fellowship)*

**Purpose:** To provide opportunities for scholars to undertake research that is both of major importance in its field and of significant benefit to Australia. **Focus:** General Studies. **Qualif.:** Applicant may be of any nationality. Candidate must be a senior lecturer, principal, senior research scientist, or hold an equivalent rank. Fellowships are tenable only at an approved Australian 'Unified National System' higher education institution that has the facilities to support the research. Fellows manage or work with a research team at the host facility.

**Funds Avail.:** A$50,225-77,900. **To Apply:** Write for application form and guidelines. **Deadline:** March 1. **Contact:** Institutional Grants Section Director at the above address (see entry 1334).

### • 1338 • Queen Elizabeth II Fellowships *(Postdoctorate/Fellowship)*

**Purpose:** To encourage research in Australia by young postdoctoral graduates. **Focus:** General Studies. **Qualif.:** Applicant may be of any nationality. Applicant must hold a Ph.D. or equivalent; have at most six years of postdoctoral experience at the time of application; preferably away from the institution where the Ph.D. was obtained; and have published in scholarly journals. Fellowships are tenable at any Australian institution, including government and industrial research organizations, that has the facilities to support the research. Fellows manage or work with a research team at the host facility.

**Funds Avail.:** A$44,075-48,688/year, plus A$10,500 research support grant. **To Apply:** Write for application form and guidelines. **Deadline:** March 1. **Contact:** Institutional Programs and Research Training Section Director at the above address (see entry 1334).

### • 1339 • Overseas Postgraduate Research Scholarships for Study in Australia *(Graduate/ Scholarship)*

**Purpose:** To support individuals who wish to conduct postgraduate research in Australia. **Focus:** General Studies. **Qualif.:** Applicants may be a citizen of any country except Australia or New Zealand who are commencing full-time study for a higher degree. Proposed research should be consistent with the priority areas of national interests of Australia. The specific areas of study for which scholarships are offered may vary, according to the courses offered by the host institution. **Criteria:** Applicants judged on academic merit.

**Funds Avail.:** Tuition and fees. **No. of Awards:** 300. **To Apply:** Detailed information and application forms should be obtained from the higher education institution at which the student is proposing to enroll. **Deadline:** Varies.

### • 1340 • Austrian Cultural Institute

950 3rd Ave., 20th Fl.      *Ph:* (212)759-5165
New York, NY 10022      *Fax:* (212)319-9636
*URL:* http://www.austriaculture.net

### • 1341 • Austrian Federal Ministry for Science and Research Grants *(Professional Development/Grant)*

**Purpose:** To provide students with the opportunity to study in Austria at an Academy of Music and Dramatic Art or Art Academy. **Focus:** Music and Fine Arts. **Qualif.:** Applicant must be 20 and 35 years old and fluent in German.

**Funds Avail.:** AS 7,400/month; Students with a master's degree AS 8,100/month. **To Apply:** Write to the above address for application form and guidelines. **Deadline:** January 31. **Contact:** Grants for Studies in Austria at the above address (see entry 1340).

### • 1342 • Automotive Booster Clubs International - Educational & Scholastic Foundation

1806 Johns Dr.      *Ph:* (708)729-2227
Glenview, IL 60025-1657      *Fax:* (708)729-3670
*URL:* http://www.aftmkt.com/MISG/associations/ASIA/boosters/

### • 1343 • ABCI Scholarships *(Undergraduate/ Scholarship)*

**Purpose:** To promote students to seek four-year degrees in automotive-related subjects. **Focus:** Automotive Industry. **Qualif.:** Applicants must be enrolled in the automotive program at Northwood Institute in Michigan or the University of Southern Colorado.

**Funds Avail.:** $800. **No. of Awards:** 2. **To Apply:** Candidates do not apply directly for these scholarships; they are selected by the university for the award. **Contact:** Molly Willett, Scholarship Program Coordinator, Northwood Institute, 3225 Cook Rd., Midland, MI 48640-2398; telephone: (517)832-4279; or Ms. Kathy McHugh, Scholarship Coordinator, University of Southern Colorado, c/o USC Foundation, 2200 Bonforte Blvd., Pueblo, CO 81001; telephone: (719)549-2380. At ABCI, contact Donn R. Proven at the above address (see entry 1342).

### • 1344 • Automotive Hall of Fame

21400 Oakwood Blvd.      *Ph:* (313)240-4000
Dearborn, MI 48121      *Fax:* (313)240-8641

### • 1345 • Automotive Hall of Fame Educational Fund Scholarships *(Undergraduate/Scholarship)*

**Focus:** General Studies. **Qualif.:** Applicants must have a sincere interest in pursuing automotive careers upon graduation. They must be enrolled full-time (a minimum of 12 credit hours per semester) in two- or four-year degree programs of study, including graduate school. They must be at least sophomores when receiving the award, and maintain satisfactory academic performance, although some scholarships designate superior academic performance. **Criteria:** Selection is based on interest in the automotive industry and academic standing.

**Funds Avail.:** From $250 to $2,000. **No. of Awards:** 16 to 24. **To Apply:** Completed applications should be accompanied by two letters of recommendation verifying interest in an automotive career and official transcript of grades. **Deadline:** June 30. Recipients are chosen in mid-October. **Contact:** The Automotive Hall of Fame at the above address (see entry 1344).

---

**• 1346 •**

## Auxiliary to Sons of Union Veterans of the Civil War

1016 Gorman St.
Philadelphia, PA 19116     **Ph:** (215)673-1688
*E-mail:* marauxsuv@aol.com
*URL:* http://suvcw.org/asuv.htm

**• 1347 • Grand Army of the Republic Memorial Scholarship** *(Undergraduate/Scholarship)*

**Purpose:** To continue interest in the history of the Grand Army of the Republic. **Focus:** History. **Qualif.:** Applicants must be studying history and must be the descendant of a Civil War veteran. **Criteria:** The national president of the auxiliary chooses the recipient.

**Funds Avail.:** $350. **No. of Awards:** 1. **To Apply:** Students may apply during their senior year of high school or any year of college by sending a resume of qualifications, the name of the college or university at which they are enrolled, or accepted, and a statement describing their lineage from a Civil War veteran. **Deadline:** November 1. **Contact:** Margaret Atkinson at the above address (see entry 1346).

---

**• 1348 •**

## Aviation Council of Pennsylvania

3111 Arcadia Ave.     **Ph:** (610)797-1133
Allentown, PA 18103     **Fax:** (610)797-8238
*URL:* http://www.acpfly.com

**• 1349 • Aviation Technology Scholarship** *(Professional Development, Undergraduate/Scholarship)*

**Purpose:** To assist applicants in the attainment of their aviation career goals. **Focus:** Aviation Technology, Maintenance, and Engineering. **Qualif.:** Applicants must be residents of Pennsylvania planning on attending school within the state.

**Funds Avail.:** $1,000. **No. of Awards:** One. **To Apply:** Applications must be typed and must include: personal background; activities; personal goals; reason financial assistance is requested; two or more recommendations from individuals within the aviation community or elsewhere; and transcripts. **Deadline:** July 30. **Contact:** Robert Rockmaker.

**• 1350 • Professional Pilot John W. "Reds" Macfarlane Scholarship** *(Professional Development, Undergraduate/Scholarship)*

**Purpose:** To assist applicants in the attainment of their aviation career goals. **Focus:** Flight. **Qualif.:** Applicants must be residents of Pennsylvania planning on attending school in Pennsylvania. Applicants must also hold at least a Student Pilot Certificate.

**Funds Avail.:** $1,000. **No. of Awards:** One. **To Apply:** Applications must be typed and must include: personal background; activities; personal goals; reason financial assistance is needed; two or more recommendations from the aviation community or from other sources; and transcripts. **Deadline:** July 30. **Contact:** Robert Rockmaker.

**• 1351 • Aviation Management Wilfred M. "Wiley" Post Scholarship** *(Professional Development, Undergraduate/Scholarship)*

**Purpose:** To promote aviation careers and to assist applicants in the attainment of their goals. **Focus:** Aviation and Aviaton Management. **Qualif.:** Applicants must be residents of Pennsylvania.

**Funds Avail.:** $1,000. **No. of Awards:** One. **To Apply:** Applications must be typed and must include: personal background; activities; personal goals; statement explaining why financial assistance is sought; two recommendations from individuals in the aviation community or the applicant's schools; and transcripts. **Deadline:** July 30. Winners are announced in October. **Contact:** Robert Rockmaker.

---

**• 1352 •**

## Charles Babbage Institute

University of Minnesota
103 Walter Library
117 Pleasant St. SE     **Ph:** (612)624-5050
Minneapolis, MN 55455     **Fax:** (612)625-8054
*E-mail:* cbi@tc.umn.edu
*URL:* http://www.cbi.umn.edu

**• 1353 • Adelle and Erwin Tomash Fellowship in the History of Information Processing** *(Doctorate, Graduate/Fellowship)*

**Purpose:** To support advanced studies in the history of information processing. **Focus:** Information Processing and Computing/History, Modern. **Qualif.:** Candidate may be of any nationality. Applicant must be a graduate student. Priority is given to candidates who have completed all requirements for the doctoral degree except the research and writing of the dissertation. Applicant must be intending to write his/her dissertation on some aspect of the history of computers and information processing. Fellowship is tenable at the home academic institution, the Babbage Institute, or any other location where there are appropriate research facilities.

**Funds Avail.:** $10,000 stipend, plus up to $2,000 for tuition, travel, and other approved research expenses. **No. of Awards:** One per year. **To Apply:** There is no application form. Submit biographical information and a detailed research plan, including evidence of faculty support for the project. Three letters of reference and certified transcripts of graduate school credits must be sent directly to the Institute. **Deadline:** Materials must be in by January 15. **Contact:** Associate Director at the above address (see entry 1352).

---

**• 1354 •**

## Leo Baeck Institute

129 E. 73rd St.     **Ph:** (212)744-6400
New York, NY 10021     **Fax:** (212)988-1305
*E-mail:* lbi1@interport.net
*URL:* http://www.ushmm.org/organizations/63.html

**• 1355 • David Baumgardt Memorial Fellowships** *(Postdoctorate/Fellowship)*

**Purpose:** To assist scholars whose research projects are related to the writings of Professor David Baumgardt or his scholarly interests. **Focus:** Ethics, Jewish Studies. **Qualif.:** Applicants may be of any nationality but must be academics affiliated with an accredited institution of higher education. Both predoctoral and

---

## Leo Baeck Institute (continued)

postdoctoral scholars are eligible. Proposed research must be relevant to the writings of Professor David Baumgardt or his scholarly interests, including ethics and the modern intellectual history of German-speaking Jewry. Research should also require extensive use of the facilities of LBI. Funds are not available for travel costs.

**Funds Avail.:** $2,000. **No. of Awards:** 1. **To Apply:** Write to LBI for application guidelines and application form. Submit four copies of the following: a curriculum vitae, transcripts, a full description of the research project, and two academic letters of reference. Evidence of enrollment in a Ph.D. program or of receipt of the doctorate is also required. **Deadline:** November 1. The fellowship will be announced in February. **Contact:** Carol Kahn Strauss, Executive Director, at the above address (see entry 1354).

### • 1356 • Fritz Halbers Fellowships (Doctorate/ Fellowship)

**Purpose:** To support doctoral research on the culture and history of German-speaking Jewry. **Focus:** Jewish Studies. **Qualif.:** Applicants may be of any nationality but must be students enrolled in a Ph.D. program at an accredited institution of higher education conducting dissertation research on the culture and history of German-speaking Jewry. The fellowship may not be applied to travel costs.

**Funds Avail.:** $3,000 maximum. **No. of Awards:** 1 or more. **To Apply:** Write to LBI for application guidelines and application form. Submit four copies of the following: a curriculum vitae, transcripts, a full description of the research project, and two academic letters of reference. Evidence of enrollment in a Ph.D. program is also required. **Deadline:** November 1. Fellow will be announced in February. **Contact:** Carol Kahn Strauss, Executive Director, at the above address (see entry 1354).

### • 1357 • LBI/DAAD Fellowships (Doctorate/ Fellowship)

**Purpose:** To support scholarly work using the resources of LBI. **Focus:** Jewish History. **Qualif.:** Applicants must be U.S. citizens and Ph.D. students under the age of 32 years, or recent recipients of the doctorate who are less than 35 years old. Award is tenable at LBI. Fellows may use the resources of the Institute for dissertation research or to prepare a scholarly essay or book. The research project must be relevant to the social, communal and intellectual history of German-speaking Jewry.

**Funds Avail.:** $2,000. **No. of Awards:** 1. **To Apply:** Write to LBI for application guidelines and application form. Submit four copies of the following: a curriculum vitae, transcripts, a full description of the research project, and two academic letters of reference. Evidence of enrollment in a Ph.D. program or of receipt of the doctorate is also required. **Deadline:** November 1. The fellow is announced in January. **Contact:** Carol Kahn Strauss, Executive Director, at the above address (see entry 1354).

### • 1358 • LBI/DAAD Fellowships for Research in Germany (Doctorate/Fellowship)

**Purpose:** To enable U.S. students and scholars to undertake research in Germany related to the interests of LBI. **Focus:** Jewish History. **Qualif.:** Applicants must be U.S. citizens and Ph.D. students under the age of 32 years, or recent recipients of the doctorate who are less than 35 years old. The fellowship is tenable at German archives, libraries, and research institutions. Fellows may use the award for dissertation research or to prepare a scholarly essay or book. The research project must be relevant to the social, communal and intellectual history of German-speaking Jewry.

**Funds Avail.:** DM1,680/month, plus DM1,000 for travel. **No. of Awards:** 1 (six month) or 2 (three-month) fellowships. **To Apply:** Write to LBI for application guidelines and application form. Submit four copies of the following: a curriculum vitae, transcripts,

a full description of the research project, and two academic letters of reference. Evidence of enrollment in a Ph.D. program or of receipt of the doctorate is also required. **Deadline:** November 1. The fellow is announced in January. **Contact:** Carol Kahn Strauss, Executive Director, at the above address (see entry 1354).

---

### • 1359 •
## The Bailey Foundation
PO Box 494            *Ph:* (864)833-1910
Clinton, SC 29325-1276      *Fax:* (864)833-7451

### • 1360 • Mercer Silas Bailey Memorial Scholarships (Undergraduate/Scholarship)

**Qualif.:** The scholarships are for graduating seniors at Laurens and Clinton High Schools accepted in an accredited degree-granting college or university. Students must be in the top quarter of their graduating class and their prospective colleges must be in the United States. **Criteria:** Financial need, academic record and participation in extracurricular activities.

**Funds Avail.:** The scholarship is paid directly to the institution over a period of four years, at a maximum of $4,000 per year. **No. of Awards:** 2 annually. **To Apply:** A formal application must be submitted to high school guidance counselors or the Foundation administrator. Application must include page one of IRS form 1040. **Deadline:** April 15. **Contact:** H. William Carter, Jr., Administrator, at the above address (see entry 1359).

---

### • 1361 •
## The Albert Baker Fund
5 Third St., Ste. 717
San Francisco, CA 94103      *Ph:* (415)543-7028

### • 1362 • The Albert Baker Fund (Graduate, Undergraduate/Loan)

**Purpose:** To provide financial assistance to members of The First Church of Christ, Scientist, in Boston, Massachusetts, who need help with their education expenses. **Focus:** General Studies, Nursing, Religion. **Qualif.:** Applicants must be students of Christian Science, members of The Mother Church, and attending (or have been accepted by) an accredited college, university, approved vocational school, Christian Science Nurses' training program, or be enrolled in a United States Armed Forces Chaplaincy Program.

**Funds Avail.:** Recipients receive long-term loans with interest that is well below the bank prime rate. Repayment of the loan begins six months after graduation by predetermined monthly installments. Lump sum repayment is acceptable at any time. **To Apply:** Application packets must be submitted. **Deadline:** The final deadline for applications is August 1. Nurse Loan application forms are accepted any time during the year.

**Remarks:** A cosigner is required for all secured loans.

• 1363 •
## J.H. Baker Trust
Student Loan Committee
Box 280
La Crosse, KS 67548                    *Ph:* (913)222-2537

• 1364 •   **J.H. Baker Trust Student Loan Program**
*(Undergraduate/Loan)*

**Focus:** General Studies. **Qualif.:** Applicants must be graduates of high schools located in Rush, Barton, Ellis, Ness, or Pawnee Counties in Kansas, less than 25 years old, full-time undergraduate students (at least 12 credit hours) at a college, university, or vocational-technical school, and maintain a cumulative grade point average of 2.0 or greater. **Criteria:** The Selection Committee bases its decisions on financial need, academic performance, motivation, character, ability, and potential.

**Funds Avail.:** Generally, loans do not exceed the cost of tuition, or $1,000 per semester, whichever is less. Total loans may not exceed $8,000. Each loan must be fully guaranteed, generally by a parent, and the interest is due semiannually while the student is still in school. Interest rates are determined by the Selection Committee and are currently six percent, but can be changed at any semiannual renewal date. Repayment of the loan must begin within six months of either graduation or failure to qualify under full-time status, and will be spread out over the same time frame as was necessary for completion of the education (generally four years). **To Apply:** Applications are available by writing to the above address. Also required are school transcripts, class rank information, and one letter of recommendation from a former teacher, guidance counselor, or principal. **Deadline:** July 1, January 1; recipients are notified by July 15 for fall loans and by January 15 for spring loans.

**Remarks:** Joseph H. Baker, a 1915 graduate of Ecletic Medical University in Kansas City, Kansas, was an active member in his community and local civic organizations, as well as the medical profession. Upon his death in 1976, Dr. Baker's will created the student loan program, which has provided nearly $1 million to qualified students. **Contact:** The J.H. Baker Trust at the above address (see entry 1363).

• 1365 •
## Balso Foundation
493 W. Main St.                        *Ph:* (203)250-6000
Cheshire, CT 06410                     *Fax:* (203)272-4150

• 1366 •   **Balso Foundation Scholarships**
*(Undergraduate/Scholarship)*

**Purpose:** To help area students attend college. **Qualif.:** Candidates must be residents of Cheshire, Connecticut, or the surrounding area and have at least a 3.0 grade point average. **Criteria:** Selection is based on academic performance and financial need.

**Funds Avail.:** $15,000 to $20,000 is distributed among 15 to 25 applicants annually. **To Apply:** Students must contact Cheshire High School. **Deadline:** April 1 for fall study. **Contact:** Guidance counselors or the Balso Foundation at the above address (see entry 1365).

• 1367 •
## Baltimore Opera Company, Inc.
110 W Mt. Royal Ave.                   *Ph:* (410)625-1600
Baltimore, MD 21201                    *Fax:* (410)625-6474
*E-mail:* hstevens@baltimoreopera.com
*URL:* http://www.baltimoreopera.com

• 1368 •   **Baltimore Opera Studio & Residency Program** *(Professional Development/Prize)*

**Purpose:** A directed training program designed to prepare young opera artists for the profession. **Focus:** Opera, voice, theatre arts, dance/movement, stage combat, and diction and language. **Qualif.:** Applicants musbe be citizens of North America between the ages of 21 and 35 who have performed or are contracted to perform a lead role with an OPERA America member company with an annual budget in excess of $5,000,000. No member of the Baltimore Opera Company Board of Trustees, or the Baltimore Opera Guild, Inc. or their families wll be eligibel.

**Funds Avail.:** Four artists receive a weekly stipend of $300. **To Apply:** A copy of the applicant's birth certificate or passport (or copies of naturalization papers for naturalized citizens); two signed and sealed letters of recommendations from recognized musical authorities (other than the applicant's vocal teacher or coach); an audiocassette of the applicant singing two arias in contrasting languages and styles; a formal biography and an 8 x 10 black and white glossy photograph (biographies should include present and past vocal teachers and coaches and recent singing engagements with dates, places, and types of engagements); and a $40 non-refundable registration fee payable by check or money ordr must be submitted. **Deadline:** Applications and accompanying materials must be submitted by April 15, 1999.

**Remarks:** If selected for a live audition, singers must be prepared to sing six arias from the standard operatic repertoire with at least one selection each in Italian, German, French, and English. All arias are to be sung from memory in the original languages and key, with preceeding recitative where appropriate. Once this repertoire list is submitted, changes may not be made. Unless the singer chooses to bring a pianist, the Baltimore Opera Company will provide an accompanist.

• 1369 •
## Banff Centre for the Arts - Office of the Registrar
PO Box 1020, Sta. 28                   *Ph:* (403)762-6180
107 Tunnel Mountain Dr.                *Fax:* (403)762-6345
Banff, AB, Canada T0L 0C0              *Free:* 800-565-9989
*E-mail:* arts_info@banffcentre.ab.ca
*URL:* http://www.banffcentre.ab.ca/cfa/

• 1370 •   **Banff Centre for the Arts Scholarships**
*(Postgraduate, Professional Development/Scholarship)*

**Purpose:** To offer dedicated artists a supportive, varied, and multidisciplinary environment in which to further their creative and technical development. **Focus:** Arts Journalism, Music and Sound, Arts Administration, Curatorial, Television Computer Support, Dance, Drama, 20th Century Opera and Song, Playwrights' Colony, Publishing, Television Co-production, Theater Production and Stage Management, Media Technologies, New Media Research, Writing, Visual Arts, Aboriginal Arts. **Qualif.:** Application requirements vary depending on the program. Generally most programs are open to the most qualified applicant, regardless of nationality. Scholarships are tenable at the Centre. **Criteria:** Candidates are selected based on demonstrated ability and commitment.

**Funds Avail.:** Scholarships vary. Stipend is also offered in some programs. **To Apply:** Write the registrar for application guidelines. **Deadline:** Varies, according to discipline.

## • 1371 •
## Bank of Sweden Tercentenary Foundation - Stiftelsen Riksbankens Jubileumsfond
Box 5675
S-114 86 Stockholm, Sweden          *Ph:* 8 24 32 15

### • 1372 • Bank of Sweden Tercentenary Foundation Project Grants *(Professional Development/Grant)*

**Purpose:** To support and promote advanced scientific research. **Focus:** Humanities, Social Sciences. **Qualif.:** Applicant may be of any nationality. Applicants from outside of Sweden must describe a defined cooperation with Swedish scholars or research institutes. Awards are tenable in Sweden.

**Funds Avail.:** 350.000skr/year average. **To Apply:** Write for preliminary application form and guidelines. Submit form and outline of project to priority committee. The committee will decide if complete research proposal is needed. **Contact:** Dr. Dan Brndstrm, Executive Director, at the above address (see entry 1371).

## • 1373 •
## Baptist General Convention of Texas
Black Church Relations Section
333 N. Washington St., Ste. 311          *Ph:* (214)828-5236
Dallas, TX 75246-1798          *Fax:* (214)828-5261
*URL:* http://www.bgct.org

### • 1374 • Texas Black Scholarships *(Undergraduate/Scholarship)*

**Purpose:** To recognize worthy, capable young men and women and offer them continuing opportunities afforded by a Christian education. **Focus:** General Studies. **Qualif.:** Candidates must be Black; hold active membership in a Baptist church; give evidence of being a genuine Christian; be graduates of Texas schools; have acceptable recommendations from pastors and teachers; have maintained a B average in high school, or have a minimum of 2.0 on a 4.0 grading scale from an accredited college or university; be residents of Texas for at least 12 months; possess a vital interest in the advance of the Kingdom of God; and attend a Texas Baptist Educational Institution, or a Baptist Institution agreed upon by the scholarship committee. **Criteria:** The scholarship committee receives recommendations from papers, mission personnel, high school teachers and advisors, and many others.

**Funds Avail.:** Grants of $400 per semester, or $266.66 per quarter; maximum of $3,200. **To Apply:** Applicants must write the Black Church Relations Section. A confidential file is compiled that includes the application, letters of recommendation, transcript, biographical data, and other basic information. If applicants qualify under scholarship policy limitations, they will be invited to meet with the scholarship committee, during which time the final decision shall be made.

**Remarks:** There are nine participating Texas Baptist institutions of higher learning: Baylor University-Waco; Dallas Baptist University-Dallas; East Texas State University-Marshall; Hardin-Simmons University-Abilene; Houston Baptist University-Houston; Howard Payne University-Brownwood; University of Mary Hardin Baylor-Belton; Wayland Baptist University-Plainview; and Southwestern Baptist Theological Seminary-Fort Worth. The scholarships are funded through the Mary Hill Davis Offering for state missions sponsored annually by the Woman's Missionary Union of Texas. **Contact:** James W. Culp, Sr., Black Churches Relations Section, Baptist General Convention of Texas at the above address (see entry 1373).

## • 1375 •
## Battelle Institute
PO Box 12297
200 Park Drive, Ste. 211
Research Triangle Park, NC 27709          *Ph:* (919)549-8291
*E-mail:* summer@aro-emh1.army.mil
*URL:* http://www.battelle.org/sfrep/tofc.html

### • 1376 • U.S. Army Summer Faculty Research and Engineering Associateships *(Postdoctorate/Fellowship)*

**Purpose:** To enable faculty members to conduct research at U.S. Army laboratories. **Focus:** Behavioral Sciences, Chemistry, Computer Science, Engineering, Mathematics, Medicine, Meteorology, Physics. **Qualif.:** Candidate must be a U.S. citizen. Applicant must be a faculty member in one of the areas of study listed above, who is employed by a U.S. institution. Awards are tenable at selected U.S. Army laboratories and research centers; a list of participating facilities is included in application materials.

**Funds Avail.:** $900/week; a $350 allowance if relocation expenses are necessary. **To Apply:** Write to the administrator for application form and guidelines. **Deadline:** Varies. **Contact:** Gary E. Hill, Program Manager, at the above address (see entry 1375).

## • 1377 •
## Bausch & Lomb Science Award Committee
University of Rochester
Director of Admissions          *Ph:* (716)275-3221
Wallis Hall          *Fax:* (716)756-8480
Rochester, NY 14627          *Free:* 800-281-6203
*E-mail:* admission@rochester.edu

### • 1378 • Bausch & Lomb Science Awards *(Undergraduate/Scholarship)*

**Purpose:** To recognize outstanding achievement in the sciences by high school students. **Focus:** General Studies. **Qualif.:** Applicants must be selected as Baush & Lomb medal winners during their junior year of high school. **Criteria:** Only students selected by their high schools are eligible to be considered for the scholarship.

**Funds Avail.:** $6,000 yearly over four years. **To Apply:** Applications are automatically sent to eligible students. **Deadline:** January 15. **Contact:** Bridget Klenk, at the above address (see entry 1377).

## • 1379 •
## Bedding Plants Foundation
PO Box 27241          *Ph:* (517)694-8537
Lansing, MI 48909          *Fax:* (517)694-9561
*URL:* http://www.BPFI.org

*The Bedding Plants Foundation was formerly known as the Professional Plant Growers Scholarship Foundation.*

### • 1380 • Jerry Baker College Freshman Scholarships *(Undergraduate/Scholarship)*

**Focus:** Horticulture. **Qualif.:** Applicants must be entering their freshman year in college and be interested in careers in horticulture, landscaping or gardening. Citizens of any country may apply.

**Funds Avail.:** $1,000. **No. of Awards:** 2. **To Apply:** Write for application forms and guidelines. **Deadline:** April 1.

**Remarks:** BPFI sponsors two scholarships through Future Farmers of America for high school seniors entering college. **Contact:** The Bedding Plants Foundation Inc. at the above address (see entry 1379).

• 1381 • **Bedding Plants Foundation Vocational Scholarships** *(Other/Scholarship)*

**Focus:** Horticulture. **Qualif.:** Applicants must be accepted in a one- or two-year vocational program and be enrolled for the entire following academic year. They must be interested in horticulture with intentions of becoming a floriculture plant producer and/or operations manager. A minimum 3.0 GPA is required. It is open to U.S. and Canadian citizens. **Criteria:** Based on financial need and scholastic record.

**Funds Avail.:** $500-1,000. **No. of Awards:** 2-4. **To Apply:** Write for an application form and guidelines. **Deadline:** April 1. **Contact:** Bedding Plants Foundation Inc. at the above address (see entry 1379).

• 1382 • **Harold Bettinger Memorial Scholarship** *(Graduate, Undergraduate/Scholarship)*

**Purpose:** To encourage the combined study of horticulture and business and/or marketing. **Focus:** Horticulture. **Qualif.:** Applicant may be of any nationality. Applicant should be an undergraduate or graduate student at an accredited college or university in the United States or Canada. Candidate must be a horticulture major with a business and/or marketing emphasis, or a business/marketing major with a horticulture emphasis. A minimum 3.0 GPA is required on a 4.0 scale.

**Funds Avail.:** $1,000. The award is given to one undergraduate or one graduate student. **No. of Awards:** 1. **To Apply:** Write for application materials. Submit application form with undergraduate and graduate transcripts, an academic letter of recommendation, and a personal letter of recommendation. **Deadline:** April 1. **Contact:** The Bedding Plants Foundation Inc. at the above address (see entry 1379).

• 1383 • **John Carew Memorial Scholarship** *(Graduate/Scholarship)*

**Purpose:** To encourage young horticulturists with a specific interest in bedding or flowering potted plants. **Focus:** Horticulture. **Qualif.:** Applicant may be of any nationality, but must be a graduate student majoring in horticulture or a related field at an accredited U.S. or Canadian university. Applicant must have a particular interest in bedding or flowering potted plants.

**Funds Avail.:** $1,500. **No. of Awards:** 1. **To Apply:** Write for application materials. Submit application form with undergraduate and graduate transcripts, an academic letter of recommendation, and a personal letter of recommendation. **Deadline:** April 1. **Contact:** The Bedding Plants Foundation Inc. at the above address (see entry 1379).

• 1384 • **Carl F. Dietz Memorial Scholarship** *(Undergraduate/Scholarship)*

**Focus:** Horticulture. **Qualif.:** Applicants must be undergraduate students majoring in horticulture, with a specific interest in bedding plants. Recipients must attend an accredited college or university in the United States or Canada during the complete next academic year. There are no citizenship requirements. A minimum 3.0 GPA is required on a 4.0 scale.

**Funds Avail.:** $1,000. **No. of Awards:** 1. **To Apply:** Applications must include the following documents: a letter of recommendation from a college faculty member who can evaluate the applicant as a student; a letter of recommendation from someone in the community who can evaluate the applicant as a citizen; a recent photograph; and a transcript of undergraduate and graduate grades from the college registrar. **Deadline:** April 1. **Contact:** The Bedding Plants Foundation Inc. at the above address (see entry 1379).

• 1385 • **Fran Johnson Scholarships** *(Graduate, Undergraduate/Scholarship)*

**Focus:** Horticulture. **Qualif.:** Applicants may be undergraduate or graduate students pursuing a degree in floriculture who are re-entering the academic setting after an absence of at least five years. Specific interest in bedding plants or other floral crops is desired. Students must be enrolled in an accredited four-year college or university program in the United States or Canada for the entire next academic year. It is open of U.S. and Canadian citizens.

**Funds Avail.:** $500-1,000. **No. of Awards:** 1. **To Apply:** Write for application forms and guidelines. **Deadline:** April 1. **Contact:** The Bedding Plants Foundation at the above address (see entry 1379).

• 1386 • **PPGA Family Member Scholarship** *(Graduate, Undergraduate/Scholarship)*

**Focus:** Horticulture. **Qualif.:** The award is open to all immediate relatives of members of PPGA who are at the undergraduate or graduate level in any program of study. A minimum 3.0 GPA is required on a 4.0 scale. Citizens of any country may apply.

**Funds Avail.:** $500-1,000. **No. of Awards:** 1. **To Apply:** Write for application forms and guidelines. **Deadline:** April 1. **Contact:** The Bedding Plants Foundation Inc. at the above address (see entry 1379).

• 1387 • **James K. Rathmell, Jr., Memorial Scholarship to Work/Study Abroad** *(Graduate, Undergraduate/Scholarship)*

**Purpose:** To encourage overseas work and study in the fields of horticulture, floriculture, and landscape architecture by U.S. students. **Focus:** Floriculture, Horticulture, Landscape Architecture. **Qualif.:** Applicant must be an undergraduate or graduate student in the United States who wishes to pursue work or study abroad. Candidate is responsible for making all arrangements for his/her overseas program. Preference will be given to applicants with well-defined objectives that will benefit the bedding and container plant industry.

**Funds Avail.:** $2,000 maximum. **No. of Awards:** 1. **To Apply:** Write for application materials. Submit application form with undergraduate and graduate transcripts, a letter of invitation from host firm/institution abroad, an academic letter of recommendation, and a personal letter of recommendation. **Deadline:** April 1. **Contact:** The Bedding Plants Foundation Inc. at the above address (see entry 1379).

• 1388 • **Earl J. Small Growers, Inc. Scholarships** *(Undergraduate/Scholarship)*

**Focus:** Horticulture. **Qualif.:** Undergraduate students of horticulture who are attending an accredited four-year college or university in the United States or Canada are eligible for this scholarship. Applicants must be U.S. or Canadian citizens. They must intend to pursue a career in greenhouse production.

**Funds Avail.:** $2,000. **No. of Awards:** 2. **To Apply:** Applications must be accompanied by the following documents: a letter of recommendation from a faculty member who can evaluate the applicant as a student; a letter of recommendation from someone in the community who can evaluate the applicant as a citizen; a recent photograph; and a transcript of undergraduate grades from the applicant's college or university. Grade point average must be calculated to a 4.0 scale. **Deadline:** April 1.

**Remarks:** The foundation generally receives approximately 65 applications. **Contact:** The Bedding Plants Foundation Inc. at the above address (see entry 1379).

## Bedding Plants Foundation (continued)

**• 1389 • Jerry Wilmot Scholarship** *(Undergraduate/ Scholarship)*

**Focus:** Horticulture, Business/Finance. **Qualif.:** Students must be pursuing a career in garden center management. It is open to all business/finance or horticulture majors in their sophomore, junior or senior year. Citizens of any country may apply but study must be conducted in the United States or Canada.

**Funds Avail.:** $2,000. **No. of Awards:** 1. **To Apply:** Write for application forms and guidelines. **Deadline:** April 1.

---

**• 1390 •**

## Frank Huntington Beebe Fund for Musicians

290 Huntington Ave.                    *Ph:* (617)585-1267
Boston, MA 02115                       *Fax:* (617)585-1270

**• 1391 • Frank Huntington Beebe Awards** *(Professional Development/Grant)*

**Purpose:** To promote advanced music study abroad. **Focus:** Music. **Qualif.:** It is expected that applicants have not previously studied abroad for an extended period. Applicants must develop a strong, well-planned project that will enhance their life work in music. Enrollment in a school or university is not required unless such study is an essential part of the project. **Criteria:** Selection is based on transcripts and recommendations, followed by tape, and then by audition.

**Funds Avail.:** $12,000. The award is intended to provide support including round trip transportation, room and board, and other expenses. **No. of Awards:** Varies. **To Apply:** Applications may be obtained starting October 1 of the preceding year by writing to the secretary of the Beebe Fund. **Deadline:** Usually mid-December; notification of semi-finalists is in February. The awarding of fellowship grants is in mid-April. **Contact:** Carol Woodworth, Executive Secretary, at the above address (see entry 1390).

---

**• 1392 •**

## Beinecke Rare Book and Manuscript Library

Yale University
PO Box 208240                          *Ph:* (203)432-2968
New Haven, CT 06520-8240               *Fax:* (203)432-4047
*E-mail:* robert.babcock@yale.edu
*URL:* http://www.library.yale.edu/beinecke/

**• 1393 • Beinecke Library Visiting Fellowships** *(Postdoctorate/Fellowship)*

**Purpose:** To support visiting scholars pursuing advanced research in the collections of the Beinecke Library. **Focus:** Cartography, History, Humanities, Literature, Natural Sciences, Theology. **Qualif.:** Applicant may be of any nationality. Scholars living anywhere in the world outside the greater New Haven area are eligible. Candidate must be pursuing postdoctoral or equivalent research that requires use of the Library's collections. The awardees must be in residence during tenure of the award and are encouraged to participate in the activities of Yale University.

**Funds Avail.:** The award is $2,500 living allowance, plus round trip travel between home and New Haven. **No. of Awards:** Varies, 12-15. **To Apply:** There is no application form; applicants should write to the director for guidelines and submit resume with brief research proposal emphasizing the relationship of the Beinecke collections to the proposed project and indicating preferred dates of residence. Two confidential letters of recommendation must be

sent directly to the director. **Deadline:** Materials must be submitted by January 15. Fellowships are announced in March.

**Remarks:** The Beinecke Library offers thirteen named fellowships: the Frederick W. Beinecke Fellowship in Western Americana, the Hermann Broch Fellowship in Modern German Literature, the Edith and Richard French Fellowship, the Donald C. Gallup Fellowship in American Literature, the Archibald Hanna, Jr., Fellowship in American History, the H.P. Kraus Fellowship in Early Books and Manuscripts, the H.D. Fellowship in English or American Literature, the A. Bartlett Giamatti Fellowship, the John D. and Rose H. Jackson Fellowship, the Jackson Brothers Fellowship, the James M. Osborn Fellowship in English Literature and History, the Frederick A. and Marion S. Pottle Fellowship in 18th Century British Studies, and the Alexander Vietor Fellowship in Cartography and Related Fields. The eligibility requirements and application procedures are the same as those listed above. **Contact:** Coordinator of Fellowship Programs at the above address (see entry 1392).

---

**• 1394 •**

## Beit Trust

PO Box CH 76
Chisipite
Harare, Zimbabwe                       *Ph:* 4 496046
                                       *Fax:* 4 494046

**• 1395 • Beit Trust Postgraduate Fellowships** *(Postgraduate/Fellowship)*

**Purpose:** To support research of benefit to Zimbabwe. **Focus:** General Studies. **Qualif.:** Applicant must be a resident of Zimbabwe and hold a good first degree (2.1 or better). Fellowships are only tenable in England, Southern Africa, and Ireland. **Criteria:** Applicant must return to Zimbabwe.

**Funds Avail.:** Tuition, room and board, books, and personal allowance. **To Apply:** Write for application form and guidelines. **Deadline:** September 30. **Contact:** Beit Trust Representative at the above address (see entry 1394).

---

**• 1396 •**

## Belgian American Educational Foundation, Inc.

195 Church St.
New Haven, CT 06510                    *Ph:* (203)777-5765

**• 1397 • BAEF Predoctoral Fellowships** *(Doctorate/Fellowship)*

**Purpose:** The purpose of the Fellowship is to allow American graduate students to pursue independent study and research in Belgium on projects for which Belgium provides special advantages. **Focus:** Area and Ethnic Studies. **Qualif.:** Candidates must be nominated by the Dean of their Graduate School, and only one candidate may be nominated by each university. Evidence of American citizenship and of a speaking and reading knowledge of French, Dutch, or German is required. Candidate must be under 30 years of age and have a Master's Degree or be working towards a Ph.D. or equivalent.

**Funds Avail.:** The amount of the stipend is $12,000 payable in the United States in four installments. Additional funds must be provided from other sources if the Fellow is to be accompanied by spouse and family. The tenure of the Fellowship is ten months. **No. of Awards:** 10. **To Apply:** Candidates must furnish a statement of the dissertation or research project and its current status; a proposed program of study to be undertaken during the period of the grant; a curriculum vitae; official transcripts of both undergraduate and graduate courses; and reasons governing the choice of the university or other institutions, including the scholars with whom they plan to study. Three letters of recommendation from professors who have knowledge of the candidate and his or her qualifications are also required. **Deadline:** Nominations and all supporting documents must be received not later than January 31; recipients are announced approximately April 1. **Contact:** Deans of Graduate Schools of American universities, or the Belgian American Education Foundation, Inc. at the above address (see entry 1396).

**• 1398 •**
## Alexander Graham Bell Association for the Deaf
3417 Volta Place, NW
Washington, DC 20007-2778          *Ph:* (202)337-5220
*URL:* http://www.agbell.com

**• 1399 •  Alexander G. Bell Scholarship Awards**
*(Graduate, Undergraduate/Scholarship)*

**Focus:** Auditory Oral college students. **Qualif.:** Candidate must be oral deaf and have a severe or profound hearing impairment from birth or before speech was learned. Speech, lip reading, or residual hearing must be the preferred and customary form of communication. Applicants are required to be accepted by or currently enrolled in a regular, full-time college or university program for hearing students. Applicants who have serious handicaps in addition to their hearing impairment are encouraged to apply. **Deadline:** All materials must be filed by March 15. **Contact:** Alexander Graham Bell Association, Financial Aid Coordinator, at the above address (see entry 1398).

**• 1400 •  Herbert P. Feibelman Jr. (IPO) Award**
*(Undergraduate/Award, Scholarship)*

**Focus:** Auditory oral college students. **Qualif.:** Applicants must be oral deaf men and women who were born with a severe or profound hearing impairment or lost their hearing before acquiring language. There are no geographic limitations. Candidates must use speech and speech-reading and/or their residual hearing as their preferred, customary form of communication; have been accepted by or currently attending a regular college or university for hearing students; and demonstrate a potential for leadership. Applicants who have serious handicaps in addition to their deafness are encouraged to apply.

**Funds Avail.:** One award of $1,000. **No. of Awards:** One. **Deadline:** All materials must be received by April 1. **Contact:** Alexander Graham Bell Association, Scholarship Committee.

**• 1401 •  Elsie Bell Grosvenor Scholarship Awards**
*(Undergraduate/Scholarship)*

**Focus:** Auditory oral college students. **Qualif.:** Candidate must be oral deaf and have had a severe or profound hearing impairment from birth or before speech was learned. Speech, lip reading, or residual hearing must be the preferred and customary form of communication. Applicants are required to be accepted by, or currently enrolled in a regular, full-time college or university program for hearing students and must demonstrate a potential for leadership. Applicants who have serious handicaps in addition to their hearing impairment are encouraged to apply. The candidate must be from Metropolitan Washington, D.C., or reside outside the area and attend college in Metropolitan Washington, D.C.

**Funds Avail.:** One $500 and one $1,000 scholarship. **No. of Awards:** Two. **Deadline:** All materials must be filed by April 1. **Contact:** Alexander Graham Bell Association, Scholarship Committee, at the above address (see entry 1398).

**• 1402 •  The Allie Raney Hunt Memorial Scholarship**
*(Undergraduate/Scholarship)*

**Focus:** Auditory oral college students. **Qualif.:** Candidates must be oral deaf and have profound hearing impairments from birth or before speech was learned. Speech, lip reading, or residual hearing must be the preferred and customary form of communication. Applicants are required to be accepted by or currently enrolled in a regular, full-time college or university program for hearing students. Applicants who have serious handicaps in addition to their hearing impairment are encouraged to apply. **Criteria:** Applicants should demonstrate a potential for leadership.

**Funds Avail.:** $250. **No. of Awards:** One **Deadline:** All material must be filed by April 1. **Contact:** Alexander Graham Bell Association, Scholarship Committee.

**• 1403 •  Oral Hearing Impaired Section Scholarship Award** *(Undergraduate/Scholarship)*

**Focus:** Auditory oral college students. **Qualif.:** Candidate must be oral deaf and have a severe or profound hearing impairment from birth or before speech was learned. Speech, lip reading, or residual hearing must be the preferred and customary form of communication. Applicants are required to be accepted by or currently enrolled in a regular, full-time college or university program for hearing students and demonstrate a potential for leadership. Applicants who have serious handicaps in addition to their hearing impairment are encouraged to apply.

**Funds Avail.:** $1000 scholarship. **No. of Awards:** One **Deadline:** All materials must be filed by April 1. **Contact:** Alexander Graham Bell Association, Scholarship Committee.

**• 1404 •  Volta Scholarship Award** *(Undergraduate/Scholarship)*

**Focus:** Auditory oral college students. **Qualif.:** Candidate must be oral deaf and have a severe or profound hearing impairment from birth or before speech was learned. Speech, lip reading, or residual hearing must be the preferred and customary form of communication. Applicants are required to be accepted by or currently enrolled in a regular, full-time college or university program for hearing students and demonstrate leadership potential. Applicants who have serious handicaps in addition to their hearing impairment are encouraged to apply.

**Funds Avail.:** $500. **No. of Awards:** 1. **Deadline:** All materials must be filed by April 1. **Contact:** Alexander Graham Bell Association, Scholarship Committee, at the above address (see entry 1398).

**• 1405 •  David J. Von Hagen Scholarship Award** *(Undergraduate/Scholarship)*

**Focus:** Science or engineering. **Qualif.:** Candidate must be oral deaf and have had a profound hearing impairment from birth or before speech was learned. Speech, lip reading, or residual hearing must be the preferred and customary form of communication. Applicants are required to be accepted by, or currently enrolled in a regular, full-time college or university program for hearing students and demonstrate potential for leadership. Applicants who have serious handicaps in addition to their hearing impairment are encouraged to apply. **Criteria:** Preference is given to science or engineering students.

**Funds Avail.:** Two scholarships of $750 are awarded. **No. of Awards:** Two **Deadline:** All materials must be filed by April 1. **Contact:** Alexander Graham Bell Association, Scholarship Committee, at the above address (see entry 1398).

**• 1406 •  Robert H. Weitbrecht Scholarship Award** *(Undergraduate/Scholarship)*

**Focus:** Science, Engineering. **Qualif.:** Applicants must be oral deaf men and women who were born with a profound hearing

*Alexander Graham Bell Association for the Deaf (continued)*

impairment or lost their hearing before acquiring language. There are no geographic limitations. Candidates must use speech and speech-reading and/or their residual hearing as their preferred, customary form of communication; have been accepted by or attend a regular college or university for hearing students; and demonstrate a potential for leadership. Applicants who have serious handicaps in addition to their deafness are encouraged to apply. **Criteria:** Preference is given to science and engineering students.

**Funds Avail.:** Two scholarships of $750 are awarded. **No. of Awards:** Two. **Deadline:** All materials must be received by April 1. **Contact:** Alexander Graham Bell, Scholarship Committee, at the above address (see entry 1398).

• 1407 • **Maude Winkler Scholarship Awards** *(Graduate, Undergraduate/Scholarship)*

**Focus:** Auditory oral college students. **Qualif.:** Candidate must be oral deaf and have a severe or profound hearing impairment from birth or before speech was learned. Speech, lip reading, or residual hearing must be the preferred and customary form of communication. Applicants are required to be accepted by or currently enrolled in a regular, full-time college or university program for hearing students and demonstrate potential for leadership. Applicants who have serious handicaps in addition to their hearing impairment are encouraged to apply.

**Funds Avail.:** Five scholarships of $1,000 each are awarded. R One year.

• 1408 •
**Bement Educational Grants Committee**
37 Chestnut St.                    *Ph:* (413)737-4786
Springfield, MA 01103              *Fax:* (413)746-9873

• 1409 • **Bement Educational Grants** *(Undergraduate/Grant)*

**Purpose:** Help young people active in the Episcopal Church to pursue their educational goals after secondary school. **Focus:** General Studies. **Qualif.:** Applicants must be single, active members of the Episcopal Diocese of Western Massachusetts, demonstrating financial need, and planning to obtain a degree in any subject at any two- or four- year college. **Criteria:** Based on qualifications and an interview with a member of the Grants Committee.

**Funds Avail.:** Up to $750 is offered to each recipient. **No. of Awards:** Varies. **To Apply:** Candidates should first obtain a form from the Committee. They must also submit a Financial Aid Form, three references (including one from a member of the clergy), transcripts, and a personal letter from the student. **Deadline:** February 15. **Contact:** Bement Educational Grants Committee at the above address (see entry 1408).

• 1410 •
**Benevolent Foundation - Scottish Rite Schitzophrenia Research Program Office**
PO Box 519
33 Marrett Road
Lexington, MA 02173                *Ph:* (617)862-4410

• 1411 • **Benevolent Foundation Dissertation Research Fellowships** *(Postdoctorate/Fellowship)*

**Purpose:** To assist doctoral students preparing dissertations in fields related to schizophrenia. **Focus:** Schizophrenia. **Qualif.:** Candidate may be of any nationality. Applicant must have completed all requirements, including course work, for the doctoral dissertation by the beginning of the fellowship year. Candidate's dissertation must be in a field relevant to schizophrenia research. Application must be initiated by letter from a scientist willing to sponsor candidate.

**Funds Avail.:** $12,000/year. **To Apply:** Sponsor should submit letter to the Program Office, including evidence of the candidate's distinction in graduate studies and an outline of the proposed research. If candidate's qualifications and interests are appropriate, application form will be forwarded. Candidate should then submit ten copies of form with collated proposal and supplementary material. Letters of recommendation and academic transcripts must be sent directly to the Program Office. **Deadline:** Sponsoring letter: February 1; application: March 15. **Contact:** Nancy L. Maxwell, Administrator, at the above address (see entry 1410).

• 1412 • **Benevolent Foundation Research Grants** *(Postdoctorate/Grant)*

**Purpose:** To support innovative research into the nature and causes of schizophrenia. **Focus:** Schizophrenia. **Qualif.:** Applicant may be of any nationality. Candidate must be conducting research in the cause, diagnosis, or prevention of schizophrenia. Grants are intended for clearly defined research projects rather than for general laboratory support or for advanced training. Pilot projects are preferred to established lines of investigation. Postdoctoral candidates may apply jointly with the senior scientist at the host laboratory.

**Funds Avail.:** $30,000/year direct costs with maximum of 15% indirect costs. **To Apply:** Submit initial letter of no more than three pages listing the project title and names of investigators (plus best mail address and telephone) and the specific aims and significance of the proposed research to Dr. Steven Matthysse, Research Director at the above address. If the Foundation is interested, application form will be forwarded. **Deadline:** Initial letter: December 15; application: March 15. **Contact:** Nancy L. Maxwell, Administrator, at the above address (see entry 1410).

• 1413 •
**Berkshire District Medical Society**
741 North St.                      *Ph:* (413)442-9900
Pittsfield, MA 01201               *Fax:* (413)499-3349

• 1414 • **Berkshire District Medical Society Medical School Scholarship Loan** *(Graduate/Loan)*

**Focus:** Medicine. **Qualif.:** Applicants must be residents of Berkshire County, Massachusetts and accepted at an approved medical school in the United States or Canada. **Criteria:** Applicants are chosen based on financial need.

**Funds Avail.:** Loans of up to $4,000. Loan is set up on a revolving basis so that repaid funds will help as many medical students as possible. Recipients sign agreements pledging to begin repayment of the scholarship loan (unsecured and bearing no interest) the year of graduation, with half the amount to be repaid in four years and the balance within the following two years. **No. of Awards:** Varies according to the amount that is available. **To Apply:** Requests for applications should be directed to the above address. **Deadline:** Applications must be in by April 1.

**Remarks:** Recipients are asked to consider serving residencies in Berkshire County Hospitals. **Contact:** Berkshire District Medical Society at the above address (see entry 1413).

---

**• 1415 •**

## Bermuda Biological Station for Research, Inc.

17 Biological Lane      *Ph:* (809)297-1880
Ferry Reach GE 01, Bermuda      *Fax:* (809)297-8143

**• 1416 • Bermuda Biological Station Grants-in-Aid**
*(Professional Development/Grant)*

**Purpose:** To support research in atmospheric and marine sciences. **Focus:** Atmospheric Sciences, Marine Sciences. **Qualif.:** Candidate may be of any nationality. Candidate must wish to conduct atmospheric or marine science research in Bermuda. Grants are intended to defray in-house charges such as laboratory fees and boat or truck rental. Grants are tenable in Bermuda.

**Funds Avail.:** $200-2,500. **To Apply:** Write to the Director for application guidelines. Submit proposal containing: abstract, curriculum vitae, budget, and background, objectives, methods, and significance of proposed research including justification for choosing Bermuda as a site. **Deadline:** March 1 and October 1, for summer or winter projects respectively. **Contact:** Dr. Anthony H. Knap, Director, at the above address (see entry 1415).

**• 1417 • Bermuda Biological Station Summer Course Scholarships** *(Graduate, Undergraduate/ Scholarship)*

**Purpose:** To provide the opportunity for summer studies at the Station. **Focus:** Environmental Sciences, Marine Sciences. **Qualif.:** Applicant may be of any nationality. Candidate must be a graduate or upper-level undergraduate engaged in studies relevant to marine chemistry, pollution, global change, or marine biology. Scholarships are tenable at the Station and provide partial support of summer course tuition and room and board.

**Funds Avail.:** Usually 60% of course costs. **To Apply:** Write to the director for application guidelines. Submit letter of application stating reason for taking course, current transcripts, two letters of recommendation, and brief statement of financial need. **Deadline:** March 1. **Contact:** Robert S. Jones, Education Director, at the above address (see entry 1415).

**• 1418 • Bermuda Biological Station Visiting Graduate Internships** *(Graduate, Postgraduate/ Internship)*

**Purpose:** To enable graduate students to conduct thesis research at the Station. **Focus:** Environmental Sciences, Marine Biology, Oceanography. **Qualif.:** Candidate may be of any nationality. Candidate must be enrolled in a Ph.D. or M.S. program. Applicant's thesis topic must be approved by his/her adviser and department. Candidate's proposed project must be relevant to the oligotrophic open ocean, coral reefs, or inshore marine environment. Internships are tenable at the station.

**Funds Avail.:** Housing and laboratory fees worth $3,000-15,000. **To Apply:** Write to the director for application guidelines. Submit letter of application, a concise research proposal, graduate transcripts, and two letters of recommendation. **Deadline:** October 1. **Contact:** Robert S. Jones, Education Director, at the above address (see entry 1415).

**• 1419 •**

## Bertelsmann A.G.

1540 Broadway, 33rd Fl.      *Ph:* (212)930-4978
New York, NY 10036      *Fax:* (212)930-4783

**• 1420 • World of Expression Scholarship Program**
*(High School, Undergraduate/Award)*

**Purpose:** To award scholarship aid based on artistic expression and overall creativity in the fields of music and literature. **Focus:** Music Composition, Creative Writing. **Qualif.:** Applicants must be New York City public high school seniors planning to continue their education in any field. Students may enter in two categories: musical composition and/or literary composition. Musical composition entries must be submitted as either a written musical composition or an instrumental and/or lyrical musical composition on audio cassette tape. Compositions submitted on cassette must be no longer than 10 minutes, labeled with the composition title, student's name, telephone number and school, and may be recorded on any type of recording equipment. Submissions on digital audio tapes as well as written lyrics without music and foreign language submissions will not be eligible. Any form of sampling is not eligible. Literary composition entries must be in the form of poetry, a short story, a scene from a play, or a satirical piece. All submissions must be double spaced, typed, no longer than 2,500 words, and must include the title on each page of the submission. Neither previously published or awarded material nor foreign language submissions will be accepted. Students with family members employed by Bertelsmann or its subsidiaries, divisions, or affiliates are not eligible. **Criteria:** Music composition - entries are judged on content and form according to the chosen genre, and on artistic expression and overall creativity. The complexity of the arrangement will not be judged unless it is a pivotal component of its form and content. The composition itself is judged and not the actual performance of it. Literary composition - entries are judged on content and form according to the chosen genre, clear and logical communication of ideas conveyed with appropriate language and usage, and on artistic expression and overall creativity.

**Funds Avail.:** First, second, and third prize scholarships are given in each category (musical and literary). First prize is $10,000; second prize $7,500; and third prize $5,000; 40 $1,000 awards are given out for runner-ups in literature; 15 $1,000 awards are given out for runner-ups in music. **No. of Awards:** 61. **To Apply:** Compositions must be accompanied by completed entry forms signed by the students, their teachers, and their parents or legal guardians. **Deadline:** March 1.

**Remarks:** Prize awards will be made by Bertelsmann directly to the student's choice of institution of higher education. If student does not enroll in any institution of higher education within two years of award, the prize is automatically forfeited. Winners agree to the use by Bertelsmann or any of its subsidiaries or divisions of their names, addresses, likenesses and entries for promotional purposes. **Contact:** Bertelsmann's World of Expression Scholarship Program at the above address (see entry 1419).

---

## • 1421 •
**Beta Phi Mu International Library Studies Honor Society**
School of Library and Information
   Studies
Florida State University
Tallahassee, FL 32306-2100
*E-mail:* beta_phi_mu@lis.fsu.edu
*URL:* http://www.cas.usf.edu/lis/bpm

*Ph:* (850)644-3907
*Fax:* (850)644-6253

### • 1422 • Doctoral Dissertation Scholarship
*(Doctorate/Scholarship)*

**Focus:** Library and Information Studies. **Qualif.:** Applicants must be completing doctoral research. **Criteria:** Based on the usefulness of the research topic to the profession.

**Funds Avail.:** $1500. **No. of Awards:** Only given when appropriate applications are received. **To Apply:** A letter from the Dean or Director indicating that the applicant is a candidate for the PhD degree with an approved dissertation topic and has completed the course work for a doctorate in library and information studies; a current vita; three letters of reference from professors indicating the importance of the research and the applicant's ability to complete the work; a work plan indicating the title and plan for the study including a time-line for completion; and a budget indicating how the grant will be used must be submitted. **Deadline:** March 15.

**Remarks:** Recipients are expected to submit a report pertaining to their study to Beta Phi Mu within one year of the completion of PhD. It also is expected that Beta Phi Mu will receive acknowledgment in the actual dissertation.

### • 1423 • Harold Lancour Scholarship for Foreign Study *(Graduate/Scholarship)*

**Purpose:** To allow U.S. library scholars to study abroad. **Focus:** Information Science, Librarianship. **Qualif.:** Applicant may be of any nationality, but must be a librarian or graduate student in library sciences. Awards are tenable outside of the United States; foreign study must relate to graduate or professional goals.

**Funds Avail.:** $1,000. **No. of Awards:** 1. **To Apply:** Write to the executive secretary, including a SASE, for application form and guidelines. Submit form and resume with statement indicating the relevance of proposed foreign study to work or studies. **Deadline:** March 15. **Contact:** Executive Director at the above address (see entry 1421).

### • 1424 • Sarah Rebecca Reed Scholarships
*(Graduate/Scholarship)*

**Purpose:** To assist graduate students in the library sciences. **Focus:** Information Science, Librarianship. **Qualif.:** Applicant may be of any nationality, but must be accepted into a program of study accredited by the American Library Association, plan to begin in the fall semester with no more than 12 hours.

**Funds Avail.:** $1,500. **No. of Awards:** 1. **To Apply:** Write to the executive director with a SASE for application form and guidelines. Submit form with five letters of reference. **Deadline:** March 1. **Contact:** Executive Director at the above address (see entry 1421).

### • 1425 • Frank B. Sessa Scholarship for Continuing Education *(Professional Development/Scholarship)*

**Purpose:** For continuing education of a Beta Phi Mu member. **Focus:** Information Science, Librarianship. **Qualif.:** Applicant may be of any nationality, but must be a member of Beta Phi Mu. Scholarship is tenable worldwide.

**Funds Avail.:** $750. **No. of Awards:** 1. **To Apply:** Write to the executive director with a SASE for application form and guidelines. Submit form with resume and an explanation of proposed study or

research. **Deadline:** March 15. **Contact:** Executive Director at the above address (see entry 1421).

### • 1426 • Blance E. Woolls Scholarship for School Library Media Service *(Masters/Scholarship)*

**Purpose:** For beginning students who intend to become school media specialists. **Qualif.:** Applicants must be accepted in ALA-accredited program, planning 12 or fewer academic hours.

**Funds Avail.:** $1,000. **No. of Awards:** 1. **To Apply:** Send SASE for information and application. **Deadline:** March 15.

## • 1427 •
**Beta Theta Pi Foundation**
5134 Bonham Rd.
PO Box 6277
Oxford, OH 45056
*E-mail:* aoffice@wooglin.com

*Ph:* (513)523-7591
*Fax:* (513)523-2381

### • 1428 • Beta Theta Pi Founders Fund Scholarship-Leadership Awards *(Graduate, Undergraduate/Award)*

**Focus:** General Studies. **Qualif.:** Any member of Beta Theta Pi who is an undergraduate or graduate student may apply for an award to assist him in pursuing his undergraduate or graduate study. There are no marriage or citizenship restrictions. The majority of the awards are made to undergraduates who will be fully active chapter members during the following academic year. Graduate Awards are made to current seniors, graduate students, or graduate school applicants. No limitation is placed on the number of Undergraduate Award and Graduate Award applicants from each chapter. However, a previous recipient of a Founders Fund Scholarship-Leadership Award may not apply for an additional award. **Criteria:** Selection is based primarily on scholarship, with further emphasis placed on service to Beta Theta Pi, leadership, and financial need.

**Funds Avail.:** $500-$2,000. **No. of Awards:** More than 80. **To Apply:** In addition to the application form, the applicant must submit a cover letter giving the reasons he desires and needs a scholarship. An official transcript of the college record and all grades received through the end of the last term is required. The applicant must supply a black-and-white glossy head-and-shoulders photograph to be used for The Beta Theta Pi Magazine article covering the awards. **Deadline:** Completed applications and accompanying material must be received no later than April 15. All applicants are notified by July 15 whether or not they receive an award. Official announcement of the awards is made at the General Convention. **Contact:** Founders Fund Scholarship Chairman at the above address (see entry 1427).

## • 1429 •
**Bibliographical Society of America**
PO Box 1537
Lenox Hill Sta.
New York, NY 10021
*E-mail:* bibsocamer@aol.com; bsa@bibsocamer.org
*URL:* http://www.bibsocamer.org

*Ph:* (212)452-2710
*Fax:* (212)452-2710

### • 1430 • Bibliographical Society of America Fellowships *(All/Fellowship)*

**Purpose:** To support bibliographic inquiry and research in the history of the book trades and in publishing history. **Focus:** Bibliography, Library and Archival Sciences, Publishing, History.

**Qualif.:** Applicant may be of any nationality. There are no formal academic or professional requirements; however, graduate degree-holders comprise the majority of candidates. Applicant may be a Ph.D. student. Candidate's proposed research may be in any discipline, but must focus on the book or manuscript (the physical object) as historical evidence. Projects that place primary emphasis on enumerative listings are not eligible for support. Funds may be used for short-term travel, living, and research expenses.

**Funds Avail.:** Up to $1,500/month. **To Apply:** Candidates should write to BSA for application form and guidelines. Submit form with a three-page summary of proposed research and three letters of reference. **Deadline:** December 1; notification February 28. **Contact:** Executive Secretary at the above address (see entry 1429).

---

• **1431** •

**Binational Agricultural Research and Development Fund**
c/o Lynn Gipe
USDA-ARS-NPS
5601 SUnnyside Ave.    *Ph:* (301)504-4584
Beltsville, MD 20705-5134    *Fax:* (301)504-4518
*E-mail:* mlg@ars.usda.gov
*URL:* http://www.bard-isus.com

• **1432** • **BARD Postdoctoral Fellowships; BARD Research Fellows Program** *(Postdoctorate/Fellowship)*

**Purpose:** To support cooperative research between agriculturalists in Israel and the United States. **Focus:** Agriculture and related disciplines, including Agricultural Economics, Agricultural Engineering, Animal Production, Soil Conservation, Veterinary Medicine, Water Conservation. **Qualif.:** Applicant must be a U.S. or Israeli citizen who has completed a Ph.D. degree within the last three years. Fellowships are designed to allow U.S. postdoctoral scientists to conduct research in Israel, and to enable Israelis to work in U.S. institutions. The award may not be used to continue any existing postdoctoral appointment; individuals already living in the host country are ineligible for support. Applicants for Research Fellows must be U.S. citizens who are research scientists affiliated with American nonprofit research institutions, universities, or government agencies. Candidate must make arrangements with a laboratory in the host country prior to submitting application. A senior scientist at the host institution must agree to supervise the proposed research project. **Criteria:** BARD's Technical Advisory Committee and Ex Director prepare recommendations for the Board of Directors.

**Funds Avail.:** $30,000 for Postdoctoral and $3,000 a month for Research Fellows. **No. of Awards:** 10 Postdoctoral Fellowships and one to five Research Fellowships. **To Apply:** Write to either address above or Dr. Edo Chalutz, BARD, PO Box 6, Bet Dagan 50250, Israel, 972-3-968-3230 (phone), 972-3-966-2506 (fax) for application form and guidelines. Submit form to either BARD office with research proposal; curriculum vitae and list of publications; authorization of the proposal by host institution and supervising scientist; and a letter from the host institution explaining relevance of proposed research to its research program. Three names of referees are also required. **Deadline:** January 15. Notification in May. **Contact:** Lynn Gipe, International Program Specialist, at the above address (see entry 1431).

---

• **1433** •
**Biochemical Society**
59 Portland Place
London W1N 3AJ, England    *Ph:* 171 580 6276

• **1434** • **Krebs Memorial Scholarships** *(Doctorate/Scholarship)*

**Purpose:** To support Ph.D. students whose careers have been interrupted for non-academic reasons beyond their control and/or who are unlikely to qualify for awards from public funds. **Focus:** Biochemistry and allied Biomedical Sciences. **Qualif.:** Candidate may be of any nationality. Scholarship must be held at a British university. Applicants are expected to have made prior arrangements with the university at which they intend to hold the scholarship.

**Funds Avail.:** Personal maintenance grant, all necessary fees. **No. of Awards:** 1. **To Apply:** Write to the Assistant Director, Personnel and Administration, for application form and guidelines. Applications must be submitted to the Society by the head of the applicant's university department. **Deadline:** The scholarship is offered biennially, in odd-numbered years. Only one scholarship is awarded at any one time. **Contact:** Personnel and Administration Manager at the above address (see entry 1433).

---

• **1435** •
**Black American Cinema Society**
3617 Montclair St.    *Ph:* (213)737-3292
Los Angeles, CA 90018    *Fax:* (213)737-2842

• **1436** • **Independent and Student Filmmakers Competition** *(Graduate, Professional Development, Undergraduate/Grant)*

**Purpose:** To encourage and support Black filmmakers to produce new and innovative works and to recognize and reward their accomplishments. **Focus:** Filmmaking. **Qualif.:** College students and independent filmmakers are eligible.

**Funds Avail.:** Awards of up to $3,000 are given. **No. of Awards:** 6. **To Apply:** Applicants must submit works on 16mm film or 3/4-inch videotape. Each film must be created, produced, and directed by black filmmakers. Contact society for application requirements. **Deadline:** February 27.

**Remarks:** Awards are given in mid-April. **Contact:** Dr. Mayme A. Clayton at the above address (see entry 1435).

---

• **1437** •
**Black College Communication Association**
Howard University
School of Communications
Dept. of Journalism    *Ph:* (202)806-7855
Washington, DC 20059    *Fax:* (202)806-4638
*Formerly known as the Association of Black College Journalism and Mass Communications.*

• **1438** • **Chips Quinn Scholars Program Internship** *(Undergraduate/Internship, Scholarship)*

**Purpose:** To increase minority participation in newspaper journalism. **Qualif.:** Internships are open to junior-level journalism students who are nominated through journalism programs that are members of the Black College Communications Association.

## Black College Communication Association (continued)

**Funds Avail.:** Winners are matched with appropriate paid summer internships at cooperating newspapers and with editors acting as mentors. In addition, they receive a travel stipend and, upon successful completion of the internship, a $1,000 scholarship. **Contact:** Dr. Lawrence Kaggwa, Dept. of Journalism at the above address (see entry 1437).

---

## • 1439 •
## Blakemore Foundation
c/o Griffith Way
1201 3rd Ave., 40th Fl.          *Ph:* (206)583-8778
Seattle, WA 98101-3099          *Fax:* (206)583-8500
*E-mail:* blakemore@perkinscoie.com

### • 1440 • Blakemore Foundation Asian Language Fellowship Grants *(Doctorate, Graduate/Grant)*

**Purpose:** To assist individuals to become fluent in Asian languages. **Focus:** Any fields which require Asian language fluency. **Qualif.:** Applicants must be pursuing an academic, professional, or business career that involves the regular use of an Asian language; have an undergraduate degree; be at or near an advanced level in the language; be able to devote oneself exclusively to the language study during the term of the grant; and be a United States citizen or permanent resident. **Criteria:** Greater weight will be given to applications where the regular use of the language plays a key part of the career program. Applications are also rated on potential to make significant contributions to the field of study or area of professional activity, prior experience in the country, a realistic study proposal and budget, and a superior academic, professional, or business background of the candidate.

**Funds Avail.:** Grants cover tuition, related educational expenses, basic living costs and transportation. **No. of Awards:** Approximately 20. **To Apply:** Application materials will be available after September 1. **Deadline:** January 15.

---

## • 1441 •
## Blind Service Association
22 W. Monroe, 11th Fl.          *Ph:* (312)236-0808
Chicago, IL 60603-2501          *Fax:* (312)236-8679

### • 1442 • Blind Service Association Scholarship Awards *(Graduate, Other, Undergraduate/Scholarship)*

**Purpose:** To promote the independence of blind and visually impaired people through education. **Focus:** General Studies. **Qualif.:** Applicants must be legally blind residents of the Metropolitan Chicago area. They must show proof of acceptance or pending acceptance at a postsecondary, accredited program. **Criteria:** Well developed personal goals and evidence of having worked toward these goals, and a good track record at school, or past school.

**Funds Avail.:** Awards are unrestricted, and may be as high as $2,500. **No. of Awards:** Varies. **To Apply:** Interested persons should call or write the Blind Service Association to ask for an application. Prior to the deadline, applicants must submit: a completed application (typed); an autobiographical sketch; certified transcripts from the school presently and/or most recently attended; two letters of recommendation from current or recent instructors; proof of acceptance at postsecondary school; and certification of visual status completed by ophthalmologist, optometrist, physician, agency executive serving the blind, or

other competent authority. Selected applicants will be interviewed by members of the Blind Service Association Scholarship Committee during March and April. Applicants should be prepared to discuss their level of need and how the educational programs for which they seek support will further their career aspirations. **Deadline:** Deadline varies every year, but is usually the end of March. Awards are announced at the Blind Service Association Annual Meeting during June. **Contact:** Anna Nessy Perlberg, Executive Director, at the above address (see entry 1441).

---

## • 1443 •
## Blinded Veterans Association
477 H St. NW          *Ph:* (202)371-8880
Washington, DC 20001-2694          *Fax:* (202)371-8258
                              *Free:* 800-669-7079

*E-mail:* cbentley@pop.erols.com
*URL:* http://www.va.gov/vso/bva.htm

### • 1444 • Kathern F. Gruber Scholarships *(Doctorate, Graduate, Undergraduate/Scholarship)*

**Purpose:** To defray a student's educational expenses and other academic fees. **Focus:** General Studies. **Qualif.:** Candidates must be the spouses or dependent children of a legally blinded veteran of the U.S. Armed Forces. The veteran need not be a member of the Blinded Veterans Association and the blindness may or may not be service connected. Veteran's blindness is defined as having central visual acuity of 20/200 or less in the better eye with corrective glasses, or central visual acuity of more than 20/200 if there is a field defect in which the peripheral field has contracted to such an extent that the widest diameter of visual field subtends an angular distance no greater than twenty degrees in the better eye. Applicants must also have been accepted for admission, or be attending an undergraduate or graduate program at an accredited institution of higher education or business, secretarial, or vocational training school as a full-time student. **Criteria:** Selection will be based on answers to questions on the application form, transcripts, letters of reference, and an essay.

**Funds Avail.:** Eight $2,000 scholarships and eight $1,000 scholarships. Recipients must reapply for subsequent years. **No. of Awards:** 16. **To Apply:** Applicants must submit completed application with high school and/or college transcripts, three letters of reference, and a 300-word essay on the applicant's post-education, lifetime career goals and aspirations. **Deadline:** April 15. **Contact:** Scholarship Coordinator, at the above address (see entry 1443).

---

## • 1445 •
## Blue Mountain Center
PO Box 109
Blue Mountain Lake, NY 12812          *Ph:* (518)352-7391
*URL:* http://www.bluemountaincenter.com/

### • 1446 • Blue Mountain Center Residencies *(Professional Development/Internship)*

**Purpose:** To provide a peaceful and comfortable environment in which writers and artists may work, without the distractions and demands of normal daily life. **Focus:** Visual Arts, Writing, Music. **Qualif.:** Applicants may be of any nationality, but must be established artists, creative writers, or nonfiction writers whose work addresses social concerns and is directed at a general audience.

**Funds Avail.:** Funds provide for room and board. **To Apply:** Send the following: brief biographical sketch; statement of proposed project; sample of work, including copies of reviews, if available; indication of preferred residency period; application fee ($20); and names of any former Blue Mountain residents known to the applicant. (There is no application form.) **Deadline:** February 1. Awards are announced March 31. **Contact:** Harriet Barlow, Director, at the above address (see entry 1445).

• **1447** •
**Blues Heaven Foundation**
249 N. Brand Blvd., No. 590       *Ph:* (818)507-8944
Glendale, CA 91203       *Fax:* (818)247-4118
*URL:* http://www.island.net/~blues/heaven.html

• **1448** • **Muddy Waters Scholarship** *(Undergraduate/ Scholarship)*

**Qualif.:** Applicants must be full-time college students in at least their first year of undergraduate study at a Chicago area college or university. They must be studying music, music education, Afro-American studies, journalism, folklore, performing arts, arts management, or radio/TV/film. **Criteria:** The applicant's academic achievements, extracurricular involvement, and financial need are considered. The scholarship selection committee includes professionals from the fields of music, journalism, education, and performing arts.

**Funds Avail.:** One $2,000 scholarship. **No. of Awards:** 1. **To Apply:** Applications are available February of each year. **Deadline:** March 31. **Contact:** Blues Heaven Foundation at the above address (see entry 1447).

• **1449** •
**BMI Foundation, Inc.**
320 W. 57th St.       *Ph:* (212)830-2520
New York, NY 10019       *Fax:* (212)246-2163
*E-mail:* pr@bmi.com
*URL:* http://bi.com/grantreg.html

• **1450** • **BMI Student Composer Awards** *(Professional Development/Award)*

**Purpose:** To encourage the creation of concert music by student composers. **Qualif.:** Applicants must be under 26 years of age, citizens of the Western Hemisphere, and engaged in the study of music. **Criteria:** Compositions are judged on evidence of true creative talent. Academic finesse, while not disregarded, will be considered secondary to vital musicality and clarity of expression.

**Funds Avail.:** $16,000 annually. **To Apply:** Write for application forms and official rules. Students may submit one score only. Tapes are allowed for electronic works only. **Deadline:** Early February.

**Remarks:** Telephone for student composer awards: (212)830-9702. Fax is: (212)262-2824. **Contact:** Ralph N. Jackson at the above address (see entry 1449).

• **1451** • **Pete Carpenter Film Composing Internship** *(Professional Development/Internship)*

**Purpose:** To give an aspiring composer of film music an opportunity for a tutorial period in Los Angeles, working with established film and television score composers. **Qualif.:** Applicants must be under the age of 35 at the time of application deadline. Candidates must have appropriate musical study background. **Criteria:** Winner is selected on basis of application

and a brief piece of music created as theme or background music for a film.

**Funds Avail.:** Up to $2,000 stipend for each year's winner. **No. of Awards:** 1-2. **To Apply:** Applications must be requested from the BMI Foundation. **Deadline:** Varies.

**Remarks:** Approximately 130 applications are filed each year. **Contact:** Theodora Zavin at the above address (see entry 1449).

• **1452** • **Lionel Newman Conducting Fellowship** *(Professional Development/Fellowship)*

**Purpose:** To enable a young conductor to work for a three-year period with the Los Angeles Young Musicians Foundation Debut Orchestra annum. **Qualif.:** Applicants must have a distinguished background in music study. **Criteria:** The winner is determined by the Los Angeles Young Musicians Foundation.

**Funds Avail.:** $5,000-6,000 per annum is provided to the scholarship program. Awards are given every three years. **Contact:** Ms. Edye Rugolo at (213) 859-7668 Information and application details should be requested from Young Musicians Foundation, 195 S. Beverly Dr. Ste. 400, Beverly Hills, CA 90212. (213)859-7668.

• **1453** • **Jean Pratt Scholarship** *(High School/ Scholarship)*

**Purpose:** To provide an annual scholarship to the Lovewell Institute summer program in Manhattan, Kansas where high school students write, compose, produce, and perform a full musical theatre work. **Qualif.:** Applicants must be between 14 and 18 years old. Talent in writing and/or performing musical theatre is necessary. **Criteria:** Student's background; audition tape or sample of writing.

**Funds Avail.:** Complete scholarship for summer program. **No. of Awards:** 1. **Deadline:** April 15. **Contact:** David Spangler, c/o Lovewell Institute for the Creative Arts, Rte. 5, Box 42F, Independence Ave., Big Pine Key, FL 33043. Telephone: (305)872-0011.

• **1454** •
**Boettcher Foundation**
Katie Kramer.
600 17th St., Ste. 2210 S.
Denver, CO 80202-5422       *Ph:* (303)285-6207
*E-mail:* info@boettcher-fdn.org

• **1455** • **Boettcher Foundation Scholarship** *(Undergraduate/Scholarship)*

**Focus:** General studies. **Qualif.:** Applicants must high school seniors ranking in the upper 7% of their graduating class and hold scores of at least 1100 in a combination of the SAT verbal and mathematics tests, or a composite of 27 or more on the ACT, and plan to attend one of the following accredited colleges and universities in the state of Colorado: Adams State College, Colorado Christian University, Colorado College, Colorado School of Mines, Colorado State University, Fort Lewis College, Mesa State College, Metropolitan State College, Regis College, University of Colorado, University of Denver, University of Northern Colorado, University of Southern Colorado, and Western State College. **Criteria:** Awards are granted based on academic promise, personality, strength of character, and potential for making a useful contribution to the people of Colorado in later life.

**Funds Avail.:** Full tuition and laboratory, health and other special fees; with 75A% of tuition provided by the Boettcher Foundation and 25% guaranteed by the college; a stipend of $2,800 to be used in defraying room and board expenses; and a reasonable allowance for books and required fees. **No. of Awards:** 40. **To Apply:** Applicants must submit a completed application form

*Boettcher Foundation (continued)*

which is available at the eligible institutions. **Deadline:** February 15. **Contact:** Boettcher Foundation at the above address (see entry 1454). Boettcher Foundation at the above address.

## • 1456 •
## The Boleslaw Monic Fund Foundation - The Netherlands Reinsurance Group
P.O. Box 141
1180 AC Amstelveen, Netherlands

### • 1457 • Boleslaw Monic Fund Prizes *(Professional Development/Prize)*

**Purpose:** To support written research on the insurance and reinsurance industry. Specific topics are assigned annually. **Focus:** Insurance and Reinsurance. **Qualif.:** The competition is open to applicants of any nationality, whether or not directly employed by the reinsurance industry. Entries must be typewritten, be in English, French, German, Italian, Spanish, or Dutch. The copyright in any entry which is awarded a prize will be vested in the Foundation.

**Funds Avail.:** D.fls50,000, which may be shared with other entries. **To Apply:** Entries must be submitted under a pseudonym. Under the same cover, but in a separate sealed envelope, a note is to be enclosed repeating the pseudonym and the name and address of the author. **Deadline:** Varies. **Contact:** Secretary/Treasurer at the above address (see entry 1456).

## • 1458 •
## The Robert Bosch Foundation Fellowship Program
c/o CDS International, Inc.
871 United Nations Plz., 15th Fl.      *Ph:* (212)497-3500
New York, NY 10017-1814                *Fax:* (212)497-3535
*E-mail:* info@cdsintl.org
*URL:* http://www.cdsintl.org

### • 1459 • Bosch Foundation Fellowships *(Postgraduate/Fellowship)*

**Purpose:** To promote United States and German relations by giving internships in Germany to young American professionals. **Focus:** Business Administration, Economics, Journalism, Law, Mass Communications, Political Science, Public Policy. **Qualif.:** Applicants must be U.S. citizens and have a master's degree or equivalent work experience. They must demonstrate outstanding professional and/or academic achievement and active participation in community and public affairs. A good command of the German language is highly recommended. Fellowships are tenable at high level German industrial and governmental organizations.

**Funds Avail.:** DM3,500/month stipend, plus travel allowances and, if necessary, language training. **No. of Awards:** 20. **To Apply:** Write for application materials and instructions. 36 candidates will be invited for an interview. **Deadline:** October 15. Fellows are announced in January. **Contact:** Elfriede Andros at the above address (see entry 1458).

## • 1460 •
## The Boston Globe
PO Box 2378
35 Morissey Blvd.                       *Ph:* (617)929-3120
Boston, MA 02107-2378                   *Fax:* (617)929-2018

### • 1461 • Boston Globe One-Year Minority Development Program *(Professional Development/Other)*

**Purpose:** To serve as a polishing program for journalists with 6 months to 3 years experience. **Focus:** Journalism. **Qualif.:** Applicants must be minority newspaper reporters, copy editors, photographers, or graphic designers with some experience. **Criteria:** Six months' newspaper experience, aptitude for and interest in newspaper work.

**Funds Avail.:** One or two positions are available each year. About 70 percent of those completing the program are offered staff positions at daily newspapers. **To Apply:** Send clips and cover letter to Daisey Harris, Assistant to the Editor, at the above address. **Contact:** Daisey Harris at the above address (see entry 1460).

## • 1462 •
## Boy Scouts of America - Eagle Scout Service
1325 W. Walnut Hill Ln.
PO Box 152079
Irving, TX 75015-2079                   *Ph:* (972)580-2431

### • 1463 • Elks National Foundation Eagle Scout Scholarship *(Undergraduate/Scholarship)*

**Focus:** General Studies. **Qualif.:** Applicants must be active members of the Boy Scouts of America holding the rank of Eagle Scout and be graduating high school seniors and entering college freshmen. They must also have SAT and/or ACT scores acceptable to standards set by the selection committee and have demonstrated strong scout leadership ability, a good record of participation in non-scout activities, and require financial assistance to pursue a college education.

**Funds Avail.:** Four scholarships of $8,000 each, one for each of the four BSA regions, are awarded annually (paid $2,000 per academic year). Additionally, four scholarships of $4,000 each, one for each of the four BSA regions, are awarded annually (paid $1,000 per academic year). **No. of Awards:** 8. **To Apply:** Applications must be obtained from local Boy Scout Councils. A transcript of high school grades including SAT or ACT test scores, a letter of recommendation from the candidate's Scoutmaster or other leaders, and a statement from the candidate on what distinguishes his need for financial aid from others must accompany the application. **Deadline:** Completed applications must be postmarked to the Eagle Scout Service, National Scout Office by February 28th and received no later than March 5th. Recipients will be notified between June 1 and June 15. **Contact:** Local Boy Scout Councils. Councils.

### • 1464 • National Eagle Scout Scholarships *(Undergraduate/Scholarship)*

**Purpose:** To assist Boy Scouts of America Eagle Scouts in attending college. **Focus:** General Studies. **Qualif.:** Applicants must be active members of the Boy Scouts of America. They must hold the rank of Eagle Scout and be graduating high school seniors and entering college as freshmen. SAT and/or ACT scores acceptable to standards set by the selection committee are also required. They must also have demonstrated strong scout leadership ability, a good record of participation in non-scout activities, and must require financial assistance to pursue a college education.

**Funds Avail.:** Various scholarships, are available for the four geographic regions annually. Each scholarship is in the amount of $3,000 (non-renewable). **To Apply:** Applications must be obtained from local Boy Scout Councils September through October. A transcript of high school grades including SAT or ACT test scores, a letter of recommendation from the candidate's Scout master or other leaders, and a statement from the candidate on what distinguishes his need for financial aid from others must accompany the application. **Deadline:** Completed applications must be sent to the National Boy Scout Office by February 28th and received by March 5. The National Office sends applications to the appropriate regional scholarship chairman. Recipients are notified between June 1st and June 15th. **Contact:** Local Boy Scout Council.

**• 1465 •**
**Boy Scouts of America - Order of the Arrow**
National Office
1325 W. Walnut Hill Ln.
PO Box 152079
Irving, TX 75015-2079
*Ph:* (214)580-2438
*Fax:* (214)580-2502

**• 1466 • E. Urner Goodman Professional Scouter Scholarship** *(Undergraduate/Scholarship)*

**Purpose:** To assist members of the Order of the Arrow BSA who are preparing for a professional Scouting career. Grants are provided to help fulfill the financial obligations of their college education. The National Order of the Arrow Committee plans through this program to furnish a corps of high caliber service-minded professionals needed by the Boy Scouts of America. **Focus:** General **Qualif.:** Applicants must be members of the Order of the Arrow BSA who are preparing to enter a career in professional Scouting. The scholarship is intended for use primarily at the undergraduate level of study.

**Funds Avail.:** The amount of the scholarship is individually determined. Usually ranges from $1,000 to $5,000 per year. **No. of Awards:** Between 5 and 10 per year. **To Apply:** Included with the application should be a 250 to 500 word essay on applicant's reasons for pursuing a professional Scouting career, past scholastic and Scouting background, and records of employment. Also included should be letters of recommendation from two knowledgeable instructors, two adult scouters (one volunteer and one professional), the Lodge Staff Advisor, and a Council Scout executive. **Deadline:** January 15. **Contact:** Clyde Mayer at the above address (see entry 1465).

**• 1467 •**
**Edward Boyle Memorial Trust**
18 Park Crescent
Leeds LS8 1DH, England
*Ph:* 532 662671

**• 1468 • Boyle Research Scholarships** *(Doctorate/Scholarship)*

**Purpose:** To provide an opportunity for doctoral students from countries outside the United Kingdom to study at a U.K. university. **Focus:** General Studies. **Qualif.:** Candidate may be of any nationality except British. Applicant must have been accepted into a Ph.D. program or the equivalent at a university in the United Kingdom selected by the trust and hold an Overseas Research Student award. **Criteria:** Selection is based on first class Honors degree and on Referees' Comments.

**Funds Avail.:** £1,000/year maximum. **To Apply:** Write for application guidelines. Submit curriculum vitae, intended study program, and the names of two academic referees. **Contact:** Professor P.L. Marsden at the above address (see entry 1467).

**• 1469 •**
**Boys and Girls Clubs of Chicago**
820 N. Orleans, Ste. 235
Chicago, IL 60610
*Ph:* (312)627-2700
*Fax:* (312)248-0006

**• 1470 • Woman's Board Scholarship** *(Undergraduate/Scholarship)*

**Purpose:** To provide members of the Boys and Girls Clubs of Chicago a financial opportunity to continue their undergraduate education at the college of their choice. **Qualif.:** Applications are limited to high school graduates who are members and past members of the Boys and Girls Clubs of Chicago and have demonstrated leadership in school, community, and Boys and Girls Club. Members of other Boys and Girls Clubs throughout the country should not apply. **Criteria:** Financial need; academic potential; demonstrated leadership; written essay; interview.

**Funds Avail.:** 15 scholarships of $1000 each are awarded annually. Each is renewable for a total of four years if satisfactory academic progress is maintained. **No. of Awards:** 15. **To Apply:** Each unit of the Chicago Boys and Girls Clubs may nominate three candidates. Applicants must submit an application that is accompanied by letters from Boys and Girls Clubs staff and high school or college faculty members and by a narrative statement of 300 words that describes their background experience and future ambition. A personal interview is required with the Selection Committee which is composed of Board members, educators, and professional staff of the Boys and Girls Clubs of Chicago. Applications must be submitted by the club director. **Deadline:** March 1.

**Remarks:** Continuing counseling and communication regarding educational progress and careers is available to recipients. **Contact:** Julie Potter administrative assistant, at the above address,(see entry 1469) or the Club Director in the community.

**• 1471 •**
**BP America**
200 Public Sq.
10-3655-E
Cleveland, OH 44114-2375
*E-mail:* usaclv/regctr002/kochtj%bp@mcimail.com
*URL:* http://solstice.crest.org/renewables/eerg/bpa.html
*Ph:* (216)586-6491
*Fax:* (216)586-4050

**• 1472 • BP America Scholarship** *(Undergraduate/Scholarship)*

**Qualif.:** Applicants must be high school seniors who are children, including adopted and stepchildren, of regular full-time employees of BP America and its designated subsidiaries. Children of retired and deceased employees and children of company dealers, distributors, and jobbers are also eligible. Students must be U.S. citizens or permanent residents in the process of becoming U.S. citizens. Students must be in their last year of high school and planning to enter a regionally-accredited U.S. college offering traditional baccalaureate degrees. Applicants must also have taken the Preliminary Scholastic Aptitude Test (PSAT/NMSQT) in their junior year of high school. **Criteria:** A group of candidates who score high on the PSAT/NMSQT will receive further consideration for a scholarship. Students and their secondary school principals then file additional biographical and academic information with the National Merit Scholarship Corporation

## BP America *(continued)*

(NMSC). Winners are selected by an NMSC committee according to merit on a competitive basis and without regard to financial need. Factors considered include test scores, high school grades and class rank, qualities of leadership, and significant accomplishments.

**Funds Avail.:** Renewable awards from $1,000 to $4,000 as determined by NMSC. Factors considered include cost of attending the college of the winner's choice and their family's financial situation. Awards cover up to four years of full-time study or until baccalaureate degree requirements are completed, whichever occurs first. **To Apply:** Applications must be sent directly to BP America; PSAT/NMSQT scores are automatically forwarded by the National Merit Scholarship Corporation. **Deadline:** Applications must be mailed before December 31 of the student's junior year in high school. Winners are usually notified in March of the student's senior year.

**Remarks:** Winners must enter college in the fall term following selection and must pursue a course of study leading to one of the traditional baccalaureate degrees. They must also remain in good academic and disciplinary standing according to the regulations of the colleges they attend. NMSC report forms indicating academic progress must be completed and returned periodically.

## • 1473 •
## Brazilian Artistic and Cultural Society
Avenida Franklin Roosevelt 23, Sala
310
Rio de Janeiro, Brazil                    *Ph:* 21 551 1468

### • 1474 • International Music Contest of Rio de Janeiro Prizes *(Professional Development/Prize)*

**Purpose:** To encourage young pianists and singers who wish to perform internationally. **Focus:** Piano, Voice. **Qualif.:** Applicant may be of any nationality. Singers must be less than 32 years old. Pianists of any age may apply. The Competition is held in odd-numbered years in June in Rio de Janiero.

**Funds Avail.:** Piano: first prize: $3,500; second prize: $2,000; third prize: $1,500. Voice: first prize: $5,000; second prize: $3,000; third prize: $2,000. **No. of Awards:** 8 per competition. **To Apply:** Write for application form and guidelines. **Deadline:** January 1. Awards are offered biennially.

**Remarks:** Number of awards includes five for voice, and three for piano. The Gulbenkian Foundation invites the first prize winner of the singing competition to the official season at the Opera House in Portugal. Winners are invited to perform in concerts in other cities of Brazil and abroad.

## • 1475 •
## Bread Loaf Writers' Conference
Middlebury College                    *Ph:* (802)443-5286
Middlebury, VT 05753                    *Fax:* (802)443-2087
*E-mail:* blwc@middlebury.edu
*URL:* http://www.middlebury.edu/~blwc

### • 1476 • Bread Loaf Writers' Conference Fellowships; Bread Loaf Writers' Conference Scholarships *(Professional Development/Fellowship, Scholarship)*

**Purpose:** To provide an opportunity for writers to attend the Conference. **Focus:** Fiction, Nonfiction, Poetry. **Qualif.:** Candidate may be of any nationality. Within four years prior to application,

fellowship applicant must have published at least one, but not more than two, original books with a major house or press. Candidate for the tuition scholarships must not have published a first book, but must have had original work published in major periodicals and/or newspapers. Applicants for both awards may apply either as contributors to or auditors of the Conference. **Criteria:** Based upon publication credentials.

**Funds Avail.:** Fellowships: full tuition, room and board; scholarships: full tuition **To Apply:** A letter of nomination from a literary agent, publisher, editor, or another writer, must support an application. Submit either fellowship form with a copy of published book or galley proofs; or submit scholarship form with original work, either published or unpublished. **Deadline:** For letter of nomination: March 1; for application form: April 1. Notification in May.

**Remarks:** Working scholarships for partial tuition are also available to candidates who have not yet begun to publish. Write for further details. **Contact:** Carol Knauss at the above address (see entry 1475).

## • 1477 •
## Brigham and Women's Hospital
75 Francis St.                    *Ph:* (617)732-5559
Boston, MA 02115                    *Fax:* (617)738-6909
*URL:* http://www.pslgroup.com/dg/2416.htm

### • 1478 • F. Stanton Deland Fellowships in Health Care and Society *(Graduate, Postgraduate/Fellowship)*

**Purpose:** To provide the opportunity to participate in the management of an eminent health care institution. **Focus:** Clinical, Financial, and Management Aspects of Health Care Administration. **Qualif.:** Applicant must hold an advanced degree. There are no other specific background requirements. Fellows will be located primarily at Brigham and Women's Hospital in Boston, Massachusetts. Fellows are expected to give occasional seminars or tutorials, and to complete a project.

**Funds Avail.:** Stipend varies, according to professional and educational experience as well as need. **No. of Awards:** Two. **To Apply:** Write for application forms. Submit completed forms with curriculum vitae, personal and professional goals statement, and a project proposal. **Deadline:** February 1. **Contact:** Bruce Goldstrom at the above address (see entry 1477).

## • 1479 •
## The British Academy
20-21 Cornwall Terrace
London NW1 4QP, England                    *Ph:* 171 487 5966

### • 1480 • British Academy Visiting Professorships for Overseas Scholars *(Postdoctorate/Other)*

**Purpose:** To enable distinguished scholars from overseas to pursue research in the United Kingdom. **Focus:** Humanities, Social Sciences. **Qualif.:** Applicant may be from any country except the United Kingdom. Candidate must be of postdoctorate or equivalent status; both young and established scholars are eligible. Application must be made by a British academic who is willing to act as a sponsor for the visit and to undertake all administrative arrangements on behalf of the scholar.

**Funds Avail.:** £2,000 maximum. **To Apply:** Write for guidelines and application form. **Deadline:** December 31.

**Remarks:** Limited funds are available from the Academy to help meet the costs of overseas scholars contributing major papers at conferences held in Britain. Write to the above address for application form and guidelines. **Contact:** The British Academy at the above address (see entry 1479).

## • 1481 • Neil Ker Memorial Fund Grants
*(Postdoctorate/Grant)*

**Purpose:** To support research on Western medieval manuscripts. **Focus:** Medieval Literature. **Qualif.:** Candidate may be of any nationality. Applicant must have a doctorate in a discipline in the humanities or social sciences. Grants support all aspects of research related to the study of medieval Western manuscripts, including travel and publication. Preference is given to research of interest to British scholars.

**Funds Avail.:** £1,000. **No. of Awards:** Four. **To Apply:** Write to the Academy for application form and guidelines. Two references are required. **Deadline:** February 28. Notification is made within three months. **Contact:** The British Academy at the above address (see entry 1479).

## • 1482 •
## The British Council, Marshall Scholarships
c/o Cultural Department
British Embassy
3100 Massachusetts Ave., NW          *Ph:* (202)588-7830
Washington, DC 20008                 *Fax:* (202)588-7918
*E-mail:* study.uk@bc-washingtondc.bcouncil.org
*URL:* http://www.britishcouncil-usa.org

### • 1483 • British Marshall Scholarships *(Graduate, Undergraduate/Scholarship)*

**Purpose:** To support degree studies by U.S. citizens at British universities. **Qualif.:** Applicant must be a U.S. citizen who has graduated within the last two years (or is about to graduate) from a four-year U.S. college or university and must have earned a grade point average of 3.7/4.0 as an undergraduate. Scholarships are tenable at all British universities. Applicant may indicate two schools of preference, but final placement is made by the Commission. Awards are not granted to students who are already studying at a British institution for the purpose of continuing those studies. Scholar must attend the British university with the intention of earning an undergraduate or graduate degree there. Awards are rarely granted to students seeking medical degrees.

**Funds Avail.:** Full tuition grant, plus living, travel, and book allowances. **No. of Awards:** Up to 40. **To Apply:** Obtain application forms and guidelines from Marshall Adviser at the college or university, or from the British Consulate General in Atlanta, Boston, Chicago, Houston, or San Francisco, or from the British Council at the above address. Submit form with supporting documents to the regional center designated on application. Shortlisted candidates will be interviewed in November. Applications are also available on-line. **Deadline:** Mid-October for initial application. Scholarships are announced in December.

## • 1484 •
## British Digestive Foundation
3 St. Andrew's Place
Regent's Park
London NW1 4LB, England          *Ph:* 171 486 0341

### • 1485 • British Digestive Foundation Project Grants
*(Professional Development/Grant)*

**Purpose:** To encourage research into the causes, prevention, and treatment of digestive diseases. **Focus:** Digestive Diseases. **Qualif.:** Applicant may be a researcher of any nationality. Candidate should have about six years of experience after qualification. Awards are tenable in the United Kingdom.

**Funds Avail.:** £30,000. **To Apply:** Refer to announcement advertised in March/April and September/October in the British Medical Journal+FA or The Lancet+FA. Announcement will set forth topics and conditions for each award. **Contact:** Geraldine Oliver at the above address (see entry 1484).

## • 1486 •
## British Information Services
845 3rd Ave.                      *Ph:* (212)745-0200
New York, NY 10022-6691           *Fax:* (212)758-5395
*URL:* http://britian.nyc.ny.us

### • 1487 • British Marshall Scholarships *(Graduate/ Scholarship)*

**Purpose:** To support study leading to a degree at a British university. **Focus:** General Studies. **Qualif.:** Applicants must be U.S. citizens who will be under 26 years of age on October 1 in the year of application. They must also have obtained a degree requiring at least three years of study from an accredited, degree-granting college or university in the United States, maintaining a minimum 3.7 grade point average (on a 4.0 scale) for academic courses after the freshman year.

**Funds Avail.:** Covers tuition, residence, and related costs, and may include a marriage allowance. **No. of Awards:** Up to 40. **To Apply:** Application forms are obtainable after June 1 of each year. Submit original plus five copies of application form, letter of endorsement from college president or dean or employer, signed personal statement, proposed academic program, and college transcripts. **Deadline:** Completed applications must be submitted by mid-October of year preceding date of beginning scholarship study. **Contact:** Information and applications are available by writing to the British Marshall Scholarships at the above address (see entry 1486)or one of the following addresses: British Consulate-General, Marquis 1 Tower, 245 Peachtree Ave., Ste. 2700, Atlanta, GA 30303; British Consulate-General, 1 Sansome St., San Francisco, CA 94104; British Consulate General, Federal Reserve Plaza, 600 Atlantic Ave., Boston, MA 02210; British Consulate-General, 33 N. Dearborn St., Chicago, IL 60602; or, British Embassy, 3100 Massachusetts Ave., NW, Washington, DC 20008.

## • 1488 •
## British Institute of Radiology
36 Portland Place                *Ph:* 171 580 4085
London W1N 4AT, England          *Fax:* 171 255 3209

### • 1489 • Stanley Melville Memorial Award
*(Professional Development/Award)*

**Purpose:** To enable junior members to visit clinics and institutions abroad. **Focus:** Diagnostic and Therapeutic Radiology. **Qualif.:**

## British Institute of Radiology (continued)

Candidate need not be a U.K. citizen or resident but must be a member of the BIR, aged 35 years or younger. Visit must be taken within one year of award date. Award is offered every three years.

**Funds Avail.:** £250. **No. of Awards:** in 1993 One **To Apply:** Direct initial enquiries to the BIR Chief Executive. **Deadline:** December of the year preceding the award. The current award year scheduled is 1996. **Contact:** Chief Executive at the above address (see entry 1488).

## • 1490 •
## British Leprosy Relief Association

Programmes and Projects
  Department
Fairfax House, Causton Road
Colchester, Essex CO1 1PU,                    *Ph:* 206562286
  England                                     *Fax:* 206762151

### • 1491 • British Leprosy Relief Association
### Research Grants *(Postdoctorate/Grant)*

**Purpose:** To support research into causes of and cures for leprosy. **Focus:** Leprosy. **Qualif.:** Applicant may be of any nationality. There are no specific academic degree requirements. Research proposals must be connected with leprosy, be of a high standard, and have the backing of any ethical committee, if relevant. Grants are tenable worldwide. **Criteria:** Applications are considered based on merit.

**Funds Avail.:** £1,000-100,000 **To Apply:** Write for application guidelines and forms. **Deadline:** March, August, November. Applications are reviewed in May, October, and January. **Contact:** The Research & Projects Officer, at the above address (see entry 1490).

## • 1492 •
## British Psychological Society

St. Andrews House
48 Princess Rd. E                             *Ph:* 116 254 9568
Leicester LEI 7DR, England                    *Fax:* 116 247 0787
*E-mail:* mail@bps.org.uk
*URL:* http://www.bps.org.uk

### • 1493 • Postgraduate Study Visits Scheme
*(Postdoctorate/Grant)*

**Purpose:** To permit postgraduate students to acquire skills directly relevant to their research training. **Focus:** Psychology. **Qualif.:** A research student who is registered for a doctoral degree at a UK university may be eligible to undertake a study visit to another institution for a minimum of two weeks if the applicant and his or her supervisor confirm in the cover letter that the student has an income which either attracts no income tax, or is taxed wholly within the lowest (20%) tax band.

**Funds Avail.:** Up to £250 is awarded for a visit to an institution in the UK; up to £400 for a visit to an institution in another European country, and up to £600 for a visit to an institution elsewhere in the world. **No. of Awards:** 6. **To Apply:** Applications should be in the form of a letter marked to the Chair of the Scientific Affairs Board at the Society's office, making it clear what the student will gain from the study visit that cannot be gained from the institution at which the student is registered for a doctoral degree. A supporting statement by the supervisor and by the proposed host institution must be included. The applicant must state the amount needed to finance the visit and how much is being requested from the

Society. An account must be given of where any additional money is to come from. **Deadline:** November 20. **Contact:** Lisa Morrison, Adm.

## • 1494 •
## Broadcast Education Association

1771 N St., NW
Washington, DC 20036-2891                     *Ph:* (202)429-5354
*URL:* http://trv.malone.edu/BEAhello.html

*The Broadcast Education Association is the professional association for professors who teach radio, television, film, and all electronic media in colleges and universities.*

### • 1495 • Broadcast Pioneers Scholarships *(Graduate, Undergraduate/Scholarship)*

**Focus:** Broadcasting. **Qualif.:** Applicants must be planning to enroll in a college or university for degree work at the junior, senior, or graduate level where at least one department on the campus is an institutional member of the Association in good standing by the application deadline. They must also be studying any area of broadcasting. Current scholarship holders are not eligible for reappointment in the year following their award. **Criteria:** Candidates must show substantial evidence of superior academic performance and the potential to be an outstanding contributor to electronic media. They should be able to communicate interest in the broadcasting industry and provide evidence that they possess high integrity and a well-articulated sense of personal and professional responsibility.

**Funds Avail.:** $1,250 each. **No. of Awards:** 2. **To Apply:** Application forms are available from BEA or college campus faculty. Applicants must provide personal and academic data, transcripts, broadcast and other experience, a written statement of goals, and three references. **Deadline:** Application requests must be made by December 15, and application materials must be returned by January 16. Winners are announced at the annual spring convention of the Broadcast Education Association.

**Remarks:** These scholarships are sponsored by the Broadcast Pioneers, New York, NY. **Contact:** To request an application or for membership information, contact BEA at the above address (see entry 1494). Application materials must be returned to Dr. Peter B. Orlik, Scholarships, 343 Moore Hall, Central Michigan University, Mt. Pleasant, MI 48859. Questions may be directed to Dr. Orlik at (517)774-7279.

### • 1496 • Harold E. Fellows Scholarships *(Graduate, Undergraduate/Scholarship)*

**Focus:** Broadcasting. **Qualif.:** Candidates, or one of their parents, must have worked at a National Association of Broadcasters (NAB)-member station as an employee of that station, or completed a formal internship for credit and/or pay at that station. Formal implies some arrangement between school and station and does not include a person who works voluntarily and for whom no evaluation is made in the form of a paycheck or grade. Applicants must be planning to enroll in a college or university for degree work at the junior, senior, or graduate level where at least one department on the campus is an institutional member of BEA in good standing by the application deadline. They must also be studying any area of broadcasting. Current scholarship holders are not eligible for reappointment in the year following their award. **Criteria:** Candidates must show substantial evidence of superior academic performance and potential to be an outstanding contributor to electronic media. They should be able to communicate interest in the broadcasting industry and provide evidence that they possess high integrity and a well-articulated sense of personal and professional responsibility.

**Funds Avail.:** $1,250 each. **No. of Awards:** 4. **To Apply:** Application forms are available from BEA or college campus faculty.

Applicants must provide personal and academic data, transcripts, broadcast and other experience, a written statement of goals, and three references. **Deadline:** Application requests must be made by December 15, and application materials must be returned by January 16. Winners are announced at the annual spring convention of the Broadcast Education Association.

**Remarks:** This scholarships is sponsored by the National Association of Broadcasters, Washington, DC. **Contact:** To request an application or for membership information, contact BEA at the above address (see entry 1494). Application materials must be returned to Dr. Peter B. Orlik, Scholarships, 343 Moore Hall, Central Michigan University, Mt. Pleasant, MI 48859. Questions may be directed to Dr. Orlik at (517)774-7279.

**• 1497 • James Lawrence Fly Scholarships** *(Graduate, Undergraduate/Scholarship)*

**Focus:** Broadcasting, Law. **Qualif.:** Applicants must be planning to enroll in a college or university for degree work at the junior, senior, or graduate level where at least one department on the campus is an institutional member of BEA in good standing by the application deadline. They must also be studying media law or policy. Current scholarship holders are not eligible for reappointment in the year following their award. **Criteria:** Candidates must show substantial evidence of superior academic performance and potential to be an outstanding contributor to electronic media. They should be able to communicate interest in the broadcasting industry and provide evidence that they possess high integrity and a well-articulated sense of personal and professional responsibility.

**Funds Avail.:** $2,500. **No. of Awards:** 1. **To Apply:** Application forms are available from BEA or college campus faculty. Applicants must provide personal and academic data, transcripts, broadcast and other experience, a written statement of goals, and supportive statements from three references. **Deadline:** Application requests must be made by December 15, and application materials must be returned by January 16. Winners are announced at the annual spring convention of the Broadcast Education Association.

**Remarks:** This scholarships is sponsored by the law firm of Fly, Shuebruk, Gaguine, Boros, Shulkind and Braun, Washington, DC. **Contact:** To request an application or for membership information, contact BEA at the above address (see entry 1494). Application materials must be returned to Dr. Peter B. Orlik, Scholarships, 343 Moore Hall, Central Michigan University, Mt. Pleasant, MI 48859. Questions may be directed to Dr. Orlik at (517)774-7279.

**• 1498 • Walter Patterson Scholarships** *(Graduate, Undergraduate/Scholarship)*

**Focus:** Communications, Broadcasting, Radio and Television. **Qualif.:** Applicants must be planning to enroll in a college or university for degree work at the junior, senior, or graduate level where at least one department on the campus is an institutional member of BEA in good standing by the application deadline. They must also be studying for a career in radio. Current scholarship holders are not eligible for reappointment in the year following their award. **Criteria:** Candidates must show substantial evidence of superior academic performance and potential to be an outstanding contributor to electronic media. They should be able to communicate interest in the broadcasting industry and provide evidence that they possess high integrity and a well-articulated sense of personal and professional responsibility.

**Funds Avail.:** $1,250 each. **No. of Awards:** 2. **To Apply:** Application forms are available from BEA or college campus faculty. Applicants must provide personal and academic data, transcripts, broadcast and other experience, a written statement of goals, and supportive statements from three references. **Deadline:** Application requests must be made by December 15, and application materials must be returned by January 16. Winners are announced at the annual spring convention of the Broadcast Education Association.

**Remarks:** This scholarships is sponsored by the National Association of Broadcasters, Washington, DC. **Contact:** To request an application or for membership information, contact BEA at the above address (see entry 1494). Application materials must be returned to Dr. Peter B. Orlik, Scholarships, 343 Moore Hall, Central Michigan University, Mt. Pleasant, MI 48859. Questions may be directed to Dr. Orlik at (517)774-7279.

**• 1499 • Shane Media Scholarships** *(Graduate, Undergraduate/Scholarship)*

**Focus:** Communications, Broadcasting, Radio and Television. **Qualif.:** Applicants must be planning to enroll in a college or university for degree work at the junior, senior, or graduate level where at least one department on the campus is an institutional member of BEA in good standing by the application deadline. They must also be studying for a career in radio. Current scholarship holders are not eligible for reappointment in the year following their award. **Criteria:** Candidates must show substantial evidence of superior academic performance and potential to be an outstanding contributor to electronic media. They should be able to communicate interest in the broadcasting industry and provide evidence that they possess high integrity and a well-articulated sense of personal and professional responsibility.

**Funds Avail.:** $3,000. **No. of Awards:** 1. **To Apply:** Application forms are available from BEA or college campus faculty. Applicants must provide personal and academic data, transcripts, broadcast and other experience, a written statement of goals, and supportive statements from three references. **Deadline:** Application requests must be made by December 15, and application materials must be returned by January 16. Winners are announced at the annual spring convention of the Broadcast Education Association.

**Remarks:** This scholarship is sponsored by Shane Media Services, Houston, TX. **Contact:** To request an application or for membership information, contact BEA at the above address (see entry 1494). Application materials must be returned to Dr. Peter B. Orlik, Scholarships, 343 Moore Hall, Central Michigan University, Mt. Pleasant, MI 48859. Questions may be directed to Dr. Orlik at (517)774-7279.

**• 1500 • Vincent T. Wasilewski Scholarships** *(Graduate, Undergraduate/Scholarship)*

**Focus:** Communications, Broadcasting. **Qualif.:** Applicants must be planning to enroll in a college or university for degree work at the junior, senior, or graduate level where at least one department on the campus is an institutional member of BEA in good standing by the application deadline. They must also be studying any area of broadcasting. Current scholarship holders are not eligible for reappointment in the year following their award. **Criteria:** Candidates must show substantial evidence of superior academic performance and potential to be an outstanding contributor to electronic media. They should be able to communicate interest in the broadcasting industry and provide evidence that they possess high integrity and a well-articulated sense of personal and professional responsibility. Graduate students are given preference.

**Funds Avail.:** $2,500. **To Apply:** Application forms are available from BEA or college campus faculty. Applicants must provide personal and academic data, transcripts, broadcast and other experience, a written statement of goals, and supportive statements from three references. **Deadline:** Application requests must be made by December 15, and application materials must be returned by January 16. Winners are announced at the annual spring convention of the Broadcast Education Association.

**Remarks:** This scholarships is sponsored by Patrick Communication Corporation, Columbia, MD. **Contact:** To request an application or for membership information, contact BEA at the above address (see entry 1494). Application materials must be returned to Dr. Peter B. Orlik, Scholarships, 343 Moore Hall, Central Michigan University, Mt. Pleasant, MI 48859. Questions may be directed to Dr. Orlik at (517)774-7279.

## • 1501 •
### George M. Brooker Collegiate Scholarship for Minorities - Institute of Real Estate Management Foundation

c/o Kay Shannon
430 N. Michigan Ave.
Chicago, IL 60611-4090
URL: http://WWW.IREM.ORG/FOUNDAITON

*Ph:* (312)329-6008
*Fax:* (312)661-0217
*Free:* 800-837-0706

#### • 1502 • George M. Brooker Collegiate Scholarship for Minorities *(Graduate/Scholarship)*

**Focus:** Finance. **Qualif.:** Applicants must currently enrolled as full-time students in a graduate program that prepares students for careers instate and local government finance, have a baccalaureate degree or its equivalent, be legal residents of the United States or Canada, and be recommended by the Dean of the graduate program studied. **Criteria:** Awards are made based on career plans, strength of past coursework, present plan of study, letters or recommendation, and undergraduate and graduate grade point averages.

**Funds Avail.:** $3,500. **To Apply:** Applicants must submit an application form, statement of proposed plan of graduate study and career plans, undergraduate and graduate grade transcripts, resume, Dean's letter of recommendation, recommendation of other graduate program faculty (optional). **Contact:** Government Finance Officers Association at the above address (see entry 1501).

## • 1503 •
### Brookhaven National Laboratory

Physics Dept.
Upton, NY 11973
URL: http://suntid.bnl.gov:8080/

*Ph:* (516)282-4063

#### • 1504 • BNL Postdoctoral Research Associateships *(Postdoctorate/Other)*

**Purpose:** To promote postdoctoral study in basic and applied research in chemistry, physics (including accelerator physics), materials science, biology, oceanography, and medical science. **Focus:** Physical and Life Sciences. **Qualif.:** A recent doctoral degree is required. Persons of U.S. or foreign nationality are invited to apply. Persons from groups traditionally under-represented are especially encouraged to apply.

**Funds Avail.:** Approximately twenty-five new awards are taken up each year. Salaries are highly competitive for postdoctoral study in each discipline, and are normally subject to state and Federal income taxes. Minimum salary is $29,000. Postdoctoral Research Associates are eligible for the same employee benefits offered to regular staff, such as twenty-four days of paid leave per year, medical/dental/life insurances, and retirement contributions to the TIAA/CREF plan. The associateships are tenable at Brookhaven National Laboratory for one or two years initially, renewable to a total of three years. **Deadline:** The associateships may be applied for and taken up at any time throughout the year. However, most applications are submitted in the spring for terms beginning in September. **Contact:** E. Gail Williams, Office of Scientific Personnel, Brookhaven National Laboratory, at the above address (see entry 1503).

#### • 1505 • BNL Research Fellowship in Physics *(Postdoctorate/Fellowship)*

**Purpose:** To support postdoctoral research training in physics at Brookhaven. **Focus:** Physics. **Qualif.:** Applicant must be a U.S. citizen or holder of immigrant visas who has recently obtained Ph.D. in physics and a member of a traditionally minority group under-represented in physics. Fellowships are tenable at the Laboratory.

**Funds Avail.:** Salary and benefits (highly competitive). **To Apply:** Write to the Chairman's Office for application guidelines. **Deadline:** February 1. **Contact:** Chairman's Office at the above address (see entry 1503).

## • 1506 •
### Brookhaven Women in Science

PO Box 183
Upton, NY 11973

*Ph:* (516)344-2307
*Fax:* (516)282-7533

#### • 1507 • Renate W. Chasman Scholarship *(Graduate, Undergraduate/Scholarship)*

**Purpose:** To encourage women whose studies have been interrupted through family, financial, or other pressures to pursue a degree in the sciences, engineering, or mathematics. **Focus:** Science technologies, Engineering, Mathematics. **Qualif.:** Candidates must be re-entry women, citizens of the United States or permanent resident aliens, and residents of Nassau or Suffolk counties of Long Island, or Brooklyn or Queens, New York City. Applicants must be accepted for credit in a degree-oriented program in the sciences, engineering, or mathematics at an accredited institution. The program of study must be at the junior or senior undergraduate level, or first-year graduate level. **Criteria:** Selection is based on academic and life/career record, letters of reference, and a short essay on career goals. Finalists will be chosen on merit.

**Funds Avail.:** One-time awards of $2,000 are made directly to recipients, to be applied towards expenses associated with an academic program pursued on a half-time or greater basis. Recipients will be required to enter into an agreement with Brookhaven Women in Science in which Brookhaven Women in Science will reserve the right of claim to the award should recipients fail to complete two consecutive sessions of formal study (half-time or greater) in good academic standing. **Deadline:** May 1. **Contact:** C. Ruth Kempf at the above address (see entry 1506).

## • 1508 •
### Brookings Institution

1775 Massachusetts Ave., NW
Washington, DC 20036-2188
E-mail: bfinlaydick@brook.edu
URL: http://www.brookings.org

*Ph:* (202)797-6044
*Fax:* (202)797-6003

#### • 1509 • Foreign Policy Research Fellowships *(Doctorate/Fellowship)*

**Purpose:** To enable doctoral candidates to benefit from access to the data, opportunities for interviewing, and consultation with senior staff members afforded by the Brookings Institution and by residence in Washington, D.C. **Focus:** U.S. Foreign Policy, International Relations. **Qualif.:** Applicant must be a doctoral candidate at any stage of his/her dissertation research. Candidate must show relevance of dissertation topic to the Brookings research program, and evidence that the research will be facilitated by access to the Institution's resources or to federal government agencies. Award is tenable at the Institution.

**Funds Avail.:** $17,500, payable on a 12-month basis, for 11 months of research at Brookings and one month of vacation. The Institution will provide supplementary assistance for typing and other essential research requirements in an amount not to exceed

$600, plus access to computer facilities. **No. of Awards:** Varies. **To Apply:** Graduate department must nominate candidate by letter. Departments should nominate no more than two persons. Write for guidelines. **Deadline:** Nomination letter: December 15; application: February 15.

**Remarks:** Fellows may participate in appropriate staff conferences and seminars of the Institution and have access to the research resources available to resident staff members. Outstanding dissertations will be considered for publication by Brookings. **Contact:** Brian Finlay-Dick at the above address (see entry 1508).

---

• 1510 •

## John Carter Brown Library
Brown University Green
PO Box 1894
Providence, RI 02912
E-mail: jcbl_fellowships@brown.edu
*Ph:* (401)863-2725
*Fax:* (401)863-3477
*URL:* http://www.brown.edu/Facilities/John_Carter_Brown_ Library

*The John Carter Brown Library, founded in 1846 at Brown University in Providence, Rhode Island, contains collections of primary materials relating to virtually all aspects of the discovery, exploration, settlement, and development of the New World.*

• 1511 • **Jeannette D. Black Memorial Fellowship**
*(Doctorate, Postdoctorate/Fellowship)*

**Purpose:** To research the history of cartography or a closely related area. **Focus:** Cartography. **Qualif.:** Candidates may be engaged in predoctoral, postdoctoral, or independent research. Fellowship research must be on some aspect of the history of cartography or a closely related area. The fellowship is open to scholars from any country. **Criteria:** Applications are evaluated by committees consisting of members of the Brown University Faculty Liaison Committee to the Library and the National Advisory Council of the Library. Fellowships are awarded on the basis of the applicant's scholarly qualifications, the merits of the project, and the appropriateness of the inquiry in relation to the holdings of the John Carter Brown Library. Recipients are expected to be in regular residence at the John Carter Brown Library and to participate in the intellectual life of Brown University. Therefore, preference may be given to applicants able to take up the Fellowship during the course of the academic year, September to May.

**Funds Avail.:** A stipend of $1,000 per month. **No. of Awards:** One. **Deadline:** January 15. Announcements of awards are made before March 15. **Contact:** The John Carter Brown Library at the above address (see entry 1510).

• 1512 • **John Carter Brown Library Associates Fellowship** *(Doctorate, Postdoctorate/Fellowship)*

**Focus:** General Studies. **Qualif.:** Candidates may be engaged in predoctoral, postdoctoral, or independent research. Scholars may be working in any area of research related to the library's holdings. The fellowship is open to scholars from any country. **Criteria:** Applications are evaluated by committees comprised of members of the Brown University Faculty Liaison Committee to the Library and the National Advisory Council of the Library. Fellowships are awarded on the basis of the applicant's scholarly qualifications, the merits of the project, and the appropriateness of the inquiry in relation to the holdings of the John Carter Brown Library.

**Funds Avail.:** A stipend of $1,000 per month. **No. of Awards:** One. **Deadline:** January 15. Announcements of awards are made before March 15.

**Remarks:** Recipients are expected to be in regular residence at the John Carter Brown Library and to participate in the intellectual life of Brown University. Therefore, preference may be given to

applicants able to take up the Fellowship during the course of the academic year, September to May. **Contact:** John Carter Brown Library at the above address (see entry 1510).

• 1513 • **Brown Library Long-Term Research Fellowships** *(Postdoctorate/Fellowship)*

**Purpose:** To support research in areas related to the Library's holdings. **Focus:** New World History. **Qualif.:** Applicant must be a U.S. citizen or a U.S. resident for the three years preceding the term of the fellowship. Graduate students are not eligible. Fellows are expected to be in regular residence at the Library and to participate in the intellectual life of Brown University.

**Funds Avail.:** $16,000. **No. of Awards:** 3. **To Apply:** Write for application form and guidelines. **Deadline:** January 15. Fellowships will be announced by March 15.

**Remarks:** The long-term fellowships are funded by the National Endowment for the Humanities. **Contact:** John Carter Brown Library at the above address (see entry 1510).

• 1514 • **John Carter Brown Library Travel Grants** *(Doctorate, Postdoctorate/Grant)*

**Purpose:** These are small, short-term travel reimbursement grants, enabling qualified scholars to use the collections of the John Carter Brown Library for periods of less than two months. **Focus:** Colonial American History. **Qualif.:** Candidates may be engaged in predoctoral, postdoctoral, or independent research. Scholars may be working in any area of research related to the library's holdings. Grants are open to scholars from any country. **Criteria:** Applications are evaluated by committees comprised of members of the Brown University Faculty Liaison Committee to the Library and the National Advisory Council of the Library. Grants are awarded on the basis of the applicant's scholarly qualifications, the merits of the project, and the appropriateness of the inquiry in relation to the holdings of the John Carter Brown Library.

**Funds Avail.:** The amount of these grants varies with the distance traveled, but will not exceed $450 in any one case; overseas $600. **Deadline:** Grants are awarded throughout the year, with a required lead time of four months. **Contact:** The John Carter Brown Library at the above address (see entry 1510).

• 1515 • **Paul W. McQuillen Memorial Fellowship** *(Doctorate, Postdoctorate/Fellowship)*

**Focus:** General Studies. **Qualif.:** Candidates may be engaged in predoctoral, postdoctoral, or independent research. Scholars may be working in any area of research related to the library's holdings. The fellowship is open to scholars from any country. **Criteria:** Applications are evaluated by committees consisting of members of the Brown University Faculty Liaison Committee to the Library and the National Advisory Council of the Library. Fellowships are awarded on the basis of the applicant's scholarly qualifications, the merits of the project, and the appropriateness of the inquiry in relation to the holdings of the John Carter Brown Library. Recipients are expected to be in regular residence at the John Carter Brown Library and to participate in the intellectual life of Brown University. Therefore, preference may be given to applicants able to take up the Fellowship during the course of the academic year, September to May.

**Funds Avail.:** A stipend of $1,000 per month. **No. of Awards:** One. **Deadline:** January 15. Announcements of awards are made before March 15. **Contact:** The John Carter Brown Library at the above address (see entry 1510).

• 1516 • **Barbara S. Mosbacher Fellowship** *(Doctorate, Postdoctorate/Fellowship)*

**Focus:** General Studies. **Qualif.:** Candidates may be engaged in predoctoral, postdoctoral, or independent research in any area of related to the library's holdings. The fellowship is open to scholars from any country. **Criteria:** Applications are evaluated by

---

## John Carter Brown Library (continued)

committees comprised of members of the Brown university Faculty Liaison Committee to the Library and the National Advisory Council of the Library. Fellowships are awarded on the basis of the applicant's scholarly qualifications, the merits of the project, and the appropriateness of the inquiry in relation to the holdings of the John Carter Brown Library.

**Funds Avail.:** A stipend of $1,000 per month. **No. of Awards:** One. **Deadline:** January 15. Announcements of awards are made before March 15.

**Remarks:** Recipients are expected to be in regular residence at the John Carter Brown Library and to participate in the intellectual life of Brown University. Therefore, preference may be given to applicants able to take up the Fellowship during the course of the academic year, September to May. **Contact:** The John Carter Brown Library at the above address (see entry 1510).

### • 1517 • Touro National Heritage Trust Fellowship
*(Doctorate, Postdoctorate/Fellowship)*

**Purpose:** To fund research in the Jewish experience in the Western Hemisphere. **Focus:** General Studies. **Qualif.:** Candidates may be engaged in predoctoral, postdoctoral, or independent research. Fellowship research must be on some aspect of the Jewish experience in the New World before 1830. The fellowship is open to scholars from any country. **Criteria:** The Touro Fellow will be selected by an academic committee comprised of representatives of Brown University, the American Jewish Historical Society, Brandeis University, the Newport Historical Society, and the John Carter Brown Library, as well as a representative of the Touro National Heritage Trust.

**Funds Avail.:** A stipend of $1,000 per month, plus a research travel reimbursement allowance of up to $300. **No. of Awards:** One. **Deadline:** January 15.

**Remarks:** The Touro Fellow must be prepared to participate in symposia or other academic activities organized by the institutions represented on the academic committee and may be called upon to deliver one or two public lectures. The John Carter Brown Library can provide moderate-cost housing for the Fellow in close proximity to Brown University. **Contact:** The John Carter Brown Library at the above address (see entry 1510).

### • 1518 • Alexander O. Vietor Memorial Fellowship
*(Doctorate, Postdoctorate/Fellowship)*

**Focus:** Maritime History. **Qualif.:** Candidates may be engaged in predoctoral, postdoctoral, or independent research. Fellowship research must be on early maritime history. The fellowship is open to scholars from any country. **Criteria:** Applications are evaluated by committees comprised of members of the Brown University Faculty Liaison Committee to the Library and the National Advisory Council of the Library. Fellowships are awarded on the basis of the applicant's scholarly qualifications, the merits of the project, and the appropriateness of the inquiry in relation to the holdings of the John Carter Brown Library. Recipients are expected to be in regular residence at the John Carter Brown Library and to participate in the intellectual life of Brown University. Therefore, preference may be given to applicants able to take up the Fellowship during the course of the academic year, September to May.

**Funds Avail.:** A stipend of $1,000 per month. **No. of Awards:** One. **Deadline:** January 15. Announcements of awards are made before March 15. **Contact:** The John Carter Brown Library at the above address (see entry 1510).

### • 1519 • Charles H. Watts Memorial Fellowship
*(Doctorate, Postdoctorate/Fellowship)*

**Focus:** General Studies. **Qualif.:** Candidates may be engaged in predoctoral, postdoctoral, or independent research. Scholars may be working in any area of research related to the library's holdings.

The fellowship is open to scholars from any country. **Criteria:** Applications are evaluated by committees consisting of members of the Brown University Faculty Liaison Committee to the Library and the National Advisory Council of the Library. Fellowships are awarded on the basis of the applicant's scholarly qualifications, the merits of the project, and the appropriateness of the inquiry in relation to the holdings of the John Carter Brown Library.

**Funds Avail.:** A stipend of $1,000 per month. **No. of Awards:** One. **Deadline:** January 15. Announcements of awards are made before March 15.

**Remarks:** Recipients are expected to be in regular residence at the John Carter Brown Library and to participate in the intellectual life of Brown University. Therefore, preference may be given to applicants able to take up the Fellowship during the course of the academic year, September to May. **Contact:** The John Carter Brown Library at the above address (see entry 1510).

---

### • 1520 •
### Gabriel J. Brown Trust
112 Ave. E West
Bismarck, ND 58501                    *Ph:* (701)223-5916

### • 1521 • Gabriel J. Brown Trust Fund Loans
*(Graduate, Undergraduate/Loan)*

**Purpose:** To make loans to residents of North Dakota in need of financial assistance to attend a college or university. **Focus:** General studies. **Qualif.:** Applicants must be residents of North Dakota and have attended a college or university for four semesters or six quarters, or have acquired 48 semester hours of credit or its equivalent in quarter hours. Students attending Bismarck State College, Medcenter One College of Nursing, or the University of Mary are required to have attended only two semesters or three quarters, or have acquired 24 semester hours of credit or its quarter hour equivalent. Students must also have at least a 2.5 grade point average (4.0 scale) and be in need of financial assistance to continue their education. **Criteria:** Loan applications are judged on the basis of the need for financial assistance.

**Funds Avail.:** Recipients must sign a promissory note providing for repayment in monthly installments commencing one year after graduating or leaving school. Interest accrues at six percent per annum. **No. of Awards:** Varies with year. **To Apply:** Loan applications are available from the registrar or student loan officer of Bismarck State College or any four-year college or university in North Dakota. They are also available by writing to the Gabriel J. Brown Trust. **Deadline:** Applications are judged on or shortly after June 15, and funds are dispersed on or about September 1. Individual applications at other times are also welcome. **Contact:** Trustees Robert H. Lundberg or Susan Lundberg, Gabriel J. Brown Trust, at the above address (see entry 1520).

---

### • 1522 •
### Dodd and Dorothy L. Bryan Foundation
PO Box 6287
1st Plaza - 2 North Main
4th Fl., Ste. 401
Sheridan, WY 82801                    *Ph:* (307)672-3535

### • 1523 • Dodd and Dorothy L. Bryan Loan
*(Undergraduate/Loan)*

**Qualif.:** All applicants must be residents of Sheridan, Campbell or Johnson County in Wyoming, Powder River, Rosebud or Big Horn County in Montana for at least on year prior to the date the application is filed. Applicants for academic loans must be under the age of twenty-five at the time of application and have a GPA of at least 2.25 at high school graduation or last semester in college. Applicants over the age of thirty applying for vocational loans requires an affirmative vote of four directors for approval. **Criteria:** Loans are made based on personal interview and academic record.

**Funds Avail.:** Up to $4,000 per year. **To Apply:** Applicants must submit a completed application form, high school transcript or most recent college grade report, and most recent Federal Tax Return form filed by applicant, parents or guardian. **Deadline:** June 15.

**Remarks:** Applicants awarded loans must maintain a minimum 2.25 grade point average while enrolled in at least twelve credit hours per semester; must have both parents co-sign the note unless applicant is living with one parent, then that parent must sign. If applicant is married, spouse must sign the note; must carry life insurance with a collateral assignment to the Dodd & Dorothy L. Bryan Foundation, in an amount at least equal to the amount the applicant will borrow until graduation, and it must be kept in force until the loan is repaid in full. Failure to do so will cause the entire loan to become due in full; must arrange with the college or university office to have a copy of the applicant's grades sent to the Foundation office at the end of each reporting period (quarter or semester) until graduation even though the applicant may not borrow for every semester or quarter; must keep the foundation informed of the applicant's current address at all times and also that of the applicant's parents, if there is a change. Loans are automatically extended for succeeding school years if grade requirements are met. Repayments, on a monthly schedule, average $25.00 per $1,000 borrowed, negotiable with borrower at time of graduation or upon leaving school. Full repayment should be made as soon as possible so that other in need may use the money. **Contact:** Rose Marie Madia.

---

• 1524 •

**Mary Ingraham Bunting Institute of Radcliffe College**
34 Concord Ave.          *Ph:* (617)495-8212
Cambridge, MA 02138      *Fax:* (617)495-8136
*E-mail:* bunting_fellowships@radcliffe.harvard.edu
*URL:* http://www.radcliffe.edu/bunting

• 1525 • **Berkshire Summer Fellowships**
*(Postdoctorate/Fellowship)*

**Purpose:** To enable women historians to pursue historical research. **Focus:** History. **Qualif.:** Applicants must be women scholars who hold a Ph.D. degree in history and are working in any field of history. Women doing historical study who do not hold a Ph.D. in history are not eligible. **Criteria:** Applications are judged on the quality and significance of the project proposal, record of significant accomplishment, and the stage in the applicant's career. Preference is given to junior scholars and those who do not normally have access to Boston-area resources.

**Funds Avail.:** One $3,500 stipend for a summer appointment, July 15 through August 31. Private office space is provided, along with access to most Harvard/Radcliffe resources. The Berkshire Summer Fellow is expected to give a seminar presentation on her project and is requested to be in residence in the Cambridge/Boston area for a minimum of one month between June 15 and August 31. Housing is not provided. **No. of Awards:** 1. **To Apply:** Applications are available from the Institute. **Deadline:** January 15.

**Remarks:** Funded by the Berkshire Conference of Women Historians.

• 1526 • **Bunting Fellowship** *(Postdoctorate, Professional Development/Fellowship)*

**Purpose:** To enable female scholars, professionals, and creative artists to pursue independent projects at Radcliffe. **Focus:** General studies. **Qualif.:** Women scholars, creative writers, and visual artists are eligible. Scholars must have held the Ph.D. or appropriate terminal degree at least two years prior to appointment. Non-academic applicants, such as artists, writers, social workers, lawyers, and journalists, need to have a significant record of accomplishment and professional experience equivalent to a doctorate and some postdoctoral work. **Criteria:** Applications go through a two-stage selection process. All applications go to a first stage committee in the applicant's field (i.e., psychology, literature, etc.), which chooses a small number of finalists. Fellows are chosen from the finalist group by an interdisciplinary final selection committee. Applications are judged on the significance and quality of the project proposal, the applicant's record of accomplishment, and on the difference the fellowship may make in the applicant's career.

**Funds Avail.:** A $36,500 stipend for an 11-month appointment, September through August. Eight fellowships are awarded annually. Private office or studio space is provided, along with access to most Harvard/Radcliffe resources. Fellows are required to present a public lecture or reading in the Institute Colloquium Series or an exhibition in the Institute gallery. Bunting fellows are required to be in residence in the Cambridge/Boston area for the entire term of appointment. Housing is not provided. **No. of Awards:** 8-10. **To Apply:** Applications are available from the Institute on June 15th. **Deadline:** Applications must be postmarked by October 1. Fellows and alternates are notified in the beginning of April. **Contact:** Paula Soares at the above address (see entry 1524).

• 1527 • **Bunting Institute Affiliation Program** *(Postdoctorate, Professional Development/Other)*

**Purpose:** To enable female scholars, professionals, and creative artists to pursue independent projects at Radcliffe. **Focus:** General Studies. **Qualif.:** Women scholars, creative writers, and visual artists are eligible. Scholars must have held the Ph.D. or appropriate terminal degree at least two years prior to appointment. Non-academic applicants, such as artists, writers, social workers, lawyers, and journalists, need to have a significant record of accomplishment and professional experience equivalent to a doctorate and some postdoctoral work. **Criteria:** Applicants go through a two-stage selection process. All applications go to a first stage committee in the applicant's field (i.e. psychology, literature, etc.) which chooses a small number of finalists. Fellows are chosen from the finalist group by an interdisciplinary final selection committee. Applications are judged on the significance and quality of the project proposal, the applicant's record of accomplishment, and on the difference the fellowship may make in the applicant's career.

**Funds Avail.:** Appointment is without stipend, but includes private office or studio space and access to most other Harvard/Radcliffe resources available to all fellows. Affiliates come with funding from another fellowship, sabbatical money, or can afford a year without stipend. Affiliates are required to be in residence in the Cambridge/Boston area for the entire term of appointment. Housing is not provided. **No. of Awards:** 10-20. **To Apply:** Applications are available from the Institute. **Deadline:** October 1. Notification is made by April. **Contact:** Linda Roach at the above address (see entry 1524).

• 1528 • **Bunting Institute Peace Fellowships** *(Postgraduate/Fellowship)*

**Purpose:** To enable women to pursue projects relevant to the peaceful resolution of conflicts between groups or nations. **Focus:** International or Domestic Relations, Peace Studies. **Qualif.:** Applicants must be women committed to domestic or international policy work or involved in finding peaceful solutions, of an active or

## Mary Ingraham Bunting Institute of Radcliffe College (continued)

scholarly nature, to conflict or potential conflict among groups or nations. **Criteria:** Selection is based on the quality and significance of the proposed project, the applicant's record of accomplishment, and the stage in the applicant's career.

**Funds Avail.:** One $32,000 stipend for a one-year appointment, from September 15 through August 15. Private office space is provided, along with access to most Harvard/Radcliffe resources. The Peace Fellow is required to present a public lecture as part of the Institute Colloquium Series and be in residence in the Cambridge/Boston area for the entire term of appointment. Housing is not provided. **No. of Awards:** 1. **To Apply:** Applications are available from the Institute. **Deadline:** January 15.

### • 1529 • Bunting Institute Science Scholars Fellowships and Biomedical Research Fellowships
*(Postdoctorate/Fellowship)*

**Purpose:** To enable female scientists to pursue research in their fields. **Focus:** Sciences. **Qualif.:** Women scientists who are U.S. citizens or permanent residents are eligible to apply. Applicants must have held a M.D. or a Ph.D. for two years prior to the date of appointment. Applications are accepted in the following fields: molecular and cellular biology; biochemistry; chemistry; cognitive and neural sciences; mathematics; physics; astronomy; computer science; electrical engineering; aerospace/mechanical engineering; materials science; geology; naval architecture and ocean engineering; oceanography; and biomedical research. **Criteria:** Applications go through a three-stage selection process. All applications are initially reviewed by two selections of committees who are expert in the field and subfield of the proposed project. Finalists are approved by a third stage interdisciplinary committee. Applications are judged on the significance and quality of the project proposal, the difference the fellowship may make in the applicant's career, and balancing scientific disciplines.

**Funds Avail.:** $41,600 stipend plus $3,000 for research expenses. Housing is not provided. Funding pending for Science Scholars Fellowship Program. **No. of Awards:** 2 (biomedical fellowships). **To Apply:** Applications are available from the Institute. **Deadline:** October 1. **Contact:** Paula Soares, at the above address (see entry 1524).

---

### • 1530 •

## Burlington Northern Santa Fe Foundation
1700 E. Golf Rd.
Schaumburg, IL 60173-5860          *Ph:* (847)995-6177

*Santa Fe Pacific Foundation's various scholarship programs are administered by several different agencies. All correspondence should be directed to the organization listed in the contact section of each award.*

### • 1531 • Burlington Northern Santa Fe Scholarships
*(High School, Undergraduate/Scholarship)*

**Focus:** General Studies. **Qualif.:** Applicants must be sons or daughters of full-time employees or retirees of Burlington Northern Santa Fe Corp and its predecessor companies who have at least two consecutive calendar years of service with the company. Students must be high school seniors in the upper one-third of their graduating class, take the Scholastic Aptitude Test (SAT), and plan to attend an accredited college or university beginning in the fall term immediately following graduation. Brothers, sisters, grandchildren, nieces, and nephews, and other relatives of the employee are not eligible. **Criteria:** Selection is based on academic achievement, aptitude, character, SAT scores, and application. Satisfactory academic progress and successful completion of

studies each quarter or semester must be maintained for continued support.

**Funds Avail.:** Twenty-five $2,500 scholarships are given each year for up to four consecutive years. **Deadline:** November 30. **Contact:** For applications, contact Scholar Program Administrators, 3314 W. End Ave., Ste. 102, Nashville, TN, 37203-0916, (615)292-4379.

### • 1532 • Future Farmers of America Scholarships
*(Undergraduate/Scholarship)*

**Focus:** Agriculture. **Qualif.:** Active members of FFA are eligible to apply during their senior year of high school. Recipients are required to attend a land-grant college withing their home state.

**Funds Avail.:** $1,000. **No. of Awards:** Two scholarships per state for the following states: Arizona, California, Colorado, Illinois, Iowa, Kansas, Minnesota, Missouri, Montana, Nebraska, New Mexico, North Dakota, Oklahoma, Oregon, South Dakota, Texas and Washington.

### • 1533 • Hispanic American Scholarship Program
*(Undergraduate/Scholarship)*

**Qualif.:** Scholarships are awarded to high school graduates of Hispanic origin through the League of Latin American Citizens National Scholarship Fund.

### • 1534 • Santa Fe Pacific Native American Scholarships *(Undergraduate/Scholarship)*

**Qualif.:** Applicants must be Native American (at least 25 percent) high school seniors residing in Arizona, Colorado, Kansas, New Mexico, Oklahoma, and San Bernardino County, California. They must also be planning to attend an accredited college or university in the United States. Affiliation with Santa Fe Pacific is not required. **Criteria:** Winners are selected on the basis of academic performance in high school, with preference given to students of any of the sciences, including medicine, engineering, natural and physical sciences.

**Funds Avail.:** Awards range from $1,000 to $2,500 each. Financial need will determine the amount of the scholarship. **No. of Awards:** 5 awards are available. Two awards are provided for members of the Navajo Tribe; the other three are available to students of any tribal affiliation. Financial need will determine the amount of each scholarship. **Contact:** American Indian Science and Engineering Society, 1630 30th St., Ste. 301, Boulder, CO 80301-1014.

### • 1535 • Santa Fe Pacific Special Scholarships
*(Undergraduate/Scholarship)*

**Qualif.:** Students who are completing high school and entering an accredited U.S. college during the same year are eligible to apply. They must also be children of employees of Santa Fe Pacific and its affiliate companies. **Criteria:** Winners are evaluated on academic record, leadership qualities, extracurricular accomplishments, recommendations, the student's statement, and test scores. Selection is made according to merit on a competitive basis without regard for financial need.

**Funds Avail.:** Awards are $2,000. **Contact:** Santa Fe Pacific Foundation, Scholarships Program, at the above address (see entry 1530).

## Burns Memorial Fund
615 Macleod, No. 1109
Trail S.E.                          *Ph:* (403)234-9396
Calgary, AB, Canada T2G 4T8         *Fax:* (403)233-0513

### • 1537 • Burns Scholarships (Undergraduate/ Scholarship)

**Purpose:** To further post-secondary educational pursuits. **Focus:** General Studies. **Qualif.:** Applicants must be the children of the City of Calgary Police Officers or the City of Calgary Fire Fighters only. **Criteria:** Applicants must be registered as full-time students, and have graduated from high school. A high school equivalency or mature adult status will be considered. Applicants must apply before they reach the age of 25 years.

**Funds Avail.:** Varies. **To Apply:** Applications available by February. **Deadline:** June 30.

**Remarks:** Sponsored by the Burns Police Fund/Burns Fire Fund, Calgary, Alberta, Canada. **Contact:** Administrative Assistant, Burns Memorial Fund, at the above address (see entry 1536).

## Bush Artist Fellows Programs
E-900 First National Bank Bldg.
332 Minnesota St.                   *Ph:* (651)227-5222
St. Paul, MN 55101                  *Free:* 800-605-7315

### • 1539 • Bush Artist Fellowships (Professional Development/Fellowship)

**Purpose:** To provide artists with significant financial support that enables them to advance their work and further their contribution to their community. **Qualif.:** Applicants must be at least 25 years old at the time of application and residents of Minnesota, North Dakota, South Dakota, or the 26 counties in western Wisconsin that lie within the Ninth Federal Reserve District. They must have lived in one of those areas for at least 12 of the 36 months preceding the application deadline. Students are not eligible. Artists working in the following categories are eligible: literature (fiction, creative non-fiction, poetry), visual arts (two and three dimensional), choreography/multimedia performance art, film and video, scriptworks (playwriting, screenwriting), and music composition. Literature applicants must be published and scriptwriters must have had their work produced. **Criteria:** Applicants must possess strong vision, creative energy, and perservance, and will be judged on past endeavors, current work, the impact a BAF may have on the applicant's work and life, and the difference the artist may make in their region because of fellowship.

**Funds Avail.:** Stipends of up to $40,000 are available. **No. of Awards:** Up to 15. **To Apply:** Write for an application form. **Deadline:** Deadlines vary according to category. They are usually mid-October to mid-November. **Contact:** Kathi Polley at the above address (see entry 1538).

## Florence Evans Bushee Foundation, Inc.
1 Beacon St., Rm. 2000              *Ph:* (617)573-0100
Boston, MA 02108                    *Fax:* (617)227-4420

### • 1541 • Florence Evans Bushee Foundation Scholarship Grants (Undergraduate/Scholarship)

**Focus:** General Studies. **Qualif.:** Applicants must be undergraduate college students who reside in the towns of Byfield, Newbury, Newburyport, Rowley, or West Newbury in Massachusetts. **To Apply:** Students who matriculate at one of the four high schools in the areas listed above are informed through their respective schools. **Deadline:** May 1. **Contact:** Danielle Meltz, Florence Evans Bushee Foundation, at the above address (see entry 1540). Alternate telephone: (617)573-0556.

## Business Press Educational Foundation
675 3rd Ave. Ste. 415
New York, NY 10017                  *Ph:* (212)661-6360

### • 1543 • Business Press Educational Foundation Student Intern Program (Graduate, Undergraduate/ Internship)

**Purpose:** Annual summer internships in business press editorial. Internships take place at specialized business magazines nationwide. **Focus:** Business journalism. **Qualif.:** Juniors, non-graduating seniors and graduate students should apply through their journalism professors. **Deadline:** Professors receive applications in October. Qualified students must apply by the last Wednesday of November.

**Remarks:** BPEF emphasizes full representation of the U.S. population and encourages minorities and mature students to apply.

## Business and Professional Women's Foundation
2012 Massachusetts Ave., NW         *Ph:* (202)293-1200
Washington, DC 20036                *Fax:* (202)861-0298

### • 1545 • Avon Products Foundation Scholarship Program for Women in Business Studies (Graduate, Professional Development, Undergraduate/Scholarship)

**Purpose:** To assist women seeking the education necessary for entry or re-entry into the work force, or career advancement in a business-related field. **Focus:** Business Administration, Management, Accounting, Marketing and Distribution, Business. **Qualif.:** Applicants must be women 25 years or older who are U.S. citizens. They must be officially accepted into an accredited program or course of study at a U.S. institution, including institutions in Puerto Rico and the Virgin Islands; graduating within 12 to 24 months; able to demonstrate critical need for financial assistance (annual gross income of 25,000 or less for family of four); and studying in a business-related field such as management, business administration, marketing, sales, or accounting. They must have a definite plan to use the desired training to upgrade skills for career advancement, to train for a new career field, or to enter or re-enter the job market. This scholarship does not cover study at the doctoral level.

**Funds Avail.:** $1,000 scholarships for full-time programs at the undergraduate and graduate level. **To Apply:** To receive

## Business and Professional Women's Foundation (continued)

application packet (available October 1 through April 1), send an application request with a business size, self-addressed envelope, double-stamped (first class) envelope, and enrollment verification to the BPW Foundation. **Deadline:** April 15. **Contact:** Business and Professional Women's Foundation, Educational Programs, at the above address (see entry 1544).

### • 1546 • BPW Career Advancement Scholarships (Graduate, Undergraduate/Scholarship)

**Purpose:** To assist women seeking the education necessary for entry or re-entry into the workforce or advancement within a career field. The program was conceived as a concrete, practical means to achieve the Foundation's mission of improving the economic status of all workingwomen. **Focus:** Computer and Information Sciences, Education, Law, Science, Engineering. **Qualif.:** Scholarships are awarded for full-time or part-time programs of study in the fields of computer science, education, paralegal, engineering, or science, and for professional degrees (health care fields are not covered). Applicants must be women 30 years of age or older; citizens of the United States; officially accepted into an accredited program or course of study at a United States institution; graduating within 12 to 24 months from August 31 of the application year; and able to demonstrate critical need for financial assistance to upgrade skills or complete education for career advancement. They must have a definite plan to use the desired training to improve chances for advancement, train for a new career field, or re-enter the job market. This scholarship program does not cover study at the doctoral level, correspondence courses, or non-degree programs.

**Funds Avail.:** Scholarships range from $500 to $1,000. **To Apply:** To receive an application packet, a scholarship application request must be submitted to the BPW Foundation. Applicants must enclose the following with the application request: a business-size, self-addressed envelope with two first class stamps. Photo copies of the application form will not be accepted. Application materials are available between October 1 and April 1. **Deadline:** April 15. **Contact:** Business and Professional Women's Foundation, Educational Programs, at the above address (see entry 1544).

### • 1547 • BPW Loans for Women in Engineering Studies (Graduate, Professional Development, Undergraduate/Loan)

**Purpose:** To assist women in their final two years of any accredited engineering program, including undergraduate, refresher, conversion, or graduate programs. **Focus:** Engineering. **Qualif.:** Applicants must be U.S. citizens, have written acceptance for a course of study in engineering accredited by the Accreditation Board of Engineering and Technology, have academic and/or work experience records showing career motivation and the technical ability to complete course of study, and demonstrate financial need. Studies may be full or part-time, but applicants must carry at least six semester hours or the equivalent during each semester for which a loan is requested.

**Funds Avail.:** Loans of up to $5,000 per academic year. Interest of seven percent per annum begins immediately after graduation. Loans are repaid in 20 quarterly equal installments commencing 12 months after graduation. **To Apply:** To receive application packet, applicants must submit an application request to the BPW Foundation (include a business-size, self-addressed envelope with two first class stamps). Application materials are available between October 1 and April 1. **Deadline:** Applications must be postmarked by April 15. **Contact:** Business and Professional Women's Foundation, Educational Programs, at the above address (see entry 1544).

### • 1548 • BPW/Sears Roebuck Loans for Women in Graduate Business Studies (Graduate/Loan)

**Purpose:** The loan fund was established in 1974 jointly by the BPW Foundation and the Sears-Roebuck Foundation for women seeking their master's degree in business administration. **Focus:** Business Administration. **Qualif.:** Studies may be full- or part-time, but applicants must carry at least six semester hours or the equivalent during each semester for which a loan is requested. Applicants must be citizens of the United States, have written notice of acceptance or enrollment at a school accredited by the American Assembly of Collegiate Schools of Business, have academic and/or work experience records showing career motivation and ability to complete course of study, and demonstrate financial need. BPW Foundation and Sears-Roebuck Foundation employees are not eligible.

**Funds Avail.:** Loans of up to $2,500 are made for tuition and fees for an academic year and are paid directly to the recipient. Interest of seven percent per annum begins immediately after graduation. Loans are repaid in 20 quarterly installments commencing 12 months after graduation. **To Apply:** To receive an application packet, applicants must submit a loan application request to the BPW Foundation. Applicants must enclose with the application request a business-size, self-addressed envelope with two first class stamps. Application materials are available between October 1 and April 1. **Deadline:** Applications must be postmarked on or before April 15. **Contact:** Business and Professional Women's Foundation, Educational Programs, at the above address (see entry 1544).

### • 1549 • Sally Butler Memorial Fund for Latina Research (Doctorate, Postdoctorate/Fellowship)

**Focus:** General Studies. **Qualif.:** Applicants must be Latin American women by descent or citizenship, including women in the Caribbean and North, South, and Central American regions, and BPW members (by the time the fellowship is awarded). They must also be postdoctoral scholars or doctoral candidates whose research proposal has been approved by academic authorities in an accredited graduate institution.

**Funds Avail.:** Awards ranging from $500 to $2,500 each are made annually. **No. of Awards:** 1-5. **To Apply:** Applicants must first send a one-page letter that includes a concise statement about the proposed research subject, applicant's academic level, and Latina background. After eligibility is ascertained from review of the proposed research statement, selected applicants will be invited to prepare a more detailed proposal for formal assessment and review. Applicants must then submit a completed application, a prospectus, detailed budget, timetable, three letters of recommendation, graduate school transcripts, and copies of all publicaitons. Applications are available betweeen September 1 and November 1. **Deadline:** January 20. **Contact:** Research Grant, BPW Foundation, at the above address (see entry 1544).

### • 1550 • Lena Lake Forrest Fellowships/BPW Research Grants (Postdoctorate/Fellowship)

**Focus:** Women's Studies. **Qualif.:** Applicants must be United States citizens and members of BPW by the time the fellowship is awarded. They must also be postdoctoral scholars or doctoral candidates whose research proposal has been approved by academic authorities in an accredited graduate institution. They must be engaged in contemporary and historical research in the U.S. on issues of importance to today's working women that will help women achieve economic equality and balance the demands of work and home and that will aid the formation of positive policies for women as permanent members and full participants in the work force. The Fund also supports feminist scholars especially by funding those in the early stages of their research.

**Funds Avail.:** Awards ranging from $500 to $2,500 each are made each year. **No. of Awards:** 1-5. **To Apply:** Applicants must first send a one-page letter including a concise statement about the proposed research subject and the applicant's academic level.

After eligibility is ascertained from review of the proposed research statement, selected applicants will be invited to prepare a more detailed proposal for formal assessment and review. Applicants must then submit a completed application, a prospectus, detailed budget, timetable, three letters of recommendation, graduate school transcripts, and copies of all publications. Applications are available between September 1 and November 1. **Deadline:** January 20. **Contact:** Research Grant, BPW Foundation, at the above address (see entry 1544).

### • 1551 • New York Life Foundation Scholarships for Women in the Health Professions (Undergraduate/Scholarship)

**Purpose:** To assist women seeking the education necessary for entry or re-entry into the workforce or advancement within a career in the health-care field. The program reflects the Foundation's belief in equal opportunity and a desire to help meet the increasing need for trained professionals in the health-care field. **Focus:** Health Care Services, Health Sciences. **Qualif.:** Scholarships are awarded for full-time or part-time programs of study in one of the health care fields. Applicants must be women 30 years of age or older; citizens of the United States; officially accepted into an accredited program or course of study at a United States institution and be graduating within 12 to 24 months from August 31 of the application year. They must also demonstrate critical need for financial assistance to upgrade skills or complete education for career advancement and have a definite plan to use the desired training to improve chances for advancement, to train for a new career field, or to re-enter the job market. This scholarship program does not cover study at the doctoral level, correspondence courses, or non-degree programs. Relatives of officials of the New York Life Insurance Company are not eligible to participate in this program.

**Funds Avail.:** Scholarships range from $500 to $1,000. **No. of Awards:** 50 scholarships are awarded each year. **To Apply:** To receive an application packet, a scholarship application request must be submitted to the BPW Foundation. Applicants must enclose a business-size, self-addressed envelope with two first class stamps. Xerox copies of the application form will not be accepted. **Deadline:** Application request forms must be received between October 1 and April 1. Completed application materials must be postmarked on or before April 15. **Contact:** The Business and Professional Women's Foundation Educational Programs at the above address (see entry 1544).

### • 1552 •
## Butler Manufacturing Company Foundation
c/o Barbara L. Fay, Foundation
  Administrator
BMA Tower, 31st and SW Trafficway
PO Box 419917
Kansas City, MO 64141-0917
*E-mail:* gmderigne@butlermfg.com
*URL:* http://www.silicon-prairie.org/MemberDir/members/butler.html

*Ph:* (816)968-3208
*Fax:* (816)968-3211

### • 1553 • Butler Manufacturing Company Foundation Scholarship (Undergraduate/Scholarship)

**Purpose:** To encourage educational, moral and social progress of the society which the company serves. **Focus:** General studies. **Qualif.:** Applicants must be children of regular, full-time employees of Butler Manufacturing or any of its wholly-owned subsidiaries who are high school seniors. **Criteria:** Awards are made based on academic achievement and potential personal repute and responsibility, and relative financial need.

**Funds Avail.:** $2,500. Renewable for up to three years. **No. of Awards:** 8. **To Apply:** Applicants must submit high school

transcript, written essays, teacher/counselor references and family financial report. **Deadline:** February.

**Remarks:** Applications are available in Human Resources departments at all Butler locations. **Contact:** Barbara Fay.

### • 1554 •
## California Chicano News Media Association
3716 S. Hope St., Rm. 301
Los Angeles, CA 90007
*E-mail:* info@ccnma.org
*URL:* http://www.ccnma.org/

*Ph:* (213)743-2440
*Fax:* (213)744-1809

### • 1555 • Joel Garcia Memorial Scholarship (Undergraduate/Scholarship)

**Purpose:** To provide Latino students who are pursuing a career in the news media a chance to further their education and get a start in their field. **Focus:** Journalism, Communications. **Qualif.:** Applicants must be Latinos preparing for a career in the news media. Scholarships are awarded to undergraduates attending a college or university. Winners must attend a school in California or be residents of California. **Criteria:** Scholarships are awarded based on financial need, commitment to the journalism profession, community service, continuing education, and academic excellence.

**Funds Avail.:** $250 to $2,000. **No. of Awards:** 15-30. **To Apply:** Students are asked to submit an autobiographical sketch or an essay explaining their interest in a career in journalism or mass communications, three reference letters (including one faculty member), academic transcripts, and samples of their work along with the application. Applicants need to include self-addressed envelope with $.52 postage. **Deadline:** March 31.

### • 1556 •
## California Farm Bureau Scholarship Foundation
2300 River Plaza Dr.
Sacramento, CA 95833

*URL:* http://www.cfbf.com

*Ph:* (916)561-5500
*Fax:* (916)561-5699
*Free:* 800-698-3276

### • 1557 • California Farm Bureau Scholarships (Undergraduate/Scholarship)

**Purpose:** To aid students with a desire to start a career in the agricultural industry. **Focus:** Agricultural Sciences. **Qualif.:** Applicants must demonstrate a commitment to study agriculture and must attend a four-year school in California. **Criteria:** Selection is based upon scholastic achievement, career goals, leadership skills, and determination.

**Funds Avail.:** The scholarship amounts vary, but most range from $1,250 to $2,000. **No. of Awards:** Varies. **To Apply:** Applications are available through the student's local County Farm Bureau or the Foundation office. **Deadline:** March 1. **Contact:** Darlene Licciardo, Scholarship Coordinator, at the above address (see entry 1556).

# • 1558 •
## California-Hawaii Elks Major Project, Inc.
5450 E. Lamona      *Ph:* (559)255-4531
Fresno, CA 93727      *Fax:* (559)456-2659

### • 1559 • California-Hawaii Elks Disabled Student Scholarships *(Undergraduate/Scholarship)*

**Purpose:** To help disabled individuals into the mainstream of the working community. **Focus:** General Studies. **Qualif.:** Candidates must qualify as disabled, defined as physically disabled, visually impaired, hearing impaired, or speech/language or neurologically impaired. They must plan to pursue undergraduate education at an accredited educational institution or licensed vocational school. Applicants must also be United States citizens and residents of California or Hawaii and sponsored by a California-Hawaii Elks Association member.

**Funds Avail.:** Community College/Vocational: $1,000 per year; $2000 at accredited four-year universities. Scholarships may be renewed for a total of four years, judged yearly. Scholarships are in the form of certificates. The money is sent to the respective college only after the State Association office has received the Verification of Enrollment by the first of November. We may also request a financial breakdown as to how money was used in the previous year. **To Apply:** Applicants must submit a formal application, sealed official transcripts, an applicant/spouse of applicant/parent financial analysis, a one-page self-evaluation essay and four letters of recommendation (one each from a physician/M.D. only, school administrator/counselor, a special educational therapist/teacher, and a friend or clergy member). Application forms may be obtained from the Elks Lodge. **Deadline:** Applications are accepted only between January 1 and March 15. Recipients are notified by June 1. **Contact:** Scholarship Committee, nearest Elks Lodge, or Elizabeth Scane at (626)963-1636 or the above address.

# • 1560 •
## California Junior Miss, Inc.
PO Box 729      *Ph:* (707)837-1900
Windsor, CA 95492      *Fax:* (707)837-9410
*E-mail:* cjm@saber.net
*URL:* http://www.ajm.org/california

### • 1561 • California Junior Miss Scholarship Program *(Undergraduate/Scholarship)*

**Focus:** General studies. **Qualif.:** Applicants must be female California residents who are high school juniors and who never been married and are U.S. citizens. **Criteria:** Awards are granted based on judges interview, creative and performing arts, scholastic achievement, presence and composure, and fitness.

**Funds Avail.:** $30,000. **No. of Awards:** 20. **To Apply:** Write for further details. **Deadline:** January 1 of junior year in high school. **Contact:** Katy Dillwood.

# • 1562 •
## California League for Nursing
c/o Lila L. Anastas
502 Wrangler Ct.      *Ph:* (916)786-3004
Roseville, CA 95661      *Fax:* (916)786-8687
*E-mail:* seperry@sfsu.edu

### • 1563 • Fay L. Bower Nursing Student Scholarship *(Graduate, Undergraduate/Scholarship)*

**Purpose:** To honor Dr. Fay Bower and to promote nursing scholarships. **Focus:** Nursing. **Qualif.:** Applicants must be enrolled in California schools of nursing and have completed at least 15 semester units of nursing courses or 23 quarter units of nursing courses with minimum grade point averages of 3.0. In case of MSN student, must have completed 1 semester of nursing courses. **Criteria:** Awards are made based on merit of essay, academic achievement and financial need.

**Funds Avail.:** $400 per award. **No. of Awards:** 3. **To Apply:** Applicants must submit a 1-2 page typewritten essay documenting need and reasons for scholarship, two letters of recommendation with one from current nursing faculty, and official transcript. **Deadline:** March. **Contact:** Lila L. Anastas, RN, MS.

# • 1564 •
## California Library Association
717 K St., Ste. 300      *Ph:* (916)447-8541
Sacramento, CA 95814-3477      *Fax:* (916)447-8394
*E-mail:* info@cla-net.org
*URL:* http://www.cla-net.org/

### • 1565 • CLA Scholarship for Minority Students in Memory of Edna Yelland *(Graduate/Scholarship)*

**Purpose:** To encourage and support ethnic minority students in the attainment of a graduate degree in library or information science. **Focus:** Library and Archival Sciences. **Qualif.:** Applicants must be enrolled or accepted for enrollment in a master's program in an ALA accredited California library school; be American Indian, African American, Mexican American, Latino/Hispanic, Asian American, Pacific Islander, or Filipino; be a California resident at the time of the application and a U.S. citizen or permanent U.S. resident; and provide evidence of financial need. **Criteria:** Individuals will be considered for oral interviews based upon the merits of the written application. Scholarship selections are based on applicant's adherence to instructions and the professional presentation of the application package.

**Funds Avail.:** The amount of each scholarship as well as the actual number granted depends upon the available funds and the financial need of the applicants. **No. of Awards:** 2. **To Apply:** Application forms can be requested from the California Library Association. **Deadline:** Applications must be received by May 31, and awards will be announced in July. Two interview sessions will be conducted in June, one in Southern California, the other in Northern California.

**Remarks:** The scholarship is in memory of Edna Yelland who graduated from the California State Library School in Sacramento and worked to promote the goals of the Association and the profession. **Contact:** California Library Association at the above address (see entry 1564).

### • 1566 • Reference Service Press Fellowships *(Graduate/Fellowship)*

**Focus:** Library and Archival Sciences. **Qualif.:** Applicants must be college seniors or college graduates who have been accepted in an accredited MLS program (documentation required). They must be California residents attending or planning to attend library school in any state, or residents of any state pursuing or planning to pursue an MLS at a school in California. In addition, they must be interested in preparing for a career in reference or information service librarianship and, if awarded the fellowship, agree to take at least three classes specifically dealing with reference or information service. Graduate students currently enrolled in an MLS program (as long as no more than eight credits have been completed by the date of the award) are also eligible to apply. **Criteria:** Selections are based on academic record, applicant essay, and letters of recommendation.

**Funds Avail.:** One $2,000 fellowship distributed in three equal payments, as the recipient completes each of three reference/information classes with a grade of B or better. **No. of Awards:** 1. **To Apply:** Candidates must include an application form, transcripts, an essay (up to 1,000 words, typed, double-spaced) on career plans and preparation, and two letters of recommendation that support applicants' interest in and potential for reference or information service. **Deadline:** May 31. The winner will be announced in July. **Contact:** California Library Association at the above address (see entry 1564).

---

• 1567 •
**California Office of the Governor**
Attn: Rosalie Zalis
300 S Spring St., 16th Fl.          *Ph:* (213)897-0322
Los Angeles, CA 90013              *Fax:* (213)897-0319

• 1568 • **Call to Action Opportunity Scholarship** *(Undergraduate/Scholarship)*

**Focus:** Education, health care, business, law enforcement, public service, mathematics, science. **Qualif.:** Applicants must be female California residents who have been accepted to accredited California institutions and have minimum grade point averages of 3.3, and who have completed at least two years of post-secondary education or who have four years of work experience. Applicants must be U.S. citizens.

**Funds Avail.:** $5,000 per award. **No. of Awards:** 5; one in each category: education, health care, business, law enforcement/public service, mathematics/science. **To Apply:** Applicants must submit a complete and typed application form, three letters of recommendation, two essays (one autobiographical and one describing career plans), and a self-addressed stamped envelope. **Deadline:** August 31. **Contact:** Rosalie Zalis at the above address (see entry 1567).

---

• 1569 •
**California Pharmacists Association - Educational Foundation Trust Fund**
1112 I St., Ste. 300
Sacramento, CA 95814              *Ph:* (916)444-7811

• 1570 • **California Pharmacists Association Educational Foundation Trust Fund** *(Graduate/Loan)*

**Focus:** Pharmacy. **Qualif.:** Applicants must be registered and have attended professional pharmaceutical study in the State of California in the last 2 years and have plans to pursue a post graduation career in California. Must be citizens of the United States, and a member of the Academy of Students of Pharmacy chapter at their school. A guarantor is required for all loans. **Criteria:** Applications will be reviewed and granted/not granted on an individual basis throughout the year. The amount of the loan is at the discretion of the loan committee.

**Funds Avail.:** Loan amounts vary. The amount ranges from $500 to $5,000 in $500 increments. Payment will be based on a repayment schedule chosen by the student , payable over a 5 year period. **To Apply:** Must have the signature of the Dean of the School of Pharmacy for each application. Repayment of the loan begins no later than 3 months after graduation, or immediately upon termination of a student's pharmaceutical education, should it occur prior to graduation.

---

• 1571 •
**California Psychological Association Foundation**
1022 G St.                          *Ph:* (916)325-9786
Sacramento, CA 95814               *Fax:* (916)325-9790
*E-mail:* sburgess@calpsychlink.org

• 1572 • **California Psychological Association Foundation Minority Scholarships** *(Doctorate/Grant)*

**Purpose:** To provide funding for minority students with interest in the field of psychology in order to increase the number of minority professional psychologists serving as teachers, administrators, practitioners, and researchers, who will fully participate in these functions in minority communities. **Focus:** Psychology, Mental Health. **Qualif.:** Applicants must be considered a member of one or more of these established ethnic minority groups: Black/African American, Hispanic/Latino, Asian/Asian American, American Indian/Alaskan Native, and Pacific Islander. They must also be graduates from a regionally accredited undergraduate institution, and have been accepted into a doctoral program in psychology at a regionally accredited or approved institution in California. **Criteria:** Applicants are selected based on written essay, activities, scholarship, references and need.

**Funds Avail.:** Awards are in the form of a grant, administered by the recipient's respective graduate school. **No. of Awards:** 2. **To Apply:** Applicants must submit a completed application form which includes an essay detailing their plans and goals for their graduate education and career; at least three, but not more than five, letters of recommendation and an official copy of the most recent transcript; a letter from the respective graduate program acknowledging acceptance; and financial information. **Deadline:** October 15. Recipients will be notified by mid-December. **Contact:** California Psychological Association Foundation, at the above address (see entry 1571).

---

• 1573 •
**California State Assembly - Jesse Marvin Unruh Assembly Fellowship Program**
Center for California Studies        *Ph:* (916)278-6906
6000 J St.                          *Fax:* (916)278-5199
Sacramento, CA 95819               *Free:* 800-776-1761
*URL:* http://www.csus.edu/calst

• 1574 • **Jesse Marvin Unruh Assembly Fellowships** *(Graduate, Postgraduate/Fellowship)*

**Purpose:** To provide first-hand knowledge of the California Legislature through work experience in the Capitol and a graduate seminar. **Focus:** Political Science. **Qualif.:** Applicants must have at least a bachelor's degree. There is no preferred major. Individuals with advanced degrees or career experience are encouraged to apply. Fellows participate in a graduate seminar held at a California university, and they receive assignments in the California legislature similar to those of legislative assistants and committee consultants.

---

## California State Assembly - Jesse Marvin Unruh Assembly Fellowship Program (continued)

**Funds Avail.:** $1,792/month, plus tuition and health insurance. **No. of Awards:** 18. **To Apply:** Write to the program director for application materials, available October 15. Semifinalists are selected and notified in April. Finalists are interviewed in May. **Deadline:** March 1. Fellows and alternates are notified in May. **Contact:** Robbin Coaxum, Assembly Fellowship Program Director, at the above address (see entry 1573).

---

## • 1575 •
## California Student Aid Commission

PO Box 419027
Rancho Cordova, CA 95741-9027
*URL:* http://www.csac.ca.gov/
*Ph:* (916)526-7590
*Fax:* (916)526-8002

### • 1576 • Robert C. Byrd Honors Scholarship
*(Undergraduate/Scholarship)*

**Purpose:** To provide merit scholarships for college bound students. **Focus:** General Studies. **Qualif.:** This federally funded program provides college scholarships to high school graduates who have demonstrated outstanding academic achievement in high school and who show promise of continued academic achievement in college. **Criteria:** Scholarships are awarded, in part, according to the congressional district in which the applicant resides.

**Funds Avail.:** These $1,500 renewable scholarships are awarded for four years of postsecondary study at any public or private nonprofit institution in the United States. Proprietary schools and military academies are excluded. **To Apply:** Applications are available after January at all California public and private secondary institutions. **Deadline:** March 31.

**Remarks:** Renewable only if federal funds are available. **Contact:** The California Student Aid Commission at the above address (see entry 1575).

### • 1577 • Cal Grant A *(Undergraduate/Grant)*

**Purpose:** To help low- and middle-income students with tuition/fee costs. **Focus:** General Studies. **Qualif.:** To qualify for a Cal Grant, a student must be a California resident attending an eligible school or college in the state. The student must be making satisfactory academic progress as determined by the institution. The applicant must not owe a refund on any state or federal educational grant or have defaulted on a student loan. To be eligible for a first-time Cal Grant A, a student must enroll at least half-time. A student may receive only one Cal Grant, either Cal Grant A, B, or C. **Criteria:** Grant recipients are selected on the basis of financial need and grade point average.

**Funds Avail.:** Awards range from $594 to $5,250 at independent schools and colleges, $3,799 at the University of California, and $1,584 at California State University. Awards are for tuition/fees only. **No. of Awards:** 17,400. **To Apply:** Applicants must complete the Federal Student Financial Aid (FAFSA) application form and return it to the U.S. Department of Education's Central Processor. Applicants must also complete a GPA Verification Form and return it to the commission by March 2. **Deadline:** A completed FAFSA must be filed by March 2. **Contact:** The California Student Aid Commission at the above address (see entry 1575).

### • 1578 • Cal Grant B *(Undergraduate/Grant)*

**Purpose:** To provide a living allowance for very low-income students. Usually, first year recipients of this award use the funds for nontuition costs of attending college. When renewed beyond the first year, funds may cover all or part of tuition and fees. **Focus:** General Studies. **Qualif.:** Students must be California residents

attending an eligible school or college in California, have financial need, and be United States citizens, permanent residents, or eligible noncitizens. They must also be in a program of study leading directly to an undergraduate degree or certificate and must not have completed more than one semester or two quarter full-time, or 16 semester units part-time college work, or over four and one-half months at a vocational school before June 30 of the award year. A student may accept only one Cal Grant. **Criteria:** Applicants are selected based on GPA and consideration of disadvantaged background.

**Funds Avail.:** There are 250 awards authorized for community college students transferring to four-year colleges each year. Living allowances ranges from $700 to $1,140. Tuition allowances are the same as for Cal Grant A. **No. of Awards:** 12,250. **To Apply:** Applicants must complete and file the Free Application for Federal Student Aid (FAFSA) and return it to the processors address listed on the FAFSA by March 2. Applicants must also complete a GPA Verification Form and submit it to the commission by March 2. **Remarks:** More than half of all new Cal Grant B recipients begin at a public community college. **Contact:** Counselors and financial aid offices have complete Cal Grant eligibility and application information.

### • 1579 • Cal Grant C *(Undergraduate/Grant)*

**Purpose:** To help students pursuing an undergraduate, vocationally-oriented program. **Focus:** Vocational/Technical. **Qualif.:** To qualify for a Cal Grant, students must be California residents attending an eligible school or college in the state and be making satisfactory academic progress as determined by the institution. Applicants must not owe a refund on any state or federal educational grant or have defaulted on a student loan. Recipients of the Cal Grant C award must be enrolled in a vocational or technical program at a community college, independent college, or vocational school, in a program of study from four months to two years in length.

**Funds Avail.:** Awards of up to $2,360 per year for tuition and up to $530 per year for training-related costs such as special clothing, tools, equipment, books, supplies, and transportation are given. Grants are limited to $530 per year at a community college. **No. of Awards:** 1,570. **To Apply:** Applicants are required to complete all appropriate sections of the Free Application for Federal Student Aid (FAFSA) and mail it to the processor's address listed on the FAFSA by March 2. It is also recommended that students also complete a GPA Verification Form and submit it to the commission by March 2. **Deadline:** To be considered for a Cal Grant, a completed FAFSA must be submitted to the processor listed on the FAFSA with a postmark no later than March 2. **Contact:** The California Student Aid Commission at the above address (see entry 1575).

### • 1580 • CSAC Assumption Program of Loans for Education *(Graduate, Undergraduate/Loan)*

**Purpose:** To encourage outstanding students to become teachers and serve in critical teacher shortage areas. **Focus:** Education. **Qualif.:** Teacher candidates may apply for the Assumption Program of Loans for Education (APLE). Applicants must have completed at least 60 semester units of undergraduate study and be currently enrolled for at least ten semester units or the equivalent, as appropriate to their employment status. To receive the maximum in loan-assumption benefits, participants must provide three consecutive years of teaching in a California public school in a designated subject matter shortage area (mathematics, science, English, foreign language, bilingual education, or special education) or in a school serving a high proportion of low-income students. **Criteria:** Participating colleges set their own standards.

**Funds Avail.:** There is a maximum of $8,000 in loan-assumption benefits. **To Apply:** Each year the Commission will accept up to 400 new APLE applicants who are selected by participating postsecondary institutions with approved teacher preparation programs. Applications may be obtained from participating institutions with teacher preparation programs. **Deadline:** Vary by college. Colleges must submit selection by June 30. **Contact:** Application Services Branch, The California Student Aid Commission, at the above address (see entry 1575). Telephone number (916)322-2294. (916)322-2294.

### • 1581 • CSAC Graduate Fellowships *(Graduate/ Fellowship)*

**Focus:** General Studies. **Qualif.:** Candidates must be pursuing recognized advanced or professional degrees at an eligible California graduate or professional school. Applicants must demonstrate their intent to become college or university faculty members. **Criteria:** Awards are made on the basis of grades, graduate test scores, and consideration of disadvantaged background.

**Funds Avail.:** 300 awards ranging from $882 to $6,490. **To Apply:** Students must file an FAFSA. Graduate test scores must be forwarded to the commission. Complete GPA Verification Form and forward to the commission. **Deadline:** March 2 each year. **Contact:** Counselors and financial aid offices have complete eligibility and application information.

### • 1582 • CSAC Law Enforcement Personnel Dependents Scholarships *(Graduate, Undergraduate/ Grant)*

**Purpose:** To enable needy dependents of deceased or 100% disabled law enforcement, fire officials to obtain a secondary education. **Focus:** General Studies. **Qualif.:** Applicants must be needy dependents and spouses of California police and other law enforcement officers (Highway Patrol, county sheriffs, correctional officers), or permanent and full-time firefighters employed by counties, cities, districts, and other political subdivisions of the state who have been killed or totally disabled in the line of duty. The death or disablement must have been the result of an accident or injury caused by external violence or physical force incurred in the performance of duty. **Criteria:** Financial need.

**Funds Avail.:** Grants at four-year colleges range from $100-$1,500 per year with a maximum of $6,000 in a six-year period. Grants at community colleges range from $100-$500 per year not to exceed a cumulative maximum of $2,000 over four years. **Deadline:** None. **Contact:** Initial Processing Branch, the California Student Aid Commission, at the above address (see entry 1575). Telephone number: (916)322-2294.

### • 1583 • Paul Douglas Teacher Scholarship *(Graduate, Undergraduate/Scholarship loan)*

**Purpose:** To provide college scholarships to outstanding high school graduates and college students who demonstrate a commitment to pursue teaching careers at the preschool, elementary, or secondary level. **Focus:** Education. **Qualif.:** An applicant must be in the top 10 percent of his or her graduating high school class, or receive an equivalent General Educational Development (GED) score and must attend an accredited postsecondary institution in the United States. Participants agree to teach two years full-time for each year the scholarship is received. This requirement may be reduced by 50 percent if teaching is done in a subject shortage area identified by the U.S. Department of Education. Recipients who fail to fulfill the teaching requirement must repay the scholarship, plus interest and collection fees. Acceptance of this scholarship may affect income tax reporting and other financial aid, including Cal Grants. **Criteria:** A 3.0 GPA is required.

**Funds Avail.:** Scholarships of up to $5,000 may be awarded for up to four academic years beginning in the recipient's sophomore year. 200 new awards are granted each year as funds allow. **To Apply:** Applications are available for college students after January 1 at participating postsecondary institutions with teacher preparation programs and at California high schools. **Deadline:** College students: varies per college. High school students: July 30.

**Contact:** Specialized Programs at the above address (see entry 1575).

### • 1584 •
## Fuller E. Callaway Foundation
209 Broome St.
PO Box 790                                    Ph: (706)884-7348
La Grange, GA 30241                            Fax: (706)884-0201

### • 1585 • Hatton Lovejoy Graduate Studies Fund *(Graduate/Scholarship)*

**Purpose:** To assist qualified students. **Focus:** Graduate studies - none specified. **Qualif.:** First priority is given to sons of former employees of Callaway Mills Company; second preference is given to applicants who reside within 50 miles of LaGrange, Georgia and who are graduates of the LaGrange public schools. Candidates must be enrolled in or accepted as a candidate for a graduate degree at an accredited school. While scholarships are normally awarded to first-year graduate students, second and later year students are also considered. **Criteria:** Recipients are selected on the basis of the selection committee's judgment of candidate's relative ability, motivation, character, and need.

**Funds Avail.:** The amount of the scholarships varies according to the needs of individual applicants. Scholarships are renewable based on satisfactory academic performances. **Deadline:** Application and supporting materials must be submitted by June 30 of each year.

**Remarks:** A bequest in the will of Fuller E. Callaway, III, endowed a fund to provide Graduate Studies scholarships in honor of the late Hatton Lovejoy, a prominent attorney and citizen of LaGrange. **Contact:** Fuller E. Callaway Foundation, Hatton Lovejoy Graduate Studies Fund Committee, at the above address (see entry 1584).

### • 1586 • Hatton Lovejoy Scholarship Plan *(Undergraduate/Scholarship)*

**Purpose:** The purpose of the Hatton Lovejoy Scholarship Plan is to encourage and help deserving young men and women to prepare themselves through college training for positions of community leadership and service. The Plan is sponsored by the Fuller E. Callaway Foundation and administered by the Hatton Lovejoy Scholarship Plan Committee. **Focus:** Undergraduate Studies. **Qualif.:** Candidates must have been residents of Troup County, Georgia for at least two years. They must be graduates of or scheduled for graduation within six months from an accredited high school with a scholastic standing in the top 25 percent of the class. Recipients may attend any college or university of their choice approved by the Committee; they are expected to pursue a full course of study during the period of the award and maintain a cumulative scholastic standing in the upper half of their college class. **Criteria:** College Board and intelligence tests, scholastic record, financial need, planned course of study, character, qualities of leadership, participation in student and community activities, co-operation with school authorities, personal interview by Scholarship Plan Committee, other information obtained through investigation by the Committee, and purposes in life.

**Funds Avail.:** A maximum of ten scholarships may be awarded annually, with no more than six being awarded to any one sex. The total maximum value per scholarship is $14,400, payable at $1,200 per quarter or $1,800 per semester for 12 quarters or 8 semesters. Recipients must forward a transcript of their grades after each quarter or semester to the Committee; payment is not made until the transcript is received. The amount of any scholarship may not exceed the expenses of tuition, room, board, books, and lab fees. Recipients may not accept any other scholarship funds or loans without specific approval of the Committee. **No. of Awards:** 10. **To Apply:** Application forms are available from Foundation. **Deadline:**

---

## Fuller E. Callaway Foundation (continued)

February 15 each year. **Contact:** J.T. Gresham, General Manager, at the above address (see entry 1584).

---

## • 1587 •
## Camargo Foundation
400 Sibley St.
125 Park Sq. Ct.
St. Paul, MN 55101-1928          *Ph:* (612)290-2237

### • 1588 • Camargo Foundation Residential Fellowships *(Graduate/Fellowship)*

**Purpose:** To benefit scholars, writers, artists, and composers who wish to pursue humanities projects related to France. **Focus:** French Studies. **Qualif.:** Grants are for residential stay at the Foundation's community in Cassis, France. There are no nationality restrictions. Applicants may be members of a university or college faculty who wish to pursue studies while on leave from their home institution; a teacher from a private or public secondary school on leave of absence; graduate students with only the dissertation left to complete who would benefit from a stay in France; or writers, photographers, visual artists or musicians with a specific project to complete. Research should be at an advanced stage. Since awards are residential grants only, fellows who need funds for living or research expenses should apply to other sources for financing. Fellows may not accept gainful employment while at Camargo.

**Funds Avail.:** Furnished apartment, plus studio and library privileges, valued at $10,000-12,000. **To Apply:** Write Ricardo Bloch at the U.S. address listed above for application form and guidelines. Submit form to the same address with curriculum vitae and a detailed description of proposed project. Samples of work are required from visual artists, composers, and creative writers. Three letters of recommendation, including two from persons outside of applicant's institution, should be forwarded directly to Ricardo Bloch. **Deadline:** February 1. **Contact:** Ricardo Bloch at the above address (see entry 1587).

---

## • 1589 •
## Cambridge Commonwealth Trust - Cambridge Overseas Trust
P.O. Box 252
Cambridge CB2 1TZ, England          *Ph:* 1223 323322

### • 1590 • Scholarships and Awards for Overseas Students *(Postgraduate/Award, Scholarship)*

**Purpose:** To support postgraduate students from the Commonwealth and other overseas nations who wish to study at the University of Cambridge. **Focus:** General Studies. **Qualif.:** Applicant must be from a country other than the United Kingdom. The Commonwealth Trust administers applications from candidates from Commonwealth countries, Burma, Pakistan, and Sudan; preference is given to applicants from developing nations. The Overseas Trust assists students from countries outside of the Commonwealth. Awards are tenable at the University of Cambridge, but the receipt of an award does not guarantee acceptance to the University or its constituent Colleges. In addition to applying to the appropriate Trust for financial assistance, candidates must apply directly to the University for admission to a pertinent postgraduate course of study or research. Awards from the Trusts are contingent upon acceptance to Cambridge. The Trusts also administer awards cosponsored by national governments, private foundations, universities, corporations, and associated local trusts. These awards are generally intended to help citizens of particular nations to attend Cambridge; fields of study and eligibility may be restricted, and application procedures can vary. Further information on all types of these more restricted Cambridge awards can be obtained from the Trusts.

**Funds Avail.:** Varies; can include fees, tuition, and/or stipend. **To Apply:** Write to the Trusts for a preliminary application form, descriptions of available awards, and application guidelines. Submit application form at least one year in advance of intended start of study. Applicants who submit a preliminary application to the Trusts for a particular scholarship will automatically be considered for all other awards offered by the Trusts for which they are eligible. **Deadline:** September 1 (for most awards).

**Remarks:** Prospective Cambridge students from Botswana, Lesotho, Malawi, Namibia, South Africa, Swaziland, Zambia, and Zimbabwe can obtain assistance from the Cambridge Livingstone Trust, care of the address listed above. U.S. citizens and permanent residents seeking funds for Ph.D. research at the University of Cambridge should also consult the American Friends of Cambridge University, which offers three tuition scholarships annually. For further information, write to the American Friends of Cambridge University, Cambridge Office, The Pitt Building, Trumpington Street, Cambridge CB2 1RP, England. **Contact:** Secretary at the above address (see entry 1589).

---

## • 1591 •
## Cambridge University Library
West Road                          *Ph:* 1223 333000
Cambridge CB3 9DR, England          *Fax:* 1223 333160

### • 1592 • Munby Fellowship in Bibliography *(Postdoctorate/Fellowship)*

**Purpose:** To undertake bibliographic research based preferably on the collections of the University of Cambridge. **Focus:** Historical Bibliography, History of the Book Trade and Book Collecting. **Qualif.:** Applicant may be a graduate of any university, and of any nationality. Preference will be given to promising young scholars already established in their careers. There is no restriction of choice of topic beyond the broad areas of study listed above. Research may concern printed or manuscript material, Western or Oriental. The fellow will not be called upon to undertake any routine departmental or other staff duties or responsibilities within the Library. A non-stipendiary visiting fellowship at Darwin College may be offered to the Munby Fellow.

**Funds Avail.:** £11,000. **To Apply:** There are no formal application forms. Submit curriculum vitae, statement outlining proposed research, list of publications, and names and addresses of two referees. There are no interviews. **Deadline:** July 31. Elections for the fellowship are usually made in the autumn of the year preceding the award. **Contact:** Deputy Librarian at the above address (see entry 1591).

---

## • 1593 •
## The Canada Council for the Arts
350 Albert St.                     *Ph:* (613)566-4414
PO Box 1047                        *Fax:* (613)566-4390
Ottawa, ON, Canada K1P 5V8          *Free:* 800-263-5588
*E-mail:* michelle.chawla@canadacouncil.ca; maria.martin@
  canadacouncil.ca
*URL:* http://www.canadacouncil.ca/

*The Canada Council for the Arts is a national arm's length agency which provides grants and services to professional Canadian artists and arts organizations in dance, media arts, music, theatre, writing and publishing, interdisciplinary work and performance art, and visual arts. The Council defines a professional artist as someone who has specialized training in the field who is recognized as such by her or his peers and who has a history of public presentation or publication.*

### • 1594 • Canadian Council for the Arts Grants Program *(Professional Development/Grant)*

**Purpose:** To help winners pursue professional development, independent artistic creation or production. **Qualif.:** Applicants must be Canadian citizens who are professional artists in one of the council's service areas.

**Funds Avail.:** Applicants can request a fixed amount of $3000, $5000, $10,000, $15,000, or $20,000 (or $34,000 for senior visual artists only) Travel grants of $500, $1000, $1500, or $2000 can also be requested. Additional fixed travel amounts of $1500 and $2000 are also available only to applicants trvelling to northern Canada or to distinations other than the United States and Europe.

### • 1595 •
### Canada - Department of Indian and Northern Affairs
10 Wellington St.                        *Ph:* (819)997-0380
Hull, PQ, Canada K1A 0H4          *Fax:* (819)953-4941

### • 1596 • Cultural Grants *(Professional Development/Grant)*

**Purpose:** To encourage projects by and about Canadian Inuit. **Focus:** Canadian Inuit Culture. **Qualif.:** Applicant must be a Canadian Inuit who wishes to undertake a project related to the promotion or preservation of his/her native culture.

**Funds Avail.:** $5,000 maximum. **To Apply:** Submit a letter of application to the Department, including an explanation of the project and a budget outline. **Deadline:** None. **Contact:** David Webster at the above address (see entry 1595).

### • 1597 •
### Canada - House of Commons
House of Commons Page
   Programme (Recruitment)
Human Resources Directorate
Rm. 538, Wellington Bldg.
House of Commons                       *Ph:* (613)996-0897
Ottawa, ON, Canada K1A 0A6        *Fax:* (613)995-1470

### • 1598 • House of Commons Page Programme *(Undergraduate/Work Study)*

**Focus:** All programs except Law, Science, and Engineering. **Qualif.:** Applicants must be bilingual Canadian citizens, graduating from a secondary school or CEGEP (with no academic interruptions), and must be commencing their first year of full-time studies at one of the universities in the National Capital Region (i.e. University of Ottawa, Carleton University, Universite du Quebec a Hull, St. Paul University) in September of the year of application. Candidates must also have an overall academic average of at least 80%. **Criteria:** In addition to meeting the basic requirements requested in the application form, candidates may be asked to write an essay or an examination. Those successful at this level will be tested for language skills and may then be invited to an interview.

**Funds Avail.:** 40 positions paying approximately $9,500 for the year are available. Costs of travel to and from Ottawa at the beginning and end of the programme year will also be borne by the House of Commons. **No. of Awards:** Approximately 40. **To Apply:** Application forms for the House of Commons Page Programme may be obtained from the Page Programme Recruitment Office at the above address after September 1. **Deadline:** First Monday in December. **Contact:** Coordinator, Page Programme, at the above address (see entry 1597).

### • 1599 •
### Canadian Association of Broadcasters
350 Sparks St., Ste. 306                 *Ph:* (613)233-4035
Ottawa, ON, Canada K1R 7S8         *Fax:* (613)233-6961
*URL:* http://www.cab-ac.ca/

### • 1600 • Jim Allard Broadcast Journalism Scholarship *(Undergraduate/Scholarship)*

**Purpose:** For the advancement of Canadian students studying in Canada. **Focus:** Broadcasting and Journalism. **Qualif.:** Applicants should be Canadian citizens and aspiring broadcasters enrolled in a broadcast journalism course at a Canadian college or university. **Criteria:** The judging committee looks for evidence of strong character and leadership qualities, a willingness to assist others in the industry, and genuine enthusiasm for a career in Canadian broadcasting as reflected in activities related to broadcasting such as home studies and part-time employment.

**Funds Avail.:** One $2,500 scholarship. **No. of Awards:** One. **To Apply:** A 500-word outline explaining why the applicant is interested in broadcast journalism, what the applicant's career goal is, and how the scholarship can help attain that goal must be submitted with the application to the course director of the applicant's institution. Each college or university is limited to three entries. **Deadline:** June 30. Applications should be submitted to the course director several weeks before the deadline. The winner is announced during the Association's annual convention in the fall.

**Remarks:** The Scholarship was established in 1983 by the Canadian Association of Broadcasters in memory of T.J. "Jim" Allard, its long-time chief executive officer. **Contact:** Angela Roberge at the above address (see entry 1599).

### • 1601 • The BBM Scholarship *(Graduate/Scholarship)*

**Purpose:** The Bureau of Broadcast Measurement (BBM) established this scholarship to honor the important role the Canadian Association of Broadcasters plays in Canada's broadcast industry while commemorating its 60th anniversary in 1986. Further, this scholarship, awarded annually by the CAB, has been created in recognition of BBM's responsibility as the industry's rating service to ensure there is an investment in the development of individuals, skilled and knowledgeable in research, who may be of future benefit to the Canadian broadcast industry. **Qualif.:** Students must be enrolled in a graduate studies program, or be in the final year of an Honours degree with the intention of entering a graduate program anywhere in Canada. Applicants must have demonstrated achievement in and knowledge of statistical and/or quantitative research methodology in a course of study at a Canadian university or postsecondary institution. **Criteria:** Essay, recommendations, and the part the scholarship will play in the further education of the recipient.

**Funds Avail.:** $2,500 cash, payable at a special presentation to be made at the fall convention of the Canadian Association of Broadcasters. Transportation to the convention, plus accommodation and meals, is provided. **No. of Awards:** 1. **To Apply:** Students should submit a 250 word essay outlining their interest in audience research. Students may also submit a copy of any course project or paper on research previously completed. Students should attach three references/recommendations from

## Canadian Association of Broadcasters (continued)

appropriate sources. One should be from the applicant's course director or advisor. **Deadline:** June 30. **Contact:** Angela Roberge at the above address (see entry 1599).

### • 1602 • Raymond Crepault Scholarship (Graduate/Scholarship)

**Qualif.:** Applicants must be French Canadian students with broadcasting experience who are presently enrolled in, or wish to begin or complete a program of studies in, communications at the university level. Candidates should meet one or more of the following requirements: university graduation in any discipline (first degree), university graduation or current studies in communications, graduation from a recognized broadcasting course or the equivalent, or desire to improve broadcasting skills. **Criteria:** The Judging Committee will consider motivation, ability to complete studies, financial need, and recommendations from professors, colleagues, and/or employers.

**Funds Avail.:** One scholarship with a $5,000 bursary is awarded annually. The bursary may be renewed. **Deadline:** June 30. The winner is announced during the CAB annual conference in the fall.

**Remarks:** The scholarship was established in 1975 by Radiomutuel, in cooperation with the Canadian Association of Broadcasters, to commemorate Raymond Crepault's special contribution to Canadian broadcasting and his deep commitment, as a French Canadian, to Canadian Unity. **Contact:** Angela Roberge at the above address (see entry 1599).

### • 1603 • Ruth Hancock Scholarships (Undergraduate/Scholarship)

**Purpose:** To encourage talented, hard working students to pursue careers in Canadian broadcasting. **Qualif.:** Applicants must be Canadian students enrolled in a recognized communications course in Canada. They are expected to demonstrate strong character and leadership qualities, a willingness to assist others, a genuine interest in pursuing a broadcasting career, as reflected in extracurricular activities related to broadcasting, and/or enthusiasm in carrying through teacher-assigned or self-initiated undertakings.

**Funds Avail.:** Three $1,500 scholarships are awarded. **No. of Awards:** 3. **To Apply:** On a separate paper, candidates should explain, in about 500 words, why they are taking a communications course, what their career goals are, and how these scholarships will help them attain those goals. An application form, the 500-word outline, and a signed recommendation from the applicant's course director, must be submitted. **Deadline:** June 30. Winners are announced at the CAB Annual Conference in the fall.

**Remarks:** The scholarship is sponsored by the CTV Television Network/Broadcast Executives Society, in cooperation with the Canadian Association of Broadcasters in memory of Ruth Hancock, who for 12 years was manager of the Toronto office of the Canadian Association of Broadcasters. **Contact:** Angela Liuzzo at the above address (see entry 1599).

### • 1604 •
## Canadian Association of University Teachers
2675 Queensview Dr.                    *Ph:* (613)820-2270
Ottawa, ON, Canada K2B 8K2            *Fax:* (613)820-7244
*E-mail:* richer@caut.ca
*URL:* http://caut.ca

### • 1605 • J. H. Stewart Reid Memorial Fellowship (Doctorate/Fellowship)

**Purpose:** To recognize and encourage an outstanding Canadian graduate student. **Focus:** General **Qualif.:** Applicant must be a Canadian citizen or have landed immigrant status from 30 April of the previous year or earlier. The fellowship is tenable in Ph.D. programs at Canadian universities. The Fellowship is available only for doctoral studies.

**Funds Avail.:** $5,000. **No. of Awards:** One. **To Apply:** Write to the Association for application form and guidelines. Submit form with letters of reference. **Deadline:** April 30. Fellowship is announced in July. **Contact:** Peggy Richer, Awards Officer, at the above address (see entry 1604).

### • 1606 •
## Canadian Aviation Historical Society
National Headquarters
PO Box 224, Sta. A
Willowdale, ON, Canada M2N 5S8        *Ph:* (416)488-2247
*URL:* http://www.canadian-aviation.com/250.html

### • 1607 • Silver Dart Aviation History Award (Undergraduate/Prize)

**Purpose:** To encourage the research and publication of Canadian aviation history. **Qualif.:** The Silver Dart Aviation History Award is offered annually to students at technical colleges, aviation schools, and universities. Canadian aviation history encompasses a wide range of topics. Papers may address any topic that relates to the development, use, or impact of aviation, aircraft, or aeronautics in Canada or by Canadians elsewhere. **Criteria:** Judging for the award is based on presentation, content, and style.

**Funds Avail.:** The author of the best essay will be awarded the Silver Dart Aviation History Award, a scroll, and a $500 cash payment. In addition, the Prize essay will be published in the Society's Journal. In case of papers of equal merit all winning papers may be published and the prize split. The Society reserves the right to withhold the prize if no appropriate entries are received. Runners-up will receive a book prize. The runner-up papers would also be available for publication in the Journal at the discretion of the editor. All prize winners and their institutions will receive a one year membership in the Society. **To Apply:** Papers should be approximately 5,000 words with an abstract of 200 words. Papers should be typed, double-spaced and meet basic academic standards. All sources should be given in end notes or a bibliography and all illustrations credited. The use of maps, photos, and drawings to enhance the paper is encouraged. The development of a clearly defined theme tying the subject of the paper to the larger picture of Canadian or aviation history and an original approach to the topic will distinguish the winning paper. The use of relevant primary material is encouraged. Each entrant should submit four copies of the paper for judging. **Deadline:** Papers must be received by the awards chairman by March 15. **Contact:** Further information is available by writing the Awards Chairman, Canadian Aviation Historical Society, at the above address (see entry 1606).

### • 1608 •
## Canadian Bar Association
50 O'Connor St., Ste. 902            *Ph:* (613)237-2925
Ottawa, ON, Canada K1P 6L2           *Fax:* (613)237-0185
                                     *Free:* 800-267-8860
*E-mail:* stephenh@cba.org
*URL:* http://www.cba.org/abc

### • 1609 • Viscount Bennett Fellowship (Graduate, Postgraduate/Fellowship)

**Purpose:** To encourage a high standard of legal education, training, and ethics. **Focus:** Law. **Qualif.:** Open to Canadian citizens who have graduated from an approved law school in Canada or who, at the time of application, are pursuing final-year studies as undergraduate students at an approved law school.

**Funds Avail.:** $20,000. **No. of Awards:** 1. **To Apply:** Write the Association for application guidelines. **Deadline:** November 15. **Contact:** Stephen Hanson, Senior Director of Communications, at the above address (see entry 1608).

## • 1610 •
### Canadian Blood Services
Head Office
Research & Development
1800 Alta Vista Drive
Ottawa, ON, Canada K1G 4J5
*E-mail:* CILLA.PERRY@BLOODSERVICES.CA
*URL:* http://WWW.BLOODSERVICES.CA

*Ph:* (613)739-2408
*Fax:* (613)739-2426

### • 1611 • Career Development Fellowships
*(Postdoctorate, Postgraduate/Fellowship)*

**Purpose:** To support Canadians who have completed their formal research training and wish to acquire further experience in a Blood Centre setting. **Focus:** Hematology. **Qualif.:** Candidates must be Canadian citizens or permanent residents who either hold a Ph.D. (or equivalent research degree), or have an M.Sc. in an appropriate health field plus an M.D., D.D.S., or D.V.M. degree. Candidates may not be registered for a higher degree at the time of application, nor may they undertake degree studies during the fellowship term. Awards are tenable at Canadian Red Cross Society Blood Centres.

**Funds Avail.:** Approximately $30,000; includes stipend and $10,000 research grant. **To Apply:** Write to the Administrator R&D for application form and guidelines, or contact one of the 17 Blood Centres in Canada for application materials. Application must be made through and with the support of the medical director of the host Blood Centre. **Deadline:** January 15.

## • 1612 •
### Canadian Cancer Society - Medical Affairs
10 Alcorn Ave., Ste. 200
Toronto, ON, Canada M4V 3B1
*URL:* http://www.cancer.ca/

*Ph:* (416)961-7223

### • 1613 • Maurice Legault Awards *(Postgraduate/Award, Fellowship)*

**Purpose:** To provide an opportunity for nurses with leadership potential to undertake training for a career in clinical oncology within the Canadian health care system. **Focus:** Oncological Nursing. **Qualif.:** Applicant must be a graduate of an approved diploma school of nursing, or of a university baccalaureate program in nursing, and hold current registration as a nurse in a province or territory of Canada. Applicant must be a resident of Canada and either a Canadian citizen or landed immigrant at the date of application, but may have trained previously in another country. Also, applicant must be committed to remaining in Canada following completion of the Fellowship.

**Funds Avail.:** $17,500/year, prorated for lesser periods. **No. of Awards:** Varies. **To Apply:** Write to the Society for an application form. **Deadline:** October 15.

**Remarks:** If tuition fees are required, a contribution to such fees of up to $1,000 may be available on application. A transportation grant of up to $1,000 may be offered upon request. **Contact:** Director, Medical Affairs, at the above address (see entry 1612).

### • 1614 • McEachern Awards *(Postdoctorate/Award, Fellowship)*

**Purpose:** To provide an opportunity for physicians with leadership potential to undertake training for careers in clinical oncology in Canada. **Focus:** Clinical Oncology. **Qualif.:** Applicant must be a graduate of an approved faculty or school of medicine, and must have completed not less than three years of postgraduate training after receipt of the M.D. degree. Also, they must be a resident of Canada and a Canadian citizen or landed immigrant, and must be committed to remaining in Canada following completion of the Fellowship.

**Funds Avail.:** $37,500. **No. of Awards:** Varies. **To Apply:** Write to the Society for application forms. **Deadline:** October 15.

**Remarks:** If tuition fees are required, a contribution to such fees of up to $1,000 may be available on application. A transportation grant of up to $1,000 may be offered upon request. **Contact:** Executive Director at the above address (see entry 1612).

## • 1615 •
### Canadian Council of Professional Engineers
116 Albert St., Ste. 401
Ottawa, ON, Canada K1P 5G3
*E-mail:* lmacdon@fox.nstn.ns.ca
*URL:* http://www.ccpe.ca/

*Ph:* (613)232-2474
*Fax:* (613)230-5759

### • 1616 • ENCON Endowment *(Postgraduate/Fellowship)*

**Purpose:** To provide financial assistance to engineers wishing to pursue studies or research in the area of engineering failure investigation. This area of engineering is concerned with the analysis of the various causes of materials failure, and the prevention of accidents, which may result from them, either in the industrial, manufacturing or construction sector. **Focus:** Engineering Failure Investigation. **Qualif.:** Applicant may be of any nationality, but must be registered as a full member of one of the 12 provincial or territorial professional engineering associations federated in the CCPE, and must be accepted for postgraduate study at a university recognized by CCPE. **Criteria:** Selection of Endowment winner will be based on all information and references provided with the application plus financial need. No restrictions are placed on Endowment winner concurrently holding other grants or awards or receiving assistance or income from other sources.

**Funds Avail.:** $5,000. **No. of Awards:** One. **To Apply:** Write to the office of CCPE for application forms. Forms are also available from the provincial and territorial associations that are constituents of CCPE. **Deadline:** May 1. Notification by mid-July. **Contact:** Lorelei Scott, Manager, Member Services, at the above address (see entry 1615).

### • 1617 • Manulife Financial Scholarships
*(Postdoctorate, Postgraduate/Scholarship)*

**Purpose:** To provide financial assistance to engineers returning to a university for further study or research. **Focus:** Engineering. **Qualif.:** Applicant may be of any nationality, but must be registered as a full member of one of the 12 provincial or territorial professional engineering associations federated in the CCPE, and must be accepted for postgraduate study at a university recognized by CCPE. **Criteria:** Selection of award winners will be based on all information and references provided with the application plus financial need. No restrictions are placed on award winners concurrently holding other grants or awards or receiving assistance or income from other sources.

**Funds Avail.:** $7,500. **No. of Awards:** Three. **To Apply:** Write to CCPE for application forms. Forms are also available from the

## Canadian Council of Professional Engineers (continued)

provincial and territorial associations that are constituents of CCPE. **Deadline:** May 1. Notification by mid-July.

**Remarks:** Formerly known as North American Life Assurance Company Scholarships. **Contact:** Lorelei Scott, Manager, Member Services, at the above address (see entry 1615).

### • 1618 • Meloche-Monnex Scholarship
*(Postdoctorate, Postgraduate/Scholarship)*

**Purpose:** To provide financial assistance to engineers returning to a university for further study or research in a field, other than engineering, that will enhance professional engineering capabilities. **Focus:** General Studies. **Qualif.:** Applicant may be of any nationality, but must be registered as a full member of one of the 12 provincial or territorial professional engineering associations federated in the CCPE, and must be accepted for postgraduate study at a university recognized by CCPE. Scholar may select any field of study other than engineering, but the field chosen should enhance the candidate's performance in engineering. **Criteria:** Selection of award winners will be based on all information and references provided with the application plus financial need. No restrictions are placed on award winners concurrently holding other grants or awards or receiving assistance or income from other sources.

**Funds Avail.:** $5,000. **No. of Awards:** Two. **To Apply:** Write to CCPE for application forms. Forms are also available from the provincial and territorial associations that are constituents of CCPE. **Deadline:** May 1. Notification by mid-July.

**Remarks:** Formerly know as OPTIMUM Scholarship. **Contact:** Lorelei Scott, Manager, Member Services, at the above address (see entry 1615).

### • 1619 •
## Canadian Diabetes Association - National Office/ Siege Social

15 Toronto St., No. 1001     *Ph:* (416)363-3373
Toronto, ON, Canada M5C 2E3    *Fax:* (416)363-3393
*E-mail:* info@diabetes.ca
*URL:* http://www.diabetes.ca/

### • 1620 • Charles H. Best Research Grants
*(Doctorate, Graduate, Postdoctorate/Grant)*

**Purpose:** To support research into the causes, treatment, and possible cure of diabetes. **Focus:** Diabetes. **Qualif.:** Applicant must be a Canadian citizen or permanent resident who is affiliated with a Canadian university or research institute and qualified to conduct independent medical research. Grants are tenable at the home institution.

**Funds Avail.:** $60,000 maximum per year. **To Apply:** Write to the research Coordinator for application materials. **Deadline:** July 31. **Contact:** Myrtella Hodge, Coordinator Grants and Personnel Awards, at the above address (see entry 1619). Toll-free number: (800)361-1306.

### • 1621 • CDA Fellowships *(Postdoctorate/Fellowship)*

**Purpose:** To support research training at the postdoctoral level in the field of diabetes. **Focus:** Diabetes. **Qualif.:** Applicant must be a Canadian citizen or permanent resident. The awardee must have a supervisor other than the person who supervised his/her doctoral research work. Award is tenable only at Canadian universities or research institutions.

**Funds Avail.:** Varies. **To Apply:** Write to the research Coordinator for application materials. **Deadline:** December 1. **Contact:** Myrtella

Hodge, Grants and Personnel Awards, at the above address (see entry 1619). Toll-free number: (800)361-1306.

### • 1622 • CDA Scholarships *(Postdoctorate/ Scholarship loan)*

**Purpose:** To provide support for newly appointed faculty members who have recently completed their training in research and show promise of ability to initiate and carry out independent research in diabetes. **Focus:** Diabetes. **Qualif.:** Applicant must be a Canadian citizen or permanent resident. Applicant must hold a doctorate (M.D., Ph.D., D.Sc., D.D.S., or D.V.M.) and must be about to take up a full-time university faculty appointment or have held such an appointment for less than 24 months.

**Funds Avail.:** $50,000 maximum; scholar receives $10,000 the first year. **To Apply:** Write to the research Coordinator for application materials. **Deadline:** December 1. **Contact:** Myrtella Hodge, Grants and Personnel Awards, at the above address (see entry 1619).

### • 1623 •
## Canadian Embassy, Washington, D.C. - Canadian Studies Grant Program

501 Pennsylvania Ave., NW
Washington, DC 20001      *Ph:* (202)682-1740
*URL:* http://www.cdnemb-washdc.org/

### • 1624 • Canadian Studies Faculty Enrichment Awards *(Professional Development/Award)*

**Purpose:** To encourage faculty members in the United States to teach courses with a substantial Canadian content. **Focus:** Canadian Studies. **Qualif.:** Applicant may be of any nationality, but must be a full-time faculty member at an accredited U.S. four-year college or university who wishes to teach courses about Canada. Candidate must have held a full-time position for at least two years at his/her present institution. Awards must be used to develop or modify courses that will be offered as a part of the awardee's regular teaching load. Candidate should be teaching or authorized to teach courses focusing substantially on Canadian studies. Courses may be in any discipline in the social sciences, business, environment, humanities, law, or fine arts. Awardees should spend at least part of the award tenure in Canada. Awards are only available for direct costs related to the project. Funds will not be paid for stipends or institutional overhead.

**Funds Avail.:** Up to $1,500/month. **To Apply:** Write to the academic relations officer for application form and guidelines. Submit six copies of the form with concise research proposal, curriculum vitae, syllabus proposal, and a letter of support from academic supervisor. Two letters of recommendation are also required. **Deadline:** October 31. Notification two months after the deadline. **Contact:** Dr. Norman T. London, Academic Relations Officer, at the above address (see entry 1623).

### • 1625 • Canadian Studies Faculty Research Grants
*(Postdoctorate/Grant)*

**Purpose:** To assist scholars in writing articles that will increase knowledge and understanding of Canada in the United States. **Focus:** Canadian Studies. **Qualif.:** Applicant may be of any nationality, but must be a full-time faculty member at an accredited four-year U.S. college or university, or a scholar at a U.S. research and policy-planning institute. Candidate must plan to undertake a significant Canadian or Canadian-U.S. research project that will result in an article-length manuscript of publishable quality. Grants are not given to support degree related research; nor are they intended for contractual or commissioned work. Awards are for direct costs only, and are not available for stipends or institutional overhead.

**Funds Avail.:** $1,000-6,000. **To Apply:** Write to the academic relations officer for application materials. Submit six copies of application form with a concise research proposal, detailed budget, and a curriculum vitae. Two letters of recommendation are also required. **Deadline:** September 30. Notification two months after the deadline. **Contact:** Dr. Norman T. London, Academic Relations Officer, at the above address (see entry 1623).

• **1626** • **Canadian Studies Graduate Student Fellowships** *(Doctorate/Fellowship)*

**Purpose:** To offer U.S. graduate students the opportunity to conduct part of their doctoral research in Canada **Focus:** Canadian Studies. **Qualif.:** Applicant must be a U.S. citizen or permanent resident. Applicant must be a full-time doctoral student at an accredited U.S. or Canadian institution who has completed all degree requirements except the dissertation. Dissertation may be in any discipline in the social sciences, business, environment, humanities, law, or fine arts, as long as it relates substantially to the study of Canada. Awards are tenable for research in Canada.

**Funds Avail.:** Up to $850/month. **To Apply:** Write to the academic relations officer for application form and guidelines. Submit six copies of form with educational information, research proposal, dissertation prospectus, transcripts, curriculum vitae, and proof of citizenship or residency status. Two letters of academic reference, including one from the dissertation advisor, are also required. **Deadline:** October 31. Notification two months after the deadline. **Contact:** Dr. Norman T. London, Academic Relations Officer, at the above address (see entry 1623).

• **1627** • **Canadian Studies Sabbatical Fellowship Program** *(Professional Development/Fellowship)*

**Purpose:** To assist scholars on their first sabbatical leave devoted to a project on Canada, write a manuscript of publishable quality and report their findings in scholarly publications. **Focus:** Business, Environment, Fine Arts, Humanities, Journalism, Law, Social Sciences as they relate to Canada, Canada-U.S., or Canada-North American relationships. **Qualif.:** Applicant must be a full-time faculty member at an accredited four-year U.S. college or university, on a first sabbatical leave, undertaking a project relating to Canada, Canada-U.S., or Canada-North American relationship. The Fellowship is for direct costs only. Fellow must spend a minimum of two months in Canada and be affiliated with a Canadian institution during the residency. Fellow is ineligible to receive two individual category Canadian Studies grants.

**Funds Avail.:** $8,000-12,000. **To Apply:** Write to the academic relations officer for application materials. Submit the original and five copies of the application form with a concise proposal, detailed budget, curriculum vitae, a letter from a Canadian institution extending an officer of affiliation, and two recommendations from scholars. **Deadline:** September 30. **Contact:** Dr. Norman T. London, Academic Relations Officer, at the above address (see entry 1623).

• **1628** • **Canadian Studies Senior Fellowships** *(Postdoctorate/Fellowship)*

**Purpose:** To provide senior scholars with an opportunity to complete and publish a major study which will significantly benefit the development of Canadian studies in the United States. **Focus:** Canadian Studies. **Qualif.:** Applicant may be of any nationality, but must be a full-time, tenured faculty member at an accredited four-year U.S. college or university who is fully involved in Canadian studies. Candidate must be in the process of completing research for a book or major monograph focusing on a subject of widespread interest to the Canadian studies community in the United States and Canada. Research must be conducted on a full-time basis; candidate's academic department must be prepared to relieve all teaching and administrative duties for the tenure of the award. Funds are provided to defray direct costs of research only.

**Funds Avail.:** $3,000/month maximum. **To Apply:** Write to the academic relations officer for application materials. Submit six

copies of the application form with statement of background and current interests in Canadian studies, detailed budget and research schedule, a presentation of the book's key issues and methodology, curriculum vitae, and a letter of support from department head. Three letters of recommendation are also required. **Deadline:** October 31. Notification two months after the deadline. **Contact:** Dr. Norman T. London, Academic Relations Officer, at the above address (see entry 1623).

• **1629** •
**Canadian Federation of University Women**
251 Bank St. 600
Ottawa, ON, Canada K2P 1X3          *Ph:* (613)234-2732
*URL:* http://www.cfuw.ca

• **1630** • **1989 Polytechnique Commemorative Award** *(Graduate/Award)*

**Purpose:** To support graduate studies. **Focus:** General studies. **Qualif.:** Applicant must be a female Canadian citizen or have held landed immigrant status for at least one year and hold a bachelor's degree or equivalent from a recognized university. Applicant must have been accepted into the proposed place of study at the time of application. **Criteria:** Based on special consideration for study of issues related particularly to women.

**Funds Avail.:** $2,400. **No. of Awards:** One. **To Apply:** For application forms and guidelines contact the Canadian Federation of University Women. A non-refundable filing fee of $20 must accompany each application. **Deadline:** November 15. **Contact:** Fellowships Secretary, at the above address (see entry 1629).

• **1631** • **CFUW Awards** *(Graduate/Award)*

**Purpose:** To support graduate study. **Focus:** Science/Technology, French Language Studies, Humanities, Social Science. **Qualif.:** Applicant must be a female Canadian citizen or landed immigrant of at least one year, with a bachelor's degree or the equivalent. Candidate must be accepted into a program of study at the time of application. There are four types of CFUW awards, each with slightly different requirements in addition to the basic restrictions listed above: The CFUW Memorial Award ($1,000) is offered to a scholar studying science and/or technology. La Bourse Georgette Lemoyne ($1,000) is awarded for study at a Canadian university where one of the languages of administration and instruction is French. Preference for Alice E. Wilson Awards ($1,000) is given to candidates returning to study after a few years. The Margaret Dale Philp Award ($1,000) is for studies in the humanities or social sciences. Philp Award recipients must study in Canada; special consideration is given to candidates in Canadian history.

**Funds Avail.:** $2,000. **No. of Awards:** 6. **To Apply:** Write to the CFUW fellowships secretary for application materials, available between August and mid-November. Submit application form with filing fee ($20). **Deadline:** November 15. Award recipients are notified by May 31. **Contact:** Fellowships Secretary.

• **1632** • **CFUW Professional Fellowship** *(Graduate/Fellowship)*

**Purpose:** To assist Canadian women with graduate studies at the Master's degree level. **Focus:** General Studies. **Qualif.:** Applicant must be a female Canadian citizen or landed immigrant of at least one year, with a bachelor's degree or the equivalent. Candidate must be accepted to a graduate program at time of application; studies should be at the Master's level and may be conducted in Canada or abroad.

**Funds Avail.:** $5,000. **No. of Awards:** One. **To Apply:** Write to the CFUW fellowships secretary for application materials, available between August and mid-November. Submit application form with filing fee ($25). **Deadline:** November 15. Applicants are notified by

*Canadian Federation of University Women (continued)*

May 31. **Contact:** Fellowships Secretary, at the above address (see entry 1629).

• **1633** • **Dr. Marion Elder Grant Fellowship**
*(Graduate/Fellowship)*

**Purpose:** To support graduate study. **Focus:** General Studies. **Qualif.:** Applicant must be a female Canadian citizen or landed immigrant of at least one year with a bachelor's degree. Candidate must be accepted t a graduate program at the time of application. **Criteria:** Preference is given to graduates of Acadia University.

**Funds Avail.:** $8,000. **No. of Awards:** One. **To Apply:** Write to the CFUW fellowships secretary for application materials, available between August and mid-November. Submit application form with filing fee ($25). **Deadline:** November 15. Award applicants are notified by May 31. **Contact:** Fellowships Secretary, at the above address (see entry 1629).

• **1634** • **Beverley Jackson Fellowship** *(Graduate/Fellowship)*

**Purpose:** To support graduate study. **Focus:** General Studies. **Qualif.:** Applicant must be a female Canadian citizen or landed immigrant of at least one year, over the age of 35 with a bachelor's degree or the equivalent. Candidate must be accepted into a program of study in an Ontario university at the time of application.

**Funds Avail.:** $3,500. **No. of Awards:** One. **To Apply:** Write to the CFUW fellowships secretary for application materials, available between August and mid-November. Submit application form with filing fee ($20). **Deadline:** November 15. Award applicants will be notified by May 31. **Contact:** Fellowships Secretary, at the above address (see entry 1629).

• **1635** • **Margaret McWilliams Predoctoral Fellowship** *(Doctorate/Fellowship)*

**Purpose:** To support doctoral studies by Canadian women. **Focus:** General Studies. **Qualif.:** Applicant must be a female Canadian citizen or landed immigrant of at least one year, with a bachelor's degree or equivalent. Candidate should have completed at least twelve months of doctoral studies at time of application. Fellowship is tenable in Canada and abroad.

**Funds Avail.:** $10,000. **No. of Awards:** One. **To Apply:** Write to the CFUW fellowships secretary for application materials, available between August and mid-November. Submit application form with filing fee ($35). **Deadline:** November 15. The applicants are notified by May 31. **Contact:** Fellowships Secretary, at the above address (see entry 1629).

• **1636** • **Alice E. Wilson Award** *(Graduate/Other)*

**Purpose:** To provide graduate level study for women. **Focus:** General studies. **Qualif.:** Applicants must hold at least a Bachelor's degree or equivalent from a recognized university; have been accepted into the proposed program and place of study; and be a Canadian citizen or have held landed immigrant status for at least one year. Special consideration is given to students returning to study after at least three years. **No. of Awards:** 3. **To Apply:** A filling fee of $20 plus a completed application (clearly indicating the fellowship or award for which the applicant is applying) must be submitted. Write for application forms and guidelines. **Deadline:** November 15.

• **1637** •
**The Canadian Foundation for the Study of Infant Deaths**
586 Eglinton Ave. E, Ste. 308                *Ph:* (416)488-3260
Toronto, ON, Canada M4P 1P2            *Fax:* (416)488-3864
                                                              *Free:* 800-363-7437
*URL:* http://www.vois.org.uk/fsid/

• **1638** • **Dr. Sydney Segal Research Grants**
*(Doctorate, Graduate/Grant)*

**Purpose:** To encourage graduate research related to Sudden Infant Death Syndrome (SIDS). **Focus:** Sudden Infant Death Syndrome. **Qualif.:** Candidates must be researchers or students enrolled at a Canadian university or teaching hospital, in a health science program leading to an M.Sc., M.D., or Ph.D. degree. A grant is tenable at the home institution, and must be applied to the cost of conducting research related to SIDS. **Criteria:** Applicants are judged on merit.

**Funds Avail.:** MRC Guidelines. **To Apply:** Write to the executive director for application guidelines and forms. **Deadline:** June 1.

**Remarks:** If funds are available, special projects my be funded for qualified applicants. Letter of intent required. **Contact:** Executive Director at the above address (see entry 1637).

• **1639** •
**Canadian Friends of the Hebrew University**
3080 Yonge St., Ste. 5024                    *Ph:* (416)485-8000
Toronto, ON, Canada M4N 3P4           *Fax:* (416)485-8565
*E-mail:* 75477.201@compuserve.com; 75477.201@ compuserve.com

• **1640** • **Grants for Canadians** *(Doctorate, Graduate, Undergraduate/Grant)*

**Purpose:** To support Canadian students studying at the Hebrew University of Jerusalem **Focus:** General. **Qualif.:** Applicant must be a Canadian citizen or landed immigrant. Grants are tenable at the Hebrew University of Jerusalem and may be used for exchange and degree programs.

**Funds Avail.:** $750-4,000. **No. of Awards:** Varies. **To Apply:** Write for application form. **Deadline:** April 1. **Contact:** Academic Affairs Officer at the above address (see entry 1639).

• **1641** •
**Canadian Golf Foundation**
Golf House
1333 Dorval Dr.
Oakville, ON, Canada L6J 4Z3              *Ph:* (905)849-9700

• **1642** • **Canadian Golf Foundation Scholarships**
*(Undergraduate/Scholarship)*

**Focus:** General Studies. **Qualif.:** Applicants must be undergraduates and demonstrate successful competitive golf experience and participation in extracurricular and community activities. **Criteria:** Selection is based on academic merit.

**Funds Avail.:** Awards up to $4,000/year. **No. of Awards:** Varies. **Deadline:** June 21. **Contact:** Scholarship committee at the above address (see entry 1641).

## • 1643 •
## Canadian Home Economics Association
151 Slater St., Ste. 901      *Ph:* (613)238-8817
Ottawa, ON, Canada K1P 5H3     *Fax:* (613)238-1677

### • 1644 • Ruth Binnie Scholarships *(Graduate/Scholarship)*

**Purpose:** To encourage outstanding Canadian home economics education students. **Focus:** Home Economics Education. **Qualif.:** Applicant must be a Canadian citizen or landed immigrant and be a member of CHEA. Candidate must hold a professional teaching degree and be enrolled in a graduate course of study related to home economics education. First consideration is given to applicants in full-time master's-in-education programs. Candidate must be committed to a career of teaching and home economics education at the high school or junior high school level.

**Funds Avail.:** $5,000. **No. of Awards:** 1 full-time, 1 part-time or 2 part-time. **To Apply:** Write to the CHEA Scholarship Fund for application form and guidelines. **Deadline:** January 15. **Contact:** Scholarship Fund at the above address (see entry 1643).

### • 1645 • CHEA Fiftieth Anniversary Scholarship *(Doctorate/Scholarship)*

**Qualif.:** Applicants must be Canadian citizens or landed immigrants and have been members of CHEA for at least two years. All candidates must be graduates in home economics or a related field such as human ecology or family and consumer sciences, who are undertaking graduate studies proceeding to a higher academic degree. Previous CHEA scholarship or award winners are eligible to reapply for awards provided they continue to be enrolled in graduate study. **Criteria:** The award is based on scholarship, personal qualities, past and/or potential contributions to the profession of home economics, and financial considerations.

**Funds Avail.:** The scholarship is worth $3,000-$4,000. **No. of Awards:** 1. **To Apply:** Application forms are available through the faculty office or from the CHEA National Office. **Deadline:** January 15. **Contact:** Faculty offices or CHEA at the above address (see entry 1643).

### • 1646 • CHEA Silver Jubilee Scholarship *(Graduate/Scholarship)*

**Qualif.:** Applicants must be Canadian citizens or landed immigrants and members of CHEA. All candidates must be graduates in home economics or a related field, such as human ecology or family and consumer sciences, who are undertaking graduate studies proceeding to a higher academic degree. Previous CHEA scholarship/award winners are eligible to reapply for awards provided they continue to be enrolled in graduate study. **Criteria:** Scholarship, personal qualities, past and/or potential contributions to the profession of home economics, and financial considerations.

**Funds Avail.:** The scholarship is worth $3,000-$4,000. **No. of Awards:** 1. **To Apply:** Application forms are available through the faculty office or from the CHEA National Office at the above address. **Deadline:** January 15. **Contact:** Canadian Home Economics Association at the above address (see entry 1643).

### • 1647 • Mary A. Clarke Memorial Scholarship *(Graduate/Scholarship)*

**Qualif.:** Applicants must be Canadian citizens or landed immigrants and members of CHEA. All candidates must be graduates in home economics or a related field such as human ecology or family of consumer sciences who are undertaking graduate studies proceeding to a higher academic degree. Previous CHEA scholarship or award winners are eligible to reapply for awards provided they continue to be enrolled in

graduate study. **Criteria:** The award will be based on scholarship, personal qualities, past and/or potential contributions to the profession of home economics, and financial considerations.

**Funds Avail.:** The scholarship is worth $3,000-$4,000. **No. of Awards:** 1. **To Apply:** Application forms are available through the faculty office or from the CHEA National Office. **Deadline:** January 15.

**Remarks:** This scholarship was established as a tribute to Mary Clarke, a valued member of the Canadian Home Economics Association, and President from 1952 to 1954. **Contact:** The Canadian Home Economics Association at the above address (see entry 1643).

### • 1648 • Federated Women's Institutes of Ontario International Scholarship *(Graduate, Undergraduate/Scholarship)*

**Focus:** Human development. **Qualif.:** Applicants must be international students from a CIDA-eligible country; studying at an Ontario university; planning to return to their home country to work in development of human potential; either graduate or undergraduate students. **Criteria:** Based on excellence in scholastic achievement, leadership, and professional potential.

**Funds Avail.:** $2500. **Deadline:** January 15.

### • 1649 • Kraft Canada Inc. Undergraduate Scholarship *(Undergraduate/Scholarship)*

**Focus:** Food services and home economics. **Qualif.:** Applicants must be Canadian citizens or landed immigrants who are third or fourth year students enrolled in a home economics or consumer- or foods-related program at a university offering a home economics perspective as approved by the Canadian Home economics Association. **Criteria:** Based on the applicants involvement, interest in foods and nutrition, leadership, volunteer activities, scholarship, and potential contribution to the profession of home economics.

**Funds Avail.:** $1500. **Deadline:** Applications must be postmarked no later than March 31.

### • 1650 • Nestle Canada Scholarship *(Graduate/Award)*

**Qualif.:** Applicants must be Canadian citizens or landed immigrants and members of CHEA. All candidates must be graduates in home economics or a related field such as Food and Nutrition who are undertaking graduate studies proceeding to a higher academic degree. Previous CHEA scholarship or award winners are eligible to reapply for awards provided they continue to be enrolled in graduate study. **Criteria:** Special consideration will be given to a student undertaking post graduate study in foods. The award is based on scholarship, personal qualities, past and/or potential contributions to the home economics profession, and financial considerations.

**Funds Avail.:** The scholarship is worth $1,000. **No. of Awards:** 1. **To Apply:** Application forms are available through the faculty office or from the CHEA National Office. **Deadline:** January 15.

**Remarks:** This award is presented by Nestle Canada Limited. **Contact:** Faculty offices or CHEA at the above address (see entry 1643).

### • 1651 • Robin Hood Multifoods Scholarship *(Graduate/Award)*

**Qualif.:** Applicants must be Canadian citizens or landed immigrants and members of CHEA. All candidates must be graduates in home economics or related field such as Consumer Sciences who are undertaking graduate studies proceeding to a higher academic degree. Previous CHEA scholarship/award winners are eligible to reapply for awards provided they continue to be enrolled in graduate study. **Criteria:** Preference is given to

---

## Canadian Home Economics Association (continued)

applicants planning a career in business, in the consumer service (foods) field, or food service management. The award is based on scholarship, personal qualities, past and/or potential contributions to the profession of home economics, and financial considerations.

**Funds Avail.:** The scholarship is worth $1,000. **No. of Awards:** 1. **To Apply:** Application forms are available through the faculty office or from the CHEA National Office. **Deadline:** January 15.

**Remarks:** This award is presented by Robin Hood Multifoods Inc. **Contact:** Faculty office or CHEA at the above address (see entry 1643).

## • 1652 •
## Canadian Hospitality Foundation

300 Adelaide St. E., Ste. 213      *Ph:* (416)363-3401
Toronto, ON, Canada M5A 1N1      *Fax:* (416)363-3403

### • 1653 • Canadian Hospitality Foundation Scholarships *(Undergraduate/Scholarship)*

**Qualif.:** Applicants must be students planning to enter a degree program in hotel and food administration, institutional food service management, food and beverage management, lodging and institutional management, or hospitality and tourism management at the University of Guelph, Ryerson Polytechnic Institute, or Mount Saint Vincent University.

**Funds Avail.:** Nine awards between $1,000 and $2,000 each. **Deadline:** March 1. **Contact:** Awards Committee, Canadian Hospitality Foundation, at the above address (see entry 1652).

## • 1654 •
## Canadian Institute for Advanced Legal Studies

4 Beechwood Ave., Ste. 203      *Ph:* (613)744-6166
Ottawa, ON, Canada K1L 8L9      *Fax:* (613)744-5766

### • 1655 • Graduate Scholarships at University of Cambridge *(Graduate/Scholarship)*

**Purpose:** To encourage the study of law by Canadian scholars. **Focus:** Law. **Qualif.:** Applicants may be of any nationality, but must be currently in a bar admission course in Canada, in articling year, or in third year in a Canadian law school. Scholarships are tenable at the University of Cambridge. **Criteria:** Selection is based on legal transcripts and undergraduate transcripts.

**Funds Avail.:** Approximately $16,000. **To Apply:** Submit statement of planned course of study and future goals, curriculum vitae, transcripts, and letters of reference from three persons. **Deadline:** December 31. **Contact:** The Institute at the above address (see entry 1654).

## • 1656 •
## Canadian Institute of Ukrainian Studies

University of Alberta
352 Athabasca Hall      *Ph:* (403)492-2972
Edmonton, AB, Canada T6G 2E8      *Fax:* (403)492-4967
*E-mail:* cius@pop.srv.ualberta.ca

### • 1657 • Helen Darcovich Memorial Doctoral Fellowship *(Doctorate, Graduate/Fellowship)*

**Purpose:** To support graduate study on Ukrainian or Ukrainian Canadian topics. **Focus:** Canadian Studies, Ukrainian Studies and related disciplines. **Qualif.:** Candidate must be a graduate student who is writing a dissertation on a Ukrainian or Ukrainian Canadian topic. Applicant may be enrolled in any of the following disciplines: education, history, law, humanities, arts, social sciences, women's studies, and library sciences. Fellowships are awarded only for the thesis/dissertation year of an academic program and only for thesis/dissertation work. Canadian citizens and landed immigrants may use the fellowships at any institution of higher learning in Canada or elsewhere. Non-Canadians must study in Canada; preference is given to students enrolled at the University of Alberta. Only in exceptional circumstances may a fellowship be held concurrently with other awards. **Criteria:** Applications will be judged on a points system based on the dissertation proposal, letters of reference, writing sample, grades, and publishing record.

**Funds Avail.:** $8,000. **To Apply:** Write to the Institute for application guidelines. **Deadline:** May 1.

**Remarks:** Write to the Institute for application forms and the Guide to Research Applications.

### • 1658 • Doctoral Thesis Fellowship in Ukrainian History *(Doctorate/Fellowship)*

**Purpose:** To assist a graduate student to complete a dissertation in Ukrainian history. **Focus:** Ukrainian History. **Qualif.:** Candidate must be a doctoral candidate with only the dissertation requirement to complete. Applicant must be writing his/her dissertation on some aspect of Ukrainian history and should be able to complete the thesis during the fellowship year. Awards are tenable at the Centre (which is part of the Institute) or elsewhere.

**Funds Avail.:** $10,000 maximum. **To Apply:** Write to the Centre for application guidelines. Submit a dissertation prospectus, a work plan for the fellowship year, information about other sources of possible funding, and copies of all work completed or in progress. Two letters of recommendation, including one from the principal dissertation advisor, are required. **Deadline:** May 1.

**Remarks:** The Institute also invites applications for research grants in Ukrainian and Ukrainian Canadian studies. Scholars in history, literature, language, education, the social sciences, and library sciences are all eligible to apply. Write to the Institute for application forms and the Guide to Research Applications. **Contact:** Khrystyna Kohut, Administrative Assistant, at the above address (see entry 1656).

### • 1659 • Marusia and Michael Dorosh Masters Fellowship *(Graduate/Fellowship)*

**Purpose:** To support a student writing a thesis on a Ukranian or Ukranian-Candaian topic. **Focus:** Education, history, law, humanities, arts, social sciences, women's studies, library sciences. **Criteria:** Applications will be judged on a point system in which the thesis proposal, grades, letters of reference, and writing sample are equally weighted. Canadian citizens, permanent residents, and foreign students enrolled at the University of Alberta will receive extra points.

**Funds Avail.:** $4,500, non-renewable. **Deadline:** May 1.

**• 1660 • Leo J. Krysa Family Foundation Undergraduate Scholarship** *(Undergraduate/Scholarship)*

**Focus:** Education, History, Humanities, Social Sciences. **Qualif.:** Applicants must be undergraduate students and Canadian citizens entering their final year of study in an Arts or Education program pursuing a degree with emphasis on Ukrainian studies, through a combination of courses in Ukrainian and East European, or Canadian studies in an arts or education program. Scholarship is tenable at any Canadian university.

**Funds Avail.:** $1,500. **To Apply:** Applications may be obtained from the Institute at the above address. **Deadline:** May 1.

**• 1661 • Neporany Research and Teaching Fellowship** *(Postdoctorate, Professional Development/ Fellowship)*

**Purpose:** To enable fellows to teach a course related to Ukrainian studies. **Qualif.:** Applicants must hold a doctoral degree or have equivalent professional achievement in Ukrainian studies. Fellowships are tenable at any university with research facilities for Ukrainian studies.

**Funds Avail.:** $20,000. **Deadline:** March 1. **Contact:** Canadian Institute of Ukrainian Studies at the above address (see entry 1656).

**• 1662 •**
**Canadian Labour Congress**
2841 Riverside Drive          Ph: (613)521-3400
Ottawa, ON, Canada K1V 8X7    Fax: (613)521-5480

**• 1663 • A. A. Heaps Scholarships** *(Graduate, Undergraduate/Scholarship)*

**Purpose:** To support study at a Canadian institution. **Focus:** General Studies. **Qualif.:** Applicants must be Canadian citizens or landed immigrants and enrolled full-time in graduate or undergraduate studies at a Canadian university during the academic year of application. They must also submit an essay that demonstrates a commitment to the social ideals characterized by the work of A.A. Heaps.

**Funds Avail.:** $3,000. **No. of Awards:** 1. **To Apply:** There is no official application form; write for application guidelines. Submit one copy of a 500-1,000 word biographical essay, statement of financial need, academic transcripts, and the names of two referees. **Deadline:** May 15. Recipient is notified by July 15. **Contact:** M. Hanratty or A.A. Heaps Scholarship Committee, at the above address (see entry 1662).

**• 1664 •**
**Canadian Library Association**
200 Elgin St., Ste. 602          Ph: (613)232-9625
Ottawa, ON, Canada K2P 1L5       Fax: (613)563-9895
*URL:* http://www.cla.amlibs.ca/

**• 1665 • CLA DaFoe Scholarships** *(Graduate/ Scholarship)*

**Focus:** Library and Archival Sciences. **Qualif.:** Applicants must be entering an accredited Canadian library school to obtain their first professional degree. They must also be Canadian citizens or landed immigrants. **Criteria:** Selection is based on academic record and financial need.

**Funds Avail.:** $1,750 for one year. **To Apply:** Applicants are required to complete CLA Scholarship Application Forms with transcripts with reference and proof of admission to a library school. **Deadline:** May 1. **Contact:** Canadian Library Association, Scholarship and Awards Committee, at the above address (see entry 1664).

**• 1666 • Library Research and Development Grants** *(Professional Development/Grant)*

**Focus:** Library and Archival Sciences. **Qualif.:** Applicants must be personal members of the Canadian Library Association conducting theoretical and applied research in library and information science. **Criteria:** The proposal for funding is judged on originality or necessity of research; appropriateness of proposed project to the goals and objectives of the Canadian Library Association; cost-effectiveness of research in terms of the expected influence and ramifications of the results; timeliness of the research; assurance of project management and control; appropriateness of the proposed research method and design; completeness of application; and availability of researcher to other funding.

**Funds Avail.:** One or more grants totalling $1,000 are awarded annually when merited. **To Apply:** Grant applications should be submitted in the form of a letter containing name and address of applicant, mailing address and date of application; a reasonable description of the research project identifying methodology and design; duration of the project, including a detailed project timetable; assessment of the potential utility of research results to the Canadian Library community; detailed assessment of costs and statement of other grants or awards received; and assessment of relevance of the research to the goals and objectives of the Canadian Library Association. **Deadline:** May 1. **Contact:** Canadian Library Association, Library Research and Development Committee, at the above address (see entry 1664).

**• 1667 • The H.W. Wilson Scholarships** *(Graduate/ Scholarship)*

**Focus:** Library and Archival Sciences. **Qualif.:** Applicants must be entering an accredited library school for their first professional degree and be Canadian citizens or landed immigrants. **Criteria:** Selection is based on academic standing and financial need.

**Funds Avail.:** $2,000. **To Apply:** Applicants are required to complete CLA Scholarship Application Forms with transcripts, references, and proof of admission to a library school. **Deadline:** May 1. **Contact:** Canadian Library Association, Scholarship and Awards Committee, at the above address (see entry 1664).

**• 1668 • World Book Graduate Scholarships in Library Science** *(Doctorate, Postgraduate/Scholarship)*

**Purpose:** To support Canadian library students. **Focus:** Library and Archival Sciences. **Qualif.:** Applicants must be Canadian citizens or landed immigrants. Normally, candidates must already hold a B.L.S. or M.L.S. degree, but in exceptional circumstances consideration will be given to outstanding candidates with a degree in another discipline who wish to obtain their first library degree. The scholarship is tenable at accredited library schools in the United States or Canada. Award must be used for a program of study or series of courses leading to a further library degree; related to library work in which the candidate is currently engaged; or relevant to library work that will be undertaken on completion of the program or courses.

**Funds Avail.:** $2,500. **No. of Awards:** One. **To Apply:** Write to the CLA Scholarships and Awards Committee for application form and guidelines. **Deadline:** May 1. **Contact:** Scholarships and Awards Committee at the above address (see entry 1664).

---

• 1669 •
## Canadian Liver Foundation
365 Bloor St. E, No. 200
Toronto, ON, Canada M4W 3L4
*E-mail:* clf@liver.ca
*URL:* http://www.liver.ca/

*Ph:* (416)964-1953
*Fax:* (416)964-0024

### • 1670 • Canadian Liver Foundation Establishment Grants *(Postdoctorate/Grant)*

**Purpose:** To provide hepatologists and scientists with funds to begin liver research projects. **Focus:** Hepatology. **Qualif.:** Candidates must be Canadian citizens and hold M.D. or Ph.D. degrees, with proven interest in the structure, function, and diseases of the liver. Applicants must have completed a minimum of two years of formal research training and have obtained additional research experience as clinical investigators or postdoctoral fellows. Candidates must be prepared to spend 80% of their time in research and to commit remaining time to active participation in teaching and/or patient care. Research must be at investigator's own laboratory at a Canadian university. **Criteria:** Based on peer review.

**Funds Avail.:** $60,000/year. **To Apply:** Obtain application guidelines and forms through the dean of the faculty of medicine at home institution or by writing to the Foundation. **Deadline:** November 1. Awards announced in April. Funding commences July 1. **Contact:** Ms. E.J. Girouard, Executive/Research Secretary, at the above address (see entry 1669).

### • 1671 • Canadian Liver Foundation Fellowships *(Postdoctorate/Fellowship)*

**Purpose:** To help Canadian doctors obtain further training in the study of liver diseases at internationally recognized centers. **Focus:** Hepatology. **Qualif.:** Applicants must have an M.D. or Ph.D. degrees and be either Canadian citizens or landed immigrant residents in Canada at time of application. Applicants must be sponsored by faculty members of medicine or health sciences. **Criteria:** Based on peer review.

**Funds Avail.:** Varies based on qualifications and seniority of applicant. **To Apply:** Write to the Foundation for application form. Submit six copies with letter of support from dean or designate, letters of recommendation, and official transcripts. **Deadline:** November 1. Awards announced in April. **Contact:** Ms. E.J. Girouard, Executive/Research Secretary, at the above address (see entry 1669).

### • 1672 • Canadian Liver Foundation Graduate Studentships *(Doctorate, Graduate/Award)*

**Purpose:** To help academically superior students to undertake full-time studies in Canadian universities. **Focus:** Hepatology. **Qualif.:** Candidate must be accepted into a full-time university graduate science program in a medically related discipline leading to an M.S. or Ph.D. degree and hold a superior academic record in studies relevant to the proposed training. Research must be conducted under the sponsorship of an experienced liver research scientist. **Criteria:** Based on peer review.

**Funds Avail.:** Approximately $16,000 per year. **No. of Awards:** in 1993 ,4 original plus 10 renewals. **To Apply:** Obtain application guidelines and forms through the office of the dean of the faculty of medicine at home institution, or by writing to the Foundation. **Deadline:** February 15. Awards announced in April. **Contact:** Ms. E.J. Girouard, Executive/Research Secretary, at the above address (see entry 1669).

### • 1673 • Canadian Liver Foundation Operating Grant Program *(Postdoctorate/Grant)*

**Purpose:** To provide support for research and education in the causes, diagnosis, prevention, and treatment of diseases of the liver. **Focus:** Hepatology. **Qualif.:** Eligible candidates are independent investigators who hold an academic appointment at a Canadian university in a Faculty of Medicine, Nursing, Pharmacy, or Veterinary Medicine. **Criteria:** Based on scientific merit and relevance of proposed research program.

**Funds Avail.:** Up to $60,000 annually for two years, although the amount funded will be established on the basis of the financial requirements of the proposed research program and whether the amount of the grant is justified by the extent and significance of the research program. These grants may be used to purchase materials, supplies, and items of equipment costing less than $5,000, to buy and maintain animals, and to support travel costs (to a limit of $1,000). It is not possible to support trainee salaries nor major equipment purchases. **To Apply:** Eight copies of the application and all attachments must be submitted. **Deadline:** November 1. Awards are announced in early April. Funding commences July 1. **Contact:** National Liver Foundation at the above address (see entry 1669).

### • 1674 • Canadian Liver Foundation Summer Studentship Award *(Graduate/Internship)*

**Purpose:** To provide support for research and education in the causes, diagnosis, prevention, and treatment of diseases of the liver. **Focus:** Hepatology. **Qualif.:** Students must be registered at a Canadian institution in an undergraduate program. A limit of two applications may be sponsored by a faculty supervisor, who must have a record of productive medical research related to the liver and adequate research funding and is prepared to provide the student with direct supervision during the term of the award. As summer students often require intensive supervision and in an attempt to meet regional needs, the Medical Advisory Board of the Canadian Liver Foundation has recommended that only one summer studentship be awarded to each supervisor. Students must be prepared to participate in the project on a full-time basis and to agree not to change supervisors during the term of the award. **Criteria:** All applications will be reviewed by the same three referees. Each application will be scored out of a maximum of ten points. Applicants will be ranked according to the average score of the three reviewers.

**Funds Avail.:** Approximately $4,000 each. **No. of Awards:** Up to ten. **To Apply:** Guidelines and application forms for Studentship awards are available at medical schools through the office of the Associate Dean of Undergraduate Affairs for Summer Studentships or from the Canadian Liver Foundation. Instructions for completing the form must be followed precisely, and applications must be typewritten. The original plus four copies of the application, complete with the candidate's up-to-date transcript and one letter of reference, must be submitted to the Foundation. When the research program with which the student will be associated involves human subjects, the use of animals, or a biohazardous material, it is the responsibility of the sponsoring faculty and/or department to ensure that the research has received the approval of the appropriate institutional committee(s). **Deadline:** February 15. **Contact:** Executive Secretary, Canadian Liver Foundation, at the above address (see entry 1669).

• 1675 •
## Canadian National Institute for the Blind - E.A. Baker Foundation - Professional Advisory Committee
1929 Bayview Ave.
Toronto, ON, Canada M4G 3E8
*URL:* http://www.cnib.ca

*Ph:* (416)480-7587
*Fax:* (416)480-7000

### • 1676 • E. A. Baker Foundation Fellowships and Research Grants *(Postgraduate/Fellowship, Grant)*

**Purpose:** To encourage research to prevent blindness. **Focus:** Ophthalmology. **Qualif.:** Applicants must be Canadian residents qualified to conduct postgraduate research related to the prevention of blindness and/or eye diseases. Awards are tenable in Canada or elsewhere if adequate research facilities are unavailable in Canada. Fellowships provide for living expenses; research grants must be applied to direct research costs. **Criteria:** Research priorityis given to scientists in the intial five years of their career.

**Funds Avail.:** Up to $40,000. **No. of Awards:** 18. **To Apply:** Write to the secretary for application guidelines or check website **Deadline:** December 1. **Contact:** The Canadian National Institute for the Blind, Baker Foundation, at the above address (see entry 1675).

---

### • 1677 •
### Canadian Northern Studies Trust - Association of Canadian Universities for Northern Studies

17 York St., Ste. 405
Ottawa, ON, Canada K1N 9J6
*E-mail:* acuns@cyberus.ca

*Ph:* (613)562-0515
*Fax:* (613)562-0533

#### • 1678 • Beverly and Qamanirjaq Caribou Management Scholarship *(Graduate, Undergraduate/ Grant)*

**Purpose:** To fund studies related to the Beverly and Qamanirjuaq Barren Ground caribou herds and their habitat. **Focus:** Caribou. **Qualif.:** Applicant must be a Canadian citizen or landed immigrant. Preference may be given to individuals who are normally resident in one of the caribou-using communities on the range of the Beverly or Qamanirjuaq caribou. Candidate must be enrolled in full-time studies at a recognized Canadian community college or university.

**Funds Avail.:** $3,000 maximum. **No. of Awards:** One. **To Apply:** Write to the secretary for application guidelines. **Deadline:** January 31. **Contact:** Administrator at the above address (see entry 1677).

#### • 1679 • James W. Bourque Studentship in Northern Geography *(Other/Scholarship)*

**Purpose:** To recognize outstanding students. **Focus:** Northern geograhpical or related research. **Qualif.:** Applicants must be students at a Canadian university.

**Funds Avail.:** $10,000. **To Apply:** Write for additional information and application materials.

**Remarks:** Sponsored by Royal Canadian Geographical Society.

#### • 1680 • Caribou Research Bursary *(Other/ Scholarship)*

**Purpose:** To contribute to the understanding of Barren Ground Caribou and its habitat in Canada. **Focus:** Agricluture. **Qualif.:** Applicants must be full-time students enrolled in a recognized Canadian community college or university. **Criteria:** Preference will be given to students normally living in one of the caribou-using communities on the range of the Beverly or Qamanirjuaq caribou.

**Funds Avail.:** Up to $3000. **To Apply:** Write for additional information and application material. **Deadline:** January 31.

**Remarks:** Funded by the Beverly and Qamanirjuaq Caribou Management Scholarship Fund.

#### • 1681 • Cooperatives Bursary *(Other/Scholarship)*

**Purpose:** To support a student whose studies will contribute to the understanding and development of cooperatives in the Northwest Territories. **Focus:** General studies. **Qualif.:** Applicants must be either residents of northern Canada or full-time students at a recognized Canadian community college or university. **Criteria:** Preference will be given to northern residents.

**Funds Avail.:** $2000. **To Apply:** Write for additional information and application material. **Deadline:** January 31.

**Remarks:** Cosponsord by Arctic Co-operatives Ltd.; the NWT Cooperative Business Development Fund; and the Canadian Northern Studies Trust.

#### • 1682 • Research Support Opportunities in Arctic Environmental Studies *(Doctorate, Graduate/Other)*

**Purpose:** To provide logistical support to graduate students for environmental research in the Arctic. **Focus:** Arctic Studies, Climatology, Environmental Sciences, Meteorology. **Qualif.:** Applicant must be a Canadian citizen or permanent resident enrolled in a master's or doctoral program at a Canadian university. Preference is given to environmental research proposals in the physical and/or biological sciences for which location at the High Arctic Weather Station in Eureka is demonstrably advantageous, but opportunities are not confined to students engaged in weather-related studies. Opportunities are tenable at the High Arctic Weather Station in Eureka. Awards provide accommodation, facilities, and research support services at the Stations. Funds to cover the cost of conducting research are not available.

**Funds Avail.:** Room and board, research facilities and support **No. of Awards:** 1 or 2 awards are offered. **To Apply:** For further information on the Weather Stations' facilities and resources, contact the Superintendent of Arctic Operations at AES. For application materials, write to the Trust. **Deadline:** January 31.

**Remarks:** The award is cosponsored by the Atmospheric Envisionment Service of Environment Canada. **Contact:** Administrator at the above address (see entry 1677).

#### • 1683 • Special Bursary For Northern Residents *(Other/Scholarship)*

**Purpose:** To permit Northerners to undertake studies in a field of interest that will further their careers in the north or assist their local communities. **Focus:** The program of studies can be flexible and may not necessarily lead to the completion of a degree or diploma. **Qualif.:** Applicants must be residents of Northern Canada.

**Funds Avail.:** $5000. **To Apply:** Write for additional information and application material. **Deadline:** January 31.

**Remarks:** It is desirable that the student have a sponsor at the institution of learning and a mutually satisfactory program of studies is agreed upon.

#### • 1684 • Studentships in Northern Studies *(Graduate, Undergraduate/Scholarship)*

**Purpose:** To encourage students to undertake research relevant to Canada's northern territories and adjacent regions. **Focus:** All subject areas. **Qualif.:** Applicant must be a Canadian citizen or permanent resident enrolled in a graduate or undergraduate degree program or other course of study at a Canadian university. Candidate may be studying in any subject, but the proposed inquiry must pertain to northern Canadian themes, problems, or issues. Preference will be given to candidates who will engage in research culminating in a thesis or similar document and whose programs will involve direct experience in the Canadian North.

**Funds Avail.:** $10,000. **No. of Awards:** Varies. **To Apply:** Write to the Trust for application materials. **Deadline:** January 31. Notification in April. **Contact:** Administrator at the above address (see entry 1677).

---

• 1685 •
## Canadian Nurses Foundation
50 Driveway
Ottawa, ON, Canada K2P 1E2

Ph: (613)237-2133
Fax: (613)237-3520
Free: 800-361-8404

E-mail: cnf@cnursesfdn.ca
URL: http://www.cna-nurses.ca/cnf

• 1686 • Canadian Nurses Foundation Small
Research Grants (Graduate/Grant)

**Purpose:** To provide support for nursing research. **Focus:** Nursing, Health Care. **Qualif.:** Applicants must be registered nurses who are Canadian citizens or landed immigrants. Candidates must also be members of the Canadian Nurses Foundation. Graduate nursing students and previous applicants are also eligible. Research proposals pertaining to nursing practice, education, or administration will be considered for funding. **Criteria:** All proposals are reviewed for scientific merit, potential contribution to the profession of nursing, feasibility, clarity, and relevance.

**Funds Avail.:** Small research grants are $5,000. An applicant is eligible to receive only one research grant from CNF at a time. CNF monies will not be given retroactively for completed research. **No. of Awards:** Varies, subject to availability of funds.

**Remarks:** Temporarily suspended.

• 1687 • Canadian Nurses Foundation Study Awards
(Doctorate, Graduate/Other)

**Focus:** Nursing, Gerontology, Maternal/Child Health. **Qualif.:** Candidates must be registered nurses who are Canadian citizens or landed immigrants, and current members of the Canadian Nurses Foundation (CNF). Unconditional university acceptance into the proposed program of study is required. **Criteria:** CNF Awards are granted to Canadian nurses who are selected in a national competition on the basis of excellence. Selection is based on proficiency in nursing, intellectual ability, leadership, applicant potential, overall ability in nursing, and potential ability to advance in nursing. Preference is given to nurses studying on a full-time basis.

**Funds Avail.:** The total number of CNF study awards granted at the doctoral and masters levels may vary from year to year subject to the availability of funds. Annual amounts to any one applicant will not usually exceed $3,000 to $3,500 for a master's program and $4,000 to $6,000 for a doctoral program. Recipients must apply the monies received solely to tuition fees, travel, and living expenses related to the program of study. They must agree to be employed in a nursing position in Canada for a period of one year for each year of financial assistance. The CNF study awards given to successful candidates may carry the name of a distinguished Canadian or sponsoring organization. Applicants are automatically considered for all the awards for which they are eligible. CNF awards are for one academic year only. Candidates may re-apply for a CNF award but awards will not exceed two years for the same degree. When a recipient fails to fulfill the commitments inherent in the award, or for any reason is unable to complete the program of study for which the award was given, the Canadian Nurses Foundation reserves the right to terminate further payments and to require repayment of funds already granted. **No. of Awards:** Varies, subject to availability of funds. **To Apply:** Application forms are available from CNF offices as of January 1 each year, or by downloading application from the website at www.cna-nurses.co/cnf. **Deadline:** Application forms must be received by April 15.

**Remarks:** An academic summary with transcripts and thesis or dissertation where applicable must be submitted to the CNF at the completion of the funded academic year. **Contact:** Executive Director at the above address (see entry 1685).

• 1688 • Dr. Dorothy J. Kergin Research Grant in
Primary Health Care (Graduate/Grant)

**Purpose:** To provide support for nursing research. **Focus:** Primary Health Care. **Qualif.:** Applicants must be registered nurses who are Canadian citizens or landed immigrants and members of the Canadian Nurses Foundation. Graduate nursing students and previous applicants are also eligible. Research proposals pertaining to nursing practice, education, or administration will be considered for funding. **Criteria:** All proposals are reviewed for scientific merit, potential contribution to the profession of nursing, feasibility, clarity, and relevance.

**Funds Avail.:** $15,000 is available. Recipients may receive only one research grant from CNF at a time. CNF monies will not be given retroactively for completed research.

**Remarks:** Temporarily suspended.

• 1689 •
## Canadian Pharmacists Association
1785 Alta Vista Dr.
Ottawa, ON, Canada K1G 3Y6

Ph: (613)523-7877
Fax: (613)523-0445
Free: 800-917-9489

E-mail: cpha@cdnpharm.ca
URL: http://www.cdnpharm.ca

• 1690 • Centennial Scholars Awards (Graduate/
Grant)

**Purpose:** To recognize academic achievement and contribution to the undergraduate life of the attending school by pharmacy students. **Focus:** Pharmacy. **Qualif.:** Applicant may be of any nationality, but must be a third-year pharmacy student at a Canadian college or university. Awards are intended to defray costs for travel and registration to the CPA conference.

**Funds Avail.:** $300, plus travel. **No. of Awards:** 9. **To Apply:** Write to the Association for guidelines. **Deadline:** End of February. **Contact:** Leroy Fevang, Executive Director, at the above address (see entry 1689).

• 1691 •
## Canadian Political Science Association
Parliamentary Internship Program
1 Stewart St., Ste. 205
Ottawa, ON, Canada K1N 6H7

Ph: (613)564-4026
Fax: (613)230-2746

URL: http://www.sfu.ca/igs/CPSA.html

• 1692 • Parliamentary Internships (Professional
Development/Internship)

**Purpose:** To provide an opportunity for university graduates to experience the day-to-day work of the Canadian Parliament. **Focus:** General Studies. **Qualif.:** Applicant must be a Canadian citizen who has recently graduated from a Canadian university. Funds apply only to internships at the Canadian Parliament. Interns' responsibilities include working with members of the House of Commons, conducting scholarly research, and undertaking study travel. Interns are not allowed to be employed elsewhere for remuneration during the term of the internship.

**Funds Avail.:** $15,500 stipend, plus travel subsidies. **To Apply:** Write to Professor Houle for application forms. Submit the original and four copies of the following: transcripts, two academic letters of reference, and one letter of reference from an employer. Applicants may be interviewed. **Deadline:** Last Friday in January.

Notification by April. **Contact:** Professor Francois Houle, Director, at the above address (see entry 1691).

---

• 1693 •
## Canadian Printing Industries Scholarship Trust Fund

906, 75 Albert St.                    *Ph:* (613)236-7208
Ottawa, ON, Canada K1P 5E7            *Fax:* (613)236-8169

• 1694 • **Canadian Printing Industries Scholarships** *(Undergraduate/Scholarship)*

**Purpose:** To prepare students for a career in the Graphics Communications industry. **Focus:** Graphic Communications. **Qualif.:** Candidates must maintain a B average or better, be enrolled in the first year of a graphic arts or printing related program of study, and show a keen interest in pursuing a career in the printing industry. The scholarship may be applied to study at a Canadian college or university with two-, three-, or four-year diploma or degree programs. **Criteria:** Applicants are judged based on an industry interview.

**Funds Avail.:** $1,000 annually. **No. of Awards:** 50 annually. **To Apply:** Available upon request. **Deadline:** June 30. **Contact:** Administrator, Canadian Printing Industries Scholarship Trust Fund, at the above address (see entry 1693).

---

• 1695 •
## Canadian-Scandinavian Foundation

c/o Dr. Hans Moller, Director of the
  Office of Libraries
McGill University
3459 McTavish St.                     *Ph:* (514)398-4740
Montreal, PQ, Canada H3A 1Y1          *Fax:* (514)398-7356
*E-mail:* moller@lib1.lan.mcgill.ca

• 1696 • **Brucebo Fine Arts Summer Scholarship** *(Professional Development/Scholarship)*

**Purpose:** To provide opportunities for studies and research in Sweden. **Qualif.:** Applicants must be promising young Canadian artists wishing to spend two summer months at the Brucebo Studio near Visby on the Island of Gotland, Sweden.

**Funds Avail.:** The approximate value of the scholarship is $2,500. **Deadline:** Applications must reach the Secretary not later than January 31, and recipients must use their scholarships or grants before May of the following year.

**Remarks:** Upon completion of the stay recipients are required to submit a report to the CSF.

• 1697 • **CSF Special Purpose Grants** *(Other/Grant)*

**Purpose:** To provide opportunities for studies and research in Scandinavian Countries. **Qualif.:** Applicants must be qualified Canadian students/researchers wishing to pursue academic studies or independent research for a short period in Scandinavia.

**Funds Avail.:** The approximate value of the scholarship is $600 to $1,000. **Deadline:** Applications must reach the Secretary no later than January 31, and recipients must use their scholarships or grants before May of the following year.

**Remarks:** Upon completion of a stay in Scandinavia, recipients are required to submit a report to the CSF.

---

• 1698 •
## Canadian Society of Exploration Geophysicists - Scholarship Committee

905, 510 5th St. SW                   *Ph:* (403)262-0015
Calgary, AB, Canada T2P 3S8           *Fax:* (403)262-7383
*E-mail:* info@cseg.org
*URL:* http://www.cseg.org

• 1699 • **Canadian Society of Exploration Geophysicists Scholarships** *(Undergraduate/Scholarship)*

**Focus:** Geophysics. **Qualif.:** Candidates must intend to pursue a program of study in geophysics at a Canadian university. **Criteria:** Selection is based upon scholastic achievement, faculty appraisal, interest in geophysics, and financial need.

**Funds Avail.:** A number of $1,500 awards. **Contact:** CSEG Scholarship Committee, at the above address (see entry 1698).

---

• 1700 •
## Canadian Society of Laboratory Technologists

PO Box 2830, LCD 1                    *Ph:* (905)528-8642
Hamilton, ON, Canada L8N 3N8          *Fax:* (905)528-4968
*URL:* http://www.cslt.com/

• 1701 • **CSLT Founders Fund Awards** *(Professional Development/Award)*

**Purpose:** To support members with advanced medical laboratory technology courses. **Focus:** Medical Laboratory Technology. **Qualif.:** Applicants must be members of CSLT, and may only apply for one CSLT award for any activity.

**Funds Avail.:** $500 maximum. **No. of Awards:** 86. **To Apply:** Write to the national office for application forms and guidelines. **Deadline:** January 1, April 1, August 1, November 1. **Contact:** Ed Hollingham, at the above address (see entry 1700).

• 1702 • **International Founders' Fund Awards** *(Other/Award)*

**Purpose:** To provide financial assistance to members for international activities. **Focus:** Medical Laboratory Technology. **Qualif.:** Applicants must be members of CSLT, and may only apply for one CSLT award for any activity. Awards are granted for direct expenses. **Criteria:** Activity must promote the image/status of Canadian medical lab techs or the CSLT at the international level.

**Funds Avail.:** $1,000 maximum. **To Apply:** Write to the national office for application forms and guidelines. **Deadline:** January 15. **Contact:** Ed Hollingham, at the above address (see entry 1700).

---

• 1703 •
## Canadian Society of Petroleum Geologists

206 7th Ave., SW, Ste. 505
Calgary, AB, Canada T2P 0W7           *Ph:* (403)264-5610

• 1704 • **Canadian Society of Petroleum Geologists Graduate Scholarships** *(Graduate/Scholarship)*

**Purpose:** To promote advanced education and research in fields relevant to the petroleum industry. **Focus:** Natural Resources—Petroleum Sciences, Geology. **Qualif.:** Applicant must be a Canadian citizen or landed immigrant, and must be accepted in the second or subsequent year of graduate study at a Western Canadian (Alberta, British Columbia, Manitoba, or Saskatchewan)

---

## Canadian Society of Petroleum Geologists (continued)

university. **Criteria:** Preference will be given to studies of geological sciences involved with coastal and shelf sediment processes, marine geotechnology, marine geochemistry, and offshore basin tectonics and sedimentology.

**Funds Avail.:** $1,500. **No. of Awards:** 3. **To Apply:** Applicants should write the CSPG office for application form and guidelines. Forms are also available at most Canadian universities with applicable programs. Applicants must submit the form with background information, academic program, appraisal by academic supervisor and one other academic member of the department, and undergraduate and graduate transcripts. **Deadline:** May 1. **Contact:** Richard Thom, Chair, at the above address (see entry 1703).

---

## • 1705 •
## Canadian Transportation Education Foundation
PO Box 64
Beachville, ON, Canada N0J 1A0     *Ph:* (519)423-6460

### • 1706 • Canadian Transportation Education Foundation Scholarships and Research Grants
*(Postdoctorate, Professional Development/Grant, Scholarship)*

**Purpose:** To encourage research on logistics distribution, and transportation in Canada. **Focus:** Canadian Transportation. **Qualif.:** Applicant must be a Canadian citizen who is researching a topic in the field of transportation. Awards are tenable worldwide but candidate's research must focus on circumstances in Canada.

**Funds Avail.:** Varies, according to research project. **No. of Awards:** 12. **To Apply:** Write to the general manager for application guidelines. Submit a detailed outline of research project and a budget. **Deadline:** September 15. **Contact:** J. Alvin White, General Manager, at the above address (see entry 1705).

---

## • 1707 •
## Canadian Water Resources Association
PO Box 1329     *Ph:* (519)622-4764
Cambridge, ON, Canada N1R 7G6     *Fax:* (519)621-4844

### • 1708 • Canadian Water Resources Association Scholarships *(Graduate/Scholarship)*

**Purpose:** To support graduate study focusing on water resources. **Focus:** Water Supply Industry, Environmental Science. **Qualif.:** Applicant must be a Canadian citizen or landed immigrant and must be enrolled full-time in a graduate program at a Canadian college or university. Study may be in any discipline or profession relating to water resources. The scholarship committee will accept only one applicant from any department or school in a Canadian university or college. **Criteria:** Selection is primarily based on academic excellence and the project relevance to water management and development.

**Funds Avail.:** $1,250 scholarship, plus one-year membership in CWRA. **No. of Awards:** 4. **To Apply:** Write to the Association for an application form or obtain forms from the awards office at a college or university. Submit with transcripts, a letter of endorsement from the program chair or director and a description of the study program and its relation to water resources in Canada. Two letters of reference from the referees must be also be submitted. **Deadline:** March 1. Results are announced by June.

---

## • 1709 •
## Cancer Federation
PO Box 1298     *Ph:* (909)849-4325
Banning, CA 92220-0009     *Fax:* (909)849-0156
*E-mail:* alene@realm.net
*URL:* http://www.realm.net/~alene

### • 1710 • Cancer Federation Scholarships
*(Undergraduate/Scholarship)*

**Purpose:** To encourage students in the fields of microbiology and immunology. **Qualif.:** Applicants must be students at the school giving the award. **Criteria:** Criteria considered are: grades; community and school service; attitude; and leadership potential. Financial need is not a factor.

**Funds Avail.:** Varies. **Contact:** The Federation at the above address (see entry 1709).

---

## • 1711 •
## Cancer Research Campaign
Cambridge House
10 Cambridge Terrace     *Ph:* 171 224 1333
London NW1 4JL, England     *Fax:* 171 487 4302

### • 1712 • Cancer Research Campaign Research Grants *(Professional Development/Grant)*

**Purpose:** To support original research on cancer. **Focus:** Oncology. **Qualif.:** Applicant may be of any nationality, although awards are usually made to U.K. citizens. Candidate must be qualified to conduct independent research. Grants are tenable at U.K. institutions. Proposed research must be endorsed by the relevant department head at the host institution. Funds support operating costs and salaries.

**Funds Avail.:** £10,000-100,000. **To Apply:** Write to the Projects Grants Administrator, Scientific Department for application form and guidelines. **Deadline:** Varies. **Contact:** Project Grants Administrator, Scientific Department, at the above address (see entry 1711).

---

## • 1713 •
## Cancer Research Institute
681 5th Ave.     *Ph:* (212)688-7515
New York, NY 10022-4209     *Fax:* (212)832-9376

### • 1714 • Cancer Research Institute Clinical Investigator Award *(Other/Grant)*

**Purpose:** To support qualified scientists working in the field of basic immunology or cancer immunology. **Focus:** Immunology and cancer immunology. **Qualif.:** Candidates must hold a doctoral degree and be a tenure-track assistant professor, or equivalent rank at the time of award activation. **Criteria:** Applications are reviewed by a panel drawn from the Scientific Advisory Council.

**Funds Avail.:** The award is $50,000 per year for 4 years ($200,000 total). **No. of Awards:** 6 per year. **To Apply:** Application forms are available upon request. **Deadline:** Materials must be in by March 1. **Contact:** Ms. Lynne Harmer, Director of Grants Administration, at the above address (see entry 1713).

## • 1715 • Cancer Research Institute Postdoctoral Fellowship (Postdoctorate/Fellowship)

**Purpose:** To offer funding to qualified scientists who wish to receive training in general immunology or cancer immunology. **Focus:** General Immunology and Cancer Immunology. **Qualif.:** Applicants must have a doctoral degree and must conduct their proposed research under a sponsor who holds a formal appointment at the host institution. **Criteria:** The Fellowship Committee, comprised of members of the Scientific Advisory Council, considers the qualifications and experience of both the applicant and the proposed sponsor, as well as the nature and feasibility of the intended line of inquiry.

**Funds Avail.:** Fellowship stipends are $32,000 for the first year and $34,000 for the second year. A third year of support at the rate of $36,000 is available for fellows who have demonstrated substantial progress in their research. An institutional allowance of $1,500 per year is provided to the host institution. **No. of Awards:** Approximately 15% of the applications received are awarded fellowships. **To Apply:** Application forms are available upon request. **Deadline:** Application materials must be in by April 1 and October 1.

**Remarks:** Funds cannot be used for indirect costs. **Contact:** Ms. Lynne Harmer, Director of Grants Administration, at the above address (see entry 1713).

## • 1716 • Cancer Research Institute Science Writing Internship (Graduate/Internship)

**Focus:** Science writing. **Qualif.:** Candidates must be good writers, capable of assimilating and organizing information. A strong science background is preferred but not required.

**Funds Avail.:** $375 per week. **No. of Awards:** 2. **To Apply:** Mail or fax a resume, three writing samples, and a cover letter to the Executive Director of the Institute. **Deadline:** May 31.

## • 1717 • Cancer Research Society, Inc.
1 Place Ville Marie, No. 2332          *Ph:* (514)861-9227
Montreal, PQ, Canada H3B 5C3          *Fax:* (514)861-9220

## • 1718 • Cancer Research Society Fellowships (Doctorate, Postdoctorate/Fellowship)

**Purpose:** To support research training in the field of cancer. **Focus:** Oncology **Qualif.:** Candidates must be predoctoral students or postdoctoral researchers of any nationality who are planning to train in a Canadian university or one of its affiliate institutions.

**Funds Avail.:** Predoctorate: $15,050/year; postdoctorate: $28,510/year **To Apply:** Inquire at the university or institution where training will take place. **Deadline:** February 15. **Contact:** The Cancer Research Society at the above address (see entry 1717).

## • 1719 • Cancer Research Society Grants (Professional Development/Grant)

**Purpose:** To support research in the field of cancer. **Focus:** Oncology **Qualif.:** Candidates, of any nationality, must be members of a recognized university and planning to conduct research in a Canadian university or at its affiliated institutions.

**Funds Avail.:** $40,000 per year. **To Apply:** Inquire at the university or institution where research will take place for an application form. **Deadline:** February 15. **Contact:** The Cancer Research Society at the above address (see entry 1717).

## • 1720 •
## Capital Cities/ABC Inc. - Newspaper Internship Program
c/o The Times Leader
15 N. Main St.                          *Ph:* (717)829-7100
Wilkes Barre, PA 18711                  *Fax:* (717)822-2762

## • 1721 • Capital Cities/ABC Inc. Newspaper Internship (Professional Development/Internship)

**Purpose:** To allow college graduates the opportunity to work for one year at three Capital Cities newspapers (four months each). **Qualif.:** Applicants must be minority college graduates.

**Funds Avail.:** Interns receive a weekly salary of $240 plus $350 for each of the three moves, but must provide their own automobile to cover work assignments and to facilitate moves. Housing is provided. Ten internships are available. **To Apply:** Applicants must provide a letter detailing qualifications and interest in the program, a resume, and three to five samples of their work. **Deadline:** October 31. **Contact:** David Daris, Program Coordinator, at the above address (see entry 1720).

## • 1722 •
## Capranica Foundation
c/o The Tompkins County Trust Co.
The Commons Trust Dept.                 *Ph:* (607)273-3210
PO Box 460                              *Fax:* (607)273-0024
Ithaca, NY 14851                        *Free:* 800-273-3210
*E-mail:* decibel@aol.com

## • 1723 • Capranica Foundation Award in Neuroethology (Doctorate, Postdoctorate/Award)

**Purpose:** To recognize an outstanding contribution to the field of neuroethology. **Qualif.:** Applicants must be U.S. citizens and graduate students in the latter stages of their doctoral thesis research, or recent postdoctoral candidates who have received their doctoral degree within four years of the deadline date for submission of applications that year. **Criteria:** The members of the selection committee rank each of the applicants. The candidate with the highest consensus ranking will be considered the most deserving recipient of the fellowship award. This selection will be based entirely on scientific and academic merit, irrespective of race, color, creed, sex, or age.

**Funds Avail.:** One award per year of up to $2,000. **To Apply:** In cases where the award will be a cash prize in recognition of the most outstanding paper published by a junior scientist in the field of neuroethology, the selection committee will announce a "call-for-nominations" by publication of a notice in appropriate scientific society newsletters. If the award will be a fellowship, the selection committee will announce a "call-for-applications" by publication of an appropriate notice in several scientific society newsletters. In addition, announcements will be sent by the committee at its discretion to key departments that are engaged in important neuroethological research at various major universities in the United States. Each of the fellowship applicants will be directed to complete an application form listing scientific background, field of interest, and planned research project. In addition, applicants must arrange to have three letters of reference sent to the Foundation Office in support of their application. **Deadline:** Variable; usually early fall each year (September through November).

**Remarks:** Fellows are eligible to apply for a continuation in subsequent years of their fellowship (up to a maximum of three years) on a competitive basis each year with all new incoming applications. Each fellow must submit a brief report to the selection committee at the end of their year of support that documents the progress made during that year of activity.

*Capranica Foundation (continued)*

**Contact:** The Tompkins Country Trust Co. at the above address (see entry 1722).

---

• 1724 •

**Career Opportunities Through Education -
Marguerite Tremblay Cote Scholarship Program**
PO Box 2810                              *Ph:* (609)573-9400
Cherry Hill, NJ 08034                    *Fax:* (609)573-9799
*E-mail:* scholars@erols.com

• 1725 • **Ida Speyrer Stahl Scholarships**
*(Undergraduate/Scholarship)*

**Focus:** Opera. **Qualif.:** Applicants must be residents of Maspeth, New York, of German descent, juniors in a SUNY college with a minimum grade point of 3.5 on a 4.0 scale (or equivalent), majoring in voice, and planning a career in opera.

**Funds Avail.:** Amounts vary. Scholarships are nonrenewable and are not always awarded yearly. **Deadline:** Applications must be requested from Career Opportunities Through Education (COTE) no later than April 15. Only recipients are notified. **Contact:** COTE at the above address (see entry 1724).

• 1726 • **Marguerite Tremblay Cote Scholarships**
*(Undergraduate/Scholarship)*

**Focus:** Education. **Qualif.:** Applicants must be residents of Biddeford or Saco, Maine, of French Canadian descent, juniors in the University of Maine system with a minimum grade point of 3.5 out of 4.0, and planning to become teachers at the elementary school level at a school located in Maine.

**Funds Avail.:** Amount varies. Scholarships are non-renewable and are not always awarded yearly. **To Apply:** Applications must be requested from Career Opportunities Through Education no later than April 15.

**Remarks:** Only recipients will be notified. **Contact:** Career Opportunities Through Education (COTE) at the above address (see entry 1724).

---

• 1727 •

**The Cargill Foundation**
15407 W. McGinty Rd.                     *Ph:* (612)742-6201
Wayzata, MN 55391                        *Fax:* (612)742-7224

• 1728 • **Cargill National Merit Scholarships**
*(Undergraduate/Scholarship)*

**Qualif.:** Applicants must be sons or daughters of employees of Cargill or one of its subsidiaries. Employees must work at least 20 hours per week and have been employed for one year or longer. Students must be citizens of the United States or intend to become one as soon as qualified to do so, high school students who will be completing or leaving secondary school and entering college the following term, and planning to attend a regionally-accredited college or university in the United States to pursue courses of study leading to one of the traditional baccalaureate degrees. The PSAT/MNSQT test must be taken while the student is still in high school. **Criteria:** Winners are chosen on the basis of PSAT/NMSQT scores, academic record, leadership qualities and extracurricular involvement, test scores, school recommendations, and the student's self-description of interests and goals.

**Funds Avail.:** Stipends range from $500 to $3,000 per year. **No. of Awards:** 5 awards per year, plus 1 or 2 National Achievement Winners. **To Apply:** Students should make arrangements with their high school principals or counselors immediately after the beginning of their junior year to take the PSAT/NMSQT test. It is administered throughout the United States in October each year. Students who accelerate the high school program and enter college early should refer to the PSAT/NMSQT Student Bulletin for information on when to take the test. Applicants must also complete a special Cargill entry form. **Deadline:** Application materials must be received by January 1.

**Remarks:** This scholarship is administered by the National Merit Scholarship Corporation (NMSC). **Contact:** Gladys Tripp, Cargill Public Affairs/50, Box 9300, Minneapolis, MN 55440.

• 1729 • **Cargill Scholars Program Scholarships**
*(Undergraduate/Scholarship)*

**Qualif.:** Candidates must be sons and daughters of employees of Cargill and its domestic divisions and subsidiaries. Employees must work at least 20 hours per week and have been employed for one year or longer. Children of employees who are retired on service or disability pensions, deceased, or retired and who have completed one year of employment are also eligible. Students must be citizens of the United States or intend to become one as soon as qualified to do so, be high school seniors, and be planning to attend a regionally accredited college, university, or vocational-technical school in the United States to pursue courses of study leading to a baccalaureate or associate degree. Applicants must also enter college as a full-time day student in the fall term following selection and remain in good academic standing. **Criteria:** Winners are selected on the basis of academic records, financial need, leadership qualities, involvement in extracurricular activities and community accomplishment, a personal statement, and a recommendation from a high school principal, teacher, or counselor. Priority is given to students who demonstrate high academic achievement and evidence of financial need.

**Funds Avail.:** Thirty $2,000, non-renewable scholarships are available annually. **To Apply:** Required materials include a completed application form, a recommendation from a school official, and a current and official transcript. **Deadline:** Application materials must be received by March 15. Recipients must notify the administering agency of acceptance of the award within three weeks of notification or the award will be forfeited. **Contact:** Career Opportunities Through Education (COTE), Cargill Scholars Program, Box 2810, Cherry Hill, NJ 08034. Telephone: (609)573-9400. FAX: (609)573-9799.

---

• 1730 •

**Nellie Martin Carman Scholarship Committee**
18223 73rd Ave., NE, No. B101
Bothell, WA 98011-2755                   *Ph:* (206)486-6575

• 1731 • **Nellie Martin Carman Scholarships**
*(Undergraduate/Scholarship)*

**Purpose:** To train and educate young people to become active and intelligent members of society. **Focus:** Courses other than music, sculpture, drawing, interior decorating or domestic science. **Qualif.:** Candidates must be U.S. citizens and graduates of public high schools in King, Snohomish, or Pierce Counties in the State of Washington in the year of appointment. Recipients must plan to attend a college or university in the state of Washington. Recipients are required to maintain at least a 3.0 GPA, continue to require financial aid, and continue to merit a renewal of the scholarship in the opinion of the scholarship committee. **Criteria:** Academic record, school activities, and financial situation.

**Funds Avail.:** Awards are individually determined and do not exceed $1,000 per year. Awards are paid in September and

January each year. **No. of Awards:** 25-30; varies according to funds available. **To Apply:** Each public high school in King, Snohomish, and Pierce Counties nominates one candidate, or if senior class enrollment is more than 400, two candidates. Application forms are sent to the high schools in January. Instructions for initial application and renewals are provided annually to the high schools and to students who are already recipients of scholarships. First time candidates must submit a birth certificate or proof of U.S. citizenship. **Deadline:** March 15.

**Remarks:** Mrs. Nellie Martin Carman was a successful Seattle businesswoman who established these scholarships in her will. The first scholarships were awarded in 1949. **Contact:** High school counselor or Secretary, Carman Scholarship Committee, at the above address (see entry 1730).

---

• **1732** •
## Carmel Music Society
PO Box 1144
Carmel, CA 93921          *Ph:* (408)625-9938
*URL:* http://www.carmelmusic.org

• **1733** • **Carmel Music Society Competition**
*(Professional Development/Prize)*

**Purpose:** To encourage young artists just beginning their careers and to give them experience in appearing before the public. **Focus:** Instrumental 1999, Vocal 2000, Piano 2001, on a rotation basis. **Qualif.:** Contestants must be residents of California or full-time students in the state of California between the ages of 18 and 30, 18-32 in vocal year. Performers currently under professional management and previous Carmel Music Society award winners are not eligible for the competition. Each contestant should prepare a recital program of not more than 25 minutes duration. Contestants may select their own program, but it must include selections from at least three of the following five style periods: baroque, classical, romantic, impressionistic, and contemporary. All selections must memorized. **Criteria:** Tapes will be auditioned by a screening committee of professional musicians to select eight finalists. The committee will listen to tapes with no knowledge of the performer's age, educational background, or racial origin. Each finalist will perform the same 25-minute program as submitted on the audition tape.

**Funds Avail.:** A $3,500 grand prize is awarded, which consists of a $1,500 cash award and a $2,000 contract to appear the following year on the Carmel Music Society's subscription series. A $1,000 second prize, a $500 third prize, and five $200 prizes will also be awarded. **To Apply:** Applications must contain a completed form, proof of age, nonrefundable application fee of $25, three high-quality cassette recordings of the program to be performed for the competition, and three 3x5 inch file cards with repertoire selections described by title and composer. The tapes should not contain the name of the contestant and will be returned. **Deadline:** Varies each year. **Contact:** Pottie Robertson, at the above address (see entry 1732).

---

• **1734** •
## Carnegie Communications
Paul D. Adams
PO Box 427                      *Ph:* (508)764-8633
Sturbridge, MA 01566            *Fax:* (508)764-4720
*E-mail:* padams@interramp.com

• **1735** • **Private Colleges & Universities Community Service Scholarship** *(Undergraduate/Scholarship)*

**Focus:** General studies. **Qualif.:** Applicants must be minority high school juniors and seniors who will matriculate at one of the 400 private institutions as published in PC&U magazine immediately after graduating from high school. **Criteria:** Awards are granted based on academic merit, and service to community.

**Funds Avail.:** $30,000. Renewable. **No. of Awards:** 20-30. **To Apply:** Applicants must submit an application, 1,000-word essay on community service involvement, high school transcripts, and a letter of recommendation. **Deadline:** November 1. **Contact:** Paul D. Adams, Scholarship Administrator.

---

• **1736** •
## Carnegie Institution of Washington
1530 P St., NW                  *Ph:* (202)939-1120
Washington, DC 20005-1910       *Fax:* (202)387-8092
*E-mail:* pcraig@science.pst.ciw.edu; rbowers@
   science.pst.ciw.edu
*URL:* http://www.ciw.edu; http://www.ciw.edu

• **1737** • **Carnegie Institution of Washington Postdoctoral and Predoctoral Fellowships** *(Doctorate, Postdoctorate/Fellowship)*

**Purpose:** To train research scientists. **Focus:** Astronomy, Developmental Biology, Earth Sciences, Planetary Sciences, Plant Biology. **Qualif.:** Candidate may be of any nationality. Applicant must have a research interest complementary to a program within one of the Institution's departments. Prior to appointment, a candidate usually must arrange for a staff member at the department to act as a sponsor. All appointments are for training and research in residence at one of the Institution's departments.

**Funds Avail.:** Varies, according to research proposal and departmental resources **No. of Awards:** 40. **To Apply:** Write to the Institution's publications office for catalogue. Submit letter of application with research proposal to the director of the appropriate department within the Institution. Three letters of recommendation are also required. **Deadline:** Varies, according to the department.

**Remarks:** The departments are: Department of Embryology (Baltimore, MD); Department of Plant Biology (Stanford, CA); Department of Terrestrial Magnetism and Geophysical Laboratory (both in Washington, D.C.); and the Observatories (Pasadena, CA and Las Campanas, Chile). **Contact:** Publications Officer at the above address (see entry 1736).

## • 1738 •
## Carnegie Trust for the Universities of Scotland
Cameron House
Abbey Park Place
Dunfermline
Fife KY12 7PZ, Scotland      *Ph:* 383 622148

### • 1739 • Carnegie Grants *(Postdoctorate, Postgraduate/Grant)*

**Purpose:** To support the pursuit and publication of personal research. **Focus:** General Studies. **Qualif.:** Applicant may be of any nationality, but must be a graduate of a Scottish university or a staff member of a Scottish university. When the applicant is a Scottish graduate, applications can normally only be considered if the project is in association with, or likely to be of specific benefit to, one or more of the Scottish universities. Grants are for personal expenditures only, and are not intended for technical or secretarial assistance, computing, bench fees, equipment, or for conference attendance.

**Funds Avail.:** £2,000. **To Apply:** Write to the Trust office for application form. **Deadline:** February 1, June 1, November 1. Applications will be considered at the executive meetings of the Trust in each of those months. **Contact:** Secretary at the above address (see entry 1738).

## • 1740 •
## Vikki Carr Scholarship Foundation
PO Box 57756
Sherman Oaks, CA 91413-2756

### • 1741 • Vikki Carr Scholarship *(Graduate, Undergraduate/Scholarship)*

**Focus:** General Studies. **Qualif.:** Applicants must be of Latino heritage and between the ages of 17 and 22. They must also be California or Texas residents and legal residents of the United States. **Criteria:** Selection is based upon need, goals, and community service.

**Funds Avail.:** Amount varies depending upon fund balance. Renewable. **No. of Awards:** 5 to 8. **To Apply:** A self-addressed, stamped envelope must accompany application requests. Two letters of recommendation, a biography of 200 words or less, most recent high school transcripts, and a photograph must be included with the completed applications. **Deadline:** April 15. **Contact:** D. Corral at the above address (see entry 1740).

## • 1742 •
## Marjorie Carter Boy Scout Scholarship Trust
PO Box 527
West Chatham, MA 02669      *Ph:* (508)945-1225

### • 1743 • Marjorie S. Carter Boy Scout Scholarship *(Undergraduate/Scholarship)*

**Purpose:** To financially assist boy scouts in their pursuit of higher education. **Focus:** General Studies. **Qualif.:** Applicants must be residents of New England States (Connecticut, Rhode Island, Massachusetts, Vermont, New Hampshire, Maine), high school seniors, and members of the Boy Scouts of America. **Criteria:** Selection is based on financial need, leadership ability, and academic record.

**Funds Avail.:** $1,500 scholarship per year for the first two years of college. **No. of Awards:** 30-35 annually. **Deadline:** April 15.

**Contact:** Mrs. B.J. Shaffer, Administrative Secretary, at the above address (see entry 1742)or the BSA Council.

## • 1744 •
## Casualty Actuarial Society
1100 N. Glen Rd., Ste. 600      *Ph:* (703)276-3100
Arlington, VA 22201      *Fax:* (703)276-3108
*E-mail:* office@casact.org
*URL:* http://www.casact.org

### • 1745 • Harold W. Schloss Memorial Scholarship *(Undergraduate/Scholarship)*

**Purpose:** To benefit deserving and academically outstanding students in the actuarial program of the Department of Statistics and Actuarial Science at the University of Iowa. **Qualif.:** Applicants must be students enrolled in the Department of Statistics and Actuarial Science at the University of Iowa.

**Funds Avail.:** $500. **To Apply:** Recipients are selected each spring by trustees of the CAS Trust, based upon the recommendation of the departmental chairman at the University of Iowa. **Deadline:** April.

**Remarks:** In November 1984, the Harold W. Schloss Scholarship was established by the Casualty Actuarial Society Trust as a memorial to Mr. Schloss, a past president of CAS. **Contact:** The Casualty Actuarial Society at the above address (see entry 1744).

## • 1746 •
## Catholic Aid Association
3499 Lexington Ave., N.      *Ph:* (651)490-0170
St. Paul, MN 55126      *Fax:* (651)490-0746
*E-mail:* caa@catholicaid.com
*URL:* http://www.catholicaid.qpg.com

### • 1747 • Catholic Aid Association Tuition Scholarships *(Undergraduate/Scholarship)*

**Purpose:** To provide financial assistance to association members for college or technical school. **Focus:** General Studies. **Qualif.:** Applicants must have been members of the Catholic Aid Association for at least two years and be entering their freshman or sophomore year in college. Membership entails holding an insurance policy or annuity with the association. **Criteria:** Selection is based upon need, scholastic achievements, and fraternal involvement.

**Funds Avail.:** $300 if attending a non-Catholic college or university; $500 if attending a Catholic college or university. **To Apply:** Applications should be requested after December 1 of each year. **Deadline:** February 15.

**Remarks:** The association generally receives approximately 200 applications. **Contact:** Fraternal Department at the above address (see entry 1746).

• 1748 •
## Catholic Kolping Society of America
248 Lakeview Ave. 131
Clifton, NJ 07011-4014          Ph: (973)478-8635

• 1749 • **Father Krewitt Scholarship Awards**
*(Undergraduate/Scholarship)*

**Purpose:** To aid members and children of members to attain educational goals. **Focus:** General Studies. **Qualif.:** Applicants must be members or children of members of the Kolping Society. **Criteria:** Submission of an essay on a topic chosen each September.

**Funds Avail.:** $1,000. **No. of Awards:** 1. **To Apply:** Must show proof of membership of parents or self, and proof of college enrollment. **Deadline:** February 15. **Contact:** Society at the above address (see entry 1748).

• 1750 •
## Catholic Library Association
100 North St., Ste. 224        Ph: (413)443-2CLA
Pittsfield, MA 01201-5109      Fax: (413)442-2CLA
*E-mail:* cla@vgernet.net
*URL:* http://www.cathla.org

• 1751 • **Reverend Andrew L. Bouwhuis Memorial Scholarship** *(Graduate/Scholarship)*

**Purpose:** To encourage college students to enter the library profession. **Focus:** Library and Archival Sciences. **Qualif.:** Applicant must be a college senior or graduate who has been accepted by a master's of library science program. Candidates are evaluated on the basis of academic scholarship and financial need.

**Funds Avail.:** $1,500. **No. of Awards:** 1. **To Apply:** Write to the Scholarship Committee for application materials. Submit application form with statement of interest in librarianship, statement of financial need, transcripts, and Graduate Record Examination, Miller, or other applicable test scores. Letters of reference and supporting financial documents are also welcome. **Deadline:** February 1. The scholarship winner is announced during the week following Easter. **Contact:** Scholarship Committee Chair at the above address (see entry 1750).

• 1752 • **World Book, Inc., Grants** *(Professional Development/Grant)*

**Purpose:** To support continuing education in school or children's librarianship. **Focus:** Library and Archival Sciences. **Qualif.:** Applicant must be a member of the Association. Awardee may use the grant for attendance at special workshops, institutes, or seminars; a summer session at institutions of higher learning; or a sabbatical. The grant may not be used to subsidize studies leading to a library science degree.

**Funds Avail.:** $1,500 maximum. **No. of Awards:** Three maximum. **To Apply:** Write to the Scholarship Committee for application form and guidelines. Submit form with a grant proposal. **Deadline:** March 15. Grant recipients are announced during the week of Easter. **Contact:** Scholarship Committee Chair at the above address (see entry 1750).

• 1753 •
## Catholic Workman
PO Box 47                      Ph: (612)758-2229
New Prague, MN 56071           Fax: (612)758-6221
                               Free: 800-346-6231

• 1754 • **Catholic Workman College Scholarships**
*(Undergraduate/Scholarship)*

**Purpose:** To assist members in furthering their education. **Focus:** General Studies. **Qualif.:** Applicants must be members of Catholic Workman's fraternal life insurance society and enrolled in an accredited college as freshmen, sophomores, juniors, or seniors. **Criteria:** Selection is based on academic achievement and potential.

**Funds Avail.:** 22 scholarships were awarded for a total of $15,000. **No. of Awards:** 22. **To Apply:** Applications must include ACT or SAT scores for freshmen and college transcripts for sophomores, juniors, and seniors. Letters of recommendation and a record of society, community, or parish involvement are also required. **Deadline:** July 1. **Contact:** Steve Bisek, CEO, at the above address,(see entry 1753) or Catholic Workman - Scholarship Dept., at the above address.

• 1755 •
## James McKeen Cattell Fund
Attn: Gregory A. Kimble, Secretary/
  Treasurer
Department of Psychology,
  Experimental
Duke University                Ph: (919)660-5739
Durham, NC 27706               Fax: (919)660-5726

• 1756 • **Psychologists Supplemental Sabbatical Awards** *(Postdoctorate/Award)*

**Purpose:** To encourage research and scholarly endeavor on the part of psychologists at colleges and universities. **Focus:** Psychology. **Qualif.:** Applicant must be a psychologist and a tenured or tenure-track faculty member at a college or university in the United States or Canada. Applicant must be eligible for a period of sabbatical leave from employing institution. Preference will be given to applicants with specific projects of research or scholarship. Awards will ordinarily be made only to assist in the support of leaves of a full academic year, and awardee must not engage in teaching or any other employment that may conflict with accomplishing the endeavors for which the award was granted. Preference will be given to applicants with specific projects of research or scholarship. **Criteria:** Selection is based on quality of the proposal and the credentials of the applicant.

**Funds Avail.:** $24,000 maximum. **No. of Awards:** 5-6. **To Apply:** Write to the secretary-treasurer for application form. Submit with academic and work history, including bibliography, proposed plan for sabbatical, Secure two letters of reference to be submitted separately. **Deadline:** December 1. Awards will be announced about March 1.

**Remarks:** There are 70-90 applicants each year.

## • 1757 •
## CDS International, Inc.
330 7th Ave., 19th Fl.  
New York, NY 10001-5010  
*E-mail:* info@cdsintl.org  
*URL:* http://www.cdsintl.org

*Ph:* (212)497-3500  
*Fax:* (212)497-5535

### • 1758 • Robert Bosch Foundation Fellowships
*(Professional Development/Internship)*

**Purpose:** To maintain ties of friendship and understanding between the U.S. and Germany by sponsoring young American professionals in full-time work internships in Germany. During the nine-month program (September-May), Fellows have the opportunity to live in Germany while working in the branches of the Federal Government as well as in high-level internships relating to their professional experience. **Focus:** Journalism, Public Affairs, Mass Communications, Law, Economics, Political Science, Business. **Qualif.:** Applicants must be U.S. citizens who have outstanding credentials, including advanced degrees or equivalent work experience in the fields of journalism, public affairs, mass communications, law, economics, political science, and/or business administration. There is no strict age limit, although the program is primarily intended for those near the start of their careers. Applicants must be active participants in their community or in public affairs. Proficiency in the German language is not required at the time of application, but it is required of all selected Fellows by the start of the program. Language training may be provided by the Foundation when necessary. **To Apply:** Contact the Foundation for further information or an application. **Deadline:** October 15. **Contact:** CDS International, Inc. at the above address.

### • 1759 • Congress-Bundestag Youth Exchange for Young Professionals *(Undergraduate/Scholarship)*

**Purpose:** To strengthen ties between younger generations of Germans and Americans. Established as part of the President's International Youth Exchange Initiative. **Focus:** Business, Technical, Vocational Studies. **Qualif.:** Applicants must be U.S. citizens, between 18 and 24 years of age, high school graduates with good records of academic achievement, and have well-defined career goals, full or part-time practical work experience related to prospective career, and the ability to communicate with others and adapt to new situations. Previous knowledge of German is not required but strongly recommended. **Criteria:** Special emphasis is placed on care-related work experience and the applicant's maturity and ability to adapt to a foreign culture.

**Funds Avail.:** $3,500 per month. **No. of Awards:** 20. **To Apply:** Application must be accompanied by resume, essay, transcript, copy of high school diploma, and recommendations from teacher and employer. **Deadline:** October 15.Rolling deadline with final deadline of December 31.

**Remarks:** The program offers a similar work/study experience for young Germans in the U.S. **Contact:** Elfriede Andros, Program Officer, at the above address (see entry 1757).

## • 1760 •
## Center for 17th- & 18th-Century Studies
Univ. of California Los Angeles  
Fellowship Coordinator  
William Andrews Clark Memorial  
  Library  
2520 Cimarron St.  
Los Angeles, CA 90018-2098  
*E-mail:* eczfra@mvs.oac.ucla.edu

*Ph:* (213)735-7605  
*Fax:* (213)731-8617

*The Clark Library is known for its collection of materials on all aspects of British culture of the seventeenth and eighteenth centuries, Oscar Wilde and the 1890s, and the history of printing.*

### • 1761 • ASECS/Clark Fellowship *(Postdoctorate/Fellowship)*

**Purpose:** To support research projects dealing with the Restoration or the eighteenth century. **Focus:** History. **Qualif.:** Applicants must hold a Ph.D. or the equivalent and be members in good standing of the American Society for Eighteenth Century Studies. **Criteria:** The proposed research is evaluated in relation to the library's collection.

**Funds Avail.:** The stipend for this one-month fellowship is $1,500. **No. of Awards:** 1. **To Apply:** A formal application must be submitted. Three letters of reference from scholars familiar with the applicant's work must be sent directly to the library. Applications are supplied upon request. **Deadline:** March 15 for fellowships that will be completed in the fiscal year following.

**Remarks:** American Society for 18th-Century Studies and the William Andrews Clark Library are cosponsors of this fellowship. **Contact:** Fran Andersen at the above address (see entry 1760).

### • 1762 • Clark Library Predoctoral Fellowship *(Doctorate/Fellowship)*

**Purpose:** To support doctoral research in subject areas appropriate to the Clark Library's holdings. **Focus:** 17th and 18th Century British Culture, Oscar Wilde in 19th Century Typography, Bookmaking, Fine Press in 19th and 20th Century. **Qualif.:** Graduate students who have been advanced to doctoral candidacy are eligible to apply. **Criteria:** The relevance of the proposed research to the Library's collection is taken into account.

**Funds Avail.:** The stipend for the three-month fellowship is $4,500. **No. of Awards:** 1. **To Apply:** A formal application must be submitted. Three letters of reference from scholars familiar with the applicant's work must be sent directly to the library. Applications are supplied upon request. **Deadline:** March 15 for all fellowships that will be completed the fiscal year following.

**Remarks:** The fellowship is supported by funds from the Ahamson Foundation and the J. Paul Getty Trust. **Contact:** Fran Andersen at the above address (see entry 1760).

### • 1763 • Clark Library Short-Term Fellowship *(Postdoctorate/Fellowship)*

**Purpose:** To support advanced research in subject areas appropriate to the Clark Library's holdings. **Focus:** 17th and 18th Century British Culture, Oscar Wilde in 19th Century Typography, Bookmaking, Fine Press in 19th and 20th Century. **Qualif.:** Scholars who hold a Ph.D degree or the equivalent are eligible to apply. **Criteria:** The relevance of the proposed research to the library's collection is taken into account.

**Funds Avail.:** Stipends are $1,500 per month. **No. of Awards:** 5-7. **To Apply:** A formal application must be submitted. Three letters of reference must be sent directly to the library. Applications are supplied upon request. **Deadline:** March 1 for all fellowships that will be completed in the fiscal year following.

**Remarks:** The fellowships are supported by funds from the Ahamson Foundation of Los Angeles and the J. Paul Getty Trust. **Contact:** Fran Andersen at the above address (see entry 1760).

• 1764 •

## Center for Advanced Study in the Behavioral Sciences

75 Alta Road
Stanford, CA 94305

Ph: (650)321-2052
Fax: (650)321-1192

### • 1765 • Center for Advanced Study in the Behavioral Sciences Fellowship *(Postdoctorate/Fellowship)*

**Focus:** General Studies. **Qualif.:** Applicants must be scientists and scholars from the United States and abroad who show exceptional accomplishment or promise in their respective fields. These fields include but are not limited to anthropology, art history, biology, classics, economics, education, history, law, linguistics, literature, mathematical and statistical specialties, medicine, musicology, philosophy, political science, psychiatry, psychology, and sociology. The Center accepts Fellows of any race, color, and national or ethnic origin. The fellowship award entails a period of residence in the vicinity of the Center, normally beginning in September and extending from seven to twelve months. This requirement specifically excludes residence in San Francisco, Berkeley, Santa Cruz, or the East Bay. **Criteria:** Evaluation of candidates is based on standing in the field rather than on the merit of a particular project under way at a given time. The normal process of selection begins with nomination and proceeds through a moderately complex set of evaluations. Any scholar is entitled to nominate another person for consideration as a Fellow, but most nominations come from well-known scholars, academic administrators, former Fellows, and directors of the Center's summer institutes. **No. of Awards:** 48. **To Apply:** Nominees are asked to provide certain background information and a short list of references who are familiar with their scholarly work. **Deadline:** None.

**Remarks:** Nominees are notified of their eligibility and asked their preference concerning the timing of their fellowship. Requests for residency several years in the future (to coincide, perhaps, with a sabbatical year) are quite common and lead to inclusion in a tentative roster. **Contact:** Robert A. Scott at the above address (see entry 1764).

• 1766 •

## Center for Advanced Study in the Visual Arts

National Gallery of Art
Washington, DC 20565

Ph: (202)842-6482
Fax: (202)842-6733

*E-mail:* advstudy@nga.gov
*URL:* http://www.nga.gov/resources/casva.htm

*The Center for Advanced Study in the Visual Arts was founded in 1979 to further the study of the history, theory, and criticism of art, architecture, and urbanism. The extensive resources of the National Gallery of Art and the Washington D.C. area are made available to recipients of these awards.*

### • 1767 • Center for Advanced Study in the Visual Arts Senior Fellowships and Senior Visiting Fellowships *(Postdoctorate/Fellowship)*

**Purpose:** To assist advanced studies of the history, theory, and criticism of art, architecture, and urbanism. **Focus:** Art History, History of Architecture, History of Urban Design. **Qualif.:** Applicant for the Senior Fellowships and Visiting Senior Fellowships may be any age and of any nationality. Candidates must have at least five years of postdoctoral experience, ordinarily in the history, theory, or criticism of the visual arts. Applicants may specialize in any geographical area or time period. Candidates from other disciplines whose work examines artifacts or has implication for the analysis and criticism of physical form, as well as those who wish to do research on the Gallery's collections, may also apply.

The Senior Fellowships and Visiting Senior Fellowships are named as the Paul Mellon Senior Fellowship, the Ailsa Mellon Bruce Fellowships, and the Samuel H. Kress Senior Fellowships. Fellowships are tenable in Washington, D.C. Fellows must devote full-time to their research and participate in the activities of the Center. Recipients of the Latin American Fellowship travel for two months also visiting other collections, libraries, and institutions in the United States.

**Funds Avail.:** Varies; includes stipend and travel. **To Apply:** Write for application forms and guidelines. **Deadline:** Senior Fellowships: October 1; Visiting Senior Fellowships and Latin America Fellowships: March 21, September 21.

**Remarks:** The Center also offers Associate Appointments to candidates with research support from other institutions who would like to be affiliated with the Center. The appointments provide study space for periods from one month to one academic year. Eligibility requirements are the same as those described above; write for application form.

### • 1768 • Center For Advanced Study in the Visual Arts Associate Appointments *(Postdoctorate/Fellowship)*

**Purpose:** To allow the extensive resources of the National Gallery of Art and of the Washington, D.C. area be made available to scholars. **Qualif.:** Candidates must have held a Ph.D. for five or more years or have a record of professional accomplishment at the time of application. Candidates must be scholars in the fields of history, theory, and criticism of the visual arts (painting, sculpture, architecture, landscape architecture, urbanism, graphics, film, photography, decorative arts, industrial design, etc.) of any geographical area and of any period. Scholars in other disciplines whose work examines physical objects or has implications for the analysis and criticism of physical form may also apply. Additionally, applications are solicited from scholars who are interested in research related to objects in painting, sculpture, graphics, and other collections of the National Gallery of Art. Applicants should have obtained awards for full-time research from other granting institutions. **Criteria:** A selection committee composed of art history scholars makes selections without regard to the age or nationality.

**Funds Avail.:** The number of awards varies each year. All recipients are expected to live in Washington, D.C. for the duration of the appointment and to participate in the activities of the Center. **To Apply:** Applicants must submit ten copies of all application materials, including application forms, supporting letters, and publications. **Deadline:** October 1 of the preceding academic year, March 21st and September 21st. **Contact:** For information and application forms, write to the Center for Advanced Study in the Visual Arts, National Gallery of Art, at the above address (see entry 1766).

### • 1769 • Chester Dale Fellowship *(Other/Fellowship)*

**Purpose:** To support the advancement of a doctoral dissertation in Western art. **Qualif.:** Candidates must be either United States citizens or enrolled in a university in the United States; have completed residence requirements and coursework for the Ph.D. and general or preliminary examinations before the date of application; must have devoted at least one-half year's full-time research to their proposed dissertation topic; and know two foreign languages. **Criteria:** After preliminary selection, several candidates will be invited to Washington in February or March for an interview.

**Funds Avail.:** Two fellowships of $16,000 each for one year is provided to support research conducted either in the United States or abroad. The Fellowship carries no stipulation for residence at the National Gallery of Art, although the Fellow may be based at the Center if desired. **To Apply:** Application must be made through chairmen of graduate art history departments, who act as sponsors for applicants from their respective schools. Nomination forms must be completed by the applicant and the department chair. Departments should limit nominations to one candidate for each named fellowship. Candidates should consult with their

## Center for Advanced Study in the Visual Arts (continued)

dissertation advisor and chairman to obtain departmental sponsorship and an application form. Applicants must submit ten copies of the application and supporting materials, which includes a letter of recommendation by the chairman and supporting letters from at least two other faculty members who have directed the work of the applicant; a statement of the dissertation project and a report of the previous year's research; a tentative schedule of the work to be accomplished during the Fellowship years; a curriculum vitae; a short personal biography; official transcripts of both undergraduate and completed graduate courses; evidence of language examinations passed and scheduled; writing samples and a list of other fellowship applications for the same period. **Deadline:** Nomination forms and supporting letters must be submitted by November 15 to the Dean, Center for Advanced Study in the Visual Arts, National Gallery of Art. **Contact:** Art History Department Chair at the applicant's university.

### • 1770 • Mary Davis Fellowship (Doctorate/ Fellowship)

**Purpose:** To support the advancement or completion of a doctoral history. **Focus:** Western art, history. **Qualif.:** Applicants must be either United States citizens or enrolled in a university in the United States; have completed their residence requirements and coursework for the Ph.D. as well as general or preliminary examinations before the date of application; and know two foreign languages. **Criteria:** After preliminary selection, several candidates will be invited to Washington in February or March for interviews.

**Funds Avail.:** One non-renewable fellowship for $16,000 is awarded. The Fellow is expected to spend one year of the fellowship period on dissertation research in the United States or abroad, and one year at the Center for Advanced Study in the Visual Arts, National Gallery of Art, completing the dissertation and devoting half-time to Gallery research projects designed to complement the subjects of the dissertation, and to provide curatorial experience. **No. of Awards:** One. **To Apply:** Application for the fellowship must be made through chairmen of graduate art history departments, who act as sponsors for applicants from their respective schools. Candidates should consult with their dissertation advisor and chairman to obtain departmental sponsorship and an application form. Applicants must submit ten copies of the application and supporting materials, which include a statement of the dissertation project; a report of the previous year's research; a tentative schedule of the work to be accomplished during the Fellowship years; a curriculum vitae; a short personal biography; official transcripts of both undergraduate and completed graduate courses; evidence of language examinations passed and scheduled; a list of other fellowship applications for the same period; and a letter of recommendation by the chairman and supporting letters from at least two other faculty members who have directed the applicant's work. **Deadline:** Applications and all supporting materials must be sent by November 15, to the Dean, Center for Advanced Study in the Visual Arts, National Gallery of Art. Recipients are announced in the spring for fellowships that become tenable September 1. **Contact:** Art History Department Chairman at the applicant's university.

### • 1771 • David E. Finley Fellowship (Doctorate/ Fellowship)

**Purpose:** To provide support to complete an already well-advanced doctoral dissertation on Western Art. **Qualif.:** Candidates must be either United States citizens or enrolled in a university in the United States; have completed residence requirements and course work for the Ph.D. and general or preliminary examinations before the date of application; have devoted at least one-half year's full-time research to their proposed dissertation topic; and know two foreign languages related to their dissertation topic. A primary requirement for this fellowship is that the candidate have a significant interest in museum work, although there is no requirement as to the candidate's subsequent choice of career. **Criteria:** After preliminary selection, several candidates will be invited to Washington in February or March for interviews.

**Funds Avail.:** $16,000 annually for three years. The Fellow must spend two-years researching their topic either elsewhere in the United States or abroad, and the third year in-residence at the National Gallery of Art, Center for the Advanced Studies in Visual Arts. Half-time of the year in residence will be devoted to Gallery research projects designed to complement the subject of the dissertation. **To Apply:** Application must be made through chairmen of graduate art history departments, who act as sponsors for applicants from their respective schools. Nomination forms must be completed by the applicant and the department chair. Departments should limit nominations to one candidate for each named fellowship. Candidates should consult with their dissertation advisor and chairman to obtain departmental sponsorship and an application form. Applicants must submit ten copies of the application form and supporting materials, which include a letter of recommendation by the chairman and supporting letters from at least two other faculty members who have directed the work of the applicant; a statement of the dissertation project and a report of the previous year's research; a tentative schedule of the work to be accomplished during the Fellowship years; a curriculum vitae; a short personal biography; official transcripts of both undergraduate and completed graduate courses; and evidence of language examinations passed and scheduled; ten offprints of each published work or typescripts of work accepted for publication with indications of the place of publication; and a list of other fellowship applications for the same period. **Deadline:** Nomination forms and supporting letters must be submitted by November 15, to the Dean, Center for Advanced Study in the Visual Arts, National Gallery of Art. **Contact:** Art History Department Chair at the applicant's university.

### • 1772 • Frese Senior Research Fellowship (Postdoctorate/Fellowship)

**Purpose:** To allow German scholars to study at the Center **Focus:** History, Theory and Criticism of the Visual Arts. **Qualif.:** Applicant must be a German citizen who has held the PhD for five or more years. Applicants may either be preparing a Habilitationsschrift or pursuing a career in museums or historic monuments. Fellows are expected to reside in Washington DC throughout the academic year.

**Funds Avail.:** $35,000. **No. of Awards:** 1. **To Apply:** For information and application forms, write to the Center at the above address. **Deadline:** October 1. **Contact:** The Center for Advanced Study in the Visual Arts at the above address (see entry 1766).

### • 1773 • Frese Senior Research Fellowship Program (Postdoctorate/Fellowship)

**Focus:** History, theory, and criticism of the visual arts (painting, sculpture, architecture, landscape architecture, urbanism, graphics, film, photography, decorative arts, industrial design, and other arts) of any geographical area and of any period. Applications are also solicited from scholars in ohter disciplines whose work examines artifacts or has implications for the analysis and criticism of physical form. In addition, applications are solicited from scholars who are interested in research related to objects in the painting, sculpture, graphics, and other collections of the National Gallery of Art. **Qualif.:** Intended for a German citizen who has held the PhD for five years or more or who possesses an equivalent record of professional accomplishment at the time of application. Applicants may either be preparing a Habilitationsschrift or pursuing a career in museums or in historic monuments commissions in Germany. **Criteria:** Applications are reviewed by an external Selection Committee composed of scholars in the history of art.

**Funds Avail.:** Each fellow receives a stipend that includes round-trip travel andlocal expenses. **Deadline:** October 1.

**Remarks:** The fellowship is for full-time research. Fellows are expected to reside in Washington throughout the academic year and participate in the activities of the Center.

**• 1774 • The Ittleson Fellowship** *(Doctorate/Fellowship)*

**Purpose:** To support the completion of doctoral dissertations in fields other than Western art. **Focus:** Non-Western Art **Qualif.:** Candidates must be either United States citizens or enrolled in a university in the United States; have completed residence requirements and coursework for the Ph.D and general or preliminary examinations before the date of application; must have devoted at least one-half year's full-time research to their proposed dissertation topic; and know two foreign languages related to the dissertation topic. **Criteria:** After preliminary selection, several candidates will be invited to Washington in February or March for an interview.

**Funds Avail.:** A fellowship of $16,000 per year for two years. The Fellow is expected to spend one year conducting research either elsewhere in the United States or abroad, and the second year in-residence at the National Gallery of Art to complete the dissertation. **To Apply:** Application must be made through chairmen of graduate art history departments, who act as sponsors for applicants from their respective schools. Nomination forms must be completed by the applicant and the department chair. Departments should limit nominations to one candidate for each named fellowship. Candidates should consult with their dissertation advisor and chairman to obtain departmental sponsorship and an application form. Applicants must submit ten copies of the application and supporting materials, which includes a letter of recommendation by the chairman and supporting letters from at least two other faculty members who have directed the work of the applicant; a statement of the dissertation project and a report of the previous year's research; a tentative schedule of the work to be accomplished during the Fellowship years; a curriculum vitae; a short personal biography; official transcripts of both undergraduate and completed graduate courses; evidence of language examinations passed and scheduled; and a list of other fellowship applications for the same period. **Deadline:** Nomination forms and supporting letters must be submitted by November 15 to the Dean, Center for Advanced Study in the Visual Arts, National Gallery of Art. **Contact:** Art History Department Chair at the applicant's university.

**• 1775 • Andrew W. Mellon Fellowship** *(Doctorate/Fellowship)*

**Purpose:** To support the completion of a doctoral dissertation in a field other than Western art. **Qualif.:** Candidates must be either United States citizens or enrolled in a university in the United States; have completed residence requirements and coursework for the Ph.D. and general or preliminary examinations before the date of application; have devoted at least one-half year's full-time research to their proposed dissertation topic; and know two foreign languages. **Criteria:** After a preliminary selection, candidates will be invited to Washington in February or March for interviews.

**Funds Avail.:** $16,000 annually for two years. Fellows are expected to spend one year conducting research elsewhere in the United States or abroad and the second year at the National Gallery of Art to complete their dissertation. **To Apply:** Application must be made through chairmen of graduate art history departments, who act as sponsors for applicants from their respective schools. Departments should limit nominations to one candidate for each named fellowship. Candidates should consult with their dissertation advisor and chairman to obtain departmental sponsorship and an application form. Nomination forms must be completed by the applicant and the department chair. Applicants must submit ten copies of the application and supporting materials, which include a letter of recommendation by the chairman and supporting letters from at least two other faculty members who have directed the work of the applicant; a statement

of the dissertation project; a report of the previous year's research; a tentative schedule of the work to be accomplished during the Fellowship years; a curriculum vitae; a short personal biography; official transcripts of both undergraduate and completed graduate courses; evidence of language examinations passed and scheduled; and a list of other fellowship applications for the same period. **Deadline:** Nomination forms and supporting letters must be submitted by November 15, to the Dean, Center for Advanced Study in the Visual Arts, National Gallery of Art. **Contact:** Art History Department Chair at the applicant's university.

**• 1776 • Paul Mellon Fellowship** *(Doctorate/Fellowship)*

**Purpose:** To support the completion of a already well-advanced doctoral dissertation on Western Art. The fellowship is intended to allow a candidate of exceptional promise to develop expertise in a specific region or locality abroad. **Qualif.:** Candidates must be either United States citizens or enrolled in a university in the United States; have completed residence requirements and course work for the Ph.D. and general or preliminary examinations before the date of application; have devoted at least one-half year's full-time research to their proposed dissertation topic; and know two foreign languages related to the dissertation subject. **Criteria:** After a preliminary selection, several candidates will be invited to Washington in February or March for interviews.

**Funds Avail.:** $16,000 annually for three years. The Fellowship usually includes a two-year period of research in Europe or elsewhere on a dissertation topic, and an additional year of residence in the National Gallery of Art, Center for the Advanced Study of Visual Arts. **To Apply:** Application must be made through chairmen of art history graduate departments, who act as sponsors for applicants from their respective schools. Nomination forms must be completed by the applicant and the department chair. Departments should limit nominations to one candidate for each named fellowship. Candidates should consult with their dissertation advisor and chairman to obtain departmental sponsorship and an application form. Applicants must submit ten copies of the application and supporting materials, which include a letter of recommendation by the chairman and supporting letters from at least two other faculty members who have directed the work of the applicant; a statement of the dissertation project and a report of the previous year's research; a tentative schedule of the work to be accomplished during the Fellowship years; a curriculum vitae; a short personal biography; official transcripts of both undergraduate and completed graduate courses; evidence of language examinations passed and scheduled; offprints of each published work or typescripts of work accepted for publication with indications of the place of publication; and a list of other fellowship applications for the same period. **Deadline:** Nomination forms and supporting letters must be submitted by November 15, to the Dean, Center for Advanced Study in the Visual Arts, National Gallery of Art. **Contact:** Art History Department Chair at the applicant's university.

**• 1777 • Samuel H. Kress/Ailsa Mellon Bruce Paired Fellowship for Research in Conservation and Art History/Archaeology** *(Postdoctorate/Fellowship)*

**Focus:** History and conservation of the visual arts (painting, sculpture, architecture, landscape architecture, urbanism, graphics, film, photography, decorative arts, industrial design, and other arts) of any geographical area and of any period. A focus on National Gallery collections is not required. **Qualif.:** Open to those who have held the appropriate terminal degree for five years or more and who possess a record of professional accomplishment at the time of application. An equivalent record of professional accomplishment, in exceptional cases, may fulfill this requirement. **Criteria:** Applications are reviewed by an external Selection Committee composed of scholars in the history of art, archaeology, conservation, and materials science.

**Funds Avail.:** $5,500 for each team member. Additional funds are available for related research travel for the first segment and for

## Center for Advanced Study in the Visual Arts (continued)

round-trip travel to Washington for the residency period. Each team may apply for a supplemental allowance for expenses related to photography for publication, the creation of drawings, maps, or charts, or other expenditures directly related to the publication of the study. **No. of Awards:** Two paired fellowships (for four individuals) will be awarded annually.

### • 1778 • Senior Fellowships (Postdoctorate/Fellowship)

**Purpose:** To allow the extensive resources of the National Gallery of Art and of the Washington, D.C. area be made available to art scholars. The Fellowship is intended primarily to support research related to objects in the collection of the National Gallery of Art. **Qualif.:** Candidates must have held a Ph.D. for five or more years or have a record of professional accomplishment at the time of application. Candidates must be scholars in the fields of history, theory, and criticism of the visual arts (painting, sculpture, architecture, landscape architecture, urbanism, graphics, film, photography, decorative arts, industrial design, etc.) of any geographical area and of any period. Scholars in other disciplines whose work examines physical objects or has implications for the analysis and criticism of physical form may also apply. In addition, applications are solicited from scholars who are interested in research related to objects in painting, sculpture, graphics, and other collections of the National Gallery of Art. Applicants should have obtained awards for full-time research from other granting institutions. **Criteria:** A selection committee composed of scholars in the history of art makes selections without regard to the age or nationality of the applicant. Awards based on individual needs.

**Funds Avail.:** One appointment is considered for periods of one academic year, semester. Fellows receive one-half of their annual salary on the expectation that they will bring sabbatical stipends or research grants from their home institutions. They also receive a monthly stipend with additional allowances for research materials, round-trip travel, and local expenses and are provided with a study and luncheon privileges. The Fellowship may not be postponed or renewed. All recipients are expected to live in Washington, D.C. for the duration of the appointment and to participate in the activities of the Center. **To Apply:** Ten copies of all materials, including application form, supporting letters, and publications must be forwarded by the application deadline. **Deadline:** October 1 of the preceding academic year. **Contact:** For information and application forms, write to the Center for Advanced Study in the Visual Arts, National Gallery of Art, at the above address (see entry 1766).

### • 1779 • Robert H. and Clarice Smith Fellowship (Doctorate/Fellowship)

**Purpose:** To support the advancement or completion either of a doctoral dissertation or a resulting publication in Dutch and Flemish art. **Qualif.:** Candidates must either be United States citizens or enrolled in a university in the United States; have completed residence requirements and course work for the Ph.D. and general or preliminary examinations before the date of application; must have devoted at least one-half year's full-time research to their proposed dissertation topic; and know two foreign languages related to the dissertation topic. **Criteria:** After preliminary selection, several candidates will be invited to Washington in February or March for an interview.

**Funds Avail.:** A fellowship of $16,000 for one year. The Fellow may use the grant to study in the United States or abroad. There are no residence requirements at the National Gallery of Art, but the Fellow may be based at the Center, if desired. **To Apply:** Application must be made through chairmen of graduate art history departments, who act as sponsors for applicants from their respective schools. Nomination forms must be completed by the applicant and the department chair. Departments should limit nominations to one candidate for each named fellowship. Candidates should consult with their dissertation advisor and

chairman to obtain departmental sponsorship and an application form. Applicants must submit ten copies of the application and supporting materials, which includes a letter of recommendation by the chairman and supporting letters from at least two other faculty members who have directed the work of the applicant; a statement of the dissertation project and a report of the previous year's research; a tentative schedule of the work to be accomplished during the Fellowship years; a curriculum vitae; a short personal biography; official transcripts of both undergraduate and completed graduate courses; evidence of language examinations passed and scheduled; offprints of each published work or typescripts of work accepted for publication with indications of the place of publication; and a list of other fellowship applications for the same period. **Deadline:** Nomination forms and supporting letters must be submitted by November 15 to the Dean, Center for Advanced Study in the Visual Arts, National Gallery of Art. **Contact:** Art History Department Chair at the applicant's university.

### • 1780 • Visiting Senior Fellowships (Postdoctorate/Fellowship)

**Purpose:** To allow the extensive resources of the National Gallery of Art and of the Washington, D.C. area be made available to scholars. **Qualif.:** Candidates must have held a Ph.D. for five or more years or have a record of professional accomplishment at the time of application. Candidates must be scholars in the fields of history, theory, and criticism of the visual arts (painting, sculpture, architecture, landscape architecture, urbanism, graphics, film, photography, decorative arts, industrial design, etc.) of any geographical area and of any period. Scholars in other disciplines whose work examines physical objects or has implications for the analysis and criticism of physical form may also apply. In addition, applications are solicited from scholars who are interested in research related to objects in painting, sculpture, graphics, and other collections of the National Gallery of Art. Applicants should have obtained awards for full-time research from other granting institutions. **Criteria:** A selection committee composed of scholars in the history of art makes selections without regard to the age or nationality of the applicant.

**Funds Avail.:** Appointments are made for a maximum of 60 days. Visiting Fellows receive a stipend that includes round-trip travel, research, and local expenses and are provided with a study and luncheon privileges. All recipients are expected to live in Washington, D.C. for the duration of the appointment and to participate in the activities of the Center. **No. of Awards:** varies, about 6 each deadline **To Apply:** Five copies of all materials, including application form, supporting letters, and publications must be forwarded by the application deadline. **Deadline:** March 21 and September 21. **Contact:** For information and application forms, write to the Center for Advanced Study in the Visual Arts, National Gallery of Art, at the above address (see entry 1766).

### • 1781 • Visiting Senior Research Fellowship Program for Scholars from East and South Asia (Other/Fellowship)

**Focus:** History, archaeology, theory, and criticism of the visual arts (painting, sculpture, architecture, landscape architecture, urbanism, graphics, film, photography, decorative arts, industrial desing, and other arts) of any geographical area and of any period. Applications are solicited from art historians, archaeologists, curators, and scholars in other disciplines who study artifacts and cultures. **Qualif.:** Open to scholars from East and South Asia who hold appropriate degrees in the field and/or possess an equivalent record of professional accomplishment. Knowledge of English is required. **Criteria:** Applications will be reviewed by a Selection Committee composed of scholars in the field.

**Funds Avail.:** The fellows receive a stipend that includes travel, research, and housing expenses. **No. of Awards:** 2. **Deadline:** March 21 and September 21.

## • 1782 • Wyeth Fellowship *(Doctorate/Fellowship)*

**Purpose:** To support the completion of a doctoral dissertation on the topic of American art. **Qualif.:** Candidates must be either United States citizens or enrolled in a university in the United States; have completed residence requirements and course work for the Ph.D. and general or preliminary examinations before the date of application; must have devoted at least one-half year's full-time research to their proposed dissertation topic; and know two foreign languages related to the dissertation topic. **Criteria:** After preliminary selection, several candidates will be invited to Washington in February or March for an interview.

**Funds Avail.:** A fellowship of $16,000 per year. The Fellow is expected to spend one year conducting research either elsewhere in the United States or abroad, and the second year in-residence at the National Gallery of Art to complete the dissertation. **To Apply:** Application must be made through chairmen of graduate art history departments, who act as sponsors for applicants from their respective schools. Nomination forms must be completed by the applicant and the department chair. Departments should limit nominations to one candidate for each named fellowship. Candidates should consult with their dissertation advisor and chairman to obtain departmental sponsorship and an application form. Applicants must submit ten copies of the application and supporting materials, which includes a letter of recommendation by the chairman and supporting letters from at least two other faculty members who have directed the work of the applicant; a statement of the dissertation project and a report of the previous year's research; a tentative schedule of the work to be accomplished during the Fellowship years; a curriculum vitae; a short personal biography; official transcripts of both undergraduate and completed graduate courses; evidence of language examinations passed and scheduled; offprints of each published work or typescripts of work accepted for publication with indications of the place of publication; and a list of other fellowship applications for the same period. **Deadline:** Nomination forms and supporting letters must be submitted by November 15 to the Dean, Center for Advanced Study in the Visual Arts, National Gallery of Art. **Contact:** Art History Department Chair at the applicant's university.

## • 1783 • Center for Afroamerican and African Studies

200 W. Engineering Bldg.
550 E. University
University of Michigan
Ann Arbor, MI 48109-1092
*E-mail:* caasinformation@umich.edu
*URL:* http://www.umich.edu~iinet/caas/

*Ph:* (734)764-5513
*Fax:* (734)763-0543

### • 1784 • Du Bois Mandela Rodney Postdoctoral Fellowships *(Postdoctorate/Fellowship)*

**Purpose:** To identify and support scholars of high ability engaged in postdoctoral work on the Afro-American, African, and Caribbean experiences of men and women of color. **Focus:** Humanities, Social Sciences, African American Studies, and African Studies. **Qualif.:** Candidate must hold a Ph.D. at the time of application and be no more than ten years beyond degree completion. Fellows will be expected to conduct a CAAS work-in-progress seminar on their research during one of their semesters in residence.

**Funds Avail.:** $30,000. Taxes and the cost of health insurance are deducted from the stipend. **To Apply:** Write to the fellowship office for application guidelines. Submission must include a full curriculum vitae, three letters of recommendation (direct from referees), research prospectus and schedule of completion, and a writing sample. **Deadline:** January 16. Notification by March 15. **Contact:** Dubois-Mandela-Rodney Fellowship at the above address (see entry 1783).

## • 1785 • Rockefeller Fellows Programs *(Postdoctorate/Fellowship)*

**Purpose:** To allow scholars the opportunity to do independent research into Africa, its peoples, and people of African descent in the Industrial Age. **Focus:** Humanities, African Studies, African American Studies. **Qualif.:** Candidates must be junior-or senior-level researchers in the humanities holding a Ph.D., and being no more than ten years beyond the completion of their degree.

**Funds Avail.:** $31,000. Taxes and part of the cost of health insurance are deducted from the stipend. **To Apply:** Write to the fellowship office for application guidelines. Submission must include a full curriculum vitae, three letters of recommendation (direct from referees), research prospectus and schedule of completion, and a writing sample. **Deadline:** January 16. Notification by March 15. **Contact:** Rockefeller Fellows Program at the above address (see entry 1783).

## • 1786 • Center for Arabic Study Abroad

c/o Johns Hopkins University
Nitze School of Advanced
  International Studies
1619 Massachusetts Ave. NW, Rm.
  330
Washington, DC 20036-1983
*E-mail:* casa@mail.jhuwash.jhu.edu
*URL:* http://www.sais-jhu.edu/languages/casa

*Ph:* (202)663-5789
*Fax:* (202)663-5764

### • 1787 • Center for Arabic Study Abroad Fellowship *(Graduate, Undergraduate/Fellowship)*

**Purpose:** To provide advanced Arabic language training. **Focus:** Language arts. **Qualif.:** Applicants must be undergraduate and graduate students with a minimum of two years of college Arabic language study or equivalent. **Criteria:** Awards are made based on exam score, grade point average, references and health.

**Funds Avail.:** Varies. **No. of Awards:** Varies. **To Apply:** Applicants must submit an application, transcript, and references, and take an exam administered by the Center for Arabic Study Abroad in February. **Deadline:** December 31. **Contact:** Diane Whaley.

## • 1788 • Center for Archaeological Investigations

Southern Illinois University
Carbondale, IL 62901-4527
*E-mail:* lnewsom@siu.edu
*URL:* http://www.siu.edu/~cai/vshist.htm

*Ph:* (618)453-5031
*Fax:* (618)453-3253

### • 1789 • Visiting Scholar Postdoctoral Stipend *(Postdoctorate/Scholarship)*

**Purpose:** To support the organization and presentation of a conference and the publication of conference proceedings. **Focus:** Archaeology and Related Disciplines. **Qualif.:** Candidate may be of any nationality. Applicant must have a Ph.D. degree, and must wish to conduct a conference at the Center.

**Funds Avail.:** $2,700/month, plus fringe benefits **To Apply:** Send letter of application, 5-page proposal, curriculum vitae, and list of referees to the chair of the visiting scholar committee. Preapplication inquiries are strongly encouraged. **Deadline:** March 1. **Contact:** Dr. Lee A. Newsom, Visiting Scholar Committee Chair, at the above address (see entry 1788).

## • 1790 •
**The Center for Field Research**
680 Mt. Auburn St.                    *Ph:* (617)926-8200
PO Box 403                            *Fax:* (617)926-8532
Watertown, MA 02471                   *Free:* 800-776-0188
*E-mail:* cfr@earthwatch.org
*URL:* http://www.earthwatch.org

### • 1791 •   The Center for Field Research Grants
*(Postdoctorate, Postgraduate/Grant)*

**Purpose:** To support field studies by scientists and humanists working to investigate and/or preserve the physical, biological and cultural heritage in our trust. **Focus:** Physical Sciences. **Qualif.:** Applicants must submit a design for field investigation that integrates non-specialists into the research (research teams must include qualified volunteers). Field Research includes scholarship in the sciences and humanities that directly addresses natural, cultural, or occasionally, archival primary resources. The Center invites scholars of all nationalities to apply for support, and there are no limits on the geographical location of projects. Women and minorities are encouraged to apply. **Criteria:** The Center favors research that promises fresh insight and significant publications to their scholarly disciplines or to the public at large. They also give particular attention to research designs of a multidisciplinary nature or those involving international collaboration. Preference is given to post-doctoral scholarship, although occasionally exceptional initiatives by younger scholars and seasoned graduate students are considered. Proposals from a full range of field disciplines will be considered.

**Funds Avail.:** Grants are paid by Earthwatch and are awarded on a per capita basis, determined by multiplying the per capita grant by the number of volunteers deployed to the project. Per capita grants average $750 (range $250-1,000) and project grants average $20,000 (range $8,000-150,000). Grants are renewable each year, contingent on the success of the project. Grants cover expenses for maintaining research staff and volunteers in the field, travel for PI's to and from the field; leased or rented field equipment; consumables and insurance; support of staff and visiting scientists; and support for associates from host country. Earthwatch does not normally provide support for capital equipment, staff salaries, university overhead or indirect costs, data analysis, or preparation of results for publication. **No. of Awards:** Approximately 140 per year. **To Apply:** Preliminary proposals can be made by telephone, fax, email, or by a two-page letter to the Director of the Center at any time. Letters should include a description of the project, its research discipline(s) and objectives, scholarly significance, and staff composition and qualifications. Also the number and use of volunteers should be specified, field dates, location and approximate budget. A typical project would utilize from 20 to 40 volunteers annually, with 6 to 10 volunteers each on 3 to 5 sequential teams. Teams normally spend 10 to 25 days in the field. **Deadline:** Preliminary proposals must be submitted at least one year before field starting date and are responded to within 30 days. If staff determines that Earthwatch support would be appropriate to the described research, applicants are invited to submit a full proposal, which is due ten to twelve months before project date. A standard full proposal application form is available from the Center. Computer submissions are encouraged. Consultation with the staff of the Center is encouraged during the process of proposal development.

**Remarks:** The Center is not the source of funds. Instead, it reviews and evaluates research proposals in a wide range of disciplines. The Center recommends approved projects to Earthwatch for funding which, in turn, raises funds from carefully selected non-specialists. **Contact:** Dr. Andrew Hudson, Acting Executive Director, at the above address (see entry 1790).

## • 1792 •
**Center for Hellenic Studies**
3100 Whitehaven St., NW               *Ph:* (202)234-3738
Washington, DC 20008                  *Fax:* (202)797-3745
*E-mail:* chs@harvard.edu
*URL:* http://chs.harvard.edu

*The Center is a project of the Trustees of Harvard University. It is a self-contained academic community with housing on the grounds and permits a full @ year of individual study and research.*

### • 1793 •   Center for Hellenic Studies Fellowships
*(Postdoctorate/Fellowship)*

**Purpose:** To advance the scholarship of outstanding Hellenists in the earlier stages of their careers. **Focus:** Greek Studies. **Qualif.:** Candidates must have a Ph.D. or its equivalent and be professionally competent in Ancient Greek, as documented by publication. **Criteria:** The candidate's scholarly accomplishments and the quality of the research project.

**Funds Avail.:** Each fellowship includes housing with all utilities and a maximum stipend of $18,000 adjusted for individual circumstances such as number of dependents accompanying fellow and the amount of support from other sources. **No. of Awards:** 12. **To Apply:** Application forms must be accompanied by at least two, but not more than three, letters of recommendation and a detailed proposal of work in the field of Ancient Greek literature, language, history, religion, or philosophy. **Deadline:** Application must be postmarked by October 15; letters of recommendation must reach the Center's Directors by early November. **Contact:** Director's office at the above address (see entry 1792).

## • 1794 •
**Center for Interdisciplinary Studies in Chemical Physics**
Centre for Chemical Physics
P&A Bldg., Rm. 102
The University of Western Ontario      *Ph:* (519)661-4088
London, ON, Canada N6A 3K7            *Fax:* (519)661-3032
*E-mail:* ccp@uwd.ca
*URL:* http://www.uwd.ca/ccp

### • 1795 •   Centre for Interdisciplinary Studies in Chemical Physics Senior Visiting Fellowships
*(Postdoctorate/Fellowship)*

**Purpose:** To provide opportunities for established senior scientists to conduct research at the Centre. **Focus:** Applied Mathematics, Chemistry, Geology, Image Techniques, Materials Engineering, Oncology, Physics, Astronomy. **Qualif.:** Applicants may be of any nationality and senior scientists who are willing to undertake interdisciplinary research in problems of interest to the Centre. Fellowships may be held concurrently with other awards or income.

**Funds Avail.:** Living and travel allowances. **No. of Awards:** 4. **To Apply:** Write to the chair of the visiting fellowships committee for application form and guidelines. **Deadline:** October 1. Fellowships are announced by the end of December. **Contact:** Dr. M. J. Stillman, Director, Center for Chemical Physics, at the above address (see entry 1794).

## • 1796 •
### Center for International Mobility - CIMO
### Scholarships for Study and Research in Finland

PO Box 343      *Ph:* 0 7 747 7033
SF-00531 Helsinki, Finland      *Fax:* 0 7 747 7064
*E-mail:* cimoinfo@cimo.fi
*URL:* http://www.cimo.fi

### • 1797 • Scholarships for Young Researchers and University Teaching Staff *(Postdoctorate, Postgraduate/ Scholarship)*

**Purpose:** To promote international cooperation in teaching and research. **Focus:** General Studies. **Qualif.:** Applicants must be young researchers at the postgraduate or postdoctorate level or university teachers preferably under the age of 35. Scholarships are granted to nationals of all countries for research in Finland. Prior contact with the staff of the receiving university department is necessary. **Criteria:** Special emphasis is laid on active participation and interaction with research and teaching at the receiving institute.

**Funds Avail.:** Scholarship duration is three to 12 months. The monthly allowance is approximately FM 3000 to 6000 depending on the academic qualifications of the applicant. **To Apply:** Scholarships may be applied for either by the foreign visitor or a staff member of the receiving institute. **Deadline:** None. **Contact:** The Centre for International Mobility at the above address (see entry 1796).

## • 1798 •
### Center for Judaic Studies

420 Walnut St.      *Ph:* (215)238-1290
Philadelphia, PA 19106      *Fax:* (215)238-1540
*URL:* http://www.cjs.upenn.edu/

*Formerly known as Annenberg Research Institute.*

### • 1799 • Center for Judaic Studies Postdoctoral Fellowships *(Postdoctorate/Fellowship)*

**Purpose:** To encourage advanced scholarship in areas of interest to the Institute. **Focus:** Judaic Studies, Near Eastern Studies. **Qualif.:** Applicant must have a Ph.D. and be conducting research in Judaic and Near Eastern Studies or a related field, including pre-Christian, Christian or Islamic History and Culture, from ancient to modern times. Candidate may propose any topic for investigation within the areas of study, but each year the Institute will announce an issue or topic about which it is particularly interested in receiving proposals.

**Funds Avail.:** $23,000-50,000; travel allowances are also available. **To Apply:** Write to the fellowship program secretary for application materials. **Deadline:** September. Awards are announced in mid-December. **Contact:** Sheila Allen, Fellowship Program Secretary, at the above address (see entry 1798).

## • 1800 •
### Center for Molecular Nutrition and Sensory Disorders

c/o Taste & Smell Clinic
5125 MacArthur Blvd. NW, Ste. 20      *Ph:* (202)364-4180
Washington, DC 20016      *Fax:* (202)304-9727
*URL:* http://www.tasteandsmell.com

### • 1801 • Taste & Clinic Fellowship *(Postdoctorate/ Fellowship)*

**Purpose:** To pursue research in the areas of taste and smell physiology, biochemistry, and pathology and the role of growth factors in saliva. **Focus:** Salivary Biochemsitry, Sensory Receptor Biochemistry, Growth Factors. **Qualif.:** Candidates must hold a Ph.D. in biochemistry or pharmacology. **Criteria:** Selection is based upon recommendation, grades, and expertise in the field.

**Funds Avail.:** $20,000 to $25,000 is available. **No. of Awards:** Two. **To Apply:** Fellowship requests should be submitted to the Taste & Smell Clinic. **Deadline:** June 30. **Contact:** R.I. Henkin, M.D. at the above address (see entry 1800).

## • 1802 •
### Center for Science in the Public Interest

1875 Connecticut Ave., NW, Ste.
300      *Ph:* (202)332-9110
Washington, DC 20009-5728      *Fax:* (202)265-4954
*E-mail:* khartzell@cspinet.org
*URL:* http://cspinet.org

### • 1803 • Public Interest Internships *(Doctorate, Graduate, Undergraduate/Internship)*

**Purpose:** To give qualified students the opportunity to focus on national health and nutrition issues. **Focus:** Consumer Affairs, Journalism, Law, Nutrition, Public Health, Public Affairs. **Qualif.:** Applicant may be of any nationality. Applicant must be an undergraduate, graduate, law, or medical student concerned with national policy-making on issues of health and nutrition. Previous experience with advocacy groups is not required, but would be advantageous. Internships are tenable at CSPI during the summer and the school year. Candidates apply to particular CSPI projects which match their interests and qualifications. Information about requirements for specific internship projects is available from the intern coordinator.

**Funds Avail.:** $5.25/hour undergraduate; $6.00/hour graduate. **No. of Awards:** 8. **To Apply:** Write to the intern coordinator for application guidelines and a list of current projects. Submit the following documents: a cover letter indicating issues of interest, future plans, and dates of availability for internship; a resume or curriculum vitae; a writing sample; two letters of recommendation; and transcripts. **Deadline:** Applications are accepted on a rolling basis. Candidates are advised to apply as early as possible. **Contact:** Intern Coordinator at the above address (see entry 1802).

## • 1804 •
### Center for Strategic And Budgetary Assessments
1730 Rhode Island Ave. NW, Ste.
912             *Ph:* (202)331-7990
Washington, DC 20036      *Fax:* (202)331-8019
*E-mail:* 102375413@compuserve.com; info@csbahome.com
*URL:* http://www.csbahome.com

### • 1805 • Center for Strategic and Budgetary Assessments Internship *(Other/Internship)*

**Purpose:** To examine the inextricable link between near-term and long-range military planning and defense investment strategies, using innovative assessment methodologies and data-based analyses. **Focus:** Military Policy, Defense Budgets, Industrial Base. **Qualif.:** Candidates must have excellent research, fact gathering, writing, and computer skills. Applicants must possess a willingness to do administrative as well as substantive tasks.

**Funds Avail.:** Stipend of $175 TO $250 per week is provided for 40 hours of work. **No. of Awards:** 1-2. **To Apply:** A letter of interest, resume, and short writing sample must be submitted. **Deadline:** April 15 for summer; July 15 for fall; November 15 for winter/spring.

**Remarks:** Interns assist staff with tracking legislative issues, preparing materials for the news media, gathering budget data, and conducting research for project reports. **Contact:** Adrianne Janus, Office Administrator, at the above address (see entry 1804).

## • 1806 •
### Center for the Study of the History of Nursing
University of Pennsylvania School of
   Nursing
307 Nursing Education Bldg.      *Ph:* (215)898-4502
Philadelphia, PA 19104-6096     *Fax:* (215)573-2168
*E-mail:* nhistory@pobox.upenn.edu
*URL:* http://www.nursing.upenn.edu/history

### • 1807 • Lillian Sholtis Brunner Summer Fellowship *(Doctorate, Postdoctorate/Fellowship)*

**Purpose:** To encourage scholarly research on the history of nursing. **Focus:** History of Nursing. **Qualif.:** Candidate may be of any nationality. Both predoctoral and postdoctoral scholars are eligible, although preference is given to candidates with Ph.D. degrees. Applicant must have experience in historical research related to nursing. The fellowship is tenable at the Center.

**Funds Avail.:** $2,500. **To Apply:** Write to the Center for application guidelines. Submit three copies of a detailed research proposal, an itemized budget, and curriculum vitae. **Deadline:** December 31. Notification by March 1. **Contact:** Center for the Study of the History of Nursing at the above address (see entry 1806).

## • 1808 •
### Center for Women in Government
University of Albany
Draper Hall, Rm. 302
135 Western Ave.          *Ph:* (518)442-3900
Albany, NY 12222        *Fax:* (518)442-3877

### • 1809 • Women and Public Policy Fellowship *(Graduate/Fellowship)*

**Purpose:** To encourage the greater participation of women in the public policy process, the development of policy specialists in areas of concern to women, and the formulation of state policy which recognizes the needs of women and families. **Focus:** Public Affairs, Women's Studies. **Qualif.:** Applicants must be graduate students from any academic discipline and matriculated in colleges and universities in the state of New York. They must have completed 12 hours of graduate work by May 1, with degree completion scheduled for May of the following year or after, and have demonstrated an interest in improving the status of women through their research, paid employment, or volunteer activities. Fellows are assigned as staff to a legislator or a state agency for 30 hours each week. They work on a wide range of issues, which have included health, insurance, labor, education, and aging. They become involved in all aspects of the policy-making process. All placements are in Albany. In addition, they are required to complete three seminars (12 credits) to complement their placements while providing a comprehensive perspective on policy making and its impact on women and families. The seminars are: The New York State Public Policy Process, Women and Public Policy: The Impact of Gender, Race, and Class, and Women in Public Policy: The Current Agenda.

**Funds Avail.:** A stipend of $9,000 for the 7-month period from January to July. Free tuition is provided for 12 credits of academic coursework at the Graduate School of Public Affairs, University of Albany, SUNY. **To Apply:** Applications are available in early Spring. **Deadline:** May 31. **Contact:** Judith R. Saidel, Director of Fellowship Programs, at the above address (see entry 1808).

## • 1810 •
### Central Intelligence Agency - Office of Student Programs
PO Box 12727
Arlington, VA 22209-8727     *Ph:* (703)613-7126
*URL:* http://www.cia.gov

### • 1811 • Central Intelligence Agency Graduate Studies Internships *(Graduate/Internship)*

**Purpose:** To attract bright scholars to the CIA. **Focus:** Area and Ethnic Studies, Economics, Engineering, Geography, International Affairs and Relations, Foreign Languages, Science, Political Science, Mathematics and Mathematical Sciences, Graphic Art and Design, Computer and Information Sciences. **Qualif.:** Applicants must be U.S. citizens entering either their first or second year of graduate studies. Applicants must have earned a minimum grade point average of 3.0/4.0, and be committed to attending graduate school on a full-time basis during the semester following the internship. Candidates must successfully complete medical and security screening by the CIA.

**Funds Avail.:** Competitive salary, plus travel and housing assistance. Applicants demonstrating financial need are eligible for tuition assistance. **To Apply:** Write or phone for application guidelines by August 31. Submit a letter of application, resume, and planned course of study to the coordinator for student programs. **Deadline:** November 1.

**Remarks:** Tuition assistance is offered to students who are already enrolled in the Graduate Studies program and who plan to return to the CIA as staff employees upon completion of their academic degree requirements.

### • 1812 • Central Intelligence Agency Undergraduate Scholars Program *(Undergraduate/Internship, Scholarship)*

**Purpose:** To offer graduating high school students, particularly minorities and people with disabilities, who have a financial need for tuition assistance, the opportunity to work in challenging positions with the CIA each college summer. **Focus:** Computer and Information Sciences, Electrical Engineering, Economics. **Qualif.:** Applicants must be U.S. citizens, 18 years of age or older by May 1 of their senior year, with SAT scores of at least 1000 and ACT scores of at least 21, and a high school GPA of at least 3.0 on a 4.0 scale. In addition, applicants must successfully complete medical and security screening, including a polygraph interview, by the CIA. For tuition assistance, applicants must demonstrate financial need.

**Funds Avail.:** Tuition, fees, books, and a salary ranging from GS-2 to GS-5 during college which raises to at least GS-7 after graduation. Housing assistance and round-trip transportation to Washington, D.C. are also provided. **Deadline:** No later than the end of the first semester of applicants' senior year in high school.

**Remarks:** CIA undergraduate scholars are expected to continue employment with the Agency after graduation for a period of 1 times the length of their college career. **Contact:** Personnel Representative, at the above address (see entry 1810).

• 1813 •
## Central Newspapers, Inc.
c/o The Indianapolis News
PO Box 145
Indianapolis, IN 46206-0145          Ph: (317)633-9121

• 1814 • **Pulliam Journalism Fellowships** (Graduate/ Fellowship)

**Purpose:** To provide specialized training in journalism to recent college graduates. **Focus:** Newspaper Journalism. **Qualif.:** Applicant must be a U.S. citizen or permanent resident who will earn a bachelor's degree during the eleven months directly prior to the start of the fellowship in June. Candidate may be a newspaper journalism major or a liberal arts major with part-time or full-time newspaper experience. Applicant must have a proven potential in reporting, writing and editing and have high scholastic attainment, especially in the liberal arts. Fellows are granted work-study internships at the Indianapolis Star, the Indianapolis News, the Arizona Republic or the Phoenix Gazette. In addition to working as reporters, editorial writers or copy editors, fellows meet with guest speakers and participate in group and individual sessions conducted by a writing coach. **Criteria:** Based on scholastic achievement, writing ability, newspaper internships and references.

**Funds Avail.:** $4,200. **To Apply:** Write to Mr. Pulliam for application form and guidelines. Submit form with samples of published writing, transcripts, a recent photograph, three letters of recommendation and a 400- to 600-word editorial written expressly for the application. **Deadline:** March 1. **Contact:** Russell B. Pulliam, Editor

• 1815 •
## The Central Scholarship Bureau
1700 Reisterstown Rd., Ste. 220       Ph: (410)358-8668
Baltimore, MD 21208                   Fax: (410)358-3217
E-mail: info@centralsb.org
URL: http://www.centralsb.org.com

• 1816 • **Central Scholarship Bureau Interest-Free Loans** (Graduate, Undergraduate/Loan)

**Purpose:** To provide "last resort" loans for students who have exhausted their financial aid resources. **Focus:** General Studies. **Qualif.:** Candidates must be residents of the city of Baltimore, or Baltimore County, or Ann Arandel, Caroll, Harford, and Howard counties and be attending an accredited post-secondary school. They must also be in good academic standing. **Criteria:**

Candidates must also meet income guidelines. Contact office for details.

**Funds Avail.:** Up to $2,500 per year is available to undergraduates and $4,500 per year for graduate students. **Deadline:** None. **Contact:** Roberta Goldman, The Central Scholarship Bureau, at the above address (see entry 1815).

• 1817 •
## Centro de Investigacion y Estudios Avanzados dep IPN - Department of Mathematics
Apartado Postal 14-740
CP 07000 Mexico 14 DF, Mexico

• 1818 • **Solomon Lefschetz Instructorships in Mathematics** (Postdoctorate/Fellowship)

**Purpose:** To provide postdoctoral mathematicians with the opportunity to research and teach in Mexico. **Focus:** Mathematics. **Qualif.:** Applicant may be of any nationality. Candidate must hold a Ph.D. in mathematics. A knowledge of Spanish is desired but not required. Instructors must teach three hours per week at the graduate level. The remainder of their time should be dedicated to research. **To Apply:** Write for application guidelines. **Deadline:** February. **Contact:** Solomon Lefschetz, Instructorships, at the above address (see entry 1817).

• 1819 •
## Centrum
Fort Worden State Park
PO Box 1158                           Ph: (360)385-3102
Port Townsend, WA 98368              Fax: (360)385-2470
E-mail: marlene@centrum.org
URL: http://www.centrum.org

• 1820 • **Centrum Residencies** (Professional Development/Other)

**Purpose:** To support and encourage writers. **Focus:** Drama, Fiction, Nonfiction, Poetry. **Qualif.:** Applicant may be any age and of any nationality. Candidate must be a poet, a playwright, or a writer of fiction or creative nonfiction. Residencies are tenable at Centrum.

**Funds Avail.:** $75/week, plus free housing. **To Apply:** Write to the director for application guidelines. Include self-addressed, stamped envelope. **Deadline:** For fall, winter and spring residencies: September 8. Notification within three months of deadline. **Contact:** Marlene Bennett at the above address (see entry 1819).

• 1821 •
## Centura Bank - Trust Division
Box 1220                              Ph: (919)977-8483
Rocky Mount, NC 27802                 Fax: (919)977-4446
URL: http://www.asheville.com/centura.html

• 1822 • **Henry N. and Sydney T. Davenport Loan Fund** (Graduate, Undergraduate/Loan)

**Purpose:** To provide financial assistance to qualified post-secondary school students in the form of loans. **Qualif.:** Applicants

## Centura Bank - Trust Division (continued)

must be residents of Nash or Edgecombe Counties, North Carolina who are U.S. citizens and are enrolled in an accredited junior college, college, or university. Students must demonstrate need, qualities of leadership, good citizenship, force of character and community spirit, and scholarship. **Criteria:** Selection is made by the Loan Committee, which is comprised of members of the Rocky Mount Foundation Distribution Committee and the Superintendents of Schools of Nash and Edgecombe Counties.

**Funds Avail.:** There are no minimum or maximum amounts for loans. Loans must be repaid within five years of date of graduation. Principal payments commence one year after date of graduation or separation from school and equal one-fifth of the unpaid balance per year. No interest is paid while the student attends school. Interest commences one year after date of graduation at the rate of 8 percent until loan is repaid. If student terminates education prior to graduation, interest commences upon date of separation from school at the rate of 8 percent until loan is repaid. One or both parents of student recipient may be required to co-sign the loan with the student. Student may reapply for additional loans for succeeding academic years subject to maintenance of satisfactory academic standing. **To Apply:** Formal application must be accompanied by official academic transcripts, copy of SAT test scores, a copy of most recent tax returns, and a recent photograph of applicant. **Deadline:** June 1.

**Remarks:** The Fund is supervised by the Rocky Mount Foundation and administered by Centura Bank Trust Division. **Contact:** Mr. Stephen E. Pullin at the above address (see entry 1821).

### • 1823 • Carrie and Luther Huffines Loan Fund
(Undergraduate/Loan)

**Purpose:** To provide financial assistance to qualified post-secondary school students in the form of loans. **Qualif.:** Residents of Nash or Edgecombe Counties, North Carolina who are citizens of the U.S. and enrolled in an accredited junior college, college, or university are eligible. Students must demonstrate need, qualities of leadership, good citizenship, force of character, community spirit, and scholarship. **Criteria:** Preference is given to qualified students studying medicine or textiles. Selections are made by the Loan Committee, which consists of members of the Rocky Mount Foundation distribution Committee and the Superintendents of Schools of Nash and Edgecombe Counties.

**Funds Avail.:** There are no minimum or maximum amounts of loans. Loans must be repaid within five years of date of graduation. Principal payments commence one year after date of graduation or separation from school and equal one-fifth of the unpaid balance per year. No interest is paid while the student attends school. Interest commences one year after date of graduation at the rate of 8 percent until loan is repaid. If student terminates education prior to graduation, interest commences upon date of separation from school at the rate of 8 percent until the loan is repaid. One or both parents of student recipients may be required to co-sign the loan with the student. **To Apply:** Formal applications must be submitted and accompanied by official academic transcripts, copies of SAT test scores, most recent tax returns, and a recent photograph of the applicant. **Deadline:** June 1.

**Remarks:** The Fund is supervised by the Rocky Mount Foundation and administered by Centura Bank Trust Division. **Contact:** Mr. Stephen E. Pullin at the above address (see entry 1821).

### • 1824 • Helen Lancaster Minton Educational Fund
(Undergraduate/Scholarship)

**Purpose:** To provide funds for worthy individuals attending North Carolina Wesleyan College. **Qualif.:** Graduates of high schools located within Nash or Edgecombe Counties, North Carolina, who are citizens of the United States and will attend North Carolina Wesleyan College are eligible to apply. Students must demonstrate need, qualities of leadership, good citizenship, force of character and community spirit, and scholarship (C-plus average or better). Students are not restricted by creed or sex. Students previously

receiving scholarship grants from the Fund may reapply, subject to continued compliance with the above guidelines. **To Apply:** Formal application accompanied by official academic transcripts, copy of SAT test scores, and a recent photograph of applicant. **Deadline:** April 1. **Contact:** Mr. Stephen E. Pullin at the above address (see entry 1821).

## • 1825 •
## Chairscholars Foundation, Inc.
c/o Hugo and Alicia Keim
Silver Dollar Ranch 38
17000 Patterson Rd.
Odessa, FL 33556       *Ph:* (813)920-2737

### • 1826 • Chairscholars Foundation Scholarship
(Undergraduate/Scholarship)

**Focus:** General studies. **Qualif.:** Applicants must be physically challenged and be chair confined; have financial difficulties which would prevent them from attending college; have histories of satisfactory academic performance in the past; be high school seniors or college freshman; and show some form of community service or social contribution in the past. **Criteria:** Awards are based on financial need. **To Apply:** Applicants must submit an application form; 300-500 word essay outlining how they became physically challenged, how their lives in wheelchairs have affected them and their families, and their goals and aspirations for the future; financial statement (previous year tax return). **Deadline:** January 15. **Contact:** Dr. Hugo and Alicia Keim.

## • 1827 •
## Chancellor's Talent Award
University of Massachusetts at
   Amherst
307 Admissions Ctr.
Amherst, MA 01003       *Ph:* (413)545-2621

### • 1828 • Chancellor's Talent Award Program
(Undergraduate/Scholarship)

**Focus:** Music, dance, art. **Qualif.:** Applicants must be Massachusetts high school seniors with minimum cumulative grade point averages of 2.5 who apply and are accepted to the University of Massachusetts. **Criteria:** Awards are made based on academic achievement and demonstrated ability in music. Art and dance awards are determined by departmental audition/portfolio.

**Funds Avail.:** $5,000 per year. **To Apply:** Write for further details. **Contact:** Sarah Hamilton, CTA Program Coordinator.

## • 1829 •
## Charcot-Marie-Tooth International
One Springbank Dr.       *Ph:* (905)687-3630
St. Catharines, ON, Canada L2S 2K1    *Fax:* (905)687-8753

### • 1830 • CMT Scholarships (Graduate/Scholarship)

**Purpose:** To assist people who have Charcot-Marie-Tooth disease to earn a graduate degree. **Qualif.:** Applicants must be diagnosed in writing as having Charcot-Marie-Tooth disease and be current members of CMT International. They must also have been accepted by a recognized college or university in any country.

**Funds Avail.:** $1,000 Canadian may be divided among two or more applicants. **To Apply:** Write for details and application. **Deadline:** May 15. **Contact:** Linda Crabtree, Executive Director, at the above address (see entry 1829).

## • 1831 •
## Charles River District Medical Society

                           *Fax:* (781)893-2105
1440 Main St.
Waltham, MA 02451-1600            *Free:* 800-944-5562

### • 1832 • Charles River District Medical Society Scholarship *(Graduate/Scholarship)*

**Focus:** Medicine. **Qualif.:** Applicants must be medical students who are legal residents of one of the five towns comprising the Charles River district: Needham, Newton, Waltham, Wellesley, and Weston. They must be enrolled at an approved U.S. institution. **Criteria:** Based on financial need.

**Funds Avail.:** $1000 per student for one year. **To Apply:** Applications must include the following: curriculum vitae; a letter that includes a statement of personal goals; the Graduate and Professional School Financial Aid Service form or a financial aid form of equivalent informational value (applications that provide the best documentation of financial need are considered first); parents' resources must be included; a letter from the financial aid officer of the medical school verifying a need for financial assistance; and a statement of academic standing from the medical school. The name of a district society member who may be contacted for a recommendation should also be included if possible. **Deadline:** April 1.

**Remarks:** Applicants must be district residents. **Contact:** Rachel R. Mahar, administrative assistant, at the above address (see entry 1831).

## • 1833 •
## Chartered Institute of Management Accountants Research Foundation

63 Portland Place             *Ph:* 171 637 2311
London W1N 4AB, England       *Fax:* 171 436 1582

### • 1834 • Chartered Institute of Management Accountants Research Foundation Grants *(All/Grant)*

**Purpose:** To promote and develop the science of management accounting and to foster and maintain investigations and research into the best means and methods of developing and applying such science. **Focus:** Management Accounting and related disciplines. **Qualif.:** There are no eligibility restrictions or requirements. Anyone with a viable research plan may submit a proposal to the Foundation. Funds are not available for fees for courses, postgraduate qualifications, or travel.

**Funds Avail.:** Approximately $55,000 U.S. maximum. **To Apply:** Write to the director of research for a copy of research plan, application forms and guidelines. Submit forms with a research proposal. **Deadline:** None. **Contact:** Andrea Jeffries, Director of Research, at the above address (see entry 1833).

## • 1835 •
## Chartered Institute of Transport

80 Portland Place             *Ph:* 171 636 9952
London W1N 4DP, England      *Fax:* 171 637 0511

### • 1836 • Henry Spurrier Scholarship *(Professional Development/Scholarship)*

**Purpose:** To assist study/research in road transport. **Focus:** Road Transport. **Qualif.:** Candidate may be of any nationality. Applicant must inform the institute of the sum required and how it would be applied to study/research in road transport.

**Funds Avail.:** $1,000-3,000, usually divided among a number of applicants. **No. of Awards:** Varies. **To Apply:** Write to the Institute for application guidelines. **Deadline:** May 25. **Contact:** Examinations Officer at the above address (see entry 1835).

## • 1837 •
## Chartered Institute of Transport, New Zealand

P.O. Box 13-635, Armagh        *Ph:* 3 365 4920
Christchurch, New Zealand      *Fax:* 3 379 4762

### • 1838 • Chartered Institute of Transport to New Zealand Scholarships *(Professional Development/Scholarship)*

**Purpose:** To promote research into transport matters in New Zealand. **Focus:** Transport. **Qualif.:** There are no restrictions on eligibility, but preference will be given to New Zealand citizens, members of the Institute, and persons intending to enroll as associates or students of the Institute. Applications will be considered from organizations for a nominated person to undertake a study project, which would ultimately benefit the industry as a whole.

**Funds Avail.:** NZ$8,000 maximum. **To Apply:** Write to the executive director for application form and guidelines. An interview may be required; attendance shall be at the candidate's own expense. **Deadline:** February 28. Awards are announced in April.

**Remarks:** A travel award of up to $5,000 funded by B.P. New Zealand Ltd. may, on the recommendation of the New Zealand Council, also be granted to the scholar to cover travel to and from the country where an accepted research project is to be carried out. **Contact:** Peter J. Goodwin, Executive Director, at the above address (see entry 1837).

## • 1839 •
## Chatham College

Office of Admissions
Woodland Rd.                *Ph:* 800-837-1290
Pittsburgh, PA 15232         *Fax:* (412)365-1609
*E-mail:* admissions@chatham.edu
*URL:* http://www.chatham.edu/

### • 1840 • Minna Kaufmann Ruud Scholarship *(Undergraduate/Scholarship)*

**Purpose:** To recognize students with outstanding vocal talent. **Focus:** Music. **Qualif.:** Applicants must major in music or have an interdisciplinary major with another department. **Criteria:** Selection is based upon an on-campus audition.

**Funds Avail.:** Awards are valued at $3,500 annually and are renewable. **To Apply:** Students must submit completed applications and arrange an on-campus interview. **Deadline:** June

*Chatham College (continued)*

1. **Contact:** Office of Admissions at the above address (see entry 1839).

---

• 1841 •

## Chautauqua Institution
PO Box 1098, Dept. 6  *Ph:* (716)357-6233
Chautauqua, NY 14722  *Fax:* (716)357-9014

### • 1842 • Chautauqua Institution Scholarship
*(Graduate, High School, Undergraduate/Scholarship)*

**Focus:** Visual and Performing Arts—Orchestra, Piano, Opera, Ballet, Drama, Fine Arts. **Qualif.:** The Institution's Summer Schools of Music, Dance, and Theater offer seven-to eight-week programs designed for talented high school, college, and graduate-level students. Students must be between the ages of 15 and 25. **Criteria:** Scholarships are awarded on the basis of merit and financial need.

**Funds Avail.:** A fund of $225,000 is available for scholarships. The number of awards varies. **To Apply:** All applicants must audition and provide a photocopy of 1040 tax forms with their application. **Deadline:** April 1. **Contact:** David E. Horn, Continuous Improvement Director, at the above address (see entry 1841).

---

• 1843 •

## Chautauqua Region Community Foundation Inc.
21 E. Third St., Ste. 301  *Ph:* (716)661-3390
Jamestown, NY 14701  *Fax:* (716)488-0387

### • 1844 • A.A.R.P. Jamestown Chapter 334 Scholarship *(Undergraduate/Scholarship)*

**Focus:** General studies. **Qualif.:** Applicants must be students of Jamestown, Southwestern, Maple Grove, Falconer, Frewsburg, Chautauqua, and Panama high schools. **Criteria:** Awards are granted based on financial need.

**Funds Avail.:** $200 to $300 per scholarship. **No. of Awards:** 1-2. **To Apply:** Apply through high school counselor. **Deadline:** Varies. **Contact:** Chautauqua Region Community Foundation.

### • 1845 • Agnes Home Scholarship *(Undergraduate/Scholarship)*

**Focus:** General studies. **Qualif.:** Applicants must be female residents of Chautauqua County and attending JBC or JCC. **Criteria:** Awards made based on financial need.

**Funds Avail.:** $500 per award. **No. of Awards:** 1. **To Apply:** Write for further details. **Deadline:** April 20. **Contact:** Chautauqua Region Community Foundation at the above address (see entry 1843).

### • 1846 • Glenn Lee Akam, Jr. Memorial Scholarship *(Undergraduate/Scholarship)*

**Focus:** General studies. **Qualif.:** Applicants must be JCC sophomore students. **Criteria:**

**Funds Avail.:** $100 to $300 for books. **No. of Awards:** 1. **To Apply:** Write for further details. **Deadline:** April 20. **Contact:** Chautauqua Region Community Foundation at the above address (see entry 1843).

### • 1847 • Allied Fire Protection System, Inc. Scholarship *(Undergraduate/Scholarship)*

**Focus:** General studies. **Qualif.:** Applicant must be residents of the Chautauqua region. **Criteria:** Awards made based on financial need, field of study. Preference given to those majoring in building/construction.

**Funds Avail.:** $1,000 per scholarship. **No. of Awards:** 1. **To Apply:** Applicants must submit completed application. Write for further details. **Deadline:** April 20. **Contact:** Chautauqua Region Community Foundation at the above address (see entry 1843).

### • 1848 • A.A. Amidon Scholarship *(Undergraduate/Scholarship)*

**Focus:** General studies. **Qualif.:** Applicants must be residents of Chautuaqua region who are business and finance majors.

**Funds Avail.:** $300 to $1,000 per award. **No. of Awards:** 1-5. **To Apply:** Write for further details. **Deadline:** April 20. **Contact:** Chautauqua Region Community Foundation at the above address (see entry 1843).

### • 1849 • William C. Arrison Memorial Scholarship *(Undergraduate/Scholarship)*

**Focus:** General studies. **Qualif.:** Applicants must be sophomores majoring in criminal justice with high grade point averages. **Criteria:** Award made based on academic achievement.

**Funds Avail.:** $100 to $300 per scholarship. **No. of Awards:** 1. **To Apply:** Write for further details. **Deadline:** Varies; contact Jamestown Community College. **Contact:** Chautauqua Region Community Foundation at the above address (see entry 1843).

### • 1850 • Wendy Sue Axelson & Theodore Moll II Frewsburg School Scholarship *(Undergraduate/Scholarship)*

**Focus:** General studies. **Qualif.:** Applicants must be Frewsburgh High School graduates. **Criteria:** Awards made based on character and financial need.

**Funds Avail.:** $200 - $500 per award. **To Apply:** Write for further details. **Deadline:** April 20. **Contact:** Chautauqua Region Community Foundation at the above address (see entry 1843).

### • 1851 • Kathleen A. Black Memorial Scholarship *(Undergraduate/Scholarship)*

**Focus:** General studies. **Qualif.:** Applicants must be Maple Grove High School graduates who are attending or planning to attend SUNY at Geneseo, majoring in education.

**Funds Avail.:** $100 to $500 per award. **To Apply:** Contact Maple Grove guidance department for further details. **Contact:** Chautauqua Region Community Foundation at the above address (see entry 1843).

### • 1852 • Charles Reed Carlson Business Education Fund *(Undergraduate/Scholarship)*

**Focus:** General studies. **Qualif.:** Applicants must be residents of the Chautauqua region who are business education majors.

**Funds Avail.:** $200 to $500. **No. of Awards:** 1. **To Apply:** Write for further details. **Deadline:** April 20. **Contact:** Chautauqua Region Community Foundation at the above address (see entry 1843).

### • 1853 • Hanna Carola Art Scholarship *(Undergraduate/Scholarship)*

**Focus:** Art. **Qualif.:** Applicants must be graduates of Southwestern, Maple Grove, Panama, Clymer, Sherman, Chautauqua, Mayville, Frewsburg, Ripley, Westfield, Pine Valley,

Forestville, Brocton, and Cassadaga Valley schools who are art majors.

**Funds Avail.:** $500 per award. **No. of Awards:** 1-10. **To Apply:** Applicants must submit sample artwork. Write for further details. **Deadline:** April 20. **Contact:** Chautauqua Region Community Foundation at the above address (see entry 1843).

**• 1854 •   Constance E. Casey Scholarship** *(Undergraduate/Scholarship)*

**Focus:** General studies. **Qualif.:** Applicants must be Fine Arts majors at Jamestown Community College.

**Funds Avail.:** $500 per award. **No. of Awards:** 2. **To Apply:** Write for further details. **Deadline:** Varies. **Contact:** Chautauqua Region Community Foundation at the above address (see entry 1843).

**• 1855 •   Chautauqua County Basketball Officials Scholarship** *(Undergraduate/Scholarship)*

**Focus:** General studies. **Qualif.:** Applicants must be Chautauqua County graduates attending Jamestown Community College.

**Funds Avail.:** $200 to $500 per award. **No. of Awards:** 1-2. **To Apply:** Apply through the Jamestown Community College financial aid office. **Deadline:** Varies. **Contact:** Chautauqua Region Community Foundation at the above address (see entry 1843).

**• 1856 •   Joan C. Chiappetta Scholarship for a Career In Practical Nursing** *(Undergraduate/Scholarship)*

**Focus:** Nursing. **Qualif.:** Applicants must Chautauqua County residents. **Criteria:** Awards granted based on applicant's potential to make contribution to health care, and financial need.

**Funds Avail.:** $100 to $500 per award. **No. of Awards:** 1. **To Apply:** Write for further details. **Deadline:** April 20. **Contact:** Chautauqua Region Community Foundation at the above address (see entry 1843).

**• 1857 •   Lance G. Colvin Memorial Scholarship** *(Undergraduate/Scholarship)*

**Focus:** General studies. **Qualif.:** Applicants must be graduating seniors of Pine Valley Central School advancing themselves into the trucking industry.

**Funds Avail.:** $200 to $400 per award. **No. of Awards:** 1. **To Apply:** Apply through Pine Valley High School. **Deadline:** April 20. **Contact:** Chautauqua Region Community Foundation at the above address (see entry 1843).

**• 1858 •   Terry Gane Coon Scholarship** *(Undergraduate/Scholarship)*

**Focus:** General studies. **Qualif.:** Applicants must be Maple Grove High School graduates.

**Funds Avail.:** $200 to $400 per award. **No. of Awards:** 1. **To Apply:** Apply through Maple Grove Central School. **Deadline:** Varies. **Contact:** Chautauqua Region Community Foundation at the above address (see entry 1843).

**• 1859 •   Emily Harrington Crane Scholarship** *(Undergraduate/Scholarship)*

**Focus:** Music. **Qualif.:** Applicants must be residents of Chautauqua County majoring in music.

**Funds Avail.:** $500 to $1,500. **No. of Awards:** 3-10. **To Apply:** Write for further details. **Deadline:** April 20. **Contact:** Chautauqua Region Community Foundation at the above address (see entry 1843).

**• 1860 •   Barbara D'Angelo Memorial Teaching Scholarship** *(Undergraduate/Scholarship)*

**Focus:** General studies. **Qualif.:** Applicants must be residents of Chautauqua region.

**Funds Avail.:** Varies. **No. of Awards:** Undetermined. **To Apply:** Write for further details. **Deadline:** April 20. **Contact:** Chautauqua Region Community Foundation at the above address (see entry 1843).

**• 1861 •   Gordon & Mabel Morse Danielson Memorial Scholarship** *(Undergraduate/Scholarship)*

**Focus:** General studies. **Qualif.:** Applicants must be members of the First Lutheran Church of Jamestown or students attending Kent State University.

**Funds Avail.:** $300 to $700 per award. **No. of Awards:** 1-5. **To Apply:** Write for further details. **Deadline:** April 20. **Contact:** Chautauqua Region Community Foundation at the above address (see entry 1843).

**• 1862 •   Verland & Doris Danielson Scholarship** *(Undergraduate/Scholarship)*

**Focus:** General studies. **Qualif.:** Applicants must be residents of Chautauqua Region attending Jamestown Business College.

**Funds Avail.:** $200 to $400 per award. **No. of Awards:** 1. **To Apply:** Write for further details. **Deadline:** April 20. **Contact:** Chautauqua Region Community Foundation at the above address (see entry 1843).

**• 1863 •   Bert Day/Acu-Rite Memorial Scholarship** *(Undergraduate/Scholarship)*

**Focus:** General studies. **Qualif.:** Applicants must be graduates of Falconer Central School who are attending junior college, trade school, business school or four-year colleges.

**Funds Avail.:** $100 to $500 per award. **No. of Awards:** 1. **To Apply:** Apply through Falconer Central School. **Deadline:** Varies. **Contact:** Chautauqua Region Community Foundation at the above address (see entry 1843).

**• 1864 •   Betty Derby Memorial Scholarship** *(Undergraduate/Scholarship)*

**Focus:** General studies. **Qualif.:** Applicants must be graduates of Frewsburg Central School and members of Fresburg First United Methodist Church. **Criteria:** Awards made based on financial need and academic achievement.

**Funds Avail.:** $500 per award. **No. of Awards:** 1-2. **To Apply:** Write for further details. **Contact:** Chautauqua Region Community Foundation at the above address (see entry 1843).

**• 1865 •   Rita A. Dunn & Mollie Dunn McKee Scholarship** *(Undergraduate/Scholarship)*

**Focus:** General studies. **Qualif.:** Applicants must be graduates of Jamestown High School. **Criteria:** Awards made based on financial need.

**Funds Avail.:** Varies. **No. of Awards:** Varies. **To Apply:** Write for further details. **Deadline:** April 20. **Contact:** Chautauqua Region Community Foundation at the above address (see entry 1843).

**• 1866 •   Barbara Mae Gustafson & Bridget Mary Drew (B&B) Scholarship** *(Undergraduate/Scholarship)*

**Focus:** General studies. **Qualif.:** Applicants must be female residents of Chautauqua, Cattaraugus, and Allegany, New York who are mother attending Jamestown Community College.

*Chautauqua Region Community Foundation Inc. (continued)*

**Funds Avail.:** $100 to $500 per award. **No. of Awards:** 1. **To Apply:** Write for further details. **Deadline:** April 20. **Contact:** Chautauqua Region Community Foundation at the above address (see entry 1843).

**• 1867 • John D. Hamilton Scholarship** *(Undergraduate/Scholarship)*

**Focus:** General studies. **Qualif.:** Applicants must be residents of Chautauqua County, New York. **Criteria:** Awards are made based on academic record and financial need.

**Funds Avail.:** $1,000 to $1,500 per award. **No. of Awards:** 1-2. **To Apply:** Write for further details. **Deadline:** April 20. **Contact:** Chautauqua Region Community Foundation at the above address (see entry 1843).

**• 1868 • Walter & Grace Hazzard Scholarship** *(Undergraduate/Scholarship)*

**Focus:** General studies. **Qualif.:** Applicants must be graduates of Chautauqua Region School.

**Funds Avail.:** $250 to $1,500 per award. **No. of Awards:** 50-75. **To Apply:** Write for further details. **Deadline:** April 20. **Contact:** Chautauqua Region Community Foundation at the above address (see entry 1843).

**• 1869 • Randy Hough Scholarship** *(Undergraduate/Scholarship)*

**Focus:** General studies. **Qualif.:** Applicants must be graduates of Southwestern High School. **Criteria:** Awards granted based on academic achievement, leadership and character.

**Funds Avail.:** $500 to $1,000 per award. **No. of Awards:** 1. **To Apply:** Write for further details. **Deadline:** April 20. **Contact:** Chautauqua Region Community Foundation at the above address (see entry 1843).

**• 1870 • Jamestown General Hospital Auxiliary Scholarship** *(Undergraduate/Scholarship)*

**Focus:** Medicine. **Qualif.:** Applicants must be residents of Chautauqua Region who are majoring in health related field in their second, third or fourth year of medical school or last two years at college or university.

**Funds Avail.:** $500 to $1,000 per award. **No. of Awards:** 1-3. **To Apply:** Write for further details. **Deadline:** April 20. **Contact:** Chautauqua Region Community Foundation at the above address (see entry 1843).

**• 1871 • Jamestown School of Practical Nursing Scholarship** *(Undergraduate/Scholarship)*

**Focus:** General studies. **Qualif.:** Applicants must be enrolled in a E2CC BOCES Practical Nursing Program. **Criteria:** Awards granted based on academic achievement and financial need.

**Funds Avail.:** $100 to $300 per award. **No. of Awards:** Varies. **To Apply:** Apply to Erie 2-Chautauqua-Cattaraugus. **Deadline:** September 8. **Contact:** Chautauqua Region Community Foundation at the above address (see entry 1843).

**• 1872 • John A. Johnson Memorial Scholarship** *(Undergraduate/Scholarship)*

**Focus:** General studies. **Qualif.:** Applicants must be enrolled or planning to enroll in Jamestown Business College. **Criteria:** Awards granted based on financial need and academic promise.

**Funds Avail.:** $500 to $1,000 per award. **No. of Awards:** 15-25. **To Apply:** Apply to Jamestown Business College. **Deadline:** May 1. **Contact:** Chautauqua Region Community Foundation at the above address (see entry 1843).

**• 1873 • Hazel A. and H. Margaret Johnson Scholarship** *(Undergraduate/Scholarship)*

**Focus:** General studies. **Qualif.:** Applicants must be Chautauqua County residents. **Criteria:** Preference given to student entering teaching, nursing or geriatric care careers in the Chautauqua County area.

**Funds Avail.:** Varies. **No. of Awards:** 1. **To Apply:** Write for further details. **Deadline:** April 20. **Contact:** Chautauqua Region Community Foundation at the above address (see entry 1843).

**• 1874 • Maude Grant Kent Scholarship** *(Undergraduate/Scholarship)*

**Focus:** General studies. **Qualif.:** Applicants must be graduates of Chautauqua Region High School. **Criteria:** Awards granted based on financial need.

**Funds Avail.:** $300 to $1,500 per award. **No. of Awards:** 10-20. **To Apply:** Write for further details. **Deadline:** April 20. **Contact:** Chautauqua Region Community Foundation at the above address (see entry 1843).

**• 1875 • William R. & Catherine Joann Krishock Scholarship** *(Undergraduate/Scholarship)*

**Focus:** General studies. **Qualif.:** Applicants must be graduates of Maple Grove High School studying technical field or business majors (yearly rotation).

**Funds Avail.:** $200 to $400 per award. **No. of Awards:** 1. **To Apply:** Apply through Maple Grove Central School. **Deadline:** Varies. **Contact:** Chautauqua Region Community Foundation at the above address (see entry 1843).

**• 1876 • Sharon Kunkel Nursing Scholarship** *(Undergraduate/Scholarship)*

**Focus:** Nursing. **Qualif.:** Applicants must be graduates of Chautauqua Region High School who are nursing majors. **Criteria:**

**Funds Avail.:** $200 to $300 per award. **No. of Awards:** 1-4. **To Apply:** Write for further details. **Deadline:** April 20. **Contact:** Chautauqua Region Community Foundation at the above address (see entry 1843).

**• 1877 • Lois T. Larson Scholarship** *(Undergraduate/Scholarship)*

**Focus:** Education, music, ministry. **Qualif.:** Applicants must be graduates of Cassadaga Valley and Falconer Central Schools.

**Funds Avail.:** $500 to $1,000 per award. **No. of Awards:** 1-5. **To Apply:** Write for further details. **Deadline:** April 20. **Contact:** Chautauqua Region Community Foundation at the above address (see entry 1843).

**• 1878 • Samuel J. Lasser Scholarship** *(Undergraduate/Scholarship)*

**Focus:** General studies. **Qualif.:** Applicants must be graduates of Chautauqua Region High School who are attending St. Bonaventure University. **Criteria:** Awards are granted based on financial need.

**Funds Avail.:** $200 to $300 per award. **No. of Awards:** 1-2. **To Apply:** Write for further details. **Deadline:** April 20. **Contact:** Chautauqua Region Community Foundation at the above address (see entry 1843).

**• 1879 •  Ruth A. & G. Elving Lundine Scholarship**
*(Undergraduate/Scholarship)*

**Focus:** Mechanical engineering, electrical engineering, computer science. **Qualif.:** Applicants must be graduates of Chautauqua Region High School who are family members of Dowcraft employees or public employees majoring in mechanical engineering, electrical engineering, or computers.

**Funds Avail.:** $400 to $700 per award. **No. of Awards:** 1-2. **To Apply:** Write for further details. **Deadline:** April 20. **Contact:** Chautauqua Region Community Foundation at the above address (see entry 1843).

**• 1880 •  Elizabeth Warner Marvin Music Scholarship**
*(Undergraduate/Scholarship)*

**Focus:** Music. **Qualif.:** Applicants must be students of any age in the Jamestown School District who are seeking education or training in music.

**Funds Avail.:** Varies. **No. of Awards:** Varies. **To Apply:** Write for further details. **Deadline:** April 20. **Contact:** Chautauqua Region Community Foundation at the above address (see entry 1843).

**• 1881 •  Joseph Mason Memorial Scholarship**
*(Undergraduate/Scholarship)*

**Focus:** General studies. **Qualif.:** Applicants must be graduates of Chautauqua Region School attending Jamestown Community College studying labor-related majors.

**Funds Avail.:** $200 to $400 per award. **No. of Awards:** 1. **To Apply:** Apply through Jamestown Community College. **Deadline:** Varies. **Contact:** Chautauqua Region Community Foundation at the above address (see entry 1843).

**• 1882 •  McFadden Family Automotive Scholarship**
*(Undergraduate/Scholarship)*

**Focus:** Mechanics and repairs. **Qualif.:** Applicants must be graduates of Chautauqua Region School attending Northwood Institute, Midland, Michigan.

**Funds Avail.:** $500 to $800 per award. **No. of Awards:** 1. **To Apply:** Write for further details. **Deadline:** April 20. **Contact:** Chautauqua Region Community Foundation at the above address (see entry 1843).

**• 1883 •  Charles D. Melhuish Scholarship**
*(Undergraduate/Scholarship)*

**Focus:** General studies. **Qualif.:** Applicants must be graduates of Chautauqua Region School.

**Funds Avail.:** $200 to $1,000 per award. **No. of Awards:** 10-20. **To Apply:** Write for further details. **Deadline:** April 20. **Contact:** Chautauqua Region Community Foundation at the above address (see entry 1843).

**• 1884 •  Memmott-Langhans Scholarship**
*(Undergraduate/Scholarship)*

**Focus:** General studies. **Qualif.:** Applicants must be graduates of Little Valley High School. **Criteria:** Awards granted based on financial need.

**Funds Avail.:** $500 per award. **No. of Awards:** 1. **To Apply:** Apply through Little Valley High School. **Deadline:** Varies. **Contact:** Chautauqua Region Community Foundation at the above address (see entry 1843).

**• 1885 •  Leon S. Miller Memorial Scholarship**
*(Undergraduate/Scholarship)*

**Focus:** General studies. **Qualif.:** Applicants must be Ashville or Chautauqua Region, New York residents in their junior year of study. **Criteria:** Preference given to Ashville residents.

**Funds Avail.:** $500 to $1,000 per award. **No. of Awards:** 1-2. **To Apply:** Write for further details. **Deadline:** April 20. **Contact:** Chautauqua Region Community Foundation at the above address (see entry 1843).

**• 1886 •  Minority Educator Scholarship**
*(Undergraduate/Scholarship)*

**Focus:** Education. **Qualif.:** Applicants must be Jamestown High School graduates who are minority students majoring in education at Jamestown Community College.

**Funds Avail.:** $1,000 to $2,500 for the last two years of schooling at Jamestown Community College. **No. of Awards:** 1 every other year. **To Apply:** Write for further details. **Deadline:** April 20. **Contact:** Chautauqua Region Community Foundation at the above address (see entry 1843).

**• 1887 •  Ted Moll Flight Scholarship**
*(Undergraduate/Scholarship)*

**Focus:** Aviation. **Qualif.:** Applicants must be Chautauqua County High School graduates entering the field of aviation at the college level.

**Funds Avail.:** Varies. **No. of Awards:** 1-2. **To Apply:** Write for further details. **Deadline:** April 20. **Contact:** Chautauqua Region Community Foundation at the above address (see entry 1843).

**• 1888 •  Brenda L. Morrow Memorial Scholarship**
*(Undergraduate/Scholarship)*

**Focus:** General studies. **Qualif.:** Applicants must be residents of South Chautauqua County who are between the ages of 15 and 18 years and going on exchange in foreign countries.

**Funds Avail.:** Varies. **No. of Awards:** Varies. **To Apply:** Write for further details. **Deadline:** April 20. **Contact:** Chautauqua Region Community Foundation at the above address (see entry 1843).

**• 1889 •  Alberta M. Morse Memorial Scholarship**
*(Undergraduate/Scholarship)*

**Focus:** General studies. **Qualif.:** Applicants must be residents of Chautauqua Region, New York, who are handicapped or adults with family working part-time and attending college or trade school.

**Funds Avail.:** $500 to $1,000 per award. **No. of Awards:** 1-5. **To Apply:** Write for further details. **Deadline:** April 20. **Contact:** Chautauqua Region Community Foundation at the above address (see entry 1843).

**• 1890 •  Mozart Club Music Scholarship**
*(Undergraduate/Scholarship)*

**Focus:** Music. **Qualif.:** Applicants must be residents of Chautauqua Region, New York, who study music.

**Funds Avail.:** $200 to $500 per award. **No. of Awards:** 1-2. **To Apply:** Audition required. Write for further details. **Deadline:** April 20. **Contact:** Chautauqua Region Community Foundation at the above address (see entry 1843).

**• 1891 •  Ruth E. Munson Music Scholarship**
*(Undergraduate/Scholarship)*

**Focus:** Music education. **Qualif.:** Applicants must be graduates of Jamestown High School who are studying music with an emphasis

*Chautauqua Region Community Foundation Inc. (continued)*

on performance or instruction of piano or organ, or any music education major.

**Funds Avail.:** $500 to $1,000 per award. **No. of Awards:** 1-2. **To Apply:** Audition required. Write for further details. **Deadline:** April 20. **Contact:** Chautauqua Region Community Foundation at the above address (see entry 1843).

**• 1892 •  Margarete E. Nelson Scholarship**
*(Undergraduate/Scholarship)*

**Focus:** Nursing. **Qualif.:** Applicants must be enrolled in an E2CC BOCES Practical Nursing Program. **Criteria:** Awards granted based on academic achievement and financial need.

**Funds Avail.:** $100 to $500 per award. **No. of Awards:** Varies. **To Apply:** Apply through Erie 2-Chautauqua-Cattaraugus. Write for further details. **Deadline:** September 8. **Contact:** Chautauqua Region Community Foundation at the above address (see entry 1843).

**• 1893 •  Margaret E. Olson Memorial Scholarship**
*(Undergraduate/Scholarship)*

**Focus:** Criminal justice, psychology. **Qualif.:** Applicants must be residents of Chautauqua County who are studying criminal justice or psychology.

**Funds Avail.:** $300 per award. **No. of Awards:** 1. **To Apply:** Write for further details. **Deadline:** April 20. **Contact:** Chautauqua Region Community Foundation at the above address (see entry 1843).

**• 1894 •  Jane Hultquist Pearson Medical Scholarship** *(Undergraduate/Scholarship)*

**Focus:** Medicine. **Qualif.:** Applicants must be residents of Chautauqua Region.

**Funds Avail.:** $1,000 to $3,000 per award. **No. of Awards:** 4-10. **To Apply:** Write for further details. **Deadline:** April 20. **Contact:** Chautauqua Region Community Foundation at the above address (see entry 1843).

**• 1895 •  Robert "Bobby" Guy Pollino II Memorial Scholarship** *(Undergraduate/Scholarship)*

**Focus:** General studies. **Qualif.:** Applicants must be graduating seniors of Jamestown High School who are members of the football team or basketball team. **Criteria:** Awards are made based on financial need.

**Funds Avail.:** $1,000 per award. **No. of Awards:** 2; one for football, one for baseball. **To Apply:** Write for further details. **Deadline:** November 1 for football applicants; May 1 for baseball applicants. **Contact:** Chautauqua Region Community Foundation at the above address (see entry 1843).

**• 1896 •  Ney Stineman Memorial Scholarship**
*(Undergraduate/Scholarship)*

**Focus:** General studies. **Qualif.:** Applicants must be graduating Jamestown High School female seniors who will attend a four-year college or university. The applicants must show evidence of school/community involvement, love of nature/environment, recognition of equal rights for women, concern of human rights, zest for life, nurturing of friends, and determination to make a difference. **Criteria:** Awards granted based on character.

**Funds Avail.:** $1000 per award. **No. of Awards:** Varies. **To Apply:** Write for further details. **Deadline:** April 20. **Contact:** Chautauqua Region Community Foundation at the above address (see entry 1843).

**• 1897 •  W.C.A. Care and Share Scholarship**
*(Undergraduate/Scholarship)*

**Focus:** General studies. **Qualif.:** Applicants must be Chautauqua and Cattaraugus, New York and Warren County, Pennsylvania residents who are immediate family members of W.C.A. employees.

**Funds Avail.:** $100 to $500 per award. **No. of Awards:** 1-4. **To Apply:** Write for further details. **Deadline:** April 20. **Contact:** Chautauqua Region Community Foundation at the above address (see entry 1843).

**• 1898 •**
**Chemical Heritage Foundation**
315 Chestnut St.                    *Ph:* (215)925-2222
Philadelphia, PA 19106              *Fax:* (215)925-1954
*URL:* http://www.chemheritage.org/

**• 1899 •  Chemical Heritage Foundation Travel Grants** *(Other/Grant)*

**Purpose:** Offers researchers the opportunity to visit Philadelphia and use the research resources of the Beckman Center for the History or Chemistry, the Othmer Library of Chemical History including its Chemists' Club Collection, the Edgar Fahs Smith Memorial Collection, and associated facilities. **Focus:** Chemistry, History. **Qualif.:** Applicants must be individuals conducting research in the history of chemistry and chemical technologies.

**Funds Avail.:** Maximum grants of $500 may be applied to travel, subsistence, and photocopying costs. **To Apply:** Applications must include a vitae, a one paragraph statement on the research proposed, a budget, and two references. **Deadline:** February 1 for April-June grant; May 1 for July-September grant; August 1 for October-December grant; and November 1 for January-March grant. **Contact:** Mary Ellen Bowden, at the above address (see entry 1898).

**• 1900 •  Edelstein International Fellowship in the History of Chemical Sciences and Technology**
*(Postdoctorate/Fellowship)*

**Focus:** Chemistry, History, Science, Medical History. **Qualif.:** Applicants must be established scholars in chemical science and technology. The Fellow must be able to divide his or her time between the Chemical Heritage Foundation (CHF) in Philadelphia, Pennsylvania, and the Edelstein Center for History and Philosophy of Science, Technology and Medicine in Jerusalem, Israel. The major portion of time is devoted to research, but the Fellow also contributes to the work of each Center in an appropriate manner. The fellowship may be held in conjunction with other research or sabbatical support.

**Funds Avail.:** A travel allowance is available along with Fellowship funding. **To Apply:** Letters of application should indicate how CHF/Edelstein Collection resources in the chemical sciences are relevant to the applicant's research. Applicants should also enclose a financial statement, a curriculum vitae, and the names of three referees. **Deadline:** Applications should be received by October 31. The Fellowship period is September 1 through June 30. **Contact:** Applications must be sent to Professor Seymour Mauskopf, Coordinator, Edelstein International Awards, Department of History, Duke University, Durham, North Carolina 27706. Telephone: (919)684-3014.

**• 1901 •**
## Chemical Industry Institute of Toxicology
6 Davis Dr.
PO Box 12137
Research Triangle Park, NC 27709-
2137

*Ph:* (919)558-1200
*Fax:* (919)541-9015

### • 1902 • CIIT Postdoctoral Trainee Fellowships *(Postdoctorate/Fellowship)*

**Purpose:** To provide the opportunity for scientists to train at CIIT. **Focus:** Toxicology. **Qualif.:** Applicants may be of any nationality and must have recently earned an M.D., D.V.M., Dr.P.H., or Ph.D. in toxicology or a related field, such as biochemistry, pharmacology, pathology, cell biology, immunology, molecular biology, genetics, or the basic sciences. Fellowships are tenable at CIIT.

**Funds Avail.:** $30,000/year minimum; plus health insurance. **To Apply:** Write for application form and guidelines. Submit form with curriculum vitae, any publications, official transcripts, and three letters of reference. Applications are accepted any time, and will be kept on file for review. **Deadline:** None.

**Remarks:** CIIT also offers a Visiting Scientist Program that enables established scientists from industry, academia, and government to come to the Institute to learn specialized research techniques in toxicology. Write for further details. **Contact:** Human Resources Manager, at the above address (see entry 1901).

### • 1903 • CIIT Summer Internships *(Graduate, Postgraduate, Undergraduate/Internship)*

**Purpose:** To provide talented science majors with an experience in contemporary toxicology research at the Chemical Industry Institute of Toxicology. Internships give students an idea of what a career in contemporary biomedical research is like. **Focus:** Toxicology, Biomedical Research. **Qualif.:** Applicants should have completed at least three years of college-level training in some aspect of the sciences.

**Funds Avail.:** Interns receive a stipend of $320 per week, paid on a biweekly basis. A travel allowance of $300 round-trip is provided for participants whose permanent residence or school is 75 miles or more from the Institute. **Deadline:** February 15. **Contact:** Manager, Human Resources, at the above address (see entry 1901). at the above address.

**• 1904 •**
## Chemical Institute of Canada
130 Slater St., Ste. 550
Ottawa, ON, Canada K1P 6E2
*E-mail:* cic_prog@fox.nstn.ca
*URL:* http://chem-inst-can.org

*Ph:* (613)232-6252
*Fax:* (613)232-5862

*The Chemical Institute of Canada (CIC) is the national scientific, educational, and professional organization of chemists, chemical engineers and chemical technologists.*

### • 1905 • Alfred Bader Scholarship *(Graduate/Scholarship)*

**Purpose:** To honor achievement in organic chemistry or biochemistry by undergraduate students completing their final year of study in an Honours program. **Qualif.:** Students must be nominated by their research advisor. Nominees must be members of the CSC (ACIC) and be continuing in a graduate program in chemistry or biochemistry at a Canadian university.

**Funds Avail.:** Up to three $1,000 scholarships. **To Apply:** Applications should include a copy of the Honours' research project report, a statement from the research supervisor describing the student's contribution at the academic and

extracurricular levels, a second letter of reference, and an official transcript of the student's academic record, all in quadruplicate. **Deadline:** May 15. Recipients are chosen in July.

**Remarks:** This award is administered by The Canadian Society for Chemistry. **Contact:** Kimberley Ross, Program Manager, Awards, at the above address (see entry 1904).

### • 1906 • Pestcon Graduate Scholarship *(Graduate/Scholarship)*

**Purpose:** To support graduate study in pesticide chemistry. **Focus:** Pesticide Science. **Qualif.:** Applicant must be a Canadian citizen or landed immigrant who is enrolled in a graduate program in chemistry or biochemistry at a Canadian university.

**Funds Avail.:** $3,000. **To Apply:** Write for application form and guidelines. **Deadline:** March 1. Scholarship is announced by June 1.

**Remarks:** The Institute also offers a number of awards to recognize outstanding achievements in the scientific and engineering community in Canada. Contact the national office at the above address for a copy of the awards booklet and further information. **Contact:** Kimberley Ross Program Manager, Awards, at the above address (see entry 1904).

### • 1907 • J.E. Zajic Postgraduate Scholarship in Biochemical Engineering *(Postgraduate/Scholarship)*

**Purpose:** To support graduate study in biochemical engineering. **Focus:** Biochemical Engineering. **Qualif.:** Applicant must be a Canadian citizen or landed immigrant who is enrolled in a graduate program in chemistry or biochemistry at a Canadian university.

**Funds Avail.:** $2,000. **To Apply:** Write for application form and guidelines. Award is offered in even number years. **Deadline:** December 1. **Contact:** Kimberley Ross, Program Manager, Awards, at the above address (see entry 1904).

**• 1908 •**
## Chenango County Medical Society and Ostego County Medical Society
210 Clinton Rd., Rte. 12-B
New Hartford, NY 13413

### • 1909 • Lee C. Van Wagner Scholarship *(Doctorate, Graduate/Scholarship)*

**Purpose:** To assist eligible students of Chenango and Otsego Counties, State of New York, who attend a medical or osteopathic school approved by the Association of American Medical Colleges. **Focus:** Medicine. **Qualif.:** Applicant must be a legal resident of either Chenango of Otsego County, State of New York. Recipient must agree to practice in the County of Chenango or Otsego for one year for each year financial assistance is received, or to pay back any monies received (plus interest) within 6 years following graduation from medical school or within 5 years following completion of residency. **Criteria:** Selected by the Van Wagner Scholarship Committee.

**Funds Avail.:** Loan amounts fluctuate depending upon the number of applications received and the amount in the Scholarship Fund. **No. of Awards:** Varies. **To Apply:** Those interested should submit an application as soon as possible. **Deadline:** July 1st of each year. **Contact:** Ms. Kathleen E. Dyman, Executive Director, Medical Society of the County of Chenango, 210 Clinton Road, PO Box 620, New Hartford, NY 13413.

## • 1910 •
## Cherokee Nation

Education Dept.                          Ph: (918)456-0671
PO Box 948                              Fax: (918)458-6286
Tahlequah, OK 74465-0948               Free: 800-256-0671
URL: http://www.eerc.und.nodak.edu/cert/cherok.html

### • 1911 • Cherokee Nation Graduate Scholarship
(Graduate/Scholarship)

**Purpose:** To assist members of the Cherokee Nation to attain graduate degrees. **Focus:** Education, Engineering, Law, Medicine. **Qualif.:** Applicant must be a certified member of the Cherokee Nation who has a bachelor's degree and is enrolled in a master's program. Candidates in fields other than those listed above may be considered, but only on a case-by-case basis.

**Funds Avail.:** $500 full-time, $250 part-time. **To Apply:** Write to the Department for application form and guidelines. Submit form with a copy of Certificate of Degree of Indian Blood and transcripts including cumulative grade point average. **Deadline:** May 1. **Contact:** Turner Bear, Jr., at the above address (see entry 1910).

### • 1912 • Cherokee National Higher Education Undergraduate Grant Program (Undergraduate/Grant)

**Purpose:** To assist Cherokee students in their quest for a post secondary education. **Focus:** Applied sciences or vocational training. **Qualif.:** Applicants must possess or be in the process of obtaining CDIB and Tribal Membership cards showing membership in the Cherokee Nation or the United Keetoowah Band of Cherokee Indians; attending or planning to attend a regionally-accredited post-secondary institution studying toward an Associates of Arts. Associate of Science, or Baccalaureate degree; and have applied for additional financial aid at the attending institution. **Deadline:** April 1.

## • 1913 •
## Cheyenne-Arapaho Tribal Offices

PO Box 38                               Ph: (405)262-0345
Concho, OK 73022                        Fax: (405)262-0745
                                        Free: 800-247-4612

### • 1914 • Cheyenne-Arapaho Higher Education Assistance Program Grant (Undergraduate/Grant)

**Purpose:** To increase educational level of Cheyenne and Arapaho students. **Focus:** General Studies. **Qualif.:** Applicants must be certified by the Concho Agency to be at least 1/4 or more degree Cheyenn-Arapaho Indian; a high school graduate or GED holder approved for admission by a college or university; show financial need; show potential of completing a four year course of study. Summer and part-time students may be considered. .

**Funds Avail.:** The amount of assistance is individually determined by need and availability of funds. Part-time students aid is limited to tuition and books. **To Apply:** A completed application requires: a Financial Needs Analysis form completed by the college or university Financial Aid Office showing an estimate of college expenses; a personal letter that indicates academic goals and financial needs; a high school or college transcript or GED certificate; and indication of having filed the ACT or FAF packet, which is obtainable from high school, college, or university financial aid offices. Recipients must maintain academic standing and social conduct acceptable to the education institution attended. They may also expect personal on-campus contact by their Native American Counselor for the purpose of providing supportive services. Grade reports or transcripts must be submitted after each term. **Deadline:** Application and all supporting materials must be filed by June 1 for the first semester;

November 1 for the second semester; and April 1 for summer semester. Late applications must be accompanied with an appeal letter...

**Remarks:** The United States Government, through the Bureau of Indian Affairs, provides funds for Indian students to obtain a college education. The Cheyenne-Arapaho Tribes of Oklahoma administer the program for enrolled tribal members.

## • 1915 •
## Chicago Association of Black Journalists

c/o Maudlyne Ihejircka                  Ph: (312)321-2345
PO Box 11425                            Fax: (312)321-3084
Chicago, IL 60611                       Free: 800-621-7782

### • 1916 • Chicago Association of Black Journalists Scholarships (Graduate, Undergraduate/Scholarship)

**Purpose:** To financially assist minorities in journalism. **Focus:** Journalism. **Qualif.:** Applicants must be minorities and full-time undergraduate juniors or seniors, or full-time graduate students attending an accredited college or university in the Chicago metropolitan area. In addition, candidates must be majoring in print or broadcast journalism, or show a strong interest in a journalism career.

**Funds Avail.:** $1,000. **To Apply:** Send a completed application form; resume, including candidate's contact information, career goals, and journalistic activities; three reference letters (two from college faculty and one from a non-faculty person), including address/telephone of writer; college transcript; and a 500-word essay discussing how and why applicant was drawn to journalism, and what applicant expects to contribute to journalism in general and as a minority journalist specifically. **Deadline:** June 30. **Contact:** Maudlyne Ihejirika, Scholarship Committee Chairman at the above address (see entry 1915).

## • 1917 •
## Chicago and Northeast Illinois District Council of Carpenters

12 E. Erie St.                          Ph: (312)787-3076
Chicago, IL 60611                       Fax: (312)951-1540

### • 1918 • Ted Kenney Memorial Scholarships
(Undergraduate/Scholarship)

**Qualif.:** Applicants must be graduating from high school the same year in which they are applying. They must be the son or daughter of a member in good standing of any local union affiliated with the Chicago and Northeast Illinois District Council of Carpenters. The scholarship awards will be available for use in any accredited college or university in the United States. **Criteria:** Selection will be made on the basis of high school transcripts, scores on college entrance examinations, and other tests. Extra-curricular activities will also be examined by an official of the scholarship committee.

**Funds Avail.:** Four scholarships at $1,000 each. **To Apply:** Applicants should contact the Scholarship Foundation for an application. They will eventually have to supply their high school transcript, certification of high school principal, scores of the College Entrance Examination Board, National Merit scholarship test or any other tests, as well as a record of extra-curricular activities. **Deadline:** July 1. **Contact:** The Chicago and Northeast Illinois District Council of Carpenters at the above address (see entry 1917).

**• 1919 •**
## The Chicago Reporter
332 S. Michigan Ave.　　　　　　　　*Ph:* (312)427-4830
Chicago, IL 60604　　　　　　　　　*Fax:* (312)427-6130
*E-mail:* chgorptr@aol.com
*URL:* http://www.bonneville.com/bonntoday/chicago.html

**• 1920 • The Chicago Reporter Minority Fellowship in Urban Journalism** *(Postgraduate, Professional Development/Fellowship)*

**Purpose:** To provide investigative reporting experience and training by giving an experienced minority journalist the opportunity to work at The Chicago Reporter for one year. **Focus:** Journalism Public Policy Issues. **Qualif.:** Applicants should be experienced minority journalists. **Criteria:** Applicants should have 3-5 years full time experience in journalism or related topic.

**Funds Avail.:** $29,000 approximate. **No. of Awards:** 1. **To Apply:** Applicants must submit a resume and five clippings. **Deadline:** July 1.

**Remarks:** The Chicago Reporter is a monthly newspaper known for its coverage of issues of race and poverty in the Chicago area. Postgraduate work will be available through Northwestern University's Medill School of Journalism and other local colleges and universities. **Contact:** Laura Washington at the above address (see entry 1919).

**• 1921 •**
## Chicago Sun-Times
401 N. Wabash Ave.　　　　　　　　*Ph:* (312)321-3000
Chicago, IL 60611　　　　　　　　　*Fax:* (312)321-2120
*URL:* http://www1.webcrawler.com/select/newsrc.55.html

**• 1922 • Chicago Sun-Times Minority Scholarships and Internships** *(Undergraduate/Internship, Scholarship)*

**Qualif.:** Open to minority college students from the Chicago metropolitan area who will be incoming juniors and have demonstrated an interest in print journalism.

**Funds Avail.:** Recipients will receive a $1,500 scholarship plus, if a B average is maintained, a paid internship. Scholarships may be used at the school of the recipient's choice. **Deadline:** December 31.

**• 1923 •**
## Chicago Tribune - Nelson Algren Short Story Comptetition
435 North Michigan Ave.
Chicago, IL 60611　　　　　　　　　*Ph:* (312)222-4540

**• 1924 • Nelson Algren Awards** *(Professional Development/Award)*

**Purpose:** To recognize superior short fiction by American writers. **Focus:** Fiction. **Qualif.:** Applicant must be a U.S. citizen. Manuscript must be an original, unpublished work of short fiction, between 2,500 and 10,000 words.

**Funds Avail.:** First prize: $5,000; runner-up prizes: $1,000. **No. of Awards:** Four **To Apply:** Submit the manuscript with a self-addressed, stamped envelope. **Deadline:** February 1. Notification in the fall.

**Remarks:** The winning stories will be published in the Chicago Tribune. **Contact:** Marcy Keno, Awards Coordinator, at the above address (see entry 1923).

**• 1925 •**
## Chicago Urban League
4510 S. Michigan Ave.　　　　　　　*Ph:* (312)451-3567
Chicago, IL 60653　　　　　　　　　*Fax:* (312)285-7772

**• 1926 • Anheuser-Busch Scholarship Fund** *(Undergraduate/Scholarship)*

**Purpose:** To help minority students attain higher academic levels, advance their career goals, and ultimately improve the quality of life for themselves and their families. **Qualif.:** Applicants must be male or female minority students who are the heads of households and are currently enrolled in the city colleges of Chicago. They must demonstrate financial need and have a GPA of at least 2.5. **Criteria:** Applicants must be Illinois residents, full-time students, and have at least 2.5 GPA.

**Funds Avail.:** From $250 to $400 per semester for up to two years. **To Apply:** An autobiographical letter of introduction indicating the academic background, career aspirations, and financial circumstances must be sent with application requests. Completed application forms must be accompanied by two letters of recommendation, transcript of grades, demonstrated financial need, tuition costs, and financial awards transcript. In addition, two interviews are required. **Deadline:** December 1 and July 15. **Contact:** Gina Blake, Scholarship Specialist, at the above address (see entry 1925).

**• 1927 • Jewel/Taylor C. Cotton Scholarship** *(Undergraduate/Scholarship)*

**Purpose:** To help minority students attain higher academic levels, advance their career goals, and ultimately improve the quality of life for themselves and their families. **Focus:** Business, Architecture, Engineering, Construction. **Qualif.:** Applicants must be minority high school seniors who have been accepted into a four-year college or university and intend to major in business or a field related to the construction industry, i.e., engineering, architecture. They must also be Illinois residents, full-time students, have a 2.5 GPA, and be able to demonstrate financial need. In addition to the award, candidates must be available for a summer internship for four years, beginning the summer following high school graduation.

**Funds Avail.:** $2,000 award. **No. of Awards:** 1 annually. **To Apply:** An autobiographical letter of introduction indicating the academic background, career aspirations, and financial circumstances must accompany application requests. Completed application forms must be accompanied by two letters of recommendation, transcript of grades, demonstrated financial need, tuition costs, and financial awards transcript. Two interviews are also required. **Deadline:** July 15.

**Remarks:** This program is supported by Jewel Food Stores and Taylor Cotton.

**• 1928 • Mercedes-Benz of North America Scholarship Program** *(Undergraduate/Scholarship)*

**Purpose:** To help minority students attain higher academic levels, advance their career goals, and ultimately improve the quality of life for themselves and their families. **Focus:** Business, Computer Science, Engineering, Communications, the Automotive Industry. **Qualif.:** Applicants must be minority high school graduates who will be or are attending a 2 year or 4 year college in a business-related field and are interested in applying education to the automotive industry. They also must be Illinois residents, and full time students. These graduates will also be eligible to participate

## Chicago Urban League (continued)

in MBNA technical training. There is also a possibility for available internships. **Criteria:** Applicants must have a 2.5 GPA.

**Funds Avail.:** Four $1,000 awards per year for four years for tuition and other educational supplies including books and tools. **No. of Awards:** 4 annually. **To Apply:** An autobiographical letter of introduction indicating the academic background, career aspirations, and financial circumstances must accompany application requests. Completed application forms must be accompanied by two letters of recommendation, transcript of grades, demonstrated financial need, tuition costs, and financial awards transcript. Two interviews are also required. **Deadline:** July 15.

**Remarks:** This award is funded by Mercedes-Benz of North America. **Contact:** Gina Blake, Scholarship Specialist, at the above address (see entry 1925).

**• 1929 • Whitney M. Young Memorial Scholarship** *(Undergraduate/Scholarship)*

**Purpose:** To financially assist minority students with their education. **Focus:** General Studies. **Qualif.:** Applicants must be minority students currently enrolled in a post-secondary institution who are able to verify outstanding financial need. They must also be Illinois residents, full-time students, and have a 2.5 GPA.

**Funds Avail.:** Awards may be granted for $250 to $400 per semester, not to exceed $2,000 for four years. Recipients must maintain a 2.5 GPA. **To Apply:** An autobiographical letter of introduction indicating the academic background, career aspirations, and financial circumstances must accompany application requests. Completed application forms must be accompanied by two letters of recommendation, transcript of grades, demonstrated financial need, tuition costs, and financial awards transcript. Two interviews are also required. **Deadline:** July 15 and December 1.

**Remarks:** These scholarships are supported primarily by the Women's Board of the Chicago Urban League, Avon Products, Inc., the Dr. Scholl Foundation, and other Chicago area corporations and contributors. **Contact:** Gina Blake, Scholarship Specialist, at the above address (see entry 1925).

## • 1930 •
## Chicana Latina Foundation
PO Box 27803
Oakland, CA 94602     *Ph:* (510)526-5861
*Formerly Known as Chicana Foundation of Northern California.*

**• 1931 • Chicana Latina Foundation Scholarships** *(Graduate, Undergraduate/Scholarship)*

**Purpose:** To assist Latina women in continuing their education. **Focus:** General Studies. **Qualif.:** Applicants must be Hispanic females who are permanent residents, or who have completed 15 semesters at a college, in the following San Francisco Bay Area counties: Alameda; Contra Costa; Marin; San Francisco, San Mateo; and Santa Clara. They must have a minimum grade point average of 2.5 and be able to demonstrate leadership, community involvement, and commitment to the Hispanic community. **Criteria:** Application and interview.

**Funds Avail.:** Individual awards are $1,000. **No. of Awards:** 10. **To Apply:** Applicants must submit an application form, two letters of recommendation, two 300- to 500-word essays on their career goals and community involvement, official transcripts, and an agreement to volunteer over the year. Graduate students must submit a supplementary application. **Deadline:** Usually in March. **Contact:** Olga E. Terrazas, Scholarship Committee Chair, 708 Lexington Ave., El Cerrito, CA 94530-3169.

## • 1932 •
## Chicano Studies Research Center
University of California, Los Angeles
Institute of American Cultures
405 Hilgard Ave.
Haines Hall     *Ph:* (310)825-2363
Los Angeles, CA 90024     *Fax:* (310)206-1784
*URL:* http://latino.sscnet.ucla.edu/UCLA.HTML

**• 1933 • Institute of American Cultures Postdoctoral Fellowship** *(Postdoctorate/Fellowship)*

**Purpose:** To support and promote relevant research in Chicano studies. **Focus:** Chicano Studies and pertinent disciplines, including Cultural Studies, Humanities, Medicine, Public Health, Social Sciences, and Women's Studies. **Qualif.:** Applicant must be a U.S. citizen or permanent resident, and must have a Ph.D. Those who have recently completed their Ph.D. as well as senior scholars are invited to apply. UCLA faculty and UCLA doctoral recepients are not eligible. Awards can be used to support sabbatical salary provided by applicant's home institution.

**Funds Avail.:** Varies, according to rank and experience; $28,000 maximum. **To Apply:** Write to the Assistant Director for application form and guidelines. **Deadline:** 31 December.

**Remarks:** Additional support may be available to grantees for specific research. Contact the Center for details.

## • 1934 •
## Chigiana Musical Academy Foundation - L'Accademia Musicale Chigiana
Via di Citta, 89
53100 Sienna, Italy     *Ph:* 5 774 6152

**• 1935 • Chigiana Summer Course Scholarships** *(Graduate, Professional Development/Scholarship)*

**Purpose:** To assist music students to attend master courses at the Academy. **Focus:** Conducting, Instrumental Music, Music Composition, Voice. **Qualif.:** Applicant may be of any nationality, but must hold an Italian music degree or foreign equivalent. Qualifications for the individual categories of master courses vary. Candidate must pass an entrance exam; scholarships are awarded solely on the basis of exam results. Candidates who have been awarded scholarships by other institutions are not eligible.

**Funds Avail.:** 16,500 lire/day, plus tuition fees. **To Apply:** Write for application form and guidelines. **Deadline:** Varies, according to musical category.

**Remarks:** The Academy also holds the biennial Alfredo Casella International Composition Contest. Write to the above address for information. **Contact:** Secretary at the above address (see entry 1934).

## · 1936 ·
## Children of Deaf Adults
c/o Robert J. Hoffmeister
(33-120)
Boston University-SED/Deaf Studies
605 Commonwealth Ave.
Boston, MA 02215
*E-mail:* RHOFF@BU.edu
*URL:* http://www.gallaudet.edu/~rgpricke/coda/index.html

### · 1937 · Children of Deaf Adults Scholarship
*(Undergraduate/Scholarship)*

**Focus:** General studies. **Qualif.:** Applicants must be high school graduates who are hearing sons or daughters of deaf adults. **Criteria:** Awards are made based on scholastic record, community involvement and written essay.

**Funds Avail.:** $1,000 to $2000 per award. **No. of Awards:** 2. **To Apply:** Applicants must submit grade transcripts and written essay. Write for further details. **Deadline:** Varies.

## · 1938 ·
## Children's Literature Association
PO Box 138                    *Ph:* (616)965-3568
Battle Creek, MI 49016        *Fax:* (616)965-3568
*E-mail:* chla@mlc.lib.mi.us
*URL:* http://ebbs.english.vt.edu/chla

### · 1939 · ChLA Research Fellowships *(Postdoctorate/Fellowship)*

**Focus:** Children's Literature. **Qualif.:** Applicants must be members of the ChLA. The fellowship is awarded for proposals dealing with criticism or original scholarship with the expectation that the undertaking will lead to publication and make a significant contribution to the field of children's literature. Members of the Executive Board of ChLA are not eligible. Previous recipients of a scholarship or research fellowship are not eligible to reapply until the third year from the date of the first award. **Criteria:** All proposals are read and judged by the ChLA Scholarship Committee.

**Funds Avail.:** Grants range from $250-1,000, depending on the number and needs of the recipients. Funds are not intended for work leading to the completion of a professional degree. The awards may be used only for research-related expenses such as travel to special collections or materials and supplies. The awards may not be used for obtaining advanced degrees, for researching or writing a thesis dissertation, for textbook writing, or for pedagogical projects. Recipients should be prepared to submit either a progress report or a summary of the completed project to the Scholarship Committee the February of the year following the award. **To Apply:** Each application must be sent in quintuplicate. Applications should include name, telephone number, and address; academic institution and academic standing, or the institution the applicant is affiliated with (library, publisher, etc.); detailed description (not exceeding three single-spaced pages) of the research proposal, indicating the nature of the project, where it will be carried out, the expected date of completion, and the projected cost of such main budget items as transportation, mailing, subsistence funds, and supplies; a vita which includes a bibliography of major publications and scholarly achievements; three letters of reference attesting specifically to the significance of the project and to the applicant's capacity to carry it out. Include a stamped, self-addressed envelope for notification. **Deadline:** February 1.

**Remarks:** Winners are encouraged to submit their completed papers to *Children's Literature* or *ChLA Quarterly* and should acknowledge ChLA in any publication resulting from the award.

**Contact:** Children's Literature Association at the above address (see entry 1938).

## · 1940 ·
## Children's Medical Research Institute
Locked Mail Bag 23            *Ph:* 2 687 2800
Wentworthville, NSW 2145, Australia    *Fax:* 2 687 2120

### · 1941 · Children's Medical Research Institute Ph.D. Scholarships; Children's Medical Research Institute Postdoctoral Research Fellowships *(Doctorate, Postdoctorate/Fellowship, Scholarship)*

**Purpose:** To assist Ph.D. candidates and postdoctoral scholars in their studies. **Focus:** Cell Adhesion Molecules in CNS Development, Early Embryonic Development, Mechanisms of Oncogenesis, Myogenesis. **Qualif.:** Applicant may be of any nationality for the Ph.D scholarship, but must be a Ph.D. candidate with a first class honors degree. Applicant for the postdoctoral fellowship must already have a Ph.D.

**Funds Avail.:** Varies. **To Apply:** Write to the director for application guidelines. **Deadline:** None. **Contact:** Professor P. B. Rowe, Director, at the above address (see entry 1940).

## · 1942 ·
## The Jane Coffin Childs Memorial Fund for Medical Research
Yale University School of Medicine
333 Cedar St.                 *Ph:* (203)785-4612
New Haven, CT 06510           *Fax:* (203)785-3301
*E-mail:* JCCFUND@Minerva.cis.yale.edu

### · 1943 · Childs Postdoctoral Fellowships
*(Postdoctorate/Fellowship)*

**Purpose:** To support research into the causes, origins, and treatments of cancer. **Focus:** Medicine. **Qualif.:** Applicant may be a citizen of any country, but awards to foreign nationals will be made only for study in the United States. Candidates must hold either the M.D. or Ph.D. degree in the field in which they propose to study, or furnish evidence of equivalent training and experience. Study must be full-time, and must be sponsored by a laboratory. Only under exceptional circumstances will an award be made to an individual who has one year or more of postdoctoral research experience.

**Funds Avail.:** $28,000 first year, $29,000 second year, $30,000 third year, plus allowances for research, travel, and dependent children. **No. of Awards:** 23-25 annually. **To Apply:** Write for application form. Strict adherence to the instructions noted within the application is required. **Deadline:** February 1. Applications are reviewed in late April or early May. **Contact:** Elizabeth Ford at the above address (see entry 1942).

## • 1944 •
## Chinese-American Librarians Association
c/o Sheila Lai
California State Univ., Sacramento
2000 Jed Smith Dr.                           Ph: (916)278-6201
Sacramento, CA 95819-6039              Fax: (916)363-0868
URL: http://www.hbz-nrw.de/hbz/tools/scholar/section2_5_
   30.html

### • 1945 • Sheila Suen Lai Scholarships (Graduate/Scholarship)

**Focus:** Library and Archival Sciences. **Qualif.:** Candidates must be of Chinese nationality or Chinese descent and must be pursuing full-time graduate studies for a Master's degree at an ALA accredited graduate library school.

**Funds Avail.:** $500 is awarded annually. **Deadline:** February 15. **Contact:** Chinese-American Librarians Association at the above address (see entry 1944).

## • 1946 •
## Christian Church (Disciples of Christ)
130 E. Washington St.
PO Box 1986                                  Ph: (317)635-3100
Indianapolis, IN 46204-3615            Fax: (317)635-4426

### • 1947 • Christian Church Hispanic Scholarship (Graduate/Scholarship)

**Qualif.:** Applicants must be Hispanic ministerial students who are members of the Christian Church (Disciples of Christ) with regional registration. They must also have at least a C++FA academic average, be able to show evidence of financial need, and be enrolled in an accredited school or seminary.

**Funds Avail.:** The amount of the awards is individually determined. Homeland Ministries of the Christian Church through its Center for Leadership & Ministry administers these funds. **To Apply:** Applicants must prepare a transcript of academic work and make a renewal application each year if eligible. Candidates are expected to provide details on career plans and background within the church, and provide detailed family financial expenditures and income information. References from the candidates' congregation pastors, regional ministers, church school superintendents, and two others who can comment on their academic ability and potential for the ministry are also required. **Deadline:** March 15. **Contact:** Homeland Ministries at the above address (see entry 1946).

### • 1948 • Disciple Chaplain's Scholarship Grant (Graduate/Scholarship)

**Qualif.:** Applicants must be a member of the Christian Church (Disciples of Christ) with regional registration who is planning to prepare for a professional ministry. They must have at least a C plus academic average and be able to show evidence of financial need. The student should be enrolled in an accredited school or seminary.

**Funds Avail.:** The amount of the awards is individually determined. Homeland Ministries of the Christian Church through its Center for Leadership & Ministry administers these funds. **To Apply:** Applicants must prepare a transcript of academic work and make a renewal application each year if eligible. Candidates are expected to fill in details on career plans and past background within the church. Detailed family financial expenditures and income information is required. References from the candidates' congregation pastors, regional ministers, church school superintendents, and two others who can vouch for them, their

academic ability, and potential for the ministry must also be submitted. **Deadline:** March 15. **Contact:** Homeland Ministries at the above address (see entry 1946).

### • 1949 • David Tamotsu Kagiwada Memorial Fund Award (Graduate/Scholarship)

**Qualif.:** Applicants must be Asian ministerial students who are members of the Christian Church (Disciples of Christ) with regional registration. They must have at least a C++FA academic average, be able to show evidence of financial need, and be enrolled in an accredited school or seminary.

**Funds Avail.:** The amount of the awards is individually determined. **To Apply:** Homeland Ministries of the Christian Church through its Center for Leadership & Ministry administers these funds. Applicants must prepare a transcript of academic work and make a renewal application each year if eligible. Candidates are expected to provide details on career plans and background within the church. Detailed information on family financial expenditures and income are required. References from the candidates' congregation pastors, regional ministers, church school superintendents, and two others who can comment on their academic ability and potential for the ministry must also be submitted. **Deadline:** March 15. **Contact:** Homeland Ministries at the above address (see entry 1946).

### • 1950 • Edwin G. and Lauretta M. Michael Scholarship (Undergraduate/Scholarship)

**Qualif.:** Candidates must be wives of ministers who are members of the Christian Church (Disciples of Christ). They must also be better than average students with at least a C++FA average, provide evidence of financial need, and be enrolled as full-time students in an accredited school or seminary. **To Apply:** Applicants must provide a transcript of academic work and references. Recipients must make a renewal application each year if eligible. **Deadline:** March 15. **Contact:** Homeland Ministries at the above address (see entry 1946).

### • 1951 • Rowley Ministerial Education Scholarship (Graduate/Scholarship)

**Focus:** Ministry studies. **Qualif.:** Applicants must be members of the Christian Church (Disciples of Christ) with regional registration and planning to prepare for a professional ministry. They must have at least a C++FA academic average, be able to show evidence of financial need, and be enrolled in an accredited school or seminary.

**Funds Avail.:** Scholarship amounts are individually determined. Homeland Ministries of the Christian Church through its Center for Leadership & Ministry administers these funds. **To Apply:** Applicants must prepare a transcript of academic work and make a renewal application each year if eligible. Candidates are expected to provide details on career plans and background within the church. Detailed information on family financial expenditures and income are required. References from the candidates' congregation pastors, regional ministers, church school superintendents and two others who can comment on their academic ability and potential for the ministry must also be submitted. **Deadline:** March 15. **Contact:** Homeland Ministries at the above address (see entry 1946).

### • 1952 • Katherine J. Schutze Memorial Scholarship (Graduate/Scholarship)

**Focus:** Seminary studies. **Qualif.:** Applicants must be women seminary students who are members of the Christian Church (Disciples of Christ) planning to prepare for the ordained ministry. They must also have at least a C++FA average, provide evidence of financial need, be enrolled full-time in an accredited school or seminary, and be under care of a regional Commission on the Ministry or in the process of coming under care. **To Apply:** Write for application. Candidates must provide transcripts of academic work, make a renewal application each year if eligible, and provide references from a regional minister, pastor, lay leaders and/or professors. **Deadline:** March 15. **Contact:** Homeland Ministries at the above address (see entry 1946).

---

### • 1953 •
### Winston Churchill Foundation of the United States
Box 1248
Gracie Station
New York, NY 10028      *Ph:* (212)879-3480
*E-mail:* churchillf@aol.com
*URL:* http://members.aol.com/churchillf/

#### • 1954 • Churchill Scholarships *(Postgraduate/ Scholarship)*

**Purpose:** To encourage the development of American talent in engineering, mathematics, and the physical and natural sciences, and to encourage Anglo-American cooperation. **Focus:** Engineering, Mathematics, Natural Sciences, Physical Sciences. **Qualif.:** Applicant must be a U.S. citizen, enrolled in one of 55 participating U.S. colleges and universities, and between the ages of 19 and 26 years. Applicant must have a bachelor's degree from a U.S. institution, but may not have attained the Ph.D. Awards are tenable at Churchill College, University of Cambridge. **Criteria:** Applicant must have achieved academic excellence, be committed to a career in science or technology, and be a volunteer or involved in extra-curricula activities.

**Funds Avail.:** Approximately $27,000: includes all tuition and fees, $7,200 or $9,000, depending on course of study, $500 travel allowance. **No. of Awards:** 11. **To Apply:** Write to the Foundation for a list of participating colleges and universities. Obtain applications through a Foundation representative at a participating institution. **Deadline:** Usually November 15 (exact deadline is determined by participating institutions). **Contact:** Harold Epstein, Executive Director.

---

### • 1955 •
### The CIBA Fellowship Trust
Hulley Road
Macclesfield, Cheshire SK10 2NX,    *Ph:* 1625 421 933
England              *Fax:* 1625 619 637

#### • 1956 • Continental European Fellowships
*(Postgraduate/Fellowship)*

**Purpose:** To encourage the interchange of ideas between United Kingdom and mainland European scholars. **Focus:** Chemistry, Biochemistry, Biology, Chemical Engineering, Chemical Technology, Chemistry, Biotechnology. **Qualif.:** Applicant may be of any nationality, but must be a lecturer, senior lecturer, or reader at a university or comparable teaching institution in the United Kingdom or Republic of Ireland. Applicant should hold a current teaching position, and must agree to return to the same job upon completion of the fellowship. Fellowships are tenable for research at approved universities and technological universities in continental Europe. Fellows working in the field of biology should be conducting research that relates to chemistry. Awards are intended to supplement academic salaries.

**Funds Avail.:** Scholars receive £15,000/year, plus traveling expenses. **To Apply:** Write to the secretary for application form and guidelines. **Deadline:** All materials must be received by November 1.

---

**Remarks:** The Trust also offers awards to U.K. and Irish research teams that wish to cooperate on a research project with their continental European colleagues. Information on Awards for Collaboration in Europe may be obtained from the secretary. **Contact:** L.A. Murray, Secretary, at the above address (see entry 1955).

---

### • 1957 •
### Citizens Research Council of Michigan
38200 W. 10 Mile, Ste. 200    *Ph:* (248)474-0044
Farmington Hills, MI 48335    *Fax:* (248)474-0090
*E-mail:* crcmich@mich.com
*URL:* http://www.crcmich.org

#### • 1958 • Lent D. Upson-Loren B. Miller Fellowships
*(Graduate/Fellowship)*

**Purpose:** To provide the facilities necessary for the training of individuals of exceptional ability and capacity for leadership for professional service with citizen agencies concerned with government, including research bureaus, taxpayer groups, citizen leagues, chambers of commerce, and civic groups. **Focus:** Public Administration. **Qualif.:** Applicants must hold a bachelor's degree and be eligible for admission to Wayne State University's Graduate School of Public Administration. **Criteria:** Scholarship, leadership qualities, and personal interest of candidates will be considered in awarding a Fellowship. Personal interviews generally are required.

**Funds Avail.:** The stipend is $550 monthly through the Fellowship period unless terminated by resignation or unsatisfactory performance. In addition, the Fellowship provides tuition and fees for graduate study at Wayne State University. **To Apply:** A formal application must be filed. Applications are processed as received. **Deadline:** March 1.

**Remarks:** The period of the Fellowships is for two years commencing in June or September. By the end of the Fellowship period, the student is expected to have completed the requirements leading to the masters degree. The course of study of a Fellow is designed to concentrate on the functions common to all governments. It is intended that Fellows receive an overall view of public administration, that their training be that of generalists rather than specialists, and that they have an understanding of the principles and philosophies underlying public administration and organized citizen concern with government. In the Fellowship program, the research internship occupies an equal role with academic instruction. A substantial part of each week must be spent at the Council engaged in work on the problems of state, county, and local government. Work training is under the supervision of a qualified full-time staff member. The Fellows are expected to perform as junior staff members. Regular work hours are maintained at the Council with an allowance for time to meet class engagements. Plans call for the class work to be taken in the Graduate School at Wayne State University in Detroit. Internship is at the Citizens Research Council of Michigan. Fellows will be enrolled for the regular courses leading to the degree of Master of Public Administration or its equivalent. The actual courses are prescribed by the Council within the requirements of the University and in accordance with the interests of the Fellow. Thesis requirements will be met through choice of a subject mutually agreeable to the Fellow, the University, and the Council. **Contact:** Earl M. Ryan, Vice President-Executive Director, at the above address (see entry 1957).

---

## • 1959 •
### Citizens' Scholarship Foundation of Wakefield, Inc.
PO Box 321
467 Main St.                                    *Ph:* (781)245-4890
Wakefield, MA 01880                             *Fax:* (781)245-6761

### • 1960 • Citizens' Scholarship Foundation of Wakefield Scholarships *(All/Scholarship)*

**Focus:** General Studies. **Qualif.:** Applicants must be full-time students who are residents of Wakefield, Massachusetts. **Criteria:** Selection is based on financial need, which is determined by Citizens Scholarship Foundation of America, Inc. in St. Peter, Minnesota.

**Funds Avail.:** Awards vary. **No. of Awards:** 250-300. **To Apply:** A completed application and financial aid questionnaire must be submitted. **Deadline:** March 15. **Contact:** Lynne P. Zervas at the above address (see entry 1959).

## • 1961 •
### Civic Service Union No. 52
Union Office
11305 - 95 St.
Edmonton, AB, Canada T5G 1L2              *Fax:* (403)479-7975

### • 1962 • Civic Service Union No. 52 Charitable Assistance Fund *(Undergraduate/Scholarship)*

**Qualif.:** Candidates must be children of Canadian Service Union No. 52 Edmonton employees who are planning to pursue post-secondary studies at an approved institution.

**Funds Avail.:** Varies. **Contact:** Civic Service Union No. 52, Union Office, at the above address (see entry 1961).

## • 1963 •
### Civitan International Foundation
PO Box 130744                                   *Ph:* (205)591-8910
Birmingham, AL 35213-0744                       *Fax:* (205)592-6307
*E-mail:* civitan@civitan.org
*URL:* http://www.civitan.org/civitan

### • 1964 • Civitan Scholarships *(Graduate, Undergraduate/Scholarship)*

**Focus:** General Studies. **Qualif.:** Candidates must be a Civitan (or a Civitan's immediate family member) and must have been a Civitan for at least two years and/or must be or have been a Junior Civitan for no less than two years. Candidates must be enrolled in a degreed or certificate program at an accredited community college, vocational school, four-year college or graduate school. If a candidate in not pursuing graduate studies, full-time attendance is required. **Criteria:** Scholarships are awarded to students pursuing careers which help further the ideals and purposes of Civitan International as embodied in its Creed.

**Funds Avail.:** $1,000. **To Apply:** Send a self-addressed, stamped envelope to the Foundation for application guidelines. **Deadline:** Postmarked January 31. Notification by mid-May.

**Remarks:** Civitan is currently revising its scholarships. Send a self-addressed, stamped envelope for final program details.

## • 1965 •
### The Cleveland Institute of Art
11141 E. Boulevard
Cleveland, OH 44106                             *Ph:* (216)223-4700
*URL:* http://www.cia.du/cia01.html

### • 1966 • The Cleveland Institute of Art Portfolio Scholarships *(Undergraduate/Scholarship)*

**Purpose:** To attract outstanding visual artists to the Cleveland Institute of Art. **Focus:** Visual Arts. **Qualif.:** Applicants must have a strong visual portfolio and at least a 2.0 grade point average on a 4.0 scale from a secondary school.

**Funds Avail.:** Awards range from $15,000-to 45,000 over a five-year BFA period, provided that the student's grades merit continued funding. **To Apply:** Applicants must submit a completed application, indicating that they are applying for the portfolio scholarship competition, and 12 to 20 slides of recent artwork. **Deadline:** March 1. **Contact:** Thomas Steffen at the above address (see entry 1965). Toll-free telephone number for Ohio residents: 800-223-6500.

## • 1967 •
### Cleveland Institute of Music
11021 East Blvd.                                *Ph:* (216)791-5000
Cleveland, OH 44106                             *Fax:* (216)791-3063
*URL:* http://www.cwru.edu/CIM/cimhome.html

### • 1968 • Cleveland International Piano Competition *(Professional Development/Prize)*

**Purpose:** To encourage the contestants to attain the finest elements of pianistic excellence, clarity of expression, maximum fidelity to the text and the fullest possible commitment to the highest level of musicianship. At the same time, the contestants are encouraged to reach into the great repertory not so generally regarded as standard. **Focus:** Pianistic studies. **Qualif.:** Applicants must be pianists between the ages of 17 and 32. The number of contestants is limited to fifty. Tapes, references, dossier.

**Funds Avail.:** Nine prizes ranging from $12,000 to $750 will be awarded. The First Prize winner will receive two years of free management services for professional engagements, a CD recording, and a New York debut. **No. of Awards:** Eight. **To Apply:** Application form must be accompanied by birth certificate; two recent glossy black and white photographs; recent cassette, audio, or video tape which includes a complete sonata by Haydn, Mozart, Beethoven, or Schubert. One virtuoso etude and one work of candidate's choice; $45 application fee; two letters of recommendation from musicians of acknowledged professional standing (one may be from current or recent teacher); list of all major public appearances within the past few years with date, place and description; copies of critical reviews and programs; list of names and addresses of principal teachers of piano, with places and dates of study; complete list of repertoire to be performed for the Preliminary, Semi-Final, and Final Rounds of the competition; and list of honors and prizes received. **Deadline:** 20 March, 1997.

**Remarks:** Formerly known as the Robert Casadesus International Piano Competition **Contact:** Karen Knowlton, Executive Director, or Sara Smith, Assistant Administrator, at the above address (see entry 1967).

## • 1969 •
## Cleveland Scholarship Programs Inc.
850 Euclid Ave., Ste. 1000           *Ph:* (216)241-5587
Cleveland, OH 44114                    *Fax:* (216)241-6184
*E-mail:* csp@cspohio.org
*URL:* http://www.cspohio.org

### • 1970 •   Cleveland Scholarship Programs
*(Undergraduate/Scholarship)*

**Focus:** General Studies. **Qualif.:** Applicants must be graduates of select high schools in the Greater Cleveland area only. Full time enrollment in a college or accredited post secondary program. **Criteria:** Selection is based on motivation, ACT/SAT scores, a high school GPA above 2.5, recommendation by CSP advisory staff in participating high schools, or qualifications set by sponsors of other awards.

**Funds Avail.:** $300 to $1,000. **To Apply:** No direct application, nominees are selected through advisory staff referral. **Contact:** Mary Louise Nixon, Director of Financial Aid, at the above address (see entry 1969).

## • 1971 •
## Van Cliburn Foundation
2525 Ridgmar Blvd., Ste. 307         *Ph:* (817)738-6536
Fort Worth, TX 76116-4593           *Fax:* (817)738-6534
*E-mail:* clistaff@cliburn.org
*URL:* http://www.cliburn.com

### • 1972 •   Van Cliburn International Piano
### Competition *(Professional Development/Prize)*

**Purpose:** To provide an opportunity for the most gifted and communicative musicians to rise to the top and gain recognition. **Qualif.:** The competition is open to pianists of all nationalities. First Prize Winners of previous Van Cliburn Competitions are not eligible to compete. Applicants should be between the ages of 18 and 30 at the time of the competition. **Criteria:** Based on performance and jury judging.

**Funds Avail.:** First prize consists of $20,000 cash award, a gold medal, New York recital, concert tours, specially arranged domestic and international air travel, compact disc recording (total value of first prize is $200,000); second prize is $15,000 cash award, silver medal, New York recital, concert tours, compact disc recording; third prize is $10,000 cash award, bronze medal, concert tours, compact disc recording; 3 finalists receive $5,000 each. **To Apply:** Application books are available in January, 2000. **Deadline:** October 15.

**Remarks:** The Competition is held every four years in Fort Worth, Texas. **Contact:** Richard Rodzinski, Executive Director.

## • 1973 •
## CN Native Educational Awards Program
Employment Equity
PO Box 8100
Montreal, PQ, Canada H3C 3N4

### • 1974 •   CN Native Education Awards
*(Undergraduate/Award)*

**Focus:** Transportation. **Qualif.:** Applicants must be Canadian native students attending post-secondary institutions. They must be in need of financial assistance, seriously interested in preparing

for a career in the transportation industry, provide proof of acceptance into post-secondary institution, maintain full-time student status, and have a good academic record. **Criteria:** Financial need is considered.

**Funds Avail.:** Five awards of $1,500 each. **To Apply:** Completed application forms must be submitted. For applications, write to: 935 De La Gaucuetiere, Montreal, Quebec H3B 2M9. **Deadline:** June 30. **Contact:** Sophie-Anne Girardin, Manager-Employment Equity, at the above address (see entry 1973).

## • 1975 •
## Ty Cobb Educational Foundation
PO Box 725
Forest Park, GA 30298
*E-mail:* tycobb@mindspring.com

### • 1976 •   Ty Cobb Scholarships *(Graduate, Undergraduate/Scholarship)*

**Purpose:** To assist capable, deserving, and needy residents of Georgia in completing their college education. **Focus:** General Studies. **Qualif.:** Applicants must be undergradute students who are residents of Georgia, have demonstrated financial need, and have completed at least 45 quarter hours or 30 semester hours of academic credits with an average of B or higher in an accredited college. Professional students in medicine, and dentistry who are residents of Georgia and who have demonstrated financial need are also eligible to apply. Although scholarships are granted only to students who are residents of Georgia, a student may be awarded a scholarship to attend an accredited college or university in Georgia or another state. **Criteria:** Students with higher academic averages and the greatest need will be given priority.

**Funds Avail.:** Scholarships are awarded for the purpose of attending a specific institution and may not be transferred to any other institution except by prior authorization of the scholarship board. Funds awarded to students are sent directly to the approved college or university. Scholarship will be revoked if the student fails to maintain the status of a full-time student in good standing, is placed on probation or suspension, or if the financial circumstances of the student no longer require funds from the Foundation. **No. of Awards:** 250. **To Apply:** Applications must include a completed application form, a letter in the applicant's handwriting indicating the specific circumstances which cause them to request financial assistance, a letter of recommendation from academic dean or advisor, and transcripts of all college studies including spring quarter or semester grades. **Deadline:** June 15. **Contact:** The Ty Cobb Educational Foundation at the above address (see entry 1975).

## • 1977 •
## Coca-Cola Scholars Foundation
PO Box 442                            *Ph:* (404)733-5420
Atlanta, GA 30301-0442               *Fax:* (404)733-5439
                                       *Free:* 800-306-2653

*E-mail:* scholars@coca-cola.com
*URL:* http://www.coca-cola.com/scholars

### • 1978 •   Coca-Cola Scholars *(Undergraduate/Award)*

**Purpose:** To reward high school seniors for outstanding leadership, merit, service, excellence in school and community. **Focus:** General Studies. **Qualif.:** Applicants must be high school seniors. **Criteria:** Selection based on academic performance,

## Coca-Cola Scholars Foundation (continued)

extracurricular activities, community involvement, employment, and leadership potential.

**Funds Avail.:** 50 national awards of $5,000 per year; 100 regional awards of $1,000 per year. Both are available for four years. **No. of Awards:** 150. **To Apply:** Applications are available through guidance counselor's office only. **Deadline:** Must be postmarked by October 31 of senior year in high school. **Contact:** High school guidance counselors.

## • 1979 •

## James W. Colgan Fund
c/o Fleet Bank of Massachusetts
PO Box 9003      *Ph:* (413)732-2858
Springfield, MA 01101      *Fax:* (413)733-8565

### • 1980 • James W. Colgan Educational Loan
*(Undergraduate/Loan)*

**Purpose:** To provide educational and business training loans. **Focus:** General Studies. **Qualif.:** Applicants must be Massachusetts residents for at least five years prior to applying for the loan. Loans are for undergraduate study only. **Criteria:** Selection is first based on financial need, then academic record.

**Funds Avail.:** Varies. **No. of Awards:** Approximately 200. **To Apply:** Send self-addressed, stamped envelope for application. **Deadline:** April 15. **Contact:** Judith Turcotte or Maria Flores at the above address (see entry 1979).

## • 1981 •

## College Art Association
275 7th Ave. 18th Fl.      *Ph:* (212)691-1051
New York, NY 10001      *Fax:* (212)627-2381
*E-mail:* nyoffice@collegeart.org
*URL:* http://www.collegeart.org

### • 1982 • Professional Development Fellowship Program for Artists and Art Historians *(Doctorate, Graduate/Fellowship)*

**Purpose:** To bridge the gap between graduate study and professional careers. **Qualif.:** Artists and art historians from culturally diverse backgrounds may apply. Applicants must also demonstrate financial need and plan to receive the M.F.A., M.A. or PhD degree in the spring of the upcoming year. Applicants must be citizens of the US or permanent residents.

**Funds Avail.:** $5,000 in first year. **To Apply:** Applications are also available in most art and history graduate departments. The second year funding provides assistance in securing employment or an internship at a museum, university, or art center, and subsidizes the position. **Deadline:** January 31.

## • 1983 •

## The College Board
1717 Massachusetts Ave., NW, Ste.
401      *Ph:* (202)332-7134
Washington, DC 20036-2093      *Fax:* (202)462-5558

*The College Board is a national nonprofit membership organization of approximately 2,600 institutions and schools, systems, and associations serving both higher and secondary education. It sponsors programs and services for guidance, college admissions, placement, and financial aid purposes.*

### • 1984 • National Hispanic Scholar Recognition Program *(Undergraduate/Scholarship)*

**Purpose:** To recognize the exceptional academic achievements of Hispanic high school seniors, to identify academically well-prepared Hispanic high school seniors to collegiate postsecondary institutions and encourage their recruitment, and to focus renewed attention on the academic preparation of all Hispanic high school students. **Qualif.:** To be eligible for preliminary consideration, students must take the Preliminary Scholastic Aptitude Test/National Merit Scholarship Qualifying Test (PSAT/NMSQT) as high school juniors, identify themselves as Hispanic at that time, and indicate that they want to participate in the program. The 3,000 highest scoring students are invited in their senior year to complete applications for the scholarship. From this group of semifinalists, 500 students are selected for the awards. Scholarships must be used for full-time day study leading to one of the traditional baccalaureate degrees at any fully accredited four-year collegiate postsecondary institution. **Criteria:** From the applicant pool, winners are chosen on the basis of grade-point average, high school record, scores on the Scholastic Aptitude Test (SAT), personal qualities and community involvement, recommendations, and a personal essay. Winners are chosen by a selection committee comprised of college admissions and financial aid administrators and secondary school representatives.

**Funds Avail.:** 500 one-year nonrenewable scholarships of $1,500 each and 500 honorable mention awards in the amount of $100. In addition, the names of all students selected as semi-finalists in the awards program are included on a roster of outstanding Hispanic scholars. The program also distributes the roster of semi-finalists' names to colleges and universities to encourage institutions to recruit these students as potential candidates for admission. **To Apply:** Interested students should contact their high school guidance counselors for details. **Deadline:** Students receive notification of their selection in April of their senior year. Award certificates are mailed in May directly to the high schools to be used in senior award ceremonies. The scholarship is mailed in September to the college indicated by the student on the award reply form.

**Remarks:** The National Hispanic Scholar Recognition Program is a continuation of the National Hispanic Scholar Awards Program, which was funded for the past ten years by the Andrew W. Mellon Foundation. **Contact:** Evelyn Davila, Director of the National Hispanic Scholar Awards Program, at the above address (see entry 1983).

## • 1985 •

## College of Family Physicians of Canada
2630 Skymark Ave.      *Ph:* (905)629-0900
Mississauga, ON, Canada L4W 5A4      *Fax:* (905)629-0893
*E-mail:* dsteen@cfpc.ca
*URL:* http://www.cfpc.ca

### • 1986 • The College of Family Physicians of Canada Awards/DM Robb Research and Family Physician Research Grants *(Professional Development/ Award)*

**Purpose:** To provide "seed money" to college members to initiate or complete appropriate research or development projects in family medicine. **Focus:** Medicine. **Qualif.:** Must be a member of the College of Family Physicians of Canada.

**Funds Avail.:** The amount of the award will vary depending on the annual contributions to the fund and the number of applicants. **Deadline:** Spring. **Contact:** D.J.C. Steen, Director of Administration, at the above address (see entry 1985).

## • 1987 • The College of Family Physicians of Canada/Family Physician Study Grants *(Professional Development/Award)*

**Purpose:** To enable CFPC members to pursue continuing medical education. **Focus:** Medicine.

**Funds Avail.:** The amount of the award will vary depending on the annual contributions to the fund and the number of applicants. **To Apply:** Formal application must be submitted. **Deadline:** Spring. **Contact:** D.J.C. Steen, Director of Administration at the above address (see entry 1985).

## • 1988 • The College of Family Physicians of Canada Practice Enrichment Awards *(Professional Development/Award)*

**Purpose:** To enable a CFPC member to pursue a practice enrichment course under the direction of a Canadian university for at least three months. **Focus:** Medicine. **Qualif.:** Applicants must be members of the College of Family Physicians of Canada.

**Funds Avail.:** $3,000. **To Apply:** Formal application must be submitted. **Deadline:** November 15. **Contact:** Director of Administration at the above address (see entry 1985).

## • 1989 • Donald I. Rice Merit Award *(Professional Development/Award)*

**Purpose:** To enable a nationally or internationally renowned leader in family medicine to travel for approximately one month to one or more Canadian provinces to pursue educational activities with the provincial chapters of CFPC, university departments of family medicine, continuing medical education programs, family physicians and other members of the medical profession, allied health professionals, and the public. **Focus:** Medicine.

**Funds Avail.:** Award provides $5,000 plus travel expenses for recipient and spouse. **To Apply:** Formal application required. **Deadline:** November 15. **Contact:** Director of Administration at the above address (see entry 1985).

## • 1990 • College Foundation Inc.

PO Box 12100 (27605)
2100 Yonkers Rd.
Raleigh, NC 27604-2252
*E-mail:* info@cfi-nc.org
*URL:* http://www.cfi.org

*Ph:* (919)821-4771
*Fax:* (919)821-3139
*Free:* 888-CFI-6400

## • 1991 • Federal PLUS Loans to Parents under the North Carolina Insured Student Loan Program *(Undergraduate/Loan)*

**Focus:** General Studies. **Qualif.:** Borrowers must be the natural or adoptive parents, or legal guardians of dependent students. Borrowers and beneficiary students must be United States citizens, nationals, or eligible non-citizens and cannot be in default on another student loan or owe a refund to an education grant program. **Criteria:** Selection for the applicant is based on parents/guardian ability to make required loan repayments and not necessarily on need. A stable credit history is also required.

**Funds Avail.:** Loan up to the difference in cost of attendance and other financial aid. Variable interest rate is adjusted annually, not to exceed 9 percent. Repayment begins 60 days after the funds are disbursed. **To Apply:** Applicants should first file the (FAFSA) for the student's college to see if student qualifies for an interest-subsidized federal Stafford Loan. If not, candidates may obtain a PLUS Loan application promissory note from CFI, a North Carolina college or university, or a North Carolina high school. **Deadline:** The completed application must reach CFI at least 30 days before

the end of the academic period covered by the loan request. **Contact:** Program Information Staff, College Foundation Inc., at the above address (see entry 1990).

## • 1992 • Federal Stafford Loan under the North Carolina Insured Student Loan Program *(Graduate, Undergraduate/Loan)*

**Focus:** General Studies. **Qualif.:** Applicants must be legal residents of North Carolina and enrolled in eligible higher education institutions in-state or out-of-state students attending North Carolina institutions of higher learning. They must be United States citizens, nationals, or other eligible non-citizens who are enrolled (or accepted for enrollment) and making satisfactory academic progress at an approved educational institution. Applicants must be enrolled at least half-time, show compliance with selective service requirements, and cannot be in default on another student loan or owe a refund to an education grant program. **Criteria:** For a subsidized loan, selection is based on financial need. The unsubsidized Stafford Loan is not based on need.

**Funds Avail.:** Up to $2,625 per year prior to completion of first year of undergraduate program, up to $3,500 per year for the second year of the program, up to $5,500 per year for the remainder of undergraduate study. Up to $8,500 per academic year for graduate or professional study. Additional amounts are available from the unsubsidized loan for eligible independent students. Interest-subsidized and unsubsidized loans are available. For subsidized loans, federal government pays interest until student begins repayment six months after graduation or termination of studies. Interest at variable rate not to exceed 8.25 percent is adjusted annually. **To Apply:** Applicants must complete and file (FAFSA) to enable the college's financial aid office to determine eligibility for a federal Pell Grant before applying for a Stafford Loan. Applications may be obtained from CFI, a North Carolina college, or a North Carolina high school. **Deadline:** Completed applications must reach CFI at least 30 days before the end of the academic period covered by the loan request. **Contact:** Program Information Staff, College Foundation Inc., at the above address (see entry 1990).

## • 1993 • Joseph Collins Foundation

787 7th Ave.
New York, NY 10019-6099

## • 1994 • Joseph Collins Foundation Scholarships *(Graduate/Scholarship)*

**Purpose:** To enable men and women, whose own resources are inadequate, to attend accredited medical schools of their choice towards an M.D. degree. **Focus:** Medicine. **Qualif.:** Applicants must demonstrate financial need and be attending an accredited medical school geographically located east of or contiguous to the Mississippi River in the United States. They must stand in the upper half of their class except in most unusual cases, demonstrate interest in arts and letters or other cultural pursuits outside the field of medicine, intend to specialize in neurology, psychiatry, or general medicine, and provide evidence of good moral character. **Criteria:** Preference is given to advanced students, however, entering students who have outstanding college records and exceptional aptitudes for medicine may be nominated and will receive careful consideration.

**Funds Avail.:** Up to $10,000 per year for an average of one year. Renewal grants will be made at the discretion of the Trustees. Grants towards the payment of tuition will be paid directly to the medical school in one payment at the beginning of each school year. **To Apply:** Applications must be made on the official application form provided by the Foundation. A limited number of forms are available to accredited medical schools or colleges upon request by the medical school authorities. Application forms are

## Joseph Collins Foundation (continued)

not distributed to students or prospective students directly. They should be obtained from the medical school authorities, completed, and returned to the medical school for forwarding to the Foundation. Each application is to be accompanied by a letter from the dean or other officer of the medical school, approving the application on the basis of qualifications, merit, and need. This letter must contain a specific recommendation as to the amount of financial assistance required by the student to enter or continue in medical school. Applicants who have completed one or more years of medical school must arrange to have transcripts of the medical school records forwarded to the Trustees. Entering first year students must furnish college transcripts. Only one application to each school. **Deadline:** March 1. **Contact:** Students should request school authorities to contact Augusta L. Packer, Secretary Treasurer, Joseph Collins Foundation, at the above address (see entry 1993).

---

• 1995 •

## The Colonial Players, Inc. Theater-in-the-Round

108 East St.                    Ph: (410)268-7373
Annapolis, MD 21401-1799        Fax: (410)267-6106

### • 1996 • Promising Playwright Award (Professional Development/Award)

**Purpose:** To recognize a promising playwright. **Focus:** Drama. **Qualif.:** Applicant must be a resident of Maryland, Washington, DC, Virginia, W. Virginia, Delaware or Pennsylvania. Candidate must have written an original full-length play, or two one-act plays, without copyright restrictions and suitable for arena production, running between 1 1/2 and 2 hours. The play's cast should not exceed 10 characters. Awardee must agree to attend rehearsals of their play(s). Colonial Players Inc. reserves the right to produce the winning play on a royalty-free basis within two years of selection.

**Funds Avail.:** $750 plus mainstage production of the play. **To Apply:** Write to Colonial Players Inc. for application guidelines and current contest rules. **Deadline:** September 1 to December 31. The Award is given biennially. **Contact:** Frank Moorman, Coordinator, at the above address (see entry 1995).

---

• 1997 •

## Colorado AFL-CIO

2460 W. 26th Ave., Bldg. C, Ste.
 350
Denver, CO 80211-5401          Ph: (303)433-2100

### • 1998 • Americo Toffoli Scholarships (Undergraduate/Scholarship)

**Purpose:** To enable graduating Colorado high school seniors to attend a university, college, or trade school of their choice. ARS General Studies. **Qualif.:** Applicants must be graduating high school seniors or their parent or guardian must be a member in good standing of the Colorado AFL-CIO. They must also have passing grades.

**Funds Avail.:** Six scholarhips will be awarded: three to young men and three to young women. Scholarships are annual one-time awards and the amount varies each year. **No. of Awards:** 12. **To Apply:** Applications must be accompanied by two letters of recommendation from teachers, counselors, or school principals. Applicants must submit an essay of 1,000 to 1,500 words on how new jobs can be created in America. **Deadline:** May 1. **Contact:** Ann Sutton at the above address (see entry 1997).

---

• 1999 •

## Colorado Society of Certified Public Accountants

7979 E. Tufts Ave., Ste. 500       Ph: (303)773-2877
Denver, CO 80237-2845              Fax: (303)773-6344

### • 2000 • Colorado Society of CPAs Educational Foundation High School Scholarship (Undergraduate/ Scholarship)

**Purpose:** To provide financial assistance to students interested in accounting. **Focus:** Accounting. **Qualif.:** Colorado high school seniors who intend to major in accounting at one of the 13 Colorado colleges or universities that offer an accounting major. Applicants must have a 3.75 or better grade point average. Students who will attend community colleges in Colorado are also eligible. **Criteria:** Based primarily on scholastic achievement.

**Funds Avail.:** Seven to ten $750 scholarships. **To Apply:** Applications, official transcript showing GPA and class rank at the end of first semester of senior year, and SAT and/or ACT test scores must be submitted. **Deadline:** March 1.

**Remarks:** There are approximately 75 applicants each year. **Contact:** Colorado Society of Certified Public Accountants at the above address (see entry 1999).

### • 2001 • Colorado Society of CPAs Educational Foundation Scholarships (Undergraduate/Scholarship)

**Focus:** Accounting. **Qualif.:** Declared Accounting majors at Colorado colleges or universities are eligible. Their GPA must be 3.0 or better, and they must have completed 8 semester hours or 12 quarter hours of accounting courses. **Criteria:** The scholarship is based primarily on scholastic achievement and secondarily on financial need.

**Funds Avail.:** Grants of up to $1,000 per semester are awarded for the fall and mid-winter sessions. Seven scholarships are offered each semester. **To Apply:** Applicants must submit an official transcript from the school of enrollment, the scholarship applications, and pages 1 and 2 of parents' and applicant's most recent Federal tax return. **Deadline:** June 30 for fall and November 30 for the winter quarter or spring semester.

**Remarks:** There are typically between 50 and 75 applicants. **Contact:** Colorado Society of Certified Public Accountants at the above address (see entry 1999).

---

• 2002 •

## Colorado Springs Osteopathic Foundation

PO Box 154                     Ph: (719)635-9057
Colorado Springs, CO 80901     Fax: (719)635-4727

### • 2003 • Osteopathic Medical Students Loans (Graduate/Loan)

**Purpose:** To assist Colorado state residents with the cost of tuition at an osteopathic medical school. **Focus:** Medicine, Osteopathic Medicine. **Qualif.:** Applicants must be residents of Colorado and attending osteopathic medical school. **Criteria:** Preference is given to seniors and Colorado Springs residents.

**Funds Avail.:** Approximately $15,000 per year. **To Apply:** Write for information. **Deadline:** May 15. **Contact:** Dee Grimes at the above address (see entry 2002).

• 2004 •

## Columbia 300, Inc.
PO Box 13430　　　　　　　　*Ph:* (210)344-9211
San Antonio, TX 78213-0430　*Fax:* (210)349-8672
*E-mail:* debbieb@columbia300.com

• 2005 • **Columbia 300 John Jowdy Scholarship**
*(Undergraduate/Scholarship)*

**Qualif.:** Applicants must be high school seniors, graduating in the current year, and actively involved in the sport of bowling.

**Funds Avail.:** $500 annually. **No. of Awards:** 1. **To Apply:** Applicants must complete an application form and send it to the Columbia 300, Inc. After finalists are selected, they will be notified and are then required to forward transcripts to the Columbia 300, Inc. **Deadline:** Applications are due April 1 and transcripts of finalists are due by June 15. **Contact:** Deborah Bibb at the above address (see entry 2004). Send request for applications to John Jowdy Scholarship c/o the Professional Bowlers Association Education Fund, 1720 Merriman Rd., PO Box 5118, Akron, OH 44334-0118. Telephone: (216)836-5568.

• 2006 •

## Columbia College Theater/Music Center
72 East 11th St.　　　　　*Ph:* (312)344-6136
Chicago, IL 60605　　　　*Fax:* (312)344-8077
*E-mail:* chigochuck@aol.com

• 2007 • **Theodore Ward Prize** *(Undergraduate/Prize)*

**Purpose:** To uncover and identify new African American plays that are promising and produceable, to encourage and aid playwrights in the development of scripts, and to offer an opportunity for emerging and established playwrights to be exposed to Chicago's professional theater community. **Focus:** Playwriting. **Qualif.:** Applicants must be of African American descent and permanent residents of the United States. Staff and faculty of Columbia College Chicago are not eligible.

**Funds Avail.:** First prize includes: $2,000; fully mounted production in the coming studio season; transportation (within the continental United States), and housing (maximum of one week) during rehearsal period and performances. The first prize winner must be willing to sign a contract with the college that obligates the playwright to travel to Chicago during production, acknowledge prize in future programs and publications, and a small percentage of future royalties. Second prize includes: $500; a staged reading in the Studio Theater that will be directed by a faculty director; and an audio tape of the reading. **No. of Awards:** 1. **To Apply:** Applicants must submit one full length, typed, securely bound, copyrighted play addressing the African-American experience. One acts and musicals are not accepted (with the exception of a play-with-music). Adaptations and translations are not eligible unless from works in the public domain. All rights for music or biographies must be secured by the entrant prior to submission. Scripts that have received professional production are ineligible. "Professional" includes Equity Showcase and Waiver productions but does not include amateur and college productions. Applicants should also include a brief personal resume, a short synopsis, and a script history about any prior productions or readings. Only scripts with self-addressed, stamped envelopes will be returned to entrants. **Deadline:** Scripts are accepted from May 1 to August 1, and must be postmarked no later than August 1.

**Remarks:** Mr. Ward was one of the most significant playwrights to emerge from the Chicago chapter of the Federal Theater Project during the mid-1930's. **Contact:** Manuscripts are sent to Mr. Chuck Smith, Columbia College, Theater/Music Center, at the above address (see entry 2006).

• 2008 •

## Columbia Journalism Review
700 Journalism Bldg.
Columbia University
New York, NY 10027　　　　*Ph:* (212)854-1881
*URL:* http://www.cjr.org

• 2009 • **Columbia Journalism Review Internship Program** *(Graduate, Undergraduate/Internship)*

**Purpose:** To offer opportunities for Graduate and Undergraduate students interested in journalism. **Focus:** Journalism.

**Funds Avail.:** Internship is unpaid with the possibility of payment for published material in the *Columbia Journalism Review*. **No. of Awards:** One internship is given each spring, summer and fall semester. **To Apply:** A cover letter, resume, clips, and names of three recommendations should be submitted. **Deadline:** The semester before the internship takes place.

• 2010 •

## Columbia University - Graduate School of Journalism
Knight-Bagehot Fellowship Program
116th St. and Broadway　　　*Ph:* (212)854-2711
New York, NY 10027　　　　*Fax:* (212)854-7837
*E-mail:* tats@columbia.edu

• 2011 • **Knight-Bagehot Fellowships in Economics and Business Journalism** *(Professional Development/Fellowship)*

**Purpose:** To improve the coverage of business, economics, and finance. **Focus:** Business, Economics, and Finance. **Qualif.:** Applicant may be of any nationality, but must be either a freelance journalist or a full-time editorial employee of a newspaper, magazine, wire service, or broadcast news program. Applicant must have at least four years of experience. The fellowship is open only to journalists whose work regularly appears in the United States or Canada. There are no age requirements, but those selected are typically between the ages of 27 and 40 years. There are no educational prerequisites. Fellowships are tenable only at the Graduate School of Journalism, Columbia University.

**Funds Avail.:** $25,000/year, plus tuition. **No. of Awards:** 8 per year. **To Apply:** Write or phone the fellowship director for application form and guidelines. Submit with four references, an essay on economics, a personal essay, and samples of work. **Deadline:** March 1. Fellowships are announced by May 1.

• 2012 •

## Committee on Institutional Cooperation
CIC Predoctoral Fellowships
　Program
Indiana University　　　　*Ph:* (812)855-0822
803 E. 8th St.　　　　　　*Fax:* (812)855-8741
Bloomington, IN 47405　　*Free:* 800-457-4420

• 2013 • **CIC Predoctoral Fellowships** *(Doctorate, Graduate/Fellowship)*

**Purpose:** To increase the representation of Native Americans, African Americans, Mexican-Americans, and Puerto Ricans among Ph.D. recipients in humanities, social sciences, natural sciences, mathematics, and engineering at select universities. **Focus:**

## Committee on Institutional Cooperation (continued)

Engineering, Humanities, Mathematics, Science, Social Sciences. **Qualif.:** Applicant must be a U.S. citizen. Candidate must be African American, American Indian, Mexican American, or Puerto Rican and must hold or receive a bachelor's degree from a regionally accredited college or university by August of the year of matriculation into a graduate program. Students who have received master's degrees or who are currently enrolled in graduate study may also apply. Fellowships are for doctoral study, and continued support is contingent upon satisfactory performance and progress toward the degree. Fellowships are tenable at any of the 11 CIC universities: University of Chicago, University of Illinois at Chicago, Indiana University, University of Iowa, University of Michigan, Michigan State University, University of Minnesota, Northwestern University, Ohio State University, Pennsylvania State University, Purdue University, University of Wisconsin, Madison, and University of Wisconsin, Milwaukee. Currently enrolled graduate students at CIC university campuses are not eligible to apply.

**Funds Avail.:** Humanities $10,500 plus tuition; Social Sciences $10,000/year plus full tuition. **To Apply:** Write or call the CIC office for brochures or application. **Deadline:** January 5. **Contact:** Professor R. F. Smith, Director, at the above address (see entry 2012). Can also be reached at 800-457-4420 (outside Indiana).

### • 2014 •
## Committee on Scholarly Communication in China
1112 16th St. NW, Ste. 340                     *Ph:* (202)337-1250
Washington, DC 20036                           *Fax:* (202)337-3109

*The Committee on Scholarly Communication China was established to facilitate scholarly exchanges with the People's Republic of China. It is a Committee of the National Research Council, the working arm of the National Academy of Sciences, a private membership organization founded in 1863 under a charter signed by President Abraham Lincoln. The Academy provides advisory services on scientific and technological matters to governmental agencies and Congress.*

### • 2015 •  National Program for Advanced Study and Research in China - General Advanced Studies
*(Graduate/Grant)*

**Purpose:** To enable graduate students in the social sciences and humanities to do coursework in an academic discipline at a Chinese university. **Focus:** Humanities. **Qualif.:** Applicants must be U.S. citizens or permanent residents proficient in Chinese language through at least three years of college-level study or its equivalent, and have an MA or equivalent. There is a minimum tenure requirement of one year.

**Funds Avail.:** Stipend and allowance amounts vary. **Deadline:** Mid-October. **Contact:** The Committee on Scholarly Communication in China at the above address (see entry 2014).

### • 2016 •  National Program for Advanced Study and Research in China - Research Program
*(Postdoctorate/Other)*

**Purpose:** To support individual research on China, the Chinese portion of a comparative study, exploratory research on an aspect of contemporary China, or limited research in Hong Kong or elsewhere in East Asia to supplement research within the People's Republic of China. **Focus:** Social Sciences, Humanities. **Qualif.:** Applicants must be United States citizens or permanent residents with a Ph.D or equivalent in the social sciences or humanities at the time of application. **Criteria:** Preference is given to those who have not previously participated in the program, but former participants are encouraged to apply on the basis of published research done during an earlier visit. **Deadline:** Mid-October.

**Remarks:** Research grantees normally spend from two months to one year in China. This program is sponsored by the U.S. Information Agency and the National Endowment for the Humanities. **Contact:** Committee on Scholarly Communication in China at the above address (see entry 2014).

### • 2017 •  National Program for Advanced Study and Research in China - Senior Advanced Studies
*(Doctorate, Graduate/Award)*

**Purpose:** To support in-depth research on China, the Chinese portion of a comparative study, or an exploratory survey of an aspect of contemporary China for dissertation research. **Focus:** Chinese Studies. **Qualif.:** Candidates must be U.S. citizens or permanent residents and have a Ph.D. or equivalent. **Criteria:** Preference is given to those who have not previously participated in the program, but former participants are encouraged to apply on the basis of publications derived from an earlier visit.

**Funds Avail.:** The amount and number of awards varies. **Contact:** The Committee on Scholarly Communication in China at the above address (see entry 2014).

### • 2018 •
## Commonwealth of Pennsylvania - Department of Military Affairs
Bureau for Veteran Affairs
Fort Indiantown Gap                            *Ph:* (717)865-8910
Annville, PA 17003-5002                        *Fax:* (717)861-8589

### • 2019 •  Commonwealth of Pennsylvania Educational Gratuity Program Grants *(Undergraduate/ Award)*

**Purpose:** To provide financial assistance to children of certain veterans. **Qualif.:** Applicants must be children of veterans who have a 100 percent disability that was war-or-armed conflict-service connected, or the children of veterans who died while on active duty during war or suffered armed conflict service connected disabilities, or as a result of hostile fire or terrorist attacks during peacetime (as determined by the Department of Military Affairs). Applicants must be between the ages of 16 and 24 and have been residents of the Commonwealth of Pennsylvania five years immediately prior to the date of filing the application. They are also required to attend a State or State-aided educational or training institution of a secondary or college level or other institutions of higher education, including business school, trade school, hospital providing training for nurses, or institutions providing courses for beauty culture, art, or radio within the Commonwealth that are approved and licensed by the Department of Education. Applicants must have financial need. **Criteria:** All applicants who meet the eligibility requirements will receive grants.

**Funds Avail.:** A $500 grant. **To Apply:** Applications are obtained from the Bureau for Veterans Affairs at the above address.

## Commonwealth Scholarship and Fellowship Plan
c/o ICCS
325 Dalhousie, S-800      *Ph:* (613)789-7828
Ottawa, ON, Canada K1N 7G2    *Fax:* (613)789-7830
*E-mail:* general@iccs-ciec.ca
*URL:* http://www.iccs-ciec.ca

### • 2021 • Commonwealth Scholarship Plan
*(Graduate/Scholarship)*

**Purpose:** To support Commonwealth students who wish to study in Commonwealth countries other than their own. **Focus:** General Studies. **Qualif.:** Applicant must be a citizen of a Commonwealth nation who will have completed his/her undergraduate education by the start of the proposed scholarship term. Awards are tenable in selected postgraduate programs in Commonwealth countries other than the students' own. Awarding agency is responsible for arranging admission to the host institution. Scholars must return to their home country upon completion of their studies. Additional requirements may vary, depending on the regulations of the home and host country.

**Funds Avail.:** Tuition, living and travel allowances. **To Apply:** Write to the Commonwealth Plan agency in home country for application guidelines. In most countries the agency is part of the national government's department or ministry of education. Citizens of Canada, New Zealand and the United Kingdom, however, must write to different organizations; the addresses are listed in the note below. Submit completed form to the national agency in home country. The agency will review all applications and nominate superior candidates to the appropriate officials in the host country. The final selection of scholarship recipients is made by the host country. **Deadline:** Usually September or October; nominations must reach the host country by December 31. **Contact:** In Canada the address for the Commonwealth Plan is: c/o ICCS, 325 Dalhousie, S-800, Ottawa, Ontario, K1N 7G2. In New Zealand write: Commonwealth Scholarship and Fellowship Committee, New Zealand Vice-Chancellors Committee, PO Box 11-915, Wellington, New Zealand. In the United Kingdom contact: Commonwealth Scholarship Commission; the Association of Commonwealth Universities; 36 Gordon Square; London WC1H OPF.

## The Community Church of New York
40 E. 35th St.
New York, NY 10016      *Ph:* (212)683-4988

### • 2023 • John Haynes Holmes Memorial Fund
*(Other/Award)*

**Purpose:** The purpose of the fund is to give financial help to students already admitted to theological school and whose goal is to prepare for work in the field of liberal religion, either as a parish minister or as a liberal religious educator. **Focus:** Religion. **Qualif.:** Awards are given to men and women who intend to enter the Unitarian Universalist ministry.

**Funds Avail.:** The amount of each award ranges from $500 to $2,000 and is individually determined. **No. of Awards:** 5-8. **To Apply:** Every applicant must answer the following: Why do you want to be a liberal minister or religious educator? Describe your attachment to and involvement in liberal religion. How did this develop? Explain your family's background, especially with regard to religion. Describe your relationship to various minority groups in the United States. Describe and evaluate your personality indicating how you expect to meet the requirements for your future career. Also to be submitted with the application are one professional recommendation from a minister, college transcripts, and two academic recommendations from college professors for

students about to begin theological school, or two academic recommendations from appropriate theological school professors or officers, and college and theological school transcripts for students continuing theological school. All applicants, including current John Haynes Holmes Fellows must file a completed financial information form prepared in consultation with the financial aid officer of the school. **Deadline:** Completed applications must be filed by April 1; recipients are announced by mid-May.

**Remarks:** The Fund was established in memory of Dr. John Haynes Holmes, a long-time Unitarian minister in New York and Boston. **Contact:** Secretary, John Haynes Holmes Memorial Fund Committee, at the above address (see entry 2022).

## Community Foundation for Palm Beach and Martin Counties
Attn: Scholarship Coordinator
324 Datura St., Ste. 340      *Ph:* (561)659-6800
West Palm Beach, FL 33401-5431    *Fax:* (561)288-2069
*E-mail:* cpfbmc2@aol.com
*URL:* http://www.cfpbmc.org

### • 2025 • Barnett Bank of Palm Beach County Minority Student Scholarship Fund *(Undergraduate/ Scholarship)*

**Focus:** General studies. **Qualif.:** Applicants must be minority students. **Criteria:** Applicants must be students who are members of a minority community who intends to major in business. Awards are made based on financial need and academic achievement. Preference given to business majors.

**Funds Avail.:** $4,000. **To Apply:** Write for further details. **Contact:** Community Foundation for Palm Beach and Martin Counties at the above address (see entry 2024).

### • 2026 • Maura and William Benjamin Scholarship *(Undergraduate/Scholarship)*

**Focus:** General studies. **Qualif.:** Applicants must be students in Palm Beach and Martin Counties. **Criteria:** Awards are made based on scholastic achievement, leadership skills, and community service.

**Funds Avail.:** $1,200. **To Apply:** Write for further details. **Contact:** Community Foundation for Palm Beach and Martin Counties at the above address (see entry 2024).

### • 2027 • Thomas William Bennett Memorial Scholarship *(Undergraduate/Scholarship)*

**Focus:** Education with an emphasis on teaching reading skills. **Qualif.:** Graduating high school senior attending a public or private school in Palm Beach or Martin county. Must have a GPA of 2.5 or higher, be a U.S. citizen, and show financial need.

### • 2028 • Lisa Bjork Memorial Scholarship *(High School, Undergraduate/Scholarship)*

**Focus:** Journalism and communications. **No. of Awards:** 2, one to a student at Jupiter High School the other to a student at another Palm Beach County high school. **To Apply:** A 500 to 750 word essay on the The Importance of the Family must be submitted.

## Community Foundation for Palm Beach and Martin Counties (continued)

### • 2029 • Walter and Adi Blum Scholarship
*(Undergraduate/Scholarship)*

**Qualif.:** Graduating high school senior attending a public or private school in Palm Beach or Martin county; maintain an overall C average; demonstrate financial need; attend an accredited college, university or voactional school in the United States as a full-time student.

### • 2030 • Allen C. Clark Memorial Scholarship *(High School/Scholarship)*

**Qualif.:** Graduating senior from Forest Hill High School who demonstrates financial need and has a GPA of 2.5 or better.

### • 2031 • Julian and Eunice Cohen Scholarship
*(Undergraduate/Scholarship)*

**Qualif.:** Based on academic excellence and financial need.

### • 2032 • Terry Darby Memorial Scholarship *(High School/Scholarship)*

**Qualif.:** Graduating senior from a Palm Beach or Martin County high school who has been actively involved in soccer during his or her high school career. This scholarship is not based on financial need. Student must attend a two or four year college or university.

### • 2033 • James H. Davis Memorial Scholarship
*(High School/Scholarship)*

**Focus:** Horticulture, agriculture or related fields. **Qualif.:** Graduating high school senior attending a public or private school in Palm Beach and Martin County, Homestead Senior High and South Dade High; must be a Florida resident; GPA of 2.0 or higher; demonstrate financial need. Students may attend any accredited college, university or vocational school in Florida. Must maintain a C average during college.

### • 2034 • Ellen Beth Eddleman Memorial Scholarship
*(High School, Undergraduate/Scholarship)*

**Qualif.:** Student at John I Leonard High School who has excelled in academics (3.0 GPA or better), leadership, service, and talent (including music, art and literary). Financial need is not considered; must be in the band, choral department or Excalibur and must be continuing their education beyond high school. Student nominated by John I Leonard Committee on Awards.

### • 2035 • Inez Peppers Lovett Scholarship
*(Undergraduate/Scholarship)*

**Focus:** General studies. **Criteria:** Applicants must be African American Palm Beach County graduating high school seniors interested in pursuing a career in elementary education; having a 3.0 or better GPA; and demonstrating financial need. **To Apply:** Write for further details. **Contact:** Community Foundation for Palm Beach and Martin Counties at the above address (see entry 2024).

### • 2036 • Palm Beach Kennel Club Scholarship
*(Undergraduate/Scholarship)*

**Focus:** General studies. **Qualif.:** Applicants must be children of Palm Beach Kennel Club employees. **Criteria:** Awarded to children or grandchildren of employees of the Palm Beach Kennel Club. Parent or grandparent must have at least two years of continuous corporate service before the deadline. Applicants must be graduating high school seniors, Florida residents, US citizens, have a 2.0-3.0 GPA, and plan to attend an accredited Florida college or university. **To Apply:** Write for further details. **Contact:** Community Foundation for Palm Beach and Martin Counties at the above address (see entry 2024).

---

### • 2037 •
## Conference of Educational Administrators Serving the Deaf
Attn: Dr. K.M. Cristebsen
San Diego State University
Department of Communication
  Disorders
Campanile Dr.
San Diego, CA 92182

### • 2038 • CEASD Ethic Student Scholarship
*(Graduate/Scholarship)*

**Purpose:** To encourage people to become teacher of deaf children. **Focus:** Teaching. **Qualif.:** Must be graduate students.

**Funds Avail.:** $1,000 per award. **No. of Awards:** 2 **To Apply:** An essay and recommendations from the faculty must be submitted each spring. **Deadline:** April 15. **Contact:** Conference of Educational Administrators Serving the Deaf at the above address (see entry 2037).

---

### • 2039 •
## Congress of the United States - Office of Technology Assessment
c/o William J. Norris
600 Pennsylvania Ave., SE          Ph: (202)224-8713
Washington, DC 20003               Fax: (202)228-6098

*The Office of Technology Assessment provides congressional committees with objective analyses of the emerging, difficult, and often highly technical issues of the late 20th century. It explores complex issues involving science and technology, helps Congress resolve uncertainties and conflicting claims, identifies alternative policy options, and provides foresight or early alert to new developments that could have important implications for future Federal policy.*

### • 2040 • OTA Congressional Fellowship *(Doctorate/Fellowship)*

**Purpose:** To provide an opportunity for individuals of proven ability to gain a better understanding of science and technology issues facing Congress and the ways in which Congress establishes national policy related to these issues. **Focus:** Government, Political Science. **Qualif.:** The program is open to individuals who have demonstrated exceptional ability in such areas as the physical or biological sciences, engineering, law, economics, environmental and social sciences, and public policy. Candidates must have significant experience in technical fields or management or have completed research at the doctoral level. Applicants must have the ability to perform objective, comprehensive analyses, to work cooperatively with individuals of diverse backgrounds, experience, and training, and to present reports in clear, concise language. **Criteria:** Applicants are considered on the basis of their records of achievement and their potential for continuing individual expertise to one or more of the Office of Technology Assessment's assessment studies.

**Funds Avail.:** Up to six fellowships are awarded with a salary range of $35,000 to $70,000 per year, based on the fellow's current salary and/or training and experience. **To Apply:** Applicants are required to submit the following: a resume limited to two pages, including education, experience, area(s) of special interest, and one page listing most recent published works; three letters of reference, including telephone numbers from individuals who know the applicant well enough to write about his or her professional competence; a statement of up to 1,000 words that either evaluates an issue with both technical and public policy content and why it is of interest to him/her or summarizes the findings of a piece of public policy related to work he/she has done. A second statement up to 250 words explaining how OTA and the fellowship fits into applicant's career objectives. **Deadline:** All materials including all reference letters must be received by January 31.

**Remarks:** OTA provides congressional committees with objective analyses of the emerging, difficult, and often highly technical issues of the late 20th century. It explores complex issues involving science and technology, helps Congress resolve uncertainties and conflicting claims, identifies alternative policy options, and provides foresight or early alert to new developments that could have important implications for future federal policy. **Contact:** Congressional Fellowships, Personnel Office, at the above address (see entry 2039).

---

## • 2041 •
## Connecticut Department of Higher Education
Office of Financial Aid
61 Woodland St.
Hartford, CT 06105
*E-mail:* dhewebmaster@commnet.edu
*URL:* http://ctdje/commnet.edu/dheweb/default.htm

*Ph:* (860)947-1855
*Fax:* (860)947-1311

### • 2042 • Robert C. Byrd Honors Scholarships
*(Undergraduate/Scholarship)*

**Focus:** General Studies. **Qualif.:** Applicants must be Connecticut high school seniors in the top two percent of their class or SAT scores above 1400. **Criteria:** SAT scores and high school ranking. **Contact:** High school counseling offices or the Connecticut Department of Higher Education at the above address (see entry 2041). A toll-free telephone number for Connecticut residents only is 800-252-3357.

### • 2043 • Connecticut Aid for Public College
Students *(Undergraduate/Other)*

**Focus:** General Studies. **Qualif.:** Applicants must be Connecticut residents attending a public Connecticut college. **Criteria:** Selection is based upon financial need.

**Funds Avail.:** Up to amount of unmet financial need. **Contact:** College financial aid offices for application and additional information.

### • 2044 • Connecticut Family Education Loan
Program (CT FELP) *(Graduate, Professional Development, Undergraduate/Loan)*

**Focus:** General Studies. **Qualif.:** Student must be enrolled at least half-time in a Connecticut non-profit college, or be a Connecticut resident enrolled at least half-time in a non-profit college anywhere in the United States. **Criteria:** Selection is based upon the recipient's ability to repay the loan.

**Funds Avail.:** From $2,000 to the total cost of education less other financial aid awarded per academic year at a fixed rate. **To Apply:** Call for an application. **Deadline:** There is no deadline. **Contact:** Mary Young at the above address or call (in Connecticut only) 800-252-3357.

### • 2045 • Connecticut Independent College Student
Grants *(Undergraduate/Grant)*

**Focus:** General Studies. **Qualif.:** Applicants must be Connecticut residents attending an independent Connecticut college. **Criteria:** Selection is based upon financial need.

**Funds Avail.:** Up to $6,384. **Contact:** College financial aid offices for applications and additional information.

### • 2046 • Connecticut Scholastic Achievement Grants
*(Undergraduate/Grant)*

**Focus:** General Studies. **Qualif.:** Applicants must be Connecticut residents and U.S. citizens or nationals who are high school seniors or graduates with ranking in the top 20 percent of their class or SAT scores of at least 1,100 or an ACT score of 27. **Criteria:** Selection is based upon financial need and academic performance.

**Funds Avail.:** Up to $2,000 per year to be used at a Connecticut college or in states that have a reciprocity agreement with Connecticut. Total amount awarded depends upon annual state appropriation. **Deadline:** February 15. **Contact:** The Connecticut Department of Higher Education at the above address (see entry 2041). A toll-free telephone number for Connecticut residents is 800-252-3357.

### • 2047 • Connecticut Tuition Aid for Needy
Students *(Undergraduate/Scholarship)*

**Focus:** General Studies. **Qualif.:** Applicants must be students attending public Connecticut colleges. **Criteria:** Based upon financial need.

**Funds Avail.:** Up to amount of unmet financial need. **To Apply:** Apply at college financial aid office. **Contact:** College financial aid offices.

### • 2048 • Connecticut Tuition Waiver for Senior
Citizens *(Undergraduate/Scholarship)*

**Focus:** General Studies. **Qualif.:** Applicants must be Connecticut residents age 62 and over who are attending a Connecticut public college.

**Funds Avail.:** Equal to tuition only. **To Apply:** Apply at the college registrar's office. **Contact:** College registrars office.

### • 2049 • Connecticut Tuition Waiver for Veterans
*(Undergraduate/Scholarship)*

**Focus:** General Studies. **Qualif.:** Applicants must be veterans who are Connecticut residents at the time of college enrollment and upon entry into the U.S. Armed Forces, or the children of Vietnam veterans who have been declared MIA/POW. They must also be attending a Connecticut public college.

**Funds Avail.:** Equal to tuition. **Contact:** College registrar offices.

### • 2050 • Supplemental Educational Opportunity
Grant *(Undergraduate/Grant)*

**Focus:** General studies. **Qualif.:** Applicants must be U.S. Citizens or nationals currently enrolled as undergraduate students.

**Funds Avail.:** Up to $4,000. **Contact:** Connecticut Department of Higher Education at the above address (see entry 2041).

---

**• 2051 •**
## Connecticut League for Nursing
393 Center St.                                    *Ph:* (203)265-4248
Wallingford, CT 06492-0365              *Fax:* (203)265-5311

**• 2052 • Connecticut League for Nursing
Scholarships** *(Graduate, Undergraduate/Scholarship)*

**Focus:** Nursing. **Qualif.:** Applicants must be Connecticut residents enrolled in undergraduate nursing education in an NLN-accredited Connecticut school of nursing that is a CLN agency member. B.S.N. applicants must have completed their third year of four; diploma applicants must have completed the second year of a three-year program or first year of a two-year program; RN students in upper division BSN programs must be entering their senior year of the nursing program. **Criteria:** Applicants are judged based upon financial need and scholastic ability.

**Funds Avail.:** Three scholarships ($500, $500, and $500) are awarded. **No. of Awards:** 3. **To Apply:** Applicants must submit an official academic transcript from current school and a completed reference form from the dean/director of their school. A personal interview may be requested at the discretion of the scholarship committee. **Deadline:** October 1. **Contact:** Diantha R. McMorrow, R.N., M.S.N., Executive Director, at the above address (see entry 2051).

**• 2053 •**
## Connecticut Library Association
Franklin Commons
106 Route 32                                      *Ph:* (860)885-2758
Franklin, CT 06254                              *Fax:* (860)889-1200
*URL:* http://www.lib.uconn.edu/cla

**• 2054 • Connecticut Library Association Education
Grants** *(Professional Development/Grant)*

**Purpose:** To provide an opportunity for library workers to keep up with advances in the profession and to become better providers at all levels. **Qualif.:** Applicants must be members of the Connecticut Library Association willing to share gained knowledge through an article in the *Connecticut Libraries*. **Criteria:** Applications are reviewed by a committee of librarians. Awards are based on the quality, appropriateness, and type of program.

**Funds Avail.:** Grants fund 50 to 75 percent of some expenses for continuing education programs, workshops, seminars, courses, institutes, and other types of study. The grants are not used to fund course work leading to, or any part of, an MLS degree program. **To Apply:** Applications may be submitted at any time prior to the beginning of the program of study. It takes at least eight weeks for the committee to determine an award. **Contact:** The Connecticut Library Association at the above address (see entry 2053).

**• 2055 •**
## Connecticut Student Loan Foundation
525 Brook St.                                      *Ph:* (860)257-4001
PO Box 1009                                      *Fax:* (860)563-3247
Rocky Hill, CT 06067                          *Free:* 800-237-9721
*E-mail:* cslfqamainel.cslf.org
*URL:* http://www.cslf.com

**• 2056 • (Connecticut) Federal Subsidized Stafford
Loans** *(Graduate, Undergraduate/Loan)*

**Purpose:** Loan eligibility will be determined by the financial aid office. **Qualif.:** Applicants must be United States citizens or eligible non-citizens who are enrolled (or accepted for enrollment) and making satisfactory academic progress at an approved educational institution. Applicants must also be enrolled at least half-time, meet all requirements mandated by State and Federal regulations, and must borrow from a CSLF participating lender. **Criteria:** Based on financial need.

**Funds Avail.:** Up to $2,625 for the first year of undergraduate study; up to $3,500 for the second year; and up to $5,500 per year for the third, fourth and fifth years of undergraduate study. Graduate students may receive up to $8,500 per year. Aggregate limit for undergraduate study cannot exceed $23,000. Aggregate limit for undergraduate and graduate study combined cannot exceed $65,000. A borrower may not, between the Stafford and Unsubsidized Stafford programs, receive more than the annual maximum permitted. Interest accrues during the in-school period and periods of authorized deferment. Loans are made co-payable to the borrower and institution. Repayment period begins six months after termination of a least half-time studies. The interest rate is variable and changes annually on July 1 and is capped at 8.25 percent. **To Apply:** Applications may be obtained at any financial aid office or lender. **Deadline:** During the academic period for which the loan is intended. **Contact:** College financial aid offices, lenders, or the Connecticut Student Loan Foundation at the above address (see entry 2055).

**• 2057 • Federal Unsubsidized Stafford Loan**
*(Graduate, Undergraduate/Loan)*

**Purpose:** Loan eligibility will be determined by the financial aid office. **Qualif.:** Applicants must be United States citizens or eligible non-citizens who are enrolled (or accepted for enrollment) and making satisfactory academic progress at an approved educational institution. Applicants must also be enrolled at least half-time, meet all requirements mandated by State and Federal regulations, and must borrow from a CSLF participating lender. **Criteria:** Students do not need to demonstrate need.

**Funds Avail.:** Loans are made co-payable to the borrower and institution. Repayment period begins six months after termination of a least half-time studies. Loan must be repaid in full within ten years. The interest rate is variable and changes annually every July 1. Currently, the rate is capped at 8.25 percent. **To Apply:** Applications may be obtained at any financial aid office bank, or by contacting CSLF Student Loan Foundation. **Deadline:** During the academic period for which the loan is intended. **Contact:** College financial aid offices, lenders, or the CSLF Student Loan Foundation at the above address (see entry 2055).

**• 2058 • Parent Loan for Undergraduate Students
(PLUS)** *(Undergraduate/Loan)*

**Purpose:** Parents may borrow on behalf of eligible dependent undergraduate students. **Qualif.:** Borrowers must be a United States citizens or eligible noncitizens and must borrow on behalf of a dependent student who is enrolled and making satisfactory progress or has been accepted for enrollment at an eligible post-secondary institution. Borrowers are subject to a credit evaluation performed by the lender.

**Funds Avail.:** Applicants may borrow up to the remaining need of the student (cost of attendance minus all other financial aid). **To Apply:** Application may be obtained at financial aid offices, banks, or from CSLF Student Loan Foundation **Contact:** CSLF Student Loan Foundation at the above address (see entry 2055).

---

• 2059 •
## Conservation Analytical Laboratory
Smithsonian Institution
Museum Support Center
MRC 534 *Ph:* (202)357-2627
Washington, DC 20560 *Fax:* (202)786-2777
*E-mail:* cal.web@cal.si.edu
*URL:* http://simsc.si.edu/cal/

• 2060 • **Conservation Science Fellowship**
*(Postdoctorate, Postgraduate/Fellowship)*

**Purpose:** To support research related to the care, preservation, and conservation of museum collections. **Focus:** Application of Materials Science and Chemistry to the care and/or study of museum objects. **Qualif.:** Applicant may be of any nationality. Applicant must either have a master's or doctoral degree, or have a degree or certificate of advanced training in the conservation of artifacts or art objects. Candidate's research proposal may be in any scientific discipline related to the composition of museum objects and their deterioration, the study of materials, deterioration mechanisms, and methods of preservation. Proposals from the perspectives of materials science, engineering, and chemistry will receive special consideration. Fellowships are tenable at CAL.

**Funds Avail.:** $21,000, plus $1,000 research/travel allowance. **To Apply:** Write for application guidelines. Candidates are encouraged to contact a staff member before submitting a formal proposal. **Deadline:** January 15. **Contact:** Dr. Marion F. Mecklenburg, Assistant Director for Conservation Research, at the above address (see entry 2059).

• 2061 • **Materials Analysis Fellowships**
*(Postdoctorate, Postgraduate, Professional Development/Fellowship)*

**Purpose:** To support advanced research in materials analysis related to archaeology, anthropology, art history, or history of technology. **Focus:** Archaelology, Anthropology, Art History. **Qualif.:** Candidate must have a degree or certificate of pre- or postdoctoral training in archaeology, anthropology, or art history. Candidate's proposed research must deal with the application of physical science techniques to problems in art history, anthropology, archaeology, or the history of technology. Fellowships are tenable at CAL.

**Funds Avail.:** $21,000, plus $1,000 research/travel allowance. **To Apply:** Write for application guidelines. Candidates are encouraged to contact a staff member before submitting a formal proposal. **Deadline:** January 15. **Contact:** Jacqueline S. Olin, Assistant Director for Archaeology, at the above address (see entry 2059).

---

• 2062 •
## Conservation and Research Foundation
Connecticut College, Box 5261
New London, CT 06320

• 2063 • **Conservation and Research Foundation Research Grants** *(Professional Development/Grant)*

**Purpose:** To support environmental research. **Focus:** Biology, Ecology, Environmental Sciences. **Qualif.:** Candidate may be of any nationality. Grants are tenable worldwide and are intended for research in areas that might have a favorable impact on environmental quality and that are usually neglected by larger funding agencies; projects that should be able to compete for funding from conventional granting agencies will not be considered by the Foundation. Indirect costs of research are usually not allowed by the Foundation.

**Funds Avail.:** $100-5,000. **No. of Awards:** 15. **To Apply:** Proposals are invited by the Foundation. Unsolicited proposals will not be accepted. **Deadline:** None. **Contact:** Richard H. Goodwin at the above address (see entry 2062).

---

• 2064 •
## Consortium of College and University Media Centers
121 Pearson Hall-JTC
Iowa State University *Ph:* (515)294-1811
Ames, IA 50011-2203 *Fax:* (515)294-8089
*E-mail:* ccumc@ccumc.org
*URL:* http://www.ccumc.org

• 2065 • **Consortium College University Media Centers Annual Research Grants** *(Doctorate, Graduate, Professional Development, Undergraduate/Grant)*

**Purpose:** To support research related to the improvement of media production, selection, cataloging, distribution, and/or utilization. **Focus:** Educational Media, Educational Video. **Qualif.:** Candidate may be of any nationality. Applicant must be an graduate student, faculty member, or staff person of an institutional member of the Consortium. Preference will be given to studies with general applications to the field of educational film and video.

**Funds Avail.:** $2,000. **No. of Awards:** 1-3. **To Apply:** Write to the Consortium for application guidelines. Application must include a brief description of study, proposed budget, and a resume of the investigator. **Deadline:** May 1 (each year). **Contact:** Don Rieck, Executive Director, at the above address (see entry 2064).

---

• 2066 •
## Consortium for Graduate Study in Management
200 S. Hanley, Ste. 1102 *Ph:* (314)935-5614
St. Louis, MO 63105-3415 *Fax:* (314)935-5014
*Free:* 888-658-6814
*E-mail:* cgsm@wuolin.wastl.edu
*URL:* http://www.cgsm.wustl.edu:8010/

• 2067 • **Consortium Graduate Study Management Fellowships for Minorities** *(Graduate/Fellowship)*

**Purpose:** To hasten the entry of minorities into managerial positions in business. **Focus:** Business Administration. **Qualif.:** Applicants must be U.S. citizens and members of one of the following minority groups: African-American, Hispanic, or Native

---

## Consortium for Graduate Study in Management (continued)

American. They must already have an undergraduate degree and be qualified for admission to an M.B.A. program at one of the Consortium universities. Fellowships are tenable at the business schools of the University of California at Berkeley, Indiana University, the University of Michigan, New York University, the University of North Carolina at Chapel Hill, University of Rochester, University of Southern California, the University of Texas at Austin, Washington University in St. Louis, University of Virginia, and University of Wisconsin. Fellows are selected on merit and are awarded full tuition and fees.

**Funds Avail.:** Tuition and fees. **No. of Awards:** 250. **Deadline:** January 15. **Contact:** Consortium for application materials at the above address (see entry 2066).

---

## • 2068 •
## Consulting Engineers Council of New Jersey
66 Morris Ave., Ste. 1A      Ph: (201)564-5848
Springfield, NJ 07081-1409      Fax: (201)564-7480

### • 2069 • Louis Goldberg Scholarship (Graduate/Scholarship)

**Purpose:** To encourage students to join the consulting engineer profession. **Qualif.:** Applicants must be United States citizens entering their junior, senior, or fifth year of a five-year program at a college or university accredited by the Accreditation Board for Engineering and Technology (ABET). **Criteria:** Selection is based on the student's GPA, professor recommendation, and essay.

**Funds Avail.:** A $1,000 scholarship is given in two parts, half upon award and half upon graduation. In addition, a $5,000 student of the year award and $2,500 and $1,000 awards are also presented. **To Apply:** Write for information. **Deadline:** January 15. **Contact:** Peter Allen or Virginia Maguire at the above address (see entry 2068).

---

## • 2070 •
## Contemporary Record Society
724 Winchester Rd.      Ph: (215)544-5920
Broomall, PA 19008      Fax: (215)544-5921

### • 2071 • Contemporary Record Society National Festival for the Performing Arts (Professional Development/Fellowship)

**Purpose:** To provide financially needy performance and visual artists, musicians, and writers the opportunity to participate in a two-week competition held at various campuses throughout Philadelphia and surrounding area institutions selected by CRS. **Focus:** Performing Arts, Visual Arts. **Qualif.:** Candidates may be composers, soloists, orchestra members, conductors and other musicians as well as dancers, authors, and visual artists. There are no age restrictions. **Criteria:** Fellowships for full or part tuition are given to a large number of applicants requesting financial assistance. Recipients receive solo appearances in concert on Festival sites and composers receive a performance of new prize winning work(s) chosen by the Festival Chamber Committee according to submission of performance and tape scores. During the Festival term, the Committee selects CRS National Competition winners from among the Festival participants. A distinguished selection of outstanding members will perform their compositions with the Chamber Society Festival and be featured in concert or commercial recording with record production costs covered by grants obtained by CRS.

**Funds Avail.:** Varies. **To Apply:** Instrumental and vocal artists must submit a performance tape including two or more compositions displaying technical proficiency and artistic maturity involving excerpts from solo, chamber, and orchestral repertoire. Composers must send scores or tapes and pertinent information on chamber works, large ensembles, or solo works. Conductors must submit a resume, recommendations, and a taped rehearsal or performance in ensemble, masterclass, or lecture. Dance applicants must submit resume, recommendations, and video taped performance and visual artists must submit resume and sample works. Art and dance exhibitions are held on festival grounds. All applicants must send a $25 registration fee and a self-addressed, stamped envelope if they want their material returned. **Deadline:** May 15. Festival begins July 3.

**Remarks:** Contestants must agree to waive all rights of said recording in return for the artistic exposure and cultural benefits gained. **Contact:** Festival Headquarters, CRS, at the above address (see entry 2070).

---

## • 2072 •
## Continental Society Daughters of Indian Wars
206 Springdale Dr.
La Grange, GA 30240

### • 2073 • Continental Society Daughters of Indian Wars Scholarships (Undergraduate/Scholarship)

**Purpose:** To assist Native Americans in pursuing higher education. **Focus:** General Studies. **Qualif.:** Candidates must be certified tribal members of any federally-recognized Native American Tribe. They must plan on working on a reservation, be accepted or attending an accredited college or university, and maintain a minimum grade point average of 3.0 while carrying at least ten quarter hours or eight semester hours. **Criteria:** Selection is based on financial need and, more importantly, dedication and academic excellence.

**Funds Avail.:** $500 per year. **To Apply:** Along with the application form, applicants must submit letters of recommendation, statements of financial need and career objectives, transcripts, and a list of extracurricular activities. **Deadline:** June 15. **Contact:** Eunice Connally, The Continental Society Daughters of Indian Wars, at the above address (see entry 2072).

---

## • 2074 •
## Carle C. Conway Scholarship Foundation, Inc.
95 Alexandra Dr.      Ph: (203)329-9622
Stamford, CT 06903      Fax: (203)322-3161

### • 2075 • Carle C. Conway Scholarships (Undergraduate/Scholarship)

**Qualif.:** Competition for the Conway Scholarships is open to children of Continental Can employees with at least six months of continuous service with the company and its domestic subsidiaries prior to the close of the yearly competition. All applicants must be enrolled in the first semester of their senior year of high school and scheduled to enter college in the fall. Current employees must be employed by the company at the time a recipient enters college. **Criteria:** Awards are given based on Scholastic Aptitude Test Scores, high school academic records, extracurricular activities, recommendations of high school principals and biographical data. Recipients are chosen on a competitive basis by a Scholarship Committee of educators appointed by the Educational Testing Service which administers the competition on behalf of the College Entrance Examination Board for the Foundation.

**Funds Avail.:** Awards include scholarship stipends that range up to $8,500 a year but do not cover more than the cost of tuition and related mandatory fees for four years or until a baccalaureate degree is earned, whichever is earlier. Annual renewal depends upon student's satisfactory progress. Each scholarship becomes effective when the recipient is enrolled in a college or university. Payment is made directly to the institution for credit to the recipient's account. **To Apply:** Recipients may select any course of study leading to a baccalaureate degree in any regionally accredited institution in the United States. **Deadline:** The Scholastic Aptitude Test must be taken no later than December of the senior year in high school. The Educational Testing Service must receive the application for a Conway Scholarship by mid-November. Recipients are notified in April. **Contact:** The Carle C. Conway Scholarship Foundation at the above address (see entry 2074).

---

• **2076** •

## Cooley's Anemia Foundation, Inc.

129-09 26th Ave., Ste. 203     Ph: (718)321-2873
Flushing, NY 11354     Fax: (718)321-3340
    Free: 800-522-7222
URL: http://www.stepstn.com/nord/org-sum/1161.htm

• **2077** • Cooley's Anemia Foundation Research Fellowship *(Postdoctorate/Fellowship)*

**Purpose:** To assist young investigators with research. **Focus:** Cooley's Anemia. **Qualif.:** Candidates may be of any nationality and should have completed training within the last five years. Junior faculty members do not need sponsors. Other candidates must seek the sponsorship of an experienced investigator who is a staff member of a research institute with adequate facilities. **Criteria:** Selection is based on scientific merit and pertinence to Cooley's anemia.

**Funds Avail.:** $20,000 maximum. **No. of Awards:** Varies **To Apply:** Write for application guidelines and forms. Submit twelve copies of the completed form to the national executive director. **Deadline:** March 11. **Contact:** Gina Cioffi, at the above address (see entry 2076).

---

• **2078** •

## John K. Cooper Foundation

1278 Laurel Road
RR No. 3
Sidney, BC, Canada V8L 5K8     Ph: (604)656-7848

• **2079** • John K. Cooper Ornithology Research Grants *(Doctorate, Graduate/Grant)*

**Purpose:** To provide assistance to graduate students for ornithological research. **Focus:** Ornithology. **Qualif.:** Applicant must be a Canadian student registered in an M.Sc. or Ph.D. program at a Canadian university. Proposed research project must relate to ornithology in Canada. Preference is given to projects with a large field research component. **Criteria:** Applicants are judged on study design; conservation or theoretical application; publication records ( past and future).

**Funds Avail.:** $1,000. **No. of Awards:** 3. **To Apply:** Submit a letter of application including research proposal, curriculum vitae, proof of citizenship and university registration, and supervisor's name. **Deadline:** April 1. Successful candidates are notified by April 30. **Contact:** John M. Cooper, at the above address (see entry 2078).

---

• **2080** •

## Cooperating Hampton Roads Organizations for Minorities in Engineering

PO Box 1394     Ph: (804)683-6032
Norfolk, VA 23501-1394     Fax: (804)683-6031
E-mail: kkuhla@whro.org
URL: http://www.whro.org/cl/chrome/

• **2081** • CHROME Scholarship *(Undergraduate/ Scholarship)*

**Purpose:** To support distinguished CHROME students in their pursuit of degrees in engineering, science, mathematics, or technology. **Focus:** Engineering, Science, Mathematics, Technology. **Qualif.:** Applicants must be graduating high school seniors and be participating in the CHROME program. **Criteria:** Selection is based on GPA, SAT scores, participation in CHROME activities, and financial need.

**Funds Avail.:** Varies. **Deadline:** Varies. **Contact:** Katura Carey-Harvey, Executive Director, at the above address (see entry 2080).

---

• **2082** •

## Cooperative Institute for Research in the Atmosphere

Colorado State University
Foothills Campus     Ph: (303)491-8448
Fort Collins, CO 80523     Fax: (303)491-8241

• **2083** • CIRA Fellowships in Atmospheric Science and Related Research *(Professional Development/ Fellowship)*

**Purpose:** To provide an active exchange of ideas between Fellows, NOAA, and CSU Scientists in CIRA. **Focus:** Atmospheric Science and/or Related Fields. **Qualif.:** Senior scientists, including those on sabbatical leave or recent Ph.D. recipients, are eligible. Those receiving the awards will pursue their own research programs, collaborate with existing programs, and participate in Institute seminars and functions. The program is open to scientists from all countries. **Criteria:** Selection is based on the likelihood of an active exchange of ideas between the fellows and the National Oceanic and Atmospheric Administration and Colorado State University scientists in CIRA.

**Funds Avail.:** Support from CIRA is limited to a maximum of $28,500 per year. Up to two awards are granted annually. **To Apply:** Applications should contain a curriculum vitae, publications list, brief outline of the intended research, a statement of estimated research support needs, and names and addresses of three professional references. **Deadline:** October 31.

**Remarks:** CIRA is jointly sponsored by Colorado State University and the National Oceanic and Atmospheric Administration. The Institute generally receives between 20 and 30 applications per year. **Contact:** DR.Thomas H. Vonder Haar at the above address (see entry 2082).

---

## • 2084 •
### Cooperative Institute for Research in Environmental Sciences
c/o CIRES Director
Campus Box 216
University of Colorado at Boulder        Ph: (303)492-1143
Boulder, CO 80309-0216                   Fax: (303)492-1149
E-mail: cires@cires.colorado.edu; cives@cives.colorado.edu
URL: http://cires.colorado.edu; http://cives.colorado.edu

#### • 2085 • CIRES Visiting Fellowships (Postdoctorate, Professional Development/Fellowship)

**Purpose:** To support research on problems related to enhancement of air and water quality, and prediction of weather and climate fluctuations, and global environmental change. **Focus:** Environmental Sciences, Atmospheric Chemistry and Physics, Atmospheric and Climate Dynamics, Cryospheric and Polar Processes, Environmental Chemistry and Biology, Environmental Measurements and Instrumentation, Geochemistry and Biology, Global Change, Remote Sensing. **Qualif.:** The program is open to scientists of all countries. Applicant must have a Ph.D. or the equivalent. Selection is based in part on the likelihood of interactions between the visiting fellow and the scientists at CIRES; applicants are encouraged to contact one or more senior investigators when preparing proposals. Fellowships are tenable at CIRES. **Criteria:** The university strongly supports the principle of diversity. They are particularly interested in receiving applications from women, ethnic minorities, disabled persons, veterans, and veterans of the Vietnam era.

**Funds Avail.:** $32,000/year average is available. **No. of Awards:** 5 per year. **To Apply:** Submit resume, publications list, and a brief description of proposed research to the director of the fellowship program. Three letters of recommendation must be submitted directly to CIRES from the referees. Junior applicants must submit undergraduate and graduate transcripts. **Deadline:** Materials must be in by December 15. **Contact:** Dr. Howard P. Hanson, Program Director, at the above address (see entry 2084).

## • 2086 •
### Corn Refiners Association, Inc.
1701 Pennsylvania Ave., NW, Ste.
  950                                    Ph: (202)331-1634
Washington, DC 20006                     Fax: (202)331-2054
E-mail: details@corn.org
URL: http://www.corn.org/

#### • 2087 • Corn Refiners Association Research Funds (Postdoctorate/Grant)

**Purpose:** To support research in the corn wet milling industry. **Focus:** Agriculture. **Qualif.:** The Association serves as a clearinghouse for investigators seeking support; research proposals are forwarded to member corporations in the corn industry. The Association itself does not offer any funds. Applicant may be of any nationality. Applicant must be an investigator conducting or planning to conduct research in areas of interest to the Association.

**Funds Avail.:** Varies, according to project. **To Apply:** Write for application form and guidelines. Submit form with a research pre-proposal, which will then be forwarded to member companies of the Association for their individual review. Any company with an interest in pursuing the research will contact the applicant directly. **Deadline:** None.

**Remarks:** Corn Refiners Association Graduate Fellowships are also offered to students at selected U.S. institutions. Participating universities vary; write for a current list of participants and the

fellowship selection procedures. **Contact:** Research Program at the above address (see entry 2086).

## • 2088 •
### Costume Society of America
55 Edgewater Dr.                         Ph: (410)275-1619
PO Box 73                                Fax: (410)275-8936
Earleville, MD 21919-2226                Free: 800-CSA-9447
E-mail: 71554,3201 Compuserve
URL: http://www.costumesocietyamerica.com

#### • 2089 • Stella Blum Research Grant (Graduate, Undergraduate/Grant)

**Purpose:** To support the study of North American costume through original research. **Focus:** Native American Studies, North American Costume. **Qualif.:** Applicant must be matriculating in a degree program at an accredited institution, and be a member of the Costume Society. Proposals must be for research in the field of North American costumes. Grants are tenable in the United States and selected other countries. Grants do not cover tuition, materials for coursework, salary, transportation to Society meetings, or institutional costs. Covered cost limited to project support including transportation to and from research site (away from home or school); living expenses at research site (away from home or school); supplies such as film photographic reproductions, books, paper, and computer disks; postage and telephone; and services such as typing, computer searches, graphics. **Criteria:** Creativity and innovation, specific awareness of and attention to costume matters, impact on the broad field of costume, awareness of interdisciplinarity of the field, ability to successfully implement the proposed project in a timely manner, and faculty advisor recommendation.

**Funds Avail.:** $3,000 maximum. **No. of Awards:** One. **To Apply:** Write to the Society for application form and guidelines, available in September. Submit with research proposal, budget, college transcripts, and proof of current student enrollment. Two letters of recommendation, including one from the project supervisor, must be sent directly to the Society from the referees. **Deadline:** February 1. Grant is announced in May. **Contact:** Kaye Kittle Boyer, Manager, at the above address (see entry 2088).

## • 2090 •
### Council for the Advancement of Science Writing
PO Box 404                               Ph: (516)757-5664
Greenlawn, NY 11740-0404                 Fax: (516)757-0069

#### • 2091 • Rennie Taylor/Alton Blakeslee Memorial Fellowship in Science Writing (Postdoctorate, Professional Development/Fellowship)

**Purpose:** To improve the quality of science writing through graduate study. **Focus:** Journalism. **Qualif.:** Applicant must be a U.S. citizen and a journalist who has a minimum of two years experience at a daily newspaper, wire service, news magazine, radio or television station or network. Applicant must also hold an undergraduate degree in journalism or science and demonstrate a desire to pursue science journalism or attend grad school.

**Funds Avail.:** $2,000. **To Apply:** Write to the Executive Director for application form and guidelines. Application must contain a resume, undergraduate transcripts, three letters of recommendation, three writing samples, and a statement of career goals. **Deadline:** July 1. **Contact:** Ben Patrusky, Executive Director, at the above address (see entry 2090).

## • 2092 •
### Council for Basic Education
1319 F St., NW, Ste. 900
Washington, DC 20004-1152
*E-mail:* info@c-b-e.org
*URL:* http://www.c-b-e.org

*Ph:* (202)347-4171
*Fax:* (202)347-5047

### • 2093 • Arts Education Fellowships *(Professional Development/Fellowship)*

**Purpose:** To promote the study of fine arts. **Focus:** Fine Arts. **Qualif.:** Applicant must be a U.S. citizen and be a teacher of fine arts, grades K-12.

**Funds Avail.:** $3,000. **To Apply:** Write to CBE at the above address for application form and guidelines. **Deadline:** January 7. **Contact:** Barbara M. Manzon, Program Manager, at the above address (see entry 2092).

### • 2094 • Fellowships for Basic Study in the Humanities/Fellowships for Principals *(Professional Development/Fellowship)*

**Purpose:** To provide principals with a concentrated opportunity to cultivate their love of learning and thus enhance the intellectual life of their schools. **Focus:** Education. **Qualif.:** Applicants must be full-time principals in grade K-12 and plan to continue as a principal at least five more years. Applicants must have the word "principal" or "head" in their title for at least two years, and must have completed three years of teaching, preferably in the humanities. A master's degree is required.

**Funds Avail.:** Approximately ten $2,100 grants to pursue four weeks of independent study in a humanities topic of their choice. Also included is $150 to purchase books for the their school library. **To Apply:** Write for an application. **Deadline:** First week in January. The deadline varies annually.

**Remarks:** Fellowships are funded by the National Endowment for the Humanities, with additional support form the Esther A. and Joseph Klingenstein Fund, and the DeWitt Wallace-Reader's Digest Fund. **Contact:** Elsa M. Little, Director of Fellowships, at the above address (see entry 2092).

### • 2095 • Fellowships for Independent Study in the Humanities *(Professional Development/Fellowship)*

**Focus:** Education. **Qualif.:** Teachers are eligible to apply if they are full-time teachers or librarians in grades K-12 in at least their fifth year of full-time teaching in the humanities. Special education, English as a Second Language, and reading teachers qualify. Applicants must hold a master's degree or show equivalent evidence of continuing professional growth in the humanities.

**Funds Avail.:** Fellows receive $3,000 stipends to pursue six weeks of independent study in humanities topics of their choice. An additional $200 is provided to purchase books for the fellows' school libraries. Approximately 180 fellowships are awarded. **To Apply:** Write for an application. **Deadline:** First week in January (actual data varies with year).

**Remarks:** Fellowships are funded by the National Endowment for the Humanities, with additional support from the Esther A. and Joseph Klingenstein Fund, and the DeWitt Wallace-Reader's Digest Fund. The council typically receives approximately 1,000 applications. **Contact:** Elsa M. Little, Director of Fellowships, at the above address (see entry 2092).

## • 2096 •
### Council of Citizens with Low Vision International
6511 26th St. W
Bradenton, FL 34207

*Ph:* (941)755-3846
*Fax:* (941)755-9721
*Free:* 800-733-2258

### • 2097 • Carl Foley Scholarships *(Professional Development/Scholarship)*

**Purpose:** To train professionals in the field of visual impairment. **Focus:** Visual Impairment. **Qualif.:** Grade point average, professional goals, commitment to the field.

**Funds Avail.:** Two $1,000 scholarships. **No. of Awards:** 2. **To Apply:** Write for applications before March 15 of each year. **Contact:** Council of Citizens with Low Vision, at the above address (see entry 2096).

### • 2098 • Telesensory Scholarship *(Undergraduate/Scholarship)*

**Purpose:** To assist students with low vision to obtain a postsecondary education. **Focus:** General Studies. **Qualif.:** Applicants must have low vision and participate in various organizations and activities.

**Funds Avail.:** $1,000 per year. **No. of Awards:** 2. **Deadline:** March 15. **Contact:** Teresa Blessing, at the above address (see entry 2096).

## • 2099 •
### Council of Energy Resource Tribes
1999 Broadway, Ste. 2600
Denver, CO 80202-3050

*Ph:* (303)297-2378
*Fax:* (303)296-5690

### • 2100 • CERT Scholarship *(Graduate, Undergraduate/Scholarship)*

**Purpose:** To assist American Indians pursuing degrees in the fields of engineering, physical sciences, and business. **Focus:** Business, Engineering, Science. **Qualif.:** Candidates must be American Indian graduate or undergraduate students in one of the above areas of study or a related field, and hold a grade point average of at least 3.0/4.0. They must have completed CERT's pre-college program for recently graduated high school seniors. Scholarships are tenable at any accredited university in the United States.

**Funds Avail.:** $1,000. **To Apply:** Write to the Student Services Coordinator for application form and guidelines. **Deadline:** Graduates: June 1; undergraduates: June 10. **Contact:** Student Services Coordinator, at the above address (see entry 2099).

## • 2101 •
### Council for European Studies
Columbia University
808-809 International Affairs Bldg.
New York, NY 10027-0044
*E-mail:* ces@columbia.edu
*URL:* http://www.europanet.org

*Ph:* (212)854-4172
*Fax:* (212)854-8808

*The overarching aim of Council-sponsored programs is to promote and sustain the study of contemporary Western European politics and society.*

## Council for European Studies (continued)

### • 2102 • Council for European Studies Pre-Dissertation Fellowships in the Social Sciences (Doctorate/Fellowship)

**Purpose:** To enable graduate students to pursue short-term exploratory research in Europe in order to determine the viability and to better define the scope of their proposed dissertation. **Focus:** Social Sciences, Anthropology, Economics, History. **Qualif.:** Applicants must be enrolled in a doctoral program at an American or Canadian university and must have completed the equivalent of at least two years of full-time graduate study prior to the beginning date of proposed research. Fellowships are restricted to citizens or permanent residents of the United States and citizens or landed immigrants of Canada. Eligible disciplines are anthropology (excluding archaeology), economics, history (post-1750 only), geography, political science, sociology, social psychology, and urban planning. **Criteria:** Students who are advanced in their dissertation research or whose dissertation prospectuses have received formal approval from their academic departments are ineligible.

**Funds Avail.:** Fellowships provide $3,000 for travel and living expenses. **No. of Awards:** About 12. **To Apply:** Applications must be requested by January 15. **Deadline:** Applications must be completed by February 1.

**Remarks:** Fellowship recipients must submit a written report to the Council upon their return, outlining their research in specific archives or libraries, their contacts with European scholars in their field, any problems encountered in the course of their research, and ways in which the experience has reshaped the dissertation project. **Contact:** The Council for European Studies at the above address (see entry 2101).

### • 2103 • Council for European Studies Pre-Dissertation Fellowships for Topics Related to the European Community (Doctorate/Fellowship)

**Purpose:** To enable graduate students to pursue short-term exploratory research in order to determine the viability and to better define the scope of their proposed dissertation. **Focus:** Political Science, History, Sociology, Economics. **Qualif.:** Candidates must be citizens of the United States. Doctoral candidates in the following disciplines are eligible: economics, history, political science, and sociology. Proposed topics may address any aspect of the process of European integration, including subjects related to the Treaties of Paris and Rome, as well as the Single European Act. **Criteria:** Students who are advanced in their dissertation research or whose dissertation prospectuses have received formal approval from their academic departments are ineligible.

**Funds Avail.:** Fellowships provide $3,000 for travel and living expenses. **No. of Awards:** 3. **To Apply:** Applications must be requested by January 15. **Deadline:** Applications must be completed by February 1.

**Remarks:** Fellowship recipients must submit a written report to the Council upon their return, outlining their research in specific archives or libraries, their contacts with European scholars in their field, any problems encountered in the course of their research, and ways in which the experience has reshaped the dissertation project. **Contact:** The Council for European Studies at the above address (see entry 2101).

### • 2104 •
## Council on Foreign Relations
Harold Pratt House
58 E. 68th St.
New York, NY 10021
E-mail: fellowships@cfr.org
URL: http://www.cfr.org

Ph: (212)434-9400
Fax: (212)861-2701

*The Council on Foreign Relations is a non-profit and non-partisan organization devoted to promoting improved understanding of internation affairs through the free exchange of ideas.*

### • 2105 • International Affairs Fellowships (Professional Development/Fellowship)

**Purpose:** To provide a contrasting career experience for the young foreign policy professional by supporting a variety of policy studies and active experiences in policy-making. **Focus:** Agriculture, Anthropology, Business, Economics, Foreign Policy, History, International Relations, Journalism, Law, Philosophy, Political Science, Sociology. **Qualif.:** Applicant must be a U.S. citizen or a permanent resident with application for citizenship pending. Applicant must be between the ages of 27 and 35 years. Candidates may come from the academic, business, government, and professional communities. While the Ph.D. degree or its equivalent is not a firm requirement for academic applicants, the Council will not grant fellowships to support the writing of dissertations or research toward the Ph.D., nor will its support be given to complete books or other projects on which substantial progress has been made prior to the fellowship period.

**Funds Avail.:** Varies, according to sources of income and research budget; normally does not exceed salary relinquished during the period of fellowship. **No. of Awards:** Varies. **To Apply:** Applications will be sent to qualified nominees. Nominators should provide a letter of recommendation and a curriculum vitae or resume, with the nominee's address. Individuals can nominate themselves by forwarding a curriculum vitae or resume. All applicants will be asked to write a fellowship proposal. **Deadline:** September 15 for nomination letter, October 31 for completed application. Fellowships are announced in April.

**Remarks:** Application for the fellowship is primarily by invitation, based on the recommendation of a national panel of experts, but others who inquire directly and who meet preliminary requirements may also be invited to apply without formal nomination. **Contact:** Elise Carlson Lewis, Director of Fellowship Affairs, at the above address (see entry 2104).

### • 2106 • Edward R. Murrow Fellowship for American Foreign Correspondents (Professional Development/Fellowship)

**Purpose:** To help journalists increase their competence to report and interpret events abroad, and to allow them a period for sustained analysis and writing free from the daily pressures of journalism. **Focus:** Journalism. **Qualif.:** Applicant must be a U.S. citizen and a mid-career correspondent, editor, or producer of an American newspaper, magazine, radio, or television station. Applicant either must be serving abroad now or, having recently served abroad, must plan to return to a foreign post. There are no set work requirements for the term of the fellowship, but preference will be given to those candidates who have a thorough plan of study and writing relating to foreign affairs. Fellows are expected to be in residence in New York City and to participate fully in the activities of the Council. The stipend granted the fellow will not normally exceed the amount of salary relinquished during the fellowship term.

**Funds Avail.:** $60,000 maximum. **No. of Awards:** 1. **To Apply:** Forward a brief outline of proposal with curriculum vitae to Elise Carlson Lewis at the Council. After internal review, an invitation to apply and application form may be forwarded. **Deadline:** January 5 for nomination letters; February 25 for completed applications.

Contact: Elise Carlson Lewis, Director of Fellowship Affairs, at the above address (see entry 2104).

## • 2107 •
## Council of the Humanities
122 East Pyne
Princeton University      Ph: (609)258-4713
Princeton, NJ 08544-5264      Fax: (609)258-2783
E-mail: humcounc@princeton.edu
URL: http://www.princeton.edu/~humcounc

### • 2108 • Alfred Hodder Fellowships (Professional Development/Fellowship)

Purpose: To promote independent projects by humanists in the early stages of a career. Focus: Humanities. Qualif.: Applicants may be of any nationality. Awards are intended to support independent research or creative work in the humanities, and may not be used to obtain a Ph.D. degree. The fellowship is tenable at Princeton University. Criteria: The Fellowship is designed to identify and nurture potential rather that to honor achievement. It is awarded to humanists at the early stages of their careers when they have demonstrated exceptional promise but have not yet received widespread recognition. Applicants will typically have published one or two works and will be undertaking a significant new project that would not be possible without the Fellowship.

Funds Avail.: $44,000. No. of Awards: Two. To Apply: Applicants must submit a resume, a sample of previous work (ten pages maximum), and a two- to three-page project proposal. Deadline: Postmarked November 1. Fellowship is announced in February via the internet. Contact: Dr. Carol Rigolot, Executive Director, at the above address (see entry 2107).

## • 2109 •
## Council for Instruction of Finnish for Foreigners
PO Box 293      Ph: 358 0 134 171
Pohjosranta 4 A 4      Fax: 358 0 134
SF-00171 Helsinki, Finland      17374

### • 2110 • Bilateral Scholarships (Postgraduate/Scholarship)

Purpose: To promote international cooperation in teaching and research. Focus: Culture. Qualif.: Applicant must not be older than 35 years of age; involved in post-graduate academic research for 3-9 months in a Finnish University.

Funds Avail.: $3,000-$6,000. Deadline: March 1. Contact: Division of Study Abroad Programs.

### • 2111 • Scholarships for Advanced Finnish Studies and Research (Postgraduate/Scholarship)

Purpose: To study and research the Finnish language, literature, Finno-Ugric linguistics, ethnology and folkloristics in a Finnish university. Qualif.: Applicants are assumed to have studied the relevant subjects at advanced university level.

Funds Avail.: $4,000 R 4-9 months.

## • 2112 •
## Council on International Educational Exchange
Attn: ISIC Fund
205 E. 42nd St.      Ph: (212)661-1414
New York, NY 10017-5706      Fax: (212)972-3231
E-mail: isicgrants@ciee.org
URL: http://www.ciee.org/

### • 2113 • International Student Identity Card Travel Grants for Educational Programs in Developing Countries (High School, Undergraduate/Grant)

Purpose: To encourage U.S. students considering an educational experience in a developing country. Focus: General Studies, African Studies, Asian Studies, Latin American Studies. Qualif.: Candidates must be U.S. citizens or permanent residents, who are at least 16 years old and high school or undergraduate students at the time of application. They must be participating in a educational program in an developing country in Asia, Africa, or Latin America including study abroad programs, internship/traineeship programs, independent research, or service projects in a group or as an individual. The student must be nominated by a nonprofit institution or organization. Students must be attending a council member institution or planning to participate in a program sponsored by council or one of its members. Criteria: Selection criteria include the quality of the proposed project or program, and the applicant's financial need.

Funds Avail.: Travel grants do not exceed the cost of minimum, round-trip transportation. They are given directly to the recipients, and the sponsoring institutions or organizations are notified. No. of Awards: Varies. To Apply: The application form must be accompanied by the Nominator's Endorsement Form, which is prepared by a faculty member/administrator/program director. Two letters of reference by two persons who can demonstrate the candidate's capability to complete the proposed project; an estimate of total expenses for the proposed project, other sources of financial support for the project, and the amount requested; background information about the project and the applicant; and most recent transcripts are also required. Seven copies of all required materials must be submitted by the nominator. All recipients are expected to submit a brief written report on their experiences within three months of the project's conclusion. Deadline: Students applying for awards granted in the fall of each year must begin their study or service project during the January 1 through July 31 period of the following year; filing date is no later than October 15. For awards granted in the spring the filing deadline is March 15 and projects must begin between June 1 and December 31.

Remarks: The International Student Identity Card Fund was established in 1981. Contact: Council on International Educational Exchange at the above address (see entry 2112).

## • 2114 •
## Council for International Exchange of Scholars
3007 Tilden St., NW, Ste. 5L      Ph: (202)686-7877
Washington, DC 20008-3009      Fax: (202)362-3442
E-mail: apprequest@cies.lle.org
URL: http://www.cies.org

The Council for International Exchange of Scholars (CIES), an affiliate of the American Council of Learned Societies (ACLS), administers the Fulbright Scholar Program for research and university lecturing abroad in cooperation with the U.S. Information Agency (USIA).

### • 2115 • Fulbright Senior Scholar Program (Postdoctorate/Grant)

Focus: General Studies. Qualif.: Candidates must be United States citizens and have a master's, Ph.D., or comparable professional/

## Council for International Exchange of Scholars (continued)

terminal degree, depending on award requirements; university or college teaching experience for lecturing awards; and proficiency in a foreign language (for selected assignments). There is no limit on the number of grants a single scholar can hold, but there must be a three-year interval between awards. Awards are granted in virtually all disciplines, and scholars in all academic ranks are eligible to apply. Applications are encouraged from retired faculty and independent scholars.

**Funds Avail.:** Benefits vary by country, but generally include a monthly stipend, a maintenance allowance, round-trip travel for the grantee and, for most full academic-year awards, one dependent. Stipends are in U.S. dollars and/or local currency. In many countries grants also include book and baggage allowances. **No. of Awards:** Above 800 awards are offered. **To Apply:** Applications are available March 1. Print copies and application diskettes may be requested from CIES. Award listings and application materials are also available online. **Deadline:** August 1 for all world areas. November 1 in institutional proposals for Scholar-in-Residence Program, International Education Administrators Program in Germany, Korea, Japan, and the Fulbright German Studies Seminar; January 1 for NATO Research Fellowships. **Contact:** Council for International Exchange of Scholars at the above address (see entry 2114).

## • 2116 •
## Council of Jewish Federations
730 Broadway       *Ph:* (212)475-5000
New York, NY 10003-9511      *Fax:* (212)529-5842
*URL:* http://jewishfedna.org

### • 2117 • Federation Executive Recruitment and Education Program (FEREP) Scholarships *(Graduate/Scholarship)*

**Purpose:** To assist students who are interested in careers with The Jewish Federation in the areas of social work and/or Jewish communal service and public administration. **Focus:** Social Work, Public Administration, Public Works. **Qualif.:** Applicants must have bachelors degrees, GPA's of at least 3.0, be enrolled in one of the schools/programs in the FEREP Consortium, and should be at the beginning of their careers in Jewish communal service or with federations. **Criteria:** Applicants are selected based on intellectual achievements, leadership ability and organizational skills, oral and written communication skills, poise and maturity, and commitment to Jewish community service.

**Funds Avail.:** Up to four full-tuition grants, including full cost of tuition for two years plus a stipend of up to $5,000 per year. Maximum amounts awarded each year cannot exceed $20,000. Up to 10 partial-tuition assistance grants of $7,500 per year for each of two years of graduate study are also offered. **To Apply:** Candidates must submit a completed application, attend a preliminary interview with a FEREP coordinator at the local federation, and participate in a full-day orientation. CFJ will arrange for the initial interview. **Deadline:** February 1. Finalists are chosen in mid-March and final interviews are held in April.

**Remarks:** The FEREP Scholarship recipient must make a commitment to work in Jewish Federation in North America for a minimum of 3 years upon completion of the graduate school program. Programs are offered at Baltimore Institute for Jewish Communal Service, University of Maryland School of Social Work and Community Planning, Baltimore Hebrew University, Case Western Reserve University - Mandel School of Applied Social Sciences, Cleveland College of Jewish Studies, Columbia University/Jewish Theological Seminary, Hebrew Union College/Jewish Institute of Religion, the University of Southern California - School of Social Work or Public Administration, Washington

University - George Warren Brown School of Social Work, Brandeis University - Hornstein Program in Jewish Communal Service, University of Pennsylvania/Gratz College, Yeshiva University Wurzweiler School of Social Work and University of Toronto - Faculty of Social Work. **Contact:** Lance Jacobs, CJF - Personnel Services, at the above address (see entry 2116). **Telephone:** (800) 899-4480.

## • 2118 •
## Council on Legal Education Opportunity
740 15th St. NW
Washington, DC 20005      *Ph:* (202)662-8630

### • 2119 • Council On Legal Education Opportunities *(Graduate/Scholarship)*

**Purpose:** To assist minority and economically disadvantaged students who wish to attend law school but hold less than "traditional" academic credentials. **Qualif.:** Applicants must be U.S. citizens, permanent residents, or citizens of U.S. Trust Territories who will have received a bachelor's degree by the beginning of the summer institute. **Criteria:** Selection based on financial and academic criteria.

**Funds Avail.:** Varies. Covers the cost of room, board, books, tuition and transportation to and from the host site. **To Apply:** All requests must be submitted in writing. **Deadline:** February 1.

## • 2120 •
## Council on Library Resources
1400 16th St. NW, Ste. 510      *Ph:* (202)483-7474
Washington, DC 20036-2217      *Fax:* (202)483-6410
*E-mail:* clr@cni.org

### • 2121 • CLR Fellows Program *(Professional Development/Award)*

**Purpose:** To support research and analytical studies pertinent to library operations and services, as well as other projects of importance to library professionals. **Focus:** Librarianship. **Qualif.:** Applicant must be a citizen or permanent resident of the United States or Canada and be a librarian or other professional working directly with libraries. Candidate must have institutional support for the proposed research project, including provision of leave with pay for at least a portion of the fellowship period. Fellowships are available for limited salary support; necessary travel; direct research costs; and, in some exceptional cases, the cost of course work that adds substantively to the fellow's knowledge of his/her specialized field. Grants may not be used for tuition in any degree program, for the purchase of equipment, or for indirect costs.

**Funds Avail.:** Varies, according to project. **To Apply:** Write to CLR for application guidelines; there is no official form. Submit five copies of a concise proposal, including a description of proposed study, duration of project, utility of research results, a detailed budget, plans for disseminating results, a curriculum vitae, and name of three referees. **Deadline:** March 1, October 1. The review process takes eight to twelve weeks. **Contact:** Julia Blixrud, Program Director, at the above address (see entry 2120).

### • 2122 •
### Council of Logistics Management
2805 Butterfield Rd. 200  
Oak Brook, IL 60523-1170  
*E-mail:* clmadmin@clm1.org  
*URL:* http://www.clm1.org  

*Ph:* (630)574-0985  
*Fax:* (630)574-0989

#### • 2123 • Council of Logistics Management Graduate Scholarships *(Graduate/Scholarship)*

**Purpose:** To make high-potential students aware of the opportunities and challenges that await them in a career in logistics management. **Focus:** Logistics Management. **Qualif.:** Applicants must be seniors at an accredited four-year college or university, or already enrolled in the first year of a logistics-related graduate program. **Criteria:** Based on merit-academic achievement, work experience, leadership skills and career commitment. Financial need will not be considered.

**Funds Avail.:** $1,500 scholarships. **No. of Awards:** 29. **Deadline:** April 1. **Contact:** Program Manager at the above address (see entry 2122)for additional information. Applications may be requested through Citizens' Scholarship Foundation of America at 1505 Riverview Rd., PO Box 297, St. Peter, MN 56082.

### • 2124 •
### Council for Tobacco Research - U.S.A., Inc.
900 3rd Ave., Ste. 400  
New York, NY 10022-4728  

*Ph:* (212)421-8885

#### • 2125 • Council for Tobacco Research Grants-in-Aid *(Professional Development/Grant)*

**Purpose:** Research support is provided to investigators who study biomedical science in order to gain a better understanding of human health and disease, especially in those areas related to tobacco use. **Focus:** Cellular and molecular biology of cancer, the cardiovascular and pulmonary systems, neuroscience, developmental biology, genetics and immunology. **Qualif.:** Applicants must be independent faculty-level scientists at not-for-profit institutions, generally hospitals and universities. Postdoctoral fellows may not apply, although funding for them may be sought by eligible applicants. **Criteria:** Peer-review.

**Funds Avail.:** Typical requests are in the $40,000 to $85,000 range. **No. of Awards:** Varies. **To Apply:** Contact the Council for preliminary application guidelines. **Deadline:** Preliminary applications are reviewed on an on-going basis, although deadlines are August 14 and February 14, in order to be included in the November 30 or May 31 full application deadlines. **Contact:** Arthur D. Eisenberg, Associate Research Director.

### • 2126 •
### County of Forty Mile No. 8
PO Box 160  
Foremost, AB, Canada T0X 0X0  

*Ph:* (403)867-3530  
*Fax:* (403)867-2242

#### • 2127 • County of Forty Mile Agricultural Committee Bursaries *(Undergraduate/Scholarship)*

**Qualif.:** Applicants must be area residents studying agriculture or home economics at the college or university level who plan to return to the County of Forty Mile upon completion of their studies.

**Funds Avail.:** Number of $200 awards varies. **Deadline:** September 1 and January 1. **Contact:** Agricultural Field Manager, County of Forty Mile No. 8, 2ATA.

### • 2128 •
### Court Aurora Borealis No. 1407
PO Box 203  
Grande Prairie, AB, Canada T8V 3A4  

*Ph:* (780)538-2488

#### • 2129 • Charlie Floyd Memorial Scholarship *(Undergraduate/Scholarship)*

**Purpose:** To assist with educational expenses. **Focus:** Open. **Qualif.:** Applicants must be members of Court Aurora Borealis No. 1407 or their children. **Criteria:** Selection is based on the standing of the member and a completed application.

**Funds Avail.:** One award of $750. **No. of Awards:** One annually. **To Apply:** The application is printed in the newsletter of the company. **Deadline:** October 31. **Contact:** Court Deputy, Court Aurora Borealis No. 1407, at the above address (see entry 2128).

### • 2130 •
### Cox Newspapers - Minority Journalism Scholarship
PO Box 4689  
Atlanta, GA 30302  

*Ph:* (404)526-5091  
*Fax:* (404)526-5199

#### • 2131 • Cox Minority Journalism Scholarship *(Undergraduate/Scholarship)*

**Focus:** Journalism, Mass Communication, Economics, English, Accounting, Political Science, History, Public Policy, Urban Studies, Advertising. **Qualif.:** Applicants must be graduating high school seniors in need of financial assistance, who are racial minorities from one of the public schools in Atlanta, Georgia. They must have at least a B average and an interest in pursuing a career in the newspaper industry. The recipient will attend either Georgia State University or one of the colleges in the Atlanta University Center (Clark, Spelman, Morehouse, Morris Brown).

**Funds Avail.:** All education expenses, including room, board, books, and tuition. **No. of Awards:** 1. **Deadline:** April 30.

**Remarks:** Recipients must intern at the Atlanta Journal and Constitution during all summer and holiday breaks throughout the four years of college. **Contact:** Booker T. Izell, at the above address (see entry 2130).

### • 2132 •
### Crestar Bank - Personal Financial Services Div.
PO Box 4911  
Martinsville, VA 24115  
*URL:* http://www.okeefe.com/work/crestar.htm  

*Ph:* (703)666-8343

#### • 2133 • Lester Educational Trust Loans *(Professional Development, Undergraduate/Loan)*

**Focus:** General Studies. **Criteria:** Students from the city of Martinsville and Henry, Patrick, and Franklin Counties, Virginia, will be given preference. Awards are based on grades and scholastic ability, and family finances.

**Funds Avail.:** The combined Lester and Rangeley Trusts provide in excess of $100,000 annually for loans. Loans must be repaid in full within five to seven years from the time repayment commences, which must be within one year after completion of a course of study. Simple interest is charged at the rate of 5 percent per annum. **To Apply:** Applicants for loans are interviewed by an Administrative Assistant of the Trust Department of the Bank. Written applications are reviewed by an advisory board, which is comprised of representatives of the school systems in Martinsville and the County of Henry, Patrick Henry Community College, and

## Crestar Bank - Personal Financial Services Div. (continued)

two local businessmen; this board meets annually in June. **Deadline:** Applications must be filed by May.

**Remarks:** The Lester Educational Trust and the Rangeley Educational Trust was established under the will of Mr. Lester, who had a deep interest in assisting young people in obtaining their educations. Crestar Bank serves as Trustee for the trust. **Contact:** Gladys Setliff at the above address (see entry 2132).

### • 2134 • Rangeley Educational Trust Loans (Professional Development, Undergraduate/Loan)

**Focus:** General Studies. **Criteria:** Students from the city of Martinsville and Henry, Patrick, and Franklin Counties, Virginia will be given preference. Awards are based on grades and scholastic ability.

**Funds Avail.:** The combined Lester and Rangeley Trusts provide in excess of $100,000 annually for loans. Loans must be repaid in full within five to seven years from the time repayment commences, which must be within one year after completion of a course of study. Simple interest is charged at the rate of 5 percent per annum. **To Apply:** Applicants for loans are interviewed by an Administrative Assistant of the Trust Department of the Bank. Written applications are reviewed by an advisory board, which is comprised of representatives of the school systems in Martinsville and the County of Henry, Patrick Henry Community College, and two local businessmen; this board meets annually in June. **Deadline:** Applications must be filed by May 1.

**Remarks:** The Rangeley Educational Trust was established under the will of Mr. Rangeley, who had a deep interest in assisting young people in obtaining their educations. Crestar Bank serves as Trustee for the trust. **Contact:** Gladys Setliff at the above address (see entry 2132).

## • 2135 •
## Croatian Music Institute
Hrvatski Glazbeni Zavod
Gunduliceva 6
41000 Zagreb, Croatia                    *Ph:* 41 271 066

### • 2136 • Vaclav Huml International Violin Competition Prizes (Professional Development/Prize)

**Purpose:** To recognize and encourage young violinists. **Focus:** Violin. **Qualif.:** Applicant may be of any nationality but must be a violinist between the ages of 16 and 30 years. The repertoire is fixed by the Competition and must be played from memory. All stages of the Competition are performed live and in public.

**Funds Avail.:** First prize: $2,000; second prize: $1,500; third prize: $1,000. **To Apply:** Write to the secretariat for application form and Competition rules. Submit form with birth certificate, certificates of musical education, a curriculum vitae, three photographs, and participation fee ($20). **Deadline:** November 15. The Competition is held every four years, and will next convene in January 1997.

**Remarks:** The first prize winner also participates in a Croatian concert tour. **Contact:** Secretariat at the above address (see entry 2135).

## • 2137 •
## Crohn's & Colitis Foundation of America, Inc.
386 Park Avenue South, 17th Fl.          *Ph:* (212)685-3440
New York, NY 10016-8804                  *Fax:* (212)779-4098
                                         *Free:* 800-932-2423

*E-mail:* info@ccfa.org
*URL:* http://www.ccfa.org/

### • 2138 • Crohn's & Colitis Foundation Career Development Awards (Postdoctorate/Award)

**Purpose:** To encourage the development of young outstanding scientists who wish to undertake careers of independent research in the areas of Crohn's disease and ulcerative colitis. **Focus:** Crohn's Disease (Ileitis), Ulcerative Colitis. **Qualif.:** Applicant must have an M.D. or Ph.D. degree, with at least two years of documented research interest and experience in a project directly relevant to inflammatory bowel disease. M.D. applicants should have between five and ten years total postdoctoral experience. Applicant must be sponsored by an experienced investigator at a public or private nonprofit institution, or at a government institution engaged in health care and/or health related research in the United States and its possessions. Awardees must devote at least 80% of their time to the projects. **Criteria:** Intellectual background of the applicant, applicant's research experience, mentor's track record, number of important techniques to be learned, importance of research area, and relevance to IBD.

**Funds Avail.:** Salary support up to $40,000/year, plus up to $20,000/year for supplies, technical support, etc. **To Apply:** Write to the Foundation for application form and guidelines. Submit form with budget, research proposal, curriculum vitae, and proof of support from sponsoring institution. **Deadline:** January 1, July 1.

**Remarks:** Ratio statistics are for career awards and research fellowships combined. **Contact:** Marjorie Merrick, Director of Research and Education at the above address (see entry 2137).

### • 2139 • Crohn's & Colitis Foundation Research Fellowships (Postdoctorate/Fellowship)

**Purpose:** To encourage the development of young outstanding scientists who wish to undertake careers of independent research in the areas of Crohn's Disease and ulcerative colitis. **Focus:** Crohn's Disease (Ileitis), Ulcerative Colitis. **Qualif.:** Applicant must have an M.D. or Ph.D. degree. All candidates must have a demonstrated interest and capability in research; M.D. applicants must have at least two years of postdoctoral experience, including one year of documented research interest and experience in projects directly relevant to inflammatory bowel disease. Applicant must be sponsored by an experienced investigator at a public or private nonprofit institution, or at a government institution engaged in health care and/or health related research in the United States and its possessions. Awardees must devote at least 95% of their time to the projects. **Criteria:** Intellectual background of the applicant, research experience, mentor's track record, number of important techniques to be learned, importance of the research area, relevance of research to IBD, and applicant's career objectives.

**Funds Avail.:** Up to $30,000/year in salary support. CCFA will also allow for fringe benefits according to institutional policy, not to exceed 25% of the salary. **To Apply:** Write to the Foundation for application form and guidelines. Submit form with budget, research proposal, curriculum vitae, and proof of support from sponsoring institution. **Deadline:** January 1, July 1.

**Remarks:** Ratio statistics are for career awards and research fellowships combined. **Contact:** Marjorie Merrick, Director of Research and Education, at the above address (see entry 2137).

## • 2140 • Crohn's & Colitis Foundation Research Grants (Postdoctorate/Grant)

**Purpose:** To provide financial support for innovative basic and clinical research relevant to the cause, pathogenesis, or treatment of inflammatory bowel disease. **Focus:** Crohn's Disease (Ileitis), Ulcerative Colitis. **Qualif.:** Applicant may be of any nationality. Applicant must be a qualified researcher employed by a public or private non-profit institution, or by a government institution engaged in health care and/or health related research. **Criteria:** Scientific merit, relevancy to IBD, and excellence of investigator and research environment.

**Funds Avail.:** Up to $80,000/year for direct costs. **To Apply:** Write to the Foundation for application form and guidelines. Submit 21 copies of the form with research proposal, budget, curriculum vitae, and pertinent references. **Deadline:** January 1 and July 1. **Contact:** Marjorie Merrick, Director of Research and Education at the above address (see entry 2137).

## • 2141 • Cummington Community of the Arts
10 Mountain St.
Haydenville, MA 01039-9733          Ph: (413)634-2172

### • 2142 • Cummington Community of the Arts Residencies (Professional Development/Fellowship)

**Purpose:** To provide work space and lodging for artists and writers in natural settings. **Focus:** Creative Writing, Music Composition, Performance Arts, Visual Arts. **Qualif.:** Candidate may be of any nationality. Applicant must be a composer, performance artist, choreographer, photographer, visual artist, or writer. Awards are tenable at the Cummington Community of the Arts. Residencies run year-round, from two weeks to three months. During July and August only full-month or two month residencies are available. **To Apply:** Write or phone for application form and guidelines. Submit resume with a work sample, application fee ($15), and the names of three professional references. Application will be subject to a blind review. **Deadline:** First day of month two months prior to the requested period, except July and August, which have April 1 deadline.

**Remarks:** Applicants have the option of bringing their children to the residency during July and August for the Children's Program. **Contact:** Kirk Stephens, Executive Director, at the above address (see entry 2141).

## • 2143 • Curtis Institute of Music
1726 Locust St.                    Ph: (215)893-5252
Philadelphia, PA 19103             Fax: (215)893-0194
E-mail: natecole@sprynet.com
URL: http://home.sprynet.com/sprynet/natecole/

### • 2144 • Curtis Institute of Music Scholarships (Other/Scholarship)

**Focus:** Music. **Qualif.:** The sole requirements for admission are that students demonstrate a native gift of music, a special aptitude for a chosen instrument, and personal characteristics that indicate the possibility of continuous further development. Age requirements vary according to department. **Criteria:** Personal audition.

**Funds Avail.:** Full tuition scholarships to all students. The institute does not provide funds for living expenses as part of the scholarship award. **To Apply:** Catalogues containing the application form may be obtained from the admissions office by telephone or written request. The following material must accompany the completed application form: written consent of the present teacher and the head of the music school or department; a certificate of health; one or two concert programs in which the applicant has participated (photocopies are acceptable); a non-refundable application fee of $60; confidential statements from two musicians, excluding relatives, who are qualified to judge the applicant's personal and musical talents; and the most current official transcript of high school or college. Students applying to the Bachelor of Music program must also submit Scholastic Aptitude Test scores (SAT) or TOEFL and TWE (Test of Written English) scores (for students whose language of instruction was not English). Personal auditions are required of every applicant with the exception of applicants to the Composition department. **Deadline:** January 15. **Contact:** Judi L. Gattone, Admissions and Financial Aid, at the above address (see entry 2143).

## • 2145 • Cuyahoga County Medical Foundation
c/o Academy of Medicine
6000 Rockside Woods Blvd., Ste.
150                                 Ph: (216)520-1000
Cleveland, OH 44131                 Fax: (216)520-0999

### • 2146 • Cuyahoga County Medical Foundation Scholarship (Graduate/Scholarship)

**Purpose:** To provide Cuyahoga County residents financial assistance to study medicine, dentistry, pharmacy, and nursing. **Focus:** Medicine. **Qualif.:** Applicants must be bona fide residents of Cuyahoga County and be attending an accredited professional school anywhere in the United States.

**Funds Avail.:** The Foundation offers a $1,500 scholarship in medicine; $1,500 in osteopathic medicine; $1,000 in dentistry; $600 in pharmacy; and $500 in nursing. Awards are payable on a semester basis with the first half paid in September and the second half paid in January. The second payment is made only after verification of the student's progress is received from the dean of the professional school. Winners may make a request to renew their award each year before June 1. **No. of Awards:** Dependent upon funds available. **To Apply:** Applicants must present evidence of high scholastic ability by submitting a transcript of their undergraduate college record and, if applicable, their last year's scholastic record in professional school. They must also submit a biographical statement including reasons for requesting a scholarship and why they have chosen their profession. They should send a snapshot and state their financial need as correctly as possible on the application form. If married, the spouse should also complete the form. **Deadline:** June 1. **Contact:** George D. Reitz, Secretary/Treasurer, at the above address (see entry 2145).

## • 2147 • Cymdei Thas Gymreig
Hen Dy Hapus
367 S. River St.
Wilkes Barre, PA 18702              Ph: (570)822-4871
URL: http://www.voicenet.com/~dalex/Welsh%20Society/
Welsh20%Society%20Home.html

### • 2148 • Cymdeithas Gymreig/Philadelphia Scholarships (Undergraduate/Scholarship)

**Purpose:** To financially assist the education of students of Welsh descent in the hope that they will seek membership and/or

## Cymdei Thas Gymreig (continued)

participate in the activities of the Welsh Society of Philadelphia. **Focus:** General Studies. **Qualif.:** Applicants must be of Welsh descent, beginning their undergraduate studies, and live within or intend to go to a college or university within 150 miles of metropolitan Philadelphia. **Criteria:** Selection is based on SAT or ACT scores, transcript and class ranking, academic potential, goals, activities, letter of recommendation, and participation in or membership of a Welsh organization or church. The organization will not respond to inquiries which fail to note Welsh descent and participation.

**Funds Avail.:** $500 to $1,000. **No. of Awards:** 4-6. **To Apply:** Applicants must send a self-addressed stamped envelope with inquiry and explain how they meet descent and participation criteria. **Deadline:** March 1.

**Remarks:** Financial need is not a criterion. Recipients are expected to be present at the St. David's Banquet the following year and must participate in Welsh activities in their community. **Contact:** Daniel E. Williams, Ysgrifennydd, at the above address (see entry 2147). An alternate telephone is (609)964-0891.

## • 2149 •
## Cystic Fibrosis Foundation - Office of Grants Management

6931 Arlington Rd.          Ph: (301)951-4422
Bethesda, MD 20814         Fax: (301)951-6378
                           Free: 800-344-4823

*E-mail:* rereundlich@cff.org
*URL:* http://www.cff.org

### • 2150 • CFF/NIH Funding Award (Other/Grant)

**Purpose:** To complement the granting mechanism of the N IH. Also to support CF-related research projects that have been submitted to and approved by the National Institutes of Health (NIH), but cannot be supported by available NIH funds. **Qualif.:** Applicants must fall within the upper 40th percentile with a priority score of 200 or better.

**Funds Avail.:** CFF support ranges fro $75,000 to $125,000 per year. R up to two years.

### • 2151 • Cystic Fibrosis Foundation Clinical Fellowships (Postdoctorate/Fellowship)

**Purpose:** To encourage specialized training early in a physician's career and prepare candidates for careers in academic medicine. **Focus:** Cystic Fibrosis. **Qualif.:** Applicants must be a U.S. citizens or permanent residents and be eligible for Board certification in pediatrics or internal medicine by the time the fellowship begins. Fellowships are tenable for training at one of the CFF care centers and must encompass diagnostic and therapeutic procedures, comprehensive care, and research related to cystic fibrosis.

**Funds Avail.:** Up to $55,000 ($45,00 for stipend and $10,00 for research costs. **To Apply:** Applicants and sponsors must submit a proposal of the research studies to be undertaken and other specialized training that will be offered during thie third year. **Deadline:** October 1.

**Remarks:** A fourth year of usdport is available as an option to highly qualified condidates who have received CFF support as Thir Year Fellows. Recipients who do not enter a career of academic medicine will be subject to payback provisions.

### • 2152 • Cystic Fibrosis Foundation Clinical Research Grants (Postgraduate/Grant)

**Purpose:** To offer support to clinical research projects directly related to CF treatment and care. **Qualif.:** Applicants must

demonstrate access to a sufficient number of CF patients and appropriate controls.

**Funds Avail.:** Up to $80,000 per year for up to three years may be requested for single-center clinical research grants. For multi-center clinical research, the potential award is up to $150,000 per year for up to three years. **To Apply:** A letter of intent must be submitted by potential applicants. **Deadline:** May 1 for letters of intent; October 1 for application.

### • 2153 • Cystic Fibrosis Foundation/National Institute of Diabetes and Digestive and Kidney Diseases Funding Award (Postdoctorate/Award)

**Purpose:** To support excellent CF-related research projects that have been submitted to and approved by the NIH, but cannot be supported by available NIH funds. **Qualif.:** Applicants must fall within the upper 40th percentile with a priority score of 200 or better.

**Funds Avail.:** Support for up to two years cannot exceed $75,000 annually. Investigators will be required to resubmit to the NIH. **To Apply:** Contact the Cystic Fibrosis Foundation for further information on application procedures. **Deadline:** Ongoing basis. **Contact:** The Cystic Fibrosis Foundation at the above address (see entry 2149).

### • 2154 • Cystic Fibrosis Foundation New Investigator Grants (Postdoctorate/Grant)

**Purpose:** To support promising new investigators as they establish themselves in research areas relevant to CF and to enable investigators to collect sufficient data to compete successfully for support from the NIH or other funding agencies. **Qualif.:** Applicants must be scientists starting their careers as independent researchers. Preference is given to candidates with at least two years relevant postdoctoral experience and a faculty appointment, who have not yet achieved the rank of associate professor or its equivalent. Applicants may not have served as a principal investigator or co-principal investigator on a previous research grant award nor have received an NIH Research Career Development Award. **Criteria:** Funding of awards is based on available funds, the priority score awarded each application, and the recommendations of the CFF Research and Research Training Committee, Medical Advisory Council, and the Board of Trustees. Relevance of the proposed study to issues in cystic fibrosis also is considered in determining awards.

**Funds Avail.:** Research grants may receive funding of up to $30,000 per year. Grants may be approved for up to a two-year period, but are funded for one year. Funding for the second year is contingent upon submission and approval of a Renewal Application and the availability of funds. Multiple CFF research grants held by a single investigator will not be permitted when the total combined funding exceeds $30,000. **To Apply:** An original and fifteen copies of each application must be submitted. A detailed Research Plan of no more than 15 pages in length must accompany the application. For research involving humans, animals, or recombinant DNA, certification in writing that an institutional committee has reviewed and approved the procedures must also accompany the application. Applicants should also include an original and three copies of two to four reprints of work relating to the general area of research. **Deadline:** September 1. **Contact:** The Cystic Fibrosis Foundation at the above address (see entry 2149).

### • 2155 • Cystic Fibrosis Foundation Research Fellowships (Postdoctorate/Fellowship)

**Purpose:** To allow MD's, PhD's and MD/PhD's to conduct basic or clinical research related to cystic fibrosis. **Qualif.:** Applicants must be US citizens.

**Funds Avail.:** $30,000 stipend first year; $31,000 stipend second year; and $33,000 stipend optional third year. **To Apply:** Each application for a Research Fellowship must include an original and fifteen copies of the form. In addition, the application form requires an abstract of the research plans; a lay information statement; a complete, detailed budget and a budget justification; a research plan; a biographical sketch and/or copy of the respective sponsor's curriculum vita; three letters of reference; and a letter of recommendation from the sponsor. **Deadline:** Applications must be postmarked by midnight September 1.

### • 2156 • Cystic Fibrosis Foundation Research Grants *(Other/Grant)*

**Purpose:** To encourage the development of new information that contributes to the understanding of the basic etiology and pathogeneses of CF. **Qualif.:** Consideraton will be given to those projects that provide insight into the development of information that may contribute to the development of new therapies for CF. **Criteria:** All proposals must be hypotheses driven, and sufficient preliminary data must be provided to justify CFF support.

**Funds Avail.:** $60,000 per annum. R Two years at which time a grant may be competitively renewed for an additioanl two years.

### • 2157 • Cystic Fibrosis Foundation Research Scholar Awards *(Postdoctorate/Award)*

**Purpose:** To encourage sustained commitment to cystic fibrosis research by scientists engaged in independent, creative research careers. **Focus:** Cystic Fibrosis. **Qualif.:** Applicant must be a U.S. citizen or permanent resident. Candidate must have qualifications equivalent to a National Institutes of Health Research Career Development Award recipient; that is, he/she must have a doctoral degree and some postdoctoral experience. Well-established independent investigators are ineligible. Awardee must be prepared to conduct research on full-time basis; studies may be carried out at the subcellular, cellular, animal, or patient level.

**Funds Avail.:** $100,000/year maximum, including up to $60,000/year for salary. **To Apply:** Write to the CFF Grants Department for application guidelines. A preliminary letter of intent is required before formal application materials will be forwarded. **Deadline:** Letter of intent: July 1; application: September 1. **Contact:** Grants Department at the above address (see entry 2149).

### • 2158 • Cystic Fibrosis Foundation Special Research Awards *(Postgraduate/Award)*

**Purpose:** To direct research efforts toward specific areas of CF-related research.

**Funds Avail.:** The amount and duration will be determined by the Cystic Fibrosis Foundation at the time of the announcement. **To Apply:** Telephone or write for further information on application details and procedures. **Contact:** The Cystic Fibrosis Foundation at the above address (see entry 2149).

### • 2159 • Cystic Fibrosis Foundation Student Traineeships *(Doctorate, Graduate/Award)*

**Purpose:** To introduce students to research related to cystic fibrosis. **Focus:** Cystic Fibrosis. **Qualif.:** Applicants must be students in or about to entera doctoral programs. Senior-level undergraduates planning to pursue graduate training may also apply.

**Funds Avail.:** $1500 ($1200 stipend and $300 lab expenses). **Deadline:** Applicants are accepted on an aon-going basis.

**Remarks:** Each applicant must work with a faculty sponsor on a research project trelated to CF.

### • 2160 • Cystic Fibrosis Foundation Third Year Clinical Fellowship Awards for Research Training *(Postdoctorate/Fellowship)*

**Qualif.:** Candidates are physicians who have completed two years of fellowship training related to cystic fibrosis, generally pulmonology or gastroenterology, and who seek support for a third year of training devoted to clinical or basic research related to cystic fibrosis. **Criteria:** Selection criteria include: the research potential of the candidate; the scientific merit of the proposed study; and the research environment of the training program and candidate's commitment to continued involvement with cystic fibrosis research and clinical care in an academic setting. Preference is given to those whose prior training was supported by the Cystic Fibrosis Foundation.

**Funds Avail.:** The basic stipend is $35,000. Up to $10,000 may be requested for equipment, technician salary, supplies, travel to national scientific meetings, or other related project expenses. **To Apply:** Candidates must apply on a special form available from the Foundation. Application requires a Research Plan of not more than ten pages single-sided and letters of recommendation. **Deadline:** Applications must be postmarked by midnight September 1. **Contact:** The Cystic Fibrosis Foundation at the above address (see entry 2149).

### • 2161 • Leroy Matthews Physician/Scientist Awards *(Postdoctorate/Award)*

**Purpose:** To assist outstanding, newly trained pediatricians and internists with research related to cystic fibrosis. **Focus:** Cystic Fibrosis. **Qualif.:** Applicant must be a U.S. citizen or permanent resident. Candidate must be a recent recipient of the M.D. or M.D./Ph.D. degree and must be a pediatrician or internist. Award may be used to complete sub-specialty training, develop skills as an independent investigator, or initiate a research program. Studies may be carried out at the subcellular, cellular, animal, or patient level.

**Funds Avail.:** Support ranges from $36,000 stipend, plus $10,000 for research and development for year one, to $60,000 stipend, plus $15,000 for research and development for year six. Awards increase in value annually. **To Apply:** Write to the CFF Grants Department for application guidelines. **Deadline:** September 1. **Contact:** Grants Department at the above address (see entry 2149).

### • 2162 • National Institute of Diabetes and Digestive and Kidney Diseases Fellowship Program-Sabbatical *(Postdoctorate/Fellowship)*

**Purpose:** To offer advanced research training with National Institutes of Health (NIH) staff interested in CF research areas. **Qualif.:** Applicants must be M.D.'s, Ph.D.'s, or M.D/Ph.D.'s interested in expanding and enhancing their research knowledge and skills.

**Funds Avail.:** Sabbatical funding will provide a stipend for living expenses. **To Apply:** Applicants should submit their applications directly to the NIH. **Deadline:** Ongoing. **Contact:** The National Institutes of Health or the Cystic Fibrosis Foundation at the above address (see entry 2149).

### • 2163 • Pilot and Feasibility Awards *(Other/Grant)*

**Purpose:** For developing and testing new hypotheses and/or new methods, and to support promising new investigators as they establish themselves in research areas relevant to CF. The award is not meant to support continuation of programs begun under other granting mechanisms. **Qualif.:** Proposed work must be hypothesis driven and must reflect innovative approaches to critical questions in CF research.

**Funds Avail.:** Up to $40,000 per year. R Two years.

### • 2164 • Harry Shwachman Clinical Investigator Award *(Postdoctorate/Award)*

**Purpose:** To provide research opportunities in cystic fibrosis to clinically trained physicians, and to facilitate the transition from postdoctoral training to a career in academic pediatrics. **Focus:** Cystic Fibrosis. **Qualif.:** Applicant must be a U.S. citizen or

## Cystic Fibrosis Foundation - Office of Grants Management (continued)

permanent resident. Candidate must have an M.D. degree and postdoctoral clinical training experience. Awards may be used for research that will help establish the recipient either as an independent biomedical investigator, or as a candidate for a career in academic pediatrics. Research must relate to cystic fibrosis; studies may be carried out at the subcellular, cellular, animal, or patient level.

**Funds Avail.:** Up to $60,000 per year plus $15,000 for supplies. **To Apply:** Write to the CFF Grants Department for application guidelines. **Deadline:** August 1. **Contact:** Grants Department at the above address (see entry 2149).

### • 2165 • Summer Scholarships in Epidemiology (Postdoctorate/Scholarship)

**Purpose:** To increase skills in epidemiology for MDs currently working in cystic fibrosis. **Focus:** Biostatistics, epidemiology, including clinical epidemiology and/or clinical trials. **Qualif.:** Applicants must be MDs currently working in cystitc fibrosis.

**Funds Avail.:** $2000. **Deadline:** April 1.

### • 2166 • Therapuetics Development Grants (Other/ Grant)

**Purpose:** To provide funds to businesses that will develop commercial products to benefit individuals with CF. Structured as a matching grants program funds will be awarded only if they are matched by the recipient. First the grantee will examine the scientific potential of new products under Component I. Component II studies will involve support for the continuation of Component I developments and the initiation of patient clinical studies.

**Funds Avail.:** Component I awards will be up to $100,000 per annum. Component II awards will be up to $750,000 per annum. Funds must be used for research prior to, but not including , Phase III clinical trails. **Deadline:** On-going basis.

## • 2167 •
## Dairy Management Inc.
Research Dept.
10255 W. Higgins Rd., Ste. 1900      Ph: (708)803-2000
Rosemont, IL 60018-5616      Fax: (708)803-2077
E-mail: douglasd@rosedmi.com

### • 2168 • Dairy Management Inc. Nutrition Research Projects (Other/Other)

**Purpose:** To support nutrition research that will identify and clarify nutritional attributes of dairy foods offering product positioning and/or promotion opportunities or to resolve or put into perspective nutrition/health-related concerns which consumers or health professionals may have about dairy foods. Priority areas include milkfat, fluid milk, cheese, and the image of dairy products. **Focus:** Dairy Foods, Nutrition. **Qualif.:** The primary investigator may be of any nationality, but must have a Ph.D., M.D., D.D.S., D.V.M., or other related degrees. Applicants must have an affiliation or appointment with a recognized university or research institution, preferably in the United States, and access to the necessary research facilities.

**Funds Avail.:** $40,000-60,000/year average. **To Apply:** Write for guidelines containing program descriptions and application forms. **Deadline:** August 1.

**Remarks:** Dairy Management, Inc. is the domestic and international planning and management organization responsible for increasing the demand for dairy products on behalf of America's dairy farmers. As part of DMI, national dairy council is responsible for reviewing and managing nutrition research funded by DMI. **Contact:** Douglas B. DiRienzo, Ph.D., Director, Nutrition Research at the above address (see entry 2167).

## • 2169 •
## Dallas-Fort Worth Association of Black Communicators
400 South Record St.
Dallas, TX 75202      Ph: (214)740-7163

### • 2170 • Dallas-Fort Worth Association of Black Communicators Scholarships (High School, Undergraduate/Scholarship)

**Qualif.:** Applicants must be high school seniors or college students planning a career in print or broadcast journalism, photojournalism, graphic arts, or public relations.

**Funds Avail.:** Several scholarships with a minimum value of $1,500 each. **Deadline:** March 1. **Contact:** Cheryl Smith, President, DFW/ABC at the above address (see entry 2169).

## • 2171 •
## Nathan and Harry Daly Scholarship
c/o Laurie Moritz
3 Mellon Bank Center Rm. 4000
Trust Dept.      Ph: (412)234-0023
Pittsburgh, PA 15258      Fax: (412)234-1073

### • 2172 • Nathan and Harry Daly Scholarship (Undergraduate/Scholarship)

**Focus:** General studies. **Qualif.:** Applicants must be residents of Butler County, Pennsylvania, attending or planning to attend Duquesne University. **Criteria:** Awards are determined by a committee of clergy from Butler County, Pennsylvania.

**Funds Avail.:** $3,500. **To Apply:** Write for further details. **Contact:** Nathan and Harry Daly Scholarship Foundation at the above address (see entry 2171).

## • 2173 •
## Danish Sisterhood in America
3429 Columbus Dr.
Holiday, FL 34691

### • 2174 • Danish Sisterhood in America National Scholarships (Undergraduate/Scholarship)

**Focus:** General Studies. **Qualif.:** Candidates must be members of the Danish Sisterhood or the son or daughter of a member. They must have attained high academic achievement.

**Funds Avail.:** Amount varies. **No. of Awards:** Varies. **To Apply:** Applications are available to members after November 1. **Deadline:** February 28. **Contact:** Elizabeth K. Hunter, National Vice President, at the above address (see entry 2173).

• 2175 •
## Daughter of Union Veterans of the Civil War
503 S. Walnut St.
Springfield, IL 62704

### • 2176 • GAR Living Memorial Scholarship
*(Undergraduate/Scholarship)*

**Purpose:** For descendants of Union Veterans of the Civil War. **Qualif.:** Applicant must be a junior or senior in college or university, a lineal descendant of a Union veteran, and have a satisfactory scholastic record. **Criteria:** Chosen by elected national committee of 5 in August.

**Funds Avail.:** Varies. Usually several awards of $200. **To Apply:** Must send SASE in request for application before February 1 in sophomore or junior college year and return with enclosures. **Deadline:** April 30.

• 2177 •
## Daughters of the Cincinnati
122 E. 58th St.
New York, NY 10022-1909          *Ph:* (212)319-6915

### • 2178 • Daughters of the Cincinnati Scholarships
*(Undergraduate/Scholarship)*

**Focus:** General Studies. **Qualif.:** Applicants must be seniors in high school and daughters of career officers commissioned in the Regular Army, navy, Air Force, Coast Guard, or Marine Corps (active, retired, or deceased). **Criteria:** Awards are given on the basis of merit and financial need.

**Funds Avail.:** Scholarships of up to $3,000. **No. of Awards:** 8. **To Apply:** In order to receive an application, interested students must send proof of parent's rank and branch of service. Also indicate current year in high school. SASE appreciated **Deadline:** March 15. **Contact:** The Scholarship Program at the above address (see entry 2177).

• 2179 •
## Daughters of Indian Wars - Scholarship Coordinator
Route 2
Locust Grove, OK 74352          *Ph:* (918)479-5670

### • 2180 • Continental Society Daughters of Indian Wars Scholarship *(Undergraduate/Scholarship)*

**Focus:** General studies. **Qualif.:** Applicants must be certified members of a federally recognized tribe of Native Americans, plan to work on a reservation, be accepted or attending an accredited college or university, and maintain at least a 3.0 grade point average while carrying at least ten quarter hours or eight semester hours. **Criteria:** Awards are granted based on financial need and academic excellence.

**Funds Avail.:** $500. Renewable. **No. of Awards:** 1. **To Apply:** Applicants must submit application, letters of recommendation, statements of financial need and career objective, transcripts, and an outline of extracurricular activities. **Deadline:** June 15. **Contact:** Miss Eunice Connally.

• 2181 •
## Daughters of Penelope
AHEPA Senior Women's Auxiliary
1909 Q St. NW, Ste. 500
Washington, DC 20009          *Ph:* (202)234-9741
*URL:* http://www.ahepa.org/dofpenelope

### • 2182 • Daughters of Penelope Graduate Student Award *(Graduate/Scholarship)*

**Focus:** General Studies. **Qualif.:** Candidates must be females accepted or currently enrolled in a post graduate degree program and taking a minimum of nine credit hours per academic year, and be members of the Daughters of Penelope or the Maids of Athena or have an immediate family member in the Daughters of Penelope or the Order of Ahepa in good standing for a minimum of two years. Applicants must be sponsored by their local or nearest Daughters of Penelope chapter; if there is no Daughters of Penelope chapter, the local or nearest Order of AHEPA chapter may recommend the candidate and verify the applicant. Applicants must also be residents of the United States, Canada, Greece or wherever there is an established Daughters of Penelope chapter in good standing. **Criteria:** The scholarship is awarded according to academic performance, without regard to other scholarships applicants may receive.

**Funds Avail.:** $1,500. **To Apply:** Applications must be accompanied by an official transcript, evidence of acceptance to graduate school, a recommendation from a faculty member, a recommendation from a community member, GRE scores or other general exams (Canadians use the equivalent type of testing), and a one-page essay on educational and vocational goals. In addition, applications must be verified by the president and secretary of the chapter in which they or their immediate family member holds membership. **Deadline:** June 20. Recipients are announced by July 15. **Contact:** Mrs. Effie Moon, National Chairman, Scholarship Committee, 2790 Marineview Dr., San Leandro, CA 94577.

### • 2183 • Daughters of Penelope Past Grand President's Award *(High School, Undergraduate/ Scholarship)*

**Focus:** General Studies. **Qualif.:** Candidates must be female high school seniors, recent high school graduates or undergraduates and members of the Daughters of Penelope or the Maids of Athena, have an immediate family member in the Daughters of Penelope or the Order of Ahepa in good standing for a minimum of two years. Applicants must be sponsored by their local or nearest Daughters of Penelope chapter; if there is no Daughters of Penelope chapter, the local or nearest Order of AHEPA chapter may recommend the candidate and verify the applicant. Applicants must also be residents of the United States, Canada, Greece or wherever there is an established Daughters of Penelope chapter in good standing. **Criteria:** Based on academic performance and financial need, without regard to other scholarships applicants may receive.

**Funds Avail.:** $1,500 scholarship, which is renewable at $500 per year for no more than two years. **No. of Awards:** 1. **To Apply:** Applications must be accompanied by an official transcript (high school seniors or recent graduates must include their SAT or ACT scores), a recommendation from a faculty or community member, a one-page essay about educational and career goals, and a copy of applicants' parents' IRS forms. In addition, applications must be verified by the president and secretary of the chapter in which they or their immediate family member holds membership. **Deadline:** June. Recipients are announced by Aug 1. **Contact:** Paula J. Alexander, National Chairman, Scholarship Committee, 1425 S. Marifpos Ave., Apt. 104, Los Angeles, CA 90006-4337.

*Daughters of Penelope (continued)*
### • 2184 • Kottis Family Scholarships *(Graduate/ Scholarship)*

**Focus:** General Studies. **Qualif.:** Candidates must be females accepted or currently enrolled in a post graduate degree program and taking a minimum of nine credit hours per academic year, and be a member of the Daughters of Penelope or the Maids of Athena, or have an immediate family member belong, in good standing, for a minimum of two years. Applicants must also be residents of the United States, Canada, Greece, or wherever there is an established chapter. **Criteria:** Academic performance.

**Funds Avail.:** $1,000. **No. of Awards:** 1. **To Apply:** Applications must be verified by the president and secretary of the chapter in which they or their immediate family member holds membership. **Deadline:** June 20. **Contact:** Daughters of Penelope at the above address (see entry 2181).

### • 2185 • Past Grand Presidents Award *(High School, Undergraduate/Scholarship)*

**Focus:** General Studies. **Qualif.:** Candidates must be female high school seniors or recent graduates or undergraduates and members of the Daughters of Penelope or the Maids of Athena, or have an immediate family member in the Daughters of Penelope or the Order of Ahepa in good standing for a minimum of two years. Applicants must be sponsored by their local or nearest Daughters of Penelope chapter. Applicants must also be residents of the United States, Canada, Greece or wherever there is an established Daughters of Penelope chapter in good standing. **Criteria:** The scholarship is awarded according to academic performance and financial need, without regard to other scholarships applicants may receive.

**Funds Avail.:** $1,500. **No. of Awards:** 1. **To Apply:** Applications must be accompanied by an official transcript (high school seniors or recent graduates must include their SAT or ACT scores), a recommendation from a faculty or community member, and a one-page essay on educational and career goals and a copy of applicants or parents IRS form. In addition, applications must be verified by the president and secretary of the chapter with which they or their immediate family member holds membership. **Deadline:** June 20. Recipients are announced by July 15. **Contact:** Paula J. Alexander, National Chairman, Scholarship Committee, 1425 S. Mariposa Ave., Apt. 104, Los Angeles, CA 90006-4337.

### • 2186 • Alexandra Apostolides Sonenfeld Award *(High School, Undergraduate/Scholarship)*

**Focus:** General Studies. **Qualif.:** Candidates must be female high school seniors or recent high school graduates or undergraduates and be members of the Daughters of Penelope or the Maids of Athena, have an immediate family member in the Daughters of Penelope or the Order of Ahepa in good standing for a minimum of two years. Applicants must be sponsored by their local or nearest Daughters of Penelope chapter. Applicants must also be residents of the United States, Canada, Greece or wherever there is an established Daughters of Penelope chapter in good standing. **Criteria:** Based on academic performance and financial need, without regard to other scholarships applicants may receive.

**Funds Avail.:** $1,500. **No. of Awards:** 1. **To Apply:** Applications must be accompanied by an official transcript (high school seniors or recent graduates must include their SAT or ACT scores), a recommendation from a faculty or community member, a one-page essay on educational and career goals, and a copy of applicants' parents' IRS forms. In addition, applications must be endorsed by the president and secretary of the chapter with which they or their immediate family member holds membership. **Deadline:** June 20.

### • 2187 • Sonja Stefanadis Graduate Student Award *(Graduate/Scholarship)*

**Focus:** General Studies. **Qualif.:** Candidates must be females accepted in or currently enrolled in a post graduate degree program and taking a minimum of nine credit hours per academic year. They must also be members of the Daughters of Penelope or the Maids of Athena, or have an immediate family member belong, in good standing, for a minimum of two years. **Criteria:** Academic performance without regard to other scholarships received by applicant.

**Funds Avail.:** $1,000. **No. of Awards:** 1. **To Apply:** Applications must be verified by the president and secretary of the chapter in which they or their immediate family member holds a membership. **Deadline:** June 20. Announcement made by August 1. **Contact:** Daughters of Penelope at the above address (see entry 2181).

### • 2188 •
### Shelby Cullom Davis Center for Historical Studies
Princeton Univ.
History Dept.
129 Dickinson Hall
Princeton, NJ 08544-1017

### • 2189 • Shelby Cullom Davis Center Research Fellowships *(Postdoctorate/Fellowship)*

**Qualif.:** Applicants must be highly recommended younger scholars who have finished their dissertations, as well as senior scholars with established reputations. Fellows are expected to live in Princeton.

**Funds Avail.:** Within the limits of its resources, it is the intent of the Davis Center to provide a salary that will equal, but not exceed, the normal salary paid to Fellows at their home university, up to a maximum of $56,000. The Center will pay transportation costs for Visiting Fellows without outside travel funds, and their spouses and children. The Center will allow each Visiting Fellow research expenses of up to $900 per semester, or $1,800 for the year. Those with outside support that amounts to less than their normal salary will receive sufficient additional funds from the Center to bring their salaries up to normal. Fellowships run from September to January and from February to June. **Deadline:** December 1. **Contact:** Inquiries and requests for Fellowship application forms should be addressed to the Manager, Shelby Cullom Davis Center for Historical Studies, Department of History, at the above address (see entry 2188).

### • 2190 •
### Kathryn W. and Shelby Cullom Davis Center for Russian Studies - Harvard University
| | |
|---|---|
| 1737 Cambridge St. | Ph: (617)495-4038 |
| Cambridge, MA 02138 | Fax: (617)495-8319 |

*E-mail:* daviscrs@fas.harvard.edu
*URL:* http://www.fas.harvard.edu/~daviscrs

### • 2191 • Davis Center for Russian Studies Postdoctoral Fellowships *(Postdoctorate/Fellowship)*

**Purpose:** To enable scholars to spend a semester or a year at the Davis Center, participating in its scholarly activities and conducting research on a project of his/her own choosing related to Russia the former Soviet Union and Eastern Europe. **Qualif.:** Applicants must have a Ph.D. degree and fluency in Russian. **Criteria:** Scholarly credentials and potential value of research project are considered.

**Funds Avail.:** $30,000. **No. of Awards:** 5. **Deadline:** December 31 of the preceding year. **Contact:** Fellowship Program, at the above address (see entry 2190).

---

• 2192 •

**Lady Davis Fellowship Trust**

Givat Ram
91904 Jerusalem, Israel
*E-mail:* ldft@vms.huji.ac.il
*URL:* http://sites.huji.ac.il/LDFT

*Ph:* 972 2 6512306
*Fax:* 972 2 5663848

• 2193 • **Lady Davis Graduate and Postdoctoral Fellowships** *(Doctorate, Graduate, Postdoctorate/ Fellowship)*

**Purpose:** To support research and study in Israel. **Focus:** General Studies. **Qualif.:** Candidate may be of any nationality. Applicant must either be studying toward a master's or Ph.D. degree or have completed his/her doctoral dissertation during the three years prior to application. Fellowships are tenable at the Hebrew University of Jerusalem or the Technion-Israel Institute of Technology in Haifa. Only graduate students who are enrolled in a Ph.D. program overseas are eligible for the Graduate Fellowship at the Hebrew University. Applicants for the Technion must have completed their studies with excellent grades. **Criteria:** Priority may be given to qualified applicants from Canada.

**Funds Avail.:** Tuition, plus travel and living expenses in Israel. **To Apply:** Write to the executive secretary for application form and guidelines. Submit form with curriculum vitae, transcripts, and three letters of reference. **Deadline:** November 30. **Contact:** Tova Wilk, Executive Secretary, at the above address (see entry 2192).

• 2194 • **Lady Davis Visiting Professorships** *(Postdoctorate/Other)*

**Purpose:** To encourage teaching and research in Israel by visiting scholars. **Focus:** General Studies. **Qualif.:** Candidate may be of any nationality, but preference may be given to qualified applicants from Canada. Applicant must be a full or associate professor at his/her home institution. Professorships are tenable at the Hebrew University of Jerusalem or the Technion-Israel Institute of Technology.

**Funds Avail.:** $2,500-2,700/month, plus $1,800 average allowance for travel costs. **To Apply:** Write to the executive secretary for application form and guidelines. Submit form with curriculum vitae, list of publications, and other relevant information. **Deadline:** November 30.

**Remarks:** Several organizations in other countries offer scholarships tenable at the Hebrew University and/or the Rothberg School at the University. For more details, see one of the following entries: Canadian Friends of the Hebrew University or the Hebrew University. Or contact the Jewish Agency office or Israel Aliyah Center in home country. Or write one of the following addresses: Australian Friends of the Hebrew University; 554 St. Kilda Road; Melbourne, Victoria 3004; Australia (phone 3-51-6921 or 3-529-4611). Friends of the Hebrew University; 3 St. John's Wood Road; London NW8 8RB; England. South African Friends of the Hebrew University; 86 Eloff Street, Royal St. Mary's Building; P.O. Box 4316; Johannesburg 2000; South Africa (phone 23-6632 or 23-6668). **Contact:** Tova Wilk, Executive Secretary, at the above address (see entry 2192).

---

• 2195 •

**Davis-Roberts Scholarship Fund, Inc.**

PO Box 1974
Cheyenne, WY 82003

*Ph:* (307)632-2948

• 2196 • **Davis-Roberts Scholarships** *(Undergraduate/ Scholarship)*

**Purpose:** To assist DeMolays and Jobs Daughters in the State of Wyoming with their education, providing they are attending or planning to attend college on a full-time basis. **Focus:** General Studies. **Qualif.:** Applicants must have belonged to a DeMolay Chapter or Jobs Daughter Bethel in Wyoming and be of good moral character and worthy of financial assistance. Scholarships are made available only to regularly-enrolled college students. Applicants must have average or better grades in their previous school term.

**Funds Avail.:** Scholarships average $350; amount is determined by availability. **No. of Awards:** 12 to 14 scholarships are awarded annually. **To Apply:** Formal applications must be accompanied by a letter of endorsement from a responsible person, not a relative, who can give an opinion as to the character, industry, disposition, and general worthiness of the applicant; a letter from Chapter Dad or Bethel Guardian substantiating worthiness and need; transcript of previous year's school grades; recent photograph; and a 200-word (or less) essay, in applicant's own handwriting, explaining why applicant wishes to continue his/her education. Appearance before the Educational Committee may be required. **Deadline:** June 15.

**Remarks:** Generally, 20 to 30 applications are submitted. **Contact:** Charles H. Moore at the above address (see entry 2195).

---

• 2197 •

**Deafness Research Foundation**

575 5th Ave., 11th Fl.
New York, NY 10017

*Ph:* (212)599-0027
*Fax:* (212)599-0039
*Free:* 800-535-3323

*E-mail:* drf@drf.org
*URL:* http://www.drf.org

• 2198 • **Deafness Research Foundation Grants** *(Postdoctorate/Grant)*

**Purpose:** To support research into the causes, treatment, and prevention of hearing loss and related ear disorders. **Focus:** Otology and related disciplines. **Qualif.:** Applicants may be of any nationality, but must be a qualified investigator employed by or formally attached to a U.S. or Canadian nonprofit institution, such as a university or hospital. Grants are tenable at the home institution and may be used for research expenses and some institutional overhead. Funds are not available for principal investigator's salary.

**Funds Avail.:** Up to $20,000 (including overhead). **To Apply:** Applicants may write to the medical director for application form and guidelines, available March 1. The home institution must submit the form to the Foundation on the candidate's behalf. A summary of the investigator's qualifications and a description of proposed research, including a budget and a listing of available resources should be sent with the application. **Deadline:** June 1. Notification in early December. **Contact:** D. Thane Cody, M.D., Medical Director, at the above address (see entry 2197).

• 2199 • **Otological Research Fellowships** *(Doctorate/Fellowship)*

**Purpose:** To support research into the causes, treatment, and prevention of hearing loss and related ear disorders. **Focus:** Otology and related disciplines **Qualif.:** Applicants may be of any

---

## Deafness Research Foundation (continued)

nationality, but must be a third-year medical student. Candidates must be sponsored by a U.S. or Canadian department of otolaryngology conducting otological research. The fellow may undertake related research in a discipline other than otology, but must maintain liaison with the sponsoring department. The fellowship is tenable at the end of the third year of medical school. Candidate must be assured of a place in the fourth-year class at the home institution upon conclusion of the fellowship.

**Funds Avail.:** $10,000 stipend, plus up to $3,500 for animals and consumable supplies. **To Apply:** Applicants must write to the medical director for application forms and guidelines. Written approval from the medical school, medical school transcripts, two letters of recommendation from members of the medical school faculty, and written acceptance from the sponsor are also required. **Deadline:** November 1. **Contact:** D. Thane Cody, M.D., Ph.D. Medical Director, at the above address (see entry 2197).

## • 2200 •
## DECA
1908 Association Dr.
Reston, VA 22091-1594          *Ph:* (703)860-5000
*URL:* http://lpsweb.lps.K12.co.us/schools/littleton/activities/deca.html

### • 2201 • Henry A. Applegate Scholarships
*(Professional Development/Scholarship)*

**Purpose:** To further education in marketing, merchandising, management, entrepreneurship. **Focus:** Marketing Education. **Qualif.:** Applicant need not be a U.S. citizen or permanent resident but must be a current member of DECA. Applicant must be planning a career in marketing or the teaching of marketing education.

**Funds Avail.:** $500-1,500. **No. of Awards:** 2 per state (through each state advisor). **To Apply:** Contact local office for application form and information. Submit application to DECA state advisor. State advisor will submit top applications to National DECA for final selection. **Deadline:** Application to local chapter: February 1. **Contact:** Tim Coffey at the above address (see entry 2200).

## • 2202 •
## Delaward Space Grant Consortium
University of Delaware
Bartol Research Institute
Newark, DE 19716-4793          *Ph:* (302)831-1094
                               *Fax:* (302)831-1843
*E-mail:* desgc@bartol.udel.edu
*URL:* http://www.bartol.udel.edu/~sherry/desgc

### • 2203 • Delaware NASA Space Grant Undergraduate Tuition Scholarships *(Undergraduate/Scholarship)*

**Focus:** Aerospace engineering and space science-related fields. **Qualif.:** Applicants must be U.S. citizens and undergraduate students at a DSGC institution. **Deadline:** March 1.

### • 2204 • NASA/DESGC Graduate Student Fellowships *(Graduate/Fellowship)*

**Focus:** Aerospace-related research, technology, or design. **Qualif.:** Applicants must be U.S. citizens and graduate students attending a DESGC consortium institution. **Deadline:** March 1.

### • 2205 • NASA/DESGC Undergraduate Summer Scholarships *(Undergraduate/Scholarship)*

**Purpose:** To assist students with a proven interest and aptitude in a related area of study. **Focus:** Space-related fields. **Qualif.:** Applicants must be U.S. citizens and undergraduates attending a member of affiliate institution. **Deadline:** March 1.

## • 2206 •
## Delaware Academy of Medicine, Inc.
1925 Lovering Ave.          *Ph:* (302)656-1629
Wilmington, DE 19806-2157   *Fax:* (302)656-0470

### • 2207 • Delaware Academy of Medicine Student Financial Aid Program *(Doctorate/Loan)*

**Purpose:** To assist Delawareans in the pursuit of a career in medicine, dentistry, or one of the allied health professions. **Qualif.:** Any resident of Delaware, or bona fide resident of Delaware who may have temporary residency in another state, who is enrolled as a full-time student in an accredited degree program of medicine, dentistry, or allied health fields is eligible. Principal emphasis is given to students enrolled in medical or dental school. Loans are not available for undergraduate students. **Criteria:** All loans are based on financial need and amount is determined by the Academy's Student Financial Aid Committee on an individual basis.

**Funds Avail.:** Loans range from $1,000 to $5,000 per year and are interest free during the recipient's studies. Following graduation, interest is charged at a moderate rate. All loans plus interest must be repaid, in full, five years following graduation. **To Apply:** Applicants must complete a Delaware Academy of Medicine application each year. In addition, all applicants are also required to complete a free application for federal student aid (FAFSA) financial statement each year. Applications may be requested after January 1 of each year. **Deadline:** May 15. Notification occurs in early August. **Contact:** W. Thomas Short at the above address (see entry 2206).

## • 2208 •
## Delaware Higher Education Commission
820 N. French St.          *Ph:* (302)577-3240
Wilmington, DE 19801       *Fax:* (302)577-6765
                           *Free:* 800-292-7935
*E-mail:* nholm@state.de.us
*URL:* http://www.doe.state.de.us

### • 2209 • Delaware Higher Education Benefits for Children of Veterans and Others *(Undergraduate/Grant)*

**Purpose:** To pay tuition for students whose parent(s) was killed in active duty military or state police service. **Focus:** General Studies. **Qualif.:** Applicants must be children of a deceased military veteran or state police officer whose cause of death was service connected. The applicants must have been residents in the state of Delaware for at least three consecutive years prior to application and must be between 16 and 24 years of age. They must also be attending or admitted for attendance at an educational institution beyond the high school level in a program of a maximum four-years duration. If the deceased parents were members of the military service of the United States, then they must have been official residents of Delaware at the time of their death.

**Funds Avail.:** Full tuition will be paid per academic year if the students attend a Delaware public college; if the student's major field of study is not offered at a Delaware public college, the student may receive full tuition per academic year to attend a private college in Delaware; if the student's major field of study is not offered at either a public or private college in Delaware, the state will pay the amount of tuition per academic year at the out-of-state college the student attends; however, if the student chooses to attend a Delaware private college when their major is offered at a Delaware public college, or if the student chooses to attend an out-of-state college when their major is offered at a Delaware public and/or private college, the state will pay benefits equal to the average tuition and fees of the Delaware public college which offers the major, or the average tuition and fees of the Delaware private college which offers the major, if it is not offered at a Delaware public college. **Contact:** Marilyn B. Quinn, Delaware Higher Education Commission, at the above address (see entry 2208).

## • 2210 •
### Delaware State Dental Society
1925 Lovering Ave.  **Ph:** (302)654-4335
Wilmington, DE 19806  **Fax:** (302)427-8657
*URL:* http://www.ada.org/states/delaware.html

#### • 2211 • G. Layton Grier Scholarship *(Graduate/Scholarship)*

**Focus:** Dentistry. **Qualif.:** Candidates should be from the state of Delaware and have successfully completed their first year of studies at an accredited dental school.

**Funds Avail.:** Three awards of approximately $1,000 each are awarded annually. Payment is made prior to the recipient's first semester of the sophomore year, and upon the student's acceptance by his/her dental college for the continuation of dental studies in the college's second semester courses or at a dental college that accepts a "good standing" transfer. Award payments are made by the American Fund for Dental Health and distributed to each participant by the Council on Dental Education Committee of the Delaware Dental Society. **No. of Awards:** 3. **To Apply:** Contact the Society for application information. **Deadline:** January 15. **Contact:** Dr. Peter Schaeffer at the above address (see entry 2210).

## • 2212 •
### Delius Association of Florida, Inc.
Jacksonville University
College of Fine Arts
Jacksonville, FL 32211  **Ph:** (904)744-3950

#### • 2213 • Delius Composition Contest *(Other/Award)*

**Purpose:** To foster creativity in both younger and older music composers. **Qualif.:** Applicants must be high school graduates or the equivalent. **Criteria:** A secret panel of judges selects winning compositions in three categories including vocal (solo or choral, alone or accompanied), keyboard (solo, duet, duo, etc.), and instrumental (solo and chamber music, including ensembles of up to eight players). Judges may also withhold awards in the event that no entry is judged worthy.

**Funds Avail.:** First prize is $500. Three best-of-category awards of $100 each will also be given. **To Apply:** A $20 entry fee per composer must accompany original compositions. Each composer may submit up to four works. Scores must conform to all contest rules and will not be returned unless a self-addressed, stamped envelope is included. **Deadline:** October 1.

**Remarks:** Winning compositions will be performed during the annual Delius Festival in Jacksonville, Florida. **Contact:** William McNeiland at the above address (see entry 2212).

#### • 2214 • Delius Composition Contest for High School Composers *(High School/Award)*

**Purpose:** To foster creativity in young music composers. **Qualif.:** Applicants must be high school students in 10th, 11th or 12th grade. **Criteria:** A secret panel of judges selects winners or may withhold awards in the event that no entry is judged worthy.

**Funds Avail.:** A $200 first prize and a $100 second prize are awarded. **To Apply:** A $5 entry fee must accompany all original compositions. Each composer may submit up to two works. Scores must conform to all contest rules and will not be returned unless a self-addressed stamped envelope is enclosed. A statement from a high school music teacher verifying applicant's grade level, compliance with contest rules, and originality of composition must also be submitted. **Deadline:** October 15.

**Remarks:** Works selected by judges may be performed at a special Delius Composition Contest during the annual Delius Festival in Jacksonville. **Contact:** William McNeiland at the above address (see entry 2212).

## • 2215 •
### Gladys Krieble Delmas Foundation
521 5th Ave., Ste. 1612  **Ph:** (212)687-0011
New York, NY 10175-1699  **Fax:** (212)687-8877
*E-mail:* DelmasFdtn@aol.com
*URL:* http://www.delmas.org

#### • 2216 • Venetian Research Program *(Postdoctorate, Postgraduate/Grant)*

**Purpose:** To support travel to and residence in Venice and the Veneto. Grants will be awarded for historical research on Venice and the former Venetian empire, and for study of contemporary Venetian society and culture. **Focus:** Archaeology, Architecture, Art, bibliography, economics, history, history of science, law, literature, music, political science, religion, and theater. **Qualif.:** Applicant must be a U.S. citizen or permanent resident; have some experience in advanced research; and, if a graduate student, have fulfilled at the time of application all doctoral requirements except for the completion of the dissertation. Funds are granted for research in Venice and the Veneto, and for transportation to, from, and within the Veneto.

**Funds Avail.:** $500-14,500 is available. **To Apply:** Write for filing procedure. **Deadline:** December 15. Awards are announced by April 1. **Contact:** No phone calls are accepted.

## • 2217 •
### The Delta Gamma Foundation
3250 Riverside Dr.
Columbus, OH 43221
*E-mail:* wgfr88d@prodigy.com
*URL:* http://www.deltagamma-hdqtrs.org/foundatn.html

#### • 2218 • Delta Gamma Foundation Fellowships *(Graduate/Fellowship)*

**Focus:** General Studies. **Qualif.:** Applicants must be members of Delta Gamma Fraternity who will have completed their undergraduate study and are interested in funding to continue their

*The Delta Gamma Foundation (continued)*

education. **Criteria:** Selection is based on scholastic ability, potential for achievement, and financial need.

**Funds Avail.:** Three or more $2,500 fellowships for graduate study in any chosen field are awarded annually. **To Apply:** Senior and alumnae members may apply. **Deadline:** Applications and all supporting materials must be filed by April 1. **Contact:** Grants and Loans Chairperson at the above address (see entry 2217).

**• 2219 • Delta Gamma Foundation Scholarships**
*(Undergraduate/Scholarship)*

**Focus:** General Studies. **Qualif.:** Applicants must be initiated members of a Delta Gamma collegiate chapter who have completed three semesters or five quarters of their college course and have maintained a B average or better. **Criteria:** Selection is based on scholarship chapter, and campus activities.

**Funds Avail.:** Scholarships of at least $1,000 are awarded annually. Delta Gamma Foundation also maintains one loan funds. Student Loans not to exceed $1,000 are available to Delta Gamma members, and family members of Delta Gammas. **To Apply:** Each year the Scholarships, Fellowships, and Loans Committee awards scholarships to outstanding collegiate members who have made significant contributions to both their chapter and their campus. **Deadline:** February 1. **Contact:** Scholarship Chairperson at the above address (see entry 2217).

**• 2220 •**
**Delta Omicron International Music Fraternity**
12297 W. Tennessee Pl.
Lakewood, CO 80228
*URL:* http://poe.acc.virginia.edu/~hlasf/do/

**• 2221 • Delta Omicron International Triennial Composition Competition** *(Other/Award)*

**Purpose:** To encourage composers to give their works an audience. **Focus:** Music composition. **Qualif.:** Applicants must be 18 years of age or older. **Criteria:** Awards are granted based on merit of composition.

**Funds Avail.:** $500. **No. of Awards:** 1. **To Apply:** Applicant must submit previously unpublished works not performed in public. Write for further details. **Deadline:** March of second year of triennium. **Contact:** Judith L. Eidson.

**• 2222 •**
**Delta Psi Kappa**
PO Box 90264                          *Ph:* (317)255-4379
Indianapolis, IN 46290-0264          *Fax:* (317)253-5067

**• 2223 • Delta Psi Kappa Research Awards**
*(Graduate/Award)*

**Purpose:** To further research in all areas of health, physical education, recreation, and dance. **Focus:** Health, Physical Education, Recreation, Dance. **Qualif.:** Members of Delta Psi Kappa doing research (unpublished) in any area of health, physical education, recreation, and dance are eligible.

**Funds Avail.:** $500 awarded biannually. **To Apply:** Write for application details. **Deadline:** November 15 in odd numbered years. **Contact:** Harriet Rodenberg at the above address (see entry 2222).

**• 2224 •**
**Cecil Delworth Foundation**
PO Box 25022                          *Ph:* (519)837-8846
Gruelph, ON, Canada N1G 4T4          *Fax:* (519)837-8886
*E-mail:* tlee@delworth.ca
*URL:* http://www.delworth.ca

**• 2225 • Dr. Allan P. Chan Scholarship** *(Doctorate, Graduate/Scholarship)*

**Purpose:** To support research that will benefit the Canadian floriculture industry. **Focus:** Floriculture and related disciplines. **Qualif.:** Applicant usually must be a Canadian citizen who is entering or engaged in M.Sc. or Ph.D. studies in an area that can benefit the Canadian floriculture industry. Candidates who are not Canadian citizens but are conducting research that is appropriate to the Foundation's interests may also be considered.

**Funds Avail.:** $2,000. **To Apply:** There is no application form; write to the Foundation for guidelines. Submit a description of objectives, summary of experience, and references from faculty members to the Research Education Program. **Deadline:** January 31, August 15. **Contact:** Research Education Program at the above address (see entry 2224).

**• 2226 •**
**Eben Demarest Trust**
c/o Eben Demarest Council
6831 Edgerton Ave.
Pittsburgh, PA 15208                  *Ph:* (412)362-8074

**• 2227 • Eben Demarest Fund** *(Professional Development/Grant)*

**Purpose:** To assist mature artists and archaeologists. **Focus:** Archaeology, Art, Dance, Music, Writing. **Qualif.:** Candidates may be of any nationality, but preference is given to U.S. citizens. They must be a archaeologists or creative artists at a mature stage in their career. Grant is never given for scholarship aid. Candidate must be sponsored by a nonprofit organization or institution; direct applications are not accepted. Grant is tenable worldwide. Recipient may not have outside income that exceeds amount of the grant.

**Funds Avail.:** $10,000/year. **No. of Awards:** One per year. **To Apply:** Representative from sponsoring organization must write to the secretary for nomination guidelines. **Deadline:** June 1.

**Remarks:** Award is made in quarterly payments that begin the March following the awarding of the June grant. **Contact:** Susan H. Brownlee, Secretary, at the above address (see entry 2226).

**• 2228 •**
**Dentistry Canada Fund**
1815 Alta Vista Drive
Ottawa, ON, Canada K1G 3Y6           *Ph:* (613)731-0493
*Formerly known as Canadian Fund for Dental Education.*

**• 2229 • Dental Teaching and Research Fellowships**
*(Graduate/Fellowship)*

**Purpose:** To support dental graduate students in furthering their education. **Focus:** Dentistry. **Qualif.:** Applicant must be a Canadian citizen or landed immigrant, and must have completed undergraduate work in dentistry or science. Candidate must be eligible for admission or accepted to a Canadian graduate school, and must plan to pursue a career in teaching and research at a university for a minimum of two years following fellowship tenure.

**Funds Avail.:** $1,000-6,500. **To Apply:** Write to the Fund for application form and guidelines. Submit form with transcripts and letters of support. **Deadline:** March 1. Successful candidates are notified in May. **Contact:** James Wegg, Executive Vice-President, at the above address (see entry 2228).

# • 2230 •
## Denver Area Labor Federation, AFL-CIO
202 Denver Labor Center
360 Acoma St.               Ph: (303)722-1306
Denver, CO 80223-1139      Fax: (303)722-0378

### • 2231 • Cletus E. Ludden Memorial Scholarships
(Undergraduate/Scholarship)

**Focus:** General Studies. **Qualif.:** Candidates must be either members or the children of members of a local union affiliated with the AFL-CIO Federation that has jurisdiction in Adams, Denver, Arapahoe, Jefferson, and Douglas Counties in Colorado. Applicants must graduate or have graduated from an accredited high school and must select an accredited institution of higher learning for further study.

**Funds Avail.:** Several scholarships of from $250 to $1,000 are awarded annually. **To Apply:** Applicants must submit a written essay of no more that 750 words on a topic announced each spring. Finalists are interviewed by the Scholarship Committee on their knowledge of the past, present and future of the American Labor Movement and on their ambitions and goals. The application and two letters of recommendation, one from a former or current teacher or employer and one from a union member, must be filed with the essay. Recipients are announced in June or July.

**Remarks:** This scholarship was established in honor of Cletus E. Ludden, the late President Emeritus of the Denver Area Labor Federation. **Contact:** Scholarship Committee at the above address (see entry 2230).

# • 2232 •
## Department of Chicano Studies
Attn: Administrative Adviser
University of California at Santa
  Barbara
Santa Barbara, CA 93106       Ph: (805)893-3012

### • 2233 • Chicana Dissertation Fellowship (Graduate/Fellowship)

**Purpose:** To assist promising Chicana scholars in completing their dissertations, preparing for university teaching and research, and achieving increased professional recognition and associations. **Qualif.:** Applicant must be advanced to candidacy by the beginning of the fellowship year and expect completion of the dissertation during their term of residence. Candidates must be of Mexican-American descent.

**Funds Avail.:** Total award is $18,000.00, plus benefits. **No. of Awards:** 2. **To Apply:** To apply, submit a letter of application describing progress toward the PhD (including date of advancement to candidacy), a dissertation proposal, a curriculum vitae, a writing sample, and arrange to have two letters of recommendation. **Deadline:** April 1. **Contact:** Dr. Chela Sandoval.

# • 2234 •
## Dermatology Foundation
1560 Sherman Ave., Ste. 870        Ph: (708)328-2256
Evanston, IL 60201-4808           Fax: (708)328-0509
E-mail: dfgen@dermfnd.org
URL: http://www.dermfnd.org/

### • 2235 • American Society for Dermatologic Surgery Grants (Postdoctorate/Grant)

**Purpose:** To encourage research related to dermatologic surgery. **Focus:** Dermatology. **Qualif.:** Applicant may be of any nationality, but must wish to initiate a research project related to dermatologic surgery or oncology. Candidate must be sponsored by his/her department or section head. A preceptor who has an academic appointment in a department of dermatology must agree to supervise proposed training. Grants are tenable in the United States and Canada. Award funds may not be used for indirect costs. **Criteria:** Proposals are reviewed by a Medical and Scientific committee established by the Dermatology Foundation. Recipients are ultimately chosen by the quality of the work and its usefulness to enhance the clinical practice of dermatology.

**Funds Avail.:** $10,000 maximum. **No. of Awards:** Varies from year to year. **To Apply:** Write for application form and guidelines. Submit two copies of form, layperson's statement, description of career goals, detailed proposal, and two or three letters of recommendation. The sponsor and preceptor must also submit letters of support describing the training and supervision to be provided. **Deadline:** October 15. Grants are announced in mid-winter. **Contact:** Sandra Rahn Goldman, Executive Director, at the above address (see entry 2234).

### • 2236 • Clinical Career Development Award (Postdoctorate/Award)

**Purpose:** To encourage dermatology research among junior investigators. **Focus:** Dermatology. **Qualif.:** Applicants must be clinician-scientists who are faculty members in a department or division of dermatology and who has completed initial training (2-3 year research fellowship or equivalent experience) in relevant research. They must also be devoted to pursuing a clinical investigation intended to improve clinical dermatology. Grants are tenable in the United States. Award funds may not be used for indirect costs. **Criteria:** A Medical and Scientific Committee established by the Dermatology Foundation reviews the proposals. Recipients are chosen by the quality of their research proposal and its usefulness to enhance the clinical practice of dermatology.

**Funds Avail.:** $40,000 maximum. **No. of Awards:** Varies from year to year. **To Apply:** For application forms, write to the Medical and Scientific Committee at the above address. **Deadline:** October 15. Grants are announced in mid-winter. **Contact:** Sandra Rahn Goldman, Executive Director, at the above address (see entry 2234).

### • 2237 • Dermatologist Investigator Research Fellowship Award (Postdoctorate, Postgraduate/Fellowship)

**Purpose:** To support dermatologists who desire research training and have a commitment to a career in academic dermatology and cutaneous biology. **Focus:** Dermatology. **Qualif.:** Applicants must hold an M.D., M.D.-Ph.D., or D.O. degree and have completed their dermatology residency training. Research must be conducted in the U.S. **Criteria:** Proposals are reviewed by a Medical and Scientific Committee established by the Dermatology Foundation. Recipients are ultimately chosen by the quality of the work and its usefulness to enhance the clinical practice of dermatology.

**Funds Avail.:** $25,000. **No. of Awards:** Varies from year to year. **To Apply:** Contact the Foundation for application information. **Deadline:** October 15. **Contact:** Dermatology Foundation at the above address (see entry 2234).

## Dermatology Foundation (continued)

### • 2238 • Dermatology Foundation Research Fellowships (Postdoctorate/Fellowship)

**Purpose:** To support postdoctoral research training in dermatology. **Focus:** Dermatology. **Qualif.:** Applicant may be of any nationality, but must be a researcher who holds an M.D., Ph.D., or equivalent, and is committed to a career in academic dermatology. Candidate should normally have no more than two years of training, or its equivalent, in skin research. Consideration will be given to candidates with substantial training in other areas who are entering into skin research. Candidate must be sponsored by his/her department or section head. A preceptor must agree to supervise training. Research must be conducted in the United States. Any recipient of a fellowship must spend at least 75% if their total effort in cutaneous research. **Criteria:** Proposals are reviewed by a Medical and Scientific Committee established by the Dermatology Foundation. Recipients are ultimately chosen by the quality of the work and its usefulness to enhance the clinical practice of dermatology.

**Funds Avail.:** $25,000 maximum. **No. of Awards:** Varies from year to year. **To Apply:** Write for application form and guidelines. Submit three copies of form, layperson's statement, description of career goals, detailed proposal, photograph, and two or three letters of recommendation. The sponsor and preceptor must also submit letters of support describing the training and supervision to be provided. **Deadline:** October 15. Fellowship is announced in mid-winter.

**Remarks:** The Foundation also offers a limited number of grants to initiate research projects in dermatology and cutaneous biology. Write for further details. **Contact:** Sandra Rahn Goldman, Executive Director, at the above address (see entry 2234).

### • 2239 • Dermatology Foundation Research Grants (Postdoctorate/Grant)

**Purpose:** To encourage projects in dermatology and cutaneous biology. **Focus:** Dermatology. **Qualif.:** Applicant may be of any nationality, but must wish to initiate a research project in dermatology or cutaneous biology. Candidate must be sponsored by his/her department or section head. A preceptor who has an academic appointment in a department of dermatology must agree to supervise proposed training. Grants are tenable in the United States. Award funds may not be used for indirect costs. **Criteria:** Proposals are reviewed by a Medical and Scientific Committee established by the Dermatology Foundation. Recipients are ultimately chosen by the quality of the work and its usefulness to enhance the clinical practice of dermatology.

**Funds Avail.:** $10,000 maximum. **No. of Awards:** Varies from year to year. **To Apply:** Write for application form and guidelines. Submit three copies of form, layperson's statement, description of career goals, detailed proposal, photograph, and two or three letters of recommendation. The sponsor and preceptor must also submit letters of support describing the training and supervision to be provided. **Deadline:** October 15. Grants are announced in mid-winter. **Contact:** Sandra Rahn Goldman, Executive Director, at the above address (see entry 2234).

### • 2240 • Health Care Policy Clinical Career Development Award (Doctorate/Other)

**Purpose:** To support the establishment and development of health policy careers for dermatologists. **Focus:** Dermatology. **Qualif.:** Applicants must be faculty members in a department or division of dermatology. **Criteria:** Proposals are reviewed by a Medical and Scientific Committee established by the Dermatology Foundation. Recipients are ultimately chosen by the quality of the work and its usefulness to health care policy and dermatology.

**Funds Avail.:** Stipend $40,000/year. **No. of Awards:** Varies from year to year. **To Apply:** Initial funding can be renewed (pending availability of funds) for up to two years (total of three years of support). **Deadline:** October 15. **Contact:** Dermatology Foundation at the above address (see entry 2234).

### • 2241 • Research Career Development Award (Postdoctorate/Award)

**Purpose:** To assist investigators in the transition to established careers. **Focus:** Dermatology. **Qualif.:** Applicant may be of any nationality, but must be a junior investigator in the early stages of an academic career. Applicant must be a faculty member in a department of dermatology who has experience in skin research and appropriate initial training in biomedical research. Candidate must be sponsored by his/her department or section head. A preceptor must agree to supervise training. Awardee is expected to spend at least 75% of his/her time in cutaneous research. A strong institutional commitment to the individual's career development is essential. Research must be conducted in the United States. **Criteria:** Proposals are reviewed by a Medical and Scientific Committee established by the Dermatology Foundation. Recipients are ultimately chosen by the quality of the work and its usefulness to enhance the clinical practice of dermatology.

**Funds Avail.:** $40,000/year. **No. of Awards:** Varies from year to year. **To Apply:** Write for application form and guidelines. Submit two copies of form, layperson's statement, description of career goals, detailed proposal, photograph, and two or three letters of recommendation. The sponsor and preceptor must also submit letters of support describing the training and supervision to be provided. **Deadline:** October 15. Award is announced in mid-winter.

**Remarks:** The Foundation also offers a limited number of grants to initiate research projects in dermatology and cutaneous biology. Write for further details. **Contact:** Sandra Rahn Goldman, Executive Director, at the above address (see entry 2234).

### • 2242 •
## Descendants of the Signers of the Declaration of Independence-Scholarship Committee
PO Box 224
Suncook, NH 03275-0224             *Ph:* (603)297-9770

### • 2243 • Descendants of the Signers of the Declaration of Independence Scholarship (Graduate, Undergraduate/Scholarship)

**Purpose:** To help young members in their quest for knowledge. **Focus:** General Studies. **Qualif.:** Applicants must be full-time students at a U.S. four-year college or university and be members of the Descendants of the Signers of the Declaration of Independence. **Criteria:** Quality of submitted materials.

**Funds Avail.:** Six to nine scholarships of $1,000-1,500 each. **To Apply:** Candidates should send a transcript of high school or college academic record, three letters of recommendation, a list of extracurricular activities, and a self-addressed, stamped envelope. Applicants must also provide proof of direct lineal descent to a Signer of the Declaration of Independence. **Deadline:** March 15. **Contact:** Mrs. Phillip F. Kennedy, Chairperson Scholarship Committee, at the above address (see entry 2242).

## • 2244 •
### Desk and Derrick Education Trust
c/o Linda P. Butler
6606 Chancellor     *Ph:* (713)656-3867
Spring, TX 77379     *Fax:* (713)656-7211

#### • 2245 • Desk and Derrick Educational Trust Scholarship *(Undergraduate/Scholarship)*

**Focus:** Petroleum, energy and allied industries. **Qualif.:** Applicants must have completed at least two year or are currently enrolled in the second year of undergraduate study at an accredited college or university; maintain a grade point average of 3.0 or above on a 4.0 grading system; demonstrate financial need for financial assistance in pursuing a college degree; be a citizen of the United States or Canada; and plan a career in the petroleum or an allied industry. **Criteria:** Awards are granted based on academic record and financial need.

**Funds Avail.:** $15,000. **No. of Awards:** 15. **To Apply:** Write for further details. **Deadline:** April 1. **Contact:** Linda P. Butler.

## • 2246 •
### Detroit Free Press
321 W. Lafayette Blvd.
Detroit, MI 48231

#### • 2247 • *Detroit Free Press* Minority Journalism Scholarships *(Undergraduate/Scholarship)*

**Focus:** Journalism. **Qualif.:** Applicants must be Black, Asian, Hispanic, or Native American high school students with a 3.0 GPA, living in the *Detroit Free Press* circulation area, and planning a career in writing, editing, or photojournalism. **Criteria:** Based an essay, journalism-related activities, recommendations, and academic achievement. **No. of Awards:** At least 3. **Deadline:** January.

## • 2248 •
### Dietitians of Canada
480 University Ave., Ste. 604     *Ph:* (416)596-0857
Toronto, ON, Canada M5G 1V2     *Fax:* (416)596-0603
*E-mail:* centralinfo@dietitians.ca
*URL:* http://www.dietitians.ca

#### • 2249 • Graduate Awards in Dietetics *(Graduate/ Award)*

**Purpose:** To encourage dietitians engaged in continuing education in the field of dietetics. **Focus:** Dietetics and Nutrition. **Qualif.:** Applicants must be members of the Association currently enrolled in a graduate program focusing on dietetics. **Criteria:** Academic excellence, personal and professional potential in the dietetic profession.

**Funds Avail.:** $1,000-2,500. **No. of Awards:** 4. **To Apply:** Write to the awards committee for application form and guidelines. **Deadline:** February 1.

**Remarks:** The Graduate Awards are also known as the Dietitians of Canada Memorial Award ($2,500), the McCain Foods Award ($2,500), the Sodexho Marriott Services Canada Award in Clinical Dietetics ($2,000), and the Dietitions of Canada Award ($1,000). The Marriot Award is reserved for students studying clinical dietetics. **Contact:** Awards Committee at the above address (see entry 2248).

## • 2250 •
### Direct Marketing Educational Foundation, Inc.
1120 Avenue of the Americas     *Ph:* (212)768-7277
New York, NY 10036-6700     *Fax:* (212)790-1561

#### • 2251 • Direct Marketing Institute for Professors Scholarships *(Professional Development/Fellowship)*

**Purpose:** To provide marketing faculty members with the opportunity to attend a DMEF Professor's Institute. **Focus:** Direct Marketing. **Qualif.:** Applicant must be a full-time educator who is teaching or who plans to teach direct marketing.

**Funds Avail.:** Tuition, room and board, and a small travel allowance. **No. of Awards:** Varies. **To Apply:** Write to the Vice President for application form and guidelines. **Deadline:** Varies. **Contact:** Laurie Spar, Vice President, at the above address (see entry 2250).

## • 2252 •
### The Dirksen Congressional Center
301 S. 4th St., Ste. A     *Ph:* (309)347-7113
Pekin, IL 61554-4219     *Fax:* (309)347-6432
*E-mail:* dirksencenter@ichange.com; fmackaman@perkin.net
*URL:* http://www.pekin.net/dirksen

#### • 2253 • Dirksen Congressional Research Grants *(Graduate, Postgraduate/Grant)*

**Purpose:** To promote better understanding of the U.S. Congress and its leaders. Grants program was developed to support work intended for publication in some form or for application in a teaching or policy-making setting. **Qualif.:** The competition is open to anyone with a serious interest in studying Congress. The Center seeks applications specifically from political scientists, historians, biographers, scholars of public administration or American studies, or journalists; graduate students may also apply. **Criteria:** Proposals are judged by the significance of the research project; project's design, plan of work and dissemination; the applicant's qualifications; the relationship of the project to the Center's program goals and to current work in the field; and the appropriateness of the budget request for the project's requirements.

**Funds Avail.:** Awards range from a few hundred dollars to $3,500. Grants will not be awarded for purchase of equipment or for subsidizing publication costs. Assistance with salaries of project principals is possible, limited to $1,500 per month. **No. of Awards:** 15-20 grants are available. **To Apply:** There is no standard application form. Applicants are responsible for showing the relationship between their work and the awards program guidelines. Applicants must submit: a cover sheet listing name, addresses, telephone numbers, social security number, institutional affiliation, project title and abstract, and total amount requested; a description of the project goals, methods, and intended results, demonstrating clearly its importance to award program priorities; a vita, including a list of publications; and a budget indicating how funds will be spent and the extent of matching funds available (if any). **Deadline:** Application materials must be postmarked by April 30; notification by June 15.

**Remarks:** Grant recipients must agree to acknowledge support in all publications or presentations incorporating research conducted with grant funds, furnish The Center with a copy of any book, article, or other publication incorporating research conducted with grant funds, and cooperate in future studies conducted by the Center to evaluate the grants program. **Contact:** Frank Mackaman, Executive Director, at the above address (see entry 2252).

*The Dirksen Congressional Center (continued)*

• 2254 • **Robert H. Michel Civic Education Grants**
*(Other/Grant)*

**Purpose:** To provide funding for practical classroom strategies to improve the quality of teaching and learning about civics. **Focus:** Education. **Qualif.:** Applicants must be teachers (4th through 12th grades), community and junior college faculty, and college and university faculty, teacher-led student teams, and individuals who develop curriculum.

**Funds Avail.:** $30,000 to be split between the eligible groups.

• 2255 •
**Disabled American Veterans - Department of New York**
PO Box 108           **Ph:** (315)635-9289
Baldwinsville, NY 13027-0108    **Fax:** (315)635-0026
*E-mail:* retiredsch@hotmail.com; Glep105815@aol.com;
  glep105815@aol.com
*URL:* http://www.eint.com/retiredsch/default.htm

• 2256 • **Department of New York Scholarship**
*(Undergraduate/Scholarship)*

**Focus:** General studies. **Qualif.:** Applicants must be honorably discharged wartime disabled veterans, their spouses, children or grandchildren. **Criteria:** Awards are granted based on academic achievement, community service, school participation (clubs/activities), and SAT/ACT scores.

**Funds Avail.:** $500 per award. **No. of Awards:** 60. **To Apply:** Applicants must submit a completed application form, grade transcript, letters of recommendation, and letter of separation (DD214). **Deadline:** April 15. **Contact:** George Le Porte, Scholarship Committee Chair.

• 2257 •
**The Walt Disney Studios**
500 S. Buena Vista St.
Burbank, CA 91521-0880      **Ph:** (818)560-6894
*E-mail:* stu-ops@disney.com
*URL:* http://stu-ops.disney.com/welcome.htm

• 2258 • **The Walt Disney Studios Fellowship Program** *(Professional Development/Fellowship)*

**Purpose:** To seek out and employ culturally and ethnically diverse new writers. **Focus:** Feature and television writing. **Qualif.:** Open to all writers. No previous experience necessary.

**Funds Avail.:** $30,000; Fellows outside Los Angeles area also will be provided with airfare and one month's accomodations. **No. of Awards:** Approximately 10 to 15. **To Apply:** Contact the program administrator for application, letter of agreement and program guidelines. **Deadline:** April 1-26.

**Remarks:** Writers with WGA credits may apply through the WGA Human Resources Department, (310)205-2548. **Contact:** Program Administrator, at the above address (see entry 2257).

• 2259 •
**District of Columbia Public Schools**
Carver Administration Bldg.
4501 Lee St., NE         **Ph:** (202)724-4934
Washington, DC 20019     **Fax:** (202)724-4940
*E-mail:* Renard@mercury.k12.dc.us
*URL:* http://www.k12.dc.us/schools.htm/

• 2260 • **Martha V. Johnson Memorial Scholarship**
*(Undergraduate/Scholarship)*

**Focus:** General Studies. **Qualif.:** Applicants must be high school students attending the District of Columbia Public Schools. They must exhibit academic potential and financial need. **Deadline:** Applications are accepted continually. **Contact:** Annabelle F. Strayhorn, Director of Student Affairs, at the above address (see entry 2259).

• 2261 •
**The Dobie-Paisano Project**
The Graduate School
The University of Texas at Austin   **Ph:** (512)471-7213
Austin, TX 78712-1191     **Fax:** (512)471-7620
*E-mail:* GSAN5@UTXDP.DP.UTEXAS.EDU

• 2262 • **Dobie-Paisano Fellowships** *(Other/Fellowship)*

**Purpose:** The fellowship is primarily for creative writing. It is not suitable for those who are looking for academic and research opportunities. **Focus:** Writing, Poetry, Journalism. **Qualif.:** This fellowship is open to native Texans, individuals who have lived in Texas at least 2 years, or individuals whose work focuses on Texas and the Southwest.

**Funds Avail.:** Awards include residence at the ranch and a stipend of approximately $7,200. The house is furnished and utilities and maintenance are provided by the University of Texas at Austin. Two fellowships are awarded annually, the Jesse Jones Writing Fellowship and the Ralph A. Johnston Memorial Fellowship. **No. of Awards:** 85-100. **To Apply:** A formal application must be filed. **Deadline:** An application and a sample of the author's work must be submitted by the fourth Friday in January. Announcement of the award is made by May 1. Recipients take up residence August 1.

**Remarks:** Since 1967, books, short stories, magazine articles, and poetry have been created by Paisano fellows. There are generally between 85 and 100 applicants for the fellowships. **Contact:** Audrey N. Slate, Coordinator, at the above address (see entry 2261).

• 2263 •
**Dog Writers' Educational Trust**
c/o Mary Ellen Tarman
D.W.E.T. Secretary
PO Box E
Hummelstown, PA 17036-0199   **Ph:** (717)566-7030

• 2264 • **Dog Writers' Educational Trust Scholarships** *(Graduate, Undergraduate/Scholarship)*

**Purpose:** To provide scholarships for young people desiring a college education who are interested in the world of dogs or who have participated in the junior handling classes at dog shows in the United States or Canada. **Focus:** General Studies, Journalism, Animal Science and Behavior, Veterinary Science and Medicine.

Qualif.: Applicants or close relatives must have been active as dog breeders, exhibitors, judges or club officers. Applicants must be enrolled in or about to enter college. Criteria: Preference is given to those students who are active in the sport of dogs. In addition, awards will be given based on involvement with dog-related activities, scholastic ability (students should be in the top third of their class), financial need, and character, including humane attitude, all-around ability and the potential to contribute to society.

Funds Avail.: Varies. Award recipients must accept within 30 days and furnish, in writing, the name and address of the college or university where the award should be sent. A check will be forwarded to the school's financial aid officer by August 15. No. of Awards: Varies. To Apply: Applicants must submit 5 copies of a complete typed application, scholastic records for the past three years, including official transcripts and academic test scores, a typed 250 word statement of the applicants personal goals in college and thoughts on a career; a typed essay of not more than 250 words entitled "Why People Own Dogs"; and a $25.00 application fee payable to the Dog Writers' Educational Trust. Deadline: December 31. Contact: Mary Ellen Tarman, Executive Secretary, at the above address (see entry 2263).

## • 2265 •
### Dolphins Scholarship Foundation
5040 Virginia Beach Blvd., Ste. 104A    Ph: (757)671-3200
Virginia Beach, VA 23462    Fax: (757)671-3330
URL: http://www.subnet.com/fdsf.htm

### • 2266 • Dolphin Scholarship (Undergraduate/ Scholarship)

Purpose: To reward academic excellence and provide financial assistance to dependent sons and daughters of members or former members of the U.S. Navy's Submarine Force. Qualif.: Candidates must be unmarried dependent sons or daughters (up to age 24) of members or former members of the Submarine Force who have qualified in submarines and served in the Submarine Force for at least five years. Children of navy members who have served in submarine support activities for a minimum of six years (the six years need not be consecutive) are also eligible. Qualifying time must have been served on active duty. There is no minimum period of service for children of personnel who died on active duty while in the Submarine Force. Students must be working toward a BA or BS degree at a four-year college. Criteria: Based equally upon academic performance, non-academic excellence, and financial need.

Funds Avail.: 100 scholarships of $2,000 each are maintained each year; approximately 25 new scholarships are awarded annually. Scholarships are renewable. To Apply: A business-sized self-addressed, stamped envelope should accompany requests for further information and/or application forms. Deadline: April 15. Contact: Tomi Roeske, Secretary, Dolphin Scholarship Foundation, at the above address (see entry 2265).

## • 2267 •
### Dong Ji Hoi Society
Scholarship Committee
142 Circle Dr.
Wahiawa, HI 96786
   Ph: (808)621-9433

### • 2268 • Dr. Syngman Rhee Scholarship (Undergraduate/Scholarship)

Purpose: To help Korean students further their education. Focus: General studies. Qualif.: Applicants must be residents of Hawaii who have 50% Korean ancestry, and must be undergraduate or college-bound high school seniors. Criteria: Awards are given based on GPA and SAT scores, and community service. No. of Awards: Approximately 10. To Apply: Applicants must write for details. Deadline: June 30. Contact: S.K. Kim.

## • 2269 •
### Donrey Media Group
c/o Jodie Long, Manager
Recruitment and Training
PO Box 17017
Fort Smith, AR 72917-7017

### • 2270 • Donrey Media Group Internships (Other/ Internship)

Focus: Journalism.

Funds Avail.: Salary equal to an entry level reporter. No. of Awards: 30. Deadline: December 31.

## • 2271 •
### Dow Chemical Canada Inc.
Corporate Benefits    Ph: (519)339-3606
Sarnia, ON, Canada N7T 7K7    Fax: (519)339-3587

### • 2272 • Dow Chemical Canada Higher Education Awards (Undergraduate/Scholarship)

Focus: General Studies. Qualif.: Applicants should be dependents of Dow Chemical Canada Inc. employees and retirees. It is intended to assist students enrolled in a Canadian university or college post-secondary program of at least two years duration leading to a degree, diploma, or certificate. Foreign institutions will be considered on an individual basis. Criteria: Based upon academic achievement. No. of Awards: As many as apply and qualify. To Apply: Applicants must submit transcripts and a copy of their acceptance letter from a Canadian university or college. Deadline: July 15. Contact: Dow Chemical Canada Inc., at the above address (see entry 2271).

## • 2273 •
### The Dow Jones Newspaper Fund
PO Box 300    Ph: (609)452-2820
Princeton, NJ 08543-0300    Fax: (609)520-5804
E-mail: newsfund@wsj.dowjones.com
URL: http://www.dj.com/newsfund

### • 2274 • Business Reporting Intern Program for College Sophomores and Juniors (Undergraduate/ Internship, Scholarship)

Focus: Journalism. Qualif.: Applicants must be minority sophomore and juniors students and US citizens.

Funds Avail.: Internship consists of regular wages from the newspapers for which they work. A $1000 scholarship is payed to the students' colleges or universities after completion of the internship. No. of Awards: Up to 12. Deadline: November 15.

Remarks: All interns attend a pre-internship training program.

## The Dow Jones Newspaper Fund (continued)

### • 2275 • Editing Internships (Graduate, Undergraduate/Internship)

**Purpose:** To provide students with the opportunity to work as copy editors for daily newspapers, online newspapers, or real-time financial news services. **Focus:** Journalism. **Qualif.:** Applicant must be a U.S. citizen. Candidate must be a full time graduate student or a junior or senior undergraduate. Internship is tenable in the summer at a U.S. daily newspaper. **Criteria:** Based on application info, essay and test.

**Funds Avail.:** $1,000 scholarship and regular wages paid by the newspaper. **No. of Awards:** Approximately 100 **To Apply:** Write for application form available between July 15 and November 1. **Deadline:** November 15. **Contact:** Dow Jones Newspaper Fund at the above address (see entry 2273).

### • 2276 • Online Newspaper Intern Program (Graduate, Undergraduate/Internship, Scholarship)

**Purpose:** Offers college students the opportunity to work for online newspapers. Allows interns to attend a preinternship training program. **Focus:** Newspaper journalism. **Qualif.:** Open to college juniors, seniors or graduate students.

**Funds Avail.:** Interns are paid whatever wage is offered by the participating newspaper. They also receive a $1000 scholarship upon returning to school. **No. of Awards:** 20. **Deadline:** Applications are available from September 1 through November 1. Deadline for receipt is November 15.

### • 2277 •
## Lord Dowding Fund for Humane Research
261 Goldhawk Road     *Ph:* 181 846 9777
London W12 9PE, England     *Fax:* 181 846 9712

### • 2278 • Lord Dowding Grant (Doctorate, Graduate/ Grant)

**Purpose:** To aid research aimed at reducing the number of animals used in laboratories. **Focus:** Biology, Medicine, Toxicology, Veterinary Medicine, Computer Sciences. **Qualif.:** Candidate may be of any nationality. Applicants must not be users of laboratory animals. There are no other restrictions placed on proposed research. Grant is tenable in the United Kingdom. M.Sc. scholars are discouraged from applying.

**Funds Avail.:** Maximum amount to date is full funding for three years, including salaries. **To Apply:** Contact the Science Researcher for "The Guidelines for Applicants" and application form. **Deadline:** January 1, April 1, July 1, and October 1. **Contact:** Ali Gray, Science Researcher, at the above address (see entry 2277).

### • 2279 •
## Dramarists Guild Fund, Inc.
330 W. 42nd St.
New York, NY 10036     *Ph:* (212)268-1208

### • 2280 • Dramatists Guild Fund Scholarships (Professional Development/Grant, Loan)

**Qualif.:** Applicants must be non-profit theater companies and workshops, playwrights, composers and lyricists facing personal emergencies. **Criteria:** Awards are granted based on financial need. Funds are not available for long-range career assistance or subsidize writing or production of plays.

**Funds Avail.:** Grants range form $7500 to $500. $35,000 available for loans. **No. of Awards:** 60. **To Apply:** Write for further details. **Deadline:** None. **Contact:** Susan Drury.

### • 2281 •
## Dublin Institute for Advanced Studies
10 Burlington Road     *Ph:* 1 668 0748
Dublin 4, Ireland     *Fax:* 1 668 0561

### • 2282 • Dublin Institute for Advanced Studies Research Scholarships (Postdoctorate/Scholarship)

**Purpose:** To train advanced scholars in methods of research. **Focus:** Astronomy, Celtic Studies, Cosmic Physics, Geophysics, Theoretical Physics. **Qualif.:** Applicant may be of any nationality, but must have a Ph.D. in a field appropriate for study at one of the Institute's three schools: Celtic Studies, Theoretical Physics, and Cosmic Physics. When appointed, each scholar is expected to pursue a definite line of research under the direction of one of the senior professors. Scholars are required to attend the Institute full time. No elementary teaching is given by the Institute. Candidate should be reasonably fluent in English.

**Funds Avail.:** $9,000-13,000/year. **To Apply:** Request application forms from the registrar. Submit with two letters of reference and evidence of ability to carry out original reference. **Deadline:** March 31.

**Remarks:** A maximum of six scholarships are awarded in each of the Institute's schools. Dublin Institute Small Grants are also available to scholars traveling from outside Great Britain and Ireland for the expense of moving to the Institute. **Contact:** Registrar at the above address (see entry 2281).

### • 2283 •
## Simone and Cino del Duca Foundation
10, rue Alfred de Vigny
75008 Paris, France     *Ph:* 1 47 66 01 21

### • 2284 • del Duca Foundation Maintenance and Travel Grants (Professional Development/Grant)

**Purpose:** To encourage biomedical research and the development of the French scientific community. **Focus:** Cardiology, Neurosciences and related disciplines, including Cellular Biology, Epidemiology, Mental Health, Molecular Biology, Pathology, Pharmacology, Psychiatry. **Qualif.:** Candidate may be of any nationality. Research workers at all levels of experience are eligible to apply, provided that their scientific activity concentrates on either the cardiovascular system or the nervous system, behavior, and mental health. Award recipients who are French must study abroad; all other awardees must conduct research in French laboratories. Travel grants and maintenance grants are rarely awarded together to a single investigator. Grants from the Foundation may not be held concurrently with similar awards from other organizations. Funds are not available for conferences or to non-French researchers already resident in France.

**Funds Avail.:** Varies, according to travel costs or experience. **To Apply:** Write to the Foundation for application form and guidelines. Submit form, including list of publications and description of proposed research. Travel grant applications must also include proof of ability to finance research. **Deadline:** March 15. Notification in June. **Contact:** Secretariat at the above address (see entry 2283).

**• 2285 •**
**Dumbarton Oaks**
1703 32nd St., NW
Washington, DC 20007          *Ph:* (202)339-6410
*URL:* http://www.doaks.org

**• 2286 • Bliss Prize Fellowship in Byzantine Studies**
*(Graduate/Fellowship)*

**Focus:** Byzantine Studies. **Qualif.:** Candidates must be in the last year of undergraduate education or have a recent B.A., have completed at least one year of ancient or medieval Greek, and be applicants to graduate school in any field of Byzantine studies. Awards are normally restricted to students currently enrolled in U.S. or Canadian universities or colleges.

**Funds Avail.:** The non-residential Bliss Prize in Byzantine studies provides graduate school tuition and living expenses (as estimated by the graduate school in which the successful candidate enrolls) for two academic years, plus up to $5,000 for study travel during the intervening summer to areas that are important to the understanding of Byzantine civilization and culture. Students who have successfully completed two years as Bliss Prize Fellows, have fulfilled all preliminary requirements for a higher degree, and are working on a dissertation are awarded a Junior Fellowship at Dumbarton Oaks, the year being determined by Dumbarton Oaks, in consultation with the student and academic advisor. **No. of Awards:** One. **To Apply:** Students must first be nominated by their advisors. Candidates must then send ten complete, collated sets of the application letter, writing sample, and personal and scholarly data. They must also send undergraduate transcripts and two letters of recommendation from scholars other than their academic advisor. **Deadline:** Candidates must be nominated by their advisors by October 15. Applications must be postmarked by November 1. Recipients are notified in February. Awards must be accepted by March 15.

**Remarks:** The Dumbarton Oaks Research Library and Collection occupies building and grounds in the Georgetown area of Washington, DC. It has important research resources in Byzantine studies, Pre-Columbian studies, and the history of landscape architecture. **Contact:** Office of the Director at the above address (see entry 2285).

**• 2287 • Dumbarton Oaks Project Grants**
*(Professional Development/Grant)*

**Focus:** Byzantine Studies, Area and Ethnic Studies, Pre-Columbian Studies, Landscape Architecture and Design, Architecture. **Qualif.:** Applicants must be conducting research in Byzantine studies, Pre-Columbian studies, or studies in landscape architecture. Support is generally for archeological research, as well as for the recovery, recording, and analysis of materials that would otherwise be lost. Eligible projects may include, but are not limited to, excavation of a site or component site, materials analysis of works of art or excavated material, and systematic campaigns to survey or photograph monuments and objects that are at risk. **Criteria:** Selection is based on the ability and preparation of the principal project personnel, including knowledge of the requisite languages, and interest and value of the project to the specific field of study.

**Funds Avail.:** Award amounts average from $3,000-10,000. **No. of Awards:** 7-10. **To Apply:** Applicants must send ten complete, collated sets of their application letter, proposal, and personal and professional data. In addition, they must have recommendations from three scholars commenting on the qualifications of the principal project personnel and the interest and value of the project to the specified field of study. **Deadline:** November 1.

**Remarks:** Project awards are not offered purely for the purpose of travel, nor for work associated with a degree, for library or archive research, for catalogues, or for conservation and restoration per se. **Contact:** Officer of the Director at the above address (see entry 2285).

**• 2288 • Fellowships in Byzantine Studies, Pre-Columbian Studies and Landscape Architecture**
*(Doctorate, Graduate, Postdoctorate, Undergraduate/Fellowship)*

**Focus:** Byzantine Studies, Pre-Columbian Studies, Landscape Architecture and Design. **Qualif.:** Residential fellowships are offered at three different levels. The junior fellowship is for students who have fulfilled all preliminary requirements for a Ph.D. and will be working on a dissertation or final project under the direction of a faculty member at their university. Regular fellowships are for scholars who hold a doctorate or have done comparable advanced work and wish to pursue independent research at Dumbarton Oaks. Applications will also be accepted from graduate students who expect to have the Ph.D. in hand prior to taking up residence at Dumbarton Oaks. Summer fellowships are for scholars at any level. All Fellows are expected to communicate satisfactorily in English. **Criteria:** Fellowships are awarded based on scholarly ability and preparation, interest and value of the study or project, and the project's relevance to the resources of Dumbarton Oaks.

**Funds Avail.:** Fellowship awards range from approximately $17,600 for an unmarried Junior Fellow to a maximum of $37,700 for a Fellow from abroad accompanied by family members. Support includes a stipend of $13,370 for a Junior Fellow or $24,315 for a Fellow for the full academic year, housing, $1,825 (if needed) to assist with the cost of bringing and supporting dependents, a research expense allowance of $860 for the year, lunch on weekdays, and the Dumbarton Oaks contribution to health insurance. Travel expense reimbursement for the lowest available airfare, up to a maximum of $1,300, may be provided for Fellows if support cannot be obtained through other sources. Awards are prorated for appointments shorter than the academic year. Summer fellowships are awarded for periods of six to nine weeks and provide a maintenance allowance of $180 per week, housing at the Fellows Building or in a Dumbarton Oaks rented apartment, lunch on weekdays, health insurance, and travel expense reimbursement up to $1,300. No housing allowances or dependents' allowances for families are available in the summer. Fellowships are not renewable, and may not be extended. **No. of Awards:** Twenty for an academic year and a semester, or approximately 12-14 for the summer semester. **To Apply:** Applicants must send ten complete, collated sets of the application letter, proposal, and personal and professional data. Junior Fellow applicants only must have their university registrar send an official transcript of their graduate record. All applicants must have three references (two for Summer Fellowships) sent. One of the three letters for Junior Fellows must be from the faculty advisor. **Deadline:** Applications are due November 1. Recipients are notified in February. Awards must be accepted by March 15.

**Remarks:** The Dumbarton Oaks Research Library and Collection occupies building and grounds in the Georgetown area of Washington, DC. It has important research resources in Byzantine studies, Pre-Columbian studies and history of landscape architecture. **Contact:** Office of the Director at the above address (see entry 2285).

**• 2289 •**
**Dunkin' Donuts Charitable Trust**
c/o Allied Domecq Retailing, USA
14 Pacella Park Dr.          *Ph:* (781)961-4000
Randolph, MA 02368-1756          *Fax:* (781)986-9954
*E-mail:* lrankin@adrus.com
*URL:* http://www.franchise1.com/comp/dunkin1.html

**• 2290 • Dunkin' Donuts Charitable Trust Scholarships** *(Undergraduate/Scholarship)*

**Purpose:** To provide educational assistance for dependent children of Dunkin' Donuts, Baskin Robbins, or Togo's corporate

## Dunkin' Donuts Charitable Trust (continued)

employees or franchise owners. **Focus:** General Studies. **Qualif.:** Candidates must be dependents of employees of Dunkin' Donuts, Baskin Robbins, or Togo's or dependents of franchise owners of these establishments in the United States. **Criteria:** Selections are based on overall academic accomplishments and financial need.

**Funds Avail.:** $1,000. **No. of Awards:** 16. **To Apply:** Application forms can be requested at the above address. **Deadline:** April 30. **Contact:** Lin Rankin, at the above address (see entry 2289).

---

## • 2291 •
### Dysautonomia Foundation Inc.

20 E. 46th St., Rm. 302　　　　　　*Ph:* (212)949-6644
New York, NY 10017　　　　　　　*Fax:* (212)682-7625
*URL:* http://www.ortge.ufl.edu/fyi/v23n11/fyi025.html

### • 2292 • Dysautonomia Research Grants
*(Postdoctorate/Grant)*

**Purpose:** To fund research into the treatment and cure for familial dysautonomia. **Focus:** Dysautonomia. **Qualif.:** Candidate may be of any nationality. Applicant must be a postdoctoral researcher. Research may be conducted at any recognized medical and/or teaching institution worldwide.

**Funds Avail.:** $10,000-20,000. **To Apply:** Write to the executive director for application form and guidelines. Submit 12 copies and one original of the application, including project summary, abstract, detailed budget, project personnel biographical data, and a research plan of no more than five pages in length. **Deadline:** March 15. Notification is made by June 30. **Contact:** Lenore F. Roseman, Executive Director, at the above address (see entry 2291).

---

## • 2293 •
### EAA Aviation Foundation

Education Office
PO Box 3065
Oshkosh, WI 54903-3065　　　　　*Ph:* (920)426-6815
*E-mail:* education@eaa.orgm
*URL:* http://web.eaa.org

### • 2294 • Herbert L. Cox Memorial Scholarship
*(Undergraduate/Scholarship)*

**Focus:** Aviation. **Qualif.:** Applicants must be accepted or attending a four-year accredited college or university in pursuit of a degree leading to an aviation profession. **Criteria:** Awards are made based on financial need.

**Funds Avail.:** $500 per award. Renewable. **No. of Awards:** 1. **To Apply:** Applicants must submit a completed application form; $5 application fee; one page letter of application describing self, activities, goals and needs for financial assistance; two or more recommendations by individuals from school, aviation community, clergy or others; transcripts; verification of financial need through college or university financial aid offices; and any other materials pertinent to the application. **Deadline:** May 1. **Contact:** EAA Aviation Foundation at the above address (see entry 2293).

### • 2295 • EAA Aviation Achievement Scholarship
*(Undergraduate/Scholarship)*

**Focus:** Aviation. **Qualif.:** Applicants must be active in sport aviation endeavors.

**Funds Avail.:** $500 per award. **No. of Awards:** 2. **To Apply:** Applicants must submit a completed application form; $5 application fee; one page letter of application describing self, activities, goals and needs for financial assistance; two or more recommendations by individuals from school, aviation community, clergy or others; transcripts; and any other materials pertinent to the application. **Deadline:** May 1. **Contact:** EAA Aviation Foundation at the above address (see entry 2293).

### • 2296 • The Payzer Scholarship *(Undergraduate/Scholarship)*

**Focus:** Engineering, mathematics, physical or biological sciences. **Qualif.:** Applicants must be students accepted or enrolled in an accredited college, university, or post-secondary school with an emphasis on technical information.

**Funds Avail.:** $5000. **No. of Awards:** 1.

### • 2297 • Spartan School of Aeronautics Scholarship
*(Undergraduate/Scholarship)*

**Focus:** Aeronautics. **Qualif.:** Applicants must be seeking careers in aeronautics and attend Spartan School of Aeronautics.

**Funds Avail.:** $1,000 - $3,000 per award. **No. of Awards:** 1. **To Apply:** Applicants must submit a completed application form; $5 application fee; one page letter of application describing self, activities, goals and needs for financial assistance; two or more recommendations by individuals from school, aviation community, clergy or others; transcripts; and any other materials pertinent to the application. **Deadline:** May 31.

**Remarks:** This scholarship will not be available in 1999/2000.

### • 2298 • Teledyne Continental Aviation Excellence
Scholarship *(Undergraduate/Scholarship)*

**Focus:** Aviation. **Qualif.:** Applicants must be pursuing careers in any field of aviation. **Criteria:** Awards are made based on excellence in personal and aviation accomplishments.

**Funds Avail.:** $500 per award. **No. of Awards:** 1. **To Apply:** Applicants must submit a completed application form; $5 application fee; one page letter of application describing self, activities, goals and needs for financial assistance; two or more recommendations by individuals from school, aviation community, clergy or others; transcripts; and any other materials pertinent to the application. **Deadline:** May 1. **Contact:** EAA Aviation Foundation at the above address (see entry 2293).

### • 2299 • Richard Lee Vernon Aviation Scholarship
*(Undergraduate/Scholarship)*

**Focus:** Aviation. **Qualif.:** Applicants must be pursuing training leading to a professional aviation occupation. **Criteria:** Awards are made based on academic achievement and financial need.

**Funds Avail.:** $500 per award. **No. of Awards:** 1. **To Apply:** Applicants must submit a completed application form; $5 application fee; one page letter of application describing self, activities, goals and needs for financial assistance; two or more recommendations by individuals from school, aviation community, clergy or others; transcripts; and any other materials pertinent to the application. **Deadline:** May 1. **Contact:** EAA Aviation Foundation at the above address (see entry 2293).

---

## • 2300 •
### Earhart Foundation

2200 Green Rd., Ste. H
Ann Arbor, MI 48105　　　　　　*Ph:* (734)761-8592

*The Earhart Foundation was incorporated in 1929 by Harry Boyd Earhart of Detroit for charitable, religious, and educational purposes.*

*The emphasis has been placed on such disciplines as the social sciences and humanities, economics, history, international affairs, and political science.*

### • 2301 • H.B. Earhart Fellowships *(Graduate/ Fellowship)*

**Purpose:** To move talented individuals through graduate study in optimum time to embark upon careers in college or university teaching or in research. **Focus:** Humanities, Economics, History, International Affairs and Relations, Political Science. **Qualif.:** Candidates must be graduate students in the social sciences and humanities, such as economics, philosophy, international affairs, and government or politics. They must be nominated by faculty sponsors who will monitor their performance.

**Funds Avail.:** Stipends range annually from $1,000 to $7,500. 41 Fellows also received tuition. Government and political science were the disciplines primarily represented. The maximum term for any appropriation is 12 months. **No. of Awards:** 53. **To Apply:** Grants are awarded only upon nomination by faculty sponsors. No applications are accepted. **Contact:** Earhart Foundation at the above address (see entry 2300).

### • 2302 • Earhart Foundation Fellowship Research Grants *(Postdoctorate/Grant)*

**Purpose:** To assist academic research. **Focus:** Humanities, Social Sciences. **Qualif.:** Applicant may be of any nationality. Candidate must have a Ph.D. degree. Applicant must be affiliated with a university or other academic institution at the time of application. Proposed project must be directly relevant to academic career goals.

**Funds Avail.:** $500-22,000; $9,500 average. **No. of Awards:** 71. **To Apply:** Write to the president for application guidelines. **Deadline:** 120 days prior to proposed start of research. **Contact:** David B. Kennedy, President, at the above address (see entry 2300).

### • 2303 •
## Early American Industries Association
c/o Ms. Justine Matalono
1324 Shallcross Ave.
Wilmington, DE 19806       *Ph:* (302)652-7297
*URL:* http://ourworld.compuserve.com/homepages/old-tools/ about.htm

### • 2304 • EAIA Research Grants Program *(Postgraduate/Grant)*

**Purpose:** To assist individuals, graduate students, and scholars with serious research leading to publications or exhibitions. Not to be used as scholarship or fellowship funds. **Focus:** Early American Industry, Preservation and Exhibition of Tools and Mechanical Devices used in Early America prior to 1900. **Qualif.:** Applicants must be U.S. citizens and must have interests paralleling those of EAIA. Undergraduates are not eligible.

**Funds Avail.:** $6,000. **No. of Awards:** 3-5. **To Apply:** Write to EAIA for guidelines and application forms. **Deadline:** March 15. **Contact:** Ms. Justine J. Mataleno, Coordinator, at the above address (see entry 2303).

### • 2305 •
## East Texas Historical Association
Box 6223
SFA Sta.       *Ph:* (409)468-2407
Nacogdoches, TX 75962       *Fax:* (409)468-2190
*E-mail:* jjackson@sfasu.edu
*URL:* http://144.211.125/ETHA.html

### • 2306 • Ottis Lock Endowment Scholarships *(Graduate, Undergraduate/Scholarship)*

**Purpose:** To encourage attendance at an institution of higher education in East Texas. **Focus:** History, Social Sciences. **Qualif.:** Applicants must be history or social science majors and attending a college or university located in East Texas. **Criteria:** Selection is merit based.

**Funds Avail.:** $500. **No. of Awards:** 1. **To Apply:** Applicants should provide transcripts of schools attended and a general statement of worthiness, need, and interest in furthering their education. Letters of recommendation are encouraged. Applications may be obtained by contacting the Association. **Deadline:** May 1. **Contact:** Dr. Archie P. McDonald at the above address (see entry 2305).

### • 2307 •
## East-West Center
1601 East-West Rd.       *Ph:* (808)944-7735
Honolulu, HI 96848-1601       *Fax:* (808)944-7730
*URL:* http://www.wec.hawaii.edu

*The East-West Center was established by the United States Congress in 1960 to promote better relations and understanding among the nations of Asia, the Pacific, and the United States through cooperative study, training, and research.*

### • 2308 • East-West Center Graduate Degree Fellowships *(Graduate/Award)*

**Focus:** General Studies. **Qualif.:** Applicants must intend to participate in the Center's educational program while studying in master's and doctorate programs of the University of Hawaii. **Criteria:** Recipients are selected through an open competition with application directly to the East-West Center or through program representatives of the applicant's country of citizenship in Asia and the Pacific. Applicants are selected who demonstrate strong professional interest in the Center's program and meet the high academic standards of the university.

**Funds Avail.:** Awards are granted each year for a period of up to 24 months. Funds are available by a monthly stipend which covers tuition, book allowance, and EWC-approved academic expenses as well. Residence hall accommodations are available. Two types of awards funding are offered. A fully-funded award covers all award provisions with Center funding. Cooperatively-funded awards share the cost of the award between the Center and the individual's institution or government. **To Apply:** Any questions on application requirements and deadlines should be directed to EWC Award Services Officer or candidate's program representative. **Contact:** Award Services Officer, Burns Hall 2066, at the above address (see entry 2307).

### • 2309 • East-West Center Internships *(Professional Development/Internship)*

**Purpose:** To attract promising researchers and professionals for problem-oriented, interdisciplinary research and professional training in specific EWC projects. **Focus:** Social Sciences.

**Funds Avail.:** Awards from one to 12 months are presented. Monthly stipends of $675 also are awarded. Transportation costs are sometimes covered. **To Apply:** Candidates are selected

## East-West Center (continued)

through EWC invitations and nominations by cooperating institutions, and in some cases, through public announcement of competition for awards. **Contact:** The East-West Center at the above address (see entry 2307).

### • 2310 • East-West Center Professional Associateships *(Professional Development/Fellowship)*

**Purpose:** To attract leaders and established professionals to EWC conferences to plan cooperative research. **Focus:** Asian and Pacific Studies and related disciplines, including Communication, Demography, Economic Development, Energy, Environmental Sciences, International Relations, International Trade. **Qualif.:** Applicant must be a citizen or permanent resident of the United States or of a country or territory within Asia or the Pacific region. Candidate must be invited by the Center or nominated by his/her home institution. Associateships are tenable at the Center. Awardees participate in seminars, workshops, conferences, and planning meetings; and are involved in the development of educational programs and materials.

**Funds Avail.:** Varies. **To Apply:** Write to the awards services officer for information. **Deadline:** Varies. **Contact:** Award Services Officer, at the above address (see entry 2307).

### • 2311 • East-West Center Visiting Fellowships *(Postdoctorate/Fellowship)*

**Purpose:** To attract international scholars and authorities to the Center for involvement in specific Center project. **Focus:** Asian and Pacific Studies and related disciplines, including Communication, Demography, Economic Development, Energy, Environmental Sciences, International Relations, International Trade. **Qualif.:** Applicant must be a citizen or permanent resident of the United States or of a country or territory within Asia or the Pacific region. Candidate must have professional and/or academic qualifications and extensive previous research experience. Candidate must be invited by the Center or nominated by his/her home institution. Fellowships are tenable at the Center.

**Funds Avail.:** Varies, according to experience. **To Apply:** Write to the awards services officer for application guidelines. **Deadline:** Varies. **Contact:** June Y. Hirano, Award Services Officer, at the above address (see entry 2307).

### • 2312 • Jefferson Fellowships *(Professional Development/Fellowship)*

**Purpose:** To enable mid-career journalists to attend briefings, seminars on major news issues, and the cultural background of the countries of Asia and the Pacific region. **Focus:** Journalism. **Qualif.:** Applicant must be a citizen of the United States or of a country in Asia or the Pacific. Candidate must have a minimum of five years experience. Fellows spend one month at the Center, after that, Asian and Pacific Islander Fellows spend one month traveling in the U.S. while the U.S. Fellows travel to Asia and the Pacific.

**Funds Avail.:** Partial travel and living expenses. **No. of Awards:** 12. **To Apply:** Write to the director or curator for application guidelines. **Contact:** Webster K. Nolan, Director, EWC Media Program Fellowships at the above address (see entry 2307).

### • 2313 •
### E. B. Eastburn Fellowship Fund

McMaster University
School of Graduate Studies
Gilmore Hall 110
1280 Main St., W.
Hamilton, ON, Canada L8S 4L8          *Ph:* (416)525-9140
*URL:* http://leroy.cc.uregina.ca/~gradstud/GradStud/
scholarships/S_and_A/E.html

### • 2314 • Eastburn Fellowships *(Postdoctorate/Fellowship)*

**Purpose:** To encourage postdoctoral research by Canadian scientists. **Focus:** Biomedical Sciences, Medicine, Natural Sciences, Physical Sciences. **Qualif.:** Applicant must be a Canadian citizen or permanent resident. Candidate must either be a recent recipient of the Ph.D. (or the equivalent), or expect to complete the degree by the spring preceding the start of the fellowship. Awards are tenable for full-time research and study at Canadian universities. No other paid employment or major academic award may be accepted during the year the Fellowship is held. **Criteria:** Preference is given to candidates who are unable to continue their studies through a lack of finances.

**Funds Avail.:** Approximately $44,000. **To Apply:** Applicants must submit six copies of the following: curriculum vitae and transcripts, and abstract of the research proposal, a statement of the research program, a budget for research expenditures, a personal financial statement, two or more letters of recommendation and a cover letter. **Deadline:** January. **Contact:** Dean of Graduate Studies at the above address (see entry 2313).

### • 2315 •
### The Easter Seal Research Institute

250 Ferrand Drive, Ste. 200          *Ph:* (416)421-8377
Don Mills, ON, Canada M3C 3P2          *Fax:* (416)696-1035

### • 2316 • ESRI Doctoral Training Grants ESRI Postdoctoral Fellowships *(Doctorate, Postdoctorate/Fellowship, Grant)*

**Purpose:** To encourage research in the prevention, treatment, and management of physical disabilities in children and young adults. **Focus:** Physical Disabilities. **Qualif.:** Applicants must be Canadian citizens or landed immigrants. Applicants for the doctoral grants should be enrolled in a Ph.D. program in Ontario. Applicants for the postdoctoral grants must hold an M.D. or Ph.D. degree. Research must investigate some aspect of physical disabilities in children and/or young adults, and must be carried out in Ontario, Canada. **Criteria:** Awards are sometimes given for study outside of Ontario.

**Funds Avail.:** $15,000-30,000. **To Apply:** Write to the director for an application form and guidelines. **Deadline:** April 15.

**Remarks:** ESRI also awards Research Grants to investigators associated with Ontario universities, hospitals, and treatment centers. Write for further details.

### • 2317 • Elizabeth St. Louis Award *(Professional Development/Award)*

**Purpose:** To encourage research into the development and/or testing of assistive or prosthetic devices for physically disabled children. **Focus:** Physical Disabilities. **Qualif.:** Applicants must be Canadian citizens or landed immigrants who have prepared a research project proposal but have not yet completed the study. The Award is by competition.

**Funds Avail.:** $5,000. **No. of Awards:** 1 per year. **To Apply:** Write to the director for application form and guidelines. **Deadline:** April 15

**Contact:** Anne Michie, Administrator, at the above address (see entry 2315).

### • 2318 •   Miriam Neveren Summer Studentship
*(Professional Development/Scholarship)*

**Purpose:** To encourage research in the prevention, treatment, and management of physical disabilities in children and young adults. **Focus:** Physical Disabilities. **Qualif.:** Applicants must be Canadian citizens or landed immigrants.

**Funds Avail.:** $3,000. **No. of Awards:** 1 per year. **To Apply:** Write to the administrator for application form and guidelines. **Deadline:** March 1. **Contact:** Administrator, The Easter Seal Research Institute, at the above address (see entry 2315).

---

### • 2319 •
### Easter Seal Society of Iowa, Inc.
PO Box 4002         *Ph:* (515)289-1933
Des Moines, IA 50333-4002    *Fax:* (515)289-1281
*E-mail:* essia@netins.net

### • 2320 •   Easter Seal Society of Iowa Disability Scholarship *(Undergraduate/Scholarship)*

**Focus:** General Studies. **Qualif.:** Applicants must be graduating high school seniors who have a permanent disability and plan to attend an accredited college or university. They must also be residents of Iowa, in the upper 40 percent of their class (equivalent to a cumulative grade point average of 2.8 or above), and able to show financial need.

**Funds Avail.:** One $750 scholarship. **No. of Awards:** 1. **To Apply:** Candidates must submit a completed application form, arrange for high school transcripts to be sent, ensure that references have been completed, and return the required forms. **Deadline:** March 1. Applications are available December 1. **Contact:** The Easter Seal Society of Iowa at the above address (see entry 2319).

### • 2321 •   Rolfe B. Karlsson Scholarships *(Graduate, Undergraduate/Scholarship)*

**Purpose:** To provide scholarships for college sophomores, juniors, seniors, and graduate students who are preparing for a career in a profession concerned with physical and/or psychological rehabilitation. **Focus:** Health Care Services. **Qualif.:** Students must be Iowa residents attending an accredited college or university on a full-time basis; have obtained sophomore, junior, senior, or graduate standing; plan a career in the broad field of rehabilitation (in the medical or dentistry fields, the student's curriculum must be rehabilitation-oriented, and students in the nursing field must be in a four-year program); be in the upper 40 percent of their class (equivalent to a cumulative grade point average of 2.8 or above); and able to show financial need.

**Funds Avail.:** One $1,000 scholarship. **To Apply:** Applicants must submit a completed application form, arrange for current transcripts to be sent by the school they are attending, ensure that cited references have completed and returned the appropriate forms, and provide the Society with copies of letters that indicate aid amounts awarded by the institution they are attending. **Deadline:** March 1. Applications are available from the Easter Seal Society after December 1 of each year. **Contact:** The Easter Seal Society of Iowa at the above address (see entry 2319).

### • 2322 •   James L. and Lavon Madden Mallory Disability Scholarship *(High School, Undergraduate/Scholarship)*

**Focus:** General Studies. **Qualif.:** Applicants must be graduating high school seniors who have a permanent disability and plan to attend an accredited college or university. They must also be residents of Iowa, in the upper 40 percent of their class (equivalent to a cumulative grade point average of 2.8 or above), and able to show financial need.

**Funds Avail.:** One $1,000 scholarship. **No. of Awards:** 1. **To Apply:** Candidates must submit a completed application form, arrange for high school transcripts to be sent, ensure that references have completed, and returned the required forms. **Deadline:** March 1.

**Remarks:** This scholarship is presented by the Board of Directors of The Easter Seal Society of Iowa, Inc. at the Society's Annual Meeting in October of each year. Applications available December 1. **Contact:** The Easter Seal Society of Iowa at the above address (see entry 2319).

### • 2323 •   E.L. Peterson Scholarships *(Graduate, Undergraduate/Scholarship)*

**Purpose:** To provide scholarships for college sophomores, juniors, seniors, and graduate students who are preparing for a career in a profession concerned with physical and/or psychological rehabilitation. **Focus:** Health Care Services. **Qualif.:** Students must be Iowa residents attending an accredited college or university on a full-time basis; have obtained sophomore, junior, senior, or graduate standing; plan a career in the broad field of rehabilitation (in the medical or dentistry fields, the student's curriculum must be rehabilitation-oriented, and students in the nursing field must be in a four-year program); be in the upper 40 percent of their class (equivalent to a cumulative grade point average of 2.8 or above); and able to show financial need.

**Funds Avail.:** One $1,000 scholarship. **No. of Awards:** 1. **To Apply:** Applicants must submit a completed application form, arrange for current transcripts to be sent by the school they are attending, ensure that cited references have completed and returned the appropriate forms, and provide the Society with copies of letters that indicate aid amounts awarded by the institution they are attending. **Deadline:** March 1. Applications are available from the Easter Seal Society after December 1 of each year. **Contact:** The Easter Seal Society of Iowa at the above address (see entry 2319).

### • 2324 •   Lynn Marie Vogel Scholarships *(Graduate, Undergraduate/Scholarship)*

**Purpose:** To provide scholarships for college sophomores, juniors, seniors, and graduate students who are preparing for a career in a profession concerned with physical and/or psychological rehabilitation. **Focus:** Health Care Services. **Qualif.:** Students must be Iowa residents attending an accredited college or university on a full-time basis; have obtained sophomore, junior, senior, or graduate standing; plan a career in the broad field of rehabilitation (in the medical or dentistry fields, the student's curriculum must be rehabilitation-oriented, and students in the nursing field must be in a four-year program); be in the upper 40 percent of their class (equivalent to a cumulative grade point average of 2.8 or above); and able to show financial need.

**Funds Avail.:** One $1,000 scholarship. **No. of Awards:** 1. **To Apply:** Applicants must submit a completed application form, arrange for current transcripts to be sent by the school they are attending, ensure that cited references have completed and returned the appropriate forms, and provide the Society with copies of letters that indicate aid amounts awarded by the institution they are attending. **Deadline:** March 1. Applications are available from the Easter Seal Society after December 1 of each year. **Contact:** The Easter Seal Society of Iowa at the above address (see entry 2319).

---

## • 2325 •
## Eastern Surfing Association

PO Box 582  
Ocean City, MD 21842  
*URL:* http://www.surfesa.org/ustream.html

Ph: (410)213-0515  
Fax: (410)213-0515

### • 2326 • Marsh Scholarship (Undergraduate/Scholarship)

**Purpose:** To offer financial aid to deserving student surfers wishing to continue their education beyond the secondary level. **Focus:** General Studies. **Qualif.:** Applicants must be current members in good standing of the Eastern Surfing Association. **Criteria:** Grants are awarded based on academics and citizenship rather than athletic ability.

**Funds Avail.:** Two or three awards annually of $750 to $1,000 each. **To Apply:** Applicants must submit completed applications, a letter of recommendation, and a typewritten letter (no longer than 500 words) detailing future goals and how applicant's choice of educational institution will help in reaching these goals. **Deadline:** April 15. Recipients are notified by June 10.

**Remarks:** The Marsh Scholarship was founded in 1981 to honor the Marsh family and their accomplishments, in particular Mike Marsh, who set a fine example for students everywhere by earning his law degree while simultaneously and successfully battling cancer. **Contact:** Kathlyn B. Phillips, ESA/Marsh Scholarship Program, c/o Henningsen, 25 Old Post Rd., Rye, New York 10580.

## • 2327 •
## Eastman Dental Center

625 Elmwood Ave.  
Rochester, NY 14620-2989  
*URL:* http://www.rrlc.org/edc.html

Ph: (716)275-5010  
Fax: (716)244-8705

### • 2328 • Clinical Dental Fellowships (Postdoctorate/Fellowship)

**Purpose:** To support postdoctoral dental training and research. **Focus:** Dentistry. **Qualif.:** Applicants must have D.D.S., D.M.D. or equivalent. Fellowships are tenable at the Center, and are intended for advanced clinical training and/or research in general or pediatric dentistry.

**Funds Avail.:** $11,000-16,000. **No. of Awards:** 20 annually. **To Apply:** Write for application form and guidelines. **Deadline:** October 15. **Contact:** Shirley J. Wallace, Registrar, at the above address (see entry 2327).

## • 2329 •
## Friedrich Ebert Foundation

342 Madison Avenue Ste. 1912  
New York, NY 10173

Ph: (212)687-0208  
Fax: (212)687-0261

### • 2330 • Friedreich Ebert Foundation Doctoral Research Fellowships (Postgraduate/Fellowship)

**Purpose:** To provide doctoral candidates with an opportunity to conduct research necessary for their thesis in the Federal Republic. **Focus:** Political science, sociology, history and economics. **Qualif.:** Applicants must be qualified PhD candidates at an American university and must have completed all of the prerequisites for a doctorate except for the thesis. Applicants must have an approved dissertation proposal and submit a recommendation from their academic advisor. Must provide evidence of knowledge of German, and must be a US citizen.

**Funds Avail.:** Monthly allowance is DM 1,390 plus airfare and tuition if applicable. **Deadline:** February 28.

### • 2331 • Friedreich Ebert Foundation, Post-Doctoral/Young Scholar Fellowships (Postdoctorate/Fellowship)

**Purpose:** To provide scholars who have already accumulated a certain amount of experience in teaching and/or research the opportunity to conduct independent research in the Federal Republic. **Qualif.:** Applicants must have a PhD or equivalent university degree and at least two years of subsequent experience in research and/or teaching at universities or in related research institutions. Must submit copies of relevant academic publications. Must be a US citizen. The applicant must also indicate a German counterpart who would be available for cooperation and assistance during their stay in the Federal Republic, and have an appropriate knowledge of German. **Criteria:** Priority will be given to applicants who wish to conduct studies on politically relevant subjects, particularly those involving a comparative approach (U.S. - Federal Republic).

**Funds Avail.:** Monthly allowance is DM 1,700, plus airfare and tuition if applicable. **Deadline:** February 28.

### • 2332 • Friedreich Ebert Stiftung Pre Dissertation/Advanced Graduate Fellowshps (Doctorate, Graduate/Fellowship)

**Purpose:** To enable the fellowship holder to engage in advanced studies at a university in the Federal Republic under the guidance of a German university professor. **Qualif.:** Applicants must be highly qualified graduate students intending to pursue doctoral degrees and/or participating in a special research projects; they must have successfully completed at least two years of graduate study at an American university before commencing the intended period of study in the Federal Republic. The application is restricted to the following disciplines: political science, sociology, history, and economics. Applicants must also be US citizens.

**Funds Avail.:** Monthly allowance is DM 1,250 plus airfare and tuition if applicable. **To Apply:** Applicants must submit a description of their study and/or research objective and a recommendation from their graduate advisor at the American university they are attending. Applicants must also provide proof that they have sufficient knowledge of German. **Deadline:** February 28. **Contact:** Friedreich-Ebert-Stiftung at the above address (see entry 2329).

## • 2333 •
## Economic History Association - Committee on Research in Economic History

Dept. of Economics  
Univ. of Kansas  
Lawrence, KS 66045  
*E-mail:* eha@falcon.cc.ukans.edu  
*URL:* http://www.eh.net/EHA

Ph: (913)864-3501  
Fax: (913)864-5270

### • 2334 • Arthur H. Cole Grants-in-Aid (Postdoctorate/Grant)

**Purpose:** To support research in economic history. **Focus:** Economic History. **Qualif.:** Applicant may be of any nationality, but preference is given to recent Ph.D. recipients. Applicants must be EHA members. Grants are tenable worldwide. Grants-in-aid are intended to be supplemental to other grants or income.

**Funds Avail.:** $1,500 maximum. **To Apply:** Write for application guidelines. Submit seven copies of a presentation of not more than five pages including a curriculum vitae, a project description, and brief budget. **Deadline:** April 1. Notification by June 1. **Contact:** Li Liang, at the above address (see entry 2333).

• 2335 •

## Economics America - National Council on Economic Education

1140 Avenue of the Americas     *Ph:* (212)730-7007
New York, NY 10036     *Fax:* (212)730-1793
    *Free:* 800-338-1192

*E-mail:* econusa@novalink.com
*URL:* http://www.bsu.edu/econed/ecohome.html

### • 2336 • National Awards for the Teaching of Economics *(Professional Development/Award)*

**Purpose:** To recognize excellence in the teaching of economics. **Focus:** Economics. **Qualif.:** Applicant must be a teacher, supervisor, administrator, guidance counselor, librarian at a U.S. elementary or secondary school. Awards recognize outstanding projects related to the teaching of economics that were carried out or implemented during the previous year. Candidate's submission must be an instructional program or activity conducted during the 12 months preceding June 30 of the year of application. Educators compete in one of five categories, depending on level of students taught.

**Funds Avail.:** First prize: $1,000; second prize: $500. **No. of Awards:** 60. **To Apply:** Write to the director for application form and guidelines. Submit form and documents describing project to the National Depository for Economic Education Awards, Milner Library 518, Illinois State University, Normal, Illinois, U.S.A. 61790-8900 **Deadline:** July 12. Notification by November 1. **Contact:** Director, National Awards for Teaching Economics, at the above address (see entry 2335).

• 2337 •

## The Editing Program

University of Arizona
Journalism Dept.
Franklin Bldg., 101 M     *Ph:* (520)621-9134
Tucson, AZ 85721     *Fax:* (520)621-9557
*E-mail:* mije@maynardije.org
*URL:* http://www.maynardije.org

### • 2338 • Editing Program for Minority Journalists *(Professional Development/Other)*

**Purpose:** To provide 12 journalists with advanced training at the University of Arizona working as editors on the program's newspaper, *Headline,* and on the copy desks of the *Tucson Citizen* and the *Arizona Daily Star.* The program covers basics in copy editing, headline writing, newsroom organization, libel laws, and newspaper layout. After completing the session, participants go on to copy desk jobs at sponsoring daily newspapers. Those not sponsored by a newspaper will be matched to newspapers and sent on one or more interviews before the end of the program. **Qualif.:** Preference will be given to journalists with at least one year of experience.

**Funds Avail.:** Successful candidates will receive tuition and housing. Transportation and expenses for interviews will be covered by sponsoring newspapers. Candidates not receiving salaries will receive a $200 per week stipend. **To Apply:** Upon request applications are distributed in November for the following year. **Deadline:** Mid-February. **Contact:** Sylvia Boemer at the above address (see entry 2337).

• 2339 •

## Education Assistance Corp.

115 1st Ave., SW     *Ph:* (605)225-6423
Aberdeen, SD 57401-4174     *Fax:* (605)225-5722
    *Free:* 800-592-1802

*E-mail:* eac@eac-easci.org
*URL:* http://www.eac-easci.org

### • 2340 • Federal Plus Loans *(Undergraduate/Loan)*

**Qualif.:** Applicants must be parents with good credit histories of dependent students enrolled at least half-time. Students must have a high school diploma or a GED certificate, be enrolled in an eligible program, and be making satisfactory academic progress. Parents must be U.S. citizens or eligible non-citizens

**Funds Avail.:** There are no annual or aggregate limits. The parent may borrow up to the amount of cost minus any aid the student has been or will be awarded during the period of enrollment. Interest rate is adjusted annually, not to exceed 9 percent. Repayment begins within 60 days after the funds are disbursed. **To Apply:** Contact the financial aid office or your lender for applications. **Contact:** College financial offices, lenders, or Lynn Murphy, Supervisor of Loan Processing, at the above address (see entry 2339).

### • 2341 • Federal Stafford Loan (Subsidized and Unsubsidized) *(Graduate, Undergraduate/Loan)*

**Qualif.:** Must be U.S. citizen, national or other eligible non-citizen who is enrolled (or accepted for enrollment) and making satisfactory academic progress at an approved educational institution. Applicant must be enrolled at least half-time, show compliance with selective service requirements, and cannot be in default on another student loan (or have made satisfactory repayment arrangements with their lender to repay the defaulted loan) or owe a refund to an education grant program. **Criteria:** Based on financial need.

**Funds Avail.:** Up to $2,625 per year for the first year of undergraduate study; up to $3,500 for the second year; and up to $5,500 per year for the remainder of undergraduate study. Aggregate for undergraduate study cannot exceed $23,000. Up to $8,500 per year for graduate or profession study. Aggregate for undergraduate and graduate study cannot exceed $65,500. Loan amount for a given year cannot exceed the student's cost of attendance minus other financial aid and (if required) the estimated family contribution. The Federal government pays interest on subsidized Federal Stafford Loans until student begins repayment six months after graduation or termination of studies. Interest accrues at a variable rate that changes yearly not to exceed 8.25 percent. **To Apply:** Contact the financial aid office or your lender for application. **Contact:** Financial aid offices, lenders, or Lynn Murphy, Supervisor of Loan Processing at the above address (see entry 2339).

• 2342 •

## Education Writers Association

1331 H St. NW 307     *Ph:* (202)637-9700
Washington, DC 20005     *Fax:* (202)637-9707
*E-mail:* ewa@crosslink.net
*URL:* http://www.ewa.org

### • 2343 • National Fellowships in Education Reporting *(Professional Development/Fellowship)*

**Purpose:** To promote the exploration of issues and problems in education at the community level and in a national context. **Qualif.:** Open to full-time print or broadcast journalists who have been covering education for at least two years, have the endorsement of

## Education Writers Association (continued)

their employer, and show that they have a likely outlet for the product of their study. Freelancers may apply if they write about education for a sunstantial portion of their time and if they submit an endorsement from a media organization indicating plans to publish or produce stories resulting from the fellowship.

**Funds Avail.:** Up to 12 reporters receive half salary plus travel expenses. **Deadline:** May 14.

**Remarks:** Supported by grants from the John D. and Catherine T. MacArthur Foundation, the Pew Charitable Trusts, and others. **Contact:** Lisa J. Walker, Exec.Dir.

---

## • 2344 •
## Educational Commission for Foreign Medical Graduates

c/o Magdalena Miranda, M.S.
2401 Pennsylvania Ave., NW, Ste.
475                                        *Ph:* (202)293-9320
Washington, DC 20037                       *Fax:* (202)457-0751
*URL:* http://www.ecfmg.org

### • 2345 • International Fellowships in Medical Education *(Professional Development/Fellowship)*

**Purpose:** To enable basic science teachers from foreign medical schools to study aspects of medical education that have the potential to improve medical education in their home country institutions. **Qualif.:** Applicant may be of any nationality, but must be a full-time faculty member presently teaching a basic medical science at a medical school outside the United States. Candidate must have at least three years of teaching experience in the basic sciences and a good command of English. Application may be submitted by the candidate or by the U.S. sponsoring institution, on behalf of the candidate. If a U.S. sponsoring institution has not been selected, ECFMG will attempt to match the candidate with an appropriate host institution. Candidate's home institution must endorse the proposed fellowship and provide the fellow a leave of absence. Fellows must return to their home institutions upon completion of the fellowship.

**Funds Avail.:** $2,200/month, plus travel and institutional grants. **No. of Awards:** 20. **To Apply:** Write to Ms. Miranda for application form and guidelines. **Deadline:** August 15.

---

## • 2346 •
## Educational Communications Scholarship Foundation

721 N. McKinley Rd.                        *Ph:* (847)295-6650
Lake Forest, IL 60045-1849                 *Fax:* (847)295-3972
*E-mail:* scholar@eclif.com

### • 2347 • Educational Communications Scholarship *(Undergraduate/Scholarship)*

**Focus:** General Studies. **Qualif.:** Candidates are current high school students who are U.S. citizens and have taken the SAT and ACT examinations. **Criteria:** Selections are based on grade point average, achievement test scores, leadership qualifications, work experience, evaluation of an essay, and financial need.

**Funds Avail.:** $1,000. **No. of Awards:** 200. **To Apply:** Application requests must be made by March 15, and may be obtained at most high school guidance offices or through a written request to the Foundation. Applicants should state their name, home address, current year in high school, and approximate grade point average.

**Deadline:** June 1. Semi-finalists only will be notified by June 15 and winners only will be notified by August 5. **Contact:** The Educational Communications Scholarship Foundation at the above address (see entry 2346).

### • 2348 • Educational Communications Scholarship Foundation *(Graduate, Undergraduate/Scholarship)*

**Focus:** General Studies. **Qualif.:** Available to undergraduate and graduate students with a GPA of B or better. **Criteria:** Recipients are selected on the basis of academic achievement, leadership activities, and honors and awards. Semi-finalists are notified by June 15 and asked to complete an essay.

**Funds Avail.:** $1,000. **No. of Awards:** 50. **To Apply:** Application requests must be made by March 15, and may be obtained at most high school guidance offices or through a written request to the Foundation. Applicants should state their name, home address, current year in high school, and approximate grade point average. **Deadline:** June 1. Semi-finalists only will be notified by June 15 and winners only will be notified by August 5. **Contact:** Educational Communications at the above address (see entry 2346).

---

## • 2349 •
## The Educational Foundation for Women in Accounting

PO Box 1925                                *Ph:* (610)407-9229
Southeastern, PA 19399-1925                *Fax:* (610)407-0286
                                           *Free:* 800-326-2163
*E-mail:* jambor@ro.com
*URL:* http://www.efwa.org

### • 2350 • Laurels Fund Scholarships *(Doctorate, Graduate/Scholarship)*

**Purpose:** To assist women seeking advanced accounting degrees. **Focus:** Accounting. **Qualif.:** Applicant may be of any nationality. Applicant must be working toward a bachelor's or master's degree in the field of accounting. Applicant does not have to be a member of either ASWA or AWSCPA.

**Funds Avail.:** $1,000-5,000. **No. of Awards:** 3. **To Apply:** Write to The Education Foundation for Women in Accounting for application form and guidelines, available in September. Submit application materials to the scholarship chair, whose address is included in the guidelines. **Deadline:** February 15.

---

## • 2351 •
## Educational Testing Service

666 Rosedale Rd.                           *Ph:* (609)921-9000
Princeton, NJ 08541-2218                   *Fax:* (609)734-5410
*E-mail:* etsinfo@ets.org
*URL:* http://www.ets.org/

### • 2352 • ETS Center for Performance Assessment Postdoctoral Fellowships *(Postdoctorate/Fellowship)*

**Purpose:** To provide research opportunities to individuals who hold doctorates in relevant fields and to increase the number of women and minority professionals with expertise in performance/ portfolio assessment in relation to the improvement of learning and teaching. **Focus:** Performance Assessment. **Qualif.:** Candidates must hold a doctorate in a relevant discipline and provide evidence of interest and prior research pertaining to performance assessment in education. The recipient will conduct research for ongoing projects at the Center. **Criteria:** Based on scholarship and relevant experience in educational settings. Affirmative action goals are also a criterion in selection.

**Funds Avail.:** $35,000 for the period; renewable for a second year. **No. of Awards:** Up to two. **To Apply:** There is no formal application form. Applicants may want to obtain a brochure from the Center prior to applying. They need to submit a resume, publications and other relevant documents and materials, transcripts, and letters of recommendation. **Deadline:** February 1. Applicants are notified by April 1. **Contact:** Linda J. DeLauro, at the above address (see entry 2351).

• **2353** • **ETS Postdoctoral Fellowships**
*(Postdoctorate/Fellowship)*

**Purpose:** To provide research opportunities for recent awardees of the doctorate and to increase the number of women and minority professionals in educational measurement and related fields. **Focus:** Psychology, Education, Minority Issues, Occupational/ Vocational Testing, Policy Studies, Psychometrics, Statistics, Computer Science, Linguistics. **Qualif.:** Candidate may be of any nationality. Applicant must hold a doctorate in a relevant discipline and provide evidence of prior research. The fellowship is tenable at ETS in Princeton, New Jersey, only. **Criteria:** Scholarship, importance and appropriateness of the proposed research will be considered.

**Funds Avail.:** $35,000 stipend, plus limited reimbursement for expenses, beginning September 1 through August 31. **No. of Awards:** Three. **To Apply:** Submit a resume of educational and employment history, honors, awards, etc; a detailed description of research interests and experience, plus a description of the research to be pursued during the fellowship year; names of three individuals who are willing to provide recommendations; and undergraduate and graduate transcripts. Specify interest in Postdoctoral Fellowship program on application. **Deadline:** February 1. All applicants will be notified by April 1. **Contact:** Linda J. DeLauro, ETS, at the above address (see entry 2351).

• **2354** • **ETS Summer Program in Research for Graduate Students** *(Doctorate/Award)*

**Purpose:** To provide research opportunities for doctoral students and increase the number of women and minority professionals in educational measurement and related fields. **Focus:** Psychology, Education, Higher Education, Minority Issues, Occupational/ Vocational Testing, Policy Studies, Psychometrics. **Qualif.:** Candidate must be a graduate student who has completed 40 or more credits in a doctoral program emphasizing one of the areas of study. **Criteria:** Scholarship as well as the match of applicant interests with participating ETS staff will be considered.

**Funds Avail.:** $3,500 and travel reimbursement. **No. of Awards:** 12. **To Apply:** Contact ETS for application materials. Submit with a letter of recommendation from advisor or committee chair, and undergraduate and graduate transcripts. **Deadline:** February 1. All applicants will be notified by April 1. **Contact:** Linda J. DeLauro, at the above address (see entry 2351).

• **2355** • **National Assessment of Educational Progress Visiting Scholar Program** *(Postdoctorate/ Award)*

**Purpose:** To provide research opportunities for recent awardees of the doctorate. **Focus:** Educational Policy and Measurement Issues associated with Black, Hispanic, or other minority students. **Qualif.:** Applicant must hold a doctorate in a relevant discipline and provide evidence of prior research relevant to the education of minorities. **Criteria:** Scholarship, importance of the research questions, and relevance will all be considered.

**Funds Avail.:** Stipends are set in relation to compensation from the scholar's home institution with reimbursement for relocation of up to $4,000. **No. of Awards:** Two maximum. **To Apply:** Submit a resume of educational and employment history, honors, awards, etc; a detailed description of research interests and experience,

plus a description of the nature of the research to be pursued during the fellowship; names of three individuals who are willing to provide recommendations; and undergraduate and graduate transcripts. Specify interest in the NAEP Visiting Scholar Program on application. **Deadline:** February 1. All applicants will be contacted by March 1. **Contact:** Linda DeLauro, at the above address (see entry 2351). Direct scientific inquiries to Dr. Eugene Johnson, Mail Stop 02-T, at the above address. **Telephone:** (609)734-5305.

• **2356** •
**Edwards Scholarship Fund**
10 Post Office Sq., Ste. 1230
Boston, MA 02109          *Ph:* (617)426-4434

• **2357** • **Edwards Scholarship** *(Graduate, Undergraduate/Scholarship)*

**Qualif.:** Only students from the city of Boston are eligible for aid. Boston includes residents from Allston, Brighton, Charlestown, Dorchester, East Boston, Forest Hills, Hyde Park, Jamaica Plain, Mattapan, Readville, Roslindale, Roxbury, South Boston, and West Roxbury. They must be under 25 years of age, about to enter undergraduate or graduate school, and show evidence of financial need, scholastic ability and good character. Undergraduates receive preference.

**Funds Avail.:** Between $250 and $5,000. Scholarships are granted for a period of one academic year but may be applied for in subsequent years. **No. of Awards:** Varies. **To Apply:** Application forms may be requested by writing or telephoning the office of the Edwards Scholarship Fund. **Deadline:** March 1.

**Remarks:** In accordance with Miss Edwards' wish, scholarship recipients are asked to repay any amount granted when they are able to do so. **Contact:** Brenda McCarthy, Executive Secretary, at the above adress.

• **2358** •
**EHA Committee on Research in Economic History**
University of Kansas
Dept. of Economics
213 G Summerfield Hall          *Ph:* (913)864-3501
Lawrence, KS 66045          *Fax:* (913)864-5270
*E-mail:* eha@falcon.cc.ukans.edu
*URL:* http://www.eh.net/EHA

• **2359** • **Arthur H. Cole Grants-In-Aid for Research in Economic History** *(Postdoctorate/Grant)*

**Focus:** Economic History. **Qualif.:** The Committee on Research in Economic History supports research regardless of time or geographic area. Preference is given to recent Ph.D. recipients.

**Funds Avail.:** Stipends up to $1,500; the grants are designed to supplement other grants or income. **To Apply:** Applicants must supply seven copies of a presentation of not more than five pages containing a description of the project, a curriculum vitae, and a brief budget. **Deadline:** Applications must be filed by April 1. Notification is made before June 1. **Contact:** Return applications to: Professor Gillian Hamilton, Department of Economics, University of Toronto, 150 St. George St., Toronto, Ontario, Canada MS8 3G7.

---

• 2360 •
## Albert Einstein Institution
50 Church St.
Cambridge, MA 02138                     *Ph:* (617)876-0837
*E-mail:* einstein@igc.apc.org
*URL:* http://hdc-www.harvard.edu/cfia/pnscs.aei.htm

### • 2361 • Albert Einstein Institution Fellowships
*(Doctorate, Postdoctorate, Professional Development/ Fellowship)*

**Purpose:** To support research, writing, and systematic reflection on the history, characteristics, and potential applications of nonviolent action, and particularly its political applications. **Qualif.:** Applicants must have demonstrated in scholarship or practice the capacity to make a significant contribution to the understanding of nonviolent action. The Program offers support to persons in one of the three categories: candidates for doctoral degrees undertaking dissertation research or writing dissertations; advanced scholars undertaking specific research projects; and practitioners in past or present nonviolent struggles preparing documentation, description, and analysis of nonviolent struggle. Independent scholars wishing to apply must demonstrate a level of preparation and scholarly promise comparable to those attained in universities.

**Funds Avail.:** Financial awards are normally made for 12-month periods, beginning September 1 of each year. The normal financial support is a stipend that takes into consideration the applicant's level of preparation, need, and prevailing academic salaries for comparable persons and projects. Applicants are encouraged to seek further support for their project from other sources as appropriate, and must inform the Institution of all additional support received. Doctoral candidates may request renewal based upon a clear demonstration of satisfactory progress, continued financial need, and the likelihood of completion of the project. Other renewals are considered only under special circumstances. **To Apply:** Applicants must submit cover sheet bearing the applicant's name, address, and affiliation, the project title and location where it will be based, and the financial request; one-page, single-spaced abstract of the proposal; the text of the proposal; a curriculum vitae and supporting documents; and two letters of recommendation from persons familiar with the applicant and able to evaluate the project. All applicants are encouraged to submit an exploratory letter of intent to the Fellows Program Director prior to applying. **Deadline:** January 1. **Contact:** Ronald M. McCarthy, Fellows Program, at the above address (see entry 2360).

• 2362 •
## Electrical Women's Round Table, Inc.
PO Box 292793                           *Ph:* (615)890-1272
Nashville, TN 37229-2793                *Fax:* (615)890-1272

### • 2363 • Julia Kiene Fellowship *(Graduate/ Fellowship)*

**Purpose:** To honor the accomplishments of women in the electrical field and to encourage high caliber women to study toward advanced degrees in preparation for leadership in fields such as electric utilities, electrical engineering, electric home appliance and home equipment manufacturing, housing, marketing, journalism, radio-television, research, education, cooperative extension service, and communications. **Qualif.:** Candidates must be women who are graduating seniors from an accredited college or university. Candidates should be planning to pursue graduate studies in any phase of electrical energy at a college or university that is approved by the EWRT Fellowship Committee. **Criteria:** Applications are judged on the basis of scholarship, character, financial need, and professional interest in electrical energy.

**Funds Avail.:** Up to $2,000 for graduate work in electrical energy. **No. of Awards:** 1. **To Apply:** Applications must include statements about the candidate's interest in graduate work and how they propose to contribute to the field of electrical energy upon completion of graduate study and should be submitted with references and official transcripts. **Deadline:** March 1. **Contact:** The Electrical Women's Round Table at the above address (see entry 2362).

### • 2364 • Lyle Mamer Fellowship *(Graduate/ Fellowship)*

**Purpose:** To honor the accomplishments of women in the electrical field and to encourage high caliber women to study toward advanced degrees in preparation for leadership in fields such as electric utilities, electrical engineering, electric home appliance and home equipment manufacturing, housing, marketing, journalism, radio-television, research, communications, cooperative extension service and education. **Qualif.:** Candidates must be women who are graduating seniors from an accredited college or university and should be planning to pursue graduate studies in any phase of electrical energy at a college or university that is approved by the EWRT Fellowship Committee. **Criteria:** Applications are judged on the basis of scholarship, character, financial need, and professional interest in electrical energy.

**Funds Avail.:** Up to $1,000 for graduate work in electrical energy. **No. of Awards:** 1. **To Apply:** Applications must include statements about the candidate's interest in graduate work and how they propose to contribute to the field of electrical energy upon completion of graduate study and should be submitted with references and official transcripts. **Deadline:** March 1. **Contact:** The Electrical Women's Round Table at the above address (see entry 2362).

• 2365 •
## The Electrochemical Society, Inc.
10 S. Main St.                          *Ph:* (609)737-1902
Pennington, NJ 08534-2896               *Fax:* (609)737-2743
*E-mail:* ecs@electrochem.org
*URL:* http://www.electrochem.org

### • 2366 • F.M. Becket Memorial Award *(Doctorate, Graduate/Fellowship)*

**Purpose:** To stimulate active and continued participation in the fields of electrochemical science and technology concerned with specialty materials and processes. **Qualif.:** Candidates should be students of science, engineering, or electrochemistry. They must be either graduating seniors from a recognized college, university, or institute of technology in the United States or Canada who are planning to seek an advanced degree, or graduate students, similarly enrolled to seek an advanced degree.

**Funds Avail.:** The Award consists of a $3,500 stipend for summer research and study in the laboratory of a recognized overseas research institute or institution of higher learning. **No. of Awards:** 1. **To Apply:** A formal application must be filed, along with transcripts of previous academic work and two copies of a letter of recommendation from the head of the college or department in which the student is enrolled. A brief biographical sketch, plus a detailed description of the student's proposed work in relation to the award, is required. The Becket Memorial Award is available every other year. **Deadline:** Applications and other materials must be received by January 1 of odd-numbered years; recipient is announced in late March.

**Remarks:** The Award commemorates the contributions of F. M. Becket, a former president of The Electrochemical Society. **Contact:** Direct questions and applications to Marc Cahay, ECECS Department, 832 Rhodes Hall, ML 30, Univ. of Cincinnati, Cincinnati, OH 45221-0030. Phone: (513)556-4754.

**• 2367 • Electrochemical Society Energy Research Fellowships** *(Doctorate, Graduate/Fellowship)*

**Qualif.:** Candidates must be graduate students pursuing work between the degrees of B.S. and Ph.D. in a college or university in the United States or Canada, and who will continue their studies after the period of the summer fellowship. Students should be pursuing advanced work in such fields of interest to the Society and to those such as energy-related aspects of electrochemical science and engineering as well as solid state engineering and science. A previous holder of an award is eligible for reappointment.

**Funds Avail.:** Approximately $15,000 is allocated for the Energy Research Fellowships. The number of fellowships awarded varies, at the discretion of the Awards Committee. Each fellowship consists of $3,000, supported by the U.S. Dept. of Energy. These fellowships may be used by graduate students pursuing work in the areas of fuel cells, batteries, photoelectrochemistry, photovoltaics, and electrochemical processes of materials aimed at reducing energy consumption. **To Apply:** A formal application must be submitted, along with transcripts of undergraduate and graduate work and two letters of recommendation, including one from the candidate's research advisor. Candidates must supply a brief statement of educational objectives and a statement of the proposed thesis research problem to be pursued during the fellowship. **Deadline:** Applications and other materials must be received by January 15. Award winners are announced in May. **Contact:** Society Summer Fellowships at the above address (see entry 2365).

**• 2368 • Electrochemical Society Summer Fellowships** *(Doctorate/Fellowship)*

**Purpose:** To assist a student in continuing graduate work during the summer months in a field of interest to The Electrochemical Society. **Focus:** Electrochemical and Solid State Science and Technology. **Qualif.:** Candidates must be graduate students pursuing work between the degrees of B.S. and Ph.D. in a college or university in the United States or Canada, and who will continue their studies after the period of the summer fellowship. Students should be pursuing advanced work in such fields of interest to the Society and to those such as energy-related aspects of electrochemical science and engineering as well as solid state engineering and science. A previous holder of an award is eligible for reappointment.

**Funds Avail.:** Approximately $12,000 is allocated for the Summer Fellowships. The number of fellowships awarded varies, at the discretion of the Awards Committee. If one award is given, it is called the Edward G. Weston Fellowship Award. If two awards are given, the second one is designated the Colin Garfield Fink Fellowship Award; if more than two awards are given, the third award shall be called the Joseph W. Richards Fellowship Award. Five additional Energy Research Summer Fellowships, each consisting of $4,000, supported by the U.S. Department of Energy, are also awarded. These fellowships may be used by graduate students pursuing work in the areas of fuel cells, batteries, photoelectrochemistry, photovoltaics, and electrochemical processes of materials aimed at reducing energy consumption. **No. of Awards:** 3. **To Apply:** A formal application must be submitted, along with transcripts of undergraduate and graduate work and two letters of recommendation, including one from the candidate's research advisor. Candidates must supply a brief statement of educational objectives and a statement of the proposed thesis research problem to be pursued during the fellowship. **Deadline:** Applications and other materials must be received by January 1. Award winners are announced April 1. **Contact:** ELS at the above address (see entry 2365).

**• 2369 •**
**Electronic Industries Foundation**
919 18th St., NW, Ste. 900
Washington, DC 20006
*URL:* http://www.eia.org/eif/

**• 2370 • Electronic Industries Foundation Scholarships** *(Graduate, Undergraduate/Scholarship)*

**Purpose:** To assist students with disabilities who are pursuing technical or science degrees. **Focus:** Sciences, Technology. **Qualif.:** Candidates must be U.S. citizens with a disabling condition and must be enrolled, or accepted to, a degree-granting program at an accredited college or university. Candidates must demonstrate that no other financial resources are available to address the particular need. Award funds must be used for tuition, books, or other fees that facilitate academic or technical training.

**Funds Avail.:** $5,000. **To Apply:** Write to the scholarship program coordinator for application form and guidelines. Submit form, statement of disabling condition, at least two letters of support, transcript and history of employment and volunteer experience. **Deadline:** February 1. Notification in May. **Contact:** Scholarship Coordinator at the above address (see entry 2369).

**• 2371 •**
**Embassy of France - Department of Science and Technology**
4101 Reservoir Rd., NW
Washington, DC 20007-2176
*E-mail:* chateaubriand_@amb-wash.fr
*Ph:* (202)944-6246
*Fax:* (202)944-6244

**• 2372 • Chateaubriand Scholarship (Scientifique)** *(Doctorate, Postdoctorate/Scholarship)*

**Purpose:** To provide the opportunity for scholars to conduct research in the exact or social sciences, engineering, and medicine at a French university, school of engineering, or state-funded laboratory. **Qualif.:** Scholarships are offered to United States citizens who are registered at an American university. They must be currently working on a doctoral degree or have completed their studies in the past three years.

**Funds Avail.:** Scholarships are available for periods of six to 12 months and carry a stipend of 9,000 Fr per month. Health insurance and a round-trip ticket to France are also provided. 12 scholarships are available each year. **To Apply:** Applicants must contact the host institution prior to application. The application must include educational background, details on the contemplated research project, and three letters of recommendation from professors acquainted with the student's talents and interests. **Deadline:** Applications must be received before December 31.

**Remarks:** Approximately 50 applications for this scholarship are received by the Embassy each year. **Contact:** Christel Stanley at the above address (see entry 2371).

## Embassy of France - French Cultural Services

972 5th Ave.  *Ph:* (212)439-1400
New York, NY 10021-0144  *Fax:* (212)439-1455
*E-mail:* new-york.culture@diplomatie.fr
*URL:* http://www.info-france-usa.org/culture

### • 2374 • Assistantships in France *(Graduate, Undergraduate/Internship)*

**Purpose:** To provide English assistant post in French schools while improving the knowledge of French and providing teaching experience. **Focus:** French. **Qualif.:** Applicants must be American citizens, under 30 years of age, graduate or undergraduate students, and majoring in French.

**Funds Avail.:** A monthly salary of 5600FF is provided. **To Apply:** Write for application forms. **Deadline:** April 15.

### • 2375 • Chateaubriand Fellowships (Humanities) *(Doctorate/Grant)*

**Focus:** Economics, History, Archeology, Law, Literature, Linguistics, Political Science. **Qualif.:** Fellowships are offered by the French government for doctoral research that would benefit from association with a French research institute or the use of French archives. Research should pertain to one of the following fields: economics, history/archeology, law, literature/linguistics, political science, philosophy, psychology, and sociology. American citizenship is required as well as sufficient proficiency in written and spoken French to be able to carry out the proposed research.

**Funds Avail.:** The grant is paid in monthly installments of about 8,600 Fr for a maximum period of nine months. In addition, health insurance and round-trip airfare are provided. **No. of Awards:** 25. **To Apply:** Application forms are available on the website. **Deadline:** January 15. **Contact:** Embassy of France, French Cultural Services, at the above address (see entry 2373).

### • 2376 • French Government Teaching Awards *(Graduate, Undergraduate/Other)*

**Purpose:** To provide teaching assistantships for the teaching of English conversation in French secondary schools. **Focus:** French Studies. **Qualif.:** Applicants must be unmarried, under the age of 30, fluent in French, and planning a career teaching French. They must also be enrolled in an American university as either senior undergraduates or graduate students. **To Apply:** Application is made through the candidate's home institution, which must accept a French teaching assistant in return. The Cultural Services will not process applications from candidates whose home institution is not participating reciprocally in the exchange. **Deadline:** February 1. **Contact:** The Embassy of France, French Cultural Services, at the above address (see entry 2373).

## Emblem Club Scholarship Foundation

PO Box 712
San Luis Rey, CA 92068  *Ph:* (619)757-0619

### • 2378 • Emblem Club Scholarship Grants *(Postgraduate/Grant)*

**Qualif.:** Applicants must hold or be working toward a master's degree. (When funds are available, applications will be accepted from senior-level students completing their studies toward a bachelor's degree with intent to continue directly into a master's program). They must be in good health, under 50 years of age, above average students, fully enrolled, and citizens of the United States (applications are accepted from non-citizen residents if it is their intent to teach in the United States).

**Funds Avail.:** Grants are awarded as funding becomes available, usually each quarter. Applicants must sign an agreement to refund monies advanced if they fail to complete the training course. **To Apply:** Applications must be made through a certified university or college that provides all necessary units for credit for graduation with a master's degree in the specialized field of the handicapped. Applicants must be screened by the university or college for grant eligibility before applications are forwarded to the Emblem Club. A letter of recommendation from an authorized person or instructor at the university or college indicating applicant is eligible must accompany applications. **Deadline:** September 1, December 1, March 1, and June 1.

**Remarks:** The foundation receives approximately 70 applications per year. **Contact:** The Emblem Club Scholarship Foundation at the above address (see entry 2377)or certified universities or colleges.

## Emigre Memorial German Internship Programs

PO Box 345
Durham, NH 03824

### • 2380 • EMGIP Internships *(Graduate, Professional Development, Undergraduate/Internship)*

**Purpose:** To allow non-Germans to study administrative procedures and policy directions while working in German federal and state governmental offices. **Focus:** German Government. **Qualif.:** Applicants may be from any non-German-speaking country. Special consideration is given to applicants from North America. Candidates must be undergraduate or graduate students or professionals who speak German well enough to perform assigned functions of the internship and to engage in discussions at all levels of German society. They must also have a background in the social sciences or humanities related to social sciences. A degree in German language or literature is normally not sufficient for internship. Internships are currently tenable in Deutscher Bundestag, Berlin; and in IV Five State (Lond) Legislatures in Germany. Interns participate in various administrative duties and observe policy making during the award tenure. Internships are not intended for research or language training, nor do they provide academic credits. **Criteria:** Awards are given based on academic credentials, language mastery, and interest in Germany.

**Funds Avail.:** Stipends vary between DM 750-2500. **No. of Awards:** 11 or more. **To Apply:** Write for application form and guidelines. **Deadline:** Usually in January of appointment year; January 15. **Contact:** Intern Selection Committee, at the above address (see entry 2379).

## Engineering Geology Foundation

c/o Dr. John W. Williams
1021 Crestview Dr.  *Ph:* (415)443-4639
San Carlos, CA 94070  *Fax:* (415)443-2948

### • 2382 • Marliave Scholarships *(Graduate/ Scholarship)*

**Purpose:** To support academic activity and reward outstanding students in engineering geology and geological engineering. **Qualif.:** Applicants must be seniors or graduate students majoring in engineering geology or geological engineering and student members of AEG. **Criteria:** Based on demonstrated ability, scholarship, potential for contribution to the profession, character, and activities in student and professional societies.

**Funds Avail.:** $1,000 grants. **To Apply:** Applications must be submitted by students' major professors, student chapter advisors, or department chairpersons and include three letters of reference, an official transcript, and a two-page report on a topic announced each year. **Deadline:** February 15. **Contact:** Dr. C. F. Watts, Radford University, Radford, VA 24142.

**• 2383 •**
## English-Speaking Union of the United States
Education Department
16 East 69th St.
New York, NY 10021

*Ph:* (212)879-6800
*Fax:* (212)772-2886

**• 2384 • The British Universities Summer Schools Scholarships** *(Graduate, Professional Development/ Scholarship)*

**Purpose:** To allow graduate students and professionals, primarily teachers, to attend courses in England at one of several universities. **Focus:** Education. **Criteria:** Applicants are selected only through participating local E-SU branches.

**Funds Avail.:** Varies. **Contact:** Contact local E-SU branch. Union of the United States at the above address (see entry 2383).

**• 2385 • Lucy Dalbiac Luard Scholarship** *(Undergraduate/Scholarship)*

**Purpose:** To enable college students to spend their junior years studying in the United Kingdom. **Focus:** General Studies. **Qualif.:** Applicants must have completed their sophomore year at Howard or Hampton university, or a United Negro College Fund school.

**Funds Avail.:** Awards cover transportation, tuition, room and board, and books at a university in the United Kingdom. **To Apply:** Applications must be submitted to a participating school in the United States. **Deadline:** November. **Contact:** College Academic Dean.

**• 2386 • Secondary School Exchange** *(High School, Undergraduate/Other)*

**Purpose:** To enable students of the United Kingdom and the United States to spend a semester or year after high school graduation in the opposite country. **Focus:** General Studies. **Qualif.:** Applicants must attend an independent school that participates in this program.

**Funds Avail.:** Funding is provided by participating independent schools. **Deadline:** November. **Contact:** The English-Speaking Union of the United States at the above address (see entry 2383).

**• 2387 •**
## Entomological Society of America
9301 Annapolis Rd., Ste. 300
Lanham, MD 20706
*E-mail:* info@entsoc.org
*URL:* http://www.msstate.edu/Entomology/esa.html

*Ph:* (301)731-4535
*Fax:* (301)731-4538

**• 2388 • John Henry Comstock Graduate Student Awards** *(Graduate/Award)*

**Purpose:** To promote interest in the science of entomology at the graduate level and to stimulate interest in attending the Society's annual meeting. **Focus:** Entomology or Related Sciences. **Qualif.:** Students must be pursuing a course leading to a graduate degree with a major in entomology; however, individuals may receive the award providing they have not graduated more than 12 months prior to the award. Active members returning for graduate study are eligible if membership status changes from active to student with two years of resuming studies. **Criteria:** Criteria for selection of award winners is the responsibility of each ESA branch president.

**Funds Avail.:** All expenses paid trip to the ESA annual meeting, plus $100 and a certificate. **No. of Awards:** 5. **To Apply:** The name of each branch awardee should be sent along with supporting documents and a black and white photograph to ESA (address above). **Deadline:** January 1. **Contact:** Executive Director at the above address (see entry 2387).

**• 2389 • ESA Undergraduate Scholarships** *(Undergraduate/Scholarship)*

**Purpose:** To encourage student interest in the science of entomology. **Focus:** Zoology, Entomology, Biology or Related Sciences. **Qualif.:** Applicants must be enrolled as undergraduate students in entomology, zoology, biology, or a related science at a college or university in the United States, Mexico, or Canada, and have accumulated a minimum of 30 semester hours at the time the award is presented. **Criteria:** Students must have demonstrated interest in entomology, and students with such interest will be given special consideration, as will students with demonstrated financial need.

**Funds Avail.:** Several awards or $1,500 are presented. **To Apply:** Potential applicants should request an application in writing. The completed application must contain a statement from the student concerning interest in entomology, career goals, financial need, and other pertinent factors that illustrate qualifications for the scholarship (limit the statement to two typewritten pages); three typewritten statements from school officials or other knowledgeable individuals attesting to entomological interests, character, aptitude, and financial need; current official college transcripts; and a black and white photograph. **Deadline:** May 31. **Contact:** The Entomological Society of America at the above address (see entry 2387).

**• 2390 • Jeffrey P. LaFage Graduate Student Research Award** *(Graduate/Award)*

**Purpose:** To promote research in control of urban pests. **Focus:** Entomology. **Qualif.:** Applicant may be of any nationality, but must be a graduate student whose proposal on the control of urban pests is innovative.

**Funds Avail.:** $2,000. **No. of Awards:** One. **To Apply:** Submit a double spaced proposal (six copies) including title, duration, and background information on the proposals significance to the Jeffrey P. LaFage, Graduate Student Research Committee, at the above address. Include a black and white picture and two letters of recommendation. **Deadline:** July 1. **Contact:** Executive Director at the above address (see entry 2387).

**• 2391 • Henry and Sylvia Richardson Research Grant** *(Postdoctorate/Award)*

**Purpose:** To promote research in selected areas of entomology. **Focus:** Entomology. **Qualif.:** Applicant may be of any nationality, but must be a postdoctoral member of the Society with at least one year of research experience. Applicant must have a GPA of 3.0. Primary consideration will be given to those postdoctoral candidates doing research in insect attractants, repellents, biological control, thermo control, or chemical control. Secondary consideration will be given to research into veterinary medicine where control of insects is important.

**Funds Avail.:** $1,000. **No. of Awards:** One. **To Apply:** Write to the Executive Director for application form and guidelines. Include a description of credentials, a two-page typewritten research

## Entomological Society of America (continued)

summary, college transcripts, and two letters of reference (one from a major professor, one from a former instructor). **Deadline:** July 1. **Contact:** Executive Director at the above address (see entry 2387).

### • 2392 • Snodgrass Memorial Research Grant
*(Graduate/Grant)*

**Purpose:** To provide research funds to graduate student members of ESA who are undertaking research in selected areas of entomology and have demonstrated a high level of scholarship. **Focus:** Entomology. **Qualif.:** Candidates must be graduate student members of ESA and must be conducting research in either arthropod morphology, systematics and taxonomy, or evolution at a recognized college or university, and must have an overall grade-point average equivalent to 3.0 on a 4.0 scale.

**Funds Avail.:** Varies. **To Apply:** Candidates should submit a letter of application describing eligibility credentials; one typewritten page describing research in one of the three areas defined above; college graduate transcripts; letters of recommendation from two faculty members from the college or university the applicant is attending; and a black and white photograph. **Deadline:** July 1. **Contact:** Executive Director at the above address (see entry 2387).

### • 2393 •
## Entomological Society of Canada
393 Winston Ave.                    *Ph:* (613)725-2619
Ottawa, ON, Canada K2A 1Y8          *Fax:* (613)725-9349
*E-mail:* entsoc.can@sympatico.ca
*URL:* http://insect-world.com/ca-ensoc.html

### • 2394 • Entomological Society Postgraduate Awards *(Graduate/Award)*

**Purpose:** To assist entomological studies by Canadian graduate students. **Focus:** Entomology. **Qualif.:** Applicant must be a Canadian citizen or landed immigrant with a bachelor's degree from a Canadian university. Candidate must be entering, or be accepted into, a graduate program in entomology at a Canadian university.

**Funds Avail.:** $2,000. **No. of Awards:** 2. **To Apply:** Write for application form and guidelines. **Deadline:** June 15. Awards are made in October.

### • 2395 •
## Epilepsy Foundation of America
Research and Professional
  Education
4351 Garden City Dr.                *Ph:* (301)459-3700
Landover, MD 20785                  *Fax:* (301)577-2684
*E-mail:* postmaster@efa.org
*URL:* http://www.efa.org

### • 2396 • Behavioral Sciences Research Training Fellowship *(Postdoctorate/Fellowship)*

**Purpose:** To offer qualified individuals an opportunity to develop expertise in the area of epilepsy research relative to behavioral sciences through a one-year training experience with involvement in an epilepsy research project. **Focus:** Sociology, social work, psychology, anthropology, nursing, political science, and others relevant to epilepsy research and practice. **Qualif.:** Applicants must have received their doctoral degree in a field of the behavioral sciences by the time the Fellowship commences and desire additional postdoctoral research experience in epilepsy. The project must be carried out at an approved facility. Women and minorities are encouraged to apply.

**Funds Avail.:** The Fellowship carries a stipend of up to $30,000 depending on the experience and qualifications of the applicant and the scope and duration of the proposed project. **No. of Awards:** 1. **To Apply:** Application forms and guidelines are available upon request. **Deadline:** February 1. **Contact:** Epilepsy Foundation of America at the above address (see entry 2395).

### • 2397 • Behavioral Sciences Student Fellowship
*(Professional Development/Fellowship)*

**Purpose:** To stimulate individuals to pursue careers in epilepsy in either research or practice settings. **Focus:** Sociology, social work, psychology, anthropology, nursing, and political science. **Qualif.:** Applicants must be students of vocational rehabilitation or rehabilitation counseling, who are able to work for a three-month period on an epilepsy project. Candidates may propose an epilepsy-related study or training project that will be carried out at a United States institution of their choice, where there are on-going programs of research, service, or training for epilepsy and where preceptors will accept responsibility for recipients' supervision and projects. Applications from women and minorities are encouraged.

**Funds Avail.:** $2,000. The amount of fellowships varies each year. **No. of Awards:** Varies. **To Apply:** The candidate must submit an original and ten copies of the application, which includes a brief description of the project, a letter from the preceptor, a letter from the applicant that states relevant experience, interests as they relate to epilepsy, and reasons for applying for the fellowship. **Deadline:** February 1. **Contact:** Epilepsy Foundation of America at the above address (see entry 2395).

### • 2398 • Clinical Research Fellowship
*(Postdoctorate/Fellowship)*

**Purpose:** To develop expertise in epilepsy research. **Focus:** Epilepsy. **Qualif.:** Candidates must be eligible to work in the United States. Applicants for a Postdoctoral Fellowship must be either physicians or neuroscientists with a Ph.D. Preference is given to project proposals that have a pediatric or developmental emphasis. Research must be conducted at a facility with an ongoing epilepsy research program. Applicants for Clinical Research Fellowships must hold an M.D. degree and have completed residency training. Fellowships are tenable at facilities where there are ongoing clinical epilepsy research programs. Research may either be basic or clinical, but they must have equal emphasis on clinical training and clinical epileptology. Applicants for a Behavioral Sciences Fellowship must have received a doctoral degree in a field of behavioral sciences by the start of the fellowship term. They must also plan to conduct a research project in epilepsy relevant to a behavioral science at an approved facility.

**Funds Avail.:** $40,000/year maximum. **No. of Awards:** Varies according to funding available. **To Apply:** Write to the Foundation for application form and guidelines. **Deadline:** September 1.

**Remarks:** The Clinical Research Fellowships are also known as the William Gowers Fellowship, the Victor Horsley Fellowship, the John Hughlings Jackson Fellowship, the Merritt-Putnam Fellowship, and the Wilder Penfield Fellowship. EFA also offers EFA Research Grants to investigators in the field of epilepsy research. Write for further details. **Contact:** Epilepsy Foundation of America, at the above address (see entry 2395).

### • 2399 • Epilepsy Foundation of America Research Grants *(Postdoctorate/Grant)*

**Purpose:** To support basic and clinical research in the biological, behavioral, and social sciences, which will advance the understanding, treatment, and prevention of epilepsy. **Qualif.:** Priority is given to young investigators who are just entering the field of epilepsy research, those who are engaged in new or innovative projects, and to investigators whose research is relevant to developmental or pediatric aspects of epilepsy. Applications in the behavioral sciences are encouraged, as are applications from women and minorities. Applications from established investigators with other sources of support are discouraged.

**Funds Avail.:** Support is limited up to $40,000. Second-year funding may be requested by re-application; first year applicants receive priority. Funds may not be applied to the purchase of permanent equipment, salary support for non-junior professional personnel, travel to present findings at meetings, or indirect costs or institutional overhead. **To Apply:** The completed application includes a list and description of duties of all personnel engaged in the project, an outline of estimated financial outlays, biographical data, and financial support from other sources. In not more than ten pages, a one-page abstract of the proposal, specific aims and anticipated significance of the research, facilities available, methods of procedure, and the principal investigator's and staffs' previous work that is related to the research must be presented. At the conclusion of the research, written reports describing research findings and funds expended must be submitted to the Foundation. Investigator reports must acknowledge the Foundation's support. Candidate must submit original and 15 copies of the application with the supporting material. **Deadline:** September 2.

**Remarks:** The program is supported in part by Parke-Davis, Geigy Pharmaceuticals, Abbott Laboratories and the Burroughs Wellcome Fund. **Contact:** Epilepsy Foundation of America at the above address (see entry 2395).

### • 2400 • Epilepsy Foundation of America Research Training Fellowships *(Doctorate/Fellowship)*

**Purpose:** To offer qualified individuals the opportunity to develop expertise in epilepsy research through a one-year training experience and involvement in an epilepsy research project. **Qualif.:** Applicants must be physicians or Ph.D. neuroscientists who desire postdoctoral research experience. The research project may be either basic or clinical but must address a question of fundamental importance. A clinical training component is not required. **Criteria:** Preference is given to applicants whose proposals have a pediatric or developmental emphasis.

**Funds Avail.:** The Fellowship carries up to $40,000 stipend and must be carried out at a facility where there is an ongoing epilepsy research program. **No. of Awards:** Varies. **To Apply:** Application forms and guidelines are available upon request. **Deadline:** September 1. **Contact:** Epilepsy Foundation of America at the above address (see entry 2395).

### • 2401 • Health Sciences Student Fellowships *(All/ Fellowship)*

**Purpose:** To stimulate individuals to pursue careers in epilepsy in either research or practice settings. **Qualif.:** Applicants must be medical or health science students, who are able to work during a three-month period on an epilepsy study project. The project may be carried out at a United States institution of the student's choice where there are on-going programs of research, service, or training in the field of epilepsy. A preceptor must accept responsibility for supervision of the student and the project.

**Funds Avail.:** The amount of each fellowship is $2,000. **No. of Awards:** Varies. **To Apply:** Application forms and guidelines are available by request. **Deadline:** February 1. **Contact:** Epilepsy Foundation of America at the above address (see entry 2395).

### • 2402 • William G. Lennox International Clinical Research Fellowship; Fritz E. Dreifuss International Visiting Professorships *(Postdoctorate/Fellowship)*

**Purpose:** To promote the exchange of medical and scientific information on epilepsy between the United States and other countries. **Focus:** Epilepsy. **Qualif.:** Applicants may be of any nationality. U.S. citizens may use the awards in any country. Citizens of other countries must use the awards in the United States. Applicants for the Lennox Fellowship must hold an M.D. or the equivalent and have completed residency training. Applicants for a Merritt-Putnam Professorship must be professors of epilepsy. EFA provides the cost of transportation and incidental expenses of the visiting professor; the host institution is expected to assume other expenses. Placements for professorships are arranged by EFA from a preselected group of institutions.

**Funds Avail.:** Lennox Fellowship: $40,000; Fritz E. Dreifuss Professorship: varies. **No. of Awards:** Varies. **To Apply:** Write for application guidelines and form. **Deadline:** All year - for Dreifuss, 9/ 1 - for Lennox. **Contact:** Epilepsy Foundation of America, at the above address (see entry 2395).

### • 2403 • Eppley Foundation for Research, Inc.
260 Madison Ave., 18th Fl.
New York, NY 10016                                    *Fax:* (212)448-0066

### • 2404 • Eppley Foundation Support for Advanced Scientific Research *(Postdoctorate/Grant)*

**Purpose:** To support and encourage post-doctoral work in the physical and biological sciences. **Focus:** Biological Sciences. **Qualif.:** Applicants must be qualified investigators conducting post-doctoral, original research in the physical and biological sciences. Candidates must have a Ph.D. or M.D., and be affiliated with a recognized educational or research institution. Persons who have recently received their doctorates are unlikely to receive funding. Grant proposals from foreign countries are considered without prejudice, but such applicants must explain in a cover letter why they are unable to obtain research funds in their own countries.

**Funds Avail.:** Up to 12 grants ranging from several thousand dollars to $25,000. The average grant is $15,000. Funds are issued to the institution for the individual. Institutions must acknowledge in writing their willingness to administer the grant. Up to 15 percent of the grant will go for institutional administration costs. Recipients must submit a final report one year after the grant period, which includes an itemized accounting of funds disbursed. **No. of Awards:** 10. **To Apply:** Five reprints of any publication arising from work sponsored by the Foundation must be sent to the Foundation office. A formal application, a proposal that is concise and states clearly the methods and goals of the researcher, a vita (proposals involving more than one investigator should include vitae for all researchers), itemized budget and a sponsoring letter from the institution must be submitted. No Phone inquiries accepted. **Deadline:** All application materials must be filed by the first of February, May, August or November.

**Remarks:** The Eppley Research Foundation was created 1947 by Captain Marion Eppley, a well-known physical chemist who guided the Eppley Laboratory for 43 years. **Contact:** Huyler C. Held at the above address (see entry 2403).

### • 2405 • Epsilon Sigma Phi
PO Box 626                                              *Ph:* (218)864-8678
Battle Lake, MN 56515                             *Fax:* (218)864-8064
*E-mail:* jscarlsm@aol.com

### • 2406 • Epsilon Sigma Phi Mini-Grants *(Graduate, Professional Development/Grant)*

**Purpose:** To increase professional competencies and enhance professionalism in the Cooperative Extension system. **Focus:**

## Epsilon Sigma Phi (continued)

General Studies. **Qualif.:** Applicant must be a member of Epsilon Sigma Phi in good standing, show evidence of financial need, present a strong professional improvement plan, and be recommended by the State Extension Director. Mini-grants are based on topics to enhance professionalism. **Criteria:** Selection is by the Member Services Committee for the Mini-grants.

**Funds Avail.:** Mini-grants for $500. **No. of Awards:** 4. **To Apply:** Applications are available from the State Chapter. **Deadline:** Mini-grant proposals must be postmarked by March 1. **Contact:** Epsilon Sigma Phi at the above address (see entry 2405).

### • 2407 • Epsilon Sigma Phi Professionalism Scholarship *(Professional Development/Scholarship)*

**Purpose:** To increase professional competencies and enhance professionalism in the Cooperative Extension system. **Focus:** General Studies. **Qualif.:** Applicants must be members of Epsilon Sigma Phi in good standing and show evidence of financial need. **Criteria:** Selection is based on the relevance of the proposed study to applicant's overall professional development and to their State's emphasis on professionalism.

**Funds Avail.:** $500 scholarships. **No. of Awards:** Up to 4. **To Apply:** Applications are available from the State Chapter. **Deadline:** Applications must be postmarked by March 1. **Contact:** Epsilon Sigma Phi at the above address (see entry 2405).

### • 2408 • Epsilon Sigma Phi Scholarship Loans *(Graduate, Professional Development/Scholarship loan)*

**Purpose:** To increase professional competencies and enhance professionalism in the Cooperative Extension system. **Focus:** General Studies. **Qualif.:** Applicants must be members of Epsilon Sigma Phi in good standing, show evidence of financial need, present a strong professional improvement plan, and be recommended by the State Extension Director. **Criteria:** Selection is through a peer review of applications.

**Funds Avail.:** Up to $2,000 is available per loan with no interest, provided that the loan is repaid before the conclusion of the first year following the closing date of study. **To Apply:** Applications are available from each state chapter. **Deadline:** Loan applications must be submitted at least four months in advance of study. **Contact:** Epsilon Sigma Phi at the above address (see entry 2405).

### • 2409 •
### Equitable Life Assurance Society of the U.S.
787 7th Ave.  
New York, NY 10019  
*URL:* http://www.law.emory.edu/11circuit/mar96/94-9401.opa.html  
*Ph:* (212)554-8591  
*Fax:* (212)554-1296

### • 2410 • Pillsbury Music Scholarship *(Undergraduate/Scholarship)*

**Focus:** Music. **Criteria:** Applicants must be Santa Barbara county residents and studying in Santa Barbara.

**Funds Avail.:** $25,000. **No. of Awards:** 20. **To Apply:** Applicants must audition. **Deadline:** May 15. **Contact:** Lisa K. Garrett.

### • 2411 •
### Esperanza, Inc.
May Dugan Multi-Service Center  
4115 Bridge Ave., Rm. 107  
Cleveland, OH 44113-3304  
*E-mail:* AnnSanchez@aol.com  
*Ph:* (216)651-7178  
*Fax:* (216)651-7183

### • 2412 • Esperanza Scholarships *(Graduate, Undergraduate/Scholarship)*

**Purpose:** To enable Hispanic students to pursue a higher education. **Focus:** Open. **Qualif.:** Applicants must be Hispanic and residents of Cuyahoga, Lake, Geauga, Portage, Summit, Medina, or Lorain County, Ohio. They must also be enrolled full-time at an accredited college or university. High school applicants must be scheduled to receive their diploma or GED certificate. **Criteria:** Selection is based on academic achievement, community involvement, income level, letters of recommendation, and an essay. All semi-finalists are interviewed by a scholarship committee.

**Funds Avail.:** A minimum $500. **No. of Awards:** 40-50. **To Apply:** Two letters of recommendation are required. **Deadline:** March 1. **Contact:** Esperanza, Inc. at the above address (see entry 2411).

### • 2413 •
### Eta Sigma Phi
Dept. of Classics  
414 E. Clark  
University of South Dakota  
Vermillion, SD 57069-2390  
*Ph:* (605)677-5468  
*Fax:* (605)677-5073

### • 2414 • The Eta Sigma Phi Summer Scholarships *(Doctorate, Graduate/Scholarship)*

**Purpose:** Six semester hours of credit may be earned at either summer session, which is applicable toward an advanced degree in Classics at most graduate schools, provided advance arrangements have been made. **Focus:** Greek, Latin, Ancient History, Classical Archeology. **Qualif.:** Candidates must be Eta Sigma Phi members and alumni who have received a bachelor's degree within five years of the deadline for submitting application or who will receive it before June of the summer the scholarship is tenable. Candidates must not yet have received a doctoral degree. **Criteria:** The quality of the applicant's work in Greek and Latin, intention to teach at the secondary school or college level, and service to Eta Sigma Phi are considered.

**Funds Avail.:** The Scholarship to the American Academy in Rome has a value of $2,600, a stipend granted by the Trustees of Eta Sigma Phi. The Scholarship to the American School of Classical Studies at Athens has a value of $3,150, including a stipend granted by the Trustees of Eta Sigma Phi and remission of the tuition fee by grant of the American School. **No. of Awards:** 2. **To Apply:** A transcript of undergraduate work, letters of recommendation and a statement, not to exceed 500 words, of purpose and reason for desiring the scholarship are required. **Deadline:** Applications must be submitted by mid December. Recipients are announced approximately January 15. **Contact:** Eta Sigma Phi, at the above address (see entry 2413).

• 2415 •

## Ole Evinrude Foundation
100 Sea Horse Dr.
Waukegan, IL 60085      *Ph:* (847)689-6200

### • 2416 • OMC Foundation Scholarship
*(Undergraduate/Scholarship)*

**Focus:** General Studies **Qualif.:** Applicants must be children of employees of Outboard Marine Corporation pursuing an education at a college or university.

**Funds Avail.:** $42,000; 42 scholarship at a value of $1,000 each. **To Apply:** Applicants must write for details. **Deadline:** Early fall. **Contact:** Outboard Marine Corporation Foundation at the above address (see entry 2415).

• 2417 •

## Evrytanian Association of America
121 Greenwich Rd.      *Ph:* (704)366-6571
Charlotte, NC 28211-2343      *Fax:* (704)366-6571

### • 2418 • Evrytanian Association Scholarship
*(Doctorate, Graduate, Undergraduate/Scholarship)*

**Qualif.:** Applicants must be students of Evrytanian background. **Criteria:** Winners are selected by a scholarship committee chosen by the board of trustees.

**Funds Avail.:** $1,000 per student. **To Apply:** Notify Association of interest. **Deadline:** June 1. **Contact:** Olga Kleto at the above address (see entry 2417).

• 2419 •

## H.T. Ewald Foundation
15175 E. Jefferson Ave.      *Ph:* (313)821-1278
Grosse Pointe, MI 48230-1312      *Fax:* (616)821-3299
*E-mail:* ewaldfndtn@aol.com

### • 2420 • H.T. Ewald Scholarships *(Undergraduate/Scholarship)*

**Purpose:** To help high school seniors finance a four-year education. **Focus:** None in particular. **Qualif.:** Applicants must be residents of Metropolitan Detroit, high school seniors in the top 50% of their classes, and show financial need. **Criteria:** Based on financial need, good grades, good character, leadership qualities, and good deeds.

**Funds Avail.:** $500-$2,500 per year. **No. of Awards:** 12 annually. **To Apply:** The completed application must be submitted along with the student's high school transcript, a 500-word autobiography, three or more letters of recommendation, and a photograph. **Deadline:** April 1. **Contact:** Ted Ewald, Shelagh Czuprenski, at the above address (see entry 2419).

• 2421 •

## Experimental Aircraft Association Foundation
Scholarship Program
PO Box 3065
Oshkosh, WI 54903-3065      *Ph:* (920)426-6815
*E-mail:* education@eaa.org
*URL:* http://ww.eaa.org

### • 2422 • EAA Aviation Achievement Scholarship *(All/Scholarship)*

**Focus:** Aviation. **Qualif.:** Applicants must be aviation majors, as well as well-rounded individuals involved in school and community activities.

**Funds Avail.:** Varies. **No. of Awards:** Two. **To Apply:** Contact the EAA Education Office for an application. **Deadline:** Early May.

### • 2423 • The Payzer Scholarship *(All/Scholarship)*

**Focus:** Engineering, Mathematics, Physical Science, Biological Science. **Qualif.:** Applicants must be majors in the subjects listed above. They must also be well-rounded individuals involved in school and community activities.

**Funds Avail.:** Varies. **No. of Awards:** One. **To Apply:** To apply, contact the EAA Education Office at the above address.

• 2424 •

## Explorers Club
46 E. 70th St.      *Ph:* (212)628-8383
New York, NY 10021-4971      *Fax:* (212)288-4449

### • 2425 • Explorers Club Exploration Fund Grants
*(Graduate, Postgraduate/Grant)*

**Purpose:** To provide grants in support of exploration and field research. **Focus:** Science. **Qualif.:** Candidates must be graduate students or researchers who will use the grants for expeditions of a scientific research nature. Mere travel to remote areas is not considered valid. In addition, the club's name or flag may not be used for any commercial purposes. Membership to the Explorers Club is not required. **Criteria:** Selection is based on the scientific and practical merit of the proposal, the competence of the investigator, and the appropriateness of the budget.

**Funds Avail.:** Grants of up to $1,200 each. Recipients are expected to provide a one or two page report on their exploration or research within the year. **No. of Awards:** 25. **To Apply:** Application form requests must be made to the Explorers Club. No application will be considered without a signed liability waiver. **Deadline:** January 31. Awards are announced in April. **Contact:** The Exploration Fund Committee at the above address (see entry 2424).

• 2426 •

## Falcon Foundation
3116 Academy Dr., Ste. 200      *Ph:* (719)333-4096
USAF Academy, CO 80840-4480      *Fax:* (719)333-3669

### • 2427 • Falcon Foundation Scholarship
*(Undergraduate/Scholarship)*

**Purpose:** To provide financial assistance for motivated young private preparatory school students seeking admission to the United States Air Force Academy and careers in the Air Force.

## Falcon Foundation (continued)

**Qualif.:** Applicants must be at least 17, but not more than 22 years of age by July 1 of the year they are admitted to the preparatory school. They must be citizens of the United States, unmarried with no dependent children, meet medical standards for a commission in the United States Air Force, and have completed the USAF Academy Precandidate Questionnaire (PCQ). **Criteria:** The foundation evaluates each candidate on the following criteria: motivation to graduate from the United States Air Force Academy and subsequently make a career in the Air Force; high literary and scholastic achievement; the qualities of maturity, truthfulness, courage, kindliness, unselfishness, fellowship, and devotion to duty; moral force of character and leadership instincts; and physical vigor demonstrated by success in sports. Applicants may be active candidates for an Academy appointment at the time the application is made.

**Funds Avail.:** $3,000. Scholarships provide a significant portion of the cost of room, board, and tuition, but are not expected to cover transportation and personal expenses. **No. of Awards:** 100. **To Apply:** Interested students must request the USAF PCQ from the Director of Admissions of the USAFA/RRS, return the completed PCQ, apply to authorized sources of nomination before January 31, and request, complete, and return the foundation's scholarship application with the signatures of both parents (if available) or legal guardian. SAT or ACT test results must be forwarded to the Director of Admissions, USAFA/RRS. **Deadline:** April 3. Test results must be at the Director's office in time for the results to be reviewed by May 1.

**Remarks:** A group of prominent Air Force Alumni organized the Foundation in 1958, three years after the Air Force Academy was established. **Contact:** Pearl L. Swofford, Administrative Assistant to President at the above address (see entry 2426)or the Director of Admissions, USAFA/RRS, USAF Academy, Colorado 80840-5651. Telephone (719)333-2520.

---

## • 2428 •
## Fancy Publications
PO Box 6050
Mission Viejo, CA 92690
*URL:* http://www.animalnetwork.com

### • 2429 • Dennis and Elizabeth Shattuck Internships
*(Undergraduate/Internship)*

**Purpose:** To provide experience for students at one or more Fancy Publications' national consumer and trade magazines in California and Hawaii. **Focus:** Journalism. **Qualif.:** Applicants must have completed their junior year and be pursuing careers in magazine editing.

**Funds Avail.:** $365 per week. **To Apply:** Applicants must submit a cover letter, resume, writing samples, non-official transcript and at least one faculty letter of recommendation.

---

## • 2430 •
## Federal Employee Education and Assistance Fund
8441 W. Bowles Ave., Ste. 200          *Ph:* (303)933-7580
Littleton, CO 80123                          *Fax:* (303)933-7587
                                                     *Free:* 800-323-4140

*E-mail:* FEEEAHQ@aol.com
*URL:* http://fpmi.com/FEEEA/FEEAhome.html

### • 2431 • FEEA Federal Plus Loan *(Graduate, Undergraduate/Loan)*

**Purpose:** To assist federal employees and their families in their search for higher education funding. A Federal Parent Plus Loan is a federally guaranteed loan available to parents of dependent undergraduate or graduate students. **Qualif.:** Applicants must be dependents of civilian federal and postal employees who are enrolled in an accredited college or university. Former employees and military are also eligible. **Criteria:** Selection is not based on financial need, but rather the ability to repay the loan.

**Funds Avail.:** Parents may borrow up to the cost of education minus any financial aid awarded. The loan must be repaid in 10 years. Interest rates are variable and do not exceed 10 percent. **To Apply:** For a complete application form, send a self-addressed, stamped envelope to the FEEA.

**Remarks:** A credit check may be performed. **Contact:** Financial Aid Offices or the FEEA at the above address (see entry 2430).

### • 2432 • FEEA Federal SLS Loan *(Graduate, Undergraduate/Loan)*

**Purpose:** To assist federal employees and their families in their search for higher education funding. A Federal SLS Loan is a federally guaranteed loan available to independent undergraduate and graduate students. **Qualif.:** Applicants must be civilian federal and postal employees and their family members who are enrolled in an accredited college or university. Former employees and military are also eligible. Applicants must apply for a Stafford Loan and a Pell Grant first. **Criteria:** Selection is not based on financial need.

**Funds Avail.:** Students may borrow up to $4,000 per year as a freshman or sophomore, $5,000 per year as a junior or senior, and $10,000 per year as a graduate or professional student. The loan must be repaid in 10 years. Interest rates are variable and do not exceed 11 percent. **To Apply:** For a complete application form, send a self-addressed, stamped envelope to the FEEA.

**Remarks:** A credit check may be performed. **Contact:** Financial Aid Offices or the FEEA at the above address (see entry 2430).

### • 2433 • FEEA Federal Stafford Loan *(Graduate, Undergraduate/Loan)*

**Purpose:** To assist federal employees and their families in their search for higher education funding. A Federal Stafford Loan is a low interest, federally subsidized loan available to help undergraduate and graduate students meet the costs of postsecondary education. **Qualif.:** Applicants must be civilian federal and postal employees and their dependent family members who are enrolled in an accredited college or university. Former employees and military are also eligible. **Criteria:** Selection is based on financial need.

**Funds Avail.:** Students may borrow up to $2,625 per year as a freshman, $3,500 as a sophomore, $5,500 per year as a junior or senior; and $8,500 per year as a graduate or professional student. The loan must be repaid in 10 years. Interest rates are variable and do not exceed 9 percent. **To Apply:** Students are required to file the Free Application for Federal Student Aid to assess their financial need. Each school may have additional requirements. For a complete application form, send a self-addressed, stamped envelope to the FEEA. **Contact:** Financial Aid Offices or FEEA at the above address (see entry 2430).

### • 2434 • FEEA Federal Unsubsidized Stafford Loan
*(Graduate, Undergraduate/Loan)*

**Purpose:** To assist federal employees and their families in their search for higher education funding. A Federal Unsubsidized Stafford Loan is a low interest non federally subsidized loan. **Qualif.:** Applicants must be civilian federal and postal employees and their dependent family members who are enrolled in an accredited college or university. Former employees and military are also eligible. **Criteria:** Selection is not based on financial need.

**Funds Avail.:** Students may borrow up to $2,625 per year as a freshman, $3,500 as a sophomore, $5,500 per year as a junior or senior; and $8,500 per year as a graduate or professional student. The loan must be repaid in 10 years. Interest rates are variable and do not exceed 9 percent. **To Apply:** Students are required to file the Free Application for Federal Student Aid to assess their financial need. Each school may have additional requirements. For a complete application form, send a self-addressed, stamped envelope to the FEEA. **Contact:** Financial Aid Offices or the FEEA at the above address (see entry 2430).

### • 2435 • FEEA Scholarship Award *(Graduate, Undergraduate/Scholarship)*

**Purpose:** To assist federal employees and their families in their search for higher education funding. **Qualif.:** Applicants must be civilian federal and postal employees with at least three years of federal service or their dependent family members (children and spouses). Active duty personnel and retirees are not eligible. Employee applicants may be part-time students; dependents must be full-time. All applicants must be enrolled or plan to enroll in an accredited post secondary school in a course of study that will lead to a two-year, four-year, or graduate degree and have a GPA of at least 3.0 on a 4.0 scale. **Criteria:** Selection is strictly based on merit, including the applicant's academic record, recommendations, extracurricular and community service activities, and an essay.

**Funds Avail.:** The awards are from $300 to $1,500 for one year and are made in August. **No. of Awards:** 400. **To Apply:** Employees must provide their most recent Standard Form 50/Notice of Personnel Action or equivalent. Applicants must send a completed application form with one reference, a list briefly describing any awards or extracurricular or community service activities, an essay (topic changes each year), and a self-addressed, stamped envelope to acknowledge receipt of application. High school seniors must provide copies of their ACT or SAT scores. To receive an application, send a self-addressed stamped envelope to the address above between February and May. **Deadline:** Last Friday in May. **Contact:** The Federal Employee Education and Assistance Fund at the above address (see entry 2430). Toll-free telephone for questions only: 800-323-4240.

### • 2436 •
## J. Hugh & Earle W. Fellows Memorial Fund
1000 College Blvd.
Pensacola Junior College
Pensacola, FL 32504-8998          *Ph:* (904)484-1700

### • 2437 • J. Hugh & Earle W. Fellows Memorial Fund Loans *(Undergraduate/Loan)*

**Purpose:** To assist deserving and qualified men and women in the pursuit of their education in the fields of medicine, nursing, medical technology, and the ministry. **Focus:** Medicine, Nursing, Medical Technology, Religion. **Qualif.:** Applicants must be bona fide residents of Escambia, Santa Rosa, Okaloosa, or Walton County, Florida. Candidates must be of good moral character and qualified scholastically and intellectually for the education desired, and must have been accepted by, or be successfully pursuing training

at, an accredited school in the appropriate area of study. **Criteria:** Based on financial need, scholastic record, and the extent of assistance reasonably required to enable individuals to complete their training.

**Funds Avail.:** Loan amounts are determined by the need of the applicant. Loans are interest-free until graduation. Interest begins to accrue on the first day of the fourth month following graduation with payments beginning on the first day of the fifth month after graduation. **Contact:** The Memorial Fund at the above address (see entry 2436).

### • 2438 •
## Fellowship of United Methodists in Music and Worship Arts
c/o GBOD Worship Section
PO Box 24787                    *Ph:* (615)749-6875
Nashville, TN 37202            *Fax:* (615)749-6874
*E-mail:* fummwa@aol.com

### • 2439 • Fellowship of United Methodists in Worship, Music and Other Arts Scholarship *(Graduate, Undergraduate/Scholarship)*

**Purpose:** To encourage students training for ministry in the United Methodist Church in the areas of music worship, drama, dance, visuals, and other liturgical arts. **Focus:** Music, Religion. **Qualif.:** Applicants must be full-time music degree candidates, either entering as freshmen or already in an accredited university, college, or school of theology; candidates may also be doing special education in worship or the arts related to worship. Applicants must be members of The United Methodist Church for one year immediately before applying, giving evidence of strong Christian character and participation in Christian activities of the church and/or campus. Evidence of exceptional musical or other artistic talent, effective leadership ability, and outstanding promise of future usefulness must be demonstrated. **Criteria:** Talent, leadership ability, and promise and intent of continued service to the United Methodist Church as a church professional.

**Funds Avail.:** Three $1,000 scholarships and the Thom Jones Scholarship, a $1,500 grant. **No. of Awards:** One. **To Apply:** The following documents must be submitted on the applicant's behalf to the Chairperson of the Scholarship Committee: a completed application form; an official transcript of the applicant's academic record from the last institution attended; a personal statement from the applicant which describes intent of church music as a vocation, or other music or arts degree in relation to worship, and evidence of enthusiasm for and commitment to the vocational choice; three letters of reference attesting to the ability of the applicant to meet the above requirements (from the applicant's major professor, the minister of the church where the applicant is affiliated and/or employed, and a third person who can support the applicant's abilities as a musician/artist/performer); and a page from the Financial Officer of the applicant's school which describes his/her financial need. **Deadline:** March 1. **Contact:** Fellowship of United Methodists in Worship, Music, and Other Arts Scholarship at the above address (see entry 2438).

---

• 2440 •
## Feminist Majority - Internship Program in Feminism and Public Policy
1600 Wilson Blvd., Ste. 801
Arlington, VA 22209
*E-mail:* femmaj@feminist.org
*URL:* http://www.feminst.org/home.html

*Ph:* (703)522-2214
*Fax:* (703)522-2219

### • 2441 • The Feminist Majority Internships
*(Graduate, Professional Development, Undergraduate/ Internship)*

**Focus:** Women's Studies. **Qualif.:** Applicants must be undergraduate, graduate, and professional school students who aspire to become leaders in the feminist movement. Any major is fine, but we are especially interested in political science and women's studies majors.

**Funds Avail.:** The internships are available year-round on either a full-time or part-time basis and run for a minimum of two months. They are served in the Feminist Majority's Washington, DC, and Los Angeles offices. Each internship is tailored to meet the needs of the individual student. Responsibilities include monitoring press conferences and congressional hearings, researching, writing, policy analysis, organizing, and outreach. Interns are responsible for their own housing. From September-May, a stipend of $70/ week is offered. **Contact:** Kimberly Schmidt and Clea Benson at the above address;(see entry 2440) Shelly Cryer, The Fund for the Feminist Majority, Los Angeles office, 8105 W. Third St., Ste. 1, Los Angeles, California. Telephone: (213)651-0495; fax: (213)653-2689. Priscilla Sanders, The Fund for the Feminist Majority, Boston office, 675 Massachusetts Ave., Cambridge, Massachusetts 02139. Telephone (617)864-0130; fax (617)864-0417.

• 2442 •
## Field Museum of Natural History
Scholarship Committee
Roosevelt Rd. at Lake Shore Dr.
Chicago, IL 60605-2496
*E-mail:* ezeiger@fmnh.org
*URL:* http://www.fmnh.org/info/scholar.htm

*Ph:* (312)922-9410
*Fax:* (312)427-7269

### • 2443 • Lester Armour Graduate Fellowships
*(Graduate/Fellowship)*

**Purpose:** To support graduate studies and research associated with the Museum. **Focus:** Natural History: Anthropology, Botany, Geology, Zoology. **Qualif.:** Candidate may be of any nationality. Graduate Fellowships are for dissertation research associated with the Museum. Normally, candidate will be expected to have formal involvement with the Museum, by having a curator serve on the student's academic committee and by utilizing the collections and facilities of the Museum. Student must be in residence in the Chicago area and is expected to spend a significant portion of his/ her research time at the Museum and should have already passed his/her preliminary exam (i.e., be working on a dissertation).

**Funds Avail.:** Stipend and limited tuition support. **To Apply:** Write to the chairperson for application form and guidelines. Submit six copies of the following: form; one- to two-page description of proposed research; current curriculum vitae; names of two references; copy of thesis proposal. **Deadline:** February 1.

**Remarks:** Applicants for all funding categories are encouraged to contact an appropriate curator at the Field Museum prior to submitting their application; curator must be on student's committee. **Contact:** Lance Grande, Chairperson, Scholarship Committee, at the above address (see entry 2442).

### • 2444 • Field Museum Graduate Fellowships
*(Graduate/Fellowship)*

**Purpose:** To support graduate studies and research associated with the Museum. **Focus:** Natural History: Anthropology, Botany, Geology, Zoology. **Qualif.:** Graduate Fellowships are for dissertation research associated with the Museum. Normally, candidate will be expected to have formal involvement with the Museum by having a curator serve on the student's academic committee and by utilizing the collections and facilities of the Museum. Student must be in residence in the Chicago area and is expected to spend a significant portion of his/her research time at the Museum and should have already passed his/her preliminary exam (i.e., be working on a dissertation).

**Funds Avail.:** Stipend and limited tuition support. **No. of Awards:** Up to two. **To Apply:** Write to the chairperson for application form and guidelines. Submit six copies of the following: form; one to two-page description of proposed research; current curriculum vitae; names of two references; copy of thesis proposal. **Deadline:** February 1.

**Remarks:** Applicants for all funding categories are required to submit a letter of support from a curator at the Field Museum prior to submitting their application; curator must be on student's committee. **Contact:** Dr. Lance Grande Chairperson, Scholarship Committee, at the above address (see entry 2442).

### • 2445 • Field Museum of Natural History Undergraduate Internships *(Undergraduate/Internship)*

**Purpose:** To allow undergraduate students or recent graduates to work directly with a Collections and Research Department staff member at the museum. **Focus:** Natural History.

**Funds Avail.:** A stipend of $964 per month. **No. of Awards:** Six. **To Apply:** Applications should include the original, plus five copies. **Deadline:** February 1. **Contact:** Tracey Pilch at (312)922-9410, ext. 522.

### • 2446 • Field Museum Visiting Scholar Funds
*(Postdoctorate/Grant)*

**Purpose:** To provide research opportunities for scientists and students who wish to utilize the research collections at the Field Museum. **Focus:** Natural History: Anthropology, Botany, Geology, Zoology. **Qualif.:** Four separate funds are available. Professionals and graduate students may apply. The Bass Fund was established to provide extended-term research opportunities for distinguished national and foreign scientists. Preference is given to projects related to the research interests of a staff member of the Field Museum.

**Funds Avail.:** Bass Fund: negotiable stipend; other Funds: travel and subsistence grants. **To Apply:** Write to the chairperson for application form and guidelines. Submit six copies of the following: form; one- to two-page description of proposed research; current curriculum vitae; detailed budget. **Deadline:** May 1, November 1.

**Remarks:** Applicants for all funding categories are required to submit a letter of support from a curator at the Field Museum prior to submitting their application. **Contact:** Dr. Lance Grande, Chairperson, Scholarship Committee, at the above address (see entry 2442).

### • 2447 • William A. and Stella M. Rowley Graduate Fellowship *(Graduate/Fellowship)*

**Purpose:** To support graduate studies and research associated with the Museum. **Focus:** Natural History: Anthropology, Botany, Geology, Zoology. **Qualif.:** Candidate may be of any nationality. Graduate Fellowships are for dissertation research associated with the Museum. Normally, candidate will be expected to have formal involvement with the Museum, by having a curator serve on the student's academic committee and by utilizing the collections and facilities of the Museum. Student must be in residence in the Chicago area and is expected to spend a significant portion of his/

her research time at the Museum and should have already passed his/her preliminary exam (i.e., be working on a dissertation).

**Funds Avail.:** Stipend and limited tuition support. **To Apply:** Write to the chairperson for application form and guidelines. Submit six copies of the following: form; one- to two-page description of proposed research; current curriculum vitae; names of two references; copy of thesis proposal. **Deadline:** February 1.

**Remarks:** Applicants for all funding categories are encouraged to contact an appropriate curator at the Field Museum prior to submitting their application; curator must be on student's committee. **Contact:** Lance Grande, Chairperson, Scholarship Committee, at the above address (see entry 2442).

---

### • 2448 •
### Fight for Sight, Inc. - Research Division, Prevent Blindness America

500 E. Remington Rd.                        *Ph:* (847)843-2020
Schaumburg, IL 60173-4557              *Fax:* (847)843-8458
*E-mail:* info@preventblindness.org
*URL:* http://www.preventblindness.org

*Fight for Sight is the Research Division of the National Society to Prevent Blindness.*

#### • 2449 • FFS-NSPB Grants-In-Aid *(Postdoctorate/ Grant)*

**Purpose:** To fund studies of priority interest and pilot projects of investigators in ophthalmology, vision, and related sciences who have limited or no research funding. **Focus:** Ophthalmology, vision and related sciences. **Qualif.:** Applications are generally not considered from residents, postdoctoral fellows, or senior investigators with significant research support.

**Funds Avail.:** $1,000 to $12,000. Support is used to help defray costs of personnel (excluding the applicant), equipment, and consumable supplies needed for specific research investigations. Institutional overhead charges are not covered by these grants. Renewal support for a second year may be available; two years is the maximum for such assistance. **No. of Awards:** 20-25. **Deadline:** March 1; grants commence between July 1 and October 1.

**Remarks:** Fight for Sight generally receives approximately 100 grant applications. **Contact:** Research Awards Coordinator at the above address (see entry 2448).

#### • 2450 • FFS-NSPB Postdoctoral Research Fellowships *(Postdoctorate/Fellowship)*

**Purpose:** To fund vision related research. **Focus:** Ophthalmology and related sciences. **Qualif.:** Applicants must be individuals with a doctorate who are interested in academic careers involving basic or clinical research in ophthalmology, vision, or related sciences. Clinical research fellows are required to spend at least 50 percent of their time on their research project, while basic researchers are expected to devote full time. Postdoctoral fellowships are not awarded to residents or persons who are receiving fellowships from other sources. Applications usually will not be considered from individuals who have had two or more years of postdoctoral training.

**Funds Avail.:** Fellows are awarded with stipends ranging from $5,000 to $14,000. Recipients may supplement FFS-NSPB postdoctoral fellowships with institutional funds providing the combined total does not exceed $28,000 per annum. **No. of Awards:** 15-20. **To Apply:** If at the time of filing the applicant does not have a doctorate, a cover letter must be submitted with the application advising that the doctorate will be conferred by the designated commencement date of the award. Should unanticipated delays occur in obtaining the doctorate, FFS-NSPB reserves the right to withdraw the award. **Deadline:** Materials must

be submitted by March 1; fellowships commence between July 1 and September 1.

**Remarks:** Fight for Sight generally receives approximately 65 fellowship applications. **Contact:** Research Awards Coordinator at the above address (see entry 2448).

#### • 2451 • FFS-NSPB Student Fellowships *(Doctorate, Graduate, Undergraduate/Fellowship)*

**Qualif.:** Applicants must be undergraduates, medical students, or graduate students interested in eye-related clinical or basic research. Advanced graduate students and others with additional stipend support are not eligible.

**Funds Avail.:** $500 monthly may be given to selected applicants. **No. of Awards:** 20-25. **Deadline:** Materials must be in by March 1. Commencement dates are variable, but usually begin June 1. **Contact:** Research Awards Coordinator at the above address (see entry 2448).

---

### • 2452 •
### FINA Oil and Chemical Company

                                            *Fax:* (972)801-4228
PO Box 2159
Dallas, TX 75221                            *Free:* 800-555-FINA
*E-mail:* scholar.athlete.program@fina.com
*URL:* http://www.rmfssi.com/pboshow/D-38.htm

#### • 2453 • FINA/Dallas Morning News All-Texas Scholar-Athlete Team Scholarships *(Undergraduate/ Scholarship)*

**Purpose:** To honor Texas high school students who excel in athletics, academic achievement, and leadership qualities, and who participate in other school and community activities. **Focus:** General Studies. **Qualif.:** Candidates should be seniors in Texas high schools who have lettered in varsity sports for their high school. Anyone may nominate an eligible senior. To become finalists, applicants must have been varsity letter winners in a UIL-approved sport, have a high school grade point average of at least 90 percent, and be in the top ten percent of their graduating class. **Criteria:** Based upon academic achievements and honors, community service, and leadership.

**Funds Avail.:** 12 scholarships of $4,000 each are awarded annually, and 32 scholarships of $500 each are also awarded. **No. of Awards:** 44. **To Apply:** Applications are sent to all Texas high schools. Nominees are sent application forms to complete. 44 finalists are selected on a geographic distribution formula. Recipients must enter college as full-time students the fall following high school graduation. They may also accept other scholarships. Recipients are announced in March. **Deadline:** Announced in mid December. **Contact:** High school coach, principal, or student advisor/counselor or Maria Martineau, FINA Public Affairs Department, at the above address (see entry 2452).

---

• 2454 •
**Finance Authority of Maine - Education Assistance Div.**

| | |
|---|---|
| 1 Weston Ct. | *Ph:* (207)287-2183 |
| State House Sta., No. 119 | *Fax:* (207)287-2233 |
| Augusta, ME 04333 | *Free:* 800-228-3734 |

*E-mail:* fwistaff@erols.com
*URL:* http://www.famemaine.com

#### • 2455 • Blaine House Scholars Loans *(Graduate, Undergraduate/Loan)*

**Purpose:** To provide interest-free loans for graduating high school seniors, college students, and teachers who are pursuing studies in education. **Focus:** Education. **Qualif.:** Applicants must be Maine residents who are one of the following: high school seniors graduating in the top half of their class or those with GED scores equivalent to the top half of scores taken at the same time; college students who have a minimum cumulative GPA of 3.0 on a 4.0 scale; post-baccalaureate students who have a minimum GPA of 3.0 on a 4.0 scale at the time of graduation or in their last semester of graduate work after completing a minimum of nine credit hours; or teachers who are certified and working as teachers at least half-time. **Criteria:** Based on an essay submitted by the applicant as well as high school or college transcripts, rank in class, SAT scores, GPA, awards, and activities related to teaching (where applicable). Teacher loans are also competitive, and based on the relevance of the loan request to the individual's teaching career.

**Funds Avail.:** Recipients may borrow a maximum of $1,500 per year up to an aggregate total of $6,000. Undergraduate students must be enrolled full-time while graduate students need not be. Each student recipient may cancel the total amount of the loan by completing four years of return service in a public or private elementary or secondary school approved for tuition purposes, or in a state-operated school. This repayment option can be accelerated to two years if the return service is conducted in a geographically isolated area or underserved subject area designated by the Finance Authority of Maine. If the recipient fails to meet the return service option, the total debt must be repaid to the state within five years of graduation. Teachers may have their loans forgiven with two years of return service in a Maine public or private elementary or secondary school approved for tuition purposes or a state-operated school. If this service is performed in a designated underserved subject or geographically isolated area, the loan will be considered canceled after one year of return service. Failure to complete the return service option will necessitate total repayment of the loan within three years of graduation or completion of the courses for which the loan was awarded. Loans are renewable if the student maintains a 2.5 GPA. **To Apply:** Applications are available at Maine high school guidance offices and college financial aid offices throughout Maine. Applicants for loan renewal need only to submit a renewal application sent to the recipient's home. **Deadline:** April 1. **Contact:** Finance Authority of Maine, Education Assistance Division, at the above address (see entry 2454). Toll-free telephone (in Maine): (800)228-3734. TDD: (207)626-2717.

• 2456 •
**Financial Women International, Inc.**

| | |
|---|---|
| 200 N. Glebe Rd., Ste. 814 | *Ph:* (703)807-2007 |
| Arlington, VA 22203-3728 | *Fax:* (703)807-0111 |

*URL:* http://www.fwi.org

#### • 2457 • Chase Manhattan Scholarship *(Professional Development/Scholarship)*

**Purpose:** To encourage women in the financial services industry to reach their career goals by helping them pursue the necessary education.

**Funds Avail.:** One award for $2,000 was given in 1992. Scholarships may be applied toward any educational program the recipient chooses. **To Apply:** A completed application must be submitted. **Deadline:** May 1. **Contact:** Write to Chase Manhattan Scholarship at the above address (see entry 2456).

• 2458 •
**Fine Arts Work Center in Provincetown**

| | |
|---|---|
| 24 Pearl St. | *Ph:* (508)487-9960 |
| Provincetown, MA 02657 | *Fax:* (508)487-8873 |

*E-mail:* fawc@capecod.net
*URL:* http://www.capecodaccess.com/fineartsworkcenter

#### • 2459 • Fine Arts Work Center Fellowships *(Professional Development/Fellowship)*

**Purpose:** To encourage and support emerging artists and writers by giving them the freedom to work without distraction in a community of peers. **Focus:** Fiction, Painting, Photography, Poetry, Sculpture. **Qualif.:** Applicants may be any age, but the Center aims to help emerging talents who have completed their formal training and are already working on their own. Fellowships are based on the quality of the applicant's work. No other restrictions apply. Fellowships include a residency at the Center.

**Funds Avail.:** Monthly stipend, plus living and studio space **No. of Awards:** 10 visual arts and 10 writing. **To Apply:** Send a self-addressed, stamped envelope with request for application form and guidelines; specify interest in writing or visual arts. Information on submission of creative works is included in the application forms. **Deadline:** Writers December 1st; Visual Artists February 1. Notification around May 1. **Contact:** Fine Arts Work Center at the above address (see entry 2458).

• 2460 •
**First Catholic Slovak Ladies Association**

| | |
|---|---|
| 24950 Chagrin Blvd. | *Ph:* (216)464-8015 |
| Beachwood, OH 44122-5615 | *Fax:* (216)464-8717 |

#### • 2461 • First Catholic Slovak Ladies Association Fraternal Scholarship Awards *(Graduate, Undergraduate/Scholarship)*

**Focus:** General Studies. **Qualif.:** Applicants must be members in good standing of the First Catholic Slovak Ladies Association, and have been beneficial members of the Association for at least three years prior to the date of application on a $1,000 legal reserve certificate, or a minimum of three years on a $5,000 Participating Estate Certificate. All candidates must select a program leading to a bachelor's degree at an accredited college or university in the United States or Canada. Applicants are eligible to win this scholarship once as an undergraduate and once as a graduate student.

**Funds Avail.:** $800. **No. of Awards:** The are 60 Fraternal Scholarship Awards (31 for freshmen, 13 for sophomores, six for juniors, five for seniors, and five for full-time graduate students). **To Apply:** Freshman candidates must submit official transcripts of high school grades, including the first half of the senior year, along with scores of College Examination Board tests. Candidates other than freshmen must furnish complete transcripts of their college or university records. For all applicants, an autobiographical statement of approximately 500 words describing the applicant's goals and aspirations, a wallet-sized photograph, and verification of membership by the secretary of their local branch must accompany the application. A certified copy of their acceptance to the college named in the application must be received by the

Committee on the Fraternal Scholarships before payment will be made. **Deadline:** March 1. Winners are notified by June. **Contact:** Director of Fraternal Scholarship Aid at the above address (see entry 2460).

**• 2462 • First Catholic Slovak Ladies Association High School Fraternal Scholarship Awards** *(High School/Scholarship)*

**Focus:** General Studies. **Qualif.:** Applicants must be members in good standing of the First Catholic Slovak Ladies Association, have been a beneficial member of the Association for at least three years prior to the date of application on a $1,000 legal reserve certificate, or a minimum of three years on a $5,000 Participating Estate Certificate, and in a program leading to a high school certificate. All candidates must select a private or Catholic accredited high school in the United States or Canada.

**Funds Avail.:** U.S. 300. **No. of Awards:** Three each for freshmen, sophomores, juniors, and seniors. Applicants are eligible to win this award once, but may later apply for a college scholarship. **To Apply:** Freshman candidates must submit an official transcript of the previous year's grades. Candidates other than freshman scholars must submit a complete transcript of the candidate's high school record. All applicants must also submit an essay of approximately 250 words on "What this High School scholarship will do for me," a wallet-sized photograph, a copy of acceptance to the high school named in the application, and verification of membership. **Deadline:** March 1. Winners are notified by June. **Contact:** Director of Fraternal Scholarship Aid at the above address (see entry 2460).

**• 2463 •**
**First Cavalry Division Association**
302 N Main
Copperas Cove, TX 76522-1799          *Ph:* (817)547-6537

**• 2464 • First Cavalry Division Association Scholarship** *(Undergraduate/Scholarship)*

**Focus:** General Studies. **Qualif.:** Applicants must be children of soldiers of the 1st Cavalry Division who died, or who were totally and permanently disabled; children of members of the 1st Cavalry Division in peacetime; children of soldiers of he 1st Cavalry Division, USA Forward Air Controllers and A1E pilots and was Correspondents who served in designated qualifying units. In addition to meeting the above criteria, applicants must be registered with the Foundation prior to applying.

**Funds Avail.:** $600/year. **To Apply:** Applicants must provide proof of relationship and death or disability of parent, and evidence relating to parent's death or disability to service with the 1st calvary division. **Contact:** The First Cavalry Division Association at the above address (see entry 2463).

**• 2465 •**
**First Commercial Corp.**
PO Box 1471
Little Rock, AR 72203-1471          *Ph:* (501)371-7000

**• 2466 • First Commercial Bank National Advisory Board Scholarship** *(Undergraduate/Scholarship)*

**Focus:** General studies. **Qualif.:** Applicants must be graduating Arkansas high school seniors with minimum ACT scores of 28, planning to attend a four-year Arkansas college. **Criteria:** Awards

are granted based on academic achievement, activities, essay, references, personal interview.

**Funds Avail.:** Varies. **No. of Awards:** 1-2. **To Apply:** Write for further details. **Deadline:** February 1. **Contact:** Marilyn Stiles.

**• 2467 •**
**First Interstate Bank of Washington**
PO Box 160
MS 803
Seattle, WA 98111-1060          *Ph:* (206)292-3111

**• 2468 • First Interstate Bank Scholarship** *(Undergraduate/Scholarship)*

**Focus:** Finance, business, economics. **Qualif.:** Applicants must be Washington residents who are freshmen students entering the following schools: Central Washington University, Eastern Washington University, Evergreen College, Gonzaga University, Heritage College, Pacific Lutheran University, St. Martin's University, Seattle Pacific University, University of Puget Sound, University of Washington, Walla Walla College, Washington State University, Western Washington University, Whitman College, and Whitworth College. **Criteria:** Awards are made based on financial need, academic and extracurricular achievement in business, finance, or economics.

**Funds Avail.:** $1,500 per award. **To Apply:** Applicants may apply directly to the financial aid offices of the eligible schools. **Contact:** First Interstate Bank Scholarship Program at the above address (see entry 2467).

**• 2469 •**
**Five Colleges, Incorporated**
97 Spring St.          *Ph:* (413)256-8316
Amherst, MA 01002          *Fax:* (413)256-0249
*URL:* http://www.fivecolleges.edu/

**• 2470 • Five Colleges Fellowship Program** *(Doctorate/Fellowship)*

**Purpose:** To support advanced minority graduate students in the completion of doctoral dissertations. **Focus:** Liberal Arts. **Qualif.:** Applicants must be members of a minority group, must have completed all of the requirements for the Ph.D. except the dissertation, and must intend to teach at the undergraduate level in a U.S. institution. Fellowships are tenable at any member of Five Colleges, Incorporated: Amherst, Hampshire, MountxHolyoke, and Smith Colleges, and the University of Massachusetts at Amherst. Fellows will have minimal teaching responsibilities.

**Funds Avail.:** The fellowship will be a $25,000 stipend, plus benefits and housing assistance. **To Apply:** Candidates should write for application forms. These should be submitted with an abstract of proposed dissertation; references; transcripts; curriculum vitae; and a statement of interest in teaching in a liberal arts context. **Deadline:** Applications are due by January 16. Awards are announced by May 1.

**Remarks:** The fellowship at Smith College is named the Mendenhall Fellowship. **Contact:** Carol Angus, Associate Coordinator, at the above address (see entry 2469).

• 2471 •

## Fleet Bank of Massachusetts

PO Box 9003  
Springfield, MA 01101

*Ph:* (413)732-2858  
*Fax:* (413)732-8565

### • 2472 • James Z. Naurison Scholarship Fund
*(Graduate, Undergraduate/Scholarship)*

**Focus:** General Studies. **Qualif.:** Applicants must have been residents for at least one year of Hampden, Hampshire, Franklin, or Berkshire counties of the state of Massachusetts or of Enfield or Suffield, Connecticut, and be unable to pursue higher education except through scholarship assistance. Candidates must be high school or other secondary school graduates and have satisfactorily completed all college or university admission requirements. Full-time college and graduate students are also eligible. **Criteria:** Selection of applicant is based on financial need, academic merit, and extra curricular activities.

**Funds Avail.:** The amount of a scholarship is individually determined. A student may receive a maximum of four scholarships. Payment is made directly to each college's financial aid office in August and January. **No. of Awards:** Varies. **To Apply:** In order for the application to be processed, a financial aid form (FAF) from the college scholarship services, must be provided. (This is not the free form). **Deadline:** Applications must be filed by April 15. Transcripts and a completed FAFSA must be received by April 15. Recipients are notified on or about July 1.

**Remarks:** Dr. James Z. Naurison was a cardiologist who practiced in the Springfield area for 56 years after emigrating from Russia in 1891. The scholarship fund was established as part of his will. **Contact:** Judith Turcotte or Maria Flores at the above address (see entry 2471).

• 2473 •

## Fleet Reserve Association

125 N. West St.  
Alexandria, VA 22314-2754  
*E-mail:* news-fra@fra.org  
*URL:* http://www.va.gov/vso/fra.htm

*Ph:* 800-FRA-1924  
*Fax:* (703)549-6610

### • 2474 • Stanley A. Doran Memorial Scholarship
*(Undergraduate/Scholarship)*

**Focus:** General studies. **Qualif.:** Applicants must be dependent children of members in good standing of the Fleet Reserve Association or of member in good standing at time of death. **Criteria:** Awards are made based on financial need, scholastic standing, character, and leadership abilities. **No. of Awards:** 3. **To Apply:** Applicants must submit sponsor's name, FRA Branch/Unit and membership number; grade transcript with overall grade point average on 4.0 scale. **Deadline:** April 15. **Contact:** FRA Scholarship Administrator at the above address (see entry 2473).

### • 2475 • Fleet Reserve Association Scholarship
*(Undergraduate/Scholarship)*

**Focus:** General studies. **Qualif.:** Applicants must be children, grandchildren, or spouses of members of the U.S. Navy, Marine Corps, and Coast Guard (regular reserve), retired with pay, or deceased while in aforementioned status, and members of the FRA. **Criteria:** Awards are made based on financial need, scholastic standing, character, and leadership qualities. **To Apply:** Applicants must submit sponsor's name, FRA Branch/Unit and membership number; grade transcript with overall grade point average on 4.0 scale. **Deadline:** April 15. **Contact:** FRA Scholarship Administrator at the above address (see entry 2473).

### • 2476 • Oliver and Esther R. Howard Scholarship
*(Undergraduate/Scholarship)*

**Focus:** General studies. **Qualif.:** Applicants must be dependent children of members in good standing of the Fleet Reserve Association or the Ladies Auxiliary of the Fleet Reserve Association or of a member in good standing at time of death. Awards are alternated annually between female dependents (in even numbered years) and male dependents (in odd numbered years). **Criteria:** Awards are made based on financial need, scholastic standing, character, and leadership qualities. **To Apply:** Applicants must submit sponsor's name, FRA Branch/Unit and membership number; grade transcript with overall grade point average on 4.0 scale. **Deadline:** April 15. **Contact:** FRA Scholarship Administrator at the above address (see entry 2473).

### • 2477 • LA FRA National President's Scholarship
*(Undergraduate/Scholarship)*

**Focus:** General studies. **Qualif.:** Applicants must be children/grandchildren of Naval, Marine Corps, and Coast Guard Personnel, active Fleet Reserve, Fleet Marine Corps Reserve, and Coast Guard Reserve, retired with pay or deceased. **Criteria:** Awards are made based on financial need, scholastic standing, character, and leadership qualities. **To Apply:** Applicants must submit sponsor's name, FRA Branch/Unit and membership number; grade transcript with overall grade point average on 4.0 scale. **Deadline:** April 15. **Contact:** FRA Scholarship Administrator at the above address (see entry 2473).

### • 2478 • Ladies Auxiliary of Fleet Reserve Association Scholarship *(Undergraduate/Scholarship)*

**Focus:** General studies. **Qualif.:** Applicants must be daughters/granddaughters of Naval, Marine Corps, and Coast Guard personnel, active Fleet Reserve, Fleet Marine Corps Reserve, and Coast Guard Reserve, retired with pay or deceased. **Criteria:** Awards are made based on financial need, scholastic standing, character, and leadership qualities. **To Apply:** Applicants must submit sponsor's name, FRA Branch/Unit and membership number; grade transcript with overall grade point average on 4.0 scale. **Deadline:** April 15. **Contact:** LA FRA Scholarship Administrator at the above address (see entry 2473).

### • 2479 • Allie Mae Oden Memorial Scholarship
*(Undergraduate/Scholarship)*

**Focus:** General studies. **Qualif.:** Applicants must be children/grandchildren of members of the FRA or LA FRA. **Criteria:** Awards are made based on financial need, scholastic standing, character, and leadership qualities. **To Apply:** Applicants must submit sponsor's name, FRA Branch/Unit and membership number; grade transcript with overall grade point average on 4.0 scale. **Deadline:** April 15. **Contact:** FRA Scholarship Administrator at the above address (see entry 2473).

### • 2480 • Schuler S. Pyle Scholarship
*(Undergraduate/Scholarship)*

**Focus:** General studies. **Qualif.:** Applicants must be dependent children/spouses of members in good standing of the Fleet Reserve Association or of a member in good standing at time of death, and members of the FRA. **Criteria:** Awards are made based on financial need, scholastic standing, character, and leadership qualities. **To Apply:** Applicants must submit sponsor's name, FRA Branch/Unit and membership number; grade transcript with overall grade point average on 4.0 scale. **Deadline:** April 15. **Contact:** FRA Scholarship Administrator at the above address (see entry 2473).

### • 2481 • Sam Rose Memorial Scholarship
*(Undergraduate/Scholarship)*

**Focus:** General studies. **Qualif.:** Applicants must be children/grandchildren of deceased FRA members or persons who were eligible to be FRA members at the time of death. **Criteria:** Awards are made based on financial need, scholastic standing, character, and leadership qualities. **To Apply:** Applicants must submit sponsor's name, FRA Branch/Unit and membership number; grade transcript with overall grade point average on 4.0 scale. **Deadline:** April 15. **Contact:** FRA Scholarship Administrator at the above address (see entry 2473).

### • 2482 •
**Flemish Community**
c/o Embassy of Belgium
3330 Garfield St. NW
Washington, DC 20008      *Ph:* (202)333-6900

### • 2483 • Ministry of the Flemish Community in Belgium Fellowships *(Doctorate, Graduate, Postgraduate/Fellowship)*

**Qualif.:** Applicants must be US Citizens, under 35 years of age. Must hold a bachelor's or master's degree, and cannot have other Belgian sources of income.

**Funds Avail.:** Winners will receive a monthly stipend of 24,800 Belgian Francs, tuition at Flemish institution up to 17.600 francs, a one-time 25.000 franc contribution towards costs of printing of doctoral dissertation or 7.500 francs towards costs of printing of licentiate thesis. Health insurance and public liability insurance in accordance with Belgian law is also provided. **No. of Awards:** 5. **To Apply:** The application must be in triplicate; a medical certificate must be submitted; a certified copy of applicant's birth certificate; a copy of diploma(s); a summary of thesis (maximum of 5 pages); official transcript(s); two recommendations from current teacher(s) or employer(s); and indicate latest GPA, if applicable. **Contact:** Flemish Community at the above address (see entry 2482).

### • 2484 •
**Peter G. Flinn Scholarship Fund**
c/o Bank One Trust Group, Ste. 1501
PO Box 7700      *Ph:* (317)321-8204
Indianapolis, IN 46277      *Fax:* (317)321-8588

### • 2485 • Peter G. Flinn Scholarships *(Undergraduate/Scholarship)*

**Qualif.:** Applicants must be Grant County, Indiana, high school seniors who have resided in Grant County for at least one year. **Criteria:** Winners are selected by a group comprised of Grant County faculty and members of local community organizations.

**Funds Avail.:** Five scholarships are awarded annually. Awards may be used for tuition or room and board for the recipient's full four years of study. **To Apply:** Applicants must include a postage-paid, self-addressed envelope for a response outside of the Grant County Indiana area. **Contact:** Jean Wheatley at the above address (see entry 2484).

### • 2486 •
**Florida Dental Association**
1111 E. Tennessee St.      *Ph:* (850)681-3629
Tallahassee, FL 32308      *Fax:* (850)561-0504
*URL:* http://www.floridadental.org/fda

### • 2487 • Florida Dental Association Dental Hygiene Scholarship Program *(Other, Professional Development/Scholarship)*

**Purpose:** To provide monetary assistance for the education of individuals seeking careers in dental hygiene in Florida. **Focus:** Dental-hygiene. **Qualif.:** Applicant must have lived in Florida for at least three years and who meets the admission requirements to an ADA accredited dental-hygiene program in Florida. Preference is given to qualified individuals who: apply from counties that the scholarship committee determines to be in the most need of dental hygienists; have been accepted or are continuing in an accredited dental hygiene program at a Florida school; are dedicated to working in a Florida county that has a shortage of dental-hygienists; show financial need.

**Funds Avail.:** The funds for this program are obtained through early contributions from the Florida Dental Hygienists' Association and FDA Services Inc. **To Apply:** Each applicant must provide a letter to the FDA/FDHA Joint Dental Hygiene Scholarship Committee. Continuing applicants must provide a letter from the program director to show the need for the scholarship. Each applicant must have a personal or telephone interview with a dentist and dental-hygienist member of the committee. **Contact:** Chairperson, FDA/FDHA Joint Committee.

### • 2488 • Florida Dental Association Student Loan Program *(Graduate/Loan)*

**Purpose:** To help needy students obtain a dental education. **Qualif.:** Any dental student who has successfully completed one academic year in any accredited dental college in the United States is eligible to apply for this loan. The student must have lived in Florida for three years prior to loan application. Academic standing, financial need and potential will be considered in granting a loan.

**Funds Avail.:** $9,000. **To Apply:** Must send an official transcript of the completed freshman year or an official transcript from the preceding year in an accredited dental college with the application. Each applicant must have a personal or telephone interview with a task group member. A letter must be provided to the chairperson of the task group outlining the reasons the applicant feels he or she deserves this loan. **Contact:** Task Group on Student Loans.

### • 2489 •
**Florida Dental Health Foundation**
1111 E. Tennessee St.      *Ph:* (850)681-3629
Tallahassee, FL 32308      *Fax:* (850)561-0504
      *Free:* 800-877-9922

### • 2490 • Florida Dental Health Foundation Dental Assisting Scholarship *(Undergraduate/Scholarship)*

**Focus:** Dental Assisting. **Qualif.:** Applicants must be residents of Florida for at least three years. They must also have completed one grading period in an accredited dental assisting program. **Criteria:** Selection is based on grades, financial need, recommendation, and geographic work preference. **To Apply:** A completed application, grade transcript from first semester of accredited dental assisting school, and a letter from a program administrator must be submitted. **Deadline:** Continuous review.

## Florida Dental Health Foundation (continued)

### • 2491 • Florida Dental Health Foundation Dental Hygiene Scholarship *(Undergraduate/Scholarship)*

**Focus:** Dental Hygiene. **Qualif.:** Applicants must be residents of Florida for at least three years. They must also be enrolled in an accredited dental hygiene program. **Criteria:** Selection is based on academic record, a telephone interview, letter of recommendation, financial need, and geographic work preference. **To Apply:** A completed application, a letter of need, and transcripts of grades must be submitted. **Deadline:** November 1 and May 1.

### • 2492 • Florida Dental Health Foundation Student Loans *(Doctorate, Postdoctorate/Loan)*

**Focus:** Dentistry. **Qualif.:** Applicants must be Florida residents for at least three years. They must also be enrolled as sophomores or above in a college of dentistry accredited by the American Dental Association Commission on Dental Accreditation. **Criteria:** Selection is based on academic record, financial need, a personal interview, and letter of recommendation. Preference is given to upperclassmen with previous loans.

**Funds Avail.:** $2,000 is awarded to sophomores, $3,000 to juniors, $4,000 to seniors, and $3,000 to post-doctoral students. **To Apply:** A completed application, copy of current transcript, and a letter from a dean or faculty advisor must be submitted. **Deadline:** March 31.

---

### • 2493 •
## Florida Department of Education - Office of Student Financial Assistance - State Programs
255 Collins
325 W. Gaines St.
Tallahassee, FL 32399-0400           Ph: (904)487-0049
*URL:* http://www.firn.edu/doe/menu/whatsnew.htm

### • 2494 • Mary McLeod Bethune Scholarship *(Graduate, Undergraduate/Grant)*

**Focus:** General Studies. **Qualif.:** Applicants must enroll at Florida Agricultue and Mechanical University, Bethune-Cookman College, Edward Waters College, or Florida Memorial College for a minimum of 12 credit hours per term. Students must have earned a minimum cumulative grade point average of 3.0 on a 4.0 scale in high school. Application for an initial award must be made during the senior year of high school. Students must meet Florida's general eligibility requirements for receipt of state aid, including residency in Florida for purposes other than education for no less than one year prior to the first day of class of the fall term of the academic year for which the funds are received; compliance with registration requirements of the Selective Service System; and participation in the college-level communication and computation testing (CLAST) program. Applicants must not owe a repayment of a grant under any state or federal grant or scholarship program, and must not be in default on any state or federal student loan program unless satisfactory arrangements to repay have been made. Eligibility for renewal is determined at the end of the second semester or third quarter of each academic year. Credits earned the previous summer can be counted toward the total number of credits required. **Criteria:** Renewal awards take precedence over new awards in years in which funds are not sufficient to award all eligible, timely applicants.

**Funds Avail.:** $3,000 per academic year for a maximum of eight semesters or 12 quarters. Awards from this fund may be made only if sufficient matching contributions are received from private sources on behalf of eligible institutions. **No. of Awards:** 180. **To Apply:** Applicants must complete a Free Application for Federal Student Aid need analysis form to demonstrate financial need.

Applications may be obtained from high school guidance offices, financial aid offices at Bethune-Cookman College, Edward Waters College, Florida Memorial College, and Florida Agricultural and Mechanical University, or the Florida Department of Education, Office of Student Financial Assistance. **Deadline:** Need analysis form must be submitted in time to be processed by the U.S. Department of Energy no later than May 15. Grant application must be submitted to the Office of Student Financial Assistance postmarked by April 30 during the senior year of high school. Applications postmarked between May 1 and June 1 will be considered for awards on a funds-available basis after all timely eligible applicants have been awarded. Renewal application must be submitted postmarked by April 30. A Florida need analysis form must also be submitted each year in time to be processed by May 15. **Contact:** Florida Department of Education, Office of Student Financial Assistance, at the above address (see entry 2493).

### • 2495 • William L. Boyd IV, Florida Resident Access Grant *(Undergraduate/Grant)*

**Qualif.:** Applicants must be Florida residents who are full-time undergraduate students attending eligible private non-profit Florida colleges or universities.

**Funds Avail.:** Varies with the number of eligible students. **No. of Awards:** 23,425 for 1999-2000. **Deadline:** Established by each institution.

### • 2496 • Robert C. Byrd Honors Scholarship *(Undergraduate/Scholarship)*

**Focus:** General Studies. **Qualif.:** Candidates must be Florida residents planning to attend any public or private non-profit, postsecondary institution for a course of study at least one year in length. Recipients must be nominated by their high school. **Criteria:** Selection is based upon promise of continued academic achievement. **No. of Awards:** 1,200. **To Apply:** Each public and private high school in Florida may nominate one applicant as a potential recipient. Applications may be obtained from high school guidance offices or the Office of Student Financial Assistance, Florida Department of Education. **Deadline:** April 30.

**Remarks:** The scholarships are offered through the U.S. Department of Education. **Contact:** Florida Department of Education, Office of Student Financial Assistance, at the above address (see entry 2493).

### • 2497 • Children of Deceased or Disabled Veterans or Children of Servicemen Classified as Prisoners of War or Missing in Action Scholarship *(Undergraduate/Scholarship)*

**Focus:** General Studies. **Qualif.:** Applicants must be the children of deceased or disabled Florida veterans or children of Florida servicemen classified as Prisoners of War or Missing in Action during one of the following wars, conflicts, or events: Persian Gulf War (August 2, 1990); Operation Just Cause in Panama (December 1989); USS Stark Attack (May 17, 1987); Newfoundland Air Tragedy (December 12, 1985); Operation Urgent Fury in Grenada (October 23 - November 2, 1983); Multinational Peace Keeping Force in Lebanon (September 17, 1982 - February 3, 1984); Operation Eagle Claw, Iranian Rescue Mission (April 25, 1980); Vietnam Era (August 4, 1964 - May 7, 1975); Korean Conflict (June 25, 1950 - January 31, 1955); World War II (December 7, 1941 - September 2, 1945); World War I (April 6, 1917 - July 2, 1921). Veterans or servicemen who served in the Vietnam Era, the Korean Conflict, World War II, World War I, or who died in the Newfoundland Air Tragedy must have entered the armed forces from the state of Florida, except those classified as prisoners of war or missing in action in the Vietnam Era or the Korean Conflict. Veterans or servicemen must also have been residents of the state of Florida on the following dates: those who died in the USS Stark Attack - May 17, 1987; Those who died or became disabled in Operation Urgent Fury in Grenada - October 23 through November 2, 1983; those who died or became disabled in the Multinational Peace Keeping Force in Lebanon - September

17, 1982 through February 3, 1984; those who died or became disabled in Operation Eagle Claw, Iranian Rescue Mission - April 25, 1980; those classified as Prisoners of War or Missing in Action during the Vietnam Era or the Korean Conflict - July 1, 1982. Additionally, the parent(s) of a dependent applying for a scholarship must have been resident(s) of Florida for five years prior to the student's application if the veteran served in Vietnam, the Korean Conflict, World War II, or World War I. If the veteran parent served in the Persian Gulf War, Operation Just Cause, USS Stark Attack, the Newfoundland Air Tragedy, Operation Urgent Fury in Grenada, or Operation Eagle Claw, the parent(s) must have been resident(s) of Florida for one year prior to the student's application. Applicant must not have previously received a bachelor's degree, and must be between the ages of 16 and 22. Student must meet Florida's general eligibility requirements for receipt of state aid, including compliance with registration requirements of the Selective Service System and participation in the college-level communication and computation testing (CLAST) program. Applicants must enroll at an eligible Florida public or eligible private university, community college, or vocational-technical center for a minimum of 12 credit hours, or the equivalent, per term, not owe a repayment of a grant under any state or federal grant or scholarship program, and must not be in default on any state or federal student loan program unless satisfactory arrangements to repay have been made. A renewal applicant must have earned a minimum cumulative grade point average of 2.0 on a 4.0 scale and have earned the equivalent of 12 credit hours for each term an award was received during the academic year. Eligibility for renewal is determined at the end of the second semester or third quarter of each academic year. Credits earned the previous summer can be counted toward the total number of credits required.

**Funds Avail.:** The amount of the scholarship is the cost of tuition and fees for two semesters at the Florida public postsecondary institution which the student plans to attend, for a maximum of eight semesters of undergraduate study. **To Apply:** Applications may be obtained from high school guidance offices or the Florida Department of Education Office of Student Financial Assistance. Letters of recommendation are required. **Deadline:** Application with letters of recommendation must be submitted to the Executive Director of the Florida Department of Veterans' Affairs postmarked by April 1. **Contact:** Florida Department of Education, Office of Student Financial Assistance, at the above address (see entry 2493).

### • 2498 • Paul Douglas Teacher Scholarship
*(Undergraduate/Scholarship loan)*

**Purpose:** To provide financial assistance to outstanding high school graduates and college students who intend to pursue teaching careers at the preschool, elementary, or secondary school levels. **Focus:** Education. **Qualif.:** Candidates must be United States citizens or eligible non-citizens; be ranked in the top 10 percent of their high school graduating class or earn a state GED score equivalent to ranking in the top 10 percent; have scored in at least in the 40th percentile on the SAT or ACT; if an initial undergraduate applicant, must have maintained a GPA of 3.0 for all previous course work; be enrolled at an eligible Florida or non-Florida postsecondary institution on a full-time basis in a course of study leading to teacher certification at the preschool, elementary, or secondary school level; submit a Florida need analysis form to ACT, CSS, or CSX; not owe a repayment of a grant under any state or federal grant or scholarship program; and not be in default on any state or federal student loan program unless satisfactory arrangements to repay have been made.

**Funds Avail.:** $5,000 per academic year of the cost of education minus other Title IV financial aid up to a maximum of $20,000, subject to Congressional appropriations. A scholarship loan recipient is required to teach in a public or private non-profit preschool, elementary, or secondary school in any state for two years for each year of a scholarship loan award. A recipient who teaches in a designated teacher shortage subject area as designated by the U.S. Department of Education is obligated to teach one year for each year of assistance. **To Apply:** Applications

may be obtained from high school counselors, college of education offices, financial aid offices at Florida universities and colleges, or the Office of Student Financial Assistance, Florida Department of Education. **Deadline:** April 15. **Contact:** Florida Department of Education, Office of Financial Assistance, at the above address (see entry 2493).

### • 2499 • Ethics in Business Scholarship Program
*(Undergraduate/Scholarship)*

**Focus:** Not restricted to any particular field of study. **Qualif.:** Applicants must be undergraduate students who enroll at community colleges and eligible private Florida colleges and universities.

### • 2500 • Florida Bright Futures Scholarship Program
*(Undergraduate/Scholarship)*

**Purpose:** To award Florida high school graduates with high academic achievement and who are enrolled in an eligible Florida postsecondary institution. **Focus:** All areas of study accepted. **Qualif.:** This scholarship has three award levels: the Florida Academic Scholars Award, the Florida Merit Scholars Award, and the Florida Gold Seal Vocational Scholars Award. Each award level has different academic criteria for eligibility.

**Funds Avail.:** Each award level receives a different award amount. The top ranked scholar from each county will receive an additional award of up to $1500. **No. of Awards:** Over 70,000.

### • 2501 • Florida Critical Teacher Shortage Scholarship Loans *(Graduate, Undergraduate/ Scholarship loan)*

**Purpose:** Provides financial assistance to upper division undergraduate and graduate students who pursue certification in critical teacher shortage subject areas, meet scholastic requirements, and agree to enter the public school teaching profession in Florida. **Focus:** Education. **Qualif.:** Undergraduate applicants must not have previously received a bachelor's degree; graduate applicants must not hold a permanent or professional Florida Teacher's (or Educator's) Certificate in the critical teacher subject area for which the award is requested. Students must meet Florida's general eligibility requirements for receipt of state aid, including compliance with registration requirements of the Selective Service System and participation in the college-level communication and computation testing (CLAST) program. Undergraduate students must have earned a minimum cumulative grade point average of 2.0 on a 4.0 scale on all previous undergraduate work and have a test score of at least 835 on the Scholastic Achievement Test (SAT) or 19 on the American College Testing Program (ACT). Graduate students must have earned a minimum cumulative grade point average of 3.0 on a 4.0 scale for all previous graduate work and have a test score of at least 1000 on the Graduate Record Examination (GRE). Undergraduate applicants must enroll in a state-approved teacher education program at an eligible Florida public or private college or university for a minimum of 12 credit hours per term; graduate students must take 9 credit hours per term. Certification must be pursued in a critical teacher subject area as designated by the State Board of Education. Recipients of the "Chappie" James Most Promising Teacher Scholarship Loan Program awards and participants in the Critical Teacher Shortage Student Loan Forgiveness Program are not eligible. Candidates must not owe repayment of a grant under any state or federal grant or scholarship program, and must not be in default on any state or federal student loan program unless satisfactory arrangements to repay have been made. Undergraduate renewal applicants must have earned a minimum cumulative grade point average of 2.0 on a 4.0 scale and the equivalent of 12 credit hours for each term an award was received during the academic year. Graduate renewal applicants must have earned a minimum cumulative grade point average of 3.0 on a 4.0 scale and the equivalent of 9 credit hours for each term an award was received during the academic year. Eligibility for renewal is

## Florida Department of Education - Office of Student Financial Assistance - State Programs (continued)

determined at the end of the second semester or third quarter of each academic year. Credits earned the previous summer can be counted toward the total number of credits required. **Criteria:** Awards are made on a funds available basis to eligible applicants ranked by unweighted grade point average (GPA), then by Scholastic Aptitude Test (SAT), American College Testing Program (ACT), or Graduate Record Examination (GRE) scores.

**Funds Avail.:** The amount of the scholarship loan is $4,000 per academic year or the cost of the student's education minus other financial aid, whichever is less, for a maximum of four semesters or six quarters. **Deadline:** Applications must be postmarked by April 1. **Contact:** Applications and a current list of Critical Teacher Shortage areas may be obtained from the Dean of Education at the postsecondary school the candidate is planning to attend or the Florida Department of Education Office of Student Financial Assistance at the above address (see entry 2493).

### • 2502 • Florida Critical Teacher Shortage Tuition Reimbursement Program *(Graduate, Professional Development/Other)*

**Purpose:** Provides financial assistance to full-time Florida public school employees who are certified to teach in Florida and who are teaching or preparing to teach in critical teacher shortage subject areas approved by the State Board of Education. **Focus:** Education. **Qualif.:** Applicants must be certified and currently teaching full-time in the Florida public school system; be taking courses either to acquire, renew, or extend certification or to acquire a graduate degree in a designated critical teacher shortage subject area; earn a minimum GPA of 3.0 on all approved courses; and meet the registration requirements of the Selective Service System. Candidates must not owe repayment of a grant under any state or federal grant or scholarship program, and must not be in default on any state or federal student loan program unless satisfactory arrangements to repay have been made. **Criteria:** Awards are made on a first-come, first-served basis.

**Funds Avail.:** Participants may receive tuition reimbursement for up to 9 semester hours, or the equivalent, per academic year, at a rate not to exceed $78 per semester hour, for a maximum of 36 semester hours. For the purposes of this program, an "academic year" begins with the summer term. **To Apply:** Applications must include verification of certification, employment, and applicability of courses for certification or graduate degree in a critical teacher shortage subject area. Applications may be obtained from the Critical Teacher Shortage contact person at the public school office in the district employed in, or from the Florida Department of Education Office of Student Financial Assistance. **Deadline:** Applications, including all required documentation, must be postmarked by deadlines indicated on the application for each term for which reimbursement is requested. **Contact:** Florida Department of Education, Office of Student Financial Assistance, at the above address (see entry 2493).

### • 2503 • Florida National Science Scholars Program *(Undergraduate/Scholarship)*

**Focus:** Science. **Qualif.:** Students must be U.S. citizens or eligible noncitizins. They must also demonstrate potential to successfully complete a postsecondary program in the physical, life, or computer sciences, math, or engineering. **Contact:** Applications may be obtained from high school guidance offices or the Florida Department of Education Office of Student Financial Assistance at the above address (see entry 2493).

### • 2504 • Florida Resident Access Grant *(Undergraduate/Other)*

**Purpose:** Provides tuition assistance to Florida undergraduate students attending eligible independent, nonprofit Florida colleges or universities. **Focus:** General Studies. **Qualif.:** Applicants must

not have previously received a bachelor's degree and meet Florida's general eligibility requirements for receipt of state aid, including residency in Florida for purposes other than education for no less than one year prior to the first day of class of the fall term of the academic year for which the funds are received. They must be in compliance with registration requirements of the Selective Service System; and have participated in the college-level communication and computation skills testing (CLAST) program. Applicants must enroll at an independent, nonprofit Florida college or university accredited by the Commission on Colleges and Schools in a program of study other than divinity or theology for a minimum of 12 credit hours per term. Candidates must not owe a repayment of a grant under any state or federal grant or scholarship program, and must not be in default on any state or federal student loan program unless satisfactory arrangements to repay have been made. A renewal applicant must have earned a minimum cumulative grade point average of 2.0 on a 4.0 scale, meet the institution's definition of satisfactory academic progress and earned the equivalent of 12 credit hours for each term an award was received during the academic year. Eligibility for renewal is determined at the end of the second semester of the third quarter of each academic year. Credits earned the previous summer can be counted toward the total number of credits required.

**Funds Avail.:** The amount of the tuition voucher is between $1,150 and $2,000 per academic year, or the amount specified in the General Appropriations Act, for a maximum of nine semesters or 14 quarters. The amount of the tuition voucher plus all other scholarships and grants specifically designated for payment of tuition and fees cannot exceed the total amount of tuition and fees charged by the institution. The college or university will adjust the amount of the tuition voucher to conform to this maximum. **Deadline:** Applicants must submit an application to the financial aid office of the institution of enrollment by the deadline established by the institution. Renewal applications must be submitted to the institution annually. **Contact:** Applications may be obtained at the financial aid offices of eligible Florida universities and colleges or the Office of Student Financial Assistance at the above address (see entry 2493).

### • 2505 • Florida Student Assistance Grants *(Undergraduate/Grant)*

**Purpose:** These grants are three separately funded student financial aid programs that are available to full-time Florida undergraduate students who demonstrate substantial financial need. **Focus:** General Studies. **Qualif.:** The Florida Public Student Assistance Grant is available to students who attend a Florida public college or university. The Florida Private Student Assistance Grant is available to students who attend an eligible Florida independent non-profit college or university that offers baccalaureate degrees. The Florida Postsecondary Student Assistance Grant is available to students who attend an eligible Florida private college or university which offers degrees and is not eligible under the Florida Private Student Assistance Grant. All grants are available to full-time Florida undergraduate students who demonstrate financial need. Applicants must be U.S. citizens or eligible non-citizens; must not have previously received a bachelor's degree; and must meet Florida's general eligibility requirement for receipt of state aid, including residency in Florida for purposes other than education for no less than one year prior to the first day of class of the fall term of the academic year for which the funds are received, compliance with registration requirements of the Selective Service System, and participation in the college-level communication and computation skills testing (CLAST) program. Students must enroll at an eligible Florida educational institution for a minimum of 12 credit hours per term. Applicants must not owe repayment of a grant under any state or federal grant or scholarship program, and must not be in default on any state or federal student loan program unless satisfactory arrangements to repay have been made. Renewal applicants must have maintained a minimum cumulative grade point average of 2.0 on a 4.0 scale and have earned the equivalent of 12 credit hours for each term an award was received during the academic year. Eligibility for renewal is determined at the end of the second semester or third quarter of each academic year. Credits earned the previous summer can be counted toward the total number of credits required. **Criteria:** Priority is given to students with the lowest total family resources.

**Funds Avail.:** The amount of these grants range from $200-1,500 per academic year or as specified in the general appropriations act based on the student's demonstrated financial need. **No. of Awards:** 40,040. **To Apply:** Candidates must apply for an FSAG and a Pell Grant by completing the Free Application for Federal Student Aid need analysis form to demonstrate financial need. Applications may be obtained by contacting high school guidance offices, college financial aid offices, or the Office of Student Financial Assistance, Florida Department of Education. **Deadline:** Need analysis form must be submitted in time to be processed by the U.S. Department of Education no later than May 15, or October 15 for community college students. **Contact:** Florida Department of Education, Office of Student Financial Assistance, at the above address (see entry 2493).

**• 2506 • Florida Teacher Scholarship and Forgivable Loan Program** *(Graduate, Undergraduate/Loan, Scholarship)*

**Purpose:** The Florida Teacher Scholarship and Forgivable Loan Program comprises the "Chappie" James Most Promising Teacher Scholarship, which provides scholarship assistance to lower division undergraduate students, and the Florida Critical Teacher Shortage Forgivable Loan, which provides loan assistance to upper division undergraduate students and to graduate students. The purpose of the program is to attract capable and promising students and teachers to teaching careers in critical teacher shortage subject areas in Florida public elementary and secondary schools. **Focus:** Education. **Qualif.:** Applicants must enroll in an eligible Florida public or private college or university for a minimum of 12 credit hours each term, if an undergraduate, or for a minimum of nine credit hours each term, if a graduate student; meet Florida's general eligibility requirements for receipt of state aid; must not owe a repayment of a grant under any federal or state grant or scholarship program; must not be in default on any state or federal student loan program unless satisfactory arrangements to repay have been made; and must not have received a Paul Douglas Teacher Scholarship, Critical Teacher Shortage Scholarship Loan, a "Chappie" James Most Promising Teacher Scholarship Loan, or a Masters' Fellowship Loan for Teachers. A scholarship applicant must also attend and eligible public or private Florida high school; have a minimum cumulative high school grade point average of 3.0 on a 4.0 scale; be ranked in the upper quarter of the high school senior class; have taken the ACT or SAT; have been an active member of a future teacher organization, if such an organization exists at the student's high school; be nominated by the high school principal; must not have previously received a bachelor's degree; must enroll in a degree program; and must not be a participant in the Florida Undergraduate Scholars' Fund or Vocational Gold Seal Scholarship. A loan applicant must be enrolled in a state-approved teacher preparation program that leads to certification in critical teacher shortage subject area; if an undergraduate student, be an upper division student, have scored at the 40th percentile or better on the SAT or ACT, and have earned a minimum cumulative grade point average of 2.5 on a 4.0 scale for all undergraduate work; and if a graduate student, have a bachelor's degree, not have a bachelor's degree in education in a critical teacher shortage subject area, have either earned a minimum cumulative grade point average of 3.0 on a 4.0 scale for all undergraduate work or scored a minimum of 1000 on the GRE, not hold a teaching certificate in a critical teacher shortage subject area, and not have received an undergraduate loan through this program.

**Funds Avail.:** The amount of the scholarship is $1,500 per year for a maximum of two years. The amount of an undergraduate loan may not exceed $4,000 per year for a maximum of two years. The amount of a graduate loan may not exceed $8,000 per year for a maximum of two years. **Deadline:** A scholarship applicant must submit the scholarship application to their high school principal by

March 1 in their senior year. A loan applicant must submit the loan application to the Dean or Director of the College of Education by March 15 for completion of Section E. The completed application must be sent to the Office of Student Financial Assistance, Florida Department of Education, by April 1. **Contact:** Florida Department of Education, Office of Student Financial Assistance, at the above address (see entry 2493).

**• 2507 • Florida Undergraduate Scholars' Fund** *(Undergraduate/Scholarship)*

**Purpose:** Provides financial assistance to Florida high school seniors who have outstanding academic achievement and who plan to attend an eligible Florida public or private college or university. **Focus:** General Studies. **Qualif.:** Applicants must not have previously received a bachelor's degree and must have received a Florida high school diploma or its equivalent. Candidates must meet one of the following requirements: have been a finalist in either the National Merit Scholarship or the National Achievement Scholarship Program for Outstanding Negro Students sponsored by the National Merit Scholarship Corporation; have a minimum cumulative unweighted grade point average of 3.5 on a 4.0 scale in high school subjects acceptable toward a diploma and have earned a minimum score of 1200 on the Scholastic Aptitude Test (SAT) or minimum score of 29 on the American College Testing Program (ACT); have received an International Baccalaureate Diploma from the International Baccalaureate Office; have participated in a state-approved home education program during grade levels 9 through 12 and have earned a minimum score of 1250 on the combined verbal and quantitative parts of the SAT or a minimum score of 30 on the ACT; or have received a certificate through the Florida Academic Scholars' Certificate Program. Applicants must meet Florida's general eligibility requirements for receipt of state aid, including residency in Florida for purposes other than education for no less than one year prior to the first day of class of the fall term of the academic year for which the funds are received; compliance with the registration requirements of the Selective Service System; and participation in the college-level communication and computation skills testing (CLAST) program. Students are required to enroll at an eligible Florida public or private college or university for a minimum of 12 credit hours per term. Students may not be recipients of a Challenger Astronauts Memorial Undergraduate Scholarship award, a Vocational Gold Seal Endorsement Scholarship award, or a Vocational Achievement Grant award. Applicants must not owe repayment of a grant under any state or federal grant or scholarship program, and must not be in default on any state or federal student loan program unless satisfactory arrangements to repay have been made. Renewal applicants must have maintained a minimum cumulative grade point average of 3.2 on a 4.0 scale and have earned the equivalent of 12 credit hours for each term an award was received during the academic year. Eligibility for renewal is determined at the end of the second semester or third quarter of each academic year.

**Funds Avail.:** All initial and renewal awards are $2,500 per academic year. The academically top-ranked Florida Undergraduate Scholars' Fund recipient from each county may receive the Challenger Astronauts Memorial Award award in addition to the FUSF award, which is worth $1,500 for a total award of $4,000 per academic year. **To Apply:** Applications may be obtained from high school guidance offices or the Florida Department of Education Office of Student Financial Assistance. **Deadline:** Application must be postmarked by April 1. **Contact:** Florida Department of Education, Office of Student Financial Assistance, at the above address (see entry 2493).

**• 2508 • Florida Vocational Gold Seal Endorsement Scholarship Program** *(Undergraduate/Scholarship)*

**Purpose:** Provides scholarships to recipients of the Vocational Gold Seal Endorsement for enrollment in postsecondary vocational-technical degree or certificate programs. **Focus:** Vocational-Technical Education. **Qualif.:** Applicants must receive a standard high school diploma with a Florida Gold Seal

## Florida Department of Education - Office of Student Financial Assistance - State Programs (continued)

Endorsement from a Florida public high school. Students must meet Florida's general eligibility requirements for receipt of state aid, including residency in Florida for purposes other than education for no less than one year prior to the first day of class of the fall term of the academic year for which the funds are received; compliance with registration requirements of the Selective Service System; and participation in the college-level communication and computation skills testing (CLAST) program. Applicants must enroll in an appropriate vocational-technical degree or certificate program at an eligible Florida public or private postsecondary vocational, technical, trade, or business school, or college or university for a minimum of 12 credit hours or 450 clock hours. Candidates must not owe a repayment of a grant under any state or federal grant or scholarship program, and must not be in default on any state or federal student loan program unless satisfactory arrangements to repay have been made. Renewal applicants must have maintained a minimum cumulative grade point average of 3.0 on a 4.0 scale and have earned the equivalent of 12 credit hours for each term an award was received during the academic year. Eligibility for renewal is determined at the end of the second semester of the third quarter of each academic year.

**Funds Avail.:** The annual award to each recipient is $2,000. Renewal awards take precedence over new awards in any year in which funds are not sufficient to award all eligible timely applicants. The first awards are contingent upon legislative appropriation. **Deadline:** Applications and renewal applications must be postmarked by April 1 of the senior year of high school. Those submitted between April 2 and June 1 will be considered for awards on a funds-available basis after all eligible, timely applicants have been awarded. **Contact:** Applications may be obtained from public high school guidance counselors or the Office of Student Financial Assistance at the above address (see entry 2493).

## • 2509 • Florida Work Experience Program
*(Undergraduate/Work Study)*

**Purpose:** To provide eligible Florida students the opportunity to secure work experiences that are complementary to and reinforce the students' education program and career goals. **Qualif.:** Applicants must not have previously received a bachelor's degree, must be enrolled in an eligible Florida public or private college or university for a minimum of six credit hours, must demonstrate financial need by completing a Free Application for Federal Student Aid by the deadline specified by the institution, must submit, if applicable, an application to the institution by the deadline established by the institution, must meet Florida's general eligibility requirements for receipt of state aid, must not owe a repayment of a grant under any federal or state grant or scholarship program, must not be in default on any state or federal student loan program unless satisfactory arrangements to repay have been made, and must have earned a minimum cumulative grade point average of 2.0 on a 4.0 for all college work.

**Funds Avail.:** The amount of the award is determined by the institution's financial aid office. This award, in combination with other financial aid, may not exceed the student's financial need. Eligibility for renewal awards is determined at the end of the second semester or third quarter each academic year. **No. of Awards:** 458. **Contact:** Florida Department of Education, Office of Student Financial Assistance, at the above address (see entry 2493).

## • 2510 • Limited Access Competitive Grant
*(Undergraduate/Grant)*

**Qualif.:** Applicants must be Florida residents who are community college graduates or transfer students from state universities, and who enroll in one of the designated limited access programs at eligible private colleges or universities in Florida. Priority is given to florida residents who graduated from Florida high schools or community colleges.

**Funds Avail.:** 50% of the state's cost per academic year to fund an undergraduate student's public postsecondary education. **No. of Awards:** 705 anticipated. **Deadline:** Established by individual institutions.

## • 2511 • Jose Marti Scholarship Challenge Grants
*(Graduate, Undergraduate/Grant)*

**Purpose:** To provide financial assistance to Hispanic-American students who meet scholastic requirements, demonstrate financial need, and enroll for undergraduate or graduate study. **Focus:** General Studies. **Qualif.:** Applicants must be U.S. citizens or eligible non-citizens and be of Spanish culture who were born in, or whose natural parent was born in, either Mexico or Spain, or a Hispanic country of the Caribbean, Central America, or South America. Students must have earned a minimum cumulative grade point average of 3.0 on a 4.0 scale in high school or, if a graduate applicant, earned a minimum cumulative grade point average of 3.0 on a 4.0 scale for undergraduate college-level courses. Applicants must meet Florida's general eligibility requirements for receipt of state aid, including: residency in Florida for purposes other than education for no less than one year prior to the first day of class of the fall term of the academic year for which the funds are received; compliance with registration requirements of the Selective Service System; and participation in the college-level communication and computation testing (CLAST) program. Applicants must enroll at an eligible Florida public or private college or university for a minimum of 12 credit hours of undergraduate study or nine credit hours of graduate study. Students must not owe a repayment of a grant under any state or federal grant or scholarship program, and must not be in default on any state or federal student loan program unless satisfactory arrangements to repay have been made. Renewal applicants must have maintained a minimum cumulative grade point average of 3.0 on a 4.0 scale and have earned the equivalent of 12 credit hours for each term an award was received during the academic year. Eligibility for renewal is determined at the end of the second semester or third quarter of each academic year. Credits earned the previous summer can be counted toward the total number of credits required.

**Funds Avail.:** $2,000 per academic year for a maximum of eight semesters or 12 quarters of undergraduate study, or a maximum of four semesters or six quarters of graduate study. Available funds are contingent upon matching contributions from private sources. **To Apply:** Applicants must complete Free Application for Federal Student Aid need analysis form and demonstrate sufficient financial need to receive the entire annual award. Applications may be obtained from high school guidance offices or the Florida Department of Education Office of Student Financial Assistance. **Deadline:** Need analysis form must be submitted in time to be processed by the U.S. Department of Education no later than May 15. Grant application must be submitted to the Office of Student Financial Assistance postmarked by April 30 during the last year of high school for undergraduate study or immediately prior to the year for which the funds are requested for graduate study. **Contact:** Florida Department of Education, Office of Student Financial Assistance, at the above address (see entry 2493).

## • 2512 • Nursing Scholarship Program *(Graduate, Undergraduate/Scholarship loan)*

**Focus:** Nursing. **Qualif.:** Applicants must be full or part-time students enrolled in the upper division of an approved nursing program leading to a baccalaureate degree in nursing, an advanced registered nurse practitioner degree, an associate degree in nursing, or a diploma in nursing.

**Funds Avail.:** $8000 per year undergraduate; $12,000 per year for advanced degrees.

**Remarks:** Loans must be repaid by working one year in a medically underserved area for each year of assistance received.

**• 2513 • Occupational Therapist and Physical Therapist Scholarship Loan Program** *(Graduate/ Scholarship loan)*

**Purpose:** Provides financial assistance to students interested in practicing in Florida public schools. **Focus:** Occupational therapy, physical therapy or therapy assistant. **Qualif.:** Applicants must be enrolled full-time in therapist or therapist assistant programs at the upper division or graduate level and declare their intent to be employed for a minimum of three years in the Florida public schools.

**Funds Avail.:** Up to $4000 minus other financial aid. **Deadline:** April 15.

**Remarks:** The scholarship loan must be repaid in cash if the recipient does not work full-time in Florida public schools for the required time period.

**• 2514 • Rosewood Family Scholarship Fund** *(Undergraduate/Scholarship)*

**Qualif.:** Applicants must be undergraduate students who are descendants of affected African American Rosewood families and be enrolled full-time in eligible programs at state universities, public community colleges, or public postsecondary vocational/ technical schools in Florida. Other minority undergraduate students will be considered for award if funds remain available after awarding Rosewood descendants. **Criteria:** Need based.

**Funds Avail.:** Tuition and fees for up to 30 credit hours not to exceed $4000. **No. of Awards:** 25. **Deadline:** Application deadline is April 1. Florida residents must submit the FAFSA in time to be processed by May 15. Non-Florida residents must submit the FAFSA in order to receive the "Student Aid Report" (SAR) which must be submitted by April 15.

**• 2515 • Seminole-Miccosukee Indian Scholarships** *(Graduate, Undergraduate/Scholarship)*

**Purpose:** Provides financial assistance to Florida Seminole or Miccosukee Indian students who are enrolled as full- or part-time undergraduate or graduate students and demonstrate financial need. **Focus:** General Studies. **Qualif.:** Applicants must be members or eligible for membership in either the Seminole Indian Tribe of Florida or the Miccosukee Indian Tribe of Florida. Candidates must meet Florida's general eligibility requirements for receipt of state aid, including: residency in Florida for purposes other than education for no less than one year prior to the first day of class of the fall term of the academic year for which the funds are received; compliance with registration requirements of the Selective Service System; and participation in the college-level communication and computation skills testing (CLAST) program. Applicants must enroll as either undergraduate or graduate students at an eligible Florida public or private college or university for a minimum of one credit hour per term. Applicants must not owe a repayment of a grant under any state or federal grant or scholarship program, and must not be in default on any state or federal student loan program unless satisfactory arrangements to repay have been made. A renewal applicant must have earned a minimum cumulative grade point average of 2.0 on a 4.0 scale. Full-time students must have earned the equivalent of 12 credit hours for each term an award was received during the academic year. Students enrolled less than full-time must earn the equivalent number of hours required for enrollment as three-quarter-time, half-time, or less than half-time students. Eligibility for renewal is determined at the end of the second semester of third quarter of each academic year. Credits earned the previous summer can be counted toward the total number of credits required. **Criteria:** Renewal awards take precedence over new awards in any year in which funds are insufficient to award all eligible, timely applicants.

**Funds Avail.:** The amount of the award is recommended by the respective tribe but may not exceed the student's annual cost of education for a maximum of eight semesters or 12 quarters of undergraduate study, or the equivalent for less than full-time enrollment. **No. of Awards:** 23. **To Apply:** Applicants must

demonstrate financial need as determined by the standards established by the respective tribes. An application must be submitted to the appropriate tribal higher education committee. A renewal application must be submitted annually. **Contact:** Applications may be obtained from the Office of Student Financial Assistance or from one of the following tribal offices: Miccosukee Tribe of Florida, c/o Higher Education Committee, PO Box 440021, Tamiami Station, Miami, FL 33144; Seminole Tribe of Florida, c/o Higher Education Committee, 6703 Sterling Rd., Hollywood, FL 33024.

**• 2516 •**
**Florida Division of Blind Services**
2540 Executive Center Circle West　　　*Ph:* (904)488-1330
Tallahassee, FL 32399-6578　　　　　　　*Fax:* (904)487-1807

**• 2517 • Florida Division of Blind Services Vocational Rehabilitation Program** *(Other/Other)*

**Focus:** General Studies. **Qualif.:** Applicants must be Florida residents, legally blind or severely visually impaired, and eligible for vocational rehabilitation services. **Criteria:** Determination is made on an individual basis according to need (except tuition) and fund availability. **Contact:** Marie Beauford at the above address (see entry 2516).

**• 2518 •**
**Florida Education Fund**
201 E. Kennedy Blvd., Ste. 1525　　　　*Ph:* (813)272-2772
Tampa, FL 33602-5828　　　　　　　　　*Fax:* (813)272-2784
*E-mail:* fef@tnt.org; mdf@fl-educ-fd.org
*URL:* http://www.fl-educ-fd.org

**• 2519 • McKnight Doctoral Fellowships** *(Doctorate/ Fellowship)*

**Purpose:** This program is specifically designed to increase the number of African-American faculty in higher education and is aimed at both public and private educational institutions. As a by-product, it is expected that employment opportunities in industry will also be expanded. **Qualif.:** These fellowships are open to all African-American graduate students who are seeking fellowships for doctoral degrees in all disciplines except Law, Medicine, and Education with the exception of Science and Math Education. Applicants must be United States citizens. Study must take place at Florida doctoral granting institutions. Upon completion of their studies, the students are encouraged to remain in Florida. The Fellowship courses of study are available at the following Universities in Florida: Barry University, Florida Agricultural and Mechanical University, Florida Atlantic University, Florida Institute of Technology, Florida International University, Florida State University, University of Central Florida, University of Florida, University of Miami, and the University of South Florida.

**Funds Avail.:** Each award provides full tuition up to $5,000 for each of three academic years plus an annual stipend of $11,000. If a fourth or fifth year is required, it will be funded by the institution. The program provides for 25 annual fellowships. Each annual renewal is contingent upon satisfactory performance and normal progress toward the Ph.D. degree. **To Apply:** These fellowships are awarded only through direct application to the Florida Education Fund. **Deadline:** All applications and application papers must be postmarked no later than January 15. **Contact:** Bettye Parker Smith at the above address (see entry 2518).

## Florida Education Fund (continued)

### • 2520 • McKnight Junior Faculty Developmment Fellowships (Graduate, Professional Development/Fellowship)

**Purpose:** The program is intended to encourage excellence in teaching and research for minority junior faculty members with special emphasis on African Americans and Women in fields where they are severely under represented by affording a full academic year to enable participants to pursue special interests or research directly related to their teaching area. **Qualif.:** The awards are open to teachers in public and private colleges, universities, and community colleges in Florida. Applicants are required to have a minimum of two years and no more than six years in a non-tenured position. Proof of legal residency in Florida is required. Candidates must be United States citizens.

**Funds Avail.:** Twenty fellowships of $15,000 are awarded annually. The recipient receives normal salary and benefits. The awardees' institution receives $15,000 to cover teaching replacement cost. **Deadline:** February 1. **Contact:** The Florida Education Fund at the above address (see entry 2518).

### • 2521 •
## Florida House of Representatives Intern Program - Legislative Staff Internship Program
B9 Historic Capitol      *Ph:* (904)487-2390
Tallahassee, FL 32399-1300      *Fax:* (904)488-4732
*URL:* http://www.leg.state.fl.us/house/intern/

### • 2522 • Florida House of Representatives Intern Program (Graduate/Internship)

**Purpose:** To provide "hands on" experience to students interested in public policy at the state level. **Qualif.:** Applicants must have received their four-year degree prior to serving as an intern, if selected. Interns must be enrolled at a State University during the internship. Applicants must either be Florida residents or attending a Florida university at the time of application. **Criteria:** Based on an evaluation of the applicant file and personal interviews.

**Funds Avail.:** Interns receive a monthly stipend and up to 36 hours of university tuition payments at State University System (SUS) rates. Approximately 35 to 40 internships are awarded each year. **To Apply:** Candidates must complete an applicant file, which consists of a formal application, writing samples, faculty recommendations, employer recommendations, work experience, personal community, civic background, and test scores. **Deadline:** November 1.

**Remarks:** There are more than 300 internship applicants each year. **Contact:** Beverly Broussard, Program Coordinator, at the above address (see entry 2521).

### • 2523 •
## John E. Fogarty International Center
National Institutes of Health
Division of International Training and
  Research
Bldg. 31, Rm. B2C39      *Ph:* (301)496-1653
Bethesda, MD 20892      *Fax:* (301)402-0779
*E-mail:* m3p@cu.nih.gov
*URL:* http://www.nih.gov/fic

*The John E. Fogarty International Center for Advanced Study in Health Sciences (FIC) is a component of the National Institutes of Health (NIH). It promotes international cooperation in the biomedical and behavioral sciences, primarily through long- and short-term fellow-ships and scientist exchanges. Postdoctoral fellowship programs are supported by the FIC or by foreign governments or organizations. Bilateral exchange programs are supported by the FIC and cooperating foreign governments.*

### • 2524 • AIDS Fellowships (Postdoctorate/Fellowship)

**Purpose:** To support collaborative research and training for United States and foreign scientists who want to expand their capabilities in the epidemiology, diagnosis, prevention, and treatment of AIDS. **Focus:** AIDS. **Qualif.:** Researchers from any country and at all career levels may apply for training through this program. Priority is given to researchers from developing countries. **Contact:** John E. Fogarty International Center at the above address (see entry 2523).

### • 2525 • FIC Bilateral Exchanges (Postdoctorate/Award)

**Purpose:** To support advanced research by scientists from selected countries. **Focus:** Biomedical Sciences, Health Sciences. **Qualif.:** Bilateral exchange programs support collaborative activities between health professionals and biomedical scientists in the United States and participating countries. The United States participates in Health Scientist Exchanges with Hungary, Poland, Romania, and the Russia. The Fogarty Center arranges Biomedical Research Exchanges for U.S. scientists and their colleagues in Austria and Mongolia. Individuals from each participating country are supported for varying periods of work in the other country. Activities may include joint research between collaborating scientists or consultation on individually conducted research. The programs do not fund formal, academic, clinical, or research training, or attendance at scientific meetings. Candidate must be from the United States or one of the other participating countries. Candidate must have an advanced degree (normally a Ph.D.) in one of the biomedical, behavioral, or clinical sciences; professional experience in the appropriate field; and a working knowledge of the language of the host country. Candidate's home government must cover the cost of travel to the host country. The host government must provide support for expenses and travel undertaken in the host country.

**Funds Avail.:** Round-trip airfare. **To Apply:** U.S. candidates should write to the above address for application form and guidelines. Candidates from other countries should contact the appropriate government authorities in their home countries. **Deadline:** None. **Contact:** International Coordination and Liaison Branch at the above address (see entry 2523).

### • 2526 • FIC Foreign-Funded Fellowships (Postdoctorate/Fellowship)

**Purpose:** To support research by U.S. scientists in selected countries. **Focus:** Biomedical Sciences. **Qualif.:** Candidate must be a U.S. citizen or permanent resident and may apply to only one of the programs during any given receipt date. Additional qualifications vary from country to country and are outlined in the booklet, "International Opportunities in Biomedical Research," which is available from the above address.

**Funds Avail.:** Varies. **To Apply:** Write for application form and guidelines. Candidates for the West German and Taiwan programs must apply directly to those countries; candidates for all other participating countries' programs apply through the NIH International Research and Awards Branch. **Deadline:** April 5, and August 5, and December 5.

**Remarks:** The Fogarty International Center administers applications for the fellowship program, which supports U.S. scientists conducting collaborative research in laboratories in ten countries: Finland, France, Germany, Ireland, Israel, Japan, Norway, Sweden, Switzerland, and Taiwan (Fogarty does not review or maintain applications for German or Taiwanese programs. In these cases, Fogarty sends out program information and material only). **Contact:** John E. Fogarty, International Center at the above address (see entry 2523).

• 2527 • **FIC International Neuroscience Fellowships**
*(Postdoctorate/Fellowship)*

**Purpose:** To support advanced research in the United States by scientists from other countries. **Focus:** Epilepsy, Neuroscience, Stroke. **Qualif.:** Applicant must be from a member country of the World Health Organization, and be proficient in English. Preference is given to applicants from developing countries. Applicant must be a junior or mid-career health professional or scientist in the neurosciences who holds a Ph.D. or the equivalent. Preference is given to candidates proposing research and research training in epilepsy and stroke. Candidate must have a sponsor in the United States, and be assured of a position at an institution in home country upon completion of the fellowship. Fellowships are tenable at laboratories in the United States.

**Funds Avail.:** $21,000-32,300. **To Apply:** For further information, write to the above address or contact the regional office of the World Health Organization in home country. Submit to same office the form with a detailed research plan and a statement indicating how the proposed plan will be used for candidate's future career. **Deadline:** February 28. **Contact:** International Neuroscience Fellowships Program at the above address (see entry 2523).

• 2528 • **FIC International Research Fellowships**
*(Postdoctorate/Fellowship)*

**Purpose:** To enable scientists from selected countries to conduct postdoctoral research in the United States. **Focus:** Behavioral Sciences, Biomedical Sciences, Health Sciences. **Qualif.:** Individuals who have received pre- or postdoctoral training in the United States or are residing in this country at the time the application is submitted or the award would be made are not eligible for the program.

**Funds Avail.:** $21,000-32,300/year, plus travel allowance. **To Apply:** Application materials can only be obtained from the Fogarty Center nominating committee in home country/region except as noted below; write to the Center at the above address to inquire about how and where to contact the appropriate committee. Submit a pre-application letter to the nominating committee, which selects applications to forward to the Fogarty Center. Scientists from the recognized republics of the former Soviet Union (except the Russian Republic) and eligible independent states of Yugoslavia may apply through a U.S. sponsor. Applications and instructions will be sent directly to the candidate from the Fogarty International Center upon request from the applicant or sponsor. **Deadline:** July 1 and October 15.

**Remarks:** Over 60 countries participate in the Fogarty Center's International Research Fellowship Program, including Eastern Europe, Africa, Asia, and Latin America. **Contact:** International Research Fellowship Program at the above address (see entry 2523).

• 2529 • **FIC Senior International Fellowships**
*(Postdoctorate/Fellowship)*

**Purpose:** To support U.S. scientists conducting advanced research abroad. **Focus:** Behavioral Sciences, Biomedical Sciences, Health Sciences. **Qualif.:** Applicant must be a U.S. citizen or permanent resident, and hold a Ph.D. degree in one of the areas of study listed above. Candidate must have at least five years of postdoctoral experience, including at least two years of professional experience during the last four years. Candidate must be a full-time staff member of a U.S. research, clinical, or educational institution; be nominated by the academic dean of home institution; and be invited to conduct research by an institution outside of the United States. Individuals who have previously held more than one Senior International Fellowship, as well as those employed by the U.S. government, are not eligible. Candidate may only apply for one Fogarty fellowship at a time.

**Funds Avail.:** Up to $1,250/month stipend, plus $2,000/month living allowance and a travel allowance. **To Apply:** Candidates are encouraged to discuss research interests with the program officer before beginning application process. Nominating dean must

request the application kit. Candidate must submit application materials with a letter of nomination from the academic dean or other official at home institution, and a letter of invitation and curriculum vitae from the foreign host. **Deadline:** April 5, August 5, and December 5. Notification is made within approximately six months. **Contact:** Program Officer at the above address (see entry 2523).

• 2530 • **FIC Senior International Fellowships in Biomedical Sciences** *(Postdoctorate/Fellowship)*

**Purpose:** To provide opportunities for research experience and the exchange of information. **Focus:** Biomedical and Behavioral Sciences. **Qualif.:** Applicants must hold a doctoral degree in one of the biomedical, behavioral, or health sciences, and have at least five years postdoctoral experience. Candidates must have professional experience in one of the biomedical, behavioral, or health sciences for at least two of the last four years and hold a full-time appointment on the staff of a public or private not-for-profit research, clinical, or educational institution. They must also be invited by a not-for-profit foreign institution and not have received more than one Senior International Fellowship previously. In addition, the program is open only to citizens or permanent residents of the United States.

**Funds Avail.:** Senior International Fellowships are awarded for a total of 3 to 12 months. The award may be divided into as many as 3 terms, used over a 3-year period, with a minimum term of 3 months. The stipend provides $1,250 per month (maximum of $15,000 per year), a foreign living allowance of $2,000 per month (or $24,000 per year maximum), economy class round-trip air travel for the fellow only on a U.S. air carrier between the U.S. city and the host city abroad, and a host institutional allowance of up to $6,000 per year or a prorated allowance for a shorter time. **Deadline:** April 5, August 5, and December 5.

**Remarks:** The foreign host is expected to provide resources to support the research project. **Contact:** Division of International Training and Research, Bldg. 31, Rm. B2C39, at the above address (see entry 2523).

• 2531 • **FIC Visiting Fellowships** *(Postdoctorate/Fellowship)*

**Purpose:** To support research in NIH centers by scientists from outside of the United States. **Focus:** Health Sciences. **Qualif.:** Applicant may be from any country except the United States, and must have a Ph.D. degree or the equivalent in the health sciences. All participants must be nominated by the host NIH facility, and be proficient in English. Candidate must have not more than three years of postdoctoral research experience at the start of the fellowship. Awards are tenable at facilities of the U.S. National Health Institutes, where fellows will conduct collaborative research in their biomedical specialties.

**Funds Avail.:** $25,000-31,000. **To Apply:** Write to the Fogarty Public Information Office at the address listed above for a copy of the "Scientific Directory and Annual Bibliography," which lists NIH staff members and their research interests. Then, send a resume and a brief description of research interests to an NIH senior staff scientist in the pertinent field of study. If proposed research meets the interests of the potential sponsor, further information will be requested. **Deadline:** None. **Contact:** International Services and Communication Branch at the above address (see entry 2523).

• 2532 • **Fogarty International Research Collaboration Award** *(Postdoctorate/Other)*

**Purpose:** To provide small grants to U.S. investigators to facilitate cooperation and collaboration between U.S. scientists and scientists in Central and Eastern European, and Latin American and Caribbean Initiatives. Awards are also provided for cancer-related collaborative research with scientists located in Sub-Saharan Africa. **Focus:** Health Sciences. **Qualif.:** Applicants must be Principal Investigators of NIH research project grants (R, P, or U-01 series) that will be active and funded during the proposed

## John E. Fogarty International Center (continued)

grant award period (up to three years). The foreign collaborator must be from a country located in the geographical regions commonly known as Central and Eastern Europe, Latin America, or the non-U.S. Caribbean. The foreign collaborator must also hold a position at a public or private non-profit institution that will allow him or her adequate time and provide appropriate facilities to conduct the proposed research.

**Funds Avail.:** Up to $32,000 in direct costs per year, for up to three years. Funds may be used for materials, supplies, and equipment and/or travel and living expenses, and their research associates, as justified by the scientific needs of the project. No salaries or stipends for any of the collaborators, students, or technical assistants will be offered under these awards. Award monies are sent to the U.S. investigator's parent institution for distribution to the recipient. **To Apply:** Applications must be submitted on an official form provided by the National Institutes of Health. Special application instructions are necessary and are available from the International Research and Awards Branch of FIC. Applications consist of portions to be completed by the U.S. Principal Investigator, and separate portions to be completed by the foreign collaborator. Both portions must be submitted as a single package. **Deadline:** Receipt dates for completed applications are March 25, July 25, and November 25. If the deadline falls on a weekend, it is automatically extended to the following Monday. **Contact:** Division of International Training and Research, Fogarty International Center, at the above address (see entry 2523).

## • 2533 • Israeli Ministry of Health Fellowships
*(Postdoctorate/Fellowship)*

**Purpose:** To allow United States scientists to conduct collaborative research in laboratories in one of five Israeli institutions: Hadassah Medical Organization, Tel Aviv University, Weizmann Institute of Science, Technion-Israel Institute of Technology, and Ben Gurion University of the Negev. **Focus:** Biomedical and Behavioral Sciences. **Qualif.:** Applicants must hold a doctoral degree in one of the biomedical or behavioral sciences and have appropriate professional experience in the proposed area of research. They must also be citizens or permanent residents of the United States.

**Funds Avail.:** Fellowships are awarded for periods of 3 to 12 months; in exceptional cases, fellowships may be extended for an additional period if mutually agreed to by the Israeli sponsor. Fellowships include a stipend equivalent to the fellow's counterpart in Israel (determined by the applicant's experience at the time of award), and accident insurance for the fellow only. **Deadline:** April 5, August 5, and December 5. **Contact:** Division of International Training and Research at the above address (see entry 2523).

## • 2534 • Japan Society for the Promotion of Science Fellowships *(Postdoctorate/Fellowship)*

**Purpose:** The Japan Society for the Promotion of Science (JSPS) provides fellowships to enable United States scientists to conduct research in Japan. **Focus:** Clinical, Biomedical and Behavioral Sciences. **Qualif.:** Applicants must hold a doctoral degree in one of the clinical, biomedical, or behavioral sciences; be 35 years old or younger at the start of the fellowship tenure; and make prior arrangements with the Japanese host researcher as to the research plan. They must also be citizens or permanent residents of the United States.

**Funds Avail.:** The Society provides a monthly stipend of 270,000 Y; monthly family allowance of 50,000 Y; monthly housing allowance not to exceed 100,000 Y; relocation allowance of 200,000 Y; round-trip airfare expenses; in-transit travel allowance (transportation from Tokyo to destination, if other than Tokyo); medical and accident insurance coverage for the fellow only; and language training allowance not to exceed 500,000 Y. Fellowships are awarded for up to 12 months; fellowships may be extended if recommended by the host institution and approved by the JSPS.

**Deadline:** April 5, August 5, and December 5. **Contact:** Division of International Training and Research at the above address (see entry 2523).

## • 2535 • Swedish Medical Research Council Fellowships *(Postdoctorate/Fellowship)*

**Purpose:** The Swedish Medical Research Council provides fellowships to enable United States scientists to conduct collaborative research in laboratories in Sweden. **Focus:** Clinical, Biomedical and Behavioral Sciences. **Qualif.:** Applicants must hold a doctoral degree in one of the clinical, biomedical, or behavioral sciences; have 10 years or less of postdoctoral experience; and have professional experience in the health sciences for at least two of the last four years. They must also be citizens or permanent residents of the United States.

**Funds Avail.:** The Council provides a stipend of between $19,000 and $23,000 per year (amounts are determined by the number of years of relevant or professional postdoctoral experience at the time of the award); round-trip air travel expenses for fellows and accompanying dependents; and health insurance coverage for fellows and accompanying family members. Fellowships are awarded for 12 months; exceptions are considered if recommended by the host institution and approved by the Council. **Deadline:** April 5. **Contact:** International Research and Awards Branch at the above address (see entry 2523).

## • 2536 • Taiwan National Science Council Fellowships *(Postdoctorate/Fellowship)*

**Purpose:** To enable United States scientists to conduct collaborative research or to lecture in Taiwan. **Focus:** Biomedical, Behavioral and Health Sciences. **Qualif.:** Applicants must hold a doctoral degree in one of the biomedical, behavioral, or health sciences. The Council offers opportunities at four career levels: Special Chair for internationally prominent scientists; Visiting Research Professor Award for scientists who are full professors; Visiting Associate Research Professor Award for scientists who are associate or assistant professors; and Visiting Specialist Award for scientists who have at least five years of postdoctoral experience or whose scientific specialty has not been fully developed in Taiwan. **Criteria:** Preference is given to applicants working in the areas of cancer, cardiovascular diseases, stroke, infectious diseases, environmental health, blood banking, and animal models.

**Funds Avail.:** Fellowships are awarded for a minimum of three months to a maximum of 12 months and may be renewed, if necessary. Fellowships cover living expenses (determined by the experience and qualifications of the applicant); one round-trip ticket for the awardee for a visit of 6 months (2 tickets for visits of from 6 to 10 months, and up to two additional single-trip tickets for fellow's children 18 years or younger if fellow stays more than 10 months); a housing allowance or a house (provided by the host institution); and 65 percent of medical insurance premium. **Deadline:** April 5, August 5, and December 5. **Contact:** CCNAA or Fogarty International at the above address (see entry 2523).

## • 2537 • Alexander von Humboldt Foundation Fellowship *(Postdoctorate/Fellowship)*

**Purpose:** To provide United States scientists the opportunity to conduct collaborative research in laboratories in Germany. **Focus:** Biomedical, Behavioral and Clinical sciences. **Qualif.:** Applicants must hold a doctoral degree in one of the biomedical, behavioral, or clinical sciences; have professional experience in the health sciences for a least two of the last four years (clinicians should have finished their specialization examination); and not be more than 40 years old.

**Funds Avail.:** Fellowships are awarded for 6 to 12 months and may be extended up to an additional 12 months if recommended by the host institution and approved by the AvH Foundation. The Foundation provides a stipend of DM 2.700 to DM 3.500 per month (levels are determined by the number of years of postdoctoral experience at the time of the award). There are additional provisions for covering spouse and children, travel expenses, and German language courses. **Deadline:** April 5, August 5, and December 5. **Contact:** Division of International Training and Research at the above address (see entry 2523).

## • 2538 •
## Donald W. Fogarty International Student Paper Competition - APICS Educational & Research Foundation

5301 Shawnee Rd.　　　　　　　　*Ph:* (703)354-8851
Alexandria, VA 22312　　　　　　*Free:* 800-444-2742
*E-mail:* h-kather@apics-ha.org
*URL:* http://www.apics.org

### • 2539 • Donald W. Fogarty International Student Paper Competition *(Graduate, Undergraduate/Other)*

**Focus:** Resource management. **Qualif.:** Applicants must be attending classes at accredited colleges or universities as full- or part-time graduate or undergraduate students at the time of submission, May 15. High school students are ineligible.

**Funds Avail.:** $250-1,500. **To Apply:** Telephone for further details. **Deadline:** May 15.

**Remarks:** An eligible paper must be the original work of one or more authors who submit a single paper to one local APICS chapter. Paper topics should pertain to the field of resource management only. Papers developed as part of normal class assignments are eligible, but theses or dissertations are not acceptable. There is no set length, but papers typically range between 10 and 20 pages. Papers should be in English and conform to the guidelines. To be eligible for this annual competition, the original and two copies of the paper must be received by the submission date. **Contact:** Heidi Kather at the new address.

## • 2540 •
## The Folger Shakespeare Library

201 E. Capital St., SE　　　　　　*Ph:* (202)544-4600
Washington, DC 20003　　　　　　*Fax:* (202)544-4623
*E-mail:* webmaster@folger.edu
*URL:* http://www.folger.edu/menu.htm

### • 2541 • Folger Library Long-Term Fellowships *(Postdoctorate/Fellowship)*

**Purpose:** To assist senior scholars with research projects appropriate to the collections of the Folger Library. **Focus:** American, Continental, and British History, 1500-1715; American, English, and European Literature and Drama, 1500-1800; History of Art, Exploration, Medicine, Music, Philosophy, Religion, and Science; Political, Economic, and Legal History, 1500-1715; Renaissance Studies; William Shakespeare. **Qualif.:** Applicant may be of any nationality, but must have a Ph.D., and should be a senior scholar. Fellows are expected to be in residence in Washington, D.C., during the term of the fellowship, and to be regular readers at the Library.

**Funds Avail.:** $1,700/month. **To Apply:** Submit seven copies each of a 500-word description of the research project and a curriculum vitae. Three letters of reference should be sent directly to the Committee on Research Fellowships at the Folger. **Deadline:** November 1. **Contact:** Carol Brobeck, Committee on Research Fellowships, at the above address (see entry 2540).

### • 2542 • Folger Library Short-Term Fellowships *(Postdoctorate/Fellowship)*

**Purpose:** To assist scholars with research projects appropriate to the collections of the Folger Library. **Focus:** American, Continental, and British History, 1500-1715; American, English, and European Literature and Drama, 1500-1800; History of Art, Exploration, Medicine, Music, Philosophy, Religion, and Science; Political, Economic, and Legal History, 1500-1715; Renaissance Studies; William Shakespeare. **Qualif.:** Applicant may be of any nationality, but must have a Ph.D., and is expected to be resident in Washington, D.C., during the term of the fellowship.

**Funds Avail.:** $1,700/month. **To Apply:** Submit four copies of a 500-word description of research project and curriculum vitae. Three letters of reference should be sent directly to the Committee on Research Fellowships. **Deadline:** March 1. **Contact:** Carol Brobeck, Committee on Research Fellowships, at the above address (see entry 2540).

### • 2543 • National Endowment for the Humanities Fellowships *(Postdoctorate/Fellowship)*

**Purpose:** To assist senior scholars with research projects appropriate to the collections of the Folger Library. **Focus:** American, Continental, and British History, 1500-1715; American, English, and European Literature and Drama, 1500-1800; History of Art, Exploration, Medicine, Music, Philosophy, Religion, and Science; Political, Economic, and Legal History, 1500-1715; Renaissance Studies; William Shakespeare. **Qualif.:** Applicant must have a Ph.D., and should be a senior scholar. NEH Fellowships are restricted to U.S. citizens. Fellows are expected to be in residence in Washington, D.C., during the term of the fellowship, and to be regular readers at the Library.

**Funds Avail.:** $30,000 maximum. The amount of the Fellowship is not to exceed one-half of the Fellow's regular academic salary for the period of the fellowship, exclusive of benefits. The Library assumes that the remainder will be covered by leave pay or some similar grant from the Fellow's institution. **To Apply:** Submit seven copies each of a 500-word description of the research project and a curriculum vitae, including a list of publications. Three letters of reference should be sent directly to the Committee on Research Fellowships at the Folger. **Deadline:** November 1.

## • 2544 •
## Fondation des Etats Unis

15, boulevard Jourdan　　　　　　*Ph:* 33 1 53806880
75690 Paris Cedex 14, France　　*Fax:* 33 1 53806899

### • 2545 • Harriet Hale Woolley Scholarships *(Graduate/Scholarship)*

**Purpose:** To support graduate study of art and music in Paris. **Qualif.:** Applicants must be United States citizens between 21 and 29 years of age who have graduated with high academic standing from an American college, university, or professional school of recognized standing. They must have the capacity for study on the graduate level, show evidence of artistic or musical accomplishment and demonstrate proficiency in French. Applicants should also possess good moral character and personality, adaptability, good physical health, and emotional stability. Since the Foundation has no accommodation for couples, only single applicants are considered. **Criteria:** Preference is given to mature students who have already done graduate study. Grants are specifically for persons doing painting, print-making, or sculpture, and for instrumentalists. They are not intended for research in art history, musicology, composition, dance, or theater.

**Funds Avail.:** Four to five scholarships of $8,500 each, payable in French francs, in five installments, during the academic year (October 1 through June 29). Recipients live at the Fondation des

## Fondation des Etats Unis (continued)

Etats-Unis, which is one of the residences of the Cite Internationale Universitaire de Paris. They are expected to participate in the cultural and social activities of the Foundation. Although Woolley scholars should remain in Paris during the full academic year, they are free to travel during the Christmas and Easter vacation periods. **No. of Awards:** 4. **To Apply:** Applicants must submit a short statement of the foreign study project including the Paris school and/or instructor preferred, a formal application, a statement of income form, a letter attesting proficiency in the French language by a qualified teacher of French, three letters of recommendation from professors, college transcripts, a medical certificate of general health, four small identification photographs, seven international postal coupons, and slides of art work (12 maximum in a sheet of flat plastic), or ten minutes of music on a cassette. **Deadline:** January 31. **Contact:** The Director, Fondation des Etats-Unis at the above address (see entry 2544).

---

### • 2546 •
### Fondation Internationale Nadia et Lili Boulanger
11, rue de Saint-Simon
75007 Paris, France

#### • 2547 • Nadia and Lili Boulanger Scholarship
*(Professional Development/Scholarship)*

**Focus:** Music. **Qualif.:** Candidates may be serious musicians of any nationality. The scholarship is open to performers, composers, and scholars (research topics can be in either music history or theory). The target age group is 20 to 35 but this requirement may be waived by the board of directors.

**Funds Avail.:** The amount of the one-year scholarship may be adjusted to the needs and scope of the proposed project. **To Apply:** A complete application file will contain an application form, a curriculum vitae, a short project statement, and three recommendations. **Deadline:** July 1. **Contact:** Mlle. Cecile Armagnac, Secretaire Generale, Fondation Nadia et Lili Boulanger at the above address (see entry 2546).

---

### • 2548 •
### Food Distribution Research Society, Inc.
c/o Roger Hinson
Dept. of Ag. Economics
101 Ag. Admin. Bldg.
LSU
Baton Rouge, LA 70803
E-mail: rhinson@agctr.lsu.edu

*Ph:* (225)388-2753
*Fax:* (225)388-2716

#### • 2549 • Applebaum Master's and Ph.D. Programs Awards *(Doctorate, Graduate, Undergraduate/Scholarship)*

**Purpose:** To promote research in food distribution. **Qualif.:** Applicants must be Master's or Doctor's candidates or outstanding seniors with a sincere interest in the food industry. **Criteria:** Quality of the paper.

**Funds Avail.:** A cash stipend of $1,250 is provided at the Ph.D level; a cash stipend of $750 is provided at the Master's degree level. Recipients are provided with complimentary registration to the annual conference of the FDRS and one year's complimentary student membership. Tourist class air fare to the annual meeting is also provided for recipients. **To Apply:** Candidates must submit a short written description of career interests, goals, and objectives,

including a biographical description listing any food industry experience and/or research experience. Copies of student reports, special problems, or other food industry research papers should also be submitted. Applicants should be in the upper half of their class, but a record below this is not to be interpreted as automatic disqualification. **Deadline:** July.

**Remarks:** Recipients will be asked to make a short presentation at the annual FDRS Conference on a food industry related topic of their choice from research and related papers submitted. **Contact:** The Food Distribution Research Society at the above address (see entry 2548).

---

### • 2550 •
### Food and Drug Law Institute
1000 Vermont Ave., NW, Ste. 200
Washington, DC 20005-4903
E-mail: jko@fdli.org
URL: http://www.fdli.org

*Ph:* (202)371-1420
*Fax:* (202)371-0649

#### • 2551 • Summer Internship Program *(Other/Internship)*

**Purpose:** To complement law, pharmacy, or biomedical engineering education. **Qualif.:** Enrollement in an ABA accredited law school or enrollment in a scientific or technical degree program addressing an area related to the food and drug field and participation in a summer internship sponsored by a government agency. **To Apply:** Submission of completed application. Brief resume and transcript of grades. Brief cover letter describing candidates qualifications/relevent coursework, experience, and long-term career goals. **Deadline:** June 5.

---

### • 2552 •
### Forest History Society
c/o Cheryl Oakes, Librarian
701 Vickers Ave.
Durham, NC 27701-3162
E-mail: coakes@duke.edu
URL: http://www.lib.duke.edu/forest/

*Ph:* (919)682-9319
*Fax:* (919)682-2349

#### • 2553 • Alfred D. Bell, Jr. Visiting Scholars Program *(Doctorate, Graduate, Postdoctorate, Professional Development/Fellowship)*

**Purpose:** To enable scholars to make use of the varied collections of the Forest History Society library and archives. **Focus:** Forest History, Conservation History, Land Use History. **Qualif.:** Applicant must be pursuing serious research on a forest or conservation history topic. **Criteria:** Selection is based upon compatibility of research topic with the collections of the Forest History Society.

**Funds Avail.:** Up to $850. **No. of Awards:** 5 to 8. **Deadline:** None. **Contact:** Cheryl Oakes, Librarian, at the above address (see entry 2552).

## • 2554 •
## Forest Products Society
2801 Marshall Court
Madison, WI 53705-2295
*E-mail:* info@forestprod.org
*URL:* http://www.forestprod.org/

*Ph:* (608)231-1361
*Fax:* (608)231-2152

### • 2555 • Wood Awards *(Graduate, Postgraduate/Award)*

**Purpose:** To recognize outstanding graduate research papers on wood and wood products. **Focus:** Wood. **Qualif.:** Applicant may be of any nationality, but must be a graduate student registered at any college or university for at least one full quarter prior to the award year. Candidate's paper should focus on some aspect of wood, and be from 2,000 to 4,000 words in length.

**Funds Avail.:** First prize: $1,000; second prize: $500. **No. of Awards:** 2. **To Apply:** Submit tentative title of entry to Forest Products Society. Four copies and the original of the completed paper must be submitted to Forest Products Society by an advisor, dean, or department head at the home institution. **Deadline:** For title submission: February 16; for paper submission: March 1.

## • 2556 •
## Fort Wayne News-Sentinel
Attn: Assistant Managing Editor
600 W Main St.
Fort Wayne, IN 46802-1498

*Ph:* (219)416-8713
*Fax:* (219)461-8749

### • 2557 • Fort Wayne News-Sentinel Minority Journalism Scholarship *(Undergraduate/Internship)*

**Focus:** Journalism. **Qualif.:** Applicants must plan to pursue a career in journalism.

**Funds Avail.:** $400 weekly stipend. **No. of Awards:** Varies. **To Apply:** Write for further details. **Deadline:** January 1. **Contact:** Carolyn DiPaolo.

## • 2558 •
## Foundation for Amateur Radio, Inc.
6903 Rhode Island Ave.
College Park, MD 20740
*URL:* http://www.seas.gwu.edu/student/hanir/mdc/far.html

### • 2559 • FAR Scholarships *(Graduate, Undergraduate/Scholarship)*

**Focus:** Engineering, General Studies. **Qualif.:** Candidates must be active licensed radio amateurs.

**Funds Avail.:** Amounts vary. **To Apply:** Scholarships vary yearly. Information must be obtained from amateur radio journals such as *QST, CQ,* or *WorldRadio.* **Contact:** Journals listed above or The Foundation for Amateur Radio, Inc. at the above address (see entry 2558).

## • 2560 •
## Foundation of the American College of Healthcare Executives
1 N. Franklin St., Ste. 1700
Chicago, IL 60606-3491
*URL:* http://www.ache.org

*Ph:* (312)424-2800
*Fax:* (312)424-0023

### • 2561 • Albert W. Dent Scholarship *(Graduate/Scholarship)*

**Purpose:** To increase the enrollment of minority students in healthcare management graduate programs and to encourage students, through structured, formalized study, to obtain positions in middle and upper levels of healthcare management. **Focus:** Health Services Management or Administration. **Qualif.:** Applicants must be Student Associates of the American College of Healthcare Executives and minority undergraduates who have been accepted for full-time study for the fall term in a healthcare management graduate program accredited by the Accrediting Commission on Education for Health Services Administration or enrolled full-time and in good academic standing in an ACEHSA-accredited graduate program in healthcare management. They must also be citizens of the United States or Canada who are receiving the scholarship for the first time and be able to demonstrate financial need.

**Funds Avail.:** $3,000. **No. of Awards:** Varies. **To Apply:** Program director at the above address. **Deadline:** Applications are accepted between January 1 and March 31.

**Remarks:** The Board of Governors of the Foundation of the American College of Healthcare Executives established and named the Scholarship in honor of its first black Fellow Dr. Dent, president emeritus of Dillard University, New Orleans, who was granted Fellowship in the College in 1939. The foundation receives between 50-100 applications annually. **Contact:** Foundation of the American College of Healthcare Executives at the above address (see entry 2560).

### • 2562 • Foster G. McGaw Student Scholarship *(Graduate/Scholarship)*

**Purpose:** To financially assist worthy persons to better prepare themselves for healthcare management, thereby contributing to improvements in the field. **Focus:** HSA/MBA. **Qualif.:** Applicants must be Student Associates of the American College of Healthcare Executives and enrolled full-time and in good academic standing in a graduate program in healthcare management that is accredited by the Accrediting Commission on Education for Health Services Administration. They must be citizens of the United States or Canada who are receiving the scholarship for the first time and able to demonstrate financial need.

**Funds Avail.:** $3,000. **No. of Awards:** Varies. **To Apply:** Application forms may be obtained from program directors or by contacting the Foundation of American College Healthcare Executives. **Deadline:** Applications are accepted between January 1 and March 31.

**Remarks:** The College has administered the Foster G. McGaw Student Loan Fund since 1969. The initial gift of $150,000 was from the Foster G. McGaw Charitable Fund. Additional gifts were made by Mr. McGaw from his personal funds before his death in 1986. He was the founder of the American Hospital Supply Corporation. Between 50-100 applications are received each year. **Contact:** The Foundation of the American College of Heathcare Executives at the above address (see entry 2560).

**• 2563 •**
**Foundation for Chiropractic Education and Research**
1701 Clarendon Blvd.                    *Ph:* (703)276-7445
Arlington, VA 22209                     *Fax:* (703)276-8178
*E-mail:* fcer@healthy.net
*URL:* http://www.healthy.net/pan/pa/fcer/Abtfcer.HTM

**• 2564 •   Foundation for Chiropractic Education and Research Fellowships, Scholarships, and Residency Stipends** *(Graduate, Professional Development/ Fellowship, Grant)*

**Purpose:** To fund research training in programs leading to doctorate degrees in scientific and non-scientific health-related areas. **Focus:** Chiropractic. **Qualif.:** Must have received a D.C. degree. Grants are awarded for research development, basic science, and clinical science projects that specifically relate to chiropractic and the principles upon which it is founded. **Criteria:** Grants are awarded to any post-baccalaureate Principal Investigator whose proposal is deemed worthy and most consistent with the mission of the Foundation.

**Funds Avail.:** Approximately $300,000 is available annually. **To Apply:** Forms, instructions, and guidelines are mailed upon request. **Deadline:** October 1 and March 1 for grants; March 1 for fellowships and residencies. **Contact:** Deborah Callahan (for fellowships and residencies) and Anthony L. Rosner (for grants) at the above address (see entry 2563).

**• 2565 •**
**Foundation for Exceptional Children**
1920 Association Dr.
Reston, VA 22091                        *Ph:* (703)620-1054
*URL:* http://www.cec.sped.org/fd-menu.htm

**• 2566 •   Stanley E. Jackson Scholarship Awards** *(Undergraduate/Scholarship)*

**Focus:** General Studies. **Qualif.:** Candidates must be entering freshmen who are disabled, disabled minority, disabled gifted, or disabled gifted minority students. They must plan to be full-time students at two- or four-year undergraduate colleges or universities or at vocational, technical, or fine arts training programs. They must provide evidence of financial need.

**Funds Avail.:** One scholarship award of $1,000 is made in each of the four categories named above. Other scholarships may be awarded if funds are available and applications merit further awards. An individual can receive no more than one award. Past recipients are ineligible. **To Apply:** Applicants apply in one category only. They must provide two copies of the following materials: completed scholarship application form, transcript(s) of academic records for grades 9-12, three letters of recommendation, a goals statement of 250 words or less, and a statement of financial need. Applications are available in the fall. **Deadline:** All materials must be postmarked by February 1. **Contact:** The Foundation for Exceptional Children at the above address (see entry 2565).

**• 2567 •**
**Foundation of the Flexographic Technical Association, Inc.**
900 Marconi Ave.                        *Ph:* (516)737-6020
Ronkonkoma, NY 11779                    *Fax:* (516)737-6813
*E-mail:* srubin@vax.fta-ffta.org

**• 2568 •   FFTA Scholarship Competition** *(High School, Undergraduate/Scholarship)*

**Purpose:** To assist students in a graphic arts program with an interest in flexography. **Qualif.:** Applicants must demonstrate an interest in a career in flexography and be high school seniors presently enrolled at a post-secondary institution offering a course of study in flexography. They must also have a GPA of at least 3.0 on a 4.0 scale and exhibit exemplary performance in their studies, particularly in the graphic arts. **Criteria:** Applications are reviewed by members of the scholarship committee.

**Funds Avail.:** $2,000. Renewal is possible provided the recipient maintains an acceptable scholastic average and continues in an approved program of study. **No. of Awards:** 19. **To Apply:** Candidates should send a completed application to a college official in the graphic arts department with a copy of their transcripts. College officials must then sign and forward applications with their comments to the Foundation. **Deadline:** March 19. **Contact:** Shelley Rubin, Educational Coordinator, at the above address (see entry 2567).

**• 2569 •   Sun Chemical Corporation Flexographic Research Scholarship** *(Graduate/Fellowship)*

**Purpose:** To enable top graduate students to conduct flexographic printing research. **Focus:** Research in Flexography. **Qualif.:** Candidates must be full-time graduate students (in the United States or abroad) enrolled in a qualified graphic arts curriculum, hold a B.S. or B.A. degree in a related discipline, and have an undergraduate GPA of at least 3.0 on a 4.0 scale. Professionals in the flexographic field are also eligible to apply. **Criteria:** Applications are reviewed by a committee.

**Funds Avail.:** $10,000 non-renewable grant disbursed directly to institution. Recipient must prepare and present to the flexographic industry a paper of substance on an approved topic as a direct result of the fellowship studies. Quarterly written updates are also required in order to monitor progress. **No. of Awards:** 1. **To Apply:** Applications may be obtained through the FFTA. **Deadline:** March 19.

**Remarks:** The fellowship program was established by Sun Chemical Corporation in conjunction with the FFTA. **Contact:** Shelly Robins, Educational Coordinator, at the above address (see entry 2567). Please indicate Sun Chemical Corporation Fellowship.

**• 2570 •**
**Foundation for Interior Design Education Research**
60 Monroe Center, NW, Ste. 300         *Ph:* (616)458-0400
Grand Rapids, MI 49503-2920            *Fax:* (616)458-0460
*E-mail:* fider@fider.org
*URL:* http://www.fider.org

**• 2571 •   Joel Polsky/Fixtures Furniture/FIDER Endowment Research Award** *(Professional Development/Award)*

**Purpose:** To encourage research in interior design. **Focus:** Interior Design. **Qualif.:** Candidates must be interior design educators or practitioners in North America. Applicants must intend to conduct research clearly related to building the body of knowledge of interior design education. Students are not eligible. Grant funds may be used for customary research expenses. Funds must not be used for indirect costs, travel expenses or equipment worth $200 or more, or for work undertaken to fulfill academic degree requirements.

**Funds Avail.:** $5,000 maximum. **No. of Awards:** 1 annually. **To Apply:** Write or phone the F.I.D.E.R. for application form and guidelines. Submit form, resume, budget, summary of research, timeline, and letters of recommendation. Applications forms can be accessed using email address: fider@fider.org **Deadline:** January 1. Grants are announced in April. **Contact:** Kayem Dunn, Executive Director, at the above address (see entry 2570).

---

## • 2572 •
### The Foundation of the National Student Nurses' Association, Inc.

555 W. 57th St., Ste. 1327     *Ph:* (212)581-2211
New York, NY 10019-2925     *Fax:* (212)581-2368
*E-mail:* nsna@nsns.org
*URL:* http://www.nsna.org

#### • 2573 • Frances Tompkins Scholarships
*(Undergraduate/Scholarship)*

**Purpose:** to promote nursing education **Qualif.:** Applicants must be students currently enrolled in a state-approved school of nursing or pre-nursing in an associate's, baccalaureate, diploma, generic doctorate, or generic master's program. **Criteria:** Selections are based on academic achievement, financial need, and involvement in nursing student organizations and community activities related to health care. All factors are equally weighed.

**Funds Avail.:** NSNA has awarded $75,000; individual scholarships ranged from $1,000 to $2,500. **To Apply:** Send a self addressed stamped legal-size envelope with 52 cents postage to the above address. Applications must include a recent nursing school and college transcript, or grade report. The application must be accompanied by a $10 processing fee. NSNA members must submit proof of membership. Applications will be available from September until mid-January. **Deadline:** February 1. Recipients will be notified in March.

**Remarks:** There is only one application for all NSNA scholarships, graduating high school seniors are not eligible. **Contact:** The Foundation of the National Student Nurses' Association, Inc. at the above address (see entry 2572).

---

## • 2574 •
### Foundation for Physical Therapy

1111 N. Fairfax St.     *Ph:* (703)684-5984
Alexandria, VA 22314-1488     *Fax:* (703)706-8519
    *Free:* 800-875-1378
*E-mail:* foundation@apta.org
*URL:* http://www.apta.org/foundation/index.html

#### • 2575 • Foundation for Physical Therapy Doctoral Award *(Doctorate/Award)*

**Focus:** Physical Therapy. **Qualif.:** Applicants must be students pursuing a doctoral degree in physical therapy or a related field with a research focus germane to the clinical practice of physical therapy. Applicants must demonstrate a commitment to teach and do research in an accredited entry-level physical therapy program upon completion of their doctoral studies. One year of teaching and research service will be expected for each year of scholarship support.

**Funds Avail.:** A maximum of $12,000 can be requested. Successful candidates may reapply for continuing funding for up to four years. **No. of Awards:** Varies every year. **To Apply:** Applicants must submit a completed application, available at the Foundation offices. Telephone or write the Foundation for an application. **Deadline:** March 1. **Contact:** Program Officer at the above address (see entry 2574).

#### • 2576 • Foundation for Physical Therapy Research Grant *(Other/Grant)*

**Focus:** Physical Therapy. **Qualif.:** The Principal Investigator must be a qualified physical therapist. Applicants' proposals must meet the objectives and priorities of the Foundation and must demonstrate ability to complete the project within the time frame designated.

**Funds Avail.:** The Foundation makes available sole or matching funds to individuals or groups of researchers to pursue scientifically-based and clinically-related physical therapy research. Projects are supported for a maximum of two calendar years. Grant requests of $30,000 per year or less are considered. Support for purchase of major pieces of equipment must be limited to 50 percent of the total award. **No. of Awards:** Varies every year. **To Apply:** Applicants must submit a completed research application, available from the Foundation office. **Deadline:** February 1. **Contact:** Program Officer at the above address (see entry 2574).

---

## • 2577 •
### Foundation for Science and Disability, Inc.

115 South Brainard Ave.
La Grange, IL 60525-2114     *Ph:* (708)352-1091

#### • 2578 • FSD Student Grant *(Graduate/Grant)*

**Purpose:** To increase the opportunities in science for physically disabled students. **Focus:** Science, Computer Science, Mathematics, Medicine, Engineering. **Qualif.:** Applicants must be fourth-year undergraduates who have been accepted to graduate or professional school, or graduate students who have some physical disability. The awards are made to these students for some special purpose in connection with a science project or thesis in any of the fields listed above. Awards may be given for an assitive device or instrument, or as financial support to work with a professor on an individual research project or for some other special need. **Criteria:** Since few grants and rehabilitation grants are given to disabled groups who wish to obtain a Master's degree in the field of science, FSD offers this award only to students who are entering or continuing a Master's Degree in one of the above fields of science.

**Funds Avail.:** $2,000-3,000. **No. of Awards:** 1-3 per year. **To Apply:** A formal application must be completed. As part of the application, the student is required to write an essay of approximately 250 words, which should include a description of professional goals and objectives, as well as the specific purpose for which the grant would be used. A copy of the applicant's official college transcripts must be submitted. Two letters of recommendation from faculty members are required, one of which should be from the faculty member who will serve as the student's academic research advisor. **Deadline:** December 1. **Contact:** Rebecca F. Smith, Co-Chairperson of the Science Student Grant Committee, 115 S. Brainard Ave., La Grange, IL 60525 for submission of application materials.

#### • 2579 • Grants for Physically Disabled Students in the Sciences *(Graduate/Grant)*

**Purpose:** To provide physically disabled students with opportunities in science. **Focus:** Computer Science, Engineering,

---

## Foundation for Science and Disability, Inc. (continued)

Mathematics, Medicine, Science. **Qualif.:** Applicants may be of any nationality, but must be physically disabled students enrolled in or accepted to a master's degree program at a graduate or professional school. Grants are intended for some special purpose, such as a science project or thesis.

**Funds Avail.:** $1,000 each. **No. of Awards:** 1-3. **To Apply:** Write to the Foundation for application form and guidelines. Submit form with official transcripts, two letters of reference from faculty members, and a 250-word statement describing goals and proposed project. **Deadline:** December 1.

**Remarks:** There are usually 5-8 applicants each year. **Contact:** Rebecca F. Smith, Science Student Grant Committee Chair, at the above address (see entry 2577).

---

## • 2580 •
## Foundation of the Wall and Ceiling Industry

803 W. Broad St., Ste 600      *Ph:* (703)534-8300
Falls Church, VA 22046      *Fax:* (703)534-8307
*URL:* http://www.awci.org/index.htm

### • 2581 • Bookbuilders West Annual Scholarship
*(Undergraduate/Scholarship)*

**Focus:** Publishing. **Qualif.:** Applicants must be entering their third or fourth year of study and have a minimum "C" grade point average. **Criteria:** Awards are made based on merit of essay.

**Funds Avail.:** $2,000. **No. of Awards:** 2. **To Apply:** Applicants must submit an essay outlining why the applicant would like to pursue a career in publishing. Applicants may also submit a portfolio, but it is not required. **Deadline:** May 3. **Contact:** Vivian Tobias at the above address (see entry 2580).

---

## • 2582 •
## Four-Shra-Nish Foundation

c/o Arcanum Lions Club
Box 126
Arcanum, OH 45304-0126

### • 2583 • Four-Shra-Nish Foundation Loan
*(Undergraduate/Loan)*

**Focus:** Medicine, Religion, Education, Business. **Qualif.:** Candidates must have been residents for at least 18 months of Darke County, Ohio, and pursuing studies in education, religion, business, or medicine. They must have successfully completed their college freshman year with a minimum grade point average of 2.0 on a 4.0 scale, or 1.5 on a 3.0 scale.

**Funds Avail.:** Up to $2,500-$3,000 in loans annually with a cap of $5,000-$6,000 for all loans granted. Repayment of loans begins on the sixth month after graduation, with a minimum of $50 per month for each individual loan received plus interest based at three percent less than the current prime rate. **To Apply:** Applicants must submit three character references and sign a promissory note with surety to pay back loans. **Deadline:** June.

**Remarks:** 1996 is the final year for the foundation. **Contact:** Four-Shra-Nish Foundation at the above address (see entry 2582).

---

## • 2584 •
## Terry Fox Humanitarian Award Program

Simon Fraser University      *Ph:* (604)291-3057
Burnaby, BC, Canada V5A 1S6      *Fax:* (604)291-3311

### • 2585 • Terry Fox Humanitarian Award
*(Undergraduate/Award)*

**Purpose:** To encourage post-secondary study at the university or college level in Canada. Award recognizes a commitment to high ideals, citizenship, humanitarian service, amateur sport and fitness, health and community service as well as academic excellence. **Qualif.:** Applicants must be Canadian citizens and be 25 years old or younger.

**Funds Avail.:** Number of awards ranging from $2,500 to $4,000 each varies. **To Apply:** Applicants must submit 3 reference letters with application form. **Deadline:** February 1. **Contact:** Terry Fox Humanitarian Award Program at the above address (see entry 2584).

---

## • 2586 •
## Parker B. Francis Fellowships

c/o Joseph D. Brain, Director
Physiology Program
Harvard School of Public Health
665 Huntington Ave.      *Ph:* (617)432-4099
Boston, MA 02115      *Fax:* (617)277-2382
*E-mail:* brain@hsph.harvard.edu; soishi@
  medicine.med.sch.ucla.edu

### • 2587 • Parker B. Francis Fellowships
*(Postdoctorate/Fellowship)*

**Purpose:** To support post-doctoral training of pulmonary researchers during the transition to becoming independent investigators. **Focus:** Pulmonary Medicine. **Qualif.:** Candidates must hold either the M.D., Sc.D., or Ph.D. degree and demonstrate evidence of research proficiency in pulmonary diseases. The researcher must be sponsored by an established faculty member who is employed or connected with accredited academic institutions located in the United States or Canada. Candidates who are not citizens of the United States or Canada must show evidence of progress towards permanent residence in the United States or Canada (preferably paperwork in process). **Criteria:** Selection is based on the applicant's qualifications, scientific merits of the research project proposal, and assessment of the sponsor's laboratory.

**Funds Avail.:** Total budget is limited to $38,000 in the first year, $40,000 for the second, and $42,000 for the third year. The totals include a stipend plus fringe benefits and may include travel funds to a maximum of $1,500. **No. of Awards:** 15. **To Apply:** The Foundation requires information on the resources and capabilities of the applicant's sponsor, and on the background and qualifications of the candidate, who must outline long-term career goals and submit budgetary requirements and other details of the research project. Applications are filed by the director of any academic training program or pulmonary division or research laboratory on behalf of a fellowship candidate. Originals and nine copies of the application form and supporting materials must be submitted. **Deadline:** Usually October 15.

**Remarks:** Parker B. Francis, founder of the Puritan Bennett Company, established this Foundation in 1951. The research fellowships program was inaugurated in 1975 and the fellowship program has supported more than 300 individuals with grants awarded to more than 80 academic medical centers in the United States and Canada. **Contact:** Arlene C. Kirsch, Administrator, at the above address (see entry 2586).

• **2588** •

**Fredrikson & Byron Foundation**
1100 International Centre
900 2nd Ave., S.                    Ph: (612)347-7000
Minneapolis, MN 55402-3397         Fax: (612)347-7077
E-mail: glarson@fredlaw.com
URL: http://www.fredlaw.com

• **2589** • **Fredrikson & Byron Minority Scholarships**
*(Graduate/Scholarship)*

**Purpose:** To promote the practice of law in Minneapolis. **Focus:** Law. **Qualif.:** Applicants must be ethnic minority students in their first year and second semester of law school. **Criteria:** Selection is based on undergraduate and law school GPA, answers on scholarship application, recommendations, extracurricular activities, and a writing sample.

**Funds Avail.:** $5,000. **No. of Awards:** 2. **To Apply:** Applications are available in January of each year. They are also mailed to various law schools and their minority organizations. **Deadline:** March 31. **Contact:** Greta M. Larson at the above address (see entry 2588).

• **2590** •

**The Freedom Forum Media Studies Center**
Columbia University
2950 Broadway                      Ph: (212)678-6600
New York, NY 10027                 Fax: (212)678-6663
URL: http://www.mediastudies.org/
*Formerly the Gannett Center for Media Studies.*

• **2591** • **Chips Quinn Scholars Program**
*(Undergraduate/Scholarship)*

**Focus:** Journalism or mass communications.

**Funds Avail.:** $1000. **To Apply:** Applications are available through the journalism or mass communications department of head of the university. University representatives may nominate one junior-level journalism student.

• **2592** • **The Freedom Forum Media Studies Center Residential Fellowships** *(Professional Development/ Fellowship)*

**Purpose:** To support advanced study of mass communication and technological change. **Focus:** Mass Communication. **Qualif.:** Applicant may be of any nationality. Candidate may be a media professional from a print or broadcast organization, a journalism or mass communication educator, or a scholar from another field with a primary interest in media studies. Fellowships are offered to applicants at three levels of attainment: senior fellowships for established candidates with substantial national reputations, fellowships for accomplished applicants at mid-career, and research fellowships for candidates with five to eight years of experience. Candidate's proposed project should examine major issues and problems facing the mass media and society, in either a domestic or global context. Investigations into broad issues are preferred to single-topic studies. Fellowships are tenable at Columbia University. Fellows are expected to participate in the general activities of the Center.

**Funds Avail.:** Stipend, plus housing allowance, and other benefits. **To Apply:** Write for application guidelines. Submit letter of application with a three- to five-page project proposal, curriculum vitae or resume, and relevant publications or work samples. Three letters of reference must be sent to the Center by the referees. **Deadline:** February 1. Fellowships are announced in April. **Contact:** Residential Fellowship Program at the above address (see entry 2590).

• **2593** • **Gannett Center Fellowships** *(Other, Professional Development/Fellowship)*

**Qualif.:** Applicants must be examining major issues and problems facing the mass media and society, in either a domestic or global context, with special attention to projects on First Amendment freedoms; the minority and ethnic press; media economics; the relationship between the media and other institutions; coverage of such topics as education, the environment, and the arts; and the advancement of journalism education. Examinations of great issues are preferred to single-topic studies. Fellowships are awarded to persons at three levels of attainment: senior fellowships for mature individuals with substantial national reputations; fellowships for accomplished persons at mid-career; and research fellowships for those with five to eight years of experience. Applicants may be media professionals from print and broadcast organizations, journalism and mass communication educators, as well as scholars from other fields with a primary interest in media studies. **Criteria:** Fellowships will be awarded on the basis of: the significance and the quality of the project; the applicant's ability to carry out the work; and the relevance of the work to the resources of the Center, Columbia University, and the New York metropolitan area.

**Funds Avail.:** Fellows will be in residence at Columbia University for periods of three months to one academic year for major scholarly or professional projects and will participate in weekly seminars and special programs and make the result of their work at the Center available to the public through publication or other public presentation. A stipend based on salary needs or matching sabbatical support, a housing allowance, and other benefits will be provided. Fellows will have office space as well as secretarial and research assistance. **To Apply:** Applicants should submit a letter of application with a three to five page summary of their proposed project. The summary should include: a title; an executive summary; a brief description of the project; delineation of the method of analysis or inquiry; explanation of the project's distinctiveness; the anticipated outcome (e.g., book or monograph); and why the project should be carried out at the Gannett Center in New York City. Applicants should also send a resume or curriculum vita and publications or work samples, if relevant. In addition, applicants should arrange to have three letters of reference sent to the Center. **Deadline:** All materials, including those sent by references, should be postmarked no later than February 1. **Contact:** The Freedom Forum Media Studies Center at the above address (see entry 2590).

• **2594** •

**Fresno County Women Lawyers**
5151 N Palm, Ste. 820
Fresno, CA 93704                   Ph: (559)226-1540

• **2595** • **Justice Pauline Davis Hanson Memorial Scholarship** *(Graduate/Scholarship)*

**Purpose:** To provide assistance for women law students. **Qualif.:** Awarded to a woman following her first year in law school. **Criteria:** Academic excellence and community service, financial need also considered, preference to current or former residents of Fresno, Madera, Kings and Tulave Counties, California.

**Funds Avail.:** Range: $500-1,000. **To Apply:** Application form and personal interview in Fresno, California required of finalists. **Deadline:** May 1.

# • 2596 •
## Fresno-Madera County Medical Society - Scholarship Foundation
PO Box 31          *Ph:* (209)224-4224
Fresno, CA 93707      *Fax:* (209)224-0276
*E-mail:* info@fmms.org
*URL:* http://www.fmms.com

### • 2597 • Fresno-Madera Medical Society Scholarships *(Doctorate/Scholarship)*

**Purpose:** To create and administer a perpetual and revolving scholarship fund for deserving residents of Fresno County and Madera County in pursuit of their education in medicine. **Qualif.:** Applicants must have been residents of Madera or Fresno counties for at least one year, and enrolled in or accepted to a medical school. **Criteria:** Need, scholastic achievement and prospects for completion of the chosen curriculum are important considerations.

**Funds Avail.:** Awards vary each year. They are generally $1,000-1,500 each. Funds are distributed to the recipient's school of matriculation. That school will administer the scholarship for tuition, laboratory fees, books and any other valid educational expense, except for room, board, or personal expenses. **No. of Awards:** Varies. **Deadline:** May 15. **Contact:** Ellen Burton, Administrative Secretary, at the above address (see entry 2596)for applications and further information.

# • 2598 •
## Friends of the Library of Hawaii
690 Pohukaina St.      *Ph:* (808)536-4174
Honolulu, HI 96813      *Fax:* (808)536-5232
*E-mail:* jms@hcc.hawaii.edu
*URL:* http://www.hcc.hawaii.edu/hspls/friends.html

### • 2599 • Friends of the Library of Hawaii Memorial Scholarship *(Graduate/Scholarship)*

**Purpose:** To assist Hawaii residents who are enrolled in the School of Library and Information Sciences at the University of Hawaii. **Focus:** Library and Information Science. **Qualif.:** Applicants must be Hawaii residents who are now enrolled or who have been accepted for enrollment in the Master's program in Library and Information Services School at the University of Hawaii at Manoa. **Criteria:** Based on financial need and merit.

**Funds Avail.:** $25,000 is available, usually awarded in $1,000 and $2,000 scholarships. **No. of Awards:** Varies. **To Apply:** Applications are available in mid-March. **Deadline:** Last day of May. **Contact:** Scholarship Chair at the above address (see entry 2598).

# • 2600 •
## Friends of Martin Fischbein, Inc.
1500 Broadway, 25th Fl.
New York, NY 10036      *Ph:* (212)704-8174

### • 2601 • Martin Fischbein Fellowship
*(Undergraduate/Fellowship)*

**Purpose:** To provide qualified students the opportunity to work on the editorial or business side of publications at News Corp. or Fox TV. **Focus:** Print or broadcast communications. **Qualif.:** Open to college juniors.

**Funds Avail.:** $250 per week. **No. of Awards:** 1. **To Apply:** Applicants must submit a two page 500 word essay describing career goals and personal qualities. **Deadline:** March 15.

# • 2602 •
## Fukunaga Scholarship Foundation
PO Box 2788      *Ph:* (808)521-6511
Honolulu, HI 96803      *Fax:* (808)523-3937
*E-mail:* eviek@lava.net

### • 2603 • Fukunaga Scholarship Foundation Annual Four-Year Scholarships in Business Administration *(Undergraduate/Scholarship)*

**Purpose:** To encourage high school students in the State of Hawaii to pursue higher education in business administration at one of the campuses of the University of Hawaii or at any accredited college. Students who are already attending college will also be considered. **Focus:** Business Administration **Qualif.:** Applicants must impress fellow students, members of the faculty, and members of the community as individuals deserving of a chance to begin or continue toward higher education and have demonstrated those personal attitudes, and scholastic aptitude needed to achieve educational goals. Applicants must have an interest in business and have participated in school activities and community services that demonstrate leadership and responsibility. They must show a true desire to further their education as a means of attaining and sustaining a career within the Pacific Ocean Islands area and must plan to return eventually to Hawaii or to employment in the Pacific Island region to contribute to their growth and welfare. **Criteria:** Applicants' class standings will be considered. A cumulative grade-point average of at least 3.0 is highly desirable. The need for financial assistance will also be taken into consideration. Semifinalist are selected based on the application and accompanying documents, and are interviewed by members of the selection committee, who then choose recipients. Applicants must be residents of Hawaii.

**Funds Avail.:** $2,000 will be awarded annually for four years; a total of $8,000 if a satisfactory record is sustained. For college students, the amount and length of the award will vary with the circumstances. **No. of Awards:** Approximately 50. Twelve to fifteen new scholarships are awarded at the end of each school year. Recipients must successfully complete a full-time course load and maintain a 3.0 GPA each year to continue to receive the scholarship. **To Apply:** Applicants must submit a formal application form, available from the Fukunaga Scholarship Foundation, that requires applicants to provide general information, personal statements on financial needs and responses to various topics, a four-year activity review, and an essay on career objectives and plans to achieve those goals. A copy of school transcripts, including cumulative grade-point and class standing as of the end of the first semester, must accompany the application. College entrance test scores (preferably SAT) should be submitted if available. Two letters of recommendation, from the high school principal, teacher, or counselor, or from a business or professional person in the community are required. Semi-finalists will be contacted for an interview. **Deadline:** Applications must be postmarked by February 15. **Contact:** Funkunaga Scholarship Foundation at the above address (see entry 2602).

• 2604 •
## Fulbright Teacher Exchange
600 Maryland Ave., SW, Rm. 320
Washington, DC 20024-2520

*Ph:* (202)314-3527
*Fax:* (202)479-6806
*Free:* 800-726-0479

### • 2605 • Fulbright Teacher Exchange Program
*(Professional Development/Grant)*

**Purpose:** Sponsored by the United States Information Agency, the program's purpose is to promote the mutual understanding between the people of the United States and the peoples of other countries through educational exchange. **Focus:** Education. **Qualif.:** The Fulbright Teacher Exchange Program is open to administrators and educators of all subjects from K-12 through college level. The tentative list of participating countries includes: Argentina, Benin, Brazil, Bulgaria, Canada, Chile, Colombia, Czech Republic, Estonia, Finland, France, Germany, Hungary, Italy, Latvia, Mexico, Morocco, Norway, Peru, Poland, Romania, Senegal, Slovakia, South Africa, Spain, Turkey, United Kingdom, and Zimbabwe. In addition, an eight-week summer seminar in Italy is open to teachers of Latin, Greek and the Classics. Applicants must: (1) be U.S. citizens; (2) hold at least a bachelor's degree; (3) have a current full-time teaching position; (4) have three years full-time teaching experience; and (5) be fluent in English. In addition to meeting the general requirements, applicants must also meet various country specific requirements which are detailed in the application booklet.

**Funds Avail.:** Grants vary. In most cases, both the U.S. and international educator remain on their respective home salaries while exchanging classrooms for the academic year. The grant includes a summer orientation program and may include round-trip transportation for the grantee. **No. of Awards:** Varies yearly. **To Apply:** Telephone or write to request the application booklet. **Deadline:** October 15 of the year preceding the grant year; grantees are notified of selection in the spring. **Contact:** Tiffany Swanson, Outreach Specialist, at the above address (see entry 2604).

• 2606 •
## Fund for Education and Training
1830 Connecticut Ave., NW
Washington, DC 20009-5732

*Ph:* (202)483-2220
*Fax:* (202)483-1246
*Free:* 800-379-2679

*E-mail:* nisbco@igc.apc.org
*URL:* http://www.nisbco.org

### • 2607 • FEAT Loans *(All/Loan)*

**Purpose:** To assist young men who believe it is wrong to comply with the law enforcing registration for the draft. **Focus:** General Studies. **Qualif.:** Priority is given to those who have no other source of aid, either from the financial aid program of their school, or from other agencies. Also eligible are individuals who are denied job training under the Job Training Partnership Act and other employment programs funded by the federal government under title IV. Applicants are asked to explain why they refuse to register for the draft and prepare for war.

**Remarks:** The Fund has been incorporated since 1985 and will remain active for as long as peacetime draft registration is national policy. **Contact:** Further information and application forms may be obtained from FEAT at the above address (see entry 2606).

• 2608 •
## Fyssen Foundation
194, rue de Rivoli
F-75001 Paris, France

*Ph:* 1 42 97 53 16
*Fax:* 1 42 60 17 95

### • 2609 • Fondation Fyssen Post-Doctoral Study Grants *(Postdoctorate/Grant)*

**Purpose:** To support and train postdoctoral researchers working on topics keeping with the Foundation's goals. **Qualif.:** Applicants must be younger than 35 years, intending to assist French scientists outside of France, and foreign scientists in France.

**Funds Avail.:** Up to Fr120,000 per year. **To Apply:** Applications should be completed according to a form obtained from the Foundation. **Deadline:** March 31.

### • 2610 • Fyssen Foundation Research Grants *(Doctorate, Postgraduate/Grant)*

**Purpose:** To provide funds for the training and support of young researchers working on topics corresponding to the Foundation's goals. **Focus:** Cognitive Mechanisms—Anthropology, Archaeology, Epistemology, Ethnology, Ethology, Logic, Neurosciences, Paleontology, Psychology. **Qualif.:** Candidate may be of any nationality. Applicant must be enrolled in a science leading to a Ph.D. degree or postgraduate. Grants to French citizens are tenable worldwide. Citizens of other countries must study at institutions or in the field in France.

**Funds Avail.:** Up to FF100,000. **To Apply:** Write to the Executive Secretary for application form and guidelines, available November through February. Submit form, five-page research project, letter of inviting laboratory, two testimonials, curriculum vitae, and list of publication in 15 copies. **Deadline:** March 31. Notification by the second week of July. **Contact:** Colette Leconte, Executive Secretary, at the above address (see entry 2608).

### • 2611 • International Scientific Prize *(Professional Development/Prize)*

**Purpose:** To provide funds for research of interest to the Foundation. **Focus:** Discipline changes each year. In 1994, the subject was Developmental Psychology in Humans. **Qualif.:** Candidate may be of any nationality, but must be nominated.

**Funds Avail.:** Up to FF200,000 **To Apply:** Write to the Executive Secretary for nomination form and guidelines, available November through February. **Deadline:** September 1. **Contact:** Colette Leconte, Executive Secretary, at the above address (see entry 2608).

• 2612 •
## Albert Gallatin Fellowship Program
University of Virginia
International Studies Office
208 Minor Hall
Charlottesville, VA 22903
*E-mail:* rgd@virginia.edu

*Ph:* (804)982-3010
*Fax:* (804)982-3011

### • 2613 • Albert Gallatin Fellowships in International Affairs *(Doctorate/Fellowship)*

**Purpose:** To provide an opportunity for Ph.D. students to engage in dissertation research at the Graduate Institute of International Studies. **Focus:** Economics, International Law, International Relations, Political Science. **Qualif.:** Applicant must be a U.S. citizen and a Ph.D. candidate whose dissertation research will be enhanced by an academic year of study at the Graduate Institute

## Albert Gallatin Fellowship Program *(continued)*

of International Studies, University of Geneva, Switzerland. Fellows must be competent in the French language.

**Funds Avail.:** $11,250, plus travel between New York and Geneva. **No. of Awards:** 1. **To Apply:** Write for application form. Submit with essay outlining research program; writing sample; curriculum vitae; transcripts; and four letters of reference, including one from the thesis supervisor, and one judging competency in French. **Deadline:** March 1. Final selection of fellows will be completed by May 1. **Contact:** Allen Lynch Executive at the above address (see entry 2612).

## • 2614 •
## Gallaudet University Alumni Association

Gallaudet University
Peikoff Alumni House, Kendall Green
800 Florida Ave., NE                    *Ph:* (202)651-5060
Washington, DC 20002-3695               *Fax:* (202)651-5062
*E-mail:* mapugin@gallua.gallaudet.edu; alumweb@
  gallux.gallaudet.edu
*URL:* http://www.gallaudet.edu/~alumweb

### • 2615 • Gallaudet University Alumni Association Graduate Fellowship Funds *(Doctorate, Graduate/ Fellowship)*

**Purpose:** To provide financial assistance to deaf graduates of Gallaudet University and other accredited colleges and universities in pursuit of doctoral study at colleges and universities. **Focus:** General Studies. **Qualif.:** Applicants must be deaf or hard of hearing and be accepted for admission to any accredited graduate program, working toward a doctorate degree. **Criteria:** Preference is given to those who show financial need and are residents of the United States.

**Funds Avail.:** The amounts of the grants vary from candidate to candidate. Fellowships are awarded for one year and may be renewed for the duration of the course of study and for dissertation expenses provided that the holder of the award maintains personal and scholastic standards required by the college or university and resubmits an application each year. **No. of Awards:** Varies. **To Apply:** Applicants must submit an audiological assessment of the status of applicant's hearing, a letter from the head of the university department or school who will supervise the applicant's program stating confirming admission, a list of courses to be taken and major field of study, official transcripts from all college and universities attended, a report of financial standing, and letters of reference. In applying for subsequent grants, applicants must submit an up-to-date official transcript, an evaluation report from applicant's academic advisor, and a new financial report. **Deadline:** April 20. **Contact:** Mary Anne Pugin, Executive Director, at the above address (see entry 2614).

## • 2616 •
## Gamma Theta Upsilson

c/o Mr. Lawrence R. Handley
U.S. Fish and Wildlife Service
National Wetlands Research Center
700 Cajundome Blvd.                     *Ph:* (318)266-8691
Lafayette, LA 70506                     *Fax:* (318)266-8513
*URL:* http://ga-mac.uncc.edu/students/gtu/aboutgtu.html

### • 2617 • Robert G. Buzzard Scholarships *(Graduate/ Scholarship)*

**Qualif.:** Applicants must be active Gamma Theta Upsilon members and superior scholars. One award is presented to a member with an outstanding undergraduate record who has enrolled in a graduate program in geography. The other award is for a student who has been in graduate school for at least a year. **Criteria:** Selection is based upon service to GTU, service to the geography department, academic performance, and recommendations.

**Funds Avail.:** Each award is $500. **To Apply:** Each geography department that has a chapter charter receives application forms each year. Contact the chapter sponsor or write to the First Vice President for an application. Two faculty member recommendations, one of which must be from the chapter sponsors, must accompany transcript copies and completed applications. **Deadline:** August 1. **Contact:** Lawrence R. Handley, First Vice President, at the above address (see entry 2616).

### • 2618 • Benjamin F. Richason III Scholarship *(Graduate, Professional Development/Scholarship)*

**Qualif.:** Candidates must be active Gamma Theta Upsilon members and have junior or senior undergraduate status at the time of the award with either career or graduate school aspirations. **Criteria:** Selection is based on service to GTU, service to the geography department, academic performance, and recommendations.

**Funds Avail.:** One award of $500. **To Apply:** Application forms must be requested. Letters of recommendation from two faculty members and official college transcripts must accompany the completed application. **Deadline:** August 1. **Contact:** Lawrence R. Handley, First Vice President, at the above address (see entry 2616).

## • 2619 •
## Garden Club of America

598 Madison Ave.                        *Ph:* (212)753-8287
New York, NY 10022                      *Fax:* (212)753-0134

### • 2620 • GCA Awards For Summer Environmental Studies; Clara Carter Higgins Scholarship *(Undergraduate/Scholarship)*

**Purpose:** To further the cause of environmental protection. **Focus:** Ecology, Environmental Sciences.

**Funds Avail.:** $1,500. **No. of Awards:** 2 or more. **To Apply:** Send self-addressed stamped envelope for application. **Deadline:** February 15. The recipient of the award is announced in May. **Contact:** Monica Freeman at the above address (see entry 2619).

### • 2621 • GCA Awards in Tropical Botany *(Doctorate/ Award)*

**Purpose:** To promote the preservation of tropical forests by enlarging the body of botanists with field experience. **Focus:** Tropical Botany. **Qualif.:** Applicants must be Ph.D. candidates. Grant is to enable field study in tropical botany.

**Funds Avail.:** $5,500. **No. of Awards:** Two annually. **Deadline:** December 31.

**Remarks:** Selection is made by a panel of botanists appointed by the World Wildlife Fund and approved by the GCA Scholarship Committee. **Contact:** For information and application, contact World Wildlife Fund, 1250 24th St. N.W., Washington, DC 20037-1175, U.S.A. (202)778-9714.

• 2622 • **Interchange Fellowship in Horticulture and Landscape Design** *(Graduate, Postgraduate/Fellowship)*

**Purpose:** To enable a British postgraduate student in horticulture or landscape architecture to study in the United States, and a U.S. postgraduate to study in the U.K. **Focus:** Horticulture, Landscape Architecture. **Qualif.:** For 1997-98 school year, fellowship may be limited to those living or attending school in Alabama, District of Columbia, Florida, Georgia, Kentucky, Maryland, North Carolina, South Carolina, Virginia, or West Virginia. Applicant must be a U.K. or U.S. citizen. Candidate must be a postgraduate or final-year undergraduate student in horticulture or landscape architecture. For British citizen, the fellowship is tenable at any U.S. university that offers relevant postgraduate courses. Fellowship candidates are responsible for arranging admission to the host institution. For U.S. citizens, applicant must be a college graduate who is not older than 27. Fellowship is tenable for one semester at any U.K. institution, other semesters will be spent in short-term study and at the Royal Botanic Garden, Edinburgh and The Royal Botanic Gardens, Kew.

**Funds Avail.:** Tuition, room and board, personal allowances, and round-trip airfare. **No. of Awards:** One. **To Apply:** Send a self-addressed, stamped envelope to the director of education for application form and guidelines. **Deadline:** November 15.

**Remarks:** Fellowships are sponsored jointly by the GCA and The Martin McLaren Fund of The English Speaking Union. **Contact:** M. Freeman at the above address (see entry 2619).

• 2623 •
**Gardner Foundation**
c/o Martha Sorrell
304 S. Highview Rd.
Middletown, OH 45044-5033     *Ph:* (513)423-0699

• 2624 • **Gardner Foundation Scholarship Grants**
*(High School, Undergraduate/Scholarship)*

**Focus:** General Studies. **Qualif.:** Applicants must be in their senior year of high school and planning to immediately enroll in a four-year baccalaureate program. Only Ohio students in Hamilton County (Ohio School Districts), Butler County (Middletown, Edgewood, and Madison School Districts), and Warren County (Franklin School District) are eligible.

**Funds Avail.:** Scholarship amount is based on need and made payable to qualified educational institutions. **To Apply:** Applications are available from guidance counselors at high schools located in the areas listed above. **Contact:** Hamilton County scholarships are distributed by the Cincinnati Scholarship Foundation, 230 E. Ninth St., Rm. 209, Cincinnati, OH 45202; all other areas are serviced by the Middletown Community Foundation, 29 City Center Plaza, Middletown, OH 45042.

• 2625 •
**Erroll Garner Memorial Foundation, Inc.**
521 5th Ave., 17th Fl.
New York, NY 10017

• 2626 • **Errol Garner Memorial Foundation Scholarship Awards** *(All/Award)*

**Purpose:** To perpetuate the music and memory of Errol Garner and to give scholarships to non-professional jazz instrumental students, who have a plan of study. **Qualif.:** Applicants must have musical ability, economic need, and plans for continued study. **Criteria:** Based on economic background and study plans. Extra consideration will be given to students who play the piano.

**Funds Avail.:** $1,5000 per scholarship. **No. of Awards:** 2 a year. **To Apply:** A cassette of the musician playing solo and two letters of reference must be submitted.

• 2627 •
**Gencorp**
c/o Joan Thompson, Dir. of
  Community Relations
175 Ghent Rd.        *Ph:* (216)869-4298
Fairlawn, OH 44333     *Fax:* (216)869-4288

• 2628 • **National Merit Scholarship** *(Undergraduate/Scholarship)*

**Qualif.:** Applicants must be children of GenCorp. employees. **To Apply:** Applicants must write for details. **Contact:** S. Theresa Carter.

• 2629 •
**General Commission on Archives and History of the United Methodist Church**
36 Madison Ave.
PO Box 127        *Ph:* (973)408-3189
Madison, NJ 07940     *Fax:* (973)408-3909
*E-mail:* gcah@gcah.org
*URL:* http://www.gcah.org

• 2630 • **Jesse Lee Prizes** *(Graduate/Prize)*

**Purpose:** To encourage the writing of serious, book-length monographs in United Methodist History, which would include the history of any antecedent bodies or offshoots of Methodism in the United States or its missions. **Focus:** Religion, Theology. **Qualif.:** Applicants are usually graduates doing work in United Methodist history. **Criteria:** The originality of the research and writing are taken in consideration.

**Funds Avail.:** A $2,000 prize is awarded every four years to assist the author with publication. **No. of Awards:** 1. **Deadline:** October 1.

• 2631 • **John Harrison Ness Memorial Awards**
*(Graduate/Award)*

**Purpose:** To recognize the best papers on some aspect of United Methodist history written each year. **Focus:** Religion, Theology. **Qualif.:** Applicants must be students enrolled in M.Div. or equivalent program in United Methodist or other accredited seminaries by the Association of Theological Schools.

**Funds Avail.:** First prize is $200; second prize is $100. The winning paper(s) may be published in Methodist History at the discretion of

### General Commission on Archives and History of the United Methodist Church (continued)

the editor. **No. of Awards:** 2. **To Apply:** The paper must have been judged by applicant's professor as one of quality. The professor will then submit three copies of the paper to the General Commission on Archives and History. The paper must be properly footnoted and bear evidence of thorough and reliable handling of sources using the annotation standards accepted at the seminary. A bibliography must also be included. Papers are generally 5,000 to 10,000 words. **Deadline:** February 1.

**Remarks:** The award is given in the memory of John Harrison Ness (1891-1980), pastor, conference superintendent, and denominational executive in the Evangelical United Brethren Church.

#### • 2632 • Women in United Methodist History Research Grants *(Other/Grant)*

**Purpose:** To provide seed money for research projects relating specifically to the history of women in the United Methodist Church or its antecedents. **Focus:** Theology, Religion, Women's Studies. **Criteria:** Selection is based on the project's potential contribution to the body of knowledge in the field, availability of the results to interested persons, and the quality of the applicant's scholarship. Proposals on women of color and history at the grass roots level are especially encouraged.

**Funds Avail.:** $1,000 for one person or $500 each for two persons is awarded each year at the discretion of the selection committee. Funds may be used for travel, secretarial services, and other such costs, but not for equipment, publications costs, or the researcher's salary. **To Apply:** Candidates must submit a curriculum vita, a description of the project, a timetable, a budget, an indication of how the research results will be disseminated, and three letters of recommendation from persons providing evidence of the scholarly capabilities of candidates. Applicants are encouraged to consider a variety of formats (written, audiovisual, oral history, bibliographies, archival guides, etc.). The final product does not necessarily have to be formally published, but the information must be made available to the public in some way. **Deadline:** December 31. Grant recipients are announced by May 1.

**Remarks:** Selection is made by a committee comprised of two historians of women in United Methodism and the Assistant General Secretary of the General Commission on Archives and History of the Methodist Church. A copy of the final product will be deposited with the General Commission on Archives and the History of the United Methodist Church. **Contact:** All materials should be submitted to Assistant General Secretary, General Commission on Archives and History, at the above address (see entry 2629).

#### • 2633 • Women in United Methodist History Writing Awards *(Other/Award)*

**Purpose:** To award excellence in research and writing in the history of women in the United Methodist Church or its antecedents. **Focus:** Religion, Theology, Women's Studies. **Criteria:** Selection is based on the quality of writing and research, and contribution to the body of knowledge in the field.

**Funds Avail.:** $250. **No. of Awards:** One or two. **To Apply:** Applicants should submit unpublished manuscripts not longer than 25 double-spaced, typewritten pages. Footnotes and bibliography should follow the *Chicago Manual of Style.* **Deadline:** May 1.

**Remarks:** Selection is made by a committee comprised of two historians of women in United Methodism and the Assistant General Secretary of the General commission on Archives and History, The United Methodist Church. The award will be announced at the annual meeting of the General Commission on Archives and History of The United Methodist Church. A copy of the winning entry will be deposited with the General Commission on Archives and History of The United Methodist Church. The winning manuscript may be published in *Methodist History,* the

Commission's journal, at the editor's discretion. **Contact:** Manuscripts should be submitted to Assistant General Secretary, General Commission on Archives and History of the Methodist Church, at the above address (see entry 2629).

### • 2634 •
### General Federation of Women's Clubs of Massachusetts
Box 679
Sudbury, MA 01776-0679                    *Ph:* (508)443-4569

#### • 2635 • Dorchester Woman's Club Scholarships *(High School, Undergraduate/Scholarship)*

**Focus:** Music, Vocal. **Qualif.:** Applicants must be undergraduates who are enroll in a four-year accredited college or university, or school of music.

**Funds Avail.:** $500. **No. of Awards:** At least 1. **To Apply:** Applications consist of a letter of endorsement from the president of the sponsoring GFWC of MA club in the community of the applicant's legal residence, a personal letter stating the applicant's need for this scholarship and other pertinent information, a letter of recommendation from high school department head or career counselor, and a transcript grades. **Deadline:** February 1. **Contact:** Alyca Burke, Coordinator, Arts Dept., at the above address (see entry 2634).

#### • 2636 • GFWC of MA Art Scholarships *(High School, Undergraduate/Scholarship)*

**Focus:** Art Institute of Boston Scholarship is for study at the Art Institute of Boston; Edith Folsom Hall Scholarship is for study at Mount Ida College, Fisher College Scholarship is for study at Fisher College. **Qualif.:** Applicants must be Massachusetts high school seniors who plan to attend the designated school for each scholarship. Edith Folsom Hall Scholarship and Fisher College Scholarship applicants must also be women. Fisher College Scholarship applicants must show financial need.

**Funds Avail.:** Art Insitute of Boston Scholarhip is $1000 for freshman year only; Edith Folsom Hall Scholarship is $500; and Fisher College Scholarship is $600. **No. of Awards:** Varies. **To Apply:** Applications include a letter of endorsement from the president of the sponsoring GFWC of MA club in the community of the applicant's legal residence, a personal letter stating goals, a letter of recommendation from the applicant's high school art instructor, and a portfolio of three examples of original work. **Deadline:** March 1. **Contact:** Marilyn Perry, Scholarship Chairman, at the above address (see entry 2634).

#### • 2637 • GFWC of MA Communication Disorder Scholarships *(Graduate/Scholarship)*

**Focus:** Speech and language pathology/audiology. **Qualif.:** Applicants must be graduate students maintaining legal residence in Massachusetts.

**Funds Avail.:** $500. **No. of Awards:** At least 1. **To Apply:** Application consist of a a completed form, a letter of endorsement from the president of the sponsoring GFWC of MA club in the community of the applicant's legal residence, a personal letter stating the reason for needing financial assistance, a letter of reference from the department head of applicant's major, and a transcript of college grades. A personal interview is required. **Deadline:** March 1.

### • 2638 • GFWC of MA International Affairs Scholarships (Graduate, Undergraduate/Scholarship)

**Purpose:** To provide the opportunity for students to study abroad. **Focus:** General Studies. **Qualif.:** Applicants must be undergraduate or graduate students maintaining legal residence in Massachusetts.

**Funds Avail.:** Scholarships of $500 to be used for a minimum of a full semester during an academic year. **No. of Awards:** 1. **To Apply:** Applications include a letter of endorsement from the president of the sponsoring GFWC of MA club in the community of the applicant's legal residence, a personal letter providing pertinent information, a letter of reference from the applicant's department head, and a transcript of college grades. An interview is required. **Deadline:** March 1. **Contact:** International Affairs Dept., at the above address (see entry 2634).

### • 2639 • GFWC of MA Memorial Education Fellowships (Graduate/Fellowship)

**Focus:** Theology, woman's health/gerontology. Fields of study change each year. **Qualif.:** Applicants must be women who have maintained legal residence in Massachusetts for at least five years and are pursuing study at the graduate level in a designated field.

**Funds Avail.:** $2000. **No. of Awards:** 8-10. **To Apply:** Send a self-addressed stamped envelope for further information and an application. Applications must be accompanied by a letter of endorsement from the president of the sponsoring GFWC of MA club in the community of the applicant's legal residence, a personal letter giving pertinent information including goals and yearly tuition, a letter of reference from college or place of employment, and transcripts of grades from college and graduate school. A personal interview is also required. **Deadline:** March 1. **Contact:** Chairman of Trustees, Memorial Education Fund, at the above address (see entry 2634).

### • 2640 • GFWC of MA Music Scholarships (High School, Undergraduate/Scholarship)

**Focus:** Music education, music therapy, instrumental music, and piano. **Qualif.:** Applicants must be Massachusetts high school seniors who plan to major in one of the required areas of study.

**Funds Avail.:** $500. **No. of Awards:** 1-3. **To Apply:** Applications consist of a completed form, a letter of endorsement from the president of the sponsoring GFWC of MA club in the community of the applicant's legal residence, a letter of recommendation from either the applicant's high school principal or music teacher, and transcripts. Personal auditions are required. Applicants must provide their own accompanist, and should have two short pieces ready to perform. **Deadline:** February 1. **Contact:** Alyce Burke, Coordinator, Arts Dept., at the above address (see entry 2634).

### • 2641 • Newtonville Woman's Club Scholarships (High School, Undergraduate/Scholarship)

**Focus:** Education/teaching. **Qualif.:** Applicants must be Massachusetts high school seniors who will enroll in a four-year accredited college or university in a teacher training program that leads to certification.

**Funds Avail.:** At least one scholarship of $600 is awarded. **To Apply:** Applications consist of a completed application form, a letter of endorsement from the president of the sponsoring GFWC of MA club in the community of the applicant's legal residence, a personal letter stating applicant's need for this scholarship and other pertinent information, a letter of recommendation from high school department head or career counselor, and transcript of high school grades. An interview is required. **Deadline:** March 1. **Contact:** Marilyn Perry, Scholarship Chariman, at the above address (see entry 2634).

### • 2642 • General Learning Communications

60 Revere Dr.      *Ph:* (847)205-3000
Northbrook, IL 60062-1563      *Fax:* (847)564-8197

### • 2643 • The DuPont Challenge: Science Essay Awards Program (High School/Award)

**Purpose:** To challenge students to create an essay describing a significant challenge in science: a development, problem, joint effort, or singular achievement that has captured their interest and expanded their horizons. **Focus:** Science. **Qualif.:** Applicants must be students in grades 7 through 12 regularly and currently enrolled in public and nonpublic schools in the United States and its territories, or any schools in Canada may submit entries. Winning essayists, their science instructor, and one parent must be available to participate in a trip to Space Center Houston. **Criteria:** Winning entries are selected based on the authors' enthusiasm for the subjects. Judges have noted that past winning essays reflect a careful choice of subject, thorough research, thoughtful contemplation, and a clear and creative written presentation.

**Funds Avail.:** Three educational grants and 24 honorable mentions are awarded in two divisions: Senior Division (grades 10, 11, and 12) and Junior Division (grades 7, 8, and 9). Winners in each division receive $1,500 for first place; $750 for second place; $500 for third place; and $50 for Honorable Mention. The top essayist in each division is flown to Houston, Texas, along with a parent and a teacher to tour the Space Center Houston. Sponsoring teachers of first-place winners also receive a $500 Educational Award. **To Apply:** Each essay must be written expressly for The Du Pont Challenge Science Essay Awards Program and be accompanied by an individual entry form. Essays must be between 700 and 1,000 words in length. For an entry blank and official student competition rules, write to the address above. Entries that do not conform to the official rules will be disqualified. **Deadline:** January 27. This date may change. Write the DuPont Challenge Science Essay Awards Program at the above address.

**Remarks:** This award is co-sponsored by Du Pont and the National Science Teachers Association (NSTA). **Contact:** General Living Corporation at the above address (see entry 2642).

### • 2644 • General Semantics Foundation

14 Charcoal Hill
Westport, CT 06880      *Ph:* (203)226-1394

### • 2645 • General Semantics Foundation Project Grants (Doctorate, Postdoctorate/Grant)

**Purpose:** To support research in general semantics. **Focus:** Semantics. **Qualif.:** Candidate may be of any nationality, and be either a graduate student or advanced scholar. Candidate must have knowledge of general semantics and present evidence to that effect. Preference is given to applicants with university support. Applicant's proposed research must be specifically in the field of general semantics or explicitly related to the field.

**Funds Avail.:** $300-4,500. **To Apply:** Send a preliminary letter of application to the president. Include project proposal and documentation of on-going work in general semantics. **Deadline:** None. **Contact:** Harry E. Maynard President, at the above address (see entry 2644).

# Geological Society of America

3300 Penrose Pl.
PO Box 9140
Boulder, CO 80301
*E-mail:* jforstro@geosociety.org
*URL:* http://www.geosociety.org

*Ph:* (303)447-2020
*Fax:* (303)447-1133
*Free:* 800-472-1988

### • 2647 • Gladys W. Cole Memorial Research Awards *(Postdoctorate/Award)*

**Focus:** Physical Sciences. **Qualif.:** Applicants must be members or fellows of the Geological Society of America between 30 and 65 years of age who will investigate the geomorphology of the semi-arid and arid terrains of the United States and Mexico. Candidates must have published one or more significant papers on geomorphology.

**Funds Avail.:** The award is given annually and is in the amount of $7,000 or more. **No. of Awards:** 1 annually. **To Apply:** An original and two photocopies of the application are required. A description of the proposed research and the names and addresses of three references are part of the application. **Deadline:** Applications must be filed by February 1st; recipients are announced in April. **Contact:** Research Grants Administrator at the above address (see entry 2646).

### • 2648 • W. Storrs Cole Memorial Research Awards *(Postdoctorate/Award)*

**Purpose:** To support research in invertebrate micropaleontology. **Qualif.:** Applicants must be members or fellows of the Geological Society of America between 30 and 65 years of age who has published one or more significant papers on micropaleontology.

**Funds Avail.:** The award is given annually and is in the amount of $7,000 or more. Funds cannot be used for work already accomplished, but recipients of a previous award may reapply if additional support is needed to complete their work. **No. of Awards:** 1 annually. **To Apply:** An original and two photocopies of the application are required. **Deadline:** Applications must be filed by February 1st; recipients are announced in April. **Contact:** Additional information may be obtained from the Executive Director, or June R. Forstrom, Research Grants Administrator, at the above address (see entry 2646).

### • 2649 • Geological Society of America Research Grants *(Graduate, Postgraduate/Grant)*

**Qualif.:** Candidates are usually graduate students at universities in the United States, Canada, Mexico, and Central America who will use the grant for doctoral or master's thesis research. Postdoctoral and faculty researchers are rarely supported, and undergraduates are ineligible. **Criteria:** Applications are judged on how the proposed investigations will contribute to the purpose for which the Society, the promotion of the science of geology, was organized.

**Funds Avail.:** Grants rarely exceed $2,000 and are given for one year. Recipients must reapply for research that extends beyond a year. In general, grants can be used for cost of travel, room and board and travel in the field, cost of materials and supplies, and other expenses directly related to the fulfillment of the research contract. Grants cannot be used for the purchase of ordinary field equipment, maintenance of families, or as reimbursement for work already accomplished and paid for. Recipients are expected to use funds prudently, to conduct their research work in accordance with scientific principles, and to confine their work within the general framework established by their application and the terms of the grant. An annual progress report and statement of expenditures is required. **No. of Awards:** 215-240 annually. **To Apply:** Grants are intended as aids to research projects. A formal application requires a concise statement of the project's objectives, a statement of why the work is important, how and

when the project will be conducted; a budget; availability of other funds, facilities, and materials and other grants that have and are supporting the project and have been applied for. Also a part of the application is a biographical sketch, appraisal by faculty members and a brief bibliography of papers related to the proposed research and of candidate's publications. If a faculty member evaluates more than one candidate, they must be ranked and their relative qualifications discussed. An original and two photocopies of the application must be postmarked by February 1st. **Deadline:** Applications and supporting letters must be submitted. Recipients are selected in April. **Contact:** Research Grants Administrator at the above address (see entry 2646).

## • 2650 •

# Georgia Library Association - Duckworth Library

Young Harris College
Young Harris, GA 30582
*E-mail:* webmaster@langate.gsu.edu
*URL:* http://www.lib.gsu.edu/gla/

### • 2651 • Hubbards Scholarships *(Graduate/Scholarship)*

**Purpose:** To encourage the study of librarianship, and to recruit excellent librarians for the state of Georgia. **Focus:** Library Science. **Qualif.:** Applicant must be a U.S. citizen accepted for admission to a master's program at a library school accredited by the American Library Association (ALA). Candidate must indicate an intention to complete the degree requirements within two years. An accepted scholar must work in a Georgia library for one year following completion of degree.

**Funds Avail.:** $3,000. **No. of Awards:** 1. **To Apply:** Write for application form. Submit with three letters of reference, transcripts, and proof of acceptance by an ALA-accredited library school. **Deadline:** May 1. Applicants will be notified by June 1. **Contact:** Executive Secretary, at the above address (see entry 2650).

## • 2652 •

# Georgia Press Educational Foundation

3066 Mercer University Dr., Ste. 200
Atlanta, GA 30341-4137
*E-mail:* mail@gapress.org
*URL:* http://gapress.org/lendinglib.html

*Ph:* (770)454-6776
*Fax:* (770)454-6778

### • 2653 • Georgia Press Education Foundation Scholarships *(Undergraduate/Scholarship)*

**Focus:** Journalism. **Qualif.:** Applicants must be high school seniors, undergraduate and graduate students of Georgia schools studying print journalism. **Criteria:** Awards are granted based on interest, grades, financial need, recommendations and experience.

**Funds Avail.:** $250 to $1500. **No. of Awards:** Varies. **To Apply:** Write for further details. **Deadline:** February 1. **Contact:** Georgia Press Educational Foundation at the above address (see entry 2652).

### • 2654 •

## Georgia Space Grant Consortium
Georgia Institute of Technology
Aerospace Engineering
Savant Bldg., Rm. 208      *Ph:* (404)853-0055
Atlanta, GA 30332-1050      *Fax:* (404)894-9313
*URL:* http://web.cad.gatech.edu/~space/trial.htmlfellow

#### • 2655 • Georgia Space Grant Consortium Fellowships *(Graduate, Undergraduate/Fellowship)*

**Focus:** All areas of engineering and science, and many areas of social science. **Qualif.:** Applicants can be graduate or undergraduate students.

### • 2656 •

## Georgia State Regents Scholarship Program
270 Washington St., SW      *Ph:* (404)656-2272
Atlanta, GA 30334      *Fax:* (404)651-5190
*E-mail:* www@westga.edu
*URL:* http://www.westga.edu/ugcat/fa/sgp.html

#### • 2657 • Georgia State Regents Scholarship *(Graduate, Undergraduate/Scholarship loan)*

**Purpose:** To help deserving students defray college expenses. **Qualif.:** Students must be residents of Georgia. They must study at a University System of Georgia Institution. Candidates should be in the upper 25 percent of their classes. **Criteria:** Both financial need and merit are taken into consideration.

**Funds Avail.:** Varies. Students may pay the loan back through service in the state or they may pay it back in cash. **To Apply:** Copies of the application are available at any of the 34 member institutions of the University System of Georgia. **Deadline:** The deadline is set by the institutions. Early application is encouraged because funds are limited.

#### • 2658 • Hope Scholarship *(Undergraduate/ Scholarship loan)*

**Qualif.:** Applicants must be graduates of a Georgia high school, with a 3.0 GPA in a college preparatory track or a 3.2 in a vocational track. **Contact:** Georgia Student Finance Commission, 2082 E. Exchange Place, Ste. 200, Tucker, GA 30084.

#### • 2659 • Regents' Opportunity Scholarship *(Graduate/Scholarship)*

**Qualif.:** Applicants must be Georgia residents enrolled in a full-time graduate program. **Contact:** Georgia State Regents Scholarship Program at the above address (see entry 2656).

#### • 2660 • Service Cancelable Student Loan *(Graduate, Undergraduate/Loan)*

**Qualif.:** Applicants must have a 2.75 GPA and must have completed at least 90 hours of course work. Nursing students must be formally accepted into a Nursing program. **Contact:** Georgia Students Finance Commission 2082 E. Exchange Place, Ste. 200 Tucker, GA 30084.

### • 2661 •

## Georgia Student Finance Commission
2082 E. Exchange Pl., Ste. 200      *Ph:* (404)414-3000
Tucker, GA 30084-5305      *Fax:* (404)414-3133
     *Free:* 800-776-6878
*URL:* http://www.gsfc.org/gsfc/frame1.htm

#### • 2662 • Georgia Student Finance Commission Governor's Scholarship *(Undergraduate/Scholarship)*

**Purpose:** To assist students selected as Georgia Scholars, STAR Students, valedictorians, and salutatorians. **Qualif.:** Recipients are selected as entering freshmen and must be Georgia residents who are planning to attend accredited institutions in Georgia.

**Funds Avail.:** Up to $1,540 a year, renewable. **Contact:** Local high school counselors.

#### • 2663 • Georgia Student Finance Commission Pell Grant *(Undergraduate/Grant)*

**Purpose:** To provide non-repayable funds to students to assist in paying for educational expenses. **Criteria:** Selection is based on financial need.

**Funds Avail.:** Up to $2,400 a year. **To Apply:** Applicants need to complete a need analysis form (e.g., FAF or AFSA) and submit a Student Aid Report to the school's financial aid administrator. **Contact:** High school guidance counselors or college financial aid offices.

#### • 2664 • Georgia Student Finance Commission Perkins Loan *(Graduate, Undergraduate/Loan)*

**Purpose:** To provide low-interest loans to students to assist in paying educational expenses. **Criteria:** Selection is based on financial need.

**Funds Avail.:** Amount varies. Interest rates are currently five percent. **To Apply:** Applicants must complete a need analysis form (e.g., FAF or AFSA ). To find out which form is necessary, contact the school or college financial aid administrator. **Contact:** For more information, contact the school or college financial aid administrator or the Georgia Student Finance Commission at the above address (see entry 2661).

#### • 2665 • Georgia Student Finance Commission PLUS Loan *(Undergraduate/Loan)*

**Purpose:** To provide loans to parents of dependent undergraduate students.

**Funds Avail.:** Up to $4,000 a year. Current interest rates are variable up to 12 percent. **To Apply:** Applicants must complete a need analysis form (e.g., FAF, AFSA, etc.) and the PLUS/SLS Loan Application. **Contact:** For more information contact the Georgia Student Finance Commission at the above address (see entry 2661).

#### • 2666 • Georgia Student Finance Commission Service-Cancellable Stafford Loan *(Graduate, Undergraduate/Loan)*

**Purpose:** To assist students enrolled in critical fields of study (e.g., Nursing, Special Education, etc.). **Qualif.:** Applicants must be Georgia residents who are planning to attend a GSFA-approved postsecondary school. Also students must be accepted for admission or enrolled in an approved program of study. Students enrolled in "pre-field" programs, such as pre-pharmacy and pre-dentistry, are not eligible. **Criteria:** Selection is based on financial need.

**Funds Avail.:** Up to $2,000 a year; up to $3,500 a year for Dentistry programs only. **To Apply:** Students must complete a need analysis form (e.g., FAF or AFSA) and the Stafford Loan Application.

---

## Georgia Student Finance Commission (continued)

**Contact:** Additional requirements, application procedures, and loan amounts information is available through the school's financial aid administrator.

### • 2667 • Georgia Student Finance Commission SLS Loan *(Graduate, Undergraduate/Loan)*

**Purpose:** To provide repayable funds to independent students.

**Funds Avail.:** Up to $4,000 a year. Current interest rates are variable up to 12 percent. There are loan amount limitations for students enrolled in short-term programs. **To Apply:** Applicants must complete a need analysis form (e.g., FAF or AFSA) and the PLUS/SLS Loan Application. **Contact:** For additional information contact the school's financial aid administrator.

### • 2668 • Georgia Student Finance Commission Stafford Loan *(Graduate, Undergraduate/Loan)*

**Purpose:** To provide low-interest loans to students to assist in paying educational expenses. **Criteria:** Selection is based on financial need.

**Funds Avail.:** Up to $2,625 a year for freshmen and sophomores; $4,000 a year for juniors and seniors; and $7,500 a year for graduate and professional students. Current interest rates are 8 to 10 percent. **To Apply:** Applicants must complete a need analysis form (e.g., FAF or AFSA) and the Stafford Loan Application.

**Remarks:** This loan was formerly known as the Guaranteed Student Loan. **Contact:** For additional requirements, application procedures, and loan amounts, contact the school's financial aid administrator.

### • 2669 • Georgia Student Finance Commission State-Sponsored Loan *(Graduate, Undergraduate/Loan)*

**Purpose:** To assist students enrolled in critical fields of study (e.g., Nursing, Special Education, etc.). **Qualif.:** Applicants must be Georgia residents who are planning to attend a GSFA-approved postsecondary school. Also students must be accepted for admission or enrolled in an approved program of study. Students enrolled in "pre-field" programs, such as pre-pharmacy and pre-dentistry, are not eligible.

**Funds Avail.:** Up to $2,000 a year; up to $3,500 a year for Dentistry programs only. **To Apply:** Students must complete a need analysis form (e.g., FAF or AFSA) and the Stafford Loan Application. **Contact:** Additional requirements, application procedures, and loan amounts information is available through the school's financial aid administrator.

### • 2670 • Georgia Student Finance Commission Student Incentive Grant *(Undergraduate/Grant)*

**Purpose:** To provide non-repayable funds to students to assist in paying educational expenses. **Qualif.:** Applicants must be Georgia residents who are planning to attend a non-profit, postsecondary school in Georgia. **Criteria:** Selection is based on financial need.

**Funds Avail.:** $300 to $2,500. Awards are not available for summer terms. **To Apply:** Students must complete a need analysis form (e.g., FAF or AFSA) to be considered.

### • 2671 • Georgia Student Finance Commission Supplemental Educational Opportunity Grant *(Undergraduate/Grant)*

**Purpose:** To provide non-repayable funds to students to assist in paying educational expenses. **Criteria:** Selection is based on exceptional financial need.

**Funds Avail.:** Amount varies. **To Apply:** Applicants must complete a need analysis form (e.g., FAF or AFSA). **Contact:** School financial aid office or the Georgia Student Finance Commission at the above address (see entry 2661).

### • 2672 • Georgia Tuition Equalization Grant *(Undergraduate/Grant)*

**Purpose:** To provide non-repayable funds to Georgia residents attending approved private, non-profit colleges in Georgia. **Qualif.:** Applicants must be Georgia residents who are attending approved private, non-profit institutions in Georgia. Also, any juniors and seniors enrolled in eligible four-year colleges located in states bordering Georgia that are within 50 miles of their home may be eligible.

**Funds Avail.:** Up to $864 a year. **To Apply:** Students must complete the Georgia Student Grant Application (GSGA). **Contact:** School financial aid administrator or the Georgia Student Finance Commission at the above address (see entry 2661).

### • 2673 • Law Enforcement Personnel Dependents Grant *(Undergraduate/Grant)*

**Purpose:** To assist children of law enforcement officers, firemen, or prison guards in Georgia who have been permanently disabled or killed in the line of duty. **Qualif.:** Applicants must be Georgia residents, planning to attend a non-profit post-secondary school in Georgia, and children of a law enforcement officer, fireman, or prison guard who has been permanently disabled or killed in the line of duty.

**Funds Avail.:** Up to $2,000 each year for up to four years of undergraduate study. **To Apply:** Students must complete the LEPD Application. **Contact:** School financial aid administrator or the Georgia Student Finance Commission at the above address (see entry 2661).

### • 2674 • North Georgia College Military Scholarship *(Undergraduate/Scholarship)*

**Purpose:** To assist outstanding students who attend and pursue military careers at North Georgia College. **Qualif.:** Applicants must be Georgia residents who are nominated by a Georgia state legislator and planning to attend North Georgia College. Recipients are obligated to serve four years in the Georgia National Guard.

**Funds Avail.:** An amount that covers the cost of tuition, fees, room and board, books, supplies, and uniform. **To Apply:** Completion of the NGC Military Scholarship Application is necessary, as well as nomination by a Georgia state legislator. **Contact:** Further information is available from North Georgia College.

### • 2675 • North Georgia College ROTC Grant *(Undergraduate/Grant)*

**Purpose:** To assist students attending North Georgia College who are enrolled in the Army ROTC program. **Qualif.:** Students must be Georgia residents who are planning to attend North Georgia College.

**Funds Avail.:** Up to $300 a year. **To Apply:** Applicants must complete the Georgia Student Grant Application (GSGA). **Contact:** For more information contact North Georgia College.

• 2676 •
## Gerber Foundation
5 S. Division Ave.            *Ph:* (616)924-3175
Fremont, MI 49412       *Fax:* (616)924-3560

### • 2677 • Gerber Companies Foundation Scholarships *(Other/Scholarship)*

**Focus:** General Studies. **Qualif.:** Applicants must be regular full-time employees, or dependent children of such employees, with Gerber Products Company or its subsidiaries. Step-children are eligible if they reside with the step-parent employee or, if in the case of a non-custodial step-parent employee, that employee claims the child as a dependent for federal income tax purposes. **Criteria:** Selection is based on academic excellence.

**Funds Avail.:** $1,500 per year for 4 years. **Deadline:** February 28. **Contact:** Barbara J. Getz, Exec.Dir.

• 2678 •
## German Academic Exchange Service
950 3rd Ave., 19th Fl.      *Ph:* (212)758-3223
New York, NY 10022     *Fax:* (212)755-5780
*E-mail:* daadny@daad.org
*URL:* http://www.daad.org

### • 2679 • Alexander von Humboldt Research Fellowships *(Doctorate/Fellowship)*

**Purpose:** To enable scholars to carry out research in Germany. **Focus:** German studies. **Qualif.:** Applicants must hold a PhD or equivalent and not be older than 40. **To Apply:** Contact Alexander von Humboldt Foundation, US Liaison, 1055 Thomas Jefferson St., NW, Ste. 2030, Washington DC 20007 for additional information.

**Remarks:** Allows fellows to conduct research in any area they choose.

### • 2680 • Leo Baeck Institute-DAAD Grants *(Doctorate/Fellowship, Grant)*

**Purpose:** To assist in research on the social, communal, and intellectual history of German speaking Jewry. **Focus:** German studies. **Qualif.:** Applicants must be doctoral students or recent PhDs. **To Apply:** Contact Leo Baeck Institute, 129 E. 73rd St., New York, NY 10021 for additional information. **Deadline:** November 1.

**Remarks:** Funds are for research at the Leo Baeck Institute or for research in Germany.

### • 2681 • Bundeskanzler Scholarships *(Other/Scholarship)*

**Purpose:** To recognize future American leaders. Also provides insite into related study areas as they related to Germany. **Focus:** Academia, business, or politics. **No. of Awards:** Up to 10 awarded annually. **To Apply:** Contact Alexander von Humboldt Foundation, US Liaison, 1055 Thomas Jefferson St., NW, Ste. 2030, Washington, DC 20007 for additional information.

**Remarks:** Designed to be an extended, self-structured study program.

### • 2682 • Contemporary Literature Grant *(Other/Grant)*

**Purpose:** To provide faculty the opportunity to work at the Center for Contemporary German Literature at Washington University in St. Louis. **Focus:** Contemporary German literature.

**Funds Avail.:** Up to $3000. **To Apply:** Forms and guidelines can be downloaded from the DAAD website or requested in writing form DAAD or Center for Contemporary German Literature, Campus Box 1104, Washington University, St. Louis, MO 63130. **Deadline:** March 1.

### • 2683 • Council of Europe Scholarships *(Undergraduate/Scholarship)*

**Purpose:** To support further academic study in Germany by young graduates. **Focus:** General Studies. **Qualif.:** Applicant must be a citizen of a member country of the Council of Europe, other than Germany. Applicant from Denmark, Finland, Iceland, Luxembourg, Malta, Norway, Sweden, Switzerland, or Cyprus must have completed two years of academic studies; applicant from any other country must have a university degree. Candidate must be 32 years old or younger, and have a good command of the German language. Write to the above address for information.

**Funds Avail.:** Selected applicants will receive DM965-1,555/month, plus travel costs and health insurance. **No. of Awards:** 32 awards are offered annually. **To Apply:** Applicants should contact the German Embassy or other local authority in home country for application form and guidelines. Submit form to same office with proof of German language ability. **Deadline:** The deadline varies according to the country of application. **Contact:** The German Embassy.

### • 2684 • DAAD-Canadian Government Grants and Grants of Quebec *(Graduate/Grant)*

**Purpose:** Provides funds for graduate study and/or research in Germany. **Focus:** Open to all academic fields. **Qualif.:** Applicants must be Canadian citizens not older than 32 enrolled full-time in a North American university degree program. Applicants also must have a good command of German. **To Apply:** Forms and guidelines can be obtained from the DAAD website or graduate studies or student award offices at the student's university, or through a written request to DAAD office.

### • 2685 • DAAD and DAAD-Fulbright Grants *(Graduate/Grant)*

**Purpose:** Provides funds for graduate study and/or research in Germany. **Focus:** General studies. **Qualif.:** Applicants must be US citizens over the age of 32 enrolled full-time in a North American university degree program and have a good command of German. **To Apply:** Applications and guidelines can be downloaded from the website or requested in writing.

### • 2686 • DAAD Young Lawyers Program *(Postdoctorate/Fellowship)*

**Purpose:** To encourage attorneys to study the German legal system. **Focus:** Law. **Qualif.:** Applicant must be a U.S. or Canadian citizen, hold the JD or LLB, passed the bar, and be under 32 years of age. Applicant must be fluent in German (defined as at least two years of college-level instruction in German). The program consists of a 2-month course in German legal terminology, 5-month course organized by the North Rhine-Westphalian Ministry of Justice, and a 3-month internship.

**Funds Avail.:** Tuition and fees, monthly allowance, travel susidy, and health insurance. **To Apply:** Address inquires to the above address. **Deadline:** March 15.

### • 2687 • German Studies Research Grant *(Doctorate, Graduate, Undergraduate/Grant)*

**Purpose:** To promote study of cultural, political, historical, economic, and social aspects of modern and contemporary German affairs from an inter- and multi-disciplinary perspective. Also offers department and/or program chairs the opportunity to nominate highly qualified candidates to DAAD. **Focus:** German

### German Academic Exchange Service (continued)

studies. **Qualif.:** Applicants must be undergraduates with at least a junior standing pursuing a German Studies track or minor, Masters and PhD candidates working on a Certificate in German Studies, or PhD candidates doing preliminayr dissertation research. **To Apply:** Forms and guidelines can be downloaded from the DAAD website or requested in writing. **Deadline:** November 1 and May 1.

**Remarks:** Grant support for projects in either North America or Germany is intended to offset possible additional research costs or summer earnings requirements.

### • 2688 • Hochschulsommerkurse at German Universities *(Graduate, Undergraduate/Scholarship)*

**Purpose:** To provide summer German language courses in Germany. **Focus:** German language. **Qualif.:** Applicants must be Canadian or US students with two years of college-level German or equivalent at the time of application. Applicants also must be undergraduates, at least junior status, or graduate students between the ages of 18 and 32 who are enrolled full-time. Students in all discipliines are eligible to apply.

**Funds Avail.:** Scholarshps cover tuition and room and board. **To Apply:** Forms and guidelines can be downloaded from the DAAD website or requested in writing. **Deadline:** January 31.

**Remarks:** Courses focus on literary, cultural, political, and economic aspect of modern and contemporary Germany.

### • 2689 • NSF-DAAD Grants for the Natural, Engineering and Social Sciences *(Other/Grant)*

**Purpose:** To provide opportunities for joint research projects between scholars and scientists at US universities as well as university affiliated research institutes and colleges at German universities and Fachhochshulen. **Focus:** Natural, engineering, and social sciences. **To Apply:** Forms and guidelines can be downloaded from the DAAD website or requested in writing from DAAD or National Science Foundation (NSF) 4201 Wilson Blvd., Arlington, VA 22230. Phone: (703)306-1702 Fax: (703)306-0476 E-mail: msuskin@nsf.gov. **Deadline:** June 15.

### • 2690 • Research Grants for Recent PhDs and PhD Candidates *(Doctorate, Postdoctorate/Grant)*

**Purpose:** To enable PhD candidates and recent PhDs to carry out dissertation or post-doctoral research at libraries, archives, institutes or laboratories in Germany. **Focus:** Open to all academic fields. **Qualif.:** Applicants must be PhDs (up to 2 years after the degree) who should not be older than 35 and PhD candidates who should not be older than 32. Applicants should possess good knowledge of the German language.

**Funds Avail.:** Consists of monthly maintenance allowance, international travel subsidy, and h ealth insurance. **To Apply:** Forms and guidelines can be downloaded from the website or requested in writing. **Deadline:** August 1 for visits during the first half of the year and February 1 for visits during the second half of the year.

### • 2691 • Study Visit Research Grants for Faculty *(Doctorate/Grant)*

**Purpose:** Provides support to scholars and scientists to pursue research at universities and other institutions in Germany. **Focus:** Open to all academic fields. **Qualif.:** Applicants must have at least two years of teaching and /or research experience after their PhD or equivalent and a research record in the proposed field.

**Funds Avail.:** Grants are for specific research projects can not be used for travel only, attendance at conferences or conventions, editorial meetings, lecture tours, or extended guest-professorships. Stipend consists of a monthly maintenance allowance. **To Apply:** Forms and guidelines can be downloaded from the DAAD website or requested in writing. **Deadline:** August 1

for visits during the first half of the year and February 1 for visits during the second half of the year.

### • 2692 • Summer Language Course at the University of Leipzig *(Graduate, Undergraduate/Scholarship)*

**Qualif.:** Applicants must be juniors, seniors, or graduate students enrolled full-time in any discipline except English, German or any other modern languages or literature. Applicants also must have completed three semesters of college-level German or equivalent at the time of application.

**Funds Avail.:** Scholarship covers course fees, excursions, room and partial board. **To Apply:** Forms and guidelines can be downloaded from the DAAD website or requested in writing. **Deadline:** January 31.

**Remarks:** Program consists of an intensive language course, guest lectures and group discussions on contemporary German and European issues, independent project work, social and cultural activities and excursions to differnt parts of the city's enfirons and the region.

### • 2693 • Summer Language Courses at Goethe Institutes *(Graduate/Scholarship)*

**Purpose:** Provides opportunities to study German at the Goethe Institutes. **Focus:** German language. **Qualif.:** Applicants must be graduate students between the ages of 18-32 who are enrolled full time and have completed three semesters of college-level German or equivalent at the time of application. Open to all disciplines except English, German, or any other modern languages or literatures.

**Funds Avail.:** Scholarship covers tuition and fees, room, and partial board. **To Apply:** Forms and guidelines can be downloaded from the DAAD website or requested in writing. **Deadline:** January 31.

### • 2694 •
### German Marshall Fund of the United States
11 Dupont Circle, NW      *Ph:* (202)745-3950
Washington, DC 20036      *Fax:* (202)265-1662

### • 2695 • German Marshall Fund Research Fellowships *(Postdoctorate/Fellowship)*

**Purpose:** To support advanced research by U.S. scholars on domestic and international issues of importance to industrial societies. **Focus:** Economics, International Relations, Political Science, Public Policy. **Qualif.:** Applicant must be a U.S. scholar who has completed all degree requirements and who normally has completed at least one research project that has received critical review. Preference is given to scholars with two to seven years of postdoctoral experience, although more senior scholars may apply. Proposed research must have the potential to improve the understanding of significant contemporary economic, political, and social developments involving the United States and Europe. Projects may focus on either comparative domestic or international issues. Fellow must devote full-time to research, which may be conducted in the United States or Europe.

**Funds Avail.:** $30,000 maximum, plus $2,000 travel allowance. **To Apply:** Write to the Fund for application form and guidelines. **Deadline:** November 15. Fellowships are announced by March 15. **Contact:** Susan Smith at the above address (see entry 2694).

**• 2696 •**

**Germanistic Society of America**
Institute of International Education
U.S. Student Programs Division
809 United Nations Plaza
New York, NY 10017          *Ph:* (212)984-5330
*E-mail:* center@amc.net
*URL:* http://www.amc.net

**• 2697 • Germanistic Society of America Quadrille Grants** *(Graduate, Postgraduate/Grant)*

**Purpose:** To provide support for prospective specialists to study for one academic year. **Focus:** German Studies, History, Art History, Philosophy, Economics, Banking, Law, Political Science, Public Affairs. **Qualif.:** For consideration, a master's degree is desirable.

**Funds Avail.:** Stipends of $11,000 each are available. Candidates selected for these awards will be considered for Fulbright travel grants. **No. of Awards:** 6. **Contact:** The U.S. Student Programs Division at the Institute of International Education at the above address (see entry 2696).

**• 2698 •**

**Getty Center for the History of Art and the Humanities - Center Fellowships**
401 Wilshire Blvd., Ste. 700          *Ph:* (310)458-9811
Santa Monica, CA 90401-1455          *Fax:* (310)395-1515
*E-mail:* fellowships@getty.edu

**• 2699 • Getty Center Postdoctoral Fellowships**
*(Postdoctorate/Fellowship)*

**Purpose:** To support recent recipients of a doctorate in the humanities or social sciences who are rewriting their dissertations for publication. **Focus:** Humanities, Social Sciences, including Anthropology, Art History, Cultural History, Economic History, Intellectual History, History of Architecture, History of Music, Literary Criticism and Theory, Philosophy, Political History, Religious History, Social History. **Qualif.:** Candidate may be of any nationality. Applicant must have earned a Ph.D. in the humanities or social sciences within the last three years, and must be rewriting the dissertation for publication. Fellows must spend the academic year in residence at the Center.

**Funds Avail.:** $22,000 stipend; some funds are also available for housing or relocation, photographic reproduction, and research-related travel.

**Remarks:** The Center also sponsors the Getty Scholar Program for already established scholars. There is no formal application procedure; each year a community of scholars with common interests is invited to participate. Write to the Center for details. **Contact:** Getty Center at the above address (see entry 2698).

**• 2700 • Getty Center Predoctoral Fellowships**
*(Doctorate/Fellowship)*

**Purpose:** To support students who expect to complete their dissertations during the fellowship year. **Focus:** Anthropology, Art History, Cultural History, Economic History, Intellectual History, History of Architecture, History of Music, Literary Criticism and Theory, Philosophy, Political History, Religious History, Social History, other fields within the Humanities and Social Sciences. **Qualif.:** Applicant may be of any nationality, but must be a Ph.D. candidate in the humanities or social sciences, and must expect to complete the dissertation during the fellowship year. Fellows must spend the academic year in residence at the Center.

**Funds Avail.:** $18,000 stipend; some funds are also available for housing or relocation, photographic reproduction, and research-related travel. **No. of Awards:** 4. **Contact:** Getty Center at the above address (see entry 2698).

**• 2701 •**

**J. Paul Getty Museum - Department of Education and Academic Affairs**
PO Box 2112          *Ph:* (310)459-7611
Santa Monica, CA 90407-2112          *Fax:* (310)454-8156
*E-mail:* aclark@getty.edu
*URL:* http://www.lacityview.com/things/museums/J_Paul_
   Getty_Museum.html

**• 2702 • Getty Museum Graduate Internships**
*(Doctorate, Graduate/Internship)*

**Purpose:** To provide graduate students with full-time, practical experience in specific departments at the Museum, the Getty Conservation Institute, the Getty Grant Program, the Getty Center for Education in the Arts, the Getty Trust Department of Public Affairs, and the Provenance Index. **Focus:** Art Conservation, Art History, Museum Studies. **Qualif.:** Applicant must be currently enrolled in a university program leading to a master's or Ph.D. degree in one of the areas of study listed above, or have completed a relevant degree within the 18 months prior to the start of the proposed internship at the Museum.

**Funds Avail.:** $18,000/year or $12,450/nine months. **To Apply:** Write or phone the intern program administrator for application form and guidelines. Submit form with graduate and undergraduate transcripts, two letters of recommendation, and a statement of goals. **Deadline:** Varies. Notification by April 15. **Contact:** Andrew J. Clark, Intern Program Administrator, at the above address (see entry 2701).

**• 2703 • Getty Museum Guest Scholar Grants**
*(Postdoctorate/Grant)*

**Purpose:** To support object-oriented research projects at the Museum. **Focus:** Art History. **Qualif.:** Applicant must have a Ph.D. Candidate's proposed project must be in art history in a field relevant to the Museum's collections of Greek and Roman antiquities; pre-20th-century Western European paintings, drawings, sculpture, illuminated manuscripts, and decorative arts; or 19th- and 20th-century American and European photographs. Applicant must demonstrate that the project is best pursued at the Museum in conjunction with its professional staff. Scholars are have access to the collection at the museum and research facilities of the Getty Center for the History of Art and the Humanities.

**Funds Avail.:** $750/week (apartment and travel provided). **No. of Awards:** Nine. **To Apply:** Write to the scholar program administrator, with a statement of project, curriculum vitae, and an estimate of time needed for project. **Deadline:** July. Notification in December/January. **Contact:** Laurie Fusco, Scholar Program Administrator, at the above address (see entry 2701).

---

Awards are arranged alphabetically below their administering organizations

## • 2704 •
### GITA
14456 E. Evans Ave.
Aurora, CO 80014
*E-mail:* staff@gita.org
*URL:* http://www.gita.org

*Ph:* (303)337-0513
*Fax:* (303)337-1001

#### • 2705 • GITA *(Graduate, Undergraduate/Scholarship)*

**Purpose:** To recognize and support outstanding students in the field of mapping or mapping-related studies. **Focus:** Automated Mapping, Facilities Management, Geographic Information Systems. **Qualif.:** Students must be juniors or higher.

**Funds Avail.:** $2,000. **No. of Awards:** 9. **To Apply:** Write for nomination form and guidelines. Submit form with transcripts, a brief statement of educational and professional goals, and four letters of recommendation. Application form can also be downloaded from the web site. **Deadline:** December 15. **Contact:** Rose Seemann at the above address (see entry 2704).

## • 2706 •
### Glass Bottle Blowers Association of America and Canada
608 East Baltimore Pike
PO Box 607
Media, PA 19063

#### • 2707 • GMP Memorial Scholarships *(Undergraduate/Scholarship)*

**Purpose:** To provide encouragement and assistance to the children of members of the Glass, Molders, Pottery, Plastics, and Allied Workers International Union (AFL-CIO, CLC) who are interested in pursuing college educations. **Qualif.:** Applicants must be the children, stepchildren, or legal wards of GMP members and rank in the top 25 percent of their high school senior class. Children of officers and employees of the International Union are not eligible. Children of deceased members are eligible to apply if the deceased was a dues-paying member at the time of death, in which case they should apply within three years after the parent's death. Children of retired members may apply if members have retained their retirement status. **Criteria:** Applicants' Scholastic Aptitude Test (SAT) scores are used to determine the top 20 candidates in the scholarship competition. These candidates are designated as semifinalists and must provide the Scholarship Selection Committee with a Biographical Questionnaire (to be sent by College Scholarship Service) and a Secondary School Report Form (to be completed by secondary school). Four winners are selected based on total high school records, including academic test scores, extracurricular activities, leadership qualities, high school recommendations, and students' own statements.

**Funds Avail.:** Four renewable scholarships in the amount of $2,500 are awarded annually. Recipients receive an additional $2,500 award each year for three additional years, providing they maintain satisfactory progress toward degree requirements. **To Apply:** To be considered, applicants must complete the official Scholarship application form supplied by the GMP Local Unions or by writing to the International Office. Applicants must also take the SAT or ACT. (When completing the Reports to Colleges and Scholarship Sponsors Section of the Registration Form, applicants should enter Code 0429 for the GMP Memorial Scholarship Program as one of the colleges or scholarship programs to which scores should be sent.) **Deadline:** Application must be received at the College Scholarship Service - Sponsored Scholarship Programs, CN6730, Princeton, NJ 08541, by November. The SAT should be taken no later than the December administration. The winners are announced in May.

**Remarks:** Recipients of GMP Memorial Scholarships may choose any accredited college or university in the United States or Canada. Although recipients are free to select any regular program of college studies leading to a degree, the GMP is hopeful they will give consideration, if their talents and interests show an inclination, to such fields as ceramic engineering, industrial relations, or fields of endeavor in which the trade union movement has had traditional interests.

## • 2708 •
### Gleaner Life Insurance Society
5200 W. U.S. 223
Box 1894
Adrian, MI 49221

*Ph:* (517)263-2244
*Fax:* (517)265-7745

#### • 2709 • Gleaner Life Insurance Society Scholarship Award *(Undergraduate/Scholarship)*

**Purpose:** To enable Society members or Gleaner family members to further their education. **Qualif.:** Applicants must either be members or in the family of a member for scholarship eligibility. Candidates should also be high school graduates and full-time students. **Criteria:** A Scholarship Committee reviews and rates by points the areas of scholarship, leadership, extracurricular activities, community involvement, financial need, and overall quality.

**Funds Avail.:** The Gleaners currently award eight $1,000 awards and one $250 technical award per year. **To Apply:** Applications should be forwarded to Mr. Frank Dick, President, Gleaner Life Insurance Society, after January 1 of each year. **Deadline:** April 30.

**Remarks:** Regarding funds available, additional scholarships are awarded through state associations of lodges. In addition, a number of lodges in Michigan, Ohio, Indiana, and Illinois have awarded scholarships. **Contact:** Janet Goulart, Coordinator, Personnel Services, at the above address (see entry 2708).

## • 2710 •
### Tony Godwin Memorial Trust
c/o Eugene H. Winick
310 Madison Ave.
New York, NY 10017

*Ph:* (212)687-6887
*Fax:* (212)687-6894

#### • 2711 • Tony Godwin Award *(Professional Development/Award)*

**Purpose:** To enable the award winner to travel to and reside for one month in Great Britain to become acquainted with the literary and publishing practices and customs of the United Kingdom of Great Britain while working as an "in-house" guest of a publisher. **Qualif.:** Applicants must be under 35 years of age, and must have been engaged in the publishing of literary works and resided continuously in the United States for a period of three years immediately preceding application. The competition is open not only to those working in publishing houses, but also to those engaged in other publishing activities, including writers and agents. **Criteria:** Based on the quality and promise of the applicant's work in the publishing field.

**Funds Avail.:** One annual award which covers traveling costs and living expenses. **To Apply:** Deadlines and submission procedures for applications are announced each spring in *Publishers Weekly*. **Contact:** Eugene H. Winick at the above address (see entry 2710).

**• 2712 •**
## Golden State Minority Foundation
333 S. Beaudry Ave., Ste. 216-C     *Ph:* (213)482-6300
Los Angeles, CA 90017     *Fax:* (213)482-6305
    *Free:* 800-666-4763

*E-mail:* gsmf@earthlink.net
*URL:* http://www.gsmf.org

### • 2713 • Golden State Minority Foundation Scholarships *(Undergraduate/Scholarship)*

**Purpose:** To provide financial assistance for minority college students. **Qualif.:** Applicants must attend school in or be a resident of southern California, study business administration, economics, or a related field; be a qualified minority (African-American, Hispanic, Native American, or other underrepresented minority); have a minimum GPA of 3.0 on a 4.0 scale; be a U.S. citizen or legal resident; be of at least junior standing (60 units of college credit); work no more than 28 hours per week; and have full-time status at an accredited four-year college, university or graduate school. **Criteria:** Based on GPA, financial need and community involvement.

**Funds Avail.:** $78,000. **No. of Awards:** 10-20. **To Apply:** Applications are on file at most schools' financial aid offices or can be obtained by sending a self-addressed stamped envelope. Applications are only sent out during application periods. **Deadline:** Southern California - February 1 to April 1.

**Remarks:** Scholarship is open to most majors. **Contact:** Elizabeth Erazo, Executive Assistant, at the above address (see entry 2712).

**• 2714 •**
## Barry M. Goldwater Scholarship and Excellence in Education Foundation
6225 Brandon Ave., No. 315     *Ph:* (703)756-6012
Springfield, VA 22150-2519     *Fax:* (703)756-6015
*E-mail:* goldh2o@erols.com
*URL:* http://www.act.org/goldwater

### • 2715 • Barry M. Goldwater Scholarship *(Undergraduate/Scholarship)*

**Purpose:** To encourage outstanding students to pursue careers in mathematics, natural sciences, and engineering and to foster excellence in those careers. **Focus:** Natural Science, Engineering, Mathematics. **Qualif.:** Applicants must be matriculated full-time sophomore or junior students pursuing a degree in mathematics, the natural sciences, or engineering at an accredited institution of higher education during the current academic year, and they must have a college grade point average of at least B (or equivalent) and be in the upper fourth of their class. Students planning to study medicine are eligible if they plan a research career rather than a career as a medical doctor in private practice. Students in two-year colleges who plan to transfer to a baccalaureate program at another institution may be nominated. Applicants must be United States citizens, resident aliens showing intent to obtain U.S. citizenship, or United States nationals. Nominations from resident aliens must include a letter of the nominee's intent to obtain United States citizenship. Students must be nominated by their college or university. Four-year institutions can nominate up to four students who are in their sophomore or junior class in the current academic year. Two-year institutions may nominate up to two students who are sophomores during the current academic year. Scholarship recipients cannot be engaged in gainful employment that interferes with the scholar's studies, and scholars may seek postponement of their award because of ill health or other mitigating circumstances. **Criteria:** The most outstanding nominees from each state are considered. The nominees are evaluated on outstanding academic performance and their demonstrated

potential for and commitment to a career in mathematics, the natural sciences, or eligible engineering disciplines. The number of scholarships awarded per state depends on the number and qualifications of nominees per state.

**Funds Avail.:** Up to 300 scholarships of up to $7,500 each are awarded annually. Junior-level scholarship recipients will be eligible for two years of scholarship support or until the baccalaureate degree is received. Senior-level scholarship recipients will be eligible for one year of scholarship support or until the baccalaureate degree is received. **To Apply:** Nominations must be submitted on the official forms, which are mailed to institution faculty representatives in early September. Application materials must include: an Institutional Nomination and Eligibility Form, which verifies the nominees' eligibility; Nomination and Supporting Information which affirms the nominees' wish to be considered for the scholarship, provides biographical information about their background, interests, and plans, and provides a statement about the nominees' intent to enter an appropriate career in the qualified areas and specifies how their educational plans will provide preparation for that career; three Independent Evaluation of Nominee forms completed by a faculty member in the nominee's field of study, an individual that can discuss the nominee's potential for a career in the qualified areas, and another individual that can attest to the nominee's potential; and transcripts. Nominees must write and submit a 600 word or less essay relating to their chosen career.

**Remarks:** Please refer to website for future revisions.

**• 2716 •**
## Good Samaritan Foundation
5615 Kirby Dr., Ste. 308
Houston, TX 77005     *Ph:* (713)529-4647

### • 2717 • Good Samaritan Foundation Scholarship for Nursing *(Undergraduate/Scholarship)*

**Purpose:** To provide financial assistance for the tuition and books of a nursing student. **Focus:** Nursing. **Qualif.:** Must be taking clinical nursing courses at a nursing school in the state of Texas. **Criteria:** Need, dedication, and academic potential.

**Funds Avail.:** Varies. **To Apply:** Write for application. **Deadline:** August 1 for spring session; December 1 for summer session; April 1 for fall session. **Contact:** Kay K. McHughes at the above address (see entry 2716).

**• 2718 •**
## Adolph and Esther Gottlieb Foundation, Inc.
380 W. Broadway     *Ph:* (212)226-0581
New York, NY 10012     *Fax:* (212)226-0584
*URL:* http://www.ecn.ca/osf/scca/cz/nabidky/g_adol.htm

### • 2719 • Emergency Assistance Grants *(Other, Professional Development/Grant)*

**Purpose:** To offer interim financial assistance to qualified artists whose needs are the result of unforeseen, catastrophic incidents such as fire, flood, or emergency medical expense. **Focus:** Painting, Printmaking, Sculpture. **Qualif.:** Candidate may be of any nationality. Applicant must be without the resources to meet the cost incurred by a recent catastrophic incident, and must demonstrate a minimum involvement of ten years in a mature phase of his or her work. Maturity is based on the level of technical, intellectual, and creative development. An artist who works within the disciplines of film, photography, or related forms is not eligible unless the work directly involves or can be

## Adolph and Esther Gottlieb Foundation, Inc. (continued)

interpreted as painting or sculpture. Grants are offered on a one-time basis.

**Funds Avail.:** $10,000 maximum; $5,000 is a typical award. **To Apply:** Telephone or write to the Foundation for an Emergency Grant application. **Deadline:** None. Applications are considered upon receipt.

**Remarks:** There is a set amount appropriated each year for emergency grants; once this budgetary limit has been reached, the Foundation will not be able to judge any additional requests.

### • 2720 • Individual Support Grants (Professional Development/Grant)

**Purpose:** To recognize and support serious, fully-committed artists regardless of their level of commercial success. **Focus:** Painting, Printmaking, Sculpture. **Qualif.:** Candidate may be of any nationality. Applicant must currently be in financial need, and must demonstrate a minimum of 20 years involvement in a mature phase of his or her art. Maturity is based on the level of technical, intellectual, and creative development. An artist who works within the disciplines of film, photography, or related forms is not eligible unless the work directly involves or can be interpreted as painting or sculpture.

**Funds Avail.:** $20,000. **No. of Awards:** 10. **To Apply:** Write for application forms, available in the late summer. The Foundation will not mail out applications in response to telephoned or second-party requests. Submit application with a written statement describing artistic and career history, including details of education, exhibitions, and changes in artistic approach through the years; proof of income; and slides or photographs of the artist's work which illustrate the progressive development of the art for at least a 20-year period. **Deadline:** December 15. **Contact:** Sheila Ross, Grants Manager, at the above address (see entry 2718).

### • 2721 •
## Government Documents Round Table
50 E. Huron St.  
Chicago, IL 60611-2729

Ph: (312)944-6780  
Fax: (312)280-3257  
Free: 800-545-2433

### • 2722 • Readex/GODORT/ALA Catherine J. Reynolds Grant (Professional Development/Grant)

**Purpose:** To enable documents librarians to travel and/or study in the field of documents librarianship or an area of study benefiting performance as documents librarians.

**Funds Avail.:** $2,000.

**Remarks:** Funding is provided by Readex Corporation. **Contact:** Jan B. Swanbeck, Doc. Dept., Library West, University of Florida, Gainesville, FL 32611, or Peggy Barber, ALA Liaison 50 E. Huron St., Chicago, IL 60611.

### • 2723 •
## The Graco Foundation
PO Box 1441  
Minneapolis, MN 55440-1441

Ph: (612)623-6684  
Fax: (612)623-6944

### • 2724 • Graco Scholarship Program (Undergraduate/Scholarship)

**Focus:** General studies. **Qualif.:** Applicants must be children of Graco, Inc. employees. **Criteria:** Awards are granted based on academic excellence, extra curricular activities, and career goals.

**Funds Avail.:** $5,000. **No. of Awards:** 3. **To Apply:** Write for further details. **Deadline:** March 15.

**Remarks:** Managed by Citizens' Scholarship Foundation of America. **Contact:** Robert M. Mattison, V.P. & Sec.

### • 2725 •
## Graham Foundation for Advanced Studies in the Fine Arts
4 W. Burton Pl.  
Chicago, IL 60610  
E-mail: info@grahamfoundation.org  
URL: http://www.grahamfoundation.org

Ph: (312)787-4071

### • 2726 • Graham Foundation Grants (Professional Development/Grant)

**Purpose:** To support research, independent study, exhibitions, and publications in educational areas directly concerned with architecture and other arts that are immediately contributive to architecture. **Focus:** Architectural History, Architecture. **Qualif.:** Candidates may be of any nationality. Grants are not awarded for construction, or for direct scholarship aid. No aid is granted for projects done in pursuit of a degree. Fellowship grants to individuals for independent study normally must have some end objective such as a book or a monograph.

**Funds Avail.:** $10,000 maximum. **To Apply:** There are no application forms. Submit project proposal with resume; budget; work plan and schedule; and specific amount requested. Three letters of reference evaluating the applicant and the proposed project should be sent directly from the referees to the Foundation. **Deadline:** January 15 and July 15. Awards are usually made approximately 120 days after the deadline. **Contact:** Richard Solomon, Director, at the above address (see entry 2725).

### • 2727 •
## Martha Graham School of Contemporary Dance, Inc.
440 Lafayette St.  
New York, NY 10003  
E-mail: clumgdc@aol.com  
URL: http://www.philclas.polygram.nl/class/ag-j/graham.htm

Ph: (212)838-5886  
Fax: (212)223-0351

### • 2728 • Martha Graham Dance Scholarships (Professional Development/Scholarship)

**Purpose:** To support study of the Martha Graham Technique in the Martha Graham School in preparation for a career as a professional dancer. **Focus:** Martha Graham Technique, Modern Dance. **Qualif.:** Candidate may be of any nationality. Applicant must be a dancer between the ages of 17 and 30 years. Scholarships are partial and full tuition waivers only. **Criteria:** Based on audition held once year only.

Funds Avail.: $1,500-3,000 in tuition. No. of Awards: Varies. To Apply: Write to the director for audition information. Deadline: Auditions are held in August. Contact: Amy Harrison, Administrative Director, at the above address (see entry 2727).

---

• 2729 •
## Grand Lodge of Alberta
Grand Secretary
A.F. & A.M., 330-12 Ave., SW
Calgary, AB, Canada T2R 0H2            Fax: (403)269-7292

• 2730 • **Masonic Bursaries** (Undergraduate/
Scholarship)

Qualif.: Applicants must be students wishing to attend a post-secondary institution in Alberta or pursue a program of studies outside the province which is not otherwise available. Criteria: Selection is based on financial need.

Funds Avail.: $1,000 awards. Deadline: April 30. Contact: Grand Lodge of Alberta at the above address (see entry 2729).

---

• 2731 •
## Grand Prairie Composite High School
11202 - 104 St.                        Ph: (403)532-7721
Grande Prairie, AB, Canada T8V 2Z1    Fax: (403)532-6036

• 2732 • **P.V. Croken Matriculation Scholarships**
(Undergraduate/Scholarship)

Qualif.: Candidates must be students from Grande Prairie high schools. Criteria: Awarded on the basis of academic achievement, personal qualities, and financial need to encourage post-secondary studies at a college or university.

Funds Avail.: Number of $700 to $1,000 awards varies. Contact: Principal, Grande Prairie Composite High School, at the above address (see entry 2731).

---

• 2733 •
## Grand Prairie District Association for the Mentally Handicaped
8702-113 St.
Grand Prairie, AB, Canada T8V 6K5

• 2734 • **Iris Pollock Memorial Scholarship**
(Undergraduate/Scholarship)

Focus: Rehabilitation. Qualif.: Applicants must be from northern Alberta and entering a post-secondary program of study related to the field of mental retardation. Recipients are expected to work with the mentally handicapped.

Funds Avail.: One $500 scholarship. No. of Awards: 1. Deadline: August 15. Contact: Grand Prairie District Association for the Mentally Handicapped at the above address (see entry 2733).

---

• 2735 •
## Granite State Management & Resources
4 Barrell Court                        Ph: (603)228-6532
PO Box 2287                            Fax: (603)226-0356
Concord, NH 03302-2287                Free: 800-719-0708
URL: http://www.gsmr.org

• 2736 • **New Hampshire Alternative Loans for Parents and Students** (All/Loan)

Purpose: To provide alternative financing options. Focus: General Studies. Qualif.: Loans are made to New Hampshire residents or students attending New Hampshire schools. Criteria: Loan selections are based on credit history and debt to income ratio.

Funds Avail.: $2,000 to $20,000 per year, and cumulative loan limit of $80,000, with a variable interest of prime rate plus two percent, repayable 30 days after disbursement in regular monthly payments, with a repayment term of one to fifteen years. To Apply: Applicants must submit credit history and income information and complete an application form. Unless students can credit qualify on their own, a credit-worthy co-maker is required. Deadline: None. Contact: Loans are administered by Granite State Management & Resources, 44 Warren St., PO Box 2287, Concord, NH 03302. Contact Vivian Larson at (603)225-5867 or 800-444-3796.

• 2737 • **New Hampshire Federal PLUS Loans**
(Undergraduate/Loan)

Purpose: To provide alternative financing options. Focus: General Studies. Qualif.: Loans are made to parents of dependent undergraduate students. Parents must be New Hampshire residents or borrowing for students attending New Hampshire schools. Criteria: Loan selections are based on credit history and debt to income ratio.

Funds Avail.: Cost of education minus financial aid with a variable interest not to exceed 12 percent, repayable 30 to 45 days after disbursement in regular monthly payments, with a repayment term of ten years. To Apply: Applicants must file required Federal loan program forms. Deadline: None. Contact: Loans are administered by NH Higher Education Assistance Foundation, 4 Barrell Court, Concord, NH 03302-0877. Contact Gina Cote at (603)225-6612. Toll-free telephone: 800-525-2577.

---

• 2738 •
## William T. Grant Foundation
570 Lexington Ave. 18th Floor          Ph: (212)752-0071
New York, NY 10022-5403               Fax: (212)752-1398
URL: http://www.fdncenter.org/grantmesker/Wtgrant/
index.html

• 2739 • **Grant Foundation Faculty Scholars Program** (Other/Grant)

Purpose: To encourage young scholars investigating topics relevant to understanding and promoting the well-being and healthy development of children, adolescents, and youth. Focus: Child Development, Mental Health. Qualif.: Candidates may be of any nationality but must be faculty members at a university or nonprofit research institution. Preference is given to investigators in their earliest postgraduate years who have a reasonably stable academic appointment and to minority scholars who can use the award to bring a broadened and multiple problem focus to their research. Awards are not intended for well-established investigators. Candidates must also have advanced research experience related to factors that compromise children's and youth's healthy development. Candidates must be nominated by their home institutions, and at least one investigator, preferably

## William T. Grant Foundation (continued)

from the home institution, must agree to act as a mentor. Awards are tenable at institutions worldwide. During tenure of the award, scholars must devote at least half of their time to research in areas of interest to the Foundation. Grant funds must be used primarily for direct research costs; some salary assistance may be provided, but it is not intended to replace university support.

**Funds Avail.:** Up to $50,000/year is available. **To Apply:** Write to the Grants Coordinator for nomination guidelines. Submit a five-page abstract of proposed research, curriculum vitae, full research plan, budget, statement of nomination from departmental chair, and letter of acceptance from designated mentor. Three letters of recommendation from supervisors or colleagues must be sent directly to the Foundation. Selected candidates will be interviewed. **Deadline:** Materials must be in by July 1. Awards are announced in March. **Contact:** Grants Coordinator, at the above address (see entry 2738).

### • 2740 • Grant Foundation Research Grants
*(Postdoctorate/Grant)*

**Purpose:** To support research on the development of children, adolescents, and youth. **Focus:** Child Development, Mental Health. **Qualif.:** Applicants may be of any nationality but must be qualified investigators from a medical or social-behavioral scientific discipline. The Foundation welcomes proposals for research on the development of children, adolescents, or youth, as well as research to evaluate community intervention programs aimed at reducing problem behavior in young people. Research may be conducted at any location worldwide. Grants are not offered to support building funds, fundraising drives, operating budgets of ongoing service agencies or educational institutions, or endowments or school scholarships.

**Funds Avail.:** $150,000/year average is available. **To Apply:** There is no official application form. Submit an initial letter of inquiry, briefly describing proposed research, to the Grants Coordinator. If the Foundation is interested, a full proposal will be invited. This proposal must include: a cover page listing the project's title (also include a title of twenty-five letters or less), the investigators, the amount of the request, and its term; and an abstract of the proposal (no more than five pages) concisely summarizing each of the items listed under. The abstract is a critically important component of the application, and should cover the details of the proposed study as thoroughly as possible within the five page limit. The full proposal (no page limit) should consist of a detailed description of the project, addressing: its unique contribution to the field of research including a review of the literature, its potential social significance, relation, of the current proposal to the investigator's past research, methods of procedure including sample characteristics and availability, instruments and measures, and analysis plans, key personnel with a full curricula vitae and a summary CV for PI, institutional resources, all other funding currently available to the investigators, plans for evaluation and/or dissemination of results, and a bibliography. **Deadline:** Letters of inquiry are accepted year-round. **Contact:** Grants Coordinator, at the above address (see entry 2738).

---

### • 2741 •
## The Grass Foundation
77 Reservoir Rd.       *Ph:* (617)843-0219
Quincy, MA 02170      *Fax:* (617)843-0474

### • 2742 • Grass Fellowships in Neurophysiology
*(Doctorate, Postdoctorate/Fellowship)*

**Purpose:** With these fellowships, the Grass Foundation seeks to encourage independent research by young investigators and to increase research opportunities for young persons trained for careers in neurophysiological investigation by providing for summer study and research at the Marine Biological Laboratory. **Focus:** Neuroscience, Marine Biology. **Qualif.:** Students in the late predoctoral or early postdoctoral categories who are academically prepared for and interested in neurophysiological research are eligible. Applicants should be close to the award of Ph.D. or M.D. and usually no more than three years postdoctoral. Preference is given to those with no prior research experience at the Marine Biological Laboratory (MBL) at Woods Hole, Massachusetts. Applicants should not attempt to combine these summer fellowships with the writing of dissertations. Full-time students are ineligible. **Criteria:** The Selection Committee judges the abilities of the applicants to organize and present pertinent information that applicants are asked to submit in three categories. Preference is given to research proposals appropriate to the facilities and organisms available at the MBL, Woods Hole.

**Funds Avail.:** These fellowships provide funds to support the fellows, their spouses, and dependent children at the Marine Biological Laboratory, Woods Hole, Massachusetts, for one summer. Laboratory research space rental, housing, and board are provided. Modest budgets for laboratory research expenses and personal expenses are also included. Travel expenses to and from MBL are covered. **No. of Awards:** 12. **To Apply:** Formal applications are required. Research proposals call for curricula vitae, summaries of previous investigations, outlines and rationales for proposed summer work, and, when possible, ten copies of one representative reprint. Candidates are asked to furnish tabulated estimates of shipping and travel expenses, living accommodations required, laboratory space required, and other information. A letter of recommendation from a senior investigator is also required. **Deadline:** December 1. **Contact:** The Grass Foundation at the above address (see entry 2741).

### • 2743 • Robert S. Morison Fellowships *(Professional Development/Fellowship)*

**Purpose:** To supplement and expand clinical residency training by exposure to research or basic mammalian neurophysiology. Expertise and perspective should be developed in one or more of the following: molecular and cell biology, developmental neurobiology, membrane physiology and biophysics, cellular and molecular neuropharmacology, computational neurobiology, and cellular correlates of behavior. **Focus:** Neuroscience, Medical Research. **Qualif.:** Applicants must be M.D.s who have been accepted into or just completed a residency in neurology or neurosurgery. They must wish to undertake a two-year program of basic research training. **Criteria:** Selection is based on the quality of preparation of the candidate and on the research proposal.

**Funds Avail.:** The Fellowship provides an annual stipend of $40,000. $4,000 a year is available for research expenses and travel to one scientific meeting. **No. of Awards:** 1. **To Apply:** The application is a joint statement of the candidate and sponsor that describes the proposed research. The sponsor must be an established investigator at a recognized North American institution. The sponsor provides space, facilities, and appropriate supervision. Candidate and sponsor each submit their curriculum vita. A letter of recommendation from the residency supervisor is also required. **Deadline:** Applications must be filed by November 1 of even-numbered years. The fellowship begins between July 1 and December 31 of the following odd-numbered year.

**Remarks:** This Fellowship was established to honor Robert S. Morison and his contributions as a founding trustee of the Foundation. **Contact:** The Grass Foundation at the above address (see entry 2741).

## • 2744 •
## Gravure Education Foundation
1200-A Scottsville Rd.                    *Ph:* (716)436-2150
Rochester, NY 14624                    *Fax:* (716)436-7689
*E-mail:* 102366.2134@compuserve.com
*URL:* http://www.gaa.org/6gaf.htm

### • 2745 • Gravure Education Foundation Cooperative Education Grant *(Undergraduate/Other)*

**Purpose:** To financially assist full-time college students in the printing field. **Focus:** Graphic Arts. **Qualif.:** Applicant must be an intern or co-op with a gravure-related company while attending school. They must be enrolled full-time as undergraduates at an accredited college or university and actively participating in a college or university-approved Co-op Educational Program. **To Apply:** Students must submit a completed application and a copy of their transcripts with 30 days of beginning co-op employment. Applications are considered in the order they are received. At the conclusion of the co-op, students must notify GEF in writing and provide evidence of completion of their work assignments.

**Remarks:** GEF also offers the Werner B. Thiele Memorial Scholarships for students who are at least juniors in an undergraduate program at a college or university designated as a Gravure Resource Center, and the GEF Technical Writing Contest for college or university students. Interested individuals should contact the Foundation for further information. **Contact:** Gravure Education Foundation at the above address (see entry 2744).

## • 2746 •
## Sidney Herbert & Mary Lois Langille Gray Family Scholarship Fund
The Massachusetts Co., Inc.
125 High St.
Boston, MA 02110-2713                    *Ph:* (617)556-2335

### • 2747 • M. Geneva Gray Scholarship *(Undergraduate/Scholarship)*

**Qualif.:** Candidates who are unable to qualify for a scholarship for a higher education degree because of minimum parental or individual income limitations or those who lack sufficient finances are eligible. **Criteria:** Preference is given to candidates from middle income families ($25,000 to $50,000) with several children to be educated.

**Funds Avail.:** Up to $1,000. **To Apply:** Applicants must submit a completed application form with letter of acceptance to the university or college being attended and a copy of the front page of either the student's or the student's parents' 1040 for the previous year. **Deadline:** June 15. **Contact:** Cynthia M. Nadai at the above address (see entry 2746).

## • 2748 •
## Greek Orthodox Ladies Philoptochos Society, Inc.
345 E. 74th St.                    *Ph:* (212)744-4390
New York, NY 10021                    *Fax:* (212)861-1956

### • 2749 • Greek Orthodox Ladies Philoptochos Society Scholarships for Hellenic College and Holy Cross Greek Orthodox School of Theology *(Graduate, Postgraduate/Scholarship)*

**Purpose:** To assist future priests. **Qualif.:** Graduate and postgraduate students are eligible. **Criteria:** Recommended by the Dean of Students.

**Funds Avail.:** The number of scholarships varies from year to year. **No. of Awards:** 30-35 annually. **To Apply:** Recommendation of Dean of Students of Holy Cross Seminary and Hellenic College is required. **Contact:** Terry Kokas at the above address (see entry 2748).

## • 2750 •
## Elizabeth Greenshields Foundation
1814 Sherbrooke St. W, Apt. 1                    *Ph:* (514)937-9225
Montreal, PQ, Canada H3H 1E4                    *Fax:* (514)937-0141
*E-mail:* egreen@total.net
*URL:* http://www.ecn.cz/osf/scca/cz/nabidky/geliz.htm

### • 2751 • The Elizabeth Greenshields Grant *(Graduate, High School, Other, Undergraduate/Grant)*

**Purpose:** To aid talented artists in the early stages of their careers. **Focus:** Fine Arts. **Qualif.:** Candidates must have already started or completed training in an established school of art and/or demonstrated, through past work and future plans, a commitment to making art a lifetime career. Each applicant must be a painter, sculptor, print-maker, drawer in figurative or representational art. Open to applicants of all nationalities.

**Funds Avail.:** $10,000 Canadian (per grant). **No. of Awards:** 45-55. **To Apply:** Abstract or non-representational art is precluded by the terms of the Foundation's charter. Applications are sent upon request either by phone, mail, or e-mail. No SASE please.

**Remarks:** Applications are judged by a Selection Committee. Foundation is not a school. **Contact:** Micheline Leduc, Administrator and Secretary.

### • 2752 • Greenshields Grants *(Other/Grant)*

**Purpose:** To assist talented artists in the early stages of their careers. **Focus:** Drawing, Painting, Printmaking, Sculpture. **Qualif.:** Applicants may be citizens of any country but must have started or completed training in an established school of art and/or be committed to making art a lifetime career. Work must be representational or figurative; abstract or non-representational art is precluded by the terms of the Foundation charter. Grants are tenable worldwide. **Criteria:** Based on application form and slides of recent works.

**Funds Avail.:** $10,000. **No. of Awards:** 45-55. **To Apply:** Write, phone, or email for application form. **Deadline:** None.

**Remarks:** When requesting an application form through email, please provide mailing address.

---

Awards are arranged alphabetically below their administering organizations

## • 2753 •
**George Grotefend Scholarship Board**
1644 Magnolia Ave.
Redding, CA 96001-1599

*Ph:* (916)225-0227
*Fax:* (916)225-0299

**• 2754 • George Grotefend Scholarships** *(All/ Scholarship)*

**Focus:** General Studies. **Qualif.:** Applicants must be high school graduates from Shasta County who have completed all of their high school experience in Shasta County.

**Funds Avail.:** Approximately 300 scholarships, totaling in excess of $70,000, are paid to recipients on an annual basis. **Deadline:** Applications are due April 20. **Contact:** Shasta County Office of Education at the above address (see entry 2753).

## • 2755 •
**William M. Grupe Foundation Inc.**
PO Box 775
Livingston, NJ 07039

*Ph:* (201)428-1190

**• 2756 • William F. Grupe Foundation Scholarships** *(Doctorate, Graduate/Scholarship)*

**Focus:** Medicine, Nursing. **Qualif.:** Applicants must be residents of Bergen, Essex, or Hudson counties in New Jersey pursuing an M.D., D.O., or nursing degree and intend to practice in the state of New Jersey at the completion of their training.

**Funds Avail.:** 20 to 30 awards are given. **No. of Awards:** 20-30. **To Apply:** March 1 of every year. Write for further information and application. **Contact:** D. Lynn Van Borkulo, President, at the above address (see entry 2755).

## • 2757 •
**Harry Frank Guggenheim Foundation**
527 Madison Ave.
New York, NY 10022-4304
*URL:* http://www.hfg.org

*Ph:* (212)644-4907
*Fax:* (212)644-5110

**• 2758 • H. F. Guggenheim Foundation Dissertation Fellowships** *(Doctorate/Fellowship)*

**Purpose:** To assist doctoral students with the completion of dissertations on aggression, dominance and violence. **Focus:** Aggression, Dominance, Violence. **Qualif.:** Candidates may be citizens of any country and may study at any college or university. Fellows are expected to complete their dissertations within the fellowship year. Fellowships may be accepted in conjunction with other awards, fellowships, or employment. The Foundation will consider research proposals from any discipline that will further the Foundation's objectives. **Criteria:** Recipients must demonstrate excellence and relevance to program interests.

**Funds Avail.:** $10,000. Fellows will be selected in June. **No. of Awards:** 10. **To Apply:** Write for application form. Submit with curriculum vitae, abstract of dissertation, letter from dissertation advisor, advisor's curriculum vitae, research plan, and a description of other facilities and resources already available for proposed research. **Deadline:** February 1. **Contact:** Any staff member at the above address (see entry 2757).

## • 2759 • H. F. Guggenheim Foundation Research Grants *(Postdoctorate/Grant)*

**Purpose:** To support projects relating to the study of dominance, aggression, and violence. **Focus:** Aggression, Dominance, Violence. **Qualif.:** Candidates may be of any nationality. The Foundation will consider research proposals from any discipline that will further the Foundation's objectives. Requests will be considered for salaries, employee benefits, research assistantships, computer time, supplies and equipment, field work, essential secretarial and technical help, and other items necessary to the successful completion of a project. The Foundation does not supply funds for overhead costs of institutions; travel to professional meetings; self-education; or support while completing the requirements for advanced degrees. **Criteria:** Recipients must demonstrate excellence and relevance to program interests.

**Funds Avail.:** $30,000 average. **No. of Awards:** 30 annually. **To Apply:** Write for application forms. Submit six copies in English with curriculum vitae, budget, and a research plan, describing the aims, methods, and significance of the project. Two referees who are not involved with the project should be solicited to evaluate research proposal; the referees' comments must be sent independently to the Foundation. **Deadline:** August 1. Final decisions are made in December for August applications. **Contact:** Any staff member at the above address (see entry 2757).

## • 2760 •
**John Simon Guggenheim Memorial Foundation**
90 Park Ave.
New York, NY 10016
*E-mail:* fellowships@gf.org
*URL:* http://www.gf.org

*Ph:* (212)687-4470
*Fax:* (212)697-3248

**• 2761 • John Simon Guggenheim Fellowships** *(Professional Development/Fellowship)*

**Purpose:** To assist research and artistic creation. **Focus:** General. **Qualif.:** Applicant must be a citizen or permanent resident of the United States, Canada, Latin America, or the Caribbean. Candidate must have already demonstrated exceptional capacity for productive scholarship or exceptional creative ability in the arts. Members of the teaching profession receiving sabbatical leave on full or partial salary are eligible for appointment, as are holders of other Fellowships or appointments at research centers.

**Funds Avail.:** Average is $31,682. **No. of Awards:** 202. **To Apply:** Write for application form and guidelines. **Deadline:** U.S. and Canada: October 1; Latin America and Caribbean: December 1. **Contact:** Send address inquiries to the above address.

## • 2762 •
**Guideposts Young Writers Contest**
16 E. 34th St.
New York, NY 10016

*Ph:* (212)251-8100
*Fax:* (212)684-0679

**• 2763 • Guideposts Magazine's Youth Writing Contest** *(Undergraduate/Scholarship)*

**Purpose:** To encourage writers to attend college. **Qualif.:** Entrants must be high school juniors or seniors, or students in equivalent grades in other countries. *Guideposts* employees and their children are not eligible.

**Funds Avail.:** Authors of the top eight manuscripts will each receive a scholarship and a portable electronic typewriter. Scholarships are in the amounts of $6,000, first prize; $5,000, second prize; $4,000, third prize; and $1,000, fourth through eighth prizes. Portable electronic typewriters are also awarded to the ninth through 25th place winners. Prizes must be used within five years after high school graduation at an accredited college or university. **No. of Awards:** 21 **To Apply:** Students must write a first-person story telling about a memorable or moving experience they have had. Stories must be true personal experiences and written as if applicants were describing it in a letter to their best friend. Manuscripts must be original, unpublished works and written in English, typed and double-spaced, with a maximum of 1,200 words. Only entries accompanied by a self-addressed, stamped envelope are returned. **Deadline:** All manuscripts must be postmarked by midnight November 30. Winners are notified by mail prior to announcement in *Guideposts*.

**Remarks:** Prizewinning manuscripts become the property of *Guideposts*. Approximately 5,000-7,000 applications are received each year. **Contact:** Youth Contest, c/o Guideposts at the above address (see entry 2762).

---

• 2764 •
## Harvard University - Minda de Gunzburg Center for European Studies
27 Kirkland St.       *Ph:* (617)495-4303
Cambridge, MA 02138      *Fax:* (617)495-8509

### • 2765 • The James Bryant Conant Fellowships for Postdoctoral Research *(Postdoctorate/Fellowship)*

**Purpose:** To support scholarly work at the post-doctoral level with a special emphasis on a German or a comparative German topic. **Qualif.:** Applicants must be United States or Canadian citizens who intend to teach in North America and who have completed their dissertation within the last five years. Harvard Ph.D.s should have taught or conducted research elsewhere for at least two years prior to application. Projects on 20th-century Germany, or on a comparative European framework that includes German components, are preferred, but topics concerned with earlier problems that have relevance for the development of contemporary culture and society will also be considered.

**Funds Avail.:** Two Conant Fellowships for $32,000 each for a 12-month period. While some research-related travel is acceptable, this is a residential fellowship at the Center for European Studies in Cambridge, and it is expected that the Conant Fellows be active in the Program for the Study of Germany and Europe. Health insurance is provided if necessary. A publishable monograph is required upon completion. **To Apply:** Applicants must submit six copies of a three-page research project description, a three-page dissertation abstract, a curriculum vitae, two 20-page writing samples (published articles or conference papers), and three letters of recommendation. **Deadline:** Varies from year to year. **Contact:** Barbara Chrenko, Minda De Gunzburg Center for European Studies, at the above address (see entry 2764).

### • 2766 • Minda de Gunzburg Center for European Studies Dissertation Exploration Grants *(Graduate/ Grant)*

**Purpose:** To allow graduate students to pursue a particular dissertation topic. **Qualif.:** Applicants must be graduate students who have completed their general examinations in the social sciences and history in the Faculty of Arts and Sciences at Harvard, or the John F. Kennedy School of Government at Harvard, or at M.I.T. **Criteria:** Topics on Germany or Germany in a comparative context are preferred, but proposals on other European issues are also considered. Dissertations should focus on 20th-century Germany or Europe, but topics concerned with earlier problems related to the development of contemporary culture and society are also considered.

**Funds Avail.:** The maximum award is $3,500. **Deadline:** March 5.

**Remarks:** These grants are funded by the Program for the Study of Germany and Europe. **Contact:** Barbara Chrenko at the above address (see entry 2764).

### • 2767 • Minda de Gunzburg Center for European Studies German Language Training Grants *(Graduate/ Grant)*

**Qualif.:** Applicants must be Harvard or M.I.T. graduate students in the social sciences or history. In most cases, students must have had one year of German or the equivalent before applying. **Criteria:** Preference is given to those who intend to do primary or comparative research in German.

**Funds Avail.:** The maximum award is $3,000. **To Apply:** Students are responsible for applying and becoming accepted to the program of their choice. Application instructions are listed on an informational sheet, which is available at the Center. **Deadline:** February 12. **Contact:** Barbara Chrenko at the above address (see entry 2764).

### • 2768 • Minda de Gunzburg Center for European Studies Graduate Summer Research Travel Grants *(Graduate/Grant)*

**Qualif.:** Applicants must be graduate level students at the John F. Kennedy School of Government who require a short period of research abroad. **Criteria:** Topics on Germany or Germany in a comparative context are preferred, but proposals on other European issues will be considered. Projects should focus on 20th-century Germany or Europe, but topics concerned with earlier problems that relate to the development of contemporary culture and society are also considered.

**Funds Avail.:** The maximum award is $3,500. **Deadline:** March 5.

**Remarks:** These grants are funded through the Program for the study of Germany and Europe (PSGE). **Contact:** Barbara Chrenko at the above address (see entry 2764).

### • 2769 • Minda de Gunzburg Center for European Studies Program for the Study of Germany and Europe Dissertation Research Fellowships *(Doctorate/ Fellowship)*

**Qualif.:** Applicants must be graduate students in doctoral programs in the social sciences and history in the faculty of Arts and Sciences of Harvard, in the John F. Kennedy School at Harvard, or at M.I.T., who have passed their general examinations. **Criteria:** Topics on Germany or Germany in a comparative context are preferred, but proposals on other European issues will be considered. Ordinarily, dissertations should focus on 20th-century Germany or Europe, but topics concerned with earlier problems relating to the development of contemporary culture and society will also be considered.

**Funds Avail.:** The Fellowship carries a stipend of $15,000, plus up to $2,000 for insurance and low-level tuition. The Fellowship may be used for research abroad or for writing subsequent to research in Europe. **To Apply:** Applications may be obtained from the Minda de Gunzburg Center for European Studies. **Deadline:** January 18. **Contact:** Barbara Chrenko at the above address (see entry 2764).

### • 2770 • Minda de Gunzburg Center for European Studies Short-Term Opportunity Grants *(Graduate/ Grant)*

**Purpose:** To enable qualified applicants to take advantage of special short-term (up to one month) opportunities related to their dissertation topics. **Qualif.:** Applicants must be Harvard or M.I.T. graduate students in the social sciences or history. Eligible activities may include travel to Europe to collect data or for observational purposes. **Criteria:** Applicants whose dissertations focus on Germany or Germany in a comparative perspective are preferred, but topics on any European subject are also considered.

---

*Awards are arranged alphabetically below their administering organizations*

## Harvard University - Minda de Gunzburg Center for European Studies (continued)

**Funds Avail.:** The maximum grant is $1,500. Funds are limited and often supplementary. **To Apply:** There is no formal application to complete. Application instructions for each grant are listed on an informational sheet, which is available at the Center. **Deadline:** November 6; February 5; and April 16. **Contact:** Barbara Chrenko at the above address (see entry 2764).

### • 2771 • Minda de Gunzburg Center for European Studies Undergraduate Summer Travel Grants (Undergraduate/Grant)

**Purpose:** To fund summer research in Europe for Harvard Faculty Arts and Sciences undergraduates. **Qualif.:** Applicants must be undergraduate students in the Faculty of Arts and Sciences at Harvard preparing senior theses on political, historical, economical, and intellectual trends in Europe since 1750. Proposals on any European topic are considered.

**Funds Avail.:** The maximum award is $3,500. **Deadline:** March 5.

**Remarks:** These grants are provided by the German government through the Program for the Study of Germany and Europe, and by the Krupp Foundation. **Contact:** Barbara Chrenko at the above address (see entry 2764).

### • 2772 • Harvard University Pre-Doctoral Fellowships in European Studies (Graduate/Fellowship)

**Qualif.:** Applicants must be advanced graduate students in the social sciences and history who are in their last year of writing and expecting to complete their dissertation at the end of the grant period. Applicants must be United States or Canadian citizens who intend to teach in North America and who are currently enrolled in graduate departments of North American universities. This Program is not offered to Harvard or M.I.T. students. **Criteria:** Projects on 20th-century Germany or on a comparative European framework that includes German components are preferred, but topics concerned with earlier periods relating to the development of contemporary culture and society are also considered.

**Funds Avail.:** A $15,000 stipend over a ten- month period and residency at the Center for European Studies. Health insurance is provided if necessary. **To Apply:** Applicants must submit six copies of a five-page dissertation abstract, a curriculum vitae, one 20-page writing sample (e.g., published article or conference paper), and two letters of recommendation, one of which should be from the dissertation adviser. **Deadline:** Applications were due February 19, and applicants were informed of the Center's decision by April 15. **Contact:** Barbara Butler at the above address (see entry 2764).

### • 2773 • Krupp Foundation Fellowship (Graduate/Fellowship)

**Purpose:** To provide funds for graduate students working on their dissertations on topics that require research in Europe and relate to contemporary concerns of European culture and society. **Qualif.:** Applicants must be graduate students in the Faculty of Arts and Sciences of Harvard who have passed their general examinations and are working on dissertation topics concerning Europe in the post-1750 period. Applications are accepted from students in the Departments of Anthropology, Economics, Government, History, Philosophy, Psychology and Social Relations, and Sociology. Recipients are required to spend a minimum of six months abroad. Highly theoretical topics, or topics that do not require research in Europe, will not be accepted. Fellowships are not intended for the purposes of writing grants.

**Funds Avail.:** The stipend is $15,000, plus $2,000 for insurance and low-level tuition. **Deadline:** January 15. **Contact:** Barbara Chrenko at the above address (see entry 2764).

### • 2774 •
## Paul and Mary Haas Foundation
PO Box 2928
Corpus Christi, TX 78403          *Ph:* (361)887-6955

### • 2775 • Paul and Mary Haas Foundation Student Scholarship Grants (Undergraduate/Scholarship)

**Purpose:** To aid persons of financially limited backgrounds in becoming economically self-sufficient and to provide the Coastal Bend area of the state of Texas with men and women who have knowledge and skills to maintain a viable pattern of economic growth. **Focus:** General Studies. **Qualif.:** Candidates must be graduating seniors of a Corpus Christi, Texas, high school planning to attend college who come from lower or middle income families. They must also have an above average attendance record and show above average academic motivation and ability as demonstrated by high school grade point or standardized test scores or who, in the opinion of counselors, will develop sufficiently to overcome existing grade deficiencies. **Criteria:** Awards are made based on financial need and academic motivation and ability.

**Funds Avail.:** The amount awarded is individually determined, based on the number of hours carried by the student. Payments are made to the student after submission of appropriate paper work and are disbursed for tuition and book fees. Maximum of $1,500 per semester. **No. of Awards:** 50 per semester. **To Apply:** A scholarship application form must be completed and submitted. All applications are evaluated by trustees of the Foundation at a meeting held approximately six weeks before the school term begins. Students are notified in person or in writing of action taken by the trustees. **Deadline:** Renewal application process must be completed by August 1 for fall and December 1 for spring semester. High school seniors are required to contact the Foundation in August of their senior year to begin "in-house" procedures. **Contact:** Karen Wesson, Director, at the above address (see entry 2774).

### • 2776 •
## Hagley Graduate Program
History Department
University of Delaware          *Ph:* (302)831-8226
Newark, DE 19716          *Fax:* (302)831-1538

### • 2777 • University of Delaware-Hagley Program Fellowship (Graduate/Fellowship)

**Purpose:** The University of Delaware-Hagley Program looks for individuals with an interest in the history of industrialization, broadly defined to include social, business, economic and labor history and especially the history of technology, and seek careers in college teaching and public history. **Focus:** Industrialization. **Qualif.:** Candidates for Plan A (terminal) master's are required to have an overall 2.5 and 3.0 in history and have a combind score of 1250 on the GRE. Candidates for the PhD entering with an MA have the same requirements as Plan B candidates. **No. of Awards:** 1-3. **Deadline:** January 30. **Contact:** Coordinator.

## • 2778 •
### Hagley Museum and Library
c/o Carol Ressler Lockman
P.O. Box 3630
Wilmington, DE 19807       *Ph:* (302)658-2400
      *Fax:* (302)655-3188
*URL:* http://www.hagley.lib.de.us

#### • 2779 • Hagley Fellowships/Grants-in-Aid *(Graduate, Postdoctorate, Postgraduate/Grant)*

**Purpose:** To provide travel grants for research of Hagley Library Collections. **Focus:** Imprint, manuscript, pictorial, and artifact collections. **Qualif.:** Grant recipients must spend their time in residence at Hagley, or travel there on a regular basis.

**Funds Avail.:** No more than $1200 per month. **To Apply:** Applicants must submit the following: fellowship application cover sheet; cover letter noting the requested period for residency and social security number; copy of current resume or curriculum vitae no more than four pages in length; and a 4-5 page description of the proposed research project. Please provide information on the significance of the work and research methodology. Competitive proposals will demonstrate the relevance of the project to Hagley's fields of interest and include a discussion of collections to be used and their importance to the plan of work. If this is an application for a second grant to continue work on a project previously supported by Hagley, include an outline of progress made to date, a timetable of expected work to be accomplished, and a description of the final product of your research. **Deadline:** March 31, June 30 and October 29.

#### • 2780 • Hagley-Winterthur Fellowship *(Doctorate, Graduate, Postdoctorate, Professional Development/ Fellowship)*

**Purpose:** To provide travel grants for research of Hagley Library Winterthur Library Collection. **Focus:** History and culture imprint, manuscript, pictorial, and artifact collections. **Qualif.:** Grant recipients must spend their time in residence at Hagley-Winterthur or travel there on a regular basis.

**Funds Avail.:** $1200 per month. **No. of Awards:** Varies, the average is 3. **To Apply:** Must submit the following: fellowship application cover sheet; cover letter noting the requested period for residency for the grant and your social security number; copy of current resume or curriculum vitae. This must be limited to no more than four pages in length: 4-5 page description of your proposed research project. Please provide information on the significance of the work and your research methodology. Competitive proposals will demonstrate the relevance of the project to Hagley-Winterthur fields of interest and include a discussion of collections to be used and their importance to the plan of work. If this is an application for a second grant to continue work on a project previously supported by Hagley-Winterthur, include an outline of progress made to date, a timetable of expected work to be accomplished, and a description of the final product of your research. **Deadline:** December 1.

## • 2781 •
### John T. Hall Student Loan Fund
c/o Dale Welch, VP
SunTrust Bank
PO Box 4655       *Ph:* (404)230-5479
Atlanta, GA 30302       *Fax:* (404)588-7491

#### • 2782 • John T. Hall Student Loan Fund *(Graduate, Undergraduate/Loan)*

**Focus:** General studies. **Qualif.:** Applicants must be Georgia residents attending colleges or universities within the state of Georgia. **Criteria:** Awards are granted based on scholastic aptitude and personal interview.

**Funds Avail.:** $1,500 maximum for undergraduates; $5,000 for graduate students. **No. of Awards:** 24. **To Apply:** Write for further details. **Deadline:** May 1. **Contact:** Dale Welch.

## • 2783 •
### Halton Foundation
PO Box 3377
Portland, OR 97208

#### • 2784 • Halton Foundation Scholarships *(All/ Scholarship)*

**Qualif.:** Students must be sons or daughters of a Halton Company employee and under the age of 28. **Contact:** S.H. Findlay at the above address (see entry 2783).

## • 2785 •
### The Hambidge Center for Creative Arts and Sciences
PO Box 339       *Ph:* (706)746-5718
Rabun Gap, GA 30568       *Fax:* (706)746-9933

*The Hambidge Center is a private nonprofit organization that provides creative people with the opportunity to work in a peaceful, remote mountain setting removed from daily chores.*

#### • 2786 • Resident Fellowships *(Professional Development/Fellowship)*

**Purpose:** To allow time in solitude to complete projects or explore new directions. **Focus:** Fine Arts, Crafts, Music, Composition, Writing, Performing Arts. **Qualif.:** Applicants may be from any discipline but should have moderate to expert-level experience in their field. However, there is also space for developing artists. Fellowships are tenable at the Center.

**Funds Avail.:** Varies; fellows are given a private cottage, which includes work area, and are granted access to several common studios equipped for work in the visual and musical arts. **To Apply:** Send a self-addressed, stamped envelope for an application form. State area of interest or discipline when requesting application. **Deadline:** January 31 for initial scheduling review. The Center accepts applications year round.

**Remarks:** Limited work-study scholarships are also available from the Center. Write for details. **Contact:** Executive Director at the above address (see entry 2785).

**• 2787 •**

**Hamilton Foundation**
Dean of Graduate Studies
1280 Main St., W.
Gilmour Hall, Rm. 110
McMaster University
Hamilton, ON, Canada L8S 4L8          Ph: (416)525-9140
*E-mail:* incze@mcmaster.ca
*URL:* http://leroy.cc.uregina.ca/~gradstud/GradStud/
scholarships/S_and_A/E.html

**• 2788 •   E. B. Eastburn Fellowships** *(Postdoctorate/
Fellowship)*

**Purpose:** To support postdoctoral studies in the sciences. **Focus:**
Medicine, Natural Sciences, Physical Sciences. **Qualif.:** Candidate
must be a Canadian citizen Permanent Resident. Applicant must
have completed a Ph.D., or be close to completion, in one of the
natural or physical sciences, including medicine. Preference will be
given to candidates with financial need. Fellowship is tenable at
any Canadian university. Awardee is expected to pursue full-time
study and research during the fellowship term. No other academic
award or employment may be accepted by the candidate during
the Fellowship. Interim written reports must be submitted in
December and April by the Fellow to briefly described progress,
and a final detailed report is required one month after conclusion
of the Fellowship.

**Funds Avail.:** $44,000. **No. of Awards:** One. **To Apply:** Applicants
should write for application form and guidelines. They should
submit six copies of the following: curriculum vitae, academic
transcripts, abstract of research proposal, a full statement of the
research proposal, budget, personal financial statement, and
cover letter. Two confidential letters of recommendation must be
sent directly to McMaster University. All envelopes containing
correspondence relating to the Fellowship must be marked E.B.
Eastburn Fellowship. **Deadline:** January 31. **Contact:** Eva Incze,
Secretary to the Dean, at the above address (see entry 2787).

**• 2789 •**

**Harness Horse Youth Foundation**
14950 Greyhound Ct., Ste. 210          Ph: (317)848-5132
Carmel, IN 46032                       Fax: (317)848-5136
*URL:* http://www.hhyf.org

**• 2790 •   Harness Horse Youth Foundation
Scholarships** *(Undergraduate/Scholarship)*

**Purpose:** To promote interest and educate young people about
harness racing. **Focus:** Equine Studies. **Qualif.:** Applicants must be
pursuing or planning a horse-related career. **Criteria:** Selection is
based upon an applicant's academic record, financial need,
experience with horses, potential for achievement, character,
recommendations, and effort.

**Funds Avail.:** $20,000 in HHYF funds are available. **To Apply:** A
formal application must be completed. An essay must accompany
the application, along with transcripts, tax information, and three
recommendations. **Deadline:** April 30.

**Remarks:** Formerly named Critchfield Oviatt Memorial
Scholarship.

**• 2791 •**

**Harness Horsemen International Foundation**
14 Main St.                            Ph: (609)259-3717
Robbinsville, NJ 08691-1410            Fax: (609)259-3778

**• 2792 •   The Jerome L. Hauck Scholarship** *(High
School, Undergraduate/Association, Scholarship)*

**Purpose:** To assist students of outstanding merit who show an
appreciation of the value of an education and who are willing to
achieve success. **Focus:** General Studies. **Qualif.:** Applicants must
be children of a full-time groom or children of members of an HHI
member association. They should be seniors in high school or high
school graduates. **Criteria:** Selection is determined by financial
need, extracurricular and community service participation,
scholarship, citizenship, and leadership.

**Funds Avail.:** Scholarships are for $1,000 per year for four years.
**To Apply:** Two letters of recommendation and school transcript
showing SAT or ACT scores must be submitted. A letter of
endorsement from the President of the HHI association sponsoring
the applicant and a recent photo of the applicant are also required.
**Deadline:** June 1. **Contact:** Michael Izzo at the above address (see
entry 2791).

**• 2793 •**

**Harness Tracks of America**
4640 E. Sunrise, Ste. 200              Ph: (520)529-2525
Tucson, AZ 85718                       Fax: (520)529-3235
*E-mail:* harness@azstarnet.com

**• 2794 •   Harness Tracks of America Scholarship**
*(Graduate, Undergraduate/Scholarship)*

**Purpose:** To promote education and to aid those people who have
worked within the harness racing industry. **Focus:** General Studies.
**Qualif.:** Sons or daughters of licensed standard bred drivers,
trainers, breeders, owners and caretakers (including retired or
deceased) or young people actively engaged in harness racing are
eligible. **Criteria:** Scholarships are awarded on the basis of merit,
financial need, harness racing involvement, and future goals.

**Funds Avail.:** Five scholarships of $4,000 each for study beyond
the high school level are awarded annually. **To Apply:** Completed
application, academic transcripts, plans or ambitions for future
education, and an essay on harness racing involvement are
required along with financial forms. **Deadline:** June 15.

**Remarks:** Approximately 250 applications are received each year.
**Contact:** Scholarship Coordinator, at the above address (see entry
2793).

**• 2795 •**

**Patricia Roberts Harris Fellowship Program**
ROB 3, Rm. 3022
7th & D Sts, SW
Washington, DC 20202-5251              Ph: (202)708-8395
*URL:* http://www.ed.gov/pubs/Biennial/54.htm/

**• 2796 •   Patricia Roberts Harris Fellowships**
*(Doctorate, Graduate/Fellowship)*

**Qualif.:** Applicants must be women, minorities, and those
underrepresented who are enrolled in graduate degree programs.

**Funds Avail.:** A fund of $21,780,000 is available. **Deadline:** To be determined. **Contact:** Charles H. Miller at the above address (see entry 2795).

---

• 2797 •

**Hartford Courant**
285 Broad St.  Ph: (203)241-6481
Hartford, CT 06115  Fax: (203)241-3865
URL: http://www.arcade.uioa.edu/proj/earth2/reviews/The_
Hartford_Courant.html

• 2798 • **Hartford Courant Minority Internship**
(Professional Development/Internship)

**Purpose:** To provide preparation for a reporting position at The Hartford Courant. **Qualif.:** Candidates must be minorities who are no longer in school. They need not have a degree, but must have a strong interest in pursuing a career in newspapers. **Criteria:** Applicants will be judged on personal interviews, clips or writing samples, letters of recommendation, and writing tests. Connecticut applicants are strongly preferred. Candidates must have a car and be prepared to live within the Courant's core circulation area.

**Funds Avail.:** Internships last approximately one year and pay $400 weekly. **To Apply:** Applicants must send a letter of application, current resume, and clips or other writing samples. **Contact:** Jeff Rivers, Associate Editor at the above address (see entry 2797).

---

• 2799 •

**Hartford Public Library**
500 Main St.  Ph: (860)543-8628
Hartford, CT 06103  Fax: (860)722-6900
E-mail: webmaster@hartfordpl.lib.ct.us
URL: http://www.hartfordpl.lib.ct.us

• 2800 • **Caroline M. Hewins Scholarship** (Graduate/
Scholarship)

**Qualif.:** Applicants must plan to specialize in library work with children. Candidates must have received a four-year undergraduate degree or be about to receive one and have made formal application for admission to a library school accredited by the American Library Association. **Criteria:** Applicants who plan to follow public library service careers receive preference.

**Funds Avail.:** One scholarship of $4,000 is awarded annually. Proof of acceptance by an accredited library school is necessary before payment of the scholarship may be made. **To Apply:** A transcript of college credits, including the first semester of the senior year, and evidence of application for admission to an accredited library school should accompany each Hewins' application or be forwarded shortly after it is made. **Deadline:** April 1. **Contact:** Caroline M. Hewins Scholarship, chief librarian, at the above address (see entry 2799).

---

• 2801 •

**Harvard Travellers Club**
PO Box H  Ph: (781)821-0400
Canton, MA 02021  Fax: (781)828-4254

• 2802 • **Harvard Travellers Club Grants** (Doctorate,
Graduate, Undergraduate/Grant)

**Purpose:** To foster research and/or exploration that involves travel and exploration. **Focus:** General Studies. **Qualif.:** Applicants may be of any nationality and should have at least college level qualifications. **Criteria:** Preference is given to individuals seeking advanced degrees.

**Funds Avail.:** $500-1,000. **No. of Awards:** 3. **To Apply:** Submit resume and a brief explanation of project not more than two pages and reasons why funds are requested. **Deadline:** Six months before proposed research.

**Remarks:** The Grants are awarded each year to persons with projects that involve intelligent travel and exploration. All travel must be intimately involved with research and/or exploration. Grants are not awarded for travel for study in a foreign city. **Contact:** George P. Bates at the above address (see entry 2801).

---

• 2803 •

**Harvard University - Center for International Affairs
- Harvard Academy in International and Area
Studies**
1737 Cambridge St.  Ph: (617)495-2137
Cambridge, MA 02138  Fax: (617)495-8292

• 2804 • **Pre- and Postdoctoral Fellowships in
International and Area Studies** (Doctorate,
Postdoctorate/Fellowship)

**Purpose:** To assist young scholars who are preparing for an academic career involving both a social science discipline and a particular area of the world. **Focus:** Area Studies, Social Sciences. **Qualif.:** Applicant may be of any nationality, although preference will be given to U.S. citizens and permanent residents. Applicant must hold a doctoral or equivalent professional degree or have completed the course work and general examinations leading to the Ph.D. Fellow is required to be in residence at the Center during the term of the Fellowship.

**Funds Avail.:** Predoctoral: $20,000-25,000, plus university facilities fees and health insurance; postdoctoral: $30,000-35,000, plus health insurance **To Apply:** Write to the Program Director for details and application guidelines which are available beginning in July. **Deadline:** October. **Contact:** Marisa Murtagh, Program Director, at the above address (see entry 2803).

---

• 2805 •

**Harvard University - Center for International Affairs
- Program on Nonviolent Sanctions**
1737 Cambridge Street  Ph: (617)495-5580
Cambridge, MA 02138  Fax: (617)495-8292

• 2806 • **Pre- and Postdoctoral Fellowships on
Nonviolent Sanctions; Visiting Scholar Affiliations**
(Doctorate, Postdoctorate/Fellowship)

**Purpose:** To support research on the degree to which, and how, nonviolent direct action provides an alternative to violence in resolving the problems of totalitarian rule, war, genocide, and

---

**Harvard University - Center for International Affairs - Program on Nonviolent Sanctions** *(continued)*

oppression. **Focus:** Nonviolent Sanctions. **Qualif.:** Applicant may be of any nationality, although preference will be given to U.S. citizens and permanent residents. Applicant must hold a doctoral or equivalent professional degree or have completed the course work and general examinations leading to the Ph.D. Applicant should contact the Program Director to discuss the research project before compiling application. Fellow is required to be in residence at the Center during the term of the Fellowship.

**Funds Avail.:** Varies. **To Apply:** Write to the Research Director for details and application guidelines which are available beginning in July. **Deadline:** January.

• 2807 •
**Harvard University - Center for International Affairs - Program on U.S.-Japan Relations**
1737 Cambridge Street               *Ph:* (617)495-1890
Cambridge, MA 02138                 *Fax:* (617)495-4921

• 2808 • **Advanced Research Fellowships in U.S.-Japan Relations** *(Postdoctorate/Fellowship)*

**Purpose:** To support the work of scholars engaged in the study of contemporary Japan and/or U.S.-Japan relations. **Focus:** Japan, U.S.-Japan Relations. **Qualif.:** Applicant may be of any nationality, although preference will be given to U.S. citizens and permanent residents. Applicant must hold a doctoral or equivalent professional degree. Fellow is required to be in residence at the Center during the term of the Fellowship.

**Funds Avail.:** $25,000. **To Apply:** Write to the Associate Director for details and application guidelines which are available beginning in October. **Deadline:** March. **Contact:** Dr. Frank Schwartz at the above address (see entry 2807).

• 2809 •
**Harvard University - Law School**
Cambridge, MA 02138               *Ph:* (617)495-3165

• 2810 • **Liberal Arts Fellowships in Law**
*(Professional Development/Fellowship)*

**Purpose:** To enable teachers in the social sciences or humanities to study fundamental techniques, concepts, and aims of law. **Focus:** Law. **Qualif.:** Applicant must be a college or university teacher in the liberal arts and sciences. There are no other restrictions on eligibility. Fellows will be expected to take two first-year courses in law, as well as advanced courses. The fellowship year of study cannot count toward a degree.

**Funds Avail.:** Tuition, health fees, and office space. **To Apply:** There is no special application form. Submit resume, including academic record, a list of publications, and a statement describing interest in the fellowship. Two letters of recommendation should be sent directly from the referees to the chair of the committee. **Deadline:** January 15. Awards are announced by February 15. **Contact:** Calls are not encouraged. Chair, Committee on Liberal Arts Fellowships, at the above address (see entry 2809).

• 2811 •
**Harvard University - Weatherhead Center for International Affairs - John M. Olin Institute for Strategic Studies**
1737 Cambridge St.                  *Ph:* (617)496-5495
Cambridge, MA 02138                 *Fax:* (617)495-1384
*E-mail:* peterson@cha.howard.edu
*URL:* http://www.data.fas.harvard.edu/cfia/olin/
havepage.htm

• 2812 • **Fellowships in National Security** *(Graduate, Postdoctorate/Fellowship)*

**Purpose:** To promote basic research in the broad area of security and strategic affairs. **Focus:** Defense, Military History, National Security. **Qualif.:** Applicants may be of any nationality and must be scholars in security affairs. Preference is given to recent Ph.D. recipients or graduate students who have made progress on their dissertations and are likely to complete them during the fellowship period. The Institute is particularly interested in research into the causes and conduct of war, military strategy and history, defense policy, and the ways in which the United States and other societies can provide for their security in a dangerous world. Fellowships are tenable at the Institute.

**Funds Avail.:** Postdoctorate: $30,000; predoctorate: $17,500 plus health insurance. **To Apply:** Submit four copies each of the following: curriculum vitae, a 1,500-word description of the proposed research project, one or two relevant writing samples (if possible), and the names of three references. **Deadline:** January 15. **Contact:** Inga Peterson, Program Coordinator, (617)496-5495

• 2813 •
**The Hastings Center**
Garrison, NY 10524-5555             *Ph:* (914)424-4040
                                    *Fax:* (914)424-4545
*URL:* http://www.thehastingscenter.org

• 2814 • **Eastern European Visiting Scholarships**
*(Postdoctorate, Professional Development/Scholarship)*

**Purpose:** To establish collaborative and mutually beneficial efforts among those working on bioethical research in Eastern Europe, Western Europe, and North America. **Focus:** Bioethics **Qualif.:** Applicants must be from a country in Central/Eastern Europe and advanced scholars or practitioners who are already working, or plan to work, in the field of bioethics. Applicants must have a working knowledge of English. Scholarships are tenable at either the Hastings Center, the Centre for the Study of Philosophy and Health Care (which cosponsors the scholarship), or both. Scholars engage in independent or directed research of bioethical issues. Formal courses of study not available at the Hastings Center. Scholars are expected to participate in the ongoing activities of the program, as well as conduct their own research. Award funds should be applied to the costs of travel, accommodations, and living expenses. **Criteria:** Center's interest in subject matter.

**Funds Avail.:** $1,000-1,500. **No. of Awards:** Depends on funding. **To Apply:** Write to the Hastings Center for application form and guidelines. Submit form, a threeto five-page detailed description of proposed project, curriculum vitae, a copy of a recent writing sample in English, a statement of rationale for the proposed fellowship, and the names and addresses of two referees. **Deadline:** At least four months prior to the proposed visit.

**Remarks:** Journalist-in-Residence Awards to journalists who concentrate on medical and scientific issues and Hastings Center Student Internships to advanced graduate students are also awarded. These awards carry no stipend. Write to the Hastings Center for further details.

• **2815** • **Hastings Center International Fellowships**
*(Postdoctorate/Fellowship)*

**Purpose:** To enable scholars to conduct advanced studies and research in comparative bioethics at the Center. **Focus:** Bioethics. **Qualif.:** Candidate may be of any nationality and advanced scholars or medical professionals who plan a research project or independent study of ethical problems in medicine, the life sciences, and the professions. Fellowships are tenable at the Hastings Center. Time is divided between research and participation in the ongoing activities of the Center. Award funds are intended to be applied to the costs of travel, accommodations, and living expenses. **Criteria:** Center's interest in subject matter.

**Funds Avail.:** $500-1,000. **No. of Awards:** Depends on funding. **To Apply:** Write to the director of education for application form and guidelines. Submit form, a three- to five-page detailed description of proposed project, curriculum vitae, a copy of a recent writing sample, a statement of rationale for the proposed fellowship, and the names and addresses of two referees. **Deadline:** At least three months prior to proposed fellowship.

**Remarks:** Hastings Center Journalist-in-Residence Awards to journalists who concentrate on medical and scientific issues and Hastings Center Student Internships to advanced graduate students are also awarded. These awards carry no stipend. Write to the Hastings Center for further details. **Contact:** Dr. Strachan Donnelly, Director of Education, at the above address (see entry 2813).

• **2816** •
**The Hauss-Helms Foundation, Inc.**
PO Box 25
Wapakoneta, OH 45895                    *Ph:* (419)738-4911

• **2817** • **The Hauss-Helms Foundation Scholarships**
*(All/Scholarship)*

**Purpose:** To aid high school and college students whose financial need makes it difficult to continue their education. **Focus:** General Studies. **Qualif.:** Applicants must be residents of either Allen or Auglaize counties in Ohio. Graduating high school students must be in the top 50 percent of their class academically, while college applicants must have at least a 2.0 grade point average.

**Funds Avail.:** Awards vary from $400- 5,000 each. **No. of Awards:** 225. **To Apply:** Applications may be requested in writing after January 1. **Deadline:** April 15. **Contact:** James E. Weger, president, at the above address (see entry 2816).

• **2818** •
**Havana National Bank**
112 S. Orange St.
Box 200                              *Ph:* (309)543-3361
Havana, IL 62655-0200                *Free:* 800-921-5538
*E-mail:* hnb@fgi.net
*URL:* http://www.outfitters.com/com/hnb/abmstar.html

• **2819** • **McFarland Charitable Foundation Scholarship** *(Undergraduate/Scholarship)*

**Focus:** Nursing. **Qualif.:** Applicants must be high school graduates or equivalent who have been accepted into an accredited registered nursing program. Recipients must contractually commit to work for a number of years in the Havana, Illinois area after graduation. **Criteria:** Awards are made based on academic record.

**Funds Avail.:** $6,000 - $10,000. **No. of Awards:** 3-5. **To Apply:** Write for further details. **Deadline:** May 1. **Contact:** Linda Butler.

• **2820** •
**Hawaii Education Loan Program**
PO Box 22187                         *Ph:* (808)593-2262
Honolulu, HI 96823-2187              *Fax:* (808)593-8268

• **2821** • **Hawaii's Federal PLUS Loans**
*(Undergraduate/Loan)*

**Focus:** General Studies. **Qualif.:** Must be natural or adoptive parents, or legal guardians of an eligible student; U.S. citizen, U.S. national, or eligible non-citizen; and not in default on another student loan or owe a refund to an education grant program. Loan is primarily for students whose financial circumstances disqualify the student for the federally subsidized loan or who still need some financial assistance.

**Funds Avail.:** May borrow up to cost of education minus financial aid each year. There is no aggregate limit. Interest rate is adjusted annually, not to exceed 9 percent. Repayment begins 60 days after the funds are disbursed. **Contact:** Financial aid office or lenders for applications and details.

• **2822** • **Hawaii's Federal Stafford Loans** *(Graduate, Undergraduate/Loan)*

**Focus:** General Studies. **Qualif.:** Applicants must be U.S. citizens, nationals, or other eligible non-citizens who are enrolled (or accepted for enrollment) and making satisfactory academic progress at an approved educational institution. They must be enrolled at least half-time, show compliance with selective service requirements, and cannot be in default on another student loan or owe a refund to an education grant program. Applicants must apply for the Pell Grant. **Criteria:** Based on financial need.

**Funds Avail.:** Up to $2,625 per year for the first year of undergraduate study; up to $3,500 for second year; and up to $5,500 per year for the remainder of undergraduate study. Aggregate for undergraduate study cannot exceed $23,000. Up to $8,500 per year for graduate or professional study. Aggregate for undergraduate and graduate study cannot exceed $65,500. Loan amount for a given year cannot exceed the student's cost of attendance minus other financial aid and (if required) the estimated family contribution. Federal government pays interest until student begins repayment six months after graduation or termination of studies. Interest rate is variable, adjusted annually with a cap of 8.25 percent. Additional amount available for independent student under unsubsidized Federal Stafford Loans. **To Apply:** Contact any financial aid office or lender for applications. **Contact:** Hawaii Education Loan Program at the above address (see entry 2820).

• **2823** •
**Hawaii Society of Professional Journalists**
c/o John Black
Trade Publishing Company
287 Mokauea St.
Honolulu, HI 96819

• **2824** • **Hawaii Society of Professional Journalists Internships** *(Other, Undergraduate/Internship)*

**Purpose:** Provides internships at newspapers, magazines, television stations, and public relations firms in Hawaii. **Focus:** Journalism. **Qualif.:** Applicants must be residents of Hawaii. If applicants are students, they must at least by a sophomore.

*Hawaii Society of Professional Journalists (continued)*

**Funds Avail.:** $2700 stipend. **No. of Awards:** 10.

---

**• 2825 •**

## Haystack Mountain School of Crafts

PO Box 518
Deer Isle, ME 04627-0518
*E-mail:* haystack@haystack-mtn.org
*URL:* http://www.haystack-mtn.org
*Ph:* (207)348-2306
*Fax:* (207)348-2307

**• 2826 • Monitor/Technical Assistant Scholarships** *(Graduate/Scholarship)*

**Purpose:** To support the investigation of the possibilities of craft in an aesthetic climate which honors both tradition and the rich potential of contemporary visual art. **Focus:** Crafts. **Qualif.:** Candidates may be of any nationality. Applicants for the Technical Assistant award must have completed one year of graduate specialization, or the equivalent, in the area for which aid is requested, and must be willing to help instructors at the School in the studios with shop maintenance and organization. **Criteria:** Selection is based on the applicant's level of accomplishment, ability to assist in teaching, and the ability to work in a supportive, closely knit community.

**Funds Avail.:** $820-$1,115/session. **No. of Awards:** Approximately 45. **To Apply:** Candidates should write for application form and then submit it with application fee ($25), three letters of reference, and ten slides of artwork. **Deadline:** March 25.

**Remarks:** Work-study and minority scholarships are also available from the School. Write to the director for details. **Contact:** Stuart Kestenbaum, Director, at the above address (see entry 2825).

---

**• 2827 •**

## Health Canada - National Health Research and Development Program

Information Analysis and
 Connectivity Branch
Tunney's Pature, Jeanne Mance
 bldg.
Ottawa, ON, Canada K1A 1B4
*E-mail:* nhrdpinfo@hc-sc.gc.ca
*URL:* http://www.hwc.sc.gc.ca/hppb/nhrdp
*Ph:* (613)954-8549
*Fax:* (613)954-7363

**• 2828 • Health Canada Research Personnel Career Awards** *(Postdoctorate, Professional Development/ Award, Fellowship)*

**Purpose:** To support investigators conducting research related to the interests of Health Canada and to allow Canadian scientists to study at other institutions, and to bring non-Canadian investigators to Canada. **Focus:** Public Health, Health Care Service. **Qualif.:** For awards available to postdoctorals, scholars, and scientists, applicant must be a Canadian citizen or a permanent resident. Candidate must be a qualified investigator who has a Ph.D. or equivalent research doctorate in a research field closely associated with public health or health services, or an M.D./D.D.S. and a master's degree. Awards are tenable at Canadian Research centers with active health services or public health research programs. Applicant must be a Canadian citizen or permanent resident for Group II Awards. There is no restriction or citizenship for Group I Awards. **Criteria:** Based on candidate's professional standing, academic qualifications, evidence of proven or potential

ability to conduct health research, and the appropriateness of the centers in which the work was performed.

**Funds Avail.:** Stipend and benefits, commensurate with experience, plus research and travel allowances **To Apply:** Write for application form and Career Awards Guide. **Deadline:** July 31. **Contact:** Information Officer at the above address (see entry 2827).

**• 2829 • Health Canada Research Personnel Training Awards (Regular Program)** *(Doctorate, Graduate/Fellowship)*

**Purpose:** To provide support to highly qualified individuals who wish to undertake full-time training leading to a M.Sc or a Ph.D. in areas related to Health Canada's research priorities. **Focus:** Public Health, Health Services. **Qualif.:** Applicants must be Canadian citizens or legally landed immigrants and hold an Honours Bachelors's (or equivalent) or a health professional degree, or already be engaged in a Master's or Ph.D. program. Preference will be given to candidates seeking training in Canada. Ph.D. candidates that can fully justify that a similar program is not available anywhere in Canada will be considered. **Criteria:** Based on academic history, choice of program, research and professional experiences, career plans, and references.

**Funds Avail.:** Stipend of $16,800/year and a travel and training allowance of $1,200/year. **To Apply:** Write for Training Awards Guide and application kit. **Deadline:** March 1. **Contact:** Information Resource Officer at the above address (see entry 2827).

---

**• 2830 •**

## Health Research Council of New Zealand

PO Box 5541
Wellesley Street
Auckland, New Zealand
*Ph:* 9 3798 227
*Fax:* 9 3779 988

**• 2831 • HRC Postdoctoral Fellowship** *(Postdoctorate/Fellowship)*

**Purpose:** To support outstanding postdoctoral students conducting research of interest to HRC. **Focus:** Health Sciences. **Qualif.:** Applicant may be of any nationality, but must hold a Ph.D. or equivalent, (or have submitted the thesis at the time of application). Applicants must have no more than three years experience at the postdoctoral level. Fellowships are tenable at New Zealand universities, hospitals, or other research institutions approved by the Council. Fellows may accept limited remuneration from the host institution and are required to submit, to the council, an annual report as well as a final report within 28 days of completion of the Fellowship. **Criteria:** Applicants are judged on academic qualifications and quality of proposal.

**Funds Avail.:** NZ$37,400-41,600/year, plus a limited allowance, including return airfare. **No. of Awards:** Varies. **To Apply:** Write to the Administrative Officer for application form and guidelines. Application must contain an overview of research undertaken within the past two years, a confidential report written by the applicant's current and/or doctoral supervisor (to be submitted directly to the Council), a confidential report written by the applicant's proposed Fellowship supervisor (to be submitted directly to the Council), an outline of the Fellowship proposal, and a description of funds available or being sought for the research. **Deadline:** April 1 and August 15.

**Remarks:** Applicants are strongly encouraged also to apply for the HRC Project Grant, a Public Health Research Limited Budget Grant, Maori Health Research Grant, or South Pacific Health Research Committee Grant (deadlines June 1, February 1, June 1 and September 1, respectively). **Contact:** Ms. Tracey Monehan at the above address (see entry 2830).

## • 2832 •

## Healthcare Information and Management Systems Society

840 N. Lake Shore Dr.
Chicago, IL 60611                    Ph: (312)280-6148
URL: http://www.himss.org/

### • 2833 • Richard P. Covert Scholarships (Doctorate, Graduate, Undergraduate/Scholarship)

**Purpose:** To encourage scholarship by students in the fields of health care information and management systems. **Focus:** Healthcare Information, Hospital Administration, and related fields. **Qualif.:** Candidate may be of any nationality. Applicant must be enrolled in an accredited undergraduate or graduate program related to health care information or management systems, such as management engineering, operations research, computer science and information systems, mathematics, business administration, or hospital administration. Candidate must be a student member of HIMSS or apply for membership. Normally, one scholarship is reserved for a graduate student and one for an undergraduate.

**Funds Avail.:** $1,000; plus all-expense-paid trip to the HIMSS annual conference. **To Apply:** Write to HIMSS for application form and guidelines. Submit form with transcripts, technical paper and/or essay, completed federal student financial aid form, and a faculty recommendation. Application for membership, including dues, may accompany the scholarship application. **Deadline:** October 15. Notification by mid-January. **Contact:** Director at the above address (see entry 2832).

## • 2834 •

## U.S. Senate Youth Program - William Randolph Hearst Foundation

90 New Montgomery St., Ste. 1212        Ph: (415)543-4057
San Francisco, CA 94105-4504            Fax: (415)243-0760
                                        Free: 800-841-7048

### • 2835 • United States Senate Youth Program (High School/Scholarship)

**Purpose:** To bring high school students to Washington, D.C. for one week for an on-site introduction to the functions of the federal government and, in particular, the United States Senate. **Qualif.:** Applicants must be high school juniors or seniors currently serving in an elected capacity in any one of the following student offices: student body president, vice president, secretary, or treasurer; class president, vice president, secretary, or treasurer; student council representative; or a student representative to district, regional, or state-level civic or educational organization. Students must be permanent residents of the United States and currently enrolled in a public or private secondary school located in the state in which either of their parents or guardians legally reside. Exceptions are made for Department of Defense (DoD) Dependent Schools' students and Interstate Compacts. **Criteria:** Selection is based solely on the outstanding ability and demonstrated qualities of leadership as elected high school student body officers. Two students from each state, the District of Columbia, and the Department of Defense Dependents Schools Overseas will be chosen as delegates by the Head of the Department of Education in each state.

**Funds Avail.:** The foundation will pay for all expenses of the Washington Week including transportation, hotel, and meals. In addition, a $2,000 scholarship will be presented to each delegate during the visit. **No. of Awards:** 104. **Deadline:** Late September or early October. **Contact:** High school principals, chief state school officers, or the Washington, D.C. Office of DoD schools for detailed application information.

## • 2836 •

## William Randolph Hearst Foundation

Journalism Awards Program            Ph: (415)543-6033
90 New Montgomery St., Ste. 1212     Fax: (415)243-0760
San Francisco, CA 94105              Free: 800-243-0760

### • 2837 • Hearst Foundation Journalism Writing Competition (Undergraduate/Award)

**Purpose:** To provide support, encouragement, and assistance to undergraduate journalism students. **Focus:** The competition is open to Journalism and Mass Communication majors only. **Qualif.:** Only undergraduate students enrolled in member colleges and universities of the Association of Schools of Journalism and Mass Communication are eligible. Entrants must be full-time undergraduate journalism majors at the time the entries are produced and submitted. Students who have had full-time professional newspaper or broadcast news experience, or its equivalent, for one year or more, are not eligible. **Criteria:** Selection is based on knowledge of subject, understandability, clarity, color, reporting in depth, and construction.

**Funds Avail.:** Awards range from $1,000 to $5,000. **No. of Awards:** 125 yearly. **To Apply:** Only students attending participating schools are eligible. Entry forms and rules are available through each school's Department of Journalism. **Deadline:** Deadlines for submission are monthly from October to March. **Contact:** Jan C. Watten at the above address (see entry 2836)for applications, guidelines, deadlines, and additional information.

## • 2838 •

## Heart and Stroke Foundation of Canada

222 Queen St. 1402                   Ph: (613)241-4361
Ottawa, ON, Canada K1P 5V9           Fax: (613)234-3278
URL: http://www.hsf.ca/

### • 2839 • HSFC Career Investigator Awards (Doctorate/Award)

**Focus:** Medicine, Medicine-Cardiology, Medical Research. **Qualif.:** The Career Investigator Award of the Heart and Stroke Foundation of Ontario is awarded to individuals with an M.D. or Ph.D. degree, or the equivalent, who hold a peer-reviewed Grant-in-Aid from the Heart and Stroke Foundation of Ontario or other research granting body, and who are established and recognized independent research workers in the field of cardiovascular and/or cerebrovascular disease and wish to make research in these fields a full-time career. Such individuals would be expected to have achieved national recognition at the time of the first application and to have achieved international stature at the time of the first renewal application. Individuals must be proposed by a university or an affiliated institution, which must guarantee career investigators an appropriate academic rate, and provide adequate space and facilities for their research commensurate with the status of the individuals in terms of experience and level of support by the Foundation. A letter must be provided by the Dean, the Chairperson of the department, and, where applicable, the Chief of Service of the hospital stating that the applicant will have 75% of his/her time allocated to research. Details as to how this 75% allocation of research time will be spent must be provided, as well as commitments in the remaining 25%. No more than ten years should have elapsed from completion of research training (first faculty appointment) and receipt of this award. The award is intended for individuals who have just completed the five-year scholarship or equivalent research experience. Applications from more senior individuals will be considered at the first renewal level (having achieved international recognition for their research) and the length of support will be at the discretion of the Committee. More senior individuals such as full Professors, Department Chairs, or Division Heads will be eligible for only one five-year

## Heart and Stroke Foundation of Canada *(continued)*

term, and the application will be considered at the first or second renewal level. Normally, this award is given to prior recipients of Research Scholarships (Heart and Stroke Foundation of Canada, Heart and Stroke Foundation of Ontario, Medical Research Council, or other funding agencies of equivalent stature) once the recipient has achieved the requisite standing as an independent investigator. The Award is a special program of the HSFO and is tenable in the Province of Ontario only.

**Funds Avail.:** The initial salary will depend on the individual's experience and qualifications. Career Investigators may apply for funds allowing them to visit other laboratories, if necessary, in the pursuit of their research. Such a visit may last for a period not to exceed one year. **To Apply:** The initial application must include a letter from the sponsoring institution appraising the candidate and the proposed research, a description of the nature and extent of any work to be carried out by the awardee apart from the research activity, and the amount and source of any income to be paid supplementary to the award. An abstract and a detailed description of the proposed research is required, and should include the objective(s), rationale, methodology, current progress, and potential significance of the intended work. New applicants should demonstrate that the research has been of high quality and significance and has received at least national recognition. In addition, three letters attesting to this national recognition should be provided. **Deadline:** September 1. The award will commence the following July 1. **Contact:** Mark Taylor, National Coordinator, Research Administration, at the above address (see entry 2838).

### • 2840 • HSFC Graduate Research Traineeships
*(Graduate, Postgraduate/Internship)*

**Purpose:** To support graduate training in the cardiovascular/cerebrovascular disease, and health education fields. **Focus:** Cardiology/Cerebrovascular Disease. **Qualif.:** Candidate should preferably be a Canadian citizen or resident. Applicant must be a graduate student with a B.Sc., M.Sc., or equivalent degree, who is undertaking full-time training research in one of the areas of study listed above. Candidate must be admitted to an approved institution before the start of the traineeship. Research must be supervised by a qualified faculty member.

**Funds Avail.:** $15,295. **To Apply:** Write to HSCF for a junior personnel application form and guidelines. Submit four copies of the form with transcripts and a research plan written by the project supervisor. Letters of recommendation from the supervisor and three other professors are also required. **Deadline:** November 15. **Contact:** Jeanne Salo, Research Department, at the above address (see entry 2838).

### • 2841 • HSFC Junior Personnel Medical Scientist Traineeships *(Doctorate/Internship)*

**Purpose:** To support outstanding candidates through medical school. It is expected to bring scientifically trained people and those with potential for independent research into a medical program in order to produce outstanding cardiovascular scientists. **Focus:** Medicine, Medicine-Cardiology, Medical Research. **Qualif.:** The candidate should not be more than 35 years of age upon entry into the program. Arrangement must be made with the institution for an appropriate training or research program and the institution or department must be fully aware of its responsibilities. **Criteria:** Priority will be given to those who have conducted independent research.

**Funds Avail.:** The number of Medical Scientists in the program will be limited. All Medical Scientists will be paid a stipend related to their qualifications at entry and not on the basis of seniority. Applicants with Ph.D. degrees receive a stipend starting at $16,237; those without the degree start at $15,295. On submission of receipts, fees and books will be paid for. When independent research is carried out, and if a Grant in Aid application is not appropriate, consideration will be given to a request for limited research support from the sponsor (by letter). **To Apply:** A

complete Junior Personnel application is required. It is expected that the Medical Scientist will carry out research related to the cardiovascular/cerebrovascular field during the M.D. training. To evaluate the program, the following are required: time requirements of the medical course, time available for research, and research protocol describing the work to be undertaken. **Deadline:** November 15. **Contact:** Mr. Mark Taylor, National Coordinator, Research Administration, at the above address (see entry 2838).

### • 2842 • HSFC Nursing Research Fellowships
*(Doctorate, Graduate/Fellowship)*

**Purpose:** To support Canadian nurses seeking higher degrees relevant to cardiovascular/cerebrovascular nursing. **Focus:** Nursing-Cardiovascular and cerebrovascular. **Qualif.:** Applicants must be qualified nurses wishing to study and/or conduct research leading to a master's or Ph.D. degree. Candidates entering a degree program, as well as those at the second- and third-year level, are eligible to apply. Awards are tenable at institutions worldwide, however, justification is needed for study abroad and fellows who study abroad must return to Canada upon completion of the award tenure. Fellows must dedicate at least 75% of their time to training, development, and research in the cardiovascular/cerebrovascular field. Purely clinical non-research or educational fellowships are not awarded. **Criteria:** Applications are evaluated on the quality of the applicant (academic record, letters of recommendation, performance to date), the academic program, duration, and setting, and the quality of the content of the plan of study for those entering a Master's or Ph.D. program or the quality of the content of the research proposal for those entering the second, or higher, year of a Master's or the third year of a Ph.D. study. Each application is considered a joint effort by the applicant and the university program. The assessment of the quality of the applicant is primary, but for nurses with less than two years research experience, assessment of the plan of study, academic program, and potential for research training takes precedence over the proposed research project.

**Funds Avail.:** $26,790 **To Apply:** Write to HSFC for application guidelines. Submit transcripts; a letter of support from the sponsor at the host institution appraising the candidate and the proposed research, describing the nature and extent of any work to be carried out by the awardee apart from the research activity, and telling the amount and source of any income to be paid supplementary to the award; three additional letters of recommendation, preferably from professors; five key words which identify the research project, and a research proposal of no more than 600 words. **Deadline:** November 15. The award will commence on July 1. **Contact:** Jeanne Salo, Research Department

### • 2843 • HSFC PhD Research Traineeships
*(Doctorate, Postdoctorate/Internship)*

**Purpose:** To encourage students enrolled in a Ph.D. program to acquire research training and become cardiovascular/cerebrovascular scientists. **Focus:** Medicine-Cardiovascular, Medicine-Cerebrovascular. **Qualif.:** Applicants must be enrolled in a Ph.D. program at the time of activation of the award. Priority will be given to candidates who have conducted independent research. Awards are tenable at medical schools that have adequate supporting facilities and a commitment to cardiovascular/cerebrovascular research. Applicant must arrange an appropriate training or research program in cardiovascular/cerebrovascular science at the host institution. **Criteria:** Applications will be evaluated on the quality of the applicant (academic record, letters of recommendation, etc.), the research environment (supervisor, department, etc.), and the quality of the research project.

**Funds Avail.:** $15,295. **To Apply:** Applicants must submit a completed Junior Personnel application form, academic transcripts, letters of recommendation from three professors or instructors under whom the candidate has studied or taken training, and a research plan written by the supervisor in full consultation with the applicant. A letter from the supervisor must be included, accepting the candidate and providing an overview of the training environment, resources, and programs which will be made available to the candidate and containing a description of the nature and extent of any work to be carried out by the awardee apart from the research activity. **Deadline:** November 15.

**Remarks:** Ontario and British Columbia residents may need to follow slightly different application procedures. Write to the HSFC national address listed above or contact the provincial chapter for further information. **Contact:** Jeanne Salo, Research Department

• 2844 • **HSFC Research Fellowships** *(Postdoctorate/ Fellowship)*

**Purpose:** To encourage young investigators to initiate and/or continue training in the scientific method. **Focus:** Medicine-Cardiovascular, Medicine-Cerebrovascular. **Qualif.:** Applicants must have completed a Ph.D., M.D., or D.V.M. degree before the start of the fellowship year. Individuals wishing to undertake postdoctoral training with their Ph.D. supervisor or in the same department in which they received their postdoctoral training are ineligible. Awards are normally tenable at Canadian research institutions but may, under exceptional circumstances and only for Canadian citizens, be awarded for study abroad. At least 75% of the awardee's time must be spent in research. The remaining time should be spent in departmental activities at the host institution that contribute to development as a research worker. Clinical non-research, residency-type fellowships (traineeships) are not awarded. **Criteria:** Applications are evaluated on the quality of the applicant (academic record, letters of recommendation, performance to date), the research environment and the person with whom the applicant intends to work, and the quality of the research project.

**Funds Avail.:** $26,790-42,585 **To Apply:** Write to HSFC for a junior personnel application form and guidelines. Submit four copies of the form with transcripts and a research plan written jointly by applicant and supervisor. A letter from the research supervisor providing an overview of the training environment, resources, and programs available to the applicant, and describing the nature and extent of any work to be carried out by the awardee apart from the research activity must be included, and three other professors are also required. **Deadline:** November 15. The award commences on July 1. **Contact:** Jeanne Salo, Research Department

• 2845 • **HSFC Research Scholarships** *(Postdoctorate/Scholarship)*

**Purpose:** To recognize and encourage individuals who have clearly demonstrated excellence during their predoctoral and postdoctoral training in cardiovascular or cerebrovascular research. **Focus:** Medicine-Cardiovascular, Medicine-Cerebrovascular. **Qualif.:** Applicant must be a Canadian citizen or resident. Candidate must have an M.D., Ph.D., or an equivalent degree and/or experience. Applicant must have completed research training within the five years prior to the application date, and must have the potential to become an independent investigator during a period of supervised research. Candidate must have the sponsorship of the host institution before submitting application; such sponsorship indicates a definite interest by the institution in the future career of the scholar. Awards are tenable at Canadian institutions. Scholars must dedicate at least 75% of their time to research. Awards are for scholar's stipend only. The scholar must hold a grant-in-aid in support of the proposed research; the grant may be from the HSFC or another granting institution. Scholarships are contingent upon the success of the grant-in-aid application.

**Funds Avail.:** $42,015-53,305/year. **To Apply:** Write to HSFC for a senior personnel application form and guidelines. Submit form with transcripts; a letter of support from sponsoring department head; an abstract of proposed research; a detailed research proposal; copies of related grant-in-aid applications; and three letters of recommendation from professors who supervised previous research training. **Deadline:** September 1.

**Remarks:** The awardee with the highest scientific rating in the Research Scholarship competition will be the recipient of the McDonald Scholarship. This award carries an additional research grant of $15,000 in the first year of tenure. **Contact:** Jeanne Salo, Research Department, at the above address (see entry 2838).

• 2846 • **HSFC Senior Personnel Research Scholarship/McDonald Scholarship** *(Postdoctorate/ Scholarship)*

**Purpose:** To assist qualified individuals to become established as fully independent investigators in the field of cerebrovascular, cardiovascular, or health education research. The Research Scholarship is the senior award offered by the HSFC to individuals who have clearly demonstrated excellence during their pre-doctoral and post-doctoral training in cardiovascular, stroke, or health education research. Research Scholars must have demonstrated the potential to become independent investigators during a period of supervised research. **Qualif.:** The applicant must have an M.D., Ph.D., or equivalent degree. No more than five years should have elapsed from completion of research training and application for this award. The Scholarship is not intended as an "in-training" award. The Research Scholar must hold at the time of this award a Grant-in-Aid in support of the proposed research; such grant(s) could be from this and/or other granting agencies. The Scholarship award is contingent upon the success of the Grant-in-Aid application. In case of a cooperative grant, the applicant must delineate specifically his or her contribution to the overall research project. An awardee is not permitted to hold another major award at the same time. **Criteria:** The scientific merit of the proposed research will receive equal weight with the merit of the applicant in the evaluation of the application. Therefore, a clear, concise, and comprehensive description of the proposed research must be given.

**Funds Avail.:** The initial stipend will depend on the qualifications and experience of the applicant. Annual increments will be provided on the basis of the Scholar's performance. The stipends range from $44,660 to $53,305. An amount of up to $1,500 per annum is available for travel for scientific purposes. Additionally, the awardee receiving the highest scientific rating in the Research Scholarship competition will be awarded the McDonald Scholarship. The McDonald Scholar will be awarded a research grant of $15,000 in addition to the stipend. **To Apply:** Applicants must complete the Senior Personnel Application Form (HSFC R2). Applications should include a transcript of the applicant's record with standing. Also included should be a letter from the sponsoring department head appraising the candidate and the proposed research and a description of the nature and extent of any work to be carried out by the awardee apart from the research activity. Also required are recommendations and evaluations from three professors or instructors with whom the candidate has taken training. An abstract and a detailed description of the proposed research must be submitted, and should include the objective(s), background, rationale, methodology, and potential significance of the intended work. An appropriate Grant in Aid research proposal, including references, should be attached to each copy of the scholarship application. A copy of any related Grant in Aid application, whether it be new or ongoing, must accompany each copy of the scholarship application. **Deadline:** The deadline for applications is September 1.

**Remarks:** The appointment will be for a period of five years. The Scholarship cannot be renewed for a second term. The Research Scholar will be considered an employee of the university or institution and monies granted as stipend will be paid to the institution for payment to the awardee. The Scholar will enjoy all the benefits of a full-time member of the staff with respect to pension, insurance, and other plans. The employer's share of any such plans will be paid by the sponsoring institution. This award will normally commence July 1 and the appointee will devote the ensuing five years to the object(s) of the award. This period will include holiday time as per University policy. An appointment may be terminated at any time for good cause by the awardee, the sponsoring institution, or the HSFC. During tenure of this award, the successful candidate may not sit for specialty qualifying

*Heart and Stroke Foundation of Canada (continued)*
examination without permission from the HSFC. **Contact:** Mr. Mark Taylor, National Coordinator, Research Administration, at the above address (see entry 2838).

**• 2847 • HSFC Visiting Scientist Program**
*(Professional Development/Award)*

**Purpose:** To encourage cardiovascular/cerebrovascular scientists to visit other institutions. **Focus:** Cardiovascular/Cerebrovascular disease. **Qualif.:** Applicant may be of any nationality. Candidate must be a senior investigator whose contribution and visit will be mutually rewarding to the host institution and the visiting scientist. Awards to Canadians are tenable at any institution worldwide (other than their own employer); awards to non-Canadians must be used at Canadian institutions.

**Funds Avail.:** $1,000/month maximum, plus traveling expenses for awardee and immediate family. **To Apply:** Write to HSFC for the visiting scientist application form and guidelines. Submit form with a research proposal and a letter of invitation from the host institution. **Deadline:** September 1. **Contact:** Jeanne Salo, Research Department, at the above address (see entry 2838).

**• 2848 •**
**Hebrew University of Jerusalem - Institute of Jewish Studies**
Joseph and Ceil Mazer Center for
  Humanities
Rm. 4110, Mount Scopus          *Ph:* 2 883504 6
Jerusalem, Israel                *Fax:* 2 322 545

**• 2849 • Moritz and Charlotte Warbourg Research Fellowships** *(Postdoctorate/Fellowship)*

**Purpose:** To encourage research in Jewish studies at the University. **Focus:** Jewish Studies. **Qualif.:** Applicant may be of any nationality. Candidate must be a postdoctoral scholar under the age of 35 years; preference is given to scholars under 30 years. Fellowships are tenable at the Hebrew University.

**Funds Avail.:** Varies. **No. of Awards:** 3-5. **To Apply:** Write to the secretariat for application materials. **Deadline:** January 4.

**Remarks:** Several other organizations offer scholarships tenable at the Hebrew University and/or the Rothberg School at the University to citizens of specific countries. Canadian citizens should consult the Canadian Friends of the Hebrew University. In Australia, write: Australian Friends of the Hebrew University; 584 St. Kilda Road; Melbourne, Victoria 3004; Australia (phone 3-51-6921 or 3-529-4611). In the United Kingdom, contact: Friends of the Hebrew University; 3 St. John's Wood Road; London NW8 8RB; England. In South Africa, the address is: South African Friends of the Hebrew University; 86 Eloff Street, Royal St. Mary's Building; P.O. Box 4316; Johannesburg 2000; South Africa (phone 23-6632 or 23-6668). Students should also refer to the Lady Davis Fellowship Trust or contact the Jewish Agency office or Israel Aliyah Center in home country for other potential sources of funding for attending the Hebrew University. **Contact:** Secretariat at the above address (see entry 2848).

**• 2850 •**
**Hebrew University of Jerusalem - Office of Academic Affairs**
11 E. 69th St.
New York, NY 10021              *Ph:* (212)472-2288
*URL:* http://www1.huji.ac.il/www_dir/dafault_e.html

**• 2851 • Scholarships for Study in Israel** *(Doctorate, Graduate, Undergraduate/Scholarship)*

**Purpose:** To assist American students who wish to attend the University in Israel. **Focus:** General Studies. **Qualif.:** Applicant must be a U.S. citizen. Candidate may either be a graduate or undergraduate student who wishes to attend the Hebrew University in Jerusalem. Scholarships, grants, and awards are offered for specific areas of study and for candidates from particular regions; education requirements and age limitations vary for each individual award. Write for a list of awards and further information. Awards are tenable at the Hebrew University and/or the Rothberg School for Overseas Students at the University.

**Funds Avail.:** Varies by program. **To Apply:** Write to the Financial Aid Officer for application form and guidelines. Candidate must also apply for admission to the University. **Deadline:** Varies.

**Remarks:** Several organizations in other countries offer scholarships tenable at the Hebrew University and/or the Rothberg School at the University. For more details, see one of the following entries: Canadian Friends of the Hebrew University or the Lady Davis Fellowship Trust. **Contact:** Financial Aid Officer at the above address (see entry 2850).

**• 2852 •**
**Hebrew University of Jerusalem - Office of University Grants**
PO Box 1255
Jerusalem, Israel              *Ph:* 2 882111

**• 2853 • Hebrew University Postdoctoral Fellowships** *(Postdoctorate/Fellowship)*

**Purpose:** To support postdoctoral studies research at the University. **Focus:** General Studies. **Qualif.:** Candidate may be of any nationality. Applicant must have completed doctoral dissertation within the three years prior to the application deadline. Award is tenable at the Hebrew University.

**Funds Avail.:** $1,000/month, plus $150-250/month rent allowance and round-trip airfare to Jerusalem. **To Apply:** Write to the Office of University Grants for application form and guidelines. **Deadline:** November 30. Notification in February or March.

**Remarks:** Several other organizations offer scholarships tenable at the Hebrew University and/or the Rothberg School at the University to citizens of specific countries. Canadian citizens should consult the Canadian Friends of the Hebrew University, 3080 Yonge St., Ste. 502, Toronto, Ontario, M4N 3P4, Canada. In Australia, write: Australian Friends of the Hebrew University, 584 St. Kilda Road, Melbourne, Victoria 3004; Australia (phone 3-51-6921 or 3-529-4611). In the United Kingdom, contact: Friends of the Hebrew University, 3 St. John's Wood Road, London NW8 8RB, England. In South Africa, the address is: South African Friends of the Hebrew University; 86 Eloff Street, Royal St. Mary's Building, P.O. Box 4316; Johannesburg 2000; South Africa (phone 23-6632 or 23-6668). In the United States, contact: American Friends of the Hebrew University of Jerusalem, 11 E. 69th St., New York, NY 10021 (phone (212)472-9800). **Contact:** Yoel Alpert, Academic Secretary, at the above address (see entry 2852).

**• 2854 •**

## Heed Ophthalmic Foundation

c/o Froncie Gutman, MD
Dept. of Ophthalmology
Cleveland Clinic Foundation
9500 Euclid Ave.
Cleveland, OH 44195

*Ph:* (216)445-8145
*Fax:* (216)444-9137

**• 2855 • Heed Ophthalmic Foundation Fellowships**
*(Postgraduate/Fellowship)*

**Purpose:** To provide assistance to promising men and women of exceptional ability who desire to further their education in the field of diseases and surgery of the eye or to conduct research work and investigation in ophthalmology. **Focus:** Medical Research, Opthamology. **Qualif.:** Applicants must be U.S. citizens and graduates of a medical school accredited by the American Medical Association. Recipients must agree to pursue their education or to conduct research in the United States. **Criteria:** Preference is given to candidates who complete the training requirements of the American Board of Opthalmology and wish additional training in a particular phase of a specialty.

**Funds Avail.:** $15,000 per year. **To Apply:** Applicant must submit application form, a minimum of three letters of recommendation, and a list of publications. **Deadline:** January 15.

**• 2856 •**

## Heiser Program for Research in Leprosy

450 East 63rd St.
New York, NY 10021

*Ph:* (212)751-6233
*Fax:* (212)688-6794

**• 2857 • Heiser Postdoctoral Research Fellowships**
*(Postdoctorate/Fellowship)*

**Purpose:** To support young biomedical scientists in beginning postdoctoral training for research in leprosy and tuberculosis. **Focus:** Leprosy, Tuberculosis. **Qualif.:** Candidate may be of any nationality. Applicant must have a Ph.D., M.D., or equivalent degree. Candidate may be of any age, but should be at an early stage of postdoctoral training. The fellowship is tenable at any institution other than that at which the awardee obtained his/her doctorate. The fellow must undertake research training directly related to the study of leprosy. Successful candidates for U.S.-based fellowships will be paid through the host institutions. Foreign-based fellows will be paid the stipend directly in quarterly installments.

**Funds Avail.:** $25,000-28,000 stipend, plus airfare to training location, $2,000 training allowance, and up to $1,500 for health insurance. **To Apply:** There is no application form; write to the director for guidelines. Submit five copies of curriculum vitae and selected bibliography on relevant topics; summary of research experience; detailed description of proposed research; specific plans for the application of knowledge and experience gained through the fellowship; name of supervisor and laboratory where fellowship is to be held, and letter of acceptance from proposed supervisor. Three referees must send letters of recommendation directly to the Program. **Deadline:** February 1. Notification by May 1. **Contact:** Barbara M. Hugonnet, Director, at the above address (see entry 2856).

**• 2858 • Heiser Research Grants** *(Postdoctorate/ Grant)*

**Purpose:** To provide support for leprosy and tuberculosis research. **Focus:** Leprosy, Tuberculosis. **Qualif.:** Candidate may be of any nationality. Applicant must be a senior investigator who is experienced in leprosy research and associated with a laboratory providing training opportunities in this field. Awards are tenable at the home institution. Proposed research project must be clearly related to leprosy. Start-up funds may be offered for new projects or facilities which show promise of receiving support from other sources within one year and of contributing to leprosy research. No more than 10% of the grant may be used for institutional overhead. Awards are not offered for clinical trials or salaries of personnel.

**Funds Avail.:** $30,000 maximum. **To Apply:** There is no application form; write to the director for guidelines. Submit five copies of curriculum vitae, relevant bibliography, research proposal, and budget. **Deadline:** February 1. Notification by May 1. **Contact:** Barbara M. Hugonnet, Director, at the above address (see entry 2856).

**• 2859 •**

## Charles R. Hemenway Scholarship Trust

c/o Hawaiian Trust Company, Ltd.
Box 3170
Honolulu, HI 96802

**• 2860 • Charles R. Hemenway Scholarship**
*(Undergraduate/Scholarship)*

**Focus:** General studies. **Qualif.:** Applicants must be undergraduates at the University of Hawaii or University of Hawaii community colleges who are enrolled at least half-time. **Criteria:** Awards are made based on financial need, academic progress and good citizenship. Preference is given to Hawaii residents.

**Funds Avail.:** $200 - $2,000 per award. **No. of Awards:** Varies. **To Apply:** Applicants must submit application through the University or Hawaii or Hawaii community college financial aid offices. **Contact:** Charles R. Hemenway Scholarship Trust at the above address (see entry 2859).

**• 2861 •**

## Herb Society of America, Inc.

9019 Kirtland Chardon Rd.
Kirtland, OH 44094
*E-mail:* herbsociet@aol.com
*URL:* http://www.herbsociety.org

*Ph:* (440)256-0514
*Fax:* (440)256-0541

**• 2862 • Herb Society Research Grants** *(Doctorate, Graduate/Grant)*

**Purpose:** To further the knowledge and use of herbs and to contribute the results of the study and research to the records of horticulture, science, literature, history, art, and/or economics. **Focus:** Herbs. **Qualif.:** Candidate may be of any nationality. Applicant must wish to conduct graduate-level research specifically on herbs. Grants are not offered for financial aid to individuals or personal travel. Grants are tenable in locations and formats which can be monitored by the grant committee chair, consultants, or designees.

**Funds Avail.:** $5,000 maximum. **No. of Awards:** Varies. **To Apply:** Write to the research grant committee chair for application form and guidelines. Submit five copies of form with 500-word proposal and a budget. Selected candidates will be interviewed. **Deadline:** January 31. Grants are announced by May 1. **Contact:** Research Grant Committee Chair at the above address (see entry 2861).

• 2863 •
## Herpetologists' League
c/o Secretary
Department of Biology
University of Richmond
Richmond, VA 23173          Ph: (804)289-8234
URL: http://128.97.40.127/Jerod/HL.html

• 2864 • **Herpetologists' League Best Student Paper**
*(Graduate/Award)*

**Purpose:** Awards the students presenting the best oral paper at the Herpetologists' League's annual meetings. **Focus:** Life Sciences, Zoology, Herpetelology. **Qualif.:** Student must be the senior author of the paper, must be a student at the time of presentation, and must be a member of the Herpetologists' League. **Criteria:** Selection is based on the quality of presentation and the importance of the scientific research.

**Funds Avail.:** $500 is awarded to the winning paper. **No. of Awards:** 1 annually. **To Apply:** Applicant must fill out registration form for the annual meeting and indicate entry in competition, as well as submit and expanded abstract before the meeting to the panel of judges. **Deadline:** Dependent upon meeting date. **Contact:** President of the society, at the above address (see entry 2863).

• 2865 •
## Fannie and John Hertz Foundation
Box 5032
Livermore, CA 94551-5032          Ph: (925)373-1642
E-mail: askhertz@aol.com
URL: http://www.hertzfoundation.org

• 2866 • **Hertz Foundation Graduate Fellowships**
*(Doctorate, Graduate/Fellowship)*

**Purpose:** To support graduate students with outstanding potential in the applied physical sciences related to the defense potential and technological status of the United States. **Focus:** Applied Physical Sciences, Engineering, Applied Mathematics. **Qualif.:** Candidates must be U.S. citizens or permanent residents, must have received a bachelor's degree by the start of proposed fellowship, and be enrolled in a program of graduate study leading to an advanced degree. Proposed field of graduate study must be concerned with applications of the physical sciences to problems, as contrasted with problems addressed in extending the basic physical sciences. Applicant's undergraduate preparation should have included at least one year of calculus and physics. Fellowships are tenable only at selected institutions in the United States; consult website or write to the Foundation for a list. A candidate who has been offered unique research opportunities at another institution and is not presently enrolled there, however, may petition the Foundation to hold the fellowship there. Grants are not offered to support studies leading to both Ph.D. and professional degrees, e.g., Ph.D./M.D.

**Funds Avail.:** $25,000 stipend per nine-month academic year, plus an educational allowance of up to $15,000 to the academic institution **No. of Awards:** 20-25 per year. **To Apply:** Applications become available from the website: www.hertzfoundation.org, beginning August 1 of each year. See website for full details. An interview may be required. **Deadline:** Second to the last Friday in October of each year. Notification is made by March 31. **Contact:** The Fannie and John Hertz Foundation at the above address (see entry 2865).

• 2867 •
## Hewlett-Packard Company Medical Products Group
3000 Minuteman Rd.
Mail Stop 210          Ph: (508)687-1501
Andover, MA 01810          Fax: (508)686-7262
URL: http://www.medical.hp.com

• 2868 • **HP/AACN Critical-Care Nursing Research Grants** *(Doctorate, Graduate/Grant)*

**Purpose:** To encourage further research in critical-care nursing. Preferred topics will address the information technology requirements of patient management in critical care. **Focus:** Nursing. **Qualif.:** Any registered nurse with current AACN membership may apply. **Criteria:** Applications are reviewed by a Selection Committee that includes AACN and Hewlett-Packard representatives.

**Funds Avail.:** The grant includes $30,000 in cash, $2,000 in travel expenses, an HP Vectra personal computer, HP LaserJet printer, and utility software. **No. of Awards:** 1 per year. **To Apply:** Applications must be requested from the Hewlett-Packard Co. **Deadline:** August 15. **Contact:** For specific questions about suitability of proposals, contact the American Association of Critical Care Nurses, Attn: Research Dept., 101 Columbia, Also Viejo, CA 92656. Toll-free telephone: 800-899-AACN. For applications, contact the Hewlett-Packard Co., Attn: Research Grant, at the above address (see entry 2867).

• 2869 •
## High Twelve International
c/o Wolcott Foundation, Inc.
3663 Lindell Blvd., Ste. 260
St. Louis, MO 63108          Ph: (314)487-3387
E-mail: roy.rasnake@juno.com
URL: http://darkstar.icdc.com/˜rrasnake/

• 2870 • **Wolcott Foundation Fellowships** *(Graduate/Fellowship)*

**Purpose:** To prepare young men and women who have a background in Masonic ideals for careers in U.S. Government service at the federal, state and local levels as well as in selected private sector international businesses. **Focus:** Government, International Affairs, International Business. **Qualif.:** Applicants must be admitted to graduate school at George Washington University (School of Business and Public Management or the Elliott School of International Affairs). **Criteria:** Leadership, academics, character, and masonic affiliation.

**Funds Avail.:** The maximum award covers tuition and fees for 36 credit hours (minimum covers 18 credit hours). Funds are deposited with the University Treasurer's Office for disbursement. The fellowship is considered a grant if, upon graduation, the recipient is employed for four years in a position as specified in the preceding section and approved by the trustees of the Wolcott Foundation. Relocation assistance loans of up to $1,800 (repayable after graduation) may be awarded on the basis of need to students moving to the Washington, D.C. area. **No. of Awards:** 10-12 annually. **To Apply:** Application requests must be made by February 1. Candidates must also file applications for university admission prior to February 1. **Deadline:** Completed fellowship applications must be received by the appropriate trustee prior to February 15. **Contact:** Beryl C. Franklin, PhD, 402 Beasley St., Monroe, LA 71203.

• **2871** •

## Higher Education Development Fund

2090 7th Ave., 10th Fl.
New York, NY 10027

• **2872** • **Herschel C. Price Scholarship**
(Undergraduate/Scholarship)

**Focus:** General Studies. **Qualif.:** Applicants must attend an accredited educational institution. **Criteria:** Awards are given based on financial need, academic record, and interviews. Preference is given to West Virginia residents attending West Virginia institutions.

**Funds Avail.:** Varies; approximately $140,000 annually. **No. of Awards:** 180.

• **2873** •

## Hilgenfeld Foundation for Mortuary Education

PO Box 4311
Fullerton, CA 92634

• **2874** • **Hilgenfeld Research and Publications Grants; Hilgenfeld Scholarship Grants** (Professional Development/Grant)

**Purpose:** To expand the knowledge and understanding of funeral service through education, research, and thanatology books publication. **Focus:** Mortuary Science, Thanatology. **Qualif.:** Applicants must be high school graduates or actively involved in the mortuary science industry. They must also be students pursuing a career in funeral service, or in the funeral service industry seeking a graduate degree. **Criteria:** A committee established by American Board of Funeral Service.

**Funds Avail.:** $250-10,000. **No. of Awards:** Approximately 30. **To Apply:** Write to the Foundation for guidelines. **Deadline:** None.

• **2875** •

## Orris C. Hirtzel Memorial Foundation

c/o Laurie Moritz
3 Mellon Bank Center, Rm. 4000          Ph: (412)234-0023
Pittsburgh, PA 15259                     Fax: (412)234-1073

• **2876** • **Orris C. and Beatrice Dewey Hirtzel Memorial Foundation Scholarship** (Undergraduate/ Scholarship)

**Focus:** General studies. **Qualif.:** Applicants must be residents of North East Borough, North East Township and Greenfield Township of Earie County, Pennsylvania, and the town of Ripley in Chautauqua County, New York. **To Apply:** Write for further details. **Contact:** Laurie Mortiz.

• **2877** •

## Hispanic Link News Service/Journalism Foundation

1420 N St., NW, Ste. 101          Ph: (202)234-0280
Washington, DC 20005              Fax: (202)234-4090
E-mail: zapoteco@aol.com

• **2878** • **Hispanic Link News Service Internships**
(Undergraduate/Internship)

**Purpose:** To provide an opportunity for talented Hispanics interested in pursuing careers in the media and to bring parity to the nation's newsrooms. **Focus:** Journalism. **Qualif.:** Applicants must have creative writing and reporting abilities (emphasis in English language) and potential, commitment to pursue journalism as a career, and general communication skills. Age and experience are not requirements and candidates may or may not be currently working as journalists. **Criteria:** Selection is based on the application form, essays, writing samples, and telephone interviews with the judging panel.

**Funds Avail.:** $20,000. **No. of Awards:** 2. **To Apply:** Applicants must fill out an application form and submit it with a short essay, writing samples, and a self-addressed, stamped envelope. **Deadline:** Varies. **Contact:** Patricia Guadalupe, telephone (202)234-0280.

• **2879** • **NAHJ Scholarships** (Graduate, Undergraduate/Scholarship)

**Purpose:** To support and encourage the study of journalism. **Focus:** Journalism. **Qualif.:** Applicants must be planning to enroll full time in college for the next school year and have a demonstrated interest in pursuing a career in journalism. High school seniors, college undergraduates, or graduate students majoring in print or broadcast journalism are eligible. **Criteria:** Academic excellence, a demonstrated interest in journalism as a career, and financial need.

**Funds Avail.:** $1,000 to $5,000. **No. of Awards:** 20-25. **To Apply:** Applicants must request an application in writing and enclose a self-addressed, stamped envelope. A completed application, along with transcript, resume (listing educational background, work history, awards, and journalism work), work samples, two reference letters, and an autobiographical essay must be submitted. **Deadline:** Entries must be postmarked no later than February 27.

• **2880** • **Mark Zambrano Scholarship** (Graduate, Undergraduate/Scholarship)

**Purpose:** To support and encourage students to pursue or continue the study of journalism. **Focus:** Journalism. **Qualif.:** Applicants must be college students majoring in print or broadcast journalism. **Criteria:** Based on academic excellence, a demonstrated interest in news media as a career, and financial need.

**Funds Avail.:** $1,000. **No. of Awards:** 1. **To Apply:** Applicants must submit: a completed application form, transcripts of grades, resume (listing educational background, work history, awards, and journalism work), three samples of their best journalism work, three letters of recommendations, an autobiographical essay, and a financial need statement. **Deadline:** January 31.

**Remarks:** This scholarship was established by the Chicago Tribune Foundation and NAHJ in memory of the Chicago Tribune general assignments reporter Mark Zambrano. **Contact:** Rebecca K. Finley at the above address (see entry 2877).

## • 2881 •
### Hispanic Office of Planning & Evaluation
165 Brookside Ave.  *Ph:* (617)524-8888
Boston, MA 02130  *Fax:* (617)524-4939
*E-mail:* hopename@aol.com

#### • 2882 • HOPE Scholarships *(Undergraduate/Scholarship)*

**Purpose:** To assist Latino and Latina college entrants from low-income families. **Qualif.:** Candidates must be Latinos and Latinas who have completed high school or the equivalent and are accepted for admission to an accredited Massachusetts college or university. They must also have a satisfactory educational background, possess a serious desire to pursue postsecondary education, demonstrate a commitment toward community development, and show financial need. **Criteria:** Selection is based on educational achievement and promise, leadership ability, and commitment toward the development of the Latino community.

**Funds Avail.:** $500. **No. of Awards:** 6. **To Apply:** Write a letter of request for application materials. **Deadline:** May 1.

**Remarks:** Scholarship funds released with proof of enrollment in PSE (college). Awards are not granted every year. **Contact:** Ofelia Pena/Lily Mendez-Morgan.

## • 2883 •
### Charles H. Hood Fund
500 Rutherford Ave.
Boston, MA 02129  *Ph:* (617)242-0600

#### • 2884 • Charles H. Hood Fund Scholarships *(Undergraduate/Scholarship)*

**Focus:** General Studies. **Qualif.:** Applicants must be sons and daughters of employees of H.P. Hood, Inc. There are two programs, one for high school seniors and one is for upperclassman.

**Funds Avail.:** $4,000 scholarships per year, per student, per program. **No. of Awards:** 3-4. **Deadline:** January 15. **Contact:** Prudence Dame, Executive Driector, at the above address (see entry 2883).

## • 2885 •
### Frances Hook Scholarship Fund
PO Box 597346  *Ph:* (847)673-2787
Chicago, IL 60659-7346  *Fax:* (847)673-2782
*E-mail:* chester@ma.ultranet.com
*URL:* http://www.thegiftgallery.com/FHOOK.HTM

#### • 2886 • Frances Hook Scholarship *(High School, Undergraduate/Scholarship)*

**Purpose:** To encourage young art students to pursue a career in two-dimensional art. **Focus:** Art—Two-dimensional, except Photography and sculpture. **Qualif.:** Applicants must be 24 years old or younger. High school students and college undergraduates are eligible.

**Funds Avail.:** $350-2,500 for art supplies and/or art-related course tuition. **No. of Awards:** 170. **To Apply:** Application forms, rules, and guidelines may be obtained by contacting the Frances Hook Scholarship Fund. **Deadline:** March 1.

**Remarks:** More than 4,000 students apply each year. **Contact:** W.L. Volchenboum at the above address (see entry 2885).

## • 2887 •
### Hoover Institution on War, Revolution and Peace
Stanford University  *Ph:* (650)723-3972
Stanford, CA 94305-6004  *Fax:* (650)723-1687
*E-mail:* Richard Hacken@byu.edu
*URL:* http://www-hoover.stanford.edu

#### • 2888 • Hoover Institution National Fellowships *(Postdoctorate/Fellowship)*

**Purpose:** To support postdoctoral research and writing on policy-related issues. **Focus:** U.S. Domestic and Foreign Policy and related disciplines, including Economics, Education, International Relations, Law, Modern History, Political Science, Sociology. **Qualif.:** Candidate may be of any nationality. Applicant must have a Ph.D. degree or its equivalent and three or four years of postdoctoral experience. Fellowships are tenable at the Hoover Institution. The fellow must undertake original research dealing with current and historical policy issues in domestic and foreign affairs, and leading to a publishable manuscript. Preference is given to proposals that consider important policy issues facing the United States today. Fellows are expected to participate in the activities of the Institution.

**Funds Avail.:** Varies, according to project. **No. of Awards:** Twelve. **To Apply:** Write to the executive secretary for application form and guidelines. Submit form with curriculum vitae; three or more letters of recommendation from leading U.S. scholars; copies of articles and books; a five- to ten-page detailed research proposal; and a working outline of the proposed manuscript with draft chapters, if available. **Deadline:** Second Monday in January. **Contact:** Dr. Thomas H. Henriksen, Executive Secretary, at the above address (see entry 2887).

## • 2889 •
### Herbert Hoover Presidential Library Association
PO Box 696  *Ph:* (319)643-5327
West Branch, IA 52358  *Fax:* (319)643-2391

#### • 2890 • Hoover Library Fellowships and Grants *(Graduate, Postdoctorate/Fellowship, Grant)*

**Purpose:** To encourage scholarly use of the holdings of the Hoover Presidential Library and to promote the study of the subjects of interest and concern to Herbert Hoover, Lou Henry Hoover, their associates, and other public figures as reflected in the Library's collections. **Focus:** History, American-Herbert Hoover, Lou Henry Hoover, Political Science, Journalism. **Qualif.:** Current graduate students, post-doctoral scholars, and qualified non-academic researchers are eligible to apply. Candidates may be of any nationality. Funds must be used for research trips to the Hoover Presidential Library. Potential candidates are urged to consult with the archival staff at 319-643-5301 concerning Hoover Library holdings. Written inquiries may be sent to PO Box 488, West Branch, IA 52358.

**Funds Avail.:** Although there is no specific dollar limit, these grants generally range up to $1500. The Library Association will consider larger requests for extended research at the Hoover Presidential Library. **No. of Awards:** Varies. **To Apply:** Call or write to the Fellowship and Grant committee chair for application form and guidelines. Submit form with a project proposal of not more than 1,200 words. **Deadline:** March 1. Awards are announced by May 1. **Contact:** Patricia A. Hand at the above address (see entry 2889).

**• 2891 •**
## Hopi Tribe Grants and Scholarship Program
PO Box 123                                    *Ph:* (520)734-3533
Kykotsmovi, AZ 86039                           *Fax:* (520)734-9575
                                               *Free:* 800-762-9630
*URL:* http://www.eerc.und.nodak.edu/cert/hopi.htm

### • 2892 • BIA Higher Education/Hopi Supplemental Grants *(Doctorate, Graduate, Postgraduate, Undergraduate/Grant)*

**Purpose:** To enable eligible Hopi students the opportunity to obtain their professional degrees with the hope that they will return to the reservation and provide care and expertise to the Hopi people. **Focus:** General Studies. **Qualif.:** Applicants must be **enrolled members of the Hopi Tribe** and be high school graduates or have earned their GED certificate. They must be admitted and enrolled at a regionally accredited college or university and pursuing a professional degree. Students pursuing vocational certification/diplomas are not eligible. They are also required to meet the minimum applicable grade point average listed as follows: entering freshmen must have a minimum 2.0 cumulative high school grade point average or a composite score of 45 percent on the GED; undergraduates must have a minimum 2.0 grade point average for all undergraduate coursework; graduates, post-graduates and professional degree students must be in good academic standing as defined by their university. Applicants must apply for all available funding sources before being considered for Hopi grants and must demonstrate financial need as determined by the school Financial Aid Office. Both full and part-time students are eligible to apply. **Criteria:** Grant is based on financial need. Eligible applicants who have completed files will be reviewed on a first-come first-serve basis.

**Funds Avail.:** Up to $2,500 per semester; up to $1,500 per summer session. Part-time students are eligible for books and tuition only; undergraduate students may be funded for a maximum of 10 semesters/15 quarters (no more than 5 terms can be funded at a community college); graduate students may be funded for a maximum of five semesters. **To Apply:** Applicants must first apply for Federal Aid and then must complete, sign, and submit a new application form for each academic year and a separate application for the summer session(s). They must submit the Financial Aid Analysis form to a school financial aid office and submit to the HTGSP a Certificate of Indian Blood form. They must also request their high school and college/university to submit official transcripts or GED scores to the HTGSP. Online transcripts are not considered official. **Deadline:** July 31 for fall semester; November 30 for spring semester; and April 30 for summer session.

### • 2893 • Educational Enrichment Grant *(All/Grant)*

**Focus:** General Studies. **Qualif.:** Applicants must be enrolled members of the Hopi Tribe and students who have been accepted to participate in special activities and events that offer unique opportunities to develop leadership/personal skills, or to acquire educational/preoccupational experiences. This grant is open to students from grade four through college. Additional qualifications are included in the application package.

**Funds Avail.:** $200 maximum. **To Apply:** Applicants are funded only once within the fiscal year. **Deadline:** Applications must be submitted at least two weeks prior to the date of activity.

### • 2894 • Hopi Scholarship *(Graduate, Postgraduate, Undergraduate/Scholarship)*

**Purpose:** To enable eligible Hopi students the opportunity to obtain their professional degrees with the hope that they will return to the reservation and provide care and expertise to the Hopi people. **Focus:** General Studies. **Qualif.:** Applicants must be enrolled members of the Hopi Tribe. Applicants must be high school graduates or have earned their GED certificate, and they must be admitted and enrolled full-time at a regionally accredited college or university and pursuing a professional degree. Students pursuing vocational certification/diplomas are not eligible. Entering freshmen must be in the top ten percent of their graduating class or score a minimum of 21 on the ACT test or 930 on the SAT test; undergraduates must have a minimum of 3.0 cumulative grade point average for all undergraduate coursework; graduates, post-graduates and professional degree students must have a minimum 3.2 cumulative grade point average for all graduate coursework. **Criteria:** Scholarship is based on academic excellence and applicants need not demonstrate financial need.

**Funds Avail.:** Up to $1,000 per semester and up to $2,000 per year. The number of terms funded follows: ten terms for undergraduates, five terms for graduates, and six terms for postgraduates. **To Apply:** Applicants first need to apply for Federal Aid and then must complete, sign, and submit an application form as well as a Certificate of Indian Blood form. They must also request their high school and college/university to submit official transcripts or GED scores to the HTGSP. Online transcripts are not considered official. Applicants must complete a statement reflecting their educational goals and plans. Graduate and postgraduate students, if not already on file, must provide written verification of admission from the graduate college and their specific program. **Deadline:** July 31.

### • 2895 • Private High School Scholarship *(High School/Scholarship)*

**Purpose:** To encourage Hopi students to achieve and maintain a high level of academic excellence. **Focus:** General Studies. **Qualif.:** Applicants must be enrolled members of the Hopi Tribe and enrolled and accepted in an accredited private high school. Entering freshmen must have a minimum 3.50 cumulative grade point average and continuing students must have a minimum 3.25 cumulative grade point average. Additional eligibility criteria is explained on the application form. **Criteria:** Scholarship is based on academic excellence.

**Funds Avail.:** $2,000 per year. **To Apply:** Applicants must submit their grade report or transcript to HTGSP within three weeks after the end of fall semester, maintain a minimum 3.25 cumulative GPA, and submit an official transcript within three weeks after the end of spring semester. They must also forward the official verification of admission to the private high school to be attended and three letters of recommendation. **Deadline:** July 31.

### • 2896 • Tuition/Book Scholarship *(Other, Undergraduate/Scholarship)*

**Purpose:** To award students who are pursuing post secondary education for reasons of career enhancement/change, and those who demonstrate zero financial need. **Focus:** General Studies. **Qualif.:** Applicants must be enrolled members of the Hopi Tribe and be high school graduates or have earned their GED certificate.

**Funds Avail.:** Up to $1,500 to be used for tuition and books. **To Apply:** Applicants first need to apply for Federal Aid and then must complete, sign, and submit an application form as well as a Certificate of Indian Blood form. They must also request their high school and college/university to submit official transcripts or GED scores to the HTGSP. Online transcripts are not considered official. Applicants must also complete a statement reflecting their educational goals and plans. **Deadline:** July 31 for the fall semester, November 30 for the spring semester, and April 30 for summer sessions.

---

## • 2897 •
## Horticultural Research Institute

1250 Eye St., NW, Ste. 500     *Ph:* (202)789-2900
Washington, DC 20005     *Fax:* (202)789-1893

### • 2898 • Horticultural Research Institute Grants
*(Postdoctorate/Grant)*

**Purpose:** To support research that will advance knowledge and progress in the garden center, landscape and nursery industry. **Focus:** Horticulture. **Qualif.:** Candidates may be of any nationality who wish to conduct research that will benefit the nursery industry. Emphasis is placed on projects that consider significant industry problems and have broad economic applications. **Criteria:** As set forth in research policy.

**Funds Avail.:** Varies, according to project: usually $15,000 maximum. **No. of Awards:** 30-40. **To Apply:** Write to the administrator for application form and guidelines. **Deadline:** May 1. Grants are announced in November. **Contact:** Director of Horticulture Research, at the above address (see entry 2897).

## • 2899 •
## The Hospital For Sick Children Foundation

Grants Program Officer
555 University Ave.     *Ph:* (416)813-6166
Toronto, ON, Canada M5G 1X8     *Fax:* (416)813-5024
*E-mail:* gwen.burrows@sickkids.on.ca
*URL:* http://sickkids.on.ca

### • 2900 • Duncan L. Gordon Fellowships
*(Postdoctorate/Fellowship)*

**Purpose:** To encourage leadership in teaching, research, and clinical care in children's health in Canada. **Focus:** Pediatrics **Qualif.:** Candidate must be a Canadian citizen or landed immigrant. Applicant should be a health scientist at the postdoctoral level. Candidate must be nominated by an institution or agency which indicates whether the nominee will be offered an appointment within the nominating Institution upon completion of training or to establish a program in the field concerned.

**Funds Avail.:** $37,000-$47,000. **No. of Awards:** Up to three per year. **To Apply:** Write for nomination form and guidelines. Three referees, including at least one from outside the candidate's department, must submit a letter and formal evaluation form to the Foundation. A list of up to five potential reviewers for this nomination is required. **Deadline:** October 1.

### • 2901 • The Hospital for Sick Children Foundation External Grants Program *(Professional Development/ Grant)*

**Purpose:** To support research with the goal of improving the health and health care of children. **Focus:** Pediatrics, Biomedical, Psychosocial and Applied Research. **Qualif.:** Applicant must be a Canadian citizen working in Canada. Grants must be used for research.

**Funds Avail.:** $5000-65,000/year **No. of Awards:** 10-13 per cycle; 2 cycles a year. **To Apply:** Write for grant application and guidelines. **Deadline:** March 1 and September 1. **Contact:** The Hospital for Sick Children Foundation at the above address (see entry 2899).

## • 2902 •
## Hotel Employees & Restaurant Employees International Union

1219 28th St., NW     *Ph:* (202)393-4373
Washington, DC 20007     *Fax:* (202)333-0468

### • 2903 • Edward T. Hanley Scholarships
*(Professional Development/Scholarship)*

**Purpose:** To support study at the Culinary Institute of America. **Focus:** Cooking. **Qualif.:** Applicant must live in one of the international districts served by the Union, and either be a member of the Union or be endorsed by a member. The scholarship is tenable at the Culinary Institute of America in Hyde Park, New York. Award funds do not support the student during the extern period, during which he/she is training under a master chef at a restaurant.

**Funds Avail.:** $4,500/year. **To Apply:** Write to the secretary-treasurer, or refer to advertisements placed in the January, February and March issues of the Union's magazine, Catering Industry Employee+FA. **Deadline:** April 1. **Contact:** Herman Leavitt, General Secretary-Treasurer, at the above address (see entry 2902).

### • 2904 • Ed S. Miller Scholarship in Industrial and Labor Relations *(Undergraduate/Scholarship)*

**Qualif.:** Candidates must be sons, daughters, grandchildren, or legal wards of members in good standing, or must be members in good standing of a local union affiliated with the International Union for at least one year prior to November 1 of the application year. The scholarship is intended only for the study of Industrial and Labor Relations.

**Funds Avail.:** One four-year scholarship providing $3,500 each academic year is available. Winners in the west attend the University of California, Los Angeles. Winners in the east attend Cornell University. **To Apply:** During even-numbered years, persons living west of the Mississippi River (including Minnesota) and in the Canadian provinces west of Ontario are eligible to apply. During odd-numbered years, persons living east of the Mississippi River are eligible to apply. Requests for application forms are published in the October, November, and December issues of the Catering Industry Employee, the official magazine of the International Union. **Contact:** Hotel Employees and Restaurant Employees International Union at the above address (see entry 2902).

## • 2905 •
## House of Humour and Satire

PO Box 104     *Ph:* 66 27229
5300 Gabrovo, Bulgaria     *Fax:* 66 26989

### • 2906 • International Biennial Competition of Humour and Satire in the Arts *(Professional Development/Award)*

**Purpose:** To recognize the creation of artistic works of merriment and cheerfulness, as well as satire on everything that hinders the development of humankind to moral perfection and progress. **Focus:** Humor, Satire. **Qualif.:** Applicant may be of any nationality. Candidate may submit work in any of the following categories: cartoon (no titles), drawings, grahics, paintings, sculpture, photography, or literature. Applicant may submit up to five works total but no more than two works in any category. Works that offend the national dignity of any country or make propaganda for violence, eroticism, and religious fanaticism are not eligible for submission. Specific entry requirements and prizes differ for each category; write to the House for details.

**Funds Avail.:** Prizes vary for each category. **To Apply:** Write to the director for application form and guidelines. **Deadline:** March 1. The Competition is held in odd-numbered years. **Contact:** Mrs. Tatyana Tsankova, Director, at the above address (see entry 2905).

---

• **2907** •

**George A. and Eliza Gardner Howard Foundation**
42 Charlesfield St.
4th Floor, Graduate School
Brown University             *Ph:* (401)863-2640
Providence, RI 02912         *Fax:* (401)863-7341
*E-mail:* howard_foundation@brown.edu

• **2908** • **Howard Foundation Fellowships**
*(Professional Development/Fellowship)*

**Purpose:** To support independent projects. **Focus:** Rotating fields each year in Anthropology, Art History, Classical and Archaeological Studies, Creative Writing, Fine Arts, History, History of Science, Language and Literature, Literary Criticism, Philosophy, Political Science, Sociology. **Qualif.:** Fellows are selected by nomination only. Nominees normally have the rank of assistant or associate professor, or their equivalents. Candidates, regardless of citizenship, must be professionally based in the United States. The areas of study rotate; write to the Foundation for categories. Fellowships are tenable worldwide. Fellows are expected to have other sources of income, such as sabbatical leave, in addition to the fellowship so they may be free from any professional responsibilities except the proposed project. No grants are available for short-term projects, or for work leading to an academic degree.

**Funds Avail.:** $18,000. **No. of Awards:** 7. **To Apply:** For individuals associated with a college or university, nominations must be submitted by the president of the institution, or a designated representative. Each academic institution may nominate two individuals. Scholars without academic institutional connections may be nominated by a university president, the president of a professional association, or by the editor of a nonacademically affiliated professional publication. **Deadline:** October 31. Fellows are announced by May 1. **Contact:** Administrative Director at the above address (see entry 2907).

---

• **2909** •

**Hudson Institute**
Herman Kahn Center
PO Box 26919                 *Ph:* (317)545-1000
Indianapolis, IN 46226-0919  *Fax:* (317)545-9639
*URL:* http://www.a1.com/hudson/abouthud.html

• **2910** • **Herman Kahn Fellowships** *(Doctorate/Fellowship)*

**Purpose:** To support Ph.D. candidates who have only their dissertation remaining. **Focus:** Educational Policy, International and Domestic Political Economy, National Security. **Qualif.:** Applicants must be Ph.D. candidates with only the dissertation left to complete. They must have completed course work within the last five years. Fellows will work on their dissertation 50% of the time with the remainder devoted to policy-oriented research projects assigned by the Institute in the fellows' general areas of interest.

**Funds Avail.:** $18,000 stipend, plus travel allowance. **To Apply:** Submit curriculum vitae, two academic and one non-academic letters of recommendation, recent university publications, and graduate school transcripts. Indicate on application desired area

of study. Selected applicants will be interviewed by the Institute. **Deadline:** April 1. All applicants will be notified by May 15. **Contact:** Gary Geipel, at the above address (see entry 2909).

---

• **2911** •

**Hudson River Foundation**
40 W. 20th St., 9th Fl.       *Ph:* (212)924-8290
New York, NY 10011           *Fax:* (212)924-8305
*E-mail:* info@hudsonriver.org
*URL:* http://www.hudsonriver.org

• **2912** • **Hudson River Fellowships** *(Doctorate, Graduate/Fellowship)*

**Purpose:** To support dissertation research on issues and matters of concern to the Hudson River its tributaries, and its drainage basin. **Focus:** Hudson River. **Qualif.:** Applicant may be of any nationality, but must be enrolled in an accredited doctoral or masters program and must have passed qualifying exams. Candidate's school must agree to waive tuition for the duration of the fellowship. Applicant's proposed research plan must be approved by advisory committee; both scientific and public policy projects relating to the Hudson River are eligible for consideration. Fellowships are not renewable.

**Funds Avail.:** $9,000 stipend, plus $750 for materials, M.S.; $12,000 stipend, plus $1,000 for materials, Ph.D. **No. of Awards:** Up to 6. **To Apply:** Submit description of thesis research, letters of recommendation from advisor and others, curriculum vitae, timetable for project completion, proposed budget summary, statement of project relevance in regards to Hudson River Foundation objectives. **Deadline:** March 8. Decisions will be made by the end of May. **Contact:** Science Director, at the above address (see entry 2911).

• **2913** • **Hudson River Research Grants**
*(Postdoctorate/Grant)*

**Purpose:** To support scientific, ecological, and related public policy research on issues and matters of concern to the Hudson River, its tributaries, and its drainage basin. **Focus:** Hudson River. **Qualif.:** Applicant must be a qualified researcher; proposals are welcome from both independent and institutionally affiliated investigators in the scientific, educational, and public policy fields. Independent researchers are encouraged to seek some institutional sponsorship to carry out the proposed research. Although most proposals have involved investigators and institutions within New York state, there are no geographic restrictions on the location of the investigator or his/her sponsoring institution.

**Funds Avail.:** Varies, according to project; grants rarely exceed $100,000/yr. **To Apply:** Write to the Foundation for application form and proposal-writing guidelines. Proposals in the formal funding cycle must be preceded by a preproposal consisting of a project description, abstract and estimated budget. **Deadline:** Preproposal: September 18; full proposal: November 23.

**Remarks:** The Foundation gives Travel Grants to support travel to or from the Hudson River region for research related to the goals of the Foundation. Executive Committee Grants are awarded to researchers who are studying emergency situations on the Hudson River or who need funds for unexpected opportunities. Eligibility requirements for both types of awards are the same as those listed above for research grants; applications are accepted year-round. Write to the Foundation for further information. **Contact:** Science Director at the above address (see entry 2911).

---

Awards are arranged alphabetically below their administering organizations

*Hudson River Foundation (continued)*
  • 2914 •  **Tibor T. Polgar Fellowships** *(Graduate, Undergraduate/Fellowship)*

**Purpose:** To provide opportunities to conduct research on the Hudson River, including gathering important information on all aspects of the Hudson River and to train students in conducting estuarine studies and public policy research. **Focus:** Environmental research. **Qualif.:** Applicants must be college students.

**Funds Avail.:** $3500 plus limited research funds. Advisors also receive a $500 stipend. **No. of Awards:** 8. **To Apply:** The original and five copies of a letter of interest, a short description (4-6 pages) of the research project, a timetable for research completion, an estivate of the cost of supplies, travel, etc; and a letter of support from an advisor must be submitted. **Deadline:** March 8.

**Remarks:** Each potential fellow must be sponsored by a primary advisor. This advisor must be willing to commit sufficient time for research supervision and to attend at least one meeting to review the progress of the research.

---

• 2915 •
**Hudson River National Estuarine Research Reserve - New York State Department of Environmental Conservation**
Bard College Field Station       *Ph:* (914)758-7010
Annandale, NY 12504-5000       *Fax:* (914)758-7033
*URL:* http://www.nos.noaa.gov/ocrm/nerr/reserves/nerrhudsonriver.html

  • 2916 •  **Tibor T. Polgar Fellowship** *(Graduate, Undergraduate/Fellowship)*

**Purpose:** To train young scientists in estuarine science and to gather information about the complex natural patterns, processes, and relationships that exist in the Hudson River Estuary (HRE). The award also supports student research in public policy that relates to the HRE. **Focus:** Wetlands Ecology. Nutrient Cycling, Natural History, Fisheries, Trophic Interactions, Sediment Dynamics, Estuarine Ecology. **Qualif.:** Applicants must be undergraduate or graduate students interested in conducting research on the Hudson River. **Criteria:** Selection is based on quality of proposal, scientific merit, availability and commitment of the academic sponsor, and ability of the student to conduct requisite work.

**Funds Avail.:** $3,500 summer fellowship plus $500 in research funds, and $200 for the sponsor. At the conclusion of their fellowship, recipients must present their research findings and submit a final report in November. **No. of Awards:** 8. **To Apply:** Applicants must submit a fourto six-page research proposal, including its significance, a schedule, and a detailed budget. They must also submit a letter of interest from themselves and their sponsor and a resume. **Deadline:** March 1. **Contact:** Elizabeth Blair or Chuck Nieder at the above address (see entry 2915) or John Waldman at (212)924-8290.

• 2917 •
**The S. S. Huebner Foundation For Insurance Education**
430 Vance Hall
3733 Spruce St.
Wharton School
University of Pennsylvania       *Ph:* (215)898-9631
Philadelphia, PA 19104-6301       *Fax:* (215)573-2218
*URL:* http://rider.wharton.upenn.edu/~sshuebne

  • 2918 •  **Huebner Foundation Doctoral Fellowships** *(Doctorate/Fellowship)*

**Purpose:** To assist scholars aspiring to insurance teaching or research careers at the college or university level. **Focus:** Insurance and Risk, Insurance Economics. **Qualif.:** Applicant must be a U.S. or Canadian citizen, and must have obtained a baccalaureate degree from an accredited college or university. A person in the senior year of undergraduate study may apply for a grant to be effective in the following year, contingent upon satisfactory completion of the degree requirements. Candidates must apply separately to the doctoral program at the Wharton School of the University of Pennsylvania, where the awards are tenable. A successful candidate must intend to follow a career as a full-time college or university faculty member with a teaching or research specialization in risk and insurance, and must major in risk and insurance for a graduate degree. Fellows may not engage in any outside work for pay or profit during the fellowship year without the consent of the Foundation.

**Funds Avail.:** $1,083/month, plus a grant for full tuition and fees. **To Apply:** Write the Foundation for application form and guidelines. Submit application with transcripts, scores from either the Graduate Management Admissions Test or the Graduate Record Examination. A personal interview with the Foundation is required. **Deadline:** February 1. **Contact:** J. David Cummins, Executive Director, at the above address (see entry 2917).

  • 2919 •  **Huebner Foundation Postdoctoral Fellowships** *(Postdoctorate/Fellowship)*

**Purpose:** To assist scholars aspiring to insurance teaching or research careers at the college or university level. **Focus:** Insurance and Risk. **Qualif.:** Applicant must be a U.S. or Canadian citizen, and have a terminal degree. Candidate must wish to develop or strengthen background in risk and insurance with the objective of teaching or conducting research in the field. College faculty in any business or economic specialty are eligible to apply. Fellowships usually involve some course work as well as independent research. Fellowships are tenable only at the Wharton School of the University of Pennsylvania, and fellows may not engage in outside work for pay or profit during the fellowship year without the consent of the Foundation.

**Funds Avail.:** $12,000 stipend. **To Apply:** Write to the Foundation for application form and guidelines. A personal interview with the Foundation is required. **Deadline:** March 15. **Contact:** J. David Cummins, Executive Director, at the above address (see entry 2917).

  • 2920 •  **Wharton Doctoral and Postdoctoral Fellowships In Risk & Insurance** *(Doctorate, Postdoctorate/Fellowship)*

**Purpose:** To increase the number of qualified teachers of risk and insurance through the provision of financial assistance to graduate students and established teachers. **Focus:** Insurance and Insurance-Related fields. **Qualif.:** Candidates must be citizens of the United States or Canada. Doctoral fellowship applicants must be in the senior year of undergraduate study or have obtained a baccalaureate degree from an accredited college or university. Applicants for postdoctoral fellowships must hold terminal degrees in fields other than risk and insurance from an accredited college or university.

**Funds Avail.:** A doctoral fellowship covers tuition and other fees of the Wharton School of the University of Pennsylvania and provides a stipend of $1,167 per month. Summer fellowships provide income at the same rate as that payable during the regular academic year as well as payment of tuition and fees for summer courses. The value of the fellowship could total approximately $34,000 per year. Fellowships are awarded for one year, and are renewable for up to three calendar years; in exceptional cases, up to four years. Research expenses in connection with the doctoral dissertation are reimbursed within limits set by the Administrative Board. A postdoctoral fellowship provides a cash stipend of $14,000 and pays all tuition and fees. **No. of Awards:** Varies. **To Apply:** Candidates must apply on a special Foundation form and provide a transcript of undergraduate and/or graduate courses. Applicants must also take the Graduate Management Admissions Test administered by the Educational Testing Service of Princeton, New Jersey, and have the results sent to the Foundation. A personal interview with the Executive Director or other officials of the Foundation is required. In addition, candidates must apply separately and directly for admission to the Wharton Doctoral Program. Applicants must also certify that they will major in risk insurance for a graduate degree, will follow a teaching career in these fields, and during the fellowship period will not engage in any outside work for pay and profit without consent of the Administrative Board of the Foundation. **Deadline:** Applications must be submitted by February 1 and supporting materials by March 1.

**Remarks:** The primary support of the Foundation comes from the annual contributions of life insurance companies. **Contact:** Executive Director at the above address (see entry 2917).

• **2921** •
**Hughes Aircraft Company**
Technical Education Center
PO Box 956
El Segundo, CA 90245-0956
*E-mail:* webmaster@link.com
*URL:* http://www.hughes.com/h_air.html

• **2922** • **Engineer Degree Fellowships; Howard Hughes Doctoral Fellowships** *(Doctorate/Fellowship)*

**Purpose:** To support doctoral studies in engineering and related sciences and to provide students with practical work experience. **Focus:** Computer Science, Engineering, Mathematics, Physics. **Qualif.:** Applicants for either type of fellowship must be U.S. citizens and have a bachelor's and master's degree or equivalent graduate experience in electrical, mechanical, systems, computer or aerospace engineering; computer science; physics; or mathematics. Engineer Degree Fellowships are reserved for candidates who have first degrees in engineering. For both awards, priority is given to individuals with experience in electronics and related disciplines. They must also have a minimum grade point average of 3.0/4.0, and be qualified for admission to an approved graduate program in the United States. Fellows are considered employees of the Hughes Aircraft Company and, in addition to their graduate studies, gain work experience in one of two programs: work-study or full-study. Fellows in the work-study program attend a university near a Hughes facility (usually in southern California) and complete coursework while working at the facility for 20 to 36 hours per week. Work-study fellows may switch to full-study status to complete their dissertations. Full-study fellows attend a university distant from Hughes and are on leave of absence from the company while studying full-time. Full-study fellows are required to spend the summer term working for the Company, and may

work eight hours a week during the school year if attending a university within commuting distance.

**Funds Avail.:** Company salary and benefits, plus tuition, book and living allowances. **To Apply:** Write to the educational coordinator for application form and guidelines. Include pertinent information regarding academic status (university, field of interest for both undergraduate and graduate work, year of graduation, and grade point average) in initial letter of interest. **Deadline:** January 10. Fellows are announced in April.

**Remarks:** Hughes also offers the Master of Science Fellowship to individuals with bachelor's degrees in science and engineering. Aside from the level of study, the benefits and requirements are essentially the same as those listed for the doctoral awards described above. Application deadlines vary. Write to the educational coordinator for further information. **Contact:** Fellowship and Rotation Programs, at the above address (see entry 2921).

• **2923** • **Engineering Rotation Program** *(Professional Development/Award)*

**Purpose:** To enable engineering and science graduates to find and develop the special field of work and the career position best suited to their interests and education. **Focus:** Computer Science, Engineering, Mathematics, Physics. **Qualif.:** Applicants must be U.S. citizens and have a bachelor's degree in electrical, mechanical, systems, computer or aerospace engineering; computer science; physics; or mathematics. They must also have a grade point average of at least 3.0/4.0, with emphasis on technical classes and related disciplines. Participants in the Rotation Program gain practical experience through up to four different work assignments at Hughes facilities, usually in southern California. Upon completion of the program, participants may be placed in permanent positions with the Company, based on their interests and assignments available.

**Funds Avail.:** Salary and company benefits. **To Apply:** Write to the educational coordinator for application form and guidelines. Include pertinent information regarding academic status (university, field of interest for both undergraduate and graduate work, year of graduation, and grade point average) in initial letter of interest. **Deadline:** March 1.

**Remarks:** Candidates for the Rotation Program are also encouraged to apply to Hughes for a work-study fellowship, which supports graduate study undertaken concurrently with the rotation assignments. **Contact:** Corporate Fellowship and Rotation Programs, at the above address (see entry 2921).

• **2924** •
**Howard Hughes Medical Institute - Office of Grants and Special Programs**
4000 Jones Bridge Rd.                    *Ph:* (301)215-8500
Chevy Chase, MD 20815-6789               *Fax:* (301)215-8888
*E-mail:* fellows@hhmi.org
*URL:* http://www.hhmi.org/fellowships

• **2925** • **Howard Hughes Medical Institute Research Training Fellowships for Medical Students** *(Graduate/Fellowship)*

**Purpose:** To strengthen and expand the pool of medically trained researchers interested in biological processes and disease mechanisms. The program is designed to enable selected medical students with an interest in fundamental research to spend a year at intensive work in a research laboratory. **Focus:** Biomedical Research, Biology. **Qualif.:** Applicants must be students currently enrolled in M.D. or D.O. degree programs in medical schools in the United States. Students may apply during any year of their medical studies, but applicants in the fourth year of medical school must

## Howard Hughes Medical Institute - Office of Grants and Special Programs (continued)

defer graduation until completion of the fellowship year. Prior research experience is not required. Students with a year of full-time research experience since entering medical school must show how further full-time research experience would strongly enhance their future research career. Students enrolled in M.D./Ph.D., Ph.D., or Sc.D. programs or holders of the Ph.D. or Sc.D. degree are not eligible. There are no citizenship requirements. **Criteria:** Fellowships are awarded on the basis of the applicant's ability and promise for a research career and the quality of the training that will be provided. Specifically, reviewers look at the mentor's plans for training the applicant, letters of reference, proposed research plan, undergraduate and medical school transcripts, and scores on the MCAT and National Board of Medical Examiners Part I examination, if available.

**Funds Avail.:** The annual stipend for fellows is $16,000. In addition, the fellowship institution receives $5,500 research allowance for the fellow and a $5,500 institutional allowance. A fellow may not accept private employment or consulting or receive funds from another external fellowship, scholarship, or similar award for the fellowship year. **No. of Awards:** Up to 60 per year. **To Apply:** Applicants are advised to write to the Institute or go to its homepage for program guidelines and applications. Applicants must send a complete application which includes background information; statement of prior research experience; two-page research plan; endorsement by the proposed research mentor; a letter from the dean of the applicant's medical school; two letters of reference; and academic transcripts. **Deadline:** Early December. **Contact:** Howard Hughes Medical Institute, Office of Grants and Special Programs at the above address (see entry 2924).

• **2926** • **Postdoctoral Research Fellowships for Physicians** *(Postdoctorate/Fellowship)*

**Purpose:** To promote excellence in biomedical research by medically trained investigators. **Focus:** Biomedical Sciences including Cell Biology, Genetics, Immunology, Neuroscience, Structural Biology, and Epidemiology and Biostatistics. **Qualif.:** Applicant must hold an M.B.B.S., M.D., D.O., or M.D./Ph.D. degree. Applicant must have at least two years of postgraduate clinical training, and no more than two years of postdoctoral research training, by the start of the fellowship. U.S. citizens may conduct research at any academic or research institution worldwide. Citizens of other countries must conduct research in the United States. Research must be full time, and must be directed toward further understanding basic biological processes or disease mechanisms. Fellow may not be enrolled in a graduate degree program or have a faculty appointment. **Criteria:** Fellowships are awarded on the basis of the applicant's ability and promise for a research career. Reviewers also consider the applicant's commitment to a career in research and the fellowship's role in furthering the applicant's career development.

**Funds Avail.:** $40,000-60,000/year, plus $16,000/year research allowance, and $13,000/year institutional allowance. **No. of Awards:** 30 per year. **To Apply:** Write to the Institute or visit its homepage for program guidelines and applications. Submit application including transcripts, summary of research experience and educational background, proposed research plan, statement of career goals, mentor's endorsement, and four letters of reference. **Deadline:** Early December. Notification in June. **Contact:** Howard Hughes Medical Institute Office of Grants and Special Programs, at the above address (see entry 2924).

• **2927** • **Predoctoral Fellowships in Biological Sciences** *(Doctorate/Fellowship)*

**Purpose:** To encourage graduate students who are beginning doctoral studies in the biological sciences. **Focus:** Biological Sciences, including Biochemistry, Biophysics, Biostatistics, Cell Biology, Developmental Biology, Epidemiology, Genetics, Immunology, Mathematical and Computational Biology, Microbiology, Molecular Biology, Neuroscience, Pharmacology,

Physiology, Structural Biology, Virology. **Qualif.:** Applicant must be entering or enrolled in a full-time Ph.D. or Sc.D. program in the biological sciences. Fellowships are intended to assist doctoral candidates at the beginning of their studies; students who will have completed the first year of postbaccalaureate graduate study by the application deadline are not eligible. U.S. citizens may study at educational institutions in the United States or abroad; citizens of other countries must enroll at institutions in the United States. **Criteria:** Fellowships are awarded on the basis of ability, as reflected by such evidence as academic records, the proposed plan of study and research, previous research experience, reference reports, and GRE scores.

**Funds Avail.:** $16,000/year, plus $15,000/year cost-of-education allowance. **No. of Awards:** 80. **To Apply:** General fellowship information and the application may be obtained from the Fellowship Office at the National Research Council. Submit to the NRC the form with proposed plan of study, transcripts, four letters of reference, and Graduate Record Examination general and subject test scores. Some foreign applicants must also submit scores from the Test of English as a Foreign Language. **Deadline:** Early November. Notification is in early April. **Contact:** Applications are available from Hughes Predoctoral Fellowships, National Research Council Fellowship Office, 2101 Constitution Avenue, N.W., Washington DC 20418, USA, 202-334-2872, or from http://fellowships.nas.edu. The NRC assists the Institute in the processing and evaluation of fellowship applications. The Institute, however, selects the fellows.

---

• **2928** •

## Human Growth Foundation

7777 Leesburg Pke., Ste. 202S
Falls Church, VA 22043

Ph: (703)883-1773
Fax: (703)883-1776
Free: 800-451-6434

*E-mail:* hgfound@erols.com
*URL:* http://www.medhelp.org/web/hgfinfo.htm

• **2929** • **Human Growth Foundation Small Grants** *(Postdoctorate/Grant)*

**Purpose:** To assist scientists researching growth and growth disorders. **Focus:** Human Growth Disorders, Genetics, Medical Research. **Qualif.:** Candidate may be of any nationality. Applicant must be a scientist working to develop knowledge of endocrine, metabolic, genetic, or orthopedic growth disorders. Grants are tenable worldwide.

**Funds Avail.:** $20,000 maximum. **To Apply:** Write to the executive director for application materials. **Deadline:** Varies. **Contact:** Kimberly Frye at the above address (see entry 2928).

---

• **2930** •

## Humanitarian Trust

64 Aberdare Gardens
London NW6 3QD, England

• **2931** • **Humanitarian Trust Research Awards** *(Professional Development/Grant)*

**Purpose:** To provide funds to supplement larger research grants. **Focus:** General **Qualif.:** Applicant may be of any nationality, but must be a qualified scholar affiliated with a U.K. academic institution. Candidate must hold a substantial basic grant at the time of application, and be in need of supplementary assistance. Awards are not made for fieldwork, overseas courses, travel, or for arts subjects such as music, theatre, journalism, etc.

Funds Avail.: £200. To Apply: Write to the Trust for application guidelines. Deadline: None Contact: M. Myers at the above address (see entry 2930).

---

• 2932 •
## Humanities Research Centre
Australian National University (ANU)
GPO Box 4
Canberra, ACT 0200, Australia

Ph: 6 249 2700
Fax: 6 248 0054

• 2933 • Humanities Research Centre Visiting
Fellowships (Postdoctorate/Fellowship)

Purpose: To support research in the humanities. Focus: Humanities. (Specific themes vary each year. For 1995 the topic was Africa.) Qualif.: Candidate may be of any nationality. Applicants must be postdoctoral scholars not working for a higher degree. Applications are welcome from scholars in any area of the humanities; a proportion of each year's fellowships is reserved for those without special interest in the year's theme. The majority of awards, however, will be given to those whose work is relevant to the annual theme. Fellows are expected to work at the Centre, but are encouraged to visit other Australian universities.

Funds Avail.: Varies, according to other resources available to fellow. Usual grant includes a weekly stipend, plus travel allowance. To Apply: Write to the HRC Administrator for application forms and details of annual theme, usually available in June. Submit application to the ANU registrar. Deadline: October 31.

Remarks: HRC also sponsors a visiting scholarship scheme for scholars within Australia and New Zealand who wish to work at the Centre for not more than three months, especially during the summer vacation, i.e. December to February. Further information and application forms are available from the Centre Administrator. Contact: Centre Administrator at the above address (see entry 2932).

---

• 2934 •
## Hungarian Arts Club
24408 Emily
Brownstown Twp., MI 48183
E-mail: csango@aol.com

Ph: (734)783-0924

• 2935 • Hungarian Arts Club Scholarships
(Undergraduate/Scholarship)

Purpose: To promote the study of fine arts through Hungarian youth. Focus: Art, Dance, Music, Painting, Sculpture, Theater Arts, Vocal Music. Qualif.: Applicants must be of Hungarian descent and studying, or planning to study, for a Fine Arts Degree in college. Criteria: A portfolio of the applicant's work history and letters of recommendations are required.

Funds Avail.: $1,000. To Apply: Students must complete an application, prove Hungarian descent, and submit a portfolio of work which can be any form of fine arts, including art, painting, sculpture, music, singing, dancing, and theatre. Deadline: First week of December. Contact: Kimberley Kish at the above address (see entry 2934).

---

• 2936 •
## Hunt Manufacturing Co.
2005 Market St.
Philadelphia, PA 19103-7085

Ph: (215)656-0300
Fax: (215)656-3700
Free: 800-955-4868

E-mail: webmaster@huntmfg.com
URL: http://www.huntmfg.com

• 2937 • Hunt Manufacturing Company Foundation
Scholarships (Undergraduate/Scholarship)

Focus: General Studies. Qualif.: Applicants must be children of Hunt Manufacturing Co. employees and high school seniors. Criteria: Selection is determined by academic scholarship, financial need, and evidence of extracurricular leadership.

Funds Avail.: Scholarships are for four years at $1,000 to $2,000 per year. To Apply: Contact Hunt Manufacturing Company Foundation for applications. Deadline: April 15. Contact: Ivy Peterson at the above address (see entry 2936).

---

• 2938 •
## Huntington Library and Art Gallery
1151 Oxford Rd.
San Marino, CA 91108
E-mail: cpowell@huntington.org
URL: http://www.huntington.org

Ph: (626)405-2194
Fax: (626)449-5703

• 2939 • Huntington Library Research Awards
(Graduate, Postdoctorate/Award)

Purpose: To support worthy scholars in the early stages of their careers when heavy teaching schedules and financial constraints reduce research time. Focus: American History, American Literature, Art History, British History, British Literature, History of Science. Qualif.: Candidates may be of any nationality and may be graduate students or postdoctoral scholars. Awards are also made to persons writing doctoral dissertations. Awardees are expected to be in residence at the library throughout their tenure. Permission must be obtained from the Huntington Library if scholars wish to hold an award from another source simultaneously.

Funds Avail.: $2,000/month. No. of Awards: 100. Deadline: Applcations are accepted from October 1 to December 15. Results are announced by April 1. Contact: Robert C. Ritchie, Chairman, or the Research Department Office via phone, e-mail or at the above address (see entry 2938).

---

• 2940 •
## Huntington's Disease Society of America
140 W. 22nd St., 6th Fl.
New York, NY 10011-2420

Ph: (212)242-1968
Fax: (212)243-2443
Free: 800-345-HDSA

E-mail: archimededc@hdsa.ttisms.com; curehd@hdsa.ttisms.com
URL: http://neuro-www2.mgh.harvard.edu/hdsa/society-nclk

• 2941 • Huntington's Disease Society Research
Fellowships (Postdoctorate/Fellowship)

Purpose: To help promising young investigators in the early stages of their careers. Focus: Huntington's Disease Qualif.: Applicants must have an M.D. or Ph.D. and must be affiliated with any accredited medical school or university worldwide. U.S. citizenship is not a requirement but citizens of other countries will be

---

## Huntington's Disease Society of America *(continued)*

evaluated, in part, on the Society's knowledge, or lack of knowledge, about the quality of research conducted at the candidate's foreign institution. All research work by a fellow must be supervised by a qualified investigator designated by the fellow's school. Awardees are expected to devote the major portion of their time to research but may include some study and clinical experience in allied fields.

**Funds Avail.:** $30,000. **No. of Awards:** Varies. **To Apply:** Write for application form and guidelines. Submit form through the medical school or university, including curriculum vitae, description of proposed medical research, and letters of recommendation from the director and/or project supervisor. **Deadline:** January 5. Final selections are made in March. **Contact:** Claudia Archimede at the above address (see entry 2940).

### • 2942 • Huntington's Disease Society Research Grants *(Professional Development/Grant)*

**Purpose:** To support new or innovative research projects. **Focus:** Huntington's Disease **Qualif.:** Grants are available to all investigators affiliated with an accredited medical school or university, in support of basic or clinical research related to Huntington's Disease. U.S. citizenship is not a requirement but citizens of other countries will be evaluated, in part, on the Society's knowledge or lack of knowledge, about the quality of research conducted at the candidate's foreign institution. Awardees are expected to devote the major portion of their time to research but may include some study and clinical experience in allied fields.

**Funds Avail.:** $35,000 maximum **To Apply:** Write for application form and guidelines. Submit form through the medical school or university, including curriculum vitae, description of proposed medical research, and letters of recommendation from the director and/or project supervisor. **Deadline:** January 5. Final selections are made in March. **Contact:** Claudia Archimede at the above address (see entry 2940).

### • 2943 •
## Edmund Niles Huyck Preserve and Biological Research Station
PO Box 189
Rensselaerville, NY 12147     *Ph:* (518)797-3440
*E-mail:* rlwyman@capital.net     *Fax:* (518)797-3440
*URL:* http://jasper.stanford.edu/OBFS/OBFS_Stations/Ny_Huyck_Preserve.html

### • 2944 • Huyck Station Research Grants *(Graduate/Grant)*

**Purpose:** To support study of the ecology, evolution, natural history, systematics, and/or behavior of flora and fauna of the Huyck Preserve. **Focus:** Botany, Ecology, Wildlife Conservation, Zoology. **Qualif.:** Candidates may be of any nationality but must be working toward or possess an advanced degree. Awards are tenable at the Preserve. **Criteria:** Applicants are chosen based on scientific merit of proposal.

**Funds Avail.:** $2,500 maximum. **To Apply:** Write for application materials and guidelines. **Deadline:** February 1. Notification by April 1. **Contact:** Dr. R. L. Wyman, at the above address (see entry 2943).

### • 2945 •
## Hydrocephalus Association
870 Market St., Ste. 955
San Francisco, CA 94102     *Ph:* (415)732-7040

### • 2946 • Gerard S. Fudge Scholarship *(Graduate, Undergraduate/Scholarship loan)*

**Purpose:** To recognize the accomplishments of yound adults with hydrocephulas and to give them assistance in obtaining a secondary education. **Focus:** General studies. **Qualif.:** Applicants must have hydrocephalus and be between the ages of 17 and 30.

**Funds Avail.:** Funds must be used for educational purposes, including , but not limited to, a four-year or junior college, a high school post-graduate year, technical or trade school, and accredited employment training program, or a post-graduate program. They may be used for tuition, books, housing, or an expense directly related to the educaitonal experience. **No. of Awards:** 1. **Deadline:** April 1. Winners announced in June.

### • 2947 •
## IBM Thomas J. Watson Research Center - Department of Mathematical Sciences
PO Box 218     *Ph:* (914)945-2409
Yorktown Heights, NY 10598     *Fax:* (914)945-3434

### • 2948 • IBM Postdoctoral Research Fellowships in Mathematical Sciences *(Postdoctorate/Fellowship)*

**Purpose:** To provide scientists of outstanding ability with an opportunity to advance their scholarship as resident department members at the Research Center. The department provides an atmosphere which combines basic research with exposure to technical problems arising in industry. **Focus:** Mathematics, Computer Science. **Qualif.:** Candidates must have a doctorate degree and not more than five years of postdoctoral professional experience when the fellowship commences. Citizens of countries defined as restricted by the U.S. Department of Commerce are required to have a green card or an equivalent visa status.

**Funds Avail.:** $70,000. There is an additional allowance for moving expenses to the Research Center located in Westchester County, New York. **To Apply:** Candidates must submit a resume, thesis summary, thesis or reprints of publicatons based on the thesis and other research, a research proposal, and visa status. Applicants are also responsible for requesting for submittal three or more letters of reference (one from thesis advisor). **Deadline:** January 9. Candidates are notified of the Committee's decision by March 17.

### • 2949 •
## IEEE Computer Society
Attn: Scholarships
1730 Massachusetts Ave. NW     *Ph:* (202)371-0103
Washington, DC 20036-1992     *Fax:* (202)728-0884
*E-mail:* swagner@computer.org
*URL:* http://www.computer.org

### • 2950 • Richard E. Merwin Scholarships *(Graduate, Undergraduate/Scholarship)*

**Purpose:** To support students in the field of computer-related engineering. **Focus:** Computer Science, Engineering. **Qualif.:** Applicant must be a full-time graduate, senior or junior in college in computer-related engineering fields and active in his/her IEEE

Computer Branch Chapter. Applicants must have a minimum grade point average of 2.5 over 4.0. **Criteria:** Evaluation criteria include involvement in chapter activities (counts 40%), academic achievement (counts 30%), other extracurricular activities in college (counts 10%), and letter of evaluation by branch chapter advisor (counts 20%). A brief statement will be submitted by each winner at the end of the academic year outlining his or her accomplishments.

**Funds Avail.:** $3,000. **No. of Awards:** Up to four per year. **To Apply:** Write to the Computer Society for application. **Deadline:** May 17. **Contact:** Volunteer Services Coordinator at the above address (see entry 2949).

### • 2951 • Lance Stafferd Larson Student Scholarship
*(Undergraduate/Scholarship)*

**Qualif.:** Applicants must be undergraduate students who are IEEE Computer Society members and maintain a minimum 3.0 GPA.

**Funds Avail.:** $500. **Contact:** IEEE Computer Society at the above address (see entry 2949).

### • 2952 • Upsilon Pi Epsilon/Computer Society Award for Academic Excellence *(Graduate, Undergraduate/Award)*

**Qualif.:** Applicants must be graduates or undergraduate full-time students who are IEEE members and maintain a minimum 3.0 GPA.

**Funds Avail.:** $500. **No. of Awards:** 4. **Deadline:** October 31. **Contact:** IEEE Computer Society at the above address (see entry 2949).

### • 2953 •
**Illinois AMVETS**
2200 South Sixth St.
Springfield, IL 62703-3496

Ph: (217)528-4713
Fax: (217)528-9896
Free: 800-638-8387

*E-mail:* amvets@warpnet.net

### • 2954 • AMVETS Auxiliary Department of Illinois Memorial Scholarship *(Undergraduate/Scholarship)*

**Focus:** General Studies. **Qualif.:** Applicants must be unmarried Illinois high school seniors and have taken the American College Test. They must also be Illinois residents. **Criteria:** The following point system is used as criteria: need, 40 percent; scholarship, 30 percent; personality, 20 percent; aims, 10 percent.

**Funds Avail.:** The Scholarship Award is $500 payable to the student and the college of his/her choice. **No. of Awards:** 2. **To Apply:** Formal applications must be filed. Candidates must describe their aims for the future in 50 words or less. Applications must include current transcripts, ACT scores, and a financial statement. High school transcripts are filed by the high school principals or counselors and must include semester averages for all courses taken in high school through the first semester of the senior year, and candidate's rank in class through the first semester of the senior year. Applicants must submit a statement regarding financial status of the family and actual need of the applicant (or 1040 form). Applications must be notarized. **Deadline:** Application materials must be received at State Headquarters postmarked on or before March 1. **Contact:** High school counselors or Executive Director at the above address (see entry 2953).

### • 2955 • Illinois AMVETS Auxiliary WORCHID Scholarships *(Undergraduate/Scholarship)*

**Focus:** General Studies. **Qualif.:** Applicants must be children of deceased veterans who served after September 15, 1940, and who were honorably discharged. The veteran parent need not have been killed in action nor died as a result of a service-connected disability. Applicants must be Illinois residents and seniors in high school and have taken the American College Test and unmarried. **Criteria:** The following point system is used as criteria: need, 40 percent; scholarship, 30 percent; personality, 20 percent; and aims, 10 percent.

**Funds Avail.:** The amount of the scholarship is $500, to be used at any college of the recipient's choice. Check is payable to the student and the college. Recipients may accept other scholarship awards without their AMVETS scholarship being affected. **No. of Awards:** 2. **To Apply:** A formal application must be filed. Candidates must write about their aims for the future in 50 words or less. Applications must be signed by the candidate and a parent or guardian and notarized. A current transcript, ACT scores, and a statement regarding the financial status of the family and the actual need of the applicant (or 1040 form) must be filed with the application. High school transcripts must be submitted by high school principals or counselors and must include semester averages for all courses taken in high school and the candidate's class rank through the first semester of the senior year. **Deadline:** Applications and all supporting materials must be received at the State Headquarters postmarked on or before March 1. **Contact:** High school counselors or Executive Director at the above address (see entry 2953).

### • 2956 • Illinois AMVETS Sad Sacks Nursing Scholarships *(Undergraduate/Scholarship)*

**Focus:** Nursing. **Qualif.:** Applicants must be students in an approved school of nursing in the State of Illinois or Illinois high school graduates who have been accepted for training in such a school. Priority is given to dependents of deceased or disabled veterans. Preference is given to student nurses in training in the following order: third year students; second year students; first year students. **Criteria:** The following point system is used as criteria: need, 40 percent; scholarship, 30 percent; personality, 20 percent; and aims, 10 percent.

**Funds Avail.:** Each scholarship is in the amount of $1,000 payable to student and School of Nursing. Recipients may accept other scholarship awards without their AMVETS scholarships being affected. **No. of Awards:** 2. **To Apply:** A formal application must be filed. High school transcripts are filed by high school principals or counselors and must include semester averages for all courses taken in high school through the first semester of the senior year, and candidate's rank in class through the first semester of the senior year. Statement forms regarding financial status of the family and actual need of the applicant are also required. Parents or guardians must sign for financial assistance or include copies of form 1040. A letter of acceptance into a school of Nursing must also be included. Applications must be notarized. **Deadline:** Applications and all supporting materials must be received at State Headquarters postmarked on or before March 1. **Contact:** High school counselors or Executive Director at the above address (see entry 2953).

### • 2957 • Illinois AMVETS Service Foundation Scholarship Award *(Undergraduate/Scholarship)*

**Focus:** General Studies. **Qualif.:** Candidates must be children of veterans who served after September 15, 1940, and were honorably discharged. Candidates must be unmarried Illinois seniors in high school and must have taken the examination given by the Illinois State Scholarship Commission, which is the American College Test. **Criteria:** The following point system is used as criteria: need, 40 percent; scholarship, 30 percent; personality, 20 percent; and aims, 10 percent.

## Illinois AMVETS (continued)

**Funds Avail.:** The amount of the scholarship is $1,000. Recipients may accept other scholarship awards without their AMVETS scholarship being affected. **No. of Awards:** 30. **To Apply:** Formal applications, current transcripts, ACT scores, and financial statements (or 1040) are required. Formal applications must be signed by candidates and parents or guardians and notarized. High school transcripts are filed by high school principals or counselors and must include semester averages for all courses taken in high school through the first semester of the senior year, and candidate's rank in class through the first semester of the senior year. Applicants must also submit a statement regarding financial status of the family and actual need of the applicant (or 1040 form). **Deadline:** Applications must be postmarked on or before March 1. **Contact:** High school counselors or Executive Director at the above address (see entry 2953).

## • 2958 • Clarence Newlun Memorial Scholarship Award *(Undergraduate/Scholarship)*

**Focus:** General Studies. **Qualif.:** Applicants must be unmarried Illinois high school seniors who are children of war veterans who served after September 15, 1940, and were honorably discharged. Students must have taken the American College Test as used by the Illinois State Scholarship Commission. They must also be Illinois residents. **Criteria:** The following point system is used as criteria: need, 40 percent; scholarship, 30 percent; personality, 20 percent; aims, 10 percent.

**Funds Avail.:** The amount of the scholarship is $500 payable to student and college. **To Apply:** Formal applications must be filed. High school transcripts are filed by high school principals or counselors and must include semester averages for all courses taken in high school through the first semester of the senior year, and candidate's rank in class through the first semester of the senior year. Applicants must submit a statement regarding financial status of the family and actual need of the applicant (or 1040 form). Applications must be signed by candidates and parents or guardians and notarized. **Deadline:** Completed applications and accompanying materials must be postmarked on or before March 1. **Contact:** High school counselors or Executive Director at the above address (see entry 2953).

## • 2959 • Paul Powell Memorial AMVETS Scholarships *(Undergraduate/Scholarship)*

**Focus:** General Studies. **Qualif.:** Applicants must be unmarried Illinois high school seniors. They must have taken the examination given by the Illinois State Scholarship Commission, which is the American College Test. They must also be Illinois residents. **Criteria:** The following point system is used as criteria: need, 40 percent; scholarship, 30 percent; personality; 20 percent; and aims, 10 percent.

**Funds Avail.:** $1,000. **No. of Awards:** 2. **To Apply:** A formal application must be filed. High school transcripts are filed by high school principals or counselors and must include semester averages of all courses taken in high school through the first semester of the senior year, and candidate's rank in class through the first semester of the senior year. Applicants must complete a statement regarding financial status of the family and actual need of the applicant (or 1040 form). Applications must be signed by the candidate and parent or guardian and notarized. **Deadline:** Applications must be received at State Headquarters postmarked on or before March 1. **Contact:** High school counselors or Executive Director at the above address (see entry 2953).

## • 2960 •
## Illinois Department of Veterans' Affairs
833 S. Spring St.
PO Box 19432
Springfield, IL 62794-9432

*Ph:* (217)782-3418
*Fax:* (217)524-0344

## • 2961 • Illinois MIA/POW Scholarship *(Undergraduate/Scholarship)*

**Focus:** General Studies. **Qualif.:** Applicants must be spouses, natural children, legally adopted children, or step-children of eligible veterans or service persons who have been declared by the U.S. Department of Defense or the U.S. Veterans Administration to be a prisoner of war or missing in action, or who have died as the result of a service-connected disability or been permanently disabled from service-connected causes with 100 percent disability, and who at the time of entering service were Illinois residents or became Illinois residents within six months of entering such service.

**Funds Avail.:** In-state and in-district tuition and certain fees for full-time enrollment (including summer terms) at any Illinois state-controlled college, university, or community college. **To Apply:** Dependents must complete a POW Form 1 and provide the following documentation when applicable: DD214/Enlistment Record, marriage certificate, birth certificate, adoption decree, letter of guardianship, death certificate or report of casualty, proof of MIA/POW status, or proof of total and permanent disability. **Deadline:** Application may be made anytime. **Contact:** Tracy Mahan at the above address (see entry 2960).

## • 2962 • Illinois Veterans' Children Educational Opportunities *(Undergraduate/Grant)*

**Purpose:** To provide educational opportunities for children of persons who served in the Armed Forces of the United States and who died or are totally and permanently disabled from a service-connected disability. **Focus:** General Studies. **Qualif.:** Veterans must have died in a period of hostilities in service, as a result of a service-connected disability, or have been awarded 100 percent service-connected disability for at least two years prior to application. Children must be attending school and have had domicile in the State of Illinois for 12 months prior to application. Children must be between ages 10 and 18.

**Funds Avail.:** Up to $250 grant for any one child for any one school year for matriculation and tuition fees, board, room rent, books, and supplies. **To Apply:** The initial claim for each child will consist of the veteran's Notice of Separation or Discharge Form DD 214 or discharge paper and the following forms and documentary evidence: Department of Veterans' Affairs Form EDI (submitted only upon original claim for each child), birth certificate of each child, adoption decree or guardianship where applicable, death certificate or casualty report (in the case of a deceased veteran), marriage certificate (in the case of remarriage of the veteran's widow), United States Veterans' Administration Form 21-22 - Power of Attorney, and Department of Veterans' Affairs Form ED II. **Contact:** Eva Palmer at the above address (see entry 2960). Telephone: (217)782-6643.

**• 2963 •**

## Illinois Federation of Business and Professional Women's Clubs

Celia M. Howard Fellowship Fund
  Committee
528 S. 5th St., Ste. 209      *Ph:* (217)528-8985
Springfield, IL 62701      *Fax:* (217)528-1625

**• 2964 •  Celia M. Howard Fellowships** *(Doctorate, Graduate/Fellowship)*

**Qualif.:** Applicants must be Illinois women who have been domiciled in the state for no less than two years prior to the granting of the award, have received a B.A. or B.S. degree or will receive it by the fall semester, and have maintained at least a B average. Fellowships are granted for study at Southern Illinois University at Carbondale, in the Master of Science in Administration of Justice program, and at the University of Illinois at Urbana, in the Juris Doctor program. International study fellowships are awarded for use at the Fletcher School of Law and Diplomacy at Medford, Massachusetts, in the Master of Arts in Law and Diplomacy program, and the American Graduate School of International Management at Glendale, Arizona, in the Master of Arts, International Management program. **Criteria:** Selection is based on financial need, previous graduate study, practical experience in business or government, and extent of supporting work in two other fields. Preference is given to economics, history, or government majors and those conversant in at least one foreign language (if applying for international study fellowship).

**Funds Avail.:** Past awards have ranged from $500 to $8,500 per year and are renewable. Payments are made directly to the school. **Deadline:** Applications, credentials, and supporting data must be on file with the Celia M. Howard Fellowship Fund Committee on or before November 1. Awards are announced by April 1. **Contact:** Chairman, Celia M. Howard Fellowship Fund Committee, at the above address (see entry 2963)for application forms and additional information.

**• 2965 •**

## Illinois State Library

300 S. 2nd St.      *Ph:* (217)782-7848
Springfield, IL 62701      *Fax:* (217)782-1877
      *Free:* 800-665-5576

*E-mail:* pnorris@library.sos.state.il.us
*URL:* http://www.sos.state.il.us/depts/library/programs/kids/
  cavd_win.html

**• 2966 •  Master of Library Science Degree Training Grants** *(Graduate/Grant)*

**Purpose:** The training grant is intended to encourage college graduates with demonstrated scholarship, talent, and potential to enter the library profession; to work in Illinois libraries; and to improve and stimulate development of public library service in Illinois. **Focus:** Library and Information Sciences. **Qualif.:** Applicants must be residents of Illinois, citizens of the United States or one of its territories, and have a bachelor's degree from an accredited four-year college or university.

**Funds Avail.:** Up to 15 scholarships of $7,500 each are awarded annually. If the program is not completed or if the recipient fails to work the equivalent of two full-time years in an Illinois public library or at the Illinois State Library, the scholarship becomes a loan and must be repaid. **No. of Awards:** Up to 15. **To Apply:** Candidates must complete an application form listing three references, and be personally interviewed by staff of the Illinois State Library and members of the Illinois State Library Advisory Committee's Subcommittee on Public Library Services. They must submit proof of acceptance in a Master of Library Science degree program in an American Library Association-accredited library school in Illinois and must notify the Illinois State Library of the name of the school, date of admission, and anticipated date of graduation. Recipients must notify the Illinois State Library immediately if scholarships and/or loans in addition to the Illinois State Library are accepted. Graduate study may be on a full-time or part-time basis. Transcripts of graduate library school courses must be forwarded for each semester to the Illinois State Library Training Grant Committee within 30 days following the semester's conclusion. A grade C average must be maintained or training grant is subject to cancellation. **Deadline:** Applications must be filed by May 1. **Contact:** Patricia Norris at the above address (see entry 2965).

**• 2967 •**

## Illinois Student Assistance Commission

1755 Lake Cook Rd.      *Ph:* (708)948-8550
Deerfield, IL 60015-5209      *Fax:* (708)831-8327
*URL:* http://www.isac1.org

**• 2968 •  Paul Douglas Teacher Scholarship (Illinois)** *(Undergraduate/Scholarship loan)*

**Qualif.:** Applicants must be undergraduate students enrolled full-time at approved public or private colleges and universities in a teacher education program. Recipients must have graduated in the top ten percent of their high school class, and must sign a teaching commitment to teach two years for each year of assistance. If the teaching commitment is not fulfilled, the scholarship becomes a loan to be repaid.

**Funds Avail.:** Up to $5,000 per year. **Contact:** Financial Aid Administrators or ISAC at the above address (see entry 2967).

**• 2969 •  Illinois Correctional Officer's Grant** *(Undergraduate/Grant)*

**Qualif.:** Applicants must be the spouse or children of Illinois Correctional Officers killed or at least 90 percent disabled in the line of duty. They must be attending approved Illinois public and private two- or four-year institutions.

**Funds Avail.:** Up to $3,500 for tuition and mandatory fees. **Contact:** Financial Aid Administrators or ISAC at the above address (see entry 2967).

**• 2970 •  Illinois Federal PLUS Loan** *(Graduate, Undergraduate/Loan)*

**Qualif.:** Applicants must be the parents of dependent undergraduate and graduate students who are Illinois residents or are attending an approved Illinois postsecondary institution.

**Funds Avail.:** Up to the difference of the cost of attendance and other financial aid received. **Contact:** Participating lenders or ISAC at the above address (see entry 2967).

**• 2971 •  Illinois Federal Subsidized Stafford Loan** *(Graduate, Undergraduate/Loan)*

**Qualif.:** Applicants must be Illinois undergraduate or graduate students or be enrolled on at least a half-time basis at approved public or private colleges or universities, hospital or vocational schools in Illinois. They must also complete a financial aid application form.

**Funds Avail.:** From $2,625 to $8,500 per academic year, depending on academic level. Loan limits will be lower for academic programs that are less than one year. Repayment, at variable interest rate not to exceed nine percent, begins six months after the student drops below half-time status. The repayment period is up to ten years. **Contact:** Financial Aid Administrators, participating lenders, or ISAC at the above address (see entry 2967).

---

Awards are arranged alphabetically below their administering organizations

## Illinois Student Assistance Commission (continued)

### • 2972 • Illinois Federal Supplemental Loans for Students (Graduate, Undergraduate/Loan)

**Qualif.:** Applicants must be graduate students or qualified independent undergraduates attending approved public or private colleges, universities, hospital, or vocational schools.

**Funds Avail.:** Up to $5,000 per year for junior and senior level undergraduates, depending on program length and up to $10,000 per year for graduate students. Repayment begins shortly after funds are disbursed. The repayment period is up to ten years. **Contact:** Participating lenders or ISAC at the above address (see entry 2967).

### • 2973 • Illinois Federal Unsubsidized Stafford Loan (Graduate, Undergraduate/Loan)

**Qualif.:** Applicants must be Illinois undergraduate or graduate students or be enrolled on at least a half-time basis at approved public or private colleges or universities, hospital or vocational schools in Illinois. They must also complete a financial aid application form.

**Funds Avail.:** From $2,625 to $8,500 per academic year, depending on academic level. Loan limits will be lower for academic programs that are less than one year. Repayment, at variable interest rate not to exceed nine percent, begins shortly after funds are disbursed but, if eligible, the principal may be deferred. The repayment period is up to ten years. **Contact:** Financial Aid Administrators, paticipating lenders, or ISAC at the above address (see entry 2967).

### • 2974 • Illinois Merit Recognition Scholarship (Undergraduate/Scholarship)

**Qualif.:** Applicants must be students who rank in the top five percent of their high school class at the end of the seventh semester. Recipients must use the award within one year of high school graduation, and must be enrolled at least half-time at approved Illinois public or private, two- or four-year universities, colleges, or hospital schools.

**Funds Avail.:** A one-time $1,000 scholarship. Availability of MRS awards is subject to state funding. **Contact:** High School Counselors or ISAC at the above address (see entry 2967).

### • 2975 • Illinois Monetary Award Program (Undergraduate/Grant)

**Qualif.:** Applicants must be attending approved Illinois public and private two- or four-year institutions at least half-time. They must be able to demonstrate financial need.

**Funds Avail.:** Up to $3,500 per year for five years to cover tuition and mandatory fees. **Contact:** Financial aid offices, high school counselors, or ISAC at the above address (see entry 2967).

### • 2976 • Illinois National Guard Grant (Graduate, Undergraduate/Grant)

**Qualif.:** Applicants must be attending Illinois public two- or four-year institutions. They must be enlistees or company grade officers up to the rank of captain who have served one year active duty or are currently on active duty status.

**Funds Avail.:** Tuition and some fees for the equivalent of 8 semesters or 12 quarters of undergraduate and graduate study. **Contact:** Local National Guard Unit, financial aid offices, or ISAC at the above address (see entry 2967).

### • 2977 • Illinois Police Officer/Fire Officer Grant (Undergraduate/Grant)

**Qualif.:** Applicants must be the spouse or children (age 25 and under) of Illinois police and fire officers who were killed in the line of duty and who are attending approved public and private two- or four-year institutions.

**Funds Avail.:** Up to $3,500 for tuition and mandatory fees. **Contact:** Financial Aid Administrators or ISAC at the above address (see entry 2967).

### • 2978 • Illinois Student-to-Student Grant (Undergraduate/Grant)

**Qualif.:** Applicants must be attending participating Illinois public two- or four-year institutions.

**Funds Avail.:** Voluntary student contributions are matched, dollar-for-dollar, by ISAC, and paid to participating institutions. Grants are then made available to needy students through procedures established by the campus financial aid administrator and the local student government. **Contact:** Financial Aid Administrators.

### • 2979 • Illinois uniLoan (Graduate, Undergraduate/Loan)

**Purpose:** To enable students to combine various educational loans into a single, manageable loan. **Qualif.:** Educational loans that may be considered include: Federal Stafford Loans, Guaranteed Student Loans (GSL), Illinois Opportunity Loans, Federal Supplemental Loans for Students (SLS), Auxiliary Loans to Assist Students (ALAS), Federal Perkins Loans, Federal Direct Loans, National Direct Student Loans (NDSL), and Health Professions Student Loans (HPSL), and Federal PLUS Loans. **Contact:** Participating lenders or ISAC at the above address (see entry 2967).

### • 2980 • Illinois Veteran Grant (Undergraduate/Grant)

**Qualif.:** Applicants must be veterans who served at least one year of honorable active duty in the U.S. Armed Forces. Veterans must have been residents of Illinois upon entering the service, and must have returned to Illinois to reside within six months of leaving the service. They must also be attending Illinois public two- or four-year institutions.

**Funds Avail.:** The grant is available for up to 120 eligibility units. **Contact:** Illinois Department of Veteran Affairs, Financial Aid Offices, or ISAC at the above address (see entry 2967).

### • 2981 • Minority Teachers of Illinois Scholarship (Undergraduate/Scholarship loan)

**Qualif.:** Applicants must be academically talented students of Black, Hispanic, Native American, or Asian American origin who plan to become teachers at the elementary or secondary level. They must be sophmores or above attending approved Illinois public or private colleges and universities, and must sign a teaching commitment to teach one year for each year assistance is received. MTI recipients must teach at an Illinois elementary or secondary school where no less than 30 percent of those enrolled are Black, Hispanic, Asian American, or Native American minority students. If the teaching commitment is not fulfilled, the scholarship becomes a loan.

**Funds Avail.:** Up to $5,000 per year. **Contact:** Financial Aid Administrators, College Minority Affairs Offices, or ISAC at the above address (see entry 2967).

# • 2982 •
## Illuminating Engineering Society of North America
Thunen Fund Committee
PO Box 77527
San Francisco, CA 94107-0527    *Ph:* (415)626-1950
*E-mail:* iesna@iesna.org
*URL:* http://www.iesna.org

### • 2983 • Robert Thunen Memorial Educational Scholarships *(Graduate, Undergraduate/Scholarship)*

**Purpose:** To further the study of light, lighting, and vision. **Focus:** Lighting and Related Fields. **Qualif.:** Student must be enrolled in an accredited institution located in northern California, northern Nevada, Oregon, or Washington state and study some field of lighting, including but not limited to theater, interior design, architecture, electrical engineering, or architectural engineering. **Criteria:** The award is based on the extent to which the grant will influence the student's work and career in the lighting field.

**Funds Avail.:** $2,000. Amount may vary according to the distribution committee's discretion. **No. of Awards:** 2. **To Apply:** A statement of purpose is required, three recommendations, and transcripts. Graduates must submit a project description. **Deadline:** March 19. **Contact:** Thunen Distribution Committee at the above address (see entry 2982).

# • 2984 •
## Imperial Cancer Research Fund
c/o Dr. Lillian Gann
PO Box 123
Lincoln's Inn Fields                *Ph:* 171 269 3090
London WC2A 3PX, England      *Fax:* 171 269 3585

### • 2985 • ICRF Postdoctoral Fellowships *(Postdoctorate/Fellowship)*

**Purpose:** To support fundamental, applied, and clinical research on cancer. **Focus:** Cancer Research. **Qualif.:** Applicants of all nationalities are eligible to apply. Applicant must be a postdoctoral scholar. Fellowships are tenable only at ICRF laboratories.

**Funds Avail.:** £19,700-23,040. **No. of Awards:** 30. **To Apply:** Write for application guidelines, or respond to advertisements placed in Nature+FA and Cell+FA twice a year. Inquiries about specific research proposals should be directed to the head of the relevant ICRF laboratory. **Deadline:** Bi-monthly. Applications are reviewed at ICRF Laboratory Research Committee meetings every two months. **Contact:** Dr. Lilian Gann, at the above address (see entry 2984).

# • 2986 •
## IMS Education Fund
1001 Grand Ave.                     *Ph:* (515)223-1401
West Des Moines, IA 50265      *Fax:* (515)223-0590
                                              *Free:* 800-747-3070

*The IMS Education Fund was formerly known as the Iowa Medical Foundation.*

### • 2987 • George Scanlon Medical Student Loans *(Doctorate/Loan)*

**Focus:** Medicine. **Qualif.:** Student borrowers must be residents of Iowa, but need not attend medical school in the state. They must maintain the academic standing required for graduation and be in their junior or senior year of college.

**Funds Avail.:** Loans are individually determined and renewable up to a level of $8,000 per year. Borrowers must sign a loan agreement that states the terms of repayment. Interest at seven percent per year accrues from the date of graduation. Repayment does not have to start until five years after graduation. If medical training is discontinued for any reason, repayment must begin immediately. **To Apply:** A financial aid form must be filed with a letter from the financial aid office that states the student's need and academic standing. **Deadline:** Applications may be submitted at any time. **Contact:** Deborah Potter at the above address (see entry 2986).

# • 2988 •
## Independent Accountants International Educational Foundation
9200 S. Dadeland Blvd., Ste. 510    *Ph:* (305)670-0580
Miami, FL 33156                           *Fax:* (305)670-3818
*URL:* http://www.iaintl.com/bylaws/htm

### • 2989 • Robert Kaufman Memorial Scholarships *(Graduate, Undergraduate/Scholarship)*

**Purpose:** To assist young people in furthering their education in the field of accounting. **Focus:** Accounting. **Qualif.:** Students who are pursuing, or planning to pursue, an education in accounting at recognized academic institutions anywhere in the world are eligible to apply. Applicants must be equivalent year college students or graduate students and have above a 3.5 GPA or equivalent in accounting. **Criteria:** Applications are evaluated on the basis of past academic achievement, standardized test scores, extracurricular activities, and courses taken. Applicants compete on an academic basis only, without reference to financial need. Financial need is considered only after the winning applicants are selected and the amount of the award is to be set.

**Funds Avail.:** An honorary award of up to $250 to assist in the purchase of textbooks may be given to any full-time student without demonstration of financial need. A scholarship of up to $1,500 may be awarded to a full-time student demonstrating financial need. The size of this award is based on the student's financial need as determined by an analysis of the student's financial circumstances. **No. of Awards:** 12 to 14. **To Apply:** Applications may be obtained from a college financial aid office, an IA member, or IA International headquarters. To be considered, the application must bear the signature of an endorsing IA member firm. If applicant is not familiar with an IA member, the IA headquarters will provide the name and address of the nearest member firm. **Deadline:** February 28.

**Remarks:** The scholarship fund was established in memory of Robert Kaufman, CPA, founder and second Chairman of Independent Accountants International. **Contact:** College financial aid offices, or the Independent Accountants International Educational Foundation at the above address (see entry 2988).

# • 2990 •
## Independent Order of Odd Fellows
22 Munsey Ave.
Livermore Falls, ME 04254       Ph: (207)897-3173
*URL:* http://www.ioof.nl

### • 2991 • Independent Order of Odd Fellows Nurses Training Scholarships *(Undergraduate/Scholarship)*

**Purpose:** To help alleviate the nursing shortage by providing assistance to students planning to become registered nurses. **Focus:** Nursing. **Qualif.:** Students must be accepted at and attending an accredited school of nursing in Maine that offers a registered nursing program. Requests from students not attending a school in Maine will not be acknowledged. **Criteria:** Awards are based on financial need, answers to application form questions, and motivation to earn and save money for education.

**Funds Avail.:** $150 to $300 per student according to the donations received and the number of scholarships awarded. **No. of Awards:** Depending on funds, between 15 and 30 scholarships are awarded. **To Apply:** Applications are available from the organization and contain requests for family details, income information, nursing school preparation, and references. **Deadline:** April 15. Selections are made the first Saturday in May. **Contact:** Ellen F. Washburn, Secretary, at the above address (see entry 2990).

# • 2992 •
## Indian Health Service Scholarship Program
Twinbrook Plaza, Ste. 100A
12300 Twinbrook Parkway       Ph: (301)443-6197
Rockville, MD 20852       Fax: (301)443-6048

*Indian Health Services is part of the U.S. Department of Health and Human Services.*

### • 2993 • IHS Health Professions Compensatory Preprofessional Scholarship *(Undergraduate/ Scholarship)*

**Qualif.:** Applicants must be American Indians or Alaska Natives, high school graduates or the equivalent, in good standing at the educational institution they are attending, have the capacity to complete a health professions course of study, and must intend to serve Indian People upon completion of professional health care degree as a health care provider in the discipline for which they are taking preparatory courses. Applicants must also be enrolled, or be accepted for enrollment, in courses that will prepare them for acceptance into health professions schools. Courses may be either compensatory (required to improve science, mathematics, or other basic skills and knowledge) or preprofessional (required in order to qualify for admission into a health professions program). **Criteria:** Previous recipients who meet the continued eligibility requirements will be given priority consideration.

**Funds Avail.:** Funding is available for a maximum of two years. Recipients must apply annually to receive continued funding beyond the initial award period. The level of scholarship benefits is contingent upon the availability of funds appropriated each fiscal year by the Congress of the United States and, therefore, is subject to yearly changes. The Scholarship Program will provide a monthly stipend to cover living expenses including room and board. Recipients will receive the stipend only during the academic period covered by their awards, August 1 to May 31. **Contact:** IHS Area Scholarship Coordinator at the above address (see entry 2992).

### • 2994 • IHS Health Professions Pre-Graduate Scholarships *(Undergraduate/Scholarship)*

**Qualif.:** Applicants must be American Indians or Alaska Natives. Candidates must be high school graduates or the equivalent, and must have the capacity to complete a health professions course of study. Applicants must be enrolled, or accepted for enrollment, in a baccalaureate degree program in specific preprofessional areas (pre-medicine and pre-dentistry). Applicants may be seniors, juniors, sophomores, or freshmen (priority is given to applicants in this order). Applicants must be in good standing at the educational institution they are attending. Candidates must intend to serve Indian People upon completion of professional health care education as health care providers in the disciplines for which the students are enrolled at the pregraduate level.

**Funds Avail.:** Funding is available for a maximum of four academic years. The level of scholarship benefits is contingent upon the availability of funds appropriated each fiscal year by the Congress of the United States and, therefore, is subject to yearly changes. The Scholarship Program will provide a monthly stipend to cover living expenses, tuition and educational expenses such as cost of books, uniforms, travel, rental of a post office box to use for receiving stipend checks, and room and board. Recipients will receive the stipend only during the academic period covered by their awards, August 1 to May 31. **Contact:** IHS Area Scholarship Coordinator at the above address (see entry 2992).

# • 2995 •
## Indiana Department of Veterans Affairs
302 W. Washington St., Rm. E-120    Ph: (317)232-3910
Indianapolis, IN 46204-2738      Fax: (317)232-7721
*URL:* http://www.va.gov/vaold.htm

### • 2996 • Child of Disabled Veteran Grant or Purple Heart Recipient, Grant *(Graduate, Other, Undergraduate/Other)*

**Purpose:** To reduce the amount of tuition paid by children of disabled or deceased veterans or Purple Heart recipients in state-supported schools. **Focus:** General Studies. **Qualif.:** Applicants must be legal Indiana residents attending state-supported universities. They must be the biological or legally adopted children of honorably discharged veterans who served during wartime and are rated with a service-connected disability or death, or received the Purple Heart medal for wounds received as a result of enemy action.

**Funds Avail.:** Recipients receive a reduction in the amount of tuition for up to four years. The reduction amount varies per university. **To Apply:** Along with an application form, applicants must fill out a remission of fees form (State Form 20234) and send it to the Indiana Department of Veteran's Affairs, attention: Education Division, at the above address. **Deadline:** None, although application must be approved prior to enrollment to be effective. **Contact:** Jon Brinkley, Indiana Department of Veterans Affairs State Service Officer, at the above address (see entry 2995).

### • 2997 • Department of Veterans Affairs Free Tuition for Children of POW/MIA's in Vietnam *(Undergraduate/Other)*

**Focus:** General Studies. **Qualif.:** Applicants must be the children of veterans who were legal residents of Indiana at the time of entrance on active duty in the U.S. Armed Forces and have since been declared Prisoners of War or Missing in Action after January 1, 1960. The applicants must have been born before or during the time the veteran was classified MIA/POW.

**Funds Avail.:** Recipients receive free tuition to obtain a bachelor's degree or certificate of completion at a state-supported institution. **To Apply:** Applicants must complete an application form and submit it to the Indiana Department of Veteran's Affairs, attention : Education Division, at the above address. **Contact:** Jon Brinkley, Indiana Department of Veterans Affairs State Service Officer, at the above address (see entry 2995).

---

**• 2998 •**
**Indianapolis Press Club**
150 W. Market St.                    *Ph:* (317)237-6222
Indianapolis, IN 46204              *Fax:* (317)237-6224

**• 2999 •  Maurice and Robert Early Scholarship**
*(Undergraduate/Scholarship)*

**Qualif.:** Applicants must be attending Indiana universities or colleges and preparing for a career in the news business. **Criteria:** It is preferred, but not required, that applicants major in journalism or broadcast journalism. Career potential is the primary consideration in awarding scholarships, but other factors, including journalistic competence and financial need are also considered. Applications are reviewed by a four-member Scholarship Committee.

**Funds Avail.:** Scholarships of up to $1,000 are awarded. The number of recipients varies depending upon funds available. **To Apply:** A formal application, an explanation of career goals and how the candidate plans to achieve them, work samples, and at least three letters of recommendation must be submitted. **Deadline:** June 1. **Contact:** Jim Hetherington, Chairman, Press Club Scholarship Committee, at the above address (see entry 2998).

---

**• 3000 •**
**Industrial Relations Council on GOALS**
PO Box 44218                         *Ph:* (612)833-1691
Eden Prairie, MN 55347              *Fax:* (612)833-1692
                                     *Free:* 800-344-
                                     GOALS

*E-mail:* rcanton999@aol.com
*URL:* http://www-cba.gsu.edu/GOALS

**• 3001 •  GOALS Fellowships** *(Graduate/Fellowship)*

**Purpose:** To recruit minority students. **Focus:** Human Resource Management/Relations. **Qualif.:** Applicants must be African American, Hispanic, Native Alaskan, Native American, or Native Hawaiian U.S. citizens. They must use the fellowship for full-time graduate study in human resource management or relations at any of the 15 participating consortium universities. Participating universities are Loyola University, Cornell University, University of Illinois (Champaign-Whara), Georgia State, University of Massachusetts—Amherst, Michigan State University, University of Minnesota, Ohio State University, Rutgers University, University of South Carolina, West Virginia University, University of Wisconsin, Texas A&M, Purdue, and American University. Candidates should also have an undergraduate degree in one of the social sciences, such as economics, psychology, sociology, or political science, or have concentrations in business administration, communications, or social work. **Criteria:** Candidates are ranked according to overall academic ability by a selection committee.

**Funds Avail.:** Fellowships include either whole or partial waiver of tuition and fees and stipends of up to $7,800 per academic year. The number of fellowships awarded each year varies depending on funds donated by corporate sponsors. **No. of Awards:** 20-25. **To Apply:** Students must be accepted at one of the 15 consortium graduate schools to be eligible. Candidates must then apply directly to the school for the GOALS fellowship and be nominated

by the school's director. **Deadline:** Depends on the university. Many graduate programs require that necessary documents be received by the middle of January for the following fall term. **Contact:** Rosana Canton, Executive Director, GOALS, at the above address (see entry 3000). Telephone: (612)833-1691. Toll-free telephone: 800-344-6257.

---

**• 3002 •**
**Infectious Diseases Society of America**
1200 19th St. N.W., Ste. 300        *Ph:* (202)857-1139
Washington, DC 20036                *Fax:* (202)223-4579

**• 3003 •  Burroughs Wellcome Young Investigator Award in Virology** *(Postdoctorate/Award)*

**Purpose:** To support virology research at the junior faculty level. **Focus:** Virology. **Qualif.:** Applicant must be a U.S. citizen or permanent resident with an M.D. degree. Candidate must be an unestablished investigator no more than three years out of a training program, working at a U.S. research institution. Candidate must be nominated and sponsored by a Fellow at the Society.

**Funds Avail.:** $90,000. **No. of Awards:** One. **To Apply:** Write to the Society for application form and guidelines. Submit seven copies of form, curriculum vitae, a letter from department chair or dean detailing institutional commitment, a letter from the sponsor, and a description of the proposed research. **Deadline:** June 1. Notification in August.

**Remarks:** The Society also offers a two-year postdoctoral research fellowship. Write for further information. **Contact:** Dr. Vincent T. Andriole at the above address (see entry 3002).

---

**• 3004 •**
**Inland Steel Industries**
c/o David C. Hawley, Sec.
30 W Monroe St.
Chicago, IL 60603                    *Ph:* (312)899-3421
*URL:* http://www.inland.com

**• 3005 •  All-Inland Scholarship** *(Undergraduate/Scholarship)*

**Purpose:** To assist the children of Inland employees in realizing their academic and career objectives. **Focus:** General Studies. **Qualif.:** Applicants must be children of Inland employees and in their senior year of high school. **Criteria:** Awards will be given based on academic records, SAT or ACT scores leadership activities in school and in the community, and future academic and career potential.

**Funds Avail.:** $500 to $2,000. **To Apply:** Applicants must write for details. **Contact:** Inland Steel-Ryerson Foundation, Inc. at the above address (see entry 3004).

---

## Institute for Advanced Studies in the Humanities
University of Edinburgh
Hope Park Square                     *Ph:* 131 650 4671
Edinburgh EH8 9NW, Scotland          *Fax:* 131 668 2252

### • 3007 • Institute for Advanced Studies Visiting Research Fellowships *(Postdoctorate/Fellowship)*

**Purpose:** To encourage advanced study and inter-disciplinary research in the humanities. **Focus:** Humanities (Archaeology Art History, Classics, English Literature, European and Oriental Languages and Literature, History, Linguistics, Philosophy, Scottish Studies and History of Science, Law, Divinity, and the Social Sciences). **Qualif.:** Applicant may be of any nationality. Applicant should have a Ph.D. and appropriate publications, or equivalent evidence of aptitude for advanced studies. Degree candidates are not eligible for fellowships. Consideration is given to academic excellence and to the need for pursuing the subject of research in Edinburgh. In addition to carrying out research, a fellow is normally required to hold one or two seminars; no regular teaching is required of fellows. While all fellows have study rooms and library privileges at the University of Edinburgh, most fellowships are honorary (i.e., without stipend). Candidates are encouraged to apply to other resources for funding their tenure at the Institute. Fellowships are tenable only at the Institute.

**Funds Avail.:** £500 maximum. **To Apply:** Write to the director for application form and guidelines. Submit application with brief curriculum vitae, research proposal and the names of two references. **Deadline:** November 30. **Contact:** Professor Peter Jones, Director, at the above address (see entry 3006).

### • 3008 •
## Institute for Advanced Study
Olden Ln.                            *Ph:* (609)734-8000
Princeton, NJ 08540                  *Fax:* (609)924-8399
*E-mail:* webmaster@.edu
*URL:* http://www.ias.edu

### • 3009 • Institute for Advanced Study Postdoctoral Research Fellowships *(Postdoctorate/Fellowship)*

**Purpose:** To provide scholars with an opportunity to conduct research at the Institute. **Focus:** History, Mathematics, Natural Sciences, Social Sciences, Physical Sciences, Theoretical Biology. **Qualif.:** Candidate may be of any nationality. Applicant must be a postdoctoral scholar in one of the areas of study. Fellowships are tenable at the Institute.

**Funds Avail.:** Varies, according to school. **To Apply:** Write to the appropriate school at the Institute for application form and guidelines. **Deadline:** History Fellowships: October 15 and November 1; Mathematics and Social Science Fellowships: December 1; and Natural Science Fellowships: December 15. **Contact:** Institute for Advanced Study at the above address (see entry 3008).

### • 3010 • Institute for Advanced Study Postdoctoral Study Awards *(Postdoctorate/Grant)*

**Purpose:** To provide the opportunity for postdoctoral research to scholars of unusual ability and achievement. **Focus:** History, Social Sciences, Physical Sciences, Mathematics, Theoretical Biology. **Qualif.:** Applicants must be postdoctoral scholars. Areas of study are: historical studies (Greek and Roman civilization, medieval history, history of art, modern European history, Near Eastern history, history of modern philosophy, and American intellectual history and the history of mathematics and sciences); pure and applied mathematics; natural sciences (theoretical physics, field

theory, and astrophysics); social sciences (emphasis on humanistic social science); and theoretical biology.

**Funds Avail.:** Varies. **No. of Awards:** 150-160. **Deadline:** For historical studies: November 15. For social sciences: November 15. For natural sciences: December 1. For mathematics: December 1. **Contact:** School Administrative Officers at the above address (see entry 3008).

### • 3011 •
## Institute of American Cultures
160 Haines Hall
405 Hilgard Ave.                     *Ph:* (310)825-7403
Los Angeles, CA 90024-1545           *Fax:* (310)206-3421
*URL:* http://www.sscnet.ucla.edu/caas/research/iac.html

### • 3012 • Institute of American Cultures Graduate and Predoctoral Fellowships *(Doctorate/Fellowship)*

**Purpose:** To support the completion of a doctoral dissertation that is related to African American, Asian American, Chicano/a, and American Indian Studies. **Focus:** American Studies. **Qualif.:** Applicants must be UCLA graduate and predoctoral students. Candidates for the predoctoral fellowship in African American studies must be advanced to candidacy by the beginning of the fellowship year. Acceptance of the award carries with it the commitment to make a contribution to the activities of the sponsoring ethnic studies center.

**Funds Avail.:** $10,000 per year plus registration fees. **To Apply:** Students should contact the sponsoring center to learn about additional possible restrictions. A completed application form, letters of recommendation from three faculty members with whom the student has worked most closely, a curriculum vitae, dissertation proposal, and a statement of purpose are required. **Deadline:** December 31. **Contact:** The Institute of American Cultures at the above address or call (310)206-2557. Department telephone numbers are as follows: African American studies (310)206-8009; American Indian studies (310)825-7315; Asian American studies (310)825-2974; and Chicano studies (310)825-2363.

### • 3013 • Institute of American Cultures Postdoctoral and Visiting Scholars Fellowships *(Postdoctorate/Fellowship)*

**Purpose:** To support research and writing in the fields of African American, Asian American, American Indian, and Chicano/a studies. **Focus:** American Studies. **Qualif.:** Senior scholars or those who have recently obtained their Ph.D. are eligible to apply. Applicants must have specific plans for their activities during the fellowship year. The Center is particularly interested in projects that advance knowledge about the nation's minorities. Applicants must be certified to have completed all requirements for the doctoral degree beginning the fellowship year. The acceptance of support carries with it the commitment to participate in the activities of the Center for Afro-American Studies. UCLA faculty and staff are not eligible for postdoctoral or visiting scholar support.

**Funds Avail.:** Recent Ph.D.s may receive up to $28,000 depending on rank and experience. Senior scholars will receive awards to supplement the sabbatical salaries provided by their own institutions. Fellowships can be renewed, but are subject to review in competition with new applications. **Deadline:** December 31. **Contact:** The appropriate UCLA ethnic studies center as follows: African American studies (310)206-8009; American Indian studies (310)825-7315; Asian American studies (310)825-2974; or Chicano studies (310)825-2363.

## • 3014 •
### Institute of Chartered Accountants in England and Wales
PO Box 433
Chartered Accountants' Hall,
  Moorgate Place
London EC2P 2BJ, England      *Ph:* 171 920 8483

#### • 3015 •   Institute of Chartered Accountants Research Grants *(Professional Development/Grant)*

**Purpose:** To sponsor projects aimed at furthering the theory and practice of accounting. **Focus:** Accounting. **Qualif.:** Candidate may be of any nationality. Research grants are normally awarded to individuals holding paid academic or professional posts in British universities. The proposed research project should be related to finance, financial accounting, auditing or management accounting. The board does not fund research undertaken in pursuit of an undergraduate or graduate degree.

**Funds Avail.:** £200-50,000. **To Apply:** Write for application form and guidelines. **Deadline:** None. **Contact:** Mr. Desmond Wright, at the above address (see entry 3014).

## • 3016 •
### Institute of Classical Studies
31334 Gordon Square
London WC1H 0PY, England      *Ph:* 171 387 7696

#### • 3017 •   Michael Ventris Memorial Award *(Postdoctorate, Postgraduate/Award)*

**Purpose:** To support projects related to Mycenaean civilization and architecture. **Focus:** Architecture, Mycenaean Civilization. **Qualif.:** Candidate may be of any nationality. Applicant must have a postgraduate degree, or the equivalent experience, in a field related to Mycenaean civilization or in architecture. Candidate should intend to undertake a specific project rather than a continuing program of study.

**Funds Avail.:** £1,000 maximum. **To Apply:** Write to the secretary for application guidelines. Submit particulars of age, qualifications, academic record (or other supporting evidence), the names of two referees, and an outline of the proposed project. Candidates for an architecture award should submit application to the secretary of the Architectural Association, 34-36 Bedford Square, London WC1B 3EG, England. **Deadline:** March 31. Award is made in June. **Contact:** Secretary at the above address (see entry 3016).

## • 3018 •
### Institute on Comparative Political and Economic Systems - Fund for American Studies
1526 18th St. NW      *Ph:* (202)986-0384
Washington, DC 20036      *Fax:* (202)986-0390
                *Free:* 800-741-6964

*E-mail:* goldy@ifas.org
*URL:* http://www.dcinternships.org/icpes.htm

#### • 3019 •   Engalitcheff Institute on Comparative Political and Economic Systems Internship *(Undergraduate/Internship)*

**Focus:** Political science, business, economics, journalism. **Qualif.:** Applicants must be undergraduate sophomores and juniors who have been accepted to the programs sponsored by the Fund for American Studies and Georgetown University. **Criteria:** Awards are made based on applicant's interest in politics, economics, business or journalism; academic achievement, leadership skills/experience, and financial need.

**Funds Avail.:** $500 (partial) to $3,450 (full). **To Apply:** Applicants must submit a resume, transcript, three letters of recommendation, 500-word essay, parents' last tax return and last FAF, if applicable, and a $15 non-refundable application fee. **Deadline:** March 15.

**Remarks:** Each day of the internship starts with work at an office on Capitol Hill, a think tank or policy group, a law fir, a foreign embassy, a government agency, or a public or private organization involved in public policy. The Fund's staff will work diligently to match the intern with an internship that best meets the intern's interests and skills and provides the intern with real-life training. The intern may also arrange their own internship, if so desired. In the afternoon, the intern with take two courses at Georgetown University, Comparative Economic Systems and Comparative Political Systems. The six credit are transferable to the intern's home institution. **Contact:** Lisa Goldy.

#### • 3020 •   Bryce Harlow Institute on Business and Government Affairs Internship *(Undergraduate/Internship)*

**Focus:** Political science, business, economics, journalism. **Qualif.:** Applicants must be undergraduate sophomores and juniors who have been accepted to the programs sponsored by the Fund for American Studies and Georgetown University. **Criteria:** Awards are made based on applicant's interest in politics, economics, business or journalism; academic achievement, leadership skills/experience, and financial need.

**Funds Avail.:** $500 (partial) to $3,450 (full). **To Apply:** Applicants must submit a resume, transcript, three letters of recommendation, 500-word essay, parents' last tax return and last FAF, if applicable, and a $15 non-refundable application fee. **Deadline:** March 15.

**Remarks:** Each weekday starts with an internship in the office of a Fortune 500 corporation, trade association, non-profit organization or consulting firm with a government affairs office. The Fund's staff will match the intern with an internship that best meets the inter's level of skill and experience, or the intern may arrange their own internship if it meets the requirements of the Institute. Two academic courses are taught each weekday afternoon on the Georgetown University campus. Courses include Business and Government Relations, and Power and Values in Organizations. Leadership Development Activities include evening panel discussions. **Contact:** Lisa Goldy.

#### • 3021 •   Institute on Political Journalism Summer Program *(Undergraduate/Internship)*

**Focus:** Political science, business, economics, journalism. **Qualif.:** Applicants must be undergraduate sophomores and juniors who have been accepted to the programs sponsored by the Fund for American Studies and Georgetown University. **Criteria:** Awards are made based on applicant's interest in politics, economics, business or journalism; academic achievement, leadership skills/experience, and financial need.

**Funds Avail.:** $500 (partial) to $3,450 (full). **To Apply:** Applicants must submit a resume, transcript, three letters of recommendation, 500-word essay, parents' last tax return and last FAF, if applicable, and a $15 non-refundable application fee. **Deadline:** March 15.

**Remarks:** For approximately forty hours a week, the intern will be in a Washington media organization. Sponsors include print and broadcast media outlets, think tanks, Congressional press offices, and public affairs offices of Federal government agencies. The staff of the Institute will match the intern with an internship that best meets the intern's interests and level of skill, or interns may arrange their own internships if they meet the requirements of the institute. The internships provide students with a firsthand look at the world of Washington journalism. Intern responsibilities vary, but often include covering Congressional hearings, writing press releases, drafting articles for publication, producing videos, and

---

*Institute on Comparative Political and Economic Systems - Fund for American Studies (continued)*

assisting with media relations. Courses include Economics in Public Policy and Ethical Perspectives on the Media. Leadership development activities include weekly lectures and dialogues. **Contact:** Lisa Goldy.

---

**• 3022 •**
## Institute of Contemporary History and Wiener Library

| 4 Devonshire Street | *Ph:* 171 636 7247 |
| London W1N 2BH, England | *Fax:* 171 436 6428 |

### • 3023 • Fraenkel Prizes in Contemporary History
*(Professional Development/Prize)*

**Purpose:** To recognize outstanding, unpublished work in a field of interest to the Wiener Library. **Focus:** Modern European History. **Qualif.:** Candidates may be of any nationality, but must have written an unpublished work in a field of contemporary history covering an area of interest to the Wiener Library. Work may be written in English, French, German, or Russian. One prize is available to all candidates (length between 50,000 and 150,000 words).The other prize is reserved for those who have yet to publish a major work (length between 25,000 and 100,000 words).

**Funds Avail.:** $5,000 or $3,000. **No. of Awards:** Two. **To Apply:** Write to the administrative secretary for application guidelines. Submit two copies of manuscript plus a brief curriculum vitae. Specify for which award you are applying. **Deadline:** May 2. Prizes are decided in the summer. **Contact:** Administrative Secretary at the above address (see entry 3022).

---

**• 3024 •**
## Institute of Current World Affairs - Crane-Rogers Foundation

| 4 W. Wheelock St. | *Ph:* (603)643-5548 |
| Hanover, NH 03755 | *Fax:* (603)643-9599 |
| *E-mail:* icwa@valley.net | |

### • 3025 • Crane-Rogers Fellowships *(Professional Development/Fellowship)*

**Purpose:** To select a young person of outstanding promise and character to study and write about an area or issue of the world outside the U.S. in need of in-depth understanding for a minimum fellowship period of two years. **Focus:** Liberal Arts. **Qualif.:** Applicant may be of any nationality, but must have completed his/her formal education, and be under the age of 36 years. Fellowships may not be used to underwrite specific research projects or advanced degree work. "Target of Opportunity" fellowships are ones where the issue or area is of the candidate's own devising. The Institute will also select certain areas it would like to see studied.

**Funds Avail.:** The Institute provides full support for its fellows and their immediate families for the two year period, requiring that they write monthly reports or newsletters to the Executive Director. **No. of Awards:** 4. **To Apply:** There are no official application forms. Write to the executive director, enclosing a curriculum vitae, a brief explanation of personal background and professional experience, and description of proposed study. This initial letter is followed by a formal written application. **Deadline:** April 1 for a June decision, and September 1 for a December decision.

**Remarks:** Occasionally, the Institute offers fellowships that focus on continuing themes of specific issues, such as John Miller

Musser Memorial Forest & Society Fellowship for people with graduate degrees in forestry or forest-related specialties, and the John O. Crane Memorial Fellowship for people who are interested in the study of Eastern Europe and the Middle East. Write for further details. **Contact:** Peter Bird Martin, Executive Director, at the above address (see entry 3024).

---

**• 3026 •**
## Institute of Developing Economies

| International Exchanges Department | |
| 42 Ichigaya-Hommura-Cho | |
| Shinjuku-ku | *Ph:* 3 353 4231 |
| Tokyo 162, Japan | *Fax:* 3 226 8475 |

### • 3027 • Institute of Developing Economies Visiting Research Fellowships *(Postdoctorate/Fellowship)*

**Purpose:** To provide post doctoral research opportunities in Japan and gain insight into the process of development issues in developing countries. **Focus:** Economic and Social Development, Economics, Politics, Sociology. **Qualif.:** Applicant may be of any nationality, but must be a specialist from a university or government institution who is engaged in research concerning the economic, political or social problems of a developing countries. Applicant must have a Ph.D. or equivalent degree, or have several years of research or administrative experience. Candidate must have a working knowledge of English. Two types of fellowships are offered: Institute-Supported Fellowships, which are limited to people from developing countries; and Self-Supporting Fellowships, which are offered to people from both developing and developed countries. Fellows are expected to spend part of the fellowship term at the Institute, as well as assisting in the research activities of the Institute.

**Funds Avail.:** Up to 396,000 yen/month, plus round-trip airfare. **To Apply:** Write for application form and guidelines. Submit form with a personal history and statement of proposed research. Three letters of recommendation, one of which must be from a representative of home organization, are also required. **Deadline:** End of December; end of June. **Contact:** Shinichi Nozoe, Director, at the above address (see entry 3026).

---

**• 3028 •**
## Institute for Education in Journalism

| Institute of Afro-American Affairs | |
| 269 Mercer St., Ste. 601 | |
| New York University | *Ph:* (212)998-2130 |
| New York, NY 10003 | *Fax:* (212)995-4109 |

### • 3029 • AEJ Summer Internships for Minorities
*(Undergraduate/Internship)*

**Focus:** Journalism. **Qualif.:** The program is for sophomore, junior, and senior undergraduates; preference is for full-time juniors. The students' credentials must reflect an interest in journalism. Students must be members of a minority group (e.g., African American, Puerto Rican, American Indian, Mexican American, Eskimo).

**Funds Avail.:** As an AEJ intern, the candidate is placed in an entry-level position with news publications, primarily in the New York/New Jersey area. As full-time writers, recipients receive a minimum stipend of $200 per week for a 35-hour week. Most broadcasting internships are non-paying. **No. of Awards:** 15-20. **To Apply:** Formal applications must be accompanied by the following: an autobiographical essay of 500 words with information about the applicant's reasons for pursuing a career in journalism and what he/she would like to gain from the internship; college transcript; samples of work; resume; and two recommendations. Applicants are also required to submit work published by local or campus publications. Broadcast majors should submit audio cassette tapes or standard VHS tapes. A staff position on either a campus publication, a radio or television station, or a previous journalism-related internship experience, as well as published writing samples, should be submitted if available. **Deadline:** Applications must be filed by December 11. Students seeking early consideration should complete and forward the application materials by October 23. Requests for applications will be accepted until October 30; however, students are recommended to make their requests by September 18 to meet the initial deadlines of the larger media organizations.

**Remarks:** The program begins the second week in June and ends the second week in August. In addition to full-time internship the student will be enrolled in a two credit course, Journalism and Minorities. The AEJ coordinator is available for counseling and support throughout the course. **Contact:** The Institute for Education in Journalism at the above address (see entry 3028).

---

• 3030 •

## Institute of Electrical and Electronics Engineers - Charles LeGeyt Fortescue Fellowship Committee

445 Hoes Lane    *Ph:* (908)562-3839
Piscataway, NJ 08855-1331    *Fax:* (908)981-9019
*E-mail:* M.Quinn@1eee.org

### • 3031 • Charles LeGeyt Fortescue Fellowship
*(Graduate/Fellowship)*

**Purpose:** To support graduate studies in electrical engineering. **Focus:** Electrical/Electronic Engineering. **Qualif.:** Candidate must have a bachelor's degree and must be starting full-time graduate studies at a recognized school of engineering in the United States or Canada. Awardee may not hold or receive other fellowships for the same academic year.

**Funds Avail.:** $24,000. **No. of Awards:** 1. **To Apply:** Write to the Secretary for application form and guidelines. Submit form, certified academic transcripts, Graduate Record Examination scores, and three letters of recommendation. **Deadline:** January 31. **Contact:** Secretary at the above address (see entry 3030).

---

• 3032 •

## Institute of Electrical and Electronics Engineers - History Center

Rutgers—The State University of
  New Jersey
39 Union St.    *Ph:* (732)932-1066
New Brunswick, NJ 08901-8538    *Fax:* (732)932-1066
*E-mail:* history@iece.org
*URL:* http://www.ieee.org/organizations/history-center

### • 3033 • IEEE Fellowship in Electrical History
*(Doctorate, Graduate, Postdoctorate/Fellowship)*

**Purpose:** To support graduate and postdoctoral studies in the history of electrical engineering and technology. **Focus:** History of Electrical Engineering and Technology. **Qualif.:** Candidate must be a full-time graduate student in electrical engineering or a postdoctoral researcher who has received his/her Ph.D. within the past three years.

**Funds Avail.:** $15,000. **No. of Awards:** One. **To Apply:** Write to the Director for application form and guidelines. **Deadline:** February 1. **Contact:** Chairman at the above address (see entry 3032).

---

• 3034 •

## Institute for European History - Institut fur Europaische Geschichte

Alte Universitatsstrasse 19    *Ph:* 61 31 399360
D-55116 Mainz, Germany    *Fax:* 61 31 237988

### • 3035 • Institute for European History Fellowships
*(Doctorate, Postdoctorate/Fellowship)*

**Purpose:** To support advanced research in European history and religions. **Focus:** European History, European Religions. **Qualif.:** Candidate may be of any nationality but must have a thorough command of the German language. Applicant must have a doctorate or be at the advanced stage of the dissertation. Candidate must wish to undertake research into the history of occidental religion or the history of Europe from the 16th to the 20th century. Fellowships are tenable at the Institute.

**Funds Avail.:** DM14,640-18,720. **No. of Awards:** 20. **To Apply:** Write to the appropriate department for application guidelines. Submit a curriculum vitae, a brief outline of the proposed research, university transcripts, and the names of two referees. **Deadline:** Varies. **Contact:** Can also be reached at 061-31-399360; Professor Dr. K.O. von Aretin at the above address (see entry 3034).

---

• 3036 •

## Institute of Food Technologists

221 N. LaSalle St.    *Ph:* (312)782-8424
Chicago, IL 60601    *Fax:* (312)782-8348
*E-mail:* pgpaglicuco@ift.org
*URL:* http://www.ift.org

### • 3037 • Institute of Food Technologists Freshman/Sophomore Scholarships *(Undergraduate/Scholarship)*

**Purpose:** To attract and encourage outstanding students to enter the field of food science and technology. **Focus:** Food Science and Technology. **Qualif.:** Candidates for the Freshman Scholarship must be scholastically outstanding high school graduates or seniors expecting to graduate from accredited high schools. Candidates must have been accepted by colleges or universities approved by the Institute of Food Technologists (IFT) and must follow programs of study in food technology or food science. First year students applying for the Sophomore Scholarship must have a G.P.A. of at least 2.5 on a 4.0 scale. Recommendations from department heads and faculty members familiar with respective candidates' work are also required.

**Funds Avail.:** The number of awards and stipend amounts varies each year; however, awards typically range form $1,000-1,500. **No. of Awards:** Approximately 50. **To Apply:** Applications must be submitted to the department head of the school being attended. Freshman and sophomore students who submit applications through approved schools and are awarded scholarships may keep the scholarships even if they subsequently transfer to other schools, as long as the other schools are approved by IFT. Department heads at the transfer schools must certify that the proposed curricula meet IFT minimum standards. Applications must be resubmitted each year. **Deadline:** Freshman applications must be submitted by February 15; sophomore applications by March 1. Each department head may submit a maximum of eight freshman and eight sophomore applications by March 1 and March 15, respectively. All applicants and department heads will

---

---

## Institute of Food Technologists (continued)

be notified by April 15. Recipients must accept in writing by May 15.

**Remarks:** The sponsoring organizations include Continental Baking Co., Nabisco Brands, Inc., and IFT Student Association George R. Foster. **Contact:** Department heads at the individual educational institutions or the Institute's Scholarship Department at the above address (see entry 3036).

### • 3038 • Institute of Food Technologists Graduate Fellowships *(Graduate/Fellowship)*

**Purpose:** To encourage graduate research in food science and technology rather than in other disciplines such as genetics, nutrition, and microbiology. **Focus:** Food Science and Technology. **Qualif.:** Applicants must be scholastically outstanding senior undergraduates or graduate students with above average interest and aptitude in research, who will be enrolled in graduate studies on the effective date of the fellowship. The school of enrollment can be any educational institution that is conducting fundamental investigations for the advancement of food science/technology.

**Funds Avail.:** $1,250 to $5,000. The number of awards and the stipend amounts of the awards vary each year. Fellowship recipients become ineligible for further payments when the degrees for which the fellowships were awarded are earned or if the students drop or substantially change the research programs during the tenure of the fellowships. **No. of Awards:** Approximately 33. **To Apply:** Applications must be submitted to the department heads of the academic institutions that the candidates attend. **Deadline:** Applications are due to department heads by February 1; department heads must submit applications to the Institute of Food Technologists by February 15.

**Remarks:** Sponsoring organizations include: Kraft General Foods Foundation, General Mills, Inc., The Coca-Cola Foundation, Nabisco Brands, Inc., Thomas J. Lipton Foundation, Inc., IFT Past-Presidents, Pfizer Speciality Chemical Group - Pfizer Lite Food Ingredients, Grocery Manufacturers of America, Inc., Proctor & Gamble Co., Frito-Lay, Inc., Kalsec, Inc., Society of Flavor Chemists Memorial, Florasynth, Inc., and IFT New York Section. **Contact:** Department heads at the individual educational institutions or the Institute's Scholarship Department at the above address (see entry 3036).

### • 3039 • Institute of Food Technologists Junior/Senior Scholarships *(Undergraduate/Scholarship)*

**Purpose:** To encourage deserving and outstanding undergraduate students to pursue or continue curricula leading to Bachelor of Science degrees in food science and technology. **Focus:** Food Science and Technology. **Qualif.:** Scholastically outstanding sophomores or juniors who are enrolled in food science or food technology curricula in colleges or universities approved by the Institute of Food Technology (IFT) are eligible. Sophomores who transfer to other approved institutions are also eligible. Students' curricula must meet or show progress toward meeting IFT minimum standards.

**Funds Avail.:** $1,000 to $2,250. The stipend amounts of the awards vary each year. **No. of Awards:** 64. **To Apply:** Students who submit applications through approved schools and are awarded scholarships may keep the scholarships even if they subsequently transfer to other schools, as long as the other schools are IFT approved schools. The department heads at the transfer schools must certify that their curricula or proposed curricula meet IFT minimum standards. **Deadline:** To department heads by February 1; department heads must submit applications to the Institute of Food Technologists by February 15. **Contact:** Department heads at the individual educational institutions or the Institute's Scholarship Department at the above address (see entry 3036).

## • 3040 •
## Institute Francais de Washington
Department of Romance Languages
University of North Carolina at
  Chapel Hill
234 Dey Hall CB 3170      *Ph:* (919)962-0154
Chapel Hill, NC 27599      *Fax:* (919)962-5457
*E-mail:* cmaley@email.unc.edu

### • 3041 • Gilbert Chinard Scholarships *(Doctorate, Postdoctorate/Scholarship)*

**Focus:** French Studies. **Qualif.:** Applicants must be Ph.D. candidates completing the final stages of their dissertations or individuals who received their Ph.D. degrees not more than six years before applying for this scholarship. Their fields of study must be French history, literature, art and music.

**Funds Avail.:** $1,000 for maintenance (not travel) during research in France. **No. of Awards:** 3. **To Apply:** Candidates must submit a two-page description of the proposed research project and planned trip (location, length of stay, etc.) and include a curriculum vitae. A letter of recommendation from the dissertation director is also required for Ph.D. candidates. Upon returning to the United States, recipients are expected to submit a brief report to the Institute. **Deadline:** January 15. **Contact:** The Institute Francais de Washington at the above address (see entry 3040).

## • 3042 •
## Institute on Global Conflict and Cooperation
University of California, San Diego
9500 Gilman Dr.      *Ph:* (619)534-3352
La Jolla, CA 92093-0158      *Fax:* (619)534-7655
*E-mail:* bhalvorsen@ucsd.edu; bhalvorsen@ucsd.edu
*URL:* http://www-igcc.ucsd.edu; http://www-igcc.ucsd.edu

### • 3043 • IGCC Dissertation Fellowships *(Doctorate, Graduate/Fellowship)*

**Purpose:** To support graduate student research at the dissertation level on the causes of international conflict and opportunities to promote international cooperation. In addition to traditional security issues, IGCC's research agenda also includes international conflict and cooperation of political, economic, environmental affairs, and ethnic conflict. **Focus:** All disciplines of study. **Qualif.:** Applicant may be of any nationality, but must be enrolled in one of the graduate programs in the University of California system. U.S. citizenship is not required. **Criteria:** Proposals are evaluated on quality, and the relevance of the project to IGCC's goal of understanding international structures and processes so as to reduce conflict and promote cooperation among nations or regions. The project must be linked to international outcomes. The project does not have to overlap IGCC's current research priorities.

**Funds Avail.:** $12,000 nine month stipend, from October to June of an academic year. Up to $4,000 in travel and research support available in the first year, when justified as critical to the project. **No. of Awards:** 20-25 per year. **To Apply:** Write for application form and guidelines. **Deadline:** February 1.

**Remarks:** IGCC also offers grants for research and teaching projects within the University of California system. Contact the IGCC Coordinator of Campus Programs. **Contact:** Bettina B. Halvorsen, Coordinator of Campus Programs, at the above address (see entry 3042).

### • 3044 •
### Institute for Health Policy Studies
Health Services Research Training
  Program
University of California, San
  Francisco
1388 Sutter St., 11th Floor
San Francisco, CA 94109     *Ph:* (415)476-0531
*E-mail:* nancy_ramsay@quickmail.ucsf.edu

#### • 3045 • Postdoctoral Fellowships in Health Policy and Health Services Research *(Postdoctorate/ Fellowship)*

**Purpose:** To support health professionals and scholars who are preparing for leadership roles in health policy and health services research. **Focus:** Health Policy, Health Services Research. **Qualif.:** Candidates must be a postdoctoral social scientist or health professional, or have an advanced professional degree in a field related to health policy. Candidates must also be citizens of the U.S. or noncitizens admitted for permanent residence. Physician candidates must have completed their clinical training and be board-certified or board-eligible.

**Funds Avail.:** $19,000-32,000. **To Apply:** Write to the program coordinator for application form and guidelines. Submit form, two written samples of work, a two-page professional statement, and three letters of reference. An interview may be required. **Deadline:** January 31. Notification by March 31. **Contact:** Nancy Ramsay at the above address (see entry 3044).

### • 3046 •
### Institute of Holy Land Studies
Mount Zion
PO Box 1276
91012 Jerusalem, Israel     *Ph:* 2 718628
    *Fax:* 2 732717

#### • 3047 • Institute of Holy Land Studies Scholarships *(Graduate/Scholarship)*

**Purpose:** To assist graduate studies at the Institute. **Focus:** Biblical Studies, Hebrew Language, Middle Eastern Studies, Religious Studies. **Qualif.:** Applicant may be of any nationality. Candidate must have a bachelor's degree in appropriate area of study and an undergraduate grade point average of 3.0/4.0. Scholarships are tenable at the Institute. Candidate may be seeking a graduate degree from the Institute, or from another institution that will accept credits earned at the Institute. Selected individuals pursuing non-degree studies at the Institute may also qualify for support. **Criteria:** The scholarships are awarded based on academic ability, promise and need.

**Funds Avail.:** $400-800. **To Apply:** North and South American applicants should write to Amelia Nakai, 4249 East State Street, Suite 203, Rockford, IL 61108, USA (815)229-5900 for application materials. Candidates from all other parts of the world should write the Institute in Jerusalem. **Deadline:** Fall semester: February 24, spring semester: October 6. Notification by April 10 and November 20, respectively. **Contact:** Mr. Maurice Helou, Chair of Scholarship Committee, Institute of Holy Land Studies PO Box 1276, Mt. Zion 91012, Jerusalem, Israel.

### • 3048 •
### Institute of Human Paleontology - Institut de Paléontologie Humaine
Fondation Prince Albert Ier de
  Monaco
1, rue René Panhard     *Ph:* 1 43 31 62 91
75013 Paris, France     *Fax:* 1 43 31 22 79

#### • 3049 • Prince Rainier III de Monaco Bursary *(Professional Development/Grant)*

**Purpose:** To support research in areas of interest to the Institute. **Focus:** Geology, Paleontology, Prehistory. **Qualif.:** Applicant may be of any nationality. Applicant must be a young researcher who plans to conduct a field or laboratory research project in one of the above areas of study.

**Funds Avail.:** 20,000Fr. **To Apply:** Write for application guidelines. Submit a letter of interest describing proposed project and a curriculum vitae. **Deadline:** October 1. The bursary is offered biennially and is awarded in June. **Contact:** Director of the Institute of Human Paleontology at the above address (see entry 3048).

### • 3050 •
### Institute for Humane Studies
4084 University Dr., Ste.101     *Ph:* (703)934-6920
Fairfax, VA 22030-6812     *Fax:* (703)352-7535
    *Free:* 800-697-3799

*E-mail:* IHS@gmu.edu
*URL:* http://osf1.gmu.edu/˜ihs/index.html

*The Institute for Humane Studies is an independent scholarly center promoting the advanced study of liberty across a broad range of @ and professional disciplines. IHS promotes the principles of classical liberalism, which includes recognition of individual rights and the worth of the individual.*

#### • 3051 • Donald Bogie Prize *(Graduate/Prize)*

**Purpose:** To honor outstanding, original, unpublished philosophical papers that reflect an interest in the classical liberal tradition. **Focus:** Philosophy, Law, Political Science. **Qualif.:** Candidates must be advanced graduate students in philosophy, law, or political science.

**Funds Avail.:** $500. **To Apply:** Applications may be submitted by either a teacher or a student. Each application must contain an original, unpublished paper on moral, legal, or social philosophy reflecting the classic liberal tradition. It must have been written within the 16 months preceding application deadline date. Candidates must also submit an updated vitae or resume, including academic honors; full undergraduate and most recent graduate transcripts; SAT and GRE or LSAT scores; and the name, address, and phone number of a faculty reference. If entries do not meet Institute standards, there may be no prizes awarded. Applicants are notified of the outcome by mail. **Deadline:** January 1. **Contact:** Bogie Prize Secretary at the above address (see entry 3050).

#### • 3052 • R.C. Hoiles and IHS Postdoctoral Fellowships *(Postdoctorate/Fellowship)*

**Purpose:** To help candidates with an interest in the classical liberal tradition pursue an intellectual/scholarly career in the social sciences, law, humanities, or journalism. Fellowships may be used to help candidates develop a Ph.D. thesis into a book or series of articles. **Qualif.:** Candidates must be Ph.D. candidates completing a dissertation in the social sciences, law, humanities, or journalism. **Criteria:** Fellowships are awarded based on academic

## Institute for Humane Studies (continued)

performance, interest in classical liberal ideas, and potential for an intellectual career.

**Funds Avail.:** Fellowships may reach $27,500. Funds may be used for educational expenses, travel, medical expenses, and relocation assistance. **To Apply:** Applicants must submit a 1,000 to 1,500 word research proposal, that should include a short section on how they could use the fellowship to further their studies; an updated resume; an annotated bibliography of the proposed research area; a writing sample, preferably discussing a topic related to the proposal; the names, addresses, and phone numbers of three faculty members willing to provide references; and a travel budget for attending professional meetings, interviews for tenure-track positions, and other such events. **Deadline:** February 1. **Contact:** Postdoctoral Fellowship Secretary at the above address (see entry 3050).

### • 3053 • Humane Studies Foundation Summer Residential Program Fellowships (Graduate/Fellowship)

**Purpose:** To support intensive interdisciplinary study within the humane sciences through participation at a summer seminar at George Mason University. **Focus:** History, Philosophy, Political Science, History-Economic, Social Sciences, Law. **Qualif.:** Candidates must be graduate students pursuing an advanced degree in areas of concern to the Institute.

**Funds Avail.:** Fellowships are worth up to $5,000, with $2,500 available for educational expenses, housing, and travel. One-third of the stipend is contingent on the submission of a paper fit for publication. **To Apply:** Candidates must submit a 1,000 to 1,500 word proposal outlining a subject of research in history, political and moral philosophy, political economy, economic history, or legal and social theory. It must have potential for original research in the classical liberal tradition and be on a topic that can result in a paper of publishable quality. The paper can be a chapter of a dissertation. Applicants must also provide an updated vitae or resume, including work experience and SAT, LSAT, and GRE scores; an annotated bibliography of the proposed research areas; writing samples; undergraduate and graduate transcripts, and the name, address, and phone number of a faculty member who is willing to provide references. **Deadline:** March 1. **Contact:** Summer Residential Fellowship Secretary at the above address (see entry 3050).

### • 3054 • IHS-Eberhard Student-Writing Competition (Graduate/Prize)

**Qualif.:** Competition is open to all law students except those at Harvard Law School.

**Funds Avail.:** A prize of $1,000 is awarded to the comment that best analyzes a case or legal topic of interest to conservatives and libertarians. A prize of $500 is given to the book review that best analyzes a publication of interest to conservatives and libertarians. **To Apply:** Comments should be between 25 and 45 double-spaced typed pages; book reviews should be between 15 and 35 double-spaced typed pages. Winning submissions are published in the *Harvard Journal of Law and Public Policy.* **Deadline:** September 30. **Contact:** Harvard Journal of Law and Public Policy, Harvard Law School, Cambridge, MA 02138.

### • 3055 • IHS Excellence in Liberty Prizes (Graduate, Undergraduate/Prize)

**Purpose:** To encourage classical liberal research in history, political theory, sociology, literature, or economics by recognizing outstanding papers in these areas. **Qualif.:** Candidates must be graduate or undergraduate students.

**Funds Avail.:** Two prizes of $500 each for term papers, one to a graduate and one to an undergraduate student. **To Apply:** Papers may be submitted by either faculty members or students. In both cases, the name and phone number of the faculty member to whom the paper was submitted must be included for reference.

**Deadline:** June 1 with winners announced by July 4. **Contact:** Liberty Prize Secretary at the above address (see entry 3050).

### • 3056 • IHS John M. Olin Fellowships (Graduate/Fellowship)

**Purpose:** Fellowships support outstanding students with a demonstrated interest in the principles of a free society. **Focus:** Economics, Law, Government, History, Political Science, Philosophy. **Qualif.:** Candidates must be U.S. citizens who have at least senior standing at an accredited university. Economics, law, government, history, political science or philosophy must be the major field of study. Applicants must be planning to pursue a graduate degree at one of three British universities: Oxford University, Cambridge University, or the University of London. Candidates must intend to pursue an intellectual or scholarly career. **Criteria:** Fellowships are awarded based on academic performance, interest in classical liberal ideas, and potential for an intellectual career.

**Funds Avail.:** Fellowships may reach $18,500, though the amount of the fellowships depends on tuition costs at the recipient's university and the status of any other scholarships awarded during the same year. Fellowships may be used for tuition, stipends, and travel expenses. Applicants who receive full tuition scholarships from other sources are eligible to receive a stipend for educational expenses of up to $8,250. **To Apply:** Applicants must submit a formal application. **Deadline:** December 31.

**Remarks:** These Fellowships are supported by the John M. Olin Foundation. **Contact:** The Institute for Humane Studies at the above address (see entry 3050).

### • 3057 • IHS Summer Faculty Fellowships (Professional Development/Fellowship)

**Purpose:** Fellowships promote research and writing in disciplines of interest to the Institute, especially history, and political and legal theory, as well as moral philosophy and political economy. **Qualif.:** Candidates must be untenured faculty members in the early stages of their careers. **Criteria:** Selection is based on the research proposal's originality and the applicant's potential to contribute to the scholarship of liberty.

**Funds Avail.:** Fellowships may reach $4,500. **To Apply:** Applicants must submit two-page research proposals, updated vitae, copies of relevant publications, and two references. Research should involve the historical expressions, institutions, or principles of a free society or spontaneous social order. **Deadline:** March 15. **Contact:** Director, F. Leroy Hill Summer Faculty Fellowships, at the above address (see entry 3050).

### • 3058 • Claude R. Lambe Fellowships (Graduate/Fellowship)

**Focus:** Social Sciences, Law, Humanities, Literature, Communications, Journalism. **Qualif.:** Candidates must have junior or senior standing at an accredited college or university by the fall term of the academic year of filing deadline. Fellowships for students who have applied to graduate programs, but have not yet been accepted, are conditional upon acceptance. Applicants' major field of study must be in the social sciences, law, the humanities, literature, communications, or journalism, and they must be planning to pursue both graduate study and an intellectual or scholarly career in these areas. **Criteria:** Fellowships are awarded based on academic performance, interest in classical liberal ideas, and potential for an intellectual career.

**Funds Avail.:** Scholarships may reach $17,500, though the amount of the fellowships depends on tuition costs at the recipient's university and the status of any other scholarships awarded during the same year. Fellowships may be used for tuition and stipends for educational expenses. Applicants who receive full tuition scholarships from other sources are eligible to receive a stipend for educational expenses of up to $8,500. **Deadline:** December 31.

**Remarks:** Funding for the program is provided by the Claude R. Lambe Foundation. **Contact:** Lambe Fellowship Secretary at the above address (see entry 3050).

---

• 3059 •

**Institute of Industrial Engineers**
25 Technology Park/Atlanta                    *Ph:* (770)449-0461
Norcross, GA 30092                            *Fax:* (770)263-8532
                                              *Free:* 800-494-0460
*E-mail:* hgilbert@www.iienet.org; webmaster@www.iienet.org
*URL:* http://www.iienet.org

• 3060 • **Dwight D. Gardner Memorial Scholarship**
*(Undergraduate/Scholarship)*

**Purpose:** To encourage and assist industrial engineering education and aid men and women in becoming qualified to practice as professional industrial engineers. **Focus:** Engineering. **Qualif.:** Candidates must be undergraduate industrial engineering students enrolled full-time in any school in the United States and its territories, Canada, or Mexico that is accredited by an agency recognized by IIE. They must be active Institute members and have a grade point average of 3.40 out of 4.00. They must also have at least five full quarters or three full semesters remaining from the date of nomination to be eligible.

**Funds Avail.:** Number of awards presented and amounts vary. **No. of Awards:** Varies. **To Apply:** Nominations are solicited each fall from the academic department heads of all accredited programs. Interested students are urged to contact their respective department head and indicate their interest. Application packets are sent directly to all nominated students for completion. **Deadline:** Nominations must be completed by November 15. **Contact:** Academic department heads at student's university or college.

• 3061 • **Frank and Lillian Gilbreth Memorial Fellowships** *(Graduate/Fellowship)*

**Purpose:** To encourage and assist industrial engineering education and aid men and women in becoming qualified to practice as professional industrial engineers. **Focus:** Engineering. **Qualif.:** Candidates must be graduate industrial engineering students enrolled full-time in any school in the United States and its territories, Canada, or Mexico. They must be active Institute members and have a grade point average of at least 3.40 out of 4.00. They must also have at least five full quarters or three full semesters remaining from the date of nomination to be eligible for consideration.

**Funds Avail.:** The number of awards presented and amount of award varies. **To Apply:** Nominations are solicited each fall from the academic department heads of all accredited programs. Interested students are urged to contact their respective department head and indicate their interest. Application packets are sent directly to all nominated students for completion. **Deadline:** Nominations must be completed by November 15. **Contact:** Academic department headers at student's college or university.

• 3062 • **MTM Fellowships** *(Undergraduate/ Fellowship)*

**Purpose:** To encourage and assist industrial engineering education and aid men and women in becoming qualified to practice as professional industrial engineers. **Focus:** Engineering. **Qualif.:** Candidates must be full-time undergraduate students who have demonstrated specific interest in the field of work measurement. They must be active Institute members, have a grade point average of 3.4 out of 4.0 and have at least five full

quarters or three full semesters remaining from the date of nomination to be eligible.

**Funds Avail.:** Two fellowships of $1,500. **To Apply:** Nominations are solicited each fall from the academic department heads of all accredited programs. Interested students are urged to contact their respective department heads and indicate their interest. Application packets are sent directly to all nominated students for completion. **Deadline:** Nominations must be completed by November 15. **Contact:** Academic department heads at student's university or college.

• 3063 • **E.J. Sierleja Memorial Fellowship**
*(Graduate/Fellowship)*

**Purpose:** To encourage research and education in the area of transportation. **Focus:** Engineering. **Qualif.:** Candidates must be full-time graduate students pursuing advanced studies in transportation with priority given to those focusing on rail transportation. They must be active Institute members and have a grade point average of 3.40 out of 4.00. They must also have at least five full quarters or three full semesters remaining from the date of nomination to be eligible for consideration.

**Funds Avail.:** $300 in 1997. **No. of Awards:** 1. **To Apply:** Nominations are solicited each fall from the academic department heads of all accredited programs. Interested students are urged to contact their respective department head and indicate their interest. Application packets are sent directly to all nominated students for completion. **Deadline:** Nominations must be completed by November 15.

**Remarks:** The fellowship was established through an endowment from Transportation and Distribution Associates, Inc. **Contact:** Academic department heads at student's college or university.

---

• 3064 •

**Institute of Internal Auditors Research Foundation**
249 Maitland Ave.                            *Ph:* (407)830-7600
Altamonte Springs, FL 32701-4201            *Fax:* (407)831-5171
*E-mail:* iiai@theiia.org
*URL:* http://www.rutgers.edu/Accounting/raw/lia

• 3065 • **Michael J. Barrett Doctoral Dissertation Grant** *(Doctorate/Grant)*

**Purpose:** To encourage internal audit research by doctoral candidates. **Focus:** Accounting. **Qualif.:** Applicants must be pursuing a doctoral degree in business with a concentration in auditing or accounting from an accredited institution. They must intend to teach in the field of auditing for at least two years and have completed or be within one year of completing the necessary course requirements and pre-dissertation examinations required by the degree-granting institution, and be at the dissertation stage at the time of the award. If all requirements have not been completed, a schedule of completion of the remaining requirements should be included in the cover letter. They should also devote full-time to the dissertation during the term of the award; however, if less than full-time work is expected, and the reason is justified on the cover letter, the candidate will not be disqualified. **Criteria:** Selection of candidates is the responsibility of the Doctoral Dissertations Committee of the IIA Research Foundation Board of Research Advisors, which includes both academicians and professionals actively involved in internal auditing.

**Funds Avail.:** Grants vary from $1,000 to $10,000 each, based on the amount required to complete the dissertation within one year. The grant is paid over a period generally not exceeding one year and usually divided into three installments corresponding with dissertation progress reports. **To Apply:** Applicants must submit two letters of recommendation, a dissertation proposal that

---

### Institute of Internal Auditors Research Foundation (continued)

includes their name, dissertation title, and name of the degree-granting institution; the objective of the research; the need for the research; the research plan; the candidate's qualifications; and a schedule that lists individual tasks and estimated completion time, in months, from the starting date. Proposals should not exceed six pages. Cover letter must be submitted discussing the degree the candidate will receive; the major and minor fields covered in the doctoral program; the full name of the degree-granting institution where they will complete their dissertation and its business school accreditations; the names and positions of the two professors who will send letters of recommendation to the IIA and who are directly involved in the supervision of the applicant's dissertation; the schedule for completion of course work, qualifying examinations, and beginning of the dissertation research; the future professional and career plans after completing the doctoral program; and a one-half page summary (abstract) of the dissertation. **Deadline:** May 15 and October 31. The Foundation reviews proposals in June and December. **Contact:** Submit applications to James H. Thompson, CIA Manager of Research at the above address (see entry 3064). For further information contact Donald E. Ricketts, DBA, Professor and Head of Accounting, University of Cincinnati, College of Business Administration, 310 Lindner Hall, Cincinnati, Ohio 45221. Telephone (513)556-7049.

---

## • 3066 •

### Institute of International Education
809 United Nations Plaza
New York, NY 10017-3580          *Ph:* (212)984-5330

#### • 3067 • Germanistic Society of America Fellowships *(Postgraduate/Fellowship)*

**Purpose:** To support Americans who wish to study in Germany. **Focus:** German Studies. **Qualif.:** Candidate must be a U.S. citizen. Applicant must ordinarily have a master's degree. Candidate's proposed plan of study must focus on Germany; preference is given to individuals specializing in German language, literature, history, art history, philosophy, economics, politics, or public affairs, and to those studying Germany's role in international law. Fellowships are tenable in Germany.

**Funds Avail.:** $10,000. **No. of Awards:** in 1993 6. **To Apply:** Write to the Institute for application guidelines. **Deadline:** October 31. **Contact:** U.S. Student Programs at the above address (see entry 3066).

---

## • 3068 •

### Institute of Irish Studies
Queen's University Belfast
8 FitzWilliam Street
Belfast BT9 6AW, Northern Ireland          *Ph:* 1232 245133

#### • 3069 • Institute of Irish Studies Junior Fellowships *(Postdoctorate/Fellowship)*

**Purpose:** To support personal research leading to publication. **Focus:** Irish Studies. **Qualif.:** Candidate may be of any nationality. Applicant must have doctoral degree or equivalent research experience. Research can be in any academic discipline relating to Ireland, and should lead to the preparation of a manuscript for publication.

**Funds Avail.:** £5,874/year. **To Apply:** Write to the Institute for application forms, available in December. **Deadline:** January 14.

**Contact:** Dr. B.M. Walker, Director, at the above address (see entry 3068).

---

## • 3070 •

### Institute for Latin American Studies
Auburn University
320A Thach                          *Ph:* (205)844-4161
Auburn, AL 36849-5258               *Fax:* (205)844-6673
*E-mail:* ilas@mail.auburn.edu; ilas@mail.auburn.edu
*URL:* http://ihr.sas.ac.uk/hr/wp/ilas.htm/

#### • 3071 • James R. Scobie Memorial Awards *(Doctorate/Grant)*

**Purpose:** To permit a short exploratory research trip abroad to determine the feasibility of a Ph.D. topic dealing with some facet of Latin American history. **Focus:** Latin American Studies.

**Funds Avail.:** Approximately $1,000 for one or more travel grants. The grant must be used during the summer following the award, unless there is prior approval from the Award Committee and the Secretariat of the Institute for Latin American Studies. Under no circumstances is the award to be combined with a research grant for an extended stay. **No. of Awards:** 1-2. **To Apply:** Applicants should submit the following: a comprehensive research prospectus, including a preliminary bibliography; three letters of recommendation, one of which should attest to the language competence (Spanish or Portuguese) of the applicant; and a curriculum vitae. **Deadline:** March 15. **Contact:** Michael Conniff, Executive Secretary, at the above address (see entry 3070).

---

## • 3072 •

### Institute of Medicine - National Academy of Sciences
2101 Constitution Ave., NW FO
  3122-G                            *Ph:* (202)334-1506
Washington, DC 20418               *Fax:* (202)334-3862
*E-mail:* hppf@nas.edu

#### • 3073 • Robert Wood Johnson Health Policy Fellowships *(Professional Development/Fellowship)*

**Purpose:** The Robert Wood Johnson Health Policy Fellowships Program has a two-fold purpose: to extend the public policy horizons of health professional schools in the United States and improve the capabilities of their faculty members to study health policy and assume leadership in health activities at all levels. **Qualif.:** Candidates are mid-career faculty members from all health and health-related professions. **Criteria:** Criteria for selection include academic and other professional achievements and potential for growth and leadership in an academic or governmental setting. Applicant's interest in public affairs and general and social cultural awareness and applicant's potential for influencing the policies and programs of the sponsoring institution are important attributes.

**Funds Avail.:** Six fellowships are awarded annually. Annual stipends are equal to the salary of the recipient prior to entering the Program up to $75,000 a year. Existing fringe benefits are maintained at levels corresponding to the stipends. Both salary and fringe benefits may be supplemented by the sponsoring institution. **No. of Awards:** 6. **To Apply:** Applications by nomination only. Applicants must be nominated by the chief executive officers at their institutions. The candidate must submit: a letter that contains his or her reasons for interest in the Program and plans for using the fellowship experience and training in career development, up-to-date curriculum vitae, and list of names and addresses of three references. References send their evaluation of candidate's qualifications for the Program directly to the Institute of Medicine. The chief executive officer of the nominating institution sends to the Institute a letter that contains an evaluation of the candidate's qualifications for the Program and outlines the institution's plan for utilizing the experience and training the Fellow will have. The Health Policy Fellowships Board pays particular attention to this letter. **Deadline:** Nominating institutions screen their applicants in September and October, and they submit to the Institute of Medicine their nominations by the middle of November. All supporting materials must be received by the Institute by the end of November. Finalists are selected in January and interviewed in February. Recipients are announced in February.

**Remarks:** The program begins in September with an eight week orientation period arranged by the Institute of Medicine. Following this, the Health Policy Fellows join the 4-week orientation for the Congressional Fellows. **Contact:** Director, Health Policy Fellowships Program, at the above address (see entry 3072).

## • 3074 •
## Institute for Mesoamerican Studies - Christopher DeCormier Scholarship Fund
Social Sciences 263
State University of New York at
 Albany                              Ph: (518)442-4722
Albany, NY 12222                     Fax: (518)442-5710
E-mail: ims@csc.albany.edu
URL: http://www.albany.edu/ims

### • 3075 • Christopher DeCormier Scholarship
*(Doctorate/Scholarship)*

**Purpose:** To enable young scholars to conduct field research on some aspect of ancient or modern Mesoamerican cultures in any of the subfields of anthropology. **Focus:** Anthropology—Mesoamerica. **Qualif.:** Scholarships are awarded to graduate students in the Department of Anthropology, State University of New York-Albany. Research projects can be in any of the subfields of anthropology and can focus on aspects of modern or ancient cultures of Mesoamerica. **Criteria:** Scholarships are awarded to one or more students based on the quality of research proposals that are evaluated by IMS faculty.

**Funds Avail.:** Awards range from $1,400 to $2,500. **No. of Awards:** 1 or 2. **To Apply:** Research proposals should be short (three pages), and they must outline the project, theoretical approach and methods, and work schedule. **Deadline:** February 1.

**Remarks:** Research is usually conducted in the spring or summer. The award was created to honor the memory of Chris DeCormier, a dedicated anthropology student. **Contact:** Michael E. Smith, Director, at the above address (see entry 3074).

## • 3076 •
## Institute of Store Planners
25 N. Broadway                       Ph: (914)332-1806
Tarrytown, NY 10591-3201             Fax: (914)332-1541
E-mail: isp@ispo.org
URL: http://www.ispo.org

### • 3077 • Student Store Interior Design Competition Prizes *(Undergraduate/Prize)*

**Purpose:** To encourage students in the field of retail store planning and design. **Focus:** Interior Design. **Qualif.:** Candidate may be of any nationality, but must be enrolled in a college-level program in architecture, interior design, industrial design or environmental design. Applicant's entry must conform to competition regulations.

**Funds Avail.:** First Prize: $1,000; Second Prize: $500; Third Prize: $300. **No. of Awards:** 3. **To Apply:** Write for application form and guidelines. **Deadline:** May 1.

**Remarks:** The First Prize winner's school also receives an award ($700).

## • 3078 •
## Institute for the Study of World Politics
1755 Massachusetts Ave., NW
Washington, DC 20036

### • 3079 • Institute for the Study of World Politics Fellowships *(Doctorate/Fellowship)*

**Purpose:** To support doctoral dissertation research in international relations. **Focus:** Economics, International Relations, Political Science, History. **Qualif.:** Applicant may be of any nationality. Applicant must be a Ph.D. candidate with only the dissertation requirement remaining to complete the degree. Fellowships are tenable at U.S. universities. **Criteria:** Applicants are based on academic record (grades and references) plus dissertation prospectus.

**Funds Avail.:** Varies. **No. of Awards:** Varies. **To Apply:** Write for application guidelines, available in September. **Deadline:** February 15.

**Remarks:** Requests for applications should include short description of dissertation topic. **Contact:** Steve Paschke, Associate Director, at the above address (see entry 3078).

## • 3080 •
## Institute of Turkish Studies, Inc.
Intercultural Center
Georgetown University                Ph: (202)687-0295
Washington, DC 20057                 Fax: (202)687-3780
E-mail: acara@gunet.georgetown.edu

### • 3081 • Institute of Turkish Studies Dissertation Writing Grants *(Doctorate/Grant)*

**Purpose:** To increase and spread knowledge of Turkey, its history, culture, and people. **Focus:** Turkish Studies. **Qualif.:** Applicant must be a Ph.D. candidate in the United States in the field of Turkish studies who has completed the research stage of the dissertation. Dissertation grants will be awarded only to applicants who certify that they will not be involved in teaching beyond the half-time level.

**Funds Avail.:** $4,000 maximum. **To Apply:** Write to the Institute for application guidelines. Submit project description and proposal, proposed budget, and a curriculum vitae. Three letters of recommendation should be sent directly to the Institute from the referees. **Deadline:** March 15. Awards will be announced by May 30.

**Remarks:** The Institute also offers graduate fellowships; post-doctoral research in Turkey; subventions towards the publication costs of manuscripts, texts, documents, translations and periodicals in the field of Turkish studies, as well as teaching aid grants for the preparation of materials relating to Turkish studies. Write to the Institute for further information. **Contact:** Dr. Sabri Sayari, Executive Director, at the above address (see entry 3080).

---

## Institute of Turkish Studies, Inc. (continued)

### • 3082 • Summer Travel/Research in Turkey Grants (Postdoctorate/Grant)

**Purpose:** To increase and spread knowledge of Turkey, its history, culture, and people. **Focus:** Turkish Studies. **Qualif.:** Applicant must be a postdoctoral scholar in the United States who wishes to conduct research in Turkey. Awards are limited to the cost of airfare to and from Turkey.

**Funds Avail.:** Not to exceed the cost of round-trip airfare between the United States and Turkey. **To Apply:** Write to the Institute for application guidelines. Submit project description and proposal, proposed budget, and a curriculum vitae. Three letters of recommendation should be sent directly to the Institute from the referees. **Deadline:** March 15. Awards will be announced by May 30.

**Remarks:** The Institute also offers dissertation writing grants; graduate fellowships; subventions towards the publication costs of manuscripts, texts, documents, translations and periodicals in the field of Turkish studies, as well as teaching aid grants for the preparation of materials relating to Turkish studies. Write to the Institute for further information. **Contact:** Dr. Sabri Sayari, Executive Director, at the above address (see entry 3080).

### • 3083 •
## Institution of Civil Engineers
Great George Street
Westminster
London SW1P 3AA, England     *Ph:* 171 222 7722
    *Fax:* 171 222 7500

### • 3084 • ICE Overseas Travel Awards (Professional Development/Award)

**Purpose:** To support overseas travel by ICE members. **Focus:** Civil Engineering. **Qualif.:** Applicant may be of any nationality, but must be a member of ICE who is planning a specific overseas project or other mid-career development. Project proposals are not necessarily restricted to technical developments; they also may be concerned with organizational, managerial, or financial aspects of civil engineering.

**Funds Avail.:** £2,000. **No. of Awards:** in 1993 28. **To Apply:** Write to the education officer for application form and guidelines. **Deadline:** End of February. **Contact:** W. H. T. Spaight, Education Officer, at the above address (see entry 3083).

### • 3085 •
## Institution of Mechanical Engineers
Educational Services
Northgate Avenue
Bury St. Edmunds, Suffolk IP32     *Ph:* 1284 763277
    6BN, England     *Fax:* 1284 704006

### • 3086 • Joseph Bramah Scholarship; Raymond Coleman Prescott Scholarship (Graduate, Professional Development/Scholarship)

**Purpose:** To encourage further study or research in areas of interest to IMechE. **Focus:** Mechanical Engineering and related Sciences. **Qualif.:** Candidate for the Bramah Scholarship may be of any nationality, but must be a member, or be in the process of applying for membership, of the IMechE. Applicants with at least two years of practical training in mechanical engineering are preferred. The Bramah Scholarship is intended for study of hydraulic mechanisms and particularly hydrostatic transmissions

and servomechanisms; or for study at approved centers and laboratories. Candidate for the Prescott Scholarship must have an approved engineering qualification or have satisfied the Institution's requirements for student membership. Applicant should have at least two years of approved industrial training. The Prescott Scholarship is intended for study for a first degree, for some special experience or training, or for pursuit of an approved program of research.

**Funds Avail.:** Bramah: £1,100 maximum; Prescott: £500 maximum **No. of Awards:** Two. **To Apply:** Write to executive officer for application form and guidelines. **Deadline:** Varies.

**Remarks:** IMechE also offers the IMechE Undergraduate Scholarships to encourage outstanding young people to study for an accredited degree; as well as Thomas Andrew Common Grants to enable members to attend conferences. Write to the executive officer for further details. IMechE offers a number of other awards to both its members and those who are not members. These awards include prizes, fellowships, scholarships, and grants. Details of these awards may be obtained from: The Council Officer, Institution of Mechanical Engineers, 1 Birdcage Walk, Westminster, London SW1H 9JJ, England (Phone: 71-222-7899 ext. 209). **Contact:** Richard Franklin, Executive Officer, at the above address (see entry 3085).

### • 3087 • Clayton Grants (Professional Development/Grant)

**Purpose:** To enable recipients to obtain special experience or training in practice to supplement that previously obtained in mechanical engineering. **Focus:** Mechanical Engineering and related sciences. **Qualif.:** Applicant for the Clayton Grants may be of any nationality, but must be over 23 years old, and have an accredited engineering degree or have satisfied the academic requirements for IMechE membership by other means. Candidate should have at least two years of approved professional training in mechanical engineering.

**Funds Avail.:** Up to £1,000. **To Apply:** Write to the executive officer for application form and guidelines. **Deadline:** Varies.

**Remarks:** IMechE offers a number of other awards to both its members and those who are not members. These awards include prizes, fellowships, scholarships, and grants. Details of these awards may be obtained from: The Council Officer, Institution of Mechanical Engineers, 1 Birdcage Walk, Westminster, London SW1H 9JJ, England (Phone: 71-222-7899 ext. 209). **Contact:** Richard Franklin, Executive Officer, at the above address (see entry 3085).

### • 3088 •
## Inter-American Foundation
IAF Fellowship Program, Dept. 222
901 N. Stuart St., 10th Floor     *Ph:* (703)841-3800
Arlington, VA 22203     *Fax:* (703)527-3529
*URL:* http://www.iaf.gov/iaf1.htm

### • 3089 • Dante B. Fascell Inter-American Fellowships (Other/Fellowship)

**Purpose:** To provide outstanding men and women support for reflection upon, analysis, and dissemination of their successful experiences in grassroots development in Latin American or Caribbean countries to audiences across the hemisphere. **Focus:** Sciences, Area Studies. **Qualif.:** Candidates should have attained notable achievements in their work well beyond professional excellence and received recognition for their past accomplishments in grassroots development. In addition, they should show great promise of future important contributions for the benefit of society at large. Fellowships are open to candidates from the social sciences, physical sciences, technical fields, and business professions. Recipients may be practictioners, non-government organization (NGO) managers, or applied researchers engaged in development work and should be distinguished Latin American leaders instrumental in developing successful approaches to grassroots development.

**Funds Avail.:** $50,000 for a period not exceeding 12 months. **No. of Awards:** 3. **To Apply:** Candidates are generally nominated by Latin American and Caribbean citizens, but individuals may also apply directly. Candidates or their nominators then submit a completed IAF-printed Candidate Information Form (available from the above address), a Fellowship Proposal, and letters of recommendation. **Deadline:** Award is given triennially. The next scheduled deadline is May 1, 1997.

**Remarks:** During the Fellowship period, a Fellow may not be employed by any government agency or any foundation contractor, nor may they maintain an individual contract with the foundation. **Contact:** Inter-American Foundation Fellowship Programs at the above address (see entry 3088).

## • 3090 • IAF Field Research Fellowships Program at the Doctoral Level *(Doctorate/Fellowship)*

**Purpose:** To allow scholars the opportunity to study Latin American and Caribbean social programs at the local level. **Focus:** Social Service Organizations. **Qualif.:** Candidate may be of any nationality, but must be enrolled in a U.S. university and studying the social sciences, physical sciences, or a field leading to a professional degree. Candidates must have fulfilled all degree requirements for the Ph.D. except the dissertation and be fluent in a language spoken in Central America or the Caribbean. Fellows are required to establish a working relationship with a Latin American or Caribbean institution. Fellowships are tenable in Central America or the Caribbean (other than Puerto Rico).

**Funds Avail.:** $10,000-$12,000 average. **To Apply:** Write to the Fellowship Officer for information and guidelines. **Deadline:** November 22. Notification in early March. **Contact:** Fellowship Officer at the above address (see entry 3088).

## • 3091 • IAF Field Research Fellowships Program at the Master's Level *(Graduate/Fellowship)*

**Purpose:** To allow graduate students the opportunity to study Latin American and Caribbean social programs at the local level. **Focus:** Social Service Organizations. **Qualif.:** Candidate may be of any nationality, but must be enrolled in a U.S. university and studying the social sciences, physical sciences, or a field leading to a professional degree. Candidates must be fluent in a language spoken in Central America or the Caribbean. The program may also cover pre-dissertation field research. Fellows are required to establish a working relationship with a Latin American or Caribbean institution. Fellowships are tenable in Central America or the Caribbean (other than Puerto Rico).

**Funds Avail.:** $2,000-$3,000 average. **To Apply:** Write to the Fellowship Officer for information and guidelines. **Deadline:** February 20. Notification by May 1. **Contact:** Fellowship Officer at the above address (see entry 3088).

## • 3092 •
**Inter-American Press Association Scholarship Fund, Inc.**
2911 NW 39th St.
Miami, FL 33142

Ph: (305)634-2465
Fax: (305)635-2272

## • 3093 • Inter-American Press Association Scholarships *(Graduate, Professional Development/Scholarship)*

**Purpose:** To support the exchange of journalists between the United States, Canada, Latin America, and the Caribbean. **Focus:**

Journalism. **Qualif.:** Applicant must be a citizen of the United States, Canada, Latin America, or the Caribbean. Applicant must be a journalist or journalism school graduate, and be between the ages of 21 and 35 years. Students must have finished their degree before beginning the scholarship term. U.S. and Canadian scholars spend the award tenure studying and reporting in Latin America and the Caribbean. Journalists from the Caribbean and Latin America use the awards to study at Canadian and U.S. journalism schools. Candidates must be fluent in the language of the host country. U.S. and Canadian candidates must have their language ability attested to by a recognized authority. Latin American candidates must take the Test of English as a Foreign Language.

**Funds Avail.:** $10,000. **To Apply:** Write for an application form and guidelines. Submit form with a study and work plan. **Deadline:** December 31.

## • 3094 •
**Inter-University Center for Japanese Language Studies - Institute for International Studies**
Littlefield Center, Rm. 14
Stanford University
300 Lasuen Street
Stanford, CA 94305-5013     Ph: (415)725-1490
E-mail: IUC.Yokohama@forsythe.stanford.edu

## • 3095 • Inter-University Center Fellowships *(Graduate, Undergraduate/Fellowship)*

**Purpose:** To assist students to attend intensive language courses at the Center in Japan. **Focus:** Japanese Language. **Qualif.:** Applicant may be of any nationality. Applicant must have completed at least two years of college-level Japanese, and be admitted to the Inter-University Center for Japanese Language Studies. Fellowships are tenable at the Center in Yokohama-shi, Japan. Participants at the Center must be college students or graduates who intend to enroll in a graduate program after completing Center training. The Center is not part of Stanford University, and does not grant degrees.

**Funds Avail.:** Full or partial tuition fees. **To Apply:** Write for application form and guidelines, available in the fall. Submit form with transcripts, letters of reference, and an application fee. A Japanese proficiency examination will be required. Admitted students must submit financial aid forms. **Deadline:** January 15. Notification of admission in late March. Notification of award in late April.

## • 3096 •
**Inter-University Program for Chinese Language Studies**
Littlefield Center, Rm. 14
Stanford University
300 Lasuen Street     Ph: (415)725-2575
Stanford, CA 94305-5013     Fax: (415)723-9972
E-mail: 1UP.TAIPEI@FORSYTHE.STANFORD.EDU

## • 3097 • Inter-University Program Fellowships *(Graduate, Undergraduate/Fellowship)*

**Purpose:** To assist students to attend intensive language courses at the Program in Taipei. **Focus:** Chinese Language. **Qualif.:** Applicant may be of any nationality but must speak English. Applicant must have completed at least two years of college-level Chinese, and be admitted to the Inter-University Program for Chinese Language Studies. Fellowships are tenable at the

## Inter-University Program for Chinese Language Studies *(continued)*

Program in Taipei, Taiwan. Participants in the Program must be college students or graduates who are enrolled or intend to enroll in a graduate program after completing Program training. The Program is not part of Stanford University, and does not grant degrees.

**Funds Avail.:** Full or partial tuition fees **No. of Awards:** 50 awards are offered. **To Apply:** Write for application form and guidelines, available in the fall. Submit form with transcripts, letters of reference, and an application fee. A Chinese proficiency examination will be required. **Deadline:** Materials must be in by February 1. Notification is by late April.

## • 3098 •
## Intercollegiate Studies Institute

PO Box 4431
Wilmington, DE 19807

*Fax:* (302)652-1760

*Free:* 800-526-7022

### • 3099 • Richard M. Weaver Fellowship *(Graduate/Fellowship)*

**Purpose:** To teach at the college level in the liberal arts or social sciences. **Qualif.:** Applicant must be a US citizen, planning to teach in humanities/social sciences at the college level, must be a member of ISI, and must be in or have been accepted to graduate school. Medicine and law students are ineligible. **Criteria:** Essays, recommendations and transcripts.

**Funds Avail.:** $5,000 stipend and full tuition. **No. of Awards:** 10. **Deadline:** January 15.

## • 3100 •
## Interlochen Arts Academy and Arts Camp

c/o Tom Bewley
Box 199
Interlochen, MI 49643

*Ph:* (616)276-7472
*Fax:* (616)276-6321

*URL:* http://www.interlochen.k12.mi.us/intro.html

### • 3101 • Interlochen Arts Academy and Arts Camp Scholarships *(High School, Postgraduate, Undergraduate/Scholarship)*

**Focus:** Music, Dance, Visual, Arts, Theatre, Creative Writing, Academics. **Qualif.:** Applicants must display artistic potential and ability, and financial need. **Criteria:** Selection is based on an audition or portfolio presentation.

**Funds Avail.:** Over $3 million total. **Deadline:** February 15. **Contact:** Academy: Lorraine Smith at (616)276-7497; Camp: Karin Schrouder at (616)276-7498.

## • 3102 •
## International Agricultural Centre

PO Box 88
6700 AB Wageningen, Netherlands

*Ph:* 8370 90111
*Fax:* 8370 18552

*E-mail:* IAC@IAC.AGRO.NL

### • 3103 • Fellowship Progamme of the Netherlands Ministry of Agriculture, Nature Management and Fisheries *(Postgraduate/Fellowship)*

**Purpose:** To establish cooperation at the postgraduate level between agricultural government institutions in the Netherlands and other industrialized nations. **Focus:** Agriculture. **Qualif.:** Applicant must be a citizen of one of the European countries (with the exception of Yugoslavia), the United States, Canada, Australia, New Zealand, Israel, or Japan. Applicant must also have a minimum degree of MSc, be employed by a governmental institution and have several years experience in the field of agriculture in which they apply. Fellowships are tenable only within the Netherlands.

**Funds Avail.:** 50f/day, plus book allowances and health insurance. **To Apply:** Write for an application form and guidelines. Submit form with two letters of recommendation and a letter of confirmation from the receiving institute in the Netherlands. **Deadline:** July 31.

**Remarks:** Fellows studying at the Centre in Wageningen receive free room and board at the Centre's hostel for up to three months. This residency is accompanied by a reduction in the daily allowance to 18 Dutch guilders. **Contact:** R. van Agen at the above address (see entry 3102).

## • 3104 •
## International Arabian Horse Foundation Scholarships

12000 Zuni St.
Westminster, CO 80234

*Ph:* (303)450-4774

### • 3105 • International Arabian Horse Foundation Scholarship Application *(Postgraduate, Undergraduate/Scholarship)*

**Qualif.:** Anyone may apply. **Criteria:** Selection is based on academic ability, leadership, financial need, and involvement in equine activities.

**Funds Avail.:** Varies. **To Apply:** At least two and not more than four letters of recommendation must be submitted with the application. Required letters include one letter from an officer of IAHA, IAHA club 4-H FFA, civic, or community leaders; and one from the applicants high school principal, counselor, or college/university faculty member. **Deadline:** May 1. **Contact:** International Arabian Horse Foundation Scholarships.

## • 3106 •
## International Association of Arson Investigators

300 S. Broadway, Ste. 100
St. Louis, MO 63102-2808

*Ph:* (314)621-1966
*Fax:* (314)621-5125

*E-mail:* firecop@ix.netcom.com
*URL:* http://www.aurorafire.gov/pres1.htm

### • 3107 • John Charles Wilson Scholarship *(Graduate/Scholarship)*

**Purpose:** To assist qualified students in financing their education. **Focus:** Law Enforcement. **Qualif.:** Applicants must be members in good standing who are pursuing studies in a field related to arson investigation. **Criteria:** Applications are reviewed by committee.

**Funds Avail.:** $3,000. **Deadline:** March 1. **Contact:** Benny King at the above address (see entry 3106).

• 3108 •

## International Association of Bridge, Structural and Ornamental Iron Workers

Attn. Scholarship Committee
1750 New York Ave., NW, Ste. 400
Washington, DC 20006                    *Ph:* (202)383-4800

**• 3109 • John H. Lyons, Sr. Scholarship Program** *(Undergraduate/Scholarship)*

**Qualif.:** Applicants must be children, stepchildren, or adopted children of members of the International Association of Bridge, Structural and Ornamental Iron Workers who have five or more years of continuous membership in the Association and who are active members at the time of their children's applications. Neither grandchildren of members, nor brothers or sisters of a scholarship recipient are eligible to apply. Children of deceased members who were in good standing at the time of their death are eligible to apply. Candidates must be in their senior year of high school, rank in the upper half of their graduating class, and plan to attend an accredited college or university. **Criteria:** Scholarship awards are competitive and are based upon academic standing, college entrance examination scores, extracurricular activities, leadership, character reference, and citizenship.

**Funds Avail.:** A maximum of $2,500 per year is awarded to each recipient. Renewal is determined by the Scholarship Committee on the basis of the recipient's scholastic record and conduct and the status of the recipient's parent or guardian. The parent must remain in good standing in the Association for the period of the scholarship. Awards are made payable to recipients, but are deposited with the college or university of their choice after they have been accepted for admission. One half of the scholarship is available each semester and applies to educational expenses first. **No. of Awards:** 2. **To Apply:** Recipients may attend any accredited college or university in the United States or Canada and must be enrolled in full-time programs leading toward a degree. The formal application contains a Secondary School Report that must be completed by the applicant's principal or academic advisor regarding the student's intellectual ability and achievement. An official transcript must be forwarded with the application. The remainder of the application is to be completed by the candidate, who must respond with biographical information including interests, special talents, activities, offices held, and employment experiences. Applicants must also respond to the question: "What person or persons have been most influential in your life and in what ways?." Completed applications and supporting materials must be filed in March; judging is in April/May; recipients are notified shortly thereafter. **Deadline:** Applications must be requested by January 20 and received by March 31.

**Remarks:** The scholarship program honors the memory of the late General President who helped numerous sons and daughters of Ironworkers to attend college. **Contact:** The International Association of Bridge, Structural and Ornamental Iron workers at the above address (see entry 3108).

• 3110 •

## International Association of Culinary Professionals Foundation

c/o Ellen McKnight
304 W. Liberty St., Ste. 201         *Ph:* (502)587-7953
Louisville, KY 40202                 *Fax:* (502)589-3602
*E-mail:* emcknight@hqtrs.com
*URL:* http://www.gstis.net/~epicure

**• 3111 • IACP Foundation Scholarships** *(Professional Development, Undergraduate/Scholarship)*

**Purpose:** To further the pursuit and recognize the achievement of culinary excellence through scholarship, research, and education. **Focus:** Culinary Arts. **Qualif.:** Applicants must be at least 18 years of age and be seeking to establish or further a career in the food industry. Applicants must have foodservice work experience. **Criteria:** Awards are based on merit, ability, and need.

**Funds Avail.:** Ranges between $500 and $10,000. Awards will take the form of tuition credit or cash. Occasionally an award will cover course-related expenses such as research, room and board, or travel. **No. of Awards:** About 60. **Deadline:** December 1. Finalists are notified April 1. **Contact:** The International Association of Culinary Professionals Foundation at the above address (see entry 3110).

• 3112 •

## International Association of Fire Chiefs Foundation

1257 Wiltshire Rd.
York, PA 17403-3408                  *Ph:* (717)741-5704
*E-mail:* IAFCHQ@connectinc.com
*URL:* http://www.ichiefs.org

**• 3113 • International Association of Fire Chiefs Foundation Scholarships** *(Professional Development/Scholarship)*

**Purpose:** To assist individuals in fire departments to further their education. **Focus:** Fire Sciences and Related Fields. **Qualif.:** Applicant may be of any nationality. Applicant must be an active member of a state, county, provincial, municipal, community, industrial, or federal fire department. Candidate must wish to continue his/her academic education through college-level courses in the fire sciences or a related field.

**Funds Avail.:** $250-4,000. **To Apply:** Write for application form and guidelines. Submit form with a statement of purpose and transcripts of any previous college-level courses. **Deadline:** August 1. **Contact:** Sue Hawkings Program Coordinator at the above address (see entry 3112).

• 3114 •

## International Association of Hospitality Accountants

9015 Mountain Ridge Dr., Ste. 350    *Ph:* (512)346-5680
Austin, TX 78759                     *Fax:* (512)346-5760
                                     *Free:* 800-856-4242

*E-mail:* iaha@iaha.org
*URL:* http://www.iaha.org

**• 3115 • Charles Fitzsimmons Award; IAHA General Scholarships; Frances Tally Award** *(Professional Development/Award, Scholarship)*

**Purpose:** To assist studies in hospitality management and accounting. **Focus:** Hospitality Accounting and Management.

*International Association of Hospitality Accountants (continued)*

**Qualif.:** Candidate must be pursuing a degree in hospitality accounting or administration at an accredited institution of higher education. Applicant must be endorsed by a local chapter of IAHA in the Bahamas, Barbados, Canada, Jamaica, or the United States. Write for a list of addresses.

**Funds Avail.:** Fitzsimmons Award: $1,500; General Scholarship and Tally Award: $1,000. **No. of Awards:** Four. **To Apply:** Write to local IAHA Chapter for application form and guidelines. Submit form, resume, academic transcripts, and three letters of reference to the IAHA Chapter president to be forwarded to the scholarship committee chair. **Deadline:** For receipt of materials by local chapter: March 1; for receipt by scholarship committee: April 1. Awards are announced by May 15. **Contact:** Scholarship Committee Chair at the above address (see entry 3114).

---

**• 3116 •**
## International Association of Machinists and Aerospace Workers
9000 Machinists Pl., Rm. 117     *Ph:* (301)967-4708
Upper Marlboro, MD 20772-2687    *Fax:* (301)967-3431

**• 3117 •** **IAM Scholarships** *(Undergraduate/ Scholarship)*

**Qualif.:** Applicants must be either IAM members, or the son, daughter, stepchild, or legally adopted child of an IAM member. Candidates must reside in the United States or Canada and plan to enroll in an accredited college on a full-time basis. Member applicants must have two years of continuous good standing membership as of December 31 of the year of filing the application and be working full-time in a company under contract with the IAM with the expectation of continuing this work until after the scholarship awards are announced (an exception is allowed if the Local Lodge certifies the member is temporarily unemployed and available for work at the time of application). Member applicants may apply whether entering college as a freshman or at a higher level with some college credits already completed. Son or daughter applicants must have one living parent with two years continuous good-standing membership as of December 31 of the year of filing the application. They must be high school seniors, or completing the last year of college preparatory work at the time of application. They may not be attending or have attended college. Son or daughter applicants are also eligible if the parent member died after the candidate entered high school and had two years continuous good-standing membership at the time of death. **Criteria:** Award recipients are chosen by an independent Selection Committee comprised of four qualified educators from the Washington, D.C., metropolitan area. The Committee attempts to select, from each IAM territory, applicants who have demonstrated learning capacity and all-around suitability for college work. In reaching this determination, many factors are taken into consideration, including grades, attitude toward study, personal references, available test scores, the opinions of counselors and teachers, and activities outside of school. For member applicants weight also is given to participation in local lodge responsibilities.

**Funds Avail.:** Awards to members are $2,000 per academic year. They are granted for a specific period from one to four years leading to a bachelor's degree. Awards to children of members are $1,000 per academic year. All awards are renewable each year until a bachelor's degree is obtained or for a maximum of four years, whichever occurs first. The annual total amount of contributions determines the number of scholarships awarded each year. **To Apply:** Applications must be requested. **Deadline:** Completed applications must be filed by December 1. Recipients and alternates are announced in the June issue of the *Machinist* newspaper. **Contact:** The International Association of Machinists and Aerospace Workers at the above address (see entry 3116).

---

**• 3118 •**
## International Association of Y's Men's Clubs
12405 W. Lewis Ave.     *Ph:* (602)935-6322
Avondale, AZ 85323-6518    *Fax:* (602)935-6322

**• 3119 •** **Alexander Scholarship Loans** *(Undergraduate/Scholarship loan)*

**Purpose:** To help staff the YMCAs of the world. **Qualif.:** Only high school seniors accepted for college, current college students, or recommended YMCA staff may apply. Applicants must agree to full-time professional employment in the YMCA upon graduation for the number of years assistance is received. A history of previous YMCA participation is favored. Recipients must attend a fully accredited, four-year college or university in the United States. **Criteria:** Selection criteria are academic achievement, character and promise, and whether or not the applicant is recommended by a Y's Men's Club and/or the YMCA.

**Funds Avail.:** Ten to fifteen scholarship loans, including new students as well as renewals, are awarded annually. Amounts vary from $500 to $1,500. Recipients who do not enter a YMCA career for the number of years assistance received must start to repay the scholarship within a year. The extent of financial resources and the statement of need completed by the applicant. In analyzing the ability of the parents to contribute toward college expenses, consideration is given to current income, assets, number of dependents, other educational expenses, debts, and situations in which both parents work. **To Apply:** A formal application must be submitted. Recommendation of a YMCA Director and/or Y's Men's Club is required. Application information and brochure may be requested by sending a SASE and $1 to the address above. **Deadline:** May 1 and October 1.

---

**• 3120 •**
## International Astronomical Union
98 bis, boulevard Arago     *Ph:* 1 43 25 83 58
75014 Paris, France    *Fax:* 1 40 51 21 00
*E-mail:* iau@iap.fr

**• 3121 •** **International Astronomical Union Travel Grants** *(Doctorate, Graduate, Postdoctorate/Grant)*

**Purpose:** To support international travel by astronomers. **Focus:** Astronomy. **Qualif.:** Candidate may be of any nationality. Applicant must be a faculty or staff member, a postdoctoral fellow, or a graduate student at a recognized educational/research institution or observatory. Candidate must have research experience and a commitment to astronomy. All visits must normally consist of a visit to a single host institution, and must be formally endorsed by the directors of the home and host institutions. Recipients are expected to return to their home country after their visits. Grants are normally intended for travel costs only. With prior approval, however, the funds can instead be used wholly or in part for subsistence costs incurred during visits. Grants are not normally made to researchers for the sole purpose of obtaining observational data.

**Funds Avail.:** Round-trip economy air fare. **To Apply:** Write to the secretariat for application guidelines and addresses for submission. A copy of the application, including a curriculum vitae, documents to support travel plans and costs, and details of support from other funds, must be submitted to both the president and vice-president of Commission 38. Two letters of endorsement from senior officials at the home and host institutions should be sent directly to the president of Commission 38. **Deadline:** None. **Contact:** Secretariat at the above address (see entry 3120).

## • 3122 •
## International Ballet Competition

8 Tzar Osvoboditel Boulevard      *Ph:* 2 83 54 10
1000 Sofia, Bulgaria      *Fax:* 2 80 18 02

### • 3123 • Ballet Prizes *(Professional Development/ Prize)*

**Purpose:** To recognize talented young ballet dancers. **Focus:** Ballet. **Qualif.:** Applicant may be of any nationality. Applicant for the Competition for Seniors must be under 26 years of age. Participants may compete in couples or as sole dancers, but in both cases the positioning will be individual. The Competition in 1990 was held in Varna, Bulgaria, for two weeks in July. Rehearsal space, room, and board are provided for all competitors for the duration of contest.

**Funds Avail.:** Varies according to outcome of competition. **To Apply:** Write for application form and guidelines and a list of the competition rules. Submit form with a statement of personal history, including ballet training data; a copy of birth certificate; a copy of document verifying ballet education; six photographs; a letter of recommendation; and application fee ($50 in 1992). **Deadline:** February 28 The Competition is held biennially, in even-numbered years.

**Remarks:** The grand prize and first price also includes a guest performance in Paris. **Contact:** Secretariat at the above address (see entry 3122).

## • 3124 •
## International Brain Research Organization

World Federation of Neuroscientists
51, boulevard de Montmorency
75016 Paris, France      *Fax:* 1 45 20 60 06

### • 3125 • IBRO/Unesco Research Fellowships *(Postdoctorate/Fellowship)*

**Purpose:** To support research outside scientist's home country. **Focus:** Neuroscience. **Qualif.:** Applicant may be of any nationality. Candidate must already be engaged in brain research, and be accepted as a visiting scientist by a laboratory in one of the countries specified by IBRO. Applicant should have sufficient knowledge of the host country's language to benefit from the proposed visit. Recipients are expected to return to home country after the fellowship term is completed.

**Funds Avail.:** Varies. **To Apply:** Write to the director for a list of participating countries, application form and guidelines. Submit form with letters of recommendation from both the receiving institution and from someone familiar with the candidate's work. The IBRO/Unesco Fellowship Committee will then forward application to the funding organization in the host country for review. **Deadline:** March 31; notification within six months.

**Remarks:** IBRO/Unesco Travel Fellowships are awarded to complement the Research Fellowships in providing support for travel expenses. Write for further details. **Contact:** Dr. E.S. Vizi, Fellowship Program Director, at the above address (see entry 3124).

## • 3126 •
## International Brotherhood of Teamsters Scholarship Fund

25 Louisiana Ave., NW      *Ph:* (202)624-8735
Washington, DC 20001      *Fax:* (202)624-6910

### • 3127 • International Brotherhood of Teamsters Scholarships *(Undergraduate/Scholarship)*

**Qualif.:** Applicants must be children or financial dependents of Teamster members who have paid dues for 12 consecutive months preceding the application deadline. Applicants must be high school seniors who rank in the top 15 percent of their class, and have excellent SAT or ACT scores. They must be able to demonstrate financial need. **Criteria:** Graduation from high school; official transcript; SAT or ACT scores; and financial need.

**Funds Avail.:** Ten $6,000 scholarships (disbursed over a four-year period) are awarded annually, as well as 15 one-time $1,000 "Bootstraps" awards. **To Apply:** Applications are available through Teamster Local Unions or the IBT Scholarship Fund. Applicants must complete the first part of the application, then forward it to parent's Local Union for membership verification. **Deadline:** February 26. **Contact:** Local Teamster unions or the Scholarship Administrator at the above address (see entry 3126).

## • 3128 •
## International Bureau of Education

Case Postale 199      *Ph:* 22 798 1455
1211 Geneva 20, Switzerland      *Fax:* 22 798 1486

### • 3129 • IBE Scholars-in-Residence Awards *(Professional Development/Award)*

**Purpose:** To enable scholars to pursue projects in comparative education at IBE. **Focus:** Education. **Qualif.:** Applicant may be of any nationality. Candidate must be a qualified educator, faculty member, or government official. Awards are tenable at IBE in Geneva, and must be used for research and writing projects related to the comparative education interests of IBE and the United Nations Educational, Scientific and Cultural Organization (UNESCO).

**Funds Avail.:** Approximately $5,000 for a period of three months. **No. of Awards:** 10-15. **To Apply:** Write to the National Commission for UNESCO in the home country for application form and guidelines. Information on the resources of IBE may be obtained from the address listed above. Beyond the IBE funds, requests for study programs may be financed by the UNESCO Participation Program. For details, contact the National Commission for UNESCO. **Deadline:** Varies, according to national requirements. **Contact:** Mr. V. Adamets at the above address (see entry 3128).

## • 3130 •
## International Center for Journalists

1616 H St. NW, 3rd Fl.      *Ph:* (202)737-3700
Washington, DC 20006      *Fax:* (202)737-0530
*E-mail:* editor@icfj.org
*URL:* http://www.icfj.org

### • 3131 • Arthur F. Burns Fellowships *(Professional Development/Fellowship)*

**Purpose:** To enable U.S. and German journalists to work with the press in the United States or Germany. **Focus:** Journalism. **Qualif.:** Applicant must be a U.S. or German citizen or permanent resident.

---

## International Center for Journalists (continued)

Candidate should be between the ages of 21 and 35 years. Applicant must be a working journalist in any news medium. U.S. citizens are placed with news organizations in Germany; German citizens are placed with U.S. news organizations.

**Funds Avail.:** $5,000. **To Apply:** Write to the ICFJ for application guidelines. **Deadline:** February 1. Notification by April 15. **Contact:** Project Director at the above address (see entry 3130).

## • 3132 •
## International Centre for Agricultural Education - Centre international d'études agricoles

Mattenhofstrasse 5       *Ph:* 31 322 2619
3003 Berne, Switzerland       *Fax:* 31 322 2634

### • 3133 • CIEA Grants-in-Aid (Professional Development/Grant)

**Purpose:** To promote agricultural education. **Focus:** Agriculture. **Qualif.:** Applicant may be of any nationality. Applicants should be teachers in the field of agriculture. Courses are offered in English, French, and German. Award is tenable at the Centre.

**Funds Avail.:** Varies. **To Apply:** Write the Secretariat for application form and guidelines. **Deadline:** May 31. **Contact:** Secretariat at the above address (see entry 3132).

## • 3134 •
## International Centre for Theoretical Physics

Strada Costiera 11
PO Box 586
34014 Trieste, Italy       *Ph:* 40 224 0211
*E-mail:* sci info@ictp.trieste.it

### • 3135 • ICTP Research Grants for Postdoctoral Students (Postdoctorate/Grant)

**Purpose:** To support research in an international environment at ICTP. **Focus:** Condensed Matter Physics, Fundamental Physics, Mathematics, Plasma Physics. **Qualif.:** Applicant may be of any nationality, but preference may be given to candidates from developing nations. Applicant must be a scientist with a Ph.D. in physics or mathematics. Grants are tenable at ICTP.

**Funds Avail.:** Monthly stipend from 1,876,000 lire. **To Apply:** Write for application guidelines. **Deadline:** None. **Contact:** Secretary of Research Group at the above address (see entry 3134).

## • 3136 •
## International College of Surgeons

1516 N. Lake Shore Dr.       *Ph:* (312)787-6274
Chicago, IL 60610       *Fax:* (312)787-9289
*E-mail:* exd@aol.com

### • 3137 • ICS Research Scholarships (Postdoctorate/Scholarship)

**Purpose:** To provide surgeons with training and research opportunities in countries other than their own. **Focus:** Surgery. **Qualif.:** Candidate may be of any nationality. Applicant must have an M.D. degree. Awards are tenable at institutions worldwide, but may not be used in the recipient's home country. **Criteria:**

Applicant must secure support of national section prior to submission to HQ.

**Funds Avail.:** $500-1,500. **No. of Awards:** 10-15. **To Apply:** Write to the research and scholarship coordinator for application guidelines. Submit application to ICS section secretary in home country. **Deadline:** None. **Contact:** Virginia Flens, Research and Scholarship Coordinator, at the above address (see entry 3136).

### • 3138 • Dr. Max Thorek Student Loans (Doctorate/Loan)

**Focus:** Medicine. **Qualif.:** Applicants must be third or fourth year medical students.

**Funds Avail.:** $5,000. **To Apply:** Write to Executive Director for details. **Contact:** J. Thomas Viall, Executive Director at the above address (see entry 3136).

## • 3139 •
## International Council for Canadian Studies

325 Dalhousie St., Ste. 800       *Ph:* (613)789-7828
Ottawa, ON, Canada K1N 7G2       *Fax:* (613)789-7830
*E-mail:* general@iccs-ciec.ca; contact@iccs-ciec.ca
*URL:* http://www.iccs-ciec.ca

### • 3140 • CCSFC Australian Scholarships (Graduate/Scholarship)

**Qualif.:** Applicants must have completed any university degree or expect to graduate prior to the tenure of the award. All applicants must be citizens of Canada who are graduates of a Canadian university and have at least a B plus GPA. Permanent residents of the awarding country are not eligible. Candidates whose native language is not English are advised to take the Princeton Test of English as a Foreign Language (TOEFL). Address inquiries to: TOEFL, Box 899, Princeton, NJ 08541. Those applying to do research toward a Canadian graduate degree must show that they have approval of the relevant authorities at the university they are presently attending. Successful applicants, as well as their spouse and children, when relevant, must meet all requirements for entry to the awarding country. **Criteria:** The CCSFC selects the nominations to be forwarded to the awarding country. The number of nominations varies, but is approximately double the number of awards made. No age restriction pertains, but preference is given to applicants who have obtained a university degree within the last five years.

**Funds Avail.:** The Australian Government offers scholarships for study or research at the graduate level normally extending over two or three academic years. Scholarships include, for the scholar only, travel to and from Australia, via the most direct route at excursion rate, as arranged by the Australian authorities. Scholars receive payment of compulsory fees and charges; an all inclusive allowance of $A19,307 a year (this includes an inbuilt component to cover the cost of books, equipment, fieldwork, thesis expenses and a contribution to the support of a scholar's dependents in Australia); limited assistance for essential research travel within Australia; and an allowance covering essential thesis expenses. **To Apply:** Application forms are available from Graduate Studies or Student Awards Offices at Canadian universities or from ICCS (CSFP Division). One original plus five copies of the application, undergraduate and graduate transcripts, and proof of citizenship must be submitted to ICCS (CSFP Division). All scholars must return to Canada at the end of the scholarship and are required to sign to this effect when making application for an award. **Deadline:** Applications must be postmarked December 31.

**Remarks:** The academic year begins in March. Recipients must follow the approved course of study and abide by the rules of the institutions in which they are registered. An award may be terminated at any time for reasons of a scholar's unsatisfactory progress or conduct, or for breaches of conditions of the award. Commonwealth Scholars cannot normally hold any other scholarships or awards. They may not, without the written consent of the awarding agency, undertake paid employment during the tenure of the award or serve on the staff of the Canadian High Commission in the awarding country. The actual offer of a scholarship will be made by the Commonwealth Scholarship Agency in the awarding country. Applicants are encouraged to seek placement in institutions of their choice and must have approval to undertake a study program from an Australian higher educational institution before a scholarship can be confirmed. **Contact:** CCSFC at the above address (see entry 3139).

### • 3141 • CCSFC India Scholarships *(Doctorate, Graduate/Scholarship)*

**Qualif.:** Applicants must have completed a university degree or expect to graduate prior to the tenure of the award. All applicants must be citizens or permanent residents of Canada who are graduates of a Canadian university. Permanent residents of the awarding country are not eligible. Candidates whose native language is not English are advised to take the Princeton Test of English as a Foreign Language (TOEFL). Address inquiries to: TOEFL, Box 899, Princeton, NJ 08541. Students from Canada who are temporarily in India, including those embarked on a course of study in India, may be considered for these awards. Scholars desiring to conduct research for a short period in India to collect material for their Ph.D programs in Canada may register with an Indian University and work under the supervision of an Indian Supervisor, subject to the rules of the university. Those applying to do research toward a Canadian graduate degree must show that they have approval of the relevant authorities at the university they are presently attending. The fields of study are unrestricted for the India Scholarships. Successful applicants, as well as their spouse and children, when relevant, must meet all requirements for entry to the awarding country. **Criteria:** The CCSFC will select the nominations to be forwarded to the awarding country. The number of nominations varies, but is approximately double the number of awards made. No age restriction pertains, but preference is given to applicants who have obtained a university degree within the last five years and have maintained a B plus average.

**Funds Avail.:** The Government of India offers scholarships for study at the graduate level for two academic years with the possibility of renewal for a third year. Travel to India and return via the most direct route tourist-economy class is provided, as arranged by the Indian High Commission, for scholars only. All compulsory tuition and examination fees are covered by the scholarship. A maintenance allowance of Rs33,600 per year for master's and doctoral degree students or Rs42,000 for post-doctoral students; plus an annual contingency grant which varies according to the programme being undertaken. Hostel accommodation is normally provided to a scholar. Where this is not available, the scholar will be reimbursed or paid an allowance for actual accommodation costs up to Rs1000 per month. There is no provision for any additional monies if scholars want to take their families to India. Rent for private accommodation is very high and it is recommended that scholars leave their families at home. A grant for expenses of approved study travel within India is paid in accordance with the rules in force. Expenses for a holiday or youth camp approved by the Government of India are also paid in accordance with the rules. All medical expenses (except those for tonics, dentures, surgical appliances, artificial aids, eyeglasses, and similar articles) incurred on the advice of the Medical Officer of the institution attended is reimbursed. **To Apply:** Application forms are available from Graduate Studies or Student Awards Offices at Canadian universities or from ICCS (CSFP Division). One original plus five copies of the application, official undergraduate and graduate transcripts, and proof of citizenship or permanent resident status must be submitted to ICCS (CSFP Division). Scholars conducting research in India for a short period to collect material for a Ph.D. program in Canada must submit, along with the application, a document confirming registration for a Ph.D degree in Canada. The Canadian universities of the scholars should agree in writing to accept the Indian supervisor as a co-supervisor for the final degree, and the authorities of those universities should give due consideration to the grades given by the Indian Supervisors for work done under their guidance. All scholars must return to Canada at the end of the scholarship and are required to sign to this effect when making application for an award. **Deadline:** Applications must be postmarked October 25.

**Remarks:** Once scholars accept the award, no requests for changes in the courses or institutions or for increases in the value of the scholarship are considered. If scholars are permitted to go home during vacation, the scholarship will be suspended from the date of leaving India until the date of return to India. All passage expenses, both ways, is borne by scholars. Recipients must follow the approved course of study and abide by the rules of the institutions in which they are placed. An award may be terminated at any time for reasons of a scholar's unsatisfactory progress or conduct; or for breaches of conditions of the award. Commonwealth Scholars cannot normally hold any other scholarships or awards. They may not, without the written consent of the awarding agency, undertake paid employment during the tenure of the award or serve on the staff of the Canadian High Commission in the awarding country. The actual offer of a scholarship will be made by the Commonwealth Scholarship Agency in the awarding country. In general, the Agency tries to place selected candidates in the institutions of their choice, however, where this is not possible, an alternative institution offering opportunities for the proposed course of study will be chosen. If, after submitting an application and before the offer of a scholarship, scholars make an independent approach to any university and are offered admission, they must inform the ICCS. **Contact:** CCSFC at the above address (see entry 3139).

### • 3142 • CCSFC New Zealand Scholarships *(Doctorate, Graduate/Scholarship)*

**Qualif.:** Applicants must have completed a university degree or expect to graduate prior to the tenure of the award. Applicants for Ph.D. study should have a minimum standard of upper second class honours. Others should have a minimum standard of a B.A. with at least an average grade of B, or they should be expected to achieve these results in coming examinations. All applicants must be citizens of Canada who are graduates of a Canadian university (proof of citizenship status must be submitted). Permanent residents of the awarding country are not eligible. Candidates whose native language is not English are advised to take the Princeton Test of English as a Foreign Language (TOEFL). Address inquiries to: TOEFL, Box 899, Princeton, NJ 08541. Those applying to do research toward a Canadian graduate degree must show that they have approval of the relevant authorities at the university they are presently attending. Successful applicants, as well as their spouse and children, when relevant, must meet all requirements for entry to the awarding country. The fields of study are unrestricted for the New Zealand Scholarships. **Criteria:** The CCSFC selects the nominations to be forwarded to the awarding country. The number of nominations varies, but is approximately double the number of awards made. No age restriction pertains, but preference is given to applicants who have obtained a university degree within the last five years.

**Funds Avail.:** The Government of New Zealand offers scholarships for graduate studies or research normally covering a period of two academic years and the intervening summer, or a shorter period when the program of study takes less than two years. Awards for Ph.D. studies are for three years with a possible extension of one more year. Travel to and from New Zealand by tourist class air passage, as arranged by the New Zealand authorities, is provided for the scholar only. However, the spouse's air fare home is provided at the most economical rate if he/she has not been able to earn while in New Zealand. Approved tuition, laboratory, and examination fees are covered. There is a personal maintenance of NZ$11,400 per year, a limited refund of up to NZ$450 a year on certified necessary books, and an establishment grant of NZ$575. Coverage for medical and hospital expenses, except for hearing aids, eye glasses, and any form of dental treatment, is provided. There is also a marriage and child allowance to a married scholar with dependents in New Zealand, provided the spouse holds

## International Council for Canadian Studies (continued)

neither a scholarship nor paid employment. This is paid at the rate of NZ$2,400 per year for first dependent, NZ$780 per year for second dependent, NZ$480 per year for third dependent, and NZ$360 per year for fourth dependent. The dependent's allowance is only a contribution towards the support of a scholar's spouse and family in New Zealand. New Zealand Immigration Authorities will require evidence of sufficient financial resources before entry visas for the spouse and family are issued. The scholarship offers assistance with thesis expenses and research travel expenses within New Zealand up to NZ$550 a year. Allowances are not taxed in New Zealand. **To Apply:** Applications forms are available from ICCS (CSFP Division). One original plus five copies of the application along with official undergraduate and graduate transcripts must be submitted to ICCS (CSFP Division). All scholars must return to Canada at the end of the scholarship and are required to sign an undertaking to this effect when making application for an award. **Deadline:** Applications must be postmarked December 31.

**Remarks:** The academic year commences in March, but a research student may start earlier if suitable arrangements can be made. No award shall last for more than four years nor less than one. Recipients must follow the approved course of study and abide by the rules of the institutions in which they are placed. An award may be terminated at any time for reasons of a scholar's unsatisfactory progress or conduct; or for breaches of conditions of the award. Commonwealth Scholars cannot normally hold any other scholarships or awards. They may not, without the written consent of the awarding agency, undertake paid employment during the tenure of the award or serve on the staff of the Canadian High Commission in the awarding country. The actual offer of a scholarship will be made by the Commonwealth Scholarship Agency in the awarding country. In general, the Agency tries to place selected candidates in the institutions of their choice; however, where this is not possible, an alternative institution offering opportunities for the proposed course of study is chosen. If, after submitting an application and before the offer of a scholarship, scholars make an independent approach to any university and are offered admission, they must inform ICCS.

## • 3143 • CCSFC Sri Lanka Scholarships (Doctorate, Graduate/Scholarship)

**Qualif.:** Applicants must have completed any university degree or expect to graduate prior to the tenure of the award. All applicants must be citizens or permanent residents of Canada who are graduates of a Canadian university with at least a B plus GPA. Permanent residents of the awarding country are not eligible. Married scholars may not be accompanied by their spouses to Sri Lanka. Candidates whose native language is not English are advised to take the Princeton Test of English as a Foreign Language (TOEFL). Address inquiries to: TOEFL, Box 899, Princeton, NJ 08541. Those applying to do research toward a Canadian graduate degree must show that they have approval of the relevant authorities at the university they are presently attending. **Criteria:** The CCSFC selects the nominations to be forwarded to the awarding country. The number of nominations varies, but is approximately double the number of awards made. No age restriction pertains, but preference is given to applicants who have obtained a university degree within the last five years. Successful applicants, as well as their spouse and children, when relevant, must meet all requirements for entry to the awarding country.

**Funds Avail.:** The Government of Sri Lanka offers scholarships for study at the graduate level and/or research in Sri Lanka for a period that normally extends over one or two academic years. Travel to Sri Lanka, as arranged by the Sri Lanka authorities, is provided for the scholar only. Scholarship includes payment of approved tuition, laboratory, and examination fees. There is a maintenance allowance up to a maximum of CRs 33,600 per year, a grant of CRs 375 per year to a maximum of CRs 750 for the entire course for approved books and apparatus, and a grant of CRs 500

per year for study travel within Sri Lanka. Free medical treatment is provided. Expenses due to treatment by a private medical practitioner or from a private hospital will not be reimbursed except under exceptional or extenuating circumstances. **To Apply:** Application forms are available from Graduate Studies or Student Awards Offices at Canadian universities or from ICCS (CSFP Division). One original plus five copies of the application, official undergraduate and graduate transcripts, and proof of citizenship or permanent resident status must be submitted to ICCS (CSFP Division). All scholars must return to Canada at the end of the scholarship and are required to sign an undertaking to this effect when making application for an award. **Deadline:** Applications must be postmarked October 25.

**Remarks:** The academic year begins in October. Recipients must follow the approved course of study and abide by the rules of the institutions in which they are placed. An award may be terminated at any time for reasons of a scholar's unsatisfactory progress or conduct or for breaches of conditions of the award. Commonwealth Scholars cannot normally hold any other scholarships or awards. They may not, without the written consent of the awarding agency, undertake paid employment during the tenure of the award or serve on the staff of the Canadian High Commission in the awarding country. The actual offer of a scholarship will be made by the Commonwealth Scholarship Agency in the awarding country. In general, the Agency tries to place selected candidates in the institutions of their choice, however, where this is not possible, an alternative institution offering opportunities for the proposed course of study is chosen. **Contact:** CCSFC at the above address (see entry 3139).

## • 3144 • CCSFC United Kingdom Scholarships (Doctorate, Graduate/Scholarship)

**Qualif.:** Applicants must have completed a university degree or expect to graduate prior to the tenure of the award. All applicants must be Canadian citizens, or those permanent residents who are graduates of a Canadian university (proof of citizenship or permanent resident status must be submitted). Permanent residents of the awarding country are not eligible. Candidates whose native language is not English are advised to take the Princeton Test of English as a Foreign Language (TOEFL). (Address inquiries to: TOEFL, Box 899, Princeton, NJ 08541.) Qualified doctors and dentists wishing to undertake graduate studies in Britain are advised to consult the prospectus of the Commonwealth Medical Awards administered under the Commonwealth Scholarship and Fellowship Plan, which may be obtained from the ICCS. Candidates for awards in medicine should possess qualifications registrable with the General Medical Council. Candidates who wish to pursue graduate study in Business and/or Management should take the Graduate Management Admission Test before applying for a Commonwealth Scholarship. (Address inquiries to: G.M.A.T. Educational Testing Service, Box 966-R, Princeton, NJ, 08541, U.S.A.) Those applying to do research toward a Canadian graduate degree must show that they have approval of the relevant authorities at the university they are presently attending. These awards may be held for research or courses at institutions other than universities for studies in such fields as adult, social, or rural education; fine art; architecture; or industrial design. **Criteria:** The CCSFC will select the nominations to be forwarded to the awarding country. The number of nominations varies, but will be approximately double the number of awards to be made. No age restriction pertains, but preference will be given to applicants who have obtained a university degree within the last five years.

**Funds Avail.:** The United Kingdom Government offers scholarships for graduate level study and/or research in the United Kingdom towards a Canadian graduate degree. Return fare to the U.K and return at student concessionary or other approved rates, as arranged in consultation with the British Council, is provided for the scholar only. There is no travel allowance for a scholar's dependents. Approved tuition and examination fees are covered. There is a personal maintenance allowance of £5,916 per year, a grant for books and apparatus of £330 during the first year of study and £198 for each year thereafter, a grant towards the cost of typing and binding one thesis, where applicable, and a grant for study travel within Britain. There is a marriage allowance of £2,964 per year provided spouses reside together at the same address. It is not paid if the spouse holds an award or is in paid employment. A child allowance of £396 per year each is payable for the first, second, and third child respectively under the age of 16, provided they live with their parents in Britain. Where a host institution has in advance declared, and the Commission has accepted, the need for fieldwork outside the U.K., a grant towards the cost of such fieldwork which shall not exceed normally the cost of one economy or tourist airfare to the fieldwork location. A scholar who is granted fieldwork fare to the home country is not entitled to the mid-term fare home. **To Apply:** Application forms are available from Graduate Studies or Student Awards Offices at Canadian universities or from ICCS (CSFP Division). One original plus five copies of the application must be submitted to ICCS (CSFP Division). **Deadline:** Applications must be postmarked by October 25.

**Remarks:** The academic year begins in October. To facilitate entry into the United Kingdom, candidates selected should apply to the nearest British High Commission or other British Government Office for an Entry Certificate (for themselves and for any dependents accompanying or following them), as long as possible before departure. While a scholar is expected to reside in Britain throughout the tenure of award, a short vacation abroad may be permitted. All scholars must return to Canada at the end of the scholarship and are required to sign an undertaking to this effect when making application for an award. Recipients must follow the approved course of study and abide by the rules of the institutions in which they are placed. An award may be terminated at any time for reasons of a scholar's unsatisfactory progress or conduct; or for breaches of conditions of the award. Commonwealth Scholars cannot normally hold any other scholarships or awards. They may not, without the written consent of the awarding agency, undertake paid employment during the tenure of the award or serve on the staff of the Canadian High Commission in the awarding country. Successful applicants, as well as their spouse and children, when relevant, must meet all requirements for entry to the awarding country. The actual offer of a scholarship will be made by the Commonwealth Scholarship Agency in the awarding country. In general, the Agency tries to place selected candidates in the institutions of their choice. However, where this is not possible, an alternative institution offering opportunities for the proposed course of study will be chosen. In addition to the countries listed above, the following Commonwealth countries offer awards in some years: Ghana, Jamaica, Sierra Leone, Trinidad and Tobago. Those interested in these countries should contact the ICCS for further information. **Contact:** The Association of Commonwealth Universities, 36 Gordon Square, London WC1H OPF, is responsible for all matters concerning selection and academic studies. The British Council, 10 Spring Gardens, London SW1A 2BN, is responsible for all matters concerning payment, travel, reception, and other support services for selected scholars.

• **3145** • **Government of Canada Awards** *(Doctorate, Graduate, Postdoctorate/Award)*

**Purpose:** To enable foreign nationals of high academic standing to undertake graduate studies or postdoctoral research in Canada. **Focus:** Arts, Engineering, Humanities, Natural Sciences, Social Sciences. **Qualif.:** Applicant must be a national of one of the following countries: France, Germany, Italy, Japan or Mexico. Candidate must not have obtained or plan to obtain landed immigrant status. Applicant for full scholarship or research scholarship must be qualified to enter a Canadian graduate program. Applicant in the fine arts must have completed basic training and have begun his/her professional career. Candidate's proposed program of study must focus on a Canadian subject or include Canadian content. Candidate must have sufficient facility in English or French. Awards are tenable at Canadian institutions. Award holders are expected to return to their respective countries at the end of tenure. **Criteria:** Academic record, relevance and interest of project.

**Funds Avail.:** Full scholarship and research scholarship: $900 monthly allowance, plus tuition and registration fees; postdoctoral fellowship: $1,200/month. Award holders are also entitled to an installation allowance of $300, as well as life insurance, hospital, medical and prescription drugs insurance coverage. **No. of Awards:** Varies. **To Apply:** Write to the Council for procedures and a list of regional agencies and deadlines. Submit application, with the required supporting documents, to the appropriate regional agency. Applications sent directly to Canada will not be considered. **Deadline:** Varies, according to country.

**Remarks:** Full scholarships are available only to citizens of France, Germany and Japan. Postdoctoral fellowships are not available to citizens of France. Hydro-Quebec offers top-awards to recipients of Government of Canada Awards from France and Germany who will undertake graduate studies or post-doctoral research at an institution located in the Provence of Quebec. Applicant's field of study must be in one of the following areas: Engineering and Technology, Energy Efficiency, Northern Technology, Environmental Studies and Northern Studies. Award holders cannot accept other awards concurrently and, unless expressly authorized, they may not accept paid employment in Canada. **Contact:** Program Officer at the above address (see entry 3139).

• **3146** • **ICCS Foreign Government Awards** *(Doctorate, Graduate/Award)*

**Purpose:** To enable Canadians to undertake advanced study and research abroad. **Focus:** General. **Qualif.:** The Council administers many fellowships, scholarships, grants and other awards for Canadians on behalf of foreign governments and international organizations. For all types of Foreign Government awards, applicant must be a Canadian citizen. For most awards, candidate must have at least a bachelor's degree. Additional requirements (including language proficiency, age restrictions, and educational/research background) vary according to the stipulations of the donor government or organization. Write to ICCS for specific information, or contact the Graduate Study Office at a Canadian university. Award recipients may study or conduct research in any discipline; however, not all countries offer awards in all disciplines. Among the countries offering awards through ICCS competition: Belgium (Flemish community), Colombia, Finland, France, Germany and Mexico, with the possible participation of Poland, Portugal and Spain. **Criteria:** Academic record, relevance and interest of project.

**Funds Avail.:** Tuition, living, research, and travel allowances. **No. of Awards:** Varies. **To Apply:** Write to ICCS for program brochure, which includes application form and guidelines. ICCS literature is also available from graduate advisors at most Canadian colleges and universities. Submit form with three supporting letters, academic transcripts, a detailed study plan or research proposal, a resume, a language certificate, and proof of Canadian citizenship. Selected applications are forwarded to the respective host countries, where the final selection of award recipients will take place. **Deadline:** October 15. **Contact:** Program Officer at the above address (see entry 3139).

• **3147** •
**International Desalination Association**
PO Box 387
Topsfield, MA 01983
*E-mail:* ida1pab@ix.netcom.com
*URL:* http://www.ida.bm
*Ph:* (978)887-0410
*Fax:* (978)887-0411

• **3148** • **International Desalination Association Scholarship** *(Undergraduate/Scholarship)*

**Purpose:** To further the studies of a student in the field of desalination. **Focus:** Engineering/Chemical/Civil/Management. **Qualif.:** Applicants must be graduates of accredited universities

## International Desalination Association (continued)

and must have ranked in the top 10% of the class in science and engineering. Candidates should have proof of admission to graduate program in desalination or water reuse. **Criteria:** Selection is based upon the recommendation of IDA members and the approval of the scholarship committee.

**Funds Avail.:** $6,000. **No. of Awards:** One or two per year. **To Apply:** Candidates must submit application documents including evidence of other sources of funding to supplement this scholarship, admission to a post-graduate program, and academic records and references.

## • 3149 •
### International Development Research Centre
PO Box 8500                     *Ph:* (613)236-6163
Ottawa, ON, Canada K1G 3H9      *Fax:* (613)563-0815
*E-mail:* cta@idrc.ca; cta@idrc.ca

#### • 3150 • John G. Bene Fellowship in Social Forestry
*(Doctorate, Graduate/Fellowship)*

**Purpose:** To encourage Canadian graduate students to pursue research focusing on the relationship of forest resources to the social, economic and environmental welfare of people, particularly in developing nations. **Focus:** Economic and Social Development, Forestry. **Qualif.:** Applicant must be a Canadian citizen enrolled in a Canadian university at the master's or doctoral level. The fellowship is open to: graduate students whose academic background combines the study of tree sciences (forestry or agroforestry) with social science (anthropology, sociology, or development economics). This may include students from interdisciplinary programs (e.g. environmental studies) provided their programs contain the specified elements; and graduate students who are interested in social forestry from an international development perspective, and who intend to conduct at least part of their thesis research in a developing country.

**Funds Avail.:** Fellows receive $7,000. **To Apply:** Write to the Corporate Services Branch for application guidelines. **Deadline:** Submission must be made by February 1.

#### • 3151 • Young Canadian Researchers Awards
*(Doctorate, Graduate/Award)*

**Purpose:** To promote the growth of Canadian capacity in research on sustainable and equitable development. **Focus:** Environmental, Social and Economic Policies; Technology and Environment; Food Systems Under Stress; Information and Communication for Environment and Development; Health and the Environment; Biodiversity; Environmental and Natural Resources; Health Sciences; Information Sciences and Systems; Gender; sustainable Development; Management of Innovation Systems; Human Resource Development. **Qualif.:** Applicant must be a Canadian citizen or permanent resident, be registered at a Canadian university, have proposed research for a master's or doctoral thesis with approval by the appropriate academic committee, be researching in one of the eligible fields of study, and provide evidence of affiliation with an institution or organization in the region which the research will take place. Master's students must provide evidence that course work will be complete and comprehensive examination passed by the time of award tenure. Applicants at the master's level are restricted to the areas of health sciences, information sciences, and environmental policy. **Criteria:** Selection is competition based on research topic and qualifications.

**Funds Avail.:** The award will be a maximum of $20,000 per year. **To Apply:** Write to the Centre Training and Awards Unit for application guidelines. **Deadline:** Application materials must be received by

January 15 and June 30. **Contact:** Corporate Services Branch, at the above address (see entry 3149).

## • 3152 •
### International Education Center, Ltd.
Bowling Green Sta., Box 843     *Ph:* (718)948-1091
New York, NY 10274             *Fax:* (718)356-1302

#### • 3153 • IEC Russia, China Study Fellowship
*(Professional Development/Fellowship)*

**Purpose:** To promote friendship between Russia and the United States and between China and the United States. Additional programs include Europe and Australia. **Focus:** Language, Culture, History, Field Research. **Qualif.:** Applicants must be teachers or in the field of education or graduate students. **Criteria:** Essay applicants are judged based on essay.

**Funds Avail.:** $50,000 total (fellowships do not exceed $1,000); or 50% of IEC program cost. **To Apply:** Fellowships are only for IEC programs. **Deadline:** Rolling acceptance.

**Remarks:** This is the twelfth program year. **Contact:** Mr. Jack Scheckner at the above address (see entry 3152).

## • 3154 •
### International Foundation of Employee Benefit Plans
18700 W. Bluemound Rd.
PO Box 69                       *Ph:* (414)786-6710
Brookfield, WI 53008-0069       *Fax:* (414)786-8670
*E-mail:* research@ifebp.org
*URL:* http://www.ifebp.org

#### • 3155 • International Foundation of Employee Benefit Plans Grants for Research *(Doctorate, Graduate, Postdoctorate/Grant)*

**Purpose:** To support original research on employee benefit topics. **Focus:** Employment, Healthcare Benefits, Industrial Relations, Labor Law, Business and Finance, Economics, Human Resources. **Qualif.:** Applicant must be a citizen of the U.S. or Canada. Candidate for the graduate or post-graduate research grant must be pursuing a graduate or post-graduate degree from an accredited university, and must have a thesis or dissertation topic approved by an advisor. Candidate for the postdoctoral research grant must hold a terminal degree from an accredited institution, and be employed by a nonprofit educational or research institution. Research should relate to employee benefits, such as health care benefits, or retirement and income security.

**Funds Avail.:** Graduate: $5,000 maximum; postdoctorate: $10,000 maximum. **To Apply:** Write, email, fax, or phone for application guidelines. Submit a curriculum vitae, most recent transcripts, and research proposal. Graduate students must also submit two letters of recommendation. **Deadline:** None. Applications are reviewed within 60 days of receipt. **Contact:** Director of Research at the above address (see entry 3154).

## International Furnishings & Design Association

1200 19th St. NW, Ste. 300      *Ph:* (202)857-1897
Washington, DC 20036-2422      *Fax:* (202)223-4579
*E-mail:* info@ifda.com
*URL:* http://www.ifda.com

### • 3157 • IFDA Educational Foundation Scholarship
*(Undergraduate/Scholarship)*

**Focus:** General studies. **Qualif.:** Applicants must be IFDA student members in good standing who are full-time students with one-half of the program's requirement completed. **Criteria:** Awards are made based on merit of essay.

**Funds Avail.:** $1,500 per award. **To Apply:** Applicants must submit an essay, two letters of recommendation (one from a professor or instructor at the student's school/institution that includes verification of the student's full-time status) and one letter from a professional currently working in the industry. Write for further details. **Deadline:** October 15. **Contact:** IFDA at the above address (see entry 3156).

## International Ladies Garment Workers Union Local 23-25

275 7th Ave.      *Ph:* (212)929-2600
New York, NY 10001      *Fax:* (212)929-2946

### • 3159 • ILGWU Local 23-25 College Textbook Scholarship *(Undergraduate/Scholarship)*

**Purpose:** To help members of the local union with their child's textbook expense. **Focus:** General Studies. **Qualif.:** Candidates must be graduating high school seniors who are children of members who have been in good standing of Local 23-25, ILGWU, for at least two years as of June 30 of the year of the applicant's high school graduation. Children of retired, permanently disabled or deceased members may also apply if the member had been in good standing for at least two years and the separation from the industry occurred within the year of the candidate's high school graduation. Candidates must be planning to enter an accredited college degree program on a full-time basis immediately after high school graduation, have a cumulative high school grade point average of at least 80 percent, and must demonstrate an active concern for the community in which they live. Such activity includes participation in clubs, community or church organizations, extra-curricular school programs, jobs, and responsibilities at home. **Criteria:** Candidates are reviewed by an independent committee of college and admissions experts based on their academic record, extra-curricular activities, personal recommendations, and their own written statements.

**Funds Avail.:** The funds are $1,000 scholarships. **To Apply:** Preliminary applications must be completed by the student and high school principal or guidance counselor and returned to the Scholarship Program. If eligible, a biographical and secondary school questionnaire and two personal evaluation forms will be sent. One of the two Personal Evaluation forms must be completed by a person who has supervised the applicant's activities. Students may also apply for the ILGWU National Scholarship, but may accept only one. **Deadline:** Materials must be in by January 15. All candidates are notified by mail in June. **Contact:** Lana Cheung at the above address (see entry 3158).

## International Ladies Garment Workers Union (New York)

1710 Broadway
New York, NY 10019

### • 3161 • ILGWU National College Award Program
*(High School, Undergraduate/Scholarship)*

**Purpose:** To financially support undergraduate students. **Focus:** General Studies. **Qualif.:** Applicants must be high school seniors who are sons or daughters of members of the ILGWU in good standing for two years and who have been accepted to an accredited two-or four-year college. **Criteria:** SAT/ACT scores and high school transcript.

**Funds Avail.:** $2,500 distributed over four years. **No. of Awards:** 20. **To Apply:** Write for application. **Deadline:** June 30. **Contact:** Ruth Trujillo at the above address (see entry 3160).

## International Lead Zinc Research Organization, Inc.

2525 Meridan Pkwy.
PO Box 12036      *Ph:* (919)361-4647
Research Triangle Park, NC 27709      *Fax:* (919)361-1957
*E-mail:* rputnam@ilzro.org
*URL:* http://www.recycle.net/recycle/assn/ilzro.html

### • 3163 • ILZRO Lead-Acid Battery Fellowship
*(Postgraduate/Fellowship)*

**Purpose:** To stimulate innovative thinking and experimental research aimed at improving the electrochemical performance of lead-acid storage batteries. **Qualif.:** Candidates must be enrolled in an accredited post-graduate program in an institution equipped to conduct lead-acid battery research under a qualified supervisor in that field. **Criteria:** Selection is based upon the novelty of proposed research, the utility of results obtainable, and the qualifications of the institution (equipment, supervision, and expertise in this field).

**Funds Avail.:** The Fellowship is in the amount of $17,000 per year over three years ($51,000 total). **To Apply:** Candidate should submit a detailed proposal identifying the area of investigation, equipment availability, and the qualifications of immediate supervisor. **Deadline:** May 1. **Contact:** Dr. Robert F. Nelson, at the above address (see entry 3162).

### • 3164 • ILZRO Postdoctoral Fellowships
*(Postdoctorate/Fellowship)*

**Purpose:** To provide training for prospective scientists seeking careers in lead and zinc research. **Focus:** Lead, Zinc and related sciences, including Chemistry, Electrochemistry, Environmental Health, Metallurgy. **Qualif.:** Candidate may be of any nationality. Applicant must have a Ph.D. in a field relevant to proposed research, and be sponsored by the college or university at which research will be done. Research must be related to either lead or zinc, depending on the stipulations of the industry providing the fellowship funds.

**Funds Avail.:** $5,000-15,000. **To Apply:** Unsolicited proposals from faculty and/or students for a research investigation in ILZRO's area of interest are welcome. Send to the president a brief outline of proposed area of investigation, including scope and objectives of proposed work and the name of sponsoring organization. A more detailed proposal will be requested. **Deadline:** June 1. **Contact:** Dr. Jerome F. Cole, President, at the above address (see entry 3162).

## • 3165 •
### International Music Centre - Internationales Musikzentrum

Lothringerstrasse 20      Ph: 1 713 0777
A-1030 Vienna, Austria      Fax: 1 713 0777

#### • 3166 •   Dance Screen Competition Awards
*(Professional Development/Award)*

**Purpose:** To recognize the innovative use of dance in the video and film media. **Focus:** Dance, Media Arts, Radio and Television, Music. **Qualif.:** Applicant may be of any nationality. The Dance Screen Competition grants awards to dance programs that set new standards in video/TV/film art. The Competition takes place annually in Lyon.

**Funds Avail.:** 100,000Fr. **No. of Awards:** 1. **To Apply:** Write to the Secretary General for application guidelines. **Deadline:** Varies. **Contact:** Eric Marinitsch, Secretary General, at the above address (see entry 3165).

#### • 3167 •   Opera Screen Competition Awards
*(Professional Development/Award)*

**Purpose:** To recognize the innovative use of music in the video and film media. **Focus:** Music, Opera, Media Arts, Radio and Television. **Qualif.:** Applicant may be of any nationality. The Opera Screen Competition recognizes innovative approaches for visualizing music: theatrical creations in the categories of stage recordings/studio adaptations and video creations. The Competition takes place biennially.

**Funds Avail.:** 100,000 Fr. **To Apply:** Write to the Secretary General for application guidelines. **Deadline:** Varies. **Contact:** Eric Marinitsch, Secretary General, at the above address (see entry 3165).

## • 3168 •
### International Order of the King's Daughters and Sons

5451 Cameo Ct.
Pleasanton, CA 94588      Ph: (510)847-0105

#### • 3169 •   International Order of the King's Daughters and Sons Health Careers Scholarships *(Graduate, Postgraduate, Undergraduate/Scholarship)*

**Purpose:** To assist students preparing for careers in the medical field. **Focus:** Medicine, Dentistry, Pharmacy, Physical Therapy, Occupational Therapy, Health Care Services, Nursing. **Qualif.:** Students preparing for careers in medicine, dentistry, pharmacy, physical or occupational therapy, medical technologies, and selected other health fields are eligible to apply. Students must be United States or Canadian citizens, enrolled full-time in a school accredited in the field involved and located in the United States or Canada. For all students, except those preparing for an R.N. degree, application must be for at least the third year of college. R.N. students must have completed the first year of schooling. Pre-med students are not eligible to apply. For those students seeking M.D. or D.D.S. degrees, application must be for at least the second year of medical or dental school. Each applicant must supply proof of acceptance at the accredited school of choice. **Criteria:** Priority will be given to applicants from areas supporting this program.

**Funds Avail.:** $1,000 or less per award. **No. of Awards:** Varies. **To Apply:** Applicants must submit a completed application, a recent photograph, resume, a personal statement detailing why the chosen field was selected and career intentions following graduation, at least two letters of recommendation, a current

official grade transcript mailed directly from the registrar's office (if grading is pass/fail system, a statement is required from the Dean of Students or a professor in regard to academic progress), and two stamped, self-addressed business envelopes. Also required are an itemized budget endorsed by the school financial aid officer that includes school and living expenses, income, loans, awards, and family contribution for the current year, and a projected estimate for the next year. Application requests must include a statement as to the field of interest and present level of study and a stamped, self-addressed, business-size envelope. Each student must request his/her own application blank between September 1 and March 1. **Deadline:** April 15. **Contact:** Mrs. Harry E. Stuard, Jr., at the above address (see entry 3168).

#### • 3170 •   M.A. Hanna Company Scholarship
*(Undergraduate/Scholarship)*

**Focus:** General studies. **Qualif.:** Applicants must be children or spouse of full-time active associates of M.A. Hanna or a business unit or subsidiary which is at least majority-owned by M.A. Hanna. **Criteria:** Awards are made based on academic achievement, financial need, achievements in areas outside academics and the geographic location of the M.A. Hanna business unit where the applicant's parent or spouse is employed.

**Funds Avail.:** $1,500 per award. **No. of Awards:** 50. **To Apply:** Applicants must submit a completed application form, grade transcript and three letters of reference. **Deadline:** June 30. **Contact:** Marcia Chipka.

## • 3171 •
### International Personnel Management Association

1617 Duke St.      Ph: (703)549-7100
Alexandria, VA 22314      Fax: (703)684-0948
E-mail: ipma@ipma-hr.org
URL: http://www.ipma-hr.org/

#### • 3172 •   IPMA Graduate Study Fellowships
*(Professional Development/Fellowship)*

**Purpose:** To assist graduate level studies related to public or business administration. **Focus:** Business Administration, Public Administration. **Qualif.:** Candidate may be of any nationality. Applicant must have been an IPMA individual member for at least one year. Candidate should have a minimum of five years of full-time professional experience in personnel-related work, a strong academic record, and a commitment to public service.

**Funds Avail.:** $2,000 maximum. **To Apply:** Write for application form and guidelines. **Deadline:** May. Notification in July. **Contact:** Sarah A.I. Shiffert at the above address (see entry 3171).

## • 3173 •
### International Radio and Television Society Foundation

420 Lexington Ave., Ste. 1714
New York, NY 10170      Ph: (212)867-6650

#### • 3174 •   College Conference and Summer Fellowship Program *(Graduate, Undergraduate/Fellowship)*

**Focus:** Communications. **Qualif.:** Full-time undergraduates who are juniors or seniors in a four-year college are eligible to apply. Applicants should either be a communications major or have demonstrated a strong interest in the field through extracurricular activities or other practical experience. Recipients of these awards must also be able to take part in the entire nine weeks of the summer program. Graduate students are not discouraged from applying and may also be selected as fellows. **Criteria:** Candidates should have academic records and extracurricular activities that suggest that they may be the communications leaders of tomorrow.

**Funds Avail.:** Recipients participate in a program that includes a one-week orientation to broadcasting, cable, and advertising, including field trips, and are assigned an eight-week fellowship in a New York-based corporation. Housing, round-trip transportation, and personal stipend are provided. IRTS also provides supervision and counseling. **To Apply:** Applications are available from IRTS. Graduate students applying for the program must submit a formal letter to the selection committee justifying exemption to the rules in addition to the application. **Contact:** IRTS at the above address (see entry 3173).

---

**• 3175 •**
**International Reading Association**
800 Barksdale Rd.     *Ph:* (302)731-1600
PO Box 8139     *Fax:* (302)731-1057
Newark, DE 19714-8139     *Free:* 800-336-READ
*E-mail:* gkeating@reading.org; 73314.1411@
    compuserve.com
*URL:* http://reading.org

**• 3176 • Jeanne S. Chall Research Fellowship** *(Doctorate/Fellowship)*

**Purpose:** To encourage and support doctoral research investigating issues in beginning research, readability, reading difficulty, and stages of reading development. **Focus:** Literacy. **Qualif.:** Applicants must be doctoral students who are members of the International Reading Association and are planning or beginning dissertations.

**Funds Avail.:** Up to $6000. **To Apply:** Inquire for details. **Deadline:** October.

**• 3177 • Elva Knight Research Grants** *(Postgraduate/Grant)*

**Purpose:** To assist researchers in reading and literacy projects. Research is defined as inquiry that addresses significant questions about literacy instruction and practice. **Focus:** Reading and literacy research. **Qualif.:** Applicants may be of any nationality, but must be members of the IRA. Each year it is expected that at least one grant will be awarded to a researcher outside the United States and Canada, and one grant will be awarded to a teacher-initiated project. Applicant's project may be carried out using any research method or approach as long as the focus of the project is research in reading. Activities such as developing new programs or instructional materials are not eligible for funding except to the extent that these activities are necessary procedures for the conduct of research. IRA retains the first rights on refusal of publication.

**Funds Avail.:** $5,000 maximum. **No. of Awards:** Up to seven awards may be offered. **To Apply:** Write for application cover sheet and guidelines. Submit two copies of the cover sheet with five copies of the research proposal and budget. **Deadline:** October 15. Grants will be awarded at the time of the IRA annual convention. **Contact:** Gail Keating at the above address (see entry 3175).

**• 3178 • Reading/Literacy Research Fellowship** *(Postdoctorate/Fellowship)*

**Purpose:** To provide support for the first five years following doctoral study for a researcher outside of the U.S and Canada.

**Focus:** Reading and literacy. **Qualif.:** Applicant must be a member of the International Reading Association who has shown exceptional promise in reading/literacy research. Applicant may be of any nationality other than American or Canadian, but must have received their Ph.D. within five years of application.

**Funds Avail.:** Fellows will receive $1,000. **No. of Awards:** One award is offered per year. **To Apply:** Write for application form and guidelines prior to August 1. **Deadline:** Deadline for receipt of proposal is October 15. **Contact:** Gail Keating at the above address (see entry 3175).

**• 3179 • Helen M. Robinson Award** *(Doctorate/Grant)*

**Purpose:** To support doctoral IRA members in the early stages of their dissertation research in the area of reading and literacy. **Focus:** Reading. **Criteria:** Decisions will be based on the quality of the dissertation proposal, relevance to the areas of correcting reading problems, and the quality of supporting materials. The award will be made only in those years when the committee concludes that there are applications of very high quality.

**Funds Avail.:** $500. **No. of Awards:** One. **To Apply:** To apply for this award, doctoral students should submit an abstract, not to exceed 1,000 words, of an approved dissertation proposal; a brief statement, not to exceed 500 words, indicating how the grant will be used to support the research; a copy of the full proposal with a cover sheet including signatures of approval by a supervisory committee; a letter from the student's advisor that includes a brief rationale as to why the grant should be awarded to this applicant as well as a statement indicating that the applicant is in the early stages of the dissertation research and that it appears that the grant will be used to support that research. **Deadline:** June 15. Applicants will be notified in November.

**Remarks:** Recipients of the grant are required to submit a brief report, within one year of receipt of the grant, to the Division of Research at IRA Headquarters. The report should outline progress toward execution or completion of the research, findings to date, and should explain briefly how the funding was expended.

**• 3180 • Nila Banton Smith Research Dissemination Support Grant** *(Professional Development/Grant)*

**Purpose:** To facilitate the dissemination of literacy research to the educational community. **Focus:** Reading and literacy research. **Qualif.:** Applicant may be a student of any nationality but must be an IRA member. Candidate's project may be a literature review, meta-analysis, monograph, or other form of research dissemination. Funds for equipment will not normally be supported. Research should result in a publishable manuscript; IRA retains the first rights of refusal on publication.

**Funds Avail.:** Student receives $5,000 maximum. **No. of Awards:** One award is offered annually. **To Apply:** Write for application cover sheet and guidelines. Submit cover sheet with a detailed research proposal (20 page, maximum) and a budget. Letters of institutional support, curriculum vitae, and other documentation may also be required. **Deadline:** Materials must be received by October 15. **Contact:** Gail Keating at the above address (see entry 3175).

**• 3181 • Teacher as Researcher Grant** *(Other/Grant)*

**Purpose:** To support teachers in their inquiries about literacy learning and instruction. **Qualif.:** Applicants must be members of the International Reading Association who are practicing K-12 teachers with full-time teaching responsibilities, include librarians, Title I teachers, classroom, and resource teachers.

**Funds Avail.:** Up to $5000 maximum, but priority is given to smaller grants (for example $1000, and $2000 grants). **No. of Awards:** Several grants are awarded annually. **To Apply:** Inquire for specific guidelines. **Deadline:** October 15.

---

• 3182 •

## International Research and Exchanges Board

1616 H St., NW

Washington, DC 20006

*E-mail:* irex@info.irex.org

*URL:* http://www.irex.org

*Ph:* (202)628-8188

*Fax:* (202)628-8189

*IREX guarantees access by American scholars to research resources in the former Soviet Union, Eastern Europe, and the Mongolian People's Republic. It encourages scholarly cooperation with the region, especially in the humanities and social sciences.*

### • 3183 • Bulgarian Studies Seminar *(Doctorate, Graduate, Postdoctorate/Fellowship)*

**Purpose:** To provide fellowships for U.S. Scholars wishing to improve their knowledge of the Bulgarian language and culture. The seminar consists of lectures on Bulgarian language, history, culture, and literature. Topics vary each year to compliment the needs and interests of each group of scholars. **Focus:** Bulgarian Language and Culture. **Qualif.:** U.S. citizenship or permanent residency. Applicants should already have begun formal study of the Bulgarian language prior to participation. Participation is open to scholars at all academic levels from graduate students to full professors. No funds will be disbursed until final reports have been received for any previous IREX grants.

**Funds Avail.:** Round-trip airfare, tuition, housing, and local stipend. **To Apply:** Contact IREX for the Grant Opportunities for U.S. Scholars booklet and an application. **Deadline:** November 1. **Contact:** IREX at the above address (see entry 3182).

### • 3184 • IREX Bulgarian Studies Seminar *(All/Grant)*

**Purpose:** To allow Fellows to improve their knowledge of the Bulgarian language at the Slavonic Studies Seminar held during the month of August at Kliment Okhridski University in Sofia, Bulgaria or at Kiril and Methodius University in Veliko Turnova, Bulgaria. **Qualif.:** Application is open to scholars at all academic levels, from graduate students to full professors who have already begun formal study of the Bulgarian language prior to participation. Applicants must be United States citizens or permanent residents. The grant is designed for students focusing on Bulgarian language and literature study.

**Funds Avail.:** Round-trip transportation, lodging, tuition, and living allowance. Eight grants were awarded for the 1992-93 academic year. **To Apply:** Applications are available from IREX. Normally, applicants are required to take an IREX-administered written test of the relevant host-country language. **Deadline:** November 1.

**Remarks:** The grants are funded by the United States Department of State through Title VIII. **Contact:** Vera Lichtenberg, Program Officer, International Research and Exchange Board, at the above address (see entry 3182).

### • 3185 • IREX Individual Advanced Research Opportunities *(Doctorate/Award)*

**Purpose:** To provide research placement and access for U.S. Scholars to study in Central and Eastern Europe, Eurasia, and Mongolia. **Focus:** Humanities, Social Sciences. **Qualif.:** U.S. citizenship or permanent residency; command of the host country language sufficient for advanced research; full-time affiliation with a college or university; and to be a faculty member or doctoral candidate who will have completed all requirements for the Ph.D. except the dissertation by the time of participation. Independent scholars or recipients of professional degrees (MLS, MFA, etc.) may also qualify. No funds will be disbursed until final reports have been received for any previous IREX grants. Applicants may be required to take an IREX-administered written and/or oral test of the relevant host country language.

**Funds Avail.:** Round-trip airfare and visa fees, dollar stipend, stipend for host country room and board, local research allowance, and excess baggage allowance. Support for

accompanying family may be available. (Provisions may vary slightly by country) **To Apply:** Contact IREX for the Grant Opportunities for U.S. Scholars booklet and an application. **Deadline:** November 1.

**Remarks:** Review by a rotating panel of scholarly experts appointed by the IREX Board, with separate panels for Central and Eastern Europe, Eurasia, and Mongolia. **Contact:** IREX at the above address (see entry 3182).

### • 3186 • IREX Research Residencies *(Postdoctorate/ Grant)*

**Purpose:** Combination research/developmental opportunities to conduct long-term research in Eurasian and East European countries previously understudied by the American scholarly community. Research residents are placed in the host country to pursue their individual research projects and improve their host country language competency. Through regular correspondence with IREX, research residents also keep the U.S. academic community abreast of developments of scholarly interest in the region of residency. **Focus:** Research residencies are available in the countries of Albania, Armenia, Azerbaijan, Belarus, Bulgaria, Croatia, Estonia, Georgia, Kazakhstan, Kyrgyzstan, Latvia, Lithuania, Macedonia, Moldova, Romania, Slovakia, Sovenia, Tajikistan, Turkmenistan, Ukraine, and Uzbekistan, as well as the Urals, Siberian and Far Eastern regions of the Russian Federation. **Qualif.:** U.S. citizenship or permanent residency. Ph.D. or equivalent professional degree. (Preference will be given to Ph.D.s awarded after January 1, 1988. In exceptional circumstances, advanced doctoral candidates may be considered). Command of host country language sufficient for advanced research. Research proposal in the humanities or social sciences encompassing one or more of the countries/regions enumerated above. Evidence of prior interest and/or commitment to develop expertise in country/ region of residency. No funds will be disbursed until final reports have been received for any previous IREX grants. Applicants may be required to take an IREX-administered written and/or oral test of the relevant host country language.

**Funds Avail.:** $25,000. **To Apply:** Contact IREX for the Grant Opportunities for U.S. Scholars booklet and an application. **Deadline:** November 1. **Contact:** IREX at the above address (see entry 3182).

### • 3187 • IREX Short-Term Travel Grants for Independent Short-Term Research *(Postdoctorate/ Grant)*

**Purpose:** To provide one to two-week stays in Central and Eastern Europe or the states of the former Soviet region for scholarly projects in the humanities and social sciences. **Qualif.:** Applicants must be scholars conducting library or archival research and carrying out interviews in either of the above regions. They must also be citizens or permanent residents of the United States, and have a Ph.D. or equivalent professional degree. Support is provided for individuals who do not require administrative assistance.

**Funds Avail.:** Grants provide trans-oceanic APEX airfare on a U.S.-flag carrier and a per diem for up to two weeks not to exceed $75 a day, in cases where the host country will not provide support. There were 61 grants awarded in February 1992 and 60 awarded in June 1992. **To Apply:** Applications may be obtained from IREX. Placement with host country is the responsibility of the grant recipient. **Deadline:** There are three annual deadlines: October 1; February 1; and June 1. Notification is approximately eight weeks after the application deadline. The proposed activities must have starting dates that follow the grant deadlines.

**Remarks:** The grants are funded by the National Endowment for the Humanities; Andrew W. Mellon Foundation; and the U.S. Department of State through Title VIII. **Contact:** Tomothy W. Blythe, Program Officer, International Research and Exchange Board, at the above address (see entry 3182).

**• 3188 • Support for Special Projects in the Study of Central and Eastern Europe, Eurasia and Mongolia** *(Postdoctorate/Grant)*

**Purpose:** To provide financial support for collaborative projects in the study of Central and Eastern Europe, Eurasia, and Mongolia, including the former German Democratic Republic (GDR). **Focus:** Humanities, Social Sciences. **Qualif.:** All projects must involve Americans and foreign participants from one or more of the above regions. Normally, affiliation with a university or research institution.

**Funds Avail.:** Travel, accommodations, per diem, fees for use of facilities, and publication costs and/or other expenses associated with presenting results to policymakers, scholarly peers, and the general public. (Grants do not normally exceed $25,000) **To Apply:** Contact IREX for the Grant Opportunities for U.S. Scholars booklet and an application. **Deadline:** March 1.

**Remarks:** Review by a rotation panel of scholarly experts appointed by the IREX Board, with separate panels for Central and Eastern Europe and Eurasia/Mongolia. Projects relating to the former GDR are limited to topics that address its communist experience, or which extend into the period of unification, and relate to the transition experience of other countries in the region. **Contact:** IREX at the above address (see entry 3182).

**• 3189 • Support for Special Projects in the Study of Library and Information Science** *(Professional Development/Award)*

**Purpose:** To provide opportunities for support librarians, archivists, and information specialists pursuing projects relating to Central and Eastern Europe, Eurasia, and Mongolia, including the former German Democratic Republic (GDR). **Focus:** Library and Informtion Science, Archives. **Qualif.:** Individuals and institutions in archival, library, and information sciences. Pilot projects to assess the current state of exchange relations and/or international acquisitions in a particular geographic area or with particular libraries, publishing houses, etc; production of directories, research guides, and other finding aids on collections, libraries, and/or archives in the region; collaborative work and joint projects, including conferences and workshopss (with particular weight given to initiatives that result in publication and other forms of public dissemination); or other initiatives that are designed to increase the knowledge of the field of library and information science and/or improve relations with libraries and archives in the region.

**Funds Avail.:** Travel, accomodations, per diem, fees for use of facilities, and publication costs and/or other expenses associated with presenting resultss to librarians, archivists, scholarly peers, and the general public. (Grants do not normally exceed $25,000). **To Apply:** Contact IREX for the Grant Opportunities for U.S. Scholar booklet. **Deadline:** January 15.

**Remarks:** Projects relating to the former GDR are limited to topics that address its communist experience, or which extend into the period of unification, and relate to the transition experience of other countries in the region.

**• 3190 • Travel Grants for Independent Short-Term Research** *(Other/Grant)*

**Purpose:** To provide grants for senior scholars who need to make brief trips, typically two weeks, to the former Soviet Union or Eastern Europe in connection with ongoing research. **Deadline:** October 1 and April 1.

**Remarks:** No host-country administrative support is provided. Grantees are expected to make their own arrangements for visas, housing, and research. This program is sponsored by the American Council of Learned Societies. **Contact:** International Research & Exchange Board at the above address (see entry 3182).

**• 3191 •**
**International Society of Arboriculture**
Research Committee
Dept. of Botany & Microbiology
Ohio Wesleyan University
Delaware, OH 43015
E-mail: brrobert@cc.owu.edu
URL: http://www.ag.uiuc.edu/~isa/

Ph: (740)368-3508
Fax: (740)368-3011

**• 3192 • Shade Tree Research Grants** *(Postdoctorate/Grant)*

**Purpose:** To support the investigation of problems encountered by arborists in caring for shade and landscape trees. **Focus:** Horticulture. **Qualif.:** Applicant may be of any nationality. Grants are not expected to cover all research costs, but to aid, stimulate, and encourage scientific studies of shade trees. Grants may be used to buy supplies or equipment, hire technical or student help, or otherwise aid the work. Funds cannot be used for tuition, books or lab fees, nor can they be applied toward the cost of administrative overhead. Grant recipients are requested to publish the results of their research in ISA's Journal of Arboriculture.

**Funds Avail.:** Up to $5,000. **To Apply:** A 2-page application form is required; write for application guidelines. **Deadline:** November 1. All applicants are notified by April 1. **Contact:** Dr. Bruce R. Roberts, Research Committee Chair, at the above address (see entry 3191).

**• 3193 •**
**International Union Against Cancer**
3, rue du Conseil General
CH-1205 Geneva, Switzerland
E-mail: baker@uicc.ch
URL: http://www.uicc.ch

Ph: 41 22 8091840
Fax: 41 22 8091810

*The International Union Against Cancer is an international non-governmental organization comprising some 250 Institutes and National Cancer Associations of scientific, medical, and lay members in more than 80 countries.*

**• 3194 • International Cancer Technology Transfer Fellowships** *(Professional Development/Fellowship)*

**Purpose:** To assist practicing cancer specialists to acquire knowledge of and experience in current clinical management practices. **Focus:** Oncology. **Qualif.:** Candidate for either a project award or a fellowship may be of any nationality. Applicant must be a medically or scientifically qualified investigator or specialist who is actively engaged in cancer research or clinical management in the cancer field. Candidate's home institution must agree to grant him/her a leave of absence for the duration of the award and hold a position till his/her return. Candidate for a research award should be in the early stages of his/her career. Applicant for a Clinical Oncology Fellowship should be an established investigator with several years of experience in oncology practice at a laboratory, cancer hospital/center, or university. Fellowships and awards are tenable at institutions outside of candidate's home country. Candidate must have a working knowledge of the host country's language.

**Funds Avail.:** $2,800 average. **No. of Awards:** 120. **To Apply:** Write to the Fellowships Department for application form and guidelines. Submit form with a letter of agreement from home institution, including confirmation of proficiency in the host language; a letter of invitation from the host institution; a description of proposed project; and a list of recent, relevant publications and copies of abstracts. All materials should be in English. **Deadline:** None. Notification within two months. **Contact:** Brita M. Baker at the above address (see entry 3193).

*International Union Against Cancer (continued)*

**• 3195 •   International Oncology Nursing Fellowships** *(Professional Development/Fellowship)*

**Purpose:** To provide an opportunity for qualified nurses to augment their professional knowledge and experience through a short-term observership at a renowned comprehensive cancer centre in North America or the United Kingdom. **Focus:** Oncology. **Qualif.:** Candidate must be an English-speaking registered nurse who is involved in the care of cancer patients in his/her home institute. Applicant must come from a country where specialist cancer nursing training is not yet widely available.

**Funds Avail.:** $2,800 average. **No. of Awards:** 5. **To Apply:** Write to the Fellowships Department for application form and guidelines. Submit form with a project description detailing the particular cancer nursing skills that the candidate wishes to observe. **Deadline:** November 15. Notification by mid-February. **Contact:** Brita M. Baker at the above address (see entry 3193).

**• 3196 •   Research Fellowships** *(Other/Fellowship)*

**Purpose:** Designed to allow highly qualified researchers from any country to work in collaboration with outstanding scientists in another country. **Focus:** Cancer research. **Qualif.:** Applicants must have been active in cancer research for at least 5 years.

**Funds Avail.:** $40,000 stipend. **Deadline:** October 1. **Contact:** International Union Against Cancer at the above address (see entry 3193).

**• 3197 •   Yamagiwa-Yoshida Memorial International Cancer Study Grants** *(Professional Development/Grant)*

**Purpose:** To enable investigators to undertake joint projects with researchers in other countries, and to train in experimental methods or special techniques. **Focus:** Oncology. **Qualif.:** Candidate may be of any nationality. Applicant must be a scientifically or medically qualified investigator who is actively engaged in cancer research. Candidate's home institution must agree to provide him/her with a leave of absence for the duration of the grant term and hold a position until his/her return. Grants are tenable at institutions outside of candidate's home country. Candidate must have adequate fluency in the language of the proposed host country.

**Funds Avail.:** $8,000 average. **To Apply:** Write to the Fellowships Department for application form and guidelines. Submit form with a letter of agreement from home institute, including confirmation of proficiency in the host language; a letter of invitation from the host institute; a description of proposed project; a list of recent, relevant publications and copies of abstracts; and two references. All materials should be in English. **Deadline:** January 1 and July 1. Notification by mid-March and mid-October respectively. **Contact:** International Union Against Cancer at the above address (see entry 3193).

**• 3198 •**
**International Union for Vacuum Science, Technique and Applications**
Advanced Technology Laboratory
c/o Dr. William Westwood
BNR
PO Box 3511, Station C
Ottawa, ON, Canada K1Y 4H7
*E-mail:* weave004@maroon.tc.umn.edu
*URL:* http://www.vacumm.org

*Ph:* (613)763-3248
*Fax:* (613)763-2404

**• 3199 •   Welch Foundation Scholarship** *(Graduate, Postdoctorate/Scholarship)*

**Purpose:** To support a promising scholar who wishes to contribute to the study of vacuum science techniques or their application in any field. **Focus:** Vacuum Science **Qualif.:** Candidate may be of any nationality. Applicant should have at least a bachelor's degree; a Ph.D. is preferred. Applicant must make arrangements for the proposed research program with a laboratory of his/her choice. Because of the international nature of the scholarship, strong preference will be given to applicants who propose to study in a foreign laboratory in which they have not yet studied. Candidate must be reasonably fluent in the language of the country of study. Scholars must receive permission from IUVSTA before accepting research funds from other organizations during the tenure of the scholarship.

**Funds Avail.:** $12,500. Awards are paid in three installments. **No. of Awards:** 1. **To Apply:** Write for application form and guidelines. Submit form with research proposal, curriculum vitae, two letters of recommendation, and evidence of support from laboratory and project supervisor. **Deadline:** 15 April. Notification by the beginning of August.

**• 3200 •**
**International Women Helicopter Pilots**
The Whirly-Girls, Inc.
Executive Towers 10-D
207 W. Clarendon Ave.
Phoenix, AZ 85013
*E-mail:* leeh426@aol.com

*Ph:* (602)263-0190
*Fax:* (602)264-5812

**• 3201 •   Bell Helicopter Scholarship** *(Other/ Scholarship)*

**Purpose:** For attendance at the Bell 206 Turbine Transition Course at the Bell Flight Training Academy in Ft. Worth, TX. **Focus:** Aviation. **Qualif.:** Applicants must be a Whirly Girl in good standing.

**Remarks:** Sponsored by the Bell Textron Co.

**• 3202 •   Flight Safety International Instrument Refresher Course Scholarship** *(Other/Scholarship)*

**Focus:** Aviation. **Qualif.:** Applicants must be Whirly Girls in good standing who posses a helicopter instrument rating. **To Apply:** Inquire for details.

**Remarks:** Sponsored by Flight Safety International in Hurst, Texas.

**• 3203 •   Doris Mullen Memorial Scholarships** *(All/ Scholarship)*

**Purpose:** To assist women pilots seeking helicopter rating or advanced helicopter training. **Focus:** Helicopter Flight Training. **Qualif.:** Candidates may be of any nationality but must be pilots. One scholarship is reserved for a woman who wishes to obtain her helicopter rating; one scholarship is intended to support advanced helicopter training.

**Funds Avail.:** Up to $4,500. **No. of Awards:** Four. **To Apply:** Write for application materials, available in June. **Deadline:** October 31. **Contact:** Lee Hixon, 3674 Andreas Hills Dr., Palm Springs, CA 92264.

• **3204** • **Whirly-Girls Memorial Flight Scholarships**
*(Professional Development/Scholarship)*

**Purpose:** To enable deserving women airplane, balloon, or glider pilots to obtain their initial helicopter rating. **Qualif.:** Applicants must be licensed women airplane, balloon, or glider pilots. They must also have proof of financial need and have demonstrated a strong desire and effort to pursue a career as a helicopter pilot.

**Funds Avail.:** $4,500. **To Apply:** Applicants must include a check for $25 payable to The Whirly-Girls Scholarship Fund, Inc. (to cover the cost of processing and mailing) with application. **Deadline:** Applications must be postmarked on or before October 15.

**Remarks:** This scholarship is funded by the Whirly-Girls' Men's Auxiliary. **Contact:** Lee Hixon, 3674 Andreas Hills Dr., Palm Springs, CA, 92264.

• **3205** •
**International Women's Fishing Association**
PO Drawer 3125
Palm Beach, FL 33480          *Ph:* (407)746-0597

• **3206** • **Scholarships for Marine Sciences**
*(Graduate/Scholarship)*

**Purpose:** To assist students earning a graduate degree in marine science. **Focus:** Marine Sciences. **Qualif.:** Candidates may be of any nationality and need not be women. Applicants must be enrolled in a graduate program at a recognized university in the United States or one of its territorial possessions, and be studying one of the marine sciences.

**Funds Avail.:** $3,000 maximum. **To Apply:** Write for application form and guidelines. Submit form with a letter of interest, college transcripts, recent photograph, names of references. Letters of recommendation should be sent directly to the chair. **Deadline:** March 1. Notification after April 1. **Contact:** Chair at the above address (see entry 3205).

• **3207** •
**Interstitial Cystitis Association**
51 Monroe St., Ste. 1402
Madison Square Station          *Ph:* (301)610-5300
Rockville, MD 20850          *Fax:* (301)610-5308
*E-mail:* ICAmail@ichelp.org
*URL:* http://www.ichelp.org

• **3208** • **ICA Pilot Research Project Grants**
*(Postdoctorate/Grant)*

**Purpose:** To support initial research projects relevant to the interests of ICA. **Focus:** Etiology of interstitial cystitis; epidermiology of the disease neurophysiology; serum or urine markers; potential IC treatment modalities; pregnancy and IC, and pain management. **Qualif.:** Candidate may be of any nationality. Applicant must be a qualified investigator proposing to conduct preliminary research on interstitial cystitis. Preference is given to proposals for research that will be undertaken in the United States.

**Funds Avail.:** $10,000 maximum. **No. of Awards:** Three. **To Apply:** Seven collated copies of the research porposal must be submitted. A complete research proposal consists of a one page cover sheet, one page extract, a hypotheses, proposed methodology, estimated time required to complete the project, a detailed budget, a curriculum vitae of principal researchers, and anu relevant articles. **Deadline:** August 1. **Contact:** James Loney c/o above address.

• **3209** •
**IntraMed**
c/o John Bayliss
1180 Avenue of the Americas
New York, NY 10036          *Free:* 800-292-7373

• **3210** • **Grover T. Cronin Memorial Scholarship**
*(Undergraduate/Scholarship)*

**Focus:** General studies. **Qualif.:** Applicants must be residents of Waltham, Massachusetts who are graduating seniors. **Criteria:** Awards are granted based on academic achievement, financial need and personal accomplishment.

**Funds Avail.:** Renewable. **No. of Awards:** 1. **To Apply:** Applications are available through the Waltham High School guidance office. **Deadline:** Early April. **Contact:** Robert J. Cronin, Trustee.

• **3211** • **Parke-Davis Epilepsy Scholarship**
*(Undergraduate/Scholarship)*

**Focus:** General studies. **Qualif.:** Applicants must have epilepsy. **Criteria:** Awards are granted based on academic achievement and essay.

**Funds Avail.:** $3,000. **No. of Awards:** 16. **To Apply:** Applicants must submit an essay, letter from doctor explaining condition, letter of recommendation, current transcript, and college acceptance letter. **Deadline:** March 1. **Contact:** John Bayliss.

• **3212** •
**Iota Lambda Sigma**
c/o Raymond L. Christensen
Iota Lambda Sigma Grand Chapter
1017 Oma          *Ph:* (318)352-8206
Natchitoches, LA 71457          *Fax:* (318)352-8206

• **3213** • **Iota Lambda Sigma Grand Chapter Scholarship** *(Doctorate, Graduate/Scholarship)*

**Purpose:** To assist promising members to obtain either a masters or doctorate degree. **Focus:** Industrial, Technical, Technology, and Engineering Technology Education. **Qualif.:** Applicants must be contributing members of the organization who have successfully completed an undergraduate degree. They must be enrolled in graduate school or accepted as doctoral candidates. A high grade point average must be maintained. **Criteria:** Scholarships, need, and recommendations.

**Funds Avail.:** Each scholarship is worth $1,000. **No. of Awards:** 2. **To Apply:** Applications may be obtained from the above address. **Deadline:** August 1.

**Remarks:** Also offers the ILS Distinguished Teacher Award, the ILS Distinguished Service Award, and the ILS Outstanding Chapter Award. **Contact:** Raymond L. Christensen, Executive Secretary, Iota Lambda Sigma at the above address (see entry 3212).

## • 3214 •
**Iota Sigma Pi**
c/o Dr. Barbara A. Sawrey
Dept. of Chemistry and
  Biochemistry, 0303
University of California, San Diego    Ph: (619)534-6479
La Jolla, CA 92093-0303    Fax: (619)534-7687
E-mail: bsawrey@ucsd.edu

### • 3215 • Gladys Anderson Emerson Scholarships
*(Undergraduate/Scholarship)*

**Focus:** Chemistry, Biochemistry. **Qualif.:** Nominees must be women undergraduate students with junior or senior standing in their curriculum at an accredited college or university, and must have at least one semester of work to complete as of August 1 following the announcement. Nominees must be members of Iota Sigma Pi. **Criteria:** Selection is based on excellence in chemistry or biochemistry.

**Funds Avail.:** $1,000. **No. of Awards:** One per year. **To Apply:** The nomination dossier must contain the name and address of the nominee, a stipulation of Chapter or MAL status, official transcript, a list of all academic honors and professional memberships, a short personal essay by the nominee describing herself, her goals, and presenting any financial need, a letter of nomination, and at least two letters of recommendation from a faculty member. **Deadline:** February 15. Award is announced April 15. **Contact:** Dr. Barbara A. Sawrey at the above address (see entry 3214).

### • 3216 • Anna Louise Hoffman Awards for Outstanding Achievement in Graduate Research
*(Graduate/Award)*

**Focus:** Chemistry, Biochemistry. **Qualif.:** Candidates must be full-time women graduate students who are candidates for a graduate degree in an accredited institution. The research presented by the candidates must be original research that can be described by one of the main chemical divisions (analytical, biochemical, inorganic, organic, physical, and/or ancillary divisions of chemistry). Nominees may, but need not be, members of Iota Sigma Pi. **Criteria:** Selection is based on excellence in original chemical research.

**Funds Avail.:** $400. **No. of Awards:** One per year. **To Apply:** Nomination forms are available from the Junior National Director. Nomination for the award must be made by members of the institution's graduate faculty, and only one nomination may be submitted by each department. The nomination dossier must contain: the candidate's permanent and school addresses; an academic history, including official transcripts from the colleges and universities attended by the nominee; a brief description of the candidate's research (prepared by the candidate, and no more than 1,000 words); a list of publications; and two recommendations (one work, and one from another person familiar with the candidate's research capabilities). Five copies of the dossier should be sent to the Junior National Director. **Deadline:** February 15. Award is announced by April 15. **Contact:** Dr. Barbara A. Sawrey at the above address (see entry 3214).

### • 3217 • Iota Sigma Pi Undergraduate Awards for Excellence in Chemistry *(Undergraduate/Award)*

**Focus:** Chemistry. **Qualif.:** Nominees must be women chemistry students in an accredited college or university that grants a four-year degree. Nominees must have attained senior standing. Nominees may be, but need not be, members of Iota Sigma Pi. **Criteria:** Selection is based on excellence in the field of chemistry.

**Funds Avail.:** $300. **No. of Awards:** One per year. **To Apply:** Nomination for the award must be made by members of the institution's undergraduate faculty. Only one nomination may be submitted by each department. The nomination dossier must contain: the nominee's permanent and school addresses; an

official transcript of the student's college record, including grade point average; Department Head certification of most recent grades if they are not included in the official transcript; a list of the student's activities while in college and a statement of plans after graduation; two or more recommendations by faculty members. Five copies of the dossier should be sent to the Junior National Director. **Deadline:** February 15. Award is announced by April 15. **Contact:** Iota Sigma Pi at the above address (see entry 3214).

## • 3218 •
**Iowa Broadcasters Association**
PO Box 71186
Des Moines, IA 50325

### • 3219 • Iowa Broadcasters Association Scholarship
*(Undergraduate/Scholarship)*

**Focus:** Broadcasting. **Qualif.:** Applicants must be graduating high school seniors of Iowa schools who plan to attend four-year Iowa colleges or universities, studying broadcasting. **Criteria:** Awards are granted based on scholastic record, financial need, broadcasting career goals, and related experience in the broadcasting field.

**Funds Avail.:** $2,5000 per year. Renewable up to four years. **No. of Awards:** 4. **To Apply:** Write for further details. **Deadline:** April 1. **Contact:** Iowa Broadcaster Association at the above address (see entry 3218).

## • 3220 •
**Iowa Commission of Veterans Affairs - Camp Dodge Office**
7700 NW Beaver Dr.    Ph: (515)242-5331
Camp Dodge    Fax: (515)242-5659
Johnston, IA 50131-1902    Free: 800-838-4692

### • 3221 • War Orphans Educational Fund
*(Undergraduate/Grant)*

**Qualif.:** Students must have lived in the state of Iowa for two years preceding application for aid, and must be children of persons who died while serving in the United States military during World War I (between the dates of April 6, 1917, and June 2, 1921), World War II (between the dates of September 16, 1940, and December 31, 1946), the Korean Conflict (between June 25, 1950, and January 31, 1955), or the Vietnam Conflict (between August 5, 1964, and May 7, 1975). Also eligible are war orphans of National Guardsmen and other members of Reserve Components who died as a result of performance of training or other duties ordered by competent Federal or State authorities.

**Funds Avail.:** Awards may not be in excess of $600 per person per calendar year. Lifetime maximum is $3,000. The fund pays expenses of tuition, matriculation, fees, books and supplies, board, lodging, and any other reasonably necessary expenses for attendance at any educational or training institution of college grade, or in any business or vocational training school of standards approved by the commission and located within the state of Iowa. **To Apply:** A copy of the war orphan's birth certificate and a copy of the death certificate of the veteran parent must accompany the application. In the case of adoption, the applicant must submit a copy of the adoption papers. **Contact:** The Commission of Veterans Affairs at the above address (see entry 3220).

• **3222** •

## Iowa Federation of Labor, AFL-CIO

2000 Walker St., Ste. A
Des Moines, IA 50317          *Ph:* (515)262-9571
*E-mail:* 71112.174@compuserve.com

• **3223** • **Iowa Federation of Labor, AFL-CIO High School Scholarships** *(Undergraduate/Scholarship)*

**Qualif.:** Applicants must be graduating high school seniors in the state of Iowa.

**Funds Avail.:** $1,500 is available. **No. of Awards: 1. To Apply:** Students must submit a cover sheet and essay on an assigned topic to the Federation. **Deadline:** March 18. **Contact:** Ken D. Sagar at the above address (see entry 3222).

• **3224** •

## Iowa School of Letters - Department of English

English-Philosophy Bldg.
The University of Iowa
Iowa City, IA 52242

• **3225** • **Iowa School of Letters Award for Short Fiction** *(Other/Award)*

**Qualif.:** Any writer who has not previously published a volume of prose fiction is eligible to enter the competition. Revised manuscripts that have been entered previously may be resubmitted. Any writer who has published a volume of poetry is also eligible. The Award is given for a collection of short stories only. Preliminary professional readings are organized by the Writers' Workshop. Final judgment is made by a prominent writer or critic. Manuscripts must be a collection of short stories of at least 150 typewritten pages. Stories previously published in periodicals are eligible for inclusion. Photocopies are acceptable. Stamped, self-addressed return packaging must accompany manuscripts.

**Funds Avail.:** The manuscript is published by the University of Iowa Press. **To Apply:** No application forms are necessary. **Deadline:** Entries should be submitted between August 1 and September 30. Announcement of the winner is made early in the next calendar year.

**Remarks:** The Award for Short Fiction is provided by the Iowa School of Letters in cooperation with the Iowa Arts Council, the Writers Workshop, and the University of Iowa Press. The Award was established in 1969 to encourage writing in a typically American literary genre. Each year more than 400 manuscripts are entered in the Short Fiction Award competition. Potential entrants wishing to read stories by previous winners may order The Iowa Award: The Best Stories from Twenty Years for $24.95 (cloth) and $14.95 (paper) plus $3.00 postage and handling from the University of Iowa Order Department, 100 Oakdale Campus M105 OH, Iowa City, IA 52242-5000. **Contact:** The Iowa School of Letters at the above address (see entry 3224).

• **3226** •

## Irish American Cultural Institute

1 Lackawanna Pl.          *Ph:* (201)605-1991
Morristown, NJ 07960      *Fax:* (201)605-8875

• **3227** • **Irish American Cultural Institute Visiting Fellowship in Irish Studies** *(Postgraduate/Fellowship)*

**Focus:** Area and Ethnic Studies. **Qualif.:** Open to scholars who are residents of the United States whose work relates to any aspect of Irish Studies. Scholars must spend a period of not less than four months in study and research at University College Galway.

**Funds Avail.:** A stipend of $13,000, plus transatlantic transportation is awarded. Recipients of the Fellowship are provided with services appropriate to a visiting faculty member during their time at University College Galway. There are certain relatively minor departmental responsibilities expected of the recipients during their time at UCG, and certain other expectations regarding publication, etc., upon completion of the Fellowship. **Deadline:** December 31. **Contact:** Colette Gorman, Office Manager, Irish American Cultural Institute, at the above address (see entry 3226).

• **3228** • **Irish Research Funds** *(Professional Development/Grant)*

**Purpose:** To support capable scholarship & research on Irish American themes. **Focus:** Area and Ethnic Studies. **Qualif.:** Applications may come from any discipline and from any part of the world. While primary research is the focus of the Irish Research Fund, projects such as museum exhibitions, curriculum development, and the compilation of bibliographies and other research tools are also eligible for these funds. Candidates must demonstrate academic competence. **Criteria:** Significance of the project and competence of the researcher. A distinguished panel of scholars reviews applications and makes recommendations to the Irish American Cultural Institute.

**Funds Avail.:** Typical grants range from $2,000 to $5,000. Total grants approximate $22,500. **Deadline:** Usually October of each year. **Contact:** Katie Finn, Coordinator-Research Funds, Irish American Cultural Institute, at the above address (see entry 3226).

• **3229** •

## Richard D. Irwin Foundation

1333 Burr Ridge Pkwy.     *Ph:* (708)789-4000
Burr Ridge, IL 60521-6423 *Fax:* (708)789-6942

• **3230** • **Richard D. Irwin Fellowship Awards** *(Doctorate/Award, Fellowship)*

**Purpose:** To help prospective teachers in the fields of business and economics to complete their dissertations. **Focus:** Business, Economics. **Qualif.:** Candidates may be of any nationality, but must be enrolled in a doctoral program in a school of business at a university located in the United States or Canada, and must be nominated by the dean of the school. Direct applications are not accepted. Nominees must have completed all requirements for the Ph.D. degree with the exception of the dissertation and final oral examinations. Students at any stage of researching or writing the dissertation are eligible. Preference is usually given to those applicants whose contribution to teaching is to be made in the United States or Canada. Awards are not granted for foreign travel, or the purchase of equipment. **Criteria:** Financial need and level of qualifications.

**Funds Avail.:** $2,000-2,500. **No. of Awards:** 10-20. **To Apply:** Write for nomination guidelines. The dean of the business school must submit the nomination with supporting recommendations from the chairman of the dissertation committee and the director of the doctoral program. **Deadline:** February 15. Successful candidates are notified in the beginning of April.

**Remarks:** Presently incative.

**• 3231 •**
**Jackson Laboratory**
Training and Education Office
600 Main St.                                 *Ph:* (207)288-6420
Bar Harbor, ME 04609              *Fax:* (207)288-6079
*E-mail:* sbs@jax.org
*URL:* http://www.jax.org/

**• 3232 •   Jackson Laboratory Postdoctoral**
**Traineeships** *(Postdoctorate/Fellowship)*

**Purpose:** To support research training at the Laboratory. **Focus:** Mammalian Biology and Genetics. **Qualif.:** Awards are tenable only at Jackson laboratory. Applicant may be of any nationality, although some traineeships are reserved for U.S. citizens and permanent residents. Applicant must have earned a doctoral degree in medicine, veterinary medicine, or the biological sciences.

**Funds Avail.:** $26,256-$41,268. **No. of Awards:** 12. **To Apply:** Write to the manager for application guidelines. **Deadline:** None. **Contact:** Suzanne Serreze, at the above address (see entry 3231).

**• 3233 •**
**Jacob's Pillow Dance Festival**
PO Box 287                                    *Ph:* (413)637-1322
Lee, MA 01238                              *Fax:* (413)243-4744
*E-mail:* jacobspillow@taconic.net
*URL:* http://www.jabobspillow.org

**• 3234 •   Jacob's Pillow Dance Festival Internships**
*(Graduate, Undergraduate/Internship)*

**Purpose:** To provide on-the-job training in arts administration and technical production. **Focus:** Operations, Press/Marketing, Technical/Theater Production, Development, Box Office, Education, Programming, Archives/Preservation, Business Office, and Documentation. **Qualif.:** Applicants may be of any nationality, but must be undergraduates or graduate students interested in dance and arts administration. Internships are tenable at the Festival. **Criteria:** Applicants must undergo a phone interview, and must have an interest in dance.

**Funds Avail.:** Awards cover room and board, plus a small stipend. **No. of Awards:** 25. **To Apply:** Applicants should submit a letter expressing interest in the internship, along with a resume and names and telephone numbers of two work-related references. **Deadline:** March 6.

**Remarks:** The Festival also offers Scholarships for Dance Study at the Festival School. Write to the company manager for further details. **Contact:** Debbie Markowitz, Company Manager, at the above address (see entry 3233).

**• 3235 •**
**Jacobs Research Fund**
Whatcom Museum of History and
Art
121 Prospect St.                             *Ph:* (360)676-6981
Bellingham, WA 98225               *Fax:* (360)738-7409
*URL:* http://www.chy0govt.ci.bellingham.wa.us/cobweb/
museum/jacobs.html

**• 3236 •   Jacobs Research Fund Grants** *(Professional Development/Grant)*

**Purpose:** To support ethnographic and linguistic fieldwork on the living indigenous peoples of Mexico, Canada, and the continental United States, particularly those of the greater Pacific Northwest. **Focus:** Native American Studies. **Qualif.:** Applicant may be of any nationality and from any educational background, although inexperienced researchers should seek the assistance of an appropriate and experienced research scholar. Research must be related to living Native Americans. Grants are made for fieldwork in the following areas: art, cultural anthropology, ethnography, history, linguistics, musicology, mythology, psychology, religious studies, and social anthropology. Projects in archaeology, physical anthropology, applied anthropology, and applied linguistics are not eligible, nor is archival research supported. Funds will not be supplied for salaries, ordinary living expenses, or for major items of equipment. **Criteria:** Based on proposal feasibility, significance, and quality, as well as the qualifications of applicant.

**Funds Avail.:** $1,200 maximum. **No. of Awards:** 16. **To Apply:** Write or fax to the museum representative for application materials. Two letters of recommendation are required. **Deadline:** February 15. Notification by late April. **Contact:** Amy Geise, Jacobs Fund Secretary, at the above address (see entry 3235).

**• 3237 •**
**Japan-America Society of Washington**
1020 19th St., NW, LL40                *Ph:* (202)833-2210
Washington, DC 20036-6101        *Fax:* (202)833-2456

**• 3238 •   U. Alexis Johnson Scholarship** *(Graduate, Undergraduate/Scholarship)*

**Purpose:** To provide partial support to a full-time student of Japanese language and culture at a college or university in Japan. **Qualif.:** Applicants must be graduate or undergraduate students currently enrolled full-time at an accredited college or university in the District or Columbia, Maryland, Virginia, or West Virginia, and have completed at least one year of college level study in the United States. They should have already begun a program of Japanese language and area studies and should have arranged a course of study in Japan. **Criteria:** Applicants will be evaluated on the basis of scholastic achievement, motivation, and financial need.

**Funds Avail.:** One or more awards of up to $10,000 and/or round-trip air travel to Japan. **No. of Awards:** 3-4. **To Apply:** Application must be made by letter and must follow application guidelines. Applications must include official transcripts and three letters of recommendation. Write for further details. **Deadline:** March 1 for studies beginning in Japan in the fall of the same year. **Contact:** The Japan-America Society at the above address (see entry 3237).

## • 3239 •
**Japan Foundation**
152 W. 57th St., 39th Fl.      *Ph:* (212)489-0299
New York, NY 10019      *Fax:* (212)489-0409
*E-mail:* info@jfny.org
*URL:* http://www.jfny.org

### • 3240 • Artists Fellowship; Japan Foundation Cultural Properties Specialists Fellowship; Japan Foundation Doctoral Fellowship; Japan Foundation Research Fellowship *(Doctorate, Postdoctorate, Professional Development/Fellowship)*

**Purpose:** To enable foreign scholars to conduct research in Japan. **Focus:** Social Sciences, Humanities, Art, Conservation and Restoration of Cultural Properties **Qualif.:** Proposed research must relate wholly or in substantial part to Japan. Proposals must be in the humanities, social sciences, or the arts. Grants are not offered for research in the natural sciences, medicine, engineering; or for training purely in the Japanese language, or in non-academic fields in sports, technology, commerce, etc. Candidates whose research projects require cooperation from Japanese professionals or institutions must make all arrangements for such assistance and should provide specific names of participants with the application. Candidate for the doctoral fellowship must have completed all requirements for the Ph.D. except the dissertation at the time of fellowship commencement. Research fellowship candidate must be an academic faculty member, or other professional with substantial training and experience in some aspect of Japanese studies; or a scholar who wishes to increase knowledge of his/her field of specialization as it relates to Japan. Fellowships are tenable only in Japan. Fellows are expected to devote full-time to research. Grantees may not accept employment or hold another major grant during tenure of the Japan Foundation Fellowship.

**Funds Avail.:** Doctoral fellowship: yen 310,000/month; other fellowships: yen 370,000-430,000/month. **To Apply:** Write to either office for application form and guidelines. **Deadline:** Research and Doctoral Fellowships: November 1; Artists and Cultural Properties Specialists Fellowships: December 1.

**Remarks:** Fellows are also awarded allowances and round-trip airfare to Tokyo. **Contact:** Mr. Chris Watanabe, Program Associate, at the above address (see entry 3239).

## • 3241 •
**Japan Society**
333 E 47th St.      *Ph:* (212)832-1155
New York, NY 10017      *Fax:* (212)755-6752
*E-mail:* gen@jpnsoc.org
*URL:* http://www.jpnsoc.org

### • 3242 • U.S. Japan Media Fellowship *(Postgraduate/Fellowship)*

**Purpose:** To increase communication skills between United States and Japan. **Focus:** Journalism, policy-making. **Qualif.:** Applicant must be a U.S. citizen between the ages of 30 and 45, with little Japan experience. Must demonstrate potential for excellence and influence.

**Funds Avail.:** Round-trip airfare, a Japan travel grant, a stipend to cover living expenses, interpreter's expenses and administrative assistance is provided. There is no salary reimbursement. **No. of Awards:** 8 per year. **To Apply:** Name and address of the applicant and a brief description of his/her qualifications should be sent to the address. Application materials will be sent to those nominated. **Deadline:** February 15. **Contact:** Ruri Kawashima at the above address (see entry 3241).

## • 3243 •
**Japanese American Citizens League**
Attn: Scholarships
1765 Sutter St.      *Ph:* (415)921-5225
San Francisco, CA 94115      *Fax:* (415)931-4671
*E-mail:* jacl@jael.org
*URL:* http://www.jael.org

### • 3244 • Japanese American Citizens League Creative Arts Award *(Other/Scholarship)*

**Purpose:** To encourage creative projects, preferably those that reflect the Japanese American experience and culture. **Qualif.:** Applicants may be JACL Members or their children.

**Funds Avail.:** $ 5,000. **No. of Awards:** (1) **To Apply:** Applicants must submit a completed application. **Deadline:** April 1. Recipient is announced in July.

**Remarks:** This scholarship was established by the estate of Henry and Chiyo Kuwahara of Los Angeles. **Contact:** Local JACL Chapters, District Offices, or National Headquarters at the above address (see entry 3243).

### • 3245 • Japanese American Citizens League Freshman Awards *(High School/Scholarship)*

**Purpose:** To perpetuate the Japanese Americans' tradition of encouraging their children to pursue knowledge in the belief that education is the door to greater opportunities and horizons. In this vein, JACL created in 1946 and still continues to support its National Scholarship and Student Aid Program. The Freshman Awards are part of that program. **Qualif.:** Japanese American Citizens League members or their children. Applicants must be graduating high school seniors who are planning to enter trade schools, business schools, colleges or universities, or any other institution of higher education in the following semester. **Criteria:** Based on scholastic achievement, extracurricular activities, community involvement, personal statement or essay, and a letter of recommendation. Preference may be given to JACL members.

**Funds Avail.:** $ 1,000 - $5,000 **No. of Awards:** 14 **To Apply:** Applicants must submit a completed application, a personal statement, transcripts, a letter of recommendation, and one copy of application and attachments. **Deadline:** Applications must be submitted to local chapters by March 1. Recipients are announced in August.

**Remarks:** The Freshman Awards include the Kenji Kasai Memorial Scholarship; the Mr. and Mrs. James Michener Scholarships; the Mr. and Mrs. Takashi Moriuchi Scholarship; the Gongoro Nakamura Memorial Scholarship; the South Park Japanese Community Scholarship; the Majiu Uyesugi Memorial Scholarship; the Mitsuyuki Yonemura Memorial Scholarship; the Sumitomo Bank of California Scholarship; the Sam S. Kuwahara Memorial Scholarship; and the Henry and Chiyo Kuwahara Memorial Scholarship.

### • 3246 • Japanese American Citizens League Graduate Scholarships *(Doctorate, Graduate, Masters/ Scholarship)*

**Purpose:** To support graduate and professional studies. **Focus:** General (see requirements). **Qualif.:** Applicant must be a JACL member a child of a member. Candidate must be enrolled in, or planning to enter, an accredited graduate or professional school. Several scholarships are reserved for particular fields of study: the Magoichi and Shizuko Kato Memorial Scholarship is given to a student of medicine or the ministry. The Chiyoko Tanaka Shimazaki Memorial Scholarship supports cancer research at the graduate level. The Dr. Kiyoshi Sonoda Memorial Scholarship is limited to dentistry students. The Thomas T. Hayashi and Sho Sato Memorial Scholarships are for law students. All other requirements are the same as those listed above.

## *Japanese American Citizens League (continued)*

**Funds Avail.:** $ 1,000 - $5,000 **No. of Awards:** 10 **To Apply:** Send a self-addressed, stamped envelope to 1765 Sitter St., San Francisco, CA 94115. **Deadline:** April 1. Scholarships are announced in July. **Contact:** Scholarship Coordinator at the above address (see entry 3243). written by and about Japanese Americans. Application materials are available from local JACL chapters. The National Headquarters offers several paid internships, as well as the Henry and Chiyo Kuwahara Creative Arts Scholarship, which supports creative projects that reflect Japanese American experience and culture. Application forms and guidelines are available from the address listed above.

## • 3247 • Japanese American Citizens League Performing Arts Award *(All/Scholarship)*

**Qualif.:** Open to JACL members or their children.

**Funds Avail.:** $ 2500 **No. of Awards:** 1 **To Apply:** Applicants must submit published performance reviews and/or evaluations by an instructor. **Deadline:** April 1. Recipients are announced in July.

**Remarks:** This scholarship was established in the memory of pianist Aiko Susanna Tashiro Hiratsuka by the estate of Abe and Esther Hagiwara. **Contact:** JACL National Headquarters at the above address (see entry 3243).

## • 3248 • Japanese American Citizens League Student Aid Award *(Graduate, High School, Undergraduate/Scholarship)*

**Purpose:** To provide financial assistance to students who, because of lack of funds, may otherwise be pressed to terminate or delay their educational goals. **Qualif.:** Applicants must be JACL members or their children.

**Funds Avail.:** $ 2500 **No. of Awards:** 1 **To Apply:** Applicants must submit a Hagiwara Student Aid application and a copy of one of the following financial aid forms: SAAC, NDSL application, FAF, or a copy of the financial aid statement submitted to the student's college or university. **Deadline:** April 1. Recipient are announced in July.

**Remarks:** This scholarship was established by the estate of Abe and Esther Hagiwara. **Contact:** Local JACL Chapters, District Offices, or JACL National Headquarters at the above address (see entry 3243).

## • 3249 • Japanese American Citizens League Undergraduate Awards *(Undergraduate/Scholarship)*

**Purpose:** To perpetuate the Japanese Americans' tradition of encouraging their children to pursue knowledge in the belief that education is the door to greater opportunities and horizons. **Qualif.:** Applicants must be Japanese American Citizens League member or a child of a family member or their children either currently enrolled or planning to re-enter a trade school, business college, college or university, or other institution of higher learning at the undergraduate level. **Criteria:** Selection is based on scholastic achievement, extracurricular activities, community involvement, personal statement or essay, and letter of recommendation. Preference may be given to JACL members. High school seniors are not Eligible for these awards.

**Funds Avail.:** A number of different scholarships are awarded annually. The amounts vary from scholarship to scholarship depending upon the terms of the various trusts and the gifts that endow the respective awards. **No. of Awards:** 12 **To Apply:** Applicants must submit a completed application with a personal statement, transcripts, letter of recommendation, one copy of application and attachments, and if student is a Hagiwara Student Aid applicant, a copy of their financial aid statement. **Deadline:** April 1. Recipients are announced in July. **Contact:** JACL National Headquarters at the above address (see entry 3243).

## • 3250 • Law Scholarships *(Juris Doctorate/Scholarship)*

**Purpose:** To perpetuate the Japanese Americans' tradition of encouraging their children to pursue knowledge in the belief that education is the door to greater opportunities and horizons. **Qualif.:** Applicants must be Japanese American Citizens League members or their children currently enrolled or planning to enroll in an accredited law school. **Criteria:** Selection is based on scholastic achievement, extracurricular activities, community involvement, personal statement or essay, and letter of recommendation.

**Funds Avail.:** $ 1,000 $ 2,500. **No. of Awards:** 2 **To Apply:** Applicants must submit a completed application with a personal statement, transcripts, letter of recommendation, and one copy of application and attachments. **Deadline:** April 1. Recipients are announced in July. **Contact:** Local JACL Chapters, District Offices, or JACL National Headquarters at the above address (see entry 3243).

## • 3251 • Sho Sato Memorial Law Scholarship *(Juris Doctorate/Scholarship)*

**Purpose:** To perpetuate the Japanese Americans' tradition of encouraging their children to pursue knowledge in the belief that education is the door to greater opportunities and horizons. **Qualif.:** Applicants must be Japanese American Citizens League members or a child of a member, who is either currently enrolled or planning to enroll in an accredited law school in the following semester. **Criteria:** Selection is based on scholastic achievement, extracurricular activities, community involvement, personal statement or essay, and letter of recommendation. Preference may be given to JACL members.

**Funds Avail.:** $ 1,000. **No. of Awards:** 1 **To Apply:** Applicants must submit a completed application with a personal statement, transcripts, letter of recommendation, and one copy of application and attachments. Hagiwara Student Aid applicants must also submit a copy of their financial aid statement. **Deadline:** April 1. Recipients are announced in July.

**Remarks:** Sho Sato, Professor of Law at the University of California, Berkeley, was one of the nation's most prominent scholars of local governmental law and a leading figure in promoting relations between the law schools of Japan and the United States. **Contact:** JACL National Headquarters at the above address (see entry 3243).

## • 3252 •
## Clem Jaunich Education Trust
c/o Joseph L. Abrahamson
7801 E. Bush Lake Rd., Ste. 260
Minneapolis, MN 55439          *Ph:* (612)546-1555

## • 3253 • Clem Jaunich Education Trust Scholarships *(Graduate, Undergraduate/Scholarship)*

**Focus:** Medicine, Religion, Theology. **Qualif.:** Applicants must be enrolled in a medical school or seminary, or they must be undergraduates enrolled in a program which constitutes a pre-medicine or pre-seminary curricula. They must also either have attended kindergarten through senior year in a public or parochial school in Delano, Minnesota, or reside within Wright County, Minnesota. **Criteria:** Qualifications are considered first, then financial need.

**Funds Avail.:** Scholarships are worth $250 to $3,000 per year. **No. of Awards:** 3-8. **To Apply:** Contact the Fund at the above address for application information. **Deadline:** July 1. **Contact:** Fund Clem Jaunich Education at the above address (see entry 3252).

• 3254 •

## Jacob K. Javits Fellowship Program

Program Manager
Portals Building
400 Maryland Ave., SW, Ste. C80     *Ph:* (202)260-3574
Washington, DC 20202-5329     *Free:* 800-433-3243

• 3255 •   **Jacob K. Javits Fellowship** *(Doctorate/ Fellowship)*

**Purpose:** To provide fellowships for doctoral study in the arts, humanities, and social sciences to individuals of superior ability. **Focus:** Arts and Humanities. **Qualif.:** Applicants must be eligible to begin or have begun graduate study at the doctoral level at an accredited institution of higher education. **Criteria:** Fellowship selections are based on demonstrated achievement and exceptional promise.

**Funds Avail.:** The number and amount of awards vary annually. Awards range from $9,000 to $23,000 per fellowship. The estimated size of awards is $21,000 per fellowship, with an estimation of 56 fellowships awarded annually. **No. of Awards:** 56. **To Apply:** Applications are available February 12. **Deadline:** March 15. **Contact:** For applications contact: The Jacob K. Javits Fellowship Program, PO Box 84, Washington, DC 20044. Toll-free telephone: (800)433-3243; individuals who are hearing impaired may call: (301)369-0518. For further information contact: Diana Hayman, U.S. Department of Education, at the above address;(see entry 3254) individuals who are hearing impaired may call the Federal Dual Part Relay Service at (800)877-3889, or, if in the Washington DC area code, telephone: 708-9300.

• 3256 •

## Jaycee War Memorial Fund

Department 94922
PO Box 7
Tulsa, OK 74194-0001     *Ph:* (918)584-2481
*URL:* http://www.usjaycees.org

• 3257 •   **Jaycee War Memorial Scholarships** *(All, Undergraduate/Scholarship)*

**Focus:** General Studies. **Qualif.:** Students must be citizens of the United States, possess academic potential and leadership traits, and show financial need.

**Funds Avail.:** $1,000. **No. of Awards:** 26. **To Apply:** To receive an application, students must submit a self-addressed, business-size stamped envelope, and a $5 application fee to: JWMF, Dept. 94922, Tulsa, OK 74194-0001. The check or money order must be made payable to JWMF. Completed applications must be sent to the Jaycee organization in their state. **Deadline:** Requests for applications must be submitted between July 1 and February 1 and completed applications must be postmarked by March 1. Recipients only are notified by May 15. **Contact:** State Jaycee organizations or JWMF at the above address (see entry 3256).

• 3258 •

## JCC of Metropolitan New Jersey

760 Northfield Ave.     *Ph:* (201)736-3200
West Orange, NJ 07052     *Fax:* (201)736-6871

• 3259 •   **JCC of Metropolitan New Jersey Patrons Award and Florence Ben-Asher Memorial Award** *(Professional Development/Award)*

**Purpose:** The Patrons Award and the Florence Ben-Asher Memorial Award are intended to promote professional performing careers. **Focus:** Music. **Qualif.:** Classical musicians (instrumentalists 16-30 years of age; singers 16-35 years of age) who are bona fide residents of New Jersey and who plan to undertake or are presently engaged in a musical career. **Criteria:** Artistry, projection of stylistic differences as required by music, stage presence, and overall excellence.

**Funds Avail.:** $500 and $250. **To Apply:** Applicants must complete an application from JCC; a list of public performances, a list of repertory, and a birth certificate must be supplied. Application fee is $10. **Deadline:** March 8. **Contact:** Ellen Musikant at the above address (see entry 3258).

• 3260 •

## Jewish Community Center Theatre - Eugene S. and Blanche R. Halle Theatre

3505 Mayfield Road     *Ph:* (216)382-4000
Cleveland Heights, OH 44118     *Fax:* (216)382-5401

• 3261 •   **Dorothy Silver Playwriting Competition Prize** *(Professional Development/Prize)*

**Purpose:** To encourage and produce new plays on the Jewish experience. **Focus:** Drama. **Qualif.:** Applicant may be of any nationality, but must have written an unpublished, unproduced play directly concerned with the Jewish experience and suitable for full-length presentation. Awardee must be in residence during the production of a staged reading of his/her play at the JCC Theatre. One half of the award funds will be paid upon announcement of the prize; the other half will be paid later and may be used to cover travel and residency expenses during the production period. JCC reserves the right to perform the first fully-staged production of the winning script following the staged reading, without payment of additional royalties.

**Funds Avail.:** $1,000. **To Apply:** Submit play with a self-addressed, stamped envelope for return of manuscript. **Deadline:** December 15. Notification in late Summer. **Contact:** Lisa Kollins, Managing Director, at the above address (see entry 3260).

• 3262 •

## Jewish Family and Children's Services

c/o Val Steinberg, Dir. of Loans and
  Grants Program
2245 Post St.     *Ph:* (415)561-1226
San Francisco, CA 94115     *Fax:* (415)449-3742
*E-mail:* lag@jfcs.org
*URL:* http://www.jcfs.org

• 3263 •   **Vivienne Camp College Scholarship Fund** *(Undergraduate/Scholarship)*

**Purpose:** To provide annual college or vocational school scholarships to students planning on attending California institutions. **Qualif.:** Applicants must be Jewish students who are

*Jewish Family and Children's Services (continued)*

residents of San Francisco, Peninsula, Marin, or Sonoma Counties in California who demonstrate financial need and have a GPA of at least 3.0.

**Funds Avail.:** $5,000 maximum per award. **No. of Awards:** 4. **To Apply:** Write for further details.

---

• 3264 •
## Jewish Federation of Metropolitan Chicago
1 S. Franklin St.         *Ph:* (312)357-4500
Chicago, IL 60606       *Fax:* (312)855-3282

### • 3265 • Jewish Federation of Metropolitan Chicago Academic Scholarships *(Doctorate, Graduate, Undergraduate/Scholarship)*

**Focus:** General Studies. **Qualif.:** Candidates must be men or women of the Jewish faith who are permanent residents of the Metropolitan Chicago area and need financial assistance for a full-time academic program in the helping professions in studies in mathematics, engineering, and other sciences or in communications within the college of communications at the University of Illinois, Urbana at the undergraduate, graduate or professional school levels or in vocational training programs. **Criteria:** Scholarships are awarded based on financial need and student promise for significant contributions in their chosen field.

**Funds Avail.:** Scholarship amounts are individually determined. **To Apply:** Formal application packages are available starting December 1. Candidates must be available for a personal interview at the Jewish Vocational Service. **Deadline:** March 1.

**Remarks:** The Jewish Vocational Service administers the following funds which provide the money for this program. The largest fund is the Marcus and Theresa Levie Educational Fund, which requires applicants to live in Cook County, IL. Other individual funds include the Katherine J. Horwich Scholarship Fund, the Charles Aaron Scholarship Fund, the Adele Kagan Scholarship Fund, the Gillian and Ellis Goodman scholarship Fund, Victor Sikevitz Scholarship Fund, the Marvin S. Corwin Fund, the Stanley N. Gore Fund, the Joseph L. Stone-Hortense Singer Fund, the Maurice Yonover Fund, which requires residency in northern Indiana. **Contact:** Scholarship Secretary at the above address (see entry 3264).

---

• 3266 •
## Jewish Social Service Agency
6123 Montrose Rd.
Rockville, MD 20852       *Ph:* (301)881-3700

### • 3267 • ACNM Scholarships *(Graduate/Scholarship)*

**Purpose:** To support individuals interested in pursuing careers as midwives. **Focus:** Midwifery. **Qualif.:** Applicant must be a student member of ACNM who is enrolled in a U.S. college or university that offers a certificate or master's degree in midwifery. Candidate must have completed at least one semester (or its equivalent) at the time of application.

**Funds Avail.:** $1,000. **To Apply:** Write or call ACNM for the name and address of the scholarship chair, from whom application materials may be obtained. Application procedures are also advertised in relevant professional journals. **Deadline:** April 1. Notification by March 1.

### • 3268 • Morton A. Gibson Memorial Scholarships *(Undergraduate/Scholarship)*

**Focus:** General Studies. **Qualif.:** Applicants must be current Jewish high school seniors from the Washington Metropolitan area who have performed significant volunteer service in the local Jewish Community or under the auspices of a Jewish organization. This volunteer service must be in addition to any high school graduation requirements. Applicants must be admitted on a full-time basis to an accredited four-year undergraduate degree program in the United States. **Criteria:** Selections are based on the student's volunteer service, financial need, and academic achievements.

**Funds Avail.:** Two $2,500 grants. **To Apply:** Applicants must request an application form from the Jewish Social Service Agency. Application materials include: personal and financial information; scholastic and/or work history; scholastic and/or career plans; and names of references. They are also required to furnish proof of acceptance to or enrollment in an accredited degree program and any financial award letters. All applicants will be sent notification that their application has been received, and they will be notified of their status. Interviews are scheduled at the Scholarship Committee's discretion. **Deadline:** June 1. Candidates will be informed of the Committee's decision by early August.

**Remarks:** Names of recipients may be made public, and they will be required to complete a questionnaire describing their educational experience. **Contact:** Applications can be requested from the Jewish Social Service Agency at the above address (see entry 3266). Telephone: (301)816-2687.

### • 3269 • Jewish Educational Loans Fund *(Graduate, Undergraduate/Loan)*

**Focus:** General Studies. **Qualif.:** Applicants must be Jewish students from the Washington Metropolitan area, 18 years old or older, U.S. citizens or permanent residents of the U.S. with the intent of obtaining U.S. citizenship. They must be in financial need and be within 18 months of completing an undergraduate, graduate, or a vocational training program. The program must be completed within a two-year period. **Criteria:** Award decisions are based on financial need.

**Funds Avail.:** This no-interest loan is a one-time award, generally not to exceed $2,000. Recipients must be willing to sign a loan agreement stipulating a $50-per-month payback beginning three months after graduation. Recipients will also be asked to complete an annual report detailing their program. **To Apply:** Application materials include personal and financial information, scholastic and/or work history, scholastic and/or work plans, and names of references. Degree candidates are required to furnish proof of acceptance to or enrollment in an accredited degree program and any financial aid award letters. All applicants will be sent notification that their application has been received, and they will be notified of their status. Interviews are scheduled at the Scholarship Committee's discretion. **Deadline:** June 1. Some applications will be considered later in the year under exceptional circumstances. **Contact:** The Jewish Social Service Agency at the above address (see entry 3266). Application requests may be made by phone: (301)816-2687.

### • 3270 • Jewish Undergraduate Scholarships *(Undergraduate/Scholarship)*

**Focus:** General Studies. **Qualif.:** Applicants must be Jewish students from the Washington Metropolitan area and no older than 30 at the time of the award. Only full-time students entering or already enrolled in an accredited four-year undergraduate program may apply. Students in community colleges, Israeli schools or year-abroad programs are not eligible to apply. Special consideration will be given to refugees. **Criteria:** Award decisions are based primarily on financial need.

**Funds Avail.:** Each grant shall not exceed $3,500 per year. Average grants are $1,500 and $2,000. **To Apply:** Application materials include personal and financial information, scholastic and/or work history, scholastic and/or work plans, and names of references. Degree candidates are required to furnish proof of acceptance to or enrollment in an accredited degree program and any financial aid award letters. All applicants will be sent notification that their application has been received, and they will be notified of their status. Interviews are scheduled at the Scholarship Committee's discretion. **Deadline:** June 1.

**Remarks:** Names of recipients will be made public, and all recipients will be required to complete an annual report detailing their academic accomplishments. Grant recipients may competitively apply for the scholarship for up to four years. **Contact:** The Jewish Social Service Agency at the above address (see entry 3266). The telephone number for application requests is (301)816-2687.

### • 3271 • Irene Stambler Vocational Opportunities Grants (Other/Grant)

**Purpose:** To assist women who need to become self-supporting after a recent separation, divorce, widowhood, or the catastrophic illness of a spouse. **Focus:** General Studies. **Qualif.:** Candidates must be Jewish women in the Washington, DC Metropolitan area who have been divorced, widowed, or separated within the last five years. They must demonstrate financial need, and they must have a specific, feasible vocational plan that can be implemented within two years. Women whose husbands have become disabled and who are financially in need may also apply.

**Funds Avail.:** One-time grants of up to $2,500 are awarded. **To Apply:** Application materials include personal and financial information, scholastic and/or work history, scholastic and/or work plans, and names of references. Degree candidates are required to furnish proof of acceptance to or enrollment in an accredited degree program and any financial aid award letters. All applicants will be sent notification that their application has been received, and they will be notified of their status. Interviews are scheduled at the Scholarship Committee's discretion. **Deadline:** Applications are considered throughout the year. **Contact:** Scholarship and Loan Coordinator at the above address (see entry 3266). Telephone: (301)816-2687.

### • 3272 •
### Jewish War Veterans of the U.S.A. - National Ladies Auxiliary

1811 R St., NW
Washington, DC 20009
*URL:* http://www.penfed.org/jwv/home.htm

*Ph:* (202)265-6280
*Fax:* (202)462-3192

### • 3273 • USA National Educational Grants
(Undergraduate/Grant)

**Qualif.:** Applicants must be direct descendants of members of the Jewish War Veterans of the USA in good standing who have been accepted into a four-year college or university or a three-year hospital school of nursing as members of the freshman class. **Contact:** Jewish War Veterans of the U.S.A. at the above address (see entry 3272).

### • 3274 • Raoul Wallenberg Scholarships
(Undergraduate/Scholarship)

**Qualif.:** Applicants must be children or grandchildren of Auxiliary Members. They must also be high school seniors who have been accepted by a qualified college or university. **Criteria:** Applicants are judged by financial need first and scholastic ability second. Transcripts, financial statements, and applications are reviewed anonymously by a Raoul Wallenberg Scholarship Committee. **To Apply:** High school transcripts and parents' financial statement must accompany applications. A letter of recommendation from a principal, teacher, or school counselor is also required. All material

requested must be mailed with the application in one packet. **Deadline:** June 30. **Contact:** Information requests and application materials must be submitted to: Lillian Rovner, PDP Scholarship Chairman, 4200 W. Lake Ave., No. 310-B, Glenview, IL 60025.

### • 3275 • XX Olympiad Memorial Award (High School/Award)

**Purpose:** Honors the memory of the 11 members of the Israeli Olympic team brutally slain at the XX Olympiad held in Munich, Germany in September 1972. **Qualif.:** Applicants must be senior high school students who excel in athletics and scholastics, demonstrate leadership, and have served the school and community.

**Funds Avail.:** $1,000 U.S. Savings Bond. **Contact:** Jewish War Veterans of the U.S.A. at the above address (see entry 3272).

### • 3276 •
### JILA

Campus Box 440
University of Colorado
Boulder, CO 80309
*E-mail:* jilavf@jila.colorado.edu
*URL:* http://jilawww.colorado.edu/

*Ph:* (303)492-7796
*Fax:* (303)492-5235

### • 3277 • JILA Postdoctoral Research Associateships for Laboratory Astrophysics (Postdoctorate/Fellowship)

**Purpose:** To promote advanced research by scientists who have recently received the Ph.D. **Focus:** Astrophysics, Atomic and Molecular Physics, Chemical Physics, Laser Physics, Optical Physics and related fields. **Qualif.:** Applicant may be of any nationality. Only scientists who have recently received the Ph.D. should apply. **Criteria:** Award is based on scholarship and research promise.

**Funds Avail.:** $24,000-30,000. **No. of Awards:** Varies. **To Apply:** Please write to the Secretary for application form and guidelines. **Deadline:** None. **Contact:** Secretary at the above address (see entry 3276).

### • 3278 • JILA Visiting Fellowships for Laboratory Astrophysics (Postdoctorate/Fellowship)

**Purpose:** To promote independent research and study for senior scientists. **Focus:** Astrophysics, Atomic and Molecular Physics, Chemical Physics, Gravitational and Geophyics, Laser Physics, Optical Physics and related fields. **Qualif.:** Applicant may be of any nationality. Only scientists with extensive experience beyond the doctorate should apply.

**Funds Avail.:** Varies according to financial support provided by the home institution. **No. of Awards:** Ten. **To Apply:** Please write to the Secretary for application form and guidelines. **Deadline:** November 1. **Contact:** Secretary at the above address (see entry 3276).

### • 3279 •
### Johnson Atelier Technical Institute of Sculpture

60 Ward Avenue Extension
Mercerville, NJ 08619

*Ph:* (609)890-7777
*Fax:* (609)890-1816

### • 3280 • Tuition Grants for Apprenticeships
(Graduate, Professional Development/Grant)

**Purpose:** To support an apprenticeship in advanced sculpture-casting techniques. **Focus:** Sculpture. **Qualif.:** Candidates may be

## Johnson Atelier Technical Institute of Sculpture (continued)

of any nationality but should preferably have a B.F.A., M.F.A., or equivalent experience. Awards are tenable at the Johnson Atelier Institute and must be used toward the cost of tuition in the apprenticeship program.

**Funds Avail.:** $4,800. **To Apply:** Write to the Academic Director for application form and guidelines. Submit form with resume, slide portfolio, college transcripts, three letters of recommendation, and application fee. TOEFL and TSE-A tests are required for foreign students whose native language is not English. **Deadline:** Applications are reviewed every two months, beginning in February. Notification in two to three weeks after review. **Contact:** Academic Director, at the above address (see entry 3279).

---

• 3281 •

## The Lyndon Baines Johnson Foundation

2313 Red River St.
Austin, TX 78705

*Ph:* (512)478-7829
*Fax:* (512)478-9104
*Free:* (180)0874-6451

### • 3282 • Johnson Foundation Grants-in-Aid of Research (Professional Development/Grant)

**Purpose:** To help scholars to defray the cost of research at the Lyndon Baines Johnson Library. **Focus:** History—American, Lyndon Baines Johnson, U.S. Politics. **Qualif.:** Candidates may be of any nationality and will usually be historians, political scientists, sociologists, or communication specialists. Grants-in-aid are intended only for living, travel, and related expenses incurred while conducting research at the Johnson Library. Funds are not awarded for secretarial or research assistance and may not be used for research that has political purposes.

**Funds Avail.:** $500-2,000, calculated on the basis of $75/day plus travel costs. **To Apply:** Interested scholars must first contact the Johnson Library's chief archivist at the above address or phone (512)916-5137 ext 257 to obtain information about available library materials related to the proposed research topic. Then they must write for application forms and guidelines. Completed application forms should be returned with a budget proposal and three names of references. **Deadline:** January 31 and July 31. Recipients are announced in March and September. **Contact:** Lawrence Reed at the above address (see entry 3281).

### • 3283 • Johnson Foundation Photocopying Grants (Graduate/Grant)

**Purpose:** To help defray costs of photocopying materials in the holdings of the Lyndon Baines Johnson Library. **Focus:** History—American, Lyndon Baines Johnson, U.S. Politics. **Qualif.:** Applicants must be graduate students enrolled at a university within a 50-mile radius of Austin, Texas.

**Funds Avail.:** $250. **To Apply:** Interested scholars must first contact the library's chief archivist at the above address to obtain information about available library materials. Then write for application forms and guidelines. **Deadline:** January 31 and July 31. Recipients are notified in March and September. **Contact:** Lawrence Reed at the above address (see entry 3281).

• 3284 •

## The Robert Wood Johnson Foundation - National Program Office

Georgetown University
5005 PHC
3800 Reservoir Rd.
Washington, DC 20007
*E-mail:* gpfsp@gunet.georgetown.edu
*URL:* http://www.rwjf.org/health/oran1.htm

*Ph:* (202)687-2937
*Fax:* (202)687-7797

### • 3285 • Generalist Physician Faculty Grants (Professional Development/Grant)

**Purpose:** To strengthen generalist physician faculty in United States medical schools by improving their research capacity while maintaining their clinical and teaching competencies. **Focus:** Generalist practice and education or national health policy. **Qualif.:** Candidates must be United States citizens who are full-time junior faculty member physicians in general internal medicine, family practice, or general pediatrics in a four-year, fully accredited medical school. They must provide evidence of research skills (research fellowship or equivalent training or experience), have at least two papers published in peer-reviewed journals, and demonstrate excellence as a generalist clinician and teacher. **Criteria:** Selection is based on the candidate's commitment to their career and participation in undergraduate and graduate medical education, quality of the research plan proposed, the availability of mentors, and the medical school's promotion criteria.

**Funds Avail.:** Up to 15 grants per year are awarded. Four-year grants of up to $60,000 annually are made to sponsoring institutions to help cover the recipient's salary and research costs. Recipients are required to spend at least 40 percent of their time in research and other scholarly pursuits. **No. of Awards:** Up to 15 per year. **To Apply:** Candidates must be nominated by the deans of their institution. **Deadline:** Mid-September for applicants. Interviews are held in January. Recipients are announced in April. **Contact:** John M. Eisenberg, M.D., Program Director, Department of Medicine, Georgetown University Medical Center, 3800 Reservoir Rd., NW, Washington, DC 20007. Telephone: (202)687-2937.

---

• 3286 •

## Edward Johnson Music Foundation

Lynn McGugigan, Gen. Mgr.
PO Box 1718
Guelph, ON, Canada N1H 6Z9
*E-mail:* GSF@FREESPACE.NET
*URL:* http://WWW.FREESPACE.NET/-GSF

*Ph:* (519)821-3210
*Fax:* (519)821-4403

### • 3287 • Edward Johnson Music Competition (Professional Development/Prize)

**Purpose:** To recognize talented singers. **Focus:** Voice. **Qualif.:** Applicant must be a Canadian citizen or permanent resident. Male singers must be between the ages of 20 and 33 years; female singers must be between 20 and 30 years old.

**Funds Avail.:** First prize: $7,000; second prize: $5,000; third prize: $3,000. **To Apply:** Write to the administrator for application guidelines. **Deadline:** Prizes are awarded every five years. The Competition will next be held in May . **Contact:** Administrator at the above address (see entry 3286).

• 3288 •

## Joint Action in Community Services
5225 Wisconsin Ave., NW, Ste. 404  Ph: (202)537-0996
Washington, DC 20015  Fax: (202)363-0239
*E-mail:* webmaster@jacs_isp.com
*URL:* http://www.jacsinc.org

• 3289 • JACS Annual Scholarship *(Undergraduate/ Scholarship)*

**Purpose:** To assist Job Corps graduates attain additional training or advanced educational opportunities. **Focus:** General Studies. **Qualif.:** Applicants must be graduates of the Job Corps program and must be accepted at an undergraduate institution or other vocational trade school. **Criteria:** Selection is based on demonstrated abilities and activities while in Job Corps and financial need.

**Funds Avail.:** The annual scholarships are worth $1,000. Payment is made directly to the institution. **To Apply:** Applicants must write an essay describing need and their activities in Job Corps and the community. Two or three letters of recommendation from instructors or employers are required. **Deadline:** February 28. **Contact:** Ana Gomez at the above address (see entry 3288).

• 3290 •

## Joint Oceanographic Institutions, Inc.
1755 Massachusetts Ave., NW, Ste.
 800  Ph: (202)232-3900
Washington, DC 20036-2102  Fax: (202)232-8203
*E-mail:* joi@brook.edu
*URL:* http://www.joneset.org/harvey-bernice.html

• 3291 • JOI/USSAC Ocean Drilling Fellowships *(Doctorate/Fellowship)*

**Purpose:** To provide outstanding doctoral students with an opportunity to conduct research compatible with the goals of The Ocean Drilling Program (ODP), and to encourage student participation on board ODP's drillship, JOIDES *Resolution*. **Focus:** Earth Sciences. **Qualif.:** Applicants must be graduate students who are enrolled in a full-time Ph.D. program at a United States university. Approval of the research project by the student's faculty advisor is necessary to begin the application process. Qualified applicants will receive consideration without regard to race, creed, sex, age, or national origin. **Criteria:** Based on competitive research proposals, letters of recommendation, and academic record.

**Funds Avail.:** $20,000 per year for one or two years, payable through the candidate's home institution, for either shipboard or shore based research. The entire amount is intended to be directly applied to the research project, student stipend, tuition, benefits, and related travel. Travel to and from the drillship and to the pre- and post-cruise meetings is paid separately. **To Apply:** Applicants must submit a formal application, a short research proposal, approval by a faculty advisor, transcripts, and three references. **Deadline:** Shipboard proposals are due April 15; shore based are due November 15.

**Remarks:** ODP is funded by the U.S. National Science Foundation (NSF) together with contributions from 19 other countries. The JOI/ USSAC Fellowships are offered by the JOI/U.S. Science Support Program (JOI/USSSP) which supports U.S. involvement in the Ocean Drilling Program. Funding for JOI/USSP is provided through a contract with NSF. The Ocean Drilling Program (ODP) is an international effort to explore the structure and history of the ocean basins. It allows scientists from around the world to participate in scientific drilling cruises. On these cruises, the scientists obtain core samples and geophysical data from beneath the ocean floor in order to better understand the ages of ocean basins and their

processes of development, the rearrangement of continents with time, the structure of the earth's interior, the evolution of life in the oceans, and the history of worldwide climatic change. **Contact:** JOI/USSAC Ocean Drilling Fellowship Program Coordinator, at the above address (see entry 3290).

• 3292 •

## Chester H. Jones Foundation
PO Box 498  Ph: (440)286-6310
Chardon, OH 44024  Fax: (440)286-6310

• 3293 • National Poetry Competition Prizes *(Professional Development/Prize)*

**Purpose:** To discover new talent in poetry. **Focus:** Poetry. **Qualif.:** Applicant must live, work, or study in the United States, or be a Canadian or U.S. citizen. Candidate may submit up to ten poems: each entry must be written in English and not have been published or broadcasted. Poems may not exceed 32 lines in length. Prize-winning poems and runner-ups will be published in an anthology by the Foundation.

**Funds Avail.:** First prize: $1,000; second prize: $750, third prize: $500; fourth prize $250; fifth prize: $100; plus honorable mention and commendation awards. **No. of Awards:** 45. **To Apply:** Write the Foundation SASE for entry form and guidelines. Submit form with three copies of poem and entry fee ($2 for the first poem, $1 all other poems up to ten). Author's name must not appear on the manuscript. **Deadline:** March 31. Prizes will be announced in the fall. **Contact:** Mary Ferris at the above address (see entry 3292).

• 3294 •

## Harvey and Bernice Jones Foundation
PO Box 233
Springdale, AR 72765-0233  Ph: (501)756-0611

• 3295 • Harvey and Bernice Jones Scholarships *(Undergraduate/Scholarship)*

**Focus:** Nursing. **Qualif.:** Applicants must be needy Springdale, Arkansas nursing students. **Deadline:** None. **Contact:** The Harvey and Bernice Jones Foundation at the above address (see entry 3294).

• 3296 •

## The Jostens Foundation, INC.
5501 Norman Center Dr.  Ph: (612)830-3235
Minneapolis, MN 55437  Fax: (612)897-4116
*URL:* http://www.jostens.com

• 3297 • Jostens Our Town Jack M. Holt Memorial Scholarship *(Undergraduate/Scholarship)*

**Focus:** General Studies. **Qualif.:** Applicants must be the children of Jostens employees or sales representatives and enrolled at an accredited institution of higher education. **Criteria:** Leadership and involvement in school and community activities, and academic excellence.

**Funds Avail.:** $1,500; renewable for up to three additional years. **No. of Awards:** 1. **To Apply:** All applicants to the Jostens Our Town Scholarship (see separate entry) are automatically eligible. **Deadline:** March 15. **Contact:** Citizens Scholarship Foundation of

*The Jostens Foundation, INC. (continued)*

America, Jostens Our Town Scholarship, PO Box 297, St. Peter, MN 56082.

**• 3298 • Jostens Our Town Scholarship**
*(Undergraduate/Scholarship)*

**Focus:** General Studies. **Qualif.:** Applicants must be dependents of a Jostens employee or sales representative and enrolled as a senior in high school. **Criteria:** Academic performance and leadership in school and community.

**Funds Avail.:** $1,000. **No. of Awards:** Up to 15. **Deadline:** March 15. **Contact:** Citizen's Scholarship Foundation of America, Jostens Scholars Program, PO Box 297, St. Peter, MN 56082. Telephone: (612) 830-3235.

---

**• 3299 •**
**Journalism Institute for Minorities**
191 Manoogian Hall
Wayne State University
Detroit, MI 48202                    *Ph:* (313)577-6304

**• 3300 • Journalism Institute for Minorities Scholarships** *(Undergraduate/Scholarship)*

**Focus:** Journalism. **Qualif.:** Applicants must have a 3.0 GPA, show talent for writing, and be attending or planning to attend Wayne State University. Candidates may apply up to the start of their junior year.

**Funds Avail.:** Full-tuition. **No. of Awards:** Up to 10. **To Apply:** Writing samples must be submitted.

---

**• 3301 •**
**Journalists in Europe Fund**
4, rue du Faubourg Montmartie        *Ph:* 33 1 55772000
F-75009 Paris, France                *Fax:* 33 1 48244002
*E-mail:* europmag@europinag.vom
*URL:* http://europmag.com

**• 3302 • Journalists in Europe Study Program**
*(Graduate/Scholarship)*

**Purpose:** To improve the reporting of European affairs by offering an eight-month program open to experienced journalists from all over the world. **Focus:** Journalism, Broadcasting. **Qualif.:** Candidates for the Journalists in Europe program should be between 25 and 35 years of age and have worked for at least four years, full-time, as journalists in a news agency, newspaper or magazine, radio or television station, or as freelancers. Participants must be able to read, understand, and speak both English and French and be able to write in one of the two languages.

**Funds Avail.:** Recipients may obtain scholarships that cover the cost of enrollment and a modest living allowance of 4,000 to 6,000 Fr per month. **To Apply:** The following is a list of requirements for program applicants. For specific information regarding scholarships, contact the Journalists in Europe Fund. Candidates should send clippings or recordings of articles or broadcasts the candidate has written or produced, with details of where and when they appeared. (It is not necessary to translate these but a short explanatory note in English or French would be appreciated). Copies of diplomas or certificates should be submitted (with explanation if not in English or French). Applicants must also submit, in English or French, the following: a statement explaining

why the candidate wants to take part in the Journalists in Europe program; a completed application form (available from the Journalists in Europe Fund); a detailed curriculum vitae, outlining current and previous employment and education, with dates and places; a description of the candidate's current level of spoken and written French and English when these are neither first language nor normal working language. For French, this should be signed by a diplomatic or consular officer or an official of the Alliance Francaise; for English, this should be signed by a diplomatic or consular officer of Great Britain or the United States or an officer of the British Council. Letters of reference, preferably in English or French, signed by directors and editors in chief of companies where the candidate has worked or works as a journalist, should be sent. Applications sent by fax are not accepted. **Deadline:** Complete dossiers must arrive in Paris by January 15. Only dossiers containing documentation will be considered. Dossiers sent by fax or e-mail are unacceptable. **Contact:** Journalists in Europe at the above address (see entry 3301).

---

**• 3303 •**
**Judicial Council of California - Trial Court Services Division**
303 Second St., South Tower          *Ph:* (415)396-9153
San Francisco, CA 94107-1366         *Fax:* (415)396-9288

**• 3304 • Family Court Services Dissertation Grant Competition** *(Doctorate/Grant)*

**Qualif.:** Students in programs relevant to family and juvenile court law, psychology, sociology, education, social work, human development, related fields seeking a Ph.D. or Psy.D. in California are eligible.

**Funds Avail.:** $8,000. **No. of Awards:** 2. **To Apply:** To apply, call (415)396-9153 for materials. **Deadline:** January 12.

---

**• 3305 •**
**Juniper Gardens Children's Project**
650 Minnesota Ave., 2nd Fl.          *Ph:* (913)321-3143
Kansas City, KS 66101                *Fax:* (913)371-8522
*URL:* http://www.lsi.ukans.edu/jg/jgcpindx.htm

**• 3306 • Juniper Gardens Post-Doctoral Fellowship in Research with Minority Handicapped Children** *(Postdoctorate/Fellowship)*

**Purpose:** To allow fellows the opportunity to study current research methods of, and participate directly in, research with minority group students currently in progress at the Juniper Gardens Children's Project. Included in the research are instruction and practicum experiences in eco-behavioral models and theory, eco-behavioral assessment methods, process-product design in research, minority issues in special education, design of instruction, computer methods, and research communications. **Qualif.:** Applicants must have a Ph.D. or Ed.D. in special education or a related field, and must be employed at the university level in teaching, research, or service to handicapped children. Dissertation or comparable proof of research competency in handicapped and minority children must be supplied. **Criteria:** Preference is given to persons with minority group background and/or extensive life experience with minority groups and the disabled.

**Funds Avail.:** 2 awards of $23,500 for a 9-month period are available. **To Apply:** Forward curriculum vitae, a letter of interest, samples of articles or documents written by the applicant, and three letters of recommendation. **Deadline:** March 15 or until filled. **Contact:** Debra Kamps at the above address (see entry 3305).

---

• **3307** •

**Juvenile Diabetes Foundation International**
120 Wall St., 19th Fl.      *Ph:* (212)785-9500
New York, NY 10005-4001      *Fax:* (212)785-9595
         *Free:* 800-JDF-CURE

*E-mail:* rmarsch@jdfcure.org
*URL:* http://www.jdfcure.org

• **3308** • **JDFI Career Development Awards**
*(Postdoctorate, Professional Development/Award, Grant)*

**Purpose:** To assist developing scientists in the transition from postdoctoral work to independent investigation and to enable individuals with a demonstrated aptitude in diabetes research to investigate a clearly described problem. **Focus:** Diabetes. **Qualif.:** Applicant may be of any nationality. Candidate must have a doctoral degree or the equivalent from an accredited institution, with at least three but not more than seven years of postdoctoral research experience in a diabetes-related field with relevant accomplishments and publications. Note that time spent in residency training is not considered equivalent to research experience. At the start of this award, the candidate must be a faculty member of junior rank (instructor, assistant professor, etc.); the candidate may not hold the position of professor or associate professor. Awards are tenable worldwide, at universities, medical schools, or comparable institutions with well-established research and training programs in the candidate's chosen areas.

**Funds Avail.:** Up to $75,000 per year in total support; up to $25,000 per year may be requested for research allowance. Non-renewable. **To Apply:** Contact the grant administrator by phone, fax, or e-mail, or consult the JDFI Research web page for guidelines and application form. Submit original signed application, plus 15 individually bound copies. **Deadline:** August 15 or January 15 for the first two pages of the application; September 1 or February 1 for the completed application. **Contact:** Ruth Marsch, Grant Administrator, at the above address (see entry 3307).

• **3309** • **JDFI Innovative Grants** *(Other/Grant)*

**Purpose:** To support highly innovative basic and clinical research that is at the developmental stage by providing "seed" money for investigative work based on sound scientific hypotheses of technologies for which preliminary data are insufficient for a regular research grant by that are likely to result in important results for the treatment of diabetes and it complications. **Focus:** All aspects of basic, clinical, or other applied research relevant to Type 1 diabetes. **Qualif.:** Applicants may be of any nationality at a college, university, medical school, company, or other research facility.

**Funds Avail.:** $50,000 in direct costs. Indirect costs of 10% (excluding equipment) can be applied to the budget, bringing the maximum total support to $55,000. **Deadline:** July 1, October 1, January 1, and April 1.

**Remarks:** Awards are tenable worldwide.

• **3310** • **JDFI Postdoctoral Fellowships**
*(Postdoctorate/Fellowship)*

**Purpose:** To attract qualified and promising scientists beginning their professional careers in fields of research related to the causes, treatment, prevention and cure of diabetes and its complications. **Focus:** Diabetes. **Qualif.:** Applicant may be of any nationality. The applicant, by the beginning of the period of support, must have a doctoral degree or the equivalent from an accredited institution, and must not be serving simultaneously an internship or residency. The applicant must be sponsored by a scientist who is affiliated full-time with an accredited institution, and who agrees to supervise the applicant's training. The institution must have adequate staff and facilities to support the proposed training.

**Funds Avail.:** Stipend will depend on the number of years of relevant research experience plus a $3,000 research allowance. Stipend levels range from $26,000 to $38,000 per year. **To Apply:** Contact the grant administrator by phone, fax, or e-mail for application form and guidelines. Submit 15 copies of application, individually bound, plus the signed original document. **Deadline:** August 15 or January 15 for the first two pages of the application; September 1 or February 1 for the completed application (with the 15 copies). **Contact:** Ruth Marsch, Grant Administrator, at the above address (see entry 3307).

• **3311** • **JDFI Research Grants** *(Postdoctorate, Professional Development/Grant)*

**Purpose:** To support research and studies relevant to diabetes. Areas of interest are prevention, maintenance of euglycemia, and treatment of complications. **Focus:** Diabetes. **Qualif.:** Applicant may be of any nationality. Candidate must have a doctoral degree or the equivalent from an accredited institution and have a full-time faculty position or equivalent at a college, university, medical school, company, or other research facility. Awards are tenable worldwide.

**Funds Avail.:** Up to $100,000 total costs per year for two years. Salary support plus fringe benefits for the principal investigator may not exceed 20% of the total budget. Indirect costs may not exceed 10%. Purchase of equipment in the second year is not permitted. **To Apply:** Contact the grant administrator by phone, fax, or e-mail. **Deadline:** August 15 or January 15 for the first two pages of the application; September 1 or February 1 for the completed application (with the 15 copies). **Contact:** Ruth Marsch, Grant Administrator, at the above address (see entry 3307).

---

• **3312** •

**Kaiser Family Foundation**
2400 Sand Hill Rd.
Menlo Park, CA 94025      *Ph:* (415)854-9400
*E-mail:* pduckham@kff.org
*URL:* http://www.kff.org

• **3313** • **Kaiser Media Internships in Urban Health Reporting** *(Other/Internship)*

**Purpose:** To provide opportunities to work with six metropolitan newspapers and three television stations. Interns attend a one week briefing on related issues before beginning the internship. **Focus:** Journalism. **Qualif.:** Applicants must by young minority journalists or graduate journalism students interested in reporting on urban health.

**Funds Avail.:** Interns receive a stipend for travel and project expenses. **No. of Awards:** 9. **To Apply:** Write for more details.

---

## • 3314 •
### Kansas Commission on Veterans' Affairs
700 SW Jackson St.
Jayhawk Towers, Ste. 701      *Ph:* (913)296-3976
Topeka, KS 66603      *Fax:* (913)296-1462

#### • 3315 • Kansas State Program of Benefits for Dependents of POWs and MIAs *(Graduate, Undergraduate/Other)*

**Focus:** General Studies. **Qualif.:** Applicants must be dependents of the prisoners of war and those servicemen declared to be missing in action in the Southeast Asia Conflict or the children of veterans who died as the result of injuries suffered in line of duty during the Vietnam Conflict. The fathers of qualified dependents must have entered the Armed Forces from the state of Kansas and, while serving, must have been declared by the Secretary of Defense to be a prisoner of war or missing in action after January 1, 1960. In the case of dependents whose fathers died as the result of injuries suffered, the dependents must have been actually living in Kansas when a new law was passed qualifying them for this aid. Dependent is defined as any child born before or during the time such child's father served as a POW or MIA, it is also defined as a child legally adopted or in the legal custody of such a person during the period of such service.

**Funds Avail.:** Waiver of tuition and fees at any state-supported college, university, community junior college, or area vocational school for a period of up to a total of 12 semesters (6 years) of higher education. **To Apply:** Contact the Kansas Commission on Veterans' Affairs, or any regional office, and request an application form and instructions for applying. **Contact:** Kansas Commission on Veterans' Affairs at the above address (see entry 3314).

## • 3316 •
### Lazare and Charlotte Kaplan Foundation, Inc.
PO Box 216
Livingston Manor, NY 12758      *Ph:* (914)439-4544

#### • 3317 • Charlotte and Lazare Kaplan Foundation Scholarship *(Undergraduate/Scholarship)*

**Focus:** General studies. **Qualif.:** Applicants must be high school seniors or graduates of Livingston Manor, Roacoe, Liberty or Jeffersonville Central schools in New York. **Criteria:** Awards are granted based on financial need, academic achievement, local involvement, and good citizenship.

**Funds Avail.:** $100,000. **No. of Awards:** 80-100. **To Apply:** Write for further details or contact local guidance department. **Deadline:** May 1. **Contact:** Irving Avery.

## • 3318 •
### Kappa Delta Epsilon
c/o Dr. Frances T. Carter, National
  Executive Director
2561 Rocky Ridge Rd.      *Ph:* (205)822-4106
Birmingham, AL 35243      *Fax:* (205)822-4106

#### • 3319 • Eva Betschart Scholarships *(Undergraduate/ Scholarship)*

**Focus:** Education. **Qualif.:** Applicant must have a very high GPA, be of good character and personality, show promise as a future teacher, and have served Kappa Delta Epsilon. **Criteria:** Winner is selected by the Scholarship Committee of Kappa Delta Epsilon.

**Funds Avail.:** $300. **To Apply:** Application with a photograph and biographical information, a transcript, a list of academic/ professional offices held and honors received, a description of service to Kappa Delta Epsilon, a personal letter of professional objectives, and two letters of recommendation must be submitted. **Deadline:** March 1. **Contact:** Dr. Frances T. Carter at the above address (see entry 3318).

#### • 3320 • Patricia Chesebro Scholarships *(Undergraduate/Scholarship)*

**Focus:** Education. **Qualif.:** Applicant must have a very high GPA, be of good character and personality, show promise as a future teacher, and have served Kappa Delta Epsilon. **Criteria:** Winner is selected by the Scholarship Committee of Kappa Delta Epsilon.

**Funds Avail.:** $300. **To Apply:** Application with a photograph and biographical information, a transcript, a list of academic/ professional offices held and honors received, a description of service to Kappa Delta Epsilon, a personal letter of professional objectives, and two letters of recommendation must be submitted. **Deadline:** March 1. **Contact:** Dr. Frances T. Carter at the above address (see entry 3318).

#### • 3321 • Margaret Holland Scholarships *(Undergraduate/Scholarship)*

**Focus:** Education. **Qualif.:** Applicant must have a very high GPA, be of good character and personality, show promise as a future teacher, and have served Kappa Delta Epsilon. **Criteria:** Winner is selected by the Scholarship Committee of Kappa Delta Epsilon.

**Funds Avail.:** $300. **To Apply:** Application with a photograph and biographical information, a transcript, a list of academic/ professional offices held and honors received, a description of service to Kappa Delta Epsilon, a personal letter of professional objectives, and two letters of recommendation must be submitted. **Deadline:** March 1. **Contact:** Dr. Frances T. Carter at the above address (see entry 3318).

#### • 3322 • Billy D. Pounds Scholarships and Bobby Jones Scholarships *(Graduate, Undergraduate/ Scholarship)*

**Focus:** Education. **Qualif.:** Applicants may be either undergraduate or graduate students who have a high GPA, good character and personality, show promise as a future teacher, and have served Kappa Delta Epsilon. **Criteria:** Winners are selected by the Scholarship Committee of Kappa Delta Epsilon.

**Funds Avail.:** $300. **To Apply:** Applications must be submitted along with a photograph and biographical information, transcripts, a list of academic/professional offices held and honors received, a description of service to Kappa Delta Epsilon, a personal letter of professional objectives, and two letters of recommendation. **Contact:** Dr. Frances T. Carter at the above address (see entry 3318).

#### • 3323 • Elizabeth Stadtlander Scholarships *(Undergraduate/Scholarship)*

**Focus:** Education. **Qualif.:** Applicants must be undergraduates and must have high GPAs, be of good character and personality, show promise as a future teacher, and have served Kappa Delta Epsilon. **Criteria:** Winner is selected by the Scholarship Committee of Kappa Delta Epsilon.

**Funds Avail.:** $300. **To Apply:** An application is required, including a photograph and biographical information, transcripts, list of academic/professional offices held and honors received, a description of service to Kappa Delta Epsilon, a personal letter of professional objectives, and two letters of recommendation. **Deadline:** March 1. **Contact:** Dr. Frances T. Carter at the above address (see entry 3318).

## • 3324 • Margaret Wight Scholarships *(Graduate/Scholarship)*

**Focus:** Education. **Qualif.:** Applicants must be graduate students with high GPAs, be of good character and personality, show promise as a future teacher, and have served Kappa Delta Epsilon. **Criteria:** Winners are selected by the Scholarship Committee of Kappa Delta Epsilon.

**Funds Avail.:** $300. **To Apply:** Applications must be submitted along with a photograph and biographical information, a transcript, a list of academic/professional offices held and honors received, a description of service to Kappa Delta Epsilon, a personal letter of professional objectives, and two letters of recommendation. **Deadline:** March 1. **Contact:** Dr. Frances T. Carter at the above address (see entry 3318).

## • 3325 •

## Kappa Kappa Gamma Foundation

PO Box 38      Ph: (614)228-6515
Columbus, OH 43216-0038      Fax: (614)228-7809

### • 3326 • Circle Key Grants of Rose McGill *(Professional Development, Undergraduate/Grant)*

**Qualif.:** These grants are specifically for Kappa Kappa Gamma Fraternity alumnae who have either interrupted their education or need further education for career advancement. The grants are awarded on the basis of need, merit, and individual goals for study at a college, university, vocational or technical school. Recipients must be members of the fraternity for at least seven years to be considered for these grants. may study at colleges, universities, career, vocational, or technical schools.

**Funds Avail.:** Grants are available in varying amounts not to exceed $750. **To Apply:** Alumnae may apply for Circle Key Grants any time during the year. Grants will be awarded throughout the year as long as funds are available. **Contact:** Chairman of Circle Key Alumnae Grants at the above address.

### • 3327 • Kansas City Speech Pathology Award *(Graduate/Award)*

**Purpose:** This scholarship is for an eight week period of clinical training in the Speech Pathology Service of the Institute of Rehabilitation Medicine, New York University Medical Center. This Advanced Clinical Practicum is a comprehensive and intensive clinical experience in the language rehabilitation of the brain-damaged adult and is especially geared toward the speech pathology student who intends to specialize in this area. **Focus:** Speech and Language Pathology. **Qualif.:** Candidates must be members of Kappa Kappa Gamma, and must have completed at least half of a master's degree program in the field of speech/language pathology. Candidates must demonstrate a need for financial assistance.

**Funds Avail.:** The amounts of the awards are determined on an individual basis. **To Apply:** Candidates should send a self-addressed stamped envelope for application forms. Candidates must write the name of their fraternity chapter on their requests. **Deadline:** Applications must be received by February 01 **Contact:** Additional information about the course of study may be obtained by writing to Dr. Martha Taylor Sarno, Institute of Rehabilitation Medicine, New York University Medical Center, New York.

### • 3328 • Kappa Kappa Gamma Chapter Consultant Scholarships *(Graduate/Scholarship)*

**Qualif.:** These scholarships are available to graduating Kappa Kappa Gamma Fraternity members who have held a major office in their own chapters and who are interested in assisting other chapters while doing additional study. Candidates must be graduate students on a campus with a chapter of Kappa Kappa Gamma Fraternity.

**Funds Avail.:** The amounts of the awards are determined on an individual basis. **To Apply:** Candidates should send a self-addressed stamped envelope, and write their chapter's name. **Deadline:** November 15. **Contact:** Director of Field Representatives at the above address.

### • 3329 • Kappa Kappa Gamma Emergency Assistance Grants *(Undergraduate/Grant)*

**Qualif.:** These grants are intended for Kappa Kappa Gamma Fraternity upperclassmen who face sudden financial emergencies. Applicants must be members of Kappa Kappa Gamma Fraternity.

**Funds Avail.:** The amounts of the grants are determined on an individual basis up to $250. **To Apply:** These emergency grants are confidential. Applicants must be recommended by the Kappa Kappa Gamma Chapter's Advisory Board. They are available during the year, and applications are accepted throughout the year. Application forms may be obtained from the Chapter Philanthropy Chair, or by calling headquarters. **Contact:** Chapter Council adviser or Chairman of Emergency Assistance Grants at the above address.

### • 3330 • Kappa Kappa Gamma Graduate Fellowships *(Graduate/Fellowship)*

**Qualif.:** Applicants must have received their bachelor's degree, or will have obtained it prior to July 1. Awards are based on academic performance, contribution to Chapter life, merit, and demonstrate a need for financial assistance.

**Funds Avail.:** Graduate Fellowships of $1,500 each are awarded annually. **To Apply:** Candidates should send a self-addressed, stamped envelope for application forms. Candidates must write the name of their chapter on their request. **Deadline:** February 1.

### • 3331 • Kappa Kappa Gamma Rehabilitation Scholarships *(Graduate, Undergraduate/Scholarship)*

**Focus:** Rehabilitation. **Qualif.:** Applicants must be Kappa Kappa Gamma Fraternity members. Undergraduate students must have completed two years of study on campuses with chapters of Kappa Kappa Gamma. Applicants for the undergraduate scholarships must be majoring in any phase of rehabilitation. Graduate student applicants must be pursuing advanced study in some field of rehabilitation. **Criteria:** Awards are based on academic performance, contribution to chapter, merit, and a need for financial assistance.

**Funds Avail.:** The undergraduate scholarships are awarded in the amount of $1,000 each. The graduate scholarships are $1,500 each. **To Apply:** Candidates should send a self-addressed, stamped envelope for application forms. Candidates must write the name of their chapter on their request. **Deadline:** Completed applications must be filed by February 1. **Contact:** Kappa Kappa Gamma Fraternity at the above address.

### • 3332 • Kappa Kappa Gamma Undergraduate Scholarships *(Undergraduate/Scholarship)*

**Focus:** General Studies. **Qualif.:** Candidates must be Kappa Kappa Gamma members. **Criteria:** Awards are based on academic performance, contribution to chapter life, merit, and a need for financial assistance.

**Funds Avail.:** The amount of each scholarship is $1,000. **To Apply:** Candidates should send a self-addressed, stamped envelope for application forms. Candidates must write their chapter name on their request. **Deadline:** February 1. **Contact:** Chairman of Undergraduate Scholarships at the above address.

## Kappa Kappa Gamma Foundation (continued)

• 3333 • **Root Foreign Language Scholarship**
*(Graduate, Undergraduate/Scholarship)*

**Qualif.:** Applicants must be Kappa Kappa Gamma Fraternity members who study a foreign language in the country of that language for one year. **Criteria:** Awards are based on academic performance, contribution to chapter life, merit, and a need for financial assistance.

**Funds Avail.:** $1,000 per undergraduate scholarship; $1,500 for graduate fellowship. **To Apply:** Candidates should send a self-addressed, stamped envelope for application forms. Candidates must include their chapter name on their request. **Deadline:** Completed applications must be filed by February 1. **Contact:** Chairman of Graduate Fellowships at the above address.

---

• 3334 •

**Kappa Omicron Nu**
4990 Northwind Dr., Ste. 140
East Lansing, MI 48823-5031
E-mail: dmitstifer@kon.org
URL: http://www.kon.org

*Ph:* (517)351-8335
*Fax:* (517)351-8336

• 3335 • **Kappa Omicron Nu Doctoral Fellowships**
*(Doctorate/Fellowship)*

**Purpose:** To promote excellence and scholarship. **Focus:** Home Economics. **Qualif.:** Applicants must be Kappa Omicron Nu members enrolled in a doctoral program. They must have demonstrated interest and competency in conducting research in home economics, show proof of scholastic achievement and evidence of potential for leadership. The college or university chosen for study must have a strong research program as well as available supportive disciplines for the chosen area of study. **Criteria:** Based on professional goals and research proposal.

**Funds Avail.:** Four $2,000 fellowships are awarded annually. **No. of Awards:** Four. **To Apply:** Applications are also available on the web. **Deadline:** Applications must be submitted by January 15; recipients and alternates are notified by April 1. **Contact:** Dorothy I. Mitstifer at the above address (see entry 3334).

• 3336 • **Kappa Omicron Nu Masters Fellowships**
*(Graduate/Fellowship)*

**Purpose:** To promote excellence and shcholarship. **Focus:** Home Economics. **Qualif.:** Applicants must be Kappa Omicron Nu members who are studying home economics in a masters program at a college or university with a strong research program and supportive disciplines for the chosen area of study. **Criteria:** Demonstrated scholarship, evidence of leadership potential, and indication of how candidate's career and study goals will promote the mission of home economics.

**Funds Avail.:** $2,000 is awarded annually; a $2,000 National Alumni Chapter Fellowship is awarded in odd numbered years. **No. of Awards:** One or two. **To Apply:** Applications are also available on the web. **Deadline:** Applications must be submitted by April 1; recipients and alternates are notified by May 15. **Contact:** Dorothy I. Mitstifer at the above address (see entry 3334).

• 3337 • **Kappa Omicron Nu Research/Project Grant**
*(Other/Grant)*

**Purpose:** To encourage cross-specialization and integrative research. **Focus:** Home Economics. **Qualif.:** Proposals must meet the criteria of the Kappa Omicron Nu research agenda. Cross-specialization and integrative research is the research priority for the honor society. The focus for 1998-2000 is targeted to leadership in home economics and its specializations. Multi-year proposals will be considered. **Criteria:** Based applicants' research proposal.

**Funds Avail.:** $500 is awarded annually as a project of the Alumni Chapter-at-Large; $3,000 is awarded annually from the Kappa Omicron Nu New Initiatives Fund. **No. of Awards:** 2 or more. **To Apply:** Applications are also available on the web. **Deadline:** Proposals must be filed by February 15; applicants are notified by April 15; grants are dispersed in August.

**Remarks:** A technical report must be submitted to Kappa Omicron Nu upon project completion. **Contact:** Dorothy I. Mitstifer at the above address (see entry 3334).

---

• 3338 •

**Ezra Jack Keats Foundation**
University of Minnesota
Kerlan Collection
109 Walter Library
117 Pleasant St., S.E.
Minneapolis, MN 55455

*Ph:* (612)624-4576
*Fax:* (612)625-5525

• 3339 • **Ezra Jack Keats/Kerlan Collection Memorial Fellowship** *(Professional Development/Fellowship)*

**Purpose:** To support a writer or illustrator of children's books who wishes to use the Kerlan Collection to advance his/her artistic development. **Focus:** Children's Literature/Illustration. **Qualif.:** Applicant must be a writer or illustrator (published or unpublished) of children's books whose artistic career would benefit from studying the Kerlan Collection of children's literature. Special consideration will be given to applicants who would otherwise find it difficult to finance studies at the Collection. The fellowship will provide transportation costs and a per-diem allotment.

**Funds Avail.:** $1,500. **To Apply:** Write to the fellowship committee for application materials. **Deadline:** First Monday in May. **Contact:** Fellowship Committee at the above address (see entry 3338).

---

• 3340 •

**Donald Keene Center of Japanese Culture**
Columbia University
407 Kent Hall
New York, NY 10027

*Ph:* (212)854-5036
*Fax:* (212)678-8629

• 3341 • **Friendship Commission Prize for the Translation of Japanese Literature** *(Professional Development/Prize)*

**Purpose:** To promote the translation of Japanese literature by Americans, and to enhance the quality of Japanese literature available in the English language. **Focus:** Japanese Literature, Translation. **Qualif.:** Applicants must be a U.S. citizens who are not widely recognized for their translations, though they may have been previously published. Candidate's translation must be book-length works of Japanese literature (novels, collections of short stories, literary essays, memoirs, drama or poetry). Translations may also include unpublished manuscripts, works in press, and translations. One award is given for modern literature; one is given for classical. **Criteria:** Submissions are judged on the literary merit of the translation and its faithfulness to the spirit of the Japanese original. Winners are selected by a panel of distinguished writers, editors, translators and scholars.

**Funds Avail.:** $2,500 each. **To Apply:** Write to the Center for application guidelines. Applications are accepted from individual translators and from publishers on behalf of eligible translators.

**Deadline:** January 31 **Contact:** Mineyo Yamaguchi at the above address (see entry 3340).

---

• 3342 •

## Lucille R. Keller Foundation
c/o Irwin Union Bank & Trust
  Company
500 Washington St.                          *Ph:* (812)376-1883
Columbus, IN 47201                          *Fax:* (812)376-1790

### • 3343 • Lucille R. Keller Foundation Loans
*(Graduate, Undergraduate/Loan)*

**Focus:** General Studies. **Qualif.:** Applicants must be residents of Bartholomew County, Indiana. They must have a minimum grade point average of 2.0, and have financial need.

**Funds Avail.:** Loans are interest-free and range from $500 to $1,000 per student. Students may reapply for loans for up to four years. **No. of Awards:** Varies. **To Apply:** Students must request an application and complete and return it with grade transcript and tax returns. **Deadline:** May 31. **Contact:** Amy Lookingbill at the above address (see entry 3342).

---

• 3344 •

## Edward Bangs Kelley and Elza Kelley Foundation, Inc.
243 South St.
PO Box M                                    *Ph:* (508)775-3117
Hyannis, MA 02601                           *Fax:* (508)775-3720

### • 3345 • Kelley Foundation Scholarships
*(Undergraduate/Scholarship)*

**Purpose:** To promote the health and welfare of Barnstable County residents. **Focus:** Health Related Fields. **Qualif.:** Applicants must be residents of Barnstable County, Massachusetts. **Criteria:** Based on merit and need.

**Funds Avail.:** $50,000 is allocated each school year. **No. of Awards:** 57. **To Apply:** Applicants should contact the Foundation for information and applications. **Deadline:** April 30. **Contact:** Henry L. Murphy Jr., Foundation Manager, at the above address (see entry 3344).

---

• 3346 •

## Helen Kellogg Institute for International Studies
University of Notre Dame
216 Hesburgh Ctr.                           *Ph:* (219)631-6580
Notre Dame, IN 46556-5677                   *Fax:* (219)631-6717
*E-mail:* mossi.1@nd.edu; bartlett.5@nd.edu
*URL:* http://www.nd.edu/~kellogg/

### • 3347 • H. Kellogg Institute Residential Fellowships
*(Postdoctorate/Fellowship)*

**Purpose:** To support advanced research in comparative international studies. **Focus:** International Studies, Latin American Studies. **Qualif.:** Applicants may be of any nationality but must have a Ph.D. or equivalent degree in any discipline of the social sciences or history. Both junior and senior scholars are eligible to apply. Fellowships are tenable at the University of Notre Dame.

Fellows undertake work on individual or joint research projects related to the Institute's themes, and take part in Institute seminars and other meetings. Awardees are given faculty status within the University and may hold joint appointments in academic departments for which they may be invited to teach a course. **Criteria:** Preference is given to the applicants whose work and presence will contribute creatively to research themes.

**Funds Avail.:** Varies, according to experience and qualifications. **No. of Awards:** 8. **To Apply:** Write to the academic coordinator for application form and guidelines. **Deadline:** November 15. Fellowships are announced by January 31. **Contact:** Grabriela Mossi, Academic Coordinator, at the above address (see entry 3346).

---

• 3348 •

## Kennedy Center American College Theatre Festival
Attn: Producing Director
Education Department
Kennedy Center
Washington, DC 20566                         *Ph:* (202)416-8850

### • 3349 • National Stage Combat Workshop Fellowship *(Professional Development/Fellowship)*

**Qualif.:** Awarded to a national finalist in the Irene Ryan Acting Awards Program.

**Funds Avail.:** Winner will attend the three week workshop involving intensive study in many aspects of the art of stage combat.

### • 3350 • Sundance Theater Laboratory Fellowship *(Professional Development/Fellowship)*

**Purpose:** To provide a playwright with the chance to meet in a mentoring situation with Sundance resource directors.

**Funds Avail.:** Winner is provided with an all-expenses paid fellowship to the Sundance Theater Lab.

---

• 3351 •

## Joseph P. Kennedy, Jr. Foundation
1325 G St. NW, Ste. 500
Washington, DC 20005                         *Ph:* (202)393-1250
*E-mail:* smeatJph@qol.com

### • 3352 • Public Policy Fellowships in Mental Retardation *(Postdoctorate/Fellowship)*

**Purpose:** To provide an opportunity for professionals in mental retardation to observe and participate in the development of public policy. **Focus:** Mental Retardation. **Qualif.:** Applicants must have at least five years of experience in the behavioral or social sciences, education, law, health care, state or local government, or the humanities. Their background should include distinguished involvement in university, local government, or association programs that assist mentally retarded individuals and their families. Fellowships do not support work toward higher degrees or independent research. Rather, fellows are brought to Washington, D.C., to work at a congressional committee or in a federal department or agency that works in the area of mental retardation. Fellows also participate in the intensive bioethics course at Georgetown University. Fellowships are intended to supplement sabbatical or leave-of-absence pay. **Criteria:** Based on demonstrated professional leadership in mental retardation.

**Funds Avail.:** Up to $60,000. **No. of Awards:** 5. **To Apply:** Write to the Foundation for application guidelines. Submit a preliminary

---

## Joseph P. Kennedy, Jr. Foundation (continued)

letter of intent describing the project, plus a budget. If the Foundation is interested, a full proposal will be requested. **Deadline:** Rotates. **Contact:** Steven M. Eidelman, Executive Director, at the above address (see entry 3351).

---

• 3353 •

## Kent Medical Foundation

| | |
|---|---|
| 1400 Michigan St. N.E. | **Ph:** (616)458-4157 |
| Grand Rapids, MI 49503-2006 | **Fax:** (616)458-3305 |

**E-mail:** chip@kcms.org
**URL:** http://www.kcms.org/kmffound.html

### • 3354 • Kent Medical Foundation Student Loans Program (Doctorate/Loan)

**Purpose:** Kent Medical Foundation (KMF) loans help students who might otherwise have to discontinue their studies for financial reasons. **Qualif.:** Candidates must be deserving students who have resided in Kent County, Michigan or nearby communities. Recipients must have excellent academic qualifications and demonstrate financial need. Residency requirements may be met if applicants and their families have lived in these communities. Medical students must have completed their first year of medical school.

**Funds Avail.:** Medical students loans range up to $6,000 per academic year. If additional loans are requested, reapplication is required. Loans are interest-free until the completion of the recipient's postgraduate year, after which the loan will bear interest at a rate of 7 percent per annum. Principal or the full amount of the note loan becomes payable five years after graduation from medical school or upon completion of the recipient's first residency program, whichever comes first. Loan repayments go to a revolving loan fund, which makes future awards possible. **To Apply:** Applicants must submit transcripts, recommendation from the school, three character references (including at least one from a doctor), and a statement of financial status clearly showing earnings, other sources of income, or financial aid and estimated expenses for the coming year. Students must agree to carry life insurance payable to the Foundation in the amount of the loan and during the time the loan is outstanding. Evidence of insurance in effect for this purpose shall be presented to the Executive Office within 30 days of the policy's anniversary date. Applicants must also arrange a personal interview with at least one member of KMF's Education Committee. **Deadline:** There are no specific application deadlines. **Contact:** William G. McClimans, Jr., Student Loans, at the above address (see entry 3353).

---

• 3355 •

## Kentucky Dept. of Veterans Affairs

| | |
|---|---|
| 545 S 3rd St., Rm. 123 | **Ph:** (502)595-4447 |
| Louisville, KY 40202 | **Fax:** (502)595-4448 |

### • 3356 • Kentucky Department of Veterans Affairs Tuition Waivers (Undergraduate/Scholarship)

**Purpose:** To recognize wartime military service of Kentucky veterans. **Focus:** General Studies. **Qualif.:** Applicant must be a spouse of any, child, or nonremarried widow of a permanently disabled national guardsmen, war veteran, prisoner of war, or serviceman missing in action. The veteran must have served during a wartime period, be rated 100 percent permanently and totally disabled, and be a resident of Kentucky or have been a resident at the time of death. There are two statutes under which

an applicant may qualify. Under statute KRS 164.505, applicants may be eligible if veteran was killed in action during a wartime period, or died as a result of a service-connected disability incurred while serving during a wartime period provided the veteran's home of record upon entry into the armed forces was the Commonwealth of Kentucky. Under Statute KRS 164.515 veterans must be rated 100 percent permanently and totally disabled, rated as 100 percent disabled for compensation purposes, or provide medical evidence showing permanent and total disability or the existence of permanent and total disability for a period of at least 30 days prior to death if this evidence is signed by a physician licensed to practice. In both statutes the parent's or spouse's service and the cause of death must be evidenced by certification from the records of the Kentucky Department of Military Affairs or the veteran's administration records, or the Department of Defense of the United States.

**Funds Avail.:** A waiver of tuition to attend any two-year, four-year, or vocational/technical school operated and funded by the Kentucky Department of Education. **To Apply:** Application forms must be completed and supported with the following types of documentation: a DD Form 1300 or death certificate and DD form 214 pertaining to veterans; for widows, a marriage certificate; for children, a birth certificate or court record of adoption. Stepchildren are not eligible. **Contact:** James E. Welch or Mary Neimeyer at the above address (see entry 3355). at the above address. at the above address.

---

• 3357 •

## Kentucky Dept. of Veterans Affairs - Kentucky Veterans Dependents Educational Assistance

| | |
|---|---|
| 545 S. 3rd St., Rm. 123 | **Ph:** (502)595-4447 |
| Louisville, KY 40202 | **Fax:** (502)595-4448 |

**URL:** http://www.state.ky.us/agencies/militarykevatxt.htm

### • 3358 • Kentucky Center for Veterans Affairs State Tuition Waivers (Undergraduate/Other)

**Purpose:** To provide educational benefits to the dependents of wartime veterans. **Focus:** General Studies. **Qualif.:** Veterans must have entered service from Kentucky and be rated 100 percent with a service connected disability, or rated 100 percent permanently and totally disabled with a non-service connected disability, or provide medical evidence from a licensed physician that the veteran is permanently and totally disabled if their is no VA rating. Applicants must meet requirements set forth in KRS 164.505 or 164.515. The tuition waiver is used at two- or four-year state supported colleges and vocational schools.

**Funds Avail.:** Tuition Waiver. **To Apply:** Applicants may obtain applications from the Kentucky Dept. of Veterans Affairs office at the above address. **Deadline:** None, but is in the best interest of the applicants to apply approximately three months before entering. **Contact:** Larry W. Garrett, Jr., Director, Kentucky Center for Veterans Affairs, at the above address (see entry 3357).

---

• 3359 •

## Kentucky Department of Vocational Rehabilitation

| | |
|---|---|
| | **Fax:** (502)564-6745 |
| c/o Marian Spencer | |
| 209 St. Clair | |
| Frankfort, KY 40601 | **Free:** 800-372-7172 |

### • 3360 • Vocational Rehabilitation Grants (Undergraduate/Scholarship)

**Focus:** General Studies. **Qualif.:** Applicant must be Kentucky resident who has a disabling condition that presents substantial handicap to employment and reasonable expectation that vocational rehabilitation services will benefit the individual in terms of employability. The individual must also demonstrate academic aptitude and economic need. **To Apply:** Applicants will be interviewed and evaluated. **Deadline:** Anytime prior to the start of training programs. **Contact:** Marian Spencer at the above address (see entry 3359).

## • 3361 •
## Kentucky Journalism Foundation
101 Consumer Ln.
Frankfort, KY 40601

### • 3362 • Kentucky School of Journalism Foundation Internships *(Undergraduate/Internship)*

**Focus:** Journalism. **Qualif.:** Applicants must be graduates of a Kentucky high school attending any college or university or students who have completed their sophomore year at a Kentucky college or university.

**Funds Avail.:** $2500. R 9 weeks during the summer.

## • 3363 •
## Kentucky Medical Association
KMA Building, Ste. 2000
4965 US Hwy. 42                    Ph: (502)426-6200
Louisville, KY 40222               Fax: (502)426-6877
*URL:* http://www.kyma.org/index.htm

### • 3364 • Rural Kentucky Medical Scholarship Fund (RKMSF) *(Doctorate/Loan, Scholarship)*

**Purpose:** To assist medical students who are willing to practice in rural areas in Kentucky, and to provide a better distribution of physicians. **Focus:** Medicine. **Qualif.:** Applicants must be residents of Kentucky who have been admitted to one of the two accredited medical schools in Kentucky. The applicant must agree to begin practice within 60 days after completing internship or approved residency. Candidate must practice in Kentucky in an approved area 12 months for each loan received. Residencies are approved in primary care fields only. These include family practice, general practice, internal medicine, OB/GYN, and pediatrics. **Criteria:** Financial need and willingness to comply with RKMSF criteria.

**Funds Avail.:** Loans of up to $12,000 per year. Practice is permitted in 87 of the state's 120 counties. The Board of Directors annually designates a selected number of counties as being in critical need of physicians. Recipients who practice in a critical county or in the Kentucky Public Health Service have one loan forgiven for each full year of practice in the approved county. All other loans must be repaid with interest at the stipulated rate to maturity and maximum allowable rate by law thereafter. Loan contracts are for one year and must be renewed annually. Market rate is charged on past due loans. The contract includes a provision for liquidated damages; a borrower who fails to fulfill the medical practice provision of the agreement pays $7,500 for each year of failure, in addition to all other sums loaned. Applicants must cover the amount of money borrowed by life insurance assigned to the Board of Directors for the duration of the loan. **No. of Awards:** No set limit at discretion of Board of Directors. **To Apply:** Request application from RKMSF staff at (502)426-6200. **Deadline:** April 1.

**Remarks:** The Fund was created in 1945-46 with money donated by interested physicians and leaders in agriculture, business, industry, and civic-minded individuals. In 1954 the State Legislature, recognizing the Fund's value to rural Kentuckians,

began providing support. The Fund is administered by a Board of Directors composed of the deans of the medical schools chartered in the State of Kentucky, the Kentucky State Bar Association, Kentucky Business, the Kentucky Farm Bureau, the Kentucky Medical Association, past RKMSF recipients and other interested citizens. The Fiscal Agent is the PNC Bank. **Contact:** Kentucky Medical Association at the above address (see entry 3363).

## • 3365 •
## Merck & Co., Inc. - James J. Kerrigan Memorial Scholarship Program
One Merck Dr.
PO Box 100
White House Station, NJ 08889-0100

### • 3366 • James J. Kerrigan Memorial Scholarships *(Undergraduate/Scholarship)*

**Focus:** General Studies. **Qualif.:** Applicants must be children of Merck employees who will graduate from high school the year the scholarship is awarded. They must be planning to attend an accredited college or university in the United States. **Criteria:** Applicants are based on academic achievement, leadership potential, and community involvement.

**Funds Avail.:** Award amounts vary from $1,500 to full tuition. **Deadline:** November 15. **Contact:** Human Resources, Personnel Relations at the above address (see entry 3365).

## • 3367 •
## The Kidney Foundation of Canada
300-5165 rue Sherbrooke Ouest     Ph: (514)369-4806
Montreal, PQ, Canada H4A 1T6      Fax: (514)369-2472
                                  Free: 800-361-7494
*E-mail:* research@kidney.ca
*URL:* http://www.kidney.ca

### • 3368 • Allied Health Doctoral Fellowships *(Doctorate, Professional Development/Fellowship)*

**Purpose:** to provide for full-time academic and research preparation at the doctoral level; To promote and enhance the development of nephrology/urology allied health investigators in Canada. **Focus:** Nephrology, Urology. **Qualif.:** Applicants must be Canadian citizens or landed immigrants. The fellowship is open to nephrology/urology nurses and technicians, social workers, dietitians, and transplant coordinators who have been accepted in a proposed course of full-time study. Applicants in related allied health care disciplines who show commitment to the area of nephrology/urology may be considered. The fellowship is tenable in Canada or overseas; however, fellows must return to Canada.

**Funds Avail.:** $31,000/year maximum; travel allowances are also provided **To Apply:** Candidates should write to or call the Foundation for application form and guidelines. **Deadline:** October 15. Notification is made before May 31. **Contact:** The Kidney Foundation of Canada at the above address (see entry 3367).

### • 3369 • Allied Health Research Grants *(Professional Development/Grant)*

**Purpose:** To encourage research relevant to clinical practice in the area of nephrology, urology and organ donation by allied health professionals. **Focus:** Nephrology, Urology, Organ Donation. **Qualif.:** Applicants must be Canadian citizens or landed immigrants who intend to conduct research at an institution in

## The Kidney Foundation of Canada (continued)

Canada. Candidates should be nephrology/urology nurses or technicians, social workers, dietitians, renal transplant coordinators, or professionals in an allied health care discipline who have demonstrated a commitment to the field of nephrology, urology or organ donation. Grants are not intended to cover the entire cost of a research project. Allowable expenses include the purchase of materials, supplies, and equipment; the payment of research and support staff; and travel funds. Funding is not provided for salaries of the applicants.

**Funds Avail.:** $40,000/year maximum **To Apply:** Candidates should write to or call the Foundation for application form and guidelines. The Foundation may request letters of intent to participate from research collaborators, medical ethic reports, or other documentation in addition to the application form. **Deadline:** October 15. Notification is made before May 31. **Contact:** The Kidney Foundation of Canada at the above address (see entry 3367).

### • 3370 • Allied Health Scholarships *(Graduate, Postgraduate/Scholarship)*

**Purpose:** To assist students pursuing education at the masters, doctoral, or nurse practitioner level. **Focus:** Nephrology, Urology, Organ donation. **Qualif.:** Applicants must be Canadian citizens or landed immigrants who have been accepted in a course of full-time graduate study leading to a master's, doctoral degree, or nurse practioner level. Candidates should be nephrology/urology nurses or technicians, social workers, dietitians, renal transplant coordinators, or professionals in an allied health care discipline who have demonstrated a commitment to the field of nephrology or urology. Applicant should have demonstrated a minimum of two years of direct clinical practice. Scholarships are tenable in Canada and in other countries, but scholars who wish to study in another country must intend to return to Canada upon completion of their education.

**Funds Avail.:** Master's scholarship: $5,000; doctoral scholarship: $5,000; nurse practitioner $5,000. **To Apply:** Candidates should write to or call the Foundation for application form and guidelines. **Deadline:** October 15. Notification is made before May 31. **Contact:** The Kidney Foundation of Canada at the above address (see entry 3367).

### • 3371 • Biomedical Fellowships *(Postdoctorate/ Fellowship)*

**Purpose:** To provide for full-time postdoctoral-research training in the renal and urinary tract field. **Focus:** Nephrology, Urology. **Qualif.:** Applicants must be Canadian citizens or landed immigrants. They must have an M.D., D.D.S., D.V.M. or Ph.D. degree and must apply through a university department or affiliated institution approved for research training by the Foundation, having an experienced researcher as a supervisor. There is a limit of two fellowships per supervisor. Fellows are expected to dedicate 80 percent of their time to the objectives of the award and may not practice medicine or hold another fellowship during the tenure of their award.

**Funds Avail.:** Up to $46,844/year; travel allowances are also provided. **To Apply:** Candidates should write to or call the Foundation for application form and guidelines, including transcripts, a letter of acceptance from supervisor, a description of research project, supervisor's recent research and list of publications, and two letters of recommendation. **Deadline:** October 15. Notification is made in April. **Contact:** The Kidney Foundation of Canada at the above address (see entry 3367).

### • 3372 • Biomedical Research Grant *(Postdoctorate/ Grant)*

**Purpose:** To encourage research that may further the current knowledge pertaining to the kidney and urinary tract. To assist in defraying the operating costs of research. **Focus:** Nephrology,

Urology. **Qualif.:** Applicants must be Canadian citizens or have landed immigrant status and must hold a staff appointment at a Canadian university or other recognized Canadian academic institution. Priority is given to young investigators who, at the time of application, have held their first faculty position for no more than 18 months. Research must be conducted within Canada. Funds may be used for the purchase and maintenance of materials, supplies, and equipment; the payment of laboratory assistants; and graduate student support. Grants do not provide for personal support of the grantee and are not intended to cover the entire cost of the research for which they are provided.

**Funds Avail.:** $40,000 maximum. Grants are paid in quarterly installments. **To Apply:** Candidates should write to or call the Foundation for application form and guidelines and must submit six copies of the form (original, plus 5 copies) to the Medical Research Program of the Foundation. Grant applications must also include letters of intent to participate from research collaborators. Letters of recommendation, medical ethics reports, and other additional documentation may also be requested. **Deadline:** October 15. Notification is made before May 31. **Contact:** The Kidney Foundation of Canada at the above address (see entry 3367).

### • 3373 • Biomedical Scholarship *(Doctorate, Postdoctorate/Scholarship)*

**Purpose:** To provide salary for up to two years of an initial faculty appointment at the rank of assistant professor or its equivalent at an approved medical school in Canada in accordance with the university's policy. **Focus:** Nephrology, Urology **Qualif.:** Applicants must be Canadian citizens or landed immigrants and should have an M.D. or Ph.D. and have completed clinical training in nephrology or urology. Applicants must have at least two years of research training at the time of the award. Application must be made through the institution employing the candidate; priority will be given to applicants from institutions at which no Kidney Foundation scholarship is currently being held. The scholars must commit at least 75 percent of their time to research during the tenure of the award. Scholars may not hold other major personnel support awards concurrently with the Foundation scholarship, nor may they hold established faculty positions supported by regular operating funds of the university, institute, or hospital.

**Funds Avail.:** $45,000/year **To Apply:** Candidates should write or call the Foundation for application form and guidelines. Submit ten copies of the form with copies of recent publications and manuscripts. Letters of recommendation are also required. **Deadline:** October 15. Notification is made in May. **Contact:** The Kidney Foundation of Canada at the above address (see entry 3367).

### • 3374 •
## Killam Program

c/o The Canada Council  
PO Box 1047  
Ottawa, ON, Canada K1P 5V8  

Ph: (613)566-4414  
Fax: (613)566-4407  
Free: 800-263-5588

### • 3375 • Killam Research Fellowships *(Postdoctorate/Fellowship)*

**Purpose:** To support advanced research in areas of interest to the Killam Program. **Focus:** Engineering, Health Sciences, Humanities, Natural Sciences, Social Sciences. **Qualif.:** Applicant must be a resident of Canada. Candidate must be an established scholar who wishes to pursue research in one of the areas of study listed above. Canadian citizens may use the fellowship in Canada and abroad; others must use the fellowship at a university or institution in Canada.

**Funds Avail.:** $53,000 maximum per year, plus full fringe benefits. **To Apply:** Write for application guidelines. **Deadline:** May 31.

**Contact:** Can also be reached at 613-566-4414 ext. 5041;Carol Bream, Director Endowment, at the above address (see entry 3374).

---

**• 3376 •**

**Kingsport Symphony Orchestra**
Renaissance Center, Box 13
1200 E. Center St.                    Ph: (423)392-8423
Kingsport, TN 37660                   Fax: (423)392-8428

**• 3377 • Elizabeth Harper Vaughn Concerto Competition Prizes** (Professional Development/Prize)

**Purpose:** To recognize outstanding musical talent. **Focus:** Brass, Percussion, Piano, String Instruments, Wind Instruments. **Qualif.:** Categories of competition rotate annually (1997-98, strings; 1998-99, Piano; 1996-97, Winds & Brass). Applicants must have been born on or before Jan.1, 1971. Awardee performs with the Kingsport Symphony Orchestra during its regular concert series. **Criteria:** A performance tape is judged.

**Funds Avail.:** $1,000. **No. of Awards:** 1 annually. **To Apply:** Write to the General Manager for application form and guidelines. Submit application with recommendation from private instructor, $20 entry fee and a cassette tape. **Deadline:** December 31. **Contact:** Debbie Robinson, General Manager, at the above address (see entry 3376). at the above address.

---

**• 3378 •**

**Esther A. and Joseph Klingenstein Center for Independent Education**
Teacher's College
Columbia University
Box 125                               Ph: (212)678-3156
New York, NY 10027                    Fax: (212)678-3254
E-mail: prk4@columbia.edu
URL: http://www.klingenstein.org

**• 3379 • Joseph Klingenstein Fellowships** (Professional Development/Fellowship)

**Purpose:** To develop leadership potential and broaden professional perspectives of independent school educators and administrators. **Focus:** Education. **Qualif.:** Applicant must be a teacher or administrator working in grades 5-12 of an independent school with a nondiscriminatory policy. Candidate must have at least five years of professional experience in schools and must propose a specific project or problem that he/she wishes to study or research. Fellowships are tenable at Teachers College, Columbia University. Awardees undertake independent projects and participate in seminars run by the Center. Fellows must return to their sponsoring schools upon completion of the award.

**Funds Avail.:** Tuition, stipend, and housing allowance. **No. of Awards:** 12 annually. **To Apply:** Write or phone the office for application form and guidelines. **Deadline:** January 15. Fellowships are announced by mid-March.

**Remarks:** All applicants must schedule a personal interview with a Klingenstein Alumni Representative prior to February 1.

---

**• 3380 •**

**Steven Knezevich Trust**
100 E. Wisconsin Ave., Ste. 1020      Ph: (414)271-6364
Milwaukee, WI 53202                   Fax: (414)271-6365

**• 3381 • Steven Knezevich Trust Grants** (Doctorate, Graduate, Postgraduate, Undergraduate/Scholarship)

**Qualif.:** Applicants must be of Serbian descent. **Criteria:** Selection is based on academic grades, extracurricular involvement, and financial need.

**Funds Avail.:** Award amounts vary. **To Apply:** Application requests must be accompanied by a self-addressed, stamped envelope. **Deadline:** November 30.

**Remarks:** Approximately 100 candidates apply each year. **Contact:** Stanley Hack at the above address (see entry 3380).

---

**• 3382 •**

**Knight Science Journalism Fellowships**
c/o Massachusetts Institute of
    Technology
Bldg. E32 - 300                       Ph: (617)253-3442
Cambridge, MA 02139                   Fax: (617)258-8100
E-mail: lmlowe@mit.edu; boyce@mit.edu
URL: http://web.mit.edu/Knight-science

**• 3383 • Knight Science Journalism Fellowships** (Professional Development/Fellowship)

**Purpose:** To increase acquaintance of science and technology journalists with leading researchers during an academic year at MIT through twice weekly seminars and attendance of courses, lectures, and workshops. **Focus:** Journalism, Science. **Qualif.:** Applicants must be full-time science and technology journalists with a minimum of three years experience as staff or free-lance writers for print or broadcast media. **Criteria:** Commitment to the profession of science journalism and evidence of outstanding work.

**Funds Avail.:** $35,000 stipend for U.S. fellows. **No. of Awards:** 6 U.S. fellows and a varying number of independently financed foreign journalists. **To Apply:** Write or phone for an application. Applicants will be expected to supply letters of recommendation, copies of work, and two essays. **Deadline:** March 1. **Contact:** Boyce Rensberger, Director, at the above address (see entry 3382).

---

**• 3384 •**

**Knights of Columbus**
PO Box 1670                           Ph: (203)772-2130
New Haven, CT 06507-0901              Fax: (203)773-3000

**• 3385 • Bishop Charles P. Greco Graduate Fellowships** (Graduate/Fellowship)

**Focus:** Education. **Qualif.:** Applicants must be members of the Knights of Columbus in good standing or the wives, sons, or daughters of such members or deceased members. Candidates must have good undergraduate records and give evidence of interest and aptitude for work with mentally retarded children. They must also be accepted into full-time graduate study that leads to a master's degree in a program designed for the preparation of classroom teachers of mentally retarded children. **Criteria:** Special consideration is given to applicants who select a Catholic graduate school.

---

## Knights of Columbus (continued)

**Funds Avail.:** The maximum amount of the fellowship is $2,000 payable to the university in amounts not to exceed $500 per semester. The fellowship is renewable each semester for a maximum of four semesters upon evidence of satisfactory performance and at the discretion of the Committee on Fellowships. **No. of Awards:** 3. **Deadline:** May 1. **Contact:** Committee on Fellowships at the above address (see entry 3384).

### • 3386 • Percy J. Johnson Scholarships (Undergraduate/Scholarship)

**Focus:** General Studies. **Qualif.:** Applicants must be young men entering their freshman year in a program leading to a bachelor's degree in a United States Catholic college or university. Recipients must be members in good standing of the Knights of Columbus, or sons of living or deceased members. **Criteria:** The scholarships are awarded on the basis of financial need.

**Funds Avail.:** Four $1,500 scholarships, renewable each year for a maximum of four years of undergraduate study subject to evidence of satisfactory academic performance and the discretion of the committee on scholarships. **No. of Awards:** 4. **To Apply:** Required application materials include a copy of the Student Aid Report (SAR). They should also submit a completed Pro Deo and Pro Patria application. Applications are available after September 1. **Deadline:** March 1. **Contact:** Director of Scholarship Aid, Knights of Columbus, at the above address (see entry 3384).

### • 3387 • Knights of Columbus Educational Trust Program Scholarships (Undergraduate/Scholarship)

**Focus:** General Studies. **Qualif.:** Candidates are children of Knights of Columbus members in good standing who were killed or permanently disabled during World War II, the Korean War, the Vietnam War, or the Persian Gulf Conflict, or within ten years following the official termination of a period of conflict from a cause directly connected with military service. Also eligible are children of members in good standing of the Order who lost their lives or became disabled as a result of criminal violence in lawful performance of duties as full-time law enforcement officers or full-time firemen.

**Funds Avail.:** Scholarships are for use at any Catholic college and include tuition, fees, room and board, and books. They are reduced by funds to which the candidates are entitled from any governmental agency or by financial aid from any other source. **Remarks:** The Educational Trust Program was established in 1944 through a special per capita tax of members. **Contact:** Director of Scholarship Aid at the above address (see entry 3384).

### • 3388 • Knights of Columbus Student Loan Program (Graduate, Undergraduate/Loan)

**Focus:** General Studies. **Qualif.:** Applicants must be widows, wives, or children of Order members who were in good standing at the time of their deaths; priests, brothers, sisters, seminarians or postulants at the college, seminary, and post-graduate levels without reference to membership in the Knights of Columbus or members of the Columbian Squires. They must also be United States citizens or resident aliens enrolled at least half-time at a school that is recognized by the United States Government under the Guaranteed Student Loan program (GSL). It includes technical and vocational schools, community and junior colleges, universities, and major seminaries within the United States and in other countries. These loans are guaranteed by the Federal Government. Candidates must meet the eligibility standards of the Federal Guaranteed Student Loan program as regards family income limits, subsidized interest, rates of interest, amounts that may be borrowed, and repayment schedules.

**Funds Avail.:** Loan maximums are $2,625 per academic year for first year, $3,500 for second-year students and $5,500 per academic year for third-and-fourth year students. Graduate students may borrow up to $8,500 for each of two academic years.

These loans are designed to cover educational costs including tuition, room and board, books, supplies, transportation, and fees. Loan requests must be renewed each year. **Contact:** Student Loan Committee at the above address (see entry 3384).

### • 3389 • Pro Deo and Pro Patria (Canada) Scholarships (Undergraduate/Scholarship)

**Focus:** General Studies. **Qualif.:** Students who are entering their first year of study leading to a baccalaureate degree at a college or university in Canada are eligible to apply. They also must be Knights of Columbus members in good standing of Canadian councils, or sons or daughters of living or deceased members in good standing. **Criteria:** Scholarships are awarded on the basis of academic excellence.

**Funds Avail.:** Twelve scholarships of $1,500 are renewable for each year of undergraduate study for up to four years, subject to satisfactory academic performance and the discretion of the Committee on Scholarships. **To Apply:** Applications are available from the Director of Scholarship Aid at the above address. **Deadline:** May 1. **Contact:** Director of Scholarship Aid Knights of Columbus, at the above address (see entry 3384).

### • 3390 • Pro Deo and Pro Patria Scholarships (Undergraduate/Scholarship)

**Focus:** General Studies. **Qualif.:** Applicants must be entering their freshman year in a program leading to a bachelor's degree. Recipients must be members of the Columbian Squires or the Knights of Columbus or sons or daughters of members currently in good standing or a deceased member who was in good standing at the time of demise. **Criteria:** The scholarships are awarded on the basis of academic excellence achieved in secondary school, including class rank, grade point average, and aptitude test results.

**Funds Avail.:** 62 $1,500 scholarships are awarded each year. They are renewable for a maximum of four years of undergraduate study providing satisfactory academic behavior is maintained. 12 of the scholarships are reserved for study at The Catholic University of America, Washington, D.C. The remaining 50 are designated for study at other Catholic colleges with Columbian Squires receiving preference for two of these. **Deadline:** Completed application forms for The Catholic University of America Scholarships must be filed by February 1; forms for scholarships to be used at other Catholic colleges are due by March 1. **Contact:** For The Catholic University of America scholarships, contact the Director of Financial Aid, The Catholic University of America, Washington, DC 20064. For other scholarships, contact the Director of Scholarship Aid, Knights of Columbus, PO Box 1670, New Haven, CT 06507-0901.

### • 3391 •
## Knights of Lithuania - Scholarship Committee
11 Hill Top Road
Pittston, PA 18640

### • 3392 • Knights of Lithuania Scholarships (Graduate, Undergraduate/Scholarship)

**Purpose:** To help worthy and deserving youths of the Knights of Lithuania obtain a college education and to encourage young Lithuanian-Americans to join and be active in the organization. **Focus:** General studies. **Qualif.:** Membership and service to the Knights of Lithuania. **Criteria:** Selection is based on scholastic ability, financial need, community service, and extent of service to the Knights of Lithuania.

**Funds Avail.:** Up to $1,500. Awards are made in two installments beginning in August of each year, and are not renewable. **To Apply:**

A formal application must be obtained and completed. Four letters of recommendation are required. **Deadline:** June 30.

**Remarks:** The Knights of Lithuania is a fraternal organization of Roman Catholic Lithuanian-Americans. **Contact:** A local Knights of Lithuania chapter at the above address (see entry 3391).

---

• 3393 •
## KNTV Television

645 Park Ave.
San Jose, CA 95110
*URL:* http://www.kntv.com

*Ph:* (408)286-1111
*Fax:* (408)295-5461

### • 3394 • KNTV Minority Scholarships
*(Undergraduate/Scholarship)*

**Purpose:** To assist local students who plan to attend or are attending a four-year college in the field of broadcast television to pay for college expenses. **Focus:** Broadcast Televison. **Qualif.:** Students must be either Black, Hispanic, Asian/Pacific Islander, or American Indian and residents of Santa Clara, Santa Cruz, Monterey, or San Benito Counties. The award is contingent on the acceptability of student for admission to an accredited California four-year college or university. The major should be broadcast televison. Students must have at least one full year of undergraduate work remaining and must carry a minimum of 12 semester units during each semester of the school year. **Criteria:** Scholarships are given to students with financial need who demonstrate interest and potential in the field of broadcast televison.

**Funds Avail.:** Two $1,000 scholarships. **No. of Awards:** 2. **To Apply:** Contact KNTV for applications. **Deadline:** April 7. **Contact:** Melba Dangerfield, at the above address (see entry 3393).

---

• 3395 •
## Kohler Co.

c/o Peter Fetterer, Mgr., Civic
  Services
444 Highland Dr.
Kohler, WI 53044
*E-mail:* FettereP@Kohlerco.com
*URL:* http://www.Kohlerco.com

*Ph:* (920)457-4441
*Fax:* (920)457-9064

### • 3396 • Kohler Co. College Scholarship
*(Undergraduate/Scholarship)*

**Purpose:** To recognize the accomplishments of children of associates of Kohler Co. and its U.S. or Canadian subsidiaries. **Focus:** General studies. **Qualif.:** Applicants must be high school seniors who are children of associates of Kohler Co. and its U.S. or Canadian subsidiaries who are college bound and who have outstanding academic and community service qualifications. **Criteria:** Scholarships are awarded based on academic record, class rank, SAT and ACT scores, recommendations, educational goals, honors and achievements, school activities, community experience and work experience.

**Funds Avail.:** Four-year renewable scholarships valued at $1,200 per year. **No. of Awards:** 15. **To Apply:** Brochure and application form available from Kohler Co. **Deadline:** February 15. **Contact:** Peter Fetterer at the above address (see entry 3395).

---

• 3397 •
## Kosciuszko Foundation

15 E. 65th St.
New York, NY 10021-6595
*E-mail:* thekf@pegasusnet.com
*URL:* http://www.kosciuszkofoundation.org

*Ph:* (212)734-2130
*Fax:* (212)628-4552

### • 3398 • Kosciuszko Foundation Chopin Piano Competition/Scholarships *(Professional Development/Scholarship)*

**Purpose:** To encourage highly talented American students of piano to study and play the works of Chopin. **Focus:** Piano. **Qualif.:** Applicant must be a U.S. citizen or permanent resident or an international student with a U.S. visa. Candidate must be a pianist between the ages of 16 and 22 years at the opening date of the Competition. The Competition is held annually in New York in mid-May.

**Funds Avail.:** First prize: $2,500; second prize: $1,500; third prize: $1,000. **No. of Awards:** Three. **To Apply:** Write to the Foundation for application guidelines. **Deadline:** April 15 in 1996. **Contact:** Grants Office at the above address (see entry 3397).

### • 3399 • Kosciuszko Foundation Domestic Scholarships *(Graduate/Scholarship)*

**Purpose:** To support graduate studies by Americans of Polish descent and to encourage the study of Polish subjects. **Focus:** Polish Studies. **Qualif.:** Applicant must be a U.S. citizen or permanent resident of Polish ancestry, enrolled in a graduate program at a U.S. university, with at least a 3.0 GPA. **Criteria:** Preference is given to candidates with a strong sense of identification with the Polish community and financial need.

**Funds Avail.:** Varies from $1,000 to $5,000. **To Apply:** Write to the Foundation for application materials. **Deadline:** January 16.

### • 3400 • Kosciuszko Foundation Graduate/Postgraduate Study and Research in Poland Scholarships *(Graduate, Postgraduate/Other)*

**Purpose:** To assist Americans in continuing their graduate and postgraduate studies at institutions of higher learning in Poland. **Qualif.:** Applicants must be U.S. graduate students who possess a working knowledge of the Polish language. **Criteria:** Selection is based upon overall academic performance, motivation for pursuing graduate studies in Poland, and a well-reasoned research proposal.

**Funds Avail.:** Students receive tuition, housing, and a monthly stipend for living expenses. No provisions are made for dependents. Grantees wishing to have family members accompany them may do so at their own expense. Transportation to and from Poland is at the expense of the participant. **To Apply:** There is a non-refundable fee of $50 due upon submission of the completed application. **Deadline:** January 15. **Contact:** The Kosciuszko Foundation, Domestic Grants Office, at the above address (see entry 3397)for additional information and application forms.

### • 3401 • The Year Abroad Program at the Jagiellonian University of Krakow *(Doctorate, Graduate/Fellowship)*

**Purpose:** To allow Canadian and U.S. students to study in Poland. **Focus:** Polish Language, Polish Studies. **Qualif.:** Applicant must be a U.S. or Canadian citizen of Polish background. Junior and senior undergraduates, master's students, and Ph.D. candidates who have not reached the dissertation stage are eligible to apply. Awards are tenable at Jagiellonian University. Students may study Polish language, literature, history, and culture; coursework in other disciplines is permitted if the student is fluent in Polish. Travel expenses are the responsibility of the student.

---

## Kosciuszko Foundation (continued)

**Funds Avail.:** Tuition, room and board, plus a monthly stipend **To Apply:** Write to the Foundation for application form and guidelines. Submit form with application and administration fee ($30 in 1989). **Deadline:** 15 January **Contact:** Grants Office

---

• 3402 •

## Samuel H. Kress Foundation

174 E. 80th St.  
New York, NY 10021     *Ph:* (212)861-4993  
*URL:* http://www.shkf.org     *Fax:* (212)628-3146

### • 3403 • Fellowships in Art Conservation
*(Professional Development/Fellowship)*

**Purpose:** To encourage the study of art conservation through advanced training internships. **Focus:** Art Conservation. **Qualif.:** Candidate may be of any nationality, but must have completed a recognized art conservation training program. U.S. citizens can participate in advanced training in any country. Foreign conservators must be accepted at U.S. institutions; cannot support foreigners working outside of U.S.

**Funds Avail.:** $1,000 to $12,000. **To Apply:** Write to the Fellowship Administrator for application form and guidelines. **Deadline:** February 28. **Contact:** The Fellowship Administrator, at the above address (see entry 3402).

### • 3404 • Kress Research Fellowship in Art History
*(Doctorate/Fellowship)*

**Purpose:** To encourage the study of European art before 1900. **Focus:** European Art History. **Qualif.:** Candidate may be of any nationality, but must have completed all requirements for the Ph.D. at a U.S. university, except the dissertation, prior to the acceptance of the Fellowship. The Fellowship is competitive.

**Funds Avail.:** $12,000. **To Apply:** Write to the Chief Administrative Officer for application form and guidelines. **Deadline:** November 30. **Contact:** Lisa M. Ackerman, Chief Administrative Officer, at the above address (see entry 3402).

### • 3405 • Kress Research Fellowships at Foreign Institutions *(Doctorate/Fellowship)*

**Purpose:** To provide the opportunity for advanced dissertation research in association with a selected art historical institute in Florence, Jerusalem, Leiden, London, Munich, Nicosia, Paris, Rome, or Zurich. **Focus:** Art History. **Qualif.:** Limited to pre-doctoral candidates at American universities and American students abroad. Applicants must be nominated by their Art History department. Limit of one applicant per department.

**Funds Avail.:** $18,000. **No. of Awards:** 4. **Deadline:** November 30. **Contact:** Art history department advisors at applicant's university.

---

• 3406 •

## Ladies Auxiliary to the Veterans of Foreign Wars

406 West 34th St.     *Ph:* (816)561-8655  
Kansas City, MO 64111     *Fax:* (816)931-4753

### • 3407 • Cancer Research Fellowship Program
*(Other/Fellowship)*

**Qualif.:** Applicant must be U.S. citizens involved in cancer research.

**Funds Avail.:** $25,000 stipend. **Contact:** Ladies Auxiliary to the Veterans of Foreign Wars at the above address (see entry 3406).

### • 3408 • Ladies Auxiliary to the VFW Junior Girls Scholarships *(Undergraduate/Scholarship)*

**Focus:** General Studies. **Qualif.:** Applicants must have been an active member for one year, holding an office in their Junior Girls Unit, and be 13 - 16 years of age. Previous prize winners are not eligible, but former unsuccessful applicants may reapply. **Criteria:** Judging is on a point system: Junior unit activities 30 points, school activities and community activities 25 points each, and scholastic grades 20 points.

**Funds Avail.:** Two scholarships, one of $5,000 and one of $3,000, are awarded annually. Scholarships are paid to the recipients' college of choice upon their acceptance. In addition, $100 is awarded to each Junior Girl who is selected as Department winner and entered in the National Championship. **To Apply:** Application must be accompanied by school grades transcript, and three letters of recommendation from a school teacher, Junior Girls leader, and one other person of applicant's choice. Applications must be submitted to the Auxiliary Junior Girls Unit Chairman for initial judging. **Deadline:** One application from each unit is sent to the Department Junior Girls chairman by April 15. The winning department application is forwarded to the National Headquarters for national competition by May 15.

**Remarks:** The first place winner will attend the Ladies Auxiliary National Convention and participate in the American Academy of Achievement's salute to excellence. **Contact:** Local Junior Unit Chairman, or Judy Millick, Administrator of Programs, at the above address (see entry 3406).

### • 3409 • Young American Creative Patriotic Art Awards *(High School/Prize)*

**Purpose:** To encourage high school students to express their artistic talents, demonstrate their patriotism, and at the same time become eligible for funds to further their art education. **Focus:** Visual and Performing Arts. **Qualif.:** Applicants must be United States citizens in high school (grades 9 through 12) and attend school in the same state as the sponsoring auxiliary. **Criteria:** Selection is based on originality of concept and patriotism expressed; the content and clarity of idea; the design, use of color, and technique; and the total impact or execution and contrast. The judging is local, state, and national. On all levels, judges are teachers, professionals, and persons knowledgeable in art.

**Funds Avail.:** First prize, $3,000; second, $2,000; third, $1,500; fourth, $1,000; and fifth, $500. First prize also includes an expense-paid weekend to the American Academy of Achievement honoring youth champions in many fields of endeavor, plus an expense-paid trip to be honored at the annual VFW Auxiliary National Convention. First-place art will be featured on the November cover of the National Auxiliary Magazine. Winners must use these funds towards their continued art education or for art supplies. Prior first- and second-place national winners may not compete again. **To Apply:** Art must be on paper or canvas and must not be framed. Water color, pencil, pastel, charcoal, tempera, crayon, acrylic, pen-and-ink, or oil may be used. Canvas entries must be submitted on stretcher frames. Other entries must be matted on heavy white paper, two inches to two and one-half inches wide. Do not use color mats. In matting, use heavy paper to reinforce back (no smaller than eight inches by ten inches but no larger than 18 inches by 24 inches not including mat). Art must be packaged so that it can be mailed without being damaged. Applicants must complete entry forms and attach to the back of the entry, which must be sponsored by an Auxiliary. If the American flag is used in the entry, it must conform to the flag code as far as color, number of stars and stripes, and other pertinent rules of the code (which can be obtained from the auxiliary). The entry must have been done sometime in the previous school year, and it must have a teacher's signature. Comments of local and state judges should be attached to paintings and forwarded with art. **Deadline:** No later than May 1. Department winners are forwarded to Ladies Auxiliary to the VFW National Headquarters by June 1. **Contact:** Judy Millick at the above address (see entry 3406)or Local Unit Chairman.

• 3410 •
## Lalor Foundation
PO Box 2493
Providence, RI 02906-0493          *Ph:* (401)272-1973

### • 3411 • Lalor Foundation Postdoctoral Research Grants *(Postdoctorate/Fellowship)*

**Purpose:** To promote intensive research and to assist and encourage able young investigators in academic positions to follow research careers in mammalian reproductive biology as related to the regulation of fertility. **Focus:** Medical Research. **Qualif.:** Applicants must have earned a doctoral degree, and preferably have held the doctoral degree no more than five years. The institution proposed for research must be tax-exempt from federal income taxes. Eligible fields of research include mammalian reproductive physiology and biochemistry for yielding improved methods of sterilization, contraception and/or termination of pregnancy.

**Funds Avail.:** Fellowships include grants of up to $22,500 and cover stipends and overhead, laboratory and miscellaneous expenses. **To Apply:** Write or call foundation for application materials. **Deadline:** January 15.

**Remarks:** The Foundation generally receives between 60 and 90 applications. **Contact:** Cynthia Patterson at the above address (see entry 3410).

• 3412 •
## Lambda Kappa Sigma - Educational Trust
2284 Diamond Point Rd.
Alpena, MI 49707-4608

### • 3413 • Dr. B. Olive Cole Graduate Educational Grant *(Graduate/Grant)*

**Focus:** Pharmaceutical Sciences. **Qualif.:** Candidates must be members of Lambda Kappa Sigma Fraternity who are enrolled in programs of graduate study and research at accredited colleges or universities in order to advance their careers in the pharmaceutical sciences. Applicants must have successfully completed one academic year of graduate study toward Master of Science, Doctor of Philosophy, or Master of Science/Doctor of Philosophy degrees and must have the endorsements of their respective department directors. Candidates must also be members in good standing with collegiate or alumni chapters, or be Stray Lambs of Lambda Kappa Sigma. They must be current in their dues. Applicants' graduate records must also be filed with the Fraternity's Educational Grant Committee.

**Funds Avail.:** One grant of $1,000 is awarded annually and may be used for tuition, books, living or travel expenses, or thesis expenses. **Deadline:** Applications must be filed by November 1. Awards are made by January 15.

**Remarks:** This grant was named for a distinguished member of the Fraternity, Dr. B. Olive Cole, who was a leader in pharmaceutical education. **Contact:** Chairman, Educational Grant Committee, at the above address (see entry 3412).

### • 3414 • Cora E. Craven Educational Grants *(Graduate/Grant)*

**Purpose:** To aid recipients in paying for tuition and/or books. **Focus:** Pharmaceutical Sciences. **Qualif.:** Candidates must be members in good standing of Lambda Kappa Sigma Fraternity. They must have scholastic standing in the upper half of their classes. Preference is given to applicants enrolled in the last two years of the professional curriculum. Applicants must provide evidence of financial need. **Criteria:** Each applicant is considered on the basis of emotional stability, self-reliance, leadership, intelligence, good health, dedication to the profession of pharmacy, citizenship, and financial need.

**Funds Avail.:** The Fraternity currently awards nine $500 grants annually. The number of grants per year is established by the Fraternity's Educational Trust Liaison Committee. **No. of Awards:** 9. **Deadline:** Completed applications must be received by November 1. Recipients are notified by January 15. **Contact:** Chairman, Educational Grant Committee, at the above address (see entry 3412).

### • 3415 • Mary Connolly Livingston Grant *(Doctorate/Grant)*

**Purpose:** To advance the careers of students in the pharmaceutical sciences. **Focus:** Pharmaceutical Science. **Qualif.:** Candidates must be members of Lambda Kappa Sigma who are enrolled in programs leading to the Pharm.D. degree at an accredited college or university. They must be in the upper half of their class. Preference is given to applicants enrolled in the last two years of the professional curriculum. Applicants must provide evidence of financial need.

**Funds Avail.:** Currently, one award of $500 is presented. **Deadline:** November 1. Recipients are notified by January 15. **Contact:** Chairman, Educational Grant Committee, at the above address (see entry 3412).

• 3416 •
## Land Improvement Foundation for Education
1300 Maybrook Dr.
PO Box 9
Maywood, IL 60153          *Ph:* (708)344-0700

### • 3417 • LIFE Scholarship Award *(Undergraduate/Scholarship)*

**Purpose:** To provide scholarship assistance to students interested in pursuing a career in the field of conservation/environmental construction. **Qualif.:** Students must display an interest in conservation/environmental construction and have maintained a 2.5 GPA. **Criteria:** Vocational pursuit of conservation/environmental construction, character worthiness, and financial need.

**Funds Avail.:** A maximum of three students per year receive $1,000 each. **To Apply:** Completed application includes an essay, GPA, financial statement, and proof of acceptance by a college or university. Students must supply letters from their communities and schools as character references. **Deadline:** March 15. **Contact:** Mary Ellen Bushnell at the above address (see entry 3416).

## • 3418 •
**Landmark Communications, Inc.**
150 W. Brambleton Ave.  *Ph:* (804)446-2538
Norfolk, VA 23510  *Fax:* (804)446-2414
*URL:* http://www.cweb.com/landmark/welcome.html

### • 3419 • Landmark Communications Minority Internships *(Professional Development/Internship)*

**Purpose:** To train participants for full-time employment at one of the Landmark daily newspapers. **Focus:** Journalism. **Qualif.:** Positions are open to minorities who have completed their undergraduate work. **Criteria:** Clips, grade point averages and SAT and ACT scores are considered.

**Funds Avail.:** Six one-year internships are available with an annual salary of $17,900 each; includes a benefits package and a moving allowance. Interns may be hired to full-time positions at any point during the scheduled training program. Interns are expected to have their own car. **To Apply:** Applicants must submit a cover letter, resume, and samples of work.

**Remarks:** Positions are available for news and sports reporters, copy editors, artists, and photographers. **Contact:** Marvin Lake, Recruiting, at the above address (see entry 3418).

## • 3420 •
**Landscape Architecture Foundation**
636 I St., NW  *Ph:* (202)898-2444
Washington, DC 20001-3736  *Fax:* (202)898-1185

### • 3421 • AILA Yamagami Hope Fellowship *(Professional Development/Fellowship)*

**Focus:** Landscape Art. **Qualif.:** Candidates must be landscape architects who have been in practice for a minimum of three years and wish to use the funds for continuing education. They must have a bachelor's degree or a master's degree in landscape architecture. **Criteria:** Submissions will be evaluated on the innovative nature of the proposed endeavor, the benefits that may accrue to other members of the profession and the profession in general, the personal goals to be achieved, and the qualifications of the applicant.

**Funds Avail.:** $1,000. The fellowship grant may be used to support credit or non-credit courses, seminars or workshops, development of a history of the American Institute of Landscape Architects from 1954 to 1982, travel or related expenses in support of an independent research project, or development of post-secondary educational materials or curriculum plans. **No. of Awards:** One. **To Apply:** Applications consist of: a summary addressing several questions supplied by the Foundation; a statement of intent detailing how the funds would be used; two letters of recommendation from licensed landscape architects; and a completed application form. **Deadline:** August 2. **Contact:** The Landscape Architecture Foundation at the above address (see entry 3420).

### • 3422 • California Landscape Architectural Student Scholarships *(Undergraduate/Scholarship)*

**Purpose:** To assist Southern California students enrolled in programs of landscape architecture and ornamental horticulture. **Focus:** Landscape architecture or ornamental horticultural studies. **Qualif.:** This award is bestowed to students in financial need who show promise and commitment to the profession. Students currently enrolled in an accredited program in landscape architecture at Southern California Community Colleges with 15 or more units are eligible.

**Funds Avail.:** Three awards of $500 each are available. **To Apply:** A formal application must be submitted. Applicants are required to give a listing of their academic, community, and professional involvement backgrounds. A 300-word (maximum) statement on the profession is required, as well as a 100-word statement (maximum) indicating the intended use of the funds. Two letters of recommendation must also accompany the application. **Deadline:** April 3.

**Remarks:** Recipients will be asked to write an article for the SCC/ASLA newsletter covering the LAF/CLASS Fund, benefits gained from the scholarship, and information on the green industry. **Contact:** The Landscape Architecture Foundation at the above address (see entry 3420).

### • 3423 • Grace and Robert Fraser Landscape Heritage Award *(Graduate, Undergraduate/Award)*

**Purpose:** To recognize innovative horticultural design as it relates to the profession of landscape architecture. **Focus:** Landscape Architecture, Horticulture. **Qualif.:** Candidate must be an undergraduate or graduate student currently pursuing research on new approaches to landscape architecture through horticulture.

**Funds Avail.:** $500. **No. of Awards:** One. **To Apply:** Write to the Foundation for application form and guidelines. Submit form with essay (500-word maximum) outlining the research or design project. **Deadline:** May 4. **Contact:** Mary Hanson, Executive Director, at the above address (see entry 3420).

### • 3424 • Edith H. Henderson Scholarship *(Graduate, Undergraduate/Scholarship)*

**Purpose:** The prize is awarded to a student committed to the goal of developing practical communication skills in her role as a landscape architect. **Focus:** Landscape Architecture. **Qualif.:** Applicants must be female landscape architecture students enrolled at the University of Georgia. They must be entering their final year of undergraduate work, or in any year of their graduate career.

**Funds Avail.:** $1,000. **No. of Awards:** One. **To Apply:** Applicants should submit the completed application form with a typed, double-spaced 500-1000 word essay describing the candidate's viewpoint on the value of a two-hour client consultation in residential design. Included in the essay should be how such a consultation would be developed and the way in which this session would be conducted. Participation in a class in public speaking or creative writing is also required. **Deadline:** April 2. **Contact:** The Landscape Architecture Foundation at the above address (see entry 3420).

### • 3425 • Ralph Hudson Environmental Fellowship *(Professional Development/Fellowship)*

**Purpose:** To advance the profession of landscape architecture through research activities with emphasis on concern for open space, parks, and recreation. **Focus:** Landscape Architecture. **Qualif.:** Applicants must hold a degree in landscape architecture, have at least five years experience in professional practice (private, public, academic, or any combination thereof), be residents of the U.S., Canada, Mexico, islands of the Caribbean, or citizens of the U.S. residing or working abroad.

**Funds Avail.:** $3,500. **No. of Awards:** One. **To Apply:** Applications may be obtained from the Foundation. **Deadline:** August 2. **Contact:** The Landscape Architecture Foundation at the above address (see entry 3420).

### • 3426 • LAF/CLASS Cal Poly Scholarships *(Undergraduate/Scholarship)*

**Purpose:** To assist Southern California students enrolled in programs of landscape architecture and ornamental horticulture. **Focus:** Landscape Architecture, Ornamental Horticulture. **Qualif.:** This award is bestowed to students in financial need who show promise and commitment to the profession. All applicants must be continuing their studies in landscape architecture or ornamental horticulture. Full-time students (12 or more credits) who are currently enrolled at Cal Poly Pomona and Cal Poly San Obispo and will be juniors or seniors in the session beginning each September are eligible.

**Funds Avail.:** $1,500. **No. of Awards:** Six. **To Apply:** A formal application must be submitted. Applicants are required to give a listing of their academic, community, and professional involvement backgrounds. A 300-word (maximum) statement on the profession is required, as well as a 100-word statement (maximum) indicating the intended use of the funds. Two letters of recommendation must also accompany the application. **Deadline:** April 2.

**Remarks:** Recipients will be asked to write an article for the SCC/ASLA newsletter covering the LAF/CLASS Fund, benefits gained from the scholarship, and information on the green industry. **Contact:** The Landscape Architecture Foundation at the above address (see entry 3420).

#### • 3427 • LAF/CLASS Fund Scholarships and Internships (Undergraduate/Internship)

**Purpose:** To provide an opportunity for full-time, supervised work experience in a design office and related industry support systems. **Focus:** Landscape Architecture. **Qualif.:** The Internship Program is open to full-time (12 or more credits) students currently enrolled at Cal Poly Pomona and San Luis Obispo who will be juniors or seniors in the sessions beginning each September and to landscape architecture program students from UCI, UCLA, and USC who have completed 15 or more units.

**Funds Avail.:** Two students will receive a grant for a nine-week internship program in the Orange County area of Southern California for three-week work segments with a landscape architect and contractor and/or manufacturer. Housing and transportation will be the responsibility of the intern. The award includes a $2,000 grant matched by the employer paying $6 per hour for a 40-hour work week. Disbursement will be $500 at the time of orientation, weekly pay checks, and $1,500 at the end of the nine weeks based on job performance. Total scholarship value is $4,160. **No. of Awards:** Two. **To Apply:** A formal application must be submitted. Applicants are required to give a listing of their academic, community, and professional involvement backgrounds. A 300-word (maximum) statement on the profession is required, as well as a 100-word statement (maximum) indicating the intended use of the funds. Two letters of recommendation must also accompany the application. **Deadline:** April 2.

**Remarks:** In the design office the candidate may be preparing base sheet materials and exercising drafting and graphic techniques. With the contractor, the intern may be performing light construction tasks, installation, and cost estimating. The time with the manufacturer may include exposure to sales, research development, and specifications. The program will begin with orientation by the LAF/CLASS Fund Scholarship chairman and conclude with the SCC/ASLA Fall Conference. Recipients will be asked to write an article for the SCC/ASLA newsletter covering the LAF/CLASS Fund, benefits gained from the scholarship, and information on the green industry. In addition, interns will be asked to submit five slides and an accompanying narrative of each office's work experience. **Contact:** The Landscape Architecture Foundation at the above address (see entry 3420).

#### • 3428 • LAF/CLASS University Program (Undergraduate/Scholarship)

**Purpose:** To assist Southern California students enrolled in programs of landscape architecture and ornamental horticulture. **Focus:** Landscape Architecture, Ornamental Horticulture. **Qualif.:** This award is bestowed to students in financial need who show promise and commitment to the profession. All applicants must be continuing their studies in landscape architecture or ornamental horticulture. Students who have completed or are currently enrolled at UCI, UCLA, or UC Davis and students who are juniors or seniors enrolled at Cal Poly Pomona and Cal Poly San Obispo are eligible.

**Funds Avail.:** $500. **No. of Awards:** Five. **To Apply:** A formal application must be submitted. Applicants are required to describe their academic, community, and professional involvement backgrounds. A 300-word (maximum) statement on the profession is required, as well as a 100-word statement (maximum) indicating the intended use of the funds. Two letters of recommendation must also accompany the application. **Deadline:** April 2.

**Remarks:** Recipients will be asked to write an article for the SCC/ASLA newsletter or LAND covering the LAF/CLASS Fund, benefits gained from the scholarship, and information on the green industry. **Contact:** The Landscape Architecture Foundation at the above address (see entry 3420).

#### • 3429 • LAF Student Research Grant (Graduate, Undergraduate/Grant)

**Purpose:** To encourage innovative, practical research projects in landscape architecture. **Focus:** Landscape Architecture. **Qualif.:** Candidate must be an undergraduate or graduate student. Applicant's research proposal must include: problem statement, procedures/methodology for collecting information and analyzing the material, and implications of the research in terms of the advancement of the knowledge base of the profession and its applicability to professional activities.

**Funds Avail.:** $1,000. **No. of Awards:** One. **To Apply:** Write to the Foundation for application form and guidelines. Submit form with statement outlining the research project, description of the research project, line-item budget for the proposed project, and two letters of recommendation relevant to the proposed project. **Deadline:** May 4. **Contact:** Mary Hanson, Executive Director, at the above address (see entry 3420).

#### • 3430 • LANDCADD, Inc. Scholarship (Graduate, Undergraduate/Scholarship)

**Purpose:** To encourage the use of emerging technologies in the study and practice of landscape architecture. **Focus:** Landscape Architecture. **Qualif.:** Candidate must be an undergraduate or graduate landscape architecture student who wishes to utilize such technological advancements as computer-aided design, video imaging or telecommunications in his/her career.

**Funds Avail.:** $500, plus $500 in LANDCADD software to the recipient's department. **No. of Awards:** One. **To Apply:** Write to the Foundation for application form and guidelines. Submit form with two recommendation letters and essay (500-word maximum) addressing one of the following: how these technologies could affect the future of landscape architecture; research plans and how research will be implemented; how the knowledge and use of emerging technologies have contributed to your studies in landscape architecture. **Deadline:** April 2. **Contact:** Mary Hanson, Executive Director, at the above address (see entry 3420).

#### • 3431 • William J. Locklin Scholarship (Graduate, Undergraduate/Scholarship)

**Purpose:** To emphasize the importance of 24-hour lighting in landscape designs. **Focus:** Landscape Architecture, Lighting Design. **Qualif.:** Candidate must be a student pursuing a program in lighting design, or a landscape architectural student focusing on lighting design in studio projects.

**Funds Avail.:** $500. **No. of Awards:** One. **To Apply:** Write to the Foundation for application form and guidelines. Submit form with letter of recommendation relevant to the proposed project, visual samples, and essay (300-word maximum) highlighting the design project. **Deadline:** April 2.

**Remarks:** For preparing submission, a full working demonstration lighting design unit is available for student use. Contact Dr. Leon Lapides at Nightscaping by Loran, 1705 E. Coltan Ave., Redlands, California 92373, (714)794-2121. **Contact:** Mary Hanson, Executive Director, at the above address (see entry 3420).

*Landscape Architecture Foundation (continued)*

### • 3432 • Raymond E. Page Scholarship *(Graduate, Undergraduate/Scholarship)*

**Purpose:** To provide students with the opportunity of following the benefactor's examples in landscape architecture. **Focus:** Landscape Architecture. **Qualif.:** Candidate must be an undergraduate or graduate student in need of financial assistance, who is currently pursuing studies in landscape architecture.

**Funds Avail.:** $500. **No. of Awards:** Two. **To Apply:** Write to the Foundation for application form and guidelines. Submit a double-spaced, two-page essay describing the need for financial assistance, how the award will be used, and a letter of recommendation from a previous or current professor or employer who is familiar with applicant's character and goals. **Deadline:** April 2. **Contact:** Mary Hanson, Executive Director, at the above address (see entry 3420).

### • 3433 • Rain Bird Company Scholarship *(Undergraduate/Scholarship)*

**Purpose:** To recognize an outstanding landscape architecture student. **Focus:** Landscape architecture. **Qualif.:** Applicants must be students in their final two years of undergraduate study (third, fourth, fifth years) in need of financial assistance. Eligible applicants include those who have demonstrated commitment to the profession through participation in extracurricular activities and exemplary scholastic achievements.

**Funds Avail.:** $1,000. **No. of Awards:** One. **To Apply:** Applicants must submit an application form, Financial Aid Form, and a 300-word essay. **Deadline:** April 2. **Contact:** The Landscape Architecture Foundation at the above address (see entry 3420).

### • 3434 • Edward D. Stone Jr. and Associates Minority Scholarship *(Undergraduate/Scholarship)*

**Purpose:** To help continue the education of students entering their final years of undergraduate study in landscape architecture. **Focus:** Landscape architecture. **Qualif.:** Applicants must be minority students in their final years of study.

**Funds Avail.:** $1,000. **No. of Awards:** Two. **To Apply:** Applications consist of the following: a typed, double-spaced 500-word essay; between four and eight 35mm color slides neatly arranged in a plastic folder or three to five 8x10 black and white or color photographs that demonstrate the student's best work; two letters of recommendation; a completed application form; and a completed Financial Aid Form. **Deadline:** April 2.

### • 3435 • Lester Walls III Scholarship *(Graduate, Undergraduate/Scholarship)*

**Purpose:** To provide funds for a disabled student pursuing a degree in landscape architecture or for a project on barrier-free design. **Focus:** Landscape Architecture. **Qualif.:** Candidate must be a disabled student of landscape architecture; or, must be interested in doing a project on barrier-free design. Project applicant does not have to be handicapped.

**Funds Avail.:** $500. **No. of Awards:** One. **To Apply:** Write to the Foundation for application form and guidelines. Submit form with two-page autobiography and statement of professional and personal goals. Submission for applicants pursuing a degree must include a maximum of 20 35mm slides depicting his/her best work completed to date. Submission for applicants interested in barrier-free design research projects must include an abstract (1,000-word maximum) of research area, with a description of the final project. **Deadline:** April 2. **Contact:** Mary Hanson, Executive Director, at the above address (see entry 3420).

### • 3436 • Harriett Barnhardt Wimmer Scholarship *(Undergraduate/Scholarship)*

**Focus:** Landscape architecture. **Qualif.:** Applicants must be women entering their final year of undergraduate landscape studies who have demonstrated excellence in design ability and sensitivity to the environment.

**Funds Avail.:** $1,000. **No. of Awards:** One. **To Apply:** Applications include a 500-word autobiography and statement of personal and professional goals, one letter of recommendation from a design instructor, a sample of design work, and a completed application form. **Deadline:** April 2. **Contact:** The Landscape Architecture Foundation at the above address (see entry 3420).

### • 3437 • David T. Woolsey Scholarship *(Graduate, Undergraduate/Scholarship)*

**Focus:** Landscape architecture. **Qualif.:** Applicants must be in their third, fourth, or fifth year, or be graduate students of landscape architecture from the state of Hawaii.

**Funds Avail.:** $1,000. **No. of Awards:** One. **To Apply:** Applications consist of a 500-word autobiography and statement of personal and professional goals, a statement of design work, two letters of recommendation (at least one from a design teacher), completed application form, and a completed Financial Aid Form. **Deadline:** April 2. **Contact:** The Landscape Architecture Foundation at the above address (see entry 3420).

### • 3438 •
### Latin American Educational Foundation
930 W. 7th Ave.                          *Ph:* (303)446-0541
Denver, CO 80204-4417                     *Fax:* (303)446-0526
*E-mail:* laef@uswest.net
*URL:* http://www.laef.org

### • 3439 • Latin American Educational Foundation Scholarships *(Graduate, Postgraduate, Undergraduate/Scholarship)*

**Qualif.:** Applicants must be Hispanic residents of Colorado. They must be planning to attend an accredited college, university, or vocational school, and have a minimum 3.0 cumulative grade point average. **Criteria:** Candidates are evaluated on academic achievement, personal qualities and strengths, financial need, and letters of recommendation.

**Funds Avail.:** Scholarships range from $500 to $1,500 per semester. Amounts may also be matched by one of 19 schools participating in the LAEF Colorado Higher Education Partnership. **No. of Awards:** Varies. **To Apply:** Applicants must submit a completed application, high school or college transcript, federal income tax returns, two letters of recommendation, personal statement, and an optional self-addressed stamped envelope to verify receipt of application. **Deadline:** March 1. **Contact:** Scholarship Selection Committee.

### • 3440 •
### L. S. B. Leakey Foundation
PO Box 29346                             *Ph:* (415)561-4646
San Francisco, CA 94129                   *Fax:* (415)561-4647
*E-mail:* grants@leakeyfoundation.org
*URL:* http://www.leakeyfoundation.org

*The Leakey Foundation was formed to further research into human origins, behavior, and survival. Recent priorities include research into environment, archaeology, and human paleontology of the Miocene,*

*Pliocene, and Pleistocene; into behavior of great Apes and other Old World primates; and into the ecology and adaptation of living hunter-gather peoples.*

### • 3441 • Fellowship for the Study of Foraging Peoples *(Doctorate, Graduate, Postdoctorate/Fellowship)*

**Purpose:** To support field research among contemporary foraging peoples. **Focus:** Anthropology of Foraging Peoples. **Qualif.:** Candidate may be of any nationality, and may be either a doctoral student or professionally qualified investigator. Graduate students must be supported by their faculty advisors. This grant may be used to initiate research in a particular area or to continue a study already underway. Priority will be given to research directed towards long-term, systematic behavioral observations and research which attempts to elucidate evolutionary theory or specific socioecological adaptations. We especially seek proposals for urgent research that might not ordinarily be funded by other granting agencies.

**Funds Avail.:** $20,000 maximum. **To Apply:** Submit copies of a curriculum vitae and a two-page statement of research goals. Eligible applicants will receive further instructions after submitting the preliminary materials. **Deadline:** October 15 for pre-application; January 5 for full proposal (if requested). Notification in May. **Contact:** Dr. Karla Savage, Grants Officer, at the above address (see entry 3440).

### • 3442 • Leakey Foundation Fellowships for Great Ape Research and Conservation *(Doctorate, Graduate, Postdoctorate/Fellowship)*

**Purpose:** To promote long-term research on wild populations of great apes. **Focus:** Primatology. **Qualif.:** Candidate may be of any nationality, and may be a professionally qualified investigator or a doctoral student. Graduate students must be supported by their faculty advisors. This special award promotes long-term research on the behavior and ecology of wild populations of great apes, especially if, in addition to the basic scientific goals of the project, the work contributes to the development or testing of models of human evolution. Both continuing and new projects will be considered. Strong preference is given to post-doctoral applicants prepared to make a long-term commitment to the study site. Awards are made for field expenses only.

**Funds Avail.:** $20,000 maximum. **No. of Awards:** 1. **To Apply:** Submit copies of a curriculum vitae and a two-page statement of research goals. Eligible applicants will receive further instructions after submitting the preliminary materials. **Deadline:** October 15 for pre-application; January 5 for full proposal (if requested). Notification in May. **Contact:** Dr. Karla Savage, Grants Officer, at the above address (see entry 3440).

### • 3443 • Leakey Foundation General Grants *(Doctorate, Graduate, Postdoctorate, Professional Development/Grant)*

**Purpose:** To support research related to human evolution. **Focus:** Human Evolution and related disciplines, including Archaeology, Paleontology, Primatology. **Qualif.:** Candidate may be of any nationality. Applicant may be a professionally qualified scientist or a graduate student working toward an advanced degree. Applications from graduate students must be supported by their faculty advisors. Preference is given to the exploratory phase of projects as well as to enable researchers to exploit novel opportunities in establishing programs. Long-term projects will be considered only if investigator estimates future requirements in the initial application. Candidates who wish to conduct research abroad must secure permission from the host government prior to applying for a grant.

**Funds Avail.:** $3,000-7,000 for graduate students; up to $12,000 for professionally qualified scientists. **To Apply:** Write to the grants officer for application form and guidelines. Submit form, three or four letters of reference, two-page curriculum vitae/publication list, and up to five pages of supplemental material. **Deadline:** August 15, January 5. **Contact:** Dr. Karla Savage, Grants Officer, at the above address (see entry 3440).

### • 3444 • Paleoanthropology Award *(Doctorate, Professional Development/Award)*

**Purpose:** To promote long-term multidisciplinary research in paleoanthropology. **Focus:** Paleoanthropology. **Qualif.:** Candidate may be of any nationality and may be a professionally qualified investigator or doctoral student. Graduate students must be supported by their faculty advisors. Awards are made for field expenses only.

**Funds Avail.:** $20,000 maximum. **No. of Awards:** 1. **To Apply:** Submit copies of a curriculum vitae and a two-page statement of research goals. Eligible applicants will receive further instructions after submitting the preliminary materials. **Deadline:** October 15 for pre-application; January 5 for full proposal (if requested). Notification in May. **Contact:** Dr. Karla Savage, Grants Officer, at the above address (see entry 3440).

---

### • 3445 •
### Learning Disabilities Association of Canada
323 Chapel St., Ste. 200     Ph: (613)238-5721
Ottawa, ON, Canada K1N 7Z2     Fax: (613)235-5391
*E-mail:* ldactaac@fox.nstn.ca
*URL:* http://educ.queensu.ca/~lda

### • 3446 • Doreen Kronick Scholarship *(Graduate/Scholarship)*

**Purpose:** To support a graduate student who wishes to assist individuals with learning disabilities. **Focus:** Learning Disabilities. **Qualif.:** Candidate must be a Canadian Citizen or landed immigrant and a full- or part-time graduate student at a Canadian university during the year for which the scholarship is received. Applicant may be studying in any discipline, but studies must help prepare him or her to assist persons with learning disabilities.

**Funds Avail.:** $500. **No. of Awards:** 1. **To Apply:** Write for application form and guidelines. Submit form with transcripts, three letters of reference, an outline of contributions to community and campus life, a statement indicating past and present educational involvement, plans for the ensuing university year's enrollment, name of university and faculty, and a description of the applicant's future academic program's component related to learning disabilities. **Deadline:** May 15. **Contact:** LDAC Scholarship Dept. at the above address (see entry 3445).

### • 3447 • Carol Thomson Memorial Fund Scholarship *(All/Scholarship)*

**Purpose:** To enable an individual with learning disabilities to attend a private vocational school or undergraduate program at at Canadian University, or college. **Focus:** General Studies. **Qualif.:** Applicant must be an individual with learning disabilities enrolling or enrolled, on a full or part-time basis, in any program of study at any Canadian university or college.

**Funds Avail.:** $500. **No. of Awards:** 1. **To Apply:** Application must include: a letter of acceptance from the college or university; three letters of reference; and a letter containing: a description of learning disability, an outline of coping skills to compensate for that learning disability, community involvement, and future goals. **Deadline:** May 15.

---

### • 3448 •
### Lehigh County Labor Council, AFL-CIO and Northampton County Labor Council
PO Box 20226
Lehigh Valley, PA 18002-0226

#### • 3449 • Lehigh Valley Workers Memorial Scholarship Fund *(High School/Scholarship)*

**Purpose:** To provide scholarships. **Qualif.:** Parent must have died on the job or have been severely injured, limiting earning abilities. **Criteria:** Grades plus essay.

**Funds Avail.:** Up to $10,000 per year with $2,500 cap for each recipient. **No. of Awards:** 4. **To Apply:** Please send high school grades, SAT scores and proof of acceptance from college. **Deadline:** February 28. **Contact:** Dawn D'Andria or Pete DePietra.

### • 3450 •
### Lemberg Scholarship Loan Fund, Inc.
60 E. 42nd St., Ste. 1814
New York, NY 10165

#### • 3451 • Samuel Lemberg Scholarship Loan Fund, Inc. *(Graduate, Undergraduate/Loan)*

**Purpose:** To aid Jewish men and women who otherwise might be unable to obtain the benefits of higher education. **Qualif.:** Candidates must be Jewish students preferably enrolled at accredited colleges and universities and engaged in, or intending to engage in, the pursuit of academic work or professional courses leading to a recognized degree. **Criteria:** Financial need, academic standing, family need, and potential for leadership in the American Jewish community.

**Funds Avail.:** Loans are granted interest-free. Successful applicants assume an obligation to repay the full amount of the loan within ten years after the completion of their course of study. Recipients of loans must communicate their progress and economic status to the secretary not less than twice per year. **No. of Awards:** 12-25. **To Apply:** Applications must be requested and submitted with transcripts and letters of recommendation. **Deadline:** April 1. Successful applicants are notified by July 1 **Contact:** Myron E. Schoen, Secretary, at the above address (see entry 3450).

### • 3452 •
### Letras de Oro
University of Miami
1531 Brescia Ave.
PO Box 248123
Coral Gables, FL 33124
Ph: (305)284-3266
Fax: (305)284-4406

#### • 3453 • Letras de Oro Spanish Speaking Literary Prizes *(Professional Development/Prize)*

**Purpose:** To recognize outstanding manuscripts written in Spanish by authors living in the United States. **Focus:** Plays, Essays, Novels, Short Stories, Poems. **Qualif.:** Applicant must be living in the United States. Candidate's submission must be an original, unpublished play, essay, novel, short story, or poem written in Spanish. Manuscripts that have previously won local, national, or international prizes are ineligible for submission. Winning manuscripts will be published in Letras de Oro literacy collection.

**Funds Avail.:** $2,500. **No. of Awards:** 5 (one in each category per year). **To Apply:** Write for submission guidelines. Three copies of the manuscript are required. **Deadline:** October 12. Awards are announced in March. **Contact:** Joaquin Roy or Maggie Hernandez at the above address (see entry 3452).

### • 3454 •
### Leukemia Society of America, Inc.
600 Third Ave., 4th Floor
New York, NY 10016
*E-mail:* lermandb@leukemia.org
*URL:* http://www.leukemia.org
*Ph:* (212)573-8484
*Fax:* (212)856-9686

#### • 3455 • Leukemia Society of America Short-term Scientific Awards *(Professional Development/Grant)*

**Focus:** Medicine. **Qualif.:** Applicants may be current Leukemia Society Fellows, Special Fellows or Scholars, or established investigators who wish to visit a laboratory/clinic of a Leukemia Society grantee's sponsor who has demonstrated expertise in a particular field of research. The nature of the information exchanged must enhance the grantee's ability to conduct the project for which the Society is already providing funds.

**Funds Avail.:** A maximum grant of $5,000 covers transportation, lodging and out-of-pocket expenses. **No. of Awards:** 7. **Deadline:** August 1, December 1, and April 1. **Contact:** Director of Research Administration at the above address (see entry 3454).

#### • 3456 • Leukemia Society Fellow Awards *(Postdoctorate/Award)*

**Purpose:** To encourage investigators dedicating their careers to research toward a cure or control of leukemia, Hodgkin's disease, the lymphomas, and multiple myeloma. **Focus:** Hodgkin's Disease, Leukemia, Lymphomas, Multiple Myeloma. **Qualif.:** Applicants may be of any nationality but must have a Ph.D., M.D., or equivalent degree. They should not have any or minimal prior postdoctoral experience working in fields relevant to leukemia and related diseases. They must also be affiliated with an academic institution at the time funding is to commence, but awards will not be made to individuals with full institutional salary support. Applicants must be sponsored by a senior investigator at the institution.

**Funds Avail.:** $93,000 total stipend. Funds for institutional overhead are also available. **No. of Awards:** Depends on funds available. **To Apply:** Write to director, research administration for application form and guidelines. Submit form with curriculum vitaes of candidate and sponsor, relevant publications by the applicant, research proposal, sponsor's letter of support, three other letters of reference, budget proposal, and statements regarding safety and ethics of project. **Deadline:** September 15 (first two pages of completed application); October 1 (complete application). Notification by March.

**Remarks:** All Leukemia Society of America grantees are eligible to apply for the Short-term Scientific Exchange Award, which provides up to $5,000 for travel to another laboratory or clinic to learn a specific technique or to share specific information. **Contact:** Director of Research Administration, at the above address (see entry 3454).

#### • 3457 • Leukemia Society Scholar Awards *(Postdoctorate/Award)*

**Purpose:** To encourage investigators dedicating their careers to research toward a cure or control of leukemia, Hodgkin's disease, the lymphomas, and multiple myeloma. **Focus:** Hodgkin's Disease, Leukemia, Lymphomas, Multiple Myeloma. **Qualif.:** Applicant may be of any nationality. Applicant must have a Ph.D., M.D., or equivalent degree. Candidate should have at least five years experience conducting original research bearing on leukemia and related diseases.

**Funds Avail.:** $40,000/year. Funds for institutional overhead are also available. **To Apply:** Write to the research grant administrator for application form and guidelines. Submit form with curriculum vitaes of candidate and sponsor, relevant publications by the applicant, research proposal, sponsor's letter of support, three other letters of reference, budget proposal, and statements regarding safety and ethics of project. **Deadline:** September 15 (first two pages of application); October 1. Notification by March.

**Remarks:** All Leukemia Society of America grantees are eligible to apply for the Short-term Scientific Exchange Award, which provides up to $5,000 for travel to another laboratory or clinic to learn a specific technique or to share specific information. **Contact:** Lewis Braham Research Grant Coordinator or the Research Program Administrator at the above address (see entry 3454).

**• 3458 • Leukemia Society Special Fellow Awards** *(Postdoctorate/Award)*

**Purpose:** To encourage investigators dedicating their careers to research toward a cure or control of leukemia, Hodgkin's disease, the lymphomas, and multiple myeloma. **Focus:** Hodgkin's Disease, Leukemia, Lymphomas, Multiple Myeloma. **Qualif.:** Applicants may be of any nationality but must have a Ph.D., M.D., or equivalent degree. They should have at least two or three years of postdoctoral training at the time of review. Applicants must be affiliated with an academic institution at the time funding is to commence, but awards will not be made to individuals with full institutional salary support. Applicant must be sponsored by a senior investigator at the institution.

**Funds Avail.:** $111,000 total stipend. Funds for institutional overhead are also available. **No. of Awards:** Depends on availability of funds. **To Apply:** Write to the Director of Research Administration for application form and guidelines. Submit form with curriculum vitaes of candidate and sponsor, relevant publications by the applicant, research proposal, sponsor's letter of support, three other letters of reference, budget proposal, and statements regarding safety and ethics of project. **Deadline:** September 15 (first two pages of completed application); October 1 (completed application). Notification by March.

**Remarks:** All Leukemia Society of America grantees are eligible to apply for the Short-term Scientific Exchange Award, which provides up to $5,000 for travel to another laboratory or clinic to learn a specific technique or to share specific information. **Contact:** Director of Research Administration at the above address (see entry 3454).

**• 3459 •**
**Library Company of Philadelphia**
1314 Locust St.                          Ph: (215)546-3181
Philadelphia, PA 19107-5698              Fax: (215)546-5167
*E-mail:* jgreen@librarycompany.org
*URL:* http://www.librarycompany.org

**• 3460 • Research Fellowships in American History and Culture** *(Doctorate, Postdoctorate/Fellowship)*

**Purpose:** To support research in residence in the collections of the Library Company. **Focus:** 18th and 19th Century American History. **Qualif.:** Candidates may be of any nationality but must have a Ph.D., or be a doctoral candidate engaged in dissertation research. They must demonstrate that the collections of the Library Company have primary sources central to the research topic. International applications are especially encouraged.

**Funds Avail.:** $1,500/month. **To Apply:** Write to the Library Company for application guidelines. Submit a curriculum vitae and a concise description of the research project, including need for the collections, to the Company, and one letter of reference.

**Deadline:** February 1. Notification by March 15. **Contact:** James Green, Assistant Librarian, at the above address (see entry 3459).

**• 3461 •**
**Library of Congress**
Collections Services, LM642
101 Independence Ave. SE                 Ph: (202)707-5000
Washington, DC 20540-4600                Fax: (202)707-6269
*E-mail:* jrfell@loc.gov
*URL:* http://lcweb.loc.gov/rr/jrfell

**• 3462 • Library of Congress Junior Fellowship** *(Graduate, Undergraduate/Fellowship)*

**Purpose:** To make the Library's collections better known and to help the Library inventory, chronicle, and make available previously unexplored material. To expose bright young Americans to the challenging career opportunities available at the Library. **Qualif.:** Must be junior or senior undergraduates, or graduate-level students enrolled in a continuing academic program.

**Funds Avail.:** A stipend of $1,200 a month is paid for a two to three-month fellowship. The fellowships are available throughout the year according to the schedules of the students. **To Apply:** Applicants should send an Application for Federal Employment (SF-171) or a resume, a transcript, letter of recommendation, and a cover letter indicating the subject areas in which they are interested to Junior Fellows Program Coordinator, Library Services, Library of Congress LM 642, Washington, DC 20540. The Special Programs Office will arrange telephone or face-to-face interviews with students who submit the most effective applications. Applicants' institutions should submit two letters: the first will identify the official status of the student, to give approval for the fellowship, and to state that the fellowship at the Library will be a direct extension of the student's educational program; the second will provide a personal recommendation by an appropriate professor attesting to the student's reliability and the feasibility of his/her carrying out the project. **Deadline:** April 15.

**• 3463 •**
**Library and Information Technology Association**
50 E. Huron St.                          Ph: (312)280-4270
Chicago, IL 60611-2729                   Fax: (312)280-3257
                                         Free: 800-545-2433
*E-mail:* lita@.ala.org
*URL:* http://www.lita.org

**• 3464 • Christian Larew Memorial Scholarship in Library Information Technology** *(Graduate/Scholarship)*

**Purpose:** To seek individuals with high academic standards and leadership ability. **Focus:** Library and information science, including Library automation. **Qualif.:** Applicants must be seeking a master's degree. **Criteria:** Based on academic standing and leadership potential.

**Funds Avail.:** $3000. **No. of Awards:** 1.

**• 3465 • LITA/GEAC Scholarships in Library and Information Technology** *(Graduate/Scholarship)*

**Purpose:** To encourage students committed to a career in library automation and information technology. **Focus:** Librarianship. **Qualif.:** Applicant must be a student entering an ALA-accredited master's program of library education, with an emphasis on library

## Library and Information Technology Association (continued)

automation, and must demonstrate potential leadership in and a strong commitment to the use of automated systems in libraries.

**Funds Avail.:** $2,500. **No. of Awards:** 1. **To Apply:** Write to the ALA at the above address for application form and guidelines. **Deadline:** April 1. **Contact:** Rebecca Felkner, Program Officer.

### • 3466 • LITA/OCLC and LITA/LSSI Minority Scholarships in Library and Information Technology (Graduate/Scholarship)

**Purpose:** To encourage minority students committed to a career in library automation and information technology. **Focus:** Librarianship. **Qualif.:** Applicant must be a U.S. or Canadian citizen, a member of a minority group, and a student entering a ALA-accredited master's program of library education, with an emphasis on library automation.

**Funds Avail.:** $2,500. **To Apply:** Write to the ALA at the above address for application form and guidelines. **Deadline:** April 1.

### • 3467 •
## Licensing Executives Society (USA and Canada), Inc.
1800 Diagonal Rd., Ste. 280          Ph: (703)836-3106
Alexandria, VA 22314                 Fax: (703)836-3107
URL: http://www.les.org

### • 3468 • LES Fellowships (Graduate/Fellowship)

**Purpose:** To encourage students to conduct research related to licensing and other transfer of technology and intellectual property rights. **Focus:** Licensing. **Qualif.:** Applicant must be a graduate degree candidate at a U.S. or Canadian university. Candidate's research must be relevant to some aspect of the licensing process and should be capable of being described in a publication quality paper.

**Funds Avail.:** $5,000 maximum. **No. of Awards:** Up to four. **To Apply:** Write to the Fellowship Selection Committee for application materials. Submit form with confidential letter from academic sponsor evaluating both candidate and project. **Deadline:** September 23. **Contact:** LES Fellowship Selection Committee at the above address (see entry 3467).

### • 3469 •
## Life Sciences Research Foundation
Lewis Thomas Laboratories
Princeton University
Princeton, NJ 08544                   Ph: (609)258-3551
E-mail: sdirenzo@molbio.princeton.edu
URL: http://lsrf.molbio.princeton.edu

### • 3470 • Life Sciences Research Foundation Fellowships (Postdoctorate, Postgraduate/Fellowship)

**Purpose:** To support postdoctoral research in the biological sciences. **Focus:** Biological Sciences. **Qualif.:** Applicant may be of any nationality, but must hold an M.D. or Ph.D. in any of the biological sciences. Fellowship is competitive and is based primarily on the quality of the applicant's past achievements. U.S. fellows are not restricted in their choice of laboratory. Foreign citizens must conduct their fellowship research in a U.S. laboratory.

**Funds Avail.:** $40,000/year. **No. of Awards:** 16-18 per year. RAT 16/580. **To Apply:** Send self-addressed return envelope to the Fellowship Coordinator for application form and guidelines or retrieve application form from the internet. **Deadline:** October 1.

**Remarks:** All inquiries to LSRF should be made by email for a timely response. **Contact:** Susan Di Renzo, Asst. Director, at the above address (see entry 3469).

### • 3471 •
## Light Work
316 Waverly Ave.                     Ph: (315)443-1300
Syracuse, NY 13244                   Fax: (315)443-9516
E-mail: edlight@syr.edu
URL: http://sumweb.syr.edu/com_dark/lw.html

### • 3472 • Light Work Artist-in-Residence Program (Professional Development/Grant)

**Purpose:** To support mid-career and emerging artists in the production of new work. **Focus:** Photography, Digital Imaging. **Qualif.:** Candidate may be of any nationality. Applicant must be a mid-career or emerging artist with a demonstrated, serious interest in photography. Students are not eligible for support. **Criteria:** Candidates are chosen based on the quality of their work.

**Funds Avail.:** $2,000 stipend, plus darkroom and apartment. **No. of Awards:** 12-15 annually. **To Apply:** Write for guidelines; there are no application forms. Submit a cover letter, 20 slides, a current resume, and other supporting documents. **Deadline:** None; review of applications is ongoing. **Contact:** Jeffrey Hoone, Director, at the above address (see entry 3471).

### • 3473 •
## Lighthouse, International
111 East 59th St.                    Ph: (212)821-9428
New York, NY 10022                   Fax: (212)821-9703
E-mail: awards@lighthouse.org
URL: http://www.lighthouse.org

### • 3474 • The Lighthouse Career Incentive Award for Adult Undergraduates (Undergraduate/Scholarship)

**Purpose:** To help blind and visually impaired students achieve their career goals, to reward excellence, and to recognize accomplishments. **Qualif.:** Applicants must be legally blind adults enrolled or planning to enroll in an undergraduate program at a college or university. They must also be United States citizens living and attending school in the Northeast (New York, New Jersey, Connecticut, Pennsylvania, New Hampshire, Vermont, Rhode Island, Maine, and Massachusetts). Employees of Lighthouse International or members of their immediate families are not eligible to apply. **Criteria:** Scholastic and other achievements.

**Funds Avail.:** $5,000 award. **To Apply:** Applicants must submit a completed application with two letters of recommendation from persons other than family members, documentation of legal blindness, an essay of no more than 500 words outlining career goals and achievements, documentation of United States citizenship, and documentation of academic record and current school status. **Deadline:** March 31; recipients are announced in the spring. **Contact:** Kelly Clark, Career Incentive Awards, at the above address (see entry 3473).

**• 3475 • The Lighthouse Career Incentive Award for College-Bound Students** (*Undergraduate/Scholarship*)

**Purpose:** To help blind and visually impaired students achieve their career goals, to reward excellence, and to recognize accomplishments. **Qualif.:** Applicants must be legally blind high school seniors or graduates planning to enroll in an institution of higher learning. They must also be United States citizens living and attending or planning to attend school in New York, New Jersey, Connecticut, Pennsylvania, Maine, Massachusetts, Rhode Island, New Hampshire, and Vermont. Employees of Lighthouse International or members of their immediate families are not eligible to apply. **Criteria:** Scholastic and other achievements.

**Funds Avail.:** $5,000 award. **To Apply:** Applicants must submit a completed application with two letters of recommendation from persons other than family members, documentation of legal blindness, an essay of no more than 500 words outlining career goals and achievements, documentation of United States citizenship, and documentation of academic record and current school status. **Deadline:** March 31; recipients are announced in the spring. **Contact:** Kelly Clark, Career Incentive Awards, at the above address (see entry 3473).

**• 3476 • The Lighthouse Career Incentive Award for Graduate Students** (*Graduate/Scholarship*)

**Purpose:** To help blind and visually impaired students achieve their career goals, to reward excellence, and to recognize accomplishments. **Qualif.:** Applicants must be legally blind students enrolled or planning to enroll in a graduate program at a university or college. They must also be United States citizens living and attending or planning to attend school in the Northeast (New York, New Jersey, Connecticut, Pennsylvania, Maine, New Hampshire, Massachusetts, Vermont, and Rhode Island). Employees of Lighthouse International or members of their immediate families are not eligible to apply. **Criteria:** Scholastic and other achievements.

**Funds Avail.:** $5,000 award. **To Apply:** Applicants must submit a completed application with two letters of recommendation from persons other than family members, documentation of legal blindness, an essay of no more than 500 words outlining career goals and achievements, documentation of United States citizenship, and documentation of academic record and current school status. **Deadline:** March 31. Recipients are announced in the spring. **Contact:** Kelly Clark, Career Incentive Awards, at the above address (see entry 3473).

**• 3477 • The Lighthouse Career Incentive Award for Undergraduates** (*Undergraduate/Scholarship*)

**Purpose:** To help blind and visually impaired students achieve their career goals, to reward excellence, and to recognize accomplishments. **Qualif.:** Applicants must be legally blind undergraduate students currently attending a university or college. They must also be United States citizens living and attending or planning to attend school in New York, New Jersey, Connecticut, Pennsylvania, Maine, Massachusetts, New Hampshire, Rhode Island, and Vermont. Employees of Lighthouse International or members of their immediate family are not eligible to apply. **Criteria:** Scholastic and other achievements.

**Funds Avail.:** $5,000 award. **To Apply:** Applicants must submit a completed application with two letters of recommendation by persons other than family members, documentation of legal blindness, an essay of no more than 500 words outlining career goals and achievements, documentation of United States citizenship, and documentation of academic record and current school status. **Deadline:** March 31; recipients are announced in the spring. **Contact:** Kelly Clark, Career Incentive Awards, at the above address (see entry 3473).

**• 3478 •**
**Eli Lilly and Company**
Lilly Corporate Center
Indianapolis, IN 46285
*E-mail:* webmaster@lilly.com
*URL:* http://www.lilly.com/

*Ph:* (317)276-6778
*Fax:* (317)277-2025

**• 3479 • Lilly International Fellowships** (*Graduate/Fellowship*)

**Purpose:** To support British, French, and Japanese individuals who wish to undertake postgraduate studies in internal medicine and related fields at U.S. and Canadian institutions. **Focus:** Internal Medicine, Pharmacology, Public Health. **Qualif.:** Applicant must be from the United Kingdom, Japan or France. Candidate must be a university graduate qualified to begin research training in internal medicine or a related field. Award is not renewable, and must be used at a single medical center in the United States or Canada.

**Funds Avail.:** $1,815/month, plus travel to and from host institution. **No. of Awards:** Up to three. **To Apply:** There is no application form; write to the Lilly affiliate in home country for application guidelines. In the United Kingdom the affiliate is: Dr. Alexandar Simpson, Lilly, Dextra Court, Chapel Hill, Basingstoke, Hampshire, RG21 2SY England. In Japan, write to: Dr. T. Kobayashi, Eli Lilly Japan K. K., Sannomiya Chuo Building, 2-20 Goko-dori 4-chome, Chuo-ku, Kobe 651, Japan. In France, contact: Dr. D. Blazy, Lilly France S. A., 203 Bureaux de la Colline, 92-213 Saint-Cloud, France. **Deadline:** Varies, according to country. **Contact:** Dr. Allan J. Weinstein, International Fellowship Program Chair, at the above address (see entry 3478).

**• 3480 •**
**James F. Lincoln Arc Welding Foundation**
PO Box 17305
Cleveland, OH 44117-0035

*Ph:* (216)481-4300

**• 3481 • Division II Arc Welding Awards** (*Professional Development/Award*)

**Purpose:** To recognize outstanding student talent in arc welding. **Focus:** Arc Welding. **Qualif.:** Applicant must be a U.S. resident who is at least 18 years old and who is engaged in arc-welding training at a vocational level. Individuals enrolled in bachelor's or master's degree courses are not eligible to apply. There are two categories of competition: in Division II-A, candidates are invited to submit designs and photos from completed arc-welded projects. In Division II-B, applicants submit a solution to a problem concerned with the use and knowledge of arc welding. For either category, project must have been completed during the year prior to the application deadline.

**Funds Avail.:** Best of the Program Prize: $1,000; Gold Award: $500; Silver Award: $250; Bronze Award: $125. **To Apply:** Write to the secretary for application guidelines; there is no application form. Submit project. **Deadline:** June 1. **Contact:** Secretary, at the above address (see entry 3480).

**• 3482 • Excellence in Arc Welding Awards; Graduate and Professional Awards for Achievement in Arc-Welded Design, Engineering and Fabrication** (*Doctorate, Graduate, Professional Development/Award*)

**Purpose:** To recognize professionals with innovative ideas in arc welding and related technologies. **Focus:** Arc Welding. **Qualif.:** Applicant must be a U.S. resident. Applicant to the Graduate Award division must be enrolled in a master's or doctoral degree program. For the Professional Awards, candidate must be employed in a design, engineering, research, fabricating, production, or maintenance group that has reduced costs or

## James F. Lincoln Arc Welding Foundation (continued)

achieved some other noteworthy objective relevant to arc welding. Individuals who do not qualify for the Graduate or Professional Awards but who use arc welding in their occupations are eligible for the Excellence Awards. Awards are given to recognize specific projects that successfully used arc welding. Submissions are judged on practicality, innovation, and presentation.

**Funds Avail.:** Best of Program Award: $2,000 (Excellence and Graduate categories), $10,000 (Professional category); Gold Award: $1,000 (Excellence and Graduate), $5,000 (Professional). **No. of Awards:** 56. (22 each in the Excellence and Professional categories; 12 in the Graduate category). **To Apply:** Write to the secretary for application form and guidelines. Submit two copies of the following: completed form, a written description of the project, appropriate photos and illustrations, and a one-page abstract. Actual projects may not be submitted. **Deadline:** May 1. Awards are made in the fall. **Contact:** Secretary, at the above address (see entry 3480).

---

## • 3483 •
## Charles A. and Anne Morrow Lindbergh Foundation

708 S. 3rd St., Ste. 110      Ph: (612)338-1703
Minneapolis, MN 55415-1141      Fax: (612)338-6826
E-mail: lindfdtn@mtn.org; lindfdtn@mtn.org
URL: http://www.mtn.org/lindfdtn; http://www.mtn.org/lindfdtn

*Charles A. Lindbergh Fund, Inc.*

### • 3484 • Lindbergh Grants (Other/Grant)

**Purpose:** To support research projects that focus on the balance between the advance of technology and the preservation of the human/natural environment. **Focus:** Aviation/Aerospace, Agriculture, Arts, Biomedical Research, Conservation of Natural Resources, Exploration, Health and Population Sciences, Intercultural Communication, Humanities/Education, Adaptive Technology, Waste Minimization and Management. **Qualif.:** Applicant may be of any nationality. Priority is given to those projects that best address the issue of the balance between environment and technology, regardless of field of study. The fund does not provide support for tuition, scholarships, fellowships, or related travel.

**Funds Avail.:** $10,580 maximum (represents the cost of the Spirit of St. Louis) **No. of Awards:** Approx. 10. **To Apply:** Send a self-addressed, stamped envelope to the grants administrator for application form and guidelines. **Deadline:** Varies. Award recipients are notified by April 15.

**Remarks:** The Jonathan Lindbergh Brown Grant may be given to a project in the above categories to support adaptive technology or biomedical research that seeks to redress imbalance between an individual and his/her environment. **Contact:** Grants Administrator at the above address (see entry 3483).

---

## • 3485 •
## Franklin Lindsay Student Aid Fund

Chase Bank of Texas
PO Box 550      Ph: (512)479-2634
Austin, TX 78789      Fax: (512)479-2656
E-mail: Chad.Goldreyer@chase.com

### • 3486 • Franklin Lindsay Student Loans (Graduate, Undergraduate/Loan)

**Purpose:** To help deserving students fulfill their college education. **Focus:** General Studies. **Qualif.:** Applicants must have at least 24 college credit hours, a 2.0 GPA, and be attending an accredited college or university within the state of Texas (full-time). Applicants must also be U.S. citizens. **Criteria:** Loans are given on a first come, first served basis.

**Funds Avail.:** $3,000 per year maximum loan; $12,000 total. **To Apply:** Applicants must have a co-signer (may be parent, guardian, or other responsible adult other than spouse), provide a transcript from the previous semester, and four recommendations. The guarantee form must be notarized. **Deadline:** July 1. **Contact:** Texas Commerce Bank at the above address (see entry 3485).

---

## • 3487 •
## Link Foundation

c/o Dr. Lee Lynd
Thayer School of Engineering
Dartmouth College
8000 Cummings Hall
Hanover, NH 0375-8000      Ph: (603)646-2231

### • 3488 • Energy Fellowships (Doctorate/Fellowship)

**Purpose:** To foster theoretical and practical energy research. **Focus:** Energy Sciences. **Qualif.:** Applicant may be of any nationality. Applicant must be working towards a Ph.D. in an academic institution. Candidate must have access to institutional research facilities adequate for research project, and must be supervised by an experienced investigator. Preference will be given to applicants conducting research dealing directly with energy and exploring ideas not yet fully tested. First priority will be given to projects which can be implemented in the relatively near future. Funds are not provided for tuition, institutional overhead, or for secretarial or clerical help.

**Funds Avail.:** $18,000 grant, including stipend, and research and publication allowances **To Apply:** Write for application form and guidelines. Submit form with a brief description of research project, letters of endorsement from supervisor and dean, two additional letters of reference, a resume, and a projected budget for use of the fellowship. **Deadline:** December 1. Awards are announced in mid-March. **Contact:** Barbara Granger, Administrative Assistant, at the above address (see entry 3487).

---

## • 3489 •
## Lisle Fellowship

433 W Sterns Rd.
Temperance, MI 48182      Ph: (313)847-7126

### • 3490 • Marion Wright Edelman Scholarship (All/Scholarship)

**Purpose:** To encourage participation in the Lisle international program. **Qualif.:** Applicant must be a person of racial or cultural diversity. **Criteria:** Applicants must commit to a just and peaceful world and work toward a world community.

**Funds Avail.:** $1,000.00. **To Apply:** Submit a letter explaining personal growth expected from getting the scholarship. Submit 3 letters of reference. **Deadline:** April 1.

---

• 3491 •
**Little Emo Music**
Box 3155
Palos Verdes Peninsula, CA 90274     *Fax:* (310)831-1635
*E-mail:* littleemo@aol.com

• 3492 •     **The Little Emo Awards** *(Professional Development/Award)*

**Purpose:** To honor musicians who have demonstrated major social, environmental, and political awareness in the origination and implementation of their musical endeavors. **Focus:** Music: Composition, Performance, Production. **Qualif.:** Applicant may be of any nationality. All categories of musicians are eligible, but applicant should have a proven record of success and substantial musical proficiency, whether classical, pop, jazz, fusion, avant-garde, aleatoric, rap, folk, electronic, computer, international, nonfunctional, choral, or orchestral. **Criteria:** Selection is based on superior performance record.

**Funds Avail.:** $1,000-10,000. **No. of Awards:** 2. **To Apply:** Submit evidence of completed or ongoing musical projects that demonstrate originality, successful implementation and a determination to advance a social, environmental, or political stance consistent with the goals of international harmony as determined by Amnesty International, The United Nations, and Greenpeace. **Deadline:** Ongoing.

**Remarks:** Purpose, musical categories, eligibility, and application procedures and submitted evidences of related endeavors may vary. Decisions regarding the nature of the prize are made every two years. **Contact:** Dr. James Sitterly at the above address (see entry 3491).

---

• 3493 •
**Lorain City Schools**
Administrative Offices
2350 Pole Ave.                    *Ph:* (216)233-2232
Lorain, OH 44052                  *Fax:* (216)282-9151

• 3494 •     **Dusendon Scholarship Grants** *(Undergraduate/Scholarship)*

**Focus:** Education. **Qualif.:** Limited to graduates of the three Lorain city high schools who are entering the field of education. **Criteria:** Financial need.

**Funds Avail.:** Varies. **No. of Awards:** Varies. **To Apply:** Applicants must submit completed applications, transcripts of grades 9 through 12, parents' confidential statements indicating financial need, and personal statements explaining applicants' goals and objectives, and how the grants would be used by the applicants to attain these goals. Financial need must be such that, without financial aid, the applicants would be unable to attend college. **Deadline:** Completed applications must be filed by May 1.

**Remarks:** The Lorain City Board of Education members are Trustees for administering the Dusendon Scholarship Grants according to the Dusendon Will. The Trustees require an evaluation of each final candidate by a high school selection committee comprised of the high school principal, a guidance counselor, and a classroom teacher. **Contact:** The High School Principal's Office at any of the three Lorain city high schools.

---

• 3495 •
**Los Angeles Times**
Times Mirror Sq.                    *Ph:* (213)237-4435
Los Angeles, CA 90053              *Fax:* (213)237-4712
*URL:* http://gpg.com/Mage/rev/sfi_latimes.html

• 3496 •     **Times Mirror Minority Editorial Training Program** *(Professional Development/Other)*

**Purpose:** To provide 18 journalists an opportunity to train for two years at Times Mirror newspapers. **Qualif.:** Applicants must be minorities (African Americans, Asian Americans, Latinos and Native Americans) who are legal residents of the United States with any amount of experience. Applicants must provide proof of eligibility to work two years at newsroom locations. They must hold a driver's and have a car in good condition. Reporters must know how to type and photographers must have basic equipment in good condition, although they will have access to METPRO camera/equipment pool. **Criteria:** Selections are based on written essays, a review of written work or photographs, college transcripts, recommendations, writing tests and personal interviews.

**Funds Avail.:** The program provides paid training for reporters, photographers, and copy editors at daily newspapers. Reporting and photography trainees spend the first year at the Los Angeles Times; editing trainees spend the first year at Newsday in Long Island, New York. Second year trainees are assigned to newsrooms of the Times Mirror newspapers and will receive the compensation and benefits applicable at the newspaper which they work and are subject to the employment terms and conditions of those newspapers. Reporting and photography trainees spend the first year at the Los Angeles Times; editing trainees spend the first year at Newsday in Long Island, New York. Second year trainees are assigned to newsrooms of Times Mirror newspapers. **Deadline:** December 1. **Contact:** Reporting and photography applications are available from METPRO/Reporting Director, Los Angeles Times at the above address (see entry 3495). Editing applications are available from METPRO/Editing Director, Newsday, 235 Pinelawn Rd., Melville, NY 11747. Telephone (516)454-3087. For additional information, contact the Times Mirror Minority Editorial Training Program at the above address.

---

• 3497 •
**Louisiana Department of Education**
626 N. 4th
PO Box 94064                      *Ph:* (504)342-4411
Baton Rouge, LA 70804             *Fax:* (504)342-3432
*E-mail:* webmaster@mail.doe.state.la.us
*URL:* http://www.doe.state.la.us/us2httpd/public/bultin/1134/ chap_6.htm

• 3498 •     **Robert C. Byrd Honors Scholarship** *(Undergraduate/Scholarship)*

**Focus:** General studies. **Qualif.:** Applicants must be residents of the state of Louisiana who are high school graduates with minimum cumulative grade point averages of 3.5 and ACT scores of 23, and demonstrate outstanding academic achievement and promise of continued achievement. Applicants must also be U.S. citizens. **Criteria:** Awards are made based on academic achievement.

---

## Louisiana Department of Education (continued)

**Funds Avail.:** $1,500 maximum per year, not to exceed the cost of attendance. Renewable up to four years. **No. of Awards:** 120-125. **To Apply:** Write for further details. **Deadline:** April. **Contact:** Phyllis Trisler, coordinator.

---

## • 3499 •
## Louisiana Department of Veteran Affairs
PO Box 94095, Capitol Sta.          *Ph:* (504)922-0500
Baton Rouge, LA 70804-9095          *Fax:* (504)922-0511
*E-mail:* ray.noland@vaonline.va.gov
*URL:* http://www.state.la.us

### • 3500 • Louisiana State Aid Dependents Educational Assistance *(Graduate, Other, Undergraduate/Scholarship)*

**Purpose:** To assist dependents and survivors of servicemen and disabled veterans attain their educational goal. **Focus:** General Studies. **Qualif.:** Applicants must be children, or surviving spouses of veterans of Louisiana who died in service in the Armed Forces of the United States, died of a service connected disability that was incurred while in military service, or who are rated 100 percent permanently disabled by the Schedule for Rating Disabilities. Deceased veterans must have been Louisiana residents for at least one year immediately preceding entry into service. Veterans who suffer from a 100 percent service connected disability must have resided in Louisiana for not less than two years immediately preceding admission of child's entry into a training institution. The child must be between the ages of 16 and 25 (marriage is not a bar). The surviving spouse has no age limit, but must use the benefit within ten years of date eligibility is established, remarriage is a bar to this benefit and a divorce after remarriage does not restore eligibility. The student must attend on a full-time basis. Applicants may attend any state supported college, university, trade, or vocational technical school in Louisiana if they meet all entrance requirements for admission at the institution and this program. **Criteria:** Must meet eligibility criteria.

**Funds Avail.:** Tuition exemption. Exemption from payment of all tuition and college-imposed fees. Tuition and fee exemption are provided for a maximum of four school years to be completed in not more than five years from the date of original entry. Also, a possible payment of cash subsistence allowance may be made for a maximum of four years of schooling. **To Apply:** Applications should be requested. They are processed through the Parish Veterans Service Office and are then mailed to the Department of Veterans Affairs for final consideration. **Deadline:** Application must be received no later than one month prior to the beginning of a semester. **Contact:** Louisiana Department of Veterans Affairs, PO Box 94095, Capitol Station, Baton Rouge, LA 70804-9095.

---

## • 3501 •
## Louisiana Library Association
Administrative Officer
PO Box 3058                         *Ph:* (504)342-4928
Baton Rouge, LA 70821               *Fax:* (225)342-3547
*E-mail:* lla@pelican.state.lib.la.us
*URL:* http://www.leeric.lsu.edu/lla

### • 3502 • Louisiana Library Association Scholarship in Librarianship *(Graduate/Scholarship)*

**Purpose:** To provide financial assistance to Louisiana students during their full-time study toward their master's degree in Library Science at Louisiana State University. **Qualif.:** Applicants must

have been born in Louisiana, or lived in Louisiana for a period of at least two years exclusive of any period of full-time enrollment in post-secondary education or, a parent of the applicant has lived in Louisiana for a period of five years exclusive of any period of full-time enrollment in post-secondary education. Applicants must have a composite undergraduate grade point average of at least 3.2 and a combined score on the verbal and quantitative portions of the GRE of at least 1050. Applicants must also have unconditional admission to the Louisiana State University School of Library and Information Science. Recommendation from at least one librarian in addition to recommendations are required for entry into the Louisiana State University School of Library and Information Science. **Criteria:** A personal interview by members of the Scholarship Committee is required for selection.

**Funds Avail.:** $3,000. **To Apply:** Return applications to Phyllis Heroy, 5768 Hyacinth Ave., Baron Rouge, LA 70808. **Deadline:** May 1.

---

## • 3503 •
## Louisiana National Guard - State of Louisiana, Military Department
Office of Adjutant General           *Ph:* (504)271-6262
Jackson Barracks                     *Fax:* (504)278-6290
New Orleans, LA 70146                *Free:* 800-899-6355

### • 3504 • Louisiana National Guard Tuition Exemption Program *(Undergraduate/Other)*

**Focus:** General Studies. **Qualif.:** Applicants must be 17 years of age or older and serving in the Louisiana National Guard. They must be a Louisiana registered voter (if 18 or over), and enrolled in a public institution of higher learning in the state of Louisiana. They must also be members in good standing of the active Louisiana National Guard at the beginning of and throughout the entire academic period for which they receive benefits, and continuously maintain satisfactory participation in the Guard as prescribed by regulations in effect and respectively promulgated by the Department of the Army, Department of the Air Force, and the Louisiana Department of Military Affairs.

**Funds Avail.:** Exemption from all tuition charges. This exemption may be claimed for five separate academic years or until the receipt of a bachelor's degree, whichever occurs first. Termination of Guard service or scholastic probation by the school results in forfeiture of free tuition charges for the current academic year. **Contact:** The Louisiana National Guard, Director of Personnel Administration, at the above address (see entry 3503).

---

## • 3505 •
## Louisiana Rehabilitation Services
8225 Florida Blvd.                   *Ph:* (225)925-4131
Baton Rouge, LA 70806-4834           *Fax:* (225)925-4184

### • 3506 • Louisiana Rehabilitation Services Award *(Other/Other)*

**Purpose:** To assist severely disabled individuals in achieving educational training in order to become employed. **Focus:** General Studies. **Qualif.:** Applicants must be severely disabled residents of Louisiana. **Criteria:** Based on need and eligibility.

**Funds Avail.:** Varies with the cost of tuition. **To Apply:** Candidates may apply through one of nine regional offices. **Contact:** The Louisiana Rehabilitation Services at the above address (see entry 3505)for details.

• 3507 •

## Louisiana Space Consortium
Louisiana State University
277 Nicholson Hall
Baton Rouge, LA 70803
*URL:* http://phacts.phys.lsu.edu/fellows/deadline.html

• **3508** • **Space and Aerospace Graduate Fellowships** *(Graduate/Fellowship)*

**Purpose:** To encourage interest in aerospace fields; to strengthen the educational base in Louisiana; and to develop the research infrastructure needed to increase aerospace research and development. **Focus:** Aerospace related fields. **Qualif.:** Applicants must be U.S. citizens; college seniors, recent graduates, or graduate students; engaged in an aerospace related curriculum; enrolled or have applied to a LaSPACE member college or university; and be a full-time student.

**Funds Avail.:** $17,500 for students seeking doctoral degrees and $15,00 for students seeking master's degrees. **No. of Awards:** 1 to 3. **Deadline:** February 5. No faxed or e-mailed applications will be accepted. To verify receipt of application, include a self-addressed stamped postcard.

**Remarks:** Continuation of funds over the 3 year period is based on availability of funds.

• 3509 •

## Amy Lowell Poetry Travelling Scholarship Trust
c/o Choate, Hall & Stewart
Exchange Place
53 State St., 35th Fl.          *Ph:* (617)248-5000
Boston, MA 02109-2891          *Fax:* (617)248-4000

• **3510** • **Amy Lowell Poetry Travelling Scholarship** *(Professional Development/Scholarship)*

**Purpose:** To support an American-born poet whose work would benefit from a year spent outside of North America. **Focus:** Poetry. **Qualif.:** Applicant must have been born in the United States. Although it is not a requirement of the scholarship, applicants should note that recipients in recent years have been published poets. Scholar must spend the scholarship year outside of North America; there are no other restrictions on the places to which the poet travels, except that it must advance his/her poetry.

**Funds Avail.:** Approximately $29,000. **To Apply:** Write for application materials. Submit four copies of one printed volume, plus no more than 20 pages of most recent work, or 40 pages of work. **Deadline:** October 1. **Contact:** F. Davis Dassori, Jr., Trustee, at the above address (see entry 3509).

• 3511 •

## The Henry Luce Foundation, Inc.
111 W. 50th St.              *Ph:* (212)489-7700
New York, NY 10020          *Fax:* (212)581-9541
*URL:* http://www.metmuseum.org/htmlfile/education/r_ luce.html

• **3512** • **Luce Scholars Program** *(Graduate, Undergraduate/Internship, Scholarship)*

**Purpose:** To provide an internship in Asia for Americans who would not, in the normal course of their careers, expect to have such exposure. **Qualif.:** Candidate must be a U.S. citizen under the age of 30 years on 1 September of the scholarship year, and be nominated by a U.S. university or college participating in the scholarship program. Participating institutions may vary from year to year; write to the Foundation for a current list. Candidate must have, or be about to receive, at least a bachelor's degree. Candidate must also have a clearly defined career interest in a specific field in which he/she has potential for professional accomplishment. Individuals who already have had significant exposure to Asian culture or who have a specific career interest in Asian affairs are not eligible. Awards are tenable in Asia, where scholars are placed in professional work assignments related to their career goals. Placements with host organizations are arranged by the scholarship administrators in Asia. **Criteria:** Academic Achievement, evidence of outstanding leadership ability, and a clearly defined career interest.

**Funds Avail.:** $18,000 stipend, plus housing and cost of living allowances (when necessary), round-trip airfare, and medical and travel insurance. **No. of Awards:** 18. **To Apply:** General application guidelines may be obtained from the Foundation, but applications must be submitted through a university or college authorized to make scholarship nominations. All nominated applicants will be interviewed by the Foundation. **Deadline:** For institution to submit nominations: early December. Notification in mid-March. **Contact:** Helene E. Redell, Program Director, at the above address (see entry 3511).

• 3513 •

## Lunar and Planetary Institute
3600 Bay Area Blvd.          *Ph:* (713)486-2139
Houston, TX 77058-1113      *Fax:* (713)486-2162
*E-mail:* lpi@cass.jsc.nasa.gov
*URL:* http://cass.jsc.nasa.gov/lpi.html

• **3514** • **LPI Summer Intern Program in Planetary Science** *(Undergraduate/Internship)*

**Purpose:** To provide research opportunities with scientists at LPI and the NASA Johnson Space Center. Aimed at exposing interns in planetary and terrestrial studies to an actual research environment in order to help them examine and focus their career goals and to encourage their development as planetary scientists. **Focus:** Planetary Science, geosciences, physics, chemistry, engineering, computer science, and mathematics. **Qualif.:** Applicants must be college undergraduates with at least 50 semester hours of credit who are interested in pursuing a career in the physical sciences. **Criteria:** Based on scholarship, curriculum, and experience; career objectives and scientific interest; and match of interest of applicant with available research projects.

**Funds Avail.:** $350 per week cost-of-living allowance, plus a maximum of $1000 toward travel expenses. **To Apply:** Name and address at school with daytime and evening telephone numbers (and time of day best for contact) Permanent address and telephone number, e-mail address, overall GPA, last semester GPA, spring semester end dates, major, work experience or training; a brief biographical sketch, a description of academic goals, career plans, and scientific interests; a summary of why you want the internship; and official transcripts and three letters of recommendation must be submitted. Letter of recommendations covering academic achievement, career potential and character and transcripts must be mailed under separate cover. **Deadline:** February 5.

• **3515** • **Lunar and Planetary Institute Visiting Graduate Fellows** *(Graduate/Fellowship)*

**Purpose:** To support graduate research at the Institute. **Focus:** Lunar and Planetary Sciences. **Qualif.:** Applicant may be of any nationality. Candidate must be actively engaged in supervised

## Lunar and Planetary Institute (continued)

research at their home institution. Fellowships are tenable at the Institute.

**Funds Avail.:** Varies, according to project and previous experience. **To Apply:** Write to the Director's office for application guidelines. **Deadline:** None. **Contact:** Director's Office at the above address (see entry 3513).

### • 3516 • Lunar and Planetary Institute Visiting Postdoctoral Fellowships *(Postdoctorate/Fellowship)*

**Purpose:** To support postdoctoral research at the Institute. **Focus:** Lunar and Planetary Sciences. **Qualif.:** Applicant may be of any nationality. Candidate must have a doctoral degree in science and be qualified to undertake planetary and lunar research. Fellowships are tenable at the Institute.

**Funds Avail.:** Varies, according to project and previous experience. **To Apply:** Write to the Director's office for application guidelines. **Deadline:** None. **Contact:** Director's Office at the above address (see entry 3513).

### • 3517 • Lunar and Planetary Institute Visiting Scientist Program *(Postdoctorate/Fellowship)*

**Purpose:** To support scientific research at the Institute. **Focus:** Lunar and Planetary Sciences. **Qualif.:** Applicant may be of any nationality. There are three programs: Visiting Staff Scientists; Visiting Senior Scientists; and Visiting Research Scientists. The Visiting Staff Scientists program allows scientists the opportunity to make repeat visits to the Institute in order to complete research. The Visiting Senior Scientists program encourages senior scientists to explore new areas of research. The Visiting Research Scientists program allows scientists holding positions at universities, government facilities, or laboratories to use the facilities at the institute. Fellowships are tenable at the Institute.

**Funds Avail.:** Varies, according to project and previous experience. **To Apply:** Write to the Director's office for application guidelines. **Deadline:** None. **Contact:** Director's Office at the above address (see entry 3513).

## • 3518 •

## Lupus Foundation of America, Inc.

1300 Picard Dr., Ste. 200  
Rockville, MD 20850-4303

*Ph:* (301)670-9292  
*Fax:* (301)670-9486  
*Free:* 800-558-0121

*E-mail:* lfanatl@aol.com  
*URL:* http://www.lupus.org/lupus

### • 3519 • Gina Finzi Memorial Student Summer Fellowships for Research *(Doctorate, Graduate, Undergraduate/Fellowship)*

**Purpose:** To help foster an interest in lupus erythematosus research. **Focus:** Basic, Clinical, or Psychosocial Research. **Qualif.:** Applicants must be undergraduate, graduate, or medical students and all projects must be sponsored by and under the supervision of an established investigator. **Criteria:** Preference is given students with an undergraduate degree.

**Funds Avail.:** Fellowship awards are $2,000. **No. of Awards:** 10. **To Apply:** Fellowship applicants must submit application forms accompanied by a two-page narrative of the research project (narratives over two pages will be rejected), a proposed budget, lay-language abstract and biographical sketch (all using LFA forms), evidence of compliance with government regulations, a statement of concurrent support from other sources, especially LFA chapters, and a statement of support by a sponsor. **Deadline:** February 1.

**Remarks:** All publications resulting from funded research must acknowledge LFA support. Recipients must comply with the Department of Health and Human Services' research rules and regulations. All work involving human subjects or animal experimentation must comply with NIH guidelines. Recipients must also agree to hold the Lupus Foundation harmless from any claims arising from the research. The Foundation has a close relationship with the National Institutes of Health. Many of the foundation's guidelines mirror federal regulations, and both grant and fellowship applications are reviewed NIH-style. **Contact:** Student Summer Fellowships, at the above address (see entry 3518).

### • 3520 • Lupus Foundation of America Research Grants *(Doctorate, Graduate/Grant)*

**Purpose:** To provide seed research monies to test new approaches that may later be presented for funding through other sources, and to promote research (basic, clinical, and psychosocial) into the causes, treatments, and cure for lupus. **Qualif.:** Research grants are awarded to junior academic or professional investigators to support clinical, basic, or psychosocial research related to lupus erythematosus (junior investigator is defined as Assistant Professor or below). **Criteria:** Recipients are chosen based on quality, originality and relevance of proposed project to lupus erythematosus.

**Funds Avail.:** Five research grants of $15,000 per year for up to two years are awarded. Funds may not be used for institutional overhead or indirect costs. **No. of Awards:** 5. **To Apply:** LFA application forms are required The application includes a budget, five-page narrative proposal, curriculum vitae, and a lay-language abstract. **Deadline:** April 1.

**Remarks:** The Foundation has a close relationship with the National Institutes of Health. Many of the foundation's guidelines mirror federal regulations, and both grant and fellowship applications are reviewed NIH-style. All research must be conducted in the United States. Grantees must inform LFA of their intended work location, and a project can be moved during the funded period only with LFA's permission. Recipients must comply with the Department of Health and Human Services' research rules and regulations. All work involving human subjects or animal experimentation must meet National Institute of Health's guidelines. Recipients must also agree to hold the Lupus Foundation harmless from any claims arising from the research. **Contact:** Research Grants Program at the above address (see entry 3518).

## • 3521 •

## Lynden Memorial Scholarship Fund

PO Box 3757  
Seattle, WA 98124-3757  
*E-mail:* dcher@lynden.com  
*URL:* http://www.lynden.com

### • 3522 • Lynden Memorial Scholarship *(Graduate, Postgraduate, Undergraduate/Scholarship)*

**Purpose:** To reward and assist students who excel academically. **Qualif.:** Applicants must be children or stepchildren of a full-time employee of one of the operating companies of Lynden Incorporated. **Criteria:** Selection is based half upon academic achievement and half upon other factors, including work experience, leadership roles, school and community participation, outside appraisal, and/or unusual circumstances.

**Funds Avail.:** $1,000. **No. of Awards:** Five or six. **To Apply:** Applications may be obtained from: Citizens' Scholarship Foundation of America, PO Box 297, St. Peter, MN, 56082. **Deadline:** March 1. **Contact:** Diane Chervenak at the above address (see entry 3521).

**• 3523 •**
## MacDowell Colony
100 High St.         *Ph:* (603)924-3886
Peterborough, NH 03458-2485    *Fax:* (603)924-9142
*E-mail:* youngd@one.mv.com
*URL:* http://www.macdowellcolony.org

### • 3524 • MacDowell Colony Residencies *(Other, Professional Development/Fellowship)*

**Purpose:** To provide artists with uninterrupted time and seclusion, enabling the concentration and intensity that are vital to the creative process. **Focus:** Architecture, Literature, Film/Video, Photography, Interdisciplinary or Mixed Media Arts, Music Composition, Visual Arts. **Qualif.:** Residencies are open to established writers, architects, composers, visual artists and filmmakers, as well as to newer artists of promise. **Criteria:** Applications are judged solely on artistic talent.

**Funds Avail.:** Room and board and the exclusive use of a studio. Also limited travel assistance is provided. **No. of Awards:** 220. **To Apply:** Write to the admissions coordinator for application form and guideline. **Deadline:** September 15; January 15 (for summer); April 15 (for fall/winter). Applicants are notified approximately two months after the deadline.

**Remarks:** The Pollock-Krasner Foundation considers applications from visual artists applying to colonies who, in order to accept and fully utilize a colony residency, will need financial help beyond that which a colony can offer. **Contact:** The MacDowell Colony at the above address (see entry 3523).

**• 3525 •**
## The MacKenzie Foundation
c/o Philip Irwin, Trustee
400 Hope St., Ste. 1861
Los Angeles, CA 90071    *Ph:* (213)669-6377

### • 3526 • The MacKenzie Foundation *(Doctorate/Scholarship)*

**Purpose:** This scholarship provides funds for students enrolled in medical schools located in the State of California. **Focus:** Medicine. **Qualif.:** Applicant must be approved by the foundation.

**Funds Avail.:** Ranges from $1,000.00 $2,500.00.

**Remarks:** The grants are actually made to the schools, which then disburse the funds to the students who have been approved by the Foundation. Most of the awards go to students who have completed at least two years of medical school. **Contact:** The Mackenzie Foundation at the above address (see entry 3525).

**• 3527 •**
## Mackenzie King Scholarships Board
c/o Faculty of Graduate Studies
University of British Columbia
Graduate Student Centre
180-6371 Crescent Rd.    *Ph:* (604)822-4556
Vancouver, BC, Canada V6T 1Z2    *Fax:* (604)822-5802
*E-mail:* grad-award@mercury.ubc.ca
*URL:* http://www.grad.ubc.ca/awards/top.htm

### • 3528 • MacKenzie King Open Scholarship *(Postgraduate/Scholarship)*

**Purpose:** To support postgraduate studies. **Focus:** General Studies. **Qualif.:** Applicants may be of any nationality, but must be graduates of a Canadian university. Award is tenable in full-time postgraduate degree programs in Canada or elsewhere. **Criteria:** Selection is based on students who have demonstrated high academic achievements, positive personal qualities and demonstrated aptitudes.

**Funds Avail.:** $8,000/year. **No. of Awards:** Two annually. **To Apply:** Write to the Scholarships Board for application form and guidelines. Submit form with transcripts and three letters of reference to the faculty of graduate studies or award office at Canadian university from which most recent degree was or will be received. Applications sent directly to the Board will not be considered. **Deadline:** February 1 for receipt by home university. Scholar is announced in May. **Contact:** Awards Administrator at the above address (see entry 3527).

### • 3529 • Mackenzie King Travelling Scholarships *(Graduate, Postgraduate/Scholarship)*

**Purpose:** To allow graduates of Canadian universities to study international affairs or industrial relations in the United States or the United Kingdom. **Focus:** Industrial Relations, International Law, International Relations. **Qualif.:** Candidates may be of any nationality, but must be graduates of a Canadian university who wish to study industrial or international relations (including relevant aspects of law, history, politics and economics). Scholarships are tenable in postgraduate programs in the United States or the United Kingdom.

**Funds Avail.:** $13,000. **No. of Awards:** 5. **To Apply:** Write to the Scholarships Board for application form and guidelines. Submit form with transcripts and three letters of reference to the faculty of graduate studies or award office at Canadian university from which most recent degree was or will be received. The university must forward the application to the Board. **Deadline:** February 1 for receipt by university. **Contact:** Susanne Schmiesing at the above address (see entry 3527).

**• 3530 •**
## James Madison Memorial Fellowship Foundation
2000 K St., NW, Ste. 303    *Ph:* (202)563-8700
Washington, DC 20006    *Fax:* (202)653-6045
    *Free:* 800-525-6928
*E-mail:* jmf@jamesmadison.com
*URL:* http://www.jamesmadison.com

### • 3531 • James Madison Fellowships *(Graduate/Fellowship)*

**Purpose:** To support graduate study of the roots, principles, framing and development of the United States Constitution. **Qualif.:** Applicant must be a U.S. Citizen or U.S. national; must qualify for study toward one of the qualifying master's degrees indicated in application; and must agree to teach full time in secondary school for no less than one year for each full academic year of study under a fellowship. If you are already a teacher, you must be a full-time teacher of American history, American government, or social studies in grades 7-12; and be under contract or prospective contract to teach full time as a secondary school teacher of the same subjects.

**Funds Avail.:** Up to $24,000 for two to five years. This pays for the actual costs of tuition, required fees, books, room, and board. **No. of Awards:** Approximately 60. **Deadline:** March 1.

**Remarks:** Fellows will be required to attend, at the Foundation's expense, a four-week, graduate-level institute on the founding of American constitutional government at a Georgetown University. **Contact:** James Madison Fellowship Program.

## • 3532 •
## Maine Osteopathic Association

RR 2, Box 1920        *Ph:* (207)623-1101
Manchester, ME 04351      *Fax:* (207)623-4228
*E-mail:* meosteo@mint.net
*URL:* http://www.me-osteo.org

### • 3533 • Beale Family Memorial Scholarship
*(Doctorate/Scholarship)*

**Qualif.:** Applicants must be well qualified students in their second, third, or fourth year of matriculation at an osteopathic college who evidence an interest in returning to Maine to practice or in teaching in an osteopathic college in New England. Students are eligible only if they can provide acceptable evidence of legal residence in the state of Maine for a period of not less than three years prior to first application. Residence in Maine for the purpose of post-secondary education only is not considered evidence of Maine residency for this program. **Criteria:** Preference is given to applicants from the Bangor, Maine area.

**Funds Avail.:** $1,000 each year. **Deadline:** May 1. **Contact:** Kellie P. Miller, Executive Director, at the above address (see entry 3532).

### • 3534 • Andrew M. Longley, Jr., D.O. Scholarship
*(Doctorate/Scholarship)*

**Qualif.:** Applicants must be Maine residents and show evidence of interest in practicing primary care in Maine. Students must be entering or attending the University of New England College of Medicine. Students are eligible only if they can provide acceptable evidence of legal residence in the state of Maine for a period of not less than three years prior to their first application. Residence in Maine for the purpose of post-secondary education only is not considered evidence of Maine residency for this program.

**Funds Avail.:** One award of $1,000 per year. **Deadline:** May 1. **Contact:** Kellie P. Miller, Executive Director, at the above address (see entry 3532).

### • 3535 • Maine Osteopathic Association Memorial Scholarship *(Doctorate, Graduate, Undergraduate/ Scholarship)*

**Qualif.:** Applicants must be second, third, or fourth year students, who are a residents of Maine, and able to present proof of enrollment at an approved osteopathic college. Students are eligible only if they can provide acceptable evidence of legal residence in the state of Maine for a period of not less than three years prior to their first application. Residence in Maine for the purpose of post-secondary education only is not considered evidence of Maine residency for this program.

**Funds Avail.:** One award of $,1,000. **Deadline:** May 1. **Contact:** Kellie P. Miller, Executive Director, at the above address (see entry 3532).

### • 3536 • Maine Osteopathic Association Scholarship
*(Doctorate, Graduate, Undergraduate/Scholarship)*

**Qualif.:** Applicants must be first year students who are residents of Maine and able to present proof of enrollment at an approved osteopathic college. Students are eligible only if they can provide acceptable evidence of legal residence in the state of Maine for a period of not less than three years prior to their first application. Residence in Maine for the purpose of post-secondary education only is not considered evidence of Maine residency for this program.

**Funds Avail.:** One award of $1,000. **Deadline:** May 1. **Contact:** Kellie P. Miller, Executive Director, at the above address (see entry 3532).

## • 3537 •
## Maine Veteran's Services

117 State House Station      *Ph:* (207)626-4464
Augusta, ME 04333       *Fax:* (207)626-4471
                    *Free:* 800-345-0116
*E-mail:* mvs@mint.net; mvs@me-arng.ngb.army.mil

### • 3538 • Maine Veterans Dependents Educational Benefits *(All/Scholarship)*

**Focus:** General Studies. **Qualif.:** Applicants must be children, step-children, or spouses of service persons who are either living and have a total and permanent disability as a result of service; who were killed in action; who died from a service-connected disability; or who, at the time of death, were totally and permanently disabled due to a service-connected disability, but whose deaths were not related to the service-connected disability; who are members of the Armed Forces on active duty who have been listed for more than 90 days as missing in action, captured, or forcibly detained or interned in the line of duty by a foreign government or power. Children must be high school graduates and younger than 22 years old when first entering a secondary school. Children who could not enter before the age of 21 because of service in the Armed Forces of the United States may enter if they are not older than 25 and able to show proof of military service. Additionally, spouses may not be divorced, and widows or widowers may not be remarried. The service person or veteran must have been a Maine resident at the time of entry into the service, or if not, have been a resident for five years preceding application. If the veteran was a resident of Maine for less than five years before death, applicant must wait the full five-year period from the date the veteran last established residency to be considered eligible.

**Funds Avail.:** Full tuition at an institution of higher education supported by the state of Maine to be used within six years.

**Remarks:** Full tuition grants may be used at all branches of the University of Maine, all state vocational technical institutions, and Maine Maritime Academy at Castine. **Contact:** Maine Veteran's Services at the above address (see entry 3537).

## • 3539 •
## Maltese-American Benevolent Society

1832 Michigan Ave.
Detroit, MI 48216

### • 3540 • Maltese-American Benevolent Society Scholarship *(Graduate, Undergraduate/Scholarship)*

**Purpose:** To reward academic excellence. **Qualif.:** Applicants must be members or children of members of the Society and must be enrolled full-time in a college or university.

**Funds Avail.:** $500.

## • 3541 •
## MANA - A National Latina Organization

1101 17th St., NW, Ste. 803
Washington, DC 20036-4704      *Ph:* (202)833-0060
*Formerly Known as the Mexican American Women's National Association.*

• **3542** • **Raquel Marquez Frankel Scholarship Fund**
*(Graduate, Undergraduate/Scholarship)*

**Purpose:** To assist Hispanic female students in completing their higher education. **Focus:** General Studies. **Qualif.:** Applicants must be undergraduate or graduate Hispanic female students enrolled in an accredited college, university, community college, or vocational program. **Criteria:** Applicants are evaluated on their academic achievements, financial need, personal qualities and strengths, and commitment to Hispanic women's progress and development, and their contribution to local/national Hispanic community and/or issues. They must also show a demonstration of overcoming unique obstacles in obtaining education.

**Funds Avail.:** Awards range from $200 to $1,000. **To Apply:** Application package includes application form, a one-page typed personal statement, grade transcripts, a letter of recommendation, and a sponsorship letter from a local MANA chapter or a Hispanic community organization. A $10 processing fee and a self-addressed, stamped envelope are also required. Five copies of the entire application package must be submitted. Incomplete applications will not be considered. The personal statement is one of the most important aspects of the application and must be addressed solely to the scholarship committee. **Deadline:** Applications have to be postmarked no later than May 31. **Contact:** Applications may be obtained through the Scholarship Director at the above address (see entry 3541).

• **3543** •
**Horace Mann Companies**
Scholarship Program
PO Box 20490
Springfield, IL 62708
*URL:* http://www.horacemann.com

• **3544** • **Horace Mann Scholarship** *(Undergraduate/Scholarship)*

**Focus:** General studies. **Qualif.:** Applicants must be high school seniors who are children or legal dependent of U.S. public education employees; have at least a "B" average; and have a score of at least 23 on the ACT or 1,100 on the SAT. **Criteria:** Awards are granted based on merit of essay, academic achievement, activities and honors, and letters of recommendation.

**Funds Avail.:** $50,000. One award at $20,000; five at $4,000; and 10 at $1,000. **No. of Awards:** 16. **To Apply:** Applicants must submit an essay up to two pages in length on an assigned topic; two letters of recommendation; and high school transcript, including ACT/SAT test scores. **Deadline:** February 28. **Contact:** Horace Mann Scholarship Program at the above address (see entry 3543).

• **3545** •
**Manomet Center for Conservation Sciences**
81 Stage Point Rd.
PO Box 1770                          *Ph:* (508)224-6521
Manomet, MA 02345              *Fax:* (508)224-9220
*URL:* http://www.manomet.org

• **3546** • **Kathleen S. Anderson Award** *(Professional Development/Award)*

**Purpose:** To encourage significant ornithological research in areas of interest to Kathleen Anderson and the Manomet Center, and to support promising biologists in their work. **Focus:** Ornithology. **Qualif.:** Applicants may be of any nationality and any age, beginning a career in biology. Enrollment in an academic program is desirable, but not required. Awards are tenable in the Americas only. **Criteria:** Awards are based on merit and feasibility of proposed research, competence of researches and reasonable compliance with guidelines.

**Funds Avail.:** $1,000, to one person or divided between two recipients. **No. of Awards:** 1-2. **To Apply:** Write for application guidelines. Submit 3- to 5-page proposal in English and two recommendations. **Deadline:** December 1. Notification by February 1. **Contact:** Jennifer Robbins at the above address (see entry 3545).

• **3547** •
**March of Dimes Birth Defects Foundation - Grants Administration**
1275 Mamaroneck Ave.                    *Ph:* (914)997-4555
White Plains, NY 10605                    *Fax:* (914)997-4560
*E-mail:* research_grants@modimes.org
*URL:* http://www.modimes.org

• **3548** • **March of Dimes Research Grants**
*(Postdoctorate, Professional Development/Grant)*

**Purpose:** To support research directed at the prevention of birth defects. **Focus:** Biology, Genetics, Clinical Studies, Reproductive Health, Environmental Toxicology, and relevant Social and Behavioral Studies. **Qualif.:** Applicants must be qualified scientists from universities, hospitals and research institutions and must hold faculty appointments or the equivalent.

**Funds Avail.:** Approximately $60,000. **To Apply:** Applicants must write a letter of intent addressed to the vice president for research. This letter, submitted in quadruplicate, should be limited to two pages, typewritten in single space on one side of bond paper, in a print no smaller than 12 point print, with one inch margins. It should be accompanied by four copies of the applicant's curriculum vitae and bibliography and should include: writer's full name, title of the proposed research, objective, relevance to birth defects or reproductive health, the hypothesis or hypotheses to be tested, statement of the methods of procedure, plan for evaluating the results, and current financial support. Applicants wishing confirmation of our receipt of the letter should include a stamped and self addressed postcard. **Deadline:** Applications must be postmarked by March 31. Faxes are not accepted.

**Remarks:** The foundations does not accept telephone inquiries. **Contact:** Vice President of Research, at the above address (see entry 3547).

• **3549** • **Basil O'Connor Starter Scholar Awards**
*(Postdoctorate/Award)*

**Purpose:** To support young scientists at the level of instructor or assistant professor who are just embarking on their independent research careers. **Focus:** Birth Defects and related Medical and Scientific disciplines. **Qualif.:** Candidates may be of any nationality, but preference is given to researchers working in the United States. They must have a Ph.D. and/or M.D. degree and should be at the level of instructor or assistant professor. They must also have completed postdoctoral training. Candidates must be nominated by a dean, faculty member, or colleague at home institution. Grants are tenable at the home institution and will cover such items as technical assistance, small equipment and supplies for research directly related to birth defects.

**Funds Avail.:** $50,000/year maximum for technical help and supplies. **To Apply:** The Deans, Chairpersons of Departments and Directors of Institutes or Centers must submit nominations of their best candidates whose research fits the mission stated above. Nominations must include curricula vitae and abstracts of the

*March of Dimes Birth Defects Foundation - Grants Administration (continued)*

proposed research. **Deadline:** Abstract, CV & Nomination: February 27; application for accepted proposals, May 31.

---

**• 3550 •**

**Marin County American Revolution (Bicentennial Scholarships)**

c/o Marin County Office of
  Education
1111 Las Gallinas Ave.
PO Box 4925
San Rafael, CA 94913

**• 3551 •  Marin County American Revolution Bicentennial Scholarship** *(Graduate, Undergraduate/ Scholarship)*

**Purpose:** To encourage communication and understanding of the concepts that are inherent in the spirit of the Bicentennial through scholarships for students to attend approved institutions of higher education. **Qualif.:** Applicants must be residents of Marin County since September 1 of the year prior to submitting the application. Applicants must plan to attend an approved institution of higher education during the year of this application.

**Funds Avail.:** $500 to $2,000. **No. of Awards:** One to two. **To Apply:** The application form must be completed in its entirety and be printed or typed. Must send proof of application/acceptance to the school you plan to attend. **Deadline:** March 31. **Contact:** Marin County American Revolution Bicentennial Committee, Beryl Buck Institute for Education.

---

**• 3552 •**

**Marin Education Fund**

1010 B St., Ste., 300         *Ph:* (415)459-4240
San Rafael, CA 94901          *Fax:* (415)459-0527

**• 3553 •  Marin Education Grant for Short-Term and Long-Term Occupational Study** *(Other, Undergraduate/ Grant)*

**Focus:** Vocational-Technical Studies. **Qualif.:** Applicants must be United States citizens or have permanent resident status and have been continuous residents of Marin County for at least one year (for dependent students the parents must meet the residence requirements). They must be accepted by a vocational training program of six months or less for short-term grants, or over six months for long-term grants. They must also prove financial need and demonstrate high employment potential or promise of a job after training, along with the ability to maintain living expenses during the training period. Applicants must be enrolled at least half-time in a program leading to a certificate or license from an accredited or state approved school.

**Funds Avail.:** Grants range from $500 -$3,000 depending on financial need, and support of up to 75 percent of direct educational expenses. **Deadline:** Applications are accepted on an on-going basis for short-term grants. The deadlines for long-term grants are May 31, August 31, November 30, and February 28. Application process time is approximately two months. **Contact:** The Resource Center, Marin Education Fund, at the above address (see entry 3552).

**• 3554 •  Marin Education Grants** *(Undergraduate/ Grant)*

**Focus:** Education. **Qualif.:** Applicants must be enrolled at least half-time in an undergraduate program leading to a degree or fifth-year teaching credential at an accredited school in the United States; have proven financial need; be United States citizens or have permanent resident alien or asylum status; and have been continuous residents of Marin County for at least one year (parents of dependent students must meet the residence requirements).

**Funds Avail.:** Annual grants vary from $500-$2,000 depending upon financial need. They are paid to the school in equal installments in September and January. Recipients must reapply each year. In determining the extent of need, the following factors are considered: income, school cost, family assets, family size, and number of dependents attending post-secondary school. **No. of Awards:** 500-600. **Deadline:** Applications must be filed by March 2 prior to the next school year. Recipients are notified in July. **Contact:** The Resource Center, Marin Education Fund, at the above address (see entry 3552).

---

**• 3555 •**

**Marine Corps Historical Center**

Coordinator, Grants and Fellowships
Bldg. 58
901 M St. SE
Washington Navy Yard
Washington, DC 20374-5040         *Ph:* (202)433-4244
*URL:* http://www.usmc.mil

**• 3556 •  Marine Corps Historical Center College Internships** *(Undergraduate/Internship)*

**Focus:** General Studies. **Qualif.:** Applicants must be registered students at a college or university that will grant them academic credit for work experience as interns in subject areas relating to their course of study. The students will be employed by the History and Museums Division. Interns are generally drawn from those majoring in history, political science, data processing, art, music, museology, and American studies.

**Funds Avail.:** The only finances available are small grants for daily expense money for interns who work at the Historical Center or Air-Ground Museum.

**Remarks:** The History and Museums Division, which incorporates the Marine Corps Museum in the Washington Navy Yard and the Air-Ground Museum at Quantico, Virginia offers a broad range of historical and museum-related responsibilities. Students work as reference and research historians, curators assistants, catalogers and in other museum positions. Internships are regarded as beginning professional-level historian, curator, librarian, or archivist positions. Interns are assigned to experienced professional members of the division's staff for supervision, instruction, and evaluation. The service can be performed at any time during the year and for at least half-a-day a week. Thus, most interns are students in colleges in the metropolitan Washington D.C. area, although students from other colleges have obtained internships during summer or while involved in Washington-study programs. The academic institution must agree to grant credit for the internship.

**• 3557 •  Marine Corps Historical Center Doctoral Dissertation Fellowship** *(Doctorate/Fellowship)*

**Qualif.:** Applicants must be enrolled in an accredited doctoral degree program and must have completed all requirements for the doctoral degree except the dissertation. A pertinent topic must be approved by the parent academic institution, and must have the potential of furthering the understanding of some aspect of Marine Corps history. Topics in United States military and naval history, and history-based studies in the social and behavioral sciences, with a direct relationship to the U.S. Marine Corps, are considered. Within this context, considerable latitude exists in choosing an appropriate study topic. Preference is given to projects covering the pre-1991 period where records are declassified or can easily be made available to scholars. Fellowships are not awarded to anyone who has received an equivalent fellowship from any other Department of Defense agency. However, recipients of the Marine Corps Master's Thesis Fellowship may apply for a Dissertation Fellowship. **Criteria:** Academic achievements, faculty recommendations, demonstrated research and writing ability, and the nature of the proposed topic and its benefit to the study and understanding of Marine Corps history. The Marine Corps Historical Foundation, the funding organization, makes the final selection. All awards are made on merit, regardless of race, color, creed or sex.

**Funds Avail.:** The U.S. Marine Corps offers one Doctoral Dissertation Fellowship per year in the amount of $7,500. Fellowship stipends are paid in two equal installments. The first comes upon acceptance of the fellowship, and upon the Marine Corps' receipt of certification from the parent academic institution that the student is currently enrolled in the appropriate graduate program and authorized to become a Marine Corps Dissertation Fellow. The second is paid at the beginning of the subsequent academic term upon receipt of confirmation of satisfactory progress from the recipient's academic advisor. **To Apply:** Preliminary application involves writing the Director of Marine Corps History and Museums, outlining the applicant's qualifications and proposing a specific topic or requesting a suggested topic based on the applicant's interests and qualifications. If the preliminary application is favorable, the applicant will be asked to make formal application on a form provided by the Historical Center, including letters of recommendation, publications or evidence of accomplishment in relevant fields. Students should provide academic transcripts. **Deadline:** Fellowship applications must be received by May 1. The Director of Marine Corps History and Museums notifies all applicants individually by letter of their selection status.

**Remarks:** Recipients are encouraged to do part of their research in Washington, DC. Desk space is available in the Marine Corps Historical Center, and recipients receive personalized assistance in gaining access to archival and library sources. This does not preclude research elsewhere. The Marine Corps Historical Center designates one of its staff to serve as the Fellow's point of contact during the fellowship period, and makes its collections and specialists available for the Fellow's research. While the Center will review and comment on the thesis or dissertation if desired, responsibility for direction, control, progress, and final approval remains solely with the Fellow's academic institution and its faculty. The Marine Corps Historical Center requests one copy of the Fellow's finished thesis or dissertation for its library. **Contact:** The chairman of the history department or the graduate school of the applicant's university, or the Director of Marine Corps History and Museums at the above address (see entry 3555).

• 3558 • **Marine Corps Historical Center Master's Thesis Fellowship** *(Graduate/Fellowship)*

**Qualif.:** Applicants must be enrolled in an accredited Master's degree program that requires a thesis. A pertinent topic must be approved by the parent academic institution, and it must have the potential of furthering the understanding of some aspect of Marine Corps history. Topics in United States military and naval history and history-based studies in the social and behavioral sciences with a direct relationship to the U.S. Marine Corps are considered. Within this context, considerable latitude exists in choosing an appropriate study topic. Preference is given to projects covering the pre-1991 period where records are declassified or can easily be made available to scholars. Fellowships are not awarded to anyone who has received an equivalent fellowship from any other Department of Defense agency. **Criteria:** Academic achievements, faculty recommendations, demonstrated research and writing ability, and the nature of the proposed topic and its benefit to the study and understanding of Marine Corps history. The Marine

Corps Historical Foundation, the funding organization, makes the final selection.

**Funds Avail.:** The U.S. Marine Corps offers two Master's Thesis Fellowships each year in the amount of $2,500 each. Stipends are paid in two equal installments. The first comes upon acceptance of the fellowship, and upon the Marine Corps' receipt of certification from the parent academic institution that the student is currently enrolled in the appropriate graduate program and authorized to become a Marine Corps Thesis Fellow. The second is paid at the beginning of the subsequent academic term upon receipt of confirmation of satisfactory progress from the recipient's academic advisor. All awards are made on merit. **To Apply:** Preliminary application involves writing the Director of Marine Corps History and Museums, outlining the applicant's qualifications and proposing a specific topic or requesting a suggested topic based on the applicant's interests and qualifications. If the preliminary application is favorable, the applicant will be asked to make formal application on a form provided by the Historical Center, including letters of recommendation and publications or evidence of accomplishment in relevant fields. Students should provide academic transcripts. **Deadline:** Fellowship applications must be received by May 1. The Director of Marine Corps History and Museums notifies all applicants individually by letter of their selection status.

**Remarks:** Recipients are encouraged to do part of their research in Washington, D.C. Desk space is available in the Marine Corps Historical Center, and recipients receive personalized assistance in gaining access to archival and library sources. This does not preclude research elsewhere. The Marine Corps Historical Center designates one of its staff to serve as the Fellow's point of contact during the fellowship period and makes its collections and specialists available for the Fellow's research. While the Center will review and comment on the thesis if desired, responsibility for direction, control, progress, and final approval remains solely with the Fellow's academic institution and its faculty. The Marine Corps Historical Center requests one copy of the Fellow's finished thesis or dissertation for its library. **Contact:** The chairman of the history department or the graduate school of the applicant's university or the Director of Marine Corps History and Museums at the above address (see entry 3555).

• 3559 • **Marine Corps Historical Center Research Grants** *(Graduate, Postgraduate/Grant)*

**Qualif.:** Research Grants are for graduate and post-graduate study by key qualified persons. Grant research must result in a finite product that directly furthers or illuminates some aspect of Marine Corp history, such as an article for a professional journal, a publishable monograph or essay, a bibliography, a work of art, a museum display, or a diorama. **Criteria:** Academic achievements, faculty recommendations, demonstrated research and writing ability, and the nature of the proposed topic and its benefit to the study and understanding of Marine Corps history. The Marine Corps Historical Foundation, the funding organization, makes the final selection. All awards are made on merit, regardless of race, color, creed or sex.

**Funds Avail.:** Grants range from $400 to $2,000 and are ordinarily paid in two installments; half on initiation of the approved project and half on its successful conclusion. The Director of Marine Corps History and Museums makes final selections for grants of less than $1,000; larger grants require the approval of the Marine Corps Historical Foundation. **To Apply:** Preliminary application for a grant involves writing the Director of Marine Corps History and Museums, outlining the applicant's qualifications and proposing a specific topic or requesting a suggested topic based on the applicant's interests and qualifications. If the preliminary application is favorable, the applicant will be asked to make formal application on a form provided by the Historical Center, including letters of recommendation and publications or evidence of accomplishment in relevant fields. Students should provide academic transcripts. **Deadline:** Fellowship applications are considered throughout the year. The Director of Marine Corps

## Marine Corps Historical Center (continued)

History and Museums notifies all applicants individually by letter of their selection status.

**Remarks:** Recipients are encouraged to do part of their research in Washington, D.C. Desk space is available in the Marine Corps Historical Center, and recipients receive personalized assistance in gaining access to archival and library sources. This does not preclude research elsewhere. **Contact:** The chairman of the history department or the graduate school of the applicant's university, or the Director of Marine Corps History and Museums.

## • 3560 •

### Marine Corps Scholarship Foundation
PO Box 3008
Princeton, NJ 08543-3008     *Ph:* (609)921-3534
*E-mail:* mcsf@aosi.com

#### • 3561 • Fifth Marine Division Association Scholarships *(Undergraduate/Scholarship)*

**Focus:** General Studies. **Qualif.:** Applicants must be children of Marine or Navy personnel who served with the Fifth Marine Division and who have a current, paid-up membership in the Fifth Marine Division Association, unless deceased. Applicants must also be high school graduates or have a high school equivalency certificate; accepted at an accredited university, college, or post secondary business, nursing, technical or trade school; and be in need of financial aid. **Criteria:** Recipients are chosen based on academic merit and financial need.

**Funds Avail.:** Up to $1,000 annually for up to four years. The total amount may not exceed the cost of eight semesters of undergraduate study. If the total amount awarded to the recipient is close to the estimated need, the Division will make an adjustment so the other needy students may benefit. **No. of Awards:** 5. **To Apply:** Completed application forms must be accompanied by evidence of financial need, proof of admission to an approved institution, SAT or ACT scores, high school rank, recommendation from a principal or teacher, and information regarding other forms of aid. Application requests should include a self-addressed, stamped envelope. **Deadline:** June 1.

#### • 3562 • Marine Corps Foundation Scholarships *(Undergraduate/Scholarship)*

**Purpose:** To encourage needy and deserving children of Marines and former Marines to develop their spiritual, intellectual, and physical capabilities through a college, vocational, or technical education. **Focus:** General Studies. **Qualif.:** Applicants must be the sons or daughters of Marines on active duty or in the Reserves, or the sons or daughters of former Marines or Marine Reservists who have been honorably and/or medically discharged or are retired or deceased. Applicants must currently be seniors in high school, high school graduates, or currently enrolled in a certified college or vocational school. The family gross income cannot exceed a prescribed limit. The limit is $43,000. Applicants are expected to have participated in civic or school activities.

**Funds Avail.:** Awards range from $500-2,500. **No. of Awards:** 950. **To Apply:** Applications are distributed only upon written request beginning in September each year. Recipients must reapply annually. **Deadline:** Feb 1.

## • 3563 •

### Marine Corps Tankers Association, Inc.
Phil Morell, Scholarship Chair
1112 Alpine Heights Rd.     *Ph:* (619)445-8423
Alpine, CA 91901     *Fax:* (619)445-8423

#### • 3564 • John Cornelius and Max English Memorial Scholarship *(Graduate, Undergraduate/Scholarship)*

**Purpose:** To support educational pursuits of marine tankers and their dependents. **Focus:** General Studies. **Qualif.:** Applicants must be survivors, dependents or under the legal guardianship of a member of the Marine Corps Tankers Association, Inc. or of a Marine Tanker eligible for membership in the Association. Eligibility for membership is extended to any person who is honorably discharged, retired, or still on active duty who was a member of, assigned or attached to, or performed duty with any Marine Tank unit, regular or reserve, or is currently serving a Marine Tank unit, regular or reserve. In addition, a marine tanker on active duty, a marine reserve tanker, or a marine tanker honorably discharged are themselves eligible to apply. Applicants must have graduated from high school by June of the year of application, have passed an approved high school equivalency test, or be currently enrolled in college. **Criteria:** Selection is based on grade point average, class rank, awards and achievements, a personal write up of goals, plans, and philosophy, school and community activities and service, letters of recommendation, and financial need.

**Funds Avail.:** Up to 10 awards of $1,500 each. **No. of Awards:** Approximately 10. **To Apply:** Applicants should request an application then send with a photograph, high school or college transcripts, a letter of recommendation from applicant's high school or college counselor, a letter of recommendation from a reputable community or church member, unrelated to applicant, and a write up of goals, plans, philosophy etc. **Deadline:** March 15. **Contact:** Phil Morell, Scholarship Chairman, at the above address (see entry 3563).

## • 3565 •

### Thurgood Marshall Scholarship Fund
100 Park Ave.     *Ph:* (917)663-2221
New York, NY 10017     *Fax:* (917)663-2988
*E-mail:* tmsf1@aol.com
*URL:* http://www.tmsf.org

#### • 3566 • Thurgood Marshall Scholarship *(Undergraduate/Scholarship)*

**Purpose:** To provide four-year scholarships to students attending historically black public colleges and universities. **Focus:** General Studies. **Qualif.:** Applicants must be entering as full-time freshmen at one of the 38 historically black public colleges and universities in the United States. They must be pursuing a bachelor's degree in any discipline, have at least a 3.0 GPA, and have an SAT score of at least 1100 and ACT score of at least 25. **Criteria:** Selection is based on academic excellence and excellence in the creative or performing arts.

**Funds Avail.:** Up to $16,800 for a four-year period. **No. of Awards:** 50. **To Apply:** Applicants should apply directly through the public black institution they wish to attend. **Deadline:** Determined by application deadline at participating schools.

**Remarks:** The Fund also awards three-year merit scholarships for men to Howard University, North Carolina Central University, Southern University and Texas Southern University. **Contact:** Johnny E. Parham Jr., Executive Director, at the above address (see entry 3565).

• 3567 •
**Maryland Higher Education Commission - State Scholarship Administration**
16 Francis St.                                  Ph: (410)974-5370
Annapolis, MD 21401-1781          Fax: (410)974-5994
                                               Free: 800-974-1024

E-mail: ssamail@mhec.state.md.us
URL: http://www.mhec.state.md.us

• 3568 • **Edward T. Conroy Memorial Scholarship**
*(Graduate, Undergraduate/Scholarship)*

**Purpose:** To provide financial assistance to sons/daughters of deceased, missing in action or prisoner of war members of the of U.S. Armed Forces and public safety personnel. Surviving spouses (those who have not remarried) of deceased or disabled public safety personnel are also eligible. **Qualif.:** Applicants must attend a Maryland postsecondary institution on at least a part-time basis (minimum six credits per semester). They must also at least 16 years old and have a parent who was one of the following: a member of the armed forces and a Maryland resident at the time of their death or permanent disablement as a result of military service after December 7, 1941; a MD resident at the time they were declared to be a prisoner of war or missing in action after January 1, 1960 as a result of the Vietnam conflict; a prisoner of war or missing in action at the time of the applicant's birth; or a State or local public safety employee killed in the line of duty. Applicants may also qualify if they were a prisoner of war on or after January 1, 1960 as a result of the Vietnam conflict and a resident of Maryland at the time the person was declared to be a prisoner of war or missing in action or if they are the surviving spouse of any local disabled public safety employee killed in the line of duty and have not remarried. Additionally, applicants may be a State or local disabled public safety employee who sustained an injury in the line of duty that precludes the individual from continuing to serve or be employed as a State or local public safety employee in the same capacity. **Criteria:** All eligible new applicants and renewal applicants who apply by the deadline are awarded and late applicants are awarded if funds are available.

**Funds Avail.:** The amount of the award may not exceed the equivalent annual tuition and mandatory fees of a registered undergraduate student at the University of Maryland College Park. The maximum length of assistance is five years of full-time study, or eight years of part-time study, or age 24 in the case of dependent children. **To Apply:** Applicants must file a completed Edward T. Conroy Memorial Scholarship application. Students applying as continuing award recipients must provide a completed Reapplication Form. Applications are available from the State Scholarship Administration. The scholarship will be canceled if the student fails to respond to the award offer, or the designated college or university reports the failure of the student to enroll for a minimum of six credits. **Deadline:** July 15. **Contact:** Margaret Crutchley at the above address (see entry 3567).

• 3569 • **Educational Assistance Grant**
*(Undergraduate/Grant, Scholarship)*

**Purpose:** To provide need-based financial aid to Maryland residents. **Qualif.:** Applicants must be full-time undergraduate students who are residents of Maryland.

**Funds Avail.:** $200-3,000. **To Apply:** Applicants must file the Free Application for Federal Student Aid (FAFSA) each year and maintain a 2.0 GPA. **Deadline:** March 1. **Contact:** State Scholarship Administration at the above address (see entry 3567).

• 3570 • **Guaranteed Access Grant** *(Undergraduate/ Grant)*

**Purpose:** To guarantee access to postsecondary education for the state's neediest students. **Qualif.:** Applicants must have completed high school with at least a 2.5 GPA in the state of Maryland, must file a GA Grant application, must have an annual total family income below 130% of the federal poverty level and be under the age of 22 at the time of the first award. **To Apply:** Applicant should file a separate GA application March 1 of senior year in high school. **Deadline:** March 1. **Contact:** State Scholarship Administration at the above address (see entry 3567).

• 3571 • **Loan Assistant Repayment Program** *(Other/ Other)*

**Purpose:** To provide educational loan repayment assistance to individuals working for state or local governments or the non-profit sector in the state of Maryland in critical manpower shortage areas. **Qualif.:** Applicants must have received a degree in any area, be full-time employees in a state or local government agency or non-profit organization, and have a salary of $40,000 or less ($100,000 combined for married couples). **Criteria:** Loans are granted within priority fields; ranked according to highest annual loan debt-to-income ratio. **Deadline:** September 30. **Contact:** Cis Whittington at the above address (see entry 3567).

• 3572 • **Loan Assistant Repayment Program for Medical Residents in Primary Care** *(Other/Other)*

**Purpose:** To provide educational loan repayment assistance to Maryland residents who are in medical residency programs, general internal medicine, family practice, pediatrics, general pediatrics, or obstetrics/gynecology. **Qualif.:** Candidate must be either a primary care physician practicing at an eligible site or a medical resident specializing in primary care who agrees to practice at an eligible site. **To Apply:** Application materials are available through the Maryland Department of Health and Mental Hygiene: (410)767-5695. **Contact:** State Scholarship Administration at the above address (see entry 3567).

• 3573 • **Maryland Child Care Provider Scholarship**
*(Undergraduate/Scholarship)*

**Purpose:** To attract qualified students into the field of child care. **Focus:** Child Development, Early Childhood Education. **Qualif.:** Applicants must be residents of Maryland who have enrolled or plan to enroll full-time or part-time in an eligible Maryland institution with eligible child care programs for undergraduate study. They are also required to have taken courses that apply toward the eligible degree or credential program. Applicant must, after graduation, serve as a senior staff member or director at a child care center/family day care provider in Maryland for each year of financial assistance.

**Funds Avail.:** $500 to $2,000 per year, renewable upon reapplication. **To Apply:** File Child Care Provider application by June 15. **Deadline:** June 30. **Contact:** Margaret Crutchley for applications and additional information at the above address (see entry 3567).

• 3574 • **Maryland Distinguished Scholar Scholarship**
*(Undergraduate/Scholarship)*

**Purpose:** To identify Maryland high school students who are highly able academically or artistically and to provide scholarship incentives for attending Maryland colleges and universities. **Qualif.:** Applicants must be residents of Maryland who plan to enroll full-time in accredited Maryland postsecondary institutions to pursue an undergraduate degree. **Criteria:** Selection is based on SAT scores and high school grade point average for the first 2 1/2 years of high school.

**Funds Avail.:** $3,000 for up to four years, renewable if a 3.0 grade point average is maintained. **No. of Awards:** 350 awards are offered. **Deadline:** Applications must be submitted during the 11th grade. **Contact:** High school guidance counselors or the Maryland Higher Education Commission at the above address (see entry 3567).

## Maryland Higher Education Commission - State Scholarship Administration (continued)

### • 3575 • Maryland House of Delegates Scholarship
(Graduate, Professional Development, Undergraduate/ Scholarship)

**Purpose:** To provide financial assistance to full-and part-time students pursuing an undergraduate, graduate, or professional education. **Qualif.:** Applicants must be residents of Maryland with financial need. They must be undergraduate or graduate students enrolled or accepted for enrollment full-time or part-time at either a degree-granting higher education institution in Maryland, an out-of-state institution with unique majors, a facility for the hearing-impaired, certain private career schools, or a nursing diploma school.

**Funds Avail.:** Renewable scholarships for up to four years with a minimum award of $200. Scholarship recipients must maintain satisfactory progress. **To Apply:** Applicants must apply to the state delegate in their district. **Deadline:** Deadlines are set by each delegate. **Contact:** State Scholarship Administration at the above address (see entry 3567).

### • 3576 • Maryland Part-Time Grant Program
(Undergraduate/Grant)

**Qualif.:** Applicants must be residents of Maryland who are enrolled in a Maryland degree-granting institution part-time (six to eleven credits per semester) and have financial need. **Criteria:** Schools select recipients.

**Funds Avail.:** $200 to $1,000 per year, renewable upon reapplication. **Contact:** College and university financial aid offices.

### • 3577 • Maryland Physical and Occupational Therapists and Assistants Scholarships
(Undergraduate/Scholarship)

**Purpose:** To reduce the shortage of physical and occupational therapists and assistants working with handicapped children in Maryland public schools or certain non-public education programs. **Qualif.:** Applicants must be residents of Maryland who are undergraduates enrolled or accepted for enrollment full-time in postsecondary institutions with approved programs of occupational or physical therapy which leads to Maryland licensing as a therapist or assistant. Upon completion of their degree, they must serve one year of service at a public school, state hospital, or other approved sites for each year the award is received.

**Funds Avail.:** $2,000, renewable up to four years if satisfactory progress is maintained. **Deadline:** July 1. **Contact:** State Scholarship Administration at the above address (see entry 3567)for applications and additional information.

### • 3578 • Maryland Professional Scholarship
(Graduate, Undergraduate/Scholarship)

**Purpose:** To provide financial assistance to full-time students in medicine, dentistry, law, pharmacy and nursing. **Qualif.:** Applicants must be residents of Maryland who have been admitted to a full-time Maryland degree-granting or diploma progam. **Criteria:** Selection is based on financial need.

**Funds Avail.:** $200 to $1,000 per year, renewable for a total of four years maximum (must reapply). **To Apply:** Applicants must complet both the Professional Scholarship Application, which can be obtained from the State Scholarship Administration, and the Free Application for Federal Student Aid (FAFSA). **Deadline:** March 1.

### • 3579 • Maryland Reimbursement of Firefighters and Rescue Squad Members
(Graduate, Undergraduate/Scholarship)

**Purpose:** To encourage members of firefighting, ambulance and rescue organizations in Maryland to improve their professional skills by reimbursing them for tuition costs of courses leading to a degree in fire services or emergency medical technology. **Qualif.:** Applicants must be firefighters or rescue squad members taking courses credited toward an eligible undergraduate or graduate degree in fire service or emergency medical technology. They may be full-time or part-time students at Maryland degree-granting institutions, and must continue to be active in Maryland as a firefighter or rescue squad member after graduation.

**Funds Avail.:** Renewable scholarship equaling up to the tuition cost at the University of Maryland College Park. Reimbursement is made one year after the completion of each course. **Deadline:** July 1. **Contact:** State Scholarship Administration at the above address (see entry 3567)for applications and additional information.

### • 3580 • Maryland Senatorial Scholarship
(Graduate, Undergraduate/Scholarship)

**Purpose:** To provide financial assistance to full-and part-time students pursuing undergraduate, graduate, and professional education. **Qualif.:** Applicants must be residents of Maryland with financial need. Undergraduate, graduate, or certain vocational program students are eligible to apply. They must enroll or be accepted for enrollment full-time or part-time in degree-granting higher education institutions in Maryland, out-of-state institutions with unique majors, facilities for the hearing-impaired, certain private career schools, or nursing diploma schools. **Criteria:** Selection is based on financial need.

**Funds Avail.:** $400 to $2,000 per year for up to four years. **To Apply:** Applicants must fill out a Free Application for Federal Student Aid (FAFSA), which can be obtained from high school guidance counselors, college financial aid offices, public libraries, or the Maryland State Scholarship Administration. Freshmen students at four-year colleges must submit their ACT or SAT scores. **Deadline:** March 1.

**Remarks:** Awards are made by State Senators to students in their districts. **Contact:** State Scholarship Administration at the above address (see entry 3567).

### • 3581 • Maryland State Nursing Scholarships
(Graduate, Undergraduate/Scholarship)

**Purpose:** To provide financial assistance to full-time or part-time nursing students, and, if financial need exists, assistance in meeting living expenses. **Qualif.:** Applicants must be residents of Maryland who are undergraduate or graduate students enrolled or accepted for enrollment full-time or part-time in a Maryland degree-granting or diploma program. They must also have a minimum 3.0 cumulative grade point average. Upon completion of their degree, recipients must serve in a Maryland nursing shortage area for one year per each year the award was received.

**Funds Avail.:** Up to $2,400 with a need-based additional grant of up to $2,400, renewable annually up to a maximum total award of $9,600, provided recipient meets eligibility requirements. **To Apply:** Applicants must complete a State Nursing Scholarship Application by June 30. Applications are available from the State Scholarship Administration. Recipients may apply for a living expense grant by filing the Free Application for Federal Student Aid (FAFSA) by March 1. **Deadline:** June 30. **Contact:** State Scholarship Administration at the above address (see entry 3567).

### • 3582 • Maryland Teacher Education Distinguished Scholar Scholarship
(Undergraduate/Scholarship)

**Purpose:** To encourage exceptionally able and talented students to enter the teaching profession. **Qualif.:** Applicants must be residents of Maryland enrolled or accepted for enrollment full-time in accredited Maryland postsecondary institutions pursuing an undergraduate degree in an approved teacher education program. They must have received a Distinguished Scholar award and must teach after graduation in a Maryland public school one year for each year, or portion thereof, the award is received. **Criteria:** Selection is based on SAT score and high school grade point average.

**Funds Avail.:** $3,000, renewable for up to four years if a 3.0 grade point average is maintained. **To Apply:** Applicant must complete Distinguished Scholar Teacher Education application which is available at the State Scholarship Administration. **Deadline:** July 1. **Contact:** State Scholarship Administration at the above address (see entry 3567)for applications and additional information.

• 3583 • **Sharon Christa McAuliffe Education Scholarship** *(Graduate, Undergraduate/Scholarship)*

**Purpose:** To certify teachers in critical shortage areas. **Focus:** Determined annually by Maryland State Department of Education. **Qualif.:** Applicants must be residents of Maryland who are undergraduate or graduate students enrolled or accepted for enrollment full-time or part-time in teacher education programs at degree-granting Maryland institutions. They must also have a minimum 3.0 grade point average and at least 60 undergraduate credits. After graduation, they must teach full-time in the designated critical shortage field in a Maryland public school one year for each year, or portion thereof, the award is received.

**Funds Avail.:** Up to $10,000 for up to four semesters, for tuition, fees, and room and board. Awards are renewable if a 3.0 grade point average is maintained. **Deadline:** Applications are accepted November through December. Awards begin the following September. **Contact:** State Scholarship Administration at the above address (see entry 3567)for applications and additional information.

• 3584 • **Tolbert Grant** *(Professional Development, Undergraduate/Grant)*

**Purpose:** To provide financial assistance to full-time students attending an approved private career school in Maryland. **Qualif.:** Applicants must be residents of Maryland with financial need. They must enroll or be accepted for enrollment full-time in Maryland private career schools. **Criteria:** Selections are based on financial need.

**Funds Avail.:** $200 to $1,500 per year, renewable for up to two years. Scholarship recipients must maintain satisfactory progress. **To Apply:** Applicants must contact the schools' financial aid officers. **Deadline:** Varies. **Contact:** State Scholarship Administration at the above address (see entry 3567).

• 3585 •
**Maryland MESA Program**
c/o Johns Hopkins University
Applied Physics Laboratory
Johns Hopkins Rd.                    *Ph:* (301)953-5382
Laurel, MD 20723-6099              *Fax:* (301)953-6123
*URL:* http://www.jhuapl.edu/mesa/content.htm

• 3586 • **Maryland MESA Scholarships** *(High School, Undergraduate/Scholarship)*

**Purpose:** To assist deserving Maryland MESA high school seniors who wish to major in mathematics, engineering, or science. **Qualif.:** Qualified applicants will have participated in the Maryland MESA program for at least one year prior to their senior year; have a B average or better in mathematics, English, and science; and be accepted into a college or university with a major in mathematics, engineering, or science for the academic year following

graduation. **Criteria:** Candidates will be judged on their academic records, nonacademic accomplishments, letters of reference, and an essay.

**Funds Avail.:** Varies. **To Apply:** Applications are available at Maryland MESA Schools. **Deadline:** April 1. **Contact:** Norma F. Boyd at the above address (see entry 3585).

• 3587 •
**Maryland Space Grant Consortium**
The John Hopkins University
Bloomberg Center for Physics and
  Astronomy
3400 N. Charles St., Rm. 203         *Ph:* (410)516-7106
Baltimore, MD 21218-2686             *Fax:* (410)516-4109
*URL:* http://msx4pha.jhu.edu/msgc

• 3588 • **Maryland Space Grant Consortium Graduate Level Fellowship** *(Graduate/Fellowship)*

**Purpose:** To provide the opportunity to operate and conduct public outreach tours of the Space Grant Observatory. **Focus:** Aerospace related fields. **Qualif.:** Applicants must be graduate students. **No. of Awards:** 1.

• 3589 • **Space Scholars Program** *(Undergraduate/Scholarship)*

**Purpose:** Provides scholarship assistance to students at various universities. **Focus:** Aerospace related fields. **Qualif.:** Applicants must be undergraduate students.

**Funds Avail.:** Full scholarship. **No. of Awards:** Varies.

• 3590 •
**Maryland State Scholarship Administration**
Maryland Distinguished Scholar
  Award
16 Francis St.                       *Ph:* (410)974-5370
Annapolis, MD 21401                  *Free:* 800-974-1024
*E-mail:* ssamail@mbec.state.md.us
*URL:* http://www.mbec.state.md.us

• 3591 • **Maryland Higher Education Commission Distinguished Scholar Program** *(Undergraduate/Scholarship)*

**Focus:** General studies. **Qualif.:** Applicants must be Maryland high school juniors who are exceptionally talented and who have clear potential for superior academic achievement in higher education, or are National Merit and National Achievement finalists. Applicants must enroll in a Maryland college or university. **Criteria:** Awards are made based on academic excellence.

**Funds Avail.:** $3,000 per award. May be used for tuition, fees, room, board, books or supplies for use at a Maryland college or university. Renewable. **No. of Awards:** 350. **To Apply:** Write for further details. **Contact:** Distinguished Scholar Program at the above address (see entry 3590).

## • 3592 •
## Massachusetts Black Librarians' Network
c/o Pearl Mosley
27 Beech Glen St.
Roxbury, MA 02119                          *Ph:* (617)442-3066

### • 3593 • Massachusetts Black Librarians Network Scholarship. *(Undergraduate/Scholarship)*

**Focus:** General studies. **Qualif.:** Applicants must be citizens of the United States of Afro-American descent who have been accepted for admission in a library school offering an ALA-accredited program toward a master's degree in library and information studies. Applicants currently attending college must not have completed twelve semester hours prior to the first of the year. **Criteria:** Awards are made based on applicant's commitment to a career in library work.

**Funds Avail.:** $500 minimum per award. **To Apply:** Applicants must submit a transcript from an accredited college and two letters of recommendation. **Contact:** Pearl Mosley.

## • 3594 •
## Massachusetts Indian Association (Scholarship Fund)
245 Rockland Rd.
Carlisle, MA 01741                          *Ph:* (978)369-1235

### • 3595 • Massachusetts Indian Association Scholarships *(Graduate, Undergraduate/Scholarship)*

**Purpose:** To help Native Americans fulfill their educational goals. **Focus:** General Studies. **Qualif.:** Applicants must be tribal members who are full-time students. **Criteria:** Applicants are judged by their educational and professional goals, and financial need.

**Funds Avail.:** $500 undergraduate scholarships and $1,000 graduate scholarships. **To Apply:** A completed application must be submitted. **Deadline:** September 15 and January 15. **Contact:** Marjorie Findlay at the above address (see entry 3594).

## • 3596 •
## Massachusetts Office of Student Financial Assistance
330 Stuart St.                             *Ph:* (617)727-9420
Boston, MA 02116                           *Fax:* (617)727-0667

### • 3597 • Gilbert Matching Scholarship *(Undergraduate/Scholarship)*

**Qualif.:** Applicants must be Massachusetts residents for at least one year before the beginning of the academic year for which state scholarship aid is received and attending an independent, regionally accredited school in Massachusetts full-time.

**Funds Avail.:** Determined by financial aid office. **To Apply:** Applications must be made through school financial aid offices. A Free Application for Federal Student Aid (FAFSA) must be filed. **Contact:** School financial aid offices.

### • 3598 • Massachusetts Family Education Loan *(Graduate, Undergraduate/Loan)*

**Qualif.:** Specific criteria available at a participating Massachusetts college or university.

**Funds Avail.:** Up to 100 percent of the cost of attendance at a fixed rate. **To Apply:** Apply at financial aid office of a participating college or university. **Contact:** School financial aid offices or the Massachusetts Educational Financing Authority at (617)338-1253 or (800)842-1531.

### • 3599 • Massachusetts Public Service Scholarship *(Undergraduate/Scholarship)*

**Qualif.:** Applicants must be the child and/or spouse of a deceased fire/police/corrections officer or just a child of a war veteran whose death was service related. They must also have been a permanent resident of Massachusetts for at least one year, or be a war orphan born in Massachusetts.

**Funds Avail.:** Up to the cost of tuition at a Massachusetts public college or university (whether the recipient is enrolled at a public or private school). The scholarship is renewable. **Contact:** Specific eligibility criteria, applications, and deadline information must be obtained from the office of student financial assistance.

### • 3600 • Massachusetts Tuition Waiver *(Undergraduate/Other)*

**Qualif.:** Candidates must have been Massachusetts residents for at least one year and be enrolled in a Massachusetts state-supported college or university.

**Funds Avail.:** Determined by financial aid office. Up to the cost of tuition. **To Apply:** Application must be made at the school's financial aid office. A Free Application for Federal Student Aid (FAFSA) must be filed. **Contact:** College or university financial aid offices.

### • 3601 • MassGrant Program *(Undergraduate/Scholarship)*

**Qualif.:** Students must be permanent residents of Massachusetts for at least 12 months before the beginning of the academic year for which state scholarship aid is received. Eligibility is limited to students who have not previously received an undergraduate degree and are enrolled full time. To qualify as a legal resident, students must have a permanent address in Massachusetts. Dependent students are considered to have the same state of legal residence as their parents. Attendance at a Massachusetts college or university does not constitute Massachusetts residency. Applicants must be attending or planning to attend a full-time, state-approved, postsecondary school in Massachusetts or the following reciprocal states: Connecticut, Maine, Maryland, New Hampshire, Pennsylvania, Rhode Island, Vermont, or the District of Columbia.

**Funds Avail.:** $250 to $2,500. **To Apply:** A Free Application for Federal Student Aid (FAFSA) must be completed. **Deadline:** Between January 1 and May 1. **Contact:** College or university financial aid offices.

## • 3602 •
## Massachusetts/Rhode Island League for Nursing
One Thompson Square                        *Ph:* (617)242-3009
Charlestown, MA 02129                      *Fax:* (617)242-3009

### • 3603 • MARILN Scholarship *(Undergraduate/Scholarship)*

**Focus:** Nursing. **Qualif.:** Candidates must have resided in the Massachusetts/Rhode Island League for Nursing geographic area for the four years immediately prior to receipt of the scholarship. Applicants may be registered nurses accepted into a program leading to a baccalaureate degree in nursing, generic students entering or completing their senior year in any undergraduate nursing program, or students who have successfully completed four months of a practical nursing program. **Criteria:** Financial need, ability to maintain satisfactory scholarship standards, and ability to contribute to the nursing profession.

**Funds Avail.:** The scholarship(s) is awarded annually, and the amount is individually determined. **No. of Awards:** Varies. **To Apply:** Requests for applications must be in writing and include a self-addressed, double stamped business size envelope. **Deadline:** For practical nursing students, completed applications must be filed by January 30; recepients only are notified by March 15. For registered nursing students, completed applications must be filed by June 15; recipients only are notified by August 15. **Contact:** Scholarship Committee at the above address (see entry 3602).

• 3604 •
## Masters, Mates & Pilots Health & Benefit Plan
5700 Hammonds Ferry Rd.        *Ph:* (410)850-8500
Linthicum Heights, MD 21090    *Fax:* (410)850-8655

• 3605 • **Masters, Mates & Pilots Health & Benefit Plan Scholarship Program** (*Undergraduate/Scholarship*)

**Focus:** General Studies. **Qualif.:** Candidates must be sons or daughters of an active or deceased member or pensioner of MM&P who meets all employee eligibility requirements. Candidates must also be high school seniors who are expecting to graduate in January or June of a current school year and plan to attend an accredited college or university. **Criteria:** An independent scholarship committee selects winners on the basis of high school records, extracurricular activities, College Entrance Examination Board test results, and other indications of character and leadership potential for success in post-college life.

**Funds Avail.:** $5,000 scholarships are awarded annually, which are renewable for up to four years. **No. of Awards:** 6. **Deadline:** November 30. **Contact:** Any port office of the organization or the MM&P Health and Benefit Plan Scholarship Program at the above address (see entry 3604).

• 3606 •
## The Material Handling Education Foundation, Inc.
8720 Red Oak Blvd., Ste. 201    *Ph:* (704)522-8644
Charlotte, NC 28217-3992        *Fax:* (704)522-7826

• 3607 • **MHEF Scholarship** (*Graduate, Undergraduate/Scholarship*)

**Purpose:** To further education and training of all persons working in the material handling field. **Qualif.:** Candidates must have a minimum of two years undergraduate education at an accredited college or university in the United States. Graduate students and transferees from junior and community colleges or other two-year postsecondary institutions may apply. Candidates must be enrolled in an accredited program of study with emphasis in material handling, and have an overall "B" grade point average. Applicants must be U.S. citizens.

**Funds Avail.:** Up to $4,500. **To Apply:** Candidates must submit a completed Scholarship Application Form with a statement outlining: method and manner in which applicants expect to emphasize material handling in his/her educational program; and projected career goals upon completion of educational program. Two additional letters of recommendation from faculty on abilities and leadership must be submitted. Applications can be obtained only from the Engineering department of pre-qualified colleges or universities. Applications from professors of pre-qualified schools

only are accepted; no applications or letters are answered by this office. **Deadline:** March 1. **Contact:** College and university engineering departments.

• 3608 •
## Maternity Center Association
281 Park Ave.
New York, NY 10010        *Ph:* (212)777-5000

• 3609 • **Hazel Corbin Assistance Fund Scholarships** (*Postgraduate/Scholarship*)

**Purpose:** To support postgraduate studies in nurse-midwifery. **Focus:** Nurse-midwifery. **Qualif.:** Applicant may be of any nationality, but must be a registered nurse who plans on practicing nurse-midwifery in the United States. Scholarships are intended to cover the daily living expenses of students enrolled in postgraduate courses in nurse-midwifery. Awards will not be given for other courses of study.

**Funds Avail.:** $50-1,000. **To Apply:** Write to the Association for application guidelines. **Deadline:** None.

**Remarks:** The Association's ability to grant scholarships depends on available funding. Currently, MCA is not awarding the scholarship due to a lack of funding. However, applicants will be placed on a waiting list to be considered as funding becomes available. Write or call for information regarding the current the current status of the Corbin Fund. **Contact:** Carolyn Ambers at the above address (see entry 3608).

• 3610 •
## Mathematical Sciences Research Institute
1000 Centennial Drive     *Ph:* (510)642-0143
Berkeley, CA 94720-5070   *Fax:* (510)642-8609
*E-mail:* inquiries@msri.org
*URL:* http://www.msri.org

• 3611 • **Mathematical Sciences Research Institute Postdoctoral Fellowships in Mathematics** (*Postdoctorate/Fellowship*)

**Purpose:** To support postdoctoral research in selected areas of mathematics. **Focus:** Mathematics. **Qualif.:** Applicants must be U.S. residents who have received the Ph.D. in mathematics within five years prior to application. Fellowships are tenable at the Institute; each year it announces particular areas of mathematics in which research proposals are invited. However, applications are encouraged in all fields of the mathematical sciences.

**Funds Avail.:** $32,500/year, plus round-trip airfare. **No. of Awards:** 18. **To Apply:** Applicants must submit completed application forms, available from the Institute. **Deadline:** November 25; notification is made February 28.

**Remarks:** Senior memberships are also available to experienced mathematicians who wish to conduct research at the Institute. Members are expected to be fully or partially supported from other sources, although the Institute can make awards to offset living expenses for visits of three months or less. Application guidelines and further information are available from the Institute. **Contact:** Program Coordinator, at the above address (see entry 3610).

*Mathematical Sciences Research Institute (continued)*

**• 3612 • Mathematical Sciences Research Institute Research Professorships in Mathematics**
*(Postdoctorate/Fellowship)*

**Purpose:** To encourage research in specific fields by mid-career mathematicians. **Focus:** Mathematics. **Qualif.:** Applicants must be U.S. residents who have received the Ph.D. in mathematics more than six years prior to the year of application. Professorships are tenable at the Institute. Applications are encouraged in all fields of the mathematical sciences.

**Funds Avail.:** Up to $40,000/year, plus round-trip airfare. Awards are intended to supplement sabbatical-leave pay and may not exceed half the applicant's normal salary. **To Apply:** Completed application forms are required. To request an application form, visit the website. **Deadline:** September 25. Notification is made by December 1.

**Remarks:** General memberships are also available to experienced mathematicians who wish to conduct research at the Institute. Members are expected to be fully or partially supported from other sources, although the Institute can make awards to offset living expenses for visits of three months or less. Application guidelines and further information are available from the Institute. **Contact:** Program Coordinator, at the above address (see entry 3610).

---

**• 3613 •**
**Edmund F. Maxwell Foundation**
c/o George V. Powell
PO Box 22537
Seattle, WA 98122-0537
*E-mail:* admin@maxwell.org
*URL:* http://www.maxwell.org

**• 3614 • Edmund F. Maxwell Foundation Scholarship** *(Undergraduate/Scholarship)*

**Purpose:** To provide assistance to those who have demonstrated financial need and have shown ability, aptitude and promise of useful citizenship. **Qualif.:** Applicants must: demonstrate financial need; be residents of western Washington state; have combined SAT scores above 1200; plan to use the scholarship for study at an accredited independent institution which receives its fundamental support from sources other than taxes; and demonstrate high scholastic and extra-curricular achievement. **Criteria:** Based upon essay, SAT score, high school transcript, employment history, extra-curriculars, and financial need.

**Funds Avail.:** $3,500 per scholarship. **No. of Awards:** 35 new and 87 renewals. **To Apply:** See website for more details. **Deadline:** April 30.

---

**• 3615 •**
**Mayo Graduate School of Medicine**
200 1st St.                    *Ph:* (507)284-5920
Rochester, MN 55905            *Fax:* (507)284-1772

**• 3616 • Mayo Foundation Postdoctoral Training Fellowships** *(Postdoctorate/Fellowship)*

**Purpose:** To support postdoctoral medical training at the School. **Focus:** Medicine. **Qualif.:** Candidates may be of any nationality but must be the recent recipient of a doctoral degree in a medical science. Fellowships are tenable at the Mayo Graduate School of

Medicine. Candidates must be sponsored by an investigator at the School prior to submitting formal application.

**Funds Avail.:** $26,200 minimum. **To Apply:** Write to the research administrator for application guidelines. A curriculum vitae and letters of recommendation are required. **Deadline:** None. **Contact:** Cheryl Nelson, Research Administrator, at the above address (see entry 3615).

---

**• 3617 •**
**Anne O'Hare McCormick Memorial Fund**
15 Gramercy Park S.
New York, NY 10003

**• 3618 • Anne O'Hare McCormick Scholarship** *(Graduate/Scholarship)*

**Purpose:** To provide assistance for women preparing for careers in the media. **Focus:** Journalism. **Qualif.:** Open only to women students who are U.S. citizens and have been accepted for enrollment at Columbia University's Graduate School of Journalism. **Criteria:** Financial need and the candidate's potential for success in the media.

**Funds Avail.:** Awards range from $2,500 to $5,000. **No. of Awards:** 2 or more. **To Apply:** Applicants must send a self-addressed, stamped envelope with request for application or information. **Deadline:** May 8.

**Remarks:** The Fund typically receives between 40 or more applications. **Contact:** The Fund at the above address (see entry 3617).

---

**• 3619 •**
**McDonnell Douglas Scholarship Foundation**
3855 Lakewood Blvd.
M/C 802-11                     *Ph:* (310)593-2612
Long Beach, CA 90846          *Fax:* (310)593-0955
*URL:* http://oft-gw.zone.org/clui/database/r%26d/medog/
html

**• 3620 • McDonnell Douglas Scholarships** *(Undergraduate/Scholarship)*

**Focus:** General Studies. **Qualif.:** Applicants must be the dependent children, stepchildren, or legally adopted children of active or former (retired, disabled, or deceased) employees of an MDC component company or subsidiary that participates in the McDonnell Douglas-West Employees Community Fund, Inc. Applicants must also be high school seniors in the upper third of their class or have graduated from high school in the upper third of their class. Applicants must intend to enter college in September and have met all scholastic or other admission requirements of the college being attended. Mid-year graduates entering college immediately after graduation are also eligible to apply. **Criteria:** Applicants are judged on a point system as outlined on application.

**Funds Avail.:** A minimum of $1,500 without regard to financial need to a maximum of $4,000 based on financial need is awarded to 30 recipients. Most awards are at the $1,500 level. **No. of Awards:** Varies. **To Apply:** Applicants must provide a scholarship application form, high school transcripts, and the results of the college entrance examinations (SAT or ACT). **Deadline:** First Friday in March.

**Remarks:** Approximately 250 applications are received each year. **Contact:** B.A. Hoskinson, Administrator, McDonnell Douglas Scholarship, Foundation, at the above address (see entry 3619).

---

• 3621 •

## Verne Catt McDowell Corporation
PO Box 1336
Albany, OR 97321-0440          *Ph:* (541)926-6829

### • 3622 • Verne Catt McDowell Corporation Scholarships *(Graduate/Scholarship)*

**Purpose:** To assist seminary students of the Christian Church (Disciples of Christ) denomination. **Focus:** Theology, Religion for Christian Church (Disciples of Christ). **Qualif.:** Applicants must be members of the Christian Church (Disciples of Christ) denomination and graduates of an accredited liberal arts college or university, receiving a bachelor's degree. They must be ordained, or studying to be ordained, as ministers in the Christian Church (Disciples of Christ). Applicants must also be accepted into a professional degree program at a graduate institution of theological education accredited by the General Assembly of the Christian Church (Disciples of Christ). **Criteria:** Applicants are interviewed following the completion of the application process. Awards are granted by the trustees of the Verne Catt McDowell Corporation, confirmed by the Pastor and Board of Trustees of First Christian Church, Albany, Oregon.

**Funds Avail.:** Grants are individually determined. They supplement a student-minister's self-support capabilities. Recipients must repay the Verne Catt McDowell Corporation if they do not complete seminary and enter the ordained ministry of the Christian Church (Disciples of Christ). **No. of Awards:** 4-6. **To Apply:** Write to the manager for application guidelines. A personal interview is required. **Deadline:** None. **Contact:** Emily Killin at the above address (see entry 3621).

---

• 3623 •

## McFarland Charitable Foundation Trust
c/o Havana National Bank
112 S. Orange
PO Box 200
Havana, IL 62644-0200          *Ph:* (309)543-3361

### • 3624 • McFarland Charitable Foundation Registered Nursing Scholarship *(Undergraduate/Scholarship loan)*

**Purpose:** To help educate nurses who will return to Havana, Illinois, to work upon completion of degree. **Qualif.:** Applicants should be high school graduates or the equivalent accepted into an accredited registered nursing program, and must have a prior employment commitment to return to Havana, Illinois, to work for a predetermined number of years. Recipients must sign written contracts with co-signers requiring them to return to Havana to work. Breach of contract results in repayment of the scholarship with interest and replacement costs.

**Funds Avail.:** Amount of funding varies. **No. of Awards:** 2-3. **To Apply:** Application forms are available from the Havana National Bank upon request. **Deadline:** May 31. **Contact:** Linda M. Butler at the above address (see entry 3623).

---

• 3625 •

## McGill University - Faculty of Law
3644 Peel St.                  *Ph:* (514)398-6604
Montreal, PQ, Canada H3A 1W9   *Fax:* (514)398-4659
*E-mail:* web-team@cim.mcgill.com
*URL:* http://www.cim.mcgill.ca/

### • 3626 • Maxwell Boulton Junior Fellowship *(Doctorate, Postdoctorate/Fellowship)*

**Purpose:** To allow a junior legal scholar to further study toward a higher degree through research. **Focus:** Canadian Legal System, Law. **Qualif.:** Candidates may be of any nationality but must be legal scholars working to fulfill the requirements of a higher degree or working on a major post-doctoral research project. Fellowships are intended to support scholars conducting significant research and are tenable at McGill University. **Criteria:** Preference is given to candidates with research projects that have significance to the Canadian legal system and legal community. Some limited teaching assignments may be required of the fellow.

**Funds Avail.:** $35,000 approximately. **No. of Awards:** Up to two. **To Apply:** Apply by letter to the Chair of the Boulton Trustees. Submit application with curriculum vitae, a detailed statement of research project, and the names of three referees. **Deadline:** February 1. **Contact:** Peter Leuprecht, Dean, at the above address (see entry 3625).

### • 3627 • Maxwell Boulton Senior Fellowship *(Professional Development/Fellowship)*

**Purpose:** To allow an established scholar to pursue, and preferably complete, a major research project. **Focus:** Canadian Legal System, Law. **Qualif.:** Candidates may be of any nationality but must be well-established legal scholars. Fellowships are intended to support scholars conducting a major research project, and are tenable at McGill University. **Criteria:** Preference is given to candidates with research projects that have significance to the Canadian legal system and legal community. Some limited teaching assignments may be required of the fellow.

**Funds Avail.:** Negotiable. **No. of Awards:** No more than one annually. **To Apply:** Apply by letter to the Chair of the Boulton Trustees. Submit application with curriculum vitae, a detailed statement of research project, and the names of three referees. **Deadline:** February 1. **Contact:** Peter Leuprecht, Dean, at the above address (see entry 3625).

---

• 3628 •

## Median School of Allied Health Careers
125 7th St.                    *Ph:* (412)391-7021
Pittsburgh, PA 15222           *Fax:* (412)232-4348
                               *Free:* 800-570-0693
*E-mail:* median@sgi.net
*URL:* http://www.medianschool.com

### • 3629 • Median School Scholarship *(High School/Scholarship)*

**Purpose:** To assist students with financial needs to attend Median School. **Focus:** Orthotics and Prosthetics, Dental, Medical, and Veterinary, Medical Billing. **Qualif.:** Applicants must be high school seniors planning on studying health at Median School. **Criteria:** Scholarship Exam.

**Funds Avail.:** Two $2,000 scholarships for dorm students; five $1,000 scholarships for commuters. **No. of Awards:** 7. **Deadline:** March 10.

**Remarks:** Based on competitive examination given at the Median School of Allied Health Careers. **Contact:** Director of Admissions.

---

# • 3630 •

**Medical Library Association**
65 E. Wacker Pl., Ste. 1900
Chicago, IL 60601
*E-mail:* mlapda@mlahg.org
*URL:* http://www.kumc.edu/MLA/secinfo.html

*Ph:* (312)419-9094
*Fax:* (312)419-8950

### • 3631 • Cunningham Memorial International Fellowship *(Professional Development/Fellowship)*

**Purpose:** To assist in the education and training of medical librarians from countries outside of the United States and Canada. **Focus:** Medical Librarianship. **Qualif.:** Applicant must be a citizen or permanent resident of a country other than the United States or Canada. Candidate must ordinarily have both an undergraduate and a library degree, although the library degree requirement may be waived under extraordinary circumstances. Applicant must currently work, or plan to work, in a medical library in his/her home country. Past Cunningham Fellows may not re-apply. Fellows spend the duration of the award working at one or more medical libraries in the United States or Canada; fellows may also attend continuing education courses at the annual meeting of the MLA.

**Funds Avail.:** $3,000 for living and tuition expenses, plus $1,000 for travel. **No. of Awards:** 1. **To Apply:** Write to the Professional Development Department for application form and guidelines. Submit form to the Cunningham Fellowship Jury chair, with three professional letters of reference; transcripts; a signed statement from a supervisor, guaranteeing a position in a medical library upon return to home country; proof of ability to speak English; a project overview; and a certificate of health. The address of the chair is included in the application materials. Candidates are encouraged to obtain personal interviews with a U.S. education or cultural affairs officer in home country. **Deadline:** December 1.

**Remarks:** MLA also offers numerous awards in recognition of distinguished service and outstanding individual achievements in medical librarianship. Write to the Professional Development Department. **Contact:** Professional Development Department at the above address (see entry 3630).

### • 3632 • MLA Continuing Education Grant *(Professional Development/Grant)*

**Purpose:** To provide qualified medical librarians with study opportunities. **Focus:** Medical Librarianship. **Qualif.:** Applicant must be a U.S. or Canadian citizen or permanent resident, a member of MLA, and a degree-holding, practicing medical librarian with at least two years of professional experience. In exceptional cases, however, consideration will be given to an outstanding candidate who does not meet the usual eligibility criteria. Continuing Education Grant provide the opportunity to increase competence in the theoretical, administrative, and/or technical aspects of librarianship. Awards are not given for work toward a degree or certificate, although relevant course work that is not part of the normal professional curriculum will be considered.

**Funds Avail.:** $500 maximum. **To Apply:** Write to the Professional Development Department for application form and guidelines. **Deadline:** December 1. Award recipients will be notified in April.

**Remarks:** MLA also offers numerous awards in recognition of distinguished service and outstanding individual achievements in medical librarianship. Write to the Program Development Department for further information. **Contact:** Professional Development Department at the above address (see entry 3630).

### • 3633 • MLA Doctoral Fellowship *(Doctorate/Fellowship)*

**Purpose:** To encourage superior students to conduct doctoral work in medical librarianship or information science. **Focus:** Library and Archival Sciences (Biomedical Related Areas). **Qualif.:** Applicants must be citizens or permanent residents of the United States or Canada and graduates of ALA-accredited schools of library science pursuing a doctoral degree. Programs must emphasize biomedical and health-related information science. Candidates should already be accepted in a doctoral program to assure acceptance of the project toward Ph.D. requirements. Previous winners of Doctoral Fellowships are not eligible. **Criteria:** Preference is given to applicants who have at least 80 percent of their course work completed and an approved dissertation prospectus.

**Funds Avail.:** One fellowship of $1,000 is awarded annually. Funds may be used for project and travel expenses, as well as augmenting larger, separately funded projects relevant to doctoral degree requirements. Funds may not be used to pay for tuition, equipment, clinical support except preparation of the final report for MLA, and living expenses. **No. of Awards:** 1. **To Apply:** Applicants must submit formal application form, two letters of reference including one from the applicant's doctoral advisor and one from a person recognized for expertise in the proposed field, official graduate transcripts, a summary and detailed budget for the doctoral project, and a signed statement of terms and conditions. **Deadline:** December 1.

**Remarks:** Scholarships are sponsored by the Institute for Scientific Information. All publications by the grantee relevant to the project should acknowledge MLA support, and MLA has the first right of review of any report deriving from the project. **Contact:** Professional Development Department at the above address (see entry 3630).

### • 3634 • MLA Research, Development, and Demonstration Project Grant *(Professional Development/Grant)*

**Purpose:** To provide qualified medical librarians with support for research opportunities. **Focus:** Medical Librarianship. **Qualif.:** Applicant must be a U.S. or Canadian citizen or permanent resident, a member of MLA, and a degree-holding, practicing medical librarian with at least two years of professional experience. In exceptional cases, however, consideration will be given to an outstanding candidate who does not meet the usual eligibility criteria. The Research, Development, and Demonstration Project Grant supports projects that promote excellence in the field of health science librarianship and the information sciences. Activities which are operational in nature or have only local usefulness are not eligible for funding.

**Funds Avail.:** $1,000 maximum. **To Apply:** Write to the Professional Development Department for application form and guidelines. **Deadline:** December 1. Award recipients will be notified in March.

**Remarks:** MLA also offers numerous awards in recognition of distinguished service and outstanding individual achievements in medical librarianship. Write to the Professional Development Department for further information. **Contact:** Professional Development Department at the above address (see entry 3630).

### • 3635 • MLA Scholarship *(Graduate/Scholarship)*

**Purpose:** To recognize and encourage students showing excellence in scholarship and potential for accomplishment in health sciences librarianship. **Focus:** Medical Librarianship. **Qualif.:** Candidate must be a citizen or permanent resident of the United States or Canada. Applicant must be entering a graduate library school accredited by the American Library Association, and have at least one-half of his/her academic requirements to complete during the year following the granting of the scholarship. Past recipients of MLA scholarships are ineligible.

**Funds Avail.:** $2,000. **No. of Awards:** 1. **To Apply:** Write to the Professional Development Department assistant for application form and guidelines. Submit form with three letters of reference, official transcripts, and a statement of career objectives. **Deadline:** December 1. Scholarship recipients are notified in April.

**Remarks:** MLA also offers numerous awards in recognition of distinguished service and outstanding individual achievements in medical librarianship. Write to the program services assistant for

further information. **Contact:** Professional Development Department at the above address (see entry 3630).

### • 3636 • MLA Scholarship for Minority Students
*(Graduate/Scholarship)*

**Purpose:** To recognize and encourage students showing excellence in scholarship and potential for accomplishment in health sciences librarianship. **Focus:** Medical Librarianship. **Qualif.:** Candidate must be a citizen or permanent resident of the United States or Canada and a member of one of the following minority groups: African-American, Asian, Hispanic, Native or Pacific Islander. Applicant must be entering a graduate library school accredited by the American Library Association, and have at least one-half of his/her academic requirements to complete during the year following the granting of the scholarship. Past recipients of MLA scholarships are ineligible.

**Funds Avail.:** $2,000. **No. of Awards:** 1. **To Apply:** Write to the Professional Development Department assistant for application form and guidelines. Submit form with three letters of reference, official transcripts, and a statement of career objectives. **Deadline:** December 1. Scholarship recipients are notified in April.

**Remarks:** MLA also offers numerous awards in recognition of distinguished service and outstanding individual achievements in medical librarianship. Write to the program services assistant for further information. **Contact:** Professional Development Department at the above address (see entry 3630).

### • 3637 •
**Medical Research Council of Canada**
Holland Cross, Tower B, 5th Fl.
1600 Scott St.
Postal Locator 3105A
Ottawa, ON, Canada K1A 0W9       *Ph:* (613)941-2672
*E-mail:* mrcinfocrm@hpb.hwc.ca      *Fax:* (613)954-1800
*URL:* http://www.hwc.ca:8100

### • 3638 • CLA/MRC Scholarships *(Postdoctorate/Scholarship)*

**Purpose:** To support a qualified investigator to work in the field of respiratory research. **Focus:** Medicine, Pulmonary Research. **Qualif.:** Applicants must be Canadian citizens or permanent residents of Canada. Candidates must have attained a M.D. or Ph.D. degree or the equivalent. Those who hold a university-level academic position are not eligible. **Criteria:** Recipients are selected by the Canadian Thoracic Society (CTS) research committee based on priority ratings provided by the MRC and subject to the approval of the CTS and the Canadian Lung Association (CLA) Board of Directors. Applicants are screened to ensure that the proposed research areas are appropriate to the goals of the CLA.

**Funds Avail.:** $50,000 plus an initial $15,000 establishment award. **No. of Awards:** 1. **To Apply:** Applications must be submitted on MRC form "19" to the MRC along with a letter of intent. Letters of intent must also be sent the CLA. **Deadline:** September 15 for applications to the MRC; August 3 for letters to the CLA.

**Remarks:** This scholarship is jointly funded by the Medical Research Council of Canada and the Canadian Lung Association.

### • 3639 • Medical Research Council Travel Grants
*(Professional Development/Grant)*

**Purpose:** To provide limited funds for Travel Grants to Canadian health scientists who wish to spend short periods of time (maximum length of stay is 30 days) in a specific laboratory for the purpose of furthering their research. **Qualif.:** The Council will not entertain applications from individual investigators for travel grants

to attend meetings, either in Canada or abroad. **To Apply:** The letter of application should include details of the planned visit, an explanation of how this visit relates to current research activity, the funds required, and current grant support. The application should also be accompanied by a letter of support from the host laboratory. **Deadline:** December 1 and March 1. **Contact:** The Medical Research Council of Canada at the above address (see entry 3637).

### • 3640 •
**Medical Society of New Jersey**
2 Princess Rd.                     *Ph:* (609)896-1766
Lawrenceville, NJ 08648            *Fax:* (609)896-1368

### • 3641 • MSNJ Medical Student Loan Fund
*(Doctorate/Loan)*

**Focus:** Medicine. **Qualif.:** Funding is available to medical students who have satisfactorily completed two years of an approved medical school in the United States or Canada. Candidates are United States citizens who have been bonafide residents of New Jersey for a minimum of five years prior to matriculation at medical school. The applicant must be a member of the Medical Society of New Jersey student association or join when the application is filed. Students must be of good moral character, of acceptable academic standing, and must be able to prove financial need.

**Funds Avail.:** Loans of up to $6,000 annually are repayable in four equal installments beginning two years after graduation from medical school. Further loans may be made with conditions similar to the initial loan repayment. Interest of 7 percent per annum is charged from the date of graduation. Each loan must be secured by a note co-signed by a responsible relative. In the event the borrower fails to complete medical school education, voluntarily or involuntarily, the loan or loans shall immediately become due and payable, with interest of 7 percent per annum from date of issuance. **No. of Awards:** 25. **Deadline:** March 31. **Contact:** David J. Greifinger, M.D., Chairman MSLF Committee at the above address (see entry 3640).

### • 3642 •
**Memorial Foundation for Jewish Culture**
15 East 26th St., Room 1703
New York, NY 10010                 *Ph:* (212)679-4074

### • 3643 • Community Service Scholarships *(Graduate, Undergraduate/Scholarship)*

**Purpose:** To support professional training for careers in Jewish education, Jewish social service, the rabbinate, shehita, and milah. **Focus:** Jewish Studies. **Qualif.:** Applicants may be of any nationality. Candidate must be pursuing professional training in a field that will prepare him/her for a career of service to the Jewish community. Scholarship recipients must commit themselves after their training to serve in a deprived Diaspora community outside Israel, The United States or Canada, where professional personnel are urgently needed.

**Funds Avail.:** $1,000-2,500. **To Apply:** Write to the Foundation for application form and guidelines. **Deadline:** November 30. Notification in August. **Contact:** Dr. Jerry Hochbaum at the above address (see entry 3642).

*Memorial Foundation for Jewish Culture (continued)*

**• 3644 • International Doctoral Scholarships for Studies Specializing in Jewish Fields** *(Doctorate/Scholarship)*

**Purpose:** To help train qualified individuals for careers in Jewish scholarship and research, and to help Jewish educational, religious, and communal workers obtain advanced training for leadership positions. **Focus:** Jewish Studies. **Qualif.:** Applicants may be of any nationality and enrolled in a doctoral program at a recognized university, and be specializing in a Jewish field. **Criteria:** Priority is given to applicants who are at the dissertation level.

**Funds Avail.:** $1,000-5,000. **To Apply:** Write to the Foundation for application materials. **Deadline:** October 31 for submission of completed application. Notification in August. **Contact:** Dr. Jerry Hochbaum at the above address (see entry 3642).

**• 3645 • International Fellowships in Jewish Studies** *(Professional Development/Fellowship)*

**Purpose:** To assist independent scholarly, literary or art projects that contribute to the understanding, preservation, enhancement, or transmission of Jewish Culture. **Focus:** Jewish Studies. **Qualif.:** Applicant may be of any nationality. Candidate must be a qualified scholar, researcher, or artist who possesses the knowledge and experience to formulate and implement a project in a field of Jewish specialization.

**Funds Avail.:** $1,000-4,000. **To Apply:** Write to the Foundation for application form and guidelines. **Deadline:** October 31. Notification in August. **Contact:** Dr. Jerry Hochbaum at the above address (see entry 3642).

**• 3646 • Post-Rabbinic Scholarships** *(Graduate, Professional Development/Scholarship)*

**Purpose:** To assist newly ordained rabbis with advanced training. **Focus:** Jewish Studies, Rabbinical Training. **Qualif.:** Applicant may be of any nationality. Candidate must be a recently ordained rabbi who is enrolled full-time in graduate study at a rabbinical seminary, yeshiva, or other institution of higher Jewish learning. Applicant must be seeking further training for a career as a judge on a rabbinical court (dayanim), a head of an institution of higher learning, or in another advanced religious leadership position.

**Funds Avail.:** $2,000-3,000. **To Apply:** Write to the Foundation for application form and guidelines. **Deadline:** November 30. **Contact:** Dr. Jerry Hochbaum at the above address (see entry 3642).

**• 3647 •**
**Mercantile Bank of Topeka**
c/o Trust Dept.
PO Box 192
Topeka, KS 66601-0192

**• 3648 • Claude & Ina Brey Scholarships** *(Undergraduate/Scholarship)*

**Focus:** General Studies. **Qualif.:** Applicants must be fourth-degree Kansas Grange members who are enrolled in an accredited college or university or an approved trade school.

**Funds Avail.:** $500. **No. of Awards:** 8. **To Apply:** Apply through local grange chapter. **Deadline:** April 15. **Contact:** Pat West, R.R. 2, Box 23, Mound City, KS 66056; or any local Kansas Grange chapter for application information.

**• 3649 •**
**Merit Gasoline Foundation**
551 W. Lancaster Ave.
Haverford, PA 19041

**• 3650 • Merit Gasoline Foundation College Scholarships** *(Undergraduate/Scholarship)*

**Qualif.:** Applicants must be children or stepchildren of full-time employees of the Merit Oil Corporation and/or its affiliates for at least two consecutive years prior to June 1 of the year in which the scholarship is to be awarded. A full-time employee is defined as one who works thirty-five hours per week or more. Also eligible are sons, daughters, or stepchildren of employees who are retired under the company's pension plan, totally disabled due to an accident or illness under the wage continuation program, or deceased yet fully qualified prior to death. Applicants must graduate from an accredited public, private, or parochial high school and be entering their first, second, third, or fourth years of college. Scholarships may be used only for full-time study in an undergraduate program of at least two years duration at an accredited United States college, university, junior college, or community college. **Criteria:** Selection is based upon financial need, academic achievement, SAT scores, evaluation of character, quality of leadership, work habits, and general interests.

**Funds Avail.:** Up to four new scholarships are awarded each year. They range in value from $1,000 to $3,000 per year, depending on the financial need of the recipient. The winners will continue to receive their awards for their sophomore, junior, and senior years, providing they remain students in good standing and advance during the previous year toward a designated degree. A total of up to $12,000 can be awarded over a period of four years to each scholarship winner. **To Apply:** Application must be requested. Students who apply but are not selected can reapply the following year by simply submitting copies of their college transcript. **Deadline:** May 15. **Contact:** Executive Director, Merit Gasoline Foundation College Scholarship Program, at the above address (see entry 3649).

**• 3651 •**
**Metropolitan Museum of Art**
1000 5th Ave.
New York, NY 10028-0198

*Ph:* (212)570-3710
*Fax:* (212)570-3972

**• 3652 • The Classical Fellowship; The Norbert Schimmel Fellowship for Mediterranean Art and Archaeology** *(Doctorate/Fellowship)*

**Purpose:** To support doctoral students who would benefit from using the resources of the Museum's Ancient Near Eastern Art or Greek and Roman Art Departments. **Focus:** Ancient Near Eastern Art and Archaeology, Greek Art, Roman Art. **Qualif.:** The Classical Fellowship is not open to students of ancient Near Eastern art; all other requirements are the same for both awards. Applicant may be of any nationality, but must be an outstanding graduate student who is enrolled in a doctoral program at a U.S. university, and who has submitted a dissertation proposal dealing with ancient Near Eastern, Greek or Roman art. The thesis outline must already have been accepted by the candidate's advisor at the time of application for the fellowship. Fellowships are tenable at the Museum's departments of Ancient Near Eastern and Greek and Roman art. The fellow will be expected to participate in ongoing activities of the sponsoring department, and will devote approximately one-half of tenure to administrative and art historical curatorial duties. The fellow will also be required to give a gallery talk.

**Funds Avail.:** $15,000/year stipend, plus a $2,500 travel grant. **No. of Awards:** Two. **To Apply:** Before applying, contact the Ancient Near Eastern or Greek and Roman department to discuss research proposal. The department must approve the proposal before application will be considered by the grants committee. There is no application form. Submit three copies of the following to the grants committee: a full resume of education and employment, undergraduate and graduate transcripts, a research proposal, a tentative schedule of work to be accomplished during the fellowship period, and a list of other applications for grants and fellowships during the same period. Three letters of recommendation (including at least one professional and one academic) should be sent directly from the referees to the committee. **Deadline:** Mid-November. Fellowships are announced in late February. **Contact:** Pia Quintano, Fellowship Program, at the above address (see entry 3651).

• **3653** • **The Cloisters Summer Internship Program for College Students** *(Undergraduate/Internship)*

**Purpose:** To provide interns with the opportunity to work with the Education Department of the Cloisters, the branch museum of the Metropolitan Museum of Art devoted to the art of medieval Europe. **Qualif.:** Undergraduate college students, in particular first or second year, who are interested in art and museum careers and who enjoy working with children. Non U.S. citizens must offer proof of alien status which permits them to work in the U.S.

**Funds Avail.:** An honorarium of $2,250 is awarded. **To Apply:** Inquiries and all correspondence should be addressed to the College Internship Program, The Cloisters, Fort Tryon Park, New York NY 10040. **Deadline:** February 6.

• **3654** • **Chester Dale Fellowships** *(Postgraduate/ Fellowship)*

**Purpose:** To support individuals whose fields of study are related to the fine arts of the western worlds and who are preferably American citizens under the age of 40.

**Funds Avail.:** Grants are given for research at the Metropolitan Museum. **To Apply:** There are no application forms. Applicants must submit a typed application in triplicate including the following: full resume of education and employment; a two-part statement (not to exceed 1,000 words)specifying what the applicant wishes to accomplish during the fellowship period and detailing how the Museum's resources can be utilized to accomplish the goals; tentative schedule of work to be accomplished and travel required during the fellowship; three letters of recommendation (at least one academic and one professional); list of other applications for fellowships or grants applied for in the same period; and official undergraduate and graduate transcripts original transcripts plus two copies (pre-doctoral applicants only).

• **3655** • **Roswell L. Gilpatric Internship** *(Graduate, Undergraduate/Internship)*

**Qualif.:** College juniors, seniors, recent graduates, and graduate students showing special interest in museum careers will receive consideration for this award. The successful candidates will participate in the college or graduate program.

**Funds Avail.:** An honorarium of $2,500 is awarded to college students; $2,750 for graduate students. **To Apply:** There is no need to submit a separate application.

**Remarks:** Made possible by the Thorne Foundation.

• **3656** • **Lifchez/Stronach Curatorial Internship** *(Graduate/Internship)*

**Purpose:** To award a student who has recently graduated from college or is enrolled in an Art History M.A. program and would use the internship to continue in a career in Art History. **Qualif.:** The student should come from a background of financial need or other disadvantage that might jeopardize his or her pursuing such a career without this support.

**Funds Avail.:** An honorarium of $15,000 is awarded. **Deadline:** January 29.

**Remarks:** Made possible by Mr. Raymond Lifchez and Mrs. Judith L. Stronach.

• **3657** • **Andrew W. Mellon Fellowships** *(Postdoctorate/Fellowship)*

**Purpose:** To support commendable research projects related to the Museum's collections. **Qualif.:** For young doctoral scholars as well as for distinguished visiting scholars from this country and abroad who can serve as teachers and advisors and make their expertise available to catalogue and refine the collections.

**Funds Avail.:** $26,000 stipend for senior fellows and $3,000 for travel. R One year or on a short-term basis.

• **3658** • **Andrew W. Mellon Fellowships in Art History** *(Doctorate, Postdoctorate/Fellowship)*

**Purpose:** To support scholars with research projects related to the Museum's collections. **Focus:** Art History, Museum Studies. **Qualif.:** Applicant may be of any nationality. Candidate should have earned the doctorate or have completed substantial work toward the degree. Fellowships are open to both promising young scholars whose research is related to the Museum's collections, and to distinguished visiting scholars who can serve as teachers and advisors and make their expertise available to catalogue and refine the collections. Fellows are expected to spend most of the award tenure at the Museum. Predoctoral fellows will be expected to participate in ongoing activities of the Museum department most closely related to their field of study, and will devote approximately one-half of their time to administrative and art historical curatorial duties. Predoctoral fellows will also be required to give a gallery talk.

**Funds Avail.:** Predoctoral fellowships: $15,000/year; senior fellowships: $25,000/year. Fellows are also granted $2,500 for travel. **No. of Awards:** 11. **To Apply:** Before applying, contact the Museum department most closely related to field of study to discuss research proposal. The department must approve the proposal before application will be considered by the grants committee. There is no application form. Submit three copies of the following to the grants committee: a full resume of education and employment, undergraduate and graduate transcripts, a research proposal, a tentative schedule of work to be accomplished during the fellowship period, and a list of other applications for grants and fellowships during the same period. Three letters of recommendation (including at least one professional and one academic) should be sent directly from the referees to the committee. **Deadline:** Varies; usually mid-November. Fellowships are announced in late February. **Contact:** Pia Quintano, Fellowship Program, at the above address (see entry 3651).

• **3659** • **Andrew W. Mellon Fellowships in Conservation** *(Postdoctorate, Professional Development/ Fellowship)*

**Purpose:** To support scholars who wish to learn conservation skills at the Museum. **Focus:** Arms and Armor Conservation, Asian Art Conservation, Costume Conservation, Musical Instrument Conservation, Objects Conservation (including Archaeological Objects, Ceramics, Furniture, Glass, Metalwork, Sculpture), Paintings Conservation, Paper Conservation, Textile Conservation. **Qualif.:** Applicant may be of any nationality. Whenever possible, applicant for the Mellon Fellowship should have reached an advanced level of experience or training in art conservation. Previous training and experience is not required for applicants in Asian Art conservation. All fellows are expected to spend the fellowship in residence in the Museum department with which they are affiliated.

**Funds Avail.:** Stipend appropriate to level of expertise. Additional funds may be available for travel, books, photographs and other

## Metropolitan Museum of Art *(continued)*

reasonable or necessary expenses incident to the fellowship. **No. of Awards:** Three. **To Apply:** Before applying, contact the Museum conservation department most closely related to field of study to discuss research proposal. The department must approve the proposal before application will be considered by the grants committee. There is no application form. Submit two copies of the following to the grants committee: a full resume of education and employment, undergraduate and graduate transcripts, a research proposal, a tentative schedule of work to be accomplished during the fellowship period, and a list of other applications for grants and fellowships during the same period. Three letters of recommendation (including at least one professional and one academic) should be sent directly from the referees to the committee. **Deadline:** January 7. Fellowships are announced mid-March. **Contact:** Fellowships Administrator, at the above address (see entry 3651).

### • 3660 • Metropolitan Museum of Art Classical Fellowship *(Doctorate/Fellowship)*

**Qualif.:** Recipient will be an outstanding graduate student who has been admitted to the doctoral program of a university in the U.S., and who has submitted an outline of a thesis dealing with either Greek or Roman art. The thesis outline must already have been accepted by the applicant's advisor at the time of application for the fellowship. **Criteria:** Preference will be given to the applicant who, in the opinion of the Grants Committee, will profit most from utilizing the resources of the Department of Greek and Roman Art. **To Apply:** There are no application forms. Applicants must submit a typed application in triplicate including the following: name, home, and present address and phone number; full resume of education and employment; official undergraduate and graduate transcripts; a two-part statement, not to exceed 1000 words, specifying what the applicant wishes to accomplish during the fellowship period, and detailing how the Museum's resources can be utilized to accomplish the applicant's goals; tentative schedule of work to be accomplished and travel required during the fellowship period; three letters of recommendation (at least one academic and one professional); list of other applications for fellowships or grants applied for in the same period. **Deadline:** November. **Contact:** Fellowship Program, Office of Academic Programs at the above address (see entry 3651).

### • 3661 • Metropolitan Museum of Art Nine-Month Internship *(Graduate, Undergraduate/Internship)*

**Qualif.:** Applicants must be disadvantaged, minority residents of New York state who are graduating seniors, recent graduates, or graduate students in art history, arts administration, conservation, or art education. Interns are assigned to one or more of the Museum's departments, where they work on projects that match their academic background, professional skills, and career goals.

**Funds Avail.:** Three internships with an honorarium of $12,000. Internships include full-time, five-day, 35-hour week work programs for nine month durations. **To Apply:** There is no official application form. A typed application, specifying the internship or internships for which they would like to be considered, should include the following: the applicant's name, home and school address, and telephone numbers; a full resume of education and employment; two academic recommendations; official transcripts of grades; a separate list of art-history courses taken; a list of knowledge of foreign languages; an essay of 500 words or less describing the applicant's career goals, interest in museum work, and reasons for applying to the internship program. **Deadline:** February 5. A small group of students are selected for an interview in March. Final notification to all applicants is in April.

**Remarks:** The internship is funded by the Edward and Sally Van Lier Fund at the New York Community Trust. **Contact:** Linda Komaroff at the above address (see entry 3651).

### • 3662 • Metropolitan Museum of Art Six Month Internship *(Graduate, Undergraduate/Internship)*

**Purpose:** To provide interns with learning experiences in the Museum's departments, where they work on projects that match their academic background, professional skills, and career goals. **Qualif.:** Graduating college seniors, recent graduates, or graduate students in art history or related fields may apply. The program is directed toward students who have demonstrated financial need and is intended to promote greater diversity in the national pool of future museum professionals.

**Funds Avail.:** $10,000. **To Apply:** The application essay should include some discussion of how the aforementioned goal of diversity may be met. **Deadline:** January 29.

**Remarks:** Made possible by The Altman Foundation.

### • 3663 • Metropolitan Museum of Art Summer Internship for College Students *(Undergraduate/Internship)*

**Qualif.:** Applicants must be college juniors, seniors, and recent graduates who have not yet entered graduate school, and who have a strong background in art history. Freshmen and sophomores are not eligible. Interns work on departmental projects (curatorial, administration, or education), give gallery talks, and work at the Visitor Information Center.

**Funds Avail.:** An honorarium of $2,500. **To Apply:** There is no official application form. A typed application, specifying the internship or internships for which one would like to be considered, should include the following: the applicant's name, home and school address, and telephone numbers; a full resume of education and employment; two academic recommendations; official transcripts of grades; a separate list of art-history courses taken; a list of knowledge of foreign languages; an essay of 500 words or less describing the applicant's career goals, interest in museum work, and reasons for applying to the internship program. **Deadline:** January 15. A small group of students are selected for an interview in March. Final notification to all applicants is in April.

**Remarks:** The internship is funded by the Altman Foundation, by Francine LeFrak, and the Ittleson Foundation, Inc.

### • 3664 • Metropolitan Museum of Art Summer Internship for Graduate Students *(Graduate/Internship)*

**Qualif.:** Applicants must have completed at least one year of graduate work in art history or in an allied field, and intend to pursue careers in art museums. The intern's work may include research and writing related to the Museum's collections or to a special exhibition. The work is based upon the applicant's background, interests, and the availability of projects.

**Funds Avail.:** An honorarium of $2,750. **To Apply:** There is no official application form. A typed application, specifying the internship or internships for which one would like to be considered, should include the following: the applicant's name, home and school address, and telephone numbers; a full resume of education and employment; two academic recommendations; an official transcripts of grades; a separate list of art-history courses taken; a list of knowledge of foreign languages; an essay of 500 words or less describing the applicant's career goals, interest in museum work, and reasons for applying to the internship program. **Deadline:** January 22.

**Remarks:** The internship is funded in part by the Solow Art and Architecture Foundation.

### • 3665 • Metropolitan Museum of Art Volunteer Internships *(Graduate, Undergraduate/Internship)*

**Qualif.:** Applicants must be college students, recent graduates, or graduate students.

**Funds Avail.:** Unpaid, volunteer internships on a full or part-time basis. The number of positions varies according to departmental needs, and opportunities range from two months to nine months. Academic credit may be arranged for interns at their schools' discretion. **To Apply:** There is no official application form. A typed application must include the following: the applicant's name, home and school address, and telephone numbers; a full resume of education and employment; two academic recommendations; official transcripts of grades; a separate list of art-history courses taken; a cover letter describing specific areas within the Museum of interest to the applicant, precise dates of proposed internship, and the number of hours per week the applicant is able to work. Some students will be selected for an interview at the Museum. **Deadline:** Applications must be made at least one month prior to the proposed starting date. **Contact:** Internship Programs at the above address (see entry 3651).

### • 3666 • J. Clawson Mills Scholarships
*(Postdoctorate/Fellowship)*

**Purpose:** To support study at the Metropolitan Museum of Art. **Qualif.:** For mature scholars of demonstrated ability in any branch of the fine arts relating to the Museum's collections.

**Funds Avail.:** Stipend of $26,000 for senior fellows. R One year, with the possibility of a second.

### • 3667 • Theodore Rousseau Fellowships *(Doctorate, Graduate/Fellowship)*

**Purpose:** To develop the skills of connoisseurship by supporting first-hand examination of paintings in major European collections rather than by supporting library research. **Qualif.:** Awarded for the training of students whose goal is to enter museums as curators of painting. Applicants should have been enrolled for at least one year in an advanced degree program in the field of art history.

**Funds Avail.:** Stipend of $18,000 for pre-doctoral fellows. R Short term fellowships of at least three months will be considered along with 12 month requests. All fellowships must take place between September 1 and August 31.

### • 3668 • Starr Fellowships in Asian Paintings Conservation *(Professional Development/Fellowship)*

**Purpose:** To provide training in the conservation and mounting of Asian paintings. **Focus:** Asian Art Conservation. **Qualif.:** Applicant may be of any nationality, but must wish to study the mounting, conservation, and restoration of hanging scrolls, handscrolls, folding screens, prints, albums, books, etc. The fellow is expected to spend the fellowship in residence in the department of Asian art conservation.

**Funds Avail.:** Varies. **No. of Awards:** Varies. **To Apply:** Before applying, contact the Museum's department of Asian art conservation to discuss research proposal. The department must approve the proposal before application will be considered. There is no application form. Submit a resume of education and professional experience and three letters of recommendation (including at least one professional and one academic) to the department of Asian art conservation. A personal interview is required. **Deadline:** None. **Contact:** Sondra M. Castile, Asian Art Conservation, at the above address (see entry 3651).

### • 3669 • Polaire Weissman Fund Fellowship
*(Doctorate, Graduate/Fellowship)*

**Purpose:** To support research by scholars who are interested in pursuing careers related to costume history and conservation. **Focus:** Costume History and Conservation. **Qualif.:** Applicant may be of any nationality, but must be a graduate student, preferable studying fine arts or costume history. Candidate must intend to pursue a museum, teaching, or other professional career (including conservation) related to costume. Fellows will be expected to participate in ongoing activities of the Costume institute and will devote approximately one-half of their time to administrative and

art historical curatorial duties. Fellows will also be required to give a gallery talk.

**Funds Avail.:** Stipend appropriate to level of training plus additional funds for travel, books, photographs and other reasonable or necessary expenses incident to the fellowship. **No. of Awards:** One. **To Apply:** Before applying, contact the Costume Institute to discuss research proposal. The Institute must approve the proposal before application will be considered by the grants committee. There are no application forms. Submit three copies of the following to the grants committee: a full resume of education and employment, undergraduate and graduate transcripts, a research proposal, a tentative schedule of work to be accomplished during the fellowship period, and a list of the applications for grants and fellowships during the same period. Three letters or recommendation (including at least one professional and one academic) should be sent directly from the referees to the committee. **Deadline:** January 7. Fellowships are given biennially. The next Fellowship will be awarded in 1996-97. **Contact:** Pia Quintano, Fellowships in Conservation, at the above address (see entry 3651).

### • 3670 • Polaire Weissman Fund *(Graduate/Fellowship)*

**Purpose:** To provide biennial fellowships to qualified graduate students. **Qualif.:** Students who preferably will have completed graduate studies in the fine arts or studies in costume, and who are interested in pursuing costume history in a museum or teaching career, or other career (including conservation) related to the field of costume.

**Funds Avail.:** A maximum stipend of $18,000 is awarded. R Nine months.

### • 3671 • Jane and Morgan Whitney Fellowships *(Graduate, Postdoctorate, Postgraduate/Fellowship)*

**Purpose:** To support study, work, or research at the Metropolitan Museum. **Qualif.:** Students of the Fine Arts whose fields are related to the Museum's collections. **Criteria:** Preference is given to students in the decorative arts who are under 40 years of age.

**Funds Avail.:** Stipend of $26,000 for senior fellows and $18,000 for pre-doctoral fellows, with an additional $3,000 for travel. R One year, with the possibility of renewal.

---

### • 3672 •
**Mexican American Grocers Association Foundation**
405 N. San Fernanado Rd.    *Ph:* (213)227-1565
Los Angeles, CA 90031    *Fax:* (213)227-6935

### • 3673 • Mexican American Grocers Association Foundation Scholarships *(Undergraduate/Scholarship)*

**Focus:** Business Administration. **Qualif.:** Applicants must be Hispanic undergraduate students attending two- or four-year accredited colleges or universities majoring in business administration or a business related field. They must also be entering at least their sophomore year of study, have a minimum GPA of 2.5, and demonstrate genuine financial need. **To Apply:** Applicants must submit a completed application with official transcripts and a copy of Student Aid Application for California, or appropriate financial aid application for state in which the student resides. **Deadline:** All applications must be postmarked between June 1 and July 31.

**Remarks:** Each applicant must submit a SASE. Fax requests will not he honored. **Contact:** Mexican American Grocers Association Foundation at the above address (see entry 3672).

**Mexican American Legal Defense and Educational Fund**
634 S. Spring St., 11th Fl.                 Ph: (213)629-8016
Los Angeles, CA 90014                       Fax: (213)629-0226
E-mail: MALDEFone@aol.com
URL: http://www.MALDEF.org

• 3675 •  MALDEF Scholarships (Graduate/
Scholarship)

**Purpose:** To support Hispanic American law students. **Focus:** Law. **Qualif.:** Applicants must be U.S. citizens or residents of Hispanic descent and enrolled in, or about to begin, a law degree program at an accredited institution. **Criteria:** Selection is based on the applicant's active work with the Latino community, financial need and academic achievement.

**Funds Avail.:** $1,000. **No. of Awards:** 15. **To Apply:** Write to the program director for application guidelines. **Deadline:** June 30.

**Remarks:** MALDEF also awards the Valerie Kantor Memorial Scholarship, valued at $2,000. There is no separate application process: all candidates for general MALDEF scholarships will also be considered for the Kantor Memorial Scholarship. **Contact:** Scholarship Program, at the above address (see entry 3674).

• 3676 •

**Allen H. Meyers Foundation**
PO Box 100
Tecumseh, MI 49286                          Ph: (517)423-7629

• 3677 •  Allen H. Meyers Scholarship
(Undergraduate/Scholarship)

**Purpose:** To encourage, support, and stimulate scientific education, teaching, research, and related efforts in areas such as engineering and aerospace studies and design, and to provide early financial support for young men and women interested in college education for scientific careers and teaching. **Qualif.:** Candidates must be students attending Lenawee County schools who are planning college studies in the sciences and allied fields; for example, the natural sciences, science teaching, medicine, chemistry, engineering, aeronautics, and space studies. Students having grades permitting college entrance may apply.

**Funds Avail.:** Amounts are variable. Awards are made once to any individual and are only renewable under unusual circumstances. **To Apply:** Application forms are available only upon request from the Lenawee intermediate School District. **Deadline:** March 15.

• 3678 •

**Michigan Association for Deaf, Hearing, and Speech Services**
2929 Covington Ct., Ste. 200               Ph: (517)487-0066
Lansing, MI 48912-4939                      Fax: (517)487-2586
                                            Free: 800-YOUR-
                                                  EAR

E-mail: yourear@pilot.msu.edu
URL: http://www.madhs.org

• 3679 •  Michigan Association for Deaf, Hearing, and Speech Services Scholarships (Undergraduate/ Scholarship)

**Purpose:** To provide financial assistance for post secondary education to students with hearing and/or speech impairments as

determined by an Individual Education Plan Committee (IEPC). **Focus:** General Studies. **Qualif.:** Applicants must be speech or hearing impaired high school seniors with United States citizenship and Michigan residency who demonstrate leadership by contributing to the community through some form of community service. **Criteria:** Selection is based on an essay discussing community service and academic achievement.

**Funds Avail.:** Two $500 scholarships annually. **No. of Awards:** 2. **To Apply:** The completed application must be signed by an IEPC representative and be accompanied by a one-page essay. **Deadline:** March 1. **Contact:** Katherine Draper at the above address (see entry 3678).

• 3680 •

**Michigan Commission for the Blind**
Michigan Department of Labor
201 N. Washington Sq.
PO Box 30015
Lansing, MI 48909                           Ph: (517)373-2062
URL: http://ncats.newaygo.mi.us/mac/agencies/local/
micommblind.html

• 3681 •  Roy Johnson Trust Graduate School Grants (Graduate/Grant)

**Purpose:** To assist blind graduate students studying in Michigan. **Focus:** General. **Qualif.:** Applicants must be legally blind and must have earned a bachelor's degree from an accredited college in the United States. Grants must be used to pursue graduate studies at an accredited institution in Michigan. Awards are made for tuition.

**Funds Avail.:** $500-1,500. **To Apply:** Candidates should write to the Commission for application form and guidelines and then submit form with proof of acceptance to a Michigan institution, a copy of bachelor's degree, graduate school transcripts, two letters of recommendation from undergraduate or graduate faculty, and an evaluation report from an ophthalmologist or optometrist stating diagnosis. **Deadline:** May 31. **Contact:** Sue Wilson, Coordinator or James Buscetta, Admin.

• 3682 •

**Michigan Commission on Indian Affairs**
741 W. Cedar St., Ste. 102                 Ph: (517)334-8632
Lansing, MI 48913                           Fax: (517)334-8641
URL: http://www2.cic.net/~dennis/mcia-2htm

• 3683 •  Michigan Indian Tuition Waiver (Graduate, Undergraduate/Other)

**Purpose:** To provide free tuition for North American Indians to attend public state community, public junior colleges, public colleges, or public universities. **Qualif.:** Applicants must be Michigan residents for 12 consecutive months and must have not less than one-quarter blood quantum as certified by the applicant's tribal association and verified by the Bureau of Indian Affairs. They must also attend a Michigan public community college or university.

**Funds Avail.:** Cost of tuition.

**Remarks:** The tuition waiver program covers part-time and summer school students. This program only guarantees tuition payment, not admission. Admission is determined by individual schools. **Contact:** College or University financial-aid office.

**• 3684 •**

## Michigan Higher Education Assistance Authority

Office of Scholarships and Grants
PO Box 30462                          *Ph:* (517)373-3394
Lansing, MI 48909                     *Free:* 888-4-GRANTS
*URL:* http://www.treas.state.mi.us/college/mheaa.htm

**• 3685 •   Michigan Competitive Scholarships**
*(Undergraduate/Scholarship)*

**Focus:** General Studies. **Qualif.:** Applicants must be United States citizens, permanent residents, or approved refugees, and Michigan residents who have achieved a qualifying score on the ACT. If a student has not taken the ACT for the Competitive Scholarship Program, they may do so if they have not had college experience. Applicants must also demonstrate financial need, attend an eligible Michigan college at least half-time, and not have a Bachelor's degree. Recipients may not concurrently receive state scholarship and tuition grant assistance. **Criteria:** Selections are based on recommendations by an appropriate educational institution, academic achievement, and financial need.

**Funds Avail.:** Awards range from a minimum of $100 to a maximum of the amount of demonstrated financial need, the school's tuition, or the stated annual maximum amount established by the Michigan Higher Education Assistance Authority. **To Apply:** Applicants must complete the Free Application for Federal Student Aid (FAFSA) from the high school guidance office or the college financial aid office. When filling out the FAFSA, applicants should list first the highest cost Michigan college they plan to attend. **Deadline:** High school seniors should mail their FAFSA by February 15 for priority consideration; college students should mail their FAFSA by March 15 for priority consideration. Late applicants are considered if the funds are available. **Contact:** Michigan Higher Education Assistance Authority at the above address (see entry 3684).

**• 3686 •   Michigan Tuition Grants** *(Graduate, Undergraduate/Grant)*

**Focus:** General Studies. **Qualif.:** Applicants must be United States citizens, permanent residents, or approved refugees, and Michigan residents. Applicants must also demonstrate financial need, attend an eligible degree-granting Michigan college at least half-time. Recipients may not concurrently receive state scholarship and tuition grant assistance. Applicants may be undergraduate or graduate students. Students enrolled in a program leading to a degree in theology, divinity, or religious education are not eligible. **Criteria:** Selections are based on financial need.

**Funds Avail.:** Awards are restricted to tuition. Undergraduate Tuition Grants are limited to attainment of a degree or up to ten semesters or fifteen terms of assistance. Graduate level students may receive up to six semesters or nine terms of assistance, and graduate dental students, eight semesters or twelve terms. **To Apply:** Applicants must complete the Free Application for Federal Student Aid (FAFSA) from the high school guidance office or the college financial aid office. When filling out the FAFSA, applicants should list first the highest cost Michigan college they plan to attend. **Deadline:** High school seniors should mail their FAFSA by February 15 for priority consideration; college students should mail their FAFSA by March 15 for priority consideration. Late applicants are considered if the funds are available. **Contact:** High school counselor, college financial aid administrator, or Michigan Higher Education Assistance Authority at the above address (see entry 3684).

**• 3687 •**

## Michigan Higher Education Assistance Authoriy - Michigan Guaranty Agency

PO Box 30047                          *Ph:* (517)373-0760
Lansing, MI 48909                     *Fax:* (517)335-5983
                                      *Free:* 800-642-5626

*E-mail:* MGA@state.mi.us

**• 3688 •   Federal Consolidation Loan Program** *(All/Loan)*

**Purpose:** To provide access to postsecondary educational opportunities through low-interest, long-term educational loans. **Focus:** General Studies. **Qualif.:** Students must be Michigan residents who are in repayment status or in the grace period preceding repayment. **To Apply:** Applications are available from any financial aid office or lender.

**Remarks:** Federal Consolidation Loans have a fixed interest rate for the term of the loan. The rate is the weighted average of all loans being consolidated, rounded up to the nearest 1/8 of one percent. This agency also services the U.S. Department of Education Federal Education Loan Programs (i.e., Stafford/PLUS, etc.). **Contact:** Michigan Guaranty Agency Customer Relations at 800-642-5626, ext. 77009 for further information.

**• 3689 •**

## Michigan League for Nursing

33150 Schoolcraft Rd., No. 201        *Ph:* (734)427-1900
Livonia, MI 48150-1646                *Fax:* (734)427-0104

**• 3690 •   Michigan League for Nursing Student Achievement Scholarship Awards** *(Undergraduate/Scholarship)*

**Purpose:** To recognize individuals who have made significant academic, professional, and community contributions. **Focus:** Nursing. **Qualif.:** Candidates must be enrolled in an undergraduate nursing program in the state of Michigan (generic or degree completion) and have successfully completed two nursing courses. They must have a minimum overall grade point average of 3.0, be a member of the MLN, and be endorsed by one nursing faculty member and one personal reference. **Criteria:** Award winners will be selected on the basis of the completed application and essay, and the entries will be judged by MLN's Council on Nursing Education. Winners will be announced at MLN's annual membership meeting.

**Funds Avail.:** Scholarship funds vary. **To Apply:** A formal application and a short essay on a topic to be determined by the MLN are required. **Deadline:** January 15. **Contact:** Michelle Henry, Michigan League For Nursing, at the above address (see entry 3689). Toll-free telephone: 800-242-0189.

## Michigan Society of Fellows
University of Michigan
915 E. Washington St.  Ph: (734)763-1259
Ann Arbor, MI 48109-1070  Fax: (734)763-2447
E-mail: society.of.fellows@umich.edu
URL: http://www.rackham.umich.edu/Faculty/society.htm

**• 3692 •  Michigan Society Postdoctoral Fellowships**
*(Postdoctorate/Fellowship)*

**Purpose:** To provide financial and intellectual support for individuals selected for outstanding achievement, professional promise, and interdisciplinary interests. **Focus:** General Studies. **Qualif.:** Candidate may be of any nationality. Applicant must have completed the Ph.D. degree, or its professional or artistic equivalent, within the three years prior to the application. Fellowships are tenable at the University of Michigan; fellows are appointed as assistant professors in an appropriate University department and as postdoctoral scholars in the Society. Fellows spend the equivalent of one academic year teaching; the balance of their time is devoted to independent scholarly research and creative work and to participation in the intellectual life of the Society.

**Funds Avail.:** $36,000/year (2/3 stipend; 1/3 salary). **No. of Awards:** Four. **To Apply:** Write to the Society for application materials. **Deadline:** October 9. **Contact:** Luan McCarty Briefer, Administrative Assistant, at the above address (see entry 3691).

## Michigan Veterans Trust Fund
611 North Ottawa Bldg., 3rd Fl.  Ph: (517)335-1629
Lansing, MI 48913  Fax: (517)335-1631

**• 3694 •  Michigan Veterans Trust Educational Tuition Grants** *(Undergraduate/Grant)*

**Focus:** General Studies. **Qualif.:** Applicants must be between the ages of 16 and 22, residents of the state of Michigan for the preceding 12 months, and the offspring of a Michigan veteran who was killed, died as a result of service-connected disabilities, or is rated at 100 percent disabled because of injuries sustained while in the Armed Forces of the U.S. Applicants must also be admitted to a Michigan tax-support institution of higher education. Students need to maintain at least a 2.25 cumulative GPA.

**Funds Avail.:** Tuition or any other fees that take the place of tuition. **Contact:** Mary Kay Flitton at the above address (see entry 3693).

## Microscopy Society of America
Fax: (312)644-8557
435 N. Michigan Ave., Ste. 1717
Chicago, IL 60611-4067  Free: 800-538-3672
E-mail: businessoffice@msa.microscopy.com
URL: http://www.msa.microscopy.com

**• 3696 •  MSA Presidential Student Awards**
*(Graduate, Undergraduate/Award)*

**Purpose:** To recognize outstanding original research by students. **Focus:** Biological and Clinical Sciences—Microscopy, Physical Sciences—Microscopy. **Qualif.:** Candidate may be of any nationality, but must be enrolled at a recognized college or university in the United States at the time of the MSA annual meeting. Applicant must be the first author of a paper based on original research in a biological or physical field of microscopy. The paper must be sponsored by a member of MSA, preferably the candidate's professor. Award recipient is required to present his/her paper at a scientific session of the MSA annual meeting.

**Funds Avail.:** Registration and round-trip travel to the MSA annual meeting, plus a stipend to defray lodging and other expenses, and a copy of the Proceedings. **No. of Awards:** Up to 20. **To Apply:** Write to MSA for application form and guidelines. Submit form with abstract to the MSA Annual Meeting Office. **Deadline:** February 15. **Contact:** Alternate phone number: 800-538-EMSA.

**• 3697 •  MSA Undergraduate Research Scholarships**
*(Undergraduate/Scholarship)*

**Purpose:** To foster the educational and research potential of full-time undergraduates interested in pursuing microscopy as a career or major research tool. **Focus:** Science Technologies, Physical Sciences, Biological and Clinical Sciences. **Qualif.:** Applicants must be full-time undergraduate students. Applicants must be juniors or seniors.

**Funds Avail.:** Up to $2,500 each. Fewer awards may be made depending on the quality of applications and applicants. The maximum total awarded will be $10,000 per year. **To Apply:** Completed application forms should include a research proposal of no more than three pages in length; a budget proposal detailing how awards will be utilized; two letters of reference from academic and/or industrial personnel familiar with the student's competence; a letter from the laboratory supervisor where the proposed research will be performed, indicating the applicant will be accepted in the laboratory to work on the proposed project; a curriculum vitae detailing previous education and/or experience in electron microscopy; and a brief statement of career goals. **Deadline:** December 30 each year; awards are granted by April 1 of the following year.

**Remarks:** Research programs for which scholarship funds are awarded must be carried out in a U.S. laboratory. **Contact:** Microscopy Society of America, at the above address (see entry 3695).

## Mid-America Consortium for Engineering & Science Advancement
Kansas State University
144 Durland Hall  Ph: (913)532-7127
Manhattan, KS 66506  Fax: (913)532-7810

**• 3699 •  MACESA Awards** *(Undergraduate/Scholarship)*

**Qualif.:** Candidates must be African American, Hispanic, or American Indian students who are members of MACESA chapters. **Criteria:** Applicants are judged on the quality of their essay, letters of recommendation, and their activities at the pre-college level.

**Funds Avail.:** $500 to cover books for a year. **Deadline:** May 1. **Contact:** MACESA at the above address (see entry 3698).

• 3700 •
## Milheim Foundation for Cancer Research
c/o US Bank
Trust and Investment Group      *Ph:* (303)316-5948
200 University Blvd.      *Fax:* (303)388-9387
Denver, CO 80206      *Free:* 800-836-8044

**• 3701 • Milheim Foundation for Cancer Research Project Grants in Oncology** *(Postdoctorate/Grant)*

**Purpose:** To provide funds for research toward the prevention, treatment, and cure of cancer. **Focus:** Oncology. **Qualif.:** Applicants must be qualified investigators affiliated with approved research institutions in the continental United States. Grants are tenable at the home institution and are intended to support research costs. Funds are not given for salaries of academic personnel, attendance at meetings, or for the presentation of papers.

**Funds Avail.:** $1,125-23,485. **No. of Awards:** 7-10. **To Apply:** Write to the trust officer for application form and guidelines. Submit seven copies of the application with research plan and letter of recommendation from department chair or sponsor. **Deadline:** March 15. Notification by mid-June. **Contact:** Barbara S. Cole, Trust Account Executive, at the above address (see entry 3700).

• 3702 •
## Mill Mountain Theatre
Center in the Square
1 Market Square      *Ph:* (540)342-5730
Roanoke, VA 24011-1437      *Fax:* (540)342-5745
*E-mail:* mmtmail@millmountain.org
*URL:* http://www.millmountain.org

**• 3703 • New Play Competition Prizes** *(Professional Development/Prize)*

**Purpose:** To identify an unpublished and unproduced play of social significance that speaks with a voice of its own. **Focus:** Drama. **Qualif.:** Candidates must be playwright residents in the United States. Submission must be an unpublished, unproduced script written in English for the theater. Plays having received developmental workshops may be submitted. Play may be full-length or one act. Subject matter and character variations are open, but cast size is limited to ten. Author may submit one play per competition. Plays may not be resubmitted unless they have had substantial structural changes. The winning play may be staged at the Theatre. After the staging, author retains all rights to the play.

**Funds Avail.:** $1,000 and $500. **No. of Awards:** 2. **To Apply:** Submit bound copy of script with a manuscript-size, self addressed, stamped envelope; a biography of author and history of play; and a cast of characters with brief descriptions. Recommendation by a literary agent, dramaturg, or artistic director must accompany or follow script. **Deadline:** Manuscripts are accepted from October 1 to January 1. Notification in early August.

**Remarks:** The theatre may choose to do a full production at a later date through the festival. **Contact:** New Play Competition Coordinator, at the above address (see entry 3702).

• 3704 •
## Glenn Miller Birthplace Society - Scholarship Program
P.O Box 61
Clarinda, IA 51632      *Ph:* (712)542-2461

**• 3705 • Ralph Brewster Vocal Scholarship/Jack Pullen Memorial Scholarship** *(High School, Undergraduate/Scholarship)*

**Purpose:** To help students who wish to pursue careers in music. **Qualif.:** Candidates must be either graduating high school seniors or college freshmen, majoring or planning to major in music.

**Funds Avail.:** $1,000 and $500. Winners must perform at the Glenn Miller Festival stage show (held some time in June), where they will also receive their checks. Scholarships are awarded without regard to other awards, and may be used for any school-related expense. **To Apply:** Applicants must submit a completed application; a $25 refundable check an appearance fee, made out to the Glenn Miller Birthplace Society; a statement that indicates applicants intention of making music performance or teaching a central part of their life, accompanied by a statement of how they plan to proceed in this direction; and a clear high-quality cassette tape to the Scholarship Committee. This tape will contain either the composition the applicant intends to perform at the competition or one similar to it in style and difficulty. It should also contain evidence of technical skills as listed below. A good length of performance would be about ten minutes; in no case should the entire tape performance exceed fifteen minutes. Those not accepted as finalists will be notified within a reasonable period of time following the closing date for applications. Finalists should be prepared to do the following things: perform a work of competition or concert quality of up to five minutes (a major work running slightly longer will be acceptable); sight read simple selections such as hymns or song of the judges choice, with or without accompaniment; and sing scales, arpeggios, or other technical exercises as directed by the judge. Applicants will also be given the opportunity to perform a selection contrasting in style to the required piece. Singers will compete without amplification. **Deadline:** March 15. To insure timely consideration, inquiries should be received by early to mid-winter. Finalist auditions are held June 8.

**Remarks:** Application deadlines, amount of awards and competition rules are all subject to annual review. Old application forms should not be used. To date, the total amount of awards has never been reduced, and tends to increase gradually, as income from the permanent scholarship fund permits. **Contact:** Dr. Gene Garrett, Chairman, Glenn Miller Scholarship Committee, at the above address (see entry 3704).

**• 3706 • Glenn Miller Birthplace Society Instrumental Scholarships** *(High School, Undergraduate/Scholarship)*

**Purpose:** To help students who wish to pursue careers in music. **Qualif.:** Candidates must be either graduating high school seniors or college freshmen, majoring or planning to major in music.

**Funds Avail.:** Two scholarships of $1,250 and $500. Winners must perform at the Glenn Miller Festival stage show (held the second weekend in June) where their checks will be presented. Scholarships are awarded without regard to other awards, and may be used for any school-related expense. **To Apply:** Applicants must submit a completed application; a check for a $25 refundable appearance fee, made out to the Glenn Miller Birthplace Society; a statement that indicates applicants intention of making music performance or teaching a central part of his/her life, accompanied by a statement of the manner in which the applicant plans to proceed in this direction; and a clear high-quality cassette tape to the Scholarship Committee. This tape should contain either the composition the applicant intends to perform at the competition or one similar to it in style and difficulty. It should also contain evidence of technical skills as listed below. A good length of

*Glenn Miller Birthplace Society - Scholarship Program (continued)*

performance would be about ten minutes; in no case should the entire tape performance exceed fifteen minutes. Those not accepted as finalists will be notified within a reasonable period of time following the closing date for applications. Finalists must perform an audition at Clarina. During the audition, finalists should be prepared to: perform a work of concert competition quality of about 5 minutes, or a movement of a major work; sight read selections of the judge's choice; and perform technical exercises such as arpeggios, scales, or rudiments, to the extent required by the judge. Applicants will also be given the opportunity to demonstrate their skill at improvising and/or performing a selection contrasting in style to the required piece, including pop, jazz, etc. There are restrictions on the use of instruments with electrically produced or amplified sound. Contestants are responsible for providing an accompanist, if needed, all equipment except a piano, and a copy of the music to be used by the judges. **Deadline:** March 15. To insure timely consideration, inquiries should be received by early to mid-winter. Finalist auditions are held June 8.

**Remarks:** Application deadlines, amount of awards and competition rules are all subject to annual review. Old application forms should not be used. To date, the total amount of awards has never been reduced, and tends to increase gradually, as income from the permanent scholarship fund permits. **Contact:** Dr. Gene Garrett, Chairman, Glenn Miller Scholarship Committee at the above address (see entry 3704).

---

• 3707 •

**Ministry of Education, Czechoslovakia**
Ministerstvo Skolstvi CSR
Karmelitska 7
1 Prague, Czech Republic            *Ph:* 2 531 6519

• 3708 • **Czech Education Scholarships** *(Doctorate, Graduate, Postdoctorate/Scholarship)*

**Purpose:** To support studies at Czech institutions. **Focus:** Agriculture, Civil Engineering, Czech Language, Czech Studies, Health Sciences, Mechanical Engineering, Medicine, Science, Slavic Language, Slavic Studies, Visual Arts. **Qualif.:** Applicant may be from any country outside of Czechoslovakia. Educational requirements and age limits vary depending on the course of study in which candidate wishes to enroll. Scholarships are tenable in Czechoslovakia for study at any of the following: vocational schools in civil engineering, mechanical engineering, agriculture, and health services; university degree programs in Czech or Slovak studies; art schools and other special schools; graduate and postgraduate training courses in the sciences and medicine. Students who do not have an adequate knowledge of the Czech or Slovak language are required to undertake language training in addition to their regular coursework.

**Funds Avail.:** Tuition fees, monthly allowance. **To Apply:** Applications are not accepted directly from individuals. Instead, candidate must be nominated by an approved organization in the home country. Write to the Ministry or the Czech diplomatic office in home country for the address of the national nominating authority, which can provide application materials. Submit two copies of the application form to the nominating authority with official transcripts, curriculum vitae, copy of birth certificate, and a certificate of good health. Endorsed applications are forwarded to the Ministry for final selection. **Deadline:** Varies. **Contact:** Can also be reached at 2-53-00419 Scholarships Program.

---

• 3709 •

**Ministry of the Flemish Community in Belgium**
c/o Embassy of Belgium
3330 Garfield St., NW            *Ph:* (202)625-5850
Washington, DC 20008            *Fax:* (202)342-8346

• 3710 • **Ministry of the Flemish Community Fellowships** *(Postdoctorate, Undergraduate/Fellowship)*

**Purpose:** To support study or research at institutions affiliated with the Flemish Community. **Focus:** Art, Economics, Humanities, Law, Medicine, Music, Political Science, Science, Social Sciences. **Qualif.:** Applicants must be U.S. citizens and under 35. Students must hold a bachelor's or master's degree. Fellowships are tenable at universities, music conservatories, and art academies affiliated with the Flemish Community in Flanders. Fellows must have no other Belgian sources of income.

**Funds Avail.:** BFr24.800 /month, plus tuition, health insurance, and a one-time contribution towards costs of printing of doctoral dissertation or towards printing of licentiate theses. **No. of Awards:** 5. **To Apply:** Students must submit application form in triplicate, a medical certificate, a certified copy of their birth certificate, copy of diplomas, summary of their thesis, official transcripts, and two letters of recommendation from current teacher or employer. **Deadline:** March 1. Notification by June.

**Remarks:** Three fellowships are offered to postgraduate students, two to sophomores who wish to spend their junior or senior year at a Flemish University. **Contact:** Attache of the Flemish Community.

---

• 3711 •

**Minnesota Physicians Foundation of the Minnesota Medical Association**
3433 Broadway St., NE, No. 300            *Ph:* (612)378-1875
Minneapolis, MN 55413            *Fax:* (612)378-3875

• 3712 • **MMA Medical Student Loans** *(Doctorate/Loan)*

**Focus:** Medicine. **Qualif.:** Candidates must be medical student members of the Minnesota Medical Association who are residents of Minnesota and currently enrolled in good standing at an accredited medical school in Minnesota. Applicants must have satisfactorily completed one semester of medical school. Financial need must be demonstrated.

**Funds Avail.:** Maximum loan a student may obtain during any one year is $3,000. Loans are interest-free until September following graduation; thereafter interest is 8 percent per year. Loans must be repaid monthly within four years of graduation. Loans become due and payable immediately if the recipient terminates studies prior to graduation. **To Apply:** Applicants are required to submit a completed application for financial aid with an attached copy of their medical school registration. Candidates must be interviewed by members of the Medical Student Financial Assistance Committee. **Contact:** Director, Medical Student Financial Assistance Program, at the above address (see entry 3711).

## • 3713 •
### Minnesota State Arts Board
Park Square Ct.
400 Sibley St., Ste. 200
St. Paul, MN 55101-1928

*Ph:* (612)215-1600
*Fax:* (612)215-1602
*Free:* 800-8MN-ARTS

*URL:* http://www.arts.state.mn.us

### • 3714 • Minnesota Artist Assistance Fellowships
*(Professional Development/Fellowship)*

**Purpose:** To assist Minnesota artists in setting aside a significant period of time for work in their chosen art forms. **Focus:** Visual Arts, Film, Video, Screenwriting, Photography, Poetry, Prose, Music, Dance, Theatre Arts and Playwriting. **Qualif.:** Candidates must be professional artists, not high school or undergraduate students. They must have been Minnesota residents for at least six months. **Criteria:** Applicants are judged on quality of the work; merit of the proposed fellowship plan.

**Funds Avail.:** $8,000. **No. of Awards:** 50. **Deadline:** Early fall. **Contact:** Lori Hindbjorgen, Artist Assistance Program Associate at the above address (see entry 3713).

### • 3715 • Minnesota Career Opportunity Grants
*(Professional Development/Grant)*

**Purpose:** Career Opportunity Grants fund short-term impending opportunities that will significantly advance the artists' work or career such as advanced study (not related to a degree) with a mentor of significant importance; travel relating to an impending concrete opportunity; rental of equipment, instruments, or work space for a unique performance opportunity; or materials to complete work for a gallery exhibition that will have a significant impact on the recipient's career. **Focus:** Visual, Performing, Literary, and Theatre Arts. **Qualif.:** Candidates must be professional artists, not high school or undergraduate students. They must have been Minnesota residents for at least six months. **Criteria:** Applicants are judged on the quality of the work; merit and feasibility of the proposed career opportunity.

**Funds Avail.:** Career Opportunity Grants are short term grants and vary from $100 to $1,500 per grant. **No. of Awards:** Varies; approximately 8-10 per deadline. **Deadline:** 3 per fiscal year. **Contact:** Lori Hindbjorgen, Artist Assistance Program Associate at the above address (see entry 3713).

### • 3716 • Minnesota Folk Arts Apprenticeship
*(Professional Development/Other)*

**Purpose:** To encourage the transmission of traditional folk arts skills from masters to promising apprentices. **Focus:** Traditional Crafts, Music, Dance, and Storytelling. **Qualif.:** Applicants must have been Minnesota residents for at least six months. **Criteria:** Applicants are judged on quality and traditionality of the artistic activity and community impact.

**Funds Avail.:** Folk Arts Apprenticeships are variable awards that can range from $100 to $4,000. **No. of Awards:** Varies; approximately 12-15 each year. **Deadline:** December 1. **Contact:** Philip Nusbaum, Folk Arts Program Associate, at the above address (see entry 3713).

## • 3717 •
### Minnesota State Department of Veterans Affairs - Deceased Veterans' Dependents Scholarships
Veterans Service Bldg.
Benefits Div.
St. Paul, MN 55155

*Ph:* (612)296-2562
*Fax:* (612)296-3954

### • 3718 • Minnesota State Department of Veterans Affairs Educational Assistance Grants *(Undergraduate/Grant)*

**Purpose:** To serve veterans of Minnesota and their dependents and survivors. **Focus:** General Studies. **Qualif.:** Applicants must be Minnesota veterans who have exhausted, through use, all of their federal educational benefits (refer to Minnesota Statute 197.447 for definition of the term "veteran"). Veterans must be currently enrolled in a post-secondary educational institution. Special education assistance is also available to children of Minnesota Veterans who died while on active duty military service or who died as a result of active duty military service. Assistance is also available for dependents of those Minnesota residents who have been declared as Prisoners of War or Missing in Action. Students must attend a Minnesota college or university, a community college, a technical college or some other institution of higher education. **Criteria:** Based solely on eligibility criteria.

**Funds Avail.:** A one-time grant to be used for payment of tuition expenses. **No. of Awards:** Unlimited. **To Apply:** Applications may be obtained through County Veterans Service Officers, the financial aid offices of any institution of higher learning, or the Department of Veterans Affairs at the above address. **Deadline:** None.

## • 3719 •
### Minnesota Teamsters Joint Council No. 32
3001 University Ave., SE
Minneapolis, MN 55414

*Ph:* (612)331-3456
*Fax:* (612)378-0496

### • 3720 • Minnesota Teamsters Joint Council No. 32 Scholarship Awards *(Undergraduate/Scholarship)*

**Focus:** General Studies. **Qualif.:** Applicants must be current graduating seniors of any high school within the jurisdiction of Minnesota Teamsters Joint Council No. 32. Applicants (or mother, father, or guardian) must be members in good standing of a Teamsters Union affiliated with Minnesota Teamsters Joint Council No. 32. Also eligible are children of deceased or disabled members of an affiliated Locals who were in good standing at the time of retirement, disablement or death. Applicants must have a straight B average or better (2.0 on a 3.0 grade point system; 3.0 on a 4.0 grade point system). **Criteria:** Recipients are selected by lot.

**Funds Avail.:** Eight $2,000 scholarships (to be received in two consecutive $1,000 payments). Scholarships may be used at any university, college, or vocational technical institute in the state of Minnesota. **No. of Awards:** 8. **To Apply:** The following must be submitted: application form, official high school transcripts, and two letters of reference (two from former teachers). **Deadline:** Application materials must be postmarked by April 30. **Contact:** Lori Angelo at the above address (see entry 3719). Applications may be requested from local union offices.

**• 3721 •**
**Minority Access to Research Careers**
National Institute of General Medical
  Sciences
45 Center Drive MSC 6200      *Ph:* (301)594-3900
Bethesda, MD 20892-6200     *Fax:* (301)480-2753

*The National Institute of General Medical Sciences is part of the U.S. Department of Health and Human Services - National Institutes of Health.*

**• 3722 •  NIH Predoctoral Fellowship Awards for Minority Students** *(Doctorate/Fellowship)*

**Purpose:** To make fellowships available to minority doctoral candidates. **Focus:** Biomedical Sciences. **Qualif.:** Applicants must be currently enrolled in a Ph.D. or M.D./Ph.D. graduate program in the biomedical sciences, or have been accepted by and agreed to enroll in such a graduate program the following academic year. **Criteria:** Selection is based upon academic records and research experience, which is evaluated for scientific merit and training potential as well as originality of proposed research.

**Funds Avail.:** 30 fellowships. **No. of Awards:** 30. **To Apply:** Fellowship application PHS 416-1 should be used when applying. It is available through the Office of Grants Inquiries, Division of Research Grants, National Institutes of Health, Westwood Bldg., Rm. 449, Bethesda, MD 20892. **Deadline:** April.

**• 3723 •**
**Minority Fellowship Programs - Council on Social Work Education**
1600 Duke St., Ste. 300      *Ph:* (703)683-8080
Alexandria, VA 22314-3421    *Fax:* (703)683-8099
*E-mail:* cswe@access.digex.net

**• 3724 •  Council on Social Work Education Minority Fellowships** *(Doctorate/Fellowship)*

**Purpose:** To increase the number of ethnic minority mental health researchers, and to equip minority individuals for the provision of leadership, teaching, consultation, training, policy development and administration in mental health and substance abuse programs. **Focus:** Mental Health, Social Welfare, Social Work. **Qualif.:** Open to U.S. citizens or those who have permanent residence status, who are members of a minority group, including (but not limited to) persons who are American Indian/Alaskan Native, Asian/Pacific Islander, Black, or Hispanic. Applicant must have a master's degree in social work and plan to begin full-time study leading to a doctoral degree in social work, or be currently enrolled full-time in a social work doctoral program.

**Funds Avail.:** Monthly stipend for living expenses; tuition support may be available. **No. of Awards:** Research 20; Clinical 10. **To Apply:** Write for application form and guidelines. Submit completed application to the national selection committee. **Deadline:** February 28. Notification by June 1. **Contact:** Minority Fellowship Program Director at the above address (see entry 3723).

**• 3725 •**
**Miss America Pageant Scholarship Foundation**
2 Ocean Way, Ste. 1000     *Ph:* (609)345-7571
Atlantic City, NJ 08401     *Fax:* (609)347-6079
                 *Free:* 800-282-6477
*URL:* http://www.missamerica.org

**• 3726 •  Miss America Pageant Scholarships**
*(Graduate, Undergraduate/Scholarship)*

**Purpose:** To encourage and foster young women in becoming the leaders of tomorrow. **Qualif.:** Entrant must be a female between the ages of 17 and 24, a high school graduate, single and never been married, of good moral character, and a citizen of the United States. A complete list of eligibility requirements is available from the local or state pageants. **Criteria:** Based on a series of pageants beginning at the local, state, and national level. Contestants are judged on talent, interview, evening wear, and swimwear competitions.

**Funds Avail.:** Over $294 million is awarded annually in scholarships presented at the local, state and national Miss America pageants. The scholarships are for tuition, room, board, supplies, and other educational expenses. The use of the scholarships must begin within one year from the date of the award unless a reasonable extension is requested and granted. Miss America must begin use of her scholarship within two years from the date of the award. Training under the scholarship should be continuous. **Contact:** Jacqueline C. Carpo, at the above address.

**• 3727 •**
**Mississippi Board of Trustees of State Institutions of Higher Learning**
Student Financial Aid
3825 Ridgewood Rd.
Jackson, MS 39211-6453     *Ph:* (601)982-6570

**• 3728 •  Southeast Asia POW/MIA Scholarship**
*(Undergraduate/Scholarship)*

**Qualif.:** Candidate must be under the age of 23, of a Mississippi veteran presently or formerly listed as MIA in Southeast Asia as a result of action against the U.S. naval vessel Pueblo.

**Funds Avail.:** Full tuition, average room fees, and additional fees. Awarded annually. Award is for a maximum of eight semesters. **Contact:** Mississippi Board of Trustees of State Institutions of Higher Learning at the above address (see entry 3727).

**• 3729 •**
**Mississippi Office of State Student Financial Aid**
3825 Ridgewood Road     *Ph:* (601)982-6633
Jackson, MS 39211-6453    *Fax:* (601)982-6527

**• 3730 •  Mississippi African-American Doctoral Teacher Loan/Scholarship Program** *(Doctorate/Scholarship loan)*

**Focus:** Education. **Qualif.:** Applicants must be African American Mississippi residents who are full-time students with the intention of teaching at an accredited public Mississippi college or university. Participants must also meet the Program's academic qualifications, be admitted to a doctoral program at an accredited public educational institution in Mississippi approved by the Board of Trustees, and meet the selection and approval of the Commissioner of Higher Education in consultation with the

Mississippi Research Consortium. **Criteria:** Priority is given to renewal students.

**Funds Avail.:** $10,000 per academic year up to three years upon renewal. Approximately five recipients will be chosen per year. **Deadline:** June 30.

**Remarks:** Obligation can be discharged on the basis of one year's teaching service at an accredited public Mississippi college or university for one year's loan/scholarship. The period of service must be a minimum of 12 consecutive months. **Contact:** Mississippi Office of State Student Financial Aid at the above address (see entry 3729).

**• 3731 • Mississippi Graduate and Professional Degree Loan/Scholarship Program** *(Doctorate/Scholarship loan)*

**Focus:** Chiropractic Medicine, Podiatry, Medicine, Orthotics/Prosthetics. **Qualif.:** Applicants must be Mississippi residents seeking a professional degree not available at a Mississippi university and who, as a result, enroll in accredited out-of-state institutions. The approved fields of study are Chiropractic Medicine, Orthotics/Prosthetics, and Podiatric Medicine. Participants must also meet the program's academic qualifications. **Criteria:** Priority is given to renewal students.

**Funds Avail.:** An average of $6,000 will be awarded per academic year dependent upon the availability of funds. **Deadline:** April 30.

**Remarks:** Obligation can be discharged on the basis of one year's service in the approved field of training in Mississippi for one year's loan/scholarship. The period cannot be less than 12 consecutive months. **Contact:** Mississippi Office of State Student Financial Aid at the above address (see entry 3729).

**• 3732 • Mississippi Health Care Professions Loan/Scholarship Program** *(Undergraduate/Scholarship loan)*

**Focus:** Health Care Services, Occupational and Physical Therapy, Audiology. **Qualif.:** Applicants must be Mississippi residents who meet the Program's academic qualifications and are enrolled full-time as a junior or senior in an accredited training program of critical need in the State of Mississippi. Approved programs of study include speech pathology, psychology, occupational therapy, physical therapy and other allied health programs in critical demand. **Criteria:** Priority is given to renewal students.

**Funds Avail.:** $1,500 per year for up to two years. Only one recipient per critical training program of study will be selected per year. **Deadline:** April 30.

**Remarks:** Obligation can be discharged on the basis on one year's service in the health profession as a full-time employee at a state health institution in Mississippi for one year's loan/scholarship. **Contact:** Mississippi Office of State Student Financial Aid at the above address (see entry 3729).

**• 3733 • Mississippi Law Enforcement Officers and Firemen Scholarship Program** *(Graduate, Undergraduate/Scholarship)*

**Focus:** General Studies. **Qualif.:** Applicants must be the spouses or children of full-time Mississippi law enforcement officers and firemen who were fatally injured or totally disabled from injuries which occurred while performing official duties. Applicants must be Mississippi residents and be enrolled or accepted for enrollment at a state-supported college or university located in Mississippi.

**Funds Avail.:** The cost of tuition and the average cost of a dormitory room plus required fees, including applicable course fees. The scholarship does not include educational expenses such as books, food, school supplies and materials, and school dues or fees for extracurricular activities. Recipients are entitled to eight semesters of scholarship assistance. Children are entitled to the scholarship until the age of 23. There are no repayment

requirements. **Contact:** Mississippi Office of State Student Financial Aid at the above address (see entry 3729).

**• 3734 • Mississippi Nursing Education BSN Program** *(Undergraduate/Scholarship loan)*

**Focus:** Nursing. **Qualif.:** Applicants must be Mississippi residents pursuing a BSN Degree. **Criteria:** Priority is given to renewal students.

**Funds Avail.:** $2,000 per academic year, not to exceed two calendar years for full-time students; a maximum of $4,000 prorated over three years for part-time students. Recipients must maintain a GPA of 2.5 or higher each semester in order to continue to receive funds under the renewal process. **Deadline:** April 30.

**Remarks:** Obligation can be discharged on the basis of one year's full-time service in nursing in Mississippi for one year's loan/scholarship. For the prorated three-calendar-year recipient, the time of service required shall be two years. **Contact:** Mississippi Office of State Student Financial Aid at the above address (see entry 3729).

**• 3735 • Mississippi Nursing Education DSN Program** *(Doctorate/Scholarship loan)*

**Focus:** Nursing. **Qualif.:** Applicants must be Mississippi residents pursuing DSN degrees. **Criteria:** Priority is given to renewal students.

**Funds Avail.:** $5,000 per academic year, not to exceed two calendar years for full-time students; a maximum of $10,000 prorated over four years for part-time students. Recipients must maintain a GPA of 3.0 or higher each semester in order to continue to receive funds under the renewal process. **Deadline:** April 30.

**Remarks:** Obligation can be discharged on the basis of one year's full-time service in nursing in Mississippi for one year's loan/scholarship. For the prorated four-calendar-year recipient, the time of service required shall be two years. **Contact:** Mississippi Office of State Student Financial Aid at the above address (see entry 3729).

**• 3736 • Mississippi Nursing Education MSN Program** *(Graduate/Scholarship loan)*

**Focus:** Nursing. **Qualif.:** Applicants must be Mississippi residents pursuing MSN Degrees. **Criteria:** Priority is given to renewal students. Applicants must have earned BSN Degree prior to applying for MSN program and must be pursuing a MSN degree. Applicants pursuing certificates are not eligible.

**Funds Avail.:** $3,000 per academic year, not to exceed one calendar year for full-time students; a maximum of $3,000 prorated over two years for part-time students. Recipients must maintain a GPA of 3.0 or higher each semester in order to continue to receive funds under the renewal process. **Deadline:** April 30.

**Remarks:** Obligation can be discharged on the basis of one year's full-time service in nursing in Mississippi for one year's loan/scholarship. For the prorated two-calendar-year recipient, the time of service required shall be one year. **Contact:** Mississippi Office of State Student Financial Aid at the above address (see entry 3729).

**• 3737 • Mississippi Nursing Education RN to BSN Program** *(Undergraduate/Scholarship loan)*

**Focus:** Nursing. **Qualif.:** Priority is given to renewal students.

**Funds Avail.:** $1,500 per academic year, not to exceed two calendar years for full-time students; a maximum of $3,000 prorated over three years for part-time students. Recipients must maintain a GPA of 2.5 or higher each semester in order to continue to receive funds under the renewal process. **Deadline:** April 30.

**Remarks:** Obligation can be discharged on the basis of one year's full-time service in nursing in Mississippi for one year's loan/scholarship. For the prorated three-calendar-year recipient, the

## Mississippi Office of State Student Financial Aid (continued)

time of service required shall be two years. **Contact:** Mississippi Office of State Student Financial Aid at the above address (see entry 3729).

### • 3738 • Mississippi Psychology Apprenticeship Program *(Graduate, Undergraduate/Internship)*

**Purpose:** To encourage students to pursue health professions in the field of psychology, to expose students to the professional practice of psychology in a Veterans Affairs Medical Center setting, and to enhance graduate education in psychology through research and applied experience. **Focus:** Physical/Psychological Rehabilitation. **Qualif.:** Applicants must be current legal Mississippi residents, enrolled full time in Psychology at one of Mississippi's accredited colleges or universities, and have a cumulative college grade point average of 3.0 or higher on a 4.0 scale.

**Funds Avail.:** $1,000 stipend per month for graduate students for three summer months; $500 per month for undergraduate students. Room and board will be provided by the Veterans Affairs Medical Center. **To Apply:** Applicants must submit letter of recommendation from an instructor in the Department of Psychology where the student is enrolled. For information and/or application packet write the Mississippi Office of State, Student Financial Aid at the above address. **Deadline:** April 1.

**Remarks:** This program is administered by the Board of Trustees in conjunction with the Biloxi, Mississippi, Veterans Affairs Medical Center.

### • 3739 • Mississippi Public Management Graduate Internship Program *(Graduate/Internship)*

**Purpose:** To allow students the opportunity to have practical experience working for a state government agency in Mississippi. **Focus:** Public Administration, Public Service, Criminal Justice. **Qualif.:** Applicants must be permanent U.S. residents or possess "green cards" and be enrolled at Jackson State University, Mississippi State University, University of Mississippi, or University of Southern Mississippi pursuing graduate degrees in Public Administration, Public Policy and Administration, or Criminal Justice Administration. They must have completed at least one semester of course work earning a grade of B or higher in a quantitative research methods course.

**Funds Avail.:** Approximately ten recipients receive a $1,000 stipend per month plus one percent fringe benefits (dependent upon the availability of funds) for no longer than eight months. All recipients must maintain a grade point average of at least 3.0 on a 4.0 scale in order to receive funds under the renewal process. **To Apply:** For information and/or application packet write Program Coordinator, Public Management Graduate Internship Program, Mississippi State University, Dept. of Political Science, PO Drawer PC, 121 Bowen Hall, Mississippi State, MS, 39762 or call (601)325-7855. **Contact:** Mississippi Office of State Student Financial Aid at the above address (see entry 3729).

### • 3740 • Mississippi Southeast Asia POW/MIA Scholarship Program *(Graduate, Undergraduate/Scholarship)*

**Focus:** General Studies. **Qualif.:** Applicants must be the children of Mississippi veterans presently or formerly listed as missing in action in Southeast Asia. Children of Mississippi veterans who have been prisoners of a foreign government as the result of a military action against the United States naval vessel Pueblo are also eligible. The POW/MIA must have been a legal Mississippi resident at the time of induction into the armed forces and at the time they were officially reported as a prisoner of war or missing in action. The spouse of the person reported as a present or former prisoner of war or missing action must also have been a legal Mississippi resident for a period of not less than ten years during their minority and a legal resident of the state at the time of the

child's enrollment. These children must be enrolled or accepted for enrollment at a state-supported college or university located in Mississippi.

**Funds Avail.:** The amount of assistance available is the cost of tuition and the average cost of a dormitory room plus required fees, including applicable course fees. The scholarship does not include educational expenses such as books, food, school supplies and materials, and school dues or fees for extracurricular activities. Recipients are entitled to eight semesters of scholarship assistance. Children are entitled to the scholarship until the age of 23. There are no repayment requirements. **To Apply:** For information and/or application packet contact Mississippi State Student Financial Aid at the above address. **Deadline:** There is no application priority date for this program.

### • 3741 • Mississippi Southern Regional Education Board Loan/Scholarship Program *(Doctorate/Scholarship loan)*

**Focus:** Osteopathic Medicine, Optometry. **Qualif.:** Applicants must be Mississippi residents enrolled in an accredited school of optometry or school of osteopathic medicine approved by the Board of Trustees and who meet the Program's academic qualifications. **Criteria:** Priority is given to renewal students.

**Funds Avail.:** The amount of the award is determined by the SREB Board and is dependent upon the availability of funds. Funding can be received for up to four years. The award is made on an annual basis. **Deadline:** April 30.

**Remarks:** Obligation can be discharged on the basis of one year's service in the field of approved training in Mississippi for one year's loan/scholarship. The period of service shall not be less than 12 consecutive months. **Contact:** Mississippi Office of State Student Financial Aid at the above address (see entry 3729).

### • 3742 • Mississippi Special Medical Education Loan/Scholarship Program *(Doctorate/Scholarship loan)*

**Focus:** Medicine. **Qualif.:** Applicants must be residents of Mississippi, enrolled in the University of Mississippi School of Medicine and be entering specialty and subspecialty areas in the field of medicine. **Criteria:** Selection is based on financial need and academic achievement.

**Funds Avail.:** Up to $6,000 per year for four academic years. **Deadline:** April 30.

**Remarks:** The loan/scholarship is discharged on the basis of one year's service in Mississippi for one year's funding. This program is privately funded by the Vicksburg Foundation. **Contact:** Mississippi Office of State Student Financial Aid at the above address (see entry 3729).

### • 3743 • Mississippi State Dental Education Loan/Scholarship Program *(Doctorate/Scholarship loan)*

**Focus:** Dentistry. **Qualif.:** Applicants must be Mississippi residents who have been accepted for admission to the University of Mississippi School of Dentistry and who meet Program academic qualifications. **Criteria:** Priority is given to renewal students.

**Funds Avail.:** $4,000 per academic year for up to four years (dependent on the availability of funds). **Deadline:** April 30.

**Remarks:** Obligation can be discharged on the basis of one year's service in a geographical area of critical need in Mississippi designated by the Mississippi State Department of Health, or entry into full-time public health work at a state health institution or community health center for one year's loan/scholarship. **Contact:** Mississippi Office of State Student Financial Aid at the above address (see entry 3729).

## • 3744 • Mississippi State Medical Education Loan/ Scholarship Program (Doctorate/Scholarship loan)

Focus: Medicine, Pediatric Medicine. Qualif.: Applicants must be Mississippi residents who have been accepted for admission in the University of Mississippi School of Medicine and who meet Program academic qualifications. Acceptable fields of study, training, and practice include Family Medicine, Internal Medicine, Pediatrics, or Obstetrics/Gynecology. Criteria: Priority is given to renewal students.

Funds Avail.: Up to $6,000 for four academic years. Deadline: April 30.

Remarks: Obligation can be discharged on the basis of one year's service in a geographical area of critical need in Mississippi designated by the Mississippi State Department of Health, or entry into full-time public health work at a state health institution or community health center for one year's loan/scholarship. Contact: Mississippi Office of State Student Financial Aid at the above address (see entry 3729).

## • 3745 • Mississippi State Student Incentive Grant Program (Undergraduate/Grant)

Focus: General Studies. Qualif.: Applicants must be Mississippi residents enrolled full-time at the undergraduate level at a nonprofit college or university located in Mississippi. They must demonstrate financial need.

Funds Avail.: Amount ranges from $100 to $1,500 per academic year. There are no repayment requirements. Deadline: Established by the financial aid office of each participating college/university. Contact: College and university financial aid offices.

## • 3746 • William Winter Teacher Scholar Loan Program (Other, Undergraduate/Loan, Scholarship)

Focus: Teacher education. Qualif.: Applicants must be Mississippi residents enrolled full-time in any accredited program that leads to a baccalaureate degree and/or a Class "A" teaching certificate at a Mississippi public or private college or university. Entering freshman must have a cumulative high school GPA of 3.0 or higher and an ACT score of 21 or higher. Sophomores, juniors, seniors and applicants seeking a second baccalaureate degree must have a cumulative college GPA of 2.5 or higher. Criteria: Priority is given to renewal students.

Funds Avail.: Up to $1,000 per academic year for freshman and sophomore participants; up to $3,000 for junior and senior participants; and up to $3,000 for recipients already with a baccalaureate degree seeking teacher certification. Approximately 50 participants per grade level will be selected. The award is made on an annual basis with priority given to renewal students and a Program participation limit of four years. Deadline: April 30.

Remarks: Obligation can be discharged on the basis of one year's teaching service in a critical subject area or in a critical teacher shortage geographic section for one year's loan/scholarship. Contact: High school counselors, college financial aid offices, or the Mississippi Office of State Student Financial Aid at the above address (see entry 3729).

## • 3747 •
## Missouri Archaeological Society
PO Box 958                          Ph: (573)882-3544
Columbia, MO 65205                  Fax: (573)882-9410
E-mail: archmg@showme.missouri.edu

## • 3748 • Jesse Wrench Scholarship (Graduate, Undergraduate/Scholarship)

Purpose: To enhance the development of a student in the field of anthropology and to help the Missouri Archaeological Society and the University of Missouri-Columbia Department of Anthropology maintain their jointly held library. Focus: Anthropology, Archaeology. Qualif.: Applicant must be enrolled at the University of Missouri-Columbia. Criteria: Selection is based on a short statement written by the applicant outlining his/her interest in the field of archaeology.

Funds Avail.: One annual award of $250 per semester for two semesters. No. of Awards: 1. To Apply: Applicants are required to prove their current status in the university. Applicants must submit their address and a short statement outlining their interests in archaeology. Deadline: Early fall. Contact: Melody Galen, Associate Editor, at the above address (see entry 3747). In Missouri call 800-472-3223.

## • 3749 •
## Missouri Department of Elementary and Secondary Education
c/o Jackie Kampeter
PO Box 480                          Ph: (573)751-1668
Jefferson City, MO 65102            Fax: (573)526-3580
E-mail: moirfal@mail.dese.state.mo.us
URL: http://service.dese.state.mo.us/divschsvc/trans/9596trans.html

## • 3750 • Missouri Minority Teacher Education Scholarship (Undergraduate/Scholarship loan)

Focus: Match or science teacher education. Qualif.: Applicants must be Missouri residents of African American, Asian American, Hispanic American or Native American descent who are high school seniors, college students or individuals with baccalaureate degrees. Applicants must rank in the top twenty-five percent of their high school class or score at or above the 75th percentile on the ACT or SAT examination or have 30 college hours with a 3.0 better grade point average. Criteria: Awards are made based on academic achievement.

Funds Avail.: $3,000 per award. Renewable up to three times. To Apply: Write for further details. Deadline: March 1. Contact: Jackie Kampefer at the above address (see entry 3749). at the above address.

## • 3751 • Missouri Teacher Education Scholarship (Undergraduate/Scholarship loan)

Focus: Education. Qualif.: Applicants must be Missouri residents who are graduating high school seniors. Criteria: Awards are made based on academic achievement.

Funds Avail.: $2,000 per award. Non-renewable. To Apply: Write for further details. Deadline: February 15. Contact: Jackie Kampefer at the above address (see entry 3749).

• 3752 •
## Missouri Department of Health
Medical Student Loan Repayment
  Program
Bureau of Health Care Access and
  Assessment
PO Box 570
Jefferson City, MO 65102
*URL:* http://health.state.mo.us

*Ph:* (573)751-6219
*Fax:* (573)522-8146
*Free:* 800-891-7415

### • 3753 • Medical Student Loan Repayment Program
*(Postgraduate/Loan)*

**Purpose:** To provide financial assistance to health care professionals. **Focus:** Physician. **Qualif.:** Family and general practice, general internists, pediatricians and OB/GYN's are eligible. Must work in a health professional shortage area. **Criteria:** Based on need and availability of funds.

**Funds Avail.:** Provides for payment up to $20,000 annually. **To Apply:** This is a repayment program. The loan is to be used for medical school education loans for a minimum of two years of service. **Deadline:** July 15. **Contact:** Cindy Cox, Bureau of Health Care Access and Assessment at listed address.

### • 3754 • Nurse Loan Repayment Program
*(Postgraduate/Other)*

**Purpose:** To provide financial assistance to health care professionals. **Focus:** Nursing. **Qualif.:** Must work at a public agency or a non-profit agency located in a health professional shortage area in Missouri. **Criteria:** Financial need, type and place of employment.

**Funds Avail.:** Provides for payment up to $5,000 annually. **No. of Awards:** Varies according to funds available. **To Apply:** The loan is to be used for nursing school education loans for a minimum of two years of service. **Deadline:** July 15. **Contact:** Cindy Cox, Bureau of Health Care Access and Assessment at listed address.

### • 3755 • The Primary Care Resource Initiative for Missouri (PRIMO) *(Doctorate, Graduate, Undergraduate/Loan)*

**Purpose:** To provide support to students pursuing primary health care professional careers in medicine and advanced practice nursing. **Focus:** Allopathic and Osteopathic Medicine, Family Nurse Practitioner. **Qualif.:** Applicants must be Missouri residents attending a Missouri school of at least one year for purposes other than attending an educational institution. **Criteria:** Priority is given to students from rural and under served areas and minority students.

**Funds Avail.:** Up to $5,000 a year for students pursuing a graduate nursing degree leading to certification as a primary care practitioner. Also provided are loans up to $20,000 for students in schools of allopathic or osteopathic medicine and $10,000 or $15,000 for primary care resident physicians in their second and third year of residency training in Missouri, respectively. **No. of Awards:** Varies according to funds available. **To Apply:** Must reapply annually. **Deadline:** July 15.

**Remarks:** The loans will be paid back at 9.5 percent interest or forgiven on a year per loan basis for services in an area of defined need within the state. **Contact:** Cindy Cox, Bureau of Health of Health Care Access and Assessment at listed address.

### • 3756 • The Professional and Practical Nursing Student Loan Program *(Graduate, Undergraduate/Loan)*

**Purpose:** To assist with expenses associated with nursing education. **Focus:** Nursing. **Qualif.:** Applicant must be a full-time nursing student pursuing a degree. Must also be a Missouri resident for more than 1 year in an academic standing and attend an approved Missouri school for purposes other than attending an educational instititution . **Criteria:** Based on financial need.

**Funds Avail.:** Annually up to $5,000 to nursing students pursuing an RN, and up to $2,500 for those pursuing an LPN license. **No. of Awards:** Varies according to funds available. **To Apply:** Must reapply annually. **Deadline:** July 15 and Dec. 15.

**Remarks:** Loans will be paid back at 9.5 percent interest or forgiven at 25 percent of the interest and principal per year for service in an area of defined need within the state. **Contact:** Cindy Cox, Bureau of Health Care Access and Assessment at listed address.

• 3757 •
## Mixed Blood Theatre Company
1501 South 4th St.
Minneapolis, MN 55454

*Ph:* (612)338-0937
*Fax:* (612)338-1851

### • 3758 • We Don't Need No Stinkin' Dramas
*(Professional Development/Prize)*

**Purpose:** To promote and develop new plays and playwrights. **Focus:** Drama. **Qualif.:** Candidate may be of any nationality. Applicant must be a playwright who has had works previously produced. Submitt full-length, contemporary comedies; particularly comedieis about race,sport or containing a political edge. Script should be 65 pages. No translationr or adaptations will be accepted All scripts entered must reamin unproduces as of September 1, 1999. Limit two submissions per author. Must be firmly bound and legibly typed on word processed.

**Funds Avail.:** $2,000. **To Apply:** Send a self-addressed, stamped envelope for submission guidelines. **Deadline:** February 1, 1999. Notification by October 1. **Contact:** David Kunz at the above address (see entry 3757).

• 3759 •
## Modesto Bee
PO Box 5256
Modesto, CA 95352
*E-mail:* dmoullette@modbee.com
*URL:* http://modbee.com

*Ph:* (209)578-2351
*Fax:* (209)578-2207

### • 3760 • Modesto Bee Summer Internships
*(Undergraduate/Internship)*

**Focus:** Journalism (Print). **Qualif.:** Applicants must have completed at least their junior year in college with either basic journalism training or newspaper experience. **Criteria:** Interns' assignments are made based on their skills and enthusiasm.

**Funds Avail.:** $420 per week. **No. of Awards:** Three reporting; one sports reporter (fall); one photographer. **To Apply:** Applicants must submit a cover letter outlining career goals, a resume, five work samples, and the names of at least three professional references. **Deadline:** November 30. **Contact:** Mark Vasche, Executive Editor at the above address (see entry 3759).

## • 3761 •
## Money for Women Fund - Barbara Deming Memorial Fund, Inc.
Money for Women
PO Box 630125
Bronx, NY 10463

### • 3762 • Grants to Individual Artists (Professional Development/Grant)

**Purpose:** To support feminists in the arts whose projects shed light upon the condition of women. **Focus:** Visual Arts, Fiction, Nonfiction and Poetry. **Qualif.:** Applicant must be a U.S. or Canadian citizen and a feminist and artist working on a project related to the lives and concerns of women. Grants will not be made for educational assistance, personal study, loans, dissertation or research projects, or for groups or business ventures. SEL Applicants are judged by board members and additional jurors.

**Funds Avail.:** Up to $1000. **No. of Awards:** Varies. **To Apply:** Send a self addressed, stamped envelope to the administrator for application guidelines. **Deadline:** June 30, December 31. Notification in May and October.

**Remarks:** The Fund offers two special grants: the Gerty Grant in the Arts is awarded to a lesbian whose work either accurately portrays the conditions of lesbians or whose project combats homophobia. The Fannie Lou Hamer Grant will be offered to a woman whose work combats racism. There are no special application procedures; recipients will be chosen from all proposals. **Contact:** Susan Pliner, Administrator, at the above address (see entry 3761).

## • 3763 •
## Thelonious Monk Institute of Jazz
5225 Wisconsin Ave, NW, Ste., 605
Washington, DC 20015
E-mail: sfischer@tmonkinst.org
URL: http://www.monkinstitute.org

*Ph:* (202)364-7272
*Fax:* (202)364-0176

### • 3764 • Thelonious Monk International Jazz Instrumental Competition (Professional Development/Scholarship)

**Purpose:** The Thelonious Monk International Jazz Instrumental Competition is a program under the auspices of the Thelonious Monk Institute of Jazz. The internationally recognized jazz education center, dedicated to the advancement of America's treasured jazz tradition, offers young artists the opportunity to study and perform with renowned jazz scholars, educators, and musicians. **Qualif.:** The Thelonious Monk International Jazz Instrumental Competition is open to all musicians who plan to pursue jazz music as a career. Applicants must have never recorded commercially as a leader with a major label. Each year the competition features a different instrument. **Criteria:** A review panel will evaluate and select each competitor based on the application and audio tape presentation.

**Funds Avail.:** $20,000 is awarded for first place; $10,000 for second; $5,000 for third. Half of the prize money is awarded at the competition, half is applied to towards the recipient's musical education. **To Apply:** An application may be obtained by writing or telephoning the Institute. It must be completed in full and returned with a current resume of musical experience with discography, and an audio cassette demonstrating musical ability. **Deadline:** All applications must be received no later than July 1. **Contact:** Shelby Fischer, Executive Producer, at the above address (see entry 3763).

## • 3765 •
## Montalvo Center for the Arts
15400 Montalvo Road
PO Box 158
Saratoga, CA 95071-0158
E-mail: kfunk@villamontalvo.org
URL: http://www.villamontalvo.org

*Ph:* (408)961-5818
*Fax:* (408)961-5850

### • 3766 • Artists Fellowships and Residencies (Professional Development/Fellowship)

**Purpose:** To give artists uninterrupted time for creative pursuits at Villa Montalvo. **Focus:** Literature, Music, Visual Arts. **Qualif.:** Applicant may be of any nationality, but must be an artist who has completed formal training or the equivalent and is engaged in the arts on a professional level. **Criteria:** Based on the quality of work submitted.

**Funds Avail.:** Housing and studio space; seven stipends are given each year on the basis of merit. **No. of Awards:** Varies from 25-35 depending on length of stays by accepted artists. **To Apply:** Send a self-addressed, stamped envelope for application materials. Fellowships and Residencies are considered under the one application; dual application is not necessary. **Deadline:** March 1 and September 1. **Contact:** Artist Residency Program, Director.

## • 3767 •
## Montana Guaranteed Student Loan Program
PO Box 203101
Helena, MT 59620-3101
E-mail: custserv@mgslp.state.mt.us
URL: http://mgslp.state.mt.us

*Ph:* (406)444-6594
*Fax:* (406)444-1869
*Free:* 800-537-7508

*Also see U.S. Department of Education for other ferally funded grants, scholarships, and loans, including the Pell Grant; Supplemental Educational Opportunity Grant; College Work Study; Perkins Loan; Stafford Loan; Parent Loans for Undergraduate Studies; and Supplemental Loans for Students.*

### • 3768 • Montana State Student Incentive Grants (Undergraduate/Grant)

**Qualif.:** Applicants must be Montana residents, full-time undergraduates, and attending participating Montana schools. **Criteria:** Awards are based on financial need.

**Funds Avail.:** The maximum award is $900 per year. **Contact:** Montana Guaranteed Student Loan Program at the above address (see entry 3767).

### • 3769 • Montana University System Fee Waivers (Undergraduate/Other)

**Qualif.:** Waivers are available to Native Americans; senior citizens; some veterans; war orphans; dependents of prisoners of war; residents of Mountain View and Pine Hill schools, and similar private and public non-sectarian Montana charitable institutions; athletes; National Merit Scholarship semi-finalists; and recipients of High School and Community College Honor Scholarships. Applicants must be enrolled at one of the Montana State University or University of Montana campuses. **Criteria:** Waivers are granted on the basis of financial need and academic or athletic achievement.

**Funds Avail.:** Fees waived vary according to the type of waiver granted. **Contact:** The financial aid offices of the schools listed above.

## • 3770 •
## Montana Space Grant Consortium
c/o Laurie Howell
261 EPS Building
MSU-Bozeman
PO Box 173835     *Ph:* (406)994-4223
Bozeman, MT 59717-3835     *Fax:* (406)994-4452
*E-mail:* msgc@montana.edu
*URL:* http://www.montana.edu/~wwwmsgc/

### • 3771 • Montana Space Grant Consortium Scholarship-Fellowship Program *(Graduate, Undergraduate/Fellowship, Scholarship)*

**Focus:** Aerospace related fields, including biological and life sciences, chemistry, geological sciences, physics and astronomy, mechanical engineering, chemical engineering, electrical engineering, computer sciences, and civil engineering. **Qualif.:** Applicants must be full-time students at a consortium campus.

**Funds Avail.:** $10,800 plus tuition and fees for graduate fellowships and $1000 for undergraduate scholarships. **To Apply:** Proof of attendance at a consortium institution must be provided when requesting application information.

## • 3772 •
## Montreal International Music Competition
Place des Arts
1501, rue Jeanne-Mance     *Ph:* (514)285-4380
Montreal, PQ, Canada H2X 1Z9     *Fax:* (514)285-4266

### • 3773 • Montreal International Music Prizes *(Undergraduate/Prize)*

**Purpose:** To recognize talented young performers. **Focus:** Piano, Violin, Voice. **Qualif.:** The category for the Competition changes annually, 1998 is a recess year. Applicants may be of any nationality. Candidates for the violin and piano prizes must be 17 to 30 years old. In the voice competition applicants must be 20 to 35 years old. **Funds Avail.:** $1,000-18,000, plus a prize of $1,000 entitled Prix du public, awarded to the candidate chosen by the public by ballot. **No. of Awards:** 8. **To Apply:** Write for application form and guidelines. Submit form with registration fee ($60). **Deadline:** February 15. **Contact:** Monique Marcil, executive director, at the above address (see entry 3772).

## • 3774 •
## Montreal Neurological Institute
3801 University St.     *Ph:* (514)398-1903
Montreal, PQ, Canada H3A 2B4     *Fax:* (514)398-8248
*E-mail:* fil@mni.lan.mcgill.ca
*URL:* http://www.mni.mcgill.ca/bic_home.html

### • 3775 • Jeanne Timmins Costello Fellowship *(Postdoctorate/Fellowship)*

**Purpose:** Candidates must have an M.D. or Ph.D. degree. Those candidates with M.D. degrees will ordinarily have completed clinical studies in neurology or neurosurgery. **Focus:** Neuroscience, Epilepsy. **Funds Avail.:** Initial appointments are for one year with a maximum value of $25,000 (Canadian) and with one renewal possible. **No. of Awards:** 4. **Deadline:** Applications must be received before October 15 of each year to be considered in the following January or July competition. **Remarks:** Research themes include: cerebrovascular disease, neuroimaging, neuroimmunology, epilepsy, neuromuscular disease, neuro-oncology, neurosurgery, neuropsychology, neurobiology, and cell and molecular biology. **Contact:** The Director at the above address (see entry 3774).

### • 3776 • Preston Robb Fellowship *(Postdoctorate/Fellowship)*

**Purpose:** Candidates must have an M.D. or Ph.D. degree. Those candidates with M.D. degrees will ordinarily have completed clinical studies in neurology or neurosurgery. **Focus:** Neuroscience—Epilepsy. **Funds Avail.:** Initial appointments are for one year with a maximum value of $25,000 (Canadian) and with one renewal possible. **To Apply:** Awards are made strictly on a competitive basis. **Deadline:** Applications must be received before October 15 of each year to be considered in the following January or July competition. **Remarks:** Research themes include: neurobiology, cerebrovascular disease, neuroimaging, neuroimmunology, epilepsy, neuromuscular disease, neuro-oncology, neurosurgery, neurophsychology, and cell and molecular biology. **Contact:** The Director at the above address (see entry 3774)for more information and application forms.

## • 3777 •
## Montreal Symphony Orchestra - Orchestre Symphonique de Montreal
260, de Maisonneuve Blvd. W     *Ph:* (514)842-3402
Montreal, PQ, Canada H2X 1Y9     *Fax:* (514)842-0728
*URL:* http://www.osm.ca

### • 3778 • OSM Competition *(Professional Development/Prize)*

**Purpose:** To help and encourage young Canadian musicians. **Focus:** Brass Instruments, Piano, Voice, Woodwinds, Strings. **Qualif.:** Applicants must be Canadian citizens or landed immigrants. Age restrictions, repertoires, and other restrictions vary according to the category of competition. Write to the education coordinator for details. Competition categories rotate annually. First-prize winners are expected to perform with OSM in one concert of a regular subscription series. **Funds Avail.:** $300-2,000. **To Apply:** Write for application form, audition schedule, and repertoire selections. Submit form to the educational coordinator with proof of age and citizenship, professional and educational resume, repertoire, and registration fee ($75). **Deadline:** October 1 (for completed application). Auditions take place in mid- November. **Contact:** Education Coordinator at the above address (see entry 3777).

## • 3779 •
## Moorman Manufacturing Co.
c/o Judy Hays, Corresponding Sec.
1000 N 30th St.     *Ph:* (217)222-7100
Quincy, IL 62301     *Fax:* (217)223-9435

### • 3780 • Moorman Scholarship in Agriculture *(Undergraduate/Scholarship)*

**Focus:** Agriculture. **Qualif.:** Applicants must be sophomores, juniors and seniors in a College of Agriculture at a participating university. **Criteria:** Awards are granted based on interest in agriculture, scholastic standing, leadership qualities, and financial need. **To Apply:** Write for further details. **Deadline:** Varies with each university.

**Remarks:** Participating universities include: University of Arkansas, Auburn University, Clemson University, Colorado State University, University of Florida, University of Georgia, University of Illinois, Iowa State University, University of Kentucky, Lincoln University, Louisiana State University, Michigan State University, University of Minnesota, Mississippi State University, University of Missouri, Montana State University, University of Nebraska, New Mexico State University, Ohio State University, Oklahoma State University, Purdue University, South Dakota State University, Southern Illinois University, University of Tennessee, Texas A&M University, Texas Tech University, University of Wisconsin, University of Wyoming. **Contact:** Moorman Manufacturing Company at the above address (see entry 3779).

---

**• 3781 •**
**Mortar Board National Foundation**
1250 Chambers Rd., No. 170    *Ph:* (614)488-4094
Columbus, OH 43212-1753    *Fax:* (614)488-4095
   *Free:* 800-989-6266
*E-mail:* selby.1@osu.edu
*URL:* http://radar.ch.ua.edu/~robin/mortarbd/mbfound.htm

**• 3782 • Mortar Board Foundation Fellowships** *(Doctorate, Graduate/Fellowship)*

**Purpose:** To promote scholarship, leadership & service. **Focus:** General Studies. **Qualif.:** Applicants must be current or former Mortar Board members who are pursuing graduate or professional degrees.
**Funds Avail.:** A varied number of $1,500 fellowships are awarded each year. **No. of Awards:** 12. **To Apply:** Applications are available each year between September 1 and January 1. **Deadline:** January 31st. **Contact:** Diane M. Selby at the above address (see entry 3781).

---

**• 3783 •**
**Mt. Desert Island Biological Laboratory**
PO Box 35, Old Bar Harbor Rd.    *Ph:* (207)288-3605
Salsbury Cove, ME 04672    *Fax:* (207)288-2130
*E-mail:* bkb@mdibl.org
*URL:* http://www.mdibl.org

**• 3784 • Hancock County Scholars Program** *(High School/Scholarship)*

**Purpose:** To interest high school students in careers in biological sciences. **Focus:** Molecular biology, cell physiology, toxicology. **Qualif.:** The program offers a ten week commuter project in basic biological research of marine organisms for eight Hancock County students entering grades 11 and 12. The core of the project is the one-on-one research laboratory experience each student will have with a trained scientist mentor. The scholars will have a one week training session prior to working in the laboratory and will have a weekly schedule which will include scientific seminars and peer discussions of individual research projects led by the Project Director. In conjunction with high school students in other science programs, students will discuss ethics in science and science as a career. Field trips are planned to examine life on the rocky shores and whale watching. The program runs from June through August. **Criteria:** Awards are given based on the applicant's strong interest and aptitude in science.

**Funds Avail.:** $2,000. **No. of Awards:** 10. **To Apply:** Application form from MDIBL. **Deadline:** April 1.

**Remarks:** Students who are not local must provide own housing or stay in MDIBL dormitories. **Contact:** Jennifer Litteral at the above address (see entry 3783).

---

**• 3785 •**
**Mountain Lake Biological Station**
University of Virginia
Gilmer Hall    *Ph:* (804)982-5486
Charlottesville, VA 22903-2477    *Fax:* (804)982-5626
*E-mail:* mtlake@virginia.edu
*URL:* http://www.virginia.edu/~mtlake

**• 3786 • NIDAY Fellowships** *(Postdoctorate, Postgraduate/Fellowship)*

**Purpose:** To support pre- or postdoctoral research at Mountain Lake. **Focus:** Biological Sciences, Ecology. **Qualif.:** Candidate may be of any nationality. Applicant must be a qualified pre- or postdoctoral investigator who would benefit from a period of field research and training at the Station.

**Funds Avail.:** $2,000 maximum **To Apply:** Write to the director for application form and guidelines. Submit form with curriculum vitae, names and phone numbers of two referees, and a brief research proposal, including a list of equipment and facilities needed. **Deadline:** March 15.

**Remarks:** Summer address is: 240 Salt Pond Rd., Pembroke, VA, 24136, (540)626-7196. **Contact:** Henry M. Wilbur, Director, at the above address (see entry 3785).

**• 3787 • Walton Scholarships** *(Graduate, Undergraduate/Scholarship)*

**Purpose:** To support students who wish to study at Mountain Lake. **Focus:** Biological Sciences, Ecology. **Qualif.:** Candidate may be of any nationality. Applicant must be an undergraduate or graduate student in good standing who has at least eight semester hours of college credit in biology. Scholarships are tenable at courses offered by the Station; the courses are designed primarily for students working toward advanced degrees. Mountain Lake is part of the summer session of the University of Virginia. Students who wish to apply credit earned at Mountain Lake toward a graduate degree from the University of Virginia must first be admitted to a graduate program at the University before enrollment at the Station. Candidates from other institutions who wish to transfer credits earned at the Station to their home university must secure approval in advance.

**Funds Avail.:** $750-1,000. **To Apply:** Write to the director for application form and guidelines. Submit form with transcripts, two letters of recommendation, informal statement of financial need, and a small photograph. **Deadline:** March 15.

**Remarks:** Numerous work-study scholarships, providing for room and board at the Station, are available to students with financial need. Summer address is: 240 Salt Pond Rd., Pembroke, VA, 24136, (703)626-7196. **Contact:** Henry M. Wilbur, Director, at the above address (see entry 3785). Wilbur, Director, at the above address.

---

## • 3788 •
### Multiple Sclerosis Society of Canada
250 Bloor St. E., Ste. 1000          *Ph:* (416)922-6065
Toronto, ON, Canada M4W 3P9          *Fax:* (416)922-7538
*E-mail:* info@mssoc.ca
*URL:* http://www.mssoc.ca/

### • 3789 •   Multiple Sclerosis Society Career Development Awards *(Postdoctorate/Award)*

**Purpose:** To stimulate and support research and training in multiple sclerosis and allied diseases. **Focus:** Multiple Sclerosis and Allied Diseases. **Qualif.:** Applicant must hold a doctoral degree and must have recently completed training in research. Research must be conducted on a full-time basis in a Canadian school of medicine. Applicants must also submit a copy of the operating grant to be used during the first year of the award.

**Funds Avail.:** Varies, according to the salary scale set by the Medical Research Council of Canada. **To Apply:** Write for application guidelines. Submit application to the chair of the grants review committee with official transcripts. A letter from the head of the university department where research is to be conducted must also be submitted to confirm that at least 75% of the candidate's time will be reserved for research and that adequate accommodation and research facilities will be provided. **Deadline:** October 1. Results of applications are available March 1. **Contact:** National Medical Advisor at the above address (see entry 3788).

### • 3790 •   Multiple Sclerosis Society Postdoctoral Fellowships *(Postdoctorate/Fellowship)*

**Purpose:** To stimulate and support research and training in multiple sclerosis and allied diseases. **Focus:** Multiple Sclerosis and Allied Diseases. **Qualif.:** Applicants must hold an M.D. or Ph.D. degree. The fellowship must be held at a recognized institution which deals with problems relevant to multiple sclerosis. Fellowships may be held outside of Canada, but fellows studying abroad must intend to return to Canada upon completion of research.

**Funds Avail.:** Varies, according to the salary scale set by the Medical Research Council of Canada plus $1,000. **No. of Awards:** Varies. **To Apply:** Write for application guidelines. Submit application to the chair of the grants review committee. Candidate must arrange to have assessments sent directly to the Society by at least three individuals. **Deadline:** October 1. Results of applications are available March 1. **Contact:** National Medical Advisor at the above address (see entry 3788).

### • 3791 •   Multiple Sclerosis Society Research Grants *(Postdoctorate/Grant)*

**Purpose:** To stimulate and support research and training in multiple sclerosis and allied diseases. **Focus:** Multiple Sclerosis and Allied Diseases. **Qualif.:** Research must be conducted in or under the auspices of an approved institution either in Canada or abroad. Fellows working outside of Canada must intend to return to Canada upon completion of research. A research report and any relevant published papers must be submitted upon completion of the grant.

**Funds Avail.:** Varies. **No. of Awards:** Varies. **To Apply:** Write for application guidelines. **Deadline:** October 1. Results of applications are available March 1. **Contact:** National Medical Advisor at the above address (see entry 3788).

### • 3792 •   Multiple Sclerosis Society Research Studentships *(Doctorate/Grant)*

**Purpose:** To stimulate and support research and training in multiple sclerosis and allied diseases. **Focus:** Multiple Sclerosis and Allied Diseases. **Qualif.:** Applicants must be working toward an M.Sc., Ph.D., or comparable degree. Research must be in

multiple sclerosis and allied diseases. Preference is given to applicants with special interest in the pathogenesis and potential treatment of multiple sclerosis. Applicants must be supervised by an experienced researcher.

**Funds Avail.:** Varies, according to the salary scale set by the Medical Research Council of Canada. **No. of Awards:** Varies. **To Apply:** Write for application guidelines. Submit application to the chair of the grants review committee with a official transcripts and supporting letter from supervisor. **Deadline:** October 1. Results of applications are available March 1. **Contact:** National Medical Advisor at the above address (see entry 3788).

## • 3793 •
### Munson Institute - Mystic Seaport
75 Greenmanville Ave.
PO Box 6000                          *Ph:* (860)572-5359
Mystic, CT 06355-0990                *Fax:* (860)572-5329
*E-mail:* munson@mysticseaport.org
*URL:* http://www.mysticseaport.org

### • 3794 •   Paul Cuffe Memorial Fellowship for the Study of Minorities in American Maritime History *(Other/Fellowship)*

**Purpose:** To encourage research that considers the participation of Native and African Americans in the maritime activities of southeastern New England. **Focus:** History, Social Sciences. **Criteria:** Selection is based on the merits of the proposed research project, the qualifications of the applicant, and the use to be made of the scholarly resources of southeastern New England.

**Funds Avail.:** Fellowships up to $2,400. Fellows are requested to write a report on their research within one year. **No. of Awards:** 2-4 annually. **To Apply:** Applicants must submit a full description of the proposed project, a preliminary bibliography, brief project budget, complete resume, and the names and addresses of three references. **Deadline:** Application deadline is March 30.

**Remarks:** Paul Cuffe, born in 1759 on Cuttyhunk Island, Massachusetts, was the son of a Wamponoag Indian mother and a former slave father. Before his death in 1817 he became a sea captain, shipowner, landowner, and respected community leader of Westport, Massachusetts. The Paul Cuffe Memorial Fellowships are made possible through the generosity of a local private foundation. **Contact:** Katrina Bercaw, Assistant to the Director, at the above address (see entry 3793).

## • 3795 •
### Henry A. Murray Research Center
Attn: Grants Administrator
Radcliffe College
10 Garden St.                        *Ph:* (617)495-8140
Cambridge, MA 02138                  *Fax:* (617)496-3993

### • 3796 •   The Jeanne Humphrey Block Dissertation Award *(Doctorate/Grant)*

**Purpose:** To support women graduate students studying girls' or women's psychological development. Proposals should focus on sex and gender differences or some developmental issue of particular concern to American girls or women. **Focus:** Female psychological development **Qualif.:** Any female student currently enrolled in a doctoral program in a relevant field is eligible to apply. Dissertation proposals must be approved by an advisor before the grant application is submitted.

**Funds Avail.:** Up to $2500 **No. of Awards:** 1-2 per year **To Apply:** Cover page, proposal curriculum vitae, social security number, permanent home address, name and address of a reference and reference letter. Seven copies of all proposal materials are requested. **Deadline:** April 1 **Contact:** Grants Administrator at the above address (see entry 3795).

## • 3797 • The Henry A. Murray Dissertation Award
*(Doctorate/Award)*

**Purpose:** To support women and men graduate students doing research in the social and behavioral sciences. The award supports research that best embodies Henry A. Murray's commitment to the in-depth study of individuals in context, over time, and from a variety of perspectives. **Focus:** Social and behavioral Studies. **Qualif.:** Applicants must be enrolled in a doctoral program in a relevant field and must have their dissertation proposal approved by an advisor or committee before the grant application is made.

**Funds Avail.:** $2500. **No. of Awards:** 4 a year. **Deadline:** April 1. **Contact:** Grants Administrator at the above address (see entry 3795).

## • 3798 • Radcliffe Research Support Program
*(Postdoctorate/Grant)*

**Purpose:** To provide small grants up to $5000 to post-doctoral investigators for research drawing on the center's data resources. **Focus:** Psychology, psychiatry, anthropology, political science, sociology, and history. **Qualif.:** Applicant must have received doctorate one year prior to application.

**Funds Avail.:** Up to $5000. Funds are provided for travel to the research center, duplication, computer time, assistance in coding data, and other research expenses. **No. of Awards:** 6 per year. **To Apply:** Cover page, proposal, curriculum vitae, social security number, permanent home address, name and address of a reference and reference letter. Seven copies of all proposal materials are requested. **Deadline:** October 15 and April 15. **Contact:** Janice Randall, Grants Administrator.

## • 3799 •
**Muscular Dystrophy Association**
3300 E. Sunrise Dr.             *Ph:* (520)529-2000
Tucson, AZ 85718                *Fax:* (520)529-5300
*E-mail:* info@mdausa.org
*URL:* http://www.mdausa.org

## • 3800 • MDA Research Grants; MDA Research Development Grants; MDA Genetics Research Grants
*(Professional Development/Grant)*

**Purpose:** To support research on the causes and effective treatments of the muscular dystrophies and related diseases. **Focus:** Muscular Dystrophy and related Neuromuscular Diseases. **Qualif.:** Candidate may be of any nationality, but must hold a doctoral degree or the equivalent; be a professional or faculty member at an appropriate U.S. educational, medical, or research institution; and be qualified to conduct and supervise a program of original research. Applicant must have access to institutional resources necessary to conduct the proposed research project. MDA administers two grant programs: neuromuscular disease research and neuromuscular disease research development. Specific research requirements may vary depending on program to which candidate applies. No more than 8% of the grant may be used for institutional overhead.

**Funds Avail.:** Varies, according research project. **No. of Awards:** Variable depending on available funds. **To Apply:** Submission of

pre-application is necessary. **Deadline:** Varies, depending on grant program.

**Remarks:** Research guidelines, pre-application and Research Grants Policy are availabel on the web. **Contact:** Karen Mashburn, Grants Manager, at the above address (see entry 3799).

## • 3801 •
**Muscular Dystrophy Association of Canada**
National Headquarters
150 Eglinton Ave. East, Ste. 400
Toronto, ON, Canada M4P 1E8          *Ph:* (416)488-0030

## • 3802 • Ruth Aziz Clinical Fellowship *(Professional Development/Fellowship)*

**Purpose:** To support clinical research and training in muscular dystrophy. **Focus:** Muscular Dystrophy. **Qualif.:** Applicant may be of any nationality, but preference is given to Canadian citizens and permanent residents. Candidate must have an M.D. or Ph.D. degree, and at least seven years of postdoctoral experience in clinical research. The fellowship is tenable at recognized Canadian research institutions.

**Funds Avail.:** $28,455/year, plus $1,000 for approved scientific travel. **No. of Awards:** One. **To Apply:** Write to the executive assistant for application guidelines. **Deadline:** November 15. **Contact:** Debra Ragbar, Executive Assistant, at the above address (see entry 3801).

## • 3803 • Dr. David Green Postdoctoral Fellowship
*(Professional Development/Fellowship)*

**Purpose:** To enable a postdoctoral investigator to acquire training in muscular dystrophy research. **Focus:** Muscular Dystrophy. **Qualif.:** Applicant may be of any nationality, but preference is given to Canadian citizens and permanent residents. Candidate must have an M.D. or Ph.D. degree, and less than three years of postdoctoral experience. The fellowship is tenable at recognized Canadian research institutions.

**Funds Avail.:** $28,130/year, plus $1,000 laboratory allowance. **No. of Awards:** One. **To Apply:** Write to the executive assistant for application guidelines. **Deadline:** November 15. **Contact:** Debra Ragbar, Executive Assistant, at the above address (see entry 3801).

## • 3804 • Arthur Minden Predoctoral Fellowship
*(Doctorate/Fellowship)*

**Purpose:** To support predoctoral training in muscular dystrophy research. **Focus:** Muscular Dystrophy. **Qualif.:** Applicant may be of any nationality, but preference is given to Canadian citizens and permanent residents. Candidate must be a predoctoral student at a Canadian research institution. The fellowship is tenable at the recipient's home institution.

**Funds Avail.:** $20,150/year, plus $1,000 laboratory allowance. **No. of Awards:** One. **To Apply:** Write to the executive assistant for application guidelines. **Deadline:** January 15. **Contact:** Debra Ragbar, Executive Assistant, at the above address (see entry 3801).

## • 3805 •
## Museum of Science, Boston
Human Resources
1 Science Park
O'Brien Hwy.                          *Ph:* (617)723-2500
Boston, MA 02114-1099                 *Fax:* (617)589-0362
*E-mail:* jobs@mos.org
*URL:* http://www.mos.org

### • 3806 • Arthur Davis Fellowship; Charles E. Merrill Trust Fellowship *(Graduate/Fellowship)*

**Purpose:** To provide the opportunity to participate in the diverse activities of the Museum's Education Programs. **Focus:** Museum Studies, Science Education. **Qualif.:** Candidate must be authorized to work in the United States. Applicant must have an undergraduate degree in science or science education, and be enthusiastic about children and science. Experience in teaching, particularly in the teaching of students in kindergarten through high school, is desirable. Fellowships are tenable at the Museum. The fellow will be expected to help develop and present programs to school groups; to develop and present exhibit hall demonstrations; to assist in presenting teacher workshops and weekend courses, as well as to aid in maintenance of the chemistry and biology laboratories. **Criteria:** Candidates are selected based on personal interviews at Museum of Science.

**Funds Avail.:** $20,020; health benefits, paid time-off, and retirement savings plan eligibility. **No. of Awards:** 2. **To Apply:** Submit resume to Ms. Pang with statement of interest in fellowship. Finalists will be interviewed. **Deadline:** June 1. **Contact:** Sherlyn Pang, Senior Recruiter, at the above address (see entry 3805).

## • 3807 •
## Music Academy of the West
1070 Fairway Rd.                      *Ph:* (805)969-4726
Santa Barbara, CA 93108-2899          *Fax:* (805)969-0686
*E-mail:* catalog@musicacademy.org
*URL:* http://www.musicacadamy.org

### • 3808 • Lotte Lehmann Fellowship in Voice/Vocal Accompanying; Gabor Rejto Fellowship in Cello *(Professional Development/Fellowship)*

**Purpose:** To allow singers, vocal accompanists, and cellists to attend the Academy's Summer Festival. **Focus:** Cello, Voice. **Qualif.:** Candidates must be at least 16 years old. Applicant must be accepted to the Festival in one of the areas of study. **Criteria:** Admission is based on audition and an application evaluation. A live audition is required for the Lehmann Award and taped audition for the Rejto.

**Funds Avail.:** Lehmann Fellowship: tuition, room, board, round-trip airfare and $1,000; Rejto Fellowship: tuition, room, board, round-trip airfare and $1,000. **No. of Awards:** 2. **To Apply:** Write for application forms and guidelines. Submit application for admission to the festival, the name of a musical reference, and application fee ($50). Instrumentalists must submit an audition tape. Vocalists must audition in person. Applicants will need also need to submit a recommendation from their most recent music teacher or the one who is most familiar with their ability on their application form. **Deadline:** Cellists: February 28; vocalist auditions are held from late January to early February.

**Remarks:** All Music Academy students are on full scholarship. **Contact:** Carleen Landes at the above address (see entry 3807).

## • 3809 •
## The Myasthenia Gravis Foundation of America, Inc.
123 W. Madison St., Ste. 800          *Ph:* (312)258-0522
Chicago, IL 60602-4503                *Fax:* (312)258-0461
                                      *Free:* 800-541-5454
*E-mail:* myastheniagravis@msn.com
*URL:* http://www.myasthenia.org

### • 3810 • Myasthenia Gravis Osserman Fellowship Grants *(Postdoctorate/Grant)*

**Purpose:** To promote Myasthenia Gravis research. **Focus:** Medical Research—Myasthenia Gravis or Myasthenia Gravis related field. **Qualif.:** Applicants must have an M.D., Ph.D., D.V.M., or equivalent degree and be conducting research pertinent to Myasthenia Gravis (MG), or a closely-related condition, in the laboratory of a qualified senior investigator. Laboratories must be approved by the Medical Advisory Board's Research and Grants Committee. Candidates must also be permanent residents of the United States who have worked in laboratories at qualified institutions in the United States or abroad, or foreign nationals who have been accepted to work in qualified laboratories in the United States. Any research results published as a result of the grant must give credit to the National Myasthenia Gravis Foundation. **Criteria:** Based on the quality of the research proposal.

**Funds Avail.:** Support is available for 12 months. **No. of Awards:** 4-8. **To Apply:** Fellowship proposals should be ten pages or less in length and include a brief statement of specific aims, description of methods and experimental design, description of laboratory resources and environment, budget, pertinent references, and applicant's curriculum vitae. The Foundation requires nine copies of the proposal. Applications should include the candidate's sponsor/mentor's curriculum vitae and a letter of recommendation from them stating acceptance of the candidate as a fellow. A letter of recommendation is also required from the applicant's past or current academic advisor. **Deadline:** November 1.

**Remarks:** There are usually 10 to 12 applicants. **Contact:** Edward S. Trainer, Executive Director of the Research and Grants Committee, The Myastenia Gravis Foundation, at the above address (see entry 3809).

### • 3811 • Nursing Research Fellowship *(Other/Fellowship)*

**Purpose:** For nurses or nursing students interested in studying problems encountered by patients with Myasthenia Gravis (MG) or related neuromuscular conditions. **Focus:** Nursing.

**Funds Avail.:** $1500 stipend. **To Apply:** Applicants must submit four copies of the following: a cover letter; summary of the research proposal and its association to Myasthenia Gravis or related neuromuscular conditions; proposed budget, curriculum vitae of applicant and sponsor preceptor (student only); letter of recommendation from preceptor that indicates acceptance of the candidate and outlines the proposed work plan for the research study (student only). All items must be submitted in one package. **Deadline:** Applications are accepted throughout the year.

### • 3812 • Dr. Henry R. Viets Medical Student Research Fellowships *(Doctorate, Graduate/Fellowship)*

**Purpose:** To support medical students seeking research training relevant to Myasthenia Gravis (MG). **Focus:** Medical Research—Myasthenia Gravis. **Qualif.:** Applicant may be of any nationality, but must be a pre-medical or medical student enrolled at a U.S. institution and proposing quality MG research. Awards are tenable at the fellow's home institution. Candidate must be sponsored by an established investigator at the institution prior to application to the Foundation.

**Funds Avail.:** $3,000. **No. of Awards:** 4-8. **To Apply:** Write to the executive director for application guidelines. Submit eight copies of cover letter, curriculum vitae, and letter of recommendation from sponsor. **Deadline:** March 15. Notification by May 15.

**Remarks:** There are usually about 12 to 15 applicants. **Contact:** Edward S. Trainer, Executive Director, at the above address (see entry 3809).

---

• **3813** •
## Mycological Society of America
Arizona State University
Department of Botany          *Ph:* (602)965-3414
Tempe, AZ 85287-1601          *Fax:* (602)965-6899
*URL:* http://www.orin.utoronto.co/soc/msa

### • 3814 • Alexopoulos Prize *(Postdoctorate/Prize)*

**Purpose:** To recognize outstanding "young" mycologists on the basis of their research. **Qualif.:** Nominees must be members of MSA and have received their last degree within the 10-year period immediately preceding January 1 of the year the award is given. Recipients normally have received their degrees seven to ten years previous. Those applicants not selected for the prize in the year they are nominated are considered for up to two additional years. Winners may receive the prize only once. **Criteria:** Evaluation is based on originality and quality of candidate's published mycological work.

**Funds Avail.:** Monetary prize presented at the MSA annual meeting awards ceremony. **To Apply:** Self-nomination is not allowed. Nominators must be members of MSA and should request that the nominee send a curriculum vitae, reprints, and a letter from the nominator detailing the candidate's merits to each member of the awards committee. Letters should be sent to the awards committee chairman who will distribute them to committee members. **Deadline:** April 1.

**Remarks:** The Alexopoulos Prize is one of the highest honors bestowed by the MSA. **Contact:** MSA Awards Committee Chairperson, Robert W. Roberson, at the above address (see entry 3813).

### • 3815 • Mycological Society of America Graduate Fellowships *(Doctorate/Fellowship)*

**Purpose:** To assist promising graduate students in mycology. **Qualif.:** Applicants must be student members of MSA and candidates for a Ph.D. degree. They must also be a resident during the tenure of the fellowship in a university in the United States or Canada. Previous MSA fellows are not eligible. **Criteria:** Scholastic merit, research ability, and promise shown as a mycologist are evaluated in the selection process.

**Funds Avail.:** Two fellowships of $1,000 each are awarded annually. These awards are intended as supplementary grants and may be used in any way to further graduate studies. **To Apply:** Applications must be sent to each member of the committee and must include a curriculum vitae, two letters of recommendation, and graduate school transcripts. A detailed plan of study must also be included, which should consist of a one-paragraph abstract at the beginning, an introduction explaining the student's intentions and why it is interesting or important, a methods section discussing the feasibility of the research, and a discussion section explaining the results and significance. Plans of study must be double-spaced and organized using section headings. **Deadline:** April 1. **Contact:** MSA Awards Committee Chairperson, Robert W. Roberson, at the above address (see entry 3813).

### • 3816 • Mycological Society of America Graduate Research Prizes *(Doctorate, Graduate/Prize)*

**Qualif.:** Applicants must be members of MSA and candidates for a master's or Ph.D. degree. Those who have received their degree

within one year of the annual meeting are also eligible. Previous recipients of the prize are not eligible. **Criteria:** Awards are given for the best research papers presented orally at the annual MSA meeting, or on the research posters presented. Evaluations are based on the significance of the work, creativity, appropriateness of the methods, clarity of presentation, and validity of conclusions.

**Funds Avail.:** Two prizes of $100 each are awarded in each of the two categories, research papers and research posters. **To Apply:** Students must indicate on the call for papers for the MSA meeting that they are interested in being considered for this prize. Application can only be made in one category. **Deadline:** April 1. **Contact:** MSA Awards Committee Chairperson, Robert W. Roberson, at the above address (see entry 3813).

---

• **3817** •
## NAACP Legal Defense and Educational Fund, Inc.
99 Hudson St., 16th Fl.          *Ph:* (212)965-2200
New York, NY 10013               *Fax:* (212)219-1595
*URL:* http://www.ldfla.org/

*LDF is not a part of the National Association for the Advancement of Colored People although LDF was founded by that organization and shares its commitment to equal rights.*

### • 3818 • Herbert Lehman Education Fund Scholarships *(Undergraduate/Scholarship)*

**Purpose:** To promote diversity in colleges and universities throughout the country and to contribute to the development of leadership among African American college students. **Qualif.:** Applicants must be highly qualified high school graduates planning to begin undergraduate study at an institution that has an enrollment of African American undergraduates of less than 8 percent of the total undergraduate enrollment for that school. They must enroll full-time and be citizens of the United States. Students who have been or are enrolled in a two- or four-year college are not eligible. Students planning to attend predominantly Black institutions are also not eligible. **Criteria:** Preference is given to students planning to attend a college or university in the south that was at one time segregated. Competition is highly competitive and only students with high academic and extracurricular credentials are encouraged to apply.

**Funds Avail.:** Between 20 and 40 scholarships are awarded each year in the amount of $2,000 each and are renewable for up to three additional years. **To Apply:** All requests for application forms must be requested in writing by the applicant before March 1. **Deadline:** April 15. **Contact:** G. Michael Bagley, Scholarship Program Director, at the above address (see entry 3817).

---

• **3819** •
## The Nansen Fund, Inc.
77 Saddlebrook Lane          *Ph:* (713)686-3963
Houston, TX 77024            *Fax:* (713)680-8255

### • 3820 • John Dana Archbold Fellowship *(Postgraduate, Professional Development/Fellowship)*

**Purpose:** To support educational exchange between the United States and Norway. **Focus:** General studies (those offered at the University of Oslo). **Qualif.:** Applicants must be citizens and residents of the United States between the ages of 20 and 35 years. They must also be in good health, and must have at least a bachelor's degree before the start of the fellowship. Fellowships are for postgraduate and postdoctoral study and research at the University of Oslo in Norway. Fellows are required to attend the

---

## The Nansen Fund, Inc. (continued)

University's International Summer School for six weeks before the start of the academic year.

**Funds Avail.:** Up to $10,000 stipend, plus tuition and round-trip travel from the United States to Norway. **No. of Awards:** 1-2. **To Apply:** Write to the Fund for application form, available from September until the end of December. Submit application with transcripts and references and proposed studies. **Deadline:** January 15 of even-numbered years. The fellowship is offered biennially.

**Remarks:** For further information about the University of Oslo, contact the Norwegian Information Service, 825 Third Avenue, 17th Floor, New York, New York 10222; Phone: (212)421-7333. **Contact:** Celine F. Womack Jr., Vice-President, at the above address (see entry 3819).

---

## • 3821 •

## The Nation Institute

c/o Peter Meyer
72 Fifth Ave.
New York, NY 10011

### • 3822 • *The Nation* Internships Program *(Other, Undergraduate/Internship)*

**Purpose:** To provide experience in editorial and business departments of the magazine. **Focus:** Journalism. **Qualif.:** Applicants must be college students or recent graduates.

**Funds Avail.:** Interns receive a small stipend and information on applying the internship to college credits or work study program. **No. of Awards:** 24.

---

## • 3823 •

## National Academic Advising Association

2323 Andersen Ave., Ste. 225
Kansas State University     Ph: (913)532-5717
Manhattan, KS 66502-2912     Fax: (913)532-7732
E-mail: nacada@ksu.edu
URL: http://www.ksu.edu/nacada

### • 3824 • NACADA Research Award *(Graduate, Professional Development/Grant)*

**Purpose:** To provide funds to individuals for research that contributes to the field of advising-related research. **Focus:** Impact of advising, retention, assessment, student development, etc. **Qualif.:** Applicants may be practicing professionals or faculty as well as graduate students seeking support for dissertation research. **Criteria:** The Committee is interested in receiving proposals concerned with developing, conducting, and reporting; empirical studies; evaluation or analysis of advising practices, models, or systems; development, evaluation, or analysis of advising-based theory; studies of history, evolution, and future of the field; development of instruments or measurements to assess advising outcomes; and integrative or field theory or practices.

**Funds Avail.:** Awards are worth up to $5,000. **To Apply:** Applications are available after January 1 for the following year's awards. **Deadline:** March 8 and July 15. Winners are notified in November. Funds are distributed in January. **Contact:** The National Academic Advising Association at the above address (see entry 3823)for additional information. For applications, write to NACADA, Kansas State University, 2323 Anderson Ave., Ste. 225, Manhattan, KS 66502.

### • 3825 • NACADA Scholarship *(Doctorate, Graduate/Scholarship)*

**Purpose:** To support NACADA members who are pursuing graduate education at either the Masters or Ph.D. level and to promote the professional training of advisors. **Qualif.:** Applicants must be current members of NACADA who have been in the association for two years. They must be currently enrolled in either a masters or doctoral program and must have worked as an academic advisor for two years with a minimum of half-time appointment.

**Funds Avail.:** One $1,000 and four $500 scholarships are awarded at the National Conference each year. **No. of Awards:** 5. **To Apply:** Applications are available after January 1. **Deadline:** May 15. Winners are notified in September. **Contact:** The National Academic Advising Association at the above address (see entry 3823)for additional information. For applications contact NACADA, Kansas State University, 2323 Anderson Ave., Ste. 225, Manhattan, Kansas 66502.

---

## • 3826 •

## National Academy of American Scholars

Scholarship Committee
1249 S. Diamond Bar Blvd., Ste.
325
Diamond Bar, CA 91765-4122     Ph: (909)621-6856
URL: http://www.naas.org

### • 3827 • Easley National Scholarship Awards *(Undergraduate/Scholarship)*

**Purpose:** To promote higher education through the awarding of a merit-based scholarship to qualified applicant. **Focus:** General Studies. **Qualif.:** Applicants must be U.S. citizens or permanent residents in their senior year of high school who have been accepted or anticipate being accepted into an accredited four-year academic institution. They must have a GPA of at least a C or higher at time of application and must have taken either the SAT or the ACT test. **Criteria:** Scholarship is awarded based on merit, essay, integrity, and leadership.

**Funds Avail.:** The following awards are available for tuition, room, board, books, and academically-related supplies: one annual four-year scholarship ranging from $8,000 to $10,000 (top ten finalists receive $200 award); one four-year scholarship of $6,000; one four-year scholarship of $4,000; and one four-year scholarship of $2,000. **No. of Awards:** 15. **To Apply:** Candidates must request an information packet and application in writing and include a self-addressed, stamped envelope and $2 handling fee. **Deadline:** February 1. **Contact:** National Academy of American Scholars at the above address (see entry 3826). Applications will not be mailed unless accompanied by handling fee and SASE.

• 3828 •

## The National Academy of Education
New York University
School of Education
726 Broadway, 5th Fl.        *Ph:* (212)998-9035
New York, NY 10003-9580      *Fax:* (212)995-4435
*E-mail:* khkzoz@b9.nyu.edu
*URL:* http://www.nae.nyu.edu

• 3829 • **Spencer Postdoctoral Fellowships**
*(Postdoctorate/Fellowship)*

**Purpose:** To support research that shows promise of yielding significant new knowledge leading to the improvement of education and to encourage the development of young scholars in educational research fields. **Focus:** Education. **Qualif.:** Candidate may be of any nationality. Applicant must have completed doctoral studies within the six years prior to application and wish to carry on research dealing with problems in education.

**Funds Avail.:** $45,000. **No. of Awards:** 30. **To Apply:** Write to the executive director for application form and guidelines, or obtain application from website. **Deadline:** December 10. **Contact:** Kerith Gardner, Executive Director, or Kate Kuo, Program Associate at the above address (see entry 3828).

• 3830 •

## National Academy of Sciences/National Research Council - Office for Central Europe and Eurasia
2101 Constitution Ave., NW (FO
2060)              *Ph:* (202)334-3680
Washington, DC 20418      *Fax:* (202)334-2614
*E-mail:* ocee@nas.edu
*URL:* http://www2.nas.edu/oia/22da.html

*The National Research Council, an independent advisor to the Federal Government on scientific and technical questions of national importance, jointly administered by the National Academy of Sciences, National Academy of Engineering, and the Institute of Medicine, seeks to bring the resources of the entire scientific and technical community to bear in national problems through its volunteer advisory committees.*

• 3831 • **NAS/NRC Collaboration in Basic Science and Engineering Long-Term Grants** *(Postdoctorate/ Grant)*

**Purpose:** To support individual American specialists who wish to collaborate with their colleagues from Central and Eastern Europe and the former Soviet Union for familiarization with research for a period of one to six months. **Focus:** Science, Engineering. **Qualif.:** Applicants must be American specialists who possess or will possess a Ph.D., or equivalent research experience, at least six months prior to the requested beginning date of their programs. They must be U.S. citizens or permanent residents. Visiting specialists must possess Central or Eastern Europe citizenship and must hold a Ph.D. (candidate) degree, or research training and experience equivalent to a doctoral degree at least six months prior to the program start date. American applicants must make all logistical and administrative arrangements directly with their Central or Eastern European colleague. Specialists who have received their doctoral degrees within the past six years are strongly encouraged to apply. Permanent residents of the United States are eligible. Accepted fields of study include all fields generally supported by the National Science Foundation, such as: environmental sciences, archaeology and anthropology, geography, biological sciences, history and philosophy of science, chemistry, mathematics, computer science, physics, earth sciences, psychology, engineering, and science and technology policy. Medical and biomedical fields are not eligible.

**Funds Avail.:** American hosts currently receive $1,500 for travel of the visiting specialist; $2,000 monthly living allowance; and a monthly research allowance (supplies) of $300 per month. American travelers receive $1,500 for travel expenses; $1,500 monthly living allowance and a monthly research allowance (supplies) of $300 per month. Recipients are entitled to 90 percent of their grant monies one month prior to the beginning of the program. The final ten percent is available within three months after completion of the visit and upon receipt of the report of the visit in accordance with NAS/NRC trip report guidelines. Grants do not cover any overhead or other indirect charges assessed by universities or by other institutional organizations. Applicants must certify in writing that such charges will be waived. Funds will not be issued for collaboration with restricted or embargoed countries as specified by U.S. government policy. **No. of Awards:** Varies. **Deadline:** July 30.

**Remarks:** Participating countries include Azerbaijan (travel only), Armenia, Belarus, Bosnia (hosting only), Bulgaria, Croatia, Czech Republic, Estonia, Georgia, Hungary, Kazakhstan, Kyrgyzstan, Latvia, Lithuania, Macedonia, Moldova, Poland, Romania, Russia, Serbia, Slovakia, Slovenia, Tajikistan, Turkmenistan, Ukraine, and Uzbekistan. **Contact:** National Academy of Sciences, Office for Central Europe and Eurasia, at the above address (see entry 3830).

• 3832 • **NAS/NRC Collaboration in Basic Science and Engineering Short-Term Project Development Grants** *(Postdoctorate/Grant)*

**Purpose:** To support individual American specialists who wish to host or visit with their colleagues from Central and Eastern Europe and the former Soviet Union for a period of two weeks in order to prepare a collaborative research proposal for submission to the National Science Foundation. **Focus:** Science, Engineering. **Qualif.:** Applicants must be American specialists who possess or will possess a Ph.D., or equivalent research experience, at least six months prior to the requested beginning date of their programs. They must be U.S. citizens or permanent residents. Visiting specialists must possess Central or Eastern Europe citizenship and must hold a Ph.D. (candidate) degree, or research training and experience equivalent to a doctoral degree at least six months prior to the program start date. American applicants must make all logistical and administrative arrangements directly with their Central or Eastern European colleague. Specialists who have received their doctoral degrees within the past six years are strongly encouraged to apply. Accepted fields of study include: archaeology and anthropology, geography, biological sciences, history and philosophy of science, chemistry, mathematics, computer science, physics, earth sciences, psychology, engineering, and science and technology policy.

**Funds Avail.:** American hosts currently receive grants for living expenses and travel for the visiting specialists in the amount of $2,750. American travelers receive grants for living expenses and travel in the amount of $2,500. Recipients are entitled to 90 percent of their grant monies one month prior to the beginning of the program. The final ten percent is available within three months after completion of the visit and upon receipt of the report of the visit in accordance with NAS/NRC trip report guidelines. Grants do not cover any overhead or other indirect charges assessed by universities or by other institutional organizations. Applicants must certify in writing that such charges will be waived. Funds will not be issued for collaboration with restricted or embargoed countries as specified by U.S. government policy. **No. of Awards:** Varies. **To Apply:** Applicants must request for guidelines and application forms. **Deadline:** Varies. Contact Academy.

**Remarks:** Participating countries include Azerbaijan (travel only), Armenia, Belarus, Bosnia (hosting only), Bulgaria, Croatia, Czech Republic, Estonia, Georgia, Hungary, Kazakhstan, Kyrgyzstan, Latvia, Lithuania, Macedonia, Moldova, Poland, Romania, Russia, Serbia, Slovakia, Slovenia, Tajikistan, Turkmenistan, Ukraine, and Uzbekistan. **Contact:** National Academy of Sciences, Office for Central Europe and Eurasia, Collaboration in Basic Science and Engineering (COBASE) Program, at the above address (see entry 3830).

## National Academy of Sciences/National Research Council - Office for Central Europe and Eurasia (continued)

### • 3833 • NAS/NRC Radioactive Waste Management Program Grants (Postdoctorate/Grant)

**Purpose:** To support individual American specialists who wish to collaborate with their colleagues in the field of radioactive waste management from the former Soviet Union by hosting their visit for a period of six to 12 months. **Focus:** Waste Management. **Qualif.:** Applicants must be American specialists who possess or will possess a Ph.D., or equivalent research experience, at least six months prior to the requested beginning date of their programs. They must be U.S. citizens or obtain U.S. citizenship at least six months prior to the requested beginning date of their programs. Visiting specialists must possess Central or Eastern Europe citizenship and must hold a Ph.D. (candidate) degree, or research training and experience equivalent to a doctoral degree at least six months prior to the program start date. American applicants must make all logistical and administrative arrangements directly with their Central or Eastern European colleague. Specialists who have received their doctoral degrees within the past six years are strongly encouraged to apply. Permanent residents of the United States are not eligible to apply. Accepted areas of research include policy and practices regarding environmental restoration and waste management association with past and current operations related to the nuclear fuel cycle; problems of process design, development and operations related to environmental remediation and control of materials contaminated by radioactive and other hazardous waste; research directed at improving the effectiveness, economics, safety, and public acceptability of methods of handling, storing, and permanently disposing of radioactive and associated hazardous waste; analysis and investigations related to waste partitioning to facility permanent disposal; and analysis and investigations related to geological disposal of wastes.

**Funds Avail.:** American hosts receive $2,000 per month for travel and living expenses of visiting specialists for a period of up to nine months. Travel funds provided on case by case basis. **No. of Awards:** Varies. **To Apply:** Applicants should request application forms and guidelines. **Deadline:** February 1.

**Remarks:** Participating countries include Armenia, Belarus, Estonia, Georgia, Kazakhstan, Kyrgyzstan, Latvia, Lithuania, Moldova, Russia, Tajikistan, Turkmenistan, Ukraine, and Uzbekistan. **Contact:** NAS/NRC, Radioactive Waste Management Program, at the above address (see entry 3830).

## • 3834 •
## National Action Council for Minorities in Engineering, Inc.
3 W. 35th St.  
New York, NY 10001-2281  
*URL:* http://www.nacme.org

*Ph:* (212)279-2626  
*Fax:* (212)629-5178

### • 3835 • NACME Corporate Scholars Program (Undergraduate/Scholarship)

**Focus:** Engineering. **Qualif.:** Applicants must be African American, Hispanic, or American Indian students who are studying engineering. **Criteria:** Students must demonstrate engineering leadership potential in areas where imminent need is anticipated.

**Funds Avail.:** Scholars receive between $12,000 and $20,000 each during their college careers. They also receive summer internship opportunities with their corporate sponsors, research and development work experience, academic and career mentoring, and professional development opportunities. **To Apply:** Scholarships are administered by participating colleges and universities. Students must be nominated through participating universities. They should apply to the dean of admissions or contact NACME. **Contact:** NACME at the above address (see entry 3834).

### • 3836 • NACME TechForce Scholarships (Undergraduate/Scholarship)

**Focus:** Engineering. **Qualif.:** Candidates must be exceptional African American, Hispanic, or American Indian high school seniors who plan to pursue careers in engineering. **Criteria:** Students must demonstrate academic excellence, leadership skills, and commitment to engineering as a career.

**Funds Avail.:** Ten primary finalists receive awards of $1,000 each per year, renewable for four years. Two top scholars receive an additional $2,500 per year for four years. Additionally, ten semifinalists each receive $500. **No. of Awards:** 20. **To Apply:** Students must be nominated through participating pre-college engineering programs. **Contact:** NACME at the above address (see entry 3834).

## • 3837 •
## National Aeronautics and Space Administration
NASA Headquarters, Code FEH  
Higher Education Branch  
Washington, DC 20546  
*E-mail:* oconnoj@ncs.gov  
*URL:* http://www.spacelink.msfc.nasa.gov

*Ph:* (202)358-1531  
*Fax:* (202)358-3048

### • 3838 • NASA Field Center Resident Research Associateships (Postdoctorate/Other)

**Purpose:** To provide postdoctoral scientists and engineers of unusual promise and ability opportunities for research on problems that are compatible with the interests of the sponsoring labs, and to contribute thereby to the overall efforts of the federal labs. **Focus:** Aeronautics Space Science and Technology, life Sciences, Earth Science. **Qualif.:** Applicants must be United States citizens or hold valid visas. Applicants must hold Ph.D., Sc.D. or equivalent degrees. Candidates must have demonstrated superior ability for creative research. **Criteria:** Based on personal qualification and merits of their proposal.

**Funds Avail.:** Stipend is $35,000-85,000 per annum, plus relocation expenses and limited travel expenditures. **No. of Awards:** Approximately 250 annually. **Deadline:** January 15, April 15, and August 15. **Contact:** Associateship Programs, GR-430-A, National Research Council, 2101 Constitution Ave. N.W., Washington, DC 20418.

### • 3839 • NASA Graduate Student Research Fellowships (Graduate/Fellowship)

**Purpose:** To cultivate additional research ties to the academic community and to support promising students pursuing advanced degrees in science and engineering. In 1985, the program was expanded to include an Underrepresented Minority Focus Component. **Focus:** Science and Engineering. **Qualif.:** Applicants must be full-time graduate students from accredited U.S. colleges or universities. Students must be U.S. citizens. Applicants may not concurrently receive other federal funds. **Criteria:** Academic qualifications; quality of proposed research or plan to study and its relevance to NASA programs; proposed utilization of Center research facilities; availability of student to accomplish proposed research.

**Funds Avail.:** $16,000 stipend, plus up to $6,000 allowance. **To Apply:** Students may apply during graduate work or prior to receiving baccalaureate degree. Applicants must be sponsored by department chair or faculty advisor. **Deadline:** February 1.

**Contact:** Ahmad Nurriddin, GSRP Prog. Mgr., at the above address (see entry 3837).

---

• *3840* •

## National Alliance for Excellence
20 Thomas Ave.
Shrewsbury, NJ 07702     *Ph:* (732)747-0028
*E-mail:* info@excellence.org
*URL:* http://www.excellence.org/

• **3841** • **National Alliance for Excellence Honored Scholars Awards** *(Graduate, Undergraduate/Scholarship)*

**Purpose:** To provide scholarships to students who have demonstrated outstanding academic achievement or who excel in the visual/performing arts regardless of financial need. **Focus:** General Studies, Performing Arts. **Qualif.:** Applicants must be U.S. citizens who are pursuing a full-time formal education at an accredited college or university in the United States. Applicants must also have taken the SAT or ACT examination and received written results prior to applying. **Criteria:** Selection is based on talent and ability without regard to financial need.

**Funds Avail.:** Awards range from $1,000 to $5,000. However, most awards are $1,000. Merit scholarships are awarded in four specific categories: technological innovations, academics, visual arts, and performing arts. Within the category of visual arts there are competitions for photography, fine arts, graphic design, jewelry, and fashion design. The performing arts category is divided into dance, vocal, theater arts, film production, and instrumental music. **No. of Awards:** Approximately 1 per week. **To Apply:** Application forms are available by telephoning or sending a self addressed stamped envelope to the Scholarship Foundation of America. Students applying in the academic category should have a minimum 1200 SAT score. Students applying for the Visual Arts category must include a minimum of 20 slides of their work marked with their name, state, type of medium used, and size of original artwork, and a teacher recommendation letter. Photography students are requested to send 20 examples of their work that will be kept for final judging and will not be returned. Students applying for the Performing Arts category should send a VHS video not longer than ten minutes, and a teacher recommendation letter. An audio cassette may also be enclosed but not in place of the video. If the applicant wishes to demonstrate more than one talent, the video may be edited into several shorter segments. There is a $5 processing fee. **Deadline:** There are no deadlines; awards are given on a continuous basis.

**Remarks:** Awards are given out at Ceremonies by senators, governors, and members of Congress to give recognition to the recipient. Internships are available to selected individuals. **Contact:** National Alliance for Excellence at the above address (see entry 3840).

• *3842* •

## National Alliance for Research on Schizophrenia and Depression
Grants Office
208 S. LaSalle St., Ste. 1431     *Ph:* (312)641-1666
Chicago, IL 60604-1003     *Fax:* (312)641-3483
*E-mail:* dcbrowne@hotmail.com
*URL:* http://www.rtnaf.org

• **3843** • **NARSAD Established Investigator Award** *(Postdoctorate/Grant)*

**Purpose:** To stimulate the development of needed scientific personnel and resources, and to facilitate the rapid pursuit of innovative or unique research opportunities. **Focus:** Medicine, Psychiatry. **Qualif.:** Applicants must be established scientists at the rank of associate professor or above. **Criteria:** Applications are first reviewed by the NARSAD Scientific Council. A small number of these are then selected for further review at which time additional information is requested. Recipients are selected on the merit of their proposals.

**Funds Avail.:** Budget requests expected range from $25,000 to $100,000 for a one year grant. **No. of Awards:** 14. **To Apply:** A one-page letter of intent, a curriculum vitae, and a bibliography stating total number of publications and listing up to 12 relevant articles are required. The purpose of the project, the budget requirements, and the longer-term implications of the short-term funding should be specified. Six copies of the letter of intent and accompanying materials should be submitted. **Deadline:** Letter of intent must be received by mid-June. Requests for further information to selected investigators are made in early September. Final applications must be received by mid-October. Selection of awardees and notification is made by March 15. **Contact:** Brenda Berman, grants administrator, at the above address (see entry 3842).

• **3844** • **NARSAD Young Investigator Award** *(Postdoctorate/Fellowship)*

**Purpose:** To enable promising investigators to either extend their research fellowship training or to begin careers as independent research faculty. **Focus:** Medicine, Psychiatry. **Qualif.:** Basic and/or clinical investigators are supported, but research must be relevant to schizophrenia, major affective disorders, or other serious mental illnesses. Applicants must have recently obtained an advanced degree (doctoral level or equivalent) and must already be a participant in active research training, or at the beginning phase of an initial faculty or independent research position. Applicants must have a mentor or senior collaborator who is an established investigator in areas relevant to schizophrenia, depression, or other serious mental illness. **Criteria:** Merit of the research proposal.

**Funds Avail.:** Applicants may request up to $30,000 per year for up to two years. **No. of Awards:** 72. **To Apply:** Applications must include the following: a letter from a mentor/sponsor stating how the award will enhance the applicant's training or facilitate the transition into an independent investigator of relevance to NARSAD's mission and describing the sponsor's commitment to the proposed work (absolute maximum of one page standard type); letter from the applicant outlining training and/or project goals that will be accomplished within the award period and including a description of one representative project in sufficient detail to elucidate hypothesis, significance, and central methodology (absolute maximum of two pages standard type with no appendices). A page listing up to ten bibliographical references may be included. Also required is a brief description of present or just completed research training, and the applicant's future career plans. (one-half page limit); a budget description specifying the amount requested with a brief justification, and indicating whether the applicant is applying for a one-year or a two-year award; a less than 250-word description of the applicant's research proposal written on an enclosed abstract form, in terms understandable to lay people; and a curriculum vitae and bibliography for the

*National Alliance for Research on Schizophrenia and Depression (continued)*

applicant and the mentor/sponsor. Current grant support of each should also be listed. **Deadline:** October 25. **Contact:** Brenda Berman, Grants Administrator, at the above address (see entry 3842).

---

• **3845** •

## National Amputation Foundation
38-40 Church St.                           *Ph:* (516)887-3600
Malverne, NY 11565                         *Fax:* (516)887-3667
*URL:* http://www.social.com/health/nhic/data/hr0300/hr0359.html

• **3846** •   **National Amputation Foundation Scholarship** *(Undergraduate/Scholarship)*

**Purpose:** To assist major limb amputated students with college tuition expenses. **Focus:** General Studies. **Qualif.:** Students who have a major limb amputation and who plan to attend college are eligible.

**Funds Avail.:** Awards are $250 for major limb amputees. If recipients continue their education, an additional award for the original amount is granted each year. **To Apply:** Eligible students must submit a letter stating the name of the college they plan to attend along with a doctor's letter verifying their amputation. **Deadline:** None. **Contact:** Sol Kaminsky at the above address (see entry 3845).

---

• **3847** •

## National Art Materials Trade Association
178 Lakeview Ave.                          *Ph:* (201)546-6400
Clifton, NJ 07011                          *Fax:* (201)546-0393
*URL:* http://www.creative-industries.com/namta/

• **3848** •   **National Art Materials Trade Association Scholarships** *(Doctorate, Graduate, Undergraduate/Scholarship)*

**Purpose:** To further the use of art materials. **Qualif.:** Applicants must be employees of NAMTA member firms, or their relatives, or in an organization related to art or the art materials industry. Candidates must also graduate from high school or its equivalent before July 1 of the year in which they will receive the scholarship, and be accepted by an accredited university, college, junior college, or technical institute. Students already in college are also eligible. Previous recipients of this scholarship are ineligible. **Criteria:** Candidates are judged on financial need, grade point average, extra-curricular activities, special interests, and career choice.

**Funds Avail.:** Three $1,000 scholarships are awarded annually. **To Apply:** A completed application form, transcript of grades, and a letter of recommendation from an employee or relative of a NAMTA member firm or an individual in an organization related to art or the art materials industry must be sent the NAMTA office. Applications are available from the NAMTA office. **Deadline:** March 1. This date may vary from year to year. **Contact:** NAMTA at the above address (see entry 3847).

---

• **3849** •

## National Association for the Advancement of Colored People - Education Department
4805 Mt. Hope Dr.
Baltimore, MD 21215-3297                    *Ph:* (410)486-9133

• **3850** •   **Agnes Jones Jackson Scholarship** *(Graduate, Undergraduate/Scholarship)*

**Qualif.:** Applicants must be undergraduate or graduate students who have been current regular members of the NAACP for at least one year or fully-paid life members. They must not have reached the age of 25 by April 30 of the year of application. Undergraduates must possess a GPA of at least 2.5 on a 4.0 scale; graduate students, a GPA of 3.0 on a 4.0 scale.

**Funds Avail.:** One undergraduate award of $1,500 and one graduate award of $2,500. **To Apply:** Application forms are available from the NAACP in January. **Deadline:** April 30. **Contact:** Andrea E. Moss, Education Department, at the above address (see entry 3849).

• **3851** •   **NAACP Willems Scholarship** *(Graduate, Undergraduate/Scholarship)*

**Qualif.:** Applicants must be majoring in engineering, chemistry, physics, or computer and mathematical sciences and possess and maintain a cumulative grade point average of at least 3.0 or B average. They must be members of the NAACP.

**Funds Avail.:** Undergraduates will receive a maximum award of $8,000 to be paid in annual installments of $2,000. Graduates will be awarded a $3,000 renewable scholarship. **To Apply:** Updated application forms are available in January. **Deadline:** April 30. **Contact:** Andrea E. Moss, Education Department, at the above address (see entry 3849).

• **3852** •   **Roy Wilkins Scholarships** *(Undergraduate/Scholarship)*

**Qualif.:** Applicants must be graduating high school seniors who are members of the NAACP. They must possess a grade point average of at least 2.5 (4.0 scale) or C plus average.

**Funds Avail.:** Awards are $1,000 each. **To Apply:** Requests for applications must be accompanied by a self-addressed, stamped envelope. **Deadline:** Requests for applications must be made after January 1. Application deadline is April 30. **Contact:** Andrea E. Moss, Education Department, at the above address (see entry 3849).

---

• **3853** •

## National Association of American Business Clubs
PO Box 5127                                *Ph:* (336)869-2166
High Point, NC 27262-5127                   *Fax:* (336)887-8451
*E-mail:* ambucs@ambucs.com
*URL:* http://www.ambucs.com

• **3854** •   **AMBUCS Scholars** *(Graduate, Undergraduate/Scholarship)*

**Purpose:** To further the field of corrective therapy. **Focus:** Physical Therapy, Occupational Therapy, Audiology, Speech and Language Pathology. **Qualif.:** Applicants must be planning to enter clinical practice in the fields of physical, occupational, or speech and language pathology, hearing audiology, in the United States immediately following completion of the course of study for which aid is being requested. They must also be in their junior or senior year in a Bachelor's degree program that qualifies the applicant for clinical practice or in a one- or two-year postgraduate program leading to a master's degree or certification in any of the above fields. Applicants must be in schools with curricula approved by the Council on Medical Education and Hospitals of the American Medical Association. Candidates must be U.S. citizens, have good scholastic standing, and be able to document financial need.

**Funds Avail.:** The number and amount of scholarships vary. Upon acceptance of a scholarship, recipients receive a set of Vouchers of Enrollment and Status, one voucher for each session for the entire period of training. Recipients must have the institutional registrar fill out the voucher at the beginning of each session and return it to the National AMBUCS office in order for the stipend to be forwarded to the appropriate financial officer. **No. of Awards:** Award range from $500 to $1,500 annually with one 2-year award for $6,000. **To Apply:** Applicants must apply online at AMBUCS.com; a transcript of grades and credits for the most recent two years of college from each institution attended, including the most recent cumulative grade point or quality point average; a typed statement of 300 words or less describing the development of their interest in their chosen field, their reasons for desiring further study, their career plans following completion of study and why they feel financial aid is needed; and notification of enrollment or acceptance from the educational institution to which they have applied. Incomplete applications will not be processed. **Deadline:** April 15. Recipients are notified in June.

**Remarks:** Paper applications are no longer accepted. Must apply online at our website: www.ambucs.com or www.fastweb.com. **Contact:** Scholarship Committee at the above address (see entry 3853).

### • 3855 • Scholarships for Therapists (Professional Development/Scholarship)

**Focus:** Occupational Therapy, Physical Therapy, Music Therapy, Speech and Language Pathology, Audiology, Recreational Therapy. **Qualif.:** Applicants must be U.S. citizens in their junior/senior year in a bachelor's degree, or graduate program leading to a master's degree. Candidates must be enrolled in, or accepted to, an accredited by the appropriate health therapy profession authority in clinical therapy and must intend to enter clinical practice in the United States upon completion of scholarship. Grades should be between 3.0-4.0. Sponsorship by an AMBUCS chapter is recommended but not necessary. Assistant programs are not eligible.

**Funds Avail.:** $1,500 maximum. **To Apply:** Send a self-addressed, stamped envelope to AMBUCS for a current application form and guidelines, available between December and March. Submit form with a narrative statement, proof of enrollment, transcripts from three semesters, and financial information, including IRS Form 1040 (both sides). **Deadline:** April 15. Notification is made by June. **Contact:** Scholarship Committee at the above address (see entry 3853).

---

### • 3856 •
### National Association of Black Accountants, Inc.
7249-A Hanover Pkwy.                    Ph: (301)474-6222
Greenbelt, MD 20770                     Fax: (301)474-3114
*E-mail:* bleonard@uc.edu; cquinn@primanet.com
*URL:* http://www.nabainc.org

### • 3857 • National Association of Black Accountants National Scholarship (Graduate, Undergraduate/Scholarship)

**Purpose:** To assist minorities in obtaining a business education. **Focus:** Accounting/finance or business major. **Qualif.:** Applicants must be minority undergraduate or graduate students majoring in accounting or finance or other business degree; be paid NABA members and have overall grade point averages of at least 2.5 on a 4.0 scale and 2.5 within their major, and be a college sophomore,

junior or first year graduate student. **Criteria:** Awards are granted based on academic achievement, involvement in NABA, leadership, and/or financial need.

**Funds Avail.:** $500-$6000. **No. of Awards:** 40. **To Apply:** Applicants must submit a personal biography not exceeding 500 words, outlining applicant's career objectives, leadership abilities, community activities and involvement in NABA; a completed application form; grade transcripts; student aid report; and financial aid transcript. **Deadline:** December 31. **Contact:** National Scholarship Committee at the above address (see entry 3856).

---

### • 3858 •
### National Association of Black Journalists
11600 Sunrise Valley Dr.                Ph: (703)648-1270
Reston, VA 22091                        Fax: (703)476-6245

### • 3859 • National Association of Black Journalists Scholarship (Graduate, Undergraduate/Scholarship)

**Focus:** Journalism-print, photography, radio and television. **Qualif.:** Applicants may be undergraduate or graduate students, but must have completed at least one full semester of college to be eligible. Students can be U.S. or foreign residents who are currently attending an accredited four-year university. Students must have a cumulative GPA of 2.50.

**Funds Avail.:** $2,500. **No. of Awards:** Ten. **Deadline:** March 22. **Contact:** NABJ Scholarship Coordinator at the above address (see entry 3858).

### • 3860 • National Association of Black Journalists Summer Internships (Undergraduate/Internship)

**Qualif.:** Candidates are black sophomores or juniors who are enrolled at an accredited four-year college or university and have a 2.5 grade point average. They must be majoring in print or broadcast journalism or planning a career in the communications field, and plan to be enrolled in school for the school year following submission of the application. **Criteria:** Applications will be considered by the NABJ Internship Committee on the basis of the candidate's writing ability, scholarship, and originality and completeness of materials submitted.

**Funds Avail.:** Internship payments vary. **To Apply:** Candidates must submit the following typewritten documents: letter of nomination from the journalism dean or appropriate faculty member; a completed application form; a resume giving basic facts of identity of the applicant; a 500-word autobiography; and a 150-200 word essay on why the candidate is interested in journalism. In addition, print candidates must submit copies of at least five published by-line stories; broadcast candidates, an audio or video cassette of at least three news oriented programs produced by the candidate from actual local happening; and photography candidates, a minimum of five published news photographs. For references, each candidate must submit two letters of recommendation from school faculty members or professional journalists. **Deadline:** Applications must be filed by November 1. Students selected for internships are notified no later than January 31. **Contact:** Internship Program at the above address (see entry 3858).

---

**• 3861 •**

## National Association of Black Women Attorneys

724 9th St., NW, Ste. 206      *Ph:* (202)637-3570
Washington, DC 20001      *Fax:* (202)637-4892

**• 3862 •** National Association of Black Women
Attorneys Scholarships *(Doctorate/Scholarship)*

**Purpose:** To recognize law students who have written outstanding essays, and to support their continued education. **Focus:** Law. **Qualif.:** Candidate must be a U.S. citizen enrolled in law school. Applicant need not be black or a woman. The theme of the essay contest varies each year. Write for current guidelines. Awards should be used for educational purposes.

**Funds Avail.:** Varies. **To Apply:** Write to the executive dir. for application guidelines, available in October. **Deadline:** February 15. **Contact:** Robinette Alexander, Exec. Dir., at the above address (see entry 3861).

**• 3863 •**

## National Association of Broadcasters

Research and Planning Dept.
1771 N St., NW
Washington, DC 20036-2891    *Ph:* (202)429-5389
*URL:* http://www.nab.org/reserach/grants.htm

**• 3864 •** Grants for Research in Broadcasting
*(Graduate, Undergraduate/Grant)*

**Purpose:** To encourage research in broadcasting, especially in economic, business, social or policy issues of importance to the U.S. commercial broadcast industry. **Focus:** Broadcasting. **Qualif.:** Program is open to all academic personnel. Graduate and senior undergraduate students may submit proposals. Applicant may be of any nationality, but must wish to conduct high quality academic research in an area of significance to the U.S. broadcast industry. Funds may not be used to pay tuition, overhead, or benefits.

**Funds Avail.:** $5,000 average. **To Apply:** Write to the Vice President Economist for application form and guidelines. Submit form and five copies with research proposal. **Deadline:** Varies. **Contact:** Dr. Mark R. Fratrik, Vice President Economist, at the above address (see entry 3863).

**• 3865 •**

## National Association for Campus Activities - Educational Foundation

13 Harbison Way      *Ph:* (803)732-6222
Columbia, SC 29212-3401    *Fax:* (803)749-1047

**• 3866 •** Donald L. McCullough Memorial
Scholarships *(Doctorate, Graduate/Scholarship)*

**Qualif.:** Applicants must be pursuing a master's or doctorate degree in student personnel services or a related area and provide proof of acceptance and matriculation into an accredited graduate school. They must have graduated from a four-year college or university with a minimum grade point average of 2.5, have demonstrated experience and involvement in campus activities, and be committed to pursuing a career as a campus activities professional.

**Funds Avail.:** Up to six $250 scholarships are awarded. **To Apply:** Candidates must file a statement on future long term professional goals and how the awarding of this scholarship will aid in their attainment; a copy of undergraduate and graduate transcript of

grades; a summary (resume or vitae) of volunteer and employment activities related to campus activities; and two to four letters of recommendation from professors, advisers or employers who are familiar with applicant's campus experiences. **Deadline:** While applications are solicited in the spring, they are accepted all year. Applications must be filed by June 30. Scholarships are awarded in August. If funds are available, additional awards may be granted throughout the year.

**Remarks:** A grant from the Foundation for Educational Programming in Higher Education made possible the establishment of the Donald L. McCullough Memorial Scholarship Fund in 1984. The fund was created in the memory of Donald M. McCullough, former Director of Student Activities at the University of Connecticut/Storrs.

**• 3867 •** NACA Multi-Cultural Scholarship
*(Professional Development/Scholarship)*

**Purpose:** To increase the participation of ethnic minorities in the field of campus activities by providing economic assistance to qualified minority group members to allow attendance at NACA-sponsored training workshops, regional conferences or national conventions. **Qualif.:** Applicants must be identified as members of African American, Hispanic American, Native American, Pacific Islander, or Asian-American ethnic minority groups who are interested in training in campus activities. **Criteria:** Financial need is considered as a criterion only to choose among applicants who have successfully met the first three criteria.

**Funds Avail.:** Up to three scholarships are available for registration to NACA-sponsored training workshops, regional conferences and national conventions. Travel is not included. **To Apply:** In addition to a completed application form, candidates must submit at least one letter of recommendation, which is to be forwarded separately to the National Office. This letter should be from someone well acquainted with the applicant and they should address their involvement in the student's activities and potential in the field. It should also affirm the applicant's ethnic minority status, financial need, and commitment to stay in the field at least one year following the program for which a scholarship is being sought. Applicants must demonstrate their minority status, their past, present, and potential involvement in activities, their professional development objectives, and their financial need. When documenting their financial need, applicants should describe their institution's procedures and policy for funding expenses, and explain why such funding is unavailable for the program being sought. **Deadline:** Applications must be filed by May 1. **Contact:** National Association for Campus Activities at the above address (see entry 3865).

**• 3868 •** NACA Prize Papers Competition *(Graduate, Professional Development, Undergraduate/Prize)*

**Purpose:** To recognize outstanding research and opinion papers in the field of campus activities, to offer undergraduate and graduate students an opportunity to write about their involvement in campus activities, and to offer professional staff added incentives to publish. **Qualif.:** The competition is open to any person or group, regardless of NACA membership status, in three categories: undergraduate students; graduate students; and faculty or staff of an institution of higher education, or business related to the college market.

**Funds Avail.:** In each category, there is a first prize of $250 and a second prize of $150 for a total of six prizes. **To Apply:** The competition papers must be original, unpublished works on an aspect of campus activities programming including management, volunteerism, leadership training, travel, recreation, etc. Submissions should not be dissertations or written in dissertation style. Papers must be 8 to 15 pages typed, double-spaced on 8x11 inch sheets, with attached appendices. Write for an application. **Deadline:** August 1. **Contact:** National Association for Campus Activities, Educational Foundation, at the above address (see entry 3865).

**• 3869 •   NACA Scholarships for Student Leaders**
*(Undergraduate/Scholarship)*

**Purpose:** To promote the achievement of excellence in the field of campus activities through the development and delivery of educational programs and services for college and university students, professional staff, and others. **Qualif.:** Applicants must be full-time, matriculated undergraduate students in good standing at the time of application and during the semester in which the scholarship is awarded; hold significant leadership positions on their campuses; have made significant contributions to their campus communities; and have demonstrated leadership skills and abilities.

**Funds Avail.:** Scholarships range from $200 to $250 each and can be used for the recipient's educational expenses. **To Apply:** Candidates must submit a completed application form giving biographical data and extra-curricular activities as well as leadership training; at least two letters of recommendation from knowledgeable persons such as administrators or faculty members; a description of leadership activities, skills and ability, training and accomplishments; and verification of current enrollment status from the registrar. **Deadline:** Applications must be filed by November 1. **Contact:** National Association for Campus Activities, Educational Foundation, at the above address (see entry 3865).

**• 3870 •**
**The National Association for Core Curriculum, Inc.**
1640 Franklin Ave., Ste. 104          *Ph:* (330)677-5008
Kent, OH 44240-4324          *Fax:* (330)677-5008
*E-mail:* GVarsNACC@aol.com

**• 3871 •   Bossing-Edwards Research Scholarships**
*(Doctorate, Graduate/Scholarship)*

**Purpose:** To promote research in core curriculum and other integrative/interdisciplinary approaches. **Focus:** Education. **Qualif.:** Applicants must be already admitted to a graduate program leading to a degree at the master's, specialist's, or doctoral level and must have at least one year's experience as a core teacher. Acceptable research may include development of audio-visual or other materials dealing with core philosophy and techniques, studies of changes in pupils resulting from core experiences, creative approaches to the use of core ideas, a project giving some new slant on core in relation to today's world, and a new collation of materials in booklet form, expounding the core philosophy.

**Funds Avail.:** The amount of the scholarship is individually determined. **No. of Awards:** Varies. **To Apply:** The applicant must submit a letter of intent and a statement outlining the research project proposed. The scholarship may be used at any university providing adequate resources for research in core curriculum. A selection committee appointed by the Association's Advisory Committee will review and make selections from applicants' research proposals. Scholarship recipients must provide a statement of research findings or a sample of materials developed to the Association. **Deadline:** None. **Contact:** Dr. Gordon F. Vars at the above address (see entry 3870).

**• 3872 •**
**National Association of the Deaf**
814 Thayer Ave.          *Ph:* (301)587-1788
Silver Spring, MD 20910          *Fax:* (301)587-1789
*E-mail:* NADinfo@nad.org
*URL:* http://www.nad.org

**• 3873 •   Stokoe Scholarships** *(Graduate/Scholarship)*

**Purpose:** To promote research by a deaf graduate student in the areas of sign language or the deaf community. **Focus:** Deafness, Sign Language. **Qualif.:** Applicant must be a deaf graduate student. Applicant's studies may be full- or part-time. The end result of the scholar's research must be a project. **Criteria:** Selection is based on how well proposed project relates to sign language or the deaf community project plan, academic record of applicant and other relevant skills.

**Funds Avail.:** $2,000. **No. of Awards:** 1 per year. **To Apply:** Write to the Association for application form and guidelines. **Deadline:** March 15. The scholarship is announced in May. **Contact:** Stokoe Scholarship Secretary at the above address (see entry 3872).

**• 3874 •**
**National Association of Executive Secretaries**
900 S. Washington St., Ste. G-13
Falls Church, VA 22046          *Ph:* (703)237-8616

**• 3875 •   National Association of Executive Secretaries Scholarships** *(Graduate, Undergraduate/Scholarship)*

**Focus:** General Studies. **Qualif.:** Applicants must be working towards any college degree, a member of NAES or a member's spouse or dependent, and have been a member in good standing for a least two years (members only). Members' dependents must be between the ages of 17 and 21 to apply. Past recipients of this award may apply again.

**Funds Avail.:** One $250 scholarship that can be used for the Certified Professional Exam or required book purchases. Scholarships are paid directly to recipient's institution or student is directly reimbursed for enrollment fees with board-approved proof of payment. **To Apply:** Applicants must submit one recommendation from a current or previous employer (if a dependent, the recommendation must be from a school counselor or another career secretary), current transcript of grades, and a completed application form. Dependent applicants must also provide proof of age. **Contact:** Address inquiries to NAES Advisory Board, Scholarship Department, at the above address (see entry 3874).

**• 3876 •**
**National Association for Gifted Children**
1707 L St. NW, No. 550          *Ph:* (202)785-4268
Washington, DC 20036          *Fax:* (202)785-4248
*URL:* http://www.NAGC.ORG

**• 3877 •   Hollingworth Award Competition** *(Doctorate, Graduate, Postdoctorate, Professional Development/Award)*

**Purpose:** To encourage educational and psychological research studies of potential benefit to the gifted and talented. **Qualif.:** The competition is open to individuals and organizations that present proposals for publishable research projects concerning gifted and/

*National Association for Gifted Children (continued)*

or talented individuals. Graduate students, teachers, educational administrators, psychologists, or other professionals, as well as educational institutions and school systems are eligible. The research projects may be sponsored by universities, school systems, individual schools, public agencies, or private nonprofit organizations. Competition is for research proposals only. Completed research is not eligible. **Criteria:** Only the proposals are evaluated; letters of application, etc., are not judged. Proposals are judged on the basis of potential significance to the field of gifted/talented education and adequacy of research design and presentation.

**Funds Avail.:** A cash award of $2,000. **No. of Awards:** 1. **To Apply:** Applicants must submit eight copies of an approved research proposal in English, which should not exceed 20 double-spaced, typed pages, excluding appendixes and other attachments. Copies should be printed on both sides of the paper if possible with the pages stapled together. They must also submit eight copies of a 200-word abstract, a signed statement of approval from the sponsoring institution, and a brief letter stating the applicant's work and home addresses and phone numbers, current position and qualifications, how the applicant learned of the award, and estimated date of completion of the study. **Deadline:** Proposals and other documents must be received by January 15.

**Remarks:** The award is named for Dr. Leta Stetter Hollingworth, a pioneer in the field of gifted education. **Contact:** Dr. Sally Reis, Chmn., at the above address (see entry 3876).

• 3878 •
**National Association of Hispanic Nurses**
1501 16th St., NW
Washington, DC 20036
URL: http://www.calumet.purdue.edu/public/finaid/nahn2.htm
*Ph:* (202)387-2477
*Fax:* (202)797-4353

• 3879 • **National Association of Hispanic Nurses National Scholarship Award** *(Graduate, Undergraduate/Scholarship)*

**Focus:** Nursing. **Qualif.:** Applicants must be outstanding Hispanic students enrolled in associate of arts, diploma, baccalaureate, or graduate nursing programs. Students must be members of the National Association of Hispanic Nurses. **Criteria:** Based on current academic standing in an NLN accredited school of nursing, promise of future professional contributions to the nursing profession, and potential to act as role models to other aspiring Hispanic nursing students. Financial need is also considered. **To Apply:** Application information is available by contacting the Association. **Deadline:** April 15. **Contact:** National Award Scholarships Chairperson at the above address (see entry 3878).

• 3880 •
**National Association of Junior Auxiliaries**
PO Box 1873
Greenville, MS 38702-1873
URL: http://www.tecinfo.com/~najanet/schapp.html
*Ph:* (601)332-3000
*Fax:* (601)332-3076

• 3881 • **NAJA Graduate Scholarships** *(Graduate/Scholarship)*

**Purpose:** To fund qualified applicants whose enhanced education and training will ultimately benefit the primary concern of NAJA, children and youth. **Focus:** Education, Child Psychology and Related Fields. **Qualif.:** Applicants must have been accepted by a

graduate school on or before April 1. Each April, scholarships are awarded for graduate-level studies for one year in counseling psychology, mental health, mental retardation, speech pathology, exceptional children, remedial skills, hearing impaired, and gifted and talented. Applicants must work directly with children. Applicants pursuing a graduate degree in Administration are not considered. Applicants must be U.S. citizens, and residents of states with NAJA chapters (AL, AR, LA, MS, MO, TN and TX). Applicants must also enroll in U.S. colleges. **Criteria:** Selection is based on potential for long-term contribution to children and youth.

**Funds Avail.:** Varies. **No. of Awards:** 10-15. **Deadline:** Completed applications and supporting documents must be postmarked by February 1. **Contact:** Chairman, NAJA Scholarship Committee, at the above address (see entry 3880).

• 3882 •
**National Association of Letter Carriers**
100 Indiana Ave., NW
Washington, DC 20001-2144
URL: http://www.nalc.org/
*Ph:* (202)393-4695
*Fax:* (202)737-1540

• 3883 • **William C. Doherty Scholarships** *(High School, Undergraduate/Scholarship)*

**Focus:** General Studies. **Qualif.:** Applicants must be high school seniors and children, or legally adopted children of active, retired, or deceased letter carriers. Stepchildren are eligible if they live with the member in a regular parent-child relationship. Parents must be members in good standing of the NALC at least one year prior to application. The scholarship must be used toward pursuing an undergraduate degree at an accredited college or university. **Criteria:** Winners are judged on the basis of secondary school records, personal qualifications, and SAT results.

**Funds Avail.:** Awards of up to $800 annually are renewable for four consecutive years providing the winner maintains satisfactory grades. Winners may accept other scholarship assistance. **No. of Awards:** 15. (Five in each of three nationwide regions.) **To Apply:** All applicants must take the Scholastic Aptitude Test (SAT) or the American College Test (ACT) in either their junior or senior year and have their scores forwarded to the NALC. Applicants must submit a scholarship application and have it signed by the parent NALC member and an officer of the member's NALC branch. Applications are disseminated only through the *The Postal Record* (NALC's official monthly periodical). **Deadline:** Application forms should be submitted by December 31. **Contact:** The National Association of Letter Carriers at the above address (see entry 3882).

• 3884 •
**National Association of Media Women - Atlanta Chapter**
1185 Niskey Lake Rd., S.W.
Atlanta, GA 30331
*Ph:* (404)344-5862

• 3885 • **National Association of Media Women Scholarship** *(Undergraduate/Scholarship)*

**Qualif.:** Applicants must be undergraduate female minority students majoring in mass communications and attending a college or university in Georgia.

**Funds Avail.:** Minimum grant $500. **Deadline:** March 15.

**Remarks:** Scholarship offered by the Atlanta chapter of the NAMW. **Contact:** Alexis Scott Reeves, National Association of Media Women, PO Box 4689, Atlanta, GA, 30302.

• 3886 •

## National Association of Plumbing, Heating, Cooling Contractors - Scholarship Program

PO Box 6808        *Ph:* (703)237-8100
Falls Church, VA 22040      *Fax:* (703)237-7442
                        *Free:* 800-533-7694

• 3887 • **NAPHCC Educational Foundation Scholarships** *(High School, Undergraduate/Scholarship)*

**Purpose:** To improve the technical and business competence of the industry by awarding scholarships to young people with extensive backgrounds and intimate knowledge of the industry. The scholarships, given each year, are to be used by the recipients to augment their backgrounds and knowledge with specialized academic pursuits. **Focus:** Industry and Trade. **Qualif.:** Candidates must have experience in the plumbing, heating, and cooling industry and be sponsored by an NAPHCC member in good standing who has retained such status without interruption for at least two years prior to the date of application. The sponsor must maintain good standing during the full term of the scholarship. Failure to maintain such status will be considered adequate reason for the committee to reevaluate the recipient's continuance in the program. Only applicants presently in their final year of high school or freshman year of college may apply for a scholarship award. The scholarship money may only be earmarked for an accredited college in the United States. **Criteria:** Selection is based upon grades and experience in the plumbing, heating, and cooling industry.

**Funds Avail.:** $2,500. **No. of Awards:** 3. **To Apply:** Sponsors must sign the student's completed application form and submit a letter of recommendation on business letterhead. Applicants under final consideration for an award will be interviewed by an NAPHCC representative of the industry. **Deadline:** April 1. **Contact:** Jackie Hansmann at the above address (see entry 3886).

• 3888 •

## National Association of Power Engineers

1 Springfield St.        *Ph:* (413)592-6273
Chicopee, MA 01013     *Fax:* (413)592-1998
*URL:* http://www.powerengineers.com

• 3889 • **Henry Cozen Scholarship** *(Undergraduate/Scholarship)*

**Qualif.:** Applicant must be a member or the child of a member of the National Association of Power Engineers.

**Funds Avail.:** $1,000 per year. **No. of Awards:** 1. **Deadline:** June 1. **Contact:** National Secretary at the above address (see entry 3888).

• 3890 •

## National Association of Professional Word Processing Technicians (G/KAM)

110 W. Byberry Rd., Ste. E2
Philadelphia, PA 19116

• 3891 • **NAPWPT Scholarships** *(Graduate, Undergraduate/Scholarship)*

**Focus:** General Studies. **Qualif.:** Applicants should be undergraduate students or graduate students. Others are also considered. Upon receipt of processing fee, confirmation and details of awards will be issued to applicant. **Criteria:** Random drawings are held in February and August each year.

**Funds Avail.:** $500. **To Apply:** Applicants must submit curriculum vitae and a $20 processing fee accompanied by a self-addressed stamped envelope. **Deadline:** February 15 and August 15.

**Remarks:** Upon receipt of processing fee, confirmation and details of awards will be issued to applicant. **Contact:** Lamont Seguro at the above address (see entry 3890).

• 3892 •

## National Association for Public Interest Law

1118 22nd St, NW, 3rd Floor    *Ph:* (202)466-3686
Washington, DC 20037        *Fax:* (202)429-9766
*E-mail:* bbeeland@napil.org
*URL:* http://www.napil.org/

• 3893 • **NAPIL Fellowships for Equal Justice** *(Postdoctorate/Fellowship)*

**Purpose:** To provide salary and loan repayment assistance to lawyers who advocate on behalf of individuals, groups, or interest that are not adequately represented by the American civil legal system. The goals of the Fellowship program are to: serve underrepresented communities; create new public interest law positions; select a diverse group of highly qualified Fellows; and develop future leaders in public interest law. **Focus:** Law. **Qualif.:** Candidate's who hold a J.D., or who will hold a J.D. by commencement of the Fellowship are eligble to apply. NAPIL Fellowships for Equal Justice is committed to selecting a group of Fellows who represent a broad range of backgrounds and experiences, and who come from a wide range of law schools.

**Funds Avail.:** NAPIL Fellowships will provide a Fellow with the starting salary at the sponsoring non-profit organization (up to $30,000). If the first year of the Fellowship is successful, then the Fellow can apply for renewal for a second year at half the salary rate for a second year lawyer (up to $15,000). NAPIL Fellowships will also provide debt service during the Fellowship to cover educational debt payments (Fellows will be required to maximize their participation in available Loan Repayment Assistance Programs) before applying for any loan repayment assistance from NAPIL Fellowships. Sponsoring organizations must agree to pay fringe benefits in both years, and to commit to seeking or providing funding for one-half of the second year salary of the Fellowship. **To Apply:** Write to the above address for application form and guidelines. **Deadline:** Early November. **Contact:** K. Jill Barr, Fellowship Program Coordinator at the above address (see entry 3892).

## • 3894 •
## National Association of Purchasing Management - Senior Research Fellowship Committee

c/o Holly LaCroix Johnson
PO Box 22160                      *Ph:* (480)752-6276
Tempe, AZ 85285-2160              *Fax:* (480)752-7890
*E-mail:* hjohnson@napm.org
*URL:* http://www.napm.org

### • 3895 •  NAPM Doctoral Grants *(Doctorate/Grant)*

**Purpose:** To support research in purchasing and materials management or related fields. **Qualif.:** Applicants must be doctoral candidates pursuing a Ph.D. or D.B.A. in purchasing, business, management, logistics, economics, industrial engineering, or related fields at an accredited U.S. university.

**Funds Avail.:** $10,000. **No. of Awards:** 4. **To Apply:** Candidates must submit application form, official transcripts, three letters of recommendation, a research proposal abstract of up to 25 pages (including literature search and research design), and a letter of endorsement from a major advisor to: NAPM Senior Research Fellowship Committee, c/o Holly LaCriox Johnson, Sr. VP, 2055 E. Centennial Cir. Tempe, AZ 85284. **Deadline:** January 31.

### • 3896 •  NAPM Senior Research Fellowship Grants *(Doctorate/Fellowship)*

**Purpose:** To promote research into the field of purchasing and materials management or related fileds. **Focus:** Institutional purchasing, materials management and related fields. **Qualif.:** Applicants must be assistant or associate professors (or of equivalent status) at their institutions and have demonstrated exceptional academic productivity in research and teaching. They also must be full-time faculty members (within or outside of the United States).

**Funds Avail.:** $5,000. **No. of Awards:** Four **To Apply:** Candidates must submit four copies of letter of application, research proposal of no more than five pages (including problem statement or hypothesis; research methodology, with data sources, collection, and analysis; and value to the field of purchasing and supply), curriculum vitae, including works in progress to NAPM Senior Research Fellowship Committee, c/o Holly LaCroix Johnson, Sr. VP, 2055 E. Centennial Cir. Tempe, AZ 85284. **Deadline:** April 11. **Contact:** Rick Boyle, Ph.D., at the above address (see entry 3894).

## • 3897 •
## National Association of Secondary School Principals

1904 Association Dr.              *Ph:* (703)860-0200
Reston, VA 22091                  *Fax:* (703)476-5432

### • 3898 •  Century Three Leaders Scholarships *(Undergraduate/Scholarship)*

**Purpose:** To inspire American youth to become involved in community and social issues; assume leadership roles; think about their roles as adults; explore America's past, present, and future; and apply responsible leadership techniques to community action. **Qualif.:** Applicants must be senior high school students enrolled in public, private, or parochial schools in the United States. Students should have good academic records, be involved in school and community activities, and have an awareness of world events. **Criteria:** Selection is based on school and community activities, work experience, a current events quiz, and preparation of a project for innovative leadership that discusses a major challenge facing the United States in the third century and how it should be handled.

**Funds Avail.:** Scholarships totaling $249,100 are awarded annually. The District of Columbia is treated as a state. From each state, two winners receive $1,500 college scholarships and all-expense-paid trips to the national Century Three Leaders conference; two alternates each receive $500 college scholarships; and six finalists each receive $100 college scholarships. The National winner receives an additional $10,000 college scholarship, and nine runners-up each receive $500. **To Apply:** The application process includes a two-page projection written by school winners concerning a problem America will face in its third century as a nation. A current events exam is also given. Each school selects one winner, who then competes on a state-by-state basis. State winners, two alternates, and six finalists are selected based on individual interviews. At the national conference, one national winner and nine runner-ups are announced. Program kits are provided to all high school principals each September. **Deadline:** Applications must be filed in mid-October of the student's senior year.

**Remarks:** The Shell Century Three program developed as an outgrowth of the 1976 bicentennial program sponsored by the Shell Oil Company Foundation and administered by the National Association of Secondary School Principals. **Contact:** Local high school principal.

### • 3899 •  National Honor Society Scholarships *(Undergraduate/Scholarship)*

**Qualif.:** Each National Honor Society Chapter can nominate two seniors for a national scholarship. Any high school senior who is a member of the National Honor Society may be nominated.

**Funds Avail.:** 250 $1,000 scholarships. **To Apply:** Nominees must be able to demonstrate on their applications that they possess outstanding character, scholarship, service, and leadership.

**Remarks:** This award is funded by (NASSP), L.G. Balfour Company, and Collegiate Cap and Gown Company. **Contact:** For additional information contact high school counselors, or The Division of Student Activities at 800-253-7746.

### • 3900 •  Principal's Leadership Award *(Undergraduate/Scholarship)*

**Qualif.:** Candidates are high school seniors nominated by their school. Each school may nominate only one senior to compete. **Criteria:** School winners compete on the basis of their application.

**Funds Avail.:** 150 $1,000 scholarships.

**Remarks:** This award is funded by Herff-Jones, Inc. **Contact:** For additional information contact high school counselors or the Division of Activities at 800-253-7746.

## • 3901 •
## National Association of Teachers of Singing, Inc.

2800 University Blvd. N., J.U. Sta.    *Ph:* (904)744-9022
Jacksonville, FL 32211                 *Fax:* (904)744-9033
*E-mail:* wmvessels@aol.com
*URL:* http://www.nats.org

### • 3902 •  NATS Artist Awards *(Postgraduate, Professional Development/Award)*

**Purpose:** To recognize qualified singers and advance their professional careers. **Focus:** Vocal Music. **Qualif.:** Applicants must be at least 21 and not more than 35 years of age on the application deadline date. They must have studied continuously for at least a year with a NATS member in good standing who must also have been their most recent teacher, or they must be a NATS members themselves. Repertoire requirements should be obtained from NATS.

**Funds Avail.:** First prize of $5,000, a second prize of $2,500, and a third prize of $2,000. **To Apply:** There are state, regional, and national auditions. Fourteen semifinalists will appear with expenses paid at the final auditions at the NATS National Convention in December or early July. **Deadline:** Applications must be filed by August 1 for December conventions and by January 10 for July conventions.

**Remarks:** Since 1978, competitions are held every 18 months. **Contact:** National Association of Teachers of Singing at the above address (see entry 3901).

---

• **3903** •

**National Association of Water Companies - New Jersey Chapter**
c/o Elizabethtown Water Co.
ATTN: Gail P. Brady
600 South Ave.                          *Ph:* (908)654-9122
Westfield, NJ 07090                     *Fax:* (908)232-2719
*E-mail:* gbrady@etownwater.com

• **3904** • **National Association of Water Companies - New Jersey Chapter Scholarship** *(Graduate, Undergraduate/Scholarship)*

**Purpose:** To encourage the pursuit of a career in the investor owned water utility business. **Focus:** Natural resource management, environmental sciences, biology, chemistry, engineering, communication, computer science, business administration, human resources, consumer affairs, law, accounting, finance and other fields related to the water utility industry. **Qualif.:** Applicants must be New Jersey residents who have lived in the state for at least five year, attending and pursuing a degree in a New Jersey college or university as undergraduate or graduate students pursuing professional careers in the water utility industry or in any field related to it with a minimum grade point average of 3.0 on a 4.0 grading scale, and be U.S. citizens. Officers or directors of NAWC, or regular representatives of NAWC member companies, or members of their immediate families are ineligible, as are officials, representatives or employees of any agency regulating the water industry, or members of their immediate families. **Criteria:** Awards are made based on academic achievement, leadership potential and initiative.

**Funds Avail.:** $2,500 per award. **No. of Awards:** 2. **To Apply:** Write for further details. **Deadline:** April 1. **Contact:** NAWC at the above address (see entry 3903).

---

• **3905** •

**National Association of Women in Construction**
3452 Loadstone Dr.
Sherman Oaks, CA 91403

• **3906** • **El Camino Real No. 158 NAWIC Scholarship** *(Undergraduate/Scholarship)*

**Purpose:** To further the education of construction students. **Qualif.:** Applicants must be United States citizens who are sophomores majoring in some phase of construction at an accredited four-year college in California. **Criteria:** Selection is based on academic record, ambitions, and financial need.

**Funds Avail.:** $1,000. **To Apply:** Materials to be submitted include a completed application, high school and college grade transcripts, letter from college dean of admissions, and a personal statement citing qualifications and goals. **Deadline:** April 30. **Contact:** Marie

Revere, Scholarship Chairperson, at the above address (see entry 3905).

---

• **3907** •

**National Association for Women in Education**
1325 18th St., NW, Ste. 210          *Ph:* (202)659-9330
Washington, DC 20036                  *Fax:* (202)457-0946

• **3908** • **National Association for Women in Education Women's Research Awards** *(Graduate/ Award)*

**Purpose:** To encourage and support excellence in research by, for, and about women. **Focus:** Women's Studies. **Qualif.:** The graduate student competition is open to any student enrolled in a graduate study program. Any person may enter the open competition.

**Funds Avail.:** $750. **To Apply:** Contact the Association for applications. **Deadline:** November 1. **Contact:** The National Association for Women in Education at the above address (see entry 3907).

---

• **3909** •

**National Black MBA Association**
180 N. Michigan Ave., Ste. 1820
Chicago, IL 60601

• **3910** • **NBMBAA National MBA Scholarship/PhD Fellowship** *(Graduate/Fellowship, Scholarship)*

**Purpose:** To provide access to funding for full-time minority business graduate students. **Focus:** Business. **Qualif.:** Minority MBA or PhD candidate enrolled full-time in a business graduate program. **Criteria:** Essay/research response; extra curricular activity/community involvement; GPA; financial need; interview. **No. of Awards:** 2- PhD; 25- MBA **To Apply:** Completed application with certified official transcripts required. **Deadline:** April 6. **Contact:** Scholarship Coordinator.

---

• **3911** •

**National Black Police Association**
3251 Mt. Pleasant St., NW, 2nd Fl.    *Ph:* (202)986-2070
Washington, DC 20010                  *Fax:* (202)986-0410
*URL:* http://www.Blackpolice.org

• **3912** • **Alphonso Deal Scholarship Award** *(Undergraduate/Scholarship)*

**Purpose:** To enhance the higher educational opportunities among qualified high school graduates in the area of law enforcement or other related fields for the betterment of the criminal justice system. **Focus:** Criminal Justice. **Qualif.:** Applicants must be U.S. citizens, high school seniors accepted by a college or university prior to the date of the award, and have maintained at least a 2.5 GPA. **Criteria:** Selection is based upon GPA, recommendations, and extra-curricular activities.

**Funds Avail.:** $500 per recipient. **No. of Awards:** 2. **To Apply:** Candidates should submit information regarding their educational background, biographical information, and transcripts. Request application in writing, include self-addressed, stamped envelope. **Deadline:** June 1. **Contact:** Ronald E. Hampton at the above address (see entry 3911).

---

## • 3913 •
## National Board Civil Air Patrol
HQ CAP/CP
105 S. Hansell St., Bldg. 714
Maxwell AFB, AL 36116-6332          *Ph:* (205)953-4238
*E-mail:* bcampbell@cap.af.mil; CPR@cap.af.mil
*URL:* http://cap.af.mil

### • 3914 •  Major General Lucas Beau Flight
Scholarship *(Other/Scholarship)*

**Purpose:** To provide ground and air training towards a FAA private pilot license.

**Funds Avail.:** $750-1500 awarded annually. **To Apply:** Applicants must submit CAP form 95. **Contact:** Lt. Col. Bruce Gunn, Cadet Special Activity.

### • 3915 •  Civil Air Patrol Graduate Scholarship
*(Doctorate, Graduate/Scholarship)*

**Focus:** Varies. **Qualif.:** Applicants must be members of the Civil Air Patrol. **Criteria:** Academic, extracurricular, Cap participation.

**Funds Avail.:** $750-1500. Awarded annually. **No. of Awards:** Varies. **To Apply:** CAP form 95 must be submitted. **Deadline:** January 31.

### • 3916 •  Civil Air Patrol Technical/Vocational
Scholarships *(Other/Scholarship)*

**Focus:** Varies. **Qualif.:** Applicant must be a member of the Civil Air Patrol and have received the Billy Mitchell Award or Senior Rating in Level II of the Senior Training Program. .

**Funds Avail.:** $750-1500. Awarded annually. **No. of Awards:** Varies. **To Apply:** CAP form 95 must be submitted. **Contact:** Major Brian Campbell, CAP, Registrar.

### • 3917 •  Col. Louisa Spruance Morse CAP
Scholarship *(Undergraduate/Scholarship)*

**Focus:** Aeronautics. **Qualif.:** Applicants must be a CAP member pursing an aviation education at Embry-Riddle Aeronautical University and have completed one semester of AFROTC.

**Funds Avail.:** $1000 awarded annually. **No. of Awards:** 5. **To Apply:** CAP form 95 must be submitted. **Deadline:** April 1. **Contact:** Major Brian Campbell, Cap, Registrar.

### • 3918 •  National Board Civil Air Patrol
Undergraduate/Advanced Undergraduate College
Scholarship *(Undergraduate/Scholarship)*

**Focus:** Varies. **Qualif.:** Applicant must be a member of the Civil Air Patrol and have received the Billy Mitchell Award or Senior Rating in Level II of the Senior Training Program.

**Funds Avail.:** $750-1500. Awarded annually. **No. of Awards:** Varies. **To Apply:** CAP form 95 must be submitted. **Deadline:** January 31. **Contact:** Major Brian Campbell, CAP, Registrar.

## • 3919 •
## National Broadcasting Society
c/o Donna R. Williams
St. Thomas Aquinas College
Rte. 340
Sparkill, NY 10976          *Ph:* (914)398-4072
*URL:* http://www.onu.edu/org/nbs/jobs.html

### • 3920 •  National Broadcasting Society Member
Scholarship *(Undergraduate/Scholarship)*

**Focus:** General studies. **Qualif.:** Applicants must be members of the National Broadcasting Society. **Criteria:** Awards are made based on academic achievement and contribution to the National Broadcasting Society. **No. of Awards:** 7. **To Apply:** Write for further details. **Contact:** National Broadcasting Society at the above address (see entry 3919).

## • 3921 •
## National Cancer Institute
National Institutes of Health
6130 Executive Blvd.          *Ph:* (301)496-8520
Bethesda, MD 20892-7346          *Fax:* (301)402-0816
*E-mail:* msears@nih.gov
*URL:* http://www.nci.nih.gov/

*The National Cancer Institute is part of the National Institutes of Health and the U.S. Department of Health and Human Services.*

### • 3922 •  Cancer Prevention and Control Research
Small Grant Program *(Doctorate, Postdoctorate, Postgraduate/Grant)*

**Purpose:** To facilitate growth of a nationwide cohort of scientists with a high level of research expertise in the field of human cancer control intervention research. **Focus:** Prevention, Screening & Early Detection, Cancer Control Science, Applications Research, Smoking Prevention and Cessation. **Qualif.:** New and experienced investigators in relevant fields and disciplines (e.g., disease prevention and control, medicine, public health, health promotion, epidemiology, social work, nursing research, nutrition, health policy, health services research, and behavioral sciences, such as psychology, health education, sociology, and community organization) are eligible to apply. Investigators must have doctoral degrees or currently be enrolled in an accredited doctoral degree program. Ineligible applicants are those who are or have previously been Principal Investigators of a cancer control Small Grant or RO1. Small grant research support may not be used to supplement research projects currently supported by Federal or non-Federal funds, or to provide interim support of projects under review by the Public Health Service. **Criteria:** Applicants are judged on scientific/technical merit of the research; potential for P.I. contribution as an investigator in the field of cancer control intervention research; adequacy of resources or facilities.

**Funds Avail.:** Total direct costs of up to $50,000 are provided. **To Apply:** Applications are available at most institutional offices of sponsored research, use standard PHS 398 research grant application. **Deadline:** January 15, May 15, and September 15. **Contact:** Applications are available by writing to the Grants Information Center for Scientific Review, National Institutes of Health, 6701 Rocklege Dr., MSG7761, Bethesda, MD 20892, Telephone: (301)435-0714. Direct inquiries may be addressed to Helen I. Meissner, Sc.M., National Cancer Institute, at (301)496-8520 or e-mail Hm36d@nih.gov.

• **3923** • **EORTC/NCI Exchange Program**
*(Postdoctorate/Grant)*

**Purpose:** To allow cancer research scientists affiliated with the European Organization for Research and Treatment of Cancer (EORTC) to receive training at the National Cancer Institute or at one of its extramural cancer research institutions in the United States, and to allow American scientists to receive training at EORTC-affiliated institutions. **Focus:** Cancer. **Qualif.:** Candidates must have completed a minimum of three years of postdoctoral cancer research and be familiar with the language of the host institution.

**Funds Avail.:** Subsistence allowance of $30,000. The exchangeship does not cover travel or insurance expenses. **Deadline:** April 15 and October 15. **Contact:** Office of International Affairs, Bldg. 31, Rm. 4B55, Bethesda, MD 20892. Telephone: (301)496-4761.

• **3924** • **NCI International Bilateral Program**
*(Postdoctorate/Other)*

**Purpose:** To promote cooperative research, exchange of individual scientists, and exchange of information on state-of-the-art of cancer research through symposia and workshops with cancer research institutes in Egypt, Germany, France, Hungary, Italy, Japan, China, Poland, Russia, Korea, and other countries. **Focus:** Cancer. **Qualif.:** U.S. scientists in the areas of basic and clinical cancer research are eligible to apply.

**Funds Avail.:** Scientists receive an APEX or government fare airline ticket from the Office of International Affairs (OIA). In-country expenses are provided by the hosting institution. **To Apply:** Applicants must submit a letter of intent, a letter of invitation, and a curriculum vitae.

• **3925** • **Oncology Research Faculty Development Program** *(Postdoctorate/Grant)*

**Purpose:** To prepare participants for independent careers as investigators and for leadership positions in cancer research. **Focus:** Cancer Research. **Qualif.:** Applicants must be sponsored by the Director of their home institution, have a minimum of three years postdoctoral experience in cancer research and be proficient in spoken and written English.

**Funds Avail.:** Subsistence allowance of $22,500 the first year, $23,500 the second year, and $24,500 the third year. The program also provides for the recipient's (and dependent's) health insurance. No dependant allowances are otherwise provided. **Deadline:** April 15. **Contact:** National Cancer Institute, Office of International Affairs, Bldg. 31, Rm. 4B55, Bethesda, MD 20892. Telephone: (301)496-4761.

• **3926** •
**National Cancer Institute of Canada - Research Programs**
10 Alcorn Ave., Ste. 200            *Ph:* (416)961-7223
Toronto, ON, Canada M4V 3B1       *Fax:* (416)961-4189
*E-mail:* research@cancer.ca
*URL:* http://www.ncic.cancer.ca

• **3927** • **National Cancer Institute of Canada Research Fellowships** *(Postdoctorate/Fellowship)*

**Purpose:** To support training and study in cancer research. **Focus:** Oncology. **Qualif.:** Applicant for a Research Fellowship must be a Canadian citizen or landed immigrant; hold an M.D. or Ph.D. degree; and be accepted for postdoctoral training in cancer research by a university laboratory or teaching hospital in Canada. Applicant for a Clinical Research Fellowship must be a Canadian

citizen or resident at time of application; hold an M.D. degree; and have qualified for admission to Fellowship of the Royal College of Physicians and Surgeons of Canada. The Clinical Research Fellowships support specialized training in clinical cancer research. All candidates with an M.D. degree must normally be licensed to practice in Canada. **Criteria:** Applicants are judged on academic record; nature of proposed program; relevance to cancer; source of research support and breadth of training in cancer research in selected environment.

**Funds Avail.:** $29,200-45,400/year. **To Apply:** Write for application form and guidelines. Submit 15 copies of the form with university transcripts and letters of recommendation. See website for details and form. **Deadline:** February 1. Notification in June.

**Remarks:** The Institute also offers funds for travel during sabbatical leaves and grants for research equipment. Write for further details.

• **3928** • **National Cancer Institute of Canada Research Grants** *(Postdoctorate/Grant)*

**Purpose:** To provide support for research projects in cancer. **Focus:** Oncology. **Qualif.:** Candidate must be a Canadian citizen or landed immigrant. Applicant must hold an appointment at a Canadian university or institution, and be conducting research relating to cancer. The institution concerned must agree to the proposed research and provide basic equipment and research facilities. Grants are intended to cover the costs of minor equipment, supplies, and payment of assistants, and do not provide for the personal support of the grantee. **Criteria:** Based on scientific merit.

**Funds Avail.:** $150,000-500,000. **To Apply:** Write for application form and guidelines. Submit 15 copies of form with a full description of the proposed research. See website for details and form. **Deadline:** October 15. Notification in March.

**Remarks:** The Institute awards Research Scientist Career Appointments to highly qualified investigators who have demonstrated their ability to conduct cancer research. Applicant must be a recipient of research grant support from the Institute. Funds for travel during sabbatical leaves are also available. Write for further details. **Contact:** Research Grants Manager.

• **3929** • **National Cancer Institute of Canada Research Scientist Career Appointments**
*(Postdoctorate/Award)*

**Purpose:** To support cancer research. **Focus:** Oncology **Qualif.:** Applicant must hold an M.D. or Ph.D. degree and should normally have completed three years of postdoctoral training in research. Individuals may be presented as candidates who have up to, but not more than, five years of research experience, counted from the beginning of their independent research career. Candidates must have experience in cancer research. Candidates must remain in Canada. Appointments are tenable at any Canadian university or institution with appropriate research facilities. These awards enable the recipient to work full-time on a research project, without involvement in major teaching duties. Application must be made by the host institution. **Criteria:** Candidates must hold a fully-funded NCIC grant, or candidates must apply for one in the grant competition of the concurrent award year.

**Funds Avail.:** $33,013-88,974. **To Apply:** Write for application guidelines. Application must be submitted by the university or institution at which candidate will conduct research; candidate must not apply directly. Short-listed candidates will be interviewed. See website for details and application forms. **Deadline:** February 1, Notification in June.

**Remarks:** The Institute also offers funds for travel during sabbatical leaves and grants for research equipment. Write for further details. **Contact:** Research Awards Manager.

**• 3930 •**
**National Center For Atmospheric Research - Advanced Study Program**
PO Box 3000                          *Ph:* (303)497-1601
Boulder, CO 80307-3000       *Fax:* (303)497-1646
*E-mail:* barbm@ucar.edu

**• 3931 • Postdoctoral Fellowships in the Atmospheric Sciences** *(Postdoctorate/Fellowship)*

**Purpose:** To support postdoctoral research, and to enrich the research talent in the atmospheric sciences. **Focus:** Atmospheric Sciences, Mathematics, and Mathematical Sciences, Biology, Chemistry, Ecology, Economics, Engineering, Geology, Geography, Oceanography. **Qualif.:** Candidate may be of any nationality. Applicant must have earned the Ph.D. degree, and must have no more than four years of postdoctoral experience. Fellowships are tenable at the Center except for special field project assignments.

**Funds Avail.:** $36,000-38,000 stipend, plus travel expenses. **No. of Awards:** 8-10. **To Apply:** There are no standard application forms. Write for application guidelines. Submit undergraduate and graduate transcripts, curriculum vitae, abstract of dissertation, list of publications, four letters of reference, summary of scientific work, and a short statement about interest in atmospheric sciences and the fellowship. Four letters of reference must be sent directly to NCAR. **Deadline:** January 5. Selections are announced by late March. **Contact:** Barbara Hansford, Coordinator, at the above address (see entry 3930).

**• 3932 •**
**National Center for Preventive Law**
1900 Olive St.                         *Ph:* (303)871-6099
Denver, CO 80220             *Fax:* (303)871-6001
*E-mail:* ncpl@adm.law.du.edu
*URL:* http://www.nepl.org/˜nepl

**• 3933 • Preventive Law Prizes (Discontinued)**
*(Graduate, Professional Development/Prize)*

**Purpose:** To recognize written work in the field of preventive law. **Focus:** Preventive Law. **Qualif.:** Applicant may be of any nationality, but must have written a manuscript on a topic related to preventive law. Applicant may be a law student, attorney, or other person, or a project submitted by a bar association, educational institution, legal service organization, or other group. Works by law students are judged separately. Manuscripts, recommendations, and project descriptions may be of any length and should be submitted in duplicate. Previously published work may be considered. Winning articles may be published in the Preventive Law Reporter.

**Funds Avail.:** $1,000/category. **No. of Awards:** 3. **To Apply:** Submit manuscript, recommendations, and project descriptions to the President. **Deadline:** December 31. Prizes are announced in February.

**Remarks:** This is not a scholarship, fellowship or loan program. It is a writing competition. **Contact:** Edward A. Dauer, President, at the above address (see entry 3932).

**• 3934 •**
**The National Chapter of Canada (IODE)**
Head Office
40 Orchard View Blvd., Ste. 254    *Ph:* (416)487-4416
Toronto, ON, Canada M4R 1B9    *Fax:* (416)487-4417

**• 3935 • War Memorial Scholarships** *(Doctorate/ Scholarship)*

**Purpose:** To honor the memory of the men and women who gave their lives for Canada in World Wars I and II. **Focus:** General Studies. **Qualif.:** Applicants must be Canadian citizens and must hold a first degree from a Canadian recognized university. At the time of application, candidates must be enrolled in a doctoral program or equivalent. Scholarships are tenable anywhere in Canada or the Commonwealth. Recipients studying in Canada must not hold more than $5,000 in support from other sources. Those studying overseas may not hold more than $9,000.

**Funds Avail.:** For study in Canada: $12,000; for study within the Commonwealth: $15,000. **No. of Awards:** A Maximum of 9. **To Apply:** Write for application form and guidelines, available in August. Submit application to the IODE convener in the province where applicant received his or her first degree. **Deadline:** Application must be received by December 1.

**Remarks:** The former name of IODE was Imperial Order Daughters of the Empire; now only the acronym is used. **Contact:** K.L. Speller, Vice President and National War Memorial Officer, at the above address (see entry 3934).

**• 3936 •**
**National Collegiate Athletic Association**
6201 College Blvd.                    *Ph:* (913)339-1906
Overland Park, KS 66211-2422    *Fax:* (913)339-0043
*URL:* http://volleyball.org/ncaa

**• 3937 • NCAA Postgraduate Scholarships**
*(Postgraduate, Undergraduate/Scholarship)*

**Purpose:** To encourage NCAA student-athletes to pursue graduate degrees. **Focus:** General Studies. **Qualif.:** Candidates may be of any nationality, but must be enrolled as student-athletes at and nominated by a NCAA member institution. They must also be in the academic year of their final season of NCAA eligibility and have a cumulative grade point average of at least a 3.0/4.0. Their performance as a varsity team athlete will be considered at least equally with their academic achievement. Awards are offered for student-athletes in football, basketball, and other varsity sports in which the NCAA sponsors national championship competition. Specific requirements and deadlines vary for each category. Grantees must undertake full-time graduate study within five years of receiving the award.

**Funds Avail.:** $5,000 is available. **No. of Awards:** 154 awards are offered, 77 each for men and women. **To Apply:** Contact institution's faculty athletic representative or director of athletics. Nomination forms are sent automatically to NCAA member institutions and only faculty athletics representatives or directors of athletics at member institutions may submit nominations. **Deadline:** The deadlines for materials to be submitted are as follows: basketball, March 4; football, October 21; other sports, April 14. **Contact:** Fannie B. Vaughan, Executive Assistant, at the above address (see entry 3936).

## • 3938 •
## National Consortium for Educational Access
Georgia Institute of Technology
Alumni Faculty House       *Ph:* (404)894-2389
Atlanta, GA 30332       *Fax:* (404)853-0446

### • 3939 • National Consortium for Educational Access Fellowship *(Doctorate/Fellowship)*

**Purpose:** To provide financial support to minorities who are pursuing Ph.D.'s, particularly in the scientific, technological, and business-related fields and to increase the number of minorities with Ph.D.'s who are teaching on the university and college level. **Qualif.:** Applicants must be enrolled full-time in Ph.D. program at a NCEA member institution. **Criteria:** Applicants will be judged on the bases of GPA, standardized test scores, recommendations, and academic discipline.

**Funds Avail.:** $3,000 for students; $5,000 for faculty members. Member schools waive tuition and fees and provide assistantships. **To Apply:** Candidates must submit original applications plus four copies directly to the NCEA. Transcripts and test scores must be forwarded when available. **Deadline:** December 1. **Contact:** Leroy Ervin, Ph.D., Executive Director, at the above address (see entry 3938).

## • 3940 •
## National Consortium for Graduate Degrees for Minorities in Engineering and Science
GEM Central Office
PO Box 537       *Ph:* (219)631-1091
Notre Dame, IN 46556       *Fax:* (219)287-1486
*E-mail:* goldman@llnl.gov
*URL:* http://edprog.llnl.gov/kjd/ncfgdfm.html

### • 3941 • GEM Master's Engineering Fellowships for Minorities *(Graduate/Fellowship)*

**Purpose:** To provide opportunities for minority students to obtain a master's degree in engineering through a program of paid summer engineering internship and financial aid. **Focus:** Engineering. **Qualif.:** Applicant must be a U.S. citizen and a member of one of the ethnic groups under-represented in engineering: American Indian, Black American, Mexican American, Puerto Rican, and other Hispanics. Fellowships are for master's study; applicant must have a minimum academic status of junior-year enrollment in an accredited engineering discipline. Master's studies must take place at a GEM member institution. Acceptance in the fellowship program does not guarantee acceptance to a graduate program. Fellows are required to spend a paid summer research internship at a GEM member employer location.

**Funds Avail.:** $20,000-40,000: includes full tuition and fees, annual stipend, and paid summer research internship **No. of Awards:** over 200. **To Apply:** Write to the Central Office for application guidelines and a list of participating academic institutions and employers. **Deadline:** December 1. Awards are announced February 1. **Contact:** Betty Jean Valdez, Manager, Admittance and Retention, at the above address (see entry 3940).

### • 3942 • GEM Ph.D. Engineering Fellowships for Minorities *(Doctorate/Fellowship)*

**Purpose:** To increase/produce members in engineering faculties and industries. **Focus:** Engineering. **Qualif.:** Applicant must be a U.S. citizen and a member of one of the ethnic groups under-represented in engineering: American Indian, Black American, Mexican American, Puerto Rican, and other Hispanics. Fellowships are for doctoral study at GEM member institutions; applicant must hold an M.S. degree in engineering and be accepted to an approved doctoral program, or have three years of graduate studying remaining to complete the Ph.D. Candidate must demonstrate financial need and a strong interest in teaching and/or industrial research. Fellowships include summer research at a research-based company. Fellows must also be willing to accept a teaching/research assistantship after the first year.

**Funds Avail.:** $60,000-100,000: includes full tuition and fees, annual stipend, and paid summer research. **No. of Awards:** 19. **To Apply:** Write to the Central Office for application guidelines and a list of participating academic institutions and employers. **Deadline:** December 1. Awards are made February 1. **Contact:** Betty Jean Valdez, Manager, Admittance and Retention, at the above address (see entry 3940).

### • 3943 • GEM Ph.D. Science Fellowship Program *(Doctorate/Fellowship)*

**Purpose:** To provide opportunities for minority students to obtain a Ph.D. degree in the natural sciences through a program of paid summer internship and financial aid. **Focus:** Life Sciences, Physical Sciences. **Qualif.:** Applicant must be a U.S. citizen and a member of one of the ethnic groups under-represented in the sciences: American Indian, Black American, Mexican American, Puerto Rican, and other Hispanics. Applicant must be a junior, senior, or baccalaureate degree recipient in an accredited science discipline with an academic record that reflects the ability to succeed in a Ph.D. program. Fellowships are tenable at a GEM Ph.D. Science Program member university. Fellow must intern with a member employer during one summer of the program.

**Funds Avail.:** Tuition, fees, and a stipend of $,12,000, plus funds earned during summer internship. **No. of Awards:** 15. **To Apply:** Write to the Central Office for application guidelines. **Deadline:** December 1. Awards are announced February 1. **Contact:** Betty Jean Valdez, Manager, Admittance and Retention, at the above address (see entry 3940).

## • 3944 •
## The National Council for Eurasian and East European Research
910 17th St., NW, Ste. 300
Washington, DC 20006       *Ph:* (202)822-6950
*E-mail:* nceeerdc@aol.com
*URL:* http://www.nceeer.org

### • 3945 • The National Council Research Contracts *(Postdoctorate/Fellowship, Grant)*

**Purpose:** To support research projects related to the economy, history, politics, and societies of Russia and the other successor states of the USSR and Eastern Europe. **Focus:** Eastern European Studies, Russian, Eurasian and Central Asian Studies. **Qualif.:** Applicants must be either U.S. citizens or permanent resident aliens, and be postdoctoral scholars qualified to conduct independent research. Application must be submitted through a nonprofit U.S. institution.

**Funds Avail.:** Varies. **No. of Awards:** Varies. **To Apply:** Call or write for application forms and guidelines. **Deadline:** January 1, February 15, March 30. **Contact:** Kimberly Righter, Program Officer, at the above address (see entry 3944).

## • 3946 •
## National Council on Family Relations

3989 Central Ave. NE, Ste. 550      *Ph:* (612)781-9331
Minneapolis, MN 55421     *Fax:* (612)781-9348
                   *Free:* 888-781-9331

*E-mail:* ncfr3989@ncfr.com
*URL:* http://www.ncfr.com

### • 3947 • National Council on Family Relations Ernest W. Burgess Award *(Doctorate, Professional Development/Award)*

**Purpose:** Recognizes outstanding scholarly achievement during the course of a career in the study of families. **Focus:** Family Research, Sociology. **Qualif.:** Applicants may be U.S. citizens, permanent U.S. residents or non U.S. citizen/residents. **Criteria:** The award will be presented to an individual who has shown a distinguished career in the field of family research and scholarship.

**Funds Avail.:** A plaque and check for $1,000. **No. of Awards:** 1. **Deadline:** April 15. **Contact:** Cindy Winter, CMP.

### • 3948 • National Council on Family Relations Student Award *(Graduate/Award)*

**Qualif.:** Applicants may be U.S. Citizens, permanent U.S. residents or non U.S. citizens/residents. **Criteria:** The award will be given to a student member who has demonstrated excellence as a student with high potential for contribution to the field of family studies.

**Funds Avail.:** $1,000. **Deadline:** April 15. **Contact:** Cindy Winter.

## • 3949 •
## National Council of Farmer Cooperatives

50 F St., NW, Ste. 900     *Ph:* (202)626-8700
Washington, DC 20001     *Fax:* (202)626-8722
*E-mail:* info@ncfe.org
*URL:* http://www.access.digex.net/~ncfc/members/

### • 3950 • Kenneth D. Naden Award *(Graduate/Award)*

**Purpose:** Award is given for the best Master's thesis. **Focus:** Cooperative Education, Agriculture. **Qualif.:** Theses must be written on topics concerned with the operations of American agricultural cooperatives. Applicants must be graduate students in economics, business, communications, sociology, or other relevant fields, who have agricultural vocational objectives. **Criteria:** A panel of leading agricultural researchers and university faculty members will evaluate the entries.

**Funds Avail.:** $1,000 and a trip to the National Institute on Cooperative Education where recipient will make an oral presentation and receive award. **No. of Awards:** One. **To Apply:** Entries must be accompanied by registration forms, which are available from NCFC. All entries will be acknowledged and retained by NCFC for its research library. **Deadline:** April 15. Winners are announced in July.

**Remarks:** In the event that NCFC receives fewer than four theses, entries will be held for consideration the following year. **Contact:** National Council of Farmer Cooperatives, Graduate Awards, at above address.

### • 3951 • NCFC Undergraduate Term Paper Awards *(Undergraduate/Award)*

**Purpose:** Awards are given to five undergraduates who write outstanding term papers. **Focus:** Agriculture. **Qualif.:** Term papers must deal with issues affecting the operations of American agricultural cooperatives. Applicants must be undergraduate students who are in their junior or senior year at a college or university or second-year students at a junior or community college or a technical institute. **Criteria:** Cooperative leaders and university faculty members will evaluate the entries.

**Funds Avail.:** Five awards of $200 each are given. **To Apply:** Entries must be accompanied by registration forms, which are available from NCFC. All entries will be acknowledged and will become the property of NCFC. Professors submitting papers written by their students should submit no more than five papers each term. **Deadline:** June 15. Winners are announced in July. **Contact:** National Council of Farmer Cooperatives, Undergraduate Awards, at the above address (see entry 3949).

### • 3952 • Edwin G. Nourse Award *(Doctorate/Award)*

**Purpose:** Award is given for the best doctoral dissertation submitted. **Focus:** Cooperative education, Agriculture. **Qualif.:** Dissertations must be written on topics concerned with the operations of American agricultural cooperatives. Applicants must be graduate students in economics, business, communications, sociology, or other relevant fields, who have agricultural vocational objectives. **Criteria:** A panel of leading agricultural researchers and university faculty members will evaluate the entries.

**Funds Avail.:** $1,500 and a trip to the annual National Institute on Cooperative Education, where the winner will make an oral presentation and receive the award. **No. of Awards:** One. **To Apply:** Entries must be accompanied by registration forms, which are available from NCFC. All entries will be acknowledged and will be retained by NCFC for its research library. **Deadline:** April 15. Winners are announced in July.

**Remarks:** In the event that NCFC receives fewer than two dissertations, the single entry will be held for consideration the following year. **Contact:** National Council of Farmer Cooperatives, Graduate Awards, at the above address (see entry 3949).

### • 3953 • E.A. Stokdyk Award *(Graduate/Award)*

**Purpose:** Award is given for the second best Master's thesis. **Focus:** Cooperative Education, Agriculture. **Qualif.:** Theses must be written on topics concerned with the operations of American agricultural cooperatives. Applicants must be graduate students in economics, business, communications, sociology, or other relevant fields, who have an agricultural vocational objective. **Criteria:** A panel of leading agricultural researchers and university faculty members will evaluate the entries.

**Funds Avail.:** $600. **No. of Awards:** One. **To Apply:** Entries must be accompanied by registration forms, which are available from NCFC. All entries will be acknowledged and retained by NCFC for its research library. **Deadline:** April 15. Winners are announced in July.

**Remarks:** In the event that NCFC receives fewer than four theses, entries will be held for consideration the following year. **Contact:** Dorothy J. Fisher, Director of Education and Training, at the above address (see entry 3949).

• 3954 •

## National Council for Geographic Education

Attn: Connie McCardle
16A Leonard Hall
Indiana University of Pennsylvania     *Ph:* (724)357-6290
Indiana, PA 15705     *Fax:* (724)357-7708
*E-mail:* ncge-org@grove.iup.edu
*URL:* http://www.ncge.org

• 3955 • **National Council for Geographic Education Committee for Women in Geographic Education Scholarship** *(Graduate, Undergraduate/Scholarship)*

**Purpose:** To encourage women in geographic education careers. **Focus:** Geography. **Qualif.:** Applicants must have a minimum cumulative grade point average of 3.0 on a 4.0 scale, and a 3.5 in their geography major (a minimum of 15 undergraduate credits or 9 graduate credits in geography is required). **Criteria:** Awards are made based on academic achievement.

**Funds Avail.:** $300. **No. of Awards:** 1. **To Apply:** Applicants must submit a completed application form, transcript including all geography courses taken and grades earned, a letter of recommendation, and a 200-word (approximately) essay. **Deadline:** April 1. **Contact:** NCGE at the above address (see entry 3954).

• 3956 •

## National Council of Jewish Women - Newton Branch

831 Beacon St., 9100-138
Newton, MA 02159     *Ph:* (617)825-9191

• 3957 • **Amelia Greenbaum Scholarships** *(Undergraduate/Scholarship)*

**Qualif.:** Applicants must be female students of the Jewish faith who reside in the Greater Boston area. Applicants must be attending or planning to attend a degree granting institution within the Commonwealth of Massachusetts on an undergraduate level. **Criteria:** The decision will be influenced by financial need and academic record. Priority will be given to women who are returning to school after at least a five-year absence, are new Americans with competency in English, and intend to pursue studies in areas related to the objectives of NCJW, such as social work, public policy and administration, law, and early childhood education.

**Funds Avail.:** Two scholarships are awarded; amounts are individually determined. **No. of Awards:** 2. **To Apply:** Applications may be requested in writing after January 1. A transcript and letter of recommendation from the applicant's principal, guidance counselor, or professor must accompany the application. **Deadline:** All application materials must be received by April 30. Interviews are held shortly thereafter. Recipients are notified the end of June. **Contact:** Administrative Director at the above address (see entry 3956).

• 3958 •

## National Council of State Garden Clubs, Inc.

4401 Magnolia Ave.
St. Louis, MO 63110-3492     *Ph:* (314)776-7574

• 3959 • **NCSGC National Scholarships** *(Graduate, Undergraduate/Scholarship)*

**Purpose:** To encourage the study of horticulture, floriculture, landscape design, city planning land management and allied subjects. **Focus:** Horticulture; Landscape Architecture and Design; Urban Affairs, Design and Planning. **Qualif.:** Applicants must be United States citizens who are studying horticulture, floriculture, landscape design, city planning, or an allied subject. They must also be endorsed by their State Garden Club. **No. of Awards:** 32. **To Apply:** Candidates should write to obtain the name of their state scholarship chairperson. **Deadline:** National deadline is March 1. State deadlines vary. **Contact:** Kathleen Romine, Administrative Secretary, at the above address (see entry 3958).

• 3960 •

## National Council of Teachers of English Research Foundation

1111 W. Kenyon Rd.     *Ph:* (217)328-3870
Urbana, IL 61801     *Fax:* (217)328-0977
    *Free:* 800-369-6283
*URL:* http://www.NCTE.org

• 3961 • **NCTE Research Foundation Research Grant-in-Aid** *(Graduate, Postgraduate/Grant)*

**Purpose:** To encourage investigation, experimentation, and research in the teaching of English. **Focus:** Education, English Language and Literature. **Qualif.:** The research project for which assistance is requested must deal with some phase of the teaching of English, including language arts and related fields. Grants are awarded to individuals and groups engaged in theoretical, basic, or applied research. An imaginative and intellectual approach shown in the conception, design, and execution of the proposals is encouraged. Candidates must demonstrate their ability to complete research projects. The Research Foundation supports research that is part of an academic program leading to a degree. Applicants must be members of NCTE.

**Funds Avail.:** Grants can range up to $12,500 and are individually determined. **To Apply:** Recipients of all grants are required to make interim and final reports and to credit the Foundation as a source of support in publications resulting from funded projects. **Deadline:** Completed application and supporting materials must be received by February 15th. Applicants are notified of decisions in early May.

**Remarks:** The National Council of Teachers of English Research Foundation was established in 1960 in honor of J.N. Hook, Executive Secretary of NCTE from 1953-1960. **Contact:** Project Coordinator at the above address (see entry 3960).

• 3962 • **NCTE Teacher-Researcher Grants** *(Postdoctorate/Grant)*

**Purpose:** To support investigation of research questions that grow out of teachers' classroom experiences and concerns. **Focus:** Education, English Language and Literature. **Qualif.:** Candidate must be a member of NCTE and a teacher of English or language arts at the pre-kindergarten to middle-school level. Proposed research must be directly relevant to the teaching work of the applicant. Grants are not awarded to support travel to professional meetings, purchase permanent equipment or commercial teaching

**National Council of Teachers of English Research Foundation** *(continued)*

materials, or conduct research for a graduate degree program. Grants are tenable worldwide.

**Funds Avail.:** $2,500 maximum. **To Apply:** Write for application form and instructions. **Deadline:** February 15. Notification of results in late May. **Contact:** Project Assistant at the above address (see entry 3960).

• 3963 •
## National Court Reporters Association

8224 Old Courthouse Rd.          *Ph:* (703)556-6272
Vienna, VA 22182-3808            *Fax:* (703)556-6291
                                 *Free:* 800-272-6272

*E-mail:* msic@ncrahq.org
*URL:* http://www.verbatimreporters.com

• 3964 •  **National Court Reporters Association Scholarships** *(Professional Development/Scholarship)*

**Purpose:** To further the study of court reporting. **Focus:** Communications. **Qualif.:** Scholarships are offered to students enrolled in NCRA-approved training programs. Candidates must be entering the second year of the program or equivalent. **Criteria:** Based on the applicant's writing speed which should be at the rate of 140-180 words per minutes.

**Funds Avail.:** Amounts are $1,500, $1,000, and $500. **No. of Awards:** Three. **To Apply:** Each NCRA-approved court reporter training program may nominate two outstanding shorthand reporting students on a nomination form that the program must fill out. The nominee must write a one-page essay on a predetermined subject. **Deadline:** April 1. **Contact:** The National Court Reporters Association at the above address (see entry 3963).

• 3965 •
## National Cowboy Hall of Fame

c/o Ed Muno
1700 NE 63rd St.                 *Ph:* (405)478-2250
Oklahoma City, OK 73111          *Fax:* (405)478-4714
*E-mail:* webmaster@www.keytech.com
*URL:* http://cowboyhalloffame.org

• 3966 •  **John F. and Anna Lee Stacey Scholarships** *(Professional Development/Scholarship)*

**Purpose:** To promote artists working in the classical or conservative tradition of western art. **Focus:** Drawing, Painting. **Qualif.:** Applicants must be U.S. citizens between 18 and 35 years old who create art in the classical or conservative western tradition. Applicant's work must be primarily drawings and/or paintings, and must be created in a realist, naturalist, or photographic style. Eligible categories for submission include painting from life, drawing form the figure (nude), composition, and landscape.

**Funds Avail.:** $3,000. **No. of Awards:** 3. **To Apply:** Write for application form and guidelines. Submit form with a letter describing plans for study, a recent photograph, slides of work, and at least four letters of reference after October 1. It is very important that the slides of paintings reproduce correctly the tone values. **Deadline:** February 1; applications are not accepted prior to October 1. Scholarships are awarded the following fall. **Contact:** Scholarship Committee at the above address (see entry 3965).

• 3967 •
## National Dairy Shrine

c/o Maurice E. Core, Exec.Dir.
1224 Alton Darby Creek Rd.         *Ph:* (614)878-5333
Columbus, OH 43228-9792            *Fax:* (614)870-2622
*E-mail:* cobass@aol.com
*URL:* http://www.dairyshrine.org

• 3968 •  **National Dairy Shrine/Dairy Management Scholarships, Inc.** *(Undergraduate/Scholarship)*

**Purpose:** To encourage qualified undergraduate students to pursue careers in the marketing of dairy products. **Focus:** Dairy Science. **Qualif.:** Applicants must be undergraduate sophomore, junior, or senior students with a grade point average of at least 2.5 on a 4.0 scale. They must demonstrate explicit interest in milk marketing in areas including dairy science, animal science, agricultural economics, agricultural communications, agricultural education, general agriculture and food, and nutrition.

**Funds Avail.:** One $1,000 scholarship and two or more $500 scholarships are awarded. **No. of Awards:** Depends upon the number and the quality of the applicants. **To Apply:** Applications must be typed on an official form accompanied by two letters of recommendation, one of which must be from a faculty member in the applicant's major department. **Deadline:** March 15.

**Remarks:** These scholarships are co-sponsored by Dairy Management, Inc., 10255 W. Higgins Rd., Rosemont, IL 60028. Telephone: (708)803-2000. Fax: (708)803-2088. **Contact:** Jim Leuenberger, secretary, National Dairy Shrine, at the above address (see entry 3967).

• 3969 •
## National Deaf Children's Society - Susan Daniels, Chief Executive

15 Dufferin St.                   *Ph:* 171 490 8656
London EC1Y 8PD, England          *Fax:* 171 251 5020
*E-mail:* ndcs@ndcs.org.uk

• 3970 •  **NDCS Scholarship Grant** *(Graduate/Scholarship)*

**Purpose:** To award a scholarship yearly to one deaf person. **Qualif.:** Must wish to train as a teacher of the deaf. **To Apply:** Someone wishing to apply must write to the Chief Executive at the NDCS office.

• 3971 •  **David Rogers Bursary** *(Graduate, Undergraduate/Grant)*

**Purpose:** To provide a course of further education for deaf students. **Qualif.:** Students must be between the ages of 19 and 25 and must be able to show that financial difficulties and needs relating to their deafness mean that they would not be able to take their place without help from the bursary. **Criteria:** Priority is given to deaf students in courses of study where deaf people are under-represented.

**Funds Avail.:** Two bursaries of £500 will be given annually for two years.

**Remarks:** This fund is contributed to by NDCS in memory of David Rogers.

## • 3972 •
## National Endowment for the Arts
Visual Arts Program/Fellowships,
Rm. 729
Nancy Hanks Center
1100 Pennsylvania Ave., NW        Ph: (202)682-5400
Washington, DC 20506-0001         Fax: (202)682-5699
E-mail: webmgr@arts.endow.gob
URL: http://arts.endow.gov/

*The National Endowment for the Arts, an independent agency of the Federal government, was created by Congress in 1965 to encourage and support American art and artists. It fullfills its mission by awarding grants and through its leadership and advocacy activities. The TDD number is (202)682-5496.*

### • 3973 • National Endowment for Arts - Choreographers' Fellowships (*Professional Development/Fellowship*)

**Purpose:** To assist the artistic growth of professional choreographers whose work has attained a level of national significance. **Qualif.:** To be eligible, choreographers must have shown work professionally for at least three years and have choreographed at least five works during their professional careers. Applicants must be United States citizens or permanent residents. **Criteria:** The Endowment places a strong emphasis on quality as the first criterion in evaluating applications.

**Funds Avail.:** The majority of grants are awarded for a two-year period at $10,000 per year. A smaller proportion are awarded for a one-year period at $7,000. The panel may also recommend a limited number of three year fellowships at $15,000 per year. Fellowship funds can be used for any project or activity that will aid a choreographer's creative development. **Deadline:** Applications must be postmarked by December 6. Announcements are made in October and the earliest project beginning date is August 1. **Contact:** The National Endowment for the Arts, Choreographers Fellowships at the above address. Telephone: (202)682-5435.

### • 3974 • National Endowment for the Arts - Design Arts Program USA Fellowships (*Professional Development/Fellowship*)

**Purpose:** To enable designers and those in design-related professions who have made significant contributions to the design field to travel and study independently within the United States. The grants provide designers the time and flexibility to explore new concepts, generate fresh ideas, or compile information for a book or study. **Qualif.:** Fellowships are awarded to professional designers and other qualified individuals working on innovative design projects. They are intended for those for whom a more extensive first-hand knowledge of the American design environment is critical to their work. Eligible fields include architecture, landscape architecture, urban design and planning, historic preservation, interior design, industrial and product design, and graphic design. Applicants must be United States citizens or permanent residents. **Criteria:** The Endowment places a strong emphasis on quality as the first criterion in evaluating applications.

**Funds Avail.:** Fellowships include awards of up to $20,000.

**Remarks:** The USA Fellowships are administered through the Design Arts Program of the National Endowment for the Arts. **Contact:** Telephone the National Endowment for the Arts, Design Arts Program at (202)682-5437 for guidelines and deadline dates. The Fax number is (202)682-5669.

### • 3975 • National Endowment for the Arts - Director Fellows (*Professional Development/Fellowship*)

**Qualif.:** Applicants must be early career stage directors of exceptional talent who work in the American not-for-profit theater. Candidates must be United States citizens or permanent residents.

**Funds Avail.:** The fellowships provide direct support for work with senior directors to develop artistic skills, or support independent fellowships including research, study, assistantships, travel, observation and/or other related activities. Four $15,000 awards are granted. **Contact:** Theatre Communications Group, Inc., 355 Lexington Ave., New York, NY 10017. Telephone: (212)697-5230.

### • 3976 • National Endowment for the Arts - Fellowships for Playwrights (*Professional Development/Fellowship*)

**Purpose:** To encourage the development of professional playwrights of exceptional talent by enabling them to set aside time for writing, research, travel, or other activities to advance their artistic vision. **Qualif.:** Playwrights are eligible if they have had a play produced by a professional theater company within the last five years. Candidates must be United States citizens or permanent residents.

**Funds Avail.:** Two-year nonmatching fellowships generally range from $10,000 to $35,000. In addition, grantees may receive $2,500 for use in defraying costs of residency at a professional theater of their choice. **To Apply:** Call or write to Theater Program for guidelines. **Contact:** Lisa Engelken, Program Specialist, National Endowment for the Arts Theater Program, Rm. 608, at the above address (see entry 3972).

### • 3977 • National Endowment for the Arts - Literature Program Creative Writing Fellowships (*Professional Development/Fellowship*)

**Purpose:** To enable published creative writers of exceptional talent to set aside time for writing, research, travel, and generally advance their careers. **Qualif.:** Applicants must be poets or authors of fiction or creative non-fiction, and must have publication histories to be eligible. Applicants must be United States citizens or permanent residents. **Criteria:** Literary quality of the manuscript submission.

**Funds Avail.:** Fellowships are $20,000. Ninety fellowships are available. **To Apply:** Contact the Literature Program for application and guidelines.

**Remarks:** The NEA receives approximately 2,400 applications for these fellowships. **Contact:** Literature Program Specialist/Creative Writing Fellowships at the above address (see entry 3972). The Literature Program can be reached by telephone at (202) 682-5451.

### • 3978 • National Endowment for the Arts - Literature Program Translators' Fellowships (*Professional Development/Fellowship*)

**Purpose:** To enable published literary translators of exceptional talent to translate works of fiction, poetry, drama, or creative nonfiction from other languages into English. **Qualif.:** Applicants should be translators involved in specific translation projects from other languages into English. Applicants must have publication histories to be eligible. They must be also United States citizens or permanent residents. **Criteria:** The primary criteria is the literary quality of the sample translations of work(s) to be translated. Consideration is then given to need for and importance of the project, and significance of author(s) and original work(s).

**Funds Avail.:** Fellowships are $10,000 or $20,000 depending upon the length and scope of the subject. **To Apply:** Contact the Literature Program for an application and guidelines. **Contact:** Literature Program Specialist/Translation Fellowships at the above address (see entry 3972). The Literature Program can be reached by telephone at (202) 682-5451.

*National Endowment for the Arts (continued)*

**• 3979 •   National Endowment for the Arts - National Heritage Fellowships** *(Professional Development/Fellowship)*

**Purpose:** To provide national recognition to exemplary master folk artists and artisans and to allow them to set aside time to pursue their art form and/or to purchase materials and equipment. **Qualif.:** Applicants must be worthy of national recognition, should have a record of ongoing artistic accomplishment, and must be actively participating in their art form, either as a practitioner or teacher. The folk arts include music, dance, poetry, tales, oratory, crafts, and various types of visual art forms. Applicants must be citizens or permanent residents of the United States. **Criteria:** Selection is based on authenticity, excellence, and significance within the particular artistic tradition.

**Funds Avail.:** Ten to fifteen $10,000 one-time-only fellowships. **To Apply:** Application must be made by nomination. Nominations are made by sending a letter to the Folk Arts Program detailing why the artist nominated should receive the Fellowship. Nominations must include a resume or short biography detailing the career of the artist; clearly labeled samples of the artistic works (visual artists must be represented by slides; musicians and storytellers by videotapes or sound recordings, and dancers by film or videotape samples); references to articles written about the nominee, titles or published works, if appropriate; a list of major appearances by the nominee, titles or published works, if appropriate; and selected letters demonstrating expert and/or community support. **Deadline:** November 1. **Contact:** National Endowment for the Arts at the above address (see entry 3972).

**• 3980 •   National Endowment for the Arts - U.S./France Exchange Fellowship** *(Professional Development/Fellowship)*

**Purpose:** To enable American visual artists to work and study in France. **Qualif.:** Applicants must be United States citizens or permanent residents well established in their fields and be recommended for a Visual Artists Fellowship. Proficiency in French is not required. **Criteria:** Selection is based on the quality of work.

**Funds Avail.:** Fellowships cover the cost of residency in France. Up to two recipients are selected each year. **To Apply:** Applicants must complete the Visual Artists Fellowship application form and add the phrase "U.S./France" to the top of the form. They must also apply to the appropriate Fellowship area, in painting, sculpture, crafts, works on paper, photography or other genres. The original application form must be accompanied by two signed copies of the application, a resume, visual documentation, and two copies of the Visual Artists Fellowship Supplementary Information Sheet. Applicants must request a copy of the guidelines each time they apply. **Deadline:** Each Fellowship area is offered in a cycle which repeats every other year. Deadlines vary according to the area and are available with application information. **Contact:** Silvio Lim, Visual Arts Program/Fellowship, at the above address (see entry 3972).

**• 3981 •   National Endowment for the Arts - U.S./Japan Exchange Fellowships** *(Professional Development/Fellowship)*

**Purpose:** To enable American artists to work and study in Japan. **Qualif.:** Creative artists must be United States citizens or permanent residents of the United States. Proficiency in Japanese is not required.

**Funds Avail.:** Fellowships provide round-trip transportation to Japan, monthly living stipend, and language training. Five fellowships are awarded each year. **Deadline:** The deadline for design/artists was December 10; for all others, it is March 11. **Contact:** International Program at the above address (see entry 3972).

**• 3982 •   National Endowment for the Arts - Visual Artists Fellowships** *(Professional Development/Fellowship)*

**Purpose:** To encourage the creative development of professional artists by enabling them to set aside time to pursue their work. **Qualif.:** Fellowships are available to practicing professional artists of exceptional talent with demonstrated ability working in a wide variety of visual media, including painting, sculpture, photography, crafts, printmaking, drawing, artists books, video, performance art, conceptual art, and new genres. Applicants must be United States citizens or permanent residents.

**Funds Avail.:** Fellowships include awards from $15,000 to $20,000. **Deadline:** Application deadlines vary. Application deadlines were mid-January for "Other Genres," February 1 for Painting, and mid-March for Works on Paper. **Contact:** The National Endowment for the Arts at the above address (see entry 3972).

**• 3983 •**

**National Endowment for the Humanities**
1100 Pennsylvania Ave., NW                        Ph: (202)606-8380
Washington, DC 20506                               Fax: (202)606-8558
*E-mail:* fellowsuniv@neh.gov; fellowscollind@neh.gov
*URL:* http://www.neh.gov

**• 3984 •   Faculty Graduate Study Fellowships for Historically Black Colleges and Universities** *(Doctorate/Fellowship)*

**Purpose:** To support doctoral studies in the humanities. **Focus:** Humanities. **Qualif.:** Applicant must be a U.S. citizen or resident for at least three years before application. Applicant must be a faculty member at a historically Black U.S. college or university. Candidate must have completed at least one year of graduate work and wish to undertake study and research toward the completion of a doctoral degree in the humanities. Proposed project must have the support of the home institution. Fellowships are not awarded for graduate study in the creative or performing arts or for study leading to a doctorate in education.

**Funds Avail.:** $30,000 maximum. **To Apply:** Write or call to discuss the proposed project. Applications forms will be forwarded. Applicants are encouraged to submit a draft proposal for informal comment by staff. **Deadline:** March 15. Fellowships are announced in September.

**Remarks:** NEH also offers many other grants and fellowships. Current guidelines and descriptive materials for all NEH programs are available from the NEH Office of Publications and Public Affairs, at the above address, two months in advance of an application deadline. **Contact:** Division of Fellowships and Seminars, at the above address (see entry 3983).

**• 3985 •   NEH Fellowship for University Teachers** *(Postdoctorate/Fellowship)*

**Purpose:** To provide opportunities for individuals to pursue advanced study and research in disciplines of the humanities. Projects proposed may contribute to scholarly knowledge or to the general public's understanding of the humanities. They may address broad topics or consist of study and research in a single field. **Qualif.:** Generally, the fellowship is open only to the faculty of Ph.D.-granting universities. Other applicants may be eligible and should write the NEH for further information. Applicants should be United States citizens, native residents of U.S. territorial possessions, or foreign nationals who have been residing in the United States or its territories for at least three years immediately preceding the application deadline. **Criteria:** The quality or the promise of quality of the applicant's work as a teacher, scholar, or interpreter of the humanities; the significance of the contribution that the proposed project will make to thought and knowledge in the field of the project and to the humanities; the conception, definition, organization, and description of the proposed project; and the likelihood that the applicant will complete the project.

**Funds Avail.:** The maximum stipend is $30,000. **No. of Awards:** 86. **Deadline:** May 1. **Contact:** Jane Aikin, Fellowships for University Teachers Program, at the above address (see entry 3983).

## • 3986 • NEH Fellowships for College Teachers and Independent Scholars *(Postdoctorate/Fellowship)*

**Purpose:** To provide opportunities for individuals to pursue advanced study and research in disciplines of the humanities. Projects proposed may contribute to scholarly knowledge or to the general public's understanding of the humanities. They may address broad topics or consist of study and research in a single field. **Qualif.:** Generally, the fellowship is open only to part-time or full-time faculty and staff members of two-year, four-year, and five-year colleges and universities that do not grant the Ph.D. degree, as well as scholars working independently. Applicants should be United States citizens, native residents of U.S. territorial possessions, or foreign nationals who have been residing in the United States or its territories for at least three years immediately preceding the application deadline. **Criteria:** The quality or the promise of quality of the applicant's work as a teacher, scholar, or interpreter of the humanities; the significance of the contribution that the proposed project will make to thought and knowledge in the field of the project and to the humanities generally; the conception, definition, organization, and description of the proposed project; and the likelihood that the applicant will complete the project.

**Funds Avail.:** Support is provided for from six to 12 months of full-time study and research. The maximum stipend is $30,000. **No. of Awards:** 86. **Deadline:** May 1. **Contact:** Joseph Neville, Program Officer, at the above address (see entry 3983).

## • 3987 • NEH Interpretive Research Grants *(Doctorate, Postdoctorate/Grant)*

**Purpose:** To support scholarly research collaborations and conferences in the humanities as well as research in archaeology and the relationship of the sciences to the humanities. **Focus:** Humanities. **Qualif.:** Applicant must be a U.S. citizen or resident for at least three years prior to application. Applicant must be planning to work in an area of the humanities. Priority is given to projects in the following fields: history; literature; philosophy; archaeology; history, theory and criticism of the arts; ethics; history and philosophy of science, technology, and medicine. Awards are for specific projects. NEH does not fund study to acquire an academic degree, original works of art, or performance or training in the arts.

**Funds Avail.:** $10,000 minimum. **To Apply:** Write or call to discuss the proposed project. Applications forms will be forwarded. Applicants are encouraged to submit a draft proposal for informal comment by staff. **Deadline:** October 15. **Contact:** George R. Lucas at the above address (see entry 3983).

## • 3988 • NEH Reference Materials Grants *(Doctorate, Postdoctorate/Grant)*

**Purpose:** To support projects that will facilitate scholarly research in the humanities by organizing essential resources and by preparing reference materials that improve scholars' access to information and collections. **Focus:** Humanities. **Qualif.:** Applicant must be a U.S. citizen or resident for at least three years prior to application. Applicant must be planning to work in one of the following fields: history; literature; philosophy; languages; linguistics; archaeology; jurisprudence; history, theory and criticism of the arts; ethics; comparative religion; or those aspects of the sciences or social sciences that employ historical or philosophical approaches. Awards are for specific projects. NEH does not fund original works of art, or performance or training in the arts.

**Funds Avail.:** $10,000 minimum. **To Apply:** Write or call to discuss the proposed project. Applications forms will be forwarded. Applicants are encouraged to submit a draft proposal for informal comment by staff. **Deadline:** September 1. **Contact:** Jane Rosenberg at the above address (see entry 3983).

## • 3989 • NEH Summer Fellowships for Foreign Language Teachers K-12 *(Professional Development/Fellowship)*

**Purpose:** To support summer study abroad by primary and secondary school teachers of languages other than English. **Focus:** Languages (except English). **Qualif.:** Candidate must have completed at least three years of full-time paid teaching before the fellowship summer begins. At least one half of the applicant's teaching schedule during those years must have been in a foreign language discipline in a U.S. primary or secondary school (i.e., grades K-12). Applicant must be under contract to teach during the year following the fellowship, and an with intention to teach foreign languages at least five more years. Fellowships are intended for six weeks of intensive summer study outside of the United States. **Criteria:** Based on intellectual content of study plan, evidence it will strengthen applicant's FL teaching, and the impact of the experience on students and fellow teachers.

**Funds Avail.:** $3,750 **To Apply:** Write the program director for application materials. **Deadline:** October 31. **Contact:** Dr. Doris Meyer Program Director

## • 3990 • NEH Summer Stipend *(Postdoctorate/Fellowship)*

**Purpose:** To provide support for college and university teachers; individuals employed by schools, museums, and libraries; and others to undertake full-time independent study and research in the humanities for two consecutive summer months. **Qualif.:** Applicants may be senior or junior scholars, writers and scholars working in the humanities either independently or at nonacademic institutions, or faculty members in two-year, four-year, and five-year colleges and universities. Applicants should be United States citizens, native residents of U.S. territorial possessions, or foreign nationals who have been residing in the United States or its territories for at least three years immediately preceding the application deadline. Also, to be considered, applicants must be nominated by the chief academic officer of the institution (only three nominations per institution). **Criteria:** Selection is based on the significance of the contribution that the proposed project will make to thought and knowledge in that field, and to interpreting and understanding the humanities in general; the quality or promise of quality of the applicant's work as a teacher, scholar, or interpreter of the humanities; the conception, definition, organization, and description of the proposed project; and if applicable, the necessity of the planned travel and the appropriateness of the specific collection for the proposed project.

**Funds Avail.:** $4,000. **No. of Awards:** 130. **Deadline:** October 1. **Contact:** Leon Bramson, Summer Stipends, National Endowment for the Humanities, at the above address (see entry 3983).

## • 3991 •
# National Federation of the Blind of Connecticut
580 Burnside Ave., Ste. 1
East Hartford, CT 06108 *Ph:* (203)289-1971

## • 3992 • Howard E. May Memorial Scholarships *(Undergraduate/Scholarship)*

**Focus:** General Studies. **Qualif.:** The scholarship is given to legally blind students attending school in, or residing in, Connecticut. Applicants must be pursuing or planning to pursue a full-time college education.

## National Federation of the Blind of Connecticut (continued)

**Funds Avail.:** $2,000. **To Apply:** Candidates must submit a completed application form, transcripts, two letters of recommendation, a letter stating goals, plans, qualifications, and educational background, and a letter from a state officer of the National Federation of the Blind of Connecticut evidencing the fact that the candidate has discussed the application. **Deadline:** September 15.

**Remarks:** Howard E. May was the founding president of the National Federation of the Blind of Connecticut. **Contact:** Scholarships office at the above address (see entry 3991).

### • 3993 • Jonathan May Memorial Scholarships
*(Undergraduate/Scholarship)*

**Focus:** General Studies. **Qualif.:** The scholarship is given to an individual pursuing or planning to pursue a full-time college education. All applicants must be legally blind students attending school in, or residing in Connecticut.

**Funds Avail.:** $1,500. **To Apply:** Candidates must complete an application form, submit transcript, two letters of recommendation, a letter stating goals, plans, qualifications, and educational background, and a letter from a state officer of the National Federation of the Blind of Connecticut evidencing the fact that the candidate has discussed the application. **Deadline:** September 15.

**Remarks:** The scholarship is given in memory of Jonathan May, a past dedicated leader of the National Federation of the Blind of Connecticut. **Contact:** Scholarships at the above address (see entry 3991).

### • 3994 • NFB of CT Academic Sholarship
*(Undergraduate/Scholarship)*

**Focus:** General Studies. **Qualif.:** Scholarship is given to an individual pursuing or planning to pursue a full-time college education. All applicants must be legally blind students attending school in, or residing in, Connecticut.

**Funds Avail.:** $1,000. **No. of Awards:** 1. **To Apply:** Candidates must complete an application form, submit transcripts, and two letters of recommendation, a letter stating goals, plans, qualifications, and educational background and a letter from a state officer of the National Foundation of the Blind of Connecticut evidencing the fact that the candidate has discussed the application. **Deadline:** September 15. **Contact:** Scholarships at the above address (see entry 3991).

### • 3995 •

## National Federation of the Blind of Maryland, Inc. - John T. McCraw Scholarship Program
9736 Basket Ring Rd.
Columbia, MD 21045          *Ph:* (410)992-9608

### • 3996 • John T. McCraw Scholarship *(Graduate, Undergraduate/Scholarship)*

**Focus:** General studies. **Qualif.:** Applicants must be legally blind Maryland residents, attending school full-time in Maryland or elsewhere, or residents of other states attending school full-time in Maryland. **Criteria:** Awards are granted based on scholastic achievement, extracurricular activities, potential for sustained achievement, and attendance at Annual Statewide Convention.

**Funds Avail.:** $3,000. **No. of Awards:** 2. **To Apply:** Applicants must submit an application, two letters of recommendation and a personal essay. **Deadline:** May 31. **Contact:** Sharon Maneki.

### • 3997 •

## National Federation of the Blind - Scholarship Committee
805 5th Ave.
Grinnell, IA 50112          *Ph:* (515)236-3366
*E-mail:* webmaster@nybar.com
*URL:* http://www.eduzone.com/Scholar;BLIND.HTM

### • 3998 • Hermione Grant Calhoun Scholarship
*(Undergraduate/Scholarship)*

**Purpose:** To recognize achievement by blind scholars. **Qualif.:** All applicants must be women who are legally blind and pursuing or planning to pursue a full-time post-secondary course of study. Recipients need not be members of the National Federation of the Blind. **Criteria:** Scholarships are awarded on the basis of academic excellence, service to the community, and financial need.

**Funds Avail.:** $3,000 and the cost travel to the National Federation of the Blind convention in July. **To Apply:** The scholarship committee requires a completed application, two letters of recommendation, current and past school transcripts, and a letter from a state officer, preferably the President, of the National Federation of the Blind evidencing that the scholarship application has been discussed with that officer. A letter detailing achievements, goals, and personal data is also required. Applications are available by writing the NFB Scholarship Committee. **Deadline:** March 31. Winners are notified by June 1 .

**Remarks:** Dr. Isabelle Grant endowed this scholarship in memory of her daughter.

### • 3999 • Ezra Davis Memorial Scholarship
*(Undergraduate/Scholarship)*

**Purpose:** To recognize achievement by blind scholars. **Qualif.:** All applicants must be legally blind and pursuing or planning to pursue a full-time post-secondary course of study. Recipients need not be members of the National Federation of the Blind. **Criteria:** Scholarships are awarded on the basis of academic excellence, service to the community, and financial need.

**Funds Avail.:** $10,000 and travel expenses for attendance at the National Federation of the Blind in July. **To Apply:** The scholarship committee requires a completed application, two letters of recommendation, current and past school transcripts, and a letter from a state officer, preferably the President, of the National Federation of the Blind evidencing the scholarship application has been discussed with that officer. A letter detailing personal achievements, goals, and personal data is also required. Applications are available by writing the NFB Scholarship Committee. **Deadline:** March 31. Winners are notified by June 1.

**Remarks:** This scholarship is endowed by Ezra Davis and given by the American Action Fund for Blind Children and Adults, a nonprofit organization that works to assist blind persons. **Contact:** Peggy Pinder, Chairman, National Federation of the Blind Scholarship Committee, at the above address (see entry 3997).

### • 4000 • Frank Walton Horn Memorial Scholarships
*(Undergraduate/Scholarship)*

**Purpose:** To recognize achievement by blind scholars. **Qualif.:** All applicants must be legally blind and pursuing or planning to pursue a full-time post-secondary course of study. Recipients need not be members of the National Federation of the Blind. **Criteria:** Scholarships are awarded on the basis of academic excellence, service to the community, and financial need. Preference is given to those studying architecture or engineering.

**Funds Avail.:** $3,000 and travel expenses for the National Federation of the Blind Convention in July. **To Apply:** The scholarship committee requires a completed application, two letters of recommendation, current and past school transcripts, and a letter from a state officer, preferably the President, of the National Federation of the Blind evidencing that the scholarship application has been discussed with that officer. A letter detailing personal achievements, goals, and personal data is also required. Applications are available by writing the NFB Scholarship Committee. **Deadline:** March 31. Winners are notified by June 1.

### • 4001 • Kuchler-Killian Memorial Scholarship
*(Undergraduate/Scholarship)*

**Purpose:** To recognize achievement by blind scholars. **Qualif.:** All applicants must be legally blind and pursuing or planning to pursue a full-time post-secondary course of study. Recipients need not be members of the National Federation of the Blind. **Criteria:** Scholarships are awarded on the basis of academic excellence, service to the community, and financial need.

**Funds Avail.:** $3,000 plus cost of travel to the National Federation of the Blind convention in July. **To Apply:** The scholarship committee requires a completed application, two letters of recommendation, current and past school transcripts, and a letter from a state officer, preferably the President, of the National Federation of the Blind evidencing that the scholarship application has been discussed with that officer. A letter detailing personal achievements, goals, and personal data is also required. Applications are available by writing or telephoning the NFB Scholarship Committee. **Deadline:** March 31. Winners are notified by June 1.

**Remarks:** Junerose Killian dedicated this scholarship in memory of her parents, Charles Albert Kuchler and Alice Helen Kuchler, members of the National Federation of the Blind of Connecticut. **Contact:** Peggy Elliott at the above address (see entry 3997).

### • 4002 • National Federation of the Blind Educator of Tomorrow Award *(Undergraduate/Award)*

**Purpose:** To recognize achievement by blind scholars. **Qualif.:** Applicants must be legally blind and pursuing or planning to pursue a career in elementary, secondary, or post-secondary teaching. Recipients need not be members of the National Federation of the Blind. **Criteria:** Scholarships are awarded on the basis of academic excellence, service to the community, and financial need.

**Funds Avail.:** $3,000 plus cost of travel to the National Federation of the Blind convention in July. **To Apply:** The scholarship committee requires a completed application, two letters of recommendation, current and past school transcripts, and a letter from a state officer, preferably the President, of the National Federation of the Blind evidencing that the scholarship application has been discussed with that officer. A letter detailing personal achievements, goals, and personal data is also required. Applications are available by writing or telephoning the NFB Scholarship Committee. **Deadline:** March 31. Winners are notified by June 1. **Contact:** Peggy Elliott at the above address (see entry 3997).

### • 4003 • National Federation of the Blind Humanities Scholarship *(Undergraduate/Scholarship)*

**Purpose:** To recognize achievement by blind scholars. **Qualif.:** All applicants must be legally blind and pursuing or planning to pursue a full-time post-secondary courses in a traditional Humanities field, such as art, English, foreign languages, history, philosophy, or religion. Recipients need not be members of the National Federation of the Blind. **Criteria:** Scholarships are awarded on the basis of academic excellence, service to the community, and financial need.

**Funds Avail.:** $3,000 plus travel expenses for attendance at the National Federation of the Blind convention in July. **To Apply:** The scholarship committee requires a completed application, two letters of recommendation, current and past school transcripts, and a letter from a state officer, preferably the President, of the National Federation of the Blind evidencing that the scholarship application has been discussed with that officer. A letter detailing personal achievements, goals, and personal data is also required.

Applications are available by writing or telephoning the NFB Scholarship Committee. **Deadline:** March 31. Winners are notified by June 1. **Contact:** Peggy Elliott at the above address (see entry 3997).

### • 4004 • National Federation of the Blind Scholarships *(Undergraduate/Scholarship)*

**Purpose:** To recognize achievement by blind scholars. **Qualif.:** All applicants must be legally blind and pursuing or planning to pursue a full-time post-secondary course of study. Recipients need not be members of the National Federation of the Blind. **Criteria:** Scholarships are awarded on the basis of academic excellence, service to the community, and financial need.

**Funds Avail.:** Two $4,000 and thirteen $3,000 scholarships. **To Apply:** The scholarship committee requires a completed application, two letters of recommendation, current and past school transcripts, and a letter from a state officer, preferably the President, of the National Federation of the Blind evidencing that the scholarship application has been discussed with that officer. A letter detailing personal achievements, goals, and personal data is also required. Applications are available by writing or telephoning the NFB Scholarship Committee. **Deadline:** March 31. Winners are notified by June 1. **Contact:** Peggy Elliott, Chairman, National Federation of the Blind Scholarship Committee, at the above address (see entry 3997).

### • 4005 • Melva T. Owen Memorial Scholarship
*(Undergraduate/Scholarship)*

**Purpose:** To recognize achievement by blind scholars. **Qualif.:** All applicants must be legally blind and pursuing or planning to pursue a full-time post-secondary course of study (excluding religion study). Recipients need not be members of the National Federation of the Blind. **Criteria:** Scholarships are awarded on the basis of academic excellence, service to the community, and financial need.

**Funds Avail.:** $4,000 and funds for travel to the National Federation of the Blind convention in July. **To Apply:** The scholarship committee requires a completed application, two letters of recommendation, current and past school transcripts, and a letter from a state officer, preferably the President, of the National Federation of the Blind evidencing that the scholarship application has been discussed with that officer. A letter detailing personal achievements, goals, and personal data is also required. Applications are available by writing or telephoning the NFB Scholarship Committee. **Deadline:** March 31. Winners are notified by June 1.

**Remarks:** Given in memory of Melva T. Owen, who was widely known and loved among the blind.

### • 4006 • Anne Pekar Memorial Scholarship
*(Undergraduate/Scholarship)*

**Qualif.:** Applicants must be women between the ages of 17 and 25 who are legally blind and pursuing or planning to pursue a full-time post-secondary course of study. Recipients need not be members of the National Federation of the Blind. **Criteria:** Scholarships are awarded on the basis of academic excellence, service to the community, and financial need.

**Funds Avail.:** $4,000 and funds for travel to the National Federation of the Blind convention in July. **To Apply:** The scholarship committee requires a completed application, two letters of recommendation, current and past school transcripts, and a letter from a state officer, preferably the President, of the National Federation of the Blind evidencing that the scholarship application has been discussed with that officer. A letter detailing personal achievements, goals, and personal data is also required. Applications are available by writing or telephoning the NFB Scholarship Committee. **Deadline:** March 31. Winners are notified by June 1.

---

Awards are arranged alphabetically below their administering organizations

## National Federation of the Blind - Scholarship Committee (continued)

**Remarks:** This scholarships is given in loving memory of Anne Pekar by her parents. **Contact:** Peggy Pinder, Chairman, National Federation of the Blind Scholarship Committee, at the above address (see entry 3997).

### • 4007 • Howard Brown Rickard Scholarship
*(Undergraduate/Scholarship)*

**Purpose:** To recognize achievement by blind scholars. **Qualif.:** All applicants must be legally blind and pursuing or planning to pursue a full-time post-secondary course of study in the fields of law, medicine, engineering, architecture, or the natural sciences. Recipients need not be members of the National Federation of the Blind. **Criteria:** Scholarships are awarded on the basis of academic excellence, service to the community, and financial need.

**Funds Avail.:** $3,000 and funds for travel to the National Federation of the Blind convention. **To Apply:** The scholarship committee requires a completed application, two letters of recommendation, current and past school transcripts, and a letter from a state officer, preferably the President, of the National Federation of the Blind evidencing that the scholarship application has been discussed with that officer. A letter detailing personal achievements, goals, and personal data is also required. Applications are available by writing or telephoning the NFB Scholarship Committee. **Deadline:** March 31. Winners are notified by June 1.

### • 4008 • Ellen Setterfield Memorial Scholarship
*(Graduate/Scholarship)*

**Purpose:** To recognize achievement by blind scholars. **Qualif.:** All applicants must be legally blind and pursuing or planning to pursue full-time graduate study in the field of social sciences. Recipients need not be members of the National Federation of the Blind. **Criteria:** Scholarships are awarded on the basis of academic excellence, service to the community, and financial need.

**Funds Avail.:** $2,000 plus funds to cover travel to the National Federation of the Blind convention in July. **To Apply:** The scholarship committee requires a completed application, two letters of recommendation, current and past school transcripts, and a letter from a state officer, preferably the President, of the National Federation of the Blind evidencing that the scholarship application has been discussed with that officer. A letter detailing personal achievements, goals, and personal data is also required. Applications are available by writing or telephoning the NFB Scholarship Committee. **Deadline:** March 31. Winners are notified by June 1.

**Remarks:** This scholarship is given in memory of Ellen Setterfield by Roy Landstrom. **Contact:** Peggy Elliott at the above address (see entry 3997).

## • 4009 •
## National Federation of State Poetry Societies, Inc.
c/o Pj Doyle
4242 Stevens Ave.                    *Ph:* (612)824-1964
Minneapolis, MN 55409                *Fax:* (612)872-3200

### • 4010 • Edna Meudt Memorial Scholarship
*(Undergraduate/Scholarship)*

**Purpose:** To encourage young poets in the study and writing of poetry. **Focus:** Poetry. **Qualif.:** Applicants must be students in an accredited college or university in the United States at the junior or senior level. There is no age limit. **Criteria:** Based solely on excellence of submitted manuscript furnished regarding scholastics and civic participation. Financial, race, and religion information is not pertinent.

**Funds Avail.:** Two $500 scholarships are offered. **No. of Awards:** Two. **To Apply:** Candidates must submit original manuscripts of ten poems. They must provide three references, a one-page autobiography, and list other activities. Grade point average should be submitted. No scatological material is accepted. Manuscripts must have a title representing the body of ten poems. Each poem in the manuscript must have a title unless it is a haiku. Specific instructions are provided in criteria sheet. No information is furnished unless inquiry is accompanied by a No. 10 (legal size) self-addressed, stamped envelope. Manuscripts must be sent unfolded in a large envelope. Spaces per line and line limit must be strictly followed and it is important that all information on the application form is typed. Manuscripts are photocopied and sent to other judges and information must be legible. **Deadline:** February 1. **Contact:** Ms. Pj Doyle, Chancellor/Scholarship Chair, at the above address (see entry 4009).

## • 4011 •
## National FFA Foundation
5632 Mt. Vernon Memorial Hwy.
PO Box 15160
Alexandria, VA 22309-0160          *Ph:* (703)360-3600

*The National FFA Foundation is the grant-making arm of the The National FFA Organization (formerly, the Future Farmers of America) which fosters character development, agricultural leadership, and responsible citizenship, and supplements training opportunities for students preparing for careers in farming and agribusiness. Awards are funded by more than 120 corporations, and are adminstered by the FFA College and Vocational/Technical Scholarship Program. A representative selection of scholarships follows; for further information, contact the FFA.*

### • 4012 • 21st Century Genetics Cooperative Scholarships *(Undergraduate/Scholarship)*

**Qualif.:** Applicants must be FFA members from Iowa, Minnesota, Nebraska, North Dakota, South Dakota, or Wisconsin and pursuing a four-year degree in dairy science.

**Funds Avail.:** Two $1,000 scholarships. **To Apply:** Application material is available from FFA. **Deadline:** February 15. **Contact:** National FFA Foundation at the above address (see entry 4011).

### • 4013 • AgRadio Network Scholarships
*(Undergraduate/Scholarship)*

**Qualif.:** Applicants must be FFA members pursuing a two-year degree in any area of agriculture from one of the following states: Connecticut, Maine, Massachusetts, New Hampshire, New York, Rhode Island, or Vermont.

**Funds Avail.:** One $500 scholarship. **To Apply:** Applications are available through FFA. **Deadline:** February 15. **Contact:** National FFA Organization Office at the above address (see entry 4011).

### • 4014 • Alfa-Laval Agri Scholarships
*(Undergraduate/Scholarship)*

**Qualif.:** Applicants must be FFA members pursuing a four-year degree in dairy science, agricultural economics, agricultural marketing, or agricultural engineering or a two-year degree in any area of agricultural technology.

**Funds Avail.:** Two $1,000 scholarships toward four-year degrees and three $500 scholarships toward two-year degrees. **To Apply:** Applications are available through FFA. **Deadline:** February 15. **Contact:** National FFA Organization Office at the above address (see entry 4011).

• **4015** • **Allflex USA Scholarship** *(Undergraduate/ Scholarship)*

**Qualif.:** Applicants must be FFA members pursuing four-year degrees in animal science.

**Funds Avail.:** One $1,000 scholarship. **To Apply:** Applications are available through FFA. **Deadline:** February 15. **Contact:** National FFA Organization Office at the above address (see entry 4011).

• **4016** • **Alpha Gamma Rho Education Foundation Scholarship** *(Undergraduate/Scholarship)*

**Qualif.:** Applicants must be pursuing a four-year degree in any area of agriculture.

**Funds Avail.:** One $1,000 scholarship. **To Apply:** Applications are available through FFA. **Contact:** National FFA Organization Office at the above address (see entry 4011).

• **4017** • **American Cyanamid Scholarship** *(Undergraduate/Scholarship)*

**Qualif.:** Applicants must be FFA members pursuing a degree in natural sciences, including biology, biotechnology, plant sciences, and agronomy.

**Funds Avail.:** One $1,000 scholarship. **To Apply:** Applications are available through FFA. **Deadline:** February 15. **Contact:** National FFA Organization Office at the above address (see entry 4011).

• **4018** • **American Family Insurance Company Scholarships** *(Undergraduate/Scholarship)*

**Qualif.:** Applicants must be FFA members from either Wisconsin, Missouri, or Minnesota who are pursuing four-year degrees in any major at an accredited university or college.

**Funds Avail.:** Three $1,000 scholarships are awarded to one recipient from each state. **To Apply:** Application material is available from the FFA. **Deadline:** The February 15. **Contact:** National FFA Organization Office at the above address (see entry 4011).

• **4019** • **American Farm Bureau Federation Scholarship** *(Undergraduate/Scholarship)*

**Qualif.:** Applicants must be FFA members from a Farm Bureau family pursuing four-year degrees in production agriculture.

**Funds Avail.:** One $1,000 scholarship. **To Apply:** Application material is available from FFA. **Deadline:** February 15. **Contact:** National FFA Organization Office at the above address (see entry 4011).

• **4020** • **American Floral Endowment Scholarship** *(Undergraduate/Scholarship)*

**Qualif.:** Applicants must be FFA members pursuing careers in floriculture and/or environmental horticulture at a four-year institution.

**Funds Avail.:** One $1,000 scholarship. **To Apply:** Application material is available from FFA. **Deadline:** February 15. **Contact:** National FFA Organization Office at the above address (see entry 4011).

• **4021** • **American Grain and Related Industries Scholarship** *(Undergraduate/Scholarship)*

**Qualif.:** Applicants must be FFA members from Iowa pursuing degrees in any area of agriculture or agribusiness at a two- or four-year institution.

**Funds Avail.:** One $1,000 scholarship to attend a four-year institution and one $500 scholarship to attend a two-year institution. **To Apply:** Application material is available from FFA.

**Deadline:** February 15. **Contact:** National FFA Organization Office at the above address (see entry 4011).

• **4022** • **American Morgan Horse Institute Scholarships** *(Undergraduate/Scholarship)*

**Qualif.:** Applicants must be FFA members pursuing a career in animal science at a two- or four-year institution.

**Funds Avail.:** Two $1,000 scholarships to study at a four-year institution and one $500 scholarship to study at a two-year institution. **To Apply:** Application material is available from FFA. **Deadline:** February 15. **Contact:** National FFA Organization Office at the above address (see entry 4011).

• **4023** • **American Seed Trade Association Scholarship** *(Undergraduate/Scholarship)*

**Qualif.:** Applicants must be FFA members pursuing a degree in any area of agriculture at a four-year or two-year institution. **Criteria:** Preference may be given to students studying Agronomy or related areas.

**Funds Avail.:** One $1,000 scholarship. **To Apply:** Application material is available from FFA. **Deadline:** February 15. **Contact:** National FFA Foundation at the above address (see entry 4011).

• **4024** • **Anchor Division Boehringer Ingelheim Animal Health Scholarship** *(Undergraduate/Scholarship)*

**Qualif.:** Applicants must be FFA members from Missouri pursuing four-year degrees in animal science or any area of agriculture.

**Funds Avail.:** One $1,000 scholarship. **To Apply:** Application material is available from FFA. **Deadline:** February 15. **Contact:** National FFA Organization Office at the above address (see entry 4011).

• **4025** • **Associated Landscape Contractors of America Scholarsip** *(Undergraduate/Scholarship)*

**Qualif.:** Applicants must be FFA members pursuing two- or four-year degrees in any field directly associated with the landscape industry.

**Funds Avail.:** One $500 scholarship. **To Apply:** Application material is available from FFA. **Deadline:** April 15. **Contact:** National FFA Organization Office at the above address (see entry 4011).

• **4026** • **Associated Milk Producers and Babson Bros. Co./SURGE Scholarships** *(Undergraduate/ Scholarship)*

**Qualif.:** Applicants must be FFA members pursuing degrees in dairy science at a four-year institution who have competed in the Dairy Contest above the local level.

**Funds Avail.:** Five $1,000 scholarships. An additional eight scholarships will be presented to high scoring individuals in the National FFA Dairy Contest. **To Apply:** An FFA Advisor must certify applicant's involvement in the contest. Application material is available from FFA. **Contact:** National FFA Organization Office at the above address (see entry 4011).

• **4027** • **Award Design Medals Scholarship** *(Undergraduate/Scholarship)*

**Qualif.:** Applicants must be FFA members pursuing a degree in any area of agriculture at a four-year institution.

**Funds Avail.:** One $1,000 scholarship. **To Apply:** Application material is available from FFA. **Deadline:** February 15. **Contact:** National FFA Organization Office at the above address (see entry 4011).

---

Awards are arranged alphabetically below their administering organizations

*National FFA Foundation (continued)*

## • 4028 • Bedding Plants Foundation Scholarship
*(Undergraduate/Scholarship)*

**Qualif.:** Applicants must be FFA members pursuing a two- or four-year degree in horticulture or floriculture.

**Funds Avail.:** One $1,000 scholarship for a four-year degree and one $500 scholarship for a two-year degree. **To Apply:** Application material is available from FFA. **Deadline:** February 15. **Contact:** National FFA Organization Office at the above address (see entry 4011).

## • 4029 • Big R. Stores and Fleet Supply Company Scholarship *(Undergraduate/Scholarship)*

**Qualif.:** Applicants must be FFA members from a northern Indiana county pursuing two- or four-year degrees in any field of agriculture at Purdue University. (For the purpose of this scholarship, Indiana northern counties are defined as north of I-74 from Covington to Indianapolis and north of I-70 from Indianapolis to Richmond.)

**Funds Avail.:** One $1,000 scholarship. **To Apply:** Application material is available from FFA. **Contact:** National FFA Foundation at the above address (see entry 4011).

## • 4030 • Biggs and Gilmore Communications Scholarships *(Graduate, Undergraduate/Scholarship)*

**Qualif.:** Applicants must be current or former FFA members entering their junior or senior undergraduate years towards a degree in agricultural communications or journalism at Iowa State University, Michigan State University, University of Illinois, or The Ohio State University. They must also intend to pursue a career in advertising, public relations, journalism, or communications upon graduation. An additional scholarship is given to a former or present FFA member pursuing a graduate degree in agricultural communications or journalism at the University of Wisconsin-Madison.

**Funds Avail.:** Four $1,500 undergraduate scholarships (one at each school) and one $1,500 graduate scholarship. **To Apply:** Application material is available from FFA. **Deadline:** February 15. **Contact:** National FFA Foundation at the above address (see entry 4011).

## • 4031 • Blue Seal Feeds Scholarship
*(Undergraduate/Scholarship)*

**Qualif.:** Applicants must be FFA members pursuing a degree in animal science at a four-year institution. They must also be from the following states: Connecticut, Maine, Maryland, Massachusetts, New Hampshire, New Jersey, New York, Ohio, Pennsylvania, Rhode Island, or Vermont. **To Apply:** Application materials are available from FFA. **Deadline:** February 15. **Contact:** National FFA Foundation at the above address (see entry 4011).

## • 4032 • Borden Foundation Scholarships
*(Undergraduate/Scholarship)*

**Qualif.:** Applicants must be FFA members pursuing degrees in food science and technology or agricultural economics at Texas A&M University or food science and technology/dairy foods or agricultural economics at Mississippi State University.

**Funds Avail.:** Two $1,000 scholarships. **To Apply:** Application material is available from the FFA. **Deadline:** February 15. **Contact:** National FFA Foundation at the above address (see entry 4011).

## • 4033 • B.R.I.D.G.E. Endowment Fund Scholarships
*(Undergraduate/Scholarship)*

**Qualif.:** Applicants must be disabled or handicapped FFA members studying any agricultural major at a two- or four-year institution.

**Funds Avail.:** Two $5,000 scholarships. (Three additional $6,000 scholarships were awarded in 1992 by the Dr. Scholl Foundation). Application material is available from the FFA. **Deadline:** March 1.

**Remarks:** B.R.I.D.G.E. stands for "Building Rural Initiative for Disabled through Group Effort." **Contact:** National FFA Foundation at the above address (see entry 4011).

## • 4034 • B.R.I.D.G.E. Kraft General Foods Scholarship *(Undergraduate/Scholarship)*

**Qualif.:** Applicants must be FFA members pursuing a two- or four-year degree and be physically disabled or handicapped.

**Funds Avail.:** Two $2,500 scholarships. **To Apply:** Advisor's statement must clarify the eligibility of the candidate. Application materials are available from FFA. **Deadline:** February 15. **Contact:** National FFA Foundation at the above address (see entry 4011).

## • 4035 • B.R.I.D.G.E. Quaker Oats Foundation Scholarship *(Undergraduate/Scholarship)*

**Qualif.:** Applicants must be physically handicapped or disabled FFA members pursuing a degree at a four-year institution.

**Funds Avail.:** Four $1,000 scholarships. **To Apply:** Advisor's statement must clarify the eligibility of candidate. Application materials are available from FFA. **Deadline:** February 15. **Contact:** National FFA Foundation at the above address (see entry 4011).

## • 4036 • Bridgestone/Firestone Agricultural Mechanics Scholarships *(Undergraduate/Scholarship)*

**Qualif.:** Applicants must be FFA members pursuing a two- or four-year degree in any area of study and must have competed in a state FFA agricultural mechanics contest.

**Funds Avail.:** Two $500 scholarships each for members attending either vocational/technical school or four-year college. An additional ten scholarships will be presented to high-scoring individuals in the National FFA Agricultural Mechanics Contest. **To Apply:** FFA advisor must certify applicant's involvement in the state contest in "chapter advisor statement" section of this form. **Deadline:** February 15. **Contact:** National FFA Foundation at the above address (see entry 4011).

## • 4037 • Bunge Corporation Scholarship
*(Undergraduate/Scholarship)*

**Qualif.:** Applicants must be pursuing a degree in any area of agriculture at a four-year institution.

**Funds Avail.:** One $1,000 scholarship. **To Apply:** Application material is available from FFA. **Deadline:** February 15. **Contact:** National FFA Foundation at the above address (see entry 4011).

## • 4038 • Business Men's Assurance Company of America Scholarships *(Undergraduate/Scholarship)*

**Qualif.:** Applicants must be FFA members pursuing a four-year degree in any area of agriculture and must be from one of the fifty U.S. states except New York, New Jersey, Connecticut, New Hampshire, Vermont Rhode Island, Hawaii, and Alaska. **Criteria:** Financial need, academic standing, and leadership ability will all be considered.

**Funds Avail.:** Five $1,000 scholarships. **To Apply:** Application material is available from FFA. **Contact:** National FFA Foundation at the above address (see entry 4011).

## • 4039 • CAL Stores Companies Scholarships
*(Undergraduate/Scholarship)*

**Qualif.:** Applicants must be FFA members pursuing a degree in any area of agribusiness at a two- or four-year institution and be from selected counties in Idaho. The following 21 eligible counties are: Bannock, Bingham, Bear lake, Blaine, Bonneville, Butte, Caribou, Cassia, Clark, Custer, Franklin, Fremont, Jefferson, Jerome, Lemhi, Lincoln, Madison, Minidoka, Oneida, Power, and Teton.

**Funds Avail.:** Two $1,000 scholarships. **To Apply:** Application material is available from FFA. **Contact:** National FFA Foundation at the above address (see entry 4011).

## • 4040 • Capital Agricultural Property Services, Inc. Scholarship *(Undergraduate/Scholarship)*

**Qualif.:** Applicants must be FFA members pursuing a four-year degree in agricultural economics.

**Funds Avail.:** One $1,000 scholarship. **To Apply:** Application material is available from FFA. **Deadline:** February 15. **Contact:** National FFA Foundation at the above address (see entry 4011).

## • 4041 • Capitol American Scholarships
*(Undergraduate/Scholarship)*

**Qualif.:** Applicants must be FFA members pursuing degrees in agriculture, dairy farming, or ranching at a two- or four-year institution and must be from one of the following thirteen states: Arkansas, Colorado, Illinois, Indiana, Iowa, Kansas, Missouri, Montana, Nebraska, North Dakota, Oklahoma, South Dakota, or Wyoming.

**Funds Avail.:** Two $1,500 scholarships for a four-year degree and four $500 scholarships for a two-year degree. **To Apply:** Application material is available from FFA. **Deadline:** February 15. **Contact:** National FFA Foundation at the above address (see entry 4011).

## • 4042 • Cargill Scholarships for Rural America
*(Undergraduate/Scholarship)*

**Qualif.:** Applicants must be high school seniors planning to pursue or pursuing a two- or four-year degree full-time in the fall after graduation. Applicants families must receive at least 50 percent of income from farming. Both members and non-members of FFA are eligible to apply. **Criteria:** Selection is based on financial need, academic record, potential to succeed, demonstrated leadership, extra-curricular accomplishments, work experience, statement of educational and career goals and an evaluation by a teacher or advisor.

**Funds Avail.:** 250 $1,000 scholarships. **To Apply:** Applicant must complete parent financial analysis page. Applications (for members) can be obtained through the FFA and for non-members at any Cargill facility. Non-members should substitute other school, community, leadership and work activities when asked for FFA activities. **Deadline:** February 15. **Contact:** National FFA Organization Office at the above address (see entry 4011).

## • 4043 • Wilson W. Carnes Scholarships
*(Undergraduate/Scholarship)*

**Qualif.:** Applicants must be FFA members pursuing a degree in agricultural communications at a four-year institution.

**Funds Avail.:** One $500 scholarship. **To Apply:** Application material is available from FFA. **Deadline:** February 15.

**Remarks:** The scholarship is given in recognition of Mr. Wilson Carnes, retired editor of FFA New Horizons magazine, by his friends and co-workers to encourage FFA members to pursue an agricultural publishing career. **Contact:** National FFA Foundation at the above address (see entry 4011).

## • 4044 • CARQUEST Corporation Scholarships
*(Undergraduate/Scholarship)*

**Qualif.:** Applicants must be FFA members from a chapter with a CARQUEST store within a 25-mile radius pursuing a four-year degree in any area of study.

**Funds Avail.:** Five $1,000 scholarships. **To Apply:** Candidates must have their application signed (on "Sponsor" line of eligibility list) by their local CARQUEST manager or owner, including the store name. Application material can be obtained from FFA. **Deadline:** February 15. **Contact:** National FFA Foundation at the above address (see entry 4011).

## • 4045 • Casey's General Stores, Inc. Scholarships
*(Undergraduate/Scholarship)*

**Qualif.:** Applicants must be FFA members pursuing degrees in any area of agriculture or agribusiness at a two-year institution and be from Illinois, Iowa, or Missouri.

**Funds Avail.:** Three $500 scholarships. **To Apply:** Application material can be obtained from FFA. **Deadline:** February 15. **Contact:** National FFA Foundation at the above address (see entry 4011).

## • 4046 • Champions Choice/AKZO Salt Scholarships
*(Undergraduate/Scholarship)*

**Qualif.:** Applicants must be FFA members in need of financial support, pursuing degrees in dairy or beef science at a two- or four-year institution. **Criteria:** Preference is given to students with outstanding leadership and ag-related work experience and those from the top ten dairy and beef states.

**Funds Avail.:** Two $1,000 scholarships. **To Apply:** Application material is available from FFA. **Deadline:** February 15. **Contact:** National FFA Foundation at the above address (see entry 4011).

## • 4047 • Chevron USA, Inc. Scholarship
*(Undergraduate/Scholarship)*

**Qualif.:** Applicants must be FFA members pursuing a four-year degree in agriculture or agribusiness and must be from Florida or Georgia. **Criteria:** Preference is given to those showing outstanding leadership.

**Funds Avail.:** One $1,000 scholarship. **To Apply:** Application material can be obtained from FFA. **Deadline:** February 15. **Contact:** National FFA Foundation at the above address (see entry 4011).

## • 4048 • Chevy Trucks Scholarships *(Undergraduate/Scholarship)*

**Qualif.:** Applicants must be current and paid-in-full FFA members who are enrolled or planning to enroll in two- or four-year institutions, have demonstrated recruitment and leadership skills that have contributed to the local FFA chapter, and have participated in a Supervised Agricultural Experience (SAE). Applicants must be recommended by their local FFA chapter Advisor.

**Funds Avail.:** Ten scholarships totaling $25,000. **To Apply:** Application materials are available from the FFA. **Deadline:** February 15. **Contact:** National FFA Foundation at the above address (see entry 4011).

## • 4049 • Chicago and North Western Transportation Company Scholarship *(Undergraduate/Scholarship)*

**Qualif.:** Applicants must be FFA members from Iowa pursuing four-year degrees in agricultural education.

**Funds Avail.:** One $1,000 scholarship. **To Apply:** Application material can be obtained from FFA. **Deadline:** February 15.

---

## National FFA Foundation *(continued)*

**Contact:** National FFA Foundation at the above address (see entry 4011).

### • 4050 • Chief Industries Inc. Scholarships
*(Undergraduate/Scholarship)*

**Qualif.:** Applicants must be FFA members from Nebraska pursuing a degree in any area of agriculture at a two- or four-year institution.

**Funds Avail.:** One $1,000 scholarship to attend a four-year institution and one $500 scholarship to attend a two-year institution. **To Apply:** Application material can be obtained from FFA. **Deadline:** February 15. **Contact:** National FFA Foundation at the above address (see entry 4011).

### • 4051 • Chilean Nitrate Corporation Scholarship
*(Undergraduate/Scholarship)*

**Qualif.:** Applicants must be FFA members from Virginia or North Carolina pursuing degrees in any area of agriculture or agribusiness and must have tobacco production as part of their SAE (Supervised Agricultural Experience). **Criteria:** Preference may be given to agronomy majors.

**Funds Avail.:** One $1,200 scholarship. **To Apply:** Advisor must certify tobacco production in Advisor Statement of application. **Deadline:** February 15. **Contact:** National FFA Foundation at the above address (see entry 4011).

### • 4052 • ConAgra Scholarships *(Undergraduate/ Scholarship)*

**Qualif.:** Applicants must be high school seniors planning to pursue four-year degrees in agribusiness in either the College of Business Administration of the College of Agriculture, Department of Agricultural Economics, at the University of Nebraska-Lincoln. They must also be enrolled full-time, in the top 15 percent of their graduating class, active members of the FFA, and participated in extracurricular activities in which they have exhibited leadership potential. Students from all 50 states are eligible. **Criteria:** Selection is based on academic achievement, activities in the FFA, and extracurricular activities. If these three criteria are equal between potential applicants, then the person with the greatest financial need will be selected.

**Funds Avail.:** Four $7,000 scholarships ($1,725 per year for four years) and may be renewed for three subsequent years. Recipients must maintain a GPA of 3.2/4.0. **To Apply:** Application material is available from the FFA. **Deadline:** February 15. **Contact:** National FFA Foundation at the above address (see entry 4011).

### • 4053 • Countrymark Cooperative, Inc. Scholarships *(Undergraduate/Scholarship)*

**Qualif.:** Applicants must be FFA members from Indiana, Michigan, or Ohio pursuing a four-year degree in any area of agriculture. **Criteria:** Preference is given to those with outstanding leadership activities and work-related experience.

**Funds Avail.:** Two $1,000 scholarships. **To Apply:** Application material can be obtained from FFA. **Deadline:** February 15. **Contact:** National FFA Foundation at the above address (see entry 4011).

### • 4054 • Creswell, Munsell, Fultz & Zirbel Scholarships *(Undergraduate/Scholarship)*

**Qualif.:** Applicants must be FFA members entering their junior or senior year in college, pursuing a degree in agricultural communications, agricultural journalism, or agricultural marketing, and upon graduation, intend to pursue a career in advertising, public relations, journalism, or communications. They must also be attending one of the following 11 universities: Clemson University, Iowa State University, Kansas State University, North Carolina State University, The Ohio State University, Purdue University, University of Illinois, University of Nebraska-Lincoln, University of Minnesota, University of Missouri, or the University of Wisconsin-Madison. **Criteria:** Selection is based on grades, high school activities, university campus activities, and community involvement.

**Funds Avail.:** Eight $1,250 scholarships. **To Apply:** Application material is available from FFA. **Deadline:** February 15. **Contact:** National FFA Foundation at the above address (see entry 4011).

### • 4055 • Curtice Burns and Pro-Fac Scholarships
*(Undergraduate/Scholarship)*

**Qualif.:** Applicants must be FFA members pursuing degrees in any area of agriculture. **Criteria:** Preference is given to members in the following states, in the order they are listed: New York, Michigan, Illinois, Pennsylvania, Washington, Oregon, Georgia, Nebraska, and Iowa.

**Funds Avail.:** Two $1,000 scholarships and one $500 scholarship. **To Apply:** Application material can be obtained from FFA. **Deadline:** February 15. **Contact:** National FFA Foundation at the above address (see entry 4011).

### • 4056 • D & B Supply Company, Inc. Scholarships
*(Undergraduate/Scholarship)*

**Qualif.:** Applicants must be FFA members from selected counties in Washington, Idaho, or Oregon who are pursuing degrees in any area of agribusiness at a two- or four-year institution. In Washington, eligible candidates must be from Asotin county. Idaho counties: Ada, Canyon, Cassia, Clearwater, Gem, Gooding, Jerome, Lewis, Lincoln, Nez Perce, Owyhee, Payette, Twin Falls, and Washington. Oregon counties: Baker, Malheur, Umatilla, and Union.

**Funds Avail.:** Two $1,000 scholarships. One award is given to applicants in the selected counties of Washington or Idaho. The other is given to a student living in one of the selected counties in Oregon. **To Apply:** Application material can be obtained from FFA. **Deadline:** February 15. **Contact:** National FFA Foundation at the above address (see entry 4011).

### • 4057 • Darigold Scholarships *(Undergraduate/ Scholarship)*

**Qualif.:** Applicants must be FFA members from California, Idaho, Oregon, or Washington who have dairy backgrounds and are pursuing four-year degrees. **Criteria:** Preference is given to students with dairy science or food technology-related major.

**Funds Avail.:** Two $1,000 scholarships. **To Apply:** Application material can be obtained from FFA. **Deadline:** February 15. **Contact:** National FFA Foundation at the above address (see entry 4011).

### • 4058 • Data Transmission Network Corporation Scholarship *(Undergraduate/Scholarship)*

**Qualif.:** Applicants must be FFA members pursuing degrees in any area of agriculture at a four-year institution.

**Funds Avail.:** One $1,000 scholarship. **To Apply:** Application material can be obtained from FFA. **Deadline:** February 15.

**Remarks:** DTN is the lead provider of agricultural news market information and quotes to over 55,000 producers nationwide. **Contact:** National FFA Foundation at the above address (see entry 4011).

### • 4059 • Harold Davis Memorial Endowment Scholarship *(Undergraduate/Scholarship)*

**Qualif.:** Applicants must be FFA members pursuing two- or four-year degrees in animal science (livestock or dairy), ag education, or agribusiness. Must have livestock background in swine, beef, dairy, or any combination. **Criteria:** Financial need is an important criterium.

**Funds Avail.:** One $500 scholarship. **To Apply:** Because the scholarship is sponsored by A. O. Smith Harvestore Products, Inc, in addition to filling out an application, candidates must visit with the authorized local Harvestore System dealer, obtain the Harvestore System dealer's signature on the appropriate line, and complete the parent financial analysis page. If no recommendation signature from a local dealer is provided, please have FFA Advisor indicate reason why. Application material can be obtained from FFA. **Deadline:** February 15. **Contact:** National FFA Foundation at the above address (see entry 4011).

• 4060 • **DEKALB Genetic Corporation Scholarships** *(Undergraduate/Scholarship)*

**Qualif.:** Applicants must be FFA members pursuing four-year degrees in ag economics, ag business, ag sales, agronomy, or a related field.

**Funds Avail.:** Five $1,000 scholarships. **To Apply:** Application material is available from FFA. **Deadline:** February 15. **Contact:** National FFA Foundation at the above address (see entry 4011).

• 4061 • **Delmar Publishers Scholarship** *(Undergraduate/Scholarship)*

**Qualif.:** Applicants must be FFA members pursuing a four-year degree in agricultural education or a two-year degree in environmental science.

**Funds Avail.:** One $1,000 scholarship for FFA members pursuing a degree in agricultural education; one $500 scholarship for FFA members pursuing a degree in environmental sciences. **To Apply:** Application material is available from FFA. **Deadline:** February 15. **Contact:** National FFA Foundation at the above address (see entry 4011).

• 4062 • **Delta and Pine Land Company Scholarship** *(Undergraduate/Scholarship)*

**Qualif.:** Applicants must be FFA members pursuing four-year degrees in any area of agriculture and must be from one of the following seventeen states: Alabama, Arizona, Arkansas, California, Florida, Georgia, Kansas, Louisiana, Mississippi, Missouri, New Mexico, North Carolina, Oklahoma, South Carolina, Tennessee, Texas, or Virginia.

**Funds Avail.:** One $1,000 scholarship. **To Apply:** Application material is available from FFA. **Deadline:** February 15. **Contact:** National FFA Foundation at the above address (see entry 4011).

• 4063 • **Dodge Trucks Scholarships** *(Undergraduate/Scholarship)*

**Qualif.:** Applicants must be FFA members pursuing a degree in agricultural mechanics/diesel engines. **Criteria:** Preference will be given to those members with established financial need.

**Funds Avail.:** One $1,250 scholarship and nine $1,000 scholarships. **To Apply:** Application material is available from FFA. Applicants must complete the parental analysis section. **Deadline:** February 15. **Contact:** National FFA Foundation at the above address (see entry 4011).

• 4064 • **Douglas Products and Packaging Scholarships** *(Undergraduate/Scholarship)*

**Qualif.:** Applicants must be FFA members from Missouri pursuing a degree in any area of agriculture at a four-year institution.

**Funds Avail.:** Two $1,000 scholarships. **To Apply:** Application material is available from FFA. **Deadline:** February 15. **Contact:** National FFA Foundation at the above address (see entry 4011).

• 4065 • **Drysdales Scholarships** *(Undergraduate/Scholarship)*

**Qualif.:** Applicants must be FFA members pursuing a two- or four-year degree in any area of agriculture.

**Funds Avail.:** One $1,000 scholarship for a four-year degree and one $500 scholarship for a two-year degree. **To Apply:** Application material is available from FFA. **Deadline:** February 15. **Contact:** National FFA Foundation at the above address (see entry 4011).

• 4066 • **Dueutz-Allis Corporation, Hesston Corporation, and White Tractor Scholarships** *(Undergraduate/Scholarship)*

**Qualif.:** Applicants must be FFA members pursuing either a four-year degree in agricultural engineering or a two-year degree in agricultural mechanics.

**Funds Avail.:** Two $2,000 scholarships for agricultural engineering and two $500 scholarships for agricultural mechanics. **To Apply:** Applications are available through FFA. **Deadline:** February 15. **Contact:** National FFA Organization Office at the above address (see entry 4011).

• 4067 • **Eastern Apiculture Society of North America Scholarship** *(Undergraduate/Scholarship)*

**Qualif.:** Applicants must be FFA members pursuing a degree in any area of agriculture or agribusiness at a two-year institution in one of the following sixteen states: Connecticut, Delaware, Maine, Maryland, Massachusetts, New Hampshire, New Jersey, New York, North Carolina, Ohio, Pennsylvania, Rhode Island, Tennessee, Vermont, Virginia, or West Virginia. **Criteria:** Preference will be given to those with apiculture background.

**Funds Avail.:** One $500 scholarship. Winner must write an article for EAS Journal. **To Apply:** Application material is available from FFA. **Deadline:** February 15. **Contact:** National FFA Foundation at the above address (see entry 4011).

• 4068 • **Environmental Science Amoco Foundation Scholarships** *(Undergraduate/Scholarship)*

**Qualif.:** Applicants must be FFA members pursuing a four-year degree in any area of environmental studies.

**Funds Avail.:** Two scholarships at $2,500 each. **To Apply:** Application material is available from FFA. **Deadline:** February 15. **Contact:** National FFA Organization Office, PO Box 15160, 5632 Mt. Vernon Memorial Highway, Alexandria, VA 22309-0160.

• 4069 • **The Ertl Company Scholarship** *(Undergraduate/Scholarship)*

**Qualif.:** Applicants must be FFA members who are graduating high school seniors planning to pursue a degree at a midwestern land grant university or a two-year institution in any area of agriculture. Applicants must be from one of the following 13 states: Illinois, Indiana, Iowa, Kansas, Kentucky, Michigan, Minnesota, Missouri, Nebraska, North Dakota, Ohio, South Dakota, and Wisconsin. **Criteria:** Academic achievement and leadership will be considered equally.

**Funds Avail.:** One $1,000 scholarship to attend a Midwest land grant university and one $500 scholarship to attend a two-year institution. **To Apply:** Application material is available from FFA. **Deadline:** February 15. **Contact:** National FFA Foundation at the above address (see entry 4011).

• 4070 • **Excel Corporation, Geo. A. Hormel & Company, and Oscar Mayer Food Corporation Scholarship** *(Undergraduate/Scholarship)*

**Qualif.:** Applicants must be FFA members pursuing a degree in meat or animal science at a four-year institution. Applicants must

---

*National FFA Foundation (continued)*

have competed in the Meats Evaluation Contest above the local level.

**Funds Avail.:** Three $1,000 scholarships and an additional six scholarships will be presented to high-scoring individuals in the National FFA Meats Evaluation and Management Contest. **To Apply:** Advisor must certify applicant's involvement in contest in Advisor's Statement section of the application form. Application material is available from FFA. **Deadline:** February 15. **Contact:** National FFA Foundation at the above address (see entry 4011).

**• 4071 • FARM AID Scholarships** *(Undergraduate/ Scholarship)*

**Qualif.:** Applicants must be FFA members who are high school seniors from farm families who are pursuing four-year degrees in any area of agriculture. They must also be FFA members and demonstrate financial need.

**Funds Avail.:** Approximately ten $3,000 scholarships ($1,500 the freshman year, $1,000 the sophomore year, and $500 the junior year). The second and third year grants will be provided if recipients maintain a GPA of 2.0 on a 4.0 scale. **To Apply:** Applicants must submit a completed parent financial analysis form with completed application. Application material is available from the FFA. **Deadline:** February 15. **Contact:** National FFA Foundation at the above address (see entry 4011).

**• 4072 • Farm King Supply Scholarship** *(Undergraduate/Scholarship)*

**Qualif.:** Applicants must be FFA members from selected counties in Illinois or Iowa pursuing a two- or four-year degree in any area of agriculture. Illinois counties are: Fulton, Hancock, Henderson, Henry, Knox, McDonough, Mason, Mercer, Peoria, Schuyler, Stark, and Warren. Iowa counties are: DesMoines and Lee.

**Funds Avail.:** $1,000. **No. of Awards:** 1. **To Apply:** Application material is available from FFA. **Deadline:** February 15. **Contact:** National FFA Foundation at the above address (see entry 4011).

**• 4073 • Farmers Mutual Hail Insurance Company of Iowa Scholarships** *(Undergraduate/Scholarship)*

**Qualif.:** Applicants must be FFA members pursuing degrees in any area of agriculture at a four-year institution and be from one of the seven regions: Iowa, Illinois, Wisconsin, Indiana/Ohio/Michigan, Minnesota/North Dakota, Nebraska, and Missouri.

**Funds Avail.:** Fourteen $1,000 scholarships (two per each region). **To Apply:** Application material is available from FFA. **Deadline:** February 15. **Contact:** National FFA Foundation at the above address (see entry 4011).

**• 4074 • Federal Cartridge Company Scholarship** *(Undergraduate/Scholarship)*

**Qualif.:** Applicants must be FFA members pursuing a degree in natural resources.

**Funds Avail.:** One $1,000 scholarship. **To Apply:** Application material is available from FFA. **Deadline:** February 15. **Contact:** National FFA Foundation at the above address (see entry 4011).

**• 4075 • Federated Genetics Scholarship** *(Undergraduate/Scholarship)*

**Qualif.:** Applicants must be FFA members pursuing a degree in dairy science at a four-year institution.

**Funds Avail.:** One $1,000 scholarship. **To Apply:** Application material is available from FFA. **Deadline:** February 15. **Contact:** National FFA Foundation at the above address (see entry 4011).

**• 4076 • Fermenta Animal Health Company Scholarships** *(Undergraduate/Scholarship)*

**Qualif.:** Applicants must be FFA members pursuing a four-year degree in any area of agriculture.

**Funds Avail.:** Two $1,000 scholarships. An additional two $1,000 scholarships will be awarded to one member each of Indiana's North and South Knox FFA chapters pursuing a four-year degree. If there are no qualifying applicants from the North Knox or South Knox chapters, the respective scholarship will be open to any eligible Indiana FFA member. **To Apply:** Application material is available from FFA. **Deadline:** February 15. **Contact:** National FFA Foundation at the above address (see entry 4011).

**• 4077 • First Mississippi Corporation Scholarships** *(Undergraduate/Scholarship)*

**Qualif.:** Applicants must be FFA members from Mississippi or Louisiana pursuing a degree in any area of agriculture at a two- or four-year institution.

**Funds Avail.:** One $1,000 scholarship to study at a four-year institution and one $500 scholarship to study at a two-year institution. **To Apply:** Application material is available from FFA. **Deadline:** February 15. **Contact:** National FFA Foundation at the above address (see entry 4011).

**• 4078 • FISCO Farm and Home Stores Scholarships** *(Undergraduate/Scholarship)*

**Qualif.:** Applicants must be graduating high school seniors pursuing a four-year degree in agriculture, agribusiness, or animal science at a college or university within the state of California and must also be members of a California FFA chapter within a 25-mile radius of a FISCO store. **Criteria:** Selection is based on involvement in local FFA chapter, leadership potential, written recommendation of FFA leader, academic achievement, and financial need.

**Funds Avail.:** Seven $1,000 scholarships. **To Apply:** Application material is available from FFA. **Deadline:** February 15. **Contact:** National FFA Foundation at the above address (see entry 4011).

**• 4079 • Fleishman-Hillard, Inc. Scholarship** *(Undergraduate/Scholarship)*

**Qualif.:** Applicants must be FFA members pursuing a degree in agricultural communications at a four-year institution, have completed their sophomore year, and have a GPA of 3.0 on a 4.0 scale.

**Funds Avail.:** One $1,000 scholarship. **To Apply:** Application material is available from FFA. **Deadline:** February 15. **Contact:** National FFA Foundation at the above address (see entry 4011).

**• 4080 • Ford Motor Company Fund Scholarship** *(Undergraduate/Scholarship)*

**Qualif.:** Applicants must be FFA members pursuing a degree at a four-year institution.

**Funds Avail.:** Two $1,200 scholarships. **To Apply:** Application material is available from FFA. **Deadline:** February 15. **Contact:** National FFA Foundation at the above address (see entry 4011).

**• 4081 • Ford New Holland Scholarship** *(Undergraduate/Scholarship)*

**Qualif.:** Applicants must be FFA members pursuing a degree in any area and demonstrate significant activity in the chapter safety program. This activity must be certified by the chapter advisor in the Advisor Statement.

**Funds Avail.:** One $1,000 scholarship. **To Apply:** Application material is available from FFA. **Deadline:** February 15. **Contact:** National FFA Foundation at the above address (see entry 4011).

### • 4082 • Golden Harvest Seeds, Inc. Scholarships
*(Undergraduate/Scholarship)*

**Qualif.:** Applicants must be United States citizens and FFA members pursuing a four-year degree in agronomy. They must also be from either Illinois, Indiana, Michigan, Ohio, or Wisconsin and be attending University of Illinois, Purdue University, Michigan State University, Ohio State University, or the University of Wisconsin. They may also be from Colorado, Iowa, Kansas, Minnesota, Missouri, Nebraska, or South Dakota and be attending Colorado State University, Iowa State University, Kansas State University, University of Minnesota, University of Nebraska, or South Dakota State University.

**Funds Avail.:** Two $1,000 scholarships (one for each region). **To Apply:** Application material is available from FFA. **Deadline:** February 15. **Contact:** National FFA Foundation at the above address (see entry 4011).

### • 4083 • Growmark, Inc. Scholarships
*(Undergraduate/Scholarship)*

**Qualif.:** Applicants must be graduating high school seniors pursuing a two-year degree in a vocational/technical school or community college in any area of agriculture. They must also be from either Illinois, Iowa, or Wisconsin and attend school in their state of residence.

**Funds Avail.:** Six $500 scholarships (two in each state). **To Apply:** Application material is available from FFA. **Deadline:** February 15.

**Remarks:** GROWMARK, Inc. is a regional cooperative doing business primarily in these states through a federated system of farm supply and grain marketing member cooperatives. **Contact:** National FFA Foundation at the above address (see entry 4011).

### • 4084 • Gustafson, Inc. Scholarship *(Undergraduate/ Scholarship)*

**Qualif.:** Applicants must be FFA members pursuing a degree in agronomy and/or seed technology at Colorado State, Mississippi State, or Iowa State. **Criteria:** Preference will be given to those with outstanding leadership and academic achievement.

**Funds Avail.:** One $2,500 scholarship. **To Apply:** Application material is available from FFA. **Deadline:** February 15. **Contact:** National FFA Foundation at the above address (see entry 4011).

### • 4085 • Hardie Irrigation Scholarships
*(Undergraduate/Scholarship)*

**Qualif.:** Applicants must be FFA members pursuing a four-year degree and have an interest in irrigation. **Criteria:** Preference will be given to those who establish financial need.

**Funds Avail.:** Two $1,000 scholarships. **To Apply:** Applicants' interest in irrigation must be confirmed in Advisor's Statement on the application. Application material is available from FFA. **Deadline:** February 15. **Contact:** National FFA Foundation at the above address (see entry 4011).

### • 4086 • Hawkeye Steel Products, Inc. Scholarship
*(Undergraduate/Scholarship)*

**Qualif.:** Applicants must be FFA members from Iowa pursuing a degree in animal science or agricultural business and attending or planning to attend Iowa State University.

**Funds Avail.:** One $1,000 scholarship. **To Apply:** Application material is available from FFA. **Deadline:** February 15. **Contact:** National FFA Foundation at the above address (see entry 4011).

### • 4087 • Helena Chemical Company Scholarships
*(Undergraduate/Scholarship)*

**Qualif.:** Applicants must be FFA members and graduating high school seniors pursuing a four-year degree in agricultural

economics or agribusiness and be from one of three regions. Region 1: Arizona, California, Idaho, Montana, Nevada, Oregon, Utah, and Washington. Region 2: Alabama, Arkansas, Florida, Georgia, Kentucky, Louisiana, Mississippi, New Mexico, North Carolina, Oklahoma, South Carolina, Tennessee, and Texas. Region 3: Colorado, Connecticut, Delaware, Illinois, Indiana, Iowa, Kansas, Maine, Maryland, Massachusetts, Michigan, Minnesota, Missouri, Nebraska, New Hampshire, New Jersey, New York, North Dakota, Ohio, Pennsylvania, South Dakota, Vermont, West Virginia, Wisconsin, and Wyoming. **Criteria:** Financial need will be considered.

**Funds Avail.:** One $1,000 scholarship for each region. **To Apply:** Parent financial analysis form must be completed. Application material is available from FFA. **Deadline:** February 15. **Contact:** National FFA Foundation at the above address (see entry 4011).

### • 4088 • Georgia M. Hellberg Memorial Scholarships
*(Undergraduate/Scholarship)*

**Qualif.:** Applicants must be FFA members pursuing a four-year degree in water and soil conservation or be majoring in a discipline leading to employment in the area of soil and water conservation.

**Funds Avail.:** Four $3,500 scholarships. **To Apply:** Application material is available from FFA. **Deadline:** February 15. **Contact:** National FFA Foundation at the above address (see entry 4011).

### • 4089 • Cheryl Dant Hennesy Scholarship
*(Undergraduate/Scholarship)*

**Qualif.:** Applicants must be female FFA members from Kentucky, Georgia, or Tennessee pursuing a two- or four-year degree in any area of study full-time. Applicants must also demonstrate financial need and personal motivation.

**Funds Avail.:** One $1,000 scholarship, renewable for three additional years if recipient maintains a GPA of 2.0 on a 4.0 scale. **To Apply:** Application material is available from FFA. **Deadline:** February 15. **Contact:** National FFA Foundation at the above address (see entry 4011).

### • 4090 • Hillshire Farm & Kahn's Scholarship
*(Undergraduate/Scholarship)*

**Qualif.:** Applicants must be FFA members from Wisconsin pursuing a degree in agriculture or food technology at a four-year institution in Wisconsin.

**Funds Avail.:** One $1,000 scholarship. **To Apply:** Application material is available from FFA. **Deadline:** February 15. **Contact:** National FFA Foundation at the above address (see entry 4011).

### • 4091 • Hoard's Dairyman Scholarship
*(Undergraduate/Scholarship)*

**Qualif.:** Applicants must be FFA members pursuing a four-year degree in dairy science. **Criteria:** Preference is given to individual with agricultural journalism emphasis.

**Funds Avail.:** One $1,000 scholarship. **To Apply:** Application material is available from FFA. **Deadline:** February 15. **Contact:** National FFA Foundation at the above address (see entry 4011).

### • 4092 • Hydro Agri North America, Inc.
Scholarships *(Undergraduate/Scholarship)*

**Qualif.:** Applicants must be FFA members pursuing a four-year degree in any area of agriculture.

**Funds Avail.:** Four $1,000 scholarships. **To Apply:** Application material is available from FFA. **Deadline:** February 15. **Contact:** National FFA Foundation at the above address (see entry 4011).

---

## National FFA Foundation (continued)

### • 4093 • Kova Fertilizer, Inc. Scholarships
(Undergraduate/Scholarship)

**Qualif.:** Applicants must be FFA members from Indiana pursuing a four-year degree in any area at Purdue University or one of its affiliates. **Criteria:** Preference is given to FFA members from Decatur and Jackson counties.

**Funds Avail.:** Two $1,000 scholarships. **To Apply:** Application material is available from FFA. **Deadline:** February 15. **Contact:** National FFA Foundation at the above address (see entry 4011).

### • 4094 • Lextron, Inc. Scholarships (Undergraduate/Scholarship)

**Qualif.:** Applicants must be FFA members pursuing a four-year degree in animal science. They must also be from one of the following 26 states: Alabama, Arizona, Arkansas, California, Colorado, Florida, Georgia, Idaho, Iowa, Kansas, Louisiana, Minnesota, Mississippi, Missouri, Montana, Nebraska, Nevada, New Mexico, North Dakota, Oklahoma, Oregon, South Dakota, Texas, Utah, Washington, or Wyoming.

**Funds Avail.:** One $1,000 scholarship. **To Apply:** Application material is available from FFA. **Deadline:** February 15. **Contact:** National FFA Foundation at the above address (see entry 4011).

### • 4095 • Livestock Marketing Association and Local LMA Member Market Scholarship (Undergraduate/Scholarship)

**Qualif.:** Applicants must be FFA members pursuing a four-year, two-year, or one-year degree in animal science and industry, with the intent of a career based on livestock production.

**Funds Avail.:** One $1,000 scholarship for a four-year degree and one $500 scholarship for a one- or two-year degree. **To Apply:** Application material is available from FFA. **Deadline:** February 15. **Contact:** National FFA Foundation at the above address (see entry 4011).

### • 4096 • Earl May Seed & Nursery L.P. Scholarship (Undergraduate/Scholarship)

**Qualif.:** Applicants must be FFA members pursuing a two- or four-year degree in horticulture in one of the following five states: Iowa, Kansas, Missouri, Nebraska, or South Dakota.

**Funds Avail.:** Two $500 scholarships. **To Apply:** Application material is available from FFA. **Deadline:** February 15. **Contact:** National FFA Foundation at the above address (see entry 4011).

### • 4097 • Metropolitan Life Foundation Scholarships (Undergraduate/Scholarship)

**Qualif.:** Applicants must be FFA members pursuing a degree in agriculture or agribusiness at the following land-grant institutions: Iowa State University, Ames, IA; Kansas State University, Manhattan, KS; University of Missouri, Columbia, MO; University of Nebraska, Lincoln, NE; or Purdue University, West Lafayette, IN.

**Funds Avail.:** Five $2,000 scholarships (one for each university). **To Apply:** Application material is available from FFA. **Deadline:** February 15. **Contact:** National FFA Foundation at the above address (see entry 4011).

### • 4098 • Mid-America Dairymen, Inc., National Dairy Promotion and Research Board and Patz Sales, Inc. Scholarships (Undergraduate/Scholarship)

**Qualif.:** Applicants must be FFA members pursuing a degree in agriculture or agribusiness at a four-year institution and must have competed in the Dairy Foods Contest above the local level.

Advisor must certify applicant's involvement in contest in the Chapter's Advisor's Statement section of the form.

**Funds Avail.:** Two $1,000 scholarships. **To Apply:** Application material is available from FFA. **Deadline:** February 15. **Contact:** National FFA Foundation at the above address (see entry 4011).

### • 4099 • Mid-State Wool Growers Cooperative Scholarship (Undergraduate/Scholarship)

**Qualif.:** Applicants must be FFA members pursuing a four-year degree in agriculture or agribusiness and who are sheep producers or from sheep-producing families with operations of 20 or more ewes. Advisor's Statement must confirm sheep involvement. They must also be from the following states: Iowa, Kansas, Kentucky, Illinois, Indiana, Michigan, Minnesota, Missouri, Nebraska, Ohio, Oklahoma, or South Dakota.

**Funds Avail.:** One $1,000 scholarship. **To Apply:** Application material is available from FFA. **Deadline:** February 15. **Contact:** National FFA Foundation at the above address (see entry 4011).

### • 4100 • Miller Meester Advertising Scholarship (Undergraduate/Scholarship)

**Qualif.:** Applicants must be former or present FFA members who have completed their sophomore year and are pursuing a degree in agricultural communications or journalism at a four-year institution. They must also intend to pursue a career in advertising, public relations, journalism or communications upon graduation.

**Funds Avail.:** One $1,000 scholarship. **To Apply:** Application material is available from FFA. **Deadline:** February 15. **Contact:** National FFA Foundation at the above address (see entry 4011).

### • 4101 • Mississippi Farm Bureau Foundation Scholarship (Undergraduate/Scholarship)

**Qualif.:** Applicants must be FFA members from Mississippi pursuing a two-year degree in agriculture or agribusiness. They must also be sons or daughters of a Mississippi Farm Bureau Federation member-family.

**Funds Avail.:** One $500 scholarship. **To Apply:** Application material is available from FFA. **Deadline:** February 15. **Contact:** National FFA Foundation at the above address (see entry 4011).

### • 4102 • Monrovia Nursery Co. Scholarship (Undergraduate/Scholarship)

**Qualif.:** Applicants must be FFA members from pursuing a four-year degree in ornamental horticulture.

**Funds Avail.:** One $1,000 scholarship. **To Apply:** Application material is available from FFA. **Deadline:** February 15. **Contact:** National FFA Foundation at the above address (see entry 4011).

### • 4103 • National FFA Alumni Scholarships (Undergraduate/Scholarship)

**Qualif.:** Applicants must be current or former FFA members entering their junior or senior year at an accredited institution and pursuing a degree in agriculture education.

**Funds Avail.:** Three $1,000 scholarships. **To Apply:** Application material is available from FFA. **Deadline:** February 15. **Contact:** National FFA Foundation at the above address (see entry 4011).

### • 4104 • National FFA Foundation Minority Scholarships (Undergraduate/Scholarship)

**Qualif.:** Applicants must be FFA members pursuing college degrees in any area of agriculture and must represent a minority ethnic group (American Indian or Alaskan Native, Asian or Pacific Islander, African American, or Hispanic). FFA members from any state, Puerto Rico, the Virgin Islands, or the District of Columbia are eligible.

**Funds Avail.:** One $10,000 scholarship and three $5,000 scholarships. Winners of the $10,000 scholarship will have to provide documentation of college expenses (tuition, books, room and board) to the National FFA in order to receive allotment of funds. They must also maintain full-time student status and a GPA of 2.0 on a 4.0 scale. A copy of quarter, trimester, or semester grades will be sent to FFA after each grading period. **To Apply:** Application material is available from the FFA. **Deadline:** March 1. **Contact:** National FFA Foundation at the above address (see entry 4011).

• **4105** • **National Mastitis Council Scholarship** *(Undergraduate/Scholarship)*

**Qualif.:** Applicants must be FFA members pursuing a degree in dairy science at a two- or four-year institution.

**Funds Avail.:** One $500 scholarship. **To Apply:** Application material is available from FFA. **Deadline:** February 15. **Contact:** National FFA Foundation at the above address (see entry 4011).

• **4106** • **National Pork Producers Council Scholarships** *(Undergraduate/Scholarship)*

**Qualif.:** Applicants must be FFA members pursuing a degree in any area of agriculture at a four-year institution and from a swine-producing family or involved in swine production.

**Funds Avail.:** Four $1,000 scholarships. **To Apply:** Application material is available from FFA. **Deadline:** February 15. **Contact:** National FFA Foundation at the above address (see entry 4011).

• **4107** • **National Suffolk Sheep Association Scholarship** *(Undergraduate/Scholarship)*

**Qualif.:** Applicants must be FFA members with sheep-related experience pursuing a degree in any area of agriculture at a two- or four-year institution. **Criteria:** Leadership activities is a primary selection criteria.

**Funds Avail.:** One $500 scholarship. **To Apply:** Application material is available from FFA. **Deadline:** February 15. **Contact:** National FFA Foundation at the above address (see entry 4011).

• **4108** • **Nationwide Foundation Scholarships** *(Undergraduate/Scholarship)*

**Qualif.:** Applicants must be FFA members pursuing a four-year degree in any area of agriculture.

**Funds Avail.:** Two $1,000 scholarships. **To Apply:** Application material is available from FFA. **Deadline:** February 15. **Contact:** National FFA Foundation at the above address (see entry 4011).

• **4109** • **NC++FA Hybrids Scholarship** *(Undergraduate/Scholarship)*

**Qualif.:** Applicants must be FFA members pursuing a two- or four-year degree in any area of agriculture and demonstrate leadership ability. They must also be from one the following 13 states: Colorado, Illinois, Iowa, Kansas, Minnesota, Missouri, Nebraska, New Mexico, Oklahoma, Pennsylvania, South Dakota, Texas, or Wyoming. **Criteria:** Financial need and leadership qualities (in areas such as soil, crop, and livestock judging, parliamentary procedure, and public speaking) are the primary criterium.

**Funds Avail.:** One $1,000 scholarship for a four-year degree and one $500 scholarship for a two-year degree. **To Apply:** Applicants must complete the parent financial analysis section of the application. Application material is available from FFA. **Deadline:** February 15. **Contact:** National FFA Foundation at the above address (see entry 4011).

• **4110** • **Kenneth and Ellen Nielsen Cooperative Scholarships** *(Undergraduate/Scholarship)*

**Qualif.:** Applicants must be pursuing a four-year degree in any area of agriculture and demonstrate leadership ability. They must also be a resident of and plan to attend school in one the following 12 states: Colorado, Illinois, Iowa, Kansas, Minnesota, Missouri, Nebraska, North Dakota, Oklahoma, South Dakota, Texas, Wisconsin or Wyoming. **Criteria:** Financial need is a consideration.

**Funds Avail.:** Six $500 scholarships. **To Apply:** Must complete the parent financial analysis section of the application. Application material is available from FFA. **Deadline:** February 15.

**Remarks:** The awards are given in memory of the late Mr. and Mrs. Kenneth Nielsen. He served as Farmland Industries, Inc. President and Chief Executive Officer from 1981-86. The Nielsens were committed to developing and strengthening agriculture through farm cooperatives. **Contact:** National FFA Foundation at the above address (see entry 4011).

• **4111** • **Norfolk Southern Foundation Scholarships** *(Undergraduate/Scholarship)*

**Qualif.:** Applicants must be pursuing a degree in agricultural education at a four-year institution or any area of agriculture at a two-year institution.

**Funds Avail.:** Three $1,000 scholarships to attend a four-year institution and one $500 scholarships to attend a two-year institution. **To Apply:** Application material is available from FFA. **Deadline:** February 15. **Contact:** National FFA Foundation at the above address (see entry 4011).

• **4112** • **North American Limousin Foundation Scholarship** *(Undergraduate/Scholarship)*

**Qualif.:** Applicants must be FFA members pursuing a four-year degree in animal science or pre-veterinary medicine.

**Funds Avail.:** One $1,000 scholarship. **To Apply:** Application material is available from FFA. **Deadline:** February 15. **Contact:** National FFA Foundation at the above address (see entry 4011).

• **4113** • **Northrup King Company Scholarships** *(Undergraduate/Scholarship)*

**Qualif.:** Applicants must be FFA members pursuing a four-year degree in any area of agriculture and be from one of the following five states: Illinois, Iowa, Minnesota, Nebraska, and Wisconsin. **Criteria:** Selection is based on academic achievement.

**Funds Avail.:** Four $1,000 scholarships. **To Apply:** Application material is available from FFA. **Deadline:** February 15. **Contact:** National FFA Foundation at the above address (see entry 4011).

• **4114** • **Oklahoma Natural Gas Company Scholarship** *(Undergraduate/Scholarship)*

**Qualif.:** Applicants must be FFA members from Oklahoma pursuing a four-year degree in any area of agriculture at an Oklahoma institution.

**Funds Avail.:** One $1,000 scholarship. **To Apply:** Application material is available from FFA. **Deadline:** February 15. **Contact:** National FFA Foundation at the above address (see entry 4011).

• **4115** • **Prairie Farms Dairy, Inc. Scholarship** *(Undergraduate/Scholarship)*

**Qualif.:** Applicants must be FFA members from Illinois, Indiana, Iowa, or Missouri pursuing a two-year degree in dairy science.

**Funds Avail.:** One $500 scholarship. **To Apply:** Application material is available from FFA. **Deadline:** February 15. **Contact:** National FFA Foundation at the above address (see entry 4011).

---

Awards are arranged alphabetically below their administering organizations

*National FFA Foundation (continued)*

### • 4116 • Precision Laboratories, Inc. Scholarship
*(Undergraduate/Scholarship)*

**Qualif.:** Applicants must be FFA members from Illinois pursuing a four-year degree in agricultural economics or agribusiness at an Illinois institution.

**Funds Avail.:** One $1,000 scholarship. **To Apply:** Application material is available from FFA. **Deadline:** February 15. **Contact:** National FFA Foundation at the above address (see entry 4011).

### • 4117 • Professional Products & Services, Inc. Scholarship *(Undergraduate/Scholarship)*

**Qualif.:** Applicants must be FFA members from Wisconsin pursuing a degree in diary science.

**Funds Avail.:** One $500 scholarship. **To Apply:** Application material is available from FFA. **Deadline:** February 15. **Contact:** National FFA Foundation at the above address (see entry 4011).

### • 4118 • Purina Mills Scholarships *(Undergraduate/Scholarship)*

**Qualif.:** Applicants must be FFA members attending four-year colleges or universities studying animal science and have competed in the FFA Livestock Contest at the district, state, or national level.

**Funds Avail.:** Five $1,000 scholarships. An additional eight scholarships will be presented to high scoring individuals at the National FFA Livestock Contest. **To Apply:** FFA Advisor must certify the applicant's involvement in the FFA Livestock Contest in the "Chapter Advisor Statement" section of the application form. Application material is available from the FFA. **Deadline:** February 15. **Contact:** National FFA Foundation at the above address (see entry 4011).

### • 4119 • Quality Stores, Inc. Scholarships *(Undergraduate/Scholarship)*

**Qualif.:** Applicants must be FFA members from Indiana, Michigan, or Ohio pursuing a degree in any area of agribusiness at a four-year institution.

**Funds Avail.:** Three $1,000 scholarships (one for each state). **To Apply:** Application material is available from FFA. **Deadline:** February 15. **Contact:** National FFA Foundation at the above address (see entry 4011).

### • 4120 • Rain Bird Sprinkler Manufacturing Corp. Scholarships *(Undergraduate/Scholarship)*

**Qualif.:** Applicants must be FFA members pursuing a four-year degree and be interested in irrigation.

**Funds Avail.:** Two $1,000 scholarships. **To Apply:** Applicants' interest in irrigation must be confirmed in Advisor's Statement on application form. Applications are available from FFA. **Deadline:** February 15. **Contact:** National FFA Organization Office at the above address (see entry 4011).

### • 4121 • Rhone-Poulenc Animal Nutrition Scholarships *(Undergraduate/Scholarship)*

**Qualif.:** Applicants must be FFA members pursuing a four-year degree in animal, poultry, or grain science. In addition to the above requirements, for the animal science/poultry science scholarship, candidates must be from either Alabama, Arkansas, California, Florida, Georgia, or North Carolina. For the grain science scholarship, candidates must attend Kansas State University but may reside anywhere in the United States. For another animal science scholarship, candidates must attend either Kansas State

University, Oklahoma State University, Texas A&M, Iowa State University, or University of Nebraska.

**Funds Avail.:** Four scholarships; two $1,000 scholarships to major in animal science/poultry science, one $1,000 scholarship to major in grain science, and one $1,000 scholarship to major in animal science. **To Apply:** Application material is available from FFA. **Deadline:** February 15. **Contact:** National FFA Organization Office, PO Box 15160, 5632 Mt. Vernon Memorial Highway, Alexandria, VA 22309-0160.

### • 4122 • Ritchie Industries, Inc. Scholarship *(Undergraduate/Scholarship)*

**Qualif.:** Applicants must be FFA members from Iowa pursuing a four-year degree in any area of agriculture.

**Funds Avail.:** One $1,000 scholarship. **To Apply:** Application material is available from FFA. **Deadline:** February 15. **Contact:** National FFA Foundation at the above address (see entry 4011).

### • 4123 • Ruetgers-Nease Chemical Company, Inc. Scholarship *(Undergraduate/Scholarship)*

**Qualif.:** Applicants must be FFA members pursuing a four-year degree in any area of agriculture at Penn State University.

**Funds Avail.:** One $1,000 scholarship. **To Apply:** Application material is available from FFA. **Deadline:** February 15. **Contact:** National FFA Foundation at the above address (see entry 4011).

### • 4124 • Sandoz Agro, Inc. Scholarships *(Undergraduate/Scholarship)*

**Qualif.:** Applicants must be FFA members studying any field of agriculture at one of the following schools: University of Illinois; Cornell University; Purdue University; Iowa State University; University of Minnesota; Michigan State University; University of Wisconsin-Madison; Texas A&M; Virginia Polytechnic Institute; University of California-Davis; or Florida A&M University.

**Funds Avail.:** Three $2,000 scholarships. **To Apply:** Application material is available from the FFA. **Deadline:** February 15. **Contact:** National FFA Foundation at the above address (see entry 4011).

### • 4125 • Santa Fe Pacific Foundation Scholarships *(Undergraduate/Scholarship)*

**Qualif.:** Applicants must be high school seniors who are FFA members planning to pursue a career in any area of agriculture at a four-year university. Applicants must be from: Arizona, California, Colorado, Illinois, Kansas, Missouri, New Mexico, Oklahoma, or Texas.

**Funds Avail.:** Two $1,000 scholarships per state. Winners will also receive a travel stipend to attend the National FFA Convention in Kansas City, where there will be a recognition dinner hosted by the sponsor. **To Apply:** Applications are available through FFA. **Deadline:** February 15. **Contact:** National FFA National FFA Organization Office at the above address (see entry 4011).

### • 4126 • SIGCO Research Scholarships *(Undergraduate/Scholarship)*

**Qualif.:** Applicants must be FFA members from North Dakota, South Dakota, or Minnesota pursuing a two- or four-year degree in any area of agriculture.

**Funds Avail.:** Five $750 scholarships; two scholarships are available for both North Dakota and South Dakota members, one two-year and one four-year; one twoor four-year scholarship is available to a Minnesota member. **To Apply:** Application material is available from FFA. **Deadline:** February 15. **Contact:** National FFA Foundation at the above address (see entry 4011).

### • 4127 • Silgan Containers Corporation Scholarships (Undergraduate/Scholarship)

**Qualif.:** Applicants must be FFA members from California, Illinois, Iowa, Kentucky, Missouri, Oregon, Pennsylvania, or Wisconsin pursuing a four-year degree in food science/technology or agribusiness.

**Funds Avail.:** One $1,000 scholarship. **To Apply:** Application material is available from FFA. **Deadline:** February 15. **Contact:** National FFA Foundation at the above address (see entry 4011).

### • 4128 • Souvenir Shirts, Etc. Scholarships (Undergraduate/Scholarship)

**Qualif.:** Applicants must be FFA members pursuing a four-year degree in any area of agriculture. **Criteria:** Financial need will be considered.

**Funds Avail.:** Two $2,000 scholarships. **To Apply:** Applicants must complete the parental financial analysis section of the application. Application material is available from FFA. **Deadline:** February 15. **Contact:** National FFA Foundation at the above address (see entry 4011).

### • 4129 • Spraying Systems Company Scholarships (Undergraduate/Scholarship)

**Qualif.:** Applicants must be FFA members pursuing a four-year degree in agronomy, agriculture engineering or mechanization, landscape or turf grass management, or horticulture.

**Funds Avail.:** One $1,000 scholarship. **To Apply:** Application material is available from FFA. **Deadline:** February 15. **Contact:** National FFA Foundation at the above address (see entry 4011).

### • 4130 • State Farm Companies Foundation Scholarships (Undergraduate/Scholarship)

**Qualif.:** Applicants must be FFA members from Illinois pursuing a degree in agriculture or agribusiness at a four-year institution.

**Funds Avail.:** Three $1,000 scholarships. **To Apply:** Application material is available from FFA. **Deadline:** February 15. **Contact:** National FFA Foundation at the above address (see entry 4011).

### • 4131 • Sun Company Scholarships (Undergraduate/Scholarship)

**Qualif.:** Applicants must be FFA members pursuing a degree in floriculture or horticulture at a four-year institution. They must have also competed in the Floriculture Contest above the local level.

**Funds Avail.:** Two $1,000 scholarships. An additional four scholarships will be presented to high-scoring individuals in the National FFA Floriculture Contest. **To Apply:** Advisor must certify applicant's involvement in the contest in the Advisor's Statement of the application form. Application material is available from FFA. **Deadline:** February 15. **Contact:** National FFA Foundation at the above address (see entry 4011).

### • 4132 • TCS, Farm, Home and Auto Stores Scholarship (Undergraduate/Scholarship)

**Qualif.:** Applicants must be high school seniors who are FFA members and who want to pursue a career in any area of agriculture at a four-year institution. Applicants must also be from one of following three regions: North Dakota, South Dakota, Minnesota, Nebraska, Iowa, Kansas, Missouri, Texas and Montana; Illinois, Indiana, Kentucky, Tennessee, Arkansas, Mississippi, and Wisconsin; or Michigan, Ohio, Pennsylvania, New York, and Maryland. **Criteria:** Financial need will be considered and is a very important criteria.

**Funds Avail.:** Three $10,000 scholarships (one for each region). Winners must provide documentation of college expenses in order to receive advancement of funds for future payments of reimbursement of post payments; maintain a GPA of 2.0/4.0 (a copy of grades must be sent after each grading period); be enrolled full-time; and be willing to allow TSC to use a photograph of recipient's family in a tasteful way in company advertising. **To Apply:** Applicants must complete a Parent Financial Analysis page. Applications are available through FFA or any TSC store. **Deadline:** February 15. **Contact:** National FFA Organization Office at the above address (see entry 4011).

### • 4133 • Tetra Park Scholarship (Undergraduate/Scholarship)

**Qualif.:** Applicants must be pursuing a two- or four-year degree in food technology or dairy science.

**Funds Avail.:** One $1,000 scholarship for a four-year degree, two $500 scholarships for a two-year degree. **To Apply:** Application material is available from FFA. **Deadline:** February 15. **Contact:** National FFA Foundation at the above address (see entry 4011).

### • 4134 • Theisen Supply, Inc. Scholarships (Undergraduate/Scholarship)

**Qualif.:** Applicants must be FFA members pursuing a two- or four-year degree in any area of agriculture. They must also be from one of the following northeast communities of Iowa: Benton, Cedar, Clayton, Clinton, Delaware, Dubuque, Jackson, Jones, Linn, or Scott.

**Funds Avail.:** One $1,000 scholarship for a four-year degree, one $500 scholarship for a two-year degree. **To Apply:** Application material is available from FFA. **Deadline:** February 15. **Contact:** National FFA Foundation at the above address (see entry 4011).

### • 4135 • Tri-State Breeders Scholarships (Undergraduate/Scholarship)

**Qualif.:** Applicants must be FFA members completing their freshman, sophomore, or junior year and pursuing a two- or four-year degree in any area of agriculture. Applicant or parents must be purchasing Tri-State semen from an authorized Tri-State representative.

**Funds Avail.:** Three $500 scholarships. **To Apply:** Application material is available from FFA. **Deadline:** February 15. **Contact:** National FFA Foundation at the above address (see entry 4011).

### • 4136 • Tyson Foods, Sanofi Animal Health and American Proteins Scholarships (Undergraduate/Scholarship)

**Qualif.:** Applicants must be FFA members pursuing a degree in agriculture or agribusiness at a four-year institution. They must also have competed in the Poultry Contest above the local level.

**Funds Avail.:** One $1,000 scholarship. **To Apply:** Advisor must certify applicant's involvement in contest in Advisor's Statement of the application. Application material is available from FFA. **Deadline:** February 15. **Contact:** National FFA Foundation at the above address (see entry 4011).

### • 4137 • Union Pacific Foundation Scholarship (Undergraduate/Scholarship)

**Qualif.:** Applicants must be FFA members pursuing a degree in any area of agriculture a four-year institution. They must also be from Arkansas, California, Colorado, Idaho, Illinois, Iowa, Kansas, Louisiana, Missouri, Nebraska, Nevada, Oklahoma, Oregon, Texas, Washington, and Wyoming.

**Funds Avail.:** Sixteen $1,000 scholarships. Application material is available from FFA. **Deadline:** February 15. **Contact:** National FFA Foundation at the above address (see entry 4011).

---

Awards are arranged alphabetically below their administering organizations

*National FFA Foundation (continued)*

### • 4138 • United Dairymen of Idaho Scholarship *(Undergraduate/Scholarship)*

**Qualif.:** Candidates must be FFA members from Idaho with a dairy background studying at a two- or four-year institution. **Criteria:** Preference will be given to a dairy-related major.

**Funds Avail.:** One $1,600 scholarship. **To Apply:** Application material is available from FFA. **Deadline:** February 15. **Contact:** National FFA Foundation at the above address (see entry 4011).

### • 4139 • United Feeds Scholarships *(Undergraduate/Scholarship)*

**Qualif.:** Applicants must be FFA members from Indiana, Ohio, Michigan or Illinois pursuing a four-year degree in animal science at either Purdue University, The Ohio State University, Michigan State University, or University of Illinois.

**Funds Avail.:** Four $1,000 scholarships (one for each state). **To Apply:** Application material is available from FFA. **Deadline:** February 15. **Contact:** National FFA Foundation at the above address (see entry 4011).

### • 4140 • Universal Dairy Equipment, Inc. Scholarships *(Undergraduate/Scholarship)*

**Qualif.:** Applicants must be FFA members graduating from Kansas City East Environmental Sciences/Agribusiness Magnet High School pursuing a four-year degree in any agriculture-related major.

**Funds Avail.:** Two $1,000 scholarships. **To Apply:** Application material is available from FFA. **Deadline:** February 15. **Contact:** National FFA Foundation at the above address (see entry 4011).

### • 4141 • Universal Leaf Tobacco Company Scholarship *(Undergraduate/Scholarship)*

**Qualif.:** Applicants must be FFA members from North Carolina pursuing a two-year degree in agribusiness.

**Funds Avail.:** One $700 scholarship. **To Apply:** Application material is available from FFA. **Deadline:** February 15. **Contact:** National FFA Foundation at the above address (see entry 4011).

### • 4142 • Valmont Irrigation Scholarships *(Undergraduate/Scholarship)*

**Qualif.:** Applicants must be FFA members pursuing a four-year degree in any area of agriculture.

**Funds Avail.:** Two $1,000 scholarships. **To Apply:** Application material is available from FFA. **Deadline:** February 15. **Contact:** National FFA Foundation at the above address (see entry 4011).

### • 4143 • Viscosity Oil Company Scholarships *(Undergraduate/Scholarship)*

**Qualif.:** Applicants must be FFA members pursuing any field of study at a two or four-year institution. **Criteria:** Financial need is a consideration.

**Funds Avail.:** One $8,000, two $3,500, and five $2,000 scholarships. **To Apply:** Applicants must complete the parent financial analysis section. Applications are available through FFA. **Deadline:** February 15.

**Remarks:** These scholarships are funded by a portion of the sales of Case IH Engine Oil products marketed through the Case IH dealer network. **Contact:** National FFA Organization Office at the above address (see entry 4011).

### • 4144 • Wal-Mart Scholarship *(Undergraduate/Scholarship)*

**Qualif.:** Applicants must be pursuing degrees in any area of agriculture at a four-year institution in any of the fifty states and Puerto Rico except Vermont, Massachusetts, Alaska, and New Jersey.

**Funds Avail.:** Forty-seven $1,000 scholarships. **To Apply:** Available through FFA. **Deadline:** February 15. **Contact:** National FFA Organization Office at the above address (see entry 4011).

### • 4145 • Walco International, Inc. Scholarship *(Undergraduate/Scholarship)*

**Qualif.:** Applicants must be FFA members pursuing a four-year degree in animal science.

**Funds Avail.:** One $1,000 scholarship. **To Apply:** Application material is available from FFA. **Deadline:** February 15. **Contact:** National FFA Foundation at the above address (see entry 4011).

### • 4146 • Wells Fargo Bank Scholarship *(Undergraduate/Scholarship)*

**Qualif.:** Applicants must be FFA members from California pursuing a four-year degree in any area of agriculture. **Criteria:** Both scholastic achievement and FFA leadership will be considered.

**Funds Avail.:** One $750 scholarship. **To Apply:** Application material is available from FFA. **Deadline:** February 15. **Contact:** National FFA Foundation at the above address (see entry 4011).

### • 4147 • Western Dairymen - John Elway - Melba FFA Scholarship Fund *(Undergraduate/Scholarship)*

**Qualif.:** Applicants must be FFA members from Idaho pursuing a degree in agriculture or agribusiness. They must also have a GPA of at 3.0 on a 4.0 scale. **Criteria:** Preference will be given to members of the Melba FFA chapter.

**Funds Avail.:** One $500 scholarship. **To Apply:** Application material is available from FFA. **Deadline:** February 15.

**Remarks:** If there are no qualifying applicants from one of the Melba Chapters, the scholarship will be open to any eligible Idaho FFA member. **Contact:** National FFA Foundation at the above address (see entry 4011).

### • 4148 • Western Seedmen's Association Scholarships *(Undergraduate/Scholarship)*

**Qualif.:** Applicants must be FFA members pursuing a four-year degree in agronomy or agricultural education, or a two-year degree in any area of agriculture. Applicants must also be from one of the following 20 states: Arizona, California, Colorado, Idaho, Iowa, Kansas, Minnesota, Missouri, Montana, Nebraska, Nevada, New Mexico, North Dakota, Oklahoma, Oregon, South Dakota, Texas, Utah, Washington, or Wyoming.

**Funds Avail.:** One $1,000 scholarship towards a four-year degree in agronomy or agricultural education and one $750 scholarship towards a two- or four-year degree in any area of agriculture. **To Apply:** Application material is available from FFA. **Deadline:** February 15. **Contact:** National FFA Foundation at the above address (see entry 4011).

### • 4149 • Who's Who Among American High School Students Scholarships *(Undergraduate/Scholarship)*

**Qualif.:** Applicants must be FFA members pursuing a degree at a four-year institution.

**Funds Avail.:** One $1,000 scholarship. **To Apply:** Application material is available from FFA. **Deadline:** February 15. **Contact:** National FFA Foundation at the above address (see entry 4011).

## • 4150 • Williams Pipe Line Company Scholarship
*(Undergraduate/Scholarship)*

**Qualif.:** Applicants must be FFA members pursuing a degree in agribusiness. They must also be from one of the following ten states: Illinois, Iowa, Kansas, Minnesota, Missouri, Nebraska, North Dakota, Oklahoma, South Dakota, or Wisconsin.

**Funds Avail.:** One $1,000 scholarship. **To Apply:** Application material is available from FFA. **Deadline:** February 15. **Contact:** National FFA Foundation at the above address (see entry 4011).

## • 4151 • WIX Corporation Scholarships
*(Undergraduate/Scholarship)*

**Qualif.:** Applicants must be FFA members pursing a two- or four-year degree in agricultural mechanics and/or agricultural engineering.

**Funds Avail.:** Four $1,000 scholarships. **To Apply:** Application material is available from FFA. **Deadline:** February 15. **Contact:** National FFA Foundation at the above address (see entry 4011).

## • 4152 • Wolf's Head Oil Company Scholarships
*(Undergraduate/Scholarship)*

**Qualif.:** Applicants must be FFA members pursing a two-year technical degree in agricultural mechanics. They must also be from one of the following 25 states: Connecticut, Delaware, Georgia, Illinois, Indiana, Kentucky, Maine, Maryland, Massachusetts, Michigan, Minnesota, Missouri, New Hampshire, New Jersey, New York, North Carolina, Ohio, Pennsylvania, Rhode Island, South Carolina, Tennessee, Vermont, Virginia, West Virginia, or Wisconsin.

**Funds Avail.:** Two $500 scholarships. **To Apply:** Application material is available from FFA. **Deadline:** February 15. **Contact:** National FFA Foundation at the above address (see entry 4011).

## • 4153 • Wyandott, Inc. Snacks and Popcorn Scholarship *(Undergraduate/Scholarship)*

**Qualif.:** Applicants must be FFA members from a chapter in Marion or Wyandot County, Ohio pursuing a degree at a two- or four-year institution.

**Funds Avail.:** One $1,000 scholarship. **To Apply:** Application material is available from FFA. **Deadline:** February 15. **Contact:** National FFA Foundation at the above address (see entry 4011).

## • 4154 • Yetter Manufacturing Co. Scholarship
*(Undergraduate/Scholarship)*

**Qualif.:** Applicants must be FFA members pursuing a two-year degree in agriculture or agribusiness.

**Funds Avail.:** One $500 scholarship. **To Apply:** Application material is available from FFA. **Deadline:** February 15. **Contact:** National FFA Foundation at the above address (see entry 4011).

## • 4155 •
## National Foster Parent Association
9 Dartmoor Dr.  Ph: (815)455-2527
Crystal Lake, IL 60014  Fax: (815)455-2527

## • 4156 • Benjamin Eaton Scholarships
*(Undergraduate/Scholarship)*

**Focus:** General Studies. **Qualif.:** Applicants should be foster children, adopted children, or birth children in foster homes affiliated with the NFPA. **Criteria:** Preference is given to those who have had a balanced experience in high school and demonstrate a degree of commitment represented in the letter of application.

**Funds Avail.:** The amount and availability of funds is determined by the Benjamin Eaton Scholarship Trust Fund. **To Apply:** Applications must be requested. **Deadline:** March 1. **Contact:** Charles Black, Chair, at the above address (see entry 4155).

## • 4157 •
## National Foundation for Advancement in the Arts
800 Brickell Ave., Ste. 500  Ph: (305)377-1140
Miami, FL 33131  Fax: (305)377-1149
  Free: 800-970-ARTS
*E-mail:* nfaa@nfaa.org

## • 4158 • Arts Recognition and Talent Search (ARTS)
*(Undergraduate/Award)*

**Purpose:** ARTS (Arts Recognition and Talent Search) is a national program of the National Foundation for Advancement in the Arts in recognition of high school seniors or other artists age 17 and 18 years old who demonstrate excellence in dance, music, music/jazz, theater, photography, visual arts, voice and writing. **Focus:** Visual and Performing Arts, and writing. **Qualif.:** Applicants must be citizens or permanent residents of the United States (except for jazz applicants) and 17 or 18 years old as of December 1 of the year of the application. If enrolled in high school, they must be seniors in September of the academic year of application. Previous winners of ARTS cash awards are not eligible to reapply.

**Funds Avail.:** Cash awards totaling up to $300,000 are available to ARTS applicants whose work has been judged as outstanding by a national panel of experts. First level awards are for $3,000 each; second level awards, $1,500 each; third level, $1,000 each; fourth level, $500 each; and honorable mentions, $100 each. **No. of Awards:** 350. **To Apply:** Depending upon the discipline entered, applicants must submit audiotapes, videotapes, films, slides, or manuscripts demonstrating artistic accomplishment. Panels or expert judges (one panel for each art discipline) evaluate applicants in a two-step process. Judges first review materials submitted by applicants and then select up to 20 candidates in dance, music, theater, visual arts and writing, 10 in voice and photography and five in dance to be invited to Miami for a week of final auditions, interviews, and master classes (at NFAA's expense). Only candidates invited to Miami are eligible for cash awards. Judges also select applicants who are not invited to Miami for Honorable Mention recognition. The National Foundation for Advancement in the Arts (NFAA) nominates selected ARTS awardees to the White House Commission on Presidential Scholars, which, in a separate process, names 20 Presidential Scholars in the Arts. These young artists attend a week of events in their honor in Washington, DC. Through the Scholarship List Service (SLS), NFAA provides names of all the ARTS applicants who are seniors in high school to approximately 100 colleges, universities, and professional institutions who actively recruit young creative and performing artists and who provide scholarship opportunities to them. Although applicants may enter in more than one category, they are encouraged to enter only in their strongest area. An official application form, together with a nonrefundable fee of $35 ($25 for early applicants who apply before June 1) for each discipline or category of entry, is required. **Deadline:** The early deadline is June 1. The regular deadline is October 1. Candidates invited to Miami are notified in December and appear in Miami in January. Awards are announced the end of January and checks are distributed in June.

**Remarks:** More than 8,000 students typically apply each year. **Contact:** National Foundation for Advancement in the Arts at the above address (see entry 4157).

# National Foundation for Infectious Diseases

4733 Bethesda Ave., Ste. 750          *Ph:* (301)656-0003
Bethesda, MD 20814-5228             *Fax:* (301)907-0878
*E-mail:* nfid@aol.com
*URL:* http://www.nfid.org

### • 4160 • Fellowship in Infectious Diseases
*(Postdoctorate/Fellowship)*

**Purpose:** To encourage and assist young qualified physicians to become specialists and investigators in the field of infectious diseases. **Focus:** Infectious Disease. **Qualif.:** Applicant must be a U.S. citizen and must have at least three years of postgraduate medical training. A university-affiliated medical laboratory must agree to act as sponsor and provide guidance, research space, and necessary equipment. Candidates who have or will receive major support from the federal government or another foundation are not eligible. **Criteria:** Priority will be given to fellows in or entering into infectious diseases training.

**Funds Avail.:** $25,000 stipend. **No. of Awards:** 1. **To Apply:** Write for guidelines. Submit six copies of the following: the abstract, a letter of acceptance from a specialist or departmental chair at host institution, a two-page curriculum vitae, and a five-page project proposal. **Deadline:** January 11. Notification by April 15.

**Remarks:** Sponsored by Glaxo Wellcome, Inc.

### • 4161 • New Investigator Matching Grants
*(Postdoctorate/Grant)*

**Purpose:** To assist young investigators who are beginning their research. **Focus:** AIDS, Respiratory Infections, including Influenza and Tuberculosis, Hospital-Acquired Infections, Sexually Transmitted Diseases, including Syphilis and Papilloma Virus, Viral Hepatitis, Infections in Cancer and Transplantation, Gastrointestinal and Diarrheal Diseases, Meningitis and Encephalitis, Tropical, Travelers' and Parasitic Diseases, Urinary Tract Infections. **Qualif.:** Applicant must be a legal resident of the U.S. or Canada and a young investigator, defined as an individual with full-time junior faculty status at a recognized and accredited institution of higher learning. **Criteria:** Priority will be given to those who do not have research grants and whose studies represent pilot work.

**Funds Avail.:** $2,000. **To Apply:** Write for application form and guidelines. Submit six copies of the following: the 4-page form, a letter of acceptance from a specialist or departmental chair at host institution, a two-page curriculum vitae. **Deadline:** February 16. Notification by May 1.

**Remarks:** Sponsored by Schering-Plough.

### • 4162 • Postdoctoral Fellowship in Emerging Infectious Diseases *(Postdoctorate/Fellowship)*

**Purpose:** To encourage and assist a qualified physician to become a recognized authority on emerging infectious diseases and epidemiology. **Qualif.:** The applicant must be a physician who is a citizen of the United States, preferably having completed an infectious diseases fellowship. Prior experience or knowledge in managing databases is desirable but not a requirement.

**Funds Avail.:** $50,000 stipend. **To Apply:** An original application and four copies must be postmarked no later than January 11.

**Remarks:** Sponsored by Merck & Co., Inc.

### • 4163 • Postdoctoral Fellowship in Nosocomial Infection Research and Training *(Postdoctorate/Fellowship)*

**Purpose:** To encourage and assist a qualified physician researcher to become a specialist and investigator in the field of nosocomial infections. **Focus:** Infectious disease-nosocomial infections.

**Qualif.:** Applicants must be physicians in training who are U.S. citizens and demonstrate aptitude and accomplishment in laboratory or epidemiologic research. They must also confirm arrangements for conducting the proposed research with a recognized host laboratory. **Criteria:** Selection criteria includes applicant's record of scholarship performance and professional qualifications, scientific merit of the proposed research project, validity of research rationale, and adequacy of facilities available. Priority is given to fellows in or entering into infectious diseases training.

**Funds Avail.:** $25,000 of which $1,000 may be used for travel and supplies expenses. **No. of Awards:** 1. **To Apply:** Applications must be completed and returned to the National Foundation for Infectious Diseases along with a letter from the Nosocomial Infection specialist, department chair, or faculty member who will oversee the applicant's work, a curriculum vitae of no more than two pages (Courier 10 point), and a description of no more than five pages in length (single-spaced) of the applicant's proposed research project. **Deadline:** January 11.

**Remarks:** Sponsored by Hoechst Marion Roussel, Inc.

### • 4164 • Colin L. Powell Minority Postdoctoral Fellowship in Tropical Disease Research *(Graduate/Fellowship)*

**Purpose:** To encourage and assist a qualified minority researcher to become a specialist and investigator in the field of tropical diseases. **Focus:** Infectious diseases. **Qualif.:** Applicants must be Black, Hispanic, American Indian, Alaska Native, or Asian or Pacific Islanders holding a doctorate from a recognized university. Applicants also must be U.S. residents or a spouse of a U.S. resident. **Criteria:** Selection criteria includes, but is not limited to, applicant's scholarship performance and professional qualifications; scientific merit of the proposed research project; validity of the research rationale; adequacy of the facilities available to the applicant; host department; and host institution.

**Funds Avail.:** $30,000. **To Apply:** The original application and four copies must be submitted. **Deadline:** January 11.

### • 4165 • John P. Utz Postdoctoral Fellowship in Medical Mycology *(Postdoctorate/Fellowship)*

**Purpose:** To encourage a qualified physician to become a specialist and investigator in medical mycology. **Focus:** Medical mycology **Qualif.:** Applicants must be physicians, citizens of the U.S., and must demonstrate aptitude and training in research. They must also confirm arrangements for conducting the proposed research in a recognized host laboratory. The laboratory director or appropriate Department Chair must attest willingness to accept the applicant and provide guidance, research space, and necessary research equipment. Candidates must be sponsored by a university-affiliated medical center. **Criteria:** Selection criteria will include, but is not limited to: applicant's record of scholarship performance and professional qualifications, scientific merit of the clinical research project proposal, validity of research rationale, and adequacy of facilities available to the applicant, host department, and host institution. Priority will be given to fellows in or entering infectious diseases training.

**Funds Avail.:** A stipend of $29,000, and an additional $1,000 for travel and supplies. The fellowship may not be awarded if the applicant has received or will receive a major fellowship, research grant, or traineeship from the federal government or another foundation in excess of the amount of this award. **No. of Awards:** 1. **To Apply:** An original and six copies of the application, including a letter from the person who will oversee the candidate's work, a curriculum vitae of no more than two pages, and a description of the proposed clinical project of no more than five pages are required. The Chairman of the Department of Infectious Diseases, in a letter that accompanies the application, must express a willingness to be responsible for the candidate's training. **Deadline:** January 11. Recipients are notified by April 15. Support starts July 1.

**Remarks:** Recipients must submit progress reports of one page, singled-spaced after six months and again after 12 months or completion of the Fellowship. Sponsored by Pfizer, Inc.

• 4166 •

## National Foundation for Jewish Culture

330 Seventh Ave., 21st Floor     *Ph:* (212)629-0500
New York, NY 10001     *Fax:* (212)629-0508
*E-mail:* rmetzger@jewishculture.org
*URL:* http://www.jewishculture.org

• 4167 • **National Foundation for Jewish Culture Doctoral Dissertation Grants** *(Doctorate/Grant)*

**Purpose:** To assist students preparing for academic careers in Jewish studies. **Focus:** Jewish Studies. **Qualif.:** Applicants must be U.S. citizens or permanent residents. They must also be Ph.D. students who have completed all degree requirements except the dissertation. Applicants must be interested in an academic career in Jewish studies or related fields in the humanities or social sciences and have knowledge of a jewish language.

**Funds Avail.:** $7,000-$10,000. **No. of Awards:** 10-13. **To Apply:** Write the grants administrator for application form and guidelines. **Deadline:** January 1. Notification in the spring. **Contact:** Rebecca Metzger, Grants Administrator, at the above address (see entry 4166).

• 4168 •

## National Foundation for Long Term Health Care

1201 L St. NW
Washington, DC 20005

• 4169 • **James D. Durante Nurse Scholarship Program** *(Undergraduate/Scholarship)*

**Focus:** Nursing. **Qualif.:** Applicants must work for a long term care facility that is a member of AHCA, and be enrolled/accepted in an accredited LPN or RN school of nursing program. **Criteria:** Awards are granted based on the quality of their personal statements and recommendations.

**Funds Avail.:** $500. **No. of Awards:** 20. 10 awarded to registered nursing students and 10 awarded to licensed practical nursing students. **To Apply:** Applicants must submit a completed and signed application; a copy of acceptance letter from nursing school; a copy of most recent transcripts with grades (enrolled students only); and two letters of recommendation: (1) One recommendation completed by a supervisory level representative of the AHCA member facility. (2) A second recommendation from an academic or professional source. Recommendations must be sealed by each reference in separate envelopes and included in the application packet. Only recommendations received in this manner will be accepted. Applications not meeting all of the above criteria will be disqualified. **Deadline:** May 31.

**Remarks:** Scholarship recipients must submit copies of transcripts for two consecutive semesters following scholarship receipt to validate continued academic enrollment. Recipients must also complete twenty-five hours of volunteer service at a long term care facility that is a member of AHCA. **Contact:** Chris Condeelis, Manager, Professional Development.

• 4170 •

## National Fourth Infantry (IVY) Division Association

2 Spring Dr.
Walkersville, MD 21793-8107     *Ph:* (516)821-7284
*URL:* http://www.4thinfantry.org

• 4171 • **National Fourth Infantry Division Association Scholarship** *(Doctorate, Graduate, Other, Undergraduate/Scholarship)*

**Qualif.:** Applicants must be children of members of the Fourth Infantry Division during the Vietnam war who died in action or in the line of duty.

**Funds Avail.:** $6000 awarded annually. **No. of Awards:** 6. **Contact:** National Fouth Infantry (IVY) Division Association at the above address (see entry 4170).

• 4172 •

## National Fraternal Society of the Deaf

1118 S. 6th St.     *Ph:* (217)789-7429
Springfield, IL 62703     *Fax:* (217)789-7489
*E-mail:* thefrat@nfsd.com
*URL:* http://www.nfsd.com/

• 4173 • **National Fraternal Society of the Deaf Scholarships** *(Doctorate, Graduate, Postgraduate, Professional Development, Undergraduate/Scholarship)*

**Purpose:** To financially assist NFSD members with their post-secondary education. **Focus:** General Studies. **Qualif.:** Applicants must be members of the Society for at least one year. Membership involves having a life insurance policy with NFSD. The scholarship is open to both deaf and hearing individuals. **Criteria:** Selection is based on academic record, goals, and financial need.

**Funds Avail.:** Ten awards of $1,000 each are given. **No. of Awards:** 10. **To Apply:** A completed application, recent transcripts and three letters of reference are required. **Deadline:** July 1.

• 4174 •

## National Heart, Lung, and Blood Institute

National Institutes of Health
2 Rockledge Center
6701 Rockledge Dr.     *Ph:* (301)435-0144
Bethesda, MD 20892     *Fax:* (301)480-3310
*URL:* http://www.amhrt.org/hs96/nhlbi.html

*The National Heart, Lung, and Blood Institute is part of the National Institutes of Health and of the U.S. Department of Health and Human Services.*

• 4175 • **National Heart, Lung, and Blood Institute's Minority School Faculty Development Award** *(Postdoctorate/Award)*

**Purpose:** To foster the development of minority school faculty researchers in subjects of study relating to hematologic, cardiovascular, and pulmonary diseases, to encourage the enhancement of research skills in the areas of interest to the NHLBI by faculty members at minority institutions, and to increase the number of minority individuals involved in research endeavors. **Qualif.:** Applicants must be minority faculty members who are either United States citizens, noncitizen nationals, or permanent residents. They must also have a biomedical or behavioral science doctoral degree, wish to receive specialized training in the areas

## National Heart, Lung, and Blood Institute (continued)

mentioned in the purpose of the award, and have the background and potential to benefit from the training. The awardee will work with a mentor at a nearby (within 100 miles) research center, who is recognized as an accomplished investigator in the research area proposed, and who will provide guidance for the awardee's development and research plan. Awardees must commit 100 percent of their effort during the summer and/or off quarter periods and at least 25 percent during the academic year. **Criteria:** Selection is based on the scientific and technical merit of the application.

**Funds Avail.:** Grants will be made to a minority institution on behalf of the awardee. Salary support of up to $50,000 plus fringe benefits per year for up to five years. Up to $20,000 in research support is also available. In addition to the candidate's salary request, support for up to ten percent of the mentor's salary during the summer experience may also be requested. **To Apply:** Applicants must forward a letter of intent that includes a descriptive title, the name and address of the research mentor, and any other participating institutions. Applicants are advised to obtain the NHLBI Guidelines before preparing an application. They must submit a completed grant application form PHS 398. The application must include statement(s) from the Dean and departmental chair indicating that the candidate will be provided with sufficient release time. Each candidate must identify and complete arrangements with a mentor. Plans for the intensive training during the summer period (two or three months) as well as during the academic year must be developed with the mentor. Details regarding the apportionment of the funds between the minority institution and the research center must be worked out with the mentor at the research center and agreed to by representatives of both institutions. **Deadline:** The letter of intent is due July 1; Applications are due by Mid-August. **Contact:** Letters of intent must be sent to Scientific Review Administrator, Research Training Review Committee, Division of Extramural Affairs, NHLBI, Westwood Building, Rm. 550, Bethesda, MD 20892. Application kits are available at most institutional business offices. Written and telephone inquires and guidelines for the program may be obtained from John Fakunding, Ph.D., Division of Heart and Vascular Diseases, National Heart, Lung and Blood Institute, Federal Bldg., Rm., 3C04, Bethesda, Maryland 20892 (telephone: (301)496-1724); Helena Mishoe, Ph.D., Division of Blood Diseases and Resources, National Heart, Lung and Blood Institute, Federal Bldg., Rm., 504, Bethesda, Maryland 20892 (telephone: (301)496-6931); and Mary Reilly, M.S., Division of Lung Diseases, National Heart, Lung and Blood Institute, Westwood Bldg., Rm., 640A, Bethesda, Maryland 20892 (telephone: (301)496-7668). For fiscal and administrative matters, contact: Jane Davis, Grants Operation Branch, Division of Extramural Affairs, National Heart, Lung and Blood Institute, Westwood Bldg., Rm., 4A15C, Bethesda, Maryland 20892 (telephone: (301)496-7257).

## • 4176 •
## National Hemophilia Foundation

116 W. 32nd St., 11th Fl.  
New York, NY 10001

Ph: (212)328-3741  
Fax: (212)328-3788  
Free: 800-424-2634

E-mail: dkenny@hemophilia.org  
URL: http://www.hemophilia.org

### • 4177 • Judith Graham Pool Postdoctoral Research Fellowships (Postdoctorate/Fellowship)

**Purpose:** To support research of high scientific merit in hemophilia, and to stimulate the life-long interest of promising investigators in hemophilia. **Focus:** Basic and Clinical Research in Hemophilia and its complications. **Qualif.:** Applicants must be U.S. citizens or permanent residents who have recently earned the doctoral degree. Candidates must also have completed doctoral

training and must enter the Judith Graham Pool Fellowship program from a doctoral, postdoctoral, internship, or residency training program. Applications from faculty members or established investigators will not be considered. Applicants must be affiliated with a U.S. institution with adequate research facilities. Research can be conducted on the biochemical, genetic, hematologic, orthopedic, psychiatric, or dental aspects of hemophilia or von Willerbrand's Disease. Research may also focus on rehabilitation, therapy, AIDS research with respect to hemophilia, or social features of these disorders. Fellows must commit at least 90% of their time to the research projects. **Criteria:** Selection is based on peer review.

**Funds Avail.:** $35,000 maximum for salary, fringe benefits, and up to $750 for travel. **No. of Awards:** Five per year plus two renewals. **To Apply:** Candidates should write to the Foundation for application form and guidelines. Information about the fellowship is also distributed to hematology/oncology departments at U.S. institutions. Please submit form with a description of proposed research. Three letters of recommendation are also required. **Deadline:** December 15. Applicants are notified in early May. **Contact:** Steven Humes, MPH, Director of Research, at the above address (see entry 4176).

## • 4178 •
## National Hispanic Scholarship Fund

1 Sansome St., Ste. 1000  
San Francisco, CA 94104  
E-mail: info@omhrc.gov  
URL: http://www.omhrc.gov/mhr2/orgs/8800249.htm

Ph: (415)445-9930

### • 4179 • NHSF Scholarships (Graduate, Undergraduate/Scholarship)

**Purpose:** To support studies by Hispanic Americans. **Focus:** General **Qualif.:** Applicant must be a U.S. citizen or permanent resident of Hispanic-American descent. Candidate must attend a U.S. or Puerto Rican college at the time of application and have completed at least fifteen units of course work.

**Funds Avail.:** $500-1,000. **To Apply:** Write for application form and guidelines. Submit form with personal statement, college transcripts, and a letter of recommendation from appropriate school official. **Deadline:** August 15 through October 1 each year. **Contact:** Selection Committee at the above address (see entry 4178).

## • 4180 •
## National Historical Publications and Records Commission

National Archives (Arch I), Rm. 106  
701 Pennsylvania Ave. NW  
Washington, DC 20408-0001  
E-mail: nhprc@arch.nara.gov  
URL: http://www.nara.gov/nara/nhprc/

Ph: (202)501-5610  
Fax: (202)501-5601

### • 4181 • NHPRC/Fellowships in Archival Administration (Professional Development/Fellowship)

**Purpose:** To give archivists actual working experience in administration. The Commission believes that workshops and other types of training, although important aspects of archival education, are not as beneficial as hands-on experience in training future administrators. **Focus:** Archives, History. **Qualif.:** Fellowship applicants should have between two and five years' experience in archival work. While not required, it is desirable that applicants have the equivalent of two semesters of full-time graduate training in a program containing an archives education component. Host institutions are encouraged to provide fellows with a series of supervisory and decision-making experiences. Included in past fellowships have been such diverse areas as appraisal, budget preparation, personnel administration, grants administration, publications, plant operation, long-range planning, disaster planning, collection policy development, committee work, and collection surveys. **Criteria:** Selection is based on interview process.

**Funds Avail.:** Fellows receive a stipend and benefits package. Applicants should check with Commission staff for the current salary and benefit levels. **No. of Awards:** 2. **To Apply:** The application process for the host institution and fellow is competitive. The Commission selects the host institution from eligible applications received against the September deadline. Institutional staff interested in applying to be host should contact Commission staff to discuss their ideas for the program and the technical project. Individual and host application materials may be requested from the Commission. **Deadline:** The deadline for host institutions is September 1 and March 1 for individual fellowships. **Contact:** Laurie A. Baty, Program Officer, at the above address (see entry 4180).

**• 4182 • NHPRC/Fellowships in Historical Editing**
*(Postdoctorate/Fellowship)*

**Purpose:** To provide specialized training in transcription, annotation, research techniques, and other activities involved in preparing historical editions for publication. **Focus:** American History. **Qualif.:** Fellowship applicants must hold a Ph.D. or have completed all requirements for degree except the dissertation. **Criteria:** Selection based on interview process.

**Funds Avail.:** Fellows receive a stipend and benefits package. Applicants should check with Commission staff for the current salary and benefit levels. **No. of Awards:** 1. **To Apply:** Details on the project may be obtained from the NHPRC. All entries must be typed on application forms. Applicants must include a copy of a dissertation prospectus, dissertation abstract, or some other evidence of the applicants' written work. Unofficial transcripts are acceptable for the competition; however, applicants must provide official copies before a fellowship can be confirmed by the Commission. Applicants may not submit an application to an editor for whom they have worked or under whom they have studied. The NHPRC prefers that editors not nominate any student from the editorial project's host institution. **Deadline:** Application materials must be received by March 1.

**Remarks:** Recipients spend 11 months in training with a designated project beginning sometime between August 1 and October 1. **Contact:** Laurie A. Baty, at the above address (see entry 4180).

**• 4183 •**
**National Humanities Center**
PO Box 12256
Research Triangle Park, NC 27709-
2256                                                    *Ph:* (919)549-0661
*E-mail:* nhc@unc.edu
*URL:* http://www.nhc.rtp.nc.us:8080

**• 4184 • National Humanities Center Residential, Advanced Postdoctoral Fellowships** *(Postdoctorate/ Fellowship)*

**Purpose:** To encourage the exchange of ideas between scholars. **Focus:** Humanities (including Fine Arts, History, Languages, Literature, Philosophy), Natural Sciences, Social Sciences. **Qualif.:** Applicant may be from any nation, and may be a senior or junior scholar. Applicant must hold a doctorate or have equivalent professional accomplishments, should be engaged in work

significantly beyond revision of a doctoral dissertation. Individuals from fields outside of the traditional realm of humanities, such as arts, the natural and social sciences, or public life, are welcome to apply if their work has humanistic dimensions. Fellowships are tenable at the Center; fellows are expected to spend the duration of the award there, pursuing writing and research. **Criteria:** Annual jured competition.

**Funds Avail.:** Up to $30,000, plus travel expenses (based on need). **No. of Awards:** Approximately 30. **To Apply:** Write to the fellowship program at the Center for application materials. Submit application form with curriculum vitae, a project proposal, and three letters of recommendation. **Deadline:** October 15. **Contact:** Fellowship Program at the above address (see entry 4183).

**• 4185 •**
**National Institute of Arthritis and Musculoskeletal and Skin Diseases**
National Institutes of Health
Bldg. 31                                                *Ph:* (301)594-2463
Bethesda, MD 20892                                       *Fax:* (301)480-4543
*The National Institute of Arthritis and Musculoskeletal and Skin Diseases (NIAMS) has primary responsibility at the National Institutes of Health (NIH) for research and research training in the three disease areas constituting its name, and on the normal structure and function of joints, muscles, bones, and skin. The institute carries out its mandate, in large part, through its Extramural Program, which includes a wide range of fundamental and clinical research. Also embodied in the Institute's extramural activities are research projects in prevention, epidemiology, and clinical applications.*

**• 4186 • NIAMS Academic Research Enhancement Awards** *(Postdoctorate/Grant)*

**Purpose:** To provide support for small-scale research projects conducted by faculty in primarily baccalaureate degree-granting institutions.

**Funds Avail.:** Awards are up to $75,000 for a period up to 36 months. **Contact:** Dr. Steven J, Hausman, Director, Extramural Program, National Institute of Arthritis and Musculoskeletal and Skin Diseases, Bldg. 45, Room 5AS-13F, Bethesda, MD 20892.

**• 4187 • NIAMS National Research Service Award (NRSA) Fellowships** *(Postdoctorate/Grant)*

**Purpose:** To provide postdoctoral research training to individuals to extend their potential for a career in research. **Qualif.:** Applicants must hold a doctoral degree (Ph.D., M.D., or equivalent). Research is to be in one or more of the following areas: arthritis, musculoskeletal diseases, and skin diseases.

**Funds Avail.:** Stipends range from $17,000 to $31,500 per year. Institutional allowance is $3,000 per year ($2,000 per year in Federal laboratories). Duration of the award is up to three years. **Deadline:** January 10, May 10, and September 10. **Contact:** Dr. Steven J. Hausman, Director, Extramural Program, National Institute of Arthritis and Musculoskeletal and Skin Diseases, Bldg. 45, Room 5AS-13F, Bethesda, MD 20892.

**• 4188 • NIAMS National Research Service Award (NRSA) Senior Fellowships** *(Postdoctorate/Grant)*

**Purpose:** To provide opportunities for experienced scientists to make major changes in the direction of research careers, to broaden scientific background, and to acquire new research capabilities. **Qualif.:** Applicants must have at least seven years of postdoctoral experience.

**Funds Avail.:** Stipend is $30,000. There are no fringe benefits. Institutional allowance is $3,000 per year ($2,000 per year in Federal laboratories). Duration of the award is up to two years.

## *National Institute of Arthritis and Musculoskeletal and Skin Diseases (continued)*

**Deadline:** January 10; May 10; and September 10. **Contact:** Dr. Steven J. Hausman, Director, Extramural Program, National Institute of Arthritis and Musculoskeletal and Skin Diseases, Bldg. 45, Room 5AS-13F, Bethesda, MD 20892.

### • 4189 • NIAMS Regular Research Grants *(Postdoctorate/Grant)*

**Purpose:** To support a specific, circumscribed project to be performed by an investigator or investigators in an area representing their specific interest and competencies. **Contact:** Dr. Steven J. Hausman, Director, Extramural Program, National Institute of Arthritis and Musculoskeletal and Skin Diseases, Bldg. 45, Room 5AS-13F, Bethesda, MD 20892.

### • 4190 • NIAMS Research Career Development Awards *(Postdoctorate/Grant)*

**Purpose:** To foster the development of young scientists with outstanding research potential for careers of independent research. **Qualif.:** Applicants must have at least three years of postdoctoral (M.D. or Ph.D.) research experience. The program is designed for candidates in the formative stages of their careers who have demonstrated outstanding potential for independent investigation but who need additional experience. Research may be in one or more of the following areas: arthritis, musculoskeletal diseases, and skin diseases.

**Funds Avail.:** Awards include a salary of up to $50,000, plus fringe benefits. The duration of the award is five years (nonrenewable). **Deadline:** February 1; June 1; and October 1. **Contact:** Dr. Steven J. Hausman, Director, Extramural Program, National Institute of Arthritis and Musculoskeletal and Skin Diseases, Bldg. 45, Room 5AS-13F, Bethesda, MD 20892.

### • 4191 •
## National Institute on Drug Abuse
6001 Executive Blvd.
Rm. 3131, MSC 9541　　　　　　　　　*Ph:* (301)443-6710
Bethesda, MD 20892-9541　　　　　　　*Fax:* (301)443-6849
*E-mail:* apl@cu.nih.gov
*URL:* http://www.aamc.org/research.adhocgp/nida.htm

### • 4192 • NIDA Individual National Research Service Awards *(Doctorate, Postdoctorate/Fellowship)*

**Purpose:** To support research training at the pre- and postdoctoral levels in biomedical, neuroscientific, clinical, psychological, epidemiological, and behavioral disciplines. Research projects range from fundamental study of the basic neurobiology of illicit drugs to the development and evaluation of new treatment and prevention strategies. Support is provided for training utilizing a variety of methodologies and approaches for developing and enhancing the skills of investigators to conduct such studies. **Focus:** Biomedical Research, Substance Abuse. **Qualif.:** Applicants must be U.S. citizens, noncitizen nationals, or lawfully admitted to the U.S. for permanent residence at the time of application. They must be willing to engage in biomedical or behavioral health-related research and/or health-related teaching within two years after termination of the Award. Such service shall be on a continuous basis and average more than 20 hours per week for a period equal to the total NRSA support in excess of 12 months. **Criteria:** Applicant qualifications and potential for both a successful career as an independent researcher and for a successful fellowship experience are assessed by consideration of applicant's academic records, honors received, research and/or clinical experience, publications, references, and training and

career goals. Research proposals are evaluated for scientific merit and training potential. Scientific merit is judged by the significance and originality of the proposed research goals, the adequacy of the proposed methods, and the adequacy of plans for protection against adverse effects on humans, animals, or the environment. Training potential is assessed according to the opportunities for the candidate to learn new theoretical approaches, techniques and methods, and/or experimental models.

**Funds Avail.:** Awards include stipends for awardees and a small allowance to the sponsoring institution to defray some of the awardee's training expenses. Individuals sponsored by foreign institutions also receive travel funds. Annual stipends at the predoctoral level have been $8,000; postdoctoral level stipends range from $18,600 to $32,300 depending on the number of years of experience (from 0 to 7 or more). **To Apply:** Formal applications are comprised of two parts (part 1 to be completed by the applicant; part 2 by the sponsor and sponsoring institution officials). Both parts must be submitted together. Applicants must use Form PHS 416-1 (revised 10/91); no other forms will be accepted. **Deadline:** April 5, August 4, and December 5 for projects to begin no earlier than January, May, and August of the following year, respectively. **Contact:** Office of Grants Inquiries, Division of Research Grants, National Institutes of Health, Bethesda, MD 20892.

### • 4193 •
## National Institute of Justice
U.S. Dept. of Justice
633 Indiana Ave., NW
Washington, DC 20531　　　　　　　　*Free:* 800-851-3420
*URL:* http://www.usdoj.gov/

### • 4194 • National Institute of Justice Graduate Research Fellowships *(Doctorate/Fellowship)*

**Purpose:** To support criminal justice related dissertations. **Focus:** Criminal Justice, Political Science, Economics, Sociology. **Qualif.:** All requirements for doctoral level except dissertation must have been met.

**Funds Avail.:** Approximately 15 fellowships are awarded. The maximum stipend is $35,000. **Deadline:** March 15, June 15, September 15, and December 15. **Contact:** NIJ at the above address (see entry 4193).

### • 4195 •
## National Institute for Labor Relations Research
5211 Port Royal Rd.
Springfield, VA 22151　　　　　　　　*Ph:* (703)321-9820
*E-mail:* nilrr@erols.com

### • 4196 • William B. Ruggles Journalism Scholarship *(Graduate, Undergraduate/Scholarship)*

**Purpose:** To foster an understanding of volunteerism and of the problems of compulsory unionism. **Focus:** Journalism, Communications. **Qualif.:** Applicants may be of any nationality, but must be graduate or undergraduate students majoring in journalism or mass communications at a U.S. institution. Members of the National Right to Work Committee and the National Institute for Labor Relations Research board of directors, staff, or their families are ineligible.

**Funds Avail.:** $2,000. **To Apply:** Write for application form and guidelines. Submit completed form with current transcripts, student financial aid form, projection of education expenses, and an essay demonstrating an interest in and knowledge of the Right to Work principle. **Deadline:** Between January 1 and March 31. **Contact:** Mary Katherine Grover, Public Research Assistant, at the above address (see entry 4195).

## • 4197 •
## National Institute of Mental Health

Henry Khachaturian, Ph.D.
6001 Executive Blvd., Rm. 8208     *Ph:* (301)443-4335
Bethesda, MD 20892     *Fax:* (301)443-3225
*E-mail:* hk11b@nih.gov
*URL:* http://www.nimh.nih.gov/grants/rtcd.htm

*The National Institute of Mental Health (NIMH), part of the Alcohol, Drug Abuse, and Mental Health Administration (ADAMHA) of the U.S. Department of Health and Human Services, endeavors to increase knowledge and improve research methods on mental and behavioral disorders, to generate information regarding basic biological and behavioral processes underlying these disorders and the maintenance of mental health, and to improve mental health services. Its Division of Basic Sciences (DBS) provides support for research training in the neurosciences, behavioral sciences, and in health and behavior through its Neurosciences Research Branch, Behavioral Sciences Research Branch, and Health and Behavior Research Branch. All three of these branches support fellowships and institutional research training grants.*

## • 4198 • NIMH Individual Postdoctoral National Research Service Awards *(Postdoctorate/Fellowship)*

**Purpose:** The National Institute of Mental Health (NIMH) supports Research and Research Training Programs to increase knowledge and improve research methods on mental and behavioral disorders; to generate information regarding basic biological and behavioral processes underlying these disorders and the maintenance of mental health; and to develop and improve mental health treatment and services. Research and research training supported by the Institute may employ theoretical, laboratory, clinical, methodological, and field studies, any of which may involve clinical, subclinical, and normal subjects and populations of all age ranges, as well as animal models appropriate to the system or disorder being investigated and to the state of the field. See website for more information. **Qualif.:** Applicants must be U.S. citizens, noncitizen nationals, or lawfully admitted to the U.S. for permanent residence at the time of application. They must have received a Ph.D., Psy.D., M.D., D.D.S., Sc.D., D.N.S., D.O., D.S.W., or equivalent degree from an accredited domestic or foreign institution as of the proposed activation date of the fellowship. Prior to formal submission of application, applicants must arrange for an appointment to an appropriate institution and acceptance by a sponsor who will supervise the research training experience. The institutional setting may be a domestic or foreign, nonprofit, private, or public instiution, including a Federal laboratory. Recipients must be willing to engage in biomedical or behavioral health-related research and/or health-related teaching for a period equal to the period of NRSA support in excess of 12 months. An individuals' intital 12 months of post-baccalaureate NRSA support is excluded from payback obligation. All subsequent NRSA support is fully obligated. **Criteria:** Selection is based on the quality of applicants' academic records, awards, and honors; the extent and quality of their previous research; demonstrated potential for a productive research career; evidence of commitment to a career in research; references; quality of the research proposal; and adequacy of the applicant's sponsor.

**Funds Avail.:** Awards include stipends for awardees and a small allowance to the sponsoring institution to defray some of the awardee's training expenses. Individuals sponsored by foreign institutions also receive travel funds. Annual stipends range from $26,256 to $41,268 depending on the number of years of experience (from 0 to 7 or more). **To Apply:** Formal applications comprised of two parts (part 1 to be completed by the applicant;

part 2 by the sponsor and sponsoring institution officials). Both parts must be submitted together. Applicants must use Form PHS 416-1; no other forms will be accepted. **Deadline:** April 5, August 5, and December 5 for projects to begin no earlier than September, January, and May respectively.

## • 4199 • NIMH Individual Predoctoral National Research Service Awards *(Doctorate/Fellowship)*

**Purpose:** The National Institute of Mental Health (NIMH) supports Research and Research Training Programs to increase knowledge and improve research methods on mental and behavioral disorders; to generate information regarding basic biological and behavioral processes underlying these disorders and the maintenance of mental health; and to develop and improve mental helath treatment and services. Research and research training supported by the Institute may employ theoretical, laboratory, clinical, methodological, and field studies, any of which may involve clinical, subclinical, and normal subjects and populations of all age ranges, as well as animal models appropriate to the system or disorder being investigated and to the state of the field. See website for more information. **Qualif.:** Applicants must be U.S. citizens, noncitizen nationals, or lawfully admitted to the U.S. for permanent residence at the time of application. They must have completed 2 or more years of graduate work and be enrolled in a doctoral degree program by the proposed activation date of the fellowship. Prior to formal submission of application, applicants must arrange for an appointment to an appropriate institution and acceptance by a sponsor who will supervise the research training experience. The institutional setting may be a domestic or foreign, nonprofit, private, or public instiution, including a Federal laboratory. Recipients must be willing to engage in biomedical or behavioral health-related research and/or health-related teaching for a period equal to the period of NRSA support in excess of 12 months. An individual' initial 12 months of post-baccalaureate NRSA support is excluded from payback obligation. All subsequent NRSA support is fully obligated. **Criteria:** Selection is based on the quality of applicants' academic records, awards, and honors; the extent and quality of their previous research; demonstrated potential for a productive research career; evidence of commitment to a career in research; references; quality of the research proposal; and adequacy of the applicant's sponsor.

**Funds Avail.:** Awards include stipends for awardees and a small allowance to the sponsoring institution to defray some of the awardee's training expenses. Individuals sponsored by foreign institutions also receive travel funds. Annual stipends are $14,688. **To Apply:** Formal applications are comprised of two parts (part 1 to be completed by the applicant; part 2 by the sponsor and sponsoring institution officials). Both parts must be submitted together. Applicants must use Form PHS 416-1; no other forms will be accepted. **Deadline:** April 5, August 5, and December 5 for projects to begin no earlier than September, January, and May respectively.

## • 4200 •
## National Institute of Nursing Research

Division of Extramural Activities
45/3AN12
45 Center Dr. - MSC 6300     *Ph:* (301)594-6906
Bethesda, MD 20892-6300     *Fax:* (301)480-8260
*E-mail:* info@opae.ninr.nih.gov; pgrady@opae.ninr.nih.gov
*URL:* http://www.nih.gov/ninr

*Formerly known as National Center for Nursing Research. The National Institute of Nursing Research (NINR), part of the National Institutes of Health (NIH), is the Federal agency responsible for funding nursing research and research training and for promoting excellence in nursing science. Research is aimed at providing a better understanding of the physiological and behavioral processes that relate to maintaining or recovering health, or coping with illness.*

## National Institute of Nursing Research (continued)

### • 4201 • NINR Individual National Research Service Awards Postdoctoral Fellowship *(Postdoctorate/ Fellowship)*

**Purpose:** To support postdoctoral training in areas related to the NINR mission. **Qualif.:** Applicants must possess a Ph.D. or equivalent degree. Applicants must have a sponsor and must identify a research project for full-time study.

**Funds Avail.:** Awards include a stipend and a modest allowance for necessary research costs. **To Apply:** Application form PHS 416-1 (Rev. 10/91) must be completed. **Deadline:** December 5, April 5, and August 5. **Contact:** Division of Extramural Programs, NINR, NIH, Bldg. 45, Rm. 3AN-12, 45 Center Dr., MSC 6300, Bethesda, MD 20892. Phone: (301)594-6906.

### • 4202 • NINR Individual National Research Service Awards Predoctoral Fellowship *(Doctorate/Fellowship)*

**Purpose:** This award is available to registered nurses for supervised research training by a sponsor, leading to a doctoral degree in areas related to the NINR mission. Applicants must have either a baccalaureate and/or a master's degree and must have been admitted to a full-time doctoral study program.

**Funds Avail.:** The award provides a stipend and an institutional allowance to partially defray training and research costs. **To Apply:** Application form PHS 416-1 (Rev. 10/91) must be completed. **Deadline:** December 5, April 5, and August 5. **Contact:** Division of Extramural Programs, NINR, NIH, Bldg. 45, Rm. 3AN-12, 45 Center Dr., Msc 6300, Bethesda, MD 20892. Telephone number: (301)594-6906.

### • 4203 • NINR Individual National Research Service Awards Senior Fellowship *(Postdoctorate/Fellowship)*

**Purpose:** To enable awardees to take time from regular professional activities to make major changes in the direction of their research careers, to broaden their scientific backgrounds, to acquire new research capabilities, and to expand their command of an allied research field. **Qualif.:** Applicants must be nurse investigators generally with at least seven years of relevant research experience beyond the doctoral degree.

**Funds Avail.:** Awards include a stipend and an institutional allowance for research costs. **To Apply:** Application form PHS 416-1 (Rev. 10/91) must be completed. **Deadline:** December 5, April 5, and August 5. **Contact:** Division of Extramural Programs, NINR, NIH, Bldg. 45, Rm. 3AN-12, 45 Center Dr., MSC 6300, Bethesda, MD 20892. Telephone number: (301)594-6906.

## • 4204 •
## National Intercollegiate Flying Association

General Aviation Manufacturers
 Association
1400 K St. NW, Ste. 801             Ph: (202)393-1500
Washington, DC 20005                Fax: (202)842-4063
*E-mail:* eadavis@generalaviation.org
*URL:* http://www.generalaviation.org

### • 4205 • Harold S. Wood Award for Excellence *(Graduate, Undergraduate/Scholarship)*

**Focus:** Flying. **Qualif.:** Applicants must have a GPA of at least 3.0, attend a National Intercollegiate Flying Association school, and must have experience in aviation and non-aviation related activities.

**Funds Avail.:** $1,000. **No. of Awards:** One. **Deadline:** February 18. **Contact:** Elizabeth Davis.

## • 4206 •
## National Italian American Foundation

c/o Dr. Maria Lombardo
Education Director
1860 19th St. NW
Washington, DC 20009                *Ph:* (202)530-5315

### • 4207 • Thomas Joseph "Willie" Ambrosole Scholarship *(Undergraduate/Scholarship)*

**Qualif.:** Available to any undergraduate student majoring in the Arts or Humanities from the New York/New Jersey area.

**Funds Avail.:** $1,000 **Deadline:** May 31.

**Remarks:** Made possible by John V. Cioffi of the John V. Cioffi Foundation.

### • 4208 • Dr. William L. Amoroso, Jr. Scholarship *(Undergraduate/Scholarship)*

**Qualif.:** Available to Italian-American students accepted to the American University of Rome.

**Funds Avail.:** $1,000. **Deadline:** May 31.

**Remarks:** In memory of his parents Rosa and William Amoroso. **Contact:** Interested candidates are to call Maria Enrico at (301) 977-2250.

### • 4209 • Angela Scholarship *(Undergraduate/ Scholarship)*

**Qualif.:** Available to an entering freshman with an exemplary academic record and demonstrating social responsibilities during high school years.

**Funds Avail.:** $2,500. **Deadline:** May 31.

**Remarks:** Student must intern at the NIAF for one semester.

### • 4210 • Marija Bileta Scholarship *(Undergraduate/ Scholarship)*

**Qualif.:** For any undergraduate student.

**Funds Avail.:** $1,000. **Deadline:** May 31.

**Remarks:** made possible by Grace E. Bileta.

### • 4211 • Bolla Wines Scholarship *(Undergraduate/ Scholarship)*

**Focus:** General studies. **Qualif.:** Applicants must be Italian Americans who are at least 21 years of age, who have grade point averages of 3.0 or higher, and degrees in International Studies with emphasis on Italian business or Italian-American history. Students must write an essay: "The Importance of Italy in Today's Business World."

**Funds Avail.:** $1000. **To Apply:** Write for further details. **Contact:** National Italian American Foundation at the above address (see entry 4206).

### • 4212 • Alyce M. Cafaro Scholarship *(Undergraduate/Scholarship)*

**Qualif.:** Available to an undergraduate student from Ohio.

**Funds Avail.:** $5,000. **Deadline:** May 31.

### • 4213 • Anthony J. Celebrezze Scholarship *(Graduate, Undergraduate/Scholarship)*

**Focus:** General studies. **Qualif.:** Applicants must be graduate and undergraduate Italian-American students who are residents of Central Ohio.

Funds Avail.: $1000. To Apply: Write for further details. Contact: National Italian American Foundation at the above address (see entry 4206).

### • 4214 • Ferdinand Cinelli Etruscan Scholarship
*(Graduate, Undergraduate/Scholarship)*

Focus: General studies. Qualif.: Applicants must be graduate and undergraduates students who are Italian-American. Criteria: Preference given to residents or students of Michigan and Michigan schools.

Funds Avail.: $1000. To Apply: Write for further details. Contact: National Italian American Foundation at the above address (see entry 4206).

### • 4215 • Communications Scholarship
*(Undergraduate/Scholarship)*

Qualif.: Journalism and Communication majors are eligible.

Funds Avail.: $5,000 To Apply: Applicants must submit an example of their best work. Deadline: May 31.

### • 4216 • Silvio Conte Internship *(Undergraduate/ Scholarship)*

Focus: General studies. Qualif.: Applicants must be Italian-American undergraduate or graduate students interested in working for one semester on Capitol Hill.

Funds Avail.: $1000. To Apply: Applicants must provide a letter of acceptance from a congressional office and prepare a two to three page typed paper on the importance of this experience to their career. Write for further details. Deadline: May 31. Contact: National Italian American Foundation at the above address (see entry 4206).

### • 4217 • Cornaro Scholarship *(Undergraduate/ Scholarship)*

Focus: General studies. Qualif.: Applicants must be Italian-American women currently enrolled or entering college.

Funds Avail.: $1000. To Apply: Write for further details. Contact: National Italian American Foundation at the above address (see entry 4206).

### • 4218 • NIAF/NOIAW Cornaro Scholarship
*(Graduate, Undergraduate/Scholarship)*

Qualif.: Available to Italian-American graduate and undergraduate women.

Funds Avail.: Three $1,000 scholarships are available. To Apply: Student must prepare a three-page paper on either a current issue of concern for Italian-American women or a famous Italian-American woman. Deadline: May 31.

Remarks: Made possible in part by the National Organization of Italian American Women.

### • 4219 • Alexander Defilippis Scholarship
*(Undergraduate/Scholarship)*

Qualif.: Available to Engineering students. Criteria: First priority given to those attending Virginia Polytechnic Institute.

Funds Avail.: $1,000. Deadline: May 31.

### • 4220 • Johnson & Wales Governor Christopher Del Sesto/NIAF Scholarship *(Undergraduate/ Scholarship)*

Qualif.: Available to freshmen of Johnson and Wales University.

Funds Avail.: $2,000 Deadline: May 31.

Remarks: In memory of Governor Christopher Del Sesto of Rhode Island, presented by his family and sponsored by Johnson & Wales University. Contact Richard Tarantino, (401) 598-1072.

### • 4221 • Frank DePietro Memorial Scholarship
*(Undergraduate/Scholarship)*

Qualif.: Available to current or entering freshmen at Harvey Mudd College of California. Criteria: Priority is given to Italian-American students.

Funds Avail.: Varies. Deadline: May 31.

Remarks: Made possible by Frances, Robert, and Dennis DePietro. Contact Barbara Bergman, (909) 621-8384.

### • 4222 • Robert J. Di Pietro Scholarship
*(Undergraduate/Scholarship)*

Focus: General studies. Qualif.: Applicants must be Italian Americans no older than 25 years of age.

Funds Avail.: $1000. To Apply: Applicants must write a 400 to 600 word essay on how they intend to use ethnicity throughout their chosen field of education to preserve and support ethnicity throughout life. Submit four copies. Write for further details.

Remarks: Made possible by Mrs. Robert J. DiPietro and the NIAF in honor of Robert, Americo, and Mary DiPietro.

### • 4223 • Rabbi Robert Feinberg Scholarship
*(Graduate, Undergraduate/Scholarship)*

Qualif.: Available to any graduate or undergraduate student interested in World War II studies.

Funds Avail.: $1,000. To Apply: Student must prepare a five page paper on the Italian assistance to Jews in Italy and its occupied territories. Deadline: May 31.

Remarks: Made possible by Jews who admire Rabbi Feinberg's work in this area of study.

### • 4224 • Cesare Fera Memorial Scholarship
*(Undergraduate/Scholarship)*

Qualif.: Available to Italian-American Architecture students attending Clemson University.

Funds Avail.: $2000. Deadline: May 31.

### • 4225 • Sergio Franchi Music Scholarship in Voice Performance *(Graduate, Undergraduate/Scholarship)*

Focus: Music. Qualif.: Applicants must be graduate or undergraduate students of voice (tenors).

Funds Avail.: $1000. To Apply: Applicants must submit a cassette tape of their work. Write for further details. Deadline: May 31.

Remarks: Made possible by Mrs. Sergio Franchi and the Sergio Franchi Music Foundation.

### • 4226 • Carmela Gagliardi Fellowship *(Graduate/ Fellowship)*

Focus: General studies. Qualif.: Applicants must be Italian American students accepted to or presently attending medical schools. Students must rank in the upper 25% of their class and demonstrate financial need.

Funds Avail.: $5000. To Apply: Write for further details. Deadline: May 31. Contact: National Italian American Foundation at the above address (see entry 4206).

---

Awards are arranged alphabetically below their administering organizations

*National Italian American Foundation (continued)*

### • 4227 •   General Undergraduate Scholarships
*(Undergraduate/Scholarship)*

**Qualif.:** Open to Italian-American students of all majors currently enrolled or entering college who are permanent residents of the United States.

**Funds Avail.:** One scholarship of $5,000 and $2,000 each are awarded for of the following 12 regions: New England, Upper Mid-Atlantic, Lower Mid-Atlantic, Capital Area, Southeast, North Central, Mid-America, South Central, North Central, Mid Pacific, Southwest, and Italian (for students accepted at Italian Universities). **To Apply:** Students must write a two to three page typed essay on a family member or a personality considered "An Italian American Hero." **Deadline:** May 31.

### • 4228 •   A.P. Giannini Scholarship *(Graduate, Undergraduate/Scholarship)*

**Focus:** Banking, international finance. **Qualif.:** Applicants must be Italian-American students majoring in banking or international finance.

**Funds Avail.:** $1000. **To Apply:** Write for further details. **Deadline:** May 31. **Contact:** National Italian American Foundation at the above address (see entry 4206).

### • 4229 •   Giargiari Fellowship *(Graduate/Fellowship)*

**Focus:** Medicine. **Qualif.:** Applicants must be second, third, and fourth year Italian-American students enrolled in an approved U.S. Medical school.

**Funds Avail.:** $5000. **To Apply:** Applicants must submit a five page, typed essay on "Italian Americans in the Medical Field." Write for further details. **Deadline:** May 31. **Contact:** National Italian American Foundation at the above address (see entry 4206).

### • 4230 •   George L. Graziadio Fellowship for Business *(Undergraduate/Scholarship)*

**Qualif.:** Available to Italian-American Students attending the George L. Graziadio School of Business and Management at Pepperdine University.

**Funds Avail.:** Two scholarships available: $5,000 and $2,500. **Deadline:** May 31.

### • 4231 •   Rose Basile Green Scholarship *(Undergraduate/Scholarship)*

**Focus:** General studies. **Qualif.:** Applicants must be Italian-American undergraduates majoring or minoring in Italian American Studies.

**Funds Avail.:** $1,000. **Deadline:** Applications must be postmarked by May 31.

### • 4232 •   GRI/ICIF Culinary Scholarships *(Professional Development/Scholarship)*

**Qualif.:** Available to culinary school graduates meeting the criteria established by the Italian Culinary Institute for Foreigners and the Gruppo Ristoratori Italiani.

**Funds Avail.:** Five $6,000 scholarships are available. **To Apply:** Please call Enrico Bazzoni (718) 875-0547 before applying. **Deadline:** May 31.

### • 4233 •   Guido-Zerilli-Marimo Scholarships *(Graduate, Undergraduate/Scholarship)*

**Qualif.:** Available to undergraduate and graduate students of New York University.

**Funds Avail.:** Three scholarships of $US1,000 each. **Deadline:** May 31.

### • 4234 •   Italian Cultural Society and NIAF Matching Scholarship *(Undergraduate/Scholarship)*

**Qualif.:** Available to undergraduate students majoring in science or the humanities in the Washington D.C, Maryland, and Virginia areas.

**Funds Avail.:** $2,000. **Deadline:** May 31.

### • 4235 •   Law Fellowship *(Graduate, Postgraduate/Fellowship)*

**Focus:** Law. **Qualif.:** Applicants must be Italian American law students.

**Funds Avail.:** $1000. **To Apply:** Applicants must submit a 750-word essay describing the maintenance of Italian culture in the U.S. in the law field or at the political level. Write for further details. **Contact:** National Italian American Foundation at the above address (see entry 4206).

### • 4236 •   Ralph Lombardi Memorial Scholarship *(Doctorate/Scholarship)*

**Qualif.:** Available to medical students of the D.C. area.

**Funds Avail.:** $1,000. **Deadline:** May 31.

### • 4237 •   Antonio M. Marinelli Founders' Scholarship *(Undergraduate/Scholarship)*

**Qualif.:** Available to the undergraduate children of members of the National Utility Contractors Association studying in the D.C. area.

**Funds Avail.:** $2,500. **Deadline:** May 31. **RMK** To be selected by the National Utility Contractors Association Scholarship Awards Committee.

### • 4238 •   Marinelli Scholarships *(Undergraduate/Scholarship)*

**Focus:** General studies. **Qualif.:** Applicants must be Italian American students who have been accepted at the American University in Rome (Antonio and Felicia Marinelli Scholarship) or are attending either Barry or Nova University in Florida (O. Mike Marinelli Scholarship).

**Funds Avail.:** $1000 to $2000. **No. of Awards:** 2 **To Apply:** Write for further details. **Deadline:** May 31.

### • 4239 •   Martino Scholars Program *(Graduate/Fellowship)*

**Focus:** Mathematics, technology. **Qualif.:** Applicants must be Italian-American Master's or Doctoral students majoring in information science, multimedia technology, and mathematics. **Criteria:** Awards granted based on academic achievement and leadership.

**Funds Avail.:** $1000. **No. of Awards:** 5. **To Apply:** Write for further details. **Contact:** National Italian American Foundation at the above address (see entry 4206).

### • 4240 •   Assunta Lucchetti Martino Scholarship for International Studies *(Undergraduate/Scholarship)*

**Qualif.:** Available to undergraduate International Studies majors.

**Funds Avail.:** $1,000. **Deadline:** May 31.

• 4241 • **Merrill Lynch Scholarship** *(Undergraduate/ Scholarship)*

**Qualif.:** Available to undergraduate Business majors of the NY state area.

**Funds Avail.:** $1,000. **Deadline:** May 31.

• 4242 • **Vincent Minnelli Scholarship** *(Undergraduate/Scholarship)*

**Qualif.:** Available to Drama majors of California.

**Funds Avail.:** $1,000. **Deadline:** May 31.

**Remarks:** Made possible by the Minnelli family.

• 4243 • **Mola Foundation of Chicago Scholarships** *(Undergraduate/Scholarship)*

**Qualif.:** Available to undergraduate students from Illinois, Indiana, Michigan, Wisconsin, Ohio, Iowa, Minnesota, Kentucky, South Dakota, and North Dakota who are majoring in Italian.

**Funds Avail.:** Nine scholarships of $1,000 are available. **Deadline:** May 31.

• 4244 • **Nerone/NIAF Matching Art Scholarship** *(Undergraduate/Scholarship)*

**Qualif.:** Available to Art majors.

**Funds Avail.:** $1,000. **Deadline:** May 31.

• 4245 • **NIAF/FIERI D.C. Matching Scholarship** *(Graduate/Scholarship)*

**Qualif.:** Available to a graduate law student.

**Funds Avail.:** $1,000. **Deadline:** May 31.

• 4246 • **NIAF/FIERI National Matching Scholarship** *(Undergraduate/Scholarship)*

**Focus:** General studies. **Qualif.:** Applicants must be Italian-Americans who are undergraduate students of FIERI.

**Funds Avail.:** $1000. **To Apply:** Write for further details. **Contact:** National Italian American Foundation at the above address (see entry 4206).

• 4247 • **NIAF/Pepperdine University Scholarship** *(Undergraduate/Scholarship)*

**Qualif.:** Available to sophomore and upperclass students at Pepperdine who are accepted into the school's International Program.

**Funds Avail.:** $2,000. **To Apply:** For information, contact William B. Phillips, (310) 456-4532.

**Remarks:** In honor of Edward DiLoreto.

• 4248 • **NIAF/Sacred Heart University Matching Scholarship** *(Undergraduate/Scholarship)*

**Focus:** General studies. **Qualif.:** Applicants must be Italian American undergraduate students at Sacred Heart University in Fairfield, CT.

**Funds Avail.:** $2,000. **To Apply:** Applicants must be screened and must meet the admissions and financial need requirements. Write for further details. **Deadline:** May 31. **Contact:** National Italian American Foundation at the above address (see entry 4206).

• 4249 • **Vennera Noto Scholarship** *(Undergraduate/ Scholarship)*

**Qualif.:** Available to any Business major undergraduate student.

**Funds Avail.:** $2,000. **Deadline:** May 31.

**Remarks:** Made possible by Karen L. Ribaro.

• 4250 • **Paragano Scholarship** *(Undergraduate/ Scholarship)*

**Qualif.:** Available to undergraduate Italian majors who are residents of New Jersey.

**Funds Avail.:** Two $4,000 scholarships are available. **Deadline:** May 31.

• 4251 • **John and Anne Parente Matching Scholarship** *(Undergraduate/Scholarship)*

**Focus:** General studies. **Qualif.:** Applicants must be Italian-American undergraduate students attending King's College in Wilkes-Barre, Pennsylvania.

**Funds Avail.:** $2,000. **To Apply:** Write for further details. **Contact:** National Italian American Foundation at the above address (see entry 4206).

• 4252 • **Pavarotti Scholarship** *(Graduate, Undergraduate/Scholarship)*

**Focus:** Music. **Qualif.:** Applicants must be undergraduate or graduate students of music from southern California.

**Funds Avail.:** $1000. **To Apply:** Must send a cassette tape of voice in performance. Write for further details. **Deadline:** May 31. **Contact:** National Italian American Foundation at the above address (see entry 4206).

• 4253 • **Norman R. Peterson Scholarship (John Cabot University)** *(Undergraduate/Scholarship)*

**Purpose:** To provide an opportunity to study at John Cabot University in Rome. **Qualif.:** Available to a Midwestern U.S. citizen who is a business, economics, or finance undergraduate student.

**Funds Avail.:** Scholarships of $5,000 and $2,500 are available. **Contact:** Francesca Gleason, Director of Admissions, 011-39-6-687-8881.

• 4254 • **Piancone Family Agriculture Scholarship** *(Graduate, Undergraduate/Scholarship)*

**Focus:** Agriculture. **Qualif.:** Applicants must be Italian-American graduate or undergraduate students from New Jersey, New York, Pennsylvania, Delaware, Virginia, Maryland, Washington D.C., or Massachusetts majoring in agriculture.

**Funds Avail.:** $2000. **To Apply:** Write for further details. **Contact:** National Italian American Foundation at the above address (see entry 4206).

• 4255 • **Alex and Henry Recine Scholarships** *(Undergraduate/Scholarship)*

**Qualif.:** Available to any undergraduate student of New York state.

**Funds Avail.:** $2,500. **Deadline:** May 31.

• 4256 • **St. Anslem's College Scholarship** *(Undergraduate/Scholarship)*

**Qualif.:** Available to any undergraduate student living outside of New England and entering St. Anslem's College, Mew Hampshire.

**Funds Avail.:** $5,000. **Deadline:** May 31.

## National Italian American Foundation (continued)

### • 4257 • Louis J. Salerno, M.D. Memorial Scholarship (Graduate, Undergraduate/Scholarship)

**Qualif.:** Available to Art History students with a minimum GPA of 3.5 to study at the American University in Rome.

**Funds Avail.:** $2,000. **To Apply:** For application information contact Maria Enrico, (202) 331-8327. **Deadline:** May 31.

### • 4258 • Peter Sammartino Scholarship (Graduate/Scholarship)

**Qualif.:** Available to teachers of Italian pursuing their Master's degree.

**Funds Avail.:** $2,000. **Deadline:** May 31.

### • 4259 • Nina Santavicca Scholarship (Undergraduate/Scholarship)

**Qualif.:** Available to a Music major. **Criteria:** Pianists are preferred.

**Funds Avail.:** $1,000. **Deadline:** May 31.

**Remarks:** Made possible by Mr. and Mrs. Quinto Vitale.

### • 4260 • Scalia Scholarship (Graduate/Scholarship)

**Qualif.:** Available to any graduate law student who is a resident of New York state.

**Funds Avail.:** $1,000. **To Apply:** Applicant must prepare a 750 word essay on Italian Americans in the law. **Deadline:** May 31.

### • 4261 • Daniel Stella Scholarship (Undergraduate/Scholarship)

**Focus:** General studies. **Qualif.:** Applicants must be Italian-American undergraduate students afflicted with Cooley's Anemia.

**Funds Avail.:** $1000. **To Apply:** Write for further details. **Contact:** National Italian American Foundation at the above address (see entry 4206).

### • 4262 • E.D. Stella Scholarship (Undergraduate/Scholarship)

**Focus:** Business. **Qualif.:** Applicants must be Italian-American undergraduate and graduate business majors.

**Funds Avail.:** $1000. **To Apply:** Write for further details.

**Remarks:** In conjunction with the Detroit Chamber of Commerce.

### • 4263 • Study Abroad Scholarships (Graduate, Undergraduate/Scholarship)

**Qualif.:** Available to any undergraduate or graduate student wishing to study in Italy (must show letter of acceptance from an accredited school).

**Funds Avail.:** Five $2,000 scholarships are awarded.

**Remarks:** Programs are available at the American University of Rome (contact Rita Leahy, 202-331-8327) and John Cabot University (contact Francesca Gleason, 11-39-6-687-8881).

### • 4264 • Joe Tangaro Memorial Athletic Scholarship (Undergraduate/Scholarship)

**Qualif.:** Available to any Italian-American high school senior who excels in athletics and resides in St. Louis.

**Funds Avail.:** $2,500. **To Apply:** A letter of recommendation from a school official is required along with a personal letter of request from the student. **Deadline:** May 31.

**Remarks:** Made possible by the St. Louis Italian Open Golf Tournament.

### • 4265 • William Toto Scholarship (Undergraduate/Scholarship)

**Focus:** Engineering, business management. **Qualif.:** Applicants must have successfully completed sophomore year in engineering and/or business management.

**Funds Avail.:** $1000. **To Apply:** Write for further details. **Contact:** National Italian American Foundation at the above address (see entry 4206).

### • 4266 • Agnes E. Vaghi-Cornaro Scholarship (Undergraduate/Scholarship)

**Focus:** General studies. **Qualif.:** Applicants must be Italian-American undergraduate women.

**Funds Avail.:** $2000. **To Apply:** Applicants must type a three-page paper on a famous Italian American woman. Write for further details. **Deadline:** May 31.

**Remarks:** Made possible by Msgr. Peter J., Dr. Vincent J., Nino R., and Joseph P. Vaghi III.

### • 4267 • Gianni Versace Scholarship in Fashion Design (Undergraduate/Scholarship)

**Qualif.:** Available to undergraduate students majoring in fashion design.

**Funds Avail.:** $1,000. **Deadline:** May 31.

### • 4268 • Vincent and Anna Visceglia Fellowship (Doctorate, Graduate/Fellowship)

**Qualif.:** Available to Italian Americans working on a master's or doctorate in Italian Studies.

**Funds Avail.:** $1,000. **Deadline:** May 31.

### • 4269 • John A. Volpe Scholarship (Undergraduate/Scholarship)

**Qualif.:** Available to undergraduate students in New England.

**Funds Avail.:** $1,000. **Deadline:** May 31.

**Remarks:** In honor of Ambassador John A. Volpe.

### • 4270 • West Virginia Italian Heritage Festival Scholarships (Undergraduate/Scholarship)

**Qualif.:** Available to any West Virginia student of Italian descent entering or enrolled in college.

**Funds Avail.:** $3,500. **Deadline:** May 31.

### • 4271 • Westchester Community Scholarship (Graduate, Undergraduate/Scholarship)

**Qualif.:** Available to undergraduate and graduate students of the Westchester, New York area.

**Funds Avail.:** Two scholarships are available at $2,000 each. **Deadline:** May 31.

**Remarks:** Made possible by Vincent Zuccarelli and the NIAF Westchester Committee.

### • 4272 • Zecchino Post-Graduate Orthopaedic Fellowship (Postdoctorate/Fellowship)

**Qualif.:** Available to a graduate M.D. at the completion of his or her four years of orthopaedic residency at a hospital approved by the American Academy of Orthopaedic Surgeons. The Fellowship is for attending the Rizzoli Orthopaedic Institute at the University of Bologna.

**Funds Avail.:** $2,000. **Deadline:** May 31.

---

• **4273** •

## National Junior Angus Association
3201 Frederick Blvd.          *Ph:* (816)383-5100
St. Joseph, MO 64506          *Fax:* (816)233-9703
*URL:* http://www.angus.org/njaa.html

### • 4274 • Certified Angus Beef Scholarship
*(Graduate, Undergraduate/Scholarship)*

**Purpose:** To support youth, education and research in the beef industry. **Focus:** Agricultural science, food science and technology. **Qualif.:** Applicants must be current or former NJAA members who are presently junior, regular or life members of the American Angus Association, and whose declared course of work must be in animal science, meat science, food science, agricultural communications or a related field. Applicants must also be graduating high school seniors or currently enrolled in a college or university. **Criteria:** Awards are given based on academic achievement, financial need, and committee interviews.

**Funds Avail.:** Ranges from $1,000 to $2,500. **To Apply:** Applicants must write for details. **Deadline:** May 15. **Contact:** National Junior Angus Association at the above address (see entry 4273).

### • 4275 • National Junior Angus Scholarships
*(Undergraduate/Scholarship)*

**Purpose:** To support youth, education and research in the beef industry. **Focus:** Agricultural science, food science and technology. **Qualif.:** Applicants must be current or former NJAA members who are presently junior, regular or life members of the American Angus Assoc., and whose declared course of work must be in animal science, meat science, food science, agricultural communications or a related field. Applicants must also be graduating high school seniors or currently enrolled in a college or university. **Criteria:** Awards are given based on academic achievement, financial need, and committee interviews.

**Funds Avail.:** Ranges from $1,000 to $2,500. **No. of Awards:** 17. **To Apply:** Applicants must write for details. **Deadline:** May 15. **Contact:** National Junior Angus Association at the above address (see entry 4273).

---

• **4276** •

## National Junior Horticultural Association
1424 N. Eighth Ave.
Durant, OK 74701-4101          *Ph:* (405)924-0771

### • 4277 • Scottish Gardening Scholarship *(Other/Scholarship)*

**Purpose:** To provide study scholarships to Scotland. **Focus:** Horticulture. **Qualif.:** Applicants must be American students and high school graduates over the age of 18 and in good academic standing who have been employed at least one full summer in a horticultural activity.

**Funds Avail.:** The program is for a year and begins the second week in August and includes transportation to and from Scotland, food, lodging, and a small stipend to help defray expenses. Students live and train with approximately 14 other students from Britain. Trainees live at The National Trust of Scotland Threave School of Practical Gardening and devote approximately ten hours

to weekly instruction in addition to full-time work and occasional weekend duty. Periodic trips are arranged to horticultural points of interest. **No. of Awards:** 1. **To Apply:** Applicants must submit a letter of application in outline or narrative form detailing present occupation, future occupational/vocational plans, horticultural experience, NJHA activities, key NJHA accomplishments, youth, school, community, and church activities, key non-NJHA accomplishments, horticultural projects, awards and special honors, other activities and services, and a commentary. A black and white glossy photo should also be included. **Deadline:** October 1.

**Remarks:** The Scottish Gardening Scholarship is offered annually by the National Junior Horticultural Association (NJHA) in conjunction with Longwood Gardens, Inc. and the Scottish-American Heritage, Inc. **Contact:** Tom Clark, 253 Batchelor St., Grandy, MA 01033. Phone: (413)467-2714.

---

• **4278** •

## National Kidney Foundation, Inc.
30 E. 33rd St.                *Ph:* (212)889-2210
New York, NY 10016           *Fax:* (212)689-9261
*E-mail:* jonathans@kidney.com
*URL:* http://www.kidney.org/

### • 4279 • National Kidney Foundation Research Fellowships *(Postdoctorate/Fellowship)*

**Purpose:** To encourage training in kidney and urologic disease research. **Focus:** Nephrology, Urology. **Qualif.:** Candidate should preferably be a U.S. citizen. Applicant must have no more than two years of postdoctoral research training. Candidate must wish to undertake training in laboratory and clinical research for a career in academic nephrology or urology.

**Funds Avail.:** $25,000. **To Apply:** Write for application form and guidelines. **Deadline:** September 15. Fellowships are announced in January. **Contact:** Dolph R. Chianchiano, Associate Director, at the above address (see entry 4278).

### • 4280 • National Kidney Foundation Young Investigator Grant *(Postdoctorate/Grant)*

**Purpose:** To prepare young investigators to compete for grants from the National Institutes of Health. **Qualif.:** Applicants must have their Ph.D. and be at the level of assistant professor. They should also not have any other grant support.

**Funds Avail.:** $20,000 per year for up to two years. **Deadline:** September 15. **Contact:** Dolph Chianchiano at the above address (see entry 4278).

---

• **4281** •

## National League of American Pen Women
c/o National Scholarship Chairman
The Pen-Arts Building
1300 17th St. NW
Washington, DC 20036-1973
*E-mail:* nlapw1@juno.com

### • 4282 • Scholarships for Mature Women
*(Professional Development/Scholarship)*

**Purpose:** To promote the creative talents of mature women. **Focus:** Art, Letters, and Music. **Qualif.:** Applicant must be a woman who is at least 35 years old in the year of application. Scholarships are offered in three categories: art, letters, and music. Candidates

---

## National League of American Pen Women (continued)

are judged on the basis of examples of their creative work. Submitted entries must be original, and should not have previously won an award or been published. Candidate must not be a member of NLAPW, nor part of the immediate family of a NLAPW member. Specific entry regulations (including submission of previous work) vary for each category; write for details.

**Funds Avail.:** $1,000 each category. **To Apply:** Specific entry regulations (including submission of previous work) vary for each category. Write for application guidelines and the addresses for sending entries. Submit to the preliminary judge a letter describing background and a project proposal; application fee ($8); and clear reproduction of work. **Deadline:** January 15. Scholarships are awarded biennially in even-numbered years. **Contact:** National Scholarship Chairman, at the above address (see entry 4281).

## • 4283 •
## National Leukemia Research Association, Inc.
585 Stewart Ave., Ste. 536      *Ph:* (516)222-1944
Garden City, NY 11530      *Fax:* (516)222-0457
*E-mail:* sheila@arbon.com
*URL:* http://www.arbon.com/nlra/

### • 4284 • National Leukemia Research Association Research Awards *(Postdoctorate/Award)*

**Purpose:** To support the developing careers of laboratory and clinical investigators dedicated to the ultimate cure of hematologic malignancies. **Focus:** Hematology, Leukemia. **Qualif.:** Applicants must hold an M.D. or Ph.D. degree and have completed postdoctoral training. They must be employed full-time at an academic institution or laboratory in the United States.

**Funds Avail.:** $20,000/year. **To Apply:** Write for application form and instructions. **Deadline:** June 30. **Contact:** National Leukemia Research Association at the above address (see entry 4283).

## • 4285 •
## National Live Stock and Meat Board
Research Department
444 North Michigan Ave.      *Ph:* (312)467-5520
Chicago, IL 60611      *Fax:* (312)467-1672

### • 4286 • Competitive Grants-in-Aid for Original Research *(Postdoctorate/Grant)*

**Purpose:** To encourage development of new technologies and products in order to create new market opportunities for beef and to develop information regarding the role of beef in the diet and its relationship to human health. **Focus:** Meat Sciences, Nutrition, Product Technology Development. **Qualif.:** Candidates must normally be U.S. citizens and qualified scientists in the areas of health and nutrition and meat science. Funding is not available for institutional overhead, principal investigator salaries, or equipment purchases. Grants are tenable at U.S. institutions.

**Funds Avail.:** $10,000-50,000; $30,000 average. Payments are made in installments. **To Apply:** Write to the director for application guidelines. Project solicitation varies according to research needs. **Deadline:** There is currently no schedule of deadlines. **Contact:** Dr. Cindy Schweitzer, Director of Nutrition Research and Technical Information, or Dr. James Reagan, Director of Product Technology, at the above address (see entry 4285).

## • 4287 •
## National Medical Fellowships, Inc.
110 W. 32nd St., 8th Fl.      *Ph:* (212)714-0933
New York, NY 10001-3205      *Fax:* (212)239-9718
*E-mail:* info@omhrc.gov
*URL:* http://www.omhrc.gov/mhr2/orgs/9201328.htm

### • 4288 • William and Charlotte Cadbury Award *(Doctorate/Award)*

**Purpose:** To recognize outstanding academic achievement, leadership and community service by medical students. **Focus:** Medicine. **Qualif.:** Candidate must be a U.S. citizen and a member of one of the following groups that are traditionally under-represented in the medical profession: African Americans, mainland Puerto Ricans, Mexican Americans, Native Americans, Native Hawaiians, and Alaskan Aleuts. Candidate must be a senior student enrolled in a medical school at a U.S. institution who is nominated for the award by the medical school dean.

**Funds Avail.:** $2,000. **To Apply:** Nominating letter from dean must be submitted to NMF with letters of recommendation and transcripts. **Deadline:** June 15. **Contact:** National Medical Fellowships at the above address (see entry 4287).

### • 4289 • Fellowship Program in Academic Medicine *(Doctorate/Fellowship)*

**Purpose:** To foster mentor relationships between outstanding minority medical students and prominent biomedical scientists through a program of laboratory training. **Focus:** Medicine. **Qualif.:** Candidate must be a U.S. citizen and a member of one of the following groups that are traditionally under-represented in the medical profession: African Americans, Mainland Puerto Ricans, Mexican Americans, Native Americans, Native Hawaiians, and Alaskan Aleuts. Candidate must be a student enrolled in a medical school at a U.S. institution who is nominated by the medical school dean. Nominee must have an interest in and talent for academic or research medicine. Preference is given to third-year students, although second-and fourth-year students may also be considered. Fellows study in research laboratories with established senior investigators in the biomedical sciences. The candidate is responsible for seeking a qualified mentor who is willing to support the fellowship application and oversee the proposed research project.

**Funds Avail.:** $6,000. **To Apply:** Write to NMF for guidelines. Medical school dean must submit letter of nomination with transcripts. Candidate must complete fellowship application, including personal statement. Mentor must submit letter of commitment in support of application with a detailed research proposal. Additional letters of recommendation from faculty are also required. **Deadline:** Nominations must be submitted by November 15. **Contact:** National Medical Fellowships, at the above address (see entry 4287).

### • 4290 • Fellowship Program in Academic Medicine for Minority Students *(Undergraduate/Fellowship)*

**Purpose:** To encourage academically outstanding students to pursue careers in biomedical research and academic medicine.

**Remarks:** Sponsored by the Bristol-Myers Squibb Company and established by the Commonwealth Fund.

### • 4291 • Gerber Prize for Excellence in Pediatrics *(Doctorate/Award)*

**Qualif.:** Candidates must be African Americans, American Indians, Mexican Americans, and mainland Puerto Ricans who are seniors at the University of Michigan Medical School, Michigan State University School of Human Medicine, or Wayne State University School of Medicine. Candidates must plan to pursue careers in pediatric medicine and must match to pediatric residency programs. Students must demonstrate academic excellence, especially in pediatrics, as well as leadership and financial need. **Criteria:** Nominations are reviewed by a special committee, the members of which individually review and rank each candidate. The student with the best average score is designated the Gerber Scholar.

**Funds Avail.:** One $2,000 non-renewable award is presented annually. **To Apply:** Candidates must be nominated by their medical school deans and the chairmen of the departments of pediatrics at their medical schools. The school's dean must submit letters of nomination that fully discuss the candidate's overall academic accomplishments and extracurricular involvement, and the pediatric's chairman must submit a recommendation that discusses the performance in pediatrics rotations and includes faculty evaluations. An official academic transcripts is also required. **Deadline:** Nominations are requested in January. **Contact:** National Medical Fellowships at the above address (see entry 4287).

### • 4292 • Benn and Kathleen Gilmore Scholarship
*(Doctorate/Scholarship)*

**Purpose:** To recognize outstanding academic achievement and leadership. **Qualif.:** Awarded annually to a third-year African American medical student. Candidates must be residents of Michigan, Illinois, Indiana, Ohio, or the District of Columbia, and must attend either the University of Michigan Medical School, Wayne State University School of Medicine, or Michigan State University College of Human Medicine.

### • 4293 • Irving Graef Memorial Scholarship
*(Doctorate/Scholarship)*

**Qualif.:** Candidates must be third-year medical students who have previously received NMF financial assistance during their second year and who have demonstrated outstanding academic achievement, leadership, and community service. They must be United States citizens enrolled in accredited medical schools in the United States. **Criteria:** Dr. Graef's family reviews candidate's dossiers and selects the student most deserving of the award.

**Funds Avail.:** One new award and one renewal. The stipend is $2,000. Scholarships are renewable in the fourth year if the award recipient continues in good academic standing. **To Apply:** Students must be nominated by medical school deans. Schools are required to submit letters of recommendation as well as official academic transcripts. **Deadline:** Nominations are requested in July.

**Remarks:** This scholarship program was established by NMF's board in 1978 and permanently endowed by the Irving Graef Medical Fund in 1980 to honor the memory of one of NMF's most active board members. **Contact:** National Medical Fellowships at the above address (see entry 4287).

### • 4294 • Henry G. Halladay Awards *(Doctorate/Scholarship)*

**Qualif.:** Candidates must be African American male first-year medical students who are enrolled in accredited medical schools in the United States and who are United States citizens. They must have overcome significant obstacles to obtain a medical education and also demonstrate exceptional financial need. **Criteria:** Staff members review NMF first-year, need-based scholarship applications and select five students who, on the bases of recommendations, personal statements, and financial need, are most deserving.

**Funds Avail.:** Five awards of $760 each are granted annually. **To Apply:** There is no special application for these awards. Students are selected from NMF first-year scholarship applicants. **Deadline:** Scholarship applications for NMF Scholarships become available in March. **Contact:** National Medical Fellowships at the above address (see entry 4287).

### • 4295 • George Hill Memorial Scholarship
*(Doctorate/Scholarship)*

**Qualif.:** Competition is open only to African American residents of Westchester County, New York who have been accepted into first-year classes of accredited United States medical schools. The candidates must demonstrate outstanding academic achievement, leadership, and community service. **Criteria:** Candidates' dossiers are reviewed by a committee of Westchester County community leaders.

**Funds Avail.:** $4,000 annually for four years or through completion of medical education, whichever comes first. The scholarships are renewable annually if the award recipient continues in good academic standing. **To Apply:** Applications are mailed with the NMF first-year scholarship applications. Information is also mailed to Westchester County residents who have registered with "Med-MAR." An interview is required.

**Remarks:** The scholarship program was established in 1975 by Chesebrough-Pond's Inc. of Greenwich, Connecticut in memory of the black physician who pioneered in the testing, screening, and counseling of persons suffering from sickle-cell anemia. **Contact:** National Medical Fellowships at the above address (see entry 4287).

### • 4296 • Hugh J. Andersen Memorial Scholarship
*(Doctorate/Scholarship)*

**Qualif.:** Presented to students attending Minnesota medical schools, or Minnesota students enrolled in any accredited medical school in the U.S. Awards are given in recognition of outstanding leadership, community service, and financial need.

### • 4297 • W. K. Kellogg Community Medicine Training Fellowship Program for Minority Medical Students *(Doctorate/Fellowship)*

**Qualif.:** Applicants must be African American, Mexican American, Native American, or mainland Puerto Rican second- and third-year medical students. They must be in good academic standing, attend accredited United States medical schools, and demonstrate outstanding leadership, community involvement, and potential for responsible roles in health care delivery. They must also have a desire to work in community-based health centers that provide high quality, managed care for those people who lack access to health services because of geographic isolation, lack of providers, or financial barriers. **Criteria:** Fellows are selected by a committee of persons prominent in community medicine and primary care.

**Funds Avail.:** Fifteen $5,000 non-renewable awards are presented annually. Students work with senior staff members and advisory boards at community and migrant health centers through the country for eight to twelve week periods. **To Apply:** Candidates must be nominated by medical school deans. Schools must submit letters of nomination and official academic transcripts for each nominee. Medical school faculty members willing to serve as academic advisors must submit letters of commitment in support of each student's application. Students are required to complete fellowship applications and include personal statements. **Deadline:** Nominations are requested in October.

**Remarks:** The fellowship program was established in 1990 with grant support from the W. K. Kellogg Foundation of Battle Creek, Michigan. NMF is sponsoring the program in cooperation with the National Association of Community Health Centers (NACHC) of Washington, D.C. **Contact:** National Medical Fellowships at the above address (see entry 4287).

### • 4298 • Franklin C. McLean Award *(Doctorate/Award)*

**Qualif.:** Presented to a senior medical student in recognition of outstanding academic achievement, leadership, and community service.

**Remarks:** This is NMF's most prestigious special merit award.

*National Medical Fellowships, Inc. (continued)*
### • 4299 • The Mead Johnson/NMA Scholarship
*(Doctorate/Scholarship)*

**Purpose:** To recognize and reward African American medical students for outstanding academic achievement and leadership. **Qualif.:** Applicants must be African American medical students who are attending accredited, M.D. or D.O. degree-granting schools in the United States. They must demonstrate academic excellence, leadership, financial need, and potential for outstanding contributions to medicine. **Criteria:** The Council on Talent Recruitment, Retention and Financial Aid of the National Medical Association reviews and selects the award winners. Awards are presented during the annual meeting of the NMA. Selections are based on need.

**Funds Avail.:** One $2,250 award. **To Apply:** Students must be nominated by their medical school deans. Schools are required to submit letters of recommendation, official academic transcripts, and financial aid transcripts for each student. All applicants are required to complete program applications, including personal essays, and provide copies of income tax forms for themselves, their parents, and their spouses. **Deadline:** Nominations are requested in May. **Contact:** National Medical Fellowships at the above address (see entry 4287).

### • 4300 • Metropolitan Life Foundation Awards for Academic Excellence in Medicine *(Doctorate/Award)*

**Qualif.:** Applicants must be African American, Mexican American, Native American, or mainland Puerto Rican second- and third-year medical students who attend medical schools or have legal residence in the following cities only: San Francisco, California; Tampa, Florida; Atlanta, Georgia; Aurora, Illinois (Chicago); Wichita, Kansas; New York, New York; Tulsa, Oklahoma; Pittsburgh, Pennsylvania; Scranton, Pennsylvania; Warwick, Rhode Island (Providence); Greenville, South Carolina; and San Antonio, Texas. Candidates must demonstrate outstanding academic achievement, leadership, and potential for distinguished contributions to medicine, as well as financial need. **Criteria:** NFL staff review the candidates' dossiers and select the students they judge most deserving of these scholarships.

**Funds Avail.:** Up to ten $2,500 nonrenewable scholarships are presented annually. **To Apply:** Candidates must be nominated by medical school deans. Schools are required to submit letters of recommendation and official academic transcripts for each nominee. Students are required to submit scholarship applications, including personal statements, and verification of financial need. **Deadline:** Nominations are requested in August. **Contact:** National Medical Fellowships at the above address (see entry 4287).

### • 4301 • NMA Merit Scholarships *(Doctorate/ Scholarship)*

**Purpose:** To recognize and reward African American medical students for academic excellence and leadership. **Qualif.:** Applicants must be African American medical students who are attending accredited, M.D. or D.O. degree-granting schools in the United States. They must demonstrate academic excellence, leadership, financial need, and potential for outstanding contributions to medicine. **Criteria:** The Council on Talent Recruitment, Retention and Financial Aid of the National Medical Association reviews and selects the award winners. Awards are presented during the annual meeting of the NMA. Selections are based on need.

**Funds Avail.:** Four $2,250 awards presented annually. **To Apply:** Students must be nominated by their medical school deans. Schools are required to submit letters of recommendation, official academic transcripts, and financial aid transcripts for each student. All applicants are required to complete program applications, including personal essays, and provide copies of income tax forms for themselves, their parents, and their spouses.

**Deadline:** Nominations are requested in May. **Contact:** National Medical Fellowships at the above address (see entry 4287).

### • 4302 • NMA Scholarships *(Graduate/Scholarship)*

**Qualif.:** Applicants must be U.S. citizens who are African American, Puerto Rican, Mexican American, or Native American. **Criteria:** Scholarship selections are based on needs. **To Apply:** Applications are available in April. **Deadline:** August 31. **Contact:** Scholarship Department at the above address (see entry 4287).

### • 4303 • The NMA Special Awards Program *(Doctorate/Scholarship)*

**Purpose:** To recognize and reward African-American medical students for special achievement and leadership. **Qualif.:** Applicants must be African American medical students who are attending accredited, M.D. or D.O. degree-granting schools in the United States. They must demonstrate academic excellence, leadership, financial need, and potential for outstanding contributions to medicine. **Criteria:** The Council on Talent Recruitment, Retention and Financial Aid of the National Medical Association reviews and selects the award winners. Awards are presented during the annual meeting of the NMA. Selections are based on need.

**Funds Avail.:** Three $1,350 awards. **To Apply:** Students must be nominated by their medical school deans. Schools are required to submit letters of recommendation, official academic transcripts, and financial aid transcripts for each student. All applicants are required to complete program applications, including personal essays, and provide copies of income tax forms for themselves, their parents, and their spouses. **Deadline:** Nominations are requested in May. **Contact:** National Medical Fellowships at the above address (see entry 4287).

### • 4304 • NMF Scholarships for Minority Students *(Doctorate/Scholarship)*

**Purpose:** To assist U.S. students from minority groups to obtain an education in medicine. **Focus:** Medicine. **Qualif.:** Applicant must be a U.S. citizen and a member of one of the following groups that are traditionally under-represented in the medical profession: African Americans, Mainland Puerto Ricans, Mexican Americans, Native Americans, Native Hawaiians, and Alaskan Aleuts. Candidate must be accepted to or enrolled in the first or second year of medical school at a U.S. institution.

**Funds Avail.:** Varies, depending on need, cost of education, and other sources of aid. **To Apply:** Write to NMF for application materials, available April through July. **Deadline:** August 31/May 31 for renewal students.

**Remarks:** Each year, five African-American males who overcame significant obstacles to obtain a medical education will be granted Henry G. Halladay Awards: $760 grants to supplement the NMF scholarship. No special application form is needed. Students who receive a scholarship from NMF during their second year of medical school are eligible to be nominated for the Irving Graef Memorial Scholarship, which supports third-and fourth-year studies, and the Baxter Foundation Scholarships, which are for third-year studies only. Nomination must come from the medical school dean. Write NMF for further information. **Contact:** Maritza Myers, Vice President, at the above address (see entry 4287).

### • 4305 • James H. Robinson Memorial Prize *(Doctorate/Prize)*

**Purpose:** To recognize outstanding performance in surgery by a student. **Focus:** Surgical Medicine. **Qualif.:** Candidate must be a U.S. citizen and a member of one of the following groups that are traditionally under-represented in the medical profession: African Americans, Mainland Puerto Ricans, Mexican Americans, Native Americans, Native Hawaiians, and Alaskan Aleuts. Candidate must be a senior student enrolled in a medical school at a U.S.

institution who is nominated by both the medical school dean and the chair of the department of surgery.

**Funds Avail.:** $500. **To Apply:** The letter of nomination from the dean should fully discuss academic and extracurricular accomplishments. The letter from the department chair should delineate performance in the surgical disciplines and include faculty evaluations. Transcripts are also required. **Deadline:** November. **Contact:** Maritza Myers, Vice President, at the above address (see entry 4287).

## • 4306 • Aura E. Severinghaus Award *(Doctorate/ Scholarship)*

**Qualif.:** Candidates must be African Americans, mainland Puerto Ricans, Mexican-Americans, and American Indians in their senior year who are enrolled at Columbia University College of Physicians and Surgeons. **Criteria:** Selections are based on academic excellence, and community service and leadership.

**Funds Avail.:** One nonrenewable award of $2,000 is presented annually. **To Apply:** Application is by nomination by the committee of faculty at Columbia University College of Physicians and Surgeons only. **Deadline:** Nominations are requested in September. **Contact:** National Medical Fellowships at the above address (see entry 4287).

## • 4307 • The Slack Award for Medical Journalism *(Doctorate/Award)*

**Purpose:** To recognize and reward African American medical students for academic excellence and leadership. **Qualif.:** Applicants must be African American medical students who are attending accredited, M.D. or D.O. degree-granting schools in the United States. They must demonstrate journalism skill, academic excellence, leadership, and potential for outstanding contributions to medicine. **Criteria:** The Council on Talent Recruitment, Retention and Financial Aid of the National Medical Association reviews and selects the award winners. Awards are presented during the annual meeting of the NMA. Selections are based on financial need.

**Funds Avail.:** One award of $2,500. **To Apply:** Students must be nominated by their medical school deans. Schools are required to submit letters of recommendation, official academic transcripts, and financial aid transcripts for each student. All applicants are required to complete program applications, including personal essays, and provide copies of income tax forms for themselves, their parents, and their spouses. They must also submit samples of their journalism work. **Deadline:** Nominations are requested in May. **Contact:** National Medical Fellowships at the above address (see entry 4287).

## • 4308 • Wyeth-Ayerst Prize in Women's Health *(Doctorate/Award)*

**Purpose:** To recognize graduating female minority medical students who will practice or conduct research in the field of women's health.

**Remarks:** Established by Wyeth-Ayerst Laboratories.

## • 4309 •
## National Merit Scholarship Corporation
1560 Sherman Ave., Ste. 200
Evanston, IL 60201-4897          *Ph:* (847)866-5100
*E-mail:* DOMINIQUE.LANGOUCHE @RUG.AC.BE

## • 4310 • National Achievement Scholarship Program for Outstanding Negro Students *(Undergraduate/ Scholarship)*

**Purpose:** The National Merit Scholarship Corporation administers the National Merit Scholarship Program and the National Achievement Scholarship Program for Outstanding Negro Students. The Achievement Program, established in 1964, is a compensatory activity that seeks to identify academically able high school students who are Black Americans and increase their college admission and financial aid opportunities. **Focus:** General Studies. **Qualif.:** Black students request consideration in the Achievement Program at the time they take the Preliminary Scholastic Aptitude Test/National Merit Scholarship Qualifying Test (PSAT/NMSQT). They indicate on the test answer sheet that they are Black Americans and wish to be considered in the Achievement Program. Such students participate simultaneously in both the Achievement Program and the Merit Program, which are separately administered by the National Merit Scholarship Corporation (NMSC). The PSAT/NMSQT performance required to receive recognition in the Merit Program is independent of the level required for a student to be honored in the Achievement Program. A student who takes the qualifying test to enter the competition for Achievement Scholarship awards must: request entry to the Achievement Program; be a United States citizen or taking steps to become a United States citizen as soon as qualified; be enrolled full-time in a secondary school progressing normally toward meeting the requirements for graduation or completion of high school requirements; plan to attend a regionally-accredited college in the United States upon completing high school and to enroll full-time in a course of study leading to one of the traditional baccalaureate degrees; and take the PSAT/NMSQT at the proper time in high school, regardless of grade classification. Students who complete grades 9 through 12 in four years take the PSAT/ NMSQT as juniors and compete for Achievement Scholarship awards to be awarded in the spring of their senior year. Students who plan to go directly to college after three years or less in grades 9 through 12 will either take the PSAT/NMSQT in their second (sophomore) year of high school and compete for scholarships awarded in the spring of their third and final year of secondary school, or take the PSAT/NMSQT in their third and final year of secondary school and compete for scholarships awarded in the spring that they complete their freshman year in college.

**Funds Avail.:** Achievement Scholarship awards are financed by Achievement Program sponsors and donors, and by the Achievement Program's own funds. 400 are National Achievement $2,000 Scholarships, single-payment awards for which all finalists compete. The remainder are Achievement Scholarship awards that are awarded to finalists who have particular qualifications of interest to award sponsors and are worth $250 to $2,000 or more for four years. **No. of Awards:** Approximately 800. **To Apply:** Black students who qualify as Achievement Program semifinalists are notified through their schools the fall after taking the PSAT/ NMSQT. Achievement Program semifinalists who meet further requirements and advance to finalist standing in the Achievement Program competition are notified of their standing through their high schools. Finalist compete for Achievement Scholarship awards on the basis of abilities, skills, accomplishments, and potential for future academic success. All Achievement Scholarship stipends must be used exclusively to pay college costs at a regionally-accredited United States college or university, and the winner must follow a course of study leading to one of the usual baccalaureate degrees. Throughout the undergraduate years the winner must continue to meet all the terms of the scholarship. **Contact:** High school guidance counselor for a PSAT/NMSQT Student Bulletin.

---

## National Merit Scholarship Corporation (continued)

### • 4311 • National Merit Scholarship Program
*(Undergraduate/Scholarship)*

**Purpose:** The purposes of the National Merit Scholarship Program are to identify and honor academically able high school students and to provide college scholarships for a sizable number of them each year. The National Merit Scholarship Program combines a yearly nationwide search for academically talented high school students with services designed to increase their opportunities for college admission and financial aid. Over 50,000 students are honored annually for their high PSAT/NMSQT performance. **Focus:** General Studies. **Qualif.:** To be considered for recognition and awards in the Merit Program, a student must: be a United States citizen or taking steps to become a United States citizen as soon as qualified; be enrolled full-time in a secondary school, progressing normally toward graduation or completion of high school requirements; plan to attend a regionally-accredited college in the United States upon completing high school and to enroll full-time in a course of study leading to one of the traditional baccalaureate degrees; and take the Preliminary Scholastic Aptitude Test/National Merit Scholarship Qualifying Test (PSAT/NMSQT) at proper time in high school, regardless of grade classification. Students who complete grades 9 through 12 in four years take the PSAT/NMSQT as juniors. Students who make plans to accelerate their high school program take the PSAT/NMSQT in their second year (normally the sophomore year) or their third and final year of secondary school. Only students who take the PSAT/NMSQT and who qualify as Semifinalists continue in the competition for Merit Scholarship awards. A semifinalist can become a finalist and be considered for a Merit Scholarship award only once. To qualify as a finalist, a semifinalist must meet the student eligibility requirements listed above and must meet other requirements relating to academic performance. All winners of the Merit Scholarship awards are chosen from the finalist group on the basis of abilities, skills, and accomplishments without regard to gender, race, ethnic origin, or religious preference.

**Funds Avail.:** Three types of Merit Scholarship awards are offered in each annual competition. These scholarships must be used to help pay educational costs of attending a regionally-accredited college or university in the United States and the winner must follow a course of study leading to one of the traditional baccalaureate degrees. The types of scholarships are the National Merit $2,000 Scholarships, corporate-sponsored scholarships, and college-sponsored Merit Scholarship awards. **To Apply:** The National Merit Scholarship Program is an annual competition for undergraduate college scholarships that is open to secondary school students who are United States citizens. The Preliminary Scholastic Aptitude Test/National Merit Scholarship Qualifying Test (PSAT/NMSQT) measures developed verbal and mathematical abilities, and is a shortened version of the College Board SAT 1. Taking the PSAT/NMSQT is the route of entry to the Merit Scholarship competition. The PSAT/NMSQT is administered in public, independent, and parochial secondary schools throughout the United States and in a number of other countries. It is given to high school juniors in October of each year. Students take the PSAT/NMSQT at their high schools.

**Remarks:** The Merit Program is administered by the National Merit Scholarship Corporation (NMSC), an independent, nonprofit organization created in 1955. Merit Scholarship awards are financed without government funding by some 600 companies, businesses, professional associations, company foundations, and colleges and universities. **Contact:** High school guidance counselor for a PSAT/NMSQT Student Bulletin, which contains information about the program.

### • 4312 •
## National Multiple Sclerosis Society
733 3rd Ave.  *Ph:* (212)986-3240
New York, NY 10017  *Fax:* (212)986-7981
*E-mail:* nat@nmss.org
*URL:* http://www.nmss.org

### • 4313 • National Multiple Sclerosis Society Advanced Postdoctoral Fellowships *(Postdoctorate/Fellowship)*

**Purpose:** To support additional postdoctoral training to unusually promising postdoctoral investigators. **Focus:** Multiple Sclerosis. **Qualif.:** Candidates must hold an M.D., Ph.D., or equivalent degree and have completed more than one year of prior postdoctoral training at the time of application. U.S. citizenship is not required for training in U.S. institutions; applicants who plan to train in other countries must be U.S. citizens.

**Funds Avail.:** Varies with qualifications and experience of candidate; only personal stipend and benefits are provided. **No. of Awards:** 9. **Deadline:** February 1 for July start. **Contact:** The National Multiple Sclerosis Society at the above address (see entry 4312).

### • 4314 • National Multiple Sclerosis Society Biomedical Research Grants *(Professional Development/Grant)*

**Purpose:** To support fundamental or applied studies, clinical or nonclinical in nature, which have a reasonable relevance to the Society's interests. **Focus:** Multiple Sclerosis. **Qualif.:** Principal investigator must be affiliated with an appropriate research institution.

**Funds Avail.:** Varies with each project. **No. of Awards:** 51. **To Apply:** A letter of intent briefly describing the proposed project and its relevance to multiple sclerosis must be submitted. **Deadline:** February 1 for October start; August 1 for April start. **Contact:** The National Multiple Sclerosis Society at the above address (see entry 4312).

### • 4315 • National Multiple Sclerosis Society Health Services Research Grants *(Professional Development/Grant)*

**Purpose:** To provide short-term support for feasibility studies or small grants in areas related to access to care and legislative and entitlement issues. **Focus:** Multiple Sclerosis. **Qualif.:** Open to principal investigators who are affiliated with academic and medical institutions, government agencies at any level, community groups, public/private coalitions, voluntary and for-profit organizations, and professionally qualified individuals.

**Funds Avail.:** Not to exceed $20,000. **No. of Awards:** 3. **To Apply:** Applicants must submit a letter of intent briefly describing the proposed project and its relevance to multiple sclerosis. **Deadline:** June 1. **Contact:** The National Mutliple Sclerosis Society at the above address (see entry 4312).

### • 4316 • National Multiple Sclerosis Society Patient Management Care and Rehabilitation Grants *(Professional Development/Grant)*

**Purpose:** To support research on new techniques to improve the quality of life for people with multiple sclerosis. **Focus:** Multiple Sclerosis. **Qualif.:** Principal investigator must be affiliated with an appropriate research institution.

**Funds Avail.:** Varies with each project. **No. of Awards:** 4. **To Apply:** Candidates must submit a letter of intent briefly describing the proposed project and its relevance to multiple sclerosis. **Deadline:** February 1 for October start; August 1 for April start. **Contact:** The

National Multiple Sclerosis Society at the above address (see entry 4312).

### • 4317 • National Multiple Sclerosis Society Pilot Research Grants *(Professional Development/Grant)*

**Purpose:** To provide limited short-term support for novel, high-risk research in areas related to the Society's interests. **Focus:** Multiple Sclerosis. **Qualif.:** Applicant must be an investigator at an established research institution. Applicant's research must be at its initial stages; funds are intended to support the development of concepts and attainment of preliminary data. Grants are tenable worldwide. Grants are for direct costs only.

**Funds Avail.:** $25,000 maximum. **No. of Awards:** 30. **To Apply:** Write or call the Society for application materials. **Deadline:** None. Candidates are notified two or three months of receipt of application. **Contact:** Dr. P. O'Looney at the above address (see entry 4312).

### • 4318 • National Multiple Sclerosis Society Postdoctoral Fellowships *(Postdoctorate/Fellowship)*

**Purpose:** To encourage young investigators to perform meaningful and independent research relevant to multiple sclerosis by providing them with training opportunities. **Focus:** Multiple Sclerosis. **Qualif.:** Applicant must hold or be a candidate for an M.D., Ph.D., or equivalent degree. Applicant may be of any nationality, but candidates from outside of the United States must train at a U.S. institution. U.S. citizens may train in the United States or elsewhere. Candidates who are reasonably assured of suitable research positions after completion of the fellowship are preferred.

**Funds Avail.:** $20,000-30,000/year. **No. of Awards:** 13. **To Apply:** Write or call the Society for application materials. **Deadline:** February 1. Notification by July 1. **Contact:** Dr. D. Avci at the above address (see entry 4312).

### • 4319 • National Multiple Sclerosis Society Research Grants *(Professional Development/Grant)*

**Purpose:** To support fundamental and applied studies that are reasonably relevant to the Society's interests. **Focus:** Multiple Sclerosis. **Qualif.:** Applicant may be of any nationality. Applicant must be affiliated with an established research institution approved by the Society. Research may be either clinical or nonclinical. Grants are tenable worldwide.

**Funds Avail.:** $85,000. **To Apply:** Write or call the Society for application materials. **Deadline:** February 1 and August 1. Notification by July 1 and February 1, respectively. **Contact:** Dr. A. Eastwood, at the above address (see entry 4312).

### • 4320 • National Multiple Sclerosis Society Senior Faculty Awards *(Professional Development/Award)*

**Purpose:** To assist established investigators who seek support to obtain specialized training in some field that will materially enhance their capacity to conduct more meaningful research in multiple sclerosis. **Focus:** Multiple Sclerosis.

**Funds Avail.:** Varies. **To Apply:** No specific application form is required. **Deadline:** February 1. **Contact:** The National Multiple Sclerosis Society at the above address (see entry 4312).

### • 4321 • Patient Management, Care and Rehabilitation Grants *(Professional Development/Grant)*

**Purpose:** To support research on new techniques of ameliorating function and the quality of life for Multiple Sclerosis patients. **Focus:** Multiple Sclerosis. **Qualif.:** Applicant may be of any nationality. Applicant must be a qualified investigator affiliated with an established institution. Grants are tenable worldwide.

**Funds Avail.:** $85,000. **To Apply:** Call or write the Society for application materials. **Deadline:** February 1, August 1. Notification by July 1 and February 1, respectively. **Contact:** Dr. Abe Eastwood at the above address (see entry 4312).

### • 4322 • Harry Weaver Neuroscience Scholarships *(Postdoctorate/Scholarship)*

**Purpose:** To support independent investigators at the beginning of their academic careers. **Focus:** Multiple Sclerosis. **Qualif.:** Applicant must have an M.D. or Ph.D. degree, or equivalent experience. Applicant must not have had more than five years of independent research experience at the time of application, and must hold or have been offered a position equivalent to assistant professor at an approved institution. The Society will provide up to 75% of the scholar's salary; the institution is expected to provide the other 25%. Scholarships are tenable in the United States.

**Funds Avail.:** $50,000/year maximum salary, plus up to $25,000 in research support. **To Apply:** Call or write the Society for application materials. **Deadline:** February 1. Notification by July 1. **Contact:** Dr. D. Avci at the above address (see entry 4312).

### • 4323 •
## National Native American Cooperative
PO Box 27626
Tucson, AZ 85726-7626                    *Ph:* (520)622-4900

### • 4324 • NNAC Gifted/Talented Artist Sponsorships *(Professional Development/Other)*

**Purpose:** To assist in the continuation of traditional or contemporary American Indian culture. **Focus:** Native American Studies. **Qualif.:** Applicants must be Native American artists. Both traditional and contemporary work is accepted. **Criteria:** Selection is based upon the applicant's ability to utilize materials provided and create art that reflects a Native American cultural experience.

**Funds Avail.:** Beads, buckskin, silver, turquoise, gold, and other raw craft materials are presented to the artist. **To Apply:** Applicants must forward a written request for application details to the National Native American Cooperative. **Deadline:** None. **Contact:** Fred Synder, Executive Director, at the above address (see entry 4323).

### • 4325 •
## National Newspaper Publishers Association
3200 13th St., NW                    *Ph:* (202)588-8764
Washington, DC 20010                 *Fax:* (202)588-5029
*E-mail:* nnpa@usbol.com
*URL:* http://www.nnpa.org

### • 4326 • National Newspaper Publishers Association Grants *(Undergraduate/Grant)*

**Qualif.:** Applicants must be minority college students pursuing careers in journalism.

**Funds Avail.:** Ten $2,000 grants are awarded annually. **Contact:** Chairman, NNPA Scholarship Committee at the above address (see entry 4325).

---

## National Oceanic and Atmospheric Administration

National Sea Grant College Program
1315 East-West Highway
Bldg. 3, 11th Fl.                         *Ph:* (301)713-2431
Silver Spring, MD 20910                  *Fax:* (301)713-0799
*E-mail:* deshon.carter@noaa.gov

### • 4328 • Dean John A. Knauss Marine Policy Fellowships *(Doctorate, Graduate/Fellowship)*

**Purpose:** To enable advanced students in marine-related fields to work in the U.S. Legislative and Executive Branches. **Focus:** Marine Policy. **Qualif.:** Candidate may be of any nationality. Applicant must be enrolled in a graduate or professional degree program in a marine-related field at an accredited U.S. institution. Fellowships are tenable in Washington, D.C. Fellows are matched with an office of the U.S. Legislative or Executive Branch, or other appropriate association or institution.

**Funds Avail.:** $30,000 stipend, plus travel funds, moving costs, and health insurance. **No. of Awards:** 30. **To Apply:** Write for application form, guidelines, and a list of state Sea Grant offices. Submit application to state Sea Grant director. **Deadline:** June-August. **Contact:** DeShon Carter, Secretary, at the above address (see entry 4327).

### • 4329 •

## National Orchestral Insititute

School of Music
2114 Tawes
University of Maryland                    *Ph:* (301)405-2317
College Park, MD 20742-1211              *Fax:* (301)314-9504
*E-mail:* noi@umdacc.umd.edu

### • 4330 • National Orchestral Institute Scholarships *(Graduate, Postgraduate, Undergraduate/Scholarship)*

**Purpose:** To encourage and train outstanding instrumentalists who are pursuing professional careers as orchestral musicians. **Focus:** Orchestral Music. **Qualif.:** Applicant may be of any nationality, but must be an orchestral musician between the ages of 18 and 28 years. Candidate may be studying at the undergraduate, graduate, or postgraduate level, but should be preparing for a professional orchestral career. Musicians are selected through regional auditions held in the United States during February and March. Scholarships are tenable at the National Orchestral Institute, conducted each June at the University of Maryland. **Criteria:** Personal audition.

**Funds Avail.:** Funds provide for tuition, room and board. **No. of Awards:** Approximately 90. **To Apply:** Write to the director for application materials and audition schedule. **Deadline:** Varies according to regional audition date. Selected musicians are notified by April 1.

**Remarks:** N.O.I. e-mail: noi@umdacc.umd.edu **Contact:** Donald Reinhold Director.

### • 4331 • The University of Maryland International Music Competitions *(Professional Development/Prize)*

**Purpose:** To recognize young artistic talent at the highest levels of musical performance and artistry for voice, piano, and cello. **Focus:** Music. **Qualif.:** Applicant may be of any nationality. For piano, applicant must be between the ages of 18-33; cello, 18-30; voice, 21-39. The competitions rotate each year and are as follows: Leonard Rose Cello Competition, William Kapell Piano Competition, and Marian Anderson Vocal Arts Competition. The competition examines solo repertoire and performance with symphony orchestra.

**Funds Avail.:** First prize: $20,000; second prize: $10,000; third prize: $5,000; semi-finalist prizes: $1,000. **No. of Awards:** 12. **To Apply:** Write to the administrative director for application form, repertoire guidelines, and competition rules. Submit form with registration fee $75; admission tape of solo repertoire; a typed copy of repertoire; biographical information; three photographs; and supporting documents, including reviews, letters of recommendation, programs, or brochures. **Deadline:** March 15. **Contact:** George Moquin, International Music Competitions/MCPA, 1125 Holzapfel Hall, U of Maryland, College Park, MD, 20742.

### • 4332 •

## National Osteopathic Foundation

5775 G Peachtree-Dunwoody Rd.,
 Ste. 500
Atlanta, GA 30342
*E-mail:* nofi@assnhq.com
*URL:* http://osteopathic.net/nof/

### • 4333 • American Osteopathic Association/National Osteopathic Foundation Student Loans *(Graduate/Loan)*

**Qualif.:** Applicants must be a third- or fourth-year medical student in an AOA-accredited college of osteopathic medicine and must maintain AOA membership throughout the life of the loan, or the loan will become immediately due and payable infull.

**Funds Avail.:** $1,000-$5,000. **Contact:** Financial Aid Office of a qualifying school.

### • 4334 • Bristol-Myers Squibb Outstanding Resident Awards *(Professional Development/Grant)*

**Purpose:** To recognize physicians in the primary care residencies of Family Practice, Internal Medicine, and Pediatrics. **Qualif.:** Applicants must be Osteopathic physicians currently in the 2nd or 3rd year of an AOA-approved residency program in the primary care specialties of Family Practice, Internal Medicine, and Pediatrics and should exhibit exemplary characteristics of a good osteopathic primary care physician such as compassion, leadership, commitment to the osteopathic philosophy, commitment to patient care and to community, and commitment to education/enrichment of self and others.

**Funds Avail.:** $2,000 plus a travel grant to attend the Annual Convention and Scientific Seminar of the American Osteopathic Association. **To Apply:** Application form, an optional letter of reference and an AOA rating sheet must be submitted. **Deadline:** March 31. **Contact:** National Osteopathic Foundation at the above address (see entry 4332). Online application and rating sheet are available.

### • 4335 • Russell C. McCaughan Education Fund Scholarship *(Doctorate, Graduate/Scholarship)*

**Qualif.:** Applicants must be second-year students at an accredited U.S. College of osteopathic medicine and show financial need, outstanding academic and extracurricular capabilities and strong motivation in osteopathic philosophy.

**Funds Avail.:** $400. **No. of Awards:** One student is selected from each qualifying school. Nominations are made through the Dean's Office. **Contact:** National Osteopathic Foundation at the above address (see entry 4332).

• **4336** • **Zeneca Pharmaceuticals Underserved Healthcare Grant** *(Doctorate/Grant)*

**Purpose:** To encourage osteopathic medical students to practice in underserved or minority populations. **Qualif.:** Applicants must be third-year student.

**Funds Avail.:** $5,000-$10,000. The amount of the award will be determined by the selection committee and will be made in two disbursements—one at the beginning of the fourth year of studies and one after the first year of practice. **To Apply:** A completed typwritten application, personal statement of 750 words or less, names of three clinical instructors (for references), and a letter of academic standing from the Academic Dean must be submitted. **Contact:** National Osteopathic Foundation at the above address (see entry 4332).

• **4337** •
**National Physical Sciences Consortium, MSC 3NPS**
New Mexico State University
O'Loughlin House
University Ave.                      *Ph:* (505)646-6038
Box 30001                           *Fax:* (505)646-6097
Las Cruces, NM 88003-8001           *Free:* 800-952-4118
*E-mail:* ebailey@nmsu.edu; npsc@nmsu.edu
*URL:* http://www.npsc.org

• **4338** • **National Physical Science Consortium Graduate Fellowships for Minorities and Women** *(Doctorate, Graduate/Fellowship)*

**Purpose:** To expand the pool of women and minorities in graduate physical science studies. **Focus:** Astronomy, Chemistry, Computer Science, Geology, Materials Science, Mathematical Sciences, Physics, and Subdisciplines. **Qualif.:** Applicants must be United States citizens. They must also have undergraduate standing as seniors with a GPA of at least 3.0 on a 4.0 scale, be eligible to pursue graduate study at a participating member university, and be an entering or returning student. Study must be in the fields of astronomy, chemistry, computer science, geology, materials science, mathematical sciences, physics, or subdisciplines. **Criteria:** Selection is based on grade point average, GRE scores, transcripts, letters of recommendation, and prior research and/or employment experience. Photocopies of each candidate's application are sent to major research laboratories, national corporations, and leading Ph.D. granting universities. Two review committees, consisting of scientists, academic deans, and sponsoring employers, review the applications.

**Funds Avail.:** Fellowships from $156,000 to $200,000 depending on the cost of graduate school for a period of six years, to cover tuition, fees, and a stipend. Stipends are $12,500 per year, for first four years, plus summer employment for the first and second year; and $15,000 per year for the fifth and sixth years. **No. of Awards:** Varies. **To Apply:** Application is on NPSC web site: www.npsc.org. Applicants must submit an electronic copy along with a printed, signed copy of the application, including official transcripts from each post-secondary school attended and GRE test scores. **Deadline:** November 5. Recipients will be announced the following January. **Contact:** L. Nan Snow, Executive Director, National Physical Science Consortium, at the above address (see entry 4337). For information about the application process, students may call the NPSC student recruitment office at: (800)952-4118, or (505)646-6038 or (505)646-6849, or email: npsc@nmsu.edu

• **4339** •
**National Press Club**
529 14th St. NW
Washington, DC 20045                 *Ph:* (202)662-7599

• **4340** • **National Press Club Ellen Masin Persina Scholarship** *(Undergraduate/Scholarship)*

**Focus:** Journalism. **Qualif.:** Applicants must be a minority high school senior with a 2.75 GPA and plans to pursue a career in journalism.

**Funds Avail.:** $2500, renewable for up to four years if a 2.75 GPA is maintained. **To Apply:** An application form and a one-page essay on why the students wants to pursue a career in journalism must be submitted. **Deadline:** February 1.

• **4341** •
**National Press Photographers Foundation**
c/o Bradley Wilson
3200 Croasdaile Dr., Ste. 306        *Ph:* (919)383-7246
Durham, NC 27705                     *Fax:* (919)383-7261
*E-mail:* nppa@mindspring.com
*URL:* http://www.nppa.org

• **4342** • **Reid Blackburn Scholarship** *(Undergraduate/Scholarship)*

**Purpose:** To encourage those who have talent and dedication to photojournalism, and who need financial help to continue their studies. **Focus:** Photojournalism. **Qualif.:** Applicants must be high school graduates and may already be in college or in the working world. **Criteria:** Those selected are most deserving of financial need and can demonstrate potential in photojournalism. The philosophy and goals statement (see below) is particularly important in the selection process.

**Funds Avail.:** $1,000. **No. of Awards:** 1. **To Apply:** Applicants must provide evidence of financial need, send a letter of recommendation from a college instructor, and submit a philosophy and goals statement along with a portfolio, which gives evidence of the applicant's academic ability and photo aptitude. For photographers, the portfolio should contain a minimum of six pictures (a picture story counts as one) with the applicant's name printed clearly on the back of each print or on the slide margins (keep caption information concise); for picture editors, three tear sheets; and for video journalists, a sample tape. Applicant's choice of school must be in the United States or Canada and the scholarship award must be used at the beginning of the next semester. Images will not be returned and should be 8x10 unmounted prints or 35mm duplicate slides. Persons may apply for as many different scholarships as they choose, but will only be awarded one in any given year. **Deadline:** March 1.

**Remarks:** Reid Blackburn was a staff photographer for the Columbian Newspaper in Vancouver, Washington until his death in 1980. He was on assignment at Mount St. Helens when it erupted and took his life. After his junior year, during a Columbian internship, he was proficient enough to make it as a professional, but he realized the importance of returning to college for his degree. **Contact:** Questions about the scholarship should be addressed to the National Press Photographers Foundation at the above address (see entry 4341). Application materials go to Steve Small, St. Petersburg Times, 490 First Ave., South, St. Petersburg, FL 33701; telephone: (813)893-8231.

• **4343** • **Bob East Scholarship** *(Graduate, Undergraduate/Scholarship)*

**Purpose:** To encourage those who have talent and dedication to photojournalism, and who need financial help to continue their

## National Press Photographers Foundation *(continued)*

studies. **Focus:** Photojournalism. **Qualif.:** Applicants must be either undergraduates in their first three and one-half years in college or offer some indication of acceptance to post-graduate work. **Criteria:** Those selected are most deserving of financial need and can demonstrate potential in photojournalism.

**Funds Avail.:** $1,000. **No. of Awards:** 1. **To Apply:** Applicants must provide evidence of financial need, send a letter of recommendation from a college instructor, and submit a portfolio that includes at least five single images in addition to a picture story. Caption information for the prints or slides is useful but should be concise. Applicant's choice of school must be in the United States or Canada and the scholarship award must be used at the beginning of the next semester. Images will not be returned and should be 8x10 unmounted prints or 35mm duplicate slides. Persons may apply for as many different scholarships as they choose but will only be awarded one in any given year. **Deadline:** March 1.

**Remarks:** Bob East was a veteran photographer for 45 years at the Miami Herald, until his death in 1985. In 1961 he built the Monthly National Clip Contest and was the National Press Photography Association National Secretary for two terms. **Contact:** Questions about the scholarship should be addressed to the National Press Photographers Foundation at the above address (see entry 4341). Application materials go to Chuck Fadely, The Miami Herald, One Herald Plaza, Miami, FL 33132; telephone: (305)376-3750.

## • 4344 • Joseph Ehrenreich Scholarships *(Undergraduate/Scholarship)*

**Purpose:** To encourage those who have talent and dedication to photojournalism, and who need financial help to continue their studies. **Focus:** Photojournalism. **Qualif.:** Students must be enrolled in a recognized four-year college or university having courses in photojournalism and must be continuing in a program leading to a bachelor's degree. They must have at least one-half year of undergraduate schooling remaining at the time of the award. The awards are intended for those with journalism potential, but with little opportunity and great need. **Criteria:** Those selected are most deserving of financial need and can demonstrate potential in photojournalism.

**Funds Avail.:** $1,000. **No. of Awards:** 5. **To Apply:** Applicants must submit an application, portfolio, and a letter of recommendation from a college instructor. The portfolio should demonstrate evidence of photo aptitude. For photographers, the portfolio should contain a minimum of six pictures (a picture story counts as one) with the applicant's name printed clearly on the back of each or on slide margins (keep caption information concise); for picture editors, three tear sheets; for video journalists, a sample tape. Images will not be returned and should be 8x10 unmounted prints or 35mm duplicate slides. Applicant's choice of school must be in the United States or Canada and the scholarship award must be used at the beginning of the next semester. **Deadline:** March 1.

**Remarks:** This scholarship is the oldest continually-offered scholarship of the NPPF. The funds for the scholarship honoring Joseph Ehrenreich have been provided by his widow, Mrs. Amelia Ehrenreich. **Contact:** Questions about the scholarship should be addressed to the National Press Photographers Foundation at the above address (see entry 4341). Application materials go to Tony Spina, 3525 Squirrel Rd., Bloomfield, MI 48304; telephone: (313)646-7286.

## • 4345 • Kit C. King Graduate Scholarship *(Graduate/Scholarship)*

**Purpose:** To encourage those who have talent and dedication to photojournalism, and who need financial help to continue their studies. **Focus:** Photojournalism. **Qualif.:** The scholarship is open to anyone pursuing an advanced degree in photojournalism and who can provide some indication of acceptance to an accredited graduate program in photojournalism. **Criteria:** Those selected are

most deserving of financial need and can demonstrate potential in photojournalism.

**Funds Avail.:** $500. **No. of Awards:** 1. **To Apply:** Applicants must provide evidence of financial need and send a letter of recommendation from a college instructor. They are also required to submit a philosophy and goals statement and a portfolio, both of which should demonstrate talent and initiative in documentary photojournalism. For photographers, the portfolio should contain a minimum of six pictures (a picture story counts as one) with the applicant's name printed clearly on the back of each print or on slide margins (keep caption information concise); for picture editors, three tear sheets; for video journalists, a sample tape. Images will not be returned and should be 8x10 mounted prints or 35mm duplicate slides. Applicant's choice of school must be in the United States or Canada and the scholarship award must be used at the beginning of the next semester. **Deadline:** March 1.

**Remarks:** Kit King was the Chief Photographer at the Spokesman-Review and Spokane Chronicle. His trademark was his gritty style of documentary photojournalism, and he twice won the title of Photographer of the Year in Region 11 of the National Press Photographers Association. **Contact:** Questions about the scholarship should be addressed to the National Press Photographers Foundation at the above address (see entry 4341). Application materials go to Scott Sines, Director of Photography and Graphics, The Spokesman-Review, W. 999 Riverside Ave., Spokane, Washington 99210.

## • 4346 • NPPF Still Scholarship *(Undergraduate/Scholarship)*

**Purpose:** To encourage those who have talent and dedication to photojournalism, and who need financial help to continue their studies. **Focus:** Photojournalism. **Qualif.:** Students must be enrolled in a recognized four-year college or university having courses in photojournalism and must be continuing in a program leading to a bachelor's degree. They must have at least one-half year of undergraduate schooling remaining at the time of the award. The awards are intended for those with journalism potential, but with little opportunity and great need. **Criteria:** Those selected are most deserving of financial need and can demonstrate potential in photojournalism.

**Funds Avail.:** $1,000. **No. of Awards:** 1. **To Apply:** Applicants must submit an application, portfolio, and a letter of recommendation from a college instructor. The portfolio should demonstrate evidence of photo aptitude, and contain the following: for photographers, a minimum of six pictures (a picture story counts as one) with the applicant's name printed clearly on each print or on the slide margins (keep captions concise); for picture editors, three tear sheets; for video journalists, a sample tape. Applicant's choice of school must be in the United States or Canada and the scholarship award must be used at the beginning of the next semester. Images will not be returned and should be 8x10 unmounted prints or 35mm duplicate slides. **Deadline:** March 1. **Contact:** Questions about the scholarship should be addressed to the National Press Photographers Foundation at the above address (see entry 4341). Application materials go to Bill Sanders, 1252 Selkirk Court, Cary, NC 27511; telephone (919)467-0888.

## • 4347 • NPPF Television News Scholarship *(Undergraduate/Scholarship)*

**Purpose:** To encourage those who have talent and dedication to photojournalism in television news, and who need financial help to continue their studies. **Focus:** Photojournalism. **Qualif.:** Students must be enrolled in a recognized four-year college or university having courses in TV news photojournalism and must be continuing in a program leading to a bachelor's degree. They must be in their junior or senior year when the award is given. **Criteria:** The awards are intended for those with television news photojournalism potential, but with little opportunity and great need.

**Funds Avail.:** $1,000. **No. of Awards:** 1. **To Apply:** Applicants must submit an entry form and submit it along with one 3/4 inch video tape containing examples of their work, which should be no more than three complete stories (each with a minimum of one and one-half minutes in length) with voice narration and natural sound. They are also required to submit a one-page biographical sketch, including a personal statement, detailing their professional goals, and a letter of recommendation from a college professor or advisor. Applicants' choice of school must be in the United States or Canada. Images will not be returned and should be duplicates of the original copies. **Deadline:** March 1. **Contact:** Questions about the scholarship should be addressed to the National Press Photographers Foundation at the above address (see entry 4341). Application materials go to David Dary, Director of the School of Journalism and Mass Communication, University of Oklahoma, Norman, OK 73019-0270.

---

**• 4348 •**
**National Puerto Rican Coalition, Inc.**
1700 K St. NW, Ste. 500        *Ph:* (202)223-3915
Washington, DC 20006          *Fax:* (202)429-2223
*E-mail:* nprc@aol.com
*URL:* http://www.incacorp.com/nprc

**• 4349 • Phillip Morris Public Policy Fellowship**
*(Professional Development/Fellowship)*

**Purpose:** To teach national political advocacy skills to recent college graduates. **Focus:** Political science, public affairs, government. **Qualif.:** Applicants must be recent undergraduates with an interest in government and public policy, excellent written and communication skills, and a demonstrated commitment to and knowledge of the Puerto Rican community.

**Funds Avail.:** $23,000 plus health, life and disability insurance. **No. of Awards:** One **To Apply:** Applicants must submit a cover letter, resume, writing sample no longer than five pages, names and addresses of three references. **Deadline:** April 14. **Contact:** Jennie Torres-Lewis.

---

**• 4350 •**
**National Radio Astronomy Observatory**
520 Edgemont Rd.               *Ph:* (804)296-0225
Charlottesville, VA 22903-2475   *Fax:* (804)296-0385
*E-mail:* pjackson @nrao.edu
*URL:* http://knidos.cc.meto.edu.tr:8002/ful/ful034

*The National Radio Astromony Observatory manages observing facilities for radio astronomical research in New Mexico, Arizona, and West Virginia.*

**• 4351 • Jansky Fellowships** *(Postdoctorate/ Fellowship)*

**Purpose:** To allow postdoctoral scholars to formulate and conduct investigations within the Observatory's wide framework of interests. **Focus:** Astronomy, Computer Science, Electrical Engineering, and Physics. **Qualif.:** Applicants may be of any nationality. Candidate must have a Ph.D. in a relevant field. Awards are tenable at research facilities managed by NRAO in Virginia, West Virginia, Arizona, and New Mexico. Scholars may conduct investigations independently or in collaboration with other scientists. A focus on topics in radio astronomy is desirable though not essential. **Criteria:** Preference is given to candidates who received their degree within the last two years.

**Funds Avail.:** Approximately $33,000/year, plus benefits. **To Apply:** Applicants must write to the director for application guidelines. Curriculum vitae, a brief statement of proposed research activity and three letters of recommendation are required. **Deadline:**

December 15 **Contact:** Phyllis Jackson or Robert Brown at the above address (see entry 4350).

**• 4352 • NRAO Summer Student Research Assistantships** *(Graduate, Undergraduate/Other)*

**Purpose:** To permit qualified students to work closely with staff scientists of NRAO on radio astronomy programs in progress at the Observatory. **Focus:** Astronomy, Computer Science, Electrical Engineering, Physics. **Qualif.:** Applicants must be U.S. citizens attending U.S. institutions and either undergraduate or graduate students. Awards are tenable in the summer at research facilities managed by NRAO in Virginia, West Virginia, Arizona, and New Mexico. The site at which a summer student will work depends on the location of the NRAO supervisor to whom the student is assigned. Student preferences will be accommodated, whenever possible. **Criteria:** Preference is given to undergraduates.

**Funds Avail.:** $1,200/month, plus travel and expenses. **No. of Awards:** 18. **To Apply:** Applicants must write to the program director for application forms and guidelines. A letter describing educational background and scientific experience, transcripts, and three or four letters of recommendation will be expected. **Deadline:** January 19. Notification by March 1. **Contact:** Summer Student Program Director at the above address (see entry 4350).

---

**• 4353 •**
**National Research Council of Canada**
Human Resources Branch
Montreal Rd., M-58            *Ph:* (613)993-9134
Ottawa, ON, Canada K1A 0R6    *Fax:* (613)990-7669
*URL:* http://www.cisti.nrc.ca/

*The National Research Council of Canada was formerly known as the Canadian International Development Agency.*

**• 4354 • National Research Council of Canada Research Associateships** *(Postdoctorate/Other)*

**Purpose:** To give promising scientists and engineers an opportunity to work on challenging research problems in fields of interest to the NRC as a stage in the development of their research careers. **Qualif.:** Applicants must have acquired, within the last five years, a PhD in natural science or engineering or expect to obtain the degree before taking up the associateship. **Criteria:** Selections are made on a competitive basis. Demonstrated ability to perform original research in the chosen field is the main criterion. Associateships are open to nationals of all countries although preference will be given to Canadians.

**Funds Avail.:** Associates are offered appointments to the staff of the NRC on a term basis and receive salaries and benefits currently available to members of the permanent staff. Salaries are taxable and subject to deductions. An allowance is provided toward the cost of travel for the associate, spouse, and children. At any given time, there are approximately 200 research associates employed by the NRC. The initial appointment is normally for a two-year term and may be renewed, subject to performance and NRC needs. **To Apply:** Application must be made on special forms, which may be obtained from the Research Associates Office, National Research Council of Canada, Ottawa, Ontario K1A 0R6. **Deadline:** No specific deadline. Applications are active for one year from the date of receipt and may be renewed. An appointment may be taken up at any mutually acceptable time within the calendar year in which the offer is made.

**Remarks:** The NRC offers research associateships tenable only in its 20 laboratories, located throughout Canada. Approximately 1,000 applications are received by NRC. **Contact:** RA Program Officer at the above address (see entry 4353). Telephone:(613)993-9134.

---

Awards are arranged alphabetically below their administering organizations

• 4355 •

# National Research Council - Fellowship Office
2101 Constitution Ave., NW
Washington, DC 20418       Ph: (202)334-2872
E-mail: infofell@nas.edu
URL: http://www.fellowships.nas.edu

## • 4356 • Ford Foundation Postdoctoral Fellowships for Minorities (Postdoctorate/Fellowship)

**Purpose:** To support postdoctoral research by U.S. minority scholars. **Focus:** Behavioral Sciences, Biological Sciences, Engineering, Humanities, Mathematics, Physical Sciences, Social Sciences. **Qualif.:** Applicant must be a U.S. citizen or national and a member of one of the following minority groups: Alaskan Native, Native American Indian, Black/African American, Mexican American/Chicano, Native Pacific Islander, or Puerto Rican. Applicant must have held a Ph.D. or Sc.D. degree for not more than seven years by the application deadline. Candidate must be engaged in, or planning to begin, a teaching or research career, and the proposed fellowship must further his/her career in education. Fellowships are intended for full-time research at an institution of higher learning, normally in the United States. Candidates must have the endorsement, as well as the support of a faculty member who is willing to act as fellowship sponsor. Awards will not be made to individuals in professions such as medicine, law, social work, or library science; or in such areas as business administration and management, fine arts, health sciences, home economics, speech pathology and audiology, personnel and guidance, or education.

**Funds Avail.:** $30,000, plus $3,000 for travel and relocation. **No. of Awards:** 20. **To Apply:** Write for application form and guidelines, available in September. Submit form with proposed plan of study or research, curriculum vitae, a list of publications and courses taught, transcripts, and an abstract of dissertation. Four letters of reference, one of which should be from the department chair at home institution, and a letter of endorsement from proposed host institution should be sent directly to the Fellowship Office. **Deadline:** January 6. Notification by early April. **Contact:** Fellowship Office at the above address (see entry 4355).

## • 4357 • Ford Foundation Predoctoral and Dissertation Fellowships for Minorities (Doctorate/Fellowship)

**Purpose:** To support graduate research by U.S. minority scholars. **Focus:** Behavioral Sciences, Biological Sciences, Engineering, Humanities, Mathematics, Physical Sciences, Social Sciences. **Qualif.:** Applicant must be a U.S. citizen or national and a member of one of the following minority groups: Alaskan Native, Native American Indian, African Americans, Mexican American/Chicano, Native Pacific Islander, or Puerto Rican. Applicant for the Predoctoral Fellowship must be beginning, or planning to begin, a Ph.D. or Sc.D. degree program in one of the fields listed above. Applicant for the Dissertation Fellowship must have finished all required coursework for the Ph.D. or Sc.D. degree except the dissertation defense, and expect to complete dissertation during the fellowship year. Awards will not be made to individuals studying in fields such as medicine, law, social work, library science, business administration and management, fine arts, health sciences, home economics, speech pathology and audiology, personnel and guidance, fine arts, performing arts, or education. Fellowships are tenable at any accredited U.S. institution of higher learning. **Criteria:** Merit-based.

**Funds Avail.:** Dissertation: $21,000; Predoctoral: $14,000/year; 7,500 to host institution. **No. of Awards:** Dissertation: 20; Predoctoral: 50. **To Apply:** Write for application materials and guidelines, available in September. First, submit a preliminary application Office Card, which will be included with application materials. The Fellowship Office will send a complete application packet to qualified candidates. Then, submit forms with proposed plan of study/research, a description of previous research

experience, and official transcripts. Predoctoral candidates must also submit Graduate Record Examination scores. Dissertation candidates must include verification of doctoral degree status, a curriculum vitae, an abstract of dissertation and reference reports from four referees. **Deadline:** Mid-November. Notification in early April. **Contact:** Fellowship Office at the above address (see entry 4355).

## • 4358 • Howard Hughes Medical Institute Predoctoral Fellowships in Biological Sciences (Postdoctorate/Fellowship)

**Purpose:** To promote excellence in biomedical research by helping prospective researchers with exceptional promise obtain high quality graduate education. **Focus:** Biological sciences, including biochemistry, bioinformatics, biophysics, biostatistics, cell biology, developmental biologoy, epidemiology, genetics, immunology, mathematical and computational biology, microbiology, molecular biology, neuroscience, pharmacology, physicology, structural biology and virology. **Qualif.:** Applicants must be students at or near the beginning of their graduate study toward a research-based doctoral degree.

**Funds Avail.:** Annual stipend of $16,000 to each fellow and an allowance of $15,000 to the fellowship institution in lieu of tuition and fees. **No. of Awards:** 80.

## • 4359 • NASA Administrator's Fellowship Program (Other/Fellowship)

**Purpose:** To enhance the professional development of NASA employees and the science and engineering faculty of Historically Black Colleges and Universities, Hispanic Serving Institutitons, and Tribal Colleges and Universities. **Focus:** Science and engineering. **Qualif.:** Applicants must be U.S. citizens, tenuretrack faculty members at an HBCU, HSI, or TCU and must hold a PhD or ScD in science, engineering, or mathematics with expertise in NASA-related fields. NASA employee applicants must be full-time career employees at the GS-13 level or above.

**Funds Avail.:** Faculty recipients receive a stipend equal to their current salary, full compensation for relocation, and other travel expenses incurred as part of the program NASA employee recipients will retain their current salaries and status as NASA employees. All relocation and other travel expenses associated with the fellowship will be provided. **No. of Awards:** Six to science and engineering faculty of HBCUs, HSIs and TCUs to conduct research at a NASA center, another government agency, a research university, or a private sector organization. Six for NASA employees to serve as exchange scientists/engineers/managers at minority-serving institutions from six months to a year. **Deadline:** January.

## • 4360 • U.S. Department of Education OERI Visiting Scholars Fellowship (Other/Fellowship)

**Purpose:** Seeks fellows to assume a 9 to 18 month residency in Washington, DC at one of the five National Research Institutes that are a part of the OERI. **Qualif.:** Awards are made to scholars, researchers, policy makers, education practitioners, librarians or statisticians engaged in the use, collection, and dissemination of information about education and educational research. **Criteria:** Topics for study will be generated by the applicants from a list of OERI Research Priorities, and mission statements from the five institutes. **No. of Awards:** Each of the five institutes will award one to tow fellowships. The five institutes are: The National Institute on Student Achievement, Curriculum, and Assessment; The National Institute on the Education of At-Risk Students; The National Institute on Educational Governance, Finance, Policy-Making, and Management; The National Institute on Early Childhood Development andEducation; and The National Institute on Postsecondary Education, Libraries, and Lifelong Learning.

• **4361** • **U.S. Department of Energy Integrated Manufacturing & Processing Predoctoral Fellowships** *(Doctorate/Fellowship)*

**Purpose:** Seeks to create a pool of PhDs trained in the integrated approach to manufacturing and processing. **Focus:** Engineering and applied science. **Qualif.:** Applicants must be U.S. citizens or national, and permanent resident aliens of the United States seeking research-based PhDs in areas related to integrated manufacturing and processing. Must also have received a master's degree, or expect to receive a master's degree before tenure would begin.

**Funds Avail.:** Annual stipend of $20,000 to each fellow and an allowance of up to $15,000 to the fellowship institution to cover tuition and fees. **No. of Awards:** 12. **Deadline:** December.

• **4362** •

**National Restaurant Association - Educational Foundation**
250 S Wacker Dr., Ste 1400
Chicago, IL 60606-5834

Ph: (312)715-6760
Fax: (312)715-0220
Free: 800-765-2122

*E-mail:* cblasius@foodtrain.org
*URL:* http://www.restaurant.org

• **4363** • **Industry Assistance Grants** *(Other/Grant)*

**Purpose:** For industry professionsl wanting to furhter their education and enhance their career opportunities. **Focus:** Foodservice and hospitality. **Qualif.:** Must not be enrolled as a student in a foodeservice/hospitality program. Have a minimun of three years foodservice supervisory, assistant management or management experience. Currently be employed in the foodservice industry. Demonstrate a commitment to the industry.

**Funds Avail.:** Valued at $1000 each. Each grant includes written materials, videos, and an exam, which upon successful passing earns a cerficiate of completion for the program. **Deadline:** July 1.

• **4364** • **National Restaurant Association Educational Foundation Undergraduate Scholarship for High School Seniors** *(Undergraduate/Scholarship)*

**Purpose:** To educate and recruit qualified students into the restaurant industry. **Focus:** Culinary, restaurant, and hospitality majors. **Qualif.:** Applicants must be high school seniors with a minimum 2.75 GPA; have taken a minimum of one foodservice-related course with a minimum B grade or have performed a minimum of 250 hours of restaurant and hospitality work experience verified by pay stubs or letter(s) form employer(s); have applied and gained acceptance to a hospitality-related post-secondary program, either full-time or part-time and plan to enroll in a minimum of three courses per term.

**Funds Avail.:** $2000. **To Apply:** A letter of recommendation on letterhead from a current or previous teacher or employer must be submitted. **Deadline:** March 1.

**Remarks:** Awards are distributed once a thank you letter from the recipient has been sent to the sponsoring organization and a copy has been forwarded to the Scholarship Program Coordinator at the Foundation.

• **4365** • **National Restaurant Association Graduate Degree Scholarship** *(Graduate/Scholarship)*

**Purpose:** To assist industry professionals pursuing a post-secondary degree in a restaurant and hospitality program. **Qualif.:** Applicants must be U.S. citizens or permanent residents attending school within the U.S. or U.S. territories, and may be graduate students (masters or doctorate). Applicants must have taken a minimum of one foodservice-related course and have received at least a B- and/or must have performed a minimum of 1,000 hours of restaurant and hospitality work.

**Funds Avail.:** $2,000. **No. of Awards:** 10. **To Apply:** Write for application form, available November 1. **Deadline:** February 15.

**Remarks:** Scholarship awards are distributed once a thank-you letter from the recipient has been sent.

• **4366** • **National Restaurant Association Teacher Work/Study Grant** *(Professional Development/Work Study)*

**Purpose:** Grants provide opportunities for full-time teachers and administrators to obtain hands-on work experience in the industry. This experience should enrich and update their knowledge of the industry and increase their capability to relate that knowledge to their students. **Focus:** Food service, Hospitality. **Qualif.:** Candidates must be full-time teachers or administrators in a hotel/restaurant/institutional management, food service, culinary arts, or commercial food program at an educational institution at secondary and post-secondary schools. Applicants must continue as full-time teachers or administrators, or be full-time students pursuing an advanced degree during the next academic year. Candidates must arrange for 80-320 hours of full-time employment with one employer, working a minimum of 35-40 hours per week. The 8-10 weeks of employment need not be consecutive, but the period of employment must be within five consecutive months of the academic year. These must be line or staff positions; consultant or researcher positions do not qualify. Former winners must allow one year to elapse before applying for another grant.

**Funds Avail.:** $700-3,000. In addition, while working, recipients must be paid by the employer at a rate commensurate with the position. Payment must be made directly to the recipients, not through their schools. **No. of Awards:** 20. **To Apply:** Candidates must submit a formal application, a letter of recommendation from their academic supervisor, and a letter from their prospective employer indicating a willingness to employ the applicant as proposed (family businesses do not qualify). Winners are selected by an independent grants committee composed of educators and industry leaders by April 15. **Deadline:** February 15. Applications are available after November 1. **Contact:** The Educational Foundation at the above address (see entry 4362).

• **4367** • **National Restaurant Association Undergraduate Scholarships** *(Undergraduate/Scholarship)*

**Purpose:** To financially benefit undergraduate students. **Focus:** Food service, Hospitality. **Qualif.:** Candidates must be full-time students working toward an undergraduate food service/hospitality degree for the full academic year. They must have 1,000 hours of work experience in the food service/hospitality industry and have a cumulative grade point average of at least 3.0 on a 4.0 scale. Eligible majors include: hotel, restaurant, and institutional management, culinary arts, dietetics, food science and technology, and other food service related curricula, including manufacturing and distribution.

**Funds Avail.:** $1,000-5,000. **No. of Awards:** 100. **To Apply:** Candidates must submit a formal application and transcripts. Applications are available after December 31. **Deadline:** March 1.

**Remarks:** The foundation typically receives approximately 1,000 applications. **Contact:** Students should contact their schools' program directors for information and applications.

• **4368** • **ProMgmt. Scholarship** *(Other/Scholarship)*

**Focus:** Foodservice or hospitality. **Qualif.:** Must attend schools which are ProMgmt. Must be a full or part-time student or a home-study student, have successfully completed at least two ProMgmt. courses, and demonstrate commitment to the industry. **Criteria:** Students are evaluated on industry related work experience, which reflects commitment to a foodservice/hospitality career.

*National Restaurant Association - Educational Foundation (continued)*

**Funds Avail.:** $850. **No. of Awards:** Up to five per school. **To Apply:** Applicants are required to write an essay on their career goals in the industry.

**• 4369 • ProStart Scholarships** *(High School/ Scholarship)*

**Focus:** Foodservice or hospitality. **Qualif.:** High school seniors enrolled in the ProStart Program and attending a ProStart Partner School. Must have successfully completed the two ProStart Programs, and have selected a two or four year college or university to pursue an undergraduate degree.

**Funds Avail.:** $1000 or $2000, based on the school selected. **Deadline:** March 15.

---

**• 4370 •**
**National Roofing Foundation**
O'Hare International Center
10255 W. Higgins, Ste. 600                    *Ph:* (847)299-9070
Rosemont, IL 60018                            *Fax:* (847)299-1183
*E-mail:* mca@mca.net
*URL:* http://www.mca.net

**• 4371 • National Roofing Foundation Scholarship Award** *(Undergraduate/Scholarship)*

**Purpose:** To provide scholarship assistance to employees immediate family of employees, or immediate family of NRCA. **Qualif.:** Applicants must be United States citizens and full-time students (high school senior, undergraduate, or graduate) undertaking architecture, engineering, or another curriculum related to the roofing industry. **Criteria:** Academic performance, faculty recommendation, extracurricular activities, employment experience, and a demonstrated interest in the construction industry.

**Funds Avail.:** $1000/year for up to four years **To Apply:** Candidates must submit an official application, which may be obtained by contacting the foundation. **Deadline:** January 31. **Contact:** Scholarship Coordinator at same address.

---

**• 4372 •**
**National Scholarship Trust Fund of the Graphic Arts**
200 Deer Run Rd.                              *Ph:* (412)741-6860
Sewickley, PA 15143                           *Fax:* (412)741-2311
*E-mail:* nstf@gatf.org
*URL:* http://www.nstf@gatf.lm.com

**• 4373 • National Scholarship Trust Fund of the Graphic Arts Fellowships** *(Graduate/Fellowship)*

**Purpose:** To promote research and study in one or more fields of study in the areas of mathematics, chemistry, physics, industrial education, engineering, and business technology, as it relates to applications in the printing, publishing, and packaging industries. **Focus:** Graphic Arts, Printing, Publishing. **Qualif.:** Applicants must plan to seek employment at the managerial or educational level in the graphic communications industry, have demonstrated ability and special aptitude for advanced education, and be enrolled in an educational institution prior to the beginning of the fellowship tenure. Recipients are required to spend full time on advanced

scientific study during the period of their awards, except for teaching or work experiences as may be assigned by the institution in order to contribute to the academic progress of the fellow. Fellows are expected to carry out the program of study and research as proposed at the time of application. **Criteria:** Fellows are selected based on academic records, recommendations, biographical records, and scientific aptitude achievement test scores.

**Funds Avail.:** Awards range from $1,500 to $3,000. Recipient's may be permitted to receive an additional fellowship, assistantship, scholarship, or similar award with the prior approval of NSTF. Permission to receive any such award is dependent upon proof that the additional stipend does not conflict with the objectives of the NSTF fellowship. **To Apply:** Acceptance to an accredited college for graduate study is required prior to application. Applicants must supply to the NSTF evidence of enrollment, college or university transcripts, recommendations, and a plan of study and advance research. Fellowship applications are available from NSTF. The fellowship may be renewed upon application provided the fellow is successfully meeting the school's requirements. The National Scholarship Trust Fund reserves the right to give no awards if it feels no suitable candidates have applied. **Deadline:** Application materials must be received by the NSTF by January 10. Applications received after this date are disqualified.

**Remarks:** The fellowship program is sponsored jointly with the Technical Association of the Graphic Arts (TAGA). **Contact:** The National Scholarship Trust Fund at the address above.

**• 4374 • The National Scholarship Trust Fund Scholarships for High School Students** *(High School, Undergraduate/Scholarship)*

**Purpose:** To financially assist qualified and interested students in the development of executive careers in the printing, publishing, and packaging industry. **Focus:** Graphic Communications/Graphic Arts. **Qualif.:** Applicants must be full-time high school seniors or graduates who have not yet started college and who are interested in a career in graphic communications. **Criteria:** Candidates are judged on their academic records; rank in class; recommendations offered from guidance counselors, teachers, or principals; biographical records indicating academic honors; extracurricular interests; and other achievements.

**Funds Avail.:** $500 to $1,500 per academic year, in most cases, for each of four years. The award is paid directly to the college selected by the winner. Students must maintain a B average, and are awarded to full-time students only. Scholarship is renewable up to four years of college. **No. of Awards:** 100. **To Apply:** Candidates should apply for and take the Scholastic Aptitude Test (SAT) (PSAT/NMSQT and ACT scores are also acceptable). Completed applications should be submitted along with high school transcript and two completed recommendation forms (provided with application). Applicant must also submit intended courses of study found in college catalogs or departmental brochures. A No. 10 self-addressed, stamped envelope must be included to notify applicant of final standing in the competition. **Deadline:** Application deadline is March 1; transcripts, recommendation forms, and SAT/ACT scores are due by March 1.

**Remarks:** Approximately 150 nationally competitive scholarships are available for both college and high school-level applicants. Current recipients are given an honorary membership in the Graphic Arts Technical Foundation for the duration of their studies. NSTF also publishes the resumes of all graduating scholars annually and sends them to industry employers to aid those seeking employment.

**• 4375 • The National Scholarship Trust Fund Scholarships for Undergraduates** *(Other, Undergraduate/Scholarship)*

**Purpose:** To financially assist qualified and interested students in the development of executive careers in the print, publishing, and

---

packaging industry. **Focus:** Graphic Communications/Graphic Arts. **Qualif.:** Applicants must be college freshmen, sophomores, or juniors enrolled in a two- or four-year year program on a full-time basis who are interested in graphic communication. **Criteria:** Candidates are judged on their high school record, class rank, recommendations, and biographical records indicating academic honors, extracurricular interests, and other achievements.

**Funds Avail.:** $500 to $1,500, in most cases, for each of four years. Funds are paid directly to the school. Students must maintain a B average. **To Apply:** Candidates must submit with their applications transcript of high school grades (freshmen only) (Photocopies are acceptable) or college grades, and two recommendations (forms included with application), one completed by a college or university instructor or advisor, the second by another school representative or employer. **Deadline:** Application deadline is April 1. Transcripts, recommendations, and SAT/ACT scores are due April 1.

**Remarks:** Approximately 100 nationally competitive scholarships are available for both college and high school-level applicants. Recipients are given an honorary membership in the Graphic Arts Technical Foundation for the duration of their studies. NSTF also publishes the resumes of all graduating scholars each year and sends them to industry employers to aid those seeking employment.

---

• **4376** •
## National Scholastic Surfing Association
PO Box 495          *Ph:* (714)536-0445
Huntington Beach, CA 92648     *Fax:* (714)960-4380
*URL:* http://www.nssa.org/htm/home.htm

• **4377** •   **NSSA Scholarship** *(Undergraduate/ Scholarship)*

**Purpose:** To assist NSSA student members in the pursuit of undergraduate education and training. **Focus:** General Studies. **Qualif.:** Candidates must be current NSSA members in good standing and full-time students with a 3.0 or higher GPA. **Criteria:** Applicants are judged on scholastic achievement and improvement, academic promise, leadership, community and/or NSSA service, and career goals.

**Funds Avail.:** Variable; dependent on donations. **To Apply:** Scholarship applications are automatically received with membership. **Deadline:** June 1. **Contact:** Janice Aragon, NSSA Executive Director, at the above address (see entry 4376).

---

• **4378** •
## National Science Education Leadership Association - Thomas Edison/Max McGraw Scholarship Program
c/o Patricia J. McWethy
PO Box 5556          *Ph:* (703)524-8646
Arlington, VA 22205      *Fax:* (703)524-3929
*URL:* http://www.careers.com/A/0066.html

• **4379** •   **Thomas Edison/Max McGraw Scholarship** *(High School, Undergraduate/Scholarship)*

**Purpose:** To recognize outstanding science and engineering students and grant awards to candidates who demonstrate the inventive genius of Thomas Edison and Max McGraw. **Qualif.:** Applicants are students in grades 7 through 12 in public, private, and parochial schools. The Senior Division is for students in grades 10 through 12 and Junior Division for grades 7 through 9. Students compete in their grade division.

**Funds Avail.:** The two Grand Award Finalists selected receive $5,000 and $3,000 respectively. The eight remaining finalists each receive $1,500 scholarships. **No. of Awards:** 10 **To Apply:** Candidates must submit no more than two copies of a 1,000-word or five-page proposal, which may be an abstract of an already completed experiment or a project idea that deals with a practical application in the fields of science and/or engineering. Applicants must also submit two copies of a letter of recommendation from their teacher/sponsor that indicates how the student exemplifies the creativity and ingenuity demonstrated by the life and work of inventors Edison and McGraw. There is no other application form, but the proposal's cover sheet must contain a title; the student's name, address, phone number, and grade level; and the teacher/sponsor's name, name of the school, school address and phone number. Ten finalists, five in each division, are chosen through their applications. Finalists present their projects before a panel of judges, who select the Grand Award Scholar finalists. Travel and housing expenses for finalists will be reimbursed. **Deadline:** December 1. **Contact:** The National Science Supervisors Association at the above address (see entry 4378).

---

• **4380** •
## National Science Teachers Association
                   *Fax:* (703)522-6193
1840 Wilson Blvd.
Arlington, VA 22201-3000     *Free:* 888-255-4242
*E-mail:* duracell@nsta.com
*URL:* http://www.nsta.org/programs/duracell

• **4381** •   **Duracell/NSTA Scholarship Competition** *(High School, Other/Prize, Scholarship)*

**Purpose:** To allow students to win U.S. Saving Bonds to use toward college by designing and building working devices powered by Duracell batteries. **Qualif.:** Students in grades 6 through 12 residing in the United States or U.S. Territories may enter either individually or in teams of two.

**Funds Avail.:** Two first place $20,000 U.S. Savings Bonds; four second place $10,000 U.S. Savings Bonds; ten third place $3,000 U.S. Savings Bonds; 24 fourth place $1,000 U.S. Savings Bonds; and 60 fifth place $500 U.S. Saving Bonds. The first and second place winners, their parents, and teacher/sponsors will be flown to the annual awards events at the NSTA National Convention. Teachers of the top six prize winners each receive $2,000 gift certificates for computers and accessories. **To Apply:** Applicants should obtain an entry form and rules from their science teacher, or write to the NSTA. To enter, students should design and build a device which runs on batteries, write a two-page description describing the device and its uses, draw a schematic (wiring diagram) of the device, and photograph the device. Once the information has been submitted, the top 100 finalists will be notified to send in their actual devices for final judging. **Deadline:** Mid-January. **Contact:** Duracell/NSTA Scholarship Competition, National Science Teachers Association, at the above address (see entry 4380).

---

**• 4382 •**
## National Sculpture Society
1177 Avenue of the Americas     *Ph:* (212)764-5645
New York, NY 10036     *Fax:* (212)764-5651
*E-mail:* nss1893@aol.com
*URL:* http://sculpturereview.com

**• 4383 • Alex J. Ettl Grant** *(Professional Development/Grant)*

**Purpose:** To recognize a realist or figurative sculptor who has demonstrated outstanding ability and a commitment to sculpture in his/her life's work. **Focus:** Sculpture. **Qualif.:** Applicant must be a U.S. citizen or resident. Applicant may not be a professional member of NSS. There are no restrictions as to how the grant funds may be used.

**Funds Avail.:** $4,000 to $5,000. **No. of Awards:** One. **To Apply:** Send SASE for application guidelines, which include a brief biographical sketch, including honors, commissions, education, exhibitions and other pertinent information, and at least ten 8" x 10" photographs of work. Photographs should be labeled on back with the sculptor's name, title of work, size, medium, and date of execution. **Deadline:** September 30. The grant is presented on the second Monday of December. **Contact:** Gwen Pier, Executive Director, at the above address (see entry 4382).

**• 4384 • National Sculpture Society Scholarships** *(Other, Professional Development/Scholarship)*

**Focus:** Figurative or Realist Sculpture. **Qualif.:** Applicants must be students of figurative or representational sculpture.

**Funds Avail.:** $6,000 ($ 1,000 each) All scholarship monies are awarded directly to the educational institution through which the student applies. Proof that course work has been successfully completed should be sent to the Society at the end of the term. It may be in the form of a report card, a progress report from a professor or administrator, or any other verifiable indication that the recipients are using the scholarship funds towards their artistic education. **No. of Awards:** 6. **To Apply:** A letter of application including a brief biography and explanation of background in sculpture, two letters of recommendation, six to ten photographs of work by the applicant, and proof of financial aid should be submitted. **Deadline:** May 31, For the next academic year. **Contact:** Gwen Pier, Executive Director, at the above address (see entry 4382).

**• 4385 •**
## National Sea Grant College Program Office
Attn: Fellowship Director
1335 E. West Highway     *Ph:* (301)713-2431
Silver Spring, MD 20910     *Fax:* (301)713-0799
*E-mail:* consert@ccmail.orst.edu
*URL:* http://www.hmsc.orst.edu/education/whales/seagrant.htm

**• 4386 • Dean John Knauss Marine Policy Fellowship** *(Graduate/Fellowship)*

**Purpose:** To provide educational experience to students who have an interest in marine, ocean, and Great Lakes resources and in the national policy decisions affecting those resources. **Focus:** Marine, ocean, and great lake biology. **Qualif.:** Applicants must be students at the master or Ph.D. level in a marine-related field at an accredited institution of higher education. **Criteria:** Selection of fellowship is based on academic ability, communication skills, diversity and appropriateness of academic background, additional qualifying experience, support of a major professor, support of a

Sea Grant Director, geographical representation, disciplinary balance and evidence of ability to work with others.

**Funds Avail.:** $36,000 per year to be disbursed between salary and living expenses. The length of the assignment is one year (non-renewable), starting usually between January 15 and February 1. **To Apply:** Applicants apply through any state Sea Grant Program. Applicants should submit applications to state Sea Grant Directors who then screen the applications for forwarding to the NSGO. Each application must include a personal and academic resume or curriculum vitae; an education and career goal statement form the applicant with emphasis on what they expect from the experiences in the way of career development (not to exceed two pages); no more than two letters of recommendation with at least one being from the student's major professor; a letter of endorsement from the sponsoring state Sea Grant Director; and copies of undergraduate and graduate student transcripts. **Deadline:** October. **Contact:** State Sea Grant Directors at the above address (see entry 4385).

**• 4387 •**
## National Slovak Society of the United States of America
333 Technology Dr., Ste. 112
Canonsburg, PA 15317     *Free:* 800-488-1890
*E-mail:* info@NSSUSA.org

**• 4388 • PVR Scholarship Award** *(Graduate/Scholarship)*

**Purpose:** To assist members of the National Slovak Society to obtain a college education. **Focus:** General Studies. **Qualif.:** Applicants must be members of the National Slovak Society for two years or more and maintain a 2.0 GPA to receive awards in their sophomore, junior, and senior years. They must also have a minimum of $3,000 of permanent insurance with the society. **Criteria:** Based on need.

**Funds Avail.:** Determined by board of directors annually. **No. of Awards:** 56. **To Apply:** Applicants must submit financial aid statement, parents' confidential financial statement, biography, and college board or SAT scores. **Deadline:** May 1. **Contact:** David G. Blazek, President, at the above address (see entry 4387).

**• 4389 •**
## The National Society of the Colonial DAMES of America - Indian Nurse Scholarship Awards
4003 Indian Hills Rd.
Decatur, AL 35603     *Ph:* (256)353-7038

**• 4390 • The National Society of the Colonial Dames of America American Indian Nurse Scholarship Awards** *(Undergraduate/Scholarship)*

**Purpose:** To help Native Americans minister to their people. **Focus:** Nursing. **Qualif.:** Applicants must be American Indian high school graduates enrolled full-time in an accredited nursing program, where they have achieved good scholastic standing in the pre-nursing courses. They must also be within two years of completing the degree, maintaining the GPA required by the their school, in need of financial assistance, and should have a career goal directly related to the needs of the Indian people. In addition, candidates may not have received an Indian Health Service Scholarship. **Criteria:** Selection is based on need, academic standing, and career objectives.

**Funds Avail.:** A limited number of $500, $750, and $1,000 scholarships. **No. of Awards:** 10-16 per year. **To Apply:** Candidates must be recommended by high school counselor or school official. **Deadline:** May 1 for fall scholarship. **Contact:** Mrs. Joe Calvin at the above address (see entry 4389).

---

• 4391 •

**National Society Daughters of The American Revolution - DAR Scholarship Committee**
1776 D St., NW
Washington, DC 20006-5392          *Ph:* (202)879-3292
*URL:* http://www.dar.org

• 4392 • American Indian Scholarship
*(Undergraduate/Scholarship)*

**Purpose:** To assist Native American students of any age, any tribe, in any state striving to get an education. **Focus:** General studies. **Qualif.:** Applicants must be Native Americans in financial need; have a GPA of at least 2.75; and plan to attend a vocational school or a college or university at an undergraduate level. Graduate students can apply, but preference is given to undergraduates. **Criteria:** Judged on financial need and academic achievement.

**Funds Avail.:** $500 sent directly to the respective school. **To Apply:** For an application, send a self-addressed stamped envelope to the above address. Letter should give family history, financial status, and education objectives; official copy of last semester transcript or last transcript obtained and sent by previous school; three letters of recommendation from persons such as teachers, clergy, or others who have personally known applicant of a minimum of two years; and proof of American Indian blood as indicated by letter or proof papers must be submitted with application. All must be submitted in one mailing. ACT or SAT scores are not required. **Deadline:** July 1 for Fall Term; November 1 for Spring Term.

• 4393 • Mildred Louise Brackney Scholarships
*(Undergraduate/Scholarship)*

**Focus:** General Studies. **Qualif.:** Applicants must be United States citizens and graduates of either the Kate Duncan Smith DAR School or the Tamassee DAR School. **Criteria:** Applicants are judged on the basis of academic excellence, commitment to field of study, and financial need.

**Funds Avail.:** $1,000. **No. of Awards:** 6. **To Apply:** Applicants must submit a formal application, a financial need form, and proof of major. Transcripts of college work should also be sent, along with a list of extra-curricular activities, honors, and academic achievements. A statement of 1,000 words or less describing career goals and explaining the relevance of the college major to future professional objectives is required also. A copy of the student's birth certificate or naturalization papers and at least two but not more than four letters of recommendation from those who know the student's work are required. A self-addressed, stamped envelope is also required. Applications are available through each school's respective Scholarship Committee. All applicants must obtain a letter of sponsorship from a local DAR chapter. **Deadline:** February 15. Awards are made in late April.

**Remarks:** There are approximately 100 applicants annually. **Contact:** DAR Scholarship Committee at the above address (see entry 4391).

• 4394 • J.E. Caldwell Centennial Scholarships
*(Graduate/Scholarship)*

**Purpose:** To provide financial assistance to deserving students. **Focus:** Historic Preservation. **Qualif.:** Applicants may be either male or female and must be United States citizens who are pursuing a course of graduate study in the subject of Historic Preservation. No affiliation with the DAR is necessary, however, all applicants must be sponsored by a local DAR chapter. **Criteria:** Applicants are judged on the basis of academic excellence, commitment to field of study, and financial need.

**Funds Avail.:** Scholarships of $2,000. **To Apply:** Applicants must submit a formal application, a financial need form, a letter of sponsorship from their local DAR chapter, and proof of major. Transcripts of college work must also be provided, along with a list of extra-curricular activities, honors, and academic achievements. A statement of 1,000 words or less describing career goals and explaining the relevance of the college major to future professional objectives is also required, as well as a copy of the student's birth certificate or naturalization papers and at least two but not more than four letters of recommendation from those who know the student's work. All requests for information must be accompanied by a self-addressed, stamped envelope. **Deadline:** Applications must be sent to the National Chairman by February 15. Awards are made in April. **Contact:** DAR Scholarship Committee at the above address (see entry 4391).

• 4395 • Madeline Pickett Halbert Cogswell Nursing Scholarships *(Undergraduate/Scholarship)*

**Focus:** Nursing. **Qualif.:** Applicants must be United States citizens who are undergraduates currently enrolled in an accredited school of nursing in the United States. Applicants must be eligible for membership in NSDAR through relationship to a member of NSDAR, SR (Sons of the Revolution), or C.A.R. **Criteria:** Applicants are judged on the basis of academic excellence, commitment to field of study, and financial need.

**Funds Avail.:** $500. **To Apply:** Applicants must submit a formal application, a financial need form, and proof of major. Transcripts of college work should also be sent, along with a list of extra-curricular activities, honors, and academic achievements. A statement of 1,000 words or less describing career goals and explaining the relevance of the college major to future professional objectives is also required. A copy of the student's birth certificate or naturalization papers and at least two, but not more than four, letters of recommendation from those who know the student's work are required. A self-addressed, stamped envelope must be enclosed. **Deadline:** Applications must be sent to the National Chairman by February 15 or August 15. **Contact:** DAR Scholarship Committee at the above address (see entry 4391).

• 4396 • Lillian and Arthur Dunn Scholarships
*(Undergraduate/Scholarship)*

**Purpose:** To provide financial assistance to children of DAR members. **Focus:** General Studies. **Qualif.:** Candidates are children of active DAR members. Applicants must be United States citizens who are graduating seniors from an accredited high school and must be planning to attend an accredited college or university in the United States. Field of study is open. Applicant must be sponsored by Mother's DAR Chapter. **Criteria:** Applicants are judged on the basis of academic excellence, commitment to field of study, and financial need.

**Funds Avail.:** Up to four scholarships are awarded in the amount of $1,000 annually for a four-year college program, subject to an annual review of grades. Outstanding students may be renewed for an additional four years beyond first four. **To Apply:** Current information and application forms are available from Office of Committees at the above address. All requests must be accompanied by a self-addressed, stamped envelope. Applicants must submit a formal application, financial need form, and a copy of their birth certificate. Applicants must send a statement of 1,000 words or less regarding their academic and professional goals, a list of extra-curricular activities and honors, and an official transcript of their high school grades and test scores. At least two and not more than four letters of recommendation from those in authority at the student's high school who know the student's work are required. **Deadline:** Applications must be sent to the National Chairman by February 15.

---

## National Society Daughters of The American Revolution - DAR Scholarship Committee (continued)

**Remarks:** Typically, approximately 200 applications are received. **Contact:** DAR Scholarship Committee at the above address (see entry 4391).

### • 4397 • Enid Hall Griswold Memorial Scholarship
*(Undergraduate/Scholarship)*

**Purpose:** To provide financial assistance to deserving students. **Focus:** Political Science, History, Government, Economics. **Qualif.:** Applicants may be either male or female and must be United States citizens entering their junior or senior year at an accredited college or university in the United States. They must be majoring in political science, history, government, or economics. No affiliation with the DAR is necessary, however, all applicants must be sponsored by a local DAR chapter. **Criteria:** Applicants are judged on the basis of academic excellence, commitment to field of study, and financial need.

**Funds Avail.:** Up to four non-renewable awards of $1,000 each are available. **To Apply:** Applicants must submit a formal application, a financial need form, letter of sponsorships from their local DAR chapter, and proof of major. Transcripts of college work must also be provided, along with a list of extra-curricular activities, honors, and academic achievements. A statement of 1,000 words or less describing career goals and explaining the relevance of the college major to future professional objectives is also required, as well as a copy of the student's birth certificate or naturalization papers and at least two but not more than four letters of recommendation from those who know the student's work. All requests for information must be accompanied by a self-addressed, stamped envelope. **Deadline:** Applications are due to the National Chairman by February 15. **Contact:** DAR Scholarship Committee at the above address (see entry 4391).

### • 4398 • Margaret Howard Hamilton Scholarships
*(Undergraduate/Scholarship)*

**Purpose:** To provide financial assistance to learning-disabled students. **Focus:** General Studies. **Qualif.:** Applicants must be high school seniors who plan to enroll in the Jones Learning Center, a special program for the learning disabled, at the University of the Ozarks. Applicants must be U.S. citizens. **Criteria:** Applications are judged on the basis of academic excellence, commitment to the field of study, and financial need.

**Funds Avail.:** $1,000 annually for up to four years, subject to yearly transcript review. **To Apply:** Applications may be requested directly from the Learning Center. All applicants must obtain a letter of sponsorship from a local DAR chapter. **Deadline:** February 15. **Contact:** University of the Ozarks, 415 College Ave., Clarksville, AR 72830; (501) 754-3839.

### • 4399 • Caroline Holt Nursing Scholarships
*(Undergraduate/Scholarship)*

**Purpose:** To provide supplementary financial aid to undergraduate nursing students. **Focus:** Nursing. **Qualif.:** Applicants must be United States citizens. The award is for any year of undergraduate study in an accredited school of nursing. No affiliation with the DAR is necessary. However, all applicants must be sponsored by a local DAR Chapter. **Criteria:** Applicants are judged on the basis of academic excellence, commitment to field of study, and financial need.

**Funds Avail.:** $500. **No. of Awards:** 20 per year; 10 each deadline. **To Apply:** Write or call Office of Committees for application forms. A self-addressed, stamped envelope must accompany application requests. Applicants must submit a formal application, along with accompanying material, including: a statement of 1,000 words or less setting forth career goals and relevance of academic program to future profession; a financial need form; an official transcript of grades and test scores from high school; and a list of all extra-curricular activities, honors, and scholastic achievements. At least

two and not more than four letters of recommendation from persons in authority at the student's high school who know the student's work, and a photocopy of the student's birth certificate or naturalization papers are also required. Proof of acceptance into a school of nursing program is required prior to payment of the scholarship. **Deadline:** Applications must be sent to the National Chairman by February 15 or August 15.

**Remarks:** Approximately 400 applications are received. **Contact:** DAR Scholarship Committee at the above address (see entry 4391).

### • 4400 • Longman-Harris Scholarship
*(Undergraduate/Scholarship)*

**Purpose:** Awarded to graduating high school seniors of Kate Duncan Smith DAR School for financial assistance. **Focus:** General Studies. **Qualif.:** Applicants must be United States citizens and graduating seniors of Kate Duncan Smith DAR School. **Criteria:** Applicants are judged on the basis of academic excellence, commitment to field of study, and financial need.

**Funds Avail.:** Two scholarships of $2,000 each year for up to four years. Annual transcript review required for renewal. **To Apply:** Applications are through the school. Applicants must submit a formal application, a financial need form, and proof of major. Transcripts of college work should also be sent, along with a list of extra-curricular activities, honors, and academic achievements. A statement of 1,000 words or less describing career goals and explaining the relevance of the college major to future professional objectives and a copy of the student's birth certificate or naturalization papers and at least two but not more than four letters of recommendation from those who know the student's work also required. Students must submit a letter of sponsorship from a local DAR chapter and a self-addressed, stamped envelope. Applications are available through the KDS scholarship committee. **Deadline:** February 15. Awards are made in June. **Contact:** Kate Duncan Smith DAR School, Grant, Alabama 35747; (205)728-4236.

### • 4401 • Irene and Daisy MacGregor Memorial Scholarship *(Doctorate/Scholarship)*

**Purpose:** To provide financial assistance to deserving students. **Focus:** Medicine. **Qualif.:** Applicants may be either male or female and must be United States citizens who have been accepted into an accredited School of Medicine to pursue an M.D. No affiliation with the DAR is necessary, however, all applicants must be sponsored by a local DAR chapter. **Criteria:** Applicants are judged on the basis of academic excellence, commitment to field of study, and financial need.

**Funds Avail.:** Scholarships of $5,000 per year for four years. **To Apply:** Applicants must submit a formal application, a financial need form, letter of sponsorships from their local DAR chapter, and proof of major. Transcripts of college work must also be provided, along with a list of extra-curricular activities, honors, and academic achievements. A statement of 1,000 words or less describing career goals and explaining the relevance of the college major to future professional objectives is also required, as well as a copy of the student's birth certificate or naturalization papers and at least two but not more than four letters of recommendation from those who know the student's work. All requests for information must be accompanied by a self-addressed, stamped envelope. **Deadline:** Applications must be sent to the National Chairman by April 15. Awards are made in June. **Contact:** DAR Scholarship Committee at the above address (see entry 4391).

### • 4402 • NSDAR American History Scholarship
*(Undergraduate/Scholarship)*

**Purpose:** To provide financial assistance to finest students of American History. **Focus:** American History. **Qualif.:** Applicants are United States citizens and high school seniors who will major in American History at an accredited college or university in the United States. Applicants must be sponsored by a local DAR chapter. **Criteria:** Financial need, commitment to study of American History, and academic excellence.

**Funds Avail.:** $2,000 per year for 4 years (first place); second place: $1,000 per year for 4 years. **To Apply:** A formal application is required. Applications may be obtained from the Office of the Committees, however, completed applications must be sent to the State Chairman of DAR Scholarship Committee. The following must accompany the application: a statement of 1,000 words or less setting forth career objectives and explaining how the major in American History relates to future professional goals, and a financial need statement. An official transcript of high school grades, including class rank/class size and scores on the Scholastic Aptitude Test or the American College Test must also be submitted. Further, the student must send a one-page listing of all extra-curricular activities, honors, and scholastic achievements. Dated and signed letters of recommendation from at least two but not more than four persons in authority from the high school who are familiar with the student's work must be completed and sent. A photocopy of the student's birth certificate or naturalization papers should also be included. **Deadline:** Completed applications must be sent to the State Chairman by February 1. **Contact:** DAR Scholarship Committee at the above address (see entry 4391).

• **4403** • **NSDAR Occupational Therapy Scholarship**
*(Graduate, Undergraduate/Scholarship)*

**Purpose:** To provide financial, supplementary assistance to students of occupational or physical therapy programs. **Focus:** Occupational or Physical Therapy. **Qualif.:** Scholarships are available to applicants who are United States citizens enrolled in an accredited school of occupational or physical therapy. No affiliation with the DAR is necessary, although candidate must be sponsored by local chapter of the DAR. **Criteria:** Applicants are judged on the basis of academic excellence, commitment to field of study, and financial need.

**Funds Avail.:** 20 nonrenewable scholarships are awarded annually. Awards of up to $1,000 may be granted if funds are available. The average award is $500. **To Apply:** Formal application must be accompanied by a financial need form, proof of acceptance into a school of occupational or physical therapy, a statement of 1,000 words or less regarding career goals and relevance of academic program to future profession, a list of extra-curricular activities, honors, and scholastic achievements, and a copy of the student's birth certificate or naturalization papers. Further, a transcript of high school grades and test scores must be sent, along with at least two and not more than four letters of recommendation from teachers or persons familiar with the applicant's work and qualifications. A letter of sponsorship from a local DAR chapter and self-addressed, stamped envelope are required (with request for information). **Deadline:** Applications must be sent to the National Chairman by August 15 for the October award and February 15 for the April award. **Contact:** DAR Awards Committee at the above address (see entry 4391).

• **4404** •
**National Society of Public Accountants Scholarship Foundation**
1010 N. Fairfax St.                        *Ph:* (703)549-6400
Alexandria, VA 22314-1574                  *Fax:* (703)549-2984
*URL:* http://utulsa.edu/Financial/Scholarships/NSPA.html

• **4405** • **NSPA Scholarship Awards** *(Undergraduate/Scholarship)*

**Purpose:** To emphasize and perpetuate the prestige and status of the public accounting profession. **Focus:** Accounting. **Qualif.:** Candidates must be US or Canadian citizens attending a US accredited school, students majoring in accounting with a B or better grade point average, and enrolled full-time in a degree program at an accredited two-year or four-year college or university. Evening program students will be considered full-time if they are pursuing an accounting degree. Only undergraduate students are eligible. Students in an accredited two-year college may apply during their first year or during their second year if transferring to a four-year institution, provided they have committed themselves to major in accounting throughout the remainder of their college career. Students in an accredited four-year college may apply for a scholarship for their second, third, or fourth year of studies, provided they have committed themselves to a major in accounting throughout the remainder of their college career. **Criteria:** Scholarships are awarded primarily for academic attainment, demonstrated leadership ability, and financial need.

**Funds Avail.:** Approximately $1,000 each for students entering their third or fourth year of studies and approximately $500 each for students entering their second year of studies. In addition, the outstanding student in the competition, designated the Charles H. Earp Memorial Scholar, receives an additional stipend. **No. of Awards:** Average of 26 per year. **To Apply:** Applications and appraisal forms may be obtained from the candidate's school or by writing the NSPA Scholarship Foundation. Completed applications must be accompanied by official transcripts bearing the official seal or registrar signature from the issuing institution from each college attended. They should also be accompanied by a completed appraisal form that can be submitted by the student or the issuing professor. **Deadline:** March 10. **Contact:** Susan E. Noell, Foundation Director, NSPA Scholarship Foundation, at the above address (see entry 4404).

• **4406** • **Stanley H. Stearman Scholarships**
*(Graduate, Undergraduate/Scholarship)*

**Purpose:** To emphasize and perpetuate the prestige and status of the public accounting profession. **Focus:** Accounting. **Qualif.:** Candidates must be enrolled in a full-time graduate or undergraduate accounting program and have a B or better grade point average in all courses. Evening program students will be considered full-time if they are pursuing an accounting degree. Undergraduate students at two-year colleges may apply during their first or second years if they will be transferring to a four-year institution for a major in accounting. Four-year undergraduate college students may apply for this scholarship for their second, third, or fourth year of study towards a major in accounting. Recipients must be sons, daughters, grandchildren, nieces, nephews, or sons- or daughters-in-law of active or deceased NSPA members. **Criteria:** Academic attainment, leadership ability, and financial need.

**Funds Avail.:** $2,000. **No. of Awards:** 1. **To Apply:** Applications and appraisal forms may be obtained by writing the NSPA Scholarship Foundation. Along with official transcripts and a completed appraisal form, applicants must include a letter of intent outlining their reasons for seeking the award, their intended career objective, and how this scholarship award would be used to accomplish that objective. **Deadline:** March 10. **Contact:** Susan E. Noell, Foundation Director, NSPA Scholarship Foundation at the above address (see entry 4404).

• **4407** •
**National Space Club**
655 Fifteenth St., NW, Ste. 300            *Ph:* (202)639-4210
Washington, DC 20005                       *Fax:* (202)347-6109
*URL:* http://jagubox.gsfe.nasa.gov/~helena/NSCSHP9.html

• **4408** • **Dr. Robert H. Goddard Scholarships**
*(Graduate, Undergraduate/Scholarship)*

**Purpose:** To encourage talented students to study Aerospace Sciences and Technology. **Focus:** Aerospace Sciences and Technology. **Qualif.:** Applicants must be U.S. citizens who are at

*National Space Club (continued)*

least juniors enrolled in a science or engineering program at an accredited university in the United States. They must also have space-related research experience and intend to pursue undergraduate or graduate studies in science or engineering during the scholarship term.

**Funds Avail.:** $10,000. **No. of Awards:** 1. **To Apply:** Write to the scholarship committee chair for application guidelines. Submit a letter of application with transcripts, academic letters of recommendation, and a self-addressed, stamped envelope. **Deadline:** January 9. Notification is made by March 1.

---

## • 4409 •
**National Speleological Society**
2813 Cave Ave.                              *Ph:* (205)852-1300
Huntsville, AL 35810-4431              *Fax:* (205)851-9241
*E-mail:* manager@caves.org; nss@caves.org
*URL:* http://www.caves.org

### • 4410 •   Ralph W. Stone Research Award
*(Graduate/Award)*

**Purpose:** To support meritorious graduate level research related to speleology. **Focus:** Speleology. **Qualif.:** Applicant must be a member of NSS who is conducting cave-related research for a thesis in the biological, social, or earth sciences. Award is tenable worldwide.

**Funds Avail.:** $1,000. **To Apply:** Submit to three copies of a six-page statement of work, transcripts, resume, and two letters of recommendation. One of the letters must come from the research advisor. **Deadline:** May 18. **Contact:** Chris Groves at the above address (see entry 4409).

---

## • 4411 •
**National Stone Association**
1415 Elliot Pl., NW                        *Ph:* (202)342-1100
Washington, DC 20007-2599          *Fax:* (202)342-0702
*URL:* http://www.aggregates.org

### • 4412 •   Samuel C. Kraus, Jr. Memorial Scholarship
*(Undergraduate/Scholarship)*

**Qualif.:** Applicants must be promising mining engineering or geology students at the University of Missouri - Rolla, who plan to pursue a career in the crushed stone industry.

**Remarks:** The Samuel C. Kraus, Jr. Memorial Scholarship honors the memory of the last Past Chairman of the National Stone Association, who at the time of his passing was President of Auxvasse Stone & Gravel Co. of St. Louis, MO. **Contact:** Don L. Warner, Dean, School of Mines and Metallurgy, University of Missouri - Rolla, 305 V.H. McNutt Hall, Rolla, MO 65401-0249. Telephone: (314)341-4153.

### • 4413 •   Quarry Engineering Scholarship Program
*(Undergraduate/Scholarship)*

**Qualif.:** Applicants must be engineering students who intend to pursue a career in the stone industry.

**Funds Avail.:** Five $2,000 scholarships. **To Apply:** Applicants should submit a completed application with a letter of recommendation from their faculty advisor and a 300- to 500-word essay on their plans for a career in the crushed stone industry. **Contact:** Website: www.AGGREGATES.ORG for application.

---

## • 4414 •
**National Strength and Conditioning Association**
1955 N. Union Blvd.                        *Ph:* (719)632-6722
Colorado Springs, CO 80909-2229     *Fax:* (719)632-6367
*E-mail:* nsca@nsca-lift.org
*URL:* http://www.nsca-lift.org

### • 4415 •   NSCA Challenge Scholarships *(All/Scholarship)*

**Purpose:** To provide NSCA members with financial assistance for an education leading toward a career in strength and conditioning, including careers in areas such as sports medicine, physical education, and physical therapy. **Focus:** Education-Physical, Medicine-Sports, Physical Therapy. **Qualif.:** Applicants must be NSCA members for at least one year prior to the application deadline. **Criteria:** Awards are based on scholarship, experience, written essay, stated objectives and career goals, recommendations, honors, and community and NSCA involvement.

**Funds Avail.:** $1,000 **No. of Awards:** One to five. **To Apply:** Students must submit a cover letter of application, resume, an essay of no more than 500 words explaining their need for the scholarship, proposed course of study, and professional goals. Also required are official transcripts from all post-secondary schools attended and three current letters of recommendation. **Deadline:** March 1. **Contact:** Karri T. Baker, Member Relations Coordinator.

### • 4416 •   NSCA Student Research Grant *(Graduate, Undergraduate/Grant)*

**Purpose:** To fund graduate student research in strength and conditioning that is directed by a graduate faculty member. **Qualif.:** Applicants must have been NSCA members for at least one year prior to application. **Criteria:** Project must fall within the mission of the NSCA.

**Funds Avail.:** Up to $2,500. **No. of Awards:** One to eight. **To Apply:** A grant application submission to the NSCA Student Grant Program should contain project information and budget, contact information and NSCA membership number, literature review, statistical analysis, consent form, and CV of faculty co-investigator. **Deadline:** Letter of intent is due February 3, grant application is due March 17.

**Remarks:** Get application from webste or write the national office.

### • 4417 •   Power Systems Inc./NSCA Strength and Conditioning Professional Scholarship *(Graduate, Undergraduate/Scholarship)*

**Purpose:** To financially assist members in their pursuit of a career as a strength and conditioning coach. **Focus:** Strength and conditioning with an emphasis on coaching. **Qualif.:** Applicants must be NSCA members for at least one year prior to application deadline. **Criteria:** Based on scholarship, experience, written essay, career goals, and recommendations.

**Funds Avail.:** $1000. **No. of Awards:** 1. **To Apply:** A letter of application; current resume; and an essay of no more than 500 words describing the applicant's career goals and objectives must be submitted by the head strength and conditioning coach from the applicant's school. The Applicant must submit an original, official transcript from all post-secondary schools attended which should be mailed directly from the school. **Deadline:** All materials must be postmarked by May 1.

• 4418 •

## National Symphony Orchestra

Education Program
The Kennedy Center                     *Ph:* (202)416-8820
Washington, DC 20566-0004              *Fax:* (202)416-8802
*URL:* http://kennedy-center.org/education/opps/music.html/
soloists

• 4419 • **National Symphony Young Soloists'
Competition, College Division** (*Professional
Development/Prize, Scholarship*)

**Purpose:** To encourage and foster the development of young
performing piano, instrumental, and vocal artists in the Washington
Metropolitan Area. **Focus:** Performing Arts. **Qualif.:** Candidates
must be high school graduates who are currently studying music in
the Washington Metropolitan Area, or who are area residents
studying elsewhere. The Washington Metropolitan Area
encompasses the District of Columbia, Alexandria, Arlington,
Fairfax, Loudoun, and Prince William counties in Virginia and,
Charles, Frederick, Montgomery and Prince George's counties in
Maryland. Upper age limit for pianists and instrumentalists is 23
and for singers, 26 as of February 11. Pianists and instrumentalists
who have an undergraduate degree, singers who have a Doctor's
Degree, previous year high school winners, former college winners,
or performers under professional management are not eligible.

**Funds Avail.:** Finalists perform in a free public concert in the
Kennedy Center Concert Hall and will be awarded the Milton W.
King Memorial Certificate. Winners perform with the National
Symphony Orchestra. Instrumentalists and pianists appear on
WQXR radio, New York. WETA FM91 is offering the Bill Cerri
$1,000 scholarship to one winner, selected by the judges. All
finalists will be invited to join the student membership of the Friday
Morning Music Club without audition. Winners receive a one year
dues-free membership. **To Apply:** The audition repertoire is listed
in the application. One selection is to be played from memory. An
official accompanist, furnished by the National Symphony
Orchestra, must be used. Applications should include teacher's
endorsement; selection chosen; a one-page, typed summary of
musical background including Solo experience; a self-addressed
stamped envelope; and a non-returnable $15 entry fee, payable to
NSO. **Contact:** Sharyn L. Byer, Competition Chairperson
(volunteer), 115 Gresham Place, Falls Church, VA 22046.

• 4420 • **National Symphony Young Soloists'
Competition, High School Division** (*High School/Prize*)

**Purpose:** To encourage and foster the development of young
performing artists in the Washington Metropolitan area. **Focus:**
Performing Arts. **Qualif.:** Candidates are students in grades 10
through 12 who are residents of, or studying with an instrumental
teacher in the Washington Metropolitan area (District of Columbia,
and Alexandria, Arlington, Fairfax, Loudoun and Price William
counties in Virginia, and Charles, Frederick, Montgomery and
Prince Georges Counties in Maryland). Former winners or
performers under professional management are not eligible.

**Funds Avail.:** Finalists perform in a free public concert in the
Kennedy Center Concert Hall, and winners perform in a concert
with the National Symphony Orchestra. WETA FM91 offers the Bill
Cerri Scholarship of $1,000 to one winner, selected by the judges.
**To Apply:** Audition repertoire is listed in the application. One
selection must be played from memory. An official accompanist is
furnished by the National Symphony Orchestra. Applications must
be accompanied by a resume of musical background including all
previous competitions, awards, and concerts, stressing solo
experience. Applicants should also send a non-refundable $15
entry fee and self-addressed, stamped envelope. **Contact:** Sharyn
L. Byer, Competition Chair (volunteer), 115 Gresham Place, Falls
Church, VA 22046.

• 4421 •

## National Tax Association - Tax Institute of America

725 15th St. NW, Ste. 600             *Ph:* (202)737-3325
Washington, DC 20005                  *Fax:* (202)737-7308

• 4422 • **National Tax Association Doctoral
Dissertation Awards** (*Doctorate/Award*)

**Purpose:** To encourage and promote scholarly research
concerning the major issues and critical problems in government
finance and taxation. **Focus:** Finance and taxation. **Qualif.:**
Applicants must attend accredited US and/or Canadian
institutions, or have recently received their degrees. Dissertations
must have been officially accepted by the filing deadline. **Criteria:**
Evaluated on the basis of originality; innovations with respect to
techniques for analyzing public finance issues; application and
significance of the analysis for scholars and practitioners of
government finance; clarity of exposition.

**Funds Avail.:** Winner receives $2,000 and two honorable mentions
receive $1,000. **To Apply:** A copy of the doctoral dissertation, an
abstract, and completed application must be submitted. Any topic
relating to general areas of government finance is acceptable, this
includes the areas of taxation, expenditures, budget policy, debt
management, and fiscal policy. A variety of approaches may be
used, including, theoretical or empirical, positive or normative, and
idealistic or practical. **Deadline:** June 1. **Contact:** Professor William
H. Oakland.

• 4423 •

## National Teenager Foundation

PO Box 610187                         *Ph:* (817)577-2220
Dallas, TX 76040                      *Fax:* (817)428-7232

• 4424 • **America's National Teenager Scholarship**
(*Undergraduate/Scholarship*)

**Purpose:** To encourage scholastic and leadership achievements of
America's teenagers and to provide cash, tuition scholarships, and
other awards to the participants. **Focus:** General Studies. **Qualif.:**
Candidates must be females between 13 and 18 years of age.
**Criteria:** Applicants are judged on leadership ability, scholastic
achievement, overall appearance, and communication skills.

**Funds Avail.:** The foundation awards more than $30,000 in cash
scholarships. Additionally, academic institutions provide state and
local winners with more than $5 million in tuition scholarship funds
annually. **To Apply:** Applications are available upon request ($15
application fee). **Deadline:** Dates vary. **Contact:** For information on
local and state programs, write to the National Teen-Ager
Foundation at the above address (see entry 4423).

• 4425 •

## National Tourism Foundation

                                      *Fax:* (606)226-4414
546 E Main St.
Lexington, KY 40508                   *Free:* 800-682-8886

• 4426 • **Academy of Travel and Tourism Award**
(*High School/Award*)

**Qualif.:** For high school seniors enrolled in an Academy of Travel &
Tourism school.

**Funds Avail.:** $500. **Deadline:** April 15.

## National Tourism Foundation (continued)

### • 4427 • Alabama/Birmingham Legacy Scholarship
(Undergraduate/Scholarship)

**Focus:** Hotel management, restaurant management, tourism. **Qualif.:** Applicants must be Alabama residents full-time students attending two- or four-year colleges or universities in North America who are entering their junior or senior year of study with at least a 3.0 grade point average on a 4.0 scale. Applicants must be pursuing study in a travel and tourism related field. **Criteria:** Awards are made based on academic achievement.

**Funds Avail.:** $500. **To Apply:** Applicants must submit a completed NTF scholarship application, two letters of recommendation (one from a tourism related faculty member and the other from a professional in the tourism industry), resume noting tourism related activities, college transcript, and an essay. Write for further details. **Deadline:** March 15. **Contact:** National Tourism Foundation at the above address (see entry 4425).

### • 4428 • Dr. Tom Anderson Memorial Scholarship
(Undergraduate/Scholarship)

**Focus:** Hotel management, restaurant management, tourism. **Qualif.:** Applicants must be full-time students attending two or four year colleges or universities in North America who are entering their junior or senior year of study with at least a 3.0 grade point average on a 4.0 scale. Applicants must be pursuing study in a travel and tourism related field. **Criteria:** Awards are made based on academic achievement.

**Funds Avail.:** $2,000. **To Apply:** Applicants must submit a completed NTF scholarship application, two letters of recommendation (one from a tourism related faculty member and the other from a professional in the tourism industry), resume noting tourism related activities, college transcript, and an essay. Write for further details. **Deadline:** March 15. **Contact:** National Tourism Foundation at the above address (see entry 4425).

### • 4429 • Bill Carpenter Memorial Certificate School Scholarship (Undergraduate/Scholarship)

**Qualif.:** For a student attending a certificate school.

**Funds Avail.:** $500.

### • 4430 • Luray Caverns Research Grant (Doctorate, Graduate/Grant)

**Purpose:** To aid a student pursuing a masters or doctorate in travel and tourism or related field in completing their thesis or dissertation.

**Funds Avail.:** $2,500.

### • 4431 • Cleveland Legacy Scholarship
(Undergraduate/Scholarship)

**Focus:** Hotel management, restaurant management, tourism. **Qualif.:** Applicants must be full-time students who are residents of Ohio and attending two- or four-year colleges or universities in North America who are entering their junior or senior year of study with at least a 3.0 grade point average on a 4.0 scale. Applicants must be pursuing study in a travel and tourism related field. **Criteria:** Awards are made based on academic achievement.

**Funds Avail.:** $1,000 and $5,000 per award. **To Apply:** Applicants must submit a completed NTF scholarship application, two letters of recommendation (one from a tourism related faculty member and the other from a professional in the tourism industry), resume noting tourism related activities, college transcript, and an essay. Write for further details. **Deadline:** March 15. **Contact:** National Tourism Foundation at the above address (see entry 4425).

### • 4432 • Weeta F. Colebank Scholarship
(Undergraduate/Scholarship)

**Focus:** Hotel management, restaurant management, tourism. **Qualif.:** Applicants must be full-time students who are residents of Mississippi attending four-year Mississippi colleges or universities in North America who are entering their junior or senior year of study with at least a 3.0 grade point average on a 4.0 scale. Applicants must be pursuing study in a travel and tourism related field. **Criteria:** Awards are made based on academic achievement.

**Funds Avail.:** $1,000. **To Apply:** Applicants must submit a completed NTF scholarship application, two letters of recommendation (one from a tourism related faculty member and the other from a professional in the tourism industry), resume noting tourism related activities, college transcript, and an essay. Write for further details. **Deadline:** March 15. **Contact:** National Tourism Foundation at the above address (see entry 4425).

### • 4433 • Louise Dessureault Memorial Scholarship
(Undergraduate/Scholarship)

**Focus:** Hotel management, restaurant management, tourism. **Qualif.:** Applicants must be full-time students attending four-year colleges or universities in North America who are entering their junior or senior year of study with at least a 3.0 grade point average on a 4.0 scale. Applicants must be pursuing study in a travel and tourism related field. All applicants must be Canadian citizens. **Criteria:** Awards are made based on academic achievement.

**Funds Avail.:** $500. **To Apply:** Applicants must submit a completed NTF scholarship application, two letters of recommendation (one from a tourism related faculty member and the other from a professional in the tourism industry), resume noting tourism related activities, college transcript, and an essay. Write for further details. **Deadline:** March 15. **Contact:** National Tourism Foundation at the above address (see entry 4425).

### • 4434 • Eric and Bette Friedheim Scholarship
(Undergraduate/Scholarship)

**Focus:** Hotel management, restaurant management, tourism. **Qualif.:** Applicants must be full-time students attending four-year colleges or universities in North America who are entering their junior or senior year of study with at least a 3.0 grade point average on a 4.0 scale. Applicants must be pursuing study in a travel and tourism related field. **Criteria:** Awards are made based on academic achievement.

**Funds Avail.:** $500. **To Apply:** Applicants must submit a completed NTF scholarship application, two letters of recommendation (one from a tourism related faculty member and the other from a professional in the tourism industry), resume noting tourism related activities, college transcript, and an essay. Write for further details. **Deadline:** March 15. **Contact:** National Tourism Foundation at the above address (see entry 4425).

### • 4435 • H. Neil Mecaskey Scholarship
(Undergraduate/Scholarship)

**Focus:** Hotel management, restaurant management, tourism. **Qualif.:** Applicants must be full-time students attending four-year colleges or universities in North America who are entering their junior or senior year of study with at least a 3.0 grade point average on a 4.0 scale. Applicants must be pursuing study in a travel and tourism related field. **Criteria:** Awards are made based on academic achievement.

**Funds Avail.:** $500. **To Apply:** Applicants must submit a completed NTF scholarship application, two letters of recommendation (one from a tourism related faculty member and the other from a professional in the tourism industry), resume noting tourism related activities, college transcript, and an essay. Write for further details. **Deadline:** March 15. **Contact:** National Tourism Foundation at the above address (see entry 4425).

• **4436** • Patrick Murphy Internship *(Undergraduate/ Internship)*

**Purpose:** To provide an internship with former congressman James D. Santini at his Washington DC office.

**Funds Avail.:** $1,000.

• **4437** • NTF Internship *(Undergraduate/Internship)*

**Qualif.:** Foundation seeks a student pursuing a degree that is travel and tourism related with excellent written, oral, and interpersonal skills.

**Funds Avail.:** $3,000. **Deadline:** April 15.

• **4438** • Quebec Scholarship *(Doctorate, Graduate/ Scholarship)*

**Focus:** Hotel management, restaurant management, tourism. **Qualif.:** Applicants must be full-time students who are Quebec residents attending two- or four-year Quebec colleges or universities in North America who are entering their junior or senior year of study with at least a 3.0 grade point average on a 4.0 scale. Applicants must be pursuing study in a travel and tourism related field. **Criteria:** Awards are made based on academic achievement.

**Funds Avail.:** $1,500. **To Apply:** Applicants must submit a completed NTF scholarship application, two letters of recommendation (one from a tourism related faculty member and the other from a professional in the tourism industry), resume noting tourism related activities, college transcript, and an essay. Write for further details. **Deadline:** March 15. **Contact:** National Tourism Foundation at the above address (see entry 4425).

• **4439** • Treadway Inns, Hotels, and Resorts Scholarship *(Undergraduate/Scholarship)*

**Focus:** Hotel management, restaurant management, tourism. **Qualif.:** Applicants must be full-time students attending four-year colleges or universities in North America who are entering their junior or senior year of study with at least a 3.0 grade point average on a 4.0 scale. Applicants must be pursuing study in a travel and tourism related field. **Criteria:** Awards are made based on academic achievement.

**Funds Avail.:** $500. **To Apply:** Applicants must submit a completed NTF scholarship application, two letters of recommendation (one from a tourism related faculty member and the other from a professional in the tourism industry), resume noting tourism related activities, college transcript, and an essay. Write for further details. **Deadline:** March 15. **Contact:** National Tourism Foundation at the above address (see entry 4425).

• **4440** • Tulsa Legacy Scholarship *(Undergraduate/ Scholarship)*

**Focus:** Hotel management, restaurant management, tourism. **Qualif.:** Applicants must be full-time students who are residents of Oklahoma and attending four-year Oklahoma colleges or universities in North America who are entering their junior or senior year of study with at least a 3.0 grade point average on a 4.0 scale. Applicants must be pursuing study in a travel and tourism related field. **Criteria:** Awards are made based on academic achievement.

**Funds Avail.:** $500. **To Apply:** Applicants must submit a completed NTF scholarship application, two letters of recommendation (one from a tourism related faculty member and the other from a professional in the tourism industry), resume noting tourism related activities, college transcript, and an essay. Write for further details. **Deadline:** March 15. **Contact:** National Tourism Foundation at the above address (see entry 4425).

• **4441** • Visiting Scholar Awards *(Professional Development/Award)*

**Purpose:** To provide the opportunity for educators to learn first hand about the NTA and the tourism industry. **Qualif.:** Travel and tourism educators at two or four year colleges and universities are eligible.

**Funds Avail.:** Room, board, and airfare is provided for a three day stay in Lexington, KY and five days in St. Louis, MO. **Deadline:** April 15.

• **4442** • Yellow Ribbon Scholarship *(Undergraduate/ Scholarship)*

**Focus:** Hotel management, restaurant management, tourism. **Qualif.:** Applicants must be full-time students with physical or sensory disabilities that are verified by accredited physicians, entering post-secondary education with at least a 3.0 grade point average on a 4.0 scale, or are maintaining at least a 2.5 grade point average at the college level. Applicants must be pursuing study in a travel and tourism related field. **Criteria:** Awards are made based on academic achievement.

**Funds Avail.:** $3,000. **To Apply:** Applicants must submit a completed NTF scholarship application, and an essay. Write for further details. **Deadline:** April 15. **Contact:** National Tourism Foundation at the above address (see entry 4425).

• **4443** •
**National Twenty and Four**
6000 Lucerne Ct., No. 2
Mequon, WI 53092
*The Twenty and Four is the Honor Society of Women Legionnaires.*

• **4444** • Twenty and Four Memorial Scholarships *(Undergraduate/Scholarship)*

**Purpose:** To recognize all women who have served in the Armed Forces in all the wars. **Focus:** General Studies. **Qualif.:** Candidates must be the children, grandchildren or great-grandchildren of members of the Twenty and Four, Honor Society of Women Legionnaires in good standing or of a deceased member, who at the time of her death was a member in good standing. Applicants must be between the ages of 16-25 by September 1st of the calendar year the application is made. Also eligible are members in good standing of any age who require further education to return to the work force or to change work fields. **Criteria:** Awards are given based on need for assistance, scholastic standing, and extra-curricular school activities.

**Funds Avail.:** Up to $500, payable at the rate of $250 at the beginning of each semester. **To Apply:** Applications should be obtained from applicant's mother, grandmother, or great-grandmother as applicable. Evidence of acceptance for admission and evidence of enrollment in a school, college, university or vocational institution beyond the high school level must be submitted by August 1 to the National Scholarship Committee or the winner risks forfeiture of the award. **Deadline:** May 1.

**Remarks:** The scholarship is a memorial to all women who have served in the Armed Forces in all wars. **Contact:** The Twenty and Four at the above address (see entry 4443).

## • 4445 •
**National Urban Fellows, Inc.**
55 W 44th St., Ste. 600
New York, NY 10036
*E-mail:* nufluis@aol.com; ednurf@aol.com
*URL:* http://www.nuf.org

*Ph:* (212)921-9400
*Fax:* (212)921-9572

### • 4446 • National Urban/Rural Fellows *(Graduate/Fellowship)*

**Purpose:** To increase the knowledge and enhance the managerial and administrative skills of mid-career minorities in the field of public administration. **Focus:** Management, Public Policy, Public Administration. **Qualif.:** Applicants must be US citizens with a bachelor's degree, leadership ability, self discipline, inter-personal and problem-solving skills, a minimum of three years work experience in a managerial or administrative capacity, and a strong work ethic.

**Funds Avail.:** $20,000 for 14 months, full payment of tuition, relocation allowance. **No. of Awards:** 20-30. **To Apply:** Application, transcript(s), two essays, and three letters of recommendation are needed. **Deadline:** Continuous. **Contact:** Myra Marin.

## • 4447 •
**National Urban League Inc.**
120 Wall St.
New York, NY 10005
*E-mail:* info@nul.org
*URL:* http://www.nul.org

*Ph:* (212)558-5300

### • 4448 • Duracell/National Urban League Scholarship and Intern Program for Minority Students *(Undergraduate/Internship, Scholarship)*

**Purpose:** To assist and encourage outstanding minority students in completing their college education, and to give them practical exposure to employment opportunities within a large corporation. **Qualif.:** Applicants must be juniors in college at the time the award commences, rank in the top 25 percent of their class, and be pursuing courses that will lead to a professional career in sales, marketing, manufacturing operation, finance, or business administration. They must also have a strong interest in summer employment with Duracell Inc. between their junior and senior years.

**Funds Avail.:** Five $10,000 awards and summer intern opportunities. The scholarship is renewable for an additional year if the recipient notifies Duracell of their academic standing after their junior year. **To Apply:** Applications are available through local Urban League Affiliate offices. Ten finalists are chosen to participate in interviews between May 15 and May 30. **Deadline:** April 15.

**Remarks:** The League maintains a scholarship hotline: 800-NUL-FUND. **Contact:** Local Urban League affiliates or the Director of Education, National Urban League, at the above address (see entry 4447).

## • 4449 •
**National Welsh-American Foundation**
c/o Warren E. Watkins, Sec.
301 Stone Ave.
Clark Summit, PA 18411

*Ph:* (717)587-4131
*Fax:* (717)586-4901

### • 4450 • National Welsh-American Foundation Exchange Scholarships *(Doctorate, Graduate, Undergraduate/Scholarship)*

**Purpose:** To provide the opportunity to study Welsh-oriented subjects at a college in Wales or University Colleges of Wales. **Focus:** Welsh Studies. **Qualif.:** Candidates must be working towards bachelor's, master's, or doctoral degrees at recognized academic institutions in the United States. They should have a clearly defined commitment of the pursual of studies at a recognized institution of higher learning in Wales (The scope of these activities should have direct relevance to Welsh-American cultural exchange). **Criteria:** Selection is based upon academic achievement and potential. It is advantageous to candidates if they have some ethnic or previous cultural connection with Wales, and working knowledge of the Welsh language.

**Funds Avail.:** $5,000. **No. of Awards:** 1. **To Apply:** Applications must be submitted to Dr. Philip Davies, Chairman, NWAF Award and Honors Committee, 24 Essex Rd., Scotch Plains, NJ 07076. Application forms are available from: NWAF, 24 Carverton Road, Trucksville, PA, 18708. **Deadline:** March 1.

**Remarks:** Recipients should make themselves available for attendance at the annual meeting of the NWAF immediately after the award of the scholarship. More importantly, awardees should be prepared to involve themselves in the activities of the NWAF after their return from Wales. Previous winners are not eligible. For administrative and legal reasons it is essential that the applicant identify a mechanism by which the award can be made payable to the host institution in Wales. **Contact:** NWAF at the above address (see entry 4449).

## • 4451 •
**National Women's Studies Association**
7100 Baltimore Ave., Ste. 301
College Park, MD 20740
*E-mail:* NWSA@UMAIL.UMD.EDU
*URL:* http://www.feminist.com/nwsa.htm

*Ph:* (301)403-0525
*Fax:* (301)403-4137

### • 4452 • NWSA Graduate Scholarships in Lesbian Studies *(Doctorate, Graduate/Scholarship)*

**Purpose:** To encourage graduate research in lesbian studies. **Focus:** Lesbian Studies. **Qualif.:** Applicants must be graduate students conducting research for or writing a master's thesis or doctoral dissertation,in lesbian studies. Candidates may be working in any relevant discipline. Preference is given to NWSA members.

**Funds Avail.:** $500. **No. of Awards:** 1. **To Apply:** Write to the program assistant for application guidelines. **Deadline:** February 15. Recipient notified by June 30.

### • 4453 • Pergamon-NWSA Graduate Scholarships in Women's Studies *(Doctorate, Graduate/Scholarship)*

**Purpose:** To support graduate studies and research on women. **Focus:** Women's Studies. **Qualif.:** Applicants must be conducting research for or writing a master's thesis or Ph.D. dissertation in the interdisciplinary field of women's studies. Preference is given to NWSA members and to those whose research projects on women examine color or class.

**Funds Avail.:** First place: $1,000; Second place: $500. **No. of Awards:** 2. **To Apply:** Write to the program assistant for application guidelines. **Deadline:** February 15. **Contact:** Program Assistant at the above address (see entry 4451).

• 4454 • **Scholarship in Jewish Women's Studies** *(Graduate/Scholarship)*

**Purpose:** To expand the boundaries and possibilities of women's studies scholarship. **Focus:** Women's Studies, Jewish Women. **Qualif.:** Applicants must be graduate students enrolled in a graduate course of study, whose area of research is Jewish women's studies.

**Funds Avail.:** $500. **No. of Awards:** 1. **To Apply:** Write the Program Assistant for application guidelines. **Deadline:** February 15.

• 4455 •

**National Zoological Park - Friends of the National Zoo - Traineeship Program**
Washington, DC 20008
Ph: (202)673-4950
Fax: (202)673-4738

• 4456 • **National Zoological Park Minority Traineeships** *(Graduate, Undergraduate/Internship)*

**Purpose:** To provide interested minority students with the opportunity to work in one of the following program areas of the Zoo: animal behavior; reproductive physiology; nutrition; genetics; husbandry; exotic animal medicine; veterinary pathology; interpretive exhibition development, design, and evaluation; appalachian mountain ecosystem studies; public affairs; education; biopark horticulture collections; facilities design; landscaping; and zoo photography. Each trainee will be responsible to an advisor while participating in ongoing or special projects. Trainees will receive guidance in research methodology. Responsibilities may include animal observation and handling, data recording, laboratory analyses, data processing, and report writing. **Qualif.:** Applicants must be undergraduates or recent college graduates. Only veterinary college students are eligible for the exotic animal medicine and veterinary pathology concentrations. **Criteria:** Applicants are judged based on their statement of interest, scholastic achievement, relevant experience, and letters of reference. Preference is given to advanced undergraduates and recent graduates, except in the exotic animal medicine area.

**Funds Avail.:** Full term (12 weeks, summer, or fall) stipend is $2,400. Students must make their own lodging arrangements in Washington D.C. (optional dormitory space is available at Front Royal). **To Apply:** Applicants need to send a typewritten letter with data in the following sequence: name, home and college addresses, and phone numbers, date of birth, social security number, name of college or university, current academic status, curriculum (major and minor), degrees held or expected (with institution names and dates conferred or anticipated date(s) of conferment), desired dates for the traineeship, program area preference, and a 500- to 1,000-word statement of interest in pursuing one of the program areas listed above (be sure to include the appropriate letter code). Statement should include relevant experience, career goals, and reason for wanting an NZP traineeship; transcripts from current and/or past institutions (may be sent separately); and the names and addresses of two or more individuals who will send letters of reference directly to the above address. Previous applicants who wish to have their formerly prepared materials considered should indicate the year they applied. **Deadline:** February 1. Applicants will be notified of selections within two months of application deadline. **Contact:** Friends of National Zoo at the above address (see entry 4455).

• 4457 • **National Zoological Park Research Traineeships** *(Graduate, Undergraduate/Internship)*

**Purpose:** To provide interested students with the opportunity to work in one of the following areas of animal research: behavior and ecology; reproductive physiology; nutrition; genetics; husbandry/exhibit interpretation; exotic animal medicine; veterinary pathology; and Appalachian mountain ecosystem studies. **Focus:** Zoology, Ecology, Veterinary Science. **Qualif.:** Applicants must be undergraduates or recent college graduates. Only veterinary college students are eligible for the Exotic Animal Medicine concentration. **Criteria:** Applicants are judged based on their statement of interest, scholastic achievement, relevant experience, and letters of reference. Preference is given to advanced undergraduates and recent graduates, except in the Exotic Animal Medicine area. Minority members and women are encouraged to apply.

**Funds Avail.:** Full term (12 weeks, summer, or fall) stipend is $2,400. Approximately ten traineeships are offered. **To Apply:** Applicants need to send a typewritten letter with data in the following sequence: name, home and college addresses and phone numbers, date of birth, social security number, name of college or university, current academic status, curriculum (major and minor), degrees held or expected (with institution names and dates conferred or anticipated date(s) of conferment), desired dates for the traineeship, program area preference, and a 500- to 1,000-word statement of interest in pursuing one of the program areas listed above (be sure to include the appropriate letter code). Statement should include relevant experience, career goals, and reason for wanting an NZP traineeship; transcripts from current and/or past institutions (may be sent separately); the names and addresses of two or more individuals who will send letters of reference directly to the above address. Previous applicants who wish to have their formerly prepared materials considered should indicate the year they applied. **Deadline:** January 31. Applicants are notified of selections within two months of application deadline. **Contact:** National Zoological Park at the above address (see entry 4455).

• 4458 • **National Zoological Park Traineeship in BioPark Horticulture** *(Graduate, Undergraduate/Internship)*

**Purpose:** To provide interested students with the opportunity to work in horticulture. The recipient will provide assistance with ongoing inventory of the arboriculture collection at the Zoo. Project time is split between field observation, literature research, and data entry. **Qualif.:** Applicants must be undergraduates or recent college graduates with a forestry, horticulture, or biology background. **Criteria:** Applicants are judged based on their statement of interest, scholastic achievement, relevant experience, and letters of reference. Preference will be given to advanced undergraduates and recent graduates.

**Funds Avail.:** Full term (12 weeks, summer, or fall) stipend of $2,400. Recipients must make their own lodging arrangements. **To Apply:** Applicants need to send a typewritten letter with data in the following sequence: name, home and college addresses and phone numbers, date of birth, social security number, name of college or university, current academic status, curriculum (major and minor), degrees held or expected (with institution names and dates conferred or anticipated date(s) of conferment), desired dates for the traineeship, program area preference, and a 500- to 1,000-word statement describing interest in horticulture. Statement should include relevant experience, career goals, and reason for wanting an NZP traineeship; transcripts from current and/or past institutions (may be sent separately); and the names and addresses of two or more individuals who will send letters of reference directly to the address above in care of Friends of the National Zoo. Previous applicants who wish to have their formerly prepared materials considered should indicate the year they applied. **Deadline:** February 22. **Contact:** Richard Hider, Horticulturist, at the above address (see entry 4455).

### National Zoological Park - Friends of the National Zoo - Traineeship Program (continued)

**• 4459 • National Zoological Park Traineeship in Education** *(Graduate, Undergraduate/Internship)*

**Purpose:** To provide interested students with the opportunity to work in education. The traineeship involved assisting in the development and running of the Reptile Discovery Center and the Amazonia Exhibit. These projects experiment with varying educational approaches by interpreters of animals and plant exhibits. **Qualif.:** Applicants must be undergraduates or recent college graduates. **Criteria:** Applicants are judged based on their statement of interest, scholastic achievement, relevant experience, and letters of reference. Preference is given to advanced undergraduates and recent graduates with some computer skills and a desire to develop program support for multicultural audiences for the Zoo.

**Funds Avail.:** Full term (12 weeks, spring, summer, or fall) stipend of $2,400. Recipients must make their own lodging arrangements. **To Apply:** Applicants need to send a typewritten letter with data in the following sequence: name, home and college addresses and phone numbers, date of birth, social security number, name of college or university, current academic status, curriculum (major and minor), degrees held or expected (with institution names and dates conferred), or anticipated date(s) of conferment, desired dates for the traineeship, program area preference, and a 500- to 1,000-word statement describing interest in education. Statement should include relevant experience, career goals, and reason for wanting an NZP traineeship; transcripts from current and/or past institutions (may be sent separately); and the names and addresses of two or more individuals who will send letters of reference directly to the address above in care of Friends of the National Zoo. Previous applicants who wish to have their formerly-prepared materials considered should indicate the year they applied. **Deadline:** February 22. **Contact:** Judith White, Office of Education, at the above address (see entry 4455).

**• 4460 • National Zoological Park Traineeship in Exhibit Interpretation** *(Graduate, Undergraduate/Internship)*

**Purpose:** To provide interested students with the opportunity to work in interpretive exhibition development. The recipient will assist with developing and designing graphic exhibits to complement and enhance the Zoo exhibits, with a focus on animals, plants, ethnobotany, specialized gardens, or other Zoo subjects. Projects may also focus on the Zoo visitor experience, by creating questionnaires and interviewing visitors, assessing the impact of the Native American and African American Heritage Gardens, or finding out what visitors know about the Amazon. **Focus:** Zoology. **Qualif.:** Applicants must be undergraduates or recent college graduates. **Criteria:** Applicants are judged based on their statement of interest, scholastic achievement, relevant experience, sample slides, and letters of reference. Preference is given to advanced undergraduates and recent graduates.

**Funds Avail.:** Full term (12 weeks, summer or fall) stipend of $2,400. Recipients must make their own lodging arrangements. **To Apply:** Applicants need to send a typewritten letter with data in the following sequence: name, home and college addresses and phone numbers, date of birth, social security number, name of college or university, current academic status, curriculum (major and minor), degrees held or expected (with institution names and dates conferred or anticipated date(s) of conferment), desired dates for the traineeship and program area preference, a 500- to 1,000-word statement describing interest in exhibit interpretation, and 20 slides of design projects. Statement should include relevant experience, career goals, and reason for wanting an NZP traineeship; transcripts from current and/or past institutions (may be sent separately); and the names and addresses of two or more individuals who will send letters of reference directly to the address above in care of Friends of the National Zoo. Previous applicants who wish to have their formerly prepared materials considered should indicate the year they applied. **Deadline:**

January 31. **Contact:** Herman Krebs at the above address (see entry 4455).

**• 4461 • National Zoological Park Traineeship in Facilities Design** *(Graduate, Undergraduate/Internship)*

**Purpose:** To provide interested students with the opportunity to work in facilities design. Major construction or renovation of Zoo exhibit buildings provides an opportunity to learn about Zoo facilities planning and construction. Project time is split between field observation, literature research, and data entry. **Qualif.:** Applicants must be enrolled in an architectural/engineering program and show special interest in zoo/museum facilities. **Criteria:** Applicants are judged based on their statement of interest, scholastic achievement, relevant experience, and letters of reference. Preference is given to advanced undergraduates and recent graduates.

**Funds Avail.:** Full term (12 weeks, summer, or fall) stipend of $2,400. Recipients must make their own lodging arrangements. **To Apply:** Applicants need to send a typewritten letter with data in the following sequence: name, home and college addresses and phone numbers, date of birth, social security number, name of college or university, current academic status, curriculum (major and minor), degrees held or expected (with institution names and dates conferred or anticipated date(s) of conferment), desired dates for the traineeship and program area preference, and a 500- to 1,000-word statement describing interest in facilities design. Statement should include relevant experience, career goals, and reason for wanting an NZP traineeship; transcripts from current and/or past institutions (may be sent separately); and the names and addresses of two or more individuals who will send letters of reference directly to the address above in care of Friends of the National Zoo. Previous applicants who wish to have their formerly prepared materials considered should indicate the year they applied. **Deadline:** February 22. **Contact:** David Boothe, Construction and Maintenance, at the above address (see entry 4455).

**• 4462 • National Zoological Park Traineeship in Landscaping** *(Graduate, Undergraduate/Internship)*

**Purpose:** To provide interested students with the opportunity to work in landscaping. The recipient will assist with the Zoo's extensive landscaping program, which includes educational exhibits of plants, plant-animal interactions, and exhibit landscaping. **Qualif.:** Applicants must be undergraduates or recent college graduates. **Criteria:** Applicants are judged based on their statement of interest, scholastic achievement, relevant experience, and letters of reference. Preference will be given to advanced undergraduates and recent graduates.

**Funds Avail.:** Full term (12 weeks, summer, or fall) stipend of $2,400. Recipients must make their own lodging arrangements. **To Apply:** Applicants need to send a typewritten letter with data in the following sequence: name, home and college addresses and phone numbers, date of birth, social security number, name of college or university, current academic status, curriculum (major and minor), degrees held or expected (with institution names and dates conferred or anticipated date(s) of conferment), desired dates for the traineeship, program area preference, and a 500- to 1,000-word statement of your interest in landscaping. Statement should include relevant experience, career goals, and reason for wanting an NZP traineeship; transcripts from current and/or past institutions (may be sent separately); and names and addresses of two or more individuals who will send letters of reference directly to the address above in care of Friends of the National Zoo. Previous applicants who wish to have their formerly prepared materials considered should indicate the year they applied. **Deadline:** February 22. **Contact:** Charles Fillah, Horticulturist, at the above address (see entry 4455).

## • 4463 • National Zoological Park Traineeship in Public Affairs *(Graduate, Undergraduate/Internship)*

**Purpose:** To provide interested students with the opportunity to work in public affairs. The recipient will assist in developing, implementing, and evaluating programs. **Qualif.:** Applicants must be undergraduates or recent college graduates. **Criteria:** Applicants are judged based on their statement of interest, scholastic achievement, relevant experience, and letters of reference. Preference is given to advanced undergraduates and recent graduates with some computer skills and a desire to develop program support for multicultural audiences for the Zoo.

**Funds Avail.:** Full term (12 weeks, summer, or fall) stipend of $2,400. Recipients must make their own lodging arrangements. **To Apply:** Applicants need to send a typewritten letter with data in the following sequence: name, home and college addresses and phone numbers; date of birth, social security number, name of college or university, current academic status, curriculum (major and minor), degrees held or expected (with institution names and dates conferred or anticipated date(s) of conferment), desired dates for the traineeship, program area preference, and a 500- to 1,000-word statement of your interest in public affairs. Statement should mention relevant experience, career goals, and reason for wanting an NZP traineeship; transcripts from current and/or past institutions (may be sent separately); and names and addresses of two or more individuals who will send letters of reference directly to the address above in care of Friends of the National Zoo. Previous applicants who wish to have their formerly prepared materials considered should indicate the year they applied. **Deadline:** February 22. **Contact:** Robert Hoage, Office of Public Affairs, at the above address (see entry 4455).

## • 4464 • National Zoological Park Traineeship in Zoo Photography *(Graduate, Undergraduate/Internship)*

**Purpose:** To provide interested students with the opportunity to work in zoo photography. **Qualif.:** Applicants must be undergraduates or recent college graduates. **Criteria:** Applicants are judged based on their statement of interest, scholastic achievement, relevant experience, and letters of reference.

**Funds Avail.:** Full term (12 weeks, summer, or fall) stipend of $2,400. Recipients must make their own lodging arrangements. **To Apply:** Applicants need to send a typewritten letter with data in the following sequence: name, home and college addresses and phone numbers, date of birth, social security number, name of college or university, current academic status, curriculum (major and minor), degrees held or expected (with institution names and dates conferred or anticipated date(s) of conferment), desired dates for the traineeship, program area preference, a 500- to 1,000-word statement describing interest in zoo photography, and 15 to 20 black and white prints of slides of applicant's work. Statements should include relevant experience, career goals, and reason for wanting an NZP traineeship; transcripts from current and/or past institutions (may be sent separately); and names and addresses of two or more individuals who will send letters of reference directly to the address above in care of Friends of the National Zoo. Previous applicants who wish to have their formerly prepared materials considered should indicate the year they applied. **Deadline:** February 22. **Contact:** Jessie Cohen, Photographer, at the above address (see entry 4455).

## • 4465 •
## Nations Bank of Texas - Minnie L. Maffett Scholarship Trust
PO Box 831515
Dallas, TX 75283-1515

### • 4466 • Minnie L. Maffett Scholarship *(Doctorate, Graduate, Undergraduate/Scholarship)*

**Purpose:** To further the education of Limestone County students pursuing undergraduate degrees. **Focus:** General Studies. **Qualif.:** Candidates must be graduates of a Limestone County, Texas, high school who plan to attend a college or university in the state of Texas.

**Funds Avail.:** Awards range from $100 to $1,000 each. **No. of Awards:** 50-75. **To Apply:** Students must submit a completed application, transcript of grades, and verification of full-time enrollment. **Deadline:** April 1. **Contact:** June Hagler at the above address (see entry 4465).

## • 4467 •
## Native American Education Unit
New York State Education Dept.
Education Bldg., Rm. 478 EBA    Ph: (518)474-0537
Albany, NY 12234    Fax: (518)474-3666

### • 4468 • New York State Indian Aid *(Undergraduate/Award)*

**Focus:** General Studies. **Qualif.:** Applicants must be New York State residents who are on an official tribal roll of a New York State tribe or children of enrolled members. New York State tribes include members of the Iroquoian tribes (St. Regis Mohawk, Oneida, Onondaga, Cayuga, Seneca Nation, Tonawanda Band of Seneca, and Tuscarora), the Shinnecock tribe, and the Poospatuck tribe. In addition, students must have graduated from an accredited high school, attained a high school equivalency diploma, or are enrolled in a special 24-credit hour program at an approved, accredited postsecondary institution that will lead to degree status and a high school equivalency diploma. Recipients must also be enrolled in an approved program offered by a college, university, technical school, school of nursing, or business or trade school located in New York State. Approved programs include collegiate and non-collegiate programs registered by the New York State Education Department. Aid is not available for graduate study, for study that is not college-level, nor for study at institutions located outside New York State. There are no age restrictions on eligibility for Native American Student Aid. **Criteria:** Funding is contingent upon the satisfactory progress (2.0 semester GPA) toward a degree or certificate requirements. Recipients are required to submit their grades to the Native American Education Unit at the end of each semester for which funding is received.

**Funds Avail.:** Up to $1,750 per year for up to four years of full-time study (five years for specific programs requiring five years to complete degree requirements). Students must be enrolled in at least 12 credit hours or more to be considered full-time. Students enrolled in institutions on the trimester or quarter system must be enrolled for at least 24 credit hours per year. Funds are pro-rated for part-time status. If funding is available, students may receive aid for summer course work. Any aid received for summer school study is deducted from the student's maximum entitlement for four years of full-time college study. Payment processing takes between four and six weeks from the receipt of the voucher to the mailing of the payment; payments are sent directly to the college. Special arrangements can be made with certain schools that have nontraditional schedules, such as Empire State College. The Unit will provide information on such arrangements. Students receiving the Tuition Assistance Program Aid (TAP) may also receive this

## Native American Education Unit (continued)

award. **To Apply:** Applicants must submit a completed application form, available from the State Education Department, along with proof of high school graduation, an official tribal certification form, and a letter of acceptance from the college to the State Education Department. Students who are minors must have the signature of a parent or guardian approving their stated educational plans. After initial approval, students must notify the Unit of their interest in aid for each subsequent semester they wish to receive the award. This may be done by completing a Request for New York State Indian Aid form, which is mailed to students' homes each semester they receive aid. Proof of satisfactory academic progress (at least 2.0 GPA) must be submitted each term preceding requests for additional aid. **Deadline:** July 15 for the fall semester; December 31 for the spring semester; and May 20 for the summer term. **Contact:** Adrian Cooke, Acting Coordinator.

---

## • 4469 •
## Native American Journalists Association
1433 E. Franklin Ave., No. 11      *Ph:* (612)874-8833
Minneapolis, MN 55404-2135      *Fax:* (612)874-9007
*E-mail:* najanut@aol.com; najanut@aol.com
*URL:* http://www.medill.nwu.edu/naja/newsletter/fall96.html

### • 4470 • Native American Journalists Association Scholarships (Undergraduate/Scholarship)

**Purpose:** To assist Native American students pursuing a degree in journalism or a related field. **Focus:** Communications. **Qualif.:** Scholarship winners must be members of NAJA (student membership fee is $10).

**Funds Avail.:** $2,000 scholarships for those studying print/photojournalism, $700 to $4,000 scholarships for broadcast. **To Apply:** Qualified applicants must send a cover letter containing name, address, phone number, parents' names, applicant's college plans, year in school, major, and statement of post-college plans; proof of tribal enrollment; official transcript; one recommendation from a school advisor, counselor, or professional familiar with applicant's background; and sample of work, if available. **Deadline:** March 31.

**Remarks:** Awards are cataloged in a newsletter available upon request, wherein different funds available (and their different requirements) are detailed. **Contact:** NAJA at the above address (see entry 4469).

---

## • 4471 •
## Native Sons of the Golden West
414 Mason St., Ste. 300
San Francisco, CA 94102
     *Ph:* (415)392-1223

### • 4472 • Native Sons of the Golden West High School Public Speaking Scholarships (High School/Prize)

**Purpose:** To further public speaking and historical knowledge of California. **Focus:** Public Speaking. **Qualif.:** Student speakers under the age of 20 must be certified by their high school to participate. Contestants must be nominated by a high school and attend a local area contest. Speeches may be made on any subject related to past or present history, geography, or cultural development of California. **Criteria:** Selection is based on organization, content, style, and delivery of the speech.

**Funds Avail.:** Prizes at statewide contest are $1,600 (first) and $600 (runners up). In May of each year, local winners attend a statewide contest. **Deadline:** January. **Contact:** Ralph Cordero, State Chairman, Public Speaking Contest, Native Sons of the Golden West, 160 Everglade Dr., San Francisco, CA, 94132.

---

## • 4473 •
## Natural Sciences and Engineering Research Council of Canada
350 Albert St.      *Ph:* (613)995-5857
Ottawa, ON, Canada K1A 1H5      *Fax:* (613)992-5337
*E-mail:* schol@nserc.ca

### • 4474 • NSERC Research Scholarships, Fellowships, and Grants (Graduate, Postdoctorate, Postgraduate, Professional Development/Fellowship, Grant, Scholarship)

**Purpose:** To support Canadians conducting research or involved in graduate study in the natural sciences or engineering in the Canadian university sector. **Focus:** Engineering, Natural Sciences. **Qualif.:** For most NSERC awards, applicant must be a Canadian citizen or landed immigrant, and be a student, postdoctoral, mid-career, or senior researcher seeking support for activities in the natural sciences or engineering and working in a university environment. Awards to Canadians are available for research and training in Canada and abroad. Types of awards administered by NSERC include: postgraduate scholarships, postdoctoral fellowships, research fellowships at government and industrial laboratories, and research grants. Funds are not available to students or researchers in the basic biomedical sciences or clinical medicine. **Criteria:** Depends on program. All awards are based on excellence and are peer reviewed.

**Funds Avail.:** Varies, according to program. **To Apply:** Literature on program is available from NSERC. Provide a description of educational/professional background, current scientific activities, and proposed field of research, training, or study. Basic information about NSERC awards is also available from university offices of graduate study in Canada. **Deadline:** Varies, according to program. **Contact:** Grants and Scholarships Directorate and Targetted Research Directorate at the above address (see entry 4473).

---

## • 4475 •
## The Walter W. Naumburg Foundation
60 Lincoln Center Plaza      *Ph:* (212)874-1150
New York, NY 10023-6588      *Fax:* (212)724-0263

### • 4476 • International Competition Prizes (Professional Development/Prize)

**Purpose:** To promote the careers of young artists. **Focus:** Cello, Piano, Violin, Voice. **Qualif.:** Each year the Competition is held in a different category: Classical Guitar in 1996. Applicant may be a musician of any nationality. Applicant must be between the ages of 17 and 33 years as of the Competition date, 35 years for voice. The winner of the Competition may not make significant professional appearances in New York City between the date of the competition and that of the first recital at Alice Tully Hall. If such a performance occurs, and the program is reviewed by the press, the Foundation will consider the recital forfeited.

**Funds Avail.:** First prize: $5,000; second prize: $2,500; third prize: $1,000. **To Apply:** Write for application form and instructions.

**Remarks:** First prize also includes two fully subsidized recitals at Alice Tully Hall, a recording with Musical Heritage Records, orchestral and recital performances, and a one-week residency by

Quad-City Arts and Bauff Summer Residency. **Contact:** Lucy Rowan Mann, at the above address (see entry 4475).

**• 4477 • Walter W. Naumburg Awards** *(Other/Award)*

**Focus:** Music, Voice 1999. **Qualif.:** The competition is open to musicians of every nationality, between the ages of 17 and 33. The competition rotates for piano, voice, cello, and violin.

**Funds Avail.:** A first-prize award of $5,000, plus two fully subsidized recitals in Alice Tully Hall at Lincoln Center, New York City; a recording with musical Heritage Records; orchestral and recital performances. The second prize is a recital. Third prize is $1,000. **To Apply:** Applicants must submit letters of recommendation from three musicians of acknowledged standing, with complete names and addresses given. Proof of age of applicants must be provided. Birth certificates or passports or certified school records are acceptable for this purpose. Along with the formal application, applicants must submit (and be prepared to perform) at least two full programs that illustrate repertory interest. There is a $100 application fee. **Deadline:** March 1. **Contact:** Lucy Rowan Mann at the above address (see entry 4475).

**• 4478 •**
**Navajo Code Talkers Association, Inc.**
103 W. 66th Ave.                    *Ph:* (505)722-2228
Gallup, NM 87301                    *Fax:* (505)863-6006

**• 4479 • Navajo Code Talkers Scholarship**
*(Graduate, Postgraduate, Professional Development, Undergraduate/Scholarship)*

**Purpose:** To meet financial needs of Navajo Code Talkers' children or grandchildren to complete an academic or vocational requirement for a degree or certificate. **Qualif.:** Applicant must be an immediate family relation of a Navajo Code Talker. **Criteria:** Students present their need to the organization in person. **To Apply:** Applicants must present their need in detail, and provide information on their academic background and the educational institution they will attend and support letters from the previously-attended schools. **Deadline:** Application must be made no later than three months prior to entry date. **Contact:** A relative who is an active Navajo Code Talker or the Association at PO Box 1182, Window Rock, Arizona, 86515 or at the above address (see entry 4478).

**• 4480 •**
**Naval Academy Women's Club**
c/o Mary R. Seymour, Scholarship
   Chairman
Box 6417
Annapolis, MD 21401                    *Ph:* (301)267-7626

**• 4481 • Naval Academy Women's Club Scholarship**
*(Undergraduate/Scholarship)*

**Qualif.:** Applicants should be one of the following: the child of a Navy or Marine Corps officer on active duty, retired or deceased who is, or has been, stationed as a commissioned officer at the U.S. Naval Academy Complex; the child of a faculty or senior staff member presently employed at the Academy; the child of a Navy or Marine Corps enlisted person presently stationed at the Academy; or a current member of the Naval Academy Women's Club.

**Funds Avail.:** Up to $1000 awarded annually. **No. of Awards:** 20. **To Apply:** Reapplication and good GPA are required to retain the scholarship. **Deadline:** March 31. **Contact:** Mary R. Seymour, Scholarship Chairman, NMPC-121D, Navy Dept., Washington, MD 20370-5121.

**• 4482 •**
**Naval Military Personnel Command**
NMPC-121D
Navy Department
Washington, DC 20370-5121                    *Ph:* (202)694-3126

**• 4483 • Armed Forces Health Professions Scholarship** *(Graduate/Scholarship)*

**Qualif.:** Applicants must be attending an accredited medical school or school of osteopathy in the U.S. Graduates become Navy medical officers.

**Funds Avail.:** Full tuition.

**Remarks:** Scholarship is awarded annually for up to four years per person. **Contact:** Local Navy Recruiter.

**• 4484 •**
**Naval Officers Association of Canada (Calgary Branch)**
PO Box 6291
Station D
Calgary, AB, Canada T2P 2C9

**• 4485 • Robert Hampton Gray Memorial Bursary**
*(Undergraduate/Scholarship)*

**Focus:** General Studies. **Qualif.:** Applicants must be direct descendants of individuals who served with the British Commonwealth naval forces or be a past or present member of the naval corps. They must also have resided in Alberta for three years and be undertaking university level studies. **Criteria:** Preference is given to students residing in or south of the Red Deer area.

**Funds Avail.:** One $600 scholarship. **No. of Awards:** 1. **To Apply:** Candidate may submit anytime prior to deadline. **Deadline:** October 31. **Contact:** The President, Naval Officers' Association of Canada (Calgary Branch), at the above address (see entry 4484).

**• 4486 •**
**Naval Officers' Spouses' Association**
PO Box 280004
Naval Station
Mayport, FL 32228

**• 4487 • Naval Officers' Spouses' Association of Mayport Scholarships** *(Graduate, Undergraduate/Scholarship)*

**Focus:** General Studies. **Qualif.:** Applicants must be dependents of Regular or Reserve Navy, Marine Corps, or Coast Guard members serving on active duty, retired-with-pay, or who died on active duty or in retired-with-pay status. The military members must currently be stationed at Naval Station Mayport, or have completed one PCS tour at Naval Station or Naval Air Station, Mayport. Spouses of military members are also eligible. Applicants must have

## Naval Officers' Spouses' Association (continued)

graduated from or expect to graduate from an accredited high school or equivalent and must intend to enter a college or university to earn an undergraduate or graduate degree. **Criteria:** Awards are based on scholastic proficiency, character, all-around ability and/or financial need.

**Funds Avail.:** The amount of the scholarship varies from year to year. **No. of Awards:** Varies. **To Apply:** Applicants must submit the official form, Dependents' Scholarship Program Competition Application (NAVPERS 1750/7). A high school transcript, family financial information, and information on the sponsor is also required, including copies of the applicant's 1040 tax forms and ID cards. Applicants must furnish results of the Scholastic Aptitude Test (SAT) or the American College Test (ACT) or the Graduate Record Exam (GRE). A maximum of two letters of recommendation will be accepted. A self-addressed post card should be mailed for receipt notification. Applicants must give specific assignments and dates of assignment at Naval Station Mayport and must also include their social security numbers. **Deadline:** Completed applications must be received by the sponsor not later than March 15.

**Remarks:** The Naval Officers' Spouses' Association established a scholarship to assist dependents in their pursuit of higher education. The Association maintains control of the funds, establishes eligibility criteria, and appoints its own selection committee. **Contact:** NOSA, PO Box 280004, Naval Station, Mayport, FL 32228 for an application or information. Completed application and transcript must be sent to NOSA PO Box 280004, Naval Station, Mayport, FL 32228, attn: Ways and Means.

## • 4488 •
## Naval Reserve Officers Training Corps Program
U.S. Navy & Marine Corps
Comdr., Navy Recruiting Command
Attn: Code 314
801 N. Randolph St.
Arlington, VA 22203

Ph: (703)696-4581
Fax: (703)696-0125
Free: 800-628-7682

### • 4489 • Navy-Marine Corps ROTC College
Scholarships *(Undergraduate/Scholarship)*

**Purpose:** To educate and train qualified men and women for service as commissioned officers in the unrestricted line Naval Reserve or Marine Corps Reserve. **Focus:** General Studies. **Qualif.:** Applicants must be United States citizens who are between the ages of 17 and 21 who will graduate from high school prior to entering college. They must also meet basic academic requirements and the minimum SAT/ACT score requirements.

**Funds Avail.:** Up to $8,000. **No. of Awards:** Varies. **To Apply:** Application information is obtained from local Navy/Marine Corps recruiters. **Deadline:** A completed form or application is due by January 31. **Contact:** Patrick Tighe, CNRC (code 314); 703-696-4581; Toll-free telephone: 800-327-Navy and ask for a brochure.

## • 4490 •
## Navy League of the United States
2300 Wilson Blvd.
Arlington, VA 22201
*URL:* http://www.navyleague.org/

Ph: (703)528-1775
Fax: (703)528-2333

### • 4491 • Navy League Scholarship Program
*(Undergraduate/Scholarship)*

**Focus:** General studies. **Qualif.:** Applicants must be high school graduates under the age of 25; be of good character, well-

motivated, and have an excellent academic record; demonstrate an appreciation of the laws, traditions and values of the United States; and be U.S. citizens. **Criteria:** Awards are made on the basis of academic achievement and financial need. Preference is given to applicants who have demonstrated an interest in, and an intention to continue their education in mathematics and/or the sciences; and those who are children of current or former members (including deceased members) of the U.S. Navy, Marine Corps, Coast Guard, and U.S.-flag merchant marine.

**Funds Avail.:** $2,000 to $2,500. **No. of Awards:** 7. **To Apply:** Applicants must submit an application form; parents' most recent Federal Income Tax Return and any information thought helpful in demonstrating financial need; high school transcript; and a typed statement of personal goals and career objectives in 200 words or less. **Deadline:** April 1. **Contact:** Scholarship Coordinator.

### • 4492 • Philippines Subic Bay-Cubi Point
Scholarship *(Undergraduate/Scholarship)*

**Focus:** General studies. **Qualif.:** Applicants must be dependents of personnel who were permanently stationed at U.S. Naval facility, Philippines or dependents of personnel attached to a ship permanently homeported at the U.S. Naval facility, Philippines from 1980 through 1992; be high school graduates or equivalent under the age of 25; be of good character, well-motivated, and have excellent academic records (minimum GPA 3.0); have demonstrated an appreciation of the laws, traditions and values of the United States, and be U.S. citizens. **Criteria:** Awards are made based on character, financial need, and academic record. Preference is given to students entering their first year of undergraduate study.

**Funds Avail.:** $2,000 to $2,500. **No. of Awards:** Varies. **To Apply:** Applicants must submit an application; parent's most recent Federal Income Tax Return and any information felt helpful in demonstrating financial need; high school transcript, and typed statement of personal goals and career objectives in 200 words or less. Send a business-sized, self-addressed stamped envelope to receive further scholarship information. **Deadline:** April 1. **Contact:** Scholarship Coordinator.

## • 4493 •
## Navy-Marine Corps Relief Society
801 N. Randolph St., Rm. 1228
Arlington, VA 22203-1978

Ph: (703)696-4960
Fax: (703)696-0144

### • 4494 • ADM Mike Boorda Seaman-to-Admiral
Educational Assistance Program *(Undergraduate/Grant, Loan)*

**Focus:** General Studies. **Qualif.:** Applicants must be service members enrolled in a Commissioning Program (NROTC, ECP, MECEP, EEAP, etc.). Grants cover undergraduate studies. NROTC must be prior active duty directly released to commissioning or NROTC program. **Criteria:** Grants are based on need.

**Funds Avail.:** Up to $2,000. **To Apply:** Applications may be made through the Professor of Naval Science or administrative commanding officer who is responsible for verifying status, need, and financial data.

**Remarks:** Interest-free loans may also be awarded when the needs and circumstances of the applicant so warrant, but award can not exceed $2,000. **Contact:** The Navy-Marine Corps Relief Society at the above address (see entry 4493).

### • 4495 • Children of Deceased Active Duty
Servicemembers Grants *(Undergraduate/Grant)*

**Purpose:** To provide a grant, awarded at the discretion of the Society, for the undergraduate studies and vocational training of children of service members who died on active duty. **Focus:** General Studies. **Qualif.:** Applicants must be high school graduates. They must be children, including step-children and legally adopted children, of Navy or Marine Corps members who died while on active duty. **Criteria:** Based on need.

**Funds Avail.:** For children of service members who died while on active duty, a grant is awarded based on the needs and circumstances of each individual applicant. **To Apply:** Applications may be obtained from NMRCS Headquarters only. **Deadline:** Applications must be made no later than 30 days prior to the end of the school year for which the loan is to be made. **Contact:** The Navy-Marine Corps Relief Society at the above address (see entry 4493).

#### • 4496 • Children of Deceased, Retired Servicemembers Grants *(Undergraduate/Grant)*

**Purpose:** These are grants based on cost of attendance for the academic year, after offset by such financial aid as social security, VA benefits, and other approved educational loans. Grants are intended for undergraduate studies and vocational training only. **Qualif.:** Applicants must be high school graduates. They must be children, including step-children and legally adopted children, of Navy or Marine Corps members who died in retired status. **Criteria:** Based on need.

**Funds Avail.:** Up to $2,000. **To Apply:** Applications may be obtained from NMRCS Headquarters only. **Contact:** The Navy-Marine Corps Relief Society at the above address (see entry 4493).

#### • 4497 • Vice Admiral E.P. Travers Scholarships and Loan Program *(Undergraduate/Grant, Loan)*

**Focus:** General Studies. **Qualif.:** Applicants must be the dependent children of active duty or retired servicemembers or the spouse of an active duty sailor or marine. A dependent is defined as a someone who possesses a valid dependent's Uniformed Services Identification and Privilege Card. All candidates must be enrolled or accepted as full-time students at post-secondary educational institutions accredited by the U.S. Department of Education and have a minimum cumulative GPA of 2.0. **Criteria:** Selection is based on financial need. Satisfactory academic progress and continued financial need are required to retain scholarship.

**Funds Avail.:** Grant up to $2,000; loan up to $3,000. **No. of Awards:** 500. **To Apply:** Applications may be obtained from NMRCS Headquarters and NMCRS Auxiliaries worldwide. **Deadline:** March 1 for grant; Oct. 1 for loan.

**Remarks:** Applicants for this award who apply by March 1 will be automatically considered for the Society's Vice Admiral E.P. Travers Interest-Free Parent Loan. **Contact:** Navy-Marine Corps Relief Society at the above address (see entry 4493).

#### • 4498 • USS Stark Memorial Scholarships *(Undergraduate/Scholarship)*

**Focus:** General Studies. **Qualif.:** Funding is limited to sons, daughters, and widows of deceased crewmembers of the USS Stark who perished as a result of the Persian Gulf missile attack on May 17, 1987. **To Apply:** Applications may be obtained from NMRCS Headquarters only. **Deadline:** Applications must be made no later than 30 days prior to the end of the school year for which the scholarship will take effect. **Contact:** The Navy-Marine Corps Relief Society at the above address (see entry 4493).

#### • 4499 • USS Tennessee Scholarships *(Undergraduate/Scholarship)*

**Focus:** General Studies. **Qualif.:** Funding is limited to dependent children of active duty personnel assigned, or previously assigned, to duty aboard the USS Tennessee and is to be used for postsecondary undergraduate education at a college or university accredited by the U.S. Department of Education.

**Funds Avail.:** $1,000 per student, per year based on need. **To Apply:** Applications may be obtained from NMRCS Headquarters and Georgia Auxiliary. **Deadline:** Applications must be postmarked by July 15. **Contact:** The Navy-Marine Corps Relief Society at the above address (see entry 4493).

---

### • 4500 •
### Navy Supply Corps Foundation
Navy Supply Corps School
1425 Prince Ave.   *Ph:* (706)354-4111
Athens, GA 30606-2205   *Fax:* (706)354-0334
*E-mail:* kmorris@athens.net
*URL:* http://www.usnscf.com

#### • 4501 • Navy Supply Corps Foundation Scholarships *(Undergraduate/Scholarship)*

**Focus:** General Studies. **Qualif.:** Applicants must be dependent sons or daughters of Navy Supply Corps Officers (including Warrant Officer) and Supply Corps associated enlisted ratings on active duty, in reserve status, retired-with-pay, or deceased (while in aforementioned categories). Recipient must attend a two- or four-year accredited college full time pursuing an undergraduate degree only. A 3.0 grade point average for high school/college is required. Some of the scholarships within the program are restricted to officer or enlisted dependents only, geographic location, education entry level, or similar factors. **Criteria:** Awards are based on scholastic ability, character, leadership, and financial need.

**Funds Avail.:** $2,500. **No. of Awards:** 60. **To Apply:** Application and high school/college transcripts must be submitted. **Deadline:** April 10. Winners are notified by May 30.

**Remarks:** The Foundation typically receives more than 150 applications. **Contact:** Kaye Morris at the above address (see entry 4500).

---

### • 4502 •
### Nebraska Department of Veterans' Affairs
301 Centennial Mall South   *Ph:* (402)471-2458
Lincoln, NE 68509   *Fax:* (402)471-2491

#### • 4503 • Nebraska Department of Veterans' Affairs Waiver of Tuition *(Undergraduate/Other)*

**Purpose:** To provide tuition assistance for the dependents of qualifying veterans at state-supported colleges in Nebraska. **Focus:** General Studies. **Qualif.:** Applicants must be the children, spouses, widows, or widowers of veterans who died of a service-connected disability, who is totally disabled as a result of military service, or who is classified missing in action or prisoner of war after August 4, 1964. Recipients must be residents of Nebraska and attend a state-supported college in Nebraska. **To Apply:** Applications may be submitted to the Nebraska Department of Veterans' Affairs through one of the recognized veterans organizations or any County Veterans Service Officer. **Deadline:** Applications must be submitted in time for proper checking and certification prior to the beginning of any school term. **Contact:** Jonathan F. Sweet at the above address (see entry 4502).

---

• 4504 •
**Nebraska Space Grant Consortium**
UNO-Allwine Hall 422       *Ph:* (402)554-3772
Omaha, NE 68182-0406      *Fax:* (402)554-3781
                        *Free:* 800-858-8648

*E-mail:* nasa@unomaha.edu
*URL:* http://unomaha.edu/~himbergr/space.html

**• 4505 • Nebraska Space Grant Scholarships and Fellowships** *(Graduate, Undergraduate/Fellowship, Scholarship)*

**Focus:** Aviation, space-related studies. **Qualif.:** Applicants must be attending participating Nebraska institutions and be U.S. citizens.

**Funds Avail.:** $100,000. **No. of Awards:** Varies. **To Apply:** Write for further details. **Contact:** Michaela Schaaf at the above address (see entry 4504).

---

**• 4506 •**
**Negro Educational Emergency Drive**
643 Liberty Ave., 17th Fl.      *Ph:* (412)566-2760
Pittsburgh, PA 15222        *Fax:* (412)471-6643
                        *Free:* 800-697-2760

**• 4507 • NEED Scholarships** *(Undergraduate/Scholarship)*

**Purpose:** To provide supplemental financial support to students with limited family resources. **Focus:** General Studies. **Qualif.:** Applicants must have a high school diploma or GED and be enrolled or plan to enroll in a state-approved program. They must be residents of Allegheny, Armstrong, Beaver, Butler, Washington, or Westmoreland county, in southwestern Pennsylvania. **Criteria:** Students must demonstrate financial need and be in good academic standing.

**Funds Avail.:** Awards range from $100 to $1,000 each. **To Apply:** Applicants must submit a NEED application form, recent high school or college transcripts (or GED test scores), a signed and notarized income form, and a signed financial aid release form. **Deadline:** April 30. **Contact:** Herman L. Reid, Jr., Executive Director, at the above address (see entry 4506).

---

**• 4508 •**
**Neighbors of Woodcraft**
PO Box 769               *Ph:* (503)656-8118
Oregon City, OR 97045-0052    *Fax:* (503)656-7656
*URL:* http://www.nowfbs.com

**• 4509 • James Conover Neighbors of Woodcraft Scholarship** *(Undergraduate/Scholarship)*

**Purpose:** To award scholarships to deserving members of Neighbors of Woodcraft for their financial help in obtaining higher education. **Focus:** General Studies. **Qualif.:** Applicants must be high school graduates and members of Neighbors of Woodcraft for at least two years. **Criteria:** Selection is made on the basis of school achievement, two letters from teachers or counselors, need, and scholastic standing.

**Funds Avail.:** $25,000 per year. **To Apply:** Applications are available from Neighbors of Woodcraft. **Deadline:** March 19. **Contact:** Judy Wright at the above address (see entry 4508).

**• 4510 •**
**Nellie Mae**
50 Braintree Hill Park      *Ph:* (617)849-1325
Braintree, MA 02184       *Free:* 800-338-5626
*E-mail:* info@nelliemae.org
*URL:* http://www.nelliemae.org

**• 4511 • Supplemental Education Loans for Families** *(Undergraduate/Loan)*

**Qualif.:** Students must be attending one of the 32 member institutions of the Consortium, which are: Amherst College, Barnard College, Brown University, Bryn Mawr College, Carleton College, Columbia University, Cornell University, Dartmouth College, Duke University, Georgetown University, Harvard University, The Johns Hopkins University, Massachusetts Institute of Technology, Mount Holyoke College, Northwestern University, Oberlin College, Pomona College, Princeton University, Radcliffe College, Rice University, Smith College, Stanford University, Swarthmore College, Trinity College, The University of Chicago, University of Pennsylvania, The University of Rochester, Washington University, Wellesley College, Wesleyan University, Williams College, and Yale University. Loan applicant may be a student, spouse, parent or other responsible person and may come from any income level. United States citizenship is required of at least one applicant (student, spouse, parent, or responsible other person). Loans must be used for only educational expenses.

**Funds Avail.:** Loans vary from $2,000 to cost of attendance per year. There are three repayment options, one of which is chosen at the time of application. Repayment begins 45 days after the loan is disbursed and must be completed within 20 years. There is no penalty for prepaying. The options are: Fixed monthly payments of interest and principal; interest is paid first and the balance is paid toward reducing the principal. Deferred principal payment; interest is paid monthly and payment of principal can be deferred up to four years. **To Apply:** Credit standards require a satisfactory credit history for each applicant and demonstration of sufficient current income to meet current liabilities including SHARE. In general, the ratio of monthly installment expenses including mortgage, auto and revolving payments to net monthly income after withheld taxes can not exceed 40 percent. Application requires credit information from the student and borrower or borrowers. Completed applications including required documentation are first sent to the financial aid office of the college or university the student attends. The school verifies student's attendance and computes the annual cost of education less any financial aid awards or certifies tuition prepayment amounts. The school then forwards the application to Nellie Mae. When the application is approved, a promissory note is signed by all the applicants. **Deadline:** There are no application deadlines, but summer application is encouraged.

**Remarks:** SHARE, the acronym for Supplemental Education Loans for Families, is a program sponsored by the New England Education Loan Marketing Corporation (Nellie Mae), and the member institutions of the Consortium on Financing Higher Education (COFHE). **Contact:** Financial aid offices of the participating institutions or Nellie Mae, 50 Braintree Hill Park, Braintree, MA 02184, or above address.

• 4512 •

**Ervin, Mary and Ida Nepage Scholarship Fund**
c/o US Bank of WWH 348, Trust
  Div.
PO Box 720                *Ph:* (206)344-5090
Seattle, WA 98111-0720     *Free:* 800-505-4545

• **4513** • Ida L., Mary L., and Ervin R. NePage
**Foundation** *(Undergraduate/Scholarship)*

**Purpose:** To help worthy students enrolled in Seattle community colleges. **Focus:** Nursing, Sociology, or Library Science. **Qualif.:** Applicants must be enrolled full time in Seattle community colleges and must have completed at least one year of study in their fields. No applicant may be related to members of the selection committee or trustees of the U.S. Bank.

**Funds Avail.:** Scholarships range from $500-$1,200. **No. of Awards:** Approximately 10. **To Apply:** Forms are available at Seattle community colleges. References from two instructors and transcripts must be submitted for consideration. **Deadline:** January 29. **Contact:** Ms. Mooi Lien Wong, Vice President.

• 4514 •

**Netz Hilai**
212 Bney Ephriam St., Apt. 1A
09985 Tel Aviv, Israel

• **4515** • Netz Hilai Visiting Artists Fellowships
*(Professional Development/Fellowship)*

**Purpose:** To provide artists with an opportunity to pursue their work in Israel. **Focus:** Arts, including Architecture, Musical Composition, Photography, Playwriting, Poetry, Writing. **Qualif.:** Candidate may be of any nationality. Applicant must be a writer, composer, architect, photographer or other artist. Fellowships are tenable at Ma'alot-Tarshiha and/or Mitzpe Ramon in Israel. Awardees pay $25/week and are expected to contribute to the community in suitable cultural and educational activities.

**Funds Avail.:** Housing. **To Apply:** Write to the director for application form and guidelines. Forms will not be sent unless a self-addressed, stamped envelope is included. Submit three copies of form, curriculum vitae, application fee and samples or reviews of work to the Admissions Committee at the above address. **Deadline:** None. Notification within ten weeks of application.

**Remarks:** The Pollack-Krasner Foundation considers applications from visual artists who, in order to accept and fully utilize a colony residency, will need financial help beyond that which a colony can offer.

• 4516 •

**The Neurosciences Institute**
10640 John Jay Hopkins Dr.     *Ph:* (619)626-2000
San Diego, CA 92121        *Fax:* (619)626-2099
*E-mail:* info@nsi.edu
*URL:* http://www.nsi.edu

• **4517** • Fellowships in Theoretical Neurobiology
*(Postdoctorate/Fellowship)*

**Purpose:** To provide research and training in theoretical neurobiology to young investigators. **Focus:** Theoretical Neurobiology. **Qualif.:** Candidate may be of any nationality, but must be at the postdoctoral or assistant professor level and have

some background in experimental or theoretical neurobiology. Fellowships are tenable only at the Institute.

**Funds Avail.:** Varies with experience. **To Apply:** Submit a statement of interest, curriculum vitae, and the names of three references to the Research Director. **Deadline:** None. **Contact:** Dr. W. Einar Gall, Research Director, at the above address (see entry 4516).

• 4518 •

**Nevada Hispanic Services Scholarship Fund**
190 E. Liberty St.
Reno, NV 89501-2209      *Ph:* (702)786-6003

• **4519** • Nevada Hispanic Services Scholarships
*(Undergraduate/Scholarship)*

**Purpose:** To help fund the undergraduate education of Hispanic students in Nevada. **Focus:** General Studies. **Qualif.:** Applicants must be high school seniors or graduates of Hispanic descent. They must also plan to work in Nevada after college graduation. **Criteria:** Selection is based on academic ability, commitment to helping the Hispanic community, and financial need.

**Funds Avail.:** $2,000. **To Apply:** Materials to be submitted include a completed application, academic transcripts from secondary or post-secondary schools attended, two letters of recommendation from the last school attended, one letter of recommendation from a non-relative, proof of acceptance to a post-secondary institution in Nevada, and a statement of financial need. **Deadline:** April 30. **Contact:** Nevada Hispanic Services Scholarship Fund at the above address (see entry 4518).

• 4520 •

**Nevada Women's Fund**
201 W. Liberty St., Ste. 201
PO Box 50428             *Ph:* (702)786-2335
Reno, NV 89513         *Fax:* (702)786-8152

• **4521** • Nevada Women's Fund Scholarships
*(Doctorate, Graduate, Other, Professional Development, Undergraduate/Scholarship)*

**Purpose:** To provide women residents of Nevada with academic study and vocational training. **Focus:** General Studies. **Qualif.:** Applicants must be women residents of Nevada. **Criteria:** Scholarship selection is based on financial need, course of study, grade point average, community service, work history, and plans for the future.

**Funds Avail.:** In on year, $92,000 in scholarships were awarded ranging from $500 to $5,000 each. **No. of Awards:** Depends on available funds. **To Apply:** Applications are usually available the first week in February. **Deadline:** Usually the first Friday in March.

**Remarks:** Scholarships awarded include: the Charlotte L. Mackenzie Scholarships; the Feltner Family Scholarships, the Public Resource Foundation Scholarships; the Louise and Bill Donovan Scholarships; the Friends of the Fund Scholarship; the Martha H. Jones Scholarships; and the Mary Davis Spirit of Enterprise Scholarship; and the Amy Biehl Memorial Scholarship. Other scholarships are available, which are funded in part with grants and private donations. **Contact:** Fristi H. Ericson, President and Chief Officer, Nevada Women's Fund, at the above address (see entry 4520).

• 4522 •

## New Dramatists
424 W. 44th St.                          *Ph:* (212)757-6960
New York, NY 10036-5298                  *Fax:* (212)265-4738
*E-mail:* newdram@aol.com
*URL:* http://www.itp.tsoa.nyu.edu/~diana/ndintro.html

• 4523 • **Arnold Weissberger Playwrighting Competition** *(Professional Development/Award)*

**Purpose:** To recognize outstanding achievement in playwriting. **Focus:** Drama. **Qualif.:** Applicant may submit only one entry. Entry must be a full length, original, and unpublished play that has not been professionally produced. Musicals, screen plays, and children's plays are ineligible.

**Funds Avail.:** $5,000 **No. of Awards:** 1. **To Apply:** Write for application guidelines. Submit manuscript with a self-addressed stamped envelope for return of entry. **Deadline:** The deadline was May 31. **Contact:** L. Arnold Weissberger at the above address (see entry 4522).

• 4524 •

## New England Board of Higher Education
45 Temple Place                          *Ph:* (617)357-9620
Boston, MA 02111                         *Fax:* (617)338-1577
*E-mail:* rsp@nebhe.org
*URL:* http://www.nebhe.org

• 4525 • **New England Regional Student Program** *(Graduate, Undergraduate/Other)*

**Qualif.:** Candidates must be residents of the New England States (Connecticut, Maine, Massachusetts, New Hampshire, Rhode Island, and Vermont). They may attend the public colleges and universities within the region at reduced tuition rates for certain degree programs that are not offered by their own state's public institutions. Also, for residents of Connecticut, Massachusetts, Rhode Island and Vermont, when a degree program is offered under this program at an in-state and out-of-state institution, if the out-of-state institution is nearer to the student's legal residence the student may apply for RSP status at the out-of-state institution. This option is only available at the two- and four-year college level. It is not applicable at the university level.

**Funds Avail.:** In addition to reduced tuition, students receive admission preference among out-of-state applicants; however, graduate students do not receive preference at state universities. Generally the reduced tuition rate is 50 percent above in-state tuition rather than full out-of-state tuition. **To Apply:** Application for RSP status is made at the same time and on the same form as the admission application.

**Remarks:** The New England Board of Higher Education was created by formal interstate compact. The Regional Student Program is one program of the Board. **Contact:** Office of the Regional Student Program at the above address (see entry 4524).

• 4526 •

## New England Education Society
745 Commonwealth Ave.                    *Ph:* (617)353-3036
Boston, MA 02215                         *Fax:* (617)353-3061

• 4527 • **New England Education Society Loan** *(Graduate/Loan)*

**Focus:** Theology. **Qualif.:** Applicants must be in degree programs at New England seminaries or theological schools. **Criteria:** Awards are granted based on financial need, character, and commitment to ministry or teaching of religion.

**Funds Avail.:** $800. **No. of Awards:** 1. **To Apply:** Write for further details. **Deadline:** None. **Contact:** Earl R. Beane.

• 4528 •

## New England Press Association
360 Huntington Ave. 428-CP
Boston, MA 02115

• 4529 • **New England Press Association Internships** *(Undergraduate/Internship)*

**Focus:** Journalism. **Qualif.:** Applicants must be a sophomore or higher enrolled in accredited programs at a college or university in Connecticut, Maine, Massachusetts, Rhode Island, New Hampshire, or Vermont. **No. of Awards:** 4 annually. **Deadline:** January 8.

• 4530 •

## New England Printing and Publishing Council
c/o WWF Paper Corp.
290 Beaver St.                           *Ph:* (617)749-8500
Franklin, MA 02038                       *Fax:* (508)520-0220

• 4531 • **New England Graphic Arts Scholarships** *(High School, Undergraduate/Scholarship)*

**Purpose:** To financially assist those pursuing an education in the graphic arts. **Focus:** Graphic Arts. **Qualif.:** Applicants must be residents of New England, high school seniors or recent graduates, or students at a college, university or school.

**Funds Avail.:** Maximum of $2,000. **To Apply:** Applicants must submit completed application form and transcipt of grades. **Deadline:** May 15.

**Remarks:** Recipients must maintain a 2.5 semester average to extend award to the following year. **Contact:** George Kaliantos at the above address (see entry 4530).

**• 4532 •**

## New Hampshire Charitable Foundation
Student Aid Program
37 Pleasant St.
Concord, NH 03301-4005          *Ph:* (603)225-6641

**• 4533 •   New Hampshire Charitable Foundation
Statewide Student Aid Program** *(Graduate,
Undergraduate/Grant)*

**Purpose:** To fill any unmet need in students' aid packages or to
reduce loans. **Qualif.:** Applicants must be New Hampshire
residents. Many of the available funds have specific eligibility
restrictions, such as field of study, which are fully described in the
brochure accompanying the application. **Criteria:** Selections are
based on financial need and merit.

**Funds Avail.:** Finalists' aid packages are individually reviewed to
determine award size. **To Apply:** Applications are available from
guidance offices and colleges or from the New Hampshire
Charitable Foundation from late January through mid April.
**Deadline:** April 23.

**Remarks:** Support comes from a variety of individuals, businesses,
and community groups. Out of the 1500 applications received, the
foundation was able to make awards to approximately 500
students. **Contact:** Judith T. Burrows, Director of Student Aid
Programs, at the above address (see entry 4532).

**• 4534 •**

## New Hampshire State Council on the Arts
40 N. Main St.
Phenix Hall                    *Ph:* (603)271-2789
Concord, NH 03301              *Fax:* (603)271-3584
*URL:* http://www.state.nh.us/nharts

**• 4535 •   New Hampshire Individual Artist
Fellowships** *(Other/Fellowship)*

**Purpose:** The awards are given in recognition of artistic excellence
and professional commitment. **Focus:** Visual Arts, Dance, Theatre,
Music, Crafts. **Qualif.:** Individual artists over 18 years of age are
eligible to apply if they are not enrolled as full-time students, have
resided in New Hampshire at least one year prior to application,
have submitted all reports on past Council grants, have not been a
Fellowship recipient in the preceding year, have a resume
demonstrating professional commitment to an artistic discipline,
and have samples of recent work (not more than five years since
completion). Applications from artists working in the following
disciplines are eligible: visual arts (includes photography), crafts,
dance (choreography and performers), music (composition and
performers), theatre (includes mime and puppet), opera/music
theatre, media arts (film, video, audio), literature (poetry, fiction,
playwriting), and multi- and interdisciplinary arts. In order for more
of the top-ranked artists in each discipline to have an opportunity
to receive an award, the committee recommended that review of
the disciplines be divided. In odd years, Literature, Music and
Crafts will be reviewed. In even years, Visual Arts, Dance, Theatre,
and Media will be reviewed. **Criteria:** Recipients will exhibit the
highest artistic quality (based on supporting materials) and
professional commitment (based on resume). Advisory panels
comprised of experts in the visual, media, literary, and performing
arts review all supporting materials. The initial review, which
eliminates all but a few applicants, is done without identification of
the artists. The work must stand on its own. Panelists then may
request biographical information to make Fellowship and Finalist
recommendations to the full Council for final decisions.

**Funds Avail.:** Maximum award is $3,000. **No. of Awards:** Up to 10
fellowships. **To Apply:** Candidates must complete an application
form, prepare a current resume (including education, publications,

and exhibitions) and gather supporting materials for submission. A
material identification sheet must accompany supporting
materials. **Deadline:** May 3.

**Remarks:** Successful applicants will be asked to make a report to
the New Hampshire community in some form during their
fellowship year to which the general public may be invited. The
selection of the event is left to the artist. **Contact:** Audrey
Sylvester, Artist Services, at the above address (see entry 4534).

**• 4536 •**

## New Jersey Academy of Science
Box B, Beck Hall, Rm. 216
Rutgers-The State University      *Ph:* (908)463-0511
Piscataway, NJ 08854             *Fax:* (908)463-0511
*URL:* http://www.shu.edu/~petersma/njas.html

**• 4537 •   New Jersey Academy of Science Research
Grants-in-Aid to High School Students** *(High School/
Grant)*

**Purpose:** To fund the purchase of equipment and supplies needed
for a research project. **Qualif.:** Candidates are New Jersey public
or private secondary school science students.

**Funds Avail.:** Up to $100 is awarded for each research project that
is approved, regardless of whether one student or a team of
students is working on the project. Awards are to be used for the
purchase of equipment and supplies needed for the research
project. **To Apply:** A formal application requests information on the
major object of the project, a project description, and a faculty
recommendation. The project description must include the
hypothesis, experimental procedure including how results will be
measured, bibliography, and a list of equipment and supplies with
cost that are needed for the project and how they are related to the
project. **Deadline:** Applications must be filed by November 1.
Awards are made in early December. **Contact:** The New Jersey
Academy of Science at the above address (see entry 4536).

**• 4538 •**

## New Jersey Department of Military and Veterans'
Affairs
Attn: Public Information Officer
101 Eggert Crossing Road, CN 340    *Ph:* (609)530-6957
Trenton, NJ 08625-0340             *Fax:* (609)530-7100
*E-mail:* CPTSNED@worldnet.att.net
*URL:* http://www.state.nj.us/military/

**• 4539 •   National Guard Association of New Jersey
Scholarship** *(Undergraduate/Scholarship)*

**Focus:** General studies. **Qualif.:** Applicants must be members of
the New Jersey National Guard, or spouses, children, legal wards,
or grandchildren of active members of retired (with at least 20
years of service), or deceased members of the New Jersey
National Guard. **To Apply:** Applicants must submit a completed
application form and official high school transcript (including first
semester of grade twelve) and a copy of high school profile (high
school seniors and graduates), or high school transcript and first
college semester/quarter transcript (college freshmen), or official
transcripts for all formal education completed after high school (all
other applicants). **Deadline:** March 15. **Contact:** National Guard
Association at the above address (see entry 4538).

## • 4540 •
### New Jersey Society for Clinical Laboratory Science
c/o Edward J Peterson
34 Diamond Dr.
Egg Harbor Twp., NJ 08234-9867

*Ph:* (609)653-3221
*Fax:* (609)653-3967

#### • 4541 • NJSCLS Scholarships *(Undergraduate/ Scholarship)*

**Purpose:** To encourage students to enter clinical laboratory science programs. **Qualif.:** Applicants must be enrolled in a medical technology (MT) or medical laboratory technician (MLT) program accredited by the National Accrediting Agency for Clinical Laboratory Science (NAACLS) at a New Jersey institute. MT applicants must be accepted into a clinical practicum and MLT applicants must be entering the final year of their MLT program.

**Funds Avail.:** Two $1,000 scholarships for medical technology students; two $500 scholarships for medical laboratory technician students. If funds permit, additional scholarships may be granted. If the applicant is granted a scholarship and does not complete the MT or MLT program, the amount of the scholarship will be considered a loan, repayable without interest within one year. **To Apply:** Applicants must complete and submit an application form, a copy of their most recent tax return or, if a dependent, their parent's tax return, an application checklist, and a stamped, self-addressed acknowledgment postcard, which will be returned to the applicant as receipt of application. They must also submit an official transcript of all academic credits at the post-secondary level from each college or university attended, and two references completed by a college professor, instructor, and/or advisor. Reference forms are included in the application. **Deadline:** June 15. The scholarships are awarded in September. **Contact:** Edward J. Peterson Jr. at the above address (see entry 4540).

## • 4542 •
### New Jersey State Federation of Women's Clubs
55 Clifton Ave.
New Brunswick, NJ 08901

*Ph:* (908)922-3230

#### • 4543 • New Jersey State Federation of Women's Clubs Margaret Yardley Fellowship *(Doctorate, Graduate/Fellowship)*

**Qualif.:** Applicant must be a New Jersey woman who is a full-time student in graduate school or a doctorate program for an uninterrupted year at an American college. **Criteria:** Selection is based on high standards of character, scholarship, ability, purpose and potential service in choice of career, as well as financial need.

**Funds Avail.:** $1,000. **To Apply:** Requests must be accompanied by a stamped, self-addressed envelope. **Deadline:** March 1.

## • 4544 •
### New Jersey State Golf Association Foundation
PO Box 6947
Freehold, NJ 07728

*Ph:* (908)780-3562

#### • 4545 • New Jersey State Golf Association Caddie Scholarships *(Undergraduate/Scholarship)*

**Purpose:** To provide financial assistance to New Jersey golf caddies who plan to attend college. **Focus:** General Studies. **Qualif.:** Applicants must have caddied for at least one year at a member golf club of the New Jersey State Golf Association. They must also be enrolled full-time at an accredited undergraduate college or university. Applicants whose parents are members of a private golf club are not eligible. **Criteria:** Selection is based on academic achievement, SAT scores, character and leadership qualities, length and quality of service as a caddie, and financial need.

**Funds Avail.:** Scholarships range from $800 to $2,500 per year. Each year there are approximately 30 to 35 new recipients. **No. of Awards:** 30-35 annually. **To Apply:** Applications are available at member golf clubs and New Jersey high schools. A Golf Professional or Caddie Master must confirm the eligibility of each applicant. College students must also submit academic transcripts and a copy of their parent(s)' federal income tax return. High school students must submit class rank, SAT scores, and a copy of their parent(s)' federal income tax return. **Deadline:** May 1. **Contact:** Jay O. Petersen, Educational Director, at the above address (see entry 4544).

## • 4546 •
### New Jersey State Opera
1020 Broad St.
Newark, NJ 07102

*Ph:* (201)623-5757

#### • 4547 • New Jersey State Opera Annual Vocal Competition *(Professional Development/Award)*

**Purpose:** To promote and recognize young talent. **Qualif.:** Applicants must be professional singers between the ages of 22 and 34; if over 27, proof of operatic experience must be presented; satisfactory completion of application form is needed to fulfill eligibility requirements. **Criteria:** Competitors appear before a panel of judges.

**Funds Avail.:** $5,000,000. **No. of Awards:** 3. **Deadline:** February 2.

## • 4548 •
### New Letters Literary Awards
University of Missouri-Kansas City
5100 Rockhill Road
Kansas City, MO 64110

*Ph:* (816)235-1168
*Fax:* (816)235-2611

#### • 4549 • New Letters Literary Awards *(Professional Development/Prize)*

**Purpose:** To recognize outstanding writers. **Focus:** Fiction, Nonfiction, Poetry. **Qualif.:** Applicant may be of any nationality, but must be the author of an original short story, essay, or series of poems. Submitted work must be previously unpublished and may not be a simultaneous submission. Candidate may enter as many times as he/she wishes but must mail all entries separately. Entries will be subject to blind review. Entries are not returned. Each genre is judged separately: The Dorothy Churchill Cappon Essay Prize is awarded for a non-expository essay under 5,000 words in length. Essayists are strongly discouraged from submitting annotated, footnoted, or academic work. The New Letters Fiction Prize is reserved for a work of fiction under 5,000 words in length. The New Letters Poetry Prize is granted for an outstanding group of three to six poems.

**Funds Avail.:** Cappon Essay Prize: $500; Fiction and Poetry Prizes: $750 each. **To Apply:** Send self-addressed, stamped envelope for entry guidelines. Submit each entry with self addressed, stamped 10 envelope and entry fee ($10). **Deadline:** May 15. Prizes are announced in the third week of September.

**Remarks:** Winners, first runners-up, and some honorable mentions are published in New Letters awards edition. **Contact:** Glenda McCrary, Awards Coordinator, at the above address (see entry 4548).

• 4550 •
## New Mexico Student Loan Guarantee Corp.
3900 Osuna Rd., NE        *Ph:* (505)345-8821
PO Box 92230        *Fax:* (505)344-3631
Albuquerque, NM 87199-2230        *Free:* 800-279-5063
*URL:* http://www.nmche.org/financialaid/nmslgc.html

### • 4551 • New Mexico Federal Stafford Loans
*(Graduate, Undergraduate/Loan)*

**Purpose:** Need based. **Focus:** All. **Qualif.:** Applicants must be New Mexico residents or non-residents attending eligible New Mexico post-secondary institutions who are U.S. citizens, nationals, or other eligible non-citizens, and enrolled (or accepted for enrollment) and making satisfactory academic progress at an approved educational institution. Applicants must be enrolled at least half-time, show compliance with selective service requirements, and cannot be in default on another student loan or owe a refund to an education grant program. **Criteria:** Based on financial need.

**Funds Avail.:** Up to $2,625 per year for first year undergraduates; up to $3,500 per year for second year undergraduates; and up to $5,500 per year for the remainder of undergraduate study. Aggregate for undergraduate study cannot exceed $23,000. Up to $8,500 per year for graduate or profession study. Aggregate for undergraduate and graduate study cannot exceed $65,500. Loan amount for a given year cannot exceed the student's cost of attendance minus other financial aid and (if required) the estimated family contribution. Federal government pays interest until student begins repayment six months after graduation, student drops below half-time study, or termination of studies. Interest accrues at a variable interest rate that changes annually and does not exceed nine percent. **Contact:** College financial aid offices, lenders, or the New Mexico Student Loan Guarantee Corp. at the above address (see entry 4550). Toll-free telephone number: (800)279-5063.

### • 4552 • New Mexico Unsubsidized Loan for Students *(Graduate, Undergraduate/Loan)*

**Qualif.:** Applicants must be U.S. citizens, nationals, or permanent residents who are graduate/professional students, independent undergraduates, or dependent undergraduates with extenuating circumstances as determined by school financial aid offices. Students must apply for a Pell Grant and Stafford loan prior to applying for the SLS. Students do not have to demonstrate need. Students cannot be in default or owe a refund on any Title IV program.

**Funds Avail.:** Up to $4,000 per year for the first and second year of undergraduate study and up to $5,000 per year for the third and fourth year. Graduate and professional students may borrow up to $10,000. Aggregate maximum is $23,000. There are no interest benefits paid by the federal government. Borrower must begin paying interest (up to 11 percent) from the day the loan is disbursed or have the interest capitalized (if available). Repayment begins upon graduating, termination of studies, or if student falls below full-time. **To Apply:** Contact financial aid office at higher learning institutions or lenders. **Contact:** College financial aid offices, lenders, or the New Mexico Student Loan Guarantee Corp. at the above address (see entry 4550). Toll-free telephone number: (800)279-5603.

• 4553 •
## New Mexico Veterans' Service Commission
PO Box 2324        *Ph:* (505)827-6300
Santa Fe, NM 87503        *Fax:* (505)827-6372
*URL:* http://www.nmche.orgfinancialaid/vetservice.html

### • 4554 • New Mexico Veterans' Service Commission Scholarships *(Undergraduate/Scholarship)*

**Purpose:** Candidates must be between 16 and 26 years of age. They must be children of those who were residents of New Mexico at the time of entry into military service and who entered the military service of the United States during World War I or II, or during any action in which the military forces of the United States were or are engaged in armed conflict, and who were killed in action or died of some other cause during such conflict or as a result of such service. In addition, children of deceased members of the New Mexico national guard who were killed while on active duty in the service of the state after having been called to active duty by the governor, and children of deceased members of the New Mexico state police who were killed while on active duty in the service of the state are eligible. **Criteria:** Based on need and merit.

**Funds Avail.:** The funds shall be used for the sole purpose of providing the matricular fees, room and board, and books and supplies for the use and benefit of the recipients. No more than $300 in addition to the free tuition shall be paid for any one child in any one year. **To Apply:** Application blanks are available at any State Field Service Office or by writing to the New Mexico Veterans' Service Commission. **Contact:** The New Mexico Veteran's Service Commission at the above address (see entry 4553).

• 4555 •
## The New School for Music Study, Inc.
PO Box 360        *Ph:* (609)921-2900
Kingston, NJ 08528-0360        *Fax:* (609)924-2536

### • 4556 • Piano Teaching Fellowship *(Professional Development/Fellowship)*

**Purpose:** To train graduate students who are already fine musicians and performers to become professional teachers of piano and piano pedagogy. **Focus:** Piano Pedagogy. **Qualif.:** Applicants may be of any nationality and must have bachelor's or master's degrees in piano pedagogy, piano performance, or music education (with a concentration in piano). Private or group teaching experience is desirable. Awards must be applied to tuition fees at the New School. Fellows will be expected to undertake a teaching internship. **Criteria:** Applicants are judged on college transcripts, letters of recommendations, performance and teaching auditions.

**Funds Avail.:** $2,500 per award. **No. of Awards:** 1-4. **To Apply:** Write to the registrar for application guidelines. Submit a resume and other credentials. A personal interview and performance and teaching auditions are required. **Deadline:** March 15. **Contact:** Director, at the above address (see entry 4555).

---

Awards are arranged alphabetically below their administering organizations

## • 4557 •
## New York Association of Black Journalists

PO Box 2446
Rockefeller Center Station      *Ph:* (212)522-6969
New York, NY 10185      *Fax:* (212)522-4425
*E-mail:* troutmp@abc.com
*URL:* http://www.nyabj.com

### • 4558 • Stephen H. Gayle Memorial Scholarship
*(High School, Undergraduate/Scholarship)*

**Purpose:** To encourage minority interest in journalism careers. **Focus:** Journalism. **Qualif.:** Applicants must be college students or graduating high school seniors from New York City, Long Island, or Westchester and planning a career in journalism. **Criteria:** Based on essay.

**Funds Avail.:** Minimum high school grant is $600; college is $1,000. Maximum grant is $3,000. **No. of Awards:** Varies. **To Apply:** Candidates must submit an autobiographical essay related to why they want to enter journalism. **Deadline:** October 19. **Contact:** Pamela Troutman.

## • 4559 •
## The New York Botanical Garden

Bronx, NY 10458-5126      *Ph:* (718)817-8230
     *Fax:* (718)220-6504
*E-mail:* dlentz@nybg.org
*URL:* http://www.nybg.org/

### • 4560 • New York Botanical Garden Fellowships for Graduate Study in Systemic and Economic Botony
*(Doctorate/Fellowship)*

**Focus:** Botany. **Qualif.:** Candidates must be students of systematic or economic botany. The fellowship requires students to devote half-time to formal graduate study leading to a Ph.D. degree in biology at Lehman College of the City University of New York (CUNY), the Biology Department of NYU, or the Biology Department at Cornell University, and half-time to herbarium or laboratory assistance and special assignments in systematic or floristic research in progress at the New York Botanical Garden.

**Funds Avail.:** The fellowship is a stipend of $12,500 a year plus tuition and health insurance and is renewable annually if satisfactory scholastic progress is maintained. **To Apply:** Candidates must submit a completed application form, transcripts, Graduate Record Examination scores, three letters of reference, and a letter telling about themselves. Application and admission to the Ph.D. program at the City University of New York is required and is conducted separately from application for the fellowship. **Deadline:** Fellowship applications must be filed by January 15. Appointments are made by March 15. **Contact:** Administrator of Graduate Studies, The New York Botanical Garden, at the above address (see entry 4559).

## • 4561 •
## New York City Dept. of Personnel

Fellowship Programs
2 Washington St., 15th Fl.      *Ph:* (212)487-5698
New York, NY 10004-1008      *Fax:* (212)487-5715

### • 4562 • Government Scholars Summer Program
*(Graduate, Undergraduate/Award)*

**Purpose:** To provide intensive fieldwork experience in urban government. **Focus:** Public Policy, Urban Government or related fields. **Qualif.:** Applicant must be a college student or recent graduate. Candidate should be interested in pursuing a career in government and willing to commit to full-time employment during the entire internship period. Fellows will participate in seminars and training sessions, and be assigned to a position in one of several city agencies in New York City.

**Funds Avail.:** $3,000. **No. of Awards:** 25. **To Apply:** Contact university placement offices for application form and guidelines, available in October. Submit to the Department the completed form, an essay, transcripts, and letters of recommendation. **Deadline:** January 13. **Contact:** Government Scholars Summer Program at the above address (see entry 4561).

### • 4563 • New York City Urban Fellowships
*(Graduate, Professional Development/Fellowship)*

**Purpose:** To provide intensive fieldwork experience in urban government. **Focus:** Public Policy, Urban Government, or related fields. **Qualif.:** Applicant must be a recent graduate, no more than 2 years out of college. Candidate should be interested in pursuing a career in government. There are no restrictions regarding previous fields of training. Fellows are assigned to one of several city agencies in New York City.

**Funds Avail.:** $18,000. **No. of Awards:** 25. **To Apply:** Write or call for application form and guidelines. Short-listed candidates will be interviewed in New York. **Deadline:** January 20. **Contact:** New York City Urban Fellows Program at the above address (see entry 4561).

### • 4564 • Summer Graduate Internships *(Graduate, Professional Development/Internship)*

**Purpose:** To provide intensive fieldwork experience in urban government. **Focus:** Public Policy, Urban Government. **Qualif.:** Applicant must be a recent graduate, or be enrolled in a graduate program. Candidate should be interested in pursuing a career in government. There are no restrictions regarding previous fields of training. Interns will be assigned a public service position in one of the city agencies in New York City.

**Funds Avail.:** $225-400/week. **To Apply:** Contact university career planning or placement office in January to review the internship directory from the Department of Personnel, which lists all hiring agencies, contact persons, telephone numbers, and areas of interest. To apply, student must send a resume to contact persons listed in the directory. Please do not contact the Department with questions about specific openings. The Department will not send individuals a copy of the directory. **Deadline:** Varies. **Contact:** Summer Graduate Internship Program at the above address (see entry 4561).

## • 4565 •
### New York Council Navy League Scholarship Fund
c/o Intrepid Museum
1 Intrepid Sq., Pier 86      Ph: (212)399-4440
New York, NY 10036      Fax: (212)399-4405
E-mail: chiefync@aol.com

#### • 4566 • New York Council Navy League Scholarships (Undergraduate/Scholarship)

**Purpose:** Support of those who supported us. **Focus:** General Studies. **Qualif.:** Applicants must be dependents of Regular/Reserve Navy, Marine Corps, or Coast Guard members who are on active duty, retired with pay, deceased, or disabled with pay and living in the tri-state area of New York, New Jersey, and Connecticut. **Criteria:** Based on grades and financial need.

**Funds Avail.:** $3,000 per year. **No. of Awards:** 4. **To Apply:** Applications are available by sending a self-addressed, stamped envelope to the above address. **Deadline:** June 15. **Contact:** Donald I. Sternberg at the above address (see entry 4565).

## • 4567 •
### New York Financial Writers' Association
     Fax: 800-533-7560
20281 Greely Sq. Sta.
New York, NY 10001-0003      Free: 800-533-7551
E-mail: nyfwa@aol.com
URL: http://www.nyfwa.org/

#### • 4568 • New York Financial Writers' Association (Undergraduate/Scholarship)

**Focus:** Journalism. **Qualif.:** Applicants must be journalism students in the Metropolitan New York area who are seriously interested in pursuing careers as business and financial journalists. **Criteria:** Awards are made based on quality of essay.

**Funds Avail.:** $2,000. **No. of Awards:** Varies. **To Apply:** Applicants must submit home address and telephone number, an essay explaining why the applicant is pursuing a career in business and financial journalism, and relevant professional information. Writing samples and clips are welcomed but not required. **Deadline:** December 22. **Contact:** Scholarship Committee at the above address (see entry 4567).

## • 4569 •
### New York Foundation for the Arts
155 Avenue of Americas, 14th Fl.      Ph: (212)366-6900
New York, NY 10013      Fax: (212)366-1778

#### • 4570 • New York Foundation for the Arts Artists' Fellowships (Other/Fellowship)

**Focus:** Architecture, Art, Performing Arts, Dance, Painting, Sculpture, Crafts, Choreography, Filmmaking, Writing, Screenwriting, Playwriting, Video, Poetry, Photography, Printmaking, Music Composition. **Qualif.:** Fellowships are awarded to individual creative artists in the following 15 categories: architecture, choreography, crafts, fiction, film, inter-arts/performance art, music composition, nonfiction literature, painting, playwriting/screenwriting, photography, poetry, printmaking/drawing/artists' books, sculpture, and video. Applicants must be artists over 18 years of age and must be residents of New York State. In addition, applicants must be able to submit supporting material showing their recent work. Public service is also a component of the Artists' Fellowships. Students matriculated in full-time degree programs are ineligible to apply for these fellowships.

**Funds Avail.:** Fellowship awards are $7,000 each, pending funding. **To Apply:** Creative artists are invited to attend application seminars, which are held in September in 30 different locations throughout New York State. These regional seminars, sponsored by local Arts Councils, provide prospective applicants with information about the fellowship program and about application procedures. The New York Foundation for the Arts can be contacted for complete listings of regional seminars. **Deadline:** Mid-October.

**Remarks:** The New York Foundation for the Arts first announced the Artists' Fellowship Program on July 1, 1984. The program, defined as a new division of the Foundation, was originally funded with an award of $1.1 million from the New York State Council on the Arts. **Contact:** New York Foundation for the Arts at the above address (see entry 4569).

## • 4571 •
### New York International Ballet Competition
250 W. 57th St., Ste. 1023      Ph: (212)956-1520
New York, NY 10107      Fax: (212)586-8406
E-mail: nyibc2000@nyibc.org
URL: http://www.nyibc.org

#### • 4572 • New York International Ballet Competition (Professional Development/Prize)

**Purpose:** To reward excellence in the field of ballet. **Qualif.:** All ballet dancers throughout the world (between 17-23 years of age for women and 18-24 years of age for men) are eligible to apply. Applicants must be trained dancers with recommendations and on the verge of discovery. **Criteria:** Based on dance education, performance experience, recommendations, and written application. Competitors will be judged by a jury of internationally recognized authorities selected by NYIBC. Scoring will be on a cumulative numerical basis.

**Funds Avail.:** Three weeks lodging in New York City is provided for all competitors. Dancers with the highest score will be awarded cash prizes, medals, and diplomas. **No. of Awards:** At least six. **To Apply:** Formal applications must be accompanied by birth certificate or other proof of age, complete dance education documentation, documentation of performance experience, three recommendations, five 8x10 glossy photographs, name and age of competing partner, name and length of prepared solo, title and composer of music, choreographer, and year choreographed. There is a non-refundable $50 application fee. **Deadline:** Materials must be in by January 15.

**Remarks:** NYIBC is held every three years. **Contact:** The New York International Ballet Competition at the above address (see entry 4571).

## • 4573 •
### New York State Assembly Intern Committee
Legislative Office Bldg., Rm 104-A      Ph: (518)455-4704
Albany, NY 12248      Fax: (518)455-4705
E-mail: intern@assembly.state.ny.us
URL: http://assembly.state.ny.us/internship/

#### • 4574 • New York State Assembly Graduate Scholarships (Postgraduate/Internship, Work Study)

**Focus:** All majors may apply. **Qualif.:** Applicants must be matriculated in or have recently completed a graduate degree

## New York State Assembly Intern Committee *(continued)*

program. They must either be New York State residents or attend a college or university in New York State. The program is open to applicants in any academic field. A strong interest in state government and legislative process is desired. **Criteria:** The Assembly Intern Committee appoints a committee of representatives of SUNY, CUNY and independent colleges to interview Graduate Scholars applicants.

**Funds Avail.:** Up to ten stipends of $11,500 each are awarded annually. Some academic institutions waive candidates' tuition during the program. **No. of Awards:** Up to 10 scholarships are awarded. **Deadline:** Completed application forms and supporting material must be sent directly to the Intern Committee before November 1.

**Remarks:** Since 1975, the New York State Assembly Graduate Scholars Program has provided candidates with in-depth research and policy development experiences. Scholars work full-time from January through June. Assembly scholars have the opportunity to develop their understanding of the legislative process and New York state government and to apply their ideas and research skills to the legislative decision-making process. Selected candidates serve as full-time Assembly researchers and policy analysts. Assignments are made according to candidate's previous experience, programs of study and fields of interest. Most scholars do not receive academic credit, although some arrange independent study credit. An orientation session, seminars, and discussion groups take place during the program. **Contact:** Campus liaison officer or Graduate Scholars Program at the above address (see entry 4573).

## • 4575 • New York State Assembly Session Internships *(Undergraduate/Internship)*

**Purpose:** The Session Intern Program has been directed by a bipartisan committee of legislators since 1971. It provides applicants with first-hand knowledge of the legislative process. Interns perform important functions, both research and administrative, in the daily operation of an Assembly office. They receive a practical educational experience while the Assembly benefits from their assistance, their new ideas, and their fresh perspectives. **Focus:** All majors may apply. **Qualif.:** Applicants must be New York State residents matriculated in a degree program as college juniors or seniors. Non-New York State residents who are juniors or seniors in degree programs at schools in New York may also apply. Students must have at least a C plus average. All applicants should have a strong interest in state government and the legislative process, but they may major in any academic field.

**Funds Avail.:** Approximately 150 internships are awarded annually. A stipend of $3,000 is awarded to help cover living and transportation costs. Some schools offer supplementary stipends, tuition waivers, work-study funds, or temporary loans to students participating in the program. **No. of Awards:** Up to 150. **To Apply:** Candidates apply through their college liaison officer who forwards applications and all supporting documents by November 1st to the Assembly Intern Committee, which makes the final selections. **Deadline:** November 1.

**Remarks:** The New York State Assembly Session Intern Program is from January through mid-May with one week allowed for a semester break. A minimum of thirty hours of work at the Capitol each week is required. Also required is participation in the educational component of the program. Candidates arrange to receive credit from appropriate faculty at their colleges. **Contact:** Campus liaison officer or Assembly Session Intern Program at the above address (see entry 4573).

## • 4576 •
## New York State Education Department
The University of the State of New
  York
Bureau of Postsecondary Grants
  Administration
Room 5B68 CEC
Albany, NY 12230

## • 4577 • New York State Regents Professional Opportunity Scholarships *(Doctorate, Graduate, Undergraduate/Scholarship)*

**Purpose:** To increase the number of minority and disadvantaged students in professions licensed by the Regents. **Qualif.:** Applicants must be United States citizens, permanent residents, or refugees approved by the Attorney General of the United States. They must also be residents of New York, qualify as a minority or economically disadvantaged students, be at the undergraduate or graduate level of study, and be accepted in an approved educational program in the state of New York. Additionally, they must be pursuing careers in one of 21 acceptable courses of study including accounting, architecture, chiropractic, dental hygiene, engineering, landscape architecture, law, nursing, occupational therapy, ophthalmology, optometry, pharmacy, physical therapy, psychology, social work, speech and language pathology and audiology, and veterinary medicine. **Criteria:** Preference is first given to minority applicants who are economically disadvantaged and members of a minority group historically under represented in the licensed professions. Secondary preference is for applicants who are members of a minority group historically under represented in the licensed professions. Applicants who are graduates of state-sponsored opportunity programs (EOP, HEOP, SEEK, and College Discovery) are then assigned preference.

**Funds Avail.:** 220 awards between $1,000 and $5,000, unless enrolled in a program recognized by the Regents as requiring more than four years to complete. No award may exceed the cost of education. **To Apply:** Application materials are usually available in October. **Deadline:** March 1.

**Remarks:** Recipients must practice in New York upon completion of their studies for a period of one year for each year of funding. **Contact:** Bureau of Postsecondary Grants Administration at the above address (see entry 4576).

## • 4578 • New York State Regents Scholarship at Cornell University *(Undergraduate/Scholarship)*

**Qualif.:** Applicants must be United States citizens or hold permanent immigration visas or refugee visas, and be legal residents of New York State for at least one year. They must plan to attend Cornell University and meet the requirements for admission to Cornell University. Students are not considered legal residents of New York State if their parents maintain legal residence in another state and the students are residing in New York State for the purpose of attending school. Applicants must also be bona fide residents of the senatorial district in which they are competing. If they have more than one residence, they must compete in the senatorial or congressional district in which they reside while attending school. Applicants should consult with their high school principal concerning the documentary proof of residence that may be required to submit with the application. **Criteria:** Scholarships are awarded on the basis of ACT or SAT test scores and grade point averages or GED test scores. The ACT/SAT test scores are weighted 25 percent and the grade point averages or GED test scores are weighted 75 percent. The grade point average for students enrolled in high school is based on ten required units: three units each for english and social studies, two units each for mathematics and science. For High School Equivalency Diploma holders, their GED total test score converts to a grade point average.

**Funds Avail.:** A minimum of 61 scholarships are awarded annually, at least one for each senatorial district of the State. The scholarships range from $100 to $1,000 per year, depending on financial need. The scholarship is valid for four or five years, depending on the length of the program for which the recipient enrolls. **To Apply:** Applicants must file a formal application for admission to Cornell University and be accepted as full-time matriculated students. They must have their ACT and/or SAT scores verified by their high school. If currently attending high school, applicants should file their application and any other supporting documents with the high school principal or guidance counselor. All applicants will be automatically entered into the competition for the Robert C. Byrd Scholarship. **Deadline:** If currently enrolled in high school, applicants must take the ACT and/or SAT tests by January 18; if competing on the basis of GED test scores, ACT and/or SAT test scores, applicants must take the tests by February 28. Applications should be completed and submitted by January and winners are announced in May. **Contact:** James A. Brown, Supervisor, Scholarship Program, at the above address (see entry 4576). If filing based upon a New York State High School Equivalency Diploma, applicants should mail completed applications to New York State Education Department, Scholarship Awards Unit, Rm. 770 Albany, NY 12234.

---

**• 4579 •**
**New York State Grange**
100 Grange Place
Cortland, NY 13045
*E-mail:* nysgrange@clarityconnect.com

Ph: (607)756-7553
Fax: (607)756-7757

**• 4580 • Howard and Marjorie DeNise Memorial Scholarships** *(Undergraduate/Scholarship loan)*

**Focus:** Agricultural sciences. **Qualif.:** Applicants are high school seniors or college undergraduates who are interested in a career within the agricultural industry. The candidates must have at least a B average and a Scholastic Aptitude Test score of at least 1000. Candidates must be New York State residents, but studies may be pursued outside the state. Recipients must be enrolled in a major within the field of agriculture and attain a B grade average for the scholarships to be extended on an annual basis.

**Funds Avail.:** The scholarship covers tuition, room, and board and is limited to the maximum expense of attending either a two- or four-year college program in New York State. **No. of Awards:** maximum of 6 **To Apply:** Applications require biographical data, estimated financial resources, projected expenses for one year of college, test results such as SAT, CEEB, and ACT, record of extra curricular activities, transcripts of school grades, summary of involvement in farm youth organizations, and an evaluation of the student's potential by the principal or superintendent of the applicant's high school. **Deadline:** Applications and supporting materials must be filed by April 15. **Contact:** New York State Grange at the above address (see entry 4579).

**• 4581 • Susan W. Freestone Vocational Education Award** *(Undergraduate/Award)*

**Focus:** Agricultural sciences. **Qualif.:** Candidate must have been a member of a Junior Grange in New York State and must be a member in good standing of a subordinate Grange in New York State. Applicant must graduate from high school and enroll in an approved two or four-year college in New York State. **Criteria:** Selection is based on the student's activities and scholarship as listed in the application and on high school transcripts. Preference is given to those candidates whose families are Grange members.

**Funds Avail.:** A maximum of one $1000 awards are made annually and are to be used to defray first year college expenses. A second $1000 for the second year may be available if school performance is satisfactory. **No. of Awards:** one **Deadline:** Applications must be filed by April 15.

**Remarks:** This award honors Mrs. Freestone for her efforts in promoting Juvenile Grange (now Junior Grange) work in New York State and nationwide. **Contact:** Any Junior Deputy or State Director of Junior Granges.

**• 4582 • New York State Grange Student Loans**
*(Undergraduate/Loan)*

**Purpose:** To assist young Grange men and women in continuing education beyond high school. **Focus:** Agricultural studies. **Qualif.:** Only members of a Subordinate Grange in New York who have been members for at least 6 months are eligible.

**Funds Avail.:** Loans are granted in the amounts of $500 per semester or a total of $1,000 per year or in lesser amounts. The loan is secured by a note signed by the student and/or parent or guardian. The maximum loaned to one person is $5,000. Repayment begins upon completion of education with interest at an annual rate of 5 percent starting when education at a formal institution ceases. Loans must be repaid within five years. **To Apply:** Applications must be signed by the subordinate master and secretary of the applicant's Grange.

**Remarks:** The Student Loan Fund is maintained by contributions from the Granges and Grange members in New York State. **Contact:** NYS Grange, 100 Grange Place, Cortland, NY 13045.

---

**• 4583 •**
**New York State Higher Education Services Corp.**
99 Washington Ave.
Albany, NY 12255
*URL:* http://assembly.state.ny.us/Reports/Green/ green36.html

Ph: (518)473-7087
Fax: (518)474-2839

**• 4584 • Robert C. Byrd Honors Scholarship**
*(Undergraduate/Scholarship)*

**Focus:** General Studies. **Qualif.:** Applicants must be U.S. citizens or must hold a permanent immigration visa or a refugee visa. They must also be New York state residents and high school graduates planning to enroll at an institution of higher learning. **Criteria:** Based on ACT and/or SAT scores and grade point average.

**Funds Avail.:** Non-renewable $1,500 scholarships for the first year of study. At least ten of these scholarships will be awarded in each of the State's 34 congressional districts, for a total of at least 340 scholarships. Scholarships may be held concurrently with any other type of scholarship. **No. of Awards:** 400. **Deadline:** November 5. **Contact:** High school guidance counselors for a test application. application.

**• 4585 • Paul Douglas Teacher Scholarship**
*(Undergraduate/Scholarship)*

**Focus:** Education. **Qualif.:** Applicants must be enrolled in a teacher certification program at a New York State college in mathematics, science, bilingual education, foreign languages, occupational education, teaching children with handicapping conditions, or teaching English to speakers of foreign languages. They must be United States citizens, permanent resident aliens, or refugees and be New York state residents who are in the top ten percent of their high school graduating class. Recipients must also agree to fulfill a service obligation to teach two years for each year of scholarship assistance. However, those who teach in an area designated by the U.S. Secretary of Education as a shortage area are obligated to teach only one year for each year of financial aid received. **Criteria:** A panel of college faculty will rank applicants on the basis of their high school and/or college work. Information concerning ACT and/or SAT score, honors, recommendations, and other information that may further substantiate the applicant's ability to complete the approved teacher certification may be submitted.

---

## New York State Higher Education Services Corp. (continued)

**Funds Avail.:** Up to $5,000 per academic year. Although scholarship winners may receive payment for up to four years of study, funding for the program is provided only one year at a time through the federal budget. Accordingly, scholarship commitments are made only for one year. **Contact:** For applications and further information, contact high school counselors, college financial aid administrators, or write to the New York State Education Department, State and Federal Scholarship and Fellowship Unit, Cultural Education Center, Albany, NY 12230. Telephone: (518)474-6394.

### • 4586 • Memorial Scholarships for Children of Deceased Police Officers and Firefighters (Undergraduate/Scholarship)

**Focus:** General Studies. **Qualif.:** Applicants must be children of deceased police officers or firefighters who died as the result of injuries sustained in the line of duty. They must also be New York State residents, U.S. citizens, and enrolled full-time in an approved program of study in New York State.

**Funds Avail.:** Awards pay tuition and nontuition costs of attendance, not to exceed SUNY tuition and nontuition costs. **Deadline:** May 1 of the academic year. **Contact:** NYSCHESC, Student Information, Albany, NY 12255 for supplemental information regarding the establishment of eligibility.

### • 4587 • New York State Child of Deceased Police Officer-Firefighter-Correction Officer Awards (Undergraduate/Award)

**Qualif.:** Applicants must be children of deceased police officers, firefighters or corrections officers. They must also be New York State residents, U.S. citizens, and enrolled full-time in an approved program of study in New York State.

**Funds Avail.:** Awards of $450. **Contact:** NYSHESC, Student Information, Albany, NY 12255.

### • 4588 • New York State Child of Veteran Awards (Undergraduate/Award)

**Focus:** General Studies. **Qualif.:** Applicants must be children of veterans who served during WWI, WWII, the Korean War, the Vietnam War, or other specified periods of war or national emergency and, as a result of service, died, suffered a 50 percent or more disability, been a prisoner of war, or be missing in action. Applicants must be New York State residents, U.S. citizens, and enrolled full-time in an approved program of study in New York State, and be in good academic standing.

**Funds Avail.:** Awards of $450 per year. **Deadline:** May 1 of the academic year. **Contact:** NYSHESC, Student Information, Albany, NY, 12255.

### • 4589 • New York State Health Service Corps Scholarships (Graduate/Scholarship)

**Focus:** Health Care. **Qualif.:** Applicants must be U.S. residents, or resident aliens eligible for employment within the United States. They must be enrolled full-time in a graduate program in any health field. If the applicant is not a New York State resident, they must attend school within New York State

**Funds Avail.:** Up to $15,000 per year. **Deadline:** Deadlines change annually. Applicants should check with college Financial Aid Offices. **Contact:** NYS Health Dept., NYS Health Service Corps, Corning Tower, Rm. 1602, Empire State Plaza, Albany, NY, 12237.

### • 4590 • New York State Higher Education Opportunity Program (Undergraduate/Grant)

**Purpose:** To provide supportive services and financial aid to economically and educationally disadvantaged New York residents attending independent colleges and universities in New York State. **Focus:** General Studies. **Qualif.:** Applicants must be New York State residents with a high school diploma, state-approved equivalency diploma, or its equivalent. They must be inadmissable at the institution by regular academic standards for admission, and they must be economically disadvantaged. They must also show also show potential for successful completion of a college degree and must apply to a participating institution.

**Funds Avail.:** Varies depending on need. **To Apply:** Applicants must apply to directly to the Higher Education Opportunity Program. **Contact:** Higher Education Opportunity Program Director at participation institutions and New York State Education Department, Rm. 5A55, Cultural Education Center, Albany, NY 12230, (518)474-5313.

### • 4591 • New York State Parent Loans for Students (Graduate, Undergraduate/Loan)

**Focus:** General Studies. **Qualif.:** Applicants must be natural or adoptive parents, or legal guardians of an eligible student; United States citizens, U.S. nationals, or eligible non-citizens; and not in default on another student loan or owe a refund to an education grant program. Students must be New York residents for at least 12 months (if attending school out of state), U.S. citizens or eligible non-citizens, and enrolled at least half-time in a program leading to a degree, certificate, or diploma. Loans are primarily for students whose financial circumstances disqualify them for the federally-subsidized loan or who still need some financial assistance. Students cannot owe a Tuition Assistance Program refund, be in default on a loan, or owe a refund on any Title IV federal program (e.g. Pell Grant, campus-based federal aid).

**Funds Avail.:** Loans of up to the cost of attendance minus other financial aid are made. The interest rate is adjusted annually, not to exceed 10 percent. Repayment begins 60 days after the funds are disbursed. **Contact:** Financial aid offices or lenders.

### • 4592 • New York State Professional Opportunity Scholarships (Doctorate, Graduate, Undergraduate/ Scholarship)

**Focus:** Accounting, Architecture, Medicine, Dentistry, Engineering, Nursing Therapy, Psychology, Veterinary Medicine, Social Work. **Qualif.:** Applicants must be pursuing a degree in one of the following fields (with indicated degree level): accountancy (baccalaureate), architecture (baccalaureate or master's), chiropractic (doctorate), dental hygiene (associate), engineering (baccalaureate), landscape architecture (baccalaureate or master's), law (J.D.), nursing (baccalaureate), occupational therapy (baccalaureate or master's), occupational therapy assistant (associate), ophthalmic dispensing (associate), optometry (doctorate), pharmacy (baccalaureate), physical therapist assistant (associate), physical therapy (baccalaureate or master's), physicians assistant (associate or baccalaureate), podiatry (doctorate), psychology (doctorate), social work (master's), speech language pathology/audiology (master's), or veterinary medicine (doctorate). Applicants must maintain an actual residence in New York State, consider New York State their permanent residence, and be U.S. citizens, permanent residents, or refugees. Applicants must be free of debt from a defaulted guaranteed student loan. **Criteria:** First priority will be given to any candidate who is economically disadvantaged and a minority group member historically under represented in the profession. Second priority will be given to any candidate who is a minority group member under represented in the profession. Third priority will be given to any candidate who is enrolled in or a graduate of one of three State-sponsored opportunity programs (SEEK at City University, EOP in the State University system, or HEOP at an independent college).

**Funds Avail.:** Scholarships range from $1,000 to $5,000 per year for up to four years, unless enrollment is in a program recognized by the Regents as requiring more than four years to complete. **No. of Awards:** 220. **To Apply:** Formal application required. **Deadline:** In the fall before year of application.

**Remarks:** Recipients must agree to practice in their chosen profession in New York State. Such practice shall mean full-time employment carrying out activities for which licensure would be required in a nonexempt setting or teaching a postsecondary program registered by the Department as licensure-qualifying in the same profession in which the teacher is licensed. The period of service is 12 months for each annual payment received. **Contact:** Applications may be obtained from any approved college in New York State or from NYS Education Department, Bureau of Grants Administration, CEC Room 5B68, Albany, NY 12230.

**• 4593 • New York State Regents Health Care Opportunity Scholarships** *(Graduate/Scholarship)*

**Focus:** Medicine, Health Care. **Qualif.:** Applicants must be New York state residents, United States citizens, or qualifying non-citizens, and full-time students in an approved program in New York state. Students must be studying medicine or dentistry and must agree to work one year for each year of financial aid received. The minimum service requirement is two years. Employment must be in the studied profession and must be in a designated physician-shortage area of New York state. If the recipient does not begin to practice within one year upon program completion, twice the amount of financial aid received must be repaid plus interest. **Criteria:** First priority will be given to any candidate who is economically disadvantaged and is a minority group member historically under represented in the profession. Second priority will be given to any candidate who is minority group member under represented in the profession (not in financial need). Third priority will be given to any candidate who is a graduate of one of three New York State sponsored opportunity programs: SEEK, College Discovery, EOP, or HEOP.

**Funds Avail.:** $1,000 to $10,000 a year for up to four years. **Contact:** New York State Education Department, Bureau of Higher and Professional Educational Testing, Cultural Education Center, Albany, NY 12230. Telephone: (518)474-6394. (518)474-6394.

**• 4594 • New York State Stafford Loan** *(Graduate, Undergraduate/Loan)*

**Focus:** General Studies. **Qualif.:** Applicants must be residents of New York for at least 12 months if they are planning to attend school out of state. They must also be U.S. citizens, national or other eligible non-citizens, enrolled or accepted for enrollment and making satisfactory academic progress at an approved educational institution. Applicants must be enrolled at least half-time, show compliance with selective service requirements, and not in default on another student loan or owe a refund to an education grant program. **Criteria:** Based on financial need.

**Funds Avail.:** For loans made on or after July 1, loans of up to $2,625 for the first year and $3,500 for the 2nd year of undergraduate study are granted. Up to $5,500 per year is available for the remainder of undergraduate study. Aggregates for undergraduate study cannot exceed $23,000. Loans of up to $8,500 per year are made for graduate or professional study. The aggregate for undergraduate and graduate study cannot exceed $65,500. Loan amounts for a given year cannot exceed student's cost of attendance minus other financial aid and (if required) the estimated family contribution. Federal government pays the interest until students begin repayment six months after graduation or upon termination of studies. Interest accrues at a variable rate. **Contact:** Contact any financial aid office or lender for an application.

**• 4595 • New York State Supplemental Loans for Students** *(Graduate, Undergraduate/Loan)*

**Focus:** General Studies. **Qualif.:** Applicants must be graduate or professional students, independent undergraduates, or dependent undergraduates with extenuating circumstances as determined by school financial aid office. Students must be New York residents for at least 12 months (if attending school out of state) and U.S. citizens or eligible non-citizens. Students must apply for a Pell Grant and Stafford loan prior to applying for the SLS. Students do not have to demonstrate need.

**Funds Avail.:** Loan of up to $4,000 for the first and second year, $5,000 for other undergraduates, and $10,000 for graduate and professional students. The aggregate undergraduate maximum is $23,000. The combined undergraduate and graduate maximum is $73,000. There are no interest benefits paid by the federal government. Borrowers must begin paying interest (up to 11 percent) from the day the loan is disbursed. Repayment begins upon graduating, termination of studies, or if student falls below full-time. **Contact:** Contact financial aid office at higher learning institutions or lenders.

**• 4596 • New York State Tuition Assistance Program** *(Graduate, Undergraduate/Grant)*

**Focus:** General Studies. **Qualif.:** Applicants must be New York state residents, United States citizens, permanent residents or refugees, and enrolled full-time at a college within the state. Applicants cannot be in default on a guaranteed education loan or have made required payments under the Renewed Eligibility for Financial Aid program. **Criteria:** Based on income and financial need.

**Funds Avail.:** Up to $4,125 annually, or tuition, whichever is less, for up to four years. Minimum award amount is $350. **Deadline:** May 1. **Contact:** College financial aid offices.

**• 4597 •**
**New York State Senate**
Senate Students Programs Office
State Capitol, 90 S. Swan/401      *Ph:* (518)455-2611
Albany, NY 12247                   *Fax:* (518)432-5470
*E-mail:* 74157,362@compuserve.com; students@
   senate.state.ny.us
*URL:* http://www.senate.state.ny.us/

**• 4598 • New York State Senate Legislative Fellows Program** *(Graduate, Postgraduate/Fellowship)*

**Purpose:** To utilize and develop the expertise of fellows, offering them an extensive view of the legislative process. **Focus:** All accredited disciplines. **Qualif.:** Applicants must be matriculated graduate students, residents of New York State, or attendees of an accredited educational institution in New York State at the time of application. They must be United States citizens and may be in any academic major. Candidates must have evidence of a strong interest in public service and outstanding skills in research, writing, and articulation. All participants are enrolled 46 weeks or more on-site in the New York State Senate, Albany, New York. **Criteria:** Selection of recipients is made by a committee historically composed of seven bipartisan representatives of the Senate and three representatives of the State academic community, one faculty member each from SUNY system, CUNY system, and from independent colleges and universities.

**Funds Avail.:** Fellowships are awarded annually. Each pays full taxable salary of $25,000 for the approximately one year duration of the appointment (September to August) in Albany. Recipients are eligible for some benefits, but without vacation credits. **No. of Awards:** 10 mos. **To Apply:** Applicants must submit official transcripts of graduate and undergraduate grades, three letters of

## New York State Senate *(continued)*

reference from persons knowledgeable about the student's academic and professional abilities, a statement of aspirations for undertaking this program, and two typewritten work samples, including an essay on a significant issue facing state government and a memorandum in support or in opposition to the legislation proposed in the essay. **Deadline:** Mid-May; recipient selection is by mid-July.

**Remarks:** After general orientation, fellows work full time as regular legislative staff members of the offices to which they are assigned. Credit for the fellowship year is a matter to be arranged between the participant and the home academic institution. Because of the demanding nature of the work, no concurrent academic course work is permitted. **Contact:** Campus Liaison Officer or Director at the above address (see entry 4597).

### • 4599 • New York State Senate Sessions Assistance Program *(Undergraduate/Work Study)*

**Purpose:** To provide talented New York State students with first-hand experience in New York State Government as part of their home campus academic curricula. **Focus:** All accredited disciplines. **Qualif.:** Candidates must be United States citizens, New York State resident citizens, and be matriculated full-time students in undergraduate degree programs at colleges and universities in New York State. Freshmen are ineligible and only outstanding sophomores are chosen. While all academic majors qualify, a strong orientation toward public service is required. Applicants must have a substantial academic record, provide evidence of strong research and communication skills, and be able to articulate purposefulness. **Criteria:** In addition to the student's background, selection of recipients depends on such balancing factors as geographic representation, academic affiliation, and equal opportunity.

**Funds Avail.:** Up to 61 session assistants can be selected annually. Each receives a stipend of $3,000 over approximately four months, January-May, to offset the costs of moving to and living in Albany. **No. of Awards:** Up to 61. **To Apply:** The formal application must include: official transcripts of completed collegiate work and courses in progress; three letters of reference from knowledgeable persons; a statement of career goals; and a campus interview. Each applicant must also submit writing samples. The first sample must either be an essay of approximately 1,200 words on a topic pertinent to the purposes of the application or an essay on a general subject evidencing the student's analysis and communications abilities. The second sample must contain two one-page memoranda; one outlines a specific policy proposal for legislative action, and one is a responsible rebuttal to the proposal. **Deadline:** Applications must be filed by mid-October. Recipient selection is made in mid-November.

**Remarks:** Recipients are assigned to offices where practical experience and an inside understanding of State Government may be acquired; they must be in placement a minimum of 30 hours weekly. Session Assistants receive orientation during the early days of the legislative session and then participate in seminars and academic activities including reading/writing assignments and projects under the direction of the Student Programs Office. This is not a scholarship program but a cooperative education/internship program on-site at he New York State Senate, Albany, New York, for approximately 17 weeks. **Contact:** Campus Liaison Officer or Director.

### • 4600 • Richard J. Roth Journalism Fellowship *(Graduate, Undergraduate/Fellowship)*

**Purpose:** To encourage better training in and understanding of governmental public relations. **Focus:** Journalism, Public Relations, Governmental Public Relations. **Qualif.:** Candidates must be United States citizens and New York State residents who are enrolled in an accredited graduate program, or citizens of other states enrolled in accredited programs in New York State. At the time of application, the student, while not necessarily enrolled in

Journalism courses, must show a clear intention to work in this field. Awarding of academic credit for the fellowship is a matter for the fellow and his/her academic institution. No concurrent course work is permitted. **Criteria:** Selection is by a committee of Senate personnel, journalism faculty, working correspondents or other appropriate persons. Selection is based on professional criteria including eligibility, orientation to a career in journalism, academic standing including research and communication skills, and abilities to meet the fellowship challenges.

**Funds Avail.:** The fellowship pays a fully taxable salary of $25,000 for approximately one year (September-August) in Albany. The fellow is eligible for some benefits, but vacation is not included. **No. of Awards:** 1. **To Apply:** Applicants must also submit at least two, but not more than three writing samples of either published work or work intended for publication. Each sample should be under 800 words. Additionally, two one-page memoranda are required. The first makes a specific policy proposal for legislative action and is written as if to be delivered by a legislator to an audience of legislative colleagues, journalists, lobbyists, or the general public. The second is a rebuttal of the policy proposal for legislation contained in the first memorandum. **Deadline:** Applications must be filed by mid-May; recipient selection is expected by mid-July.

**Remarks:** The Roth Fellow normally serves in the Office of the Press Secretary, and after preliminary orientation, is expected to participate in the programs promoting the legislative process and in journalism/governmental public relations. Roth applicants may also be considered for the Richard A. Wiebe Public Service Fellowship, the recipient of which serves approximately 46 weeks, on-site at the New York State Senate in Albany, New York. **Contact:** Campus Liaison Officer or Director.

## • 4601 •
### Newberry Library - Committee on Awards
60 W. Walton St.       Ph: (312)255-3666
Chicago, IL 60610-3380     Fax: (312)255-3513
*E-mail:* research@newberry.org
*URL:* http://www.newberry.org

### • 4602 • Lester J. Cappon Fellowship in Documentary Editing *(Postdoctorate/Fellowship)*

**Purpose:** To support editing projects based on Newberry materials and carried out while in residence at the Library. **Qualif.:** Must hold a Ph.D. or equivalent.

**Funds Avail.:** $800 per month is awarded. **Deadline:** March 1.

### • 4603 • President Francisco Cossiga Fellowship *(Postdoctorate/Fellowship)*

**Purpose:** To provide opportunities for research in any field appropriate to the Newberry's collections. **Qualif.:** Open to Italian nationals or residents holding the *dottorato di recerca* or its equivalent. **Criteria:** Preference is given to scholars whose work includes the historical study of cartography.

**Funds Avail.:** $1,500 per month, plus round trip airfare from Rome or Milan to Chicago. **To Apply:** Application forms may be obtained by contacting the Ministero delgi Affari Esteri, Direzione Generale delle relazioni culturali, Ufficio IX, Rome.

### • 4604 • Ecole des Chartes Exchange Fellowship *(Doctorate/Fellowship, Scholarship)*

**Purpose:** To provide a monthly stipend and free tuition for an American graduate student at the Ecole Nationale des Chartes in Paris. **Qualif.:** Must be a Ph.D. candidate and a U.S. citizen. **Criteria:** Preference is given to students from schools supporting the Center for Renaissance Studies.

Funds Avail.: Variable. Deadline: December 15.

• 4605 • **Audrey Lumsden-Kouvel Fellowship** *(Postdoctorate/Fellowship)*

**Purpose:** To provide research opportunities to scholars who wish to use the Newberry's holdings in late medieval and Renaissance history and literature. **Qualif.:** Applicants must hold a Ph.D. or equivalent and must plan to be in continuous residence for at least three months. **Criteria:** Preference will be given to those who plan longer stays during the academic year or who wish to use the fellowship to extend a sabbatical.

**Funds Avail.:** $3,000 is awarded. **Deadline:** March 1.

• 4606 • **D'Arcy McNickle Center for the History of the American Indian Fellowships** *(Postgraduate/Fellowship)*

**Purpose:** To encourage study in the humanities and social sciences. **Qualif.:** Frances C. Allen Fellowships are available to women of American Indian heritage who are pursuing an academic program at any stage beyond the undergraduate degree. Candidates may be working in any graduate or pre-professional field. Candidates are expected to spend a significant amount of their fellowship term in residence at the McNickle Center.

**Funds Avail.:** Varies according to need. **Deadline:** February 1.

**Remarks:** Documentary workshops and fellowships are also available to encourage faculty who would like to include Native American materials in their teaching.

• 4607 • **Mellon Postdoctoral Research Fellowships** *(Postdoctorate/Fellowship)*

**Purpose:** To support postdoctoral scholars at any stage of their career in conducting research in any field relevant to the Library's collections. Fellows will become part of the Newberry's community of scholars, participating in biweekly fellows' seminars, colloquia, and other events.

**Funds Avail.:** Up to $30,800. **To Apply:** Completed applications must include three letters of recommendation. **Deadline:** January 20.

**Remarks:** Applicants may combine this award with sabbatical or other stipendry support. Individuals applying for National Endowment for the Humanities and Lloyd Lewis Fellowships at the Library will also be considered for Mellon Research Fellowships and need not submit a second application.

• 4608 • **Rockefeller Foundation Residential Fellowships in Gender Studies in Early Modern Europe** *(Postdoctorate/Fellowship)*

**Purpose:** To provide research opportunities in literature, history, and other humanities fields. **Qualif.:** Must hold a Ph.D. or equivalent, and be exploring a topic related to issues of gender in European Cultures from the late middle ages through the seventeenth century.

**Funds Avail.:** $30,000 is awarded.

**Remarks:** Administered by the Newberry's Center for Renaissance Studies. Fellows will participate in Library seminars and activities as well as programs of the Center for Renaissance Studies.

• 4609 • **Short-Term Fellowships in the History of Cartography** *(Postdoctorate/Fellowship)*

**Purpose:** To provide work in residence at the Newberry on projects related to the history of cartography focused on cartographic materials in the Library's collection. **Qualif.:** Must hold a Ph.D. or equivalent.

**Funds Avail.:** $800 per month. **Deadline:** March 1.

• 4610 • **South Central Language Association Fellowship** *(Postdoctorate/Fellowship)*

**Purpose:** To provide a work in residence opportunity for a member of the South Central Modern Language Association. **Qualif.:** Must hold a Ph.D. or equivalent. **Criteria:** Preference will be given to those who have a particular need for the Newberry's collections.

**Funds Avail.:** $800 is available. **Deadline:** March 1.

• 4611 • **Spencer Foundation Fellowships in the History of Education** *(Postdoctorate/Fellowship)*

**Purpose:** To provide research opportunities for projects in the history of education appropriate to the Newberry's collections. Topics may range from the history of instruction to educational philosophy to the history of literacy and beyond. **Qualif.:** Applicants must hold a Ph.D. or equivalent.

**Funds Avail.:** $25,000 for a Junior Fellowhip, $35,000 for Senior. **Deadline:** January 20.

**Remarks:** Grants support individual research and opportunities to pursue projects in an interdisciplinary setting.

• 4612 • **Arthur Weinberg Fellowship for Independent Scholars** *(Professional Development/Fellowship)*

**Purpose:** To recognize independent scholars who have demonstrated excellence through publications. **Qualif.:** For scholars working outside the academy in a field appropriate to the Newberry's collections. **Criteria:** Preference is given to scholars working on historical issues related to social justice and/or reform.

**Funds Avail.:** $800 is awarded. **Deadline:** March 1.

• 4613 • **Harry and Sarah Zelzer Fellowship and Prize** *(Professional Development/Fellowship, Prize)*

**Purpose:** To recognize musicians in the early stage of their careers. **Qualif.:** Applicants will be judged on their artistic merit and the quality of their research proposal.

**Funds Avail.:** A cash prize of $1,500 and a stipend of $500 per week to conduct research will be awarded.

**Remarks:** The winner will also present a public recital in the Library.

---

• 4614 •
**The Newberry Library - Division of Research and Education**
60 W. Walton St.
Chicago, IL 60610-3380          *Ph:* (312)943-9090
*URL:* http://www.familytreemaker.com/00000125.html
*Formerly known as The Newberry Library - Center for Renaissance Studies.*

• 4615 • **Frances C. Allen Fellowships** *(Doctorate, Graduate, Postgraduate/Fellowship)*

**Purpose:** To support women of Native American heritage who are pursuing advanced education. **Focus:** General Studies. **Qualif.:** Applicant must be a woman of American Indian heritage who is pursuing an academic program beyond the undergraduate degree. Candidate may be working in any graduate or pre-professional field, but the particular purpose of the fellowship is to encourage study in the humanities and social sciences. Fellows are expected to spend a significant amount of the fellowship term in residence at the McNickle Center, which is part of the Newberry Library.

---

Awards are arranged alphabetically below their administering organizations

## The Newberry Library - Division of Research and Education (continued)

**Funds Avail.:** Varies. **To Apply:** Write or call the Center for application guidelines. **Deadline:** February 1. **Contact:** Committee on Awards, at the above address (see entry 4614).

### • 4616 • American Society for 18th-Century Studies Fellowships (Postdoctorate/Fellowship)

**Focus:** History. **Qualif.:** Applicants must be post-doctoral scholars and members in good standing of the American Society for Eighteenth-Century Studies at the time of application. Studies must cover the period from 1660 to 1815.

**Funds Avail.:** Fellowships are available for one to three months in residence at the Newberry Library with a monthly stipend of $800. **Deadline:** March 1 or October 15. **Contact:** Committee on Awards at the above address (see entry 4614).

### • 4617 • Lloyd Lewis Fellowships in American History (Postdoctorate/Fellowship)

**Focus:** American history in any area appropriate to Newberry's collection. **Qualif.:** Applicants must have the Ph.D. or its equivalent, and must have demonstrated, through their publications, particular excellence in a field of American history. Lewis Fellows are expected to participate actively in the Newberry's scholarly community.

**Funds Avail.:** Two or three awards are made each year, with a maximum stipend of $30,000. Applicants may combine grants with sabbaticals or other stipendiary support. **Deadline:** January 20.

### • 4618 • The Audrey Lumsden-Kouvel Fellowship (Postdoctorate/Fellowship)

**Focus:** General Studies. **Qualif.:** Applicants must be post-doctoral scholars for research in late Medieval-Renaissance studies.

**Funds Avail.:** $3,000. **Deadline:** January 20. **Contact:** Division of Research and Education at the above address (see entry 4614).

### • 4619 • Monticello College Foundation Fellowship for Women (Postdoctorate/Fellowship)

**Purpose:** The award is primarily for women at an early stage in their professional careers whose work gives clear promise of scholarly productivity and whose career would be significantly enhanced by six months of research and writing. **Focus:** General Studies. **Qualif.:** Applicants must have the Ph.D. at the time of application, and must be a U.S. citizen or permanent resident. Applicants may propose a study in any field appropriate to the Newberry's collections. **Criteria:** Preference, other matters being equal, will be given to an applicant whose scholarship is particularly concerned with the study of women.

**Funds Avail.:** This six month fellowship carries a stipend of $12,500. **Deadline:** January 20. **Contact:** The Committee on Awards at the above address (see entry 4614).

### • 4620 • Newberry-British Academy Fellowship (Postdoctorate/Fellowship)

**Purpose:** To offer an exchange fellowship for three months' study in Great Britain in any field in the humanities in which the Newberry's collections are strong. **Focus:** General Studies, Humanities. **Qualif.:** Applicants must be established scholars at the post-doctoral level, or its equivalent. Preference is given to readers and staff of the Newberry and to scholars who have previously used the Newberry.

**Funds Avail.:** The stipend is £30 per day while the fellow is in Great Britain. The fellow's home institution is expected to continue to pay his or her salary. **Deadline:** January 20. **Contact:** The Committee on Awards at the above address (see entry 4614).

### • 4621 • Newberry Library Joint Fellowships with the American Antiquarian Society (Graduate/Fellowship)

**Purpose:** To provide the opportunity for scholars to use collections at both the Newberry Library and the American Antiquarian Society. **Focus:** General Studies. **Qualif.:** Applicants must have the Ph.D. or have completed all requirements except the dissertation. **Criteria:** Decisions will be made independently at each institution.

**Funds Avail.:** Stipends at the Newberry are $800 per month for up to two months. **Deadline:** January 20. **Contact:** The Committee on Awards at the above address (see entry 4614).

### • 4622 • Newberry Library National Endowment for the Humanities Fellowships (Postdoctorate/Fellowship)

**Purpose:** To encourage the individual scholar's research in any field appropriate to the Newberry's collection, but also to deepen and enrich the opportunities for serious intellectual exchange through the active participation of fellows in the Newberry community. **Focus:** General Studies. **Qualif.:** Grants are for scholars at the post-doctoral level, or its equivalent. Applicants should be U.S. citizens or nationals, or foreign nationals who have been living in the U.S. for at least three years. **Criteria:** Preference is given to applicants who have not held major fellowships or grants for three years preceding the proposed period of residency.

**Funds Avail.:** From four to six fellowships are available for six to eleven months' of research with stipends of up to $30,000. Applicants may combine grants with sabbaticals or other stipendiary support. **Deadline:** January 20.

**Remarks:** Approximately 60 applications are received by the committee each year. **Contact:** The Committee on Awards at the above address (see entry 4614).

### • 4623 • Newberry Library Short-Term Resident Fellowships (Postdoctorate/Fellowship)

**Purpose:** To help provide access to Newberry resources for people who live beyond commuting distance. **Focus:** General Studies. **Qualif.:** Applicants must have the Ph.D. or have completed all requirements except the dissertation. **Criteria:** Preference is given to applicants from outside the greater Chicago area whose research particularly requires study at the Newberry.

**Funds Avail.:** Stipends of $800 per month for periods of up to two months, or three months when travel from a foreign country is involved. **Deadline:** March 1 or October 15. **Contact:** The Committee on Awards at the above address (see entry 4614).

### • 4624 • South Central Modern Languages Association Fellowship (Postdoctorate/Fellowship)

**Purpose:** To allow post doctoral scholars to study at the Newberry Library. **Focus:** General Studies. **Qualif.:** Applicants must be post-doctoral scholars and members of the South Central Modern Languages Association (SCMLA).

**Funds Avail.:** A one-month stipend of $800 is available for work in residence. **Deadline:** March 1. **Contact:** The Committee on Awards at the above address (see entry 4614).

### • 4625 • John N. Stern Fellowships for Oberlin College Faculty (Professional Development/Fellowship)

**Focus:** General Studies. **Qualif.:** Applicants must be regular faculty members of Oberlin College who wish to spend up to three months in residence at the Newberry.

**Funds Avail.:** $1,000 per month. **To Apply:** Application should be made to the Dean of the College. **Contact:** Dean at Oberlin College.

• **4626** •

## Newcomen Society of the United States

412 Newcomen Rd.                    *Ph:* (215)363-6600
Exton, PA 19341-1999               *Fax:* (215)363-0612
*URL:* http://rampages.onramp.net/~harral/newcomen.html

• **4627** • **Harvard-Newcomen Postdoctoral**
**Fellowship** *(Postdoctorate/Fellowship)*

**Purpose:** To enable scholars to improve their professional acquaintance with business and economic history and to increase their skills as they relate to this field while engaging in research that will benefit from the resources of the Harvard Business School and the Boston scholarly community. **Focus:** Business and Management. **Qualif.:** Applicants must have received a Ph.D. in history, economics, or a related discipline within the ten years prior to application.

**Funds Avail.: No. of Awards:** 1. **Contact:** The Newcomen Society of the United States at the above address (see entry 4626).

• **4628** •

## News-Sentinel

600 W. Main St.
Ft. Wayne, IN 46802

• **4629** • **News-Sentinel Minority Scholarship**
*(Undergraduate/Scholarship)*

**Focus:** Journalism. **Qualif.:** Applicants must be minority high school seniors planning to pursue a career in journalism.

**Funds Avail.:** $500 cash plus the opportunity to compete for the $5000 Knight-Ridder Scholarship. **Deadline:** December 1.

• **4630** •

## Newspaper Association of America Foundation

1921 Gallows Rd., Ste. 600
Vienna, VA 22182                    *Ph:* (703)902-1725

*The Newspaper Association of America Foundation was formerly known as the American Newspaper Publishers Association Foundation.*

• **4631** • **NAA Foundation Minority Fellowships**
*(Professional Development/Fellowship)*

**Purpose:** To widen opportunities for racial and ethnic minority professionals to enter into or advance in newspaper management. **Focus:** Journalism, Business Administration. **Criteria:** Based on supervisors' recommendations and panel's belief that the applicants are candidates for advancement in newspaper management.

**Funds Avail.:** Covers seminar and workshop registration fees, travel, meals, and hotel expenses. **To Apply:** Newspaper executives are asked to nominate candidates who demonstrate managerial potential. Self-nomination, with a supervisor's recommendation, also is encouraged. Application must be submitted.

• **4632** •

## Niccum Educational Trust Foundation

c/o Midwest Commerce Banking Co.
PO Box 27
Goshen, IN 46526                    *Ph:* (219)533-2175

• **4633** • **Niccum Educational Trust Foundation**
**Scholarship** *(Undergraduate/Scholarship)*

**Focus:** General studies. **Qualif.:** Applicants must be graduates of public schools of the counties of Elkhart, St. Joseph, Marshall, Noble, Kosciusko, and LaGrange in the State of Indiana who are in the upper third of their graduating class. Those who graduated from high school more than two years before application are ineligible. **Criteria:** Awards are made based on financial need.

**Funds Avail.:** Renewable for a maximum of six years of undergraduate study. Scholarships may only be used at accredited colleges and universities. **To Apply:** Applicants' high school counselors must submit student application, proper information, and letters of recommendation. **Contact:** Niccum Educational Trust Foundation at the above address (see entry 4632).

• **4634** •

## James R. Nicholl Memorial Foundation

Bank One Trust Co.
Trust Department
1949 Broadway                       *Ph:* (440)242-3258
Lorain, OH 44052                    *Fax:* (440)242-3226

• **4635** • **James R. Nicholl Memorial Grant**
*(Postgraduate/Grant)*

**Purpose:** To assist needy and worthy students of Lorain County with scholarships for postgraduate study. **Focus:** Medicine. **Qualif.:** Must be a Lorain County resident. **Criteria:** In determination of needy and worthy postgraduate scholarship grants, the Trustee considers the applicant's prior academic performance, recommendations from instructors, test scores, personal interviewing, financial need, the importance to society of the applicant's field of study, and whether the applicant intends to return to Lorain County to practice in his or her chosen profession.

**Funds Avail.:** $1,000-2,000 per year. Renewable. **Deadline:** None. **Contact:** Charles S. Tashjian, Trust Officer, at the above address (see entry 4634).

• **4636** •

## Nieman Foundation at Harvard University

Walter Lippmann House
1 Francis Ave.                      *Ph:* (617)495-2237
Cambridge, MA 02138-2098           *Fax:* (617)495-8976
*E-mail:* nieman@harvard.edu
*URL:* http://nieman.harvard.edu/nieman.html

• **4637** • **Nieman Fellowships for Journalists**
*(Professional Development/Fellowship)*

**Purpose:** To provide a mid-career opportunity to journalists who wish to broaden their intellectual horizons. **Focus:** General Studies. **Qualif.:** Applicants must be full-time staff or freelance journalists working for the news or editorial department of newspapers, news services, radio, television, or magazines of general public interest. Applicants must have at least three years of professional experience in the media and must obtain employer's consent for a leave of absence for the academic year. There are no educational

## Nieman Foundation at Harvard University (continued)

prerequisites or age limits; candidates may be of any nationality. Fellowships are tenable at Harvard University. Fellows may audit graduate and undergraduate courses in the University's schools and departments; they also participate in the program's ongoing seminars. No course credits are given or degree granted for work done during the fellowship. **Criteria:** Applicants are judged on past achievement, future promise, and appropriate time in career for a sabbatical.

**Funds Avail.:** $35,000 for U.S. journalists; funding arrangements vary for international journalists. **No. of Awards:** 12 for American journalists; 10 to 12 for international journalists. **To Apply:** Write to the program officer for application materials. An interview is required of all U.S. finalists. **Deadline:** January 31 for U.S. applicants; March 1 for international applicants. Fellowships are publicly announced in May.

**Remarks:** As funding for fellows from countries other than the United States is limited, international candidates are encouraged to seek outside funding. **Contact:** Program Officer at the above address (see entry 4636).

---

• 4638 •

## Non Commissioned Officers Association of the United States of America

NCOA International Headquarters
PO Box 33610
San Antonio, TX 78265          *Ph:* (210)653-6161
*URL:* http://www.kols.com/ncoa.html

• 4639 • **NCOA Scholarships** *(High School, Undergraduate/Scholarship)*

**Focus:** General Studies, Vocational-Technical Education. **Qualif.:** Candidates must be the children or spouses of members of the Non Commissioned Officers Association. Spouses are eligible, regardless of age; sons and daughters who apply must be under age 25 to receive the initial grant. Applicants must have demonstrated high scholastic accomplishment, a strong sense of patriotism, and intend to further their education at an accredited vocational institute or college. **Criteria:** NCOA scholarships are awarded based on the student's grades, other academic achievements, demonstrated sense of patriotism, and recommendations. Only persons selected for the scholarship will be notified.

**Funds Avail.:** 19 academic and four vocational scholarships of $900-$1,000 each are awarded to children of members; nine academic and one vocational for spouses. Any spouse who is awarded a grant must apply for membership in one of the NCOA Membership Categories (i.e., Regular, Associate, Veteran, or Auxiliary). Scholarships are renewable by reapplication and academic students must carry a minimum of 15 hours and maintain a B average to reapply. **No. of Awards:** 36. **To Apply:** Children of members must submit an application with two letters of recommendation from teachers; a personal recommendation from an adult who is not a relative; a handwritten autobiography; certified transcript of high school or college grades; ACT or SAT scores (vocational students are exempt); and a composition (of no less than 200 words) on Americanism. Spouses must submit an application with a copy of their high school diploma or GED equivalent; a certified transcript of all college courses completed, if any; a certificate of completion for any other courses of training; a brief biographical background; a letter of intent describing degree course of study, plans for completion of a degree program, and a closing paragraph on "What a College Degree Means to Me." **Deadline:** March 31.

• 4640 • **Bettsy Ross Educational Grants** *(Undergraduate/Grant)*

**Purpose:** To assist NCOA Auxiliary Division members in preparing for employment or improving their existing job skills by attending a local business or technical school. **Focus:** General Studies, Vocational-Technical Education. **Qualif.:** Applicants must be NCOA Auxiliary members.

**Funds Avail.:** Twelve grants of up to $250 each are awarded at the beginning of each quarter (January 1, April 1, July 1, and October 1). They may be used to defray the cost of attending a local business or technical school. NCOA forwards the grant to the school of the recipient's choice to be applied to the total cost of the course. **No. of Awards:** 12/quarter-48/year. **Deadline:** Applications must be received 30 days prior to the start of a new quarter in order to be considered for that quarter's grants.

**Remarks:** The program is named for Bettsy Ross, who was a past NCOA International Auxiliary president. **Contact:** NCOA Scholarship Administrator at the above address (see entry 4638).

---

• 4641 •

## North American Bluebird Society

PO Box 74                          *Ph:* (608)329-6403
Darlington, WI 53522               *Fax:* (608)329-7057
*E-mail:* nabluebird@aol.com
*URL:* http://www.nabluebirdsociety.org

• 4642 • **North American Bluebird Society Research Grants** *(Graduate, Professional Development/Grant)*

**Purpose:** To conduct research on cavity-nesting birds. **Focus:** Ornithology. **Qualif.:** Applicants must be competent in biological research techniques. There are three different classifications of the scholarship: a Student Research Grant available to full-time college graduate students for suitable projects focusing on a North American avian cavity-nesting species; a Bluebird Research Grant available to a student, professional, or individual researcher for projects focused on any of three species of bluebird from the genus Sialia; and a General Research Grant available to graduate students, professionals, or individual researchers for projects focused on a North American cavity-nesting species. **Criteria:** Selection is based on numerically rated categories on each proposal: project design (25); quality of presentation (15); relevance of topic (10); applicant ability (5).

**Funds Avail.:** Varies per year. $1,000 is the maximum award per individual. **No. of Awards:** Varies. **To Apply:** Application form and guidelines must be requested. **Deadline:** December 1. **Contact:** Kevin Berner at the above address (see entry 4641).

---

• 4643 •

## North American Loon Fund

6 Lily Pond Rd.
Gilford, NH 03246                  *Ph:* (603)528-4711
*E-mail:* loonfund@lr.net
*URL:* http://facstaff.uww.edu/wentzl/nalf/
    analfhomepage.html

• 4644 • **North American Loon Fund Grants** *(Other/ Grant)*

**Purpose:** To support the research, management, and educational projects related to conservation of loons. **Focus:** Ornithology, Wildlife Conservation. **Criteria:** Selection is based upon research priorities, such as capture techniques, winter ecology, migration, and subadults.

**Funds Avail.:** Awards range from $500 to $3,000. **To Apply:** Send SASE for guidelines. **Deadline:** December 15, yearly. **Contact:** Linda O'Bara at the above address (see entry 4643).

---

• **4645** •

## North American Society of Pacing and Electrophysiology
Natick Executive Park
2 Vision Drive                    *Ph:* (508)647-1000
Natick, MA 01760-2059             *Fax:* (508)647-0124
*URL:* http://www.pslgroup.com/dg/420a.htm

### • 4646 • Wilfred G. Bigelow Traveling Fellowship
*(Postdoctorate/Fellowship, Grant)*

**Purpose:** To provide the opportunity for experience in a specific technique or method in cardiac pacing or electrophysiology that is not available in the ordinary clinical or academic setting. **Focus:** Medical research in cardiology. **Qualif.:** Doctors of medicine, philosophy, osteopathy, and science, or nurses or engineers with equivalent training in biomedical engineering who are permanent residents of Canada or who plan to train in Canada.

**Funds Avail.:** Educational grant. **Deadline:** November 1.

**Remarks:** Established in 1983.

### • 4647 • Michael Bilitch Fellowship in Cardiac Pacing and Electrophysiology *(Postdoctorate/Fellowship)*

**Purpose:** To provide the opportunity for additional training in cardiac pacing. **Focus:** Cardiology and electrophysiology. **Qualif.:** Doctors of medicine, philosophy, osteopathy, and science, or individuals with equivalent training in biomedical engineering who are citizens or permanent residents of North America.

**Funds Avail.:** $35,000 annually. **Deadline:** November 1.

**Remarks:** Established in 1982 to honor Albert S. Hyman. Renamed in 1988 to honor Michael Bilitch.

### • 4648 • Leonard W. Horowitz Fellowship in Cardiac Pacing and Electrophysiology *(Postdoctorate/Fellowship, Grant)*

**Purpose:** To provide the opportunity for additional training in cardiac pacing or electrophysiology. **Qualif.:** Doctors of medicine, philosophy, osteopathy, and science, or individuals with equivalent training in biomedical engineering who are citizens or permanent residents of North America may apply.

**Funds Avail.:** An educational grant of $35,000 is awarded annually. **Deadline:** November 1.

### • 4649 • NASPE Full-Year Fellowships
*(Postdoctorate/Fellowship)*

**Purpose:** To encourage individuals seeking training in cardiac pacing and cardiac electrophysiology. **Focus:** Cardiac Electrophysiology, Cardiac Pacing. **Qualif.:** Applicants must be citizens or permanent residents of a North American country (i.e., any Western Hemisphere country north of Colombia). They must also have a Ph.D., M.D., or D.O. degree, or equivalent training in the field of biomedical engineering. Awards are intended for individuals who are seeking specialty education following their residency programs. Individuals with faculty, even junior faculty, appointments are not eligible. Applicants are responsible for making all arrangements with the host research institution and with the supervising investigator. Research may be conducted outside of North America, but applicant must demonstrate why the

overseas site chosen is best suited for the purposes of the fellowship.

**Funds Avail.:** Up to $35,000/year, including salary, benefits, and institutional overhead. **To Apply:** Write for application materials. **Deadline:** November 1. Notification by mid-February.

**Remarks:** Ratio includes statistics for both full-year and traveling fellowships. **Contact:** Janet M. Giroux at the above address (see entry 4645).

### • 4650 • NASPE Traveling Fellowships
*(Postdoctorate/Fellowship)*

**Purpose:** To encourage individuals seeking training in cardiac pacing and cardiac electrophysiology. **Focus:** Cardiac Electrophysiology, Cardiac Pacing. **Qualif.:** Applicants must be citizens or permanent residents of a North American country (i.e., any Western Hemisphere country north of Colombia). They must also have a Ph.D., M.D., or D.O. degree in biomedical engineering or nursing. Awards are intended for individuals who are seeking to obtain special training in a specific technique or method which could not otherwise be provided in the fellow's usual clinical or academic setting. Fellowships may also be used for collaborative research, teaching, or to enhance clinical skills. Applicants are responsible for making all arrangements with the host research institution and with the supervising investigator. Research may be conducted outside of North America, but applicants must demonstrate why the overseas site chosen is best suited for the purposes of the fellowship.

**Funds Avail.:** Up to $7,000; including salary, benefits, and institutional overhead. **To Apply:** Write for application materials. **Deadline:** November 1. Notification within two months. **Contact:** Janet M. Giroux at the above address (see entry 4645).

### • 4651 • Kenneth M. Rosen Fellowship in Cardiac Pacing and Electrophysiology *(Postdoctorate/Fellowship, Grant)*

**Purpose:** To provide the opportunity for additional training in cardiac pacing or electrophysiology. **Qualif.:** Doctors of medicine, philosophy, osteopathy, and science, or individuals with the equivalent training in biomedical engineering who are citizens or permanent residents of North America may apply.

**Funds Avail.:** An educational grant of $35,000 is awarded. **Deadline:** November 1.

**Remarks:** Established in 1982 in honor of Kenneth M. Rosen.

---

• **4652** •

## North Atlantic Treaty Organization - Committee on the Challenges of Modern Society
Scientific Affairs Division         *Ph:* 32 2 707 4850
B-1110 Brussels, Belgium            *Fax:* 32 2 707 4232
*E-mail:* ccms@hq.nato.int
*URL:* http://www.nato.int/ccms

### • 4653 • CCMS Fellowships *(Postdoctorate/Fellowship)*

**Purpose:** To encourage participation in CCMS pilot studies of problems relating to the natural and social environment. **Focus:** Environmental Studies. **Qualif.:** Applicant must be a citizen of a NATO-member state, and be qualified to participate in research related to one of the pilot studies conducted by CCMS. The CCMS program consists of a number of on-going pilot studies related to the natural and social environment. Topics of the pilot studies, and the sites where they are conducted, vary from year to year. Typical projects investigate the effects that pollution and modern technology have on the environment, human health, or man-made

---

*North Atlantic Treaty Organization - Committee on the Challenges of Modern Society (continued)*

structures. Write to the address listed above, or to the CCMS representative in home country, for descriptions of active studies. Fellows work under the guidance of the pilot study director. Candidates must meet the qualifications stipulated by the director, and should have a good working knowledge of English, French, or the language of the director. Awards are intended to cover living and travel expenses.

**Funds Avail.:** $2,500-6,000. **To Apply:** Write to the National CCMS coordinator in home country for application form and guidelines. The Canadian, U.K. and U.S. national CCMS coordinators may be contacted at the following addresses: Canada: Professor Howard Alper, University of Ottawa, Faculty of Sciences, Chemistry Department, 10 Marie Curie, Ottawa, Ontario K1N 6N5 Canada; United Kingdom: Brian Oliver, Department of the Environment, Environmental Protection International Division, Romney House, 43 Marsham St., London SW1P 3PY, England (phone: 71-276-8160). United States: Ms Wendy Grieder, Office of International Activities, Environmental Protection Agency, Washington, D.C. 20460, U.S.A. (phone: (202)564-6462). Addresses for other countries may be obtained from CCMS in Belgium. **Deadline:** February 28. **Contact:** Mrs. M. Deweer at the above address (see entry 4652).

---

• 4654 •

**North Atlantic Treaty Organization - NATO Information Service**
Academic Affairs Officer
Office of Information and Press
B-1110 Brussels, Belgium
*URL:* http://www.nato.int

*Ph:* 2 707 5014
*Fax:* 2 707 4743

• 4655 • **NATO Euro-Atlantic Partnership Council Fellowships Programme** *(Postdoctorate/Fellowship)*

**Purpose:** To promote study and research leading to publication in areas of particular interest to the Organization, primarily Alliance security and political issues. This program is not intended to support research in aid of obtaining an academic degree. The programme comprises Individual Fellowships and Institutional Fellowships. **Qualif.:** A limited number of advanced research fellowships will be offered to candidates from both member countries (Albania, Armenia, Azerbaijan, Belarus, Belgium, Bulgaria, Czech Republic, Denmark, Estonia, Finland, France, Georgia, Germany, Greece, Hungary, Iceland, Italy, Kazakhstan, Kyrghyz Republic, Latvia, Lithuania, Luxembourg, Moldova, Netherlands, Norway, Poland, Portugal, Romania, Russia, Slovakia, Slovenia, Spain, Sweden, Switzerland, Tajikistan, the former Yugoslav Republic of Macedonia, Turkey, Turkmenistan, Ukraine, United Kingdom, United States, and Uzbekistan) and cooperation partners. Fellowships are intended for scholars of established reputation. Research in one or more of the European member countries of NATO, with time spent at NATO headquarters, is strongly encouraged.

**Funds Avail.:** A fixed-sum grant of approximately 240,000 Belgian francs or the equivalent in the currency of any other member country for individual fellowship awards. All travel costs are included (subject to NATO approval). **To Apply:** Applications may be obtained from appropriate national authorities. **Deadline:** February 15. **Contact:** In the United States, write to the following address for an application: Program Officer, Council for International Exchange of Scholars, 3400 International Dr. NW, Ste. M-500, Washington DC 20008-3097.

• 4656 • **NATO Senior Guest Fellowships** *(Professional Development/Fellowship)*

**Purpose:** To assist senior scientists from NATO-member countries to visit and work in France, Italy, Luxembourg, Spain, or Turkey. **Focus:** Engineering, Mathematics, Natural Sciences, Social Sciences, Technology. **Qualif.:** Candidate must be a senior scientist of high professional standing who wishes to lecture and/or conduct research in France, Italy, Luxembourg, Spain, or Turkey. Candidate must be invited to visit by a scientist or research institute in the host country before an application is submitted.

**Funds Avail.:** Travel, living and research allowances. **To Apply:** Applications are not accepted directly from the visiting scientist. Instead, the host scientist or research institute must submit the application to the Science Fellowship Program administrator in the host country. The French, Italian, Luxembourg, Portuguese, and Spanish national Science Fellowship Program administrators may be contacted at the addresses listed below. France: Professor R. Saint-Paul; Conservatoire National des Arts et Metiers; Secretariat des Bourses de l'OTAN; 2, rue Conte; F-75141 Paris, Cedex 03 (phone: 33-1-40-27-23-66). Italy: Dr. A. Donadio; Direzione Centrale Personale e Administrazione; Consiglio Nazionale delle Ricerche; Piazzale Aldo Moro, 7; 1-00100 Rome (phone: 6-4993-3245). Luxembourg: Professor J.P. Pier, Centre Universitaire de Luxembourg, 162A Avenue de la Faiencerie, L-1511, Luxembourg. Portugal: Professor A. Leao Rodrigues; Junta Nacional de Investigacao Cientifica e Technologica; Av. D. Carlos 1, 126, 2; 1200 Lisbon (phone: 351-1-397-9021). Spain: Dr. Daniel Saez Alvarez, Ministerio de Educacion y Ciencia, Secretaria General Tecnica, Subdireccion General de Cooperacion Internacional, Paseo de Prado 28 - 2, E-28014 Madrid, Tel: (34-1) 420 36 93, Telex 23801 MECIS E, Fax (34-1) 420 3325. Turkey: Professor Dr. Ersin Yurtsever, The Scientific and Technical Research Council of Turkey; Tubitak, Ataturk Bulvari, 221, Kavaklidere, TR-00680 Ankara (phone: 4-426-68-46). **Deadline:** Varies. **Contact:** Scientific Affairs Division at the above address (see entry 4654).

• 4657 • **Manfred Worner Fellowship** *(Doctorate, Postdoctorate, Professional Development/Fellowship)*

**Purpose:** To honor the memory of the late Secretary General by focusing attention on his leadership in the transformation of the Alliance, including efforts at extending NATO's relations with CEE countries and promoting the principles and image of the Transatlantic partnership. **Qualif.:** The fellowship is open to candidacies from the academic community and the media. Applicants must be citizens of the EAPC countries. **Criteria:** Granted to individuals or institutions on the merit of a proposal for work to be completed within one year after the awarding of the fellowship on a topic of particular interest to the Alliance.

**Funds Avail.:** BFr 800,000. **Deadline:** February 15.

**Remarks:** Established in 1995.

---

• 4658 •

**North Carolina Academy of Family Physicians Foundation**
PO Box 27605
Raleigh, NC 27605

*Ph:* (919)833-2110
*Fax:* (919)833-1801
*Free:* 800-872-9482

*E-mail:* cjaffe@ncafp.com
*URL:* http://www.ncafp.com

• 4659 • **NCAFP Foundation Medical Student Loan** *(Postgraduate/Fellowship, Loan)*

**Purpose:** To assist medical students attending medical school in North Carolina in their medical education by offering low interest loans that can be converted to a scholarship upon successfully completing a residency in medicine. **Qualif.:** Applicants must be enrolled or attending one of the following medical schools in North Carolina: Wake Forest University School of Medicine; Duke University Medical Center; East Carolina University School of Medicine; and University of North Carolina at Chapel Hill. Applicants must be first, second, or third year medical students. **Criteria:** When granting the loan, selection is based on the applicant's involvement and interest in family medicine, financial need, and their membership in organizations that support the specialty of family medicine.

**Funds Avail.:** $2,000 per loan. **No. of Awards:** 4/year. **To Apply:** Applications may be requested from January through April. **Deadline:** Varies between April 30 and May 30 (not set until January of each year). **Contact:** Cyndy Jaffe, Director of Development, at the above address (see entry 4658).

---

## • 4660 •
## North Carolina Arts Council
c/o Nancy Trovillion
Department of Cultural Resources
Raleigh, NC 27601-2812
*E-mail:* ncarts@ncacmail.dcr.state.nc.us
*URL:* http://www.ncarts.org

*Ph:* (919)733-2111
*Fax:* (919)733-7897

**• 4661 • Choreographers Fellowship** (*Professional Development/Fellowship*)

**Qualif.:** North Carolina choreographers of ballet, modern, jazz, folk, or ethnic dance may apply.

**Funds Avail.:** $8,000. **To Apply:** Applicants must submit five copies of the application form, copies of a resume, and one typed page explaining how the fellowship will affect artistic development. A videotape with examples of at least two recent works and a description of the video must also be submitted. **Deadline:** November 1. **Contact:** Karen Wells.

**• 4662 • Community Arts Administration Internships** (*Graduate/Internship*)

**Purpose:** To provide supervised internships with one of the state's community arts councils or multicultural arts organizations. **Qualif.:** Applicants must possess at least a four-year college degree and demonstrate a strong interest in a career in community arts administration.

**Funds Avail.:** $3,000 stipend. **Deadline:** May 1. **Contact:** Jack LeSueur.

**• 4663 • Film/Video Artists Fellowship** (*Professional Development/Fellowship*)

**Qualif.:** North Carolina filmmakers and video artists who have completed at least one film or video may apply.

**Funds Avail.:** $8,000. **To Apply:** Applicants must submit five copies of the application form, a typed page explaining how the fellowship will be utilized, one videotape featuring a ten-minute film segment, a description of the segment, and five copies of a resume. **Deadline:** November 1. **Contact:** Jeff Pettus.

**• 4664 • Folklife Documentary Program** (*Professional Development/Fellowship*)

**Qualif.:** South Carolina traditional and revivalist folk artists, folklorists, and nonprofit organizations that are knowledgeable about North Carolina's folk arts traditions may apply. **To Apply:** Applicants must submit a project budget, application narrative,

description of the project, work samples, and resumes of project personnel. **Deadline:** March 1.

**• 4665 • Folklife Internships** (*Graduate/Internship*)

**Purpose:** To introduce an intern to a range of issues and activities, including planning and implementing public programs, organizing original field research in support of folklife projects, grantsmanship, financial planning and administration, publicity and promotion of public programs, advising local organizations and arts agencies, and fostering interagency relationships.

**Funds Avail.:** $4,000 stipend. **Deadline:** February 1. **Contact:** Wayne Martin.

**• 4666 • Headlands Center for the Arts Residency** (*Professional Development/Fellowship*)

**Purpose:** To provide support for North Carolina's visual artists and writers to participate in a residency program in Sausalito, California.

**Funds Avail.:** $500 per month is provided, plus evening meals. **No. of Awards:** 2. **To Apply:** For more information, contact Headlands Center for the Arts, 944 Fort Barry, Sausalito, CA, 94965, (415)331-2787.

**• 4667 • La Napoule Residency for Visual Artists and Writers** (*Professional Development/Fellowship*)

**Purpose:** To provide support for a visual artist and writer to be in residence for ten weeks in southern France with international artists. **Qualif.:** North Carolina visual artists and writers may apply.

**Funds Avail.:** $1,000 stipend plus meals and round-trip travel. **No. of Awards:** 2. **Deadline:** November 1.

**• 4668 • North Carolina Arts Council Artist Fellowships** (*Professional Development/Fellowship*)

**Purpose:** To recognize achievement and support the artistic development of North Carolina's artists. **Focus:** Visual Arts, Music, Choreography, Playwriting, Literature, Film/Video, Screenwriting. **Qualif.:** Applicants must have been North Carolina residents for one year, and have made a career commitment to their art. Artists may not apply while enrolled in a degree-granting program. **Criteria:** Based on artistic excellence.

**Funds Avail.:** $8,000. **To Apply:** In addition to completed application, artists are asked to submit samples of their work. **Deadline:** November 1.

**• 4669 • Regional Artist Project Grants Program** (*Professional Development/Grant*)

**Purpose:** To award project grants to artists in any discipline. **Qualif.:** Regional consortia of North Carolina's local arts councils may apply.

**Funds Avail.:** Grants to artists range from $500 to $3,000; grants to consortia range from $2,000 to $8,000. **Deadline:** March 1.

**• 4670 • Visual Artists Fellowship** (*Professional Development/Fellowship*)

**Qualif.:** North Carolina craft artisans, installation artists, painters, photographers, printmakers, sculptors, and visual performance artists may apply.

**Funds Avail.:** $8,000. **To Apply:** Applicants must include seven copies of the completed application form, ten slides in a plastic slide sheet, and/or audio or videotape for performance or experimental art, and seven copies pf a list describing the work samples submitted. Seven copies of a resume are also required. **Deadline:** November 1.

---

• 4671 •
## North Carolina Association of Educators
PO Box 27347
700 S. Salisbury St.  *Ph:* (919)832-3000
Raleigh, NC 27611  *Fax:* (919)829-1626
*URL:* http://www.ncae.org

• 4672 •  **Mary Morrow-Edna Richards Scholarships**
*(Undergraduate/Scholarship)*

**Purpose:** To aid potential North Carolina teachers. **Focus:** Education. **Qualif.:** Applicants must be North Carolina residents enrolled in a teacher-education program. They must be college juniors who are willing to teach in the North Carolina public schools for at least two years following graduation. **Criteria:** Selection is based on character, personality, scholastic achievement, evidence of promise as a teacher, and financial need.

**Funds Avail.:** Award amounts vary. **To Apply:** A completed application, photograph, official transcript, and three recommendations must be submitted. Application should be made through a college or university. The head of the department of education in teacher training institutions is requested by the State NCAE president to select two juniors to receive application forms. Other qualified applicants may request application forms from the State NCAE office. **Deadline:** Second Monday of January. **Contact:** Karen Archia at the above address (see entry 4671).

• 4673 •
## North Carolina Department of Administration - Division of Veterans Affairs
325 N. Salisbury St.
Albemarle Bldg., Ste. 1065
Raleigh, NC 27603  *Ph:* (919)733-3851
 *Fax:* (919)733-2834

• 4674 •  **North Carolina Scholarships for Children of War Veterans** *(Undergraduate/Scholarship)*

**Purpose:** These scholarships are given in appreciation for the service and sacrifices of North Carolina's war veterans and as evidence of the State's concern for the children of these veterans. **Focus:** General Studies. **Qualif.:** Applicants must either have been born in North Carolina or be children of veterans who were North Carolina residents at the time of their entrance into the service. The birth requirement may be waived in certain circumstances for children whose mothers were native-born residents of North Carolina. Children meeting any of the requirements who were adopted before the age of 15 are also eligible. There are five different classifications of the scholarships. Children of veteran parents who were killed or died in wartime service, or died as a result of service-connected condition incurred in wartime service as defined by the law, are eligible for Class I-A scholarships. Those with veteran parents rated by USDVA as 100 percent disabled due to wartime service as defined by law, and currently or at the time of death were drawing compensation for such disabilities, are eligible for Class I-B scholarships. If the veteran parents are rated by USDVA as much as 20 percent but less than 100 percent disabled due to wartime service as defined in the law, or a statutory award for arrested pulmonary tuberculosis and currently or at time of death was drawing compensation, children are eligible for the Class II scholarships. Eligibility for Class III scholarships requires that applicants have either: a veteran parent who is or was at time of death drawing pension for total and permanent disability as rated by the USDVA, or a veteran parent who is a deceased war veteran who was honorably discharged and who does not qualify under any of other provisions, provided that the applicant is less than 23 years of age at the time of application. Class IV

scholarships are for children whose veteran parents were Prisoners of War or Missing in Action.

**Funds Avail.:** Class I-A scholarships provide free tuition, a room allowance, a board allowance, and exemption from certain mandatory fees as set forth in the law for students attending public, community, and technical colleges or institutes. The scholarship provides $4,500 per nine-month academic year for those attending private colleges and junior colleges. The award's duration is for four academic years and there is no limit to the number of awards given; anyone who qualifies will receive the scholarship. Class I-B scholarships provide free tuition and exemption from certain mandatory fees as set forth in the law for students attending public, community, and technical colleges or institutes. The scholarship provides $1,500 per nine-month academic year for those attending private colleges and junior colleges. There is no limit to the number of these scholarships, and the duration is four years. Class II and Class III scholarships provide the same services as Class I-A scholarships, but only a limited number are offered (100 each). Class IV scholarships provide the same services as Class I-A scholarships, and there is no limit to the number of awards given. **No. of Awards:** Varies. **To Apply:** A formal application form and financial questionnaire must be obtained and completed. Applicants must send copies of their birth certificates, Selective Service registration acknowledgement letters, and parent discharges from the Armed Services. Applicants may send letters of recommendation if they so desire. However, this is not asked of Class I-A, I-B, or IV applicants. A transcript of high school grades are absolutely essential for any consideration to be given to the applicant. **Deadline:** May 31.

**Remarks:** If the applicant is living in North Carolina, his or her Service Officer will forward the papers. If the applicant is not living in North Carolina, he or she should submit one copy of all papers directly to the Assistant Secretary's Office in Raleigh. **Contact:** Charles F. Smith, Assistant Secretary, at the above address (see entry 4673).

• 4675 •
## North Carolina Division of Veterans Affairs
c/o Charles F. Smith, Assistant
  Secretary
Albemarle Bldg., Ste. 1065
325 N. Salisbury St.
Raleigh, NC 27603  *Ph:* (919)733-3851

• 4676 •  **Scholarship for Children of Disabled, Deceased and POW/MIA Veterans** *(Graduate, Undergraduate/Scholarship)*

**Qualif.:** Candidate must be the child of a deceased or disabled veteran or one listed as a POW or MIA who had been a legal resident of North Carolina at time of enlistment. **No. of Awards:** 400. **To Apply:** Awarded annually. **Deadline:** May 31. **Contact:** Charles F. Smith, Assistant Secretary.

### • 4677 •

**North Carolina Division of Vocational Rehabilitation Services**
805 Ruggles Dr.
PO Box 26053     *Ph:* (919)733-3364
Raleigh, NC 27611     *Fax:* (919)733-7968
*E-mail:* tkemp@dhr.state.nc.us

#### • 4678 • Vocational Rehabilitation Assistance for Postsecondary Training *(Undergraduate/Other)*

**Focus:** General Studies. **Qualif.:** Candidates must be North Carolina residents who have either a mental or physical disability and are determined eligible for vocational rehabilitation services. **Contact:** Terry Kemp, Specialist for Cooperative School Program and Transition Services, at the above address (see entry 4677).

### • 4679 •

**North Carolina State Education Assistance Authority**
PO Box 13663     *Ph:* (919)549-8614
Research Triangle Park, NC 27709-     *Fax:* (919)549-8481
3663     *Free:* 800-700-1775
*E-mail:* jdmartin@ga.unc.edu
*URL:* http://www.ncseaa.edu

#### • 4680 • North Carolina State Legislative Tuition Grants *(Undergraduate/Grant)*

**Purpose:** For tuition equalization. **Qualif.:** Applicants must be North Carolina residents attending eligible private colleges or universities located in North Carolina. Students must be enrolled full time as undergraduates in a program that is not designed by the school primarily for career preparation in a religious vocation.

**Funds Avail.:** Maximum amount granted is $1,600 each year. Awards are not made for summer terms. **No. of Awards:** Approximately 27,000. **To Apply:** Applications are available at eligible schools. **Contact:** Each participating eligible institution administers the program for and on behalf of the eligible students it enrolls.

### • 4681 •

**North Dakota Department of Transportation - Human Resources Division**
608 East Blvd.     *Ph:* (701)328-3116
Bismarck, ND 58505-0700     *Fax:* (701)328-1415
*E-mail:* mlarson@state.nd.us
*URL:* http://www.state.nd.us/dot/

#### • 4682 • NDDOT Educational Grants *(Undergraduate/ Scholarship loan)*

**Purpose:** To help the NDDOT develop a technical and professional workforce. **Focus:** Civil Engineering, Construction Engineering, Survey Technology. **Qualif.:** Applicants must have completed one year of study at a higher education institution in one of the following fields: civil engineering, civil engineering and survey technology, or construction engineering. Present NDDOT employees are eligible if they have completed one year of study or have worked for the NDDOT as classified employees for at least two years. Recipients must attend a higher education institution in North Dakota and may only use funds for educational expenditures including tuition, required fees, books, materials, and necessary

personal expenses while attending college. Upon graduation, recipients must agree to work for the NDDOT for a period of time at least equal to the study period funded, or pay back the money according to specified terms. **Criteria:** Candidates are judged on their potential to contribute to NDDOT, financial need, academic achievement, and relevant experience. Preference is given to applicants who are available for summer employment with the NDDOT.

**Funds Avail.:** $1,000 annually. **No. of Awards:** 2-3. **To Apply:** Applications are distributed to North Dakota colleges and universities that have related curricula. These institutions are responsible for distributing applications to qualified candidates. **Deadline:** Spring. **Contact:** Marlene Larson, Personnel Office, Human Resources Division, at the above address (see entry 4681).

### • 4683 •

**North Dakota University System**
600 East Blvd.
State Capitol Bldg.     *Ph:* (701)328-2166
Bismarck, ND 58505-0300     *Fax:* (701)328-2961
*E-mail:* rhonda_schauer@ndus.nodak.edu
*URL:* http://toons.cc.ndsu.nodak.edu/

#### • 4684 • North Dakota Indian Scholarships *(Undergraduate/Scholarship)*

**Purpose:** To assist Native American students in obtaining a basic college education. **Focus:** General Studies. **Qualif.:** Applicants must be either residents of North Dakota with one quarter degree Native American blood or enrolled members of a tribe now resident in North Dakota. They must also have been accepted for admission at an institution of higher learning or state vocational education program within North Dakota, be enrolled full-time (12 credits or more), and have a GPA of at least 2.0 on a 4.0 scale. Students participating in internships, student teaching, teaching assistance, or cooperative education programs may be eligible for a scholarship award only if participation in that program is required for the degree and only if tuition must be paid for the credits earned. **Criteria:** Full-time students with a 3.5 average will be given priority in funding.

**Funds Avail.:** $700. **No. of Awards:** Varies. **To Apply:** Applications must include certification of Native American blood or tribal enrollment, a budget form completed by a financial aid officer at the institution attended by the applicant, and most recent transcript. **Deadline:** July 15. **Contact:** The Administrator for the Indian Scholarship Program at the above address (see entry 4683).

### • 4685 •

**Northeastern Consortium for Engineering Education**
1101 Massachusetts Ave.     *Ph:* (407)892-6146
St. Cloud, FL 34769     *Fax:* (407)892-0406
*E-mail:* stcloudof1@aol.com; stcloudof1@aol.com

#### • 4686 • U.S. Air Force Phillips Laboratory Scholar Program *(Postdoctorate/Other)*

**Purpose:** To provide a productive means for scholars to participate in research at the Air Force Phillips Laboratory Scholar Program, to foster professional association among the scholars and their counterparts in the Air Force, and to further the research objectives of the USAF. Six technical tasks of current interest to the Laboratory are: atmospheric science, earth science, infrared technology, ionospheric physics, optical physics, and space physics. **Focus:** Geophysics. **Qualif.:** Applicants must be United States citizens and holders of a Ph.D. degree or equivalent in an

## Northeastern Consortium for Engineering Education (continued)

appropriate technical field including the basic and applied science fields of physics, particularly geophysics and atmospheric physics, meteorology, chemistry, mathematics, computer science, and engineering. Applicants must be willing to pursue research work of limited time duration at the U.S. Air Force Geophysics Directorate at the Hanscom Air Force Base in Massachusetts and the advanced weapons and survivability directorate at Kirtland AFB in New Mexico. Candidates must be able to obtain Department of Defense SECRET clearance to insure access to work areas.

**Funds Avail.:** The planned stipend is $120 per day, plus a 10 percent salary increment payable at the completion of the program, 26 days vacation, and 13 days of sick leave per year. Unused vacation and sick leave is reimbursed at the end of the year. There are 10 paid holidays during the year. Travel expenses are reimbursed for one trip from the scholar's normal location to the Air Force facility at the start of the appointment, and one return trip at the close of the appointment. The period of the appointment is 12 months. **Deadline:** Applications are processed as they are received.

**Remarks:** The Air Force Geophysics Laboratory at Hanscom Air Force Base, Bedford, Massachusetts sponsors this program which is conducted by the Southeastern Center for Electrical Engineering Education. At the end of the twelve month research period, the scholar is obligated to prepare a report describing research accomplishments. **Contact:** Director, AF Geophysics Scholar Program, SCEEE Management Office, at the above address (see entry 4685).

---

## • 4687 •
## Northeastern Loggers' Association

PO Box 69  
Old Forge, NY 13420-0069  
*E-mail:* nela@telenet.net  

*Ph:* (315)369-3078  
*Fax:* (315)369-3736  

### • 4688 • Northeastern Loggers' Association Annual Scholarships *(High School, Undergraduate/Scholarship)*

**Purpose:** To promote good writing skills among students. **Qualif.:** Candidates must be college-bound high school students or undergraduates and family members of an association member or family member of an employee of an association member. **Criteria:** Primarily based on essay submission.

**Funds Avail.:** $500 each. **No. of Awards:** 3. **To Apply:** Students must submit a typewritten essay on a predetermined topic, an application, and academic transcripts. **Deadline:** March 31.

**Remarks:** One award is given in each of three categories: High School Senior, Student in Associate/Technical Degree Program, and Student in Your-Year Program. **Contact:** The Northwestern Logger's Association at the above address (see entry 4687).

---

## • 4689 •
## Northern California Scholarship Foundations

1547 Lakeside Dr.  
Oakland, CA 94612  

*Ph:* (510)451-1906  
*Fax:* (510)451-0626  

### • 4690 • Herbert Frank and Bertha Maude Laird Memorial Foundation Scholarships *(Undergraduate/Scholarship)*

**Qualif.:** Candidates must be seniors in the public high schools of Northern and Central California. Applicants must be in good health and have been recommended because of high moral character by

their high school principal or counselor. They must also have a superior high school grade point average, high scores on the Scholastic Aptitude Test, financial need, and be willing to earn a portion of their expenses while in college. **Criteria:** Applicants planning a career in engineering receive preference.

**Funds Avail.:** Scholarships are $3,500 per year for a total of four years of undergraduate study. Recipients who attend junior college and live at home may receive a lesser amount until they transfer to a four-year college. **To Apply:** Scholarship announcements are sent to high school principals in January. Trustees, at Foundation expense, invite applicants they wish to interview to Oakland. Candidates should have a clear idea of the courses they intend to pursue at college and some idea of what they intend to do for their life work. **Deadline:** Completed applications must be filed by March 17. Recipients are selected by the second week in May. **Contact:** High school principals or Northern California Scholarship Foundations at the above address (see entry 4689).

### • 4691 • Helen Wegman Parmalee Educational Foundation Scholarships *(Undergraduate/Scholarship)*

**Qualif.:** Candidates must be seniors in the public high schools of Northern and Central California. Applicants must be in good health, recommended because of high moral character by their high school principal or counselor, have a superior high school grade point average, high scores on the Scholastic Aptitude Test, financial need, and be willing to earn a portion of their expenses while in college. There are no limitations on fields of study.

**Funds Avail.:** Scholarships are $3,500 per year for a total of four years of undergraduate study. Recipients who attend junior college and live at home may receive a lesser amount until they transfer to a four-year college. **To Apply:** Trustees at Foundation expense invite applicants they wish to interview to Oakland. Candidates should have a clear idea of the courses they intend to pursue at college and some idea of what they intend to do for their life work. Scholarship announcements are sent to high school principals in January. **Deadline:** Completed applications must be filed by March 17. Recipients are selected by the second week in May. **Contact:** High school principals or Northern California Scholarship Foundations at the above address (see entry 4689).

### • 4692 • Scaife Foundation Scholarships *(Undergraduate/Scholarship)*

**Qualif.:** Candidates must be seniors in the public high schools of Northern and Central California. Applicants must be in good health, recommended because of high moral character by their high school principal or counselor, have a superior high school grade point average, high scores on the Scholastic Aptitude Test, financial need, and be willing to earn a portion of their expenses while in college. Applicants must be the sons of American-born parents, and may not study medicine or theology.

**Funds Avail.:** Scholarships are $3,500 per year for a total of four years of undergraduate study. Recipients who attend junior college and live at home may receive a lesser amount until they transfer to a four-year college. **To Apply:** Trustees, at Foundation expense, invite applicants they wish to interview to Oakland. Candidates should have a clear idea of the courses they intend to pursue at college and some idea of what they intend to do for their life work. Scholarship announcements are sent to high school principals in January. **Deadline:** Completed application must be filed by March 17. Recipients are selected by the second week in May. **Contact:** High school principal or Northern California Scholarship Foundations at the above address (see entry 4689).

• **4693** •
## Northwest Ohio Black Media Association
PO Box 9232
Toledo, OH 43697-0232 *Ph:* (419)837-2716

• **4694** • **William A. Brower Scholarship**
*(Undergraduate/Scholarship)*

**Purpose:** To assist students attending colleges or universities in northwest Ohio. **Focus:** Journalism and mass communications. **Qualif.:** Candidates must be minority residents of northwest Ohio.

**Funds Avail.:** $1500. **No. of Awards:** 1. **To Apply:** Write for details.

• **4695** •
## Northwest Pharmacists Coalition Scholarships
PO Box 22975
Seattle, WA 98122 *Ph:* (206)746-9618

• **4696** • **Northwest Pharmacist Coalition Pre-Pharmacy Scholarship** *(Undergraduate/Scholarship)*

**Focus:** Pharmacology. **Qualif.:** Applicants must be African Americans planning a career in pharmacy and enrolled in community college or university prepharmacy programs. **Criteria:** Awards are made based on academic achievement, merit of written essay and personal interview. **To Apply:** Applicants must submit high school or college transcripts, completed application, and a type written essay expressing the applicant's desire to be a pharmacist and reason why the applicant should receive the scholarship. **Contact:** Northwest Pharmacist Coalition at the above address (see entry 4695).

• **4697** •
## Northwestern University
Department of Philosophy
Brentano Hall *Ph:* (708)491-3656
Evanston, IL 60208-1315 *Fax:* (708)491-2547

• **4698** • **Northwestern University Journalism Minority Scholarships** *(Graduate/Scholarship)*

**Focus:** Journalism. **Qualif.:** Candidates are graduate students enrolled in Northwestern's Wedill School of Journalism. **Criteria:** Based on writing ability, journalistic potential, academic performance and extracurricular involvement.

**Funds Avail.:** $5000 to $24,000. **To Apply:** All enrolled minority students are automatically considered. No additional applications are necessary.

• **4699** • **Postdoctoral Fellowships in the History and Philosophy of Science** *(Postdoctorate/Fellowship)*

**Purpose:** To support postdoctoral research in the history or philosophy of science. **Focus:** History of Science, Philosophy of Science. **Qualif.:** Candidate may be of any nationality. Applicant must be a recent Ph.D. recipient who wishes to specialize or train in the history or philosophy of science. Fellowships are tenable at Northwestern University. Fellows must teach one class or workshop during the year and participate in other program activities.

**Funds Avail.:** $25,000. **To Apply:** Submit curriculum vitae, a project proposal less than four pages long, and one published or unpublished paper. Three confidential letters of recommendation

are also required. **Deadline:** December 1. Notification by March 30. **Contact:** Prof. David Hull, Department of Philosophy, at the above address (see entry 4697).

• **4700** •
## Norwich Jubilee Esperanto Foundation
37 Granville Court
Oxford OX3 0HS, England *Ph:* 1865 245509

• **4701** • **Norwich Jubilee Esperanto Foundation Travel Grants** *(Graduate/Grant)*

**Purpose:** To promote education for international understanding through Esperanto. **Focus:** Esperanto. **Qualif.:** Candidate may be of any nationality. Applicant must be under 26 years old and in need of financial help to use Esperanto for travel purposes. Non-British candidates must travel in the United Kingdom, and will be expected to speak Esperanto to British schools or clubs. **Criteria:** Satisfactory nature of travel plan; level of Esperanto shown; preference given to those whose native language is not English.

**Funds Avail.:** £100-500. **No. of Awards:** 10. **To Apply:** Write a letter in the Esperanto language to request an application form. Submit form with a character reference and reference attesting to competence in Esperanto. **Deadline:** None. **Contact:** Dr. Kathleen M. Hall, Secretary, at the above address (see entry 4700).

• **4702** •
## Nurses' Educational Funds, Inc.
555 West 57th St., Ste. 1327 *Ph:* (212)399-1428
New York, NY 10019 *Fax:* (212)581-2368
*E-mail:* BBNEF@aol.com
*URL:* http://www.N-E-F.org

• **4703** • **NEF Scholarships** *(Doctorate, Graduate/Scholarship)*

**Purpose:** To assist registered nurses with advanced study. **Focus:** Nursing. **Qualif.:** Applicant must be a U.S. citizen or permanent resident with the intent to become a citizen. Applicant must be a full-time masters graduate student or a full or part-time doctoral student. Applicant must be a registered nurse and a member of a professional nursing association, and be enrolled in or applying to a master's or doctoral level program accredited by the National League for Nursing. **Criteria:** NEF scholarships are competitive. NEF considers academic excellence the first criteria for its awards. The other criteria for the award are scholarship, academic standing, and potential for leadership and service to the nursing profession.

**Funds Avail.:** Funds of $2,500-10,000 are available. **To Apply:** Write to NEF for an application kit. The application requires GRE or MAT scores, official transcripts, letters of reference, a goal-statement essay, as well as additional professional information. Include a $10.00 check. The kits are available between August 1 and February 1. **Deadline:** All application materials must be received by March 1. Successful applicants will be notified at the end of April or the beginning of May.

**Remarks:** The M. Elizabeth Carnegie Scholarship is available from NEF to a Black nurse pursuing a doctoral degree in nursing or a related field. The Estelle Massey Osborne Memorial Scholarship is awarded annually to a Black nurse pursuing a master's degree in nursing. All other requirements, deadlines, and application procedures are the same as those for general NEF scholarships. **Contact:** Barbara Butler, Scholarship Coordinator, at the above address (see entry 4702).

# • 4704 •

## Oak Ridge Institute - Science Education Division
PO Box 117
Oak Ridge, TN 37831-0117     *Ph:* (615)576-3000
*URL:* http://www.orau.gov/orise.htm

### • 4705 • DOE Student Research Participation
*(Graduate, Postdoctorate, Undergraduate/Award)*

**Purpose:** To increase interaction and flow of information between universities and DOE laboratories, to familiarize engineers and scientists with energy sciences and techniques, and to stimulate transfer of knowledge from DOE laboratories to academic institutions for incorporation into their education and training curricula. **Qualif.:** Applicants must be undergraduate students, graduate students, or faculty in the fields of science and engineering. Candidates must be United States citizens or permanent residents.

**Funds Avail.:** Approximately 1,100 undergraduate awards, 200 graduate awards, and 200 faculty awards are given. Duration of awards is 10 weeks to one year. Stipend varies with level of appointment. **Deadline:** December/January.

**Remarks:** Approximately 3,500 applications are received each year. **Contact:** The U.S. Department of Energy at the above address (see entry 4704).

### • 4706 • Alexander Hollaender Distinguished Postdoctoral Fellowships *(Postdoctorate/Fellowship)*

**Purpose:** To provide research opportunities in energy-related life, biomedical, and environmental sciences. **Qualif.:** Applicants must have a doctoral degree (Ph.D., M.D., D.V.M., or equivalent) in an appropriate discipline (or completed all internship or residency requirements) within two years of desired starting date or expect to complete all such requirements prior to desired starting date. Disciplines appropriate to the program include those in the life, biomedical, and environmental sciences, and other supporting scientific disciplines. Candidates must be United Stated citizens or permanent residents. **Criteria:** Selection is based on academic records, recommendations, scientific interests, and compatibility of applicant's background and interests with the needs of the research center.

**Funds Avail.:** Up to ten fellowships with a stipend of $37,500 each are awarded each year for up to two years. **To Apply:** Applicants must submit an application form, a resume, a research proposal, three references, graduate transcripts, and a list and copies of publications. **Deadline:** January 15.

**Remarks:** The Fellowship is sponsored by the U.S. Department of Energy, Office of Energy Research and administered by the Oak Ridge Institute for Science and Education. **Contact:** Applicants may request application packets from Barbara Dorsey, Science/Engineering Education Division, Oak Ridge Institute for Science and Education, PO Box 117, Oak Ridge, Tennessee 37831-0117. Telephone: (615)576-9975.

# • 4707 •

## Oak Ridge Institute for Science and Education - Education and Training Division
PO Box 117     *Ph:* (423)576-3192
Oak Ridge, TN 37831-0117     *Fax:* (423)241-5219
*URL:* http://www.orau.gov/

### • 4708 • U.S. Department of Energy Distinguished Postdoctoral Research Fellowship *(Postdoctorate/ Fellowship)*

**Focus:** Physical Sciences, Computer Sciences, Engineering. **Qualif.:** Applicants must have received a doctoral degree (Ph.D.,

M.D., D.V.M., or equivalent) in an appropriate scientific or engineering discipline (or completed all internship or residency requirements) within three years of desired starting date or expect to complete all such requirements prior to desired starting date. Candidates must be United States citizens or permanent residents. Proposal must relate to an energy specific field. **Criteria:** Selection is based on academic records, recommendations, scientific interests, and compatibility of applicant's background and interests with the needs of the research center.

**Funds Avail.:** Up to ten fellowships with a stipend of $52,800 each per year for up to two years. **To Apply:** Applicants must submit an application form, a resume, a research proposal, three references, graduate transcripts, and a list and copies of publications. **Deadline:** July 1.

**Remarks:** The Fellowship is sponsored by the U.S. Department of Energy, Office of Health and Environmental Research, and administered by the Oak Ridge Institute for Science and Education. **Contact:** Applicants may request application packets from Barbara Dorsey at the above address (see entry 4707).

### • 4709 • U.S. Department of Energy Global Change Distinguished Postdoctoral Fellowships *(Postdoctorate/ Fellowship)*

**Purpose:** To provide research opportunities in problems related to global change. **Focus:** Life, Physical, Earth, Computer, and Environmental Sciences. **Qualif.:** Applicants must have received a doctoral degree (Ph.D., M.D., D.V.M., or equivalent) in an appropriate scientific or engineering discipline (or completed all internship or residency requirements) within three years of desired starting date or expect to complete all such requirements prior to desired starting date. Fields supported are disciplines in the life, physical, earth, computer, and environmental sciences. Candidates must be United States citizens or permanent residents. **Criteria:** Selection is based on academic records, recommendations, scientific interests, and compatibility of applicant's background and interests with the needs of the research center.

**Funds Avail.:** Up to 12 fellowships with a stipend of $35,000 each per year for up to two years. **To Apply:** Applicants must submit an application form, a resume, a research proposal, three references, graduate transcripts, and a list and copies of publications. **Deadline:** February 15.

**Remarks:** The Fellowship is sponsored by the U.S. Department of Energy, Office of Health and Environment Research, and administered by the Oak Ridge Institute for Science and Education. **Contact:** Applicants may request application packets from Barbara Dorsey at the above address (see entry 4707).

### • 4710 • U.S. Department of Energy Human Genome Distinguished Postdoctoral Fellowships *(Postdoctorate/Fellowship)*

**Purpose:** To improve current methods and develop new ones for determining DNA sequences; construct complete physical maps for each human chromosome and determining sequences of selected DNA regions; develop new instrumentation, effective software, and database designs to support large-scale mapping and sequencing projects; and support investigations and activities aimed at understanding the ethical, legal, and social implications of the Human Genome Program. **Focus:** Genetics, Biochemistry. **Qualif.:** Applicants must have a doctoral degree (Ph.D., M.D., D.V.M., or equivalent) in an appropriate discipline (or completed all internship or residency requirements) within two years of desired starting date or expect to complete all such requirements prior to desired starting date (which must be between May 1 and September 30). Applicants must choose mentors who are funded by Office of Health and Environmental Research of DOE. **Criteria:** Selection is based on academic records, recommendations, scientific interests, and compatibility of applicant's background and interests with the needs of the research center.

**Funds Avail.:** Up to six fellowships with a stipend of $37,500 each per year. **To Apply:** Applicants must submit an application form, a resume, a research proposal, three references, graduate transcripts, and a list and copies of publications. **Deadline:** February 1.

**Remarks:** The Fellowship is sponsored by the U.S. Department of Energy, Office of Health and Environmental Research, and administered by the Oak Ridge Institute for Science and Education. **Contact:** Applicants may request application packets from Barbara Dorsey at the above address (see entry 4707).

## • 4711 • U.S. Department of Energy Internship
*(Undergraduate/Internship)*

**Purpose:** To provide hands-on research experience with state-of-the-art equipment. **Focus:** Science, Mathematics, Engineering. **Qualif.:** Applicants must be United States citizens or permanent resident aliens who are currently at the junior or senior level at a college or university, are majoring in computer sciences, mathematics, engineering, environmental/life sciences, or physical sciences, and have a minimum grade point average of 3.0 or higher on a 4.0 scale. A limited number of appointments are available for first semester after graduation. **Criteria:** Participants are selected on the basis of academic merit, future research interests, and an availability of the position at the National Laboratory.

**Funds Avail.:** A stipend of $225 per week, plus complimentary housing (or housing allowance) and round trip transportation to the laboratory. Recipients are given internships as student research participants at one of the following locations: Argonne National Laboratory, Illinois; Brookhaven National Laboratory, New York; Lawrence Berkeley Laboratory, California; Lawrence Livermore Laboratory, California; Los Alamos National Laboratory, New Mexico; Oak Ridge National Laboratory, Tennessee; or Pacific Northwest Laboratory, Washington. Students will participate with National Laboratory scientists in ongoing research and will have access to state-of-the-art equipment and facilities. Seminars, workshops, and coursework are also conducted in the student's chosen field of study. Student appointments are normally for one academic term; however, extension of appointments through the summer are encouraged. Tuition and fees for the academic credit to be received for the semester experience are the responsibility of the participants. **To Apply:** Applications are mailed to the Department of Energy (DOE) for processing and review. Completed, eligible files are sent to the students laboratories of choice, and are forwarded to the laboratory scientists for review and selection. Laboratory decisions are forwarded back to DOE, which, in turn, sends decision letters to the students. Students may receive offers from both their first- and second-choice laboratories. Subsequent placement of students is attempted as student responses are received. **Deadline:** March 15 for the fall semester and October 20 for the spring semester.

**Remarks:** Participants are encouraged to arrange for academic credit by their home institutions for the research performed during their appointment period. **Contact:** Donna J. Prokop, Science and Engineering Research Semester Program Manager, U.S. Department of Energy, PO Box 23575, Washington, D.C. 20026-3575. Telephone: (202)488-2426 or (202)586-4570.

## • 4712 •
## The Observatories of the Carnegie Institution of Washington
813 Santa Barbara St.     *Ph:* (818)577-1122
Pasadena, CA 91101-1292   *Fax:* (818)795-8136
*URL:* http://www.ociw.edu/

## • 4713 • Carnegie Postdoctoral Research Fellowship in Astronomy *(Postgraduate/Fellowship)*

**Purpose:** To encourage long-term observational research programs in optical or infra-red astronomy. **Focus:** Physical

Science, Astronomy. **Qualif.:** The Institution is particularly interested in people who have received their Ph.D. degree within the past three years. Successful applicants must have completed their Ph.D. requirements before assuming the fellowship. **To Apply:** Applicants are requested to have letters of recommendation sent from three professional scientists. The application itself should include a brief curriculum vitae and a list of papers published and submitted. Applicants are also required to write a brief essay in which they describe their recent astronomical research and present a research proposal that shows how they would hope to take advantage of the opportunities presented by the observatories. Carnegie Fellowships are awarded for one year and may be renewed for two additional years. **Deadline:** December 15.

**Remarks:** Carnegie Fellows have access to the observatories' telescopes on Cerro Las Campanas, Chile. **Contact:** Chair, Fellowship Committee, at the above address (see entry 4712).

## • 4714 •
## Official Languages Program
9th Fl., Sterling Pl.
9940-106th St.     *Ph:* (403)427-5538
Edmonton, AB, Canada T5J 4R4   *Fax:* (403)422-4516

## • 4715 • French Fellowships *(Undergraduate/ Scholarship)*

**Qualif.:** Applicants for the Out-of-Province Fellowships must be Alberta students who wish to pursue full-time post-secondary studies taught in French at a designated institution. Applicants for the In-Province Fellowships must be Alberta students wishing to pursue full-time post-secondary studies taught in French at the Faculte Saint-Jean.

**Funds Avail.:** Up to $1,000; plus an additional $400 stipend for out-of-province fellowships. **Deadline:** July 15. **Contact:** Senior Consultant, Official Languages Program, at the above address (see entry 4714).

## • 4716 • Official Languages Part-Time Monitor Program *(Undergraduate/Scholarship)*

**Purpose:** To enable post-secondary students to pursue full-time studies while working as part-time resource persons to second language minority language teachers. **Qualif.:** Applicants must be full-time post-secondary students. Monitors are required to provide services for a minimum of eight hours per week for one full academic year. **Criteria:** Awards are given on the basis of personal interviews.

**Funds Avail.:** $3,500 scholarship. Additional allowances may be provided for justifiable related expenses. **Deadline:** February 15. **Contact:** Senior Consultant, Official Languages Program, at the above address (see entry 4714).

## • 4717 • Summer Language Bursary Program
*(Undergraduate/Award)*

**Qualif.:** Applicants must be full-time students who have attained post-secondary status and who wish to learn their official second language during a six-week immersion program at a participating Canadian institution.

**Funds Avail.:** Tuition, room and board costs. **Deadline:** February 15. **Contact:** Senior Consultant, Official Languages Program, at the above address (see entry 4714).

*Official Languages Program (continued)*

### • 4718 • Summer Language Bursary Program for Francophones *(Undergraduate/Scholarship)*

**Qualif.:** Applicants must be full-time Francophone students who have completed a minimum of Grade 11 (67 credits). The six-week program is available at designated Canadian institutions.

**Funds Avail.:** Varies. Students who successfully complete the course may have a part of their travel costs subsidized by the institution. **Deadline:** February 15. **Contact:** Senior Consultant, Official Languages Program, at the above address (see entry 4714).

---

## • 4719 •
## Ohio Baptist Education Society

248 Pine Tree Dr.
Granville, OH 43023-9548          Ph: (614)587-2274

### • 4720 • Lett Scholarships *(Graduate, Undergraduate/Scholarship)*

**Purpose:** To assist members of churches affiliated with the American Baptist Churches of Ohio to acquire education in preparation for professional Christian leadership in ministry or church-related ministries. **Qualif.:** Applicants must be members of a church affiliated with the American Baptist Churches of Ohio or a church dually aligned with ABC/OH; African Americans; be pursuing a course of study at an accredited institution or one approved by the Ohio Baptist Education Society Board of Trustees; and be pursuing a course of study leading to a degree or appropriate to, or required by, a chosen Christian ministry with the framework of the American Baptist Church in the USA. **Criteria:** The scholarship is awarded based on financial need.

**Funds Avail.:** $500. The scholarship will continue through the completion of the student's program if conditions do not change. Recipients are expected to maintain a good academic record, to submit a renewal application for aid and financial statements each year, and to submit an official transcript at the end of each grading period with a statement from the institution that the student is enrolled in for the next term. **To Apply:** Applications are available from the Ohio Baptist Education Society. **Deadline:** April. **Contact:** Dr. Ralph K. Lamb, Executive Secretary, Ohio Baptist Education Society at the above address (see entry 4719).

### • 4721 • Ohio Baptist Education Society Scholarships *(Graduate, Undergraduate/Scholarship)*

**Purpose:** To help members of the Ohio Baptist Convention Churches prepare for professional leadership in Christian ministries as endorsed by the Board of Trustees. **Focus:** Religion, General Studies. **Qualif.:** Applicants must be members of a church affiliated with the American Baptist Churches of Ohio or a church dually aligned with ABC/OH; hold permanent residence in Ohio; acknowledge a personal commitment to the Gospel; be in the process of preparing for a career in professional Christian ministries; intend to work within the framework of the American Baptist Churches, USA; have completed two years of study at an accredited undergraduate school; and prove financial need.

**Funds Avail.:** $500. The scholarship will continue through the completion of the student's program if conditions do not change. Recipients are expected to maintain a good academic record, to submit a renewal application for aid and financial statements each year, and to submit an official transcript at the end of each grading period with a statement from the institution that the student is enrolled in for the next term. **To Apply:** Application forms are available from the above address. **Deadline:** April 1. **Contact:** Dr. Ralph K. Lamb, Executive Secretary, Ohio Baptist Education Society at the above address (see entry 4719).

## • 4722 •
## Ohio Board of Regents

State Grants and Scholarships          Ph: (614)466-1190
PO Box 182452                         Fax: (614)752-5903
Columbus, OH 43218-2452               Free: 888-833-1133

### • 4723 • Ohio Academic Scholarships *(Undergraduate/Scholarship)*

**Focus:** General Studies. **Qualif.:** Applicants must be Ohio residents and one of the top five students in their high school graduating class. They must take the appropriate ACT test and plan to study at a participating Ohio college or university.

**Funds Avail.:** $2,000 per academic year for a maximum of four years. **To Apply:** Official applications must be completed and given to high school guidance counselors who then submit them to the Ohio Board of Regents. **Deadline:** February 23. **Contact:** Sue Minturn, Program Administrator, at the above address (see entry 4722).

### • 4724 • Ohio Instructional Grants *(Undergraduate/Grant)*

**Focus:** General Studies. **Qualif.:** Applicants must be Ohio residents enrolled full-time at an approved college or university in the state of Ohio or Pennsylvania, Total family income must be below $30,000.

**Funds Avail.:** Varies. **To Apply:** Applications are usually available in January or February. **Deadline:** October 1.

**Remarks:** Applicants must complete the Federal Application. There is no longer a separate application. **Contact:** David Bastian, Supervisor, at the above address (see entry 4722).

### • 4725 • Ohio Regents Graduate/Professional Fellowships *(Graduate/Fellowship)*

**Focus:** General Studies. **Qualif.:** Applicants must have received their undergraduate degree and started graduate school within the same year. They must have taken any one of the graduate exams and be in the upper ranking of their graduating class. Applicants must be attending approved graduate schools in the state of Ohio.

**Funds Avail.:** $3,500 per recipient. **To Apply:** Undergraduate institutions nominate students. Each college or university may nominate up to three candidates. If three are nominated, one must be a minority. Required applications must be submitted with three letters of recommendation and a written essay. **Deadline:** March 1. **Contact:** Barbara Metheney, Program Administrator, at the above address (see entry 4722).

### • 4726 • Ohio Student Choice Grants *(Undergraduate/Grant)*

**Purpose:** To help equalize the tuition costs between private and public colleges or universities. **Focus:** General Studies. **Qualif.:** Applicants must be Ohio residents enrolled fulltime in a bachelor's degree program, and not have attended any college or university on a full-time basis prior to July 1, 1984. The private non-profit college or university must be approved and in the state of Ohio.

**Funds Avail.:** Varies. **To Apply:** There is no set application. Some private colleges or universities have their own application. **Deadline:** Varies at each institution. **Contact:** Barbara Metheney, Program Administrator, at the above address (see entry 4722).

### • 4727 • Ohio War Orphans Scholarships *(Undergraduate/Scholarship)*

**Focus:** General Studies. **Qualif.:** Applicants must be Ohio residents over 16 but under 21 years of age who are planning to attend a participating Ohio college or university. The Veteran parent must have served for at least 90 days during a period of war and must have been killed in action or be at least a minimum of 60 percent service-connected disabled or 100 percent non-service-connected disabled. Disabled veterans must be receiving VA benefits.

**Funds Avail.:** Full tuition at a state school. Awarded annually. **To Apply:** A formal application is required and can be obtained from high school counselor. Academic progress and full-time status are required to retain the scholarship. **Deadline:** July 1. **Contact:** Sue Minturn, Program Administrator, at the above address (see entry 4722).

---

• 4728 •
**Ohio National Guard**
Adjutant General's Dept., AGOH-TG
2825 W. Dublin Granville Rd.　　　**Ph:** (614)889-7032
Columbus, OH 43235　　　　　　　**Fax:** (614)793-3261

• 4729 • **Ohio National Guard Tuition Grant**
*(Undergraduate/Grant, Scholarship)*

**Focus:** General Studies. **Qualif.:** Applicants must be Ohio residents who are high school graduates and are not already in possession of a baccalaureate degree. They must be enlisted in the Ohio National Guard for six years and successfully complete the advanced military training.

**Funds Avail.:** The program provides 60 percent of tuition and general fees at any state-assisted institution, or an amount equal to 60 percent of the annual average tuition charges of an Ohio state-assisted university for proprietary degree-granting institutions. **To Apply:** Candidates must submit AGOH Form 621-1 and 621-2, which may be obtained for the applicant's military unit for initial entry into the program. AGOH Form 621-3 is used to apply for subsequent terms. **Deadline:** July 1 for fall term; November 1 for winter term; February 1 for spring term; April 1 for summer term. **Contact:** The Ohio National Guard at the above address (see entry 4728).

---

• 4730 •
**Ohio Newspaper Women's Association - Dayton Daily News**
4th and Ludlow
Dayton, OH 45401

• 4731 • **Ohio Newspaper Women's Association Scholarship** *(Undergraduate/Scholarship)*

**Purpose:** To assist women attending Ohio journalism schools who promise to work on Ohio newspapers at least one year after graduation. **Focus:** Journalism. **Qualif.:** Applicants must be Ohio women entering their junior or senior year in an accredited Ohio school of journalism.

**Funds Avail.:** $500. **No. of Awards:** 1. **To Apply:** Information available from journalism departments of accredited institutions.

---

• 4732 •
**Ohio State University Extension**
Agricultural Administration Bldg.
2120 Fyffe Rd.　　　　　　　　**Ph:** (614)292-6169
Columbus, OH 43210　　　　　　**Fax:** (614)292-1240
*E-mail:* datacenter@agvax2.ga.ohio-state
*URL:* http://www.ag.ohio.edu/~dataunit/profiles/profiles.html

• 4733 • **Ohio State University Extension Internship**
*(Graduate, Undergraduate/Internship)*

**Purpose:** To provide interns with a working knowledge of Extension Programs. **Qualif.:** Preference is given to individuals who have completed a bachelor's degree and be engaged in, or have plans for, graduate work, in agriculture, home economics, youth development, community development, or related areas. **Criteria:** Applicants with strong communication skills, interest in planning and teaching, and a desire to work in a voluntary educational program are preferred .

**Funds Avail.:** $1,500 or more per month for 3 months. **Deadline:** Completed applications are due at least 6 weeks prior to preferred start date.

**Remarks:** Internships are tailored to each person. They are available on an irregular basis and are not posted. **Contact:** John Stitzlein at the above address (see entry 4732).

---

• 4734 •
**Oklahoma State Regents for Higher Education**
500 Education Bldg.
Oklahoma City, OK 73105-4503　　　**Ph:** (405)552-4312
*URL:* http://www.osrhe.edu/legislative_updates/docs/
　　March_29.html

• 4735 • **Paul Douglas Teacher Scholarships**
*(Undergraduate/Scholarship)*

**Purpose:** To enable and encourage outstanding high school graduates to pursue teaching careers in public or private nonprofit preschool, elementary, or secondary education programs. **Focus:** Education. **Qualif.:** Applicants must rank in the top ten percent of their high school graduating class and be enrolled full-time in an approved teacher education program. **Criteria:** Priority will be given to renewal applicants, New high school graduates, and applicants enrolled in a program of study leading to teacher certification in Oklahoma in critical shortage areas. Preferential programs of study include early childhood education, mathematics, science, special education (all areas), foreign languages, speech-language pathology, and library media specialist studies.

**Funds Avail.:** Up to $5,000 per year each, not to exceed the cost of attendance for more than four years. **No. of Awards:** 45. **Deadline:** June 15. **Contact:** Sheila Joyner, Paul Douglas Teacher Scholarship Program, at the above address (see entry 4734).

• 4736 • **Oklahoma State Regents Academic Scholars Scholarships** *(Graduate, Undergraduate/ Scholarship)*

**Purpose:** To encourage students of high academic ability to attend institutions of higher education in Oklahoma. **Focus:** General Studies. **Qualif.:** Applicants must have graduated from high school within five years of application and will attend an approved public or private Oklahoma college or university. Students will be either a National Merit Scholar, a National Merit Finalist, a National Achievement Scholar, a National Achievement Finalist, a National Hispanic Scholar, a National Hispanic Honorable Mention Awardee, a Presidential Scholar, or qualify as an Individual

---

## Oklahoma State Regents for Higher Education (continued)

Applicant Student whose enhanced ACT score or whose SAT equivalent composite score falls within the 99.5 to 100 percentile levels based on the sum of individual scores as administered in the state of Oklahoma.

**Funds Avail.:** There are approximately 225 annual scholarships awarded for up to five years for undergraduate and/or graduate study at accredited institutions in Oklahoma. The awards range from $2,950 to $4,500. **No. of Awards:** 225 **Deadline:** None. **Contact:** For application information contact Maryanne Maletz, Academic Scholars Program, at the above address (see entry 4734).

## • 4737 • Oklahoma State Regents Chiropractic Education Assistance *(Other, Undergraduate/Award)*

**Focus:** Medicine, Chiropractic. **Qualif.:** Applicants must be residents of Oklahoma who are studying chiropractic at accredited schools and making satisfactory academic progress.

**Funds Avail.:** Up to $3,000 each. **No. of Awards:** 35. **Deadline:** July 1.

**Remarks:** The Oklahoma Legislature has provided funds to the Oklahoma State Regents for Higher Education for this award. **Contact:** Maryanne Maletz, Chiropractic Education Assistance Program, at the above address (see entry 4734).

## • 4738 • Oklahoma State Regents Future Teacher Scholarships *(Undergraduate/Scholarship)*

**Focus:** Education. **Qualif.:** Applicants must rank in the top 15 percent of their high school graduating class and must score at or above the 85th percentile on the ACT or other similar tests. They must also agree to teach in shortage areas identified by the State Department of Education. Students are nominated for program participation by their college or university.

**Funds Avail.:** Up to $1,500 annually for full-time students. **No. of Awards:** 120. **Deadline:** Early August. **Contact:** For application information contact Maryanne Maletz, the Future Teacher Scholarship Program, at the above address (see entry 4734).

## • 4739 • Oklahoma State Regents for Higher Education Doctoral Study Grants *(Doctorate/Grant)*

**Purpose:** To increase the number of qualified and available college teachers from minority races to enhance minority representation on the faculties of institutions in the Oklahoma State System of Higher Education. **Focus:** Education. **Qualif.:** Applicants must be minority graduate students pursuing doctoral studies in Oklahoma institutions of higher education with college teaching as an objective, and with a commitment to teach in Oklahoma colleges and universities.

**Funds Avail.:** $6,000 each per year. **No. of Awards:** 20. **Deadline:** May 1 for fall semester study. **Contact:** Joe E. Hagy, Oklahoma State Regents for Higher Education, Doctoral Study Grant Program, at the above address (see entry 4734).

## • 4740 • Oklahoma State Regents for Higher Education Professional Study Grants *(Graduate/Grant)*

**Focus:** Medicine, Dentistry, Law, Veterinary, Optometry. **Qualif.:** Applicants must be full-time minority students in the above-mentioned professional areas. These grants are designed to provide the initial financial assistance necessary to enter a professional school.

**Funds Avail.:** $4,000 each year. **No. of Awards:** 30. **Deadline:** June 1. **Contact:** Joe E. Hagy, Oklahoma State Regents for Higher Education, Professional Study Grant Program, at the above address (see entry 4734).

## • 4741 • Oklahoma State Regents Tuition Aid Grants *(Undergraduate/Grant)*

**Focus:** General Studies. **Qualif.:** Applicants must be Oklahoma residents attending two- or four-year institutions in the state with a demonstrated financial need. They must carry at least six credit hours per semester in a curriculum leading to a degree or certificate. **Criteria:** The grants are based on financial need, according to the family income and size and the costs associated with attending school.

**Funds Avail.:** The maximum annual award is 75 percent of enrollment costs or $1,000, whichever is less. **No. of Awards:** About 16,000. **To Apply:** Candidates must complete and file a student Needs Analysis form, available from high school guidance offices and college financial aid offices. **Deadline:** Applicants should apply as early as possible after January 1, but applications are accepted through May 31. **Contact:** Sheila Joyner, Oklahoma Tuition Aid Grant Program, at the above address (see entry 4734).

## • 4742 • William P. Willis Scholars Scholarships *(Undergraduate/Scholarship)*

**Focus:** General Studies. **Qualif.:** Applicants must be low-income undergraduate students attending college full-time at one of Oklahoma's public colleges and universities. Individuals who are residents of the state of Oklahoma, enrolled full-time in an undergraduate program at a member institution of The Oklahoma State System of Higher Education, or have an Effective Gross Income of less than $20,000 are eligible.

**Funds Avail.:** The average award for students attending the comprehensive universities was $3,000; four-year and two-year college students received an average of $2,000. **No. of Awards:** 26. **Contact:** For application information contact Maryanne Maletz, William P. Willis Scholars Program, at the above address (see entry 4734).

---

## • 4743 •
## Olfactory Research Fund

145 E. 32nd St.　　　　　　　　　*Ph:* (212)725-2755
New York, NY 10016　　　　　　*Fax:* (212)779-9058
*E-mail:* olfactory@fragrance.org
*URL:* http://www.fragrance.org/olfactor/

## • 4744 • Olfactory Research Fund Grants *(Postdoctorate/Grant)*

**Purpose:** To support non-commercial scientific research in olfactory related matters. **Focus:** Medical Research, Psychology, Sociology, and Biology. **Qualif.:** Applicants must possess a doctoral degree. Submission of proposals by individuals who are currently devoting much of their research effort to the study of olfaction is encouraged. However, proposals from investigators who wish to redirect their research into this area are welcomed and the Olfactory Research Fund will help them in preparing their applications. **Criteria:** The Fund is especially interested in research that seeks to integrate the study of olfaction with current issues in developmental, social, and cognitive psychology. Researchers in allied disciplines such as anthropology and sociology are encouraged to apply. New approaches to the study of human olfaction are particularly welcome.

**Funds Avail.:** Grants are determined by the Olfactory Research Fund. **No. of Awards:** Varies annually. **To Apply:** Research proposals should be a maximum of five single-spaced pages and should include a description of the study's rationale, significance, protocol, proposed methodology, and length. A budget should be included that provides details and justification of costs for personnel, supplies, and equipment. An abbreviated curriculum vitae of the applicant and all significant collaborators should be attached. Twenty copies of the proposal and curriculum vitae should be sent. A signed IRB approval must be included with the proposal. **Deadline:** January 15.

**Remarks:** The Olfactory Research Fund was formerly known as the Fragrance Research Fund. Applicants should contact Fund prior to submitting proposals to determine priority area of interest for funding in current year. **Contact:** The Olfactory Research Fund at the above address (see entry 4743).

### • 4745 • The Tova Fellowship *(Graduate/Fellowship)*

**Purpose:** To encourage graduate students to pursue studies that will enhance their understanding of human odor perception. **Focus:** Aroma-Chology. **Qualif.:** Applicants must be in the dissertation stage of a masters or doctoral program.

**Funds Avail.:** 10,000. **No. of Awards:** 1. **To Apply:** A one to two page proposal or statement describing the applicant's academic involvement with the study of aroma-chology and olfaction; a letter of recommendation from the applicant's faculty advisor; and transcripts or other evidence that the student is enrolled in an accredited course of study in a related field must be submitted. **Deadline:** May 29.

---

### • 4746 •
### Sigurd Olson Environmental Institute

| | |
|---|---|
| Northland College | *Ph:* (715)682-1223 |
| Ashland, WI 54806-9989 | *Fax:* (715)682-1218 |

*URL:* http://bobb.northland.edu/soei/CALENDA.HTML

#### • 4747 • Sigurd T. Olson Common Loon Research Awards *(Graduate, Postgraduate, Professional Development/Award)*

**Purpose:** To partially fund research that leads to better understanding and management of Upper Great Lakes populations of Common Loons. **Focus:** Ornithology. **Qualif.:** Candidates must be principal investigators or graduate students.

**Funds Avail.:** $500-1,000 **To Apply:** Write to the Institute for application forms and guidelines. Applicants must submit brief description (10-page maximum) of the proposed research program and curriculum vitae. **Deadline:** January 19. **Contact:** The Sigurd Olson Environmental Institute at the above address (see entry 4746).

---

### • 4748 •
### Omaha World Herald
1334 Dodge St.
Omaha, NE 68102

#### • 4749 • *Omaha World-Herald* Intern Scholarships *(Other/Internship, Scholarship)*

**Purpose:** To provide scholarships money to those completing the editorial internship at the *World-Herald*. **Focus:** Journalism.

**Funds Avail.:** $1000, internship is also paid. **No. of Awards:** 6. **Deadline:** November 1.

### • 4750 •
### Omohundro Institute of Early American History and Culture
PO Box 8781
Williamsburg, VA 23187-8781
*E-mail:* ieahc1@facstaff.wm.edu

#### • 4751 • Institute Postdoctoral NEH Fellowship *(Doctorate, Graduate/Fellowship)*

**Purpose:** To give a scholar a two-year research opportunity in the field of early American Studies. **Qualif.:** Candidate's dissertation or other manuscript must have significant potential as a distinguished, book-length contribution to scholarship. A substantial portion of the work must be submitted with the application. Applicants may not have previously published or have under contract a scholarly monograph, and they must have met all requirements for the doctorate before commencing the fellowship. Those who have earned a Ph.D. and begun careers are encouraged to apply.

**Funds Avail.:** $30,000.

**Remarks:** The fellow will be supported principally by the National Endowment for the Humanities through its program of fellowships at independent research institutions. During that year he or she will be designated both an NEH and an Institute fellow.

#### • 4752 • Institute Andrew W. Mellon Postdoctoral Research Fellowship *(Doctorate, Postdoctorate/Fellowship)*

**Purpose:** To provide support with which a candidate may revise his or her first book manuscript for later publication. **Focus:** Early American studies (all aspects of the lives of North America's indigenous and immigrant peoples during the colonial, Revolutionary, and early national periods). **Qualif.:** The candidate's manuscript must have significant potential for publication as a distinguished, book-length contribution to scholarship. Applicants must not have previously published a book or have a book under contract. Applicants must have received their Ph.D. 12 months prior to the application deadline.

**Funds Avail.:** $30,000. **Deadline:** November 1.

**Remarks:** Made possible by a grant to the Institute by the Andrew W. Mellon Foundation. This award will be offered annually over the years to come.

### • 4753 •
### Omohundro Institute of Early American History and Culture

| | |
|---|---|
| PO Box 8781 | *Ph:* (804)221-1116 |
| Williamsburg, VA 23187-8781 | *Fax:* (804)221-1047 |

*URL:* http://violet.berkeley.edu:4223/earlyamhist.html

*The Institute of Early American History and Culture, founded in 1943, is partially supported by the College of William and Mary and the Colonial Williamsburg Foundation.*

#### • 4754 • Institute Postdoctoral Fellowship *(Postdoctorate/Fellowship)*

**Purpose:** To support research by junior scholars who might otherwise be encumbered by a burdensome teaching load. **Focus:** Early American History. **Qualif.:** Applicants must be U.S. citizens, or have been a residents of the United States for three years immediately before the fellowship term. They must have earned a Ph.D. by the beginning of the fellowship, and must have written a highly promising dissertation on some aspect of early American history (from the European and African backgrounds to

---

*Omohundro Institute of Early American History and Culture (continued)*

approximately 1815). Candidates may not apply simultaneously for the fellowship and the Jamestown Prize. The fellowship is intended to allow junior scholars to revise their dissertations or other research projects for publication; candidates must not have published a book previously. The Institute holds first claim to the publishing rights on any book manuscripts resulting from the fellowship. Fellows hold a concurrent appointment as assistant professor in the appropriate discipline at the College of William and Mary, and are required to teach a total of six semester hours during the two-year term of the fellowship. Fellowships may not be renewed.

**Funds Avail.:** $30,000/year, plus some travel and research funds. **To Apply:** Write to the director for application form and guidelines, available in September. Submit form with a copy of doctoral dissertation or other research project, and three letters of recommendation. **Deadline:** November 1. Fellows will be selected by February.

**• 4755 • Jamestown Prize** *(Postdoctorate/Prize)*

**Purpose:** To recognize and publish an outstanding book-length scholarly manuscript concerning early American history or culture. **Focus:** Early American History and related topics in the History of the Caribbean, British Isles, Europe, or West Africa. **Qualif.:** Applicant must not have previously published a book. Manuscript must pertain to some aspect of early American history or culture (before 1815) or to the related history of the British Isles, Europe, West Africa, or Caribbean. Past or present holders of postdoctoral fellowships from the Institute are ineligible. The Institute holds first claim to the publication of all manuscripts submitted.

**Funds Avail.:** $1,500 prize, plus royalties earned on the sale of the winning book. **To Apply:** Write to the editor of publications for guidelines. Submit manuscript with a letter indicating that the manuscript has been sent as a Jamestown Prize entry. **Deadline:** None. An author will be notified of the prize committee's preliminary decision within two months of the receipt of the manuscript at the Institute.

**Remarks:** The Jamestown Prize may not be offered every year. Winning manuscripts are published by the University of North Carolina Press in conjunction with the Institute. **Contact:** Fredrika J. Teute, Editor of Publications, at the above address (see entry 4753).

**• 4756 • Institute Andrew W. Mellon Postdoctoral Research Fellowship** *(Postdoctorate/Fellowship)*

**Purpose:** To provide support for the revision of a first book manuscript and to aid in the publishing of the resulting study. **Qualif.:** Principal criterion for selection is that the candidate's manuscript must have significant potential for publication as a distinguished, book-length contribution to scholarship. Applicants may not have previously published a book or have a book under contract. Applicants must have met all requirements for the doctorate at least 18 months prior to the application deadline.

**Funds Avail.:** $30,000 stipend and benefits package. **To Apply:** Applicants must submit a completed manuscript along with application forms.

**• 4757 •**
**Oncology Nursing Foundation**
501 Holiday Dr.                             *Ph:* (412)921-7373
Pittsburgh, PA 15220-2749                   *Fax:* (412)921-6565

**• 4758 • Oncology Nursing Foundation/Amgen, Inc. Research Grant** *(Professional Development/Grant)*

**Purpose:** To support clinically focused oncology nursing research. **Focus:** Oncology nursing research **Qualif.:** Applicants must be registered nurses actively involved in some aspect of cancer patient care, education, or research.

**Funds Avail.:** Up to $8,500 for one-year. Projects can be extended for a second year without additional funding. Recipients are requested to attend the Annual Oncology Nursing Society Congress to receive their award. **No. of Awards:** One **To Apply:** Applications outlining official project guidelines are available from the Oncology Nursing Foundation or the Oncology Nursing Society. Five copies must accompany the complete application, along with a $5 application fee. Applicants may apply for more than one grant (see separate entries), but awards are made under only one grant category. A separate budget must be submitted for each category. **Deadline:** December 1. **Contact:** The Oncology Nursing Society, 501 Holiday Dr., Pittsburgh, PA 15220-2749, or the Oncology Nursing Foundation at the above address (see entry 4757).

**• 4759 • Oncology Nursing Foundation Bachelors Scholarship** *(Undergraduate/Scholarship)*

**Focus:** Oncology nursing. **Qualif.:** Applicants must currently be licensed to practice as a registered nurse, and have an interest in and commitment to cancer nursing. They must currently be enrolled in an undergraduate nursing degree program in a NLN accredited school of Nursing.

**Funds Avail.:** $2,000 each. **No. of Awards:** 16. **Deadline:** February 1. **Contact:** The Oncology Nursing Foundation at the above address (see entry 4757).

**• 4760 • Oncology Nursing Foundation/Bristol-Myers Oncology Chapter Research Grant** *(Professional Development/Grant)*

**Purpose:** To encourage oncology research by ONS Chapters. **Focus:** Oncology nursing to improve cancer patient care. **Qualif.:** Applicants must be registered nurses actively involved in some aspect of cancer patient care, education, or research. They must also have support of a local ONS Chapter. The study should address a problem related to oncology nursing practice.

**Funds Avail.:** Up to $5,000 for one year, plus round trip coach airfare to the annual ONS Congress where the research grant is announced. Projects can be extended a second year without additional funding. **No. of Awards:** One **To Apply:** Applications outlining official project guidelines are available from the Oncology Nursing Foundation or the Oncology Nursing Society. Five copies must accompany the completed application, along with a letter of support indicating the Chapter's involvement in the planning and implementation of the study, and a $25 application fee. Applicants may apply for more than one grant (see separate entries), but awards are made under only one grant category. A separate budget must be submitted for each category. **Deadline:** November 1. **Contact:** The Oncology Nursing Society, 501 Holiday Dr., Pittsburgh, PA 15220-2749, or the Oncology Nursing Foundation at the above address (see entry 4757).

**• 4761 • Oncology Nursing Foundation/Bristol-Myers Oncology Division Community Health Research Grant** *(Professional Development/Grant)*

**Purpose:** To encourage community health nursing research. **Focus:** Nursing research in community-based health agencies.

**Qualif.:** Applicants must be registered nurses actively involved in some aspect of cancer patient care, education, or research. The site of the study must be a community agency, such as community hospitals, physician's office, nursing homes, home health agencies, or hospices. Submission of both quantitative and qualitative research is encouraged, including descriptive studies, surveys, experimental, and quasi-experimental studies.

**Funds Avail.:** Up to $5,000 for one year plus round trip airfare to the annual ONS Congress where the research grant is announced. Projects can be extended a second year without additional funding. **No. of Awards:** One **To Apply:** Applications outlining official project guidelines are available from the Oncology Nursing Foundation or the Oncology Nursing Society. Five copies must accompany the completed application, along with a $5 application fee. Applicants may apply for more than one grant (see separate entries), but awards are made under only one grant category. A separate budget must be submitted for each category. **Deadline:** November 1. **Contact:** The Oncology Nursing Society, 501 Holiday Dr., Pittsburgh, PA 15220-2749, or the Oncology Nursing Foundation at the above address (see entry 4757).

**• 4762 • Oncology Nursing Foundation/Bristol-Myers Oncology Division Research Grant** (Professional Development/Grant)

**Purpose:** To stimulate quality research in oncology nursing with the hope of further improving cancer patient care. **Focus:** Oncology nursing to improve cancer patient care. **Qualif.:** Applicants must be registered nurses actively involved in some aspect of cancer patient care, education, or research.

**Funds Avail.:** Up to $7,500 for one year plus one round-trip coach airfare to attend the annual Oncology Nursing Society Congress where research grant is announced. Projects can be extended a second year without additional funding. **No. of Awards:** One **To Apply:** Applications outlining official project guidelines are available from the Oncology Nursing Foundation or the Oncology Nursing Society. Five copies must accompany the completed application, along with a $25 application fee. Applicants may apply for more than one grant (see separate entries), but awards are made under only one grant category. A separate budget must be submitted for each category. **Deadline:** November 1. **Contact:** The Oncology Nursing Society, 501 Holiday Dr., Pittsburgh, PA 15220-2749, or the Oncology Nursing Foundation at the above address (see entry 4757).

**• 4763 • Oncology Nursing Foundation/Cetus Oncology Grants for Research Involving Biotherapy or Immunotherapy** (Professional Development/Grant)

**Purpose:** To encourage nursing research in the area of immunotherapy or biotherapy. **Qualif.:** Applicants must be registered nurses actively involved in some aspect of cancer patient care, education, or research. Research areas may include toxicity management with immunomodulators or biological response modifiers, patient education, nursing care, and patient outcomes associated with biological response modifiers.

**Funds Avail.:** Two awards of up to $4,250 for one-year. Projects may be extended for two years without additional funding. Recipients are requested to attend the Annual Oncology Nursing Society Congress to receive their awards. **To Apply:** Applications outlining official project guidelines are available from the Oncology Nursing Foundation or the Oncology Nursing Society. Five copies must accompany the completed application, along with a $25 application fee. Applicants may apply for more than one grant (see separate entries), but awards are made under only one grant category. A separate budget must be submitted for each category. **Deadline:** November 1. **Contact:** The Oncology Nursing Society, 501 Holiday Dr., Pittsburgh, PA 15220-2749, or the Oncology Nursing Foundation at the above address (see entry 4757).

**• 4764 • Oncology Nursing Foundation Doctoral Scholarship** (Doctorate/Scholarship)

**Focus:** Oncology nursing. **Qualif.:** Applicants must currently be licensed to practice as a registered nurse, and have an interest in and commitment to cancer nursing. They must currently be enrolled in or applying to a doctoral nursing degree or related program.

**Funds Avail.:** Five scholarships at $3,000 are awarded. **No. of Awards:** Five **Deadline:** February 1. **Contact:** The Oncology Nursing Foundation.

**• 4765 • Oncology Nursing Foundation/Glaxo Research Grants** (Professional Development/Grant)

**Purpose:** To support clinically focused oncology nursing research. **Focus:** Oncology nursing **Qualif.:** Applicants must be registered nurses actively involved in some aspect of cancer patient care, education, or research.

**Funds Avail.:** Two awards of up to $8,500 for one year. Projects may be extended a second year without additional funding. Recipients are requested to attend the Annual Oncology Nursing Society Congress to receive their awards. **No. of Awards:** Two **To Apply:** Applications outlining official project guidelines are available from the Oncology Nursing Foundation or the Oncology Nursing Society. Five copies must accompany the completed application, along with a $5 application fee. Applicants may apply for more than one grant (see separate entries), but awards are made under only one grant category. A separate budget must be submitted for each category. **Deadline:** December 1. **Contact:** The Oncology Nursing Society, 501 Holiday Dr., Pittsburgh, PA 15220-2749, or the Oncology Nursing Foundation at the above address (see entry 4757).

**• 4766 • Oncology Nursing Foundation Masters Scholarship** (Graduate/Scholarship)

**Purpose:** To improve oncology nursing by assisting nurses in furthering their education. **Focus:** Oncology nursing. **Qualif.:** Applicants must currently be licensed to practice as a registered nurse and have an interest in and commitment to cancer nursing. They must currently be enrolled in a graduate degree program in a NLN accredited school of Nursing.

**Funds Avail.:** Sixteen scholarships of $3,000 are awarded. **No. of Awards:** Sixteen **Deadline:** February 1. **Contact:** The Oncology Nursing Foundation at the above address (see entry 4757).

**• 4767 • Oncology Nursing Foundation/Oncology Nursing Certification Corporation Nursing Education Research Grants** (Professional Development/Grant)

**Purpose:** To stimulate quality research in oncology nursing education. **Focus:** Oncology nursing. **Qualif.:** Applicants must be registered nurses actively involved in some aspect of cancer patient care, education, or research.

**Funds Avail.:** Up to $7,500 for one year. Projects may be extended a second year without additional funding. Recipients are requested to attend the Annual Oncology Nursing Society Congress to receive their awards. **No. of Awards:** One. **To Apply:** Applications outlining official project guidelines are available from the Oncology Nursing Foundation or the Oncology Nursing Society. Five copies must accompany the completed application, along with a $5 application fee. Applicants may apply for more than one grant (see separate entries), but awards are made under only one grant category. A separate budget must be submitted for each category. **Deadline:** December 1. **Contact:** The Oncology Nursing Society, 501 Holiday Dr., Pittsburgh, PA 15220-2749, or the Oncology Nursing Foundation.

## Oncology Nursing Foundation (continued)

### • 4768 • Oncology Nursing Foundation/Oncology Nursing Society Research Grant (Professional Development/Grant)

**Purpose:** To stimulate quality research in oncology nursing. **Focus:** Oncology nursing. **Qualif.:** Applicants must be registered nurses actively involved in some aspect of cancer patient care, education, or research.

**Funds Avail.:** Up to $10,000 for one year. Projects may be extended a second year without additional funding. Recipients are requested to attend the Annual Oncology Nursing Society Congress to receive their awards. **No. of Awards:** One **To Apply:** Applications outlining official project guidelines are available from the Oncology Nursing Foundation or the Oncology Nursing Society. Five copies must accompany the completed application, along with a $5 application fee. Applicants may apply for more than one grant (see separate entries), but awards are made under only one grant category. A separate budget must be submitted for each category. **Deadline:** December 1. **Contact:** The Oncology Nursing Society, 501 Holiday Dr., Pittsburgh, PA 15220-2749, or the Oncology Nursing Foundation at the above address (see entry 4757).

### • 4769 • Oncology Nursing Foundation/Ortho Biotech Research Grant (Professional Development/Grant)

**Purpose:** To promote oncology nursing research in the area of symptom assessment and management. **Focus:** Oncology nursing **Qualif.:** Applicants must be registered nurses actively involved in some aspect of cancer patient care, education, or research.

**Funds Avail.:** Up to $8,500 for one year. Projects may be extended a second year without additional funding. Recipients are requested to attend the Annual Oncology Nursing Society Congress to receive their awards. Projects may be extended a second year without additional funding. Recipients are requested to attend the Annual Oncology Nursing Society Congress to receive their awards. **No. of Awards:** One **To Apply:** Applications outlining official project guidelines are available from the Oncology Nursing Foundation or the Oncology Nursing Society. Five copies must accompany the completed application, along with a $5 application fee. Applicants may apply for more than one grant (see separate entries), but awards are made under only one grant category. A separate budget must be submitted for each category. **Deadline:** December 1. **Contact:** The Oncology Nursing Society, 501 Holiday Dr., Pittsburgh, PA 15220-2749, or the Oncology Nursing Foundation at the above address (see entry 4757).

### • 4770 • Oncology Nursing Foundation/Purdue Frederick Research Grant (Professional Development/Grant)

**Purpose:** To promote oncology nursing research in the area of pain assessment. If drug therapy is part of the research design, a Purdue Frederick product must be employed in at least one arm of the treatment being employed. **Focus:** Oncology nursing. **Qualif.:** Applicants must be registered nurses actively involved in some aspect of cancer patient care, education, or research.

**Funds Avail.:** Up to $6,000 for one year. Recipient is requested to attend the Annual Oncology Nursing Society Congress to receive his/her award. Projects can be extended a second year without additional funding. **No. of Awards:** One **To Apply:** Applications outlining official project guidelines are available from the Oncology Nursing Foundation or the Oncology Nursing Society. Five copies must accompany the completed application, along with a $25 application fee. Applicants may apply for more than one grant (see separate entries), but awards are made under only one grant category. A separate budget must be submitted for each category. **Deadline:** November 1. **Contact:** The Oncology Nursing Society, 501 Holiday Dr., Pittsburgh, PA 15220-2749, or the Oncology Nursing Foundation at the above address (see entry 4757).

### • 4771 • Oncology Nursing Foundation/Rhone Poulenc Rorer New Investigator Research Grants (Doctorate, Graduate/Grant)

**Purpose:** To encourage new researchers in the exploration of oncology nursing. **Focus:** Oncology nursing **Qualif.:** Applicants must be registered nurses who are principal investigators or co-investigators, have not obtained a doctoral degree, and have received no previous research funding. Students are eligible to seek funding for thesis or dissertation.

**Funds Avail.:** Two awards of up to $4,250 for one year are given. Projects can be extended a second year without additional funding. Recipients are requested to attend the Annual Oncology Nursing Society Congress to receive their awards. **No. of Awards:** Ten. **To Apply:** Applications outlining official project guidelines are available from the Oncology Nursing Foundation or the Oncology Nursing Society. Five copies must accompany the completed application, along with a $5 application fee. Applicants may apply for more than one grant (see separate entries), but awards are made under only one grant category. A separate budget must be submitted for each category. **Deadline:** December 1. **Contact:** The Oncology Nursing Society, 501 Holiday Dr., Pittsburgh, PA 15220-2749, or the Oncology Nursing Foundation at the above address (see entry 4757).

### • 4772 • Oncology Nursing Foundation/Sigma Theta Tau International and Oncology Nursing Society Research Grant (Professional Development/Grant)

**Purpose:** To stimulate oncology nursing research. **Focus:** Oncology Nursing. **Qualif.:** Applicants must be registered nurses actively involved in some aspect of cancer patient care, education, or research.

**Funds Avail.:** Up to $10,000 for one year. Recipient is requested to attend the Annual Oncology Nursing Society Congress to receive his/her award. Projects can be extended a second year without additional funding. **No. of Awards:** One **To Apply:** Applications outlining official project guidelines are available from the Oncology Nursing Foundation or the Oncology Nursing Society. Five copies must accompany the completed application, along with a $25 application fee. Applicants may apply for more than one grant (see separate entries), but awards are made under only one grant category. A separate budget must be submitted for each category. **Deadline:** November 1. **Contact:** The Oncology Nursing Society, 501 Holiday Dr., Pittsburgh, PA 15220-2749, or the Oncology Nursing Foundation at the above address (see entry 4757).

### • 4773 • Oncology Nursing Society/SmithKline Beecham Research Grant (Professional Development/Grant)

**Purpose:** To promote oncology nursing research in the area of nausea and vomiting. **Focus:** Oncology Nursing. **Qualif.:** Applicants must be members of the Oncology Nursing Society who are registered nurses actively involved in some aspect of cancer patient care, education, or research. If drug therapy is part of the research design, a SmithKline product must be employed.

**Funds Avail.:** Up to $10,000 for one year (two awards with a smaller budget may be given), plus round trip airfare to the ONS Congress for presentation of the award. Projects can be extended a second year without additional funding. **No. of Awards:** Up to two awards annually. **To Apply:** Applications outlining official project guidelines are available from the Oncology Nursing Foundation or the Oncology Nursing Society. Five copies must accompany the completed application, along with a $5 application fee. Applicants may apply for more than one grant (see separate entries), but awards are made under only one grant category. A separate budget must be submitted for each category. **Deadline:** December 1. **Contact:** The Oncology Nursing Society, 501 Holiday Dr., Pittsburgh, PA 15220-2749, or the Oncology Nursing Foundation at the above address (see entry 4757).

## • 4774 •
### Eugene O'Neill Theater Center - National Playwrights Conference
234 West 44th St., Ste. 901  Ph: (212)382-2790
New York, NY 10036  Fax: (212)921-5538

### • 4775 • Herbert and Patricia Brodkin Scholarship
(Professional Development/Scholarship)

**Focus:** Drama. **Qualif.:** Awarded to a playwright "with a unique way with words, a perspective cognizance and responsible concern for the current struggle of human beings to survive and progress in a world created by the Creator but reshaped by man."

**Funds Avail.:** $1,000 stipend, plus transportation, room and board. **To Apply:** Write for guidelines for submitting manuscripts. **Contact:** Mary F. McCabe, Managing Director.

## • 4776 •
### Ontario Arts Council
151 Bloor St. W., 6th Fl.  Ph: (416)969-7450
Toronto, ON, Canada M5S 1T6  Fax: (416)961-7796
 Free: 800-387-0058

*URL:* http://www.arts.on.ca/

### • 4777 • Leslie Bell Scholarship for Choral Conducting (Professional Development/Scholarship)

**Qualif.:** Awarded every two years to aspiring Canadian choral conductors who reside in Ontario. **Criteria:** Aspirants lead a test choir through set works and are judged by a three-member jury.

**Funds Avail.:** Approximately $2,000. **Contact:** Ontario Choral Federation, 20 St. Joseph St., Toronto, ON M4Y 1J9. Telephone: (416)925-5525.

### • 4778 • Chalmers Performing Arts Training Grants
(Professional Development/Grant)

**Purpose:** To assist qualified performing artists to undertake intensive study projects or professional upgrading, either with outstanding master teachers or at highly regarded institutions. **Qualif.:** Candidates must be Ontario residents and have completed basic artistic training. **Criteria:** Artistic excellence, value and relevance of proposed training, and resume.

**Funds Avail.:** The maximum grant is $18,000. Between 15 and 25 grants are awarded each year. **To Apply:** Application forms may be requested by telephone. **Deadline:** February 15.

**Remarks:** This program is administered by the Dance Office, which coordinates the Chalmers Fund. Between 75 and 100 applications are received each year. **Contact:** The Dance Office at (800)387-0058 (Ontario toll-free).

### • 4779 • Heinz Unger Award for Conducting
(Professional Development/Award)

**Purpose:** To encourage and highlight the career of a young, or mid-career Canadian orchestra conductor. **Deadline:** May 12.

**Remarks:** The award is administered by the Ontario Arts Council in co-operation with the Association of Canadian Orchestras. **Contact:** The Association of Canadian Orchestras, 56 The Esplanade, Ste. 311, Toronto, ON M5E 1A7. Telephone: (416)366-8834.

## • 4780 •
### Ontario Ministry of Education & Training - Student Affairs
PO Box 4500
189 Red River Road  Ph: (807)343-7257
4th Floor  Fax: (807)343-7278
Thunder Bay, ON, Canada P7B 6G9  Free: 800-465-3957
*E-mail:* vibertge@epo.gov.on.ca
*URL:* http://www.edu.gov.on.ca/eng/welcome.html

### • 4781 • Ontario Graduate Scholarships (Graduate/Scholarship)

**Purpose:** To encourage excellence in graduate studies. **Focus:** General Studies. **Qualif.:** Applicants must be Canadian citizens, landed immigrants, or residents on a student visa. They must also plan to be enrolled in a graduate program leading to a Master's or Doctoral degree, and must have maintained at least an A-plus average over each of the last two years. Scholarships are tenable at Ontario universities.

**Funds Avail.:** $3,953/term. **No. of Awards:** 1300. **To Apply:** Write to the Ministry for application materials. The application form must be submitted with transcripts and academic letters of reference. **Deadline:** November 15. **Contact:** Gerry Vibert.

## • 4782 •
### OPERA America
1156 15th St. NW, Ste. 810  Ph: (202)293-4466
Washington, DC 20005  Fax: (202)393-0735
*E-mail:* frontdesk@operaam.org

### • 4783 • OPERA America Fellowship Program
(Postgraduate/Fellowship)

**Purpose:** To provide highly specialized training for entry- and mid-level arts administrators and technical and production personnel. **Focus:** Arts. **Qualif.:** Fellowships are offered to individuals who are; opera personnel with limited experience who wish to enhance or augment their skills; individuals entering opera administration or production from other fields or disciplines; and graduates of arts administration or technical/production training programs. **Criteria:** Candidates must have a commitment to a career in North American opera and be able to articulate clear goals for the Fellowship. Applicants should manifest a high degree of personal maturity and motivation. Candidates must be lawfully eligible by virtue of citizenship or authorization from US and/or Canadian government agencies to receive a stipend payment.

**Funds Avail.:** Fellows receive a stipend of $1,200.00 per month, travel and housing. **No. of Awards:** 4 per year. **To Apply:** All applicants must submit a completed application form, current resume, and three professional and/or academic letters of reference. Contact OPERA America to request an application. **Deadline:** Spring of each year. **Contact:** Eve Smith, Professional Development Director.

## • 4784 •
## Opportunities for the Blind, Inc.
PO Box 510
Leonardtown, MD 20650      *Ph:* (301)862-1990

### • 4785 • Opportunities for the Blind, Inc. Grants
*(Doctorate, Graduate, Postgraduate, Professional Development, Undergraduate/Grant)*

**Purpose:** To help blind citizens secure employment. Grants may be used for college expenses, vocational training, job counseling, employment referrals, and job placement services, special equipment, or seed money for the blind who want to be self-employed. **Qualif.:** Applicants must be legally blind U.S. citizens.

**Funds Avail.:** Grants are usually between $1,000 and $5,000. **To Apply:** A completed five-page application must be submitted in addition to three letters of reference, proof of blindness, citizenship, school enrollment (if requesting a scholarship), and tax return or financial statement. **Deadline:** February 15, May 15, August 15, and November 15 of each year. **Contact:** Robert Johnson or Sharon Johnson at the above address (see entry 4784).

## • 4786 •
## Optical Society of America
2010 Massachusetts Ave, NW    *Ph:* (202)223-8130
Washington, DC 20036      *Fax:* (202)223-1096
*E-mail:* kdavis@osa.org; osamem@osa.org
*URL:* http://www.osa.org

### • 4787 • New Focus Research Awards *(Doctorate/Award)*

**Purpose:** To encourage the development of new technology in the field of lasers and electro-optics and the effective transfer of that technology into applications. **Focus:** Electro-Optics, Lasers. **Qualif.:** Applicant must be a doctoral candidate at a U.S. university. Candidate must be conducting thesis research on lasers and electro-optics, or be making technological advances in another field through the application of lasers and electro-optics.

**Funds Avail.:** $14,400 stipend, plus $8,600 for department expenses. **No. of Awards:** 2. **To Apply:** Write, fax or e-mail the Society for application form and guidelines. Submit form with transcripts, letters of reference, and a description of proposed research. **Deadline:** April 18. Awards are announced in mid-June. **Contact:** Administrative Assistant at the above address (see entry 4786).

## • 4788 •
## Order of Alhambra
Scholarships Committee
4200 Leeds Ave.      *Ph:* (410)242-0660
Baltimore, MD 21229-5496    *Fax:* (410)536-5729

### • 4789 • Order of Alhambra Scholarships *(Graduate, Undergraduate/Scholarship)*

**Purpose:** To assist students studying special education. **Focus:** Special Education. **Qualif.:** Applicant must be enrolled at least part-time at an accredited U.S. university or college. Applicant should be an undergraduate in their third or fourth year of college. Graduate students must be clergy, religious, or come from the state of California. Students must be studying some aspect of special education, including mental, physical, or emotional disabilities.

**Funds Avail.:** Up to $400/semester. **To Apply:** Write for application form and guidelines. **Deadline:** None. **Contact:** Anthony J. Ozarowski Executive Secretary, at the above address (see entry 4788).

## • 4790 •
## Order of Eastern Star
c/o Miss Diane Dixon, Grand Sec.
870 Market St., Ste. 722
San Francisco, CA 94102

### • 4791 • Eastern Star Educational and Religious Scholarship *(Undergraduate/Scholarship)*

**Purpose:** To encourage college graduates to attend Theological School or Seminary. **Qualif.:** Applicant must be graduates from high school, and be in the 1st year of college, those who have not been able to go directly to college from high school or those needing financial assistance with college. Must be a US citizen residing in California and attending a college or university in California. **Criteria:** The award will be given on the basis of scholastic record (3.5 minimum GPA), financial need, the purpose and need for higher education, and the character of the applicant. The choice of school indicated must be approved by the committee.

**Funds Avail.:** $500 $1,000 **To Apply:** Completed application must be submitted on the current official application form. **Deadline:** May 1. **Contact:** Grand Secretary, Grand Chapter of California, Order of Eastern Star.

## • 4792 •
## Order of United Commercial Travelers of America
632 N. Park St.      *Ph:* (614)228-3276
PO Box 159019      *Fax:* (614)228-1898
Columbus, OH 43215-8619    *Free:* 800-848-0123

### • 4793 • Retarded Citizens Teachers Scholarships
*(Graduate, Postgraduate, Professional Development, Undergraduate/Scholarship)*

**Purpose:** To help teachers of the mentally retarded in the continental United States and Canada obtain a degree and/or additional certification. **Focus:** Education—Special Needs. **Qualif.:** Applicants must be teachers of the mentally handicapped who need additional course work to be certified or to retain certification, or experienced teachers who wish to become certified to teach the mentally handicapped. Also eligible are students who have bachelor's or master's degrees and plan to pursue graduate work in the field of mental retardation, and college juniors and seniors who are in courses of study leading to the teaching of the mentally handicapped, or planning to teach under a structured trade, vocational, or recreational program at a facility for the mentally retarded. These applicants need to obtain a letter of recommendation from the instructor of the facility at which the person intends to teach. Recipients must plan to teach in the U.S. or Canada. **Criteria:** Preference is given to UCT members.

**Funds Avail.:** Up to $750 annually. No more than $3,000 total is awarded to any recipient. **To Apply:** Required materials include a completed application, a brief resume of work experience in the mentally handicapped field, class rank or standing information, and a statement of educational and professional goals. Applications are available by contacting local UCT offices. Office locations are available by writing or calling the UCT. Photographs are also requested for publicity purposes only. **Deadline:** Prior to class registration. **Contact:** Dianna Duhs, Scholarship Coordinator, at the above address;(see entry 4792) toll-free telephone: 800-848-0123.

Remarks: The school sponsors residencies for emerging artists during the academic year & for mid-career artists during the summer. Contact: Coordinator, Residency Program, at the above address (see entry 4796).

• **4794** •

## Oregon AFL-CIO Asa. T. May Darling Scholarship

c/o A.S. Beany Kunis, Research/
  Education Dir.
2110 State St.                          *Ph:* (503)585-6320
Salem, OR 97301                         *Fax:* (503)585-1668
*E-mail:* beany@oraflcio.org
*URL:* http://www.oraflcio.org

### • 4795 • May Darling Scholarship/Asa T. Williams/ N.W. Labor Press Scholarship *(Undergraduate/ Scholarship)*

**Purpose:** To assist deserving Oregon high school seniors in pursuing their educational goals. **Focus:** General studies. **Qualif.:** Applicants must be graduating high school seniors from Oregon high schools planning to enroll in a full-time, undergraduate course of study at any 2- or 4-year, pubic or private, non-profit or for-profit, postsecondary institution which is eligible to participate in federal Title IV student financial aid programs. **Criteria:** Awards are made based on academic promise, financial need and merit of essay written. Preference given to applicants from union families.

**Funds Avail.:** $850-$3,000 per award. **No. of Awards:** 4. **To Apply:** Applicants must submit a completed Oregon State Scholarship Application for Private Awards and Selected Federal Programs available through the high school counseling office or the Oregon State Scholarship Commission; seventh semester high school transcripts with cumulative grade point average and SAT/ACT scores, and a federally approved need analysis form. General Education Development (GED) certificate recipients who have never attended college must send a "Transcript of GED" available to Oregon residents from the Oregon Office of Community College Services. **Deadline:** March 1. **Contact:** Oregon AFL-CIO Asa T./ May Darling Scholarship at the above address (see entry 4794).

• **4796** •

## Oregon College of Art and Craft

8245 Southwest Barnes Road              *Ph:* (503)297-5544
Portland, OR 97225                      *Fax:* (503)297-9651
                                        *Free:* 800-390-0632

*URL:* http://www.ocac.edu

### • 4797 • Oregon College of Art & Craft Artists-in-Residence Program *(Postgraduate/Grant)*

**Purpose:** To provide postgraduate artists with the opportunity to work and flourish within a community of students and artists. **Focus:** Visual Arts. **Qualif.:** Applicants must be U.S. citizens or permanent residents with an outstanding portfolio and sense of artistic purpose. They must ordinarily have completed the M.F.A. degree before beginning the residency. Awards are tenable at the Oregon School. Artists are expected to work 12 hours/week on campus; exact assignments are arranged between the School and the artist. **Criteria:** Applicants are judged on excellence of portfolio and strength of proposal.

**Funds Avail.:** $500/month, plus tuition credits, studio space, travel and materials allowance, and housing. **No. of Awards:** 2 per term. **To Apply:** Send a self-addressed stamped envelope to the College for application form and guidelines. Submit form and proposal with ten slides of work and two letters of recommendation. **Deadline:** Junior residents: April 15. Notification is made in May; senior residents: December 1. Notification is made in February.

• **4798** •

## Oregon Department of Veterans' Affairs

700 Summer St., NE, Ste. 150           *Ph:* (503)373-2085
Salem, OR 97310-1270                   *Fax:* (503)373-2392
                                       *Free:* 800-692-9666

### • 4799 • Oregon Educational Aid for Veterans *(Doctorate, Graduate, Undergraduate/Other)*

**Purpose:** To assist combat theater veterans to meet educational goals. **Focus:** General Studies. **Qualif.:** Applicants must have been in active duty in the Armed Forces of the United States for not less than 90 days. They must have served during the Korean War, or received the Armed Forces Expeditionary Medal or the Vietnam Service Medal for services after July 1, 1958, and have been released from military service under honorable conditions. Candidates must also have been living in and have been a resident of Oregon for one year immediately before entering the service, and must now be a resident of Oregon and a U.S. citizen.

**Funds Avail.:** Maximum of $50 per month. **No. of Awards:** Varies. **To Apply:** Applications and further information are available upon request and from registrar's offices in most schools. **Deadline:** Each semester.

**Remarks:** This is not a scholarship, but a benefit for combat theater veterans. **Contact:** The Oregon Department of Veterans' Affairs toll-free telephone number for Oregon residents is 800-692-9666.

• **4800** •

## Oregon PTA

531 S.E. 14th Ave., Rm. 205            *Ph:* (503)234-3928
Portland, OR 97214                     *Fax:* (503)234-6024
*E-mail:* or_office@pta.org

### • 4801 • Oregon PTA Teacher Education Scholarships *(Undergraduate/Scholarship)*

**Purpose:** The Oregon Congress of Parents and Teachers established the OPTA Teacher Education Scholarships in 1946 to encourage outstanding young people to select elementary teaching as a career. Secondary teaching was added in 1960. **Focus:** Education. **Qualif.:** Candidates are Oregon residents with a high school diploma or CAM, a GED certificate, or attending a public Oregon college or university that prepares teachers for the elementary and secondary levels. They must be preparing or planning to prepare for teaching in Oregon's schools.

**Funds Avail.:** Each scholarship is in the amount of $500 a year. **No. of Awards:** 4. **To Apply:** Candidates must complete a formal application and submit two references. Application forms are available January 1. Applicants should enclose a stamped, self-addressed envelope with their request. **Deadline:** The application and references must be received by March 1. **Contact:** The Oregon PTA at the above address (see entry 4800).

## Oregon State Bar - Affirmative Action Program
5200 SW Meadows Rd.
PO Box 1689         *Ph:* (503)620-0222
Lake Oswego, OR 97035-0889     *Fax:* (503)684-1366

### • 4803 • Oregon State Bar Scholarships *(Graduate/ Scholarship)*

**Purpose:** To help minority students meet the financial obligation of law school. **Focus:** Law. **Qualif.:** Applicants must be minority (African-American, Asian, Hispanic, Native-American) law students with financial need who are attending an Oregon law school and planning to practice law in Oregon upon graduation.

**Funds Avail.:** Varies from year to year. **No. of Awards:** 20. **To Apply:** Applicants must submit a completed, signed Oregon State Bar Scholarship Application, a copy of their resume, a one-page statement on how a legal education fits with professional endeavors, and a copy of the face page of last years IRS 1040 form. **Deadline:** March 31.

**Remarks:** Recipients are encouraged, upon obtaining employment after graduation, to contribute to the Oregon State Bar Affirmative Action Program scholarship fund. The goal is to contribute in providing adequate funding for future minority law students. **Contact:** The Oregon State Bar Affirmative Action Program at the above address (see entry 4802).

## The Oregonian
1320 SW Broadway
Portland, OR 97201         *Ph:* (503)221-8039

### • 4805 • The Oregonian Minority Internship Program *(Other/Internship)*

**Purpose:** To give experience and mentoring in various areas. **Focus:** Journalism. **Qualif.:** Applicants must be minority students with an interest in journalism. Recipients may apply for actual staff positions midway in second year. **To Apply:** Write for details. **Deadline:** January 15.

## Orentreich Foundation for the Advancement of Science, Inc.
Biomedical Research Station
855 Rte. 301         *Ph:* (914)265-4200
Cold Spring, NY 10516     *Fax:* (914)265-4210
*E-mail:* OFAS1@Juno.com

### • 4807 • OFAS Research Grants *(Postdoctorate/ Grant)*

**Purpose:** To conduct research in fields of substantial OFAS research interest. **Focus:** Biomedical Sciences, Dermatology, Endocrinology, Geriatrics, Serum Markers. **Qualif.:** Applicants may be of any nationality, must have a Ph.D. or above in medicine or science, and be conducting research in an area of interest to OFAS at an accredited university or research institution.

**Funds Avail.:** Varies depending on needs **To Apply:** Submit an outline of proposed joint or collaborative research, including, as a minimum, a brief overview of the current research in the field of interest, a statement of scientific objectives, a protocol summary, curriculum vitae of prinicipal investigator, needed funding, and

total estimated project budget. Conforming applications are reviewed at least quarterly. **Deadline:** None.

**Remarks:** OFAS is a private foundation conducting its own research. Grants are usually at invitation of OFAS for collaborative research. **Contact:** Dr. R. Krajcik, Asst.Dir. Scientific Affairs, at the above address (see entry 4806).

## Organization of American States General Secretariat
17th St. and Constitution Ave., NW    *Ph:* (202)458-3446
Washington, DC 20006     *Fax:* (202)458-3897

### • 4809 • OAS-PRA Fellowships *(Doctorate, Graduate, Postdoctorate/Fellowship)*

**Purpose:** To promote the economic, social, scientific, and cultural development of the Member States in order to achieve a stronger bond and better understanding among the peoples of the Americas through the advance training of its citizens in the priority areas requested by the countries. **Focus:** General Studies. **Qualif.:** Applicants must be citizens or permanent residents of an OAS member country. They must possess a university degree or have demonstrated ability to pursue advanced studies in the chosen field except the medical sciences and related areas and introductory language studies. Knowledge of the language of the country in which the study is to be pursued is required. Candidates can apply to study at any country except the country of which they are citizens or permanent residents.

**Funds Avail.:** The fellowship provides sufficient funds to cover travel expenses, tuition fees, study materials, and subsistence allowances at the chosen university, study center, or research site. Fellowships are granted for a minimum of three months up to a maximum of two years. **To Apply:** Candidates must choose the university, study center, or research site, and make the necessary contacts to secure an acceptance, a copy of which is to be attached to the application. Applicants must submit transcripts that show professional degree awarded; detailed research or study plan; medical certificate; certificate of language proficiency; certificate of admission or evidence that the facilities needed are available; and three letters of reference from persons familiar with their work. Applications may be obtained from OAS Headquarters at the above address. **Deadline:** No later than March 1 for the selection of recipients in June. The Fellowship begins in September.

**Remarks:** There are two kinds of fellowships: one for advanced study at the graduate level and one for research. The OAS member countries are: Antigua and Barbuda, Argentina, Bahamas, Barbados, Belize, Bolivia, Brazil, Canada, Chile, Columbia, Costa Rica, Dominica, Dominican Republic, Ecuador, El Salvador, Granada, Guatemala, Guyana, Haiti, Honduras, Jamaica, Mexico, Nicaragua, Panama, Paraguay, Peru, Saint Kitts and Nevis, Saint Lucia, Saint Vincent and the Granadines, Suriname, United States, Trinidad and Tobago, Uruguay, and Venezuela. **Contact:** Colin E. Martinez at the above address (see entry 4808).

### • 4810 • Leo S. Rowe Pan American Fund *(All/Loan)*

**Purpose:** To financially assist students, professionals, or researchers studying or wishing to study in colleges, universities, or research centers in the United States and contribute to the higher education of competent persons, who, upon completion of their studies in the United States, will be in a position to give their country the benefits of their training. **Qualif.:** Candidates must be citizens of member countries of the OAS, have meritorious personal and academic records, have financial need, be enrolled in or accepted by an accredited institution in the United States, be in a position to complete within two years maximum the studies for which the loan is requested, have a visa and be a legal resident of the United States, and have good financial standing. **Criteria:** Preference will be given to courses that lead to the awarding of degrees or diplomas.

**Funds Avail.:** Up to $5,000 per year. The fund renders assistance through supplementary loans (intended to meet only part of the financial need of the applicant), without interest, repayable within five years at most. **To Apply:** Write the fund for an application. The processing of an application takes approximately six weeks and does not imply that the loan will necessarily be granted.

**Remarks:** The fund fulfills the will of Dr. Leo Stanton Rowe, Director General of the Pan American Union from 1920 until his death in 1946. Rowe devoted the greater part of his life to the service of the Pan American cause, showing special interest in the education of Pan American youth. Member countries of the OAS are Antigua and Barbuda, Argentina, the Bahamas, Barbados, Belize, Bolivia, Brazil, Canada, Chile, Colombia, Costa Rica, Dominica, Dominican Republic, Ecuador, El Salvador, Grenada, Guatemala, Guyana, Haiti, Honduras, Jamaica, Mexico, Nicaragua, Panama, Paraguay, Peru, Saint Christopher and Neves, Saint Lucia, Saint Vincent and the Grenadines, Suriname, the United Sates, Trinidad and Tobago, Uruguay, and Venezuela. **Contact:** Secretariat of the Leo S. Rowe Pan American Fund at the above address (see entry 4808).

• **4811** •

## Orphan Foundation of America

380 Maple W., Ste. LL5      *Ph:* (703)281-4226
Vienna, VA 20180      *Fax:* (703)281-0116
     *Free:* 800-950-4673

*E-mail:* orphans@.com
*URL:* http://www.orphan.org

• **4812** •   **Orphan Foundation of America Scholarship**
*(Undergraduate/Scholarship)*

**Focus:** General Studies. **Qualif.:** Applicants must be orphans as defined by the Orphan Foundation of America. That is, anyone who has lost the love and care of his or her natural parents, whether through death, abandonment, abuse, neglect, and has not been adopted. They must be or have been in Foster Care for at least 1 year at the time of their 18th birthday or high school graduation. They must currently be enrolled or accepted in a post-secondary education program such as college, trade school, or a communmity college.

**Funds Avail.:** Scholarships are in the amounts of $800, $2,000 and $5,000. This is an annual award with one-half paid in the fall semester and the other half in the spring semester. The student must complete one semester and be registered for the coming semester to receive the balance of monies, which are payable to the student and the school. **To Apply:** Applicants must show proof that they have applied for a U.S. Department of Education Pell Grant and other student aid programs. Students attending a four-year college or a community college will have to submit a 400- to 500-word essay on an annually selected topic. Students attending a technical program must write a paragraph on a annually selected topic. Application must be accompanied with a letter from a licensed social worker. **Deadline:** April 15. **Contact:** The Orphan Foundation of America at their website: www.orphan.org. Foundation of America at their website: www.orphan.org.

• **4813** •

## Orthopaedic Research and Education Foundation

6300 N. River Rd., Ste. 700      *Ph:* (847)698-9980
Rosemont, IL 60018-4261      *Fax:* (847)698-9767
*E-mail:* mcguire@oref.org
*URL:* http://www.oref.org

• **4814** •   **Career Development Awards in Orthopaedic Surgery** *(Professional Development/Grant)*

**Purpose:** To encourage a commitment to scientific research in orthopaedic surgery. **Focus:** Orthopaedic Medicine, Orthapedic Surgery. **Qualif.:** Candidate must be an orthopedic surgeon working at a U.S. institution. Applicant must have completed a residency in orthopaedic surgery and have demonstrated a sustained interest in research as well as excellence in clinical training. **Criteria:** Selection is based on the results of the peer review process.

**Funds Avail.:** Up to $75,000 per year is available. **No. of Awards:** 1-3 awards are offered yearly. **To Apply:** Contact the Foundation for application materials. Application must be accompanied by letters of nomination and support. **Deadline:** Materials must be in by August 1. Awards are announced in February.

**Remarks:** Ratio is for all Foundation awards to individuals and orthopaedic societies. **Contact:** Jean McGuire, VP, Grants at the above address (see entry 4813).

• **4815** •   **Research Grants in Orthopaedic Surgery** *(Postdoctorate/Grant)*

**Purpose:** To encourage young investigators by providing seed money and start-up funding. **Focus:** Orthopaedic Surgery, Orthopaedic Medicine. **Qualif.:** Candidate must be working at a medical center in the U.S. Applicant must be an orthopaedic surgeon, Ph.D, or D.V.M. investigator affiliated with an orthopaedic surgery program approved by the Foundation. Grants are tenable at medical institutions in the United States. **Criteria:** Selection is based on results from peer review process.

**Funds Avail.:** $50,000 is available per year. **No. of Awards:** 8-12 awards are offered yearly. **To Apply:** Contact the Foundation for application materials. **Deadline:** Materials must be in by August 1. Grants are announced in February. **Contact:** Jean McGuire, VP, Grants, at the above address (see entry 4813).

• **4816** •   **Resident Research Fellowships in Orthopaedic Surgery** *(Postdoctorate/Fellowship)*

**Purpose:** To encourage the development of research interests in orthopaedic surgery. **Focus:** Orthopaedic Surgery. **Qualif.:** Candidate must be a resident in a orthopaedic program approved by the Foundation. Fellowships provide funds for supplies and expenses, but not for resident salary. Fellowship is tenable at a medical institution in the United States.

**Funds Avail.:** $15,000 is available. **No. of Awards:** 9-12 awards are offered yearly. **To Apply:** Contact the Foundation for application materials. **Deadline:** Materials must be in by August 1. Fellowships are announced in February. **Contact:** Jean McGuire, VP of Grants at the above address (see entry 4813).

## • 4817 •
## Oshkosh Foundation
PO Box 1726
Oshkosh, WI 54902-1726          *Ph:* (414)426-3993

### • 4818 • Oshkosh Foundation Scholarships
*(Undergraduate/Scholarship)*

**Focus:** General Studies. **Qualif.:** Applicants must be graduating high school seniors who are residents of Oshkosh or Winnebago Counties, Wisconsin. **Criteria:** Awards are given based on need, ability, and extracurricular involvement.

**Funds Avail.:** Varies. **No. of Awards:** 30. **To Apply:** Applications are available through local high schools. **Deadline:** Varies with high school. **Contact:** The Oshkosh Foundation at the above address (see entry 4817).

## • 4819 •
## The Francis Ouimet Caddie Scholarship Fund
190 Park Rd.                     *Ph:* (617)891-6400
Weston, MA 02193                 *Fax:* (617)891-9471

### • 4820 • The Francis Ouimet Scholarships
*(Undergraduate/Scholarship)*

**Qualif.:** Applicants must have three years (seasons) of service to golf at a golf or country club in the Commonwealth of Massachusetts. **Criteria:** Financial need and service to golf are taken into consideration.

**Funds Avail.:** $500 to $4,500 is offered annually per student renewable for four years. 200 to 250 students per year receive the awards. **To Apply:** Qualified applicants should call or write the Ouimet Fund in the summer of their senior year in high school. **Deadline:** December 1. **Contact:** Deborah Sherman, Scholarship Administrator at the above address (see entry 4819).

## • 4821 •
## Our World - Underwater Scholarship Society
PO Box 4428                      *Ph:* (312)666-6525
Chicago, IL 60680                *Fax:* (312)666-6846

### • 4822 • Our World - Underwater Scholarships
*(Undergraduate/Scholarship)*

**Purpose:** To further the recipient's education through practical exposure to underwater-related disciplines. **Focus:** Underwater and Underwater-Related. **Qualif.:** Applicants must be certified divers with a national certification agency, at least 21 years of age and not exceeding 24 years of age by March 1 at the time the scholarship is awarded, hold high academic standing, and pass a diving fitness medical examination.

**Funds Avail.:** One $12,000 maximum cash award each year to be used for transportation and minimal living expenses. Complete expense accounting is required for all expenditures. Funds may be withdrawn at any time if the requirements are not met. Recipients travel extensively from May to May with very little time at their home bases. Some of the travel may include international destinations. Programs vary according to experience and availability of expeditions and may include experiences in field studies, underwater research, expeditions, scientific exploration, laboratory assignments, equipment testing and design, and photographic instruction. Additional scholarships may be awarded to outstanding finalists at the discretion of the Scholarship Voting Committee. **No. of Awards:** 1. **To Apply:** Applicants must submit an application form, $25 non-refundable fee, photocopy of current Diving Certification Card (both sides), transcript of academic record (sent directly from high school or college), and statement of sufficient funds for personal needs signed by a parent and/or applicant. The Society also requires a medical examination and release by medical doctor (using form supplied by the Society), two letters of recommendation from teachers or professors, two letters of recommendation from applicant's community, a statement from certifying instructor (or school) regarding diving proficiency, resume, personal biography (300 words or less), and a statement (300 words or less) specifying goals and contribution ability to the underwater world. **Deadline:** Completed applications must be received no later than November 30.

**Remarks:** This scholarship was established in 1974. Past programs have involved such groups as the Brooks Institute of Photographic Arts and Sciences, The Cousteau Society, the Monteray Bay Aquarium, the National Geographic Society, and Woods Hole Oceanographic Institute. **Contact:** Scholarship Coordinator at the above address (see entry 4821).

## • 4823 •
## Overseas Research Students Awards Scheme
Committee of Vice-Chancellors and
  Principals
of the Universities of the U.K.
29 Tavistock Sq.                 *Ph:* 171 387 9231
London WC1H 9EZ, England         *Fax:* 171 383 4573

### • 4824 • ORS Awards *(Doctorate, Graduate, Postgraduate/Award)*

**Purpose:** To provide awards for partial remission of tuition fees to postgraduate students of outstanding merit and research potential. **Focus:** General Studies. **Qualif.:** Applicants must be accepted as registered research students at institutions in England approved by the ORS and planning to attend, or already attending, full-time. They must be liable to pay tuition fees at the rate for overseas students and propose a research project that offers good scope for intellectual training and, where relevant, the acquisition of manipulative technique and skills. It should also, where possible, provide the recipient in the first year with an opportunity to prove superior research ability. An award may be used at the academic institution at which the applicant has already obtained a degree, provided that it, and any other institution, has adequate resources for the research project. Students who have already taken three or more years of research at the postgraduate level or who have already held an ORS Award in any previous year(s) are not eligible. **Criteria:** Selection is based on ability for research work based on the results of applicants' first or recent degree examination, recommendations, and where applicable, reports on any postgraduate work already undertaken. A high level of academic ability is expected of all applicants. Students who obtained their first degree with good upper second class honors are preferred.

**Funds Avail.:** The value of each award is the difference between the tuition fee for a home postgraduate student and the rate charged to an overseas postgraduate student for the particular full-time research course being taken by the recipient. The recipient pays the home-student rate fees and the difference between this and the overseas rate is reimbursed from the ORS to the academic institution. No money is paid directly to the award holder. Each award is for a period of one year, but is renewable for up to three years, subject to satisfactory academic progress. However, deferment of the award to a later session is not permitted. An ORS award cannot be held concurrently with either a Commonwealth Scholarship or a Marshall Scholarship. **To Apply:** Applications must be made on the ORS official form and sent directly to the institution they plan to attend. In addition, each applicant must ensure that proposed research programs and institutions are acceptable. Students must not apply for this award through more than one institution. Each academic institution selects the applicants it chooses to support and forwards these candidates names to the ORS committee for final selection. Applicants who are applying for other scholarships must declare this on the ORS application form. **Deadline:** April 29. **Contact:** Additional information is available from the ORS at the above address (see entry 4823).

---

### • 4825 •
### Pacific Printing and Imaging Association

5319 SW Westgate Dr., Ste. 117
Portland, OR 97221-2488

*Ph:* (503)297-3328
*Fax:* (503)297-3320
*Free:* 800-762-7698

#### • 4826 • Pacific Printing and Imaging Association Scholarship *(Undergraduate/Scholarship)*

**Purpose:** To promote entry into the printing industry. **Focus:** Printing Technology, Electronic Prepress, Computer Graphics, Print Management. **Qualif.:** Applicants must be residents of the six-state area of Pacific Printing Industries. **Criteria:** Based on interest and involvement in printing and G.P.A.

**Funds Avail.:** From two to six scholarships are awarded. **No. of Awards:** 5 four-year scholarships; 7 two-year scholarships. **Deadline:** April 1. **Contact:** Laura Ellis at the above address (see entry 4825).

---

### • 4827 •
### Packaging Education Foundation

481 Carisle Dr.
Herndon, VA 20170
*E-mail:* pef@pkematters.com
*URL:* http://packagingeducation.org

#### • 4828 • Packaging Education Forum (PEF) Packaging Scholarships *(Undergraduate/Scholarship)*

**Purpose:** To attract young people to careers in packaging and to assist those with ambition and credible scholastic performance with their financial needs. **Focus:** Packaging. **Qualif.:** Applicants must be incoming undergraduate sophomores, juniors or seniors who are enrolled in a packaging program, demonstrate above average incentive in packaging through participation in student chapters of one or more professional organization and have above average potential to develop professionally in packaging, and are U.S. citizens or hold permanent visas. **Criteria:** Awards are made based on applicant's ambition, scholastic performance and financial need.

**Funds Avail.:** $10,000. **No. of Awards:** $500-$1,000. **To Apply:** Applicant must apply thru the university when packaging is offered. **Contact:** Packaging Education Forum at the above address (see entry 4827).

---

### • 4829 •
### Paralyzed Veterans of America - Spinal Cord Research Foundation

801 18th St., NW
Washington, DC 20006

*Ph:* (202)416-7651
*Fax:* (202)416-7641
*Free:* 800-424-8200

*E-mail:* scrf@pua.org
*URL:* http://www.pua.org

*The Spinal Cord Research Foundation was established in 1976 by the Paralyzed Veterans of America for the purpose of supporting basic and clinical sciences research directed to spinal cord injury and dysfunction and for furthering related technological advances in rehabilitative methods and devices.*

#### • 4830 • Fellowships in Spinal Cord Injury Research *(Postdoctorate/Fellowship)*

**Purpose:** To encourage young investigators to pursue research in the area of spinal cord dysfunction. **Focus:** Spinal Cord Injuries and related disciplines, including Biomedical Technology, Medicine, Neuroscience, Psychology. **Qualif.:** Applicants may be of any nationality and must be postdoctoral or postresidency investigators affiliated with or sponsored by a university, hospital, or other research institution in the U.S. and Canada. Proposed research must be relevant to spinal cord dysfunction. Fellowships are tenable at institutions worldwide.

**Funds Avail.:** $20,000-50,000/year. **To Apply:** Write or call PVA for application materials or check website. **Deadline:** December 1 and June 1. Notification by June 1 and December 1, respectively. **Contact:** Administrative Officer of Research, at the above address (see entry 4829).

---

### • 4831 •
### Parapsychology Foundation, Inc.

228 East 71st St.
New York, NY 10021
*URL:* http://www.parapsychologyy.org

*Ph:* (212)628-1550
*Fax:* (212)628-1559

#### • 4832 • Eileen J. Garrett Scholarship *(Graduate, Undergraduate/Scholarship)*

**Purpose:** To encourage and support the academic pursuit of parapsychology. **Focus:** Parapsychology. **Qualif.:** Candidate may be of any nationality. Applicant must be an undergraduate or graduate student who wishes to pursue studies in Parapsychology. Applicant must attend an accredited college or university in the United States or elsewhere.

**Funds Avail.:** $3,000. **No. of Awards:** One. **To Apply:** Write the Foundation for application guidelines. Submit biographical information, study plan, names of three references, and a description of educational background, including previous parapsychology courses and research. **Deadline:** July 15. Selected applicants will be notified by August 1. **Contact:** Michelle Whitfield at the above address (see entry 4831).

---

**Parenteral Drug Association Foundation for
Pharmaceutical Sciences, Inc.**
PO Box 242
Garden City, NY 11530          *Ph:* (516)248-6713

• **4834** • **Grant in Biotechnology** (*Postdoctorate/
Grant*)

**Purpose:** To stimulate research and development in the area of
biotechnology. **Qualif.:** Candidate must be a U.S. citizen
or permanent resident. Applicant must be a qualified investigator
associated with a tax-exempt U.S. research institution.

**Funds Avail.:** $15,000 per year. **No. of Awards:** One. **To Apply:**
Write to the Foundation for application form and guidelines.
Submit form with eight copies of research proposal, curriculum
vitae of principal investigator, and detailed budget. **Deadline:** July
15.

• **4835** • **Parenteral Drug Association Foundation
Research Grants** (*Graduate/Grant*)

**Purpose:** To stimulate research in the parenteral sciences through
the support of graduate students. **Focus:** Parenteral Sciences and
Technologies, including Biology, Chemistry, Engineering,
Formulation and Stability Studies, Manufacturing, Microbiology,
Pharmaceutics, Pharmacology, Pharmacy, Quality Assurance.
**Qualif.:** Candidate must be a U.S. citizen or permanent resident.
Applicant must be a graduate student associated with a tax-
exempt U.S. research institution.

**Funds Avail.:** $15,000. **No. of Awards:** Two. **To Apply:** Write to the
Foundation for application form and guidelines. Submit form with
eight copies of research proposal, curriculum vitae of principal
investigator, and detailed budget. **Deadline:** June 1. Successful
applicants are notified by September 15. **Contact:** Dr. Stephen M.
Olin, President, at the above address (see entry 4833).

**Parents Without Partners**
401 N. Michigan Ave.          *Ph:* (312)644-6610
Chicago, IL 60611-4212          *Fax:* (312)321-6869

• **4837** • **Parents Without Partners International
Scholarship** (*Undergraduate/Scholarship*)

**Purpose:** To further the education of the recipient. **Focus:** General
Studies. **Qualif.:** Applicants must be children of members of
Parents Without Partners and high school seniors or
undergraduates under the age of 25. **Deadline:** March 15. **Contact:**
Parents Without Partners at the above address (see entry 4836).

**The Paris Review**
Editorial Office
541 East 72nd St.
New York, NY 10021          *Ph:* (212)861-0016

• **4839** • **Bernard F. Conners Poetry Prize**
(*Professional Development/Prize*)

**Purpose:** To recognize excellence in poetry. **Focus:** Poetry.
**Qualif.:** Applicants may be of any nationality, but submission must
be an unpublished poem that is at least 200 lines long. Poem must
be written in English; translations from other languages are
accepted. The winning poem is published in the fall issue of The
Paris Review+FA.

**Funds Avail.:** $1,000. **No. of Awards:** One. **To Apply:** Submit the
manuscript with a self-addressed, stamped envelope. **Deadline:**
None. Every piece submitted is considered for the prize. **Contact:**
Poetry Editor, at the above address (see entry 4838).

**Parkinson's Disease Foundation**
William Black Medical Research
   Bldg.
Columbia-Presbyterian Medical
   Center
650 W. 168th          *Ph:* (212)923-4700
New York, NY 10032          *Fax:* (212)923-4778

• **4841** • **Viola Kerr Fellowship** (*Postdoctorate/
Fellowship*)

**Funds Avail.:** Up to $35,000 per year for up to two years. The
Foundation does not pay indirect or overhead costs. **To Apply:**
Grant application forms should be accompanied by the
investigator's curriculum vitae, an outline of work to be
undertaken, including the method to be followed (two to five
pages), a budget and a budget justification. **Deadline:** April 1.

**Remarks:** The Foundation requires the grant recipient to account
for all expenditures. The second year's funding is dependent on
submission of a satisfactory report covering the first year's work.
The Foundation requires that acknowledgment of its support is
made on all scientific papers resulting from the work undertaken.
Three copies of any such papers are to be forwarded to the
Executive Director. **Contact:** Parkinson's Disease Foundation at
the above address (see entry 4840).

• **4842** • **H. Houston Merritt Fellowship**
(*Postdoctorate/Fellowship*)

**Purpose:** For established scientist (associate professor or above)
to do advanced work relating to Parkinsonism for 6 or 12 months
at the College of Physicians and Surgeons, Columbia University.
**To Apply:** No application form is required, but candidate should
submit a curriculum vitae. **Deadline:** April 1. **Contact:** Dr. Stanley
Fahn, 710 W. 168th St., New York, NY 10032.

• **4843** • **Parkinson's Disease Foundation
Postdoctoral Fellowship** (*Postdoctorate/Fellowship*)

**Qualif.:** Applicants must be physicians who have completed their
residency in neurology and who wish to receive further training in
the movement disorders. Fellowships are usually awarded for work
at Columbia's College of Physicians and Surgeons, although some
fellowships are available for work at other institutions for research
having a direct bearing on Parkinsonism. **To Apply:** No application
form required, but applicants must submit a curriculum vitae.
**Deadline:** April 1. **Contact:** Executive Director of PDF at the above
address (see entry 4840).

• **4844** • **Parkinson's Disease Foundation Research
Grants** (*Postdoctorate/Grant*)

**Funds Avail.:** Research grants of up to $25,000 per year for up to
two years. The Foundation does not pay indirect or overhead
costs. **To Apply:** The grant application form should be
accompanied by the investigator's curriculum vitae, an outline of
work to be undertaken, including the method to be followed (two to
five pages), a budget, and a budget justification. **Deadline:** April 1.

**Remarks:** The Foundation requires the grant recipient to account
for all expenditures. The second year's funding is dependent on

submission of a satisfactory report covering the first year's work. The Foundation requires that acknowledgment of its support is made on all scientific papers resulting from the work undertaken. Three copies of any such papers are to be forwarded to the Executive Director. **Contact:** The Parkinson's Disease Foundation at the above address (see entry 4840).

• 4845 • **Parkinson's Disease Foundation Summer Fellowship** *(Graduate, Undergraduate/Fellowship)*

**Qualif.:** Candidates must be medical students and undergraduates.

**Funds Avail.:** Fellowships provide a stipend for ten weeks' study under the supervision of an established investigator. **To Apply:** Applications must be requested. **Deadline:** April 1. **Contact:** The Parkinson's Disease Foundation at the above address (see entry 4840).

• 4846 • **Lillian Shorr Fellowship** *(Postdoctorate/Fellowship)*

**Funds Avail.:** Up to $35,000 per year for up to two years. The Foundation does not pay indirect or overhead costs. **To Apply:** The grant application form should be accompanied by the investigator's curriculum vitae, an outline of work to be undertaken, including the method to be followed (two to five pages), a budget, and a budget justification. **Deadline:** April 1.

**Remarks:** The Foundation requires the grant recipient to account for all expenditures. The second year's funding is dependent on submission of a satisfactory report covering the first year's work. The Foundation requires that acknowledgment of its support is made on all scientific papers resulting from the work undertaken. Three copies of any such papers are to be forwarded to the Executive Director. **Contact:** The Parkinson's Disease Foundation at the above address (see entry 4840).

• 4847 •
**Arthur & Doreen Parrett Scholarship Fund**
c/o US Bank of WWH 348, Trust
  Dept.
PO Box 720                        *Ph:* (206)344-5090
Seattle, WA 98111-0720            *Free:* 800-505-4545

• 4848 • **Arthur & Doreen Parrett Scholarship Fund** *(Graduate, Postgraduate, Undergraduate/Scholarship)*

**Purpose:** To help men and women attend an accredited college/university in the schools of medicine, dentistry, engineering, or other sciences. **Qualif.:** Applicants must be residents of the state of Washington, must have completed at least the first year of higher education at the time of application, must be enrolled full-time in engineering, science, medicine or dentistry, and may not be related to an employee of any trustee of the bank. **Criteria:** Selection is based on financial need, scholastic record and extracurricular activities.

**Funds Avail.:** Scholarships range from $2,000-$4,000. **No. of Awards:** Approximately 15. **To Apply:** Inquiries may be made to the U.S. Bank. Applications will be provided to qualifiers after January 31. **Deadline:** July 31. **Contact:** Mooi Lien Wong, Vice President.

• 4849 •
**Pastel Society of America**
15 Gramercy Park, S.
New York, NY 10003

• 4850 • **Pastel Society of America Scholarships** *(Professional Development/Scholarship)*

**Purpose:** To help pastel artists to become more professional in their work and to promote excellence in this medium. **Focus:** Drawing, Art. **Qualif.:** Artists must be experienced in pastel painting. **Criteria:** Submissions are judged on the basis of color, line, composition, values, drawing ability, and subject matter.

**Funds Avail.:** Scholarships are in the form of workshops in art schools or artist's studios. **To Apply:** Applicants must submit three slides of artwork to be judged by the scholarship committee. **Deadline:** End of May. **Contact:** Christina Debarry, Scholarship Chairperson, Pastel Society of America, at the above address (see entry 4849).

• 4851 •
**Alicia Patterson Foundation**
1730 Pennsylvania Ave., NW, Ste.
  850                              *Ph:* (202)393-5995
Washington, DC 20006             *Fax:* (301)951-8512
*E-mail:* apfengel@charm.net
*URL:* http://www.aliciapatterson.org

• 4852 • **Patterson Fellowships** *(Professional Development/Fellowship)*

**Purpose:** To enable working journalists to pursue independent projects. **Focus:** Journalism. **Qualif.:** Applicant must be a U.S. citizen. Candidate must currently be a newspaper, magazine, freelance, on-line or wire-service journalist with at least five years of professional experience. Applicant must be able to take a leave of absence from work for the fellowship period. Fellows are expected to write four magazine-length articles based on investigations in topics of their own choosing for the *APF Reporter*. Grants are not offered for academic study.

**Funds Avail.:** $35,000. **No. of Awards:** 8-10. **To Apply:** Write or phone the executive director for application form and guidelines. Submit form, two-page autobiographical essay, three-page research proposal, three samples of journalistic work, and four letters of reference. **Deadline:** October 1. **Contact:** Margaret Engel Executive Director

• 4853 •
**Paul H. Nitze School of Advanced International Studies - Johns Hopkins University - Pew Fellowships in International Journalism**
1619 Massachusetts Ave., NW      *Ph:* (202)663-7761
Washington, DC 20036             *Fax:* (202)663-7762
*E-mail:* info@pewfellowships.org
*URL:* http://pewfellowships.org

• 4854 • **Pew Fellowships in International Journalism** *(Other/Fellowship)*

**Purpose:** To educate early-career U.S. journalists in international issues and to increase and improve the coverage of international topics in the U.S. media. **Focus:** International studies, including history, economics, international relations, political science, public

*Paul H. Nitze School of Advanced International Studies - Johns Hopkins University - Pew Fellowships in International Journalism (continued)*

policy. **No. of Awards:** 2. **To Apply:** On-line application available. Applicantion also available by contacting the above address.

**Remarks:** Fellows travel for five weeks to the country or region of their choice. While overseas, journalists work on global story which is discussed with other fellows upon returning to Washington. Funded by Pew Charitable Trusts.

---

## • 4855 •
### PEN American Center
568 Broadway, Room 401     *Ph:* (212)334-1660
New York, NY 10012     *Fax:* (212)334-2181

#### • 4856 • PEN Writers Fund *(Professional Development/Grant)*

**Purpose:** To assist experienced writers facing serious financial difficulties. **Focus:** Writing **Qualif.:** Applicant must be a writer resident in the United States who has previously had works published or produced. Candidate must be in a state of financial emergency that cannot be resolved through other sources. Grants are not made for research or the completion of projects.

**Funds Avail.:** Up to $1,000 **To Apply:** Write to the administrator for application guidelines. **Deadline:** None **Contact:** PEN American Center at the above address (see entry 4855).

---

## • 4857 •
### PEN Fund for Writers and Editors with AIDS
568 Broadway, Rm. 401     *Ph:* (212)334-1660
New York, NY 10012     *Fax:* (212)334-2181

#### • 4858 • PEN Fund for Writers and Editors with AIDS Grants and Loans *(Professional Development/ Grant, Loan)*

**Purpose:** To assist professional writers and editors through acute financial emergencies due to AIDS or HIV-related illness. **Focus:** Language and Literature. **Qualif.:** Candidates must be published writers, produced playwrights, or editors with serious financial difficulties. The fund is not intended to enable writers to complete projects or fund writing publications or organizations; it is for unexpected emergencies only. **Criteria:** Award selections are based on the acuteness of the emergency and experience of the applicant.

**Funds Avail.:** Loans of up to $500 each. Approximately $25,000 are given per year in grants. **To Apply:** An application, published writing samples, documentation of the financial emergency, and a professional resume (optional) must be submitted. **Deadline:** Every six to eight weeks. **Contact:** For applications contact Vicki Vinton, coordinator, at the above address (see entry 4857).

---

## • 4859 •
### Pennsylvania Department of Military Affairs
Bureau for Veteran's Affairs
Fort Indiantown Gap     *Ph:* (717)861-8910
Annville, PA 17003-5002     *Fax:* (717)861-8589

#### • 4860 • Pennsylvania Bureau for Veteran's Affairs Educational Gratuity *(Undergraduate/Other)*

**Purpose:** To provide financial assistance to eligible children of certain veterans. **Focus:** General Studies. **Qualif.:** Applicants must be 16-23 years of age, the child of an eligible disabled or deceased veteran (100 percent), resident of Pennsylvania for a period of five years immediately preceding the date the application was filed, and attending any college or university of the State System of Higher Education, a State-aided educational or training institution of a secondary or college grade or other institution of higher education, a business school, a trade school, a hospital school providing training for nurses, an institution providing courses in beauty culture, art, radio or undertaking or embalming, or such other educational training within Pennsylvania approved by the commission. Applicants must demonstrate financial need.

**Funds Avail.:** Educational gratuity payments not to exceed $500 per term or semester upon submission of proof that bills have been incurred or contracted covering matriculation fees and other necessary fees, tuition, board, books, and supplies. Whenever a qualified child is completing an educational or training course and becomes 23 years of age before completing the course, the educational gratuity payment may be paid until the course is completed. No educational gratuity payments may be made for any period longer than four scholastic years. **Contact:** The Pennsylvania Department of Military Affairs at the above address (see entry 4859).

---

## • 4861 •
### Pennsylvania Higher Education Assistance Agency
1200 N. 7th St.     *Ph:* (717)257-2850
Harrisburg, PA 17102     *Fax:* (717)720-3904
*E-mail:* ssobezak@pheaa.org
*URL:* http://www.pheaa.com

#### • 4862 • Robert C. Byrd Honors Scholarships *(Undergraduate/Scholarship)*

**Purpose:** This federally-funded program promotes student excellence and achievement by recognizing exceptionally able students who show promise of continued academic achievement. **Qualif.:** Applicants must be high school graduates who have been accepted for enrollment at an eligible institution of higher education. Students must be residents of Pennsylvania and must meet citizenship requirements of the federal government. Applicants must meet all three of the following three criteria: rank in the top five percent of graduating class; grade point average of 3.5 or above on a 4.0 scale (unweighted); have a combined verbal and math SAT score of at least 1,200, or a composite ACT score of at least 27, or a GED score of 289 or above. This must be the students' first enrollment at an institution of higher education following high school graduation. **Criteria:** Qualified applicants are selected at random by county.

**Funds Avail.:** Approximately 260 awards of $1,500 renewable for up to the first four years at an eligible institution of higher education. **To Apply:** A letter of acceptance from the school or college must accompany application and does not have to be from the institution of final choice. A certification of eligibility for Federal assistance is also required. Applications and certification forms may be obtained from high school guidance counselors, school authorities, or by writing to the PHEAA. **Deadline:** Postmarked by May 1. **Contact:** High school guidance counselor, school authority,

---

or the Pennsylvania Higher Education Assistance Agency at the above address (see entry 4861).

### • 4863 • Keystone Stafford and Keystone Direct Student Loans *(Graduate, Undergraduate/Loan)*

**Purpose:** To provide additional monies to students to complete their education by allowing students to borrow their remaining eligibility under the Stafford Student Loan Program. **Focus:** General Studies. **Qualif.:** Applicants must be United States citizens or nationals or other eligible non-citizens who are enrolled (or accepted for enrollment) and making satisfactory academic progress at educational institutions approved by the U.S. Department of Education and the state of Pennsylvania. Applicants must be enrolled at least half-time, show compliance with selective service requirements, and cannot be in default on another student loan or owe a refund to an education grant program. **Criteria:** Based on financial need.

**Funds Avail.:** Up to $2,625 for the first and second undergraduate year, $4,000 for remaining years, and $7,500 for graduate students. A 3% Guaranty Fee is deducted from the principal of the unsubsidized Stafford Loan amount. The interest must be paid on a quarterly basis while the student is enrolled in school and during the grace period following the school period. **To Apply:** Applicants must obtain a Stafford application form from a participating lender in Pennsylvania or contact the school's financial aid office. The unsubsidized Stafford Loan is generated from the Stafford Loan application at PHEAA. **Contact:** Nancy Heil, Manager, Loan Origination, at the above address (see entry 4861).

### • 4864 • (Pennsylvania) Federal PLUS Loans *(Undergraduate/Loan)*

**Focus:** General Studies. **Qualif.:** Applicants must be natural or adoptive parents, or legal guardians of eligible students; U.S. citizens, U.S. nationals, or eligible non-citizens; and cannot be in default on another student loan or owe a refund to an education grant program. Loans are primarily for students whose financial circumstances disqualify them for the federally subsidized loan or who still need some financial assistance. Students cannot be in default on another student loan or owe a refund to an education grant program. Students must be enrolled at an educational institution approved by the United States Department of Education and the state of Pennsylvania.

**Funds Avail.:** There are no annual or aggregate loan limits. Interest rate is variable, but may not exceed ten percent. Repayment begins 60 days after the funds are disbursed. **To Apply:** Contact the financial aid office or lenders for applications. **Contact:** Loan Division at the above address (see entry 4861). Toll-free telephone number: (800)692-7392.

### • 4865 • (Pennsylvania) Federal Stafford Loans *(Undergraduate/Loan)*

**Focus:** General Studies. **Qualif.:** Applicants must be U.S. citizens, nationals or other eligible non-citizens who are enrolled (or accepted for enrollment) and making satisfactory academic progress at an educational institution approved by the United States Department of Education and the state of Pennsylvania. Applicants must be enrolled at least half-time, show compliance with selective service requirements, and cannot be in default on another student loan or owe a refund to an education grant program. **Criteria:** Selection is based on financial need.

**Funds Avail.:** Up to $2,625 for the first year of undergraduate study; up to $3,500 for the second year of undergraduate study; up to $5,500 for the third, fourth, and fifth years of undergraduate study. Aggregate for undergraduate study cannot exceed $23,000. Up to $8,500 per year for graduate or professional study is available. Aggregate for undergraduate and graduate study cannot exceed $65,500. Loan amount for a given year cannot exceed the student's cost of attendance minus other financial aid and (if required) the estimated family contribution. Federal government pays interest until student begins repayment six months after graduation or termination of studies. Interest rate is variable but may not exceed nine percent. **To Apply:** Contact any financial aid office or lender for application. **Contact:** Loan Division at the above address (see entry 4861). Toll-free telephone number: (800)692-7392.

---

### • 4866 •
**Pennsylvania Library Association**
1919 N. Front St.                    *Ph:* (717)233-3113
Harrisburg, PA 17102               *Fax:* (717)233-3121
*E-mail:* plassn@hslc.org

### • 4867 • Pennsylvania Library Association Library Science Continuing Education Grants *(Professional Development, Undergraduate/Grant)*

**Focus:** Library and Archival Sciences. **Qualif.:** Applicants must be members of the Pennsylvania Library Association.

**Funds Avail.:** The Association annually awards five grants of $200 each, which must be used within 12 months of the award. These grants are intended to be used for tuition or fees for formal course work, for an institute sponsored by an institution of higher education, for registration fees for seminars or workshops offered by continuing education providers other than institutions of higher education, or for reimbursement of receipted expenses for individual research projects that demonstrate continuing education benefits for the applicants. **No. of Awards:** 5. **To Apply:** Candidates must submit letters of application outlining the purposes of the requests as well as letters from immediate supervisors documenting the value of the requests and providing evaluations of candidates' work performance. Applicants must also enclose descriptions of the intended projects. **Deadline:** Applications must be filed by March 15. Recipients are announced by June 1.

**Remarks:** In the case of individual projects, written reports suitable for publication in the *PaLA Bulletin* must accompany receipted expenses. The *PaLA Bulletin* is to have first printing rights to reports. **Contact:** Administrative Assistant at the above address (see entry 4866).

### • 4868 • Pennsylvania Library Association Library Science Scholarships *(Graduate/Scholarship)*

**Focus:** Library and Archival Sciences. **Qualif.:** Candidates must be residents of Pennsylvania. **Criteria:** Scholastic ability and financial need, both important, are not the only basis for awarding the scholarship. Other factors, such as character, interests, motivation, emotional maturity, leisure time activities, and potential as a librarian, will be considered.

**Funds Avail.:** The annual scholarship is $1,000 for graduate study toward a master's degree in library science. **No. of Awards:** 2. **To Apply:** For final consideration applicants may be required to appear for personal interviews and to present, at the time of the interviews, letters of acceptance for admission to American Library Association accredited graduate library schools. **Deadline:** A formal application must be filed by March 30. Recipients are announced by June 1. **Contact:** Mary F. Eckard, Administrative Assistant, at the above address (see entry 4866).

---

## Pennsylvania Medical Society Educational and Scientific Trust

777 E. Park Dr.                          *Ph:* (717)558-7750
PO Box 8820                              *Fax:* (717)558-7830
Harrisburg, PA 17105-8820                *Free:* 800-228-7823
*E-mail:* studentloans-foundation@pamedsoc.org
*URL:* http://www.pitt.edu/home/ghnet/pmsfoundation

### • 4870 •   Allied Health Student Loans
*(Undergraduate/Loan)*

**Focus:** Anesthesiology-Assistant, Medical Laboratory Technology, Medical Assisting, Medical Record Administration/Technology, Occupational Therapy, Respiratory Therapy, Blood Banking, Nursing. **Qualif.:** Applicants must be residents of Pennsylvania for at least 12 months before admission to an approved institution of higher learning, be enrolled full-time (some exceptions apply) in specified allied health curricula in an approved Pennsylvania institution of higher learning, and be enrolled in a course that leads to the first certification, licensure, or degree, except for career mobility in the same discipline (e.g. a nurse with an Associate degree enrolled in a bachelor degree nursing program). Loans are granted to married students; however no allowance will be made to finance any expenses or debts of the spouse. All applicants are expected to fully exhaust all available financial resources (i.e. other loan sources, relatives) before receiving a Trust loan. Loans are not awarded for pre-medical education, masters degree programs, or to those who have an advanced degree in another field and are now making a second career choice in allied health. **Criteria:** Renewal applications, from qualified students receive first consideration.

**Funds Avail.:** The average loan amount is $1,500 per year with a course maximum of $6,000, except where there is extreme financial need. An interest at the rate of six percent (rate may vary per year) is assessed from January 1 of the school year in which the loan is granted through November 30 of the year the loan recipient graduates, completes a required internship, or terminates enrollment. Interest is seven percent during pay back. **To Apply:** Applicants are expected to provide the Trust with a full and accurate account of their financial status (this is part of the loan application), and a completed financial aid application must be submitted to the school and the school notified that a loan application was submitted to the Pennsylvania Higher Education Assistance Agency's loan programs. **Deadline:** March1 through June 1.

### • 4871 •   Medical Student Loans *(Professional Development/Loan)*

**Purpose:** To provide financial aid to students to help them complete their allied health career education. **Focus:** Medicine. **Qualif.:** Applicants must be a medical student (loans are not awarded for pre-medical or undergraduate education), be residents of Pennsylvania for at least 12 months before registration as a medical student (these 12 months could not have been for the purpose of attending undergraduate/graduate school in a Pennsylvania institution), and be enrolled in an approved medical school in the United States. Loans are granted to married students; however no allowance will be made to finance any expenses or debts of the spouse. All applicants are expected to fully exhaust all available financial resources (i.e. other loan sources, relatives), before receiving a Trust loan. **Criteria:** Students attending Pennsylvania Medical schools receive higher priority.

**Funds Avail.:** Up to $5000. **To Apply:** Applicants are expected to provide the Trust with a full and accurate account of their financial status (this is part of the loan application), and a completed financial aid application must be submitted to the medical school and the school notified that a loan application was submitted to the Pennsylvania Higher Education Assistance Agency's loan programs. **Deadline:** April 1 to July 1. **Contact:** The Educational

and Scientific Trust of the Pennsylvania Medical Society at the above address (see entry 4869).

## Pennsylvania Steel Foundry Foundation

Third and Arch Sts.                      *Ph:* (610)562-7533
Hamburg, PA 19526                        *Fax:* (610)562-7554

### • 4873 •   Pennsylvania Steel Foundry Foundation Awards *(Undergraduate/Scholarship)*

**Focus:** General Studies. **Qualif.:** Applicants must be employees of Pennsylvania Steel Foundry & Machine Company or their children. They must also attend an accredited four-year college or university.

**Funds Avail.:** An average of $7,000 is awarded annually. **To Apply:** A completed application, personal letter, and academic transcript must be submitted. **Deadline:** May 1. **Contact:** Elizabeth N. Clapper, Chairperson, at the above address (see entry 4872).

## Penquis Valley High School

West Main St.                            *Ph:* (207)943-7346
Milo, ME 04463                           *Fax:* (207)943-5333

### • 4875 •   Milo High School Alumni Scholarships
*(Undergraduate/Scholarship)*

**Qualif.:** Applicants must be seniors or graduates of Penquis Valley High School, Milo, Maine, and be accepted at an institution of higher education. **Criteria:** Selection of recipients is based on merit.

**Funds Avail.:** Scholarships are from $100 to $500, depending on the individual college, the student's financial situation, and the amount of donations received. **Deadline:** Applications are due May 31.

**Remarks:** Milo (Maine) High School ceased to exist in 1968 with the formation of a new administrative school district. Penquis Valley High School is its successor. The Alumni Association donates these scholarships yearly to Penquis Valley graduates. The scholarship fund depends upon donations from local sources and alumni. **Contact:** Penquis Valley High School at the above address (see entry 4874).

## P.E.O. Sisterhood - P.E.O. International Peace Scholarship

3700 Grand Ave.                          *Ph:* (515)255-3153
Des Moines, IA 50312-2899                *Fax:* (515)255-3820

### • 4877 •   International Peace Scholarships *(Graduate/Scholarship)*

**Purpose:** To assist women from other countries undertaking graduate studies in the United States and Canada. **Focus:** General Studies. **Qualif.:** Applicant must be a woman and a citizen of a country other than the United States or Canada. Applicant must have a U.S. or Canadian citizen act as sponsor and nonacademic adviser. Awards are tenable in full-time graduate programs in the United States and Canada. Scholarships are not given for research. Doctoral candidates with only the dissertation to complete, and students with less than one academic year of graduate study remaining are also ineligible. Scholars must return to their native countries upon completion of the degree program. **Criteria:** Selection is based on need.

**Funds Avail.:** $5,000 is available. **No. of Awards:** 150-170. **To Apply:** Write for eligibility guidelines. Eligibility must be established before P.E.O. will send application materials. **Deadline:** Materials for eligibility must be in between August 15 and December 15. Application due January 31. Admission to grad program by April 1. Scholarships are announced in May. **Contact:** International Peace Scholarship Fund at the above address (see entry 4876).

## • 4878 •
## Persian Heritage Foundation
Committee on Awards
450 Riverside Drive, No. 4
New York, NY 10027                    *Ph:* (212)280-4366

### • 4879 •  Grants-in-Aid of Publication *(Postdoctorate/ Grant)*

**Purpose:** To provide assistance toward the publication of completed manuscripts in Iranian studies. **Focus:** Iranian Studies. **Qualif.:** Applicants may be of any nationality. Grants are awarded for works in three categories: scholarly works dealing with Iranian humanities based on original or highly advanced research; translations of works of merit from Persian or other Iranian languages; and critical editions of texts in Iranian languages. Works may be written in English, French, or German. Funds must be applied toward publication costs. Awards are not offered for research or revision work; manuscript must be ready for printing in every respect, including introduction and notes. Accepted books will be published under a special arrangement with the Foundation's Publisher. **Criteria:** Applicants will be reviewed by a screening committee.

**Funds Avail.:** Varies. **No. of Awards:** Varies. **To Apply:** Write for application guidelines. Submit two copies of manuscript in publishable form. Doctoral dissertations must be accompanied by recommendations from two scholars stating that the work is publishable in book form. **Deadline:** March 1, October 1. **Contact:** D. Amin, Editorial Coordinator, at the above address (see entry 4878).

## • 4880 •
## Petro-Canada Inc.
PO Box 2844
Calgary, AB, Canada T2P 3E3

### • 4881 •  Petro-Canada Education Awards for Native Students *(Undergraduate/Award)*

**Qualif.:** Candidates must be of Canadian or Inuit ancestry and pursuing full-time studies in disciplines applicable to the oil and gas industry. **Criteria:** Financial need, grades, applicability of course of studies.

**Funds Avail.:** A number of awards valued up to $5,000 are available. **To Apply:** Letter, resume, transcript of grades, and proof of enrollment. **Deadline:** June 15 each year. **Contact:** Employment Equity Office at the above address (see entry 4880).

## • 4882 •
## Pfizer, Inc. - U.S. Pharmaceuticals Group
Department of Medical Affairs
 Programs
235 E. 42nd St.                        *Ph:* (212)573-2880
New York, NY 10017-5755                *Fax:* (212)916-7156

### • 4883 •  The Pfizer American Geriatrics Society Postdoctoral Outcomes Research Fellowships
*(Postdoctorate/Fellowship)*

**Purpose:** To encourage research training in geriatric medicine, to provide opportunities for the scientific and academic development of promising investigators, and to help furnish additional time for them to devote to research training. **Focus:** Geriatric Medicine. **Qualif.:** Applicants must hold an M.D. or D.O. degree, have completed fellowship training in geriatrics and not have a full-time faculty appointment at the level of assistant professor for more than two years at the time the fellowship becomes effective. They must also be sponsored at a United States institution by a full-time medical school faculty member and have obtained permission to apply by the dean of that school. Each school dean may authorize no more than three applicants and no school will receive more than one award per year. Candidates must be U.S. citizens, permanent residents, or have legally declared intent to become citizens. Fellows must not have principal investigator status nor be the sole awardee of a national research grant, fellowship, or career development award, public or private. They must devote a minimum of 50 percent of professional time to research; or if the requirements for clinical training in geriatrics have been substantially fulfilled, then at least 75 percent of professional time should be committed to research. Visiting scientists on "J" visas are not eligible. **Criteria:** Applications are reviewed by an independent academic Advisory Board which evaluates: qualifications of the applicant; evidence of the applicant's commitment to, and qualifications for, an academic career in geriatric medicine or geriatric psychiatry; documentation presented by the sponsor of a commitment to, as well as experience in, research and training in the applicant's area of interest; availability of appropriate facilities for conducting the proposed research; and the training plan provided by the sponsor.

**Funds Avail.:** Two awards provide $40,000 annually. **No. of Awards:** 2. **To Apply:** Applicants must submit a completed application, curriculum vitae and bibliography, sponsor's curriculum vitae and bibliography (no more than three pages), a letter from the applicant stating previous training and experience and how the proposal relates to the applicant's projected career, and a letter from the sponsor detailing a research training plan, availability of research facilities and environment, comments on the applicant's qualifications, and a list of the sponsor's recent research trainees. Also required are letters from the department chairperson and the geriatrics program director, a research proposal, a description of the clinical training program or appropriate accreditation documentation, and the applicant's relevant scientific publications (maximum of three) if available. **Deadline:** December 2 of 1997. **Contact:** Program Coordinator, Pfizer/AGS Postdoctoral Fellowships Psymark Communications, PO Box 627, 33 Main St., Old Saybrook, CT, 06475. Telephone (800)201-1214.

### • 4884 •  The Pfizer Postdoctoral Fellowships
*(Postdoctorate/Fellowship)*

**Purpose:** To provide financial support to promising physicians who wish to conduct original clinical or basic research. **Focus:** Biological Psychiatry, Neuroscience, Cardiovascular Medicine, Diabetes, Endocrinology, Infectious Diseases, Rheumatology, Immunology. **Qualif.:** Applicants must be citizens or noncitizen nationals of the United States, hold an M.D. or D.O. degree, and have no more than one year post-residency experience at the time the award is given. A strong academic career interest in biological psychiatry, neuroscience, cardiovascular medicine, diabetes/ endocrinology, infectious diseases, or rheumatology/immunology

## Pfizer, Inc. - U.S. Pharmaceuticals Group *(continued)*

must be demonstrated. Applicants must have arranged for an appointment to an appropriate U.S. institution and acceptance by a sponsor who is a full-time faculty member of a U.S. medical school. They must not be the sole awardee of a national research grant, fellowship, career development award, or other award of equivalent designation, at the time of the granting of the award, or any other named award funded by private- sector companies in the pharmaceutical industry, or their foundations which together with the Pfizer Fellowship total more than $80,000 annually. They must plan to devote a minimum of 90% of professional time to research. Applicants should obtain permission to prepare an application from the dean of the medical school (Pfizer will accept only one application per specialty category from each medical school). **Criteria:** Applications are reviewed by an independent academic Advisory Board. Final selection of Scholars is made by the Pfizer Pharmaceuticals Group based on the recommendation of the Advisory Board. The Advisory Board evaluates: qualifications of the applicant; evidence of the applicant's interest in and qualifications for an academic research career; scientific merit of the research proposal; relevance of proposed research to specialty area; demonstrated ability of the sponsor to prepare trainees for academic research careers; experience of the sponsor; training environment available to the applicant; and the training plan provided by the sponsor. One winner is selected in each of the following areas: biological psychiatry/neuroscience; cardiovascular medicine; diabetes/endocrinology; infectious diseases; and rheumatology/immunology.

**Funds Avail.:** Five fellowships of $40,000 per year awarded in two installments on or about July 1 and January 1. **No. of Awards:** 5. **To Apply:** Applicants must complete a Pfizer Identification and Checklist Form, a Pfizer Application Form, including all required signatures, and a Pfizer Postdoctoral Fellowship Statement of Other Funding Form. Applicants must also include six copies of the following: curriculum vitae, bibliographies, a letter discussing previous training/experience and how the proposed research training relates to the applicants projected career, letters of recommendation, sponsor's curriculum vitae and bibliography, a letter from the department chairman discussing the resources available, and a research proposal. Applicants who have scientific publications should submit their single most relevant article. **Contact:** Program Coordinator Pfizer/AGS Postdoctoral Fellowships, Psymark Communications, PO Box 627, 33 Main St., Old Saybrook, CT, 06475. Telephone (800)201-1214.

### • 4885 • The Pfizer Scholars Program for New Faculty *(Postdoctorate/Award)*

**Purpose:** To encourage and provide opportunities for developing the research potential of physicians during the years just after completing their clinical and research training. **Focus:** Biological Psychiatry, Neuroscience, Cardiovascular Medicine, Diabetes, Endocrinology, Infectious Diseases, Rheumatology, Immunology. **Qualif.:** Applicants must have held an M.D. or D.O. degree for a period not exceeding ten years at the time of application and must obtain permission to apply from the dean of the medical school. Formal scientific and clinical training must be completed. Applicants must have a full-time faculty appointment below the level of associate professor and have no more than three years cumulative full-time faculty experience at the assistant professor level at the time of the initiation of the award. A proven research interest in biological psychiatry/neuroscience, cardiovascular medicine, diabetes/endocrinology, infectious diseases, or rheumatology/immunology is also required. Candidates must not have principal investigator status on, nor be the sole awardee of, a national research or training award at the time of application, nor hold a research grant, career development award, or any other named award, public or private. Recipients must devote a minimum of 75 percent of professional time to research. They must also be U.S. citizens, permanent residents, or have legally declared intent to become U.S. citizens. Visiting scientists on "J" visas are not eligible. **Criteria:** Applications are reviewed by an independent

Advisory Board. Final selections are made by the Pfizer Pharmaceuticals Group based on the recommendations of the Advisory Board. The Advisory Board evaluates research experience and clinical training of applicants, evidence of commitment to an academic career in one of the five stated areas of clinical medicine; evidence of the interest, initiative, and ability of the applicants to do original research in one of these areas; depth, originality, and feasibility of the research proposal, and commitment of the department to the area of research outlined in the research proposals of the applicants, including provision of facilities by the department to enable applicants to conduct the research.

**Funds Avail.:** Each Pfizer Scholar award provides $65,000 annually. **No. of Awards:** Five. **To Apply:** Applicants must submit a completed application, a curriculum vitae and bibliography, a letter describing previous research training and experience, how the proposed research relates to the applicants' career, estimated teaching, research, and patient care responsibilities assumed as a faculty member during the period of the award, and a letter from the applicant's prospective department chairman or division director. They must also submit a research proposal and up to three reprints of the applicant's relevant scientific publications. **Contact:** Program Coordinator Pfizer/AGS Postdoctoral Fellowships, Psymark Communications, PO Box 627, 33 Main St., Old Saybrook, CT, 06475. Telephone (800)201-1214.

---

## • 4886 •
## Pharmaceutical Manufacturers Association Foundation

| | |
|---|---|
| 1100 15th St., NW | *Ph:* (202)835-3470 |
| Washington, DC 20005 | *Fax:* (202)467-4823 |

### • 4887 • Faculty Development Awards in Clinical Pharmacology and Toxicology *(Postdoctorate/Award)*

**Purpose:** To encourage physicians, dentists and veterinarians in the pursuit of careers in clinical pharmacology. **Focus:** Clinical Pharmacology. **Qualif.:** Applicant must be a U.S. citizen, or intend to remain in the U.S., who is beyond the postdoctoral stage of their career and has demonstrated a strong desire to pursue a career in pharmacology and toxicology. Assistant professors are eligible to apply. Applicant must be sponsored by a U.S. institution. Facilities must be made available for the training.

**Funds Avail.:** $40,000. **No. of Awards:** Three. **To Apply:** Write to the above address for application form and guidelines. **Deadline:** October 1.

### • 4888 • Fellowships for Careers in Clinical Pharmacology *(Postdoctorate/Fellowship)*

**Purpose:** To encourage physicians, dentists and veterinarians in the pursuit of careers in clinical pharmacology. **Focus:** Clinical Pharmacology. **Qualif.:** Applicant must be a U.S. citizen, or intend to remain in U.S., who is at least two years beyond the doctoral degree and has demonstrated a strong desire to pursue the study of clinical pharmacology. Applicant must have a firm commitment for study from a U.S. university.

**Funds Avail.:** $24,000-30,000. **No. of Awards:** 3 or 4. **To Apply:** Write to the above address for application form and guidelines. **Deadline:** October 1.

• 4889 •
## Phi Alpha Theta History Honor Society, Inc.
50 College Dr.  *Ph:* (610)433-4140
Allentown, PA 18104-6100  *Fax:* (610)433-4661

• 4890 • **Annual Grants; Dr. John Pine Memorial Award; Dr. A. F. Zimmerman Award** *(Doctorate, Graduate/Award, Grant)*

**Purpose:** To provide support for graduate and advanced graduate study in history. **Focus:** History. **Qualif.:** Candidates for all three awards must be Phi Alpha Theta members. Applicants for the Zimmerman Award must be entering graduate school for the first time for work leading to a master's degree in history. Applicants for the Pine Award must be graduate students in advanced graduate study. Students in both graduate and advanced graduate study qualify for the annual grants.
**Funds Avail.:** Zimmerman: $1,250; Pine: $1,000; annual grants: $750. **No. of Awards:** Zimmerman and Pine: one each; annual grants: four. **To Apply:** Write to the Society for application form and guidelines. **Deadline:** March 15. **Contact:** Graydon A. Tunstall, Jr., Executive Secretary-Treasurer, at the above address (see entry 4889).

• 4891 • **Phi Alpha Theta Faculty Advisor Research Grant** *(Postdoctorate/Grant)*

**Purpose:** To provide support for any special activity of the advisor, including research, writing assistance, travel for career advancement, or other programs involving further participation by the faculty member. **Focus:** History. **Qualif.:** Candidates must be faculty members of Phi Alpha Theta who have served for at least five years as faculty advisors.
**Funds Avail.:** $1,000. **No. of Awards:** One. **To Apply:** Write to the Society for application form and guidelines. Submit a letter of recommendation from the chairperson or dean. **Deadline:** June 1. Award will be announced by August 15. **Contact:** Graydon A. Tunstall, Jr., Executive Secretary-Treasurer, at the above address (see entry 4889).

• 4892 • **Phi Alpha Theta Graduate Scholarship** *(Doctorate, Graduate/Grant)*

**Purpose:** To provide support for projects connected with the completion of the doctorate degree. **Focus:** History. **Qualif.:** Candidates must be advanced graduate-student members of Phi Alpha Theta. Awards is intended for research travel, purchase of research material, expenses for the final copy of the dissertation, and other projects connected with degree completion.
**Funds Avail.:** $1,000. **No. of Awards:** One. **To Apply:** Write to the Society for application form and guidelines. Submit a letter of recommendation from the chairman of the department of history or the graduate advisor. **Deadline:** June 1. Award will be announced by August 15. **Contact:** Graydon A. Tunstall, Jr., Executive Secretary-Treasurer, at the above address (see entry 4889).

• 4893 •
## Phi Beta Kappa
50 College Dr.
Allentown, PA 18104-6186

• 4894 • **Mary Isabel Sibley Fellowships** *(Doctorate, Postdoctorate/Fellowship)*

**Purpose:** To assist a female scholar who has demonstrated an ability to carry on original research. **Focus:** French Language and Literature (in even-numbered years); Greek Archaeology, History,

Language, and Literature (in odd-numbered years). **Qualif.:** Candidates may be of any nationality but must be unmarried women between the ages of 25 and 35 years who have earned a Ph.D., or who have completed all doctoral degree requirements except the dissertation. Applicants must also be prepared to work full-time on research during the tenure of the fellowship. Areas of study alternate each year between French and Greek studies.
**Funds Avail.:** $10,000. **To Apply:** Write to the MISF Committee for application materials. **Deadline:** January 15. Notification by April 1. **Contact:** Linda D. Surles, Program Officer, at the above address (see entry 4893).

• 4895 •
## Phi Chi Theta Foundation
1704 Hanks St.
Lufkin, TX 75904

• 4896 • **Phi Chi Theta Scholarships** *(Graduate, Postgraduate, Undergraduate/Scholarship)*

**Purpose:** To support the higher education of women in business administration or economics. **Focus:** Business Administration, Economics. **Qualif.:** Applicants must be female and full-time students who have completed at least one year of a bachelor's, master's, or doctoral degree program in business administration or economics. Candidates must demonstrate scholastic achievement, financial need, leadership, and motivation, and must be members of Phi Chi Theta.
**Funds Avail.:** $1,000. **No. of Awards:** 1-3. **To Apply:** Send self-addressed, stamped business-size envelope to the Foundation for application form and guidelines, available January 1. Submit form with two letters of recommendation and official transcripts. **Deadline:** May 1.

• 4897 •
## Phi Delta Kappa International
PO Box 789  *Ph:* (812)339-1156
Bloomington, IN 47402-0789  *Fax:* (812)339-0018

• 4898 • **Phi Delta Kappa Scholarship Grant for Prospective Educators** *(Undergraduate/Scholarship)*

**Focus:** Education. **Qualif.:** Applicants must be high school seniors who plan to pursue careers as professional educators or teachers. **Criteria:** The primary determinant is the applicant's essay response to a question related to the field of education. Other criteria include scholarship, recommendations, written expression, interest in teaching or professional education as a career, and school and community activities.
**Funds Avail.:** 46 $1,000 grants and one $2,000 grant. The grants are sent directly to the college or university indicated by the recipient and deducted from his or her registration and tuition costs during the first year of enrollment, or awarded to the recipients. **No. of Awards:** 47. **To Apply:** These grants are awarded jointly by Phi Delta Kappa, Inc., and the Phi Delta Kappa Educational Foundation. Applications are available from local PDK chapters only. The applicants' typewritten essays should not exceed 750 words. Phi Delta Kappa publishes the responses of the 47 recipients. Applications must include the names and addresses of two references. One should be a teacher who is familiar with the candidate's academic ability and the other should be a personal reference. Transcripts of high school records should be sent directly to the Phi Delta Kappa chapters that distributed the applications by the candidate's high school counselor. Class size, class rank and grade point average must be included. **Deadline:**

---

### Phi Delta Kappa International (continued)

Applications must be submitted to local PDK chapters by January 31; recipients are announced in May. **Contact:** Phi Delta Kappa International at the above address (see entry 4897).

---

• 4899 •

## Phi Kappa Phi Honor Society
PO Box 16000
Louisiana State University      *Ph:* (504)388-4917
Baton Rouge, LA 70893-6000      *Fax:* (504)388-4900
*E-mail:* pkppam@aol.com

### • 4900 • Phi Kappa Phi Graduate Fellowships
*(Graduate/Fellowship)*

**Focus:** General Studies. **Qualif.:** Candidates must be active members of Phi Kappa Phi or expect to be accepted for membership on the date the fellowship awards are made. Application should be made during the senior year of college. These fellowships are for support the first year of full-time graduate or professional study, preferably in an American college or university. **Criteria:** Preference is given to candidates who plan to obtain their doctorate or other advanced professional degree.

**Funds Avail.:** The number of fellowships awarded annually is determined by the Board of Directors based on funds available. Normally 50 fellowships worth up to $7,000 are awarded. Thirty Honorable Mention awards of $1000 each are also made. Fellowships are awarded upon receipt of certificate of registration. Recipients may accept the fellowship with full stipend, a reduced stipend (adjusted on the basis of other support), or with no stipend, dependent upon other awards, grants, fellowships, scholarships, and remuneration. Certain scholarships, tuition waivers, and other essential aid may be approved. **No. of Awards:** 80/years. **To Apply:** Each active institutional chapter of the Honor Society of Phi Kappa Phi is encouraged to submit the application of its most outstanding candidate for the national competition. While the awards are intended for the support of students undertaking graduate study within twelve months of receipt of the baccalaureate degree, persons having delayed graduate study for a year or more may compete through their chapter of initiation or chapter of current membership. Candidates are required to submit five copies of the application and all required supplementary documents. Evaluation report forms must be completed by three university professors who can attest to the applicant's scholastic and academic ability and qualification for the fellowships. Evaluation report forms must be returned to the chapter secretary before the established deadline. Applicants must provide college or university transcripts; overall grade-point average and GRE or other appropriate test scores; documentation of participation in any honors or curriculum enrichment programs; and a list of scholastic honors, and information on cultural, social, athletic, political, employment or other activities in which they are involved, as well as offices held, and honors or prizes. Graduate plans of the applicant must be indicated by listing, in order of preference, three institutions of higher education that the applicant is prepared to attend. Applicants must also briefly describe their purpose in pursuing graduate or professional study and its relation to their career objectives. **Deadline:** Applications and all supporting documents must be submitted to the Secretary of the applicant's chapter by February 1, to allow time for chapter review and forwarding to the Society's National Office by March 1. Recipients are announced around April 1. **Contact:** Chapter Secretaries on campus.

---

• 4901 •

## Phi Kappa Theta National Foundation
3901 W. 86th St., Ste 125      *Ph:* (317)872-9934
Indianapolis, IN 46268      *Fax:* (317)879-1880

### • 4902 • Phi Kappa Theta National Foundation Scholarships *(Undergraduate/Scholarship)*

**Purpose:** To assist needy undergraduate members of Phi Kappa Theta Fraternity in paying college expenses. **Focus:** General Studies. **Qualif.:** Applicants must be initiated members of Phi Kappa Theta Fraternity attending schools where there is an active chapter. **Criteria:** Financial need and satisfactory progress towards graduation are the primary criteria.

**Funds Avail.:** Six to eight grants of between $300 and $1,000 are offered. **To Apply:** Applications are sent to active chapters February 15 and March 15. **Deadline:** April 15.

**Remarks:** There are usually approximately 25 scholarship applicants. **Contact:** Phi Kappa Theta Fraternity at the above address (see entry 4901).

---

• 4903 •

## Phi Sigma Iota
5211 Essen Ln., Ste. 2      *Ph:* (504)769-7100
Baton Rouge, LA 70809-3593      *Fax:* (504)769-7105

### • 4904 • Phi Sigma Iota Scholarships *(Graduate, Undergraduate/Scholarship)*

**Purpose:** To assist students pursuing studies in the field of foreign languages. **Focus:** Foreign Languages. **Qualif.:** Applicants must be active members of Phi Sigma Iota. **Criteria:** Selection is based upon GPA and a commitment to pursue and complete foreign language studies.

**Funds Avail.:** $500 is awarded for each of the scholarships. **No. of Awards:** 15. **To Apply:** Applications must be filed on a PSI application form and signed by chapter's advisor. **Deadline:** February 1. **Contact:** Dr. Marie France, President, Foreign Language Department, University of Nevada at Las Vegas, Las Vegas, NV 89154.

---

• 4905 •

## Phi Theta Kappa International Honor Society
1625 Eastover Dr.      *Ph:* (601)957-2241
Jackson, MS 39211-6431      *Fax:* (601)957-2625
    *Free:* 800-647-7662

### • 4906 • Guistwhite Scholar Program
*(Undergraduate/Scholarship)*

**Purpose:** To encourage the completion of baccalaureate studies and to recognize outstanding work towards the completion of an associates degree. **Focus:** General Studies. **Qualif.:** Applicants must be Phi Theta Kappa members in good standing who will complete an associates degree during the academic year. They must transfer as a junior within a major field of study to a regionally accredited four-year or senior-level institution. Full time enrollment at time of transfer is required. **Criteria:** Selection is based on the strength of the application including an official college transcript, three letters of recommendation, and a 500-word essay.

**Funds Avail.:** Scholarships of $5,000 are dispersed at $2,500 per year. **No. of Awards:** 10. **To Apply:** Applications may be obtained from Phi Theta Kappa Headquarters. **Deadline:** May 31. **Contact:**

Saralyn Quinn, Special Programs, at the above address (see entry 4905).

### • 4907 • Mosal Scholar Program *(Professional Development/Scholarship)*

**Purpose:** To recognize outstanding long-term contributions to Phi Theta Kappa by a chapter advisor. **Focus:** General Studies. **Qualif.:** Candidates must currently be serving as a Phi Theta Kappa advisor and have served in that capacity for a minimum of five years. They must also have been previously selected as a Giles Distinguished Advisor.

**Funds Avail.:** Five scholarships of $2,000. **No. of Awards:** 5. **To Apply:** Applications are provided to all previous Giles Distinguished Advisors in January. **Deadline:** February. **Contact:** Mr. Billy Wilson, Director of Honors Programs, at the above address (see entry 4905).

### • 4908 • Steve Orlowski Memorial Scholarships *(Undergraduate/Scholarship)*

**Purpose:** To recognize and honor the candidate for Phi Theta Kappa's International Office who best demonstrates and embodies the ideals of Phi Theta Kappa during the campaign process. **Focus:** General Studies. **Qualif.:** Candidate must be a member of Phi Theta Kappa and a candidate for the International Office. **Criteria:** Chosen by candidates for International Office.

**Funds Avail.:** $1,000. **Contact:** Mr. Mike Watson, Director of Development and Public Affairs, at the above address (see entry 4905).

### • 4909 • Parnell Scholar Programs *(Professional Development/Scholarship)*

**Purpose:** To provide funds for a Phi Theta Kappa advisor to participate in the Society's Annual International Convention and to serve as a seminar leader at the Honors Institute. **Focus:** General Studies. **Qualif.:** Candidate must currently be serving as a Phi Theta Kappa advisor and cannot have previously attended an Honors Institute. Candidate must be selected as a finalist to serve as an Honors Institute seminar leader. **Criteria:** Selection is based on the strength of the application.

**Funds Avail.:** $2,000. **To Apply:** Applications will be mailed to each chapter advisor in January. **Deadline:** February. **Contact:** Mr. Billy Wilson, Director of Honors Programs, at the above address (see entry 4905).

### • 4910 •
**Phi Upsilon Omicron - National Honor Society in Family and Consumer Sciences**
PO Box 329
Fairmont, WV 26555-0329          *Ph:* (304)368-0612
*E-mail:* rickards@mountain.net
*URL:* http://ianrwww.unl.edu/phiu

### • 4911 • Candle Fellowships *(Graduate/Fellowship)*

**Focus:** Family and consumer sciences. **Qualif.:** Applicants must be Phi U members who are enrolled or plan to enroll in a graduate school. **Criteria:** Based on scholastic record; honors and recognitions; participation in honor society; professional, community, and religious organizations; scholarly work; statement of professional aims and goals; and recommendations.

**Funds Avail.:** $1000 each. **No. of Awards:** 2.

### • 4912 • Geraldine Clewell Fellowship I *(Graduate/Fellowship)*

**Focus:** Family and consumer sciences with preference given to students desiring to teach at the college/university level. **Qualif.:** Applicants must be Phi U members who are doctoral students. **Criteria:** Based on scholastic records; honors and recognitions; participation in honor society, professional, community, and religious organizations; scholarly work; statement of professional aims and goals; and recommendations.

**Funds Avail.:** $1500.R **No. of Awards:** 1. **To Apply:** At least one recommendation from a major advisor must be submitted.

### • 4913 • Geraldine Clewell Scholarship *(Undergraduate/Scholarship)*

**Focus:** Family and consumer sciences or related fields. **Qualif.:** Applicants must be PHI U members seeking a baccalaureate degree. **Criteria:** Based on scholastic records, participation in Phi U activities, professionals goals, and recommendations.

**Funds Avail.:** $650. **Deadline:** February 1.

### • 4914 • Closs/Parnitzke/Clarke Scholarship *(Undergraduate/Scholarship)*

**Focus:** Family and consumer sciences or related areas. **Qualif.:** Applicants must be Phi U members working toward a baccalaureate degree.

**Funds Avail.:** $650. **Deadline:** February 1.

### • 4915 • Diamond Anniversary Fellowships *(Graduate/Fellowship)*

**Focus:** Family or consumer sciences. **Qualif.:** Applicants must be Phi U members who are students at a master's or doctoral level who have been accepted into or currently enrolled in a graduate program. **Criteria:** Based on scholastic records; honors and recognitions; participation in honor society, professional, community, and religious organizations; scholarly work; statement of professional aims and goals; and recommendations.

**Funds Avail.:** $1000 each. **No. of Awards:** 2.

### • 4916 • Jean Dearth Dickerscheid Fellowship *(Graduate/Fellowship)*

**Focus:** Family and consumer sciences or related fields. **Qualif.:** Applicants must be Phi U members who have already earned one degree in family or consumer sciences. **Criteria:** Based on scholastic records; honors and recognitions; participation in honor society, professional, community, and religious organizations; scholarly work; statement of professional aims and goals; and recommendations.

**Funds Avail.:** $1000. **No. of Awards:** 1.

### • 4917 • Margaret Drew Alpha Fellowship *(Graduate/Fellowship)*

**Focus:** Family and consumer sciences with preferences given to dietetics or food and nutrition. **Qualif.:** Applicants must be Phi U members pursuing a graduate degree. **Criteria:** Based on scholastic records; honors and recognitions; participation in honor society, professional, community, and religious organizations; scholarly work; statement of professional aims and goals; and recommendations.

**Funds Avail.:** $1000. **No. of Awards:** 1.

### • 4918 • Founders Fellowship *(Graduate/Fellowship)*

**Focus:** Family and consumer sciences or related fields. **Qualif.:** Applicants must be Phi U members who are studying for advanced

## Phi Upsilon Omicron - National Honor Society in Family and Consumer Sciences (continued)

graduate study. **Criteria:** Based on scholastic records; honors and recognitions; participation in honor society, professional, community, and religious organizations; scholarly work; statement of professional aims and goals; and recommendations.

**Funds Avail.:** $1000 each. **No. of Awards:** 2.

### • 4919 • Geraldine Clewell Fellowship II (Graduate/Fellowship)

**Focus:** Family and consumer sciences with a preference to family and consumer sciences education and desiring to teach at the elementary/secondary school levels. **Qualif.:** Applicants must be Phi U members pursuing a master's degree. **Criteria:** Based on scholastic records; honors and recognitions; participation in honor society, professional, community, and religious organizations; scholarly work; statement of professional aims and goals; and recommendations.

**Funds Avail.:** $1000. **No. of Awards:** 1. **To Apply:** At least one recommendation must be from the student's major advisor.

### • 4920 • Tommie J. Hamner Scholarship (Undergraduate/Scholarship)

**Focus:** Family and consumer sciences or related fields. **Qualif.:** Applicants must be Phi U members who have shown exemplary commitments to the organization.

**Funds Avail.:** $650. **Deadline:** February 1.

### • 4921 • Treva C. Kintner Scholarships (Undergraduate/Scholarship)

**Focus:** Family and consumer sciences or related fields. **Qualif.:** Applicants must be Phi U members over 30 years of age who have completed at least half of the required academic work.

**Funds Avail.:** $1000 each. **No. of Awards:** 2.

### • 4922 • Margaret Jerome Sampson Scholarships (Undergraduate/Scholarship)

**Focus:** Family and consumer sciences with a preference given to those in dietetics or food and nutrition. **Qualif.:** Applicants must be Phi U members pursuing baccalaureate degrees. **Criteria:** Based on scholastic records, participation in Phi U activities, and professional aims and goals.

**Funds Avail.:** $3000 each. **No. of Awards:** 2. **To Apply:** Applicants must have at least one recommendation from the Phi U chapter advisor. **Deadline:** February 1.

### • 4923 • Presidents Research Fellowship (Graduate/Fellowship)

**Purpose:** To provide funding for research. **Focus:** Family and consumer sciences or related fields. **Qualif.:** Applicants must be Phi U members seeking to conduct research at the master's, doctoral, or post-doctoral level. **Criteria:** Based on scholastic records; honors and recognitions; participation in honor society, professional, community, and religious organizations; scholarly work; statement of professional aims and goals; and recommendations.

**Funds Avail.:** $1000. **No. of Awards:** 1. **To Apply:** Research prospectus exhibiting organization and need for the research must be submitted.

### • 4924 • Lillian P. Schoephoerster Scholarship (Undergraduate/Scholarship)

**Focus:** Family and consumer sciences or related fields. **Qualif.:** Applicants must be non-traditional students who are members of Phi U working toward a baccalaureate degree.

**Funds Avail.:** $1000. **Deadline:** February 1.

### • 4925 • Sutherland/Purdy Scholarship (Undergraduate/Scholarship)

**Focus:** Clothing and textile, apparel design, fashion merchandising, or related areas. **Qualif.:** Applicants must be Phi U members who have held leadership positions in their chapters and earned at least a 3.0 overall GPA.

**Funds Avail.:** $650. **Deadline:** February 1.

### • 4926 • Mary Welking Franken Scholarship (Undergraduate/Scholarship)

**Focus:** Family and consumer sciences with preference to those in child and/or family or family and consumer science education. **Qualif.:** Applicants must be Phi U members.

**Funds Avail.:** $650. **Deadline:** February 1.

### • 4927 •
## Philadelphia Inquirer
Director of Internships and
 Recruiting
Ste 100, 1100 E. Hector St.
Conshohocken, PA 19428      *Ph:* (610)832-8304

### • 4928 • Knight-Ridder Minority Specialty Development Program (Professional Development/Other)

**Purpose:** To train promising minority journalists in specialized areas of news gathering and production. **Qualif.:** Open to young minority journalists who have committed themselves to a newspaper career and are already focused on a specialty field. It is recommended that candidates obtain prior experience through internships, stringing, and freelance assignments.

**Funds Avail.:** Salaries match the experience rate of the host newspapers. Training lasts two years, the first year at The Philadelphia Inquirer, Miami Herald, San Jose Mercury News, or Detroit Free Press and the second at a mid-size Knight-Ridder newspaper. **To Apply:** Applicants are requested to send a resume, Three letters of recommendation, an essay describing qualifications, 10 to 12 clips, and cover letter explaining why a specific field has been selected. Ten to 12 finalists will be invited for interviews. Final selection will be made in mid-April. **Deadline:** December 31. **Contact:** Paul Jablow, Director of Internships, at the above address,(see entry 4927) or Joe Grimm, Detroit Free Press Hiring Director, 321 W. Lafayette Blvd., Detroit, MI 48231, (313)222-6490.

### • 4929 • Art Peters Minority Internships (Undergraduate/Internship)

**Purpose:** To provide minority college students with the opportunity to participate in a 10-week course of instruction and practical work in copy-editing at the Philadelphia Inquirer. After a week of intensive instruction, students are assigned to copy desks. **Qualif.:** Minority students from all college classes are eligible for these internships.

**Funds Avail.:** $573 per week. **To Apply:** Applicants should send a cover letter, resume, three journalistic references, and clips. **Deadline:** November 15.

**Remarks:** Assistance is given to interns in finding full-time employment after graduation. Established in 1979.

---

## • 4930 •
## Phillips Exeter Academy
Exeter, NH 03833-1104                    *Ph:* (603)772-4311
*URL:* http://www.exeter.edu

### • 4931 • George Bennett Fellowships *(Professional Development/Fellowship)*

**Purpose:** To provide freedom from material considerations to a person seriously contemplating or embarking on a career as a writer of fiction, poetry, or creative non-fiction. **Focus:** Writing-Fiction, Literary Nonfiction, Poetry, Playwriting. **Qualif.:** Candidates may be of any nationality, but must have begun a manuscript that they intend to complete during the fellowship. Preference is given to candidates who have not published a full-length book with a major publisher. Manuscripts must be in English. The fellow must live at the Academy and be available in an informal and unofficial way to students interested in writing. **Criteria:** Awards are given based on quality of submitted manuscript.

**Funds Avail.:** $6,000 stipend, plus housing and meals while school is in session. **No. of Awards:** One annually. **To Apply:** Send a stamped, self-addressed envelope for application form and guidelines. Submit form, manuscript, and the names and addresses of two references. Information and form are also available from the academy website. **Deadline:** December 1. Fellowship is awarded around March 15. **Contact:** Charles Pratt at the above address (see entry 4930).

---

## • 4932 •
## Phoenix Budget and Research Department
200 W. Washington St., 14th Fl.          *Ph:* (602)262-4800
Phoenix, AZ 85003                        *Fax:* (602)251-3918
*URL:* http://www.ci.phoenix.az.us

### • 4933 • Phoenix Management Internships *(Postgraduate/Internship)*

**Purpose:** To attract, develop, and retain innovative people in local government. **Qualif.:** Applicants must have completed coursework towards a master's degree in public administration or closely related field.

**Funds Avail.:** $27,851 salary plus comprehensive benefits. **No. of Awards:** 3. **To Apply:** Applications must be requested. To obtain an application write Management Intern Search, 135 N 2nd Ave., Phoenix, AZ 85003 or call (602)262-6277. **Deadline:** Recruitment begins in mid-November. Applications must be postmarked no later than January 26.

**Remarks:** This is a municipal apprenticeship program that does not award financial assistance or scholarships. **Contact:** Andrea Tevlin, Budget and Research Director, at the above address (see entry 4932)for applications.

---

## • 4934 •
## Phoenix Indian Medical Center Auxiliary
4212 N. 16th St.                         *Ph:* (602)263-1576
Phoenix, AZ 85016                        *Fax:* (602)263-1699

### • 4935 • Indian Health Career Awards *(Doctorate, Graduate, Undergraduate/Scholarship)*

**Purpose:** To encourage Indian students to pursue careers in health-related fields. **Focus:** Health Sciences, Health Care Services, Medicine. **Qualif.:** Candidates must be Native American Indian students who are already studying in a health-related field. **Criteria:** Grades and financial need are considered.

**Funds Avail.:** Awards are up to $700. The number of awards is dependent on available funds. **No. of Awards:** Varies. **Deadline:** July 15 for fall; November 15 for spring. **Contact:** The Phoenix Indian Medical Auxiliary at the above address (see entry 4934).

---

## • 4936 •
## Physician Assistant Foundation of the American Academy of Physician Assistants
c/o Barbara Shahbaz, Development
  Coordinator
950 N. Washington St.                    *Ph:* (703)836-2272
Alexandria, VA 22314                     *Fax:* (703)684-1924
*URL:* http://www.aapa.org

### • 4937 • Physician Assistant Foundation Annual Scholarship Program *(Undergraduate/Scholarship)*

**Focus:** Physician assistant. **Qualif.:** Applicants must be currently enroled in a CAAHEP/CAHEA accredited program and a member of the AAPA. **Criteria:** Awards are granted based on financial need, academic status as a PA, career goals and extra-curricular activities.

**Funds Avail.:** $90,000 to $110,000. **No. of Awards:** 35-45. **To Apply:** Write for further details. **Deadline:** February 1. **Contact:** PA Foundation.

---

## • 4938 •
## Physician Manpower Training Commission
1140 Northwest 63rd St., Ste. 302        *Ph:* (405)843-5667
Oklahoma City, OK 73116                  *Fax:* (405)843-5792
*E-mail:* pmtc@oklaosf.state.ok.us

### • 4939 • Oklahoma Resident Rural Scholarship Loans *(Doctorate/Scholarship loan)*

**Purpose:** To provide financial assistance to residents enrolled in an accredited Family Practice or Family Medicine Residency Program in Oklahoma. **Qualif.:** Applicants must be currently enrolled in an accredited Oklahoma Family Practice or General Practice program and have no other conflicting service obligations. Recipients must select and match with a participating rural community within 12 months of joining the program and spend one month during each of the second and third year of residency on elective rotation in the selected community. They must also return to the community upon completion of residency training at least one month for each month the loan was received for a minimum of 12 months. If the physician does not fulfill the service obligation, repayment must be made of the principal amount plus interest and a penalty of up to 100 percent of the principal. **Criteria:** Provide financial assistance to residents

## Physician Manpower Training Commission *(continued)*

enrolled in an accredited Family Practice or Family Medicine Residency Program. Interviews are not required.

**Funds Avail.:** $1,000 per month. **No. of Awards:** Varies. **To Apply:** Resident would need to apply during the first or second year of FP Residency training.

**Remarks:** FP resident cannot match with the metropolitan statistical areas of Oklahoma City or Tulsa. **Contact:** Jim Bishop and Charlotte Jiles at the above address (see entry 4938).

### • 4940 • Oklahoma Rural Medical Education Scholarship Loans *(Doctorate/Scholarship loan)*

**Purpose:** To assist Oklahoma's rural communities with populations of 7,500 or less and to provide financial assistance to residents attending medical or osteopathic colleges. **Focus:** Primary Care Medicine. **Qualif.:** Applicants must be residents of Oklahoma and currently enrolled in or accepted at a medical or osteopathic college. They must practice in an Oklahoma community with a population of less than 7,500 for one year of each year of scholarship loans received, providing a minimum of two years of service. Students entering a residency program other than in primary care must repay three times the principal and accrued interest will be due immediately. If the physician decides not to repay his/her obligated scholarship loan by practicing medicine in rural Oklahoma, he/she will be required to repay three times the principal amount, plus interest in accordance with the terms of the contract. Recipients must also plan to do an internship/residency in a primary care speciality and have no other conflicting service obligations. **Criteria:** A screening panel interviews the applicant and spouse if applicable. Scholarship awards are competitive since the amount of appropriated funding is limited.

**Funds Avail.:** Loans are made in the amounts of $6,000 for the first year of medical or osteopathic school, and $12,000 for each second, third, and fourth year. Payments are made monthly. **No. of Awards:** Overall 16 yearly. **To Apply:** Applications are mailed each January. Three letters of recommendation and a photo are to be attached to the completed application. **Deadline:** March 31. **Contact:** Jim Bishop and Charlotte Jiles at the above address (see entry 4938).

### • 4941 •
## Pi Lambda Theta - Intl. Honor and Professional Assoc. in Education
4101 E. 3rd St.
PO Box 6626
Bloomington, IN 47407-6626
URL: http://www.pilambda.org/

Ph: (812)339-3411
Fax: (812)339-3462

### • 4942 • Pi Lambda Theta Distinguished Student Scholar Award *(Undergraduate/Scholarship)*

**Focus:** Education. **Qualif.:** Applicants must be education majors who are at least second-semester sophomores with a grade point average of 3.5 or better on a 4.0 scale. Applicants belonging to a chapter must have their nomination endorsed by the chapter. **Criteria:** Selection is based on leadership potential, dedication to the future of education, and contributions to local/national/international endeavors, including volunteer work, committee work, and leadership appointments or elections.

**Funds Avail.:** $500 scholarship, an unframed certificate, and one year's paid membership in Pi Lambda Theta. Scholarship is presented every other year. **No. of Awards:** 1. **To Apply:** Applicants must be nominated by a college instructor with a written recommendation discussing the selection criteria in detail. Applicants must complete a nomination form, and send their

resume, transcripts, and letters of recommendation from two additional faculty members. **Deadline:** November in even-numbered years. Winners are selected in February and the award is presented in the month of August in odd-numbered years. **Contact:** Pi Lambda Theta at the above address (see entry 4941).

### • 4943 • Pi Lambda Theta Graduate Student Scholar Award *(Graduate/Scholarship)*

**Focus:** Education. **Qualif.:** Applicants must be education majors who have completed at least 12 semester credit hours, or the equivalent, of graduate work toward their graduate degree, with a grade point average of 3.5 or better on a 4.0 scale on all undergraduate work and a grade point average of 3.75 or better on all graduate work. Applicants may not be current Pi Lambda Theta Board members or Trustees. **Criteria:** Selection is based on moral character, service at the local/regional/international level which enhances the educational community, including volunteer work, committee work, or positions of leadership, and unique performance for the betterment of the applicant's chosen discipline.

**Funds Avail.:** $1,000 scholarship, an unframed certificate, and one year's paid membership in Pi Lambda Theta. The scholarship is presented every other year. **No. of Awards:** 1. **To Apply:** Applicants must be nominated by any member or chapter of Pi Lambda Theta, or by a college instructor, with a written recommendation discussing the selection criteria in detail. Applicants must complete a nomination form and a written statement discussing their qualifications in relation to the selection criteria. Applicants must send three additional letters of recommendation, their current transcripts, and transcripts from the college where they received their most recent degree. **Deadline:** November in even-numbered years. Winners are selected in February and the award is presented in the month of August in odd-numbered years.

**Remarks:** The award money is to be used solely for books, tuition, or other education materials. Receipts are to be sent to the International Office of Pi Lambda Theta within one year of receiving the award. **Contact:** Pi Lambda Theta at the above address (see entry 4941).

### • 4944 •
## Pickett & Hatcher Educational Fund, Inc.
PO Box 8169
Columbus, GA 31908

Ph: (706)327-6586
Fax: (706)324-6788
Free: 800-864-8308

E-mail: applications@phef.org
URL: http://www.phef.org

### • 4945 • Pickett & Hatcher Educational Loans *(Undergraduate/Loan)*

**Focus:** General Studies, Baccalaureate Degree. **Qualif.:** Applicants must be U.S. citizens and legal residents of Alabama, Florida, Georgia, Kentucky, Mississippi, North Carolina, South Carolina, Tennessee, or Virginia. They must be, or plan to be, enrolled in a college or university offering a broad, liberal, undergraduate education, and located in one of the aforementioned southeastern states. This means that the applicant's course of study must include a substantial number of regular academic degree courses in English, natural and social sciences, mathematics, and history. A loan cannot be made to candidates enrolled in a developmental or remedial studies program, a vocational or technical school or a two-year college, or to those planning to enter the professions of law, medicine, or the ministry. Applicants must be of good moral character, in sound health, and possess good citizenship. **Criteria:** Consideration is given to applicants who are limited by financial resources to the point that a college education cannot be obtained without a loan. Consideration is also given to applicant's attitude, seriousness of purpose, industry, academic achievement and ability, initiative, determination, reliability, and cooperation. Minimum SAT scores of 950 or ACT scores of 20 are required.

**Funds Avail.:** Maximum of $5,500 per academic year. Cumulative loan maximum is $22,000. The loan may be applied toward tuition, fees, food, and room rent. Interest accrues at the rate of two percent per annum while enrolled in college for the required academic load. The rate advances to six percent per annum upon graduation or if the recipient ceases to be enrolled for the required load. The interest advances to six percent if the recipient makes plans to enter the professions of law, medicine, or the ministry. A credit-worthy person of legal age must be approved as an endorser. **No. of Awards:** 450-500. **To Apply:** A formal application is required. First-time applicants must send official high school transcripts, official transcripts from each college or university attended, and if entering a college or university for the first time, a photocopy of an official admissions acceptance statement. If transcripts do not include ACT or SAT college entrance scores, arrangements should be made to have the scores sent. **Deadline:** Varies.

**Remarks:** Recipients are required to earn 12 or more hours of regular academic credit during each quarter or semester. **Contact:** Pickett & Hatcher Educational Fund at the above address (see entry 4944).

• **4946** •
**Pike Institute on Law and Disability**
Boston University Law School
765 Commonwealth Ave.          Ph: (617)353-2904
Boston, MA 02215               Fax: (617)353-2906
E-mail: pikeinst@bu.edu

• **4947** • **N. Neal Pike Prize for Service to People with Disabilities** (Other/Prize)

**Focus:** General studies. **Qualif.:** Applicants must me individuals who, despite a physical or mental disability, have achieved notable success, or to able-bodied persons or organizations that have been of great service to people with disabilities.

**Funds Avail.:** Varies. **No. of Awards:** 1 per year. **To Apply:** Applicants are nominated. **Deadline:** Varies, usually around September 1. **Contact:** H.A. Beyer.

• **4948** •
**Pipe Line Contractors Association of Canada**
775 St. Andrews Rd.
W. Vancouver, BC, Canada V7F 1V5    Ph: (604)925-2520

• **4949** • **Cal Callahan Memorial Bursary** (Undergraduate/Scholarship)

**Qualif.:** Applicants must be beginning undergraduate students who are sons, daughters, or legal wards of persons who derive their principal income from the pipeline industry and whose employers are members of the Association.

**Funds Avail.:** A total of $2,000 is awarded each year. **Contact:** The Pipeline Contractors Association of Canada at the above address (see entry 4948).

• **4950** •
**Minnie Stevens Piper Foundation**
GPM South Tower, Ste. 200-S
800 NW Loop 410               Ph: (210)525-8494
San Antonio, TX 78216-5699    Fax: (210)341-6627

• **4951** • **Minnie Stevens Piper Foundation Student Loan** (Graduate, Undergraduate/Loan)

**Focus:** General Studies. **Qualif.:** Candidates must be U.S. citizens and Texas residents, attending Texas colleges/universities on a full-time basis, and classified by the registrar as junior, senior, or graduate students. Financial need must be established by a college/university financial aid officer.

**Funds Avail.:** Per-semester amounts are from $1,000 for undergraduates and $2,000 for graduates, with a maximum amount of $10,000 available to any one student. Interest is at the rate of six percent per annum, compounded annually. Loans are made on a semester-to-semester basis. Re-application must be made for each semester. Loans are due and payable one year after graduation by lump-sum repayment or four-year installment schedule. Loans are covered by note and may be renewed. **To Apply:** Applicants must submit a completed application form and references. **Contact:** The Student Loan Department at the above address (see entry 4950).

• **4952** •
**Pittsburgh New Music Ensemble, Inc.**
Duquesne University School of
  Music                       Ph: (412)261-0554
Pittsburgh, PA 15282-1803     Fax: (412)396-5479

• **4953** • **Harvey Gaul Composition Contest** (Professional Development/Award)

**Purpose:** To promote new music compositions. **Focus:** Music Composition. **Qualif.:** Applicants must be U.S. citizens. Applicants must send a score and cassette of a work for chamber ensemble (five players and up) or orchestra and a current biography.

**Funds Avail.:** $3,000. **No. of Awards:** 1. **To Apply:** Write for entry form and guidelines. Submit form, sealed in a separate envelope, with composition and entry fee ($20). Competition is held in even-numbered years. **Deadline:** Varies; usually in April. **Contact:** Eva Tumiel-Kozak, Executive Director, at the above address (see entry 4952).

• **4954** •
**Planned Parenthood Federation of Canada**
1 Nicholas St., Ste. 430      Ph: (613)241-4474
Ottawa, ON, Canada K1N 7B7    Fax: (613)241-7550

• **4955** • **Norman Barwin Scholarships** (Graduate/Scholarship)

**Purpose:** To encourage and support graduate studies in reproductive health. **Focus:** Human Reproduction **Qualif.:** Applicants must be Canadian citizens or landed immigrants. They must also hold an honors degree or its equivalent from a recognized university, and intend to pursue a graduate degree in a field related to reproductive health, such as biology, Canadian studies, education, history, medicine, political science, psychology, social work, sociology, or women's studies. Scholarships are tenable at Canadian universities.

*Planned Parenthood Federation of*
*Canada (continued)*

**Funds Avail.:** $2,500 **No. of Awards:** 1. **To Apply:** Write for application guidelines; there is no official form. Submit transcripts, names of two referees, and a 500- to 700-word essay describing education and background in health/women's issues. Referees must submit letters of support directly to the Scholarship Committee. **Deadline:** April 1. The awardee will be notified by June 30. **Contact:** Planned Parenthood Federation of Canada at the above address (see entry 4954).

### • 4956 • Phyllis P. Harris Scholarships *(All/ Scholarship)*

**Purpose:** To encourage and support studies in family planning or population issues. **Focus:** Family Planning. **Qualif.:** Applicants must be Canadian citizens or landed immigrants who have worked or volunteered in the general field of human sexuality who intend to work for a degree in the field of family planning or population issues. The field is broadly defined to include aspects of biology, education, history, medicine, political science, psychology, international studies, or sociology.

**Funds Avail.:** $2,500. **No. of Awards:** 1. **To Apply:** Applicants should submit by the deadline a typed essay of about 500 words, outlining relevant background education, objectives, and plans for the future. The applicant's name, address, and telephone number should appear at the top of the application, as well as the names, addresses, and telephone numbers of two referees who have been asked to support the applicant. Referees should send their supporting letters to the office of Planned Parenthood Federation of Canada. **Deadline:** Applicants must be received April 1. Recipients are notified by June 30. **Contact:** Phyllis Harris Scholarship Committee at the above address (see entry 4954).

### • 4957 •
## Plastic Surgery Educational Foundation

444 East Algonquin Road      *Ph:* (708)228-9900
Arlington Heights, IL 60005      *Fax:* (708)228-9131

### • 4958 • Plastic Surgery Educational Foundation Scholarships *(Professional Development/Prize, Scholarship)*

**Purpose:** To recognize outstanding original work in plastic and reconstructive surgery, and to support future research projects by the authors. **Focus:** Plastic and Reconstructive Surgery. **Qualif.:** Candidates may be of any nationality and must describe an original research project related to plastic and reconstructive surgery. Scholarships are given in two categories: basic science and clinical research for a junior winner and senior winner. One prize will be offered in an essay category. Manuscripts submitted in the essay category will focus on theory, history, ethics, and socioeconomic issues related to the art and science of plastic and reconstructive surgery. First, second, and third prizes will be offered in the investigator category. Scholarships should be applied to new research projects. **Criteria:** Criteria for judging is originality, value to plastic surgery, methodology, depth and completeness, organization, clarity, artistry, and neatness of the presentation.

**Funds Avail.:** Varies, according to category. **No. of Awards:** 8. **To Apply:** Write to the Society for application guidelines. **Deadline:** March 1. **Contact:** Scholarship Contest Committee at the above address (see entry 4957).

### • 4959 •
## Plastics Institute of America

University Massachusetts Lowell
333 Aiken St.      *Ph:* (508)934-3130
Lowell, MA 01854-3686      *Fax:* (508)459-9420
*E-mail:* pia@cae.uml.edu
*URL:* http://www.eng.uml.edu/Dept/PIA

### • 4960 • Plastic Pioneers Association Scholarships *(Undergraduate/Scholarship)*

**Purpose:** To assist students pursuing two-year or four-year degrees in plastics technology at U.S. universities and colleges. **Focus:** Plastics Processing, Testing, Mold Making. **Qualif.:** Applicants must be U.S. citizens with strong interests in plastics industry. **Criteria:** Selections are based on grade point averages, recommendations of student advisors, and letters from students on their interests in plastics.

**Funds Avail.:** Approximately ten scholarships of $1,500 each. **No. of Awards:** 20. **To Apply:** Application forms and submission requirements may be obtained from the Plastics Institute of America. Applications must come from the school and school advisor. **Deadline:** April 1. **Contact:** Aldo Crugnola, Plastics Institute of America, at the above address (see entry 4959).

### • 4961 •
## The Playwrights' Center

2301 Franklin Ave., E.      *Ph:* (612)332-7481
Minneapolis, MN 55406-1099      *Fax:* (612)332-6037
*E-mail:* pwcenter@mtn.org
*URL:* http://www.pwcenter.org

### • 4962 • Jerome Playwright-in-Residence Fellowships *(Professional Development/Fellowship)*

**Purpose:** To provide emerging playwrights with funds and services to help them develop their craft. **Focus:** Playwriting. **Qualif.:** Applicant must be a U.S. citizen or permanent resident. Applicant must be a playwright who has not had more than two different works fully produced by professional theaters. Fellowships are tenable at the Center.

**Funds Avail.:** $7,000 is available. **No. of Awards:** 5 annually. **To Apply:** Applicants should send a self-addressed, stamped envelope for application guidelines. **Deadline:** Materials should be in by September 15 (approximate). Fellowships are announced around January 15.

**Remarks:** The Center also offers four to six awards for playwrights to attend its annual summer workshop conference, the PlayLabs. Write for further information.

### • 4963 • McKnight Advancement Grants *(Professional Development/Grant)*

**Purpose:** To recognize playwrights whose work demonstrates exceptional artistic merit and potential and to significantly advance recipients' art and careers. **Focus:** Playwriting **Qualif.:** Applicants must be citizens or permanent residents of the United States and legal residents of Minnesota since August 1 of the year the grant is awarded. They must have had a minimum of one different work fully produced by a professional theater. Applicants must not have received a McKnight Advancement Grant from the Playwrights' Center, nor can they receive any other Playwrights' Center fellowships or grants during the grant year. Applicants may apply to more than one of the seven organizations offering fellowships that are supported by McKnight Foundation funds; however, they may not receive more than $45,000 in McKnight Foundation fellowship support in any three year period. Fellows participate actively in the Center's outreach or educational programming (at least 20 hours), including teaching classes, artist-in-the-schools residencies, and serving as a mentor and they must designate two months out of the grant year to participate actively in Center programs, including mandatory weekly attendance and critical participation in readings or workshops of other members' work.

**Funds Avail.:** Three advancement grants of $8,500. Additional funds of up to $1,500 per grant recipient are available for workshops and staged readings using the Center's developmental program or may be designated to a partner organization for joint development and/or production purposes anywhere in the world. **No. of Awards:** 3 annually. **To Apply:** Only submissions received with completed application materials will be accepted. Applications are available December 1. Applicants should send a SASE. **Deadline:** All application materials and an envelope with postage for return of the manuscript must be postmarked by February 1. Recipients are announced by May 1.

**Remarks:** These grants are funded by the McKnight Foundation Arts Funding Plan.

## • 4964 • McKnight Fellowships (Professional Development/Fellowship)

**Purpose:** To provide support to American playwrights whose work has made a significant impact on contemporary theater. **Focus:** Contemporary Theater (Playwriting). **Qualif.:** Applicant must be a U.S. citizen and have had a minimum of two different works fully produced by professional theaters. Fellows must spend one month or more in residence at the Center during the fellowship year (July 1 through June 30).

**Funds Avail.:** $10,000 is available, plus $2,000 for workshops and readings while in residence. **No. of Awards:** 2 annually. **To Apply:** By nomination only. **Deadline:** Materials should be in by January 15 (approximate). Fellowships are announced April 15 (approximate).

**Remarks:** The Center also offers four to six awards for playwrights to attend its annual summer workshop conference, PlayLabs. Write for further information. **Contact:** The Playwrights' Center at the above address (see entry 4961).

## • 4965 • Playwrights' Center PlayLabs (Professional Development/Other)

**Purpose:** To serve playwrights and their plays. **Focus:** Playwriting. **Qualif.:** Applicants must be citizens or permanent residents of the United States. Submitted scripts must be unproduced and unpublished. Participants are required to attend of the Conference and Pre-conference Weekend. The Conference is scheduled in August, and the Pre-Conference Weekend is in May/June. **Criteria:** Scripts will be selected by an independent panel of three nationally recognized playwrights.

**Funds Avail.:** Four or more selected writers will receive 30 to 40 hours of workshop time to explore, refine, and test their scripts with their choice of distinguished directors, dramaturgs, and a professional company of actors. The recipients will be awarded honoraria, travel expenses, and room and board. **No. of Awards:** 4 to 6. **To Apply:** Only submissions received with completed application materials will be accepted. Applications are available October 15. Send a self-addressed stamped envelope for application, or a check for a $40 Playwright Membership . **Deadline:** All application materials must be postmarked by December 15. Final selections are announced by May 1.

**Remarks:** Playlabs is sponsored by the Playwrights' Center in association with the University of Minnesota Department of Theater Arts and Dance. **Contact:** The Playwrights' Center, at the above address (see entry 4961).

## • 4966 •
## PNC Bank

Trust Department
222 Delaware Ave.
Wilmington, DE 19899-0791
*URL:* http://www.eduloans.pncbank.com/Homepage.html

*Ph:* (302)429-1186
*Fax:* (302)429-5658
*Free:* 800-722-1172

## • 4967 • H. Fletcher Brown Scholarship (Doctorate, Graduate, Undergraduate/Scholarship)

**Purpose:** To provide Delaware residents with financial assistance for study in the fields of chemistry, engineering, dentistry, law, or medicine. **Focus:** Chemistry, Engineering, Dentistry, Law, or Medicine. **Qualif.:** Candidates must be natives of the state of Delaware (born in Deleware) of "good moral character" who have graduated from a Delaware high school or secondary school, or a college in or out of state. They must be able to demonstrate that financial assistance outside the family is necessary. Study must lead to a degree that will enable the applicant to practice in the fields of chemistry, engineering, dentistry, law, or medicine. **Criteria:** Candidates are judged on grades, test scores, financial statement, and personal interview.

**Funds Avail.:** Varies. **No. of Awards:** Varies. **To Apply:** New applications available each February. **Deadline:** Mid April. **Contact:** Donald W. Davin, Senior, Trust Officer, at the above address (see entry 4966).

## • 4968 •
## Poetry Center of the 92nd St. Y - "Discovery"/The Nation

1395 Lexington Ave.
New York, NY 10128
*URL:* http://echonyc.com:70/1/Cul/Uberg

*Ph:* (212)415-5759

## • 4969 • Discovery/The Nation Contest; The Joan Leiman Jacobson Poetry Prizes (Professional Development/Prize)

**Purpose:** To recognize unpublished poets. **Focus:** Poetry. **Qualif.:** Candidate may be of any nationality. Applicant must not have previously published a book of poetry, including chapbooks and self-published works. Single poems which have been previously published elsewhere may be submitted. All poems must be original and in English, no translations. The submission must comply with application procedures and may not exceed 500 lines in length. Winning poems will be published in *The Nation* and read at the Center.

**Funds Avail.:** $300. **No. of Awards:** 4. **To Apply:** Write to the Center for application guidelines. Submit four identical sets of the ten-page manuscript with a cover letter. Biographical information is not necessary. **Deadline:** Late January.

**Remarks:** Applicants must note their day and evening telephone numbers or their manuscript will not be processed. No personal identification may appear on any of the poems. No phone queries please.

• 4970 •

## Polaroid Foundation

549 Technology Sq.
Cambridge, MA 02139          *Ph:* (617)386-2000

### • 4971 • Polaroid Foundation National Merit Scholarship *(Undergraduate/Scholarship)*

**Focus:** General studies. **Qualif.:** Applicants must be children of employees of the Polaroid Corporation. **To Apply:** Write for further details. **Contact:** Polaroid Foundation at the above address (see entry 4970).

• 4972 •

## Polish Music Reference Center

University of Southern California
School of Music
840 W. 34th St.          *Ph:* (213)740-9369
Los Angeles, CA 90089-0851          *Fax:* (818)509-8435
*E-mail:* polmusic@usc.edu
*URL:* http://www.usc.edu/go/polish_music/

### • 4973 • Stefan and Wanda Wilk Prizes for Research in Polish Music *(All/Prize)*

**Purpose:** To stimulate research on Polish music in academic circles outside of Poland. **Focus:** Polish Music. **Qualif.:** Applicants may be students or musicologists from any nation except Poland. Prizes are awarded to the authors of the best unpublished papers reflecting original research on some aspect of the music of Poland or its composers. Students are judged separately. Essays must be written in English, and be of suitable length for publication in a scholarly journal.

**Funds Avail.:** Student category: $500; musicologist category: $1,000. **To Apply:** Write to the Center for competition rules and submission guidelines. **Deadline:** September 30. Notification by the end of December. **Contact:** Bruce Brown, Chair, at the above address (see entry 4972).

• 4974 •

## Pollock-Krasner Foundation, Inc.

725 Park Ave.          *Ph:* (212)517-5400
New York, NY 10021-5025          *Fax:* (212)288-2836
*E-mail:* grants@pkf.org
*URL:* http://www.pkf.org

### • 4975 • Pollock-Krasner Grants *(Professional Development/Grant)*

**Purpose:** To assist painters, sculptors, and printmakers with personal and professional expenses. **Focus:** Painting, Printmaking, Sculpture. **Qualif.:** Candidate may be of any nationality. Applicant must be a working professional painter, printmaker, or sculptor. Students, commercial artists, photographers, video artists, filmmakers, performance artists, and craft-makers are ineligible. Grants are offered for work, medical, and personal living expenses and for catastrophic emergency assistance. The Foundation also considers applications from artists applying to colonies who will need financial help beyond what a colony can offer. The Foundation does not ordinarily award travel grants, nor does it make grants to pay for past debts; legal fees; the purchase of real estate; moves to other cities; or the cost of installations, commissions, or projects ordered by others.

**Funds Avail.:** $1,000-30,000. **To Apply:** Write to the Foundation for application guidelines. **Deadline:** None. Candidates are notified three to nine months after application. **Contact:** Charles C. Bergman, Executive Vice President, at the above address (see entry 4974).

• 4976 •

## Poncin Scholarship Fund

c/o Seattle-First National Bank
Charitable Trust, Administration
PO Box 3586
Seattle, WA 98124          *Ph:* (206)442-3388

### • 4977 • Poncin Scholarship Fund *(Graduate, Postdoctorate/Scholarship)*

**Purpose:** To assist young people engaged in advanced medical research in the state of Washington. **Focus:** Medical research. **Qualif.:** Applicant must be conducting advanced medical research at a learning institution in the state of Washington. Preference for individual with an MD. **Criteria:** Proposals will be reviewed by a medical board for scientific merit, stated goals, student capability to accomplish goal.

**Funds Avail.:** $15,600. **No. of Awards:** 3. **To Apply:** Write for application form. **Deadline:** May 1. **Contact:** Jennifer Sorensen.

• 4978 •

## Pontifical Institute of Mediaeval Studies

59 Queen's Park Crescent E.          *Ph:* (416)926-7142
Toronto, ON, Canada M5S 2C4          *Fax:* (416)926-7292
*E-mail:* jeanette.jardine@utoronto.ca
*URL:* http://www.ehass.utoronto.ca:8080/~pontifex/ newindex/html

### • 4979 • Pontifical Institute of Mediaeval Studies Research Associateships *(Postdoctorate/Award)*

**Purpose:** To support postdoctoral scholars who wish to use the Institute collections for research. **Focus:** Medieval Studies. **Qualif.:** Candidates may be of any nationality but must have received a Ph.D., or equivalent degree, during the five years prior to application. Candidates must also be conducting a project appropriate to research at the Institute library. **Criteria:** Applicants must demonstrate outstanding promise.

**Funds Avail.:** $40,000 each. **No. of Awards:** 4. **To Apply:** Write to the President's office for application guidelines. **Deadline:** January 15. Notification by February 28.

**Remarks:** Council of the Institute Bursaries and Scholarships are also available to junior associates of the Institute who need support to continue research in medieval studies. Write to the secretary for further information. **Contact:** Secretary at the above address (see entry 4978).

## • 4980 •
### Population Council - Fellowship Program in the Social Sciences, PRD

1 Dag Hammarskjold Plz.      *Ph:* (212)339-0671
New York, NY 10017-2201      *Fax:* (212)755-6052
*E-mail:* jlam@popcouncil.org
*URL:* http://www.popcouncil.org

### • 4981 • Population Council Fellowships in the Social Sciences *(Postdoctorate/Fellowship)*

**Purpose:** To support advanced training or research related to population studies. **Focus:** Anthropology, Demography, Economics, Public Health, Sociology. **Qualif.:** Candidate may be of any nationality but strong preference is given to applicants from developing nations who have a firm commitment to return to their home countries upon completion of the proposed fellowship. Applicant must have completed all course work toward a Ph.D. in the social sciences. Awards are open to persons who wish to undertake postdoctoral training and research at an institution other than the one at which he/she completed the Ph.D. Awards are open to person with at least five years of professional experience in the population field and wish to undertake training and study to update his/her skills. Fellowships are tenable at any research or training institution with a strong program in population studies. **Criteria:** Fellowships are awarded based on academic excellence, suitability of proposed research to the population field and prospective support by the proposed visititation.

**Funds Avail.:** Stipend, transportation expenses for fellows only, and health insurance. **No. of Awards:** 19. **To Apply:** Write to the fellowship assistant for application guidelines or download them from the website. Submit a letter of application, including a brief description of academic, and professional qualifications, and short statement about the research or study plans for the proposed fellowship period. (No attachments required). **Deadline:** December 15. Notification in March. **Contact:** Jude H. Lam, Fellowship Coordinator, at the above address (see entry 4980).

## • 4982 •
### Portuguese Continental Union of the USA - Scholarship Committee

899 Boylston St.      *Ph:* (617)536-2916
Boston, MA 02115-3114      *Fax:* (617)536-8301

### • 4983 • Portuguese Continental Union Scholarships *(Undergraduate/Scholarship)*

**Focus:** General Studies. **Qualif.:** Applicants must have been members of the Portuguese Continental Union of the USA for at least one year. They must also be enrolled or plan to enroll at an accredited college or university. **Criteria:** Selection is based on character, academic record, recommendations, student's own statement, scholastic aptitude test scores, and financial need. **To Apply:** Applicants must submit a completed application and membership documentation. They will then receive a biographical questionnaire and secondary school report to be filled out by authorities at the secondary school or college attended. **Deadline:** February 15. **Contact:** Scholarship Committee at the above address (see entry 4982).

## • 4984 •
### Leslie T. Posey and Frances U. Posey Foundation

1800 Second St., Ste. 750      *Ph:* (941)957-0442
Sarasota, FL 34236      *Fax:* (941)957-3135

### • 4985 • Posey Foundation Graduate Art Scholarships *(Graduate/Scholarship)*

**Purpose:** To provide graduate students interested in painting or sculpture of the traditional kind with scholarships. **Focus:** Painting, Sculpture. **Qualif.:** Applicants must be full-time art students majoring in either painting or sculpture of the "traditional kind," and must have completed their bachelors degree or its equivalent prior to receiving the scholarship. Evidence of acceptance at a college or university must be presented to the Foundation before distribution of funds can be made. **Criteria:** Scholarships are given based on the quality of applicants' works.

**Funds Avail.:** Scholarships range from $1,000 to $4,000. **To Apply:** Applicants must provide four copies of the completed application, an official transcript of undergraduate studies, three letters of recommendation from recognized artists familiar with applicants' work, and a minimum of ten to a maximum of 20 color slides showing work completed in the last two years. The slides must represent at least five different works for the sculptor, or ten paintings, or a combination of ten different sculptures and paintings. The media, dimensions, and date of completion of the art work must be clearly marked on each slide. In addition, applicants must also submit three one-page essays (four copies of each) responding to the following topics: my definition of traditional art and how I feel about it; my personal goals; and why I chose the above college for the continuation of my studies. **Deadline:** March 1. Recipients will be notified on or before May 1.

**Remarks:** Scholarship recipients must provide a four-month progress report to the foundation and, an instructor's statement describing students' progress. The second half of the grant distribution will depend on receipt of these reports, both of which must indicate satisfactory progress. **Contact:** Debra Jacobs at the above address (see entry 4984).

## • 4986 •
### Potlatch Foundation for Higher Education

PO Box 193591
San Francisco, CA 94119-3591      *Ph:* (510)947-4725

### • 4987 • Potlatch Foundation for Higher Education Scholarships *(Undergraduate/Scholarship)*

**Purpose:** To assist students pursuing higher education. **Qualif.:** Candidates must live within 30 miles of Potlatch Corporation facilities in Arkansas, Idaho or Minnesota. They must be high school seniors or undergraduate students currently attending an accredited higher education institution. **Criteria:** The trustees of the Foundation select scholarship award recipients primarily on the basis of character, leadership qualities, scholastic achievement and ability, and financial need.

**Funds Avail.:** Award amounts are determined by the trustees and may be renewed. **No. of Awards:** 70. **To Apply:** Applicants must request an information packet between October 1 and December 15. A return envelope should not be included in the request. Applicants must also submit high school grade transcripts, ACT or SAT test results, a confidential report from a principal or counselor, and two confidential letters of reference. The Foundation will send renewal applications to undergraduate recipients who are maintaining satisfactory academic progress. Renewal applicants must also submit official transcripts. **Deadline:** All materials must be received in one complete package on or before February 15. **Contact:** Potlatch Foundation for Higher Education at the above address (see entry 4986).

## • 4988 •
**Preferred Hotels Association**
1901 S. Meyers Rd.                    *Ph:* (630)953-0404
Oakbrook Terrace, IL 60181-5243       *Fax:* (630)953-0176

### • 4989 • Edwin P. Shaunessy Memorial Scholarships
*(Graduate/Scholarship)*

**Focus:** Hospitality Services. **Qualif.:** Applicants should be students who have served an internship or have been employed by a member of Preferred Hotels, entering their senior year of college, and who are otherwise ineligible for financial assistance. **Criteria:** Mrs. Shaunessy or her son will select the recipient.

**Funds Avail.:** Annual amount averages $3,200. **To Apply:** Applications may be obtained from the Director of Admissions, Financial Aid & Student Records, Cornell University, Ithaca, New York.

**Remarks:** The scholarship was established to honor the memory of the late Edwin P. Shaunessy, the first president of Preferred Hotels & Resorts Worldwide. **Contact:** Preferred Hotels Association at the above address (see entry 4988).

## • 4990 •
**Presbyterian Church (U.S.A.)**
Office of Financial Aid for Studies
100 Witherspoon St.                   *Ph:* (502)569-5745
Louisville, KY 40202-1396             *Fax:* (502)569-8766
*E-mail:* tim_mccallister.parti@ecunet.org
*URL:* http://198.70.54.2/

### • 4991 • National Presbyterian College Scholarships
*(Undergraduate/Scholarship)*

**Purpose:** To aid high school seniors preparing to enter a Presbyterian-related college. **Focus:** General Studies. **Qualif.:** Candidates must be confirmed members of the Presbyterian Church (U.S.A.) who are United States citizens or permanent residents. They must be high school seniors who are preparing to enter one of the participating colleges related to the Presbyterian Church (U.S.A.) as full-time incoming freshmen. Applicants also must demonstrate financial need. Additional qualifications are listed in the application brochure that becomes available each September 1. In general they relate to superior academic and personal qualities, and service to the community.

**Funds Avail.:** Depending upon need and availability of funds, scholarships range from $100 to $1,400 an academic year. **No. of Awards:** 185. **Deadline:** December 1 of the candidate's senior year in high school. **Contact:** Kathy Smith at the above address (see entry 4990).

### • 4992 • Native American Education Grants
*(Graduate, Undergraduate/Grant)*

**Focus:** General Studies. **Qualif.:** Candidates must be Alaskan natives or Native American pursuing full-time post-secondary education. They also must be members of the Presbyterian Church, US citizens or permanent residents, high school graduates or GED holders, and in financial need.

**Funds Avail.:** Grants range from $200 to $1,500 annually depending on financial need and availability of funds. **No. of Awards:** 85. **To Apply:** Candidates must apply to their colleges for financial aid as well as filing an application with the Presbyterian Church (U.S.A.). **Deadline:** June 1. **Contact:** Marie Alvarez at the above address (see entry 4990).

### • 4993 • Native American Seminary Scholarships
*(Graduate/Scholarship)*

**Purpose:** To assist Native American graduate students preparing for professional church occupations in the Presbyterian Church. **Focus:** Presbyterian Theology. **Qualif.:** Applicant must be a U.S. citizen or permanent resident and be a Native American, Aleut, or Eskimo who is a communicant member of the Presbyterian Church (U.S.A.). Candidate must be a full-time seminary student; be enrolled in a program of Theological Education by Extension; or be employed in a professional Church occupation while pursuing a program of continuing education. Applicant should demonstrate a financial need that cannot be met through other loans, grants, scholarships, savings, and employment. Grants are tenable at schools and programs approved or administered by the Church.

**Funds Avail.:** $1,000-3,000. **To Apply:** Write to the Financial Aid for Studies Office for application materials. **Contact:** Tim McCallister, Associate, at the above address (see entry 4990).

### • 4994 • Presbyterian Church Native American Seminary Scholarships *(Graduate/Scholarship)*

**Focus:** Religion. **Qualif.:** Candidates are American Indians, Aleuts, and Eskimos who are certified by the candidate's presbytery or the Presbyterian Native American Consulting Committee. Applicants must be seminary students preparing for a church occupation and enrolled in a seminary fully accredited by the Association of Theological Schools in the United States and Canada. They may also be registered with, or under the care of, a presbytery and enrolled in a college program on Track 1 of the Native American Theological Association Program; or they may be members of the Presbyterian Church (U.S.A.) from a former UPCUSA congregation enrolled in a program of Theological Education by extension, such as the NATA Track III which is approved by a seminary fully accredited by the Association of Theological Schools in the United States and Canada. Candidates, ministers or members (former UPCUSA) in other church occupations pursuing an approved program of continuing education are also eligible.

**Funds Avail.:** The amount of the scholarship is determined by the Office of Financial Aid for Studies based upon recommendation by the student's Financial Officer, analysis of the applicant's financial needs, and other resources and available funds. **No. of Awards:** 60. **To Apply:** Candidates must first contact the Financial Aid Officer of the school or seminary they attend. The officer makes a recommendation to the Office of Financial Aid for Studies. **Contact:** College financial aid officers or Marie Alvarez, Office of Financial Aid for Studies, at the above address (see entry 4990).

### • 4995 • Presbyterian Church Student Loans
*(Graduate, Undergraduate/Loan)*

**Focus:** Religion. **Qualif.:** Candidates must be communicant members of the Presbyterian Church (U.S.A.) and United States citizens. They must be able to demonstrate financial need. Undergraduate applicants must be full-time candidates for a baccalaureate degree in good academic standing at a regionally accredited institution. Theological students must be under care of Presbytery for a church occupation, in good academic standing, enrolled full-time in regionally accredited institutions or in seminaries accredited by the Association of Theological Schools in the United States and Canada, and enrolled in a program approved by their Presbytery for the first professional degree. Christian Education students must plan to work within the Presbyterian Church (U.S.A.), and be in good academic standing at a regionally accredited institution or in a seminary accredited by the Association of Theological Schools in the United States and Canada. The school's financial aid officer must certify that the candidate is enrolled in a prescribed full-time program. Continuing Education applicants must be Presbyterian ministers or lay professionals in Church occupations with the Presbyterian Church (U.S.A.) and already hold the first professional degree. They must normally be enrolled on at least a half-time basis and taking prescribed courses of study that will maintain or improve their skills for church work.

**Funds Avail.:** Undergraduates $200-4000. Graduates $200-4,5000. **Contact:** Frances Cook, Office of Financial Aid for Studies, at the above address (see entry 4990).

## • 4996 • Presbyterian Church Student Opportunity Scholarships (Undergraduate/Scholarship)

**Purpose:** Designed to assist racial ethnic undergraduate students finance their undergraduate education. **Focus:** General Studies. **Qualif.:** Applicants must be Asian American, African American, Hispanic American, Native American, or Native Alaskan and members of the Presbyterian Church (U.S.A.). Candidates must be entering college as incoming full-time freshmen and must have applied to the college for financial aid. They must also be United States citizens or permanent residents and demonstrate financial need.

**Funds Avail.:** Scholarships range from $100 to $1,400 and are individually determined based on financial need and funds available. **Deadline:** April 1 of the candidate's senior year in high school.

**Remarks:** Program suspended for 1999-2000 academic year. **Contact:** Marie Alvarez, Student Opportunity Scholarships, at the above address (see entry 4990).

## • 4997 • Presbyterian Study Grants (Graduate/Grant)

**Purpose:** To assist graduate students preparing for professional church occupations in the Presbyterian Church. **Focus:** Presbyterian Theology. **Qualif.:** Applicant must be a U.S. citizen or permanent resident and a communicant member of the Presbyterian Church (U.S.A.). Candidate must be a full-time graduate student preparing for a professional career either within the Church or with an ecumenical agency in which the Church participates. Applicant should demonstrate a financial need that cannot be met through other loans, grants, scholarships, savings, and employment. Grants are tenable at U.S. and Canadian seminaries and theological institutions administered or approved by the Church. Funds are awarded for the first professional degree only, and are not available for doctoral study, summer terms, or internships.

**Funds Avail.:** $500-2,000. **To Apply:** Write to the Financial Aid for Studies Office for application materials, or contact school financial aid office. **Deadline:** None. **Contact:** Marie Alvarez, Associate, at the above address (see entry 4990).

## • 4998 • Racial/Ethnic Leadership Supplemental Grants (Graduate/Grant)

**Purpose:** To assist minority graduate students preparing for professional church occupations in the Presbyterian Church. **Focus:** Presbyterian Theology. **Qualif.:** Applicant must be a U.S. citizen or permanent resident and be an African American, Native Alaskan, Asian American, Hispanic American, or Native American who is a communicant member of the Presbyterian Church (U.S.A.). Candidate must be enrolled at least half-time in a graduate program which prepares him/her for a professional career with the Church. Applicant should demonstrate a financial need that cannot be met through other loans, grants, scholarships, savings, and employment. Grants are tenable at U.S. and Canadian seminaries and theological institutions administered or approved by the Church. Funds are awarded for the first professional degree only, and are not available for doctoral study, summer terms, or internships.

**Funds Avail.:** $500-1,000. **To Apply:** Write to the Financial Aid for Studies Office for application materials, or contact school financial aid office. Application forms must be submitted to the Church by the school financial aid officer on behalf of the candidate. **Contact:** Marie Alvarez, Associate, at the above address (see entry 4990). Information also available at http://www.collegeboard.org.

## • 4999 • Samuel Robinson Scholarships (Undergraduate/Scholarship)

**Focus:** General Studies. **Qualif.:** Applicants must be undergraduates junior or senior at one of the 69 colleges related to the Presbyterian Church (U.S.A.). They must be able to successfully recite the 107 answers of the Westminister Shorter Catechism and write a 2,000-word original essay on an assigned topic related to the Shorter Catechism.

**Funds Avail.:** $1,000. A scholarship may be received only once. **To Apply:** Students should contact the financial aid officer at their college for a description of the competition, which includes the essay topic. **Deadline:** April 1. **Contact:** Kathy Smith at the above address (see entry 4990)or college financial aid officers.

---

## • 5000 •
## President's Committee on Employment of People with Disabilities

1331 F St., NW       *Ph:* (202)376-6200
Washington, DC 20004-1107      *Fax:* (202)376-6859

## • 5001 • President's Committee on Employment of People with Disabilities Scholarships for Students with Disabilities (Undergraduate/Scholarship)

**Purpose:** To provide supplemental financial assistance to enable students with disabilities to pursue courses in higher education leading to business career opportunities. **Focus:** Business. **Qualif.:** Applicants must be current high school seniors or undergraduates at four-year colleges or universities who have documented disabilities.

**Funds Avail.:** $2,000 paid directly to the educational institution by Nordstrom to be used for tuition, room, and board. **No. of Awards:** 5. **To Apply:** Applicants must submit documentation verifying disability, letters of recommendation from a teacher, counselor or faculty member, and two 500-word essays. **Deadline:** Announced annually.

**Remarks:** A pledge of $10,000 in financial support by Nordstrom makes possible the scholarships for students with disabilities. **Contact:** Ellen Daly at the above address (see entry 5000).

---

## • 5002 •
## Press Club of Dallas Foundation

400 N. Olive, LB 218       *Ph:* (214)740-9988
Dallas, TX 75201-4048      *Fax:* (214)740-9989
*E-mail:* dallaspc@aol.com

## • 5003 • Press Club of Dallas Foundation Scholarship (Undergraduate/Scholarship)

**Focus:** Mass communications. **Qualif.:** Applicants must be mass communications majors of sophomore status attending Texas schools. **Criteria:** Awards are made based on academic achievement, financial need, essay, recommendations and work samples.

**Funds Avail.:** $500 - $2,000. **No. of Awards:** 15 approximately. **To Apply:** Write for further details. **Deadline:** May 1. **Contact:** Executive Director at the above address (see entry 5002).

---

## • 5004 •
**Pro Bowlers Association**
1720 Merriman Rd.
PO Box 5118   *Ph:* (330)836-5568
Akron, OH 44334-0118   *Fax:* (330)836-2107
*URL:* http://www.pba.org/

### • 5005 • Coca-Cola Youth Bowling Championships Scholarships *(Undergraduate/Scholarship)*

**Focus:** General studies. **Qualif.:** Applicants must be between the ages of 8 and 22, be members of YABA, participate in a local YABA league, and be in YABA level leagues.

**Funds Avail.:** $400,000. $100 - $5,000 per award. **To Apply:** Write for further details and an application form. Enclose a self-addressed and stamped envelope. **Deadline:** January 15. **Contact:** Local bowling center youth coordinator.

### • 5006 • Alberta E. Crowe Star of Tomorrow Scholarship *(Undergraduate/Scholarship)*

**Focus:** General studies. **Qualif.:** Applicants must be female amateur bowler 22 years of age or young who are high school seniors or college students.

**Funds Avail.:** $1,000. Renewable up to four years. **To Apply:** Write for further details and an application form. Provide self addressed stamped envelope. **Deadline:** January 15. **Contact:** Young American Bowling Alliance at the above address (see entry 5004).

### • 5007 • Chuck Hall Star of Tomorrow Scholarship *(Undergraduate/Scholarship)*

**Focus:** General studies. **Qualif.:** Applicants must be male amateur bowlers 21 years of age and younger who are high school seniors or college attendees.

**Funds Avail.:** $1,000 per award. Renewable up to four years. **To Apply:** Write for further information and an application form. Include self-addressed stamped envelope with request. **Deadline:** January 15. **Contact:** Young American Bowling Alliance at the above address (see entry 5004).

### • 5008 • Al Thompson Junior Bowler Scholarships *(Undergraduate/Scholarship)*

**Focus:** General studies. **Qualif.:** Applicants must be high school seniors carrying a minimum grade point average of 2.5 or equivalent, and have a current season bowling average of 170 for women and 190 for men.

**Funds Avail.:** $1,000 $1,500. **No. of Awards:** 2. **To Apply:** Write for further details and an application form. Include a self-addressed and stamped envelope. **Deadline:** January 15. **Contact:** Young American Bowling Alliance at the above address (see entry 5004).

### • 5009 • Billy Welu Scholarship *(Undergraduate/Scholarship)*

**Focus:** General studies. **Qualif.:** Applicants must be 22 years of age or younger who have a minimum grade point average of 2.5 or equivalent with a current bowling season average of 170 for women and 190 for men.

**Funds Avail.:** $500. **No. of Awards:** 1. **To Apply:** Write for further details and an application form. Enclose a self-addressed stamped envelope. **Deadline:** January 15. **Contact:** Young American Bowling Alliance.

## • 5010 •
**Professional Secretaries International**
10502 NW Ambassador Dr.
PO Box 20404   *Ph:* (816)891-6600
Kansas City, MO 64153-1278   *Fax:* (816)891-9118

### • 5011 • Professional Secretaries International Scholarships *(Undergraduate/Scholarship)*

**Focus:** Office Professions. **Qualif.:** Applicants must be high school graduates who are interested in studying office courses at the postsecondary level, and plan to attend a two- or four-year college or vocational/technical school.

**Funds Avail.:** Stipends range from $500 to $2,000 annually. **To Apply:** Students should apply through one of the 740 Professional Secretaries International chapters in the United States and Canada. **Deadline:** March. **Contact:** Local chapters of Professional Secretaries International or PSI at the above address (see entry 5010).

## • 5012 •
**Program for Cultural Cooperation Between Spain's Ministry of Culture and U.S. Universities**
University of Minnesota
106 Nicholson Hall
216 Pillsbury Dr. S.E.   *Ph:* (612)625-9888
Minneapolis, MN 55455   *Fax:* (612)626-8009
*E-mail:* zimme001@tc.umn.edu

### • 5013 • Research Grants for Cultural Cooperation *(Postdoctorate/Grant)*

**Purpose:** To allow Spanish and U.S. scholars to conduct projects in the United States or Spain. **Focus:** Spanish Studies, including Humanities and Social Sciences. **Qualif.:** Candidate must be either a Spanish or a scholar studying in the U.S. who wishes to undertake or complete a research project related to the dissemination of Spanish culture in the United States. Spanish citizens must use the grant in the United States. Scholars in the U.S. must use the grant in Spain.

**Funds Avail.:** $1,500-5,000 average. **To Apply:** Applicants should write or e-mail the general coordinator for application form and guidelines and should submit ten copies of form, curriculum vitae, two letters of evaluation, and supporting materials. **Deadline:** April 1.

**Remarks:** Grants for the Dissemination of Spanish Culture are also offered, to help defray publication and production costs of projects related to Spanish culture. Write to the general coordinator for further information. Additional awards are offered for publications focusing on the historical contributions of Spaniards to the independence and formation of the United States. **Contact:** Holly Zimmerman, Program Coordinator.

## • 5014 •

**Program in Ethics and the Professions - Harvard University**
Taubman-407
79 John F. Kennedy St.                    *Ph:* (617)495-9386
Cambridge, MA 02138                       *Fax:* (617)496-9053
*E-mail:* MCVEIGH@FAS.HARVARD.EDU

### • 5015 • Fellowships in Ethics *(Postdoctorate, Postgraduate/Fellowship)*

**Purpose:** To support teachers and scholars who wish to develop their ability to address questions of moral choice in the professions, and public life generally. **Focus:** Ethics and Bioethics, Business, Government, Law, Medicine, Philosophy, Political Science, Theology. **Qualif.:** Candidate may be of any nationality. Applicant must have a professional degree or a doctorate. Fellows normally hold a postgraduate degree in business, government, law, or medicine; or a doctorate in philosophy, political theory, theology or other relevant disciplines. Awards are tenable at Harvard University. Fellows must devote full-time to the activities of the Program during the fellowship period. **Criteria:** Fellows are selected on the basis of the quality of their achievements in their field of specialization and their ability to benefit from work in the Program; the contributions they are likely to make in the future in higher education through teaching and writing about ethical issues; and the probable significance of the research they propose to conduct and its relevance to the purposes of the Program.

**Funds Avail.:** Varies; fellows on academic leave receive up to one-half of their annual salary to a ceiling of $34,000. Awards also include library and study privileges and a modest research allowance. **To Apply:** Write to the program administrator for application guidelines; there is no application form. Submit a curriculum vitae; a scholarly paper written or published within the past two years; a brief statement describing interest in professional ethics and plans for using the fellowship; a research proposal; and a statement of financial resources. One letter of recommendation should be sent directly from the referee to the program director and applicants should provide the names and addresses of two other persons whom the Program may consult for further information about their teaching and scholarship. **Deadline:** December 29. Recipients are named in mid-March. **Contact:** Jean McVeigh, Program Administrator, at the above address (see entry 5014).

## • 5016 •

**Public Employees Roundtable**
PO Box 44801                              *Ph:* (202)401-4344
Washington, DC 20026-4801                 *Fax:* (202)401-4433
*E-mail:* permail@patroit.net
*URL:* http://www.theroundtable.org

### • 5017 • Public Employees Roundtable Public Service Scholarships *(Graduate, Undergraduate/ Scholarship)*

**Purpose:** To assist students pursuing government careers at federal, state and local levels. **Focus:** Public Service, Government. **Qualif.:** Applicants must have a cumulative 3.5 GPA, intend to enter a public service career, and be enrolled in a baccalaureate program with at least sophomore standing. They must be pursuing a four-year undergraduate degree full-time or a graduate degree. Students enrolled in community colleges are not eligible **Criteria:** Preference is given to applicants with some public service work experience. Scholarships are awarded on the basis of merit to students planning careers in government.

**Funds Avail.:** $1,000 for full-time undergraduate and graduate students; $500 for part-time graduate students. **No. of Awards:** 8

to 10. **To Apply:** Candidates should send a self-addressed, stamped envelope for application. Applications are available from website and from Public Employees Roundtable as of February 1. A two-page essay is required and the topic of the essay changes yearly. **Deadline:** May 12. **Contact:** Public Employees Roundtable at the above address (see entry 5016).

## • 5018 •

**Pueblo of Acoma**
Higer Education Program
PO Box 307                                *Ph:* (505)552-6621
Pueblo of Acoma, NM 87034-0307            *Fax:* (505)552-6604
*E-mail:* acomahe@unm.edu

### • 5019 • Acoma Higher Education Grants *(Undergraduate/Grant)*

**Qualif.:** Applicants must be Acoma Tribal members enrolled on the Pueblo of Acoma Census Roll. **Criteria:** Awards are given based on academic record, AHE application and letters of recommendation. **To Apply:** Applicants must submit an AHE grant application, Letter of Undergraduate Admission, Certificate of Indian Blood and Tribal Enrollment, two letters of recommendation, official high school or post-secondary transcript, ACT/SAT scores, student aid reports and a class schedule. **Deadline:** March 1 for fall semester or September 1 for spring semester. **Contact:** Pueblo of Acoma at the above address (see entry 5018).

## • 5020 •

**Puerto Rican Bar Association, Inc.**
111 Centre St., 2nd Fl.
New York, NY 10013

### • 5021 • The Puerto Rican Bar Association Scholarship Fund, Inc. *(Graduate/Scholarship)*

**Qualif.:** All full-and part-time law school students are eligible. **Criteria:** Applicants must have: good academic standing; community service; financial need; a statement as to future intentions, and two recommendations.

**Funds Avail.:** Averaging $1,250.00. **Contact:** Puerto Rican Bar Association, Inc. at the above address (see entry 5020).

## • 5022 •

**Puerto Rican Legal Defense and Education Fund**
Legal Education Division
99 Hudson St., 14th Fl.                   *Ph:* (212)219-3360
New York, NY 10013-2815                   *Fax:* (212)431-4276

### • 5023 • PRLDEF Scholarship *(Graduate/Scholarship)*

**Purpose:** To increase the number of Latino attorneys serving the interests of the Latino community by providing financial assistance to those demonstrating a commitment to public interest legal work. **Qualif.:** Applicants must be of Hispanic descent and attending law school. **Criteria:** Candidates are judged on their academic ability, financial need, and commitment to public interest.

**Funds Avail.:** $5,000. **No. of Awards:** 5. **To Apply:** Applications are available each October. **Deadline:** Annual deadline determined and

*Puerto Rican Legal Defense and Education Fund (continued)*

specified on application. **Contact:** K. Browno at the above address (see entry 5022).

---

## • 5024 •
### Puerto Rico Council on Higher Education

Box 23305-UPR Station
Rio Piedras, PR 00931                                    *Ph:* (809)758-3350

#### • 5025 •   Puerto Rico Council on Higher Education Educational Funds *(Undergraduate/Grant)*

**Purpose:** To provide financial aid to students who qualify, have a financial need, and are enrolled in private and public higher education institutions. **Qualif.:** A student must have resided in Puerto Rico during the 12 months immediately preceding the application with the intention of establishing permanent residence in the Island for an indefinite time; must be enrolled and taking courses leading to an academic degree or other studies above the degree in the same speciality; have financial aid needs; have a 2.00 minimum general index from high school; be within the time frame scheduled by the institution for completing the corresponding degree; and be able to complete graduation requirements with a 2.00 minimum index. **Criteria:** According to each institution analysis system for the studies expense budget.

**Funds Avail.:** $10,000,000.00 per year. **No. of Awards:** Varies annually. **To Apply:** Applies through the institutions financial aid office. **Deadline:** Stated by each institution. **Contact:** Puerto Rico Council on Higher Education at the above address (see entry 5024).

#### • 5026 •   Puerto Rico Council on Legislative Funds *(Undergraduate/Grant)*

**Purpose:** To provide grants and financial aid to eligible students to pursue studies at private higher education institutions. **Qualif.:** A student must be a United States citizen or residing in Puerto Rico; have been admitted to a higher education institution duly accredited by the state; be enrolled in a program with 6 or more credits per academic session; prove to have financial need; keep a cumulative average of "C" or above (academic index of 2.0 or more); show good behavior according to the corresponding institutional regulations; and not be subject to any disciplinary action. **Criteria:** According to each institution analysis system for the studies expense budget.

**Funds Avail.:** Approximately $2,000,000 is given per year. **No. of Awards:** Varies annually. **To Apply:** Through the institution's financial aid office. **Deadline:** As stated by each institution.

**Remarks:** Cannot be awarded for more than four semesters or its equivalent in associate degree programs or eight semesters or its equivalent in bachelor's degree programs.

#### • 5027 •   Puerto Rico Council State Student Incentive Grant *(Undergraduate/Grant)*

**Purpose:** To provide grants and work-study assistance to eligible students with substantial financial need, enrolled in higher education institutions. **Qualif.:** The student must: be a United States citizen; prove the intention to be a permanent resident of the United States, its territories or trust territories; be enrolled or accepted for enrollment at an undergraduate program at least as a part time student; and prove to have substantial economic need. **Criteria:** According to each institution analysis system for the studies expense budget.

**Funds Avail.:** Depending on the federal award each year. **No. of Awards:** Varies annually. **To Apply:** Only through the institutions

financial aid office. **Deadline:** As stated by each institution pursuant to the federal deadline.

**Remarks:** Subject to US Congress budget cuts for next year. **Contact:** Puerto Rico Council on Higher Education at the above address (see entry 5024).

---

## • 5028 •
### Pulp and Paper Foundation

Paper Science & Engineering Dept.
242 Gaskill Hall
Miami University                                          *Ph:* (513)529-6531
Oxford, OH 45056                                         *Fax:* (513)529-1530

#### • 5029 •   Miami University Pulp and Paper Foundation Scholarships *(Undergraduate/Scholarship)*

**Purpose:** To support outstanding scholars preparing for careers in paper related industries. **Focus:** Physical Sciences. **Qualif.:** Candidates must be freshmen admitted to Paper Science and Engineering, upperclassmen majoring in Paper Science with a cumulative grade point average of 3.0 or more, or transfer students majoring in Paper Science with a 3.0 average for all work taken at Miami University. Scholarships will be renewed each semester if recipients maintain at least a 3.0 cumulative grade point average for a Basic Scholarship, a 3.25 for a Plus Scholarship, a 3.5 cumulative grade point average for a Premium Scholarship, or a 3.9 average for a Summa Cum Laude Scholarship. For each term in which a scholarship is held, recipients must register for at least 12 hours of course work approved by the Paper Science and Engineering Department. **Criteria:** Admission information, ACT scores, and academic record will be evaluated.

**Funds Avail.:** The values of the scholarship will be as follows: Basic (3.000-3.499) $2,200/year; Premium (3.500-3.899) $3,200/year; and Summa cum laude (3.900-4.000) $5,660/year. The Foundation also provides a $1,000 per semester subsidy for non-Ohio residents. **To Apply:** Freshman should submit the university's scholarship application indicating a Paper Science and Engineering major. **Deadline:** January 31. **Contact:** William J. Copeland, Executive Director, at the above address (see entry 5028).

---

## • 5030 •
### Pulp and Paper Foundation, Inc.

North Carolina State University
PO Box 8005                                              *Ph:* (919)515-5661
Raleigh, NC 27695-8005                                   *Fax:* (919)515-6302
*E-mail:* jane_howe@ncsu.edu
*URL:* http://www.cfr.ncsu.edu.wps

#### • 5031 •   NCSU - Pulp & Paper Merit Scholarships *(Undergraduate/Scholarship)*

**Purpose:** To encourage students to select a career in the pulp and paper-related industries. **Focus:** Pulp and Paper Science. **Qualif.:** Candidates must be strong in math and science. **Criteria:** Selection is based on SAT scores, grade point average, and class rank.

**Funds Avail.:** Awards are $4,050 per year for out-of-state residents, and $2,000 per year for North Carolina residents. **No. of Awards:** Approximately 85 scholarships. **To Apply:** Completed applications must be submitted. **Deadline:** January 15. **Contact:** Ben Chilton at the above address (see entry 5030).

## • 5032 •
## Purina Mills, Inc.
Purina Research Awards Committee
PO Box 66812     *Ph:* (314)768-4100
St. Louis, MO 63166-6812     *Fax:* (314)768-4433
*URL:* http://www.purina-mills.com/

### • 5033 • Purina Research Fellowships *(Graduate/ Fellowship)*

**Purpose:** To assist in the training of personnel for leadership in the nutritional sciences of food and companion animals. **Focus:** Animal Science, Dairy Science, Poultry Science. **Qualif.:** Candidates may be of any nationality but must be qualified for graduate study in an agricultural college, and should be prepared to study full-time during the fellowship year. Fellowships are tenable worldwide.

**Funds Avail.:** $12,500. **To Apply:** Write for application form and guidelines. Submit form with transcripts, financial information, and research/study plans. Three letters of recommendation and a resume are also required. **Deadline:** First Monday in February. **Contact:** Susan Spiess at the above address (see entry 5032).

## • 5034 •
## Pymatuning Lab of Ecology
University of Pittsburgh
13142 Hartstown Rd.     *Ph:* (814)683-5813
Linesville, PA 16424     *Fax:* (814)683-2302
*E-mail:* pymatuning@gremlan.org; ple@toolcity.net
*URL:* http://www.pitt.edu/~blueeye/pym.html

### • 5035 • McKinley Research Fund Scholarships *(Graduate/Scholarship)*

**Purpose:** To enable graduate students and post-doctoral fellows to conduct research in the Pymatuning area. **Focus:** Ecological Sciences. **Qualif.:** Applicant may be of any nationality. Research must be based in the Pymatuning region.

**Funds Avail.:** Varies; $3,500 maximum. **To Apply:** Write to the Grants Award Committee for application guidelines. **Deadline:** The deadline is February 13.

**Remarks:** The Lab may also award the Darbaker Prize in Botany to a graduate student interested in attending the summer program and conducting research in some aspect of plant ecology ($1,500 maximum). **Contact:** Pymatuning Lab of Ecology, at the above address (see entry 5034).

## • 5036 •
## Quaker Chemical Foundation
Elm & Lee St.     *Ph:* (610)832-4000
Conshohocken, PA 19428     *Fax:* (610)832-4497

### • 5037 • Quaker Chemical Foundation Scholarships *(Other, Undergraduate/Scholarship)*

**Focus:** General Studies. **Qualif.:** Children of employees may compete for a scholarship leading to a baccalaureate or non-baccalaureate degree. **Criteria:** Selections are made by an independent group of educators. Members of the Foundation do not participate in the selection process.

**Funds Avail.:** $4,000 annually per scholarship. **No. of Awards:** 3. **Contact:** The Quaker Chemical Foundation at the above address (see entry 5036).

## • 5038 •
## Queen's University
Assistant Registrar, Student Awards     *Ph:* (613)545-2216
Kingston, ON, Canada K7L 3N6     *Fax:* (613)545-6409

### • 5039 • The National Bursaries *(Undergraduate/ Scholarship)*

**Qualif.:** Applicants must be Canadian citizens residing in Western and Atlantic Canada as well as the territories who plan to attend Queen's University in Ontario.

**Funds Avail.:** Fifteen $2,425 scholarships. Applicants will also be given automatic consideration for six other awards which range from $1,585 to $3,300. The awards include the Alumni National Scholarship; the Anniversary Scholarships; the Provincial Scholarships; the Queen's Honour Matriculation Scholarships; and the Tricolor Scholarships. **Deadline:** April 30. **Contact:** Assistant Registrar, Student Awards, Queen's University, Kingston, Ontario K7L 3N6.

### • 5040 • Royal Canadian Legion Camrose Branch No. 57 Bursaries *(Undergraduate/Scholarship)*

**Qualif.:** Applicants must be the children or grandchildren of Legion members and members of the Legion Ladies Auxiliary. Also eligible are members of the community who are attending or have completed high school and plan to pursue post-secondary education.

**Funds Avail.:** Six awards of $600 each are given to children and grandchildren of Legion members and members of the Legion Ladies Auxiliary; four awards are given to members of the community who are attending or have completed high school and plan to pursue post-secondary education. **Deadline:** August 15. **Contact:** Royal Canadian Legion Camrose Branch 57, 5703-48 Ave., Camrose, Alberta T4V 0J9.

### • 5041 • Royal Canadian Legion Ladies Auxiliary Alberta-N.W.T. Command Awards *(Undergraduate/ Scholarship)*

**Qualif.:** Applicants must be first year post-secondary students who are children or grandchildren of ex-service personnel. Children of personnel currently serving in the forces are also eligible. All candidates must be Grade 12 graduates from a high school in Alberta or the Northwest Territories.

**Funds Avail.:** $500 each. The number of awards varies. August 29. **Contact:** Ladies Auxiliary Alberta-N.W.T. Command, The Royal Canadian Legion, Box 3067, Station B, Calgary, Alberta T2A 3E7.

### • 5042 • Royal Canadian Legion Ladies Auxiliary Camrose Branch No. 57 Bursaries *(Undergraduate/ Scholarship)*

**Qualif.:** Applicants must children of ex-service personnel, veterans, or Auxiliary members from the city or the county of Camrose.

**Funds Avail.:** One $300 award. **Deadline:** September 15. **Contact:** Scholarship Chairman, Royal Canadian Legion Camrose Branch 57, 5703-48 Ave., Camrose, Alberta T4V 0J9.

### • 5043 • The Spina Bifida Association of Northern Alberta Scholarship *(Undergraduate/Scholarship)*

**Qualif.:** Applicants must disabled with Spina Bifida and Canadian citizens or land immigrants enrolled in a Canadian post-secondary institution. Candidates must also reside in Alberta, north of Red Deer for at least two years. **Criteria:** Award recipients are selected on the basis of motivation, maturity, and academic background.

**Funds Avail.:** One $500 scholarship. **Deadline:** August 31. **Contact:** The Spina Bifida Association of Northern Alberta Scholarship

*Queen's University (continued)*

Committee, PO Box 9501, Postal Station SE, Edmonton, Alberta T6E 5X2. Telephone: (403)479-9018.

**• 5044 • Honourable W.C. Woodward Scholarships** *(Undergraduate/Scholarship)*

**Qualif.:** Applicants must be dependents of full-time, regular part-time, retired or deceased employees. **Criteria:** Award recipients are selected on the basis of scholastic standing, extra-curricular activities, leadership and citizenship qualities, and service to the community.

**Funds Avail.:** Five $1,000 annual scholarship (for a maximum of five years). Recipients may apply the scholarships toward post-secondary study at universities or selected colleges offering university transfer programs in Alberta and British Columbia or university transfer programs available through B.C.I.T, N.A.I.T, and S.A.I.T. **Deadline:** July 15. **Contact:** Human Resources Offices of Woodwards Department Stores.

**• 5045 •**
**QuikTrip Corporation Scholarship Program**
PO Box 2810
Cherry Hill, NJ 08034                    *Ph:* (609)573-9400
*URL:* http://www.dial.net/users/blackdog/QT.html

*All phases of the QuickTrip Corporation scholarship program are independently managed by Career Opportunities Through Education Inc. (Cote), a national non-profit scholarship service organization. All correspondence should be addressed to Cote, PO Box 2810, Cherry Hill, NJ 08034. Telephone (609)573-9400.*

**• 5046 • QuikTrip Scholarships** *(Graduate, Undergraduate/Scholarship)*

**Focus:** General Studies. **Qualif.:** Applicants must be children of full-time employees with a minimum of one year of continuous service to QuikTrip Corporation or its subsidiaries. Children of retired, disabled, or deceased employees are also eligible. Students must be enrolled or planning to enroll as full-time students at an accredited two- or four-year university, vocational-technical school, hospital school of nursing, or graduate school. Children of the president, vice presidents, directors, and division operations managers are not eligible. **Criteria:** Winners are chosen competitively on the basis of school records and personal achievements.

**Funds Avail.:** Awards range from $750 to $1,250, depending on financial need. Students whose parents do not wish to complete the financial data section of the application are eligible for the minimum award of $750 only. These scholarships are renewable annually, but on a competitive basis with other applicants. **To Apply:** Applications are available from Career Opportunities Through Education, Inc. (Cote), PO Box 2810, Cherry Hill, NJ 08034. Students must return completed applications to Cote, along with a current and official transcript and a letter of recommendation. **Deadline:** April 15. All applicants are notified by June 1. Recipients must notify Cote of acceptance of the award within three weeks or the award is forfeited.

**• 5047 •**
**Quill and Scroll**
School of Journalism and Mass
  Communication
University of Iowa
Iowa City, IA 52242-1528                    *Ph:* (319)335-5795
*E-mail:* quill-scroll@uiowa.edu
*URL:* http://www.uiowa.edu/~quill-sc

**• 5048 • Edward J. Nell Memorial Scholarships in Journalism** *(Undergraduate/Scholarship)*

**Focus:** Journalism. **Qualif.:** Scholarship applicants must be National Winners in Quill and Scroll's National Writing/Photo Contest or Yearbook Excellence Contest who are in their senior year in high school. Applicants must sign a statement of intent to major in journalism; and attend a college or university that offers a major in journalism. Sophomore and junior Gold Key winners are eligible to apply their senior year.

**Funds Avail.:** Ten scholarships of $500. **To Apply:** Application forms are automatically sent to all senior national winners. **Deadline:** May 17. **Contact:** Send a self-addressed stamped envelope to Quill and Scroll, at the above address (see entry 5047).

**• 5049 • Quill and Scroll National Writing/Photo Contest** *(High School/Award)*

**Qualif.:** Competition is open to all high school students; Quill and Scroll membership is not required. Each school may submit two entries in each of 10 categories: Editorial, Editorial Cartoon, In-Depth Reporting (Individual and Team), News Story, Feature Story, Sports Story, Advertisement, and Photography (News/Feature and Sports). **To Apply:** Contest rules are sent in late December to all schools on the Society's mailing list. Guidelines and entry forms also appear in the Dec/Jan issue of Quill & Scroll magazine. A $2.00 fee must accompany each entry. **Deadline:** February 5.

**Remarks:** National Winners are notified by mail through their advisers.

**• 5050 •**
**Radio and Television News Directors Foundation**
1000 Connecticut Ave., NW, Ste.              *Ph:* (202)659-6510
  615                                        *Fax:* (202)223-4007
Washington, DC 20036-5302                    *Free:* 800-80-RTNDA
*E-mail:* gwenl@rtndf.org; dcbrowne@hotmail.com
*URL:* http://www.rtndaf.org

**• 5051 • Len Allen Award of Merit for Radio News** *(Graduate, Undergraduate/Grant)*

**Focus:** Journalism. **Qualif.:** Candidates must be undergraduate (sophomore and above) or graduate students enrolled at an accredited or nationally recognized college or university. They must have a career objective of radio news or news management.

**Funds Avail.:** $2,000 grant paid in two installments for one year. **No. of Awards:** 1. **To Apply:** Applications may be obtained from the applicant's faculty advisor, dean's office, or from the Foundation. **Deadline:** May 3. **Contact:** Scholarships/Internships, Radio and Television News Directors Foundation, at the above address (see entry 5050).

**• 5052 • Sherlee Barish Fellowship** *(Professional Development/Fellowship)*

**Focus:** Electronic Journalism. **Qualif.:** Applicants must be reporters or anchors interested in improving their on-air skills.

Funds Avail.: $1,000. No. of Awards: 1. To Apply: Applicants must submit a cover letter stating the reasons for seeking this award; a letter of recommendation from a news director; and a 15 minute audio or video sample tape with a script. Deadline: April 1. Contact: Radio and Television News Directors Foundation at the above address (see entry 5050).

**• 5053 • Ed Bradley Scholarships** (Undergraduate/ Scholarship)

Focus: Journalism. Qualif.: Applicants must be minority undergraduate students. They must be attending full-time with a career objective of electronic journalism. Applicants must have at least one full year of school remaining. Criteria: Minority undergraduate students will receive preference.

Funds Avail.: $5,000. No. of Awards: 1. To Apply: Entries must include completed application forms, one to three examples of work, a statement of purpose, and a letter of endorsement. Deadline: May 3.

**• 5054 • Jim Byron Scholarship** (Undergraduate/ Scholarship)

Purpose: Designed for students whose career objectives are radio or television news. Focus: Electronic journalism.

Funds Avail.: $1,000. No. of Awards: 1. Deadline: May 3. Contact: Radio and Television News Directors Foundation at the above address (see entry 5050).

**• 5055 • Ben Chatfield Scholarship** (Undergraduate/ Scholarship)

Purpose: Designed for students whose career objective is radio or television news. Focus: Electronic Journalism.

Funds Avail.: $1,000. No. of Awards: 1. Deadline: May 3. Contact: Radio and Television News Directors Foundation at the above address (see entry 5050).

**• 5056 • Richard Cheverton Scholarship** (Undergraduate/Scholarship)

Focus: Electronic Journalism. Qualif.: Awarded to sophomores, or more advanced undergraduates whose career objective is radio or television news and who have declared a major in electronic journalism.

Funds Avail.: $1,000. No. of Awards: 1. Deadline: May 3. Contact: Radio and Televisions News Directors Foundation at the above address (see entry 5050).

**• 5057 • Michele Clark Fellowship** (Professional Development/Fellowship)

Focus: Journalism. Qualif.: Candidates must be employed in electronic news and have fewer than ten years full-time experience. Criteria: Minorities are given preference.

Funds Avail.: $1,000 to be applied to any legitimate educational purpose. No. of Awards: 1. To Apply: Applicants should submit a letter, endorsed by their news director, setting forth the reasons for seeking the fellowship and how they intend to use the grant money. This letter should be accompanied by supporting material exemplifying the applicant's best work as a member of the news staff. Format and length are not prescribed. Script, tape, or preferably both, are acceptable. Entry materials, including tapes, become the property of RTNDF and cannot be returned. Deadline: April 1. Contact: RTNDF Fellowship Program at the above address (see entry 5050).

**• 5058 • Bruce Dennis Scholarship** (Undergraduate/ Scholarship)

Focus: Electronic Journalism. Qualif.: Applicants must have 1 or more years left to study.

Funds Avail.: $1,000. No. of Awards: 1. To Apply: Applicants must submit 1 to 3 samples of reporting skills; a statement of why a degree in electronic journalism is being sought; and a letter of endorsement from a dean or faculty sponsor stating remaining time in program. Deadline: May 3. Contact: Radio and Television News Directors Foundation at the above address (see entry 5050).

**• 5059 • Sandra Freeman Geller and Alfred Geller Fellowship** (Professional Development/Fellowship)

Focus: Electronic Journalism. Qualif.: Applicants must be anchors and reporters interested in improving their on-air skills.

Funds Avail.: $2,000. No. of Awards: 1. To Apply: Applicants must submit a cover letter stating the reasons for seeking the award; a letter of recommendation from a news director; and a 15 minute audio or video sample with a script. Deadline: April 1. Contact: Radio and Television News Directors Foundation at the above address (see entry 5050).

**• 5060 • John Hogan Scholarship** (Undergraduate/ Scholarship)

Focus: Electronic Journalism. Qualif.: Applicants must have 1 or more years of study remaining in an electronic journalism field.

Funds Avail.: $1,000. No. of Awards: 1. To Apply: Applicants must submit one to three 15-minute samples of their broadcasting ability; a statement for their reasons of selecting electronic journalism as a major; and an endorsement from a dean or faculty sponsor stating length of study remaining. Deadline: May 3. Contact: Radio and Television News Directors Foundation at the above address (see entry 5050).

**• 5061 • Theodore Koop Scholarship** (Undergraduate/Scholarship)

Focus: Electronic Journalism.

Funds Avail.: $1,000. No. of Awards: 1. To Apply: Applicants must provide a cover letter stating the reasons for seeking this award; a letter of recommendation from a news director; a script; and a 15 minute audio or video sample tape. Deadline: May 3. Contact: Radio and Television News Directors Foundation at the above address (see entry 5050).

**• 5062 • James McCulla Scholarship** (Undergraduate/Scholarship)

Focus: Electronic Journalism.

Funds Avail.: $1,000. No. of Awards: 1. To Apply: Applicants must provide a cover letter stating the reason for seeking this award; a letter of recommendation from a news director; a script; and a 15 minute audio or video sample tape. Deadline: May 3. Contact: Radio and Television News Directors Foundation at the above address (see entry 5050).

**• 5063 • Vada and Barney Oldfield Fellowship for National Security Reporting** (Professional Development/ Fellowship)

Focus: Journalism. Qualif.: Candidates must be employed in electronic news with no more than ten years experience. They must also declare an interest in pursuing the reporting of military affairs and have either ROTC or other military experience.

Funds Avail.: $1,000. No. of Awards: 1. To Apply: Applicants submit a letter, endorsed by their news director, setting forth the reasons for seeking the fellowship and how they intend to use the grant money. This letter should be accompanied by supporting

## Radio and Television News Directors Foundation (continued)

material exemplifying the applicant's best work as a member of the news staff. Format and length are not prescribed. Script, tape, or preferably both, are acceptable. Entry materials, including tapes, become the property of RTNDF and cannot be returned. **Deadline:** April 1. **Contact:** RTNDF Fellowship Program at the above address (see entry 5050).

### • 5064 • Bruce Palmer Scholarship (Undergraduate/Scholarship)

**Focus:** Electronic Journalism.

**Funds Avail.:** $1,000. **No. of Awards:** 1. **To Apply:** Applicants must submit a cover letter stating their reasons for seeking this award; a letter of recommendation from a news director; a script; and a 15 minute sample audio or video tape. **Deadline:** May 3. **Contact:** Radio and Television News Directors Foundation at the above address (see entry 5050).

### • 5065 • RTNDF Environmental and Science Reporting Fellowship (Professional Development/Fellowship)

**Focus:** Journalism. **Qualif.:** Applicants must be employed in electronic news and have fewer than 10 years experience, and must declare an interest in pursuing the reporting of environmental and science stories.

**Funds Avail.:** $1,000 grant may be applied to any legitimate educational purpose. **No. of Awards:** 1. **To Apply:** Applicants must submit a letter, endorsed by their director, setting forth the reasons for seeking the fellowship and how they intend to use the grant money. This letter should be accompanied by supporting material exemplifying the applicant's best work as a member of the news staff. Format and length are not prescribed. Script, tape, or preferably both, are acceptable. Entry materials, including tapes, become the property of RTNDF and cannot be returned. **Deadline:** Early April. **Contact:** RTNDF Fellowship Program at the above address (see entry 5050).

### • 5066 • RTNDF Presidential Memorial Scholarship (Graduate, Undergraduate/Scholarship)

**Purpose:** Created in honor of all past RTNDA presidents, chairmen, and chairwomen. **Focus:** Electronic journalism. **Qualif.:** Application is open to sophomores, advanced undergraduates or graduate students.

**Funds Avail.:** $2,000. **No. of Awards:** 1. **Deadline:** May 3. **Contact:** Radio and Television News Directors Foundation at the above address (see entry 5050).

### • 5067 • RTNDF Six-Month Entry Level Internships for Minority Students (Graduate/Internship)

**Focus:** Journalism. **Qualif.:** Minority students who have recently graduated with a degree in electronic journalism and who are pursuing a career in news management may apply.

**Funds Avail.:** $1300 per month. **To Apply:** Applications may be obtained from the applicant's faculty advisor, dean's office, or from the Foundation. **Deadline:** March 1. **Contact:** Scholarships/Internships, Radio and Television News Directors Foundation, at the above address (see entry 5050).

### • 5068 • RTNDF Summer Internships for Minority Students (Undergraduate/Internship)

**Focus:** Journalism. **Qualif.:** Minority students in their junior year who have declared a major in broadcast or cable news and are interested in a career in news management may apply.

**Funds Avail.:** Three paid summer internships in production or news management are available, with a monthly stipend. **No. of Awards:** 3. **To Apply:** Applications may be obtained from the applicant's faculty advisor, dean's office, or from the Foundation. **Deadline:** March 1. **Contact:** Scholarships/Internships, Radio and Television News Directors Foundation, at the above address (see entry 5050).

### • 5069 • RTNDF Undergraduate Scholarships (Graduate, Undergraduate/Scholarship)

**Qualif.:** Any sophomore or more advanced undergraduate or graduate student whose career objective is broadcast or cable news and who has declared a major in electronic journalism may apply. All recipients must have at least one full year of school remaining. Previous winners are not eligible.

**Funds Avail.:** Nine $1,000 scholarships are awarded. **No. of Awards:** 9. **To Apply:** Applications may be obtained from the applicant's faculty advisor, dean's office, or from the Foundation. Entries must include a completed application form, three to five examples of reporting or producing skills, a statement explaining why the applicant seeks a career in broadcast or cable journalism, and a letter of endorsement from applicant's faculty sponsor that includes a description of available facilities for electronic news production. **Deadline:** May 3.

**Remarks:** These scholarship were established in honor of Radio-Television New Directors Association past presidents Ben Chatfield, Bruce Palmer, James McCulla, Bruce Dennis, Richard Cheverton, Jim Byron, John Salisbury, John Hogan, and Ted Koop. **Contact:** Scholarships/Internships, Radio and Television News Directors Foundation, at the above address (see entry 5050).

### • 5070 • Abe Schechter Graduate Scholarship (Graduate/Scholarship)

**Focus:** Journalism. **Qualif.:** Any continuing or incoming graduate student whose career objective is broadcast or cable news or electronic journalism research or teaching may apply. Applicants must have at least one full year of school remaining.

**Funds Avail.:** $1,000 for one year of study. **No. of Awards:** 1. **To Apply:** Applications may be obtained from faculty advisors, dean's offices, or from the RTNDF. **Deadline:** May 3. **Contact:** Scholarships/Internships, Radio and Television News Directors Foundation, at the above address (see entry 5050).

### • 5071 • Carole Simpson Scholarship (Graduate, Undergraduate/Scholarship)

**Focus:** Journalism. **Qualif.:** Applicants may be any undergraduate or graduate minority student whose career objectives are broadcast or cable news, and who have declared a major in electronic journalism at an accredited or nationally recognized college or university. Applicants must have at least one full year of school remaining.

**Funds Avail.:** $2,000 for one year of study. **No. of Awards:** 1. **To Apply:** Applications may be obtained from faculty advisors, dean's offices, or from the Foundation. **Deadline:** May 3. **Contact:** Scholarships/Internships, Radio and Television News Directors Foundation, at the above address (see entry 5050).

## • 5072 •
**Ragdale Foundation**
1260 N. Green Bay Rd.
Lake Forest, IL 60045-1106
*E-mail:* ragdale1@aol.com
*URL:* http://nsn.nslsilus.org/lfkhome/ragdale

*Ph:* (847)234-1063
*Fax:* (847)234-1075

### • 5073 • Frances Shaw Fellowship *(Professional Development/Scholarship)*

**Purpose:** To encourage and support emerging older women writers. **Focus:** Writing. **Qualif.:** Applicants must be females over the age of fifty-five at the beginning of the writing careers. **Criteria:** Awards are granted based on talent and financial need.

**Funds Avail.:** Recipient is offered two months free residency at the Ragdale Foundation. Travel paid from anywhere in the United States. **No. of Awards:** 1. **To Apply:** Applicants must submit twelve poems or about twenty pages of prose or non-fiction in manuscript form. **Deadline:** February 1. **Contact:** Sylvia Brown.

## • 5074 •
**Jennings Randolph Program for International Peace**
U.S. Institute of Peace
1200 17th St. NW, Ste. 200
Washington, DC 20036-3006
*E-mail:* essay-contest@usip.org
*URL:* http://www.usip.org

*Ph:* (202)457-1700
*Fax:* (202)429-6063

*The Jennings Randolph Program for International Peace was created by the United States Congress to provide fellowships and other forms of support to scholars and leaders of peace from the United States and abroad to pursue scholarly inquiry and other appropriate forms of communication on international peace and conflict resolution.*

### • 5075 • National Peace Essay Contest *(High School/Scholarship)*

**Purpose:** To encourage students to consider peace as an international goal, and to grasp an understanding of the methods by which conflicts are resolved and avoided. **Qualif.:** High school students from U.S. states, territories, the District of Columbia, and overseas schools. **Criteria:** National judges select first, second, and third place state winners. The U.S.I.P. board selects national winners. Criteria includes knowledge and depth of understanding, intellectual quality and originality, and style and mechanics.

**Funds Avail.:** First-place state level scholarship is $1,000; at the national level prizes are $10,000, $5,000, and $2,500. **No. of Awards:** 56. **To Apply:** Student and school or sponsoring organization must register. **Deadline:** Varies, applicant should call for new deadlines.

**Remarks:** We can be contacted via e-mail and updated information can be found on our website: www.usip.org/et.html. **Contact:** The United States Institute of Peace at the above address (see entry 5074).

### • 5076 • Peace Fellowships *(Postgraduate, Professional Development/Fellowship)*

**Purpose:** To encourage professionals or scholars who demonstrate substantial accomplishment or promise of exceptional leadership to undertake research and education projects regarding the nature of violent international conflict and the full range of ways to deal with it peacefully. **Focus:** Diplomacy, International Relations, Peace and Conflict Studies, Political Science. **Qualif.:** Candidate may be of any nationality. Applicant should have a minimum of an undergraduate degree, supplemented by higher education or career experience. A small number of fellowships may be allocated specifically to outstanding candidates who have completed doctoral degrees in recent years. Fellows work in residence at the Institute in Washington, D.C. Fellowships are full-time appointments. Awards will not be given to support partisan political activity, policy advocacy, or policymaking for any government or private organization.

**Funds Avail.:** Up to $66,609 stipend, plus research funds. **To Apply:** Write for application form and guidelines. Submit form with a project proposal and three letters of recommendation. An interview may be required. **Deadline:** October 15. Fellowships are announced in the spring. **Contact:** Barbara Cullicott at the above address (see entry 5074).

### • 5077 • Peace Scholars Award *(Doctorate/Award)*

**Purpose:** Peace Scholar awards are intended to inspire and enable students to undertake dissertation research that significantly advances the state of existing knowledge or education regarding international peace and conflict management. **Focus:** Social Sciences and Humanities. **Qualif.:** Competition is open to outstanding students in recognized United States university doctoral programs, regardless of citizenship. Applicants must have completed all graduate work toward doctoral degrees except their dissertations. Peace Scholars do fellowship work at their universities or other sites appropriate to their research. Dissertation projects with innovative approaches and from a broad range of disciplines are accepted.

**Funds Avail.:** Stipends are set at $14,000 for one year. Ten awards are granted. **No. of Awards:** Approximately 10. **To Apply:** Candidates must submit a formal application and a letter of support from the student's dissertation supervisor. **Deadline:** November 15. **Contact:** The Jennings Randolph Program at the above address (see entry 5074).

### • 5078 • Jennings Randolph Senior Fellow Award *(Professional Development/Fellowship)*

**Purpose:** The Jennings Randolph Program for International Peace was created by the United States Congress to provide fellowships to scholars and practitioners from the U.S. and abroad to pursue scholarly inquiry and other appropriate forms of communication on international peace and conflict resolution. **Focus:** All fields of study. **Qualif.:** Candidates must be practitioners, scholars, and other professionals with extraordinary scholarly or practical achievements and have specific interest or experience in international peace and conflict management. Applications are encouraged from persons with backgrounds in government, diplomacy, higher education, international affairs, law, military service, the media, business, labor, religion, humanitarian affairs, and others. They must have at least a bachelors degree from a recognized university. **Criteria:** Based on an independent review process.

**Funds Avail.:** Fellowships are for twelve months and stipends are determined individually in relation to the recipient's earned income during the twelve months preceding the fellowship but will not exceed the Federal pay rate established for the GS-15, Step 10 level, which is currently capped at $83,520. All fellowship recipients are expected to devote full attention to their work, to provide periodic reports as their project unfolds, and to take part as appropriate in the intellectual life and public outreach efforts of the Institute. **No. of Awards:** Approximately 10. **To Apply:** Candidates must be nominated on an Institute nomination form by another person well acquainted with nominee's career and achievements. **Deadline:** October 1. **Contact:** Jennings Randolph Program for International Peace at the above address (see entry 5074).

### • 5079 • United States Institute of Peace Distinguished Fellows *(Professional Development/Fellowship)*

**Purpose:** To enable internationally recognized statespersons, scholars, and other professionals to undertake research and

## Jennings Randolph Program for International Peace (continued)

education projects regarding the nature of violent international conflict and the full range of ways to deal with it peacefully. **Focus:** Diplomacy, International Relations, Peace and Conflict Studies, Political Science. **Qualif.:** Candidate may be of any nationality. Candidate should be a highly experienced statesperson, scholar, or other professional whose scholarly or practical accomplishments in international peace and conflict management (or a related field) are widely recognized. Fellows work in residence at the Institute in Washington, D.C. Fellowships are full-time appointments. Awards will not be given to support partisan political activity, policy advocacy, or policymaking for any government or private organization.

**Funds Avail.:** Up to $86,589 stipend. **To Apply:** Write for nomination form and guidelines. An interview may be required. **Deadline:** October 15. Fellowships are announced in the spring. **Contact:** Barbara Cullicott at the above address (see entry 5074).

## • 5080 •
## Jeannette Rankin Foundation
PO Box 6653
Athens, GA 30604          *Ph:* (706)208-1211
*URL:* http://www.wmst.unt.edu/jrf/

### • 5081 • Jeannette Rankin Award *(Undergraduate/ Award)*

**Purpose:** To assist women who must reenter the workplace or retrain for work to support themselves and their families. **Focus:** General Studies, Vocational-Technical Education. **Qualif.:** Applicants must be women 35 years or older, U.S. citizens, and accepted or enrolled in a certified program of technical/vocational training or an undergraduate program. **Criteria:** Critical financial need is the major factor in selecting awardees, although merit is also a consideration.

**Funds Avail.:** $1,500. **No. of Awards:** 25. **To Apply:** To receive an application, send a self-addressed stamped business envelope to the Foundation no earlier than September 1 and no later than January 15. This envelope must be labeled with JRF and the year in the lower left-hand corner. Note on the envelope or cover letter sex, age, and level of study or training. **Deadline:** Completed applications are due March 1.

## • 5082 •
## Real Estate Educators Association
740 Florida Central Pkwy., Ste. 1020
Longwood, FL 32750-7652
*E-mail:* reea@washingtongroupinc.com
*URL:* http://www.holonet.net/realed/

### • 5083 • Harwood Memorial Real Estate Scholarship *(Graduate, Other, Undergraduate/Scholarship)*

**Focus:** Real Estate. **Qualif.:** Applicants must be enrolled in an undergraduate or graduate program specializing in real estate, have a GPA of at least 3.2 on a 4.0 scale, have attained an A or B in real estate courses, be at least a sophomore, and plan to pursue a career in some phase of real estate.

**Funds Avail.:** $250 each. **No. of Awards:** Less than 10. **To Apply:** Applicants must submit an application, resume, official transcripts, and a letter of recommendation from their real estate instructor. **Deadline:** December.

**Remarks:** There must be at least one member of the REEA on applicant's campus. **Contact:** College real estate departments, financial aid offices, or Scholarship Coordinator, Real Estate Educators Association at the above address (see entry 5082)for application or additional information.

## • 5084 •
## Realty Foundation of New York
551 5th Ave., Ste. 1105          *Ph:* (212)697-2510
New York, NY 10176-0001          *Fax:* (212)949-9319

### • 5085 • Realty Foundation of New York Scholarships *(Graduate, Undergraduate/Scholarship)*

**Purpose:** To assist employees and children of employees of the real estate industry. **Focus:** General Studies. **Qualif.:** Applicants must be employees or children of employees of a real estate firm in New York City, and member ferm of the Board of Directors. **To Apply:** Contact Realty Foundation of New York. **Deadline:** None. **Contact:** Mrs. Patricia Frank, Executive Vice President, Realty Foundation of New York at the above address (see entry 5084).

## • 5086 •
## Red River Valley Association
National Office
2 Carlton Dr.          *Ph:* (408)393-2025
Del Rey Oaks, CA 93940          *Fax:* (408)393-2043
*E-mail:* afbridger@aol.com

### • 5087 • Red River Valley Fighter Pilot Association Scholarships *(Graduate, Undergraduate/Scholarship)*

**Focus:** General Studies. **Qualif.:** Applicants must be the sons, daughters, or the spouse of members of U.S. military forces engaged in armed conflicts who were Killed in Action (KIA) or Missing in Action (MIA) during the period from Southeast Asia (1964) through the present. Candidates must attend accredited colleges and universities. **Criteria:** Scholarship awards are based on scholarship and demonstrated need.

**Funds Avail.:** The amount of scholarships is individually determined. All money is paid on invoice directly to the institution. **Deadline:** March 15.

**Remarks:** The Scholarship Program was established in 1970 out of concern for the families of aircrews who flew on the Red River Valley of North Vietnam and were killed or missing in action. These men were also known as "River Rats". **Contact:** Executive Director at the above address (see entry 5086).

## • 5088 •
## Spence Reese Foundation
c/o Boys & Girls Clubs of San
  Diego
3760 4th Ave., Ste. 1          *Ph:* (619)298-3520
San Diego, CA 92103          *Fax:* (619)298-3615

### • 5089 • Spence Reese Scholarship *(High School, Undergraduate/Scholarship)*

**Focus:** Law, Medicine, Engineering, Political Science. **Qualif.:** Applicants must be graduating United States male high school seniors planning on majoring in the field of law, medicine, engineering, or political science. Since finalists must, at their own expense, come to San Diego for a personal interview, students within a 250 mile radius of San Diego are especially encouraged to apply. **Criteria:** Awards are based on academic standing, academic ability, financial ability, and potential for good citizenship.

**Funds Avail.:** $2,000. **No. of Awards:** 4. **To Apply:** Interested students should send a self-addressed, stamped envelope with a written application request to the Foundation after January 1 of their graduating year. **Deadline:** May 15 of graduating year. **Contact:** Jean Pilley, at the above address (see entry 5088).

**• 5090 •**
**REFORMA - National Association to Promote Library Service to the Spanish Speaking**
El Paso Community College
Library Technical Services
Luis Chaparro, Director
PO Box 20500
El Paso, TX 79998-0500
*E-mail:* luisc@laguna.epcc.edu
*URL:* http://latino.sscnet.ucla.edu/library/reforma.html

*Ph:* (915)594-2132
*Fax:* (915)594-2592

**• 5091 •** **REFORMA Scholarships** *(Graduate/Scholarship)*

**Purpose:** To encourage and enable Spanish-speakers to pursue careers in library and information science. **Focus:** Information Science, Librarianship. **Qualif.:** Applicant must be a U.S. citizen or permanent resident who is a bilingual speaker of Spanish. Candidate must be enrolled in an accredited graduate school of library and information science by the start of the fellowship term. Applicant must demonstrate a commitment to a career in librarianship, preferably in service to the Spanish-speaking community.

**Funds Avail.:** Varies $1,000 minimum. **No. of Awards:** Varies. **To Apply:** Write for application form and guidelines. Submit form, copies of academic transcripts, curriculum vitae, and two letters of recommendation. **Deadline:** May 15. **Contact:** Orlando Archibegi, Chair, at the above address (see entry 5090).

**• 5092 •**
**The Reporters Committee for Freedom of the Press**
1815 N. Fort Myer Dr., Ste. 900
Arlington, VA 22209-1817
*E-mail:* rcfp@rcfp.org
*URL:* http://www.rcfp.org/rcfp

*Ph:* (703)807-2100
*Fax:* (703)807-2109

**• 5093 •** **Reporters Committee Fellowship** *(Professional Development/Fellowship)*

**Purpose:** To provide one year of legal experience working with a non-profit public interest law group in Washington, D.C. Fellows monitor legal issues, provide legal advice and assistance to working journalists, write legal briefs and memoranda, and write for committee publications. **Focus:** Law, Journalism. **Qualif.:** Applicants must have earned a law degree by August in the year the fellowship begins. Fellowships run from September to August. Background in journalism, including undergraduate or graduate journalism degree and/or reporting experience is greatly preferred. Preference is given to those who have taken any state bar examination by August. **Criteria:** Based on quality and quantity of

journalism/media law background, writing and research ability, and commitment to public interest law.

**Funds Avail.:** Two $25,000 stipends and fully paid health insurance. **No. of Awards:** 2. **To Apply:** No formal application is required. A cover letter, resume, and legal and non-legal writing samples must be submitted with names, addresses, and phone numbers of three references. **Deadline:** January 4.

**Remarks:** There are generally between 30 and 35 applicants. **Contact:** Jane E. Kirtley, Executive Director, at the above address (see entry 5092).

**• 5094 •** **Reporters Committee for Freedom of the Press Clinical Internship Program** *(Graduate, Undergraduate/Internship)*

**Purpose:** To provide the opportunity to assist in the editing and production of the Committee's publications. Some schools accept internships for credit. **Focus:** Journalism. **Qualif.:** Candidates must be qualified junior, senior or graduate journalism students interested in the legal aspect of the press. **To Apply:** Applicants must submit a resume, short writing sample, and cover letter describing their interest. **Deadline:** Late March, late October, and late January.

**• 5095 •**
**Research Corporation - Science Advancement Program**
101 N. Wilmot Rd., Ste. 250
Tucson, AZ 85711-3332
*E-mail:* awards@rescorp.org
*URL:* http://www.rescorp.org/

*Ph:* (602)571-1111
*Fax:* (602)571-1119

**• 5096 •** **Cottrell Scholars Science Awards** *(Professional Development/Award)*

**Purpose:** To support excellence in both research and teaching in chemistry, astronomy and physics in Ph.D. granting departments. **Focus:** Astronomy, Chemistry, Physics. **Qualif.:** Applicant must be a faculty member in the third year of a tenure-track appointment. **Criteria:** Based on scientific merit and originality of the candidate's research plan, and contributions to, and aspirations for teaching.

**Funds Avail.:** $50,000 each award. **No. of Awards:** No fixed number. **To Apply:** Write or call for information. **Deadline:** September 1.

**Remarks:** No budget is required, and funds can be used at the discretion of the awardee for most direct costs. There is no provision for indirect costs. **Contact:** Science Advancement Program at the above address (see entry 5095).

**• 5097 •** **Research Opportunity Awards** *(Professional Development/Award)*

**Purpose:** For mid-career faculty members seeking to explore new areas of research. **Focus:** Astronomy, Chemistry, Physics. **Qualif.:** Applicant must be a mid-career tenured scientist in a Ph.D.-granting department in the United States. Candidate must be nominated by department chair. **Criteria:** For scientists of demonstrated productivity without other funding.

**Funds Avail.:** Varies. Typical awards are in the range of $10,000 to $25,000. **No. of Awards:** No fixed number. **To Apply:** Write for guidelines. **Deadline:** May 1 and October 1. **Contact:** Science Advancement Program at the above address (see entry 5095).

## Research and Engineering Council of the Graphic Arts Industry, Inc.

Box No. 639                                  *Ph:* (610)388-7394
Chadds Ford, PA 19317-0610                   *Fax:* (610)388-2708
*E-mail:* recouncil@aol.com
*URL:* http://www.recouncil.org

**• 5099 •   William D. Krenkler Working Scholar Program** *(Undergraduate/Scholarship)*

**Purpose:** To assist working scholars in the graphic arts field. **Qualif.:** Must attend Drexel University in Philadelphia, Pennsylvania. **Contact:** Ronald L. Mihills, Managing Director.

**• 5100 •   William J. Mariner Working Scholar Program** *(Undergraduate/Scholarship)*

**Purpose:** To financially assist working scholars in the graphic arts field. **Qualif.:** Applicants must attend Rochester Institute of Technology in Rochester, New York. **Contact:** Ronald L. Mihills, Managing Director, at the above address (see entry 5098).

**• 5101 •   R & E Council Graphic Arts Educators' Programs** *(Professional Development/Grant)*

**Purpose:** To enable professional educators to attend each of the four technical seminars sponsored by the R&E Council. **Qualif.:** Applicants must be a college-level faculty members.

**Remarks:** Scholarships are awarded with the assistance of the International Graphic Arts Educators Association (IGAEA). **Contact:** Ronald L. Mihills, at the above address (see entry 5098).

## Research Science Institute - The Center for Excellence in Education

7710 Old Springhouse Rd., Ste.
  1000                                        *Ph:* (703)448-9062
Mc Lean, VA 22102                            *Fax:* (703)442-9513

**• 5103 •   Research Science Institute Internship** *(Undergraduate/Internship)*

**Focus:** Science. **Qualif.:** Applicants must have completed the equivalant of three years of high school. **Criteria:** Internships are granted based on high school academic record, recommendations, PSAT scores, and personal essays. **To Apply:** Applicants must send a self-addressed envelope with extra postage to Ms. Maite Ballestero, Director of Student Programs. **Deadline:** February 1.

**Remarks:** Sponsored by the Center for Excellence in Education, in collaboration with Massachusetts Institute of Technology, the thirteenth annual Research Science Institute combines classroom lectures and tutoring with off-campus internships in scientific research. On-campus instruction stresses mathematics and the biological and physical sciences, as well as the humanities. Classes in quantitative analysis, scientific communication, computer use and research methods prepare students for internships. Participants are matched with leading scientists at M.I.T., Harvard research organizations and private industries. The Guest Lecture Series features nationally recognized figures in science and the humanities. Field trips to cultural and scientific sites occur on weekends. Students and teachers come from all states and are joined by international students on weekends. Students and teachers come from all states and are joined by international students for the six-week program. In prior years, professors from M.I.T., Harvard University, University of Washington, Yale University, and Emory University have led the professorial staff.

## Reserve Officers Association of the United States

1 Constitution Ave. NE                       *Ph:* (202)479-2200
Washington, DC 20002-5624                    *Fax:* (202)479-0416
                                             *Free:* 800-809-9448
*E-mail:* 71154.1267@compuserve.com
*URL:* http://www.roa.org/

*The Reserve Officers Association is a professional association that represents all military officers in the Army, Navy, Air Force, Marine Corps, Coast Guard, Public Health Service and NOAA.*

**• 5105 •   Henry J. Reilly Memorial Graduate Scholarships** *(Doctorate, Graduate/Scholarship)*

**Focus:** General Studies. **Qualif.:** Applicants must be active or associate ROA members accepted for graduate study at a regionally accredited four-year United States university or college where they are enrolled in two graduate courses. If applicants are employed full-time during the period of proposed doctoral study, they may be enrolled in one course. If pursuing a Master's degree, candidates must have an undergraduate GPA of 3.2 on a 4.0 scale. If continuing in a doctoral program, they must have a Master's degree or be accepted into a doctoral program. If applicants have completed some graduate work and are continuing in the same program, they must have a 3.3 GPA on 4.0 scale in the graduate work previously undertaken.

**Funds Avail.:** The number of annual scholarships varies. The maximum annual scholarship is $500 and can not exceed one half of the total annual cost of tuition or institutional fees charged by the institution attended. **To Apply:** Applicants must submit a completed application with three letters of recommendation, one from a military reporting senior or a civilian "reporting senior" regarding leadership ability or potential and two from persons qualified to assess academic ability. A curriculum vitae is also required. **Deadline:** April 15. **Contact:** Reserve Officers Association of the United States at the above address (see entry 5104).

**• 5106 •   Henry J. Reilly Memorial Undergraduate Scholarship for College Attendees** *(Undergraduate/ Scholarship)*

**Focus:** General Studies. **Qualif.:** Applicants must be active or associate ROA or ROAL members or the children or grandchildren, age 26 or under, of such members. Children age 21 or under of deceased members who were active and paid up at the time of their death are also eligible. Spouses are not eligible unless they are members of ROA or ROAL. ROTC members do not qualify as sponsors. Legal guardians are eligible sponsors. Candidates must have registered for the draft (if eligible), be enrolled for full-time college study at a regionally accredited four-year United States university or college, and show evidence of good moral character and appropriate leadership qualities. Applicants who are first-year college attendees must have a minimum 3.3 high school GPA and a minimum 3.0 college GPA (based on a 4.0 scale). Applicants in their second and subsequent undergraduate years must have a 3.0 college GPA and have completed 30 or more semester units or 48 or more quarter units annually. A minimum combined verbal/math SAT score of 1200 and a minimum combined English/math ACT score of 57 (test before October 1989) or 62 (test in October 1989 or later) is also required.

**Funds Avail.:** The maximum annual scholarship is $500 and can not exceed one half of the total annual cost of tuition or institutional fees charged by the institution attended. **No. of Awards:** Varies. **To Apply:** Applicants must submit a copy of their final high school transcripts, a copy of the most recent college transcripts, SAT or ACT scores, and an essay of approximately 500 words (in the student's own handwriting) on career goals. **Deadline:** April 15. **Contact:** Reserve Officers Association of the United States at the above address (see entry 5104).

### • 5107 • Henry J. Reilly Memorial Undergraduate Scholarship for Graduating High School Students
*(Undergraduate/Scholarship)*

**Focus:** General Studies. **Qualif.:** Applicants must be children or grandchildren of active or associate ROA or ROAL members. Children, age 21 or under, of deceased members who were active and paid up at the time of their death are also eligible. Candidates must have registered for the draft (if eligible) and be attending or accepted for full-time undergraduate study at a regionally accredited four-year United States university or college. They must show evidence of good moral character and demonstrate appropriate leadership qualities. Only applicants who are in the top quarter of their graduating class will be considered. A minimum combined verbal/math SAT score of 1200 and a minimum combined English/math ACT score of 55 are required. Applicants must have a minimum GPA of 3.3 on a 4.0 scale (for the previous 5 semesters, including the first semester of the senior year).

**Funds Avail.:** The maximum annual scholarship is $500 and can not exceed one half of the total annual cost of tuition or institutional fees charged by the institution attended. **No. of Awards:** Varies. **To Apply:** Applicants must submit an essay of approximately 500 words (in the student's own handwriting) on career goals. **Deadline:** April. **Contact:** Reserve Officers Association of the United States at the above address (see entry 5104).

---

### • 5108 •
### Resort and Commercial Recreation Association
PO Box 1998
Tarpon Springs, FL 34688-1998     *Ph:* (813)845-7373

#### • 5109 • RCRA Internship Program *(Undergraduate/ Internship)*

**Focus:** Parks and Recreation. **Qualif.:** Applicants must be fully enrolled as juniors or seniors in a college or university recreation curriculum. **Criteria:** Selection is based upon the recommendation of student's college advisor, as well as career goals and past experience.

**Funds Avail.:** $100 per week. **To Apply:** Applicant should submit a resume and three work references with phone numbers, allowing four to six months for application and interview process to be completed. **Contact:** Frank Oliveto, Executive Director, at the above address (see entry 5108).

---

### • 5110 •
### Resources for the Future
1616 P St., NW     *Ph:* (202)328-5067
Washington, DC 20036     *Fax:* (202)939-3460
*URL:* http://www.rff.org

#### • 5111 • Joseph L. Fisher Dissertation Awards
*(Doctorate/Fellowship)*

**Purpose:** To support doctoral dissertation research in economics on issues related to the environment, natural resources, or energy. **Focus:** Economics, Energy-related Areas, Natural History, Environmental Science. **Qualif.:** Applicants must be graduate students in their final year of their dissertation research. Candidates must have completed the preliminary examinations for

the doctorate not later than February 1, or the year of the award. Women and members of minority groups are especially encouraged to apply.

**Funds Avail.:** The fellowship includes a stipend of $12,000 for the academic year. It is expected that the fellowship recipients will engage in no employment during the period of fellowship tenure and that RFF will be notified immediately of financial assistance made available from any other source for support of doctoral work. **To Apply:** Applicants must submit a letter of application, a graduate transcript, a one-page abstract of the dissertation, a technical summary of the dissertation not to exceed 2,500 words in length (not including the bibliography), a letter from the department chair or other university official certifying the student's Ph.D. candidacy, and two letters or recommendation from faculty members on the student's dissertation committee. The technical summary should describe the specific aims of the dissertation, the significance of the project, and why its results may be important, the research methods to be used, and how the research builds on existing literature on the topic. **Deadline:** February 27. **Contact:** Coordinator for Academic Programs at the above address (see entry 5110).

#### • 5112 • Gilbert F. White Postdoctoral Fellowships
*(Postdoctorate/Fellowship)*

**Purpose:** To promote and develop scholarly work on social science or public policy programs in the areas of natural resources, energy, or the environment. **Focus:** Energy-related Areas—Conservation, Environmental Science. **Qualif.:** Applicant may be of any nationality, but must have completed the Ph.D. by the start of the fellowship year. Applicant may be from any discipline, but research must relate to the concerns and projects of RFF. Awards are tenable at RFF in Washington, D.C. **Criteria:** Teaching and/or research at the postdoctoral level is preferred though not essential.

**Funds Avail.:** Fellows receive an annual stipend commensurate with experience, plus research support, office facilities at RFF, and up to $1,000 for moving/living expenses. **To Apply:** Write to Chris Mendes for application materials. **Deadline:** February 27. Awards are announced in April. **Contact:** Coordinator for Academic Programs at the above address (see entry 5110).

---

### • 5113 •
### Retired Officers Association - Cape Canaveral Chapter
PO Box 4708
Patrick AFB, FL 32925

#### • 5114 • Cape Canaveral Chapter Scholarships
*(Graduate, Undergraduate/Scholarship)*

**Purpose:** To assist worthy and outstanding students in disciplines critical to the Nation's Security. **Focus:** Mathematics, Science, General Studies. **Qualif.:** Applicants must be descendants of officers or enlisted members of the armed forces on active duty, in reserve status, retired or deceased. Applicants must be legal residents of Brevard County, Florida, and have successfully completed sufficient college-level credit hours acceptable to an accredited college or university for entry into the junior or senior year of a four-year program that will lead to a Bachelor's degree in science, engineering, mathematics, or liberal arts. Freshman and sophomore credits may be earned either at a two-or four-year institution of higher learning. **Criteria:** Awards are made on the basis of citizenship, merit, moral character, attitude, scholarship, leadership, and extracurricular activities.

**Funds Avail.:** Six awards of $2,000 each. **To Apply:** Applications are sent upon request. **Deadline:** May 31. **Contact:** Chairman, Scholarship Committee, at the above address (see entry 5113).

---

## • 5115 •
### The Retired Officers Association EAP
201 North Washington St.
Alexandria, VA 22314                    Ph: (703)549-2311
*URL:* http://www.troa.org

#### • 5116 • The Retired Officers Association Educational Assistance Program *(Undergraduate/Loan)*

**Purpose:** To help children from military families attain a higher education. **Focus:** General Studies. **Qualif.:** Applicants must be military dependents (with an ID card) who are unmarried and enrolled in an undergraduate program. Service personnel may be either active or retired. **Criteria:** Selection is based on academics, activities, and need.

**Funds Avail.:** Repayment on the interest free renewable loans must begin within three months after graduation or withdrawal from school. **No. of Awards:** Approximately 1100 loans are available annually including 600-800 renewals. **To Apply:** Formal application required. The telephone number for application requests is 1-800-245-8762. **Deadline:** Completed application must be postmarked on or before March 1. **Contact:** The Retired Officers Association at the above address (see entry 5115).

## • 5117 •
### Charles H. Revson Fellows Program on the Future of the City of New York
Columbia University
420 West 116th St., No. 1-A          Ph: (212)280-4023
New York, NY 10027                   Fax: (212)663-7537

#### • 5118 • Revson Fellowships *(Professional Development/Fellowship)*

**Purpose:** To allow mid-career individuals to study at Columbia University to enhance their understanding of and ability to contribute to the improvement of New York City and other large metropolitan centers. **Focus:** No restrictions; New York City, Urban Studies, or any area of the candidate's choosing. **Qualif.:** Candidates should preferably be U.S. citizens or permanent residents. They may be any age although successful candidates have ranged from 25 to 55 years old. Candidates must demonstrate a record of achievement in some aspect of urban affairs in New York City or another large U.S. city. There are no educational prerequisites but candidates must demonstrate suitable intellectual interest and capacity. The Program expects to choose at least one fellow who does not hold a college degree. Fellowships are tenable at Columbia University. Fellows must spend four days a week at the University engaged in a program of study and research.

**Funds Avail.:** $18,000 stipend plus tuition, fees, and medical insurance. **No. of Awards:** 10. **To Apply:** Call or write to the director for application form and guidelines. Submit form with a 1,000-word essay describing contributions to urban affairs, and an essay outlining proposed research program and its expected benefits. **Deadline:** February 1. Notification by March 30.

## • 5119 •
### Z. Smith Reynolds Foundation
101 Reynolda Village              Ph: (919)725-7541
Winston-Salem, NC 27106-5199      Fax: (919)725-6069

#### • 5120 • Z. Smith Reynolds Fellowship *(Professional Development/Fellowship)*

**Purpose:** To offer the experience of working in a private charitable foundation to individuals in early stages of their careers. **Qualif.:** Applicant must be a resident or native of North Carolina and/or recent graduate from an institution of higher learning in the state. **Criteria:** This position is appropriate for persons with an interest in philanthropy, public policy, the nonprofit sector, or community service.

**Funds Avail.:** The position is salaried and includes benefits. **No. of Awards:** 1 per year. **To Apply:** Applications may be obtained from North Carolina college placement offices or by writing to the Foundation. **Deadline:** Currently March 1, but subject to change.

**Remarks:** Fellowship will begin in August, although the Foundation will consider modest adjustments.

## • 5121 •
### Rhode Island Commission on State Government - Internships
8AA State House                   Ph: (401)277-6782
Providence, RI 02903              Fax: (401)277-6142

#### • 5122 • Rhode Island Commission on State Government Summer Internships *(Graduate, Undergraduate/Internship)*

**Purpose:** To enable students to participate in State Government while interning in a department or agency that will provide a knowledgeable experience relative to an intern's major course of study or interest. **Focus:** Government. **Qualif.:** Applicants must be Rhode Island residents attending an out of state college or university or handicapped college students enrolled in a 2- or 4-year college or university. They must have completed their sophomore year by June 1 or have senior status in a 2-year college. Students enrolled in law school or graduate school are also eligible. A minimum 2.5 of 4.0 GPA is required. **Criteria:** Eligibility is a major factor in acceptance. Students are interviewed by the internship staff.

**Funds Avail.:** A stipend is awarded on a monthly basis for a two month period. Work study students are also eligible. **No. of Awards:** 160. **To Apply:** Candidates must submit an application accompanied by a resume, letter of interest, and letter of recommendation from a state senator or representative. **Deadline:** May 15.

**Remarks:** Intern responsibilities include a 35 hour work week within chosen field placement, time sheet responsibilities, mandatory student progress reports, and final assessment. Internships are for 8 weeks in July and August. The Commission also offers a Spring internship for class credit only. **Contact:** Robert W. Gemma, Executive Director, at the above address (see entry 5121).

• 5123 •
## Rhode Island Space Grant
Brown University
Lincoln Field Bldg.
Box 1846
Providence, RI 02912          *Ph:* (401)863-2889
*E-mail:* RISpaceGrant@brown.edu
*URL:* http://www.spacegrant.brown.edu/RI_Space_Grant/

### • 5124 • Brown-NASA Space Grant Scholars Program *(Undergraduate/Scholarship)*

**Purpose:** To aissist students in financial need. **Focus:** Math, science, or engineering.

### • 5125 • Space Grant Graduate Fellowship Program *(Graduate/Fellowship)*

**Purpose:** To provide study opportunities for students. **Focus:** Space related research in science, math, or engineering. **Qualif.:** Applicants must be graduate students.

### • 5126 • Space Grant Undergraduate Scholar Program *(Undergraduate/Scholarship)*

**Focus:** Space-related science, math, and engineering; or education. **Qualif.:** Applicants must be undergraduate students.

### • 5127 • Space Grant Undergraduate Summer Scholar Program *(Undergraduate/Scholarship)*

**Focus:** Science, math, and engineering. **Qualif.:** Applicants must be undergraduate students, especially those who are uncertain about their career choices.

**Remarks:** Provides outreach activities in addition to research experience in the awardees department or field of interest.

• 5128 •
## The Rhodes Scholarship Trust
American Secretary
Pomona College
Claremont, CA 91711-6305          *Ph:* (909)621-8138
                                   *Fax:* (909)621-9609

*Initiated in 1903, the Rhodes Scholarship Program owes its existence to Cecil J. Rhodes, a British colonial pioneer and statesman who took his degree from Oxford University in 1881. He established the Trust through his will in the hopes of "bettering the lot of mankind through the diffusion of leaders motivated to serve their contemporaires, trained in the contemplative life of the mind, and broadened by their acquaintance with one another and by their exposure to cultures different from their own." To this end, scholarships are granted to scholars from the United States, Australia, Canada, New Zealand, Kenya, Nigeria, South Africa, Zimbabwe, India, Malaysia, Pakistan, Singapore, Hong Kong, Bermuda, the Commonwealth Caribbean, Jamaica, and Germany. Scholarships are granted only for study at Oxford University to individuals considered likely to make substantial contributions to the world. Typically, there are approximately 200 Rhodes Scholars in residence during a term.*

### • 5129 • Rhodes Scholarships *(Graduate, Undergraduate/Scholarship)*

**Purpose:** To enable outstanding post baccalaureate students to study for up to three years at Oxford University in any field of study available through the Oxford colleges. **Focus:** General Studies. **Qualif.:** Candidates must be U.S. citizens between the ages of 18 and 24 on October 1 in the year of application (Canadian scholars are eligible to apply for the 11 Rhodes Scholarships reserved for

Canadians through the Office of the Canadian Secretary.) Applicants must have academic standing sufficient to assure completion of a Bachelor's degree before going into residence in Oxford the following October. Scholars are expected to maintain full-time status at Oxford for the duration of their degree programs. Deferment is not allowed except for medical internships. **Criteria:** Selection committees look for proven intellectual and academic achievement of a high standard and evidence of integrity of character, an interest in and respect for others, the ability to lead, and the energy to use their talents to the full. Committee members judge the above based on academic transcripts, candidate's application essay, reference letters, and personal interviews.

**Funds Avail.:** Stipends include all tuition fees (paid directly to the college), an annual maintenance allowance adequate to meet necessary expenses for term-time and vacations, and assistance with travel expenses to and from Oxford. Scholars are appointed for two years with the possibility of renewal for a third year. Scholarship tenure is dependent upon the maintenance of a standard of work and conduct, which, in the opinion of the Trustees, justifies the Scholarship. Tenure of other awards in conjunction with a Rhodes Scholarship is not permitted without prior consultation with the Warden of Rhodes House in Oxford. 32 Scholarships are awarded annually in the United States. **To Apply:** Candidates must apply either through the state in which they legally reside or in the state in which they have received two or more years of college or university training. Applications must include academic transcripts, medical examination report, photocopy of applicant's birth certificate or proof of citizenship, a thousand-word essay on applicant's interests and reasons for wishing to attend Oxford University, and a brief description of college honors and activities. Candidates are also required to list the names and full addresses of at least five and no more than eight persons who have agreed to write letters of recommendation. No fewer than four of these must be persons under whom the candidate has done academic work at a college or university. Committees of Selection also welcome letters from persons competent to comment on aspects of the candidate's character and interests as revealed in non-academic activities. The candidate is personally responsible for insuring that the individuals named as referees receive reproductions of the information form for referees that is provided as part of the application package. No letter of recommendation submitted directly by a candidate will be considered. **Deadline:** October (exact date to be announced).

**Remarks:** Candidates from 288 American colleges and universities had been selected as Rhodes Scholars. **Contact:** Application forms and current issues of the Memorandum of Regulations are distributed in late summer to representatives of the Rhodes Scholarships on campuses throughout the country. Additional copies of application forms can be obtained by writing to the Office of the American Secretary at the above address (see entry 5128). Completed applications and accompanying materials must be submitted directly to the secretary of the appropriate State Committee before the October deadline. Canadian applicants should contact A.R.A. Scace, Esq. Q.C., General Secretary, PO Box 48, Toronto Dominion Centre, Toronto, Ontario, Canada M5K 1E6.

• 5130 •
## Richard III Society, Inc.
Schallek Awards Office
303 Vine St., Ste. 106
Philadelphia, PA 19106-1143          *Ph:* (215)574-1570
                                     *Fax:* (215)574-1571
*E-mail:* lblanchard@aol.com
*URL:* http://www.webcom.com/blanchrd/index.html

### • 5131 • David Carlyle Richards III Scholarships *(Undergraduate/Scholarship)*

**Focus:** General Studies. **Qualif.:** Applicants must be beginning their senior year at a high school in Carroll County, Illinois and

## Richard III Society, Inc. (continued)

accepted by an institution giving four years of post-high school education. A junior college is acceptable if a student intends to enroll for the third or fourth year at a college or university. No exceptions to the above qualifications are made. **Criteria:** Financial need.

**Funds Avail.:** Minimum $1,000 per semester. The trustees pay the tuition and fees of the college or university chosen by the recipient directly to the institution. Students must carry the minimum number of hours required by the college of choice to be considered a full-time student. **No. of Awards:** 1 every 4 years. **To Apply:** Applications must be accompanied by a transcript of grades (for seven semesters), letters of recommendation from the high school principal and the guidance counselor, and a biographical sketch. **Deadline:** March 31. The recipient and alternate will be notified by April 30. The alternate will be eligible for that year's award in the event that it is not used by the recipient for the next academic year. **Contact:** Donald S. Wolfe Jr., Trustee Manager, 353 Chicago Ave., Savanna, IL 61074. Telephone: (815)273-2839.

### • 5132 • William B. Schallek Memorial Graduate Study Fellowships (Doctorate, Graduate/Fellowship)

**Focus:** History. **Qualif.:** Candidates must be pursuing graduate education in fields relating to the life and times of King Richard III (1483-1485) or to late 15th century England. They must be U.S. citizens or have made application for first citizenship papers, enrolled at a recognized educational institution, and making normal progress toward a graduate degree (typically the M.A. or Ph.D.)

**Funds Avail.:** $500-$1000. **To Apply:** Candidates should submit application, transcripts of previous undergraduate and/or graduate record, four letters of recommendation (at least two should be from college or university instructors), personal statement, and estimate of expenses and resources for graduate study. An original and four photo copies of all material are needed. **Deadline:** February 28. Candidates will be notified by June 1. **Contact:** Laura Blanchard at the above address (see entry 5130).

### • 5133 •
## Sid Richardson Memorial Fund
309 Main St.
Ft. Worth, TX 76102          Ph: (817)336-0494
E-mail: jhrosacker@sidrichardson.org

### • 5134 • Sid Richardson Memorial Fund Scholarship (Graduate, Undergraduate/Scholarship)

**Focus:** General studies. **Qualif.:** Applicants must be direct descendants (children or grandchildren) of persons presently employed or retired with a minimum of three years' full time service for one or more of the following companies: Sid Richardson Carbon Co., Sid Richardson Gasoline Co., Richardson Products II Co., SRCG Aviation, Inc., Leapartners, L.P. (dba Sid Richardson Gasoline Co. - Jal), Bass Enterprises Production Company, Bass Brothers Enterprises, Inc., Richardson Oils, Inc., Perry R. Bass, Inc. Sid W. Richardson Foundation, San Jose Cattle Company, City Center Development Company and Richardson Aviation. **Criteria:** Awards are granted based on academic achievement and financial need.

**Funds Avail.:** Varies. **No. of Awards:** Varies. **To Apply:** Write for further details. **Deadline:** March 29. **Contact:** Jo Helen Rosacker at the above address (see entry 5133).

### • 5135 •
## Richland County Foundation
24 W. 3rd St., Ste. 100
Mansfield, OH 44902-1209          Ph: (419)525-3020
                                   Fax: (419)525-1590

### • 5136 • Richland County Foundation Scholarships (Undergraduate/Scholarship)

**Purpose:** To cover educational expenses for Richland County full-time undergraduate students. **Focus:** General Studies. **Qualif.:** Applicants must be residents of Richland County, Ohio, and full-time undergraduate students with a 2.5 grade point average. **Criteria:** Selections are based on financial need.

**Funds Avail.:** Up to $150,000 is given annually. The average grant is $525. **To Apply:** Candidates must file an application form and send a transcript of grades and a copy of Student Aid Report. **Deadline:** Deadline for application is May 1; deadline for transcript of grades and Student Aid Report is May 1. **Contact:** Amy Marinelli, Program Officer, at the above address (see entry 5135).

### • 5137 •
## Ripon Educational Fund
501 Capitol Court, NE, Ste. 300
Washington, DC 20002          Ph: (202)543-5466
                               Fax: (202)547-6560

### • 5138 • Mark O. Hatfield Scholarship (Graduate/ Scholarship)

**Purpose:** To encourage work by young scholars in the areas of civil liberties, war and peace, environmental stewardship, federalism and economic priorities. **Focus:** Civil Liberties, Economics, Environmental Policy, Federalism, International Relations, Law, Peace and Conflict Studies. **Qualif.:** Applicants must be graduate students prepared to write a paper of publishable quality on a topic reflecting the Fund's interests. Scholarships are intended to assist writers while they work on the paper; awards are not given for already completed works. Scholars are also encouraged to publish their material in journals.

**Funds Avail.:** $2,000 average. **To Apply:** Write for application guidelines. Submit a one or two page outline of proposed area of study, a resume, and one writing sample. **Deadline:** May 31, August 31, December 31. **Contact:** Michael Dubke, at the above address (see entry 5137).

### • 5139 •
## Robert S. McNamara Fellowships Program - The World Bank
c/o Shobha Kumar
Room G3-175
1818 H St. NW
Washington, DC 20433          Ph: (202)473-6441
                               Fax: (202)676-0962
E-mail: skumar@worldbank.org
URL: http://www.worldbank.org

### • 5140 • Robert S. McNamara Fellowships (Postgraduate/Fellowship)

**Purpose:** To support innovative and imaginative postgraduate work that contributes to the general knowledge of economic development. **Focus:** Economic Development. **Qualif.:** Applicant must be a national or resident of a country eligible to borrow from the World Bank; be under the age of 35 years; and posess a master's degree at time of application.

Funds Avail.: $7,500 to cover research costs. **To Apply:** Write to the fellowship program's assistant administrator for application materials. **Deadline:** November 15.

**Remarks:** Established in 1982.

---

• 5141 •
**Rockefeller Archive Center**
Pocantico Hills
15 Dayton Ave.                                    *Ph:* (914)631-4505
North Tarrytown, NY 10591-1598          *Fax:* (914)631-6017
*E-mail:* archive@rockvax.rockefeller.edu
*URL:* http://www.rockefeller.edu/archive.ctr

• 5142 • **Rockefeller Archive Center Research Grants** *(Graduate, Postdoctorate, Professional Development/Grant)*

**Purpose:** To foster research in the holdings of the Center. **Focus:** African American History, Agricultural History, Art History, Demography, Economic Development, Education, History, History of Medicine, History of Science, International Relations, Labor, Philanthropy, Political Science, Religious Studies, Rockefeller Family, Rockefeller Foundation, Rockefeller University, Social Sciences, Social Welfare, Women's Studies. **Qualif.:** Candidate may be of any nationality. Applicant may be from any discipline and may be a graduate student, postdoctoral scholar, or other researcher whose work requires substantial use of the Center's collections. Recipients are asked to submit a report upon completion of their research and provide a copy of the resulting publications. Grants are tenable only for research at the Center.

**Funds Avail.:** $2,500 maximum; applicants from outside U.S. and Canada may request up to $3,000. **No. of Awards:** Up to 50/yr. **To Apply:** Write for application forms and guidelines. Submit form with two letters of reference. **Deadline:** November 30. Awardees are announced in March. **Contact:** Darwin H. Stapleton, director, at the above address (see entry 5141).

---

• 5143 •
**Rockefeller Brothers Fund**
437 Madison Ave., 37th Fl.                   *Ph:* (212)812-4200
New York, NY 10022-7001                     *Fax:* (212)812-4299
*E-mail:* rock@rbf.org
*URL:* http://www.rbf.org/

• 5144 • **Rockefeller Brothers Fund Fellowships for Minority Students** *(Undergraduate/Fellowship)*

**Purpose:** To increase the number of minority teachers in American public education. **Focus:** Education. **Qualif.:** Applicants must be undergraduate minority students in the arts and sciences who are in their junior year at one of the 25 participating institutions and plan to pursue a master's degree in education or a related field. **Criteria:** Each participating institution recruits and screens eligible students on campus, and the institution nominates up to three candidates to the program. Finalists are interviewed by a selection committee.

**Funds Avail.:** $18,100 maximum. **No. of Awards:** 25. **To Apply:** Write for further details. **Deadline:** December 31.

**Remarks:** Fellows are expected to move continuously through the final year of undergraduate work leading to a B.A., through one or two years of full-time graduate program, and into a public school teaching position, and each Fellow is required to submit an annual report describing the year's accomplishments and plans for the following year, on a form provided by the Fund, in order to remain

eligible for the Fellowship. **Contact:** Miriam Aneses at the above address (see entry 5143).

---

• 5145 •
**Rockefeller Foundation**
Communications Office
420 5th Ave.                                      *Ph:* (212)869-8500
New York, NY 10018                           *Fax:* (212)764-3468
*URL:* http://www.rockfound.org/

• 5146 • **Bellagio Residencies for Scholars and Artists** *(Professional Development/Fellowship)*

**Purpose:** To provide the opportunity for scholars and artists to work at the Bellagio Center in Italy. **Focus:** General Studies. **Qualif.:** Applicant may be of any nationality. Candidate must be an artist, composer, practitioner, scholar, scientist, or writer, who has produced significant publications, compositions, or shows. Applicant should be engaged in a major project that relates to the Foundation's own program interests and that does not require laboratory or extensive library resources. Preference is given to candidates that expect their projects to result in publication or exhibition. Grants are tenable at the Bellagio Study and Conference Center in northern Italy.

**Funds Avail.:** Residency; travel allowance provided for developing country residents. **To Apply:** Write to the Bellagio Center Office for application form and guidelines. Submit form, a project summary, a detailed description of the project, and curriculum vitae. Include a list of publications and one sample of published work, if applicable. **Deadline:** At least one year prior to proposed residency.

**Remarks:** Pre-and postdoctoral fellowships may also be offered in conjunction with on-going science programs of the Foundation. Areas of study and requirements vary from program to program. Specific inquiries should be addressed to the appropriate division head, but basic guidelines are available from the Communications Department. **Contact:** Bellagio Center Office at the above address (see entry 5145).

• 5147 • **Biotechnology Career Fellowships** *(Postdoctorate/Fellowship)*

**Purpose:** To enable scientists from developing countries to conduct investigations requiring periodic residence at research institutions in other countries. **Focus:** Biotechnology as applied to Agriculture, Environmental Protection, Health Sciences, and Reproductive Biology. **Qualif.:** Applicant must be a citizen of a developing country and must have a Ph.D. or M.D. in a field of biotechnology. Candidate must be under 45 years old at the time of application. Applicant must hold a permanent position at a research or teaching institution in home country and must have both the proposed host laboratory's and the home institution's endorsements. Fellows are expected to spend approximately three months of each fellowship year at the host institution, which is expected to support most of the research costs.

**Funds Avail.:** Travel and living allowances; $70/day for U.S. fellowships. **To Apply:** Write for application guidelines. Submit a letter of application outlining career goals and previous and current scientific activities, curriculum vitae, letters of recommendation, and a project proposal to be prepared jointly by the candidate and the host laboratory. **Deadline:** At least six months in advance of proposed fellowship.

**Remarks:** Pre- and postdoctoral fellowships may also be offered in conjunction with on-going science programs of the Foundation. Areas of study and requirements vary from program to program. Specific inquiries should be addressed to the appropriate division head, but basic guidelines are available from the Communications

---

*Rockefeller Foundation (continued)*

Department. **Contact:** Jan Tensen at the above address (see entry 5145).

### • 5148 • Multi-Arts Production Fund Grants
*(Professional Development/Grant)*

**Purpose:** To provide artists with development and production support for projects in the performing arts. **Focus:** Performing Arts. **Qualif.:** Candidate may be of any nationality. Applicant must be a professional performing artist who is engaged in a project that reflects a creative approach to international or intercultural representation in contemporary art. Awards are not intended to provide total project support.

**Funds Avail.:** $5,000-9,500. **To Apply:** Write to the Division of the Arts and Humanities for current application guidelines. **Deadline:** Late July. **Contact:** Fellowship Coordinator at the above address (see entry 5145).

### • 5149 • Population Sciences Fellowships *(Graduate, Postdoctorate/Fellowship)*

**Purpose:** To support advanced training and research in the population sciences of developing countries. **Focus:** Demography. **Qualif.:** Applicant may be of any nationality. Candidate must be admitted to a graduate or postdoctoral program in population studies. Preference is given to candidates affiliated with institutions in developing nations who are firmly committed to returning to their home country after completing the fellowship term. Fellowships are tenable at institutions worldwide.

**Funds Avail.:** Predoctoral fellowship: $900/month; postdoctoral fellowship: $1,450/month. **To Apply:** Write for application guidelines. Submit curriculum vitae, a detailed study proposal, a letter from advisor under whom work is to be conducted, a letter of sponsorship from the home institution, three letters of recommendation, and a statement of long-term career interests and objectives. **Deadline:** November 15.

**Remarks:** Pre-and postdoctoral fellowships may also be offered in conjunction with on-going science programs of the Foundation. Areas of study and requirements vary from program to program. Specific inquiries should be addressed to the appropriate division head, but basic guidelines are available from the Communications Department. **Contact:** Jan Tensen at the above address (see entry 5145).

### • 5150 • Reflections on Development Fellowships
*(Postdoctorate/Fellowship)*

**Purpose:** To enable scholars and practitioners from Africa and Southeast Asia to undertake social and historical analyses of development issues. **Focus:** Economic and Social Development. **Qualif.:** Applicant must be an English-speaking citizen or permanent resident of an African or Southeast Asian country. Candidate must have completed academic or professional training, have pertinent publications, and be qualified to conduct social research on basic development issues. Scholars and practitioners from social science fields and other disciplines involving social and economic analysis are eligible to apply. Finalists in the fellowship competition receive a $1,000 grant to develop a detailed framework for their study program; subsequent funding varies and is based on the quality of the full study outline. Fellows should spend at least six months in residence at a relevant regional or international research center, where they may be expected to participate in workshops.

**Funds Avail.:** $30,000 maximum. **To Apply:** Write for application guidelines. Submit an outline of proposed study, a budget, a curriculum vitae, a writing sample of scholarly work, and references. **Deadline:** Varies; May 15.

**Remarks:** Pre- and postdoctoral fellowships may also be offered in conjunction with on-going science programs of the Foundation. Areas of study and requirements vary from program to program.

Specific inquiries should be addressed to the appropriate division head, but basic guidelines are available from the Communications Department. **Contact:** Jan Tensen at the above address (see entry 5145).

### • 5151 • Rockefeller Humanities Fellowship
*(Postdoctorate/Fellowship)*

**Purpose:** To further understanding of contemporary social and cultural issues and to promote scholarship in the humanities focused on international or transnational issues, foreign languages and literatures, the cultures of non-Western nations, and the diverse cultural heritage of the United States. **Qualif.:** Host institutions include academic departments, area studies, and other interdisciplinary programs, museums, and research libraries. Qualifications for individuals vary according to host institution and program.

**Funds Avail.:** Average stipend is $35,000 plus $2,000 toward travel, benefit, and relocation costs. Fellowships usually last between eight and ten months. **No. of Awards:** 75. **To Apply:** Information about eligibility, stipends, and procedures for individual applications is available directly from current host institutions. (List available from the Foundation). **Deadline:** Varies. Contact host institution directly. **Contact:** Lynn Szwaja at the above address (see entry 5145).

### • 5152 • Social Science Research Fellowships in Agriculture *(Postdoctorate/Fellowship)*

**Purpose:** To enable postdoctoral scholars in the social sciences to conduct research in international agricultural development. **Focus:** Agriculture, Rural Development. **Qualif.:** Applicant must be a citizen of the United States, Canada, or a sub-Saharan African country. Candidate must have completed requirements for a Ph.D. in a discipline of the social sciences by the start of the fellowship term, but may not have held the degree for more than four years. Fellowships are tenable at international agricultural institutions based in developing countries.

**Funds Avail.:** $37,000/year. **To Apply:** Write to the Foundation for application guidelines and a list of participating institutions. Submit curriculum vitae; doctoral transcripts; three letters of reference; and a two- to three- page letter describing proposed research, work experience, and general areas of interest under the program. **Deadline:** For persons applying from North America: 31 December; for persons applying from Africa: January 31.

**Remarks:** Pre-and postdoctoral fellowships may also be offered in conjunction with on-going science programs of the Foundation. Areas of study and requirements vary from program to program. Specific inquiries should be addressed to the appropriate division head, but basic guidelines are available from the Communications Department. **Contact:** Jan Tensen at the above address (see entry 5145).

### • 5153 • Social Science Research Fellowships in Population *(Postdoctorate/Fellowship)*

**Purpose:** To enable young U.S. professionals in the social sciences to conduct research in the international population and development field. **Focus:** Demography, Economic and Social Development. **Qualif.:** Applicant must be a citizen or resident of the United States or Canada. Candidate must have received a Ph.D. during the ten years prior to application and must currently hold a faculty position at a U.S. university. Knowledge of French or Spanish is recommended. Fellowships are tenable at selected population and research and training centers in developing countries. Fellows undertake interdisciplinary research in collaboration with the staff at the host institution. Fellows may be required to teach a course in their areas of special interest.

**Funds Avail.:** $37,000/year. **No. of Awards:** Up to four. **To Apply:** Write for application form and guidelines and a list of participating institutions. Submit curriculum vitae; doctoral transcripts; the names and addresses of three or four referees; and a letter describing relevant research and work experience, the type of work for which support is sought, and regional preferences for proposed fellowship. **Deadline:** December 31.

**Remarks:** Pre- and postdoctoral fellowships may also be offered in conjunction with on-going science programs of the Foundation. Areas of study and requirements vary from program to program. Specific inquiries should be addressed to the appropriate division head, but basic guidelines are available from the Communications Department. **Contact:** Jan Tensen at the above address (see entry 5145).

#### • 5154 • Sub-Saharan African Dissertation Internship Award (Doctorate/Internship)

**Purpose:** To enable African doctoral students enrolled at U.S. and Canadian universities to undertake supervised dissertation research in Africa. **Focus:** Economic and Social Development and related disciplines, including Agriculture, Health Sciences, Life Sciences. **Qualif.:** Applicant must be a citizen of a sub-Saharan African country who is currently enrolled in a doctoral program at a university in the United States or Canada. Candidate must have completed coursework for the Ph.D. and be preparing to begin dissertation research on a topic related to the economic development or reduction of poverty in Africa. Preference will be given to project proposals in the areas of study listed above. Applicant must be accepted by an institution in Africa with adequate supervision and facilities for proposed research. Internships are tenable at institutions in Africa. Award funds must be applied to travel, living expenses, and other research-related costs.

**Funds Avail.:** Up to $24,000 stipend, plus $2,500 institutional grant. **To Apply:** Write for application guidelines. Submit a dissertation proposal approved by student's advisor, three letters of reference, a letter of sponsorship from the proposed host institution, postgraduate transcripts, curriculum vitae, and a budget. **Deadline:** March 2, October 1.

**Remarks:** Pre- and postdoctoral fellowships may also be offered in conjunction with on-going science programs of the Foundation. Areas of study and requirements vary from program to program. Specific inquiries should be addressed to the appropriate division head, but basic guidelines are available from the Communications Department. Students are strongly encouraged to plan to be in the field for at least twelve months.

#### • 5155 • Warren Weaver Fellowships (Postdoctorate/ Fellowship)

**Purpose:** To provide residencies at the Foundation's New York office for individuals working on special projects. **Focus:** General Studies. **Qualif.:** Applicant may be of any nationality. Candidate must have completed academic or professional training and be in the early stages of his/her career. Applicants from any professional field are eligible to apply but must have the basic qualifications for undertaking their projects. There are no specific limitations for projects, other than that they relate to the interests of the Foundation. Fellowships are available at the Foundation.

**Funds Avail.:** $40,000-55,000 stipend, plus moving and assignment-related expenses, group life, and medical benefits for fellow and immediate family members. **To Apply:** Write to the Foundation for application information packet. Submit resume, transcripts, a short statement regarding current career options, and three short responses to questions contained in the information packet. Three letters of recommendation must be sent directly from the referees to the Foundation. **Deadline:** March 1.

**Remarks:** The Foundation awards Intercultural Film/Video Fellowships to nominated artists whose projects experiment with form and issues of cultural diversity within the United States and abroad. Write to the Arts and Humanities Division for further details. Pre-and postdoctoral fellowships may also be offered in conjunction with on-going science programs of the Foundation. Areas of study and requirements vary from program to program. Specific inquiries should be addressed to the appropriate division

head, but basic guidelines are available from the Communications Department. Fellowship shall commence approximately September 15. **Contact:** Jan Tensen at the above address (see entry 5145).

#### • 5156 •
### Rocky Mountain Coal Mining Institute

3000 Youngfield St., No. 324       Ph: (303)238-9099
Lakewood, CO 80215-6553       Fax: (303)238-0509
*E-mail:* RMCoalMine@online.com

#### • 5157 • Rocky Mountain Coal Mining Institute Scholarships (Undergraduate/Scholarship)

**Purpose:** To assist students who have chosen a career in the mining industry. **Focus:** Engineering, Physical Sciences. **Qualif.:** Candidates must be sophomores in good academic standing, U.S. citizens and residents of one of the member states (Arizona, Colorado, Montana, North Dakota, New Mexico, Texas, Utah, and Wyoming), pursuing a degree in a mining-related field or in engineering disciplines such as geology or mineral processing and metallurgy, and have expressed an interest in western coal as a possible career. **Criteria:** Based on completed application and personal interview.

**Funds Avail.:** Sixteen students from the Institute's eight member states receive $1,500 annually. **No. of Awards:** 16 annually. **To Apply:** The RMCMI Scholarship Chairman contacts the various colleges and universities in the member states and requests nominations from students and each dean of the mining department. The chairman and the RMCMI state vice president interview the various nominees. The scholarship is presented at the end of the recipient's sophomore year and renewed, upon recommendation from the dean of the college or university involved, at the close of the recipient's junior year. **Deadline:** February 1. **Contact:** Doris G. Finnie, RMCMI Executive Director, at the above address (see entry 5156).

#### • 5158 •
### Rocky Mountain Mineral Law Foundation

Porter Admin. Bldg.
7039 E. 18th Ave.       Ph: (303)321-8100
Denver, CO 80220       Fax: (303)321-7657
*E-mail:* sherwood@rmmlf.org
*URL:* http://www.rmmlf.org

#### • 5159 • Rocky Mountain Mineral Law Foundation Scholarship Program Including the Joe Rudd Scholarship (Graduate/Scholarship)

**Purpose:** To encourage the study of natural resources law by students who have the potential to make a significant contribution to the field of natural resources law. **Focus:** Natural Resources Law. **Qualif.:** Applicants must be law students pursuing the study of natural resources law. The scholarship must be used towards a degree program at one of the Governing Law School members of the Rocky Mountain Mineral Law Foundation. **Criteria:** Selection is based on applicants' potential to make a significant contribution to the field of natural resources law and their academic ability, leadership skills, and financial need.

**Funds Avail.:** Total funding is $30,000 per year. **To Apply:** A formal application must be obtained from the foundation's trustee on the law school campus. **Deadline:** October 15 and April 1. **Contact:** RMMLF, at the above address (see entry 5158).

# • 5160 •
## Franklin and Eleanor Roosevelt Institute
Franklin D. Roosevelt Library
511 Albany Post Rd.            Ph: (914)229-5321
Hyde Park, NY 12538-1927      Fax: (914)229-9046
*E-mail:* emurphy@idsi.net
*URL:* http://newdeal.feri.org/feri

### • 5161 • Roosevelt Institute Grants-in-Aid *(Graduate, Postdoctorate/Grant)*

**Purpose:** To encourage and support research on the Roosevelt period or related subjects. **Focus:** Franklin and Eleanor Roosevelt and their period. **Qualif.:** Candidate may be of any nationality. Applicant must be a qualified researcher with a viable plan of work. Grants are tenable for research at the FDR Library only. **Criteria:** Priority is given to proposals which expand the knowledge of the Roosevelt period and have greatest usefulness to educators, students and policy makers.

**Funds Avail.:** A maximum of $2,500. **No. of Awards:** 15-25. **To Apply:** Application form and guideline are available on the website, or by writing to the chair. Submit three copies of application, including form; curriculum vitae; details of proposed research project; budget for travel, lodging, and other research expenses; and three letters of references. **Deadline:** February 15 and September 15. Grants are awarded in the spring and fall. **Contact:** Chairman, Grants Committee, at the above address (see entry 5160).

# • 5162 •
## Roscoe Pound Foundation
1050 31st St. NW              Ph: (202)965-3500
Washington, DC 20007         Fax: (202)965-0355

### • 5163 • Elaine Osborne Jacobson Award for Women in Health Care *(Doctorate, Graduate/Award)*

**Purpose:** To encourage women law students to pursue careers in advocacy law on behalf of women, children, and the elderly. **Qualif.:** Applicants must be women currently enrolled in an accredited American law school on a full-or part-time basis who through her law school academic and clinical work and other related activities demonstrates her aptitude for and a long-term commitment to a legal career of advocacy on behalf of the health care needs of children, women, the elderly or the disabled.

**Funds Avail.:** $2,000 first place; $1,000 second place. **No. of Awards:** 2. **To Apply:** A letter from the Dean, clinical program director, or law school professor teaching in a related area nominating the candidate and setting forth the basis for the nomination, including a description of the purposes and content of clinical program and/or class must be submitted. Applicants must send their current vitae and. Must submit a personal statement of no more than two pages which includes how they plan to use their current law school/clinical experience. At least one, but no more than 3 letters of recommendation from a law school faculty and/or practicing attorney who has personally taught or supervised the nominee's work. One example of written work in the health care area. **Deadline:** mid-January. **Contact:** Maeghan Donohoe.

# • 5164 •
## Charles M. Ross Trust
PO Box 160
Fairbury, IL 61739           Ph: (815)692-4336

### • 5165 • Charles M. Ross Trust *(Graduate/Other)*

**Purpose:** To provide graduate training for promising and gifted students who are committed to world service. **Qualif.:** Applicant must attend one of the following universities: Lexington Theological Seminary, Lexington, KY; Vanderbilt University, Nashville, TN; University of Chicago, Chicago IL; Marquette University, Milwaukee, WI; Brite Divinity School at Texas Christian University, Fort Worth, TX; Centenary College of Louisiana, Shreveport, LA. The applicant must also be an active member of a local church who can give evidence that he/she understands the world mission of the church. The applicant must also have earned grades in undergraduate education, which are within the first ten percent of the class.

**Funds Avail.:** From $500 to $1,200. **No. of Awards:** Varies. **Deadline:** August 1. **Contact:** Paul G. Mason.

# • 5166 •
## Rotary International - The Rotary Foundation
Scholarships Program
1 Rotary Center
1560 Sherman Ave.            Ph: (847)866-4459
Evanston, IL 60201-3698      Fax: (847)328-8554
*URL:* http://www.rotary.org

### • 5167 • Academic-Year Ambassadorial Scholarship *(Graduate, Other, Undergraduate/Scholarship)*

**Purpose:** To further international understanding and friendly relations among people of different countries. **Qualif.:** Applicants must have completed two years of university work or appropriate professional experience before starting scholarship studies. Spouses or descendants of Rotarians may not apply. Applicants must be citizens of the countries in which there are Rotary clubs. During the study year, scholars are expected to be outstanding ambassadors of goodwill through appearances before Rotary clubs, schools, civic organizations, and other forums. Ambassadorial Scholarships are available for undergraduate, graduate, or vocational study, and are available to individuals of all ages.

**Funds Avail.:** The award provides funding to cover tuition, fees, room and board, round-trip transportation and one month of language training (if necessary) not to exceed $23,000. Upon completion of the scholarship, scholars are expected to share the experiences of understanding acquired during the study year with the people of their home countries. **To Apply:** Applicants must contact their local Rotary club for specific application information. **Deadline:** Applications for the academic year are available from local Rotary clubs by November. Deadline for receipt of completed applications by local clubs may be as early as March or as late as July 15, or one year befor the scholarship year. Check with local Rotary clubs for exact dates.

**Remarks:** Not all Rotary districts will offer scholarships every year; nor will all types of scholarships be available in a given year. **Contact:** Local Rotary clubs for further information and availability of particular scholarships or the Rotary Foundation at the above address (see entry 5166).

### • 5168 • Cultural Ambassadorial Scholarship *(Graduate, Undergraduate/Scholarship)*

**Purpose:** The scholarship is designed specifically for intensive language study and cultural immersion. **Focus:** Foreign Language.

**Qualif.:** Applicants must have completed two years of university work or appropriate professional experience before starting scholarship studies. Spouses or descendants of Rotarians may not apply. Applicants must be citizens of the countries in which there are Rotary clubs. Applications will be considered for candidates interested in studying the following languages: English, French, German, Italian, Japanese, Mandarin Chinese, Polish, Portuguese, Russian, Spanish, and Swahili. Whenever possible, scholars will reside with host families.

**Funds Avail.:** The award provides funding, as determined appropriate by The Rotary Foundation, for tuition, room and board, and round-trip transportation. **To Apply:** Applicants must contact their local Rotary club for specific application information. **Deadline:** Applications for the academic year are available from local Rotary clubs by November. Deadline for receipt of completed applications by local clubs may be as early as March or as late as July 15, one year before sholarship studies. Check with local Rotary clubs for exact dates.

**Remarks:** Not all Rotary districts will offer scholarships every year; nor will all types of scholarships be available in a given year. **Contact:** Local Rotary clubs for further information and availability of particular scholarships or the Rotary Foundation at the above address (see entry 5166).

• 5169 • **Grants for University Teachers to Serve in Developing Countries** (Professional Development/Grant)

**Purpose:** To subsidize expenses of a university teacher to teach at a university in a low-income country. **Qualif.:** Rotarians and relatives of Rotarians are eligible.

**Funds Avail.:** $10,000 or $20,000. **To Apply:** Prospective applicants must contact the nearest Rotary club to obtain an application and to inquire about local deadlines. **Deadline:** Deadlines for receipt of completed applications by local Rotary clubs may be as early as March or as late as July 15, one year befor the teaching period.

• 5170 • **Multi-Year Ambassadorial Scholarship** (Graduate, Other, Undergraduate/Scholarship)

**Purpose:** To further international understanding and assist students in the cost of degree-oriented study in another country. **Qualif.:** Applicants must have completed two years of university work or appropriate professional experience before starting scholarship studies. Spouses or descendants of Rotarians may not apply. Applicants must be citizens of the countries in which there are Rotary clubs. Ambassadorial Scholarships are available for undergraduate, graduate, or vocational study, and are available to individuals of all ages. The Multi-Year Ambassadorial Scholarship expands upon the premise of the Academic-Year Ambassadorial Scholarship (see separate entry) by lengthening the period of study from one year to two or three years.

**Funds Avail.:** The award provides assistance in the cost of degree-oriented study in another country. The scholarship provides a flat award of $11,000 or its equivalent per year. All additional costs must be absorbed by the scholars. **To Apply:** Applicants must contact their local Rotary club for specific application information. **Deadline:** Applications for the academic year are available from local Rotary clubs by November. Deadline for receipt of completed applications by local clubs may be as early as March or as late as July 15, one year before studies begin. Check with local Rotary clubs for exact dates.

**Remarks:** Not all Rotary districts will offer scholarships every year; nor will all types of scholarships be available in a given year. **Contact:** Local Rotary clubs for further information and availability of particular scholarships or the Rotary Foundation at the above address (see entry 5166).

• 5171 •
**Roundalab**
4825-B Valley View Ave.                        Ph: (714)572-0480
Yorba Linda, CA 92686-3645              Fax: (714)572-0931

• 5172 • **Wayne Wylie Scholarship** (Professional Development/Scholarship)

**Purpose:** To assist the professional development of round dance instructors. **Qualif.:** Applicants must be members of Roundlab. **Criteria:** Winners are selected through a drawing.

**Funds Avail.:** Up to $200. **Deadline:** June 1. **Contact:** Pat Rardin, Executive Secretary, Roundlab at the above address (see entry 5171).

• 5173 •
**Leo S. Rowe Pan American Fund**
General Secretariat
Organization of American States
17th St. and Constitution Ave., NW        Ph: (202)458-3754
Washington, DC 20006                        Fax: (202)458-6421
*URL:* http://www.oas.org/EN/PROG/OTHER/BECAS/eorowe.htm

• 5174 • **The Leo S. Rowe Pan American Fund Loan** (Graduate, Undergraduate/Loan)

**Purpose:** To contribute to the education of competent persons, who, upon completing their studies in the United States, will be in a position to give their respective countries the benefit of their training. **Qualif.:** Applicants must be United States residents with a student visa in the United States; have meritorious personal and academic records; be enrolled or accepted for admission by an accredited institution of higher education of the United States of America; and be able to complete successfully, within two years, the studies or research for which the loan is requested. The applicant must also have financial need and the necessary financial resources, or a scholarship or fellowship, to cover the greater part of the study expenses, since the loan is intended to meet only part of the applicant's need. The applicant must also assume the obligation of reimbursing the loan within a period of five years from the date of termination of studies for which the loan has been requested. Repayment starts three months after the termination of study. The Fund also extends to citizens of member countries of the Organization of American States who are already studying or wish to study as undergraduate or graduate students at universities or colleges in the United States, and students or professional persons who are already carrying out or wish to carry out advanced studies, research, or technical activities at institutions in the United States. **Criteria:** Selection of loan recipients is based on candidates' merit and financial need. Preference will be given to students enrolled in courses that lead to the awarding of degrees or diplomas.

**Funds Avail.:** The maximum amount of a loan is $5,000 per year for helping with expenses related to tuition and fees, indispensable books and study materials, room and board, transportation, certified emergency expenses, and miscellaneous costs. Holders of fellowships of the OAS and other institutions or governments may resort to the fund solely for the purpose of covering expenses that are not anticipated in the fellowship grants or other emergency expenses that the committee considers it appropriate to cover. **To Apply:** A completed application form must be delivered or mailed to the Secretariat of the Fund, together with the guarantor's contract and other documents supporting the request. Scientific research workers should present a program of study and evidence of the usefulness of their studies and research to their own countries. Candidates who seek technical training are required to show evidence of their vocation and the degree of their

*Leo S. Rowe Pan American Fund (continued)*

training in their chosen fields. **Contact:** Orlando Thomas at the above address (see entry 5173).

---

## • 5175 •
## Royal Bath & West of England Society

The Showground                          *Ph:* 44 1749 822200
Shepton Mallet, Somerset BA4 6QN,       *Fax:* 44 1749
England                                             823169
*E-mail:* general.office@bathandwest.co.uk

### • 5176 •  Royal Bath & West of England Society Scholarships *(Undergraduate/Scholarship)*

**Focus:** Agriculture.

**Funds Avail.:** Various. **No. of Awards:** Three. **To Apply:** Write for further details. **Deadline:** December 31. **Contact:** Paul Hoover, Adm.

---

## • 5177 •
## Royal College of Obstetricians and Gynaecologists

27 Sussex Pl.
Regent's Park                           *Ph:* 071 2625425
London NW1 4RG, England                 *Fax:* 071 7239575

### • 5178 •  Bernhard Baron Traveling Scholarship *(Professional Development/Scholarship)*

**Purpose:** To provide funds for short-term travel to expand the applicant's knowledge in areas in which he or she already has experience.

### • 5179 •  William Blair-Bell Memorial Lectureships in Obstetrics and Gynecology *(Doctorate, Postdoctorate/Other)*

**Qualif.:** Applicants must be either Members of the Royal College of Obstetricians and Gynaelcologists or Fellows of not more than two years standing. **To Apply:** Two lectures may be delivered each year. The subject must be either obstetrics or gynecology, or closely related. Candidates must indicate what part of the work submitted has been previously published, if any. The whole lecture should be submitted in typescript on A4 paper (original plus three copies), including prints of any slides. Successful candidates will be asked to give written permission for their manuscripts to be copied and sent out upon request to Fellows and Members of the College, unless, or until, the paper is published elsewhere. No assessment of any lecture will be made before the closing date for applications.

### • 5180 •  Eden Traveling Fellowship in Obstetrics and Gynecology *(Doctorate, Postdoctorate/Fellowship)*

**Purpose:** To enable the holder to visit, for a specified period of time, another department of obstetrics and gynecology, or closely related disciplines, where the applicant may gain additional knowledge and experience in a specific research project in which he or she is currently engaged. **Focus:** Medicine **Qualif.:** Must be a medical graduate of not less than two years' standing in an approved university. **Contact:** College Secretary.

### • 5181 •  Edgar Gentilli Prize *(Doctorate, Postdoctorate/Prize)*

**Focus:** Obstetrics and Gynecology. **Qualif.:** Candidates not restricted to Fellows and members of the college. **To Apply:** Candidates must submit results of research in the form of an essay or article, written in English, adequately referenced and written in a format comparable to that used for submission to a learned journal. **Contact:** College Secretary.

### • 5182 •  USA British Isles Traveling Fellowship *(Doctorate, Postdoctorate/Fellowship)*

**Purpose:** To enable the recipient to visit, make contact with and gain knowledge from a specific center offering new techniques or methods of clinical management within the specialty of obstetrics and gynecology. **Focus:** Gynecology **Qualif.:** Applicant must be a registrars or senior registrars in the British Isle, junior fellows in the US and medical graduates of not less than two years standing of any approved British or Commonwealth University. **To Apply:** Must include the following details: qualifications, including university; a short written account of the reasons for and benefits of such a visit; area of interest and/or publications in the specified area; individuals and center to be visited, their particular expertise and confirmation of the proposed arrangements from the head of the center; the estimated cost of travel and subsistence, together with details of any other financial assistance being obtained or requested; the names of two references; expected date of travel and confirmation that the program will be completed within the specified time; and confirmation that a written report will be submitted to the college after the visit. **Contact:** College Secretary at the above address (see entry 5177).

---

## • 5183 •
## The Royal College of Physicians and Surgeons of Canada

Awards and Grants, Office of
  Fellowship Affairs                    *Ph:* (613)730-8177
774 promenade Echo Dr.                  *Fax:* (613)730-8260
Ottawa, ON, Canada K1S 5N8              *Free:* 800-668-3740
*E-mail:* diane.sarrazin@rcpsc.edu
*URL:* http://rcpsc.medical.org

*The Royal College of Physicians and Surgeons of Canada was founded in 1929 by an Act of the Canadian Parliament to to promote the highest possible standard of specialist medical care for the people of Canada by setting high standards for post-graduate medical training and education based upon the knowledge, skills, and attitudes necessary for specialist physicians and surgeons; encouraging research in biomedical sciences, medical education and health services; promoting the continuing professional competence of specialist physicians and surgeons; encouraging and supporting scholarly approaches to the enhancement of the art and science of medicine. medicine.*

### • 5184 •  Detweiler Travelling Fellowships *(Postdoctorate/Fellowship)*

**Purpose:** To improve the quality of medical and surgical practice in Canada. The fellowship enables recipients to visit medical centers in Canada or abroad, to study or gain experience in the use or application of new knowledge or techniques in their fields, or to further the pursuit of a fundamental or clinical research project. **Focus:** Medicine, Surgery. **Qualif.:** Applicants must be Fellows (active members) of the Royal College in any medical or surgical specialty in good standing at the time of application and who reside in Canada. **Criteria:** The Awards Committee selects Fellows based on an assessment of the overall merit of the application, including the benefits to the individual and the community, the quality of the program to be undertaken, and the financial need of the applicant. Special consideration is given to Fellows who have been in private practice for three years after certification.

**Funds Avail.:** Up to $21,000 ($1,750/month), tenable for visits of 4 to 12 months. Seventy-five percent of the award is provided at the beginning of the fellowship, and the remainder is provided upon receipt of the final report at the end of the fellowship. The fellowship may be used to supplement financial assistance granted from other resources. **No. of Awards:** 6. **Deadline:** Applications must be postmarked by September 30.

**Remarks:** The RCPSC Detweiter Travel Fellowships are supported by income from the Royal College's Education Endowment Fund. **Contact:** Office of Fellowship Affairs at the above address (see entry 5183).

**• 5185 • Walter C. MacKenzie, Johnson and Johnson Fellowship** *(Postdoctorate/Fellowship)*

**Purpose:** To enable Fellows to visit one or more centers to acquire surgical research or clinical surgical training. Knowledge gained should have a direct application to the recipient's clinical surgical practice. **Focus:** Medicine, Surgery. **Qualif.:** Applicants must be practicing surgeons who are Fellows (active members) of the Royal College in good standing and who reside in Canada. Practicing surgeons are those who have spent at least 50 percent of their professional time in active clinical surgery over the last five years. **Criteria:** The Awards Committee selects a fellow based on the overall merit of the application, such as the benefits to the individual and the community, the quality of the program to be undertaken, and the financial need of the applicant.

**Funds Avail.:** One $21,000 fellowship is offered annually for visits of six to 12 months. Seventy-five percent of the award is provided at the beginning of the fellowship, and the remainder is provided upon receipt of the final report at the end of the fellowship. The fellowship may be used to supplement financial assistance granted from other sources. **No. of Awards:** 1. **Deadline:** Applications must be postmarked by September 30.

**Remarks:** The fellowship was named after Dr. Walter C. MacKenzie, a renowned Canadian surgeon, former Dean of Medicine at the University of Alberta, and former President of the Royal College. **Contact:** Office of Fellowship Affairs at the above address (see entry 5183).

**• 5186 • Medical Education Travelling Fellowship** *(Postdoctorate/Fellowship)*

**Purpose:** To enable the recipient to acquire knowledge and expertise in the field of medical education. **Focus:** Medicine, Surgery. **Qualif.:** Applicants must be Fellows (active members) of the Royal College in good standing at the time of application and who reside in Canada. Applicants need not be from university centers, although they must be sponsored (and provide a letter of support) either by a medical school, a clinical department of a hospital, or a national specialty society. **Criteria:** The Awards Committee selects a Fellow based on overall merit of the application, including the benefits to the individual and the community, the quality of the program to be undertaken, and the financial need of the applicant.

**Funds Avail.:** $21,000 maximum. The fellowship provides $1,750 per month. Seventy-five percent of the award is provided at the beginning of the fellowship, and the remainder is provided upon receipt of the final report at the end of the fellowship. The fellowship may be used to supplement financial assistance granted from other sources. **No. of Awards:** 1. **Deadline:** Applications must be postmarked by September 30. **Contact:** Office of Fellowship Affairs at the above address (see entry 5183)for details.

**• 5187 • RCPSC International Travelling Fellowship** *(Doctorate/Fellowship)*

**Purpose:** To enable Fellows residing outside of Canada to study in a Canadian medical centre in order to acquire new knowledge and skills applicable to clinical practice, or to enable Fellows residing in Canada to practice or teach in a less developed country. **Qualif.:** Applicants must be Fellows of the Royal College in good standing. **Criteria:** The selection is based on the overall merit of the application and the degree to which the proposal meets the described objectives. Considered are the benefits to the individual and to the community, the quality of the program to be undertaken, and the financial need and funds available to the applicant.

**Funds Avail.:** Maximum of $21,000. **No. of Awards:** 1. **Deadline:** September 30.

**• 5188 • RCPSC-MRC/PMAC-Novartis Clinical Research Fellowship** *(Doctorate/Fellowship)*

**Purpose:** To enable recently trained physicians to acquire appropriate knowledge and skills in the research field including clinical investigation for further application as a career clinical scientist. **Qualif.:** Candidates must have completed the requirements in one of the specialties recognized by the Royal College and must be eligible for the certification exams of the RC, or must be Fellows of the Royal College in good standing. They must also intend to complete two years of research and be Canadian citizens or landed immigrants. **Criteria:** Preference is given to those who train in Canada and intend to remain in Canada. Selection is based upon the benefits of the fellowship to the individual and the community, the quality of the program, and the financial need and funds available to the applicant.

**Funds Avail.:** $40,000 per year. **No. of Awards:** 1. **Deadline:** September 30.

**• 5189 • Royal College Fellowship for Studies in Medical Education** *(Doctorate, Graduate, Postdoctorate/Fellowship)*

**Purpose:** To increase the number and quality of professionally trained medical educators in Canada by providing training in the science of medical education to selected promising candidates. **Qualif.:** Applicants must register in a university program in Canada or outside of Canada leading to an M.A., Ph.D., or doctorate degree in education. The candidate must be registered and attending university as a full-time student for the duration of the fellowship. Applicants must be Canadian citizens or landed immigrants, and Fellows of the Royal College in good standing. Applicants must be sponsored by a Canadian Faculty of Medicine and have a commitment for a faculty appointment upon completion of studies. **Criteria:** Candidates are selected on the basis of the benefits to the individual and the university centre where he/she returns, the quality of the program, and the financial need and funds available to the applicant.

**Funds Avail.:** $45,000 per year. **No. of Awards:** 1. **Deadline:** September 30.

**• 5190 •**
**Royal Geographic Society With the Institute of British Geographers**
1 Kensington Gore
London SW7 2AR, England
*E-mail:* grants@rgs.org
Ph: 171 589 5466
Fax: 171 823 7200

**• 5191 • Monica Cole Research Grant** *(Graduate, Undergraduate/Grant)*

**Qualif.:** For a female physical geographer undertaking original field research outside of England.

**Funds Avail.:** £1,000 is awarded biennially. **Deadline:** March 31.

**Royal Geographic Society With the Institute of British Geographers** (continued)

• 5192 • **Violet Cressey-Marcks Fisher Travel Fellowship** (Graduate, Undergraduate/Scholarship)

**Purpose:** To recognize the best undergraduate or post graduate geographical research project which involves a period of overseas field research or more than six months.

**Funds Avail.:** £500 awarded every three years. **Deadline:** March 31.

• 5193 • **Dudley Stamp Memorial Trust** (Professional Development/Grant)

**Purpose:** To assist in research or study travel leading to the advancement of geography and international cooperation in the study of the subject. **Qualif.:** For young geographers; most awards are to applicants under the age of 30.

**Funds Avail.:** £3,500 is awarded each May among a number of projects. **To Apply:** Application forms from the Royal Society, 6 Carlton House Terrace, London SW1Y 5AG, England. **Deadline:** February 28.

• 5194 • **Grants for Overseas Scientific Expeditions** (Professional Development/Grant)

**Qualif.:** For scientific teams (over the age of 19) carrying out field research outside of England. The expedition's research should have a significant geographical component and advance the frontiers of scientific knowledge. **Criteria:** Preference is given to those projects involving Host country nationals.

**Funds Avail.:** Approximately £40,000 per annum is available. **Deadline:** January 25 and August 25.

• 5195 •
**Royal Society of Canada**
225 Metcalfe St., Ste. 308          *Ph:* (613)991-6990
Ottawa, ON, Canada K2P 1P9          *Fax:* (613)991-6996
*E-mail:* adminrsc@rsc.ca; lvachon@rsc.ca
*URL:* http://library.utoronto.ca/www/rsc/

• 5196 • **Sir Arthur Sims Scholarships** (Postgraduate/Scholarship)

**Purpose:** To encourage Canadian students to undertake postgraduate study in Great Britain. **Focus:** Humanities, Natural Sciences, Social Sciences. **Qualif.:** Applicants must be Canadian citizens with an undergraduate degree from a Canadian institution. They must also have completed at least one year of postgraduate study toward an advanced degree and must demonstrate outstanding merit and promise in their field of study. Scholarships are tenable at approved institutions in Great Britain and are awarded for two years based on satisfactory progress.

**Funds Avail.:** $700 per year. **No. of Awards:** 1. **To Apply:** Write to the Society for application form and guidelines. **Deadline:** February 15 in odd numbered years only. Recipients are announced in April. **Contact:** Linda Vachon, awards coordinator, at the above address (see entry 5195).

• 5197 •
**RTCA**
1140 Connecticut Ave., NW, Ste.
1020                                *Ph:* (202)833-9339
Washington, DC 20036-4001          *Fax:* (202)833-9434
*E-mail:* hmoses@rtca.org
*URL:* http://www.rtca.org

• 5198 • **William E. Jackson Award** (Graduate/Award)

**Purpose:** To recognize outstanding research by a student in the field of aviation electronics and telecommunications. **Focus:** Aviation Electronics, Telecommunications. **Qualif.:** Applicants may be of any nationality, but must be graduate-level students pursuing an advanced degree in the field of aviation electronics and telecommunications. Submissions must be in the form of a thesis, project report, or technical journal paper. The work on which the submission is based must have been completed within the three years preceding the application deadline, and the papers submitted for consideration must be written in English and provided without publication restrictions. The sole basis for selection will be the submitted written report.

**Funds Avail.:** $2,000. **No. of Awards:** 1. **To Apply:** Write to RTCA for rules for submissions. There are no application forms. Submit two copies of the research report with a one- or two-page summary of the written material, a biographical sketch, and a letter of endorsement from instructor or department head. **Deadline:** June 30. **Contact:** William E. Jackson, Award Committee, at the above address (see entry 5197).

• 5199 •
**Cancer Research Fund of the Damon Runyon-Walter Winchell Foundation**
675 3rd Ave. 25th Fl.              *Ph:* (212)697-9100
New York, NY 10017                 *Fax:* (212)697-4050
                                   *Free:* 877-7-CANCER
*E-mail:* fellowship@cancerresearchfund.org
*URL:* http://www.cancerresearchfund.org

• 5200 • **Postdoctoral Research Fellowships for Basic and Physician Scientists** (Postdoctorate/Fellowship)

**Purpose:** To advance all theoretical and experimental research that is relevant to the study of cancer and the search for cancer causes, mechanisms, therapies, and preventions. **Focus:** Oncology. **Qualif.:** Applicants may be of any nationality, but non-U.S. candidates may only apply to conduct research in the United States. They must have an M.D., Ph.D., D.D.S., or D.V.M. degree or an equivalent, and must not have previously undertaken a full-time postdoctoral fellowship. To qualify for level I funding, applicants must be basic or clinical scientists who have received a doctoral degree within the year before application. To qualify for level II funding, they must have completed residency or clinical fellowship training within three years before application. Applicants must be sponsored by a senior member of the scientific research community. The proposed investigation must be conducted at a university, hospital, or research institution. Postdoctoral research at the same institution where the candidate received his/her degree is discouraged. Research must be full-time.

**Funds Avail.:** Level I funding is $35,000, plus $2,000 for expenses, first year; $40,500 plus $2,000 for expenses, second year; $44,000, plus $2,000 for expenses, third year. Level II funding: $55,000, plus $2,000 for expenses, first year; $56,000, plus $2,000 for expenses, second year; $57,000, plus $2,000 for expenses, third year. **To Apply:** Obtain application from our website. Submit form with applicant and sponsor's curriculum vitae, research proposal, and letters of support. **Deadline:** March 15, August 15, and December 15. Fellows are selected in May, November, and February, respectively. **Contact:** Clare M. Cahill or Sarah J. Caddick, PhD at the above address (see entry 5199).

---

• 5201 •
## Edward Rutledge Charity
PO Box 758
Chippewa Falls, WI 54729                    *Ph:* (715)723-6618

### • 5202 • Edward Rutledge Charity Scholarships
*(Undergraduate/Scholarship)*

**Focus:** General Studies. **Qualif.:** Candidates must be graduates of a Chippewa County, Wisconsin, high school, and must be Chippewa County residents. **Criteria:** Selection is based on financial need. **No. of Awards:** Varies. **Deadline:** May 1, each year.

**Remarks:** We will answer replies to those who include a self-addressed, stamped envelope only. **Contact:** Gerald J. Naiberg at the above address (see entry 5201).

---

• 5203 •
## Sachs Foundation
90 S. Cascade Ave., Ste. 1410
Colorado Springs, CO 80903-1691          *Ph:* (719)633-2353
*E-mail:* sachs@fru.com
*URL:* http://www.fru.com/~sachs

### • 5204 • Sachs Foundation Grants *(Undergraduate/Grant)*

**Focus:** General Studies. **Qualif.:** Applicants must be Black residents of Colorado for 5 or more years with a GPA of about 3.5 or higher. **Criteria:** Preference will be given to those who demonstrate financial need.

**Funds Avail.:** The amount of scholarships is dependent on the Board of Directors. Approximately 50 are awarded each year. **No. of Awards:** 50 per semester. **To Apply:** Applications are available from the Foundation and from Colorado high school counselors between January 1 and February 15. **Deadline:** March 1.

**Remarks:** More than 1,000 applications are made annually. **Contact:** Lisa Harris at the above address (see entry 5203).

---

• 5205 •
## Sacramento Bee
Community Relations Department
PO Box 15779                               *Ph:* (916)321-1880
Sacramento, CA 95852-0779                  *Fax:* (916)321-1783

### • 5206 • Sacramento Bee Journalism Scholarships for Community College Students *(High School, Undergraduate/Scholarship)*

**Purpose:** To encourage students who are actively pursuing courses of study leading to a degree in journalism to remain in school. **Focus:** Journalism. **Qualif.:** Applicants must have completed at least 30 units at one of the following community colleges: Sierra College, American River College, Sacramento City College, or Cosumnes River College. Applicants must have at least a 3.0 grade point average and intend to transfer to a four-year

institution and major in journalism. **Criteria:** Selection is based upon the stringbook or portfolio of the student's published work, a letter of the student's career objectives, resume, letters of recommendation, and transcripts.

**Funds Avail.:** Awards range from $2,000 to $4,000. **No. of Awards:** 4. **To Apply:** Applications are available at community colleges and by writing to the Sacramento Bee. **Deadline:** March 1. **Contact:** Robbi Van Diest, Community Relations Coordinator, at the above address (see entry 5205).

### • 5207 • Sacramento Bee Minority Media Scholarships *(Undergraduate/Scholarship)*

**Focus:** Journalism. **Qualif.:** Applicants must be minority students living in the Sacramento circulation area. They may be entering freshmen or currently enrolled students and attending any college, but must have interest in pursuing a career in mass media. Students should have a 3.0 cumulative grade point average, but exceptions may be made for applicants who have maintained a minimum 3.0 grade point average over their most recent term. Full-time McClatchy employees or relatives are not eligible. **Criteria:** Selection is based on a three page essay, financial needs letter, letters of recommendation, resume, and transcripts.

**Funds Avail.:** $1,000-$4,000. **No. of Awards:** 10. **To Apply:** Applications are available at area high schools, community colleges, state universities, and by writing to the Sacramento Bee. **Deadline:** March 15. **Contact:** Robbi Van Diest, Community Relations Coordinator, at the above address (see entry 5205).

---

• 5208 •
## Sacramento Black Nurses Association
PO Box 5171
Sacramento, CA 95817                       *Ph:* (916)689-3255

### • 5209 • SBNA Scholarship *(Undergraduate/Scholarship)*

**Purpose:** To help African American nursing students further their education. **Qualif.:** Applicants must be African Americans currently enrolled in nursing programs. **Criteria:** Selection is based on financial need, academic records, an essay, and a personal interview.

**Funds Avail.:** $1,000. **To Apply:** Applicants must submit an essay explaining the need for the scholarship, and appear for a committee interview. **Deadline:** September 30. **Contact:** Alice Baber-Banks, President, at the above address (see entry 5208).

---

• 5210 •
## The Sacramento Bodies Ancient and Accepted Scottish Rite of Freemasonry
6151 H St., PO Box 19497
Sacramento, CA 95819                       *Ph:* (916)452-5881

### • 5211 • Charles M. Goethe Memorial Scholarships *(Undergraduate/Grant)*

**Focus:** General Studies. **Qualif.:** Applicants must be enrolled at any accredited college or university. They must also be members or senior members of the Order of DeMolay or the children of a member or deceased member of a constituent Masonic Lodge of the Grand Lodge of Free and Accepted Masons of California. **Criteria:** Any academic major is acceptable but preference is given to students majoring in eugenics or similar studies such as genetics and the biological or life sciences. Grants are awarded on

---

Awards are arranged alphabetically below their administering organizations

*The Sacramento Bodies Ancient and Accepted Scottish Rite of Freemasonry (continued)*

a competitive basis and applicants are required to meet with a screening committee. **Deadline:** June 10. **Contact:** Francis Stoffels, Sacramento Bodies Ancient and Accepted Scottish Rite of Freemasonry, at the above address (see entry 5210).

## • 5212 •
## Sacramento-El Dorado Medical Society
5380 Elvas Ave.  *Ph:* (916)452-2671
Sacramento, CA 95819-2333  *Fax:* (916)452-2690
*E-mail:* info@sedms.org
*URL:* http://www.sedms.org

### • 5213 •  William E. Dochterman Medical Student Scholarship *(Graduate/Grant)*

**Purpose:** To provide financial assistance to medical students. **Focus:** Medicine. **Qualif.:** Candidates do not have to be current residents of Sacramento or El Dorado counties but they must have graduated from a high school located in Sacramento or El Dorado counties. At the time of application, they must be enrolled in an accredited American medical school on a full-time basis (12 units or more). This grant does not apply to summer enrollment or to correspondence schools. **Criteria:** Applications are evaluated primarily on the basis of financial need and academic achievement. Financial data is analyzed according to family/student resources and household size. Given limited funds, not all eligible applicants will be recipients.

**Funds Avail.:** Grants begin at $1,000. **No. of Awards:** 3-4. **To Apply:** Application form requests family financial information, applicant's income and expenses, previous loans received, scholarships received, three letters of recommendation and a personal statement indicating the reason for applying for the scholarship. **Deadline:** July 15. Grants are awarded the following September. **Contact:** Scholarship Secretary, Sacramento-El Dorado Medical Society, at the above address (see entry 5212).

### • 5214 •  William W. Tucker Medical Student Scholarship *(Graduate/Grant)*

**Purpose:** To provide financial assistance to medical students. **Focus:** Medicine. **Qualif.:** Candidates do not have to be current residents of Sacramento or El Dorado counties but they must have graduated from a high school located in Sacramento or El Dorado counties. At the time of application, they must be enrolled in an accredited American medical school on a full-time basis (12 units or more). This grant does not apply to summer enrollment or to correspondence schools. **Criteria:** Applications are evaluated primarily on the basis of financial need and academic achievement. Financial data is analyzed according to family/student resources and household size.

**Funds Avail.:** Grants begin at $1,000. **No. of Awards:** 1. **To Apply:** Application form requests family financial information, applicant's income and expenses, previous loans received, scholarships received, three letters of recommendation, and a personal statement indicating the reasons for applying for the scholarship. **Deadline:** July 15. Grants are awarded the following September.

**Remarks:** The Tucker Scholarship is sponsored by Mercy Hospital. **Contact:** Scholarship Secretary, Sacramento-El Dorado Medical Society, at the above address (see entry 5212).

## • 5215 •
## Sacramento Hispanic Chamber of Commerce
1804 Tribute Rd.
PO Box 161933  *Ph:* (916)925-1925
Sacramento, CA 95815-4313  *Fax:* (916)925-5270
*E-mail:* sachispcc@aol.com
*URL:* http://www.shccplaza.org

### • 5216 •  Sacramento Hispanic Chamber of Commerce Scholarships *(Undergraduate/Scholarship)*

**Focus:** Business, Engineering, Computer and Information Sciences. **Qualif.:** Candidates must be high school seniors of Hispanic background who have been accepted, are in the process of acquiring acceptance, or are enrolled in an accredited college or university on a full-time basis in California. Applicants must be pursuing an education in engineering, business, computer science, or related fields. **Criteria:** Selections are based on application forms, personal statements, letters of recommendation, and grade transcripts.

**Funds Avail.:** Awards range from $500 to $750. 17 scholarships of $500 each were awarded, in one year. **To Apply:** Applicants must submit a one- or two-page typed personal statement giving a brief history of their ethnic background, achievements, financial support and need, current education status, business-related career goals, involvement in school, employment and/or community work, interests, plan of commitment to the community, and any other circumstances or information relevant to the application. The personal statement is equivalent to an interview. Applicants must also submit one letter of recommendation from an employer, teacher, counselor, or a business or community person commenting on the applicant's academic potential, public service, financial need, leadership qualities, and other factors indicating potential for future success. Applicants also must submit an official transcript of high school work or latest college transcript. The application package must be sent in the following order: application form; personal statement; transcript; letter of recommendation. Applications must be sent to the Scholarship Fund Selection Committee. **Deadline:** March; candidates are notified of their application status in April. **Contact:** For further information, contact Gloria Juarez-Schubert, Education Committee Chair, at the above address (see entry 5215).

## • 5217 •
## Saint Andrew's Society of the State of New York
3 W. 51st St.  *Ph:* (212)397-4849
New York, NY 10019  *Fax:* (212)397-4846

### • 5218 •  St. Andrews Society of the State of New York Scholarships *(Graduate/Scholarship)*

**Purpose:** To promote cultural and intellectual exchange between Scotland and the USA and enable students to obtain their master's degree. **Qualif.:** Applicant must be of Scottish-American descent, a resident of the New York area, and a graduate of an American university. **Criteria:** Only one candidate per school is considered.

**Funds Avail.:** $13,000 per scholarship. **No. of Awards:** Two. **Deadline:** December 1.

**Remarks:** Amount usually covers tuition and board, not flights and personal expenses.

---

• 5219 •
## St. David's Society of the State of New York
3 W. 51st St.
New York, NY 10019                    *Ph:* (212)397-1346

**• 5220 • St. David's Scholarship** *(Graduate, Professional Development, Undergraduate/Scholarship)*

**Focus:** Welsh Language and Literature, General Studies. **Qualif.:** To qualify for scholarship assistance, applicants must be either of Welsh descent, a student in Wales, or studying the Welsh language or literature. **Criteria:** Application, transcripts, and letters of recommendation.

**Funds Avail.:** The amount of funds available varies. **To Apply:** Academic transcripts of work to date and two letters of recommendation from faculty must be provided with the application forms. **Deadline:** May 15. **Contact:** Nancy Williams at the above address (see entry 5219).

---

• 5221 •
## St. Johns College, Cambridge - Harper-Wood Studentship
The Master's Lodge
Cambridge CB2 1TP, England

**• 5222 • The Harper-Wood Studentship for English Poetry and Literature** *(Postgraduate/Other)*

**Qualif.:** Candidates must be graduates of any University of Great Britain, Ireland, the Commonwealth, or the United States, and must not be over 30 years of age. Students are required to pursue a subject of study or research which would preferably enable the holder to engage in creative writing, within the field of English poetry and literature, and to spend all or part of the period of tenure in a foreign country of the student's choice.

**Funds Avail.:** The amount of compensation will be determined by the College Council in the light of the student's qualifications and financial circumstances, including monies from other sources. **To Apply:** Applications should be accompanied by the candidate's curriculum vitae, a plan of the proposed study or research and of the proposed travel, and the names and addresses of not more than two references. Short-listed candidates may be invited to submit examples of their work, up to a limit of 5,000 words. Details of any other research plans or applications which might relate to the tenure of the Harper-Wood Studentship should also be supplied. **Deadline:** May 31. **Contact:** The Master's Secretary, St. John's College, at the above address (see entry 5221).

---

• 5223 •
## Samsum Medical Research Institute
2219 Bath St.
Santa Barbara, CA 93105-4321          *Ph:* (805)682-7638
                                      *Fax:* (805)682-3332
*E-mail:* Sveboda@sansumres.com; leis@sansum.org
*URL:* http://www.sansum.org

**• 5224 • Samsun Medical Research Institute Student Internships** *(Doctorate, Graduate, Undergraduate/Internship)*

**Purpose:** To provide experience for students in a research laboratory while challenging and inspiring them to choose a career in medical research. **Focus:** Diabetes, Pregnancy, Physiology. **Qualif.:** Applicants must have a strong background in biology and chemistry. **Criteria:** Selection is based on letter of

recommendation, laboratory skills, science courses, GPA in the sciences, and familiarity with assays and/or equipment.

**Funds Avail.:** Recipients receive a $200 per week stipend. **No. of Awards:** 2-4. **To Apply:** Applicants must send a completed application form with at least one recommendation from a faculty member. **Deadline:** Application materials must be received by mid-March. **Contact:** A. Svoboda, M.D., at the above address (see entry 5223).

---

• 5225 •
## San Angelo Symphony Society
PO Box 5922                           *Ph:* (915)658-5877
San Angelo, TX 76902                  *Fax:* (915)653-1045
*E-mail:* symphony@wcc.net
*URL:* http://www.lynnalexander.com/symphony.html

**• 5226 • Sorantin Young Artist Award** *(Professional Development/Award)*

**Purpose:** To recognize outstanding young singers and musicians. **Focus:** Instrumental (Orchestral) Music, Piano, Voice. **Qualif.:** Candidate may be of any nationality. Applicants to the instrumental and piano categories must be 28 years old or younger at the date of the competition; vocalists may not be older than 31 years. Each category also has specific requirements pertaining to selections for repertoire; send a self-addressed stamped business size envelope to the Society for details. Contestants must perform their repertoires from memory.

**Funds Avail.:** First prize: $3,000. **No. of Awards:** 1. **To Apply:** Write or call the Society for application form and competition rules, available in late August. Submit form with entry fee ($60). **Deadline:** October 19. The competition is held annually in mid-November, on the weekend before Thanksgiving.

**Remarks:** The first prize winner also performs with the San Angelo Symphony Orchestra. This contest will not be held in 1999. It is being revised.

---

• 5227 •
## San Bernardino County Department of Mental Health
700 East Gilbert St., Building 1      *Ph:* (909)387-7171
San Bernardino, CA 92415-0920         *Fax:* (909)387-7134

**• 5228 • Psychology Internships** *(Doctorate/Internship)*

**Purpose:** To provide graduate students with practical training and experience in a comprehensive community mental health organization. **Focus:** Clinical Psychology. **Qualif.:** Candidate may be of any nationality. Applicant must be a doctoral candidate who has completed at least two years of graduate study in psychology. Candidate should both classroom and practicum background in giving and interpreting tests, as well as psychotherapeutic work. Applicant must receive permission from his/her institution to undertake the internship. Internships are intended to provide basic, rather than specialized, training in clinical psychology, and are tenable at the Department. Interns may participate on a full-time (40 hours/week) or half-time basis.

**Funds Avail.:** Full-time: $13,148 stipend; half-time: $6,920 (for on-site participation, not graduate school classes). **To Apply:** Write to the training coordinator for application form and guidelines. Submit with graduate transcripts in psychology, curriculum vitae, two letters of reference, and other supporting documents.

---

## San Bernardino County Department of Mental Health (continued)

Selected applicants will be interviewed. **Deadline:** January 8. Internships are announced in mid-February.

**Remarks:** Six internships are full-time; two are half-time. **Contact:** Dr. Christopher Ebbe, Mental Health Intern Program Supervisor, at the above address (see entry 5227).

---

## • 5229 •
### San Francisco Chronicle
901 Mission St.
San Francisco, CA 94103          *Ph:* (415)777-7185

#### • 5230 • San Francisco Chronicle Summer Newsroom Internships *(Graduate, Undergraduate/ Internship)*

**Purpose:** Provides opportunities in the areas of copy editing, reporting, photography, librarian, and graphic arts. **Focus:** Journalism. **Qualif.:** Applicants must be college students or new graduates (can not have graduated more than one year before start of internship). **To Apply:** Applicants must submit a biographical letter, a resume, three letters of reference, and writing samples. **Deadline:** All applications must be postmarked between October 1 and November 16.

#### • 5231 • San Francisco Chronicle Two-Year Editing Internships *(Graduate/Internship)*

**Focus:** Journalism. **Qualif.:** Candidates must be new college graduates (not more than one year before start of internship) with copy editing experience. **To Apply:** Applicants must submit a biographical letter, a resume, three letters of recommendation, and work samples. **Deadline:** Applications must be postmarked between October 1 and November 16.

#### • 5232 • San Francisco Chronicle Two-Year Newsroom Internships *(Graduate/Internship)*

**Purpose:** To provide experience in the areas of reporting, photography, librarians, and graphic arts. **Focus:** Journalism. **Qualif.:** Candidates must be recent graduates (less than one year before the start of the internship). **To Apply:** Applicants must submit a biographical letter, a resume, three letters of reference, and writing samples. **Deadline:** Applications must be postmarked between October 1 and November 1.

---

## • 5233 •
### The San Francisco Foundation
225 Bush St., Ste 500          *Ph:* (415)733-8500
San Francisco, CA 94104-4224          *Fax:* (415)477-2783
*E-mail:* rec@sff.org
*URL:* http://www.igc.org/sff

#### • 5234 • Joseph Henry Jackson Award *(Professional Development/Award)*

**Purpose:** To encourage young writers of unpublished manuscripts in progress. **Qualif.:** Applicants must be residents of Northern California or Nevada for three consecutive years immediately prior to the closing date of the competition and be between the ages of 20 and 35. They must be authors of an unpublished, partly completed, book-length work of fiction or non-fictional prose, short story, or poetry.

**Funds Avail.:** One annual award of $2,000. **No. of Awards:** One. **To Apply:** At the same time applicants compete for the Jackson Award, they may, if eligible, compete for the James D. Phelan Award in Literature, but they may win only one award in one year. **Deadline:** January 31.

**Remarks:** Joseph Henry Jackson was book reviewer, critic, author and editor of numerous volumes in San Francisco. **Contact:** Awards Coordinator at the above address (see entry 5233). An alternate telephone number: (510)436-3100.

#### • 5235 • James D. Phelan Award in Literature *(Professional Development/Award)*

**Purpose:** To encourage young writers of unpublished manuscripts in progress. **Focus:** Literature. **Qualif.:** Candidates must have been born in California, be between 20 and 35 years of age on the closing date of the competition, and be able to provide proof of birth date and birthplace. Applicant must be the author of an unpublished, incomplete work of fiction or non-fictional prose, short story, poetry, or drama.

**Funds Avail.:** One award of $2,000. **No. of Awards:** One. **To Apply:** At the same time applicants compete for the Phelan Award, they may compete for the Joseph Henry Jackson Award, if eligible, but they may win only one award in one year. **Deadline:** January 31.

**Remarks:** A bequest of James D. Phelan, former Senator of California and Mayor of San Francisco, established the Award to bring about further development of California native talent. **Contact:** Awards Coordinator at the above address (see entry 5233).

---

## • 5236 •
### San Francisco Opera Center
War Memorial Opera House
301 Van Ness Ave.          *Ph:* (415)861-4008
San Francisco, CA 94102-4509          *Fax:* (415)255-6774
*URL:* http://www.sfopera.com

#### • 5237 • Adler Fellowships *(Professional Development/Fellowship)*

**Focus:** Opera. **Qualif.:** Applicants must be young professional singers between the ages of 20 and 34 in any vocal style or type. Applicants may not audition more than 3 times. **Criteria:** Singers are chosen on the basis of outstanding vocal and musical talent, and career potential; singers are chosen from participants in the Merola Opera Program.

**Funds Avail.:** Eight or more singers are chosen. The Fellowship is a performance-oriented contract providing individualized advanced training as well as roles in special productions and in the company's international seasons. Fellows are on salary during the 11-month residency. Under the guidance of the San Francisco Opera Center staff, they are also directed towards roles of increasing importance in future sessions of the San Francisco Opera. **To Apply:** Candidates must submit a formal application for Opera Center Programs/Merola Opera Program, a $30.00 non-refundable application fee; references from two musical authorities with whom the applicant has worked regularly for at least one year; a copy of the applicant's birth certificate; and a recent 8x10 photo. Applicants must list on the application six operatic arias (no oratorio arias accepted) they are prepared to sing. Arias must meet repertoire requirements listed in the application. Preliminary auditions are held in New York, Bloomington, Los Angeles, San Francisco, and Dallas during October, November and December. Applications are screened by Opera Center staff, who chose those who may audition for final selection. Failure to appear for scheduled auditions can lead to elimination. Application are available after August 1. Application deadline, preliminary audition dates, and final auditions dates vary according to city. **Deadline:** To be announced.

**Remarks:** Only singers who have been selected for the Merola Opera Program are considered for fellowships. **Contact:** Robert Cable, Auditions Coordinator, at the above address (see entry 5236).

**• 5238 • Merola Opera Program** (*Professional Development/Other*)

**Purpose:** To offer a continuing sequence of performance and career development opportunities for the best young professional singers and coaches. **Focus:** Opera. **Qualif.:** Applicants must be young professional singers or coaches between the ages of 20 and 34 in any vocal style or type. Applicants may not audition more than three times. **Criteria:** Singers will be chosen on the basis of outstanding vocal and musical talent, and career potential.

**Funds Avail.:** Approximately 20 award recipients are invited to join an intensive 11-week training and development program at the San Francisco Opera from mid-June to mid-August. The program pays a living stipend plus round-trip airfare and accommodations. Study grants totaling over $30,000 will be given to outstanding participants. **To Apply:** Singers must take part in the San Francisco Opera Center auditions to be eligible for the Merola Opera Program, the Western Opera Theater, and the Adler Fellowships. Candidates must submit: a formal application; a $30 nonrefundable application fee; references from two musical authorities with whom the applicant has worked regularly for at least one year; a copy of the applicant's birth certificate; and a recent 8x10 photo. Applicants must list on the application six operatic arias (no oratorio arias accepted) they are prepared to sing. Two foreign languages, plus English, must be represented in the six operatic arias. Preliminary auditions are held in New York, Bloomington, Los Angeles, San Francisco and Dallas, during October, November, and December. Applications are screened by Opera Center staff, who choose those who may audition for final selection. Failure to appear for scheduled auditions can lead to elimination. Applications are available after August 1. **Deadline:** vary by audition location **Contact:** Robert Cable, Auditions Coordinator, at the above address (see entry 5236).

**• 5239 • Western Opera Theater Program** (*Professional Development/Other*)

**Focus:** Opera. **Qualif.:** Applicants must be young professional singers between the ages of 20 and 34 in any vocal style or type. Applicants may not audition more than three times. **Criteria:** Singers are chosen on the basis of outstanding vocal and musical talent, and career potential.

**Funds Avail.:** Singers who are accepted into the Western Opera Theater, which is the touring affiliate of the San Francisco Opera, are paid according to the AGMA agreement with Western Opera Theater. **To Apply:** Candidates must submit a formal application, a $30 non-refundable application fee, references from two musical authorities with whom the applicant has worked regularly for at least one year, a copy of the applicant's birth certificate, and a recent 8x10 photo. Applicants must list on the application six operatic arias (no oratorio arias accepted) they are prepared to sing. Arias must meet repertoire requirements listed in application. Preliminary auditions are held in New York, Bloomington, Los Angeles, San Francisco, and Dallas, during October, November and December. Applications are screened by Opera Center staff, who chose those who may audition for final selection. Failure to appear for scheduled auditions can lead to elimination. **Deadline:** Application deadline, preliminary audition, and final audition dates vary according to city. Applications are available beginning August 1. All non U.S. citizens must possess valid work authorization from the INS. **Contact:** Robert Cable, Auditions Coordinator, at the above address (see entry 5236).

**• 5240 •**
**San Joaquin County Medical Society - Scholarship Loan Fund**
3031 W. March Lne., No. 222W
PO Box 230
Stockton, CA 95201

*Ph:* (209)952-5299
*Fax:* (209)952-5298

**• 5241 • San Joaquin County Medical Society Scholarship Loans** (*Graduate/Loan*)

**Focus:** Medicine, Nursing. **Qualif.:** Only residents of San Joaquin County, California, who have been accepted to medical or nursing school are eligible. **Criteria:** Based on financial need.

**Funds Avail.:** Up to $10,000 for medical students; $6,000 for nursing students. **No. of Awards:** Varies. **To Apply:** A parental co-signer is required. **Deadline:** June 1 and December 1. **Contact:** Ellen Badley at the above address (see entry 5240).

**• 5242 •**
**San Mateo County Farm Bureau**
765 Main St.
Half Moon Bay, CA 94019-1924

*Ph:* (415)726-4485
*Fax:* (415)726-4495

**• 5243 • San Mateo County Farm Bureau Scholarships** (*All/Scholarship*)

**Focus:** General Studies. **Qualif.:** Candidates must be members, or member dependents, of the San Mateo County Farm Bureau. **Criteria:** Selection is based on academic grades, community involvement, and financial need.

**Funds Avail.:** Award amounts vary. **Deadline:** May 1. **Contact:** Jack Olsen at the above address (see entry 5242).

**• 5244 •**
**Sara Lee Corporation**
Scholarship Dept.
Three 1st National Plaza
Chicago, IL 60602-4260

*Ph:* (312)558-8690
*Fax:* (312)419-3175
*Free:* 800-SARA-LEE

**• 5245 • Nathan Cummings Scholarships (Canada)** (*Undergraduate/Scholarship*)

**Qualif.:** Applicants must be high school students at a Canadian secondary school and children of regular, full-time employees of Sarah Lee Corporation or its divisions. Employees must have completed one year of continuous service at the time of application. They must have completed the last two years of schooling required for admission to a university in not more than two years. In each of these two years, students must have obtained an average of 70 percent or higher, and be prepared to enter a university in the year they complete entrance examinations. Children of retired and deceased employees are also eligible. **Criteria:** Recipients are chosen on a competitive basis by the Association of Universities and Colleges of Canada. Judges consider scholastic ability, character, and leadership qualities.

**Funds Avail.:** Two scholarships up to $1,500 each per year for up to four years, or until the requirements for a bachelor's degree have been completed. The scholarship winner is expected to make normal progress from year to year and must remain in good academic and disciplinary standing. **To Apply:** Application requests should be directed to AUCC. **Deadline:** June 1. Winners are notified by September 1.

## Sara Lee Corporation *(continued)*

**Remarks:** Scholarships will only be granted to students attending a Canadian University or college which is a member of the Association of Universities and Colleges of Canada. **Contact:** Canadian Award Officer, Association of Universities and Colleges of Canada, 151 Slater St., Ottawa, Canada KIP 5N1.

### • 5246 • Nathan Cummings Scholarships (United States) *(Undergraduate/Scholarship)*

**Qualif.:** Applicants must be in their junior year at a United States secondary school, children of regular, full-time employees of Sarah Lee Corporation or its divisions, and planning to attend an accredited college in the United States. Children of retired and deceased employees are also eligible. **Criteria:** Recipients are chosen on a competitive basis according to test scores, high school grades and class rank, qualities of leadership, and other significant accomplishments by the National Merit Scholarship Corporation.

**Funds Avail.:** Ten scholarships of $500 to $2,000 per year for up to four years, or until the requirements for a bachelor's degree have been completed. The amount of the stipend depends upon both the family's financial circumstances and the costs of attending the U.S. college of the recipient's choice. The scholarship winner is expected to make normal progress from year to year and must remain in good academic and disciplinary standing. **To Apply:** Students must take the Preliminary Scholastic Aptitude Test/ National Merit Scholarship Qualifying Test (PSAT/NMSQT) prior to applying for the scholarship. **Deadline:** January 31. **Contact:** Sara Lee Corporation, Scholarship Program, at the above address (see entry 5244). Telephone: (312)726-2600.

### • 5247 • Sara Lee Corporation Student Loan Program *(Undergraduate/Loan)*

**Qualif.:** Applicants must be either full-time employees of Sara Lee Corporation and its U.S. Divisions or their spouses or dependents. The employee must have completed one year of continuous service at the time of application. They must also be United States citizens or permanent residents, enrolled or accepted for enrollment on at least a half-time basis at a post-secondary institution approved by the U.S. Department of Education and USA Funds, in good academic standing, able to demonstrate financial need, and not be in default on a student loan or owe a refund on an educational grant.

**Funds Avail.:** The amount of a student's loan may never exceed the actual cost of education and must be agreed on by the student, the institution and the lender. Under the Sara Lee Corporation Student Loan Program, a student may borrow up to $2,625 for the first academic year, $3,500 his or her sophomore year and $5,500 for the remaining years of undergraduate study. The aggregate undergraduate loam limit is $23,000. Graduate students may borrow up to $8,500 per academic year to an aggregate limit of $65,000. **To Apply:** Applicants should complete Section A of the Request for Student Loan Application and submit it to their Human Resource Department, where they will complete section B and forward it to the Student Loan Program. Upon receipt of the request, an application, a needs test form, and instructions will be forwarded by the Corporate office to eligible applicants. **Deadline:** Loan application processing takes a minimum of eight to 12 weeks after applications are received by the bank, which will not be accept applications more than three months prior to the date the loan is needed. **Contact:** Student Loan Program, Sara Lee Corporation, at the above address (see entry 5244). Telephone: (312)726-2600.

### • 5248 • Sara Lee National Achievement Scholarships *(Undergraduate/Scholarship)*

**Qualif.:** Applicants must be black students who are the children of Sara Lee employees and who meet the selection criteria of the

National Merit Scholarship Corporation. **Contact:** Katie Altman at the above address (see entry 5244).

---

## • 5249 •
## Abbie Sargent Memorial Scholarship, Inc.
295 Sheep Davis Rd.      *Ph:* (603)224-1934
Concord, NH 03301      *Fax:* (603)228-8432

### • 5250 • Abbie Sargent Memorial Scholarships *(Graduate, Undergraduate/Scholarship)*

**Focus:** Agriculture, Veterinary Studies, Home Economics. **Qualif.:** Applicants must be New Hampshire residents who are studying agriculture, veterinary medicine, or home economics. **No. of Awards:** Varies. **Deadline:** March. **Contact:** Abbie Sargent Memorial Scholarship, Inc. at the above address (see entry 5249).

---

## • 5251 •
## Savoy Foundation
C.P. 69
230 Foch St.
St-Jean-sur-Richelieu, PQ, Canada     *Ph:* (450)358-9779
   J3B 6Z1               *Fax:* (450)346-1045
*E-mail:* epilepsy@savoy.foundation.ca
*URL:* http://www.savoy.foundation.ca

### • 5252 • Savoy Foundation Postdoctoral and Clinical Research Fellowships; Savoy Foundation Research Grants; Savoy Foundation Studentships *(Doctorate, Graduate/Fellowship, Grant, Internship)*

**Purpose:** To assist research and training in epilepsy or related subjects. **Focus:** Epilepsy. **Qualif.:** Candidate may be of any nationality. Applicant must be a clinician, established scientist, or graduate student who plans to conduct a research project in the biological, behavioral, or social sciences in the field of epilepsy. For research grants, preference is given to the initial stages of research and projects in need of limited, short-term funding. Studentships are reserved for inexperienced scientists seeking research training. Awards are tenable at Canadian institutions with the facilities necessary for research. Studentship recipients must be supervised by a qualified investigator at the host institution.

**Funds Avail.:** Fellowships: $25,000 minimum; Grants: $25,000; studentships: $12,000-$15,000. **No. of Awards:** 18. **To Apply:** Write for application form and guidelines. **Deadline:** January 15. **Contact:** Caroline Savoy, Secretary, at the above address (see entry 5251).

---

## • 5253 •
## Karla Scherer Foundation
737 N. Michigan Ave., Ste. 2330     *Ph:* (312)943-9191
Chicago, IL 60611           *Fax:* (312)943-9271
*URL:* http://www.comnet.org/KSCHERERF

*The Karla Scherer Foundation was established in 1989 to provide scholarships for women wishing to pursue business careers.*

• 5254 •   **Karla Scherer Foundation Scholarships**
*(Graduate, Undergraduate/Scholarship)*

**Purpose:** To help women take their places in the corporate business world. **Focus:** Economics, Finance. **Qualif.:** Scholarship recipients may be any age, but must be candidates for an undergraduate or graduate degree at a four-year accredited college or university and must maintain an acceptable scholarship level. **Criteria:** Scholarships are granted only to women studying economics and finance for careers in the manufacturing-based sector. Drive, desire and determination to succeed are important criteria as well. **No. of Awards:** 20-25/year upon initial grants and renewals. **To Apply:** Applicants must write to the Foundation offices before March 1 to request an application and they must enclose a stamped self-addressed envelope. They must include the name of the school(s) to which they are applying (or attending), the courses they plan to take, and how they intend to use their education in their chosen careers. If their request meets the Foundation's preliminary criteria, the applicants will be sent an application package, including an application form, a request for pertinent academic transcripts and standardized test scores, a statement (not to exceed 500 words) of aspirations and goals, two or more letters of recommendation from employers and/or academics (none from friends or relatives), a copy of their financial aid award letter from the university they will be attending, a recent photograph (optional), and a Financial Aid Form. If the completed application file meets Foundation criteria, a personal interview will be scheduled. **Deadline:** May 1. The Board of Trustees meets throughout the year to accommodate flexible academic schedules. Applicants who are invited to interview will be considered at the next regularly scheduled board meeting and will be notified of their acceptance or rejection soon thereafter.

**Remarks:** The Foundation requires that academic transcripts be received by its office at the end of each marking period so that it can keep track of its recipients' progress. An update of the applicant's financial picture may be requested before renewal is granted. The Foundation encourages recipients to keep in touch on a more informal basis throughout the year. **Contact:** Karla Scherer Foundation at the above address (see entry 5253).

---

• 5255 •

**Arthur and Elizabeth Schlesinger Library**
Radcliffe College
10 Garden St.                    *Ph:* (617)495-8647
Cambridge, MA 02138              *Fax:* (617)496-8340
*E-mail:* slref@radcliffe.edu
*URL:* http://www.radcliffe.edu.schles

• 5256 •   **Schlesinger Library, Radcliffe College
Dissertation Grants** *(Doctorate/Grant)*

**Purpose:** To support graduate students using the holdings of the Arthur and Elizabeth Schlesinger Library on the History of Women in America. **Focus:** History, women's history and women's studies. **Criteria:** Applicants must be enrolled in a doctoral program in a relevant field, have completed their course work toward the doctoral degree, and have an approved dissertation topic by the time the application is submitted. Proposals will be evaluated on the significance of the research to be undertaken, the extent to which the project makes creative use of Schlesinger Library holdings, and the potential contribution of the candidate and the research to scholarship.

**Funds Avail.:** Up to $1,500. **To Apply:** Each proposal should include a cover page with the applicant's name, address, affiliation (if any), and the title of the proposed project. A proposed timetable for the research and a brief explanation of how the grant funds will be used should be included. A curriculum vitae and the names and addresses of two references who have been asked to send letters

of recommendation directly to the Schlesinger Library should be attached to the proposal. **Deadline:** February 1.

• 5257 •   **Schlesinger Library, Radcliffe College
Honorary Visiting Scholar Appointments** *(Doctorate,
Postdoctorate/Other)*

**Purpose:** For visiting faculty from other colleges and universities and unaffiliated scholars who are actively pursuing research that requires or will benefit from access to the holdings of the Schesinger Library. **Focus:** Women's history, women's studies, and history. **Criteria:** Priority will be given to scholars who have demonstrated research productivity and who are at work on projects that require access to unique resources at the Schlesinger Library.

**Funds Avail.:** Scholars will be provided with office space in the library and will have library privileges at Radcliffe College and Harvard University. **No. of Awards:** 3-6. **To Apply:** Each application for appointment as an honorary visiting scholar should include a cover page giving the applicant's name, address, affiliation if any, and the working title of the proposed research. The application should include a vitae and the names of two references who have been asked to send supporting letters directly to the Schlesinger Library. **Deadline:** February.

**Remarks:** Application is no longer than 7 pages. CV must be no more than 2 pages. **Contact:** Visiting Scholar Program.

• 5258 •   **Schlesinger Library, Radcliffe College
Research Support Grants** *(Postdoctorate/Grant)*

**Qualif.:** Scholars must have completed a PhD or other doctoral degree at least a year before the time of application, or have equivalent research and writing experience. **Criteria:** Priority will be given to scholars who have demonstrated research productivity and who are at work on projects that require access to resources available only at the Schlesinger Library.

**Funds Avail.:** Ranges from $100 to $2,000. **To Apply:** Applicants must include a cover page with their name, address, affiliation, if any, and the working title of the proposed research. The application should also include a budget for the expenses for which support is being requested. **Deadline:** February. **Contact:** Research Support Program.

---

• 5259 •

**Conrad & Marcel Schlumberger Scholarship
Program**
PO Box 19610
Houston, TX 77224-9610

• 5260 •   **Conrad & Marcel Schlumberger
Scholarships** *(Undergraduate/Scholarship)*

**Purpose:** To assist students in the pursuit of an undergraduate university degree. **Focus:** General Studies. **Qualif.:** Candidates must be sons or daughters of North America Schlumberger employees. **Criteria:** Selection is based on scholastic achievement and leadership ability.

**Funds Avail.:** Awards vary. **To Apply:** Applicants should write to the scholarship committee for information. **Deadline:** March 1. **Contact:** Venitta Logan at the above address (see entry 5259).

---

Awards are arranged alphabetically below their administering organizations

## • 5261 •
### Scholarship Foundation of St. Louis
8215 Clayton Rd.
St. Louis, MO 63117-1107          *Ph:* (314)725-7990

**• 5262 •** Scholarship Foundation of St. Louis Loan
*(Graduate, Undergraduate/Loan)*

**Focus:** General studies. **Qualif.:** Applicants must be residents of St. Louis, Missouri, or the following counties: Jefferson, St. Louis, Franklin, and St. Charles who have minimum cumulative grade point averages of 2.0 at accredited colleges, universities or technical/vocational schools. Ministry students ineligible. **Criteria:** Awards are made based on financial need and credit history.

**Funds Avail.:** Interest-free loan. **No. of Awards:** 250 approximately. **To Apply:** Send a self-addressed stamped envelope between January 1 and April 15 to the Scholarship Foundation for more information. **Deadline:** April 15. **Contact:** Scholarship Foundation of St. Louis at the above address (see entry 5261).

## • 5263 •
### Scholarship Research Institute
PO Box 1146                        *Ph:* (507)454-1644
Winona, MN 55987                   *Fax:* (507)454-1644
*E-mail:* ttupac@aol.com
*URL:* http://www.angelfire.com/biz/funding

**• 5264 •** SRI Multi-Cultural Scholarship *(All/ Scholarship)*

**Focus:** General studies. **Qualif.:** Application open to all. **Criteria:** Awards are made based on academic achievement, personal statement and financial need.

**Funds Avail.:** $600 per award. **No. of Awards:** Varies. **To Apply:** Applicants must submit a personal statement describing community service, career goals, personal experiences and interaction with people of color. Send a self-addressed and stamped envelope with a $4 application fee. **Deadline:** March 31, July 1, October 31. **Contact:** Valjean Adams.

## • 5265 •
### Scholarships for Children of American Military Personnel
c/o Leora M. Ostrow, Chairman of
  the Board
136 S. Fuller Ave.
Los Angeles, CA 90036              *Ph:* (213)934-2288

**• 5266 •** SCAMP Grants & Scholarships *(Graduate, Undergraduate/Grant, Scholarship)*

**Qualif.:** Candidate must be the child of an American Armed Forces serviceperson who is a POW, MIA or KIA in the Vietnam or Desert Storm conflicts or who died challenging space or implementing national policy objectives. **Criteria:** A minimum 2.0 GPA and civic and community activities are required to renew this scholarship. Awarded annually. **No. of Awards:** 8. **Deadline:** July 31. **Contact:** Leora M. Ostrow, Chairman of the Board.

## • 5267 •
### Scholastic Art and Writing Awards
555 Broadway, 4th Fl.              *Ph:* (212)343-6892
New York, NY 10012-3999            *Fax:* (212)343-6484

**• 5268 •** Scholastic Art and Writing Awards *(High School/Award, Scholarship)*

**Purpose:** To recognize outstanding talent among high school students. **Focus:** Visual Arts, Creative Writing. **Qualif.:** Applicants must be in grades 7-12. **Criteria:** Scholarships are given to graduating seniors based on submitted art/photo or writing portfolio. Individual awards are also given based on submitted single works.

**Funds Avail.:** $5,000 cash grants to graduating seniors for the best five art portfolios and to the best five writing portfolios, as well as cash awards to students in 7-12 for individual works. **To Apply:** Send a self-addressed stamped envelope for applications by September/October. **Deadline:** Most fall between December 15 and January 5.

**Remarks:** About 200,000 applications are received each year.

## • 5269 •
### Scholastic Research Institute
850 E Front St.
Winona, MN 55987

**• 5270 •** Multi-Cultural Scholarship *(High School, Undergraduate/Scholarship)*

**Purpose:** To aid students entering higher education. **Qualif.:** Applicants must be planning to attend or attending a two or four year college university, technical school, trade school or voc-tech school. **To Apply:** A $4.00 application fee and SASE must be sent.

## • 5271 •
### Schomburg Center for Research in Black Culture
New York Public Library
515 Malcolm X Blvd.                *Ph:* (212)491-2203
New York, NY 10037-1801            *Fax:* (212)491-6760
*URL:* http://www.nypl.org

**• 5272 •** Schomburg Center Scholars-in-Residence *(Professional Development/Scholarship)*

**Purpose:** To encourage research and writing in Black history and culture. **Focus:** African American Studies. **Qualif.:** Candidates must be American citizens and scholars in the humanities studying Black history or culture, or professionals in a field related to the Center's collections and program activities. Studies in the social sciences, the arts, science and technology, psychology, education, and religion are eligible if they use a humanistic approach and contribute to humanistic knowledge. Persons seeking support for research leading to degrees are not eligible for residencies. Fellowships are tenable at the Center, and must be held on a full-time basis. Fellows may not be employed or hold other major fellowships or grants during the period in residence.

**Funds Avail.:** $15,000 to $30,000/year. **To Apply:** Write to the co-directors for application materials. **Deadline:** January 1. Notification by April 5. **Contact:** Dr. Colin Palmer, at the above address (see entry 5271).

• 5273 •

## School of American Research - Resident Scholarship Program

PO Box 2188
660 Garcia St.
Santa Fe, NM 87504-2188
*E-mail:* scholar@sarsf.org
*URL:* http://www.sarweb.org

*Ph:* (505)954-7201
*Fax:* (505)989-9809

• 5274 • **Katrin H. Lamon Resident Scholarship for Native Americans** *(Doctorate, Postdoctorate/ Scholarship)*

**Purpose:** To foster the intellectual growth of Native American scholars pursuing significant research and writing. **Focus:** Anthropology and all Allied Fields **Qualif.:** Applicant must be a Native American and be either a postdoctoral scholar, a retired scholar, or a Ph.D. candidate who has completed all requirements for the degree except the dissertation. Candidate may be working in any world area and on any topic within anthropology or a related discipline in the humanities, social sciences, or arts. Preference is given to applicants who have completed field work or basic research and analysis, and need time to write up their results. Awards are tenable at the School of American Research. **Criteria:** Applications are evaluated primarily on the basis of overall excellence and significance of the project, in addition to such factors as clarity of presentation and the applicant's record of academic accomplishments. Preference will also be given to applicants whose fieldwork or basic research and analysis are complete and who need time to write up their results. Fellowships are awarded competitively on the basis of evaluations by a specially convened panel of scholars who represent a broad spectrum of intellectual expertise.

**Funds Avail.:** Housing, office, monthly stipend, and library assistance. **No. of Awards:** 1. **To Apply:** Write to the resident scholar coordinator for application guidelines. Submit six copies of curriculum vitae and a research proposal of up to four pages. Three letters of recommendation are also required. **Deadline:** November 15. Awards are announced in March. **Contact:** Resident Scholar Coordinator at the above address (see entry 5273).

• 5275 • **National Endowment for the Humanities Fellowships** *(Postdoctorate/Fellowship)*

**Purpose:** To support scholars pursuing significant research and writing in anthropology and related disciplines. **Focus:** Anthropology and allied humanistic fields. **Qualif.:** Applicants must have Ph.D. at time of application. Proposed project must have a humanistic focus. The school is looking for scholars whose work is of the broadest, most synthetic, and most interdisciplinary nature. It seeks applicants whose research promises to yield some significant advance in understanding human culture, behavior, history, or evolution. Projects that are narrowly focused both geographically and theoretically, or that are primarily methodological, seldom receive strong consideration. **Criteria:** Applications are evaluated primarily on the basis of overall excellence and significance of the project, in addition to such factors as clarity of presentation and the applicant's record of academic accomplishments. Preference will also be given to applicants whose fieldwork or basic research and analysis are complete and who need time to write up their results. Fellowships are awarded competitively on the basis of evaluations by a specially convened panel of scholars who represent a broad spectrum of intellectual expertise.

**Funds Avail.:** Each resident scholar receives an apartment, an office on the School's campus, and a maximum stipend of $30,000. **No. of Awards:** Three annually. **To Apply:** The following must accompany the application form: six copies of a proposal no more than four pages in length, double-spaced (summarizing what is to be accomplished under the fellowship, describing the status of the applicant's research on the topic, and demonstrating the significance of the work); six copies of the applicant's curriculum

vitae; six copies of a separate statement, no more than one page in length, explaining why the project should be considered to fall within the humanities; and three letters of recommendation. **Deadline:** November 15. **Contact:** Academic Programs Coordinator at the above address (see entry 5273).

• 5276 • **Weatherhead Fellowships** *(Doctorate, Postdoctorate/Fellowship)*

**Purpose:** To support scholars pursuing significant research and writing in anthropology and related disciplines. **Focus:** Anthropology and allied fields. **Qualif.:** Applicants may be pre- or post-doctorate at time of application. Proposed project may have a humanistic or scientific focus. Pre-doctorates must have completed all requirements for degree except dissertation and must be nominated by their department as their only nominee. The school is looking for scholars whose work is of the broadest, most synthetic, and most interdisciplinary nature. It seeks applicants whose research promises to yield some significant advance in understanding human culture, behavior, history, or evolution. Projects that are narrowly focused both geographically and theoretically, or that are primarily methodological, seldom receive strong consideration. **Criteria:** Applications are evaluated primarily on the basis of overall excellence and significance of the project, in addition to such factors as clarity of presentation and the applicant's record of academic accomplishments. Preference will also be given to applicants whose fieldwork or basic research and analysis are complete and who need time to write up their results. Fellowships are awarded competitively on the basis of evaluations by a specially convened panel of scholars who represent a broad spectrum of intellectual expertise.

**Funds Avail.:** Each resident scholar receives an apartment, an office on the School's campus, and a stipend. **No. of Awards:** Two annually. **To Apply:** The following must accompany the application form: six copies of a proposal no more than four pages in length, double-spaced (the proposal should summarize what is to be accomplished under the fellowship, describe the status of the applicant's research on the topic, and demonstrate the significance of the work); six copies of the applicant's curriculum vitae; and three letters of recommendation. **Deadline:** November 15. **Contact:** Academic Programs Coordinator, at the above address (see entry 5273).

• 5277 •

## School Food Service Foundation

c/o American School Food Service
  Association
1600 Duke St., 7th Fl.
Alexandria, VA 22314-3421
*URL:* http://www.asfsa.org/foundation

*Ph:* (703)739-3900
*Fax:* (703)739-3915
*Free:* 800-877-8822

• 5278 • **Tony's Foodservice Scholarships** *(Graduate, Professional Development, Undergraduate/Scholarship)*

**Purpose:** To help eligible students pursue additional education and to enhance the school foodservice profession. **Focus:** Food Service Management, Food Science, Nutrition, Dietetics. **Qualif.:** Applicants must be members of ASFSA or children of members, be high school graduates or have passed the GED, have at least 2.7 GPA, express a desire to make school foodservice a career, and be taking courses in a related field. **Criteria:** Based on school performance, and intention to work in school foodservice.

**Funds Avail.:** Awards range from $100 to $1,000. **No. of Awards:** Varies. **To Apply:** Need two letters of recommendation, official transcripts, copy of degree/course requirements, completed and signed application, and essay. **Deadline:** April 15.

---

## • 5279 •
**Robert Schreck Memorial Fund**
c/o Texas Commerce Bank-Trust
Department
P.O. Drawer 140
El Paso, TX 79980

*Ph:* (915)546-6515
*Fax:* (915)546-2423

### • 5280 • Robert Schreck Memorial Fund Scholarship
*(Graduate, Undergraduate/Scholarship)*

**Qualif.:** Applicants must be El Paso County, Texas, residents. They must be juniors or seniors studying the Episcopal clergy, medicine, veterinary medicine, physics, chemistry, engineering, or architecture. **Criteria:** Candidates who have a high scholastic standing and exhibit financial need are preferred.

**Funds Avail.:** Awards range from $500 to $1,000 each. **To Apply:** Those who wish to apply must request an application from the Schreck Memorial Fund. **Deadline:** The deadlines are July 15 and November 15. **Contact:** Terry Crenshaw at the above address (see entry 5279).

## • 5281 •
**Science Service, Inc.**
1719 N St. NW
Washington, DC 20036
*E-mail:* youth@sciserv.org

*Ph:* (202)785-2255
*Fax:* (202)785-1243

### • 5282 • Westinghouse Science Talent Search
*(Undergraduate/Scholarship)*

**Purpose:** To discover, in close cooperation with educational institutions, the youth of America whose scientific and engineering skills, talent and ability, indicate potential creative originality. **Qualif.:** Candidates are students in the last year of public, private, or parochial secondary schools in the United States, Puerto Rico, Guam, the Virgin Islands, American Samoa, Wake and Midway Islands, and the Marianas. Candidates can also be American students in the last year of secondary school who are attending Department of Defense schools, an accredited overseas American or International school, foreign schools as exchange students or as the children of parents who work and live abroad. Completion of college entrance requirements by the October 1 following application deadline is required. Prior Science Talent competition is not permitted. There are no age limitations.

**Funds Avail.:** The forty top contestants attend a five day, all-expense paid visit to Washington, D.C. Of these 40, ten receive four-year Westinghouse Science Scholarships. The ten awards include one of $40,000 ($10,000 a year); one of $30,000 ($7,500); one of $20,000 ($5,000 a year); three of $15,000 each ($3,750 a year); and four of $10,000 each ($2,500 a year). Each of the remaining 30 contestants receive a $1,000 Westinghouse Science Scholarship. Three hundred semifinalists are brought to the attention of higher education schools in the United States. Hundreds of students receive recommendations and other aid toward a college education in states holding State Science Talent Searches concurrently with the National Competition. **To Apply:** Official entry materials must be requested. Candidates submit a written report on an independent research project in the physical sciences, behavioral and social sciences, engineering, mathematics or biological sciences. Live vertebrate experimentation is not permitted (with the exception of behavioral observation of the animals in their natural habitats), unless: the student has no physical contact with the animals; the materials on which the student is working is supplied to the student by the supervising scientist; or if the animals are sacrificed for purposes other than the research being done by the student. In these cases, a statement from the supervising scientist attesting to the above must be included with the application. All proposed human contact studies, including surveys and questionnaires, must be evaluated for risk (psychological and physical) by an institutional review board. An entry form blank filled in by student, teachers, and school officials, standardized test scores, and high school transcripts must accompany each research report, as well as a statement from the supervising scientist giving descriptive and explanatory evidence of independence and creativity for students who attended summer institutes, science training programs, or worked in a scientist's laboratory and who use material from that experience as part of their project. The research must be the work of a single student. **Deadline:** Early December. The exact date is provided annually.

**Remarks:** The Science Talent Search is administered by Science Service and funded by Westinghouse Electric Corporation and the Westinghouse Foundation. Scholarships must be applied toward a course in science or engineering at a degree-granting institution of higher education in the United States that is approved by the Scholarship Committee. Acceptable science and engineering courses are those fields of activity of the National Academy of Sciences, the National Research Council, and the National Academy of Engineering. **Contact:** Karen Sullivan, Program Director, Westinghouse Science Talent Search, at the above address (see entry 5281).

## • 5283 •
**Scleroderma Federation**
89 Newbury St., Ste. 201
Danvers, MA 01923-1075
*URL:* http://www.scleroderma.org/

*Ph:* (508)535-6600
*Fax:* (508)535-6696

*The Scleroderma Federation was formerly known as the Scleroderma Association.*

### • 5284 • Scleroderma Research Grants
*(Postgraduate/Grant)*

**Purpose:** To fund research projects specifically directed to Scleroderma. Studies may be carried out at the molecular, cellular, animal, or patient level in relevant scientific disciplines. **Focus:** Medical Research.

**Funds Avail.:** Up to $35,000 per grant with funds totaling approximately $1 million. **To Apply:** Grant application/instructions and specific information concerning grant criteria may be obtained by writing the Federation. **Deadline:** Variable. **Contact:** Marie A. Coyle, Research Grant Administrator at the above address (see entry 5283).

## • 5285 •
**Scott Paper Company Foundation**
Scott Plaza One
Philadelphia, PA 19113

*Ph:* (215)522-5617

### • 5286 • McCabe Awards *(Undergraduate/Award)*

**Purpose:** To recognize the accomplishments of Scott employees' children and to encourage them to further their education. **Qualif.:** Parent of applicant must be a regular, full-time employee of Scott Paper Company Foundation or its wholly-owned subsidiaries and have worked with the Company or its wholly-owned subsidiaries for at least one continuous year prior to the January 1 deadline date. Applicants must be a dependent children (unmarried, natural or legally adopted children or stepchildren under the age of 23 and primarily supported by parent); either current high school seniors or high school graduates who have never enrolled in a full-time program of post-secondary school studies; and planning to enroll in a full-time course of study at an accredited institution of learning beyond the high school level such as an accredited college, university, vocational/technical school, or other skill development institution. **Criteria:** Citizens Scholarship Foundation of America bases its selection criteria on all aspects of the student as a person. Specifically, CSFA will consider work experience, extra-curricular activities, personal honors and achievements, counselors' recommendations, class ranking, test scores, and GPA. Academic performance is weighted equally with non-academic performance. PSAT and SAT scores are not considered for vo-tech applications.

**Funds Avail.:** Awards range from $1,000 to $3,500 annually in increments of $500 and are available for up to four years of full-time study in any post-high school education program, provided it is offered by an accredited institution. The award may be used to pay for education-related expenses such as tuition, books, lab fees, materials, and room and board. Awards are renewable each year as long as satisfactory academic performance is maintained. **To Apply:** Application must be accompanied by official high school transcripts and the completed Applicant Appraisal Section from the application (to be completed by the student's high school counselor or another authority figure who is familiar with the applicant's accomplishments). **Deadline:** January 1. **Contact:** Patricia A. Mooney, Scott Paper Company Foundation, at the above address (see entry 5285).

---

**• 5287 •**
**Scoville Peace Fellowship Program**
110 Maryland Ave., N.E., Ste. 211          *Ph:* (202)546-0795
Washington, DC 20002                       *Fax:* (202)546-5142
*URL:* http://149.43.25.250/scoville.html

**• 5288 •   Herbert Scoville Jr. Peace Fellowship**
*(Professional Development/Fellowship)*

**Purpose:** To provide an opportunity to work in Washington, D.C. for peace, disarmament, or nuclear arms control organization. **Focus:** Peace Studies, Political Science, International Relations. **Qualif.:** Applicant must be a U.S. citizen. Candidate must hold a bachelor's degree and have a strong interest in peace issues. Preference will be given to individuals without substantial experience in the Washington, D.C. area. Award is tenable in Washington, D.C. Fellow will serve as special project assistant on the staff of one of the participating organizations.

**Funds Avail.:** $1,300/month, plus travel expenses and health insurance. **No. of Awards:** 2-3 per semester. **To Apply:** Write for application form and list of participating organizations. Submit two references, transcripts, curriculum vitae and other items as described in application. **Deadline:** March 15 for fall fellowship and October 15 for spring fellowship.

**Remarks:** The fellowship encourages attendance at important Congressional hearings, seminars, and major speeches on war and peace issues. **Contact:** Program Director at the above address (see entry 5287).

---

**• 5289 •**
**Seafarers International Union - Seafarers Welfare Plan**
5201 Auth Way                              *Ph:* (301)899-0675
Suitland, MD 20746-4211                    *Fax:* (301)423-0634

**• 5290 •   Charlie Logan Scholarship for Dependents**
*(Undergraduate/Scholarship)*

**Focus:** General Studies. **Qualif.:** Applicants must be eligible for dependent (spouse) benefits under the Seafarers Welfare Plan, unmarried at the time of application, and under the age of 19.

**Funds Avail.:** Four scholarships in the amount of $15,000 each are awarded annually. They are paid at the rate of $3,750 per year over a four year period. **To Apply:** Along with a formal application, applicants must submit a certified copy of their birth certificate and an autobiographical statement in which their educational and vocational plans and reasons for these plans are described. Inclusion of a black and white passport-type photograph is optional. The following must be sent directly to the scholarship committee: high school transcripts and certification of graduation by the high school or official copy of high school equivalency (GED) examination scores by the Board of Education, official college transcripts by the college, SAT or ACT results, and three or four letters of reference. SAT or ACT tests must be taken no later than February of the year of application deadline. Letters of reference must include one from the candidate's high school principal or from one of the high school teachers, and if already in college, a fourth letter from the Dean of Students or major advisor. **Deadline:** April 15. **Contact:** Scholarship Program at the above address (see entry 5289).

**• 5291 •   Charlie Logan Scholarship for Seafarers**
*(Undergraduate/Scholarship)*

**Focus:** General Studies. **Qualif.:** Applicants must be high school graduates or equivalent. They must: have credit for a total of 730 days of employment with an employer who is obligated to make contributions to the Seafarers Welfare Plan on the employee's behalf prior to the date of application; have one day of employment on a vessel in the six-month period immediately preceding the date of application; and have 120 days of employment on a vessel in the previous calendar year. **Criteria:** Award selections are based on high school equivalency scores or secondary records, SAT or ACT scores, college transcripts (if any), and references on character and personality.

**Funds Avail.:** Three scholarships are awarded annually. Two are for $6,000 each and are designed for two-year courses of study in the United States at an accredited college, university, post-secondary vocational school, or community college. They are paid at the rate of $3,000 per year. The third scholarship is for $15,000, paid at the rate of $3,750 per year, and is intended to cover a four-year, college-level course of study. In a year with exceptionally qualified seafarer applicants, a second award of $15,000 may be disbursed. Applicants must maintain good scholastic standing in order to keep the scholarship on a yearly basis. **To Apply:** Along with a formal application, the applicant must submit a certified copy of his/her birth certificate and an autobiographical statement in which the candidate's educational and vocational plans and reasons for the applicant's choice are stated. Inclusion of a black and white passport type photograph is required. The following must be sent directly to the scholarship committee: high school transcript and certification of graduation by the high school or official copy of high school equivalency (GED) examination scores by the Board of Education; official college transcript by the college; SAT or ACT results; and three or four letters of reference. **Deadline:** April 15. **Contact:** Scholarship Program, Seafarer's Welfare Plan, at the above address (see entry 5289).

---

**• 5292 •**
**Seaspace**
PO Box 3753
Houston, TX 77253-3753                     *Ph:* (713)499-7096
*URL:* http://www.seaspace.org

**• 5293 •   Seaspace Scholarship** *(Graduate, Undergraduate/Scholarship)*

**Purpose:** To assist qualified, financially needy students who are enrolled in marine related programs in U.S. colleges and universities. **Focus:** Marine and Aquatic Sciences. **Qualif.:** Applicants must be enrolled in, or accepted for enrollment in a

---

## Seaspace (continued)

marine related curriculum in an accredited U.S. college or university as juniors, seniors, or graduate students for the fall term of the year in which the award is granted. Undergraduates must have a grade point average of at least 3.5 or the equivalent. Graduate students must have a grade point average of at least 3.0 on a 4.0 scale. **Criteria:** Selection is based upon financial need, academic excellence, and demonstrated course or research direction.

**Funds Avail.:** Variable, depending on individual need and number of qualifying candidates. In the past, scholarships have ranged from $500 to $3,000. **No. of Awards:** 20. **To Apply:** Applications available from website only. **Deadline:** February 1.

**Remarks:** Application for next year should be online by late October. **Contact:** Carolyn Peterson at the above address (see entry 5292).

---

## • 5294 •
## Seattle Times
Newsroom Intern Coordinator
PO Box 70
Seattle, WA 98111-0070
*E-mail:* bmat-new@seatimes.com

*Ph:* (206)464-3274
*Fax:* (206)382-6760

### • 5295 • Blethen Family Newspaper Internship Program for Minorities *(Graduate, Professional Development/Internship)*

**Focus:** Journalism. **Qualif.:** The program is open to African American, Asian American, Latino, Native American or Pacific Islander college graduates who are committed to print journalism and have a desire to work in the Pacific Northwest. Interns are required to have a car.

**Funds Avail.:** Housing, medical coverage, and full-time salary (ranging from $260-320 per week) is provided. **No. of Awards:** 3. **To Apply:** Applicants must submit a cover letter, resume, and clippings. **Deadline:** Applications are accepted year-round.

**Remarks:** This award was formerly known as the Seattle Times Quarterly Internships for Minority Journalists.

### • 5296 • The *Seattle Times* Summer Newsroom Internships *(Graduate, Undergraduate/Internship)*

**Purpose:** To provide experience in areas of journalism such as (but not limited to) general reporting, copydesk editors, photography, artists, and page designers. **Focus:** Journalism. **Qualif.:** Applicants must be sophomores, juniors, seniors, or graduate students attending a four-year college or university. Applicants must also be journalism majors or have demonstrated a commitment to print journalism. Previous experience is recommended but not necessary. **Criteria:**.

**Funds Avail.:** Internships are paid. **No. of Awards:** 12 each summer.

---

## • 5297 •
## Second Marine Division Association
PO Box 8180
Camp Lejeune, NC 28547-8180

*Ph:* (919)451-3167
*Fax:* (919)451-3167

### • 5298 • Second Marine Division Memorial Scholarships *(Undergraduate/Scholarship)*

**Purpose:** To assist eligible students to obtain an undergraduate education. **Focus:** General Studies. **Qualif.:** Applicants must be

unmarried dependent sons or daughters of persons who have served or are serving in the Second Marine Division, United States Marine Corps. Parents may also have served in the Second Marine Division or a unit attached to it, and died while so serving or subsequently died in the service of the United States or have been severely disabled as a result of such service. Candidates must currently be high school seniors, high school graduates, or enrolled as full time undergraduate students in an accredited college or vocational/technical school. Family income normally cannot exceed $42,000 in the year preceding the school year for which assistance is required.

**Funds Avail.:** Scholarships are $800 per year, and are available for up to four years. Students must maintain a C-plus average and take at least twelve units to qualify for continued support. **No. of Awards:** 35. **To Apply:** Candidates must submit a formal application, a family financial statement, evidence of a parent's service with the Second Marine Division, and a Selective Service Registration Statement. **Deadline:** Applications must be submitted by April 1 with all supporting documents due by July 1. **Contact:** Second Marine Division Association, PO Box 8180, Camp Lejeune, NC 28547.

---

## • 5299 •
## SEG Foundation
PO Box 702740
Tulsa, OK 74170-2740

*Ph:* (918)493-3516
*Fax:* (918)497-5558

### • 5300 • SEG Scholarships *(Graduate, Undergraduate/Scholarship)*

**Purpose:** To support studies directed toward a career in exploration geophysics. **Focus:** Exploration Geophysics. **Qualif.:** Applicants may be of any nationality, but must be graduate or undergraduate students whose studies are directed toward a career in exploration geophysics. Scholarships are tenable at U.S. colleges and universities. Administration of the scholarship is given to the college or university attended by the scholar. The institution retains custody of the funds. Certain scholarships administered by the Foundation carry additional requirements; write for further information.

**Funds Avail.:** $500-3,000; $1,200 average. **No. of Awards:** 82. **To Apply:** Write for application form and guidelines. **Deadline:** March 1.

---

## • 5301 •
## Abe and Annie Seibel Foundation
c/o United States National Bank,
  Trust Department
PO Box 8210
Galveston, TX 77553-8210

*Ph:* (409)763-1151

### • 5302 • Seibel Foundation Interest Free Educational Loan *(Undergraduate/Loan)*

**Qualif.:** Applicants must be Texas residents who are graduates of Texas high schools, and who are attending or will be attending when the scholarship is tenable, a college or university in Texas. They must be working toward their first four-year degree. The loan needs two co-signers in good credit standing. **Criteria:** Grade performance is the primary criterion.

**Funds Avail.:** Approximately 700 interest-free loans, averaging $2,500, are awarded for one school year at a time. Recipients are expected to repay their loans as quickly as possible. **To Apply:** Initial loan applications are made either by telephone or by mail. A student loan package is mailed to the candidate, and a personal interview is arranged. The completed application is returned at the time of the interview. If a personal interview cannot be arranged, the candidate files a carefully prepared self-explanatory application form. **Deadline:** Loan requests are usually accepted only during January and February. **Contact:** The Siebel Foundation at the above address (see entry 5301).

• 5303 •

**Marie Selby Botanical Garden**

| 811 S. Palm Ave. | *Ph:* (914)366-5131 |
| Sarasota, FL 34236-7726 | *Fax:* (914)366-9807 |

• 5304 • **Marie Selby Internships** *(Graduate, Undergraduate/Internship)*

**Purpose:** To provide experience in all aspects and phases of a botanical garden including maintenance and development of the grounds and the living collections, scientific research, and herbarium management. The internship lasts three months and is available three times per year. Students receive training in practical gardening, orchid growing, bromeliad culture, greenhouse practices, plant nursery, plant propagation and growing techniques, herbarium procedures, and opportunities for special projects. Interns may also attend classes, seminars, plant society meetings, and field trips. **Focus:** Botany. **Qualif.:** Applicants must be upperclass or graduate students majoring in botany, horticulture, science education, or related fields, who demonstrate a strong interest in pursuing a career in some aspect of botanical gardening, plant biology, horticulture, or gardening.

**Funds Avail.:** Housing and an $11/day stipend. Utilities, local phone calls, and bicycles are also provided. Long distance phone calls, transportation, and all other expenses will be the responsibility of the intern. **No. of Awards:** 12 per year. **To Apply:** Write for details. **Deadline:** Applications for fall, spring and summer sessions accepted year round.

**Remarks:** Selby Gardens is situated on 15 acres which includes a seven acre public garden along Sarasota Bay. The climate is subtropical and the grounds are landscaped with subtropical and tropical plants. In addition, the Gardens maintain as display greenhouse with permanent tropical plantings and colorful seasonal displays. The non-public portions of the Gardens include five research greenhouses, and administration building, herbarium, intern quarters, and laboratory facilities. **Contact:** Dr. Raul Rivero, Director of Education, at the above address (see entry 5303).

• 5305 •

**Seminole Nation Higher Education Program**

| PO Box 1498 | *Ph:* (405)257-6629 |
| Wewoka, OK 74884 | *Fax:* (405)257-7051 |
| *E-mail:* oskem_highered@nemet.com | |

• 5306 • **Louie LeFlore/Grant Foreman Scholarship** *(Undergraduate/Scholarship)*

**Qualif.:** Candidates must be members of one of the Five Civilized Tribes (Cherokee, Creek, Choctaw, Chickasaw, or Seminole) and majoring in nursing or pre-health and health professions, with a letter of acceptance to such a program as evidence. Only Oklahoma residents living within the respective tribal service area at the time of application are eligible. Applicants must also apply for financial aid and demonstrate financial need, if required by respective tribe.

**Funds Avail.:** $800 to one student from one of the five tribes each year. Scholarships are not renewable. **Deadline:** July 1. **Contact:** Higher Education Program of respective tribe at one of the

following addresses: Choctaw Tribe Higher Education Program, PO Box 1210, Durant, OK 74701; Seminole Nation Higher Education Program, PO Box 1498, Wewoka, OK 74884; Chicksaw Tribe Higher Education Program, PO Box 1548, Ada, OK 74820; Creek (Muscogee) Tribe Higher Education Program, PO Box 580, Okmulgee, OK 74447; Cherokee Tribe Higher Education, PO Box 948, Tahlequah, OK 74465.

• 5307 •

**Service Employees International Union - California State Council of Service Employees**

| 1007 7th St., 4th Fl. | *Ph:* (916)442-3838 |
| Sacramento, CA 95814-3407 | *Fax:* (916)442-0976 |

• 5308 • **Charles Hardy Memorial Scholarship Awards** *(Undergraduate/Scholarship)*

**Qualif.:** Applicants must be sons and daughters of members of any local union affiliated with the California State Council of Service Employees. A parent of the candidate must have been a member of a local union in good standing for at least one year immediately preceding the application. Entering freshmen applicants must have achieved not less than a B average in their high school work. There are no restrictions of any kind on the course of study to be taken by scholarship recipients, or on the place of study. There are no obligations imposed on recipients except that they conduct themselves in a manner worthy of the person in whose name their scholarship is awarded.

**Funds Avail.:** Scholarships in the amount of $750 annually are awarded. They commence with the fall term. Recipients may receive aid for up to four years of school provided satisfactory ability and progress has been made. This must be approved by the Executive Board of the State Council. **Deadline:** Application forms are accepted between November 1 and February 1 for scholarship awards to begin the following fall semester. **Contact:** Any local union affiliated with the California State Council of Service Employees. Applications may be obtained through the Service Employees International Union at the above address (see entry 5307). Toll-free telephone: 800-424-8592.

• 5309 •

**Service Merchandise Company Inc.**

| 7100 Service Merchandise Dr. | *Ph:* (615)660-7232 |
| Brentwood, TN 37027-2927 | *Fax:* (615)377-7329 |

*Service Merchandise programs are managed by Career Opportunities Through Education, Inc. (COTE), PO Box 2810, Cherry Hill, NJ 08034.*

• 5310 • **Service Merchandise Scholarship Program** *(High School, Undergraduate/Scholarship)*

**Purpose:** To reward individuals who have achieved academic excellence while also being involved in school and community activities. **Focus:** Business, Marketing and Distribution, Economics, Accounting, General Studies. **Qualif.:** Applicants must be high school seniors or high school graduates who are now planning to enroll in an accredited four-year program leading to a bachelor's degree. Preference is given to business, marketing, merchandising, economics, or accounting majors. Associates of Service Merchandise Co., Inc. and its affiliates, and their dependents, are not eligible. **Criteria:** Selection is based on the applicants' academic achievement, participation in school and community activities, work experience, statement of plans and goals, and recommendation by a high school faculty member. Financial need is not a consideration.

## Service Merchandise Company Inc. (continued)

**Funds Avail.:** $500. Awards are mailed directly to the recipients' home addresses and must be used to pay for tuition, room and board, books, or lab fees. **No. of Awards:** 100. **To Apply:** Applicants must submit a completed application form and current, official transcript. **Deadline:** The first 2,500 completed applications post-marked no later than January 15 will be processed. Scholarship winners will be notified by April 15. Award recipients must notify COTE (see address below) of acceptance no later than April 30 or the award will be forfeited. **Contact:** Service Merchandise Program Manager, Career Opportunities Through Education, Inc. (COTE), PO Box 2810, Cherry Hill, NJ 08034. Telephone: (609)573-9400.

### • 5311 • Mary & Harry Zimmerman Scholarship Program *(High School, Undergraduate/Scholarship)*

**Purpose:** The scholarship was created to serve as a lasting tribute to Mary and Harry Zimmerman, who along with their son Raymond, founded the company in 1960. Their concern for the associates at Service Merchandise and for quality education served as the inspiration for the establishment of this program. **Focus:** General Studies. **Qualif.:** Applicants must be associates or dependent children (unmarried and under the age of 23) of associates of Service Merchandise Co., Inc. or its affiliates, up to and including children of operating vice presidents. Associates must have worked for the company at least 90 days prior to the application deadline. Applicants must also be high school seniors or high school graduates planning to enroll in an accredited four-year program leading to a Bachelor's degree. **Criteria:** Scholarships are awarded based on the applicants' academic achievement, participation in school and community activities, work experience, statement of plans and goals, and recommendation by a high school faculty member. Financial need is not a consideration.

**Funds Avail.:** $1,000 each. Awards are mailed directly to the recipients' home addresses in two equal installments in July and December, and must be used to pay for tuition, room and board, books, or lab fees. Recipients may apply annually for renewal of their awards provided they demonstrate satisfactory academic performance and submit an official transcript at the end of each semester. Scholarships may be held for a reasonable period of time in the case of an approved leave of absence, serious illness, or injury that interrupts studies. Cote, the administering organization, must be notified immediately in any such circumstance. **No. of Awards:** 12. **To Apply:** Applicants must submit a completed application form and a current, official transcript. **Deadline:** March 1. Winners will be notified no later than April 15 and must notify Cote of acceptance of the award by April 30, or the award will be forfeited. **Contact:** Questions may be directed to Mary & Harry Zimmerman Program Manager, Career Opportunities Through Education, Inc., PO Box 2810, Cherry Hill, NJ 08034. Telephone (609)573-9400.

### • 5312 •
## Shaklee U.S.

c/o Karin Topping, Dir., Public
  Relations
444 Market St.
San Francisco, CA 94111
*E-mail:* ktopping@shaklee.com
*URL:* http://www.shaklee.com

*Ph:* (415)954-2007
*Fax:* (415)954-2280
*Free:* 800-SHA-KLEE

### • 5313 • Dr. Forrest Shaklee Memorial Scholarship
*(Undergraduate/Scholarship)*

**Purpose:** To make available financial assistance to undergraduate students for the completion of their college education. **Focus:** General studies. **Qualif.:** Applicants must be sons or daughters of Sales Leaders and employees of the Shaklee Corporation and its

U.S. subsidiaries who are completing high school requirements and entering college in the same year. Applicants must take a qualifying test, the Preliminary Scholastic Aptitude Test/National merit Scholarships Qualifying Test (PSAT/NMSQT) during the proper year in high school. The highest-scoring eligible candidates will be informed in the fall of their senior year that they will receive further consideration for a scholarship by meeting several academic and other requirements set by NMSC. **Criteria:** Awards are granted on a competitive basis, including academic record throughout high school, significant activities and contributions to the school and community, the school's recommendation, test scores, and the student's self-description of interests and goals.

**Funds Avail.:** $1,000 to $3,000 per award. Renewable. NMSC may increase or decrease the winner's annual stipend, within the minimum and maximum limits set for the scholarship. **No. of Awards:** eight per year. **To Apply:** Qualifying students and their high school principals file additional biographical and academic information with NMSC. **Deadline:** December 31. **Contact:** Shaklee Scholarship Program at the above address (see entry 5312).

### • 5314 •
## Shastri Indo-Canadian Institute

1402 Education Tower
2500 University Dr. NW
Calgary, AB, Canada T2N 1N4
*E-mail:* sici@ucalgary.ca
*URL:* http://www.ucalgary.ca/~sici

*Ph:* (403)220-7467
*Fax:* (403)289-0100

### • 5315 • Canadian Studies for Indian Scholars
*(Doctorate, Professional Development/Fellowship)*

**Purpose:** To assist and promote Indian scholars studying Canada. **Focus:** Canadian Studies. **Qualif.:** There are three Fellowships: Faculty Research Fellowships are intended for Indian scholars promoting Canadian studies at their home institutions; Faculty Enrichment Fellowships are designed to assist selected academic staff of Indian universities to gather information and materials in Canada in order to develop and teach course on Canada at their home institutions; Doctoral Research Awards are intended to promote research leading specifically to a better knowledge and understanding of Canada. Applicant must be a citizen of India doing research on Canada.

**Funds Avail.:** Faculty Research Fellowship includes up to $2,000 for international travel and up to $700 weekly living allowance for a maximum of 5 weeks. **To Apply:** Write to the Vice President in the India office for application form and guidelines. Each Fellowship has slightly different requirements. **Deadline:** Varies. **Contact:** Vice President of the institute at the above address (see entry 5314).

### • 5316 • India Studies Faculty Fellowships
*(Professional Development/Fellowship)*

**Purpose:** To support research and training in India by Canadian scholars. **Focus:** Humanities, Indian Languages, Indian Studies, Performing Arts, Social Sciences, Management, Education, Law. **Qualif.:** The Institute offers two different Fellowships: Faculty Research Fellowship and Faculty Training Fellowship. Applicant must be a Canadian citizen or landed immigrant who plans to study or conduct research in India. Candidate must have a full or part-time appointment in a Canadian institution of higher education. Candidate must intend to return to Canada upon completion of the fellowship term.

**Funds Avail.:** RS 12,000 allowance per month or the difference between leave and regular salary whichever is less and RS 3,000 for research per month. **To Apply:** Write, phone, or email the Institute for application form and guidelines. **Deadline:** June 30. **Contact:** Programme Officer, India Studies at the above address (see entry 5314).

## • 5317 • India Studies Performing Arts Fellowships
*(Professional Development/Fellowship)*

**Purpose:** To support junior or senior artists who have demonstrated a sustained commitment to one or more of the performing arts of India. **Focus:** Performing Arts. **Qualif.:** Applicant must be a Canadian citizen or landed immigrant who plans to study or conduct research in India. Candidate must intend to return to Canada upon completion of the fellowship term.

**Funds Avail.:** Senior and Junior Fellowships: 12,000 rupees/month, plus 3,000 rupees/month for instructional expenses. **To Apply:** Write, phone, or email the Institute for application form and guidelines. **Deadline:** June 30. **Contact:** Programme Officer, India Studies at the above address (see entry 5314).

## • 5318 • India Studies Postdoctoral Research Fellowships *(Professional Development/Fellowship)*

**Purpose:** To support research and training in India by Canadian scholars. **Focus:** Humanities, Indian Languages, Indian Studies, Performing Arts, Social Sciences, Management, Education, Law. **Qualif.:** Applicant must be a Canadian citizen or landed immigrant who plans to study or conduct research in India. Candidate need not be affiliated with a Canadian university. Candidate must intend to return to Canada upon completion of the fellowship term.

**Funds Avail.:** 12,000 rupees/month, plus 3,000 rupees/month for research. **To Apply:** Write, phone, or email the Institute for application form and guidelines. **Deadline:** June 30. **Contact:** Programme Officer at the above address (see entry 5314).

## • 5319 • India Studies Student Fellowships
*(Graduate/Fellowship)*

**Purpose:** To support graduate students entering a programme leading to specialization in India. **Focus:** Humanities, Indian Languages, Indian Studies, Performing Arts, Social Sciences, Management, Education, Law. **Qualif.:** There are three different Fellowships: Graduate Degree from an Indian University; Student Research Fellowship; and Student Language Training Fellowship. Applicant must be a Canadian citizen or landed immigrant who plans to study or conduct research in India. Candidate must intend to return to Canada upon completion of the fellowship term.

**Funds Avail.:** 12,000 rupees/month, plus 3,000 rupees/month for research. **To Apply:** Write, phone or email the Institute for application form and guidelines. **Deadline:** June 30. **Contact:** Programme Officer, India Studies at the above address (see entry 5314).

## • 5320 •
## Sheet Metal Workers' International Scholarship Fund
1750 New York Ave. NW
Washington, DC 20006
*URL:* http://www.amwia.org

Ph: (202)783-5880
Fax: (202)662-0891

### • 5321 • Sheet Metal Workers' International Scholarship *(Undergraduate/Scholarship)*

**Focus:** General studies. **Qualif.:** Applicants must be SMWIA members, covered employees or dependent spouses or children of SMWIA members or covered employees. Grandchildren are ineligible. All applicants must be enrolled or accepted as full-time students at accredited colleges or universities. **Criteria:** Awards are made based on achievement, recommendations and written essay.

**Funds Avail.:** $4,000. **No. of Awards:** 30 per year. **To Apply:** Applicants must submit a completed application form; full information on their or family members' SMWIA membership,

including International Association membership number, the number of the local to which they belong, the local union in whose jurisdiction they was employed during the preceding calendar year; high school transcript; SAT or ACT scores; letter of recommendation; and an essay on the importance of the Sheet Metal Workers' International Association to the applicant's family. **Deadline:** March 1. **Contact:** Terri Sodero, at the above address (see entry 5320).

## • 5322 •
## ShenaArts Inc.
Pennyroyal Farm
Rte. 5, Box 167F
Staunton, VA 24401
*E-mail:* shenarts@cfw.com

Ph: (540)248-1868
Fax: (540)248-1868

### • 5323 • ShenanArts Fellowships *(Professional Development/Fellowship)*

**Purpose:** To encourage and support projects by stage and screen writers. **Focus:** Drama, Screenwriting. **Qualif.:** Applicants may be stage or screen writers. Fellowships are tenable at the Shenandoah International Playwrights' Retreat where writers develop proposed projects in collaboration with directors, dramaturgs, and actors.

**Funds Avail.:** Room, board, tuition, transportation. **No. of Awards:** 10-12. **To Apply:** Write to the director for application guidelines. Submit two copies of a draft of proposed project, a personal statement describing background as a writer, a self-addressed, stamped postcard, and an envelope for return of manuscript. **Deadline:** February 1. Notification after June 1. **Contact:** Robert Graham Small, Director, at the above address (see entry 5322).

## • 5324 •
## Siena College
Theatre Program
515 Loudon Rd.
Loudonville, NY 12211-1462
*E-mail:* maciag@siena.edu
*URL:* http://www.siena.edu/theatre

Ph: (518)783-2381
Fax: (518)783-4293

### • 5325 • International Playwrights' Competition *(Professional Development/Prize)*

**Purpose:** To recognize and produce superior new scripts. **Focus:** Drama. **Qualif.:** Candidates may be of any nationality. Submission must be an unpublished and unproduced play that is free of royalty and copyright restrictions. Prizes are not offered for one-act plays or musicals. Prize winner is required to be in residence at the College during the production of script.

**Funds Avail.:** $2,000; plus a maximum $1,000 for traveling and housing. **No. of Awards:** 1. **To Apply:** Write for application form and guidelines. **Deadline:** February 1 to June 30 of even-numbered years. Competition is held biennially. The prize is announced by September 30. **Contact:** Gary Maciag, at the above address (see entry 5324).

---

*Awards are arranged alphabetically below their administering organizations*

## • 5326 •

### Sigma Alpha Iota
165 West 82nd St.
New York, NY 10024          *Ph:* (212)724-2809

#### • 5327 • Inter-American Music Awards (*Professional Development/Award*)

**Purpose:** To encourage American composers. **Focus:** Music Composition. **Qualif.:** Candidates must be citizens of North, South, or Central America. They must be composers. Winning composition is performed at Sigma Alpha Iota's national convention.

**Funds Avail.:** $750 honorarium, publication, plus lodging and transportation to convention. **To Apply:** Write to the director for application guidelines. **Deadline:** April 30. Award is offered triennially.

**Remarks:** Inter-American Music Awards, 165 W. 82nd St., Apt 10, New York, NY 10024. **Contact:** Euginie L. Dengel, Director, at the above address (see entry 5326).

## • 5328 •

### Sigma Delta Epsilon, Graduate Women in Science
PO Box 240726
Apple Valley, MN 55124-0726

#### • 5329 • Eloise Gerry Fellowships (*Postgraduate/ Fellowship*)

**Purpose:** To increase knowledge in the chemical and biological sciences and to encourage research by women. **Focus:** Science. **Qualif.:** Candidates must be women holding a science degree from an accredited college or university. Gerry Fellowships are for research in the biological and chemical sciences. Applicants must have demonstrated outstanding ability and potential in research. **Criteria:** Applications are reviewed based on scientific question, presentation, methodology, experience and budget.

**Funds Avail.:** The amount of the fellowship varies from $1,500-3,000 and is based on a tentative budget that indicates the amount of money needed and outlines how the funds are to be used. Grants may not be used for tuition, administrative overhead, or equipment of general use. The fellowship period depends upon the option exercised at the time the fellowship is granted. If it extends beyond a year, submission of an annual progress report is required. **To Apply:** Candidates must submit a formal application, a 4-page description of the project, evidence of research ability and experience (these may include a list of publications, short papers or reports, but not grade transcripts), a detailed budget, statement of other financial support, two letters of recommendation and two self-addressed, stamped envelopes. **Deadline:** Applications are due December 1; awards are announced on June 1.

**Remarks:** Any publications resulting from the grant must acknowledge support of Sigma Delta Epsilon. Two reprints of each publication should be submitted to the National Office. At termination of the fellowship, a report must be sent to the National Secretary of Sigma Delta Epsilon and an abstract of 100 words or less must be prepared for SDE/GWIS publication in their Bulletin as soon as possible after completion of the project. **Contact:** Chairman, Eloise Gerry Fellowships Committee, at the above address (see entry 5328).

#### • 5330 • SDE Fellowships (*Postgraduate/Fellowship*)

**Purpose:** To increase knowledge in the fundamental sciences and to encourage research by women. **Focus:** Science. **Qualif.:** Candidates must be women holding a science degree from an accredited college or university. SDE Fellowships are for research in the natural sciences (i.e., physical, environmental, mathematical, computer, and life sciences). Applicants must have demonstrated outstanding ability and potential in research. **Criteria:** Applications are reviewed based on scientific question, presentation, methodology, experience, and budget.

**Funds Avail.:** The amount of the fellowship varies from $1,500-3,000 and is based on a tentative budget that indicates the amount of money needed and outlines how the funds are to be used. Grants may not be used for tuition, administrative overhead, or equipment of general use. The fellowship period depends upon the option exercised at the time the fellowship is granted. If it extends beyond a year, submission of an annual progress report is required. **To Apply:** Candidates must submit a formal application, a four-page description of the project, evidence of research ability and experience (these may include a list of publications, short papers or reports; not grade transcripts), a detailed budget, statement of other financial support, two letters of recommendation, and two self-addressed, stamped envelopes. **Deadline:** Applications are due December 1; awards are announced on June 1.

**Remarks:** Any publications resulting from the grant must acknowledge support of Sigma Delta Epsilon and two reprints of each publication should be submitted to the National Office. At termination of the fellowship, a report must be sent to the National Secretary of Sigma Delta Epsilon and an abstract of 100 words or less must be prepared for SDE/GWIS publication in their Bulletin as soon as possible after completion of the project. **Contact:** Sigma Delta Epsilon Graduate Women in Science at the above address (see entry 5328).

## • 5331 •

### Sigma Gamma Rho
8800 S. Stony Island Ave.          *Ph:* (312)873-9000
Chicago, IL 60617                 *Fax:* (312)731-9642
*URL:* http://shrike.depaul.edu/~ccalbert/sgrho/nationals.html

#### • 5332 • Sigma Gamma Rho National Education Fund Scholarship (*Undergraduate/Scholarship*)

**Purpose:** To promote scholarship aid to needy students, both male and female of all races, and to conduct community educational programs that will aid in educational and vocational improvement in individual and community living. **Qualif.:** Students or prospective students must have a sincere interest in achieving a higher education, be enrolled in or qualified for admission to an institution of higher education, and demonstrate need and scholastic ability.

**Funds Avail.:** Determined annually by the Board of Trustees. **To Apply:** Students may request an application by writing or calling Sigma Gamma Rho. Completed applications must be submitted with proof of enrollment. **Deadline:** April 28. **Contact:** Evelyn H. Hood, Chair, at the above address (see entry 5331).

## • 5333 •

### Sigma Iota Epsilon
214 Westcott Bldg.
Florida State University          *Ph:* (904)644-4444
Tallahassee, FL 32306             *Fax:* (904)644-4447

#### • 5334 • Keith Davis Graduate Scholarship Awards (*Graduate/Award*)

**Purpose:** To recognize outstanding scholarship at the graduate level in the management discipline. **Focus:** Management. **Qualif.:** Applicants must be active graduate SIE members at any one of the 63 chapters and should be studying management. **Criteria:**

Members of the SIE National Executive Board review submissions and choose first-and-second place winners.

**Funds Avail.:** First place wins a $1,250 prize and a plaque; second and third place win $500. **To Apply:** Students must submit a scholarly paper on an appropriate management subject. The paper may be one previously written for a class assignment; however, a clean copy (without grades or comments) must be sent. **Deadline:** May 12.

**Remarks:** Only SIE student members are eligible. **Contact:** Mike Hankin, SIE National Administrator, at the above address (see entry 5333).

### • 5335 • Sigma Iota Epsilon Undergraduate Scholarship Awards (Undergraduate/Scholarship)

**Purpose:** To recognize outstanding scholarship and commitment to the SIE mission on the part of undergraduate student members. **Focus:** Management. **Qualif.:** Applicants must be active undergraduate SIE members at any of the 63 chapters. **Criteria:** Members of the SIE National Executive Board review applications and assign point weightings. The top seven applications (those with the highest number of points) win scholarships.

**Funds Avail.:** Seven $1,000 scholarships. **Deadline:** The May 12.

**Remarks:** Only SIE student members are eligible. **Contact:** Mike Hankin, SIE National Administrator, at the above address (see entry 5333). An alternate telephone number is (904)644-4772.

### • 5336 •
### Sigma Theta Tau International
550 W. North St.
Indianapolis, IN 46202-3162
*URL:* http://stti-web.iupui.edu/

*Ph:* (317)634-8171
*Fax:* (317)634-8188

### • 5337 • Mead Johnson Nutritional Perinatal Research Grants Program (Doctorate, Postdoctorate, Postgraduate/Grant)

**Purpose:** To support nursing research focused on perinatal issues spanning the prenatal period through the first year of life. **Focus:** Nursing. **Qualif.:** Applicants must be registered nurses with current licenses who have their master's or doctorate degree and are conducting perinatal research. Topics may include, but are not limited to, low and high-risk maternal and neonatal care practices; and innovative patient care delivery systems. Applicants must be U.S. citizens. **Criteria:** Preference is given to Sigma Theta Tau members, if all other requirements are equal. Allocation of funds is based on the quality of the proposed research, the future promise of the applicant, and the applicant's research budget.

**Funds Avail.:** The maximum grant is $10,000. Proposals and budgets requesting in excess of $10,000 will not be reviewed. **To Apply:** Applicants must submit seven copies of the application in seven binders and should include application form, abstract, proposal narrative, appendices, and checklist. They must also submit two references from persons who can support the applicant's potential to carry out the project. For doctoral students, one of the letters must be from the research advisor/ chairperson indicating approval of the research plan by the entire dissertation committee. If the research project is a doctoral dissertation, a biosketch of the dissertation chairperson is required. If applicable, human subject or animal protection forms must be submitted by the institutional review board of the institution where the data collection will occur. **Deadline:** June 1. Grants are awarded September 15.

**Remarks:** Funds for this grant are supported by Mead Johnson Nutritional. **Contact:** Sigma Theta Tau International at the above address (see entry 5336).

### • 5338 • Sigma Theta Tau International/American Association of Diabetes Educators Grant (Professional Development/Grant)

**Purpose:** To encourage qualified nurses to contribute to the enhancement of quality and increase the availability of diabetes education and care. **Qualif.:** Research must be related to diabetes education and care.

**Funds Avail.:** Up to $6,000. **To Apply:** For application and general instructions, call (312) 644-AADE. **Deadline:** October 1.

### • 5339 • Sigma Theta Tau International/American Nephrology Nurses' Association Grant (Professional Development/Grant)

**Purpose:** To encourage research related to nephrology nursing practice. **Qualif.:** Registered nurses with a masters degree are eligible.

**Funds Avail.:** Up to $6,000. **To Apply:** For application and general instructions, call (609) 256-2320. **Deadline:** November 1.

### • 5340 • Sigma Theta Tau International/American Nurses' Foundation Grant (Professional Development/ Grant)

**Purpose:** To encourage the research career development of nurses through support of research conducted by beginning researchers or experienced researchers who are entering a new field of study. **Qualif.:** Registered nurses who have received a master's degree are eligible.

**Funds Avail.:** $6,000. **To Apply:** Submit applications to STTI in even numbered years; to AFN in odd numbered years - (202) 651-7000. **Deadline:** May 1.

### • 5341 • Sigma Theta Tau International/Emergency Nursing Foundation Grant (Professional Development/ Grant)

**Purpose:** To provide money for research which will advance the specialized practice of emergency nursing. **Criteria:** Priority will be given to studies which relate to the ENF research initiatives.

**Funds Avail.:** $6,000 **To Apply:** For application and general instructions, call (708) 698-9400 ext. 3350. **Deadline:** March 1.

### • 5342 • Sigma Theta Tau International/Glaxo Wellcome New Investigator/Mentor Grant (Professional Development/Grant)

**Qualif.:** Award will be given to a novice investigator and an experienced researcher practicing full time in an adult clinical setting focusing on nursing issues related to medication and medication administration.

**Funds Avail.:** $5,500. **Deadline:** October 1.

### • 5343 • Sigma Theta Tau International/Glaxo Wellcome Prescriptive Practice Grant (Professional Development/Grant)

**Purpose:** To recognize research related to prescribing practices of advanced practice nurses.

**Funds Avail.:** $5,000. **Deadline:** October 1.

### • 5344 • Sigma Theta Tau International Small Research Grant (Postgraduate/Grant)

**Purpose:** To encourage qualified nurses to contribute to the advancement of nursing through research. **Qualif.:** Applicants must be registered nurses with current licenses who have master's degrees and who have already chosen or started their research projects. Proposals for pilot and/or developmental research may

## Sigma Theta Tau International (continued)

be submitted. Multidisciplinary and international research is encouraged. **Criteria:** Preference is given to members of Sigma Theta Tau and to novice researchers who have received no other national research funds, when all other attributes are equal. Allocation of funds is based on the quality of the proposed research, the future promise of the applicant, and the applicant's research budget.

**Funds Avail.:** The amount of a grant depends on the amount requested, the number of requests, and funds available. The maximum award is $3,000. **To Apply:** Applicants must submit seven copies of the application in seven binders and should include application form, abstract, proposal narrative, appendices, and checklist. They must also submit two references from persons who can support applicants potential to carry out the project. For doctoral students, one of the letters must be from the research advisor/chairperson indicating approval of the research plan by the entire dissertation committee. If the research project is a doctoral dissertation, a biosketch of the dissertation chairperson is required. If applicable, human subject or animal protection forms by the institutional review board of the institution where the data collection will occur must be submitted. **Deadline:** March 1. Grants are awarded September 15. **Contact:** Sigma Theta Tau International at the above address (see entry 5336).

### • 5345 • STTI Scholarships (Graduate/Scholarship)

**Focus:** Maternal, child or pediatric nursing. **Qualif.:** Applicants must demonstrate a potential for advanced study and research and currently be a Licensed Registered Nurse.

**Funds Avail.:** $1,000 awarded every two years. **Contact:** Sigma Theta Tau International at the above address (see entry 5336).

### • 5346 •
## Sigma Xi, The Scientific Research Society
99 Alexander Dr.  Ph: (919)549-4691
PO Box 13975  Fax: (919)549-0090
Durham, NC 27709-3975  Free: 800-243-6534
E-mail: giar@sigmaxi.org
URL: http://www.sigmaxi.org/

*Sigma Xi, The Scientific Research Society was founded in 1886 as an honor society for scientists and engineers. There are over 500 chapters and clubs at universities, government laboratories, and industry research centers.*

### • 5347 • Sigma Xi Grants-in-Aid of Research (Graduate, Undergraduate/Grant)

**Purpose:** To support scientific investigation. **Focus:** Physical Science, Engineering, Behavioral and Life Sciences. **Qualif.:** Applicant may be of any nationality. Candidate must be an undergraduate or graduate with a clearly outlined program of scientific investigation. Priority is normally given to applicants who are in the early stages of their careers. Award funds must be used for direct research expenses.

**Funds Avail.:** Up to $1,000; $600 average; up to $2,500 for astronomy, eye, or vision research. **To Apply:** Write to the Committee on Grants-in-Aid of Research for application form and guidelines. Submit form and two letters of recommendation. **Deadline:** February 1, May 1, November 1. Notification is made 12 weeks after the deadline. **Contact:** Deborah Donati at the above address (see entry 5346).

### • 5348 •
## Sikh Education Aid Fund
P.O. Box 140  Ph: (804)541-9290
Hopewell, VA 23860  Fax: (804)452-1270
E-mail: asp@maboli.com
URL: http://www.maboli.com/asp/projects

### • 5349 • Sikh Education Aid Fund Scholarship (Doctorate, Graduate, Undergraduate/Scholarship)

**Purpose:** To help immigrants finance undergraduate, graduate, and post-graduate studies. **Qualif.:** Must be high school graduates and enrolled in a recognized college. **Criteria:** Preference goes to those in professional courses, demonstrating financial need and knowledge of Punjabi. Consideration is also given to Sikh activities and/or courses and academic performance.

**Funds Avail.:** up to $3,500 is available per year. **No. of Awards:** 10-15. **To Apply:** Applicants should request form by writing to PO Box 140, Hopewell, VA 23860. **Deadline:** June 20. **Contact:** Gurpal S. Bhuller, at the above address (see entry 5348).

### • 5350 •
## The Lois and Samuel Silberman Fund
133 E. 79th St.  Ph: (212)737-8500
New York, NY 10021-0398  Fax: (212)737-6397

### • 5351 • The Lois and Samuel Silberman Awards (Professional Development/Award)

**Purpose:** To contribute to the knowledge base and methodology of the education process by undertaking research and preparing articles for publication that deal with emerging social problems, and to allow full-time faculty of accredited professional social work programs to undertake meaningful research in the interest of their own professional development. **Focus:** Social Work. **Qualif.:** Awards are given to full-time faculty in a social work program accredited by CSWE who show promise of making significant contributions to social work knowledge and practice and at the same time contribute to their own professional development and advancement. **Criteria:** When awarding, selection is based solely on the awards meeting the stated research objectives of the Program and on the qualifications of the candidates.

**Funds Avail.:** $6,000 to produce articles for publication in refereed journals. No more than $3,000 is allowed for compensation, with the balance available for expenses, or the full amount of the award may be budgeted for expenses by sacrificing compensation. The award is made in the form of a contract between the Fund and the awardee. Each awardee is required to account for all expenditures against an approved budget. **No. of Awards:** 7. **To Apply:** Grant applications with five copies should include the title of the project and an abstract of not more than 500 words clearly identifying the emerging issue, problem, or concern to be addressed and the implications for social work education and/or practice that flow from the outcome; a general background summary for the project citing work done by others, relevant literature, and how the outcome will integrate with previous knowledge to benefit future study; a vita, personal and professional, including a copy of a most recently published article, if any, and work previously done in related areas; faculty status and a list of courses taught in the last three years; information on the status of the project (if already started) and whether the applicant is receiving release time and/or support; a schedule for the project by phases, including the completion date; and a complete line by line budget, including anticipated timing of expenditures by three-month intervals. There is no special application form. **Deadline:** Applications must be postmarked by October 31. Decisions concerning awards will be made before March. **Contact:** Eleanor F. Gallagher, Administrator, at the above address (see entry 5350).

**• 5352 •**
**Sinfonia Foundation**
10600 Old State Road
Evansville, IN 47711-1399          *Ph:* (812)867-2433
*URL:* http://www.sinfonia.org

**• 5353 • Sinfonia Foundation Research Assistance Grant** *(Professional Development/Grant)*

**Purpose:** To assist qualified individuals conducting scholarly research in music. **Focus:** American Music History and Theory. **Qualif.:** Candidate may be of any nationality. Applicant must show evidence of previous successful writing and research by means of publications, thesis, Ph.D. dissertation, or M.A. degree; or demonstrate unusual knowledge or competence in the field to be researched.

**Funds Avail.:** $1,000 maximum. **To Apply:** Write for application form and guidelines. Submit completed form with biographical details, resume, project proposal and budget. If applicant is a student or faculty member, an endorsement from an official of home institution must be submitted. **Deadline:** April 1. Awardees are selected September 1.

**• 5354 •**
**Skowhegan School of Painting and Sculpture**
200 Park Ave. South, Ste. 1116      *Ph:* (212)529-0505
New York, NY 10003-1503          *Fax:* (212)473-1342
*E-mail:* mail@skowheganart.org
*URL:* http://www.skowheganart.org

**• 5355 • Skowhegan School Fellowships**
*(Professional Development/Fellowship)*

**Purpose:** To provide young artists with the opportunity to work independently in a communal environment with a community of renowned senior artists who critique work one-on-one. **Focus:** Art, Painting, Sculpture, Installation, Fresco, Video Performance. **Qualif.:** Applicants may be of any nationality but must be at least 19 years old and painters or sculptors with advanced skills. Fellowships are available for the Skowhegan summer residency in Maine. **Criteria:** Selection is determined by the applicant's slide portfolio.

**Funds Avail.:** Varies according to need. Residents of New Jersey, Kansas and Maine as well as African-Americans, Latin Americans, Native Americans, Asian Americans have specific fellowships offering full tuition, room and board. Valued at $5,200, these fellowships are available through special gifts. **No. of Awards:** 45-55 of the 65 students receive financial aid. **To Apply:** Application for scholarship must be made simultaneously with application for admission to the School. Candidates should write to the administrator for updated application forms and guidelines. Applicants must submit forms, slides, slide list, and documentation of financial need along with the application fee ($35). Names for recommendation are also required; no letters of recommendation. **Deadline:** Application materials must be submitted by early February. Notification is in early April. **Contact:** Larry Levine, Administrator, at the above address (see entry 5354).

**• 5356 •**
**C. Bascom Slemp Foundation**
c/o Patricia L. Durbin, STAR Bank,
 N.A. Cincinnati
PO Box 5208
ML 5145                    *Ph:* (513)762-8878
Cincinnati, OH 45201-5208       *Fax:* (513)632-5556

**• 5357 • C. Bascom Slemp Scholarship**
*(Undergraduate/Scholarship)*

**Qualif.:** Scholarships are available only to residents, or descendants of residents, of Lee and Wise counties in Virginia. **Criteria:** Selection is based upon scholarship, need, and achievement.

**Funds Avail.:** $2,000 annually. **Deadline:** October 1. **Contact:** Patricia L. Durbin at the above address (see entry 5356).

**• 5358 •**
**Slocum-Lunz Foundation**
c/o Jeff Scott
National Marine Fishery Service
Charleston Lab
PO Box 12559               *Ph:* (803)762-8500
Charleston, SC 29412-2559      *Fax:* (803)762-8700

**• 5359 • Slocum-Lunz Foundation Scholarships and Grants** *(Graduate/Grant, Scholarship)*

**Purpose:** To support students from South Carolina in the fields of marine biology and closely related natural sciences. **Focus:** Marine Biology and related fields. **Qualif.:** Applicant must be a graduate or advanced undergraduate student in an institution of higher education in South Carolina. Academic work must be performed in South Carolina. Awards may not be used for tuition or living expenses.

**Funds Avail.:** $2,000 maximum. **To Apply:** Write to the scholarship committee for application form and guidelines. Submit form with research proposal, detailed budget, transcripts, confirmation of enrollment in an accredited academic program, and at least two letters of reference. **Deadline:** April 1. **Contact:** Scholarship Committee Chair at the above address (see entry 5358).

**• 5360 •**
**Slovenian Women's Union of America**
52 Oakridge Dr.
Marquette, MI 48855          *Ph:* (906)249-4288
*E-mail:* mturvey@aol.com

**• 5361 • Slovenian Women's Union Scholarships**
*(Undergraduate/Scholarship)*

**Purpose:** To encourage Union members to pursue a college education. **Focus:** General Studies. **Qualif.:** Applicants must be members of the Slovenian Women's Union for a minimum of three years. **Criteria:** Selection is based on grade point average, extracurricular activities, and involvement in the Slovenian Women's Union.

**Funds Avail.:** Four $1,000 scholarships are awarded annually. **To Apply:** Application information can be found in *Zarja* (Slovenian Women's Union magazine). **Deadline:** March 20. **Contact:** Mary Turvey, Scholarship Program Director, at the above address (see entry 5360).

**Horace Smith Fund**
Springfield Institution for Savings
1441 Main St.
Springfield, MA 01102          *Ph:* (413)739-4222

• 5363 • **Walter S. Barr Fellowships** (*Graduate/ Fellowship*)

**Purpose:** To provide full-time study opportunities beyond the Bachelor's degree. **Qualif.:** Applicants must be Hampden County residents selected by the fellowship committee. **Criteria:** Awards are made on the basis of scholastic record, available resources, and need. **Deadline:** Applications become available after September 15; due February 1.

• 5364 • **Walter S. Barr Scholarships** (*Undergraduate/Scholarship*)

**Purpose:** To help deserving senior students residing in Agawam, Chicopee, East Long meadow, Long meadow, Ludlow, Springfield, West Springfield, and Wilbraham counties finance their undergraduate education. **Focus:** General Studies. **Criteria:** The competition is decided on the basis of school records, college entrance exams, general attainments, and financial need.

**Funds Avail.:** Varies. **To Apply:** Applications are available after September 15. **Deadline:** December 31.

• 5365 • **Horace Smith Fund Loans** (*Undergraduate/ Loan*)

**Purpose:** To help deserving students finance full-time undergraduate education. **Focus:** General Studies. **Qualif.:** All graduates of secondary schools in Hampden County, Massachusetts, are eligible to apply. **Criteria:** Financial need is of primary importance in selecting recipients. If loans are repaid within one year after the student graduates, no interest is charged. Interest begins to accrue at the end of one year. **To Apply:** Loan applications are available after April 1 in the Horace Smith Loan Fund office. **Deadline:** College students must file completed applications before June 15. Graduating high school seniors must file by July 1 before the beginning of the next academic year. **Contact:** The Executive Secretary of the Horace Smith Fund at the above address (see entry 5362).

• 5366 •
**W. Eugene Smith Memorial Fund**
c/o International Center of
  Photography
1130 5th Ave.                    *Ph:* (212)860-1777
New York, NY 10128               *Fax:* (212)360-1482

• 5367 • **Howard Chapnick Grant** (*Professional Development/Grant*)

**Purpose:** To encourage and support leadership in fields ancillary to photojournalism such as editing research, education, and management. **Criteria:** Special consideration will be given to projects that promote social change and/or serve significant concerns of photojournalism.

**Funds Avail.:** $5,000 to finance a program of further education, research, a long-term sabbatical project, or an internship. **To Apply:** Applications may be obtained by writing to the Chapnick Grant c/o Yukiko Launois, 125 E. 87th St. 4B, New York, NY 10128. **Deadline:** July 15.

• 5368 • **Grant in Humanistic Photography** (*Professional Development/Grant*)

**Purpose:** To identify, encourage, and support works-in-progress of photojournalists engaged in humanistic documentary photography. **Focus:** Photojournalism. **Qualif.:** Candidates may be of any nationality. They must also be highly qualified photojournalists interested in recording aspects of human life. The project proposal must be cogent, concise, journalistically realizable, visually translatable, and justifiable in humanistic terms. **Criteria:** A candidate must prove worthiness of project and demonstrated ability.

**Funds Avail.:** $20,000. **To Apply:** Write for application form and guidelines. Submit completed form with photographic prints or duplicate transparencies and project proposals. Finalists will be asked to submit a comprehensive portfolio. **Deadline:** July 15. Notification by October 15.

**Remarks:** Additional smaller awards (for a total of $5,000) may be granted at the discretion of the Fund. The W. Eugene Smith Grant in Humanistic Photography is funded by a grant from Nikon Inc. **Contact:** Alternate phone number: 212-879-6903. Helen Marcus, President, or Anna Winand, ICP, at the above address (see entry 5366).

• 5369 •
**Smithsonian Astrophysical Observatory**
60 Garden St.
Mail Stop 47                     *Ph:* (617)495-7103
Cambridge, MA 02138              *Fax:* (617)495-7105
*E-mail:* postdoc@cfa.harvard.edu
*URL:* http://cfa-www.harvard.edu/postdoc

• 5370 • **SAO Postdoctoral Fellowships** (*Postdoctorate/Fellowship*)

**Purpose:** To support advanced independent research at SAO. **Focus:** Astronomy, Astrophysics. **Qualif.:** Applicant may be of any nationality. Applicant must have a Ph.D. in the area of proposed research. Fellowships are tenable at the Observatory, beginning in the summer or fall of each year. Research programs include both theory and observation over the range from atomic physics through the solar system, other stars, and galaxies to cosmology. **Criteria:** Applicants are selected based on their research proposals and letters or recommendation.

**Funds Avail.:** $42,000. **No. of Awards:** 2-3. **To Apply:** Write for application form, guidelines, and information about current research programs. **Deadline:** November 15. **Contact:** Secretary, Postdoctoral Fellowship Committee, at the above address (see entry 5369).

• 5371 • **SAO Predoctoral Fellowships** (*Doctorate/ Fellowship*)

**Purpose:** To enable graduate students to conduct dissertation research at SAO. **Focus:** Astronomy, Astrophysics. **Qualif.:** Applicant may be of any nationality. Candidate must be enrolled in a Ph.D. program at a recognized university in the United States or abroad, and have completed all requirements for the degree except the dissertation. Fellowships are tenable at SAO. **Criteria:** Applicants are selected based on research proposals, and letters of recommendation.

**Funds Avail.:** $18,000. **No. of Awards:** 3-5. **To Apply:** Write to the Secretary of the Predoctoral Fellowship Committee for application form and guidelines. **Deadline:** April 15. **Contact:** Secretary, Predoctoral Fellowship Committee, at the above address (see entry 5369).

**• 5372 •**   **SAO Visiting Scientist Awards**
*(Postdoctorate/Award)*

**Purpose:** To encourage scholars to conduct research at SAO. **Focus:** Astronomy, Astrophysics. **Qualif.:** Candidate may be a citizen of any country including the United States. Applicant must have a Ph.D., or be enrolled in a degree program, and be qualified to conduct research at the Observatory.

**Funds Avail.:** Varies. **To Apply:** Write the Secretary for information.

---

**• 5373 •**
**Smithsonian Environmental Research Center**
Work/Learn Program
PO Box 28                          *Ph:* (301)798-4424
Edgewater, MD 21037                *Fax:* (301)261-7954
*E-mail:* intern@serc.si.edu
*URL:* http://www.serc.si.edu

**• 5374 •**   **Smithsonian Environmental Research Center Work-Learn Opportunities in Environmental Studies** *(Graduate, Undergraduate/Internship)*

**Purpose:** To allow students to gain exposure to and experience in environmental studies. **Focus:** Zoology, Chemistry, Botany, Ecology, Mathematics and Mathematical Sciences, Microbiology, Environmental Science, Terrestrial, Estuarine and Marine Ecology. **Qualif.:** Candidates must be undergraduate or beginning graduate students at academic institutions in the United States and abroad with training or experience in the area of the terrestrial and estuarine environmental research within the disciplines of mathematics, chemistry, microbiology, botany, and zoology. Environmental education opportunities are also available. Minority students are encouraged to apply. **Criteria:** Based on personal essay, letters of referral and academic transcripts.

**Funds Avail.:** A weekly stipend of $300 is awarded. A limited onsite dormitory is available. Board is not provided. Seminars and field trips are available for a fee of $60 per week. In many instances, students arrange to receive academic credit for this work/study plan. **No. of Awards:** 15-20 during the summer season (May-August), varies during other times of the year. **To Apply:** Two copies of the entire application packet are required. Applications should include school transcripts, an essay of two to three pages that indicates past and present interests, academic and non-academic experience, and an explanation how work at SERC will further educational and intellectual goals and two letters of reference. While the work/learn program is not designed to sponsor independent projects, applications from mature students who wish to pursue a more independent course of study within the context of the Center's projects are considered. **Deadline:** November 1 for projects between February and May; and March 1 for projects between May and August.

**Remarks:** The Smithsonian Institution encourages universities to waive tuition or to require only nominal tuition for students on internship. **Contact:** Smithsonian Institution, Office of Fellowships and Grants, Washington, DC 20560 or Work/Learn Program at the above address (see entry 5373).

**• 5375 •**
**Smithsonian Institution**
Office of Fellowships and Grants
955 L'Enfant Plaza, Ste. 7000      *Ph:* (202)287-3271
Washington, DC 20560-0902          *Fax:* (202)287-3691
*E-mail:* siofg@ofg.si.edu
*URL:* http://www.si.edu/researchstudy

**• 5376 •**   **Smithsonian Institution Graduate Fellowships** *(Graduate/Fellowship)*

**Purpose:** To conduct research in association with research staff members of the Smithsonian. **Focus:** Animal Science and Behavior, Ecology, Environmental Science, Anthropology, Archaeology, Art History, Crafts, Social Sciences, Technology. **Qualif.:** Applicants must be graduate students.

**Funds Avail.:** Fellowships provide for research in-residence using Smithsonian collections and facilities. **No. of Awards:** Varies. **To Apply:** Contact office of Fellowships and grants. **Deadline:** January 15 annually. **Contact:** The Smithsonian Institution, Office of Fellowships and Grants, at the above address (see entry 5375).

**• 5377 •**   **Smithsonian Institution Postdoctoral Fellowships** *(Postdoctorate/Fellowship)*

**Purpose:** To conduct research in residence at the Smithsonian Institution. **Qualif.:** Applicants must ordinarily have completed a doctoral degree less than seven years before the application deadline. Candidates with the equivalent of a doctorate in experience, training, and accomplishment may be considered.

**Funds Avail.:** Fellowships provide for research in-residence using Smithsonian collections and facilities. The stipend amounts to $27,000. **No. of Awards:** Varies. **To Apply:** Contact the Office of Fellowships and Grants. **Deadline:** January 15. **Contact:** The Smithsonian Institution, Office of Fellowships and Grants, at the above address (see entry 5375).

**• 5378 •**   **Smithsonian Institution Predoctoral Fellowships** *(Doctorate/Fellowship)*

**Purpose:** To conduct research at the Smithsonian Institution. **Qualif.:** Applicants must have completed preliminary coursework and examinations for a Ph.D. and be engaged in dissertation research. They must be seeking training supplemental to university instruction and have the approval of their university to conduct research at the Smithsonian Institution.

**Funds Avail.:** Fellowships provide for research in-residence using Smithsonian collections and facilities. The stipend is $15,000 per year. **No. of Awards:** Varies. **To Apply:** Contact the Office of Fellowships and Grants. **Deadline:** January 15. **Contact:** The Smithsonian Institution, Office of Fellowships and Grants, at the above address (see entry 5375).

---

**• 5379 •**
**Smithsonian Institution - National Air and Space Museum**
Aeronautics Dept. Fellowships Rep.
Rm. 3312                           *Ph:* (202)357-2515
Washington, DC 20560-0312          *Fax:* (202)786-2447

**• 5380 •**   **Guggenheim Fellowships** *(Doctorate/Fellowship)*

**Purpose:** To support historical and scientific research related to aviation and space. **Focus:** Aeronautics, Aerospace. **Qualif.:** Candidate may be of any nationality. Applicant must be a doctoral student who has completed all preliminary coursework and

---

### Smithsonian Institution - National Air and Space Museum *(continued)*

examinations and is engaged in dissertation research; or a scholar with preferably no more than seven years of postdoctoral experience. Fellowships are tenable at the National Air and Space Museum.

**Funds Avail.:** Predoctoral fellowship: $14,000; postdoctoral fellowship: $25,000. **No. of Awards:** 1. **To Apply:** Write to the program specialist for application guidelines. **Deadline:** January 15. Notification by April 30. **Contact:** Smithsonian at the above address (see entry 5379).

#### • 5381 • A. Verville Fellowship *(Other/Fellowship)*

**Purpose:** To support research and writing related to the history of aviation. **Focus:** History of Aviation and Aerospace. **Qualif.:** Candidate may be of any nationality. Applicant must wish to conduct research into the history of aviation or space studies. An advanced degree in history, engineering, or a related field is not required. Fellowship is tenable at the National Air and Space Museum.

**Funds Avail.:** $35,000/year. **No. of Awards:** 1. **To Apply:** Write to the program specialist for application guidelines. **Deadline:** 15 January. Notification by April 30. **Contact:** Smithsonian at the above address (see entry 5379).

---

#### • 5382 •
### Smithsonian Institution National Design Museum
Cooper-Hewitt Museum
2 East 91st St.
New York, NY 10128-9990

*Ph:* (212)849-8400
*Fax:* (212)849-8328

#### • 5383 • Cooper-Hewitt Museum Internships *(Undergraduate/Internship)*

**Purpose:** To acquaint participants with the programs, policies, procedures, and operations of the Cooper-Hewitt Museum and of museums in general. **Focus:** Museum Science. **Qualif.:** Applicants must have completed at least two years of college education before the start of the internship program.

**Funds Avail.:** Internships are unpaid. **To Apply:** There is no application form. Each candidate must submit the following materials: resume; college transcript; two letters of recommendation with at least one letter from a recent or current instructor; and a brief essay defining potential career plans and areas of interest within the Cooper-Hewitt Museum. **Deadline:** March 31.

**Remarks:** Through assignment in a specific museum department, an intern becomes fully acquainted with that department and also gains a general overview of the Museum. Summer internships are usually 40 hours per week. It may be possible to arrange a part-time summer internship. Fall-Spring Internships last at least 10 weeks at 20 hours per week during the fall and spring semesters and four weeks full-time during the January break. **Contact:** Niria Leyva-Gutierrez, Internship Coordinator at the above address (see entry 5382).

#### • 5384 • Peter Krueger Summer Internships *(Graduate, Undergraduate/Internship)*

**Purpose:** To encourage promising young students of art history, architectural history museum studies, museum education, and design to pursue careers in the museum profession. Interns are assigned to specific curatorial, education, or administrative departments where they will assist on special research or exhibition projects, as well as participate in daily museum activities. **Focus:** Museum Science, Art History. **Qualif.:** Applicants

must be college students considering a career in art history, design, museum studies, and museum education as well as graduate students who have not yet completed their M.A. degree.

**Funds Avail.:** $2,500 stipend. Housing is not provided. **No. of Awards:** 6 each summer. **To Apply:** A resume, a letter stating the applicant's goals, two letters of recommendation, and a list of courses or transcripts should be submitted. **Deadline:** March 31.

**Remarks:** The Internship honors the memory of Peter A. Krueger, who was an intern at Cooper-Hewitt. Interns will be assigned to specific curatorial, education, or administrative departments where they will assist on special research or exhibition projects, as well as participate in daily museum activities. The program has been structured to include visits and special meetings with other New York museum professionals as a way to introduce the breadth and diversity of the field. **Contact:** Niria Leyva-Guiterrez, Intern Coordinator, at the above address (see entry 5382).

#### • 5385 • The Lippincott and Margulies Summer Internship *(Graduate, Undergraduate/Internship)*

**Purpose:** To encourage students of design as well as design history/criticism to explore careers in the museum or corporate design profession. **Focus:** Design or design history/criticism. **Qualif.:** College students dedicated to one of the necessary areas of study or graduate students who have not completed their Masters degree.

**Funds Avail.:** $2500 stipend. **No. of Awards:** 1 per summer.

#### • 5386 • Smithsonian Institution Minority Internship *(Graduate, Undergraduate/Internship)*

**Focus:** General studies. **Qualif.:** Applicants must be minority undergraduate or graduate students.

**Funds Avail.:** A cash stipend of $300 per week is awarded in addition to a travel allowance. **To Apply:** Write the Office of Fellowships and Grants at the Smithsonian Institution, 955 L'Enfant Plaza, Ste. 7300, Washington, D.C. 20560. **Deadline:** February 15. **Contact:** Office of Fellowships and Grants at the above address (see entry 5382).

---

#### • 5387 •
### Smithsonian Institution National Museum of American Art
Rm. 270, MPC 210
Washington, DC 20560
*E-mail:* nmaa.judith@ic.si.edu
*URL:* http://www.nmaa.si.edu/deptdir/ressub/rscprgdir/ internships.html

*Ph:* (202)357-2714

#### • 5388 • National Museum of American Art Summer Internships *(Graduate, Undergraduate/Internship)*

**Focus:** Art History, Art, American History, American Studies. **Qualif.:** The program is open to students who are entering or have completed their second year of college, or are graduate students. Applicants must have a strong educational background in art history, studio art, or American studies, with little or no previous museum experience. **To Apply:** Applicants must submit a statement of purpose expressing personal career goals in the museum field, what skills they hope to acquire, and why the National Museum of Art has been chosen as a learning center. The application must also include a resume of relevant educational and work experience, three letters of recommendation (academic and/ or professional), and transcripts from all schools attended above the high school level. Applicants must send one original and four copies of each item (except recommendations or transcripts sent directly by a university). Applicants should call to make sure all items have been received. **Deadline:** March 1.

**Remarks:** Interns concentrate on one aspect of museum work, working in an office matched to each intern's individual interests and career goals. **Contact:** Intern Program Officer, Research and Scholars Center, National Museum of American Art at the above address (see entry 5387).

---

• **5389** •
## SOCAN Foundation
41 Valleybrook Dr.       *Ph:* (416)445-8700
Don Mills, ON, Canada M3B 2S6    *Fax:* (416)442-3371
                          *Free:* 800-557-6226

*E-mail:* foundation@socan.ca
*URL:* http://www.socan.ca

### • 5390 • Gordon F. Henderson/SOCAN Copyright Competition Award *(Professional Development/Award)*

**Purpose:** To encourage Canadian law students to consider copyright law as it relates to music. **Focus:** Law. **Qualif.:** Applicants must be Canadian citizens or landed immigrants and must be registered in the law faculty at a Canadian university, or be a graduate who is articling in law in Canada. They must have written an essay or study dealing with copyright law.

**Funds Avail.:** $2,000. **No. of Awards:** One. **To Apply:** Write for application form and guidelines. **Deadline:** May 1. **Contact:** Administrator, at the above address (see entry 5389).

---

• **5391** •
## Social Science Research Council
810 Seventh Ave.
810 Seventh Ave.       *Ph:* (212)377-2700
New York, NY 10158      *Fax:* (212)377-2727

*The Social Science Research Council is an nongovernmental, not-for-profit international association devoted to the advancement of interdisciplinary research in the social sciences. It does this through a wide variety of workshops and conferences, fellowships and grants, summer training institutes, scholarly exchanges, and publications.*

### • 5392 • SSRC Abe Fellowship Program *(Postdoctorate/Fellowship)*

**Purpose:** To support Japanese and American research professionals with a doctorate or equivalent level of professional training, as well as third country nationals affiliated with an American or Japan institution. **Focus:** Humanities, Social Sciences. **Qualif.:** Applicants must hold a Ph.D. or have attained an equivalent level of professional experience, as evaluated in the candidate's country of residence. Applications from researchers in non-academic professions are encouraged as well as from academic research professionals. They should be interested in conducting research in the social sciences and humanities as applied to themes specific to global issues, problems common to advanced industrial societies, and issues that relate to improving United States-Japanese relations. Fellowship recipients are expected to affiliate with an American or Japanese institution appropriate to their research aims. Fellowship tenure should include (but need not be restricted to) residence in the country of study and research.

**Funds Avail.:** Terms of the fellowships include base awards and supplementary research and travel expenses as necessary for completion of the research project. In addition to receiving the awards, fellows will attend annual Abe Fellows Conferences that promote the development of an international network of scholars concerned with researching contemporary policy issues. **To Apply:**

Applications sent by FAX are not accepted. **Deadline:** September 1.

**Remarks:** Funds for the fellowships are provided by the Japan Foundation Center for Global Partnership. **Contact:** SSRC at the above address (see entry 5391).

### • 5393 • SSRC Advanced Postdoctoral Training and Research Awards *(Doctorate, Postdoctorate/Award, Fellowship, Grant)*

**Purpose:** To support scholars undertaking advanced field research in the United States and abroad. **Focus:** Area Studies, Humanities, Social Sciences. **Qualif.:** There are two types of support available: awards to provide maintenance, travel, and research expenses for postdoctoral scholars; and awards for doctoral dissertation research. For most grant programs, candidate must be a U.S. citizen or permanent resident, and have a Ph.D. degree or equivalent research experience. Applicant for a fellowship must be a U.S. citizen or permanent resident, and/or be enrolled in a full-time doctoral program at a U.S. institution. Fellowship candidate must have completed all the requirements for the Ph.D. except the dissertation by the start of the fellowship period. Additional requirements for fellowships and grants vary, depending on the host country. Write for further details. Research must be conducted in the United States or abroad, depending on the program. Preference is given to projects in the beginning stages, and to those that focus on relatively neglected regions or subjects. Some countries require prior approval of research projects by government or academic agencies. Awardees usually are expected to be associated with a university, research institute, or other appropriate institution in the country that is the subject of his/her research. Fellows are also expected to have a working knowledge of the language of host country, where pertinent. Fellows may apply for additional support for up to six months in which to write the dissertation upon return to the United States.

**Funds Avail.:** Living, research, and travel allowances. **To Apply:** Write for a list of available programs, application form and guidelines. **Deadline:** Varies. **Contact:** Office of Fellowships and Grants at the above address (see entry 5391).

### • 5394 • SSRC Africa Predissertation Fellowships *(Doctorate/Fellowship)*

**Purpose:** To support short-term field trips to sub-Saharan Africa to encourage preliminary field activities, the identification of local scholars and contacts, and other planning for students preparing for dissertation research on Africa. **Focus:** Social Sciences, Humanities, Area and Ethnic Studies. **Qualif.:** Applicants must have completed one year of graduate study in the social sciences or humanities at a university located in the United States, or be United States citizens or permanent residents who have completed equivalent study abroad. They also must be accepted into a full-time Ph.D. program.

**Funds Avail.:** Up to $2,500. **Deadline:** November 1. **Contact:** SSRC at the above address (see entry 5391).

### • 5395 • SSRC African Advanced Research Grants *(Postdoctorate/Grant)*

**Focus:** Literature, Philosophy, Religion, Art History, Area and Ethnic Studies. **Qualif.:** Applicants must be scholars who hold a Ph.D. or an equivalent degree and are United States citizens or have been residents for at least three years at the time of application. Scholars in the areas of literature, philosophy, religion, and art history, areas previously under represented in African studies, are especially encouraged to apply. If travel to Africa is planned, applicants must try to arrange for affiliation with an African university or research institute. Collaborative research efforts with African scholars is also encouraged.

**Funds Avail.:** Funds of up to $15,000 may be used for field research as well as for comparative, theoretical research that proposes more than the analysis of previously gathered materials.

---

*Social Science Research Council (continued)*

**Deadline:** December 1. **Contact:** SSRC at the above address (see entry 5391).

### • 5396 • SSRC African Humanities Fellowships
*(Doctorate, Postdoctorate/Fellowship)*

**Purpose:** To provide students with the opportunity to attend the Institute for Advanced Study and Research in the African Humanities yearly residential seminar that examines defined topics at Northwestern University. **Qualif.:** Applicants must be postdoctoral scholars or advanced predoctoral students in the final stages of dissertation write-up. Citizenship, residence, or affiliations are not considerations.

**Funds Avail.:** Fellowship provides for year-long residencies at Northwestern University. **Deadline:** Fall. **Contact:** SSRC at the above address (see entry 5391).

### • 5397 • SSRC Bangladesh Studies Fellowships
*(Doctorate, Graduate/Fellowship)*

**Qualif.:** Fellowships are available for doctoral dissertation research in the social sciences and humanities, and for the advanced research of students in programs in which the doctoral degree is not usually offered, such as law, architecture, and urban or regional planning. Comparative research involving Bangladesh and West Bengal (India) is encouraged. Applicants are expected to be proficient in Bengali, but may request support for study of the language locally. There are no citizenship requirements. However, applicants must be enrolled in full-time graduate study for an advanced degree either in the United States or Canada, or be American citizens enrolled at an accredited foreign university. Citizens of Bangladesh currently enrolled in a graduate program at an American, Canadian, European, or Australian university, and ready to conduct field research for the dissertation, are especially encouraged to apply. **Deadline:** November 1.

**Remarks:** Fellows will be expected to spend at least nine months on the fellowship and a minimum of six months in Bangladesh. The total period of support for field research and additional language training normally cannot exceed 18 months. Support for this program is provided by the Ford Foundation.

### • 5398 • SSRC Berlin Program for Advanced German and European Studies Fellowships *(Doctorate, Postdoctorate/Fellowship)*

**Purpose:** To encourage the comparative and interdisciplinary study of the economic, political, and social aspects of modern and contemporary German and European affairs. **Focus:** Social Sciences, Cultural Studies, History. **Qualif.:** The program supports anthropologists, economists, political scientists, sociologists, and all scholars in appropriate social science and cultural studies fields, including historians working on the period since the mid-19th century. Applicants must be citizens or permanent residents of the United States. At the dissertation level, applicants must have completed all requirements (except the dissertation) for the Ph.D. at the time the fellowship begins. At the postdoctorate level, the program is open to scholars who have received the Ph.D. degree or its equivalent within the last two years. Fellows are expected to produce a research monograph (doctoral dissertation, book manuscript, etc.) dealing with some aspect(s) of German or European affairs, including U.S.-European relations. **To Apply:** When requesting an application form, applicants must provide: the date on which they will or did receive the Ph.D., their citizenship, and a brief summary of proposed research. **Deadline:** February 1.

**Remarks:** The program is administered by the Council and based at the Free University of Berlin. The program is funded by the Volkswagen Foundation and the German Marshall Fund of the United States.

### • 5399 • SSRC Grants for Advanced Area Research
*(Doctorate, Other/Grant)*

**Purpose:** To support research in one country, comparative research between countries in an area, and comparative research between areas. **Qualif.:** Grants are offered to scholars whose competence for research in the social sciences or humanities has been demonstrated by their previous work and who hold the Ph.D. degree or have equivalent research experience. Applications are especially encouraged from humanists, including those in the following disciplines: history; philosophy; languages; linguistics; literature; archeology; jurisprudence; the history, theory, and criticism of the arts; ethics; comparative religion; and those aspects of the social sciences that employ historical or philosophical approaches. Studies in the social sciences that involve questions of interpretation or criticism traditionally in the humanities are also eligible for support. These grants are generally not for training and candidates for academic degrees are not eligible.

**Funds Avail.:** Grants are normally made for periods of two months to one year. Budgetary limitations may make it impossible to provide full maintenance for the duration of an award. The grants may be used for travel and research expenses as well as for maintenance. Grants may be held concurrently with grants from other organizations. **To Apply:** Application forms are mailed in response to written requests from applicants. In requesting forms, an applicant should give the following information: a brief statement of the proposed research project; geographical area or areas of interest; proposed site research; occupation or current activity; university or other affiliation; country of citizenship and/or permanent residence; academic degrees held, specifying disciplines or fields of study; if currently working for a doctoral degree, the date of completion of all requirements except the dissertation; proposed date for beginning tenure of the award and the duration requested; and, for advanced research grants, the approximate amount of support needed. If requesting forms for a collaborative grant, the academic qualifications of the collaborator must be included. Application forms are available in September. **Deadline:** December 1.

**Remarks:** Funds for this program are provided by the National Endowment for the Humanities and the Ford Foundation.

### • 5400 • SSRC Grants for Collaborative Activities between American and Japanese Scholars *(Professional Development/Grant)*

**Purpose:** To support research, workshops, seminars, or conferences carried out in Japan, the United States, and/or other countries between individual, or teams of, American and Japanese scholars. **Qualif.:** Principal organizers of collaborative activities must be Japanese nationals and United States citizens or permanent residents. **Criteria:** Special attention is given to projects that concern specific themes as determined by the Japan Society for the Promotion of Science/Social Science Research Council steering committee. **Deadline:** July 31.

**Remarks:** The program especially encourages cooperation between younger scholars and more mature scholars on a single project. **Contact:** SSRC at the above address (see entry 5391).

### • 5401 • SSRC International Peace and Security Research Workshop Competition *(Professional Development/Grant)*

**Purpose:** To offer grants to support small, topical workshops. **Focus:** Peace Studies, International Affairs and Relations. **Qualif.:** Candidates must be individual recipients of either the SSRC-MacArthur Foundation Fellowships in International Peace and Security, MacArthur Foundation Grants for Research and Writing, MacArthur Collaborative Studies Grants, or any other direct or indirect grants from the MacArthur Program on Peace and International Cooperation. Grant recipients must initiate workshops on topics that test established assumptions about peace and security. Workshops must allow for small groups of junior faculty members and other junior scholars to meet for two or three days of intensive discussions and involve formal papers, leading to further collaborations and publication of research findings. The workshops should include individuals who may otherwise have not had the opportunity to obtain workshop funding. Cosponsorship of workshops by MacArthur grantees and others is permitted, and a limited number of individuals who have not received support from the programs listed above may be invited to participate. Participation by researchers based outside the United States is encouraged. Grants are not made to institutional sponsors of projects.

**Funds Avail.:** Up to $5,000. **Deadline:** September 15, February 15. Award winners announced November 15, April 15. **Contact:** SSRC at the above address (see entry 5391).

**• 5402 • SSRC International Predissertation Fellowships** *(Doctorate/Fellowship)*

**Purpose:** To increase the flow of talented graduate students in the social sciences into research and teaching careers oriented to the developing world. **Focus:** Social Sciences, Area and Ethnic Studies, Economics, Political Science, Sociology, International Trade. **Qualif.:** The program is aimed primarily at graduate students in economics, political science, psychology, and sociology, but is open to students in the other social science disciplines as well. Applicants must be students enrolled in Ph.D. programs in the social sciences at one of 23 universities participating in the program. Students should be in the early phases of their training and should demonstrate an interest in supplementing their strong disciplinary skills with interdisciplinary area and language studies.

**Funds Avail.:** Fellowships provide support for language training, overseas study, and course work in area studies, in addition to living stipends. Applicants will be expected to work with their disciplinary advisor and an area specialist in the design of a 12-month training program, which will prepare them to develop and provide them with a cultural context for the development of a dissertation research project focusing on a part of the developing world. Awards will not be tenable for dissertation research itself.

**Remarks:** The intent will be to encourage students to undertake dissertation research in or on Africa, China, Latin America and the Caribbean, the Near and Middle East, South Asia, and Southeast Asia. Funds for the program are provided by the Ford Foundation. **Contact:** Ellen Perecman, Director, at the above address (see entry 5391).

**• 5403 • SSRC Japan Advanced Research Grants** *(Postdoctorate/Grant)*

**Purpose:** To support individual postdoctoral research in Japan, the United States, and/or other countries. **Focus:** Social Sciences, Humanities, Japanese Studies. **Qualif.:** Candidates must be scholars who hold a Ph.D. or an equivalent degree. They must be United States citizens or have been residents for at least three consecutive years at the time of application. **Criteria:** Study is encouraged in traditional, area studies-oriented research in the humanities and social sciences, as well as in projects that are comparative and contemporary in nature and have long-term applied policy implications, or that engage Japan in wider regional and global debates. Special attention is given to Japanese who are interested in broadening their skills and expertise through additional training or comparative work in an additional geographic area, and to non-Japanese who use Japan as a case study or who draw Japan into wider global debates. **Deadline:** December 1. **Contact:** SSRC at the above address (see entry 5391).

**• 5404 • SSRC Japan Fellowships for Dissertation Write-Up** *(Doctorate/Fellowship)*

**Purpose:** To support advanced graduate students during the writing of their dissertations in the United States. **Focus:** Social Sciences, Japanese Studies. **Qualif.:** Students must be enrolled full-time in a doctoral program in the United States. They must also have completed research on a Japan-related topic and have begun to write their dissertations. Citizenship is not a consideration. **Deadline:** January 1. **Contact:** SSRC at the above address (see entry 5391).

**• 5405 • SSRC Japan Grants for Research Planning Activities** *(Postdoctorate/Grant)*

**Purpose:** To advance research concerning Japan in the social sciences and humanities. **Focus:** Japanese Studies, Social Sciences. **Qualif.:** Applicants must be interested in engaging in collaborative research planning activities and projects that promote comparative or interdisciplinary perspectives concerning Japanese studies, especially by involving scholars from outside North America.

**Funds Avail.:** Up to $6,000. **Deadline:** November 1, February 15. **Contact:** SSRC Japan Program at the above address (see entry 5391).

**• 5406 • SSRC Korea Advanced Research Grants** *(Postdoctorate/Grant)*

**Purpose:** To support research on Korea in the social sciences and humanities. **Focus:** Area and ethnic studies, Social Sciences, Literature, Philosophy, Religion, Performing Arts, Art History, Humanities, Asian Studies. **Qualif.:** Applicants must have either a Ph.D. or equivalent research experience and be United States citizens or residents for at least three consecutive years at the time of application. Depending on the nature of the proposed research, the project may be carried out in Korea, the United States, and/or other countries. Proposals to revise doctoral dissertations for publication are also eligible for support. **Criteria:** Candidates must demonstrate competence in the field of Korean studies, and the proposed research must promise to contribute to the further development of scholarship of Korea. Researchers in disciplines previously under represented in the competition are especially encouraged, such as literature, philosophy, religion, art history, and performance studies.

**Funds Avail.:** Maximum grants are $15,000. **Deadline:** December 1. **Contact:** SSRC Korea program at the above address (see entry 5391).

**• 5407 • SSRC Korea Grants for Research Planning Activities** *(Postdoctorate/Grant)*

**Purpose:** To identify topics that the SSRC Korea committee considers to be of particular interest and significance concerning Korea in the areas of social science and humanities. **Focus:** Social Sciences, Humanities, Asian Studies. **Qualif.:** Applicants must have either a Ph.D. or equivalent research experience. Citizenship is not a consideration. **Criteria:** Although the committee welcomes proposals in all fields, it is particularly receptive to new work on the following themes: projects that exploit newly available American, Japanese, Russian, or Chinese archival sources on Korea; all aspects of Korean women; the determinants and consequences of democratization; popular culture, including oral traditions and cinema; business history, and law and economic development; and Korean crisis management, such as how Koreans have responded to regime changes, coup's d'etat, war, etc. **To Apply:** Candidates must submit a 10 to 15 page proposal describing the substantive problem, broad trends found in the literature on the topic, the particular research questions to be addressed, the theoretical and methodological approaches to be taken, a budget, a list of the scholars to be involved, and curricula vitae for all scholars involved. **Deadline:** Varies. **Contact:** SSRC Korea program at the above address (see entry 5391).

**• 5408 • SSRC Latin America and the Caribbean Advanced Research Grants** *(Postdoctorate/Grant)*

**Purpose:** To support research by social scientists and humanists on all aspects of the societies and cultures of Latin America or the

## Social Science Research Council (continued)

Caribbean. **Focus:** Social Sciences, Humanities, Latin American Studies. **Qualif.:** Candidates must have a Ph.D. or equivalent degree and be United States citizens or residents who have lived in the United States for at least three consecutive years at the time of application. Recipients are expected to devote all or a major part of their time during the grant period to research, which may involve partial or full-time leaves from current obligations. Other proposed arrangements for allocating research time is considered, provided that at least two months of the grantee's own time is committed. Scholars who have accepted an advanced research grant from the SSRC in the last five years are not eligible, although individuals who received doctoral fellowships are eligible. Research proposals may be on any topic.

**Funds Avail.:** Grant amounts vary up to $15,000 according to project requirements. Travel expenses of dependents may be funded only for field stays of six months or more. Applicants are encouraged to seek additional funding support from other sources, but if a substantial overlap occurs, the program reserves the right to reduce the level of funding awarded. Grants for major projects as well as shorter visits to research sites are also considered. **To Apply:** Application materials are available as of August 1. **Deadline:** December 1. **Contact:** SSRC Latin America and the Caribbean program at the above address (see entry 5391).

### • 5409 • SSRC-MacArthur Foundation Dissertation Fellowships on Peace and Security in a Changing World (Doctorate/Fellowship)

**Purpose:** To support research on the implications for security issues of worldwide cultural, social, economic, and political changes. **Focus:** International Affairs and Relations, Social Sciences, Humanities, History, Behavioral Sciences. **Qualif.:** The competition is open to researchers who are finishing course work, examinations, or similar requirements for the Ph.D. or its equivalent. Applicants should expect to complete all requirements for the doctoral degree except the dissertation by the spring of the award year. The competition is open to researchers in the social and behavioral sciences (including history and area studies), the humanities, or the physical and biological sciences. Persons doing their research in nonacademic settings are welcome to apply. There are no citizenship, residency, or nationality requirements. The council especially encourages women and members of minority groups to apply.

**Funds Avail.:** Fellowships pay a stipend appropriate for the cost of living in the area where the recipient will be working. Following the award of the fellowship, the Council will negotiate the stipend. It will rarely exceed $17,500 per year, but will not be less than $12,500 per year. **No. of Awards:** Approximately 7. **Deadline:** December 1.

**Remarks:** Funding for this program is provided by the John D. and Catherine T. MacArthur Foundation. **Contact:** The Social Science Research Council at the above address (see entry 5391).

### • 5410 • SSRC-MacArthur Foundation Postdoctoral Fellowships on Peace and Security in a Changing World (Postdoctorate/Fellowship)

**Purpose:** To support research on the implications for security issues of worldwide cultural, social, economic, and political changes. **Focus:** Urban Affairs/Design/Planning, Social Sciences, International Development. **Qualif.:** In most cases, successful applicants will hold the Ph.D. or its equivalent. However, possession of that degree is not a requirement for lawyers, public servants, journalists, or others who can demonstrate comparable research experience and an ability to contribute to the research literature. The competition is designed for researchers in the first ten years of their postdoctoral careers; most senior researchers are discouraged from applying. Fellows are required to devote full time to the Fellowship; they are not permitted to be otherwise employed or to hold this Fellowship concurrently with other grants or fellowships.

**Funds Avail.:** Fellowships pay a stipend appropriate for the cost of living in the area where the recipient will be working. Following the award of the fellowship, the Council will negotiate the stipend. It will rarely exceed $35,000 per year, but it will not be less than $25,000 per year. **No. of Awards:** Approximately 7. **Deadline:** December 1.

**Remarks:** Funding is provided for this program by the John D. and Catherine T. MacArthur Foundation. **Contact:** The Social Science Research Council at the above address (see entry 5391).

### • 5411 • SSRC Near and Middle East Advanced Research Fellowships (Postdoctorate/Fellowship)

**Purpose:** To support humanists and social scientists conducting research on the Near and Middle East. **Focus:** Near Eastern Studies, Middle Eastern Studies. **Qualif.:** Applicants must be United States citizens or residents holding a Ph.D. in a social science or humanities discipline. **Criteria:** Scholars must demonstrate competence for research on the area. Preference is given to individuals without access to other major research support and to projects that are in the early stages of preparation. Research in disciplines or regions that have been previously under represented in the competition, such as literature, philosophy, religion, art history, and performance studies, are also preferred.

**Funds Avail.:** $15,000 maximum grant. Funds may be used for maintenance, travel, and research expenses. **Deadline:** December 1. **Contact:** SSRC NME Program at the above address (see entry 5391).

### • 5412 • SSRC Near and Middle East Dissertation Research Fellowships (Doctorate/Fellowship)

**Purpose:** To provide support for doctoral dissertation research on the Near and Middle East in the humanities and the social sciences. **Focus:** Near Eastern Studies, Middle Eastern Studies, Social Sciences. **Qualif.:** Applicants must be full-time students, regardless of citizenship, who are enrolled in doctoral programs in the United States, or are United States citizens or permanent residents enrolled in full-time doctoral programs abroad. Research projects must focus on the regions of North Africa, the Middle East, Afghanistan, Iran, and Turkey concerning the period since the beginning of Islam. Applicants are expected to devote a minimum of nine and a maximum of 18 months to field research in one or more countries in the area of research.

**Funds Avail.:** In addition to funding for field research, limited dissertation write-up support for not more than six months may be available. **Deadline:** November 1. **Contact:** SSRC NME Program at the above address (see entry 5391).

### • 5413 • SSRC Predoctoral and Dissertation Training and Research Awards (Doctorate/Award, Fellowship, Grant)

**Purpose:** To support scholars undertaking advanced field research in the United States and abroad. **Focus:** Area Studies, Humanities, Social Sciences. **Qualif.:** There are two types of support available: awards to provide maintenance, travel, and research expenses for postdoctoral scholars; and awards for doctoral dissertation research. For most grant programs, candidate must be a U.S. citizen or permanent resident, and have a Ph.D. degree or equivalent research experience. Applicant for a fellowship must be a U.S. citizen or permanent resident, and/or be enrolled in a full-time doctoral program at a U.S. institution. Fellowship candidate must have completed all the requirements for the Ph.D. except the dissertation by the start of the fellowship period. Additional requirements for fellowships and grants vary, depending on the host country. Write for further details. Research must be conducted in the United States or abroad, depending on the program. Preference is given to projects in the beginning stages, and to those that focus on relatively neglected regions or subjects. Some countries require prior approval of research projects by government or academic agencies. Awardees usually are expected to be associated with a university, research institute, or other appropriate institution in the country that is the subject of his/her research. Fellows are also expected to have a working knowledge of the language of host country, where pertinent. Fellows may apply for additional support for up to six months in which to write the dissertation upon return to the United States.

**Funds Avail.:** Living, research, and travel allowances. **To Apply:** Write for a list of available programs, application form and guidelines. **Deadline:** Varies. **Contact:** Office of Fellowships and Grants at the above address (see entry 5391).

**• 5414 • SSRC South Asia Advanced Research Grants** *(Postdoctorate/Grant)*

**Purpose:** To support humanists and social scientists in conducting research on Bangladesh, India, Nepal, Pakistan, and Sri Lanka. **Qualif.:** Applicants must be scholars who hold a Ph.D. or equivalent degree and be U.S. citizens or residents for at least three consecutive years at the time of applying. Research topics are open to all aspects of historical and contemporary South Asia, including politics, economics, culture, and society. Research may be carried out in Bangladesh, Nepal, Pakistan, and Sri Lanka, at major collections of Southeast Asian materials, or at any other appropriate locations. Scholars whose normal place of work is isolated from major centers of South Asian studies or other important research collections may include requests for support at such locations in their proposals. Applicants should not request support for travel to or research in India (see SSRC South Asia Dissertation Fellowships for India). However, support is provided for research on India carried out in other locations.

**Funds Avail.:** $15,000 maximum. Grants are available for any period up to 12 months and may be used for travel, research expenses, and maintenance. Maintenance and travel of dependents may be included if full-time research is conducted outside the grantee's home country for more than six months. Grants may be used to supplement sabbatical salaries or awards from other sources. Summer awards are not granted to those remaining at home institutions. **Deadline:** December 1. **Contact:** SSRC at the above address (see entry 5391).

**• 5415 • SSRC South Asia Dissertation Fellowships for Bangladesh** *(Doctorate/Fellowship)*

**Purpose:** To support doctoral dissertation research in the social sciences and humanities on Bangladesh. **Qualif.:** Applicants must be enrolled full-time in doctoral programs in the United States or Canada, or they are Bangladesh citizens enrolled in full-time graduate programs in Europe. All requirements for the Ph.D. must be met before receiving the fellowship, except for the dissertation. Scholars pursuing pan-Bengal research of a comparative nature can divide their research time between Bangladesh and India, but are expected to spend at least six months in Bangladesh.

**Funds Avail.:** Fellowships provide for nine to 12 months of research in Bangladesh, with extensions of up to 18 months where proven necessary for additional language or other training. **Deadline:** November 1.

**Remarks:** This program is supported by the Ford Foundation. **Contact:** Information is available from the SSRC South Asia program at the above address (see entry 5391).

**• 5416 • SSRC Southeast Asia Advanced Research Grants** *(Postdoctorate/Grant)*

**Purpose:** To support social scientists, humanists, and other professionals in conducting research or analyzing previously gathered research materials on Brunei, Burma (Myanmar), Indonesia, Cambodia, Laos, Malaysia, the Philippines, Thailand, Singapore, and Vietnam. **Qualif.:** Candidates must be scholars who hold a Ph.D. or an equivalent degree and are U.S. citizens or have been residents in the United States for at least three consecutive years at the time of application. Research proposals may be on all aspects of historical and contemporary Southeast Asia, including

politics, economics, culture, and society. Research may be carried out in Southeast Asia, at major collections of Southeast Asian materials, or at any other appropriate locale, such as a major center of Southeast Asian Studies in the United States or abroad. Collaboration and team research projects among scholars of different disciplines, nationalities, or levels of seniority are encouraged, as is comparative research between countries in the region.

**Funds Avail.:** $15,000 maximum awards for periods up to 12 months. Funds may be used for travel, research expenses, and maintenance. Maintenance and travel of dependents may also be included if full-time research is conducted outside the grantee's home country for more than six months. Summer awards are not granted to those remaining at their home institutions. Grants may be used to supplement sabbatical salaries or awards from other sources. **Deadline:** December 1. **Contact:** SSRC Southeast Asia program at the above address (see entry 5391).

**• 5417 • SSRC Southeast Asia Predissertation Fellowships** *(Doctorate/Fellowship)*

**Purpose:** To support short-term (two- to three-month) field trips to Southeast Asia for preliminary dissertation field activities. **Qualif.:** Students must have completed at least one year of graduate study in a program leading to a Ph.D. in the social sciences or humanities at a university in the United States, or be a U.S. citizen or permanent resident who has completed this study at an accredited institution abroad. Candidates' potential field activities may include investigating potential research sites, archival and other research materials, training in Southeast Asian languages not available in the United States, and establishing local research contacts. Applications are also considered for preliminary research in archives outside the United States and Southeast Asia.

**Funds Avail.:** Up to $4,000. **Deadline:** November 1. **Contact:** SSRC Southeast Asia program at the above address (see entry 5391).

**• 5418 • SSRC Soviet Union and Its Successor States Dissertation Fellowships** *(Doctorate/Fellowship)*

**Qualif.:** Candidates must have completed research for their doctoral dissertations and expect to complete the writing of their dissertations during the next academic year. They must be U.S. citizens specializing in any discipline of the social sciences and humanities relating to the Soviet Union and its successor states.

**Funds Avail.:** Up to $15,000 for one fellowship year each. **Deadline:** December 1. **Contact:** SSRC Soviet Union and Its Successor States program at the above address (see entry 5391).

**• 5419 • SSRC Soviet Union and Its Successor States Graduate Training Fellowships** *(Graduate/ Fellowship)*

**Qualif.:** Applicants must be U.S. citizens who are currently enrolled in their first, second, or third year of a graduate program and are interested in acquiring competency in the study of the Soviet Union and its successor states. They must also have completed at least one year of graduate work in the study of the Soviet Union and its successor states and wish to enhance their training in the area, or in related disciplines.

**Funds Avail.:** Up to $15,000 for periods of 12 months each. A performance review is conducted at the end of the first six months. The fellowship may also include extensive language training in the relevant languages of the region. **Deadline:** December 1. **Contact:** SSRC Soviet Union and Its Successor States program at the above address (see entry 5391).

**• 5420 • SSRC Soviet Union and Its Successor States Institutional Awards for First-Year Fellowships** *(Graduate/Award)*

**Purpose:** To provide first-year fellowships to students in under represented fields in Soviet studies through university

## Social Science Research Council (continued)

departments. **Qualif.:** Applications must come from sociology and anthropology departments at universities that also have other departments offering courses in Soviet studies. The selected departments must also have faculty able to support dissertations related to the Soviet Union and its successor states. Students receiving the fellowships must have a minimum two years of college-level Russian, or any other language of the former Soviet Union, and have relevant Soviet-area preparation and interest in pursuing research in Soviet studies. **Criteria:** Students are selected by the graduate departments at universities that receive this grant.

**Funds Avail.:** The award is for $15,000; $8,500 of the grant is paid to the student, and the remainder is paid to the institution in lieu of tuition. The recipient institution must participate in cost sharing by agreeing to waive overhead and tuition in excess of $6,500. **To Apply:** Students may not apply directly for these fellowships. **Deadline:** December 1. **Contact:** SSRC Soviet Union and Its Successor States program at the above address (see entry 5391).

### • 5421 • SSRC Soviet Union and Its Successor States Postdoctoral Fellowships *(Postdoctorate/Fellowship)*

**Purpose:** To improve the academic employment and tenure opportunities of new Ph.D. recipients in any discipline of the social sciences and humanities related to the study of the Soviet Union and its successor states. **Qualif.:** Applicants must be U.S. citizens who have defended their dissertations by September 1 before the deadline date and are untenured.

**Funds Avail.:** Stipends of $27,000 are available for three years of summer support plus one semester free of teaching. **Deadline:** December 1. **Contact:** SSRC Soviet Union and Its Successor States program at the above address (see entry 5391).

### • 5422 • SSRC Soviet Union and Its Successor States Workshop Grants *(Doctorate, Postdoctorate/Grant)*

**Purpose:** To counteract the isolation of many graduate students and junior scholars in Soviet-related disciplines by providing an opportunity to interact with peers, discuss their research and matters of mutual concern, establish contact, learn new methodologies, discuss sources, and promote innovative research. **Qualif.:** Applicants must be enrolled in Ph.D. programs or be junior scholars who received their Ph.D. degrees after June 1987. **Criteria:** Participants are selected on the basis of an international competition administered by the SSRC.

**Funds Avail.:** The workshop costs, including transportation, housing, and meals, is provided. The program is subject to the availability of funds. **Deadline:** February 1.

**Remarks:** Workshops are currently on the topics of Post-Soviet Domestic Politics and Society, Sociology and Anthropology, and Early East Slavic Culture. **Contact:** Information is available from the SSRC Soviet Union and Its Successor States program at the above address (see entry 5391).

### • 5423 •
## Social Sciences and Humanities Research Council of Canada
350 Albert St.
PO Box 1610
Ottawa, ON, Canada K1P 6G4
*E-mail:* cpe@sshrc.ca
*URL:* http://www.sshrc.ca

Ph: (613)992-0530
Fax: (613)992-1787

### • 5424 • Queen's Fellowship *(Doctorate/Fellowship)*

**Purpose:** To provide funding to a student who intends to earn a Ph.D. in Canadian Studies at a Canadian university. **Focus:** Canadian Studies. **Qualif.:** Applicants must be citizens of Canada or permanent residents at the time of application. The award is offered to one or two outstanding, successful doctoral fellowship candidates.

**Funds Avail.:** Can$15,000 plus an allowance to cover tuition fees, travel to the main place of tenure, and travel for research purposes. **No. of Awards:** 1-2. **To Apply:** Applications must be submitted to the Doctoral Fellowships program. Write to the Communications Division for Doctoral Fellowship application forms and guidelines. **Deadline:** November 15 for applicants not registered at a Canadian university. Contact university of registration for students registered at a Canadian university. **Contact:** Carole Ann Murphy, Director of Fellowships Division, at the above address (see entry 5423).

### • 5425 • Social Sciences and Humanities Research Council Doctoral Fellowships *(Doctorate/Fellowship)*

**Purpose:** To provide funding to Ph.D. students in the social sciences and humanities. **Focus:** Humanities, Social Sciences. **Qualif.:** Applicants must be citizens of Canada or permanent residents at the time of application. The Fellowship is intended for full-time students only.

**Funds Avail.:** Can$15,000. **No. of Awards:** 572. **To Apply:** Write to the Communications Division for application form and guidelines. **Deadline:** November 15 for applicants not registered at a Canadian university. Contact university of registration for students registered at a Canadian university. **Contact:** Carole Ann Murphy, Director of Fellowships Division, at the above address (see entry 5423).

### • 5426 • Social Sciences and Humanities Research Council Postdoctoral Fellowships *(Postdoctorate/Fellowship)*

**Purpose:** To promote and assist research and scholarship at the postdoctoral level. **Focus:** Humanities, Social Sciences. **Qualif.:** Applicants must be Canadian citizens or permanent residents of Canada.

**Funds Avail.:** Can$28,428 plus a research allowance of up to Can$5,000. **No. of Awards:** 100. **To Apply:** Write to the Council for application form and guidelines. **Deadline:** October 1.

**Remarks:** In addition to the programs open to all Canadian humanities and social science researchers, the Council also sponsors research grants and several strategic grant competitions available to researchers in targeted fields. Descriptions of these grants are included in the SSHRC Granting Programs: Detailed Guide. Specialized fellowships are also described in the SSHRC Granting Programs: Detailed Guide. **Contact:** Carole Ann Murphy, at the above address (see entry 5423).

## • 5427 •
## Sociedad Honoraria Hispanica
Glendale Community College
6000 W. Olive Ave.
Glendale, AZ 85302-3006          *Ph:* (602)939-1840

### • 5428 • Joseph Adams Scholarships
*(Undergraduate/Scholarship)*

**Purpose:** To encourage the study of the Spanish and Portuguese languages and to gain an understanding of the culture. **Focus:** Spanish or Portuguese Studies. **Qualif.:** Applicant must be high school senior and a member of an SHH chapter studying the language at the time of application submission. **Criteria:** Each chapter enters its best student. A national selection committee awards the winners based on four national regions.

**Funds Avail.:** Eight $2,000 and twenty $1,000 scholarships are awarded. **No. of Awards:** 28. **To Apply:** The Becas Packet containing applications and information is sent to chapter sponsors in December. **Deadline:** February 15. **Contact:** Sociedad Honoraria Hispanica at the above address (see entry 5427)for additional information.

## • 5429 •
## Society of Actuaries
475 N. Martingale Rd., Ste. 800     *Ph:* (847)706-3500
Schaumburg, IL 60173-2226           *Fax:* (847)706-3599
*URL:* http://www.soa.org

### • 5430 • Casualty Actuarial Scholarships for Minority Students *(Undergraduate/Scholarship)*

**Purpose:** The scholarship program is designed to aid minority students interested in pursuing actuarial careers. **Focus:** Actuarial Science. **Qualif.:** Candidates must be members of a minority group (i.e., African Americans, Hispanics, or Native Americans). They must be either U.S. citizens or have permanent resident visas. Candidates must also be undergraduate students admitted to an accredited college or university offering either a program in actuarial science or courses that will serve to prepare the student for an actuarial career. Applicants must have demonstrated mathematical ability and evidence some understanding of the field, and must have taken the Scholastic Aptitude Test (SAT) or the ACT. **Criteria:** Scholarships are awarded on the basis of individual merit and financial need.

**Funds Avail.:** The number and amount of the scholarships are determined by a committee of members of the Society of Actuaries and the Casualty Actuarial Society. The number and amount of the awards vary from year to year. **No. of Awards:** 20-30. **To Apply:** Applicants must submit the Financial Aid Form (FAF) to the College Scholarship Service (CSS) of the College Board not later than March 31 and give CSS permission to forward information to the Society. Applicants must also submit two nomination forms, completed by their instructors or academic advisors, a financial statement, and a transcript of grades. **Deadline:** May 1.

### • 5431 • Society of Actuaries Ph.D. Grants
*(Doctorate/Grant)*

**Purpose:** To encourage doctoral research in actuarial science and education. **Focus:** Actuarial Sciences. **Qualif.:** Candidate may be of any nationality. Applicant must be admitted to a Ph.D. program with the thesis on actuarial science. **Criteria:** Grants are awarded on the basis of individual merit.

**Funds Avail.:** $10,000. Renewable up to three times. **To Apply:** Contact Society for Actuaries at the above address for application form and guidelines. **Deadline:** March 15. Recipients will be notified by June. **Contact:** Warren R. Luckner, Director of Research, at the above address (see entry 5429).

## • 5432 •
## Society of American Registered Architects
1245 S. Highland Ave.          *Ph:* (630)932-4622
Lombard, IL 60148-4543         *Fax:* (630)495-3054
*URL:* http://www.protonet.com/sara/

### • 5433 • Society of American Registered Architects Student Design Competition/Emily Munson Memorial Student Award *(Graduate, Undergraduate/Award)*

**Qualif.:** Competition is open to undergraduates attending accredited architectural schools who are enrolled in a Bachelor of Arts or a Bachelor of Science in Architecture program, or undergraduate students in a Bachelor of Architecture program or graduate students in a Master of Architecture program in pursuit of a professional degree. Submissions may be the product of work for a design studio, a technical course, or an independent effort completed since January 1. Students must also secure the sponsorship of a faculty member. **Criteria:** The jury seeks submissions that clearly demonstrate a response to typical architectural concepts such as human activity needs, climatic considerations, structural integrity, cultural influences, site planning, creative insight, and coherence of architectural vocabulary. They must also be able to recognize and resolve situational problems of mechanical and electrical systems, environmental context, and external support systems, and to integrate functional aspects of the problem in an appropriate manner.

**Funds Avail.:** First prize is a $4,000 U.S savings bond, second prize is a $2,000 U.S. savings bond, and third prize is a $1,000 U.S. savings bond. **To Apply:** Applicants must complete and return a registration form, which is available from the Dean's offices or from the Society of American Registered Architects. Submissions may be any medium-sized architectural project other than a single-family home or vacation residence. Faculty and students are encouraged to select design problems pertaining to buildings that are representative of a significant functional type, such as schools, libraries, and museums. Projects must be of sufficient scale and complexity to present an appropriate challenge to design and technical skills. Site information and the original program statement must be clearly communicated as part of the presentation, in detail sufficient to be understood by persons completely unfamiliar with the project. Faculty sponsors must provide a copy of the problem statement. Students must include a concise description of the design problem on the Project Summary Form. Participants must address the climate conditions consistent with their chosen site. Sites need not be local, but entrants are encouraged to work with site specific conditions. Climatic conditions must be clearly communicated in all cases. Local regulations should be applied to the design problem. Submissions should reflect reasonable regard for the health and safety of occupants. Design drawings are limited to four display boards with sufficient graphics to explain the solution completely. **Deadline:** Entries must be received by October 13. Recipients are announced October 26. **Contact:** All questions and requests for registration forms should be directed to the Student Design Chairman, SARA National Headquarters, at the above address (see entry 5432).

---

## Society of Automotive Engineers - Scholarship Program

400 Commonwealth Dr.  
Warrendale, PA 15096-0001  
*E-mail:* lorile@sae.org  
*URL:* http://www.SAE.org/

*Ph:* (412)772-8534  
*Fax:* (412)776-1615

### • 5435 • SAE Doctoral Scholars Program *(Graduate/ Loan)*

**Purpose:** The program is designed to help alleviate the increasing shortage of engineering college faculty by providing funding to assist and encourage promising engineering graduate students to pursue careers in teaching at the college level. **Focus:** Engineering. **Qualif.:** Applicants must hold a degree from an ABET accredited undergraduate program and must be citizens of North America. They must also be admitted to a doctoral program with the avowed purpose of teaching at the college level.

**Funds Avail.:** $5,000 a year for up to 3 years. Loans will be forgiven if candidate teaches at an accredited university. **To Apply:** Applications are available after January 1. **Deadline:** End of April. **Contact:** Lori Pail, SAE Educational Relations, (412)772-8534, at the above address (see entry 5434).

### • 5436 • SAE Engineering Scholarships *(Undergraduate/Scholarship)*

**Purpose:** The program is designed to encourage interest in the study of engineering and other sciences. **Focus:** Engineering. **Qualif.:** Applicants must be high school seniors who are planning to major in engineering. **Criteria:** Preference will be given to those with a 3.75 GPA who have scored in the 99th percentile on their SAT/ACT's.

**Funds Avail.:** Scholarships range from $500 to $6,000. **No. of Awards:** 50. **To Apply:** Applications are available in September. **Deadline:** First week of January. **Contact:** Lori Pail, SAE Educational Relations, (412)772-8534, at the above address (see entry 5434).

## Society of Biological Psychiatry

c/o Elliott Richelson, M.D,  
Departments of Psychiatry and  
  Pharmacology  
4500 San Pablo Rd.  
Jacksonville, FL 32224  
*E-mail:* maggie@mayo.edu; maggie@mayo.edu  
*URL:* http://www.sobp.org; http://www.sobp.org

*Ph:* (904)953-2842  
*Fax:* (904)953-7117

### • 5438 • A. E. Bennett Research Awards *(Postdoctorate/Award)*

**Purpose:** To stimulate international research in biological psychiatry by young investigators. **Focus:** Biological Psychiatry **Qualif.:** Candidate may be of any nationality, but must be less than 35 years old in the year the award is given. Applicant must have written a manuscript that describes studies recently completed but not published or currently under consideration. Candidate must be still actively involved in the area of research described in the submission. Applicant need not be a current member of the Society. **Criteria:** Although the research is not to be judged in comparison with the work of the more senior investigators, special consideration will be given to the originality of the approach and independence of thought evident in the submission.

**Funds Avail.:** $1,500. **No. of Awards:** 2. **To Apply:** Write for application guidelines. Submit eight copies of a 15 to 25-page manuscript and biographical sketch. Refer to the Society's journal, *Biological Psychiatry,* for manuscript guidelines. **Deadline:** January 31.

**Remarks:** Lilly Travel Fellowships are also offered to help defray the cost of attending the Society's annual meeting. Candidate must be nominated by a department of psychiatry at a U.S. institution. For further information, write to Dr. Donna Giles, Western Psychiatric Institute and Clinic, 3811 O'Hara St., Pittsburgh, PA, 15213. **Contact:** Robert M. Post, MD, (301) 496-4805.

## Society of Biological Psychiatry

Department of Psychiatry  
Univ. of Pittsburgh Medical Center  
Western Psychiatric Institute and  
  Clinic  
3811 O'Hara St.  
Pittsburgh, PA 15213  
*URL:* http://www.sobp.org/

*Ph:* (412)624-2353

### • 5440 • Ziskind-Sommerfeld Research Award *(Postdoctorate/Award)*

**Purpose:** To stimulate international research in biological psychiatry by senior investigators. **Focus:** Biological Psychiatry. **Qualif.:** Candidates may be of any nationality, but must be at least 35 years old at the time of application. They must have written a manuscript that describes studies recently completed but not published or currently under consideration. They must also still be actively involved in the area of research described in the submission and current members of the Society.

**Funds Avail.:** $2,500. **To Apply:** Write for application guidelines. Submit eight copies of a manuscript no more than 30 pages in length with a biographical sketch. Refer to the Society's journal *Biological Psychiatry* for manuscript guidelines. **Deadline:** March 31.

**Remarks:** Dista Travel Fellowships are also offered to help defray the cost of attending the Society's annual meeting. Candidates must be nominated by a department of psychiatry at a U.S. institution. For further information, write to Dr. John F. Greden, Chair, Department of Psychiatry, University of Michigan Medical Center, 1500 E. Medical Center Dr., Box 0704, Ann Arbor, Michigan 48109, U.S.A. **Contact:** Dr. Paula J. Clayton, Chair, at the above address (see entry 5439).

## Society of Broadcast Engineers, Inc.

8445 Keystone Crossing, Ste. 140  
Indianapolis, IN 46240-2454  
*E-mail:* lgodby@sbe.org  
*URL:* http://www.sbe.org

*Ph:* (317)253-1640  
*Fax:* (317)253-0418

### • 5442 • Harold E. Ennes Scholarship *(Undergraduate/Scholarship)*

**Purpose:** To perpetuate the flow of qualified entrants into broadcast engineering. **Focus:** Broadcasting, Communications Technologies. **Qualif.:** Applicants must have a career interest in the technical aspects of broadcasting and must be recommended by two members of the Society. Preference is given to members of the SBE. At the conclusion of educational training, the recipient is expected to submit a 400-500 word technical paper for potential use in a Society of Broadcast Engineers' publication.

Funds Avail.: $1,000 to be used within one school year. Upon completion of admission, the educational institution obtains one-half of the award. At the end of the first semester, quarter, or trimester, if the recipient has maintained passing grades in all subjects, the remaining half of the award may be obtained by the educational institution. **No. of Awards:** 1 to 2. **To Apply:** The candidate must submit a brief autobiography that includes candidate's interest and goals in broadcasting and a summary of the changes the applicant anticipates in broadcasting within the following five years. A self-addressed, stamped envelope must be included. **Deadline:** July 1.

**Remarks:** Harold E. Ennes was an active society member and the author of broadcast maintenance books. **Contact:** The Society of Broadcast Engineers at the above address (see entry 5441).

## • 5443 •
## Society of Children's Book Writers and Illustrators
22736 Vanowen St., No. 106
Canoga Park, CA 91306  *Ph:* (818)888-8760

### • 5444 • Don Freeman Memorial Grant-in-Aid
*(Professional Development/Grant)*

**Purpose:** To enable picture-book artists to further their understanding, training, and work in the picture-book genre. **Focus:** Children's Literature/Illustration. **Qualif.:** Applicant must be a full or associate member of SCBW who intends to make picture-books his/her chief contribution to children's literature.

**Funds Avail.:** $1,000 and $500. **To Apply:** Send a self-addressed, stamped envelope to the executive director for application form and guidelines. Submit five copies of form with samples of work in picture-book illustration. **Deadline:** January 15 to February 15. Grant is announced June 15. **Contact:** The Society at the above address (see entry 5443).

### • 5445 • SCBWI Work-in-Progress Grants
*(Professional Development/Grant)*

**Purpose:** To help writers of children's books to complete specific projects. **Focus:** Children's Literature/Illustration. **Qualif.:** Applicant must be a full or associate member of SCBWI who is currently writing a book for children. Grants are awarded in three categories: general work-in-progress, contemporary novels for young people, and nonfiction research. Grants are not offered for projects on which there is already a publishing contract. Previous grant recipients are not eligible to apply.

**Funds Avail.:** $500 or $1,000. **No. of Awards:** Eight. **To Apply:** Send a self-addressed, stamped envelope to the executive director for application form and guidelines, available October 1. **Deadline:** February 1 to May 1. Grants are announced in September.

**Remarks:** SCBWI offers two grants to authors who have not been previously published. There are no special application procedures; recipients are selected from applicants to the Work-In-Progress Grants competition. **Contact:** The Society at the above address (see entry 5443).

## • 5446 •
## Society of Daughters of United States Army
c/o Janet B. Otto
7717 Rockledge Court
Springfield, VA 22152

### • 5447 • Society of Daughters of the United States Army Scholarship Program *(Undergraduate/Scholarship)*

**Qualif.:** Must be the daughter or granddaughter only (including adopted or stepdaughter) of a career warrant officer or commissioned officer of the US Army, with the following status:currently on active duty in the Army; medically retired from the Army; retired from the Army after at least 20 years on active duty; or having died while on active duty in the Army. **Criteria:** A board of judges selects recipients based on a combination of financial need and personal record. Three references, current transcripts which show SAT and/or ACT scores, a resume and essays on designated subjects are required. Minimum GPA is 3.0.

**Funds Avail.:** $1000. **No. of Awards:** Varies. **To Apply:** First consideration is given each year to current recipients who are still eligible. Letters must include a self-addressed, stamped business envelope. Must include the name, rank, social security number, duty status component, and inclusive dates of active duty of the qualifying parents(s) or grandparent(s). Send only one inquiry in a business envelope. **Deadline:** Accepted between November 1 and March 1.

**Remarks:** Inquiries which do not include a stamped, self-addressed envelope will not receive a reply. **Contact:** Janet B. Otto DUSA Memorial & Scholarship Funds, 7717 Rockledge Court, West Springfield, VA 22152-3584.

## • 5448 •
## Society Farsarotul
799 Silver Ln.
PO Box 753
Trumbull, CT 06611  *Ph:* (203)375-0600

*Founded in 1903, the Society Farsarotul is the oldest and largest Vlach Society in America. The Vlachs (also known as Arumanians and Macedo-Romanians) are a Romance-speaking population from the southern Balkan Peninsula.*

### • 5449 • Society Farsarotul Grants *(Graduate, Undergraduate/Grant)*

**Purpose:** To encourage study of the culture and history of the Vlachs (also known as Arumanians and Macedo-Romanians of the southern Balkan Peninsula.) **Focus:** Romanian Studies. **Qualif.:** Candidates can be students, scholars, or professionals who are engaged in the study of the Vlachs specifically and Eastern European Latinity in general. Undergraduate candidates must demonstrate that at least one parent or grandparent was Arumanian, and have completed at least four semesters of full-time study. All candidates must have a GPA of at least 3.0 on a 4.0 scale. Membership in the Society Farsarotul is not required unless the applicant is an undergraduate. Undergraduate applicants attending an accredited American institution on a full-time basis, must have a major in European History, Sociology, Anthropology, Linguistics, or Eastern Romance Languages. Previous grant winners are not eligible. **Criteria:** Selection is based on the applicant's GPA, letters of reference, and a written request. If there are no applicants, or if none meet the requirements, no awards will be made that year.

**Funds Avail.:** $1,000. **No. of Awards:** 2. **To Apply:** Applicants must submit three reference letters written by professors who are personally acquainted with the applicant's work and three copies of a written request of not more than 2,000 words explaining the reason for applying for the grant as well as a planned use of funds.

## Society Farsarotul (continued)

Reference letters must be sent directly to the Society Farsarotul. **Deadline:** February 1. Grants are awarded June 1. **Contact:** Nicholas Balamaci, Secretary, at the above address (see entry 5448).

---

• 5450 •
## Society of the First Division
5 Montgomery Ave.
Philadelphia, PA 19038-8283

**• 5451 •  Society of the First Division Foundation Scholarships** (Undergraduate/Scholarship)

**Focus:** General Studies. **Qualif.:** Applicants must be high school seniors who are the children or grandchildren of any soldier who has served in the First Infantry Division. **Criteria:** Selection of recipients is based on the applicant's scholastic accomplishments and on an original essay on a subject to be announced.

**Funds Avail.:** The award is $3,000 payable to the school in four annual installments of not more than $750 per year. Three scholarships are awarded each year. **To Apply:** Application forms, scholastic records, essays, letters of recommendation, letters of acceptance from college, and proof of parent's or grandparent's service with the First Infantry Division must be submitted. **Deadline:** June 1. **Contact:** Scholarship Committee at the above address (see entry 5450).

**• 5452 •  Sons of the First Division Scholarship Fund** (Undergraduate/Scholarship)

**Qualif.:** The single requirement for eligibility is that a child's father was killed while serving with the First Infantry Division in Vietnam, in on-the-job accidents, or in Operation Desert Storm.

**Funds Avail.:** Each scholarship is payable up to $2,500 over a four year period. Payments are made directly to the school to be applied to the recipient's account. The scholarship is normally awarded for courses taken at the college level. Vocational or technical courses taken in lieu of high school training are considered suitable. Payment of subsequent installments of the scholarship award is based on evidence of satisfactory completion of the preceding scholastic period and continuation of the education program. No payments are made by the fund on any scholarship after the recipient's 26th birthday. **To Apply:** Candidates must submit proof of admission to a VA approved college, vocational, or technical school. **Contact:** The Society of the First Division at the above address (see entry 5450).

---

• 5453 •
## Society of Hispanic Professional Engineers Foundation
5400 E. Olympic Blvd., Ste. 210      Ph: (213)725-3970
Los Angeles, CA 90022                Fax: (213)888-2089
E-mail: shpe@address.com
URL: http://www.incacorp.com/shpe

**• 5454 •  SHPE Foundation Education Grant** (Graduate, Undergraduate/Grant)

**Purpose:** To provide educational grants to students majoring in engineering and science. **Focus:** Engineering, Science. **Qualif.:** Applicants must be undergraduate or graduate college students, or high school students entering college enrolled full-time, and majoring in science or engineering. **Criteria:** Selection is based on

counselor recommendation, grade point average, financial need, and commitment to education and community.

**Funds Avail.:** $500-$2,000. **No. of Awards:** 250. **To Apply:** Must send self-addressed stamped envelope to request application. **Deadline:** April 15. **Contact:** Kathy Borunda at the above address (see entry 5453)for information and applications.

---

• 5455 •
## Society for the Humanities
Andrew D. White House
27 East Ave.                         Ph: (607)255-9274
Ithaca, NY 14853-1101                Fax: (607)255-1422
E-mail: as63@cornell.edu; mea4@cornell.edu
URL: http://www.arts.cornell.edu/sochum

*The Society for the Humanities was established at Cornell University in 1966 to support research and encourage imaginative teaching in the humanities. It is intended to be at once a research institute, a stimulus to educational innovation, and a continuing society of scholars. In addition to promoting research on central concepts, methods, or problems in the humanities, the Society seeks to encourage serious and sustained discussion between teachers and learners at all levels of maturity.*

**• 5456 •  Society for the Humanities Postdoctoral Fellowships** (Postdoctorate, Professional Development/Fellowship)

**Purpose:** To promote research on central concepts, methods, or problems in the humanities, and to encourage serious and sustained discussion between teachers and learners at all levels of maturity. **Focus:** Humanities (Specific themes vary from year to year) **Qualif.:** Candidates may be of any nationality but must have a Ph.D. degree and at least one year of college teaching experience, but scientists, writers, composers, artists, jurists, public servants, and others who have equivalent experience and a strong commitment to the humanities may also apply. Fellowships are tenable at Cornell University. In addition to their independent research projects, fellows are invited to conduct one seminar each term, on a topic of the fellow's choosing. Applicants must have received the PhD degree by the time of application.

**Funds Avail.:** $32,000/year. **No. of Awards:** 8-10. **To Apply:** Write to the program administrator for application form and guidelines. Submit form, curriculum vitae, samples of scholarly writing, a detailed statement of current research interests, and a two- to four-page teaching proposal. Three letters of recommendation from senior colleagues evaluating the research and teaching proposals should be submitted directly to the Society. **Deadline:** Applications must be postmarked by October 20. Fellowships are announced in late December.

**Remarks:** Applications are not accepted via fax. **Contact:** Lisa Patti, Program Administrator, at the above address (see entry 5455).

• 5457 •
## Society for the Humanities
Cornell University
Andrew D. White Center for the
  Humanities
27 East Ave.                          Ph: (607)255-9274
Ithaca, NY 14853-1101                 Fax: (607)255-1422
E-mail: as63@cornell.edu

### • 5458 • Mellon Postdoctoral Fellowships
(Postdoctorate/Fellowship)

**Purpose:** To encourage the academic growth of promising humanists with recent Ph.D. degrees. **Focus:** Humanities **Qualif.:** Applicants must have completed requirements for the Ph.D. degree before applying. Fellowships are limited to citizens of the U.S. and Canada or those with permanent residency cards. Applicants must be eligible in the fields of specialization.

**Funds Avail.:** Three fellowships are awarded and offer an annual stipend of $30,000 each. **No. of Awards:** 4-5. **To Apply:** Applicants should submit a completed application form, specifying the discipline and area of specialization in which they wish to be considered. They should also be prepared to submit a curriculum vitae, a detailed statement of current research interests, copies of two or three papers or scholarly publications, a two- to four-page statement of teaching interests and two course proposals, and three letters of recommendation. **Deadline:** Application must be postmarked on or before January 4.

**Remarks:** Between 50 and 60 applications are submitted each year. **Contact:** The Mellon Post-Doctoral Fellowship Program at the above address (see entry 5457).

### • 5459 • Society for the Humanities Fellowships
(Postdoctorate/Fellowship)

**Focus:** Humanities **Qualif.:** Applicants must have completed the Ph.D degree by the time of their application. They must also have one or more years of college teaching experience, which may include teaching as a graduate student. Fellows should be working on topics related to the year's theme, taking an approach that is broad enough to appeal to students and scholars in several humanistic disciplines. Fellows spend most of their time at Cornell in research and writing but are encourage to offer a seminar related to their research.

**Funds Avail.:** $32,000. **No. of Awards:** 6-10. **To Apply:** Applicants must send a curriculum vitae and copies of two or three papers on scholarly publications, a one-page abstract as well as a detailed statement (1,000-3,000 words) of current research interests, a two- to four-page discussion of the kind of teaching the applicant would like to pursue, and three letters of recommendation from senior colleagues, to whom candidates should send their research proposals. Letters of recommendation should include an evaluation of the candidate's statement of current research interests and teaching proposal. **Deadline:** October 21.

• 5460 •
## The Society for Imaging Science & Technology
7003 Kilworth Ln.                     Ph: (703)642-9090
Springfield, VA 22151                 Fax: (703)642-9094
E-mail: info@imaging.org
URL: http://www.imagining.org/

### • 5461 • Raymond Davis Scholarship (Graduate, Undergraduate/Scholarship)

**Focus:** Photographic Sciences, Engineering. **Qualif.:** Applicants must be graduate or undergraduate students who have completed or will complete two academic years of college. They must be pursuing a degree at an accredited institution on a full-time basis in photographic science or engineering. Grants are for academic study or research in the theory or practice of photographic science, which is broadly interpreted to include any kind of image formation initiated by radiant energy. **Criteria:** Recipients are selected by the Board of Directors of the Society on the recommendation of the Honors and Awards Committee.

**Funds Avail.:** One or more grants of $1,000 or more are made annually, depending on funds available. **To Apply:** Applications must be submitted to the Honors and Awards Committee of the Society for Imaging Science and Technology. **Deadline:** December 15. **Contact:** The Society for Imaging Science and Technology at the above address (see entry 5460).

• 5462 •
## Society of Logistics Engineers
8100 Professional Pl., Ste. 211       Ph: (301)459-8446
New Carrollton, MD 20785              Fax: (301)459-1522
                                      Free: 800-695-7653
E-mail: solehq@aol.com
URL: http://ftp.telebyte.com/sole/edu.html

### • 5463 • Logistics Education Foundation Scholarship
(Graduate, Undergraduate/Scholarship)

**Focus:** Logistics or related areas. **Qualif.:** Applicants must be students of logistics or related areas. **Criteria:** Awards are made based on scholastic achievement, overall career goals and related interests in logistics, and recommendations. **To Apply:** Applicants must submit completed application, two letters of recommendation, and transcripts of all college/university level work completed. **Deadline:** April 15. **Contact:** Society of Logistics Engineers at the above address (see entry 5462).

• 5464 •
## Society of Manufacturing Engineers - Education Foundation
1 SME Dr.                             Ph: (313)271-1500
PO Box 930                            Fax: (313)240-6095
Dearborn, MI 48121-0930              Free: 800-733-4763
E-mail: murrdor@sme.org
URL: http://www.sme.org/foundation

### • 5465 • Caterpillar Scholars Award (Undergraduate/Scholarship)

**Purpose:** To provide tuition, books, and supplies for recipients. **Focus:** Manufacturing engineering undergraduate studies. **Qualif.:** Applicants must be full-time enrolled in a degree program in manufacturing engineering and manufacturing engineering technology; have completed a minimum of 30 credit hours in a manufacturing engineering or manufacturing engineering technology curriculum; and must possess a GPA of at least 3.0 on a 4.0 scale. Students may submit a scholarship application in more than one year. Minority freshmen are encouraged to apply. **Criteria:** Need is a consideration only when two or more applicants have equal qualifications.

**Funds Avail.:** Five $2,000 scholarships. Scholarship will be deposited directly into an account at the recipient's institution in June of the award year for the fall term. If all applicants are unqualified during any given year, the scholarship award will be deferred until the following year. **No. of Awards:** 5. **To Apply:** Applicants must submit one original and three copies of the following materials: cover sheet with applicant's statement letter

## Society of Manufacturing Engineers - Education Foundation (continued)

regarding student's career objectives in manufacturing engineering or manufacturing engineering technology and explaining how the receipt of the scholarship will aid in achieving goals (250 words maximum); current official transcript and resume; and recommendations from two faculty and/or current/former employers. There is no pre-printed application form, except the Scholarship Application Cover Sheet. **Deadline:** March 1. **Contact:** Dora Murray, grants coordinator extension 1709 or Teresa Macias, grants secretary extension 1707, at the above address (see entry 5464).

### • 5466 • Wayne Kay Graduate Fellowships (Graduate/Fellowship)

**Purpose:** To provide tuition, books, and supplies for recipients. **Focus:** Manufacturing engineering or industrial engineering. **Qualif.:** Applicants must be full-time students accepted in an advanced degree program (M.S. or Ph.D.) in the field of manufacturing engineering or industrial engineering with a minimum grade point of 3.5 on a 4.0 scale. **Criteria:** Fellowship awards are made only to those students who have proven scholastic ability, exemplary character, and leadership capability and who have demonstrated their potential for future leadership in the profession. Need is a consideration only when two or more applicants have equal qualifications.

**Funds Avail.:** $4,000-12,000 each. **No. of Awards:** The number of awards each year will be determined by the financial growth of the fund. If all applicants are unqualified during any given year, the fellowship awards will be deferred until the following year. **To Apply:** Applicants must submit one original and three sets of the following materials: completed application cover sheet; statement letter regarding student's career objectives in manufacturing engineering or manufacturing engineering technology and explaining how the receipt of the scholarship will aid in achieving their goals (250 words maximum); student resume; official transcript; and letters of recommendation from two faculty and/or current/former employers. The only pre-printed application form is the Student Application Cover Sheet. **Deadline:** March 1. **Contact:** Dora Murray, grants coordinator extension 1709 or Teresa Macias, grants secretary extension 1707, at the above address (see entry 5464).

### • 5467 • Wayne Kay Scholarship (Undergraduate/Scholarship)

**Purpose:** To provide tuition, books, and supplies for recipients. **Focus:** Manufacturing engineering. **Qualif.:** Applicants must be full-time enrolled in a degree program in manufacturing engineering and manufacturing engineering technology; have completed a minimum of 30 credit hours in a manufacturing engineering or manufacturing engineering technology curriculum; and must possess a GPA of at least 3.5 on a 4.0 scale. Students may submit a scholarship application in more than one year. **Criteria:** Need is a consideration only when two or more applicants have equal qualifications.

**Funds Avail.:** Ten $2,500 scholarships. Scholarship will be paid directly to each recipient in June of the award year for the fall term. If all applicants are unqualified during any given year, the scholarship award will be deferred until the following year. **No. of Awards:** 10. **To Apply:** Applicants must submit one original and three copies of the following materials: cover sheet; statement letter regarding student's career objectives in manufacturing engineering or manufacturing engineering technology and explaining how the receipt of the scholarship will aid in achieving goals (250 words maximum); current transcript and resume; recommendations from two faculty and/or current/former employers. There is no pre-printed application form, except the Scholarship Application Cover Sheet. **Deadline:** March 1. **Contact:** Dora Murray, grants coordinator extension 1709 or Teresa Macias, grants secretary extension 1707, at the above address (see entry 5464).

### • 5468 • St. Louis SME Chapter No. 17 Scholarships (Undergraduate/Scholarship)

**Purpose:** To provide tuition, boos, and supplies for recipients. **Focus:** Manufacturing engineering; industrial technology, or other manufacturing related programs. **Qualif.:** Applicants must be full-time students from an institution with a student chapter sponsored by SME Chapter No. 17. They must have completed 30 credit hours and be enrolled in a manufacturing engineering or manufacturing technology program with a minimum grade point average of 3.5 on a 4.0 scale. **Criteria:** When two or more applicants have equal qualifications, financial need is considered.

**Funds Avail.:** Five $1,000 scholarships. **No. of Awards:** 4. **To Apply:** Applicants must submit one original and three copies of the following materials: cover sheet; statement letter regarding student's career objectives in robotics/automated systems engineering or manufacturing engineering technology and explaining how the receipt of the scholarship will aid in achieving goals (250 words maximum); current transcript and resume; and recommendations from two faculty and/or current/former employers. There is no pre-printed application form except the Scholarship Application Cover Sheet. **Deadline:** March 1. **Contact:** Dora Murray, grants coordinator extension 1709 or Teresa Macias, grants secretary extension 1707, at the above address (see entry 5464).

### • 5469 • Myrtle and Earl Walker Scholarships (Undergraduate/Scholarship)

**Purpose:** To provide tuition, books, and supplies to recipients. **Focus:** Manufacturing engineering or technology undergraduate studies. **Qualif.:** Applicants must be full-time students seeking careers in manufacturing engineering or technology and attending degree-granting institutions or accredited trade schools. They must also have completed a minimum of 30 credit hours in a manufacturing engineering technology curriculum and possess a GPA of at least 3.5 on a 4.0 scale. Students may submit a scholarship application in more than one year. **Criteria:** When two or more applicants have equal qualifications, financial need is considered.

**Funds Avail.:** At least twenty $1,000 scholarships, depending on the financial growth of the individual. Scholarships will be deposited directly into an account at the recipient's institution in June of the award year for the fall term. If all applicants are unqualified during any given year, the scholarship awards will be deferred until the following year. **No. of Awards:** 34. **To Apply:** Applicants must submit one original and three copies of the following materials: cover sheet; with applicant's statement letter regarding student's career objectives in manufacturing engineering or manufacturing technology and explaining how the receipt of the scholarship will aid in achieving their goals (250 words maximum); current transcript and resume; recommendations from two faculty and/or current/former employers. There is no pre-printed application form, except the Scholarship Application Cover Sheet. **Deadline:** March 1. **Contact:** Dora Murray, grants coordinator, extension 1709 or Teresa Macias, grants secretary, extension 1707 at the above address (see entry 5464).

### • 5470 • William E. Weisel Scholarship (Undergraduate/Scholarship)

**Purpose:** To provide tuition, books, and supplies to recipients. **Focus:** Manufacturing, robotics or automated systems. **Qualif.:** Applicants must be United States or Canadian citizens; full-time students seeking careers in robotics, manufacturing, or automated systems and attending regionally accredited school in engineering or technology; have completed a minimum of 30 credit hours in a manufacturing/robotic/automated systems curriculum; and must possess a GPA of at least 3.5 on a 4.0 scale. Students may submit a scholarship application in more than one year. **Criteria:** When two or more applicants have equal qualifications, financial need is considered.

**Funds Avail.:** One $1,000 scholarship. Scholarship will be paid directly to each recipient in June of the award year for the fall term. If all applicants are unqualified during any given year, the scholarship award will be deferred until the following year. **No. of Awards:** One award annually. **To Apply:** Applicants must submit one original and seven copies of the following materials: cover sheet; statement letter regarding student's career objectives in robotics/automated systems engineering or manufacturing technology and explaining how the receipt of the scholarship will aid in achieving goals (250 words maximum); current official transcript and resume; recommendations from two faculty and/or current/former employers. There is no pre-printed application form, except the Scholarship Application Cover Sheet. **Deadline:** March 1.

**Remarks:** Recipients will be asked to agree to contribute $1,000 to the William E. Weisel Scholarship Fund at some time in the future as their careers become successful in order to guarantee the same educational opportunity to other worthy students. **Contact:** Dora Murray, grants coordinator extension 1709 or Teresa Macias, grants secretary extension 1707, at the above address (see entry 5464).

---

• **5471** •

## Society of Naval Architects and Marine Engineers
601 Pavonia Ave., Ste. 400      *Ph:* (201)798-4800
Jersey City, NJ 07306           *Fax:* (201)798-4975
*URL:* http://www.sname.org

### • 5472 • Society of Naval Architects and Marine Engineers Scholarships *(Professional Development/ Scholarship)*

**Purpose:** To encourage graduates to pursue studies in naval architecture, marine engineering, or related fields. **Focus:** Marine Engineering, Naval Architecture. **Qualif.:** Applicants must be U.S. or Canadian citizens. In addition to scholastic ability, applicants must demonstrate leadership qualities and the capacity to pursue advanced study. For at least one scholarship, preference will be given to a candidate who has been recently employed for at least five years in the marine field.

**Funds Avail.:** $2,000-12,000. **To Apply:** Write for application form and guidelines. **Deadline:** February 1. **Contact:** Philip B. Kimball, Executive Director, at the above address (see entry 5471).

---

• **5473** •

## Society of Nuclear Medicine - Education and Research Foundation
1850 Samuel Morse Dr.          *Ph:* (703)708-9000
Reston, VA 22090-5316          *Free:* 800-513-6853
*E-mail:* sweiss@nwu.edu
*URL:* http://www.pet.upenn.edu/snmerf

### • 5474 • Cassen Postdoctoral Fellowship *(Postdoctorate/Fellowship)*

**Purpose:** To allow recent doctoral degree recipients to broaden their research experience. **Focus:** Nuclear Medicine. **Qualif.:** Candidates must be recent doctoral degree recipients who have demonstrated exceptional research ability. Awards are tenable at an institution other than the candidate's degree-granting one.

**Funds Avail.:** $25,000. **To Apply:** Write to the Foundation for application guidelines and forms. **Contact:** Secretary at the above address (see entry 5473).

### • 5475 • Paul C. Cole Scholarships *(Doctorate/ Scholarship)*

**Purpose:** To assist nuclear medicine technology students in the field of nuclear medicine. **Focus:** Nuclear Medicine. **Qualif.:** Applicant may be of any nationality, but must be a medical technology student who wishes to specialize in nuclear medicine and is enrolled in an accredited U.S. Nuclear Medicine program. Scholarships are tenable at the recipients' home institutions.

**Funds Avail.:** $1,000. **To Apply:** Write to the Foundation for application guidelines. **Deadline:** May 1. **Contact:** Secretary at the above address (see entry 5473).

### • 5476 • Society of Nuclear Medicine Pilot Research Grants *(Postdoctorate, Postgraduate/Grant)*

**Purpose:** To provide limited sums of money to young investigators to support deserving projects that are pilot in nature. The grants are intended to fund initial clinical or basic research while other major grant support is being sought. **Focus:** Medicine. **Qualif.:** Applicants must be young investigators who have their master's, doctorate, or M.D. degrees and are currently working in the nuclear medicine field.

**Funds Avail.:** $5,000 grants. The grants do not support salaries, major equipment purchases, institutional overhead or travel, but are designed to provide essential materials so that innovative ideas can be quickly tested. Recipients must submit a written summary of work accomplished at the end of the grant year to the ERF President. Continued support is contingent upon submitting the summary. Also, no recipient may receive more than one grant in any one year. **To Apply:** To receive an application and instructions, send a self-addressed stamped envelope to the Education and Research Foundation. **Deadline:** Five copies of the application form must be submitted by December 1 or May 1 of each year. **Contact:** Education and Research Foundation at the above address (see entry 5473).

### • 5477 • Society of Nuclear Medicine Student Fellowship Awards *(Doctorate, Graduate, Undergraduate/Fellowship)*

**Purpose:** To provide financial support for students to spend time assisting in clinical and basic research activities in Nuclear Medicine, with the expectation that this exposure will serve as an incentive to consider a career in some aspect of nuclear medicine. **Focus:** Medicine. **Qualif.:** Applicants must be either medical students or graduate students. Undergraduate students who are able to demonstrate competence in the physical and/or biological aspects of radioactivity are also eligible.

**Funds Avail.:** A maximum of $3,000 for at least three months of full-time research effort. Lesser durations of fellowships are considered at a stipend rate of $1,000 per month. The minimum fellowship period is two months. These awards are not renewable except under special circumstances. **To Apply:** Applications must include a letter addressed to the Education and Research Foundation requesting support, a detailed documentation of the proposed work (not to exceed five pages) that clearly delineates the student's role in the project, and a brief summary highlighting the proposed work. Applicants must also include letters of support from the nuclear medicine faculty advisor and at least one (preferably two) others, a preceptor form, and a curriculum vitae. **Deadline:** March 1. **Contact:** Education and Research Foundation at the above address (see entry 5473).

### • 5478 • Tetalman Award *(Postdoctorate/Award)*

**Purpose:** To recognize promising young physicians. **Focus:** Medicine. **Qualif.:** Applicants must be young investigators who are pursuing a career in nuclear medicine. They must be 36 years of age or younger as of July 1 of the year for which the application is submitted, or no more than seven years may have elapsed since obtaining certification in nuclear medicine or nuclear radiology or completing a Ph.D. program. **Criteria:** Selection is based on

---

## Society of Nuclear Medicine - Education and Research Foundation (continued)

research accomplishments, teaching, clinical service, administration, service to the Society, and a commitment to academic nuclear medicine.

**Funds Avail.:** $2,000-2,500. **To Apply:** Applicants must submit a curriculum vitae, a maximum of four letters of recommendation of which two must come from the applicant's institution, a maximum of three manuscripts or grant applications describing current research efforts, and a letter stating why applicant is seeking this award. **Deadline:** March 1. Recipients will be notified prior to the Society of Nuclear Medicine Annual meeting each June. **Contact:** President, Education and Research Foundation, at the above address (see entry 5473).

## • 5479 •
## Society for Pediatric Dermatology

c/o Seth J. Orlow, M.D., Ph.D
530 1st Ave., Ste. 7R
New York, NY 10016

*Ph:* (212)263-5070
*Fax:* (212)263-5819

### • 5480 • Society for Pediatric Dermatology Grant
*(Postgraduate/Grant)*

**Purpose:** To foster research in pediatric dermatology. **Focus:** Pediatric Skin Disease, Medicine, Dermatology. **Qualif.:** Applicants should have completed training in pediatrics or dermatology and be active in investigation in the field of pediatric dermatology. **Criteria:** Importance of the project and realistic assessment of its feasibility within the time frame selected.

**Funds Avail.:** Approximately $10,000-$15,000 per year per grant; one to two grants are given each year. **No. of Awards:** 1-2. **To Apply:** Application information may be obtained by writing to the address above. **Deadline:** April 15.

**Remarks:** The Society receives about 15 applications each year. **Contact:** Dr. Seth Orlow, M.D., Ph.D., at the above address (see entry 5479).

## • 5481 •
## Society of Physics Students

American Institute of Physics
1 Physics Ellipse
College Park, MD 20740-3843
*E-mail:* sps@aip.org
*URL:* http://www.aip.org

*Ph:* (301)209-3100
*Fax:* (301)209-0843

### • 5482 • Society of Physics Students Scholarships
*(Undergraduate/Scholarship)*

**Purpose:** To support a member of the Society of Physics Students in his/her final year of study. **Focus:** Physics. **Qualif.:** Applicants must be college juniors majoring in physics and be active members of the Society of Physics Students. **Criteria:** Applicants are judged on the basis of high scholastic performance, both in physics and overall studies; the potential for continued scholastic development in physics; and active participation in Society programs.

**Funds Avail.:** $1,000 each. Scholarships are payable in equal installments at the beginning of each semester or quarter if recipients are enrolled full-time in the final year of study leading to a baccalaureate degree. **No. of Awards:** 14. **To Apply:** Letters in support of a candidate's application from at least two full-time members must be sent directly to the Scholarship Committee as must official certified current transcripts from the college. The

formal application requires essays on career objectives and active participation in the Society. **Deadline:** January 31. Recipients are notified by April 30.

**Remarks:** Support for these scholarships comes from the American Institute of Physics, which administers them, and the Sigma Pi Sigma Trust Fund. Approximately 50 to 75 applications are made each year. **Contact:** Chapter Advisor, Society of Physics Students, at the college or university attended.

## • 5483 •
## Society of Plastics Engineers Foundation

c/o Gail R. Bristol, Development
  Director
14 Fairfield Dr.
Brookfield, CT 06804
*URL:* http://www.4spe.org

*Ph:* (203)740-5434
*Fax:* (203)775-8490

### • 5484 • Society of Plastics Engineers Foundation Scholarships *(Undergraduate/Scholarship)*

**Purpose:** To provide college scholarships to students who have shown a career interest in the plastics industry. **Focus:** Engineering. **Qualif.:** Applicants must be full-time students at either a four-year college or in a two-year technical program, and they must be graduates of public or private high schools. **Criteria:** Applicants must have demonstrated or expressed interest in the plastics industry, be majoring in or taking courses that would be beneficial to a career in the plastics industry, and be in good academic standing with their college. Financial need will be considered.

**Funds Avail.:** Scholarships range up to $4,000 annually at the discretion of the SPE Foundation Scholarship Committee. **To Apply:** Applicants must submit a completed application form, three recommendation forms including two from a teacher or school official and one from an employer or non-relative, a high school and/or institution transcript, and a one to two-page typed statement telling why they are applying for the scholarship, their qualifications, and their educational and career goals in the plastics industry. **Deadline:** To request an application is November 15; to submit one is December 15. **Contact:** Gail R. Bristol, Development Director at the above address (see entry 5483).

## • 5485 •
## Society of Professional Journalists - Indiana Chapter

16 S. Jackson
PO Box 77
Greencastle, IN 46135-0077

### • 5486 • Indiana Professional Chapter of SPJ Minority Scholarship *(Undergraduate/Scholarship)*

**Focus:** Journalism. **Qualif.:** Applicants must be undergraduate, minority, Indiana resident majoring in journalism. **Criteria:** Applicants must show high academic performance.

**Funds Avail.:** $2000 awarded annually. **No. of Awards:** 1.

## • 5487 •
## Society of Professional Journalists - Los Angeles Professional Chapter
c/o Linda Seebach
SPJ Scholarship Chair
Los Angeles Daily News
PO Box 4200
Woodland Hills, CA 91365-4200          *Ph:* (818)713-3645

### • 5488 • Ken Inouye Scholarship *(Graduate, Undergraduate/Scholarship)*

**Qualif.:** Applicants must be undergraduate junior, senior, or graduate minority students who live or study in Los Angeles, Ventura, or Orange counties, who intend to pursue a journalism career with an emphasis in news work. **Criteria:** The scholarship is awarded based on accomplishments, potential, and need.

**Funds Avail.:** $1,000. **Deadline:** February 15.

## • 5489 •
## Society of Professional Journalists - South Florida Chapter
c/o Sylvia Gurinsky
WPLG-TV
3100 Biscayne Blvd.
Miami, FL 33137          *Ph:* (305)826-0022

### • 5490 • Garth Reeves Jr. Memorial Scholarships *(Graduate, Undergraduate/Scholarship)*

**Purpose:** To assist undergraduate and graduate-level minority students majoring in journalism. **Focus:** Journalism. **Qualif.:** Applicants must be South Florida residents. **Criteria:** Applicants are chosen based on need, scholastic achievement, and extracurricular journalism activity.

**Funds Avail.:** Minimum grant $500; amount of each scholarship is determined by need. **To Apply:** Applications are available in January. **Deadline:** March 1. **Contact:** Sylvia Gurinsky at the above address (see entry 5489).

## • 5491 •
## The Society for the Psychological Study of Social Issues
PO Box 1248          *Ph:* (734)662-9130
Ann Arbor, MI 48106-1248          *Fax:* (734)662-5607
*E-mail:* spssi@spssi.org
*URL:* http://www.spssi.org

### • 5492 • Gordon Allport Intergroup Relations Prize *(Graduate, Postgraduate/Prize)*

**Purpose:** To recognize the best paper or article of the year in intergroup relations. **Focus:** Social Sciences. **Qualif.:** Applicants for the Allport prize should be researchers in the field of intergroup relations. Graduate students are especially encouraged to submit papers for this award. Members and non-members are eligible. **Criteria:** Originality of the contribution, whether theoretical or empirical, is given special weight.

**Funds Avail.:** The award is a prize of $1000. **No. of Awards:** One. **To Apply:** Entries can be either papers published during the current year or unpublished manuscripts. Applicants may contact the SPSSI Central Office for instructions. **Deadline:** December 31.

**Remarks:** The award is co-sponsored by the Gordon W. Allport Memorial Fund of Harvard University. **Contact:** SPSSI Central Office, Gordon Allport Prize, at the above address (see entry 5491).

### • 5493 • The Applied Social Issues Internship Program *(Graduate, Postdoctorate, Undergraduate/Internship)*

**Purpose:** To encourage intervention projects, non-partisan advocacy projects, applied research, and writing and implementing of public policy. **Qualif.:** Applicants must be college seniors, graduate students, or first-year postdoctorates in psychology, applied social science, and related disciplines.

**Funds Avail.:** Range from $1,500 to $2,500. **To Apply:** Applicants must submit two copies of the following: a 2-5 page proposal including budget; a short resume; a letter from a faculty sponsor/supervisor of the project, including a statement concerning protection for participants if relevant; and a letter from an organizational sponsor (waived if applicant is proposing to organize a group). **Deadline:** November 10. **Contact:** SPSSI Central Office, Attn: Applied Social Issues Internship program.

### • 5494 • The Clara Mayo Grant *(Graduate/Grant)*

**Purpose:** To support masters' theses or pre-dissertation research on aspects of sexism, racism, or prejudice, with preference given to students enrolled in a terminal master's program. **Focus:** Sexism, racism, prejudice, psychology, applied social science, and related disciplines. **Qualif.:** Applicants must have matriculated in graduate programs and seek support of their master's thesis or pre-dissertation research.

**Funds Avail.:** $1000. **No. of Awards:** 4. **To Apply:** Applicants should include 5 copies of a cover sheet stating title of thesis proposal, anem of investigator, address, phone, and if possible, fax and e-mail; an abstract of no more than 100 words summarizing the proposed research; project purposes.

### • 5495 • The Louise Kidder Early Career Award *(Postdoctorate/Award)*

**Purpose:** To recognize social issues researchers who have made substantial contributions to the field early in their careers, SPSSI Council has established this new award. **Qualif.:** Nominees should be investigators who have made substantial contributions to social issues research within five years of receiving a graduate degree and who have demonstrated the potential to continue such contributions. Nominees need not be current SPSSI members.

**Funds Avail.:** $500 and a plaque. **No. of Awards:** 1. **To Apply:** Applicants must send the following: a cover letter outlining the nominee's accomplishments to date and anticipated future contributions; the nominee's current curriculum vitae, and three letters of support. **Deadline:** May 1 **Contact:** SPSSI Central office, ATTN: Kidder Award Committee.

### • 5496 • Otto Klineberg Intercultural and International Relations Award *(Graduate, Postgraduate/Award)*

**Purpose:** To recognize the best paper or article of the year on intercultural or international relations. **Qualif.:** Candidates must be researchers in intercultural and international relations. Graduate students are especially encouraged to submit papers for this award. The competition is open to both members and non-members. **Criteria:** Originality of the contribution, whether theoretical or empirical, is given special weight.

**Funds Avail.:** $1000 award. **No. of Awards:** 1. **To Apply:** Entries can be either papers published during the current year or unpublished manuscripts on intercultural or international relations. Contact SPSSI Central Office for instructions on how to apply. **Deadline:** February 1. **Contact:** SPSSI Central Office, Klineberg Award Committee, at the above address (see entry 5491).

*The Society for the Psychological Study of Social Issues (continued)*

**• 5497 • Society for the Psychological Study of Social Issues Grants-In-Aid Program** *(Graduate, Postgraduate/Grant)*

**Qualif.:** Applicant must be a student or in graduate or post-graduate psychology as it relates to the social studies. Preference is given to students at the dissertation stage of their studies. Proposals for the Grant in the areas of sexism and racism are highly encouraged.

**Funds Avail.:** Up to 2,000. **No. of Awards:** 6-12. **To Apply:** Applicants must submit the following: cover sheet stating title of proposal, name of investigator, address, phone, and fax number; an abstract of 100 words or less summarizing the proposed research; project purposes, theoretical rationale, and specific procedures to be employed; relevance of research to SPSSI goals and Grants-in-Aid criteria; status of human subjects review process; resume of investigator; and specific amount requested including a budget. **Deadline:** Post marked by November 13 and April 1. **Contact:** SPSSI Central Office, ATTN: Grants-in-aid Committee.

**• 5498 • SPSSI Social Issues Dissertation Award** *(Doctorate/Award)*

**Focus:** Psychology, Social Science. **Qualif.:** Applicants must have had their doctoral dissertation in psychology or in a social science with a psychological subject matter accepted during the previous year. **Criteria:** Selection is based on scientific excellence and potential application to social problems.

**Funds Avail.:** First prize is $600; second prize is $400. **No. of Awards:** 2. **To Apply:** Contact SPSSI Central Office for application instructions. **Deadline:** Materials must be postmarked by April 1. **Contact:** SPSSI Central Office, Dissertation Award Committee.

**• 5499 •**

**Society for Range Management**
1839 York St.                           **Ph:** (303)355-7070
Denver, CO 80206                    **Fax:** (303)355-5059
*E-mail:* srmden@ix.netcom.com
*URL:* http://cnrit.tamu.edu/srm/

**• 5500 • Masonic-Range Science Scholarship** *(Undergraduate/Scholarship)*

**Focus:** Range science. **Qualif.:** Applicants must be high school seniors sponsored by members of the SRM, National Association of Conservation Districts or the Soil and Water Conservation Society. Applicants must plan to major in range science.

**Funds Avail.:** $1,400. **No. of Awards:** 1. **To Apply:** Write for further details. **Deadline:** January 15. **Contact:** Society for Range Management at the above address (see entry 5499).

**• 5501 •**

**The Society for the Scientific Study of Sexuality**
PO Box 208                              **Ph:** (319)895-8407
Mount Vernon, IA 52314            **Fax:** (319)895-6203
*URL:* http://www.ssc.wisc.edu/ssss/home.htm

**• 5502 • Student Research Grants for the Scientific Study of Sex** *(Doctorate, Graduate/Grant)*

**Purpose:** To support research in the area of human sexuality. **Focus:** Human Sexuality. **Qualif.:** Candidate may be of any nationality. Applicant must be enrolled in a degree-granting program. Grants may support work not yet begun towards a master's thesis or doctoral dissertation, or other research.

**Funds Avail.:** $750. **To Apply:** Write for application form and guidelines. Submit form with research proposal, budget, and letter from department chair. Applications will be subject to blind review. **Deadline:** February 1 and September 1. **Contact:** Ilsa Loffes, Ph.D., at the above address (see entry 5501).

**• 5503 •**

**Society for Technical Communication**
901 N. Stuart St., Ste. 904        **Ph:** (703)522-4114
Arlington, VA 22203-1854          **Fax:** (703)522-2075
*E-mail:* stc@stc-va.org
*URL:* http://www.stc-va.org

**• 5504 • Della A. Whittaker Scholarships** *(Doctorate, Graduate, Undergraduate/Scholarship)*

**Purpose:** To assist students who are pursuing established degree programs for careers in some area of technical communication. **Focus:** Technical Communications. **Qualif.:** Applicants must be full-time undergraduate students having upper-class standing in a two- or four-year degree program in technical communication or full-time graduate students working toward a master's or doctoral degree in technical communication. **Criteria:** Selection criteria is based upon academic record, potential for contributing to the profession of technical communication, and financial need.

**Funds Avail.:** $2,500. **No. of Awards:** 14. Seven to undergraduate and seven to graduate students. **Deadline:** February 15. Notification by April 15. **Contact:** Buffy McDonagh at the above address (see entry 5503)for more information and applications.

**• 5505 •**

**Society of Women Engineers**
120 Wall St., 11th Fl.               **Ph:** (212)509-9577
New York, NY 10005-3902        **Fax:** (212)509-0224
                                            **Free:** 800-666-4793
*E-mail:* 71764.743@compuserve.com
*URL:* http://swe.org

**• 5506 • Anne Maureen Whitney Barrow Memorial Scholarship** *(Undergraduate/Scholarship)*

**Purpose:** To attract entering freshmen women to the field of engineering or engineering technology. **Focus:** Engineering. **Qualif.:** Applicants must be U.S. citizens and women majoring in engineering at an accredited college or university who will be freshmen during the academic year following presentation of the grant.

**Funds Avail.:** Approximately $5,000. **To Apply:** Scholarship information and applications are sent to the deans of accredited engineering schools in March of each year. Applications are also available through SWE Headquarters March through May. Application requests must be accompanied by a self-addressed, stamped envelope. **Deadline:** May 15. Recipients are notified by September 15. **Contact:** Society of Women Engineers at the above address (see entry 5505).

### • 5507 • Digital Equipment Corporation Scholarship
*(Undergraduate/Scholarship)*

**Focus:** Engineering. **Qualif.:** Applicants must be women at the end of their freshman year majoring in electrical, mechanical, or computer engineering at a university in New York or New England. Applicants must be United States citizens or permanent residents and SWE student members.

**Funds Avail.:** $1,000. The scholarship is renewable for two consecutive years, contingent upon maintaining an appropriate grade point average. **No. of Awards:** 1. **To Apply:** Scholarship information and applications are available from Deans of accredited engineering schools or SWE Headquarters in New York October through January. Application requests to SWE Headquarters must be accompanied by a self-addressed, stamped envelope. Because of the large number of applications received, and limited volunteer and staff resources, only applicants who enclose a self-addressed, stamped envelope will be notified if not selected for a scholarship. **Deadline:** Completed applications, including all supportive materials, must be postmarked no later than February 1. Recipient will be notified by May 1. **Contact:** Society of Women Engineers at the above address (see entry 5505).

### • 5508 • General Electric Foundation Scholarships
*(Undergraduate/Scholarship)*

**Purpose:** To promote the field of engineering to women. **Focus:** Engineering. **Qualif.:** Applicants must be United States citizens and female students who will be incoming freshmen in a school, college, or university accredited by the Accreditation Board for Engineering and Technology.

**Funds Avail.:** Three $1,000 awards and one $500 award to attend the annual National Convention/Student Conference and/or to provide support to her local section. The scholarships are renewable for three years with continued academic achievement. **To Apply:** Scholarship information and applications are sent to the deans of accredited engineering schools in March of each year. Applications are also available through SWE Headquarters March through May. Applications must be sent with a self-addressed, stamped envelope. **Deadline:** May 15. Recipients are notified by September 15. **Contact:** Society of Women Engineers at the above address (see entry 5505).

### • 5509 • General Motors Foundation Scholarships for Graduates *(Undergraduate/Scholarship)*

**Purpose:** To promote women in the field of engineering. **Focus:** Engineering. **Qualif.:** Applicants must be female students who are first-year master level students. They must maintain a minimum cumulative GPA of 3.2 on a 4.0 scale, demonstrate leadership characteristics by holding a position of responsibility in a student organization and exhibit a career interest in the automotive industry and/or manufacturing environment. They must also be United States citizens or permanent residents. **Criteria:** Applicants are chosen based on academic performance.

**Funds Avail.:** One $1,000 award. **To Apply:** Scholarship information and applications are sent to the deans of accredited engineering schools in October of each year. Applications are available through SWE Headquarters October through January. Application requests must be accompanied by a self-addressed, stamped envelope. **Deadline:** February 1. Recipients are notified by May 1. **Contact:** Society of Women Engineers at the above address (see entry 5505).

### • 5510 • General Motors Foundation Scholarships for Undergraduates *(Undergraduate/Scholarship)*

**Purpose:** To promote women in the field of engineering. **Focus:** Engineering. **Qualif.:** Applicants must be female students entering their junior year at selected universities with a declared major in one of the following disciplines: mechanical, electrical, chemical, industrial, materials, automotive, or manufacturing engineering or engineering technology. They must have a minimum cumulative GPA of 3.2 on a 4.0 scale, demonstrate leadership characteristics by holding a position of responsibility in a student organization, and exhibit a career interest in the automotive industry and/or manufacturing environment. They must also be United States citizens or permanent residents. **Criteria:** Applicants are chosen based on academic performance.

**Funds Avail.:** Two $1,000 awards. It is renewable for the student's senior year. **To Apply:** Scholarship information and applications are sent to the deans of accredited engineering schools in October of each year (available through January). Applications are also available through SWE Headquarters during the same period. Application requests must be accompanied by a self-addressed, stamped envelope. **Deadline:** February 1. Recipients will be notified by May 1. **Contact:** Society of Women Engineers at the above address (see entry 5505).

### • 5511 • Lillian Moller Gilbreth Scholarship
*(Undergraduate/Scholarship)*

**Focus:** Engineering. **Qualif.:** Applicants must be junior or senior women engineering students of outstanding potential and achievement.

**Funds Avail.:** $5,000. **No. of Awards:** 1. **To Apply:** Scholarship information and applications are available from Deans of accredited engineering schools and SWE Headquarters in New York October through January. Application requests to SWE Headquarters must be accompanied by a self-addressed, stamped envelope. Because of the large number of applications received, and limited volunteer and staff resources, only applicants who enclose a self-addressed, stamped envelope will be notified if not selected for a scholarship. **Deadline:** Completed applications, including all supportive materials, must be postmarked no later than February 1. Recipient only will be notified by May 1.

**Remarks:** Dr. Gilbreth, in whose honor the scholarship was named, was well known for the many contributions that she made to the field of industrial engineering and management. **Contact:** Society of Women Engineers at the above address (see entry 5505).

### • 5512 • Hewlett-Packard Scholarships
*(Undergraduate/Scholarship)*

**Purpose:** To promote women in the field of engineering and computer science. **Focus:** Engineering, Computer Science. **Qualif.:** Applicants must be United States citizens and women in their junior or senior year in good standing who are majoring in electrical engineering or computer sciences at an accredited engineering school. Applicants should also be active supporters and contributors to SWE.

**Funds Avail.:** Seven $1,000 awards. **To Apply:** Scholarship information and applications are sent to the deans of accredited engineering schools in October of each year. Applications are also available through SWE Headquarters October through January. Application requests to must be accompanied by a self-addressed, stamped envelope. **Deadline:** February 1. Recipients are notified by May 1. **Contact:** Society of Women Engineers at the above address (see entry 5505).

### • 5513 • Admiral Grace Murray Hopper Scholarship
*(Undergraduate/Scholarship)*

**Purpose:** To attract entering freshman women to the field of engineering or computer science. **Focus:** Engineering, Computer Science. **Qualif.:** Applicants must be United States citizens and

*Society of Women Engineers (continued)*

women majoring in engineering or computer science at an accredited college or university who will be freshmen during the academic year following presentation of the grant.

**Funds Avail.:** Two $1,000 awards. **To Apply:** Scholarship information and applications are sent to the deans of accredited engineering schools in October and March of each year. Applications are available through SWE Headquarters. Application requests must be accompanied by a self-addressed, stamped envelope. **Deadline:** May 15. Recipients are notified by September 15. **Contact:** Society of Women Engineers at the above address (see entry 5505).

• 5514 • **Dorothy Lemke Howarth Scholarship**
*(Undergraduate/Scholarship)*

**Purpose:** To promote women in the field of engineering. **Focus:** Engineering. **Qualif.:** Applicants must be United States citizens and women in their sophomore year majoring in engineering at an accredited college or university.

**Funds Avail.:** Two $2,000 awards and one $1,000 awards. **To Apply:** Scholarship information and applications are sent to the deans of accredited engineering schools in October each year. Applications are also available through SWE Headquarters October through January. Application requests must be accompanied by a self-addressed, stamped envelope. **Deadline:** February 1. Recipients are notified by May 1. **Contact:** Society of Women Engineers at the above address (see entry 5505).

• 5515 • **MASWE Memorial Scholarships**
*(Undergraduate/Scholarship)*

**Focus:** Engineering. **Qualif.:** Applicants must be women majoring in engineering or computer science in a college or university with an ABET-accredited program or in a SWE-approved school, and who maintain a 3.5 GPA on a 4.0 scale. **Criteria:** Based on scholarship and financial need.

**Funds Avail.:** Two $2,000 awards. **To Apply:** Applications are available from October through January only. **Deadline:** February 1. Recipients are notified by May 1. **Contact:** Society of Women Engineers at the above address (see entry 5505).

• 5516 • **Microsoft Corporation Scholarships**
*(Graduate, Undergraduate/Scholarship)*

**Focus:** Computer Science, Computer Engineering. **Qualif.:** Applicants must be women entering their sophomore, junior, or senior year, or be in the first year of a master's program pursuing a degree in computer science or computer engineering and exhibit interest in the field of microcomputer software.

**Funds Avail.:** Ten $1,000 awards. **To Apply:** Applications are available October through January. Application requests must be accompanied by a self-addressed, stamped envelope. **Deadline:** February 1. Winners are notified by May 1. **Contact:** Society of Women Engineers at the above address (see entry 5505).

• 5517 • **Northrop Corporation Founders Scholarship**
*(Undergraduate/Scholarship)*

**Focus:** Engineering. **Qualif.:** Applicants must be sophomore women pursuing an engineering degree and SWE student members. United States citizens are preferred.

**Funds Avail.:** $1,000. **No. of Awards:** 1. **To Apply:** Applications are available from Deans of Engineering or SWE Headquarters in New York October through January. Application requests to SWE Headquarters must be accompanied by a self-addressed, stamped envelope. **Deadline:** Completed applications, including all supportive materials, must be postmarked no later than February 1. Recipient only will be notified by May 1. **Contact:** Society of Women Engineers at the above address (see entry 5505).

• 5518 • **Ivy Parker Memorial Scholarship**
*(Undergraduate/Scholarship)*

**Focus:** Engineering. **Qualif.:** Applicants must be women engineering students entering their junior or senior year who demonstrate financial need.

**Funds Avail.:** $2,000. If awarded to a junior student, the recipient may reapply for continued support the following year. **No. of Awards:** 1. **To Apply:** Scholarship information and applications are available from Deans of accredited engineering schools and SWE Headquarters in New York October through January each year. Requests to SWE Headquarters must be accompanied by a self-addressed, stamped envelope. Because of the large number of applications received, and limited volunteer and staff resources, only applicants who enclose a self-addressed, stamped envelope will be notified if not selected for a scholarship. **Deadline:** Completed applications, including all supportive materials, must be postmarked no later than February 1. Recipient will be notified by May 1. **Contact:** Society of Women Engineers at the above address (see entry 5505).

• 5519 • **Judith Resnik Memorial Scholarship**
*(Undergraduate/Scholarship)*

**Focus:** Engineering. **Qualif.:** Applicants must be rising women seniors majoring in space-related engineering fields who intend to pursue careers in the space industry. Applicants must also be SWE members.

**Funds Avail.:** $2,000. **No. of Awards:** 1. **To Apply:** Scholarship information and applications are available from Deans of accredited engineering schools and SWE Headquarters in New York October through January each year. Requests to SWE Headquarters must be accompanied by a self-addressed, stamped envelope. Because of the large number of applications received, and limited volunteer and staff resources, only applicants who enclose a self-addressed, stamped envelope will be notified if not selected for a scholarship. **Deadline:** Completed applications, including all supportive materials, must be postmarked no later than February 1. Recipient will be notified by May 1.

**Remarks:** The award was established in honor of SWE member Judith Resnik who was killed aboard the Challenger space shuttle.

• 5520 • **Olive Lynn Salembier Scholarship**
*(Graduate, Undergraduate/Scholarship)*

**Focus:** Engineering. **Qualif.:** Applicants must be women who have been out of the engineering job market a minimum of two years and seek to to obtain the credentials necessary to re-enter the job market as an engineer. Applicants may be any year undergraduate or graduate.

**Funds Avail.:** $2,000. **No. of Awards:** 1. **To Apply:** Applications are available from the Deans of accredited engineering schools or SWE Headquarters in New York March through May each year. Requests to SWE Headquarters must be accompanied by a self-addressed, stamped envelope. **Deadline:** Completed applications, including all supportive materials, must be postmarked no later than May 15. Recipient will be notified by September 15.

**Remarks:** This award was developed in 1978 in honor of a deceased past president. **Contact:** Society of Women Engineers at the above address (see entry 5505).

• 5521 • **Texaco Scholarships** *(Undergraduate/ Scholarship)*

**Purpose:** To promote women in the field of engineering. **Focus:** Engineering. **Qualif.:** Applicants must be SWE student members in their junior years majoring in chemical, civil, electrical, environmental, or petroleum engineering and ranked in the top 20 percent of their class. They must also be United States citizens or authorized to work in the United States. **Criteria:** Recipients are chosen based on academic performance.

**Funds Avail.:** Two $2,000 awards renewable with continued ranking in the top 20 percent of their class. A $500 travel grant is also provided for recipients to attend the annual National Convention/Student Conference. **To Apply:** Scholarship information and applications are sent to the deans of accredited engineering schools in October each year. Applications are also available through SWE Headquarters October through January. Application requests must be accompanied by a self-addressed, stamped envelope. **Deadline:** February 1. Recipients are notified by May 1. **Contact:** Society of Women Engineers at the above address (see entry 5505).

### • 5522 • TRW Scholarships (Undergraduate/Scholarship)

**Purpose:** To encourage freshmen women to major in engineering. **Focus:** Engineering. **Qualif.:** Applicants must be women students who will be incoming freshmen in an accredited school, college or university. **Criteria:** Scholarship winners are chosen by the Best National, Regional, and New Student Sections.

**Funds Avail.:** Awards total $2,500. **To Apply:** Applications are available from the Deans of accredited engineering schools or SWE Headquarters in New York March through May each year. Requests to SWE Headquarters must be accompanied by a self-addressed, stamped envelope. **Deadline:** Completed applications, including all supportive materials, must be postmarked no later than May 15. Recipients only will be notified by September 15.

**Remarks:** Scholarships are supported by the TRW Foundation. **Contact:** Society of Women Engineers at the above address (see entry 5505).

### • 5523 • Westinghouse Bertha Lamme Scholarships (Undergraduate/Scholarship)

**Purpose:** To attract entering freshmen women to the field of engineering. **Focus:** Engineering. **Qualif.:** Applicants must be United States citizens and women who are majoring in engineering at a school, college or university with an accredited engineering program and who will be freshmen during the academic year following presentation of the grant.

**Funds Avail.:** $1,000. **No. of Awards:** 3. **To Apply:** Scholarship information and applications are sent to the deans of accredited engineering schools in March of each year. Applications are also available through SWE Headquarters March through May. Application requests must be accompanied by a self-addressed, stamped envelope. **Deadline:** May 15. Recipients are notified by September 15.

**Remarks:** The Bertha Lamme Scholarships are supported by the Westinghouse Educational Foundation in memory of the first woman engineer employed by Westinghouse. **Contact:** Society of Women Engineers at the above address (see entry 5505).

### • 5524 •
## Sociologists for Women in Society
c/o Barbara Tomaskovic-Devey,
  Executive Officer
North Carolina University
Box 8107
Raleigh, NC 27695-8107          *Ph:* (919)515-4227

### • 5525 • Barbara Rosenblum Cancer Dissertation Award (Doctorate/Award)

**Purpose:** To encourage doctoral research in the social and behavioral sciences on women's experiences of breast cancer and cancer prevention. **Qualif.:** Applicants must be an SWS member.

**Funds Avail.:** $1,500 **Deadline:** February 1.

**Remarks:** Awarded for ongoing doctoral research and/or publication and presentation of results. **Contact:** Rachel Kahn-Hut, Sociology, SFSU, San Francisco, CA 94132.

### • 5526 •
## Solar Energy Society of Canada Inc.
116 Lisgar St., Ste. 702          *Ph:* (613)234-4151
Ottawa, ON, Canada K2P 0C2          *Fax:* (613)234-2988
*E-mail:* sesci@cyberus.ca
*URL:* http://solarenergysociety.ca/index.html

### • 5527 • J. Bolton Scholarships (Graduate/Scholarship)

**Purpose:** To promote and encourage the research and development of Canadian renewable energy and energy conservation technologies. **Focus:** Energy Science. **Qualif.:** Applicant must have a bachelor's degree from a recognized Canadian college or university. Applicant must be enrolled in or entering a full-time graduate program at a Canadian institution. Doctoral candidates are eligible for the scholarship, but preference will be given to master's degree candidates. Scholarship funds are paid directly to the institution.

**Funds Avail.:** $1,000 **To Apply:** Write for application form and guidelines. Submit application in triplicate to SESCI. **Deadline:** June 1. Successful applicants are notified in October. **Contact:** Executive Director at the above address (see entry 5526).

### • 5528 •
## Annie Sonnenblick Scholarship Fund, Inc.
c/o Republic National Bank of New
  York
452 5th Ave.
New York, NY 10018-2706          *Ph:* (212)930-6648

### • 5529 • Annie Sonnenblick Scholarship (Undergraduate/Scholarship)

**Focus:** General studies. **Qualif.:** Applicants must be dependent children of Republic National Bank employees with one or more years of service. **No. of Awards:** 15. **To Apply:** Write for further details. **Deadline:** December 1. **Contact:** Rose Perrotti, V.P.

### • 5530 •
## Sons of the American Revolution
1000 S. 4th St.
Louisville, KY 40203-3208          *Ph:* (502)589-1776
*URL:* http://www.sar.org/

### • 5531 • National Society of the Sons of the American Revolution George S. and Stella M. Knight Essay Contest (High School/Prize)

**Focus:** General studies. **Qualif.:** Applicants must be junior or senior high school students attending public, parochial or private schools. **Criteria:** Awards are granted based on merit of essay.

**Funds Avail.:** $3,500. **No. of Awards:** 3. **To Apply:** Applicants must submit an original essay written in English, not exceeding 500 words, excluding the title page and references. The topic, which varies from year to year, is available from the local SAR chapter.

---

Awards are arranged alphabetically below their administering organizations

## Sons of the American Revolution (continued)

Applicants may only enter the contest through the SAR chapter located in the state where they attend school. **Deadline:** Contest must be entered between October 1 and January 15. **Contact:** COL Charles S. Wingate, Contest Chairman.

---

## • 5532 •
### Sons of Italy Foundation

219 E St., NE      *Ph:* (202)547-5106
Washington, DC 20002      *Fax:* (202)546-8168

*The Sons of Italy Foundation is the grant-making arm of the Order Sons of Italy in America (OSIA).*

#### • 5533 • Sons of Italy Foundation National Leadership Grants *(Graduate, Undergraduate/Grant)*

**Focus:** General Studies. **Qualif.:** Applicants must be of Italian descent and enrolled as full-time students in an undergraduate or graduate program at an accredited university. **Criteria:** Applicants are chosen based on academic accomplishment and leadership potential.

**Funds Avail.:** 13 awards of between $2,000-5,000 each were awarded. **No. of Awards:** 10-15. **To Apply:** Candidates should send a completed application form with one copy of an official transcript. Transcripts should be stamped by the school or university and enclosed in separated sealed envelopes. High school students should also include their ACT or SAT scores; undergraduate students should include both high school and college transcripts (seniors should only include college transcripts). Graduate students should include both undergraduate and graduate college transcripts. In addition, applicants should include official results of all standardized tests taken in the last five years, an essay discussing the principal contribution of Italian-Americans in the United States, two letters of recommendation from administrators, instructors, and supervisors, and a non-refundable $10 processing fee. **Deadline:** March 15.

**Remarks:** In addition to grants given at the national level, hundreds of grants are given at the state and local levels.

---

## • 5534 •
### Sons of Norway Foundation

1455 W. Lake St.      *Ph:* (612)827-3611
Minneapolis, MN 55408      *Fax:* (612)827-0658
     *Free:* 800-945-8851

*URL:* http://www.sofn.com/

#### • 5535 • King Olav Norwegian-American Heritage Fund *(Graduate, Undergraduate/Grant, Scholarship)*

**Purpose:** To fund activities in which the American and Norwegian heritages are explored, studied and shared by qualified grant and scholarship recipients. **Focus:** American studies, Norwegian studies. **Qualif.:** Applicants must be at least 18 years of age; and, if American, have demonstrated a keen and sincere interest in the Norwegian heritage or, if Norwegian, have demonstrated an interest in American heritage. **Criteria:** Awards are granted based on academic standing, participation in school and community activities, work experience, educational and career goals, and personal and school references.

**Funds Avail.:** $250 - $3,000 per award. Renewable up to two time within a five-year period. **To Apply:** Applicants must submit an application form; an essay, setting forth in 500 words or less, the applicant's reasons for applying for a scholarship/grant, the course of study to be pursued, the length of the course, the name

of the institution which the applicant will attend and its tuition and costs, and the amount of financial assistance desired. Essays should also state how the planned course of study will benefit their community and be in accord with the goals and objectives of the Sons of Norway Foundation: to promote improved international relationships, provide people-to-people enrichment program, promote cultural exchange, promote and implement health sports and improved lifestyle concepts and promote humanitarian causes; and three letters of recommendation. **Deadline:** March of each year. **Contact:** Sons of Norway Foundation at the above address (see entry 5534).

---

## • 5536 •
### Sons of the Republic of Texas

1717 8th St.      *Ph:* (409)245-6644
Bay City, TX 77414      *Fax:* (409)245-6644
     *Free:* 800-624-5079

*E-mail:* srttexas@alphainternet.net
*URL:* http://www.tgn.net/~srttexas

#### • 5537 • Texas History Essay Contest *(High School/Award)*

**Purpose:** To encourage students to explore the pioneer spirit of Texans. **Focus:** General studies. **Qualif.:** Applicants must be high school graduating seniors. **Criteria:** Awards are granted based on depth of research, originality of thought and expression, and organization.

**Funds Avail.:** $1,000 - $3,000. **No. of Awards:** 3. **To Apply:** Write for further details. **Deadline:** February 1. **Contact:** Melinda Williams, Executive Secretary.

---

## • 5538 •
### Soroptimist Foundation of Canada

c/o Doreen Dodd
St. Paul's College
Westmount Road, N.
Waterloo, ON, Canada N2L 3G5

#### • 5539 • Canadian Soroptimist Grants for Women *(Graduate, Undergraduate/Grant)*

**Purpose:** To assist female students who are preparing for careers in human services. **Focus:** Community Services, Vocational Training. **Qualif.:** Applicants must be female and either Canadian citizens or permanent residents. They must be registered graduate students at an accredited university in Canada pursuing studies that will lead to a career in service to people and plan to spend at least two years in such a career in Canada. Several grants will be made annually to residents of Eastern and Western Canada regions.

**Funds Avail.:** $5,000. **No. of Awards:** 4. **To Apply:** Write for application form and guidelines. Submit form, academic transcripts, resume, and three letters of reference. **Deadline:** January 31. Successful candidates are notified by May 15. **Contact:** Marilyn Fenwick, at the above address (see entry 5538).

---

## • 5540 •
### Soroptimist International of the Americas
2 PennCenter Plz., Ste. 1000     *Ph:* (215)557-9300
Philadelphia, PA 19102-1883    *Fax:* (215)568-5200
                        *Free:* 800-942-4629

*E-mail:* siahq@omni.voicenet.com
*URL:* http://www.siahq.com/

#### • 5541 • Soroptimist Women's Opportunity Award
*(Professional Development/Award)*

**Purpose:** To assist mature women to broaden their career choices. **Focus:** General Studies. **Qualif.:** Applicant must be a resident of one of Soroptimist International's member countries: Argentina, Bolivia, Brazil, Canada, Chile, Costa Rica, El Salvador, Guatemala, Guam, Indonesia, Japan, Korea, Malaysia, Mexico, Nicaragua, Northern Marinas, Panama, Paraguay, Peru, the Philippines, the United States, or Venezuela. Candidate must be a mature woman who is entering or returning to the job market because of financial necessity, or who wishes to further her skills and training in order to improve her employment status. **Criteria:** Recipients are chosen on the basis of financial need, as well as the statement of clear career goals.

**Funds Avail.:** $3,000 is available. **No. of Awards:** 54 awards are offered. **To Apply:** Write for the address of the nearest Soroptimist chapter in home country. Then write to the local chapter for application guidelines. Applications must be submitted to the local authority. Applicant may send SASE to the headquarters address above. **Deadline:** Materials must be submitted between September 1 and December 15. Awardees are selected in April.

**Remarks:** An award of $10,000 is offered to a candidate chosen from the 54 regional recipients. **Contact:** Coordinator at the above address (see entry 5540).

## • 5542 •
### South Carolina Governor's Office - Division of Veteran's Affairs
1205 Pendleton St.
226 Edgar Brown Bldg.     *Ph:* (803)255-4317
Columbia, SC 29201     *Fax:* (803)255-4257

#### • 5543 • South Carolina Tuition Program
*(Undergraduate/Scholarship)*

**Purpose:** To provide free tuition to the children of certain war veterans in South Carolina state supported schools. **Focus:** General studies. **Qualif.:** Applicants must be children of war veterans who were residents of South Carolina at the time of enter into service and during service; who have resided in South Carolina for one year and, in the event he or she is disabled but still living, still resides in the state; who either died in action or from other causes while in the service or of disease or disability resulting from such service; who was a POW during such a war period; or who has been awarded the Congressional Medal of Honor. The veteran-parent must reside within the border of South Carolina if still living and permanently and totally disabled from either service-connected or nonservice-connected causes as rated by the Veteran's Administration. If the parent was a POW during a war period, he or she need not reside within the state but must have entered service from South Carolina. Eligibility terminates at the age of 26.

**Funds Avail.:** Full tuition to a South Carolina state-supported college, university or post-high school technical educational institution. Renewable scholarship is awarded annually. **To Apply:** Write for further details. **Contact:** Stanley E. Thornburg, Field Office Supervisor, at the above address (see entry 5542).

## • 5544 •
### South Carolina Press Association Foundation, Inc.
PO Box 11429     *Ph:* (803)750-9561
Columbia, SC 29211     *Fax:* (803)551-0903
*E-mail:* scpress@scpress.org
*URL:* http://www.scpress.org

#### • 5545 • South Carolina Press Association Foundation Scholarships *(Undergraduate/Scholarship)*

**Focus:** Journalism. **Qualif.:** Applicants must be students preparing for careers in the newspaper industry who will be entering their junior or senior year next fall in any four-year South Carolina college or university program. **Criteria:** Selection of scholarship winners is based on participation in newspaper activities in college, recommendations of faculty members, commitment to a newspaper career, grades, and financial need.

**Funds Avail.:** $1,000 for each of the two junior semesters and $1,000 for each of the two senior semesters. No work is required at the school in return for the scholarship funds. The recipient does agree to work in the newspaper field in the United States for two years, within five years of graduation; if not, the applicant agrees to pay back the scholarship to the Foundation. Scholarship winners may study at any four-year South Carolina college approved by the Foundation. **To Apply:** Applicants must complete an application form with a written description of: the newspaper work they are interested in, and why; the work they have done on scholastic publications, including their position, the type of publication, and the amount of time worked; any internships or part-time newspaper jobs; and any journalism or other awards won in high school, college, or elsewhere. They must also describe (or document) their financial need, if any. **Deadline:** March 31. **Contact:** For application forms contact William C. Rogers at the above address (see entry 5544).

## • 5546 •
### South Carolina Teacher Loan Program
Interstate Center, No. 210
PO Box 21487     *Ph:* (803)798-0916
Columbia, SC 29221     *Fax:* (803)772-9410

#### • 5547 • South Carolina Teachers Loan Program
*(Graduate, Undergraduate/Loan)*

**Focus:** Education. **Qualif.:** Entering freshmen must have been ranked in the top 40% of their high school class and have a SAT or ACT score equal to or greater than the South Carolina average for the year of graduation from high school. Enrolled undergraduates must have a cumulative grade point average of at least 2.75 on a 4.0 scale and have taken and passed the PRAXIS 1. Entering graduate students must have at least a 2.75 cumulative grade point average on a 4.0 scale. **Criteria:** Awards are granted based on academic achievement and financial need.

**Funds Avail.:** $2500 for freshmen and sophomores; $5000 for juniors, seniors and graduate students. Loans are canceled at the rate of 20% for each year a borrower teaches a critical subject or in a geographic area. Recipients teaching in both a critical subject and in a geographic area will receive a 33 1/3% rate of cancellation. **No. of Awards:** 1140. **To Apply:** Applicants should request an application form from their college financial aid office. **Deadline:** June 1. **Contact:** South Carolina Student Loan Corporation at the above address (see entry 5546).

# • 5548 •
## South Carolina Tuition Grants Commission

1310 Lady St., Ste. 811
PO Box 12159                           Ph: (803)734-1200
Columbia, SC 29211-2159                Fax: (803)734-1426
*E-mail:* eddie@scsn.net; earl@scsn.net
*URL:* http://www.icusc.org/iscgrant.htm

### • 5549 • South Carolina Tuition Grant Awards
*(Undergraduate/Grant)*

**Purpose:** To provide undergraduate grant assistance to eligible South Carolina residents attending on a full-time basis certain independent non-profit colleges located in the state. **Focus:** General Studies. **Qualif.:** Freshman level applicants must graduate in the upper three quarters of their high school class or score 900 or above on the Re-centered Scholastic Aptitude Test (SAT) or its equivalent on the ACT. Upperclassmen must complete a minimum of 24 semester hours each year. **Criteria:** Applicants with financial need who meet the academic qualifications and the deadline.

**Funds Avail.:** Maximum grants in ranged up to $3,420 based on participating colleges' budgets. No tuition grant may be applied toward room and board charges, summer school, or graduate work. **No. of Awards:** More than 14,0000. **To Apply:** Application for a South Carolina Tuition Grant is made by completing the Free Application for Federal Student Aid (FAFSA), which is available at high schools and colleges. **Deadline:** June 30. **Contact:** Regina Hailey, Financial Aid Counselor, at the above address (see entry 5548).

# • 5550 •
## South Dakota Board of Regents

207 E. Capitol Ave.                    Ph: (605)773-3455
Pierre, SD 57501-3159                  Fax: (605)773-5320
*E-mail:* info@bor.state.sd.us
*URL:* http://www.ris.sdbor.edu/

### • 5551 • Ardell Bjugstad Memorial Scholarships
*(Undergraduate/Scholarship)*

**Focus:** Agricultural Science. **Qualif.:** Applicants must be entering freshman students who are majoring in agricultural production, agribusiness, agricultural sciences, or natural resources. Eligible participants are South Dakota or North Dakota residents who are enrolled members of a federally recognized tribe whose reservations are located either in South or North Dakota. Students may attend any post secondary institution that offers programs in the majors specified.

**Funds Avail.:** $500 scholarship is awarded annually. **No. of Awards:** 1. **Contact:** South Dakota high school guidance counselors or South Dakota Public University Financial Aid Offices.

### • 5552 • Haines Memorial Scholarships
*(Undergraduate/Scholarship)*

**Focus:** Education. **Qualif.:** Applicants must be students of sophomore, junior, or senior standing who have a combination of financial need and evident promise for postsecondary work, and who are majoring in elementary or secondary education at one of the public institutions under the governance of the Board of Regents.

**Funds Avail.:** The amount of the award is set by the board and is non-renewable. **No. of Awards:** 1 or 2 annually. **To Apply:** Application forms are available through financial aid offices at public institutions of higher education offering teacher education programs. **Contact:** South Dakota Public University Financial Aid Offices.

### • 5553 • Annis Kaden-Fowler Scholarships
*(Undergraduate/Scholarship)*

**Focus:** Education—Elementary. **Qualif.:** Applicants must be entering freshman students who are majoring in elementary education at one of the public institutions under the governance of the South Dakota Board of Regents. They must also have a cumulative grade point average of 3.0 or better.

**Funds Avail.:** $1,000. **No. of Awards:** 1. **To Apply:** Application forms are available through high school guidance offices or through the Board of Regents. **Contact:** South Dakota High school guidance counselors or South Dakota Public University Financial Aid Offices.

### • 5554 • Marlin Scarborough Memorial Scholarship
*(Undergraduate/Scholarship)*

**Focus:** General Studies. **Qualif.:** Applicants must be junior undergraduate students who graduated from a South Dakota high school. They must have attained a college grade point average of at least 3.5 at a public institution governed by the Board of Regents, and be nominated by their university. **Criteria:** Nominees are evaluated on their leadership, academic, and community service qualities.

**Funds Avail.:** $1,500. **No. of Awards:** 1. **To Apply:** Application forms are available through financial aid offices at public institutions of higher education.

**Remarks:** There are six nominees; one from each South Dakota Public University. **Contact:** South Dakota Public University Financial Aid Offices.

### • 5555 • South Dakota Board of Regents National Guard Tuition Assistance *(Undergraduate/Other)*

**Focus:** General Studies. **Qualif.:** Applicants must be members of the South Dakota army national guard unit or air national guard unit throughout each semester or vocational program in which applicant has applied for benefits; have satisfactorily completed required initial active duty service; have satisfactorily performed duty upon return from initial active duty training, including a minimum ninety percent attendance on scheduled drill dates and at annual training with parent unit; maintained satisfactory academic progress; and provided proper notice to the institution at the time of registration for the term in which the benefits are sought. They must attend any state educational institution under the control and management of the board of regents. Candidates cannot be accepting benefits equal to or greater than the tuition cut, under act of Congress, by the United States; but state benefits shall be available to supplement any lesser benefits from federal sources.

**Funds Avail.:** 50 percent tuition reduction or reimbursement for no more than four academic years or one program of vo-tech study. **Contact:** Director of Financial Aid at the university applicant is attending.

### • 5556 • South Dakota Board of Regents Senior Citizens Tuition Assistance *(Undergraduate/Other)*

**Focus:** General Studies. **Qualif.:** Applicants must be persons 65 years of age or older and attend a South Dakota public university.

**Funds Avail.:** 75 percent reduction in the cost of resident tuition, provided the university is not over-enrolled. **Contact:** Financial aid director of the university being attended.

### • 5557 • South Dakota Board of Regents State Employee Tuition Assistance *(Undergraduate/Other)*

**Focus:** General Studies. **Qualif.:** Applicants must be residents and full-time employees of the state of South Dakota who have been continuously employed for a period of three years (disregarding leave without pay); have received a merit rating of competent or better in their most recent appraisal or be otherwise certified as competent by an immediate supervisor; be pursuing an undergraduate or graduate degree at any state educational institution under the control and management of the board of regents; and maintain a GPA of at least a 2.0 on a 4.0 scale. They must also not be entitled to other reduced tuition benefits by law.

**Funds Avail.:** Tuition for up to six credit hours each semester at one-half the regular tuition rate (plus full amount of any required fees), provided employees register on or after the first day of classes for the semester. Any courses for which employees register prior to the first day of classes require full tuition.

**Remarks:** The right of any employee of the state to participate in the reduced tuition program is limited to the space available, as determined by the instructor, in any course after all of the full-time or full tuition paying students have registered. **Contact:** Financial aid directors of the university being attended.

### • 5558 • South Dakota Board of Regents Veterans Tuition Exemption *(Undergraduate/Other)*

**Focus:** General Studies. **Qualif.:** Applicants must be residents of South Dakota who are veterans or who have performed active war service, such as nursing or assisting in the care of soldiers and sailors in any government hospital, field, or camp, as a member of the Red Cross or any other similar organization engaged in relief work. The qualifying periods for active duty military service must be at least one day between the dates of: April 6, 1917 to November 11, 1918; December 7, 1941 to December 31, 1946; and June 25, 1950 to May 7, 1975. The veteran must have been discharged under other than dishonorable conditions. Applicants must be attending a public institution under the control and management of the board of regents. Applicants must not be entitled to federal benefits (e.g. G.I. Bill exhausted).

**Funds Avail.:** Eligible students may attend undergraduate classes tuition-free one month in academic time for each month of qualified service for up to four years. The benefits must be used within 20 years from and after the date proclaimed for cessation of hostilities (May 7, 1975) or within six years from and after the date of discharge from the military service, whichever is later. **Contact:** Financial Aid Director at the institution applicant is attending.

### • 5559 • South Dakota Space Grant Consortium
South Dakota School of Mines and
  Technology
Rapid City, SD 57701-3995　　Ph: (605)394-3995
*E-mail:* sfarwell@silver.sdsmt.edu
*URL:* http://www.sdsmt.edu/space/space.html; http://
  www.tsgc.utexas.edu/tsgc

#### • 5560 • Graduate Student Fellowships *(Graduate/Fellowship)*

**Purpose:** To provide educational opportunities. **Focus:** Aerospace-related fields. **Qualif.:** Applicants must be graduate who are SDSGC members or affiliates.

#### • 5561 • Summer Faculty Fellowships *(Other/Fellowship)*

**Purpose:** To provide opportunities to study at the EROS Data Center. **Focus:** Aerospace-related. **Qualif.:** Applicants must be SDSGC members or affiliates.

#### • 5562 • Undergraduate Student Assistantships and Scholarships *(Undergraduate/Scholarship)*

**Focus:** Aerospace. **Qualif.:** Applicants must be undergraduate students attending a SDSGC member or affiliate member institution.

### • 5563 •
**Southern California Edison Company - The Howard P.Allen Scholarships for Edison International**
2244 Walnut Grove Ave., GO1, Quad
  1A　　　　　　　　　　　Ph: (626)302-3512
Rosemead, CA 91770　　　Free: 800-456-1044
*URL:* http://www.edisonx.com/

#### • 5564 • Robert A. Hine Memorial Scholarship *(Undergraduate/Scholarship)*

**Purpose:** To recognize and reward the achievement of an outstanding student from an underrepresented ethnic group. **Focus:** General Studies. **Qualif.:** Applicants must be high school seniors who are members of an underrepresented ethnic group, live in or attend school in an area served by Southern California Edison, and be a citizen or a permanent resident of the United States. Students must also plan to attend a four-year college or university in California as a full-time student and demonstrate academic achievement. **Criteria:** Candidates are ranked by SAT scores. The 100 highest scoring candidates are asked to complete an application and return it to an independent scholarship organization. A judging panel selects the winner based on educational performance, leadership skills, extracurricular activities, and potential to succeed.

**Funds Avail.:** $20,000 ($ 5,000 per year for 4 years.) **No. of Awards:** 1. **To Apply:** Candidates must take the Scholastic Aptitude Test (SAT) of the College Board Admissions Testing Program by the first Saturday in December of their senior year. Scores may be released by marking "No. 0043—Robert A. Hine Memorial Scholarship" on the registration form. Applications are sent to the top-scoring 100 students. **Deadline:** January 16.

**Remarks:** Robert A. Hine was the Manager of Equal Opportunity at Southern California Edison (SCE) for 19 years and helped the Edison Company achieve new levels in building a diverse work force. **Contact:** The Edison Scholarship Committee at the above address (see entry 5563).

#### • 5565 • Southern California Edison Company College Scholarships *(Undergraduate/Scholarship)*

**Purpose:** To offer (4) $20,000 scholarships for high school seniors who will attend a 4 year college or university in California and who show promise of becoming tomorrows leaders. **Focus:** General Studies **Qualif.:** Candidates must be high school seniors who live in, or attend school in, an area serviced by Southern California Edison. Students should also be U.S. citizens or permanent residents and plan to enter a 4 year college or university in California as full-time undergraduate students. Dependents of Edison International employees are not eligible. **Criteria:** Applicants are ranked by SAT scores. The highest scoring candidates in each of Edison's five regions are asked to submit applications. Ten finalists from this group are chosen; four winners then are selected by a panel of community leaders to receive awards.

**Funds Avail.:** $20,000 ($ 5,000 per year for 4 years). **No. of Awards:** 4. **To Apply:** Interested students must take the Scholastic Aptitude Test (SAT) of the College Board Admissions Testing program by the first Saturday in December of their senior year. SAT tests taken prior to March of the junior year are not accepted. Scores should be marked for release, "No. 0175—Edison College Scholarship," on the SAT registration form. **Deadline:** January 16.

## Southern California Edison Company - The Howard P.Allen Scholarships for Edison International (continued)

**Remarks:** Recipients 18 years or older may also be eligible to participate in the Edison Summer Employment Program. **Contact:** The Edison Scholarship Committee at the above address (see entry 5563).

### • 5566 • Southern California Edison Company Community College Achievement Awards *(Undergraduate/Scholarship)*

**Purpose:** To encourage under represented & disadvantaged students to become teachers. **Focus:** General Studies leading to teaching credentials. **Qualif.:** Applicants must be full-time community college students who live in, or attend a community college in, an area serviced by Southern California Edison. Students should also be U.S. citizens or permanent residents and plan to enter an eligible college as a full-time undergraduate student, with the purpose of attained a teaching credential. A minimum 2.5 GPA and sufficient transferable units to enter a four-year college or university as a junior are additional requirements, as well as begin ethnically under represented or economically or physically disadvantaged. Dependents of Edison International employees are not eligible. **Criteria:** Awardees are selected by a panel of community leaders. Selection is based on the candidate's career objectives, academic achievements in the subjects related to their major, and desire for a continued education. The awards are divided among Edison's five regions.

**Funds Avail.:** $6,000, $ 2,000 per year for 2 years toward a baccalaureate degree and one post-graduate year to year a single or multiple subject teaching credential . **No. of Awards:** 20. **To Apply:** Eligible Community colleges nominate one candidates each. Applications are available from eligible local community college financial aid offices. Financial aid officers must submit applications for nominees by March 1. **Deadline:** February 2.

**Remarks:** Recipients 18 years or older may also be eligible to participate in the Edison Summer Employment Program. **Contact:** The Edison Scholarship Committee, at the above address (see entry 5563).

### • 5567 • Southern California Edison Company Educational Grants *(Undergraduate/Grant)*

**Purpose:** To help qualified students attend an eligible California community college, business school, or trade school. **Qualif.:** Applicants must be high school seniors in good standing who live in, or attend school in, an area serviced by Southern California Edison. Students must have finished a four-year high school program within five years. Students should also have a minimum 2.5 GPA, be U.S. citizens or permanent residents, and plan to attend an eligible community college as a full-time student. Four-year college students and dependents of Edison International employees are not eligible. **Criteria:** A selection committee reviews the nominations and selects winners based on financial need, leadership and citizenship abilities, and desire for a continued education. Recipients are matched with Edison employees who have volunteered to be mentors. They will remain in contact with the students for two years.

**Funds Avail.:** $1000 ($ 500 available for two years). **No. of Awards:** 100. **To Apply:** Area high schools nominate one student each. For consideration, students must obtain and complete an application, which is available from their school scholarship counselor. **Deadline:** February 9. **Contact:** The Edison Scholarship Committee at the above address (see entry 5563).

### • 5568 • Southern California Edison Company Independent Colleges of Southern California Scholarships *(Undergraduate/Scholarship)*

**Purpose:** To recognize and reward the achievements of outstanding students from underrepresented ethnic groups, who are the 1st in their families to attend college. **Focus:** General studies **Qualif.:** Applicants must be members of an under represented minority group living in an area serviced by Southern California Edison. Students should also be U.S. citizens or permanent residents planning to enter college as full-time undergraduate students at an Independent Colleges of Southern California (ICSC) school, in one of its regular programs, and under its usual academic standards. Each applicant must demonstrate financial need, as verified by college administration, and academic achievement, and must be the first generation in their immediate family to attend college. Dependents of Edison International employees are not eligible. **Criteria:** Applicants are requested from high school scholarship counselor or the ICSC office. Their names are submitted to ICSC for selection of finalists. The finalists are interviewed by a panel of community leaders, who select two recipients based on educational performance, leadership skills, extracurricular activities, and potential to succeed.

**Funds Avail.:** $20,000 ($ 5000 per year for 4 years). **No. of Awards:** 2. **To Apply:** Interested students must obtain an application from the Financial Aid Office at their high school, or the ICSC office. **Deadline:** March 2. **Contact:** The Edison Scholarship Committee at the above address (see entry 5563).

### • 5569 •
## Spalding Trust
56 Carlyle Rd.
Cambridge CB4 3DH, England          Ph: 223 322054

### • 5570 • The Spalding Trust *(Other/Other)*

**Purpose:** To promote a better understanding between the cultures of the world by encouraging the study of religious principles on which they are based. **Contact:** Spaulding Trust at the above address (see entry 5569).

### • 5571 • Spalding Trust Postgraduate Scholarship/ Grant *(Postgraduate/Grant)*

**Purpose:** To promote a better understanding of the great cultures of the world by study of religious principles. **Qualif.:** Applicant must have a degree in Religious Studies. **Criteria:** Comparative interfaith projects.

**Funds Avail.:** Limited **To Apply:** Apply through secretary; address as listed research proposal requested. **Deadline:** Awards made throughout the year. **Contact:** Tessa Rodgers.

### • 5572 •
## Spanish Speaking Citizens' Foundation
1900 Fruitvale Ave., Ste. 1B          Ph: (510)261-7839
Oakland, CA 94601                     Fax: (510)261-2968

### • 5573 • Aztec Scholarship *(Undergraduate/ Scholarship)*

**Focus:** General studies. **Qualif.:** Applicants must be Oakland, California, residents who are graduating seniors. **Criteria:** Awards are made based on academic achievement and financial need.

**Funds Avail.:** $500 per award. **No. of Awards:** 3. **To Apply:** Applicants must submit a completed application, copy of parents' last income tax statement, and grade transcript. **Contact:** Aztec Scholarship Committee at the above address (see entry 5572).

---

• 5574 •
**Special Libraries Association - Scholarship Committee**
Membership Dept.
1700 18th St. NW
Washington, DC 20009
E-mail: sla1@capcon.net
URL: http://www.sla.org/

*Ph:* (202)234-4700
*Fax:* (202)265-9317

• 5575 • **Affirmative Action Scholarship Program**
*(Graduate/Scholarship)*

**Purpose:** To support individuals pursuing Master's degrees in library and information sciences. **Focus:** Information Sciences, Librarianship. **Qualif.:** Candidate must be enrolled, or about to enroll, as a graduate student in an accredited library or information science program in the United States or Canada. Preference is given to individuals interested in careers in special librarianship and to students in financial need. In addition to the requirements listed above, applicant for an Affirmative Action Scholarship must be a member of a minority group (African-American, Hispanic, Asian or Pacific Islander, American Indian or Alaskan Native).

**Funds Avail.:** $6,000. **No. of Awards:** 1. **To Apply:** Write to the manager for application guidelines. **Deadline:** October 31. **Contact:** Scholarship Committee at the above address (see entry 5574).

• 5576 • **Mary Adeline Connor Professional Development Scholarship Program** *(Postgraduate/Scholarship)*

**Purpose:** To support individuals pursuing a post-M.L.S. certificate or degree that is relevant to career needs and goals. **Focus:** General Studies. **Qualif.:** Candidate must be a member of the Special Libraries Association who has an M.L.S. degree and who has worked in special libraries at least five years. Applicant must be accepted into a certificate or degree program offered by an accredited college or university, or by a professional association or society. **Criteria:** Preference is given to study program proposals to be completed within 2 years from the date of the awarded.

**Funds Avail.:** Not to exceed $6,000. May include a travel stipend. **No. of Awards:** 1 or more. **To Apply:** Write to the manager for application guidelines. **Deadline:** October 31. Winners are notified in May. **Contact:** Scholarship Committee at the above address (see entry 5574).

• 5577 • **ISI Scholarship** *(Doctorate/Scholarship)*

**Qualif.:** Applicants must be beginning doctoral candidates accepted into a recognized program in library or information science in the United States or Canada. They should be members of the Special Library Association and have worked in a special library. Evidence of financial need and high academic achievement are required.

**Funds Avail.:** $1,000. **To Apply:** The application requires a detailed estimate of expenses and income. A statement of 500 to 1,000 words must discuss the candidate's experience in special libraries and the contributions he or she expects to make in special librarianship. Official transcripts of complete college scholastic records certified by the registrar of each college attended are also required. Additionally, references from three persons who are not relatives must be sent directly to the Association. **Deadline:** Application and all supporting material must be received at SLA by October 15 with the exception of references, which must be received by November 6. Recipients are announced in May.

**Remarks:** Persons planning careers in medical librarianship cannot be considered. **Contact:** The Special Libraries Association at the above address (see entry 5574).

• 5578 • **Plenum Scholarship** *(Postdoctorate/Scholarship)*

**Qualif.:** Candidates must complete all course work for the Ph.D. by the time the scholarship is received. They must be members of the Special Library Association and have worked in a special library. Evidence of financial need and high academic achievement are required.

**Funds Avail.:** $1,000. **To Apply:** The application requires a detailed estimate of expenses and income. A statement of 500 to 1,000 words must discuss the candidate's experience in special libraries and the contributions he or she expects to make in special librarianship. Official transcripts of complete college scholastic record certified by the registrar of each college attended are required. Additionally, references from three persons who are not relatives must be sent directly to the Association. **Deadline:** Application and all supporting material must be received at SLA by October 15 with the exception of references, which must be received by November 15. Recipients are announced in early June.

**Remarks:** The Plenum Scholarship is made possible by the Plenum Publishing Corporation. **Contact:** The Special Libraries Association at the above address (see entry 5574).

• 5579 • **SLA Scholarships** *(Graduate/Scholarship)*

**Qualif.:** Scholarships are awarded for graduate study leading to a master's degree at a recognized school of library or information science in the United States or Canada. Applicant must be a college graduate or college senior with a good academic record and a definite interest in and aptitude for special library work. Evidence of financial need is necessary. Preference is given to those applicants interested in pursuing a career in special librarianship and to members of the Special Library Association. Work experience in a special library is helpful.

**Funds Avail.:** A maximum of $6,000. **No. of Awards:** Up to six. **To Apply:** The application requires a detailed estimate of expenses, income, and plans for self-support during the year enrolled in library school. A statement of 500 to 1,000 words must discuss candidate's interest in special librarianship; reason for the interest; type of library of most interest and why; preference for cataloging, reference, administration or other; and future plans. Transcripts and provisional acceptance from a recognized library school or information science program must also accompany the application. References from three persons who are not relatives, which must be sent directly to the Association. **Deadline:** Application and all supporting material must be received at SLA by October 31. Recipients are announced in early June. **Contact:** Scholarship Committee at the above address (see entry 5574).

---

• 5580 •
**Specialty Equipment Market Association**
PO Box 4910
Diamond Bar, CA 91765-0910

*Ph:* (909)396-0289
*Fax:* (909)860-0184

• 5581 • **SEMA Scholarship** *(Graduate, Postgraduate, Undergraduate/Scholarship)*

**Purpose:** To further the education of students interested in careers in the specialty automotive aftermarket. **Focus:** Industry are Trade, Transportation. **Qualif.:** Any student currently enrolled in an accredited college or university and who plans a career in the specialty automotive aftermarket may apply. **Criteria:** Intention to enter the automotive field, GPA, rigor of curriculum, and recommendations.

---

## Specialty Equipment Market Association (continued)

**Funds Avail.:** $1,000 to $2,000 scholarships per year. **Deadline:** April 15.

**Remarks:** Approximately 100 applications are received. **Contact:** Harry Perdew, PH. DJ at the above address (see entry 5580).

---

### • 5582 •
### Specs Howard School of Broadcast Arts

19900 W. 9 Mile     *Ph:* (248)358-9000
Southfield, MI 48075     *Fax:* (248)746-9777
*URL:* http://www.specshoward.com

#### • 5583 • Specs Howard High School Scholarships
*(High School, Undergraduate/Scholarship)*

**Purpose:** To provide financial assistance to students interested in pursuing a career in radio and television broadcasting. **Focus:** Radio and Television Broadcasting. **Qualif.:** Applicants must be graduating high school seniors with a minimum grade point average of 2.0. **Criteria:** High school seniors must take the standard examination at Specs Howard School. The highest scorers are invited back as finalists to submit an essay and to be interviewed by a panel of professionals.

**Funds Avail.:** Three scholarships ranging from $1,500 to full tuition. **No. of Awards:** 3. **To Apply:** Applications are available through the high school guidance office or through the Specs Howard Admissions Department. **Deadline:** March 15. **Contact:** Nancy Shiner at the above address (see entry 5582).

#### • 5584 • Specs Howard School of Broadcast Arts Industry Scholarships *(Undergraduate/Scholarship)*

**Focus:** Electronics Technology, Radio and Television Broadcasting. **Qualif.:** Applicants must either be working in the fields for which Specs Howard provides training or have immediate family members working in these fields.

**Funds Avail.:** $500. **To Apply:** Applications are available through the admissions department at the Specs Howard School. **Deadline:** Rolling. **Contact:** Nancy Shiner at the above address (see entry 5582).

---

### • 5585 •
### Spencer Foundation

900 North Michigan Ave., Ste. 2800     *Ph:* (312)337-7000
Chicago, IL 60611     *Fax:* (312)337-0282

#### • 5586 • Spencer Foundation Dissertation Fellowships for Research Related to Education
*(Doctorate/Fellowship)*

**Purpose:** To support individuals whose dissertations show potential for bringing fresh and constructive perspectives to the history, theory, or practice of formal or informal education anywhere in the world. **Focus:** Education. **Qualif.:** Applicants must be candidates for the doctoral degree at a graduate school in the United States, however applicants need not be citizens of the United States. Applicant must fulfill all pre-dissertation requirements before the start of the fellowship. Fellowships are not intended to finance data collection or completion of doctoral course work, but rather to support the final analysis of the research topic and the writing of the dissertation.

**Funds Avail.:** $15,000. **No. of Awards:** 30. **To Apply:** Write to the Foundation for application materials. Application must be supported by current graduate transcripts, letters of reference, a brief personal statement, a dissertation abstract, and a narrative discussion of and work-plan for the dissertation. **Deadline:** Requests for required application forms must be received in or by October. Completed applications must be postmarked by November 7. **Contact:** Catherine A. Lacey, Program Officer, The Spencer Foundation, 900 N Michigan Avenue, Ste. 2800, Chicago, Illinois 60611-1542; (312)337-7000.

#### • 5587 • Spencer Foundation Small Grants
*(Postdoctorate/Grant)*

**Purpose:** To provide assistance to scholars pursuing exploratory, problem-finding, or pilot research, and to support modest research projects and the initial phases of larger investigations. **Focus:** Education. **Qualif.:** Candidate may be of any nationality. Applicant must have a Ph.D. in an academic discipline or in the field of education. Candidate must hold an appointment in a college, university, research facility, or cultural institution in the United States or abroad. Research project must relate directly to the field of education. Grant is made to the institution with which the investigator is affiliated.

**Funds Avail.:** $1,000-12,000. **No. of Awards:** Varies. **To Apply:** Write to the Small Grants Program administrator for application guidelines. **Deadline:** None.

**Remarks:** Larger grants for major research projects are also available from the Foundation. Write to the vice president for further information. The Foundation also sponsors a predoctoral dissertation fellowship administered by the Spencer Foundation, and a postdoctoral fellowship, administered by the National Academy of Education. **Contact:** Small Grants Program, The Spencer Foundation, at the above address (see entry 5585).

---

### • 5588 •
### SPIE - The International Society for Optical Engineering

PO Box 10     *Ph:* (360)676-3290
Bellingham, WA 98227-0010     *Fax:* (360)647-1445
*E-mail:* pascale@spie.org
*URL:* http://www.spie.org/

#### • 5589 • SPIE Educational Scholarships and Grants in Optical Engineering *(Graduate, Undergraduate/Scholarship)*

**Purpose:** To fund any activity in the field of optics. **Focus:** Optical and Science Engineering, Optics, Phonetics, Electro-optics, and Optoelectronics. **Qualif.:** Applicants must be undergraduate or graduate students in the field of optical or optoelectronics science and engineering. **Criteria:** Based upon long-range contribution possibilities to optics and optical science.

**Funds Avail.:** $1,000-$10,000. **No. of Awards:** 20-30. **To Apply:** Write for application. Two short (one page) letters of recommendation must be included with completed applications. **Deadline:** April 7. **Contact:** Pascale Barnett at the above address (see entry 5588).

• 5590 •
## Spinsters Ink
32 E. First St., 330
Duluth, MN 55802-2202

Ph: (218)727-3222
Fax: (218)727-3119
Free: 800-301-6860

E-mail: claire@spinsters-ink.com

• 5591 • **Young Feminist Scholarship Program** (High School, Undergraduate/Scholarship)

**Purpose:** To encourage and recognize young feminists interested in writing. **Qualif.:** Awarded to a student in her last year of high school who submits the best essay on feminism and what it means to her.

**Funds Avail.:** $1,000 for college plus publication of the essay and invitation to a writing retreat for women. **Deadline:** January 1. Winner is announced on March 8.

**Remarks:** Established in 1998 in honor of the 20th anniversary of Spinsters Ink.

• 5592 •
## Sport Fishing Institute Fund
1033 N. Fairfax St., Ste. 200
Alexandria, VA 22314

Ph: (703)519-9691

• 5593 • **Sport Fishery Research Grants and Fellowships** (Postgraduate, Professional Development/Fellowship, Grant)

**Purpose:** To support the training of fishery scientists; to augment presently limited biological research on sport fisheries and their environmental requirements; and to promote the development of all aspects of sport fisheries management practices. **Focus:** Fishery Sciences, Marine Biology. **Qualif.:** Applicant must be a U.S. citizen and a graduate student or practicing scientist. Awards are tenable at U.S. institutions. No direct applications from students will be considered; student applicants must be sponsored by a professor. Funds are paid to the awardee's university department or to the institution at which the research is being performed. Funds may not be used to defray any part of agency, institutional, organizational, or departmental overhead.

**Funds Avail.:** Varies. **To Apply:** Write for proposal guidelines and application form. Submit form with research proposal, names of supervisory professor and/or principal investigator, and a summary of principal investigator's qualifications. **Deadline:** March 1. Notification in April. **Contact:** Christine Altman, Grants Administrator, at the above address (see entry 5592).

• 5594 •
## Sports Illustrated For Kids
c/o Amy Lennard Goehner
Senior Editor
Time & Life Bldg.
New York, NY 10020

• 5595 • *Sports Illustrated* for Kids Internships (Undergraduate/Internship)

**Purpose:** To provide experience as fact-checkers. **Focus:** Journalism. **Qualif.:** Applicants must be college graduates interested in sports and sports journalism.

**Funds Avail.:** Internships are paid. **No. of Awards:** Available throughout the year. **To Apply:** Applicants must submit a resume and clips. **Contact:** Chief of Reporters.

• 5596 •
## Stanford University - School of Humanities and Sciences
Building One
Stanford, CA 94305-2070

Ph: (650)723-9785
Fax: (650)723-3235

E-mail: mcahill@leland.stanford.edu
URL: http://www.leland.stanford.edu/dept/humsci/office/humanities/mellon.html

• 5597 • **Andrew W. Mellon Postdoctoral Fellowships in the Humanities** (Postdoctorate/Fellowship)

**Purpose:** To provide the opportunity to undertake scholarly work at Stanford. **Focus:** Humanities. **Qualif.:** Applicant may be of any nationality, but must have received a doctorate in the humanities during the six years prior to the year of application, or expect to complete the Ph.D. degree before the start of the fellowship. Fellowships are tenable at Stanford University.

**Funds Avail.:** $40,900 plus health insurance. **To Apply:** Write to the Mellon Fellowship coordinator for application materials, available after July. **Deadline:** November 13. Notification in mid February. **Contact:** Mellon Postdoctoral Fellowship Coordinator, at the above address (see entry 5596).

• 5598 •
## Stanhome, Inc.
333 Western Ave.
Westfield, MA 01085

Ph: (413)562-3631
Fax: (413)568-2820

• 5599 • **Stanhome Scholarship** (Undergraduate/Scholarship)

**Focus:** General Studies. **Qualif.:** Candidates must be current year high school juniors, seniors, or graduates and children of full-time or regular part-time Associate of Stanhome or a participating affiliated company. **Criteria:** Selections are based on the results of the Scholastic Aptitude Test (or PSAT), the applicant's grades in school, prepared essays, class standing, and teachers' comments.

**Funds Avail.:** One $10,000 award, one $7,500 award, one $5,000 award and several $2,500 awards. **To Apply:** Submit application before November 1. **Deadline:** December 31. **Contact:** Karen Boisvert-Gallo at the above address (see entry 5598).

• **5600** •

**Star Bank, N.A.**
c/o Peggy Woods, Dir., Public
  Affairs
PO Box 1038
Mail Location 5165          **Ph:** (513)632-4610
Cincinnati, OH 45201      **Fax:** (513)632-5512
*E-mail:* customerservice@fuse.net
*URL:* http://www.starbank.com

• **5601** • **Star Bank, N.A. Scholarship**
*(Undergraduate/Scholarship)*

**Focus:** General studies. **Qualif.:** Applicants must be residents of the Cincinnati region.

**Funds Avail.:** Varies. **To Apply:** Write for further details. **Contact:** Cincinnati Scholarship Foundation at the above address (see entry 5600).

• **5602** •

**Star Publications**
PO Box 157          **Ph:** (708)755-6161
Chicago Heights, IL 60411   **Fax:** (708)755-0095

• **5603** • **Chicago Heights Star Publications Minority Internship** *(Undergraduate/Internship)*

**Purpose:** To assist in development of minority journalists. **Focus:** Journalism. **Qualif.:** The internship is open to minority students who have completed their junior year in college and have a major or minor concentration in print journalism. **Criteria:** Quality of published material and reasonably strong academic standing.

**Funds Avail.:** The paid internship includes supervised training and experience in a variety of reporting skills. The length of the internship is based on the needs of the college or university. **No. of Awards:** 2 in summer, and 1 at other seasons. **To Apply:** Write or call Dennis Shook, human resources director. **Deadline:** March 15 for summer. **Contact:** Star Publications at above address.

• **5604** •

**State Council of Higher Education for Virginia**
James Monroe Bldg.
101 N. 14th St.
Richmond, VA 23219     **Ph:** (804)786-1690
*URL:* http://www.schev.edu

• **5605** • **Undergraduate Student Financial Aid Program Grant** *(Undergraduate/Grant)*

**Qualif.:** Applicants must be minority undergraduate students enrolled for the first time in state-supported colleges or universities in Virginia. **Criteria:** Awards are made based on financial need.

**Funds Avail.:** $400 to the cost of full-time tuition and fees. **To Apply:** The applicant should contact the Financial Aid Office of the Virginia public college or university he/she plans on attending.

• **5606** • **Virginia Student Financial Assistance Award** *(Graduate, Undergraduate/Award)*

**Focus:** General studies. **Qualif.:** Applicants must be must be domiciliary residents of Virginia and be enrolled at least half-time in a university or college. **Criteria:** Awards are made based on financial need and academic record.

**Funds Avail.:** Up to full tuition, including required fees and books. **To Apply:** Applicant should contact the public college or university in Virginia he/she plans on attending.

• **5607** • **Lee-Jackson Foundation Award**
*(Undergraduate/Award)*

**Focus:** General Studies. **Qualif.:** Applicants must be high school juniors or seniors in a Virginia high school who plan on attending a Virginia public or private college. **Criteria:** Awards are given to winners of an essay contest.

**Funds Avail.:** $1,000 to each of the three best essays in eight regions of the state. Additional awards are made for those essays that are exceptional in nature. **To Apply:** Applicants should contact their high school guidance office for further information.

• **5608** • **Virginia Transfer Grant** *(Undergraduate/ Grant)*

**Focus:** General Studies. **Qualif.:** Applicants must be minority students enrolled in a traditionally white or any transfer student at a black four-year Virginia public college or university. Applicants must also qualify for first-time transfer student entry. **Criteria:** Grants are made based on minimum merit criteria.

**Funds Avail.:** Up to full tuition, including required fees. **To Apply:** Applicants must write for details. **Contact:** The Financial Aid Office at the four year public Virginia college of choice.

• **5609** • **Virginia Tuition Assistance Grant** *(Graduate, Undergraduate/Grant)*

**Focus:** General Studies. **Qualif.:** Applicants must be domiciliary residents of Virginia and attend accredited private, non-profit colleges or universities in Virginia.

**Funds Avail.:** Varies; average is $2,600. **To Apply:** Applicants must write for details. **Contact:** The Financial Aid Office at the participating Virginia private, non-profit college of choice.

• **5610** • **Virginia College Scholarship**
*(Undergraduate/Scholarship)*

**Focus:** General Studies. **Qualif.:** Applicants must be domiciliary residents of Virginia, and enrolled at least half-time at one of Virginia's public or private colleges and universities. **Criteria:** Scholarships are awarded based on financial need.

**Funds Avail.:** $400 to $5,000. **To Apply:** Applicants must write for details. **Contact:** The Financial Aid Office at the Virginia college of choice.

• **5611** • **Virginia Graduate and Undergraduate Assistance Award** *(Undergraduate/Scholarship)*

**Focus:** General Studies. **Qualif.:** Applicants must be full-time students attending Virginia public colleges or universities. **Criteria:** Awards are made based on academic record. **To Apply:** Applicants must write for more details.

**Remarks:** The program is funded from a combination of institutional endowment income and state appropriations. **Contact:** The Financial Aid Office at the Virginia public college of choice.

**• 5612 •**

**State Farm Mutual Automobile Insurance Co.**
c/o Dave Polzin, Asst. VP
1 State Farm Plz.                        *Ph:* (309)766-2161
Bloomington, IL 61710              *Fax:* (309)766-3700
*URL:* http://www.statefarm.com

**• 5613 • Exceptional Student Fellowship Award**
*(Undergraduate/Scholarship)*

**Purpose:** To identify, aid, and encourage high-potential college students majoring in business-related fields. **Focus:** Business administration, accounting, actuarial science, computer science, economics, finance, insurance, investments, management, marketing, mathematics, statistics. **Qualif.:** Applicants must have a minimum grade point average of 3.4 on a 4.0 scale, be majoring in a business-related field, currently be enrolled at a college or university as a junior or senior at time of application, and must be U.S. citizen. **Criteria:** Awards are made based on academic achievement, leadership abilities, character, potential business administrative capacity, and the nomination and recommendation of professors and advisors.

**Funds Avail.:** $150,000. **No. of Awards:** 50. **To Apply:** Applications and nomination forms are available from November 1 to February 1 from business school deans, business departments, directors of scholarships and grants, and directors of financial aid at colleges and universities. Forms are also available from the State Farm Companies Foundations. Write for more details. **Deadline:** February 15. **Contact:** Lynn Tammeus at the above address (see entry 5612).

**• 5614 •**

**The State Historical Society of Wisconsin**
816 State St.                             *Ph:* (608)264-6464
Madison, WI 53706-1488           *Fax:* (608)264-6486

**• 5615 • John C. Geilfuss Fellowship** *(Graduate, Postgraduate/Fellowship)*

**Purpose:** To support research in Wisconsin business and economic history. **Focus:** History. **Qualif.:** Applicants must be conducting research at the graduate level and beyond in Wisconsin business and economic history or for research in business and economic history using the collections of the society.

**Funds Avail.:** A stipend of $2,000 will be awarded. **No. of Awards:** 1. **To Apply:** Applicants should submit four copies of a current resume and four copies of a two-page, single-spaced letter of application. The letter should describe the applicant's background and current research project, including sources to be used, possible conclusions, and significance of work. **Deadline:** February 1.

**Remarks:** The Fellowship is offered in conjunction with the Wisconsin History Foundation. The State Historical Society of Wisconsin reserves the right not to award the fellowship in any given year. **Contact:** Dr. Michael Stevens, State Historian, State Historical Society of Wisconsin, at the above address (see entry 5614).

**• 5616 • Amy Louise Hunter Fellowship** *(Graduate, Postgraduate/Fellowship)*

**Purpose:** To support research on topics related to the history of women and public policy **Focus:** Women's Studies. **Qualif.:** Applicant should be at the graduate level or beyond doing research in the history of women and public policy with preference given to Wisconsin topics and/or for research using the collections of the State Historical Society of Wisconsin.

**Funds Avail.:** $2,500. **No. of Awards:** 1. **To Apply:** Applicants must submit four copies of a letter that is not more than two pages, describing their background and training in historical research and a description of their current research work. Descriptions should include the proposal, types of sources to be used, possible conclusions, and the applicant's conception of the work's significance. **Deadline:** May 1 of even-numbered years. **Contact:** State Historian at the above address (see entry 5614).

**• 5617 • Alice E. Smith Fellowship** *(Graduate/Fellowship)*

**Qualif.:** Women conducting research in American history are eligible to apply. **Criteria:** Preference is given to applicants involved in graduate research in the history of Wisconsin of the Middle West. Fellows are chosen by a committee of the State Historical Society of Wisconsin.

**Funds Avail.:** A grant of $2,000 is awarded. Recipients are generally not eligible for more than one award. **No. of Awards:** 1. **To Apply:** Applicants must submit four copies of a 2-page, single spaced letter describing their background or interest in historical research, and in some detail, descriptions of current research work, which should include a proposal, sources to be used, possible conclusions, and applicant's conception of the work's significance. The society does not require nor seek references, transcripts, or examples of previous work. **Deadline:** July 15. Notification is sent to all applicants in September. **Contact:** Michael E. Steven, State Historian, at the above address (see entry 5614).

**• 5618 •**

**State Medical Education Board of Georgia**
244 Washington St., SW, Rm. 574 J    *Ph:* (404)656-2226
Atlanta, GA 30334                              *Fax:* (404)651-5788

**• 5619 • "Country Doctor" Scholarship Program**
*(Graduate/Scholarship)*

**Purpose:** To promote the practice of medicine in rural Georgia. **Focus:** Medicine—Primary Care. **Qualif.:** Applicants must be residents of Georgia and students interested in practicing primary health care in rural areas (population 15,000 or less) in Georgia. **Criteria:** Selection is based on financial need of the applicant and a commitment to rural Georgia.

**Funds Avail.:** Recipients will receive up to $10,000 per year, not to exceed $40,000. **No. of Awards:** 25-30 annually. **To Apply:** Applicants must submit personal and parental financial statements. Six references (three professional) are required. An essay must also be submitted. Two interviews, one informal and one formal, are held. **Deadline:** May 15.

**Remarks:** The Board generally receives between 50 and 60 applications. **Contact:** Dr. Joe B. Lawley at the above address (see entry 5618).

**• 5620 • Georgia State Loan Repayment Program**
*(Postdoctorate/Loan)*

**Purpose:** To increase the number of physicians in underserved rural areas of Georgia by making loans to physicians who have recently completed their medical education. **Focus:** Medicine, Osteopathic Medicine. **Qualif.:** Primary care physicians with degrees in allopathic (M.D.) or osteopathic (D.O.) medicine who have completed or are in their final year of an approved graduate program in the United States may apply. They must have a license to practice allopathic or osteopathic medicine in the United States. At the time the loan is made, applicants must be licensed to practice in Georgia and have graduated from an accredited four-year medical school located in the United States. **Criteria:** Priority is given to applicants who are physicians specializing in and

## State Medical Education Board of Georgia (continued)

actively practicing obstetrics. Second-level preference is given, in the order listed, to those specializing in OB/GYN, family practice, general practice, general internal medicine, general pediatrics, general surgery, psychiatry, and other Board-approved specialties. Also considered are the ability, character, and qualifications of each applicant and the amount of their outstanding medical education loans.

**Funds Avail.:** Loans may be as high as $50,000 and may be renewable at a similar amount for two additional years. Loan recipients are required to sign a contract with the Board that affirms the recipient's commitment to practice medicine full-time in an approved physician underserved rural area. For each such year of practice, recipients will receive credit for the amount of loan which he or she received during any one year of practice. Recipients who breach the contract are liable for twice the total uncredited amount of all loans. **No. of Awards:** 8-10. **To Apply:** Application forms must be accompanied by a signed acknowledgment of conditions of the program, declaration of specialty qualifications, and a statement detailing the length of service commitment and date of availability. Applicants must attend two interviews, an informal interview with Board staff, and a formal interview with Board members. **Deadline:** May 15. **Contact:** Application forms may be obtained by writing the Executive Director of the Board at the above address (see entry 5618) beginning January.

---

• 5621 •
## Statler Foundation
107 Delaware Ave., Ste. 508      *Ph:* (716)852-1104
Buffalo, NY 14202                *Fax:* (716)852-3968

• 5622 • **Statler Foundation Scholarship** *(Graduate, Undergraduate/Scholarship)*

**Purpose:** To further education in the field of hospitality. **Qualif.:** Applicants must students of western New York who are enrolled in culinary arts or hotel/motel management programs on a full-time basis.

**Funds Avail.:** $500.00 annually. **To Apply:** Students must be co-sponsored by the hotel/motel association in their state of residence. Write for details. **Deadline:** April 15. **Contact:** Statler Foundation at the above address (see entry 5621).

---

• 5623 •
## Taylor Statten Memorial Fund
University of Toronto
315 Bloor St. West
Toronto, ON, Canada M5S 1A3      *Ph:* (416)978-7956

• 5624 • **Statten Fellowship** *(Graduate/Fellowship)*

**Purpose:** To assist graduate study in any professional field related to youth service. **Focus:** Youth Services, including Health Education, Ministry, Physical Education, Psychology, Social Work, Teaching. **Qualif.:** Applicant must be under 25 years old and a graduate of a Canadian university. Fellowships are tenable at Canadian universities **Criteria:** Preference is given to candidates whose career goals and experience indicate a serious commitment to working with young people.

**Funds Avail.:** $2,000. **No. of Awards:** One. **To Apply:** Write for application form and guidelines. Submit form with academic transcripts. Three letters of recommendation must be sent directly

from the referees to the Committee. **Deadline:** February 2. **Contact:** Admissions & Awards at the above address (see entry 5623).

---

• 5625 •
## Steedman Governing Committee
Washington University in St. Louis
School of Architecture
Box 1079                         *Ph:* (314)935-6293
St. Louis, MO 63130-4899         *Fax:* (314)935-8520

• 5626 • **Steedman Traveling Fellowship in Architecture** *(Professional Development/Fellowship)*

**Purpose:** To assist well qualified architectural graduate students to travel and study abroad. **Qualif.:** Applicants must hold a professional degree in architecture from an accredited school and have at least one year in the office of a practicing architect. There is no age limit, but professional degree must have been received up to eight years after receiving degree. **Criteria:** Based on a competition in which candidates are required to submit their presentation through drawings that solve a designated problem in architectural design.

**Funds Avail.:** One $20,000 fellowship is awarded biannually. **To Apply:** Information is available in August and can be requested by writing. **Deadline:** Early December (so that design is completed during late December/January).

**Remarks:** The Committee typically receives approximately 200 applications. **Contact:** Margaret T. Grant, Executive Assistant, at the above address (see entry 5625).

---

• 5627 •
## Emanuel Sternberger Educational Fund
PO Box 1735                      *Ph:* (910)275-6316
Greensboro, NC 27402             *Fax:* (910)379-0479

• 5628 • **Emanuel Sternberger Educational Loan** *(Graduate, Undergraduate/Loan)*

**Focus:** General Studies. **Qualif.:** Applicants must be legal residents of Triad counties North Carolina entering their junior or senior year of college, or be in graduate school. Students must be enrolled full-time and take hours sufficient to complete programs in the normal time frame. **Criteria:** Grades, economic situation, references, and credit rating.

**Funds Avail.:** Loans are limited to $1,000 for the first year and $2,000 for subsequent years for a maximum total of $5,000. **No. of Awards:** Varies. **To Apply:** Candidates must submit formal application (available upon request), transcript of college grades, and small photograph. A personal interview is also required with four references. **Deadline:** March 31. **Contact:** The Emanuel Sternberger Educational Fund at the above address (see entry 5627).

• 5629 •

**Margaret & Charles E. Stewart Scholarship Fund, Inc.**
c/o Phila Foundation
1234 Market St., Ste. 1900
Philadelphia, PA 19107-3794

• 5630 • **Margaret & Charles E. Stewart Grant** *(Other/Grant)*

**Purpose:** To aid in pastorate preparation in the Black church of any Protestant denomination. **Qualif.:** Applicants must be attending or planning to attend seminary school or a school of theology.

**Funds Avail.:** Up to four grants for $700 per semester each. **To Apply:** Applicants must submit letter of recommendation from their Pastor, an informal letter from the applicant, and proof of admission into a Seminary or School of Theology. **Contact:** Rev. E.K. Nichols, Jr., the Margaret & Charles E. Stewart Scholarship Fund, at the above address (see entry 5629).

• 5631 •

**Ann Bradshaw Stokes Foundation**
2514 Potomac Dr., Apt. G
Houston, TX 77057-4550                Ph: (214)528-1924

• 5632 • **Anne Bradshaw Stokes Foundation Scholarships** *(Undergraduate/Scholarship)*

**Purpose:** To advance and encourage the study of the drama and the performance of dramatic production. **Qualif.:** Applicants must be outstanding students in a drama department or departments of any Texas college or university.

**Funds Avail.:** Scholarships for tuition and college fees vary. Grants may be made for single disbursements or for disbursement over periods of time. A maximum of $4,000 is awarded. **To Apply:** Applications must be completed by Texas colleges and universities on behalf of qualified students, accompanied with a description of how the funds are to be spent and a summarization of student's previous theatre achievements. Applications are submitted to trustee with copies enclosed for scholarships and needs of the department. **Deadline:** none. **Contact:** William N. Stokes, Jr., Trustee, Ann Bradshaw Stokes Foundation, PO Box 878, Lake Dallas, TX 75065. Telephone: (817)497-2225, or at the above address (see entry 5631).

• 5633 •

**Lord Strathcona Trust Fund Alberta**
c/o Prarie Region Cadet
  Detachment, Edmonton
Canadian Forces Base Edmonton
PO Box 10500
Edmonton, AB, Canada T5J 4J5

• 5634 • **Lord Strathcona Trust Fund Scholarship Alberta** *(Undergraduate/Scholarship)*

**Qualif.:** Applicants must be students entering the field of education, physical education, or physical fitness. Candidates must also have served with a cadet program for a minimum of three years.

**Funds Avail.:** $900. **To Apply:** Applicants must submit a copy of latest school transcripts, list of cadet service and achievements, letter of acceptance from an education facility or application thereto, and letters of recommendation. **Deadline:** June 1. **Contact:** Secretary, Lord Strathcona Trust Fund Alberta, at the above address (see entry 5633).

• 5635 •

**Levi Strauss & Co.**
1155 Battery St.                     Ph: (415)544-7375
San Francisco, CA 94120              Fax: (415)544-3945
*URL:* http://www.levi.com

• 5636 • **Levi Strauss Foundation Scholarship Program** *(Undergraduate/Scholarship)*

**Purpose:** To recognize the outstanding achievements of employees' and retirees' children and encourage their higher education goals. **Focus:** General Studies. **Qualif.:** Applicants must be children or wards of Levi Strauss & Co. employees, either active, retired, or on long-term disability, who have a minimum of one year of employment with the company as of the application deadline date. Candidates must also be high school seniors or high school graduates who have maintained a minimum 2.5 GPA on a 4.0 scale and have enrolled or be planning to enroll as undergraduates in a full-time course of study at an accredited four-year college or university, two-year college, or vocational-technical school. **Criteria:** Recipients are selected based on academic records, potential to succeed, and participation in school and community activities, honors, work experience, a statement of education and career goals, and an appraisal by an adult professional. Students must also demonstrate financial need to be considered for this award.

**Funds Avail.:** Scholarships are awarded each year. Four awards of $2,000 each are given to students attending four-year colleges who demonstrate the greatest accomplishment and financial need, and awards of $1,500 each are given to other students attending four-year colleges. Awards of $750 each are given to students attending two-year colleges or vocational-technical schools. Payments are made in two installments, on August 15 and December 30, and mailed to each recipient's home address. Awards are renewable for up to three additional years or until the course of study is completed, whichever occurs first. Renewal is contingent upon the student maintaining a 2.0 GPA on a 4.0 scale and full-time enrollment. Students planning to transfer from a two-year college or a vocational-technical school to a four-year college must notify CSFA and request a renewal application. **Deadline:** February 15. Applicants are notified by mid April. **Contact:** Meg Franklin at the above address (see entry 5635).

• 5637 •

**Hattie M. Strong Foundation**
1620 Eye St., NW, Ste. 700          Ph: (202)331-1619
Washington, DC 20006                 Fax: (202)466-2894

• 5638 • **Hattie M. Strong College Loan Program** *(Graduate, Undergraduate/Loan)*

**Purpose:** To make student loans available to qualified applicants. **Focus:** General Studies. **Qualif.:** Eligibility is limited to American students who are within one year of a final degree from an accredited four-year college or graduate school. Applicants may be studying either in the United States or abroad and enrolled as full-time students. **Criteria:** Loans are made on a competitive basis, taking into consideration applicant's motivation, need, self-reliance, and scholastic record.

## Hattie M. Strong Foundation *(continued)*

**Funds Avail.:** The Foundation provides loans of up to a maximum of $3,000 per year. Loans are interest-free and do not require collateral. Repayment is based on monthly income after graduation. Arrangements are made with each individual in order to avoid undue hardship. **No. of Awards:** 250. **To Apply:** Applicants must apply in writing between Jan 1 and March 31 giving a brief personal history, name of the educational institution attended, subjects studied, date of completion, and amount of funds needed. The enclosure of a SASE will reduce the process response time. Applicants qualifying for consideration will receive formal application blanks. **Deadline:** Applications are accepted from January through March for the scholastic year beginning the following September. Recipients are notified during the summer. **Contact:** The Hattie M. Strong Foundation at the above address (see entry 5637).

### • 5639 •
**Student Loan Fund of Idaho, Inc.**
6905 Hwy. 95      *Ph:* (208)452-4058
PO Box 730      *Fax:* (208)452-5848
Fruitland, ID 83619      *Free:* 800-528-9447

#### • 5640 • Idaho Guaranteed Student Loans
*(Undergraduate/Loan)*

**Qualif.:** Applicants must meet federal needs test. Loans are open to bona fide students.

**Funds Avail.:** Unlimited funds from commercial lenders. **To Apply:** Financial aid offices at educational institutions provide applications and financial need requirements. **Contact:** College financial aid offices or Kris Hurd, Student Loan Fund of Idaho, Inc. at the above address (see entry 5639).

### • 5641 •
**Students for America Foundation**
PO Box 10469      *Ph:* (704)535-7321
Charlotte, NC 28212      *Fax:* (704)535-8507

#### • 5642 • Roger Milliken Scholarships
*(Undergraduate/Scholarship)*

**Focus:** Public policy/any. **Qualif.:** Applicants must hold membership in Students for America, attend an accredited college or university full-time, and have 2.5 or above GPA.

**Funds Avail.:** Between six and eight awards totaling $10,000. **Contact:** Paul A. McDonnough, Executive Director at the above address (see entry 5641).

### • 5643 •
**CDR William S. Stuhr Scholarship Fund**
1200 5th Ave.
New York, NY 10029

#### • 5644 • CDR William S. Stuhr Scholarship
*(Undergraduate/Scholarship)*

**Qualif.:** Candidates must be high school seniors who are dependents of active duty or retired career officers, or active duty or career enlisted persons of one of the five military Services: the

U.S. Army, U.S. Marine Corps, U.S. Coast Guard, U.S. Air Force, and Department of the Navy. The applicants' junior and senior year average grades in the first semester must place them in the top 10 percent of the class. Applicants must also demonstrate financial need, participation in extracurricular activities, leadership potential, and plan to attend a four-year accredited college (no geographic limitation).

**Funds Avail.:** One scholarship of $4,500, divided into $565 for eight semesters, for each of the five Services, is available for dependents of that particular service. Funds are paid directly to the institution for the student. One new four-year scholarship is awarded annually for each of the five Services. **No. of Awards:** 5 annually. **To Apply:** Recipients may attend colleges and universities throughout the United States. Applications may be obtained at the beginning of November at the above address. **Deadline:** The closing date for submission of applications is February 15. **Contact:** CDR William S. Stuhr Scholarship Fund, at the above address (see entry 5643).

### • 5645 •
**Walter C. Sumner Foundation**
c/o Montreal Trust Company
PO Box 2187      *Ph:* (902)420-2978
Halifax, NS, Canada B3J 3C5      *Fax:* (902)420-2978

#### • 5646 • Sumner Memorial Fellowships *(Graduate, Postgraduate/Fellowship)*

**Purpose:** To support doctoral study in the fields of chemistry, physics, and electronics. **Focus:** Chemistry, Electronics, Physics. **Qualif.:** Applicants must be Canadian citizens domiciled in Canada. They must also hold a degree from a Canadian university other than the one at which doctoral studies will be undertaken. Candidates who have only a bachelor's degree must also have at least two years of teaching or professional experience in the chosen field of study. Fellowships are tenable at Dalhousie University, McGill University, Queen's University (Kingston), University of British Columbia, University of Saskatchewan, and University of Toronto.

**Funds Avail.:** $4,000-5,000. **To Apply:** Applications must be made through the university where the fellowship is to be held. Write to the faculty of graduate studies at the university for application form and guidelines. Submit application to the university, which will forward it to the Foundation with a recommendation. **Deadline:** April 15. Fellowships are announced April 30. **Contact:** Susan Byrne Vice-President, at the above address (see entry 5645).

### • 5647 •
**Supporters of USS Lake Champlain - USS Lake Champlain Scholarship Fund**
PO Box 233      *Ph:* (518)834-7660
Keeseville, NY 12944      *Fax:* (518)834-7660

#### • 5648 • USS Lake Champlain Foundation Scholarships *(Undergraduate/Scholarship)*

**Focus:** General Studies. **Qualif.:** Applicants must be past and present crew members of the USS Lake Champlain (CG-57), dependent children and spouses of crew members currently serving aboard the USS Lake Champlain, or dependent children and spouses of crew members who previously served aboard the USS Lake Champlain and remain on active duty with, or retired from, the United States Navy, or who are deceased.

**Funds Avail.:** Awards are $250 or more for one year and are paid in two increments, the first upon the selection of the award and the second at the beginning of the second semester pending verification of satisfactory completion of the first semester and continued enrollment. **To Apply:** Applicants must provide verification of the sponsor's assignment aboard the USS Lake Champlain (CG-57), verification of the dependency status of the applicant with regard to the sponsor, evidence of acceptance in a program of study at a fully-accredited institution of higher education, a transcript of high school grades, a statement of financial need, verification of SAT and ACT scores, and two letters of recommendation, including one from a former teacher. **Deadline:** June 1. **Contact:** Supporters of USS Lake Champlain at the above address (see entry 5647).

• 5649 •
**Supreme Court of the United States**
Judicial Fellows Program
One 1st St., N.E., Room 5
Washington, DC 20543          *Ph:* (202)479-3415

• 5650 • **Judicial Fellowships** *(Professional Development/Fellowship)*

**Purpose:** To provide the opportunity for select individuals to work in the judicial branch of the U.S. Government. **Focus:** Law, Legal History, Political Science, Public Administration, U.S. Government, Behavioral Sciences, Business Administration. **Qualif.:** Applicants must have at least one postgraduate degree or more and at least two years of professional experience. Candidates should also be familiar with the judicial process and be able to contribute to the improvement of the judiciary during the fellowship period. Administrative ability may be desirable for some assignments. Fellows are assigned positions within the judicial system: one fellow serves at the Supreme Court in the Office of the Administrative Assistant to the Chief Justice; one fellow is assigned to the Federal Judicial Center; a third fellow may be selected and assigned to the Administrative Office of the United States Courts; and one fellow is assigned to the U.S. Sentencing Commission.

**Funds Avail.:** $71,049 maximum **No. of Awards:** 3-4. **To Apply:** Write for application guidelines. Submit a resume, an essay expressing interest in the Program, and copies of two publications or writing samples. Three letters of reference should be sent directly to the Program. Eight finalists will be chosen to interview in Washington, D.C. **Deadline:** November.

**Remarks:** Each year, one of the Judicial Fellows is designated the Justice Tom C. Clark Fellow. **Contact:** Vanessa Yarnall at the above address (see entry 5649).

• 5651 •
**James A. Swan Fund**
Pitt Rivers Museum
Oxford University
South Parks Rd.
Oxford OX1 3PP, England          *Ph:* 01865 270927

• 5652 • **James A. Swan Fund Grants** *(Graduate, Postgraduate/Grant)*

**Purpose:** To support field research about past and present African hunter-gatherer peoples. Awarded to archaeological and anthropoligal field reaserach with area of interest to the lat James A. Swan: the Later Stone Age perhistory of southern Africa and the study of the contemporary Bushman and Pygmy perople of Africa. **Focus: Criteria:** Applicants must have a sound, realistic research project. Application must consist of three copies of statement of

proposed research; an itemized budget; a full CV, including publications; and the names and addresses of two referees.

**Funds Avail.:** £500-2,000. **No. of Awards:** Varies. **Deadline:** March 1st of each year.

**Remarks:** The James A. Swan fund can only provide financial assistance to projects which are already funded from some other source; it cannot fund entire projects. **Contact:** Inquires about the fund may also be made to the Secretary of the Fund by e-mail at peter.mitchell@prm.ox.ac.uk.

• 5653 •
**The Swann Foundation Fund**
c/o Harry Katz, Curator, Swann
  Collection
Prints and Photographs Div.
Library of Congress          *Ph:* (202)707-5836
Washington, DC 20540          *Fax:* (202)707-1486
*E-mail:* Swann@loc.gov
*URL:* http://lcweb.loc.gov/rr/print/swann/swannhome.html

• 5654 • **Swann Foundation Fellowship** *(Graduate, Postgraduate/Fellowship)*

**Purpose:** To support dissertation and postgraduate research and writing on the history of caricature and cartoon. **Focus:** History of Caricature and Cartoon. **Qualif.:** Applicant must be a candidate for MA or Ph.D. degree at a U.S., Mexican, or Canadian university, or within 3 years of receiving a graduate degree. Candidate's dissertation topic must be directly concerned with caricature and/ or cartoon as visual art, but may relate to any period, culture, or geographical location. **Criteria:** Scholarly validity and degree of contributions to the Humanities.

**Funds Avail.:** Stipend of $15,000. **No. of Awards:** 1. **To Apply:** Write for application form and guidelines. Submit form, resume, a four- to five-page description of proposed project, and the names of three referees. **Deadline:** February 15. Notification is made in April. **Contact:** Harry L. Katz at the above address (see entry 5653).

• 5655 •
**Swedish Information Service**
1 Dag Hammarskjold Plaza, 45th Fl.
2nd Ave. & 48th St.          *Ph:* (212)583-2550
New York, NY 10017-2201          *Fax:* (212)752-4789
*E-mail:* swedinfo@ix.netcom.com
*URL:* http://www.swedeninfo.com

• 5656 • **Bicentennial Swedish-American Exchange Fund Travel Grants** *(Professional Development/Grant)*

**Purpose:** To provide financial support to Americans for intensive research trips to Sweden. **Focus:** Business, Cultural Studies, Education, Human Environment, Industry, Mass Media, Politics, Public Administration, Working Life. **Qualif.:** Applicant must be a citizen or permanent resident of the United States. Candidates who have visited Sweden many times before will be considered only under exceptional circumstances. There are no set educational prerequisites, but applicants should have the necessary experience and education for fulfilling their projects. Study visits involving interviews with Swedish experts and members of official bodies cannot be arranged during June, July, or August, due to the normal Swedish vacation period.

**Funds Avail.:** 10,000-20,000 Swedish kronor. **No. of Awards:** Approximately 10. **To Apply:** Send a stamped self-addressed envelope marked "Bicentennial Fund" for application form and

*Swedish Information Service (continued)*

guidelines. Submit form with detailed description of study project. Two letters of recommendation must be sent directly from the referees to the Swedish Information Service. **Deadline:** First Friday in February. Notification in May.

**Remarks:** Application must be made on current year form. **Contact:** Bicentennial Fund, at the above address (see entry 5655).

---

• 5657 •

## Lloyd D. Sweet Education Foundation

Box 548
c/o Mrs. Bonnie Webber
Chinook, MT 59523                    Ph: (406)357-3374

• 5658 • **Lloyd D. Sweet Education Scholarships**
*(All/Scholarship)*

**Purpose:** To further the education of graduates of Chinook High School so that they may become productive members of society and good citizens. **Focus:** General Studies. **Qualif.:** Applicants must be graduates of Chinook High School (Chinook, MT) and be enrolled in enough quarter or semester hours to be considered full-time students at school of choice (usually 12 hours of college-level courses). Applicants must additionally have maintained a grade average of at least a C.

**Funds Avail.:** Awards totaling approximately $100,000 are given for all levels of study and are paid to students upon the successful completion of a quarter or semester of post secondary work. **To Apply:** Formal applications must be submitted along with three letters of recommendation, a financial statement, and complete high school or college transcript. **Deadline:** March 1. **Contact:** Financial aid offices of Montana schools or the Counselor, Chinook High School, Chinook, Montana 59523.

---

• 5659 •

## Swiss Benevolent Society of Chicago

6440 N. Bosworth Ave.
Chicago, IL 60626                    Ph: (312)262-8336

• 5660 • **SBS Scholarships** *(Undergraduate/Scholarship)*

**Qualif.:** Applicants must be of proven Swiss descent and residents of Illinois or Southern Wisconsin. **Criteria:** Selection is based on GPA, ACT, SAT, and/or class rank and degree of Swiss ancestry.

**Funds Avail.:** $30,000 annually. Approximately 30 scholarships are awarded for tuition only. **No. of Awards:** Approximately 30 **To Apply:** Requests for applications must be between November 15 and February 1. **Deadline:** Applications are due March 1. **Contact:** Swiss Benevolent Society of Chicago at the above address (see entry 5659).

---

• 5661 •

## Swiss Benevolent Society of New York - Pellegrini Scholarship Fund

608 5th Ave., Ste. 309
New York, NY 10020-2303

• 5662 • **Pellegrini Scholarship Grants** *(Graduate, Undergraduate/Scholarship)*

**Focus:** General Studies. **Qualif.:** Applicants must be qualified students of Swiss descent residing in New York, New Jersey, Connecticut, Pennsylvania, or Delaware who are obtaining an education in any field of formal education above high school or for vocational training. They must also demonstrate financial need and be in good academic standing with an aptitude in their chosen field. To be considered of Swiss descent, one of the applicant's parents must be a Swiss national. **Criteria:** Scholarships are granted on the basis of need and merit, and will be limited to partial financial assistance. In addition to these awards, the Pellegrini Scholarship Fund may grant a special award for Outstanding Scholastic Achievement (OSA) which is based entirely upon merit. The OSA is given in recognition of outstanding achievement at the upper college or the graduate level. **No. of Awards:** Varies. **To Apply:** Applications are available before January 31. **Deadline:** March 3. **Contact:** Pellegrini Scholarship Fund at the above address (see entry 5661).

---

• 5663 •

## The Syracuse Newspapers

PO Box 4915                    Ph: (315)470-2131
Syracuse, NY 13221                    Fax: (315)470-6001

• 5664 • **Syracuse Newspapers Journalism Scholarship** *(Undergraduate/Scholarship)*

**Purpose:** To enable minority students attending Syracuse high schools to attend Syracuse University and study print journalism. **Focus:** Journalism. **Qualif.:** Students must attend a special journalism course taught by the Syracuse Newspapers staff prior to enrolling in Syracuse University as a journalism major. **Criteria:** A committee of professional journalists and college professors will select students based on potential and interest in making newspaper journalism a career.

**Funds Avail.:** The scholarship covers the entire cost of a four-year undergraduate degree program at Syracuse University, valued at approximately $80,000. **To Apply:** Students may check with their English teachers or contact The Syracuse Newspaper. **Contact:** Charles B. Hickey, Assistant Managing Editor, at the above address (see entry 5663).

---

• 5665 •

## Syracuse Pulp and Paper Foundation, Inc.

SUNY/College of Environmental
  Science and Forestry
1 Forestry Dr.
State University                    Ph: (315)470-6592
Syracuse, NY 13210-2778                    Fax: (315)470-6945

• 5666 • **Syracuse Pulp and Paper Foundation Scholarship** *(Undergraduate/Scholarship)*

**Purpose:** To educate students who can strengthen the paper industry. **Focus:** Paper Science and Engineering. **Qualif.:** Students must be accepted into the Paper Science and Engineering (PSE) program at the College of Environmental Science and Forestry at the State University of New York at Syracuse. They must also be United States citizens or have permanent resident status. Transfer students must have a minimum cumulative grade point average of 2.75 on a 4.0 scale. Foreign students are ineligible. **Criteria:** Grade point average is a consideration for renewing the scholarship. It must be at least 2.75 each semester, or be brought back up to 2.75 if it falls below, before receiving additional aid. Recipients must be approved by the SPPF Scholarship Committee. Selection is not based on financial need.

**Funds Avail.:** Up to full tuition each semester contingent upon grade point average. **To Apply:** Students accepted into the program receive application forms that they must complete and return to the Financial Aid Office within 30 days following acceptance. **Deadline:** Renewal applications must be completed each year by May 15. **Contact:** Syracuse Pulp and Paper Foundation at the above address (see entry 5665).

---

### • 5667 •
### Syracuse University Press
1600 Jamesville Ave.
Syracuse, NY 13244-5160          *Ph:* (315)443-5541

#### • 5668 • John Ben Snow Prize *(Professional Development/Prize)*

**Purpose:** To encourage the writing of books that will augment knowledge of New York state and its unique characteristics. **Focus:** New York **Qualif.:** Candidate may be of any nationality. Applicant must have written a nonfiction manuscript dealing with some aspect of New York state and based on personal experience or scholarly research. No substantial part of the manuscript may have been previously published, or be under consideration by another publisher. Prizes are not offered for poetry, books written specifically for children, edited collections, anthologies, or unrevised theses and dissertations. Winning manuscript will be published by the Press.

**Funds Avail.:** $1,500 advance against royalties **No. of Awards:** One **To Apply:** Send a letter of inquiry describing details of the manuscript and biographical/professional information. If the Press is interested, a copy of the manuscript will be requested for review. **Deadline:** December 31. Prize is announced in the spring. **Contact:** Andrea Garza Pflug at the above address (see entry 5667).

---

### • 5669 •
### Robert A. Taft Institute of Government
420 Lexington Ave., Ste. 2458          *Ph:* (212)682-1530
New York, NY 10170                     *Fax:* (212)953-1927

#### • 5670 • Fellowships for Taft Seminar for Teachers *(Professional Development/Fellowship)*

**Purpose:** To provide teachers with the opportunity to attend the Taft Seminars. **Focus:** Political Science, Social Studies, U.S. Government. **Qualif.:** Candidate may be of any nationality. Applicant must be an elementary, secondary school or community college instructor, a librarian, or an administrator who is actively involved in teaching social studies, government, politics, or related subjects. Fellowships are tenable at Taft Seminars held at various U.S. colleges and universities, which change annually.

**Funds Avail.:** Graduate credits, tuition, housing, meals, materials, and texts. **No. of Awards:** 1,200. **To Apply:** Write for a list of participating universities, available in January. Candidate should contact directly the university that he/she plans to attend for application guidelines. **Deadline:** Varies, according to sponsoring

institution. **Contact:** Maryann M. Feeney, President, at the above address (see entry 5669).

---

### • 5671 •
### Tandy Technology Scholars
TCU
PO Box 298-990                         *Ph:* (817)924-4087
Fort Worth, TX 76129                   *Fax:* (817)927-1942
*E-mail:* tandyscholar@tcu.edu
*URL:* http://www.tandy.com/text/scholars/

#### • 5672 • Tandy Technology Scholars *(Undergraduate/Scholarship)*

**Purpose:** To recognize academic performance and outstanding achievements by mathematics, science, and computer science students. **Qualif.:** Applicants must be high school seniors who are nominated by their high schools. **Criteria:** Selection is made based on grade point average (GPA) or class rank (based on work in grades 9, 10, and 11); mathematics, science, and computer science courses already taken and those in progress; standardized test scores (PSAT, SAT, or ACT), with emphasis on mathematics and science subscores; honors, special awards, and recognition; and service to school and community, especially in activities related to mathematics, science, or computer science.

**Funds Avail.:** $1,000 each is awarded to 100 student Tandy Prize recipients for use at the college or university of the student's choice. In addition, the top two percent of high school students from each participating high school receive certificates of recognition. **No. of Awards:** 100 students; 100 teachers. **To Apply:** Applicants can contact their high schools or the Tandy Technology Scholars Program. **Deadline:** Mid-October.

**Remarks:** This scholarship is endorsed by the National Association of Secondary School Principals and administered by Texas Christian University. Approximately 6,000 students apply each year. Schools may also nominate outstanding mathematic, science, or computer science teachers for academic excellence both in and out of the classroom. Each of 100 teacher Tandy Prize recipients receives a cash award of $2,500. **Contact:** Kaye Thornton, Director, Tandy Technology Scholars, at the above address (see entry 5671).

---

### • 5673 •
### Tartt Scholarship Fund
PO Box 1964
Marshall, TX 75671

#### • 5674 • Hope Pierce Tartt Scholarship *(Undergraduate/Scholarship)*

**Focus:** General studies. **Qualif.:** Applicants must be full-time students will at least a "C" grade point average or better on high school courses for first year students, and 2.0 or better grade point average for continuing students. **Criteria:** Awards are made based on financial need. Preference given to residents of Harrison, Gregg, Marion, Panola and Upshur counties in Texas.

**Funds Avail.:** $500 - $1,250 per award. Maximum $2,500 per year. Renewable. **To Apply:** Applicants must submit a completed application form and applicant's and/or parents' IRS 1040s. **Contact:** Hope Pierce Tartt Scholarship Fund at the above address (see entry 5673).

---

## • 5675 •
### Tau Beta Pi Association
PO Box 2697
Knoxville, TN 37901-2697
*E-mail:* tbp@tbp.org
*URL:* http://www.tbp.org

*Ph:* (423)546-4578
*Fax:* (423)546-4579

### • 5676 • Robert H. Nagel Scholarships
*(Undergraduate/Scholarship)*

**Purpose:** To advance the interest of the engineering profession. **Focus:** Engineering. **Qualif.:** Applicants must be full time undergraduate students planning to remain in or return to school for a senior year in engineering and also be Tau Beta Pi members. **Criteria:** Based on high scholarship. Strong faculty recommendations, definite extracurricular contributions, unusual promise of substantial achievement through a definite plan or purpose, and a program through which accomplishment will advance the interest of the engineering profession.

**Funds Avail.:** $2000 award in two increments (one in September and one in January). **To Apply:** An official application form and two letters of reference must be submitted. Write for official form and detailed guidelines. **Deadline:** January 15.

### • 5677 • Tau Beta Pi Fellowships for Graduate Study in Engineering *(Graduate/Fellowship)*

**Purpose:** Recipients of Fellowships are expected to advance their profession by service in the engineering field of research, practice, or teaching. **Focus:** Engineering, Public Policy. **Qualif.:** Only Tau Beta Pi members, including members already graduated, are eligible. **Criteria:** The Board considers the applicant's academic standing, plan for advanced study, contribution to campus or community activities, and references. Preference is given to those who show unusual promise of substantial achievement, particularly those who have some definite plan or purpose.

**Funds Avail.:** Each award is in the amount of $10,000 payable in ten monthly installments. The value of the fellowship may be considerably enhanced by remission of most or all of the tuition fees, which has been arranged by Fellows in the majority of cases. Up to 20 fellowships with stipends are granted. Fellows may receive up to $8,000 in other aid in excess of tuition and still receive a full stipend. **No. of Awards:** 20. **To Apply:** Candidates should give detailed information regarding extra-curricular activities, financial need, and plans for the future to assist the Board in its appraisal. Letters from at least two qualified members of the faculty must be filed in support of the application. These faculty members, who do not necessarily have to be members of the Association, should know the candidate and her qualifications. Generally they should be familiar with the line of advanced work along which the candidate wishes to concentrate. Complete application materials are available from the applicant's chapter president. They may also be obtained by sending a 4 x 9 self-addressed, stamped envelope to Tau Beta Pi Headquarters in Knoxville. **Deadline:** Applications and all supporting material must be filed by January 15.

**Remarks:** More than 220 applications are received each year. In addition to its own awards, Tau Beta Pi selects recipients for several sponsored fellowships. They are administered like other Tau Beta Pi fellowships. **Contact:** Mr. Stephen Pierre, Jr., Alabama Power Co., PO Box 2247, Mobile, AL 36652-2247.

## • 5678 •
### Teachers of English to Speakers of Other Languages
1600 Cameron St., Ste. 300
Alexandria, VA 22314-2751
*E-mail:* tesol@tesol.edu
*URL:* http://www.tesol.edu

*Ph:* (703)836-0774
*Fax:* (703)836-7864

### • 5679 • Ruth Crymes Fellowship *(Professional Development/Fellowship)*

**Purpose:** To support a teacher who wishes to attend the TESOL Academics and spend the summer renewing and expanding abilities. **Qualif.:** Applicants must be members of TESOL who are classroom teachers, trainers or supervisors. **Criteria:** Based on reasons for wishing to attend the TESOL Summer Institute, participation in and on behalf of TESOL or other similar professional organizations, and professional preparation, goals, and experience.

**Funds Avail.:** The amount varies according to estimated costs, and a waiver of Summer Institute tuition fees may be negotiated. Past awards have ranged up to $1,500. **To Apply:** Applicants must send five copies of a personal statement that includes biographical information, a description of reasons for attending the institute, and the ways in which attendance will enhance performance in the work place. Two sealed letters of recommendation written by two professionals should accompany the application. **Deadline:** October 22. **Contact:** TESOL at the above address (see entry 5678).

### • 5680 • Albert H. Marckwardt Travel Grants *(Graduate/Grant)*

**Purpose:** To assist graduate students traveling to a TESOL convention. **Focus:** ESL/EFL. **Qualif.:** Applicants must be TESOL members who are graduate students enrolled in a program preparing them to teach English to speakers of other languages and who are not eligible for USIA/IIE Travel Grants. **Criteria:** Based on scholarship, personal attributes, involvement in and commitment to ESL/EFL teaching and the profession, and financial need.

**Funds Avail.:** Approximately $500; convention registration fees are waived. **To Apply:** Applicants must submit a letter of application, a biographical summary, and a sealed letter of recommendation from a faculty member. **Deadline:** October 22. **Contact:** TESOL at the above address (see entry 5678).

## • 5681 •
### Technical Minority Scholarship Program
c/o Eleanor J. Krieger
800 Phillips Rd., Bldg. 205-99E
Webster, NY 14580

*Ph:* (716)422-7689
*Fax:* (716)422-7726

### • 5682 • Xerox Technical Minority Scholarship *(Graduate, Professional Development, Undergraduate/ Scholarship)*

**Focus:** General studies. **Qualif.:** Applicants must be minorities enrolled in technical degree programs as full-time students at bachelor or above level. **Criteria:** Awards are granted based on academic excellence. **To Apply:** Applicants must submit a completed application, resume, college verification and grade transcript. **Deadline:** September 15. **Contact:** Cheryl L. Williams at (716) 422-7689.

## • 5683 •
## Teen Magazine
6420 Wilshire Blvd.
Los Angeles, CA 90048-5515          *Ph:* (213)782-2950
*URL:* http://www.teenmag.com

### • 5684 •   Athletes of the Year (*Undergraduate/ Scholarship*)

**Purpose:** To encourage teenage females who are interested in pursuing postsecondary education and are outstanding athletes. **Focus:** General Studies. **Qualif.:** Applicants must be athletes between 12 and 18 years old who excel in sports, have strong leadership skills, and have satisfactory academic progress. Applicants must also still be in secondary school the school year prior to the announcement of the winner.

**Funds Avail.:** The winner receives a $5,000 scholarship that may be used at the school of her choice. **No. of Awards:** One. **To Apply:** Applications are available in the November through March issues of 'Teen Magazine. The winner is announced the following November. **Deadline:** March 15. **Contact:** Teen Magazine at the above address.

## • 5685 •
## TELACU Education Foundation
5400 E. Olympic Blvd., Ste. 300          *Ph:* (213)721-1655
Los Angeles, CA 90022          *Fax:* (213)724-3372

### • 5686 •   TELACU/Richard Alatorre Fellowship (*Graduate/Fellowship*)

**Focus:** Law or Public Administration. **Qualif.:** Applicants must live in the Los Angeles communities of Boyle Heights, City Terrace, El Sereno, Highland Park, Lincoln Heights, or Eagle Rock. They must be full-time students of law or public administration, and may attend any school of law or public administration in the United States. **Criteria:** Fellowship selections are based on academic records and community service, two letters of recommendation, financial need, a personal statement, and an interview.

**Funds Avail.:** $10,000. **No. of Awards:** 1. **To Apply:** Applications are available in February. **Deadline:** April 3. **Contact:** Michael E. Alvarado, Scholarship Program Director, TELACU Education Foundation, at the above address (see entry 5685).

### • 5687 •   Cesar Chavez Memorial Leadership Award (*Undergraduate/Scholarship*)

**Focus:** General Studies. **Qualif.:** Applicants must exhibit outstanding leadership abilities through the student's academic and community records, and must qualify for a TELACU Scholarship (see separate entry). **Criteria:** Scholarship selections are based on leadership exhibited in school and the community.

**Funds Avail.:** $2,500. **No. of Awards:** 1. **To Apply:** Applicants must apply for the TELACU Scholarship to be further considered for the Cesar Chavez Memorial Leadership Award. Applications for the TELACU Scholarships are available in February. **Deadline:** April 3. **Contact:** Michael E. Alvarado, Scholarships Program Director, TELACU Education Foundation, at the above address (see entry 5685).

### • 5688 •   Kodak Scholarship Award (*Undergraduate/ Scholarship*)

**Purpose:** To address the low number of underrepresented students seeking engineering degrees. **Focus:** Computer Science, Engineering. **Qualif.:** Applicants must qualify for a TELACU Scholarship (see separate entry). They must be majoring in engineering and must maintain a grade point average of at least 3.0. They must also be citizens or permanent resident aliens of the United States. **Criteria:** Scholarship selections are based on academic and community records, two letters of recommendation, financial need, a personal statement, and an interview.

**Funds Avail.:** Up to $10,000. **No. of Awards:** 1. **To Apply:** Applicants must apply for the TELACU Scholarship to be further considered for the Kodak award. Applications are available in February. **Deadline:** April 3. **Contact:** TELACU Education Foundation, at the above address (see entry 5685).

### • 5689 •   TELACU Arts Award (*Undergraduate/ Scholarship*)

**Purpose:** To encourage Latino students to study and major in the fine and performing arts. **Focus:** Fine Arts, Music, Dance, Drama or Theater. **Qualif.:** Applicants must qualify for a TELACU Scholarship (see separate entry). They must be majoring in either fine arts, music, dance, drama, or theater. **Criteria:** Scholarship selections are based on academic and community records, two letters of recommendation, financial need, a personal statement, and an audition.

**Funds Avail.:** $1,000. **No. of Awards:** 1. **To Apply:** Applicants must apply for the TELACU Scholarship to be further considered for the Arts Award. **Deadline:** April 3. **Contact:** TELACU Education Foundation, at the above address (see entry 5685).

### • 5690 •   TELACU Scholarships (*Undergraduate/ Scholarship*)

**Purpose:** To rebuild East Los Angeles by investing in its future leaders. **Focus:** General Studies. **Qualif.:** Applicants must be full-time undergraduate students with a minimum 2.5 grade point average. They must permanently reside in The City of Los Angeles, the cities of Bell Gardens, Commerce, Montebello, Monterey Park, Huntington Park, or Southgate. Students must be attending one of the following colleges or universities: East Los Angeles Community College; California State University, Fullerton, Los Angeles, Long Beach, or Northridge; Loyola Marymount University; Mount St. Mary's College; Harvey Mudd College; University of Southern California; Whittier College; Occidental College; Pepperdine University; University of California, Irvine or Los Angeles. **Criteria:** Scholarship selections are based on academic and community records, two letters of recommendation, financial need, a personal statement, and an interview.

**Funds Avail.:** $500 to $1,500. **To Apply:** Applications are available in February. **Deadline:** April 3. **Contact:** Michael E. Alvarado, Scholarship Program Director, TELACU Education Foundation, at the above address (see entry 5685).

## • 5691 •
## Teledyne Continental Motors
Scholarship Program
PO Box 3065
Oshkosh, WI 54903-3065          *Ph:* (920)426-6815
*E-mail:* education@eaa.org
*URL:* http://www.eaa.org

### • 5692 •   Herbert L. Cox Memorial Scholarship (*All/ Scholarship*)

**Focus:** Aviation. **Qualif.:** Applicants must be well-rounded individuals involved in school and community activities as well as in aviation.

**Funds Avail.:** Varies. **No. of Awards:** One. **To Apply:** Applicants must provide verification of financial need from the financial aid office of their college or university. To apply, contact the EAA Education Office at the above address. **Deadline:** Early May.

## Teledyne Continental Motors (continued)

### • 5693 • Teledyne Continental Aviation Excellence Scholarship *(All/Scholarship)*

**Qualif.:** Applicants must be well-rounded individuals involved in school and community activities as well as aviation, and must be majoring in aviation.

**Funds Avail.:** Varies. **No. of Awards:** One. **To Apply:** Contact the EAA Education Office at the above address. **Deadline:** Early May.

### • 5694 • Richard Lee Vernon Aviation Scholarship *(All/Scholarship)*

**Focus:** Aviation. **Qualif.:** Applicants must be able to provide verification of financial need and must be majoring in aviation. They must also be involved in school and community activities in addition to aviation.

**Funds Avail.:** Varies. **No. of Awards:** One. **To Apply:** To apply, contact the EAA Education Office at the above address. **Deadline:** Early May.

### • 5695 •
## Telluride Association
217 West Ave.
Ithaca, NY 14850      *Ph:* (607)273-5011
*URL:* http://www.telluride.cornell.edu

### • 5696 • Telluride Association Summer Program Scholarships *(High School/Scholarship)*

**Purpose:** To seek out young men and women who have the desire and potential ability to contribute something to society, and aid in their development by placing them in the company of associates of high purpose and intellect. **Focus:** Humanities, Social Science. **Qualif.:** Applications are sent only to high school juniors whose scores on the PSAT/NMSQT, reported to Telluride Association at their request, exceed a certain cut-off point, and to students recommended in writing by a teacher, counselor, principal, or other relevant authority.

**Funds Avail.:** Full scholarships to Telluride Association Summer Program. It is the policy of Telluride Association that any person awarded a scholarship to a TASP should not be prevented from accepting the award for financial reasons. Though students are normally expected to bear the cost of transportation to and from the program, the Association is willing to make special financial arrangements in difficult cases. Two six-week Telluride summer sessions are held at Cornell University, one six-week session is held at Kenyon, and one six-week session is held in conjunction with St. John's College. **No. of Awards:** 64. **To Apply:** Letters of recommendation, which must include the student's home address, should be sent to the Telluride Association Office, Ithaca, NY 14850 before December 15. Essays that permit applicants to demonstrate their intellectual curiosity, independence of thought, and concern for social and political issues are part of the application process. Geographic, economic, and sociological diversity among participants is sought. While need is not a factor, what a student has accomplished with available resources is taken into consideration. **Deadline:** Applications for summer programs must be filed by the beginning of February. Recipients are announced in late April. **Contact:** Administrative Director at the above address (see entry 5695).

### • 5697 •
## Tennessee Space Grant Consortium
Vanderbilt University
Box 1592, Station B.      *Ph:* (615)343-1148
Nashville, TN 37235      *Fax:* (615)343-6687
*E-mail:* eweiss@vuse.vanderbilt.edu
*URL:* http://www.vuse.vanderbilt.edu/~tnsg/homepage.html

### • 5698 • Tennessee Space Grant Consortium Fellowships and Scholarships *(Graduate, Undergraduate/Fellowship, Scholarship)*

**Purpose:** To promote space and science education. **Qualif.:** Qualifications are decided by member institutions. Applicants must be U.S. citizens.

**Funds Avail.:** Varies. **To Apply:** Contact the Tennessee Space Grant Office to receive contact information for individual member institutions. **Contact:** Ellie Weiss Rosenbloon at the above address (see entry 5697).

### • 5699 •
## Tennessee Student Assistance Corp.
Parkway Towers, Ste. 1950
404 James Robertson Pkwy.
Nashville, TN 37219-5097      *Ph:* (615)741-1346

### • 5700 • Tennessee Federal Parent Loan for Undergraduate Students *(Undergraduate/Loan)*

**Purpose:** The Federal PLUS program is a joint venture between lender, institutions, the federal government, and TSAC to enable parents of dependent students to obtain loans to assist in their children's postsecondary educational expenses. **Focus:** General Studies. **Qualif.:** Applicants must be the natural or adoptive parents and legal guardians of dependent students. They must also be U.S. citizens and residents of Tennessee whose dependent child is also a resident of Tennessee. Parents who are non-residents and whose child is attending an eligible Tennessee institution is also qualified. Parents and dependent children must not be in default on an educational loan or owe a refund on an educational grant.

**Funds Avail.:** Parents of dependent students may borrow the difference between the cost of attendance and the estimated financial assistance that the student will receive to attend college. PLUS loans will have a variable interest rate not to exceed 10 percent. In addition to variable interest rate, a guarantee fee of up to 5 percent is calculated on the principal amount. Parent borrowers must begin repaying their PLUS loans immediately. **To Apply:** There are sections to be completed by the parent borrower, the student, the institution, and the lender before the application can be submitted by the lender to TSAC for approval. The student for whom the parent is borrowing is the co-maker on the Federal PLUS loan. Not all lenders participate in the Federal PLUS program. Contact TSAC for a list of participating lenders. Federal PLUS loan applications may be obtained from the institution's financial aid office or from a participating lender. **Contact:** College financial aid offices, lenders, or TSAC at the above address (see entry 5699).

**• 5701 •**
**Tesla Memorial Society**
453 Martin Rd.                                    *Ph:* (716)822-0281
Lackawanna, NY 14218                    *Fax:* (716)822-0281

**• 5702 •   Tesla Award** *(Doctorate/Award)*

**Purpose:** To provide financial assistance to doctoral students in the field of electro-science. **Focus:** Science. **Qualif.:** Applicants must be doctoral students approved by their school and faculty advisors. **Criteria:** Nominees for the award are selected by the Society's Science Committee from recommendations by the Executive Committee.

**Funds Avail.:** Varies from year to year. **No. of Awards:** 1. **To Apply:** Students should submit a resume, area of study and certified work, and grades as approved by their faculty advisor. **Deadline:** September of every odd year. **Contact:** Dr. Richard E. Dollinger, Chairman, Science Committee, at the above address (see entry 5701).

**• 5703 •**
**Texas Electric Cooperatives Inc. - Ann Lane**
**Homemaker Scholarship**
PO Box 9589                                      *Ph:* (512)454-0311
Austin, TX 78766                              *Fax:* (512)454-3587
*E-mail:* engelke@texas-ec.org
*URL:* http://www.texas-ec.org/

**• 5704 •   Ann Lane Home Economics Scholarships**
*(Undergraduate/Scholarship)*

**Focus:** General Studies. **Qualif.:** Applicants must be graduating Texas high school seniors who are active members of a local chapter of the Texas Association, Future Homemakers of America, and who will enroll in an accredited Texas college, university, or trade school. **Criteria:** Based on FHA leadership activities, academics, involvement in school and community organizations, and financial need.

**Funds Avail.:** $1,000. **No. of Awards:** 1. **To Apply:** Write or call for application. Applicants must submit a 200-word essay on "The Role of the Homemaker." **Deadline:** March 1. **Contact:** Dennis Engelke at the above address (see entry 5703).

**• 5705 •**
**Texas Graphic Arts Education Foundation**
1770 Regal Row, No. 150                *Ph:* (214)630-8277
Dallas, TX 75235                            *Fax:* (214)637-1508
*E-mail:* director@thedallasshow.com
*URL:* http://www.thedallasshow.com

**• 5706 •   Texas Graphic Arts Education Foundation**
**Scholarships** *(Undergraduate/Scholarship)*

**Purpose:** To financially assist those working toward a degree in graphic arts management, education, or technology. **Focus:** Graphic Arts. **Qualif.:** Must be an undergraduate working toward a B.A. in the state of Texas. **Criteria:** Students in Texas secondary or post-secondary.

**Funds Avail.:** Annual grants up to $1,000. **No. of Awards:** Unlimited. **To Apply:** Apply by December 1 and April 1. Send recommendations, transcripts, and personal letter. **Contact:** Jim Weinstein, Director, at the above address (see entry 5705).

**• 5707 •**
**Texas Higher Education Coordinating Board**
PO Box 12788                                   *Ph:* (512)427-6340
Austin, TX 78711-2788                    *Fax:* (512)427-6420
                                                          *Free:* 800-242-3062
*URL:* http://www.thecb.state.tx.us/

**• 5708 •   College Access Loan** *(Graduate,*
*Undergraduate/Loan)*

**Purpose:** To help families who were excluded from the federal Guaranteed Student Loan Program due to the program changes made in 1986. It is a Hinson-Hazlewood College Student Loan administered by the Texas Higher Education Coordinating Board. **Focus:** General Studies.

**Funds Avail.:** The amount a student can receive cannot exceed the lesser of the following: the cost of education less financial aid; or $3,750 per semester to an aggregate maximum of $30,000. Promissory notes must be cosigned, and the credit worthiness of cosigners will be investigated. The repayment period begins six months after the student ceases to be enrolled at least half-time. The loans are not eligible for federal interest subsidy. The repayment period is no more than 10 years. **Contact:** For an application and more information, contact the financial aid office at the Texas institution attended.

**• 5709 •   Health Education Loan Program** *(Doctorate,*
*Graduate/Loan)*

**Focus:** Medicine. **Qualif.:** Applicants must be enrolled in a course of study leading to a doctor of medicine, osteopathy, dentistry, optometry, or, veterinary medicine; or in a course of study leading to a bachelor or master of science degree in pharmacy or to a graduate or equivalent degree in public health.

**Funds Avail.:** Eligible nonstudent borrowers in the field of medicine, osteopathy, dentistry, veterinary medicine, optometry, may borrow up to $20,000 in a 12-month period. Eligible student borrowers in the field of pharmacy or public health may borrow up to $12,500 in a 12-month period. Certain calculations are required to determine an applicant's eligibility and may limit the amount borrowed during an academic year. Interest is not subsidized by the federal government. **To Apply:** Once the applicant and the HEAL institution have completed respective parts of the application, the applicant is responsible for finding a lender in the HEAL program. For more information and applications, contact the director of financial aid at participating institutions. **Contact:** Financial aid directors at the above address (see entry 5707).

**• 5710 •   Hinson-Hazlewood College Student Loan**
**Program/Federal Stafford Student Loan Program**
*(Graduate, Undergraduate/Loan)*

**Focus:** General Studies. **Qualif.:** Students from all accredited public and independent nonprofit institutions of higher education in Texas are eligible to participate. Certain students from proprietary schools may also be eligible. Individual applicants must be eligible to pay Texas resident tuition rates, meet the academic requirements of the participating college or university, and demonstrate insufficient financial resources to pay for an education. Student eligibility requirements vary depending on the guarantor or source of insurance. Students must be enrolled on at least a half time basis.

**Funds Avail.:** The annual Maximum award varies from $2,625 to $8,500.

**Remarks:** The program was originally known as the Texas Opportunity Plan and is sometimes referred to as the TOP Loan. Under certain circumstances, persons currently in the military who have Guaranteed Student Loans through the Hinson-Hazlewood College Student Loan Program may have their loans repaid by the Secretary of Defense. **Contact:** Texas Higher Education Coordinating Board at the above address (see entry 5707).

## Texas Higher Education Coordinating Board *(continued)*

### • 5711 • Physician Student Loan Repayment Program *(Postdoctorate/Other)*

**Purpose:** To encourage qualified physicians to practice medicine in economically depressed and medically underserved areas of Texas or for certain state agencies. **Focus:** Medicine. **Qualif.:** Physicians in allopathic and osteopathic medicine are eligible. Depending on availability of federal funds, a physician practicing in certain high need areas of Texas in the fields of family practice, osteopathic general practice, and obstetrics/gynecology may qualify. Completion of a postgraduate program approved by the Accreditation Council on Graduate Medical Education or the American Osteopathic Association in an appropriate field of medicine and a license from the Texas State Board of Medical Examiners is required. Eligible physicians must have completed one year of private medical practice in an economically depressed or rural medically underserved area of Texas or one year of service with the Texas Department of Health, the Texas Department of Mental Health and Mental Retardation, the Texas Department of Corrections, or the Texas Youth Commission. Loans that have an existing service obligation or that are subject to another repayment program, and loans made to oneself from one's own insurance policy or pension plan or that of a spouse or relative are not eligible for repayment through the program. **Criteria:** Priority is given to renewal applicants, Texas residents, and physicians trained in psychiatry and in primary care specialties as defined by the Coordinating Board. Conditional approval of applicants can be given at the beginning of the final year of postgraduate training or at the beginning of the first year's service.

**Funds Avail.:** Loans for graduate or professional education repaid to one or more Texas lenders at a rate not to exceed $9,000 annually for up to five years. **Contact:** Applications and additional information about the program may be obtained through the financial aid office at Texas institutions offering graduate or professional programs in medicine or osteopathy or by writing the Texas Higher Education Coordinating Board.

### • 5712 • State Student Incentive Grant For Students at Private Non-Profit Institutions *(Graduate, Undergraduate/Grant)*

**Purpose:** To assist needy students attending private colleges. **Focus:** General Studies. **Qualif.:** Applicants must be Texas residents or National Merit Scholarship finalists enrolled at least half-time in an approved independent college or university, show financial need, not receive any form of athletic scholarship, and not be enrolled in a religion degree program. Applicants must also be registered for the draft and need assessment using a federally-approved system.

**Funds Avail.:** Grants vary up to $1,250. **No. of Awards:** Varies. **To Apply:** Applications may be obtained through the director of financial aid at any participating independent college or university in Texas.

**Remarks:** Grant can not be used for religious studies. **Contact:** Financial aid directors.

### • 5713 • State Student Incentive Grant For Students at Public Institutions *(Graduate, Undergraduate/Grant)*

**Purpose:** To help financially needy students attend public institutions of higher education in Texas. **Focus:** General Studies. **Qualif.:** Applicants must be enrolled in a participating institution at least half-time.

**Funds Avail.:** Maximum grant is $2,500, including both state and federal funds, per academic year. **To Apply:** Applications may be obtained through the director of financial aid at any participating public institution. **Deadline:** Varies by school.

### • 5714 • Texas Health Education Loan *(Graduate/Loan)*

**Purpose:** To provide non-federally guaranteed loans to medical and other health professions students whenever the overall state demand exceeds the levels authorized by the federal Health Educational Assistance Loan (HEAL) program. **Focus:** Medicine, Health Sciences. **Qualif.:** Applicants must be medical or other health professions students.

**Funds Avail.:** Eligible student borrowers in the field of medicine, osteopathy, dentistry, veterinary medicine or optometry may borrow up to $20,000 in a 12-month period. Eligible student borrowers in the field of pharmacy or public health, may borrow up to $12,500 in a 12-month period. These loans are not federally guaranteed. **To Apply:** Applications and information can be acquired through the financial aid offices at Texas colleges. **Contact:** Texas college financial aid offices at the above address (see entry 5707).

### • 5715 • Texas Public Educational Grant Program *(Undergraduate/Grant)*

**Purpose:** To provide grant aid to financially needy students. **Focus:** General Studies. **Qualif.:** Applicants must show financial need and be enrolled in a public institution participating in the TPEG program.

**Funds Avail.:** Varies. **No. of Awards:** Varies. **To Apply:** Applications may be obtained through the director of financial aid at any participating public institution.

### • 5716 • Texas State Scholarship Program for Ethnic Recruitment *(Undergraduate/Scholarship)*

**Purpose:** Encourage student integration. **Focus:** General Studies. **Qualif.:** Applicants must be resident minority students enrolling for the first time either as freshmen or new transfer students and whose ethnic group comprises less than 40 percent of the enrollment at a particular school. Entering freshmen must score at least 750 on the SAT or at least 17 on the ACT, and transfer students must have a GPA of at least 2.50. **Criteria:** A judgement of financial need by the financial aid director at the institution and recommendations of the admissions officer or minority affairs officer help determine eligibility for the scholarship.

**Funds Avail.:** One time awards range from $500 to $1,000. **To Apply:** Interested students should contact the financial aid director at the public senior college. **Deadline:** Varies by school. (Discontinued)

### • 5717 • Texas Tuition Equalization Grant *(Graduate, Undergraduate/Grant)*

**Purpose:** To help students attending independent colleges meet the higher tuition charges at their schools as compared to public institutions in the state of Texas. **Focus:** General Studies. **Qualif.:** Applicants must be Texas residents or National Merit Scholarship finalists enrolled at least half-time in an approved independent college or university, show financial need, not receive any form of athletic scholarship, and not be enrolled in a religion degree program. Both undergraduate and graduate students are eligible.

**Funds Avail.:** Grants vary according to financial need up to $2,834 for the academic year. **Contact:** Information and application forms may be obtained through the director of financial aid at any participating independent college or university in Texas.

• 5718 •

## Texas Space Grant Consotriuim

Fax: (512)471-3538

3925 W. Braker Ln., Ste. 200
Austin, TX 78759
URL: http://www.tsgc.utexas.edu/tsgc

Free: 800-248-8742

### • 5719 • TSGC Fellowship and Scholarship
(Undergraduate/Fellowship, Scholarship)

**Focus:** Aerospace related fields. **Qualif.:** Applicants must be students in a related field of study. NonTSGC institution students are eligible to apply. **To Apply:** Online eligibility verification form is available. Print copy also is available upon request. A completed form and a copy of the applicants social security card must be submitted.

**Remarks:** Over the last six years Texas Space Grant Consortium has awarded over $670,00 in scholarships and fellowships.

• 5720 •

## Texas Veterans Commission
Headquarters
PO Box 12277
Austin, TX 78711
E-mail: texas.veterans.commission@tvc.state.tx.us
URL: http://www.main.org/tvc

Ph: (512)463-5538
Fax: (512)475-2395

### • 5721 • Texas Veterans Educational Benefits
(Undergraduate/Grant)

**Focus:** General studies. **Qualif.:** Applicants must be officers, enlisted men or women, selectees or draftees of the Army, Army Reserve, Army National Guard, Air National Guard, Texas State Guard, Air Force, Air Force Reserve, Navy, Navy Reserve, Marine Corps, Marine Corps Reserve ,Coast Guard, or Coast Guard Reserve of the United States, who are assigned to duty in Texas, and their spouses and children. Out-of state Army National Guard or Air National Guard members attending training with Texas Army or Air National Guard units under National Guard Bureau regulations may not be exempted from nonresident tuition by virtue of that training status nor may out-of-state Army, Air Force, Navy, Marine Corps or Coast Guard Reserves training with units in Texas under similar regulations be exempted from nonresident tuition by virtue of that training status. **To Apply:** Write for further details. **Contact:** Texas Veterans Commission at the above address (see entry 5720).

• 5722 •

## Theatre Communications Group
355 Lexington Ave., 4th Fl.
New York, NY 10017
E-mail: grants@tcg.org
URL: http://www.tmn.com/Community/teg/home.html

Ph: (212)697-5230
Fax: (212)983-4847

### • 5723 • National Theatre Artist Residency Grants
(Professional Development/Grant)

**Purpose:** To foster continuing relationships between theatres and individual artists and to provide the expanded time necessary to develop artistic partnerships, as well as to enhance the level of artistic compensation. **Focus:** Theatre. **Qualif.:** The residencies may involve, but are not limited to playwrights, directors, designers, composers, choreographers, and/or actors working alone or in collaboration. Proposals may be initiated either by artists or not-for-profit professional theatre institutions, but they must be developed and submitted jointly to demonstrate the program's goals. The program is intended for experienced artists who have created a significant body of work and exemplary theatres that have the organizational capacity to provide substantial support services to artists.

**Funds Avail.:** Grants of $ 25,000, $ 50,000 and $100,000 are available. **To Apply:** Write to TCG for application after August 1. **Deadline:** Deadlines are TBA. Past deadlines have been in December. **Contact:** Emilya Cachapero, Director of Grant Programs, at the above address (see entry 5722).

### • 5724 • NEA/TCG Career Development Program for Designers (Other/Grant)

**Purpose:** To initiate opportunities for early-career set, costume, and lighting designers to work beside senior designers, develop their craft, and increase their knowledge of the field. **Focus:** Costume Design, Lighting Design, Scenic Design. **Qualif.:** Applicant must be a U.S. citizen or permanent resident with two to five years of professional stage design experience. Individuals enrolled in, or on leave from, training programs are not eligible to apply. Salaried staff designers at professional theaters are only eligible under exceptional circumstances. Candidates must be prepared to relocate during the program period. Recipients work with one or more senior stage designers, as well as directors and other artists. Recipients may participate in assisting, pre-production planning, and day-to-day artistic activities. Stipends cannot be used to underwrite designing jobs. **Criteria:** Selection is based on talent, skills, and professional experience; potential for future excellence; commitment to a career in the not-for-profit professional theatre; potential for the program to contribute to the applicant's artistic growth; and capacity to carry out the program.

**Funds Avail.:** Recipients receive a $17,500 stipend, in 7 monthly installments. **No. of Awards:** 6 awards are offered yearly. **To Apply:** Write to TCG for application form and guidelines. To apply, submit application form with a detailed resume and specified art from two productions. Art work may be in the form of slides, drawings, plots, and/or photographs. Finalists must present a full portfolio and three letters of recommendation at an interview with the selection panel. **Deadline:** Deadline are TBA. The program is offered every year. **Contact:** Emilya Cachapero, Director of Grant Programs, at the above address (see entry 5722).

### • 5725 • NEA/TCG Career Development Program for Directors (Other/Grant)

**Purpose:** To accelerate the artistic growth of early-career professional stage directors, developing their potential for future excellence. **Focus:** Stage Directing. **Qualif.:** Applicant must be a U.S. citizen who has directed at least three fully staged professional productions. Individuals enrolled in, or on leave from, university training programs and previous participants in National Endowment for the Arts (NEA) or TCG director fellowship programs are not eligible to apply. Salaried staff directors at professional theaters are only eligible under exceptional circumstances. Candidates must be prepared to relocate during the program period. Recipients may be assigned by TCG to work with one or more senior directors/mentors, or may elect to undertake an independent program designed to develop an aspect of his/her directing craft and expand his/her knowledge of the field. The program may include study, travel, research, observation, and other related activities. Stipends cannot be used to underwrite fees for directing jobs. **Criteria:** Selection is based on talent, skills, and professional experience; potential for future excellence; commitment to a career in the not-for-profit professional theatre; potential for the fellowship to contribute to the applicant's artistic growth; and capacity to carry out the program.

**Funds Avail.:** Recipients receive a $17,500 stipend, in 7 monthly installments of $2,500. **No. of Awards:** 6 **To Apply:** Write to TCG for application form and guidelines. To apply, submit application form with resume and a description of goals for the program. Semi-finalists must submit three letters of recommendation. Finalists will

*Theatre Communications Group (continued)*

be interviewed. **Deadline:** Deadlines are TBA. The program is offered every year. **Contact:** Emilya Cachapero, Director of Grant Programs, at the above address (see entry 5722).

• 5726 •
**Thomson Newspapers**
c/o Basil Marraffa, Senior Vice
  President
Human Resources and Industrial
  Relations
One Station Pl.                    *Ph:* (203)425-2520
Stamford, CT 06902                 *Fax:* (203)425-2516

• 5727 • **Thomson Fellowship** *(Graduate/Fellowship)*

**Focus:** Journalism. **Qualif.:** Applicants must be of racial or ethnic minorities and be recent college or university graduates who plan to pursue careers in journalism.

**Funds Avail.:** $20,000. Thomson Newspapers pays moving expenses. **No. of Awards:** 3. Two in the U.S. and one in Canada. **To Apply:** Applicants must submit a resume, short essay on the roles of newspapers in their communities, five clippings or other work samples, three references, and a letter explaining what they can contribute and hope to gain from the fellowship. **Deadline:** December 31.

**Remarks:** During the year, each Fellow is assigned to a daily newspaper as a member of its editorial staff. Training and evaluation are provided. Upon successful completion of the fellowship, Fellows are assisted in seeking a full-time position with a newspaper within the organization. Thomson Newspapers publishes daily and non-daily newspapers across Canada and the United States. The company is an equal opportunity employer. **Contact:** Basil Marraffa.

• 5728 •
**Thoroughbred Racing Associations**
420 Fair Hill Dr., No.1            *Ph:* (410)392-9200
Elkton, MD 21921-2573              *Fax:* (410)398-1366

• 5729 • **Fred Russell-Grantland RICE TRA Sports Writing** *(Undergraduate/Scholarship)*

**Purpose:** To further careers in sports writing. **Focus:** Any major offered through the College of Arts and Science. **Qualif.:** Applicants must be high school seniors and meet the entrance requirements of Vanderbilt University. **Criteria:** Winner is selected by a committee from the Thoroughbred Racing Associations and Vanderbilt University.

**Funds Avail.:** $10,000 per year. **No. of Awards:** 1. **To Apply:** Applicants must contact Coordinator of Special Scholarships, Undergraduate Admissions, Vanderbilt University, 2305 West End Ave., Nashville, Tennessee 37203-1727. Telephone: (615)322-2561. **Deadline:** January 1. **Contact:** Garrett Klein at the above address (see entry 5728).

• 5730 •
**Thurber House**
77 Jefferson Ave.                  *Ph:* (614)464-1032
Columbus, OH 43215                 *Fax:* (614)228-7445

• 5731 • **Thurber House Residencies** *(Professional Development/Award)*

**Purpose:** To support and encourage novelists, poets, playwrights, and journalists. Writer-in Residence will teach M.F.A candidates in a tutorial setting in the Creative Writing Program at the Ohio State University; participate in a writing residency with a community agency, and offer a public reading; Playwright-in-Residence will teach one playwriting class in the Department of Theatre at the Ohio State University and will be involved with a staged reading or full production of the playwright's own work; and Journalist-inResidence will teach a writing course in the Ohio State University journalism program and will conduct a writing workshop in a community setting. **Focus:** Drama, Fiction, Journalism, Nonfiction, Poetry. **Qualif.:** Writer candidates must have published at least one book with a major publisher and should possess some experience in teaching; Playwright candidates should have had at least one play published and/or produced by a significant company, and show some aptitude for teaching aspects of the position; Journalist candidates should have experience in reporting, feature writing, reviewing, or other ares of journalism as well as significan publications teaching or writing coaching experience helpful.

**Funds Avail.:** Writer: $6,000 stipend; Playwright: $6000 stipend; Journalist: $6000 stipend. All residencies include room accomidations which include a furnished one-bedroom-lus-studio apartment in the third floor of the restored Thurber House. **No. of Awards:** 3-4 per year. **To Apply:** Send a letter of interest and curriculum vitae. **Deadline:** January 1. Awards are announced by March 15. **Contact:** Michael J. Rosen, Literary Director at the above address (see entry 5730). at the above address.

• 5732 •
**Rosalie Tiles Nonsectarian Charity Fund**
c/o Mercantile Bank of St. Louis,
  N.A., Tran 15-8
PO Box 387
St. Louis, MO 63166               *Ph:* (314)418-2992

• 5733 • **Rosalie Tiles Scholarship** *(Undergraduate/Scholarship)*

**Focus:** General studies. **Qualif.:** Applicants must be residents of the city and county of St. Louis, Missouri, in need of physical and educational assistance, who have grade point averages of 3.0 on a 4.0 scale. **Criteria:** Each Missouri college and university may nominate one freshman and one alternate freshman as scholarship candidates. Awards are granted based on candidate's academic achievement, likelihood of community success, unique non-academic interests, and unique background.

**Funds Avail.:** Students selected to receive a scholarship will receive full tuition for a normal undergraduate course of study (in most cases), this will be eight consecutive semesters, but may be 12 consecutive trimesters or 10 consecutive semesters depending on school attended and elected course of study. **No. of Awards:** Varies. **To Apply:** Applicants must apply though their financial aid office. **Deadline:** Schools must submit nominations by May 1.

**Remarks:** The applicant must maintain a semester and cumulative GPA of 2.75 or better to keep the scholarship award. **Contact:** The Financial Officer at the Missouri college or university.

• **5734** •
## Tourette Syndrome Association, Inc.
42-40 Bell Blvd.
Bayside, NY 11361-2861
*E-mail:* tourette@ix.netcom.com
*URL:* http://tsa.mgh.harvard.edu

*Ph:* (718)224-2999
*Fax:* (718)279-9596

• **5735** • **TSA Clinical Studies Grants; TSA Postdoctoral Training Fellowships; TSA Research Grants** *(Postdoctorate/Grant)*

**Purpose:** To provide assistance to investigators from all areas of science who can contribute to the knowledge and treatment of Tourette Syndrome. **Focus:** Tourette Syndrome. **Qualif.:** Candidate may be of any nationality. Applicant must have at least a Ph.D. degree. Applicant must be an investigator in an area of science that can contribute to the understanding of the genetics, pathogenesis, pathophysiology, or treatment of Tourette Syndrome. Awards are made for basic and clinical research, as well as postdoctoral training. TSA supports indirect costs at the level of 10%.

**Funds Avail.:** Clinical Studies Grant: $5,000-40,000; Postdoctoral Training Fellowships: $15,000-25,000; Research Grants: $5,000-40,000. **No. of Awards:** 10-16. **To Apply:** Write to the chairperson for application guidelines. Submit a letter of intent briefly describing the scientific basis of the proposed project and an estimate of project funding. Applicant may then be invited to submit a final proposal. **Deadline:** Letter of intent: October; final proposal: December. Awards are announced in March. **Contact:** Neal Swerdlow, M.D., Ph.D. Chair, at the above address (see entry 5734).

• **5736** •
## Transport Workers Union of America, AFL-CIO
80 West End Ave.
New York, NY 10023
*URL:* http://www.twu.com

*Ph:* (212)873-6000

• **5737** • **Michael J. Quill Scholarship** *(Undergraduate/Scholarship)*

**Qualif.:** Applicants must be high school seniors who are children of Transport Workers Union members or pensioners in good standing, including retired, disabled, or deceased members. Dependent brothers or sisters of such members under the age of 21 are also eligible (must be claimed as dependent with Internal Revenue Service). The scholarships must be used for the Fall term following high school graduation. **Criteria:** Winners are selected from among eligible candidates by a public drawing.

**Funds Avail.:** $1,200. **No. of Awards:** 15. **To Apply:** Official application forms must be filed. **Deadline:** May 1. **Contact:** Trustees, Michael J. Quill Scholarship Fund, at the Transport Workers Union of America at the address above.

• **5738** •
## Transportation Association of Canada
2323 St. Laurent Blvd.
Ottawa, ON, Canada K1G 4K6
*URL:* http://www.tac-atc.ca/

*Ph:* (613)736-1350
*Fax:* (613)736-1395

• **5739** • **TAC Scholarships** *(Graduate/Scholarship)*

**Purpose:** To support postgraduate studies in transportation-related fields. **Focus:** Transportation. **Qualif.:** Applicants must be Canadian citizens or landed immigrants who hold a bachelor's degree and plan to earn a higher degree in a field related to transportation. Preference is given to candidates with relevant work experience. Scholarships may be awarded to individuals receiving other scholarships. Applicants must be in the top quarter of their class in addition to having a minimum GPA of B.

**Funds Avail.:** $3,000-5,000. **To Apply:** Write for application form and guidelines. **Deadline:** March 1. Notification in May.

**Remarks:** Scholarships are sponsored by members of TAC: Stanley Associates, Pavement Management Systems, DELCAN Corporation, John Emery Geotechnical Engineering Ltd., Lea Associates Group, Federal/Provincial/Territorial Governments of Canada, and EBA Engineering Consultants. **Contact:** Marc Conneau, Public Communications Manager, at the above address (see entry 5738).

• **5740** •
## Transportation Clubs International
PO Box 52
Arabi, LA 70032-0052
*E-mail:* gay.fielding@kaiseral.com
*URL:* http://www.trans-clubs.org

*Ph:* (504)278-1107
*Fax:* (504)278-1110

• **5741** • **Ginger & Fred Deines Canada Scholarships** *(Graduate, Undergraduate, Other/Scholarship)*

**Purpose:** To encourage advanced vocational, undergraduate, and graduate study. **Focus:** Transportation, Traffic Management, Logistics, and related fields. **Qualif.:** Applicants must be Canadian citizens who are enrolled in a school in Canada or the U.S. **Criteria:** Based on scholastic ability and potential, professional interest, character, and financial need.

**Funds Avail.:** $1500. **To Apply:** Completed application, supporting papers, documents, and photograph must be submitted. /DLN April 30.

• **5742** • **Ginger and Fred Deines Mexico Scholarships** *(Graduate, Professional Development, Undergraduate/Scholarship)*

**Purpose:** To encourage advanced vocational, undergraduate, and graduate study in the field of transportation and traffic management. **Focus:** Transportation. **Qualif.:** Applicants must be students of Mexican nationality enrolled in a school in Mexico or the United States offering accredited courses in transportation, traffic management, and related fields, preparing for a career in these areas. **Criteria:** Scholarship is based upon scholastic ability and potential, professional interest, character, and financial need.

**Funds Avail.:** $1,500. **No. of Awards:** One. **To Apply:** Application forms are obtained by writing to the Transportation Clubs International at the above address or through local transportation and traffic clubs. **Deadline:** April 30.

• **5743** • **Hooper Memorial Scholarship(s)** *(Graduate, Undergraduate/Scholarship)*

**Purpose:** To encourage advanced vocational, undergraduate, and graduate study in the field of transportation and traffic management. **Focus:** Transportation. **Qualif.:** Applicants must be enrolled in an educational program in an accredited institution of higher learning, offering courses in transportation, traffic management, and related fields and who intend to prepare for a career in these areas. **Criteria:** Scholarship is based upon scholastic ability and potential, professional interest, character, and financial need.

**Funds Avail.:** $1,500. **No. of Awards:** One. **To Apply:** Application forms are obtained by writing to the Transportation Clubs

## Transportation Clubs International (continued)

International at the above address or through local transportation and traffic clubs. **Deadline:** April 30.

### • 5744 • Denny Lydic Scholarship (Graduate, Undergraduate, Other/Scholarship)

**Purpose:** To encourage advanced vocational undergraduate and graduate study. **Focus:** Transportation, Traffic Management, Logistics, and related fields. **Qualif.:** Applicants must be enrolled in an educational program in an accredited institution of higher learning offering courses in one of the required areas of study. **Criteria:** Based on scholastic ability and potential; professional interest; character; and financial need.

**Funds Avail.:** $500. **To Apply:** Completed application, supporting papers, documents, and photograph must be submitted. **Deadline:** April 30.

### • 5745 • Texas Transportation Scholarship (Graduate, Undergraduate/Scholarship)

**Purpose:** To encourage advanced vocational, undergraduate, and graduate study. **Focus:** Transportation, Traffic Management, Logistics, and related fields. **Qualif.:** Applicants must be enrolled in a school in Texas during some phase of their education (elementary, secondary or high school). **Criteria:** Based on scholastic ability and potential, professional interest, character, and financial need.

**Funds Avail.:** $1000 **To Apply:** Completed application, supporting papers, documents, and photograph must be submitted. **Deadline:** April 30.

### • 5746 • Charlotte Woods Memorial Scholarship (Graduate, Undergraduate/Scholarship)

**Purpose:** To encourage advanced vocational, undergraduate and graduate study in the field of transportation and traffic management. **Focus:** Transportation. **Qualif.:** Applicants must be TCI members, or dependents of a member, who are enrolled in an educational program in an accredited institution of higher learning, offering courses in transportation, traffic management, and related fields and who intend to prepare for a career in these areas. **Criteria:** Scholarship is based upon scholastic ability and potential, professional interest, character, and financial need.

**Funds Avail.:** $1,000. **No. of Awards:** One. **To Apply:** Application forms are obtained by writing to the Transportation Clubs International at the above address or through local transportation and traffic clubs. **Deadline:** April 30.

### • 5747 • Triangle Native American Society
PO Box 26841
Raleigh, NC 27611-6841                    *Ph:* (919)779-5936

### • 5748 • Mark Ulmer Native American Scholarships (Undergraduate/Scholarship)

**Purpose:** To help North Carolina's American Indian students obtain a college education. **Qualif.:** Applicants must be American Indians who are residents of North Carolina for at least 12 months, be attending one of the four-year institutions that comprise the University of North Carolina system, have at least a 2.0 GPA, and be enrolled for the next quarter or semester. **Criteria:** Selection is based on financial need, leadership and community involvement, and academic success.

**Funds Avail.:** Two $500 scholarships per year. **To Apply:** Candidates must send a completed application with official postsecondary transcripts. **Deadline:** June 15. **Contact:** Panthia Chavis, telephone: (919)662-9197, or write to the above address.

### • 5749 • Truck Renting and Leasing Association
1725 Duke St., Ste. 600                    *Ph:* (703)299-9120
Alexandria, VA 22314                       *Fax:* (703)299-9115
*E-mail:* mpayne@trala.org
*URL:* http://www.trala.org

### • 5750 • Larry Miller Transportation Scholarship Program (Undergraduate/Scholarship)

**Purpose:** To aid in the undergraduate study of deserving students. **Qualif.:** Applicants must be high school seniors and dependents of employees of TRALA member companies.

**Funds Avail.:** $5,000 per scholarship annually; renewable for up to $20,000. **No. of Awards:** Up to four.

**Remarks:** Program was established in 1995.

### • 5751 • Harry S. Truman Scholarship Foundation
712 Jackson Pl., NW                       *Ph:* (202)395-4831
Washington, DC 20006                      *Fax:* (202)395-6995
*E-mail:* staff@truman.gov
*URL:* http://www.truman.gov

### • 5752 • Truman Scholarships (Graduate, Undergraduate/Scholarship)

**Purpose:** To honor President Truman's contributions to the nation, his commitment to public service, and his interest in education. Awards are given to college students who have outstanding leadership potential, plan to pursue careers in government or elsewhere in public service, and wish to attend graduate school to help prepare for their careers. **Focus:** Public Service, Public Policy, Public Administration. **Qualif.:** Applicants must be full-time students at a four-year institution and pursuing a bachelor's degree. Students must also be in the upper quarter of their class, be United States citizens or nationals, and be committed to a career in public service. Recipients may attend graduate schools in the United States or in foreign countries. **Criteria:** Awards are based on student's public and community service records, commitment to careers in government or elsewhere in the public sector, public policy goals, and leadership potential. Judging criteria also includes suitability of the nominee's proposed program of study for a career in public service, writing skills, academic performance, and potential for success in graduate school. Priority is given to candidates proposing to enroll in graduate programs specifically oriented to careers in public service.

**Funds Avail.:** Up to 85 scholarships are available in amounts up to $3,000 each for the senior year of undergraduate education and $27,000 for graduate studies. Scholars in graduate programs planning to receive degrees in one to two years are eligible to receive $13,500 per year. Scholars in graduate programs requiring three or more years of academic study are eligible to receive $9,000 per year for a maximum of three years. In addition, each year one "state" scholarship is available to a qualified resident nominee in each of the 50 states, the District of Columbia, Puerto Rico, and (considered as a single entity) Guam, the Virgin Islands, American Samoa, and the Commonwealth of the Northern Mariana Islands. **No. of Awards:** 75-80 per year. **To Apply:** Candidates must be nominated by their institution of higher education. Applications are not accepted directly from candidates. **Deadline:** Completed nomination packages must be received by February 1. **Contact:** The Truman Faculty Representative at individual colleges and institutions.

---

• 5753 •

## Richard Tucker Music Foundation

1790 Broadway, Ste. 715
New York, NY 10019-1412
*E-mail:* info@rtucker.com
*URL:* http://www.rtucker.com

Ph: (212)757-2218
Fax: (212)757-2347

### • 5754 • RTMF Career Grants/Sara Tucker Study Grant *(Professional Development/Grant)*

**Purpose:** To bestow special recognition on American opera singers. **Focus:** Opera. **Qualif.:** For Career Grants, applicants must already have an established career in opera with a fair amount of experience. For Sara Tucker Study Grants, applicants must be emerging artists making the transition from student to professional. While candidates may have already appeared on stage, their participation should be at an apprentice or secondary level rather than a major role. **Criteria:** Singers are selected to audition after nomination by opera professionals.

**Funds Avail.:** Four cash prizes of $7,500 each for Career Grants; four $5,000 Sara Tucker Study Grants. **No. of Awards:** Four study grants and four career grants. **To Apply:** Singers must be recommended by a professional with whom they have worked; they cannot apply directly. **Deadline:** Recommendations must be made by November 30 of each year.

**Remarks:** Those chosen may be of talent equal to the Richard Tucker Award winner (see separate entry) but their careers are not poised at that same critical moment. **Contact:** Ms. Ellen C. Moran, Executive Director, at the above address (see entry 5753).

### • 5755 • Richard Tucker Award *(Professional Development/Award)*

**Purpose:** To recognize and bestow special distinction on an American opera singer who is on the verge of a major national and international career. **Focus:** Opera. **Qualif.:** Applicants must be United States citizens who have already demonstrated a capacity for a career of international stature both in the United States and abroad. **Criteria:** The recipient is chosen by conferral of a panel of professionals, rather than by audition.

**Funds Avail.:** Cash prize of $30,000 and the opportunity to appear at the annual Foundation Gala, in concert with many of the profession's major stars. The Gala is heard live on WQXR and is taped for a future PBS telecast, affording the winner tremendous public exposure. **No. of Awards:** 1. **To Apply:** Singers cannot apply directly, but must be recommended by one or more professionals in the operatic field with whom they have worked, such as a conductor, company head, or stage director. Managers cannot recommend their artists. **Deadline:** November 30 of the preceding year. **Contact:** Ms. Ellen C. Moran , Executive Director, at the above address (see entry 5753).

---

• 5756 •

## Turner, May and Shepherd

185 High St., N.E.
Warren, OH 44481-1219

Ph: (330)399-8801
Fax: (330)399-8805

### • 5757 • Frank F. Bentley Scholarship *(Undergraduate/Scholarship)*

**Qualif.:** Applicants must be residents of Trunbull County, Ohio, whose family circumstances are such that they cannot afford to attend college or technical or trade school without financial assistance. **Criteria:** Preference is given to orphans, then to persons from foster homes, broken homes, and then to needy persons in general.

**Funds Avail.:** Scholarships up to $3,000 per student per year are awarded. Generally, they are renewable for up to three years. Scholarships are paid directly to the school the recipient attends and are used primarily for tuition and fees. **To Apply:** A completed, formal application must be submitted to the applicant's high school guidance counselor with a high school transcript that shows grade average, class rank, and college test scores. Also required are two letters of reference from teachers, counselors, or school administrators, and the most recent W-2 form of parent(s) and/or guardian and self. **Deadline:** Counselors must submit applications to the scholarship chairperson by the beginning of April. **Contact:** School guidance counselors.

---

• 5758 •

## Two/Ten International Footwear Foundation

Attn: Scholarship Program
56 Main St.
Watertown, MA 02172

Ph: (617)923-4500
Fax: (617)923-8414
Free: 800-346-3210

### • 5759 • Two/Ten International Footwear Foundation Scholarships *(Undergraduate/Scholarship)*

**Focus:** General Studies. **Qualif.:** Candidates must be natural, step, or adopted children of current employees in the footwear, leather, and allied industries or students who have worked at least 500 hours in these industries in the year before a scholarship will be used. Employee parent must have been employed in these industries for at least one year before the student's registration in a college, nursing program, or vocational/technical school that is regionally or professionally accredited. All applicants must be either high school seniors who will graduate during the current academic year and enter college in the fall following graduation, high school graduates within the preceding four years who will enter college the fall following application, or currently enrolled students in an approved and fully accredited college or university who will return to college the fall following application. Financial need is a requirement. **Criteria:** Based on academic excellence, community and school-related activities, and financial need.

**Funds Avail.:** $200 to $2,000. **No. of Awards:** 200. **To Apply:** Eligibility postcards must be filed before applicants are sent final application materials. **Deadline:** December 15 to request eligibility postcard, January 15 for the final application. **Contact:** Scholarship Coordinator at the above address (see entry 5758).

---

## • 5760 •
**Tyson Foundation, Inc.**
2210 Oaklawn Dr.                     *Ph:* (501)290-4955
Springdale, AR 72762-6999            *Fax:* (501)290-7984
                                     *Free:* 800-643-3410

*E-mail:* comments@tysonfoundation.org
*URL:* http://www.tysonfoundation.org

### • 5761 • Tyson Scholarship *(Undergraduate/ Scholarship)*

**Focus:** Business, computer science, agriculture, engineering and nursing. **Qualif.:** Applicants must reside near a Tyson Operating Facility located in one of the following states: Alaska, Arkansas, Alabama, Florida, Georgia, Illinois,Indiana, Minnesota, Mississippi, Missouri, North Carolina, Oklahoma, Oregon, Pennsylvania, Tennessee, Texas, Virginia, Washington, or Kentucky; be US citizens; maintain a 2.5 GPA; and attend school full-time. **Criteria:** Based on financial need.

**Funds Avail.:** $200-1800 per semester for tuition, fees, and or book expenses. . **No. of Awards:** Varies. **To Apply:** Applicants must write for further details and application form.Applicaitions must be requested by the last day of February **Deadline:** Applications must be requested by the last day of February. Completed applications must be returned by April 20. **Contact:** Cheryl Tyson at the above address (see entry 5760).

## • 5762 •
**U. The National College Magazine**
1800 Century Park E., No. 820
Los Angeles, CA 90067-1503           *Ph:* (310)551-1381

### • 5763 • *U* The National College Magazine
Internships/Fellowships *(Graduate/Fellowship, Internship)*

**Purpose:** Provides the opportunity to work as an assistant editor for the magazine. **Focus:** Journalism. **Qualif.:** Applicants must have graduated the June before the internship and worked on a college publication as an editor or section editor.

**Funds Avail.:** $1650 per month. **No. of Awards:** 4. **To Apply:** Write for application details. **Deadline:** February 13.

## • 5764 •
**Jimmie Ullery Charitable Trust**
Scholarship Committee
Christian Education Dept.
1st Presbyterian Church
709 S. Boston                        *Ph:* (918)586-5845
Tulsa, OK 74119                      *Fax:* (918)584-5233
*URL:* http://www.firstchurchtulsa.org

### • 5765 • Ullery Charitable Trust Scholarship
*(Undergraduate/Scholarship)*

**Focus:** Religious studies. **Qualif.:** Applicants must be seminary students pursuing full-time Christian work with the Presbyterian Church (USA).

**Funds Avail.:** Varies. **No. of Awards:** Varies. **To Apply:** Write for further details. **Deadline:** June 1. **Contact:** Ullery Charitable Trust at the above address (see entry 5764).

## • 5766 •
**UNICO National, Inc.**
72 Burroughs Place
Bloomfield, NJ 07003                 *Ph:* (201)748-9144

### • 5767 • William C. Davini Scholarship
*(Undergraduate/Scholarship)*

**Focus:** General studies. **Qualif.:** Applicants must be of Italian origin, reside in the corporate limits or in the adjoining suburbs of a city wherein an active chapter of UNICO National is located, and be a senior at any public or private secondary school located within these limits. **Criteria:** Awards are made based on scholarship, citizenship and leadership.

**Funds Avail.:** $1,000. **No. of Awards:** 1. **To Apply:** Applicants must submit a completed application form, formal letter of endorsement and presentation signed by the President and/or Scholarship Chairman of the local Chapter sponsoring applicant, two letters of recommendation (one from a school official and one form a member of the community), and a transcript with SAT or ACT scores. Exhibits evidencing notable achievement in leadership, literature, athletics, dramatics, community service or other activities may be attached, but the applicant should avoid submitting repetitious accounts. **Deadline:** April 15 **Contact:** UNICO Foundation at the above address (see entry 5766).

### • 5768 • Major Don S. Gentile Scholarship
*(Undergraduate/Scholarship)*

**Focus:** General studies. **Qualif.:** Applicants must be of Italian origin, reside in the corporate limits or in the adjoining suburbs of a city wherein an active chapter of UNICO National is located, and be a senior at any public or private secondary school located within these limits. **Criteria:** Awards are made based on scholarship, citizenship financial need and leadership.

**Funds Avail.:** $1,000. **No. of Awards:** 1. **To Apply:** Applicants must submit a completed application form, formal letter of endorsement and presentation signed by the President and/or Scholarship Chairman of the local Chapter sponsoring applicant, two letters of recommendation (one from a school official and one form a member of the community), and a transcript with SAT or ACT scores. Exhibits evidencing notable achievement in leadership, literature, athletics, dramatics, community service or other activities may be attached, but the applicant should avoid submitting repetitious accounts. **Deadline:** April 15 **Contact:** UNICO Foundation at the above address (see entry 5766).

### • 5769 • Theodore Mazza Scholarship
*(Undergraduate/Scholarship)*

**Focus:** Architecture, art history, music, studio art and theatre arts. **Qualif.:** Applicants must reside in the corporate limits or in the adjoining suburbs of a city wherein an active chapter of UNICO National is located, and be a senior at any public or private secondary school located within these limits. **Criteria:** Awards are made based on scholarship, citizenship and leadership.

**Funds Avail.:** $1,000. **No. of Awards:** 1. **To Apply:** Applicants must submit a completed application form, formal letter of endorsement and presentation signed by the President and/or Scholarship Chairman of the local Chapter sponsoring applicant, two letters of recommendation (one from a school official and one form a member of the community), and a transcript with SAT or ACT scores. Exhibits evidencing notable achievement in leadership, literature, athletics, dramatics, community service or other activities may be attached, but the applicant should avoid submitting repetitious accounts. **Deadline:** April 15 **Contact:** UNICO Foundation at the above address (see entry 5766).

### • 5770 • Alphonse A. Miele Scholarship
*(Undergraduate/Scholarship)*

**Focus:** General studies. **Qualif.:** Applicants must reside in the corporate limits or in the adjoining suburbs of a city wherein an active chapter of UNICO National is located, and be a senior at any public or private secondary school located within these limits. **Criteria:** Awards are made based on scholarship, citizenship and leadership.

**Funds Avail.:** $1,000. **No. of Awards:** 1. **To Apply:** Applicants must submit a completed application form, formal letter of endorsement and presentation signed by the President and/or Scholarship Chairman of the local Chapter sponsoring applicant, two letters of recommendation (one from a school official and one form a member of the community), and a transcript with SAT or ACT scores. Exhibits evidencing notable achievement in leadership, literature, athletics, dramatics, community service or other activities may be attached, but the applicant should avoid submitting repetitious accounts. **Deadline:** April 15 **Contact:** UNICO Foundation at the above address (see entry 5766).

### • 5771 •
### Unicorn Theatre
3828 Main St.  
Kansas City, MO 64111  
*Ph:* (816)531-7529  
*Fax:* (816)531-0421

### • 5772 • National Playwrights' Award *(Professional Development/Award)*

**Purpose:** To recognize and produce outstanding original scripts. **Focus:** Drama. **Qualif.:** Candidates may be of any nationality. Submissions must be original, full-length scripts that have not been previously produced or published. The setting of the play must be modern (post-1950), and the cast may not exceed ten actors. Musicals, one-acts, and historical plays are not eligible for submission. Award-winning plays will be produced by the Unicorn Theatre.

**Funds Avail.:** $1,000. **To Apply:** Send a letter of application, including a synopsis of the play and sample dialogue, with a self-addressed, stamped envelope for notification of Theatre's decision. If the Theatre is interested, it will request a copy of the manuscript for review. **Deadline:** April 30 each year, for the next year's production. **Contact:** Unicorn Theatre National Playwright Award at the above address (see entry 5771).

### • 5773 •
### UNIMA-USA
c/o Vincent Anthony, Gen. Sec.  
1404 Spring St. NW  
Atlanta, GA 30309  
*Ph:* (404)873-3089  
*Fax:* (404)873-9907  
*E-mail:* unima@mindspring.com  
*URL:* http://www.unima-usa.org

*UNIMA-USA, American Center of the Union Internationale de la Marionette promotes world friendship through puppetry.*

### • 5774 • UNIMA-USA Scholarship *(Professional Development/Scholarship)*

**Purpose:** To encourage the international exchange of students and artists and encourage and reward excellence in the field of puppetry. **Focus:** Puppetry. **Qualif.:** Applicants must be puppeteers of second-level experience and have been accepted at the International Institute of Puppetry in Charleville-Meziere, France for one summer course or at a recognized institute of puppetry abroad. Applicants must be members in good standing of UNIMA-USA.

**Funds Avail.:** $400 to $500. **No. of Awards:** Varies. **To Apply:** Applicants must apply through the center of UNIMA-USA. **Deadline:** January 15. **Contact:** UNIMA-USA, Scholarship Fund, Joann Siegrist, WVU-Puppet Mobile, PO Box 6111, Morgantown. WV 26506-6111.

### • 5775 •
### Union of Needletrades and Textile Employees (Philadelphia)
35 S. 4th St.  
Philadelphia, PA 19106  
*Ph:* (215)351-0750  
*Fax:* (215)351-0178

### • 5776 • UNITE Scholarships *(Undergraduate/Scholarship)*

**Focus:** General Studies. **Qualif.:** Applicants must be children of two-year members only of the Philadelphia South Jersey District Council as of April 15 of the award year, or of Union members who have died within the last two calendar years and were two-year members at the time of death. Applicants must be graduates of accredited high schools within two calendar years preceding the award year, or have graduated within the award year. Currently enrolled college students are not eligible. In any one award year, only one student from a family will be eligible for a scholarship. However, a second member of a family may be considered for an award if there are no other eligible applicants. Students may choose any undergraduate course in any accredited college, university, or post-high school institution, subject to the approval of the Scholarship Selection Committee. **Criteria:** Flexible.

**Funds Avail.:** Up to $1,000 per year, or up to $500 per year at the Selection Committee's discretion. The money will go toward the tuition, fees, and room and board costs to the student, for a maximum of four years if the student maintains satisfactory grades. Any scholarship applicant who has regular scholarship aid from another source shall be entitled to the full award each year, as long as the combined value of the awards does not exceed the total tuition, fees, and room and board costs to that student for one year. When such combined values do exceed these combined costs, the Scholarship Fund shall grant an award for the difference between the student's other award and total school charges for the year. **No. of Awards:** Depends on availability and amount of funds. **To Apply:** Applications must include high school transcripts, principal's evaluation of student, a letter of recommendation from one person other than a teacher or relative, reports of Scholastic Aptitude Test scores from the College Board Examination, any Achievement Test scores, and a statement explaining student's plans and reason for applying. Each applicant is required to take the SAT. **Deadline:** April 15.

**Remarks:** The scholarships are provided by the Philadelphia South Jersey District Council, UNITE, in cooperation with the Knitted Outerwear Manufacturers' Association. **Contact:** UNITE at the above address (see entry 5775).

### • 5777 •
### Union Pacific Railroad - Scholarship Program
1416 Dodge St., Rm. 320  
Omaha, NE 68179  
*Ph:* (402)271-3489  
*Fax:* (402)271-3345  
*URL:* http://www.uprr.com/

### • 5778 • Union Pacific Railroad Employee Dependent Scholarships *(Undergraduate/Scholarship)*

**Focus:** General Studies. **Qualif.:** Applicants must be children of Union Pacific employees or retired/deceased employees. They

## Union Pacific Railroad - Scholarship Program (continued)

must be seniors in high school, rank in the upper 25 percent of their class, and meet college admission requirements. **Criteria:** Selection is determined by high school grades, ACT/SAT scores, class ranking, vocational goals, and extracurricular activities.

**Funds Avail.:** 50 scholarships worth $750 per year, renewable for four years if a 2.75 grade point average is maintained. **No. of Awards:** 50. **To Apply:** Contact Union Pacific Railroad for applications. **Deadline:** February 1. **Contact:** Nancy Somervell, at the above address (see entry 5777).

## • 5779 •
## Unitarian Universalist Association
c/o Worship and Diversity
  Resources Office
25 Beacon St.                                    *Ph:* (617)742-2100
Boston, MA 02108                          *Fax:* (617)367-3237
*URL:* http://www.uua.org/

### • 5780 • Children of Unitarian Universalist Ministers Scholarship *(Undergraduate/Scholarship)*

**Funds Avail.:** Limited funding is available.

**Remarks:** Contact Office of Church Staff Finances.

### • 5781 • Pauly D'Orlando Memorial Art Scholarship *(Graduate, Undergraduate/Scholarship)*

**Purpose:** To encourage art students. **Focus:** Drawing, Enameling, Painting, Printmaking. **Qualif.:** Applicants must be members of a Unitarian Universalist church, or be sponsored by a member. They must also be enrolled as visual art students at an accredited school. Both undergraduate and M.F.A. students are eligible. The scholarship is intended for tuition fees and is paid directly to the student's school. If the award exceeds the cost of tuition, the remaining funds may be used to purchase art supplies. Scholarship selection is based on financial need and artistic merit.

**Funds Avail.:** $750. **No. of Awards:** One annually. **To Apply:** Write to UUA for application form. Send completed application to Dolores Gall, Chief Judge, 75 Charlton Hill, Hamden, Connecticut 06158, U.S.A. Completed application should include the form, a short essay explaining background and goals, six slides of artwork, statement of annual tuition, and a letter of recommendation from the minister or officer of sponsoring Unitarian Universalist congregation. **Deadline:** March 31. Notification by May 15.

**Remarks:** This award will not be given to the same student for two consecutive years. **Contact:** Jacqui James, at the above address (see entry 5779).

### • 5782 • Ministerial Education Scholarship *(Graduate/Scholarship)*

**Qualif.:** For students enrolled full-time in a Masters of Divinity program leading to ordination as a UU minister.

**Remarks:** Contact the Office of Ministerial Education.

### • 5783 • Joseph Sumner Smith Scholarship *(Undergraduate/Scholarship)*

**Qualif.:** For UU students enrolled at Antioch, Yellow Springs, Ohio, or Harvard. **Deadline:** April 15.

**Remarks:** Contact the Treasurer's Office.

### • 5784 • Marion Barr Stanfield Art Scholarship *(Undergraduate/Scholarship)*

**Qualif.:** For students in the fine arts of painting, drawing, or sculpting. **Deadline:** February 15.

**Remarks:** Contact the Publications Department.

### • 5785 • Otto M. Stanfield Legal Scholarship *(Graduate/Scholarship)*

**Qualif.:** For graduate law students. **Deadline:** February 15.

**Remarks:** Contact the Publications Department.

## • 5786 •
## United Commercial Travelers
PO Box 159019
Columbus, OH 43215

### • 5787 • United Commercial Travelers Retarded Citizens Teacher Scholarship *(Doctorate, Graduate, Postgraduate, Undergraduate/Scholarship)*

**Purpose:** To study mental retardation at the college junior, senior, bachelor's, master's, doctoral, or postgraduate levels. **Focus:** Mental Retardation. **Qualif.:** Application must be a teacher of the mentally handicapped or be an experienced teacher who wishes to become certified to teach the mentally retarded. Open to those who have a bachelor's or master's degree, and to college juniors or seniors who are studying mental retardation and plan to teach the mentally handicapped. **Criteria:** Selection is based on applicants being able to provide service to the mentally handicapped in the US or Canada. Prime consideration will be given to UCT members.

**Funds Avail.:** $750 per year, maximum of $3,000 per lifetime. **No. of Awards:** Varies. **To Apply:** Applicants must provide: a brief resume of work experience in the mentally handicapped field; indication of current college rank or standing; and a statement of further education and/or career plans. A photograph must also be submitted, this is to be used for publicity purposes, if the scholarship is awarded. **Contact:** United Commercial Travelers (UCT) at listed address.

## • 5788 •
## United Daughters of the Confederacy
328 North Blvd.                                  *Ph:* (804)355-1636
Richmond, VA 23220-4057               *Fax:* (804)353-1396
*URL:* http://www.hsv.tis.net/~maxs/udc/

### • 5789 • Confederate Memorial Scholarships *(Undergraduate/Scholarship)*

**Purpose:** Provides financial assistance to students who are lineal descendants of Confederate soldiers or sailors. **Focus:** General Studies. **Qualif.:** Applicants must not have previously received a bachelor's degree, and must be certified as a lineal descendant of a Confederate soldier or sailor by a chapter of the United Daughters of the Confederacy. Students must meet Florida's general eligibility requirements for receipt of state aid, including compliance with registration requirements of the Selective Service System and participation in the college-level communication and computation testing (CLAST) program. Applicants must enroll at Florida public universities or community colleges for a minimum of 12 credit hours per term. They must not owe repayment of a grant under any state or federal grant or scholarship program, and must not be in default on any state or federal student loan program unless satisfactory arrangements to repay have been made. A renewal applicant must have earned a minimum cumulative grade point average of 2.0 on a 4.0 scale and have earned the equivalent of 12 credit hours for each term an award was received during the academic year. Eligibility for renewal is determined at the end of the second semester or third quarter of each academic year. Credits earned the previous summer can be counted toward the total number of credits required.

**Funds Avail.:** The amount of the scholarship is $150 per academic year for a maximum of eight semesters. Renewal awards take precedence over new awards in any year in which funds are insufficient to award all eligible, timely applicants. **To Apply:** Applications may be obtained at college financial aid offices or the Florida Department of Education Office of Student Financial Assistance. Letters of recommendation are required. **Deadline:** Applications, and renewal requests must be postmarked by April 1. **Contact:** Daughters of the Confederacy at the above address (see entry 5788).

### • 5790 • United Daughters of the Confederacy Scholarships *(Graduate, Undergraduate/Scholarship)*

**Focus:** General Studies. **Qualif.:** Applicants must be descendants of confederate veterans. **Criteria:** Selection is based on application, SAT scores, and financial need.

**Funds Avail.:** Awards vary from $400 to $800 per year. **To Apply:** Requests for applications and educational curricula forms must be accompanied by a size 10 self-addressed, stamped envelope. Applicants must submit proof of lineage and be sponsored by a UDC chapter. **Deadline:** February 15. **Contact:** Scholarship Coordinator at the above address (see entry 5788).

### • 5791 •
## United Food and Commercial Workers International Union - AFL-CIO, CLC
1775 K St., NW
Washington, DC 20006
*URL:* http://ufcw.org

*Ph:* (202)223-3111
*Fax:* (202)466-1562

### • 5792 • UFCW Scholarships *(Undergraduate/Scholarship)*

**Focus:** General Studies. **Qualif.:** Candidates must be American or Canadian UFCW members, or unmarried children of members, who have been in good standing for at least one year prior to December 31 of the school year in which the application is made. All applicants must be less than 20 years of age as of March 15 of the same school year. Candidates must be graduating high school students in the same year and intend to pursue a college or university education. **Criteria:** Recipients are selected on the basis of College Board testing scores, secondary school scholastic performance and achievements, personal qualifications, and merit.

**Funds Avail.:** Seven college scholarships worth $4,000 each over a four-year period are awarded. Payment of the first $1,000 is dependent on written evidence of enrollment at an accredited college or university. Further payments are contingent upon continued satisfactory academic progress. **No. of Awards:** 7. **To Apply:** Except for Canadian students who plan to attend Canadian colleges or universities, applicants must take either the Scholastic Aptitude Test (SAT) or the American College Test (ACT). Applicants must complete a biographical questionnaire and submit it to the high school principal or guidance counselor for completion and submission with transcript. **Deadline:** Candidate must complete and submit a preliminary application before December 31. Final applications and all supporting material must be filed by March 15. **Contact:** The United Food and Commercial Workers International Union at the above address (see entry 5791).

### • 5793 •
## United Methodist Communications
c/o Scholarship Committee
PO Box 320
Nashville, TN 37202-0320
*E-mail:* scholarships@umcom.umc.org
*URL:* http://www.umcom.org/about.scholarships.html

*Ph:* (615)742-5140
*Fax:* (615)742-5404

### • 5794 • Leonard M. Perryman Communications Scholarship for Ethnic Minority Students *(Undergraduate/Scholarship)*

**Focus:** Journalism, Communications. **Qualif.:** Applicants must be college juniors or seniors who are members of an ethnic minority, intend to pursue a career in religious communication in an accredited institution of higher education, and are United States citizens. Communications includes various mediums such as audiovisual and electric and print journalism. **Criteria:** Applicants are judged on five criteria: Christian commitment and involvement in the life of the church; academic achievement as revealed by transcripts, grade point averages, and letters of reference; journalistic experience and/or evidence of journalistic talent; clarity of purpose in plans and goals for the future; and potential professional usefulness as a journalist in the field of religion.

**Funds Avail.:** $2,500 scholarship. Half of the award will be paid in August or September after the recipient is enrolled in an undergraduate program in an accredited school or department of journalism in the United States, and the remainder of the grant will be paid in December. There are no grants for summer sessions. **No. of Awards:** One annually; not renewable. **To Apply:** A formal application must be submitted with official transcripts from the institution of higher learning that the applicant is attending or any previously attended colleges or universities; an essay of no more than 500 words about the candidate's interest in religious journalism; three samples of applicant's work; and a recent black and white glossy photograph, preferably head and shoulders, suitable for publicity use should the applicant win. In addition, three letters of recommendation must also be submitted: one from the applicant's local church pastor or a denominational official, one from the chairperson of the department in which the candidate is majoring as an undergraduate, and one from an employer for whom the applicant has worked as a journalist. If any of these are not available, a letter from a knowledgeable person related to journalism may be substituted. All letters of recommendation should be sent by the writer directly to New York. **Deadline:** February 15.

**Remarks:** The scholarship honors Leonard M. Perryman, a journalist for the United Methodist Church for nearly 30 years. **Contact:** The Scholarship Committee at the above address (see entry 5793).

### • 5795 • Stoody-West Fellowship in Journalism *(Graduate/Fellowship)*

**Focus:** Religious Journalism. **Qualif.:** Candidates are members of the Christian faith who are engaged in religious journalism or are planning to enter the field by taking graduate studies in an accredited school or department of journalism. **Criteria:** Applicants are judged on Christian commitment and involvement in the life of the church, academic achievement as revealed by transcripts, grade point averages, and certain letters of reference, journalistic experience and/or evidence of journalistic talent, clarity of purpose in plans and goals for the future, and potential professional usefulness as a religious journalist.

**Funds Avail.:** The fellowship is $6,000. Half of the award will be paid in August or September after the recipient is enrolled in a graduate program in an accredited school or department of journalism in the United States. The remainder of the grant will be paid in December. Grants will not be paid for summer sessions. **No. of Awards:** One annually; not renewable. **To Apply:** A formal application must be submitted. Three letters of recommendation are required: one from the candidate's local church pastor or a

## United Methodist Communications (continued)

denominational officer; one from the chairperson of the department in which major work as an undergraduate was done; and one from an employer or supervisor for whom the applicant has worked professionally as a journalist. If any of these are not available, a letter from a knowledgeable person related to journalism may be substituted. All letters of recommendation should be sent by the writer directly to New York. Transcripts from all institutions at which the candidate has taken previous academic work should be sent from the schools directly to New York. A statement of not more than 500 words about the applicant's interest in religious journalism should be submitted along with four examples of journalistic work and a list of all published articles (if requested in writing these materials will be returned after the Stoody-West Fellowship has completed its work). Applicants must also submit evidence of an application to or acceptance by an accredited graduate school of communications or journalism and a recent black and white glossy photograph, preferably head and shoulders, suitable for publicity use should the applicant win the award. **Deadline:** February 15.

**Remarks:** The Fellowship honors two prominent leaders in public relations and information, Dr. Ralph Stoody and Dr. Arthur West. Religious journalism is broadly interpreted to include audiovisual, electronics and print journalism. Approximately 20 applications are received each year. **Contact:** Fellowship Committee at the above address (see entry 5793).

### • 5796 • UMF Annual Conference Scholars Program (Undergraduate/Scholarship)

**Purpose:** To foster value-centered education in a Christian context in United Methodist-related educational institutions. **Focus:** Theology. **Qualif.:** Applicants must be nominated and must be a member of the United Methodist Church for at least 1 year.

**Funds Avail.:** $1,000. **Deadline:** June 1. **Contact:** United Methodist Communications at the above address (see entry 5793).

### • 5797 •

## United Nations - Department of Development Support and Management Services
New York, NY 10017                     *Ph:* (212)963-6038
                                        *Fax:* (212)963-1273

*URL:* http://www.un.org/

### • 5798 • United Nations Educational Training Scholarships for Southern Africans (Graduate, Undergraduate/Scholarship)

**Purpose:** To encourage individuals from South Africa to undertake training in technical fields of study. **Focus:** Agriculture, Education, Engineering, Medicine, Science, Social Sciences. **Qualif.:** Applicant must be from South Africa or. Candidate must be studying at the vocational or university level in one of the subjects listed above or in another technical field vital to the economic and social development of his/her home country. Scholarships are mainly tenable in fields South Africa. Priority is given to students undertaking training related to the reconstruction and Development program (RDP) of the government. **Criteria:** Based on academic merit and financial need.

**Funds Avail.:** Maintenance, tuition, and book allowances. **No. of Awards:** Depends on level of voluntary contributions from member states. **To Apply:** Write to the Fellowships Service for application guidelines. **Deadline:** Varies. **Contact:** Angela M. Masithela, Officer in Charge, UNETPSA, at the above address (see entry 5797).

### • 5799 • United Nations Fellowships (Professional Development/Fellowship)

**Purpose:** To provide training opportunities for professionals in developing nations. **Focus:** Integrated Development, Public Management. **Qualif.:** Candidate must be a citizen of a developing nation who is, or is about to become, entrusted with functions important for the development of his/her home country. Candidate must be nominated by the national government in home country within an offered project. Fellowships are tenable worldwide at institutions that have appropriate facilities to train fellows for their professional duties. Fellows may use the awards to attend academic institutions or special courses, to undertake in-service training, or to participate in workshops and seminars. The nature of the training program must be fixed at the time of application, and candidate must agree to return to home country upon completion of the award term.

**Funds Avail.:** Maintenance, tuition, travel, and book allowances. **No. of Awards:** 4,000. **To Apply:** General information on the fellowship program may be obtained from the address listed above. For application guidelines, contact the United Nations Development Programme (UNDP) office in home country. Application must be submitted to the United Nations by the national government on the candidate's behalf, within an UNDP-approved project. **Deadline:** Varies. **Contact:** Fellowships Service at the above address (see entry 5797).

### • 5800 •

## United Nations Development Programme
Summer Internship Programme
Division of Personnel
One United Nations Plaza, DC/1802
New York, NY 10017                     *Ph:* (212)906-5221
*URL:* http://www.undp.org/

### • 5801 • UNDP Summer Internships (Postgraduate/ Internship)

**Purpose:** To enable students to obtain first-hand practical experience in the operations of the world's largest program of multilateral technical assistance in developing countries. **Focus:** Economic and Social Development, United Nations. **Qualif.:** Applicant may be of any nationality. Candidate must be studying at the postgraduate level in development-related studies and be proficient in two of UNDP's main working languages (English, French, and Spanish). Internships are tenable with UNDP. Each intern gains on-the-job training in a UNDP field office in a developing country, or with a bureau or division at the headquarters in New York City. Training assignments are full-time.

**Funds Avail.:** See note. **To Apply:** Write to the chief of the Recruitment Section for application guidelines. **Deadline:** January 31.

**Remarks:** UN interns are not paid. Travel costs, travel arrangements, and living accommodations are the responsibility of the intern and his/her sponsoring institution. **Contact:** Mark Farnsworth, Recruitment Associate, at the above address (see entry 5800).

## • 5802 •
## United Nations Institute for Training and Research
1 United Nations Plz.  *Ph:* (212)963-9196
New York, NY 10017  *Fax:* (212)963-9686
*URL:* http://www.unitar.org/ny/

### • 5803 • UNITAR Internships *(Postdoctorate/Internship)*

**Purpose:** To enable scholars to work with UNITAR. **Focus:** International Relations, United Nations. **Qualif.:** Applicant may be a graduate student or more advanced scholar of any nationality. Candidate's application must be endorsed by his/her home institution. Internships are tenable with UNITAR; interns undertake work in research, training, or administration.

**Funds Avail.:** See note. **To Apply:** Write to the chief for application guidelines, or contact the UN Permanent Mission in home country. Applications may either be submitted to the executive director directly from the home university or institute, or through the Permanent Mission. **Deadline:** None.

**Remarks:** UN interns are not paid. Travel costs, travel arrangements, and living accommodations are the responsibility of the intern and his/her sponsoring institution.

## • 5804 •
## United Nations Internship Office Staffing Services - Specialist Services Division
Rm. 259OC
Office of Human Resources
   Management
Specialist Services Div.  *Ph:* (212)963-4437
New York, NY 10017  *Fax:* (212)963-3683
*URL:* http://www.un-org

### • 5805 • Internships *(Graduate/Internship)*

**Purpose:** To provide students with a better of understanding of international problems through work assignments with the United Nations. **Focus:** International Relations, Political Science, Humanitarian Affairs, Law of the Sea, Adminstration and Management, Accounting and Auditing, Development Planning and Analysis, Disarmament Affairs, Economic and Social Research, Environmental Affairs, Information Systems, Legal Affairs, Library Science, Political Affairs, Peace-keeping Operations, Population Affairs, Public Information and Journalism, Sustainable Development, Translation and Terminology, and Women's Issues. **Qualif.:** Applicant may be of any nationality. Candidate must be a graduate student in a field related to the work of the United Nations. Awards are tenable primarily at the UN Headquarters in New York City. Interns are placed with a department or office, and must devote at least one-half of each work week to assignments made by their supervisor. The remainder of the intern's time may be spent in study or research in topics relevant to the United Nations.

**Funds Avail.:** See note. **To Apply:** Write to the Internship coordinator for application form and guidelines. Application forms are also available from the office of the dean at relevant graduate schools, and from the Permanent Mission to the UN in the home country. Submit form to the coordinator with transcripts, an endorsement from home institution, and a sample of research work, if available. **Deadline:** None.

**Remarks:** UN interns are not paid. Travel costs, travel arrangements, and living accommodations are the responsibility of the student and his/her sponsoring institution. **Contact:** Ad Hoc Internship Coordinator at the above address (see entry 5804).

## • 5806 •
## United Ostomy Association
19772 MacArthur Blvd., Ste. 200
Irvine, CA 92612  *Free:* 800-826-0826
*URL:* http://www.uoa.org/

### • 5807 • Archie Vinitsky ET Scholarship *(Professional Development/Scholarship)*

**Purpose:** To help cut the cost of attending school for specialized training in enterostomal therapy nursing. **Focus:** Nursing. **Qualif.:** Applicants must be registered nurses. **Criteria:** Selection is based on the area and need of the applicant.

**Funds Avail.:** $500. **No. of Awards:** 6. **To Apply:** Applications are available by written request. **Deadline:** October 15 and March 30.

## • 5808 •
## United Paperworkers International Union
PO Box 1475  *Ph:* (615)834-8590
Nashville, TN 37202  *Fax:* (615)781-0428

### • 5809 • United Paperworkers International Union Scholarships *(Undergraduate/Scholarship)*

**Focus:** General Studies. **Qualif.:** Applicants must be high school seniors who are children of active members in good standing. **Criteria:** Awards are given on the basis of scholastic achievement, character, and financial need.

**Funds Avail.:** Twenty-two awards of $1,000 each are given annually. Winners are limited to two awards per region. **To Apply:** Upon receipt of a completed and accepted preliminary application form, a supplemental packet of forms is sent to the applicant. **Deadline:** April 15. **Contact:** The United Paperworkers International Union at the above address (see entry 5808).

### • 5810 • Nicholas C. Vrataric Scholarships *(All/Scholarship)*

**Focus:** General Studies. **Qualif.:** Candidates must be members of the United Paperworkers International Union who are currently enrolled in a program to further their education and will be attending school the fall semester following application. **Criteria:** Recipients are selected by a random drawing made by an independent panel of educators.

**Funds Avail.:** Two awards of $1,000 each are given annually. **To Apply:** Applications must be obtained from UPIU. **Deadline:** March 15. **Contact:** The United Paperworkers International Union at the above address (see entry 5808).

## • 5811 •
## United South & Eastern Tribes, Inc.
711 Stewarts Ferry Pike, No. 100  *Ph:* (615)872-7900
Nashville, TN 37214-2634  *Fax:* (615)872-7417
*E-mail:* uset@bellsouth.net
*URL:* http://oneida-nation.net/uset

### • 5812 • USET Scholarships *(Undergraduate/Scholarship)*

**Purpose:** To help Native Americans obtain a college education. **Focus:** General Studies. **Qualif.:** Candidates must be enrolled or accepted at a post-secondary educational institution. They must also be enrolled members of one of the following tribes:

## *United South & Eastern Tribes, Inc. (continued)*

Chitimacha Tribe of Louisiana, Coushatta Tribe of Louisiana, Eastern Band of Cherokees, Mississippi Band of Choctaws, Miccosukee Tribe of Florida, Passamaquoddy—Indian Township, Passamaquoddy—Pleasant Point, Penobscot Nation, Seminole Tribe of Florida, Seneca Nation of Indians of New York, St. Regis Mohawks, Houlton Band of Maliseet, Poarch Band of Creeks, Narragansett Tribe, Tunica-Biloxi Tribe, Mashantucket Pequot Tribe, Gay Head Wampanoag Tribe, Oneida Nation of New York, Alabama-Coushatta, Aroostook Micmac, Catawba Nation, Jena Band of Choctaws, and Mohegan Tribe of Connecticut. **Criteria:** Selection is based on financial need and scholastic standing.

**Funds Avail.:** Four awards of $500 are given annually. **To Apply:** Applicants must submit certification of tribal affiliation, college acceptance letter or proof of current enrollment, and a letter citing the proposed use of scholarship funds. **Deadline:** April 30. **Contact:** Write to Scholarship Fund at the above address (see entry 5811).

---

## • 5813 •
## U.S. Air Force
Office of the Air Force Historian
110 Luke Ave., Ste. 405
Bolling AFB, DC 20332-8050

*Ph:* (202)767-5088
*Fax:* (202)767-5527

### • 5814 • U.S. Air Force Dissertation Year Fellowship in U.S. Military Aerospace History *(Doctorate/Fellowship)*

**Purpose:** To stimulate research and study in the field of U.S. military aerospace history, and to promote the use of the major archival library and other information centers in and around the nation's capital. Accordingly, fellows will be expected to spend a substantial portion of their fellowship year in Washington, D.C. They will be provided with desk space in the Office of the Air Force Historian, and will be assisted in obtaining access to the several archival and library facilities in the area. **Focus:** Aerospace Sciences, Military History. **Qualif.:** Applicants must be United States citizens, enrolled in a recognized graduate school, have completed all requirements for the Ph.D. except the dissertation, and have an approved dissertation topic in the field of United States military aerospace history. Any applicant who has accepted an award from any other Department of Defense agency for a period concurrent with this fellowship is not eligible. **Criteria:** Selection is based on evidence of ability, including academic records, faculty recommendations, the nature of the proposed topic and research work, and the benefit of the topic to aerospace history.

**Funds Avail.:** Two fellowships with stipends of $10,000 each are awarded each year. **No. of Awards:** 2. **To Apply:** Completed application form, official transcripts of undergraduate and graduate course work, letter of recommendation from the dissertation director, three additional letters of reference, and a proposed plan for research must be submitted. **Deadline:** Applications and all supporting documents are due by March 15. Applications may be obtained from the Chairman of the candidate's History Department or from the Office of the Air Force Historian at the above address. Applicants will be notified of decisions on or about April 30. **Contact:** Col. George Williams, at the above address (see entry 5813).

---

## • 5815 •
## U.S. Air Force Reserve Officers Training Corps
HQ AFROTC/RRO (Recruiting
Division)
551 E. Maxwell Blvd.
Maxwell AFB, AL 36112-6106
URL: http://stratofortress.tamu.edu/scholarships.html

*Ph:* (205)953-2091
*Fax:* (205)953-6167
*Free:* 800-522-0033

### • 5816 • Air Force ROTC Scholarships
*(Undergraduate/Scholarship)*

**Purpose:** To educate and prepare college students to be Air Force officers. **Focus:** General Studies. **Qualif.:** Applicants must be high school seniors, high school graduates not enrolled full-time in college who want to work toward certain (mostly technical) degrees, or college students. They must enroll in Air Force ROTC to receive scholarships. **Criteria:** High school students and high school graduates are selected on the basis of grade point average, interview evaluation, SAT and ACT scores, recommendations from high school officials, extracurricular activities, medical examination, and acceptance and attendance at a college or university offering Air Force ROTC. College students competing for scholarships will also be selected on the basis of scores on the Air Force Officer Qualifying Test, college GPA, extracurricular activities, and medical examination.

**Funds Avail.:** One- to four-year college scholarship. In selected majors scholarships may be extended to meet a five-year degree program requirement. The one-year scholarship is offered to students majoring in career fields in which the Air Force has a shortage, such as nursing. Two- to four-year scholarships are for students pursuing degrees in certain technical fields such as engineering, science, math, and nursing, as well as students enrolled in certain non-technical degree programs, such as business administration, accounting, economics, and management. **No. of Awards:** Varies. **To Apply:** Application packages are available from high school officials, admissions liaison officers, Air Force recruiters, Air Force ROTC admissions counselors, professors of aerospace studies at colleges and universities, and the Air Force ROTC Recruiting Division at the above address. **Deadline:** December 1 of the high school senior year for high school seniors and graduates, and during the freshman, sophomore, or junior years for college students.

---

## • 5817 •
## U.S. Arms Control and Disarmament Agency
Operations Analysis, Rm. 5726
320 21st St., NW
Washington, DC 20451

### • 5818 • William C. Foster Fellows Visiting Scholars Competition *(Postdoctorate, Professional Development/Fellowship)*

**Purpose:** To give specialists in the physical sciences and other disciplines relevant to the agency's activities an opportunity for active participation in the arms control and disarmament activities of the agency, and to gain for the agency the perspective and expertise such persons can offer. **Focus:** Chemistry, Engineering, Physics, Mathematics, Statistics, Operations Research, Political Science, International Affairs and Relations, Economics, Geosciences, National Security. **Qualif.:** Candidates must be United States citizens, on the faculty of a recognized institution of higher learning, and tenured or on a tenure track or equivalent. They also must have served as a permanent career employee of the institution for at least ninety days before selection for the program. Areas of study may include chemistry, engineering, physics, mathematics, statistics, operations research, political science, international relations, economics, and geophysics. Prior to appointment, applicants are subject to a full-field background security investigation for a Top Secret security clearance. Scholars are also subject to applicable Federal conflict of interest laws and standards of conduct. **Criteria:** Evaluation focuses upon the scholars' potential for providing expertise or performing services needed by ACDA, rather than on the scholars' previously displayed interests in arms control. Support of the scholars' personal research pursuits is not the primary purpose of the program.

**Funds Avail.:** Visiting scholars are provided with salaries and benefits in accordance with the Intergovernmental Personnel Act and within the agency limitations. They also receive reimbursement for travel to and from the Washington, DC area for their one-year assignment and either a per diem allowance during the one-year assignment or relocation costs. **To Apply:** Applicants must submit a letter indicating the position desired and the perspective and expertise the scholar offers to that position. Also required are a curriculum vitae, letters of reference, and no more than two samples of published articles. Twelve copies of each article are required. **Deadline:** January 31.

**Remarks:** Positions are available in the Bureau of Strategic and Euroasian Affairs (SEA), the Bureau of Multilateral Affairs (MA), the Bureau of Intelligence, Verification and Information Support (IVI), and the Bureau of Nonproliferation Policy and Regional Arms Control (NP). **Contact:** Visiting Scholars Program at the above address (see entry 5817).

**• 5819 • Hubert H. Humphrey Doctoral Fellowships in Arms Control and Disarmament** *(Doctorate/ Fellowship)*

**Purpose:** To encourage specialized training and research in the arms control field. **Focus:** Peace Studies. **Qualif.:** Fellows must be graduate students who have completed all their doctoral requirements except for the dissertation at a U.S. college or university. Dissertation proposals must have been approved in accordance with university procedures. J.D. candidates preparing to enter their third or final year of law school are eligible if the proposed research project represents a substantial amount of credit toward third-year requirements and would result in a paper that would, for example, be appropriate for publication in a law review. Students must also be citizens or nationals of the United States. Employees of ACDA or their relatives are not eligible for this program. **Criteria:** Proposals are evaluated according to the clarity of research goals, soundness of research design, originality, and relevance. Additional factors include overall feasibility of the project, graduate courses grades, and letters of recommendation. Selection may also be based on institutional, geographical, and disciplinary distribution. Although special attention is paid to research with direct policy or technical implications, innovative theoretical or empirical efforts are also considered. Historical, quantitative and policy analyses are appropriate for this program. Applicants should note that if they are selected, they are required to submit to ACDA quarterly progress reports, approved by the dissertation adviser, beginning three months after commencement of the fellowship.

**Funds Avail.:** Stipends are $8,000 each. Awards also include payment of any applicable tuition and fees for one year. For J.D. candidates who do not devote a full year to research, the award amounts are prorated by dividing the number of credits assigned to the writing of the J.D. paper by the total number of credits required to be taken during the final year. In no case, however, is the stipend less than $1,000, nor the tuition payment less than 20 percent of the total cost of tuition up to $6,000. In exceptional cases, doctoral candidates may request extensions of up to three months (prorated at $420 per month). **No. of Awards:** 6. **To Apply:** Applicants must submit a dissertation or J.D. research proposal, not exceeding five pages in length, describing the topic, research design, and methodology to be employed in the research. Its relevance to arms control, nonproliferation, and disarmament issues and policies must be outlined. The relevance of the research to arms control issues and policy is an essential criterion. Any research dealing with foreign relations or with foreign areas and people must be approved in advance by the Department of

State (if research involves foreign travel or contact). In addition, a completed application, bibliography of works related to research, official graduate school transcripts, three letters of recommendation, and a signed approval of the student's proposed dissertation topic must be submitted for review. **Deadline:** March 15.

**Remarks:** Fellows will not have access to classified information or to conduct research on ACDA premises. **Contact:** ACDA at the above address (see entry 5817).

**• 5820 •**
**U.S. Army Center of Military History**
c/o Dissertation Fellowship
   Committee, Exec.Sec.
Bldg. 35
103 3rd Ave., Fort McNair          Ph: (202)685-2278
Washington, DC 20319-5058          Fax: (202)685-2077
*E-mail:* BIRTLAJ@HQDA.ARMY.MIL
*URL:* http://www.army.mil/cmh-pg

**• 5821 • U.S. Army Center of Military History Dissertation Year Fellowships** *(Doctorate/Fellowship)*

**Purpose:** To stimulate the study of military history. **Focus:** Military History. **Qualif.:** Applicants must be civilian citizens of the United States who are qualified graduate students writing their Ph.D. dissertations on the history of war on land, especially the history of the United States Army. For the purposes of this program, the history of war on land is broadly defined, including such areas as biography, military campaigns, military organization and administration, policy, strategy, tactics, weaponry, technology, training, logistics, and the evolution of civil-military relations. At the time the Fellowship becomes tenable, all requirements for the Ph.D., except the dissertation, must be completed. There are no restrictions as to race, creed, color, or sex, but anyone who has held or accepted an equivalent fellowship from any other Department of Defense agency is not eligible. **Criteria:** Applicants are evaluated on the basis of academic achievement, faculty recommendation, demonstrated writing ability, and the nature and location of the proposed research. In the selection of proposals for funding, preference is given to topics on the history of the U.S. Army. Topics should complement rather than duplicate the Center's existing projects.

**Funds Avail.:** $9,000. From this sum, the recipient must meet travel, typing, and all other expenses connected with the fellowship. **No. of Awards:** Up to four. **To Apply:** Applicants must complete an official application form and submit a 10-25 page sample of their writing, the proposed plan of the dissertation research and reasons for their interest in the topic, and official undergraduate and graduate transcripts. Letters of recommendation from two persons who know the candidates and their work and a letter from the director of the Ph.D. dissertation that sets forth the director's judgment of the candidate's proposal, potential for research in military history, and the significance of the dissertation project must be sent directly to the Center. Although CMH may review the dissertation, responsibility for its content remains with the fellow's academic institution. CMH requires one copy of the completed dissertation for its collection. **Deadline:** Postmarked by January 15. Applicants are notified of competition results by April 1.

---

## • 5822 •
### U.S. Army Military History Institute
22 Ashburn Dr.
Carlisle Barracks
Carlisle, PA 17013-5008
*URL:* http://carlisle-www.army.mil/usamhi/

*Ph:* (717)245-3089
*Fax:* (717)245-3045

### • 5823 • Advanced Research Grants in Military History *(Graduate, Postgraduate/Grant)*

**Purpose:** To support individual research based on holdings of the Institute. **Focus:** Military History. **Qualif.:** Candidates may be non-U.S. citizens, but must be scholars at the graduate or postgraduate level or must have comparable qualifications based on experience. Applicants are required to describe the subject, scope, and character of the proposed project, estimated time to completion, and how the Institute will aid the research. Awards are tenable at the U.S. Military History Institute only.

**Funds Avail.:** $750 grant. **No. of Awards:** One or two. **To Apply:** Write for application form and guidelines. Submit the form and any supporting documents to the Assistant Director for Educational Services. **Deadline:** January 1. **Contact:** Assistant Director for Educational Services, at the above address (see entry 5822).

## • 5824 •
### U.S. Army Reserve
PO Box 3219
Warminster, PA 18974-9844
*URL:* http://www.usa.army.mil

*Free:* 800-USA-ARMY

### • 5825 • Montgomery GI Bill *(Undergraduate/Scholarship)*

**Criteria:** Candidates must enlist in the Army Reserve for 6 years.

**Funds Avail.:** Up to $6,840. **To Apply:** Awarded annually. **Contact:** U.S. Army Reserve at the above address (see entry 5824).

### • 5826 • Montgomery G.I. Bill and U.S. Army College Fund *(Undergraduate/Scholarship)*

**Purpose:** To provide financial support for college, university, or vocational school after completion of service in the U.S. Army. **Focus:** General Studies. **Qualif.:** Applicants must enlist in the Army for training in selected skills for two to four years. During active duty, soldiers contribute $100 a month from their pay for one year for a total of $1,200. The Montgomery G.I. Bill and the Army College Fund contributes the rest. Following service, the individual enrolls in a Veteran's Administration approved college, university, or vocational school, and receives a monthly payment based on the course load and the amount in their fund. Prior to enlistment, applicants must not have previously served in the military. In addition, they must be a high school graduates, score in the upper half of the Armed Forces Qualification Test, and meet the regular qualifications for U.S. military service.

**Funds Avail.:** For Army enlistees, $20,000 for a two-year enlistment; $25,000 for three years; and $30,000 for four years. **To Apply:** Individuals may apply at any U.S. Army recruiting station. For information call 800-USA-ARMY. **Deadline:** None. **Contact:** Gil Apa at the above address (see entry 5824).

## • 5827 •
### United States Association for Blind Athletes
33 N. Institute St.
Colorado Springs, CO 80903
*E-mail:* usainfo@iex.net
*URL:* http://www.usaba.org

*Ph:* (719)630-0422
*Fax:* (719)630-0616

### • 5828 • Arthur E. and Helen Copeland Scholarships *(Undergraduate/Scholarship)*

**Focus:** General Studies. **Qualif.:** Applicants must be legally blind persons who have participated in USABA sports programs and have been USABA members for the past two years. They must also have been admitted to an academic, vocational, technical, professional, or certification program at the post-secondary level. **Criteria:** Based upon demonstrated academic record, involvement in extracurricular or civic activities, academic goals and objectives, and USABA involvement at various levels. Leading scholarship candidates may be interviewed personally and/or by telephone.

**Funds Avail.:** One Arthur E. Copeland Scholarship of $500 will be awarded to a male; one Helen Copeland Scholarship of $500 will be awarded to a female. **No. of Awards:** 2. **To Apply:** A completed application must be submitted along with an autobiographical sketch of not more than three pages outlining USABA involvement and academic goals and objective for which the scholarship funds will be used, official transcripts from the school the applicant is presently attending, or most recently attended, the names, addresses, and phone numbers of three individuals from whom recommendations can be obtained (one from USABA, one academic, and one personal), and proof of acceptance into the program for which the scholarship funds will be used. **Deadline:** June 15. Notification is in August. **Contact:** Charlie Huebnee, Executive Director, at the above address (see entry 5827).

## • 5829 •
### U.S. Bank of Oregon Trust Group
321 SW 6th Ave.
PO Box 3168
Portland, OR 97208

*Scholarships offered by the U.S. Bank of Oregon Trust Group are administered by the Oregon State Scholarship Commission, 1445 Willamette St., Eugene, OR 97401-7706. Telephone 1-800-452-8807.*

### • 5830 • Campbell-Non-Linfield Scholarship Fund *(Graduate, Undergraduate/Scholarship)*

**Focus:** General Studies. **Qualif.:** Applicants must be Oregon residents who are undergraduate or graduate students at Oregon colleges or universities other than Linfield College, McMinnville, Oregon. The required minimum cumulative grade point average for high school seniors is 3.75, 1100 SAT, and for college students is 3.75 GPA. **Deadline:** Applications are processed between June 1 and June 15 only. **Contact:** Oregon State Scholarship Commission, 1500 Valley River Dr., Ste. 100, Eugene, OR 97401-7706. Telephone: (503)687-7395.

### • 5831 • Crawford Scholarship Fund *(Graduate, Undergraduate/Scholarship)*

**Focus:** General Studies. **Qualif.:** Applicants must be Oregon residents enrolled as full-time undergraduate or graduate students at accredited colleges, universities, trade or technical schools in the United States. The loan does not apply for programs of medicine, law, theology, teaching, and music. The required minimum cumulative grade point average for high school seniors is 3.50 and for college students is 3.50. Graduate students, doctoral candidates, and trade/technical school students must maintain satisfactory academic progress. **Deadline:** Applications are processed between June 1 and June 15 only. **Contact:** Oregon State Scholarship Commission, 1500 Valley River Dr., Ste. 100, Eugene, OR 97401-7706. Telephone: (503)687-7395.

### • 5832 • Franks Foundation Loan *(Graduate, Undergraduate/Loan)*

**Focus:** Nursing. **Qualif.:** Applicants must be Oregon residents enrolled as full-time undergraduate or graduate students in a nursing or theology program at an accredited school of nursing or theology in the United States. The required minimum cumulative grade point average for high school seniors is 2.50 and for college students is 2.00. **Criteria:** Selections are based on financial need and satisfactory academic progress as defined by the institution. First priority is given to applications from Deschutes, Jefferson, and Cook counties; second priority to Grant, Lake, Harney, and Klamath counties; and third priority to any other Oregon county.

**Funds Avail.:** Loans are repaid with four-and-one-half percent interest, with payments beginning six months after graduation or immediately if no longer a full-time student. **Deadline:** Applications are processed between June 1 and June 15 only. **Contact:** Oregon State Scholarship Commission, 1500 Valley River Dr., Ste. 100, Eugene, OR 97401-7706. Telephone: (503)687-7395.

### • 5833 • Maria C. Jackson & General George A. White Scholarships *(Undergraduate/Scholarship)*

**Focus:** General Studies. **Qualif.:** Applicants for the Maria C. Jackson and General George A. White Scholarships must be Oregon residents who served, or whose parent(s) served or are currently serving, in the United States Armed Forces. Applicants must enroll full-time at any two- or four-year college or university in Oregon that qualifies under Title IV of the federal student financial aid program. A cumulative grade point average of 3.75 is required for high school and college students and satisfactory academic progress for graduate and trade/technical school students. **Criteria:** Applications are reviewed based on financial need and academic promise. Renewal candidates are given preference.

**Funds Avail.:** The committee determines award amounts. The awards are renewable. **No. of Awards:** 50-75. **To Apply:** Applicants must complete a federally-approved need analysis form and mark "yes" to the question giving the U.S. Department of Education permission to send information to the state financial aid agency. Scholarship applications are available from January 1 through March 15 through participating schools or by writing to the Oregon State Scholarship Commission (see address below) and requesting the "Private Award Application." Graduating high school seniors must also submit seventh semester high school transcripts displaying cumulative grade point average and SAT scores. College students must submit transcripts of all college work completed through January 1 of the application year. **Deadline:** All materials and applications must be returned to the Oregon State Scholarship Commission by March 15. **Contact:** The Oregon State Scholarship Commission, 1500 Valley River Dr., Ste. 100, Eugene, OR 97401-7706. Telephone: (503)687-7395.

### • 5834 • Jenkins Loan *(Graduate, Undergraduate/ Loan)*

**Focus:** General Studies. **Qualif.:** Applicants must be high school graduates enrolled as full-time undergraduate or graduate students at accredited colleges and universities in the United States. The required minimum cumulative grade point average for high school seniors is 2.50 and for college students is 2.00. **Criteria:** Priority is given to renewal applicants; second priority to Oregon residents attending schools in the United States; and third priority to Oregon students who are Washington or Idaho residents.

**Funds Avail.:** Loans are renewable, with an expected fund availability of $150,000. Repayment, with seven percent interest, begins six months after graduation or immediately if no longer a full-time student. **Deadline:** Applications are processed between June 1 and June 15 and throughout the school year if funds are

available. Closed from June 16 through September 15. **Contact:** Oregon State Scholarship Commission, 1500 Valley River Dr., Ste. 100, Eugene, OR 97401-7706. Telephone: (503)687-7395.

### • 5835 • Bertha B. Singer Nurses Scholarship *(Graduate, Undergraduate/Scholarship)*

**Qualif.:** Applicants must be graduates of accredited Oregon high schools or residents who have lived in Oregon at least one full year prior to the beginning of the academic year for which assistance is needed. They must be accepted for enrollment in a full-time undergraduate or graduate nursing program at any publicly or privately accredited school of nursing or nursing program in the state of Oregon. A cumulative grade point average of 3.0 is also required. **Criteria:** Candidates are selected for interviews based on financial need and grade point average. Selected applicants interview with the Singer Committee and must supply copies of the Student Aid Report (SAR) and the college financial aid award letter. Previous recipients are considered on the same basis as first-time applicants.

**Funds Avail.:** Twenty scholarships ranging from $700 to $1,200 are awarded annually. **To Apply:** Applicants must complete a federally-approved need analysis form and mark "yes" to the question giving the U.S. Department of Education permission to send information to the state financial aid agency. Scholarship applications are available from January 1 through March 15 through participating schools or by writing to the Oregon State Scholarship Commission and requesting the "Private Award Application." Graduating high school seniors must also submit seventh semester high school transcripts displaying cumulative grade point averages and SAT scores. College students must submit transcripts of all college work completed through January 1 of the application year. Previous recipients of this scholarship must reapply each year. **Deadline:** All materials and applications must be returned to the Oregon State Scholarship Commission by March 15.

**Remarks:** Approximately 70 applications are received each year. **Contact:** The Oregon State Scholarship Commission, 1500 Valley River Dr., Ste. 100, Eugene, OR 97401-7706. Toll-free telephone: 800-452-8807.

### • 5836 • Jerome B. Steinbach Scholarship *(Undergraduate/Scholarship)*

**Qualif.:** Applicants must be Oregon residents who are American citizens by birth and planning to enroll as sophomores, juniors, or seniors in a full-time undergraduate course of study at any two- or four-year postsecondary institution in the United States that qualifies under Title IV of the federal student financial aid program. A cumulative grade point average of 3.25 is also required. **Criteria:** The Steinbach Committee reviews applications and, based on financial need and academic promise, interviews candidates. Applicants selected to be interviewed must supply the committee with copies of the Student Aid Report (SAR) and the college financial Aid award letter. **No. of Awards:** 50-60. **To Apply:** Applicants must complete a federally-approved need analysis form and mark "yes" to the question giving the U.S. Department of Education permission to send information to the state financial aid agency. Scholarship applications are available from January 1 through March 15 through participating schools or by writing to the Oregon State Scholarship Commission at the address listed below and requesting the "Private Award Application." **Deadline:** All materials and applications must be returned to the Oregon State Scholarship Commission by March 15. **Contact:** The Oregon State Scholarship Commission, 1500 Valley River Dr., Ste. 100, Eugene, OR 97401-7706. Telephone: (503)687-7395.

### • 5837 • Harley & Mertie Stevens Memorial Fund *(Undergraduate/Loan, Scholarship)*

**Focus:** General Studies. **Qualif.:** Applicants must be Oregon residents who are graduates of accredited Clackamas County high schools and are enrolling in their first year of undergraduate study

---

Awards are arranged alphabetically below their administering organizations

## U.S. Bank of Oregon Trust Group (continued)

at any two- or four-year state-supported or private, Protestant-owned and operated college or university in Oregon. A cumulative grade point average of 3.50 is also required. **Criteria:** Candidates are selected for interviews based on financial need and academic promise. Selected students must supply copies of the Student Aid Report (SAR) and the college financial aid award letter to the interview committee.

**Funds Avail.:** $400 to $2,500. **No. of Awards:** 25-30. **To Apply:** Applicants must apply for the first and fourth year scholarships. Loans are available to second and third year students who received scholarships the first year at an interest rate of three percent. Loan applications are processed June 1 through June 15 through the U.S. Bank Trust Group. Scholarships are available to fourth-year students if they received a scholarship award as a first-year student, enroll as a fourth-year student, continue to qualify for financial need, and have a 3.25 grade point average. Every new applicant must complete a federally-approved need analysis form and mark "yes" to the question giving the U.S. Department of Education permission to send information to the state financial aid agency. Scholarship applications are available from January 1 through March 15 through participating schools or by writing to the Oregon State Scholarship Commission and requesting the "Private Award Application." Graduating high school seniors must also submit seventh semester high school transcripts displaying cumulative grade point averages and SAT scores. College students must submit transcripts of all college work completed through January 1 of the application year. Previous recipients of this scholarship must apply each year. **Deadline:** All materials and applications must be returned to the Oregon State Scholarship Commission by March 15. **Contact:** The Oregon State Scholarship Commission, 1500 Valley River Dr., Ste. 100, Eugene, OR 97401-7706 (for scholarship applications and information). Telephone: (503)687-7395. For loan applications and information for second and third year students, contact the U.S. Bank Trust Group, PO Box 3168, Portland, OR 97208.

## • 5838 • Flora M. Von Der Ahe Scholarship
*(Graduate, Undergraduate/Scholarship)*

**Focus:** General Studies. **Qualif.:** Candidates must be from accredited high schools in Umatilla County, Oregon, and plan to enroll full-time in an undergraduate or graduate course of study at any accredited college, university, or technical school in Oregon. A cumulative grade point average of 2.50 is also required. **Criteria:** Awards are given based on information contained in the applications. No interviews are required. Renewal candidates are considered on the same basis as first-time applicants.

**Funds Avail.:** $200 to $750. They are renewable upon application. **No. of Awards:** 20-22. **To Apply:** Applicants must complete a federally-approved need analysis form and mark "yes" to the question giving the U.S. Department of Education permission to send information to the state financial aid agency. Scholarship applications are available from January 1 through March 15 through participating schools or by writing to the Oregon State Scholarship Commission at the address listed below and requesting the "Private Award Application." Graduating high school seniors must also submit seventh semester high school transcripts displaying cumulative grade point average and SAT scores. College students must submit transcripts of all college work completed through January 1 of the application year. **Deadline:** All materials and applications must be returned to the Oregon State Scholarship Commission by March 15. **Contact:** The Oregon State Scholarship Commission, 1500 Valley River Dr., Ste. 100, Eugene, OR 97401-7706. Telephone: (503)687-7395.

## • 5839 • Constance Dorothea Weinman Scholarship Trust for Graduate Study in Instructional Technology
*(Doctorate, Graduate/Scholarship)*

**Focus:** Education. **Qualif.:** Applicants must be qualified graduate students currently attending a college or university and who are seeking a master's or doctoral degree in the field of instructional

systems. Instructional systems technology includes the following areas specialization: instructional design, instructional film and television, school library media management, audiovisual media production, and computers-in-education. **Criteria:** Candidates must have demonstrated genuine interest, aptitude, excellence in scholarship, and potential for leadership in research, teaching, and practice within the professional field of instructional systems technology. Preference is given to residents of the State of Oregon.

**Funds Avail.:** Up to $5,000 each. **To Apply:** Three letters of reference, transcripts of completed undergraduate and graduate course work, and verification of current enrollment in a graduate program of study must be included with the application. **Deadline:** May 30. **Contact:** U.S. Bank of Oregon at the above address (see entry 5829).

## • 5840 •
## U.S. Bureau of Alcohol, Tobacco, and Firearms
Office of Liaison and Public
  Information, Rm. 8290
650 Massachusetts Ave., NW      Ph: (202)927-8500
Washington, DC 20226      Fax: (202)927-8868
E-mail: affmail@atfhg.atf.treas.gov
URL: http://atf.ustreas.gov/welcome1.htm

## • 5841 • ATF Special Agents' Scholarships
*(Undergraduate/Scholarship)*

**Purpose:** To recognize and assist outstanding law enforcement Explorers in their undergraduate studies in preparation for a career in law enforcement. **Qualif.:** Applicants must be registered Explorer scouts active in a law enforcement post. They must be at least a high school senior by March 1 of the year for which they are being considered.

**Funds Avail.:** The number of scholarships varies from year to year. The amount of the award is $1,000 payable to an accredited college or university for tuition only. The scholarship does not cover room and board or other expenses. It is available from the date of selection until two years later, expiring on December 31. **To Apply:** Applicants must submit grade transcripts; background information on Explorer experience; three letters of recommendation from a Post Advisor, employer, or coach; an essay on three personal skills necessary in law enforcement and how these skills will be developed in undergraduate studies; and certification by the Post Advisor and local Boy Scout Council. **Deadline:** April of even numbered years. **Contact:** Local Boy Scout Council or Liaison Program Manager at the above address (see entry 5840).

## • 5842 •
## U.S. Bureau of Indian Affairs
Office of Indian Education Programs
1849 C St., NW      Ph: (202)208-4871
Washington, DC 20240      Fax: (202)208-3312
E-mail: garry_martin@ios.doi.gov

## • 5843 • U.S. Bureau of Indian Affairs Scholarship Grant *(Undergraduate/Grant)*

**Qualif.:** Candidates must be Native Americans, Eskimos, or Alaska natives and be members of federally recognized tribes. They must also have been accepted at an accredited college or university. **Criteria:** Based on financial need.

**Funds Avail.:** Appropriated yearly by Congress with each tribe specifying the amount they wish to receive. **No. of Awards:** Varies. **To Apply:** All application information is available from the Tribal Contractor or the Bureau Agency serving that tribe. There are no funds or applications available from the above address or the Central Office of the Bureau of Indian Affairs. **Deadline:** Set by each Tribal Contractor. **Contact:** Branch of Post Secondary Education at the above address (see entry 5842).

• 5844 •

## U.S. Coast Guard Academy
Scholarship Department     *Ph:* (203)444-8500
New London, CT 06320-4195     *Fax:* (203)437-6700
                       *Free:* 800-883-8724

*E-mail:* uscgatr@dcseq.uscga.edu
*URL:* http://www.dot.gov/dotinfo/uscg/hq/uscga/uscga.html

### • 5845 • U.S. Coast Guard Academy Appointment
*(Undergraduate/Scholarship)*

**Purpose:** To offer cost of undergraduate education toward a degree and commission in the U.S Coast Guard. **Focus:** Civil Engineering, Electrical Engineering, Marine Engineering, Mechanical Engineering, Government, Mathematics, Marine Science, Management. **Qualif.:** Applicants must be between the ages of 17 and 21, high school graduates, and in excellent physical condition. **Criteria:** Selections are based on ACT/SAT test scores and interview. **Deadline:** December 15. **Contact:** R.W. Thorne, Captain, U.S. Coast Guard, at the above address (see entry 5844). For applications, call (203)444-8501.

• 5846 •

## U.S. Coast Guard - Chief Petty Officer's Association - Captain Caliendo College Assistance Fund
5520 G. Hempstead Way
Springfield, VA 22151

### • 5847 • USCG Chief Petty Officers Association Captain Caliendo College Assistance Fund Scholarship Program *(High School, Undergraduate/Scholarship)*

**Purpose:** To assist dependent children of CPOA regular/associate members and deceased US Coast Guard enlisted association members. **Qualif.:** Applicant must be under the age of 23, or be a handicapped, dependent child. All applicants must have applied for enrollment or, be currently enrolled in an accredited college, university or vocational school; must be enrolled in a full-time course of instruction; must submit an essay of not less than 300 or more than 500 words on the current year's topic; must provide a copy of the official grade transcripts for the scholastic year prior to application, and a copy of a letter indicating college, university or vocational school acceptance. **Criteria:** The sponsor must have served honorably in the United States Coast Guard. The five most deserving dependent sons/daughters who meet the application requirements listed.

**Funds Avail.:** There are several grants in the following amount: One $1,500 grant for the most deserving candidate who is or will be attending an accredited college, university or vocational school. One $1,250 grant for the best qualified candidate remaining who is or will be attending an accredited college, university or vocational school. One $1,000 grant for the best qualified candidate remaining who is or will be attending an accredited college, university or vocational school. One $750 grant for the best qualified candidate remaining who is or will be attending an

accredited college, university or vocational school. 5. One $500 grant for the best qualified candidate remaining who is or will be attending an accredited college, university or vocational school. **No. of Awards:** 5. **Deadline:** March 1.

**Remarks:** The receipt of one grant does not exclude students from submitting applications for additional grants during subsequent years. **Contact:** USCG Chief Petty Officers Association at the above address (see entry 5846).

• 5848 •

## U.S. Coast Guard Mutual Assistance (G-ZMA)
Coast Guard Headquarters, No. 4611    *Ph:* (202)267-1683
2100 2nd St., S.W.                  *Fax:* (202)267-4823
Washington, DC 20593-0001     *Free:* 800-881-2462

### • 5849 • Admiral Roland Student Loan *(Graduate, Postgraduate, Undergraduate/Loan)*

**Purpose:** To provide a convenient way for Coast Guard Mutual Assistance members and their families to borrow money. **Focus:** General Studies. **Qualif.:** Applicants must be members of Coast Guard Mutual Assistance, their spouses, or their children and be eligible financially for the corresponding loan they are applying for (as determined by the "financial need analysis" secured through the college financial aid office). Students must also be U.S. citizens or nationals or eligible permanent residents of the United States, enrolled at an eligible school and be in good standing at least half-time (maintaining a "C" grade average or higher by the end of the second academic year).

**Funds Avail.:** Two loans are available (Stafford Loans and PLUS Loans) in varying amounts ranging from $2,625/freshman; $3,500 second year; $5,500 for remaining years for a maximum of $23,000. Students may borrow up to $8,500 per year for graduate study. The interest rate for Federal Stafford loans is an annual variable rate not to exceed 8.25%, Federal Plus Stafford Loan not to exceed 9%. **Deadline:** March 8.

**Remarks:** A benefit of receiving a federal loans through this program is that students are not assessed a 3 percent guarantee fee generally required for Stafford and PLUS loans. Also, loans are typically processed within three days from the date of receipt. **Contact:** Contact Coast Guard Mutual Assistance for applications at the above address,(see entry 5848) or contact the financial aid office at an eligible institution.

• 5850 •

## U.S. Congress - Office of Technology Assessment
c/o William Norris, Personnel
  Director
600 Pennsylvania Ave., SE       *Ph:* (202)228-6131
Washington, DC 20003         *Fax:* (202)228-6098
*URL:* http://thomas.loc.gov/

*The Office of Technology Assessment is a nonpartisan analytical support agency that provides expertise to congressional committees in various technical and scientific fields that have important implications for future Federal policy.*

### • 5851 • Morris K. Udall OTA Congressional Fellowship *(Postdoctorate/Fellowship)*

**Purpose:** To provide an opportunity for individuals of proven ability to assist Congress in its deliberations of science and technology issues affecting public policy and to gain a better understanding of the ways in which Congress establishes national policy related to these issues. **Focus:** Science and Technology. **Qualif.:** Applicants

## U.S. Congress - Office of Technology Assessment *(continued)*

must have demonstrated exceptional ability in such areas as the physical or biological sciences, engineering, law, economics, environmental and social sciences, and public policy. They must also have completed research at the doctoral level or have experience equivalent to a doctoral degree. **Criteria:** Selection is based on applicants' records of achievement and their potential for contributing individual expertise to one or more of OTA's studies.

**Funds Avail.:** Up to six Fellows will be chosen for a one-year appointment in Washington D.C., usually beginning in September. The salary range is from $35,000-$70,000 per annum based on the applicant's current salary and/or training and experience. In some cases, the Fellow may accept a salary supplement from the parent organization. **No. of Awards:** Up to 6. **To Apply:** Applicants for the Fellowship are required to submit the following documentation: a resume not to exceed two pages listing educational experience, areas of special interest, and a one-page listing of their most recently published works; three letters of reference, including telephone numbers, from individuals well acquainted with applicant's professional competence to be sent directly to OTA; a statement of up to 1000 words that either evaluates an issue with technical and public policy content and its importance to the applicant or summarizes the public policy findings of work the applicant has done; and a brief statement of up to 250 words explaining how OTA and the Fellowship fit into the applicant's career objectives. **Deadline:** The deadline for applications and letters of reference is February 1. Interviews of finalists are at the end of March. Awards are announced at the beginning of April.

**Remarks:** The Fellowship honors former Congressman Morris K. Udall of Arizona, who retired in 1991 after a long, distinguished career of public service. Mr. Udall was one of the founders of OTA and served on OTA's Technology Assessment Board since 1973 including several terms as Chairman. **Contact:** William Norris, Personnel Director, at the above address (see entry 5850).

---

• 5852 •
## U.S. Customs Service
c/o Carolyn J. Dankel
1301 Constitution Ave., NW          Ph: (202)927-2207
Washington, DC 20229                 Fax: (202)927-5408
URL: http://www.customs.ustreas.gov/

### • 5853 • Law Enforcement Explorer Scholarships *(Undergraduate/Scholarship)*

**Purpose:** The scholarships are funded from contributions by officers of the U.S. Customs Service. They are intended to recognize and assist Explorer scouts with exceptional potential to pursue undergraduate studies in preparation for a career in law enforcement. **Focus:** Law Enforcement. **Qualif.:** Applicants must be registered Explorer scouts active in a Law Enforcement Post. They must be at least a high school senior by March 1 of the year for which they are being considered. **Criteria:** Based on an essay and grade point average.

**Funds Avail.:** The number of scholarships varies. The amount of the award is $1000, payable to an accredited college or university for tuition only. The scholarship does not cover room and board or other expenses. It is available from the date of selection until two years later, expiring on December 31. **No. of Awards:** 1. **To Apply:** Applicants must submit grade transcripts, personal data and information on Law Enforcement Explorer experience, letters of recommendation from an Advisor or employer, and certifications from the Post Advisor and local Boy Scout Council. An essay describing three personal skills necessary in a law enforcement career and relating these skills to proposed undergraduate studies is also required. **Deadline:** Applications must be received by April

1. **Contact:** Local Boy Scout Council or Law Enforcement Liaison Officer at the above address (see entry 5852).

---

• 5854 •
## U.S. Department of Defense
NDSEG Fellowship Program
200 Park Drive, Ste. 211
PO Box 13444                         Ph: (919)549-8505
Research Triangle Park, NC 27709     Fax: (919)549-8205
E-mail: ndseg@aro-emh1.army.mil
URL: http://www.battelle.org/ndseg/ndseg.html

### • 5855 • National Defense Science and Engineering Graduate Fellowship Program *(Graduate/Fellowship)*

**Purpose:** To support research and study leading to doctoral degrees. **Focus:** Behavioral Sciences, Biological Sciences, Engineering, Mathematics, Oceanography, Physical Sciences. **Qualif.:** Applicant must be a U.S. citizen or national, and be at or near the beginning of graduate study in a science or engineering department at a U.S. university. Preference will be given to candidates who intend to specialize in one of the following fields: aeronautical and astronautical engineering; biosciences; chemical engineering; chemistry; cognitive, neural, and behavioral sciences; computer science, electrical engineering; geosciences; manufacturing sciences and engineering; materials science and engineering; mathematics, mechanical engineering, naval architecture and ocean engineering; oceanography; and physics.

**Funds Avail.:** $18,000/year, plus tuition and fees. **No. of Awards:** approximately 90. **To Apply:** Write for application form and guidelines. Submit form with official transcripts, and three letters of reference, and GRE scores. **Deadline:** The third Wednesday in January, Notification on or about March 31. **Contact:** Dr. George Outterson, Program Manager.

---

• 5856 •
## U.S. Department of Energy - Oak Ridge Institute for Science Education
PO Box 117                           Ph: (423)576-3000
Oak Ridge, TN 37831-0117             Fax: (423)576-3643
E-mail: pescep@orau.gov
URL: http://www.orau.gov/oris.educ.htm

### • 5857 • Advanced Industrial Concepts (AIC) Materials Science Program *(Graduate/Fellowship)*

**Purpose:** To establish and maintain cooperative linkages between Oak Ridge National Laboratory (ORNL) and universities with program that lead to degrees or degree options in materials science and related disciplines. **Focus:** Materials science, materials engineering, metallurgical engineering, chemical engineering, ceramic engineering, chemical engineering, and chemistry. **Qualif.:** Applicants must be African American or Native American graduating seniors and graduate students who have not completed their first year.

**Funds Avail.:** Tuition and fees up to $6,000 per year; $1,200 per month in stipends plus $300 dislocation allowance during research appointment. Renewable for up to 24 months. **No. of Awards:** Varies. **To Apply:** Write or telephone for further details. **Deadline:** Late February.

**Remarks:** Research sites include any accredited U.S. institution. Funds available through the Conservation and Renewable Energy, Office of Industrial Technologies. **Contact:** Deborah McCleary,

Program Manager, at (615)576-4813, or Denise Novak, Program Specialist, at (615)576-5300.

### • 5858 • Agency for Toxic Substances and Disease Registry Clinical Fellowships in Environmental Medicine *(Postdoctorate/Fellowship)*

**Purpose:** To provide support for fellows to engage in applied environmentally-related clinical research that helps prevent or mitigate the adverse human health effects and diminished quality of life that may result from exposure to hazardous substances in the non-workplace environment. **Focus:** Occupational medicine, clinical or environmental toxicology. **Qualif.:** Applicants must have medical degree and be board eligible in a clinical specialty with one or more years of additional training in occupational medicine and/or clinical (environmental) toxicology.

**Funds Avail.:** $26,000 stipend for 50 percent time. Renewable. **To Apply:** Telephone for further details. **Deadline:** February 1.

**Remarks:** Location sites include recognized Association of Occupational and Environmental Health facilities (hospitals, clinics, medical schools). Funds made available through an interagency agreement between U.S. Department of Energy and the Agency for Toxic Substances and Disease Registry (Public Health Service). **Contact:** Priscilla Campbell, Program Manager, at (615) 241-2875 or Cindy Sheldon, Program Specialist, at (165) 576-3456.

### • 5859 • Agency for Toxic Substances and Disease Registry Postgraduate Research Program *(Postgraduate/Fellowship)*

**Purpose:** To provide opportunities and support for research in exposure and disease registries, health investigations, public health assessments, toxicological profiles, emergency response, and health education. **Focus:** Toxicology, epidemiology, environmental or public health, medicine, pharmacology. **Qualif.:** Applicants should have completed their graduate degree within the last three years; others considered on a case-by-case basis.

**Funds Avail.:** Stipend based on research area and degree; reimbursement for inbound travel and moving. Renewable. **No. of Awards:** Varies. **To Apply:** Write or telephone for further details. **Deadline:** Continuous.

**Remarks:** Research site: Agency for Toxic Substances and Disease Registry, Atlanta, Georgia. Funds available through an interagency agreement between the U.S. Department of Energy and the Agency for Toxic Substances and Disease Registry. **Contact:** Priscilla Campbell, Program Manager, at (615) 241-2875, or Cindy Sheldon, Program Specialist, at (615) 576-3456.

### • 5860 • Agency for Toxic Substances and Disease Registry Student Internship Program *(Doctorate, Graduate/Internship)*

**Focus:** Toxicology, epidemiology, environmental or public health, medicine, pharmacology, related scientific disciplines in the biological, medical and physical sciences. **Qualif.:** Applicants must be master's or doctoral students.

**Funds Avail.:** $1,650 to $2,150 monthly stipend (full-time), depending on academic status and research area; limited travel reimbursement; off-campus tuition and fees required by home institution. **To Apply:** Write or telephone for further details. **Deadline:** Continuous.

**Remarks:** Research location: Agency for Toxic Substances and Disease Registry. Funds available through an interagency agreement between the U.S. Department of Energy and the Agency for Toxic Substances and Disease Registry. **Contact:** Kathy Ketner, Program Manager, at (615) 576-3426, or Pat Pressley, Program Specialist, at (615) 576-1083.

### • 5861 • Applied Health Physics Fellowship Program *(Graduate/Fellowship)*

**Focus:** Engineering, mathematics, physical and life sciences. **Qualif.:** Applicants must be graduate students pursuing degrees in health physics.

**Funds Avail.:** $14,400 stipend; additional $300 per month during practicum; $1,000 allowance to the university. **No. of Awards:** 10. **To Apply:** Write or telephone for further details. **Deadline:** End of January.

**Remarks:** Research sites include all participating universities with practicums at various DOE research facilities. Funds available through the U.S. Department of Energy, Office of Environment, Safety and Health. **Contact:** Tom Richmond, Program Manager, at (615)576-2194, or Rose Etta Cox, Program Specialist, at (615)576-9279.

### • 5862 • Bureau of Engraving and Printing Graduate Student Research Participation Program *(Graduate, Postgraduate/Fellowship)*

**Purpose:** To provide opportunities to conduct collaborative research that complements ongoing Bureau of Engraving and Printing (BE) research projects; R&D efforts aimed at improving the quality of products, reducing manufacturing costs, and strengthening deterrents to counterfeiting. **Focus:** Physical science, graphic arts, artificial intelligence, computer science, engineering. **Qualif.:** Applicants must be master's or doctoral students.

**Funds Avail.:** Stipend based on academic status and research area; limited travel reimbursement. **To Apply:** Write or telephone for further details. **Deadline:** Continuous.

**Remarks:** Research locations include the Bureau of Engraving and Printing (Washington, D.C.) and other laboratories carrying out BE research. Funds available through an interagency agreement between the U.S. Department of Energy and the U.S. Department of the Treasury. **Contact:** Kathy Kenter, Program Manager, at (615) 576-3426 or Pat Pressley, Program Specialist, at (615) 576-1083.

### • 5863 • Bureau of Engraving and Printing Postgraduate Research Program *(Postgraduate/Fellowship)*

**Purpose:** to provide opportunities to conduct collaborative research that complements ongoing Bureau of Engraving and Printing BE research projects; R&D efforts aimed at improving the quality of products, reducing manufacturing costs, and strengthening deterrents to counterfeiting. **Focus:** Physical science, graphic arts, computer science, engineering. **Qualif.:** Applicants must have completed their graduate degree within the last three years.

**Funds Avail.:** Stipend based on research area and degree; reimbursement for inbound travel and moving. Renewable. **No. of Awards:** Varies. **To Apply:** Write or telephone for further details. **Deadline:** Continuous.

**Remarks:** Research sites include the Bureau of Engraving and Printing (Washington, D.C.) and other laboratories carrying out BE Research. Funds available through an interagency agreement between the U.S. Department of Energy and the U.S. Department of Energy. **Contact:** Priscilla Campbell, Program Manager, at (615) 241-2875, or Cindy Sheldon, Program Specialist, at (615) 576-3456.

### • 5864 • Center for Devices and Radiological Health Postgraduate Research Program *(Postgraduate/Fellowship)*

**Purpose:** To provide opportunities and support for research concerning medical devices and radiation. **Focus:** Life science, physics, engineering, medical electronics, medical imaging and computer applications, human epidemiology, biostatistics. **Qualif.:**

## U.S. Department of Energy - Oak Ridge Institute for Science Education (continued)

Applicants must have completed their master's or doctoral degrees with the last three years.

**Funds Avail.:** Stipend based on research and degree; reimbursement for inbound travel and moving. Renewable. **No. of Awards:** Varies. **To Apply:** Write or telephone for further details. **Deadline:** Continuous.

**Remarks:** Research site: Center for Devices and Radiological Health, Rockville, Maryland. Funds available through an interagency agreement between the U.S. Department of Energy and the U.S. Food and Drug Administration. **Contact:** Priscilla Campbell, Program Manager, at (615) 241-2875, or Cindy Sheldon, Program Specialist, at (615) 576-3456.

### • 5865 • Center for Drug Evaluation and Research Postgraduate Research (Postgraduate/Fellowship)

**Purpose:** To provide opportunities and support for research concerning drug evaluation. **Focus:** Life science, physical science, materials sciences and engineering, medical imagining and computer applications, human epidemiology, biostatistics. **Qualif.:** Applicants must have completed their master's or doctoral degree within the last three years.

**Funds Avail.:** Stipend based on research area and degree; reimbursement for inbound travel and moving. Renewable. **No. of Awards:** Varies. **To Apply:** Write or telephone for further details. **Deadline:** Continuous.

**Remarks:** Research site: Center for Drug Evaluation and Research, Rockville, Maryland. Funds made available through an interagency agreement between the U.S. Department of Energy and the U.S. Food and Drug Administration. **Contact:** Priscilla Campbell, Program Manager, at (615) 241-2875, or Cindy Sheldon, Program Specialist, at (615) 576-3456.

### • 5866 • Civilian Radioactive Waste Management Fellowship Program (Graduate/Fellowship)

**Purpose:** To offer fellowships for graduate work in field related to the management of spent nuclear fuel and high-level radioactive wastes. **Focus:** Earth science, engineering, materials science, radiation science. **Qualif.:** Applicants must be master's or doctoral students.

**Funds Avail.:** $14,400 minimum stipend; additional $300 per month during practicum; some travel expense; tuition and fees up to $8,000 per year. Renewable for up to four years. **No. of Awards:** Varies. **To Apply:** Write or telephone for further details. **Deadline:** Last Monday in January.

**Remarks:** Research sites include participating universities; practicum at various DOE research facilities. **Contact:** Sandra Johnson, Program Manager, at (615) 576-2600, or Cheryl Terry, Program Specialist, at (615) 576-9558.

### • 5867 • Civilian Radioactive Waste Management/ Historically Black Colleges and Universities Faculty Fellowship Program (Professional Development/ Fellowship)

**Focus:** Engineering, geology, chemistry, biology, physics. **Qualif.:** Applicants must be faculty members at historically black colleges and universities for research related to high-level radioactive waste management.

**Funds Avail.:** $3,000 per month stipend; travel expenses. **To Apply:** Write for further details. **Contact:** Sandra Johnson, Program Manager, at (615) 576-2600 or Cheryl Terry, Program Specialist, at (615) 576-9558.

### • 5868 • Department of Energy Distinguished Postdoctoral Research Program (Postdoctorate/ Fellowship)

**Focus:** Physical science, computer science, engineering. **Qualif.:** Applicants must have completed doctoral degree within last three years.

**Funds Avail.:** $52,800 stipend, reimbursement for inbound travel and moving, medical insurance, and travel to up to three domestic scientific meetings per year of appointment. **To Apply:** Telephone for further details. **Deadline:** Early July.

**Remarks:** Location sites include participating DOE laboratories. Funds made available throughout U.S. Department of Energy, Office of University and Science Education Programs. **Contact:** Linda Holmes, Program Manager, at (615) 576-3192, or Cheryl Guthrie, Program Specialist, at (615) 576-9934.

### • 5869 • Environmental Monitoring Systems Laboratory Research Participation Program (Postdoctorate, Postgraduate/Fellowship)

**Purpose:** To provide opportunities and support for research concerning environmental monitoring systems. **Focus:** Environmental science, engineering, physical science. **Qualif.:** Applicants must have completed their bachelor's, master's or doctoral degree within the last three years; others considered on a case-by-case basis.

**Funds Avail.:** Stipend based on research area and degree; reimbursement for inbound travel and moving. Renewable. **To Apply:** Write or telephone for further details. **Deadline:** Continuous.

**Remarks:** Research site: Environmental Monitoring Systems Laboratory, Cincinnati, Ohio. Funds available through an interagency agreement between the U.S. Department of Energy and the U.S. Environmental Protection Agency Environmental Monitoring Systems Laboratory. **Contact:** Priscilla Campbell, Program Manager, at (615) 241-2875, or Cindy Sheldon, Program Specialist, at (615) 576-3456.

### • 5870 • Environmental Restoration/Waste Management Fellowship Program (Graduate, Postgraduate/Fellowship)

**Purpose:** To offer fellowships for graduate study in various engineering and scientific fields related to environmental restoration and the safe handling and disposal of hazardous, mixed and radioactive wastes. **Focus:** Applied science and engineering disciplines. **Qualif.:** Applicants must be master's or doctoral students.

**Funds Avail.:** $14,400 minimum annual stipend; tuition and fees; additional $00 per month during practicum; travel expenses. Renewable up to four years. **No. of Awards:** Varies. **To Apply:** Write or telephone for further details. **Deadline:** End of January.

**Remarks:** Research sites include all participating universities; practicum at various DOE locations. Funds made available through the U.S. Department of Energy, Office of Environmental Restoration and Waste Management. **Contact:** Colleen Babcock, Program Manager, at (615) 576-9272, or Debra Lawson, Program Specialist, at (615) 576-0128.

### • 5871 • Environmental Restoration/Waste Management Technical Degree Scholarship Program (Undergraduate/Scholarship)

**Focus:** Health physics, industrial hygiene, radiochemistry. **Qualif.:** Applicants must be undergraduate students pursuing associate's and bachelor's engineering technology degrees.

**Funds Avail.:** Tuition and fees paid; monthly stipend of $600; additional $300 per month during practicum. **No. of Awards:** 25. **To Apply:** Write or telephone for further details. **Deadline:** January.

**Remarks:** Research locations include accredited U.S. community colleges, technical schools, two-year and four-year undergraduate institutions; practicums are at various DOE facilities engaged in environmental restoration/waste management research. Funds available through U.S. Department of Energy, Office of Environmental Restoration/Waste Management. **Contact:** Colleen Babcock, Program Manager, at (615) 576-9272, or Debra Lawson, Program Specialist, at (615) 576-0128.

• **5872** • **Faculty Research Participation Program at the Agency for Toxic Substances and Disease Registry** *(Professional Development/Fellowship)*

**Purpose:** To provide opportunities and support for research in exposure and disease registries, health assessments, health effects, toxicological profiles, emergency response, and health education. **Focus:** Toxicology, epidemiology, environmental or public health, education, medicine, pharmacology. **Qualif.:** Applicants must be college or university full-time faculty members.

**Funds Avail.:** Varies. Negotiable stipend based on regular salary; reimbursement for travel. **To Apply:** Telephone for further details. **Deadline:** Continuous.

**Remarks:** Funded by an interagency agreement between the U.S. Department of Energy and the Agency for Toxic Substances and Disease Registry. **Contact:** Harold Rider, Program Manager, at (615) 576-8158 or Kay Ball, Program Specialist, at (615) 576-8807.

• **5873** • **Faculty Research Participation Program at the Bureau of Engraving and Printing** *(Professional Development/Fellowship)*

**Purpose:** To provide opportunities to conduct collaborative research that complements ongoing Bureau of Engraving and Printing (BE) research projects; R&D efforts aimed at improving the quality of products, reducing manufacturing costs, and strengthening deterrents to counterfeiting. **Focus:** Physical sciences, graphic arts, artificial intelligence, computer science, engineering. **Qualif.:** Applicants must be college or university full-time faculty members.

**Funds Avail.:** Negotiable stipend based on regular salary; reimbursement for travel. **To Apply:** Telephone for further details. **Deadline:** Continuous; three months prior to requested starting date.

**Remarks:** Locations include Bureau of Engraving and Printing (Washington, D.C.) and other laboratories carrying out BE research. **Contact:** Harold Rider, Program Manager, at (615) 576-8158 or Kay Ball, Program Specialist, at (615) 576-8807.

• **5874** • **Faculty Research Participation Program at the National Center for Toxicological Research** *(Professional Development/Fellowship)*

**Purpose:** To provide opportunities and support for research in biological effects of potentially toxic chemicals and deriving solutions to problems in toxicology that have a major impact on human health and the environment. **Focus:** Toxicology, pharmacology, chemistry, biological sciences, mathematics, computer science, medicine. **Qualif.:** Applicants must be college or university full-time faculty members.

**Funds Avail.:** Negotiable stipend based on regular salary; reimbursement for travel and moving. **To Apply:** Telephone for further details. **Deadline:** Continuous.

**Remarks:** National Center for Toxicological Research (Jefferson, AR). Funds available through interagency agreement between the U.S. Department of Energy and the U.S. Food and Drug Administration. **Contact:** Harold Rider, Program Manager, at (615) 576-8158 or Kay Ball, Program Specialist, at (615) 576-8807.

• **5875** • **Faculty Research Participation Program at the Naval Air Warfare Center Training Systems Division.** *(Professional Development/Fellowship)*

**Purpose:** To provide opportunities and support for research participation in advanced simulation and training systems technology. **Focus:** Behavioral sciences, computer science, engineering. **Qualif.:** Applicants must be college or university full-time faculty members.

**Funds Avail.:** Stipend based on university salary; reimbursement for inbound and outbound travel. **To Apply:** Telephone for further details. **Deadline:** Continuous.

**Remarks:** Naval Air Warfare Center Training Systems Division (Orlando, FL) location. Funds available through an interagency agreement between U.S. Department of Energy and the Naval Air Warfare Training Systems Division. **Contact:** Harold Rider, Program Manager, at (615) 576-8158 or Kay Ball, Program Specialist, at (615) 576-8807.

• **5876** • **Fossil Energy Faculty Research Participation** *(Professional Development/Fellowship)*

**Purpose:** To provide cooperative participation in ongoing fossil energy research and development using advanced technologies and procedures with access to extensive research facilities. **Focus:** Physical and natural sciences, engineering, mathematics, computer science. **Qualif.:** Applicants must be college or university full-time faculty members.

**Funds Avail.:** Negotiable stipend based on regular salary; reimbursement for travel; participants with sabbatical leave appointments are expected to have at least one-half of their salaries paid by their home. **To Apply:** Telephone for further details. **Deadline:** Continuous.

**Remarks:** Locations include Pittsburgh Energy Technology Center (PA), Pittsburgh Research Center (PA), Morgantown Energy Technology Center (WV). Funds available through the U.S. Department of Energy, Office of Fossil Energy. **Contact:** Harold Rider, Program Manager, at (615) 576-8158 or Kay Ball, Program Specialist, at (615) 576-8807.

• **5877** • **Fossil Energy Postgraduate Research Training Program** *(Postgraduate/Fellowship)*

**Purpose:** To provide opportunities and support for research and training in advanced fossil energy technologies and procedures as well as access to modern and extensive fossil energy research facilities. **Focus:** Engineering, physical science, earth science, computer science, mathematics. **Qualif.:** Applicants must have earned graduate degrees within the last three years.

**Funds Avail.:** Stipend based on research area and degree; reimbursement for inbound travel and moving. Renewable. **To Apply:** Write or telephone for further details. **Deadline:** Continuous.

**Remarks:** Location sites include Pittsburgh Energy Technology Center (PA), and Morgantown Energy Technology Center (WV). Funding made available by the U.S. Department of Energy, Office of Fossil Energy, funded through Pittsburgh Energy Technology Center and Morgantown Energy Technology Center. **Contact:** Priscilla Campbell, Program Manager, at (615) 241-2875, or Cindy Sheldon, Program Specialist, at (615) 576-3456.

• **5878** • **Fossil Energy Professional Internship Program** *(Graduate, Postgraduate/Fellowship)*

**Focus:** Chemistry, computer science, engineering, environmental science, geology, mathematics, physics, statistics. **Qualif.:** Applicants must be master's or doctoral students.

**Funds Avail.:** $1,300 to $1,400 monthly stipend; travel (one round trip) to center/campus; off-campus tuition and fees required by the home institution. **No. of Awards:** 15. **To Apply:** Write or telephone for further details. **Deadline:** December 1, February 1, June 1, October 1.

---

## U.S. Department of Energy - Oak Ridge Institute for Science Education (continued)

**Remarks:** Research site: Pittsburgh Energy Technology Center. **Contact:** Kathy Ketner, Program Manager, at (615) 576-3426, or Betty Brewster, Program Specialist, at (615) 576-3427.

### • 5879 • Fossil Energy Professional Internship Program (Undergrad) (Undergraduate/Internship)

**Focus:** Chemistry, physics, engineering, computer science, environmental science, geology, mathematics, statistics. **Qualif.:** Applicants must be undergraduate students.

**Funds Avail.:** $1,000 to $1,300 monthly stipend; travel (one round trip) to center/campus; off-campus tuition and fees required by the home institution. **No. of Awards:** 30. **To Apply:** Write or telephone for further details. **Deadline:** December 1, February 1, June 1, October 1.

**Remarks:** Research location: Pittsburgh Energy Technology Center (PA). Funded by U.S. Department of Energy, Office of Fossil Energy, funded through Pittsburgh Energy Technology Center. **Contact:** Kathy Ketner, Program Manager, at (615) 576-3426, or Betty Brewster, Program Specialist, at (615) 576-3427.

### • 5880 • Fossil Energy Technology Internship Program (Undergraduate/Internship)

**Focus:** Chemistry, physics, engineering, mathematics, computer science, safety and health. **Qualif.:** Applicants must be associate degree candidates.

**Funds Avail.:** $1,000 monthly stipend (pro-rated for part-time); transportation to the center; any normal tuition and fees required by the home institution for an off-campus program. **No. of Awards:** 5. **To Apply:** Write or telephone for further details. **Deadline:** December 1, February 1, June 1, October 1.

**Remarks:** Research location: Pittsburgh Energy Technology Center. Funding available through the U.S. Department of Energy, Office of Fossil Energy, funded through Pittsburgh Energy Technology Center. **Contact:** Kathy Ketner, Program Manager, at (615) 576-3426, or Pat Pressley, Program Specialist, at (615) 576-1083.

### • 5881 • Fusion Energy Postdoctoral Research Program (Postdoctorate/Fellowship)

**Purpose:** To provide opportunities and support to conduct collaborative research in fusion energy research and development programs. **Focus:** Science, engineering. **Qualif.:** Applicants must have completed their doctoral degrees within the last three years.

**Funds Avail.:** $37,000 stipend plus limited reimbursement for health insurance costs; reimbursement for inbound travel and moving. Renewable. **No. of Awards:** Varies. **To Apply:** Write or telephone for further details. **Deadline:** February 1.

**Remarks:** Research sites include DOE Office of Fusion Energy-supported laboratories and contractor sites. Funds made available through the U.S. Department of Energy, Office of Fusion Energy. **Contact:** Priscilla Campbell, Program Manager, at (615) 241-2875, or Cindy Sheldon, Program Specialist, at (615) 576-3456.

### • 5882 • Global Change Distinguished Postdoctoral Fellowships (Postdoctorate/Fellowship)

**Purpose:** To provide opportunities and support for research and training in problems related to global change. **Focus:** Life science, physical science, earth science, environmental science, computer science, engineering. **Qualif.:** Applicants must have completed doctoral degrees within the last three years.

**Funds Avail.:** $35,000 annual stipend; reimbursement for inbound travel, moving, and medical insurance. Renewable. **No. of Awards:** Varies. **To Apply:** Write or telephone for further details. **Deadline:** Mid-December.

**Remarks:** Research sites include participating laboratories in the United States. Funds made available through the U.S. Department of Energy, Office of Health and Environmental Research. **Contact:** Linda Holmes, Program Manager, at (615) 576-3192, or Cheryl Guthrie, Program Specialist, at (615) 576-9934.

### • 5883 • Graduate Fellowships for Global Change (Graduate, Postgraduate/Fellowship)

**Focus:** Atmospheric science, meteorology, ecology, ocean science. **Qualif.:** Applicants must be master's and doctoral students.

**Funds Avail.:** $14,400 stipend; tuition and fees; additional $300 per month during RCRE assignment; some travel expenses. Renewable. **No. of Awards:** Varies. **To Apply:** Write or telephone for further details. **Deadline:** End of January.

**Remarks:** Research sites include participating universities; a required collaborative research experience (RCRE) must be completed at either a DOE or other government agency research facility. Funds made available through the U.S. Department of Energy, Office of Energy Research, Environmental Sciences Division, Office of Health and Environmental Research. **Contact:** Milton Constantin, Program Manager, at (615) 576-7009 or Mary Kinney, Program Specialist, at (615) 576-9655.

### • 5884 • Graduate Student Research Participation Program (Graduate, Postgraduate/Fellowship)

**Purpose:** To provide opportunities and support for research and training in advanced energy technologies and procedures, as well as access to modern and extensive energy research facilities. **Focus:** Life science, physical science, social science, mathematics, engineering. **Qualif.:** Applicants must be currently enrolled in graduate degree programs.

**Funds Avail.:** $1,600 to $1,700 monthly stipend, plus travel reimbursement. **To Apply:** Write or telephone for further details. **Deadline:** Continuous.

**Remarks:** Research sites include Atmospheric Turbulence and Diffusion Division (Oak Ridge, TN); Continuous Electron Beam Accelerator Facility (Newport News, VA); Martin Marietta Energy Systems, Inc. (Oak Ridge, TN); Oak Ridge Institute for Science and Education (TN); Oak Ridge National Laboratory (TN); Pittsburgh Energy Technology Center (PA); Pittsburgh Research Center/U.S. Bureau of Mines (PA); Savannah River Archaeological Research Program, Savannah River Ecology Laboratory, and Savannah River Technology Center (Aiken, SC). Funds made available through the U.S. Department of Energy, Office of Energy Research and Office of Fossil Energy. **Contact:** Kathy Kenter, Program Manager, at (615) 576-3426 or Pat Pressley, Program Specialist, at (615) 576-1083.

### • 5885 • Graduate U.S. Army Environmental Hygiene Internship Program (Graduate/Fellowship)

**Purpose:** To provide opportunities and support for applied research and development in the areas of environmental health engineering programs, projects and activities. **Focus:** Physical science, biological science, medicine, computer science, engineering. **Qualif.:** Applicants must be enrolled in graduate degree programs.

**Funds Avail.:** Stipend based on research areas and academic classification. **To Apply:** Write or telephone for further details. **Deadline:** Continuous.

**Remarks:** Research location: U.S. Army Environmental Hygiene Agency, Aberdeen Proving Ground, Maryland. Funds available through an interagency agreement between the U.S. Department of Energy and the U.S. Army Environmental Hygiene Agency. **Contact:** Kathy Kenter, Program Manager, at (615) 576-3426 or Pat Pressley, Program Specialist, at (615) 576-1083.

**• 5886 •   Health Physics Faculty Research Award Program** *(Professional Development/Fellowship)*

**Focus:** Health physics, radiation protection. **Qualif.:** Applicants must be full-time faculty at accredited U.S. academic institutions.

**Funds Avail.:** Up to $50,000. Renewable for two additional years. **To Apply:** Telephone for further details. **Deadline:** Late February.

**Remarks:** Supports research or education activities in applied health physics related technical areas that are supportive of the DOE mission; particular emphasis is placed on radiation safety and protection, including radiation dosimetry, risk assessment, and ALARA (As Low As Reasonably Achievable) concepts, radiological emergency management, radiation protection standards and regulation, environmental monitoring and assessment, and air monitoring and sampling. Funds made available through the U.S. Department of Energy, Office of Environment, Safety and Health, Office Health. **Contact:** Jim Wright, Senior Program Manager, at (615) 576-1716 or Leila Gosslee, Program Specialist, at (615) 576-1078.

**• 5887 •   High Temperature Materials Laboratory Faculty Fellowship** *(Professional Development/Fellowship)*

**Purpose:** To provide opportunity for faculty members to increase their understanding of DOE's research program objectives and needs. **Focus:** Ceramics. **Qualif.:** Applicants must be full-time academic staff members of Accreditation Board for Engineering and Technology (ABET)accredited university departments.

**Funds Avail.:** Stipend based on regular salary; round-trip travel reimbursement; some moving expenses. **To Apply:** Telephone for further details. **Deadline:** Continuous.

**Remarks:** High Temperature Materials Laboratory, Oak Ridge National Laboratory (TN) location. Funding through U.S. Department of Energy, Conservation and Renewable Energy, Office of Transportation Technologies. **Contact:** Ernestine Friedman, Program Manager, at (615) 576-2358 or Shirley Ellison, Program Specialist, at (615) 576-2310.

**• 5888 •   High Temperatures Materials Laboratory (HTML) Graduate Student Fellowships** *(Graduate/Fellowship)*

**Purpose:** To provide financial support for Ph.D. candidates at the university and/or while performing research for their dissertations at the HTML located at the Oak Ridge National Laboratory. **Focus:** Ceramics materials technical areas. **Qualif.:** Applicants must have an approved dissertation topic related to one of the DOE ceramics materials technical areas.

**Funds Avail.:** $2,104 month stipend; reimbursement for inbound travel and moving; benefits for full-time temporary employees of Oak Ridge Associated Universities; tuition and fees reimbursement up to a maximum of $5,000 per year. Renewable for up to four years. **To Apply:** Write or telephone for further details. **Deadline:** Continuous.

**Remarks:** Research sites include Oak Ridge National Laboratory's High Temperature Materials Laboratory, Oak Ridge, Tennessee. Funds available through Oak Ridge National Laboratory. **Contact:** Kathy Kenter, Program Manager, at (615) 576-3426 or Betty Brewster, Program Specialist, at (615) 576-3427.

**• 5889 •   Historically Black Colleges and Universities Building Technology Summer Research Participation Program** *(Graduate/Fellowship)*

**Focus:** Chemical engineering, mechanical engineering, environmental engineering, applied physics, and architectural engineering. **Qualif.:** Applicants must be full-time, upper-level students from historically black colleges and universities.

**Funds Avail.:** $1,600 per month for graduate students, $1,200 for seniors, and $1,100 for juniors. **To Apply:** Write or telephone for further details. **Deadline:** February 25.

**Remarks:** Research sites include Oak Ridge National Laboratory, Energy Division, Efficiency and Renewable research section. Funds available through the Oak Ridge National Laboratory. **Contact:** Deborah McCleary, Program Manager, at (615) 576-4813, or Denise Novak, Program Specialist, at (615) 576-5300.

**• 5890 •   Historically Black Colleges and Universities Faculty and Student Research Participation Program in Fusion.** *(Graduate, Professional Development, Undergraduate/Fellowship)*

**Focus:** Physics, chemistry, engineering. **Qualif.:** Applicants must be HBCU faculty and graduate students with an interest in fusion-related research (undergraduates will be considered if accompanied by a faculty member).

**Funds Avail.:** Faculty stipend equal to salary on campus, plus dislocation allowance based on geographic assignment; stipends of $1,200 per month for graduate students and $200 per week for undergraduates, plus round-trip travel expenses. **To Apply:** Telephone for further details. **Deadline:** Early December. **Contact:** Harold Rider, Program Manager, at (615)576-8158 or Angela Palmer, Program Specialist, at (615) 576-2494.

**• 5891 •   Historically Black Colleges and Universities Fossil Energy Faculty and Student Research Training** *(Graduate, Professional Development, Undergraduate/Fellowship)*

**Purpose:** To provide cooperative participation in ongoing fossil energy research and development by using advanced technologies and procedures with access to extensive research facilities. **Focus:** Engineering, physical sciences, earth sciences. **Qualif.:** Applicants must be full-time faculty members and students of historically black colleges and universities.

**Funds Avail.:** Faculty stipend of $3,400 per month or normal monthly salary rate, whichever is great; $225 to $250 weekly stipend for undergraduate students; $1,600 per month for graduate students. **To Apply:** Telephone for further details. **Deadline:** February 28. **Contact:** Deborah McCleary, Program Manager, at (615) 576-4813 or Denise Novak, Program Specialist, at (615) 576-5300.

**• 5892 •   Historically Black Colleges and Universities Health and Environmental Research Opportunities for Faculty and Students** *(Postgraduate, Professional Development/Fellowship)*

**Focus:** Life science, biomedical science, environmental science. **Qualif.:** Applicants must be full-time faculty members and students from historically black colleges.

**Funds Avail.:** Faculty stipend of $3,400 per month or equivalent to monthly salary, whichever is greater; $1,600 per month stipend for graduate students; $225 to $250 weekly stipend for undergraduate students; travel reimbursement. **No. of Awards:** Varies. **To Apply:** Write or telephone for further details. **Deadline:** January 17.

**Remarks:** Research locations include any of the 18 participating multiprogram or dedicated laboratories nationwide. Funded by the U.S. Department of Energy, Office of Health and Environmental Research. **Contact:** Deborah McCleary, Program Manager, at (615) 576-4813, or Denise Novak, Program Specialist, at (615) 576-5300.

**• 5893 •   Historically Black Colleges and Universities Nuclear Energy Faculty Research Participation Program** *(Professional Development/Fellowship)*

**Focus:** Nuclear science, nuclear and mechanical engineering, physics, chemistry. **Qualif.:** Applicants must be full-time permanent faculty at HBCUs who hold degrees in life or physical

---

### U.S. Department of Energy - Oak Ridge Institute for Science Education (continued)

sciences or engineering and who have ongoing interest in nuclear energy-related research; applicants must be U.S. citizens or permanent resident aliens.

**Funds Avail.:** Faculty stipend of $3,400 per month or normal monthly salary rate, whichever is greater. **To Apply:** Telephone for further details. **Deadline:** January 17.

**Remarks:** Location sites include participating DOE multiprogram or dedicated laboratories nationwide. Funds made available through U.S. Department of Energy, Office of Nuclear Energy. **Contact:** Deborah McCleary, Program Manager, at (615) 576-4813 or Denise Novak, Program Specialist, at (615) 576-5300.

### • 5894 • Historically Black Colleges and Universities Nuclear Energy Training Program *(Graduate/Fellowship)*

**Purpose:** To provide competitive fellowships for study and research careers in nuclear energy-related technologies, including an off campus research opportunity at a DOE-designated laboratory. **Focus:** Nuclear science, nuclear engineering, mechanical engineering, physics, chemistry, nuclear technology. **Qualif.:** Applicants must be first-year graduate students seeking fellowship support.

**Funds Avail.:** Tuition and fees, plus up to $14,400 per year in stipends; dislocation allowance during summer research appointment. Renewable for 24 to 48 months. **To Apply:** Write or telephone for further details. **Deadline:** January 17.

**Remarks:** Research locations include Howard University (DC), North Carolina A&T State University, Lincoln University (PA), South Carolina State University, Tennessee State University, and Virginia State University. Funds available through the U.S. Department of Energy, Office of Nuclear Energy. **Contact:** Deborah McCleary, Program Manager, at (615) 576-4813, or Denise Novak, Program Specialist, at (615) 576-5300.

### • 5895 • Historically Black Colleges and Universities Nuclear Energy Training Program (Undergrad) *(Undergraduate/Fellowship)*

**Focus:** Nuclear science, nuclear and mechanical engineering, physics, chemistry, nuclear technology. **Qualif.:** Applicants must be undergraduate juniors and seniors.

**Funds Avail.:** Tuition and fees; up to $9,600 per year in stipends; dislocation allowance during summer research appointment. **To Apply:** Write or telephone for further details. **Deadline:** January 17.

**Remarks:** Research locations include Howard University (DC), North Carolina A&T State University, Lincoln University (PA), South Carolina State University, Tennessee State University, Virginia State University. Funded through the U.S. Department of Energy, Office of Nuclear Energy. **Contact:** Deborah McCleary, Program Manager, at (615) 576-4813, or Denise Novak, Program Specialist, at (615) 576-5300.

### • 5896 • Human Genome Distinguished Postdoctoral Fellowships *(Postdoctorate/Fellowship)*

**Purpose:** To provide opportunities and support for research to develop the tools, technologies, and resources to decipher the human genome. **Focus:** Molecular biology, computational biology, technology development, related scientific disciplines. **Qualif.:** Applicants must have completed their doctoral degree within the last three years.

**Funds Avail.:** $37,500 annual stipend; reimbursement for inbound travel, moving, and medical insurance. Renewable. **No. of Awards:** Varies. **To Apply:** Write or telephone for further details. **Deadline:** Early February.

**Remarks:** Research sites include all participating laboratories in the United States. Funds made available through the U.S. Department of Energy, Office of Health and Environmental Research. **Contact:** Linda Holmes, Program Manager, at (615) 576-3192, or Barbara Dorsey, Program Specialist, at (615) 576-9975.

### • 5897 • Industrial Hygiene Graduate Fellowship Program *(Graduate/Fellowship)*

**Focus:** Industrial hygiene. **Qualif.:** Applicants must be pursuing master's degrees in industrial hygiene.

**Funds Avail.:** $15,600 stipend ($1,300 monthly); additional $400 monthly during practicum; $1,500 academic allowance. **To Apply:** Write or telephone for further details. **Deadline:** End of January.

**Remarks:** Research locations include designated participating universities with practicums at U.S. Department of Energy research facilities. Funds available through the U.S. Department of Energy, Office of Health, Industrial Hygiene Programs Division. **Contact:** Milton J. Constantin, Program Manager, at (615) 576-7009 or email at CONSTANM@ORAU.GOV, or Mary Kinney, Program Specialist, at (615)576-9655 or e-mail at KINNEYM@RAU.GOV.

### • 5898 • Laboratory Cooperative Postgraduate Research Training Program *(Postgraduate/Fellowship)*

**Purpose:** To provide opportunities and support for research and training in a broad range of energy research and engineering activities as well as access to modern and extensive research facilities. **Focus:** Engineering, life science, physical science, earth science, environmental science, mathematics, computer science. **Qualif.:** Applicants must have completed their graduate degrees within the last three years.

**Funds Avail.:** Stipend based on research area and degree; reimbursement for inbound travel and moving. Renewable. **No. of Awards:** Varies. **To Apply:** Write or telephone for further details. **Deadline:** Continuous.

**Remarks:** Research locations include Atmospheric Turbulence and Diffusion Division (Oak Ridge, TN), Continuous Electron Beam Accelerator Facility (Newport News, VA), Oak Ridge Institute for Science and Education (TN), and Savannah River Technology Center (Aiken, SC). Funds made available through the U.S. Department of Energy and host laboratories. **Contact:** Linda McCamant, Program Director, at (615) 576-1089, or Cindy Sheldon, Program Specialist, at (615) 576-3456.

### • 5899 • Laboratory Graduate Participation Program *(Graduate/Fellowship)*

**Focus:** Life science, physical science, social science, mathematics, engineering. **Qualif.:** Applicants must be graduate students who have completed all degree requirements except thesis or dissertation research.

**Funds Avail.:** $12,000 to $14,400 annual stipend; and allowance for dependents; tuition and fees reimbursement to a maximum of $3,500 per year. Renewable. **To Apply:** Write or telephone for further details. **Deadline:** Continuous.

**Remarks:** Research sites include Atmospheric Turbulence and Diffusion Division (Oak Ridge, TN), Continuous Beam Accelerator Facility (Newport News, VA); Oak Ridge Institute for Science and Education (TN); Pittsburgh Energy Technology Center (PA); Savannah River Ecology Laboratory, Savannah River Technology Center, and Savannah River Archaeological Research Program (Aiken, SC). Funds available through the U.S. Department of Energy, Office of Energy Research and Office of Fossil Energy. **Contact:** Kathy Ketner, Program Manager, at (615)576-3426, or Betty Brewster, Program Specialist, at (615)576-3427.

### • 5900 • Law Internship Program *(Graduate/ Internship)*

**Focus:** Environmental and patent law. **Qualif.:** Applicants must have completed their first year of law school.

**Funds Avail.:** $2,000 monthly stipend; travel reimbursement. **To Apply:** Write or telephone for further details. **Deadline:** February 15.

**Remarks:** Research locations include Oak Ridge National Laboratory (TN), and Savannah River Technology Center (SC) **Contact:** Kathy Ketner, Program Manager, at (615)576-3426, or Betty Brewster, Program Specialist, at (615)576-3427.

**• 5901 • Magnetic Fusion Energy Technology Fellowship Program** *(Doctorate/Fellowship)*

**Purpose:** To offer graduate work in magnetic fusion energy technology. **Focus:** Physical science, mathematics, engineering. **Qualif.:** Applicants must be doctoral students.

**Funds Avail.:** $15,600 stipend; additional $200 per month during practicum; tuition and fees; some travel expenses. Renewable for up to four years. **To Apply:** Write or telephone for further details. **Deadline:** Last Monday in January.

**Remarks:** Research locations include participating universities with practicum sat various DOE research facilities. Funds available through the U.S. Department of Energy, Office of Fusion Energy. **Contact:** Sandra Johnson, Program Manager, at (615) 576-2600, or Cheryl Terry, Program Specialist, at (615) 576-9558.

**• 5902 • Magnetic Fusion Science Fellowship Program** *(Doctorate/Fellowship)*

**Focus:** Physical science, mathematics, engineering. **Qualif.:** Applicants must be doctoral students.

**Funds Avail.:** $15,600 stipend; some travel expenses; additional $200 per month during the practicum; tuition and fees. Renewable up to three years. **To Apply:** Write or telephone for further details. **Deadline:** Last Monday in January.

**Remarks:** Research locations include participating universities with practicums at various DOE research facilities. Funds available through the U.S. Department of Energy, Office of Fusion Energy. **Contact:** Sandra Johnson, Program Manager, at (615) 576-2600, or Cheryl Terry, Program Specialist, at (615) 576-9558.

**• 5903 • Minority Student Administrative Summer Internship Program** *(Graduate, Undergraduate/ Internship)*

**Focus:** Business administration, management, finance, accounting, human resources, training, economics, public administration, computer science, and instructional technology. **Qualif.:** Applicants must be minority students with a minimum grade point average of 3.0 on a 4.0 scale, who have completed their junior or senior years in college or their first year of graduate school.

**Funds Avail.:** Salary based on educational level completed, $326 to $406 per week; travel reimbursement. **To Apply:** Write or telephone for further details. **Deadline:** Early February.

**Remarks:** Research location: Oak Ridge Institute for Science and Education (TN). Funded by the U.S. Department of Energy. **Contact:** John Hicks, Manager, Employment and Placement, at (615) 5763164, or Sherry Scircle, Employment Officer, at (615) 576-3165.

**• 5904 • Minority Students Hazardous Materials Management Training Program** *(Undergraduate/ Internship)*

**Focus:** Health physics, environmental health, hazardous waste management. **Qualif.:** Applicants must be full-time minority students in Roane State Community College associate degree program in hazardous waste management.

**Funds Avail.:** Tuition and fees and a monthly stipend while enroled in school; $1,000 stipend per month during the summer internship.

**To Apply:** Write or telephone for further details. **Deadline:** February.

**Remarks:** Research locations include participating DOE laboratories. Funded by the U.S. Department of Energy. **Contact:** Harold Rider, Program Manager, at (615) 576-8158, or Angela Palmer, Program Specialist, at (615) 576-2494.

**• 5905 • National Association for the Advancement of Colored People Scholarship Program** *(Undergraduate/Scholarship)*

**Focus:** Engineering, science, computer science, mathematics, environmental studies and other scientific and technical disciplines related to DOE mission goals. **Qualif.:** Applicants must be undergraduate students.

**Funds Avail.:** Tuition/fees and stipend payments (not to exceed $10,000); additional allowance during summer internship assignments. **To Apply:** Write or telephone for details. **Deadline:** Spring.

**Remarks:** Research locations include accredited colleges and/or universities within the United States. Funded by the U.S. Department of Energy. **Contact:** Colleen Babcock, Program Manager, at (615) 576-9272, or Debra Lawson, Program Specialist, at (615) 576-0128. 576-0128.

**• 5906 • National Center for Toxicological Research Graduate Student Research Participation** *(Graduate, Postgraduate/Fellowship)*

**Purpose:** To provide opportunities and support for research participation in biological effects of potentially toxic chemicals and deriving solutions to problems in toxicology that have a major impact on human health and the environment. **Focus:** Toxicology, pharmacology, chemistry, biological science, mathematics, computer science, medicine. **Qualif.:** Applicants must be currently enrolled in graduate degree programs.

**Funds Avail.:** Stipend based on research areas and academic classification. **To Apply:** Write or telephone for further details. **Deadline:** Continuous.

**Remarks:** Research site: National Center for Toxicological Research, Jefferson, Arkansas. Funds made available by the interagency agreement between the U.S. Department of Energy and the National Center for Toxicological Research. **Contact:** Kathy Kenter, Program Manager, at (615) 576-3426 or Pat Pressley, Program Specialist, at (615) 576-1083.

**• 5907 • National Center for Toxicological Research Postgraduate Research Program** *(Postgraduate/ Fellowship)*

**Purpose:** To provide opportunities and support for research in biological effects of potentially toxic chemicals and deriving solutions to toxicological problems that have a major impact on human health and the environment. **Focus:** Toxicology, pharmacology, chemistry, biological sciences, mathematics, computer science, medicine. **Qualif.:** Applicants should have completed their graduate degree within the last three years; others considered on case-by-case basis.

**Funds Avail.:** Stipend based on research area and degree. Renewable. **No. of Awards:** Varies. **To Apply:** Write or telephone for further details. **Deadline:** Continuous.

**Remarks:** Research site: National Center for Toxicological Research, Jefferson, Arkansas. Funds made available through an interagency agreement between the U.S. Department of Energy and the U.S. Food and Drug Administration. **Contact:** Priscilla Campbell, Program Manager, at (615) 241-2875, or Marlene Mayton, Program Specialist, at (615) 576-3190.

---

**U.S. Department of Energy - Oak Ridge Institute for Science Education** *(continued)*

## • 5908 • National Center for Toxicological Research Undergraduate Program *(Undergraduate/Internship)*

**Purpose:** To provide opportunities and support for participation in research of biological effects of potentially toxic chemicals and deriving solutions to toxicology problems that have a major impact on human health and environment. **Focus:** Toxicology, pharmacology, chemistry, biological sciences, mathematics, computer science, medicine, other related scientific disciplines. **Qualif.:** Applicants must be undergraduate students.

**Funds Avail.:** Stipend based on research areas and academic classification. **To Apply:** Write or telephone for further details. **Deadline:** Continuous.

**Remarks:** Research site: National Center for Toxicological Research (Jefferson, AR). Funds available through an interagency agreement between the U.S. Department of Energy and the National Center for Toxicological Research. **Contact:** Kathy Ketner, Program Manager, at (615) 576-3426, or Pat Pressley, Program Specialist, at (615) 576-1083.

## • 5909 • National Library of Medicine Undergraduate Research Study Program *(Undergraduate/Internship)*

**Focus:** Electrical engineering. **Qualif.:** Applicants must be juniors and seniors at designated historically black colleges and universities; currently participating institutions are Morgan State University, North Carolina A&T State University, and Southern University in Baton Rouge.

**Funds Avail.:** Full tuition and fees; $600 monthly stipend during the academic year; prepaid housing, round-trip travel and monthly stipend and allowance of $1,350 during summer internship; $2,000 annual academic allowance to university; during school year, monthly honorariums of $500 to academic preceptors. Renewable for up to 24 months. **No. of Awards:** 5. **To Apply:** Write or telephone for further details. **Deadline:** Biannually in February.

**Remarks:** Research location includes summer internships at the Lister Hill National Center for Biomedical Communications; during the academic year, research is on campus. Funded by the National Library of Medicine. **Contact:** M. Elizabeth Kittrell, Program Manager, at (615) 241-3319.

## • 5910 • National Oceanic and Atmospheric Administration/Historically Black Colleges and Universities Faculty/Student Research Participation Program *(Graduate, Professional Development, Undergraduate/Fellowship)*

**Purpose:** To support research and development activities at National Oceanic and Atmospheric Administration (NOAA)-approved sites; collaborate with senior professionals to become trained in disciplines related to the mission of NOAA. **Focus:** Life sciences, physical sciences, engineering. **Qualif.:** Applicants must be full-time faculty and students at historically black colleges and universities.

**Funds Avail.:** Faculty receive stipend equal to university salary or $1,000 per week, whichever is greater; students receive a stipend of $300 to $400 per week, depending on academic standing; faculty and students receive some reimbursement for travel. **To Apply:** Telephone for further details. **Deadline:** Continuous.

**Remarks:** Location sites include the National Oceanic and Atmospheric Administration and field centers. Funds available through an interagency agreement between the U.S. Department of Energy and the National Oceanic and Atmospheric Administration. **Contact:** Harold Rider, Program Manager, at (615) 576-8158 or Angela Palmer, Program Specialist, at (615) 576-2494.

## • 5911 • National Oceanic and Atmospheric Administration Scholar in Residence Program *(Professional Development/Fellowship)*

**Purpose:** To support research and development activities at National Oceanic and Atmospheric Administration (NOAA)-approved sites by historically black colleges and universities. **Focus:** Engineering, physical science, life science. **Qualif.:** Applicants must be full-time faculty and students at historically black colleges and universities.

**Funds Avail.:** Faculty stipend negotiable based on regular salary; student stipend $300 to $400 per week based on academic standing. **To Apply:** Write or telephone for further details. **Deadline:** Continuous.

**Remarks:** Research site: NOAA and NOAA field centers. **Contact:** Harold Rider, Program Manager, at (615) 576-8158, or Angela Palmer, Program Specialist, at (615) 576-2494.

## • 5912 • Naval Air Warfare Center Training Systems Division Graduate Research Participation Program *(Graduate, Postgraduate/Fellowship)*

**Purpose:** To provide opportunities and support for research participation in advanced simulation and training systems technology. **Focus:** Behavioral science, computer science, engineering. **Qualif.:** Applicants must be master's or doctoral students.

**Funds Avail.:** Stipend based on research areas and academic classification. **To Apply:** Write or telephone for further details. **Deadline:** Continuous.

**Remarks:** Research site: Naval Air Warfare Center Training Systems Division, Orlando, Florida. Funds made available through an interagency agreement between the U.S. Department of Energy and the Naval Air Warfare Center Training Systems Division. **Contact:** Kathy Kenter, Program Manager, at (615) 576-3426 or Pat Pressley, Program Specialist, at (615) 576-1083.

## • 5913 • Naval Air Warfare Center Training Systems Division Postgraduate Research Participation Program *(Postgraduate/Fellowship)*

**Purpose:** To provide opportunities and support for research participation in advanced simulation and training systems technology. **Focus:** Behavioral science, computer science, engineering. **Qualif.:** Applicants must have completed their master's or doctoral degree within the last three years.

**Funds Avail.:** Stipend based on research area and degree; reimbursement for inbound travel and moving. Renewable. **No. of Awards:** Varies. **To Apply:** Write or telephone for further details. **Deadline:** Continuous.

**Remarks:** Research site: Naval Air Warfare Center Training Systems Division, Orlando, Florida. **Contact:** Priscilla Campbell, Program Manager, at (615) 241-2875, or Cindy Sheldon, Program Specialist, at (615) 576-3456.

## • 5914 • Naval Air Warfare Center Training Systems Division Undergraduate Research Participation Program *(Undergraduate/Internship)*

**Purpose:** To provide opportunities and support for research participation in advanced simulation and training systems technology. **Focus:** Behavioral science, computer science, engineering. **Qualif.:** Applicants must be undergraduate students.

**Funds Avail.:** Stipend based on research areas and academic classification. **To Apply:** Write or telephone for further details. **Deadline:** Continuous.

**Remarks:** Research site: Naval Air Warfare Center Training Systems Division (Orlando, FL). Funds available through an interagency agreement between the U.S. Department of Energy and the Naval Air Warfare Center Training Systems Division.

**Contact:** Kathy Ketner, Program Manager, at (615) 576-3426, or Pat Pressley, Program Specialist, at (615) 576-1083.

### • 5915 • Nuclear Engineering/Health Physics Fellowship Program *(Doctorate, Graduate/Fellowship)*

**Focus:** Physical science, life science, engineering. **Qualif.:** Applicants must be pursuing master's or doctoral degrees in nuclear engineering or health physics.

**Funds Avail.:** $14,400 stipend; additional $300 per month during practicum; some travel expenses; tuition and fees. Renewable up to four years. **To Apply:** Write or telephone for further details. **Deadline:** Last Monday in January.

**Remarks:** Research locations include participating universities with practicums at various DOE research facilities. Funds available through the U.S. Department of Energy, Office of Nuclear Energy, Office of Energy Research. **Contact:** Sandra Johnson, Program Manager, at (615) 576-2600, or Cheryl Terry, Program Specialist, at (615) 576-9558.

### • 5916 • Nuclear Regulatory Commission Graduate Fellowship Program *(Graduate/Internship)*

**Focus:** Nuclear engineering, health physics, and specialty engineering disciplines with emphasis in instrumentation and control systems; materials science, materials engineering, metallurgy. **Qualif.:** Applicants must be Nuclear Regulatory Commission (NRC) employees or graduate students pursuing master's degrees.

**Funds Avail.:** $1,800 per month stipend or salary; full tuition and fees; $5,000 per year academic allowance to university. **To Apply:** Write or telephone for further details. **Deadline:** End of January.

**Remarks:** Research locations include universities and NRC facilities. Funds available through the U.S. Nuclear Regulatory Commission. **Contact:** Tom Richmond, Program Manager, at (615) 576-2194, or Rose Etta Cox, Program Specialist, at (615) 576-9279.

### • 5917 • Oak Ridge National Laboratory Postdoctoral Research Associates Program *(Postdoctorate/Fellowship)*

**Purpose:** To provide opportunities and support for research and training in a broad range of science and engineering activities related to basic sciences, energy and environment, as well as access to modern and extensive research facilities. **Focus:** Engineering, life science, physical science, earth science, environmental science, mathematics, computer science. **Qualif.:** Applicants must have completed their doctoral degrees within the last five years. Other considered on a case-by-case basis.

**Funds Avail.:** Stipend based on research area and degree; reimbursement for inbound travel and moving; benefits for full-time temporary employees of Oak Ridge Associated Universities. Renewable. **No. of Awards:** Varies. **To Apply:** Write or telephone for further details. **Deadline:** Continuous.

**Remarks:** Research site: Oak Ridge National Laboratory (TN). Funds made available through Oak Ridge National Laboratory. **Contact:** Janet Scott, Program Manager, at (615) 576-4805, or Linda Lea, Program Specialist, at (615) 241-2877.

### • 5918 • Oak Ridge National Laboratory Professional Internship Program *(Doctorate, Graduate/Internship)*

**Purpose:** To provide opportunities to participate in hazardous waste management and other energy-related research projects that correlate with academic and career goals. **Focus:** Chemistry, environmental science, geology, hydrogeology, hydrology, chemical engineering, mechanical engineering, computer science. **Qualif.:** Applicants must be master's or doctoral students.

**Funds Avail.:** $1,300 to $1,400 monthly stipend; travel (one round trip) to center/campus; off-campus tuition and fees required by the home institution. **To Apply:** Write or telephone for further details. **Deadline:** December 1, February 1, June 1, October 1.

**Remarks:** Research location: Oak Ridge National Laboratory (TN). **Contact:** Kathy Kenter, Program Manager, at (615) 576-3426, or Betty Brewster, Program Specialist, at (615) 576-3427.

### • 5919 • Oak Ridge National Laboratory Professional Internship Program (Undergrad) *(Undergraduate/Internship)*

**Focus:** Chemistry, environmental science, geology, hydrogeology, hydrology, chemical engineering, civil engineering, environmental engineering, mechanical engineering, computer science. **Qualif.:** Applicants must be undergraduate students.

**Funds Avail.:** Monthly stipend of $1,000 to $1,300; travel (one round trip) to center/campus; off-campus tuition and fees required by the home institution. **To Apply:** Write or telephone for further details. **Deadline:** December 1, February 1, June 1, October 1.

**Remarks:** Research site: Oak Ridge National Laboratory. **Contact:** Kathy Ketner, Program Manager, at (615) 756-3426, or Betty Brewster, Program Specialist, (615) 576-3427.

### • 5920 • Oak Ridge National Laboratory Technology Internship Program *(Undergraduate/Internship)*

**Focus:** Chemical engineering, electrical engineering, health physics, mechanical engineering, technology. **Qualif.:** Applicants must be associate degree students. **Criteria:**

**Funds Avail.:** Monthly stipend of $1,000 (pro-rated for part-time). **To Apply:** Write or telephone for further details. **Deadline:** Continuous.

**Remarks:** Research sites include Oak Ridge National Laboratory (TN) and sites of the Hazardous Waste Remedial Actions Program. **Contact:** Kathy Ketner, Program Manager, at (615) 576-3426, or Pat Pressley, Program Specialist, at (615) 576-1083.

### • 5921 • Office of Ground Water and Drinking Water Postgraduate Internship Program *(Postgraduate/Internship)*

**Purpose:** To provide opportunities and support for studies related to development and implementation of drinking water regulations. **Focus:** Environmental science, engineering, physical science. **Qualif.:** Applicants must have completed their bachelor's, master's or doctoral degree within the last three years; others considered on a case-by-case basis.

**Funds Avail.:** Stipend based on research area and degree; reimbursement for inbound travel and moving. Renewable. **To Apply:** Write or telephone for further details. **Deadline:** Continuous.

**Remarks:** Research site: Office of Ground Water and Drinking Water, Cincinnati, Ohio. Fund made available through an interagency agreement between the U.S. Department of Energy and the Office of Ground Water and Drinking Water. **Contact:** Priscilla Campbell, Program Manager, at (615) 241-2875, or Cindy Sheldon, Program Specialist, at (615) 576-3456.

### • 5922 • Part-time Fossil Energy Faculty Research Participation Program *(Professional Development/Fellowship)*

**Purpose:** To provide cooperative participation in ongoing fossil energy research and development by using advanced technologies with access to extensive research facilities. **Focus:** Engineering, physical sciences, earth sciences. **Qualif.:** Applicants must be college or university full-time faculty members.

**Funds Avail.:** Negotiable stipend based on regular salary; reimbursement for travel. **To Apply:** Telephone for further details. **Deadline:** Continuous.

**Remarks:** Location sites include Pittsburgh Energy Technology Center (PA), Pittsburgh Research Center (PA), and Morgantown

---

## U.S. Department of Energy - Oak Ridge Institute for Science Education *(continued)*

Energy Technology Center (WV). Funds made available through the U.S. Department of Energy, Office of Fossil Energy. **Contact:** Harold Rider, Program Manager, at (615) 576-8158 or Angela Palmer, Program Specialist, at (615) 576-2494.

### • 5923 • Risk Reduction Engineering Research Laboratory Research Participation Program *(Postdoctorate, Postgraduate/Fellowship)*

**Purpose:** To provide opportunities and support for research related to environmental and physical sciences concerns. **Focus:** Environmental science, engineering, physical science. **Qualif.:** Applicants must have completed their bachelor's, master's or doctoral degrees within the last three years.

**Funds Avail.:** Stipend based on research area and degree; reimbursement for inbound travel and moving. Renewable. **No. of Awards:** Varies. **To Apply:** Write or telephone for further details. **Deadline:** Continuous.

**Remarks:** Research site: Risk Reduction Engineering Research Laboratory, Cincinnati, Ohio. Funds available through an interagency agreement between the U.S. Department of Energy and the U.S. Environmental Protection Agency Risk Reduction Engineering Research Laboratory. **Contact:** Priscilla Campbell, Program Manager, at (615) 241-2875, or Cindy Sheldon, Program Specialist, at (615) 576-3456.

### • 5924 • Savannah River Technology Center Professional Internship Program *(Doctorate, Graduate/Internship)*

**Focus:** Chemistry, computer science, engineering, environmental science, geology, physics. **Qualif.:** Applicants must be master's or doctoral students.

**Funds Avail.:** $1,300 to $1,400 monthly stipend; travel (one round trip) to center/campus; off-campus tuition and fees by the home institution. **To Apply:** Write or telephone for further details. **Deadline:** February 1, June 1, September 1.

**Remarks:** Research location: Savannah River Technology Center (SC). Funds available through the Savannah River Technology Center. **Contact:** Kathy Kenter, Program Manager, at (615) 576-3426, or Betty Brewster, Program Specialist, at (615) 576-3427.

### • 5925 • Savannah River Technology Center Professional Internship Program (Undergrad) *(Undergraduate/Internship)*

**Focus:** Chemistry, computer science, engineering, environmental science, geology, physics. **Qualif.:** Applicants must be high school seniors and undergraduate students.

**Funds Avail.:** Monthly stipend of $900 to $1,300; travel (one round trip) to center/campus; off-campus tuition and fees required by the home institution. **To Apply:** Write or telephone for further details. **Deadline:** February 1, June 1, September 1.

**Remarks:** Research site: Savannah River Technology Center (SC). Funds available through the Savannah River Technology Center. **Contact:** Kathy Ketner, Program Manager, at (615) 756-3426, or Betty Brewster, Program Specialist, (615) 576-3427.

### • 5926 • Shared Research Equipment Program *(Graduate, Postdoctorate, Professional Development/Fellowship)*

**Purpose:** To provide an opportunity to conduct research by using sophisticated microanalytical facilities in the areas of transmission electron microscopy, surface analysis, and nuclear microanalysis. **Focus:** Energy-related areas. **Qualif.:** Applicants must be faculty members, graduate students, and postdoctoral fellows.

**Funds Avail.:** Travel and living expenses while conducting research. **To Apply:** Telephone for further details. **Deadline:** Early fall.

**Remarks:** Oak Ridge National Laboratory location site. Funds made available through the U.S. Department of Energy, Office of Energy Research. **Contact:** Ernestine Friedman, Program Manager, at (615) 576-2358 or Program Specialist at (615) 576-3425.

### • 5927 • Tennessee Valley Authority Research Participation Program *(Postdoctorate, Postgraduate/Fellowship)*

**Purpose:** To provide opportunities and support for research related to environmental issues. **Focus:** Environmental science, engineering, physical science. **Qualif.:** Applicants must have completed a graduate degree within the last three years.

**Funds Avail.:** Stipend based on research area and degree; reimbursement for inbound travel and moving. Renewable. **No. of Awards:** Varies. **To Apply:** Write or telephone for further details. **Deadline:** Continuous.

**Remarks:** Research site: U.S. Army Construction Engineering Research Laboratory, Champaign, Illinois. Funds made available through an interagency agreement between the U.S. Department of Energy and the Tennessee Valley Authority. **Contact:** Priscilla Campbell, Program Manager, at (615) 241-2875, or Cindy Sheldon, Program Specialist, at (615) 576-3456.

### • 5928 • Tyndall Air Force Base Research Participation Program *(Postdoctorate, Postgraduate/Fellowship)*

**Purpose:** To provide research opportunities in the environmental quality program, which investigates regulations and environmental problems, especially hazardous wastes. **Focus:** Physical science, environmental science, life science, engineering. **Qualif.:** Applicants must have completed their graduate degree within the last three years.

**Funds Avail.:** Stipend based on research area and degree; reimbursement for inbound travel and moving. Renewable. **No. of Awards:** Varies. **To Apply:** Write or telephone for further details. **Deadline:** Continuous.

**Remarks:** Research site: Tyndall Air Force Base, Panama City, Florida. Funds made available through an interagency agreement between the U.S. Department of Energy and Tyndall Air Force Base. **Contact:** Priscilla Campbell, Program Manager, at (615) 241-2875, or Cindy Sheldon, Program Specialist, at (615) 576-3456.

### • 5929 • Undergraduate U.S. Army Environmental Hygiene Internship Program *(Undergraduate/Internship)*

**Purpose:** To provide opportunities and support for applied research and development in the areas of environmental health engineering programs, projects and activities. **Focus:** Physical science, biological science, medicine, computer science, engineering. **Qualif.:** Applicants must be associate and baccalaureate degree students.

**Funds Avail.:** Stipend based on research areas and academic classification. **To Apply:** Write or telephone for further details. **Deadline:** Continuous.

**Remarks:** Research site: U.S. Army Environmental Hygiene Agency (Aberdeen Proving Ground, MD). Funds available through an interagency agreement between the U.S. Department of Energy and the U.S. Army Environmental Hygiene Agency. **Contact:** Kathy Ketner, Program Manager, at (615) 576-3426, or Pat Pressley, Program Specialist, at (615) 576-1083.

**• 5930 • U.S. Army Construction Engineering Research Laboratory Research Participation Program** *(Postdoctorate, Postgraduate/Fellowship)*

**Purpose:** To provide opportunities and support for research and training supportive of the military construction efforts, environmental issues. **Focus:** Appropriate science or engineering disciplines. **Qualif.:** Applicants must have completed their bachelor's, master's, or doctoral degrees within the last three years.

**Funds Avail.:** Stipend based on research area and degree; reimbursement for inbound travel and moving. Renewable. **No. of Awards:** Varies. **To Apply:** Write or telephone for further details. **Deadline:** Continuous.

**Remarks:** Research site: U.S. Army Construction Engineering Research Laboratory, Champaign, Illinois. Funds made available through an interagency agreement between the U.S. Department of Energy and the U.S. Army Construction Engineering Research Laboratory. **Contact:** Priscilla Campbell, Program Manager, at (615) 241-2875, or Cindy Sheldon, Program Specialist, at (615) 576-3456.

**• 5931 • U.S. Army Environmental Hygiene Agency Internship Program** *(Postdoctorate, Postgraduate/Internship)*

**Purpose:** To provide opportunities and support for applied clinical research and training activities in such areas as environmental health, entomological sciences, radiation, industrial hygiene, and other environmental concerns. **Focus:** Science, engineering. **Qualif.:** Applicants must have completed a bachelor's, master's or doctoral degree within the last three years.

**Funds Avail.:** Stipend based on research area and degree; reimbursement for inbound travel and moving. Renewable. **No. of Awards:** Varies. **To Apply:** Write or telephone for further details. **Deadline:** Continuous.

**Remarks:** Research site is U.S. Army Environmental Hygiene Agency, Aberdeen Proving Ground, MD. Funds made available through an interagency agreement between the U.S. Department of Energy and the U.S. Army Environmental Hygiene Agency. **Contact:** Priscilla Campbell, Program Manager, at (615) 241-2875, or Cindy Sheldon, Program Specialist, at (615) 576-3456.

**• 5932 • U.S. Department of Energy Faculty Research Participation Fellowship** *(Professional Development/Fellowship)*

**Purpose:** To provide cooperative participation in ongoing energy research with access to modern research facilities. **Focus:** Physical and natural sciences, engineering, mathematics, computer science. **Qualif.:** Applicants must be college and university full-time faculty members.

**Funds Avail.:** Varies. Negotiable stipend based on regular salary; some reimbursement for travel. **To Apply:** Telephone for further details. **Deadline:** Late January.

**Remarks:** Research locations include Atmospheric Turbulence and Diffusion Division (Oak Ridge, TN); Continuous Electron Beam Accelerator Facility (Newport News, VA); Oak Ridge Institute for Science and Education (TN); Oak Ridge National Laboratory (TN); Savannah River Ecology Laboratory, Savannah River Technology Center, and Savannah River Archaeological Research Program (Aiken, SC); Triangle Universities Nuclear Laboratory (Research Triangle Park, NC). **Contact:** Harold Rider, Program Manager, at (615) 576-8158 or Kay Ball, Program Specialist, at (615) 576-8807.

**• 5933 • U.S. Department of Energy Student Research Participation Program** *(Undergraduate/Internship)*

**Purpose:** To offer independent research under the guidance of DOE staff members in energy production, use, conservation, and

societal implications. **Focus:** Life science, physical science, social science, mathematics, engineering. **Qualif.:** Applicants must be college juniors and seniors.

**Funds Avail.:** Weekly stipend of $200 to $250; travel reimbursement. **To Apply:** Write or telephone for further details. **Deadline:** Mid-January.

**Remarks:** Research sites: Atmospheric Turbulence and Diffusion Division (Oak Ridge, TN); Continuous Electron Beam Accelerator Facility (Newport News, VA)p Martin Marietta Energy Systems, Inc. (Oak Ridge, TN); Oak Ridge Institute for Science and Education (TN); Oak Ridge National Laboratory (TN); Pittsburgh Energy Technology Center (PA); Pittsburgh Research Center/U.S. Bureau of Mines (PA); Savannah River Archaeological Research Program, Savannah River Ecology Laboratory, and Savannah River Technology Center (Aiken, SC). **Contact:** Kathy Ketner, Program Manager, at (615) 576-3426, or Pat Pressley, Program Specialist, at (615) 576-1083.

**• 5934 • U.S. Nuclear Regulatory Commission Historically Black Colleges and Universities Faculty Research Participation** *(Professional Development/Fellowship)*

**Focus:** Energy sciences, engineering, geosciences, health physics, computer science, mathematics. **Qualif.:** Applicants must be full-time faculty members from historically black institutions.

**Funds Avail.:** Summer stipend of $3,400 per month or normal monthly salary rate, whichever is greater; travel reimbursement. **To Apply:** Telephone for further details. **Deadline:** Third Tuesday in February.

**Remarks:** Location sites include any designated federal facility; some on-campus appointments. Funds made available through the U.S. Nuclear Regulatory Commission. **Contact:** M. Elizabeth Kittrell, Program Manager, (615) 214-3310 or Jeannie Robinson, Program Specialist, at (615) 241-2878.

**• 5935 • U.S. Nuclear Regulatory Commission Historically Black Colleges and Universities Graduate Student Research Participation** *(Graduate/Fellowship)*

**Focus:** Basic energy sciences, engineering, geoscience, health physics, computer science, mathematics systems analysis, risk and performance assessment, human factors. **Qualif.:** Applicants must be graduate students attending historically black institutions.

**Funds Avail.:** $400 weekly stipend; travel reimbursement. **To Apply:** Write or telephone for further details. **Deadline:** Third Tuesday in February.

**Remarks:** Research locations include any designated federal facility; some on-campus appointments during the academic year. Funded by the U.S. Nuclear Regulatory Commission. **Contact:** M. Elizabeth Kittrell, Program Manager, at (615) 241-3319, or Jeannie Robinson, Program Specialist, at (615) 241-2878.

**• 5936 • U.S. Nuclear Regulatory Commission Historically Black Colleges and Universities Student Research Participation** *(Undergraduate/Internship)*

**Focus:** Energy science, engineering, geoscience, health physics, computer science, mathematics, systems analysis, risk and performance assessment, human factors. **Qualif.:** Applicants must be undergraduate students at historically black institutions.

**Funds Avail.:** $300 per week; travel reimbursement. **To Apply:** Write or telephone for further details. **Deadline:** Third Tuesday in February.

**Remarks:** Research sites include any designated federal facility; some on-campus appointments during the academic year. Funds available through the U.S. Nuclear Regulatory Commission. **Contact:** M. Elizabeth Kittrell, Program Manager, at (615) 241-3310, or Jeannie Robinson, Program Specialist, at (615) 241-2878.

## • 5937 •
**U.S. Department of Health and Human Services - Health Resources and Service Administration - Bureau of Primary Health Care**
The Division of Scholarships and
    Loan Repayments
Loan Repayment Programs Branch
4350 East West Highway                 *Ph:* (301)594-4400
10th Floor                             *Fax:* (301)594-4981
Bethesda, MD 20814                     *Free:* 800-435-6464
*E-mail:* DSLR@HRSA.DHHS.GOV

### • 5938 • Nursing Education Loan Repayment
*(Graduate, Undergraduate/Loan)*

**Purpose:** To encourage nurses to work in certain facilities in geographic areas with a shortage of nurses. **Focus:** Nursing. **Qualif.:** Eligible applicants should have a diploma or degree in nursing education; be registered (licensed) as a nurse in State of employment; and be willing to commit to two years of full-time clinical service at certain eligible health facilities (EHFs) that have a critical shortage of nurses. **Criteria:** Based on financial need, EHF in geographic area with shortage of nurses.

**Funds Avail.:** Assistance in repaying 60% of eligible unpaid nursing education loan balance: 30% repaid in each of the 2 years of service commitment. Funding for program is pending as of October 1, 1998 due to Congressional negotiation of the Federal government's budget appropriation. **No. of Awards:** 200. **Deadline:** June 30.

**Remarks:** Eligible health facilities include Indian Health Service Health centers, Native Hawaiian Health Centers, public hospitals, migrant health centers, community health centers, rural clinics, or public or non-profit health facilities determined by the Secretary of Health and Human Services to have a critical shortage of nurses. **Contact:** To receive an application and related materials concerning the NELR Program, contact The Division Scholarships and Loan Repayments at the above address (see entry 5937). Toll-free telephone: (800)435-6464.

## • 5939 •
**U.S. Environmental Protection Agency**
401 M St., SW                          *Ph:* (202)260-5260
Washington, DC 20460                   *Fax:* (202)260-1828

### • 5940 • Environmental Protection Agency Fellowships *(Professional Development/Fellowship)*

**Purpose:** To provide training for and upgrading of personnel in the areas of pollution abatement and control. **Qualif.:** Applicants must be present or prospective employees of regional, state, or local environmental pollution control or regulatory agencies. Fellowships are awarded for education and training in pollution control science, engineering, and technology, and in specialty areas that are supportive of pollution abatement and control efforts. **To Apply:** Applicants must complete and return an application kit available through the EPA and include copies of transcripts of undergraduate and graduate courses taken within the last 10 years. All forms must carry original signatures of officials as requested. Applications are not processed until all materials are completed and submitted as requested. Originals and two copies of the application and transcripts are also requested. **Contact:** Grants Administration Division, Grants Operations Branch (PM-216F), Environmental Protection Agency, 401 M St., SW, Washington, D.C. 20460. Alternate telephone: (202)260-5255.

## • 5941 •
**U.S. Junior Chamber of Commerce**
4 W. 21st St.
Tulsa, OK 74114-1116

### • 5942 • Baldridge Scholarship *(All/Scholarship)*

**Qualif.:** Must be a member of the Jaycees or immediate family. **Criteria:** Citizen of United States, possessing academic potential leadership traits and financial need.

**Funds Avail.:** $2,500. **No. of Awards:** 1. **To Apply:** Send a SASE to the above address with a $5.00 application fee (check or money order). **Deadline:** February 1.

### • 5943 • Jaycee War Memorial Fund Scholarship *(All/Scholarship)*

**Criteria:** Citizen of the United States, possessing academic potential leadership traits and financial need.

**Funds Avail.:** $1,000. **To Apply:** Send SASE to JWMF, Dept. 94922, Tulsa, OK 74194-0001 with a $5 application fee (check or money order payable to JWMF). **Deadline:** February 1.

## • 5944 •
**U.S. Marine Corps Historical Center**
Washington Navy Yard, Bldg. 58
901 M St., SE
Washington, DC 20374-5040             *Ph:* (202)433-4244

### • 5945 • U.S. Marine Corps Historical Center College Internships *(Graduate, Undergraduate/ Internship)*

**Purpose:** To give college students a chance to earn college credit, while giving them opportunities to gain experience on a professional level in the fields they pursue. **Focus:** Library and Archival Sciences, Museum Science, Military History. **Qualif.:** Applicants must be registered students at a college or university which will grant academic credit for work experience as interns in subject areas related to the student's course of study. **Criteria:** Internships are based upon an agreement between the sponsoring institution, the student, and the History and Museums Division. While there are no restrictions on individuals applying for intern positions, successful interns have had major or minor fields of study in history, American studies, political science, museology, data processing, art, and music.

**Funds Avail.:** A small grant of daily expense money is provided to each intern. **To Apply:** The History and Museums Division welcomes inquiries from students regarding the intern program. The division would prefer that prospective interns and academic sponsors visit the Marine Corps Historical Center, see its facilities and collections, and meet prospective supervisors of interns.

**Remarks:** All internships are served either at the Marine Corps Historical Center or the Marine Corps Airground Museum, located in Quantico, Virginia. **Contact:** Marine Corps Historical Center, Attn: Coordinator, Grants and Fellowships.

**• 5946 •**
## United States Naval Academy Class of 1963 Foundation
c/o J. Michael Lents, Chairman of
  Scholarship Committee
3309 Parkside Ter.
Fairfax, VA 22031                    *Ph:* (703)893-8753
*E-mail:* lents@osg.saic.com

**• 5947 •** **United States Naval Academy Class of 1963 Foundation Scholarship** *(Graduate, Undergraduate/Scholarship)*

**Focus:** General studies. **Qualif.:** Applicants must be dependents of deceased members of the United States Naval Academy Class of 1963 who are attending accredited colleges, universities, technical or vocational schools. **Criteria:** Awards are granted based on moral character. Academic progress is required to retain scholarship.

**Funds Avail.:** $3,750 per award. Renewable up to $15,000. **No. of Awards:** 17. **To Apply:** Write for further details. **Deadline:** Ongoing. **Contact:** J. Michael Lents at the above address (see entry 5946).

**• 5948 •**
## U.S. Naval Institute
Essay Contest
118 Maryland Ave.
Annapolis, MD 21402-5035          *Ph:* (410)268-6110

**• 5949 •** **Vincent Astor Memorial Leadership Essay Contest** *(Other/Prize)*

**Purpose:** To encourage junior officers and trainees to develop writing skills which demonstrate research and new thinking. Entry is limited to certain personnel within the US Navy, Marine Corps, and Coast Guard. **Qualif.:** Must be commissioned officers, regular and reserve, in pay grades 0-1, 0-2 and 0-3 (ensign/2nd lieutenant; lieutenant (junior grade)/1st lieutenant; and lieutenant/captain); and officer trainees within one year of receiving their commissions. **Criteria:** Essays are judged anonymously.

**Funds Avail.:** First prize winner will receive $1,500, a Naval Institute Gold Medal, and a life membership in the Naval Institute. The first honorable-mention winner will receive $1,000 and a Naval Institute Silver Medal. The Institute also will award $500 and a Naval Institute Bronze Medal to each of two second honorable mention winners. **To Apply:** Essays must be postmarked on or before the deadlines. Essays must be original, analytical and/or interpretive, and must be 3,500 words in length. The author's name must not appear on the essay. The title and motto must appear on the title page of the essay in lieu of the author's name, as well as on the outside of an accompanying sealed envelope containing the name, address, telephone number, social security number, a short biography of the essayist, the title of the essay, and the motto. Essay must be typewritten, double spaced, on paper approximately 8 1/2 X 11. Please submit 2 copies. If typed on computer, please submit an IBM-compatible disk and specify software used.

**• 5950 •** **Coast Guard Essay Contest** *(Other/Prize)*

**Qualif.:** Anyone may enter. **Criteria:** Essays will be judged anonymously.

**Funds Avail.:** Prizes are in the amount of $1,000, $750, and $500. **No. of Awards:** 3 **To Apply:** Essays must discuss current issues and new directions for the Coast Guard. Winning essays are published in the December issue of Proceedings. Essays must be postmarked on or before the deadline indicated. Essays must be

original, analytical and/or interpretive, and must not exceed 3,000 words. An exact word count must appear on the title page. Please do not put author's name on the essay. A title and motto must appear on the title page instead of the author's name. This information must also be on the outside of an accompanying sealed envelope containing the name, address, telephone number, social security number, and a short biography of the essayist. The essay must be typewritten, double-spaced, on paper approximately 8 1/2 X 11. Please submit 2 copies. If typed on a computer, please submit an IBM-compatible disk and specify software used. **Deadline:** June 1. **Contact:** Valry Fetrow.

**• 5951 •** **Enlisted Essay Contest** *(Other/Prize)*

**Qualif.:** This contest is not restricted by service, country, or subject. Must be submitted by enlisted personnel only, including active duty, reserve and retired. **Criteria:** Essays are judged anonymously.

**Funds Avail.:** Cash prizes in the amount of: $1,000, $750 and $500. **No. of Awards:** 3. **To Apply:** Essays can be up to 2,500 words. Essays must be postmarked on or before the deadline indicated. Essays must be original, analytical and/or interpretive. An exact word count must appear on the title page. The author's name must not appear on the essay. Each author must assign a title and motto to the essay. The title and motto must appear on the title page of the essay in lieu of the author's name, as well as on the outside of an accompanying sealed envelope containing the name, address, telephone number, social security number, a short biography of the essayist, the title of the essay, and the motto. The essay must be typewritten, double-spaced, on paper approximately 8 1/2 x 11. Please submit 2 copies. If typed on a computer, please submit an IBM-compatible disk and specify software used. **Contact:** Valry Fetrow.

**• 5952 •** **International Navies Essay Contest** *(Other/Prize)*

**Qualif.:** Anyone may enter.

**Funds Avail.:** Awards in the amount of: $1,000, $750, and $500. **No. of Awards:** 3. **To Apply:** The essay must discuss strategic, geographic, and cultural influences on individual or regional navies, their commitments and capabilities, and relationships with other navies. Essays must not exceed 3,000 words, and an exact word count must appear on the title page. The author's name must not appear on the essay. Instead, each author must assign a title and a motto to the essay. The title and motto must appear on the title page of the essay instead of the author's name. This must also appear on the outside of an accompanying sealed envelope containing the name, address, telephone number, social security number, and a short biography of the essayist. All essays must be typewritten and double-spaced, on paper approximately 8 1/2 X 11. Please submit two copies. If typed on a computer, please submit an IBM-compatible disk and specify software used. **Contact:** Valry Fetrow.

**• 5953 •** **International Navies Photo Contest** *(Other/Prize)*

**Qualif.:** Photographers, amateur or professional are eligible to enter.

**Funds Avail.:** $200 to the winner, $100 to two first honorable mentions, and $50 to two second honorable mentions. **No. of Awards:** 5. **To Apply:** All photo entries must be images of international naval and maritime subjects (from countries other than the United States). There is a limit of five entries per person. All five will be published in the annual March International Navies issue of Proceedings. **Deadline:** August 1. **Contact:** Valry Fetrow.

**• 5954 •** **Marine Corps Essay Contest** *(Other/Prize)*

**Qualif.:** Anyone may enter the contest. **Criteria:** Essays will be judged anonymously.

## U.S. Naval Institute (continued)

**Funds Avail.:** Prizes are in the amount of $1,000, $750, and $500. **No. of Awards:** 3. **To Apply:** Essays must discuss current issues and new directions for the Marine Corps. Winning essays are published in the November issue of Proceedings. Essays must be postmarked on or before the deadline. Essay must be original, analytical and/or interpretive, and must not exceed 3,000 words. Essay must be original. An exact word count must appear on the title page. The author's name must not appear on the essay. The title and motto must appear on the title page of the essay in lieu of the author's name, as well as on the outside of an accompanying sealed envelope containing the name, address, telephone number, social security number, a short biography of the essayist, the title of the essay, and the motto. The essay must be typewritten, double-spaced, on paper approximately 8 x 11. Submit two copies. If typed on a computer, please submit an IBM-compatible disk and specify software. **Deadline:** May 1. **Contact:** Valry Fetrow.

### • 5955 • Naval and Maritime Photo Contest (Other/ Prize)

**Qualif.:** Amateur and professional photographers may enter.

**Funds Avail.:** Cash prizes of $500, $350 and $250 will be awarded. 15 honorable mention winners will each receive $100. **No. of Awards:** 3. **To Apply:** All photos must pertain to naval or maritime subjects. The limit is five entries per person. **Deadline:** December 31. **Contact:** Valry Fetrow.

### • 5956 • Colin L. Powell Joint Warfighting Essay Contest (Other/Prize)

**Qualif.:** Applicants can be military professionals or civilians. **Criteria:** Essay will be judged anonymously.

**Funds Avail.:** Cash prizes of $2,500, $2,000 and $1,000 to the authors of the three best essays entered. **No. of Awards:** 3. **To Apply:** Essay must be postmarked on or before the deadline indicated. An exact word count must appear on the title page. The author's name must not appear on the essay. The author must assign a title and a motto to the essay. The title and motto must appear on the title page of the essay in lieu of the author's name, as well as on the outside of an accompanying sealed envelope containing the name, address, telephone number, social security number, a short biography of the essayist, the title of the essay, and the motto. The essay must be typewritten, double-spaced, on paper approximately 8 X 11. Please submit 2 copies. If the essay is typed on a computer, please submit an IBM-compatible disk and specify software used. **Deadline:** April 1. **Contact:** Valry Fetrow.

## • 5957 •
## U.S. Navy - Navy, Marine Corps, Coast Guard Dependents' Scholarship Program
Naval Military Personnel Command
(NMPC 641 D.)
Washington, DC 20370-5641

*A number of Navy-oriented organizations offer scholarship funds to dependents of current or former members of the Navy, Marine Corps, and Coast Guard. The following are a few examples of the scholarships that are currently offered. Contact the Navy, Marine Corps, Coast Guard Dependents' Scholarship Program for a complete list of available scholarships.*

### • 5958 • Gamewardens of Vietnam Association Scholarships (Undergraduate/Award)

**Qualif.:** Applicants must be high school students or college freshmen who are dependent children, step-children, or adopted children of living or deceased U.S. Navy River Patrol Force (TF-116) members or former members who served in Vietnam in "Operation Gamewarden" between (1966 and 1971). Applicants must be unmarried and under 21 years of age. They must be under the age of 23 if currently enrolled full-time at an approved institution of higher learning. **Criteria:** Selection is based on financial need and scholastic abilities. **To Apply:** Applicants must file an Application for Dependent's Scholarship Program (NAVPERS 1750/7). **Deadline:** April 15. **Contact:** Gamewardens of Vietnam Association, Inc., PO Box 5523, Virginia Beach, VA 23455-0523 for an application and brochure with complete description of award requirements.

### • 5959 • Marianas Naval Officers' Wives' Club Scholarships (Undergraduate/Scholarship)

**Qualif.:** Applicants must be the children or spouses of officers or enlisted members of the Navy, Marine Corps, or Coast Guard on active duty or retired with pay (or who died while on active duty or retired with pay). Applicants must be local residents of Guam who are graduating seniors from accredited high schools, spouses who are planning to return to school, or currently enrolled college students. Students must be, or plan to be, enrolled full-time in accredited institutions of higher learning. **Criteria:** Selection is based on character, scholastic proficiency, community involvement, leadership ability, and financial need.

**Funds Avail.:** Funds are to be used for academic purposes only. **To Apply:** Applicants must file an Application for Dependent's Scholarship Program (NAVPERS 1750/7). Reapplication is required annually. **Deadline:** April 1. **Contact:** Scholarship Chairman, Marinas Naval Officers' Wives' Club, COMNAVMAR, Box 49, FPO AP 96630 (671)477-5405 for an application and brochure describing award requirements.

### • 5960 • Navy Wives Club of America Scholarships (Undergraduate/Scholarship)

**Purpose:** To provide access to college education, vocational, business or other training, which will enable the recipient to make a more valuable contribution to society. **Qualif.:** Applicants must be the dependent children, step-children, or adopted children of regular or reserve Navy, Marine Corps or Coast Guard enlisted members on active duty, retired with pay, or who died while on active duty or retired with pay. Applicants must be unmarried and under 21 years of age, or under the age of 23 if currently enrolled full-time at an approved institution of higher learning.

**Funds Avail.:** Grants are paid directly to the institution. Renewal is dependent on academic record. **To Apply:** Applicants must file an Application for Dependent's Scholarship Program (NAVPERS 1750/7). **Contact:** Diana Bower, Navy Wives Club of America Scholarship Foundation, 16015 Terry St., Belton, MO 64012 for an application and brochure describing award requirements.

### • 5961 • Seabee Memorial Association Scholarships (Undergraduate/Scholarship)

**Qualif.:** Applicants must be the dependent children, step-children, and adopted children of officers or enlisted members of the Seabee Memorial Association who have served with the Naval Construction Force (Seabees) or Naval Civil Engineer Corps. Members may be regular, reserve, retired, honorably discharged, or deceased. Applicants must be unmarried and under 21 years of age, or under the age of 23 if currently enrolled full-time at an approved institution of higher learning. **Criteria:** Selection is based on financial need, character, academics, citizenship, and leadership abilities.

**Funds Avail.:** Scholarships are renewable for up to four years. Fulfillment of scholarship contract is required to retain funding. **No. of Awards:** 17. **To Apply:** Applicants must file an Application for Dependent's Scholarship Program (NAVPERS 1750/7). **Deadline:** April 15. **Contact:** Chairman, Seabee Memorial Scholarship Association, Inc., Naval Facilities Engineering Command (Code OOE), 200 Stovall St., Alexandria, VA 22332 for an application and brochure describing award requirements.

## • 5962 • U.S. Submarine Veterans of World War II Scholarships (Undergraduate/Scholarship)

**Qualif.:** Applicants must be the dependent children, step-children, or adopted children of enlisted members or officers of U.S. Submarines or U.S. Submarine Relief Crews who served in World War II and are regular members in good standing of United States Submarine Veterans of WWII. Applicants must be unmarried and be under 21 years of age, or under the age of 23 if currently enrolled full-time at an approved institution of higher learning.

**Funds Avail.:** $600 scholarships are awarded directly to the institution. **To Apply:** Applicants must file an Application for Dependent's Scholarship Program (NAVPERS 1750/7). **Deadline:** April 15. **Contact:** Robert "Ben" Benites, Assistant Scholarship Director, U.S. Submarine Veterans of Word War II, 160 Lido Circle, Sacramento, CA 95826-1615; telephone: (916)381-3255 for an application and brochure describing award requirements.

---

## • 5963 •
## United States Pharmacopia
Office of External Affairs
12601 Twinbrook Pkwy.                    **Ph:** (301)816-8282
Rockville, MD 20852                      **Fax:** (301)998-6806
*URL:* http://www.usp.org

### • 5964 • USP Fellowship Award (Postgraduate/Award)

**Purpose:** To promote research related to compendial standards or medical and drug use information. **Focus:** Drug standards and drug information. **Qualif.:** Applicants must be sponsored by a faculty who is a current member of the USP Committee. **Criteria:** Selection is based on expertise in drug standards and drug information sciences.

**Funds Avail.:** $15,000. **No. of Awards:** 12 awards. **To Apply:** Each application must include the following: fully complete application that includes signatures of the applicant, USP sponsor, faculty advisor, and university official; curriculum vitae and transcript; progress report for the first months of research, if application is for a second year; and research proposal. **Deadline:** January. **Contact:** USP Office of External Affairs at the above address (see entry 5963).

---

## • 5965 •
## U.S. Public Health Service - Health Resources and Services Administration - Bureau of Health Professions
Parklawn Bldg., Rm. 8-38
5600 Fishers Ln.                         **Ph:** (301)443-5798
Rockville, MD 20857                      **Fax:** (301)443-2111
*The Health Resources and Services Administration is part of the U.S. Department of Health and Human Services.*

### • 5966 • HRSA-BHP Exceptional Financial Need Scholarship (Doctorate/Scholarship)

**Purpose:** To support students who are pursuing careers in medicine, osteopathy, and dentistry. **Qualif.:** Applicants must be citizens, nationals, or permanent residents of the United States or the District of Columbia, Puerto Rico, American Somoa, Virgin Islands, Guam, the Republic of Palua, the Republic of the Marshall Islands, the Federated State of Micronesia, the Trust Territory of the Pacific Islands, or the Mariana Islands who show exceptional financial need, which means that the student's resources do not

exceed the lesser of $5,000 or one-half the cost of attendance at the school.

**Funds Avail.:** Scholarships cover tuition and other reasonable educational expenses and provide a stipend for 12 months. **Contact:** The Director of Student Financial Aid at the participating school.

### • 5967 • HRSA-BHP Health Professions Student Loans (Doctorate, Graduate/Loan)

**Purpose:** To assist students with need for financial assistance to undertake the course of study required to become physicians, dentists, osteopathic physicians, optometrists, pharmacists, podiatrists, or veterinarians. **Qualif.:** Applicants must be enrolled or accepted for enrollment as full-time students in a program leading to a doctoral degree in medicine, dental surgery or equivalent degree, pharmacy, osteopathic medicine, optometry or equivalent degree, podiatric medicine or equivalent degree, or veterinary medicine or equivalent degree; or a bachelor of science in pharmacy or equivalent degree. Applicants must also be citizens, nationals, or permanent residents of the United States or the District of Columbia, the Commonwealths of Puerto Rico or the Marianna Islands, the Virgin Islands, Guam, The American Samoa, the Trust Territory of the Pacific Islands, the Republic of Palau, the Republic of the Marshall Islands, and the Federated State of Micronesia. Applicants must also demonstrate financial need. Professional students, interns, residents, and students seeking advanced training are not eligible.

**Funds Avail.:** Up to the cost of tuition plus $2,500 or the amount of financial need, whichever is less. The interest rate is five percent and accrues during the repayment period. Loans are repayable over a ten year period and beginning one year after the student graduates or ceases to enroll full-time in a health program.

**Remarks:** Loan repayment may be deferred during active military duty, service under the Peace Corps Act, or the Public Health Service for up to three years. Students pursuing advanced professional training, including internships and residencies, are also eligible for deferment. **Contact:** The director of student financial aid at the school the applicant intends to apply for admission will provide applications and other information.

### • 5968 • HRSA-BHP Loans for Disadvantaged Students (Undergraduate/Loan)

**Purpose:** To assist students who need financial assistance to pursue careers in medicine, osteopathic medicine, dentistry, optometry, podiatric medicine, pharmacy, or veterinary medicine. **Qualif.:** Applicants must be citizens, nationals, or lawful permanent residents of the United States or the District of Columbia, the Commonwealths of Puerto Rico or the Marianna Islands, the Virgin Islands, Guam, American Samoa, the Trust Territory of the Pacific Islands, the Republic of Palau, the Republic of the Marshall Islands, or the Federated State of Micronesia. They must also be enrolled or accepted for enrollment at a participating health professionals school full-time. Students must be determined by their school's financial aid director to meet financial need and "disadvantaged background" criteria. Those enrolled in schools of medicine or osteopathic medicine must demonstrate exceptional financial need. Preprofessional students, interns, residents, and students seeking advanced training are not eligible. **Criteria:** Schools are responsible for selecting recipients and for determining the amount of assistance.

**Funds Avail.:** The maximum loan amount allowed for each school year is the cost of tuition plus $2,500, or the amount of financial need, whichever is lesser. The repayment interest rate is five percent over a ten-year period, which begins one year after completion of cessation of full-time study. Interest begins accruing at the time the loan becomes repayable. Repayment may be deferred under special circumstances, and interest does not accrue during periods of deferment.

**Remarks:** Disadvantaged background means that a student comes from an environment that has inhibited them from obtaining

---

**U.S. Public Health Service - Health Resources and Services Administration - Bureau of Health Professions** *(continued)*

the knowledge, skills, and abilities required to enroll in and graduate from a school of medicine, osteopathic medicine, dentistry, pharmacy, podiatric medicine, optometry, or veterinary medicine, or the student's family annual income is below federally-determined thresholds according to family size. **Contact:** Students should contact the director of the financial aid office at the school they are planning to attend.

## • 5969 • HRSA-BHP National Health Service Corps Scholarships *(Doctorate/Scholarship)*

**Qualif.:** Must be full-time students enrolled or accepted for enrollment in accredited U.S. schools or allopathic or osteopathic medicine, dentistry, and other health related programs. Applicants must be U.S. citizens.

**Funds Avail.:** School tuition and a monthly stipend. **Deadline:** June 15.

**Remarks:** There is a one-year service obligation for each year of support with a minimum of two years. Obligation consists of full-time service in selected federally designated Health Manpower Shortage Areas. **Contact:** NHSC Scholarships, Parklawn Bldg., Rm. 7-29, 5600 Fishers Ln. Rockville, MD, MD 20857, (301)443-1650 or for a toll-free message (800)638-0824.

## • 5970 • HRSA-BHP Nursing Student Loan *(Other, Undergraduate/Loan)*

**Qualif.:** Applicants must be students accepted for enrollment or enrolled as full-time or half-time in a course leading to a diploma in nursing, a bachelor's degree in nursing or an equivalent degree, or an associate or graduate degree in nursing. They must also be citizens, nationals, or permanent residents of the United States or the District of Columbia, the Commonwealths of Puerto Rico or the Marianna Islands, the Virgin Islands, Guam, The American Samoa, the Trust Territory of the Pacific Islands, the Republic of Palau, the Republic of the Marshall Islands, and the Federated State of Micronesia. **Criteria:** The amount of assistance is determined by the amount of financial resources available to the applicant. They must demonstrate financial need.

**Funds Avail.:** Up to $2,500 per year depending on available funds and need, and up to $4,000 for each of the final two years. No individual may receive more than $13,000 for all years of support. Repayment begins one year after graduation or if the student ceases to pursue nursing studies and must be completed within ten years. Interest rate on the loans is 5 percent. Loan repayment may be deferred during military duty, service in the Peace Corps or advanced professional nursing training. **Contact:** Director of Student Financial Aid at a participating school.

## • 5971 • HRSA-BHP Professional Nurse Traineeship *(Doctorate, Graduate/Other)*

**Purpose:** To meet the cost of traineeships for individuals in advanced degree nursing education programs, and to educate individuals to serve in and prepare for practice as nurse practitioners, nurse midwives, nurse educators, public health nurses, or in any other clinical nursing specialties. **Qualif.:** Candidates must be United States citizens, non-citizen nationals, or foreign nationals who possess a visa permitting permanent residence in the United States. They must be currently licensed as a registered nurse in a state, or have completed basic nursing preparations in a masters of nursing program (as determined by the school). They are also required to be enrolled full-time in eligible graduate programs and be pursuing a masters or doctoral degree. Preference will be given to individuals who are residents of health professional shortage areas designated under Section 332 of the Public Health Service Act. **Criteria:** Recipients are selected by the participating institutions in accordance with the institutions' admission policies and the purpose of the traineeship program.

**Funds Avail.:** Stipend up to $8,800 for tuition, books, fees and reasonable living expenses for a maximum of 36 months of study. **Contact:** Dean of Nursing at the participating institution or Division of Nursing, Bureau of Health Professions, Health Resources and Services Administration, at the above address (see entry 5965).

## • 5972 • HRSA-BHP Scholarships for Disadvantaged Students *(Doctorate, Graduate, Undergraduate/ Scholarship)*

**Purpose:** To provide financial assistance without obligation to disadvantaged health professions and nursing students to enable them to pursue a degree in medicine, osteopathic medicine, dentistry, and nursing. **Qualif.:** Applicants must be citizens, nationals, or lawful permanent residents of the United States or the District of Columbia, the Commonwealths of Puerto Rico or the Marianna Islands, the Virgin Islands, Guam, American Samoa, the Trust Territory of the Pacific Islands, the Republic of Palau, the Republic of the Marshall Islands, or the Federated State of Micronesia. They must also be enrolled or be accepted for enrollment at a participating health professions or nursing school full-time. Students must be determined by their school's financial aid director to meet financial need and "disadvantaged background" criteria. **Criteria:** Schools are responsible for selecting recipients and for determining the amount of assistance.

**Funds Avail.:** Scholarships cover the costs of tuition, other reasonable educational expenses, and reasonable living expenses.

**Remarks:** Disadvantaged background means that a student comes from an environment that has inhibited them from obtaining the knowledge, skills, and abilities required to enroll in and graduate from a school of medicine, osteopathic medicine, dentistry, or nursing, or they are from families with annual incomes below federally-determined thresholds according to family size. **Contact:** Students should contact the director of the financial aid office at the school they are planning to attend.

---

## • 5973 •
### United States Space Foundation
2860 S. Circle Dr., Ste. 2301  
Colorado Springs, CO 80906-4184

Ph: (719)576-8000  
Fax: (719)576-8801  
Free: 800-691-4000

*E-mail:* 76702.2036@compuserve.com

## • 5974 • United States Space Foundation Teacher Course Fellowship *(Professional Development/ Fellowship)*

**Purpose:** To provide an opportunity for teachers who would not otherwise be able to attend this course to do so. The course provides teachers with an understanding of how to infuse space and aviation information into their daily lessons. It also introduces teachers to the basic concepts and resources necessary to teach using space and aviation examples. **Focus:** Education. **Qualif.:** Candidates must be educators/teachers wishing to enroll in the Foundation's teacher course. **Criteria:** Based on financial need.

**Funds Avail.:** Partial awards of up to $200 per individual. Teachers can earn two semester hours of graduate credit from the University of Colorado. **No. of Awards:** Varies, usually 100-120. **To Apply:** Further information and application forms may be requested. **Deadline:** Four to six weeks prior to course.

**Remarks:** Annual courses are held in Colorado, Arizona, or California. **Contact:** J. Sunseri at the above address (see entry 5973).

## • 5975 •
## University of Arizona - Hispanic Alumni Association
111 N. Cherry Ave.
Tucson, AZ 85721

#### • 5976 • Concerned Media Professionals Scholarships *(Undergraduate/Scholarship)*

**Focus:** Journalism. **Qualif.:** Applicants must be Hispanic Arizona residents enrolled or planning to enroll in journalism at the University of Arizona. **No. of Awards:** 2.

## • 5977 •
## University of California
President's Postdoctoral Fellowship
  Program
300 Lakeside Dr., 18th Fl.      *Ph:* (510)987-9500
Oakland, CA 94612-3550      *Fax:* (510)987-9612
*E-mail:* jane.gonzales.@ucop.edu
*URL:* http://www.ucop.edu/acadav/fgsaa/f-conts.html

#### • 5978 • University of California President's Postdoctoral Fellowship *(Postdoctorate/Fellowship)*

**Purpose:** To enhance the competitiveness of outstanding minority and women scholars for academic appointments at major research universities. **Focus:** General Studies. **Qualif.:** Applicants must be U.S. citizens or permanent residents who hold a Ph.D. from an accredited university. **Criteria:** Applications are encouraged from African Americans, American Indians, Asian Americans, Filipinos, Mexican Americans, and Latinos, and from all women in physical sciences, mathematics, and engineering.

**Funds Avail.:** Stipends are $29,112-30,360 plus health benefits and up to $4,000 for research expenses. Awards are for one academic year with the possibility of renewal for a second year pending demonstration of satisfactory progress. **No. of Awards:** 20-25. **To Apply:** Must submit application form, two essays, curriculum vitae, member form and references. **Deadline:** December 1. **Contact:** Application materials and information are available by contacting Jane A. Gonzalez, President's Postdoctoral Fellowship Program, at the above address (see entry 5977).

## • 5979 •
## University of California, Berkeley - Committee on Legal Education Exchange with China
272 Boalt Hall      *Ph:* (510)642-6150
Berkeley, CA 94720      *Fax:* (510)642-7273

#### • 5980 • Junior Research Program Grants Exchange with China *(Postdoctorate/Grant)*

**Purpose:** To facilitate study and research at selected Chinese law faculties by qualified American scholars. **Focus:** Chinese Law. **Qualif.:** Applicant must be a U.S. citizen and be either a recent graduate of law school or a law student who will graduate by the start of the award tenure. Applicant should have a strong academic record and be proficient in Mandarin. Awards are tenable for non-degree legal research at the law faculties of Peking, People's, Wuhan, or Jilin Universities or the Chinese Academy of Social Sciences Institute of Law.

**Funds Avail.:** Modest stipend and round-trip airfare. **To Apply:** Write to CLEEC for application guidelines. Submit research proposal, transcripts, and two letters of recommendation from law faculty members. Interviews are required for finalists. **Deadline:**

October 1. Award recipients are selected by CLEEC in mid-March. Final placement is made by the Chinese State Education Commission by early May. **Contact:** Mary Powell, Program Coordinator, at the above address (see entry 5979).

#### • 5981 • Specialist Program Grants Exchange with China *(Postdoctorate/Grant)*

**Purpose:** To facilitate study and research at selected Chinese law faculties by qualified American scholars. **Focus:** Chinese Law. **Qualif.:** Applicant must be a U.S. citizen who is an academic specialist in Chinese law. Candidate must be proficient in Mandarin. Awards are intended to assist original research in China on some aspect of Chinese law. Candidates are responsible for making arrangements with host institutions in China.

**Funds Avail.:** International travel and living expenses. **To Apply:** Write to CLEEC for application guidelines. Submit a research proposal written in the form of a letter. Include specific research objectives, methodology, and long-term goals. Letters of recommendation, curriculum vitae, copies of relevant publications, a statement of Chinese language proficiency, and an invitation from the Chinese host institution indicating acceptance of research program are required. **Deadline:** Applications are processed year-round. **Contact:** Mary Powell, Program Coordinator, at the above address (see entry 5979).

#### • 5982 • Teaching/Research Program Grants Exchange with China *(Postdoctorate/Grant)*

**Purpose:** To facilitate study and research at selected Chinese law faculties by qualified American scholars. **Focus:** Chinese Law. **Qualif.:** Applicant must be a U.S. citizen and a law teacher with at least five years of teaching experience. Candidate must not currently specialize in Chinese law but should wish to add a significant Chinese law component to his/her teaching and research. A grant may be used at any one of the eight key law schools and institutes in the People's Republic of China. CLEEC will assist in arranging for awardees to teach and conduct research at one of the institutions while in China. Award recipients are expected to return to their home institution and to apply Chinese experience to teaching curriculum. Grants provide only modest support and are not adequate to serve as salary and fringe benefit substitutes. CLEEC expects that most scholars will derive principal support from their home institution during a sabbatical leave.

**Funds Avail.:** Stipend and round-trip airfare. **To Apply:** Write to CLEEC for application guidelines. Submit a resume, copies of relevant publications, and a research proposal in the form of a letter. Include proposed research methodology, previous training in Chinese law, and relevance of study in China to long-term teaching goals. Letters of recommendation and interviews are also required. **Deadline:** Applications are processed year-round.

## • 5983 •
## University of California, Berkeley - Miller Institute for Basic Research in Science
2536 Channing Way      *Ph:* (510)642-4088
Berkeley, CA 94720-5190      *Fax:* (510)643-7393
*E-mail:* 4mibrs@socrates.berkeley.edu; 4mibrs@
  garnet.berkeley.edu
*URL:* http://socrates.berkeley.edu/~4mibrs

#### • 5984 • Miller Institute Research Fellowships *(Postdoctorate/Fellowship)*

**Purpose:** To discover scientists of great talent or promise. **Focus:** Science. **Qualif.:** The fellowship is awarded to brilliant young men and women of great promise who have recently taken or who are about to take the doctoral degree. Nominees may be United States

**University of California, Berkeley - Miller Institute for Basic Research in Science (continued)**

citizens or aliens. **Criteria:** Selection is by nomination only. No direct applications will be accepted.

**Funds Avail.:** The annual stipend is currently $43,000. The institute pays travel expenses to Berkeley for each recipient and his or her immediate family, plus a limited allowance for removal expenses. The Institute also provides an individual contingency fund of $5,000 to be used for research or clerical assistance, travel to attend professional meetings, to consult with investigators, or for any other essential research needs. Health benefits are included. **No. of Awards:** 8-10. **To Apply:** Candidates may not enter competition on their own initiative. Candidates are invited to do so on the basis of nominations made by a world-wide panel of outstanding scientists, former Miller Professors and Fellows, and the science faculty at the University of California. **Deadline:** Early October. **Contact:** Kathryn Day-Huh, Executive Assistant, Miller Institute for Basic Research in Science at the above address (see entry 5983).

---

• 5985 •
**University of California, Los Angeles - Center for International Relations**
11381 Bunche Hall
405 Hilgard Avenue                        *Ph:* (310)825-0604
Los Angeles, CA 90024-1486               *Fax:* (310)206-2582
*E-mail:* rosecran@polisci.sscnet.ucla.edu

• 5986 • **CIR Postdoctoral Fellowship**
*(Postdoctorate/Fellowship)*

**Purpose:** To allow a scholar to revise his/her dissertation into a book manuscript. **Focus:** Economics, Environmental Policy, International Relations, International Security. **Qualif.:** Candidate may be of any nationality. Applicant must have completed dissertation prior to the academic year in which the fellowship is held. Fellow must spend the year in residence at CIR.

**Funds Avail.:** Approximately $22,000. **No. of Awards:** One. **To Apply:** Submit curriculum vitae, abstract of dissertation, transcripts, and three letters of recommendation to CIR. **Deadline:** February 15. **Contact:** Richard Rosecrance, Director, at the above address (see entry 5985).

---

• 5987 •
**University of California, Los Angeles - Center for Medieval and Renaissance Studies**
212 Royce Hall
405 Hilgard Ave.                          *Ph:* (310)825-1880
Los Angeles, CA 90024-1485               *Fax:* (310)825-0655
*E-mail:* CMRS@HUMNET.UCLA.EDU

• 5988 • **CMRS Summer Fellowships** *(Postdoctorate/Fellowship)*

**Purpose:** To support scholarship in Medieval and Renaissance studies. **Focus:** Medieval Studies, Renaissance Studies. **Qualif.:** Candidate may be of any nationality. Applicant must be a research scholar, preferably with a Ph.D. The award is intended for those who have a special need for the resources UCLA and Los Angeles-area libraries offer. Fellows must be in residence at the Center during the fellowship tenure, which must occur during one of two summer sessions.

**Funds Avail.:** $500 stipend and temporary membership in the Center with attendant campus privileges. **To Apply:** Submit curriculum vitae, a Biography for Academic Personnel form available at any University, a 200-word description of proposed summer project, and one letter of recommendation. Indicate in application how project would benefit from residency at Center, and preferred dates of attendance. (June 26 to August 4 or August 7 to September 16). **Deadline:** February 10. Recipients of fellowships will be notified by March 10.

**Remarks:** The Center also offers visiting fellowships to scholars in the medieval and renaissance fields who wish to pursue research at UCLA. These fellowships include campus privileges, but do not carry stipends. Contact the Center for details. **Contact:** Patrick J. Geary, Director, at the above address (see entry 5987).

---

• 5989 •
**University of Denver - Rocky Mountain Women's Institute**
7150 Montview Blvd.
Denver, CO 80220                          *Ph:* (303)871-6923

• 5990 • **Brown University, The Future of Gender**
*(Postdoctorate/Fellowship)*

**Purpose:** To encourage interest in minority issues. **Qualif.:** Third world and minority scholars are encouraged to apply. Recipients may not hold a tenured position in an American college or university.

**Funds Avail.:** The stipend is $25,000. **Deadline:** Post-marked by December 15. **Contact:** University of Denver at the above address (see entry 5989).

---

• 5991 •
**University Film and Video Association**
c/o Prof. Julie Simon
School of Communications Design
University of Baltimore
1420 N. Charles St.                       *Ph:* (410)837-6061
Baltimore, MD 21201                       *Fax:* (410)837-6029
*E-mail:* jsimon@ubmail.ubalt.edu

• 5992 • **University Film and Video Association Student Grants** *(Graduate, Undergraduate/Grant)*

**Purpose:** To provide financial support for film or video productions and research projects in historical, critical, theoretical, and experimental studies of film and video. **Qualif.:** Applicants must be graduate or undergraduate students and sponsored by a faculty member who is an active member of the University Film and Video Association.

**Funds Avail.:** Up to $4,000 for film or video productions and up to $1,000 for research projects. **To Apply:** Three copies of each of the following must be postmarked by January 1: one-page resume; a one-page description of the production or research project that includes a statement of purpose, an indication of the resources available to complete the work, and a summary of the proposed production or research project; a statement by the sponsoring UFVA member assessing the feasibility of the project and indicating his or her willingness to serve as faculty supervisor or consultant (this is not a recommendation); and a one-page budget indicating what portion of the total project will be supported by this grant. Additional requirements for research projects include a description of the methodology to be employed and a statement indicating the relationship of the proposed study to previous research in the field. Requirements for specific productions are as follows: Narrative, a copy of the script (under 30 minutes); Documentary, a short treatment (under 60 minutes); Experimental or animated, a treatment (or script) and/or storyboard. **Deadline:** January 1. Awards are announced by March 15.

**Remarks:** The grants are cosponsored by the University Film and Video Foundation (UFVF). UFVA reserves the right to publish funded work in the UFVA Journal or UFVA Video Journal. The judges reserve the right to refrain from awarding grants or to fund more than one project per year based on the quantity or quality of submissions. Additional materials may be requested from applicants. **Contact:** Julie Simon at the above address (see entry 5991).

---

**• 5993 •**
**University of Georgia Press**
330 Research Dr.                          *Ph:* (706)369-6130
Athens, GA 30602                          *Fax:* (706)369-6131

**• 5994 •  Flannery O'Connor Awards for Short Fiction** *(Professional Development/Award)*

**Purpose:** To recognize and publish outstanding collections of short fiction. **Focus:** Fiction. **Qualif.:** Applicant may be of any nationality, but must write in English. Candidate's submission must be a collection of short fiction between 200 and 250 pages in length. Stories that have been previously published in magazines or anthologies may be included, but should be clearly labeled. Collections that contain long stories or novellas are eligible, but novels will not be considered. Award-winning manuscripts will be published by the University of Georgia Press.

**Funds Avail.:** $1,000. **No. of Awards:** 2 **To Apply:** Send self-addressed, stamped envelope for application form and guidelines. Submit typewritten manuscript with entry fee ($15 in 1990). Manuscripts will not be returned. **Deadline:** April 1 to May 31. Notification by December. **Contact:** Editorial Assistant at the above address (see entry 5993).

---

**• 5995 •**
**University of Hawaii at Manoa - The Freedom Forum Asia Fellowships Program for Journalists**
2530 Dole St.
Sakamaki Hall A203                        *Ph:* (808)956-7733
Honolulu, HI 96822                        *Fax:* 800-956-9600

**• 5996 •  The Freedom Forum Asia Studies Fellowships** *(Professional Development/Fellowship)*

**Purpose:** To encourage better, more informed coverage of developments related to Asia and its people by American news media. **Focus:** Asian Studies in the Humanities and Social Sciences. **Qualif.:** Candidate must be a citizen or permanent resident of the United States or an Asian country. Applicant must be a mid-career journalist. Print and broadcast journalists are eligible. Fellows must engage in intense academic study in Asian cultures and institutions.

**Funds Avail.:** Varies. **To Apply:** Write to the Fellowship Program for application form and guidelines.

**Remarks:** Two fellowships are reserved for journalists from Asian countries. **Contact:** The Freedom Forum Asia Studies Fellowships at the above address (see entry 5995). An alternate telephone number is (808)956-7123.

---

**• 5997 •**
**University of Illinois - College of Fine and Applied Arts**
608 E. Lorado Taft Dr. 115
Champaign, IL 61820                        *Ph:* (217)333-1661

**• 5998 •  Kate Neal Kinley Memorial Fellowshsip** *(Graduate/Fellowship)*

**Focus:** Architecture, Art, Music. **Qualif.:** Applicants must be graduates of the College of Fine and Applied Arts of the University of Illinois at Urbana-Champaign or graduates of similar institutions of equal educational standing whose principal or major studies have been in the fields of architecture, art, or music. **Criteria:** Preference is given to students under the age of 25. Fellowships are awarded on the basis of achievement in the applicant's chosen field, as evidenced by academic marks, suitability of the proposed program of study, and the candidate's character, personality, and seriousness of purpose.

**Funds Avail.:** Three fellowships of $7,000 each will be awarded to defray the expenses of advanced Fine Arts study in America or abroad. Additional fellowships of $1,000 may also be awarded based upon committee recommendations. **To Apply:** Three substantiating letters of reference from scholars under whom the candidate has studied must be mailed to the fellowship committee separate from the application. Applications are available in November. **Deadline:** February 1.

**Remarks:** The fellowship is partially funded by the John Robert Gregg Fund.

---

**• 5999 •**
**University of Maine Pulp and Paper Foundation**
5737 Jenness Hall                         *Ph:* (207)581-2295
Orono, ME 04469-5737                      *Fax:* (207)581-2000
*E-mail:* pulpaper@maine.maine.edu
*URL:* http://www.umecheme.maine.edu/ppfl

**• 6000 •  University of Maine Pulp and Paper Foundation Scholarships** *(Undergraduate/Scholarship)*

**Purpose:** To recognize students of high ability and career promise who are interested in paper-related technical careers with industry producers or suppliers. **Focus:** Engineering. **Qualif.:** Candidates must be admitted to or enrolled in the University of Maine College of Engineering, or the School of Engineering Technology, and demonstrate interest in paper-related careers. Entering freshmen must be in the top 10 percent of their graduating class and score at least 1,100 on the SAT exam. Upperclass applicants must have at least a 2.6 cumulative GPA. The GPA requirement applies at the beginning of the semester for which an award is made. **Criteria:** All applicants interview with an industrial member of the selection committee.

**Funds Avail.:** Awards of $1,000 each are offered in the Spring to new students upon completion of 14 credit hours with a 2.8 GPA. Upperclass students are eligible for Full Maine Resident Tuition Awards (valued at about $3,500 per year). Five full non-resident tuition scholarships are also available. **No. of Awards:** 25 first-year, 100 upper-class, and 5 out of state tuition scholarships are available. **To Apply:** New students are encouraged to apply before February 1 in the year of admission to the University of Maine College of Engineering. Applications are available to upperclassmen between January 15 and March 15. **Deadline:** Applications must be in by February 1 for new students and March 15 upperclass students. **Contact:** Stanley N. Marshall, Jr., Executive Director at the above address (see entry 5999).

---

# • 6001 •

## University of Michigan - Center for the Education of Women

330 E. Liberty St.                          *Ph:* (734)998-7080
Ann Arbor, MI 48104-2289                     *Fax:* (734)998-6203
*URL:* http://www.umich.edu/~cew

### • 6002 • CEW Scholarships for Returning Women
*(Graduate, Professional Development, Undergraduate/ Scholarship)*

**Purpose:** To honor the academic performance and potential of women whose education has been interrupted. **Focus:** Open. **Qualif.:** Applicants must be undergraduate, graduate, or professional women whose education has been interrupted for at least 48 consecutive months or a total of 60 months not counting interruptions of 12 months. They must also be pursuing any academic or professional program, full or part time, with a clear educational goal, at any campus of the University of Michigan. Women in business, chemistry, engineering, mathematics, and other less traditional fields are encouraged to apply. **Criteria:** Selection is based on merit.

**Funds Avail.:** Scholarships are not renewable and range from $1,000 to $4,500. One $11,000 scholarship (for undergraduate study) and one $10,000 scholarship are given to students majoring in engineering, computer science or a related field. **No. of Awards:** 32. **Deadline:** January, awards are announced in April. Applications are available in October.

**Remarks:** Formerly known as the Margaret Dow Towsley Scholarships for Women. **Contact:** Carol Hollenshead, director, at the above address (see entry 6001).

# • 6003 •

## University of Minnesota - Program for Cultural Cooperation Between Spain's Ministry of Culture and United States' Universities

106 Nicholson Hall
216 Pillsbury Dr., SE                        *Ph:* (612)625-9888
Minneapolis, MN 55455-0138                   *Free:* (612)626-8009
*E-mail:* zimme001@maroon.tc.umn.edu

### • 6004 • Cultural Cooperation Grants *(Doctorate, Graduate, Postgraduate, Professional Development/ Grant)*

**Purpose:** To spread awareness about Spanish culture throughout the United States. **Qualif.:** Applicants must be graduate students, professors, researchers, or publishers of non-commercial presses.

**Funds Avail.:** $150,000 twice per year. **No. of Awards:** Varies. **To Apply:** Applicants must write for details. **Deadline:** December 1 and April 30. **Contact:** Holly Zimmerman LeVoir.

# • 6005 •

## University of Missouri - School of Journalism

138 Neff Annex                               *Ph:* (573)882-2042
Columbia, MO 65211                           *Fax:* (573)882-5431

### • 6006 • Investigative Reporters and Editors Minority Conference Fellowships *(Other/Fellowship)*

**Purpose:** To assist minority professional journalists or student journalists attend IRE's annual conference, computer-assisted reporting conference, computer boot camps, or various other conferences. **Focus:** Journalism. **Qualif.:** Applicants must be minority professional journalists or student journalists. **Criteria:** Based on financial need, racial and ethnic diversity, ability, and experience.

**Funds Avail.:** Conference expenses and a stipend for travel related expenses. **Deadline:** Applications available October 15 and due December 28.

# • 6007 •

## University of Notre Dame - Cushwa Center for the Study of American Catholicism

Hesburgh Library, Room 614                   *Ph:* (219)631-5441
Notre Dame, IN 46556                         *Fax:* (219)631-5441

### • 6008 • Cushwa Center Research Travel Grants
*(Postdoctorate/Grant)*

**Purpose:** To help scholars to defray the cost of using the University of Notre Dame's library and archival collections. **Focus:** American Catholicism. **Qualif.:** Applicant may be of any nationality, but must be a postdoctoral scholar conducting research that requires the use of the University library collections. The project must relate to the American Catholic community. Grants are only tenable at the University of Notre Dame.

**Funds Avail.:** $1,000 maximum. **To Apply:** Write for application form and guidelines. Submit three copies of form with curriculum vitae, description of proposed research project, and a listing of projected expenses for travel, lodging, and research. **Deadline:** December 31.

**Remarks:** The Center also offers Cushwa Center Research Fellowships to postdoctoral scholars to provide access to resources at the University of Notre Dame. Scholars must seek other forms of support for research costs. These fellowships are not available for dissertation or thesis research. Write to the Center for further information. **Contact:** Dr. Jay P. Dolan, Director, at the above address (see entry 6007).

### • 6009 • Irish in America Publication Award Notre Dame Studies in Catholicism Publication Award
*(Professional Development/Award)*

**Purpose:** To support the publication of documents in areas of interest to the Center. **Focus:** American Catholicism, Irish in the United States. **Qualif.:** Candidate may be of any nationality. Applicant for the Irish in America Publication Award must have written an unpublished document that focuses on some aspect of the Irish people in the United States. Applicant for the Notre Dame Studies in Catholicism Publication Award must have written an unpublished document that somehow relates to the American Catholic community. Entry submissions must be in manuscript form. Unrevised dissertations will not be accepted. Manuscript may not be submitted to another publisher during the competition.

**Funds Avail.:** $500 advance on royalties. **No. of Awards:** Two. **To Apply:** Submit two copies of the manuscript and a curriculum vitae. **Deadline:** Irish in America Award: January 15; Notre Dame Studies in Catholicism Award: December 15. **Contact:** Dr. Jay P. Dolan, Director, at the above address (see entry 6007).

## • 6010 •
### University of Oregon - Oregon Humanities Center
5211 University of Oregon　　　　　　　*Ph:* (541)346-3934
Eugene, OR 97403-5211　　　　　　　　*Fax:* (541)346-5822
*E-mail:* hcampbel@oregon.uoregon.edu
*URL:* http://darkwing.uoregon.edu/~humanctr/

#### • 6011 • Oregon Humanities Center Summer Visiting Research Fellowships *(Professional Development/Fellowship)*

**Purpose:** To assist scholars who wish to conduct humanistic research at the Center. **Focus:** Humanities, including Archaeology, Art Criticism, Art History, Ethics, History, Languages, Law, Linguistics, Literature, Philosophy, Religion. **Qualif.:** Candidates may be of any nationality but must be faculty members or independent scholars. The University of Oregon invites candidates to apply for a four-week research fellowship in conjunction with the residency of a distinguished visiting scholar on a theme to be announced. From approximately June 15 through July 15, research fellows will also participate in a faculty seminar presented by this distinguished scholar. Check for information on this program on our web site. **Criteria:** Selection is based on the decision of the review panel.

**Funds Avail.:** $2,500 maximum, plus office space, computer use, and library access. **No. of Awards:** Up to Two. **To Apply:** Write for application guidelines, available in early-October. Submit six copies of application, including proposal and curriculum vitae. **Deadline:** October 15. Fellowships are announced by January 15. **Contact:** Julia J. Heydon, Assistant Director, at the above address (see entry 6010).

## • 6012 •
### University of Virginia - Darden School
PO Box 6550　　　　　　　　　　　*Ph:* (804)924-4784
Charlottesville, VA 22906-6550　　　　*Free:* 800-UVA-MBA1

#### • 6013 • Batten Fellowships *(Graduate/Fellowship)*

**Purpose:** To encourage journalists to study management. Provides funding for the MBA program at the University of Virginia's Darden Graduate School of Business Administration. **Focus:** Business. **Qualif.:** Applicants must be U.S. citizens, full-time employees of a newspaper or other news gathering organization, and have at least three years experience.

**Funds Avail.:** Provides tuition, fees, and a stipend to cover part of other expenses. **To Apply:** Inquire for details.

## • 6014 •
### W. E. Upjohn Institute for Employment Research
300 S. Westnedge Ave.　　　　　　　*Ph:* (616)343-5541
Kalamazoo, MI 49007-4686　　　　　*Fax:* (616)343-3308
*E-mail:* eberts@we.upjohninst.org
*URL:* http://www.upjohninst.org

#### • 6015 • Upjohn Institute Grants *(Postdoctorate/Grant)*

**Purpose:** To support policy-relevant research on employment and unemployment at national, state, and local levels in the United States. **Focus:** Economics, Employment, Industry, Labor, Social Security, Workers' Compensation. **Qualif.:** Applicant may be of any nationality, but must be conducting research in an area of interest to the Institute; research must be relevant to policy makers in the United States. Projects comparing U.S. and foreign markets that require international travel for the purposes of collecting data may be funded. Individuals seeking dissertation research support are not eligible to apply. Research should result in a publishable monograph. The Institute assumes all manuscripts and copyrights deriving from grant-funded projects. **Criteria:** Policy relevance, technical merit, professional qualifications.

**Funds Avail.:** $45,000 maximum. **No. of Awards:** Varies. **To Apply:** Submit a preliminary 10-page summary of the dissertation and a letter of endorsement from dissertation advisor. **Deadline:** Third week in January. **Contact:** Randall W. Eberts at the above address (see entry 6014).

## • 6016 •
### US Aircraft Insurance Group
c/o Annie Brown　　　　　　　　　*Ph:* (202)783-9000
1200 18th St., NW, Ste. 400　　　　*Fax:* (202)331-8364
Washington, DC 20036　　　　　　　*Free:* 800-FYI-NBAA
*E-mail:* info@nbaa.org
*URL:* http://www.nbaa.org

#### • 6017 • USAIG PDP Scholarships *(Postgraduate, Undergraduate/Scholarship)*

**Focus:** Aviation. **Qualif.:** Applicants must be undergraduates enrolled full-time in a college or university offering the NBAA Professional Development Program (PDP) and must be U.S. citizens. They must also maintain at least a 3.0 GPA.

**Funds Avail.:** $1,000. **No. of Awards:** Three. **To Apply:** Candidates must submit a scholarship application form, an official transcript, a letter of recommendation from a member of the aviation faculty, a resume, and a 250-word essay describing interest and goals for a career in the business aviation field. **Deadline:** August 31.

**Remarks:** NBAA/UAA member colleges and universities offering PDP curricula include: Central Missouri State University, Eastern Michigan University, Embry-Riddle Aeronautical University, Mercer County Community College, Purdue University, University of North Dakota, and University of Oklahoma. **Contact:** Annie Brown.

## • 6018 •
### Utah Higher Education Assistance Authority
355 W. N. Temple　　　　　　　　*Ph:* (801)321-7188
3 Triad Ste. 550　　　　　　　　　*Fax:* (801)321-7299
Salt Lake City, UT 84180-1205　　　*Free:* 800-418-2551
*E-mail:* uheaa@utahsbr.edu
*URL:* http://www.uheaa.org

#### • 6019 • Utah State Student Incentive Grant *(Graduate, Undergraduate/Grant)*

**Focus:** General Studies. **Qualif.:** Applicants must have substantial need and be attending a participating Utah institution.

**Funds Avail.:** A maximum of $2,500 per student per academic year is awarded. **To Apply:** Students may request an application directly from their institution's financial aid office. **Contact:** The financial aid office of any participating Utah institution.

• 6020 •
## Utility Workers Union of America
815 16th St. NW
Washington, DC 20006

*Ph:* (202)347-8105
*Fax:* (202)347-4872

### • 6021 • UWUA Scholarships *(Undergraduate/ Scholarship)*

**Focus:** General Studies. **Qualif.:** Applicants must be sons or daughters of a UWUA member. **Criteria:** The National Merit Scholarship Corporation determines semifinalists based on PSAT scores. Names of semifinalists are then given to the UWUA to select recipients.

**Funds Avail.:** A maximum of $2,000 is awarded annually for a four-year period. **No. of Awards:** 2. **To Apply:** Application details are contained in the UWUA bi-monthly magazine mailed to members. **Deadline:** January 1. **Contact:** Donald E. Wightman at the above address (see entry 6020).

### • 6022 •
## Van Alen Institute: Projects in Public Architecture
30 W. 22nd St.
New York, NY 10010
*E-mail:* vanalen@designsys.com
*URL:* http://www.vanalen.org/

*Ph:* (212)924-7000
*Fax:* (212)366-5836

### • 6023 • John Dinkeloo Bequests/American Academy in Rome Traveling Fellowship in Architectural Technology *(Graduate, Postgraduate/ Fellowship)*

**Focus:** Architecture. **Qualif.:** Applicants must be U.S. citizens who have received a professional degree in architecture from an accredited United States program between June 1992 and June 1997. **Criteria:** Applicants are selected based on their portfolio and project statement.

**Funds Avail.:** $7,000 total. The fellowship is used for approximately four months of travel abroad and two months room/board at the American Academy in Rome, which must begin within one year of receipt of the fellowship. **No. of Awards:** 1. **To Apply:** The applicant's presentation must include a portfolio detailing work and a brief written description of the proposed architectural project. Official application forms and programs must be requested from the Institute. **Deadline:** Application and all supporting materials must be filed by March 1997. **Contact:** Van Alen Institute: Projects in Public Architecture at the above address (see entry 6022).

### • 6024 • NIAE/ATBCB Student Design Competition Prizes *(Graduate, Undergraduate/Prize)*

**Purpose:** To recognize U.S. architectural students with outstanding design ability, and to encourage architecture that is accessible to physically challenged individuals. **Focus:** Architecture. **Qualif.:** Each year, the NIAE announces a student design competition; although specific projects vary annually, the theme is always architecture that is accessible to all individuals, regardless of physical disabilities. Competitor must be working full- or part-time toward a degree at a U.S. architectural or engineering school. Students in the final year of their first professional degree program are ineligible.

**Funds Avail.:** First prize: $1,000; second prize: $500; third prize: $300; six honorable mentions of $100, two Spirit of Accessibility Awards of $300. **No. of Awards:** Nine. **To Apply:** Write to the NIAE for registration application form and competition guidelines, available from mid-October to early June. Or contact dean of home institution for registration materials. Completed forms may be

submitted to the Institution anytime before the final registration deadline. After submitting registration form, candidate has three weeks during which he/she must complete and submit project. **Deadline:** Mid-June. Winners will be selected in July. **Contact:** Dr. Joan Bassin, Executive Director, at the above address (see entry 6022).

### • 6025 • Traveling Fellowships in Architectural Design and Technology *(Postdoctorate/Fellowship)*

**Purpose:** To support young U.S. architects who would benefit from European study and travel. **Focus:** Architecture. **Qualif.:** Applicant must be a U.S. citizen. Candidate must either have received his/her first professional degree in architecture during the three years prior to the application deadline, or complete the degree during the current academic year. Candidates are judged on the basis of their existing portfolio and the nature of their proposed fellowship project. At least two months of the fellowship must be spent in residence at the American Academy in Rome. Awardees begin the fellowship with a month-long orientation at the Academy; the timing of the other period of residency is arranged between the director of the Academy and the fellow. The remaining time should be spent in research/study-related travel.

**Funds Avail.:** $3,500 travel allowance, plus $1,500 to be applied to room and board expenses at the Academy. **No. of Awards:** Three. **To Apply:** Write to NIAE for application form and guidelines. Submit completed form with portfolio and a brief description of proposed project. **Deadline:** May 1. **Contact:** Dr. Joan Bassin, Executive Director, at the above address (see entry 6022).

### • 6026 • Van Alen Institute Fellowship in Public Architecture (Loyd Warren Fellowships/Paris Prize) *(Graduate, Postgraduate/Fellowship, Prize)*

**Purpose:** To encourage creative architectural designs, and to support study and travel by architectural students and recent graduates. **Focus:** Architecture. **Qualif.:** Applicants must have received their first professional degree in Architecture from an accredited U.S. program. Recipients are selected from participants in an annual architectural design competition. Each year NIAE selects a project for which competitors must submit designs. Competitor must be a U.S. permanent resident. Recipients must use the award to travel outside of the United States for study or research. Travel must begin within one year of winning competition. **Criteria:** Applicants selected based on design competition.

**Funds Avail.:** Approximately $16,000 total. **To Apply:** Official application forms and programs must be requested from the Institute.

### • 6027 •
## Venture Clubs of the Americas
1616 Walnut St., Ste. 700
Philadelphia, PA 19103

*Ph:* (215)732-0512
*Fax:* (215)732-7508

### • 6028 • Venture Student Aid Award for Physically Disabled Students *(Other/Award)*

**Qualif.:** Applicants must be physically disabled and between the ages of 15 and 35 years old at the time of application. **Criteria:** Selection is based on financial need and the capacity to profit from further education.

**Funds Avail.:** One $1,500 and one $1,000 award. **To Apply:** Candidates should apply to the Venture Club within whose boundaries they reside or, for those living outside the territorial limits of a club, to the nearest club. The completed application is returned to a designated member of that club. The formal application requests biographical information, type and extent of disability, education, annual family income, projected educational and special expenses of candidate, educational goal, and the way in which the Venture Student Aid will help. References from two individuals that include when and how long they have known the candidate and their opinion on how the applicant will profit from further education must also be submitted. **Contact:** Local Venture Clubs.

---

## • 6029 •
### Vermont Historical Society

109 State St.        *Ph:* (802)828-2291
Montpelier, VT 05609-0901    *Fax:* (802)828-3638

### • 6030 • Weston A. Cate, Jr. Annual Research Fellowship *(Other/Fellowship)*

**Purpose:** To encourage original research in the field of Vermont history. **Focus:** American History. **Criteria:** The committee will favor applications that address topics designed to fill research gaps in the state's history. Because the Society's purpose is to encourage worthwhile original research in Vermont history that might not otherwise be undertaken, segments of larger studies may be at a competitive disadvantage—the research contemplated by the applicant must stand by itself. As much as possible, the grantee should use the library and/or museum collections of the Society. The fellowship is expected to result in either a paper that can be considered for publication in *Vermont History* magazine or in a product of some other form that might be appropriate for exhibition or viewing.

**Funds Avail.:** $1,200. **To Apply:** Completed application form is required. Applicants must request two letters of recommendation from individuals familiar with their abilities. Originals plus five copies of all materials must be submitted. **Deadline:** April 1. **Contact:** Director, Vermont Historical Society, at the above address (see entry 6029).

---

## • 6031 •
### Vermont National Guard - Office of the Adjutant General

ESO, GMA
Camp Johnson          *Ph:* (802)654-0346
Colchester, VT 05446-3004    *Fax:* (802)655-5015

### • 6032 • General Buxton/St. Michael's Scholarships *(Graduate, Undergraduate/Scholarship)*

**Purpose:** To assist Vermont National Guard members in their pursuit of a degree. **Focus:** General Studies. **Qualif.:** Applicants must be members of the Vermont National Guard, Air or Army. **Criteria:** Selection is based on academic record, letter of recommendation from unit commander, and letter from applicant requesting the scholarship.

**Funds Avail.:** Varies. **No. of Awards:** 1 full-time scholarship (4 courses); remainder are awarded in one or two course blocks. **Deadline:** July 15 for fall semester, November 15 for spring semester. **Contact:** Cpt. Daniel F. Pipes at the above address (see entry 6031).

---

## • 6033 •
### Vermont Studio Center

PO Box 613           *Ph:* (802)635-2727
Johnson, VT 05656        *Fax:* (802)635-2730
*E-mail:* VSCVT@pwshift.com
*URL:* http://www.vermontstudiocenter.com

### • 6034 • Vermont Studio Center Residency Fellowships *(Professional Development/Fellowship)*

**Purpose:** To recognize artistic achievement and to offer visual artists and writers an opportunity for intensive creative studio time. **Focus:** Painting, Sculpture, Writing, Monoprinting and Etching, Photography. **Qualif.:** Candidates may be of any nationality but must be established visual artists or writers. Awards are tenable at the Center. **Criteria:** Based on juried review of application including portfolio.

**Funds Avail.:** Full fellowships covering room, board and studio space are available as well as financial assistance based on work-exchange covering up to 50% of the fee. **To Apply:** Write to the Center for application guidelines. Submit samples of work, letters of reference, and application fee. **Deadline:** None. **Contact:** Roger Kowalsky, Administrative Director, at the above address (see entry 6033).

---

## • 6035 •
### Vertical Flight Foundation

American Helicopter Society Int'l.
217 North Washington St.    *Ph:* (703)684-6777
Alexandria, VA 22314      *Fax:* (703)739-9279
*E-mail:* ahs703@aol.com
*URL:* http://www.vtol.org

### • 6036 • Vertical Flight Foundation Scholarships *(Graduate, Undergraduate/Scholarship)*

**Purpose:** To support engineering students interested in pursuing careers in the helicopter or vertical flight industry. **Focus:** Helicopter Aviation, Vertical Flight, and related disciplines. **Qualif.:** Applicants may be of any nationality but must be full-time students at an accredited school of engineering. Membership in the American Helicopter Society is not required. Scholarships should be applied to the cost of attending a degree-granting program at a college or university. **Criteria:** Based on academic achievement and pursuit of an aerospace engineering degree.

**Funds Avail.:** $1,500-$3,000 depending on endowment earnings. maximum. **No. of Awards:** 8-12. **To Apply:** Write to the scholarship committee for an application form and guidelines. Submit form with transcripts, a personal statement, and academic and personal recommendations. **Deadline:** February 1. Scholarship recipients are notified in early summer. **Contact:** Scholarship Committee at the above address (see entry 6035).

---

## • 6037 •
### Veterans of Foreign Wars Ladies Auxiliary
406 W 34th St.  *Ph:* (816)561-8655
Kansas City, MO 64111  *Fax:* (816)931-4753
*E-mail:* info@ladiesauxvfw.com
*URL:* http://www.ladiesauxvtw.com

#### • 6038 • Young American Creative Patriot Art Award *(All/Award)*

**Purpose:** To encourage high school students to express their artistic talents, demonstrate their patriotism. **Focus:** General studies. **Qualif.:** Applicants must be high school students sponsored by members of the Ladies Auxiliary to the Veterans of Foreign Wars of the United States. **Criteria:** Awards are made based on originality of concept and patriotism expressed, content and clarity of ideas, design, use of color and technique, and impact or execution.

**Funds Avail.:** $500 - $3,000. **To Apply:** Applicants must submit artwork on paper or canvas, using watercolor, pencil, pastel, charcoal, tempera, crayon, acrylic, pen-and-ink, or oil. No frames. Canvases should be submitted on stretcher frames, or matted on white. No color mats. Art should be no smaller than 8" x 10" but no larger than 18" x 24," not including mat. **Deadline:** Varies. **Contact:** Veterans of Foreign Wars Ladies Auxiliary at the above address (see entry 6037).

## • 6039 •
### Veterans of Foreign Wars of the United States - Voice of Democracy Scholarship Program
National Headquarters
406 W. 34th St.  *Ph:* (816)968-1117
Kansas City, MO 64111  *Fax:* (816)968-1149
*E-mail:* info@vfw.org
*URL:* http://www.vfw.org

#### • 6040 • Voice of Democracy Scholarship Contest *(High School, Other/Scholarship)*

**Focus:** General studies. **Qualif.:** Applicants must be in ninth, tenth, eleventh, or twelfth grade. **Criteria:** Applicants will be judged on an audio-cassette essay (annual theme each year).

**Funds Avail.:** $1,000 to $20,000. **No. of Awards:** 56. **To Apply:** Applicants may contact a high school counselor or local VFW Post for further details. **Deadline:** November 1. **Contact:** Your high school teacher, counselor, principal; or contact your local VFW Post to enter. A listing of state headquarters (call to find the location of your local VFW Post) can be found on our home page: www.vfw.org.

## • 6041 •
### Viennese Culture Club
c/o Mady Shone, Director
3358 Scadlock Ln.
Sherman Oaks, CA 91403  *Ph:* (818)990-2847

#### • 6042 • V.C.C. Fuchs Scholarship Award *(Professional Development/Scholarship)*

**Purpose:** To further a professional career in opera for young, talented singers. **Qualif.:** Applicants must be between the ages of 20 and 33 (tenors, baritones, and bass may be up to 35 years of age) and residents of California. Candidates must have voices of operatic potential. Vocal training, a musical background, and artistic aptitude are required.

**Funds Avail.:** Approximately $12,000 in funds is available. Ten scholarships are awarded. **To Apply:** A formal application must be completed. Applicants should be careful in choosing their four arias so that their voice category is properly represented. Later changes will not be accepted. Candidates must be prepared to sing those four arias from memory in the original key and original language. Contestants will be permitted to sing the aria of their choice, after which the judges may request a different type of aria for the purpose of comparison. Each applicant will be assigned a definite time to audition. **Deadline:** March 8.

**Remarks:** There are generally approximately 100 applicants. **Contact:** Mady Shone, Director, at the above address (see entry 6041).

## • 6043 •
### Villa I Tatti
Harvard University
University Place
124 Mt. Auburn St.  *Ph:* (617)495-8042
Cambridge, MA 02138  *Fax:* (617)495-8041

#### • 6044 • Villa I Tatti Fellowships *(Postdoctorate/Fellowship)*

**Qualif.:** Must be a post-doctoral scholar doing advance research in any aspect of the Italian Renaissance. **Criteria:** Applicants are selected by an international committee of distinguished senior scholars in Italian Renaissance studies, representing such fields as literature, history, fine arts, music, philosophy, and the history of ideas.

**Funds Avail.:** Up to $30,000 **No. of Awards:** 15 per year **To Apply:** Applicants must provide the following: a fellowship application form, a curriculum vitae, a statement of no more than ten pages describing their proposed research, and, three confidential letters of recommendation, which should be mailed directly by their authors. **Deadline:** October 15 **Contact:** Professor Walter Kaiser, Director.

## • 6045 •
### Virgin Islands Board of Education
PO Box 11900  *Ph:* (809)774-4546
St. Thomas, VI 00801  *Fax:* (809)774-3384

#### • 6046 • Virgin Islands Territorial Loan/Grant Program and Special Legislative Grants *(Graduate, Undergraduate/Grant, Loan)*

**Qualif.:** Applicants must be residents of the Virgin Islands, in need of financial aid, maintain an average of C or better, and be accepted by an accredited institution of higher education.

**Funds Avail.:** Varies. **To Apply:** Write for further details. **Deadline:** March 31 for fall semester and October 31 for spring. **Contact:** Mrs. Livia Turnbull at the above address (see entry 6045).

## • 6047 •
## Virginia Department of Health
Public Health Nursing
1500 E. Main St., Rm. 108
PO Box 2448
Richmond, VA 23218

### • 6048 • Mary Marshall Nurse Practitioner/Nurse Midwife Scholarship Program *(Undergraduate/ Scholarship)*

**Focus:** Nursing. **Qualif.:** Applicants must be residents of the state of Virginia for at least one year who are accepted or enrolled as a full-time student in a nurse practitioner program in the State of Virginia or a nurse midwifery program in a nearby state who demonstrate cumulative grade point averages of at least 3.0. **Criteria:** Scholarships are awarded on the basis of scholastic achievement, character, and stated commitment to post-graduate employment in a medically underserved area of Virginia and in an employment setting that provides services to persons who are unable to pay for the service and that will participate in all government sponsored insurance programs designed to assure access of covered persons to medical care services in Virginia.

**Funds Avail.:** $150 minimum per award; $1,000 maximum. graduate students. **To Apply:** Applicants must submit a completed application form signed by both the Dean/Director of the School of Nursing and the Financial Aid Officer/Authorized Person, and an official grade transcript to the Office of Public Health Nursing. Applicants must also file the Financial Aid Form (FAF) of the College Scholarship Service, The Family Financial Statement (FFS) of the American College Testing, or the Application for Federal STUDENT Aid (AFSA) with the institution they will attend in order that the financial needs can be determined. **Deadline:** July 30. Applications are available from the Dean/Director of the applicant's school financial aid office.

**Remarks:** Recipients must agree to engage in full-time practice for a period of years equal to the number of annual scholarships received, in a current (at time of employment) Virginia Medically Underserved Area (VMUA), and in an employment setting that provides services to persons who are unable to pay for the service and that will participate in all government sponsored insurance programs designed to assure access of covered persons to medical care services in Virginia. Full-time employment must begin within two years of the recipient's graduation date from the program. Voluntary military service, even if stationed in Virginia, cannot be used to repay scholarship awards. If for any reason a scholarship recipient fails to complete studies, or to engage in full-time nurse practitioner/nurse midwife practice in Virginia in an approved area and employment setting, the full amount of money represented in the scholarship(s) received, plus an annual interest charge as established by the Commonwealth of Virginia, must be repaid immediately. The recipient must write the first scheduled licensing examination following graduation. If the exam is failed it may be taken again. If failure happens a second time, the recipient must repay all scholarship money received plus an annual interest charge as stated above. If a recipient leaves the State or ceases to engage in full-time practice as a nurse practitioner/nurse midwife before all employment conditions of the scholarship award are fulfilled, the recipient must repay the balance on account plus an annual interest charge. **Contact:** Virginia Department of Health at the above address (see entry 6047).

### • 6049 • Mary Marshall Nursing Scholarship for Student Nurses Practical Nursing Program *(Undergraduate/Scholarship)*

**Focus:** Nursing. **Qualif.:** Applicants must be residents of the state of Virginia for at least one year who are accepted or enrolled in a school of nursing the State of Virginia. **Criteria:** Scholarships are awarded on the basis of scholastic attainment and financial need.

**Funds Avail.:** $150 minimum per award; $1,000 maximum. graduate students. **To Apply:** Applicants must submit a completed application form signed by both the Dean/Director of the School of Nursing and the Financial Aid Officer/Authorized Person, and an official grade transcript to the Office of Public Health Nursing. Applicants must also file the Financial Aid Form (FAF) of the College Scholarship Service, The Family Financial Statement (FFS) of the American College Testing, or the Application for Federal STUDENT Aid (AFSA) with the institution they will attend in order that the financial needs can be determined. **Deadline:** July 30. Applications are available from the Dean/Director of the applicant's school financial aid office.

**Remarks:** Recipients must agree to engage in full-time nursing practice in Virginia for one month for every $100 received. Therefore, if a student receives $500 in scholarship awards, they must repay that amount by working continuously for five months. Full-time employment must begin within 60 days of the recipient's graduation date. Voluntary military service, even if stationed in Virginia, cannot be used to repay scholarship awards. If, for any reason, a scholarship recipient fails to complete the course of study or engage in full-time nursing practice in Virginia, the full amount of money represented in the scholarship(s) received, plus 10% per annum from the date the award was received, must be paid immediately. Recipients must write the licensing examination within 90 days of graduation. If they do not pass, they may retake the examination. If they do not pass the second examination, they must repay all scholarship money received plus an annual interest charge as stated above. **Contact:** Virginia Department of Health at the above address (see entry 6047).

### • 6050 • Mary Marshall Nursing Scholarship for Student Nurses Registered Nurse Program *(Undergraduate/Scholarship)*

**Focus:** Nursing. **Qualif.:** Applicants must be residents of the state of Virginia for at least one year who are accepted or enrolled in a school of nursing the State of Virginia with grade point averages of 3.0 in required courses, not electives. **Criteria:** Scholarships are awarded on the basis of scholastic attainment and financial need.

**Funds Avail.:** $2000 maximum for undergraduates; $4000 maximum for graduate students. **To Apply:** Applicants must submit a completed application form signed by both the Dean/Director of the School of Nursing and the Financial Aid Officer/Authorized Person, and an official grade transcript to the Office of Public Health Nursing. Applicants must also file the Financial Aid Form (FAF) of the College Scholarship Service, The Family Financial Statement (FFS) of the American College Testing, or the Application for Federal Student Aid (AFSA) with the institution they will attend in order that the financial needs can be determined. **Deadline:** July 30. Applications are available from the Dean/Director of the applicant's school financial aid office.

**Remarks:** Recipients must agree to engage in full-time nursing practice in Virginia for one month for every $100 received. Therefore, if a student receives $500 in scholarship awards, they must repay that amount by working continuously for five months. Full-time employment must begin within 60 days of the recipient's graduation date. Voluntary military service, even if stationed in Virginia, cannot be used to repay scholarship awards. If, for any reason, a scholarship recipient fails to complete the course of study or engage in full-time nursing practice in Virginia, the full amount of money represented in the scholarship(s) received, plus 10% per annum from the date the award was received, must be paid immediately. Recipients must write the licensing examination within 90 days of graduation. If they do not pass, they may retake the examination. If they do not pass the second examination, they must repay all scholarship money received plus an annual interest charge as stated above. **Contact:** Virginia Department of Health at the above address (see entry 6047).

---

# • 6051 •

**Virginia Department of Transportation**
Attn: Federal Highway Administration
National Highway Institute
6300 Georgetown Pike     *Ph:* (703)285-2785
Mc Lean, VA 22101-2296     *Fax:* (703)285-2791

### • 6052 • Dwight David Eisenhower Transportation Fellowship *(Doctorate, Graduate/Fellowship)*

**Purpose:** To attract the nation's brightest minds to the field of transportation. **Qualif.:** Applicant must be US citizens attending US accredited colleges. Applicants may be in their senior year or baccalaureate or PhD/ScD candidates. **Criteria:** Applicants are evaluated on their academic records, letters of recommendation and a completed application. **No. of Awards:** 115. **To Apply:** Announcements are available in mid December. **Deadline:** February 15.

# • 6053 •

**Virginia Department of Veterans' Affairs - Virginia War Orphans Education Program**
270 Franklin Rd. SW, Rm. 503     *Ph:* (540)857-7104
Roanoke, VA 24011-2217     *Fax:* (540)857-7573

### • 6054 • Virginia War Orphans Education Program *(Graduate, Undergraduate/Other)*

**Focus:** General Studies. **Qualif.:** One of the applicant's parents must have served in the armed forces of the United States and must be permanently and totally disabled due to war or other armed conflict, have died as a result of war or other armed conflict, or be listed as a prisoner of war or missing in action. This parent must also have been a resident of the Commonwealth of Virginia at the time of entry into active military service and have been a resident of the Commonwealth of Virginia for at least five consecutive years immediately prior to the date of application or death. The other parent also must, at some time previous to marrying the disabled, deceased, or missing parent, have been a citizen of Virginia for at least five years immediately prior to the date on which the application was submitted by or on behalf of such child for admission to any education or training institution of collegiate or secondary grade in Virginia. Applicants must be no less than 16 years of age and no more than 25, and use this entitlement to attend either a state-supported secondary or post-secondary educational institution.

**Funds Avail.:** Eligible individuals are entitled to a maximum of 48 months of tuition-free education and required fees at any state-supported educational or training institution. **Contact:** The Virginia War Orphans Education Program at the above address (see entry 6053).

# • 6055 •

**Virginia Foundation for the Humanities**
145 Ednam Dr.     *Ph:* (804)924-3296
Charlottesville, VA 22903     *Fax:* (804)296-4714
*E-mail:* cah@virginia.edu
*URL:* http://www.virginia.edu/vfh

### • 6056 • Rockefeller Fellowships in Violence, Culture and Survival *(Professional Development/Fellowship)*

**Focus:** Liberal studies. **Qualif.:** Applicants must be independent or affiliated scholars, professionals, and others working in the humanities or wishing to pursue projects in the humanities. All applicants must have advanced degrees, though the center does not support work toward a degree. **Criteria:** Selection for funding is based on students who are currently studying subjects related to VFH areas of interest.

**Funds Avail.:** $10,000. **No. of Awards:** 4. **To Apply:** Applicants must submit six copies of the following: a completed application form, proposal of work to be done while in residence (no more than seven pages long, double-spaced), a curriculum vitae or resume, and three letters of recommendation. **Deadline:** December 1.

**Remarks:** Positions are available for research on the experience of violence, and religious experience. **Contact:** Roberta Anne Culbertson.

### • 6057 • VFH Center for the Humanities Affiliate Fellowships *(Professional Development/Fellowship)*

**Focus:** Liberal studies. **Qualif.:** Applicants must be independent or affiliated scholars, professionals, and others working in the humanities or wishing to pursue projects in the humanities. All applicants must have advanced degrees, though the center does not support work toward a degree.

**Funds Avail.:** $1,000 for relocation costs. **No. of Awards:** 3. **To Apply:** Applicants must submit six copies of the following: a completed application form, proposal of work to be done while in residence (no more than seven pages long, double-spaced), a curriculum vitae or resume, and three letters of recommendation. **Deadline:** Ongoing. **Contact:** Roberta Anne Culbertson. Culbertson.

# • 6058 •

**Virginia Library Association**
PO Box 8277     *Ph:* (757)583-0041
Norfolk, VA 23503-0277     *Fax:* (757)583-5041
*E-mail:* hahne@bellatlantic.net
*URL:* http://www.vla.org/

### • 6059 • Virginia Library Association Scholarships *(Graduate/Scholarship)*

**Focus:** Library Studies. **Qualif.:** Applicants must be pursuing a master's degree in library science at an A.L.A.-accredited school. **Criteria:** The major factors considered in making the awards are evidence of commitment to a career in librarianship in Virginia, financial need, potential for outstanding achievement in the library profession, academic excellence, and membership in the Virginia Library Association. **To Apply:** Applicants must submit an application form and give copies of the reference form to two persons, who will return them to the applicant in a provided envelope marked to the attention of the Scholarship Committee. **Deadline:** May 1. Applications are reviewed in the summer, and applicants are notified of the committee's decisions in early August. **Contact:** For more information or application packets, contact Susan McCarthy, Chair, at the above address (see entry 6058). Telephone: (703)358-6545.

• 6060 •

**Virginia Musuem of Fine Arts**
Education and Outreach Fellowships
Div.
2800 Grove Ave.
Richmond, VA 23221-2466
*URL:* http://vmfa.state.va.us

*Ph:* (804)367-0844

• 6061 • **Virginia Museum of Fine Arts Fellowship**
*(Professional Development/Fellowship)*

**Purpose:** To further develop virginia artists and art students in their careers and education. **Focus:** Crafts, drawing, filmmaking, mixed media, painting, photography, printmaking, sculpture, video, and art history.(graduate students only) **Qualif.:** Applicants must be legal residents of Virginia or registered in-state students for at least one year prior to the application deadline who are enrolled or planning to enroll full-time at an accredited school of the arts, college or university. **Criteria:** Selection is based on artistic merit.

**Funds Avail.:** $6,000 per graduate fellowship; $4,000 per undergraduate fellowship. **To Apply:** Applicants must submit an application; ten high-quality 35mm slides representing recent works, five of which were completed within the last three years, or three films or three videos (3/4 or VHS), one of which was completed within the last three years. Film must be transferred to VHS tape. No additions accepted; transcript officially stamped and sealed; two references; self-addressed envelope with accurate postage and packaging for the return of slides or videos; and a self-addressed, stamped postcard marked "Entry Received" to confirm receipt of application. No phone calls. **Deadline:** March 1. Notified by letter the second week of May.

**Remarks:** Submit 2"x2" slides in paper or plastic mounts for carousel projection. No glass slides accepted. Slides must be placed in a 9"x11" clear plastic slide-viewing sleeve. Mark each slide directly on paper or plastic mounts. Each slide must be numbered according to the application form, labeled with artist's name and title of work, and have a dot in the lower left-hand corner to ensure proper viewing. Do not use masking tape or other adhesive tape to label slides. Slides will be projected in two groups of five; each group of five slides should enhance the juror's understanding of the direction or development of your work. Video must be labeled with name, title of work, running time, and counter numbers for starts and ends. Send copy tapes only. Cue the tape to the starting point of the segment that you want reviewed. Generally, the juror(s) will view five minutes of each applicant's work at the initial screening; the juror(s) will decide whether or not to view the entire work. **Contact:** Virginia Museum of Fine Arts at the above address (see entry 6060).

• 6062 •

**Virginia Press Association**
c/o Ray Hall
PO Box 85613
Richmond, VA 23285-5613

• 6063 • **Virginia Press Association Minority Internship** *(Graduate, Undergraduate/Internship)*

**Focus:** Journalism. **Qualif.:** Applicants must be Virginia residents or attending a college or university in Virginia. Applicants must also be juniors through graduate students.

**Funds Avail.:** $2500 stipend. **No. of Awards:** 1. **Deadline:** March 15.

• 6064 •

**Virginia State Department of Health - Division of Dental Health**
PO Box 2448
Richmond, VA 23218
*URL:* http://www.vdh.state.va.us/

*Ph:* (804)786-3556
*Fax:* (804)371-4004

• 6065 • **Virginia Dental Scholarships** *(Doctorate/ Scholarship)*

**Purpose:** To encourage individuals to provide dental care to indigent or institutionalized persons or serve in an area of need in the state. **Focus:** Dentistry. **Criteria:** Based on scholastic achievement, character, financial need, and the adaptability of the applicant to the service contemplated.

**Funds Avail.:** $5,000. **No. of Awards:** 5. **To Apply:** Applications available from Mesical College of Virginia School of Dentistry. **Contact:** MCV School of Dentistry, Office of Admissions and Student Affairs, PO Box 566, MCV Station, Richmond, VA 23298; telephone: (804)828-9196.

• 6066 •

**Visionares**
c/o Mrs. Gussie Campbell
3531 NW 41st Terrace
Gainesville, FL 32606

*Ph:* (352)955-6702
*Fax:* (352)955-7285

• 6067 • **Visionaries Achievement Award**
*(Undergraduate/Scholarship)*

**Focus:** General studies. **Qualif.:** Applicants must be Gainesville, Florida, high school seniors with minimum grade point average of 3.0 who are involved in extracurricular and/or co-curricular activities. **Criteria:** Awards are made based on academic excellence, extracurricular involvement and financial need.

**Funds Avail.:** $500 - $1,000 per award. Non-renewable. **No. of Awards:** 1. **To Apply:** Write for further details. **Deadline:** May. **Contact:** Mrs. Gussie Campbell.

• 6068 •

**Voice of Democracy Program**
VFW National Headquarters
406 W. 34th St.
Kansas City, MO 64111
*URL:* http://www.vfw.org

*Ph:* (816)968-1117
*Fax:* (816)968-1149

• 6069 • **Voice of Democracy Scholarships** *(High School, Undergraduate/Award)*

**Focus:** General Studies. **Criteria:** Judging and selection is based on high school students' interpretations of a 3-5 minute annual patriotic theme recorded on an audio tape.

**Funds Avail.:** $1,000-$20,000. **No. of Awards:** 56. **To Apply:** Students must tape a three- to five-minute audio essay onto a cassette tape. For application instructions, applicants may contact their high school counselor or teacher, local VFW Post, or National Headquarters, at the above address. **Deadline:** November 1. **Contact:** Gordon Thorson, National Director, at the above address (see entry 6068).

## • 6070 •
### Alexander von Humboldt Foundation
US Liaison Office
1035 Thomas Jefferson St., NW.,
Ste. 2030
Washington, DC 20007
*E-mail:* humboldt@umail.umd.edu

*Ph:* (202)296-2990
*Fax:* (202)833-8514

### • 6071 • Konrad Adenauer Research Award *(Other/ Award)*

**Purpose:** To promote academic relations between Canada and the Federal Republic of Germany. **Focus:** Humanities, Social Sciences. **Qualif.:** Awards are made to highly qualified Canadian scholars whose research work in the humanities or social sciences has brought them international recognition and who also belongs to the group of leading scholars in their respective area of specialization. Recipients are entitled to carry out research work of their own choice at German Research Institutes for a period of up to one year. The research stay in Germany can be divided into several periods, but must commence within one year of the announcement of the award. Awards are made without regard to age, race, religion, or sex of the applications. Applicants who hold, or have held, another research award from the Alexander von Humboldt Foundation within the previous three years are not eligible. Recipients are not allowed to receive financial support from any other German source during tenure of the award. There is, however, no restrictions on support received from the home institution of the award winners.

**Funds Avail.:** Up to DM 100,000 each. Awards also pay for travel costs between Canada and Germany for the recipients and their family members, provided they stay with the scholar for at least six months in Germany. Medical and accident insurance may be provided for the award winners (and family members) if requested. **To Apply:** Self-application cannot be made. Candidates should be nominated by their universities and the dossiers should be sent to the Royal Society of Canada. At least two nominations each year are made jointly by the Royal Society of Canada and the University of Toronto and submitted to the Humboldt Foundation. The Humboldt Foundation's appropriate selection committee selects award winners and announces them in early summer each year. Nominations should include a letter from the candidate's institution indicating their qualifications, a list of publications and three or four of their most recent research works, a curriculum vitae, a brief statement of the candidate's research proposal, at least three names and addresses of internationally recognized scholars who can provide information of the nominee's academic qualifications, and the names of German scholars who would provide expert guidance to the Canadian scholar during their stay in Germany. Candidates should also indicate their marital status, number of children, and the number of family members who will travel to Germany should they win the award. Also required is the name of the principal German host institution and a written approval from a German scholar at this institution. **Deadline:** December 1.

**Remarks:** The award is administered by the Alexander von Humboldt Foundation in Germany in cooperation with the Royal Society of Canada and the University of Toronto. **Contact:** Executive Director, Royal Society of Canada, 225 Metcalfe St., Ste. 308, Ottawa, ON Canada K2P 1P9.

## • 6072 •
### Von Karman Institute for Fluid Dynamics
72 Chaussee de Waterloo
1640 Rhode-St-Genese, Belgium
*E-mail:* secretariat@vki.ac.be
*URL:* http://www.vki.ac.be

*Ph:* 322 359 96 11
*Fax:* 322 359 96 00

### • 6073 • Von Karman Institute Doctoral Fellowship *(Doctorate/Fellowship)*

**Focus:** Fluid Dynamics: Aerospace/Turbomachinery/Industrial. **Qualif.:** Applicants must have an engineering degree with a strong background in fluid mechanics. **Criteria:** Selection is determined on the strength of two required recommendations and college transcript.

**Funds Avail.:** 44,000DF (approximately $1,200 per month). Doctoral Fellows who have the VKI diploma will begin at 49,000DF (approximately $1,325) and in the following years will receive 56,000DF per month (approximately $1,500 per month). **No. of Awards:** 2-4. **To Apply:** Applications may be obtained by writing to the director. **Deadline:** Early in the calendar year.

**Remarks:** Fellowship awards are also available for a nine-month Diploma Course in Fluid Dynamics; the prerequisite is an engineering degree. The stipend for this award has a value of approximately $950 per month. **Contact:** Prof. Mario Carbonaro, Director, at the above address (see entry 6072).

## • 6074 •
### Wagner College - Department of Humanities - Stanley Drama Award
Howard Ave. & Campus Rd.
Staten Island, NY 10301-4495
*URL:* http://www.wagner.edu/

*Ph:* (718)390-3256

### • 6075 • Stanley Drama Award *(Professional Development/Award)*

**Purpose:** To encourage excellence in playwriting. **Focus:** Drama. **Qualif.:** Candidate may be of any nationality. Applicant must have written a full-length play, a musical, or a series of two or three thematically connected one-act plays. The works must not have been professionally produced or received trade book publication. Former Stanley Award winners are not eligible to compete. Plays must be recommended by a theater professional, such as a teacher of drama or writing, a critic, an agent, a director, or another playwright or composer. The person recommending must have read or seen the play in question and address the recommendation to that specific play. Self-recommendations are not accepted.

**Funds Avail.:** $2,000. **No. of Awards:** One. **To Apply:** Write to the director for application form and brochure. Submit form with recommendation, script, and musical recordings, if applicable. **Deadline:** September 1. Judging is normally completed by March. **Contact:** Bill Bly, Director, at the above address (see entry 6074).

## • 6076 •
**Wilbur H.H. Ward Educational Trust, Inc.**
c/o Anne B. Peramba
Financial Aid Office, Rm. 243
Whitmore Bldg.
University of Massachusetts
Amherst, MA 01003
E-mail: a.peramba@umassp.edu

Ph: (413)545-2886
Fax: (413)545-1722

### • 6077 • Wilbur H.H. Ward Educational Trust
**Scholarship** (Undergraduate/Scholarship)

**Qualif.:** Applicants must be male residents of Hampshire County, Massachusetts who will attend or are attending the University of Massachusetts or the Stockbridge School of Agriculture. Candidates must maintain a 2.0 cumulative grade point average each semester. **Criteria:** Scholarships are based on financial need.

**Funds Avail.:** $200-$1,000 per semester. The scholarships are paid in two installments early each semester. **To Apply:** No scholarship will be awarded unless the applicant has filed an application and supporting information including financial aid form. The financial aid form must be filed each year that an applicant applies for this scholarship. If applying for the first time, two supporting letters should also be sent. **Deadline:** July 1. **Contact:** Anne B. Peramba at the above address (see entry 6076).

## • 6078 •
**Mary Ellen Warner Educational Trust**
10371 Rochester Ave.
Los Angeles, CA 90024-5362

Ph: (310)275-9389
Fax: (310)274-0422

### • 6079 • Warner Trust Loan Program (Doctorate, Graduate, Other/Loan)

**Purpose:** To provide loan funds for upper division students. **Qualif.:** Applicant must be permanent resident of California and attend an accredited college or university in California. Loan funds to be used only for tuition, books and supplies. **Criteria:** Personal interview in Los Angeles with the Trustees to determine need and criteria compliance.

**Funds Avail.:** Maximum of $10,000 per student. **No. of Awards:** 4-10 per year. **To Apply:** Send letter requesting loan to the Trustees at the above address, outlining need for funds. Based on a review by the Trustees, an application will be sent.

## • 6080 •
**Earl Warren Legal Training Program, Inc.**
99 Hudson St., Ste. 1600
New York, NY 10013

Ph: (212)219-1900
Fax: (212)226-7592

### • 6081 • Earl Warren Legal Training Scholarships
(Graduate/Scholarship)

**Purpose:** To increase the number of black lawyers in the U.S. by roughly one-third the current number. **Qualif.:** Must be an entering law student and a U.S. citizen. Emphasis is placed on scholarships for applicants who wish to enroll in law schools in the South. Preferred consideration is given to applicants in financial need, under 35 years of age, and to those who plan to participate where there is a dearth of black lawyers. Each recipient must attend law school full-time and will be expected to graduate within the normally prescribed time of three years. Applicants must take the Law School Admission Test (LSAT). **Criteria:** High LSAT score, undergraduate record, and need. Because these scholarships are

highly competitive, only students with outstanding academic records are encouraged to apply. Applicants who have a well-defined interest in public.

**Funds Avail.:** Between 50 to 60 $1,500 scholarships per year are available. They are renewable for the remaining two years of law school, if the student remains in good standing and complies with all program requirements. **To Apply:** Unconditional acceptance in an accredited law school is necessary for review of the application. A copy of the acceptance letter must accompany the application. Write for an application form. **Deadline:** March 15.

## • 6082 •
**Washington Center for Politics and Journalism**
c/o Terry Michael
Executive Director
PO Box 15201
Washington, DC 20003-0201
E-mail: pol-jrn@ix.netcom.com

Ph: (202)296-8455

### • 6083 • Politics and Journalism Internship
(Graduate, Undergraduate/Internship)

**Purpose:** To provide work experience at news bureaus in Washington DC. **Focus:** Journalism. **Qualif.:** Applicants must be college student journalists, graduate students or recent graduates interested in political reporting.

**Funds Avail.:** $1750 stipend spring semester; $2000 stipend fall semester for living expenses. **No. of Awards:** 12. **Deadline:** April 1 for fall semester; November 1 for spring semester.

## • 6084 •
**Washington Crossing Foundation**
PO Box 503
Levittown, PA 19058
URL: http://www.gwcf.org

Ph: (215)949-8841

### • 6085 • Washington Crossing Foundation
**Scholarships** (Undergraduate/Scholarship)

**Purpose:** To encourage the most qualified students to consider careers in government service. **Qualif.:** Applicants must be high school seniors who are United States citizens and planning government service at the local, state, or federal levels. **Criteria:** Judges' decisions are based on student's understanding of career requirements, purpose in choice of career, preparation for such a career, leadership qualities, sincerity, and historical perspective. Semi-finalists may be interviewed by telephone as part of the selection process. All finalists are interviewed by telephone.

**Funds Avail.:** Scholarships range from $2,500 to $10,000. One $20,000 award is reserved for PA counties; Bucks, Delaware, Chester, Montgomery, and Philadelphia. **No. of Awards:** Minimum of 6. **To Apply:** Students must write a one-page essay stating why they are planning a career in government service, including any inspiration to be derived from the leadership of George Washington in his famous crossing of the Delaware. The essays must also be accompanied by a recommendation from a high school principal or guidance counselors transcript and test scores. Information regarding additional application requirements is available by writing to the Washington Crossing Foundation at the above address. **Deadline:** January 15. **Contact:** Eugene C. Fish, Vice Chairman, Washington Crossing Foundation at the above address (see entry 6084).

# • 6086 •
## Washington Osteopathic Foundation, Inc.
PO Box 16486      *Ph:* (206)937-5358
Seattle, WA 98116      *Fax:* (206)933-6529

### • 6087 • Washington Osteopathic Foundation Student Loans *(Doctorate/Loan)*

**Purpose:** To advance the presence of osteopathic medicine in Washington State. **Focus:** Osteopathic Medicine. **Qualif.:** Any osteopathic student after completion of one semester or quarter of osteopathic training in any of the AOA accredited schools of osteopathic medicine and surgery may apply for a loan. Applicants must be of legal age or have a co-signer of legal age to execute a promissory note. The Washington Osteopathic Foundation reserves the right to select loan recipients on the basis of Washington residence or any other criteria within its sole discretion. The grant of any loan is conditioned upon faithful attendance of classes and performance of duties as a student and upon maintenance of passing marks and honorable conduct without discredit to the school, the profession of osteopathic medicine and surgery, or the Foundation.

**Funds Avail.:** Students may receive one loan of a maximum of $5,000 per academic year (actual amount to be determined by the Foundation Board of Directors). Loans will be made directly to the student's tuition credit at their osteopathic college. Students receiving a loan shall begin to repay the loan three years after finishing their internship and one residency, which shall immediately follow internship. Students receiving a loan or loans must practice for three years in the state of Washington commencing within 30 days of completion of their internship and/or residency. (The Foundation may waive the requirement for practice within the State of Washington during obligatory military or public health service assignment out of the State of Washington when such service is not also part of an approved internship or residency.) The interest on student loans shall be six percent per annum computed from the date of graduation from college. If the student leaves school, the loan plus ten percent interest must be repaid within one year. If recipient fails to practice in the state of Washington or violates any of the loan guidelines, the loan(s) become immediately subject to repayment plus interest of ten percent per annum on the unpaid balance of principal and interest computed from date loan was granted. **No. of Awards:** Depends on funds available. **To Apply:** Applications for loans must be made on the official form provided by the Foundation office and must be fully completed. Applications must be accompanied by a letter of recommendation from an instructor in the osteopathic college attended, a letter of recommendation from a physician member of the Washington Osteopathic Medical Association practicing in Washington State, and the most recent transcript of grades from the osteopathic school attended. **Deadline:** February 15, May 15, August 15, and November 15. **Contact:** The Washington Osteopathic Foundation at the above address (see entry 6086).

# • 6088 •
## Washington Post
1150 15th St., NW      *Ph:* (202)334-6100
Washington, DC 20071      *Fax:* (202)334-5051

### • 6089 • Thomas Ewing Memorial Educational Grants for Newspaper Carriers *(Undergraduate/Scholarship)*

**Purpose:** To recognize the importance of newspaper carriers to the success of the Washington Post. **Qualif.:** Candidates must be current Washington Post carriers who have been employed a minimum of 18 months, and high school seniors, graduates, or GED holders. **Criteria:** Selection is based on a carrier performance evaluation, academic ability, and extra-curricular and community activities.

**Funds Avail.:** Four scholarships of $2,000 each, eight scholarships of $1,500 each, and 23 scholarships of $1,000 each are awarded. **To Apply:** Students must submit a completed application form and provide official high school/college transcripts. **Deadline:** Last business day of January. **Contact:** Mary McElroy at the above address (see entry 6088).

### • 6090 • *The Washington Post* Summer Journalism Internships *(Graduate, Undergraduate/Internship)*

**Purpose:** To provide reporting, copy editing, photography, and graphic designs experience. **Focus:** Journalism. **Qualif.:** Applicants must be juniors, seniors, or graduate students enrolled in a degree program. Previous experience is preferred but not required.

**Funds Avail.:** Internships are paid. **To Apply:** Write for application details.

# • 6091 •
## Washington Press Association
14243 156th Ave., SE      *Ph:* (206)228-5903
Renton, WA 98059      *Fax:* (206)277-8584

### • 6092 • Rae Mitsuoka Photography Scholarships *(Undergraduate/Scholarship)*

**Focus:** Photography. **Qualif.:** Applicants must be high school seniors entered in WPA's High School Photography Contest. **Criteria:** Scholarship award is based on talent, financial need, and academic performance and must be used for a photography workshop or tuition at a college or university in the state. Preference is given to Washington students.

**Funds Avail.:** $250. **No. of Awards:** 1. **To Apply:** Applicants must submit a completed application form, a letter including education and career goals and how the funds would be used, two samples of work, a high school transcript, and a self-addressed, stamped envelope. **Deadline:** April 1.

**Remarks:** Scholarships will be presented at the WPA Youth Forum, in conjunction with the Academic Journalism Contest. **Contact:** Barbara Nilson at the above address (see entry 6091).

### • 6093 • Washington Press Association Annual Scholarships *(Professional Development, Undergraduate/Scholarship)*

**Focus:** Communications. **Qualif.:** Students must be upperclass communication majors at two- and four-year state colleges in Washington and universities or Washington Press Association members who seek additional training. **Criteria:** Scholarship awards are based on scholastic achievement in communications, financial need, and career potential.

**Funds Avail.:** Two $500 scholarships or one $1,000 scholarship. **No. of Awards:** 2. **To Apply:** Candidates must submit a WPA application form; two samples of published or broadcast work, including date of work, name of publication or station (students may send class papers if no work has been published); two letters of recommendation from persons acquainted with applicant's work; and a transcript. A self-addressed, stamped envelope of suitable size should be included in the application packet if materials are to be returned. **Deadline:** April 1.

**Remarks:** Scholarships will be presented at the WPA Youth Forum in conjunction with the Academic Journalism Contest. **Contact:** Barbara Nilson at the above address (see entry 6091).

• 6094 •
## Washington Printing Guild
7 W. Tower
1333 H St. NW
Washington, DC 20005-4707          Ph: (202)682-3001

**• 6095 • Washington Printing Guild Scholarships**
*(Undergraduate/Scholarship)*

**Purpose:** To financially assist students pursuing an education in the graphic arts. **Focus:** Printing, Graphic Arts. **Qualif.:** Applicants must be United States citizens, have and maintain a cumulative grade point average of 2.5 or better, able to demonstrate financial need, and be eligible for acceptance in a graphic arts program. **To Apply:** Candidates should submit a current school transcript with application and be recommended by their supervisor, department chairperson, school counselor, or a PGCA-member employer. **Deadline:** February 28 every year. **Contact:** Printing and Graphic Communications Association, at the above address (see entry 6094).

• 6096 •
## Washington Pulp & Paper Foundation
c/o University of Washington
PO Box 352100                      Ph: (206)543-2763
Seattle, WA 98195-2100             Fax: (206)685-3091
E-mail: WPPF@U.WASHINGTON.EDU
URL: http://WEBER.U.WASHINGTON.EDU/~WPPF

**• 6097 • Washington Pulp & Paper Foundation Scholarships** *(Undergraduate/Scholarship)*

**Purpose:** To provide financial support for undergraduate paper science and engineering majors at the University of Washington. **Focus:** Forestry, Natural Resources, Chemical Engineering. **Qualif.:** Applicants must be enrolled in a pulp and paper engineering curriculum at the College of Forest Resources at the University of Washington, Seattle. **Criteria:** SAT scores, GPA, recommendations, and communications skills.

**Funds Avail.:** $1,000-6,000 each. **No. of Awards:** About 50. **To Apply:** Applications are available by writing to the Foundation. **Deadline:** February 1 to the Foundation; January 15 to the University of Washington. **Contact:** The Washington Pulp & Paper Foundation at the above address (see entry 6096).

• 6098 •
## Washington State Higher Education Coordinating Board
917 Lakeridge Way
PO Box 43430                        Ph: (360)753-7844
Olympia, WA 98504-3430             Fax: (206)753-1784

**• 6099 • Washington Health Professional Loan Repayment and Scholarship Program** *(Doctorate, Postdoctorate/Scholarship loan)*

**Purpose:** To recruit health professionals to serve in rural and/or medically-underserved areas of Washington State. **Focus:** Health Science. **Qualif.:** Applicants must be accepted or enrolled in an accredited program leading to eligibility for licensure in Washington State and training to be primary care professionals. Scholarship recipients must agree to serve a minimum of three years in a shortage area or repay the loan plus interest. **Criteria:** Loan repayment awards will be made on a competitive basis, to the limit of funds available, where a match between a qualifying facility and eligible candidate has been achieved.

**Funds Avail.:** Participants may receive loan repayment to a maximum of $15,000 per year for a minimum of three years of service in a Washington State health professional shortage area. **No. of Awards:** Varies. **To Apply:** Scholarship application materials are available after January 15. **Deadline:** Usually April/May. Recipients are notified by mail in early June for scholarship program. **Contact:** Kathy McVay, Program Administrator, at the above address (see entry 6098).

**• 6100 • Washington Scholars Grants**
*(Undergraduate/Grant)*

**Purpose:** To recognize and honor the accomplishments of three high school seniors from each legislative district; to encourage and facilitate privately-funded scholarship awards; and to stimulate recruitment of outstanding students to Washington public and independent colleges and universities. **Focus:** General Studies. **Qualif.:** Applicants must be Washington residents. **Criteria:** High school principals nominate the top one percent of the graduating senior class based upon academic accomplishments, leadership, and community service.

**Funds Avail.:** Scholars attending Washington public colleges and universities may receive a four-year undergraduate tuition and fee waiver based upon maintenance of a 3.30 GPA. Scholars attending Washington independent colleges and universities may receive a grant that must be matched on a dollar-for-dollar basis with either money or tuition and fee waiver by the institution. **To Apply:** Candidates must be nominated by their high school principals. **Contact:** Ann McLendon at the above address (see entry 6098).

**• 6101 • Washington State Educational Opportunity Grant** *(Undergraduate/Grant)*

**Purpose:** To provide an incentive to eligible placebound financially needy students who have completed an Associate of Arts degree, or its equivalent, by enabling them to complete their upper-division study at eligible institutions that have existing enrollment capacity. **Focus:** General Studies. **Qualif.:** Applicants must be residents of the state of Washington who have completed an Associate of Arts degree, or its equivalent, live in an eligible county, are financially needy and meet the "placebound" definition. **Criteria:** Financial need and "placebound" condition.

**Funds Avail.:** The grant amount is $2,500. **No. of Awards:** Varies. **To Apply:** Apply through school's financial aid office. **Deadline:** March 31. **Contact:** Barbara Theiss at the above address (see entry 6098).

**• 6102 • Washington State Need Grant**
*(Undergraduate/Grant)*

**Purpose:** To assist low income Washington residents who attend participating public or private two- or four-year or vocational-technical institutions, or selected proprietary schools. The premise of the grant is that no Washington resident should be denied postsecondary education for financial reasons. **Focus:** General Studies. **Qualif.:** Applicants must show financial need, enroll at a participating institution, and pursue a degree other than theology. Both full- and part-time students are eligible to apply. Candidates must also be Washington state residents and apply for a Pell grant.

**Funds Avail.:** Varies. The average grant has been $1,250. Students with dependents can receive an additional allowance for dependent care. **To Apply:** Students are automatically considered for the grant if they make full financial aid application at the admitting school and the institution has the funds to make an award.

**Remarks:** The program was established in 1969. Funding for the program is provided from state appropriations and matching monies from the federal government through the state student incentive grant program. **Contact:** Mrs. Terri May at the above address (see entry 6098).

*Washington State Higher Education Coordinating Board (continued)*

**• 6103 • Washington State Student Financial Aid Programs State Need Grant** *(All/Other)*

**Purpose:** To assist low and lower-middle income Washington residents who attend participating institutions.

**• 6104 • Washington State Student Financial Aid Programs Washington Scholars** *(High School, Undergraduate/Scholarship)*

**Purpose:** To recognize and honor the accomplishments of three high school seniors from each legislative district; encourage and facilitate privately-funded scholarship awards; and stimulate recruitment of outstanding students to Washington public and independent colleges and universities. **Qualif.:** Students must be in the top 1 percent of the graduating class. This is based on academic accomplishments, leadership, and community service. **Criteria:** Students are nominated by the principals of the schools.

**Funds Avail.:** The maximum grant fund is $3,021. **Contact:** The Board at the above address (see entry 6098).

**• 6105 • Washington State Work Study** *(Graduate, Undergraduate/Work Study)*

**Purpose:** To provide financial assistance to needy part-time and full-time students by stimulating and promoting their part-time employment. An equally important goal is the relationship of that employment to the student's academic pursuits or career goals. **Focus:** General Studies. **Qualif.:** Priority is given to Washington residents. **Criteria:** Awards are given based on financial need. **To Apply:** Contact local educational institution for application information. **Deadline:** Contact local educational institution for deadlines. **Contact:** Cindy McBeth at the above address (see entry 6098).

**• 6106 •**
**Washington State PTA - Scholarship Foundation**
2003 65th Ave., W.                   *Ph:* (253)565-2153
Tacoma, WA 98466-6215                 *Fax:* (253)565-7753
*E-mail:* wapta@wastatepta.org
*URL:* http://www.wastatepta.org

**• 6107 • Washington State PTA Scholarships** *(Undergraduate/Scholarship)*

**Purpose:** To assist students who might ordinarily be eliminated in academic scholastic competition. **Qualif.:** Students must be graduates of a Washington State public high school who are entering their freshman year of undergraduate studies. They must be able to meet the post-secondary institution's entrance standards for full-time students and maintain full-time student status. **Criteria:** Awards are based on financial need.

**Funds Avail.:** Awards for students entering four-year institutions are $1,000. Students attending community colleges, vocational-technical school, or other accredited institutions may receive $500. **No. of Awards:** Approximately 60. **To Apply:** Application forms are available from high school counselors or directly from the foundation. **Deadline:** March 1. **Contact:** Washington State PTA Scholarship Foundation at the above address (see entry 6106).

**• 6108 •**
**Wasie Foundation**
601 2nd Ave., Ste. 4700
Minneapolis, MN 55402-4319            *Ph:* (612)332-3883

**• 6109 • Wasie Foundation Scholarships** *(Graduate, Undergraduate/Scholarship)*

**Qualif.:** Students must be non-communists of Polish ancestry. They must also be full-time students at one of the following institutions: College of Saint Benedict, College of Saint Catherine, College of Saint Scholastica, Dunwoody Institute, Hamline University School of Law, Saint John's University, Saint Mary's University of Minnesota, University of Minnesota—Twin Cities Campus, University of Saint Thomas, or William Mitchell College of Law. **Criteria:** Selection is based on academic ability, educational goals, leadership qualities, involvement in extra-curricular activities, social conduct, and financial need.

**Funds Avail.:** Based on need. **No. of Awards:** 40. **To Apply:** Candidates may request an application from the Wasie Foundation or the institution's financial aid office. **Deadline:** April 15. **Contact:** Wasie Office at the above address (see entry 6108).

**• 6110 •**
**David Wasserman Scholarship Fund**
Adirondack Center
4722 St. Hwy. 30                      *Ph:* (518)843-2800
Amsterdam, NY 12010                   *Fax:* (518)843-2801

**• 6111 • David Wasserman Scholarships** *(Undergraduate/Scholarship)*

**Focus:** General Studies. **Qualif.:** Candidates must be residents of Montgomery County, New York, and be enrolled as undergraduates. **Criteria:** Based on academic achievement.

**Funds Avail.:** $300. **No. of Awards:** 20-30. **Deadline:** Written request for an application must be received by April 15. **Contact:** Norman J. Sherbunt.

**• 6112 •**
**Waste Management Education and Research Consortium**
New Mexico State University
Box 30001                            *Ph:* (505)646-2038
Department WERC                      *Fax:* (505)646-4149
Las Cruces, NM 88003-8001            *Free:* 800-523-5996
*E-mail:* were@mmsu.edu
*URL:* http://www.nmsu.edu/~werc

**• 6113 • WERC Undergraduate Scholarships** *(Undergraduate/Scholarship)*

**Focus:** Environmental Management. **Qualif.:** Applicants must be undergraduates with a 2.5 GPA or better pursuing a minor in environmental management. They must also attend New Mexico State University, University of New Mexico, or New Mexico Institute of Mining and Technology. **Criteria:** Preference is given to underprivileged students.

**Funds Avail.:** $200,000. **To Apply:** Applicants must submit a complete application with an essay on career goals. **Deadline:** April 15. **Contact:** Ricardo B. Jacquez, (505)646-2397, or write the above address.

• 6114 •

## Water Pollution Control Federation

601 Wythe St.  
Alexandria, VA 22314-1994

*Ph:* (703)684-2400  
*Fax:* (703)684-2492

### • 6115 • Annual Student Paper Competition
*(Postgraduate/Prize)*

**Qualif.:** Applicants must be any recent college graduate (within one year). Papers may deal with any aspect of water pollution control, water quality problems, water-related concerns, or hazardous wastes.

**Funds Avail.:** There are four applicant categories and three prizes within each category. The four categories are Operations Students, Bachelors Students, Masters Students, and Ph.D. Students. First prize is $1,000; second prize $500 and third prize $250. Winning authors will also have an opportunity to present their papers during either a technical or poster session at the Water Environment Federation's Annual Conference. **To Apply:** Applicants must submit a 500- to 1,000-word abstract. **Deadline:** February 1. **Contact:** Dianne Crilley, Program Specialist, Member Association Programs at the above address (see entry 6114).

### • 6116 • Annual Travel Fellowship *(Postdoctorate/Fellowship)*

**Qualif.:** Applicants must be young practicing engineers, either in environmental engineering or one of its allied fields.

**Funds Avail.:** $3,300 for a minimum three week study tour at the Water Research Centre, Inc. in the United Kingdom. The recipient is required to submit to the Water Environment Federation a written report suitable for publication, on the study tour, within 90 days of their return. **To Apply:** Applicants must submit a completed application with a detailed statement of career goals and aspirations in the environmental field (750 words minimum, 1000 words maximum) and three letters or recommendation. They should also indicate their intent to work in the environmental field for at least two years. **Deadline:** March 1. **Contact:** Water Environment Federation at the above address (see entry 6114).

### • 6117 • Robert A. Canham Scholarship *(Graduate/Scholarship)*

**Focus:** Water environment related fields. **Qualif.:** Applicants must be pursuing post-baccalaureate degrees in and agree to work for at least two years in the environmental field upon completion of the degree. Award recipient should be in good health and under the age of 41. **Criteria:** Special consideration is given to those applicants who have practical experience in the environmental field.

**Funds Avail.:** $2500, a one-year Water Environment Federation membership, and a plaque. **To Apply:** Applicants must submit a completed application with a detailed statement of career goals and aspirations in the environmental field (750 words minimum, 1000 words maximum) Must be amember of the Water Environment Federation Offical college transcripts, Letter of acceptance to a graduate program in the water environment field, Recommendations from three persons who can attest to applicants academic and/or practical experience, A detailed statement of degree objectives as related to applciant's career goasl., Requires a two year commitment to work in the environmental field after completion of degree. **Deadline:** March 1. **Contact:** Water Environment Federation at the above address (see entry 6114).

• 6118 •

## Thomas J. Watson Foundation

293 S. Main St.  
Providence, RI 02903

*Ph:* (401)274-1952  
*Fax:* (401)274-1954

*URL:* http://www.watsonfellowship.org

### • 6119 • Watson Fellowships *(Other/Fellowship)*

**Purpose:** To enable U.S. college graduates of unusual promise to engage in independent study and travel abroad. **Focus:** General Studies. **Qualif.:** Applicants may be of any nationality, but must be graduating seniors at one of the 50 colleges participating in the fellowship program. All of the colleges are private institutions in the United States with enrollments of less than 3,000 students; write for a complete list. They must be nominated by their home institution. Fellowships are tenable immediately after graduation from college, and may be used in countries outside of the United States. Candidate's proposed project may be in any discipline and may be directed toward any goal that is creative, feasible, and personally significant. Formal studies at universities are not supported.

**Funds Avail.:** $22,000. **No. of Awards:** Up to 60 annually. **To Apply:** Interested students should check with their College whether it is on the roster of schools who participate in the program. If on the list, college can give the student a guide to application procedures. Submit a preliminary application to the nominator, who will select two to four students to send formal applications to the Foundation. All nominees are interviewed by the Foundation after reviewing the written application. **Deadline:** For nomination to reach the Foundation: first Tuesday in November. Notification in mid-March. **Contact:** Noreen Tuross, Executive Director, at the above address (see entry 6118).

• 6120 •

## Watts Health Foundation, Inc.

Watts Health Charities  
1335 North Lake Ave., Ste. 200  
Pasadena, CA 91104

*Ph:* (626)296-7727  
*Fax:* (626)791-4090

*E-mail:* wattschrtg@aol.com  
*URL:* http://eureka.his.com/public_html/mentors/whf.html

### • 6121 • Birdell Chew Moore Scholarships
*(Undergraduate/Scholarship)*

**Purpose:** To assist students who have chosen to pursue careers in health and human services, science or mathematics. **Focus:** Health Care Services. **Qualif.:** Applicants must be residents of Los Angeles, Orange or Riverside Counties who are graduating high school seniors with an overall grade point average of at least 2.5. They must present proof of admission to an accredited college, university or technical school. Applicants must also establish evidence of financial need. Scholarships may be renewed if recipients present evidence of continued enrollment in a college/university program, a minimum grade point average of 2.5, and financial need. **Criteria:** Selection is based on merit, scholastic ability, letters of recommendation, financial need, and a personal interview conducted by the scholarship committee.

**Funds Avail.:** A total of $50,000. **No. of Awards:** 10-15. **To Apply:** Candidates must submit a completed application, academic transcripts, proof of admission to a college or university, proof of financial need, three letters of recommendation, official high school transcripts, four essays, and an autobiographical statement. **Deadline:** April 1. **Contact:** Terri Williams, Scholarship Coordinator, at the above address (see entry 6120).

## • 6122 •
### WCVB-TV
c/o Human Resources Department
5 TV Place
Needham, MA 02194
*E-mail:* lmwalsh@hearst.com
*URL:* http://www.wcvb.com/wcvb/webmate/wcvb/page/
wcvb/index-htm

*Ph:* (617)449-0400
*Fax:* (617)449-6682

#### • 6123 • WCVB TV Leo L. Beranek Fellowship for Newsreporting *(Graduate, Undergraduate/Fellowship)*

**Purpose:** To develop writing, editing, producing, and reporting skills. **Qualif.:** Applicants must have at least a BA or BS degree and proved interest in broadcast journalism demonstrated through past internships and extracurricular activities associated with the communications and journalism field. **To Apply:** Applicants must submit a grade transcript and three letters of recommendation, as well as a statement detailing why the applicant deserves the fellowship and the candidate's future career objectives. **Deadline:** March 31.

**Remarks:** One person will be selected each year for a salaried, nine-month fellowship that begins in September. WCVB-TV Boston, will conduct an on-the-job training program in broadcast journalism for those who belong to a minority or disadvantaged by economic social conditions and encounter substantial difficulty in gaining access to broadcast careers as a result. **Contact:** Human Resources, WCVB-TV.

#### • 6124 • WCVB TV 5 Broadcasting Internships *(Undergraduate/Internship)*

**Purpose:** To provide an opportunity for a student to obtain an overview of the television broadcasting field in news, programming, public affairs, or sales. **Qualif.:** Applicants must: have completed junior year and must be entering their senior year; major in some field of broadcasting; and be a US citizen.

**Funds Avail.:** Interns will be paid $150 per week. **Deadline:** April 30. **Contact:** Summer Minority Intern Program at the above address (see entry 6122).

#### • 6125 • WCVB TV Hearst Broadcast News Fellowship *(Graduate, Undergraduate/Fellowship)*

**Focus:** Broadcasting **Qualif.:** Applicant must belong to a minority or be disadvantaged with a desire to gain access to a broadcast carers. Applicants must be at least a BA or BS degree and demonstrated high interest through past internships and extracurricular activities associated with the communications and journalism field. **To Apply:** A grade transcript and three letters of recommendation are required as well as a statement detailing why the applicant chose to pursue broadcast journalism and why he/she deserves the fellowship. **Deadline:** April 30

**Remarks:** The goal of the program is to expose the fellow to all areas of news gathering and news production. The emphasis is on the development of writing skills and on the fundamentals of newscast production. **Contact:** Human Resources, WCVB-TV 5.

## • 6126 •
### Rob and Bessie Welder Wildlife Foundation
PO Drawer 1400
Sinton, TX 78387-1400

*Ph:* (512)364-2643

#### • 6127 • Welder Wildlife Fellowships *(Doctorate, Graduate/Fellowship)*

**Purpose:** To provide financial support for advanced degree candidates. **Focus:** Ecology, Wildlife Conservation. **Qualif.:**

Applicant must be an advanced degree candidate registered in an accredited university or college in the United States or Canada. Candidate must have received a combined score of at least 1100 on the verbal and quantitative sections of the Graduate Record Examination, and maintained a B grade average in either a bachelor's or master's program. Fellowships are intended to support research projects necessary to satisfy thesis or dissertation requirements.

**Funds Avail.:** Master's candidates: $850/month; Ph.D. candidates: $900/month. **To Apply:** Write to the Foundation for application form. Submit form with a preliminary research proposal. If the project is within the priorities of the Foundation's programs, a full proposal will be invited. **Deadline:** October 15.

## • 6128 •
### Well Being
27 Sussex Place
London NW1 4SP, England

*Ph:* 171 262 5337
*Fax:* 171 724 7725

#### • 6129 • Well Being *(Professional Development/Grant)*

**Purpose:** To support medical research for the better health of women and babies, with emphasis on all aspects of childbirth and the prevention of disability. **Focus:** Gynecology, Infertility, Obstetrics, Prenatal and Postnatal Health. **Qualif.:** Candidate may be of any nationality. No application will be accepted without evidence of ethical committee support. Grant is tenable at an established medical department. Funding is not available for study, travel abroad, undergraduate education, or travel to scientific meetings.

**Funds Avail.:** £75,000 maximum. **To Apply:** Write the administrator for application guidelines. **Deadline:** December. **Contact:** Administrator at the above address (see entry 6128).

## • 6130 •
### Charles Wells Memorial Aviation Scholarship Inc.
c/o Jim Walker
1835 S. 4th St.
Springfield, IL 62703-3146
*E-mail:* jimwalker@springnet1.com
*URL:* http://www.wellsscholarship.com

#### • 6131 • Charlie Wells Memorial Aviation Scholarship *(Undergraduate/Scholarship)*

**Purpose:** To promote aviation. **Qualif.:** Applicants must be enrolled in full-time study in an aviation program.

**Funds Avail.:** $1,800. **No. of Awards:** One to three. **To Apply:** Application forms may be downloaded from the website or requested from the above address with a SASE.

• 6132 •

## Wenner-Gren Foundation for Anthropological Research, Inc.

220 5th Ave., 16th Fl.  
New York, NY 10001-7708  
*E-mail:* info@wennergren.org  
*URL:* http://www.wennergren.org  

*Ph:* (212)683-5000  
*Fax:* (212)683-9151

### • 6133 • Developing Countries Training Fellowships
*(Graduate/Fellowship)*

**Purpose:** To allow scholars and advanced students from developing countries to improve their training, skills, and expertise in anthropology. **Focus:** Archaeology, Biological/Physical Anthropology, Cultural Anthropology, Linguistic Anthropology. **Qualif.:** Candidate must be from a developing nation, as defined in the Foundation's application guidelines. Applicant must be either a scholar or advanced student who is affiliated with an educational or research institution in his/her home country. Applicant must demonstrate that the training sought is unavailable in the home country, and that a qualified institution in another country has agreed to provide such training. Candidate must be sponsored by members of both the home and host institution. The host sponsor must be willing to assume responsibility for overseeing the fellow's training. Fellows may pursue either a course of studies leading to a degree or a specific non-degree plan for obtaining advanced training. Fellowships may be used to cover travel, living expenses, tuition, student fees, insurance, books, and any other relevant categories or expenditure. Funds are not available for salary or family expenses. Awards are tenable at any qualified institution in the world. Fellows must intend to return and work in their home country upon the completion of their training.

**Funds Avail.:** Up to $12,500/year. **To Apply:** Inquiries should be made by means of a one-page Summary Statement of Purpose. The statement should briefly describe the following: 1. scholary goals; 2. proposed training plan to be undertaken; 3. institutional affiliation at home and at intended institution abroad; 4. beginning date and estimated duration of training; 5. estimated budget for first year of studies/training; 6. itemized budget for amount requested for first academic year of studies/training; 7. other sources of aid; 8. prospects for employment and research upon return to Home Country. Please also include a copy of curriculum vitae or brief biography. If a candidate is considered eligible, an application will be sent. **Deadline:** Nine months before the start of training. **Contact:** The Foundation at the above address (see entry 6132).

### • 6134 • Richard Carley Hunt Memorial Postdoctoral Fellowships *(Postdoctorate/Fellowship)*

**Purpose:** To aid write-up or follow-up research in preparation for publication. **Focus:** Archaeology, Biological/Physical Anthropology, Cultural Anthropology, Linguistic Anthropology. **Qualif.:** Applicants for Hunt Fellowships may be of any nationality. There are no restrictions regarding the candidate's institutional affiliation for this award, but applicant must have a Ph.D. in hand in anthropology or a related discipline at the time application is made. Candidates for Hunt Fellowships must have received their Ph.D. within five years of applying for the award, and must use the funds for the write-up of research results for publication. Priority is given to projects that employ comparative perspectives or integrate more than one subfield of anthropology. Grants are intended for direct research and writing expenses; funds are not available for tuition, salary of awardee, non-project personnel, institutional overhead and support, or travel to meetings. Low priority is given to publication assistance and filmmaking.

**Funds Avail.:** $15,000 maximum. **To Apply:** Those eligible should write to the Foundation for application form and guidelines. No sample applications are available. **Deadline:** May 1 and November 1. Applicants are notified six to eight months after the deadline. **Contact:** The Foundation at the above address (see entry 6132).

### • 6135 • International Collaborative Research Grants
*(Postdoctorate/Grant)*

**Purpose:** To assist two or more investigators from different countries to jointly undertake anthropological research projects. **Focus:** Anthropological Research. **Qualif.:** Priority is given to projects with at least one applicant from outside North America and Western Europe. Applicants must each hold a doctorate or equivalent in anthropology or related discipline.

**Funds Avail.:** Grants will cover research expenses related directly to the project only. **To Apply:** Inquiries should be made by means of a preliminary statement, which should briefly cover the following points: names of investigators, their institutions, and biographical data; topic, aims, and scope of research project; what each investigator would bring to the collaboration; proposed schedule of research; and proposed budget. If a project is considered eligible for this program, formal application materials are sent. **Deadline:** None. **Contact:** The Foundation at the above address (see entry 6132).

### • 6136 • Wenner-Gren Foundation Predoctoral Grants *(Doctorate/Grant)*

**Purpose:** Predoctoral Grants are awarded to individuals to aid doctoral dissertation or thesis research in all branches of anthropology. Grants are made to seed innovative approaches and ideas, to cover specific expenses or phases of a project, and/or to encourage aid from other funding agencies. The Foundation particularly invites projects employing comparative perspectives or integrating two or more subfields of anthropology. **Focus:** Anthropology. **Qualif.:** Applicants must be scholars working on their doctoral dissertation or thesis research. They must be enrolled for a doctoral degree. Those seeking support for postdoctoral research who have not received the degree at the time of application should file a predoctoral application; if an award is approved it will be made after the Ph.D. is in hand. Qualified students of all nationalities are eligible.

**Funds Avail.:** Up to $20,000. **To Apply:** Application forms will be sent upon request. Application must be made jointly with a thesis advisor or other scholar who will undertake responsibility for supervising the project. Awards are contingent upon the applicant's successful completion of all requirements for the degree other than the dissertation/thesis. Applications may be submitted before such requirements have been met; should an award be approved, the Foundation will at that time request evidence of the applicant's fulfillment of degree requirements. **Deadline:** There are two deadlines, May 1 and November 1, for applications for funding during the calendar year following. Applicants who will require funds during the first half of the year should meet the May 1 deadline. Projects scheduled to begin in July or later may be submitted by the November 1 deadline. Decisions will be announced six to eight months after the deadline date. Only one application may be submitted during any twelve-month period. **Contact:** The Foundation at the above address (see entry 6132).

### • 6137 • Wenner-Gren Regular Grants
*(Postdoctorate/Grant)*

**Purpose:** To aid anthropological research projects. **Focus:** Archaeology, Biological/Physical Anthropology, Cultural Anthropology, Ethnology, Evolution, Linguistic Anthropology. **Qualif.:** Applicants may be of any nationality. There are no restrictions regarding the candidate's institutional affiliation, but applicant must have a Ph.D. in anthropology or a related discipline at the time of the award. Priority is given to projects that employ comparative perspectives or integrate more than one subfield of anthropology. Grants are intended for direct research expenses; funds are not available for tuition, salary of awardee, non-project personnel, institutional overhead and support, or travel to meetings, publication subvention, or filmmaking.

**Funds Avail.:** $20,000 maximum. **To Apply:** Those eligible should write to the Foundation for application form and guidelines.

*Wenner-Gren Foundation for Anthropological Research, Inc. (continued)*

**Deadline:** May 1 and November 1. Applicants are notified six to eight months after the deadline. **Contact:** The Foundation at the above address (see entry 6132).

---

## • 6138 •

**Wesleyan Writers Conference - Wesleyan University**
279 Court St.                          *Ph:* (860)685-3604
Middletown, CT 06459              *Fax:* (860)685-2441
*E-mail:* egreene@wesleyan.edu

### • 6139 • Barach Teaching Fellowships in Non-Fiction *(Other/Fellowship)*

**Purpose:** To give the opportunity to work with award-winning journalists, fiction writers, and film makers at the Wesleyan Writers Conference. **Focus:** Journalism.

**Funds Avail.:** $400 honorarium plus all conference related expenses. **To Apply:** Inquire for details. **Deadline:** April 12.

---

## • 6140 •

**West Virginia Department of Veterans' Affairs**
Charleston Human Resource Center      *Ph:* (304)558-3661
1321 Plaza E., Ste. 101                     *Fax:* (304)558-3662
Charleston, WV 25301-1400               *Free:* 888-838-2332
*E-mail:* wvvetaff@aol.com

### • 6141 • West Virginia War Orphans Education Benefits *(High School, Undergraduate/Grant)*

**Purpose:** To assist in the education of orphans of war veterans. **Focus:** General Studies **Qualif.:** Must be a resident of West Virginia at least 16 and not more than 23 years old. Applicants must be attending school within the state of West Virginia, (if a college or university, it must be state-supported). They must be children of deceased veterans who served on active duty in the armed forces during wartime. The death of the veteran must have occurred during active duty or have been a result of a disability incurred during a wartime period. Candidates must maintain a 2.0 GPA.

**Funds Avail.:** Under state law, student receives waiver of tuition and registration fees at college level; $250 per semester for college students and up to $225 per semester for high school students. **Deadline:** Third Monday in July for the fall semester and first Monday in December for the spring semester. **Contact:** The West Virginia Department of Veterans' Affairs at the above address (see entry 6140).

---

## • 6142 •

**West Virginia Space Grant Consortium**
West Virginia University
College of Engineering and Mineral
  Resources
PO Box 6070
G60 ESB
Morgantown, WV 26506-6070
*URL:* http://www.cemr.wvu.edu˜wwwnasa/

### • 6143 • Undergraduate NASA Space Grant Fellowship *(Undergraduate/Fellowship)*

**Purpose:** To encourage students to pursue aerospace related careers and allow them the opportunity to be connected with NASA related activities. **Focus:** Aerospace science. **Qualif.:** Applicants must be U.S. citizens; West Virginia residents; and undergraduate students in a Consortium affiliated institution. **Criteria:** Based on academic record and interest in the field.

**Funds Avail.:** Full tuition, fees, and room and board. R 4 years.

### • 6144 • West Virginia Space Consortium Graduate Fellowship Program *(Graduate/Fellowship)*

**Purpose:** To provide students the opportunity to work on a research project, enhance their education, and work directly with NASA activities. **Focus:** Aerospace-related fields. **Qualif.:** Applicants must be U.S. citizens attending graduate level courses at a Consortium institution. **Criteria:** Fellows are chosen by the faculty member they will work with.

**Funds Avail.:** Varies with the amount of the research grant.

### • 6145 • West Virginia Space Grant Consortium Undergraduate Scholarship Program *(Undergraduate/Scholarship)*

**Purpose:** To support students while giving them the opportunity to participate in Consortium activities. **Focus:** Aerospace or science related fields. **Qualif.:** Applicants must be U.S. citizens, West Virginia residents, and undergraduate students at a Consortium member institution. **Criteria:** Based on academic records and the desire to pursue a career in science or engineering.

**Funds Avail.:** $1000 and $2000.

**Remarks:** Recipients are given the opportunity to work with faculty members in their major department on a research project.

---

## • 6146 •

**Western Association of Women Historians**
2513 NE Skidmore
Portland, OR 97211
                                                      *Ph:* (503)282-9470

### • 6147 • WAWH Graduate Student Fellowship *(Doctorate/Fellowship)*

**Purpose:** To encourage a woman in the western states area working on a dissertation in any field of history. **Focus:** History. **Qualif.:** Applicants must be members of WAWH. Information about joining WAWH is included in the note below. Candidates must be graduate students in history who are writing their Ph.D. dissertation at the time of application. Students who expect to receive their Ph.D. degrees before December of the year of application are not eligible. The fellowship may be used for any activities directly or indirectly related to the dissertation, including research expenses, attendance at scholarly conferences, and the preparation of the dissertation. Preference may be given to those who reside in the region served by the WAWH (any topic) and nonresidents who are writing on topics relevant to the western states.

**Funds Avail.:** Approximately $1000. **No. of Awards:** 1 annually. **To Apply:** Write to the fellowships chair for application form and guidelines, or to become a member write: Nupur Chaudhuri, 1737 Vaughan Dr. Manhattan, KS 66502. Submit form with a prospectus on the dissertation. Three letters of recommendation must be sent directly from the referees to the chair. **Deadline:** March 1. The fellow is announced in May.

**Remarks:** Individuals interested in becoming members of WAWH should write to Dr. Carol Gold, Dept. of History, University of Alaska, Fairbanks, AK 99775. **Contact:** The addresses listed previous or the Western Association of Women Historians at the above address (see entry 6146).

---

**• 6148 •**
**Western Dredging Association**
PO Box 5797
Vancouver, WA 98668-5797
*URL:* http://jaws.tamu.edu/~oecds/weda.html

**• 6149 •   Western Dredging Association Scholarships**
*(Graduate/Scholarship)*

**Purpose:** To allow a graduate student to study at the Center for Dredging Studies. **Focus:** Dredging. **Qualif.:** Applicants must be graduate students enrolled in the Texas A&M University, Civil Engineering Department. **Criteria:** Recipient is selected by the University.

**Funds Avail.:** $1,200. **No. of Awards:** 1. **Contact:** The Western Dredging Association at the above address (see entry 6148).

---

**• 6150 •**
**Western Golf Association - Evans Scholars Foundation**
1 Briar Rd.
Golf, IL 60029                    *Ph:* (708)724-4600

**• 6151 •   Evans Caddie Scholarships** *(Undergraduate/ Scholarship)*

**Focus:** General Studies. **Qualif.:** Candidates must have completed their junior year in high school and rank in the upper 25 percent of their class, have a superior caddie record for at least two years in a club that is a member of the Western Golf Association, require financial assistance in order to attend college, and possess an outstanding personal character. Candidates must be recommended by club officials. **Criteria:** Scholarships are awarded based on overall record and financial need. Candidates who reach the finals will be asked to appear before a Scholarship Committee at Selection Meetings held in late fall or early winter.

**Funds Avail.:** The scholarship covers tuition and housing at the 14 universities where the Evans Scholars Foundation maintains an Evans Scholars Chapter House. In states where there is not an Evans Scholar Chapter House, tuition and room-rent costs are covered at the candidate's state university. An Evans Scholarship is a one-year grant that can be renewed for four years. **No. of Awards:** 273. **To Apply:** Candidates must file a formal application with a letter of recommendation from each of the four following officials at the club: President, Caddie Committee Chairman, Golf Professional, and Caddie Superintendent. A transcript of grades for the first three years, and their SAT or ACT scores are also required. A Parents Confidential Financial Statement must be requested from Western Golf Association and submitted by

applicants' parents. Candidates may obtain an application from their sponsoring club or Western Golf Association, Evans Scholarship Foundation. **Deadline:** Applications are accepted between July 1 and November 1 after candidate's junior year.

**Remarks:** Chick Evans, veteran Chicago amateur golfer, is the father of the caddie-scholarship program which began in 1930 under the administration of the Western Golf Association. The Golf Associations that sponsor the Evans Scholarship program with the Western Golf Association are; Arizona, Buffalo District, Colorado, Michigan, Greater Cincinnati, Illinois Women, Indiana, Kansas City, Kentucky State, Minnesota, Northeast Wisconsin, Northern California, Ohio, Oregon, Pacific Northwest, South Dakota, St. Louis District, Syracuse District, Toledo District, and Wisconsin State. The Chapter Houses are at Colorado, Illinois, Indiana, Marquette, Miami of Ohio, Michigan, Michigan State, Minnesota, Missouri, Northern Illinois, Northwestern, Ohio State, Purdue, and Wisconsin Universities. **Contact:** Western Golf Association, Evans Scholars Foundation, at the above address (see entry 6150).

---

**• 6152 •**
**Western Growers Association**
PO Box 2130                    *Ph:* (714)863-1000
Newport Beach, CA 92658        *Fax:* (714)863-9028

**• 6153 •   Ed Taylor Memorial Scholarship** *(Graduate, Undergraduate/Scholarship)*

**Purpose:** To promote students in California agricultural studies. **Qualif.:** Applicants must be following an agricultural course of study in conjunction with Cal Poly, San Luis Obispo enrollment. They need not reside in California. **Criteria:** GPA (minimum 3.0), financial need, and agriculture studies or major.

**Funds Avail.:** $1,000 annually. **To Apply:** Write for an application. **Deadline:** June 1. **Contact:** Randy Hause at the above address (see entry 6152).

---

**• 6154 •**
**Western History Association**
University of New Mexico
1080 Mesa Vista Hall          *Ph:* (505)277-5234
Albuquerque, NM 87131-1181    *Fax:* (505)277-6023
*E-mail:* whaunm@unm.edu

**• 6155 •   Rundell Graduate Student Award**
*(Doctorate/Award)*

**Purpose:** To support research on dissertation topics. **Qualif.:** Applicants must be graduate students nominated by a graduate advisor in western history from Ph.D. granting institutions. They should be doctoral candidates who have completed comprehensive examinations and are in the process of researching a dissertation topic.

**Funds Avail.:** Recipients are granted a $1,000 cash award. **No. of Awards:** 1. **To Apply:** Nominations are made directly to the award committee. **Deadline:** Nominations must be received by July 31. The winner is announced in October.

**Remarks:** A new award committee is announced in February of each award year. **Contact:** The Western History Association at the above address (see entry 6154).

---

## • 6156 •
## Western New York League for Nursing
PO Box 93220
Rochester, NY 14692

### • 6157 • Lucretia H. Richter Nursing Scholarship
*(Undergraduate/Scholarship)*

**Qualif.:** Applicants must be enrolled in a New York League for Nursing accredited school in Western New York State and have completed two nursing courses. **Criteria:** Selections are based on the candidate's commitment to nursing, grade point average, financial need, and faculty recommendations.

**Funds Avail.:** The amount of the scholarship awards is determined annually. **To Apply:** Application materials can be obtained from the schools of nursing by October 15. **Deadline:** December 1. **Contact:** Judith Kiley, 96 Coachman Dr., Penfield, NY 14526-1206.

## • 6158 •
## Western Regional Graduate Program - Western Interstate Commission for Higher Education
PO Box 9752      *Ph:* (303)541-0210
Boulder, CO 80301-9752      *Fax:* (303)541-0291
*E-mail:* info-sep@wiche.edu
*URL:* http://www.wiche.edu

### • 6159 • Western Regional Graduate Program
*(Graduate/Other)*

**Purpose:** To promote sharing of higher education resources among western states. **Focus:** General Studies. **Qualif.:** Applicants must be graduate students who are residents of one of the fourteen participating states in the WICHE Program. These states are: Alaska, Arizona, Colorado, Hawaii, Idaho, Montana, Nevada, New Mexico, North Dakota, Oregon, South Dakota, Utah, Washington, and Wyoming. The Western Regional Graduate Program makes many high-quality graduate programs available to WICHE-state students at a reasonable cost. **Criteria:** Institution makes decision.

**Funds Avail.:** Students selected for the program may enroll in the participating graduate programs participating institutions in participating states. Students pay reduced tuition rates. At public institutions, students pay resident rates. At private institutions, tuition rates are reduced. **No. of Awards:** Varies. **To Apply:** Applicants should contact the Participating program or they may contact WICHE directly. **Deadline:** Varies with institutions. Students make application directly to the participating institution. Applicants should identify themselves as WICHE Western Regional Graduate Program applicants.

**Remarks:** A brochure is available from WICHE at above address. **Contact:** WICHE Western Regional Graduate Program at the above address (see entry 6158)or a participating graduate department. department.

## • 6160 •
## Western States Arts Federation
1543 Champa St., Ste. 220      *Ph:* (303)629-1166
Denver, CO 80202      *Fax:* (303)629-9717

### • 6161 • WESTAF/NEA Regional Fellowships for Visual Artists *(Professional Development/Fellowship)*

**Purpose:** To honor outstanding artistic achievement by artists living and working in the region. **Focus:** Even Numbered Years: Painting, New Genres, and Works on Paper (including Drawing, Printmaking, and Artists Books); Odd Numbered Years: Sculpture, Photography, and Crafts. **Qualif.:** Applicant must be a professional artist, a citizen or legal resident of the United States, and a resident of Alaska, Arizona, California, Colorado, Hawaii, Idaho, Montana, Nevada, New Mexico, Oregon, Utah, Washington, or Wyoming from the application deadline (February) through the panel review period (July). Artists are not eligible to apply if they: have received an NEA/regional visual arts fellowship in any discipline during the preceding five years, have received an NEA national visual arts fellowship in any discipline during the preceding ten years, or are full-time students enrolled in a degree program. **Criteria:** Each discipline area is reviewed by a panel of distinguished artists, curators, and arts professionals. Selection criteria includes the quality of the work, the record of professional activity and achievement as reflected in the application materials submitted, evidence that the work reflects a continued, serious, and exceptional aesthetic investigation, and the potential impact the fellowship will have on the artist's professional growth and development.

**Funds Avail.:** $5,000 **No. of Awards:** 30. **To Apply:** Artists must contact the WESTAF to request an application for their specific discipline each time they wish to apply. To receive an application, send a stamped, self-addressed 6 by 9 inch envelope with 52 cents postage in September before the year you wish to apply. Include your name, address, and discipline area. **Deadline:** February 6. Dates vary. **Contact:** Fellowship Coordinator at the above address (see entry 6160).

## • 6162 •
## Western States Black Research/Educational Center
3617 Montclair St.      *Ph:* (213)737-3292
Los Angeles, CA 90018      *Fax:* (213)737-2842

### • 6163 • Black American Cinema Society Award
*(Professional Development/Award)*

**Focus:** Filmmaking. **Qualif.:** Applicants must be black students and independent filmmakers. **Criteria:** Awards are made based on quality of work.

**Funds Avail.:** $3,000. **To Apply:** Applicants must submit a 3/4 inch or 16mm film. Write for further details. **Deadline:** March 1. **Contact:** Western States Black Research Center at the above address (see entry 6162).

## • 6164 •
## Weyerhaeuser Company Foundation
c/o Penny Paul, Program Manager
CHIF31
Tacoma, WA 98477      *Ph:* (206)924-2629

### • 6165 • Weyerhaeuser Company Foundation College Scholarship *(Undergraduate/Scholarship)*

**Focus:** General studies. **Qualif.:** Applicants must be children of Weyerhaeuser employees who are high school juniors planning to enter a four-year institution to complete a baccalaureate degree.

**Funds Avail.:** $1,000 to $4,000 per award. **To Apply:** Applicants must submit a completed application form. **Deadline:** January 1. **Contact:** Weyerhaeuser Company Foundation at the above address (see entry 6164).

### • 6166 • Weyerhaeuser Company Foundation Community Education Scholarship *(Undergraduate/ Scholarship)*

**Focus:** General studies. **Qualif.:** Applicants must be children of Weyerhaeuser employees who are high school seniors planning to attend a community/junior college or vocational-technical institution to complete a degree or certificate program.

**Funds Avail.:** $1,000 per award. **To Apply:** Applicants must submit a completed application form. **Deadline:** January 1. **Contact:** Weyerhaeuser Company Foundation at the above address (see entry 6164).

---

### • 6167 •
## Whitehall Foundation, Inc.
251 Royal Palm Way, Ste. 211     *Ph:* (407)655-4474
Palm Beach, FL 33480     *Fax:* (407)659-4978

*The Whitehall Foundation, through its program of grants and grants-in-aid, assists scholarly research in the life sciences. It is the Foundation's policy to assist those dynamic areas of basic biological research that are not heavily supported by federal agencies or other foundations with specialized missions.*

### • 6168 • Whitehall Foundation Grants-in-Aid *(Postdoctorate/Grant)*

**Purpose:** To provide aid to researchers at the assistant professor level who experience difficulty in competing for research funds because they have not yet become firmly established. The Foundation is currently interested in basic research in neurobiology, specifically invertebrate and vertebrate neurobiology (exclusive of human beings) investigations of neural mechanisms involved in sensory, motor, or other complex functions of the whole organisms as these relate to behavior. **Focus:** Life Sciences. **Qualif.:** Although the Foundation prefers to support scientists at the beginning of their careers, senior scientists who have maintained productivity are also given consideration. **Criteria:** All applications will be judged on the scientific merit of the proposal as well as on past performance and evidence of continued productivity of the applicant.

**Funds Avail.:** Grants-in-aid do not exceed $15,000. **To Apply:** Applicants must submit a one-page letter of intent to the Foundation, written in technical language, identifying the nature of the research proposal and indicating whether the request is for a research grant (see separate entry) or a one-year grant-in-aid. Grant application forms will be sent to those applicants whose proposed project matches the Foundation's current funding interests. **Deadline:** Letters of intent are accepted throughout the year. Deadlines will be defined when the application is sent to the investigator.

### • 6169 • Whitehall Foundation Research Grants *(Postdoctorate/Grant)*

**Purpose:** To assist those areas of basic biological research that are not heavily supported by federal agencies or other foundations with specialized missions. The Foundation is currently interested in basic research in neurobiology, specifically invertebrate and vertebrate neurobiology (exclusive of human beings) investigations of neural mechanisms involved in sensory, motor, or other complex functions of the whole organisms as these relate to behavior. **Focus:** Life Sciences. **Qualif.:** Applicants must be established scientists of all ages working at accredited institutions who hold no less than the position of assistant professor, or the equivalent. Research grants will not be awarded to investigators who have already received or expect to receive substantial support from other sources, even if it is for an unrelated purpose. **Criteria:** Applications will be judged on the scientific merit of the proposal and on the competence of the applicant.

**Funds Avail.:** Research grants normally range from $10,000 to $40,000 per year. **To Apply:** Applicants must submit a one-page letter of intent to the Foundation, written in technical language, identifying the nature of the research proposal and indicating whether the request is for a research grant or a one-year grant-in-aid (see separate entry). Grant application forms will be sent to those applicants whose proposed project matches the Foundation's current funding interests. **Deadline:** Letters of intent are accepted throughout the year. Deadlines will be defined when the application is sent to the investigator. The Foundation plans to hold three grant review sessions per year.

**Remarks:** As of December 1995, no foreign institutions are eligible. **Contact:** Laurel Baker, Corporate secretary, Whitehall Foundation, Inc., at the above address (see entry 6167).

---

### • 6170 •
## Mrs. Giles Whiting Foundation
c/o Kellye Rosenheim, Assistant
Director
1133 Avenue of the Americas, 22nd
Floor
New York, NY 10036-6710     *Ph:* (212)336-2138

### • 6171 • Whiting Fellowships in the Humanities *(Doctorate/Fellowship)*

**Purpose:** To provide fellowships to students in the humanities during their final year of dissertation writing. **Focus:** Humanities. **Qualif.:** Applicants must be students at Bryn Mawr, University of Chicago, Columbia, Harvard, Princeton, Stanford, or Yale. **Criteria:** Based on merit alone. Each university appoints a selection committee to determine the recipients.

**Funds Avail.:** Fellowships begin at $14,500. The amounts are set by the individual schools. **To Apply:** Applications should be made directly to the school; they are not accepted by the Foundation. **Contact:** One of the universities mentioned above.

---

### • 6172 •
## Lillian E. Whitmore Educational Foundation
2200 6th Ave., No. 535
Seattle, WA 98121

### • 6173 • Lillian E. Whitmore Scholarship *(Graduate, Undergraduate/Scholarship)*

**Purpose:** To encourage the study of the Christian ministry. **Focus:** Religion. **Qualif.:** Applicants must live in Western Washington State. **Criteria:** Based on dedication to Christian ideals and serving in the ministry; character; ability and aptitude for college work; motivation; and financial need.

**Funds Avail.:** $1000 to 2000. **No. of Awards:** 2. **To Apply:** An essay stating the reasons the applicants feels he or she should receive the scholarship, a completed official application form; and letters of recommendation must be submitted. **Deadline:** March 31.

---

# • 6174 •

## Helen Hay Whitney Foundation, Inc.
450 East 63rd St.
New York, NY 10021-7999          *Ph:* (212)751-8228

### • 6175 • Whitney Postdoctoral Research Fellowships
*(Postdoctorate/Fellowship)*

**Purpose:** To further the careers of young scholars engaged in biological or medical research by broadening their laboratory training and experience. **Focus:** Biological Sciences, Medicine. **Qualif.:** Applicant may be of any nationality, but must be a resident of North America under the age of 35 years. Applicant must have an M.D., Ph.D., or equivalent degree. Awards are intended for early postdoctoral training only; established scientist and fellows with a year of postdoctoral laboratory training at deadline date are not eligible. U.S. citizens may use the fellowship to conduct research at any academic laboratory in the world, except those at which he/she has already trained on a pre- or postdoctoral level. Fellowships to resident non-citizens are granted only for training at academic laboratories in the United States. Commercial or industrial laboratories are not acceptable sites for the fellowship.

**Funds Avail.:** $25,000 first year; $27,000 second year; $29,000 third year; plus laboratory allowance and travel costs to the fellowship location. **To Apply:** Write to the administrative director for application materials, available March 15. An interview is required of selected candidates. **Deadline:** August 15. Applicants not selected for the interview are notified October 1; all interviewed candidates are notified by mid-December. **Contact:** Administrative Director at the above address (see entry 6174).

# • 6176 •

## Wildlife Conservation International
New York Zoological Society
185th ST. and Southern Blvd.          *Ph:* (718)220-5251
Bronx, NY 10460-1099          *Fax:* (718)364-4275
*E-mail:* fellowship@wcs.org
*URL:* http://www.wcs.org/science/rfplink.html

### • 6177 • NYZS/Wildlife Conservation Society Research Fellowship Program (RFP) *(Doctorate, Graduate, Postdoctorate/Grant)*

**Purpose:** The RFP awards small grants to field research projects leading directly to the conservation of threatened wildlife. RFP applicants must demonstrate strong scientific achievement as well as direct relevance to conservation. **Focus:** Conservation biology, ecology, and zoology. **Criteria:** Proposals are evaluated on a competitive basis. Applications are screened by outside reviewers and by WCS staff. Preference is given to proposals by nationals of the country of research. Wildlife Conservation Society does not sponsor research in North America, Australia, and Europe.

**Funds Avail.:** Awards are limited to $20,000 with a median of $5,000. **To Apply:** Prospective applicants should contact WCS for information. **Deadline:** July 1 and January 1. Start up time for awards are the end of October and April. **Contact:** Research Fellowship Program Coordinator at the above address (see entry 6176).

### • 6178 • Research Grants in Wildlife Conservation
*(Postdoctorate/Grant)*

**Purpose:** To support research that is directly related to the conservation of wildlife and the wilderness. **Focus:** Wildlife Conservation, Zoology. **Qualif.:** Candidate may be of any nationality. Applicant must wish to conduct a research project that will lead to concrete advances in the conservation of threatened wildlife, communities, or ecosystems. Preference is given to

proposed research in one of the following biogeographic areas: East African savannas, Central and West African forests, temperate South America, tropical South America, Mesoamerica and the Caribbean, tropical Asia and the Pacific, and temperate Asia. Fellowship funds may not be used for travel to scientific meetings, legal actions, erection of permanent field stations, salaries at institutions, overhead costs, or expensive laboratory analyses. Stipends are awarded only when the investigator has no other source of support.

**Funds Avail.:** Usually $20,000 maximum; $5,000 median. **To Apply:** Write to the director for application materials. Application must include a description of proposed project, a detailed budget, a time table, and a curriculum vitae. **Deadline:** July 1, and January 1. Notification by October 1 and April 1. **Contact:** Dr. William Weber, Program Coordinator, Research Fellowship Program, at the above address (see entry 6176).

# • 6179 •

## John M. Will Memorial Journalism Scholarship Program
c/o Secretary
PO Box 290
Mobile, AL 36601

### • 6180 • John M. Will Memorial Journalism Scholarships *(Graduate, High School, Undergraduate/Scholarship)*

**Focus:** Journalism. **Qualif.:** Applicants must be residents of one of the following areas: Mobile, Baldwin, Escambia, Clarke, Conecuh, Washington or Monroe County in Alabama; Santa Rosa or Escambia County in Florida; or Jackson or George County in Mississippi. They must also be high school seniors who will be enrolled full time in a degree program at an accredited college; full time students who are currently enrolled or will be enrolled in a degree program at an accredited college; and/or current employees in journalism and wishing to become full time students at an accredited college.

**Funds Avail.:** $5000. **No. of Awards:** 1. **To Apply:** Applicants must complete and submit an application form prescribed by the Foundation Committee. Applicants must also submit to the Foundation Committee cover letters furnishing pertinent information not included in the application. There will be a conference that will be arranged at the discretion of the Foundation Committee, requiring applicant participation. Applicants will submit copies of their high school or college transcript and a letter of recommendation from their principals, counselors, journalism teachers or professors. **Deadline:** Must be postmarked on or before March 8. address.

# • 6181 •

## Williams College - Mystic Seaport - Maritime Studies Program
75 Greenmanville Ave.
PO Box 6000          *Ph:* (860)572-5359
Mystic, CT 06355-0990          *Fax:* (860)572-5329
*E-mail:* munson@mysticseaport.org
*URL:* http://www.mysticseaport.org

### • 6182 • Robert G. Stone Fellowships in American Maritime History *(Doctorate, Postdoctorate/Fellowship)*

**Focus:** American History, American Studies, Maritime Studies. **Qualif.:** Candidates must have completed or be near completion of their Ph.D.

**Funds Avail.:** $27,500 per year. **No. of Awards:** 1. **To Apply:** Candidates must submit application letter, curriculum vitae, graduate dossier, and contact information for three references. **Deadline:** January 10.

**Remarks:** During this two-year appointment the fellow will teach American Maritime History each semester at the Williams-Mystic Maritime Studies Program. The course traces the development of American mercantile enterprise from colonial times to the present, and examines its relationship to American political, economic, and cultural history. The Maritime Studies Program brings together twenty-four outstanding students, with a variety of majors, from small liberal arts colleges across the country. These students come to Mystic for a semester to study marine science, literature of the sea, and marine policy as well as maritime history. Scholarly pursuits, such as publication of the dissertation, would be expected for the fellow as well. **Contact:** Dr. James T. Carlton, Director, at the above address (see entry 6181).

• **6183** •

**Woodrow Wilson International Center for Scholars**
The Woodrow Wilson Center
1000 Jefferson Drive, SI MRC 022
S.W.                                     Ph: (202)357-2841
Washington, DC 20560                Fax: (202)357-4439
E-mail: WWCEM104

• **6184** • **Woodrow Wilson Center Residential Fellowship** *(Postdoctorate/Fellowship)*

**Purpose:** To commemorate both the scholarly depth and the public concerns of Woodrow Wilson through the Center's program of advanced research. **Qualif.:** Applicants must be at the postdoctoral level, (it is normally expected that academic candidates will have demonstrated their scholarly development by publication beyond the Ph.D. dissertation). For non-academics, an equal degree of professional achievement is expected. Candidates must present outstanding project proposals representing the entire range of scholarship in the humanities and social sciences. **Criteria:** Selection is based on the importance and originality of the project; the applicant's scholarly promise, capabilities, achievement, and ability to accomplish the proposed project; and the likelihood that the work, when completed, will advance basic understanding of the topic under study.

**Funds Avail.:** Average yearly stipend is $42,000. The Center awards approximately 30 fellowships annually. Limited funds make it desirable for most applicants to seek supplementary sources of funding. Travel expenses will be provided. **To Apply:** Write for application materials. **Deadline:** October 1.

**Remarks:** The center typically receives 800 applications. **Contact:** The Woodrow Wilson International Center for Scholars at the above address (see entry 6183).

• **6185** •

**Woodrow Wilson National Fellowship Foundation**
CN 5329                              Ph: (609)452-7007
Princeton, NJ 08543-5329           Fax: (609)452-0066
                                     Free: 800-899-9963

E-mail: mellon@woodrow.org
URL: http://www.woodrow.org/mellon

• **6186** • **Doctoral Dissertation Grants in Women's Studies** *(Doctorate/Grant)*

**Purpose:** To encourage doctoral research and writing on women in history, literature and society. **Focus:** Women's Studies and related disciplines, including History, Literature, Social Sciences. **Qualif.:** Applicant may be of any nationality, but must be enrolled in a doctoral program at a U.S. graduate school. Applicant may be a degree candidate in any discipline, as long as he/she is conducting dissertation research on a topic related to the study of women.

**Funds Avail.:** $1,000. **To Apply:** Write to the Foundation for application guidelines. **Deadline:** November 4; deadline for overseas material, October 23 postmarked.

**Remarks:** The Foundation also sponsors a number of programs for high school and college teachers, as well as educational administrators and minority scholars. For further information, write to the Foundation at the above address.

• **6187** • **Andrew W. Melon Fellowships in Humanistic Studies** *(Graduate/Fellowship)*

**Purpose:** To attract exceptionally promising students to prepare for careers in college teaching and scholarship in humanistic studies. **Focus:** Humanities and related disciplines (art history, area studies, comparative literature, history, musicology, philosophy, religion). **Qualif.:** Applicants must be college seniors or graduates; US citizens or permanent residents; entering a program leading to a PhD in humanities; not currently enrolled in graduate or professional study. **Criteria:** GRE scores, transcripts, 3 letters of recommendation by faculty and a statement of intellectual interest will be used to identify and encourage persons committed to teaching who have a broad vision of learning.

**Funds Avail.:** 80 awards of $14,500.00, plus tuition and mandated fees. **No. of Awards:** 80. **To Apply:** Must provide the following information: full name; permanent address; social security number; current mailing address and telephone; physical address in late February and early March; undergraduate institution, city, state; undergraduate major; year of graduation; intended discipline in graduate school; e-mail address (if available); and how you would like the application sent (e-mail or regular mail) or would you like to complete the application over the internet? **Deadline:** November 19 to request an application, December 15 to return application. **Contact:** Teresa Stevens or Sue Lloyd.

• **6188** • **Charlotte W. Newcombe Fellowships** *(Doctorate/Fellowship)*

**Purpose:** To encourage original and significant study of ethical or religious values in all fields of the humanities and social sciences. **Focus:** Ethics, Religious Studies, and related areas in the Humanities, Social Sciences. **Qualif.:** Applicant may be of any nationality, but must be a candidate for the Ph.D or Th.D in a doctoral program at a graduate school in the United States. Candidate should be in the final writing stage and writing on a topic of ethical or religious values.

**Funds Avail.:** $15,000 stipend. **No. of Awards:** 35. **To Apply:** Applications available on the internet at www.woodrow.org/ newcombe. **Deadline:** Mid-December.

**Remarks:** The Foundation also sponsors a number of programs for high school and college teachers, as well as educational administrators and minority scholars. For further information, write to the Foundation at the above address. **Contact:** Sheila Walker.

• 6189 •
## The David and Dovetta Wilson Scholarship Fund

115-67 237th St.  
Elmont, NY 11003-3926

*Ph:* (516)285-8532  
*Fax:* (516)285-8532  
*Free:* 800-759-7512

*URL:* http://www.wilsonfund.org

### • 6190 • David and Dovetta Wilson Scholarship
*(Undergraduate/Scholarship)*

**Focus:** General studies. **Qualif.:** Applicants must be high school seniors with "B" averages who attend public schools and are active participants in community and religious service. **Criteria:** Awards are based on financial need.

**Funds Avail.:** Up to $1,000. **No. of Awards:** 9. **To Apply:** Three letters of reference must accompany completed application form. There is also a $20 fee for processing the completed application form. Awardees must submit proof of attendance (registration) at an accredited college or university before award is dispensed. **Deadline:** March 1.

**Remarks:** Requests for applications must be accompanied by a self addressed stamped envelope. **Contact:** David and Dovetta Wilson Scholarship Fund at the above address (see entry 6189).

### • 6191 • David & Dovetta Wilson Scholarship Fund
*(High School/Scholarship)*

**Purpose:** To award scholarship funds to selected seniors attending high schools. **Qualif.:** Applicant must be high school seniors; attending a public high school; "B" average; active participants in community and religious service; demonstrate financial need; demonstrated leadership abilities in religious and civic organizations.

**Funds Avail.:** Up to $1,000 each. **To Apply:** Recipients will be notified by mail; acceptance of scholarship constitutes permission to use recipients name and/or likeness for purposes of advertising and trade; no transfer of scholarship is permitted. Offer open to residents of the 50 states and the District of Columbia who plan to attend an accredited college or university in the fall. **Deadline:** Completed applications must be received on or before March 1. **Contact:** DDWSF at listed address.

---

## • 6192 •
## Windham Foundation Inc.

PO Box 70  
Grafton, VT 05146

### • 6193 • Windham Foundation Scholarship
*(Undergraduate/Scholarship)*

**Focus:** General Studies. **Qualif.:** Applicants must be residents of Windham County, Vermont and enrolled in a college or university at the undergraduate level. **Criteria:** Priority is given to candidates demonstrating financial need.

**Funds Avail.:** $1,000 per student. **No. of Awards:** Varies. **Deadline:** April 1.

**Remarks:** The foundation receives approximately 425 applications each year. **Contact:** Paula Sheehan, The Windham Foundation, at the above address (see entry 6192).

## • 6194 •
## The Winston-Salem Foundation

860 W. 5th St.  
Winston-Salem, NC 27101-2889

*Ph:* (336)725-2382  
*Fax:* (336)727-0581

### • 6195 • Mary Rowena Cooper Scholarship Fund
*(All/Scholarship)*

**Purpose:** To provide college scholarships for orphans of Vietnam veterans of the 101st Airborne Division of the U.S. Army. **Focus:** Pediatric Medicine, Engineering, Teaching, and Law. **Qualif.:** Candidates should be pursuing a degree in pediatric medicine. **Contact:** The Winston-Salem Foundation at the above address (see entry 6194).

### • 6196 • Oliver Joel and Ellen Pell Denny Student Loan Fund *(Undergraduate/Loan)*

**Focus:** Allied Health Fields. **Qualif.:** Applicants must be North Carolina residents planning to become technicians and practitioners in the allied health fields. They must attend an accredited North Carolina institution and be able to complete their training within four years.

**Funds Avail.:** Loans are available at 7.5% interest rate for new borrowers. **Contact:** The Winston-Salem Foundation at the above address (see entry 6194).

### • 6197 • Virginia Elizabeth and Alma Vane Taylor Fund *(Undergraduate/Loan)*

**Focus:** Nursing. **Qualif.:** Applicants must be North Carolina state residents attending North Carolina school accredited by the North Carolina Board of Nursing. Students must complete their training period within four years.

**Funds Avail.:** Loans are available at 7.5% interest rate for new borrowers. **Contact:** The Winston-Salem Foundation at the above address (see entry 6194).

### • 6198 • The Winston-Salem Foundation Loans
*(Undergraduate/Loan)*

**Purpose:** To help students fund their post high school education. **Focus:** General Studies. **Qualif.:** Candidates must live in one of the following North Carolina counties: Forsyth, Davidson, Davie, Stokes, Yadkin, or Surry. They must be enrolled in any program leading to a degree, certificate, or diploma from an accredited institution. They must also have an acceptable academic record, show a financial need, and be endorsed by two North Carolina residents. **Criteria:** Priority is given to students who show that they and their families wish to help themselves and have planned for the future.

**Funds Avail.:** Loans are the primary source of aid available. Students may receive one-half of their total expenses or $2,500 per year, whichever is less. No more than $10,000 may be received per person, and recipients must reapply each year. A repayment schedule is arranged after borrowers leave school. Loans can be obtained at 7.5% interest rate for new borrowers. **To Apply:** A $20 application fee must be submitted with each application. Candidates must then contact the Foundation to arrange an interview. Applications for new candidates are available each year in February. **Deadline:** Generally on a first-come, first-served basis for new applicants. **Contact:** The Director of Student Aid at the above address (see entry 6194).

### • 6199 •
## Winterthur Museum, Garden, and Library
Advanced Studies Office      *Ph:* (302)888-4649
Winterthur, DE 19735      *Fax:* (302)888-4870
*E-mail:* pelliott@winterthur.org
*URL:* http://www.winterthur.com

#### • 6200 • NEH Fellowships *(Doctorate/Fellowship)*

**Purpose:** To support advanced research in America's artistic, cultural, intellectual, and social history. **Focus:** American History—Artistic, Cultural, Intellectual, Social. **Qualif.:** Candidate must be a U.S. citizen or resident for 3 years prior to application and be interested in residential research, using Winterthur's collections. Awards are not intended for dissertation research. Fellows will be chosen according to relevance of project topic to the Library's collections.

**Funds Avail.:** Up to $30,000, depending on duration. **To Apply:** Call or write the director for application form and guidelines, available after August 1. **Deadline:** January 15. Notification by April 1.

**Remarks:** Research fellows are welcome to participate in activities at the University of Delaware, located 30 minutes from Winterthur. **Contact:** Gretchen Duggeln, Research Fellowship Program.

#### • 6201 • Winterthur Research Fellowships *(Doctorate/Fellowship)*

**Purpose:** To support research by academic, museum, and independent scholars, and to support dissertation research. **Focus:** American History—Artistic, Cultural, Intellectual, Social. **Qualif.:** Candidate may be of any nationality. Applicant must be interested in residential research, using Winterthur's collections. Fellows will be chosen according to relevance of project topic to the Library's collections.

**Funds Avail.:** $1,500/month. **To Apply:** Call or write the director for application form and guidelines, available after July 1. **Deadline:** January 15. Notification by April 1.

**Remarks:** Research Fellows are welcome to participate in activities at the University of Delaware, located 30 minutes from Winterthur. **Contact:** Director, Research Fellowship Program, at the above address (see entry 6199).

### • 6202 •
## Wisconsin Congress of Parents and Teachers, Inc.
4797 Hayes Rd., Ste. 2
Madison, WI 53704-3256      *Ph:* (608)244-1455

#### • 6203 • Brookmire-Hastings Scholarship *(Undergraduate/Scholarship)*

**Focus:** Education. **Qualif.:** Applicants must be seniors from Wisconsin public high schools who are entering college to study in the field of education with the goal of becoming teachers. **Criteria:** Committee reads all applications and interviews the top five applicants.

**Funds Avail.:** Two $1,000 scholarships are awarded; $250 per year for four years. **To Apply:** Applications and appropriate information is sent to each Wisconsin public high school in early November. **Deadline:** February 15. **Contact:** Wisconsin PTA at the above address (see entry 6202).

### • 6204 •
## Wisconsin Dental Foundation, Inc.
111 E. Wisconsin Ave., No. 1300
Milwaukee, WI 53202

#### • 6205 • Wisconsin Dental Foundation Achievement Scholarship *(Graduate/Scholarship)*

**Qualif.:** Applicants must be Wisconsin residents enrolled in an ADA-accredited dental school as junior dental students and have a minimum cumulative grade point average of 3.2. **Criteria:** Selection is based on academic record, extracurricular and personal activities, a personal statement, and letters of recommendation.

**Funds Avail.:** One $2,000 scholarship and one $1,000 scholarship. **To Apply:** Applicants must submit a complete application and two letters of recommendation, one from a current dental school instructor and the other from a community leader, professional person, or former employer familiar with the students qualifications. Recommendations should be typed on professional letterhead, include a telephone number, and be submitted directly to the Wisconsin Dental Foundation. **Deadline:** June 1. Winners are notified in September. **Contact:** Selection Committee at the above address (see entry 6204).

#### • 6206 • Wisconsin Dental Foundation/Marquette University Dental Scholarships *(Graduate/Scholarship)*

**Focus:** Dentistry, Dental Hygiene. **Qualif.:** Applicants must be Wisconsin residents enrolled in dentistry or dental hygiene programs at Marquette University. Application is limited to juniors and seniors ranking in the upper 25 percent of their class. **Criteria:** Selection is based on scholarship, motivation, character, and financial need.

**Funds Avail.:** Two $500 scholarships, one to a junior and one to a senior dental student, and two $250 scholarships one to a junior and one to a senior dental hygiene student. **No. of Awards:** 4. **To Apply:** Applicants must submit to the Office of the Dean of the School of Dentistry a biographical statement which assesses the student's motivation, extracurricular activities of a service nature, and initiative in securing financial support, a breif statement discussing the reasons for choosing the dental profession and future plans (practice, location, and specialization, etc.), and a statement of financial need. **Contact:** Office of Student Financial Aids of Marquette University or Selection Committee, Wisconsin Dental Foundation, at the above address (see entry 6204).

#### • 6207 • Wisconsin Dental Foundation Two-Year Scholarships *(Undergraduate/Scholarship)*

**Focus:** Dental Hygiene. **Qualif.:** Applicants must be Wisconsin residents who have completed at least one semester in one of the four technical colleges in Wisconsin in a two-year dental hygiene program with a minimum grade point average of 3.0. **Criteria:** Selection is made by each college based on scholastic achievement, motivation, character, and financial need.

**Funds Avail.:** Four scholarships of $500 each are awarded, one to each technical college. **To Apply:** Applicants must submit a biographical statement discussing motivation, extracurricular activities of a service nature, and initiative in securing financial support, a statement discussing the reasons for choosing dental hygiene as a profession and future career plans, and a breif statement of financial need. Applications must be submitted to the Office of the Chairperson of the Health Sciences Department at the attended college. **Contact:** Selection Committee, Wisconsin Dental Foundation, at the above address (see entry 6204).

## • 6208 •
### Wisconsin Department of Veterans Affairs
PO Box 7843        *Ph:* (608)266-1311
Madison, WI 53707-7843      *Fax:* (608)267-0403
*E-mail:* wdva@mail.state.wi.us

#### • 6209 • Wisconsin Department of Veterans Affairs Part-Time Study Grants *(Graduate, Undergraduate/ Grant)*

**Focus:** General Studies. **Qualif.:** Applicants must be Wisconsin veterans or un-remarried widows or widowers of deceased Wisconsin veterans. The children of living veterans are not eligible, however, dependent children of deceased veterans can generally qualify for a grant during summer or interim sessions. Applicants must be part-time students; 11 credits or less is considered part-time for undergraduates. Eight credits or less is considered part-time for graduate students. Students holding a Bachelor's degree or its equivalent are considered graduate students. Enrollment during summer sessions is considered part-time study. Income limits may be imposed. Generally, schools must be located in Wisconsin but there are very limited exceptions. Persons with a Master's degree or its equivalent are not eligible. Eligible veterans must either have been residents of Wisconsin upon entry into military service or have been continuous residents of Wisconsin for at least five years immediately preceding the date of application. In addition, applicants must be residents of and living in Wisconsin at the time they apply for benefits. The maximum qualifying income limit (Veteran plus spouse) is $47,500 plus $500 for each dependent in excess of two.

**Funds Avail.:** Reimbursement is made following successful course completion. Except as provided in sub. (9), the reimbursement may not exceed 50% of the cost of tuition and fees and shall also be limited to a maximum of 50% of the standard cost for a state resident for tuition and fees for an equivalent undergraduate course at the University of Wisconsin-Madison per course and may not be provided to an individual more that 4 times during any consecutive 12 month period. **To Apply:** Apply through the local County Veterans Service Officer. **Contact:** Local county veterans offices or the Wisconsin Department of Veterans Affairs at the above address (see entry 6208).

#### • 6210 • Wisconsin Department of Veterans Affairs Retraining Grant *(Other/Grant)*

**Purpose:** To provide a recently unemployed or underemployed veteran with financial assistance for employment retraining. **Qualif.:** Applicants must be Wisconsin veterans or widows, widowers, or minor or dependent children of deceased eligible Wisconsin veterans. Applicants must be living in Wisconsin at the time of application and must have been laid-off within the year preceding the date that the application is received. The combined income limit (veteran and spouse) is $36,600. The limit is increased by $500 per dependent in excess of two dependents (income limits are revised periodically).

**Funds Avail.:** The maximum grant is $3,000 for a one-year period. The size of an individual grant will be based on the applicant's need. The funds may be used for books, fees and tuition, and also living expenses. **To Apply:** The local County Veterans Service Officer can assist veterans in establishing eligibility and applying. **Contact:** Local veterans offices or the Wisconsin Department of Veterans Affairs at the above address (see entry 6208).

## • 6211 •
### Wisconsin League for Nursing
2121 E. Newport Ave.
Milwaukee, WI 53211      *Ph:* (414)332-6271

#### • 6212 • Wisconsin League for Nursing Scholarships *(Undergraduate/Scholarship)*

**Focus:** Nursing. **Qualif.:** All applicants must be residents of Wisconsin. Those already enrolled in nursing school must be enrolled in a NLN accredited Wisconsin school of nursing; have at least one half the hours necessary for graduation completion; show financial need; show achievement in quality of attainment, both in scholastics and personal characteristics. High school seniors must already be accepted into an NLN accredited school of nursing, show financial need, demonstrate scholastic excellence and leadership potential. **Criteria:** Awards are granted based on financial need, scholastic achievement and personal characteristics.

**Funds Avail.:** $500. **To Apply:** Applicants must write for further details.

**Remarks:** Potential applicants who are currently enrolled in an accredited nursing school must NOT contact the WLN. Award availability and applications are forwarded to and distributed from accredited schools. Potential high school senior applicants must contact the WLN office by mail to request application materials.

## • 6213 •
### Wisconsin Space Grant Consortium
University of Wisconsin-Milwaukee
333 Architecture and Urban Planning
   Bldg.
PO Box 413      *Ph:* (414)229-3878
Milwaukee, WI 53201-0413      *Fax:* (414)229-6976
*E-mail:* wsgc@uwm.edu
*URL:* http://www.uwm.edu/dept/WSGC

#### • 6214 • Wisconsin Space Grant Consortium Graduate Fellowships *(Graduate/Fellowship)*

**Purpose:** To provide research opportunities. **Focus:** Science related fields. **Qualif.:** Applicants must be U.S. citizens, enrolled full-time in a graduate degree program at a WSGC institution; have a minimum 3.0 GPA and good GRE scores. **Criteria:** Based on potential in the field and programs of research, scholarship, or design related to space.

**Funds Avail.:** Up to $5000 stipend. **To Apply:** A completed application, including a resume; research, technology, or design proposal; name of an advisor/mentor to supervise the research; and two letters of recommendation must be submitted. An application can be downloaded from the WSGC website.

#### • 6215 • Wisconsin Space Grant Consortium Undergraduate Research Awards *(Undergraduate/ Grant)*

**Purpose:** To allow students to conduct small research projects of their own. **Focus:** Aerospace-related fields. **Qualif.:** Applicants must be U.S. citizens attending a WSGC institution full-time; have a minimum 3.0 GPA and good SAT/ACT scores. Students from small colleges and universities, and from departments with newly developing space research infrastructure, are especially encouraged to apply.

**Funds Avail.:** Up to $3000 stipend. **To Apply:** Completed application, a brief proposal, and two letters of recommendation must be submitted. The official application can be downloaded from the WSGC website.

**• 6216 • Wisconsin Space Grant Consortium Undergraduate Scholarships** *(Undergraduate/ Scholarship)*

**Focus:** Aerospace, space science or related fields. **Qualif.:** Applicants must be U.S. citizens and full-time students in an undergraduate program at a WSGC institution; have a minimum 3.0 GPA and good SAT/ACT scores.

**Funds Avail.:** Up to $2000 stipend. **To Apply:** Completed application and two letters of recommendation must be submitted.

**• 6217 •**
**Women Band Directors National Association**
345 Overlook Dr.
West Lafayette, IN 47906
*E-mail:* agwright@gte.net

**• 6218 • Kathryn G. Siphers Scholarships** *(Undergraduate/Scholarship)*

**Purpose:** To support young college women presently preparing to be band directors. **Focus:** Music Education. **Qualif.:** Applicants must be female instrumental music majors enrolled as juniors or seniors in a university and working toward a degree in music education with the intention of becoming band directors. **Criteria:** Grade point average must be acceptable.

**Funds Avail.:** $300. **No. of Awards:** 1. **To Apply:** Applications must be requested. **Deadline:** November 15. **Contact:** Women Band Directors National Association at the above address (see entry 6217).

**• 6219 • Virginia Volkwein Memorial Scholarships** *(Undergraduate/Scholarship)*

**Purpose:** To support young college women presently preparing to be band directors. **Focus:** Music Education. **Qualif.:** Applicants must be female instrumental music majors enrolled as juniors or seniors in a university and working toward a degree in music education with the intention of becoming band directors.

**Funds Avail.:** $300. **No. of Awards:** 1. **To Apply:** Applications must be requested. **Deadline:** November 15. **Contact:** Women Band Directors National Association at the above address (see entry 6217).

**• 6220 •**
**Women in Communications, Inc. - Detroit Chapter**
1659 Dennet Ln.
Rochester Hills, MI 48307          *Ph:* (810)652-1460

**• 6221 • Mary Butler Scholarship** *(Graduate, Undergraduate/Scholarship)*

**Focus:** Journalism, Communications. **Qualif.:** Applicants must be Michigan residents attending a Michigan college or university. They must also be junior, senior, or graduate students majoring in journalism or communications. Applicants must be recommended by a faculty member, department chairman, and/or a communications professional with whom the applicant has a working relationship. They must be first-rate students who have already demonstrated communications skills. **Criteria:** The scholarship is awarded to a student who has faced a personal challenge.

**Funds Avail.:** $500. **No. of Awards:** 1. **To Apply:** Applicants must provide a description of career goals and any personal challenges

experienced, examples of how communications skills are practiced outside the classroom, recommendations from journalism or communications faculty members and/or professionals, and three samples of work (published, broadcast, or completed for a class). A self-addressed, stamped envelope must be included for return requests. **Deadline:** Beginning of April. **Contact:** Application forms may be obtained from WICI Scholarship Chair at the above address (see entry 6220).

**• 6222 • Lucy Corbett Scholarship** *(Graduate, Undergraduate/Scholarship)*

**Focus:** Journalism, Communications. **Qualif.:** Applicants must be Michigan residents and juniors, seniors, or graduate students majoring in journalism or communications at a Michigan college or university. They must be recommended by a faculty member, department chairman, and/or a communications professional with whom the applicant has a working relationship.

**Funds Avail.:** $500-$1,000 depending on funding. **No. of Awards:** 1. **To Apply:** Applicants must provide a description of career goals and strategy, examples of how communications skills are practiced outside the classroom, and recommendations from journalism or communications faculty members and/or professionals. They must also submit three samples of their work (published, broadcast, or completed for a class). A self-addressed, stamped envelope must be included for return requests. **Deadline:** Beginning of April. **Contact:** Application forms may be obtained from the WICI Scholarship Chair at the above address (see entry 6220).

**• 6223 •**
**Women in Communications, Inc. - Seattle Chapter**
217 9th Ave. N
Seattle, WA 98109          *Ph:* (206)682-9424

**• 6224 • Seattle Professional Chapter of Women in Communications Annual Communications Scholarship** *(Graduate, Undergraduate/Scholarship)*

**Focus:** Communications. **Qualif.:** Applicants must be Washington state residents and/or registered students at Washington state four-year colleges; and juniors, seniors or graduate students with declared majors in communications. **Criteria:** Awards are made based on excellence in communications, positive contribution toward communications on campus or in the community, scholastic achievement, financial need, and samples of writing, tapes, portfolios, campaigns, clips, etc. available from students.

**Funds Avail.:** $1000 per award. **No. of Awards:** 2. **To Apply:** Applicants must submit a completed application form, transcripts of post-high school academic work, current resume, and any samples of work. **Deadline:** March 2. **Contact:** Susanna Tull, WICI Scholarship Chair.

**• 6225 •**
**Women of the Evangelical Lutheran Church in America - Scholarship Program**
8765 W. Higgins Rd.
Chicago, IL 60631-4189          *Ph:* (312)380-2700

**• 6226 • Women of the ELCA Scholarship** *(Graduate, Postgraduate, Undergraduate/Scholarship)*

**Purpose:** To provide financial assistance to ELCA women who wish to pursue postsecondary school education. **Qualif.:** Applicants must be ELCA laywomen, 21 years or older, and post

## Women of the Evangelical Lutheran Church in America - Scholarship Program (continued)

high school students with a two-year interruption in schooling. They cannot be studying for ordination, deaconess, or church-certified positions. Applicants also must provide some academic record beyond high school, have clear educational goals, and demonstrate Christian commitment, scholastic ability, and financial need.

**Funds Avail.:** $500 to $2,000 available in two installments. **To Apply:** Applications are sent out after October 1 of each year. Official transcripts and/or evidence of admission to school and pastoral and academic references are among the requirements. **Deadline:** March 1. Notification is made May through June. **Contact:** Women of ELCA at the above address (see entry 6225). Toll-free telephone: 800-638-3522.

## • 6227 •
## Women in Scholarly Publishing
c/o Kim Sutherland
University of Nevada Press
MS 166
Reno, NV 89557                    Ph: (702)784-6573

### • 6228 •  Women in Scholarly Publishing Career Development Fund (Professional Development/Other)

**Purpose:** To assist members of Women in Scholarly Publishing in workshops, seminars, and other meetings aimed at professional development in scholarly publishing. **Focus:** Publishing. **Qualif.:** Applicants must be a member of WISP for at least one year before applying for a grant.

**Funds Avail.:** Up to 75 percent of total costs of meeting, not to exceed $400.

**Remarks:** WISP does not award traditional scholarships and does not administer loans. **Contact:** Sian Hunter White.

## • 6229 •
## Women's Army Corps Veterans Association
PO Box 5577
Fort Mc Clellan, AL 36205         Ph: (205)820-6824

### • 6230 •  Edith Nourse Rogers Scholarship Fund (Undergraduate/Scholarship)

**Purpose:** To assist selected students at Boston University in the completion of their studies. **Qualif.:** Female dependents of U.S. veterans majoring in Government or Political Science who are enrolled full-time at Boston University. **Criteria:** The award is based on merit with need as a secondary factor.

**Funds Avail.:** One $1,500 scholarship. **Deadline:** April 1. **Contact:** Mary Callahan at the above address (see entry 6229).

## • 6231 •
## Women's Medical Association of New York Financial Assistance Fund
33 E. 70th St.                     Ph: (212)744-3473
New York, NY 10021-4946           Fax: (212)744-3483

### • 6232 •  Women's Medical Association of New York Financial Assistance Fund Loans (Doctorate/Award, Loan)

**Purpose:** Provide loans to third and fourth year women students attending medical school in the New York City area, and travel awards for fourth year medical students. **Focus:** Medicine. **Criteria:** Students in good standing in medical school with an interest in women's health.

**Funds Avail.:** Loans currently $2,500; $500 for Travel Awards. **No. of Awards:** 8. **To Apply:** Submit application, 100 word essay, financial aid history, transcript, and faculty letter of recommendation. **Deadline:** March 15. **Contact:** Anne C. Carter, MD.

## • 6233 •
## Women's National Farm and Garden Association, Inc.
13 Davis Drive
Saginaw, MI 48602                  Ph: (517)793-1714

### • 6234 •  Sarah B. Tyson Fellowship (Professional Development/Fellowship)

**Purpose:** To support advanced study by women in agriculture or horticulture. **Focus:** Agriculture, Horticulture, and allied subjects. **Qualif.:** Applicant must be a woman with several years of experience in agriculture, horticulture, or a related field. The fellowship supports advanced study at recognized educational institutions in the United States.

**Funds Avail.:** $1,000. **To Apply:** Write to the chairperson for application guidelines; there is no application form. Submit letter of application, including a description of educational background, study proposal, writing samples, health certificate, and a small photograph. Letters of reference are also required. **Deadline:** April 15. **Contact:** Mrs. Elmer Braun, Chairperson, at the above address (see entry 6233).

## • 6235 •
## Women's Research and Education Institute
1750 New York Ave. NW, Ste. 350    Ph: (202)628-0444
Washington, DC 20006-5301         Fax: (202)628-0458
E-mail: wrei@wrei.org
URL: http://www.wrei.org

The Women's Research and Education Institute is a nonprofit organization that provides information, research and policy analysis to the bipartisan Congressional Caucus for Women's Issues and to other members of Congress.

### • 6236 •  Congressional Fellowships on Women and Public Policy (Doctorate, Graduate/Fellowship)

**Purpose:** To provide opportunities for graduate students to work with Congress on policy issues affecting women. **Focus:** Public Policy, U.S. Congress, Women's Studies. **Qualif.:** Applicant must be enrolled full-time in a master's or doctoral degree program at an accredited institution in the United States. Preference is given to candidates who have completed at least nine hours of graduate coursework and who have a demonstrated interest in research and political activity related to women's social and political status. The department chair at candidate's home institution must endorse the application and agree to give graduate credit for the fellowship. Fellowships are tenable in Washington, D.C., where fellows work as legislative aides in Congressional offices and on committee staffs.

**Funds Avail.:** $9,500 stipend, plus $500 health insurance allowance and up to $1,500 tuition reimbursement. **No. of Awards:** Varies between 6-10. **To Apply:** Send a self-addressed, stamped envelope to WREI, along with a request for an application. Submit application in triplicate with a 1,500-word essay and transcripts. Four letters of recommendation must be sent directly to WREI from the referees. Semi-finalists are interviewed. **Deadline:** Mid-March. Fellowships are announced by June 1.

**Remarks:** Applicant is required to work as office personnel in the Congressional Office in Washington, DC, from August through April. **Contact:** Fellowship Program Director at the above address (see entry 6235).

• 6237 •
## Women's Southern California Golf Association - Gloria Fecht Memorial Scholarship Fund
402 W. Arrow Hwy., Ste. 10          *Ph:* (714)592-1281
San Dimas, CA 91773                 *Fax:* (909)592-7542
*E-mail:* wscga@womensgolf.org
*URL:* http://www.womensgolf.org

• 6238 • **Gloria Fecht Memorial Scholarship**
*(Undergraduate/Scholarship)*

**Purpose:** To financially support a female student golfer in her chosen educational career. **Focus:** General Studies. **Qualif.:** Candidates must be female, Southern California residents pursuing a degree in a four-year accredited college or university, have a minimum 3.0 GPA, and have an interest in golf.

**Funds Avail.:** $1,000-3,000 per year; renewable. 15 to 28 academic scholarships are given annually and are renewable for four years; eligibility must be proven each year. **No. of Awards:** 15-20. **To Apply:** Applications must include academic records; college entrance exam and SAT scores; letters of recommendation depicting character, sportsmanship, leadership potential, and outlining the candidate's extracurricular activities; and proof of financial need that considers personal circumstances, but is not intended to preclude students from middle class families. **Deadline:** March 1. **Contact:** The Women's Southern California Golf Association at the above address (see entry 6237).

• 6239 •
## Women's Sports Foundation
Eisenhower Park              *Ph:* (516)542-4700
East Meadow, NY 11554        *Fax:* (516)542-4716
                             *Free:* 800-227-3988
*E-mail:* wosport@aol.com
*URL:* http://www.womenssportsfoundation.org

• 6240 • **Travel and Training Grant** *(Undergraduate/Grant)*

**Purpose:** To provide direct assistance to aspiring female athletes with successful competitive records who have the potential to achieve even higher performance levels and rankings. **Focus:** General Studies. **Qualif.:** Applicants must be female athletes with a regional and/or national ranking or successful record within their sports group. **Criteria:** Selection is based on financial need, present and potential level of ranking, lack of support from traditional sources, role of award in continued participation and advancement, contribution to the greater visibility of female athletes, and ability to present a plan for reimbursing the grant in the future whether financially or through coaching, administering, or otherwise contributing to women's sports.

**Funds Avail.:** Up to $1,500. Assistance is available for coaching, specialized training, equipment and/or travel. Grants are offered one time per year. **No. of Awards:** 30-100. **To Apply:** An informational brochure, current applications, and guidelines are available from the Foundation. **Deadline:** Applications must be received at least four months in advance of when the funds are to be used. Deadlines are November 15 for the February 15 grant. **Contact:** The Women's Sports Foundation at the above address (see entry 6239).

• 6241 • **The Women's Sports Foundation Minority Internship Program** *(Graduate, Postgraduate, Undergraduate/Internship)*

**Purpose:** To provide interns with practical experience in a not-for-profit organizational setting and to foster opportunity for uncovering and utilizing resources, forming business contacts, and clarifying personal goals and objectives. **Focus:** General Studies. **Qualif.:** Applicants must be women of color who are undergraduate, college graduate, or graduate students or women in a career change. They must be highly motivated individuals interested in pursuing a sports-related career.

**Funds Avail.:** Full-time interns work 35 hours per week for six to twelve months and receive a stipend of $1,000 per month. Special arrangements may be made for shorter or longer periods of time. Part-time internships are also available. All interns work out of the national office. **No. of Awards:** Four to six. **To Apply:** Applicants must send a completed application with two letters of recommendation. **Deadline:** Applications should be received at least two months before desired starting date.

**Remarks:** This program is named for two exemplary athletes, Olympian Jackie Joyner-Kersee and tennis great Zina Garrison. **Contact:** The Women's Sports Foundation at the above address (see entry 6239).

• 6242 •
## Women's Transportation Seminar
WTS National Headquarters
The Engineering Center
One Walnut St.              *Ph:* (617)367-3273
Boston, MA 02108           *Fax:* (617)227-6783

• 6243 • **Helene Overly Scholarship** *(Graduate/Scholarship)*

**Purpose:** To support studies related to transportation by female graduate students. **Focus:** Transportation. **Qualif.:** Applicants must be women enrolled in a graduate program at an accredited U.S. institution, and have a grade point average of at least 3.0/4.0. They must also intend to pursue a transportation-related career.

**Funds Avail.:** $3,000. **No. of Awards:** One nationally. **To Apply:** Application materials are available from, and should be submitted to, the chapter of Women's Transportation Seminar in candidate's home state. After reviewing applications, each chapter may nominate one candidate for consideration by the national scholarship committee. If a candidate lives in a state that does not have a chapter, then she may write to the national headquarters at the above address for application form and guidelines. **Deadline:** February 15. **Contact:** Anne Poole, National Scholarships Chair, at the above address (see entry 6242).

• 6244 •
## Women's Western Golf Foundation
393 Ramsay Rd.
Deerfield, IL 60015                    *Ph:* (708)945-0451

### • 6245 • Women's Western Golf Foundation Scholarship *(Undergraduate/Scholarship)*

**Purpose:** To provide financial support for college to female high school seniors who are involved in golf. **Focus:** General Studies. **Qualif.:** Graduating, female high school seniors who are accepted at an accredited university are eligible. **Criteria:** Applicants will be judged on academic records, financial status, involvement with (not excellence in) the sport of golf, and character.

**Funds Avail.:** Stipend of $8,000 may be renewed given satisfactory academic progress. **No. of Awards:** 17 **To Apply:** Two application forms must be filled out: a preliminary form followed by a second form if the applicant qualifies. **Deadline:** April 5. **Contact:** Women's Western Golf Foundation at the above address (see entry 6244).

### • 6246 •
## Woods Hole Oceanographic Institution
The Fellowship Committee
Education Office, Clark Laboratory
360 Woods Hole Rd.                    *Ph:* (508)289-2219
Woods Hole, MA 02543                  *Fax:* (508)457-2188
*E-mail:* education@whoi.edu
*URL:* http://www.whoi.edu

### • 6247 • Postdoctoral Fellowships in Ocean Science and Engineering *(Postdoctorate/Fellowship)*

**Purpose:** To further the education and training of scientists with an interest in oceanography/oceanographic engineering. **Focus:** Biology, Molecular Biology, Microbiology, Chemistry, Engineering, Geology, Geophysics Mathematics, Meteorology, Physics. **Qualif.:** Applicant may be of any nationality, but must be a new or recent recipient of the Ph.D. who has an interest in oceanographic sciences or engineering. Scientists with more than three or four years of postdoctoral experience are not normally eligible to apply. Awards are tenable at the Institute.

**Funds Avail.:** Fellows receive an 18-month stipend at $42,000 per year, plus health insurance, research, relocation, and travel allowances. **No. of Awards:** 6-10. **To Apply:** Write to the fellowship committee or see website for application form and guidelines. Submit form with transcripts, at least three recommendations, one page abstract of doctoral dissertation, and a concise statement of research interests, including both general career plans and specific interest in the award. **Deadline:** Materials must be received by January 15. Awards are announced in early March. **Contact:** Fellowship Committee at the above address (see entry 6246).

### • 6248 • Research Fellowships in Marine Policy *(Postdoctorate/Fellowship)*

**Purpose:** To allow qualified individuals in the social and natural sciences to apply their training and expertise to the economic, legal, and political issues that arise from uses of the world's oceans. **Focus:** Oceanography and related disciplines, including Anthropology, Economics, Engineering, Environmental Studies, Geography, International Law, International Relations, Marine Policy, Marine Sciences, Political Science, Public Policy, Sociology, Statistics. **Qualif.:** Applicant may be of any nationality, but must have a Ph.D. or have earned equivalent professional qualifications through career experience. Applicant may be a recent degree recipient or a senior scholar on sabbatical leave.

Emphasis is placed on multidisciplinary research to advance the conservation and management of coastal and marine resources.

**Funds Avail.:** $42,000 per year, plus health insurance and research and travel funds. **No. of Awards:** One per year. **To Apply:** Write to the dean of graduate studies or see website for application form and guidelines. Submit form with transcripts, at least three professional references, abstract of doctoral dissertation, and a preliminary research proposal. **Deadline:** January 15. Notification by March 31. **Contact:** Dean of Graduate Studies at the above address (see entry 6246).

### • 6249 • Woods Hole Oceanographic Institution Summer Student Fellowships *(Undergraduate/Fellowship)*

**Purpose:** To allow upper-class undergraduates to pursue independent research projects in oceanography and/or marine policy. **Focus:** Marine Policy, Marine Sciences, Oceanography, Applied Ocean Physics, Engineering, Biology, Chemistry, Geology, Geophysics, Physics, Meteorology. **Qualif.:** Applicant may be of any nationality, but must be a junior or senior in college majoring in one of the areas of study listed above. Candidate should have at least a tentative interest in a career in oceanography and/or marine policy. Awards are tenable at the Institution.

**Funds Avail.:** Fellows receive a $4,020 stipend, plus travel allowance. **To Apply:** Write to the fellowship committee for application forms and guidelines. **Deadline:** March 1. Notification is by mid-April. **Contact:** Fellowship Committee at the above address (see entry 6246).

### • 6250 •
## Carter G. Woodson Institute - University of Virginia
102 Minor Hall                        *Ph:* (804)924-3109
Charlottesville, VA 22903             *Fax:* (804)924-8820

### • 6251 • Afro-American and African Studies Fellowships *(Doctorate, Postdoctorate/Fellowship)*

**Purpose:** To support projects about Africa, Africans, and peoples of African descent in North, Central, and South America, and the Caribbean, past and present. **Focus:** African American Studies, African Studies. **Qualif.:** Applicant may be of any nationality. Candidate may be either a predoctoral student who has completed all degree requirements except the dissertation, or a postdoctoral scholar. Employees of the University of Virginia are not eligible to apply. Awards are tenable at the University of Virginia. Predoctoral fellows become visiting graduate students attached to their respective disciplinary departments. Postdoctoral fellows receive the status of visiting scholars in their fields. There are no formal service or teaching requirements, but fellows are expected to be in residence at the University and participate in its intellectual activities.

**Funds Avail.:** Predoctoral: $12,500/year; postdoctoral: $25,000. **No. of Awards:** Varies. **To Apply:** There is no application form. Submit a letter of interest in the fellowship program; curriculum vitae; a seven-page project description, including project title, a detailed research plan, and significance of the project to Afro-American or African studies; and a statement of plans for publication of research results. Three letters of recommendation must be sent directly to the Woodson Institute. Predoctoral applicants must also send graduate transcripts. **Deadline:** December 2. Notification in March. **Contact:** William E. Jackson, Associate Director for Research, at the above address (see entry 6250).

## • 6252 •
## Woodstock School of Art

Route 212, PO Box 338   *Ph:* (914)679-2388
Woodstock, NY 12498   *Fax:* (914)679-2388
*E-mail:* precipice@ulster.net

### • 6253 • Artists Workplace Fellowships *(Professional Development/Fellowship)*

**Purpose:** To provide fellowships on a competitive basis for work in drawing, painting, sculpture, or graphics. **Qualif.:** Any artist may apply. Recipients are expected to work a minimum of five hours per day in the allotted work space.

**Funds Avail.:** Each fellow will be provided work space appropriate to his or her requirements. Each fellow will also receive a $500 stipend. **No. of Awards:** 4. **To Apply:** Applicants must write for an application. **Deadline:** March 9.

**Remarks:** Sponsored in part through a grant given by the decentralization program of the New York State Council on the Arts administered by the Dutchess Country Arts Council. **Contact:** Paula Nelson.

## • 6254 •
## Woodswomen, Inc.

25 W. Diamond Lake Rd.   *Ph:* (612)822-3809
Minneapolis, MN 55419-1926   *Fax:* (612)822-3814
  *Free:* 800-279-0555

### • 6255 • Woodswomen Scholarship Fund *(Other/ Grant, Scholarship)*

**Purpose:** To foster the development of emotional, social, physical, and intellectual skills in women through involvement in outdoor activities. **Qualif.:** Must be a member of Woodswomen. **Criteria:** Includes financial need, outdoor experience, residency, trip selection.

**Funds Avail.:** Limited, but all applications are reviewed.

**Remarks:** Woodswomen trips are open to all women, and some include children too. Average award $20-125.

## • 6256 •
## Worcester County Horticultural Society

Tower Hill Botanic Garden
PO Box 598   *Ph:* (508)869-6111
Boylston, MA 01505-0598   *Fax:* (508)869-0314
*E-mail:* thbg@towerhillbg.org
*URL:* http://www.towerhillbg.org

### • 6257 • Worcester County Horticultural Society Scholarship *(Graduate, Undergraduate/Scholarship)*

**Focus:** Horticulture. **Qualif.:** Applicants must be entering their junior or senior year of an undergraduate or graduate degree program. They must be residents of New England or attending a New England college or university and majoring in horticulture or a horticulture-related field. **Criteria:** Selections are based upon the candidate's interest in horticulture, sincerity of purpose, academic performance, and financial need.

**Funds Avail.:** Scholarships range in value from $500 to $2,000. **Deadline:** May 1. Notification is made in June. **Contact:** Sue Cayford at the above address (see entry 6256)for more information and applications.

## • 6258 •
## World Health Organization

Human Resources Management
Avenue Appia   *Ph:* 22 791 2111
CH-1211 Geneva 27, Switzerland   *Fax:* 22 791 0746
*The World Health Organization is the international health agency of the United Nations.*

### • 6259 • WHO Fellowships *(Postdoctorate, Professional Development/Fellowship)*

**Purpose:** To provide international opportunities for training and study in health matters. **Focus:** Health Education, Health Sciences, Medical Technology, Medicine, Public Health Administration. **Qualif.:** Applicant may be of any nationality whose government is a member of the United Nations. Applicant should be a doctor, nurse, sanitarian, or other health professional working in his/her native country who wishes to pursue international studies on a topic directly connected to the home country's health program. Candidate must have at least two years of experience in the proposed health subject and must have exhausted all opportunities available in the home country for study of that subject. Applicant must be sponsored by the home country's national health organization (i.e., the ministry of health or equivalent authority). The study program must be approved by the home government, as well as by WHO. Fellows may use their awards to attend courses organized or assisted by WHO; to support postgraduate certificate, degree, or diploma study; to observe services and practices in other countries; or to participate in studies and research. Awards are not available for attendance at conferences, meetings, or congresses; or for studies that complement or supplement programs sponsored by other agencies. Fellows are required to return to the home country for at least three years immediately following the fellowship to serve the national health administration.

**Funds Avail.:** Varies; includes tuition fees, travel and living allowances. **To Apply:** Write to the Ministry of Health in home country for application form and guidelines. **Deadline:** Varies; applications must reach WHO regional offices at least six months before the proposed start of fellowship.

**Remarks:** WHO Regional Office for Southeast Asia, World Health House, Indraprastha Estate, Ring Road new Delhi-1, India. Candidates are strongly discouraged from writing to Geneva office.

### • 6260 • WHO Fellowships for Canadian Citizens *(Postdoctorate/Fellowship)*

**Purpose:** To provide observation and travel related to health matters outside Canada and to promote the international exchange of scientific knowledge and techniques related to health. **Focus:** Health, Public Health. **Qualif.:** Applicants must have completed formal education and training and have not less than two years professional experience. Applicants must be in a position to have an impact on others through teaching and/or Public Health Service upon return.

**Funds Avail.:** $5,000 to be applied to travel and living expenses. **To Apply:** Apply to Mr. Mark Hundman, Canadian Society for International Health, 170 Laurier Ave. W., Ste. 902, Ottawa, Ontario K1P 5V5 Canada.

### • 6261 • WHO Fellowships and Research Training Grants *(Graduate, Other, Postdoctorate/Fellowship)*

**Purpose:** To provide training or study not available in candidate's own country, and to allow them to attend formal courses or to study the services and practices in other countries. **Focus:** Medicine, Health Sciences. **Qualif.:** Applicants must be citizens of member countries of the World Health Organization. To receive research training grants and visiting scientist grants from the WHO at the Headquarter's level, applicants must be working in

## World Health Organization (continued)

collaboration with the Special Programme of Research, Development and Research Training in Human Reproduction and the Special Programme for Research and Training in Tropical Diseases. Fellowships in other areas of study are available through the governments of member states. Common subjects of study include public health, teacher training in health sciences, postgraduate studies in medicine, and surgery.

**Funds Avail.:** Fellowships provide for attendance at formal courses or study of services and practices in other countries. **To Apply:** Candidates should contact the Ministry of Health, or the corresponding national health administration, of their country of origin, which will advise them on the procedure for application. **Contact:** The Health Department of the applicant's own country. WHO discourages contacting their Geneva office.

### • 6262 • WHO Fellowships for U.S. Citizens (Postdoctorate/Fellowship)

**Purpose:** To provide observation and travel related to health matters outside the U.S. and to promote the international exchange of scientific knowledge and techniques related to health. **Focus:** Health, Public Health. **Qualif.:** Applicants must have completed formal education and training and have not less than two years professional experience. Applicants must be in a position to have an impact on others through teaching and/or Public Health Service upon return.

**Funds Avail.:** Cost of travel as well as modest monthly living allowance. **To Apply:** Apply to Mr. Lyndall G. Beamer, Secretary, WHO Fellowships Selection Committee, Office of International Health Affairs, Health Resources and Services Administration, Parklawn Bldg., Rm. 14-14, 5600 Fishers Ln., Rockville, Maryland 20857. **Deadline:** September 30.

### • 6263 •
## World Leisure and Recreation Association

c/o Dr. A.H. Grossman
New York University
Education Building, Ste. 1200
35 West 4 St.
New York, NY 10012-1172          *Ph:* (212)998-5600
                                  *Fax:* (212)995-4192
*E-mail:* arnold.grossman@nyu.edu

### • 6264 • Tom and Ruth Rivers International Scholarships (Graduate, Undergraduate/Scholarship)

**Purpose:** To provide opportunities for students to expand their understanding of world leisure and recreation trends, issues, philosophies, and problems. **Focus:** Leisure, Recreation. **Qualif.:** Applicant may be of any nationality. Applicant must be a senior undergraduate with a grade point average of 3.2/4.0, or a graduate student with a grade point average of 3.5/4.0, in a college or university program with a major in recreation, leisure studies/ services, or resources. Candidate must have a demonstrated interest in recreation and leisure on an international level, and should have either volunteer or paid work experience in the recreation/leisure services field. Scholarships are tenable at pre-selected international meetings, conferences, and conventions. **Criteria:** Qualifications are rated and ranked on a yearly basis by selection committee. Top ranked students are selected.

**Funds Avail.:** Varies; includes registration fee, housing, and round-trip airfare. **No. of Awards:** 2-4 per year. **To Apply:** Write for application form and instructions. Submit application with letter of recommendation from faculty member or advisor. Candidates who are not U.S. or Canadian citizens must also submit a letter of recommendation from WLRA member in home country. **Deadline:** February 1. **Contact:** Dr. Arnold H. Grossman, Chair, at the above address (see entry 6263).

### • 6265 •
## World Modeling Association

212 E. Waldburg St. Apt. A
Savannah, GA 31401-6550

### • 6266 • World Model Awards (Other, Professional Development/Scholarship)

**Purpose:** To assist individuals interested in fashion modeling and/ or show business. **Focus:** Fashion Merchandising, Distributive Education, Theater. **Qualif.:** Applicants must be at least 16 years old. **Criteria:** Based on potential to succeed and the desire for a future in the field of modeling or entertainment.

**Funds Avail.:** $500 per award. **To Apply:** Applicants must submit a photograph, a short 100-word essay, and a recommendation from a guidance counselor or teacher. **Deadline:** February.

**Remarks:** Both sexes may apply. **Contact:** Ruth Tolman at the above address (see entry 6265).

### • 6267 •
## World Press Institute

1635 Summit Ave.
Macalester College                *Ph:* (612)696-6360
St. Paul, MN 55105                 *Fax:* (612)696-6306
*E-mail:* WIP@MAC.CC.MACALSTR.EDU; WPI@
    MACALESTER.EDU
*URL:* http://www.MACALESTER.EDU/~WPI

### • 6268 • World Press Institute Fellowships (Professional Development/Fellowship)

**Purpose:** To help international journalists report about the United States from a personally informed background through a rigorous four-month schedule of study, travel and interviews. **Focus:** American History, Journalism, Economics, Government, Politics, Business and Culture. **Qualif.:** Applicant must be a national of a country other than the United States. Applicant must be a journalist with five years of full-time professional experience. Candidate must be fluent in written and spoken English. Fellowships are restricted to international journalists selected as WPI Fellows at Macalester College.

**Funds Avail.:** $25,000 **No. of Awards:** 10. **To Apply:** Applicants should write or call the Institute for application form and guidelines. **Deadline:** December 31. **Contact:** John Hodowanic at the above address (see entry 6267).

### • 6269 •
## WRKL

PO Box 910
Pomona, NY 10970                   *Ph:* (914)354-2000

### • 6270 • Nelson A. Rockefeller Minority Internships (Undergraduate/Internship)

**Purpose:** To give applicants an opportunity to work in the broadcasting industry and identify potential areas of specialization. **Focus:** Communications. **Qualif.:** Candidates must be Black, Hispanic, American Indian, Aleut, or Asiatic. They must be high school or undergraduate students between the ages of 17 and 21. Candidates must also be residents of New York, or students attending school in New York, who are first-time entrants in the internship program and the broadcasting industry. **Criteria:** Applicants are judged on written and verbal communication skills.

**Funds Avail.:** Interns are paid by the hour based on the current minimum wage. **To Apply:** Applicants must submit a personalized letter of application expressing their area of interest. Finalists are then chosen for an interview. **Deadline:** April 30. **Contact:** Morton M. Siegel, General Manager, at the above address (see entry 6269).

---

## • 6271 •
### Xerox Corporation Scholarship Program
University of Rochester
Wallis Hall
Director of Admissions
Rochester, NY 14627
*E-mail:* admit@macmail.cc.rochester.edu; admission@rochester.edu
*URL:* http://www.rochester.edu

*Ph:* (716)275-3221
*Fax:* (716)756-8480
*Free:* 888-822-2256

### • 6272 • Xerox Scholarships *(Undergraduate/Scholarship)*

**Purpose:** To recognize an outstanding social sciences/humanities student. **Focus:** Humanities, Social Sciences. **Qualif.:** Candidates must be recipients of the Xerox Award to be eligible for the Xerox Scholarship. **Criteria:** Selection is based on academic merit.

**Funds Avail.:** A minimum $6,000 over four years. **To Apply:** Students must submit a completed University of Rochester application. **Deadline:** January 15. **Contact:** Pam Roth, at the above address (see entry 6271).

---

## • 6273 •
### Yaddo
PO Box 395
Union Ave.
Saratoga Springs, NY 12866-0395
*E-mail:* yaddo@yaddo.org

*Ph:* (518)584-0746
*Fax:* (518)584-1312

### • 6274 • Yaddo Residencies *(Professional Development/Other)*

**Purpose:** To challenge writers, visual artists, composers, choreographers, performance artists, and film and video artists to challenge themselves by providing them uninterrupted time to work, good working conditions, and a supportive community. **Focus:** Writing, Visual Arts, Musical Composition, Choreography, Performance Art, Film and Video Art. **Qualif.:** Candidate may be of any nationality. Applicant must have achieved professional standing by having work published, exhibited, or (in the case of composers) performed. Residencies are tenable at Yaddo and are available year-round. **Criteria:** Guests are selected on the basis of review by other professional artists.

**Funds Avail.:** Room, board, studio space. **No. of Awards:** 190-200 annually. **To Apply:** Write for application guidelines. Submit application with fee ($20). **Deadline:** January 15, August 1. **Contact:** Admission Committee at the above address (see entry 6273).

---

## • 6275 •
### Yale Center for British Art
1080 Chapel St.
PO Box 208280
New Haven, CT 06520-8280
*E-mail:* bacinfo@minerva.cis.yale.edu
*URL:* http://www.cis.yale.edu/yups/bac/entrance/html

*Ph:* (203)432-2850
*Fax:* (203)432-9628

### • 6276 • Paul Mellon Centre Fellowship *(Doctorate, Graduate/Fellowship)*

**Purpose:** To support research in any field of British art or architecture before 1960. **Focus:** Art History, British Art, British Architecture. **Qualif.:** Candidates may be of any nationality but must normally be enrolled in a graduate program at a U.S. university and be a resident outside of Great Britain. Graduates of U.S. universities who are enrolled elsewhere or who are pursuing more advanced research in the field may also be considered. Fellowships are tenable at the Paul Mellon Centre for Studies in British Art, London. Fellows are expected to be in residence in or near London for at least eight months during the tenure of the award.

**Funds Avail.:** Predoctoral: $17,500 stipend plus research and travel allowances, up to $500, health insurance, round-trip airfare from the U.S., and staff and library privileges. **No. of Awards:** 1. **To Apply:** Applications should be submitted to the Director of the Yale Center for British Art. There are no application forms. Submit to the Yale Center a curriculum vitae, listing educational background, professional experience and publications, and a brief outline of the research proposal. Two confidential letters of recommendation must be sent directly from the referees to the Yale Center. An interview either at the Yale Center or the Paul Mellon Centre in London will be required. **Deadline:** January 15.

**Remarks:** The Paul Mellon Centre for the Studies in British Art and the Yale Center for British Art are sister institutions. General information on any of the fellowships may be obtained from either organization. **Contact:** Brian Allen, Director of Studies, at the above address (see entry 6275).

### • 6277 • Lewis Walpole Library Fellowship *(Graduate, Postdoctorate/Fellowship)*

**Purpose:** The Lewis Walpole Library, a department of the Yale University Library devoted to 18th-century British prints, paintings, books, and manuscripts, offers a one-month fellowship to support research in its collections. **Focus:** British 18th century from contemporary sources. **Qualif.:** Candidates may be of any nationality and must be pursuing an advanced degree or engaged in postdoctoral or equivalent research.

**Funds Avail.:** $1,500 fellowship with a modest travel allowance. A limited number of smaller research grants will be available as well. **No. of Awards:** 2. **To Apply:** There are no application forms. Candidates should send name, address, and telephone number; curriculum vitae listing educational background, professional experience, and publications; a brief outline of research proposal not to exceed three pages; and two confidential letters of recommendation. **Deadline:** January 15. **Contact:** Requests for information and applications should be submitted to the Librarian, Lewis Walpole Library, 154 Main St., Farmington, CT 06032. Telephone: (203)677-2140. Fax: (203)677-6369.

### • 6278 • Yale Center for British Art Fellowships *(Postdoctorate, Professional Development/Fellowship)*

**Purpose:** To allow scholars to study the Yale Center's holdings of paintings, drawings, prints and rare books, and to make use of its research facilities (photograph archive and art reference library). **Focus:** British Art, British History, British Literature. **Qualif.:** Applicants must be scholars in postdoctoral or equivalent research related to British art or museum professionals whose responsibilities and research interests include British art. Fellows

---

## Yale Center for British Art *(continued)*

are expected to be in residence in New Haven for the duration of the award. One fellowship each year is reserved for members of the American Society for Eighteenth-Century Studies. By arrangement with the Huntington Library, San Marino, California, scholars may apply for tandem awards.

**Funds Avail.:** Travel to and from New Haven, accommodation, and a living allowance. **No. of Awards:** 12. **To Apply:** Submit to the Director of the Yale Center a curriculum vitae, listing educational background, professional experience and publications, a brief outline of the research proposal; an indication of preferred dates of study. Two confidential letters of recommendation must be sent directly from the referees to the Yale Center. **Deadline:** January 15. **Contact:** Director, at the above address (see entry 6275).

---

• 6279 •
## Yale University Press
PO Box 209040
Yale Series of Younger Poets     *Ph:* (203)432-0900
New Haven, CT 06520-9040     *Fax:* (203)432-2394
*E-mail:* richard.miller@yale.edu
*URL:* http://www.yale.edu/yup/

### • 6280 • Yale Series of Younger Poets Prizes
*(Professional Development/Prize)*

**Purpose:** To recognize and publish an outstanding first book by an American poet. **Focus:** Poetry. **Qualif.:** Candidate must be an American writer under the age of 40 years at the time of submission of manuscript. Applicant may not have previously published a volume of poetry. Submitted verse may be written in any form and on any subject, but must be original. Translations are not accepted. The manuscript should be between 48 and 64 pages in length, with no more than one poem on a page. Poems that have been previously published in newspapers or periodicals, as well as privately published manuscripts, are eligible for submission. Candidate may submit one manuscript per year. There is an $15 submission fee. The winning manuscript is published by Yale University Press.

**Funds Avail.:** Royalties. **No. of Awards:** 1. **To Apply:** Write to the editor for submission guidelines. **Deadline:** Submissions are only accepted in February. Notification by July. **Contact:** Richard Miller, sponsoring editor, at the above address (see entry 6279).

---

• 6281 •
## The Yard
PO Box 405     *Ph:* (508)645-9662
Chilmark, MA 02535     *Fax:* (508)645-3176
*E-mail:* theyard@tiac.net
*URL:* http://www.tiac.net/users/theyard

### • 6282 • The Yard Residencies for Choreographers
*(Professional Development/Fellowship)*

**Purpose:** To provide choreographers with the opportunity to create new works and to enable dancers to assist the selected choreographers. **Focus:** Choreography, Dance. **Qualif.:** Candidates may be of any nationality but must be professional artists in one of the fields listed above. In addition to this general requirement, choreographers must have a minimum of three years of professionally produced work; dancers should be adaptable to a number of movement styles. Candidates in dance audition by invitation and are selected based on the various needs of the participating choreographers. Residencies are tenable at the

Yard's summer facilities on Martha's Vineyard, where artists-in-residence work together to create, rehearse, and perform new works.

**Funds Avail.:** Stipend varies plus room and board, studio space, performance fees, and travel allowance. Choreographers also receive a $400 production budget. **To Apply:** Write for application guidelines. Choreographers, must submit a video tape of their work. Dancers must audition. Finalists are interviewed. **Deadline:** Choreographers: mid-December; dancers: mid-January.

**Remarks:** Artist-in-School Residency teacher/choreographers will be selected by the Yard for a two to four week residency in the spring and autumn to teach dance/movement in the Martha's Vineyard public schools. Recipients teach 20 hours per week and are free to devote the rest of their time to choreographic work. The Yard may also offer internships to individuals interested in working as administrative and production assistants at the Martha's Vineyard facilities. Write for further information. Other Residency programs are also offered. **Contact:** Ernest W. Iannaccone, Administrative Associate, at the above address (see entry 6281).

---

• 6283 •
## YIVO Institute for Jewish Research
Max Weinreich Center for Advanced
  Jewish Studies
555 W. 57th St., Ste. 1100     *Ph:* (212)246-6080
New York, NY 10019     *Fax:* (212)292-1892

### • 6284 • Rose and Isidore Drench Fellowships
*(Postdoctorate/Fellowship)*

**Purpose:** To support postdoctoral research in American Jewish history at the YIVO Library and Archives. **Focus:** American Jewish History. **Qualif.:** Applicant may be of any nationality, but must be a postdoctoral scholar. Preference will be given to scholars researching aspects of the Jewish labor movement. Fellow is expected to give a public lecture based on his/her research, and to submit a paper based on the research for possible publication in the YIVO Annual.

**Funds Avail.:** $2,000 **To Apply:** Submit curriculum vitae, two letters of recommendation, and a detailed research proposal no more than three pages long. **Deadline:** January 1 for following academic year. **Contact:** Dr. Allan Nadler, Research Director, at the above address (see entry 6283).

### • 6285 • Vivian Lefsky Hort Fellowship
*(Postdoctorate/Fellowship)*

**Purpose:** To support postdoctoral research in Yiddish literature at the YIVO Library and Archives. **Focus:** Yiddish Literature. **Qualif.:** Applicant may be of any nationality, but must be a postdoctoral scholar. Fellow is expected to give a public lecture based on his/her research, in Yiddish or English, and submit a paper based on the research for possible publication in the YIVO Annual (if in English) or the YIVO-bleter (if in Yiddish).

**Funds Avail.:** $1,500. **No. of Awards:** 1. **To Apply:** Submit curriculum vitae, two letters of recommendation, and a detailed research proposal no more than three pages long. **Deadline:** September 30, for following spring semester.

**Remarks:** Scholarships are available to those who wish to attend YIVO's six-week, intensive, summer language program, the Uriel Weinreich Program in Yiddish Language, Literature and Culture. Contact YIVO for further information. **Contact:** Dr. Allan Nadler, Research Director, at the above address (see entry 6283).

• **6286** •

## YLD-North Carolina Bar Association

Scholarship Committee
PO Box 3688
Cary, NC 27519
*E-mail:* jtfount@mail.barlinc.org
*URL:* http://www.barlinc.org

*Ph:* (919)677-0561
*Fax:* (919)677-0761
*Free:* 800-662-7407

• **6287** • **YLD Scholarships** *(Graduate, Other, Undergraduate/Scholarship)*

**Focus:** General Studies. **Qualif.:** Applicants must be children of North Carolina law enforcement officers killed or disabled in the line of duty, and they must be attending or planning to attend an accredited school. **Criteria:** Selection based on need, school attendance, and circumstances.

**Funds Avail.:** Varies each year. **No. of Awards:** Varies. **To Apply:** Formal applications are required and must be submitted before the applicant reaches the age of 27. **Deadline:** Usually April 1 but varies each year. **Contact:** YLD Scholarships at the above address (see entry 6286). An in-state toll-free number is (800)662-7407.

• **6288** •

## Yoshiyama Awards

c/o Hitachi Foundation
PO Box 19247
Washington, DC 20036-9247

*Ph:* (202)457-0588
*Fax:* (202)296-1098

• **6289** • **Yoshiyama Award for Exemplary Service to the Community** *(Undergraduate/Award)*

**Purpose:** To recognize exemplary service rather than academic achievement. **Focus:** General Studies. **Qualif.:** Applicants must be graduating high school seniors who have distinguished themselves through extensive service and leadership in their communities. **Criteria:** Selection is based on the significance and extent of the community service and the relevance of these activities to solving profound community and societal problems.

**Funds Avail.:** $5,000 over a two-year period. **No. of Awards:** 6-10. **To Apply:** Applicants may be nominated by anyone other than a family member or relative. The nominator must complete and submit a nomination form, a letter of nomination, and two supporting letters. **Deadline:** April 1. **Contact:** Renata Hron, Program Officer, at the above address (see entry 6288).

• **6290** •

## Young Adult Library Services Association

50 E. Huron St.
Chicago, IL 60611-2729

*Ph:* (312)280-4390
*Fax:* (312)664-7459
*Free:* 800-545-2433

*E-mail:* yalsa@ala.org
*URL:* http://www.ala.org/yalsa

• **6291** • **Baker & Taylor Conference Grants** *(Professional Development/Grant)*

**Purpose:** To enable recipients to attend the ALA Annual Conference for the first time. **Focus:** Library and Archival Sciences. **Qualif.:** Applicants must be YALSA members (preferably for at least two years) who are young adult librarians in public or school libraries and have 1 to 10 years experience working with teenagers. The applicant must not have previously attended an Annual ALA Conference.

**Funds Avail.:** Two grants of $1000 each. **To Apply:** Applicants must submit one original and three copies of completed applications, and supporting statements completed by a supervisor (principal, department head, director, etc.) who is familiar with the applicant's work. **Deadline:** December 1.

**Remarks:** Funding is provided by Baker & Taylor Company. **Contact:** Linda Waddle, Deputy Executive Director, the American Library Association, at the above address (see entry 6290).

• **6292** •

## The Coleman A. Young Foundation

243 W. Congress, Ste. 490
Detroit, MI 48226

*Ph:* (313)963-3030
*Fax:* (313)963-1644

• **6293** • **Coleman A. Young Scholarship** *(Undergraduate/Scholarship)*

**Focus:** General studies. **Qualif.:** Applicants must be Detroit residents, graduating high school seniors planning to attend a Michigan college or any Black college in the country, and have overcome personal trauma or crisis. **Criteria:** Awards are granted based on application and interview. Selection committee looks for applicants must are independent, articulate, tenacious despite the odds, and determined.

**Funds Avail.:** $1,000. Renewable for up to eight semesters if recipient maintains eligibility. **No. of Awards:** 10. **To Apply:** Write for further details. **Deadline:** April 1. **Contact:** Pamela J. Jackson, Executive Director.

• **6294** •

## Young Menswear Association

1328 Broadway
New York, NY 10001

*Ph:* (212)594-6422
*Fax:* (212)594-9349

• **6295** • **YMA Scholarships** *(Graduate/Scholarship)*

**Purpose:** To encourage and support talent with financial needs. **Focus:** Textiles and Apparel. **Qualif.:** Applicants must be college students attending one of the following schools: Fashion Institute of Technology; Pratt Institute; North Carolina State/College of Textiles; Philadelphia College of Textiles/Parsons School of Design/NY College of Textiles. Applicants must be pursuing a career in men's or women's apparel and/or textiles. **Criteria:** Selection is made by college's financial aid office and is determined by academic record.

**Funds Avail.:** $45,000. **No. of Awards:** 10 annually. **To Apply:** Application must be made directly to above listed colleges.

• **6296** •

## Youth for Understanding International Exchange

3501 Newark St., NW
Washington, DC 20016-3199

*Ph:* (202)895-1122
*Fax:* (202)895-1104
*Free:* 800-TEEN-AGE

*URL:* http://www.yfu.org

*The Youth for Understanding (YFU) International Exchange Scholarship Program administers both government and corporate-sponsored merit scholarships that provide funding for students wishing to spend a school year or a summer overseas. In addition to the scholarships listed below, YFU also administers a number of corporate-sponsored community scholarship programs, including programs for students in communities in Maryland, Virginia, Michigan, Kentucky, Illinois, Cali-*

## Youth for Understanding International Exchange (continued)

fornia, Wisconsin, New York, Oregon, New Jersey, and the Washington D.C. metropolitan area. For information on these programs, contact the scholarship administration department at 800-833-6243.

### • 6297 • Congress Bundestag Youth Exchange Program Scholarships (High School/Scholarship)

**Purpose:** To expand perspectives and awareness of German social, economic and political institutions. **Focus:** General Studies. **Qualif.:** Applicants must be high school sophomores, juniors, or seniors with at least a 3.0 GPA and able to spend a full year in Germany. They must be U.S. citizens.

**Funds Avail.:** 300 full-year scholarships are awarded, which allow students to attend German high schools and live with host families. **No. of Awards:** 300. **Deadline:** Mid-November.

**Remarks:** This scholarship is sponsored by the U.S. Congress and the German Bundestag. **Contact:** For applications and information contact the scholarship administration department at the above address (see entry 6296).

### • 6298 • Finland U.S. Senate Youth Exchange Scholarships (High School/Scholarship)

**Purpose:** To strengthen U.S.-Finnish relationships through young people. **Focus:** General Studies. **Qualif.:** Only applicants from California, Florida, Massachusetts, Michigan, Minnesota, Oregon, and Washington are eligible to apply. In addition, the program is only offered to high school juniors with at least a 3.2 GPA. They must be U.S. citizens.

**Funds Avail.:** 14 recipients are awarded scholarships which allow them to spend the summer in Finland. **Deadline:** Late October.

**Remarks:** This program is sponsored by the government of Finland in conjunction with the United States Senate.

### • 6299 • Mazda National Scholarship (High School/Scholarship)

**Purpose:** To strengthen U.S.-Japan relationships through young people. **Focus:** General Studies. **Qualif.:** Applicants must be United States high school students with at least a 2.0 GPA.

**Funds Avail.:** Awards fund summer homestay program in Japan. **No. of Awards:** 10. **Deadline:** Mid-November.

**Remarks:** This scholarship is sponsored by Mazda North American Operations.

### • 6300 •
## Loren L. Zachary Society for the Performing Arts
2250 Gloaming Way      Ph: (310)276-3721
Beverly Hills, CA 90210      Fax: (310)275-8245

### • 6301 • National Vocal Competition for Young Opera Singers (Professional Development/Prize)

**Purpose:** To discover promising young opera singers and to assist in launching their careers in European opera houses. **Focus:** Opera. **Qualif.:** Applicant may be of any nationality. Female applicants must be between the ages of 21 and 33 years; male singers must be between the ages of 21 and 35 years. Applicants must have completed proper operatic training, be prepared to pursue a professional stage career, and be present at all phases of auditions. Candidates are required to audition in New York or Los Angeles.

**Funds Avail.:** First prize: $10,000; finalists: $1,000 plus additional cash awards. **No. of Awards:** 10. **To Apply:** Send self-addressed,

stamped envelope to the director of auditions for application guidelines, available in November. An application fee of approximately $35 is required. **Deadline:** New York: February, Los Angeles: April. Finals are held in June in Los Angeles. Winners of the Eastern Regional Auditions in New York will receive air transportation to Los Angeles and housing.

**Remarks:** A round-trip flight is also awarded to Europe for auditioning purposes. **Contact:** Nedra Zachary, Director of Auditions, at the above address (see entry 6300).

### • 6302 •
## Zeta Phi Beta Sorority - National Education Foundation
Executive Office
1734 New Hampshire Ave., NW      Ph: (202)387-3103
Washington, DC 20009      Fax: (202)232-4593
E-mail: zetanatlhq@worldnet.att.net
URL: http://zpb1920.org

For all awards: a completed application; three letters of recommendation (from a college professor or high school teacher, minister or community leader, and one other person—for sorority members the third letter must be from a graduate chapter Basileus or Advisor); a university or high school transcript; and a 150 word or more essay containing information about yourself, your educaitonal goals and professional aspirations, how this award can help you achieve you goals and aspirations, and why you should receive this award must be submitted. Applications forms must be requested from the Foundation in writing. Request envelopes should be clearly marked with NEP-AR in the bottom left corner.

### • 6303 • Mildred Cater Bradham Social Work Fellowship (Doctorate, Graduate/Fellowship)

**Qualif.:** Candidates must be members of Zeta Phi Beta Sorority who are pursuing a graduate or professional degree full-time in social work at an accredited college or university.

**Funds Avail.:** $500 to $1,000 for one academic year. **Deadline:** February 1. Recipients are notified by August 15.

**Remarks:** Documentation of academic study must be sent directly from the university to the Scholarship Chairperson.

### • 6304 • Lullelia W. Harrison Scholarship in Counseling (Graduate, Undergraduate/Scholarship)

**Qualif.:** Applicants must be graduate or undergraduate students enrolled in a degree program in counseling.

**Funds Avail.:** $500 to $1,000. **To Apply:** Completed applications must be returned along with references and an official university transcript. **Deadline:** February 1. Recipients are notified by August 15.

### • 6305 • Isabel M. Herson Scholarship in Education (Graduate, Undergraduate/Scholarship)

**Qualif.:** Students must be graduates or undergraduates enrolled in a degree program either in elementary or secondary education.

**Funds Avail.:** $500 to $1,000 for one academic year. **Deadline:** February 1. Recipients are notified by August 15.

### • 6306 • S. Evelyn Lewis Memorial Scholarship in Medical Health Sciences (Graduate, Undergraduate/Scholarship)

**Qualif.:** Students must be graduate or undergraduate women enrolled full-time in a program leading to a degree in medicine or health sciences.

Funds Avail.: $500 to $1,000. Deadline: February 1. Recipients are notified by August 15.

### • 6307 • Deborah Partridge Wolfe International Fellowship (Graduate, Undergraduate/Fellowship)

Purpose: To encourage U.S. women to study abroad, and to encourage women from other countries to study in the United States. Focus: General. Qualif.: Applicant may be a woman of any nationality, and may be a graduate or undergraduate student. Candidate need not be a member of the Sorority. The fellowship supports full-time academic study. U.S. citizens must use the award outside of the United States. Citizens of other countries may only use the award at U.S. institutions.

Funds Avail.: $500-1000. Deadline: February 1. Notification by August 15.

### • 6308 • Nancy B. Woolridge Graduate Fellowship (Doctorate, Graduate/Fellowship)

Qualif.: Candidates must be members of Zeta Phi Beta Sorority pursuing a graduate or professional degree full-time in an accredited college or university program and be able to demonstrate scholarly distinction or unusual ability in their chosen field.

Funds Avail.: $500 to $1,000 each academic year. Deadline: February 1. Recipients are notified no later than August 15.

### • 6309 • Zeta Phi Beta General Graduate Fellowship (Doctorate, Graduate, Postdoctorate/Fellowship)

Purpose: To encourage advanced study by women. Focus: General. Qualif.: Applicant must be woman who is either pursuing a professional, master's, or doctoral degree, or undertaking postdoctoral study. Candidate need not be a member of the Sorority. Fellowships may be used for full-time study, travel study, or research.

Funds Avail.: Not to exceed $2,500 per year-paid directly to recipient. Deadline: February 1. Notification by August 15.

### • 6310 • Zeta Phi Beta General Undergraduate Scholarship (Undergraduate/Scholarship)

Qualif.: College freshmen, sophomores, juniors, and seniors, and high school seniors planning to enter college in the Fall are eligible to apply.

Funds Avail.: $500 to $1,000 paid directly to the college or university to be applied to tuition or fees. Deadline: February 1. Recipients are notified by August 15.

### • 6311 • Zonta International Foundation

Attn: Ana Ubides, Foundation
  Services Assoc.          Ph: (312)930-5848
Chicago, IL 60661-2206    Fax: (312)930-0951

Zonta is a service organization of executive women in business and the professions.

### • 6312 • Amelia Earhart Fellowship Awards (Graduate/Fellowship)

Focus: Aerospace Sciences, Engineering, Science. Qualif.: Candidates must be women who hold a bachelor's degree in a qualifying area of science or engineering which is closely related to advanced studies in the aerospace-related sciences. They must have also completed one year of graduate school at a well recognized institution of higher learning or show evidence of a well defined research and development program as demonstrated by publications or a senior research project. They must have a superior academic record, career goals, and show evidence of potential. Criteria: Selection is based on transcripts, recommendations, and professional information and grants. The successful candidate clearly defines the relevance of her field of study to aerospace-related science or aerospace-related engineering, demonstrates outstanding academic credentials, and specifically outlines her professional or career goals as well as detailing an original focus in her research project.

Funds Avail.: $6,000 each, awarded annually, and renewable for an additional year upon reapplication. No. of Awards: 35-40. To Apply: Applications should include biographical information, list of schools attended and degrees received, transcripts of grades, employment history, plans for intended study, essay on academic and professional goals, a photograph, and three recommendations. Deadline: Applications must be filed by November 1 with all supporting material received by November 7. Recipients are announced by May 15. Contact: Ana L. Ubides, Foundation Services Associate, at the above address (see entry 6311).

### • 6313 • Zuni Higher Education and Employment Assistance

PO Box 339                Ph: (505)782-2191
Zuni, NM 87327            Fax: (505)782-2700
E-mail: zunihe@unm.edu

The Zuni Higher Education Program and the Employment Assistance Program are consolidated under the Department of Labor for the Zuni Tribe.

### • 6314 • Zuni Higher Education Scholarships (Doctorate, Graduate, Undergraduate/Scholarship)

Purpose: To provide supplemental funds to qualified Zuni tribal members who are in need of financial assistance. Focus: General Studies. Qualif.: Applicants must be enrolled members of the Zuni tribe who are full-time students enrolled for a minimum of 12 credit hours, be in good academic standing with a cumulative GPA of 2.0 on a 4.0 scale, and be admitted to a regionally accredited institution of higher learning in pursuit of college degrees, including the A.A., B.A., Master's, or Ph.D. Students must also apply to other financial aid sources, as the scholarship funds are intended to supplement other awards. Criteria: Selection is based on financial need.

Funds Avail.: The Higher Education Department has counselors available for any student outreach services that may be required. To Apply: Students need to complete and return a Financial Aid Form to the College Scholarship Service. The program and the institutions' offices of financial aid then consider financial aid packages relevant to each student's needs. Deadline: For the fall semester, applications must be returned by June 1 and supporting documents by June 31; for the spring semester, applications must be returned by October 1 and supporting documents by October 31; and for summer classes, applications are due April 1 and supporting documents by April 30.

Remarks: The Pueblo of Zuni is contracted with the Bureau of Indian Affairs to administer the Higher Education Scholarship Program. Funds are appropriated by Congress. Contact: Shelly Chimoni, Director, at the above address (see entry 6313). An alternate telephone number is (505)782-4481.

# Field of Study Index

This index classifies awards by one or more of some 330 specific subject categories, and includes "see" and "see also" references. Citations are arranged alphabetically under all appropriate subject categories. Each citation is followed by the study level and award type, which appear in parentheses. The number following the parenthetical information indicates the book entry number for a particular award, not a page number.

## Accounting
AAHCPA Scholarship *(Undergraduate/Scholarship)* 308
Air Force ROTC Scholarships *(Undergraduate/Scholarship)* 5816
American Accounting Association Fellowship Program in Accounting *(Doctorate/Fellowship)* 246
Andersen Fellowships for Doctoral Candidates at the Dissertation Stage *(Doctorate/Fellowship)* 1039
Andersen Foundation Faculty Residencies *(Professional Development/Award)* 1040
Avon Products Foundation Scholarship Program for Women in Business Studies *(Graduate, Professional Development, Undergraduate/Scholarship)* 1545
Michael J. Barrett Doctoral Dissertation Grant *(Doctorate/Grant)* 3065
Central Intelligence Agency Graduate Studies Internships *(Graduate/Internship)* 1811
Chartered Institute of Management Accountants Research Foundation Grants *(All/Grant)* 1834
Colorado Society of CPAs Educational Foundation High School Scholarship *(Undergraduate/Scholarship)* 2000
Colorado Society of CPAs Educational Foundation Scholarships *(Undergraduate/Scholarship)* 2001
Cox Minority Journalism Scholarship *(Undergraduate/Scholarship)* 2131
Exceptional Student Fellowship Award *(Undergraduate/Scholarship)* 5613
Institute of Chartered Accountants Research Grants *(Professional Development/Grant)* 3015
Robert Kaufman Memorial Scholarships *(Graduate, Undergraduate/Scholarship)* 2989
Laurels Fund Scholarships *(Doctorate, Graduate/Scholarship)* 2350
National Association of Black Accountants National Scholarship *(Graduate, Undergraduate/Scholarship)* 3857
New York State Professional Opportunity Scholarships *(Doctorate, Graduate, Undergraduate/Scholarship)* 4592
New York State Regents Professional Opportunity Scholarships *(Doctorate, Graduate, Undergraduate/Scholarship)* 4577
NSPA Scholarship Awards *(Undergraduate/Scholarship)* 4405
Service Merchandise Scholarship Program *(High School, Undergraduate/Scholarship)* 5310
Stanley H. Stearman Scholarships *(Graduate, Undergraduate/Scholarship)* 4406
Harry and Angel Zerigian Scholarship *(Undergraduate/Scholarship)* 1130

## Acquired immune deficiency syndrome
AIDS Fellowships *(Postdoctorate/Fellowship)* 2524
AmFAR Pediatric AIDS Foundation Grants *(Postdoctorate/Grant)* 471
AmFAR Research Grants *(Postdoctorate/Grant)* 472
AmFAR Scholar Awards *(Postdoctorate/Award)* 473

AmFAR Small Grants *(Postdoctorate/Grant)* 474
New Investigator Matching Grants *(Postdoctorate/Grant)* 4161
Judith Graham Pool Postdoctoral Research Fellowships *(Postdoctorate/Fellowship)* 4177
Summer Fellowship Grants *(Doctorate/Fellowship)* 215

## Actuarial science
AERF Individual Grants *(Professional Development/Grant)* 33
Casualty Actuarial Scholarships for Minority Students *(Undergraduate/Scholarship)* 5430
Harold W. Schloss Memorial Scholarship *(Undergraduate/Scholarship)* 1745
Society of Actuaries Ph.D. Grants *(Doctorate/Grant)* 5431

## Advertising (See also: Public relations)
AAAA Minority Advertising Internships *(Undergraduate/Internship)* 270
Biggs and Gilmore Communications Scholarships *(Graduate, Undergraduate/Scholarship)* 4030
College Conference and Summer Fellowship Program *(Graduate, Undergraduate/Fellowship)* 3174
Cox Minority Journalism Scholarship *(Undergraduate/Scholarship)* 2131
Creswell, Munsell, Fultz & Zirbel Scholarships *(Undergraduate/Scholarship)* 4054
Miller Meester Advertising Scholarship *(Undergraduate/Scholarship)* 4100

## Aeronautics (See also: Aviation)
AIAA/Gordon C. Oates Air Breathing Propulsion Award *(Doctorate, Graduate/Award)* 566
AIAA Liquid Propulsion Award *(Graduate/Scholarship)* 567
AIAA Scholarship Program *(Undergraduate/Scholarship)* 568
AIAA/William T. Piper, Sr. General Aviation Systems Award *(Graduate/Scholarship)* 569
Amelia Earhart Fellowship Awards *(Graduate/Fellowship)* 6312
Guggenheim Fellowships *(Doctorate/Fellowship)* 5380
Lindbergh Grants *(Other/Grant)* 3484
Allen H. Meyers Scholarship *(Undergraduate/Scholarship)* 3677
Col. Louisa Spruance Morse CAP Scholarship *(Undergraduate/Scholarship)* 3917
Silver Dart Aviation History Award *(Undergraduate/Prize)* 1607
Spartan School of Aeronautics Scholarship *(Undergraduate/Scholarship)* 2297
Tennessee Space Grant Consortium Fellowships and Scholarships *(Graduate, Undergraduate/Fellowship, Scholarship)* 5698

## Aerospace sciences
AIAA/William T. Piper, Sr. General Aviation Systems Award *(Graduate/Scholarship)* 569

## Aerospace sciences (continued)

Alabama Space Grant Consortium Graduate Student Fellowship Program *(Graduate/Fellowship)* 123

Alabama Space Grant Consortium Undergraduate Fellowship Program *(Undergraduate/Fellowship)* 124

Alaska Space Grant Program Graduate Research Assistantships *(Graduate/Grant)* 138

Alaska Space Grant Program Internships *(Graduate, Undergraduate/Internship)* 139

Brown-NASA Space Grant Scholars Program *(Undergraduate/Scholarship)* 5124

Civil Air Patrol Graduate Scholarship *(Doctorate, Graduate/Scholarship)* 3915

Delaware NASA Space Grant Undergraduate Tuition Scholarships *(Undergraduate/Scholarship)* 2203

Amelia Earhart Fellowship Awards *(Graduate/Fellowship)* 6312

Fellowship in Aerospace History *(Doctorate, Postdoctorate/Fellowship)* 537

Georgia Space Grant Consortium Fellowships *(Graduate, Undergraduate/Fellowship)* 2655

Dr. Robert H. Goddard Scholarships *(Graduate, Undergraduate/Scholarship)* 4408

Graduate Student Fellowships *(Graduate/Fellowship)* 5560

Guggenheim Fellowships *(Doctorate/Fellowship)* 5380

Maryland Space Grant Consortium Graduate Level Fellowship *(Graduate/Fellowship)* 3588

Allen H. Meyers Scholarship *(Undergraduate/Scholarship)* 3677

Montana Space Grant Consortium Scholarship-Fellowship Program *(Graduate, Undergraduate/Fellowship, Scholarship)* 3771

NASA Administrator's Fellowship Program *(Other/Fellowship)* 4359

NASA/DESGC Graduate Student Fellowships *(Graduate/Fellowship)* 2204

NASA/DESGC Undergraduate Summer Scholarships *(Undergraduate/Scholarship)* 2205

National Board Civil Air Patrol Undergraduate/Advanced Undergraduate College Scholarship *(Undergraduate/Scholarship)* 3918

Judith Resnik Memorial Scholarship *(Undergraduate/Scholarship)* 5519

Space and Aerospace Graduate Fellowship *(Graduate/Fellowship)* 3508

Space Grant Graduate Fellowship Program *(Graduate/Fellowship)* 5125

Space Grant Undergraduate Scholar Program *(Undergraduate/Scholarship)* 5126

Space Grant Undergraduate Summer Scholar Program *(Undergraduate/Scholarship)* 5127

Space Scholars Program *(Undergraduate/Scholarship)* 3589

Summer Faculty Fellowships *(Other/Fellowship)* 5561

Tennessee Space Grant Consortium Fellowships and Scholarships *(Graduate, Undergraduate/Fellowship, Scholarship)* 5698

TSGC Fellowship and Scholarship *(Undergraduate/Fellowship, Scholarship)* 5719

UA/NASA Space Grant Graduate Fellowship Program *(Graduate/Fellowship)* 1086

Undergraduate NASA Space Grant Fellowship *(Undergraduate/Fellowship)* 6143

Undergraduate Student Assistantships and Scholarships *(Undergraduate/Scholarship)* 5562

U.S. Air Force Dissertation Year Fellowship in U.S. Military Aerospace History *(Doctorate/Fellowship)* 5814

The University of Arizona/NASA Space Grant Undergraduate Research Internship Program *(Undergraduate/Grant, Internship)* 1087

West Virginia Space Consortium Graduate Fellowship Program *(Graduate/Fellowship)* 6144

West Virginia Space Grant Consortium Undergraduate Scholarship Program *(Undergraduate/Scholarship)* 6145

Wisconsin Space Grant Consortium Graduate Fellowships *(Graduate/Fellowship)* 6214

Wisconsin Space Grant Consortium Undergraduate Research Awards *(Undergraduate/Grant)* 6215

Wisconsin Space Grant Consortium Undergraduate Scholarships *(Undergraduate/Scholarship)* 6216

## African studies (See also: Area and ethnic studies)

AIMS Small Grants *(Doctorate, Postdoctorate/Grant)* 590

American Research Center in Egypt Research Fellowships for Study in Egypt *(Doctorate, Postdoctorate/Fellowship)* 843

American Research Center in Egypt Research Fellowships for Study in the U.S. or Canada *(Doctorate/Fellowship)* 844

Du Bois Mandela Rodney Postdoctoral Fellowships *(Postdoctorate/Fellowship)* 1784

International Student Identity Card Travel Grants for Educational Programs in Developing Countries *(High School, Undergraduate/Grant)* 2113

Rockefeller Fellows Programs *(Postdoctorate/Fellowship)* 1785

Sub-Saharan African Dissertation Internship Award *(Doctorate/Internship)* 5154

James A. Swan Fund Grants *(Graduate, Postgraduate/Grant)* 5652

## African-American studies (See also: Area and ethnic studies)

Afro-American and African Studies Fellowships *(Doctorate, Postdoctorate/Fellowship)* 6251

Brown University, The Future of Gender *(Postdoctorate/Fellowship)* 5990

Du Bois Mandela Rodney Postdoctoral Fellowships *(Postdoctorate/Fellowship)* 1784

Institute of American Cultures Graduate and Predoctoral Fellowships *(Doctorate/Fellowship)* 3012

Institute of American Cultures Postdoctoral and Visiting Scholars Fellowships *(Postdoctorate/Fellowship)* 3013

Rockefeller Fellows Programs *(Postdoctorate/Fellowship)* 1785

Schomburg Center Scholars-in-Residence *(Professional Development/Scholarship)* 5272

Muddy Waters Scholarship *(Undergraduate/Scholarship)* 1448

## Aggression and violence (See also: Sociology)

The Clara Mayo Grant *(Graduate/Grant)* 5494

H. F. Guggenheim Foundation Dissertation Fellowships *(Doctorate/Fellowship)* 2758

H. F. Guggenheim Foundation Research Grants *(Postdoctorate/Grant)* 2759

## Agribusiness (See also: Agricultural sciences)

Alberta Salers Association Scholarship *(Undergraduate/Scholarship)* 146

Alberta Wheat Pool Scholarships *(Undergraduate/Scholarship)* 148

Alfa-Laval Agri Scholarships *(Undergraduate/Scholarship)* 4014

Alpha Gamma Rho Education Foundation Scholarship *(Undergraduate/Scholarship)* 4016

American Grain and Related Industries Scholarship *(Undergraduate/Scholarship)* 4021

American Seed Trade Association Scholarship *(Undergraduate/Scholarship)* 4023

Award Design Medals Scholarship *(Undergraduate/Scholarship)* 4027

Big R. Stores and Fleet Supply Company Scholarship *(Undergraduate/Scholarship)* 4029

Ardell Bjugstad Memorial Scholarships *(Undergraduate/Scholarship)* 5551

Borden Foundation Scholarships *(Undergraduate/Scholarship)* 4032

Bunge Corporation Scholarship *(Undergraduate/Scholarship)* 4037

Business Men's Assurance Company of America Scholarships *(Undergraduate/Scholarship)* 4038

CAL Stores Companies Scholarships *(Undergraduate/Scholarship)* 4039

Capital Agricultural Property Services, Inc. Scholarship *(Undergraduate/Scholarship)* 4040

Capitol American Scholarships *(Undergraduate/ Scholarship)* 4041

Casey's General Stores, Inc. Scholarships *(Undergraduate/ Scholarship)* 4045

Chevron USA, Inc. Scholarship *(Undergraduate/ Scholarship)* 4047

Chief Industries Inc. Scholarships *(Undergraduate/ Scholarship)* 4050

Chilean Nitrate Corporation Scholarship *(Undergraduate/ Scholarship)* 4051

Competitive Grants-in-Aid for Original Research *(Postdoctorate/Grant)* 4286

ConAgra Scholarships *(Undergraduate/Scholarship)* 4052

Countrymark Cooperative, Inc. Scholarships *(Undergraduate/ Scholarship)* 4053

Curtice Burns and Pro-Fac Scholarships *(Undergraduate/ Scholarship)* 4055

D & B Supply Company, Inc. Scholarships *(Undergraduate/ Scholarship)* 4056

Data Transmission Network Corporation Scholarship *(Undergraduate/Scholarship)* 4058

Harold Davis Memorial Endowment Scholarship *(Undergraduate/Scholarship)* 4059

DEKALB Genetic Corporation Scholarships *(Undergraduate/ Scholarship)* 4060

Delta and Pine Land Company Scholarship *(Undergraduate/ Scholarship)* 4062

Douglas Products and Packaging Scholarships *(Undergraduate/Scholarship)* 4064

Drysdales Scholarships *(Undergraduate/Scholarship)* 4065

Eastern Apiculture Society of North America Scholarship *(Undergraduate/Scholarship)* 4067

The Ertl Company Scholarship *(Undergraduate/ Scholarship)* 4069

Farm King Supply Scholarship *(Undergraduate/ Scholarship)* 4072

Farmers Mutual Hail Insurance Company of Iowa Scholarships *(Undergraduate/Scholarship)* 4073

Fermenta Animal Health Company Scholarships *(Undergraduate/Scholarship)* 4076

First Mississippi Corporation Scholarships *(Undergraduate/ Scholarship)* 4077

FISCO Farm and Home Stores Scholarships *(Undergraduate/ Scholarship)* 4078

Golden Harvest Seeds, Inc. Scholarships *(Undergraduate/ Scholarship)* 4082

Gustafson, Inc. Scholarship *(Undergraduate/Scholarship)* 4084

Hawkeye Steel Products, Inc. Scholarship *(Undergraduate/ Scholarship)* 4086

Helena Chemical Company Scholarships *(Undergraduate/ Scholarship)* 4087

Hydro Agri North America, Inc. Scholarships *(Undergraduate/ Scholarship)* 4092

Metropolitan Life Foundation Scholarships *(Undergraduate/ Scholarship)* 4097

Mid-America Dairymen, Inc., National Dairy Promotion and Research Board and Patz Sales, Inc. Scholarships *(Undergraduate/Scholarship)* 4098

Mid-State Wool Growers Cooperative Scholarship *(Undergraduate/Scholarship)* 4099

Mississippi Farm Bureau Foundation Scholarship *(Undergraduate/Scholarship)* 4101

Kenneth D. Naden Award *(Graduate/Award)* 3950

National Dairy Shrine/Dairy Management Scholarships, Inc. *(Undergraduate/Scholarship)* 3968

National Pork Producers Council Scholarships *(Undergraduate/ Scholarship)* 4106

National Suffolk Sheep Association Scholarship *(Undergraduate/Scholarship)* 4107

Nationwide Foundation Scholarships *(Undergraduate/ Scholarship)* 4108

NC++FA Hybrids Scholarship *(Undergraduate/ Scholarship)* 4109

NCFC Undergraduate Term Paper Awards *(Undergraduate/ Award)* 3951

Kenneth and Ellen Nielsen Cooperative Scholarships *(Undergraduate/Scholarship)* 4110

Norfolk Southern Foundation Scholarships *(Undergraduate/ Scholarship)* 4111

Northrup King Company Scholarships *(Undergraduate/ Scholarship)* 4113

Edwin G. Nourse Award *(Doctorate/Award)* 3952

Oklahoma Natural Gas Company Scholarship *(Undergraduate/ Scholarship)* 4114

Precision Laboratories, Inc. Scholarship *(Undergraduate/ Scholarship)* 4116

Quality Stores, Inc. Scholarships *(Undergraduate/ Scholarship)* 4119

Ritchie Industries, Inc. Scholarship *(Undergraduate/ Scholarship)* 4122

Ruetgers-Nease Chemical Company, Inc. Scholarship *(Undergraduate/Scholarship)* 4123

Santa Fe Pacific Foundation Scholarships *(Undergraduate/ Scholarship)* 4125

SIGCO Research Scholarships *(Undergraduate/ Scholarship)* 4126

Silgan Containers Corporation Scholarships *(Undergraduate/ Scholarship)* 4127

Souvenir Shirts, Etc. Scholarships *(Undergraduate/ Scholarship)* 4128

State Farm Companies Foundation Scholarships *(Undergraduate/Scholarship)* 4130

E.A. Stokdyk Award *(Graduate/Award)* 3953

TCS, Farm, Home and Auto Stores Scholarship *(Undergraduate/Scholarship)* 4132

Theisen Supply, Inc. Scholarships *(Undergraduate/ Scholarship)* 4134

Tri-State Breeders Scholarships *(Undergraduate/ Scholarship)* 4135

Tyson Foods, Sanofi Animal Health and American Proteins Scholarships *(Undergraduate/Scholarship)* 4136

Union Pacific Foundation Scholarship *(Undergraduate/ Scholarship)* 4137

Universal Dairy Equipment, Inc. Scholarships *(Undergraduate/ Scholarship)* 4140

Universal Leaf Tobacco Company Scholarship *(Undergraduate/ Scholarship)* 4141

Valmont Irrigation Scholarships *(Undergraduate/ Scholarship)* 4142

Wal-Mart Scholarship *(Undergraduate/Scholarship)* 4144

Wells Fargo Bank Scholarship *(Undergraduate/ Scholarship)* 4146

Western Dairymen - John Elway - Melba FFA Scholarship Fund *(Undergraduate/Scholarship)* 4147

Western Seedmen's Association Scholarships *(Undergraduate/ Scholarship)* 4148

Williams Pipe Line Company Scholarship *(Undergraduate/ Scholarship)* 4150

Yetter Manufacturing Co. Scholarship *(Undergraduate/ Scholarship)* 4154

## Agricultural sciences (See also: specific areas of study, e.g. Horticulture)

AgRadio Network Scholarships *(Undergraduate/ Scholarship)* 4013

AIBS Congressional Science Fellowship *(Postdoctorate/ Fellowship)* 476

Airline Pilots Association Scholarship *(Undergraduate/ Scholarship)* 96

Alberta Salers Association Scholarship *(Undergraduate/ Scholarship)* 146

Alberta Wheat Pool Scholarships *(Undergraduate/ Scholarship)* 148

Alfa-Laval Agri Scholarships *(Undergraduate/ Scholarship)* 4014

Alpha Gamma Rho Education Foundation Scholarship *(Undergraduate/Scholarship)* 4016

American Farm Bureau Federation Scholarship *(Undergraduate/Scholarship)* 4019

**Agricultural sciences (See also: specific areas of study, e.g. Horticulture) (continued)**

American Grain and Related Industries Scholarship *(Undergraduate/Scholarship)* 4021

American Seed Trade Association Scholarship *(Undergraduate/Scholarship)* 4023

American Society for Enology and Viticulture Scholarships *(Graduate, Undergraduate/Scholarship)* 928

Anchor Division Boehringer Ingelheim Animal Health Scholarship *(Undergraduate/Scholarship)* 4024

Award Design Medals Scholarship *(Undergraduate/Scholarship)* 4027

BARD Postdoctoral Fellowships; BARD Research Fellows Program *(Postdoctorate/Fellowship)* 1432

Big R. Stores and Fleet Supply Company Scholarship *(Undergraduate/Scholarship)* 4029

Biggs and Gilmore Communications Scholarships *(Graduate, Undergraduate/Scholarship)* 4030

Biotechnology Career Fellowships *(Postdoctorate/Fellowship)* 5147

Ardell Bjugstad Memorial Scholarships *(Undergraduate/Scholarship)* 5551

Howard S. Brembeck Scholarship in Agricultural Engineering *(Graduate/Scholarship)* 892

B.R.I.D.G.E. Endowment Fund Scholarships *(Undergraduate/Scholarship)* 4033

Bunge Corporation Scholarship *(Undergraduate/Scholarship)* 4037

Business Men's Assurance Company of America Scholarships *(Undergraduate/Scholarship)* 4038

California Farm Bureau Scholarships *(Undergraduate/Scholarship)* 1557

A & E Capelle LN Herfords Scholarship *(Doctorate, Graduate, Undergraduate/Scholarship)* 150

Capitol American Scholarships *(Undergraduate/Scholarship)* 4041

Caribou Research Bursary *(Other/Scholarship)* 1680

Wilson W. Carnes Scholarships *(Undergraduate/Scholarship)* 4043

Casey's General Stores, Inc. Scholarships *(Undergraduate/Scholarship)* 4045

Celanese Canada Inc. Scholarships *(Undergraduate/Scholarship)* 1269

Certified Angus Beef Scholarship *(Graduate, Undergraduate/Scholarship)* 4274

Chevron USA, Inc. Scholarship *(Undergraduate/Scholarship)* 4047

Chicago and North Western Transportation Company Scholarship *(Undergraduate/Scholarship)* 4049

Chief Industries Inc. Scholarships *(Undergraduate/Scholarship)* 4050

Chilean Nitrate Corporation Scholarship *(Undergraduate/Scholarship)* 4051

CIEA Grants-in-Aid *(Professional Development/Grant)* 3133

Corn Refiners Association Research Funds *(Postdoctorate/Grant)* 2087

Countrymark Cooperative, Inc. Scholarships *(Undergraduate/Scholarship)* 4053

County of Forty Mile Agricultural Committee Bursaries *(Undergraduate/Scholarship)* 2127

Curtice Burns and Pro-Fac Scholarships *(Undergraduate/Scholarship)* 4055

Czech Education Scholarships *(Doctorate, Graduate, Postdoctorate/Scholarship)* 3708

Data Transmission Network Corporation Scholarship *(Undergraduate/Scholarship)* 4058

Harold Davis Memorial Endowment Scholarship *(Undergraduate/Scholarship)* 4059

Delmar Publishers Scholarship *(Undergraduate/Scholarship)* 4061

Delta and Pine Land Company Scholarship *(Undergraduate/Scholarship)* 4062

Howard and Marjorie DeNise Memorial Scholarships *(Undergraduate/Scholarship loan)* 4580

Dodge Trucks Scholarships *(Undergraduate/Scholarship)* 4063

Douglas Products and Packaging Scholarships *(Undergraduate/Scholarship)* 4064

Drysdales Scholarships *(Undergraduate/Scholarship)* 4065

Dueutz-Allis Corporation, Hesston Corporation, and White Tractor Scholarships *(Undergraduate/Scholarship)* 4066

Eastern Apiculture Society of North America Scholarship *(Undergraduate/Scholarship)* 4067

The Ertl Company Scholarship *(Undergraduate/Scholarship)* 4069

FARM AID Scholarships *(Undergraduate/Scholarship)* 4071

Farm King Supply Scholarship *(Undergraduate/Scholarship)* 4072

Farmers Mutual Hail Insurance Company of Iowa Scholarships *(Undergraduate/Scholarship)* 4073

Fellowship Progamme of the Netherlands Ministry of Agriculture, Nature Management and Fisheries *(Postgraduate/Fellowship)* 3103

Fermenta Animal Health Company Scholarships *(Undergraduate/Scholarship)* 4076

First Mississippi Corporation Scholarships *(Undergraduate/Scholarship)* 4077

FISCO Farm and Home Stores Scholarships *(Undergraduate/Scholarship)* 4078

Growmark, Inc. Scholarships *(Undergraduate/Scholarship)* 4083

Gustafson, Inc. Scholarship *(Undergraduate/Scholarship)* 4084

Hardie Irrigation Scholarships *(Undergraduate/Scholarship)* 4085

Georgia M. Hellberg Memorial Scholarships *(Undergraduate/Scholarship)* 4088

Hillshire Farm & Kahn's Scholarship *(Undergraduate/Scholarship)* 4090

Hoechst Canada Bursary *(Undergraduate/Scholarship)* 155

Hydro Agri North America, Inc. Scholarships *(Undergraduate/Scholarship)* 4092

International Affairs Fellowships *(Professional Development/Fellowship)* 2105

Ladies of the ABBA American Junior Brahman Association Scholarships *(Undergraduate/Scholarship)* 602

Lindbergh Grants *(Other/Grant)* 3484

Metropolitan Life Foundation Scholarships *(Undergraduate/Scholarship)* 4097

Mid-America Dairymen, Inc., National Dairy Promotion and Research Board and Patz Sales, Inc. Scholarships *(Undergraduate/Scholarship)* 4098

Mid-State Wool Growers Cooperative Scholarship *(Undergraduate/Scholarship)* 4099

Mississippi Farm Bureau Foundation Scholarship *(Undergraduate/Scholarship)* 4101

Moorman Scholarship in Agriculture *(Undergraduate/Scholarship)* 3780

NAS/NRC Collaboration in Basic Science and Engineering Long-Term Grants *(Postdoctorate/Grant)* 3831

NAS/NRC Collaboration in Basic Science and Engineering Short-Term Project Development Grants *(Postdoctorate/Grant)* 3832

National Dairy Shrine/Dairy Management Scholarships, Inc. *(Undergraduate/Scholarship)* 3968

National FFA Foundation Minority Scholarships *(Undergraduate/Scholarship)* 4104

National Junior Angus Scholarships *(Undergraduate/Scholarship)* 4275

National Pork Producers Council Scholarships *(Undergraduate/Scholarship)* 4106

National Suffolk Sheep Association Scholarship *(Undergraduate/Scholarship)* 4107

National Wool Growers Memorial Fellowships *(Graduate/Fellowship)* 887

National Zoological Park Minority Traineeships *(Graduate, Undergraduate/Internship)* 4456

Nationwide Foundation Scholarships *(Undergraduate/Scholarship)* 4108

NC++FA Hybrids Scholarship *(Undergraduate/Scholarship)* 4109

Kenneth and Ellen Nielsen Cooperative Scholarships *(Undergraduate/Scholarship)* 4110

Norfolk Southern Foundation Scholarships *(Undergraduate/Scholarship)* 4111

Northrup King Company Scholarships *(Undergraduate/Scholarship)* 4113

Ohio State University Extension Internship *(Graduate, Undergraduate/Internship)* 4733

Oklahoma Natural Gas Company Scholarship *(Undergraduate/Scholarship)* 4114

Outstanding Doctoral and Master's Thesis Awards *(Doctorate, Postgraduate/Award)* 248

Pennington Memorial Scholarships *(Undergraduate/Scholarship)* 162

Piancone Family Agriculture Scholarship *(Graduate, Undergraduate/Scholarship)* 4254

Rain Bird Sprinkler Manufacturing Corp. Scholarships *(Undergraduate/Scholarship)* 4120

Rhone-Poulenc Animal Nutrition Scholarships *(Undergraduate/Scholarship)* 4121

Ritchie Industries, Inc. Scholarship *(Undergraduate/Scholarship)* 4122

Royal Bath & West of England Society Scholarships *(Undergraduate/Scholarship)* 5176

Ruetgers-Nease Chemical Company, Inc. Scholarship *(Undergraduate/Scholarship)* 4123

Sandoz Agro, Inc. Scholarships *(Undergraduate/Scholarship)* 4124

Santa Fe Pacific Foundation Scholarships *(Undergraduate/Scholarship)* 4125

Abbie Sargent Memorial Scholarships *(Graduate, Undergraduate/Scholarship)* 5250

SIGCO Research Scholarships *(Undergraduate/Scholarship)* 4126

Social Science Research Fellowships in Agriculture *(Postdoctorate/Fellowship)* 5152

Souvenir Shirts, Etc. Scholarships *(Undergraduate/Scholarship)* 4128

Spraying Systems Company Scholarships *(Undergraduate/Scholarship)* 4129

State Farm Companies Foundation Scholarships *(Undergraduate/Scholarship)* 4130

Sub-Saharan African Dissertation Internship Award *(Doctorate/Internship)* 5154

Sun Company Scholarships *(Undergraduate/Scholarship)* 4131

Ed Taylor Memorial Scholarship *(Graduate, Undergraduate/Scholarship)* 6153

TCS, Farm, Home and Auto Stores Scholarship *(Undergraduate/Scholarship)* 4132

Theisen Supply, Inc. Scholarships *(Undergraduate/Scholarship)* 4134

Tri-State Breeders Scholarships *(Undergraduate/Scholarship)* 4135

Sarah B. Tyson Fellowship *(Professional Development/Fellowship)* 6234

Tyson Foods, Sanofi Animal Health and American Proteins Scholarships *(Undergraduate/Scholarship)* 4136

Union Pacific Foundation Scholarship *(Undergraduate/Scholarship)* 4137

United Dairymen of Idaho Scholarship *(Undergraduate/Scholarship)* 4138

United Farmers of Alberta Scholarship *(Undergraduate/Scholarship)* 165

United Nations Educational Training Scholarships for Southern Africans *(Graduate, Undergraduate/Scholarship)* 5798

Universal Dairy Equipment, Inc. Scholarships *(Undergraduate/Scholarship)* 4140

Valmont Irrigation Scholarships *(Undergraduate/Scholarship)* 4142

Wal-Mart Scholarship *(Undergraduate/Scholarship)* 4144

Wells Fargo Bank Scholarship *(Undergraduate/Scholarship)* 4146

Western Dairymen - John Elway - Melba FFA Scholarship Fund *(Undergraduate/Scholarship)* 4147

Western Seedmen's Association Scholarships *(Undergraduate/Scholarship)* 4148

WIX Corporation Scholarships *(Undergraduate/Scholarship)* 4151

Wolf's Head Oil Company Scholarships *(Undergraduate/Scholarship)* 4152

Wyandott, Inc. Snacks and Popcorn Scholarship *(Undergraduate/Scholarship)* 4153

Yetter Manufacturing Co. Scholarship *(Undergraduate/Scholarship)* 4154

Young Canadian Researchers Awards *(Doctorate, Graduate/Award)* 3151

## Allergies (See also: Asthma)

Allergy and Clinical Immunology Fellowship Program *(Postdoctorate/Fellowship)* 1300

Combined AAOA/AAO-HNSF Research Grant *(Postdoctorate/Grant)* 234

Summer Fellowship Grants *(Doctorate/Fellowship)* 215

Underrepresented Minority Investigators Award in Asthma and Allergy *(Postdoctorate/Award)* 216

## Alzheimer's disease

Alzheimer's Association Faculty Scholar Awards *(Postdoctorate/Award)* 204

Alzheimer's Association Investigator Initiated Research Grants *(Postdoctorate/Grant)* 205

Alzheimer's Association Pilot Research Grants for New Investigators *(Postdoctorate/Grant)* 206

Alzheimer's Association Pioneer Award for Alzheimer's Disease Research *(Doctorate, Postdoctorate/Grant)* 207

Senator Mark Hatfield Award for Clinical Research in Alzheimer's Disease *(Doctorate, Postdoctorate/Grant)* 208

Zenith Fellows Award Program *(Doctorate, Postdoctorate/Grant)* 209

## Amyotrophic lateral sclerosis

ALSA Research Grants *(Postdoctorate/Grant)* 1033

## Anesthesiology

Allied Health Student Loans *(Undergraduate/Loan)* 4870

Georgia Student Finance Commission Service-Cancellable Stafford Loan *(Graduate, Undergraduate/Loan)* 2666

Georgia Student Finance Commission State-Sponsored Loan *(Graduate, Undergraduate/Loan)* 2669

## Animal science and behavior (See also: Zoology)

Allflex USA Scholarship *(Undergraduate/Scholarship)* 4015

American Morgan Horse Institute Scholarships *(Undergraduate/Scholarship)* 4022

Anchor Division Boehringer Ingelheim Animal Health Scholarship *(Undergraduate/Scholarship)* 4024

Animal Health Trust of Canada Research Grants *(Doctorate/Award)* 1046

Beverly and Qamanirjaq Caribou Management Scholarship *(Graduate, Undergraduate/Grant)* 1678

Blue Seal Feeds Scholarship *(Undergraduate/Scholarship)* 4031

Capranica Foundation Award in Neuroethology *(Doctorate, Postdoctorate/Award)* 1723

Caribou Research Bursary *(Other/Scholarship)* 1680

Champions Choice/AKZO Salt Scholarships *(Undergraduate/Scholarship)* 4046

Harold Davis Memorial Endowment Scholarship *(Undergraduate/Scholarship)* 4059

Dog Writers' Educational Trust Scholarships *(Graduate, Undergraduate/Scholarship)* 2264

Excel Corporation, Geo. A. Hormel & Company, and Oscar Mayer Food Corporation Scholarship *(Undergraduate/Scholarship)* 4070

FISCO Farm and Home Stores Scholarships *(Undergraduate/Scholarship)* 4078

Hawkeye Steel Products, Inc. Scholarship *(Undergraduate/Scholarship)* 4086

Lextron, Inc. Scholarships *(Undergraduate/Scholarship)* 4094

**Animal science and behavior (See also: Zoology) (continued)**

Livestock Marketing Association and Local LMA Member Market Scholarship *(Undergraduate/Scholarship)* 4095

National Dairy Shrine/Dairy Management Scholarships, Inc. *(Undergraduate/Scholarship)* 3968

National Zoological Park Minority Traineeships *(Graduate, Undergraduate/Internship)* 4456

National Zoological Park Research Traineeships *(Graduate, Undergraduate/Internship)* 4457

North American Limousin Foundation Scholarship *(Undergraduate/Scholarship)* 4112

Tibor T. Polgar Fellowship *(Graduate, Undergraduate/ Fellowship)* 2916

Professional Products & Services, Inc. Scholarship *(Undergraduate/Scholarship)* 4117

Purina Mills Scholarships *(Undergraduate/Scholarship)* 4118

Purina Research Fellowships *(Graduate/Fellowship)* 5033

Rhone-Poulenc Animal Nutrition Scholarships *(Undergraduate/ Scholarship)* 4121

Smithsonian Institution Graduate Fellowships *(Graduate/ Fellowship)* 5376

Smithsonian Institution Postdoctoral Fellowships *(Postdoctorate/Fellowship)* 5377

Smithsonian Institution Predoctoral Fellowships *(Doctorate/ Fellowship)* 5378

United Feeds Scholarships *(Undergraduate/Scholarship)* 4139

Walco International, Inc. Scholarship *(Undergraduate/ Scholarship)* 4145

**Anthropology**

American Museum of Natural History Collection Study Grants *(Doctorate, Postdoctorate/Grant)* 712

American Museum of Natural History Research and Museum Fellowships *(Postdoctorate/Fellowship)* 713

Lester Armour Graduate Fellowships *(Graduate/ Fellowship)* 2443

Behavioral Sciences Research Training Fellowship *(Postdoctorate/Fellowship)* 2396

Behavioral Sciences Student Fellowship *(Professional Development/Fellowship)* 2397

CIBC Youthvision Graduate Research Award Program *(Graduate/Award)* 1270

Council for European Studies Pre-Dissertation Fellowships in the Social Sciences *(Doctorate/Fellowship)* 2102

Christopher DeCormier Scholarship *(Doctorate/ Scholarship)* 3075

Developing Countries Training Fellowships *(Graduate/ Fellowship)* 6133

Fellowship for the Study of Foraging Peoples *(Doctorate, Graduate, Postdoctorate/Fellowship)* 3441

Field Museum Graduate Fellowships *(Graduate/ Fellowship)* 2444

Field Museum Visiting Scholar Funds *(Postdoctorate/ Grant)* 2446

Fyssen Foundation Research Grants *(Doctorate, Postgraduate/ Grant)* 2610

Howard Foundation Fellowships *(Professional Development/ Fellowship)* 2908

Richard Carley Hunt Memorial Postdoctoral Fellowships *(Postdoctorate/Fellowship)* 6134

IGCC Dissertation Fellowships *(Doctorate, Graduate/ Fellowship)* 3043

International Affairs Fellowships *(Professional Development/ Fellowship)* 2105

International Collaborative Research Grants *(Postdoctorate/ Grant)* 6135

Krupp Foundation Fellowship *(Graduate/Fellowship)* 2773

Katrin H. Lamon Resident Scholarship for Native Americans *(Doctorate, Postdoctorate/Scholarship)* 5274

Leakey Foundation Fellowships for Great Ape Research and Conservation *(Doctorate, Graduate, Postdoctorate/ Fellowship)* 3442

Leakey Foundation General Grants *(Doctorate, Graduate, Postdoctorate, Professional Development/Grant)* 3443

Materials Analysis Fellowships *(Postdoctorate, Postgraduate, Professional Development/Fellowship)* 2061

Mesopotamian Fellowship *(Doctorate, Postdoctorate/ Fellowship)* 878

NAS/NRC Collaboration in Basic Science and Engineering Long-Term Grants *(Postdoctorate/Grant)* 3831

NAS/NRC Collaboration in Basic Science and Engineering Short-Term Project Development Grants *(Postdoctorate/ Grant)* 3832

National Endowment for the Humanities Fellowships *(Postdoctorate/Fellowship)* 5275

Olfactory Research Fund Grants *(Postdoctorate/Grant)* 4744

Paleoanthropology Award *(Doctorate, Professional Development/Award)* 3444

Population Council Fellowships in the Social Sciences *(Postdoctorate/Fellowship)* 4981

Radcliffe Research Support Program *(Postdoctorate/ Grant)* 3798

Research Fellowships in Marine Policy *(Postdoctorate/ Fellowship)* 6248

William A. and Stella M. Rowley Graduate Fellowship *(Graduate/Fellowship)* 2447

Kenneth W. Russell Fellowship *(Graduate/Fellowship)* 883

SSRC Soviet Union and Its Successor States Institutional Awards for First-Year Fellowships *(Graduate/Award)* 5420

James A. Swan Fund Grants *(Graduate, Postgraduate/ Grant)* 5652

Weatherhead Fellowships *(Doctorate, Postdoctorate/ Fellowship)* 5276

Wenner-Gren Foundation Predoctoral Grants *(Doctorate/ Grant)* 6136

Wenner-Gren Regular Grants *(Postdoctorate/Grant)* 6137

Jesse Wrench Scholarship *(Graduate, Undergraduate/ Scholarship)* 3748

**Archeology**

American Numismatic Society Graduate Seminar *(Graduate/ Other)* 737

Ancient India and Iran Trust Travel and Research Grants *(Doctorate, Graduate, Postdoctorate/Grant)* 1035

Australian Institute of Archaeology Grants *(Postdoctorate/ Grant)* 1329

Richard Barnett Memorial Travel Awards *(Postgraduate/ Award)* 1042

Chateaubriand Fellowships (Humanities) *(Doctorate/ Grant)* 2375

Anna C. and Oliver C. Colburn Fellowship *(Doctorate, Postdoctorate/Fellowship)* 1064

Eben Demarest Fund *(Professional Development/Grant)* 2227

Developing Countries Training Fellowships *(Graduate/ Fellowship)* 6133

Endowment for Biblical Research, Summer Research and Travel Grants *(Doctorate, Graduate, Postdoctorate/ Grant)* 868

Kenan T. Erim Award *(Doctorate, Postdoctorate/ Fellowship)* 1065

Fyssen Foundation Research Grants *(Doctorate, Postgraduate/ Grant)* 2610

Jennifer C. Groot Fellowship *(Graduate, Undergraduate/ Fellowship)* 869

Harrell Family Fellowship *(Graduate/Fellowship)* 870

Jacob Hirsch Fellowship *(Doctorate, Graduate/ Fellowship)* 859

Howard Foundation Fellowships *(Professional Development/ Fellowship)* 2908

Humanities Fellowships *(Doctorate, Postdoctorate/ Fellowship)* 1179

Richard Carley Hunt Memorial Postdoctoral Fellowships *(Postdoctorate/Fellowship)* 6134

Islamic Studies Fellowship *(Doctorate/Fellowship)* 872

Olivia James Traveling Fellowship *(Doctorate, Postdoctorate/ Fellowship)* 1066

Samuel H. Kress Foundation Fellowship *(Doctorate/ Fellowship)* 874

Samuel H. Kress Joint Athens-Jerusalem Fellowship *(Postdoctorate/Fellowship)* 875

Leakey Foundation General Grants *(Doctorate, Graduate, Postdoctorate, Professional Development/Grant)* 3443

Materials Analysis Fellowships *(Postdoctorate, Postgraduate, Professional Development/Fellowship)* 2061

Andrew W. Mellon Foundation Fellowships *(Doctorate, Postdoctorate/Fellowship)* 877

Mesopotamian Fellowship *(Doctorate, Postdoctorate/Fellowship)* 878

NAS/NRC Collaboration in Basic Science and Engineering Long-Term Grants *(Postdoctorate/Grant)* 3831

NAS/NRC Collaboration in Basic Science and Engineering Short-Term Project Development Grants *(Postdoctorate/Grant)* 3832

NEH Fellowships for Research in Turkey *(Postdoctorate/Fellowship)* 847

Oregon Humanities Center Summer Visiting Research Fellowships *(Professional Development/Fellowship)* 6011

Harriet and Leon Pomerance Fellowship *(Professional Development/Fellowship)* 1067

Kenneth W. Russell Fellowship *(Graduate/Fellowship)* 883

SSRC Grants for Advanced Area Research *(Doctorate, Other/Grant)* 5399

James A. Swan Fund Grants *(Graduate, Postgraduate/Grant)* 5652

Visiting Scholar Postdoctoral Stipend *(Postdoctorate/Scholarship)* 1789

Wenner-Gren Regular Grants *(Postdoctorate/Grant)* 6137

Elizabeth A. Whitehead Visiting Professorships *(Professional Development/Award)* 862

Helen M. Woodruff Fellowship of the Archaeological Institute of America *(Doctorate, Postdoctorate/Fellowship)* 1068

Woodruff Traveling Fellowship *(Doctorate/Fellowship)* 1069

Jesse Wrench Scholarship *(Graduate, Undergraduate/Scholarship)* 3748

## Architecture (See also: Landscape architecture and design)

AAUW Educational Foundation Selected Professions Fellowship *(Graduate/Fellowship)* 336

AHA/American Institute of Architects Fellowships in Health Facilities Design *(Graduate/Fellowship)* 547

AIA/AAF Scholarship for Advanced Study and Research *(Graduate, Postgraduate, Professional Development/Scholarship)* 571

AIA/AAF Scholarship for Professional Degree Candidates *(Graduate, Undergraduate/Scholarship)* 572

AIA/AHA Fellowship in Health Facilities Design *(Graduate, Undergraduate/Fellowship)* 573

The American Architectural Foundation Minority/Disadvantaged Scholarship *(Graduate, Undergraduate/Scholarship)* 574

APA Planning & the Black Community Division Scholarship *(Undergraduate/Scholarship)* 775

Architects League Scholastic Award *(Undergraduate/Scholarship)* 1075

Architects Registration Council Student Maintenance Grants *(Undergraduate/Grant)* 1079

Asian Cultural Council Fellowship Grants *(Postdoctorate/Fellowship)* 1177

Association for Women in Architecture Scholarship *(Graduate, Undergraduate/Scholarship)* 1292

Center for Advanced Study in the Visual Arts Senior Fellowships and Senior Visiting Fellowships *(Postdoctorate/Fellowship)* 1767

Cintas Fellowships *(Professional Development/Fellowship)* 1163

John Dinkeloo Bequests/American Academy in Rome Traveling Fellowship in Architectural Technology *(Graduate, Postgraduate/Fellowship)* 6023

Dumbarton Oaks Project Grants *(Professional Development/Grant)* 2287

Cesare Fera Memorial Scholarship *(Undergraduate/Scholarship)* 4224

Graham Foundation Grants *(Professional Development/Grant)* 2726

Albert Halse Memorial Scholarship *(Undergraduate/Scholarship)* 1076

Frank Walton Horn Memorial Scholarships *(Undergraduate/Scholarship)* 4000

Humanities Fellowships *(Doctorate, Postdoctorate/Fellowship)* 1179

Islamic Studies Fellowship *(Doctorate/Fellowship)* 872

Olivia James Traveling Fellowship *(Doctorate, Postdoctorate/Fellowship)* 1066

Japan-United States Art Fellowships *(Postdoctorate, Professional Development/Fellowship)* 1180

Jewel/Taylor C. Cotton Scholarship *(Undergraduate/Scholarship)* 1927

Kate Neal Kinley Memorial Fellowhsip *(Graduate/Fellowship)* 5998

Samuel H. Kress Foundation Fellowship *(Doctorate/Fellowship)* 874

Samuel H. Kress Joint Athens-Jerusalem Fellowship *(Postdoctorate/Fellowship)* 875

MacDowell Colony Residencies *(Other, Professional Development/Fellowship)* 3524

Theodore Mazza Scholarship *(Undergraduate/Scholarship)* 5769

Paul Mellon Centre Fellowship *(Doctorate, Graduate/Fellowship)* 6276

Mesopotamian Fellowship *(Doctorate, Postdoctorate/Fellowship)* 878

National Endowment for the Arts - Design Arts Program USA Fellowships *(Professional Development/Fellowship)* 3974

National Roofing Foundation Scholarship Award *(Undergraduate/Scholarship)* 4371

National Zoological Park Traineeship in Facilities Design *(Graduate, Undergraduate/Internship)* 4461

Netz Hilai Visiting Artists Fellowships *(Professional Development/Fellowship)* 4515

New York Foundation for the Arts Artists' Fellowships *(Other/Fellowship)* 4570

New York State Professional Opportunity Scholarships *(Doctorate, Graduate, Undergraduate/Scholarship)* 4592

New York State Regents Professional Opportunity Scholarships *(Doctorate, Graduate, Undergraduate/Scholarship)* 4577

NIAE/ATBCB Student Design Competition Prizes *(Graduate, Undergraduate/Prize)* 6024

Howard Brown Rickard Scholarship *(Undergraduate/Scholarship)* 4007

RTKL Traveling Fellowship *(Graduate, Undergraduate/Fellowship)* 576

Robert Schreck Memorial Fund Scholarship *(Graduate, Undergraduate/Scholarship)* 5280

Society of American Registered Architects Student Design Competition/Emily Munson Memorial Student Award *(Graduate, Undergraduate/Award)* 5433

Steedman Traveling Fellowship in Architecture *(Professional Development/Fellowship)* 5626

Clarence Tabor Memorial Scholarship *(Undergraduate/Scholarship)* 1077

George Tanaka Memorial Scholarship Program *(Undergraduate/Scholarship)* 1288

Robert Thunen Memorial Educational Scholarships *(Graduate, Undergraduate/Scholarship)* 2983

Traveling Fellowships in Architectural Design and Technology *(Postdoctorate/Fellowship)* 6025

Van Alen Institute Fellowship in Public Architecture (Loyd Warren Fellowships/Paris Prize) *(Graduate, Postgraduate/Fellowship, Prize)* 6026

Michael Ventris Memorial Award *(Postdoctorate, Postgraduate/Award)* 3017

## Architecture, Naval

American Society of Naval Engineers Scholarships *(Graduate, Undergraduate/Scholarship)* 959

## Architecture, Naval (continued)

Bunting Institute Science Scholars Fellowships and Biomedical Research Fellowships *(Postdoctorate/Fellowship)* 1529

Society of Naval Architects and Marine Engineers Scholarships *(Professional Development/Scholarship)* 5472

## Area and ethnic studies (See also: specific areas of study, e.g. Asian studies)

AIMS Small Grants *(Doctorate, Postdoctorate/Grant)* 590

Lorraine Allison Scholarships; Jennifer Robinson Scholarships *(Graduate/Scholarship)* 1081

BAEF Predoctoral Fellowships *(Doctorate/Fellowship)* 1397

Bilateral Scholarships *(Postgraduate/Scholarship)* 2110

Brown University, The Future of Gender *(Postdoctorate/ Fellowship)* 5990

Bulgarian Studies Seminar *(Doctorate, Graduate, Postdoctorate/Fellowship)* 3183

Central Intelligence Agency Graduate Studies Internships *(Graduate/Internship)* 1811

Council of American Overseas Research Centers Fellowships *(Postdoctorate/Fellowship)* 866

Crane-Rogers Fellowships *(Professional Development/ Fellowship)* 3025

Czech Education Scholarships *(Doctorate, Graduate, Postdoctorate/Scholarship)* 3708

Dublin Institute for Advanced Studies Research Scholarships *(Postdoctorate/Scholarship)* 2282

Dumbarton Oaks Project Grants *(Professional Development/ Grant)* 2287

Dante B. Fascell Inter-American Fellowships *(Other/ Fellowship)* 3089

Louise Wallace Hackney Fellowship for the Study of Chinese Art *(Doctorate, Postdoctorate/Fellowship)* 757

IEC Russia, China Study Fellowship *(Professional Development/Fellowship)* 3153

India Studies Faculty Fellowships *(Professional Development/ Fellowship)* 5316

India Studies Postdoctoral Research Fellowships *(Professional Development/Fellowship)* 5318

India Studies Student Fellowships *(Graduate/Fellowship)* 5319

Institute of American Cultures Postdoctoral Fellowship *(Postdoctorate/Fellowship)* 1933

Institute of Irish Studies Junior Fellowships *(Postdoctorate/ Fellowship)* 3069

IREX Research Residencies *(Postdoctorate/Grant)* 3186

Irish in America Publication Award Notre Dame Studies in Catholicism Publication Award *(Professional Development/ Award)* 6009

Irish American Cultural Institute Visiting Fellowship in Irish Studies *(Postgraduate/Fellowship)* 3227

Irish Research Funds *(Professional Development/Grant)* 3228

Juniper Gardens Post-Doctoral Fellowship in Research with Minority Handicapped Children *(Postdoctorate/ Fellowship)* 3306

Kosciuszko Foundation Domestic Scholarships *(Graduate/ Scholarship)* 3399

Neporany Research and Teaching Fellowship *(Postdoctorate, Professional Development/Fellowship)* 1661

Pew Fellowships in International Journalism *(Other/ Fellowship)* 4854

Pre- and Postdoctoral Fellowships in International and Area Studies *(Doctorate, Postdoctorate/Fellowship)* 2804

Bernadette Schmitt Grants *(Professional Development/ Grant)* 541

SSRC Advanced Postdoctoral Training and Research Awards *(Doctorate, Postdoctorate/Award, Fellowship, Grant)* 5393

SSRC Africa Predissertation Fellowships *(Doctorate/ Fellowship)* 5394

SSRC African Advanced Research Grants *(Postdoctorate/ Grant)* 5395

SSRC African Humanities Fellowships *(Doctorate, Postdoctorate/Fellowship)* 5396

SSRC Bangladesh Studies Fellowships *(Doctorate, Graduate/ Fellowship)* 5397

SSRC Grants for Advanced Area Research *(Doctorate, Other/ Grant)* 5399

SSRC International Predissertation Fellowships *(Doctorate/ Fellowship)* 5402

SSRC Korea Advanced Research Grants *(Postdoctorate/ Grant)* 5406

SSRC Near and Middle East Advanced Research Fellowships *(Postdoctorate/Fellowship)* 5411

SSRC Predoctoral and Dissertation Training and Research Awards *(Doctorate/Award, Fellowship, Grant)* 5413

SSRC Soviet Union and Its Successor States Dissertation Fellowships *(Doctorate/Fellowship)* 5418

SSRC Soviet Union and Its Successor States Graduate Training Fellowships *(Graduate/Fellowship)* 5419

SSRC Soviet Union and Its Successor States Institutional Awards for First-Year Fellowships *(Graduate/Award)* 5420

SSRC Soviet Union and Its Successor States Postdoctoral Fellowships *(Postdoctorate/Fellowship)* 5421

SSRC Soviet Union and Its Successor States Workshop Grants *(Doctorate, Postdoctorate/Grant)* 5422

Studentships in Northern Studies *(Graduate, Undergraduate/ Scholarship)* 1684

Travel Grants for Independent Short-Term Research *(Other/ Grant)* 3190

U.S. Japan Media Fellowship *(Postgraduate/Fellowship)* 3242

The Year Abroad Program at the Jagiellonian University of Krakow *(Doctorate, Graduate/Fellowship)* 3401

## Armenian studies (See also: Area and ethnic studies)

AGBU Education Loan Program in the U.S. *(Graduate/ Loan)* 1133

AGBU Graduate Loan Program *(Graduate/Loan)* 1134

## Art (See also: Performing arts; Visual arts; specific areas of study, e.g. Painting)

Gladys Agell Award for Excellence in Research *(Graduate/ Award)* 258

Albee Foundation Residencies *(Professional Development/ Other)* 141

Thomas Joseph "Willie" Ambrosole Scholarship *(Undergraduate/Scholarship)* 4207

Armenian Allied Arts Association Scholarship *(Undergraduate/ Award)* 1104

Artists Fellowship; Japan Foundation Cultural Properties Specialists Fellowship; Japan Foundation Doctoral Fellowship; Japan Foundation Research Fellowship *(Doctorate, Postdoctorate, Professional Development/ Fellowship)* 3240

Artists Workplace Fellowships *(Professional Development/ Fellowship)* 6253

Arts Education Fellowships *(Professional Development/ Fellowship)* 2093

Asian Art and Religion Fellowships *(Postdoctorate/ Fellowship)* 1176

Austrian Federal Ministry for Science and Research Grants *(Professional Development/Grant)* 1341

Brucebo Fine Arts Summer Scholarship *(Professional Development/Scholarship)* 1696

Canadian Council for the Arts Grants Program *(Professional Development/Grant)* 1594

Hanna Carola Art Scholarship *(Undergraduate/ Scholarship)* 1853

Constance E. Casey Scholarship *(Undergraduate/ Scholarship)* 1854

Chautauqua Institution Scholarship *(Graduate, High School, Undergraduate/Scholarship)* 1842

The Classical Fellowship; The Norbert Schimmel Fellowship for Mediterranean Art and Archaeology *(Doctorate/ Fellowship)* 3652

Community Arts Administration Internships *(Graduate/ Internship)* 4662

Chester Dale Fellowship *(Other/Fellowship)* 1769

Helen Darcovich Memorial Doctoral Fellowship *(Doctorate, Graduate/Fellowship)* 1657

Mary Davis Fellowship *(Doctorate/Fellowship)* 1770

## Art, Caricatures and cartoons

## Art conservation

## Art history

## Art history (continued)

Getty Museum Graduate Internships *(Doctorate, Graduate/ Internship)* 2702

Getty Museum Guest Scholar Grants *(Postdoctorate/ Grant)* 2703

Roswell L. Gilpatric Internship *(Graduate, Undergraduate/ Internship)* 3655

Henry Luce Foundation/ACLS Dissertation Fellowship Program in American Art *(Graduate/Fellowship)* 411

Howard Foundation Fellowships *(Professional Development/ Fellowship)* 2908

Humanities Fellowships *(Doctorate, Postdoctorate/ Fellowship)* 1179

Huntington Library Research Awards *(Graduate, Postdoctorate/Award)* 2939

Japan-United States Art Fellowships *(Postdoctorate, Professional Development/Fellowship)* 1180

Kress Fellowship in the Art and Archaeology of Jordan *(Doctorate/Fellowship)* 873

Samuel H. Kress Foundation Fellowship *(Doctorate/ Fellowship)* 874

Samuel H. Kress Joint Athens-Jerusalem Fellowship *(Postdoctorate/Fellowship)* 875

Kress Research Fellowship in Art History *(Doctorate/ Fellowship)* 3404

Kress Research Fellowships at Foreign Institutions *(Doctorate/ Fellowship)* 3405

Peter Krueger Summer Internships *(Graduate, Undergraduate/ Internship)* 5384

Lifchez/Stronach Curatorial Internship *(Graduate/ Internship)* 3656

Materials Analysis Fellowships *(Postdoctorate, Postgraduate, Professional Development/Fellowship)* 2061

Paul Mellon Centre Fellowship *(Doctorate, Graduate/ Fellowship)* 6276

Andrew W. Mellon Fellowships *(Postdoctorate/ Fellowship)* 3657

Andrew W. Mellon Fellowships in Art History *(Doctorate, Postdoctorate/Fellowship)* 3658

Mesopotamian Fellowship *(Doctorate, Postdoctorate/ Fellowship)* 878

Metropolitan Museum of Art Classical Fellowship *(Doctorate/ Fellowship)* 3660

Metropolitan Museum of Art Nine-Month Internship *(Graduate, Undergraduate/Internship)* 3661

Metropolitan Museum of Art Six Month Internship *(Graduate, Undergraduate/Internship)* 3662

Metropolitan Museum of Art Summer Internship for College Students *(Undergraduate/Internship)* 3663

Metropolitan Museum of Art Summer Internship for Graduate Students *(Graduate/Internship)* 3664

Metropolitan Museum of Art Volunteer Internships *(Graduate, Undergraduate/Internship)* 3665

National Endowment for the Humanities Fellowships *(Postdoctorate/Fellowship)* 2543

National Museum of American Art Summer Internships *(Graduate, Undergraduate/Internship)* 5388

Oregon Humanities Center Summer Visiting Research Fellowships *(Professional Development/Fellowship)* 6011

Professional Development Fellowship Program for Artists and Art Historians *(Doctorate, Graduate/Fellowship)* 1982

Theodore Rousseau Fellowships *(Doctorate, Graduate/ Fellowship)* 3667

Louis J. Salerno, M.D. Memorial Scholarship *(Graduate, Undergraduate/Scholarship)* 4257

Robert H. and Clarice Smith Fellowship *(Doctorate/ Fellowship)* 1779

Smithsonian Institution Graduate Fellowships *(Graduate/ Fellowship)* 5376

Smithsonian Institution Postdoctoral Fellowships *(Postdoctorate/Fellowship)* 5377

Smithsonian Institution Predoctoral Fellowships *(Doctorate/ Fellowship)* 5378

SSRC African Advanced Research Grants *(Postdoctorate/ Grant)* 5395

SSRC Korea Advanced Research Grants *(Postdoctorate/ Grant)* 5406

Villa I Tatti Fellowships *(Postdoctorate/Fellowship)* 6044

Virginia Museum of Fine Arts Fellowship *(Professional Development/Fellowship)* 6061

Lewis Walpole Library Fellowship *(Graduate, Postdoctorate/ Fellowship)* 6277

Yale Center for British Art Fellowships *(Postdoctorate, Professional Development/Fellowship)* 6278

## Art therapy

NSDAR Occupational Therapy Scholarship *(Graduate, Undergraduate/Scholarship)* 4403

Rawley Silver Scholarship *(Graduate/Award)* 261

## Arthritis (See also: Rheumatology)

Arthritis Biomedical Science Grants *(Postdoctorate/ Grant)* 1147

Arthritis Foundation Doctoral Dissertation Award for Arthritis Health Professionals *(Doctorate/Award)* 1148

Arthritis Foundation New Investigator Grant for Arthritis Health Professionals *(Postdoctorate/Grant)* 1149

Arthritis Foundation Physician Scientist Development Award *(Postdoctorate/Award)* 1150

Arthritis Investigator Awards *(Postdoctorate/Award)* 1152

Arthritis Society Clinical Fellowships *(Doctorate/ Fellowship)* 1154

Arthritis Society Research Fellowships *(Postdoctorate/ Fellowship)* 1155

Arthritis Society Research Scholarships *(Postdoctorate/ Scholarship)* 1157

Arthritis Society Research Scientist Award *(Postdoctorate/ Award)* 1158

## Asian studies (See also: Area and ethnic studies)

AIIS Fellowship for Senior Scholarly Development *(Postdoctorate/Fellowship)* 585

AIIS Junior Fellowships *(Doctorate/Fellowship)* 586

AIIS Senior Research Fellowships *(Postdoctorate/ Fellowship)* 587

American Institute of Pakistan Studies Predoctoral and Postdoctoral Fellowships *(Doctorate, Postdoctorate/ Fellowship)* 596

APDC Visiting Fellowships *(Postdoctorate/Fellowship)* 1182

Asian Art and Religion Fellowships *(Postdoctorate/ Fellowship)* 1176

Asian Cultural Council Fellowship Grants *(Postdoctorate/ Fellowship)* 1177

Harry J. Benda Prize *(Postdoctorate/Prize)* 1223

Blakemore Foundation Asian Language Fellowship Grants *(Doctorate, Graduate/Grant)* 1440

Council of American Overseas Research Centers Fellowships *(Postdoctorate/Fellowship)* 866

Crane-Rogers Fellowships *(Professional Development/ Fellowship)* 3025

East-West Center Professional Associateships *(Professional Development/Fellowship)* 2310

East-West Center Visiting Fellowships *(Postdoctorate/ Fellowship)* 2311

Ford Foundation Fellowships *(Doctorate, Graduate, Postdoctorate/Fellowship)* 1178

The Freedom Forum Asia Studies Fellowships *(Professional Development/Fellowship)* 5996

Humanities Fellowships *(Doctorate, Postdoctorate/ Fellowship)* 1179

International Student Identity Card Travel Grants for Educational Programs in Developing Countries *(High School, Undergraduate/Grant)* 2113

IREX Research Residencies *(Postdoctorate/Grant)* 3186

Luce Scholars Program *(Graduate, Undergraduate/Internship, Scholarship)* 3512

The National Council Research Contracts *(Postdoctorate/ Fellowship, Grant)* 3945

SSRC Korea Advanced Research Grants *(Postdoctorate/ Grant)* 5406

## Aviation (See also: Aeronautics) (continued)

Lowell Gaylor Memorial Scholarship *(Other/Scholarship)* 85

Gulf Coast Avionics Scholarships to Fox Valley Technical College *(Undergraduate/Scholarship)* 86

William E. Jackson Award *(Graduate/Award)* 5198

Russell Leroy Jones Memorial Scholarship to Colorado Aero Tech *(Undergraduate/Scholarship)* 87

Leon Harris/Les Nichols Memorial Scholarship to Spartain School of Aeronautics *(Undergraduate/Scholarship)* 88

Lindbergh Grants *(Other/Grant)* 3484

Professional Pilot John W. "Reds" Macfarlane Scholarship *(Professional Development, Undergraduate/ Scholarship)* 1350

McAllister Memorial Scholarship *(Undergraduate/ Scholarship)* 1048

Mid-Continent Instrument Scholarship *(Undergraduate/ Scholarship)* 89

Ted Moll Flight Scholarship *(Undergraduate/Scholarship)* 1887

Monte Mitchell Global Scholarship *(Undergraduate/ Scholarship)* 90

Col. Louisa Spruance Morse CAP Scholarship *(Undergraduate/ Scholarship)* 3917

Doris Mullen Memorial Scholarships *(All/Scholarship)* 3203

National Board Civil Air Patrol Undergraduate/Advanced Undergraduate College Scholarship *(Undergraduate/ Scholarship)* 3918

Nebraska Space Grant Scholarships and Fellowships *(Graduate, Undergraduate/Fellowship, Scholarship)* 4505

Northeast Chapter of the American Association of Airport Executives (AAAE) Post Scholarship *(Undergraduate/ Scholarship)* 272

Northern Airborne Technology Scholarship *(Undergraduate/ Scholarship)* 91

Plane & Pilot Magazine Germin Scholarship *(Undergraduate/ Scholarship)* 92

Aviation Management Wilfred M. "Wiley" Post Scholarship *(Professional Development, Undergraduate/ Scholarship)* 1351

Silver Dart Aviation History Award *(Undergraduate/ Prize)* 1607

Lee Tarbox Memorial Scholarship *(Undergraduate/ Scholarship)* 93

Teledyne Continental Aviation Excellence Scholarship *(Undergraduate/Scholarship)* 2298

Teledyne Continental Aviation Excellence Scholarship *(All/ Scholarship)* 5693

USAIG PDP Scholarships *(Postgraduate, Undergraduate/ Scholarship)* 6017

Richard Lee Vernon Aviation Scholarship *(Undergraduate/ Scholarship)* 2299

Vertical Flight Foundation Scholarships *(Graduate, Undergraduate/Scholarship)* 6036

A. Verville Fellowship *(Other/Fellowship)* 5381

Charlie Wells Memorial Aviation Scholarship *(Undergraduate/ Scholarship)* 6131

Whirly-Girls Memorial Flight Scholarships *(Professional Development/Scholarship)* 3204

Harold S. Wood Award for Excellence *(Graduate, Undergraduate/Scholarship)* 4205

Paul and Blanche Wulfsberg Scholarship *(Undergraduate/ Scholarship)* 94

## Banking (See also: Accounting; Finance)

Germanistic Society of America Quadrille Grants *(Graduate, Postgraduate/Grant)* 2697

## Behavioral sciences

Behavioral Sciences Research Training Fellowship *(Postdoctorate/Fellowship)* 2396

The Jeanne Humphrey Block Dissertation Award *(Doctorate/ Grant)* 3796

Faculty Research Participation Program at the Naval Air Warfare Center Training Systems Division. *(Professional Development/Fellowship)* 5875

FIC International Research Fellowships *(Postdoctorate/ Fellowship)* 2528

FIC Senior International Fellowships *(Postdoctorate/ Fellowship)* 2529

FIC Senior International Fellowships in Biomedical Sciences *(Postdoctorate/Fellowship)* 2530

Ford Foundation Postdoctoral Fellowships for Minorities *(Postdoctorate/Fellowship)* 4356

Ford Foundation Predoctoral and Dissertation Fellowships for Minorities *(Doctorate/Fellowship)* 4357

Israeli Ministry of Health Fellowships *(Postdoctorate/ Fellowship)* 2533

Japan Society for the Promotion of Science Fellowships *(Postdoctorate/Fellowship)* 2534

Judicial Fellowships *(Professional Development/ Fellowship)* 5650

The Louise Kidder Early Career Award *(Postdoctorate/ Award)* 5495

The Henry A. Murray Dissertation Award *(Doctorate/ Award)* 3797

National Defense Science and Engineering Graduate Fellowship Program *(Graduate/Fellowship)* 5855

National Heart, Lung, and Blood Institute's Minority School Faculty Development Award *(Postdoctorate/Award)* 4175

Naval Air Warfare Center Training Systems Division Graduate Research Participation Program *(Graduate, Postgraduate/ Fellowship)* 5912

Olfactory Research Fund Grants *(Postdoctorate/Grant)* 4744

Barbara Rosenblum Cancer Dissertation Award *(Doctorate/ Award)* 5525

Sigma Xi Grants-in-Aid of Research *(Graduate, Undergraduate/Grant)* 5347

SSRC-MacArthur Foundation Dissertation Fellowships on Peace and Security in a Changing World *(Doctorate/ Fellowship)* 5409

Swedish Medical Research Council Fellowships *(Postdoctorate/Fellowship)* 2535

Taiwan National Science Council Fellowships *(Postdoctorate/ Fellowship)* 2536

U.S. Army Summer Faculty Research and Engineering Associateships *(Postdoctorate/Fellowship)* 1376

Alexander von Humboldt Foundation Fellowship *(Postdoctorate/Fellowship)* 2537

## Bible studies (See also: Religion; Theology)

Australian Institute of Archaeology Grants *(Postdoctorate/ Grant)* 1329

Endowment for Biblical Research, Summer Research and Travel Grants *(Doctorate, Graduate, Postdoctorate/ Grant)* 868

Institute of Holy Land Studies Scholarships *(Graduate/ Scholarship)* 3047

Mesopotamian Fellowship *(Doctorate, Postdoctorate/ Fellowship)* 878

## Biochemistry (See also: Chemistry)

American Foundation for Aging Research Predoctoral Awards *(Doctorate, Graduate, Undergraduate/Award)* 469

Alfred Bader Scholarship *(Graduate/Scholarship)* 1905

Bunting Institute Science Scholars Fellowships and Biomedical Research Fellowships *(Postdoctorate/Fellowship)* 1529

Continental European Fellowships *(Postgraduate/ Fellowship)* 1956

Gladys Anderson Emerson Scholarships *(Undergraduate/ Scholarship)* 3215

Anna Louise Hoffman Awards for Outstanding Achievement in Graduate Research *(Graduate/Award)* 3216

Krebs Memorial Scholarships *(Doctorate/Scholarship)* 1434

Pestcon Graduate Scholarship *(Graduate/Scholarship)* 1906

Predoctoral Fellowships in Biological Sciences *(Doctorate/ Fellowship)* 2927

Taste & Clinic Fellowship *(Postdoctorate/Fellowship)* 1801

U.S. Department of Energy Human Genome Distinguished Postdoctoral Fellowships *(Postdoctorate/Fellowship)* 4710

## Biological and clinical sciences (See also: Biology)

American Society for Clinical Laboratory Science Scholarships (*Graduate/Scholarship*) 908

Archbold Biological Station Undergraduate and Graduate Internships (*Graduate, Undergraduate/Internship*) 1071

A. E. Bennett Research Awards (*Postdoctorate/Award*) 5438

del Duca Foundation Maintenance and Travel Grants (*Professional Development/Grant*) 2284

Environmental Protection Agency Tribal Lands Science Scholarship (*Doctorate, Graduate, Postgraduate/Scholarship*) 560

Eppley Foundation Support for Advanced Scientific Research (*Postdoctorate/Grant*) 2404

Faculty Research Participation Program at the National Center for Toxicological Research (*Professional Development/Fellowship*) 5874

FIC Senior International Fellowships in Biomedical Sciences (*Postdoctorate/Fellowship*) 2530

Ford Foundation Postdoctoral Fellowships for Minorities (*Postdoctorate/Fellowship*) 4356

Ford Foundation Predoctoral and Dissertation Fellowships for Minorities (*Doctorate/Fellowship*) 4357

Hancock County Scholars Program (*High School/Scholarship*) 3784

Howard Hughes Medical Institute Predoctoral Fellowships in Biological Sciences (*Postdoctorate/Fellowship*) 4358

Japan Society for the Promotion of Science Fellowships (*Postdoctorate/Fellowship*) 2534

Life Sciences Research Foundation Fellowships (*Postdoctorate, Postgraduate/Fellowship*) 3470

MSA Presidential Student Awards (*Graduate, Undergraduate/Award*) 3696

MSA Undergraduate Research Scholarships (*Undergraduate/Scholarship*) 3697

NAS/NRC Collaboration in Basic Science and Engineering Long-Term Grants (*Postdoctorate/Grant*) 3831

NAS/NRC Collaboration in Basic Science and Engineering Short-Term Project Development Grants (*Postdoctorate/Grant*) 3832

National Defense Science and Engineering Graduate Fellowship Program (*Graduate/Fellowship*) 5855

The Payzer Scholarship (*Undergraduate/Scholarship*) 2296

Predoctoral Fellowships in Biological Sciences (*Doctorate/Fellowship*) 2927

Research Science Institute Internship (*Undergraduate/Internship*) 5103

Swedish Medical Research Council Fellowships (*Postdoctorate/Fellowship*) 2535

Morris K. Udall OTA Congressional Fellowship (*Postdoctorate/Fellowship*) 5851

Alexander von Humboldt Foundation Fellowship (*Postdoctorate/Fellowship*) 2537

Whitney Postdoctoral Research Fellowships (*Postdoctorate/Fellowship*) 6175

## Biology (See also: Biological and clinical sciences)

AAAS-EPA Environmental Science and Engineering Fellowships (*Postdoctorate/Fellowship*) 265

AIBS Congressional Science Fellowship (*Postdoctorate/Fellowship*) 476

American Cyanamid Scholarship (*Undergraduate/Scholarship*) 4017

BNL Postdoctoral Research Associateships (*Postdoctorate/Other*) 1504

Bunting Institute Science Scholars Fellowships and Biomedical Research Fellowships (*Postdoctorate/Fellowship*) 1529

Carnegie Institution of Washington Postdoctoral and Predoctoral Fellowships (*Doctorate, Postdoctorate/Fellowship*) 1737

Civilian Radioactive Waste Management/Historically Black Colleges and Universities Faculty Fellowship Program (*Professional Development/Fellowship*) 5867

Conservation and Research Foundation Research Grants (*Professional Development/Grant*) 2063

Continental European Fellowships (*Postgraduate/Fellowship*) 1956

ESA Undergraduate Scholarships (*Undergraduate/Scholarship*) 2389

Eloise Gerry Fellowships (*Postgraduate/Fellowship*) 5329

Phyllis P. Harris Scholarships (*All/Scholarship*) 4956

Jackson Laboratory Postdoctoral Traineeships (*Postdoctorate/Fellowship*) 3232

NIDAY Fellowships (*Postdoctorate, Postgraduate/Fellowship*) 3786

Olfactory Research Fund Grants (*Postdoctorate/Grant*) 4744

Postdoctoral Fellowships in the Atmospheric Sciences (*Postdoctorate/Fellowship*) 3931

Postdoctoral Fellowships in Ocean Science and Engineering (*Postdoctorate/Fellowship*) 6247

Postdoctoral Research Fellowships for Physicians (*Postdoctorate/Fellowship*) 2926

James A. Swan Fund Grants (*Graduate, Postgraduate/Grant*) 5652

Walton Scholarships (*Graduate, Undergraduate/Scholarship*) 3787

## Biology, Marine

Bermuda Biological Station Grants-in-Aid (*Professional Development/Grant*) 1416

Bermuda Biological Station Summer Course Scholarships (*Graduate, Undergraduate/Scholarship*) 1417

Bermuda Biological Station Visiting Graduate Internships (*Graduate, Postgraduate/Internship*) 1418

Conchologists of America Grants (*Graduate/Grant*) 25

Grass Fellowships in Neurophysiology (*Doctorate, Postdoctorate/Fellowship*) 2742

Hudson River Fellowships (*Doctorate, Graduate/Fellowship*) 2912

Hudson River Research Grants (*Postdoctorate/Grant*) 2913

Dean John Knauss Marine Policy Fellowship (*Graduate/Fellowship*) 4386

Lerner-Gray Grants (*Postdoctorate/Grant*) 715

Olin Fellowships (*Professional Development/Fellowship*) 1312

Our World - Underwater Scholarships (*Undergraduate/Scholarship*) 4822

Scholarships for Marine Sciences (*Graduate/Scholarship*) 3206

Seaspace Scholarship (*Graduate, Undergraduate/Scholarship*) 5293

Slocum-Lunz Foundation Scholarships and Grants (*Graduate/Grant, Scholarship*) 5359

Sport Fishery Research Grants and Fellowships (*Postgraduate, Professional Development/Fellowship, Grant*) 5593

Woods Hole Oceanographic Institution Summer Student Fellowships (*Undergraduate/Fellowship*) 6249

## Biology, Molecular

American Foundation for Aging Research Predoctoral Awards (*Doctorate, Graduate, Undergraduate/Award*) 469

Postdoctoral Fellowships in Ocean Science and Engineering (*Postdoctorate/Fellowship*) 6247

Predoctoral Fellowships in Biological Sciences (*Doctorate/Fellowship*) 2927

## Biomedical research (See also: Medical research)

Action Research Program and Project Grants (*Postdoctorate/Grant*) 30

Action Research Training Fellowships (*Postgraduate/Fellowship*) 31

American Foundation for Aging Research Predoctoral Awards (*Doctorate, Graduate, Undergraduate/Award*) 469

CIIT Summer Internships (*Graduate, Postgraduate, Undergraduate/Internship*) 1903

del Duca Foundation Maintenance and Travel Grants (*Professional Development/Grant*) 2284

Gina Finzi Memorial Student Summer Fellowships for Research (*Doctorate, Graduate, Undergraduate/Fellowship*) 3519

## Biomedical research (See also: Medical research) (continued)

Lupus Foundation of America Research Grants *(Doctorate, Graduate/Grant)* 3520

NIDA Individual National Research Service Awards *(Doctorate, Postdoctorate/Fellowship)* 4192

OFAS Research Grants *(Postdoctorate/Grant)* 4807

## Biomedical sciences

AFAR Fellowships *(Graduate, Undergraduate/Fellowship)* 468

American Heart Association, California Affiliate - Grants-in-Aid *(Postdoctorate/Grant)* 530

American Heart Association, California Affiliate - Predoctoral Fellowship *(Doctorate/Fellowship)* 532

Eastburn Fellowships *(Postdoctorate/Fellowship)* 2314

FIC Bilateral Exchanges *(Postdoctorate/Award)* 2525

FIC Foreign-Funded Fellowships *(Postdoctorate/Fellowship)* 2526

FIC International Research Fellowships *(Postdoctorate/Fellowship)* 2528

FIC Senior International Fellowships *(Postdoctorate/Fellowship)* 2529

FIC Senior International Fellowships in Biomedical Sciences *(Postdoctorate/Fellowship)* 2530

Alexander Hollaender Distinguished Postdoctoral Fellowships *(Postdoctorate/Fellowship)* 4706

International Fellowships in Medical Education *(Professional Development/Fellowship)* 2345

Israeli Ministry of Health Fellowships *(Postdoctorate/Fellowship)* 2533

Japan Society for the Promotion of Science Fellowships *(Postdoctorate/Fellowship)* 2534

Krebs Memorial Scholarships *(Doctorate/Scholarship)* 1434

Lindbergh Grants *(Other/Grant)* 3484

MLA Doctoral Fellowship *(Doctorate/Fellowship)* 3633

NIH Predoctoral Fellowship Awards for Minority Students *(Doctorate/Fellowship)* 3722

OFAS Research Grants *(Postdoctorate/Grant)* 4807

Postdoctoral Research Fellowships for Physicians *(Postdoctorate/Fellowship)* 2926

Predoctoral Fellowships in Biological Sciences *(Doctorate/Fellowship)* 2927

Swedish Medical Research Council Fellowships *(Postdoctorate/Fellowship)* 2535

Taiwan National Science Council Fellowships *(Postdoctorate/Fellowship)* 2536

Alexander von Humboldt Foundation Fellowship *(Postdoctorate/Fellowship)* 2537

## Biophysics (See also: Physics)

American Foundation for Aging Research Predoctoral Awards *(Doctorate, Graduate, Undergraduate/Award)* 469

Howard Hughes Medical Institute Predoctoral Fellowships in Biological Sciences *(Postdoctorate/Fellowship)* 4358

## Blood banking

Allied Health Student Loans *(Undergraduate/Loan)* 4870

Taiwan National Science Council Fellowships *(Postdoctorate/Fellowship)* 2536

## Botany

Alexopoulos Prize *(Postdoctorate/Prize)* 3814

American Cyanamid Scholarship *(Undergraduate/Scholarship)* 4017

Lester Armour Graduate Fellowships *(Graduate/Fellowship)* 2443

Carnegie Institution of Washington Postdoctoral and Predoctoral Fellowships *(Doctorate, Postdoctorate/Fellowship)* 1737

Field Museum Graduate Fellowships *(Graduate/Fellowship)* 2444

Field Museum Visiting Scholar Funds *(Postdoctorate/Grant)* 2446

GCA Awards in Tropical Botany *(Doctorate/Award)* 2621

U.P. Hedrick Award *(Graduate, Undergraduate/Award)* 786

Huyck Station Research Grants *(Graduate/Grant)* 2944

Mycological Society of America Graduate Fellowships *(Doctorate/Fellowship)* 3815

Mycological Society of America Graduate Research Prizes *(Doctorate, Graduate/Prize)* 3816

NAS/NRC Collaboration in Basic Science and Engineering Long-Term Grants *(Postdoctorate/Grant)* 3831

NAS/NRC Collaboration in Basic Science and Engineering Short-Term Project Development Grants *(Postdoctorate/Grant)* 3832

New York Botanical Garden Fellowships for Graduate Study in Systemic and Economic Botany *(Doctorate/Fellowship)* 4560

Theodore Roosevelt Memorial Grants *(Doctorate, Graduate, Postdoctorate/Grant)* 716

William A. and Stella M. Rowley Graduate Fellowship *(Graduate/Fellowship)* 2447

Marie Selby Internships *(Graduate, Undergraduate/Internship)* 5304

Smithsonian Environmental Research Center Work-Learn Opportunities in Environmental Studies *(Graduate, Undergraduate/Internship)* 5374

## British studies (See also: Scottish studies; Welsh studies)

Folger Library Long-Term Fellowships *(Postdoctorate/Fellowship)* 2541

Folger Library Short-Term Fellowships *(Postdoctorate/Fellowship)* 2542

National Endowment for the Humanities Fellowships *(Postdoctorate/Fellowship)* 2543

Lewis Walpole Library Fellowship *(Graduate, Postdoctorate/Fellowship)* 6277

Yale Center for British Art Fellowships *(Postdoctorate, Professional Development/Fellowship)* 6278

## Broadcasting (See also: Media arts)

Jim Allard Broadcast Journalism Scholarship *(Undergraduate/Scholarship)* 1600

Len Allen Award of Merit for Radio News *(Graduate, Undergraduate/Grant)* 5051

Alpha Epsilon Rho Scholarships *(Graduate, Undergraduate/Scholarship)* 196

Asbury Park Press Scholarships for Minority Students *(Undergraduate/Scholarship)* 1168

Ed Bradley Scholarships *(Undergraduate/Scholarship)* 5053

Broadcast Pioneers Scholarships *(Graduate, Undergraduate/Scholarship)* 1495

Michele Clark Fellowship *(Professional Development/Fellowship)* 5057

College Conference and Summer Fellowship Program *(Graduate, Undergraduate/Fellowship)* 3174

Raymond Crepault Scholarship *(Graduate/Scholarship)* 1602

Dallas-Fort Worth Association of Black Communicators Scholarships *(High School, Undergraduate/Scholarship)* 2170

Harold E. Ennes Scholarship *(Undergraduate/Scholarship)* 5442

Harold E. Fellows Scholarships *(Graduate, Undergraduate/Scholarship)* 1496

James Lawrence Fly Scholarships *(Graduate, Undergraduate/Scholarship)* 1497

Gannett Center Fellowships *(Other, Professional Development/Fellowship)* 2593

Joel Garcia Memorial Scholarship *(Undergraduate/Scholarship)* 1555

Grants for Research in Broadcasting *(Graduate, Undergraduate/Grant)* 3864

Ruth Hancock Scholarships *(Undergraduate/Scholarship)* 1603

Iowa Broadcasters Association Scholarship *(Undergraduate/Scholarship)* 3219

Journalists in Europe Study Program *(Graduate/Scholarship)* 3302

KNTV Minority Scholarships *(Undergraduate/Scholarship)* 3394

National Fellowships in Education Reporting *(Professional Development/Fellowship)* 2343

Vada and Barney Oldfield Fellowship for National Security Reporting *(Professional Development/Fellowship)* 5063

Walter Patterson Scholarships *(Graduate, Undergraduate/Scholarship)* 1498

Nelson A. Rockefeller Minority Internships *(Undergraduate/Internship)* 6270

RTNDF Environmental and Science Reporting Fellowship *(Professional Development/Fellowship)* 5065

RTNDF Six-Month Entry Level Internships for Minority Students *(Graduate/Internship)* 5067

RTNDF Summer Internships for Minority Students *(Undergraduate/Internship)* 5068

RTNDF Undergraduate Scholarships *(Graduate, Undergraduate/Scholarship)* 5069

Abe Schechter Graduate Scholarship *(Graduate/Scholarship)* 5070

Shane Media Scholarships *(Graduate, Undergraduate/Scholarship)* 1499

Carole Simpson Scholarship *(Graduate, Undergraduate/Scholarship)* 5071

Specs Howard High School Scholarships *(High School, Undergraduate/Scholarship)* 5583

Specs Howard School of Broadcast Arts Industry Scholarships *(Undergraduate/Scholarship)* 5584

Vincent T. Wasilewski Scholarships *(Graduate, Undergraduate/Scholarship)* 1500

## Business

Airline Pilots Association Scholarship *(Undergraduate/Scholarship)* 96

AISES A.T. Anderson Memorial Scholarship *(Graduate, Undergraduate/Scholarship)* 559

A.A. Amidon Scholarship *(Undergraduate/Scholarship)* 1848

Avon Products Foundation Scholarship Program for Women in Business Studies *(Graduate, Professional Development, Undergraduate/Scholarship)* 1545

Batten Fellowships *(Graduate/Fellowship)* 6013

Harold Bettinger Memorial Scholarship *(Graduate, Undergraduate/Scholarship)* 1382

Bicentennial Swedish-American Exchange Fund Travel Grants *(Professional Development/Grant)* 5656

Business Press Educational Foundation Student Intern Program *(Graduate, Undergraduate/Internship)* 1543

Call to Action Opportunity Scholarship *(Undergraduate/Scholarship)* 1568

CERT Scholarship *(Graduate, Undergraduate/Scholarship)* 2100

Engalitcheff Institute on Comparative Political and Economic Systems Internship *(Undergraduate/Internship)* 3019

Ethics in Business Scholarship Program *(Undergraduate/Scholarship)* 2499

Fellowships in Ethics *(Postdoctorate, Postgraduate/Fellowship)* 5015

First Interstate Bank Scholarship *(Undergraduate/Scholarship)* 2468

Four-Shra-Nish Foundation Loan *(Undergraduate/Loan)* 2583

Golden State Minority Foundation Scholarships *(Undergraduate/Scholarship)* 2713

George L. Graziadio Fellowship for Business *(Undergraduate/Scholarship)* 4230

John Grenzebach Awards for Outstanding Research in Philanthropy for Education *(Doctorate, Postdoctorate/Award)* 12

Bryce Harlow Institute on Business and Government Affairs Internship *(Undergraduate/Internship)* 3020

Institute on Political Journalism Summer Program *(Undergraduate/Internship)* 3021

International Affairs Fellowships *(Professional Development/Fellowship)* 2105

IPMA Graduate Study Fellowships *(Professional Development/Fellowship)* 3172

Richard D. Irwin Fellowship Awards *(Doctorate/Award, Fellowship)* 3230

Jacob's Pillow Dance Festival Internships *(Graduate, Undergraduate/Internship)* 3234

Jewel/Taylor C. Cotton Scholarship *(Undergraduate/Scholarship)* 1927

Merrill Lynch Scholarship *(Undergraduate/Scholarship)* 4241

NAPM Doctoral Grants *(Doctorate/Grant)* 3895

NBMBAA National MBA Scholarship/PhD Fellowship *(Graduate/Fellowship, Scholarship)* 3910

Vennera Noto Scholarship *(Undergraduate/Scholarship)* 4249

Edwin G. Nourse Award *(Doctorate/Award)* 3952

Packaging Education Forum (PEF) Packaging Scholarships *(Undergraduate/Scholarship)* 4828

President's Committee on Employment of People with Disabilities Scholarships for Students with Disabilities *(Undergraduate/Scholarship)* 5001

Professional Secretaries International Scholarships *(Undergraduate/Scholarship)* 5011

Sacramento Hispanic Chamber of Commerce Scholarships *(Undergraduate/Scholarship)* 5216

Karla Scherer Foundation Scholarships *(Graduate, Undergraduate/Scholarship)* 5254

Service Merchandise Scholarship Program *(High School, Undergraduate/Scholarship)* 5310

E.D. Stella Scholarship *(Undergraduate/Scholarship)* 4262

Sutherland/Purdy Scholarship *(Undergraduate/Scholarship)* 4925

William Toto Scholarship *(Undergraduate/Scholarship)* 4265

Jerry Wilmot Scholarship *(Undergraduate/Scholarship)* 1389

Wolcott Foundation Fellowships *(Graduate/Fellowship)* 2870

Young Canadian Researchers Awards *(Doctorate, Graduate/Award)* 3151

## Business administration

AAUW Educational Foundation Selected Professions Engineering Dissertation Fellowship *(Graduate/Fellowship)* 335

Air Force ROTC Scholarships *(Undergraduate/Scholarship)* 5816

AISES A.T. Anderson Memorial Scholarship *(Graduate, Undergraduate/Scholarship)* 559

Andersen Fellowships for Doctoral Candidates at the Dissertation Stage *(Doctorate/Fellowship)* 1039

Andersen Foundation Faculty Residencies *(Professional Development/Award)* 1040

Aspen Systems Graduate Scholarship *(Graduate/Scholarship)* 515

Avon Products Foundation Scholarship Program for Women in Business Studies *(Graduate, Professional Development, Undergraduate/Scholarship)* 1545

Bosch Foundation Fellowships *(Postgraduate/Fellowship)* 1459

BPW/Sears Roebuck Loans for Women in Graduate Business Studies *(Graduate/Loan)* 1548

Central Intelligence Agency Graduate Studies Internships *(Graduate/Internship)* 1811

CIBC Youthvision Graduate Research Award Program *(Graduate/Award)* 1270

Community Arts Administration Internships *(Graduate/Internship)* 4662

Consortium Graduate Study Management Fellowships for Minorities *(Graduate/Fellowship)* 2067

Duracell/National Urban League Scholarship and Intern Program for Minority Students *(Undergraduate/Internship, Scholarship)* 4448

Exceptional Student Fellowship Award *(Undergraduate/Scholarship)* 5613

Fukunaga Scholarship Foundation Annual Four-Year Scholarships in Business Administration *(Undergraduate/Scholarship)* 2603

Golden State Minority Foundation Scholarships *(Undergraduate/Scholarship)* 2713

Judicial Fellowships *(Professional Development/Fellowship)* 5650

Mercedes-Benz of North America Scholarship Program *(Undergraduate/Scholarship)* 1928

## Business administration (continued)

Mexican American Grocers Association Foundation Scholarships *(Undergraduate/Scholarship)* 3673

NAA Foundation Minority Fellowships *(Professional Development/Fellowship)* 4631

NAPM Senior Research Fellowship Grants *(Doctorate/ Fellowship)* 3896

Petro-Canada Inc. Graduate Research Awards *(Doctorate, Graduate/Award)* 1284

Phi Chi Theta Scholarships *(Graduate, Postgraduate, Undergraduate/Scholarship)* 4896

Santa Fe Pacific Foundation Scholarships *(Undergraduate/ Scholarship)* 563

## Byzantine studies (See also: Area and ethnic studies)

Bliss Prize Fellowship in Byzantine Studies *(Graduate/ Fellowship)* 2286

Dumbarton Oaks Project Grants *(Professional Development/ Grant)* 2287

Fellowships in Byzantine Studies, Pre-Columbian Studies and Landscape Architecture *(Doctorate, Graduate, Postdoctorate, Undergraduate/Fellowship)* 2288

## Canadian studies (See also: Area and ethnic studies)

Canadian Studies Faculty Enrichment Awards *(Professional Development/Award)* 1624

Canadian Studies Faculty Research Grants *(Postdoctorate/ Grant)* 1625

Canadian Studies Graduate Student Fellowships *(Doctorate/ Fellowship)* 1626

Canadian Studies for Indian Scholars *(Doctorate, Professional Development/Fellowship)* 5315

Canadian Studies Sabbatical Fellowship Program *(Professional Development/Fellowship)* 1627

Canadian Studies Senior Fellowships *(Postdoctorate/ Fellowship)* 1628

Cultural Grants *(Professional Development/Grant)* 1596

Helen Darcovich Memorial Doctoral Fellowship *(Doctorate, Graduate/Fellowship)* 1657

Marusia and Michael Dorosh Masters Fellowship *(Graduate/ Fellowship)* 1659

Queen's Fellowship *(Doctorate/Fellowship)* 5424

Research Support Opportunities in Arctic Environmental Studies *(Doctorate, Graduate/Other)* 1682

Studentships in Northern Studies *(Graduate, Undergraduate/ Scholarship)* 1684

## Cartography/Surveying

ACA Scholarship Award *(Undergraduate/Scholarship)* 390

American Association for Geodetic Surveying Graduate Fellowship *(Graduate/Fellowship)* 391

Beinecke Library Visiting Fellowships *(Postdoctorate/ Fellowship)* 1393

Jeannette D. Black Memorial Fellowship *(Doctorate, Postdoctorate/Fellowship)* 1511

Central Intelligence Agency Graduate Studies Internships *(Graduate/Internship)* 1811

Central Intelligence Agency Undergraduate Scholars Program *(Undergraduate/Internship, Scholarship)* 1812

Joseph F. Dracup Scholarship Award *(Undergraduate/ Scholarship)* 392

GITA *(Graduate, Undergraduate/Scholarship)* 2705

LH Systems Internship *(Graduate/Internship)* 965

The Schonstedt Scholarship in Surveying *(Undergraduate/ Scholarship)* 393

The Wild Leitz Surveying Scholarship *(Undergraduate/ Scholarship)* 394

## Central European studies (See also: East European studies; European studies)

IREX Research Residencies *(Postdoctorate/Grant)* 3186

IREX Short-Term Travel Grants for Independent Short-Term Research *(Postdoctorate/Grant)* 3187

## Chemistry (See also: Biochemistry; Electrochemistry)

AT & T Bell Laboratories Cooperative Research Fellowships for Minorities *(Graduate/Fellowship)* 1302

AT & T Bell Laboratories Graduate Research Fellowships for Women *(Doctorate/Fellowship)* 1303

AT & T Bell Laboratories Graduate Research Grants for Women *(Doctorate, Graduate/Grant)* 1304

AT & T Bell Laboratories Summer Research Program for Minorities & Women *(Undergraduate/Fellowship)* 1305

AT & T Bell Laboratories University Relations Summer Program *(Doctorate, Graduate, Undergraduate/Work Study)* 1306

Alfred Bader Scholarship *(Graduate/Scholarship)* 1905

BNL Postdoctoral Research Associateships *(Postdoctorate/ Other)* 1504

H. Fletcher Brown Scholarship *(Doctorate, Graduate, Undergraduate/Scholarship)* 4967

Bunting Institute Science Scholars Fellowships and Biomedical Research Fellowships *(Postdoctorate/Fellowship)* 1529

Celanese Canada Inc. Scholarships *(Undergraduate/ Scholarship)* 1269

Centre for Interdisciplinary Studies in Chemical Physics Senior Visiting Fellowships *(Postdoctorate/Fellowship)* 1795

Chemical Heritage Foundation Travel Grants *(Other/ Grant)* 1899

Civilian Radioactive Waste Management/Historically Black Colleges and Universities Faculty Fellowship Program *(Professional Development/Fellowship)* 5867

Conservation Science Fellowship *(Postdoctorate, Postgraduate/Fellowship)* 2060

Continental European Fellowships *(Postgraduate/ Fellowship)* 1956

Cottrell Scholars Science Awards *(Professional Development/ Award)* 5096

Edelstein International Fellowship in the History of Chemical Sciences and Technology *(Postdoctorate/Fellowship)* 1900

Gladys Anderson Emerson Scholarships *(Undergraduate/ Scholarship)* 3215

Faculty Research Participation Program at the National Center for Toxicological Research *(Professional Development/ Fellowship)* 5874

Fellowships in Cereal Chemistry *(Doctorate, Graduate/ Fellowship)* 275

William C. Foster Fellows Visiting Scholars Competition *(Postdoctorate, Professional Development/Fellowship)* 5818

Eloise Gerry Fellowships *(Postgraduate/Fellowship)* 5329

Historically Black Colleges and Universities Faculty and Student Research Participation Program in Fusion. *(Graduate, Professional Development, Undergraduate/ Fellowship)* 5890

Historically Black Colleges and Universities Nuclear Energy Faculty Research Participation Program *(Professional Development/Fellowship)* 5893

Anna Louise Hoffman Awards for Outstanding Achievement in Graduate Research *(Graduate/Award)* 3216

ILZRO Postdoctoral Fellowships *(Postdoctorate/ Fellowship)* 3164

Iota Sigma Pi Undergraduate Awards for Excellence in Chemistry *(Undergraduate/Award)* 3217

LARS Scholarships *(Doctorate, Graduate/Scholarship)* 1020

LPI Summer Intern Program in Planetary Science *(Undergraduate/Internship)* 3514

Allen H. Meyers Scholarship *(Undergraduate/ Scholarship)* 3677

Miami University Pulp and Paper Foundation Scholarships *(Undergraduate/Scholarship)* 5029

NAACP Willems Scholarship *(Graduate, Undergraduate/ Scholarship)* 3851

NAS/NRC Collaboration in Basic Science and Engineering Long-Term Grants *(Postdoctorate/Grant)* 3831

NAS/NRC Collaboration in Basic Science and Engineering Short-Term Project Development Grants *(Postdoctorate/ Grant)* 3832

National Physical Science Consortium Graduate Fellowships for Minorities and Women *(Doctorate, Graduate/ Fellowship)* 4338

National Scholarship Trust Fund of the Graphic Arts Fellowships *(Graduate/Fellowship)* 4373

Pestcon Graduate Scholarship *(Graduate/Scholarship)* 1906

Postdoctoral Fellowships in the Atmospheric Sciences *(Postdoctorate/Fellowship)* 3931

Postdoctoral Fellowships in Ocean Science and Engineering *(Postdoctorate/Fellowship)* 6247

Research Opportunity Awards *(Professional Development/ Award)* 5097

Robert Schreck Memorial Fund Scholarship *(Graduate, Undergraduate/Scholarship)* 5280

Smithsonian Environmental Research Center Work-Learn Opportunities in Environmental Studies *(Graduate, Undergraduate/Internship)* 5374

Sumner Memorial Fellowships *(Graduate, Postgraduate/ Fellowship)* 5646

U.S. Air Force Phillips Laboratory Scholar Program *(Postdoctorate/Other)* 4686

U.S. Army Summer Faculty Research and Engineering Associateships *(Postdoctorate/Fellowship)* 1376

## Chinese studies (See also: Area and ethnic studies)

Louise Wallace Hackney Fellowship for the Study of Chinese Art *(Doctorate, Postdoctorate/Fellowship)* 757

Joseph Levenson Prizes *(Postdoctorate/Prize)* 1218

National Program for Advanced Study and Research in China - Research Program *(Postdoctorate/Other)* 2016

National Program for Advanced Study and Research in China - Senior Advanced Studies *(Doctorate, Graduate/ Award)* 2017

## Choreography (See also: Dance)

Bush Artist Fellowships *(Professional Development/ Fellowship)* 1539

Canadian Council for the Arts Grants Program *(Professional Development/Grant)* 1594

Choreographers Fellowship *(Professional Development/ Fellowship)* 4661

National Endowment for Arts - Choreographers' Fellowships *(Professional Development/Fellowship)* 3973

National Stage Combat Workshop Fellowship *(Professional Development/Fellowship)* 3349

New York Foundation for the Arts Artists' Fellowships *(Other/ Fellowship)* 4570

The Yard Residencies for Choreographers *(Professional Development/Fellowship)* 6282

## Classical studies (See also: Area and ethnic studies)

American Numismatic Society Graduate Seminar *(Graduate/ Other)* 737

Oscar Broneer Fellowship *(Doctorate, Graduate, Postdoctorate/Fellowship)* 856

Anna C. and Oliver C. Colburn Fellowship *(Doctorate, Postdoctorate/Fellowship)* 857

The Eta Sigma Phi Summer Scholarships *(Doctorate, Graduate/Scholarship)* 2414

Alison M. Frantz Fellowship *(Doctorate/Fellowship)* 858

Jacob Hirsch Fellowship *(Doctorate, Graduate/ Fellowship)* 859

Howard Foundation Fellowships *(Professional Development/ Fellowship)* 2908

Olivia James Traveling Fellowship *(Doctorate, Postdoctorate/ Fellowship)* 1066

Samuel H. Kress Joint Athens-Jerusalem Fellowship *(Postdoctorate/Fellowship)* 875

Thomas Day Seymour Fellowship *(Graduate/Fellowship)* 860

Summer Session Awards *(Graduate, Professional Development, Undergraduate/Scholarship)* 861

Thesaurus Linguae Latinae Fellowship *(Doctorate/ Fellowship)* 764

Michael Ventris Memorial Award *(Postdoctorate, Postgraduate/ Award)* 3017

Helen M. Woodruff Fellowship of the Archaeological Institute of America *(Doctorate, Postdoctorate/Fellowship)* 1068

## Clinical laboratory sciences

American Heart Association, California Affiliate - Predoctoral Fellowship *(Doctorate/Fellowship)* 532

NJSCLS Scholarships *(Undergraduate/Scholarship)* 4541

Alexander von Humboldt Foundation Fellowship *(Postdoctorate/Fellowship)* 2537

## Communications

AEJMC Communication Theory and Methodology Division Minority Doctoral Scholarships *(Doctorate/ Scholarship)* 1232

AGBU Education Loan *(Graduate/Loan)* 1136

AGBU Education Loan Program in the U.S. *(Graduate/ Loan)* 1133

AIAA/Command, Control, Communications and Intelligence Graduate Scholarship Award *(Graduate/Scholarship)* 565

American Bankers Association Fellowships *(Other/ Fellowship)* 346

American Political Science Association-MCI Communications Fellowships for Scholars and Journalists *(Other/ Fellowship)* 778

American Press Institute Minority Journalism Educators Fellowship *(Other/Fellowship)* 791

American Society of Newspaper Editors Institute for Journalism Excellence *(Other/Fellowship)* 961

Atlanta Association of Media Women Scholarship *(Undergraduate/Scholarship)* 1308

Barach Teaching Fellowships in Non-Fiction *(Other/ Fellowship)* 6139

Sherlee Barish Fellowship *(Professional Development/ Fellowship)* 5052

Batten Fellowships *(Graduate/Fellowship)* 6013

WCVB TV Leo L. Beranek Fellowship for Newsreporting *(Graduate, Undergraduate/Fellowship)* 6123

Biggs and Gilmore Communications Scholarships *(Graduate, Undergraduate/Scholarship)* 4030

Bosch Foundation Fellowships *(Postgraduate/ Fellowship)* 1459

Robert Bosch Foundation Fellowships *(Professional Development/Internship)* 1758

William A. Brower Scholarship *(Undergraduate/ Scholarship)* 4694

Business Reporting Intern Program for College Sophomores and Juniors *(Undergraduate/Internship, Scholarship)* 2274

Mary Butler Scholarship *(Graduate, Undergraduate/ Scholarship)* 6221

Jim Byron Scholarship *(Undergraduate/Scholarship)* 5054

Ben Chatfield Scholarship *(Undergraduate/Scholarship)* 5055

Richard Cheverton Scholarship *(Undergraduate/ Scholarship)* 5056

Chicago FM Club Scholarship *(Undergraduate/ Scholarship)* 818

Chips Quinn Scholars Program *(Undergraduate/ Scholarship)* 2591

Cissy Patterson Fellowship *(Other/Fellowship)* 792

College Conference and Summer Fellowship Program *(Graduate, Undergraduate/Fellowship)* 3174

Concerned Media Professionals Scholarships *(Undergraduate/ Scholarship)* 5976

Irving W. Cook, WA0CGS Scholarship *(Undergraduate/ Scholarship)* 820

Lucy Corbett Scholarship *(Graduate, Undergraduate/ Scholarship)* 6222

Creswell, Munsell, Fultz & Zirbel Scholarships *(Undergraduate/ Scholarship)* 4054

*Detroit Free Press* Minority Journalism Scholarships *(Undergraduate/Scholarship)* 2247

Donrey Media Group Internships *(Other/Internship)* 2270

Walter Everett Fellowship *(Other/Fellowship)* 793

Martin Fischbein Fellowship *(Undergraduate/Fellowship)* 2601

Charles N. Fisher Memorial Scholarship *(Undergraduate/ Scholarship)* 822

AT & T Bell Laboratories Graduate Research Fellowships for Women *(Doctorate/Fellowship)* 1303

AT & T Bell Laboratories Graduate Research Grants for Women *(Doctorate, Graduate/Grant)* 1304

AT & T Bell Laboratories Summer Research Program for Minorities & Women *(Undergraduate/Fellowship)* 1305

AT & T Bell Laboratories University Relations Summer Program *(Doctorate, Graduate, Undergraduate/Work Study)* 1306

Cable Telecommunications Research Fellowship Program *(Graduate/Fellowship)* 1267

Creswell, Munsell, Fultz & Zirbel Scholarships *(Undergraduate/Scholarship)* 4054

Harold E. Ennes Scholarship *(Undergraduate/Scholarship)* 5442

General Emmett Paige Scholarship *(Undergraduate/Scholarship)* 1101

Della A. Whittaker Scholarships *(Doctorate, Graduate, Undergraduate/Scholarship)* 5504

## Computer and information sciences

AAUW Educational Foundation Selected Professions Fellowship *(Graduate/Fellowship)* 336

The AFCEA Educational Foundation Fellowship *(Doctorate, Graduate/Fellowship)* 1099

AFCEA ROTC Scholarship Program *(Undergraduate/Scholarship)* 1100

Airline Pilots Association Scholarship *(Undergraduate/Scholarship)* 96

Andersen Fellowships for Doctoral Candidates at the Dissertation Stage *(Doctorate/Fellowship)* 1039

Andersen Foundation Faculty Residencies *(Professional Development/Award)* 1040

Argonne National Laboratory Faculty Research Leave; Faculty Research Participation Awards *(Postdoctorate/Award)* 1083

ASIS Doctoral Dissertation Scholarships *(Doctorate/Scholarship)* 933

ASIS Doctoral Forum Awards *(Postdoctorate/Award)* 934

ASIS Student Paper Award *(Doctorate, Graduate, Undergraduate/Award)* 935

Aspen Systems Graduate Scholarship *(Graduate/Scholarship)* 515

AT & T Bell Laboratories Cooperative Research Fellowships for Minorities *(Graduate/Fellowship)* 1302

AT & T Bell Laboratories Graduate Research Fellowships for Women *(Doctorate/Fellowship)* 1303

AT & T Bell Laboratories Graduate Research Grants for Women *(Doctorate, Graduate/Grant)* 1304

AT & T Bell Laboratories Summer Research Program for Minorities & Women *(Undergraduate/Fellowship)* 1305

AT & T Bell Laboratories University Relations Summer Program *(Doctorate, Graduate, Undergraduate/Work Study)* 1306

BPW Career Advancement Scholarships *(Graduate, Undergraduate/Scholarship)* 1546

Bunting Institute Science Scholars Fellowships and Biomedical Research Fellowships *(Postdoctorate/Fellowship)* 1529

Bureau of Engraving and Printing Graduate Student Research Participation Program *(Graduate, Postgraduate/Fellowship)* 5862

Central Intelligence Agency Graduate Studies Internships *(Graduate/Internship)* 1811

Central Intelligence Agency Undergraduate Scholars Program *(Undergraduate/Internship, Scholarship)* 1812

Department of Energy Distinguished Postdoctoral Research Program *(Postdoctorate/Fellowship)* 5868

Digital Equipment Corporation Scholarship *(Undergraduate/Scholarship)* 5507

Engineering Rotation Program *(Professional Development/Award)* 2923

Faculty Research Participation Program at the Bureau of Engraving and Printing *(Professional Development/Fellowship)* 5873

Faculty Research Participation Program at the National Center for Toxicological Research *(Professional Development/Fellowship)* 5874

Faculty Research Participation Program at the Naval Air Warfare Center Training Systems Division. *(Professional Development/Fellowship)* 5875

Florida National Science Scholars Program *(Undergraduate/Scholarship)* 2503

Fossil Energy Faculty Research Participation *(Professional Development/Fellowship)* 5876

FSD Student Grant *(Graduate/Grant)* 2578

Grants for Physically Disabled Students in the Sciences *(Graduate/Grant)* 2579

Hewlett-Packard Scholarships *(Undergraduate/Scholarship)* 5512

Admiral Grace Murray Hopper Scholarship *(Undergraduate/Scholarship)* 5513

Engineer Degree Fellowships; Howard Hughes Doctoral Fellowships *(Doctorate/Fellowship)* 2922

IBM Postdoctoral Research Fellowships in Mathematical Sciences *(Postdoctorate/Fellowship)* 2948

IGCC Dissertation Fellowships *(Doctorate, Graduate/Fellowship)* 3043

Jansky Fellowships *(Postdoctorate/Fellowship)* 4351

Dr. Theodore von Karman Graduate Scholarship *(Graduate/Scholarship)* 45

Laboratory-Graduate Participantships Thesis Parts Appointment *(Doctorate, Graduate/Grant)* 1084

LPI Summer Intern Program in Planetary Science *(Undergraduate/Internship)* 3514

Ruth A. & G. Elving Lundine Scholarship *(Undergraduate/Scholarship)* 1879

Richard E. Merwin Scholarships *(Graduate, Undergraduate/Scholarship)* 2950

NAACP Willems Scholarship *(Graduate, Undergraduate/Scholarship)* 3851

NAS/NRC Collaboration in Basic Science and Engineering Long-Term Grants *(Postdoctorate/Grant)* 3831

NAS/NRC Collaboration in Basic Science and Engineering Short-Term Project Development Grants *(Postdoctorate/Grant)* 3832

National Physical Science Consortium Graduate Fellowships for Minorities and Women *(Doctorate, Graduate/Fellowship)* 4338

Naval Air Warfare Center Training Systems Division Postgraduate Research Participation Program *(Postgraduate/Fellowship)* 5913

NRAO Summer Student Research Assistantships *(Graduate, Undergraduate/Other)* 4352

General Emmett Paige Scholarship *(Undergraduate/Scholarship)* 1101

Sacramento Hispanic Chamber of Commerce Scholarships *(Undergraduate/Scholarship)* 5216

SDE Fellowships *(Postgraduate/Fellowship)* 5330

The SHL Systemhouse President's Award for Education Technology Program *(Undergraduate/Scholarship)* 1286

Lance Stafferd Larson Student Scholarship *(Undergraduate/Scholarship)* 2951

Tandy Technology Scholars *(Undergraduate/Scholarship)* 5672

U.S. Air Force Phillips Laboratory Scholar Program *(Postdoctorate/Other)* 4686

U.S. Army Summer Faculty Research and Engineering Associateships *(Postdoctorate/Fellowship)* 1376

U.S. Department of Energy Distinguished Postdoctoral Research Fellowship *(Postdoctorate/Fellowship)* 4708

U.S. Department of Energy Global Change Distinguished Postdoctoral Fellowships *(Postdoctorate/Fellowship)* 4709

U.S. Department of Energy Internship *(Undergraduate/Internship)* 4711

U.S. Nuclear Regulatory Commission Historically Black Colleges and Universities Faculty Research Participation *(Professional Development/Fellowship)* 5934

Upsilon Pi Epsilon/Computer Society Award for Academic Excellence *(Graduate, Undergraduate/Award)* 2952

## Construction

AGC Foundation Graduate Awards *(Graduate, Undergraduate/Award)* 1193

O.H. Ammann Research Fellowship in Structural Engineering *(Professional Development/Fellowship)* 902

Associated General Contractors Education Research Foundation Graduate Scholarship *(Graduate/Scholarship)* 401

Associated General Contractors Education and Research Foundation Undergraduate Scholarship *(Undergraduate/Scholarship)* 402

Henry Boh Memorial Scholarships *(Undergraduate/Scholarship)* 51

The Build America Scholarships *(Undergraduate/Scholarship)* 52

G.E. Byrne Memorial Scholarships *(Undergraduate/Scholarship)* 53

Billy R. Carter Memorial Scholarships *(Undergraduate/Scholarship)* 54

CCC Scholarships *(Undergraduate/Scholarship)* 55

Construction Education Foundation Scholarship Awards *(Undergraduate/Scholarship)* 16

El Camino Real No. 158 NAWIC Scholarship *(Undergraduate/Scholarship)* 3906

Historically Black Colleges and Universities Building Technology Summer Research Participation Program *(Graduate/Fellowship)* 5889

Jewel/Taylor C. Cotton Scholarship *(Undergraduate/Scholarship)* 1927

Vernie G. Lindstron, Jr. Memorial Scholarships *(Undergraduate/Scholarship)* 56

Robert B. McEachem Memorial Scholarships *(Undergraduate/Scholarship)* 57

National Roofing Foundation Scholarship Award *(Undergraduate/Scholarship)* 4371

NDDOT Educational Grants *(Undergraduate/Scholarship loan)* 4682

Stanley F. Pepper Memorial Scholarships *(Undergraduate/Scholarship)* 58

Pitcock Scholarships *(Undergraduate/Scholarship)* 59

Paul B. Richards Memorial Scholarship *(Undergraduate/Scholarship)* 60

U.S. Army Construction Engineering Research Laboratory Research Participation Program *(Postdoctorate, Postgraduate/Fellowship)* 5930

Richard Lee Vernon Aviation Scholarship *(All/Scholarship)* 5694

## Consumer affairs

Candle Fellowships *(Graduate/Fellowship)* 4911

Geraldine Clewell Fellowship I *(Graduate/Fellowship)* 4912

Geraldine Clewell Scholarship *(Undergraduate/Scholarship)* 4913

Closs/Parnitzke/Clarke Scholarship *(Undergraduate/Scholarship)* 4914

Diamond Anniversary Fellowships *(Graduate/Fellowship)* 4915

Jean Dearth Dickerscheid Fellowship *(Graduate/Fellowship)* 4916

Margaret Drew Alpha Fellowship *(Graduate/Fellowship)* 4917

Founders Fellowship *(Graduate/Fellowship)* 4918

Geraldine Clewell Fellowship II *(Graduate/Fellowship)* 4919

Tommie J. Hamner Scholarship *(Undergraduate/Scholarship)* 4920

Treva C. Kintner Scholarships *(Undergraduate/Scholarship)* 4921

Kraft Canada Inc. Undergraduate Scholarship *(Undergraduate/Scholarship)* 1649

Margaret Jerome Sampson Scholarships *(Undergraduate/Scholarship)* 4922

Presidents Research Fellowship *(Graduate/Fellowship)* 4923

Public Interest Internships *(Doctorate, Graduate, Undergraduate/Internship)* 1803

Lillian P. Schoephoerster Scholarship *(Undergraduate/Scholarship)* 4924

Mary Welking Franken Scholarship *(Undergraduate/Scholarship)* 4926

## Cooley's anemia

Cooley's Anemia Foundation Research Fellowship *(Postdoctorate/Fellowship)* 2077

## Counseling/Guidance

Lullelia W. Harrison Scholarship in Counseling *(Graduate, Undergraduate/Scholarship)* 6304

Donald L. McCullough Memorial Scholarships *(Doctorate, Graduate/Scholarship)* 3866

NACA Multi-Cultural Scholarship *(Professional Development/Scholarship)* 3867

NACADA Research Award *(Graduate, Professional Development/Grant)* 3824

NACADA Scholarship *(Doctorate, Graduate/Scholarship)* 3825

NAJA Graduate Scholarships *(Graduate/Scholarship)* 3881

## Crafts

Folklife Documentary Program *(Professional Development/Fellowship)* 4664

Monitor/Technical Assistant Scholarships *(Graduate/Scholarship)* 2826

National Endowment for the Arts - National Heritage Fellowships *(Professional Development/Fellowship)* 3979

National Endowment for the Arts - Visual Artists Fellowships *(Professional Development/Fellowship)* 3982

New Hampshire Individual Artist Fellowships *(Other/Fellowship)* 4535

New York Foundation for the Arts Artists' Fellowships *(Other/Fellowship)* 4570

NNAC Gifted/Talented Artist Sponsorships *(Professional Development/Other)* 4324

Resident Fellowships *(Professional Development/Fellowship)* 2786

Smithsonian Institution Graduate Fellowships *(Graduate/Fellowship)* 5376

Smithsonian Institution Postdoctoral Fellowships *(Postdoctorate/Fellowship)* 5377

Smithsonian Institution Predoctoral Fellowships *(Doctorate/Fellowship)* 5378

Virginia Museum of Fine Arts Fellowship *(Professional Development/Fellowship)* 6061

## Criminal justice

Alphonso Deal Scholarship Award *(Undergraduate/Scholarship)* 3912

GFWC of MA Memorial Education Fellowships *(Graduate/Fellowship)* 2639

Mississippi Public Management Graduate Internship Program *(Graduate/Internship)* 3739

National Institute of Justice Graduate Research Fellowships *(Doctorate/Fellowship)* 4194

Margaret E. Olson Memorial Scholarship *(Undergraduate/Scholarship)* 1893

## Criminology

American Society of Crime Laboratory Scholarship Award *(Graduate, Undergraduate/Scholarship)* 916

## Criticism (Art, Drama, Literary)

Asian Cultural Council Fellowship Grants *(Postdoctorate/Fellowship)* 1177

ChLA Research Fellowships *(Postdoctorate/Fellowship)* 1939

Folger Library Long-Term Fellowships *(Postdoctorate/Fellowship)* 2541

Folger Library Short-Term Fellowships *(Postdoctorate/Fellowship)* 2542

Howard Foundation Fellowships *(Professional Development/Fellowship)* 2908

Humanities Fellowships *(Doctorate, Postdoctorate/Fellowship)* 1179

Japan-United States Art Fellowships *(Postdoctorate, Professional Development/Fellowship)* 1180

National Endowment for the Humanities Fellowships *(Postdoctorate/Fellowship)* 2543

Oregon Humanities Center Summer Visiting Research Fellowships *(Professional Development/Fellowship)* 6011

SSRC Grants for Advanced Area Research *(Doctorate, Other/Grant)* 5399

TELACU Arts Award *(Undergraduate/Scholarship)* 5689

## Cross-cultural studies

AFS Intercultural Global Teenager Program Scholarships *(High School/Other)* 49

Bicentennial Swedish-American Exchange Fund Travel Grants *(Professional Development/Grant)* 5656

East-West Center Internships *(Professional Development/Internship)* 2309

IEC Russia, China Study Fellowship *(Professional Development/Fellowship)* 3153

International Navies Essay Contest *(Other/Prize)* 5952

Rockefeller Foundation Residential Fellowships in Gender Studies in Early Modern Europe *(Postdoctorate/Fellowship)* 4608

U.S. Japan Media Fellowship *(Postgraduate/Fellowship)* 3242

## Culinary arts

American Institute of Baking and Maintenance Engineering Scholarships *(Professional Development/Scholarship)* 578

GRI/ICIF Culinary Scholarships *(Professional Development/Scholarship)* 4232

Edward T. Hanley Scholarships *(Professional Development/Scholarship)* 2903

IACP Foundation Scholarships *(Professional Development, Undergraduate/Scholarship)* 3111

National Restaurant Association Undergraduate Scholarships *(Undergraduate/Scholarship)* 4367

## Cystic fibrosis

CFF/NIH Funding Award *(Other/Grant)* 2150

Cystic Fibrosis Foundation Clinical Fellowships *(Postdoctorate/Fellowship)* 2151

Cystic Fibrosis Foundation Research Grants *(Other/Grant)* 2156

Cystic Fibrosis Foundation Research Scholar Awards *(Postdoctorate/Award)* 2157

Cystic Fibrosis Foundation Student Traineeships *(Doctorate, Graduate/Award)* 2159

Leroy Matthews Physician/Scientist Awards *(Postdoctorate/Award)* 2161

Pilot and Feasibility Awards *(Other/Grant)* 2163

Harry Shwachman Clinical Investigator Award *(Postdoctorate/Award)* 2164

Summer Scholarships in Epidemiology *(Postdoctorate/Scholarship)* 2165

Therapuetics Development Grants *(Other/Grant)* 2166

## Dairy science

21st Century Genetics Cooperative Scholarships *(Undergraduate/Scholarship)* 4012

Alfa-Laval Agri Scholarships *(Undergraduate/Scholarship)* 4014

Associated Milk Producers and Babson Bros. Co./SURGE Scholarships *(Undergraduate/Scholarship)* 4026

Borden Foundation Scholarships *(Undergraduate/Scholarship)* 4032

Capitol American Scholarships *(Undergraduate/Scholarship)* 4041

Champions Choice/AKZO Salt Scholarships *(Undergraduate/Scholarship)* 4046

Dairy Management Inc. Nutrition Research Projects *(Other/Other)* 2168

Darigold Scholarships *(Undergraduate/Scholarship)* 4057

Harold Davis Memorial Endowment Scholarship *(Undergraduate/Scholarship)* 4059

Federated Genetics Scholarship *(Undergraduate/Scholarship)* 4075

Hoard's Dairyman Scholarship *(Undergraduate/Scholarship)* 4091

National Dairy Shrine/Dairy Management Scholarships, Inc. *(Undergraduate/Scholarship)* 3968

National Mastitis Council Scholarship *(Undergraduate/Scholarship)* 4105

Prairie Farms Dairy, Inc. Scholarship *(Undergraduate/Scholarship)* 4115

Purina Research Fellowships *(Graduate/Fellowship)* 5033

Tetra Park Scholarship *(Undergraduate/Scholarship)* 4133

United Dairymen of Idaho Scholarship *(Undergraduate/Scholarship)* 4138

## Dance (See also: Choreography; Performing arts)

Arts Recognition and Talent Search (ARTS) *(Undergraduate/Award)* 4158

Ballet Prizes *(Professional Development/Prize)* 3123

Chautauqua Institution Scholarship *(Graduate, High School, Undergraduate/Scholarship)* 1842

Dance Screen Competition Awards *(Professional Development/Award)* 3166

Delta Psi Kappa Research Awards *(Graduate/Award)* 2223

Eben Demarest Fund *(Professional Development/Grant)* 2227

Martha Graham Dance Scholarships *(Professional Development/Scholarship)* 2728

Hungarian Arts Club Scholarships *(Undergraduate/Scholarship)* 2935

Minnesota Artist Assistance Fellowships *(Professional Development/Fellowship)* 3714

National Alliance for Excellence Honored Scholars Awards *(Graduate, Undergraduate/Scholarship)* 3841

National Endowment for the Arts - National Heritage Fellowships *(Professional Development/Fellowship)* 3979

New Hampshire Individual Artist Fellowships *(Other/Fellowship)* 4535

New York Foundation for the Arts Artists' Fellowships *(Other/Fellowship)* 4570

New York International Ballet Competition *(Professional Development/Prize)* 4572

North Carolina Arts Council Artist Fellowships *(Professional Development/Fellowship)* 4668

TELACU Arts Award *(Undergraduate/Scholarship)* 5689

Wayne Wylie Scholarship *(Professional Development/Scholarship)* 5172

Yaddo Residencies *(Professional Development/Other)* 6274

The Yard Residencies for Choreographers *(Professional Development/Fellowship)* 6282

## Data processing (See also: Computer and information sciences)

Marine Corps Historical Center College Internships *(Undergraduate/Internship)* 3556

## Demography

Population Council Fellowships in the Social Sciences *(Postdoctorate/Fellowship)* 4981

Population Sciences Fellowships *(Graduate, Postdoctorate/Fellowship)* 5149

Social Science Research Fellowships in Population *(Postdoctorate/Fellowship)* 5153

## Dental hygiene

ADHA Certificate/Associate Degree, Baccalaureate and Graduate Scholarships *(Graduate, Undergraduate/Scholarship)* 418

ADHA Institute Research Grants *(Professional Development/Grant)* 419

ADHA Part-Time Scholarship *(Graduate, Undergraduate/Scholarship)* 420

Carol Bauhs Benson Memorial Scholarship *(Undergraduate/Scholarship)* 421

John O. Butler Scholarships *(Graduate/Scholarship)* 422

Colgate "Bright Smile, Bright Futures" Minority Scholarship/ADHA Institute Minority Scholarship *(Undergraduate/Scholarship)* 423

Health Care Policy Clinical Career Development Award
(Doctorate/Other) 2240
OFAS Research Grants (Postdoctorate/Grant) 4807
Research Career Development Award (Postdoctorate/
Award) 2241
Society for Pediatric Dermatology Grant (Postgraduate/
Grant) 5480

## Diabetes
ADA Career Development Awards (Postdoctorate/Grant) 435
ADA Medical Student Diabetes Research Fellowship Program
(Doctorate/Fellowship) 437
ADA Mentor-Based Postdoctoral Fellowship Program
(Postdoctorate/Fellowship) 438
ADA Research Awards (Postdoctorate/Grant) 439
Charles H. Best Research Grants (Doctorate, Graduate,
Postdoctorate/Grant) 1620
CDA Fellowships (Postdoctorate/Fellowship) 1621
CDA Scholarships (Postdoctorate/Scholarship loan) 1622
JDFI Career Development Awards (Postdoctorate, Professional
Development/Award, Grant) 3308
JDFI Innovative Grants (Other/Grant) 3309
JDFI Postdoctoral Fellowships (Postdoctorate/
Fellowship) 3310
JDFI Research Grants (Postdoctorate, Professional
Development/Grant) 3311
Lions SightFirst Diabetic Retinopathy Research Program -
LCIF Clinical Research Grant Program (Postdoctorate/
Grant) 440
Lions SightFirst Diabetic Retinopathy Research Program -
LCIF Equipment Grant Program (Postdoctorate/Grant) 441
Lions SightFirst Diabetic Retinopathy Research Program -
LCIF Training Grant Program (Postdoctorate/Grant) 442
Medical Student Diabetes Research Fellowships (Doctorate/
Fellowship) 443
The Pfizer Postdoctoral Fellowships (Postdoctorate/
Fellowship) 4884
The Pfizer Scholars Program for New Faculty (Postdoctorate/
Award) 4885
Sigma Theta Tau International/American Association of
Diabetes Educators Grant (Professional Development/
Grant) 5338

## Drawing (See also: Art; Visual arts)
Artists Workplace Fellowships (Professional Development/
Fellowship) 6253
Bush Artist Fellowships (Professional Development/
Fellowship) 1539
Greenshields Grants (Other/Grant) 2752
National Endowment for the Arts - Visual Artists Fellowships
(Professional Development/Fellowship) 3982
Pastel Society of America Scholarships (Professional
Development/Scholarship) 4850
John F. and Anna Lee Stacey Scholarships (Professional
Development/Scholarship) 3966
Marion Barr Stanfield Art Scholarship (Undergraduate/
Scholarship) 5784
Virginia Museum of Fine Arts Fellowship (Professional
Development/Fellowship) 6061
Young American Creative Patriotic Art Awards (High School/
Prize) 3409

## Dysautonomia
Dysautonomia Research Grants (Postdoctorate/Grant) 2292

## Earth sciences
Carnegie Institution of Washington Postdoctoral and
Predoctoral Fellowships (Doctorate, Postdoctorate/
Fellowship) 1737
Trent R. Dames and William W. Moore Fellowship
(Postdoctorate/Fellowship) 903
Historically Black Colleges and Universities Fossil Energy
Faculty and Student Research Training (Graduate,
Professional Development, Undergraduate/Fellowship) 5891

NAS/NRC Collaboration in Basic Science and Engineering
Long-Term Grants (Postdoctorate/Grant) 3831
NAS/NRC Collaboration in Basic Science and Engineering
Short-Term Project Development Grants (Postdoctorate/
Grant) 3832
Part-time Fossil Energy Faculty Research Participation
Program (Professional Development/Fellowship) 5922
U.S. Air Force Phillips Laboratory Scholar Program
(Postdoctorate/Other) 4686
U.S. Department of Energy Global Change Distinguished
Postdoctoral Fellowships (Postdoctorate/Fellowship) 4709
Young Canadian Researchers Awards (Doctorate, Graduate/
Award) 3151

## East European studies (See also: European studies; Central European studies)
ACLS Grants for East European Studies - Dissertation
Fellowships (Doctorate/Fellowship) 407
ACLS Grants for East European Studies - Fellowships for
Postdoctoral Research (Postdoctorate/Fellowship) 408
Helen Darcovich Memorial Doctoral Fellowship (Doctorate,
Graduate/Fellowship) 1657
Marusia and Michael Dorosh Masters Fellowship (Graduate/
Fellowship) 1659
IREX Research Residencies (Postdoctorate/Grant) 3186
IREX Short-Term Travel Grants for Independent Short-Term
Research (Postdoctorate/Grant) 3187
The National Council Research Contracts (Postdoctorate/
Fellowship, Grant) 3945

## Ecology (See also: Environmental science)
Archbold Biological Station Undergraduate and Graduate
Internships (Graduate, Undergraduate/Internship) 1071
ASN Young Investigator's Award (Professional Development/
Award) 957
CCMS Fellowships (Postdoctorate/Fellowship) 4653
The Center for Field Research Grants (Postdoctorate,
Postgraduate/Grant) 1791
Conservation and Research Foundation Research Grants
(Professional Development/Grant) 2063
GCA Awards For Summer Environmental Studies; Clara Carter
Higgins Scholarship (Undergraduate/Scholarship) 2620
Huyck Station Research Grants (Graduate/Grant) 2944
McKinley Research Fund Scholarships (Graduate/
Scholarship) 5035
National Zoological Park Minority Traineeships (Graduate,
Undergraduate/Internship) 4456
National Zoological Park Research Traineeships (Graduate,
Undergraduate/Internship) 4457
NIDAY Fellowships (Postdoctorate, Postgraduate/
Fellowship) 3786
NYZS/Wildlife Conservation Society Research Fellowship
Program (RFP) (Doctorate, Graduate, Postdoctorate/
Grant) 6177
Tibor T. Polgar Fellowship (Graduate, Undergraduate/
Fellowship) 2916
Postdoctoral Fellowships in the Atmospheric Sciences
(Postdoctorate/Fellowship) 3931
Smithsonian Environmental Research Center Work-Learn
Opportunities in Environmental Studies (Graduate,
Undergraduate/Internship) 5374
Smithsonian Institution Graduate Fellowships (Graduate/
Fellowship) 5376
Smithsonian Institution Postdoctoral Fellowships
(Postdoctorate/Fellowship) 5377
Smithsonian Institution Predoctoral Fellowships (Doctorate/
Fellowship) 5378
Walton Scholarships (Graduate, Undergraduate/
Scholarship) 3787
Welder Wildlife Fellowships (Doctorate, Graduate/
Fellowship) 6127

## Economics
AFL-CIO Research Internship (Graduate/Internship) 464
AFLSE Scholarships (Graduate/Scholarship) 506

Haines Memorial Scholarships (Undergraduate/
Scholarship) 5552

Isabel M. Herson Scholarship in Education (Graduate,
Undergraduate/Scholarship) 6305

Oregon PTA Teacher Education Scholarships (Undergraduate/
Scholarship) 4801

## Education, Special

ACRSE Scholarships (Professional Development/
Scholarship) 414

CEASD Ethic Student Scholarship (Graduate/
Scholarship) 2038

CSAC Assumption Program of Loans for Education (Graduate,
Undergraduate/Loan) 1580

Delta Gamma Foundation - Florence Margaret Harvey
Memorial Scholarship (Graduate, Undergraduate/
Scholarship) 480

Rudolph Dillman Scholarship (Graduate, Undergraduate/
Scholarship) 481

Paul Douglas Teacher Scholarship (Undergraduate/
Scholarship) 4585

Paul Douglas Teacher Scholarships (Undergraduate/
Scholarship) 4735

Emblem Club Scholarship Grants (Postgraduate/Grant) 2378

Georgia Student Finance Commission Service-Cancellable
Stafford Loan (Graduate, Undergraduate/Loan) 2666

Georgia Student Finance Commission State-Sponsored Loan
(Graduate, Undergraduate/Loan) 2669

Bishop Charles P. Greco Graduate Fellowships (Graduate/
Fellowship) 3385

Wilma Hoyal/Maxine Chilton Scholarships (Undergraduate/
Scholarship) 614

Juniper Gardens Post-Doctoral Fellowship in Research with
Minority Handicapped Children (Postdoctorate/
Fellowship) 3306

Doreen Kronick Scholarship (Graduate/Scholarship) 3446

NAJA Graduate Scholarships (Graduate/Scholarship) 3881

NDCS Scholarship Grant (Graduate/Scholarship) 3970

Order of Alhambra Scholarships (Graduate, Undergraduate/
Scholarship) 4789

Retarded Citizens Teachers Scholarships (Graduate,
Postgraduate, Professional Development, Undergraduate/
Scholarship) 4793

United Commercial Travelers Retarded Citizens Teacher
Scholarship (Doctorate, Graduate, Postgraduate,
Undergraduate/Scholarship) 5787

## Education, Vocational-technical

AFSA Scholarship Awards (Undergraduate/Scholarship) 68

Airmen Memorial Scholarships (Undergraduate/
Scholarship) 98

American Council of the Blind Scholarship Program (All/
Scholarship) 399

American Postal Workers Union Vocational Scholarship
(Undergraduate/Scholarship) 788

AMF/Signet Bank Educational Loans (All/Loan) 99

AMT's Two-Year Scholarships (Undergraduate/
Scholarship) 1248

Cal Grant C (Undergraduate/Grant) 1579

Circle Key Grants of Rose McGill (Professional Development,
Undergraduate/Grant) 3326

Civil Air Patrol Technical/Vocational Scholarships (Other/
Scholarship) 3916

Division II Arc Welding Awards (Professional Development/
Award) 3481

Excellence in Arc Welding Awards; Graduate and Professional
Awards for Achievement in Arc-Welded Design, Engineering
and Fabrication (Doctorate, Graduate, Professional
Development/Award) 3482

Florida Vocational Gold Seal Endorsement Scholarship
Program (Undergraduate/Scholarship) 2508

Susan W. Freestone Vocational Education Award
(Undergraduate/Award) 4581

Iota Lambda Sigma Grand Chapter Scholarship (Doctorate,
Graduate/Scholarship) 3213

Japanese American Citizens League Freshman Awards (High
School/Scholarship) 3245

Marin Education Grant for Short-Term and Long-Term
Occupational Study (Other, Undergraduate/Grant) 3553

McCabe Awards (Undergraduate/Award) 5286

NCOA Scholarships (High School, Undergraduate/
Scholarship) 4639

Jeannette Rankin Award (Undergraduate/Award) 5081

Bettsy Ross Educational Grants (Undergraduate/Grant) 4640

Second Marine Division Memorial Scholarships
(Undergraduate/Scholarship) 5298

Sons of the First Division Scholarship Fund (Undergraduate/
Scholarship) 5452

## Educational administration

AASA and Convention Exhibitors Scholarships (Graduate/
Scholarship) 321

ACE Fellows Program (Professional Development/
Fellowship) 404

AGBU Education Loan (Graduate/Loan) 1136

AGBU Education Loan Program in the U.S. (Graduate/
Loan) 1133

AGBU Graduate Loan Program (Graduate/Loan) 1134

Exhibitor Scholarships (Professional Development/Scholarship
loan) 1258

Donald L. McCullough Memorial Scholarships (Doctorate,
Graduate/Scholarship) 3866

NACA Prize Papers Competition (Graduate, Professional
Development, Undergraduate/Prize) 3868

## Electrochemistry (See also: Chemistry)

F.M. Becket Memorial Award (Doctorate, Graduate/
Fellowship) 2366

Electrochemical Society Energy Research Fellowships
(Doctorate, Graduate/Fellowship) 2367

Electrochemical Society Summer Fellowships (Doctorate/
Fellowship) 2368

ILZRO Lead-Acid Battery Fellowship (Postgraduate/
Fellowship) 3163

## Electronics

The AFCEA Educational Foundation Fellowship (Doctorate,
Graduate/Fellowship) 1099

AFCEA ROTC Scholarship Program (Undergraduate/
Scholarship) 1100

Irving W. Cook, WA0CGS Scholarship (Undergraduate/
Scholarship) 820

Charles N. Fisher Memorial Scholarship (Undergraduate/
Scholarship) 822

Paul and Helen L. Grauer Scholarship (Undergraduate/
Scholarship) 826

Julia Kiene Fellowship (Graduate/Fellowship) 2363

Lyle Mamer Fellowship (Graduate/Fellowship) 2364

Mississippi Scholarship (Undergraduate/Scholarship) 832

General Emmett Paige Scholarship (Undergraduate/
Scholarship) 1101

Sumner Memorial Fellowships (Graduate, Postgraduate/
Fellowship) 5646

L. Phil Wicker Scholarship (Undergraduate/Scholarship) 841

## Endocrinology

ACOG/Ethicon Research Award for Innovations in Gynecologic
Surgery (Postdoctorate/Award) 378

ACOG/Novartis Pharmaceuticals Fellowship for Research in
Endocrinology of the Postreproductive Woman
(Postdoctorate/Fellowship) 380

OFAS Research Grants (Postdoctorate/Grant) 4807

## Energy-related areas

Argonne National Laboratory Faculty Research Leave; Faculty
Research Participation Awards (Postdoctorate/Award) 1083

AWU Faculty Fellowships (Postdoctorate/Fellowship) 1199

AWU Faculty Sabbatical Fellowships (Postdoctorate/
Fellowship) 1200

**Engineering (See also: specific areas of study, e.g. Engineering, Chemical) (continued)**

NACME TechForce Scholarships *(Undergraduate/ Scholarship)* 3836

Robert H. Nagel Scholarships *(Undergraduate/ Scholarship)* 5676

NAS/NRC Collaboration in Basic Science and Engineering Long-Term Grants *(Postdoctorate/Grant)* 3831

NAS/NRC Collaboration in Basic Science and Engineering Short-Term Project Development Grants *(Postdoctorate/ Grant)* 3832

NASA-ASEE Summer Faculty Fellowship *(Professional Development/Fellowship)* 923

NASA Field Center Resident Research Associateships *(Postdoctorate/Other)* 3838

NASA Graduate Student Research Fellowships *(Graduate/ Fellowship)* 3839

National Board Civil Air Patrol Undergraduate/Advanced Undergraduate College Scholarship *(Undergraduate/ Scholarship)* 3918

National Defense Science and Engineering Graduate Fellowship Program *(Graduate/Fellowship)* 5855

National Oceanic and Atmospheric Administration/Historically Black Colleges and Universities Faculty/Student Research Participation Program *(Graduate, Professional Development, Undergraduate/Fellowship)* 5910

National Research Council of Canada Research Associateships *(Postdoctorate/Other)* 4354

National Roofing Foundation Scholarship Award *(Undergraduate/Scholarship)* 4371

National Scholarship Trust Fund of the Graphic Arts Fellowships *(Graduate/Fellowship)* 4373

NATO Senior Guest Fellowships *(Professional Development/ Fellowship)* 4656

Naval Air Warfare Center Training Systems Division Postgraduate Research Participation Program *(Postgraduate/ Fellowship)* 5913

Naval Research Laboratory Postdoctoral Fellowship Program *(Postdoctorate/Fellowship)* 924

New York State Professional Opportunity Scholarships *(Doctorate, Graduate, Undergraduate/Scholarship)* 4592

New York State Regents Professional Opportunity Scholarships *(Doctorate, Graduate, Undergraduate/ Scholarship)* 4577

Northrop Corporation Founders Scholarship *(Undergraduate/ Scholarship)* 5517

NSERC Research Scholarships, Fellowships, and Grants *(Graduate, Postdoctorate, Postgraduate, Professional Development/Fellowship, Grant, Scholarship)* 4474

NSF-DAAD Grants for the Natural, Engineering and Social Sciences *(Other/Grant)* 2689

Nuclear Engineering/Health Physics Fellowship Program *(Doctorate, Graduate/Fellowship)* 5915

Ivy Parker Memorial Scholarship *(Undergraduate/ Scholarship)* 5518

Arthur & Doreen Parrett Scholarship Fund *(Graduate, Postgraduate, Undergraduate/Scholarship)* 4848

Part-time Fossil Energy Faculty Research Participation Program *(Professional Development/Fellowship)* 5922

The Payzer Scholarship *(Undergraduate/Scholarship)* 2296

The Payzer Scholarship *(All/Scholarship)* 2423

Petro-Canada Inc. Graduate Research Awards *(Doctorate, Graduate/Award)* 1284

Postdoctoral Fellowships in the Atmospheric Sciences *(Postdoctorate/Fellowship)* 3931

Al Qoyawayma Award *(Graduate, Undergraduate/Award)* 561

Quarry Engineering Scholarship Program *(Undergraduate/ Scholarship)* 4413

Spence Reese Scholarship *(High School, Undergraduate/ Scholarship)* 5089

Research Fellowships in Marine Policy *(Postdoctorate/ Fellowship)* 6248

Howard Brown Rickard Scholarship *(Undergraduate/ Scholarship)* 4007

Risk Reduction Engineering Research Laboratory Research Participation Program *(Postdoctorate, Postgraduate/ Fellowship)* 5923

G.A. Roberts Scholarship *(Undergraduate/Scholarship)* 1187

Eleanor Roosevelt Teacher Fellowships *(Doctorate, Other/ Fellowship)* 338

Sacramento Hispanic Chamber of Commerce Scholarships *(Undergraduate/Scholarship)* 5216

SAE Doctoral Scholars Program *(Graduate/Loan)* 5435

SAE Engineering Scholarships *(Undergraduate/ Scholarship)* 5436

St. Louis SME Chapter No. 17 Scholarships *(Undergraduate/ Scholarship)* 5468

Olive Lynn Salembier Scholarship *(Graduate, Undergraduate/ Scholarship)* 5520

Robert Schreck Memorial Fund Scholarship *(Graduate, Undergraduate/Scholarship)* 5280

The SHL Systemhouse President's Award for Education Technology Program *(Undergraduate/Scholarship)* 1286

SHPE Foundation Education Grant *(Graduate, Undergraduate/ Grant)* 5454

Sigma Xi Grants-in-Aid of Research *(Graduate, Undergraduate/Grant)* 5347

Society of Plastics Engineers Foundation Scholarships *(Undergraduate/Scholarship)* 5484

SPIE Educational Scholarships and Grants in Optical Engineering *(Graduate, Undergraduate/Scholarship)* 5589

Spraying Systems Company Scholarships *(Undergraduate/ Scholarship)* 4129

Student Engineer of the Year Scholarship *(Undergraduate/ Scholarship)* 893

Tau Beta Pi Fellowships for Graduate Study in Engineering *(Graduate/Fellowship)* 5677

William Toto Scholarship *(Undergraduate/Scholarship)* 4265

TRW Scholarships *(Undergraduate/Scholarship)* 5522

Morris K. Udall OTA Congressional Fellowship *(Postdoctorate/ Fellowship)* 5851

United Nations Educational Training Scholarships for Southern Africans *(Graduate, Undergraduate/Scholarship)* 5798

U.S. Air Force Phillips Laboratory Scholar Program *(Postdoctorate/Other)* 4686

U.S. Army Construction Engineering Research Laboratory Research Participation Program *(Postdoctorate, Postgraduate/Fellowship)* 5930

U.S. Army Summer Faculty Research and Engineering Associateships *(Postdoctorate/Fellowship)* 1376

U.S. Department of Energy Distinguished Postdoctoral Research Fellowship *(Postdoctorate/Fellowship)* 4708

U.S. Department of Energy Faculty Research Participation Fellowship *(Professional Development/Fellowship)* 5932

U.S. Department of Energy Internship *(Undergraduate/ Internship)* 4711

U.S. Navy-ASEE Summer Faculty Research Program *(Professional Development/Fellowship)* 925

U.S. Navy ONR-ASEE Postdoctoral Fellowship *(Postdoctorate/ Fellowship)* 926

U.S. Nuclear Regulatory Commission Historically Black Colleges and Universities Faculty Research Participation *(Professional Development/Fellowship)* 5934

U.S. Nuclear Regulatory Commission Historically Black Colleges and Universities Graduate Student Research Participation *(Graduate/Fellowship)* 5935

U.S. Nuclear Regulatory Commission Historically Black Colleges and Universities Student Research Participation *(Undergraduate/Internship)* 5936

University of Maine Pulp and Paper Foundation Scholarships *(Undergraduate/Scholarship)* 6000

Von Karman Institute Doctoral Fellowship *(Doctorate/ Fellowship)* 6073

Western Dredging Association Scholarships *(Graduate/ Scholarship)* 6149

Westinghouse Bertha Lamme Scholarships *(Undergraduate/ Scholarship)* 5523

Westinghouse Science Talent Search *(Undergraduate/ Scholarship)* 5282

William Winter Teacher Scholar Loan Program *(Other, Undergraduate/Loan, Scholarship)* 3746

WIX Corporation Scholarships *(Undergraduate/ Scholarship)* 4151

Young Canadian Researchers Awards *(Doctorate, Graduate/ Award)* 3151

## Engineering, Aerospace/Aeronautical/Astronautical

AIAA/William T. Piper, Sr. General Aviation Systems Award *(Graduate/Scholarship)* 569

American Society of Naval Engineers Scholarships *(Graduate, Undergraduate/Scholarship)* 959

Bunting Institute Science Scholars Fellowships and Biomedical Research Fellowships *(Postdoctorate/Fellowship)* 1529

Amelia Earhart Fellowship Awards *(Graduate/Fellowship)* 6312

General Motors Foundation Scholarships for Graduates *(Undergraduate/Scholarship)* 5509

Dr. Robert H. Goddard Scholarships *(Graduate, Undergraduate/Scholarship)* 4408

NASA Field Center Resident Research Associateships *(Postdoctorate/Other)* 3838

Vertical Flight Foundation Engineering Scholarships *(Graduate, Undergraduate/Scholarship)* 534

## Engineering, Automotive

Mercedes-Benz of North America Scholarship Program *(Undergraduate/Scholarship)* 1928

## Engineering, Biomedical

Action Research Program and Project Grants *(Postdoctorate/ Grant)* 30

Biotechnology Career Fellowships *(Postdoctorate/ Fellowship)* 5147

## Engineering, Chemical

AT & T Bell Laboratories Cooperative Research Fellowships for Minorities *(Graduate/Fellowship)* 1302

AT & T Bell Laboratories Graduate Research Fellowships for Women *(Doctorate/Fellowship)* 1303

AT & T Bell Laboratories Graduate Research Grants for Women *(Doctorate, Graduate/Grant)* 1304

AT & T Bell Laboratories Summer Research Program for Minorities & Women *(Undergraduate/Fellowship)* 1305

AT & T Bell Laboratories University Relations Summer Program *(Doctorate, Graduate, Undergraduate/Work Study)* 1306

Celanese Canada Inc. Scholarships *(Undergraduate/ Scholarship)* 1269

Continental European Fellowships *(Postgraduate/ Fellowship)* 1956

General Motors Foundation Scholarships for Graduates *(Undergraduate/Scholarship)* 5509

General Motors Foundation Scholarships for Undergraduates *(Undergraduate/Scholarship)* 5510

Oak Ridge National Laboratory Technology Internship Program *(Undergraduate/Internship)* 5920

Pestcon Graduate Scholarship *(Graduate/Scholarship)* 1906

Syracuse Pulp and Paper Foundation Scholarship *(Undergraduate/Scholarship)* 5666

Texaco Scholarships *(Undergraduate/Scholarship)* 5521

University of Maine Pulp and Paper Foundation Scholarships *(Undergraduate/Scholarship)* 6000

J.E. Zajic Postgraduate Scholarship in Biochemical Engineering *(Postgraduate/Scholarship)* 1907

## Engineering, Civil

AGC Foundation Graduate Awards *(Graduate, Undergraduate/ Award)* 1193

American Society of Naval Engineers Scholarships *(Graduate, Undergraduate/Scholarship)* 959

O.H. Ammann Research Fellowship in Structural Engineering *(Professional Development/Fellowship)* 902

Henry Boh Memorial Scholarships *(Undergraduate/ Scholarship)* 51

The Build America Scholarships *(Undergraduate/ Scholarship)* 52

G.E. Byrne Memorial Scholarships *(Undergraduate/ Scholarship)* 53

Cable Telecommunications Research Fellowship Program *(Graduate/Fellowship)* 1267

Billy R. Carter Memorial Scholarships *(Undergraduate/ Scholarship)* 54

CCC Scholarships *(Undergraduate/Scholarship)* 55

Czech Education Scholarships *(Doctorate, Graduate, Postdoctorate/Scholarship)* 3708

Trent R. Dames and William W. Moore Fellowship *(Postdoctorate/Fellowship)* 903

Freeman Fellowship *(Professional Development/ Fellowship)* 904

ICE Overseas Travel Awards *(Professional Development/ Award)* 3084

Vernie G. Lindstron, Jr. Memorial Scholarships *(Undergraduate/Scholarship)* 56

Robert B. McEachem Memorial Scholarships *(Undergraduate/ Scholarship)* 57

NDDOT Educational Grants *(Undergraduate/Scholarship loan)* 4682

Stanley F. Pepper Memorial Scholarships *(Undergraduate/ Scholarship)* 58

Pitcock Scholarships *(Undergraduate/Scholarship)* 59

Paul B. Richards Memorial Scholarship *(Undergraduate/ Scholarship)* 60

J. Waldo Smith Hydraulic Fellowship *(Postdoctorate/ Fellowship)* 905

Texaco Scholarships *(Undergraduate/Scholarship)* 5521

Arthur S. Tuttle Memorial National Scholarship *(Graduate/ Scholarship)* 906

Western Dredging Association Scholarships *(Graduate/ Scholarship)* 6149

## Engineering, Electrical

The AFCEA Educational Foundation Fellowship *(Doctorate, Graduate/Fellowship)* 1099

AFCEA ROTC Scholarship Program *(Undergraduate/ Scholarship)* 1100

AFSA Scholarship Awards *(Undergraduate/Scholarship)* 68

American Society of Naval Engineers Scholarships *(Graduate, Undergraduate/Scholarship)* 959

AT & T Bell Laboratories Cooperative Research Fellowships for Minorities *(Graduate/Fellowship)* 1302

AT & T Bell Laboratories Graduate Research Fellowships for Women *(Doctorate/Fellowship)* 1303

AT & T Bell Laboratories Graduate Research Grants for Women *(Doctorate, Graduate/Grant)* 1304

AT & T Bell Laboratories Summer Research Program for Minorities & Women *(Undergraduate/Fellowship)* 1305

AT & T Bell Laboratories University Relations Summer Program *(Doctorate, Graduate, Undergraduate/Work Study)* 1306

Bunting Institute Science Scholars Fellowships and Biomedical Research Fellowships *(Postdoctorate/Fellowship)* 1529

Central Intelligence Agency Undergraduate Scholars Program *(Undergraduate/Internship, Scholarship)* 1812

DEED Scholarships *(Graduate, Undergraduate/ Scholarship)* 811

Digital Equipment Corporation Scholarship *(Undergraduate/ Scholarship)* 5507

Charles LeGeyt Fortescue Fellowship *(Graduate/ Fellowship)* 3031

General Motors Foundation Scholarships for Graduates *(Undergraduate/Scholarship)* 5509

General Motors Foundation Scholarships for Undergraduates *(Undergraduate/Scholarship)* 5510

Perry F. Hadlock Memorial Scholarship *(Undergraduate/ Scholarship)* 828

Hewlett-Packard Scholarships *(Undergraduate/ Scholarship)* 5512

IEEE Fellowship in Electrical History *(Doctorate, Graduate, Postdoctorate/Fellowship)* 3033

## Engineering, Electrical (continued)

Jansky Fellowships *(Postdoctorate/Fellowship)* 4351

Julia Kiene Fellowship *(Graduate/Fellowship)* 2363

Lyle Mamer Fellowship *(Graduate/Fellowship)* 2364

NRAO Summer Student Research Assistantships *(Graduate, Undergraduate/Other)* 4352

Oak Ridge National Laboratory Technology Internship Program *(Undergraduate/Internship)* 5920

General Emmett Paige Scholarship *(Undergraduate/ Scholarship)* 1101

SPIE Educational Scholarships and Grants in Optical Engineering *(Graduate, Undergraduate/Scholarship)* 5589

Texaco Scholarships *(Undergraduate/Scholarship)* 5521

Robert Thunen Memorial Educational Scholarships *(Graduate, Undergraduate/Scholarship)* 2983

## Engineering, Geological

Marliave Scholarships *(Graduate/Scholarship)* 2382

Petroleum Research Fund Grants *(Graduate, Postdoctorate, Professional Development, Undergraduate/Grant)* 369

Quarry Engineering Scholarship Program *(Undergraduate/ Scholarship)* 4413

WAAIME Scholarship Loans *(Graduate, Undergraduate/ Scholarship loan)* 592

## Engineering, Industrial

Caterpillar Scholars Award *(Undergraduate/Scholarship)* 5465

Dwight D. Gardner Memorial Scholarship *(Undergraduate/ Scholarship)* 3060

General Motors Foundation Scholarships for Graduates *(Undergraduate/Scholarship)* 5509

General Motors Foundation Scholarships for Undergraduates *(Undergraduate/Scholarship)* 5510

Frank and Lillian Gilbreth Memorial Fellowships *(Graduate/ Fellowship)* 3061

Wayne Kay Scholarship *(Undergraduate/Scholarship)* 5467

MTM Fellowships *(Undergraduate/Fellowship)* 3062

NAPM Doctoral Grants *(Doctorate/Grant)* 3895

E.J. Sierleja Memorial Fellowship *(Graduate/Fellowship)* 3063

Myrtle and Earl Walker Scholarships *(Undergraduate/ Scholarship)* 5469

William E. Weisel Scholarship *(Undergraduate/ Scholarship)* 5470

## Engineering, Marine

American Society of Naval Engineers Scholarships *(Graduate, Undergraduate/Scholarship)* 959

Seaspace Scholarship *(Graduate, Undergraduate/ Scholarship)* 5293

Society of Naval Architects and Marine Engineers Scholarships *(Professional Development/Scholarship)* 5472

## Engineering, Mechanical

The American Society of Mechanical Engineers Auxiliary Student Loans *(Graduate, Undergraduate/Loan)* 948

American Society of Naval Engineers Scholarships *(Graduate, Undergraduate/Scholarship)* 959

ASME Federal Government Fellowships *(Professional Development/Fellowship)* 942

ASME Graduate Teaching Fellowships *(Doctorate/ Fellowship)* 943

ASME Student Assistance Loans *(Undergraduate/Loan)* 944

AT & T Bell Laboratories Cooperative Research Fellowships for Minorities *(Graduate/Fellowship)* 1302

AT & T Bell Laboratories Graduate Research Fellowships for Women *(Doctorate/Fellowship)* 1303

AT & T Bell Laboratories Graduate Research Grants for Women *(Doctorate, Graduate/Grant)* 1304

AT & T Bell Laboratories Summer Research Program for Minorities & Women *(Undergraduate/Fellowship)* 1305

AT & T Bell Laboratories University Relations Summer Program *(Doctorate, Graduate, Undergraduate/Work Study)* 1306

Joseph Bramah Scholarship; Raymond Coleman Prescott Scholarship *(Graduate, Professional Development/ Scholarship)* 3086

Bunting Institute Science Scholars Fellowships and Biomedical Research Fellowships *(Postdoctorate/Fellowship)* 1529

Clayton Grants *(Professional Development/Grant)* 3087

Czech Education Scholarships *(Doctorate, Graduate, Postdoctorate/Scholarship)* 3708

Digital Equipment Corporation Scholarship *(Undergraduate/ Scholarship)* 5507

Sylvia W. Farny Scholarships *(Undergraduate/ Scholarship)* 949

General Motors Foundation Scholarships for Graduates *(Undergraduate/Scholarship)* 5509

General Motors Foundation Scholarships for Undergraduates *(Undergraduate/Scholarship)* 5510

John and Elsa Gracik Scholarships *(Undergraduate/ Scholarship)* 945

Historically Black Colleges and Universities Nuclear Energy Faculty Research Participation Program *(Professional Development/Fellowship)* 5893

Elisabeth M. and Winchell M. Parsons Scholarships *(Doctorate/Scholarship)* 950

Rice-Cullimore Scholarships *(Graduate/Scholarship)* 951

Kenneth Andrew Roe Scholarships *(Undergraduate/ Scholarship)* 946

Marjorie Roy Rothermel Scholarships *(Graduate/ Scholarship)* 952

## Engineering, Metallurgical

Rocky Mountain Coal Mining Institute Scholarships *(Undergraduate/Scholarship)* 5157

WAAIME Scholarship Loans *(Graduate, Undergraduate/ Scholarship loan)* 592

## Engineering, Mining and Mineral

Samuel C. Kraus, Jr. Memorial Scholarship *(Undergraduate/ Scholarship)* 4412

Rocky Mountain Coal Mining Institute Scholarships *(Undergraduate/Scholarship)* 5157

Texaco Scholarships *(Undergraduate/Scholarship)* 5521

WAAIME Scholarship Loans *(Graduate, Undergraduate/ Scholarship loan)* 592

## Engineering, Naval

U.S. Navy-ASEE Summer Faculty Research Program *(Professional Development/Fellowship)* 925

U.S. Navy ONR-ASEE Postdoctoral Fellowship *(Postdoctorate/ Fellowship)* 926

## Engineering, Nuclear

ANS Environmental Sciences Division Scholarship *(Undergraduate/Scholarship)* 720

ANS Fuel Cycle and Waste Management Scholarship *(Undergraduate/Scholarship)* 721

ANS Graduate Scholarships *(Graduate/Scholarship)* 722

ANS Nuclear Operations Division Scholarship *(Undergraduate/ Scholarship)* 723

ANS Power Division Scholarship *(Undergraduate/ Scholarship)* 724

ANS Undergraduate Scholarships *(Undergraduate/ Scholarship)* 725

Robert A. Dannels Scholarships *(Graduate/Scholarship)* 726

Verne R. Dapp Scholarship *(Graduate/Scholarship)* 727

Delayed Education for Women Scholarship *(Undergraduate/ Scholarship)* 728

Joseph R. Dietrich Scholarships *(Undergraduate/ Scholarship)* 729

Paul A. Greebler Scholarship *(Graduate/Scholarship)* 730

Historically Black Colleges and Universities Nuclear Energy Faculty Research Participation Program *(Professional Development/Fellowship)* 5893

John R. Lamarsh Scholarship *(Undergraduate/ Scholarship)* 731

## Environmental science (See also: Ecology) (continued)

National Association of Water Companies - New Jersey Chapter Scholarship *(Graduate, Undergraduate/ Scholarship)* 3904

National Oceanic and Atmospheric Administration Scholar in Residence Program *(Professional Development/ Fellowship)* 5911

Office of Ground Water and Drinking Water Postgraduate Internship Program *(Postgraduate/Internship)* 5921

Tibor T. Polgar Fellowship *(Graduate, Undergraduate/ Fellowship)* 2916

Tibor T. Polgar Fellowships *(Graduate, Undergraduate/ Fellowship)* 2914

Research Support Opportunities in Arctic Environmental Studies *(Doctorate, Graduate/Other)* 1682

Risk Reduction Engineering Research Laboratory Research Participation Program *(Postdoctorate, Postgraduate/ Fellowship)* 5923

SDE Fellowships *(Postgraduate/Fellowship)* 5330

Smithsonian Environmental Research Center Work-Learn Opportunities in Environmental Studies *(Graduate, Undergraduate/Internship)* 5374

Smithsonian Institution Graduate Fellowships *(Graduate/ Fellowship)* 5376

Smithsonian Institution Postdoctoral Fellowships *(Postdoctorate/Fellowship)* 5377

Smithsonian Institution Predoctoral Fellowships *(Doctorate/ Fellowship)* 5378

Tennessee Valley Authority Research Participation Program *(Postdoctorate, Postgraduate/Fellowship)* 5927

Texaco Scholarships *(Undergraduate/Scholarship)* 5521

Tyndall Air Force Base Research Participation Program *(Postdoctorate, Postgraduate/Fellowship)* 5928

Morris K. Udall OTA Congressional Fellowship *(Postdoctorate/ Fellowship)* 5851

Undergraduate U.S. Army Environmental Hygiene Internship Program *(Undergraduate/Internship)* 5929

U.S. Army Environmental Hygiene Agency Internship Program *(Postdoctorate, Postgraduate/Internship)* 5931

U.S. Department of Energy Global Change Distinguished Postdoctoral Fellowships *(Postdoctorate/Fellowship)* 4709

U.S. Department of Energy Internship *(Undergraduate/ Internship)* 4711

WERC Undergraduate Scholarships *(Undergraduate/ Scholarship)* 6113

Gilbert F. White Postdoctoral Fellowships *(Postdoctorate/ Fellowship)* 5112

## Epidemiology (See also: Infectious diseases)

American Heart Association, California Affiliate - Predoctoral Fellowship *(Doctorate/Fellowship)* 532

del Duca Foundation Maintenance and Travel Grants *(Professional Development/Grant)* 2284

Howard Hughes Medical Institute Predoctoral Fellowships in Biological Sciences *(Postdoctorate/Fellowship)* 4358

Postdoctoral Fellowship in Emerging Infectious Diseases *(Postdoctorate/Fellowship)* 4162

Summer Scholarships in Epidemiology *(Postdoctorate/ Scholarship)* 2165

## Epilepsy

AES/EFA Research Grants *(Postdoctorate/Grant)* 455

AES Research Fellowships *(Postdoctorate/Fellowship)* 456

Behavioral Sciences Student Fellowship *(Professional Development/Fellowship)* 2397

Clinical Research Fellowship *(Postdoctorate/Fellowship)* 2398

Jeanne Timmins Costello Fellowship *(Postdoctorate/ Fellowship)* 3775

Epilepsy Foundation of America Research Grants *(Postdoctorate/Grant)* 2399

Faculty Research Participation Program at the Agency for Toxic Substances and Disease Registry *(Professional Development/Fellowship)* 5872

FIC International Neuroscience Fellowships *(Postdoctorate/ Fellowship)* 2527

Health Sciences Student Fellowships *(All/Fellowship)* 2401

William G. Lennox International Clinical Research Fellowship; Fritz E. Dreifuss International Visiting Professorships *(Postdoctorate/Fellowship)* 2402

Preston Robb Fellowship *(Postdoctorate/Fellowship)* 3776

Savoy Foundation Postdoctoral and Clinical Research Fellowships; Savoy Foundation Research Grants; Savoy Foundation Studentships *(Doctorate, Graduate/Fellowship, Grant, Internship)* 5252

## Equine studies

Harness Horse Youth Foundation Scholarships *(Undergraduate/Scholarship)* 2790

International Arabian Horse Foundation Scholarship Application *(Postgraduate, Undergraduate/ Scholarship)* 3105

Marilyn Sue Lloyd Memorial Scholarship *(Undergraduate/ Scholarship)* 158

## Ethics and bioethics

David Baumgardt Memorial Fellowships *(Postdoctorate/ Fellowship)* 1355

Eastern European Visiting Scholarships *(Postdoctorate, Professional Development/Scholarship)* 2814

Fellowships in Ethics *(Postdoctorate, Postgraduate/ Fellowship)* 5015

Hastings Center International Fellowships *(Postdoctorate/ Fellowship)* 2815

Charlotte W. Newcombe Fellowships *(Doctorate/ Fellowship)* 6188

## Ethnology

Fyssen Foundation Research Grants *(Doctorate, Postgraduate/ Grant)* 2610

Phillips Grants for North American Indian Research *(Doctorate, Postdoctorate/Grant)* 769

Wenner-Gren Regular Grants *(Postdoctorate/Grant)* 6137

## European studies (See also: East European studies; Central European studies)

Minda de Gunzburg Center for European Studies Dissertation Exploration Grants *(Graduate/Grant)* 2766

Minda de Gunzburg Center for European Studies Graduate Summer Research Travel Grants *(Graduate/Grant)* 2768

Minda de Gunzburg Center for European Studies Program for the Study of Germany and Europe Dissertation Research Fellowships *(Doctorate/Fellowship)* 2769

Minda de Gunzburg Center for European Studies Short-Term Opportunity Grants *(Graduate/Grant)* 2770

Minda de Gunzburg Center for European Studies Undergraduate Summer Travel Grants *(Undergraduate/ Grant)* 2771

The National Council Research Contracts *(Postdoctorate/ Fellowship, Grant)* 3945

Pew Fellowships in International Journalism *(Other/ Fellowship)* 4854

## Family/Marital therapy (See also: Rehabilitation, Physical/Psychological)

Candle Fellowships *(Graduate/Fellowship)* 4911

Geraldine Clewell Fellowship I *(Graduate/Fellowship)* 4912

Diamond Anniversary Fellowships *(Graduate/Fellowship)* 4915

Jean Dearth Dickerscheid Fellowship *(Graduate/ Fellowship)* 4916

Founders Fellowship *(Graduate/Fellowship)* 4918

Geraldine Clewell Fellowship II *(Graduate/Fellowship)* 4919

Tommie J. Hamner Scholarship *(Undergraduate/ Scholarship)* 4920

Treva C. Kintner Scholarships *(Undergraduate/ Scholarship)* 4921

National Council on Family Relations Student Award *(Graduate/Award)* 3948

Presidents Research Fellowship *(Graduate/Fellowship)* 4923

Mary Welking Franken Scholarship *(Undergraduate/ Scholarship)* 4926

## General studies (continued)

Robert C. Byrd Honors Scholarship (Undergraduate/ Scholarship) 3498

Robert C. Byrd Honors Scholarship (Undergraduate/ Scholarship) 4584

Robert C. Byrd Honors Scholarships (Undergraduate/ Scholarship) 2042

Robert C. Byrd Honors Scholarships (Undergraduate/ Scholarship) 4862

Alyce M. Cafaro Scholarship (Undergraduate/ Scholarship) 4212

Cal Grant A (Undergraduate/Grant) 1577

Cal Grant B (Undergraduate/Grant) 1578

Hermione Grant Calhoun Scholarship (Undergraduate/ Scholarship) 3998

California-Hawaii Elks Disabled Student Scholarships (Undergraduate/Scholarship) 1559

California Junior Miss Scholarship Program (Undergraduate/ Scholarship) 1561

Cal Callahan Memorial Bursary (Undergraduate/ Scholarship) 4949

Vivienne Camp College Scholarship Fund (Undergraduate/ Scholarship) 3263

Campbell-Non-Linfield Scholarship Fund (Graduate, Undergraduate/Scholarship) 5830

Canada Trust Scholarship Program for Outstanding Community Leadership (Undergraduate/Scholarship) 1268

Canadian Golf Foundation Scholarships (Undergraduate/ Scholarship) 1642

Cargill National Merit Scholarships (Undergraduate/ Scholarship) 1728

Cargill Scholars Program Scholarships (Undergraduate/ Scholarship) 1729

Cargill Scholarships for Rural America (Undergraduate/ Scholarship) 4042

Charles Reed Carlson Business Education Fund (Undergraduate/Scholarship) 1852

Nellie Martin Carman Scholarships (Undergraduate/ Scholarship) 1731

Carnegie Grants (Postdoctorate, Postgraduate/Grant) 1739

CARQUEST Corporation Scholarships (Undergraduate/ Scholarship) 4044

Vikki Carr Scholarship (Graduate, Undergraduate/ Scholarship) 1741

Karen D. Carsel Memorial Scholarship (Graduate/ Scholarship) 479

Marjorie S. Carter Boy Scout Scholarship (Undergraduate/ Scholarship) 1743

Thomas Caryk Memorial Scholarship (Undergraduate/ Scholarship) 151

Catholic Aid Association Tuition Scholarships (Undergraduate/ Scholarship) 1747

Catholic Workman College Scholarships (Undergraduate/ Scholarship) 1754

CCSFC Australian Scholarships (Graduate/Scholarship) 3140

CCSFC India Scholarships (Doctorate, Graduate/ Scholarship) 3141

CCSFC New Zealand Scholarships (Doctorate, Graduate/ Scholarship) 3142

CCSFC Sri Lanka Scholarships (Doctorate, Graduate/ Scholarship) 3143

CCSFC United Kingdom Scholarships (Doctorate, Graduate/ Scholarship) 3144

Anthony J. Celebrezze Scholarship (Graduate, Undergraduate/ Scholarship) 4213

Center for Advanced Study in the Behavioral Sciences Fellowship (Postdoctorate/Fellowship) 1765

Central Scholarship Bureau Interest-Free Loans (Graduate, Undergraduate/Loan) 1816

Century Three Leaders Scholarships (Undergraduate/ Scholarship) 3898

CEW Scholarships for Returning Women (Graduate, Professional Development, Undergraduate/ Scholarship) 6002

CFUW Professional Fellowship (Graduate/Fellowship) 1632

Chairscholars Foundation Scholarship (Undergraduate/ Scholarship) 1826

Chase Manhattan Scholarship (Professional Development/ Scholarship) 2457

Chautauqua County Basketball Officials Scholarship (Undergraduate/Scholarship) 1855

Cesar Chavez Memorial Leadership Award (Undergraduate/ Scholarship) 5687

Cherokee National Higher Education Undergraduate Grant Program (Undergraduate/Grant) 1912

Chevy Trucks Scholarships (Undergraduate/Scholarship) 4048

Cheyenne-Arapaho Higher Education Assistance Program Grant (Undergraduate/Grant) 1914

Chicago FM Club Scholarship (Undergraduate/ Scholarship) 818

Chicana Dissertation Fellowship (Graduate/Fellowship) 2233

Chicana Latina Foundation Scholarships (Graduate, Undergraduate/Scholarship) 1931

Child of Disabled Veteran Grant or Purple Heart Recipient, Grant (Graduate, Other, Undergraduate/Other) 2996

Children of Deaf Adults Scholarship (Undergraduate/ Scholarship) 1937

Children of Deceased Active Duty Servicemembers Grants (Undergraduate/Grant) 4495

Children of Deceased or Disabled Veterans or Children of Servicemen Classified as Prisoners of War or Missing in Action Scholarship (Undergraduate/Scholarship) 2497

Children of Deceased, Retired Servicemembers Grants (Undergraduate/Grant) 4496

Children of Unitarian Universalist Ministers Scholarship (Undergraduate/Scholarship) 5780

CIBC Youthvision Scholarship Program (Undergraduate/ Scholarship) 1271

Ferdinand Cinelli Etruscan Scholarship (Graduate, Undergraduate/Scholarship) 4214

Circle Key Grants of Rose McGill (Professional Development, Undergraduate/Grant) 3326

Citizens' Scholarship Foundation of Wakefield Scholarships (All/Scholarship) 1960

Civic Service Union No. 52 Charitable Assistance Fund (Undergraduate/Scholarship) 1962

Civitan Scholarships (Graduate, Undergraduate/ Scholarship) 1964

Allen C. Clark Memorial Scholarship (High School/ Scholarship) 2030

Cleveland Scholarship Programs (Undergraduate/ Scholarship) 1970

CMSAF Richard D. Kisling Scholarships (Undergraduate/ Scholarship) 100

CMT Scholarships (Graduate/Scholarship) 1830

Coca-Cola Scholars (Undergraduate/Award) 1978

Coca-Cola Youth Bowling Championships Scholarships (Undergraduate/Scholarship) 5005

Julian and Eunice Cohen Scholarship (Undergraduate/ Scholarship) 2031

James W. Colgan Educational Loan (Undergraduate/ Loan) 1980

College Access Loan (Graduate, Undergraduate/Loan) 5708

Lance G. Colvin Memorial Scholarship (Undergraduate/ Scholarship) 1857

Commonwealth of Pennsylvania Educational Gratuity Program Grants (Undergraduate/Award) 2019

Commonwealth Scholarship Plan (Graduate/Scholarship) 2021

Communications Scholarship (Undergraduate/ Scholarship) 4215

Tom and Judith Comstock Scholarship (Undergraduate/ Scholarship) 819

Jimmie Condon Athletic Scholarships (Undergraduate/ Scholarship) 175

Confederate Memorial Scholarships (Undergraduate/ Scholarship) 5789

Congress Bundestag Youth Exchange Program Scholarships (High School/Scholarship) 6297

Congress-Bundestag Youth Exchange for Young Professionals (Undergraduate/Scholarship) 1759

## General studies (continued)

## General studies (continued)

## General studies (continued)

Herbert Frank and Bertha Maude Laird Memorial Foundation Scholarships *(Undergraduate/Scholarship)* 4690

Ann Lane Home Economics Scholarships *(Undergraduate/ Scholarship)* 5704

Samuel J. Lasser Scholarship *(Undergraduate/ Scholarship)* 1878

Latin American Educational Foundation Scholarships *(Graduate, Postgraduate, Undergraduate/Scholarship)* 3439

Law Enforcement Personnel Dependents Grant *(Undergraduate/Grant)* 2673

Dr. James L. Lawson Memorial Scholarship *(Undergraduate/ Scholarship)* 829

Lehigh Valley Workers Memorial Scholarship Fund *(High School/Scholarship)* 3449

Herbert Lehman Education Fund Scholarships *(Undergraduate/ Scholarship)* 3818

Samuel Lemberg Scholarship Loan Fund, Inc. *(Graduate, Undergraduate/Loan)* 3451

Lester Educational Trust Loans *(Professional Development, Undergraduate/Loan)* 2133

The Lighthouse Career Incentive Award for Adult Undergraduates *(Undergraduate/Scholarship)* 3474

The Lighthouse Career Incentive Award for College-Bound Students *(Undergraduate/Scholarship)* 3475

The Lighthouse Career Incentive Award for Graduate Students *(Graduate/Scholarship)* 3476

The Lighthouse Career Incentive Award for Undergraduates *(Undergraduate/Scholarship)* 3477

Lilydale Co-operative Scholarship *(Undergraduate/ Scholarship)* 157

Limited Access Competitive Grant *(Undergraduate/ Grant)* 2510

Franklin Lindsay Student Loans *(Graduate, Undergraduate/ Loan)* 3486

Lindstrom Foundation Student Service Scholarships *(Graduate, Undergraduate/Scholarship)* 876

Loan Assistant Repayment Program *(Other/Other)* 3571

Charlie Logan Scholarship for Dependents *(Undergraduate/ Scholarship)* 5290

Charlie Logan Scholarship for Seafarers *(Undergraduate/ Scholarship)* 5291

Longman-Harris Scholarship *(Undergraduate/ Scholarship)* 4400

Louisiana National Guard Tuition Exemption Program *(Undergraduate/Other)* 3504

Louisiana Rehabilitation Services Award *(Other/Other)* 3506

Louisiana State Aid Dependents Educational Assistance *(Graduate, Other, Undergraduate/Scholarship)* 3500

Inez Peppers Lovett Scholarship *(Undergraduate/ Scholarship)* 2035

Lucy Dalbiac Luard Scholarship *(Undergraduate/ Scholarship)* 2385

Cletus E. Ludden Memorial Scholarships *(Undergraduate/ Scholarship)* 2231

The Audrey Lumsden-Kouvel Fellowship *(Postdoctorate/ Fellowship)* 4618

Lutheran Life University Scholarships *(Undergraduate/ Scholarship)* 1314

Lynden Memorial Scholarship *(Graduate, Postgraduate, Undergraduate/Scholarship)* 3522

John H. Lyons, Sr. Scholarship Program *(Undergraduate/ Scholarship)* 3109

M.A. Hanna Company Scholarship *(Undergraduate/ Scholarship)* 3170

MACESA Awards *(Undergraduate/Scholarship)* 3699

MacKenzie King Open Scholarship *(Postgraduate/ Scholarship)* 3528

Minnie L. Maffett Scholarship *(Doctorate, Graduate, Undergraduate/Scholarship)* 4466

Maine Veterans Dependents Educational Benefits *(All/ Scholarship)* 3538

James L. and Lavon Madden Mallory Disability Scholarship *(High School, Undergraduate/Scholarship)* 2322

Maltese-American Benevolent Society Scholarship *(Graduate, Undergraduate/Scholarship)* 3540

Horace Mann Scholarship *(Undergraduate/Scholarship)* 3544

Marianas Naval Officers' Wives' Club Scholarships *(Undergraduate/Scholarship)* 5959

Marin County American Revolution Bicentennial Scholarship *(Graduate, Undergraduate/Scholarship)* 3551

Marine Corps Essay Contest *(Other/Prize)* 5954

Marine Corps Foundation Scholarships *(Undergraduate/ Scholarship)* 3562

Antonio M. Marinelli Founders' Scholarship *(Undergraduate/ Scholarship)* 4237

Marinelli Scholarships *(Undergraduate/Scholarship)* 4238

Inga Marr Memorial Scholarship *(Undergraduate/ Scholarship)* 159

Marsh Scholarship *(Undergraduate/Scholarship)* 2326

Thurgood Marshall Scholarship *(Undergraduate/ Scholarship)* 3566

Jose Marti Scholarship Challenge Grants *(Graduate, Undergraduate/Grant)* 2511

Maryland Distinguished Scholar Scholarship *(Undergraduate/ Scholarship)* 3574

Maryland Higher Education Commission Distinguished Scholar Program *(Undergraduate/Scholarship)* 3591

Maryland House of Delegates Scholarship *(Graduate, Professional Development, Undergraduate/ Scholarship)* 3575

Maryland Part-Time Grant Program *(Undergraduate/ Grant)* 3576

Maryland Senatorial Scholarship *(Graduate, Undergraduate/ Scholarship)* 3580

Masonic Bursaries *(Undergraduate/Scholarship)* 2730

Massachusetts Black Librarians Network Scholarship. *(Undergraduate/Scholarship)* 3593

Massachusetts Family Education Loan *(Graduate, Undergraduate/Loan)* 3598

Massachusetts Indian Association Scholarships *(Graduate, Undergraduate/Scholarship)* 3595

Massachusetts Public Service Scholarship *(Undergraduate/ Scholarship)* 3599

Massachusetts Tuition Waiver *(Undergraduate/Other)* 3600

MassGrant Program *(Undergraduate/Scholarship)* 3601

Masters, Mates & Pilots Health & Benefit Plan Scholarship Program *(Undergraduate/Scholarship)* 3605

Don Matthews Scholarship *(Undergraduate/Scholarship)* 160

Mattinson Endowment Fund Scholarship for Disabled Students *(Undergraduate/Scholarship)* 1282

Edmund F. Maxwell Foundation Scholarship *(Undergraduate/ Scholarship)* 3614

Howard E. May Memorial Scholarships *(Undergraduate/ Scholarship)* 3992

Jonathan May Memorial Scholarships *(Undergraduate/ Scholarship)* 3993

Mazda National Scholarship *(High School/Scholarship)* 6299

McCabe Awards *(Undergraduate/Award)* 5286

John T. McCraw Scholarship *(Graduate, Undergraduate/ Scholarship)* 3996

Fred R. McDaniel Memorial Scholarship *(Undergraduate/ Scholarship)* 830

McDonnell Douglas Scholarships *(Undergraduate/ Scholarship)* 3620

Louise McKinney Post-Secondary Scholarships *(Graduate, Undergraduate/Scholarship)* 177

McKnight Doctoral Fellowships *(Doctorate/Fellowship)* 2519

Paul W. McQuillen Memorial Fellowship *(Doctorate, Postdoctorate/Fellowship)* 1515

Margaret McWilliams Predoctoral Fellowship *(Doctorate/ Fellowship)* 1635

Charles D. Melhuish Scholarship *(Undergraduate/ Scholarship)* 1883

Mellon Resident Research Fellowships *(Other/Fellowship)* 767

Meloche-Monnex Scholarship *(Postdoctorate, Postgraduate/ Scholarship)* 1618

Memmott-Langhans Scholarship *(Undergraduate/ Scholarship)* 1884

ORS Awards *(Doctorate, Graduate, Postgraduate/ Award)* 4824

Oshkosh Foundation Scholarships *(Undergraduate/ Scholarship)* 4818

The Francis Ouimet Scholarships *(Undergraduate/ Scholarship)* 4820

Overseas Postgraduate Research Scholarships for Study in Australia *(Graduate/Scholarship)* 1339

Melva T. Owen Memorial Scholarship *(Undergraduate/ Scholarship)* 4005

Palm Beach Kennel Club Scholarship *(Undergraduate/ Scholarship)* 2036

Parent Loan for Undergraduate Students (PLUS) *(Undergraduate/Loan)* 2058

John and Anne Parente Matching Scholarship *(Undergraduate/ Scholarship)* 4251

Parents Without Partners International Scholarship *(Undergraduate/Scholarship)* 4837

Parke-Davis Epilepsy Scholarship *(Undergraduate/ Scholarship)* 3211

Helen Wegman Parmalee Educational Foundation Scholarships *(Undergraduate/Scholarship)* 4691

Parnell Scholar Programs *(Professional Development/ Scholarship)* 4909

Past Grand Presidents Award *(High School, Undergraduate/ Scholarship)* 2185

The Lionel Pearson Fellowship *(Undergraduate/ Fellowship)* 763

Anne Pekar Memorial Scholarship *(Undergraduate/ Scholarship)* 4006

Pellegrini Scholarship Grants *(Graduate, Undergraduate/ Scholarship)* 5662

Pennsylvania Bureau for Veteran's Affairs Educational Gratuity *(Undergraduate/Other)* 4860

(Pennsylvania) Federal PLUS Loans *(Undergraduate/ Loan)* 4864

(Pennsylvania) Federal Stafford Loans *(Undergraduate/ Loan)* 4865

Pennsylvania Steel Foundry Foundation Awards *(Undergraduate/Scholarship)* 4873

"Persons Case" Scholarships *(Undergraduate/ Scholarship)* 183

Norman R. Peterson Scholarship (John Cabot University) *(Undergraduate/Scholarship)* 4253

Petro-Canada Education Awards for Native Students *(Undergraduate/Award)* 4881

PHD Scholarship *(Undergraduate/Scholarship)* 836

Phi Kappa Phi Graduate Fellowships *(Graduate/ Fellowship)* 4900

Phi Kappa Theta National Foundation Scholarships *(Undergraduate/Scholarship)* 4902

Philippines Subic Bay-Cubi Point Scholarship *(Undergraduate/ Scholarship)* 4492

Pickett & Hatcher Educational Loans *(Undergraduate/ Loan)* 4945

N. Neal Pike Prize for Service to People with Disabilities *(Other/Prize)* 4947

George Pimm Memorial Scholarship *(Undergraduate/ Scholarship)* 163

Minnie Stevens Piper Foundation Student Loan *(Graduate, Undergraduate/Loan)* 4951

Polaroid Foundation National Merit Scholarship *(Undergraduate/Scholarship)* 4971

Robert "Bobby" Guy Pollino II Memorial Scholarship *(Undergraduate/Scholarship)* 1895

Portuguese Continental Union Scholarships *(Undergraduate/ Scholarship)* 4983

Potlatch Foundation for Higher Education Scholarships *(Undergraduate/Scholarship)* 4987

Colin L. Powell Joint Warfighting Essay Contest *(Other/ Prize)* 5956

Paul Powell Memorial AMVETS Scholarships *(Undergraduate/ Scholarship)* 2959

PPGA Family Member Scholarship *(Graduate, Undergraduate/ Scholarship)* 1386

Presbyterian Church Student Opportunity Scholarships *(Undergraduate/Scholarship)* 4996

Herschel C. Price Scholarship *(Undergraduate/ Scholarship)* 2872

Principal's Leadership Award *(Undergraduate/ Scholarship)* 3900

Private Colleges & Universities Community Service Scholarship *(Undergraduate/Scholarship)* 1735

Private High School Scholarship *(High School/ Scholarship)* 2895

Pro Deo and Pro Patria (Canada) Scholarships *(Undergraduate/Scholarship)* 3389

Pro Deo and Pro Patria Scholarships *(Undergraduate/ Scholarship)* 3390

Puerto Rico Council on Higher Education Educational Funds *(Undergraduate/Grant)* 5025

Puerto Rico Council on Legislative Funds *(Undergraduate/ Grant)* 5026

Puerto Rico Council State Student Incentive Grant *(Undergraduate/Grant)* 5027

PVR Scholarship Award *(Graduate/Scholarship)* 4388

Schuler S. Pyle Scholarship *(Undergraduate/ Scholarship)* 2480

Quaker Chemical Foundation Scholarships *(Other, Undergraduate/Scholarship)* 5037

Queen Elizabeth Silver Jubilee Endowment Fund for Study in a Second Official Language Awards *(Undergraduate/ Scholarship)* 1285

QuikTrip Scholarships *(Graduate, Undergraduate/ Scholarship)* 5046

Michael J. Quill Scholarship *(Undergraduate/ Scholarship)* 5737

Radcliffe Research Support Program *(Postdoctorate/ Grant)* 3798

Rangeley Educational Trust Loans *(Professional Development, Undergraduate/Loan)* 2134

Jeannette Rankin Award *(Undergraduate/Award)* 5081

Realty Foundation of New York Scholarships *(Graduate, Undergraduate/Scholarship)* 5085

Alex and Henry Recine Scholarships *(Undergraduate/ Scholarship)* 4255

Red River Valley Fighter Pilot Association Scholarships *(Graduate, Undergraduate/Scholarship)* 5087

Regents' Opportunity Scholarship *(Graduate/ Scholarship)* 2659

J. H. Stewart Reid Memorial Fellowship *(Doctorate/ Fellowship)* 1605

Henry J. Reilly Memorial Graduate Scholarships *(Doctorate, Graduate/Scholarship)* 5105

Henry J. Reilly Memorial Undergraduate Scholarship for College Attendees *(Undergraduate/Scholarship)* 5106

Henry J. Reilly Memorial Undergraduate Scholarship for Graduating High School Students *(Undergraduate/. Scholarship)* 5107

Research Grants for Recent PhDs and PhD Candidates *(Doctorate, Postdoctorate/Grant)* 2690

The Retired Officers Association Educational Assistance Program *(Undergraduate/Loan)* 5116

Z. Smith Reynolds Fellowship *(Professional Development/ Fellowship)* 5120

Dr. Syngman Rhee Scholarship *(Undergraduate/ Scholarship)* 2268

David Carlyle Richards III Scholarships *(Undergraduate/ Scholarship)* 5131

Sid Richardson Memorial Fund Scholarship *(Graduate, Undergraduate/Scholarship)* 5134

Richland County Foundation Scholarships *(Undergraduate/ Scholarship)* 5136

Donald R. Riebhoff Memorial Scholarship *(Undergraduate/ Scholarship)* 837

Samuel Robinson Scholarships *(Undergraduate/ Scholarship)* 4999

David Rogers Bursary *(Graduate, Undergraduate/Grant)* 3971

Admiral Roland Student Loan *(Graduate, Postgraduate, Undergraduate/Loan)* 5849

## General studies (continued)

Sam Rose Memorial Scholarship (*Undergraduate/ Scholarship*) 2481

Rosewood Family Scholarship Fund (*Undergraduate/ Scholarship*) 2514

Leo S. Rowe Pan American Fund (*All/Loan*) 4810

The Leo S. Rowe Pan American Fund Loan (*Graduate, Undergraduate/Loan*) 5174

Royal Canadian Legion Camrose Branch No. 57 Bursaries (*Undergraduate/Scholarship*) 5040

Royal Canadian Legion Ladies Auxiliary Alberta-N.W.T. Command Awards (*Undergraduate/Scholarship*) 5041

Royal Canadian Legion Ladies Auxiliary Camrose Branch No. 57 Bursaries (*Undergraduate/Scholarship*) 5042

F. Charles Ruling/N6FR Memorial Scholarship (*Undergraduate/ Scholarship*) 838

Rutherford Scholars (*High School/Scholarship*) 184

Alexander Rutherford Scholarships for High School Achievement (*Undergraduate/Scholarship*) 185

Edward Rutledge Charity Scholarships (*Undergraduate/ Scholarship*) 5202

Sachs Foundation Grants (*Undergraduate/Grant*) 5204

St. Andrews Society of the State of New York Scholarships (*Graduate/Scholarship*) 5218

St. Anslem's College Scholarship (*Undergraduate/ Scholarship*) 4256

St. David's Scholarship (*Graduate, Professional Development, Undergraduate/Scholarship*) 5220

St. James Armenian Church Memorial Scholarship (*Undergraduate/Scholarship*) 1127

Eugene "Gene" Sallee, W4YFR Memorial Scholarship (*Undergraduate/Scholarship*) 839

Peter Sammartino Scholarship (*Graduate/Scholarship*) 4258

San Mateo County Farm Bureau Scholarships (*All/ Scholarship*) 5243

Santa Fe Pacific Foundation Scholarships (*Undergraduate/ Scholarship*) 563

Santa Fe Pacific Native American Scholarships (*Undergraduate/Scholarship*) 1534

Santa Fe Pacific Special Scholarships (*Undergraduate/ Scholarship*) 1535

Sara Lee Corporation Student Loan Program (*Undergraduate/ Loan*) 5247

Sara Lee National Achievement Scholarships (*Undergraduate/ Scholarship*) 5248

SBS Scholarships (*Undergraduate/Scholarship*) 5660

Scaife Foundation Scholarships (*Undergraduate/ Scholarship*) 4692

SCAMP Grants & Scholarships (*Graduate, Undergraduate/ Grant, Scholarship*) 5266

Marlin Scarborough Memorial Scholarship (*Undergraduate/ Scholarship*) 5554

Schlesinger Library, Radcliffe College Research Support Grants (*Postdoctorate/Grant*) 5258

Conrad & Marcel Schlumberger Scholarships (*Undergraduate/ Scholarship*) 5260

Scholarship for Children of Disabled, Deceased and POW/MIA Veterans (*Graduate, Undergraduate/Scholarship*) 4676

Scholarship Foundation of St. Louis Loan (*Graduate, Undergraduate/Loan*) 5262

Scholarships and Awards for Overseas Students (*Postgraduate/Award, Scholarship*) 1590

Scholarships for Study in Israel (*Doctorate, Graduate, Undergraduate/Scholarship*) 2851

Seabee Memorial Association Scholarships (*Undergraduate/ Scholarship*) 5961

Second Marine Division Memorial Scholarships (*Undergraduate/Scholarship*) 5298

Secondary School Exchange (*High School, Undergraduate/ Other*) 2386

Seibel Foundation Interest Free Educational Loan (*Undergraduate/Loan*) 5302

Seminole-Miccosukee Indian Scholarships (*Graduate, Undergraduate/Scholarship*) 2515

Sequoyah Graduate Fellowships (*Graduate/Fellowship*) 1215

Service Merchandise Scholarship Program (*High School, Undergraduate/Scholarship*) 5310

Dr. Forrest Shaklee Memorial Scholarship (*Undergraduate/ Scholarship*) 5313

Sheet Metal Workers' International Scholarship (*Undergraduate/Scholarship*) 5321

Sig Memorial Scholarship (*Undergraduate/Scholarship*) 20

Sigma Gamma Rho National Education Fund Scholarship (*Undergraduate/Scholarship*) 5332

Sikh Education Aid Fund Scholarship (*Doctorate, Graduate, Undergraduate/Scholarship*) 5349

Six Meter Club of Chicago Scholarship (*Undergraduate/ Scholarship*) 840

C. Bascom Slemp Scholarship (*Undergraduate/ Scholarship*) 5357

Slovenian Women's Union Scholarships (*Undergraduate/ Scholarship*) 5361

Horace Smith Fund Loans (*Undergraduate/Loan*) 5365

Joseph Sumner Smith Scholarship (*Undergraduate/ Scholarship*) 5783

Smithsonian Institution Minority Internship (*Graduate, Undergraduate/Internship*) 5386

Society of Daughters of the United States Army Scholarship Program (*Undergraduate/Scholarship*) 5447

Society of the First Division Foundation Scholarships (*Undergraduate/Scholarship*) 5451

Alexandra Apostolides Sonenfeld Award (*High School, Undergraduate/Scholarship*) 2186

Annie Sonnenblick Scholarship (*Undergraduate/ Scholarship*) 5529

Sons of the First Division Scholarship Fund (*Undergraduate/ Scholarship*) 5452

Sons of Italy Foundation National Leadership Grants (*Graduate, Undergraduate/Grant*) 5533

Soroptimist Women's Opportunity Award (*Professional Development/Award*) 5541

South Carolina Press Association Foundation Scholarships (*Undergraduate/Scholarship*) 5545

South Carolina Tuition Grant Awards (*Undergraduate/ Grant*) 5549

South Carolina Tuition Program (*Undergraduate/ Scholarship*) 5543

South Dakota Board of Regents National Guard Tuition Assistance (*Undergraduate/Other*) 5555

South Dakota Board of Regents Senior Citizens Tuition Assistance (*Undergraduate/Other*) 5556

South Dakota Board of Regents State Employee Tuition Assistance (*Undergraduate/Other*) 5557

South Dakota Board of Regents Veterans Tuition Exemption (*Undergraduate/Other*) 5558

Southeast Asia POW/MIA Scholarship (*Undergraduate/ Scholarship*) 3728

Southern California Edison Company College Scholarships (*Undergraduate/Scholarship*) 5565

Southern California Edison Company Community College Achievement Awards (*Undergraduate/Scholarship*) 5566

Southern California Edison Company Educational Grants (*Undergraduate/Grant*) 5567

Southern California Edison Company Independent Colleges of Southern California Scholarships (*Undergraduate/ Scholarship*) 5568

The Spalding Trust (*Other/Other*) 5570

Special Bursary For Northern Residents (*Other/ Scholarship*) 1683

Spencer Foundation Dissertation Fellowships for Research Related to Education (*Doctorate/Fellowship*) 5586

The Spina Bifida Association of Northern Alberta Scholarship (*Undergraduate/Scholarship*) 5043

SRI Multi-Cultural Scholarship (*All/Scholarship*) 5264

Irene Stambler Vocational Opportunities Grants (*Other/ Grant*) 3271

Stanhome Scholarship (*Undergraduate/Scholarship*) 5599

Star Bank, N.A. Scholarship (*Undergraduate/ Scholarship*) 5601

State Student Incentive Grant For Students at Private Non-Profit Institutions *(Graduate, Undergraduate/Grant)* 5712

State Student Incentive Grant For Students at Public Institutions *(Graduate, Undergraduate/Grant)* 5713

Sonja Stefanadis Graduate Student Award *(Graduate/Scholarship)* 2187

Jerome B. Steinbach Scholarship *(Undergraduate/Scholarship)* 5836

Daniel Stella Scholarship *(Undergraduate/Scholarship)* 4261

John N. Stern Fellowships for Oberlin College Faculty *(Professional Development/Fellowship)* 4625

Emanuel Sternberger Educational Loan *(Graduate, Undergraduate/Loan)* 5628

Harley & Mertie Stevens Memorial Fund *(Undergraduate/Loan, Scholarship)* 5837

Ney Stineman Memorial Scholarship *(Undergraduate/Scholarship)* 1896

Levi Strauss Foundation Scholarship Program *(Undergraduate/Scholarship)* 5636

Hattie M. Strong College Loan Program *(Graduate, Undergraduate/Loan)* 5638

Student Access Awards Program *(Undergraduate/Scholarship)* 1287

Study Visit Research Grants for Faculty *(Doctorate/Grant)* 2691

CDR William S. Stuhr Scholarship *(Undergraduate/Scholarship)* 5644

Supplemental Education Loans for Families *(Undergraduate/Loan)* 4511

Supplemental Educational Opportunity Grant *(Undergraduate/Grant)* 2050

Lloyd D. Sweet Education Scholarships *(All/Scholarship)* 5658

Joe Tangaro Memorial Athletic Scholarship *(Undergraduate/Scholarship)* 4264

Hope Pierce Tartt Scholarship *(Undergraduate/Scholarship)* 5674

Edith Taylor Memorial Scholarship *(Undergraduate/Scholarship)* 164

TELACU Scholarships *(Undergraduate/Scholarship)* 5690

Telesensory Scholarship *(Undergraduate/Scholarship)* 2098

Telluride Association Summer Program Scholarships *(High School/Scholarship)* 5696

Tennessee Federal Parent Loan for Undergraduate Students *(Undergraduate/Loan)* 5700

Texas Black Scholarships *(Undergraduate/Scholarship)* 1374

Texas History Essay Contest *(High School/Award)* 5537

Texas Public Educational Grant Program *(Undergraduate/Grant)* 5715

Texas State Scholarship Program for Ethnic Recruitment *(Undergraduate/Scholarship)* 5716

Texas Tuition Equalization Grant *(Graduate, Undergraduate/Grant)* 5717

Texas Veterans Educational Benefits *(Undergraduate/Grant)* 5721

Al Thompson Junior Bowler Scholarships *(Undergraduate/Scholarship)* 5008

Carol Thomson Memorial Fund Scholarship *(All/Scholarship)* 3447

Rosalie Tiles Scholarship *(Undergraduate/Scholarship)* 5733

Americo Toffoli Scholarships *(Undergraduate/Scholarship)* 1998

Tolbert Grant *(Professional Development, Undergraduate/Grant)* 3584

Virginia Transfer Grant *(Undergraduate/Grant)* 5608

Travel and Training Grant *(Undergraduate/Grant)* 6240

Vice Admiral E.P. Travers Scholarships and Loan Program *(Undergraduate/Grant, Loan)* 4497

Virginia Tuition Assistance Grant *(Graduate, Undergraduate/Grant)* 5609

Tuition/Book Scholarship *(Other, Undergraduate/Scholarship)* 2896

Twenty and Four Memorial Scholarships *(Undergraduate/Scholarship)* 4444

Two/Ten International Footwear Foundation Scholarships *(Undergraduate/Scholarship)* 5759

Tyson Scholarship *(Undergraduate/Scholarship)* 5761

UFCW Scholarships *(Undergraduate/Scholarship)* 5792

Mark Ulmer Native American Scholarships *(Undergraduate/Scholarship)* 5748

Union of Hadjin Fund *(Undergraduate/Scholarship)* 1128

Union of Marash Fund *(Undergraduate/Scholarship)* 1129

Union Pacific Railroad Employee Dependent Scholarships *(Undergraduate/Scholarship)* 5778

UNITE Scholarships *(Undergraduate/Scholarship)* 5776

United Daughters of the Confederacy Scholarships *(Graduate, Undergraduate/Scholarship)* 5790

United Paperworkers International Union Scholarships *(Undergraduate/Scholarship)* 5809

U.S. Air Force Academy Graduate Dependent Scholarship *(Graduate, Undergraduate/Scholarship)* 1240

U.S. Bureau of Indian Affairs Scholarship Grant *(Undergraduate/Grant)* 5843

U.S. Coast Guard Academy Appointment *(Undergraduate/Scholarship)* 5845

United States Naval Academy Class of 1963 Foundation Scholarship *(Graduate, Undergraduate/Scholarship)* 5947

U.S. Submarine Veterans of World War II Scholarships *(Undergraduate/Scholarship)* 5962

United World College Scholarships *(High School/Scholarship)* 186

University of California President's Postdoctoral Fellowship *(Postdoctorate/Fellowship)* 5978

University of Delaware-Hagley Program Fellowship *(Graduate/Fellowship)* 2777

USCG Chief Petty Officers Association Captain Caliendo College Assistance Fund Scholarship Program *(High School, Undergraduate/Scholarship)* 5847

USET Scholarships *(Undergraduate/Scholarship)* 5812

USS Lake Champlain Foundation Scholarships *(Undergraduate/Scholarship)* 5648

USS Stark Memorial Scholarships *(Undergraduate/Scholarship)* 4498

USS Tennessee Scholarships *(Undergraduate/Scholarship)* 4499

Utah State Student Incentive Grant *(Graduate, Undergraduate/Grant)* 6019

UWUA Scholarships *(Undergraduate/Scholarship)* 6021

Agnes E. Vaghi-Cornaro Scholarship *(Undergraduate/Scholarship)* 4266

Adolph Van Pelt Special Fund for Indian Scholarships *(Graduate, Undergraduate/Scholarship)* 1216

Venetian Research Program *(Postdoctorate, Postgraduate/Grant)* 2216

Venture Student Aid Award for Physically Disabled Students *(Other/Award)* 6028

Vermilion River 4-H District Scholarship *(Undergraduate/Scholarship)* 166

Virgin Islands Territorial Loan/Grant Program and Special Legislative Grants *(Graduate, Undergraduate/Grant, Loan)* 6046

Virginia College Scholarship *(Undergraduate/Scholarship)* 5610

Virginia Graduate and Undergraduate Assistance Award *(Undergraduate/Scholarship)* 5611

Virginia War Orphans Education Program *(Graduate, Undergraduate/Other)* 6054

Viscosity Oil Company Scholarships *(Undergraduate/Scholarship)* 4143

Visionaries Achievement Award *(Undergraduate/Scholarship)* 6067

Vocational Rehabilitation Assistance for Postsecondary Training *(Undergraduate/Other)* 4678

Vocational Rehabilitation Grants *(Undergraduate/Scholarship)* 3360

Voice of Democracy Scholarships *(High School, Undergraduate/Award)* 6069

John A. Volpe Scholarship *(Undergraduate/Scholarship)* 4269

Volta Scholarship Award *(Undergraduate/Scholarship)* 1404

Flora M. Von Der Ahe Scholarship *(Graduate, Undergraduate/Scholarship)* 5838

## General studies (continued)

David J. Von Hagen Scholarship Award *(Undergraduate/Scholarship)* 1405

Nicholas C. Vrataric Scholarships *(All/Scholarship)* 5810

Wallace-Folsom Prepaid College Tuition Program *(Undergraduate/Other)* 117

Raoul Wallenberg Scholarships *(Undergraduate/Scholarship)* 3274

War Memorial Scholarships *(Doctorate/Scholarship)* 3935

War Orphans Educational Fund *(Undergraduate/Grant)* 3221

Wilbur H.H. Ward Educational Trust Scholarship *(Undergraduate/Scholarship)* 6077

Warner Trust Loan Program *(Doctorate, Graduate, Other/Loan)* 6079

Washington Crossing Foundation Scholarships *(Undergraduate/Scholarship)* 6085

Washington Scholars Grants *(Undergraduate/Grant)* 6100

Washington State Educational Opportunity Grant *(Undergraduate/Grant)* 6101

Washington State Need Grant *(Undergraduate/Grant)* 6102

Washington State PTA Scholarships *(Undergraduate/Scholarship)* 6107

Washington State Student Financial Aid Programs State Need Grant *(All/Other)* 6103

Washington State Student Financial Aid Programs Washington Scholars *(High School, Undergraduate/Scholarship)* 6104

Washington State Work Study *(Graduate, Undergraduate/Work Study)* 6105

Wasie Foundation Scholarships *(Graduate, Undergraduate/Scholarship)* 6109

David Wasserman Scholarships *(Undergraduate/Scholarship)* 6111

Watson Fellowships *(Other/Fellowship)* 6119

Charles H. Watts Memorial Fellowship *(Doctorate, Postdoctorate/Fellowship)* 1519

W.C.A. Care and Share Scholarship *(Undergraduate/Scholarship)* 1897

Warren Weaver Fellowships *(Postdoctorate/Fellowship)* 5155

Robert H. Weitbrecht Scholarship Award *(Undergraduate/Scholarship)* 1406

Billy Welu Scholarship *(Undergraduate/Scholarship)* 5009

West Virginia Italian Heritage Festival Scholarships *(Undergraduate/Scholarship)* 4270

West Virginia War Orphans Education Benefits *(High School, Undergraduate/Grant)* 6141

Westchester Community Scholarship *(Graduate, Undergraduate/Scholarship)* 4271

Western Interstate Commission for Higher Education Western Regional Graduate Program *(Doctorate, Graduate/Other)* 136

Wetaskiwin District 4-H Scholarships *(Undergraduate/Scholarship)* 167

Weyerhaeuser Company Foundation College Scholarship *(Undergraduate/Scholarship)* 6165

Weyerhaeuser Company Foundation Community Education Scholarship *(Undergraduate/Scholarship)* 6166

Wheat Board Surplus Monies Trust Scholarships *(Undergraduate/Scholarship)* 168

Who's Who Among American High School Students Scholarships *(Undergraduate/Scholarship)* 4149

Roy Wilkins Scholarships *(Undergraduate/Scholarship)* 3852

William P. Willis Scholars Scholarships *(Undergraduate/Scholarship)* 4742

Alice E. Wilson Award *(Graduate/Other)* 1636

David and Dovetta Wilson Scholarship *(Undergraduate/Scholarship)* 6190

Windham Foundation Scholarship *(Undergraduate/Scholarship)* 6193

Maude Winkler Scholarship Awards *(Graduate, Undergraduate/Scholarship)* 1407

The Winston-Salem Foundation Loans *(Undergraduate/Loan)* 6198

Wisconsin Department of Veterans Affairs Part-Time Study Grants *(Graduate, Undergraduate/Grant)* 6209

Wisconsin Department of Veterans Affairs Retraining Grant *(Other/Grant)* 6210

Deborah Partridge Wolfe International Fellowship *(Graduate, Undergraduate/Fellowship)* 6307

Woman's Board Scholarship *(Undergraduate/Scholarship)* 1470

Women of the ELCA Scholarship *(Graduate, Postgraduate, Undergraduate/Scholarship)* 6226

The Women's Sports Foundation Minority Internship Program *(Graduate, Postgraduate, Undergraduate/Internship)* 6241

Women's Western Golf Foundation Scholarship *(Undergraduate/Scholarship)* 6245

Woodgrove Unifarm Local Scholarship *(Undergraduate/Scholarship)* 169

Honourable W.C. Woodward Scholarships *(Undergraduate/Scholarship)* 5044

Nancy B. Woolridge Graduate Fellowship *(Doctorate, Graduate/Fellowship)* 6308

World of Expression Scholarship Program *(High School, Undergraduate/Award)* 1420

Xerox Technical Minority Scholarship *(Graduate, Professional Development, Undergraduate/Scholarship)* 5682

XX Olympiad Memorial Award *(High School/Award)* 3275

YLD Scholarships *(Graduate, Other, Undergraduate/Scholarship)* 6287

Yoshiyama Award for Exemplary Service to the Community *(Undergraduate/Award)* 6289

Young American Creative Patriot Art Award *(All/Award)* 6038

Whitney M. Young Memorial Scholarship *(Undergraduate/Scholarship)* 1929

Coleman A. Young Scholarship *(Undergraduate/Scholarship)* 6293

Zeta Phi Beta General Graduate Fellowship *(Doctorate, Graduate, Postdoctorate/Fellowship)* 6309

Zeta Phi Beta General Undergraduate Scholarship *(Undergraduate/Scholarship)* 6310

Mary & Harry Zimmerman Scholarship Program *(High School, Undergraduate/Scholarship)* 5311

Charles K. and Pansy Pategian Zlokovich Scholarship *(Undergraduate/Scholarship)* 1131

Zuni Higher Education Scholarships *(Doctorate, Graduate, Undergraduate/Scholarship)* 6314

## Genetics

Howard Hughes Medical Institute Predoctoral Fellowships in Biological Sciences *(Postdoctorate/Fellowship)* 4358

Human Growth Foundation Small Grants *(Postdoctorate/Grant)* 2929

Jackson Laboratory Postdoctoral Traineeships *(Postdoctorate/Fellowship)* 3232

March of Dimes Research Grants *(Postdoctorate, Professional Development/Grant)* 3548

Postdoctoral Research Fellowships for Physicians *(Postdoctorate/Fellowship)* 2926

Predoctoral Fellowships in Biological Sciences *(Doctorate/Fellowship)* 2927

U.S. Department of Energy Human Genome Distinguished Postdoctoral Fellowships *(Postdoctorate/Fellowship)* 4710

## Geography (See also: Cartography/Surveying)

AAG General Fund Research Grants *(Professional Development/Grant)* 1207

James W. Bourque Studentship in Northern Geography *(Other/Scholarship)* 1679

Robert G. Buzzard Scholarships *(Graduate/Scholarship)* 2617

Central Intelligence Agency Graduate Studies Internships *(Graduate/Internship)* 1811

Central Intelligence Agency Undergraduate Scholars Program *(Undergraduate/Internship, Scholarship)* 1812

CIBC Youthvision Graduate Research Award Program *(Graduate/Award)* 1270

Monica Cole Research Grant *(Graduate, Undergraduate/Grant)* 5191

Council for European Studies Pre-Dissertation Fellowships in the Social Sciences *(Doctorate/Fellowship)* 2102

Violet Cressey-Marcks Fisher Travel Fellowship *(Graduate, Undergraduate/Scholarship)* 5192

Dudley Stamp Memorial Trust *(Professional Development/ Grant)* 5193

Grants for Overseas Scientific Expeditions *(Professional Development/Grant)* 5194

Robert D. Hodgson Memorial Ph.D. Dissertation Grant *(Doctorate/Grant)* 1208

NAS/NRC Collaboration in Basic Science and Engineering Long-Term Grants *(Postdoctorate/Grant)* 3831

NAS/NRC Collaboration in Basic Science and Engineering Short-Term Project Development Grants *(Postdoctorate/ Grant)* 3832

Postdoctoral Fellowships in the Atmospheric Sciences *(Postdoctorate/Fellowship)* 3931

Benjamin F. Richason III Scholarship *(Graduate, Professional Development/Scholarship)* 2618

Otis Paul Starkey Grant *(Doctorate/Grant)* 1209

Paul Vouras Grant *(Doctorate/Grant)* 1210

## Geology

APEGGA Entrance Scholarships *(Undergraduate/Award)* 1254

Lester Armour Graduate Fellowships *(Graduate/ Fellowship)* 2443

Bunting Institute Science Scholars Fellowships and Biomedical Research Fellowships *(Postdoctorate/Fellowship)* 1529

Canadian Society of Petroleum Geologists Graduate Scholarships *(Graduate/Scholarship)* 1704

Centre for Interdisciplinary Studies in Chemical Physics Senior Visiting Fellowships *(Postdoctorate/Fellowship)* 1795

Civilian Radioactive Waste Management/Historically Black Colleges and Universities Faculty Fellowship Program *(Professional Development/Fellowship)* 5867

Gladys W. Cole Memorial Research Awards *(Postdoctorate/ Award)* 2647

Field Museum Graduate Fellowships *(Graduate/ Fellowship)* 2444

Field Museum Visiting Scholar Funds *(Postdoctorate/ Grant)* 2446

Geological Society of America Research Grants *(Graduate, Postgraduate/Grant)* 2649

Samuel C. Kraus, Jr. Memorial Scholarship *(Undergraduate/ Scholarship)* 4412

Minority Geoscience Scholarships *(Graduate, Undergraduate/ Scholarship)* 508

National Physical Science Consortium Graduate Fellowships for Minorities and Women *(Doctorate, Graduate/ Fellowship)* 4338

Postdoctoral Fellowships in the Atmospheric Sciences *(Postdoctorate/Fellowship)* 3931

Postdoctoral Fellowships in Ocean Science and Engineering *(Postdoctorate/Fellowship)* 6247

Prince Rainier III de Monaco Bursary *(Professional Development/Grant)* 3049

Rocky Mountain Coal Mining Institute Scholarships *(Undergraduate/Scholarship)* 5157

William A. and Stella M. Rowley Graduate Fellowship *(Graduate/Fellowship)* 2447

WAAIME Scholarship Loans *(Graduate, Undergraduate/ Scholarship loan)* 592

## Geophysics (See also: Physics)

APEGGA Entrance Scholarships *(Undergraduate/Award)* 1254

Canadian Society of Exploration Geophysicists Scholarships *(Undergraduate/Scholarship)* 1699

Dublin Institute for Advanced Studies Research Scholarships *(Postdoctorate/Scholarship)* 2282

Hydrology (Horton) Research Grant *(Doctorate/Grant)* 511

JOI/USSAC Ocean Drilling Fellowships *(Doctorate/ Fellowship)* 3291

Minority Geoscience Scholarships *(Graduate, Undergraduate/ Scholarship)* 508

Postdoctoral Fellowships in Ocean Science and Engineering *(Postdoctorate/Fellowship)* 6247

SEG Scholarships *(Graduate, Undergraduate/ Scholarship)* 5300

U.S. Air Force Phillips Laboratory Scholar Program *(Postdoctorate/Other)* 4686

## Geosciences

American Association of Petroleum Geologists Foundation Grants-in-Aid *(Doctorate, Graduate/Grant)* 319

Association for Women Geoscientists Thesis Support Scholarships (Chrysalis) *(Doctorate, Graduate/ Scholarship)* 1296

William C. Foster Fellows Visiting Scholars Competition *(Postdoctorate, Professional Development/Fellowship)* 5818

LPI Summer Intern Program in Planetary Science *(Undergraduate/Internship)* 3514

Minority Geoscience Scholarships *(Graduate, Undergraduate/ Scholarship)* 508

Ralph W. Stone Research Award *(Graduate/Award)* 4410

U.S. Nuclear Regulatory Commission Historically Black Colleges and Universities Faculty Research Participation *(Professional Development/Fellowship)* 5934

## German studies (See also: Area and ethnic studies)

AATG/PAD Travel/Study Awards *(High School/Award)* 327

Alexander von Humboldt Research Fellowships *(Doctorate/ Fellowship)* 2679

Leo Baeck Institute-DAAD Grants *(Doctorate/Fellowship, Grant)* 2680

Bundeskanzler Scholarships *(Other/Scholarship)* 2681

The James Bryant Conant Fellowships for Postdoctoral Research *(Postdoctorate/Fellowship)* 2765

Contemporary Literature Grant *(Other/Grant)* 2682

DAAD Young Lawyers Program *(Postdoctorate/ Fellowship)* 2686

Minda de Gunzburg Center for European Studies Dissertation Exploration Grants *(Graduate/Grant)* 2766

Minda de Gunzburg Center for European Studies Program for the Study of Germany and Europe Dissertation Research Fellowships *(Doctorate/Fellowship)* 2769

Minda de Gunzburg Center for European Studies Short-Term Opportunity Grants *(Graduate/Grant)* 2770

Minda de Gunzburg Center for European Studies Undergraduate Summer Travel Grants *(Undergraduate/ Grant)* 2771

EMGIP Internships *(Graduate, Professional Development, Undergraduate/Internship)* 2380

German Studies Research Grant *(Doctorate, Graduate, Undergraduate/Grant)* 2687

Germanistic Society of America Fellowships *(Postgraduate/ Fellowship)* 3067

Germanistic Society of America Quadrille Grants *(Graduate, Postgraduate/Grant)* 2697

Hochschulsommerkurse at German Universities *(Graduate, Undergraduate/Scholarship)* 2688

SSRC Berlin Program for Advanced German and European Studies Fellowships *(Doctorate, Postdoctorate/ Fellowship)* 5398

Summer Language Course at the University of Leipzig *(Graduate, Undergraduate/Scholarship)* 2692

Summer Language Courses at Goethe Institutes *(Graduate/ Scholarship)* 2693

## Gerontology

ACOG/Ethicon Research Award for Innovations in Gynecologic Surgery *(Postdoctorate/Award)* 378

AFAR Fellowships *(Graduate, Undergraduate/Fellowship)* 468

American Foundation for Aging Research Predoctoral Awards *(Doctorate, Graduate, Undergraduate/Award)* 469

Canadian Nurses Foundation Study Awards *(Doctorate, Graduate/Other)* 1687

Creative Investigator Grants *(Professional Development/ Grant)* 458

Ella H. McNaughton Memorial Fellowship *(Graduate/ Fellowship)* 298

## Government (See also: Political science)
AAAS Congressional Science and Engineering Fellowships (*Postdoctorate, Professional Development/Fellowship*) 263

AIBS Congressional Science Fellowship (*Postdoctorate/Fellowship*) 476

APA Congressional Fellowships (*Postdoctorate/Fellowship*) 809

APSA Congressional Fellowships for Federal Executives (*Professional Development/Fellowship*) 779

APSA Congressional Fellowships for Journalists (*Professional Development/Fellowship*) 780

Center for Strategic and Budgetary Assessments Internship (*Other/Internship*) 1805

Council for European Studies Pre-Dissertation Fellowships in the Social Sciences (*Doctorate/Fellowship*) 2102

Council for European Studies Pre-Dissertation Fellowships for Topics Related to the European Community (*Doctorate/Fellowship*) 2103

Minda de Gunzburg Center for European Studies Graduate Summer Research Travel Grants (*Graduate/Grant*) 2768

Dirksen Congressional Research Grants (*Graduate, Postgraduate/Grant*) 2253

EMGIP Internships (*Graduate, Professional Development, Undergraduate/Internship*) 2380

Fellowships in Ethics (*Postdoctorate, Postgraduate/Fellowship*) 5015

Fellowships for Taft Seminar for Teachers (*Professional Development/Fellowship*) 5670

Enid Hall Griswold Memorial Scholarship (*Undergraduate/Scholarship*) 4397

AGBU Hirair and Anna Hovnanian Fellowship (*Graduate/Fellowship*) 1123

IHS John M. Olin Fellowships (*Graduate/Fellowship*) 3056

Krupp Foundation Fellowship (*Graduate/Fellowship*) 2773

James Madison Fellowships (*Graduate/Fellowship*) 3531

National High School Oratorical Contest (*High School/Award, Scholarship*) 631

National Tax Association Doctoral Dissertation Awards (*Doctorate/Award*) 4422

NATO Euro-Atlantic Partnership Council Fellowships Programme (*Postdoctorate/Fellowship*) 4655

New York State Assembly Graduate Scholarships (*Postgraduate/Internship, Work Study*) 4574

New York State Assembly Session Internships (*Undergraduate/Internship*) 4575

OTA Congressional Fellowship (*Doctorate/Fellowship*) 2040

Public Employees Roundtable Public Service Scholarships (*Graduate, Undergraduate/Scholarship*) 5017

Rhode Island Commission on State Government Summer Internships (*Graduate, Undergraduate/Internship*) 5122

Edith Nourse Rogers Scholarship Fund (*Undergraduate/Scholarship*) 6230

Roosevelt Institute Grants-in-Aid (*Graduate, Postdoctorate/Grant*) 5161

Truman Scholarships (*Graduate, Undergraduate/Scholarship*) 5752

United States Senate Youth Program (*High School/Scholarship*) 2835

Washington Crossing Foundation Scholarships (*Undergraduate/Scholarship*) 6085

Wolcott Foundation Fellowships (*Graduate/Fellowship*) 2870


## Graphic art and design (See also: Art)
Artists Workplace Fellowships (*Professional Development/Fellowship*) 6253

Boston Globe One-Year Minority Development Program (*Professional Development/Other*) 1461

Bureau of Engraving and Printing Graduate Student Research Participation Program (*Graduate, Postgraduate/Fellowship*) 5862

Bureau of Engraving and Printing Postgraduate Research Program (*Postgraduate/Fellowship*) 5863

Canadian Printing Industries Scholarships (*Undergraduate/Scholarship*) 1694

Central Intelligence Agency Graduate Studies Internships (*Graduate/Internship*) 1811

Central Intelligence Agency Undergraduate Scholars Program (*Undergraduate/Internship, Scholarship*) 1812

Dallas-Fort Worth Association of Black Communicators Scholarships (*High School, Undergraduate/Scholarship*) 2170

Pauly D'Orlando Memorial Art Scholarship (*Graduate, Undergraduate/Scholarship*) 5781

Faculty Research Participation Program at the Bureau of Engraving and Printing (*Professional Development/Fellowship*) 5873

FFTA Scholarship Competition (*High School, Undergraduate/Scholarship*) 2568

Gravure Education Foundation Cooperative Education Grant (*Undergraduate/Other*) 2745

The Elizabeth Greenshields Grant (*Graduate, High School, Other, Undergraduate/Grant*) 2751

International Biennial Competition of Humour and Satire in the Arts (*Professional Development/Award*) 2906

William J. Mariner Working Scholar Program (*Undergraduate/Scholarship*) 5100

National Alliance for Excellence Honored Scholars Awards (*Graduate, Undergraduate/Scholarship*) 3841

National Endowment for the Arts - Design Arts Program USA Fellowships (*Professional Development/Fellowship*) 3974

The National Scholarship Trust Fund Scholarships for High School Students (*High School, Undergraduate/Scholarship*) 4374

The National Scholarship Trust Fund Scholarships for Undergraduates (*Other, Undergraduate/Scholarship*) 4375

New England Graphic Arts Scholarships (*High School, Undergraduate/Scholarship*) 4531

Pollock-Krasner Grants (*Professional Development/Grant*) 4975

Sun Chemical Corporation Flexographic Research Scholarship (*Graduate/Fellowship*) 2569


## Greek studies (See also: Area and ethnic studies)
American School of Classical Studies Summer Sessions Scholarships (*Graduate, Professional Development/Scholarship*) 855

Center for Hellenic Studies Fellowships (*Postdoctorate/Fellowship*) 1793

The Eta Sigma Phi Summer Scholarships (*Doctorate, Graduate/Scholarship*) 2414

Alison M. Frantz Fellowship (*Doctorate/Fellowship*) 858

Thomas Day Seymour Fellowship (*Graduate/Fellowship*) 860

Mary Isabel Sibley Fellowships (*Doctorate, Postdoctorate/Fellowship*) 4894

Elizabeth A. Whitehead Visiting Professorships (*Professional Development/Award*) 862


## Health care services
AHCPR Individual National Research Service Awards (*Postdoctorate/Grant*) 62

AISES A.T. Anderson Memorial Scholarship (*Graduate, Undergraduate/Scholarship*) 559

AMBUCS Scholars (*Graduate, Undergraduate/Scholarship*) 3854

John D. Archbold Scholarship (*Graduate, Undergraduate/Scholarship*) 1073

Arthritis Foundation New Investigator Grant for Arthritis Health Professionals (*Postdoctorate/Grant*) 1149

Albert W. Dent Scholarship (*Graduate/Scholarship*) 373

Florida Dental Association Dental Hygiene Scholarship Program (*Other, Professional Development/Scholarship*) 2487

Florida Dental Association Student Loan Program (*Graduate/Loan*) 2488

GFWC of MA Memorial Education Fellowships (*Graduate/Fellowship*) 2639

Health Canada Research Personnel Career Awards (*Postdoctorate, Professional Development/Award, Fellowship*) 2828

Health Canada Research Personnel Training Awards (Regular Program) *(Doctorate, Graduate/Fellowship)* 2829

Indian Health Career Awards *(Doctorate, Graduate, Undergraduate/Scholarship)* 4935

International Order of the King's Daughters and Sons Health Careers Scholarships *(Graduate, Postgraduate, Undergraduate/Scholarship)* 3169

Oliver Joel and Ellen Pell Denny Student Loan Fund *(Undergraduate/Loan)* 6196

Robert Wood Johnson Health Policy Fellowships *(Professional Development/Fellowship)* 3073

Rolfe B. Karlsson Scholarships *(Graduate, Undergraduate/ Scholarship)* 2321

W. K. Kellogg Community Medicine Training Fellowship Program for Minority Medical Students *(Doctorate/ Fellowship)* 4297

Louie LeFlore/Grant Foreman Scholarship *(Undergraduate/ Scholarship)* 5306

Foster G. McGaw Student Scholarship *(Graduate/ Scholarship)* 374

Mississippi Health Care Professions Loan/Scholarship Program *(Undergraduate/Scholarship loan)* 3732

Birdell Chew Moore Scholarships *(Undergraduate/ Scholarship)* 6121

New York Life Foundation Scholarships for Women in the Health Professions *(Undergraduate/Scholarship)* 1551

New York State Health Service Corps Scholarships *(Graduate/ Scholarship)* 4589

E.L. Peterson Scholarships *(Graduate, Undergraduate/ Scholarship)* 2323

Scholarships for Therapists *(Professional Development/ Scholarship)* 3855

USP Fellowship Award *(Postgraduate/Award)* 5964

Lynn Marie Vogel Scholarships *(Graduate, Undergraduate/ Scholarship)* 2324

Washington Health Professional Loan Repayment and Scholarship Program *(Doctorate, Postdoctorate/Scholarship loan)* 6099

WHO Fellowships and Research Training Grants *(Graduate, Other, Postdoctorate/Fellowship)* 6261

Ray Woodham Visiting Fellowship Program *(Professional Development/Fellowship)* 549

## Health sciences

Biotechnology Career Fellowships *(Postdoctorate/ Fellowship)* 5147

Career Development Fellowships *(Postdoctorate, Postgraduate/Fellowship)* 1611

Czech Education Scholarships *(Doctorate, Graduate, Postdoctorate/Scholarship)* 3708

Delaware Academy of Medicine Student Financial Aid Program *(Doctorate/Loan)* 2207

Endowment Fund Dental Hygiene Scholarship Program *(Graduate/Scholarship)* 42

FIC Bilateral Exchanges *(Postdoctorate/Award)* 2525

FIC International Research Fellowships *(Postdoctorate/ Fellowship)* 2528

FIC Senior International Fellowships *(Postdoctorate/ Fellowship)* 2529

FIC Visiting Fellowships *(Postdoctorate/Fellowship)* 2531

Health Sciences Student Fellowships *(All/Fellowship)* 2401

HRC Postdoctoral Fellowship *(Postdoctorate/Fellowship)* 2831

IHS Health Professions Compensatory Preprofessional Scholarship *(Undergraduate/Scholarship)* 2993

Indian Health Career Awards *(Doctorate, Graduate, Undergraduate/Scholarship)* 4935

Oliver Joel and Ellen Pell Denny Student Loan Fund *(Undergraduate/Loan)* 6196

Kelley Foundation Scholarships *(Undergraduate/ Scholarship)* 3345

Killam Research Fellowships *(Postdoctorate/Fellowship)* 3375

Louie LeFlore/Grant Foreman Scholarship *(Undergraduate/ Scholarship)* 5306

S. Evelyn Lewis Memorial Scholarship in Medical Health Sciences *(Graduate, Undergraduate/Scholarship)* 6306

Lindbergh Grants *(Other/Grant)* 3484

March of Dimes Research Grants *(Postdoctorate, Professional Development/Grant)* 3548

Median School Scholarship *(High School/Scholarship)* 3629

New York Life Foundation Scholarships for Women in the Health Professions *(Undergraduate/Scholarship)* 1551

New York State Health Service Corps Scholarships *(Graduate/ Scholarship)* 4589

Sub-Saharan African Dissertation Internship Award *(Doctorate/ Internship)* 5154

Texas Health Education Loan *(Graduate/Loan)* 5714

WHO Fellowships *(Postdoctorate, Professional Development/ Fellowship)* 6259

WHO Fellowships for Canadian Citizens *(Postdoctorate/ Fellowship)* 6260

WHO Fellowships and Research Training Grants *(Graduate, Other, Postdoctorate/Fellowship)* 6261

WHO Fellowships for U.S. Citizens *(Postdoctorate/ Fellowship)* 6262

Young Canadian Researchers Awards *(Doctorate, Graduate/ Award)* 3151

## Health services administration

Richard P. Covert Scholarships *(Doctorate, Graduate, Undergraduate/Scholarship)* 2833

F. Stanton Deland Fellowships in Health Care and Society *(Graduate, Postgraduate/Fellowship)* 1478

Albert W. Dent Scholarship *(Graduate/Scholarship)* 373

Albert W. Dent Scholarship *(Graduate/Scholarship)* 2561

FORE Graduate Scholarships *(Doctorate, Graduate/ Scholarship)* 517

Foundation of Research and Education (FORE) of AHIMA Graduate Scholarship *(Graduate/Scholarship)* 693

Foundation of Research and Education (FORE) of AHIMA Undergraduate Scholarship *(Undergraduate/ Scholarship)* 694

Foundation of Research and Education Loan *(Graduate, Undergraduate/Loan)* 695

Graduate Awards in Dietetics *(Graduate/Award)* 2249

Robert Wood Johnson Health Policy Fellowships *(Professional Development/Fellowship)* 3073

Foster G. McGaw Student Scholarship *(Graduate/ Scholarship)* 374

Foster G. McGaw Student Scholarship *(Graduate/ Scholarship)* 2562

New York State Health Service Corps Scholarships *(Graduate/ Scholarship)* 4589

Postdoctoral Fellowships in Health Policy and Health Services Research *(Postdoctorate/Fellowship)* 3045

Santa Fe Pacific Foundation Scholarships *(Undergraduate/ Scholarship)* 563

Warren H Pearse/Wyeth-Ayerst Women's Health Policy Research Award *(Postdoctorate/Grant)* 386

WHO Fellowships and Research Training Grants *(Graduate, Other, Postdoctorate/Fellowship)* 6261

David A. Winston Fellowship *(Graduate, Undergraduate/ Fellowship)* 1290

## Hematology

Career Development Fellowships *(Postdoctorate, Postgraduate/Fellowship)* 1611

## Hemophilia

Judith Graham Pool Postdoctoral Research Fellowships *(Postdoctorate/Fellowship)* 4177

## Hepatology

ADHF/Industry Research Scholar Awards *(Postdoctorate/ Award)* 446

American Liver Foundation Postdoctoral Supplementary Fellowships *(Postdoctorate/Fellowship)* 673

American Liver Foundation Student Research Fellowships *(Doctorate, Graduate, Other/Fellowship)* 674

Astra/Merck Fellowship/Faculty Transition Award *(Postdoctorate/Award)* 450

## Hepatology (continued)

Canadian Liver Foundation Establishment Grants *(Postdoctorate/Grant)* 1670

Canadian Liver Foundation Fellowships *(Postdoctorate/Fellowship)* 1671

Canadian Liver Foundation Graduate Studentships *(Doctorate, Graduate/Award)* 1672

Liver Scholar Awards *(Postdoctorate/Grant)* 675

## Herpetology

Herpetologists' League Best Student Paper *(Graduate/Award)* 2864

## Historic preservation

Artists Fellowship; Japan Foundation Cultural Properties Specialists Fellowship; Japan Foundation Doctoral Fellowship; Japan Foundation Research Fellowship *(Doctorate, Postdoctorate, Professional Development/Fellowship)* 3240

The Richard Morris Hunt Fellowship *(Professional Development/Fellowship)* 575

National Endowment for the Arts - Design Arts Program USA Fellowships *(Professional Development/Fellowship)* 3974

## History

American Numismatic Society Graduate Seminar *(Graduate/Other)* 737

American Society for 18th-Century Studies Fellowships *(Postdoctorate/Fellowship)* 4616

Annual Grants; Dr. John Pine Memorial Award; Dr. A. F. Zimmerman Award *(Doctorate, Graduate/Award, Grant)* 4890

ASECS/Clark Fellowship *(Postdoctorate/Fellowship)* 1761

Beinecke Library Visiting Fellowships *(Postdoctorate/Fellowship)* 1393

Berkshire Summer Fellowships *(Postdoctorate/Fellowship)* 1525

The Albert J. Beveridge Grant *(Postdoctorate, Professional Development/Grant)* 536

John Carter Brown Library Travel Grants *(Doctorate, Postdoctorate/Grant)* 1514

Lillian Sholtis Brunner Summer Fellowship *(Doctorate, Postdoctorate/Fellowship)* 1807

J.E. Caldwell Centennial Scholarships *(Graduate/Scholarship)* 4394

Center For Advanced Study in the Visual Arts Associate Appointments *(Postdoctorate/Fellowship)* 1768

Chateaubriand Fellowships (Humanities) *(Doctorate/Grant)* 2375

Chemical Heritage Foundation Travel Grants *(Other/Grant)* 1899

Clark Library Predoctoral Fellowship *(Doctorate/Fellowship)* 1762

Clark Library Short-Term Fellowship *(Postdoctorate/Fellowship)* 1763

Arthur H. Cole Grants-In-Aid for Research in Economic History *(Postdoctorate/Grant)* 2359

Council for European Studies Pre-Dissertation Fellowships in the Social Sciences *(Doctorate/Fellowship)* 2102

Council for European Studies Pre-Dissertation Fellowships for Topics Related to the European Community *(Doctorate/Fellowship)* 2103

Cox Minority Journalism Scholarship *(Undergraduate/Scholarship)* 2131

Paul Cuffe Memorial Fellowship for the Study of Minorities in American Maritime History *(Other/Fellowship)* 3794

Helen Darcovich Memorial Doctoral Fellowship *(Doctorate, Graduate/Fellowship)* 1657

Shelby Cullom Davis Center Research Fellowships *(Postdoctorate/Fellowship)* 2189

Minda de Gunzburg Center for European Studies Dissertation Exploration Grants *(Graduate/Grant)* 2766

Minda de Gunzburg Center for European Studies German Language Training Grants *(Graduate/Grant)* 2767

Minda de Gunzburg Center for European Studies Program for the Study of Germany and Europe Dissertation Research Fellowships *(Doctorate/Fellowship)* 2769

Minda de Gunzburg Center for European Studies Short-Term Opportunity Grants *(Graduate/Grant)* 2770

Dirksen Congressional Research Grants *(Graduate, Postgraduate/Grant)* 2253

Doctoral Thesis Fellowship in Ukrainian History *(Doctorate/Fellowship)* 1658

Marusia and Michael Dorosh Masters Fellowship *(Graduate/Fellowship)* 1659

H.B. Earhart Fellowships *(Graduate/Fellowship)* 2301

Friedreich Ebert Foundation Doctoral Research Fellowships *(Postgraduate/Fellowship)* 2330

Friedreich Ebert Stiftung Pre Dissertation/Advanced Graduate Fellowhps *(Doctorate, Graduate/Fellowship)* 2332

Edelstein International Fellowship in the History of Chemical Sciences and Technology *(Postdoctorate/Fellowship)* 1900

Albert Einstein Institution Fellowships *(Doctorate, Postdoctorate, Professional Development/Fellowship)* 2361

Rabbi Robert Feinberg Scholarship *(Graduate, Undergraduate/Scholarship)* 4223

Fellowship in Aerospace History *(Doctorate, Postdoctorate/Fellowship)* 537

Fraenkel Prizes in Contemporary History *(Professional Development/Prize)* 3023

Germanistic Society of America Quadrille Grants *(Graduate, Postgraduate/Grant)* 2697

Graham Foundation Grants *(Professional Development/Grant)* 2726

Grand Army of the Republic Memorial Scholarship *(Undergraduate/Scholarship)* 1347

Enid Hall Griswold Memorial Scholarship *(Undergraduate/Scholarship)* 4397

Phyllis P. Harris Scholarships *(All/Scholarship)* 4956

Harvard-Newcomen Postdoctoral Fellowship *(Postdoctorate/Fellowship)* 4627

Harvard University Pre-Doctoral Fellowships in European Studies *(Graduate/Fellowship)* 2772

Hoover Library Fellowships and Grants *(Graduate, Postdoctorate/Fellowship, Grant)* 2890

Howard Foundation Fellowships *(Professional Development/Fellowship)* 2908

Humane Studies Foundation Summer Residential Program Fellowships *(Graduate/Fellowship)* 3053

IEC Russia, China Study Fellowship *(Professional Development/Fellowship)* 3153

IGCC Dissertation Fellowships *(Doctorate, Graduate/Fellowship)* 3043

IHS Excellence in Liberty Prizes *(Graduate, Undergraduate/Prize)* 3055

IHS John M. Olin Fellowships *(Graduate/Fellowship)* 3056

IHS Summer Faculty Fellowships *(Professional Development/Fellowship)* 3057

Institute for Advanced Study Postdoctoral Research Fellowships *(Postdoctorate/Fellowship)* 3009

Institute for Advanced Study Postdoctoral Study Awards *(Postdoctorate/Grant)* 3010

Institute for European History Fellowships *(Doctorate, Postdoctorate/Fellowship)* 3035

International Affairs Fellowships *(Professional Development/Fellowship)* 2105

Olivia James Traveling Fellowship *(Doctorate, Postdoctorate/Fellowship)* 1066

Jamestown Prize *(Postdoctorate/Prize)* 4755

Krupp Foundation Fellowship *(Graduate/Fellowship)* 2773

Lloyd Lewis Fellowships in American History *(Postdoctorate/Fellowship)* 4617

The Littleton-Griswold Research Grant *(Professional Development/Grant)* 540

Ottis Lock Endowment Scholarships *(Graduate, Undergraduate/Scholarship)* 2306

Audrey Lumsden-Kouvel Fellowship *(Postdoctorate/Fellowship)* 4605

Marine Corps Historical Center College Internships
(Undergraduate/Internship)  3556
Marine Corps Historical Center Doctoral Dissertation
Fellowship (Doctorate/Fellowship)  3557
Marine Corps Historical Center Master's Thesis Fellowship
(Graduate/Fellowship)  3558
Marine Corps Historical Center Research Grants (Graduate,
Postgraduate/Grant)  3559
Mesopotamian Fellowship (Doctorate, Postdoctorate/
Fellowship)  878
National Federation of the Blind Humanities Scholarship
(Undergraduate/Scholarship)  4003
Near and Middle East Research and Training Program Pre-
Doctoral Fellowships (Doctorate/Fellowship)  880
NEH Fellowships for Research in Turkey (Postdoctorate/
Fellowship)  847
NHPRC/Fellowships in Historical Editing (Postdoctorate/
Fellowship)  4182
Oregon Humanities Center Summer Visiting Research
Fellowships (Professional Development/Fellowship)  6011
Pew Fellowships in International Journalism (Other/
Fellowship)  4854
Phi Alpha Theta Faculty Advisor Research Grant
(Postdoctorate/Grant)  4891
Phi Alpha Theta Graduate Scholarship (Doctorate, Graduate/
Grant)  4892
Postdoctoral Fellowships in the History and Philosophy of
Science (Postdoctorate/Fellowship)  4699
Radcliffe Research Support Program (Postdoctorate/
Grant)  3798
Rockefeller Archive Center Research Grants (Graduate,
Postdoctorate, Professional Development/Grant)  5142
Rockefeller Foundation Residential Fellowships in Gender
Studies in Early Modern Europe (Postdoctorate/
Fellowship)  4608
Roosevelt Institute Grants-in-Aid (Graduate, Postdoctorate/
Grant)  5161
Rundell Graduate Student Award (Doctorate/Award)  6155
William B. Schallek Memorial Graduate Study Fellowships
(Doctorate, Graduate/Fellowship)  5132
Schlesinger Library, Radcliffe College Dissertation Grants
(Doctorate/Grant)  5256
Bernadette Schmitt Grants (Professional Development/
Grant)  541
James R. Scobie Memorial Awards (Doctorate/Grant)  3071
Thomas Day Seymour Fellowship (Graduate/Fellowship)  860
Silver Dart Aviation History Award (Undergraduate/
Prize)  1607
John Clarke Slater Fellowship (Doctorate/Fellowship)  770
SSRC Grants for Advanced Area Research (Doctorate, Other/
Grant)  5399
SSRC-MacArthur Foundation Dissertation Fellowships on
Peace and Security in a Changing World (Doctorate/
Fellowship)  5409
Robert G. Stone Fellowships in American Maritime History
(Doctorate, Postdoctorate/Fellowship)  6182
Touro National Heritage Trust Fellowship (Doctorate,
Postdoctorate/Fellowship)  1517
U.S. Air Force Dissertation Year Fellowship in U.S. Military
Aerospace History (Doctorate/Fellowship)  5814
A. Verville Fellowship (Other/Fellowship)  5381
Alexander O. Vietor Memorial Fellowship (Doctorate,
Postdoctorate/Fellowship)  1518
Muddy Waters Scholarship (Undergraduate/Scholarship)  1448
Elizabeth A. Whitehead Visiting Professorships (Professional
Development/Award)  862
Yale Center for British Art Fellowships (Postdoctorate,
Professional Development/Fellowship)  6278

## History, American

AAS/American Society for Eighteenth Century Studies
Fellowships (Professional Development/Fellowship)  252
AAS Joint Fellowships with the Newberry Library (Doctorate,
Postdoctorate/Fellowship)  253

American Jewish Studies Fellowships (Doctorate,
Postdoctorate/Award, Fellowship)  598
Stephen Botein Fellowships (Doctorate, Professional
Development/Fellowship)  254
Weston A. Cate, Jr. Annual Research Fellowship (Other/
Fellowship)  6030
Folger Library Long-Term Fellowships (Postdoctorate/
Fellowship)  2541
Folger Library Short-Term Fellowships (Postdoctorate/
Fellowship)  2542
Hoover Library Fellowships and Grants (Graduate,
Postdoctorate/Fellowship, Grant)  2890
Huntington Library Research Awards (Graduate,
Postdoctorate/Award)  2939
Institute Postdoctoral Fellowship (Postdoctorate/
Fellowship)  4754
Institute Postdoctoral NEH Fellowship (Doctorate, Graduate/
Fellowship)  4751
Irish in America Publication Award Notre Dame Studies in
Catholicism Publication Award (Professional Development/
Award)  6009
J. Franklin Jameson Fellowship in American History
(Postdoctorate/Fellowship)  538
Jamestown Prize (Postdoctorate/Prize)  4755
Johnson Foundation Grants-in-Aid of Research (Professional
Development/Grant)  3282
Johnson Foundation Photocopying Grants (Graduate/
Grant)  3283
Michael Kraus Research Grant in History (Professional
Development/Grant)  539
Lloyd Lewis Fellowships in American History (Postdoctorate/
Fellowship)  4617
Marine Corps Historical Center College Internships
(Undergraduate/Internship)  3556
Institute Andrew W. Mellon Postdoctoral Research Fellowship
(Doctorate, Postdoctorate/Fellowship)  4752
Institute Andrew W. Mellon Postdoctoral Research Fellowship
(Postdoctorate/Fellowship)  4756
National Endowment for the Humanities Fellowships
(Postgraduate/Fellowship)  255
National Endowment for the Humanities Fellowships
(Postdoctorate/Fellowship)  2543
Native Sons of the Golden West High School Public Speaking
Scholarships (High School/Prize)  4472
NEH Fellowships (Doctorate/Fellowship)  6200
NSDAR American History Scholarship (Undergraduate/
Scholarship)  4402
Kate B. and Hall J. Peterson Fellowships (Doctorate,
Professional Development/Fellowship)  256
Research Fellowships in American History and Culture
(Doctorate, Postdoctorate/Fellowship)  3460
Alice E. Smith Fellowship (Graduate/Fellowship)  5617
Robert G. Stone Fellowships in American Maritime History
(Doctorate, Postdoctorate/Fellowship)  6182
U.S. Army Center of Military History Dissertation Year
Fellowships (Doctorate/Fellowship)  5821
WAWH Graduate Student Fellowship (Doctorate/
Fellowship)  6147
Winterthur Research Fellowships (Doctorate/Fellowship)  6201
World Press Institute Fellowships (Professional Development/
Fellowship)  6268

## History, Economic

American Numismatic Society Graduate Seminar (Graduate/
Other)  737
Arthur H. Cole Grants-in-Aid (Postdoctorate/Grant)  2334
Minda de Gunzburg Center for European Studies
Undergraduate Summer Travel Grants (Undergraduate/
Grant)  2771
Folger Library Long-Term Fellowships (Postdoctorate/
Fellowship)  2541
Folger Library Short-Term Fellowships (Postdoctorate/
Fellowship)  2542
John C. Geilfuss Fellowship (Graduate, Postgraduate/
Fellowship)  5615

## History, Economic (continued)

Humane Studies Foundation Summer Residential Program Fellowships *(Graduate/Fellowship)* 3053

National Endowment for the Humanities Fellowships *(Postdoctorate/Fellowship)* 2543

## History, Medical

Edelstein International Fellowship in the History of Chemical Sciences and Technology *(Postdoctorate/Fellowship)* 1900

## History, Military

Advanced Research Grants in Military History *(Graduate, Postgraduate/Grant)* 5823

Marine Corps Historical Center Doctoral Dissertation Fellowship *(Doctorate/Fellowship)* 3557

Marine Corps Historical Center Master's Thesis Fellowship *(Graduate/Fellowship)* 3558

Marine Corps Historical Center Research Grants *(Graduate, Postgraduate/Grant)* 3559

U.S. Air Force Dissertation Year Fellowship in U.S. Military Aerospace History *(Doctorate/Fellowship)* 5814

U.S. Army Center of Military History Dissertation Year Fellowships *(Doctorate/Fellowship)* 5821

U.S. Marine Corps Historical Center College Internships *(Graduate, Undergraduate/Internship)* 5945

## Hodgkins disease

Leukemia Society Fellow Awards *(Postdoctorate/Award)* 3456

Leukemia Society Special Fellow Awards *(Postdoctorate/ Award)* 3458

## Home Economics

Alberta Wheat Pool Scholarships *(Undergraduate/ Scholarship)* 148

All Saints Educational Trust Grants *(Professional Development/Grant)* 190

AVA Home Economics Education Graduate Fellowships *(Doctorate, Graduate/Fellowship)* 1013

Ruth Binnie Scholarships *(Graduate/Scholarship)* 1644

A & E Capelle LN Herfords Scholarship *(Doctorate, Graduate, Undergraduate/Scholarship)* 150

CHEA Fiftieth Anniversary Scholarship *(Doctorate/ Scholarship)* 1645

CHEA Silver Jubilee Scholarship *(Graduate/Scholarship)* 1646

Mary A. Clarke Memorial Scholarship *(Graduate/ Scholarship)* 1647

Commemorative Lecture Award *(Professional Development/ Award)* 292

County of Forty Mile Agricultural Committee Bursaries *(Undergraduate/Scholarship)* 2127

Jeannette H. Crum Fellowship; Jewell L. Taylor Fellowships *(Graduate/Fellowship)* 293

Freda A. DeKnight Memorial Fellowship *(Graduate/ Fellowship)* 295

General Fellowship *(Graduate/Fellowship)* 296

Kappa Omicron Nu Doctoral Fellowships *(Doctorate/ Fellowship)* 3335

Kappa Omicron Nu Masters Fellowships *(Graduate/ Fellowship)* 3336

Kappa Omicron Nu Research/Project Grant *(Other/ Grant)* 3337

Flemmie P. Kittrell Memorial Fellowship for Minorities *(Graduate/Fellowship)* 297

Kraft Canada Inc. Undergraduate Scholarship *(Undergraduate/ Scholarship)* 1649

Maryland Child Care Provider Scholarship *(Undergraduate/ Scholarship)* 3573

James D. Moran Memorial Research Award *(Professional Development/Award)* 299

Nestle Canada Scholarship *(Graduate/Award)* 1650

Ruth O'Brien Project Grants *(Professional Development/ Grant)* 300

Ohio State University Extension Internship *(Graduate, Undergraduate/Internship)* 4733

Ethel L. Parker International Memorial Fellowship; Marion K. Piper Fellowship *(Graduate/Fellowship)* 301

Inez Eleanor Radell Sole Donor Memorial Fellowship *(Graduate/Fellowship)* 302

Effie I. Raitt Memorial Fellowship *(Graduate/Fellowship)* 303

Ellen H. Richards Fellowship *(Graduate/Fellowship)* 304

Hazel Putnam Roach Memorial Fellowships *(Graduate/ Fellowship)* 305

Robin Hood Multifoods Scholarship *(Graduate/Award)* 1651

Abbie Sargent Memorial Scholarships *(Graduate, Undergraduate/Scholarship)* 5250

Wiley-Berger Memorial Award for Volunteer Service *(Professional Development/Award)* 306

## Horticulture

American Floral Endowment Scholarship *(Undergraduate/ Scholarship)* 4020

American Horticultural Society Horticultural Career Internship *(Graduate, Professional Development, Undergraduate/ Internship)* 545

Jerry Baker College Freshman Scholarships *(Undergraduate/ Scholarship)* 1380

Bedding Plants Foundation Scholarship *(Undergraduate/ Scholarship)* 4028

Bedding Plants Foundation Vocational Scholarships *(Other/ Scholarship)* 1381

Harold Bettinger Memorial Scholarship *(Graduate, Undergraduate/Scholarship)* 1382

California Landscape Architectural Student Scholarships *(Undergraduate/Scholarship)* 3422

John Carew Memorial Scholarship *(Graduate/ Scholarship)* 1383

Dr. Allan P. Chan Scholarship *(Doctorate, Graduate/ Scholarship)* 2225

Carl F. Dietz Memorial Scholarship *(Undergraduate/ Scholarship)* 1384

Grace and Robert Fraser Landscape Heritage Award *(Graduate, Undergraduate/Award)* 3423

Grants for Orchid Research *(Professional Development/ Grant)* 750

U.P. Hedrick Award *(Graduate, Undergraduate/Award)* 786

Herb Society Research Grants *(Doctorate, Graduate/ Grant)* 2862

Horticultural Research Institute Grants *(Postdoctorate/ Grant)* 2898

Interchange Fellowship in Horticulture and Landscape Design *(Graduate, Postgraduate/Fellowship)* 2622

Fran Johnson Scholarships *(Graduate, Undergraduate/ Scholarship)* 1385

LAF/CLASS Cal Poly Scholarships *(Undergraduate/ Scholarship)* 3426

LAF/CLASS University Program *(Undergraduate/ Scholarship)* 3428

Earl May Seed & Nursery L.P. Scholarship *(Undergraduate/ Scholarship)* 4096

Monrovia Nursery Co. Scholarship *(Undergraduate/ Scholarship)* 4102

National Zoological Park Minority Traineeships *(Graduate, Undergraduate/Internship)* 4456

National Zoological Park Traineeship in BioPark Horticulture *(Graduate, Undergraduate/Internship)* 4458

NCSGC National Scholarships *(Graduate, Undergraduate/ Scholarship)* 3959

James K. Rathmell, Jr., Memorial Scholarship to Work/Study Abroad *(Graduate, Undergraduate/Scholarship)* 1387

Scottish Gardening Scholarship *(Other/Scholarship)* 4277

Marie Selby Internships *(Graduate, Undergraduate/ Internship)* 5304

Shade Tree Research Grants *(Postdoctorate/Grant)* 3192

Earl J. Small Growers, Inc. Scholarships *(Undergraduate/ Scholarship)* 1388

Spraying Systems Company Scholarships *(Undergraduate/ Scholarship)* 4129

Sun Company Scholarships *(Undergraduate/Scholarship)* 4131

Sarah B. Tyson Fellowship *(Professional Development/ Fellowship)* 6234

Jerry Wilmot Scholarship *(Undergraduate/Scholarship)* 1389

Worcester County Horticultural Society Scholarship *(Graduate, Undergraduate/Scholarship)* 6257

## Hotel, institutional, and restaurant management

Alabama/Birmingham Legacy Scholarship *(Undergraduate/ Scholarship)* 4427

Dr. Tom Anderson Memorial Scholarship *(Undergraduate/ Scholarship)* 4428

Canadian Hospitality Foundation Scholarships *(Undergraduate/ Scholarship)* 1653

Cleveland Legacy Scholarship *(Undergraduate/ Scholarship)* 4431

Weeta F. Colebank Scholarship *(Undergraduate/ Scholarship)* 4432

Louise Dessureault Memorial Scholarship *(Undergraduate/ Scholarship)* 4433

Charles Fitzsimmons Award; IAHA General Scholarships; Frances Tally Award *(Professional Development/Award, Scholarship)* 3115

Eric and Bette Friedheim Scholarship *(Undergraduate/ Scholarship)* 4434

H. Neil Mecaskey Scholarship *(Undergraduate/ Scholarship)* 4435

National Restaurant Association Educational Foundation Undergraduate Scholarship for High School Seniors *(Undergraduate/Scholarship)* 4364

Quebec Scholarship *(Doctorate, Graduate/Scholarship)* 4438

Edwin P. Shaunessy Memorial Scholarships *(Graduate/ Scholarship)* 4989

Statler Foundation Scholarship *(Graduate, Undergraduate/ Scholarship)* 5622

Treadway Inns, Hotels, and Resorts Scholarship *(Undergraduate/Scholarship)* 4439

Tulsa Legacy Scholarship *(Undergraduate/Scholarship)* 4440

Yellow Ribbon Scholarship *(Undergraduate/Scholarship)* 4442

## Human relations

Bicentennial Swedish-American Exchange Fund Travel Grants *(Professional Development/Grant)* 5656

Federated Women's Institutes of Ontario International Scholarship *(Graduate, Undergraduate/Scholarship)* 1648

GOALS Fellowships *(Graduate/Fellowship)* 3001

International Foundation of Employee Benefit Plans Grants for Research *(Doctorate, Graduate, Postdoctorate/Grant)* 3155

Student Research Grants for the Scientific Study of Sex *(Doctorate, Graduate/Grant)* 5502

## Humanities

ACLS Fellowships *(Postdoctorate/Fellowship)* 406

ACLS Grants for East European Studies - Dissertation Fellowships *(Doctorate/Fellowship)* 407

ACLS Grants for East European Studies - Fellowships for Postdoctoral Research *(Postdoctorate/Fellowship)* 408

Konrad Adenauer Research Award *(Other/Award)* 6071

Frances C. Allen Fellowships *(Doctorate, Graduate, Postgraduate/Fellowship)* 4615

Thomas Joseph "Willie" Ambrosole Scholarship *(Undergraduate/Scholarship)* 4207

ARIT Fellowships *(Doctorate, Postdoctorate/Fellowship)* 846

Artists Fellowship; Japan Foundation Cultural Properties Specialists Fellowship; Japan Foundation Doctoral Fellowship; Japan Foundation Research Fellowship *(Doctorate, Postdoctorate, Professional Development/ Fellowship)* 3240

Australian National University Visiting Fellowships *(Postdoctorate/Fellowship)* 1333

Beinecke Library Visiting Fellowships *(Postdoctorate/ Fellowship)* 1393

British Academy Visiting Professorships for Overseas Scholars *(Postdoctorate/Other)* 1480

Lester J. Cappon Fellowship in Documentary Editing *(Postdoctorate/Fellowship)* 4602

CFUW Awards *(Graduate/Award)* 1631

Chinese Fellowships for Scholarly Development *(Other/ Fellowship)* 409

CIC Predoctoral Fellowships *(Doctorate, Graduate/ Fellowship)* 2013

President Francisco Cossiga Fellowship *(Postdoctorate/ Fellowship)* 4603

Council of American Overseas Research Centers Fellowships *(Postdoctorate/Fellowship)* 866

Helen Darcovich Memorial Doctoral Fellowship *(Doctorate, Graduate/Fellowship)* 1657

Marusia and Michael Dorosh Masters Fellowship *(Graduate/ Fellowship)* 1659

Du Bois Mandela Rodney Postdoctoral Fellowships *(Postdoctorate/Fellowship)* 1784

H.B. Earhart Fellowships *(Graduate/Fellowship)* 2301

Earhart Foundation Fellowship Research Grants *(Postdoctorate/Grant)* 2302

Ecole des Chartes Exchange Fellowship *(Doctorate/Fellowship, Scholarship)* 4604

Faculty Graduate Study Fellowships for Historically Black Colleges and Universities *(Doctorate/Fellowship)* 3984

Fellowships for Basic Study in the Humanities/Fellowships for Principals *(Professional Development/Fellowship)* 2094

Fellowships for Independent Study in the Humanities *(Professional Development/Fellowship)* 2095

Ford Foundation Postdoctoral Fellowships for Minorities *(Postdoctorate/Fellowship)* 4356

Ford Foundation Predoctoral and Dissertation Fellowships for Minorities *(Doctorate/Fellowship)* 4357

Alison M. Frantz Fellowship *(Doctorate/Fellowship)* 858

Getty Center Postdoctoral Fellowships *(Postdoctorate/ Fellowship)* 2699

Getty Center Predoctoral Fellowships *(Doctorate/ Fellowship)* 2700

Government of Canada Awards *(Doctorate, Graduate, Postdoctorate/Award)* 3145

Alfred Hodder Fellowships *(Professional Development/ Fellowship)* 2108

R.C. Hoiles and IHS Postdoctoral Fellowships *(Postdoctorate/ Fellowship)* 3052

Humanities Research Centre Visiting Fellowships *(Postdoctorate/Fellowship)* 2933

India Studies Faculty Fellowships *(Professional Development/ Fellowship)* 5316

India Studies Postdoctoral Research Fellowships *(Professional Development/Fellowship)* 5318

India Studies Student Fellowships *(Graduate/Fellowship)* 5319

Institute for Advanced Studies Visiting Research Fellowships *(Postdoctorate/Fellowship)* 3007

IREX Individual Advanced Research Opportunities *(Doctorate/ Award)* 3185

IREX Short-Term Travel Grants for Independent Short-Term Research *(Postdoctorate/Grant)* 3187

Italian Cultural Society and NIAF Matching Scholarship *(Undergraduate/Scholarship)* 4234

Jacob K. Javits Fellowship *(Doctorate/Fellowship)* 3255

Killam Research Fellowships *(Postdoctorate/Fellowship)* 3375

Leo J. Krysa Family Foundation Undergraduate Scholarship *(Undergraduate/Scholarship)* 1660

Claude R. Lambe Fellowships *(Graduate/Fellowship)* 3058

Lindbergh Grants *(Other/Grant)* 3484

D'Arcy McNickle Center for the History of the American Indian Fellowships *(Postgraduate/Fellowship)* 4606

Mellon Postdoctoral Fellowships *(Postdoctorate/ Fellowship)* 5458

Andrew W. Mellon Postdoctoral Fellowships in the Humanities *(Postdoctorate/Fellowship)* 5597

Mellon Postdoctoral Research Fellowships *(Postdoctorate/ Fellowship)* 4607

Andrew W. Melon Fellowships in Humanistic Studies *(Graduate/Fellowship)* 6187

Ministry of the Flemish Community Fellowships *(Postdoctorate, Undergraduate/Fellowship)* 3710

## Humanities (continued)

National Endowment for the Humanities Fellowships
(Postdoctorate/Fellowship) 5275

National Endowment for the Humanities Post-Doctoral
Fellowships, Nicosia (Postdoctorate/Fellowship) 879

National Federation of the Blind Humanities Scholarship
(Undergraduate/Scholarship) 4003

National Humanities Center Residential, Advanced
Postdoctoral Fellowships (Postdoctorate/Fellowship) 4184

National Program for Advanced Study and Research in China
- General Advanced Studies (Graduate/Grant) 2015

National Program for Advanced Study and Research in China
- Research Program (Postdoctorate/Other) 2016

Near and Middle East Research and Training Program Senior
Research Grants (Postdoctorate/Grant) 881

NEH Fellowship for University Teachers (Postdoctorate/
Fellowship) 3985

NEH Fellowships for College Teachers and Independent
Scholars (Postdoctorate/Fellowship) 3986

NEH Fellowships for Research in Turkey (Postdoctorate/
Fellowship) 847

NEH Interpretive Research Grants (Doctorate, Postdoctorate/
Grant) 3987

NEH Post-Doctoral Research (Postdoctorate/Fellowship) 882

NEH Reference Materials Grants (Doctorate, Postdoctorate/
Grant) 3988

NEH Summer Stipend (Postdoctorate/Fellowship) 3990

Newberry-British Academy Fellowship (Postdoctorate/
Fellowship) 4620

Charlotte W. Newcombe Fellowships (Doctorate/
Fellowship) 6188

Oregon Humanities Center Summer Visiting Research
Fellowships (Professional Development/Fellowship) 6011

Research Science Institute Internship (Undergraduate/
Internship) 5103

Rockefeller Fellows Programs (Postdoctorate/Fellowship) 1785

Rockefeller Humanities Fellowship (Postdoctorate/
Fellowship) 5151

Sir Arthur Sims Scholarships (Postgraduate/Scholarship) 5196

Social Sciences and Humanities Research Council Doctoral
Fellowships (Doctorate/Fellowship) 5425

Social Sciences and Humanities Research Council
Postdoctoral Fellowships (Postdoctorate/Fellowship) 5426

Society for the Humanities Fellowships (Postdoctorate/
Fellowship) 5459

Society for the Humanities Postdoctoral Fellowships
(Postdoctorate, Professional Development/Fellowship) 5456

South Central Language Association Fellowship
(Postdoctorate/Fellowship) 4610

Spencer Foundation Fellowships in the History of Education
(Postdoctorate/Fellowship) 4611

SSRC Abe Fellowship Program (Postdoctorate/
Fellowship) 5392

SSRC Advanced Postdoctoral Training and Research Awards
(Doctorate, Postdoctorate/Award, Fellowship, Grant) 5393

SSRC Africa Predissertation Fellowships (Doctorate/
Fellowship) 5394

SSRC African Humanities Fellowships (Doctorate,
Postdoctorate/Fellowship) 5396

SSRC Bangladesh Studies Fellowships (Doctorate, Graduate/
Fellowship) 5397

SSRC Berlin Program for Advanced German and European
Studies Fellowships (Doctorate, Postdoctorate/
Fellowship) 5398

SSRC Grants for Advanced Area Research (Doctorate, Other/
Grant) 5399

SSRC Japan Advanced Research Grants (Postdoctorate/
Grant) 5403

SSRC Korea Advanced Research Grants (Postdoctorate/
Grant) 5406

SSRC Korea Grants for Research Planning Activities
(Postdoctorate/Grant) 5407

SSRC Latin America and the Caribbean Advanced Research
Grants (Postdoctorate/Grant) 5408

SSRC-MacArthur Foundation Dissertation Fellowships on
Peace and Security in a Changing World (Doctorate/
Fellowship) 5409

SSRC Near and Middle East Dissertation Research
Fellowships (Doctorate/Fellowship) 5412

SSRC Predoctoral and Dissertation Training and Research
Awards (Doctorate/Award, Fellowship, Grant) 5413

SSRC South Asia Dissertation Fellowships for Bangladesh
(Doctorate/Fellowship) 5415

SSRC Southeast Asia Advanced Research Grants
(Postdoctorate/Grant) 5416

SSRC Southeast Asia Predissertation Fellowships (Doctorate/
Fellowship) 5417

SSRC Soviet Union and Its Successor States Dissertation
Fellowships (Doctorate/Fellowship) 5418

SSRC Soviet Union and Its Successor States Postdoctoral
Fellowships (Postdoctorate/Fellowship) 5421

Support for Special Projects in the Study of Central and
Eastern Europe, Eurasia and Mongolia (Postdoctorate/
Grant) 3188

Villa I Tatti Fellowships (Postdoctorate/Fellowship) 6044

Richard M. Weaver Fellowship (Graduate/Fellowship) 3099

Arthur Weinberg Fellowship for Independent Scholars
(Professional Development/Fellowship) 4612

Whiting Fellowships in the Humanities (Doctorate/
Fellowship) 6171

Woodrow Wilson Center Residential Fellowship
(Postdoctorate/Fellowship) 6184

Xerox Scholarships (Undergraduate/Scholarship) 6272

## Huntington's disease

Huntington's Disease Society Research Fellowships
(Postdoctorate/Fellowship) 2941

Huntington's Disease Society Research Grants (Professional
Development/Grant) 2942

## Hydrology

AMS/Industry Government Graduate Fellowships (Graduate/
Fellowship) 701

AMS/Industry Undergraduate Scholarship (Undergraduate/
Scholarship) 703

Howard H. Hanks, Jr. Scholarship in Meteorology
(Undergraduate/Scholarship) 705

Hydrology (Horton) Research Grant (Doctorate/Grant) 511

Paul H. Kutschenreuter Scholarship (Undergraduate/
Scholarship) 706

Minority Geoscience Scholarships (Graduate, Undergraduate/
Scholarship) 508

Howard T. Orville Scholarship in Meteorology (Undergraduate/
Scholarship) 708

## Ileitis and colitis

Crohn's & Colitis Foundation Career Development Awards
(Postdoctorate/Award) 2138

Crohn's & Colitis Foundation Research Fellowships
(Postdoctorate/Fellowship) 2139

Crohn's & Colitis Foundation Research Grants (Postdoctorate/
Grant) 2140

## Immunology

Cancer Federation Scholarships (Undergraduate/
Scholarship) 1710

Cancer Research Institute Clinical Investigator Award (Other/
Grant) 1714

Cancer Research Institute Postdoctoral Fellowship
(Postdoctorate/Fellowship) 1715

Howard Hughes Medical Institute Predoctoral Fellowships in
Biological Sciences (Postdoctorate/Fellowship) 4358

Oncology Nursing Foundation/Cetus Oncology Grants for
Research Involving Biotherapy or Immunotherapy
(Professional Development/Grant) 4763

Summer Fellowship Grants (Doctorate/Fellowship) 215

## Industrial design
National Endowment for the Arts - Design Arts Program USA Fellowships *(Professional Development/Fellowship)* 3974
Plastic Pioneers Association Scholarships *(Undergraduate/ Scholarship)* 4960

## Industrial and labor relations
AFL-CIO Research Internship *(Graduate/Internship)* 464
GOALS Fellowships *(Graduate/Fellowship)* 3001
International Foundation of Employee Benefit Plans Grants for Research *(Doctorate, Graduate, Postdoctorate/Grant)* 3155
Mackenzie King Travelling Scholarships *(Graduate, Postgraduate/Scholarship)* 3529
Ed S. Miller Scholarship in Industrial and Labor Relations *(Undergraduate/Scholarship)* 2904
William B. Ruggles Journalism Scholarship *(Graduate, Undergraduate/Scholarship)* 4196
Upjohn Institute Grants *(Postdoctorate/Grant)* 6015

## Industry and trade
AAAS Technology Policy Science and Engineering Fellowships *(Postdoctorate, Professional Development/Fellowship)* 267
Bicentennial Swedish-American Exchange Fund Travel Grants *(Professional Development/Grant)* 5656
EAIA Research Grants Program *(Postgraduate/Grant)* 2304
NAPHCC Educational Foundation Scholarships *(High School, Undergraduate/Scholarship)* 3887
Upjohn Institute Grants *(Postdoctorate/Grant)* 6015

## Infectious diseases (See also: Epidemiology)
Fellowship in Infectious Diseases *(Postdoctorate/ Fellowship)* 4160
New Investigator Matching Grants *(Postdoctorate/Grant)* 4161
Postdoctoral Fellowship in Emerging Infectious Diseases *(Postdoctorate/Fellowship)* 4162

## Information science and technology
The AFCEA Educational Foundation Fellowship *(Doctorate, Graduate/Fellowship)* 1099
AFCEA ROTC Scholarship Program *(Undergraduate/ Scholarship)* 1100
Affirmative Action Scholarship Program *(Graduate/ Scholarship)* 5575
AIAA/Command, Control, Communications and Intelligence Graduate Scholarship Award *(Graduate/Scholarship)* 565
AT & T Bell Laboratories Cooperative Research Fellowships for Minorities *(Graduate/Fellowship)* 1302
AT & T Bell Laboratories Graduate Research Fellowships for Women *(Doctorate/Fellowship)* 1303
AT & T Bell Laboratories Graduate Research Grants for Women *(Doctorate, Graduate/Grant)* 1304
AT & T Bell Laboratories Summer Research Program for Minorities & Women *(Undergraduate/Fellowship)* 1305
AT & T Bell Laboratories University Relations Summer Program *(Doctorate, Graduate, Undergraduate/Work Study)* 1306
Mary Adeline Connor Professional Development Scholarship Program *(Postgraduate/Scholarship)* 5576
Doctoral Dissertation Scholarship *(Doctorate/ Scholarship)* 1422
FORE Graduate Scholarships *(Doctorate, Graduate/ Scholarship)* 517
HP/AACN Critical-Care Nursing Research Grants *(Doctorate, Graduate/Grant)* 2868
Harold Lancour Scholarship for Foreign Study *(Graduate/ Scholarship)* 1423
Microsoft Corporation Scholarships *(Graduate, Undergraduate/ Scholarship)* 5516
General Emmett Paige Scholarship *(Undergraduate/ Scholarship)* 1101
Sarah Rebecca Reed Scholarships *(Graduate/ Scholarship)* 1424
REFORMA Scholarships *(Graduate/Scholarship)* 5091
Frank B. Sessa Scholarship for Continuing Education *(Professional Development/Scholarship)* 1425

Adelle and Erwin Tomash Fellowship in the History of Information Processing *(Doctorate, Graduate/ Fellowship)* 1353
Young Canadian Researchers Awards *(Doctorate, Graduate/ Award)* 3151

## Insurance and insurance-related fields
Boleslaw Monic Fund Prizes *(Professional Development/ Prize)* 1457
Exceptional Student Fellowship Award *(Undergraduate/ Scholarship)* 5613
Huebner Foundation Doctoral Fellowships *(Doctorate/ Fellowship)* 2918
Huebner Foundation Postdoctoral Fellowships *(Postdoctorate/ Fellowship)* 2919
Wharton Doctoral and Postdoctoral Fellowships In Risk & Insurance *(Doctorate, Postdoctorate/Fellowship)* 2920

## Interdisciplinary studies
Bossing-Edwards Research Scholarships *(Doctorate, Graduate/ Scholarship)* 3871
New Hampshire Individual Artist Fellowships *(Other/ Fellowship)* 4535

## Interior design
ASID Educational Foundation/S Harris Memorial Scholarship *(Undergraduate/Scholarship)* 937
Association for Women in Architecture Scholarship *(Graduate, Undergraduate/Scholarship)* 1292
Mabelle Wilhelmina Boldt Memorial Scholarship *(Graduate/ Scholarship)* 938
The Lippincott and Margulies Summer Internship *(Graduate, Undergraduate/Internship)* 5385
National Endowment for the Arts - Design Arts Program USA Fellowships *(Professional Development/Fellowship)* 3974
Joel Polsky/Fixtures Furniture/FIDER Endowment Research Award *(Professional Development/Award)* 2571
Student Store Interior Design Competition Prizes *(Undergraduate/Prize)* 3077
Robert Thunen Memorial Educational Scholarships *(Graduate, Undergraduate/Scholarship)* 2983

## International affairs and relations
Advanced Research Fellowships in U.S.-Japan Relations *(Postdoctorate/Fellowship)* 2808
AGBU Education Loan *(Graduate/Loan)* 1136
AGBU Education Loan Program in the U.S. *(Graduate/ Loan)* 1133
AGBU Graduate Loan Program *(Graduate/Loan)* 1134
Canadian Studies Sabbatical Fellowship Program *(Professional Development/Fellowship)* 1627
Central Intelligence Agency Graduate Studies Internships *(Graduate/Internship)* 1811
Central Intelligence Agency Undergraduate Scholars Program *(Undergraduate/Internship, Scholarship)* 1812
CIR Postdoctoral Fellowship *(Postdoctorate/Fellowship)* 5986
Crane-Rogers Fellowships *(Professional Development/ Fellowship)* 3025
H.B. Earhart Fellowships *(Graduate/Fellowship)* 2301
East-West Center Internships *(Professional Development/ Internship)* 2309
Foreign Policy Research Fellowships *(Doctorate/ Fellowship)* 1509
William C. Foster Fellows Visiting Scholars Competition *(Postdoctorate, Professional Development/Fellowship)* 5818
Albert Gallatin Fellowships in International Affairs *(Doctorate/ Fellowship)* 2613
German Marshall Fund Research Fellowships *(Postdoctorate/ Fellowship)* 2695
Phyllis P. Harris Scholarships *(All/Scholarship)* 4956
Mark O. Hatfield Scholarship *(Graduate/Scholarship)* 5138
Hoover Institution National Fellowships *(Postdoctorate/ Fellowship)* 2888
AGBU Hirair and Anna Hovnanian Fellowship *(Graduate/ Fellowship)* 1123

## International affairs and relations (continued)

Celia M. Howard Fellowships (*Doctorate, Graduate/ Fellowship*) 2964

Institute for the Study of World Politics Fellowships (*Doctorate/Fellowship*) 3079

International Affairs Fellowships (*Professional Development/ Fellowship*) 2105

Internships (*Graduate/Internship*) 5805

H. Kellogg Institute Residential Fellowships (*Postdoctorate/ Fellowship*) 3347

Otto Klineberg Intercultural and International Relations Award (*Graduate, Postgraduate/Award*) 5496

Mackenzie King Travelling Scholarships (*Graduate, Postgraduate/Scholarship*) 3529

Assunta Lucchetti Martino Scholarship for International Studies (*Undergraduate/Scholarship*) 4240

Near and Middle East Research and Training Program Pre-Doctoral Fellowships (*Doctorate/Fellowship*) 880

Peace Fellowships (*Postgraduate, Professional Development/ Fellowship*) 5076

Peace Scholars Award (*Doctorate/Award*) 5077

Pew Fellowships in International Journalism (*Other/ Fellowship*) 4854

Pre- and Postdoctoral Fellowships on Nonviolent Sanctions; Visiting Scholar Affiliations (*Doctorate, Postdoctorate/ Fellowship*) 2806

Jennings Randolph Senior Fellow Award (*Professional Development/Fellowship*) 5078

Research Fellowships in Marine Policy (*Postdoctorate/ Fellowship*) 6248

Rockefeller Humanities Fellowship (*Postdoctorate/ Fellowship*) 5151

SSRC International Peace and Security Research Workshop Competition (*Professional Development/Grant*) 5401

SSRC-MacArthur Foundation Dissertation Fellowships on Peace and Security in a Changing World (*Doctorate/ Fellowship*) 5409

UNITAR Internships (*Postdoctorate/Internship*) 5803

United States Institute of Peace Distinguished Fellows (*Professional Development/Fellowship*) 5079

Wolcott Foundation Fellowships (*Graduate/Fellowship*) 2870

Manfred Worner Fellowship (*Doctorate, Postdoctorate, Professional Development/Fellowship*) 4657

## International development

American Research Center in Egypt Research Fellowships for Study in the U.S. or Canada (*Doctorate/Fellowship*) 844

Dante B. Fascell Inter-American Fellowships (*Other/ Fellowship*) 3089

SSRC-MacArthur Foundation Postdoctoral Fellowships on Peace and Security in a Changing World (*Postdoctorate/ Fellowship*) 5410

## International trade

SSRC International Predissertation Fellowships (*Doctorate/ Fellowship*) 5402

## Interstitial cystitis

ICA Pilot Research Project Grants (*Postdoctorate/Grant*) 3208

## Italian studies (See also: Area and ethnic studies)

AATI National College Essay Contest (*Undergraduate/ Prize*) 329

John Dinkeloo Bequests/American Academy in Rome Traveling Fellowship in Architectural Technology (*Graduate, Postgraduate/Fellowship*) 6023

The Eta Sigma Phi Summer Scholarships (*Doctorate, Graduate/Scholarship*) 2414

Mola Foundation of Chicago Scholarships (*Undergraduate/ Scholarship*) 4243

Paragano Scholarship (*Undergraduate/Scholarship*) 4250

Study Abroad Scholarships (*Graduate, Undergraduate/ Scholarship*) 4263

Vincent and Anna Visceglia Fellowship (*Doctorate, Graduate/ Fellowship*) 4268

## Japanese studies (See also: Area and ethnic studies)

AAS-NEAC U.S. Research Travel Grants (*Postdoctorate/ Grant*) 1220

Advanced Research Fellowships in U.S.-Japan Relations (*Postdoctorate/Fellowship*) 2808

Friendship Commission Prize for the Translation of Japanese Literature (*Professional Development/Prize*) 3341

Inter-University Center Fellowships (*Graduate, Undergraduate/ Fellowship*) 3095

U. Alexis Johnson Scholarship (*Graduate, Undergraduate/ Scholarship*) 3238

Short-term Travel Grants to Japan (*Postdoctorate/ Grant*) 1221

SSRC Japan Advanced Research Grants (*Postdoctorate/ Grant*) 5403

SSRC Japan Fellowships for Dissertation Write-Up (*Doctorate/ Fellowship*) 5404

SSRC Japan Grants for Research Planning Activities (*Postdoctorate/Grant*) 5405

U.S. Japan Media Fellowship (*Postgraduate/Fellowship*) 3242

## Jewish studies (See also: Area and ethnic studies)

American Jewish League for Israel University Scholarship Fund (*Graduate, Undergraduate/Scholarship*) 600

American Jewish Studies Fellowships (*Doctorate, Postdoctorate/Award, Fellowship*) 598

David Baumgardt Memorial Fellowships (*Postdoctorate/ Fellowship*) 1355

Center for Judaic Studies Postdoctoral Fellowships (*Postdoctorate/Fellowship*) 1799

Community Service Scholarships (*Graduate, Undergraduate/ Scholarship*) 3643

Rose and Isidore Drench Fellowships (*Postdoctorate/ Fellowship*) 6284

Fritz Halbers Fellowships (*Doctorate/Fellowship*) 1356

International Doctoral Scholarships for Studies Specializing in Jewish Fields (*Doctorate/Scholarship*) 3644

International Fellowships in Jewish Studies (*Professional Development/Fellowship*) 3645

LBI/DAAD Fellowships (*Doctorate/Fellowship*) 1357

LBI/DAAD Fellowships for Research in Germany (*Doctorate/ Fellowship*) 1358

National Foundation for Jewish Culture Doctoral Dissertation Grants (*Doctorate/Grant*) 4167

Post-Rabbinic Scholarships (*Graduate, Professional Development/Scholarship*) 3646

Scholarship in Jewish Women's Studies (*Graduate/ Scholarship*) 4454

Dorothy Silver Playwriting Competition Prize (*Professional Development/Prize*) 3261

Touro National Heritage Trust Fellowship (*Doctorate, Postdoctorate/Fellowship*) 1517

Moritz and Charlotte Warbourg Research Fellowships (*Postdoctorate/Fellowship*) 2849

## Journalism

AEJ Summer Internships for Minorities (*Undergraduate/ Internship*) 3029

AEJMC Communication Theory and Methodology Division Minority Doctoral Scholarships (*Doctorate/ Scholarship*) 1232

AGBU Graduate Loan Program (*Graduate/Loan*) 1134

Jim Allard Broadcast Journalism Scholarship (*Undergraduate/ Scholarship*) 1600

Len Allen Award of Merit for Radio News (*Graduate, Undergraduate/Grant*) 5051

American Bankers Association Fellowships (*Other/ Fellowship*) 346

American Political Science Association-MCI Communications Fellowships for Scholars and Journalists (*Other/ Fellowship*) 778

American Society of Magazine Editors Magazine Internship Program (*Undergraduate/Internship*) 940

American Society of Newspaper Editors Institute for Journalism Excellence (*Other/Fellowship*) 961

Field of Study Index

## Journalism (continued)

Journalists in Europe Study Program *(Graduate/ Scholarship)* 3302

Kaiser Media Internships in Urban Health Reporting *(Other/ Internship)* 3313

Kentucky School of Journalism Foundation Internships *(Undergraduate/Internship)* 3362

Kit C. King Graduate Scholarship *(Graduate/ Scholarship)* 4345

Knight-Bagehot Fellowships in Economics and Business Journalism *(Professional Development/Fellowship)* 2011

Knight-Ridder Minority Specialty Development Program *(Professional Development/Other)* 4928

Knight Science Journalism Fellowships *(Professional Development/Fellowship)* 3383

Claude R. Lambe Fellowships *(Graduate/Fellowship)* 3058

Landmark Communications Minority Internships *(Professional Development/Internship)* 3419

Anne O'Hare McCormick Scholarship *(Graduate/ Scholarship)* 3618

Rollan D. Melton Fellowship *(Professional Development/ Fellowship)* 796

Miller Meester Advertising Scholarship *(Undergraduate/ Scholarship)* 4100

Modesto Bee Summer Internships *(Undergraduate/ Internship)* 3760

Edward R. Murrow Fellowship for American Foreign Correspondents *(Professional Development/ Fellowship)* 2106

NAA Foundation Minority Fellowships *(Professional Development/Fellowship)* 4631

NAHJ Scholarships *(Graduate, Undergraduate/ Scholarship)* 2879

The Nation Internships Program *(Other, Undergraduate/ Internship)* 3822

National Association of Black Journalists Scholarship *(Graduate, Undergraduate/Scholarship)* 3859

National Association of Black Journalists Summer Internships *(Undergraduate/Internship)* 3860

National Fellowships in Education Reporting *(Professional Development/Fellowship)* 2343

National Newspaper Publishers Association Grants *(Undergraduate/Grant)* 4326

National Press Club Ellen Masin Persina Scholarship *(Undergraduate/Scholarship)* 4340

Native American Journalists Association Scholarships *(Undergraduate/Scholarship)* 4470

Near and Middle East Research and Training Program Pre-Doctoral Fellowships *(Doctorate/Fellowship)* 880

Edward J. Nell Memorial Scholarships in Journalism *(Undergraduate/Scholarship)* 5048

New England Press Association Internships *(Undergraduate/ Internship)* 4529

New York Financial Writers' Association *(Undergraduate/ Scholarship)* 4568

News-Sentinel Minority Scholarship *(Undergraduate/ Scholarship)* 4629

Northwestern University Journalism Minority Scholarships *(Graduate/Scholarship)* 4698

NPPF Still Scholarship *(Undergraduate/Scholarship)* 4346

NPPF Television News Scholarship *(Undergraduate/ Scholarship)* 4347

Ohio Newspaper Women's Association Scholarship *(Undergraduate/Scholarship)* 4731

Vada and Barney Oldfield Fellowship for National Security Reporting *(Professional Development/Fellowship)* 5063

Omaha World-Herald Intern Scholarships *(Other/Internship, Scholarship)* 4749

Online Newspaper Intern Program *(Graduate, Undergraduate/ Internship, Scholarship)* 2276

The Oregonian Minority Internship Program *(Other/ Internship)* 4805

James H. Ottaway Sr. Fellowships *(Other/Fellowship)* 797

Patterson Fellowships *(Professional Development/ Fellowship)* 4852

Leonard M. Perryman Communications Scholarship for Ethnic Minority Students *(Undergraduate/Scholarship)* 5794

Art Peters Minority Internships *(Undergraduate/ Internship)* 4929

Politics and Journalism Internship *(Graduate, Undergraduate/ Internship)* 6083

The Poynter Fellowship *(Professional Development/ Fellowship)* 784

Public Interest Internships *(Doctorate, Graduate, Undergraduate/Internship)* 1803

Pulliam Journalism Fellowships *(Graduate/Fellowship)* 1814

Quill and Scroll National Writing/Photo Contest *(High School/ Award)* 5049

Chips Quinn Scholars Program Internship *(Undergraduate/ Internship, Scholarship)* 1438

Garth Reeves Jr. Memorial Scholarships *(Graduate, Undergraduate/Scholarship)* 5490

Rennie Taylor/Alton Blakeslee Memorial Fellowship in Science Writing *(Postdoctorate, Professional Development/ Fellowship)* 2091

Reporters Committee Fellowship *(Professional Development/ Fellowship)* 5093

Reporters Committee for Freedom of the Press Clinical Internship Program *(Graduate, Undergraduate/ Internship)* 5094

Richard J. Roth Journalism Fellowship *(Graduate, Undergraduate/Fellowship)* 4600

RTNDF Environmental and Science Reporting Fellowship *(Professional Development/Fellowship)* 5065

RTNDF Six-Month Entry Level Internships for Minority Students *(Graduate/Internship)* 5067

RTNDF Summer Internships for Minority Students *(Undergraduate/Internship)* 5068

RTNDF Undergraduate Scholarships *(Graduate, Undergraduate/Scholarship)* 5069

William B. Ruggles Journalism Scholarship *(Graduate, Undergraduate/Scholarship)* 4196

Fred Russell-Grantland RICE TRA Sports Writing *(Undergraduate/Scholarship)* 5729

Sacramento Bee Journalism Scholarships for Community College Students *(High School, Undergraduate/ Scholarship)* 5206

Sacramento Bee Minority Media Scholarships *(Undergraduate/ Scholarship)* 5207

San Francisco Chronicle Summer Newsroom Internships *(Graduate, Undergraduate/Internship)* 5230

Abe Schechter Graduate Scholarship *(Graduate/ Scholarship)* 5070

Dennis and Elizabeth Shattuck Internships *(Undergraduate/ Internship)* 2429

Carole Simpson Scholarship *(Graduate, Undergraduate/ Scholarship)* 5071

The Slack Award for Medical Journalism *(Doctorate/ Award)* 4307

South Carolina Press Association Foundation Scholarships *(Undergraduate/Scholarship)* 5545

Stoody-West Fellowship in Journalism *(Graduate/ Fellowship)* 5795

Syracuse Newspapers Journalism Scholarship *(Undergraduate/ Scholarship)* 5664

Thomson Fellowship *(Graduate/Fellowship)* 5727

Thurber House Residencies *(Professional Development/ Award)* 5731

Times Mirror Minority Editorial Training Program *(Professional Development/Other)* 3496

Virginia Press Association Minority Internship *(Graduate, Undergraduate/Internship)* 6063

Muddy Waters Scholarship *(Undergraduate/Scholarship)* 1448

Philip S. Weld Sr. Fellowship *(Other/Fellowship)* 798

World Press Institute Fellowships *(Professional Development/ Fellowship)* 6268

Young Canadian Researchers Awards *(Doctorate, Graduate/ Award)* 3151

Mark Zambrano Scholarship *(Graduate, Undergraduate/ Scholarship)* 2880

## Landscape architecture and design

AILA Yamagami Hope Fellowship (*Professional Development/ Fellowship*) 3421

APA Planning & the Black Community Division Scholarship (*Undergraduate/Scholarship*) 775

Associated Landscape Contractors of America Scholarsip (*Undergraduate/Scholarship*) 4025

Association for Women in Architecture Scholarship (*Graduate, Undergraduate/Scholarship*) 1292

California Landscape Architectural Student Scholarships (*Undergraduate/Scholarship*) 3422

Dumbarton Oaks Project Grants (*Professional Development/ Grant*) 2287

Fellowships in Byzantine Studies, Pre-Columbian Studies and Landscape Architecture (*Doctorate, Graduate, Postdoctorate, Undergraduate/Fellowship*) 2288

Grace and Robert Fraser Landscape Heritage Award (*Graduate, Undergraduate/Award*) 3423

Edith H. Henderson Scholarship (*Graduate, Undergraduate/ Scholarship*) 3424

Ralph Hudson Environmental Fellowship (*Professional Development/Fellowship*) 3425

Interchange Fellowship in Horticulture and Landscape Design (*Graduate, Postgraduate/Fellowship*) 2622

LAF/CLASS Cal Poly Scholarships (*Undergraduate/ Scholarship*) 3426

LAF/CLASS Fund Scholarships and Internships (*Undergraduate/Internship*) 3427

LAF/CLASS University Program (*Undergraduate/ Scholarship*) 3428

LAF Student Research Grant (*Graduate, Undergraduate/ Grant*) 3429

LANDCADD, Inc. Scholarship (*Graduate, Undergraduate/ Scholarship*) 3430

William J. Locklin Scholarship (*Graduate, Undergraduate/ Scholarship*) 3431

National Endowment for the Arts - Design Arts Program USA Fellowships (*Professional Development/Fellowship*) 3974

National Zoological Park Traineeship in Landscaping (*Graduate, Undergraduate/Internship*) 4462

NCSGC National Scholarships (*Graduate, Undergraduate/ Scholarship*) 3959

New York State Professional Opportunity Scholarships (*Doctorate, Graduate, Undergraduate/Scholarship*) 4592

New York State Regents Professional Opportunity Scholarships (*Doctorate, Graduate, Undergraduate/ Scholarship*) 4577

Raymond E. Page Scholarship (*Graduate, Undergraduate/ Scholarship*) 3432

Rain Bird Company Scholarship (*Undergraduate/ Scholarship*) 3433

James K. Rathmell, Jr., Memorial Scholarship to Work/Study Abroad (*Graduate, Undergraduate/Scholarship*) 1387

Spraying Systems Company Scholarships (*Undergraduate/ Scholarship*) 4129

Edward D. Stone Jr. and Associates Minority Scholarship (*Undergraduate/Scholarship*) 3434

George Tanaka Memorial Scholarship Program (*Undergraduate/Scholarship*) 1288

Lester Walls III Scholarship (*Graduate, Undergraduate/ Scholarship*) 3435

Harriett Barnhardt Wimmer Scholarship (*Undergraduate/ Scholarship*) 3436

David T. Woolsey Scholarship (*Graduate, Undergraduate/ Scholarship*) 3437

## Latin American studies (See also: Area and ethnic studies)

Crane-Rogers Fellowships (*Professional Development/ Fellowship*) 3025

Dante B. Fascell Inter-American Fellowships (*Other/ Fellowship*) 3089

IAF Field Research Fellowships Program at the Doctoral Level (*Doctorate/Fellowship*) 3090

IAF Field Research Fellowships Program at the Master's Level (*Graduate/Fellowship*) 3091

International Student Identity Card Travel Grants for Educational Programs in Developing Countries (*High School, Undergraduate/Grant*) 2113

H. Kellogg Institute Residential Fellowships (*Postdoctorate/ Fellowship*) 3347

Helen M. Robinson Award (*Doctorate/Grant*) 3179

James R. Scobie Memorial Awards (*Doctorate/Grant*) 3071

SSRC Latin America and the Caribbean Advanced Research Grants (*Postdoctorate/Grant*) 5408

## Law

AAUW Educational Foundation Selected Professions Engineering Dissertation Fellowship (*Graduate/ Fellowship*) 335

ABA Mini-Grants (*Postdoctorate, Undergraduate/Grant*) 350

ABF Summer Research Fellowships in Law and Social Science for Minority Undergraduate Students (*Undergraduate/Fellowship*) 352

AGBU Education Loan Program in the U.S. (*Graduate/ Loan*) 1133

Air Force ROTC Scholarships (*Undergraduate/ Scholarship*) 5816

TELACU/Richard Alatorre Fellowship (*Graduate/ Fellowship*) 5686

Ida and Benjamin Alpert Scholarships (*Graduate/ Scholarship*) 192

American Jewish League for Israel University Scholarship Fund (*Graduate, Undergraduate/Scholarship*) 600

APSA Congressional Fellowships for Federal Executives (*Professional Development/Fellowship*) 779

APSA Congressional Fellowships for Journalists (*Professional Development/Fellowship*) 780

AT & T Bell Laboratories Summer Research Program for Minorities & Women (*Undergraduate/Fellowship*) 1305

Viscount Bennett Fellowship (*Graduate, Postgraduate/ Fellowship*) 1609

Donald Bogie Prize (*Graduate/Prize*) 3051

Bosch Foundation Fellowships (*Postgraduate/ Fellowship*) 1459

Robert Bosch Foundation Fellowships (*Professional Development/Internship*) 1758

Maxwell Boulton Junior Fellowship (*Doctorate, Postdoctorate/ Fellowship*) 3626

Maxwell Boulton Senior Fellowship (*Professional Development/ Fellowship*) 3627

BPW Career Advancement Scholarships (*Graduate, Undergraduate/Scholarship*) 1546

H. Fletcher Brown Scholarship (*Doctorate, Graduate, Undergraduate/Scholarship*) 4967

Call to Action Opportunity Scholarship (*Undergraduate/ Scholarship*) 1568

Chateaubriand Fellowships (Humanities) (*Doctorate/ Grant*) 2375

Cherokee Nation Graduate Scholarship (*Graduate/ Scholarship*) 1911

Council On Legal Education Opportunities (*Graduate/ Scholarship*) 2119

DAAD Young Lawyers Program (*Postdoctorate/ Fellowship*) 2686

Helen Darcovich Memorial Doctoral Fellowship (*Doctorate, Graduate/Fellowship*) 1657

Marusia and Michael Dorosh Masters Fellowship (*Graduate/ Fellowship*) 1659

Family Court Services Dissertation Grant Competition (*Doctorate/Grant*) 3304

Fellowships in Ethics (*Postdoctorate, Postgraduate/ Fellowship*) 5015

James Lawrence Fly Scholarships (*Graduate, Undergraduate/ Scholarship*) 1497

FORE Graduate Scholarships (*Doctorate, Graduate/ Scholarship*) 517

Fredrikson & Byron Minority Scholarships (*Graduate/ Scholarship*) 2589

## Law (continued)

Albert Gallatin Fellowships in International Affairs *(Doctorate/ Fellowship)* 2613

Garikian University Scholarship Fund *(Undergraduate/ Scholarship)* 1119

Germanistic Society of America Quadrille Grants *(Graduate, Postgraduate/Grant)* 2697

GFWC of MA Memorial Education Fellowships *(Graduate/ Fellowship)* 2639

Graduate Scholarships at University of Cambridge *(Graduate/ Scholarship)* 1655

Justice Pauline Davis Hanson Memorial Scholarship *(Graduate/Scholarship)* 2595

Mark O. Hatfield Scholarship *(Graduate/Scholarship)* 5138

Gordon F. Henderson/SOCAN Copyright Competition Award *(Professional Development/Award)* 5390

R.C. Hoiles and IHS Postdoctoral Fellowships *(Postdoctorate/ Fellowship)* 3052

Celia M. Howard Fellowships *(Doctorate, Graduate/ Fellowship)* 2964

Humane Studies Foundation Summer Residential Program Fellowships *(Graduate/Fellowship)* 3053

IGCC Dissertation Fellowships *(Doctorate, Graduate/ Fellowship)* 3043

IHS-Eberhard Student-Writing Competition *(Graduate/ Prize)* 3054

IHS John M. Olin Fellowships *(Graduate/Fellowship)* 3056

International Affairs Fellowships *(Professional Development/ Fellowship)* 2105

Elaine Osborne Jacobson Award for Women in Health Care *(Doctorate, Graduate/Award)* 5163

Judicial Fellowships *(Professional Development/ Fellowship)* 5650

Junior Research Program Grants Exchange with China *(Postdoctorate/Grant)* 5980

Claude R. Lambe Fellowships *(Graduate/Fellowship)* 3058

Law Fellowship *(Graduate, Postgraduate/Fellowship)* 4235

Law Internship Program *(Graduate/Internship)* 5900

Law Scholarships *(Juris Doctorate/Scholarship)* 3250

LES Fellowships *(Graduate/Fellowship)* 3468

Liberal Arts Fellowships in Law *(Professional Development/ Fellowship)* 2810

Hatton Lovejoy Graduate Studies Fund *(Graduate/ Scholarship)* 1585

Mackenzie King Travelling Scholarships *(Graduate, Postgraduate/Scholarship)* 3529

MALDEF Scholarships *(Graduate/Scholarship)* 3675

Maryland Professional Scholarship *(Graduate, Undergraduate/ Scholarship)* 3578

Ministry of the Flemish Community Fellowships *(Postdoctorate, Undergraduate/Fellowship)* 3710

Michael Murphy Memorial Scholarship Loans *(Graduate, Undergraduate/Loan)* 132

NAPIL Fellowships for Equal Justice *(Postdoctorate/ Fellowship)* 3893

National Association of Black Women Attorneys Scholarships *(Doctorate/Scholarship)* 3862

New York State Regents Professional Opportunity Scholarships *(Doctorate, Graduate, Undergraduate/ Scholarship)* 4577

NIAF/FIERI D.C. Matching Scholarship *(Graduate/ Scholarship)* 4245

Oklahoma State Regents for Higher Education Professional Study Grants *(Graduate/Grant)* 4740

Oregon Humanities Center Summer Visiting Research Fellowships *(Professional Development/Fellowship)* 6011

Oregon State Bar Scholarships *(Graduate/Scholarship)* 4803

Henry M. Phillips Grants in Jurisprudence *(Postdoctorate/ Grant)* 768

Post-Rabbinic Scholarships *(Graduate, Professional Development/Scholarship)* 3646

Preventive Law Prizes (Discontinued) *(Graduate, Professional Development/Prize)* 3933

PRLDEF Scholarship *(Graduate/Scholarship)* 5023

Public Interest Internships *(Doctorate, Graduate, Undergraduate/Internship)* 1803

The Puerto Rican Bar Association Scholarship Fund, Inc. *(Graduate/Scholarship)* 5021

Spence Reese Scholarship *(High School, Undergraduate/ Scholarship)* 5089

Reporters Committee Fellowship *(Professional Development/ Fellowship)* 5093

Howard Brown Rickard Scholarship *(Undergraduate/ Scholarship)* 4007

Rocky Mountain Mineral Law Foundation Scholarship Program Including the Joe Rudd Scholarship *(Graduate/ Scholarship)* 5159

Sho Sato Memorial Law Scholarship *(Juris Doctorate/ Scholarship)* 3251

Scalia Scholarship *(Graduate/Scholarship)* 4260

Specialist Program Grants Exchange with China *(Postdoctorate/Grant)* 5981

SSRC Grants for Advanced Area Research *(Doctorate, Other/ Grant)* 5399

Otto M. Stanfield Legal Scholarship *(Graduate/ Scholarship)* 5785

Teaching/Research Program Grants Exchange with China *(Postdoctorate/Grant)* 5982

Morris K. Udall OTA Congressional Fellowship *(Postdoctorate/ Fellowship)* 5851

Earl Warren Legal Training Scholarships *(Graduate/ Scholarship)* 6081

Young Canadian Researchers Awards *(Doctorate, Graduate/ Award)* 3151

## Law enforcement

ATF Special Agents' Scholarships *(Undergraduate/ Scholarship)* 5841

Alphonso Deal Scholarship Award *(Undergraduate/ Scholarship)* 3912

Mark O. Hatfield Scholarship *(Graduate/Scholarship)* 5138

Law Enforcement Career Scholarships *(Graduate, Undergraduate/Scholarship)* 1238

Law Enforcement Explorer Scholarships *(Undergraduate/ Scholarship)* 5853

Michael Murphy Memorial Scholarship Loans *(Graduate, Undergraduate/Loan)* 132

John Charles Wilson Scholarship *(Graduate/Scholarship)* 3107

## Leadership, Institutional and community

Federation Executive Recruitment and Education Program (FEREP) Scholarships *(Graduate/Scholarship)* 2117

E. Urner Goodman Professional Scouter Scholarship *(Undergraduate/Scholarship)* 1466

Hatton Lovejoy Scholarship Plan *(Undergraduate/ Scholarship)* 1586

NACA Prize Papers Competition *(Graduate, Professional Development, Undergraduate/Prize)* 3868

## Leprosy

Heiser Postdoctoral Research Fellowships *(Postdoctorate/ Fellowship)* 2857

Heiser Research Grants *(Postdoctorate/Grant)* 2858

## Leukemia

Leukemia Society of America Short-term Scientific Awards *(Professional Development/Grant)* 3455

Leukemia Society Fellow Awards *(Postdoctorate/Award)* 3456

Leukemia Society Scholar Awards *(Postdoctorate/ Award)* 3457

Leukemia Society Special Fellow Awards *(Postdoctorate/ Award)* 3458

National Leukemia Research Association Research Awards *(Postdoctorate/Award)* 4284

## Liberal arts

102nd Infantry Division Scholarship *(All/Scholarship)* 6

American Jewish League for Israel University Scholarship Fund *(Graduate, Undergraduate/Scholarship)* 600

## Library and archival sciences (continued)

MLA Scholarship for Minority Students *(Graduate/
Scholarship)* 3636

Gerd Muehsam Memorial Award *(Graduate, Postgraduate/
Award)* 1145

Munby Fellowship in Bibliography *(Postdoctorate/
Fellowship)* 1592

National Museum of American Art Summer Internships
*(Graduate, Undergraduate/Internship)* 5388

Ida L., Mary L., and Ervin R. NePage Foundation
*(Undergraduate/Scholarship)* 4513

NHPRC/Fellowships in Archival Administration *(Professional
Development/Fellowship)* 4181

Martinus Nijhoff International West European Specialist Study
Grant *(Professional Development/Grant)* 1227

NMRT EBSCO Scholarship *(Graduate/Scholarship)* 656

Shirley Olofson Memorial Award *(Professional Development/
Grant)* 657

Pennsylvania Library Association Library Science Continuing
Education Grants *(Professional Development,
Undergraduate/Grant)* 4867

Pennsylvania Library Association Library Science Scholarships
*(Graduate/Scholarship)* 4868

Plenum Scholarship *(Postdoctorate/Scholarship)* 5578

Putnam & Grosset Group Award *(Professional Development/
Award)* 650

Readex/GODORT/ALA Catherine J. Reynolds Grant
*(Professional Development/Grant)* 2722

Sarah Rebecca Reed Scholarships *(Graduate/
Scholarship)* 1424

Reference Service Press Fellowships *(Graduate/
Fellowship)* 1566

REFORMA Scholarships *(Graduate/Scholarship)* 5091

David Rozkuszka Scholarship (Godort) *(Graduate/
Scholarship)* 668

School Librarian's Workshop Scholarship *(Graduate/
Scholarship)* 646

School Librarian's Workshop Scholarship *(Graduate/
Scholarship)* 669

Frank B. Sessa Scholarship for Continuing Education
*(Professional Development/Scholarship)* 1425

Short-Term Fellowships in the History of Cartography
*(Postdoctorate/Fellowship)* 4609

SLA Scholarships *(Graduate/Scholarship)* 5579

George A. Strait Minority Stipend *(Graduate/Award)* 315

Support for Special Projects in the Study of Library and
Information Science *(Professional Development/
Award)* 3189

U.S. Marine Corps Historical Center College Internships
*(Graduate, Undergraduate/Internship)* 5945

The H.W. Wilson Scholarships *(Graduate/Scholarship)* 1667

Blance E. Woolls Scholarship for School Library Media
Service *(Masters/Scholarship)* 1426

World Book Graduate Scholarships in Library Science
*(Doctorate, Postgraduate/Scholarship)* 1668

World Book, Inc., Grants *(Professional Development/
Grant)* 1752

## Life sciences (See also: specific areas of study, e.g. Biology)

Air Force Civilian Cooperative Work-Study Program *(Graduate,
Undergraduate/Work Study)* 66

Air Force ROTC Scholarships *(Undergraduate/
Scholarship)* 5816

AISES A.T. Anderson Memorial Scholarship *(Graduate,
Undergraduate/Scholarship)* 559

American Cyanamid Scholarship *(Undergraduate/
Scholarship)* 4017

Argonne National Laboratory Faculty Research Leave; Faculty
Research Participation Awards *(Postdoctorate/Award)* 1083

Army Research Laboratory Postdoctoral Fellowship Program
*(Postdoctorate/Fellowship)* 922

ASET Scholarships *(Professional Development/
Scholarship)* 920

Chateaubriand Scholarship (Scientifique) *(Doctorate,
Postdoctorate/Scholarship)* 2372

Fondation Fyssen Post-Doctoral Study Grants *(Postdoctorate/
Grant)* 2609

FSD Student Grant *(Graduate/Grant)* 2578

GEM Ph.D. Science Fellowship Program *(Doctorate/
Fellowship)* 3943

Graduate Student Research Participation Program *(Graduate,
Postgraduate/Fellowship)* 5884

Alexander Hollaender Distinguished Postdoctoral Fellowships
*(Postdoctorate/Fellowship)* 4706

Italian Cultural Society and NIAF Matching Scholarship
*(Undergraduate/Scholarship)* 4234

Laboratory-Graduate Participantships Thesis Parts
Appointment *(Doctorate, Graduate/Grant)* 1084

Allen H. Meyers Scholarship *(Undergraduate/
Scholarship)* 3677

National Oceanic and Atmospheric Administration/Historically
Black Colleges and Universities Faculty/Student Research
Participation Program *(Graduate, Professional Development,
Undergraduate/Fellowship)* 5910

Oak Ridge National Laboratory Postdoctoral Research
Associates Program *(Postdoctorate/Fellowship)* 5917

Olfactory Research Fund Grants *(Postdoctorate/Grant)* 4744

Arthur & Doreen Parrett Scholarship Fund *(Graduate,
Postgraduate, Undergraduate/Scholarship)* 4848

The Payzer Scholarship *(All/Scholarship)* 2423

Santa Fe Pacific Foundation Scholarships *(Undergraduate/
Scholarship)* 563

SDE Fellowships *(Postgraduate/Fellowship)* 5330

Sigma Xi Grants-in-Aid of Research *(Graduate,
Undergraduate/Grant)* 5347

Sub-Saharan African Dissertation Internship Award *(Doctorate/
Internship)* 5154

Tyndall Air Force Base Research Participation Program
*(Postdoctorate, Postgraduate/Fellowship)* 5928

U.S. Department of Energy Global Change Distinguished
Postdoctoral Fellowships *(Postdoctorate/Fellowship)* 4709

U.S. Department of Energy Internship *(Undergraduate/
Internship)* 4711

Virginia Library Association Scholarships *(Graduate/
Scholarship)* 6059

Whitehall Foundation Grants-in-Aid *(Postdoctorate/
Grant)* 6168

Whitehall Foundation Research Grants *(Postdoctorate/
Grant)* 6169

## Linguistics

Ancient India and Iran Trust Travel and Research Grants
*(Doctorate, Graduate, Postdoctorate/Grant)* 1035

Bulgarian Studies Seminar *(Doctorate, Graduate,
Postdoctorate/Fellowship)* 3183

Chateaubriand Fellowships (Humanities) *(Doctorate/
Grant)* 2375

Fellowship in Latin Lexicography *(Postdoctorate/
Fellowship)* 762

General Semantics Foundation Project Grants *(Doctorate,
Postdoctorate/Grant)* 2645

NEH Fellowships for Research in Turkey *(Postdoctorate/
Fellowship)* 847

Phillips Grants for North American Indian Research
*(Doctorate, Postdoctorate/Grant)* 769

SSRC Grants for Advanced Area Research *(Doctorate, Other/
Grant)* 5399

The Year Abroad Program at the Jagiellonian University of
Krakow *(Doctorate, Graduate/Fellowship)* 3401

## Literature

Nelson Algren Awards *(Professional Development/
Award)* 1924

Artists Fellowships and Residencies *(Professional
Development/Fellowship)* 3766

Beinecke Library Visiting Fellowships *(Postdoctorate/
Fellowship)* 1393

Stephen Botein Fellowships (Doctorate, Professional Development/Fellowship) 254

Chateaubriand Fellowships (Humanities) (Doctorate/ Grant) 2375

Cintas Fellowships (Professional Development/ Fellowship) 1163

Contemporary Literature Grant (Other/Grant) 2682

Folger Library Long-Term Fellowships (Postdoctorate/ Fellowship) 2541

Folger Library Short-Term Fellowships (Postdoctorate/ Fellowship) 2542

R.L. Gillette Scholarship (Undergraduate/Scholarship) 482

Vivian Lefsky Hort Fellowship (Postdoctorate/Fellowship) 6285

Howard Foundation Fellowships (Professional Development/ Fellowship) 2908

Huntington Library Research Awards (Graduate, Postdoctorate/Award) 2939

IHS Excellence in Liberty Prizes (Graduate, Undergraduate/ Prize) 3055

Japan-United States Art Fellowships (Postdoctorate, Professional Development/Fellowship) 1180

Neil Ker Memorial Fund Grants (Postdoctorate/Grant) 1481

Claude R. Lambe Fellowships (Graduate/Fellowship) 3058

Audrey Lumsden-Kouvel Fellowship (Postdoctorate/ Fellowship) 4605

Mesopotamian Fellowship (Doctorate, Postdoctorate/ Fellowship) 878

Minnesota Artist Assistance Fellowships (Professional Development/Fellowship) 3714

Minnesota Career Opportunity Grants (Professional Development/Grant) 3715

National Endowment for the Humanities Fellowships (Postdoctorate/Fellowship) 2543

NEH Fellowships for Research in Turkey (Postdoctorate/ Fellowship) 847

New Hampshire Individual Artist Fellowships (Other/ Fellowship) 4535

North Carolina Arts Council Artist Fellowships (Professional Development/Fellowship) 4668

Oregon Humanities Center Summer Visiting Research Fellowships (Professional Development/Fellowship) 6011

The Lionel Pearson Fellowship (Undergraduate/ Fellowship) 763

Rockefeller Foundation Residential Fellowships in Gender Studies in Early Modern Europe (Postdoctorate/ Fellowship) 4608

Thomas Day Seymour Fellowship (Graduate/Fellowship) 860

SSRC African Advanced Research Grants (Postdoctorate/ Grant) 5395

SSRC Grants for Advanced Area Research (Doctorate, Other/ Grant) 5399

SSRC Korea Advanced Research Grants (Postdoctorate/ Grant) 5406

SSRC Near and Middle East Advanced Research Fellowships (Postdoctorate/Fellowship) 5411

Thesaurus Linguae Latinae Fellowship (Doctorate/ Fellowship) 764

Villa I Tatti Fellowships (Postdoctorate/Fellowship) 6044

Elizabeth A. Whitehead Visiting Professorships (Professional Development/Award) 862

Women in Scholarly Publishing Career Development Fund (Professional Development/Other) 6228

Yale Center for British Art Fellowships (Postdoctorate, Professional Development/Fellowship) 6278

## Literature, Children's

ChLA Research Fellowships (Postdoctorate/Fellowship) 1939

Don Freeman Memorial Grant-in-Aid (Professional Development/Grant) 5444

Ezra Jack Keats/Kerlan Collection Memorial Fellowship (Professional Development/Fellowship) 3339

SCBWI Work-in-Progress Grants (Professional Development/ Grant) 5445

## Management

Air Force ROTC Scholarships (Undergraduate/ Scholarship) 5816

Avon Products Foundation Scholarship Program for Women in Business Studies (Graduate, Professional Development, Undergraduate/Scholarship) 1545

Chartered Institute of Management Accountants Research Foundation Grants (All/Grant) 1834

Council of Logistics Management Graduate Scholarships (Graduate/Scholarship) 2123

Keith Davis Graduate Scholarship Awards (Graduate/ Award) 5334

Exceptional Student Fellowship Award (Undergraduate/ Scholarship) 5613

Donald W. Fogarty International Student Paper Competition (Graduate, Undergraduate/Other) 2539

India Studies Faculty Fellowships (Professional Development/ Fellowship) 5316

India Studies Postdoctoral Research Fellowships (Professional Development/Fellowship) 5318

India Studies Student Fellowships (Graduate/Fellowship) 5319

NAPM Doctoral Grants (Doctorate/Grant) 3895

Orchestra Management Fellowships (Professional Development/Fellowship) 1006

Sigma Iota Epsilon Undergraduate Scholarship Awards (Undergraduate/Scholarship) 5335

## Manufacturing

U.S. Department of Energy Integrated Manufacturing & Processing Predoctoral Fellowships (Doctorate/ Fellowship) 4361

Myrtle and Earl Walker Scholarships (Undergraduate/ Scholarship) 5469

William E. Weisel Scholarship (Undergraduate/ Scholarship) 5470

## Maritime studies

Paul Cuffe Memorial Fellowship for the Study of Minorities in American Maritime History (Other/Fellowship) 3794

Dean John A. Knauss Marine Policy Fellowships (Doctorate, Graduate/Fellowship) 4328

Naval and Maritime Photo Contest (Other/Prize) 5955

Robert G. Stone Fellowships in American Maritime History (Doctorate, Postdoctorate/Fellowship) 6182

Alexander O. Vietor Memorial Fellowship (Doctorate, Postdoctorate/Fellowship) 1518

Woods Hole Oceanographic Institution Summer Student Fellowships (Undergraduate/Fellowship) 6249

## Marketing and distribution

Henry A. Applegate Scholarships (Professional Development/ Scholarship) 2201

Avon Products Foundation Scholarship Program for Women in Business Studies (Graduate, Professional Development, Undergraduate/Scholarship) 1545

Harold Bettinger Memorial Scholarship (Graduate, Undergraduate/Scholarship) 1382

Council of Logistics Management Graduate Scholarships (Graduate/Scholarship) 2123

Direct Marketing Institute for Professors Scholarships (Professional Development/Fellowship) 2251

Duracell/National Urban League Scholarship and Intern Program for Minority Students (Undergraduate/Internship, Scholarship) 4448

Jacob's Pillow Dance Festival Internships (Graduate, Undergraduate/Internship) 3234

National Dairy Shrine/Dairy Management Scholarships, Inc. (Undergraduate/Scholarship) 3968

Service Merchandise Scholarship Program (High School, Undergraduate/Scholarship) 5310

## Materials research/science

Advanced Industrial Concepts (AIC) Materials Science Program (Graduate/Fellowship) 5857

## Materials research/science (continued)

AT & T Bell Laboratories Cooperative Research Fellowships for Minorities *(Graduate/Fellowship)* 1302

AT & T Bell Laboratories Graduate Research Fellowships for Women *(Doctorate/Fellowship)* 1303

AT & T Bell Laboratories Graduate Research Grants for Women *(Doctorate, Graduate/Grant)* 1304

AT & T Bell Laboratories Summer Research Program for Minorities & Women *(Undergraduate/Fellowship)* 1305

AT & T Bell Laboratories University Relations Summer Program *(Doctorate, Graduate, Undergraduate/Work Study)* 1306

BNL Postdoctoral Research Associateships *(Postdoctorate/Other)* 1504

Bunting Institute Science Scholars Fellowships and Biomedical Research Fellowships *(Postdoctorate/Fellowship)* 1529

Centre for Interdisciplinary Studies in Chemical Physics Senior Visiting Fellowships *(Postdoctorate/Fellowship)* 1795

Conservation Science Fellowship *(Postdoctorate, Postgraduate/Fellowship)* 2060

ACI Fellowships: ACI/W.R. Grace Fellowship; V. Mohan Malhotra Fellowship; Katherine Bryant Mather Fellowship; Stewart C. Watson Fellowship *(Graduate/Fellowship)* 388

MHEF Scholarship *(Graduate, Undergraduate/Scholarship)* 3607

National Physical Science Consortium Graduate Fellowships for Minorities and Women *(Doctorate, Graduate/Fellowship)* 4338

Plastic Pioneers Association Scholarships *(Undergraduate/Scholarship)* 4960

James F. Schumar Scholarship *(Graduate/Scholarship)* 733

WAAIME Scholarship Loans *(Graduate, Undergraduate/Scholarship loan)* 592

Wood Awards *(Graduate, Postgraduate/Award)* 2555

## Mathematics and mathematical sciences

AAUW Educational Foundation Selected Professions Fellowship *(Graduate/Fellowship)* 336

The AFCEA Educational Foundation Fellowship *(Doctorate, Graduate/Fellowship)* 1099

AFCEA ROTC Scholarship Program *(Undergraduate/Scholarship)* 1100

Air Force ROTC Scholarships *(Undergraduate/Scholarship)* 5816

Argonne National Laboratory Faculty Research Leave; Faculty Research Participation Awards *(Postdoctorate/Award)* 1083

AT & T Bell Laboratories Cooperative Research Fellowships for Minorities *(Graduate/Fellowship)* 1302

AT & T Bell Laboratories Graduate Research Fellowships for Women *(Doctorate/Fellowship)* 1303

AT & T Bell Laboratories Graduate Research Grants for Women *(Doctorate, Graduate/Grant)* 1304

AT & T Bell Laboratories Summer Research Program for Minorities & Women *(Undergraduate/Fellowship)* 1305

AT & T Bell Laboratories University Relations Summer Program *(Doctorate, Graduate, Undergraduate/Work Study)* 1306

Bunting Institute Science Scholars Fellowships and Biomedical Research Fellowships *(Postdoctorate/Fellowship)* 1529

Cape Canaveral Chapter Scholarships *(Graduate, Undergraduate/Scholarship)* 5114

Centennial Research Fellowships *(Postdoctorate/Fellowship)* 686

Central Intelligence Agency Graduate Studies Internships *(Graduate/Internship)* 1811

Central Intelligence Agency Undergraduate Scholars Program *(Undergraduate/Internship, Scholarship)* 1812

Centre for Interdisciplinary Studies in Chemical Physics Senior Visiting Fellowships *(Postdoctorate/Fellowship)* 1795

Renate W. Chasman Scholarship *(Graduate, Undergraduate/Scholarship)* 1507

CHROME Scholarship *(Undergraduate/Scholarship)* 2081

Churchill Scholarships *(Postgraduate/Scholarship)* 1954

CIC Predoctoral Fellowships *(Doctorate, Graduate/Fellowship)* 2013

Engineering Rotation Program *(Professional Development/Award)* 2923

Faculty Research Participation Program at the National Center for Toxicological Research *(Professional Development/Fellowship)* 5874

Florida National Science Scholars Program *(Undergraduate/Scholarship)* 2503

Ford Foundation Postdoctoral Fellowships for Minorities *(Postdoctorate/Fellowship)* 4356

Ford Foundation Predoctoral and Dissertation Fellowships for Minorities *(Doctorate/Fellowship)* 4357

Fossil Energy Faculty Research Participation *(Professional Development/Fellowship)* 5876

William C. Foster Fellows Visiting Scholars Competition *(Postdoctorate, Professional Development/Fellowship)* 5818

FSD Student Grant *(Graduate/Grant)* 2578

Georgia Student Finance Commission Service-Cancellable Stafford Loan *(Graduate, Undergraduate/Loan)* 2666

Georgia Student Finance Commission State-Sponsored Loan *(Graduate, Undergraduate/Loan)* 2669

Barry M. Goldwater Scholarship *(Undergraduate/Scholarship)* 2715

Grants for Physically Disabled Students in the Sciences *(Graduate/Grant)* 2579

Hertz Foundation Graduate Fellowships *(Doctorate, Graduate/Fellowship)* 2866

Howard Hughes Medical Institute Predoctoral Fellowships in Biological Sciences *(Postdoctorate/Fellowship)* 4358

Engineer Degree Fellowships; Howard Hughes Doctoral Fellowships *(Doctorate/Fellowship)* 2922

IBM Postdoctoral Research Fellowships in Mathematical Sciences *(Postdoctorate/Fellowship)* 2948

ICTP Research Grants for Postdoctoral Students *(Postdoctorate/Grant)* 3135

Institute for Advanced Study Postdoctoral Research Fellowships *(Postdoctorate/Fellowship)* 3009

Institute for Advanced Study Postdoctoral Study Awards *(Postdoctorate/Grant)* 3010

Dr. Theodore von Karman Graduate Scholarship *(Graduate/Scholarship)* 45

Laboratory-Graduate Participantships Thesis Parts Appointment *(Doctorate, Graduate/Grant)* 1084

Solomon Lefschetz Instructorships in Mathematics *(Postdoctorate/Fellowship)* 1818

LPI Summer Intern Program in Planetary Science *(Undergraduate/Internship)* 3514

Maryland MESA Scholarships *(High School, Undergraduate/Scholarship)* 3586

Mathematical Sciences Research Institute Postdoctoral Fellowships in Mathematics *(Postdoctorate/Fellowship)* 3611

Mathematical Sciences Research Institute Research Professorships in Mathematics *(Postdoctorate/Fellowship)* 3612

NAACP Willems Scholarship *(Graduate, Undergraduate/Scholarship)* 3851

NAS/NRC Collaboration in Basic Science and Engineering Long-Term Grants *(Postdoctorate/Grant)* 3831

NAS/NRC Collaboration in Basic Science and Engineering Short-Term Project Development Grants *(Postdoctorate/Grant)* 3832

National Defense Science and Engineering Graduate Fellowship Program *(Graduate/Fellowship)* 5855

National Physical Science Consortium Graduate Fellowships for Minorities and Women *(Doctorate, Graduate/Fellowship)* 4338

National Scholarship Trust Fund of the Graphic Arts Fellowships *(Graduate/Fellowship)* 4373

NATO Senior Guest Fellowships *(Professional Development/Fellowship)* 4656

General Emmett Paige Scholarship *(Undergraduate/Scholarship)* 1101

The Payzer Scholarship *(Undergraduate/Scholarship)* 2296

The Payzer Scholarship *(All/Scholarship)* 2423

Postdoctoral Fellowships in the Atmospheric Sciences *(Postdoctorate/Fellowship)* 3931

Postdoctoral Fellowships in Ocean Science and Engineering *(Postdoctorate/Fellowship)* 6247

Polingaysi Qoyawayma Scholarship *(Graduate/Scholarship)* 562

Research Fellowships in Marine Policy *(Postdoctorate/Fellowship)* 6248

Edith Nourse Rogers Scholarship Fund *(Undergraduate/Scholarship)* 6230

SDE Fellowships *(Postgraduate/Fellowship)* 5330

Smithsonian Environmental Research Center Work-Learn Opportunities in Environmental Studies *(Graduate, Undergraduate/Internship)* 5374

Tandy Technology Scholars *(Undergraduate/Scholarship)* 5672

U.S. Air Force Phillips Laboratory Scholar Program *(Postdoctorate/Other)* 4686

U.S. Army Summer Faculty Research and Engineering Associateships *(Postdoctorate/Fellowship)* 1376

U.S. Department of Energy Faculty Research Participation Fellowship *(Professional Development/Fellowship)* 5932

U.S. Department of Energy Internship *(Undergraduate/Internship)* 4711

U.S. Nuclear Regulatory Commission Historically Black Colleges and Universities Faculty Research Participation *(Professional Development/Fellowship)* 5934

Westinghouse Science Talent Search *(Undergraduate/Scholarship)* 5282

## Mechanics and repairs

AMT's Two-Year Scholarships *(Undergraduate/Scholarship)* 1248

Dodge Trucks Scholarships *(Undergraduate/Scholarship)* 4063

McFadden Family Automotive Scholarship *(Undergraduate/Scholarship)* 1882

Mercedes-Benz of North America Scholarship Program *(Undergraduate/Scholarship)* 1928

U.S. Army Summer Faculty Research and Engineering Associateships *(Postdoctorate/Fellowship)* 1376

## Media arts

Artists Workplace Fellowships *(Professional Development/Fellowship)* 6253

Banff Centre for the Arts Scholarships *(Postgraduate, Professional Development/Scholarship)* 1370

Sherlee Barish Fellowship *(Professional Development/Fellowship)* 5052

WCVB TV Leo L. Beranek Fellowship for Newsreporting *(Graduate, Undergraduate/Fellowship)* 6123

Bicentennial Swedish-American Exchange Fund Travel Grants *(Professional Development/Grant)* 5656

Jim Byron Scholarship *(Undergraduate/Scholarship)* 5054

Canadian Council for the Arts Grants Program *(Professional Development/Grant)* 1594

Ben Chatfield Scholarship *(Undergraduate/Scholarship)* 5055

Richard Cheverton Scholarship *(Undergraduate/Scholarship)* 5056

Consortium College University Media Centers Annual Research Grants *(Doctorate, Graduate, Professional Development, Undergraduate/Grant)* 2065

Dance Screen Competition Awards *(Professional Development/Award)* 3166

Film/Video Artists Fellowship *(Professional Development/Fellowship)* 4663

Gannett Center Fellowships *(Other, Professional Development/Fellowship)* 2593

Sandra Freeman Geller and Alfred Geller Fellowship *(Professional Development/Fellowship)* 5059

John Hogan Scholarship *(Undergraduate/Scholarship)* 5060

Theodore Koop Scholarship *(Undergraduate/Scholarship)* 5061

MacDowell Colony Residencies *(Other, Professional Development/Fellowship)* 3524

James McCulla Scholarship *(Undergraduate/Scholarship)* 5062

New Hampshire Individual Artist Fellowships *(Other/Fellowship)* 4535

Opera Screen Competition Awards *(Professional Development/Award)* 3167

Bruce Palmer Scholarship *(Undergraduate/Scholarship)* 5064

RTNDF Presidential Memorial Scholarship *(Graduate, Undergraduate/Scholarship)* 5066

Virginia Museum of Fine Arts Fellowship *(Professional Development/Fellowship)* 6061

WCVB TV Hearst Broadcast News Fellowship *(Graduate, Undergraduate/Fellowship)* 6125

Yaddo Residencies *(Professional Development/Other)* 6274

## Medical assisting

Allied Health Student Loans *(Undergraduate/Loan)* 4870

American Medical Technologists Scholarships *(Undergraduate/Scholarship)* 697

Hazel Corbin Assistance Fund Scholarships *(Postgraduate/Scholarship)* 3609

Occupational Therapist and Physical Therapist Scholarship Loan Program *(Graduate/Scholarship loan)* 2513

Maxine Williams Scholarships *(Other/Scholarship)* 317

## Medical laboratory technology

Allied Health Student Loans *(Undergraduate/Loan)* 4870

American Society of Clinical Pathologists Scholarships *(Undergraduate/Scholarship)* 910

CSLT Founders Fund Awards *(Professional Development/Award)* 1701

Georgia Student Finance Commission Service-Cancellable Stafford Loan *(Graduate, Undergraduate/Loan)* 2666

Georgia Student Finance Commission State-Sponsored Loan *(Graduate, Undergraduate/Loan)* 2669

International Founders' Fund Awards *(Other/Award)* 1702

NJSCLS Scholarships *(Undergraduate/Scholarship)* 4541

WHO Fellowships and Research Training Grants *(Graduate, Other, Postdoctorate/Fellowship)* 6261

## Medical record administration/technology

Allied Health Student Loans *(Undergraduate/Loan)* 4870

Aspen Systems Graduate Scholarship *(Graduate/Scholarship)* 515

FORE Graduate Loan *(Graduate/Loan)* 516

FORE Graduate Scholarships *(Doctorate, Graduate/Scholarship)* 517

FORE Undergraduate Loan *(Undergraduate/Loan)* 518

FORE Undergraduate Scholarships *(Undergraduate/Scholarship)* 519

Georgia Student Finance Commission Service-Cancellable Stafford Loan *(Graduate, Undergraduate/Loan)* 2666

Georgia Student Finance Commission State-Sponsored Loan *(Graduate, Undergraduate/Loan)* 2669

Grace Whiting Myers/Malcolm T. MacEachern Student Loans *(Doctorate, Graduate, Undergraduate/Loan)* 520

SMART Corporation Scholarship *(Undergraduate/Scholarship)* 521

Barbara Thomas Enterprises, Inc. Scholarship *(Undergraduate/Scholarship)* 522

Transcriptions, Ltd. Scholarship *(Undergraduate/Scholarship)* 523

Transcriptions, Ltd. Scholarship for Health Information Management and Graduate Students *(Graduate, Undergraduate/Scholarship)* 524

## Medical research (See also: Biomedical research)

ACOG/3M Pharmaceuticals Research Awards in Lower Genital Infections *(Postdoctorate/Award)* 376

Action Research Program and Project Grants *(Postdoctorate/Grant)* 30

Action Research Training Fellowships *(Postgraduate/Fellowship)* 31

ADA Career Development Awards *(Postdoctorate/Grant)* 435

ADA Clinical Research Grant Program *(Postdoctorate/Grant)* 436

**Medical research (See also: Biomedical research) (continued)**

ADA Medical Student Diabetes Research Fellowship Program *(Doctorate/Fellowship)* 437

ADA Mentor-Based Postdoctoral Fellowship Program *(Postdoctorate/Fellowship)* 438

ADA Research Awards *(Postdoctorate/Grant)* 439

American Brain Tumor Association Fellowships *(Postdoctorate/ Fellowship)* 356

American Heart Association, California Affiliate - Grants-in-Aid *(Postdoctorate/Grant)* 530

American Heart Association, California Affiliate - Postdoctoral Research Fellowships *(Postdoctorate/Fellowship)* 531

American Heart Association, California Affiliate - Predoctoral Fellowship *(Doctorate/Fellowship)* 532

American Liver Foundation Postdoctoral Supplementary Fellowships *(Postdoctorate/Fellowship)* 673

American Liver Foundation Student Research Fellowships *(Doctorate, Graduate, Other/Fellowship)* 674

American Otological Society Research Fellowship and Medical Student Training Grants *(Postdoctorate/Grant)* 759

American Otological Society Research Grants *(Postdoctorate/ Grant)* 760

Apex Foundation Research Grants *(Professional Development/ Grant)* 1050

Arthritis Biomedical Science Grants *(Postdoctorate/ Grant)* 1147

Arthritis Foundation Doctoral Dissertation Award for Arthritis Health Professionals *(Doctorate/Award)* 1148

Arthritis Foundation New Investigator Grant for Arthritis Health Professionals *(Postdoctorate/Grant)* 1149

ASHA Postdoctoral Fellowships *(Postdoctorate/ Fellowship)* 889

Norman Barwin Scholarships *(Graduate/Scholarship)* 4955

Behavioral Sciences Student Fellowship *(Professional Development/Fellowship)* 2397

Wilfred G. Bigelow Traveling Fellowship *(Postdoctorate/ Fellowship, Grant)* 4646

Michael Bilitch Fellowship in Cardiac Pacing and Electrophysiology *(Postdoctorate/Fellowship)* 4647

Burroughs Wellcome Young Investigator Award in Virology *(Postdoctorate/Award)* 3003

Canadian Liver Foundation Operating Grant Program *(Postdoctorate/Grant)* 1673

Canadian Liver Foundation Summer Studentship Award *(Graduate/Internship)* 1674

Cancer Prevention and Control Research Small Grant Program *(Doctorate, Postdoctorate, Postgraduate/Grant)* 3922

CLA/MRC Scholarships *(Postdoctorate/Scholarship)* 3638

The College of Family Physicians of Canada Awards/DM Robb Research and Family Physician Research Grants *(Professional Development/Award)* 1986

Cystic Fibrosis Foundation Clinical Fellowships *(Postdoctorate/ Fellowship)* 2151

Cystic Fibrosis Foundation Clinical Research Grants *(Postgraduate/Grant)* 2152

Cystic Fibrosis Foundation/National Institute of Diabetes and Digestive and Kidney Diseases Funding Award *(Postdoctorate/Award)* 2153

Cystic Fibrosis Foundation New Investigator Grants *(Postdoctorate/Grant)* 2154

Cystic Fibrosis Foundation Research Fellowships *(Postdoctorate/Fellowship)* 2155

Cystic Fibrosis Foundation Research Scholar Awards *(Postdoctorate/Award)* 2157

Cystic Fibrosis Foundation Special Research Awards *(Postgraduate/Award)* 2158

Cystic Fibrosis Foundation Third Year Clinical Fellowship Awards for Research Training *(Postdoctorate/ Fellowship)* 2160

Detweiler Travelling Fellowships *(Postdoctorate/ Fellowship)* 5184

EORTC/NCI Exchange Program *(Postdoctorate/Grant)* 3923

Epilepsy Foundation of America Research Grants *(Postdoctorate/Grant)* 2399

ESRI Doctoral Training Grants ESRI Postdoctoral Fellowships *(Doctorate, Postdoctorate/Fellowship, Grant)* 2316

FFS-NSPB Grants-In-Aid *(Postdoctorate/Grant)* 2449

FFS-NSPB Postdoctoral Research Fellowships *(Postdoctorate/ Fellowship)* 2450

FFS-NSPB Student Fellowships *(Doctorate, Graduate, Undergraduate/Fellowship)* 2451

Gina Finzi Memorial Student Summer Fellowships for Research *(Doctorate, Graduate, Undergraduate/ Fellowship)* 3519

Fogarty International Research Collaboration Award *(Postdoctorate/Other)* 2532

Generalist Physician Faculty Grants *(Professional Development/Grant)* 3285

Health Sciences Student Fellowships *(All/Fellowship)* 2401

Heed Ophthalmic Foundation Fellowships *(Postgraduate/ Fellowship)* 2855

Leonard W. Horowitz Fellowship in Cardiac Pacing and Electrophysiology *(Postdoctorate/Fellowship, Grant)* 4648

HSFC Career Investigator Awards *(Doctorate/Award)* 2839

HSFC Junior Personnel Medical Scientist Traineeships *(Doctorate/Internship)* 2841

HSFC Senior Personnel Research Scholarship/McDonald Scholarship *(Postdoctorate/Scholarship)* 2846

Howard Hughes Medical Institute Research Training Fellowships for Medical Students *(Graduate/ Fellowship)* 2925

Human Growth Foundation Small Grants *(Postdoctorate/ Grant)* 2929

Viola Kerr Fellowship *(Postdoctorate/Fellowship)* 4841

Lalor Foundation Postdoctoral Research Grants *(Postdoctorate/Fellowship)* 3411

Leukemia Society of America Short-term Scientific Awards *(Professional Development/Grant)* 3455

Lions SightFirst Diabetic Retinopathy Research Program - LCIF Clinical Research Grant Program *(Postdoctorate/ Grant)* 440

Lions SightFirst Diabetic Retinopathy Research Program - LCIF Equipment Grant Program *(Postdoctorate/Grant)* 441

Lions SightFirst Diabetic Retinopathy Research Program - LCIF Training Grant Program *(Postdoctorate/Grant)* 442

Liver Scholar Awards *(Postdoctorate/Grant)* 675

Lupus Foundation of America Research Grants *(Doctorate, Graduate/Grant)* 3520

Walter C. MacKenzie, Johnson and Johnson Fellowship *(Postdoctorate/Fellowship)* 5185

March of Dimes Research Grants *(Postdoctorate, Professional Development/Grant)* 3548

Medical Education Travelling Fellowship *(Postdoctorate/ Fellowship)* 5186

Medical Research Council Travel Grants *(Professional Development/Grant)* 3639

H. Houston Merritt Fellowship *(Postdoctorate/ Fellowship)* 4842

Robert S. Morison Fellowships *(Professional Development/ Fellowship)* 2743

Myasthenia Gravis Osserman Fellowship Grants *(Postdoctorate/Grant)* 3810

National Heart, Lung, and Blood Institute's Minority School Faculty Development Award *(Postdoctorate/Award)* 4175

National Institute of Diabetes and Digestive and Kidney Diseases Fellowship Program-Sabbatical *(Postdoctorate/ Fellowship)* 2162

National Kidney Foundation Young Investigator Grant *(Postdoctorate/Grant)* 4280

National Multiple Sclerosis Society Advanced Postdoctoral Fellowships *(Postdoctorate/Fellowship)* 4313

National Multiple Sclerosis Society Biomedical Research Grants *(Professional Development/Grant)* 4314

National Multiple Sclerosis Society Health Services Research Grants *(Professional Development/Grant)* 4315

National Multiple Sclerosis Society Patient Management Care and Rehabilitation Grants *(Professional Development/ Grant)* 4316

National Multiple Sclerosis Society Senior Faculty Awards *(Professional Development/Award)* 4320

NCAFP Foundation Medical Student Loan *(Postgraduate/ Fellowship, Loan)* 4659

NCI International Bilateral Program *(Postdoctorate/ Other)* 3924

NIAMS Academic Research Enhancement Awards *(Postdoctorate/Grant)* 4186

NIAMS National Research Service Award (NRSA) Fellowships *(Postdoctorate/Grant)* 4187

NIAMS National Research Service Award (NRSA) Senior Fellowships *(Postdoctorate/Grant)* 4188

NIAMS Regular Research Grants *(Postdoctorate/Grant)* 4189

NIAMS Research Career Development Awards *(Postdoctorate/ Grant)* 4190

NIMH Individual Postdoctoral National Research Service Awards *(Postdoctorate/Fellowship)* 4198

NIMH Individual Predoctoral National Research Service Awards *(Doctorate/Fellowship)* 4199

Basil O'Connor Starter Scholar Awards *(Postdoctorate/ Award)* 3549

Olfactory Research Fund Grants *(Postdoctorate/Grant)* 4744

Oncology Nursing Foundation/Amgen, Inc. Research Grant *(Professional Development/Grant)* 4758

Oncology Nursing Foundation/Bristol- Myers Oncology Chapter Research Grant *(Professional Development/ Grant)* 4760

Oncology Nursing Foundation/Bristol- Myers Oncology Division Community Health Research Grant *(Professional Development/Grant)* 4761

Oncology Nursing Foundation/Bristol- Myers Oncology Division Research Grant *(Professional Development/Grant)* 4762

Oncology Nursing Foundation/Cetus Oncology Grants for Research Involving Biotherapy or Immunotherapy *(Professional Development/Grant)* 4763

Oncology Nursing Foundation/Glaxo Research Grants *(Professional Development/Grant)* 4765

Oncology Nursing Foundation/Oncology Nursing Certification Corporation Nursing Education Research Grants *(Professional Development/Grant)* 4767

Oncology Nursing Foundation/Oncology Nursing Society Research Grant *(Professional Development/Grant)* 4768

Oncology Nursing Foundation/Ortho Biotech Research Grant *(Professional Development/Grant)* 4769

Oncology Nursing Foundation/Purdue Frederick Research Grant *(Professional Development/Grant)* 4770

Oncology Nursing Foundation/Rhone Poulenc Rorer New Investigator Research Grants *(Doctorate, Graduate/ Grant)* 4771

Oncology Nursing Foundation/Sigma Theta Tau International and Oncology Nursing Society Research Grant *(Professional Development/Grant)* 4772

Oncology Nursing Society/SmithKline Beecham Research Grant *(Professional Development/Grant)* 4773

Oncology Research Faculty Development Program *(Postdoctorate/Grant)* 3925

Parkinson's Disease Foundation Postdoctoral Fellowship *(Postdoctorate/Fellowship)* 4843

Parkinson's Disease Foundation Summer Fellowship *(Graduate, Undergraduate/Fellowship)* 4845

The Pfizer Postdoctoral Fellowships *(Postdoctorate/ Fellowship)* 4884

The Pfizer Scholars Program for New Faculty *(Postdoctorate/ Award)* 4885

Postdoctoral Fellowship in Nosocomial Infection Research and Training *(Postdoctorate/Fellowship)* 4163

Colin L. Powell Minority Postdoctoral Fellowship in Tropical Disease Research *(Graduate/Fellowship)* 4164

Public Policy Fellowships in Mental Retardation *(Postdoctorate/Fellowship)* 3352

Kenneth M. Rosen Fellowship in Cardiac Pacing and Electrophysiology *(Postdoctorate/Fellowship, Grant)* 4651

Elizabeth St. Louis Award *(Professional Development/ Award)* 2317

Samsun Medical Research Institute Student Internships *(Doctorate, Graduate, Undergraduate/Internship)* 5224

Scleroderma Research Grants *(Postgraduate/Grant)* 5284

Lillian Shorr Fellowship *(Postdoctorate/Fellowship)* 4846

Society of Nuclear Medicine Pilot Research Grants *(Postdoctorate, Postgraduate/Grant)* 5476

Society of Nuclear Medicine Student Fellowship Awards *(Doctorate, Graduate, Undergraduate/Fellowship)* 5477

Miriam Neveren Summer Studentship *(Professional Development/Scholarship)* 2318

Tetalman Award *(Postdoctorate/Award)* 5478

John P. Utz Postdoctoral Fellowship in Medical Mycology *(Postdoctorate/Fellowship)* 4165

## Medical technology

American Medical Technologists Scholarships *(Undergraduate/ Scholarship)* 697

American Society for Clinical Laboratory Science Scholarships *(Graduate/Scholarship)* 908

American Society of Clinical Pathologists Scholarships *(Undergraduate/Scholarship)* 910

J. Hugh & Earle W. Fellows Memorial Fund Loans *(Undergraduate/Loan)* 2437

Fellowships in Spinal Cord Injury Research *(Postdoctorate/ Fellowship)* 4830

Georgia Student Finance Commission Service-Cancellable Stafford Loan *(Graduate, Undergraduate/Loan)* 2666

Georgia Student Finance Commission State-Sponsored Loan *(Graduate, Undergraduate/Loan)* 2669

NJSCLS Scholarships *(Undergraduate/Scholarship)* 4541

Basil O'Connor Starter Scholar Awards *(Postdoctorate/ Award)* 3549

WHO Fellowships *(Postdoctorate, Professional Development/ Fellowship)* 6259

## Medicine (See also: specific areas of study, e.g. Oncology; specific diseases, e.g. Diabetes)

AAUW Educational Foundation Selected Professions Engineering Dissertation Fellowship *(Graduate/ Fellowship)* 335

ABMAC/Clerkship in Taiwan Award *(Doctorate/Other)* 358

ACOG/Merck Award for Research in Migraine Management in Women's Health Care *(Postdoctorate/Grant)* 379

ACOG/Organon Inc. Research Award in Contraception *(Postdoctorate/Grant)* 381

ACOG/Pharmacie & Upjohn Research Award in Urognecology of the Postreproductive Woman *(Postdoctorate/Grant)* 383

ACOG/Solvay Pharmaceuticals Research Award in Menopause *(Postdoctorate/Fellowship)* 384

AGBU Education Loan Program in the U.S. *(Graduate/ Loan)* 1133

Agency for Toxic Substances and Disease Registry Clinical Fellowships in Environmental Medicine *(Postdoctorate/ Fellowship)* 5858

Agency for Toxic Substances and Disease Registry Postgraduate Research Program *(Postgraduate/ Fellowship)* 5859

AIBS Congressional Science Fellowship *(Postdoctorate/ Fellowship)* 476

American Heart Association, California Affiliate - Grants-in-Aid *(Postdoctorate/Grant)* 530

American Heart Association, California Affiliate - Predoctoral Fellowship *(Doctorate/Fellowship)* 532

American Jewish League for Israel University Scholarship Fund *(Graduate, Undergraduate/Scholarship)* 600

American Kidney Fund Clinical Scientist in Nephrology *(Postdoctorate/Fellowship)* 606

American Osteopathic Association/National Osteopathic Foundation Student Loans *(Graduate/Loan)* 4333

American Otological Society Research Fellowship and Medical Student Training Grants *(Postdoctorate/Grant)* 759

American Otological Society Research Grants *(Postdoctorate/ Grant)* 760

**Medicine (See also: specific areas of study, e.g. Oncology; specific diseases, e.g. Diabetes) (continued)**

AMWA Medical Education Loans *(Doctorate/Loan)* 699

Applied Health Physics Fellowship Program *(Graduate/ Fellowship)* 5861

John D. Archbold Scholarship *(Graduate, Undergraduate/ Scholarship)* 1073

Armed Forces Health Professions Scholarship *(Graduate/ Scholarship)* 4483

Armenian American Medical Association Scholarship *(Undergraduate/Scholarship)* 1106

Berkshire District Medical Society Medical School Scholarship Loan *(Graduate/Loan)* 1414

William Blair-Bell Memorial Lectureships in Obstetrics and Gynecology *(Doctorate, Postdoctorate/Other)* 5179

BNL Postdoctoral Research Associateships *(Postdoctorate/ Other)* 1504

British Leprosy Relief Association Research Grants *(Postdoctorate/Grant)* 1491

H. Fletcher Brown Scholarship *(Doctorate, Graduate, Undergraduate/Scholarship)* 4967

William and Charlotte Cadbury Award *(Doctorate/ Award)* 4288

Celanese Canada Inc. Scholarships *(Undergraduate/ Scholarship)* 1269

Center for Devices and Radiological Health Postgraduate Research Program *(Postgraduate/Fellowship)* 5864

Center for Drug Evaluation and Research Postgraduate Research *(Postgraduate/Fellowship)* 5865

Charles River District Medical Society Scholarship *(Graduate/ Scholarship)* 1832

Chateaubriand Scholarship (Scientifique) *(Doctorate, Postdoctorate/Scholarship)* 2372

Cherokee Nation Graduate Scholarship *(Graduate/ Scholarship)* 1911

Children's Medical Research Institute Ph.D. Scholarships; Children's Medical Research Institute Postdoctoral Research Fellowships *(Doctorate, Postdoctorate/Fellowship, Scholarship)* 1941

Childs Postdoctoral Fellowships *(Postdoctorate/ Fellowship)* 1943

CLA/MRC Scholarships *(Postdoctorate/Scholarship)* 3638

Ty Cobb Scholarships *(Graduate, Undergraduate/ Scholarship)* 1976

The College of Family Physicians of Canada Awards/DM Robb Research and Family Physician Research Grants *(Professional Development/Award)* 1986

The College of Family Physicians of Canada/Family Physician Study Grants *(Professional Development/Award)* 1987

The College of Family Physicians of Canada Practice Enrichment Awards *(Professional Development/Award)* 1988

Joseph Collins Foundation Scholarships *(Graduate/ Scholarship)* 1994

"Country Doctor" Scholarship Program *(Graduate/ Scholarship)* 5619

Cuyahoga County Medical Foundation Scholarship *(Graduate/ Scholarship)* 2146

Czech Education Scholarships *(Doctorate, Graduate, Postdoctorate/Scholarship)* 3708

Delaware Academy of Medicine Student Financial Aid Program *(Doctorate/Loan)* 2207

Detweiler Travelling Fellowships *(Postdoctorate/ Fellowship)* 5184

William E. Dochterman Medical Student Scholarship *(Graduate/Grant)* 5213

Lord Dowding Grant *(Doctorate, Graduate/Grant)* 2278

Eastburn Fellowships *(Postdoctorate/Fellowship)* 2314

E. B. Eastburn Fellowships *(Postdoctorate/Fellowship)* 2788

Epilepsy Foundation of America Research Training Fellowships *(Doctorate/Fellowship)* 2400

Eppley Foundation Support for Advanced Scientific Research *(Postdoctorate/Grant)* 2404

Faculty Research Participation Program at the National Center for Toxicological Research *(Professional Development/ Fellowship)* 5874

J. Hugh & Earle W. Fellows Memorial Fund Loans *(Undergraduate/Loan)* 2437

Fellowship Program in Academic Medicine *(Doctorate/ Fellowship)* 4289

Fellowship Program in Academic Medicine for Minority Students *(Undergraduate/Fellowship)* 4290

Fellowships in Ethics *(Postdoctorate, Postgraduate/ Fellowship)* 5015

Morris Fishbein Fellowship in Medical Journalism *(Graduate, Postgraduate/Fellowship)* 688

Folger Library Long-Term Fellowships *(Postdoctorate/ Fellowship)* 2541

Folger Library Short-Term Fellowships *(Postdoctorate/ Fellowship)* 2542

Four-Shra-Nish Foundation Loan *(Undergraduate/Loan)* 2583

Fresno-Madera Medical Society Scholarships *(Doctorate/ Scholarship)* 2597

FSD Student Grant *(Graduate/Grant)* 2578

Generalist Physician Faculty Grants *(Professional Development/Grant)* 3285

Georgia State Loan Repayment Program *(Postdoctorate/ Loan)* 5620

Giargiari Fellowship *(Graduate/Fellowship)* 4229

Benn and Kathleen Gilmore Scholarship *(Doctorate/ Scholarship)* 4292

Glenn Foundation/AFAR Scholarships for Research in the Biology of Aging *(Doctorate/Scholarship)* 459

Irving Graef Memorial Scholarship *(Doctorate/ Scholarship)* 4293

Grants for Physically Disabled Students in the Sciences *(Graduate/Grant)* 2579

William F. Grupe Foundation Scholarships *(Doctorate, Graduate/Scholarship)* 2756

Henry G. Halladay Awards *(Doctorate/Scholarship)* 4294

Phyllis P. Harris Scholarships *(All/Scholarship)* 4956

H. William Harris Visiting Professorship *(Other/Other)* 359

John A. Hartford Afar Medical Student Geriatric Scholarship Program *(Graduate/Scholarship)* 460

Health Care Policy Clinical Career Development Award *(Doctorate/Other)* 2240

Health Education Loan Program *(Doctorate, Graduate/ Loan)* 5709

George Hill Memorial Scholarship *(Doctorate/ Scholarship)* 4295

Historically Black Colleges and Universities Health and Environmental Research Opportunities for Faculty and Students *(Postgraduate, Professional Development/ Fellowship)* 5892

HRSA-BHP Exceptional Financial Need Scholarship *(Doctorate/Scholarship)* 5966

HRSA-BHP Health Professions Student Loans *(Doctorate, Graduate/Loan)* 5967

HRSA-BHP Loans for Disadvantaged Students *(Undergraduate/Loan)* 5968

HRSA-BHP National Health Service Corps Scholarships *(Doctorate/Scholarship)* 5969

HRSA-BHP Scholarships for Disadvantaged Students *(Doctorate, Graduate, Undergraduate/Scholarship)* 5972

HSFC Career Investigator Awards *(Doctorate/Award)* 2839

HSFC Junior Personnel Medical Scientist Traineeships *(Doctorate/Internship)* 2841

HSFC Senior Personnel Research Scholarship/McDonald Scholarship *(Postdoctorate/Scholarship)* 2846

Hugh J. Andersen Memorial Scholarship *(Doctorate/ Scholarship)* 4296

IHS Health Professions Pre-Graduate Scholarships *(Undergraduate/Scholarship)* 2994

Indian Health Career Awards *(Doctorate, Graduate, Undergraduate/Scholarship)* 4935

International Order of the King's Daughters and Sons Health Careers Scholarships *(Graduate, Postgraduate, Undergraduate/Scholarship)* 3169

## Medicine (See also: specific areas of study, e.g. Oncology; specific diseases, e.g. Diabetes) (continued)

Arthur N. Wilson, M.D. Scholarship *(Doctorate, Graduate/ Scholarship)* 691

Women's Medical Association of New York Financial Assistance Fund Loans *(Doctorate/Award, Loan)* 6232

Wyeth-Ayerst Prize in Women's Health *(Doctorate/ Award)* 4308

Zeneca Pharmaceuticals Underserved Healthcare Grant *(Doctorate/Grant)* 4336

## Medicine, Cardiology

AHA Grant-in-Aid *(Postdoctorate/Grant)* 526

American Heart Association, California Affiliate - Grants-in-Aid *(Postdoctorate/Grant)* 530

American Heart Association, California Affiliate - Postdoctoral Research Fellowships *(Postdoctorate/Fellowship)* 531

American Heart Association, California Affiliate - Predoctoral Fellowship *(Doctorate/Fellowship)* 532

Wilfred G. Bigelow Traveling Fellowship *(Postdoctorate/ Fellowship, Grant)* 4646

Michael Bilitch Fellowship in Cardiac Pacing and Electrophysiology *(Postdoctorate/Fellowship)* 4647

Council for Tobacco Research Grants-in-Aid *(Professional Development/Grant)* 2125

del Duca Foundation Maintenance and Travel Grants *(Professional Development/Grant)* 2284

Established Investigator Grant *(Doctorate/Grant)* 527

Leonard W. Horowitz Fellowship in Cardiac Pacing and Electrophysiology *(Postdoctorate/Fellowship, Grant)* 4648

HP/AACN Critical-Care Nursing Research Grants *(Doctorate, Graduate/Grant)* 2868

HSFC Career Investigator Awards *(Doctorate/Award)* 2839

HSFC Junior Personnel Medical Scientist Traineeships *(Doctorate/Internship)* 2841

HSFC Research Scholarships *(Postdoctorate/ Scholarship)* 2845

HSFC Senior Personnel Research Scholarship/McDonald Scholarship *(Postdoctorate/Scholarship)* 2846

NASPE Full-Year Fellowships *(Postdoctorate/Fellowship)* 4649

NASPE Traveling Fellowships *(Postdoctorate/Fellowship)* 4650

National Heart, Lung, and Blood Institute's Minority School Faculty Development Award *(Postdoctorate/Award)* 4175

Kenneth M. Rosen Fellowship in Cardiac Pacing and Electrophysiology *(Postdoctorate/Fellowship, Grant)* 4651

Scientist Development Grant *(Doctorate/Grant)* 528

## Medicine, Cardiovascular (See also: Medicine, Cardiology)

HSFC Graduate Research Traineeships *(Graduate, Postgraduate/Internship)* 2840

HSFC PhD Research Traineeships *(Doctorate, Postdoctorate/ Internship)* 2843

HSFC Research Fellowships *(Postdoctorate/Fellowship)* 2844

HSFC Visiting Scientist Program *(Professional Development/ Award)* 2847

## Medicine, Cerebrovascular

HSFC Graduate Research Traineeships *(Graduate, Postgraduate/Internship)* 2840

HSFC PhD Research Traineeships *(Doctorate, Postdoctorate/ Internship)* 2843

HSFC Research Fellowships *(Postdoctorate/Fellowship)* 2844

HSFC Research Scholarships *(Postdoctorate/ Scholarship)* 2845

HSFC Visiting Scientist Program *(Professional Development/ Award)* 2847

## Medicine, Chiropractic

Foundation for Chiropractic Education and Research Fellowships, Scholarships, and Residency Stipends *(Graduate, Professional Development/Fellowship, Grant)* 2564

Health Education Loan Program *(Doctorate, Graduate/ Loan)* 5709

Mississippi Graduate and Professional Degree Loan/ Scholarship Program *(Doctorate/Scholarship loan)* 3731

New York State Professional Opportunity Scholarships *(Doctorate, Graduate, Undergraduate/Scholarship)* 4592

New York State Regents Professional Opportunity Scholarships *(Doctorate, Graduate, Undergraduate/ Scholarship)* 4577

Oklahoma State Regents Chiropractic Education Assistance *(Other, Undergraduate/Award)* 4737

## Medicine, Geriatric

Creative Investigator Grants *(Professional Development/ Grant)* 458

Glenn Foundation/AFAR Scholarships for Research in the Biology of Aging *(Doctorate/Scholarship)* 459

John A. Hartford Afar Medical Student Geriatric Scholarship Program *(Graduate/Scholarship)* 460

OFAS Research Grants *(Postdoctorate/Grant)* 4807

The Pfizer American Geriatrics Society Postdoctoral Outcomes Research Fellowships *(Postdoctorate/Fellowship)* 4883

## Medicine, Gynecological and obstetrical

ACOG/Cytyc Corporation Research Award for the Prevention of Cervical Cancer *(Postdoctorate/Grant)* 377

ACOG/Ethicon Research Award for Innovations in Gynecologic Surgery *(Postdoctorate/Award)* 378

ACOG/Novartis Pharmaceuticals Fellowship for Research in Endocrinology of the Postreproductive Woman *(Postdoctorate/Fellowship)* 380

ACOG/Organon Inc. Research Award in Contraception *(Postdoctorate/Grant)* 381

ACOG/Ortho-McNeil Academic Training Fellowships in Obstetrics and Gynecology *(Doctorate/Fellowship)* 382

ACOG/Pharmacie & Upjohn Research Award in Urognecology of the Postreproductive Woman *(Postdoctorate/Grant)* 383

ACOG/Solvay Pharmaceuticals Research Award in Menopause *(Postdoctorate/Fellowship)* 384

Bernhard Baron Traveling Scholarship *(Professional Development/Scholarship)* 5178

William Blair-Bell Memorial Lectureships in Obstetrics and Gynecology *(Doctorate, Postdoctorate/Other)* 5179

Eden Traveling Fellowship in Obstetrics and Gynecology *(Doctorate, Postdoctorate/Fellowship)* 5180

Edgar Gentilli Prize *(Doctorate, Postdoctorate/Prize)* 5181

Loan Assistant Repayment Program for Medical Residents in Primary Care *(Other/Other)* 3572

Medical Student Loan Repayment Program *(Postgraduate/ Loan)* 3753

USA British Isles Traveling Fellowship *(Doctorate, Postdoctorate/Fellowship)* 5182

Well Being *(Professional Development/Grant)* 6129

## Medicine, Internal

Loan Assistant Repayment Program for Medical Residents in Primary Care *(Other/Other)* 3572

Medical Student Loan Repayment Program *(Postgraduate/ Loan)* 3753

## Medicine, Nuclear

Cassen Postdoctoral Fellowship *(Postdoctorate/ Fellowship)* 5474

Paul C. Cole Scholarships *(Doctorate/Scholarship)* 5475

## Medicine, Orthopedic

Career Development Awards in Orthopaedic Surgery *(Professional Development/Grant)* 4814

Research Grants in Orthopaedic Surgery *(Postdoctorate/ Grant)* 4815

Resident Research Fellowships in Orthopaedic Surgery *(Postdoctorate/Fellowship)* 4816

Zecchino Post-Graduate Orthopaedic Fellowship *(Postdoctorate/Fellowship)* 4272

## Medicine, Osteopathic

AMWA Medical Education Loans *(Doctorate/Loan)* 699

Armed Forces Health Professions Scholarship *(Graduate/Scholarship)* 4483

Beale Family Memorial Scholarship *(Doctorate/Scholarship)* 3533

Bristol-Myers Squibb Outstanding Resident Awards *(Professional Development/Grant)* 4334

Cuyahoga County Medical Foundation Scholarship *(Graduate/Scholarship)* 2146

Georgia State Loan Repayment Program *(Postdoctorate/Loan)* 5620

Health Education Loan Program *(Doctorate, Graduate/Loan)* 5709

HRSA-BHP Health Professions Student Loans *(Doctorate, Graduate/Loan)* 5967

HRSA-BHP Loans for Disadvantaged Students *(Undergraduate/Loan)* 5968

HRSA-BHP National Health Service Corps Scholarships *(Doctorate/Scholarship)* 5969

HRSA-BHP Scholarships for Disadvantaged Students *(Doctorate, Graduate, Undergraduate/Scholarship)* 5972

Andrew M. Longley, Jr., D.O. Scholarship *(Doctorate/Scholarship)* 3534

Maine Osteopathic Association Memorial Scholarship *(Doctorate, Graduate, Undergraduate/Scholarship)* 3535

Maine Osteopathic Association Scholarship *(Doctorate, Graduate, Undergraduate/Scholarship)* 3536

The Mead Johnson/NMA Scholarship *(Doctorate/Scholarship)* 4299

Mississippi Southern Regional Education Board Loan/Scholarship Program *(Doctorate/Scholarship loan)* 3741

NMA Merit Scholarships *(Doctorate/Scholarship)* 4301

The NMA Special Awards Program *(Doctorate/Scholarship)* 4303

Oklahoma Rural Medical Education Scholarship Loans *(Doctorate/Scholarship loan)* 4940

Osteopathic Medical Students Loans *(Graduate/Loan)* 2003

The Primary Care Resource Initiative for Missouri (PRIMO) *(Doctorate, Graduate, Undergraduate/Loan)* 3755

The Slack Award for Medical Journalism *(Doctorate/Award)* 4307

Washington Osteopathic Foundation Student Loans *(Doctorate/Loan)* 6087

Western Interstate Commission for Higher Education Student Exchanges *(Doctorate, Graduate/Other)* 135

## Medicine, Pediatric

AAP Residency Scholarships *(Postdoctorate/Scholarship)* 238

Ambulatory Pediatric Association Special Projects Program *(Postdoctorate/Grant)* 213

Mary Rowena Cooper Scholarship Fund *(All/Scholarship)* 6195

Generalist Physician Faculty Grants *(Professional Development/Grant)* 3285

Gerber Prize for Excellence in Pediatrics *(Doctorate/Award)* 4291

Duncan L. Gordon Fellowships *(Postdoctorate/Fellowship)* 2900

The Hospital for Sick Children Foundation External Grants Program *(Professional Development/Grant)* 2901

Loan Assistant Repayment Program for Medical Residents in Primary Care *(Other/Other)* 3572

Medical Student Loan Repayment Program *(Postgraduate/Loan)* 3753

Mississippi State Medical Education Loan/Scholarship Program *(Doctorate/Scholarship loan)* 3744

Society for Pediatric Dermatology Grant *(Postgraduate/Grant)* 5480

Well Being *(Professional Development/Grant)* 6129

## Medicine, Pulmonary

ALA Career Investigator Awards *(Postdoctorate/Award)* 677

ALA Research Grants *(Postdoctorate/Grant)* 678

Behavioral Science Dissertation Grants (Cancelled) *(Doctorate/Grant)* 679

CLA/MRC Scholarships *(Postdoctorate/Scholarship)* 3638

Council for Tobacco Research Grants-in-Aid *(Professional Development/Grant)* 2125

Dalsemer Research Scholar Award *(Postdoctorate/Award)* 680

Parker B. Francis Fellowships *(Postdoctorate/Fellowship)* 2587

National Heart, Lung, and Blood Institute's Minority School Faculty Development Award *(Postdoctorate/Award)* 4175

Pediatric Pulmonary Research Training Fellowships (Cancelled) *(Postdoctorate/Fellowship)* 682

Research Training Fellowships *(Postdoctorate/Fellowship)* 683

Edward Livingston Trudeau Scholar Awards (Cancelled) *(Postdoctorate/Award)* 684

## Medicine, Sports

NSCA Challenge Scholarships *(All/Scholarship)* 4415

Power Systems Inc./NSCA Strength and Conditioning Professional Scholarship *(Graduate, Undergraduate/Scholarship)* 4417

## Medieval studies

CMRS Summer Fellowships *(Postdoctorate/Fellowship)* 5988

Neil Ker Memorial Fund Grants *(Postdoctorate/Grant)* 1481

Pontifical Institute of Mediaeval Studies Research Associateships *(Postdoctorate/Award)* 4979

## Meniere's disease

American Otological Society Research Grants *(Postdoctorate/Grant)* 760

## Mental health

Albert Ellis Institute Clinical Fellowships, Internships *(Graduate, Postdoctorate, Postgraduate/Fellowship)* 143

American Sociological Association Minority Fellowships *(Doctorate/Fellowship)* 986

Council on Social Work Education Minority Fellowships *(Doctorate/Fellowship)* 3724

del Duca Foundation Maintenance and Travel Grants *(Professional Development/Grant)* 2284

Fellowship Program in Academic Medicine *(Doctorate/Fellowship)* 4289

Grant Foundation Faculty Scholars Program *(Other/Grant)* 2739

Grant Foundation Research Grants *(Postdoctorate/Grant)* 2740

NAJA Graduate Scholarships *(Graduate/Scholarship)* 3881

NIMH Individual Postdoctoral National Research Service Awards *(Postdoctorate/Fellowship)* 4198

NIMH Individual Predoctoral National Research Service Awards *(Doctorate/Fellowship)* 4199

Iris Pollock Memorial Scholarship *(Undergraduate/Scholarship)* 2734

## Metallurgy

ILZRO Postdoctoral Fellowships *(Postdoctorate/Fellowship)* 3164

Rocky Mountain Coal Mining Institute Scholarships *(Undergraduate/Scholarship)* 5157

## Meteorology (See also: Atmospheric science)

Minority Geoscience Scholarships *(Graduate, Undergraduate/Scholarship)* 508

Postdoctoral Fellowships in Ocean Science and Engineering *(Postdoctorate/Fellowship)* 6247

Research Support Opportunities in Arctic Environmental Studies *(Doctorate, Graduate/Other)* 1682

U.S. Air Force Phillips Laboratory Scholar Program *(Postdoctorate/Other)* 4686

U.S. Army Summer Faculty Research and Engineering Associateships *(Postdoctorate/Fellowship)* 1376

## Microbiology (See also: Biology)

ASM Predoctoral Minority Fellowships *(Doctorate/Fellowship)* 954

Cancer Federation Scholarships *(Undergraduate/Scholarship)* 1710

## Microbiology (See also: Biology) (continued)

Howard Hughes Medical Institute Predoctoral Fellowships in Biological Sciences *(Postdoctorate/Fellowship)* 4358

Ortho/McNeil Predoctoral Minority Fellowship in Antimicrobial Chemotherapy *(Doctorate/Fellowship)* 955

Postdoctoral Fellowships in Ocean Science and Engineering *(Postdoctorate/Fellowship)* 6247

Smithsonian Environmental Research Center Work-Learn Opportunities in Environmental Studies *(Graduate, Undergraduate/Internship)* 5374

## Midwifery

ACNM Scholarships *(Graduate/Scholarship)* 3267

## Military science and education

ADM Mike Boorda Seaman-to-Admiral Educational Assistance Program *(Undergraduate/Grant, Loan)* 4494

Army Research Laboratory Postdoctoral Fellowship Program *(Postdoctorate/Fellowship)* 922

Coast Guard Essay Contest *(Other/Prize)* 5950

Department of National Defense Security and Defense Forum Internships *(Postgraduate/Internship)* 1272

Department of National Defense Security and Defense Forum MA and Ph.D Scholarships *(Doctorate, Graduate/ Scholarship)* 1273

Enlisted Essay Contest *(Other/Prize)* 5951

Falcon Foundation Scholarship *(Undergraduate/ Scholarship)* 2427

International Navies Essay Contest *(Other/Prize)* 5952

International Navies Photo Contest *(Other/Prize)* 5953

Naval Research Laboratory Postdoctoral Fellowship Program *(Postdoctorate/Fellowship)* 924

North Georgia College Military Scholarship *(Undergraduate/ Scholarship)* 2674

U.S. Army Center of Military History Dissertation Year Fellowships *(Doctorate/Fellowship)* 5821

Washington Crossing Foundation Scholarships *(Undergraduate/Scholarship)* 6085

## Mineralogy

American Museum of Natural History Collection Study Grants *(Doctorate, Postdoctorate/Grant)* 712

American Museum of Natural History Research and Museum Fellowships *(Postdoctorate/Fellowship)* 713

Rocky Mountain Coal Mining Institute Scholarships *(Undergraduate/Scholarship)* 5157

## Mining (See also: Engineering, Mining and Mineral)

Rocky Mountain Coal Mining Institute Scholarships *(Undergraduate/Scholarship)* 5157

WAAIME Scholarship Loans *(Graduate, Undergraduate/ Scholarship loan)* 592

## Mortuary science (See also: Funeral services)

Hilgenfeld Research and Publications Grants; Hilgenfeld Scholarship Grants *(Professional Development/Grant)* 2874

## Multiple sclerosis

Multiple Sclerosis Society Career Development Awards *(Postdoctorate/Award)* 3789

Multiple Sclerosis Society Postdoctoral Fellowships *(Postdoctorate/Fellowship)* 3790

Multiple Sclerosis Society Research Grants *(Postdoctorate/ Grant)* 3791

Multiple Sclerosis Society Research Studentships *(Doctorate/ Grant)* 3792

National Multiple Sclerosis Society Advanced Postdoctoral Fellowships *(Postdoctorate/Fellowship)* 4313

National Multiple Sclerosis Society Biomedical Research Grants *(Professional Development/Grant)* 4314

National Multiple Sclerosis Society Health Services Research Grants *(Professional Development/Grant)* 4315

National Multiple Sclerosis Society Patient Management Care and Rehabilitation Grants *(Professional Development/ Grant)* 4316

National Multiple Sclerosis Society Pilot Research Grants *(Professional Development/Grant)* 4317

National Multiple Sclerosis Society Postdoctoral Fellowships *(Professional Development/Fellowship)* 4318

National Multiple Sclerosis Society Research Grants *(Professional Development/Grant)* 4319

National Multiple Sclerosis Society Senior Faculty Awards *(Professional Development/Award)* 4320

Patient Management, Care and Rehabilitation Grants *(Professional Development/Grant)* 4321

Harry Weaver Neuroscience Scholarships *(Postdoctorate/ Scholarship)* 4322

## Muscular dystrophy

Ruth Aziz Clinical Fellowship *(Professional Development/ Fellowship)* 3802

Dr. David Green Postdoctoral Fellowship *(Professional Development/Fellowship)* 3803

MDA Research Grants; MDA Research Development Grants; MDA Genetics Research Grants *(Professional Development/ Grant)* 3800

Arthur Minden Predoctoral Fellowship *(Doctorate/ Fellowship)* 3804

## Museum science

AIMHS Scholarship *(Professional Development/ Scholarship)* 1242

American Museum of Natural History Research and Museum Fellowships *(Postdoctorate/Fellowship)* 713

Asian Cultural Council Fellowship Grants *(Postdoctorate/ Fellowship)* 1177

Conservation Science Fellowship *(Postdoctorate, Postgraduate/Fellowship)* 2060

Cooper-Hewitt Museum Internships *(Undergraduate/ Internship)* 5383

Arthur Davis Fellowship; Charles E. Merrill Trust Fellowship *(Graduate/Fellowship)* 3806

EAIA Research Grants Program *(Postgraduate/Grant)* 2304

Getty Museum Graduate Internships *(Doctorate, Graduate/ Internship)* 2702

Humanities Fellowships *(Doctorate, Postdoctorate/ Fellowship)* 1179

Japan-United States Art Fellowships *(Postdoctorate, Professional Development/Fellowship)* 1180

Peter Krueger Summer Internships *(Graduate, Undergraduate/ Internship)* 5384

Marine Corps Historical Center College Internships *(Undergraduate/Internship)* 3556

Andrew W. Mellon Fellowships in Art History *(Doctorate, Postdoctorate/Fellowship)* 3658

National Museum of American Art Summer Internships *(Graduate, Undergraduate/Internship)* 5388

Frances M. Schwartz Fellowships *(Graduate/Fellowship)* 741

Smithsonian Institution Graduate Fellowships *(Graduate/ Fellowship)* 5376

Smithsonian Institution Postdoctoral Fellowships *(Postdoctorate/Fellowship)* 5377

Smithsonian Institution Predoctoral Fellowships *(Doctorate/ Fellowship)* 5378

U.S. Marine Corps Historical Center College Internships *(Graduate, Undergraduate/Internship)* 5945

## Music

American Orff Schulwerk Association Research Grants *(Professional Development/Grant)* 752

Gladys C. Anderson Scholarship *(Undergraduate/ Scholarship)* 478

AOSA Tap Fund *(Postgraduate/Scholarship)* 753

Armenian Allied Arts Association Scholarship *(Undergraduate/ Award)* 1104

Artists Fellowships and Residencies *(Professional Development/Fellowship)* 3766

Arts Recognition and Talent Search (ARTS) *(Undergraduate/ Award)* 4158

Associated Board of the Royal Schools of Music International Scholarships (Postgraduate, Undergraduate/Scholarship) 1191

Associated Male Choruses of America Scholarship (Undergraduate/Scholarship) 1195

Austrian Federal Ministry for Science and Research Grants (Professional Development/Grant) 1341

Banff Centre for the Arts Scholarships (Postgraduate, Professional Development/Scholarship) 1370

Frank Huntington Beebe Awards (Professional Development/Grant) 1391

Leslie Bell Scholarship for Choral Conducting (Professional Development/Scholarship) 4777

Nadia and Lili Boulanger Scholarship (Professional Development/Scholarship) 2547

CFGP Radio Station Scholarships (Undergraduate/Scholarship) 8

Chautauqua Institution Scholarship (Graduate, High School, Undergraduate/Scholarship) 1842

Chigiana Summer Course Scholarships (Graduate, Professional Development/Scholarship) 1935

Van Cliburn International Piano Competition (Professional Development/Prize) 1972

Emily Harrington Crane Scholarship (Undergraduate/Scholarship) 1859

Curtis Institute of Music Scholarships (Other/Scholarship) 2144

Dance Screen Competition Awards (Professional Development/Award) 3166

Eben Demarest Fund (Professional Development/Grant) 2227

Fellowship of United Methodists in Worship, Music and Other Arts Scholarship (Graduate, Undergraduate/Scholarship) 2439

Folger Library Long-Term Fellowships (Postdoctorate/Fellowship) 2541

Folger Library Short-Term Fellowships (Postdoctorate/Fellowship) 2542

Sergio Franchi Music Scholarship in Voice Performance (Graduate, Undergraduate/Scholarship) 4225

Garikian University Scholarship Fund (Undergraduate/Scholarship) 1119

GFWC of MA Music Scholarships (High School, Undergraduate/Scholarship) 2640

R.L. Gillette Scholarship (Undergraduate/Scholarship) 482

Hungarian Arts Club Scholarships (Undergraduate/Scholarship) 2935

International Competition Prizes (Professional Development/Prize) 4476

JCC of Metropolitan New Jersey Patrons Award and Florence Ben-Asher Memorial Award (Professional Development/Award) 3259

Kate Neal Kinley Memorial Fellowshsip (Graduate/Fellowship) 5998

Lois T. Larson Scholarship (Undergraduate/Scholarship) 1877

The Little Emo Awards (Professional Development/Award) 3492

Marine Corps Historical Center College Internships (Undergraduate/Internship) 3556

Elizabeth Warner Marvin Music Scholarship (Undergraduate/Scholarship) 1880

Joseph Mason Memorial Scholarship (Undergraduate/Scholarship) 1881

Theodore Mazza Scholarship (Undergraduate/Scholarship) 5769

Glenn Miller Birthplace Society Instrumental Scholarships (High School, Undergraduate/Scholarship) 3706

Ministry of the Flemish Community Fellowships (Postdoctorate, Undergraduate/Fellowship) 3710

Minnesota Artist Assistance Fellowships (Professional Development/Fellowship) 3714

Thelonious Monk International Jazz Instrumental Competition (Professional Development/Scholarship) 3764

Mozart Club Music Scholarship (Undergraduate/Scholarship) 1890

Ruth E. Munson Music Scholarship (Undergraduate/Scholarship) 1891

Pillsbury Music Scholarship (Undergraduate/Scholarship) 2410

National Endowment for the Arts - National Heritage Fellowships (Professional Development/Fellowship) 3979

National Endowment for the Humanities Fellowships (Postdoctorate/Fellowship) 2543

National Symphony Young Soloists' Competition, College Division (Professional Development/Prize, Scholarship) 4419

National Symphony Young Soloists' Competition, High School Division (High School/Prize) 4420

New Hampshire Individual Artist Fellowships (Other/Fellowship) 4535

New Jersey State Opera Annual Vocal Competition (Professional Development/Award) 4547

North Carolina Arts Council Artist Fellowships (Professional Development/Fellowship) 4668

OPERA America Fellowship Program (Postgraduate/Fellowship) 4783

Opera Screen Competition Awards (Professional Development/Award) 3167

Pavarotti Scholarship (Graduate, Undergraduate/Scholarship) 4252

Minna Kaufmann Ruud Scholarship (Undergraduate/Scholarship) 1840

Nina Santavicca Scholarship (Undergraduate/Scholarship) 4259

Shields-Gillespie Scholarships (Postgraduate, Professional Development/Scholarship) 755

Sinfonia Foundation Research Assistance Grant (Professional Development/Grant) 5353

Kathryn G. Siphers Scholarships (Undergraduate/Scholarship) 6218

TELACU Arts Award (Undergraduate/Scholarship) 5689

Heinz Unger Award for Conducting (Professional Development/Award) 4779

The University of Maryland International Music Competitions (Professional Development/Prize) 4331

Virginia Volkwein Memorial Scholarships (Undergraduate/Scholarship) 6219

Muddy Waters Scholarship (Undergraduate/Scholarship) 1448

Stefan and Wanda Wilk Prizes for Research in Polish Music (All/Prize) 4973

Harriet Hale Woolley Scholarships (Graduate/Scholarship) 2545

Harry and Sarah Zelzer Fellowship and Prize (Professional Development/Fellowship, Prize) 4613

## Music, Bass

Fine Arts Grants (Professional Development/Grant) 194

Walter W. Naumburg Awards (Other/Award) 4477

## Music, Cello

Fine Arts Grants (Professional Development/Grant) 194

## Music, Classical

Gladys C. Anderson Scholarship (Undergraduate/Scholarship) 478

## Music composition

Albee Foundation Residencies (Professional Development/Other) 141

ASCAP Foundation Grants to Young Composers (Professional Development/Grant) 912

ASCAP Foundation Morton Gould Awards to Young Composers (Professional Development/Grant) 913

BMI Student Composer Awards (Professional Development/Award) 1450

Bush Artist Fellowships (Professional Development/Fellowship) 1539

Pete Carpenter Film Composing Internship (Professional Development/Internship) 1451

Chigiana Summer Course Scholarships (Graduate, Professional Development/Scholarship) 1935

## Music composition (continued)

Cintas Fellowships (*Professional Development/ Fellowship*) 1163

Composer's Composition Prizes (*Professional Development/ Prize*) 244

Cummington Community of the Arts Residencies (*Professional Development/Fellowship*) 2142

Delius Composition Contest (*Other/Award*) 2213

Delius Composition Contest for High School Composers (*High School/Award*) 2214

Delta Omicron International Triennial Composition Competition (*Other/Award*) 2221

Dramatists Guild Fund Scholarships (*Professional Development/Grant, Loan*) 2280

Harvey Gaul Composition Contest (*Professional Development/ Award*) 4953

Inter-American Music Awards (*Professional Development/ Award*) 5327

Margaret Fairbank Jory Copying Assistance Program (*Professional Development/Award*) 718

The Little Emo Awards (*Professional Development/ Award*) 3492

MacDowell Colony Residencies (*Other, Professional Development/Fellowship*) 3524

Glenn Miller Birthplace Society Instrumental Scholarships (*High School, Undergraduate/Scholarship*) 3706

MISSIM/ASCAP Composers Competition (*Professional Development/Award*) 914

Netz Hilai Visiting Artists Fellowships (*Professional Development/Fellowship*) 4515

New York Foundation for the Arts Artists' Fellowships (*Other/ Fellowship*) 4570

Jean Pratt Scholarship (*High School/Scholarship*) 1453

Resident Fellowships (*Professional Development/ Fellowship*) 2786

Scholarships for Mature Women (*Professional Development/ Scholarship*) 4282

World of Expression Scholarship Program (*High School, Undergraduate/Award*) 1420

Yaddo Residencies (*Professional Development/Other*) 6274

## Music, Jazz

Arts Recognition and Talent Search (ARTS) (*Undergraduate/ Award*) 4158

Errol Garner Memorial Foundation Scholarship Awards (*All/ Award*) 2626

Glenn Miller Birthplace Society Instrumental Scholarships (*High School, Undergraduate/Scholarship*) 3706

Thelonious Monk International Jazz Instrumental Competition (*Professional Development/Scholarship*) 3764

## Music, Orchestral

Music Assistance Fund Orchestral Fellowships (*Professional Development/Fellowship*) 1005

National Orchestral Institute Scholarships (*Graduate, Postgraduate, Undergraduate/Scholarship*) 4330

Lionel Newman Conducting Fellowship (*Professional Development/Fellowship*) 1452

Orchestra Management Fellowships (*Professional Development/Fellowship*) 1006

OSM Competition (*Professional Development/Prize*) 3778

Sorantin Young Artist Award (*Professional Development/ Award*) 5226

Heinz Unger Award for Conducting (*Professional Development/Award*) 4779

Elizabeth Harper Vaughn Concerto Competition Prizes (*Professional Development/Prize*) 3377

## Music, Piano

Carmel Music Society Competition (*Professional Development/ Prize*) 1733

Cleveland International Piano Competition (*Professional Development/Prize*) 1968

Van Cliburn International Piano Competition (*Professional Development/Prize*) 1972

Errol Garner Memorial Foundation Scholarship Awards (*All/ Award*) 2626

GFWC of MA Music Scholarships (*High School, Undergraduate/Scholarship*) 2640

International Music Contest of Rio de Janeiro Prizes (*Professional Development/Prize*) 1474

Kosciuszko Foundation Chopin Piano Competition/ Scholarships (*Professional Development/Scholarship*) 3398

Glenn Miller Birthplace Society Instrumental Scholarships (*High School, Undergraduate/Scholarship*) 3706

Montreal International Music Prizes (*Undergraduate/ Prize*) 3773

National Symphony Young Soloists' Competition, College Division (*Professional Development/Prize, Scholarship*) 4419

Walter W. Naumburg Awards (*Other/Award*) 4477

OSM Competition (*Professional Development/Prize*) 3778

Piano Teaching Fellowship (*Professional Development/ Fellowship*) 4556

Nina Santavicca Scholarship (*Undergraduate/ Scholarship*) 4259

Sorantin Young Artist Award (*Professional Development/ Award*) 5226

The University of Maryland International Music Competitions (*Professional Development/Prize*) 4331

Elizabeth Harper Vaughn Concerto Competition Prizes (*Professional Development/Prize*) 3377

## Music therapy

AMBUCS Scholars (*Graduate, Undergraduate/ Scholarship*) 3854

American Orff Schulwerk Association Research Grants (*Professional Development/Grant*) 752

GFWC of MA Music Scholarships (*High School, Undergraduate/Scholarship*) 2640

NSDAR Occupational Therapy Scholarship (*Graduate, Undergraduate/Scholarship*) 4403

Scholarships for Therapists (*Professional Development/ Scholarship*) 3855

## Music, Viola

Fine Arts Grants (*Professional Development/Grant*) 194

## Music, Violin

Fine Arts Grants (*Professional Development/Grant*) 194

Vaclav Huml International Violin Competition Prizes (*Professional Development/Prize*) 2136

Glenn Miller Birthplace Society Instrumental Scholarships (*High School, Undergraduate/Scholarship*) 3706

Montreal International Music Prizes (*Undergraduate/ Prize*) 3773

National Symphony Young Soloists' Competition, College Division (*Professional Development/Prize, Scholarship*) 4419

Walter W. Naumburg Awards (*Other/Award*) 4477

## Music, Vocal

Academy of Vocal Arts Scholarships (*Professional Development/Scholarship*) 28

Associated Male Choruses of America Scholarship (*Undergraduate/Scholarship*) 1195

Ralph Brewster Vocal Scholarship/Jack Pullen Memorial Scholarship (*High School, Undergraduate/Scholarship*) 3705

Carmel Music Society Competition (*Professional Development/ Prize*) 1733

Chigiana Summer Course Scholarships (*Graduate, Professional Development/Scholarship*) 1935

Dorchester Woman's Club Scholarships (*High School, Undergraduate/Scholarship*) 2635

Hungarian Arts Club Scholarships (*Undergraduate/ Scholarship*) 2935

International Competition Prizes (*Professional Development/ Prize*) 4476

International Music Contest of Rio de Janeiro Prizes (*Professional Development/Prize*) 1474

Edward Johnson Music Competition (*Professional Development/Prize*) 3287

Lotte Lehmann Fellowship in Voice/Vocal Accompanying; Gabor Rejto Fellowship in Cello *(Professional Development/ Fellowship)* 3808

Montreal International Music Prizes *(Undergraduate/ Prize)* 3773

National Alliance for Excellence Honored Scholars Awards *(Graduate, Undergraduate/Scholarship)* 3841

National Symphony Young Soloists' Competition, College Division *(Professional Development/Prize, Scholarship)* 4419

NATS Artist Awards *(Postgraduate, Professional Development/ Award)* 3902

Walter W. Naumburg Awards *(Other/Award)* 4477

OSM Competition *(Professional Development/Prize)* 3778

Sorantin Young Artist Award *(Professional Development/ Award)* 5226

The University of Maryland International Music Competitions *(Professional Development/Prize)* 4331

## Musicology

Sinfonia Foundation Research Assistance Grant *(Professional Development/Grant)* 5353

## Myasthenia Gravis

Dr. Henry R. Viets Medical Student Research Fellowships *(Doctorate, Graduate/Fellowship)* 3812

## National security

R. B. Byers Postdoctoral Fellowship Program *(Postdoctorate/ Fellowship)* 1266

Department of National Defense Security and Defense Forum MA and Ph.D Scholarships *(Doctorate, Graduate/ Scholarship)* 1273

Fellowships in National Security *(Graduate, Postdoctorate/ Fellowship)* 2812

William C. Foster Fellows Visiting Scholars Competition *(Postdoctorate, Professional Development/Fellowship)* 5818

Herman Kahn Fellowships *(Doctorate/Fellowship)* 2910

U.S. Navy-ASEE Summer Faculty Research Program *(Professional Development/Fellowship)* 925

## Native American studies

Stella Blum Research Grant *(Graduate, Undergraduate/ Grant)* 2089

Brown University, The Future of Gender *(Postdoctorate/ Fellowship)* 5990

Institute of American Cultures Graduate and Predoctoral Fellowships *(Doctorate/Fellowship)* 3012

Institute of American Cultures Postdoctoral and Visiting Scholars Fellowships *(Postdoctorate/Fellowship)* 3013

Jacobs Research Fund Grants *(Professional Development/ Grant)* 3236

D'Arcy McNickle Center for the History of the American Indian Fellowships *(Postgraduate/Fellowship)* 4606

NNAC Gifted/Talented Artist Sponsorships *(Professional Development/Other)* 4324

Phillips Grants for North American Indian Research *(Doctorate, Postdoctorate/Grant)* 769

## Natural history

Field Museum of Natural History Undergraduate Internships *(Undergraduate/Internship)* 2445

Joseph L. Fisher Dissertation Awards *(Doctorate/ Fellowship)* 5111

Barry M. Goldwater Scholarship *(Undergraduate/ Scholarship)* 2715

## Natural resources

Ardell Bjugstad Memorial Scholarships *(Undergraduate/ Scholarship)* 5551

Canadian Society of Petroleum Geologists Graduate Scholarships *(Graduate/Scholarship)* 1704

Federal Cartridge Company Scholarship *(Undergraduate/ Scholarship)* 4074

Donald W. Fogarty International Student Paper Competition *(Graduate, Undergraduate/Award)* 1052

Rocky Mountain Mineral Law Foundation Scholarship Program Including the Joe Rudd Scholarship *(Graduate/ Scholarship)* 5159

Washington Pulp & Paper Foundation Scholarships *(Undergraduate/Scholarship)* 6097

## Natural sciences

Beinecke Library Visiting Fellowships *(Postdoctorate/ Fellowship)* 1393

Churchill Scholarships *(Postgraduate/Scholarship)* 1954

Eastburn Fellowships *(Postdoctorate/Fellowship)* 2314

E. B. Eastburn Fellowships *(Postdoctorate/Fellowship)* 2788

Fossil Energy Faculty Research Participation *(Professional Development/Fellowship)* 5876

Government of Canada Awards *(Doctorate, Graduate, Postdoctorate/Award)* 3145

Institute for Advanced Study Postdoctoral Research Fellowships *(Postdoctorate/Fellowship)* 3009

Jessup and McHenry Awards *(Doctorate, Postdoctorate/ Award)* 26

Killam Research Fellowships *(Postdoctorate/Fellowship)* 3375

Mass Media Science and Engineering Fellowships *(Graduate/ Fellowship)* 268

Allen H. Meyers Scholarship *(Undergraduate/ Scholarship)* 3677

National Research Council of Canada Research Associateships *(Postdoctorate/Other)* 4354

NATO Senior Guest Fellowships *(Professional Development/ Fellowship)* 4656

NSERC Research Scholarships, Fellowships, and Grants *(Graduate, Postdoctorate, Postgraduate, Professional Development/Fellowship, Grant, Scholarship)* 4474

NSF-DAAD Grants for the Natural, Engineering and Social Sciences *(Other/Grant)* 2689

Howard Brown Rickard Scholarship *(Undergraduate/ Scholarship)* 4007

Sir Arthur Sims Scholarships *(Postgraduate/Scholarship)* 5196

U.S. Department of Energy Faculty Research Participation Fellowship *(Professional Development/Fellowship)* 5932

## Near Eastern studies

AIMS Small Grants *(Doctorate, Postdoctorate/Grant)* 590

American Research Center in Egypt Research Fellowships for Study in Egypt *(Doctorate, Postdoctorate/Fellowship)* 843

Ancient India and Iran Trust Travel and Research Grants *(Doctorate, Graduate, Postdoctorate/Grant)* 1035

Annual Professorship in Jerusalem *(Postdoctorate/ Fellowship)* 864

ARIT Fellowships *(Doctorate, Postdoctorate/Fellowship)* 846

George A. Barton Fellowship *(Doctorate, Postdoctorate/ Fellowship)* 865

Center for Judaic Studies Postdoctoral Fellowships *(Postdoctorate/Fellowship)* 1799

Council of American Overseas Research Centers Fellowships *(Postdoctorate/Fellowship)* 866

Dorot Research Fellowship *(Postdoctorate/Fellowship)* 867

Grants-in-Aid of Publication *(Postdoctorate/Grant)* 4879

Charles U. and Janet C. Harris Fellowship *(Doctorate, Postdoctorate/Fellowship)* 871

Institute of Holy Land Studies Scholarships *(Graduate/ Scholarship)* 3047

Institute of Turkish Studies Dissertation Writing Grants *(Doctorate/Grant)* 3081

Islamic Studies Fellowship *(Doctorate/Fellowship)* 872

Kress Fellowship in the Art and Archaeology of Jordan *(Doctorate/Fellowship)* 873

Near and Middle East Research and Training Program Pre-Doctoral Fellowships *(Doctorate/Fellowship)* 880

Near and Middle East Research and Training Program Senior Research Grants *(Postdoctorate/Grant)* 881

NEH Fellowships for Research in Turkey *(Postdoctorate/ Fellowship)* 847

SSRC Near and Middle East Advanced Research Fellowships *(Postdoctorate/Fellowship)* 5411

## Near Eastern studies (continued)

SSRC Near and Middle East Dissertation Research Fellowships *(Doctorate/Fellowship)* 5412

Summer Travel/Research in Turkey Grants *(Postdoctorate/ Grant)* 3082

United States Information Agency (USIA) Fellowships *(Doctorate, Postdoctorate/Fellowship)* 884

USIA Fellowships, AIAR, Jerusalem *(Doctorate, Postdoctorate/ Fellowship)* 885

## Nephrology

Allied Health Doctoral Fellowships *(Doctorate, Professional Development/Fellowship)* 3368

Allied Health Research Grants *(Professional Development/ Grant)* 3369

Allied Health Scholarships *(Graduate, Postgraduate/ Scholarship)* 3370

American Kidney Fund Clinical Scientist in Nephrology *(Postdoctorate/Fellowship)* 606

Biomedical Fellowships *(Postdoctorate/Fellowship)* 3371

Biomedical Research Grant *(Postdoctorate/Grant)* 3372

Biomedical Scholarship *(Doctorate, Postdoctorate/ Scholarship)* 3373

National Kidney Foundation Research Fellowships *(Postdoctorate/Fellowship)* 4279

## Neuroscience

Behavioral Sciences Student Fellowship *(Professional Development/Fellowship)* 2397

Bunting Institute Science Scholars Fellowships and Biomedical Research Fellowships *(Postdoctorate/Fellowship)* 1529

Capranica Foundation Award in Neuroethology *(Doctorate, Postdoctorate/Award)* 1723

Jeanne Timmins Costello Fellowship *(Postdoctorate/ Fellowship)* 3775

del Duca Foundation Maintenance and Travel Grants *(Professional Development/Grant)* 2284

Epilepsy Foundation of America Research Grants *(Postdoctorate/Grant)* 2399

Epilepsy Foundation of America Research Training Fellowships *(Doctorate/Fellowship)* 2400

Fellowships in Spinal Cord Injury Research *(Postdoctorate/ Fellowship)* 4830

Fellowships in Theoretical Neurobiology *(Postdoctorate/ Fellowship)* 4517

FIC International Neuroscience Fellowships *(Postdoctorate/ Fellowship)* 2527

Fyssen Foundation Research Grants *(Doctorate, Postgraduate/ Grant)* 2610

Grass Fellowships in Neurophysiology *(Doctorate, Postdoctorate/Fellowship)* 2742

Health Sciences Student Fellowships *(All/Fellowship)* 2401

Howard Hughes Medical Institute Predoctoral Fellowships in Biological Sciences *(Postdoctorate/Fellowship)* 4358

IBRO/Unesco Research Fellowships *(Postdoctorate/ Fellowship)* 3125

MDA Research Grants; MDA Research Development Grants; MDA Genetics Research Grants *(Professional Development/ Grant)* 3800

Minority Fellowships in Neuroscience *(Doctorate/ Fellowship)* 806

Robert S. Morison Fellowships *(Professional Development/ Fellowship)* 2743

Postdoctoral Research Fellowships for Physicians *(Postdoctorate/Fellowship)* 2926

Predoctoral Fellowships in Biological Sciences *(Doctorate/ Fellowship)* 2927

Preston Robb Fellowship *(Postdoctorate/Fellowship)* 3776

## Nuclear science

ANS Environmental Sciences Division Scholarship *(Undergraduate/Scholarship)* 720

ANS Fuel Cycle and Waste Management Scholarship *(Undergraduate/Scholarship)* 721

ANS Graduate Scholarships *(Graduate/Scholarship)* 722

ANS Nuclear Operations Division Scholarship *(Undergraduate/ Scholarship)* 723

ANS Power Division Scholarship *(Undergraduate/ Scholarship)* 724

ANS Undergraduate Scholarships *(Undergraduate/ Scholarship)* 725

Robert A. Dannels Scholarships *(Graduate/Scholarship)* 726

Verne R. Dapp Scholarship *(Graduate/Scholarship)* 727

Delayed Education for Women Scholarship *(Undergraduate/ Scholarship)* 728

Joseph R. Dietrich Scholarships *(Undergraduate/ Scholarship)* 729

Paul A. Greebler Scholarship *(Graduate/Scholarship)* 730

Historically Black Colleges and Universities Nuclear Energy Faculty Research Participation Program *(Professional Development/Fellowship)* 5893

John R. Lamarsh Scholarship *(Undergraduate/ Scholarship)* 731

John and Muriel Landis Scholarships *(Graduate, Undergraduate/Scholarship)* 732

NAS/NRC Radioactive Waste Management Program Grants *(Postdoctorate/Grant)* 3833

James F. Schumar Scholarship *(Graduate/Scholarship)* 733

James R. Vogt Scholarship *(Graduate, Undergraduate/ Scholarship)* 734

## Numismatics

American Numismatic Society Graduate Fellowships *(Doctorate/Fellowship)* 736

American Numismatic Society Graduate Seminar *(Graduate/ Other)* 737

American Numismatic Society Grants-in-Aid *(Graduate, Postgraduate/Grant)* 738

ANS Fellowship in Roman Studies *(Graduate/Fellowship)* 739

Donald Groves Fellowship *(Professional Development/ Fellowship)* 740

Frances M. Schwartz Fellowships *(Graduate/Fellowship)* 741

## Nursing

AACN Clinical Practice Grant *(Professional Development/ Grant)* 277

AACN Educational Advancement Scholarships for Graduates *(Doctorate, Graduate/Scholarship)* 278

AACN Educational Advancement Scholarships for Undergraduates *(Undergraduate/Scholarship)* 279

AACN-Sigma Theta Tau Critical Care Grant *(Professional Development/Grant)* 280

Air Force ROTC Scholarships *(Undergraduate/ Scholarship)* 5816

Airline Pilots Association Scholarship *(Undergraduate/ Scholarship)* 96

Alabama Nursing Scholarship *(Undergraduate/Loan, Scholarship)* 105

Allied Health Student Loans *(Undergraduate/Loan)* 4870

American Legion Auxiliary Nurses, Physical Therapists and Respiratory Therapists Scholarship *(Undergraduate/ Scholarship)* 626

American Legion Auxiliary Past Presidents' Parley Nurses Scholarships *(Undergraduate/Scholarship)* 613

AORN Scholarships *(Doctorate, Graduate/Scholarship)* 1252

The Albert Baker Fund *(Graduate, Undergraduate/Loan)* 1362

Behavioral Sciences Research Training Fellowship *(Postdoctorate/Fellowship)* 2396

Behavioral Sciences Student Fellowship *(Professional Development/Fellowship)* 2397

Fay L. Bower Nursing Student Scholarship *(Graduate, Undergraduate/Scholarship)* 1563

Lillian Sholtis Brunner Summer Fellowship *(Doctorate, Postdoctorate/Fellowship)* 1807

Canadian Nurses Foundation Small Research Grants *(Graduate/Grant)* 1686

Canadian Nurses Foundation Study Awards *(Doctorate, Graduate/Other)* 1687

Joan C. Chiappetta Scholarship for a Career In Practical Nursing *(Undergraduate/Scholarship)* 1856

Madeline Pickett Halbert Cogswell Nursing Scholarships
(Undergraduate/Scholarship) 4395

Connecticut League for Nursing Scholarships (Graduate,
Undergraduate/Scholarship) 2052

Cuyahoga County Medical Foundation Scholarship (Graduate/
Scholarship) 2146

Data-Driven Clinical Practice Grant (Professional Development/
Grant) 281

James D. Durante Nurse Scholarship Program
(Undergraduate/Scholarship) 4169

J. Hugh & Earle W. Fellows Memorial Fund Loans
(Undergraduate/Loan) 2437

Franks Foundation Loan (Graduate, Undergraduate/
Loan) 5832

Georgia Student Finance Commission Service-Cancellable
Stafford Loan (Graduate, Undergraduate/Loan) 2666

Georgia Student Finance Commission State-Sponsored Loan
(Graduate, Undergraduate/Loan) 2669

Good Samaritan Foundation Scholarship for Nursing
(Undergraduate/Scholarship) 2717

William F. Grupe Foundation Scholarships (Doctorate,
Graduate/Scholarship) 2756

Caroline Holt Nursing Scholarships (Undergraduate/
Scholarship) 4399

HP/AACN Critical-Care Nursing Research Grants (Doctorate,
Graduate/Grant) 2868

HRSA-BHP Nursing Student Loan (Other, Undergraduate/
Loan) 5970

HRSA-BHP Professional Nurse Traineeship (Doctorate,
Graduate/Other) 5971

HRSA-BHP Scholarships for Disadvantaged Students
(Doctorate, Graduate, Undergraduate/Scholarship) 5972

Illinois AMVETS Sad Sacks Nursing Scholarships
(Undergraduate/Scholarship) 2956

Independent Order of Odd Fellows Nurses Training
Scholarships (Undergraduate/Scholarship) 2991

International Order of the King's Daughters and Sons Health
Careers Scholarships (Graduate, Postgraduate,
Undergraduate/Scholarship) 3169

Harvey and Bernice Jones Scholarships (Undergraduate/
Scholarship) 3295

KCI-AACN Critical Care Research Grant (Professional
Development/Grant) 282

Dr. Dorothy J. Kergin Research Grant in Primary Health Care
(Graduate/Grant) 1688

Sharon Kunkel Nursing Scholarship (Undergraduate/
Scholarship) 1876

Louie LeFlore/Grant Foreman Scholarship (Undergraduate/
Scholarship) 5306

Minnie L. Maffett Scholarship (Doctorate, Graduate,
Undergraduate/Scholarship) 4466

MARILN Scholarship (Undergraduate/Scholarship) 3603

Mary Marshall Nurse Practitioner/Nurse Midwife Scholarship
Program (Undergraduate/Scholarship) 6048

Mary Marshall Nursing Scholarship for Student Nurses
Practical Nursing Program (Undergraduate/
Scholarship) 6049

Mary Marshall Nursing Scholarship for Student Nurses
Registered Nurse Program (Undergraduate/
Scholarship) 6050

Maryland House of Delegates Scholarship (Graduate,
Professional Development, Undergraduate/
Scholarship) 3575

Maryland Professional Scholarship (Graduate, Undergraduate/
Scholarship) 3578

Maryland Senatorial Scholarship (Graduate, Undergraduate/
Scholarship) 3580

Maryland State Nursing Scholarships (Graduate,
Undergraduate/Scholarship) 3581

Marguerite Mc Alpin Memorial Scholarships (Graduate,
Undergraduate/Scholarship) 640

McFarland Charitable Foundation Registered Nursing
Scholarship (Undergraduate/Scholarship loan) 3624

McFarland Charitable Foundation Scholarship (Undergraduate/
Scholarship) 2819

Charlotte McGuire Scholarships (Graduate, Undergraduate/
Scholarship) 543

Mead Johnson Nutritional Perinatal Research Grants Program
(Doctorate, Postdoctorate, Postgraduate/Grant) 5337

Michigan League for Nursing Student Achievement
Scholarship Awards (Undergraduate/Scholarship) 3690

Mississippi Nursing Education BSN Program (Undergraduate/
Scholarship loan) 3734

Mississippi Nursing Education DSN Program (Doctorate/
Scholarship loan) 3735

Mississippi Nursing Education MSN Program (Graduate/
Scholarship loan) 3736

Mississippi Nursing Education RN to BSN Program
(Undergraduate/Scholarship loan) 3737

National Association of Hispanic Nurses National Scholarship
Award (Graduate, Undergraduate/Scholarship) 3879

The National Society of the Colonial Dames of America
American Indian Nurse Scholarship Awards (Undergraduate/
Scholarship) 4390

NEF Scholarships (Doctorate, Graduate/Scholarship) 4703

Nellcor Puritan Bennett Inc. AACN Mentorship Grant
(Professional Development/Grant) 283

Margarete E. Nelson Scholarship (Undergraduate/
Scholarship) 1892

Ida L., Mary L., and Ervin R. NePage Foundation
(Undergraduate/Scholarship) 4513

New York State Professional Opportunity Scholarships
(Doctorate, Graduate, Undergraduate/Scholarship) 4592

New York State Regents Professional Opportunity
Scholarships (Doctorate, Graduate, Undergraduate/
Scholarship) 4577

NINR Individual National Research Service Awards
Postdoctoral Fellowship (Postdoctorate/Fellowship) 4201

NINR Individual National Research Service Awards Predoctoral
Fellowship (Doctorate/Fellowship) 4202

NINR Individual National Research Service Awards Senior
Fellowship (Postdoctorate/Fellowship) 4203

Nurse Loan Repayment Program (Postgraduate/Other) 3754

Nursing Education Loan Repayment (Graduate,
Undergraduate/Loan) 5938

Nursing Research Fellowship (Other/Fellowship) 3811

Nursing Scholarship Program (Graduate, Undergraduate/
Scholarship loan) 2512

Oncology Nursing Foundation/Amgen, Inc. Research Grant
(Professional Development/Grant) 4758

Oncology Nursing Foundation Bachelors Scholarship
(Undergraduate/Scholarship) 4759

Oncology Nursing Foundation/Bristol- Myers Oncology
Chapter Research Grant (Professional Development/
Grant) 4760

Oncology Nursing Foundation/Bristol- Myers Oncology Division
Community Health Research Grant (Professional
Development/Grant) 4761

Oncology Nursing Foundation/Bristol- Myers Oncology Division
Research Grant (Professional Development/Grant) 4762

Oncology Nursing Foundation/Cetus Oncology Grants for
Research Involving Biotherapy or Immunotherapy
(Professional Development/Grant) 4763

Oncology Nursing Foundation Doctoral Scholarship (Doctorate/
Scholarship) 4764

Oncology Nursing Foundation/Glaxo Research Grants
(Professional Development/Grant) 4765

Oncology Nursing Foundation Masters Scholarship (Graduate/
Scholarship) 4766

Oncology Nursing Foundation/Oncology Nursing Certification
Corporation Nursing Education Research Grants
(Professional Development/Grant) 4767

Oncology Nursing Foundation/Oncology Nursing Society
Research Grant (Professional Development/Grant) 4768

Oncology Nursing Foundation/Ortho Biotech Research Grant
(Professional Development/Grant) 4769

Oncology Nursing Foundation/Purdue Frederick Research
Grant (Professional Development/Grant) 4770

## Nursing (continued)

Oncology Nursing Foundation/Rhone Poulenc Rorer New Investigator Research Grants *(Doctorate, Graduate/Grant)* 4771

Oncology Nursing Foundation/Sigma Theta Tau International and Oncology Nursing Society Research Grant *(Professional Development/Grant)* 4772

Oncology Nursing Society/SmithKline Beecham Research Grant *(Professional Development/Grant)* 4773

Past Presidents Parley Nursing Scholarship *(Undergraduate/Scholarship)* 635

The Primary Care Resource Initiative for Missouri (PRIMO) *(Doctorate, Graduate, Undergraduate/Loan)* 3755

PRN Grants *(Graduate, Undergraduate/Scholarship)* 202

The Professional and Practical Nursing Student Loan Program *(Graduate, Undergraduate/Loan)* 3756

Lucretia H. Richter Nursing Scholarship *(Undergraduate/Scholarship)* 6157

San Joaquin County Medical Society Scholarship Loans *(Graduate/Loan)* 5241

SBNA Scholarship *(Undergraduate/Scholarship)* 5209

Sigma Theta Tau International/American Association of Diabetes Educators Grant *(Professional Development/Grant)* 5338

Sigma Theta Tau International/American Nephrology Nurses' Association Grant *(Professional Development/Grant)* 5339

Sigma Theta Tau International/American Nurses' Foundation Grant *(Professional Development/Grant)* 5340

Sigma Theta Tau International/Emergency Nursing Foundation Grant *(Professional Development/Grant)* 5341

Sigma Theta Tau International/Glaxo Wellcome Prescriptive Practice Grant *(Professional Development/Grant)* 5343

Sigma Theta Tau International Small Research Grant *(Postgraduate/Grant)* 5344

Bertha B. Singer Nurses Scholarship *(Graduate, Undergraduate/Scholarship)* 5835

STTI Scholarships *(Graduate/Scholarship)* 5345

Virginia Elizabeth and Alma Vane Taylor Fund *(Undergraduate/Loan)* 6197

Frances Tompkins Scholarships *(Undergraduate/Scholarship)* 2573

USA National Educational Grants *(Undergraduate/Grant)* 3273

Archie Vinitsky ET Scholarship *(Professional Development/Scholarship)* 5807

M. K. Wang Visiting Professorships *(Other/Other)* 360

WHO Fellowships and Research Training Grants *(Graduate, Other, Postdoctorate/Fellowship)* 6261

Wisconsin League for Nursing Scholarships *(Undergraduate/Scholarship)* 6212

Young Canadian Researchers Awards *(Doctorate, Graduate/Award)* 3151

## Nursing administration

Canadian Nurses Foundation Small Research Grants *(Graduate/Grant)* 1686

HRSA-BHP Professional Nurse Traineeship *(Doctorate, Graduate/Other)* 5971

Dr. Dorothy J. Kergin Research Grant in Primary Health Care *(Graduate/Grant)* 1688

## Nursing, Cardiovascular and cerebrovascular

HSFC Nursing Research Fellowships *(Doctorate, Graduate/Fellowship)* 2842

## Nursing, Oncological

Maurice Legault Awards *(Postgraduate/Award, Fellowship)* 1613

## Nursing, Pulmonary

Eight and Forty Nurses Scholarships *(Graduate/Scholarship)* 630

Nursing Research Training Award (Cancelled) *(Doctorate/Award)* 681

## Nutrition

AIN Predoctoral Fellowships *(Graduate/Fellowship)* 594

Astra/Merck Fellowship/Faculty Transition Award *(Postdoctorate/Award)* 450

Malcolm Bird Commemorative Award *(Professional Development/Award)* 1331

Borden Award *(Professional Development/Award)* 290

Competitive Grants-in-Aid for Original Research *(Postdoctorate/Grant)* 4286

Dairy Management Inc. Nutrition Research Projects *(Other/Other)* 2168

Mildred B. Davis Memorial Fellowship *(Graduate/Fellowship)* 294

Margaret Drew Alpha Fellowship *(Graduate/Fellowship)* 4917

Georgia Student Finance Commission Service-Cancellable Stafford Loan *(Graduate, Undergraduate/Loan)* 2666

Georgia Student Finance Commission State-Sponsored Loan *(Graduate, Undergraduate/Loan)* 2669

GFWC of MA Memorial Education Fellowships *(Graduate/Fellowship)* 2639

Graduate Awards in Dietetics *(Graduate/Award)* 2249

Grant in Biotechnology *(Postdoctorate/Grant)* 4834

Margaret Jerome Sampson Scholarships *(Undergraduate/Scholarship)* 4922

National Dairy Shrine/Dairy Management Scholarships, Inc. *(Undergraduate/Scholarship)* 3968

National Restaurant Association Undergraduate Scholarships *(Undergraduate/Scholarship)* 4367

Parenteral Drug Association Foundation Research Grants *(Graduate/Grant)* 4835

Public Interest Internships *(Doctorate, Graduate, Undergraduate/Internship)* 1803

## Occupational therapy

Allied Health Student Loans *(Undergraduate/Loan)* 4870

AMBUCS Scholars *(Graduate, Undergraduate/Scholarship)* 3854

AOTF Dissertation Research Award for Occupational Therapists *(Doctorate/Grant)* 743

AOTF Research Grants *(Professional Development/Grant)* 744

Georgia Student Finance Commission Service-Cancellable Stafford Loan *(Graduate, Undergraduate/Loan)* 2666

Georgia Student Finance Commission State-Sponsored Loan *(Graduate, Undergraduate/Loan)* 2669

International Order of the King's Daughters and Sons Health Careers Scholarships *(Graduate, Postgraduate, Undergraduate/Scholarship)* 3169

Maryland Physical and Occupational Therapists and Assistants Scholarships *(Undergraduate/Scholarship)* 3577

Mississippi Health Care Professions Loan/Scholarship Program *(Undergraduate/Scholarship loan)* 3732

New York State Professional Opportunity Scholarships *(Doctorate, Graduate, Undergraduate/Scholarship)* 4592

New York State Regents Professional Opportunity Scholarships *(Doctorate, Graduate, Undergraduate/Scholarship)* 4577

Occupational Therapist and Physical Therapist Scholarship Loan Program *(Graduate/Scholarship loan)* 2513

Scholarships for Therapists *(Professional Development/Scholarship)* 3855

Western Interstate Commission for Higher Education Student Exchanges *(Doctorate, Graduate/Other)* 135

Arizona WICHE Professional Student Exchange Program *(Professional Development/Work Study)* 1089

## Ocean management

Research Fellowships in Marine Policy *(Postdoctorate/Fellowship)* 6248

Woods Hole Oceanographic Institution Summer Student Fellowships *(Undergraduate/Fellowship)* 6249

## Oceanography

AMS/Industry Government Graduate Fellowships *(Graduate/Fellowship)* 701

AMS/Industry Undergraduate Scholarship (Undergraduate/ Scholarship) 703

Bermuda Biological Station Visiting Graduate Internships (Graduate, Postgraduate/Internship) 1418

BNL Postdoctoral Research Associateships (Postdoctorate/ Other) 1504

Bunting Institute Science Scholars Fellowships and Biomedical Research Fellowships (Postdoctorate/Fellowship) 1529

Howard H. Hanks, Jr. Scholarship in Meteorology (Undergraduate/Scholarship) 705

JOI/USSAC Ocean Drilling Fellowships (Doctorate/ Fellowship) 3291

Paul H. Kutschenreuter Scholarship (Undergraduate/ Scholarship) 706

Minority Geoscience Scholarships (Graduate, Undergraduate/ Scholarship) 508

National Defense Science and Engineering Graduate Fellowship Program (Graduate/Fellowship) 5855

Howard T. Orville Scholarship in Meteorology (Undergraduate/ Scholarship) 708

Postdoctoral Fellowships in the Atmospheric Sciences (Postdoctorate/Fellowship) 3931

Postdoctoral Fellowships in Ocean Science and Engineering (Postdoctorate/Fellowship) 6247

Research Fellowships in Marine Policy (Postdoctorate/ Fellowship) 6248

Woods Hole Oceanographic Institution Summer Student Fellowships (Undergraduate/Fellowship) 6249

## Oncology

ACOG/Cytyc Corporation Research Award for the Prevention of Cervical Cancer (Postdoctorate/Grant) 377

ACOG/Zeneca Pharmaceuticals Research Award in Breast Cancer (Postdoctorate/Grant) 385

American Brain Tumor Association Fellowships (Postdoctorate/ Fellowship) 356

American Cancer Society Clinical Oncology Social Work Training Grants (Postgraduate/Grant) 362

American Cancer Society Clinical Research Professorships (Postdoctorate/Grant) 363

American Cancer Society Postdoctoral Fellowships (Postdoctorate/Award, Fellowship) 364

American Society for Dermatologic Surgery Grants (Postdoctorate/Grant) 2235

Cancer Prevention and Control Research Small Grant Program (Doctorate, Postdoctorate, Postgraduate/Grant) 3922

Cancer Research Campaign Research Grants (Professional Development/Grant) 1712

Cancer Research Fellowship Program (Other/Fellowship) 3407

Cancer Research Institute Clinical Investigator Award (Other/ Grant) 1714

Cancer Research Institute Postdoctoral Fellowship (Postdoctorate/Fellowship) 1715

Cancer Research Institute Science Writing Internship (Graduate/Internship) 1716

Cancer Research Society Fellowships (Doctorate, Postdoctorate/Fellowship) 1718

Cancer Research Society Grants (Professional Development/ Grant) 1719

Centre for Interdisciplinary Studies in Chemical Physics Senior Visiting Fellowships (Postdoctorate/Fellowship) 1795

Council for Tobacco Research Grants-in-Aid (Professional Development/Grant) 2125

EORTC/NCI Exchange Program (Postdoctorate/Grant) 3923

Faculty Research Award in Oncology (Postdoctorate/ Award) 365

R. Robert and Sally Funderburg Research Scholar Award in Gastric Biology Related to Cancer (Postdoctorate/ Award) 451

ICRF Postdoctoral Fellowships (Postdoctorate/ Fellowship) 2985

International Cancer Technology Transfer Fellowships (Professional Development/Fellowship) 3194

International Oncology Nursing Fellowships (Professional Development/Fellowship) 3195

Leukemia Society of America Short-term Scientific Awards (Professional Development/Grant) 3455

Leukemia Society Fellow Awards (Postdoctorate/Award) 3456

Leukemia Society Scholar Awards (Postdoctorate/ Award) 3457

Leukemia Society Special Fellow Awards (Postdoctorate/ Award) 3458

McEachern Awards (Postdoctorate/Award, Fellowship) 1614

Milheim Foundation for Cancer Research Project Grants in Oncology (Postdoctorate/Grant) 3701

National Cancer Institute of Canada Research Fellowships (Postdoctorate/Fellowship) 3927

National Cancer Institute of Canada Research Grants (Postdoctorate/Grant) 3928

National Cancer Institute of Canada Research Scientist Career Appointments (Postdoctorate/Award) 3929

NCI International Bilateral Program (Postdoctorate/ Other) 3924

Oncology Nursing Foundation/Amgen, Inc. Research Grant (Professional Development/Grant) 4758

Oncology Nursing Foundation Bachelors Scholarship (Undergraduate/Scholarship) 4759

Oncology Nursing Foundation/Bristol- Myers Oncology Chapter Research Grant (Professional Development/ Grant) 4760

Oncology Nursing Foundation/Bristol- Myers Oncology Division Community Health Research Grant (Professional Development/Grant) 4761

Oncology Nursing Foundation/Bristol- Myers Oncology Division Research Grant (Professional Development/Grant) 4762

Oncology Nursing Foundation/Cetus Oncology Grants for Research Involving Biotherapy or Immunotherapy (Professional Development/Grant) 4763

Oncology Nursing Foundation Doctoral Scholarship (Doctorate/ Scholarship) 4764

Oncology Nursing Foundation/Glaxo Research Grants (Professional Development/Grant) 4765

Oncology Nursing Foundation Masters Scholarship (Graduate/ Scholarship) 4766

Oncology Nursing Foundation/Oncology Nursing Certification Corporation Nursing Education Research Grants (Professional Development/Grant) 4767

Oncology Nursing Foundation/Oncology Nursing Society Research Grant (Professional Development/Grant) 4768

Oncology Nursing Foundation/Ortho Biotech Research Grant (Professional Development/Grant) 4769

Oncology Nursing Foundation/Purdue Frederick Research Grant (Professional Development/Grant) 4770

Oncology Nursing Foundation/Rhone Poulenc Rorer New Investigator Research Grants (Doctorate, Graduate/ Grant) 4771

Oncology Nursing Foundation/Sigma Theta Tau International and Oncology Nursing Society Research Grant (Professional Development/Grant) 4772

Oncology Nursing Society/SmithKline Beecham Research Grant (Professional Development/Grant) 4773

Oncology Research Faculty Development Program (Postdoctorate/Grant) 3925

Postdoctoral Research Fellowships for Basic and Physician Scientists (Postdoctorate/Fellowship) 5200

Research Fellowships (Other/Fellowship) 3196

Taiwan National Science Council Fellowships (Postdoctorate/ Fellowship) 2536

Yamagiwa-Yoshida Memorial International Cancer Study Grants (Professional Development/Grant) 3197

## Opera

Adler Fellowships (Professional Development/Fellowship) 5237

Baltimore Opera Studio & Residency Program (Professional Development/Prize) 1368

Merola Opera Program (Professional Development/ Other) 5238

National Vocal Competition for Young Opera Singers (Professional Development/Prize) 6301

## Opera (continued)

New Jersey State Opera Annual Vocal Competition *(Professional Development/Award)* 4547

OPERA America Fellowship Program *(Postgraduate/Fellowship)* 4783

Opera Screen Competition Awards *(Professional Development/Award)* 3167

RTMF Career Grants/Sara Tucker Study Grant *(Professional Development/Grant)* 5754

Ida Speyrer Stahl Scholarships *(Undergraduate/Scholarship)* 1725

Richard Tucker Award *(Professional Development/Award)* 5755

V.C.C. Fuchs Scholarship Award *(Professional Development/Scholarship)* 6042

Western Opera Theater Program *(Professional Development/Other)* 5239

## Operations research

AT & T Bell Laboratories Cooperative Research Fellowships for Minorities *(Graduate/Fellowship)* 1302

AT & T Bell Laboratories Graduate Research Fellowships for Women *(Doctorate/Fellowship)* 1303

AT & T Bell Laboratories Graduate Research Grants for Women *(Doctorate, Graduate/Grant)* 1304

AT & T Bell Laboratories Summer Research Program for Minorities & Women *(Undergraduate/Fellowship)* 1305

AT & T Bell Laboratories University Relations Summer Program *(Doctorate, Graduate, Undergraduate/Work Study)* 1306

William C. Foster Fellows Visiting Scholars Competition *(Postdoctorate, Professional Development/Fellowship)* 5818

Microsoft Corporation Scholarships *(Graduate, Undergraduate/Scholarship)* 5516

## Ophthalmology

E. A. Baker Foundation Fellowships and Research Grants *(Postgraduate/Fellowship, Grant)* 1676

FFS-NSPB Grants-In-Aid *(Postdoctorate/Grant)* 2449

FFS-NSPB Postdoctoral Research Fellowships *(Postdoctorate/Fellowship)* 2450

Heed Ophthalmic Foundation Fellowships *(Postgraduate/Fellowship)* 2855

New York State Regents Professional Opportunity Scholarships *(Doctorate, Graduate, Undergraduate/Scholarship)* 4577

## Optics

New Focus Research Awards *(Doctorate/Award)* 4787

SPIE Educational Scholarships and Grants in Optical Engineering *(Graduate, Undergraduate/Scholarship)* 5589

U.S. Air Force Phillips Laboratory Scholar Program *(Postdoctorate/Other)* 4686

## Optometry

AFVA(MOA) Scholarships *(Graduate/Scholarship)* 504

William C. Ezell Fellowship *(Doctorate, Graduate/Fellowship)* 746

Georgia Student Finance Commission Service-Cancellable Stafford Loan *(Graduate, Undergraduate/Loan)* 2666

Georgia Student Finance Commission State-Sponsored Loan *(Graduate, Undergraduate/Loan)* 2669

Health Education Loan Program *(Doctorate, Graduate/Loan)* 5709

HRSA-BHP Health Professions Student Loans *(Doctorate, Graduate/Loan)* 5967

HRSA-BHP Loans for Disadvantaged Students *(Undergraduate/Loan)* 5968

Mississippi Southern Regional Education Board Loan/Scholarship Program *(Doctorate/Scholarship loan)* 3741

New York State Professional Opportunity Scholarships *(Doctorate, Graduate, Undergraduate/Scholarship)* 4592

New York State Regents Professional Opportunity Scholarships *(Doctorate, Graduate, Undergraduate/Scholarship)* 4577

Oklahoma State Regents for Higher Education Professional Study Grants *(Graduate/Grant)* 4740

Vincent Salierno Scholarship *(Doctorate, Graduate/Scholarship)* 747

Student Travel Fellowships *(Doctorate, Graduate/Fellowship)* 748

Western Interstate Commission for Higher Education Student Exchanges *(Doctorate, Graduate/Other)* 135

Arizona WICHE Professional Student Exchange Program *(Professional Development/Work Study)* 1089

## Ornithology

Kathleen S. Anderson Award *(Professional Development/Award)* 3546

Frank M. Chapman Memorial Fellowships and Grants *(Doctorate, Postdoctorate/Fellowship, Grant)* 714

John K. Cooper Ornithology Research Grants *(Doctorate, Graduate/Grant)* 2079

North American Bluebird Society Research Grants *(Graduate, Professional Development/Grant)* 4642

North American Loon Fund Grants *(Other/Grant)* 4644

Sigurd T. Olson Common Loon Research Awards *(Graduate, Postgraduate, Professional Development/Award)* 4747

## Otolaryngology

AAO-HNSF Academy Resident Research Grant *(Postdoctorate/Grant)* 233

Combined AAOA/AAO-HNSF Research Grant *(Postdoctorate/Grant)* 234

Combined PSEF/AAO-HNSF Research Grant *(Postdoctorate/Grant)* 235

Percy Memorial Research Award *(Postdoctorate/Award)* 236

## Otology

Deafness Research Foundation Grants *(Postdoctorate/Grant)* 2198

Otological Research Fellowships *(Doctorate/Fellowship)* 2199

Stokoe Scholarships *(Graduate/Scholarship)* 3873

## Otosclerosis

American Otological Society Research Grants *(Postdoctorate/Grant)* 760

## Painting (See also: Art)

Albee Foundation Residencies *(Professional Development/Other)* 141

American Watercolor Society Scholarship Award *(Graduate, Undergraduate/Scholarship)* 1022

Artists Workplace Fellowships *(Professional Development/Fellowship)* 6253

Bush Artist Fellowships *(Professional Development/Fellowship)* 1539

Pauly D'Orlando Memorial Art Scholarship *(Graduate, Undergraduate/Scholarship)* 5781

Emergency Assistance Grants *(Other, Professional Development/Grant)* 2719

Fine Arts Grants *(Professional Development/Grant)* 194

Fine Arts Work Center Fellowships *(Professional Development/Fellowship)* 2459

The Elizabeth Greenshields Grant *(Graduate, High School, Other, Undergraduate/Grant)* 2751

Hungarian Arts Club Scholarships *(Undergraduate/Scholarship)* 2935

Individual Support Grants *(Professional Development/Grant)* 2720

National Endowment for the Arts - Visual Artists Fellowships *(Professional Development/Fellowship)* 3982

New York Foundation for the Arts Artists' Fellowships *(Other/Fellowship)* 4570

Pollock-Krasner Grants *(Professional Development/Grant)* 4975

Posey Foundation Graduate Art Scholarships *(Graduate/Scholarship)* 4985

Resident Fellowships *(Professional Development/Fellowship)* 2786

Theodore Rousseau Fellowships *(Doctorate, Graduate/
Fellowship)* 3667
John F. and Anna Lee Stacey Scholarships *(Professional
Development/Scholarship)* 3966
Marion Barr Stanfield Art Scholarship *(Undergraduate/
Scholarship)* 5784
Vermont Studio Center Residency Fellowships *(Professional
Development/Fellowship)* 6034
Virginia Museum of Fine Arts Fellowship *(Professional
Development/Fellowship)* 6061
Harriet Hale Woolley Scholarships *(Graduate/
Scholarship)* 2545
Young American Creative Patriotic Art Awards *(High School/
Prize)* 3409

## Paleontology
American Museum of Natural History Research and Museum
Fellowships *(Postdoctorate/Fellowship)* 713
W. Storrs Cole Memorial Research Awards *(Postdoctorate/
Award)* 2648
Fyssen Foundation Research Grants *(Doctorate, Postgraduate/
Grant)* 2610
Prince Rainier III de Monaco Bursary *(Professional
Development/Grant)* 3049

## Parapsychology
Eileen J. Garrett Scholarship *(Graduate, Undergraduate/
Scholarship)* 4832

## Parkinson's disease
Viola Kerr Fellowship *(Postdoctorate/Fellowship)* 4841
H. Houston Merritt Fellowship *(Postdoctorate/
Fellowship)* 4842
Parkinson's Disease Foundation Postdoctoral Fellowship
*(Postdoctorate/Fellowship)* 4843
Parkinson's Disease Foundation Research Grants
*(Postdoctorate/Grant)* 4844
Parkinson's Disease Foundation Summer Fellowship
*(Graduate, Undergraduate/Fellowship)* 4845
Lillian Shorr Fellowship *(Postdoctorate/Fellowship)* 4846

## Parks and recreation
Delta Psi Kappa Research Awards *(Graduate/Award)* 2223
Ralph Hudson Environmental Fellowship *(Professional
Development/Fellowship)* 3425
RCRA Internship Program *(Undergraduate/Internship)* 5109
Tom and Ruth Rivers International Scholarships *(Graduate,
Undergraduate/Scholarship)* 6264

## Pathology
del Duca Foundation Maintenance and Travel Grants
*(Professional Development/Grant)* 2284

## Peace studies
Bunting Institute Peace Fellowships *(Postgraduate/
Fellowship)* 1528
Marion Wright Edelman Scholarship *(All/Scholarship)* 3490
Albert Einstein Institution Fellowships *(Doctorate,
Postdoctorate, Professional Development/Fellowship)* 2361
Mark O. Hatfield Scholarship *(Graduate/Scholarship)* 5138
Hubert H. Humphrey Doctoral Fellowships in Arms Control
and Disarmament *(Doctorate/Fellowship)* 5819
IGCC Dissertation Fellowships *(Doctorate, Graduate/
Fellowship)* 3043
National Peace Essay Contest *(High School/
Scholarship)* 5075
Peace Fellowships *(Postgraduate, Professional Development/
Fellowship)* 5076
Peace Scholars Award *(Doctorate/Award)* 5077
Pre- and Postdoctoral Fellowships on Nonviolent Sanctions;
Visiting Scholar Affiliations *(Doctorate, Postdoctorate/
Fellowship)* 2806
Jennings Randolph Senior Fellow Award *(Professional
Development/Fellowship)* 5078
Herbert Scoville Jr. Peace Fellowship *(Professional
Development/Fellowship)* 5288

SSRC International Peace and Security Research Workshop
Competition *(Professional Development/Grant)* 5401
United States Institute of Peace Distinguished Fellows
*(Professional Development/Fellowship)* 5079

## Performing arts
Artpark Residencies *(Professional Development/Award)* 1161
Asian Cultural Council Fellowship Grants *(Postdoctorate/
Fellowship)* 1177
Banff Centre for the Arts Scholarships *(Postgraduate,
Professional Development/Scholarship)* 1370
Bush Artist Fellowships *(Professional Development/
Fellowship)* 1539
Canadian Council for the Arts Grants Program *(Professional
Development/Grant)* 1594
Chalmers Performing Arts Training Grants *(Professional
Development/Grant)* 4778
Chancellor's Talent Award Program *(Undergraduate/
Scholarship)* 1828
Contemporary Record Society National Festival for the
Performing Arts *(Professional Development/
Fellowship)* 2071
Cummington Community of the Arts Residencies *(Professional
Development/Fellowship)* 2142
Fine Arts Grants *(Professional Development/Grant)* 194
Ford Foundation Fellowships *(Doctorate, Graduate,
Postdoctorate/Fellowship)* 1178
The Fund for U.S. Artists at International Festivals and
Exhibitions *(Other/Other)* 1164
Errol Garner Memorial Foundation Scholarship Awards *(All/
Award)* 2626
Humanities Fellowships *(Doctorate, Postdoctorate/
Fellowship)* 1179
India Studies Faculty Fellowships *(Professional Development/
Fellowship)* 5316
India Studies Performing Arts Fellowships *(Professional
Development/Fellowship)* 5317
India Studies Postdoctoral Research Fellowships *(Professional
Development/Fellowship)* 5318
India Studies Student Fellowships *(Graduate/Fellowship)* 5319
Interlochen Arts Academy and Arts Camp Scholarships *(High
School, Postgraduate, Undergraduate/Scholarship)* 3101
Japan-United States Art Fellowships *(Postdoctorate,
Professional Development/Fellowship)* 1180
Japanese American Citizens League Performing Arts Award
*(All/Scholarship)* 3247
Minnesota Artist Assistance Fellowships *(Professional
Development/Fellowship)* 3714
Minnesota Career Opportunity Grants *(Professional
Development/Grant)* 3715
Multi-Arts Production Fund Grants *(Professional Development/
Grant)* 5148
National Alliance for Excellence Honored Scholars Awards
*(Graduate, Undergraduate/Scholarship)* 3841
New Jersey State Opera Annual Vocal Competition
*(Professional Development/Award)* 4547
New York Foundation for the Arts Artists' Fellowships *(Other/
Fellowship)* 4570
OPERA America Fellowship Program *(Postgraduate/
Fellowship)* 4783
Senior Performing Arts Fellowships *(Professional Development/
Fellowship)* 588
SSRC Korea Advanced Research Grants *(Postdoctorate/
Grant)* 5406
Muddy Waters Scholarship *(Undergraduate/Scholarship)* 1448
World Model Awards *(Other, Professional Development/
Scholarship)* 6266
Yaddo Residencies *(Professional Development/Other)* 6274

## Personnel administration
Canadian Soroptimist Grants for Women *(Graduate,
Undergraduate/Grant)* 5539

## Pharmaceutical sciences

AIHP Grant-in-Aid Toward Thesis Expenses Related to the History of Pharmacy *(Doctorate, Graduate/Grant)* 583

California Pharmacists Association Educational Foundation Trust Fund *(Graduate/Loan)* 1570

Dr. B. Olive Cole Graduate Educational Grant *(Graduate/Grant)* 3413

Cora E. Craven Educational Grants *(Graduate/Grant)* 3414

Mary Connolly Livingston Grant *(Doctorate/Grant)* 3415

Sigma Theta Tau International/Glaxo Wellcome New Investigator/Mentor Grant *(Professional Development/Grant)* 5342

Sigma Theta Tau International/Glaxo Wellcome Prescriptive Practice Grant *(Professional Development/Grant)* 5343

## Pharmacology

Academia-Oriented "Springboard to Teaching" Fellowship *(Doctorate/Fellowship)* 487

AIHP Grant-in-Aid Toward Thesis Expenses Related to the History of Pharmacy *(Doctorate, Graduate/Grant)* 583

Armenian American Pharmacists' Association Scholarship *(Graduate, Undergraduate/Scholarship)* 1108

Centennial Scholars Awards *(Graduate/Grant)* 1690

del Duca Foundation Maintenance and Travel Grants *(Professional Development/Grant)* 2284

Faculty Development Awards in Clinical Pharmacology and Toxicology *(Postdoctorate/Award)* 4887

Faculty Research Participation Program at the National Center for Toxicological Research *(Professional Development/Fellowship)* 5874

Fellowships for Careers in Clinical Pharmacology *(Postdoctorate/Fellowship)* 4888

Grant in Biotechnology *(Postdoctorate/Grant)* 4834

Howard Hughes Medical Institute Predoctoral Fellowships in Biological Sciences *(Postdoctorate/Fellowship)* 4358

Lilly International Fellowships *(Graduate/Fellowship)* 3479

Northwest Pharmacist Coalition Pre-Pharmacy Scholarship *(Undergraduate/Scholarship)* 4696

Parenteral Drug Association Foundation Research Grants *(Graduate/Grant)* 4835

Predoctoral Fellowships in Biological Sciences *(Doctorate/Fellowship)* 2927

Regular AFPE Fellowships and Scholarships in the Pharmaceutical Sciences *(Doctorate/Fellowship, Scholarship)* 492

Summer Fellowship Grants *(Doctorate/Fellowship)* 215

Taste & Clinic Fellowship *(Postdoctorate/Fellowship)* 1801

## Pharmacy

AACP-AFPE Gateway Scholarships *(Graduate/Scholarship)* 485

AAPS-AFPE Gateway Scholarships *(Graduate, Undergraduate/Scholarship)* 486

Academia-Oriented "Springboard to Teaching" Fellowship *(Doctorate/Fellowship)* 487

AFPE Graduate Fellowships *(Doctorate/Fellowship)* 488

AIHP Grant-in-Aid Toward Thesis Expenses Related to the History of Pharmacy *(Doctorate, Graduate/Grant)* 583

Celanese Canada Inc. Scholarships *(Undergraduate/Scholarship)* 1269

Centennial Scholars Awards *(Graduate/Grant)* 1690

Cuyahoga County Medical Foundation Scholarship *(Graduate/Scholarship)* 2146

Georgia Student Finance Commission Service-Cancellable Stafford Loan *(Graduate, Undergraduate/Loan)* 2666

Georgia Student Finance Commission State-Sponsored Loan *(Graduate, Undergraduate/Loan)* 2669

GLAXO AACP-AFPE Graduate Studies Scholarships *(Graduate/Scholarship)* 489

Grant in Biotechnology *(Postdoctorate/Grant)* 4834

Health Education Loan Program *(Doctorate, Graduate/Loan)* 5709

HRSA-BHP Health Professions Student Loans *(Doctorate, Graduate/Loan)* 5967

HRSA-BHP Loans for Disadvantaged Students *(Undergraduate/Loan)* 5968

International Order of the King's Daughters and Sons Health Careers Scholarships *(Graduate, Postgraduate, Undergraduate/Scholarship)* 3169

Maryland Professional Scholarship *(Graduate, Undergraduate/Scholarship)* 3578

MERCK-AFPE Gateway Scholarships *(Graduate, Undergraduate/Scholarship)* 490

New York State Professional Opportunity Scholarships *(Doctorate, Graduate, Undergraduate/Scholarship)* 4592

New York State Regents Professional Opportunity Scholarships *(Doctorate, Graduate, Undergraduate/Scholarship)* 4577

Parenteral Drug Association Foundation Research Grants *(Graduate/Grant)* 4835

Gustavus A. Pfeiffer Faculty Development Postdoctoral Research Fellowship *(Postdoctorate/Fellowship)* 491

Regular AFPE Fellowships and Scholarships in the Pharmaceutical Sciences *(Doctorate/Fellowship, Scholarship)* 492

Sandoz-AFPE First Year Graduate Scholarships *(Doctorate/Scholarship)* 493

G. D. Searle & Co. Faculty Development Research Fellowship in Pharmacoeconomics *(Postdoctorate/Fellowship)* 494

SYNTEX-AFPE Gateway Scholarships *(Graduate, Undergraduate/Scholarship)* 495

UpJohn-AFPE First Year Graduate Scholarships *(Doctorate/Scholarship)* 496

## Philosophy

Donald Bogie Prize *(Graduate/Prize)* 3051

Chateaubriand Fellowships (Humanities) *(Doctorate/Grant)* 2375

Fellowships in Ethics *(Postdoctorate, Postgraduate/Fellowship)* 5015

Folger Library Long-Term Fellowships *(Postdoctorate/Fellowship)* 2541

Folger Library Short-Term Fellowships *(Postdoctorate/Fellowship)* 2542

Germanistic Society of America Quadrille Grants *(Graduate, Postgraduate/Grant)* 2697

Howard Foundation Fellowships *(Professional Development/Fellowship)* 2908

Humane Studies Foundation Summer Residential Program Fellowships *(Graduate/Fellowship)* 3053

IGCC Dissertation Fellowships *(Doctorate, Graduate/Fellowship)* 3043

IHS John M. Olin Fellowships *(Graduate/Fellowship)* 3056

IHS Summer Faculty Fellowships *(Professional Development/Fellowship)* 3057

International Affairs Fellowships *(Professional Development/Fellowship)* 2105

Krupp Foundation Fellowship *(Graduate/Fellowship)* 2773

National Endowment for the Humanities Fellowships *(Postdoctorate/Fellowship)* 2543

National Federation of the Blind Humanities Scholarship *(Undergraduate/Scholarship)* 4003

Oregon Humanities Center Summer Visiting Research Fellowships *(Professional Development/Fellowship)* 6011

Postdoctoral Fellowships in the History and Philosophy of Science *(Postdoctorate/Fellowship)* 4699

SSRC African Advanced Research Grants *(Postdoctorate/Grant)* 5395

SSRC Grants for Advanced Area Research *(Doctorate, Other/Grant)* 5399

SSRC Korea Advanced Research Grants *(Postdoctorate/Grant)* 5406

SSRC Near and Middle East Advanced Research Fellowships *(Postdoctorate/Fellowship)* 5411

## Photogrammetry

Robert E. Altenhofen Memorial Scholarship *(Graduate, Undergraduate/Scholarship)* 963

Raymond Davis Scholarship (Graduate, Undergraduate/
Scholarship) 5461
William A. Fischer Memorial Scholarship (Graduate/
Scholarship) 964
LH Systems Internship (Graduate/Internship) 965

## Photography

Reid Blackburn Scholarship (Undergraduate/Scholarship) 4342
Boston Globe One-Year Minority Development Program
(Professional Development/Other) 1461
Bush Artist Fellowships (Professional Development/
Fellowship) 1539
Central Intelligence Agency Graduate Studies Internships
(Graduate/Internship) 1811
Central Intelligence Agency Undergraduate Scholars Program
(Undergraduate/Internship, Scholarship) 1812
Howard Chapnick Grant (Professional Development/
Grant) 5367
Dallas-Fort Worth Association of Black Communicators
Scholarships (High School, Undergraduate/
Scholarship) 2170
Bob East Scholarship (Graduate, Undergraduate/
Scholarship) 4343
Joseph Ehrenreich Scholarships (Undergraduate/
Scholarship) 4344
Fine Arts Work Center Fellowships (Professional Development/
Fellowship) 2459
Grant in Humanistic Photography (Professional Development/
Grant) 5368
International Biennial Competition of Humour and Satire in the
Arts (Professional Development/Award) 2906
International Navies Photo Contest (Other/Prize) 5953
Kit C. King Graduate Scholarship (Graduate/
Scholarship) 4345
Landmark Communications Minority Internships (Professional
Development/Internship) 3419
Light Work Artist-in-Residence Program (Professional
Development/Grant) 3472
MacDowell Colony Residencies (Other, Professional
Development/Fellowship) 3524
Rae Mitsuoka Photography Scholarships (Undergraduate/
Scholarship) 6092
National Alliance for Excellence Honored Scholars Awards
(Graduate, Undergraduate/Scholarship) 3841
National Endowment for the Arts - Visual Artists Fellowships
(Professional Development/Fellowship) 3982
National Zoological Park Minority Traineeships (Graduate,
Undergraduate/Internship) 4456
National Zoological Park Traineeship in Zoo Photography
(Graduate, Undergraduate/Internship) 4464
Naval and Maritime Photo Contest (Other/Prize) 5955
Edward J. Nell Memorial Scholarships in Journalism
(Undergraduate/Scholarship) 5048
Netz Hilai Visiting Artists Fellowships (Professional
Development/Fellowship) 4515
New York Foundation for the Arts Artists' Fellowships (Other/
Fellowship) 4570
NPPF Still Scholarship (Undergraduate/Scholarship) 4346
NPPF Television News Scholarship (Undergraduate/
Scholarship) 4347
Times Mirror Minority Editorial Training Program (Professional
Development/Other) 3496
Vermont Studio Center Residency Fellowships (Professional
Development/Fellowship) 6034
Virginia Museum of Fine Arts Fellowship (Professional
Development/Fellowship) 6061

## Physical sciences

AAAS-EPA Environmental Science and Engineering
Fellowships (Postdoctorate/Fellowship) 265
AAAS Science, Engineering, and Diplomacy Fellows Program
(Postdoctorate/Fellowship) 266
ACPSEM Scholarship (Professional Development/
Scholarship) 1316

Air Force Civilian Cooperative Work-Study Program (Graduate,
Undergraduate/Work Study) 66
Air & Waste Management Scholarship Endowment Trust Fund
(Graduate/Scholarship) 75
AISES A.T. Anderson Memorial Scholarship (Graduate,
Undergraduate/Scholarship) 559
Alaska Space Grant Program Graduate Research
Assistantships (Graduate/Grant) 138
Alaska Space Grant Program Internships (Graduate,
Undergraduate/Internship) 139
Argonne National Laboratory Faculty Research Leave; Faculty
Research Participation Awards (Postdoctorate/Award) 1083
Army Research Laboratory Postdoctoral Fellowship Program
(Postdoctorate/Fellowship) 922
AWU Faculty Fellowships (Postdoctorate/Fellowship) 1199
AWU Faculty Sabbatical Fellowships (Postdoctorate/
Fellowship) 1200
AWU Graduate Research Fellowships (Doctorate, Graduate/
Fellowship) 1201
AWU Post-Graduate Fellowship (Doctorate, Postdoctorate/
Fellowship) 1202
AWU Student Research Fellowships (Graduate,
Undergraduate/Fellowship) 1203
Brown-NASA Space Grant Scholars Program (Undergraduate/
Scholarship) 5124
Central Intelligence Agency Undergraduate Scholars Program
(Undergraduate/Internship, Scholarship) 1812
CERT Scholarship (Graduate, Undergraduate/
Scholarship) 2100
Chateaubriand Scholarship (Scientifique) (Doctorate,
Postdoctorate/Scholarship) 2372
Churchill Scholarships (Postgraduate/Scholarship) 1954
Delaware NASA Space Grant Undergraduate Tuition
Scholarships (Undergraduate/Scholarship) 2203
Department of Energy Distinguished Postdoctoral Research
Program (Postdoctorate/Fellowship) 5868
Eastburn Fellowships (Postdoctorate/Fellowship) 2314
E. B. Eastburn Fellowships (Postdoctorate/Fellowship) 2788
Eppley Foundation Support for Advanced Scientific Research
(Postdoctorate/Grant) 2404
Faculty Research Participation Program at the Bureau of
Engraving and Printing (Professional Development/
Fellowship) 5873
Florida National Science Scholars Program (Undergraduate/
Scholarship) 2503
Ford Foundation Postdoctoral Fellowships for Minorities
(Postdoctorate/Fellowship) 4356
Ford Foundation Predoctoral and Dissertation Fellowships for
Minorities (Doctorate/Fellowship) 4357
Fossil Energy Faculty Research Participation (Professional
Development/Fellowship) 5876
GEM Ph.D. Science Fellowship Program (Doctorate/
Fellowship) 3943
Georgia Space Grant Consortium Fellowships (Graduate,
Undergraduate/Fellowship) 2655
Graduate Student Research Participation Program (Graduate,
Postgraduate/Fellowship) 5884
Hertz Foundation Graduate Fellowships (Doctorate, Graduate/
Fellowship) 2866
Historically Black Colleges and Universities Fossil Energy
Faculty and Student Research Training (Graduate,
Professional Development, Undergraduate/Fellowship) 5891
Laboratory-Graduate Participantships Thesis Parts
Appointment (Doctorate, Graduate/Grant) 1084
LPI Summer Intern Program in Planetary Science
(Undergraduate/Internship) 3514
Maryland Space Grant Consortium Graduate Level Fellowship
(Graduate/Fellowship) 3588
Allen H. Meyers Scholarship (Undergraduate/
Scholarship) 3677
Miami University Pulp and Paper Foundation Scholarships
(Undergraduate/Scholarship) 5029
MSA Presidential Student Awards (Graduate, Undergraduate/
Award) 3696

## Physical sciences (continued)

MSA Undergraduate Research Scholarships *(Undergraduate/ Scholarship)* 3697

NASA/DESGC Graduate Student Fellowships *(Graduate/ Fellowship)* 2204

NASA/DESGC Undergraduate Summer Scholarships *(Undergraduate/Scholarship)* 2205

National Defense Science and Engineering Graduate Fellowship Program *(Graduate/Fellowship)* 5855

National Oceanic and Atmospheric Administration/Historically Black Colleges and Universities Faculty/Student Research Participation Program *(Graduate, Professional Development, Undergraduate/Fellowship)* 5910

Naval Research Laboratory Postdoctoral Fellowship Program *(Postdoctorate/Fellowship)* 924

Arthur & Doreen Parrett Scholarship Fund *(Graduate, Postgraduate, Undergraduate/Scholarship)* 4848

Part-time Fossil Energy Faculty Research Participation Program *(Professional Development/Fellowship)* 5922

The Payzer Scholarship *(Undergraduate/Scholarship)* 2296

The Payzer Scholarship *(All/Scholarship)* 2423

Research Science Institute Internship *(Undergraduate/ Internship)* 5103

Risk Reduction Engineering Research Laboratory Research Participation Program *(Postdoctorate, Postgraduate/ Fellowship)* 5923

Santa Fe Pacific Foundation Scholarships *(Undergraduate/ Scholarship)* 563

SDE Fellowships *(Postgraduate/Fellowship)* 5330

Sigma Xi Grants-in-Aid of Research *(Graduate, Undergraduate/Grant)* 5347

John Clarke Slater Fellowship *(Doctorate/Fellowship)* 770

Space and Aerospace Graduate Fellowships *(Graduate/ Fellowship)* 3508

Space Grant Graduate Fellowship Program *(Graduate/ Fellowship)* 5125

Space Grant Undergraduate Scholar Program *(Undergraduate/ Scholarship)* 5126

Space Grant Undergraduate Summer Scholar Program *(Undergraduate/Scholarship)* 5127

Space Scholars Program *(Undergraduate/Scholarship)* 3589

Summer Faculty Fellowships *(Other/Fellowship)* 5561

Tennessee Valley Authority Research Participation Program *(Postdoctorate, Postgraduate/Fellowship)* 5927

TSGC Fellowship and Scholarship *(Undergraduate/Fellowship, Scholarship)* 5719

UA/NASA Space Grant Graduate Fellowship Program *(Graduate/Fellowship)* 1086

Morris K. Udall OTA Congressional Fellowship *(Postdoctorate/ Fellowship)* 5851

Undergraduate NASA Space Grant Fellowship *(Undergraduate/ Fellowship)* 6143

Undergraduate Student Assistantships and Scholarships *(Undergraduate/Scholarship)* 5562

U.S. Department of Energy Distinguished Postdoctoral Research Fellowship *(Postdoctorate/Fellowship)* 4708

U.S. Department of Energy Faculty Research Participation Fellowship *(Professional Development/Fellowship)* 5932

U.S. Department of Energy Global Change Distinguished Postdoctoral Fellowships *(Postdoctorate/Fellowship)* 4709

U.S. Department of Energy Internship *(Undergraduate/ Internship)* 4711

The University of Arizona/NASA Space Grant Undergraduate Research Internship Program *(Undergraduate/Grant, Internship)* 1087

West Virginia Space Consortium Graduate Fellowship Program *(Graduate/Fellowship)* 6144

West Virginia Space Grant Consortium Undergraduate Scholarship Program *(Undergraduate/Scholarship)* 6145

Wisconsin Space Grant Consortium Graduate Fellowships *(Graduate/Fellowship)* 6214

Wisconsin Space Grant Consortium Undergraduate Research Awards *(Undergraduate/Grant)* 6215

Wisconsin Space Grant Consortium Undergraduate Scholarships *(Undergraduate/Scholarship)* 6216

## Physical therapy

AMBUCS Scholars *(Graduate, Undergraduate/ Scholarship)* 3854

American Legion Auxiliary Nurses, Physical Therapists and Respiratory Therapists Scholarship *(Undergraduate/ Scholarship)* 626

Foundation for Physical Therapy Doctoral Award *(Doctorate/ Award)* 2575

Foundation for Physical Therapy Research Grant *(Other/ Grant)* 2576

Georgia Student Finance Commission Service-Cancellable Stafford Loan *(Graduate, Undergraduate/Loan)* 2666

Georgia Student Finance Commission State-Sponsored Loan *(Graduate, Undergraduate/Loan)* 2669

International Order of the King's Daughters and Sons Health Careers Scholarships *(Graduate, Postgraduate, Undergraduate/Scholarship)* 3169

Maryland Physical and Occupational Therapists and Assistants Scholarships *(Undergraduate/Scholarship)* 3577

Mississippi Health Care Professions Loan/Scholarship Program *(Undergraduate/Scholarship loan)* 3732

New York State Professional Opportunity Scholarships *(Doctorate, Graduate, Undergraduate/Scholarship)* 4592

New York State Regents Professional Opportunity Scholarships *(Doctorate, Graduate, Undergraduate/ Scholarship)* 4577

NSCA Challenge Scholarships *(All/Scholarship)* 4415

NSDAR Occupational Therapy Scholarship *(Graduate, Undergraduate/Scholarship)* 4403

Occupational Therapist and Physical Therapist Scholarship Loan Program *(Graduate/Scholarship loan)* 2513

Power Systems Inc./NSCA Strength and Conditioning Professional Scholarship *(Graduate, Undergraduate/ Scholarship)* 4417

Scholarships for Therapists *(Professional Development/ Scholarship)* 3855

## Physics

The AFCEA Educational Foundation Fellowship *(Doctorate, Graduate/Fellowship)* 1099

AFCEA ROTC Scholarship Program *(Undergraduate/ Scholarship)* 1100

AT & T Bell Laboratories Cooperative Research Fellowships for Minorities *(Graduate/Fellowship)* 1302

AT & T Bell Laboratories Graduate Research Fellowships for Women *(Doctorate/Fellowship)* 1303

AT & T Bell Laboratories Graduate Research Grants for Women *(Doctorate, Graduate/Grant)* 1304

AT & T Bell Laboratories Summer Research Program for Minorities & Women *(Undergraduate/Fellowship)* 1305

AT & T Bell Laboratories University Relations Summer Program *(Doctorate, Graduate, Undergraduate/Work Study)* 1306

BNL Postdoctoral Research Associateships *(Postdoctorate/ Other)* 1504

BNL Research Fellowship in Physics *(Postdoctorate/ Fellowship)* 1505

Bunting Institute Science Scholars Fellowships and Biomedical Research Fellowships *(Postdoctorate/Fellowship)* 1529

Central Intelligence Agency Undergraduate Scholars Program *(Undergraduate/Internship, Scholarship)* 1812

Centre for Interdisciplinary Studies in Chemical Physics Senior Visiting Fellowships *(Postdoctorate/Fellowship)* 1795

Civilian Radioactive Waste Management/Historically Black Colleges and Universities Faculty Fellowship Program *(Professional Development/Fellowship)* 5867

Corporate Sponsored Scholarships for Minority Undergraduate Physics Majors *(Undergraduate/Scholarship)* 772

Cottrell Scholars Science Awards *(Professional Development/ Award)* 5096

Dublin Institute for Advanced Studies Research Scholarships *(Postdoctorate/Scholarship)* 2282

Engineering Rotation Program *(Professional Development/ Award)* 2923

William C. Foster Fellows Visiting Scholars Competition *(Postdoctorate, Professional Development/Fellowship)* 5818

Health Physics Faculty Research Award Program *(Professional Development/Fellowship)* 5886

Historically Black Colleges and Universities Faculty and Student Research Participation Program in Fusion. *(Graduate, Professional Development, Undergraduate/Fellowship)* 5890

Historically Black Colleges and Universities Nuclear Energy Faculty Research Participation Program *(Professional Development/Fellowship)* 5893

Engineer Degree Fellowships; Howard Hughes Doctoral Fellowships *(Doctorate/Fellowship)* 2922

ICTP Research Grants for Postdoctoral Students *(Postdoctorate/Grant)* 3135

IGCC Dissertation Fellowships *(Doctorate, Graduate/Fellowship)* 3043

Institute for Advanced Study Postdoctoral Study Awards *(Postdoctorate/Grant)* 3010

Jansky Fellowships *(Postdoctorate/Fellowship)* 4351

JILA Postdoctoral Research Associateships for Laboratory Astrophysics *(Postdoctorate/Fellowship)* 3277

JILA Visiting Fellowships for Laboratory Astrophysics *(Postdoctorate/Fellowship)* 3278

Dr. Theodore von Karman Graduate Scholarship *(Graduate/Scholarship)* 45

LPI Summer Intern Program in Planetary Science *(Undergraduate/Internship)* 3514

NAACP Willems Scholarship *(Graduate, Undergraduate/Scholarship)* 3851

NAS/NRC Collaboration in Basic Science and Engineering Long-Term Grants *(Postdoctorate/Grant)* 3831

NAS/NRC Collaboration in Basic Science and Engineering Short-Term Project Development Grants *(Postdoctorate/Grant)* 3832

National Physical Science Consortium Graduate Fellowships for Minorities and Women *(Doctorate, Graduate/Fellowship)* 4338

NRAO Summer Student Research Assistantships *(Graduate, Undergraduate/Other)* 4352

General Emmett Paige Scholarship *(Undergraduate/Scholarship)* 1101

Postdoctoral Fellowships in Ocean Science and Engineering *(Postdoctorate/Fellowship)* 6247

Research Opportunity Awards *(Professional Development/Award)* 5097

Robert Schreck Memorial Fund Scholarship *(Graduate, Undergraduate/Scholarship)* 5280

Society of Physics Students Scholarships *(Undergraduate/Scholarship)* 5482

Sumner Memorial Fellowships *(Graduate, Postgraduate/Fellowship)* 5646

Tesla Award *(Doctorate/Award)* 5702

U.S. Air Force Phillips Laboratory Scholar Program *(Postdoctorate/Other)* 4686

U.S. Army Summer Faculty Research and Engineering Associateships *(Postdoctorate/Fellowship)* 1376

U.S. Nuclear Regulatory Commission Historically Black Colleges and Universities Faculty Research Participation *(Professional Development/Fellowship)* 5934

## Plastic surgery
Combined PSEF/AAO-HNSF Research Grant *(Postdoctorate/Grant)* 235

## Playwriting
Albee Foundation Residencies *(Professional Development/Other)* 141

George Bennett Fellowships *(Professional Development/Fellowship)* 4931

Herbert and Patricia Brodkin Scholarship *(Professional Development/Scholarship)* 4775

Bush Artist Fellowships *(Professional Development/Fellowship)* 1539

Centrum Residencies *(Professional Development/Other)* 1820

Dramatists Guild Fund Scholarships *(Professional Development/Grant, Loan)* 2280

International Playwrights' Competition *(Professional Development/Prize)* 5325

Jerome Playwright-in-Residence Fellowships *(Professional Development/Fellowship)* 4962

Letras de Oro Spanish Speaking Literary Prizes *(Professional Development/Prize)* 3453

McKnight Advancement Grants *(Professional Development/Grant)* 4963

McKnight Fellowships *(Professional Development/Fellowship)* 4964

National Endowment for the Arts - Fellowships for Playwrights *(Professional Development/Fellowship)* 3976

National Playwrights' Award *(Professional Development/Award)* 5772

Netz Hilai Visiting Artists Fellowships *(Professional Development/Fellowship)* 4515

New Play Competition Prizes *(Professional Development/Prize)* 3703

New York Foundation for the Arts Artists' Fellowships *(Other/Fellowship)* 4570

North Carolina Arts Council Artist Fellowships *(Professional Development/Fellowship)* 4668

PEN Fund for Writers and Editors with AIDS Grants and Loans *(Professional Development/Grant, Loan)* 4858

Playwrights' Center PlayLabs *(Professional Development/Other)* 4965

Promising Playwright Award *(Professional Development/Award)* 1996

ShenanArts Fellowships *(Professional Development/Fellowship)* 5323

Dorothy Silver Playwriting Competition Prize *(Professional Development/Prize)* 3261

Stanley Drama Award *(Professional Development/Award)* 6075

Sundance Theater Laboratory Fellowship *(Professional Development/Fellowship)* 3350

Thurber House Residencies *(Professional Development/Award)* 5731

Theodore Ward Prize *(Undergraduate/Prize)* 2007

We Don't Need No Stinkin' Dramas *(Professional Development/Prize)* 3758

Arnold Weissberger Playwrighting Competition *(Professional Development/Award)* 4523

## Podiatry
Health Education Loan Program *(Doctorate, Graduate/Loan)* 5709

HRSA-BHP Health Professions Student Loans *(Doctorate, Graduate/Loan)* 5967

HRSA-BHP Loans for Disadvantaged Students *(Undergraduate/Loan)* 5968

Mississippi Graduate and Professional Degree Loan/Scholarship Program *(Doctorate/Scholarship loan)* 3731

Zelda Walling Vicha Memorial Scholarship *(Graduate/Scholarship)* 967

Western Interstate Commission for Higher Education Student Exchanges *(Doctorate, Graduate/Other)* 135

## Poetry
Albee Foundation Residencies *(Professional Development/Other)* 141

AWP Award in Poetry, Short Fiction, Novel, and Creative Nonfiction *(Professional Development/Award)* 1205

George Bennett Fellowships *(Professional Development/Fellowship)* 4931

Bread Loaf Writers' Conference Fellowships; Bread Loaf Writers' Conference Scholarships *(Professional Development/Fellowship, Scholarship)* 1476

Bush Artist Fellowships *(Professional Development/Fellowship)* 1539

Centrum Residencies *(Professional Development/Other)* 1820

Bernard F. Conners Poetry Prize *(Professional Development/Prize)* 4839

## Poetry (continued)

Discovery/*The Nation* Contest; The Joan Leiman Jacobson Poetry Prizes *(Professional Development/Prize)* 4969

Dobie-Paisano Fellowships *(Other/Fellowship)* 2262

Fine Arts Work Center Fellowships *(Professional Development/Fellowship)* 2459

The Harper-Wood Studentship for English Poetry and Literature *(Postgraduate/Other)* 5222

Joseph Henry Jackson Award *(Professional Development/Award)* 5234

Letras de Oro Spanish Speaking Literary Prizes *(Professional Development/Prize)* 3453

Amy Lowell Poetry Travelling Scholarship *(Professional Development/Scholarship)* 3510

Edna Meudt Memorial Scholarship *(Undergraduate/Scholarship)* 4010

Minnesota Artist Assistance Fellowships *(Professional Development/Fellowship)* 3714

National Endowment for the Arts - Literature Program Creative Writing Fellowships *(Professional Development/Fellowship)* 3977

National Endowment for the Arts - National Heritage Fellowships *(Professional Development/Fellowship)* 3979

National Poetry Competition Prizes *(Professional Development/Prize)* 3293

Netz Hilai Visiting Artists Fellowships *(Professional Development/Fellowship)* 4515

New Letters Literary Awards *(Professional Development/Prize)* 4549

New York Foundation for the Arts Artists' Fellowships *(Other/Fellowship)* 4570

James D. Phelan Award in Literature *(Professional Development/Award)* 5235

Thurber House Residencies *(Professional Development/Award)* 5731

Yale Series of Younger Poets Prizes *(Professional Development/Prize)* 6280

## Political science

AFLSE Scholarships *(Graduate/Scholarship)* 506

APSA Congressional Fellowships for Federal Executives *(Professional Development/Fellowship)* 779

APSA Congressional Fellowships for Journalists *(Professional Development/Fellowship)* 780

APSA Graduate Fellowships for African-American Students *(Doctorate/Fellowship)* 781

APSA Graduate Fellowships for Latino Students *(Doctorate/Fellowship)* 782

The Joan Shorenstein Barone Congressional Fellowship *(Professional Development/Fellowship)* 783

Behavioral Sciences Research Training Fellowship *(Postdoctorate/Fellowship)* 2396

Behavioral Sciences Student Fellowship *(Professional Development/Fellowship)* 2397

Bicentennial Swedish-American Exchange Fund Travel Grants *(Professional Development/Grant)* 5656

Donald Bogie Prize *(Graduate/Prize)* 3051

Bosch Foundation Fellowships *(Postgraduate/Fellowship)* 1459

Robert Bosch Foundation Fellowships *(Professional Development/Internship)* 1758

Central Intelligence Agency Graduate Studies Internships *(Graduate/Internship)* 1811

Central Intelligence Agency Undergraduate Scholars Program *(Undergraduate/Internship, Scholarship)* 1812

Chateaubriand Fellowships (Humanities) *(Doctorate/Grant)* 2375

CIBC Youthvision Graduate Research Award Program *(Graduate/Award)* 1270

Council for European Studies Pre-Dissertation Fellowships in the Social Sciences *(Doctorate/Fellowship)* 2102

Council for European Studies Pre-Dissertation Fellowships for Topics Related to the European Community *(Doctorate/Fellowship)* 2103

Cox Minority Journalism Scholarship *(Undergraduate/Scholarship)* 2131

Minda de Gunzburg Center for European Studies Undergraduate Summer Travel Grants *(Undergraduate/Grant)* 2771

Department of National Defense Security and Defense Forum MA and Ph.D Scholarships *(Doctorate, Graduate/Scholarship)* 1273

Dirksen Congressional Research Grants *(Graduate, Postgraduate/Grant)* 2253

H.B. Earhart Fellowships *(Graduate/Fellowship)* 2301

Friedreich Ebert Foundation Doctoral Research Fellowships *(Postgraduate/Fellowship)* 2330

Friedreich Ebert Stiftung Pre Dissertation/Advanced Graduate Fellowshps *(Doctorate, Graduate/Fellowship)* 2332

Albert Einstein Institution Fellowships *(Doctorate, Postdoctorate, Professional Development/Fellowship)* 2361

EMGIP Internships *(Graduate, Professional Development, Undergraduate/Internship)* 2380

Engalitcheff Institute on Comparative Political and Economic Systems Internship *(Undergraduate/Internship)* 3019

Fellowships in Ethics *(Postdoctorate, Postgraduate/Fellowship)* 5015

Fellowships for Taft Seminar for Teachers *(Professional Development/Fellowship)* 5670

Folger Library Long-Term Fellowships *(Postdoctorate/Fellowship)* 2541

Folger Library Short-Term Fellowships *(Postdoctorate/Fellowship)* 2542

Foreign Policy Research Fellowships *(Doctorate/Fellowship)* 1509

William C. Foster Fellows Visiting Scholars Competition *(Postdoctorate, Professional Development/Fellowship)* 5818

Albert Gallatin Fellowships in International Affairs *(Doctorate/Fellowship)* 2613

Garikian University Scholarship Fund *(Undergraduate/Scholarship)* 1119

German Marshall Fund Research Fellowships *(Postdoctorate/Fellowship)* 2695

Germanistic Society of America Quadrille Grants *(Graduate, Postgraduate/Grant)* 2697

Enid Hall Griswold Memorial Scholarship *(Undergraduate/Scholarship)* 4397

Bryce Harlow Institute on Business and Government Affairs Internship *(Undergraduate/Internship)* 3020

Phyllis P. Harris Scholarships *(All/Scholarship)* 4956

Mark O. Hatfield Scholarship *(Graduate/Scholarship)* 5138

Hoover Library Fellowships and Grants *(Graduate, Postdoctorate/Fellowship, Grant)* 2890

AGBU Hirair and Anna Hovnanian Fellowship *(Graduate/Fellowship)* 1123

Howard Foundation Fellowships *(Professional Development/Fellowship)* 2908

Wilma Hoyal/Maxine Chilton Scholarships *(Undergraduate/Scholarship)* 614

Humane Studies Foundation Summer Residential Program Fellowships *(Graduate/Fellowship)* 3053

IGCC Dissertation Fellowships *(Doctorate, Graduate/Fellowship)* 3043

IHS Excellence in Liberty Prizes *(Graduate, Undergraduate/Prize)* 3055

IHS John M. Olin Fellowships *(Graduate/Fellowship)* 3056

IHS Summer Faculty Fellowships *(Professional Development/Fellowship)* 3057

Institute of Developing Economies Visiting Research Fellowships *(Postdoctorate/Fellowship)* 3027

Institute on Political Journalism Summer Program *(Undergraduate/Internship)* 3021

Institute for the Study of World Politics Fellowships *(Doctorate/Fellowship)* 3079

International Affairs Fellowships *(Professional Development/Fellowship)* 2105

Internships *(Graduate/Internship)* 5805

Johnson Foundation Grants-in-Aid of Research *(Professional Development/Grant)* 3282

Johnson Foundation Photocopying Grants *(Graduate/ Grant)* 3283

Judicial Fellowships *(Professional Development/ Fellowship)* 5650

James Madison Fellowships *(Graduate/Fellowship)* 3531

Marine Corps Historical Center College Internships *(Undergraduate/Internship)* 3556

Ministry of the Flemish Community Fellowships *(Postdoctorate, Undergraduate/Fellowship)* 3710

Phillip Morris Public Policy Fellowship *(Professional Development/Fellowship)* 4349

National Endowment for the Humanities Fellowships *(Postdoctorate/Fellowship)* 2543

National Institute of Justice Graduate Research Fellowships *(Doctorate/Fellowship)* 4194

National Tax Association Doctoral Dissertation Awards *(Doctorate/Award)* 4422

NATO Euro-Atlantic Partnership Council Fellowships Programme *(Postdoctorate/Fellowship)* 4655

Near and Middle East Research and Training Program Pre-Doctoral Fellowships *(Doctorate/Fellowship)* 880

OTA Congressional Fellowship *(Doctorate/Fellowship)* 2040

Parliamentary Internships *(Professional Development/ Internship)* 1692

Peace Fellowships *(Postgraduate, Professional Development/ Fellowship)* 5076

Pew Fellowships in International Journalism *(Other/ Fellowship)* 4854

The Poynter Fellowship *(Professional Development/ Fellowship)* 784

Radcliffe Research Support Program *(Postdoctorate/ Grant)* 3798

Spence Reese Scholarship *(High School, Undergraduate/ Scholarship)* 5089

Research Fellowships in Marine Policy *(Postdoctorate/ Fellowship)* 6248

Edith Nourse Rogers Scholarship Fund *(Undergraduate/ Scholarship)* 6230

Roosevelt Institute Grants-in-Aid *(Graduate, Postdoctorate/ Grant)* 5161

Herbert Scoville Jr. Peace Fellowship *(Professional Development/Fellowship)* 5288

SSRC International Predissertation Fellowships *(Doctorate/ Fellowship)* 5402

United States Institute of Peace Distinguished Fellows *(Professional Development/Fellowship)* 5079

Jesse Marvin Unruh Assembly Fellowships *(Graduate, Postgraduate/Fellowship)* 1574

Washington Crossing Foundation Scholarships *(Undergraduate/Scholarship)* 6085

## Portuguese studies (See also: Area and ethnic studies)

Joseph Adams Scholarships *(Undergraduate/ Scholarship)* 5428

## Poultry science

Howard S. Brembeck Scholarship in Agricultural Engineering *(Graduate/Scholarship)* 892

## Pre-Columbian studies

Dumbarton Oaks Project Grants *(Professional Development/ Grant)* 2287

Fellowships in Byzantine Studies, Pre-Columbian Studies and Landscape Architecture *(Doctorate, Graduate, Postdoctorate, Undergraduate/Fellowship)* 2288

## Primatology

Leakey Foundation Fellowships for Great Ape Research and Conservation *(Doctorate, Graduate, Postdoctorate/ Fellowship)* 3442

## Printmaking

Bush Artist Fellowships *(Professional Development/ Fellowship)* 1539

Emergency Assistance Grants *(Other, Professional Development/Grant)* 2719

Gravure Education Foundation Cooperative Education Grant *(Undergraduate/Other)* 2745

Individual Support Grants *(Professional Development/ Grant)* 2720

William D. Krenkler Working Scholar Program *(Undergraduate/ Scholarship)* 5099

National Endowment for the Arts - Visual Artists Fellowships *(Professional Development/Fellowship)* 3982

National Scholarship Trust Fund of the Graphic Arts Fellowships *(Graduate/Fellowship)* 4373

The National Scholarship Trust Fund Scholarships for High School Students *(High School, Undergraduate/ Scholarship)* 4374

The National Scholarship Trust Fund Scholarships for Undergraduates *(Other, Undergraduate/Scholarship)* 4375

New England Graphic Arts Scholarships *(High School, Undergraduate/Scholarship)* 4531

New York Foundation for the Arts Artists' Fellowships *(Other/ Fellowship)* 4570

Pacific Printing and Imaging Association Scholarship *(Undergraduate/Scholarship)* 4826

R & E Council Graphic Arts Educators' Programs *(Professional Development/Grant)* 5101

Texas Graphic Arts Education Foundation Scholarships *(Undergraduate/Scholarship)* 5706

Vermont Studio Center Residency Fellowships *(Professional Development/Fellowship)* 6034

Virginia Museum of Fine Arts Fellowship *(Professional Development/Fellowship)* 6061

Washington Printing Guild Scholarships *(Undergraduate/ Scholarship)* 6095

Harriet Hale Woolley Scholarships *(Graduate/ Scholarship)* 2545

## Protective services

Maryland Reimbursement of Firefighters and Rescue Squad Members *(Graduate, Undergraduate/Scholarship)* 3579

## Psychiatry

APA/Lilly Psychiatric Research Fellowship *(Graduate/ Fellowship)* 800

APA/SmithKline Beecham Junior Faculty Fellowship for Research Development in Biological Psychiatry *(Postdoctorate/Fellowship)* 801

APA/Wyeth-Ayerst M.D. Ph.D. Psychiatric Research Fellowship *(Postdoctorate/Fellowship)* 802

The Applied Social Issues Internship Program *(Graduate, Postdoctorate, Undergraduate/Internship)* 5493

A. E. Bennett Research Awards *(Postdoctorate/Award)* 5438

Center for Mental Health Services Minority Fellowship Program *(Doctorate/Fellowship)* 803

del Duca Foundation Maintenance and Travel Grants *(Professional Development/Grant)* 2284

Fellowship Program in Academic Medicine *(Doctorate/ Fellowship)* 4289

NARSAD Established Investigator Award *(Postdoctorate/ Grant)* 3843

NARSAD Young Investigator Award *(Postdoctorate/ Fellowship)* 3844

Presidential Scholar Awards *(Doctorate/Award)* 218

Program for Minority Research Training in Psychiatry *(Doctorate, Graduate/Fellowship)* 804

Radcliffe Research Support Program *(Postdoctorate/ Grant)* 3798

Robinson/Cunningham Awards *(Postdoctorate/Award)* 219

Rock Sleyster Memorial Scholarship *(Postdoctorate/ Scholarship)* 690

Simon Wile Awards *(Postdoctorate/Award)* 220

Ziskind-Sommerfeld Research Award *(Postdoctorate/ Award)* 5440

## Real estate

APA Planning & the Black Community Division Scholarship *(Undergraduate/Scholarship)* 775

Appraisal Institute Education Trust Scholarships *(Graduate, Undergraduate/Scholarship)* 1060

Harwood Memorial Real Estate Scholarship *(Graduate, Other, Undergraduate/Scholarship)* 5083

## Rehabilitation, Physical/Psychological

Delta Gamma Foundation - Florence Margaret Harvey Memorial Scholarship *(Graduate, Undergraduate/Scholarship)* 480

Rudolph Dillman Scholarship *(Graduate, Undergraduate/Scholarship)* 481

ESRI Doctoral Training Grants ESRI Postdoctoral Fellowships *(Doctorate, Postdoctorate/Fellowship, Grant)* 2316

William and Dorothy Ferrell Scholarship *(Graduate, Undergraduate/Scholarship)* 1235

Kappa Kappa Gamma Rehabilitation Scholarships *(Graduate, Undergraduate/Scholarship)* 3331

Rolfe B. Karlsson Scholarships *(Graduate, Undergraduate/Scholarship)* 2321

Mississippi Health Care Professions Loan/Scholarship Program *(Undergraduate/Scholarship loan)* 3732

Mississippi Psychology Apprenticeship Program *(Graduate, Undergraduate/Internship)* 3738

E.L. Peterson Scholarships *(Graduate, Undergraduate/Scholarship)* 2323

Elizabeth St. Louis Award *(Professional Development/Award)* 2317

Scholarships for Blind and Visually Impaired Postsecondary Students *(Graduate, Undergraduate/Scholarship)* 483

Miriam Neveren Summer Studentship *(Professional Development/Scholarship)* 2318

Telesensory Scholarship *(Graduate, Undergraduate/Scholarship)* 1236

Lynn Marie Vogel Scholarships *(Graduate, Undergraduate/Scholarship)* 2324

## Religion

American Academy of Religion Research Assistance and Collaborative Research Grants *(Other/Grant)* 242

ARIL Research Colloquium Fellowships *(Professional Development/Fellowship)* 1256

Asian Art and Religion Fellowships *(Postdoctorate/Fellowship)* 1176

The Albert Baker Fund *(Graduate, Undergraduate/Loan)* 1362

Frank S. and Elizabeth D. Brewer Prize *(Professional Development/Prize)* 897

Christian Church Hispanic Scholarship *(Graduate/Scholarship)* 1947

Cushwa Center Research Travel Grants *(Postdoctorate/Grant)* 6008

Disciple Chaplain's Scholarship Grant *(Graduate/Scholarship)* 1948

Jane Dempsey Douglass Prize *(Professional Development/Prize)* 898

Eastern Star Educational and Religious Scholarship *(Undergraduate/Scholarship)* 4791

J. Hugh & Earle W. Fellows Memorial Fund Loans *(Undergraduate/Loan)* 2437

Fellowship of United Methodists in Worship, Music and Other Arts Scholarship *(Graduate, Undergraduate/Scholarship)* 2439

Folger Library Long-Term Fellowships *(Postdoctorate/Fellowship)* 2541

Folger Library Short-Term Fellowships *(Postdoctorate/Fellowship)* 2542

Four-Shra-Nish Foundation Loan *(Undergraduate/Loan)* 2583

John Haynes Holmes Memorial Fund *(Other/Award)* 2023

IGCC Dissertation Fellowships *(Doctorate, Graduate/Fellowship)* 3043

Institute for European History Fellowships *(Doctorate, Postdoctorate/Fellowship)* 3035

Institute of Holy Land Studies Scholarships *(Graduate/Scholarship)* 3047

Irish in America Publication Award Notre Dame Studies in Catholicism Publication Award *(Professional Development/Award)* 6009

Clem Jaunich Education Trust Scholarships *(Graduate, Undergraduate/Scholarship)* 3253

David Tamotsu Kagiwada Memorial Fund Award *(Graduate/Scholarship)* 1949

Jesse Lee Prizes *(Graduate/Prize)* 2630

Lett Scholarships *(Graduate, Undergraduate/Scholarship)* 4720

Verne Catt McDowell Corporation Scholarships *(Graduate/Scholarship)* 3622

Sidney E. Mead Prize *(Doctorate, Postdoctorate/Prize)* 899

Ministerial Education Scholarship *(Graduate/Scholarship)* 5782

National Endowment for the Humanities Fellowships *(Postdoctorate/Fellowship)* 2543

National Federation of the Blind Humanities Scholarship *(Undergraduate/Scholarship)* 4003

John Harrison Ness Memorial Awards *(Graduate/Award)* 2631

Charlotte W. Newcombe Fellowships *(Doctorate/Fellowship)* 6188

Ohio Baptist Education Society Scholarships *(Graduate, Undergraduate/Scholarship)* 4721

Oregon Humanities Center Summer Visiting Research Fellowships *(Professional Development/Fellowship)* 6011

Albert C. Outler Prize in Ecumenical Church History *(Professional Development/Prize)* 900

Leonard M. Perryman Communications Scholarship for Ethnic Minority Students *(Undergraduate/Scholarship)* 5794

Presbyterian Church Native American Seminary Scholarships *(Graduate/Scholarship)* 4994

Presbyterian Church Student Loans *(Graduate, Undergraduate/Loan)* 4995

Rockefeller Archive Center Research Grants *(Graduate, Postdoctorate, Professional Development/Grant)* 5142

Charles M. Ross Trust *(Graduate/Other)* 5165

Rowley Ministerial Education Scholarship *(Graduate/Scholarship)* 1951

Robert Schreck Memorial Fund Scholarship *(Graduate, Undergraduate/Scholarship)* 5280

Katherine J. Schutze Memorial Scholarship *(Graduate/Scholarship)* 1952

Service Cancelable Student Loan *(Graduate, Undergraduate/Loan)* 2660

The Spalding Trust *(Other/Other)* 5570

SSRC African Advanced Research Grants *(Postdoctorate/Grant)* 5395

SSRC Grants for Advanced Area Research *(Doctorate, Other/Grant)* 5399

SSRC Korea Advanced Research Grants *(Postdoctorate/Grant)* 5406

SSRC Near and Middle East Advanced Research Fellowships *(Postdoctorate/Fellowship)* 5411

Stoody-West Fellowship in Journalism *(Graduate/Fellowship)* 5795

UMF Annual Conference Scholars Program *(Undergraduate/Scholarship)* 5796

Lillian E. Whitmore Scholarship *(Graduate, Undergraduate/Scholarship)* 6173

Women in United Methodist History Research Grants *(Other/Grant)* 2632

Women in United Methodist History Writing Awards *(Other/Award)* 2633

## Renaissance studies

CMRS Summer Fellowships *(Postdoctorate/Fellowship)* 5988

Folger Library Long-Term Fellowships *(Postdoctorate/Fellowship)* 2541

Folger Library Short-Term Fellowships *(Postdoctorate/Fellowship)* 2542

Audrey Lumsden-Kouvel Fellowship *(Postdoctorate/Fellowship)* 4605

National Endowment for the Humanities Fellowships *(Postdoctorate/Fellowship)* 2543
Villa I Tatti Fellowships *(Postdoctorate/Fellowship)* 6044

## Respiratory therapy
Allied Health Student Loans *(Undergraduate/Loan)* 4870
American Legion Auxiliary Nurses, Physical Therapists and Respiratory Therapists Scholarship *(Undergraduate/Scholarship)* 626
Morton B. Duggan Jr. Memorial Education Recognition Award *(Undergraduate/Scholarship)* 849
Georgia Student Finance Commission Service-Cancellable Stafford Loan *(Graduate, Undergraduate/Loan)* 2666
Georgia Student Finance Commission State-Sponsored Loan *(Graduate, Undergraduate/Loan)* 2669
Jimmy A. Young Memorial Education Recognition Award *(Undergraduate/Scholarship)* 850

## Rheumatology (See also: Arthritis)
Arthritis Biomedical Science Grants *(Postdoctorate/Grant)* 1147
Arthritis Foundation Doctoral Dissertation Award for Arthritis Health Professionals *(Doctorate/Award)* 1148
Arthritis Foundation New Investigator Grant for Arthritis Health Professionals *(Postdoctorate/Grant)* 1149
Arthritis Foundation Physician Scientist Development Award *(Postdoctorate/Award)* 1150
Arthritis Foundation Postdoctoral Fellowships *(Postdoctorate/Fellowship)* 1151
Arthritis Investigator Awards *(Postdoctorate/Award)* 1152
Arthritis Society Clinical Fellowships *(Doctorate/Fellowship)* 1154
Arthritis Society Research Grants *(Postdoctorate/Grant)* 1156
Metro A. Ogryzlo International Fellowship *(Postdoctorate/Fellowship)* 1159

## Romanian studies (See also: Area and ethnic studies)
Society Farsarotul Grants *(Graduate, Undergraduate/Grant)* 5449

## Schizophrenia
Benevolent Foundation Dissertation Research Fellowships *(Postdoctorate/Fellowship)* 1411
Benevolent Foundation Research Grants *(Postdoctorate/Grant)* 1412

## Science
AAAS Directorate for Science & Policy Administrative Internship *(Graduate, Undergraduate/Internship)* 264
AAAS Technology Policy Science and Engineering Fellowships *(Postdoctorate, Professional Development/Fellowship)* 267
AGU Congressional Science Fellowship Program *(Postdoctorate/Fellowship)* 510
American Water Works Association Scholarship Program *(Doctorate, Graduate/Scholarship)* 1017
F.M. Becket Memorial Award *(Doctorate, Graduate/Fellowship)* 2366
BPW Career Advancement Scholarships *(Graduate, Undergraduate/Scholarship)* 1546
Cape Canaveral Chapter Scholarships *(Graduate, Undergraduate/Scholarship)* 5114
Central Intelligence Agency Graduate Studies Internships *(Graduate/Internship)* 1811
CFUW Awards *(Graduate/Award)* 1631
CHROME Scholarship *(Undergraduate/Scholarship)* 2081
CIC Predoctoral Fellowships *(Doctorate, Graduate/Fellowship)* 2013
Czech Education Scholarships *(Doctorate, Graduate, Postdoctorate/Scholarship)* 3708
Arthur Davis Fellowship; Charles E. Merrill Trust Fellowship *(Graduate/Fellowship)* 3806
DOE Student Research Participation *(Graduate, Postdoctorate, Undergraduate/Award)* 4705
The DuPont Challenge: Science Essay Awards Program *(High School/Award)* 2643

Edelstein International Fellowship in the History of Chemical Sciences and Technology *(Postdoctorate/Fellowship)* 1900
Thomas Edison/Max McGraw Scholarship *(High School, Undergraduate/Scholarship)* 4379
Electronic Industries Foundation Scholarships *(Graduate, Undergraduate/Scholarship)* 2370
Explorers Club Exploration Fund Grants *(Graduate, Postgraduate/Grant)* 2425
Folger Library Long-Term Fellowships *(Postdoctorate/Fellowship)* 2541
Folger Library Short-Term Fellowships *(Postdoctorate/Fellowship)* 2542
Georgia Student Finance Commission Service-Cancellable Stafford Loan *(Graduate, Undergraduate/Loan)* 2666
Georgia Student Finance Commission State-Sponsored Loan *(Graduate, Undergraduate/Loan)* 2669
Grants for Physically Disabled Students in the Sciences *(Graduate/Grant)* 2579
International Scientific Prize *(Professional Development/Prize)* 2611
Logistics Education Foundation Scholarship *(Graduate, Undergraduate/Scholarship)* 5463
Maryland MESA Scholarships *(High School, Undergraduate/Scholarship)* 3586
Masonic-Range Science Scholarship *(Undergraduate/Scholarship)* 5500
Mass Media Science and Engineering Fellowships *(Graduate/Fellowship)* 268
Allen H. Meyers Scholarship *(Undergraduate/Scholarship)* 3677
Miller Institute Research Fellowships *(Postdoctorate/Fellowship)* 5984
Ministry of the Flemish Community Fellowships *(Postdoctorate, Undergraduate/Fellowship)* 3710
NAS/NRC Collaboration in Basic Science and Engineering Long-Term Grants *(Postdoctorate/Grant)* 3831
NAS/NRC Collaboration in Basic Science and Engineering Short-Term Project Development Grants *(Postdoctorate/Grant)* 3832
NASA-ASEE Summer Faculty Fellowship *(Professional Development/Fellowship)* 923
NASA Field Center Resident Research Associateships *(Postdoctorate/Other)* 3838
NASA Graduate Student Research Fellowships *(Graduate/Fellowship)* 3839
National Endowment for the Humanities Fellowships *(Postdoctorate/Fellowship)* 2543
New Jersey Academy of Science Research Grants-in-Aid to High School Students *(High School/Grant)* 4537
Petro-Canada Inc. Graduate Research Awards *(Doctorate, Graduate/Award)* 1284
Postdoctoral Fellowships in the History and Philosophy of Science *(Postdoctorate/Fellowship)* 4699
Polingaysi Qoyawayma Scholarship *(Graduate/Scholarship)* 562
SHPE Foundation Education Grant *(Graduate, Undergraduate/Grant)* 5454
SSRC Grants for Collaborative Activities between American and Japanese Scholars *(Professional Development/Grant)* 5400
Tandy Technology Scholars *(Undergraduate/Scholarship)* 5672
United Nations Educational Training Scholarships for Southern Africans *(Graduate, Undergraduate/Scholarship)* 5798
Westinghouse Science Talent Search *(Undergraduate/Scholarship)* 5282

## Science technologies
Bank of Sweden Tercentenary Foundation Project Grants *(Professional Development/Grant)* 1372
Renate W. Chasman Scholarship *(Graduate, Undergraduate/Scholarship)* 1507
High Temperatures Materials Laboratory (HTML) Graduate Student Fellowships *(Graduate/Fellowship)* 5888
MSA Undergraduate Research Scholarships *(Undergraduate/Scholarship)* 3697

## Social sciences (continued)

United Nations Educational Training Scholarships for Southern Africans *(Graduate, Undergraduate/Scholarship)* 5798

United Nations Fellowships *(Professional Development/ Fellowship)* 5799

Richard M. Weaver Fellowship *(Graduate/Fellowship)* 3099

Woodrow Wilson Center Residential Fellowship *(Postdoctorate/Fellowship)* 6184

Woodswomen Scholarship Fund *(Other/Grant, Scholarship)* 6255

Xerox Scholarships *(Undergraduate/Scholarship)* 6272

Young Canadian Researchers Awards *(Doctorate, Graduate/ Award)* 3151

## Social work

American Cancer Society Clinical Oncology Social Work Training Grants *(Postgraduate/Grant)* 362

Behavioral Sciences Research Training Fellowship *(Postdoctorate/Fellowship)* 2396

Mildred Cater Bradham Social Work Fellowship *(Doctorate, Graduate/Fellowship)* 6303

Council on Social Work Education Minority Fellowships *(Doctorate/Fellowship)* 3724

Federation Executive Recruitment and Education Program (FEREP) Scholarships *(Graduate/Scholarship)* 2117

Jewish Federation of Metropolitan Chicago Academic Scholarships *(Doctorate, Graduate, Undergraduate/ Scholarship)* 3265

New York State Professional Opportunity Scholarships *(Doctorate, Graduate, Undergraduate/Scholarship)* 4592

New York State Regents Professional Opportunity Scholarships *(Doctorate, Graduate, Undergraduate/ Scholarship)* 4577

The Lois and Samuel Silberman Awards *(Professional Development/Award)* 5351

Statten Fellowship *(Graduate/Fellowship)* 5624

## Sociology (See also: Aggression and violence)

Gordon Allport Intergroup Relations Prize *(Graduate, Postgraduate/Prize)* 5492

American Sociological Association Minority Fellowships *(Doctorate/Fellowship)* 986

American Sociological Association Research Doctoral Fellowships in Sociology *(Doctorate/Fellowship)* 987

APA Planning & the Black Community Division Scholarship *(Undergraduate/Scholarship)* 775

Asian American Studies Center Postdoctoral Fellowship/ Visiting Scholars Awards *(Postdoctorate/Award, Fellowship)* 1174

Behavioral Sciences Research Training Fellowship *(Postdoctorate/Fellowship)* 2396

Chateaubriand Fellowships (Humanities) *(Doctorate/ Grant)* 2375

CIBC Youthvision Graduate Research Award Program *(Graduate/Award)* 1270

The Clara Mayo Grant *(Graduate/Grant)* 5494

Council for European Studies Pre-Dissertation Fellowships in the Social Sciences *(Doctorate/Fellowship)* 2102

Council for European Studies Pre-Dissertation Fellowships for Topics Related to the European Community *(Doctorate/ Fellowship)* 2103

Friedreich Ebert Foundation Doctoral Research Fellowships *(Postgraduate/Fellowship)* 2330

Friedreich Ebert Stiftung Pre Dissertation/Advanced Graduate Fellowshps *(Doctorate, Graduate/Fellowship)* 2332

H. F. Guggenheim Foundation Dissertation Fellowships *(Doctorate/Fellowship)* 2758

H. F. Guggenheim Foundation Research Grants *(Postdoctorate/Grant)* 2759

Phyllis P. Harris Scholarships *(All/Scholarship)* 4956

Howard Foundation Fellowships *(Professional Development/ Fellowship)* 2908

IGCC Dissertation Fellowships *(Doctorate, Graduate/ Fellowship)* 3043

---

IHS Excellence in Liberty Prizes *(Graduate, Undergraduate/ Prize)* 3055

Institute of Developing Economies Visiting Research Fellowships *(Postdoctorate/Fellowship)* 3027

International Affairs Fellowships *(Professional Development/ Fellowship)* 2105

Krupp Foundation Fellowship *(Graduate/Fellowship)* 2773

Ida L., Mary L., and Ervin R. NePage Foundation *(Undergraduate/Scholarship)* 4513

Edwin G. Nourse Award *(Doctorate/Award)* 3952

Olfactory Research Fund Grants *(Postdoctorate/Grant)* 4744

Population Council Fellowships in the Social Sciences *(Postdoctorate/Fellowship)* 4981

Radcliffe Research Support Program *(Postdoctorate/ Grant)* 3798

Research Fellowships in Marine Policy *(Postdoctorate/ Fellowship)* 6248

SSRC International Predissertation Fellowships *(Doctorate/ Fellowship)* 5402

Arthur Weinberg Fellowship for Independent Scholars *(Professional Development/Fellowship)* 4612

## Soviet studies

Davis Center for Russian Studies Postdoctoral Fellowships *(Postdoctorate/Fellowship)* 2191

IREX Short-Term Travel Grants for Independent Short-Term Research *(Postdoctorate/Grant)* 3187

SSRC Soviet Union and Its Successor States Dissertation Fellowships *(Doctorate/Fellowship)* 5418

SSRC Soviet Union and Its Successor States Graduate Training Fellowships *(Graduate/Fellowship)* 5419

SSRC Soviet Union and Its Successor States Institutional Awards for First-Year Fellowships *(Graduate/Award)* 5420

SSRC Soviet Union and Its Successor States Postdoctoral Fellowships *(Postdoctorate/Fellowship)* 5421

SSRC Soviet Union and Its Successor States Workshop Grants *(Doctorate, Postdoctorate/Grant)* 5422

## Space and planetary sciences (See also: Astronomy and astronomical sciences)

Carnegie Institution of Washington Postdoctoral and Predoctoral Fellowships *(Doctorate, Postdoctorate/ Fellowship)* 1737

Lunar and Planetary Institute Visiting Graduate Fellows *(Graduate/Fellowship)* 3515

Lunar and Planetary Institute Visiting Postdoctoral Fellowships *(Postdoctorate/Fellowship)* 3516

Lunar and Planetary Institute Visiting Scientist Program *(Postdoctorate/Fellowship)* 3517

Judith Resnik Memorial Scholarship *(Undergraduate/ Scholarship)* 5519

Tennessee Space Grant Consortium Fellowships and Scholarships *(Graduate, Undergraduate/Fellowship, Scholarship)* 5698

U.S. Air Force Phillips Laboratory Scholar Program *(Postdoctorate/Other)* 4686

## Spanish studies (See also: Area and ethnic studies)

Joseph Adams Scholarships *(Undergraduate/ Scholarship)* 5428

Cultural Cooperation Grants *(Doctorate, Graduate, Postgraduate, Professional Development/Grant)* 6004

Research Grants for Cultural Cooperation *(Postdoctorate/ Grant)* 5013

## Speech and language pathology/Audiology

AMBUCS Scholars *(Graduate, Undergraduate/ Scholarship)* 3854

American Speech-Language-Hearing Foundation Graduate Student Scholarships *(Doctorate, Graduate/ Scholarship)* 989

American Speech-Language-Hearing Foundation Research Grants for New Investigators *(Doctorate, Graduate, Postdoctorate, Postgraduate/Grant)* 990

American Speech-Language-Hearing Foundation Student Research Grant in Audiology *(Graduate, Postgraduate/ Grant)* 991

GFWC of MA Communication Disorder Scholarships *(Graduate/Scholarship)* 2637

Leslie Isenberg Graduate Scholarship *(Doctorate, Graduate/ Scholarship)* 992

Kansas City Speech Pathology Award *(Graduate/Award)* 3327

Mississippi Health Care Professions Loan/Scholarship Program *(Undergraduate/Scholarship loan)* 3732

NAJA Graduate Scholarships *(Graduate/Scholarship)* 3881

New York State Professional Opportunity Scholarships *(Doctorate, Graduate, Undergraduate/Scholarship)* 4592

New York State Regents Professional Opportunity Scholarships *(Doctorate, Graduate, Undergraduate/ Scholarship)* 4577

Research Grant in Speech Science *(Postdoctorate/Grant)* 993

Scholarships for Therapists *(Professional Development/ Scholarship)* 3855

Kala Singh Graduate Scholarship *(Doctorate, Graduate/ Scholarship)* 994

Stokoe Scholarships *(Graduate/Scholarship)* 3873

Student Research Grant in Early Childhood Language Development *(Graduate, Postgraduate/Grant)* 995

## Spinal cord injuries and research

Fellowships in Spinal Cord Injury Research *(Postdoctorate/ Fellowship)* 4830

## Sports writing

Edward J. Nell Memorial Scholarships in Journalism *(Undergraduate/Scholarship)* 5048

Fred Russell-Grantland RICE TRA Sports Writing *(Undergraduate/Scholarship)* 5729

## Statistics

AAUW Educational Foundation Selected Professions Fellowship *(Graduate/Fellowship)* 336

ASA/NCES/NSF Research Fellowships *(Postdoctorate/ Fellowship)* 997

ASA/NSF/BLS Senior Research Fellowship *(Postdoctorate/ Fellowship)* 998

ASA/NSF/Census Research Fellowship *(Postdoctorate/ Fellowship)* 999

ASA/NSF/NIST Senior Research Fellowships and Associateships *(Postdoctorate/Fellowship)* 1000

ASA/USDA/NASS Research Fellowships and Associateships *(Doctorate, Postdoctorate/Fellowship)* 1001

AT & T Bell Laboratories Cooperative Research Fellowships for Minorities *(Graduate/Fellowship)* 1302

AT & T Bell Laboratories Graduate Research Fellowships for Women *(Doctorate/Fellowship)* 1303

AT & T Bell Laboratories Graduate Research Grants for Women *(Doctorate, Graduate/Grant)* 1304

AT & T Bell Laboratories Summer Research Program for Minorities & Women *(Undergraduate/Fellowship)* 1305

AT & T Bell Laboratories University Relations Summer Program *(Doctorate, Graduate, Undergraduate/Work Study)* 1306

The BBM Scholarship *(Graduate/Scholarship)* 1601

ETS Center for Performance Assessment Postdoctoral Fellowships *(Postdoctorate/Fellowship)* 2352

ETS Postdoctoral Fellowships *(Postdoctorate/ Fellowship)* 2353

ETS Summer Program in Research for Graduate Students *(Doctorate/Award)* 2354

William C. Foster Fellows Visiting Scholars Competition *(Postdoctorate, Professional Development/Fellowship)* 5818

Research Associateships and Fellowships in Statistics *(Postdoctorate/Fellowship)* 1321

Research Fellowships in Marine Policy *(Postdoctorate/ Fellowship)* 6248

## Substance abuse

NIDA Individual National Research Service Awards *(Doctorate, Postdoctorate/Fellowship)* 4192

## Sudden infant death syndrome

Dr. Sydney Segal Research Grants *(Doctorate, Graduate/ Grant)* 1638

## Surgery

Career Development Awards in Orthopaedic Surgery *(Professional Development/Grant)* 4814

Detweiler Travelling Fellowships *(Postdoctorate/ Fellowship)* 5184

ICS Research Scholarships *(Postdoctorate/Scholarship)* 3137

Walter C. MacKenzie, Johnson and Johnson Fellowship *(Postdoctorate/Fellowship)* 5185

Medical Education Travelling Fellowship *(Postdoctorate/ Fellowship)* 5186

Plastic Surgery Educational Foundation Scholarships *(Professional Development/Prize, Scholarship)* 4958

Research Grants in Orthopaedic Surgery *(Postdoctorate/ Grant)* 4815

Resident Research Fellowships in Orthopaedic Surgery *(Postdoctorate/Fellowship)* 4816

James H. Robinson Memorial Prize *(Doctorate/Prize)* 4305

## Swedish studies

Bicentennial Swedish-American Exchange Fund Travel Grants *(Professional Development/Grant)* 5656

## Taxonomy

National Tax Association Doctoral Dissertation Awards *(Doctorate/Award)* 4422

## Technology

AAAS Congressional Science and Engineering Fellowships *(Postdoctorate, Professional Development/Fellowship)* 263

AAAS Directorate for Science & Policy Administrative Internship *(Graduate, Undergraduate/Internship)* 264

AAAS Technology Policy Science and Engineering Fellowships *(Postdoctorate, Professional Development/Fellowship)* 267

Anne Maureen Whitney Barrow Memorial Scholarship *(Undergraduate/Scholarship)* 5506

CFUW Awards *(Graduate/Award)* 1631

CHROME Scholarship *(Undergraduate/Scholarship)* 2081

Electronic Industries Foundation Scholarships *(Graduate, Undergraduate/Scholarship)* 2370

General Motors Foundation Scholarships for Graduates *(Undergraduate/Scholarship)* 5509

General Motors Foundation Scholarships for Undergraduates *(Undergraduate/Scholarship)* 5510

IEEE Fellowship in Electrical History *(Doctorate, Graduate, Postdoctorate/Fellowship)* 3033

Iota Lambda Sigma Grand Chapter Scholarship *(Doctorate, Graduate/Scholarship)* 3213

Wayne Kay Graduate Fellowships *(Graduate/Fellowship)* 5466

Martino Scholars Program *(Graduate/Fellowship)* 4239

Mass Media Science and Engineering Fellowships *(Graduate/ Fellowship)* 268

Microsoft Corporation Scholarships *(Graduate, Undergraduate/ Scholarship)* 5516

National Scholarship Trust Fund of the Graphic Arts Fellowships *(Graduate/Fellowship)* 4373

NATO Senior Guest Fellowships *(Professional Development/ Fellowship)* 4656

NDDOT Educational Grants *(Undergraduate/Scholarship loan)* 4682

St. Louis SME Chapter No. 17 Scholarships *(Undergraduate/ Scholarship)* 5468

Smithsonian Institution Graduate Fellowships *(Graduate/ Fellowship)* 5376

Smithsonian Institution Postdoctoral Fellowships *(Postdoctorate/Fellowship)* 5377

Smithsonian Institution Predoctoral Fellowships *(Doctorate/ Fellowship)* 5378

## Telecommunications systems
William E. Jackson Award *(Graduate/Award)* 5198

## Textile science
Stella Blum Research Grant *(Graduate, Undergraduate/ Grant)* 2089

Mary Josephine Cochran Fellowship *(Graduate/ Fellowship)* 291

National Wool Growers Memorial Fellowships *(Graduate/ Fellowship)* 887

Polaire Weissman Fund Fellowship *(Doctorate, Graduate/ Fellowship)* 3669

YMA Scholarships *(Graduate/Scholarship)* 6295

## Theater arts
Arts Recognition and Talent Search (ARTS) *(Undergraduate/ Award)* 4158

Banff Centre for the Arts Scholarships *(Postgraduate, Professional Development/Scholarship)* 1370

CFGP Radio Station Scholarships *(Undergraduate/ Scholarship)* 8

Chautauqua Institution Scholarship *(Graduate, High School, Undergraduate/Scholarship)* 1842

Hungarian Arts Club Scholarships *(Undergraduate/ Scholarship)* 2935

Jacob's Pillow Dance Festival Internships *(Graduate, Undergraduate/Internship)* 3234

Vincent Minnelli Scholarship *(Undergraduate/ Scholarship)* 4242

Minnesota Artist Assistance Fellowships *(Professional Development/Fellowship)* 3714

Minnesota Career Opportunity Grants *(Professional Development/Grant)* 3715

National Alliance for Excellence Honored Scholars Awards *(Graduate, Undergraduate/Scholarship)* 3841

National Endowment for the Arts - Director Fellows *(Professional Development/Fellowship)* 3975

National Theatre Artist Residency Grants *(Professional Development/Grant)* 5723

NEA/TCG Career Development Program for Designers *(Other/ Grant)* 5724

NEA/TCG Career Development Program for Directors *(Other/ Grant)* 5725

New Hampshire Individual Artist Fellowships *(Other/ Fellowship)* 4535

Jean Pratt Scholarship *(High School/Scholarship)* 1453

Anne Bradshaw Stokes Foundation Scholarships *(Undergraduate/Scholarship)* 5632

TELACU Arts Award *(Undergraduate/Scholarship)* 5689

Robert Thunen Memorial Educational Scholarships *(Graduate, Undergraduate/Scholarship)* 2983

World Model Awards *(Other, Professional Development/ Scholarship)* 6266

## Theology (See also: Religion)
Beinecke Library Visiting Fellowships *(Postdoctorate/ Fellowship)* 1393

Christian Church Hispanic Scholarship *(Graduate/ Scholarship)* 1947

Disciple Chaplain's Scholarship Grant *(Graduate/ Scholarship)* 1948

Eastern Star Educational and Religious Scholarship *(Undergraduate/Scholarship)* 4791

Fellowships in Ethics *(Postdoctorate, Postgraduate/ Fellowship)* 5015

Franks Foundation Loan *(Graduate, Undergraduate/ Loan)* 5832

Greek Orthodox Ladies Philoptochos Society Scholarships for Hellenic College and Holy Cross Greek Orthodox School of Theology *(Graduate, Postgraduate/Scholarship)* 2749

John Haynes Holmes Memorial Fund *(Other/Award)* 2023

Clem Jaunich Education Trust Scholarships *(Graduate, Undergraduate/Scholarship)* 3253

David Tamotsu Kagiwada Memorial Fund Award *(Graduate/ Scholarship)* 1949

Lois T. Larson Scholarship *(Undergraduate/Scholarship)* 1877

Jesse Lee Prizes *(Graduate/Prize)* 2630

Verne Catt McDowell Corporation Scholarships *(Graduate/ Scholarship)* 3622

Ministerial Education Scholarship *(Graduate/Scholarship)* 5782

Native American Seminary Scholarships *(Graduate/ Scholarship)* 4993

John Harrison Ness Memorial Awards *(Graduate/Award)* 2631

New England Education Society Loan *(Graduate/Loan)* 4527

Presbyterian Church Native American Seminary Scholarships *(Graduate/Scholarship)* 4994

Presbyterian Church Student Loans *(Graduate, Undergraduate/ Loan)* 4995

Presbyterian Study Grants *(Graduate/Grant)* 4997

Racial/Ethnic Leadership Supplemental Grants *(Graduate/ Grant)* 4998

Rowley Ministerial Education Scholarship *(Graduate/ Scholarship)* 1951

Robert Schreck Memorial Fund Scholarship *(Graduate, Undergraduate/Scholarship)* 5280

Katherine J. Schutze Memorial Scholarship *(Graduate/ Scholarship)* 1952

Service Cancelable Student Loan *(Graduate, Undergraduate/ Loan)* 2660

Spalding Trust Postgraduate Scholarship/Grant *(Postgraduate/ Grant)* 5571

Ullery Charitable Trust Scholarship *(Undergraduate/ Scholarship)* 5765

Women in United Methodist History Research Grants *(Other/ Grant)* 2632

Women in United Methodist History Writing Awards *(Other/ Award)* 2633

## Tourette syndrome
TSA Clinical Studies Grants; TSA Postdoctoral Training Fellowships; TSA Research Grants *(Postdoctorate/ Grant)* 5735

## Toxicology
Agency for Toxic Substances and Disease Registry Postgraduate Research Program *(Postgraduate/ Fellowship)* 5859

Agency for Toxic Substances and Disease Registry Student Internship Program *(Doctorate, Graduate/Internship)* 5860

CIIT Postdoctoral Trainee Fellowships *(Postdoctorate/ Fellowship)* 1902

CIIT Summer Internships *(Graduate, Postgraduate, Undergraduate/Internship)* 1903

Lord Dowding Grant *(Doctorate, Graduate/Grant)* 2278

Faculty Research Participation Program at the Agency for Toxic Substances and Disease Registry *(Professional Development/Fellowship)* 5872

Faculty Research Participation Program at the National Center for Toxicological Research *(Professional Development/ Fellowship)* 5874

National Center for Toxicological Research Graduate Student Research Participation *(Graduate, Postgraduate/ Fellowship)* 5906

National Center for Toxicological Research Postgraduate Research Program *(Postgraduate/Fellowship)* 5907

National Center for Toxicological Research Undergraduate Program *(Undergraduate/Internship)* 5908

## Translating
Arabic Translation Contest *(Other/Prize)* 323

Friendship Commission Prize for the Translation of Japanese Literature *(Professional Development/Prize)* 3341

International Book Translation and Publishing Program *(Professional Development/Award)* 1318

International Magazine Publishing Program *(Professional Development/Award)* 1319

National Endowment for the Arts - Literature Program Translators' Fellowships *(Professional Development/ Fellowship)* 3978

## Transportation

ABCI Scholarships (*Undergraduate/Scholarship*) 1343

APA Planning & the Black Community Division Scholarship (*Undergraduate/Scholarship*) 775

Canadian Transportation Education Foundation Scholarships and Research Grants (*Postdoctorate, Professional Development/Grant, Scholarship*) 1706

Chartered Institute of Transport to New Zealand Scholarships (*Professional Development/Scholarship*) 1838

CN Native Education Awards (*Undergraduate/Award*) 1974

Ginger & Fred Deines Canada Scholarships (*Graduate, Undergraduate, Other/Scholarship*) 5741

Ginger and Fred Deines Mexico Scholarships (*Graduate, Professional Development, Undergraduate/ Scholarship*) 5742

Dwight David Eisenhower Transportation Fellowship (*Doctorate, Graduate/Fellowship*) 6052

Hooper Memorial Scholarship(s) (*Graduate, Undergraduate/ Scholarship*) 5743

Denny Lydic Scholarship (*Graduate, Undergraduate, Other/ Scholarship*) 5744

Helene Overly Scholarship (*Graduate/Scholarship*) 6243

SEMA Scholarship (*Graduate, Postgraduate, Undergraduate/ Scholarship*) 5581

E.J. Sierleja Memorial Fellowship (*Graduate/Fellowship*) 3063

Henry Spurrier Scholarship (*Professional Development/ Scholarship*) 1836

TAC Scholarships (*Graduate/Scholarship*) 5739

Texas Transportation Scholarship (*Graduate, Undergraduate/ Scholarship*) 5745

Charlotte Woods Memorial Scholarship (*Graduate, Undergraduate/Scholarship*) 5746

## Travel and tourism

Academy of Travel and Tourism Award (*High School/ Award*) 4426

Air Travel Card Grant (*Undergraduate/Grant*) 969

American Express Travel Scholarship (*Undergraduate/ Scholarship*) 970

Arizona Chapter Dependent Employee Membership Scholarship (*Undergraduate/Scholarship*) 971

Avis Rent a Car Scholarship (*Doctorate, Graduate, Professional Development, Undergraduate/Scholarship*) 972

Canadian Hospitality Foundation Scholarships (*Undergraduate/ Scholarship*) 1653

Bill Carpenter Memorial Certificate School Scholarship (*Undergraduate/Scholarship*) 4429

Luray Caverns Research Grant (*Doctorate, Graduate/ Grant*) 4430

David Hallissey Memorial Scholarships (*Graduate, Postgraduate/Scholarship*) 973

Healy Scholarship (*Undergraduate/Scholarship*) 974

Holland-America Line Westours Scholarships (*Undergraduate/ Scholarship*) 975

Patrick Murphy Internship (*Undergraduate/Internship*) 4436

Northern California/Richard Epping Scholarships (*Undergraduate/Scholarship*) 976

NTF Internship (*Undergraduate/Internship*) 4437

Orange County Chapter/Harry Jackson Scholarship (*Undergraduate/Scholarship*) 977

Pollard Scholarships (*Undergraduate/Scholarship*) 978

Princess Cruises and Princess Tours Scholarship (*Undergraduate/Scholarship*) 979

George Reinke Scholarships (*Undergraduate/Scholarship*) 980

Simmons Scholarship (*Doctorate, Graduate/Scholarship*) 981

Southern California Chapter/Pleasant Hawaiian Holidays Scholarship (*Undergraduate/Scholarship*) 982

A.J. (Andy) Spielman Scholarships (*Undergraduate/ Scholarship*) 983

Joseph R. Stone Scholarships (*Undergraduate/ Scholarship*) 984

Visiting Scholar Awards (*Professional Development/ Award*) 4441

## Tuberculosis

Heiser Postdoctoral Research Fellowships (*Postdoctorate/ Fellowship*) 2857

Heiser Research Grants (*Postdoctorate/Grant*) 2858

## Urban affairs/design/planning

Charles Abrams Scholarships (*Graduate/Scholarship*) 774

APA Planning & the Black Community Division Scholarship (*Undergraduate/Scholarship*) 775

APA Planning Fellowships (*Graduate/Fellowship*) 776

Association for Women in Architecture Scholarship (*Graduate, Undergraduate/Scholarship*) 1292

Center for Advanced Study in the Visual Arts Senior Fellowships and Senior Visiting Fellowships (*Postdoctorate/ Fellowship*) 1767

Council for European Studies Pre-Dissertation Fellowships in the Social Sciences (*Doctorate/Fellowship*) 2102

Cox Minority Journalism Scholarship (*Undergraduate/ Scholarship*) 2131

Emergency Preparedness Canada Research Fellowship Program (*Graduate/Fellowship*) 1274

Government Scholars Summer Program (*Graduate, Undergraduate/Award*) 4562

National Endowment for the Arts - Design Arts Program USA Fellowships (*Professional Development/Fellowship*) 3974

NCSGC National Scholarships (*Graduate, Undergraduate/ Scholarship*) 3959

New York City Urban Fellowships (*Graduate, Professional Development/Fellowship*) 4563

Revson Fellowships (*Professional Development/ Fellowship*) 5118

SSRC-MacArthur Foundation Postdoctoral Fellowships on Peace and Security in a Changing World (*Postdoctorate/ Fellowship*) 5410

Summer Graduate Internships (*Graduate, Professional Development/Internship*) 4564

## Urology

AFUD/NKF Resident Fellowship (*Postdoctorate/ Fellowship*) 498

AFUD/Ph.D. Research Scholar Program (*Postdoctorate/ Award*) 499

AFUD Research Scholars Program (*Postdoctorate/Award*) 500

AFUD Summer Student Fellowships (*Doctorate/ Fellowship*) 501

Allied Health Doctoral Fellowships (*Doctorate, Professional Development/Fellowship*) 3368

Allied Health Research Grants (*Professional Development/ Grant*) 3369

Allied Health Scholarships (*Graduate, Postgraduate/ Scholarship*) 3370

Biomedical Fellowships (*Postdoctorate/Fellowship*) 3371

Biomedical Research Grant (*Postdoctorate/Grant*) 3372

Biomedical Scholarship (*Doctorate, Postdoctorate/ Scholarship*) 3373

National Kidney Foundation Research Fellowships (*Postdoctorate/Fellowship*) 4279

Practicing Urologist's Research Award (*Postdoctorate/ Award*) 502

## Vacuum science and technology

AVS Student Prize; Russel and Sigurd Varian Fellowship (*Graduate/Fellowship, Prize*) 1008

Welch Foundation Scholarship (*Graduate, Postdoctorate/ Scholarship*) 3199

Nellie Yeoh Whetten Award (*Graduate/Award*) 1009

## Veterinary science and medicine

American Kennel Clubs Veterinary Scholarship (*Undergraduate/Scholarship*) 604

American Liver Foundation Student Research Fellowships (*Doctorate, Graduate, Other/Fellowship*) 674

Animal Health Trust of Canada Research Grants (*Doctorate/ Award*) 1046

## Veterinary science and medicine (continued)

Association for Women Veterinarians Student Scholarships *(Graduate/Scholarship)* 1298

AVMF Auxiliary Student Loan *(Graduate, Postgraduate/Loan)* 1011

BARD Postdoctoral Fellowships; BARD Research Fellows Program *(Postdoctorate/Fellowship)* 1432

A & E Capelle LN Herfords Scholarship *(Doctorate, Graduate, Undergraduate/Scholarship)* 150

Career Development Fellowships *(Postdoctorate, Postgraduate/Fellowship)* 1611

Celanese Canada Inc. Scholarships *(Undergraduate/Scholarship)* 1269

Dog Writers' Educational Trust Scholarships *(Graduate, Undergraduate/Scholarship)* 2264

Lord Dowding Grant *(Doctorate, Graduate/Grant)* 2278

Georgia Student Finance Commission Service-Cancellable Stafford Loan *(Graduate, Undergraduate/Loan)* 2666

Georgia Student Finance Commission State-Sponsored Loan *(Graduate, Undergraduate/Loan)* 2669

Health Education Loan Program *(Doctorate, Graduate/Loan)* 5709

HRSA-BHP Health Professions Student Loans *(Doctorate, Graduate/Loan)* 5967

HRSA-BHP Loans for Disadvantaged Students *(Undergraduate/Loan)* 5968

National Zoological Park Minority Traineeships *(Graduate, Undergraduate/Internship)* 4456

National Zoological Park Research Traineeships *(Graduate, Undergraduate/Internship)* 4457

New York State Professional Opportunity Scholarships *(Doctorate, Graduate, Undergraduate/Scholarship)* 4592

New York State Regents Professional Opportunity Scholarships *(Doctorate, Graduate, Undergraduate/Scholarship)* 4577

North American Limousin Foundation Scholarship *(Undergraduate/Scholarship)* 4112

Oklahoma State Regents for Higher Education Professional Study Grants *(Graduate/Grant)* 4740

Abbie Sargent Memorial Scholarships *(Graduate, Undergraduate/Scholarship)* 5250

Robert Schreck Memorial Fund Scholarship *(Graduate, Undergraduate/Scholarship)* 5280

Western Interstate Commission for Higher Education Student Exchanges *(Doctorate, Graduate/Other)* 135

Arizona WICHE Professional Student Exchange Program *(Professional Development/Work Study)* 1089

## Video

Bush Artist Fellowships *(Professional Development/Fellowship)* 1539

MacDowell Colony Residencies *(Other, Professional Development/Fellowship)* 3524

National Endowment for the Arts - Visual Artists Fellowships *(Professional Development/Fellowship)* 3982

New York Foundation for the Arts Artists' Fellowships *(Other/Fellowship)* 4570

University Film and Video Association Student Grants *(Graduate, Undergraduate/Grant)* 5992

Virginia Museum of Fine Arts Fellowship *(Professional Development/Fellowship)* 6061

## Visual arts

Artists Fellowships and Residencies *(Professional Development/Fellowship)* 3766

Artpark Residencies *(Professional Development/Award)* 1161

Arts Recognition and Talent Search (ARTS) *(Undergraduate/Award)* 4158

Asian Cultural Council Fellowship Grants *(Postdoctorate/Fellowship)* 1177

Banff Centre for the Arts Scholarships *(Postgraduate, Professional Development/Scholarship)* 1370

Blue Mountain Center Residencies *(Professional Development/Internship)* 1446

Bunting Fellowship *(Postdoctorate, Professional Development/Fellowship)* 1526

Bunting Institute Affiliation Program *(Postdoctorate, Professional Development/Other)* 1527

Canadian Council for the Arts Grants Program *(Professional Development/Grant)* 1594

Center for Advanced Study in the Visual Arts Senior Fellowships and Senior Visiting Fellowships *(Postdoctorate/Fellowship)* 1767

Center For Advanced Study in the Visual Arts Associate Appointments *(Postdoctorate/Fellowship)* 1768

Cintas Fellowships *(Professional Development/Fellowship)* 1163

The Cleveland Institute of Art Portfolio Scholarships *(Undergraduate/Scholarship)* 1966

Contemporary Record Society National Festival for the Performing Arts *(Professional Development/Fellowship)* 2071

Cummington Community of the Arts Residencies *(Professional Development/Fellowship)* 2142

Czech Education Scholarships *(Doctorate, Graduate, Postdoctorate/Scholarship)* 3708

Pauly D'Orlando Memorial Art Scholarship *(Graduate, Undergraduate/Scholarship)* 5781

Fine Arts Grants *(Professional Development/Grant)* 194

Ford Foundation Fellowships *(Doctorate, Graduate, Postdoctorate/Fellowship)* 1178

Frese Senior Research Fellowship *(Postdoctorate/Fellowship)* 1772

Frese Senior Research Fellowship Program *(Postdoctorate/Fellowship)* 1773

GFWC of MA Art Scholarships *(High School, Undergraduate/Scholarship)* 2636

Grants to Individual Artists *(Professional Development/Grant)* 3762

The Elizabeth Greenshields Grant *(Graduate, High School, Other, Undergraduate/Grant)* 2751

Greenshields Grants *(Other/Grant)* 2752

Humanities Fellowships *(Doctorate, Postdoctorate/Fellowship)* 1179

Interlochen Arts Academy and Arts Camp Scholarships *(High School, Postgraduate, Undergraduate/Scholarship)* 3101

International Biennial Competition of Humour and Satire in the Arts *(Professional Development/Award)* 2906

Japan-United States Art Fellowships *(Postdoctorate, Professional Development/Fellowship)* 1180

Japanese American Citizens League Creative Arts Award *(Other/Scholarship)* 3244

Lindbergh Grants *(Other/Grant)* 3484

Henry Luce Foundation/ACLS Dissertation Fellowship in American Art *(Doctorate/Fellowship)* 412

MacDowell Colony Residencies *(Other, Professional Development/Fellowship)* 3524

Minnesota Artist Assistance Fellowships *(Professional Development/Fellowship)* 3714

Minnesota Career Opportunity Grants *(Professional Development/Grant)* 3715

Gerd Muehsam Memorial Award *(Graduate, Postgraduate/Award)* 1145

National Alliance for Excellence Honored Scholars Awards *(Graduate, Undergraduate/Scholarship)* 3841

National Endowment for the Arts - National Heritage Fellowships *(Professional Development/Fellowship)* 3979

National Endowment for the Arts - Visual Artists Fellowships *(Professional Development/Fellowship)* 3982

New Hampshire Individual Artist Fellowships *(Other/Fellowship)* 4535

North Carolina Arts Council Artist Fellowships *(Professional Development/Fellowship)* 4668

Oregon College of Art & Craft Artists-in-Residence Program *(Postgraduate/Grant)* 4797

Pollock-Krasner Grants *(Professional Development/Grant)* 4975

Professional Development Fellowship Program for Artists and Art Historians *(Doctorate, Graduate/Fellowship)* 1982

## Writing (continued)

Bush Artist Fellowships (*Professional Development/ Fellowship*) 1539

Cancer Research Institute Science Writing Internship (*Graduate/Internship*) 1716

Centrum Residencies (*Professional Development/Other*) 1820

Cummington Community of the Arts Residencies (*Professional Development/Fellowship*) 2142

Eben Demarest Fund (*Professional Development/Grant*) 2227

The Walt Disney Studios Fellowship Program (*Professional Development/Fellowship*) 2258

Dobie-Paisano Fellowships (*Other/Fellowship*) 2262

Fine Arts Work Center Fellowships (*Professional Development/ Fellowship*) 2459

Morris Fishbein Fellowship in Medical Journalism (*Graduate, Postgraduate/Fellowship*) 688

Grants to Individual Artists (*Professional Development/ Grant*) 3762

The Harper-Wood Studentship for English Poetry and Literature (*Postgraduate/Other*) 5222

Hearst Foundation Journalism Writing Competition (*Undergraduate/Award*) 2837

International Biennial Competition of Humour and Satire in the Arts (*Professional Development/Award*) 2906

International Book Translation and Publishing Program (*Professional Development/Award*) 1318

International Magazine Publishing Program (*Professional Development/Award*) 1319

Iowa School of Letters Award for Short Fiction (*Other/ Award*) 3225

Joseph Henry Jackson Award (*Professional Development/ Award*) 5234

Letras de Oro Spanish Speaking Literary Prizes (*Professional Development/Prize*) 3453

Lindbergh Grants (*Other/Grant*) 3484

MacDowell Colony Residencies (*Other, Professional Development/Fellowship*) 3524

National Endowment for the Arts - Literature Program Creative Writing Fellowships (*Professional Development/ Fellowship*) 3977

National High School Oratorical Contest (*High School/ Prize*) 619

Netz Hilai Visiting Artists Fellowships (*Professional Development/Fellowship*) 4515

New Letters Literary Awards (*Professional Development/ Prize*) 4549

New York Foundation for the Arts Artists' Fellowships (*Other/ Fellowship*) 4570

NHPRC/Fellowships in Historical Editing (*Postdoctorate/ Fellowship*) 4182

Flannery O'Connor Awards for Short Fiction (*Professional Development/Award*) 5994

PEN Fund for Writers and Editors with AIDS Grants and Loans (*Professional Development/Grant, Loan*) 4858

PEN Writers Fund (*Professional Development/Grant*) 4856

James D. Phelan Award in Literature (*Professional Development/Award*) 5235

Resident Fellowships (*Professional Development/ Fellowship*) 2786

Scholarships for Mature Women (*Professional Development/ Scholarship*) 4282

Scholastic Art and Writing Awards (*High School/Award, Scholarship*) 5268

Frances Shaw Fellowship (*Professional Development/ Scholarship*) 5073

John Ben Snow Prize (*Professional Development/Prize*) 5668

Thurber House Residencies (*Professional Development/ Award*) 5731

Vermont Studio Center Residency Fellowships (*Professional Development/Fellowship*) 6034

W.D. Weatherford Award (*Other/Award*) 1054

World of Expression Scholarship Program (*High School, Undergraduate/Award*) 1420

Yaddo Residencies (*Professional Development/Other*) 6274

Young Feminist Scholarship Program (*High School, Undergraduate/Scholarship*) 5591

## Zoology

American Museum of Natural History Collection Study Grants (*Doctorate, Postdoctorate/Grant*) 712

American Museum of Natural History Research and Museum Fellowships (*Postdoctorate/Fellowship*) 713

Lester Armour Graduate Fellowships (*Graduate/ Fellowship*) 2443

ESA Undergraduate Scholarships (*Undergraduate/ Scholarship*) 2389

Field Museum Graduate Fellowships (*Graduate/ Fellowship*) 2444

Field Museum Visiting Scholar Funds (*Postdoctorate/ Grant*) 2446

Herpetologists' League Best Student Paper (*Graduate/ Award*) 2864

Huyck Station Research Grants (*Graduate/Grant*) 2944

Lerner-Gray Grants (*Postdoctorate/Grant*) 715

National Zoological Park Minority Traineeships (*Graduate, Undergraduate/Internship*) 4456

National Zoological Park Research Traineeships (*Graduate, Undergraduate/Internship*) 4457

National Zoological Park Traineeship in Education (*Graduate, Undergraduate/Internship*) 4459

National Zoological Park Traineeship in Exhibit Interpretation (*Graduate, Undergraduate/Internship*) 4460

Research Grants in Wildlife Conservation (*Postdoctorate/ Grant*) 6178

William A. and Stella M. Rowley Graduate Fellowship (*Graduate/Fellowship*) 2447

Smithsonian Environmental Research Center Work-Learn Opportunities in Environmental Studies (*Graduate, Undergraduate/Internship*) 5374

# Legal Residence Index

This index lists awards that are restricted by the applicant's residence of legal record. Award citations are arranged alphabetically by country and subarranged by state or province (for the U.S. and Canada). Each citation is followed by the study level and award type, which appear in parentheses. The numbers following the parenthetical information indicate book entry numbers for particular awards, not page numbers.

## UNITED STATES

AAAS-EPA Environmental Science and Engineering Fellowships *(Postdoctorate/Fellowship)* 265

AAP Residency Scholarships *(Postdoctorate/Scholarship)* 238

AASA and Convention Exhibitors Scholarships *(Graduate/ Scholarship)* 321

AAUW Educational Foundation Career Development Grants *(Masters, Professional Development/Grant)* 332

AAUW Postdoctoral Fellowships *(Postdoctorate/Fellowship)* 337

ACNM Scholarships *(Graduate/Scholarship)* 3267

AIGC Fellowships *(Graduate/Fellowship)* 553

American Accounting Association Fellowship Program in Accounting *(Doctorate/Fellowship)* 246

The American Architectural Foundation Minority/Disadvantaged Scholarship *(Graduate, Undergraduate/Scholarship)* 574

American Express Travel Scholarship *(Undergraduate/ Scholarship)* 970

American Numismatic Society Grants-in-Aid *(Graduate, Postgraduate/Grant)* 738

American Otological Society Research Grants *(Postdoctorate/ Grant)* 760

American Research Center in Egypt Research Fellowships for Study in Egypt *(Doctorate, Postdoctorate/Fellowship)* 843

American School of Classical Studies Summer Sessions Scholarships *(Graduate, Professional Development/ Scholarship)* 855

American Sociological Association Minority Fellowships *(Doctorate/Fellowship)* 986

American Water Works Association Scholarship Program *(Doctorate, Graduate/Scholarship)* 1017

Dr. William L. Amoroso, Jr. Scholarship *(Undergraduate/ Scholarship)* 4208

Arby's Scholarships *(Undergraduate/Scholarship)* 1062

Argonne National Laboratory Faculty Research Leave; Faculty Research Participation Awards *(Postdoctorate/Award)* 1083

Army Emergency Relief Scholarships *(Undergraduate/ Scholarship)* 1140

ASHA Postdoctoral Fellowships *(Postdoctorate/Fellowship)* 889

Brown Library Long-Term Research Fellowships *(Postdoctorate/ Fellowship)* 1513

Canadian Studies Faculty Enrichment Awards *(Professional Development/Award)* 1624

Canadian Studies Faculty Research Grants *(Postdoctorate/ Grant)* 1625

Canadian Studies Graduate Student Fellowships *(Doctorate/ Fellowship)* 1626

Canadian Studies Sabbatical Fellowship Program *(Professional Development/Fellowship)* 1627

Canadian Studies Senior Fellowships *(Postdoctorate/ Fellowship)* 1628

Career Development Awards in Orthopaedic Surgery *(Professional Development/Grant)* 4814

Vikki Carr Scholarship *(Graduate, Undergraduate/ Scholarship)* 1741

Century Three Leaders Scholarships *(Undergraduate/ Scholarship)* 3898

Churchill Scholarships *(Postgraduate/Scholarship)* 1954

The Classical Fellowship; The Norbert Schimmel Fellowship for Mediterranean Art and Archaeology *(Doctorate/ Fellowship)* 3652

Anna C. and Oliver C. Colburn Fellowship *(Doctorate, Postdoctorate/Fellowship)* 1064

Communications Scholarship *(Undergraduate/Scholarship)* 4215

ConAgra Scholarships *(Undergraduate/Scholarship)* 4052

Congressional Fellowships on Women and Public Policy *(Doctorate, Graduate/Fellowship)* 6236

Consortium College University Media Centers Annual Research Grants *(Doctorate, Graduate, Professional Development, Undergraduate/Grant)* 2065

Cottrell Scholars Science Awards *(Professional Development/ Award)* 5096

Division II Arc Welding Awards *(Professional Development/ Award)* 3481

Duracell/NSTA Scholarship Competition *(High School, Other/ Prize, Scholarship)* 4381

Endodontic Faculty Grants *(Postdoctorate, Professional Development/Grant)* 287

Endodontic Graduate Student Grants *(Doctorate/Grant)* 288

Excellence in Arc Welding Awards; Graduate and Professional Awards for Achievement in Arc-Welded Design, Engineering and Fabrication *(Doctorate, Graduate, Professional Development/Award)* 3482

Fellowships in Spinal Cord Injury Research *(Postdoctorate/ Fellowship)* 4830

General Undergraduate Scholarships *(Undergraduate/ Scholarship)* 4227

John Simon Guggenheim Fellowships *(Professional Development/Fellowship)* 2761

GCA Awards For Summer Environmental Studies; Clara Carter Higgins Scholarship *(Undergraduate/Scholarship)* 2620

Jacob Hirsch Fellowship *(Doctorate, Graduate/Fellowship)* 859

Howard Foundation Fellowships *(Professional Development/ Fellowship)* 2908

Ralph Hudson Environmental Fellowship *(Professional Development/Fellowship)* 3425

IAM Scholarships *(Undergraduate/Scholarship)* 3117

International Order of the King's Daughters and Sons Health Careers Scholarships *(Graduate, Postgraduate, Undergraduate/ Scholarship)* 3169

International Travel Grants *(Doctorate, Postdoctorate/Grant)* 344

Irish American Cultural Institute Visiting Fellowship in Irish Studies *(Postgraduate/Fellowship)* 3227

Jefferson Fellowships *(Professional Development/ Fellowship)* 2312

Johnson Foundation Photocopying Grants *(Graduate/ Grant)* 3283

Laboratory-Graduate Participantships Thesis Parts Appointment (Doctorate, Graduate/Grant) 1084

Letras de Oro Spanish Speaking Literary Prizes (Professional Development/Prize) 3453

Amy Lowell Poetry Travelling Scholarship (Professional Development/Scholarship) 3510

Mathematical Sciences Research Institute Postdoctoral Fellowships in Mathematics (Postdoctorate/Fellowship) 3611

Mathematical Sciences Research Institute Research Professorships in Mathematics (Postdoctorate/Fellowship) 3612

Mazda National Scholarship (High School/Scholarship) 6299

Russell C. McCaughan Education Fund Scholarship (Doctorate, Graduate/Scholarship) 4335

Frederic G. Melcher Scholarships (Graduate/Scholarship) 649

James D. Moran Memorial Research Award (Professional Development/Award) 299

MSA Presidential Student Awards (Graduate, Undergraduate/Award) 3696

The National Council Research Contracts (Postdoctorate/Fellowship, Grant) 3945

National Leukemia Research Association Research Awards (Postdoctorate/Award) 4284

National Poetry Competition Prizes (Professional Development/Prize) 3293

NCAA Postgraduate Scholarships (Postgraduate, Undergraduate/Scholarship) 3937

NEH Fellowships (Doctorate/Fellowship) 6200

Olin Fellowships (Professional Development/Fellowship) 1312

Orchestra Management Fellowships (Professional Development/Fellowship) 1006

Helene Overly Scholarship (Graduate/Scholarship) 6243

Elisabeth M. and Winchell M. Parsons Scholarships (Doctorate/Scholarship) 950

PEN Writers Fund (Professional Development/Grant) 4856

Norman R. Peterson Scholarship (John Cabot University) (Undergraduate/Scholarship) 4253

Petroleum Research Fund Grants (Graduate, Postdoctorate, Professional Development, Undergraduate/Grant) 369

Harriet and Leon Pomerance Fellowship (Professional Development/Fellowship) 1067

Judith Graham Pool Postdoctoral Research Fellowships (Postdoctorate/Fellowship) 4177

Promising Playwright Award (Professional Development/Award) 1996

James K. Rathmell, Jr., Memorial Scholarship to Work/Study Abroad (Graduate, Undergraduate/Scholarship) 1387

REFORMA Scholarships (Graduate/Scholarship) 5091

Research Grants in Orthopaedic Surgery (Postdoctorate/Grant) 4815

Research Opportunity Awards (Professional Development/Award) 5097

Leo S. Rowe Pan American Fund (All/Loan) 4810

The Leo S. Rowe Pan American Fund Loan (Graduate, Undergraduate/Loan) 5174

Senior Performing Arts Fellowships (Professional Development/Fellowship) 588

Thomas Day Seymour Fellowship (Graduate/Fellowship) 860

Shields-Gillespie Scholarships (Postgraduate, Professional Development/Scholarship) 755

Slocum-Lunz Foundation Scholarships and Grants (Graduate/Grant, Scholarship) 5359

Smithsonian Environmental Research Center Work-Learn Opportunities in Environmental Studies (Graduate, Undergraduate/Internship) 5374

Sub-Saharan African Dissertation Internship Award (Doctorate/Internship) 5154

Summer Fellowship Grants (Doctorate/Fellowship) 215

Summer Travel/Research in Turkey Grants (Postdoctorate/Grant) 3082

Thesaurus Linguae Latinae Fellowship (Doctorate/Fellowship) 764

Dr. Henry R. Viets Medical Student Research Fellowships (Doctorate, Graduate/Fellowship) 3812

Elizabeth A. Whitehead Visiting Professorships (Professional Development/Award) 862

David & Dovetta Wilson Scholarship Fund (High School/Scholarship) 6191

## UNITED STATES (by state)

### Alabama

Alabama Library Association Scholarships and Loans (Graduate/Loan, Scholarship) 121

Alabama Nursing Scholarship (Undergraduate/Loan, Scholarship) 105

Alabama Scholarships for Dependents of Blind Parents (Undergraduate/Award) 107

Alabama Senior Adult Scholarships (Undergraduate/Scholarship) 108

Alabama Student Assistance Program (Undergraduate/Grant) 110

Alabama Student Grant Program (Undergraduate/Grant) 111

American Legion Auxiliary Scholarships (Undergraduate/Grant) 113

American Legion Scholarships (Undergraduate/Scholarship) 114

Delta and Pine Land Company Scholarship (Undergraduate/Scholarship) 4062

John M. Will Memorial Journalism Scholarships (Graduate, High School, Undergraduate/Scholarship) 6180

Lextron, Inc. Scholarships (Undergraduate/Scholarship) 4094

Longman-Harris Scholarship (Undergraduate/Scholarship) 4400

NAJA Graduate Scholarships (Graduate/Scholarship) 3881

Pickett & Hatcher Educational Loans (Undergraduate/Loan) 4945

Tyson Scholarship (Undergraduate/Scholarship) 5761

### Alaska

Alaska Family Education Loans (Graduate, Undergraduate/Loan) 127

Alaska State Educational Incentive Grants (Undergraduate/Grant) 128

Alaska Student Loans (Graduate, Undergraduate/Loan) 129

Alaska Teacher Loans (Undergraduate/Loan) 130

Mary Lou Brown Scholarship (Undergraduate/Scholarship) 817

Capitol American Scholarships (Undergraduate/Scholarship) 4041

Michael Murphy Memorial Scholarship Loans (Graduate, Undergraduate/Loan) 132

Tyson Scholarship (Undergraduate/Scholarship) 5761

WAMI Medical Education Program (Doctorate/Other) 134

WESTAF/NEA Regional Fellowships for Visual Artists (Professional Development/Fellowship) 6161

Western Interstate Commission for Higher Education Student Exchanges (Doctorate, Graduate/Other) 135

Western Interstate Commission for Higher Education Western Regional Graduate Program (Doctorate, Graduate/Other) 136

Western Regional Graduate Program (Graduate/Other) 6159

### Arizona

American Legion Auxiliary Past Presidents' Parley Nurses Scholarships (Undergraduate/Scholarship) 613

Delta and Pine Land Company Scholarship (Undergraduate/Scholarship) 4062

Evans Caddie Scholarships (Undergraduate/Scholarship) 6151

Charles N. Fisher Memorial Scholarship (Undergraduate/Scholarship) 822

Future Farmers of America Scholarships (Undergraduate/Scholarship) 1532

Wilma Hoyal/Maxine Chilton Scholarships (Undergraduate/Scholarship) 614

Lextron, Inc. Scholarships (Undergraduate/Scholarship) 4094

Rocky Mountain Coal Mining Institute Scholarships (Undergraduate/Scholarship) 5157

Legal Residence Index

## California (continued)

Wells Fargo Bank Scholarship *(Undergraduate/ Scholarship)* 4146

WESTAF/NEA Regional Fellowships for Visual Artists *(Professional Development/Fellowship)* 6161

Western Seedmen's Association Scholarships *(Undergraduate/ Scholarship)* 4148

## Colorado

Capitol American Scholarships *(Undergraduate/ Scholarship)* 4041

Evans Caddie Scholarships *(Undergraduate/Scholarship)* 6151

Future Farmers of America Scholarships *(Undergraduate/ Scholarship)* 1532

Golden Harvest Seeds, Inc. Scholarships *(Undergraduate/ Scholarship)* 4082

Latin American Educational Foundation Scholarships *(Graduate, Postgraduate, Undergraduate/Scholarship)* 3439

Lextron, Inc. Scholarships *(Undergraduate/Scholarship)* 4094

Cletus E. Ludden Memorial Scholarships *(Undergraduate/ Scholarship)* 2231

Kenneth and Ellen Nielsen Cooperative Scholarships *(Undergraduate/Scholarship)* 4110

Osteopathic Medical Students Loans *(Graduate/Loan)* 2003

Rocky Mountain Coal Mining Institute Scholarships *(Undergraduate/Scholarship)* 5157

Sachs Foundation Grants *(Undergraduate/Grant)* 5204

Santa Fe Pacific Foundation Scholarships *(Undergraduate/ Scholarship)* 563

Santa Fe Pacific Foundation Scholarships *(Undergraduate/ Scholarship)* 4125

Santa Fe Pacific Native American Scholarships *(Undergraduate/Scholarship)* 1534

Americo Toffoli Scholarships *(Undergraduate/ Scholarship)* 1998

Union Pacific Foundation Scholarship *(Undergraduate/ Scholarship)* 4137

WESTAF/NEA Regional Fellowships for Visual Artists *(Professional Development/Fellowship)* 6161

Western Regional Graduate Program *(Graduate/Other)* 6159

Western Seedmen's Association Scholarships *(Undergraduate/ Scholarship)* 4148

## Connecticut

AgRadio Network Scholarships *(Undergraduate/ Scholarship)* 4013

Balso Foundation Scholarships *(Undergraduate/ Scholarship)* 1366

Blue Seal Feeds Scholarship *(Undergraduate/ Scholarship)* 4031

Robert C. Byrd Honors Scholarships *(Undergraduate/ Scholarship)* 2042

Marjorie S. Carter Boy Scout Scholarship *(Undergraduate/ Scholarship)* 1743

Connecticut Aid for Public College Students *(Undergraduate/ Other)* 2043

Connecticut Family Education Loan Program (CT FELP) *(Graduate, Professional Development, Undergraduate/ Loan)* 2044

Connecticut Independent College Student Grants *(Undergraduate/Grant)* 2045

Connecticut League for Nursing Scholarships *(Graduate, Undergraduate/Scholarship)* 2052

Connecticut Library Association Education Grants *(Professional Development/Grant)* 2054

Connecticut Scholastic Achievement Grants *(Undergraduate/ Grant)* 2046

Connecticut Tuition Waiver for Senior Citizens *(Undergraduate/Scholarship)* 2048

Connecticut Tuition Waiver for Veterans *(Undergraduate/ Scholarship)* 2049

The Lighthouse Career Incentive Award for Adult Undergraduates *(Undergraduate/Scholarship)* 3474

The Lighthouse Career Incentive Award for College-Bound Students *(Undergraduate/Scholarship)* 3475

The Lighthouse Career Incentive Award for Graduate Students *(Graduate/Scholarship)* 3476

The Lighthouse Career Incentive Award for Undergraduates *(Undergraduate/Scholarship)* 3477

James Z. Naurison Scholarship Fund *(Graduate, Undergraduate/Scholarship)* 2472

New England Graphic Arts Scholarships *(High School, Undergraduate/Scholarship)* 4531

New England Regional Student Program *(Graduate, Undergraduate/Other)* 4525

New York Council Navy League Scholarships *(Undergraduate/ Scholarship)* 4566

Pellegrini Scholarship Grants *(Graduate, Undergraduate/ Scholarship)* 5662

Wolf's Head Oil Company Scholarships *(Undergraduate/ Scholarship)* 4152

## Delaware

H. Fletcher Brown Scholarship *(Doctorate, Graduate, Undergraduate/Scholarship)* 4967

Delaware Academy of Medicine Student Financial Aid Program *(Doctorate/Loan)* 2207

Delaware Higher Education Benefits for Children of Veterans and Others *(Undergraduate/Grant)* 2209

G. Layton Grier Scholarship *(Graduate/Scholarship)* 2211

Pellegrini Scholarship Grants *(Graduate, Undergraduate/ Scholarship)* 5662

Piancone Family Agriculture Scholarship *(Graduate, Undergraduate/Scholarship)* 4254

Wolf's Head Oil Company Scholarships *(Undergraduate/ Scholarship)* 4152

## District of Columbia

Benn and Kathleen Gilmore Scholarship *(Doctorate/ Scholarship)* 4292

Jewish Educational Loans Fund *(Graduate, Undergraduate/ Loan)* 3269

Jewish Undergraduate Scholarships *(Undergraduate/ Scholarship)* 3270

Ralph Lombardi Memorial Scholarship *(Doctorate/ Scholarship)* 4236

National Symphony Young Soloists' Competition, College Division *(Professional Development/Prize, Scholarship)* 4419

Piancone Family Agriculture Scholarship *(Graduate, Undergraduate/Scholarship)* 4254

Irene Stambler Vocational Opportunities Grants *(Other/ Grant)* 3271

Washington Printing Guild Scholarships *(Undergraduate/ Scholarship)* 6095

## Florida

American Legion Auxiliary Memorial Scholarship *(Undergraduate/Scholarship)* 617

Barnett Bank of Palm Beach County Minority Student Scholarship Fund *(Undergraduate/Scholarship)* 2025

Maura and William Benjamin Scholarship *(Undergraduate/ Scholarship)* 2026

Thomas William Bennett Memorial Scholarship *(Undergraduate/Scholarship)* 2027

Mary McLeod Bethune Scholarship *(Graduate, Undergraduate/ Grant)* 2494

Lisa Bjork Memorial Scholarship *(High School, Undergraduate/ Scholarship)* 2028

Walter and Adi Blum Scholarship *(Undergraduate/ Scholarship)* 2029

William L. Boyd IV, Florida Resident Access Grant *(Undergraduate/Grant)* 2495

Robert C. Byrd Honors Scholarship *(Undergraduate/ Scholarship)* 2496

Cape Canaveral Chapter Scholarships *(Graduate, Undergraduate/Scholarship)* 5114

Chevron USA, Inc. Scholarship *(Undergraduate/ Scholarship)* 4047

Children of Deceased or Disabled Veterans or Children of Servicemen Classified as Prisoners of War or Missing in Action Scholarship *(Undergraduate/Scholarship)* 2497

Allen C. Clark Memorial Scholarship *(High School/ Scholarship)* 2030

Julian and Eunice Cohen Scholarship *(Undergraduate/ Scholarship)* 2031

Terry Darby Memorial Scholarship *(High School/ Scholarship)* 2032

James H. Davis Memorial Scholarship *(High School/ Scholarship)* 2033

Delta and Pine Land Company Scholarship *(Undergraduate/ Scholarship)* 4062

Paul Douglas Teacher Scholarship *(Undergraduate/Scholarship loan)* 2498

Ellen Beth Eddleman Memorial Scholarship *(High School, Undergraduate/Scholarship)* 2034

J. Hugh & Earle W. Fellows Memorial Fund Loans *(Undergraduate/Loan)* 2437

Finland U.S. Senate Youth Exchange Scholarships *(High School/Scholarship)* 6298

Florida Bright Futures Scholarship Program *(Undergraduate/ Scholarship)* 2500

Florida Chapter of the Association of Women in Communications Christina Saralegui Scholarship *(Graduate, Undergraduate/Scholarship)* 1294

Florida Dental Association Dental Hygiene Scholarship Program *(Other, Professional Development/ Scholarship)* 2487

Florida Dental Association Student Loan Program *(Graduate/ Loan)* 2488

Florida Dental Health Foundation Dental Assisting Scholarship *(Undergraduate/Scholarship)* 2490

Florida Dental Health Foundation Dental Hygiene Scholarship *(Undergraduate/Scholarship)* 2491

Florida Division of Blind Services Vocational Rehabilitation Program *(Other/Other)* 2517

Florida House of Representatives Intern Program *(Graduate/ Internship)* 2522

Florida National Science Scholars Program *(Undergraduate/ Scholarship)* 2503

Florida Resident Access Grant *(Undergraduate/Other)* 2504

Florida Undergraduate Scholars' Fund *(Undergraduate/ Scholarship)* 2507

Florida Vocational Gold Seal Endorsement Scholarship Program *(Undergraduate/Scholarship)* 2508

John M. Will Memorial Journalism Scholarships *(Graduate, High School, Undergraduate/Scholarship)* 6180

Lextron, Inc. Scholarships *(Undergraduate/Scholarship)* 4094

Limited Access Competitive Grant *(Undergraduate/ Grant)* 2510

Inez Peppers Lovett Scholarship *(Undergraduate/ Scholarship)* 2035

Jose Marti Scholarship Challenge Grants *(Graduate, Undergraduate/Grant)* 2511

Naval Officers' Spouses' Association of Mayport Scholarships *(Graduate, Undergraduate/Scholarship)* 4487

Palm Beach Kennel Club Scholarship *(Undergraduate/ Scholarship)* 2036

Pickett & Hatcher Educational Loans *(Undergraduate/ Loan)* 4945

Garth Reeves Jr. Memorial Scholarships *(Graduate, Undergraduate/Scholarship)* 5490

Seminole-Miccosukee Indian Scholarships *(Graduate, Undergraduate/Scholarship)* 2515

Tyson Scholarship *(Undergraduate/Scholarship)* 5761

Visionaries Achievement Award *(Undergraduate/ Scholarship)* 6067

## Georgia

Chevron USA, Inc. Scholarship *(Undergraduate/ Scholarship)* 4047

Ty Cobb Scholarships *(Graduate, Undergraduate/ Scholarship)* 1976

"Country Doctor" Scholarship Program *(Graduate/ Scholarship)* 5619

Cox Minority Journalism Scholarship *(Undergraduate/ Scholarship)* 2131

Delta and Pine Land Company Scholarship *(Undergraduate/ Scholarship)* 4062

Georgia State Regents Scholarship *(Graduate, Undergraduate/ Scholarship loan)* 2657

Georgia Student Finance Commission Governor's Scholarship *(Undergraduate/Scholarship)* 2662

Georgia Student Finance Commission Pell Grant *(Undergraduate/Grant)* 2663

Georgia Student Finance Commission Perkins Loan *(Graduate, Undergraduate/Loan)* 2664

Georgia Student Finance Commission PLUS Loan *(Undergraduate/Loan)* 2665

Georgia Student Finance Commission Service-Cancellable Stafford Loan *(Graduate, Undergraduate/Loan)* 2666

Georgia Student Finance Commission SLS Loan *(Graduate, Undergraduate/Loan)* 2667

Georgia Student Finance Commission Stafford Loan *(Graduate, Undergraduate/Loan)* 2668

Georgia Student Finance Commission State-Sponsored Loan *(Graduate, Undergraduate/Loan)* 2669

Georgia Student Finance Commission Student Incentive Grant *(Undergraduate/Grant)* 2670

Georgia Student Finance Commission Supplemental Educational Opportunity Grant *(Undergraduate/Grant)* 2671

Georgia Tuition Equalization Grant *(Undergraduate/ Grant)* 2672

John T. Hall Student Loan Fund *(Graduate, Undergraduate/ Loan)* 2782

Cheryl Dant Hennesy Scholarship *(Undergraduate/ Scholarship)* 4089

Hope Scholarship *(Undergraduate/Scholarship loan)* 2658

Law Enforcement Personnel Dependents Grant *(Undergraduate/Grant)* 2673

Lextron, Inc. Scholarships *(Undergraduate/Scholarship)* 4094

Hatton Lovejoy Scholarship Plan *(Undergraduate/ Scholarship)* 1586

North Georgia College Military Scholarship *(Undergraduate/ Scholarship)* 2674

North Georgia College ROTC Grant *(Undergraduate/ Grant)* 2675

Pickett & Hatcher Educational Loans *(Undergraduate/ Loan)* 4945

Eugene "Gene" Sallee, W4YFR Memorial Scholarship *(Undergraduate/Scholarship)* 839

Tyson Scholarship *(Undergraduate/Scholarship)* 5761

Wolf's Head Oil Company Scholarships *(Undergraduate/ Scholarship)* 4152

## Guam

Marianas Naval Officers' Wives' Club Scholarships *(Undergraduate/Scholarship)* 5959

## Hawaii

California-Hawaii Elks Disabled Student Scholarships *(Undergraduate/Scholarship)* 1559

Friends of the Library of Hawaii Memorial Scholarship *(Graduate/Scholarship)* 2599

Fukunaga Scholarship Foundation Annual Four-Year Scholarships in Business Administration *(Undergraduate/ Scholarship)* 2603

Hawaii Society of Professional Journalists Internships *(Other, Undergraduate/Internship)* 2824

Hawaii's Federal PLUS Loans *(Undergraduate/Loan)* 2821

Dr. Syngman Rhee Scholarship *(Undergraduate/ Scholarship)* 2268

WESTAF/NEA Regional Fellowships for Visual Artists *(Professional Development/Fellowship)* 6161

Western Regional Graduate Program *(Graduate/Other)* 6159

David T. Woolsey Scholarship *(Graduate, Undergraduate/ Scholarship)* 3437

## Idaho

Mary Lou Brown Scholarship *(Undergraduate/ Scholarship)* 817

CAL Stores Companies Scholarships *(Undergraduate/ Scholarship)* 4039

D & B Supply Company, Inc. Scholarships *(Undergraduate/ Scholarship)* 4056

Darigold Scholarships *(Undergraduate/Scholarship)* 4057

Jenkins Loan *(Graduate, Undergraduate/Loan)* 5834

Lextron, Inc. Scholarships *(Undergraduate/Scholarship)* 4094

Potlatch Foundation for Higher Education Scholarships *(Undergraduate/Scholarship)* 4987

Union Pacific Foundation Scholarship *(Undergraduate/ Scholarship)* 4137

United Dairymen of Idaho Scholarship *(Undergraduate/ Scholarship)* 4138

WESTAF/NEA Regional Fellowships for Visual Artists *(Professional Development/Fellowship)* 6161

Western Dairymen - John Elway - Melba FFA Scholarship Fund *(Undergraduate/Scholarship)* 4147

Western Regional Graduate Program *(Graduate/Other)* 6159

Western Seedmen's Association Scholarships *(Undergraduate/ Scholarship)* 4148

## Illinois

American Legion Boy Scout Scholarships *(Undergraduate/ Scholarship)* 608

American Legion Oratorical Contest *(Undergraduate/ Award)* 609

Americanism Essay Contest Scholarships *(High School/ Award)* 610

AMVETS Auxiliary Department of Illinois Memorial Scholarship *(Undergraduate/Scholarship)* 2954

Anheuser-Busch Scholarship Fund *(Undergraduate/ Scholarship)* 1926

Blind Service Association Scholarship Awards *(Graduate, Other, Undergraduate/Scholarship)* 1442

Capitol American Scholarships *(Undergraduate/ Scholarship)* 4041

Casey's General Stores, Inc. Scholarships *(Undergraduate/ Scholarship)* 4045

Chicago FM Club Scholarship *(Undergraduate/ Scholarship)* 818

Chicago Sun-Times Minority Scholarships and Internships *(Undergraduate/Internship, Scholarship)* 1922

Paul Douglas Teacher Scholarship (Illinois) *(Undergraduate/ Scholarship loan)* 2968

The Ertl Company Scholarship *(Undergraduate/ Scholarship)* 4069

Evans Caddie Scholarships *(Undergraduate/Scholarship)* 6151

Farm King Supply Scholarship *(Undergraduate/ Scholarship)* 4072

Farmers Mutual Hail Insurance Company of Iowa Scholarships *(Undergraduate/Scholarship)* 4073

Michael J. Flosi Memorial Scholarship *(Undergraduate/ Scholarship)* 823

Future Farmers of America Scholarships *(Undergraduate/ Scholarship)* 1532

Benn and Kathleen Gilmore Scholarship *(Doctorate/ Scholarship)* 4292

Golden Harvest Seeds, Inc. Scholarships *(Undergraduate/ Scholarship)* 4082

Growmark, Inc. Scholarships *(Undergraduate/ Scholarship)* 4083

Celia M. Howard Fellowships *(Doctorate, Graduate/ Fellowship)* 2964

Illinois American Legion Scholarships *(Undergraduate/ Scholarship)* 611

Illinois AMVETS Auxiliary WORCHID Scholarships *(Undergraduate/Scholarship)* 2955

Illinois AMVETS Service Foundation Scholarship Award *(Undergraduate/Scholarship)* 2957

Illinois Federal PLUS Loan *(Graduate, Undergraduate/ Loan)* 2970

Illinois Federal Supplemental Loans for Students *(Graduate, Undergraduate/Loan)* 2972

Illinois Merit Recognition Scholarship *(Undergraduate/ Scholarship)* 2974

Illinois Police Officer/Fire Officer Grant *(Undergraduate/ Grant)* 2977

Illinois unILoan *(Graduate, Undergraduate/Loan)* 2979

Illinois Veteran Grant *(Undergraduate/Grant)* 2980

Illinois Veterans' Children Educational Opportunities *(Undergraduate/Grant)* 2962

Jewel/Taylor C. Cotton Scholarship *(Undergraduate/ Scholarship)* 1927

Jewish Federation of Metropolitan Chicago Academic Scholarships *(Doctorate, Graduate, Undergraduate/ Scholarship)* 3265

Ted Kenney Memorial Scholarships *(Undergraduate/ Scholarship)* 1918

Master of Library Science Degree Training Grants *(Graduate/ Grant)* 2966

Mercedes-Benz of North America Scholarship Program *(Undergraduate/Scholarship)* 1928

Mid-State Wool Growers Cooperative Scholarship *(Undergraduate/Scholarship)* 4099

Mola Foundation of Chicago Scholarships *(Undergraduate/ Scholarship)* 4243

Clarence Newlun Memorial Scholarship Award *(Undergraduate/Scholarship)* 2958

Kenneth and Ellen Nielsen Cooperative Scholarships *(Undergraduate/Scholarship)* 4110

Northrup King Company Scholarships *(Undergraduate/ Scholarship)* 4113

Paul Powell Memorial AMVETS Scholarships *(Undergraduate/ Scholarship)* 2959

Prairie Farms Dairy, Inc. Scholarship *(Undergraduate/ Scholarship)* 4115

Precision Laboratories, Inc. Scholarship *(Undergraduate/ Scholarship)* 4116

Santa Fe Pacific Foundation Scholarships *(Undergraduate/ Scholarship)* 4125

SBS Scholarships *(Undergraduate/Scholarship)* 5660

Silgan Containers Corporation Scholarships *(Undergraduate/ Scholarship)* 4127

Six Meter Club of Chicago Scholarship *(Undergraduate/ Scholarship)* 840

State Farm Companies Foundation Scholarships *(Undergraduate/Scholarship)* 4130

Tyson Scholarship *(Undergraduate/Scholarship)* 5761

Union Pacific Foundation Scholarship *(Undergraduate/ Scholarship)* 4137

United Feeds Scholarships *(Undergraduate/Scholarship)* 4139

Williams Pipe Line Company Scholarship *(Undergraduate/ Scholarship)* 4150

Wolf's Head Oil Company Scholarships *(Undergraduate/ Scholarship)* 4152

Woman's Board Scholarship *(Undergraduate/ Scholarship)* 1470

Whitney M. Young Memorial Scholarship *(Undergraduate/ Scholarship)* 1929

## Indiana

Big R. Stores and Fleet Supply Company Scholarship *(Undergraduate/Scholarship)* 4029

Capitol American Scholarships *(Undergraduate/ Scholarship)* 4041

Chicago FM Club Scholarship *(Undergraduate/ Scholarship)* 818

Child of Disabled Veteran Grant or Purple Heart Recipient, Grant *(Graduate, Other, Undergraduate/Other)* 2996

Countrymark Cooperative, Inc. Scholarships *(Undergraduate/ Scholarship)* 4053

Department of Veterans Affairs Free Tuition for Children of POW/MIA's in Vietnam *(Undergraduate/Other)* 2997

The Ertl Company Scholarship *(Undergraduate/ Scholarship)* 4069

Evans Caddie Scholarships *(Undergraduate/Scholarship)* 6151

## Kentucky (continued)

Mola Foundation of Chicago Scholarships (*Undergraduate/ Scholarship*) 4243

Pickett & Hatcher Educational Loans (*Undergraduate/ Loan*) 4945

Rural Kentucky Medical Scholarship Fund (RKMSF) (*Doctorate/Loan, Scholarship*) 3364

Silgan Containers Corporation Scholarships (*Undergraduate/ Scholarship*) 4127

Vocational Rehabilitation Grants (*Undergraduate/ Scholarship*) 3360

Wolf's Head Oil Company Scholarships (*Undergraduate/ Scholarship*) 4152

## Louisiana

Robert C. Byrd Honors Scholarship (*Undergraduate/ Scholarship*) 3498

Delta and Pine Land Company Scholarship (*Undergraduate/ Scholarship*) 4062

First Mississippi Corporation Scholarships (*Undergraduate/ Scholarship*) 4077

Lextron, Inc. Scholarships (*Undergraduate/Scholarship*) 4094

Louisiana Library Association Scholarship in Librarianship (*Graduate/Scholarship*) 3502

Louisiana National Guard Tuition Exemption Program (*Undergraduate/Other*) 3504

Louisiana Rehabilitation Services Award (*Other/Other*) 3506

Louisiana State Aid Dependents Educational Assistance (*Graduate, Other, Undergraduate/Scholarship*) 3500

NAJA Graduate Scholarships (*Graduate/Scholarship*) 3881

Union Pacific Foundation Scholarship (*Undergraduate/ Scholarship*) 4137

## Maine

AgRadio Network Scholarships (*Undergraduate/ Scholarship*) 4013

Beale Family Memorial Scholarship (*Doctorate/ Scholarship*) 3533

Blaine House Scholars Loans (*Graduate, Undergraduate/ Loan*) 2455

Blue Seal Feeds Scholarship (*Undergraduate/ Scholarship*) 4031

Marjorie S. Carter Boy Scout Scholarship (*Undergraduate/ Scholarship*) 1743

Hancock County Scholars Program (*High School/ Scholarship*) 3784

The Lighthouse Career Incentive Award for Adult Undergraduates (*Undergraduate/Scholarship*) 3474

The Lighthouse Career Incentive Award for College-Bound Students (*Undergraduate/Scholarship*) 3475

The Lighthouse Career Incentive Award for Graduate Students (*Graduate/Scholarship*) 3476

The Lighthouse Career Incentive Award for Undergraduates (*Undergraduate/Scholarship*) 3477

Andrew M. Longley, Jr., D.O. Scholarship (*Doctorate/ Scholarship*) 3534

Maine Osteopathic Association Memorial Scholarship (*Doctorate, Graduate, Undergraduate/Scholarship*) 3535

Maine Osteopathic Association Scholarship (*Doctorate, Graduate, Undergraduate/Scholarship*) 3536

Maine Veterans Dependents Educational Benefits (*All/ Scholarship*) 3538

Milo High School Alumni Scholarships (*Undergraduate/ Scholarship*) 4875

New England Graphic Arts Scholarships (*High School, Undergraduate/Scholarship*) 4531

New England Regional Student Program (*Graduate, Undergraduate/Other*) 4525

Marguerite Tremblay Cote Scholarships (*Undergraduate/ Scholarship*) 1726

Wolf's Head Oil Company Scholarships (*Undergraduate/ Scholarship*) 4152

## Maryland

Blue Seal Feeds Scholarship (*Undergraduate/ Scholarship*) 4031

Central Scholarship Bureau Interest-Free Loans (*Graduate, Undergraduate/Loan*) 1816

Educational Assistance Grant (*Undergraduate/Grant, Scholarship*) 3569

Guaranteed Access Grant (*Undergraduate/Grant*) 3570

Jewish Educational Loans Fund (*Graduate, Undergraduate/ Loan*) 3269

Jewish Undergraduate Scholarships (*Undergraduate/ Scholarship*) 3270

Loan Assistant Repayment Program (*Other/Other*) 3571

Loan Assistant Repayment Program for Medical Residents in Primary Care (*Other/Other*) 3572

Maryland Child Care Provider Scholarship (*Undergraduate/ Scholarship*) 3573

Maryland Distinguished Scholar Scholarship (*Undergraduate/ Scholarship*) 3574

Maryland Higher Education Commission Distinguished Scholar Program (*Undergraduate/Scholarship*) 3591

Maryland House of Delegates Scholarship (*Graduate, Professional Development, Undergraduate/ Scholarship*) 3575

Maryland MESA Scholarships (*High School, Undergraduate/ Scholarship*) 3586

Maryland Part-Time Grant Program (*Undergraduate/ Grant*) 3576

Maryland Physical and Occupational Therapists and Assistants Scholarships (*Undergraduate/Scholarship*) 3577

Maryland Professional Scholarship (*Graduate, Undergraduate/ Scholarship*) 3578

Maryland Reimbursement of Firefighters and Rescue Squad Members (*Graduate, Undergraduate/Scholarship*) 3579

Maryland Senatorial Scholarship (*Graduate, Undergraduate/ Scholarship*) 3580

Maryland State Nursing Scholarships (*Graduate, Undergraduate/Scholarship*) 3581

Maryland Teacher Education Distinguished Scholar Scholarship (*Undergraduate/Scholarship*) 3582

Sharon Christa McAuliffe Education Scholarship (*Graduate, Undergraduate/Scholarship*) 3583

Piancone Family Agriculture Scholarship (*Graduate, Undergraduate/Scholarship*) 4254

Irene Stambler Vocational Opportunities Grants (*Other/ Grant*) 3271

Tolbert Grant (*Professional Development, Undergraduate/ Grant*) 3584

Wolf's Head Oil Company Scholarships (*Undergraduate/ Scholarship*) 4152

## Massachusetts

AgRadio Network Scholarships (*Undergraduate/ Scholarship*) 4013

Walter S. Barr Fellowships (*Graduate/Fellowship*) 5363

Walter S. Barr Scholarships (*Undergraduate/ Scholarship*) 5364

Berkshire District Medical Society Medical School Scholarship Loan (*Graduate/Loan*) 1414

Blue Seal Feeds Scholarship (*Undergraduate/ Scholarship*) 4031

Florence Evans Bushee Foundation Scholarship Grants (*Undergraduate/Scholarship*) 1541

Marjorie S. Carter Boy Scout Scholarship (*Undergraduate/ Scholarship*) 1743

Chancellor's Talent Award Program (*Undergraduate/ Scholarship*) 1828

Charles River District Medical Society Scholarship (*Graduate/ Scholarship*) 1832

Citizens' Scholarship Foundation of Wakefield Scholarships (*All/Scholarship*) 1960

James W. Colgan Educational Loan (*Undergraduate/ Loan*) 1980

Grover T. Cronin Memorial Scholarship (*Undergraduate/ Scholarship*) 3210

## Minnesota (continued)

Minnesota Folk Arts Apprenticeship *(Professional Development/Other)* 3716

Mola Foundation of Chicago Scholarships *(Undergraduate/Scholarship)* 4243

Kenneth and Ellen Nielsen Cooperative Scholarships *(Undergraduate/Scholarship)* 4110

Northrup King Company Scholarships *(Undergraduate/Scholarship)* 4113

Potlatch Foundation for Higher Education Scholarships *(Undergraduate/Scholarship)* 4987

SIGCO Research Scholarships *(Undergraduate/Scholarship)* 4126

Tyson Scholarship *(Undergraduate/Scholarship)* 5761

Western Seedmen's Association Scholarships *(Undergraduate/Scholarship)* 4148

Williams Pipe Line Company Scholarship *(Undergraduate/Scholarship)* 4150

Wolf's Head Oil Company Scholarships *(Undergraduate/Scholarship)* 4152

## Mississippi

Weeta F. Colebank Scholarship *(Undergraduate/Scholarship)* 4432

Delta and Pine Land Company Scholarship *(Undergraduate/Scholarship)* 4062

First Mississippi Corporation Scholarships *(Undergraduate/Scholarship)* 4077

John M. Will Memorial Journalism Scholarships *(Graduate, High School, Undergraduate/Scholarship)* 6180

Mississippi African-American Doctoral Teacher Loan/Scholarship Program *(Doctorate/Scholarship loan)* 3730

Mississippi Farm Bureau Foundation Scholarship *(Undergraduate/Scholarship)* 4101

Mississippi Graduate and Professional Degree Loan/Scholarship Program *(Doctorate/Scholarship loan)* 3731

Mississippi Health Care Professions Loan/Scholarship Program *(Undergraduate/Scholarship loan)* 3732

Mississippi Law Enforcement Officers and Firemen Scholarship Program *(Graduate, Undergraduate/Scholarship)* 3733

Mississippi Nursing Education BSN Program *(Undergraduate/Scholarship loan)* 3734

Mississippi Nursing Education DSN Program *(Doctorate/Scholarship loan)* 3735

Mississippi Nursing Education MSN Program *(Graduate/Scholarship loan)* 3736

Mississippi Nursing Education RN to BSN Program *(Undergraduate/Scholarship loan)* 3737

Mississippi Psychology Apprenticeship Program *(Graduate, Undergraduate/Internship)* 3738

Mississippi Public Management Graduate Internship Program *(Graduate/Internship)* 3739

Mississippi Scholarship *(Undergraduate/Scholarship)* 832

Mississippi Southeast Asia POW/MIA Scholarship Program *(Graduate, Undergraduate/Scholarship)* 3740

Mississippi Southern Regional Education Board Loan/Scholarship Program *(Doctorate/Scholarship loan)* 3741

Mississippi Special Medical Education Loan/Scholarship Program *(Doctorate/Scholarship loan)* 3742

Mississippi State Dental Education Loan/Scholarship Program *(Doctorate/Scholarship loan)* 3743

Mississippi State Medical Education Loan/Scholarship Program *(Doctorate/Scholarship loan)* 3744

Mississippi State Student Incentive Grant Program *(Undergraduate/Grant)* 3745

NAJA Graduate Scholarships *(Graduate/Scholarship)* 3881

Pickett & Hatcher Educational Loans *(Undergraduate/Loan)* 4945

Tyson Scholarship *(Undergraduate/Scholarship)* 5761

William Winter Teacher Scholar Loan Program *(Other, Undergraduate/Loan, Scholarship)* 3746

## Missouri

American Family Insurance Company Scholarships *(Undergraduate/Scholarship)* 4018

Capitol American Scholarships *(Undergraduate/Scholarship)* 4041

Casey's General Stores, Inc. Scholarships *(Undergraduate/Scholarship)* 4045

Delta and Pine Land Company Scholarship *(Undergraduate/Scholarship)* 4062

Douglas Products and Packaging Scholarships *(Undergraduate/Scholarship)* 4064

The Ertl Company Scholarship *(Undergraduate/Scholarship)* 4069

Evans Caddie Scholarships *(Undergraduate/Scholarship)* 6151

Farmers Mutual Hail Insurance Company of Iowa Scholarships *(Undergraduate/Scholarship)* 4073

Future Farmers of America Scholarships *(Undergraduate/Scholarship)* 1532

Golden Harvest Seeds, Inc. Scholarships *(Undergraduate/Scholarship)* 4082

Paul and Helen L. Grauer Scholarship *(Undergraduate/Scholarship)* 826

Lextron, Inc. Scholarships *(Undergraduate/Scholarship)* 4094

Mid-State Wool Growers Cooperative Scholarship *(Undergraduate/Scholarship)* 4099

Missouri Minority Teacher Education Scholarship *(Undergraduate/Scholarship loan)* 3750

Missouri Teacher Education Scholarship *(Undergraduate/Scholarship loan)* 3751

NAJA Graduate Scholarships *(Graduate/Scholarship)* 3881

Kenneth and Ellen Nielsen Cooperative Scholarships *(Undergraduate/Scholarship)* 4110

Nurse Loan Repayment Program *(Postgraduate/Other)* 3754

Prairie Farms Dairy, Inc. Scholarship *(Undergraduate/Scholarship)* 4115

The Primary Care Resource Initiative for Missouri (PRIMO) *(Doctorate, Graduate, Undergraduate/Loan)* 3755

The Professional and Practical Nursing Student Loan Program *(Graduate, Undergraduate/Loan)* 3756

Santa Fe Pacific Foundation Scholarships *(Undergraduate/Scholarship)* 4125

Scholarship Foundation of St. Louis Loan *(Graduate, Undergraduate/Loan)* 5262

Silgan Containers Corporation Scholarships *(Undergraduate/Scholarship)* 4127

Joe Tangaro Memorial Athletic Scholarship *(Undergraduate/Scholarship)* 4264

Rosalie Tiles Scholarship *(Undergraduate/Scholarship)* 5733

Tyson Scholarship *(Undergraduate/Scholarship)* 5761

Union Pacific Foundation Scholarship *(Undergraduate/Scholarship)* 4137

Western Seedmen's Association Scholarships *(Undergraduate/Scholarship)* 4148

Williams Pipe Line Company Scholarship *(Undergraduate/Scholarship)* 4150

Wolf's Head Oil Company Scholarships *(Undergraduate/Scholarship)* 4152

## Montana

Mary Lou Brown Scholarship *(Undergraduate/Scholarship)* 817

Dodd and Dorothy L. Bryan Loan *(Undergraduate/Loan)* 1523

Capitol American Scholarships *(Undergraduate/Scholarship)* 4041

Future Farmers of America Scholarships *(Undergraduate/Scholarship)* 1532

Lextron, Inc. Scholarships *(Undergraduate/Scholarship)* 4094

Montana State Student Incentive Grants *(Undergraduate/Grant)* 3768

Rocky Mountain Coal Mining Institute Scholarships *(Undergraduate/Scholarship)* 5157

WESTAF/NEA Regional Fellowships for Visual Artists *(Professional Development/Fellowship)* 6161

Western Regional Graduate Program *(Graduate/Other)* 6159

Western Seedmen's Association Scholarships *(Undergraduate/
Scholarship)* 4148

## Nebraska

21st Century Genetics Cooperative Scholarships
*(Undergraduate/Scholarship)* 4012

Capitol American Scholarships *(Undergraduate/
Scholarship)* 4041

Chief Industries Inc. Scholarships *(Undergraduate/
Scholarship)* 4050

The Ertl Company Scholarship *(Undergraduate/
Scholarship)* 4069

Farmers Mutual Hail Insurance Company of Iowa Scholarships
*(Undergraduate/Scholarship)* 4073

Future Farmers of America Scholarships *(Undergraduate/
Scholarship)* 1532

Golden Harvest Seeds, Inc. Scholarships *(Undergraduate/
Scholarship)* 4082

Paul and Helen L. Grauer Scholarship *(Undergraduate/
Scholarship)* 826

Lextron, Inc. Scholarships *(Undergraduate/Scholarship)* 4094

Mid-State Wool Growers Cooperative Scholarship
*(Undergraduate/Scholarship)* 4099

Nebraska Department of Veterans' Affairs Waiver of Tuition
*(Undergraduate/Other)* 4503

Kenneth and Ellen Nielsen Cooperative Scholarships
*(Undergraduate/Scholarship)* 4110

Northrup King Company Scholarships *(Undergraduate/
Scholarship)* 4113

Union Pacific Foundation Scholarship *(Undergraduate/
Scholarship)* 4137

Western Seedmen's Association Scholarships *(Undergraduate/
Scholarship)* 4148

Williams Pipe Line Company Scholarship *(Undergraduate/
Scholarship)* 4150

## Nevada

Joseph Henry Jackson Award *(Professional Development/
Award)* 5234

Lextron, Inc. Scholarships *(Undergraduate/Scholarship)* 4094

Nevada Hispanic Services Scholarships *(Undergraduate/
Scholarship)* 4519

Nevada Women's Fund Scholarships *(Doctorate, Graduate,
Other, Professional Development, Undergraduate/
Scholarship)* 4521

Union Pacific Foundation Scholarship *(Undergraduate/
Scholarship)* 4137

WESTAF/NEA Regional Fellowships for Visual Artists
*(Professional Development/Fellowship)* 6161

Western Regional Graduate Program *(Graduate/Other)* 6159

Western Seedmen's Association Scholarships *(Undergraduate/
Scholarship)* 4148

## New Hampshire

AgRadio Network Scholarships *(Undergraduate/
Scholarship)* 4013

Blue Seal Feeds Scholarship *(Undergraduate/
Scholarship)* 4031

Marjorie S. Carter Boy Scout Scholarship *(Undergraduate/
Scholarship)* 1743

The Lighthouse Career Incentive Award for Adult
Undergraduates *(Undergraduate/Scholarship)* 3474

The Lighthouse Career Incentive Award for College-Bound
Students *(Undergraduate/Scholarship)* 3475

The Lighthouse Career Incentive Award for Graduate Students
*(Graduate/Scholarship)* 3476

The Lighthouse Career Incentive Award for Undergraduates
*(Undergraduate/Scholarship)* 3477

New England Graphic Arts Scholarships *(High School,
Undergraduate/Scholarship)* 4531

New England Regional Student Program *(Graduate,
Undergraduate/Other)* 4525

New Hampshire Charitable Foundation Statewide Student Aid
Program *(Graduate, Undergraduate/Grant)* 4533

New Hampshire Federal PLUS Loans *(Undergraduate/
Loan)* 2737

New Hampshire Individual Artist Fellowships *(Other/
Fellowship)* 4535

Abbie Sargent Memorial Scholarships *(Graduate,
Undergraduate/Scholarship)* 5250

Wolf's Head Oil Company Scholarships *(Undergraduate/
Scholarship)* 4152

## New Jersey

Thomas Joseph "Willie" Ambrosole Scholarship
*(Undergraduate/Scholarship)* 4207

Architects League Scholastic Award *(Undergraduate/
Scholarship)* 1075

Asbury Park Press Scholarships for Minority Students
*(Undergraduate/Scholarship)* 1168

Blue Seal Feeds Scholarship *(Undergraduate/
Scholarship)* 4031

Albert Halse Memorial Scholarship *(Undergraduate/
Scholarship)* 1076

JCC of Metropolitan New Jersey Patrons Award and Florence
Ben-Asher Memorial Award *(Professional Development/
Award)* 3259

The Lighthouse Career Incentive Award for Adult
Undergraduates *(Undergraduate/Scholarship)* 3474

The Lighthouse Career Incentive Award for College-Bound
Students *(Undergraduate/Scholarship)* 3475

The Lighthouse Career Incentive Award for Graduate Students
*(Graduate/Scholarship)* 3476

The Lighthouse Career Incentive Award for Undergraduates
*(Undergraduate/Scholarship)* 3477

MSNJ Medical Student Loan Fund *(Doctorate/Loan)* 3641

National Association of Water Companies - New Jersey
Chapter Scholarship *(Graduate, Undergraduate/
Scholarship)* 3904

New Jersey Academy of Science Research Grants-in-Aid to
High School Students *(High School/Grant)* 4537

New Jersey State Federation of Women's Clubs Margaret
Yardley Fellowship *(Doctorate, Graduate/Fellowship)* 4543

New Jersey State Golf Association Caddie Scholarships
*(Undergraduate/Scholarship)* 4545

New York Council Navy League Scholarships *(Undergraduate/
Scholarship)* 4566

Father Anthony J. O'Driscoll Memorial Scholarship Award
*(Undergraduate/Scholarship)* 633

Paragano Scholarship *(Undergraduate/Scholarship)* 4250

Pellegrini Scholarship Grants *(Graduate, Undergraduate/
Scholarship)* 5662

Piancone Family Agriculture Scholarship *(Graduate,
Undergraduate/Scholarship)* 4254

Clarence Tabor Memorial Scholarship *(Undergraduate/
Scholarship)* 1077

Wolf's Head Oil Company Scholarships *(Undergraduate/
Scholarship)* 4152

## New Mexico

Albuquerque Amateur Radio Club Scholarship *(Undergraduate/
Scholarship)* 815

Delta and Pine Land Company Scholarship *(Undergraduate/
Scholarship)* 4062

Future Farmers of America Scholarships *(Undergraduate/
Scholarship)* 1532

Lextron, Inc. Scholarships *(Undergraduate/Scholarship)* 4094

New Mexico Federal Stafford Loans *(Graduate,
Undergraduate/Loan)* 4551

Rocky Mountain Coal Mining Institute Scholarships
*(Undergraduate/Scholarship)* 5157

Santa Fe Pacific Foundation Scholarships *(Undergraduate/
Scholarship)* 563

Santa Fe Pacific Foundation Scholarships *(Undergraduate/
Scholarship)* 4125

Santa Fe Pacific Native American Scholarships
*(Undergraduate/Scholarship)* 1534

WESTAF/NEA Regional Fellowships for Visual Artists
*(Professional Development/Fellowship)* 6161

W.C.A. Care and Share Scholarship *(Undergraduate/ Scholarship)* 1897

Westchester Community Scholarship *(Graduate, Undergraduate/Scholarship)* 4271

Wolf's Head Oil Company Scholarships *(Undergraduate/ Scholarship)* 4152

World of Expression Scholarship Program *(High School, Undergraduate/Award)* 1420

## North Carolina

Chilean Nitrate Corporation Scholarship *(Undergraduate/ Scholarship)* 4051

Choreographers Fellowship *(Professional Development/ Fellowship)* 4661

Community Arts Administration Internships *(Graduate/ Internship)* 4662

Henry N. and Sydney T. Davenport Loan Fund *(Graduate, Undergraduate/Loan)* 1822

Delta and Pine Land Company Scholarship *(Undergraduate/ Scholarship)* 4062

Film/Video Artists Fellowship *(Professional Development/ Fellowship)* 4663

Folklife Documentary Program *(Professional Development/ Fellowship)* 4664

Folklife Internships *(Graduate/Internship)* 4665

Headlands Center for the Arts Residency *(Professional Development/Fellowship)* 4666

Carrie and Luther Huffines Loan Fund *(Undergraduate/ Loan)* 1823

Oliver Joel and Ellen Pell Denny Student Loan Fund *(Undergraduate/Loan)* 6196

La Napoule Residency for Visual Artists and Writers *(Professional Development/Fellowship)* 4667

Helen Lancaster Minton Educational Fund *(Undergraduate/ Scholarship)* 1824

Mary Morrow-Edna Richards Scholarships *(Undergraduate/ Scholarship)* 4672

North Carolina Arts Council Artist Fellowships *(Professional Development/Fellowship)* 4668

North Carolina State Legislative Tuition Grants *(Undergraduate/Grant)* 4680

Pickett & Hatcher Educational Loans *(Undergraduate/ Loan)* 4945

Z. Smith Reynolds Fellowship *(Professional Development/ Fellowship)* 5120

Scholarship for Children of Disabled, Deceased and POW/MIA Veterans *(Graduate, Undergraduate/Scholarship)* 4676

Emanuel Sternberger Educational Loan *(Graduate, Undergraduate/Loan)* 5628

Virginia Elizabeth and Alma Vane Taylor Fund *(Undergraduate/ Loan)* 6197

Tyson Scholarship *(Undergraduate/Scholarship)* 5761

Mark Ulmer Native American Scholarships *(Undergraduate/ Scholarship)* 5748

Universal Leaf Tobacco Company Scholarship *(Undergraduate/ Scholarship)* 4141

Visual Artists Fellowship *(Professional Development/ Fellowship)* 4670

Vocational Rehabilitation Assistance for Postsecondary Training *(Undergraduate/Other)* 4678

L. Phil Wicker Scholarship *(Undergraduate/Scholarship)* 841

The Winston-Salem Foundation Loans *(Undergraduate/ Loan)* 6198

Wolf's Head Oil Company Scholarships *(Undergraduate/ Scholarship)* 4152

## North Dakota

21st Century Genetics Cooperative Scholarships *(Undergraduate/Scholarship)* 4012

Carol Bauhs Benson Memorial Scholarship *(Undergraduate/ Scholarship)* 421

Ardell Bjugstad Memorial Scholarships *(Undergraduate/ Scholarship)* 5551

Gabriel J. Brown Trust Fund Loans *(Graduate, Undergraduate/ Loan)* 1521

Bush Artist Fellowships *(Professional Development/ Fellowship)* 1539

Capitol American Scholarships *(Undergraduate/ Scholarship)* 4041

The Ertl Company Scholarship *(Undergraduate/ Scholarship)* 4069

Farmers Mutual Hail Insurance Company of Iowa Scholarships *(Undergraduate/Scholarship)* 4073

Future Farmers of America Scholarships *(Undergraduate/ Scholarship)* 1532

Lextron, Inc. Scholarships *(Undergraduate/Scholarship)* 4094

Mola Foundation of Chicago Scholarships *(Undergraduate/ Scholarship)* 4243

Kenneth and Ellen Nielsen Cooperative Scholarships *(Undergraduate/Scholarship)* 4110

Rocky Mountain Coal Mining Institute Scholarships *(Undergraduate/Scholarship)* 5157

SIGCO Research Scholarships *(Undergraduate/ Scholarship)* 4126

Western Regional Graduate Program *(Graduate/Other)* 6159

Western Seedmen's Association Scholarships *(Undergraduate/ Scholarship)* 4148

Williams Pipe Line Company Scholarship *(Undergraduate/ Scholarship)* 4150

## Ohio

Armenian Cultural Society of Akron/Canton Scholarship *(Undergraduate/Scholarship)* 1110

Frank F. Bentley Scholarship *(Undergraduate/ Scholarship)* 5757

Blue Seal Feeds Scholarship *(Undergraduate/ Scholarship)* 4031

William A. Brower Scholarship *(Undergraduate/ Scholarship)* 4694

Alyce M. Cafaro Scholarship *(Undergraduate/ Scholarship)* 4212

Anthony J. Celebrezze Scholarship *(Graduate, Undergraduate/ Scholarship)* 4213

Cleveland Legacy Scholarship *(Undergraduate/ Scholarship)* 4431

Countrymark Cooperative, Inc. Scholarships *(Undergraduate/ Scholarship)* 4053

Cuyahoga County Medical Foundation Scholarship *(Graduate/ Scholarship)* 2146

Dusendon Scholarship Grants *(Undergraduate/ Scholarship)* 3494

The Ertl Company Scholarship *(Undergraduate/ Scholarship)* 4069

Esperanza Scholarships *(Graduate, Undergraduate/ Scholarship)* 2412

Evans Caddie Scholarships *(Undergraduate/Scholarship)* 6151

Farmers Mutual Hail Insurance Company of Iowa Scholarships *(Undergraduate/Scholarship)* 4073

Fifty Men and Women of Toledo Scholarships *(Undergraduate/Scholarship)* 4

Four-Shra-Nish Foundation Loan *(Undergraduate/Loan)* 2583

Gardner Foundation Scholarship Grants *(High School, Undergraduate/Scholarship)* 2624

Benn and Kathleen Gilmore Scholarship *(Doctorate/ Scholarship)* 4292

Golden Harvest Seeds, Inc. Scholarships *(Undergraduate/ Scholarship)* 4082

The Hauss-Helms Foundation Scholarships *(All/ Scholarship)* 2817

Mid-State Wool Growers Cooperative Scholarship *(Undergraduate/Scholarship)* 4099

Mola Foundation of Chicago Scholarships *(Undergraduate/ Scholarship)* 4243

James R. Nicholl Memorial Grant *(Postgraduate/Grant)* 4635

Ohio Academic Scholarships *(Undergraduate/ Scholarship)* 4723

Ohio Instructional Grants *(Undergraduate/Grant)* 4724

Ohio National Guard Tuition Grant *(Undergraduate/Grant, Scholarship)* 4729

## Ohio (continued)

Ohio Newspaper Women's Association Scholarship *(Undergraduate/Scholarship)* 4731

Ohio Student Choice Grants *(Undergraduate/Grant)* 4726

Ohio War Orphans Scholarships *(Undergraduate/Scholarship)* 4727

Quality Stores, Inc. Scholarships *(Undergraduate/Scholarship)* 4119

Star Bank, N.A. Scholarship *(Undergraduate/Scholarship)* 5601

John N. Stern Fellowships for Oberlin College Faculty *(Professional Development/Fellowship)* 4625

United Feeds Scholarships *(Undergraduate/Scholarship)* 4139

Wolf's Head Oil Company Scholarships *(Undergraduate/Scholarship)* 4152

Wyandott, Inc. Snacks and Popcorn Scholarship *(Undergraduate/Scholarship)* 4153

## Oklahoma

Capitol American Scholarships *(Undergraduate/Scholarship)* 4041

Cheyenne-Arapaho Higher Education Assistance Program Grant *(Undergraduate/Grant)* 1914

Delta and Pine Land Company Scholarship *(Undergraduate/Scholarship)* 4062

Future Farmers of America Scholarships *(Undergraduate/Scholarship)* 1532

Louie LeFlore/Grant Foreman Scholarship *(Undergraduate/Scholarship)* 5306

Lextron, Inc. Scholarships *(Undergraduate/Scholarship)* 4094

Mid-State Wool Growers Cooperative Scholarship *(Undergraduate/Scholarship)* 4099

North Texas - Bob Nelson KB5BNU Memorial Scholarship *(Undergraduate/Scholarship)* 833

Kenneth and Ellen Nielsen Cooperative Scholarships *(Undergraduate/Scholarship)* 4110

Oklahoma Natural Gas Company Scholarship *(Undergraduate/Scholarship)* 4114

Oklahoma Resident Rural Scholarship Loans *(Doctorate/Scholarship loan)* 4939

Oklahoma Rural Medical Education Scholarship Loans *(Doctorate/Scholarship loan)* 4940

Oklahoma State Regents Academic Scholars Scholarships *(Graduate, Undergraduate/Scholarship)* 4736

Oklahoma State Regents Chiropractic Education Assistance *(Other, Undergraduate/Award)* 4737

Oklahoma State Regents Future Teacher Scholarships *(Undergraduate/Scholarship)* 4738

Oklahoma State Regents Tuition Aid Grants *(Undergraduate/Grant)* 4741

Santa Fe Pacific Foundation Scholarships *(Undergraduate/Scholarship)* 563

Santa Fe Pacific Foundation Scholarships *(Undergraduate/Scholarship)* 4125

Santa Fe Pacific Native American Scholarships *(Undergraduate/Scholarship)* 1534

Tulsa Legacy Scholarship *(Undergraduate/Scholarship)* 4440

Tyson Scholarship *(Undergraduate/Scholarship)* 5761

Union Pacific Foundation Scholarship *(Undergraduate/Scholarship)* 4137

Western Seedmen's Association Scholarships *(Undergraduate/Scholarship)* 4148

Williams Pipe Line Company Scholarship *(Undergraduate/Scholarship)* 4150

## Oregon

Mary Lou Brown Scholarship *(Undergraduate/Scholarship)* 817

Campbell-Non-Linfield Scholarship Fund *(Graduate, Undergraduate/Scholarship)* 5830

Crawford Scholarship Fund *(Graduate, Undergraduate/Scholarship)* 5831

D & B Supply Company, Inc. Scholarships *(Undergraduate/Scholarship)* 4056

Darigold Scholarships *(Undergraduate/Scholarship)* 4057

May Darling Scholarship/Asa T. Williams/N.W. Labor Press Scholarship *(Undergraduate/Scholarship)* 4795

Finland U.S. Senate Youth Exchange Scholarships *(High School/Scholarship)* 6298

Franks Foundation Loan *(Graduate, Undergraduate/Loan)* 5832

Future Farmers of America Scholarships *(Undergraduate/Scholarship)* 1532

Maria C. Jackson & General George A. White Scholarships *(Undergraduate/Scholarship)* 5833

Jenkins Loan *(Graduate, Undergraduate/Loan)* 5834

Lextron, Inc. Scholarships *(Undergraduate/Scholarship)* 4094

Oregon Educational Aid for Veterans *(Doctorate, Graduate, Undergraduate/Other)* 4799

Oregon PTA Teacher Education Scholarships *(Undergraduate/Scholarship)* 4801

Silgan Containers Corporation Scholarships *(Undergraduate/Scholarship)* 4127

Bertha B. Singer Nurses Scholarship *(Graduate, Undergraduate/Scholarship)* 5835

Jerome B. Steinbach Scholarship *(Undergraduate/Scholarship)* 5836

Harley & Mertie Stevens Memorial Fund *(Undergraduate/Loan, Scholarship)* 5837

Tyson Scholarship *(Undergraduate/Scholarship)* 5761

Union Pacific Foundation Scholarship *(Undergraduate/Scholarship)* 4137

Flora M. Von Der Ahe Scholarship *(Graduate, Undergraduate/Scholarship)* 5838

WESTAF/NEA Regional Fellowships for Visual Artists *(Professional Development/Fellowship)* 6161

Western Regional Graduate Program *(Graduate/Other)* 6159

Western Seedmen's Association Scholarships *(Undergraduate/Scholarship)* 4148

## Pennsylvania

Allied Health Student Loans *(Undergraduate/Loan)* 4870

Aviation Technology Scholarship *(Professional Development, Undergraduate/Scholarship)* 1349

Blue Seal Feeds Scholarship *(Undergraduate/Scholarship)* 4031

Robert C. Byrd Honors Scholarships *(Undergraduate/Scholarship)* 4862

Commonwealth of Pennsylvania Educational Gratuity Program Grants *(Undergraduate/Award)* 2019

Orris C. and Beatrice Dewey Hirtzel Memorial Foundation Scholarship *(Undergraduate/Scholarship)* 2876

The Lighthouse Career Incentive Award for Adult Undergraduates *(Undergraduate/Scholarship)* 3474

The Lighthouse Career Incentive Award for College-Bound Students *(Undergraduate/Scholarship)* 3475

The Lighthouse Career Incentive Award for Graduate Students *(Graduate/Scholarship)* 3476

The Lighthouse Career Incentive Award for Undergraduates *(Undergraduate/Scholarship)* 3477

Professional Pilot John W. "Reds" Macfarlane Scholarship *(Professional Development, Undergraduate/Scholarship)* 1350

Medical Student Loans *(Professional Development/Loan)* 4871

NEED Scholarships *(Undergraduate/Scholarship)* 4507

Pellegrini Scholarship Grants *(Graduate, Undergraduate/Scholarship)* 5662

Pennsylvania Bureau for Veteran's Affairs Educational Gratuity *(Undergraduate/Other)* 4860

Pennsylvania Library Association Library Science Scholarships *(Graduate/Scholarship)* 4868

Piancone Family Agriculture Scholarship *(Graduate, Undergraduate/Scholarship)* 4254

Aviation Management Wilfred M. "Wiley" Post Scholarship *(Professional Development, Undergraduate/Scholarship)* 1351

Silgan Containers Corporation Scholarships *(Undergraduate/Scholarship)* 4127

Tyson Scholarship *(Undergraduate/Scholarship)* 5761

Legal Residence Index

## Utah (continued)

WESTAF/NEA Regional Fellowships for Visual Artists *(Professional Development/Fellowship)* 6161

Western Regional Graduate Program *(Graduate/Other)* 6159

Western Seedmen's Association Scholarships *(Undergraduate/ Scholarship)* 4148

## Vermont

AgRadio Network Scholarships *(Undergraduate/ Scholarship)* 4013

Blue Seal Feeds Scholarship *(Undergraduate/ Scholarship)* 4031

Marjorie S. Carter Boy Scout Scholarship *(Undergraduate/ Scholarship)* 1743

The Lighthouse Career Incentive Award for Adult Undergraduates *(Undergraduate/Scholarship)* 3474

The Lighthouse Career Incentive Award for College-Bound Students *(Undergraduate/Scholarship)* 3475

The Lighthouse Career Incentive Award for Graduate Students *(Graduate/Scholarship)* 3476

The Lighthouse Career Incentive Award for Undergraduates *(Undergraduate/Scholarship)* 3477

New England Graphic Arts Scholarships *(High School, Undergraduate/Scholarship)* 4531

New England Regional Student Program *(Graduate, Undergraduate/Other)* 4525

Past Presidents Parley Nursing Scholarship *(Undergraduate/ Scholarship)* 635

Windham Foundation Scholarship *(Undergraduate/ Scholarship)* 6193

Wolf's Head Oil Company Scholarships *(Undergraduate/ Scholarship)* 4152

## Virgin Islands

Virgin Islands Territorial Loan/Grant Program and Special Legislative Grants *(Graduate, Undergraduate/Grant, Loan)* 6046

## Virginia

Chilean Nitrate Corporation Scholarship *(Undergraduate/ Scholarship)* 4051

Delta and Pine Land Company Scholarship *(Undergraduate/ Scholarship)* 4062

Virginia Student Financial Assistance Award *(Graduate, Undergraduate/Award)* 5606

Jewish Educational Loans Fund *(Graduate, Undergraduate/ Loan)* 3269

Jewish Undergraduate Scholarships *(Undergraduate/ Scholarship)* 3270

Lester Educational Trust Loans *(Professional Development, Undergraduate/Loan)* 2133

Mary Marshall Nurse Practitioner/Nurse Midwife Scholarship Program *(Undergraduate/Scholarship)* 6048

Mary Marshall Nursing Scholarship for Student Nurses Practical Nursing Program *(Undergraduate/ Scholarship)* 6049

Mary Marshall Nursing Scholarship for Student Nurses Registered Nurse Program *(Undergraduate/ Scholarship)* 6050

Piancone Family Agriculture Scholarship *(Graduate, Undergraduate/Scholarship)* 4254

Pickett & Hatcher Educational Loans *(Undergraduate/ Loan)* 4945

Rangeley Educational Trust Loans *(Professional Development, Undergraduate/Loan)* 2134

Irene Stambler Vocational Opportunities Grants *(Other/ Grant)* 3271

Virginia Tuition Assistance Grant *(Graduate, Undergraduate/ Grant)* 5609

Tyson Scholarship *(Undergraduate/Scholarship)* 5761

Virginia College Scholarship *(Undergraduate/ Scholarship)* 5610

Virginia Press Association Minority Internship *(Graduate, Undergraduate/Internship)* 6063

Virginia War Orphans Education Program *(Graduate, Undergraduate/Other)* 6054

L. Phil Wicker Scholarship *(Undergraduate/Scholarship)* 841

Wolf's Head Oil Company Scholarships *(Undergraduate/ Scholarship)* 4152

## Washington

American Indian Endowed Scholarships *(Graduate, Undergraduate/Scholarship)* 551

American Legion Auxiliary Department Gift Scholarships *(Undergraduate/Scholarship)* 637

Mary Lou Brown Scholarship *(Undergraduate/ Scholarship)* 817

Susan Burdett Scholarhips *(Undergraduate/Scholarship)* 638

Nellie Martin Carman Scholarships *(Undergraduate/ Scholarship)* 1731

D & B Supply Company, Inc. Scholarships *(Undergraduate/ Scholarship)* 4056

Darigold Scholarships *(Undergraduate/Scholarship)* 4057

Finland U.S. Senate Youth Exchange Scholarships *(High School/Scholarship)* 6298

First Interstate Bank Scholarship *(Undergraduate/ Scholarship)* 2468

Future Farmers of America Scholarships *(Undergraduate/ Scholarship)* 1532

Jenkins Loan *(Graduate, Undergraduate/Loan)* 5834

Florence Lemke Memorial Scholarships in Fine Arts *(Undergraduate/Scholarship)* 639

Lextron, Inc. Scholarships *(Undergraduate/Scholarship)* 4094

Edmund F. Maxwell Foundation Scholarship *(Undergraduate/ Scholarship)* 3614

Marguerite Mc Alpin Memorial Scholarships *(Graduate, Undergraduate/Scholarship)* 640

Ida L., Mary L., and Ervin R. NePage Foundation *(Undergraduate/Scholarship)* 4513

Arthur & Doreen Parrett Scholarship Fund *(Graduate, Postgraduate, Undergraduate/Scholarship)* 4848

Tyson Scholarship *(Undergraduate/Scholarship)* 5761

Union Pacific Foundation Scholarship *(Undergraduate/ Scholarship)* 4137

Washington Osteopathic Foundation Student Loans *(Doctorate/Loan)* 6087

Washington Scholars Grants *(Undergraduate/Grant)* 6100

Washington State Educational Opportunity Grant *(Undergraduate/Grant)* 6101

Washington State Need Grant *(Undergraduate/Grant)* 6102

Washington State PTA Scholarships *(Undergraduate/ Scholarship)* 6107

Washington State Student Financial Aid Programs State Need Grant *(All/Other)* 6103

Washington State Work Study *(Graduate, Undergraduate/Work Study)* 6105

WESTAF/NEA Regional Fellowships for Visual Artists *(Professional Development/Fellowship)* 6161

Western Regional Graduate Program *(Graduate/Other)* 6159

Western Seedmen's Association Scholarships *(Undergraduate/ Scholarship)* 4148

## West Virginia

Undergraduate NASA Space Grant Fellowship *(Undergraduate/ Fellowship)* 6143

West Virginia Italian Heritage Festival Scholarships *(Undergraduate/Scholarship)* 4270

West Virginia Space Grant Consortium Undergraduate Scholarship Program *(Undergraduate/Scholarship)* 6145

West Virginia War Orphans Education Benefits *(High School, Undergraduate/Grant)* 6141

L. Phil Wicker Scholarship *(Undergraduate/Scholarship)* 841

Wolf's Head Oil Company Scholarships *(Undergraduate/ Scholarship)* 4152

## Wisconsin

21st Century Genetics Cooperative Scholarships *(Undergraduate/Scholarship)* 4012

## CANADA (by province)

### Alberta

Legal Residence Index

# Place of Study Index

This index lists awards that carry restrictions on where study may take place. Award citations are arranged alphabetically under the following geographic headings: United States, United States (by state), Canada, Canada (by province), International, International (by region), and International (by country). Each citation is followed by the study level and award type, which appear in parentheses. Numbers following the parenthetical information indicate book entry numbers for particular awards, not page numbers.

## UNITED STATES

AAAS Congressional Science and Engineering Fellowships *(Postdoctorate, Professional Development/Fellowship)* 263

AAAS Technology Policy Science and Engineering Fellowships *(Postdoctorate, Professional Development/Fellowship)* 267

AAS/American Society for Eighteenth Century Studies Fellowships *(Professional Development/Fellowship)* 252

AAS-NEAC U.S. Research Travel Grants *(Postdoctorate/Grant)* 1220

AATF Summer Institute in France *(Professional Development/Fellowship)* 325

Charles Abrams Scholarships *(Graduate/Scholarship)* 774

Academia-Oriented "Springboard to Teaching" Fellowship *(Doctorate/Fellowship)* 487

Academy of Vocal Arts Scholarships *(Professional Development/Scholarship)* 28

ACI Fellowships: ACI/W.R. Grace Fellowship; V. Mohan Malhotra Fellowship; Katherine Bryant Mather Fellowship; Stewart C. Watson Fellowship *(Graduate/Fellowship)* 388

ACNM Scholarships *(Graduate/Scholarship)* 3267

ACOG/Ortho-McNeil Academic Training Fellowships in Obstetrics and Gynecology *(Doctorate/Fellowship)* 382

ACS Congressional Fellowship Program *(Postdoctorate, Professional Development/Fellowship)* 367

Advanced Research Fellowships in U.S.-Japan Relations *(Postdoctorate/Fellowship)* 2808

Advanced Research Grants in Military History *(Graduate, Postgraduate/Grant)* 5823

AES/EFA Research Grants *(Postdoctorate/Grant)* 455

AES Research Fellowships *(Postdoctorate/Fellowship)* 456

AFAR Fellowships *(Graduate, Undergraduate/Fellowship)* 468

Affirmative Action Scholarship Program *(Graduate/Scholarship)* 5575

AFL-CIO Research Internship *(Graduate/Internship)* 464

African Graduate Fellowships *(Graduate, Postgraduate/Fellowship)* 47

Afro-American and African Studies Fellowships *(Doctorate, Postdoctorate/Fellowship)* 6251

AFUD/NKF Resident Fellowship *(Postdoctorate/Fellowship)* 498

AFUD Research Scholars Program *(Postdoctorate/Award)* 500

AFUD Summer Student Fellowships *(Doctorate/Fellowship)* 501

AGA Foundation Advanced Research Training Awards (Discontinued) *(Postdoctorate/Award)* 448

AGA Foundation/SmithKline Beecham Clinical Research Awards (Discontinued) *(Postdoctorate/Award)* 449

AIBS Congressional Science Fellowship *(Postdoctorate/Fellowship)* 476

AIER Summer Fellowships *(Graduate, Undergraduate/Fellowship)* 580

AIHP Grant-in-Aid Toward Thesis Expenses Related to the History of Pharmacy *(Doctorate, Graduate/Grant)* 583

ALA Career Investigator Awards *(Postdoctorate/Award)* 677

ALA Research Grants *(Postdoctorate/Grant)* 678

TELACU/Richard Alatorre Fellowship *(Graduate/Fellowship)* 5686

Albee Foundation Residencies *(Professional Development/Other)* 141

Albert Ellis Institute Clinical Fellowships, Internships *(Graduate, Postdoctorate, Postgraduate/Fellowship)* 143

Alexander Scholarship Loans *(Undergraduate/Scholarship loan)* 3119

Frances C. Allen Fellowships *(Doctorate, Graduate, Postgraduate/Fellowship)* 4615

Alpha Kappa Alpha Educational Advancement Foundation Scholarships *(Undergraduate/Scholarship)* 198

American Accounting Association Fellowship Program in Accounting *(Doctorate/Fellowship)* 246

American Association for Dental Research-Student Research Fellowships *(Doctorate/Fellowship)* 285

American Foundation for Aging Research Predoctoral Awards *(Doctorate, Graduate, Undergraduate/Award)* 469

American Fund for Dental Health Dental Teacher Training Fellowships *(Postdoctorate/Fellowship)* 36

American Fund for Dental Health/Hillenbrand Fellowship in Dental Administration *(Postdoctorate/Fellowship)* 38

American Jewish Studies Fellowships *(Doctorate, Postdoctorate/Award, Fellowship)* 598

American Kennel Clubs Veterinary Scholarship *(Undergraduate/Scholarship)* 604

American Museum of Natural History Collection Study Grants *(Doctorate, Postdoctorate/Grant)* 712

American Museum of Natural History Research and Museum Fellowships *(Postdoctorate/Fellowship)* 713

American Numismatic Society Graduate Seminar *(Graduate/Other)* 737

American Numismatic Society Grants-in-Aid *(Graduate, Postgraduate/Grant)* 738

American Otological Society Research Fellowship and Medical Student Training Grants *(Postdoctorate/Grant)* 759

American Research Center in Egypt Research Fellowships for Study in the U.S. or Canada *(Doctorate/Fellowship)* 844

American Society for Dermatologic Surgery Grants *(Postdoctorate/Grant)* 2235

American Speech-Language-Hearing Foundation Graduate Student Scholarships *(Doctorate, Graduate/Scholarship)* 989

American Speech-Language-Hearing Foundation Research Grants for New Investigators *(Doctorate, Graduate, Postdoctorate, Postgraduate/Grant)* 990

American Water Works Association Thomas R. Camp Scholarship *(Graduate/Scholarship)* 1019

Amity Institute Internships *(Professional Development/Internship)* 1026

Amoco Canada Petroleum Company Scholarships *(Undergraduate/Scholarship)* 1028

APA Congressional Fellowships *(Postdoctorate/Fellowship)* 809

APA Planning Fellowships *(Graduate/Fellowship)* 776

Argonne National Laboratory Faculty Research Leave; Faculty Research Participation Awards *(Postdoctorate/Award)* 1083

Place of Study Index

## UNITED STATES (by state)

### Alabama

*Place of Study Index*

## California (continued)

U.S. Navy-ASEE Summer Faculty Research Program *(Professional Development/Fellowship)* 925

U.S. Navy ONR-ASEE Postdoctoral Fellowship *(Postdoctorate/ Fellowship)* 926

Warner Trust Loan Program *(Doctorate, Graduate, Other/ Loan)* 6079

Whiting Fellowships in the Humanities *(Doctorate/ Fellowship)* 6171

## Colorado

ABCI Scholarships *(Undergraduate/Scholarship)* 1343

AWU Faculty Fellowships *(Postdoctorate/Fellowship)* 1199

AWU Faculty Sabbatical Fellowships *(Postdoctorate/ Fellowship)* 1200

AWU Graduate Research Fellowships *(Doctorate, Graduate/ Fellowship)* 1201

AWU Post-Graduate Fellowship *(Doctorate, Postdoctorate/ Fellowship)* 1202

AWU Student Research Fellowships *(Graduate, Undergraduate/Fellowship)* 1203

Boettcher Foundation Scholarship *(Undergraduate/ Scholarship)* 1455

Colorado Society of CPAs Educational Foundation High School Scholarship *(Undergraduate/Scholarship)* 2000

Colorado Society of CPAs Educational Foundation Scholarships *(Undergraduate/Scholarship)* 2001

Evans Caddie Scholarships *(Undergraduate/Scholarship)* 6151

Golden Harvest Seeds, Inc. Scholarships *(Undergraduate/ Scholarship)* 4082

Gustafson, Inc. Scholarship *(Undergraduate/Scholarship)* 4084

Kenneth and Ellen Nielsen Cooperative Scholarships *(Undergraduate/Scholarship)* 4110

United States Space Foundation Teacher Course Fellowship *(Professional Development/Fellowship)* 5974

Western Interstate Commission for Higher Education Western Regional Graduate Program *(Doctorate, Graduate/ Other)* 136

## Connecticut

Connecticut Aid for Public College Students *(Undergraduate/ Other)* 2043

Connecticut Family Education Loan Program (CT FELP) *(Graduate, Professional Development, Undergraduate/ Loan)* 2044

Connecticut Independent College Student Grants *(Undergraduate/Grant)* 2045

Connecticut League for Nursing Scholarships *(Graduate, Undergraduate/Scholarship)* 2052

Connecticut Tuition Aid for Needy Students *(Undergraduate/ Scholarship)* 2047

Connecticut Tuition Waiver for Senior Citizens *(Undergraduate/Scholarship)* 2048

Connecticut Tuition Waiver for Veterans *(Undergraduate/ Scholarship)* 2049

Digital Equipment Corporation Scholarship *(Undergraduate/ Scholarship)* 5507

Eastern Apiculture Society of North America Scholarship *(Undergraduate/Scholarship)* 4067

The Lighthouse Career Incentive Award for Adult Undergraduates *(Undergraduate/Scholarship)* 3474

The Lighthouse Career Incentive Award for College-Bound Students *(Undergraduate/Scholarship)* 3475

The Lighthouse Career Incentive Award for Graduate Students *(Graduate/Scholarship)* 3476

The Lighthouse Career Incentive Award for Undergraduates *(Undergraduate/Scholarship)* 3477

MassGrant Program *(Undergraduate/Scholarship)* 3601

Jonathan May Memorial Scholarships *(Undergraduate/ Scholarship)* 3993

New England Education Society Loan *(Graduate/Loan)* 4527

New England Press Association Internships *(Undergraduate/ Internship)* 4529

New England Regional Student Program *(Graduate, Undergraduate/Other)* 4525

NFB of CT Academic Sholarship *(Undergraduate/ Scholarship)* 3994

Robert G. Stone Fellowships in American Maritime History *(Doctorate, Postdoctorate/Fellowship)* 6182

U.S. Navy-ASEE Summer Faculty Research Program *(Professional Development/Fellowship)* 925

U.S. Navy ONR-ASEE Postdoctoral Fellowship *(Postdoctorate/ Fellowship)* 926

Lewis Walpole Library Fellowship *(Graduate, Postdoctorate/ Fellowship)* 6277

Whiting Fellowships in the Humanities *(Doctorate/ Fellowship)* 6171

## Delaware

Eastern Apiculture Society of North America Scholarship *(Undergraduate/Scholarship)* 4067

## District of Columbia

APSA Congressional Fellowships for Federal Executives *(Professional Development/Fellowship)* 779

APSA Congressional Fellowships for Journalists *(Professional Development/Fellowship)* 780

Center For Advanced Study in the Visual Arts Associate Appointments *(Postdoctorate/Fellowship)* 1768

Center for Hellenic Studies Fellowships *(Postdoctorate/ Fellowship)* 1793

Center for Strategic and Budgetary Assessments Internship *(Other/Internship)* 1805

Central Intelligence Agency Undergraduate Scholars Program *(Undergraduate/Internship, Scholarship)* 1812

Fellowships in Byzantine Studies, Pre-Columbian Studies and Landscape Architecture *(Doctorate, Graduate, Postdoctorate, Undergraduate/Fellowship)* 2288

Frese Senior Research Fellowship Program *(Postdoctorate/ Fellowship)* 1773

Elsie Bell Grosvenor Scholarship Awards *(Undergraduate/ Scholarship)* 1401

Italian Cultural Society and NIAF Matching Scholarship *(Undergraduate/Scholarship)* 4234

U. Alexis Johnson Scholarship *(Graduate, Undergraduate/ Scholarship)* 3238

Marine Corps Historical Center College Internships *(Undergraduate/Internship)* 3556

Antonio M. Marinelli Founders' Scholarship *(Undergraduate/ Scholarship)* 4237

MassGrant Program *(Undergraduate/Scholarship)* 3601

National Symphony Young Soloists' Competition, College Division *(Professional Development/Prize, Scholarship)* 4419

Reporters Committee Fellowship *(Professional Development/ Fellowship)* 5093

Senior Fellowships *(Postdoctorate/Fellowship)* 1778

U.S. Air Force Dissertation Year Fellowship in U.S. Military Aerospace History *(Doctorate/Fellowship)* 5814

U.S. Navy-ASEE Summer Faculty Research Program *(Professional Development/Fellowship)* 925

U.S. Navy ONR-ASEE Postdoctoral Fellowship *(Postdoctorate/ Fellowship)* 926

United States Senate Youth Program *(High School/ Scholarship)* 2835

Visiting Senior Fellowships *(Postdoctorate/Fellowship)* 1780

Gilbert F. White Postdoctoral Fellowships *(Postdoctorate/ Fellowship)* 5112

David A. Winston Fellowship *(Graduate, Undergraduate/ Fellowship)* 1290

Wolcott Foundation Fellowships *(Graduate/Fellowship)* 2870

## Florida

American Legion Auxiliary Memorial Scholarship *(Undergraduate/Scholarship)* 617

Earl I. Anderson Scholarship *(Undergraduate/Scholarship)* 816

Mary McLeod Bethune Scholarship *(Graduate, Undergraduate/ Grant)* 2494

William L. Boyd IV, Florida Resident Access Grant *(Undergraduate/Grant)* 2495

## Illinois (continued)

Illinois Federal Subsidized Stafford Loan *(Graduate, Undergraduate/Loan)* 2971

Illinois Federal Supplemental Loans for Students *(Graduate, Undergraduate/Loan)* 2972

Illinois Federal Unsubsidized Stafford Loan *(Graduate, Undergraduate/Loan)* 2973

Illinois Merit Recognition Scholarship *(Undergraduate/ Scholarship)* 2974

Illinois MIA/POW Scholarship *(Undergraduate/ Scholarship)* 2961

Illinois Monetary Award Program *(Undergraduate/Grant)* 2975

Illinois National Guard Grant *(Graduate, Undergraduate/ Grant)* 2976

Illinois Police Officer/Fire Officer Grant *(Undergraduate/ Grant)* 2977

Illinois Student-to-Student Grant *(Undergraduate/Grant)* 2978

Illinois uniLoan *(Graduate, Undergraduate/Loan)* 2979

Illinois Veteran Grant *(Undergraduate/Grant)* 2980

Lloyd Lewis Fellowships in American History *(Postdoctorate/ Fellowship)* 4617

The Audrey Lumsden-Kouvel Fellowship *(Postdoctorate/ Fellowship)* 4618

Master of Library Science Degree Training Grants *(Graduate/ Grant)* 2966

Minority Teachers of Illinois Scholarship *(Undergraduate/ Scholarship loan)* 2981

Monticello College Foundation Fellowship for Women *(Postdoctorate/Fellowship)* 4619

Newberry Library National Endowment for the Humanities Fellowships *(Postdoctorate/Fellowship)* 4622

Newberry Library Short-Term Resident Fellowships *(Postdoctorate/Fellowship)* 4623

Kenneth and Ellen Nielsen Cooperative Scholarships *(Undergraduate/Scholarship)* 4110

Precision Laboratories, Inc. Scholarship *(Undergraduate/ Scholarship)* 4116

Charles M. Ross Trust *(Graduate/Other)* 5165

Sandoz Agro, Inc. Scholarships *(Undergraduate/ Scholarship)* 4124

Six Meter Club of Chicago Scholarship *(Undergraduate/ Scholarship)* 840

South Central Modern Languages Association Fellowship *(Postdoctorate/Fellowship)* 4624

SSRC African Humanities Fellowships *(Doctorate, Postdoctorate/Fellowship)* 5396

John N. Stern Fellowships for Oberlin College Faculty *(Professional Development/Fellowship)* 4625

United Feeds Scholarships *(Undergraduate/Scholarship)* 4139

U.S. Department of Energy Internship *(Undergraduate/ Internship)* 4711

Muddy Waters Scholarship *(Undergraduate/Scholarship)* 1448

Whiting Fellowships in the Humanities *(Doctorate/ Fellowship)* 6171

## Indiana

Earl I. Anderson Scholarship *(Undergraduate/Scholarship)* 816

David Arver Memorial Scholarship *(Undergraduate/ Scholarship)* 77

Big R. Stores and Fleet Supply Company Scholarship *(Undergraduate/Scholarship)* 4029

Child of Disabled Veteran Grant or Purple Heart Recipient, Grant *(Graduate, Other, Undergraduate/Other)* 2996

Creswell, Munsell, Fultz & Zirbel Scholarships *(Undergraduate/ Scholarship)* 4054

Department of Veterans Affairs Free Tuition for Children of POW/MIA's in Vietnam *(Undergraduate/Other)* 2997

Maurice and Robert Early Scholarship *(Undergraduate/ Scholarship)* 2999

Evans Caddie Scholarships *(Undergraduate/Scholarship)* 6151

Golden Harvest Seeds, Inc. Scholarships *(Undergraduate/ Scholarship)* 4082

Indiana Professional Chapter of SPJ Minority Scholarship *(Undergraduate/Scholarship)* 5486

Kova Fertilizer, Inc. Scholarships *(Undergraduate/ Scholarship)* 4093

Metropolitan Life Foundation Scholarships *(Undergraduate/ Scholarship)* 4097

Sandoz Agro, Inc. Scholarships *(Undergraduate/ Scholarship)* 4124

United Feeds Scholarships *(Undergraduate/Scholarship)* 4139

## Iowa

David Arver Memorial Scholarship *(Undergraduate/ Scholarship)* 77

Biggs and Gilmore Communications Scholarships *(Graduate, Undergraduate/Scholarship)* 4030

Creswell, Munsell, Fultz & Zirbel Scholarships *(Undergraduate/ Scholarship)* 4054

GOALS Fellowships *(Graduate/Fellowship)* 3001

Golden Harvest Seeds, Inc. Scholarships *(Undergraduate/ Scholarship)* 4082

Paul and Helen L. Grauer Scholarship *(Undergraduate/ Scholarship)* 826

Growmark, Inc. Scholarships *(Undergraduate/ Scholarship)* 4083

Gustafson, Inc. Scholarship *(Undergraduate/Scholarship)* 4084

Hawkeye Steel Products, Inc. Scholarship *(Undergraduate/ Scholarship)* 4086

Iowa Broadcasters Association Scholarship *(Undergraduate/ Scholarship)* 3219

Earl May Seed & Nursery L.P. Scholarship *(Undergraduate/ Scholarship)* 4096

Metropolitan Life Foundation Scholarships *(Undergraduate/ Scholarship)* 4097

Kenneth and Ellen Nielsen Cooperative Scholarships *(Undergraduate/Scholarship)* 4110

Sandoz Agro, Inc. Scholarships *(Undergraduate/ Scholarship)* 4124

Harold W. Schloss Memorial Scholarship *(Undergraduate/ Scholarship)* 1745

War Orphans Educational Fund *(Undergraduate/Grant)* 3221

## Kansas

David Arver Memorial Scholarship *(Undergraduate/ Scholarship)* 77

Creswell, Munsell, Fultz & Zirbel Scholarships *(Undergraduate/ Scholarship)* 4054

Golden Harvest Seeds, Inc. Scholarships *(Undergraduate/ Scholarship)* 4082

Paul and Helen L. Grauer Scholarship *(Undergraduate/ Scholarship)* 826

Earl May Seed & Nursery L.P. Scholarship *(Undergraduate/ Scholarship)* 4096

Metropolitan Life Foundation Scholarships *(Undergraduate/ Scholarship)* 4097

Kenneth and Ellen Nielsen Cooperative Scholarships *(Undergraduate/Scholarship)* 4110

Jean Pratt Scholarship *(High School/Scholarship)* 1453

## Kentucky

Evans Caddie Scholarships *(Undergraduate/Scholarship)* 6151

Kentucky Center for Veterans Affairs State Tuition Waivers *(Undergraduate/Other)* 3358

Kentucky Department of Veterans Affairs Tuition Waivers *(Undergraduate/Scholarship)* 3356

Pickett & Hatcher Educational Loans *(Undergraduate/ Loan)* 4945

Charles M. Ross Trust *(Graduate/Other)* 5165

Rural Kentucky Medical Scholarship Fund (RKMSF) *(Doctorate/Loan, Scholarship)* 3364

## Louisiana

Louisiana Library Association Scholarship in Librarianship *(Graduate/Scholarship)* 3502

Louisiana National Guard Tuition Exemption Program *(Undergraduate/Other)* 3504

Louisiana State Aid Dependents Educational Assistance *(Graduate, Other, Undergraduate/Scholarship)* 3500

Place of Study Index

## Michigan (continued)

David Arver Memorial Scholarship *(Undergraduate/ Scholarship)* 77

Biggs and Gilmore Communications Scholarships *(Graduate, Undergraduate/Scholarship)* 4030

Mary Butler Scholarship *(Graduate, Undergraduate/ Scholarship)* 6221

CEW Scholarships for Returning Women *(Graduate, Professional Development, Undergraduate/ Scholarship)* 6002

Lucy Corbett Scholarship *(Graduate, Undergraduate/ Scholarship)* 6222

Evans Caddie Scholarships *(Undergraduate/Scholarship)* 6151

Gerber Prize for Excellence in Pediatrics *(Doctorate/ Award)* 4291

Benn and Kathleen Gilmore Scholarship *(Doctorate/ Scholarship)* 4292

GOALS Fellowships *(Graduate/Fellowship)* 3001

Golden Harvest Seeds, Inc. Scholarships *(Undergraduate/ Scholarship)* 4082

Interlochen Arts Academy and Arts Camp Scholarships *(High School, Postgraduate, Undergraduate/Scholarship)* 3101

McFadden Family Automotive Scholarship *(Undergraduate/ Scholarship)* 1882

Michigan Competitive Scholarships *(Undergraduate/ Scholarship)* 3685

Michigan Indian Tuition Waiver *(Graduate, Undergraduate/ Other)* 3683

Michigan Tuition Grants *(Graduate, Undergraduate/ Grant)* 3686

Sandoz Agro, Inc. Scholarships *(Undergraduate/ Scholarship)* 4124

Specs Howard High School Scholarships *(High School, Undergraduate/Scholarship)* 5583

Specs Howard School of Broadcast Arts Industry Scholarships *(Undergraduate/Scholarship)* 5584

United Feeds Scholarships *(Undergraduate/Scholarship)* 4139

Lent D. Upson-Loren B. Miller Fellowships *(Graduate/ Fellowship)* 1958

## Minnesota

David Arver Memorial Scholarship *(Undergraduate/ Scholarship)* 77

Creswell, Munsell, Fultz & Zirbel Scholarships *(Undergraduate/ Scholarship)* 4054

Evans Caddie Scholarships *(Undergraduate/Scholarship)* 6151

GOALS Fellowships *(Graduate/Fellowship)* 3001

Golden Harvest Seeds, Inc. Scholarships *(Undergraduate/ Scholarship)* 4082

Hugh J. Andersen Memorial Scholarship *(Doctorate/ Scholarship)* 4296

Minnesota State Department of Veterans Affairs Educational Assistance Grants *(Undergraduate/Grant)* 3718

Minnesota Teamsters Joint Council No. 32 Scholarship Awards *(Undergraduate/Scholarship)* 3720

Kenneth and Ellen Nielsen Cooperative Scholarships *(Undergraduate/Scholarship)* 4110

Sandoz Agro, Inc. Scholarships *(Undergraduate/ Scholarship)* 4124

## Mississippi

Borden Foundation Scholarships *(Undergraduate/ Scholarship)* 4032

Weeta F. Colebank Scholarship *(Undergraduate/ Scholarship)* 4432

Gustafson, Inc. Scholarship *(Undergraduate/Scholarship)* 4084

Mississippi African-American Doctoral Teacher Loan/ Scholarship Program *(Doctorate/Scholarship loan)* 3730

Mississippi Health Care Professions Loan/Scholarship Program *(Undergraduate/Scholarship loan)* 3732

Mississippi Law Enforcement Officers and Firemen Scholarship Program *(Graduate, Undergraduate/ Scholarship)* 3733

Mississippi Psychology Apprenticeship Program *(Graduate, Undergraduate/Internship)* 3738

Mississippi Public Management Graduate Internship Program *(Graduate/Internship)* 3739

Mississippi Scholarship *(Undergraduate/Scholarship)* 832

Mississippi Southeast Asia POW/MIA Scholarship Program *(Graduate, Undergraduate/Scholarship)* 3740

Mississippi Special Medical Education Loan/Scholarship Program *(Doctorate/Scholarship loan)* 3742

Mississippi State Dental Education Loan/Scholarship Program *(Doctorate/Scholarship loan)* 3743

Mississippi State Medical Education Loan/Scholarship Program *(Doctorate/Scholarship loan)* 3744

Mississippi State Student Incentive Grant Program *(Undergraduate/Grant)* 3745

Pickett & Hatcher Educational Loans *(Undergraduate/ Loan)* 4945

U.S. Navy-ASEE Summer Faculty Research Program *(Professional Development/Fellowship)* 925

U.S. Navy ONR-ASEE Postdoctoral Fellowship *(Postdoctorate/ Fellowship)* 926

William Winter Teacher Scholar Loan Program *(Other, Undergraduate/Loan, Scholarship)* 3746

## Missouri

David Arver Memorial Scholarship *(Undergraduate/ Scholarship)* 77

Creswell, Munsell, Fultz & Zirbel Scholarships *(Undergraduate/ Scholarship)* 4054

Evans Caddie Scholarships *(Undergraduate/Scholarship)* 6151

Golden Harvest Seeds, Inc. Scholarships *(Undergraduate/ Scholarship)* 4082

Paul and Helen L. Grauer Scholarship *(Undergraduate/ Scholarship)* 826

Earl May Seed & Nursery L.P. Scholarship *(Undergraduate/ Scholarship)* 4096

Metropolitan Life Foundation Scholarships *(Undergraduate/ Scholarship)* 4097

Kenneth and Ellen Nielsen Cooperative Scholarships *(Undergraduate/Scholarship)* 4110

St. Louis SME Chapter No. 17 Scholarships *(Undergraduate/ Scholarship)* 5468

Jesse Wrench Scholarship *(Graduate, Undergraduate/ Scholarship)* 3748

## Montana

AWU Faculty Fellowships *(Postdoctorate/Fellowship)* 1199

AWU Faculty Sabbatical Fellowships *(Postdoctorate/ Fellowship)* 1200

AWU Graduate Research Fellowships *(Doctorate, Graduate/ Fellowship)* 1201

AWU Student Research Fellowships *(Graduate, Undergraduate/Fellowship)* 1203

Montana Indian Student Fee Waiver *(Doctorate, Graduate, Professional Development, Undergraduate/Scholarship)* 557

Montana University System Fee Waivers *(Undergraduate/ Other)* 3769

Western Interstate Commission for Higher Education Western Regional Graduate Program *(Doctorate, Graduate/ Other)* 136

## Nebraska

ConAgra Scholarships *(Undergraduate/Scholarship)* 4052

Creswell, Munsell, Fultz & Zirbel Scholarships *(Undergraduate/ Scholarship)* 4054

Golden Harvest Seeds, Inc. Scholarships *(Undergraduate/ Scholarship)* 4082

Paul and Helen L. Grauer Scholarship *(Undergraduate/ Scholarship)* 826

Earl May Seed & Nursery L.P. Scholarship *(Undergraduate/ Scholarship)* 4096

Metropolitan Life Foundation Scholarships *(Undergraduate/ Scholarship)* 4097

Nebraska Department of Veterans' Affairs Waiver of Tuition *(Undergraduate/Other)* 4503

Kenneth and Ellen Nielsen Cooperative Scholarships *(Undergraduate/Scholarship)* 4110

## Nevada

AWU Faculty Fellowships *(Postdoctorate/Fellowship)* 1199

AWU Faculty Sabbatical Fellowships *(Postdoctorate/Fellowship)* 1200

AWU Graduate Research Fellowships *(Doctorate, Graduate/Fellowship)* 1201

AWU Student Research Fellowships *(Graduate, Undergraduate/Fellowship)* 1203

Robert Thunen Memorial Educational Scholarships *(Graduate, Undergraduate/Scholarship)* 2983

Western Interstate Commission for Higher Education Western Regional Graduate Program *(Doctorate, Graduate/Other)* 136

## New Hampshire

Digital Equipment Corporation Scholarship *(Undergraduate/Scholarship)* 5507

Eastern Apiculture Society of North America Scholarship *(Undergraduate/Scholarship)* 4067

The Lighthouse Career Incentive Award for Adult Undergraduates *(Undergraduate/Scholarship)* 3474

The Lighthouse Career Incentive Award for College-Bound Students *(Undergraduate/Scholarship)* 3475

The Lighthouse Career Incentive Award for Graduate Students *(Graduate/Scholarship)* 3476

The Lighthouse Career Incentive Award for Undergraduates *(Undergraduate/Scholarship)* 3477

MassGrant Program *(Undergraduate/Scholarship)* 3601

New England Education Society Loan *(Graduate/Loan)* 4527

New England Press Association Internships *(Undergraduate/Internship)* 4529

New England Regional Student Program *(Graduate, Undergraduate/Other)* 4525

New Hampshire Federal PLUS Loans *(Undergraduate/Loan)* 2737

New Hampshire Individual Artist Fellowships *(Other/Fellowship)* 4535

## New Jersey

AEJ Summer Internships for Minorities *(Undergraduate/Internship)* 3029

AT & T Bell Laboratories Cooperative Research Fellowships for Minorities *(Graduate/Fellowship)* 1302

AT & T Bell Laboratories Graduate Research Fellowships for Women *(Doctorate/Fellowship)* 1303

AT & T Bell Laboratories Graduate Research Grants for Women *(Doctorate, Graduate/Grant)* 1304

AT & T Bell Laboratories Summer Research Program for Minorities & Women *(Undergraduate/Fellowship)* 1305

Shelby Cullom Davis Center Research Fellowships *(Postdoctorate/Fellowship)* 2189

Eastern Apiculture Society of North America Scholarship *(Undergraduate/Scholarship)* 4067

ETS Center for Performance Assessment Postdoctoral Fellowships *(Postdoctorate/Fellowship)* 2352

ETS Postdoctoral Fellowships *(Postdoctorate/Fellowship)* 2353

ETS Summer Program in Research for Graduate Students *(Doctorate/Award)* 2354

GOALS Fellowships *(Graduate/Fellowship)* 3001

The Lighthouse Career Incentive Award for Adult Undergraduates *(Undergraduate/Scholarship)* 3474

The Lighthouse Career Incentive Award for College-Bound Students *(Undergraduate/Scholarship)* 3475

The Lighthouse Career Incentive Award for Graduate Students *(Graduate/Scholarship)* 3476

The Lighthouse Career Incentive Award for Undergraduates *(Undergraduate/Scholarship)* 3477

National Assessment of Educational Progress Visiting Scholar Program *(Postdoctorate/Award)* 2355

National Association of Water Companies - New Jersey Chapter Scholarship *(Graduate, Undergraduate/Scholarship)* 3904

New Jersey Academy of Science Research Grants-in-Aid to High School Students *(High School/Grant)* 4537

NJSCLS Scholarships *(Undergraduate/Scholarship)* 4541

Whiting Fellowships in the Humanities *(Doctorate/Fellowship)* 6171

## New Mexico

AWU Faculty Fellowships *(Postdoctorate/Fellowship)* 1199

AWU Faculty Sabbatical Fellowships *(Postdoctorate/Fellowship)* 1200

AWU Graduate Research Fellowships *(Doctorate, Graduate/Fellowship)* 1201

AWU Post-Graduate Fellowship *(Doctorate, Postdoctorate/Fellowship)* 1202

AWU Student Research Fellowships *(Graduate, Undergraduate/Fellowship)* 1203

New Mexico Federal Stafford Loans *(Graduate, Undergraduate/Loan)* 4551

U.S. Department of Energy Internship *(Undergraduate/Internship)* 4711

WERC Undergraduate Scholarships *(Undergraduate/Scholarship)* 6113

Western Interstate Commission for Higher Education Western Regional Graduate Program *(Doctorate, Graduate/Other)* 136

## New York

AAAA Minority Advertising Internships *(Undergraduate/Internship)* 270

AEJ Summer Internships for Minorities *(Undergraduate/Internship)* 3029

American Numismatic Society Graduate Fellowships *(Doctorate/Fellowship)* 736

BNL Postdoctoral Research Associateships *(Postdoctorate/Other)* 1504

Herbert and Patricia Brodkin Scholarship *(Professional Development/Scholarship)* 4775

Constance E. Casey Scholarship *(Undergraduate/Scholarship)* 1854

Chautauqua County Basketball Officials Scholarship *(Undergraduate/Scholarship)* 1855

College of Aeronautics Scholarship *(Undergraduate/Scholarship)* 81

Cooper-Hewitt Museum Internships *(Undergraduate/Internship)* 5383

Christopher DeCormier Scholarship *(Doctorate/Scholarship)* 3075

Digital Equipment Corporation Scholarship *(Undergraduate/Scholarship)* 5507

Paul Douglas Teacher Scholarship *(Undergraduate/Scholarship)* 4585

Eastern Apiculture Society of North America Scholarship *(Undergraduate/Scholarship)* 4067

Susan W. Freestone Vocational Education Award *(Undergraduate/Award)* 4581

Gannett Center Fellowships *(Other, Professional Development/Fellowship)* 2593

GOALS Fellowships *(Graduate/Fellowship)* 3001

Government Scholars Summer Program *(Graduate, Undergraduate/Award)* 4562

Guido-Zerilli-Marimo Scholarships *(Graduate, Undergraduate/Scholarship)* 4233

Barbara Mae Gustafson & Bridget Mary Drew (B&B) Scholarship *(Undergraduate/Scholarship)* 1866

Perry F. Hadlock Memorial Scholarship *(Undergraduate/Scholarship)* 828

IBM Postdoctoral Research Fellowships in Mathematical Sciences *(Postdoctorate/Fellowship)* 2948

Kansas City Speech Pathology Award *(Graduate/Award)* 3327

Peter Krueger Summer Internships *(Graduate, Undergraduate/Internship)* 5384

The Lighthouse Career Incentive Award for Adult Undergraduates *(Undergraduate/Scholarship)* 3474

The Lighthouse Career Incentive Award for College-Bound Students *(Undergraduate/Scholarship)* 3475

The Lighthouse Career Incentive Award for Graduate Students *(Graduate/Scholarship)* 3476

## New York (continued)

The Lighthouse Career Incentive Award for Undergraduates *(Undergraduate/Scholarship)* 3477

William J. Mariner Working Scholar Program *(Undergraduate/Scholarship)* 5100

Joseph Mason Memorial Scholarship *(Undergraduate/Scholarship)* 1881

Anne O'Hare McCormick Scholarship *(Graduate/Scholarship)* 3618

Memorial Scholarships for Children of Deceased Police Officers and Firefighters *(Undergraduate/Scholarship)* 4586

H. Houston Merritt Fellowship *(Postdoctorate/Fellowship)* 4842

Metropolitan Museum of Art Classical Fellowship *(Doctorate/Fellowship)* 3660

Metropolitan Museum of Art Nine-Month Internship *(Graduate, Undergraduate/Internship)* 3661

Ed S. Miller Scholarship in Industrial and Labor Relations *(Undergraduate/Scholarship)* 2904

Minority Educator Scholarship *(Undergraduate/Scholarship)* 1886

Edward R. Murrow Fellowship for American Foreign Correspondents *(Professional Development/Fellowship)* 2106

National Museum of American Art Summer Internships *(Graduate, Undergraduate/Internship)* 5388

New York Botanical Garden Fellowships for Graduate Study in Systemic and Economic Botony *(Doctorate/Fellowship)* 4560

New York City Urban Fellowships *(Graduate, Professional Development/Fellowship)* 4563

New York Financial Writers' Association *(Undergraduate/Scholarship)* 4568

New York State Assembly Graduate Scholarships *(Postgraduate/Internship, Work Study)* 4574

New York State Assembly Session Internships *(Undergraduate/Internship)* 4575

New York State Child of Deceased Police Officer-Firefighter-Correction Officer Awards *(Undergraduate/Award)* 4587

New York State Child of Veteran Awards *(Undergraduate/Award)* 4588

New York State Health Service Corps Scholarships *(Graduate/Scholarship)* 4589

New York State Higher Education Opportunity Program *(Undergraduate/Grant)* 4590

New York State Indian Aid *(Undergraduate/Award)* 4468

New York State Professional Opportunity Scholarships *(Doctorate, Graduate, Undergraduate/Scholarship)* 4592

New York State Regents Professional Opportunity Scholarships *(Doctorate, Graduate, Undergraduate/Scholarship)* 4577

New York State Regents Scholarship at Cornell University *(Undergraduate/Scholarship)* 4578

New York State Senate Sessions Assistance Program *(Undergraduate/Work Study)* 4599

New York State Tuition Assistance Program *(Graduate, Undergraduate/Grant)* 4596

Tibor T. Polgar Fellowships *(Graduate, Undergraduate/Fellowship)* 2914

Realty Foundation of New York Scholarships *(Graduate, Undergraduate/Scholarship)* 5085

Lucretia H. Richter Nursing Scholarship *(Undergraduate/Scholarship)* 6157

Richard J. Roth Journalism Fellowship *(Graduate, Undergraduate/Fellowship)* 4600

Sandoz Agro, Inc. Scholarships *(Undergraduate/Scholarship)* 4124

Ida Speyrer Stahl Scholarships *(Undergraduate/Scholarship)* 1725

Statler Foundation Scholarship *(Graduate, Undergraduate/Scholarship)* 5622

Summer Graduate Internships *(Graduate, Professional Development/Internship)* 4564

Syracuse Newspapers Journalism Scholarship *(Undergraduate/Scholarship)* 5664

Syracuse Pulp and Paper Foundation Scholarship *(Undergraduate/Scholarship)* 5666

Telluride Association Summer Program Scholarships *(High School/Scholarship)* 5696

U.S. Department of Energy Internship *(Undergraduate/Internship)* 4711

Warren Weaver Fellowships *(Postdoctorate/Fellowship)* 5155

Whiting Fellowships in the Humanities *(Doctorate/Fellowship)* 6171

Women and Public Policy Fellowship *(Graduate/Fellowship)* 1809

Women's Medical Association of New York Financial Assistance Fund Loans *(Doctorate/Award, Loan)* 6232

YMA Scholarships *(Graduate/Scholarship)* 6295

## North Carolina

CIIT Summer Internships *(Graduate, Postgraduate, Undergraduate/Internship)* 1903

Creswell, Munsell, Fultz & Zirbel Scholarships *(Undergraduate/Scholarship)* 4054

Eastern Apiculture Society of North America Scholarship *(Undergraduate/Scholarship)* 4067

Oliver Joel and Ellen Pell Denny Student Loan Fund *(Undergraduate/Loan)* 6196

Helen Lancaster Minton Educational Fund *(Undergraduate/Scholarship)* 1824

Mary Morrow-Edna Richards Scholarships *(Undergraduate/Scholarship)* 4672

NCAFP Foundation Medical Student Loan *(Postgraduate/Fellowship, Loan)* 4659

North Carolina State Legislative Tuition Grants *(Undergraduate/Grant)* 4680

Pickett & Hatcher Educational Loans *(Undergraduate/Loan)* 4945

Z. Smith Reynolds Fellowship *(Professional Development/Fellowship)* 5120

Virginia Elizabeth and Alma Vane Taylor Fund *(Undergraduate/Loan)* 6197

Mark Ulmer Native American Scholarships *(Undergraduate/Scholarship)* 5748

L. Phil Wicker Scholarship *(Undergraduate/Scholarship)* 841

YLD Scholarships *(Graduate, Other, Undergraduate/Scholarship)* 6287

YMA Scholarships *(Graduate/Scholarship)* 6295

## North Dakota

David Arver Memorial Scholarship *(Undergraduate/Scholarship)* 77

AWU Faculty Fellowships *(Postdoctorate/Fellowship)* 1199

AWU Faculty Sabbatical Fellowships *(Postdoctorate/Fellowship)* 1200

AWU Graduate Research Fellowships *(Doctorate, Graduate/Fellowship)* 1201

AWU Post-Graduate Fellowship *(Doctorate, Postdoctorate/Fellowship)* 1202

AWU Student Research Fellowships *(Graduate, Undergraduate/Fellowship)* 1203

NDDOT Educational Grants *(Undergraduate/Scholarship loan)* 4682

Kenneth and Ellen Nielsen Cooperative Scholarships *(Undergraduate/Scholarship)* 4110

North Dakota Indian Scholarships *(Undergraduate/Scholarship)* 4684

Western Interstate Commission for Higher Education Western Regional Graduate Program *(Doctorate, Graduate/Other)* 136

## Ohio

Biggs and Gilmore Communications Scholarships *(Graduate, Undergraduate/Scholarship)* 4030

William A. Brower Scholarship *(Undergraduate/Scholarship)* 4694

The Cleveland Institute of Art Portfolio Scholarships *(Undergraduate/Scholarship)* 1966

Creswell, Munsell, Fultz & Zirbel Scholarships (*Undergraduate/Scholarship*) 4054

Eastern Apiculture Society of North America Scholarship (*Undergraduate/Scholarship*) 4067

Evans Caddie Scholarships (*Undergraduate/Scholarship*) 6151

GOALS Fellowships (*Graduate/Fellowship*) 3001

Golden Harvest Seeds, Inc. Scholarships (*Undergraduate/Scholarship*) 4082

Miami University Pulp and Paper Foundation Scholarships (*Undergraduate/Scholarship*) 5029

Ohio Academic Scholarships (*Undergraduate/Scholarship*) 4723

Ohio Instructional Grants (*Undergraduate/Grant*) 4724

Ohio National Guard Tuition Grant (*Undergraduate/Grant, Scholarship*) 4729

Ohio Newspaper Women's Association Scholarship (*Undergraduate/Scholarship*) 4731

Ohio Regents Graduate/Professional Fellowships (*Graduate/Fellowship*) 4725

Ohio Student Choice Grants (*Undergraduate/Grant*) 4726

Ohio War Orphans Scholarships (*Undergraduate/Scholarship*) 4727

Richland County Foundation Scholarships (*Undergraduate/Scholarship*) 5136

United Feeds Scholarships (*Undergraduate/Scholarship*) 4139

## Oklahoma

AWU Faculty Fellowships (*Postdoctorate/Fellowship*) 1199

AWU Faculty Sabbatical Fellowships (*Postdoctorate/Fellowship*) 1200

AWU Graduate Research Fellowships (*Doctorate, Graduate/Fellowship*) 1201

AWU Post-Graduate Fellowship (*Doctorate, Postdoctorate/Fellowship*) 1202

AWU Student Research Fellowships (*Graduate, Undergraduate/Fellowship*) 1203

Paul Douglas Teacher Scholarships (*Undergraduate/Scholarship*) 4735

Leon Harris/Les Nichols Memorial Scholarship to Spartain School of Aeronautics (*Undergraduate/Scholarship*) 88

Kenneth and Ellen Nielsen Cooperative Scholarships (*Undergraduate/Scholarship*) 4110

Oklahoma Natural Gas Company Scholarship (*Undergraduate/Scholarship*) 4114

Oklahoma Resident Rural Scholarship Loans (*Doctorate/Scholarship loan*) 4939

Oklahoma State Regents Academic Scholars Scholarships (*Graduate, Undergraduate/Scholarship*) 4736

Oklahoma State Regents Chiropractic Education Assistance (*Other, Undergraduate/Award*) 4737

Oklahoma State Regents for Higher Education Doctoral Study Grants (*Doctorate/Grant*) 4739

Oklahoma State Regents for Higher Education Professional Study Grants (*Graduate/Grant*) 4740

Oklahoma State Regents Tuition Aid Grants (*Undergraduate/Grant*) 4741

Tulsa Legacy Scholarship (*Undergraduate/Scholarship*) 4440

William P. Willis Scholars Scholarships (*Undergraduate/Scholarship*) 4742

## Oregon

Campbell-Non-Linfield Scholarship Fund (*Graduate, Undergraduate/Scholarship*) 5830

GOALS Fellowships (*Graduate/Fellowship*) 3001

Maria C. Jackson & General George A. White Scholarships (*Undergraduate/Scholarship*) 5833

Oregon College of Art & Craft Artists-in-Residence Program (*Postgraduate/Grant*) 4797

Oregon PTA Teacher Education Scholarships (*Undergraduate/Scholarship*) 4801

Oregon State Bar Scholarships (*Graduate/Scholarship*) 4803

Bertha B. Singer Nurses Scholarship (*Graduate, Undergraduate/Scholarship*) 5835

Harley & Mertie Stevens Memorial Fund (*Undergraduate/Loan, Scholarship*) 5837

Robert Thunen Memorial Educational Scholarships (*Graduate, Undergraduate/Scholarship*) 2983

Flora M. Von Der Ahe Scholarship (*Graduate, Undergraduate/Scholarship*) 5838

Western Interstate Commission for Higher Education Western Regional Graduate Program (*Doctorate, Graduate/Other*) 136

## Pennsylvania

Advanced Research Grants in Military History (*Graduate, Postgraduate/Grant*) 5823

Allied Health Student Loans (*Undergraduate/Loan*) 4870

Aviation Technology Scholarship (*Professional Development, Undergraduate/Scholarship*) 1349

Chemical Heritage Foundation Travel Grants (*Other/Grant*) 1899

Commonwealth of Pennsylvania Educational Gratuity Program Grants (*Undergraduate/Award*) 2019

Curtis Institute of Music Scholarships (*Other/Scholarship*) 2144

Eastern Apiculture Society of North America Scholarship (*Undergraduate/Scholarship*) 4067

Edelstein International Fellowship in the History of Chemical Sciences and Technology (*Postdoctorate/Fellowship*) 1900

Huebner Foundation Doctoral Fellowships (*Doctorate/Fellowship*) 2918

Huebner Foundation Postdoctoral Fellowships (*Postdoctorate/Fellowship*) 2919

The Lighthouse Career Incentive Award for Adult Undergraduates (*Undergraduate/Scholarship*) 3474

The Lighthouse Career Incentive Award for College-Bound Students (*Undergraduate/Scholarship*) 3475

The Lighthouse Career Incentive Award for Graduate Students (*Graduate/Scholarship*) 3476

The Lighthouse Career Incentive Award for Undergraduates (*Undergraduate/Scholarship*) 3477

Professional Pilot John W. "Reds" Macfarlane Scholarship (*Professional Development, Undergraduate/Scholarship*) 1350

MassGrant Program (*Undergraduate/Scholarship*) 3601

Ohio Instructional Grants (*Undergraduate/Grant*) 4724

Pennsylvania Bureau for Veteran's Affairs Educational Gratuity (*Undergraduate/Other*) 4860

Art Peters Minority Internships (*Undergraduate/Internship*) 4929

Ruetgers-Nease Chemical Company, Inc. Scholarship (*Undergraduate/Scholarship*) 4123

U.S. Navy-ASEE Summer Faculty Research Program (*Professional Development/Fellowship*) 925

U.S. Navy ONR-ASEE Postdoctoral Fellowship (*Postdoctorate/Fellowship*) 926

Wharton Doctoral and Postdoctoral Fellowships In Risk & Insurance (*Doctorate, Postdoctorate/Fellowship*) 2920

Whiting Fellowships in the Humanities (*Doctorate/Fellowship*) 6171

YMA Scholarships (*Graduate/Scholarship*) 6295

## Rhode Island

Jeannette D. Black Memorial Fellowship (*Doctorate, Postdoctorate/Fellowship*) 1511

John Carter Brown Library Associates Fellowship (*Doctorate, Postdoctorate/Fellowship*) 1512

John Carter Brown Library Travel Grants (*Doctorate, Postdoctorate/Grant*) 1514

Digital Equipment Corporation Scholarship (*Undergraduate/Scholarship*) 5507

Eastern Apiculture Society of North America Scholarship (*Undergraduate/Scholarship*) 4067

The Lighthouse Career Incentive Award for Adult Undergraduates (*Undergraduate/Scholarship*) 3474

The Lighthouse Career Incentive Award for College-Bound Students (*Undergraduate/Scholarship*) 3475

The Lighthouse Career Incentive Award for Graduate Students (*Graduate/Scholarship*) 3476

Place of Study Index

The Lighthouse Career Incentive Award for Undergraduates *(Undergraduate/Scholarship)* 3477
MassGrant Program *(Undergraduate/Scholarship)* 3601
New England Education Society Loan *(Graduate/Loan)* 4527
New England Press Association Internships *(Undergraduate/Internship)* 4529
New England Regional Student Program *(Graduate, Undergraduate/Other)* 4525

## Virgin Islands
Sandoz Agro, Inc. Scholarships *(Undergraduate/Scholarship)* 4124

## Virginia
Eastern Apiculture Society of North America Scholarship *(Undergraduate/Scholarship)* 4067
Undergraduate Student Financial Aid Program Grant *(Undergraduate/Grant)* 5605
Virginia Student Financial Assistance Award *(Graduate, Undergraduate/Award)* 5606
Elsie Bell Grosvenor Scholarship Awards *(Undergraduate/Scholarship)* 1401
Humane Studies Foundation Summer Residential Program Fellowships *(Graduate/Fellowship)* 3053
Italian Cultural Society and NIAF Matching Scholarship *(Undergraduate/Scholarship)* 4234
Lee-Jackson Foundation Award *(Undergraduate/Award)* 5607
U. Alexis Johnson Scholarship *(Graduate, Undergraduate/Scholarship)* 3238
Marine Corps Historical Center College Internships *(Undergraduate/Internship)* 3556
Mary Marshall Nurse Practitioner/Nurse Midwife Scholarship Program *(Undergraduate/Scholarship)* 6048
Mary Marshall Nursing Scholarship for Student Nurses Practical Nursing Program *(Undergraduate/Scholarship)* 6049
Mary Marshall Nursing Scholarship for Student Nurses Registered Nurse Program *(Undergraduate/Scholarship)* 6050
Pickett & Hatcher Educational Loans *(Undergraduate/Loan)* 4945
Virginia Transfer Grant *(Undergraduate/Grant)* 5608
Virginia Tuition Assistance Grant *(Graduate, Undergraduate/Grant)* 5609
U.S. Navy ONR-ASEE Postdoctoral Fellowship *(Postdoctorate/Fellowship)* 926
Virginia College Scholarship *(Undergraduate/Scholarship)* 5610
Virginia Dental Scholarships *(Doctorate/Scholarship)* 6065
Virginia Graduate and Undergraduate Assistance Award *(Undergraduate/Scholarship)* 5611
Virginia Press Association Minority Internship *(Graduate, Undergraduate/Internship)* 6063
Virginia War Orphans Education Program *(Graduate, Undergraduate/Other)* 6054
L. Phil Wicker Scholarship *(Undergraduate/Scholarship)* 841

## Washington
American Indian Endowed Scholarships *(Graduate, Undergraduate/Scholarship)* 551
AWU Faculty Fellowships *(Postdoctorate/Fellowship)* 1199
AWU Faculty Sabbatical Fellowships *(Postdoctorate/Fellowship)* 1200
AWU Graduate Research Fellowships *(Doctorate, Graduate/Fellowship)* 1201
AWU Student Research Fellowships *(Graduate, Undergraduate/Fellowship)* 1203
Blethen Family Newspaper Internship Program for Minorities *(Graduate, Professional Development/Internship)* 5295
Nellie Martin Carman Scholarships *(Undergraduate/Scholarship)* 1731
First Interstate Bank Scholarship *(Undergraduate/Scholarship)* 2468
Ida L., Mary L., and Ervin R. NePage Foundation *(Undergraduate/Scholarship)* 4513

Poncin Scholarship Fund *(Graduate, Postdoctorate/Scholarship)* 4977
Robert Thunen Memorial Educational Scholarships *(Graduate, Undergraduate/Scholarship)* 2983
U.S. Department of Energy Internship *(Undergraduate/Internship)* 4711
WAMI Medical Education Program *(Doctorate/Other)* 134
Washington Press Association Annual Scholarships *(Professional Development, Undergraduate/Scholarship)* 6093
Washington Pulp & Paper Foundation Scholarships *(Undergraduate/Scholarship)* 6097
Washington Scholars Grants *(Undergraduate/Grant)* 6100
Washington State Need Grant *(Undergraduate/Grant)* 6102
Washington State Student Financial Aid Programs State Need Grant *(All/Other)* 6103
Washington State Student Financial Aid Programs Washington Scholars *(High School, Undergraduate/Scholarship)* 6104
Washington State Work Study *(Graduate, Undergraduate/Work Study)* 6105
Western Interstate Commission for Higher Education Western Regional Graduate Program *(Doctorate, Graduate/Other)* 136

## West Virginia
Eastern Apiculture Society of North America Scholarship *(Undergraduate/Scholarship)* 4067
GOALS Fellowships *(Graduate/Fellowship)* 3001
U. Alexis Johnson Scholarship *(Graduate, Undergraduate/Scholarship)* 3238
West Virginia War Orphans Education Benefits *(High School, Undergraduate/Grant)* 6141
L. Phil Wicker Scholarship *(Undergraduate/Scholarship)* 841

## Wisconsin
David Arver Memorial Scholarship *(Undergraduate/Scholarship)* 77
Biggs and Gilmore Communications Scholarships *(Graduate, Undergraduate/Scholarship)* 4030
Creswell, Munsell, Fultz & Zirbel Scholarships *(Undergraduate/Scholarship)* 4054
Evans Caddie Scholarships *(Undergraduate/Scholarship)* 6151
GOALS Fellowships *(Graduate/Fellowship)* 3001
Golden Harvest Seeds, Inc. Scholarships *(Undergraduate/Scholarship)* 4082
Growmark, Inc. Scholarships *(Undergraduate/Scholarship)* 4083
Gulf Coast Avionics Scholarships to Fox Valley Technical College *(Undergraduate/Scholarship)* 86
Hillshire Farm & Kahn's Scholarship *(Undergraduate/Scholarship)* 4090
Kenneth and Ellen Nielsen Cooperative Scholarships *(Undergraduate/Scholarship)* 4110
Charles M. Ross Trust *(Graduate/Other)* 5165
Sandoz Agro, Inc. Scholarships *(Undergraduate/Scholarship)* 4124
Wisconsin Dental Foundation/Marquette University Dental Scholarships *(Graduate/Scholarship)* 6206
Wisconsin Dental Foundation Two-Year Scholarships *(Undergraduate/Scholarship)* 6207
Wisconsin Department of Veterans Affairs Part-Time Study Grants *(Graduate, Undergraduate/Grant)* 6209
Wisconsin Department of Veterans Affairs Retraining Grant *(Other/Grant)* 6210
Wisconsin League for Nursing Scholarships *(Undergraduate/Scholarship)* 6212

## Wyoming
AWU Faculty Fellowships *(Postdoctorate/Fellowship)* 1199
AWU Faculty Sabbatical Fellowships *(Postdoctorate/Fellowship)* 1200
AWU Graduate Research Fellowships *(Doctorate, Graduate/Fellowship)* 1201
AWU Student Research Fellowships *(Graduate, Undergraduate/Fellowship)* 1203

**Place of Study Index**

Psychologists Supplemental Sabbatical Awards *(Postdoctorate/ Award)* 1756

Quebec Scholarship *(Doctorate, Graduate/Scholarship)* 4438

Racial/Ethnic Leadership Supplemental Grants *(Graduate/ Grant)* 4998

J. H. Stewart Reid Memorial Fellowship *(Doctorate/ Fellowship)* 1605

Research Career Development Award *(Postdoctorate/ Award)* 2241

Research Support Opportunities in Arctic Environmental Studies *(Doctorate, Graduate/Other)* 1682

Resident Research Fellowships in Orthopaedic Surgery *(Postdoctorate/Fellowship)* 4816

Donald I. Rice Merit Award *(Professional Development/ Award)* 1989

Kenneth Andrew Roe Scholarships *(Undergraduate/ Scholarship)* 946

Savoy Foundation Postdoctoral and Clinical Research Fellowships; Savoy Foundation Research Grants; Savoy Foundation Studentships *(Doctorate, Graduate/Fellowship, Grant, Internship)* 5252

Dr. Sydney Segal Research Grants *(Doctorate, Graduate/ Grant)* 1638

SLA Scholarships *(Graduate/Scholarship)* 5579

Rock Sleyster Memorial Scholarship *(Postdoctorate/ Scholarship)* 690

Earl J. Small Growers, Inc. Scholarships *(Undergraduate/ Scholarship)* 1388

Statten Fellowship *(Graduate/Fellowship)* 5624

Lord Strathcona Trust Fund Scholarship Alberta *(Undergraduate/ Scholarship)* 5634

Student Access Awards Program *(Undergraduate/ Scholarship)* 1287

Studentships in Northern Studies *(Graduate, Undergraduate/ Scholarship)* 1684

Summer Language Bursary Program *(Undergraduate/ Award)* 4717

Summer Language Bursary Program for Francophones *(Undergraduate/Scholarship)* 4718

Sumner Memorial Fellowships *(Graduate, Postgraduate/ Fellowship)* 5646

TAC Scholarships *(Graduate/Scholarship)* 5739

George Tanaka Memorial Scholarship Program *(Undergraduate/ Scholarship)* 1288

Carol Thomson Memorial Fund Scholarship *(All/ Scholarship)* 3447

Edward Livingston Trudeau Scholar Awards (Cancelled) *(Postdoctorate/Award)* 684

United Farmers of Alberta Scholarship *(Undergraduate/ Scholarship)* 165

War Memorial Scholarships *(Doctorate/Scholarship)* 3935

Welder Wildlife Fellowships *(Doctorate, Graduate/ Fellowship)* 6127

Jerry Wilmot Scholarship *(Undergraduate/Scholarship)* 1389

World Book Graduate Scholarships in Library Science *(Doctorate, Postgraduate/Scholarship)* 1668

J.E. Zajic Postgraduate Scholarship in Biochemical Engineering *(Postgraduate/Scholarship)* 1907

## CANADA (by province)

### Alberta

Alberta Treasury Branches Scholarship *(Undergraduate/ Scholarship)* 147

Alberta Wheat Pool Scholarships *(Undergraduate/ Scholarship)* 148

APEGGA Entrance Scholarships *(Undergraduate/Award)* 1254

Greater Peace Alberta Teachers' Associatioin No. 13 Scholarship *(Undergraduate/Scholarship)* 188

Hoechst Canada Bursary *(Undergraduate/Scholarship)* 155

Anna & John Kolesar Memorial Scholarships *(Undergraduate/ Scholarship)* 176

Masonic Bursaries *(Undergraduate/Scholarship)* 2730

Charles S. Noble Junior A Hockey Scholarships *(Undergraduate/Scholarship)* 179

Charles S. Noble Junior Football Scholarships *(Undergraduate/Scholarship)* 180

Woodgrove Unifarm Local Scholarship *(Undergraduate/ Scholarship)* 169

Honourable W.C. Woodward Scholarships *(Undergraduate/ Scholarship)* 5044

### British Columbia

Honourable W.C. Woodward Scholarships *(Undergraduate/ Scholarship)* 5044

### New Brunswick

David Arver Memorial Scholarship *(Undergraduate/ Scholarship)* 77

### Nova Scotia

Canadian Hospitality Foundation Scholarships *(Undergraduate/ Scholarship)* 1653

### Ontario

Canadian Hospitality Foundation Scholarships *(Undergraduate/ Scholarship)* 1653

Federated Women's Institutes of Ontario International Scholarship *(Graduate, Undergraduate/Scholarship)* 1648

HSFC Career Investigator Awards *(Doctorate/Award)* 2839

The National Bursaries *(Undergraduate/Scholarship)* 5039

## INTERNATIONAL

AFS Intercultural Global Teenager Program Scholarships *(High School/Other)* 49

CFUW Professional Fellowship *(Graduate/Fellowship)* 1632

John Dinkeloo Bequests/American Academy in Rome Traveling Fellowship in Architectural Technology *(Graduate, Postgraduate/Fellowship)* 6023

IBRO/Unesco Research Fellowships *(Postdoctorate/ Fellowship)* 3125

ICCS Foreign Government Awards *(Doctorate, Graduate/ Award)* 3146

International Cancer Technology Transfer Fellowships *(Professional Development/Fellowship)* 3194

International Travel Grants *(Doctorate, Postdoctorate/Grant)* 344

Harold Lancour Scholarship for Foreign Study *(Graduate/ Scholarship)* 1423

Amy Lowell Poetry Travelling Scholarship *(Professional Development/Scholarship)* 3510

Margaret McWilliams Predoctoral Fellowship *(Doctorate/ Fellowship)* 1635

Stanley Melville Memorial Award *(Professional Development/ Award)* 1489

NEH Summer Fellowships for Foreign Language Teachers K-12 *(Professional Development/Fellowship)* 3989

James K. Rathmell, Jr., Memorial Scholarship to Work/Study Abroad *(Graduate, Undergraduate/Scholarship)* 1387

Tom and Ruth Rivers International Scholarships *(Graduate, Undergraduate/Scholarship)* 6264

Spencer Foundation Small Grants *(Postdoctorate/Grant)* 5587

Steedman Traveling Fellowship in Architecture *(Professional Development/Fellowship)* 5626

Van Alen Institute Fellowship in Public Architecture (Loyd Warren Fellowships/Paris Prize) *(Graduate, Postgraduate/ Fellowship, Prize)* 6026

Watson Fellowships *(Other/Fellowship)* 6119

WHO Fellowships for Canadian Citizens *(Postdoctorate/ Fellowship)* 6260

WHO Fellowships for U.S. Citizens *(Postdoctorate/ Fellowship)* 6262

Yamagiwa-Yoshida Memorial International Cancer Study Grants *(Professional Development/Grant)* 3197

## INTERNATIONAL (by Region)

### Africa

AIMS Small Grants *(Doctorate, Postdoctorate/Grant)* 590

SSRC Africa Predissertation Fellowships *(Doctorate/ Fellowship)* 5394

SSRC African Advanced Research Grants (Postdoctorate/ Grant) 5395

Sub-Saharan African Dissertation Internship Award (Doctorate/ Internship) 5154

## Asia

Asian Art and Religion Fellowships (Postdoctorate/ Fellowship) 1176

Asian Cultural Council Fellowship Grants (Postdoctorate/ Fellowship) 1177

Blakemore Foundation Asian Language Fellowship Grants (Doctorate, Graduate/Grant) 1440

Humanities Fellowships (Doctorate, Postdoctorate/ Fellowship) 1179

Jefferson Fellowships (Professional Development/ Fellowship) 2312

Luce Scholars Program (Graduate, Undergraduate/Internship, Scholarship) 3512

## Asia Minor

Olivia James Traveling Fellowship (Doctorate, Postdoctorate/ Fellowship) 1066

## Central America

Geological Society of America Research Grants (Graduate, Postgraduate/Grant) 2649

IAF Field Research Fellowships Program at the Doctoral Level (Doctorate/Fellowship) 3090

IAF Field Research Fellowships Program at the Master's Level (Graduate/Fellowship) 3091

## Commonwealth Countries

Association of Commonwealth Universities Fellowships (Postdoctorate/Fellowship) 1229

Commonwealth Scholarship Plan (Graduate/Scholarship) 2021

War Memorial Scholarships (Doctorate/Scholarship) 3935

## Eastern Europe

IREX Short-Term Travel Grants for Independent Short-Term Research (Postdoctorate/Grant) 3187

Travel Grants for Independent Short-Term Research (Other/ Grant) 3190

## Europe

Frank Huntington Beebe Awards (Professional Development/ Grant) 1391

Continental European Fellowships (Postgraduate/ Fellowship) 1956

Council for European Studies Pre-Dissertation Fellowships for Topics Related to the European Community (Doctorate/ Fellowship) 2103

Minda de Gunzburg Center for European Studies Program for the Study of Germany and Europe Dissertation Research Fellowships (Doctorate/Fellowship) 2769

Minda de Gunzburg Center for European Studies Undergraduate Summer Travel Grants (Undergraduate/ Grant) 2771

Journalists in Europe Study Program (Graduate/ Scholarship) 3302

Krupp Foundation Fellowship (Graduate/Fellowship) 2773

Martinus Nijhoff International West European Specialist Study Grant (Professional Development/Grant) 1227

Traveling Fellowships in Architectural Design and Technology (Postdoctorate/Fellowship) 6025

## Great Britain

British Marshall Scholarships (Graduate, Undergraduate/ Scholarship) 1483

Newberry-British Academy Fellowship (Postdoctorate/ Fellowship) 4620

## Latin America

Inter-American Press Association Scholarships (Graduate, Professional Development/Scholarship) 3093

## North America

ADHF Student Research Fellowship Awards (Graduate, High School, Undergraduate/Fellowship) 447

American Society for Enology and Viticulture Scholarships (Graduate, Undergraduate/Scholarship) 928

AVS Student Prize; Russel and Sigurd Varian Fellowship (Graduate/Fellowship, Prize) 1008

Robert S. Morison Fellowships (Professional Development/ Fellowship) 2743

Nellie Yeoh Whetten Award (Graduate/Award) 1009

## Scandinavia

Awards for Advanced Study and Research in Scandinavia (Graduate, Postgraduate/Fellowship, Grant) 852

CSF Special Purpose Grants (Other/Grant) 1697

## South America

Kathleen S. Anderson Award (Professional Development/ Award) 3546

## United Kingdom

Action Research Program and Project Grants (Postdoctorate/ Grant) 30

Action Research Training Fellowships (Postgraduate/ Fellowship) 31

All Saints Educational Trust Grants (Professional Development/Grant) 190

Anglo-Jewish Association Grants (Postgraduate/Grant) 1044

Architects Registration Council Student Maintenance Grants (Undergraduate/Grant) 1079

Boyle Research Scholarships (Doctorate/Scholarship) 1468

British Digestive Foundation Project Grants (Professional Development/Grant) 1485

Cancer Research Campaign Research Grants (Professional Development/Grant) 1712

Lord Dowding Grant (Doctorate, Graduate/Grant) 2278

Institute of Chartered Accountants Research Grants (Professional Development/Grant) 3015

Interchange Fellowship in Horticulture and Landscape Design (Graduate, Postgraduate/Fellowship) 2622

Krebs Memorial Scholarships (Doctorate/Scholarship) 1434

Sharon Kunkel Nursing Scholarship (Undergraduate/ Scholarship) 1876

Mackenzie King Travelling Scholarships (Graduate, Postgraduate/Scholarship) 3529

Sir Arthur Sims Scholarships (Postgraduate/Scholarship) 5196

USA British Isles Traveling Fellowship (Doctorate, Postdoctorate/Fellowship) 5182

## INTERNATIONAL (by country)

## Australia

AIATSIS Research Grants (Postdoctorate, Professional Development/Grant) 1327

Apex Foundation Research Grants (Professional Development/ Grant) 1050

Australian National University Visiting Fellowships (Postdoctorate/Fellowship) 1333

Australian Postdoctoral Research Fellowships (Postdoctorate/ Fellowship) 1335

Australian Research Fellowship (Postdoctorate/ Fellowship) 1336

Australian Senior Research Fellowships (Postdoctorate/ Fellowship) 1337

Freda Bage Fellowships; Commemorative Fellowships (Postgraduate/Fellowship) 1323

CCSFC Australian Scholarships (Graduate/Scholarship) 3140

Queen Elizabeth II Fellowships (Postdoctorate/ Fellowship) 1338

Humanities Research Centre Visiting Fellowships (Postdoctorate/Fellowship) 2933

Overseas Postgraduate Research Scholarships for Study in Australia (Graduate/Scholarship) 1339

Research Associateships and Fellowships in Statistics (Postdoctorate/Fellowship) 1321

Institute for European History Fellowships *(Doctorate, Postdoctorate/Fellowship)* 3035

Kress Research Fellowships at Foreign Institutions *(Doctorate/Fellowship)* 3405

LBI/DAAD Fellowships for Research in Germany *(Doctorate/Fellowship)* 1358

NSF-DAAD Grants for the Natural, Engineering and Social Sciences *(Other/Grant)* 2689

SSRC Berlin Program for Advanced German and European Studies Fellowships *(Doctorate, Postdoctorate/Fellowship)* 5398

Study Visit Research Grants for Faculty *(Doctorate/Grant)* 2691

Summer Language Course at the University of Leipzig *(Graduate, Undergraduate/Scholarship)* 2692

Summer Language Courses at Goethe Institutes *(Graduate/Scholarship)* 2693

Alexander von Humboldt Foundation Fellowship *(Postdoctorate/Fellowship)* 2537

### Greece

American School of Classical Studies Summer Sessions Scholarships *(Graduate, Professional Development/Scholarship)* 855

Oscar Broneer Fellowship *(Doctorate, Graduate, Postdoctorate/Fellowship)* 856

Anna C. and Oliver C. Colburn Fellowship *(Doctorate, Postdoctorate/Fellowship)* 857

Anna C. and Oliver C. Colburn Fellowship *(Doctorate, Postdoctorate/Fellowship)* 1064

The Eta Sigma Phi Summer Scholarships *(Doctorate, Graduate/Scholarship)* 2414

Jacob Hirsch Fellowship *(Doctorate, Graduate/Fellowship)* 859

Olivia James Traveling Fellowship *(Doctorate, Postdoctorate/Fellowship)* 1066

Thomas Day Seymour Fellowship *(Graduate/Fellowship)* 860

Elizabeth A. Whitehead Visiting Professorships *(Professional Development/Award)* 862

### Guam

American Water Works Association Thomas R. Camp Scholarship *(Graduate/Scholarship)* 1019

LARS Scholarships *(Doctorate, Graduate/Scholarship)* 1020

### Guatemala

NYZS/Wildlife Conservation Society Research Fellowship Program (RFP) *(Doctorate, Graduate, Postdoctorate/Grant)* 6177

### Honduras

NYZS/Wildlife Conservation Society Research Fellowship Program (RFP) *(Doctorate, Graduate, Postdoctorate/Grant)* 6177

### India

AIIS Fellowship for Senior Scholarly Development *(Postdoctorate/Fellowship)* 585

AIIS Junior Fellowships *(Doctorate/Fellowship)* 586

AIIS Senior Research Fellowships *(Postdoctorate/Fellowship)* 587

CCSFC India Scholarships *(Doctorate, Graduate/Scholarship)* 3141

India Studies Faculty Fellowships *(Professional Development/Fellowship)* 5316

India Studies Performing Arts Fellowships *(Professional Development/Fellowship)* 5317

India Studies Postdoctoral Research Fellowships *(Professional Development/Fellowship)* 5318

India Studies Student Fellowships *(Graduate/Fellowship)* 5319

Senior Performing Arts Fellowships *(Professional Development/Fellowship)* 588

### Ireland

Beit Trust Postgraduate Fellowships *(Postgraduate/Fellowship)* 1395

Dublin Institute for Advanced Studies Research Scholarships *(Postdoctorate/Scholarship)* 2282

FIC Foreign-Funded Fellowships *(Postdoctorate/Fellowship)* 2526

Irish American Cultural Institute Visiting Fellowship in Irish Studies *(Postgraduate/Fellowship)* 3227

### Israel

BARD Postdoctoral Fellowships; BARD Research Fellows Program *(Postdoctorate/Fellowship)* 1432

Richard Barnett Memorial Travel Awards *(Postgraduate/Award)* 1042

Lady Davis Graduate and Postdoctoral Fellowships *(Doctorate, Graduate, Postdoctorate/Fellowship)* 2193

Lady Davis Visiting Professorships *(Postdoctorate/Other)* 2194

Edelstein International Fellowship in the History of Chemical Sciences and Technology *(Postdoctorate/Fellowship)* 1900

FIC Foreign-Funded Fellowships *(Postdoctorate/Fellowship)* 2526

Grants for Canadians *(Doctorate, Graduate, Undergraduate/Grant)* 1640

Hebrew University Postdoctoral Fellowships *(Postdoctorate/Fellowship)* 2853

Institute of Holy Land Studies Scholarships *(Graduate/Scholarship)* 3047

Israeli Ministry of Health Fellowships *(Postdoctorate/Fellowship)* 2533

Kress Research Fellowships at Foreign Institutions *(Doctorate/Fellowship)* 3405

Netz Hilai Visiting Artists Fellowships *(Professional Development/Fellowship)* 4515

Scholarships for Study in Israel *(Doctorate, Graduate, Undergraduate/Scholarship)* 2851

Moritz and Charlotte Warbourg Research Fellowships *(Postdoctorate/Fellowship)* 2849

### Italy

Bellagio Residencies for Scholars and Artists *(Professional Development/Fellowship)* 5146

Chigiana Summer Course Scholarships *(Graduate, Professional Development/Scholarship)* 1935

John Dinkeloo Bequests/American Academy in Rome Traveling Fellowship in Architectural Technology *(Graduate, Postgraduate/Fellowship)* 6023

The Eta Sigma Phi Summer Scholarships *(Doctorate, Graduate/Scholarship)* 2414

ICTP Research Grants for Postdoctoral Students *(Postdoctorate/Grant)* 3135

Olivia James Traveling Fellowship *(Doctorate, Postdoctorate/Fellowship)* 1066

Kress Research Fellowships at Foreign Institutions *(Doctorate/Fellowship)* 3405

NATO Senior Guest Fellowships *(Professional Development/Fellowship)* 4656

Study Abroad Scholarships *(Graduate, Undergraduate/Scholarship)* 4263

Traveling Fellowships in Architectural Design and Technology *(Postdoctorate/Fellowship)* 6025

Venetian Research Program *(Postdoctorate, Postgraduate/Grant)* 2216

Zecchino Post-Graduate Orthopaedic Fellowship *(Postdoctorate/Fellowship)* 4272

### Japan

Artists Fellowship; Japan Foundation Cultural Properties Specialists Fellowship; Japan Foundation Doctoral Fellowship; Japan Foundation Research Fellowship *(Doctorate, Postdoctorate, Professional Development/Fellowship)* 3240

FIC Foreign-Funded Fellowships *(Postdoctorate/Fellowship)* 2526

Institute of Developing Economies Visiting Research Fellowships *(Postdoctorate/Fellowship)* 3027

**Japan (continued)**
Inter-University Center Fellowships *(Graduate, Undergraduate/ Fellowship)* 3095
Japan Society for the Promotion of Science Fellowships *(Postdoctorate/Fellowship)* 2534
Japan-United States Art Fellowships *(Postdoctorate, Professional Development/Fellowship)* 1180
U. Alexis Johnson Scholarship *(Graduate, Undergraduate/ Scholarship)* 3238
Mazda National Scholarship *(High School/Scholarship)* 6299
National Endowment for the Arts - U.S./Japan Exchange Fellowships *(Professional Development/Fellowship)* 3981
Short-term Travel Grants to Japan *(Postdoctorate/ Grant)* 1221
SSRC Abe Fellowship Program *(Postdoctorate/ Fellowship)* 5392

**Luxembourg**
NATO Senior Guest Fellowships *(Professional Development/ Fellowship)* 4656

**Malaysia**
APDC Visiting Fellowships *(Postdoctorate/Fellowship)* 1182

**Mexico**
American Water Works Association Thomas R. Camp Scholarship *(Graduate/Scholarship)* 1019
Ginger and Fred Deines Mexico Scholarships *(Graduate, Professional Development, Undergraduate/ Scholarship)* 5742
ESA Undergraduate Scholarships *(Undergraduate/ Scholarship)* 2389
Dwight D. Gardner Memorial Scholarship *(Undergraduate/ Scholarship)* 3060
Geological Society of America Research Grants *(Graduate, Postgraduate/Grant)* 2649
Frank and Lillian Gilbreth Memorial Fellowships *(Graduate/ Fellowship)* 3061
LARS Scholarships *(Doctorate, Graduate/Scholarship)* 1020
Solomon Lefschetz Instructorships in Mathematics *(Postdoctorate/Fellowship)* 1818
Kenneth Andrew Roe Scholarships *(Undergraduate/ Scholarship)* 946

**Netherlands**
Fellowship Progamme of the Netherlands Ministry of Agriculture, Nature Management and Fisheries *(Postgraduate/Fellowship)* 3103
Kress Research Fellowships at Foreign Institutions *(Doctorate/ Fellowship)* 3405

**New Zealand**
CCSFC New Zealand Scholarships *(Doctorate, Graduate/ Scholarship)* 3142
Chartered Institute of Transport to New Zealand Scholarships *(Professional Development/Scholarship)* 1838
HRC Postdoctoral Fellowship *(Postdoctorate/Fellowship)* 2831

**Nicaragua**
NYZS/Wildlife Conservation Society Research Fellowship Program (RFP) *(Doctorate, Graduate, Postdoctorate/ Grant)* 6177

**Norway**
John Dana Archbold Fellowship *(Postgraduate, Professional Development/Fellowship)* 3820
FIC Foreign-Funded Fellowships *(Postdoctorate/ Fellowship)* 2526

**Pakistan**
American Institute of Pakistan Studies Predoctoral and Postdoctoral Fellowships *(Doctorate, Postdoctorate/ Fellowship)* 596

**Panama**
NYZS/Wildlife Conservation Society Research Fellowship Program (RFP) *(Doctorate, Graduate, Postdoctorate/ Grant)* 6177

**People's Republic of China**
ABMAC/Clerkship in Taiwan Award *(Doctorate/Other)* 358
Inter-University Program Fellowships *(Graduate, Undergraduate/Fellowship)* 3097
Junior Research Program Grants Exchange with China *(Postdoctorate/Grant)* 5980
National Program for Advanced Study and Research in China - General Advanced Studies *(Graduate/Grant)* 2015
National Program for Advanced Study and Research in China - Research Program *(Postdoctorate/Other)* 2016
National Program for Advanced Study and Research in China - Senior Advanced Studies *(Doctorate, Graduate/ Award)* 2017
Specialist Program Grants Exchange with China *(Postdoctorate/Grant)* 5981
Teaching/Research Program Grants Exchange with China *(Postdoctorate/Grant)* 5982

**Poland**
Kosciuszko Foundation Graduate/Postgraduate Study and Research in Poland Scholarships *(Graduate, Postgraduate/ Other)* 3400
The Year Abroad Program at the Jagiellonian University of Krakow *(Doctorate, Graduate/Fellowship)* 3401

**Puerto Rico**
LARS Scholarships *(Doctorate, Graduate/Scholarship)* 1020

**Republic of South Africa**
Beit Trust Postgraduate Fellowships *(Postgraduate/ Fellowship)* 1395

**Scotland**
Carnegie Grants *(Postdoctorate, Postgraduate/Grant)* 1739
Institute for Advanced Studies Visiting Research Fellowships *(Postdoctorate/Fellowship)* 3007
Scottish Gardening Scholarship *(Other/Scholarship)* 4277

**Slovakia**
Czech Education Scholarships *(Doctorate, Graduate, Postdoctorate/Scholarship)* 3708

**Spain**
NATO Senior Guest Fellowships *(Professional Development/ Fellowship)* 4656
Research Grants for Cultural Cooperation *(Postdoctorate/ Grant)* 5013

**Sri Lanka**
CCSFC Sri Lanka Scholarships *(Doctorate, Graduate/ Scholarship)* 3143

**Sweden**
Bank of Sweden Tercentenary Foundation Project Grants *(Professional Development/Grant)* 1372
Brucebo Fine Arts Summer Scholarship *(Professional Development/Scholarship)* 1696
FIC Foreign-Funded Fellowships *(Postdoctorate/ Fellowship)* 2526
Swedish Medical Research Council Fellowships *(Postdoctorate/Fellowship)* 2535

**Switzerland**
CIEA Grants-in-Aid *(Professional Development/Grant)* 3133
FIC Foreign-Funded Fellowships *(Postdoctorate/ Fellowship)* 2526
Albert Gallatin Fellowships in International Affairs *(Doctorate/ Fellowship)* 2613
IBE Scholars-in-Residence Awards *(Professional Development/ Award)* 3129

Kress Research Fellowships at Foreign Institutions *(Doctorate/ Fellowship)* 3405

## Taiwan
FIC Foreign-Funded Fellowships *(Postdoctorate/ Fellowship)* 2526
H. William Harris Visiting Professorship *(Other/Other)* 359
Taiwan National Science Council Fellowships *(Postdoctorate/ Fellowship)* 2536
M. K. Wang Visiting Professorships *(Other/Other)* 360

## Turkey
ARIT Fellowships *(Doctorate, Postdoctorate/Fellowship)* 846
NATO Senior Guest Fellowships *(Professional Development/ Fellowship)* 4656
NEH Fellowships for Research in Turkey *(Postdoctorate/ Fellowship)* 847
Summer Travel/Research in Turkey Grants *(Postdoctorate/ Grant)* 3082

## Union of Soviet Socialist Republics
IREX Short-Term Travel Grants for Independent Short-Term Research *(Postdoctorate/Grant)* 3187

Travel Grants for Independent Short-Term Research *(Other/ Grant)* 3190

## United Kingdom
British Marshall Scholarships *(Graduate, Postgraduate/ Scholarship)* 1230
The British Universities Summer Schools Scholarships *(Graduate, Professional Development/Scholarship)* 2384
CCSFC United Kingdom Scholarships *(Doctorate, Graduate/ Scholarship)* 3144
Kress Research Fellowships at Foreign Institutions *(Doctorate/ Fellowship)* 3405
Lucy Dalbiac Luard Scholarship *(Undergraduate/ Scholarship)* 2385
Secondary School Exchange *(High School, Undergraduate/ Other)* 2386

## Wales
Eastern European Visiting Scholarships *(Postdoctorate, Professional Development/Scholarship)* 2814
National Welsh-American Foundation Exchange Scholarships *(Doctorate, Graduate, Undergraduate/Scholarship)* 4450

**Place of Study Index**

# Special Recipient Index

This index arranges awards according to qualifying factors related to membership or affiliation. Awards are listed under all appropriate headings. Awards that are designated for minorities in general appear under the "Minority" heading, not under headings for specific minorities. Each citation is followed by the study level and award type, which appear in parentheses. Numbers following the parenthetical information indicate the book entry number for particular awards, not page numbers.

## African American

ABF Summer Research Fellowships in Law and Social Science for Minority Undergraduate Students *(Undergraduate/Fellowship)* 352

Advanced Industrial Concepts (AIC) Materials Science Program *(Graduate/Fellowship)* 5857

AEJ Summer Internships for Minorities *(Undergraduate/Internship)* 3029

Affirmative Action Scholarship Program *(Graduate/Scholarship)* 5575

Alabama Space Grant Consortium Graduate Student Fellowship Program *(Graduate/Fellowship)* 123

Alabama Space Grant Consortium Undergraduate Fellowship Program *(Undergraduate/Fellowship)* 124

Alpha Kappa Alpha Educational Advancement Foundation Scholarships *(Undergraduate/Scholarship)* 198

American Economic Association/Federal Reserve System Minority Graduate Fellowships in Economics *(Graduate, Postgraduate/Fellowship)* 453

AMS/Industry Minority Scholarships *(Undergraduate/Scholarship)* 702

APA Planning & the Black Community Division Scholarship *(Undergraduate/Scholarship)* 775

APA Planning Fellowships *(Graduate/Fellowship)* 776

APSA Graduate Fellowships for African-American Students *(Doctorate/Fellowship)* 781

AT & T Bell Laboratories Cooperative Research Fellowships for Minorities *(Graduate/Fellowship)* 1302

AT & T Bell Laboratories Summer Research Program for Minorities & Women *(Undergraduate/Fellowship)* 1305

ATA Undergraduate Scholarships *(Undergraduate/Scholarship)* 1093

William and Charlotte Cadbury Award *(Doctorate/Award)* 4288

CIC Predoctoral Fellowships *(Doctorate, Graduate/Fellowship)* 2013

CLA Scholarship for Minority Students in Memory of Edna Yelland *(Graduate/Scholarship)* 1565

Consortium Graduate Study Management Fellowships for Minorities *(Graduate/Fellowship)* 2067

Corporate Sponsored Scholarships for Minority Undergraduate Physics Majors *(Undergraduate/Scholarship)* 772

Council on Social Work Education Minority Fellowships *(Doctorate/Fellowship)* 3724

Alphonso Deal Scholarship Award *(Undergraduate/Scholarship)* 3912

Freda A. DeKnight Memorial Fellowship *(Graduate/Fellowship)* 295

*Detroit Free Press* Minority Journalism Scholarships *(Undergraduate/Scholarship)* 2247

Fellowship Program in Academic Medicine *(Doctorate/Fellowship)* 4289

Ford Foundation Predoctoral and Dissertation Fellowships for Minorities *(Doctorate/Fellowship)* 4357

GEM Master's Engineering Fellowships for Minorities *(Graduate/Fellowship)* 3941

GEM Ph.D. Engineering Fellowships for Minorities *(Doctorate/Fellowship)* 3942

GEM Ph.D. Science Fellowship Program *(Doctorate/Fellowship)* 3943

Gerber Prize for Excellence in Pediatrics *(Doctorate/Award)* 4291

Benn and Kathleen Gilmore Scholarship *(Doctorate/Scholarship)* 4292

GOALS Fellowships *(Graduate/Fellowship)* 3001

Henry G. Halladay Awards *(Doctorate/Scholarship)* 4294

George Hill Memorial Scholarship *(Doctorate/Scholarship)* 4295

Independent and Student Filmmakers Competition *(Graduate, Professional Development, Undergraduate/Grant)* 1436

W. K. Kellogg Community Medicine Training Fellowship Program for Minority Medical Students *(Doctorate/Fellowship)* 4297

Herbert Lehman Education Fund Scholarships *(Undergraduate/Scholarship)* 3818

Lett Scholarships *(Graduate, Undergraduate/Scholarship)* 4720

MACESA Awards *(Undergraduate/Scholarship)* 3699

Thurgood Marshall Scholarship *(Undergraduate/Scholarship)* 3566

McKnight Doctoral Fellowships *(Doctorate/Fellowship)* 2519

The Mead Johnson/NMA Scholarship *(Doctorate/Scholarship)* 4299

Metropolitan Life Foundation Awards for Academic Excellence in Medicine *(Doctorate/Award)* 4300

Minority Dental Student Scholarship Program *(Doctorate, Graduate/Scholarship)* 43

Minority Geoscience Scholarships *(Graduate, Undergraduate/Scholarship)* 508

Mississippi African-American Doctoral Teacher Loan/Scholarship Program *(Doctorate/Scholarship loan)* 3730

MLA Scholarship for Minority Students *(Graduate/Scholarship)* 3636

Music Assistance Fund Orchestral Fellowships *(Professional Development/Fellowship)* 1005

NACME Corporate Scholars Program *(Undergraduate/Scholarship)* 3835

NACME TechForce Scholarships *(Undergraduate/Scholarship)* 3836

National Achievement Scholarship Program for Outstanding Negro Students *(Undergraduate/Scholarship)* 4310

National Association of Black Journalists Summer Internships *(Undergraduate/Internship)* 3860

National Consortium for Educational Access Fellowship *(Doctorate/Fellowship)* 3939

## African American (continued)

National FFA Foundation Minority Scholarships *(Undergraduate/Scholarship)* 4104

National Physical Science Consortium Graduate Fellowships for Minorities and Women *(Doctorate, Graduate/ Fellowship)* 4338

NMA Merit Scholarships *(Doctorate/Scholarship)* 4301

NMA Scholarships *(Graduate/Scholarship)* 4302

The NMA Special Awards Program *(Doctorate/ Scholarship)* 4303

NMF Scholarships for Minority Students *(Doctorate/ Scholarship)* 4304

Colin L. Powell Minority Postdoctoral Fellowship in Tropical Disease Research *(Graduate/Fellowship)* 4164

Presbyterian Church Student Opportunity Scholarships *(Undergraduate/Scholarship)* 4996

Racial/Ethnic Leadership Supplemental Grants *(Graduate/ Grant)* 4998

James H. Robinson Memorial Prize *(Doctorate/Prize)* 4305

Nelson A. Rockefeller Minority Internships *(Undergraduate/ Internship)* 6270

Sachs Foundation Grants *(Undergraduate/Grant)* 5204

Sara Lee National Achievement Scholarships *(Undergraduate/ Scholarship)* 5248

SBNA Scholarship *(Undergraduate/Scholarship)* 5209

Aura E. Severinghaus Award *(Doctorate/Scholarship)* 4306

The Slack Award for Medical Journalism *(Doctorate/ Award)* 4307

Texas Black Scholarships *(Undergraduate/Scholarship)* 1374

Underrepresented Minority Investigators Award in Asthma and Allergy *(Postdoctorate/Award)* 216

Theodore Ward Prize *(Undergraduate/Prize)* 2007

Earl Warren Legal Training Scholarships *(Graduate/ Scholarship)* 6081

Jimmy A. Young Memorial Education Recognition Award *(Undergraduate/Scholarship)* 850

## Asian American

AEJ Summer Internships for Minorities *(Undergraduate/ Internship)* 3029

Affirmative Action Scholarship Program *(Graduate/ Scholarship)* 5575

Alabama Space Grant Consortium Graduate Student Fellowship Program *(Graduate/Fellowship)* 123

Alabama Space Grant Consortium Undergraduate Fellowship Program *(Undergraduate/Fellowship)* 124

Alpha Kappa Alpha Educational Advancement Foundation Scholarships *(Undergraduate/Scholarship)* 198

Asian American Journalists Association Fellowships *(Professional Development/Fellowship)* 1170

Asian American Journalists Association National Internship Grant *(Other, Undergraduate/Grant)* 1171

CLA Scholarship for Minority Students in Memory of Edna Yelland *(Graduate/Scholarship)* 1565

Council on Social Work Education Minority Fellowships *(Doctorate/Fellowship)* 3724

*Detroit Free Press* Minority Journalism Scholarships *(Undergraduate/Scholarship)* 2247

Ford Foundation Predoctoral and Dissertation Fellowships for Minorities *(Doctorate/Fellowship)* 4357

David Tamotsu Kagiwada Memorial Fund Award *(Graduate/ Scholarship)* 1949

Sheila Suen Lai Scholarships *(Graduate/Scholarship)* 1945

MLA Scholarship for Minority Students *(Graduate/ Scholarship)* 3636

National FFA Foundation Minority Scholarships *(Undergraduate/Scholarship)* 4104

Colin L. Powell Minority Postdoctoral Fellowship in Tropical Disease Research *(Graduate/Fellowship)* 4164

Presbyterian Church Student Opportunity Scholarships *(Undergraduate/Scholarship)* 4996

Racial/Ethnic Leadership Supplemental Grants *(Graduate/ Grant)* 4998

Nelson A. Rockefeller Minority Internships *(Undergraduate/ Internship)* 6270

Jimmy A. Young Memorial Education Recognition Award *(Undergraduate/Scholarship)* 850

## Association

3M/NMRT Professional Development Grant *(Professional Development/Grant)* 655

21st Century Genetics Cooperative Scholarships *(Undergraduate/Scholarship)* 4012

AACN Clinical Practice Grant *(Professional Development/ Grant)* 277

AACN Educational Advancement Scholarships for Undergraduates *(Undergraduate/Scholarship)* 279

AACN-Sigma Theta Tau Critical Care Grant *(Professional Development/Grant)* 280

AAG General Fund Research Grants *(Professional Development/Grant)* 1207

AALL Law Librarians in Continuing Education Courses Scholarship *(Graduate/Scholarship)* 310

AAS/American Society for Eighteenth Century Studies Fellowships *(Professional Development/Fellowship)* 252

AASL/Highsmith Research Grant *(Other/Grant)* 642

AATF Summer Institute in France *(Professional Development/ Fellowship)* 325

AAUW Educational Foundation International Fellowships *(Graduate/Fellowship, Grant)* 334

ABC-CLIO Leadership Grant *(Other/Grant)* 643

ACNM Scholarships *(Graduate/Scholarship)* 3267

ACOG/3M Pharmaceuticals Research Awards in Lower Genital Infections *(Postdoctorate/Award)* 376

ACOG/Cytyc Corporation Research Award for the Prevention of Cervical Cancer *(Postdoctorate/Grant)* 377

ACOG/Ethicon Research Award for Innovations in Gynecologic Surgery *(Postdoctorate/Award)* 378

ACOG/Merck Award for Research in Migraine Management in Women's Health Care *(Postdoctorate/Grant)* 379

ACOG/Novartis Pharmaceuticals Fellowship for Research in Endocrinology of the Postreproductive Woman *(Postdoctorate/Fellowship)* 380

ACOG/Organon Inc. Research Award in Contraception *(Postdoctorate/Grant)* 381

ACOG/Ortho-McNeil Academic Training Fellowships in Obstetrics and Gynecology *(Doctorate/Fellowship)* 382

ACOG/Pharmacie & Upjohn Research Award in Urognecology of the Postreproductive Woman *(Postdoctorate/Grant)* 383

ACOG/Solvay Pharmaceuticals Research Award in Menopause *(Postdoctorate/Fellowship)* 384

ACOG/Zeneca Pharmaceuticals Research Award in Breast Cancer *(Postdoctorate/Grant)* 385

ACPSEM Scholarship *(Professional Development/ Scholarship)* 1316

ACS Congressional Fellowship Program *(Postdoctorate, Professional Development/Fellowship)* 367

ACS Science Policy Fellowship *(Professional Development/ Fellowship)* 368

Joseph Adams Scholarships *(Undergraduate/ Scholarship)* 5428

AEJMC Communication Theory and Methodology Division Minority Doctoral Scholarships *(Doctorate/ Scholarship)* 1232

AERF Individual Grants *(Professional Development/Grant)* 33

AgRadio Network Scholarships *(Undergraduate/ Scholarship)* 4013

AGU Congressional Science Fellowship Program *(Postdoctorate/Fellowship)* 510

AIAA Scholarship Program *(Undergraduate/Scholarship)* 568

AIBS Congressional Science Fellowship *(Postdoctorate/ Fellowship)* 476

AIMHS Scholarship *(Professional Development/ Scholarship)* 1242

AIMS Small Grants *(Doctorate, Postdoctorate/Grant)* 590

Airline Pilots Association Scholarship *(Undergraduate/ Scholarship)* 96

AISES A.T. Anderson Memorial Scholarship *(Graduate, Undergraduate/Scholarship)* 559

## Association (continued)

Special Recipient Index

## Association (continued)

North American Limousin Foundation Scholarship *(Undergraduate/Scholarship)* 4112

Northeastern Loggers' Association Annual Scholarships *(High School, Undergraduate/Scholarship)* 4688

Northrop Corporation Founders Scholarship *(Undergraduate/Scholarship)* 5517

Northrup King Company Scholarships *(Undergraduate/Scholarship)* 4113

NSCA Challenge Scholarships *(All/Scholarship)* 4415

NSSA Scholarship *(Undergraduate/Scholarship)* 4377

Oak Ridge National Laboratory Technology Internship Program *(Undergraduate/Internship)* 5920

Ruth O'Brien Project Grants *(Professional Development/Grant)* 300

Allie Mae Oden Memorial Scholarship *(Undergraduate/Scholarship)* 2479

Oklahoma Natural Gas Company Scholarship *(Undergraduate/Scholarship)* 4114

Shirley Olofson Memorial Award *(Professional Development/Grant)* 657

Oncology Nursing Society/SmithKline Beecham Research Grant *(Professional Development/Grant)* 4773

Orange County Chapter/Harry Jackson Scholarship *(Undergraduate/Scholarship)* 977

Our World - Underwater Scholarships *(Undergraduate/Scholarship)* 4822

Parents Without Partners International Scholarship *(Undergraduate/Scholarship)* 4837

Parke-Davis Teacher Development Awards *(Postdoctorate/Award)* 227

Elisabeth M. and Winchell M. Parsons Scholarships *(Doctorate/Scholarship)* 950

Past Grand Presidents Award *(High School, Undergraduate/Scholarship)* 2185

Pennington Memorial Scholarships *(Undergraduate/Scholarship)* 162

Pennsylvania Library Association Library Science Continuing Education Grants *(Professional Development, Undergraduate/Grant)* 4867

Percy Memorial Research Award *(Postdoctorate/Award)* 236

Phi Chi Theta Scholarships *(Graduate, Postgraduate, Undergraduate/Scholarship)* 4896

Physician Assistant Foundation Annual Scholarship Program *(Undergraduate/Scholarship)* 4937

George Pimm Memorial Scholarship *(Undergraduate/Scholarship)* 163

Plenum Scholarship *(Postdoctorate/Scholarship)* 5578

Portuguese Continental Union Scholarships *(Undergraduate/Scholarship)* 4983

Power Systems Inc./NSCA Strength and Conditioning Professional Scholarship *(Graduate, Undergraduate/Scholarship)* 4417

PPGA Family Member Scholarship *(Graduate, Undergraduate/Scholarship)* 1386

Prairie Farms Dairy, Inc. Scholarship *(Undergraduate/Scholarship)* 4115

Precision Laboratories, Inc. Scholarship *(Undergraduate/Scholarship)* 4116

Pro Deo and Pro Patria (Canada) Scholarships *(Undergraduate/Scholarship)* 3389

Pro Deo and Pro Patria Scholarships *(Undergraduate/Scholarship)* 3390

Professional Products & Services, Inc. Scholarship *(Undergraduate/Scholarship)* 4117

Professional Secretaries International Scholarships *(Undergraduate/Scholarship)* 5011

Purina Mills Scholarships *(Undergraduate/Scholarship)* 4118

Putnam & Grosset Group Award *(Professional Development/Award)* 650

PVR Scholarship Award *(Graduate/Scholarship)* 4388

Schuler S. Pyle Scholarship *(Undergraduate/Scholarship)* 2480

Quality Stores, Inc. Scholarships *(Undergraduate/Scholarship)* 4119

Rain Bird Sprinkler Manufacturing Corp. Scholarships *(Undergraduate/Scholarship)* 4120

RCPSC International Travelling Fellowship *(Doctorate/Fellowship)* 5187

RCPSC-MRC/PMAC-Novartis Clinical Research Fellowship *(Doctorate/Fellowship)* 5188

Reading/Literacy Research Fellowship *(Postdoctorate/Fellowship)* 3178

Judith Resnik Memorial Scholarship *(Undergraduate/Scholarship)* 5519

Rhone-Poulenc Animal Nutrition Scholarships *(Undergraduate/Scholarship)* 4121

Ellen H. Richards Fellowship *(Graduate/Fellowship)* 304

Henry and Sylvia Richardson Research Grant *(Postdoctorate/Award)* 2391

Ritchie Industries, Inc. Scholarship *(Undergraduate/Scholarship)* 4122

Robin Hood Multifoods Scholarship *(Graduate/Award)* 1651

Helen M. Robinson Award *(Doctorate/Grant)* 3179

Kenneth Andrew Roe Scholarships *(Undergraduate/Scholarship)* 946

Sam Rose Memorial Scholarship *(Undergraduate/Scholarship)* 2481

Barbara Rosenblum Cancer Dissertation Award *(Doctorate/Award)* 5525

Bettsy Ross Educational Grants *(Undergraduate/Grant)* 4640

Marjorie Roy Rothermel Scholarships *(Graduate/Scholarship)* 952

Royal Canadian Legion Camrose Branch No. 57 Bursaries *(Undergraduate/Scholarship)* 5040

Royal College Fellowship for Studies in Medical Education *(Doctorate, Graduate, Postdoctorate/Fellowship)* 5189

Ruetgers-Nease Chemical Company, Inc. Scholarship *(Undergraduate/Scholarship)* 4123

San Mateo County Farm Bureau Scholarships *(All/Scholarship)* 5243

Sandoz Agro, Inc. Scholarships *(Undergraduate/Scholarship)* 4124

Santa Fe Pacific Foundation Scholarships *(Undergraduate/Scholarship)* 563

SCBWI Work-in-Progress Grants *(Professional Development/Grant)* 5445

Bernadette Schmitt Grants *(Professional Development/Grant)* 541

Seabee Memorial Association Scholarships *(Undergraduate/Scholarship)* 5961

Sheet Metal Workers' International Scholarship *(Undergraduate/Scholarship)* 5321

Shields-Gillespie Scholarships *(Postgraduate, Professional Development/Scholarship)* 755

E.J. Sierleja Memorial Fellowship *(Graduate/Fellowship)* 3063

Sig Memorial Scholarship *(Undergraduate/Scholarship)* 20

SIGCO Research Scholarships *(Undergraduate/Scholarship)* 4126

Silgan Containers Corporation Scholarships *(Undergraduate/Scholarship)* 4127

Slovenian Women's Union Scholarships *(Undergraduate/Scholarship)* 5361

J. Waldo Smith Hydraulic Fellowship *(Postdoctorate/Fellowship)* 905

Nila Banton Smith Research Dissemination Support Grant *(Professional Development/Grant)* 3180

Snodgrass Memorial Research Grant *(Graduate/Grant)* 2392

Society of Physics Students Scholarships *(Undergraduate/Scholarship)* 5482

Alexandra Apostolides Sonenfeld Award *(High School, Undergraduate/Scholarship)* 2186

South Central Language Association Fellowship *(Postdoctorate/Fellowship)* 4610

South Central Modern Languages Association Fellowship *(Postdoctorate/Fellowship)* 4624

Souvenir Shirts, Etc. Scholarships *(Undergraduate/Scholarship)* 4128

Spraying Systems Company Scholarships *(Undergraduate/Scholarship)* 4129

## Association (continued)

Lance Stafferd Larson Student Scholarship *(Undergraduate/ Scholarship)* 2951

Otis Paul Starkey Grant *(Doctorate/Grant)* 1209

State Farm Companies Foundation Scholarships *(Undergraduate/Scholarship)* 4130

Stanley H. Stearman Scholarships *(Graduate, Undergraduate/ Scholarship)* 4406

Sonja Stefanadis Graduate Student Award *(Graduate/ Scholarship)* 2187

Ralph W. Stone Research Award *(Graduate/Award)* 4410

Sun Company Scholarships *(Undergraduate/Scholarship)* 4131

Margaret E. Swanson Scholarships *(Doctorate, Graduate, Undergraduate/Scholarship)* 432

Edith Taylor Memorial Scholarship *(Undergraduate/ Scholarship)* 164

Teacher as Researcher Grant *(Other/Grant)* 3181

Telesensory Scholarship *(Graduate, Undergraduate/ Scholarship)* 1236

Texaco Scholarships *(Undergraduate/Scholarship)* 5521

Theisen Supply, Inc. Scholarships *(Undergraduate/ Scholarship)* 4134

Tony's Foodservice Scholarships *(Graduate, Professional Development, Undergraduate/Scholarship)* 5278

Tri-State Breeders Scholarships *(Undergraduate/ Scholarship)* 4135

Arthur S. Tuttle Memorial National Scholarship *(Graduate/ Scholarship)* 906

Tyson Foods, Sanofi Animal Health and American Proteins Scholarships *(Undergraduate/Scholarship)* 4136

UNIMA-USA Scholarship *(Professional Development/ Scholarship)* 5774

Union Pacific Foundation Scholarship *(Undergraduate/ Scholarship)* 4137

UNITE Scholarships *(Undergraduate/Scholarship)* 5776

United Dairymen of Idaho Scholarship *(Undergraduate/ Scholarship)* 4138

United Farmers of Alberta Scholarship *(Undergraduate/ Scholarship)* 165

United Feeds Scholarships *(Undergraduate/Scholarship)* 4139

United States Naval Academy Class of 1963 Foundation Scholarship *(Graduate, Undergraduate/Scholarship)* 5947

U.S. Submarine Veterans of World War II Scholarships *(Undergraduate/Scholarship)* 5962

Universal Leaf Tobacco Company Scholarship *(Undergraduate/ Scholarship)* 4141

Upsilon Pi Epsilon/Computer Society Award for Academic Excellence *(Graduate, Undergraduate/Award)* 2952

USCG Chief Petty Officers Association Captain Caliendo College Assistance Fund Scholarship Program *(High School, Undergraduate/Scholarship)* 5847

Valmont Irrigation Scholarships *(Undergraduate/ Scholarship)* 4142

Vermilion River 4-H District Scholarship *(Undergraduate/ Scholarship)* 166

Paul Vouras Grant *(Doctorate/Grant)* 1210

Walco International, Inc. Scholarship *(Undergraduate/ Scholarship)* 4145

Warren H Pearse/Wyeth-Ayerst Women's Health Policy Research Award *(Postdoctorate/Grant)* 386

Vincent T. Wasilewski Scholarships *(Graduate, Undergraduate/ Scholarship)* 1500

WAWH Graduate Student Fellowship *(Doctorate/ Fellowship)* 6147

Wells Fargo Bank Scholarship *(Undergraduate/ Scholarship)* 4146

Western Dairymen - John Elway - Melba FFA Scholarship Fund *(Undergraduate/Scholarship)* 4147

Western Seedmen's Association Scholarships *(Undergraduate/ Scholarship)* 4148

Wetaskiwin District 4-H Scholarships *(Undergraduate/ Scholarship)* 167

Wheat Board Surplus Monies Trust Scholarships *(Undergraduate/Scholarship)* 168

Who's Who Among American High School Students Scholarships *(Undergraduate/Scholarship)* 4149

Roy Wilkins Scholarships *(Undergraduate/Scholarship)* 3852

Williams Pipe Line Company Scholarship *(Undergraduate/ Scholarship)* 4150

John Charles Wilson Scholarship *(Graduate/Scholarship)* 3107

WIX Corporation Scholarships *(Undergraduate/ Scholarship)* 4151

Wolf's Head Oil Company Scholarships *(Undergraduate/ Scholarship)* 4152

Woman's Board Scholarship *(Undergraduate/ Scholarship)* 1470

Women in Scholarly Publishing Career Development Fund *(Professional Development/Other)* 6228

Woodgrove Unifarm Local Scholarship *(Undergraduate/ Scholarship)* 169

Charlotte Woods Memorial Scholarship *(Graduate, Undergraduate/Scholarship)* 5746

Woodswomen Scholarship Fund *(Other/Grant, Scholarship)* 6255

World Book, Inc., Grants *(Professional Development/ Grant)* 1752

Wyandott, Inc. Snacks and Popcorn Scholarship *(Undergraduate/Scholarship)* 4153

Wayne Wylie Scholarship *(Professional Development/ Scholarship)* 5172

Yetter Manufacturing Co. Scholarship *(Undergraduate/ Scholarship)* 4154

Young American Creative Patriot Art Award *(All/Award)* 6038

Ziskind-Sommerfeld Research Award *(Postdoctorate/ Award)* 5440

## Employer

Clara Abbott Foundation Scholarships *(Undergraduate/ Scholarship)* 14

AEJMC Correspondence Fund Scholarships *(Undergraduate/ Scholarship)* 1233

All-Inland Scholarship *(Undergraduate/Scholarship)* 3005

Amoco Canada Petroleum Company Scholarships *(Undergraduate/Scholarship)* 1028

AOSC Scholarships *(Graduate, Undergraduate/ Scholarship)* 1250

APSA Congressional Fellowships for Federal Executives *(Professional Development/Fellowship)* 779

BP America Scholarship *(Undergraduate/Scholarship)* 1472

Burlington Northern Santa Fe Scholarships *(High School, Undergraduate/Scholarship)* 1531

Burns Scholarships *(Undergraduate/Scholarship)* 1537

Butler Manufacturing Company Foundation Scholarship *(Undergraduate/Scholarship)* 1553

Cal Callahan Memorial Bursary *(Undergraduate/ Scholarship)* 4949

Cargill National Merit Scholarships *(Undergraduate/ Scholarship)* 1728

Cargill Scholars Program Scholarships *(Undergraduate/ Scholarship)* 1729

Children of Air Traffic Control Specialists *(Undergraduate/ Scholarship)* 73

Carle C. Conway Scholarships *(Undergraduate/ Scholarship)* 2075

CSAC Law Enforcement Personnel Dependents Scholarships *(Graduate, Undergraduate/Grant)* 1582

Nathan Cummings Scholarships (Canada) *(Undergraduate/ Scholarship)* 5245

Nathan Cummings Scholarships (United States) *(Undergraduate/Scholarship)* 5246

Delaware Higher Education Benefits for Children of Veterans and Others *(Undergraduate/Grant)* 2209

William C. Doherty Scholarships *(High School, Undergraduate/ Scholarship)* 3883

Dow Chemical Canada Higher Education Awards *(Undergraduate/Scholarship)* 2272

Dunkin' Donuts Charitable Trust Scholarships *(Undergraduate/ Scholarship)* 2290

Environmental Protection Agency Fellowships (*Professional Development/Fellowship*) 5940

Thomas Ewing Memorial Educational Grants for Newspaper Carriers (*Undergraduate/Scholarship*) 6089

FEEA Federal Plus Loan (*Graduate, Undergraduate/ Loan*) 2431

FEEA Federal SLS Loan (*Graduate, Undergraduate/ Loan*) 2432

FEEA Federal Stafford Loan (*Graduate, Undergraduate/ Loan*) 2433

FEEA Federal Unsubsidized Stafford Loan (*Graduate, Undergraduate/Loan*) 2434

FEEA Scholarship Award (*Graduate, Undergraduate/ Scholarship*) 2435

Harold E. Fellows Scholarships (*Graduate, Undergraduate/ Scholarship*) 1496

Gerber Companies Foundation Scholarships (*Other/ Scholarship*) 2677

Gleaner Life Insurance Society Scholarship Award (*Undergraduate/Scholarship*) 2709

Graco Scholarship Program (*Undergraduate/Scholarship*) 2724

Halton Foundation Scholarships (*All/Scholarship*) 2784

Jostens Our Town Jack M. Holt Memorial Scholarship (*Undergraduate/Scholarship*) 3297

Charles H. Hood Fund Scholarships (*Undergraduate/ Scholarship*) 2884

Hunt Manufacturing Company Foundation Scholarships (*Undergraduate/Scholarship*) 2937

International Association of Fire Chiefs Foundation Scholarships (*Professional Development/Scholarship*) 3113

Robert Wood Johnson Health Policy Fellowships (*Professional Development/Fellowship*) 3073

Jostens Our Town Scholarship (*Undergraduate/ Scholarship*) 3298

James J. Kerrigan Memorial Scholarships (*Undergraduate/ Scholarship*) 3366

Kohler Co. College Scholarship (*Undergraduate/ Scholarship*) 3396

Law Enforcement Personnel Dependents Grant (*Undergraduate/Grant*) 2673

Ruth A. & G. Elving Lundine Scholarship (*Undergraduate/ Scholarship*) 1879

Lynden Memorial Scholarship (*Graduate, Postgraduate, Undergraduate/Scholarship*) 3522

M.A. Hanna Company Scholarship (*Undergraduate/ Scholarship*) 3170

Horace Mann Scholarship (*Undergraduate/Scholarship*) 3544

Maryland Reimbursement of Firefighters and Rescue Squad Members (*Graduate, Undergraduate/Scholarship*) 3579

Massachusetts Public Service Scholarship (*Undergraduate/ Scholarship*) 3599

Masters, Mates & Pilots Health & Benefit Plan Scholarship Program (*Undergraduate/Scholarship*) 3605

McCabe Awards (*Undergraduate/Award*) 5286

McDonnell Douglas Scholarships (*Undergraduate/ Scholarship*) 3620

Merit Gasoline Foundation College Scholarships (*Undergraduate/Scholarship*) 3650

Larry Miller Transportation Scholarship Program (*Undergraduate/Scholarship*) 5750

National Art Materials Trade Association Scholarships (*Doctorate, Graduate, Undergraduate/Scholarship*) 3848

National Merit Scholarship (*Undergraduate/Scholarship*) 2628

New York State Child of Deceased Police Officer-Firefighter-Correction Officer Awards (*Undergraduate/Award*) 4587

OMC Foundation Scholarship (*Undergraduate/ Scholarship*) 2416

Pennsylvania Steel Foundry Foundation Awards (*Undergraduate/Scholarship*) 4873

Polaroid Foundation National Merit Scholarship (*Undergraduate/Scholarship*) 4971

Quaker Chemical Foundation Scholarships (*Other, Undergraduate/Scholarship*) 5037

QuikTrip Scholarships (*Graduate, Undergraduate/ Scholarship*) 5046

Realty Foundation of New York Scholarships (*Graduate, Undergraduate/Scholarship*) 5085

Santa Fe Pacific Special Scholarships (*Undergraduate/ Scholarship*) 1535

Sara Lee Corporation Student Loan Program (*Undergraduate/ Loan*) 5247

Sara Lee National Achievement Scholarships (*Undergraduate/ Scholarship*) 5248

Conrad & Marcel Schlumberger Scholarships (*Undergraduate/ Scholarship*) 5260

Dr. Forrest Shaklee Memorial Scholarship (*Undergraduate/ Scholarship*) 5313

Edwin P. Shaunessy Memorial Scholarships (*Graduate/ Scholarship*) 4989

Annie Sonnenblick Scholarship (*Undergraduate/ Scholarship*) 5529

South Dakota Board of Regents State Employee Tuition Assistance (*Undergraduate/Other*) 5557

Southern California Chapter/Pleasant Hawaiian Holidays Scholarship (*Undergraduate/Scholarship*) 982

Stanhome Scholarship (*Undergraduate/Scholarship*) 5599

John N. Stern Fellowships for Oberlin College Faculty (*Professional Development/Fellowship*) 4625

Joseph R. Stone Scholarships (*Undergraduate/ Scholarship*) 984

Levi Strauss Foundation Scholarship Program (*Undergraduate/ Scholarship*) 5636

Two/Ten International Footwear Foundation Scholarships (*Undergraduate/Scholarship*) 5759

Union Pacific Railroad Employee Dependent Scholarships (*Undergraduate/Scholarship*) 5778

UWUA Scholarships (*Undergraduate/Scholarship*) 6021

W.C.A. Care and Share Scholarship (*Undergraduate/ Scholarship*) 1897

Weyerhaeuser Company Foundation College Scholarship (*Undergraduate/Scholarship*) 6165

Weyerhaeuser Company Foundation Community Education Scholarship (*Undergraduate/Scholarship*) 6166

Honourable W.C. Woodward Scholarships (*Undergraduate/ Scholarship*) 5044

YLD Scholarships (*Graduate, Other, Undergraduate/ Scholarship*) 6287

Mary & Harry Zimmerman Scholarship Program (*High School, Undergraduate/Scholarship*) 5311

## Ethnic

AGBU Education Loan (*Graduate/Loan*) 1136

AGBU Education Loan Program in the U.S. (*Graduate/ Loan*) 1133

K. Arakelian Foundation Scholarship (*Undergraduate/ Scholarship*) 1103

Armenian Allied Arts Association Scholarship (*Undergraduate/ Award*) 1104

Armenian-American Citizens' League Scholarship (*Undergraduate/Scholarship*) 1105

Armenian American Medical Association Scholarship (*Undergraduate/Scholarship*) 1106

Armenian American Middle East Club Scholarship (*Graduate, Undergraduate/Scholarship*) 1107

Armenian American Pharmacists' Association Scholarship (*Graduate, Undergraduate/Scholarship*) 1108

Armenian Bible College Scholarship (*Undergraduate/ Scholarship*) 1109

Armenian Cultural Society of Akron/Canton Scholarship (*Undergraduate/Scholarship*) 1110

Armenian General Athletic Union Scholarship (*Undergraduate/ Scholarship*) 1111

Armenian General Benevolent Union (AGBU) Loans and Grants (*Graduate, Undergraduate/Loan*) 1112

Armenian Professional Society of the Bay Area Scholarship (*Undergraduate/Scholarship*) 1113

Armenian Professional Society Scholarship (*Doctorate, Graduate/Scholarship*) 1114

Armenian Relief Society of North America Scholarship (*Undergraduate/Scholarship*) 1115

## Ethnic (continued)

Armenian Students Association of America, Inc. Grant *(Graduate, Undergraduate/Grant)* 1116

Armenian Students' Association of America Reading Scholarships *(Doctorate, Graduate, Undergraduate/Scholarship)* 1138

Asian American Journalists Association Scholarship *(Graduate, Undergraduate/Scholarship)* 1172

Hagop Bogigian Scholarship Fund *(Undergraduate/Scholarship)* 1117

Bolla Wines Scholarship *(Undergraduate/Scholarship)* 4211

Vivienne Camp College Scholarship Fund *(Undergraduate/Scholarship)* 3263

Anthony J. Celebrezze Scholarship *(Graduate, Undergraduate/Scholarship)* 4213

Ferdinand Cinelli Etruscan Scholarship *(Graduate, Undergraduate/Scholarship)* 4214

Cintas Fellowships *(Professional Development/Fellowship)* 1163

Constantinople Armenian Relief Society (CARS) Scholarship *(Undergraduate/Scholarship)* 1118

Silvio Conte Internship *(Undergraduate/Scholarship)* 4216

Cornaro Scholarship *(Undergraduate/Scholarship)* 4217

Cymdeithas Gymreig/Philadelphia Scholarships *(Undergraduate/Scholarship)* 2148

Daughters of Penelope Graduate Student Award *(Graduate/Scholarship)* 2182

Robert J. Di Pietro Scholarship *(Undergraduate/Scholarship)* 4222

Acoma Higher Education Grants *(Undergraduate/Grant)* 5019

Evrytanian Association Scholarship *(Doctorate, Graduate, Undergraduate/Scholarship)* 2418

Sergio Franchi Music Scholarship in Voice Performance *(Graduate, Undergraduate/Scholarship)* 4225

Carmela Gagliardi Fellowship *(Graduate/Fellowship)* 4226

Garikian University Scholarship Fund *(Undergraduate/Scholarship)* 1119

A.P. Giannini Scholarship *(Graduate, Undergraduate/Scholarship)* 4228

Giargiari Fellowship *(Graduate/Fellowship)* 4229

Morton A. Gibson Memorial Scholarships *(Undergraduate/Scholarship)* 3268

Thomas Googooian Memorial Scholarship *(Undergraduate/Scholarship)* 1120

Rose Basile Green Scholarship *(Undergraduate/Scholarship)* 4231

Calouste Gulbenkian Foundation *(Undergraduate/Grant)* 1121

Hai Guin Scholarship Association *(Undergraduate/Scholarship)* 1122

AGBU Hirair and Anna Hovnanian Fellowship *(Graduate/Fellowship)* 1123

Hungarian Arts Club Scholarships *(Undergraduate/Scholarship)* 2935

Indian Health Career Awards *(Doctorate, Graduate, Undergraduate/Scholarship)* 4935

Japanese American Citizens League Creative Arts Award *(Other/Scholarship)* 3244

Japanese American Citizens League Freshman Awards *(High School/Scholarship)* 3245

Japanese American Citizens League Performing Arts Award *(All/Scholarship)* 3247

Japanese American Citizens League Student Aid Award *(Graduate, High School, Undergraduate/Scholarship)* 3248

Japanese American Citizens League Undergraduate Awards *(Undergraduate/Scholarship)* 3249

Jewish Educational Loans Fund *(Graduate, Undergraduate/Loan)* 3269

Steven Knezevich Trust Grants *(Doctorate, Graduate, Postgraduate, Undergraduate/Scholarship)* 3381

Knights of Lithuania Scholarships *(Graduate, Undergraduate/Scholarship)* 3392

Knights of Varton, Fresno Lodge 9 Scholarship *(Undergraduate/Scholarship)* 1124

Peter and Alice Koomruian Armenian Education Fund *(Graduate, Undergraduate/Scholarship)* 1125

Law Fellowship *(Graduate, Postgraduate/Fellowship)* 4235

Law Scholarships *(Juris Doctorate/Scholarship)* 3250

Samuel Lemberg Scholarship Loan Fund, Inc. *(Graduate, Undergraduate/Loan)* 3451

Marinelli Scholarships *(Undergraduate/Scholarship)* 4238

Martino Scholars Program *(Graduate/Fellowship)* 4239

National Association for Armenian Studies and Research, Inc. Fund *(Graduate, Postgraduate/Fellowship, Grant)* 1126

National FFA Foundation Minority Scholarships *(Undergraduate/Scholarship)* 4104

National Welsh-American Foundation Exchange Scholarships *(Doctorate, Graduate, Undergraduate/Scholarship)* 4450

NIAF/FIERI National Matching Scholarship *(Undergraduate/Scholarship)* 4246

NIAF/Sacred Heart University Matching Scholarship *(Undergraduate/Scholarship)* 4248

John and Anne Parente Matching Scholarship *(Undergraduate/Scholarship)* 4251

Pavarotti Scholarship *(Graduate, Undergraduate/Scholarship)* 4252

Pellegrini Scholarship Grants *(Graduate, Undergraduate/Scholarship)* 5662

Piancone Family Agriculture Scholarship *(Graduate, Undergraduate/Scholarship)* 4254

Dr. Syngman Rhee Scholarship *(Undergraduate/Scholarship)* 2268

St. Andrews Society of the State of New York Scholarships *(Graduate/Scholarship)* 5218

St. David's Scholarship *(Graduate, Professional Development, Undergraduate/Scholarship)* 5220

St. James Armenian Church Memorial Scholarship *(Undergraduate/Scholarship)* 1127

Sho Sato Memorial Law Scholarship *(Juris Doctorate/Scholarship)* 3251

SBS Scholarships *(Undergraduate/Scholarship)* 5660

Sons of Italy Foundation National Leadership Grants *(Graduate, Undergraduate/Grant)* 5533

Ida Speyrer Stahl Scholarships *(Undergraduate/Scholarship)* 1725

Irene Stambler Vocational Opportunities Grants *(Other/Grant)* 3271

Daniel Stella Scholarship *(Undergraduate/Scholarship)* 4261

E.D. Stella Scholarship *(Undergraduate/Scholarship)* 4262

William Toto Scholarship *(Undergraduate/Scholarship)* 4265

Marguerite Tremblay Cote Scholarships *(Undergraduate/Scholarship)* 1726

Union of Hadjin Fund *(Undergraduate/Scholarship)* 1128

Union of Marash Fund *(Undergraduate/Scholarship)* 1129

Agnes E. Vaghi-Cornaro Scholarship *(Undergraduate/Scholarship)* 4266

Wasie Foundation Scholarships *(Graduate, Undergraduate/Scholarship)* 6109

Harry and Angel Zerigian Scholarship *(Undergraduate/Scholarship)* 1130

Charles K. and Pansy Pategian Zlokovich Scholarship *(Undergraduate/Scholarship)* 1131

## Female

1989 Polytechnique Commemorative Award *(Graduate/Award)* 1630

AAUW Educational Foundation American Fellowships *(Postdoctorate/Fellowship)* 331

AAUW Educational Foundation Career Development Grants *(Masters, Professional Development/Grant)* 332

AAUW Educational Foundation Community Action Grants *(Other/Grant)* 333

AAUW Educational Foundation International Fellowships *(Graduate/Fellowship, Grant)* 334

AAUW Educational Foundation Selected Professions Engineering Dissertation Fellowship *(Graduate/Fellowship)* 335

AAUW Educational Foundation Selected Professions Fellowship *(Graduate/Fellowship)* 336

AAUW Postdoctoral Fellowships *(Postdoctorate/Fellowship)* 337

Special Recipient Index

## Female (continued)

Hewlett-Packard Scholarships *(Undergraduate/ Scholarship)* 5512

Anna Louise Hoffman Awards for Outstanding Achievement in Graduate Research *(Graduate/Award)* 3216

Admiral Grace Murray Hopper Scholarship *(Undergraduate/ Scholarship)* 5513

Celia M. Howard Fellowships *(Doctorate, Graduate/ Fellowship)* 2964

Dorothy Lemke Howarth Scholarship *(Undergraduate/ Scholarship)* 5514

International Peace Scholarships *(Graduate/Scholarship)* 4877

Iota Sigma Pi Undergraduate Awards for Excellence in Chemistry *(Undergraduate/Award)* 3217

Beverley Jackson Fellowship *(Graduate/Fellowship)* 1634

Elaine Osborne Jacobson Award for Women in Health Care *(Doctorate, Graduate/Award)* 5163

Kansas City Speech Pathology Award *(Graduate/Award)* 3327

Kappa Kappa Gamma Chapter Consultant Scholarships *(Graduate/Scholarship)* 3328

Kappa Kappa Gamma Emergency Assistance Grants *(Undergraduate/Grant)* 3329

Kappa Kappa Gamma Graduate Fellowships *(Graduate/ Fellowship)* 3330

Kappa Kappa Gamma Rehabilitation Scholarships *(Graduate, Undergraduate/Scholarship)* 3331

Kappa Kappa Gamma Undergraduate Scholarships *(Undergraduate/Scholarship)* 3332

Julia Kiene Fellowship *(Graduate/Fellowship)* 2363

Ladies Auxiliary of Fleet Reserve Association Scholarship *(Undergraduate/Scholarship)* 2478

Ladies Auxiliary to the VFW Junior Girls Scholarships *(Undergraduate/Scholarship)* 3408

Laurels Fund Scholarships *(Doctorate, Graduate/ Scholarship)* 2350

S. Evelyn Lewis Memorial Scholarship in Medical Health Sciences *(Graduate, Undergraduate/Scholarship)* 6306

Mary Connolly Livingston Grant *(Doctorate/Grant)* 3415

Lyle Mamer Fellowship *(Graduate/Fellowship)* 2364

MASWE Memorial Scholarships *(Undergraduate/ Scholarship)* 5515

Anne O'Hare McCormick Scholarship *(Graduate/ Scholarship)* 3618

D'Arcy McNickle Center for the History of the American Indian Fellowships *(Postgraduate/Fellowship)* 4606

Margaret McWilliams Predoctoral Fellowship *(Doctorate/ Fellowship)* 1635

Edwin G. and Lauretta M. Michael Scholarship *(Undergraduate/Scholarship)* 1950

Microsoft Corporation Scholarships *(Graduate, Undergraduate/ Scholarship)* 5516

Miss America Pageant Scholarships *(Graduate, Undergraduate/Scholarship)* 3726

Monticello College Foundation Fellowship for Women *(Postdoctorate/Fellowship)* 4619

Doris Mullen Memorial Scholarships *(All/Scholarship)* 3203

National Association of Media Women Scholarship *(Undergraduate/Scholarship)* 3885

National Council for Geographic Education Committee for Women in Geographic Education Scholarship *(Graduate, Undergraduate/Scholarship)* 3955

National Physical Science Consortium Graduate Fellowships for Minorities and Women *(Doctorate, Graduate/ Fellowship)* 4338

Nevada Women's Fund Scholarships *(Doctorate, Graduate, Other, Professional Development, Undergraduate/ Scholarship)* 4521

New Jersey State Federation of Women's Clubs Margaret Yardley Fellowship *(Doctorate, Graduate/Fellowship)* 4543

New York Life Foundation Scholarships for Women in the Health Professions *(Undergraduate/Scholarship)* 1551

Northrop Corporation Founders Scholarship *(Undergraduate/ Scholarship)* 5517

Ohio Newspaper Women's Association Scholarship *(Undergraduate/Scholarship)* 4731

Helene Overly Scholarship *(Graduate/Scholarship)* 6243

Ivy Parker Memorial Scholarship *(Undergraduate/ Scholarship)* 5518

Past Grand Presidents Award *(High School, Undergraduate/ Scholarship)* 2185

Anne Pekar Memorial Scholarship *(Undergraduate/ Scholarship)* 4006

Phi Chi Theta Scholarships *(Graduate, Postgraduate, Undergraduate/Scholarship)* 4896

Jeannette Rankin Award *(Undergraduate/Award)* 5081

Judith Resnik Memorial Scholarship *(Undergraduate/ Scholarship)* 5519

Edith Nourse Rogers Scholarship Fund *(Undergraduate/ Scholarship)* 6230

Eleanor Roosevelt Teacher Fellowships *(Doctorate, Other/ Fellowship)* 338

Root Foreign Language Scholarship *(Graduate, Undergraduate/Scholarship)* 3333

Olive Lynn Salembier Scholarship *(Graduate, Undergraduate/ Scholarship)* 5520

Karla Scherer Foundation Scholarships *(Graduate, Undergraduate/Scholarship)* 5254

Scholarships for Mature Women *(Professional Development/ Scholarship)* 4282

Katherine J. Schutze Memorial Scholarship *(Graduate/ Scholarship)* 1952

SDE Fellowships *(Postgraduate/Fellowship)* 5330

Frances Shaw Fellowship *(Professional Development/ Scholarship)* 5073

Mary Isabel Sibley Fellowships *(Doctorate, Postdoctorate/ Fellowship)* 4894

Kathryn G. Siphers Scholarships *(Undergraduate/ Scholarship)* 6218

Alice E. Smith Fellowship *(Graduate/Fellowship)* 5617

Society of Daughters of the United States Army Scholarship Program *(Undergraduate/Scholarship)* 5447

Alexandra Apostolides Sonenfeld Award *(High School, Undergraduate/Scholarship)* 2186

Soroptimist Women's Opportunity Award *(Professional Development/Award)* 5541

Irene Stambler Vocational Opportunities Grants *(Other/ Grant)* 3271

Ney Stineman Memorial Scholarship *(Undergraduate/ Scholarship)* 1896

Texaco Scholarships *(Undergraduate/Scholarship)* 5521

Travel and Training Grant *(Undergraduate/Grant)* 6240

TRW Scholarships *(Undergraduate/Scholarship)* 5522

Sarah B. Tyson Fellowship *(Professional Development/ Fellowship)* 6234

Agnes E. Vaghi-Cornaro Scholarship *(Undergraduate/ Scholarship)* 4266

Virginia Volkwein Memorial Scholarships *(Undergraduate/ Scholarship)* 6219

WAWH Graduate Student Fellowship *(Doctorate/ Fellowship)* 6147

Westinghouse Bertha Lamme Scholarships *(Undergraduate/ Scholarship)* 5523

Nellie Yeoh Whetten Award *(Graduate/Award)* 1009

Whirly-Girls Memorial Flight Scholarships *(Professional Development/Scholarship)* 3204

Alice E. Wilson Award *(Graduate/Other)* 1636

Harriett Barnhardt Wimmer Scholarship *(Undergraduate/ Scholarship)* 3436

Deborah Partridge Wolfe International Fellowship *(Graduate, Undergraduate/Fellowship)* 6307

Women of the ELCA Scholarship *(Graduate, Postgraduate, Undergraduate/Scholarship)* 6226

Women in Scholarly Publishing Career Development Fund *(Professional Development/Other)* 6228

Women's Medical Association of New York Financial Assistance Fund Loans *(Doctorate/Award, Loan)* 6232

The Women's Sports Foundation Minority Internship Program *(Graduate, Postgraduate, Undergraduate/Internship)* 6241

Women's Western Golf Foundation Scholarship *(Undergraduate/Scholarship)* 6245

## Handicapped (continued)

B.R.I.D.G.E. Kraft General Foods Scholarship *(Undergraduate/ Scholarship)* 4034

B.R.I.D.G.E. Quaker Oats Foundation Scholarship *(Undergraduate/Scholarship)* 4035

Hermione Grant Calhoun Scholarship *(Undergraduate/ Scholarship)* 3998

California-Hawaii Elks Disabled Student Scholarships *(Undergraduate/Scholarship)* 1559

Karen D. Carsel Memorial Scholarship *(Graduate/ Scholarship)* 479

Central Intelligence Agency Undergraduate Scholars Program *(Undergraduate/Internship, Scholarship)* 1812

Chairscholars Foundation Scholarship *(Undergraduate/ Scholarship)* 1826

Arthur E. and Helen Copeland Scholarships *(Undergraduate/ Scholarship)* 5828

Ezra Davis Memorial Scholarship *(Undergraduate/ Scholarship)* 3999

Delta Gamma Foundation - Florence Margaret Harvey Memorial Scholarship *(Graduate, Undergraduate/ Scholarship)* 480

Rudolph Dillman Scholarship *(Graduate, Undergraduate/ Scholarship)* 481

Easter Seal Society of Iowa Disability Scholarship *(Undergraduate/Scholarship)* 2320

Electronic Industries Foundation Scholarships *(Graduate, Undergraduate/Scholarship)* 2370

Herbert P. Feibelman Jr. (IPO) Award *(Undergraduate/Award, Scholarship)* 1400

Florida Division of Blind Services Vocational Rehabilitation Program *(Other/Other)* 2517

FSD Student Grant *(Graduate/Grant)* 2578

Gallaudet University Alumni Association Graduate Fellowship Funds *(Doctorate, Graduate/Fellowship)* 2615

R.L. Gillette Scholarship *(Undergraduate/Scholarship)* 482

Grants for Physically Disabled Students in the Sciences *(Graduate/Grant)* 2579

Elsie Bell Grosvenor Scholarship Awards *(Undergraduate/ Scholarship)* 1401

Margaret Howard Hamilton Scholarships *(Undergraduate/ Scholarship)* 4398

Frank Walton Horn Memorial Scholarships *(Undergraduate/ Scholarship)* 4000

The Allie Raney Hunt Memorial Scholarship *(Undergraduate/ Scholarship)* 1402

Imasco Scholarships for Disabled Students *(Undergraduate/ Scholarship)* 1278

Leslie Isenberg Graduate Scholarship *(Doctorate, Graduate/ Scholarship)* 992

Stanley E. Jackson Scholarship Awards *(Undergraduate/ Scholarship)* 2566

Roy Johnson Trust Graduate School Grants *(Graduate/ Grant)* 3681

Kentucky Center for Veterans Affairs State Tuition Waivers *(Undergraduate/Other)* 3358

Kuchler-Killian Memorial Scholarship *(Undergraduate/ Scholarship)* 4001

The Lighthouse Career Incentive Award for Adult Undergraduates *(Undergraduate/Scholarship)* 3474

The Lighthouse Career Incentive Award for College-Bound Students *(Undergraduate/Scholarship)* 3475

The Lighthouse Career Incentive Award for Graduate Students *(Graduate/Scholarship)* 3476

The Lighthouse Career Incentive Award for Undergraduates *(Undergraduate/Scholarship)* 3477

Louisiana Rehabilitation Services Award *(Other/Other)* 3506

James L. and Lavon Madden Mallory Disability Scholarship *(High School, Undergraduate/Scholarship)* 2322

Mattinson Endowment Fund Scholarship for Disabled Students *(Undergraduate/Scholarship)* 1282

Howard E. May Memorial Scholarships *(Undergraduate/ Scholarship)* 3992

Jonathan May Memorial Scholarship *(Undergraduate/ Scholarship)* 3993

John T. McCraw Scholarship *(Graduate, Undergraduate/ Scholarship)* 3996

Michigan Association for Deaf, Hearing, and Speech Services Scholarships *(Undergraduate/Scholarship)* 3679

National Amputation Foundation Scholarship *(Undergraduate/ Scholarship)* 3846

National Federation of the Blind Educator of Tomorrow Award *(Undergraduate/Award)* 4002

National Federation of the Blind Humanities Scholarship *(Undergraduate/Scholarship)* 4003

National Federation of the Blind Scholarships *(Undergraduate/ Scholarship)* 4004

National Fraternal Society of the Deaf Scholarships *(Doctorate, Graduate, Postgraduate, Professional Development, Undergraduate/Scholarship)* 4173

NDCS Scholarship Grant *(Graduate/Scholarship)* 3970

NFB of CT Academic Sholarship *(Undergraduate/ Scholarship)* 3994

Opportunities for the Blind, Inc. Grants *(Doctorate, Graduate, Postgraduate, Professional Development, Undergraduate/ Grant)* 4785

Oral Hearing Impaired Section Scholarship Award *(Undergraduate/Scholarship)* 1403

Melva T. Owen Memorial Scholarship *(Undergraduate/ Scholarship)* 4005

Anne Pekar Memorial Scholarship *(Undergraduate/ Scholarship)* 4006

N. Neal Pike Prize for Service to People with Disabilities *(Other/Prize)* 4947

President's Committee on Employment of People with Disabilities Scholarships for Students with Disabilities *(Undergraduate/Scholarship)* 5001

Howard Brown Rickard Scholarship *(Undergraduate/ Scholarship)* 4007

David Rogers Bursary *(Graduate, Undergraduate/Grant)* 3971

Scholarships for Blind and Visually Impaired Postsecondary Students *(Graduate, Undergraduate/Scholarship)* 483

Ellen Setterfield Memorial Scholarship *(Graduate/ Scholarship)* 4008

Stokoe Scholarships *(Graduate/Scholarship)* 3873

Student Access Awards Program *(Undergraduate/ Scholarship)* 1287

Teacher Education Scholarship Program *(Undergraduate/ Scholarship)* 125

Telesensory Scholarship *(Undergraduate/Scholarship)* 2098

Carol Thomson Memorial Fund Scholarship *(All/ Scholarship)* 3447

USCG Chief Petty Officers Association Captain Caliendo College Assistance Fund Scholarship Program *(High School, Undergraduate/Scholarship)* 5847

Venture Student Aid Award for Physically Disabled Students *(Other/Award)* 6028

Vocational Rehabilitation Assistance for Postsecondary Training *(Undergraduate/Other)* 4678

Vocational Rehabilitation Grants *(Undergraduate/ Scholarship)* 3360

Volta Scholarship Award *(Undergraduate/Scholarship)* 1404

David J. Von Hagen Scholarship Award *(Undergraduate/ Scholarship)* 1405

Lester Walls III Scholarship *(Graduate, Undergraduate/ Scholarship)* 3435

Robert H. Weitbrecht Scholarship Award *(Undergraduate/ Scholarship)* 1406

Maude Winkler Scholarship Awards *(Graduate, Undergraduate/ Scholarship)* 1407

## Hispanic American

AAHCPA Scholarship *(Undergraduate/Scholarship)* 308

ABF Summer Research Fellowships in Law and Social Science for Minority Undergraduate Students *(Undergraduate/Fellowship)* 352

AEJ Summer Internships for Minorities *(Undergraduate/ Internship)* 3029

Affirmative Action Scholarship Program *(Graduate/ Scholarship)* 5575

Alabama Space Grant Consortium Graduate Student Fellowship Program *(Graduate/Fellowship)* 123

Alabama Space Grant Consortium Undergraduate Fellowship Program *(Undergraduate/Fellowship)* 124

Alpha Kappa Alpha Educational Advancement Foundation Scholarships *(Undergraduate/Scholarship)* 198

American Economic Association/Federal Reserve System Minority Graduate Fellowships in Economics *(Graduate, Postgraduate/Fellowship)* 453

AMS/Industry Minority Scholarships *(Undergraduate/Scholarship)* 702

APA Planning & the Black Community Division Scholarship *(Undergraduate/Scholarship)* 775

APA Planning Fellowships *(Graduate/Fellowship)* 776

APSA Graduate Fellowships for Latino Students *(Doctorate/Fellowship)* 782

AT & T Bell Laboratories Cooperative Research Fellowships for Minorities *(Graduate/Fellowship)* 1302

AT & T Bell Laboratories Summer Research Program for Minorities & Women *(Undergraduate/Fellowship)* 1305

Sally Butler Memorial Fund for Latina Research *(Doctorate, Postdoctorate/Fellowship)* 1549

William and Charlotte Cadbury Award *(Doctorate/Award)* 4288

Vikki Carr Scholarship *(Graduate, Undergraduate/Scholarship)* 1741

Chicana Dissertation Fellowship *(Graduate/Fellowship)* 2233

Chicana Latina Foundation Scholarships *(Graduate, Undergraduate/Scholarship)* 1931

Christian Church Hispanic Scholarship *(Graduate/Scholarship)* 1947

CIC Predoctoral Fellowships *(Doctorate, Graduate/Fellowship)* 2013

CLA Scholarship for Minority Students in Memory of Edna Yelland *(Graduate/Scholarship)* 1565

Concerned Media Professionals Scholarships *(Undergraduate/Scholarship)* 5976

Consortium Graduate Study Management Fellowships for Minorities *(Graduate/Fellowship)* 2067

Corporate Sponsored Scholarships for Minority Undergraduate Physics Majors *(Undergraduate/Scholarship)* 772

Council on Social Work Education Minority Fellowships *(Doctorate/Fellowship)* 3724

Ginger and Fred Deines Mexico Scholarships *(Graduate, Professional Development, Undergraduate/Scholarship)* 5742

*Detroit Free Press* Minority Journalism Scholarships *(Undergraduate/Scholarship)* 2247

Esperanza Scholarships *(Graduate, Undergraduate/Scholarship)* 2412

Fellowship Program in Academic Medicine *(Doctorate/Fellowship)* 4289

Florida Chapter of the Association of Women in Communications Christina Saralegui Scholarship *(Graduate, Undergraduate/Scholarship)* 1294

Ford Foundation Predoctoral and Dissertation Fellowships for Minorities *(Doctorate/Fellowship)* 4357

Raquel Marquez Frankel Scholarship Fund *(Graduate, Undergraduate/Scholarship)* 3542

Joel Garcia Memorial Scholarship *(Undergraduate/Scholarship)* 1555

GEM Master's Engineering Fellowships for Minorities *(Graduate/Fellowship)* 3941

GEM Ph.D. Engineering Fellowships for Minorities *(Doctorate/Fellowship)* 3942

GEM Ph.D. Science Fellowship Program *(Doctorate/Fellowship)* 3943

Gerber Prize for Excellence in Pediatrics *(Doctorate/Award)* 4291

GOALS Fellowships *(Graduate/Fellowship)* 3001

Hispanic American Scholarship Program *(Undergraduate/Scholarship)* 1533

Hispanic Link News Service Internships *(Undergraduate/Internship)* 2878

HOPE Scholarships *(Undergraduate/Scholarship)* 2882

W. K. Kellogg Community Medicine Training Fellowship Program for Minority Medical Students *(Doctorate/Fellowship)* 4297

Latin American Educational Foundation Scholarships *(Graduate, Postgraduate, Undergraduate/Scholarship)* 3439

MACESA Awards *(Undergraduate/Scholarship)* 3699

Metropolitan Life Foundation Awards for Academic Excellence in Medicine *(Doctorate/Award)* 4300

Mexican American Grocers Association Foundation Scholarships *(Undergraduate/Scholarship)* 3673

Minority Dental Student Scholarship Program *(Doctorate, Graduate/Scholarship)* 43

Minority Geoscience Scholarships *(Graduate, Undergraduate/Scholarship)* 508

MLA Scholarship for Minority Students *(Graduate/Scholarship)* 3636

NACME Corporate Scholars Program *(Undergraduate/Scholarship)* 3835

NACME TechForce Scholarships *(Undergraduate/Scholarship)* 3836

National Association of Hispanic Nurses National Scholarship Award *(Graduate, Undergraduate/Scholarship)* 3879

National FFA Foundation Minority Scholarships *(Undergraduate/Scholarship)* 4104

National Hispanic Scholar Recognition Program *(Undergraduate/Scholarship)* 1984

National Physical Science Consortium Graduate Fellowships for Minorities and Women *(Doctorate, Graduate/Fellowship)* 4338

Nevada Hispanic Services Scholarships *(Undergraduate/Scholarship)* 4519

NHSF Scholarships *(Graduate, Undergraduate/Scholarship)* 4179

NMA Scholarships *(Graduate/Scholarship)* 4302

NMF Scholarships for Minority Students *(Doctorate/Scholarship)* 4304

Colin L. Powell Minority Postdoctoral Fellowship in Tropical Disease Research *(Graduate/Fellowship)* 4164

Presbyterian Church Student Opportunity Scholarships *(Undergraduate/Scholarship)* 4996

PRLDEF Scholarship *(Graduate/Scholarship)* 5023

Racial/Ethnic Leadership Supplemental Grants *(Graduate/Grant)* 4998

James H. Robinson Memorial Prize *(Doctorate/Prize)* 4305

Nelson A. Rockefeller Minority Internships *(Undergraduate/Internship)* 6270

Sacramento Hispanic Chamber of Commerce Scholarships *(Undergraduate/Scholarship)* 5216

Aura E. Severinghaus Award *(Doctorate/Scholarship)* 4306

Underrepresented Minority Investigators Award in Asthma and Allergy *(Postdoctorate/Award)* 216

Jimmy A. Young Memorial Education Recognition Award *(Undergraduate/Scholarship)* 850

## Male

American Legion Boy Scout Scholarships *(Undergraduate/Scholarship)* 608

Beta Theta Pi Founders Fund Scholarship-Leadership Awards *(Graduate, Undergraduate/Award)* 1428

Elks National Foundation Eagle Scout Scholarship *(Undergraduate/Scholarship)* 1463

FEAT Loans *(All/Loan)* 2607

E. Urner Goodman Professional Scouter Scholarship *(Undergraduate/Scholarship)* 1466

Chuck Hall Star of Tomorrow Scholarship *(Undergraduate/Scholarship)* 5007

Henry G. Halladay Awards *(Doctorate/Scholarship)* 4294

Percy J. Johnson Scholarships *(Undergraduate/Scholarship)* 3386

National Eagle Scout Scholarships *(Undergraduate/Scholarship)* 1464

Spence Reese Scholarship *(High School, Undergraduate/Scholarship)* 5089

Scaife Foundation Scholarships *(Undergraduate/Scholarship)* 4692

## Male (continued)

Sons of the First Division Scholarship Fund *(Undergraduate/ Scholarship)* 5452

Wilbur H.H. Ward Educational Trust Scholarship *(Undergraduate/Scholarship)* 6077

## Military

ADM Mike Boorda Seaman-to-Admiral Educational Assistance Program *(Undergraduate/Grant, Loan)* 4494

AFCEA ROTC Scholarship Program *(Undergraduate/ Scholarship)* 1100

AFSA Scholarship Awards *(Undergraduate/Scholarship)* 68

Air Force Aid Society Education Grants *(Undergraduate/ Grant)* 64

Air Force ROTC Scholarships *(Undergraduate/ Scholarship)* 5816

Airmen Memorial Scholarships *(Undergraduate/ Scholarship)* 98

Alabama National Guard Educational Assistance Program *(Undergraduate/Award)* 104

American Legion Auxiliary Nurses, Physical Therapists and Respiratory Therapists Scholarship *(Undergraduate/ Scholarship)* 626

AMF/Signet Bank Educational Loans *(All/Loan)* 99

Armed Forces Health Professions Scholarship *(Graduate/ Scholarship)* 4483

Army Emergency Relief Scholarships *(Undergraduate/ Scholarship)* 1140

Army Engineer Memorial Awards *(Undergraduate/ Scholarship)* 1143

Vincent Astor Memorial Leadership Essay Contest *(Other/ Prize)* 5949

Major General Lucas Beau Flight Scholarship *(Other/ Scholarship)* 3914

General Buxton/St. Michael's Scholarships *(Graduate, Undergraduate/Scholarship)* 6032

Children of Air Traffic Control Specialists *(Undergraduate/ Scholarship)* 73

CMSAF Richard D. Kisling Scholarships *(Undergraduate/ Scholarship)* 100

Edward T. Conroy Memorial Scholarship *(Graduate, Undergraduate/Scholarship)* 3568

John Cornelius and Max English Memorial Scholarship *(Graduate, Undergraduate/Scholarship)* 3564

Daughters of the Cincinnati Scholarships *(Undergraduate/ Scholarship)* 2178

Department of New York Scholarship *(Undergraduate/ Scholarship)* 2256

Department of Veterans Affairs Free Tuition for Children of POW/MIA's in Vietnam *(Undergraduate/Other)* 2997

Dolphin Scholarship *(Undergraduate/Scholarship)* 2266

Enlisted Essay Contest *(Other/Prize)* 5951

Gamewardens of Vietnam Association Scholarships *(Undergraduate/Award)* 5958

Robert Hampton Gray Memorial Bursary *(Undergraduate/ Scholarship)* 4485

Illinois National Guard Grant *(Graduate, Undergraduate/ Grant)* 2976

Maria C. Jackson & General George A. White Scholarships *(Undergraduate/Scholarship)* 5833

Dr. Theodore von Karman Graduate Scholarship *(Graduate/ Scholarship)* 45

Louisiana National Guard Tuition Exemption Program *(Undergraduate/Other)* 3504

Marianas Naval Officers' Wives' Club Scholarships *(Undergraduate/Scholarship)* 5959

Marine Corps Foundation Scholarships *(Undergraduate/ Scholarship)* 3562

Mississippi Southeast Asia POW/MIA Scholarship Program *(Graduate, Undergraduate/Scholarship)* 3740

Montgomery G.I. Bill and U.S. Army College Fund *(Undergraduate/Scholarship)* 5826

Col. Louisa Spruance Morse CAP Scholarship *(Undergraduate/ Scholarship)* 3917

National Guard Association of New Jersey Scholarship *(Undergraduate/Scholarship)* 4539

Naval Academy Women's Club Scholarship *(Undergraduate/ Scholarship)* 4481

Naval Officers' Spouses' Association of Mayport Scholarships *(Graduate, Undergraduate/Scholarship)* 4487

Navy Supply Corps Foundation Scholarships *(Undergraduate/ Scholarship)* 4501

Navy Wives Club of America Scholarships *(Undergraduate/ Scholarship)* 5960

NCOA Scholarships *(High School, Undergraduate/ Scholarship)* 4639

New York Council Navy League Scholarships *(Undergraduate/ Scholarship)* 4566

North Georgia College Military Scholarship *(Undergraduate/ Scholarship)* 2674

North Georgia College ROTC Grant *(Undergraduate/ Grant)* 2675

Ohio American Legion Scholarship *(Undergraduate/ Scholarship)* 621

Ohio National Guard Tuition Grant *(Undergraduate/Grant, Scholarship)* 4729

Philippines Subic Bay-Cubi Point Scholarship *(Undergraduate/ Scholarship)* 4492

Henry J. Reilly Memorial Graduate Scholarships *(Doctorate, Graduate/Scholarship)* 5105

Henry J. Reilly Memorial Undergraduate Scholarship for College Attendees *(Undergraduate/Scholarship)* 5106

Henry J. Reilly Memorial Undergraduate Scholarship for Graduating High School Students *(Undergraduate/ Scholarship)* 5107

The Retired Officers Association Educational Assistance Program *(Undergraduate/Loan)* 5116

Bettsy Ross Educational Grants *(Undergraduate/Grant)* 4640

Royal Canadian Legion Ladies Auxiliary Alberta-N.W.T. Command Awards *(Undergraduate/Scholarship)* 5041

Royal Canadian Legion Ladies Auxiliary Camrose Branch No. 57 Bursaries *(Undergraduate/Scholarship)* 5042

Society of Daughters of the United States Army Scholarship Program *(Undergraduate/Scholarship)* 5447

South Dakota Board of Regents National Guard Tuition Assistance *(Undergraduate/Other)* 5555

CDR William S. Stuhr Scholarship *(Undergraduate/ Scholarship)* 5644

Texas Veterans Educational Benefits *(Undergraduate/ Grant)* 5721

Vice Admiral E.P. Travers Scholarships and Loan Program *(Undergraduate/Grant, Loan)* 4497

U.S. Air Force Academy Graduate Dependent Scholarship *(Graduate, Undergraduate/Scholarship)* 1240

USS Lake Champlain Foundation Scholarships *(Undergraduate/Scholarship)* 5648

## Minority

AAAA Minority Advertising Internships *(Undergraduate/ Internship)* 270

AACP-AFPE Gateway Scholarships *(Graduate/ Scholarship)* 485

AAUW Educational Foundation Selected Professions Engineering Dissertation Fellowship *(Graduate/ Fellowship)* 335

AEJ Summer Internships for Minorities *(Undergraduate/ Internship)* 3029

Alabama Space Grant Consortium Graduate Student Fellowship Program *(Graduate/Fellowship)* 123

Alabama Space Grant Consortium Undergraduate Fellowship Program *(Undergraduate/Fellowship)* 124

TELACU/Richard Alatorre Fellowship *(Graduate/ Fellowship)* 5686

The American Architectural Foundation Minority/Disadvantaged Scholarship *(Graduate, Undergraduate/Scholarship)* 574

American Press Institute Minority Journalism Educators Fellowship *(Other/Fellowship)* 791

American Sociological Association Minority Fellowships *(Doctorate/Fellowship)* 986

American Sociological Association Research Doctoral Fellowships in Sociology *(Doctorate/Fellowship)* 987

American Water Works Association Holy A. Cornell Grant *(Graduate/Scholarship)* 1016

AMS/Industry Minority Scholarships *(Undergraduate/Scholarship)* 702

Anheuser-Busch Scholarship Fund *(Undergraduate/Scholarship)* 1926

Asbury Park Press Scholarships for Minority Students *(Undergraduate/Scholarship)* 1168

ASM Predoctoral Minority Fellowships *(Doctorate/Fellowship)* 954

Associated Press Summer Minority Internships *(Undergraduate/Internship)* 1197

Atlanta Association of Media Women Scholarship *(Undergraduate/Scholarship)* 1308

Black American Cinema Society Award *(Professional Development/Award)* 6163

Blethen Family Newspaper Internship Program for Minorities *(Graduate, Professional Development/Internship)* 5295

BNL Research Fellowship in Physics *(Postdoctorate/Fellowship)* 1505

Boston Globe One-Year Minority Development Program *(Professional Development/Other)* 1461

Ed Bradley Scholarships *(Undergraduate/Scholarship)* 5053

William A. Brower Scholarship *(Undergraduate/Scholarship)* 4694

Business Reporting Intern Program for College Sophomores and Juniors *(Undergraduate/Internship, Scholarship)* 2274

California Psychological Association Foundation Minority Scholarships *(Doctorate/Grant)* 1572

Cape Canaveral Chapter Scholarships *(Graduate, Undergraduate/Scholarship)* 5114

Capital Cities/ABC Inc. Newspaper Internship *(Professional Development/Internship)* 1721

Casualty Actuarial Scholarships for Minority Students *(Undergraduate/Scholarship)* 5430

Central Intelligence Agency Undergraduate Scholars Program *(Undergraduate/Internship, Scholarship)* 1812

Cesar Chavez Memorial Leadership Award *(Undergraduate/Scholarship)* 5687

Chicago Association of Black Journalists Scholarships *(Graduate, Undergraduate/Scholarship)* 1916

Chicago Heights Star Publications Minority Internship *(Undergraduate/Internship)* 5603

The Chicago Reporter Minority Fellowship in Urban Journalism *(Postgraduate, Professional Development/Fellowship)* 1920

Chicago Sun-Times Minority Scholarships and Internships *(Undergraduate/Internship, Scholarship)* 1922

Council On Legal Education Opportunities *(Graduate/Scholarship)* 2119

Cox Minority Journalism Scholarship *(Undergraduate/Scholarship)* 2131

Dallas-Fort Worth Association of Black Communicators Scholarships *(High School, Undergraduate/Scholarship)* 2170

Albert W. Dent Scholarship *(Graduate/Scholarship)* 2561

*Detroit Free Press* Minority Journalism Scholarships *(Undergraduate/Scholarship)* 2247

Cay Drachnik Minorities Fund *(Graduate/Award)* 259

Duracell/National Urban League Scholarship and Intern Program for Minority Students *(Undergraduate/Internship, Scholarship)* 4448

Marion Wright Edelman Scholarship *(All/Scholarship)* 3490

Editing Program for Minority Journalists *(Professional Development/Other)* 2338

Fellowship Program in Academic Medicine for Minority Students *(Undergraduate/Fellowship)* 4290

Undergraduate Student Financial Aid Program Grant *(Undergraduate/Grant)* 5605

Five Colleges Fellowship Program *(Doctorate/Fellowship)* 2470

Ford Foundation Postdoctoral Fellowships for Minorities *(Postdoctorate/Fellowship)* 4356

Fredrikson & Byron Minority Scholarships *(Graduate/Scholarship)* 2589

Stephen H. Gayle Memorial Scholarship *(High School, Undergraduate/Scholarship)* 4558

Louise Giles Minority Scholarship *(Graduate/Scholarship)* 664

Golden State Minority Foundation Scholarships *(Undergraduate/Scholarship)* 2713

Hartford Courant Minority Internship *(Professional Development/Internship)* 2798

Robert A. Hine Memorial Scholarship *(Undergraduate/Scholarship)* 5564

Indiana Professional Chapter of SPJ Minority Scholarship *(Undergraduate/Scholarship)* 5486

Ken Inouye Scholarship *(Graduate, Undergraduate/Scholarship)* 5488

Investigative Reporters and Editors Minority Conference Fellowships *(Other/Fellowship)* 6006

Agnes Jones Jackson Scholarship *(Graduate, Undergraduate/Scholarship)* 3850

Jewel/Taylor C. Cotton Scholarship *(Undergraduate/Scholarship)* 1927

*Arizona Daily Star* Frank E. Johnson Scholarship *(Other/Scholarship)* 795

Journalism Institute for Minorities Scholarships *(Undergraduate/Scholarship)* 3300

Kaiser Media Internships in Urban Health Reporting *(Other/Internship)* 3313

Flemmie P. Kittrell Memorial Fellowship for Minorities *(Graduate/Fellowship)* 297

Knight-Ridder Minority Specialty Development Program *(Professional Development/Other)* 4928

KNTV Minority Scholarships *(Undergraduate/Scholarship)* 3394

Kodak Scholarship Award *(Undergraduate/Scholarship)* 5688

Landmark Communications Minority Internships *(Professional Development/Internship)* 3419

LITA/OCLC and LITA/LSSI Minority Scholarships in Library and Information Technology *(Graduate/Scholarship)* 3466

Massachusetts Black Librarians Network Scholarship. *(Undergraduate/Scholarship)* 3593

Rollan D. Melton Fellowship *(Professional Development/Fellowship)* 796

Mercedes-Benz of North America Scholarship Program *(Undergraduate/Scholarship)* 1928

Metropolitan Museum of Art Nine-Month Internship *(Graduate, Undergraduate/Internship)* 3661

Minority Dental Student Scholarship Program *(Doctorate, Graduate/Scholarship)* 43

Minority Fellowships in Neuroscience *(Doctorate/Fellowship)* 806

Minority Fellowships in Psychology *(Doctorate/Fellowship)* 807

Minority Student Administrative Summer Internship Program *(Graduate, Undergraduate/Internship)* 5903

Minority Students Hazardous Materials Management Training Program *(Undergraduate/Internship)* 5904

Minority Teachers of Illinois Scholarship *(Undergraduate/Scholarship loan)* 2981

Missouri Minority Teacher Education Scholarship *(Undergraduate/Scholarship loan)* 3750

NAA Foundation Minority Fellowships *(Professional Development/Fellowship)* 4631

NAACP Willems Scholarship *(Graduate, Undergraduate/Scholarship)* 3851

NACA Multi-Cultural Scholarship *(Professional Development/Scholarship)* 3867

National Association of Black Accountants National Scholarship *(Graduate, Undergraduate/Scholarship)* 3857

National Association of Black Journalists Scholarship *(Graduate, Undergraduate/Scholarship)* 3859

National Association of Media Women Scholarship *(Undergraduate/Scholarship)* 3885

National FFA Foundation Minority Scholarships *(Undergraduate/Scholarship)* 4104

## Minority (continued)

National Newspaper Publishers Association Grants *(Undergraduate/Grant)* 4326

National Press Club Ellen Masin Persina Scholarship *(Undergraduate/Scholarship)* 4340

NBMBAA National MBA Scholarship/PhD Fellowship *(Graduate/Fellowship, Scholarship)* 3910

News-Sentinel Minority Scholarship *(Undergraduate/Scholarship)* 4629

NIH Predoctoral Fellowship Awards for Minority Students *(Doctorate/Fellowship)* 3722

NMA Scholarships *(Graduate/Scholarship)* 4302

Northwest Pharmacist Coalition Pre-Pharmacy Scholarship *(Undergraduate/Scholarship)* 4696

Northwestern University Journalism Minority Scholarships *(Graduate/Scholarship)* 4698

Nursing Scholarship Program *(Graduate, Undergraduate/Scholarship loan)* 2512

Oklahoma State Regents for Higher Education Doctoral Study Grants *(Doctorate/Grant)* 4739

Oklahoma State Regents for Higher Education Professional Study Grants *(Graduate/Grant)* 4740

Oregon State Bar Scholarships *(Graduate/Scholarship)* 4803

The Oregonian Minority Internship Program *(Other/Internship)* 4805

Ortho/McNeil Predoctoral Minority Fellowship in Antimicrobial Chemotherapy *(Doctorate/Fellowship)* 955

Leonard M. Perryman Communications Scholarship for Ethnic Minority Students *(Undergraduate/Scholarship)* 5794

Art Peters Minority Internships *(Undergraduate/Internship)* 4929

Private Colleges & Universities Community Service Scholarship *(Undergraduate/Scholarship)* 1735

Program for Minority Research Training in Psychiatry *(Doctorate, Graduate/Fellowship)* 804

Chips Quinn Scholars Program Internship *(Undergraduate/Internship, Scholarship)* 1438

Garth Reeves Jr. Memorial Scholarships *(Graduate, Undergraduate/Scholarship)* 5490

Rockefeller Brothers Fund Fellowships for Minority Students *(Undergraduate/Fellowship)* 5144

Rosewood Family Scholarship Fund *(Undergraduate/Scholarship)* 2514

RTNDF Six-Month Entry Level Internships for Minority Students *(Graduate/Internship)* 5067

RTNDF Summer Internships for Minority Students *(Undergraduate/Internship)* 5068

Sacramento Bee Minority Media Scholarships *(Undergraduate/Scholarship)* 5207

Carole Simpson Scholarship *(Graduate, Undergraduate/Scholarship)* 5071

Smithsonian Institution Minority Internship *(Graduate, Undergraduate/Internship)* 5386

Southern California Edison Company Independent Colleges of Southern California Scholarships *(Undergraduate/Scholarship)* 5568

Edward D. Stone Jr. and Associates Minority Scholarship *(Undergraduate/Scholarship)* 3434

George A. Strait Minority Stipend *(Graduate/Award)* 315

Syracuse Newspapers Journalism Scholarship *(Undergraduate/Scholarship)* 5664

Teacher Education Scholarship Program *(Undergraduate/Scholarship)* 125

TELACU Arts Award *(Undergraduate/Scholarship)* 5689

TELACU Scholarships *(Undergraduate/Scholarship)* 5690

Texas State Scholarship Program for Ethnic Recruitment *(Undergraduate/Scholarship)* 5716

Thomson Fellowship *(Graduate/Fellowship)* 5727

Times Mirror Minority Editorial Training Program *(Professional Development/Other)* 3496

Virginia Transfer Grant *(Undergraduate/Grant)* 5608

Virginia Press Association Minority Internship *(Graduate, Undergraduate/Internship)* 6063

WCVB TV Hearst Broadcast News Fellowship *(Graduate, Undergraduate/Fellowship)* 6125

Roy Wilkins Scholarships *(Undergraduate/Scholarship)* 3852

The Women's Sports Foundation Minority Internship Program *(Graduate, Postgraduate, Undergraduate/Internship)* 6241

Wyeth-Ayerst Prize in Women's Health *(Doctorate/Award)* 4308

Xerox Technical Minority Scholarship *(Graduate, Professional Development, Undergraduate/Scholarship)* 5682

Jimmy A. Young Memorial Education Recognition Award *(Undergraduate/Scholarship)* 850

Whitney M. Young Memorial Scholarship *(Undergraduate/Scholarship)* 1929

Mark Zambrano Scholarship *(Graduate, Undergraduate/Scholarship)* 2880

## Native American

ABF Summer Research Fellowships in Law and Social Science for Minority Undergraduate Students *(Undergraduate/Fellowship)* 352

Advanced Industrial Concepts (AIC) Materials Science Program *(Graduate/Fellowship)* 5857

Affirmative Action Scholarship Program *(Graduate/Scholarship)* 5575

AIGC Fellowships *(Graduate/Fellowship)* 553

AISES A.T. Anderson Memorial Scholarship *(Graduate, Undergraduate/Scholarship)* 559

Alabama Space Grant Consortium Graduate Student Fellowship Program *(Graduate/Fellowship)* 123

Alabama Space Grant Consortium Undergraduate Fellowship Program *(Undergraduate/Fellowship)* 124

Frances C. Allen Fellowships *(Doctorate, Graduate, Postgraduate/Fellowship)* 4615

Alpha Kappa Alpha Educational Advancement Foundation Scholarships *(Undergraduate/Scholarship)* 198

American Economic Association/Federal Reserve System Minority Graduate Fellowships in Economics *(Graduate, Postgraduate/Fellowship)* 453

American Indian Scholarship *(Undergraduate/Scholarship)* 4392

AMS/Industry Minority Scholarships *(Undergraduate/Scholarship)* 702

APA Planning & the Black Community Division Scholarship *(Undergraduate/Scholarship)* 775

APA Planning Fellowships *(Graduate/Fellowship)* 776

Association on American Indian Affairs Displaced Homemaker Scholarships *(Other, Undergraduate/Scholarship)* 1212

AT & T Bell Laboratories Cooperative Research Fellowships for Minorities *(Graduate/Fellowship)* 1302

AT & T Bell Laboratories Summer Research Program for Minorities & Women *(Undergraduate/Fellowship)* 1305

BIA Higher Education/Hopi Supplemental Grants *(Doctorate, Graduate, Postgraduate, Undergraduate/Grant)* 2892

Ardell Bjugstad Memorial Scholarships *(Undergraduate/Scholarship)* 5551

William and Charlotte Cadbury Award *(Doctorate/Award)* 4288

CERT Scholarship *(Graduate, Undergraduate/Scholarship)* 2100

Cherokee Nation Graduate Scholarship *(Graduate/Scholarship)* 1911

Cheyenne-Arapaho Higher Education Assistance Program Grant *(Undergraduate/Grant)* 1914

CIC Predoctoral Fellowships *(Doctorate, Graduate/Fellowship)* 2013

CLA Scholarship for Minority Students in Memory of Edna Yelland *(Graduate/Scholarship)* 1565

Consortium Graduate Study Management Fellowships for Minorities *(Graduate/Fellowship)* 2067

Continental Society Daughters of Indian Wars Scholarship *(Undergraduate/Scholarship)* 2180

Continental Society Daughters of Indian Wars Scholarships *(Undergraduate/Scholarship)* 2073

Corporate Sponsored Scholarships for Minority Undergraduate Physics Majors *(Undergraduate/Scholarship)* 772

Council on Social Work Education Minority Fellowships *(Doctorate/Fellowship)* 3724

Cultural Grants *(Professional Development/Grant)* 1596

*Detroit Free Press* Minority Journalism Scholarships *(Undergraduate/Scholarship)* 2247

Educational Enrichment Grant *(All/Grant)* 2893

Emergency Aid and Health Professions Scholarships *(Graduate, Undergraduate/Scholarship)* 1214

Environmental Protection Agency Tribal Lands Science Scholarship *(Doctorate, Graduate, Postgraduate/Scholarship)* 560

Fellowship Program in Academic Medicine *(Doctorate/Fellowship)* 4289

Ford Foundation Predoctoral and Dissertation Fellowships for Minorities *(Doctorate/Fellowship)* 4357

GEM Master's Engineering Fellowships for Minorities *(Graduate/Fellowship)* 3941

GEM Ph.D. Engineering Fellowships for Minorities *(Doctorate/Fellowship)* 3942

GEM Ph.D. Science Fellowship Program *(Doctorate/Fellowship)* 3943

Gerber Prize for Excellence in Pediatrics *(Doctorate/Award)* 4291

GOALS Fellowships *(Graduate/Fellowship)* 3001

Hopi Scholarship *(Graduate, Postgraduate, Undergraduate/Scholarship)* 2894

IHS Health Professions Compensatory Preprofessional Scholarship *(Undergraduate/Scholarship)* 2993

IHS Health Professions Pre-Graduate Scholarships *(Undergraduate/Scholarship)* 2994

W. K. Kellogg Community Medicine Training Fellowship Program for Minority Medical Students *(Doctorate/Fellowship)* 4297

Katrin H. Lamon Resident Scholarship for Native Americans *(Doctorate, Postdoctorate/Scholarship)* 5274

Louie LeFlore/Grant Foreman Scholarship *(Undergraduate/Scholarship)* 5306

MACESA Awards *(Undergraduate/Scholarship)* 3699

Massachusetts Indian Association Scholarships *(Graduate, Undergraduate/Scholarship)* 3595

Metropolitan Life Foundation Awards for Academic Excellence in Medicine *(Doctorate/Award)* 4300

Michigan Indian Tuition Waiver *(Graduate, Undergraduate/Other)* 3683

Minority Dental Student Scholarship Program *(Doctorate, Graduate/Scholarship)* 43

Minority Geoscience Scholarships *(Graduate, Undergraduate/Scholarship)* 508

MLA Scholarship for Minority Students *(Graduate/Scholarship)* 3636

Montana Indian Student Fee Waiver *(Doctorate, Graduate, Professional Development, Undergraduate/Scholarship)* 557

Montana University System Fee Waivers *(Undergraduate/Other)* 3769

NACME Corporate Scholars Program *(Undergraduate/Scholarship)* 3835

NACME TechForce Scholarships *(Undergraduate/Scholarship)* 3836

National FFA Foundation Minority Scholarships *(Undergraduate/Scholarship)* 4104

National Miss Indian U.S.A. Scholarship *(Graduate, Undergraduate/Scholarship)* 555

National Physical Science Consortium Graduate Fellowships for Minorities and Women *(Doctorate, Graduate/Fellowship)* 4338

The National Society of the Colonial Dames of America American Indian Nurse Scholarship Awards *(Undergraduate/Scholarship)* 4390

Native American Education Grants *(Graduate, Undergraduate/Grant)* 4992

Native American Journalists Association Scholarships *(Undergraduate/Scholarship)* 4470

Native American Seminary Scholarships *(Graduate/Scholarship)* 4993

Navajo Code Talkers Scholarship *(Graduate, Postgraduate, Professional Development, Undergraduate/Scholarship)* 4479

New York State Indian Aid *(Undergraduate/Award)* 4468

NMA Scholarships *(Graduate/Scholarship)* 4302

NMF Scholarships for Minority Students *(Doctorate/Scholarship)* 4304

NNAC Gifted/Talented Artist Sponsorships *(Professional Development/Other)* 4324

North Dakota Indian Scholarships *(Undergraduate/Scholarship)* 4684

Petro-Canada Education Awards for Native Students *(Undergraduate/Award)* 4881

Colin L. Powell Minority Postdoctoral Fellowship in Tropical Disease Research *(Graduate/Fellowship)* 4164

Presbyterian Church Native American Seminary Scholarships *(Graduate/Scholarship)* 4994

Presbyterian Church Student Opportunity Scholarships *(Undergraduate/Scholarship)* 4996

Private High School Scholarship *(High School/Scholarship)* 2895

Al Qoyawayma Award *(Graduate, Undergraduate/Award)* 561

Polingaysi Qoyawayma Scholarship *(Graduate/Scholarship)* 562

Racial/Ethnic Leadership Supplemental Grants *(Graduate/Grant)* 4998

James H. Robinson Memorial Prize *(Doctorate/Prize)* 4305

Nelson A. Rockefeller Minority Internships *(Undergraduate/Internship)* 6270

Santa Fe Pacific Foundation Scholarships *(Undergraduate/Scholarship)* 563

Santa Fe Pacific Native American Scholarships *(Undergraduate/Scholarship)* 1534

Seminole-Miccosukee Indian Scholarships *(Graduate, Undergraduate/Scholarship)* 2515

Sequoyah Graduate Fellowships *(Graduate/Fellowship)* 1215

Aura E. Severinghaus Award *(Doctorate/Scholarship)* 4306

Mark Ulmer Native American Scholarships *(Undergraduate/Scholarship)* 5748

Underrepresented Minority Investigators Award in Asthma and Allergy *(Postdoctorate/Award)* 216

U.S. Bureau of Indian Affairs Scholarship Grant *(Undergraduate/Grant)* 5843

USET Scholarships *(Undergraduate/Scholarship)* 5812

Adolph Van Pelt Special Fund for Indian Scholarships *(Graduate, Undergraduate/Scholarship)* 1216

Jimmy A. Young Memorial Education Recognition Award *(Undergraduate/Scholarship)* 850

Zuni Higher Education Scholarships *(Doctorate, Graduate, Undergraduate/Scholarship)* 6314

## Other

Alabama Scholarships for Dependents of Blind Parents *(Undergraduate/Award)* 107

Arby's Scholarships *(Undergraduate/Scholarship)* 1062

ASCAP Foundation Grants to Young Composers *(Professional Development/Grant)* 912

Mercer Silas Bailey Memorial Scholarships *(Undergraduate/Scholarship)* 1360

Oscar Broneer Fellowship *(Doctorate, Graduate, Postdoctorate/Fellowship)* 856

Susan Burdett Scholarhips *(Undergraduate/Scholarship)* 638

California Junior Miss Scholarship Program *(Undergraduate/Scholarship)* 1561

Canadian Golf Foundation Scholarships *(Undergraduate/Scholarship)* 1642

CIBC Youthvision Scholarship Program *(Undergraduate/Scholarship)* 1271

CLA Scholarship for Minority Students in Memory of Edna Yelland *(Graduate/Scholarship)* 1565

Cleveland Scholarship Programs *(Undergraduate/Scholarship)* 1970

CMT Scholarships *(Graduate/Scholarship)* 1830

Anna C. and Oliver C. Colburn Fellowship *(Doctorate, Postdoctorate/Fellowship)* 857

Jimmie Condon Athletic Scholarships *(Undergraduate/Scholarship)* 175

Verne Catt McDowell Corporation Scholarships *(Graduate/Scholarship)* 3622

Edwin G. and Lauretta M. Michael Scholarship *(Undergraduate/Scholarship)* 1950

Ministerial Education Scholarship *(Graduate/Scholarship)* 5782

National Presbyterian College Scholarships *(Undergraduate/Scholarship)* 4991

Native American Seminary Scholarships *(Graduate/Scholarship)* 4993

John Harrison Ness Memorial Awards *(Graduate/Award)* 2631

Ohio Baptist Education Society Scholarships *(Graduate, Undergraduate/Scholarship)* 4721

Order of Alhambra Scholarships *(Graduate, Undergraduate/Scholarship)* 4789

Leonard M. Perryman Communications Scholarship for Ethnic Minority Students *(Undergraduate/Scholarship)* 5794

Presbyterian Church Native American Seminary Scholarships *(Graduate/Scholarship)* 4994

Presbyterian Church Student Loans *(Graduate, Undergraduate/Loan)* 4995

Presbyterian Church Student Opportunity Scholarships *(Undergraduate/Scholarship)* 4996

Presbyterian Study Grants *(Graduate/Grant)* 4997

Pro Deo and Pro Patria (Canada) Scholarships *(Undergraduate/Scholarship)* 3389

Pro Deo and Pro Patria Scholarships *(Undergraduate/Scholarship)* 3390

Racial/Ethnic Leadership Supplemental Grants *(Graduate/Grant)* 4998

Samuel Robinson Scholarships *(Undergraduate/Scholarship)* 4999

Rowley Ministerial Education Scholarship *(Graduate/Scholarship)* 1951

St. James Armenian Church Memorial Scholarship *(Undergraduate/Scholarship)* 1127

Katherine J. Schutze Memorial Scholarship *(Graduate/Scholarship)* 1952

Joseph Sumner Smith Scholarship *(Undergraduate/Scholarship)* 5783

Marion Barr Stanfield Art Scholarship *(Undergraduate/Scholarship)* 5784

Otto M. Stanfield Legal Scholarship *(Graduate/Scholarship)* 5785

Stoody-West Fellowship in Journalism *(Graduate/Fellowship)* 5795

Texas Black Scholarships *(Undergraduate/Scholarship)* 1374

UMF Annual Conference Scholars Program *(Undergraduate/Scholarship)* 5796

Raoul Wallenberg Scholarships *(Undergraduate/Scholarship)* 3274

David & Dovetta Wilson Scholarship Fund *(High School/Scholarship)* 6191

Women of the ELCA Scholarship *(Graduate, Postgraduate, Undergraduate/Scholarship)* 6226

## Union

American Postal Workers Union Vocational Scholarship *(Undergraduate/Scholarship)* 788

Civic Service Union No. 52 Charitable Assistance Fund *(Undergraduate/Scholarship)* 1962

GMP Memorial Scholarships *(Undergraduate/Scholarship)* 2707

E.C. Hallbeck Memorial Scholarship *(Undergraduate/Scholarship)* 789

Charles Hardy Memorial Scholarship Awards *(Undergraduate/Scholarship)* 5308

IAM Scholarships *(Undergraduate/Scholarship)* 3117

ILGWU Local 23-25 College Textbook Scholarship *(Undergraduate/Scholarship)* 3159

ILGWU National College Award Program *(High School, Undergraduate/Scholarship)* 3161

International Brotherhood of Teamsters Scholarships *(Undergraduate/Scholarship)* 3127

Ted Kenney Memorial Scholarships *(Undergraduate/Scholarship)* 1918

Charlie Logan Scholarship for Dependents *(Undergraduate/Scholarship)* 5290

Charlie Logan Scholarship for Seafarers *(Undergraduate/Scholarship)* 5291

Cletus E. Ludden Memorial Scholarships *(Undergraduate/Scholarship)* 2231

John H. Lyons, Sr. Scholarship Program *(Undergraduate/Scholarship)* 3109

Ed S. Miller Scholarship in Industrial and Labor Relations *(Undergraduate/Scholarship)* 2904

Minnesota Teamsters Joint Council No. 32 Scholarship Awards *(Undergraduate/Scholarship)* 3720

Michael J. Quill Scholarship *(Undergraduate/Scholarship)* 5737

Americo Toffoli Scholarships *(Undergraduate/Scholarship)* 1998

UFCW Scholarships *(Undergraduate/Scholarship)* 5792

UNITE Scholarships *(Undergraduate/Scholarship)* 5776

United Paperworkers International Union Scholarships *(Undergraduate/Scholarship)* 5809

Nicholas C. Vrataric Scholarships *(All/Scholarship)* 5810

## Veteran

37th Infantry Division Award *(Undergraduate/Award)* 2

102nd Infantry Division Scholarship *(All/Scholarship)* 6

Airmen Memorial Scholarships *(Undergraduate/Scholarship)* 98

Alabama G.I. Dependents' Scholarships *(Graduate, Undergraduate/Scholarship)* 119

American Legion Auxiliary Department Gift Scholarships *(Undergraduate/Scholarship)* 637

American Legion Auxiliary Department of Minnesota Scholarships *(Undergraduate/Scholarship)* 628

American Legion Auxiliary Memorial Scholarship *(Undergraduate/Scholarship)* 617

American Legion Auxiliary Scholarships *(Undergraduate/Grant)* 113

American Legion Scholarships *(Undergraduate/Scholarship)* 114

AMF/Signet Bank Educational Loans *(All/Loan)* 99

AMVETS National Scholarship for Graduate Students *(Graduate/Scholarship)* 1030

AMVETS National Scholarships for Undergraduate Students *(Undergraduate/Scholarship)* 1031

Army Emergency Relief Scholarships *(Undergraduate/Scholarship)* 1140

Child of Disabled Veteran Grant or Purple Heart Recipient, Grant *(Graduate, Other, Undergraduate/Other)* 2996

Children of Deceased Active Duty Servicemembers Grants *(Undergraduate/Grant)* 4495

Children of Deceased or Disabled Veterans or Children of Servicemen Classified as Prisoners of War or Missing in Action Scholarship *(Undergraduate/Scholarship)* 2497

Children of Deceased, Retired Servicemembers Grants *(Undergraduate/Grant)* 4496

Commonwealth of Pennsylvania Educational Gratuity Program Grants *(Undergraduate/Award)* 2019

Confederate Memorial Scholarships *(Undergraduate/Scholarship)* 5789

Connecticut Tuition Waiver for Veterans *(Undergraduate/Scholarship)* 2049

Edward T. Conroy Memorial Scholarship *(Graduate, Undergraduate/Scholarship)* 3568

Mary Rowena Cooper Scholarship Fund *(All/Scholarship)* 6195

Delaware Higher Education Benefits for Children of Veterans and Others *(Undergraduate/Grant)* 2209

Dependent Children of Soldiers Scholarship Program *(Undergraduate/Scholarship)* 1141

Fifth Marine Division Association Scholarships *(Undergraduate/Scholarship)* 3561

First Cavalry Division Association Scholarship *(Undergraduate/Scholarship)* 2464

Gamewardens of Vietnam Association Scholarships *(Undergraduate/Award)* 5958

## Veteran (continued)

# Sponsor and Scholarship Index

This index lists, in a single alphabetic sequence, all of the administering and sponsoring organizations and awards covered in the "Sponsors and Their Scholarships" section. Also included are co-sponsoring organizations and organization acronyms. The numbers that follow citations indicate the book entry numbers for particular organizations and awards, not page numbers. Book entry numbers for administering organizations appear in boldface type.

Sponsor and Scholarship Index

Sponsor and Scholarship Index

Early American Industries Association **2303**
Early Scholarship; Maurice and Robert 2999
Earthwatch 1791, 1791
Easley National Scholarship Awards 3827
East Scholarship; Bob 4343
East Texas Historical Association **2305**
East-West Center **2307**
East-West Center Graduate Degree Fellowships 2308
East-West Center Internships 2309
East-West Center Professional Associateships 2310
East-West Center Visiting Fellowships 2311
Eastburn Fellowship Fund; E. B. **2313**
Eastburn Fellowships 2314
Eastburn Fellowships; E. B. **2788**
The Easter Seal Research Institute **2315**
Easter Seal Society of Iowa Disability Scholarship 2320
Easter Seal Society of Iowa, Inc. **2319**
Eastern Apiculture Society of North America Scholarship 4067
Eastern European Visiting Scholarships 2814
Eastern Star Educational and Religious Scholarship 4791
Eastern Surfing Association **2325**
Eastman Dental Center **2327**
Eaton Scholarships; Benjamin 4156
Ebert Foundation Doctoral Research Fellowships; Friedreich 2330
Ebert Foundation; Friedrich **2329**
Ebert Foundation, Post-Doctoral/Young Scholar Fellowships; Friedreich 2331
Ebert Stiftung Pre Dissertation/Advanced Graduate Fellowshps; Friedreich 2332
EBSCO/NMRT Scholarship 663
EBSCO Subscription Services 656
ECFMG (Educational Commission for Foreign Medical Graduates) **2344**
ECLA (Women of the Evangelical Lutheran Church in America) **6225**
Ecole des Chartes Exchange Fellowship 4604
Economic History Association **2333**
Economics America **2335**
Eddleman Memorial Scholarship; Ellen Beth 2034
Edelman Scholarship; Marion Wright 3490
Edelstein International Fellowship in the History of Chemical Sciences and Technology 1900
Eden Traveling Fellowship in Obstetrics and Gynecology 5180
Edgerton Memorial Scholarship; Ken 152
Edison/Max McGraw Scholarship; Thomas 4379
Edith Folsom Hall Scholarship 2636
Edith and Richard French Fellowship 1393
Editing Internships 2275
The Editing Program **2337**
Editing Program for Minority Journalists 2338
Education Assistance Corp. **2339**
Education Grants; Acoma Higher 5019
Education Writers Association **2342**
Educational Assistance Grant 3569
Educational Commission for Foreign Medical Graduates **2344**
Educational Communications Scholarship 2347
Educational Communications Scholarship Foundation **2346, 2348**
Educational Enrichment Grant 2893
The Educational Foundation for Women in Accounting **2349**
Educational Testing Service **2351**
Edward and Sally Van Lier Fund 3661
Edwards Scholarship 2357
Edwards Scholarship Fund **2356**
EFA Research Grants 2398
EHA Committee on Research in Economic History **2358**
Ehrenreich Scholarships; Joseph 4344
Eight and Forty Nurses Scholarships 630
Einstein Institution; Albert **2360**
Einstein Institution Fellowships; Albert 2361
Eisenhower Transportation Fellowship; Dwight David 6052
El Camino Real No. 158 NAWIC Scholarship 3906
Electrical Women's Round Table, Inc. **2362**
Electrochemical Society Energy Research Fellowships 2367
The Electrochemical Society, Inc. **2365**

Electrochemical Society Summer Fellowships 2368
Electronic Industries Foundation **2369**
Electronic Industries Foundation Scholarships 2370
Elizabeth II Fellowships; Queen 1338
Elks National Foundation Eagle Scout Scholarship 1463
Elva Knight Research Grants 3177
Embassy of France **2371, 2373**
Emblem Club Scholarship Foundation **2377**
Emblem Club Scholarship Grants 2378
Embry-Riddle Aeronautical University 79
Emergency Aid and Health Professions Scholarships 1214
Emergency Assistance Grants 2719
Emergency Preparedness Canada Research Fellowship Program 1274
Emerson Scholarships; Gladys Anderson 3215
EMGIP (Emigre Memorial German Internship Programs) **2379**
EMGIP Internships 2380
Emigre Memorial German Internship Programs **2379**
ENCON Endowment 1616
Endodontic Faculty Grants 287
Endodontic Graduate Student Grants 288
Endowment for Biblical Research, Summer Research and Travel Grants 868
Endowment Fund Dental Hygiene Scholarship Program 42
Energy Fellowships 3488
Engalitcheff Institute on Comparative Political and Economic Systems Internship 3019
Engineering Geology Foundation **2381**
Engineering Rotation Program 2923
The English Speaking Union 2622
English-Speaking Union of the United States **2383**
Enlisted Essay Contest 5951
Ennes Scholarship; Harold E. 5442
Entomological Society of America **2387**
Entomological Society of Canada **2393**
Entomological Society Postgraduate Awards 2394
Environmental Monitoring Systems Laboratory Research Participation Program 5869
Environmental Protection Agency Fellowships 5940
Environmental Protection Agency Tribal Lands Science Scholarship 560
Environmental Restoration/Waste Management Fellowship Program 5870
Environmental Restoration/Waste Management Technical Degree Scholarship Program 5871
Environmental Science Amoco Foundation Scholarships 4068
EORTC/NCI Exchange Program 3923
EPA (U.S. Environmental Protection Agency) **5939**
Epilepsy Foundation of America 455, 456, **2395**
Epilepsy Foundation of America Research Grants 2399
Epilepsy Foundation of America Research Training Fellowships 2400
Episcopal Diocese of Western Massachusetts 1409
Epping Scholarships; Richard 976
Eppley Foundation for Research, Inc. **2403**
Eppley Foundation Support for Advanced Scientific Research 2404
Epsilon Sigma Phi **2405**
Epsilon Sigma Phi Mini-Grants 2406
Epsilon Sigma Phi Professionalism Scholarship 2407
Epsilon Sigma Phi Scholarship Loans 2408
Equitable Life Assurance Society of the U.S. **2409**
Erim Award; Kenan T. 1065
EROS Data Center 5561
The Ertl Company Scholarship 4069
ESA (Eastern Surfing Association) **2325**
ESA Undergraduate Scholarships 2389
Esperanza, Inc. **2411**
Esperanza Scholarships 2412
ESRI Doctoral Training Grants ESRI Postdoctoral Fellowships 2316
ESRI Postdoctoral Fellowships; ESRI Doctoral Training Grants 2316
Established Investigator Grant 527
Estelle Massey Osborne Memorial Scholarship 4703

Sponsor and Scholarship Index

Louisiana Rehabilitation Services Award 3506
Louisiana Space Consortium 3507
Louisiana State Aid Dependents Educational Assistance 3500
Lovejoy Graduate Studies Fund; Hatton 1585
Lovejoy Scholarship Plan; Hatton 1586
Lovett Scholarship; Inez Peppers 2035
Lowell Poetry Travelling Scholarship; Amy 3510
Lowell Poetry Travelling Scholarship Trust; Amy 3509
LPI Summer Intern Program in Planetary Science 3514
Luard Scholarship; Lucy Dalbiac 2385
Luce Foundation/ACLS Dissertation Fellowship in American Art;
　Henry 412
Luce Foundation, Inc.; The Henry 3511
Luce Scholars Program 3512
Ludden Memorial Scholarships; Cletus E. 2231
Lumsden-Kouvel Fellowship; Audrey 4605
Lumsden-Kouvel Fellowship; The Audrey 4618
Lunar and Planetary Institute 3513
Lunar and Planetary Institute Visiting Graduate Fellows 3515
Lunar and Planetary Institute Visiting Postdoctoral
　Fellowships 3516
Lunar and Planetary Institute Visiting Scientist Program 3517
Lundine Scholarship; Ruth A. & G. Elving 1879
Lupus Foundation of America, Inc. 3518
Lupus Foundation of America Research Grants 3520
Lutheran Life University Scholarships 1314
Lydic Scholarship; Denny 5744
Lynden Memorial Scholarship 3522
Lynden Memorial Scholarship Fund 3521
Lyons, Sr. Scholarship Program; John H. 3109
M.A. Hanna Company Scholarship 3170
MacDowell Colony 3523
MacDowell Colony Residencies 3524
MacEachern; Malcolm T. 520
Macelwane Annual Awards; Father James B. 707
MACESA (Mid-America Consortium for Engineering & Science
　Advancement) 3698
MACESA Awards 3699
Macfarlane Scholarship; Professional Pilot John W. "Reds" 1350
MacGregor Memorial Scholarship; Irene and Daisy 4401
The MacKenzie Foundation 3525, 3526
MacKenzie, Johnson and Johnson Fellowship; Walter C. 5185
MacKenzie King Open Scholarship 3528
Mackenzie King Scholarships Board 3527
Mackenzie King Travelling Scholarships 3529
Madison Fellowships; James 3531
Madison Memorial Fellowship Foundation; James 3530
Maffett Scholarship; Minnie L. 4466
Magnetic Fusion Energy Technology Fellowship Program 5901
Magnetic Fusion Science Fellowship Program 5902
Magoichi and Shizuko Kato Memorial Scholarship 3246
Maine Osteopathic Association 3532
Maine Osteopathic Association Memorial Scholarship 3535
Maine Osteopathic Association Scholarship 3536
Maine Veterans Dependents Educational Benefits 3538
Maine Veteran's Services 3537
Majiu Uyesugi Memorial Scholarship 3245
MALDEF (Mexican American Legal Defense and Educational
　Fund) 3674
MALDEF Scholarships 3675
Malhotra Fellowship; Katherine Bryant Mather Fellowship;
　Stewart C. Watson Fellowship; ACI Fellowships: ACI/W.R.
　Grace Fellowship; V. Mohan 388
Mallory Disability Scholarship; James L. and Lavon
　Madden 2322
Maltese-American Benevolent Society 3539
Maltese-American Benevolent Society Scholarship 3540
Mamer Fellowship; Lyle 2364
MANA - A National Latina Organization 3541
Mann Companies; Horace 3543
Mann Scholarship; Horace 3544
Manomet Center for Conservation Sciences 3545
Manulife Financial Scholarships 1617
Maori Health Research Grant 2831
March of Dimes Birth Defects Foundation 3547

March of Dimes Research Grants 3548
Marckwardt Travel Grants; Albert H. 5680
Marcus and Theresa Levie Educational Fund 3265
Margaret Dale Philp Award 1631
Margaret Dow Towsley Scholarships for Women 6002
Margaret Jerome Sampson Scholarships 4922
Margaret Yardley Fellowship; New Jersey State Federation of
　Women's Clubs 4543
Marguerite R. Jacobs Memorial Fellow in American Jewish
　Studies 598
Marian Anderson Vocal Arts Competition 4331
Marianas Naval Officers' Wives' Club Scholarships 5959
MARILN Scholarship 3603
Marin County American Revolution Bicentennial
　Scholarship 3551
Marin County American Revolution (Bicentennial
　Scholarships) 3550
Marin Education Fund 3552
Marin Education Grant for Short-Term and Long-Term
　Occupational Study 3553
Marin Education Grants 3554
Marine Corps Essay Contest 5954
Marine Corps Foundation Scholarships 3562
Marine Corps Historical Center 3555
Marine Corps Historical Center College Internships 3556
Marine Corps Historical Center Doctoral Dissertation
　Fellowship 3557
Marine Corps Historical Center Master's Thesis Fellowship 3558
Marine Corps Historical Center Research Grants 3559
Marine Corps Historical Foundation 3559
Marine Corps Scholarship Foundation 3560
Marine Corps Tankers Association, Inc. 3563
Marinelli Founders' Scholarship; Antonio M. 4237
Marinelli Scholarships 4238
Mariner Working Scholar Program; William J. 5100
Marliave Scholarships 2382
Marr Memorial Scholarship; Inga 159
Marsh Scholarship 2326
Marshall Nurse Practitioner/Nurse Midwife Scholarship Program;
　Mary 6048
Marshall Nursing Scholarship for Student Nurses Practical
　Nursing Program; Mary 6049
Marshall Nursing Scholarship for Student Nurses Registered
　Nurse Program; Mary 6050
Marshall Scholarship Fund; Thurgood 3565
Marshall Scholarship; Thurgood 3566
Martha H. Jones Scholarships 4521
Marti Scholarship Challenge Grants; Jose 2511
Martino Scholars Program 4239
Martino Scholarship for International Studies; Assunta
　Lucchetti 4240
Marvin Music Scholarship; Elizabeth Warner 1880
Marvin S. Corwin Fund 3265
Mary Davis Spirit of Enterprise Scholarship 4521
Maryland Child Care Provider Scholarship 3573
Maryland Distinguished Scholar Scholarship 3574
Maryland Higher Education Commission 3567
Maryland Higher Education Commission Distinguished Scholar
　Program 3591
Maryland House of Delegates Scholarship 3575
Maryland MESA Program 3585
Maryland MESA Scholarships 3586
Maryland Part-Time Grant Program 3576
Maryland Physical and Occupational Therapists and Assistants
　Scholarships 3577
Maryland Professional Scholarship 3578
Maryland Reimbursement of Firefighters and Rescue Squad
　Members 3579
Maryland Senatorial Scholarship 3580
Maryland Space Grant Consortium 3587
Maryland Space Grant Consortium Graduate Level
　Fellowship 3588
Maryland State Nursing Scholarships 3581
Maryland State Scholarship Administration 3590

Sponsor and Scholarship Index

Sponsor and Scholarship Index

Sponsor and Scholarship Index

Sigma Gamma Rho 5331
Sigma Gamma Rho National Education Fund Scholarship 5332
Sigma Iota Epsilon 5333
Sigma Iota Epsilon Undergraduate Scholarship Awards 5335
Sigma Phi Alpha Graduate Scholarship 430
Sigma Phi Alpha Undergraduate Scholarship 431
Sigma Pi Sigma Trust Fund 5482
Sigma Theta Tau International 5336
Sigma Theta Tau International/American Association of Diabetes Educators Grant 5338
Sigma Theta Tau International/American Nephrology Nurses' Association Grant 5339
Sigma Theta Tau International/American Nurses' Foundation Grant 5340
Sigma Theta Tau International/Emergency Nursing Foundation Grant 5341
Sigma Theta Tau International/Glaxo Wellcome New Investigator/ Mentor Grant 5342
Sigma Theta Tau International/Glaxo Wellcome Prescriptive Practice Grant 5343
Sigma Theta Tau International Small Research Grant 5344
Sigma Xi Grants-in-Aid of Research 5347
Sigma Xi, The Scientific Research Society 5346
Sikh Education Aid Fund 5348
Sikh Education Aid Fund Scholarship 5349
Silberman Awards; The Lois and Samuel 5351
Silberman Fund; The Lois and Samuel 5350
Silgan Containers Corporation Scholarships 4127
Silver Dart Aviation History Award 1607
Silver Playwriting Competition Prize; Dorothy 3261
Silver Scholarship; Rawley 261
Simmons Scholarship 981
Simpson Scholarship; Carole 5071
Sims Scholarships; Sir Arthur 5196
Sinfonia Foundation 5352
Sinfonia Foundation Research Assistance Grant 5353
Singer Nurses Scholarship; Bertha B. 5835
Singh Graduate Scholarship; Kala 994
Siphers Scholarships; Kathryn G. 6218
Six Meter Club of Chicago Scholarship 840
Skowhegan School Fellowships 5355
Skowhegan School of Painting and Sculpture 5354
SLA Scholarships 5579
The Slack Award for Medical Journalism 4307
Slater Fellowship; John Clarke 770
Slemp Foundation; C. Bascom 5356
Slemp Scholarship; C. Bascom 5357
Sleyster Memorial Scholarship; Rock 690
Slocum-Lunz Foundation 5358
Slocum-Lunz Foundation Scholarships and Grants 5359
Slovenian Women's Union of America 5360
Slovenian Women's Union Scholarships 5361
Small Growers, Inc. Scholarships; Earl J. 1388
SMART Corporation Scholarship 521
SMC (Service Merchandise Company Inc.) 5309
SME (Society of Manufacturing Engineers) 5464
Smith Fellowship; Alice E. 5617
Smith Fellowship; Robert H. and Clarice 1779
Smith Fund; Horace 5362
Smith Fund Loans; Horace 5365
Smith Hydraulic Fellowship; J. Waldo 905
Smith Memorial Fund; W. Eugene 5366
Smith Research Dissemination Support Grant; Nila Banton 3180
Smith Scholarship; Joseph Sumner 5783
Smithsonian Astrophysical Observatory 5369
Smithsonian Environmental Research Center 5373
Smithsonian Environmental Research Center Work-Learn Opportunities in Environmental Studies 5374
Smithsonian Institution 5375, 5379
Smithsonian Institution Graduate Fellowships 5376
Smithsonian Institution Minority Internship 5386
Smithsonian Institution National Design Museum 5382
Smithsonian Institution National Museum of American Art 5387
Smithsonian Institution Postdoctoral Fellowships 5377
Smithsonian Institution Predoctoral Fellowships 5378

Snodgrass Memorial Research Grant 2392
Snow Prize; John Ben 5668
SOCAN (SOCAN Foundation) 5389
SOCAN Foundation 5389
Social Science Research Council 5391
Social Science Research Fellowships in Agriculture 5152
Social Science Research Fellowships in Population 5153
Social Sciences and Humanities Research Council of Canada 5423
Social Sciences and Humanities Research Council Doctoral Fellowships 5425
Social Sciences and Humanities Research Council Postdoctoral Fellowships 5426
Sociedad Honoraria Hispanica 5427
Society of Actuaries 5429
Society of Actuaries Ph.D. Grants 5431
Society of American Registered Architects 5432
Society of American Registered Architects Student Design Competition/Emily Munson Memorial Student Award 5433
Society of Automotive Engineers 5434
Society of Biological Psychiatry 5437, 5439
Society of Broadcast Engineers, Inc. 5441
Society of Children's Book Writers and Illustrators 5443
Society of Daughters of United States Army 5446
Society of Daughters of the United States Army Scholarship Program 5447
Society Farsarotul 5448
Society Farsarotul Grants 5449
Society of the First Division 5450
Society of the First Division Foundation Scholarships 5451
Society of Flavor Chemists Memorial 3038
Society of Hispanic Professional Engineers Foundation 5453
Society for the Humanities 5455, 5457
Society for the Humanities Fellowships 5459
Society for the Humanities Postdoctoral Fellowships 5456
The Society for Imaging Science & Technology 5460
Society of Logistics Engineers 5462
Society of Manufacturing Engineers 5464
Society of Naval Architects and Marine Engineers 5471
Society of Naval Architects and Marine Engineers Scholarships 5472
Society of Nuclear Medicine 5473
Society of Nuclear Medicine Pilot Research Grants 5476
Society of Nuclear Medicine Student Fellowship Awards 5477
Society for Pediatric Dermatology 5479
Society for Pediatric Dermatology Grant 5480
Society of Physics Students 5481
Society of Physics Students Scholarships 5482
Society of Plastics Engineers Foundation 5483
Society of Plastics Engineers Foundation Scholarships 5484
Society of Professional Journalists 5485, 5487, 5489
The Society for the Psychological Study of Social Issues 5491
Society for the Psychological Study of Social Issues Grants-In-Aid Program 5497
Society for Range Management 5499
The Society for the Scientific Study of Sexuality 5501
Society for Technical Communication 5503
Society of Women Engineers 5505
Sociologists for Women in Society 5524
Sodexho Marriott Services Canada Award in Clinical Dietetics 2249
Solar Energy Society of Canada Inc. 5526
Solow Art and Architecture Foundation 3664
Solvay Pharmaceuticals Research Award in Menopause; ACOG/ 384
Sonenfeld Award; Alexandra Apostolides 2186
Sonnenblick Scholarship; Annie 5529
Sonnenblick Scholarship Fund, Inc.; Annie 5528
Sons of the American Revolution 5530
Sons of the First Division Scholarship Fund 5452
Sons of Italy Foundation 5532
Sons of Italy Foundation National Leadership Grants 5533
Sons of Norway Foundation 5534
Sons of the Republic of Texas 5536
Sorantin Young Artist Award 5226

Sponsor and Scholarship Index

Sponsor and Scholarship Index